COMMENTARY
on the
New Testament Use
of the Old Testament

COMMENTARY
on the
NEW TESTAMENT USE
of the OLD TESTAMENT

EDITED BY
G. K. BEALE *and* D. A. CARSON

Baker Academic
Grand Rapids, Michigan

APOLLOS

© 2007 by G. K. Beale and D. A. Carson

Published by Baker Academic
a division of Baker Publishing Group
P.O. Box 6287, Grand Rapids, MI 49516-6287
www.bakeracademic.com

and Apollos
(an imprint of Inter-Varsity Press)
Norton Street
Nottingham NG7 3HR England
email: ivp@ivpbooks.com
website: www.ivpbooks.com

Printed in the United States of America

Library of Congress Cataloging-in-Publication Data is on file at the Library of Congress, Washington, DC.

ISBN 10: 0-8010-2693-8
ISBN 978-0-8010-2693-5

British Library Cataloguing in Publication Data
A catalogue record for this book is available from the British Library.

UK ISBN 978-1-84474-196-0

Unless otherwise indicated, Scripture quotations are the authors' translations.

Contents

PREFACE

When the two editors of this volume began the project almost a decade ago, neither of us anticipated that it would take this long to bring it to completion. Unrealistic expectations, illness among the contributors and their families, and shifting and competing obligations all conspired to delay the project. We are profoundly grateful for the patience of the contributors who managed to submit their work in a timely manner, some of whom updated their work later, and of Baker Academic, whose editorial staff encouraged and even cajoled editors and contributors alike, but never nagged.

Yet we would also be the first to acknowledge how privileged we are to have worked on this. With many other Christians, we have thought long and hard about how the Bible hangs together, how later parts use earlier parts, and how in particular the NT documents cite or allude to the OT. Both of us have devoted a considerable part of our academic lives to these questions. So to labor with a team of scholars who have systematically worked through the evidence and to read and interact with what they have written and prepare it for the press has left us feeling enriched, and we are grateful.

Many of the quotations and allusions studied in these many hundreds of pages have been probed in greater detail elsewhere—sometimes in learned essays and monographs, sometimes in long and technical commentaries. But some of the treatments are fresh, and, perhaps more importantly, nowhere has all of this kind of material been brought together in one place. Readers will be helped to think through how a particular NT book or writer habitually uses the OT; they will be stimulated to see how certain OT passages and themes keep recurring in the various NT corpora. Moreover, even if some contemporary readers do not think the Bible holds together in any theological sense (as the editors and contributors do), every thoughtful reader must acknowledge that the biblical books themselves have been read that way from the time of their early circulation, and that the writers of the NT books saw themselves not (in some Marcionite fashion) as originators who could cheerfully dispense with whatever they wanted from the OT, but as those who stood under the authority of those OT documents even as they promulgated fresh interpretations of those documents. Whether we think the books of Scripture are the word of God or not, we ought at least to begin by extending to the writers of the NT the courtesy of trying to understand how they saw their task as they cited and explained the documents associated with the old covenant, the documents that they revered as *hē graphē* ("the Scripture").

If this volume helps some scholars and preachers to think more coherently about the Bible and teach "the whole counsel of God" with greater understanding, depth, reverence, and edification for fellow believers, contributors and editors alike will happily conclude that the thousands of hours invested in this book were a very small price to pay. We shall thank God for the privilege of spending so much time studying his word and see ourselves, once again, as debtors to grace.

G. K. Beale
D. A. Carson

CONTRIBUTORS

Peter Balla (PhD, University of Edinburgh) is the chair of New Testament studies at Károli Gáspár Reformed University in Budapest, Hungary.

G. K. Beale (PhD, University of Cambridge) is Kenneth T. Wessner Chair of Biblical Studies and professor of New Testament at Wheaton College Graduate School.

Craig L. Blomberg (PhD, University of Aberdeen) is distinguished professor of New Testament at Denver Seminary.

D. A. Carson (PhD, University of Cambridge) is research professor of New Testament at Trinity Evangelical Divinity School.

Roy E. Ciampa (PhD, University of Aberdeen) is associate professor of New Testament at Gordon-Conwell Theological Seminary.

George H. Guthrie (PhD, Southwestern Baptist Theological Seminary) is Benjamin W. Perry Professor of Bible at Union University.

Andreas J. Köstenberger (PhD, Trinity Evangelical Divinity School) is professor of New Testament at Southeastern Baptist Theological Seminary.

I. Howard Marshall (PhD, University of Aberdeen) is emeritus professor of New Testament exegesis and honorary research professor at the University of Aberdeen.

Sean M. McDonough (PhD, University of St. Andrews) is assistant professor of New Testament at Gordon-Conwell Theological Seminary.

David W. Pao (PhD, Harvard University) is assistant professor of New Testament at Trinity Evangelical Divinity School.

Brian S. Rosner (PhD, University of Cambridge) is professor of New Testament and ethics at Moore Theological College.

Eckhard J. Schnabel (PhD, University of Aberdeen) is professor of New Testament at Trinity Evangelical Divinity School.

Mark A. Seifrid (PhD, Princeton Theological Seminary) is Mildred and Ernest Hogan Professor of New Testament Interpretation at Southern Baptist Theological Seminary.

Moisés Silva (PhD, University of Manchester) has taught New Testament at Westmont College, Westminster Theological Seminary, and Gordon-Conwell Theological Seminary.

Frank S. Thielman (PhD, Duke University) is Presbyterian Professor of Divinity at Beeson Divinity School.

Contributors

Philip H. Towner (PhD, University of Aberdeen) is director of translation services at United Bible Societies.

Rikk E. Watts (PhD, University of Cambridge) is associate professor of New Testament at Regent College.

Jeffrey A. D. Weima (PhD, Wycliffe College, University of Toronto) is professor of New Testament at Calvin Theological Seminary.

ABBREVIATIONS

General

ad loc.	*ad locum* (at the place discussed)
Akk.	Akkadian
Aram.	Aramaic
b.	Babylonian Talmud
ca.	circa
chap(s).	chapter(s)
col(s).	column(s)
esp.	especially
ET	English translation
frg(s.)	fragment(s)
Gk.	Greek
Heb.	Hebrew
Lat.	Latin
lit.	literally
m.	Mishnah
mg.	margin
NT	New Testament
OT	Old Testament
par(s).	parallel(s)
pl.	plural
sg.	singular
t.	Tosefta
v.l.	*varia lectio* (variant reading)
y.	Jerusalem Talmud

Bible Versions

LXX	Septuagint
MT	Masoretic Text
ESV	English Standard Version
HCSB	Holman Christian Standard Bible
KJV	King James Version
NA²⁶	*Novum Testamentum Graece.* Edited by [E. and E. Nestle], K. Aland, et al. 26th ed. Stuttgart: Deutsche Bibelgesellschaft, 1979
NA²⁷	*Novum Testamentum Graece.* Edited by [E. and E. Nestle], B. Aland, et al. 27th rev. ed. Stuttgart: Deutsche Bibelgesellschaft, 1993
NASB	New American Standard Bible
NEB	New English Bible
NETB	New English Translation Bible
NETS	New English Translation of the Septuagint
NIV	New International Version
NJB	New Jerusalem Bible
NJPS	Tanakh: The Holy Scriptures: The New JPS Translation according to the Traditional Hebrew Text
NKJV	New King James Version
NLT	New Living Translation
NRSV	New Revised Standard Version
REB	Revised English Bible
RSV	Revised Standard Version
TNIV	Today's New International Version
Θ	Theodotion
UBS³	*The Greek New Testament.* Edited by K. Aland et al. 3rd ed. Stuttgart: Deutsche Bibelgesellschaft and United Bible Societies, 1983.
UBS⁴	*The Greek New Testament.* Edited by B. Aland et al. 4th rev. ed. 1994

Apocrypha and Septuagint

Add. Esth.	Additions to Esther
Bar.	Baruch
Bel	Bel and the Dragon
1–2 Esd.	1–2 Esdras
Jdt.	Judith
1–2 Kgdms.	1–2 Kingdoms
1–4 Macc.	1–4 Maccabees
Odes	Odes
Pr. Azar.	Prayer of Azariah
Pr. Man.	Prayer of Manasseh
Sir.	Sirach
Tob.	Tobit
Wis.	Wisdom of Solomon

Dead Sea Scrolls and Related Texts

1. Qumran

CD-A	*Damascus Document*[a]
CD-B	*Damascus Document*[b]
1QapGen ar	*1QGenesis Apocryphon*
1QHᵃ	*1QHodayot*[a]
1QIsaᵃ	*1QIsaiah*[a]
1QIsaᵇ	*1QIsaiah*[b]
1QM	*1QWar Scroll*
1QpHab	*1QPesher to Habakkuk*
1QS	*1QRule of the Community*
1Q13	*1QMelchizedek*
1Q14	*1QPesher to Micah*
1Q19 + 2Q19 bis	*1QBook of Noah*
1Q22	*1QWords of Moses*
1Q27	*1QMysteries*
1Q28a	*1QRule of the Congregation*
1Q28b	*1QRule of Benedictions*
4Q10	*4QGenesis*[k]
4Q13	*4QExodus*[b]
4Q44	*4QDeuteronomy*[q]
4Q51	*4QSamuel*[a]
4Q54	*4QKings*
4Q55	*4QIsaiah*[a]
4Q83	*4QPsalms*[a]
4Q84	*4QPsalms*[b]
4Q88	*4QPsalms*[f]
4Q158	*4QReworked Pentateuch*[a]
4Q161	*4QIsaiah Pesher*[a]
4Q162	*4QIsaiah Pesher*[b]
4Q163	*4QIsaiah Pesher*[c]
4Q164	*4QIsaiah Pesher*[d]
4Q165	*4QIsaiah Pesher*[e]
4Q167	*4QHosea Pesher*[b]
4Q169	*4QNahum Pesher*
4Q171	*4QPsalms Pesher*[a]

4Q174	*4QFlorilegium*
4Q175	*4QTestimonia*
4Q176	*4QTanhumim*
4Q177	*4QCatena A*
4Q181	*4QAges of Creation B*
4Q182	*4QCatena B*
4Q185	*4QSapiential Work*
4Q213a	*4QAramaic Levi*[b]
4Q226	*4QPseudo-Oubilees*[b]
4Q242	*4QPrayer of Nabonidus ar*
4Q244	*4QPseudo-Daniel*[b] *ar*
4Q246	*4QAramaic Apocalypse*
4Q252	*4QCommentary on Genesis A*
4Q259	*4QRule of the Community*[e]
4Q265	*4QMiscellaneous Rules*
4Q266	*4QDamascus Document*[a]
4Q270	*4QDamascus Document*[e]
4Q272	*4QDamascus Document*[g]
4Q285	*4QSefer ha-Milhamah*
4Q286	*4QBlessings*[a]
4Q365	*4QReworked Pentateuch*[c]
4Q372	*4QApocryphon of Joseph*[b]
4Q374	*4QDiscourse on the Exodus/Conquest Tradition*
4Q376	*4QApocryphon of Moses*[b]?
4Q379	*4QApocryphon of Joshua*[b]
4Q385a	*4QPseudo-Moses*[a]
4Q386	*4QPseudo-Ezekiel*[b]
4Q396	*4QHalakhic Letter*[c]
4Q397	*4QHalakhic Letter*[d]
4Q398	*4QHalakhic Letter*[e]
4Q400	*4QSongs of the Sabbath Sacrifice*[a]
4Q401	*4QSongs of the Sabbath Sacrifice*[b]
4Q403	*4QSongs of the Sabbath Sacrifice*[d]
4Q416	*4QInstruction*[b]
4Q418	*4QInstruction*[d]
4Q423	*4QInstruction*[g]
4Q427	*4QHodayot*[a]
4Q430	*4QHodayot*[d]
4Q431	*4QHodayot*[e]
4Q433a	*4QHodayot-like text B*
4Q462	*4QNarrative C*[a]
4Q473	*4QThe Two Ways*
4Q491	*4QWar Scroll*[a]
4Q491c	*4QSelf-Glorification Hymn*[b]
4Q500	*4QBenediction*
4Q504	*4QWords of the Luminaries*[a]
4Q521	*4QMessianic Apocalypse*
4Q522	*4QProphecy of Joshua*
4Q524	*4QTemple Scroll*
4Q525	*4QBeatitudes*
4Q541	*4QApocryphon of Levi*[b]? *ar*
4Q552	*4QFour Kingdoms*[a] *ar*
4Q553	*4QFour Kingdoms*[b] *ar*
4Q558	*4QVision*[b] *ar*

11Q5	*11QPsalms^a*
11Q10	*11QTargum of Job*
11Q11	*11QApocryphal Psalms^a*
11Q13	*11QMelchizedek*
11Q19	*11QTemple^a*
11Q20	*11QTemple^b*

2. Wadi Murabbaʿat

Mur 20	*papMarriage Contract ar*

3. Naḥal Ḥever

8ḤevXII gr	*Greek Scroll of the Minor Prophets*
5/6Ḥev 40	Ps [P.Yadin 40] (= 5/6Ḥev 1b)

Mishnah and Talmud Tractates

ʾAbod. Zar.	*ʾAbodah Zarah*
ʾAbot	*ʾAbot*
ʿArak.	*ʿArakin*
B. Bat.	*Baba Batra*
B. Meṣiʿa	*Baba Meṣiʿa*
B. Qam.	*Baba Qamma*
Ber.	*Berakot*
Beṣah	*Beṣah (= Yom Ṭob)*
Bik.	*Bikkurim*
ʿEd.	*ʿEduyyot*
ʿErub.	*ʿErubin*
Giṭ.	*Giṭṭin*
Ḥag.	*Ḥagigah*
Hor.	*Horayot*
Ḥul.	*Ḥullin*
Ker.	*Kerithot*
Ketub.	*Ketubbot*
Maʿaś.	*Maʿaśerot*
Maʿaś. Š.	*Maʿaśer Šeni*
Mak.	*Makkot*
Meg.	*Megillah*
Meʿil.	*Meʿilah*
Menaḥ.	*Menaḥot*
Mid.	*Middot*
Moʿed Qaṭ.	*Moʿed Qaṭan*
Naz.	*Nazir*
Ned.	*Nedarim*
Neg.	*Negaʿim*
Nid.	*Niddah*
ʾOhal.	*ʾOhalot*
Parah	*Parah*
Peʾah	*Peʾah*
Pesaḥ.	*Pesaḥim*
Qidd.	*Qiddušin*
Roš Haš.	*Roš Haššanah*
Šabb.	*Šabbat*
Sanh.	*Sanhedrin*

Šeb.	*Šebiʿit*
Šebu.	*Šebuʿot*
Šeqal.	*Šeqalim*
Soṭah	*Soṭah*
Sukkah	*Sukkah*
Taʿan.	*Taʿanit*
Tamid	*Tamid*
Ṭehar.	*Ṭeharot*
Ter.	*Terumot*
Yebam.	*Yebamot*
Yoma	*Yoma (= Kippurim)*
Zabim	*Zabim*
Zebaḥ.	*Zebaḥim*

Targumic Texts

Frg. Tg.	*Fragmentary Targum*
Tg. Esth. I, II	*First or Second Targum of Esther*
Tg. Isa.	*Targum Isaiah*
Tg. Neof.	*Targum Neofiti*
Tg. Onq.	*Targum Onqelos*
Tg. Ps.	*Targum Psalms*
Tg. Ps.-J.	*Targum Pseudo-Jonathan*
Tg. Qoh.	*Targum Qohelet*

Other Rabbinic Works

ʾAbot R. Nat.	*ʾAbot de Rabbi Nathan*
ʾAg. Ber.	*ʾAggadat Berešit*
Der. Er. Zuṭ.	*Derek Ereṣ Zuṭa*
Meg. Taʿan.	*Megillat Taʿanit*
Mek. Exod.	*Mekilta Exodus*
Mek. R. Ish.	*Mekilta de Rabbi Ishmael*
Mek. R. Sim.	*Mekilta de Rabbi Simeon*
Midr.	*Midrash* (+ biblical book)
Midr. Rab.	*Midrash Rabbah*
Pesiq. Rab.	*Pesiqta Rabbati*
Pesiq. Rab Kah.	*Pesiqta de Rab Kahana*
Pirqe R. El.	*Pirqe Rabbi Eliezer*
Rab.	(biblical book +) *Rabbah*
S. Eli. Rab.	*Seder Eliyahu Rabbah*
S. Eli. Zut.	*Seder Eliyahu Zuta*
Sipra Qed.	*Sipra Qedoshim*
Sipre	*Sipre*
Sop.	*Soperim*
Tanḥ.	*Tanḥuma*
Yal.	*Yalquṭ*

Old Testament Pseudepigrapha

Apoc. Ab.	*Apocalypse of Abraham*
Apoc. Adam	*Apocalypse of Adam*
Apoc. El. (C)	Coptic *Apocalypse of Elijah*
Apoc. Ezek.	*Apocryphon of Ezekiel*

Apoc. Sedr.	*Apocalypse of Sedrach*
Apoc. Zeph.	*Apocalypse of Zephaniah*
Aristob.	Aristobulus
As. Mos.	*Assumption of Moses*
Ascen. Isa.	*Martyrdom and Ascension of Isaiah 6–11*
2 Bar.	*2 Baruch (Syriac Apocalypse)*
3 Bar.	*3 Baruch (Greek Apocalypse)*
4 Bar.	*4 Baruch (Paraleipomena Jeremiou)*
1 En.	*1 Enoch (Ethiopic Apocalypse)*
2 En.	*2 Enoch (Slavonic Apocalypse)*
3 En.	*3 Enoch (Hebrew Apocalypse)*
Ezek. Trag.	Ezekiel the Tragedian
Gk. Apoc. Ezra	*Greek Apocalypse of Ezra*
Hel. Syn. Pr.	*Hellenistic Synagogal Prayers*
Jos. Asen.	*Joseph and Aseneth*
Jub.	*Jubilees*
L.A.B.	*Liber antiquitatum biblicarum* (Pseudo-Philo)
L.A.E.	*Life of Adam and Eve*
Lad. Jac.	*Ladder of Jacob*
Let. Aris.	*Letter of Aristeas*
Liv. Pro.	*Lives of the Prophets*
Mart. Isa.	*Martyrdom and Ascension of Isaiah 1–5*
Odes Sol.	*Odes of Solomon*
Pr. Man.	*Prayer of Manasseh*
Ps.-Phoc.	Pseudo-Phocylides
Pss. Sol.	*Psalms of Solomon*
Sib. Or.	*Sybilline Oracles*
Syr. Men.	Sentences of the Syriac Menander
T. Ab.	*Testament of Abraham*
T. Adam	*Testament of Adam*
T. Ash.	*Testament of Asher*
T. Benj.	*Testament of Benjamin*
T. Dan	*Testament of Dan*
T. Gad	*Testament of Gad*
T. Isaac	*Testament of Isaac*
T. Iss.	*Testament of Issachar*
T. Jac.	*Testament of Jacob*
T. Job	*Testament of Job*
T. Jos.	*Testament of Joseph*
T. Jud.	*Testament of Judah*
T. Levi	*Testament of Levi*
T. Mos.	*Testament of Moses*
T. Naph.	*Testament of Naphtali*
T. Reub.	*Testament of Reuben*
T. Sim.	*Testament of Simeon*
T. Sol.	*Testament of Solomon*
T. Zeb.	*Testament of Zebulun*

Apostolic Fathers

Barn.	*Barnabas*

1–2 Clem.	*1–2 Clement*
Did.	*Didache*
Diogn.	*Diognetus*
Herm. *Mand.*	Shepherd of Hermas, *Mandate*
Herm. *Sim.*	Shepherd of Hermas, *Similitude*
Mart. Pol.	*Martyrdom of Polycarp*
Pol. *Phil.*	Polycarp, *To the Philippians*

Nag Hammadi Codices

Gos. Truth	I,3 *Gospel of Truth*
Trim. Prot.	XIII,1 *Trimorphic Protennoia*

New Testament Apocrypha and Pseudepigrapha

Acts Pil.	*Acts of Pilate*
Gos. Thom.	*Gospel of Thomas*
Prot. Jas.	*Protevangelium of James*
Ps.-Mt.	*Gospel of Pseudo-Matthew*

Papyri

P.Lond.	*Greek Papyri in the British Museum*

Greek and Latin Works

Apuleius

Apol.	*Apologia (Pro se de magia)*

Augustine

Civ.	*De civitate Dei*
Serm. Dom.	*De sermone Domini in monte*

Aulus Gellius

Noct. att.	*Noctes atticae*

Cicero

Pis.	*In Pisonem*

Clement of Alexandria

Paed.	*Paedagogus*

Herodotus

Hist.	*Histories*

Hippolytus

Comm. Dan.	*Commentarium in Danielem*

Homer

Od.	*Odyssey*

Irenaeus

Haer.	*Against Heresies*

Jerome

Epist.	*Epistulae*

Josephus

Ag. Ap.	*Against Apion*
Ant.	*Jewish Antiquities*
J.W.	*Jewish War*
Life	*The Life*

Justin

1 Apol.	*First Apology*
Dial.	*Dialogue with Trypho*

Origen

Cels.	*Contra Celsum*
Comm. Matt.	*Commentarium in evangelium Matthaei*

Philo

Abraham	*On the Life of Abraham*
Agriculture	*On Agriculture*
Alleg. Interp.	*Allegorical Interpretation*
Cherubim	*On the Cherubim*
Confusion	*On the Confusion of Tongues*
Creation	*On the Creation of the World*
Decalogue	*On the Decalogue*
Dreams	*On Dreams*
Drunkenness	*On Drunkenness*
Embassy	*On the Embassy to Gaius*
Flaccus	*Against Flaccus*
Flight	*On Flight and Finding*
Giants	*On Giants*
Good Person	*That Every Good Person Is Free*
Heir	*Who Is the Heir?*
Hypothetica	*Hypothetica*
Joseph	*On the Life of Joseph*
Migration	*On the Migration of Abraham*
Moses	*On the Life of Moses*
Names	*On the Change of Names*
Planting	*On Planting*
Posterity	*On the Posterity of Cain*
Prelim. Studies	*On the Preliminary Studies*
QE	*Questions and Answers on Exodus*
QG	*Questions and Answers on Genesis*
Rewards	*On Rewards and Punishments*
Sacrifices	*On the Sacrifices of Cain and Abel*

Sobriety	*On Sobriety*
Spec. Laws	*On the Special Laws*
Unchangeable	*That God Is Unchangeable*
Virtues	*On the Virtues*
Worse	*That the Worse Attacks the Better*

Plato

Ep.	*Epistulae*
Resp.	*Respublica*
Leg.	*Leges*

Pliny the Elder

Nat.	*Naturalis historia*

Plutarch

Alex.	*Alexander*
Luc.	*Lucullus*
Quaest. rom.	*Quaestiones romanae et graecae (Aetia romana et graeca)*
Quaest. conv.	*Quaestionum convivialium libri IX*

Seneca

Ben.	*De beneficiis*
Clem.	*De clementia*
Ep.	*Epistulae morales*

Suetonius

Aug.	*Divus Augustus*
Cal.	*Gaius Caligula*
Dom.	*Domitianus*
Nero	*Nero*

Tacitus

Ann.	*Annales*
Hist.	*Historiae*

Xenophon

Cyr.	*Cyropaedia*
Mem.	*Memorabilia*

Modern Works

AB	Anchor Bible
ABD	*Anchor Bible Dictionary*. Edited by D. N. Freedman. 6 vols. New York: Doubleday, 1992
ABRL	Anchor Bible Reference Library
AcBib	Academia biblica
ACNT	Augsburg Commentaries on the New Testament

ADP	Abhandlungen des Deutschen Palästinavereins	BCOT	Biblical Commentary on the Old Testament
AGJU	Arbeiten zur Geschichte des antiken Judentums und des Urchristentums	BCOTWP	Baker Commentary on the Old Testament Wisdom and Psalms
AJT	*Asia Journal of Theology*	BDAG	Bauer, W., F. W. Danker, W. F. Arndt, and F. W. Gingrich. *Greek-English Lexicon of the New Testament and Other Early Christian Literature.* 3rd ed. Chicago: University of Chicago Press, 2000
ALGHJ	Arbeiten zur Literatur und Geschichte des hellenistischen Judentums		
AnBib	Analecta biblica		
ANET	*Ancient Near Eastern Texts Relating to the Old Testament.* Edited by J. B. Pritchard. 3rd ed. Princeton: Princeton University Press, 1969	BDB	Brown, F., S. R. Driver, and C. A. Briggs. *A Hebrew and English Lexicon of the Old Testament.* Oxford: Clarendon, 1906
ANETSt	*Ancient Near Eastern Texts and Studies*	BDF	Blass, F., A. Debrunner, and R. W. Funk. *A Greek Grammar of the New Testament and Other Early Christian Literature.* Chicago: University of Chicago Press, 1961
ANRW	*Aufstieg und Niedergang der römischen Welt: Geschichte und Kultur Roms im Spiegel der neueren Forschung.* Edited by H. Temporini and W. Haase. Berlin: de Gruyter, 1972–*		
		BDS	BIBAL Dissertation Series
		BECNT	Baker Exegetical Commentary on the New Testament
ANTC	Abingdon New Testament Commentaries	BETL	Bibliotheca ephemeridum theologicarum lovaniensium
ANTJ	Arbeiten zum Neuen Testament und Judentum	BEvT	Beiträge zur evangelischen Theologie
AOTC	Abingdon Old Testament Commentaries	BFCT	Beiträge zur Förderung christlicher Theologie
ApOTC	Apollos Old Testament Commentary	BHS	*Biblia Hebraica Stuttgartensia.* Edited by K. Elliger and W. Rudolph. Stuttgart: Deutsche Bibelgesellschaft, 1983
ApSem	Approaches to Semiotics		
ArBib	The Aramaic Bible		
ARJ	*Annual of Rabbinic Judaism*	BHT	Beiträge zur historischen Theologie
ASNU	Acta seminarii neotestamentici upsaliensis	*Bib*	*Biblica*
AsTJ	*Asbury Theological Journal*	*BibInt*	*Biblical Interpretation*
ATD	Das Alte Testament Deutsch	BibSem	The Biblical Seminar
ATDan	Acta theologica danica	BIS	Biblical Interpretation Series
ATR	*Anglican Theological Review*	*BJRL*	*Bulletin of the John Rylands University Library of Manchester*
AUS	American University Studies		
AUSS	*Andrews University Seminary Studies*	BJS	Brown Judaic Studies
		BKAT	Biblischer Kommentar, Altes Testament. Edited by M. Noth and H. W. Wolff
AUSDDS	Andrews University Seminary Doctoral Dissertation Series		
BAG	Bauer, W., W. F. Arndt, and F. W. Gingrich. *Greek-English Lexicon of the New Testament and Other Early Christian Literature.* Chicago: University of Chicago Press, 1957	*BL*	*Bibel und Liturgie*
		BMI	The Bible and Its Modern Interpreters
		BN	*Biblische Notizen*
BAR	*Biblical Archaeology Review*	BNTC	Black's New Testament Commentaries
BBB	Bonner biblische Beiträge		
BBMS	Baker Biblical Monograph Series	*BR*	*Biblical Research*
BBR	*Bulletin for Biblical Research*	*BRev*	*Bible Review*
BCBC	Believers Church Bible Commentary	BRS	Biblical Resource Series
		BSac	*Bibliotheca sacra*
		BSem	Biblical Seminar

BSL	Biblical Studies Library		*Shamra-Ugarit de 1929 à 1939.*
BSR	Biblioteca di scienze religiose		Edited by A. Herdner. Mission de
BTAT	Beiträge zur Theologie des Alten Testaments		Ras Shamra 10. Paris: P. Geuthner, 1963
BTh	Bibliothèque de théologie	*CTJ*	*Calvin Theological Journal*
BTB	*Biblical Theology Bulletin*	*CTM*	*Concordia Theological Monthly*
BU	Biblische Untersuchungen	*CTR*	*Criswell Theological Review*
BWANT	Beiträge zur Wissenschaft vom Alten und Neuen Testament	*CurBS*	*Currents in Research: Biblical Studies*
BZ	*Biblische Zeitschrift*	*DBSJ*	*Detroit Baptist Seminary Journal*
BZAW	Beihefte zur Zeitschrift für die alt-testamentliche Wissenschaft	DJD	Discoveries in the Judean Desert
BZNW	Beihefte zur Zeitschrift für die neu-testamentliche Wissenschaft	*DJG*	*Dictionary of Jesus and the Gospels.* Edited by J. B. Green, S. McKnight, and I. H. Marshall. Downers Grove: InterVarsity, 1992
CBC	Cambridge Bible Commentary		
CBET	Contributions to Biblical Exegesis and Theology	*DLNTD*	*Dictionary of the Later New Testament and Its Developments.* Edited by R. P. Martin and P. H. Davids. Downers Grove: InterVarsity, 1997
CBQ	*Catholic Biblical Quarterly*		
CBQMS	Catholic Biblical Quarterly Monograph Series		
CBSC	Cambridge Bible for Schools and Colleges	*DNTB*	*Dictionary of New Testament Background.* Edited by C. A. Evans and S. E. Porter. Downers Grove: InterVarsity, 2000
CBSS	Continuum Biblical Studies Series		
CBR	*Currents in Biblical Research*	*DPL*	*Dictionary of Paul and His Letters.* Edited by G. F. Hawthorne, R. P. Martin, and D. G. Reid. Downers Grove: InterVarsity, 1993
CC	Continental Commentaries		
CCCE	Changing Continuity of Christian Ethics		
CCL	Classic Commentary Library	*DRev*	*Downside Review*
CEB	Commentaire Évangélique de la Bible	*DSD*	*Dead Sea Discoveries*
		DSSCOL	The Dead Sea Scrolls and Christian Origins Library
CEJL	Commentaries of Early Jewish Literature	EBCNIV	The Expositor's Bible Commentary with the New International Version
CGTC	Cambridge Greek Testament Commentary	EBib	Études bibliques
CGTSC	Cambridge Greek Testament for Schools and Colleges	EBS	Encountering Biblical Studies
		ECC	Eerdmans Critical Commentary
CIJ	*Corpus inscriptionum judaicarum*	*EDNT*	*Exegetical Dictionary of the New Testament.* Edited by H. Balz and G. Schneider. ET. 3 vols. Grand Rapids: Eerdmans, 1990–1993
CM	Christianity in the Making		
CNT	Commentaire du Nouveau Testament		
ConBNT	Coniectanea neotestamentica or Coniectanea biblica: New Testament Series	EGGNT	Exegetical Guide to the Greek New Testament
		EKKNT	Evangelisch-katholischer Kommentar zum Neuen Testament
ConBOT	Coniectanea biblica: Old Testament Series	*EL*	*Ephemerides liturgicae*
COP	Cambridge Oriental Publications	*EncJud*	*Encyclopedia Judaica.* 16 vols. Jerusalem, 1972
COT	Commentaar op het Oude Testament	ERel	Études religieuses
CorpCh	*Corpus Christianorum* (Series Latina)	*ETL*	*Ephemerides theologicae lovanienses*
		ETR	*Études théologiques et religieuses*
CovQ	*Covenant Quarterly*	EUS	European University Studies
CSHJ	Chicago Studies in the History of Judaism	*EvQ*	*Evangelical Quarterly*
		EvT	*Evangelische Theologie*
CTA	*Corpus des tablettes en cunéiforms alphabétiques découvertes à Ras*	*ExpTim*	*Expository Times*
		FAT	Forschungen zum Alten Testament

FB	Forschung zur Bibel	IVPNTC	IVP New Testament Commentaries
FBBS	Facet Books, Biblical Series		
FF	Foundations and Facets	*JAAR*	*Journal of the American Academy of Religion*
FN	*Filología neotestamentaria*		
FoiVie	*Foi et vie*	*JANESCU*	*Journal of the Ancient Near Eastern Society of Columbia University*
FOTL	Forms of the Old Testament Literature		
		JBL	*Journal of Biblical Literature*
FRLANT	Forschungen zur Religion und Literatur des Alten und Neuen Testaments	JBLMS	Journal of Biblical Literature Monograph Series
		JC	Judaica et christiana
FTS	Frankfurter theologische Studien	JCPS	Jewish and Christian Perspective Series
GNC	Good News Commentary		
GNS	Good News Studies	*JE*	*The Jewish Encyclopedia.* Edited by I. Singer. 12 vols. New York: Funk and Wagnalls, 1925
GTJ	*Grace Theological Journal*		
HALOT	Koehler, L., W. Baumgartner, and J. J. Stamm. *The Hebrew and Aramaic Lexicon of the Old Testament.* Translated and edited under the supervision of M. E. J. Richardson. 4 vols. Leiden: Brill, 1994–1999		
		JEPTA	*Journal of the European Pentecostal Theological Association*
		JETS	*Journal of the Evangelical Theological Society*
		JGCJ	*Journal of Greco-Roman Christianity and Judaism*
HAR	*Hebrew Annual Review*		
HBT	*Horizons in Biblical Theology*	*JJS*	*Journal of Jewish Studies*
HDR	Harvard Dissertations in Religion	*JOTT*	*Journal of Translation and Textlinguistics*
HNT	Handbuch zum Neuen Testament		
HNTC	Harper's New Testament Commentaries	*JPC*	*Journal of Psychology and Christianity*
Hor	*Horizons*	JPSTC	Jewish Publication Society Torah Commentary
HT	Helps for Translators		
HTKAT	Herders theologischer Kommentar zum Alten Testament	JPTSup	Journal of Pentecostal Theology: Supplement Series
		JQR	*Jewish Quarterly Review*
HTKNT	Herders theologischer Kommentar zum Neuen Testament	*JR*	*Journal of Religion*
		JSHJ	*Journal for the Study of the Historical Jesus*
HTR	*Harvard Theological Review*		
HUCA	*Hebrew Union College Annual*	*JSJ*	*Journal for the Study of Judaism in the Persian, Hellenistic, and Roman Periods*
HUT	Hermeneutische Untersuchungen zur Theologie		
IBC	Interpretation: A Bible Commentary for Teaching and Preaching	*JSNT*	*Journal for the Study of the New Testament*
IBS	*Irish Biblical Studies*	JSNTSup	Journal for the Study of the New Testament: Supplement Series
ICC	International Critical Commentary		
ILPTBTS	International Library of Philosophy and Theology: Biblical and Theological Studies	*JSOT*	*Journal for the Study of the Old Testament*
		JSOTSup	Journal for the Study of the Old Testament: Supplement Series
Int	*Interpretation*		
IRT	Issues in Religion and Theology	*JSP*	*Journal for the Study of the Pseudepigrapha*
ISBE	*International Standard Bible Encyclopedia.* Edited by G. W. Bromiley. 4 vols. Grand Rapids: Eerdmans, 1979–1988	JSPSup	Journal for the Study of the Pseudepigrapha: Supplement Series
		JSS	*Journal of Semitic Studies*
ISBL	Indiana Studies in Biblical Literature	*JTS*	*Journal of Theological Studies*
		KEK	Kritisch-exegetischer Kommentar über das Neue Testament (Meyer-Kommentar)
ITC	International Theological Commentary		
ITS	International Theological Studies	KNT	Kommentar zum Neuen Testament

LBS	Library of Biblical Studies	*NIDNTT*	*New International Dictionary of New Testament Theology.* Edited by C. Brown. 4 vols. Grand Rapids: Regency Reference Library, 1975–1985
LCL	Loeb Classical Library		
LD	Lectio divina		
LEC	Library of Early Christianity		
LEH	J. Lust, E. Eynikel, and K. Hauspie, eds. *A Greek-English Lexicon of the Septuagint.* 2 vols. Stuttgart: Deutsche Bibelgesellschaft, 1992–1996	*NIDOTTE*	*New International Dictionary of Old Testament Theology and Exegesis.* Edited by W. A. VanGemeren. 5 vols. Grand Rapids: Zondervan, 1997
LLJC	Littman Library of Jewish Civilization	NIGTC	New International Greek Testament Commentary
LSJ	Liddell, H. G., R. Scott, and H. S. Jones, *A Greek-English Lexicon.* 9th ed. with rev. supplement. Oxford: Clarendon, 1996	NIVAC	NIV Application Commentary
		NovT	*Novum Testamentum*
		NovTSup	Supplements to Novum Testamentum
LSTS	Library of Second Temple Studies		
LTPM	Louvain Theological and Pastoral Monographs	*NRTh*	*La nouvelle revue théologique*
		NSBT	New Studies in Biblical Theology
LWCOT	Living Word Commentary on the Old Testament	NTAbh	Neutestamentliche Abhandlungen
		NTC	The New Testament in Context
MBCNTS	Mellen Biblical Commentary: New Testament Series	NTD	Das Neue Testament Deutsch
		NTG	New Testament Guides
MdB	Le monde de la Bible	NTL	New Testament Library
MLBS	Mercer Library of Biblical Studies	NTOA	Novum Testamentum et Orbis Antiquus
MNTC	Moffatt New Testament Commentary	NTR	New Testament Readings
		NTS	*New Testament Studies*
MNTS	McMaster New Testament Studies	NTSI	The New Testament and the Scriptures of Israel
MSt	Monographien und Studienbucher		
MTS	Marburger theologische Studien	*NTT*	*Norsk Teologisk Tidsskrift*
NABPRDS	National Association of Baptist Professors of Religion Dissertation Series	NTTS	New Testament Tools and Studies
		NVBS	New Voices in Biblical Studies
NAC	New American Commentary	*NW*	*Neuer Wettstein: Texte zum Neuen Testament aus Griechentum und Hellenismus.* Edited by G. Strecker and U. Schnelle. 3 vols. Berlin: de Gruyter, 2001–
NBD	*New Bible Dictionary.* Edited by J. D. Douglas, N. Hillyer, and D. R. W. Wood. 3rd ed. Downers Grove: InterVarsity, 1996		
NCB	New Cambridge Bible	OBO	Orbis biblicus et orientalis
NCBC	New Century Bible Commentary	OBT	Overtures to Biblical Theology
NClB	New Clarendon Bible	*OGIS*	*Orientis graeci inscriptiones selectae.* Edited by W. Dittenberger. 2 vols. Leipzig: S. Hirzel, 1903–1905
NDBT	*New Dictionary of Biblical Theology.* Edited by D. Alexander and B. S. Rosner. Downers Grove: InterVarsity, 2000		
		OTE	*Old Testament Essays*
		ÖTK	Ökumenischer Taschenbuch-Kommentar
NEchtB	Neue Echter Bibel		
Neot	*Neotestamentica*	OTL	Old Testament Library
NIBCNT	New International Biblical Commentary: New Testament Series	OTM	Oxford Theological Monographs
		OTP	*Old Testament Pseudepigrapha.* Edited by J. H. Charlesworth. 2 vols. Garden City, NY: Doubleday, 1983–1985
NIBCOT	New International Biblical Commentary: Old Testament Series		
NICNT	New International Commentary on the New Testament		
		OTS	Old Testament Studies
NICOT	New International Commentary on the Old Testament	*OTWSA*	*Die Oud Testamentiese Werkgemeenskap in Suid-Afrika*

PBTM	Paternoster Biblical and Theological Monographs	SBLSCS	Society of Biblical Literature Septuagint and Cognate Studies
PFES	Publications of the Finnish Exegetical Society	*SBLSP*	*Society of Biblical Literature Seminar Papers*
PG	Patrologia graeca [= Patrologiae cursus completus: Series graeca]. Edited by J.-P. Migne. 162 vols. Paris, 1857–1886	SBS	Sources for Biblical Study
		SBT	Studies in Biblical Theology
		ScrHier	Scripta hierosolymitana
		ScrM	Scripta minora
PGC	Pelican Gospel Commentaries	SDSSRL	Studies in the Dead Sea Scrolls and Related Literature
PIBA	Proceedings of the Irish Biblical Association	*SE*	*Studia evangelica I, II, III* (= TU 73 [1959], 87 [1964], 88 [1964], etc.)
PilNTC	Pillar New Testament Commentary		
PNTC	Pelican New Testament Commentaries		
POuT	De Prediking van het Oude Testament	*SEÅ*	*Svensk exegetisk årsbok*
		SFSHJ	South Florida Studies in the History of Judaism
PRSt	*Perspectives in Religious Studies*	SHJ	Studying the Historical Jesus
PTMS	Pittsburgh Theological Monograph Series	SJLA	Studies in Judaism in Late Antiquity
QC	*Qumran Chronicle*	*SJT*	*Scottish Journal of Theology*
RB	*Revue biblique*	SKKNT	Stuttgarter kleiner Kommentar, Neues Testament
ResQ	*Restoration Quarterly*		
RevExp	*Review and Expositor*	SMBen	Serie monografica di Benedictina: Sezione biblico-ecumenica
RevQ	*Revue de Qumran*		
RGW	Religions in the Graeco-Roman World	SNT	Studien zum Neuen Testament
		SNTA	Studiorum Novi Testamenti Auxilia
RHPR	*Revue d'histoire et de philosophie religieuses*		
		SNTSMS	Society for New Testament Studies Monograph Series
RivB	*Rivista biblica italiana*		
RNBC	Readings: A New Biblical Commentary	SNTSU	Studien zum Neuen Testament und seiner Umwelt
RNT	Regensburger Neues Testament	SNTW	Studies of the New Testament and Its World
RSR	*Recherches de science religieuse*		
RTL	*Revue théologique de Louvain*	SOTBT	Studies in Old Testament Biblical Theology
RTP	*Revue de theologie et de philosophie*		
RThom	*Revue thomiste*	SP	Sacra Pagina
RTR	*Reformed Theological Review*	SSN	Studia semitica neerlandica
RVV	Religionsgeschichtliche Versuche und Vorarbeiten	*SR*	*Studies in Religion*
		ST	*Studia theologica*
SANT	Studien zum Alten und Neuen Testaments	STDJ	Studies on the Texts of the Desert of Judah
SB	Sources bibliques	StPatr	Studia Patristica
SBB	Stuttgarter biblische Beiträge	StPB	Studia post-biblica
SBG	Studies in Biblical Greek	Str-B	Strack, H. L., and P. Billerbeck. *Kommentar zum Neuen Testament aus Talmud und Midrasch.* 6 vols. Munich: Beck, 1922–1961
SBEC	Studies in the Bible and Early Christianity		
SBib	Stuttgarter Bibelstudien		
SBL	Studies in Biblical Literature	StudNeot	Studia neotestamentica
SBLDS	Society of Biblical Literature Dissertation Series	SUNT	Studien zur Umwelt des Neuen Testaments
SBLEJL	Society of Biblical Literature Early Judaism and Its Literature	*SwJT*	*Southwestern Journal of Theology*
		SWR	Studies in Women and Religion
SBLMS	Society of Biblical Literature Monograph Series	TANZ	Texte und Arbeiten zum neutestamentlichen Zeitalter

TB	Theologische Bücherei: Neudrucke und Berichte aus dem 20. Jahrhundert	TSAJ	Texte und Studien zum antiken Judentum
TBC	Torch Bible Commentaries	*TTKi*	*Tidsskrift for Teologi og Kirke*
TBei	*Theologische Beiträge*	TUGAL	Texte und Untersuchungen zur
TBN	Themes in Biblical Narrative		Geschichte der altchristlichen
TBT	*The Bible Today*		Literatur
TDNT	*Theological Dictionary of the New Testament*. Edited by G. Kittel and G. Friedrich. Translated by G. W. Bromiley. 10 vols. Grand Rapids: Eerdmans, 1964–1976	*TWOT*	*Theological Wordbook of the Old Testament*. Edited by R. L. Harris and G. L. Archer Jr. 2 vols. Chicago: Moody, 1980
		TynBul	*Tyndale Bulletin*
		TZ	*Theologische Zeitschrift*
TDOT	*Theological Dictionary of the Old Testament*. Edited by G. J. Botterweck and H. Ringgren. Translated by J. T. Willis, G. W. Bromiley, and D. E. Green. 14 vols. Grand Rapids: Eerdmans, 1974–	UBSMS	United Bible Societies Monograph Series
		USQR	*Union Seminary Quarterly Review*
		VC	*Vigiliae christianae*
		VT	*Vetus Testamentum*
		VTSup	Supplements to Vetus Testamentum
TF	Theologische Forschung	WBC	Word Biblical Commentary
TGST	Tesi Gregoriana: serie teologia	WBT	Wienar Beiträge zur Theologie
THKNT	Theologischer Handkommentar zum Neuen Testament	WestBC	Westminster Bible Companion
		WLQ	*Wisconsin Lutheran Quarterly*
THS	Tyndale House Studies	WMANT	Wissenschaftliche Monographien zum Alten und Neuen Testament
ThWAT	*Theologisches Wörterbuch zum Alten Testament*. Edited by G. J. Botterweck and H. Ringgren. Stuttgart, 1970–	*WTJ*	*Westminster Theological Journal*
		WUNT	Wissenschaftliche Untersuchungen zum Neuen Testament
TI	Theological Inquiries	*ZAW*	*Zeitschrift für die alttestamentliche Wissenschaft*
TJ	*Trinity Journal*		
TJT	*Toronto Journal of Theology*	ZBK	Züricher Bibelkommentare
TLNT	*Theological Lexicon of the New Testament*. By C. Spicq. Translated and edited by J. Ernest. 3 vols. Peabody, MA: Hendrickson, 1994	*ZDMG*	*Zeitschrift der deutschen morgenländischen Gesellschaft*
		ZNW	*Zeitschrift für die neutestamentliche Wissenschaft und die Kunde der älteren Kirche*
TLZ	*Theologische Literaturzeitung*		
TNTC	Tyndale New Testament Commentaries	*ZRGG*	*Zeitschrift für Religions- und Geistesgeschichte*
TOTC	Tyndale Old Testament Commentaries	*ZTK*	*Zeitschrift für Theologie und Kirche*
TPINTC	Trinity Press International New Testament Commentaries	ZWB	Zürcher Werkkommentare zur Bibel

INTRODUCTION

G. K. BEALE AND D. A. CARSON

It might be the part of wisdom to say what this book is not, so as to clarify what it is and how it works.

Nowhere does this volume survey contemporary debates over the use of the OT in the NT. The many subdisciplines that contribute to this enterprise have not been canvassed. For example, we do not systematically compare non-Christian Jewish exegetical methods with the exegetical methods on display in the NT. We do not review the ongoing debate between (a) those who argue that the NT writers usually respect the entire context of the OT texts they cite or to which they allude and (b) those who argue that the NT writers engage in a kind of "prooftexting" that takes OT passages out of their contexts so as to "prove" conclusions that belong to the commitments of NT Christians but not to the antecedent Scriptures they cite. We have not summarized the extraordinarily complex developments in the field of typology since Leonhard Goppelt wrote his 1939 book *Typos*. We could easily lengthen this list of important topics that have not been systematically addressed in this book.

One of the reasons we have not surveyed these topics is that all of them have been treated elsewhere. Though it might be useful to canvass them again, we decided that it was more urgent to put together a book in which all the contribu-tors would be informed by such discussions but would focus their attention on the places where NT writers actually cite or allude to the OT. Understandably, even elegant discussions of one of the subdisciplines, discussions one finds in other works—comparisons between Jewish and Christian exegetical techniques, for instance, or studies in typology—inevitably utilize only a small percentage of the actual textual evidence. By contrast, what we have attempted is a reasonably comprehensive survey of all the textual evidence. Even a casual reader of this volume will quickly learn that each contributor brings to bear many of the contemporary studies as he works his way through his assigned corpus, so along the way many of the contributors make shrewd comments on particular techniques and hermeneutical discussions. Accordingly, contributors have been given liberty to determine how much introductory material to include (i.e., prior discussions of the use of the OT in their particular NT book). Nevertheless, the focus of each contributor is on the NT's use of the OT. All OT citations in the NT are analyzed as well as all probable allusions. Admittedly there is debate about what constitutes an allusion. Consequently not every ostensible OT allusion that has ever been proposed will be studied but only those deemed to be probable allusions.

The editors have encouraged each contributor to keep in mind six separate questions where the NT cites or clearly alludes to the OT (though they have not insisted on this organization).

1. What is the NT context of the citation or allusion? In other words, without (yet) going into the details of the exegesis, the contributor seeks to establish the topic of discussion, the flow of thought, and, where relevant, the literary structure, genre, and rhetoric of the passage.

2. What is the OT context from which the quotation or allusion is drawn? Even at its simplest, this question demands as much care with respect to the OT as the first question demands of the study of the NT. Sometimes energy must be expended simply to demonstrate that a very brief phrase really does come from a particular OT passage, and from nowhere else. Yet sometimes this second question becomes even more complex. Under the assumption that Mark's Gospel picks up exodus themes (itself a disputed point), is it enough to go to the book of Exodus to examine those themes as they first unfold? Or are such OT exodus themes, as picked up by Mark, filtered through Isaiah? In that case, surely it is important to include reflection not only on the use of the OT in the NT but also on the use of the OT within the OT. Or again, how does the Genesis flood account (Gen. 6–9) get utilized in the rest of the OT and in earlier parts of the NT before it is picked up by 2 Peter? Sometimes a NT author may have in mind the earlier OT reference but may be interpreting it through the later OT development of that earlier text, and if the lens of that later text is not analyzed, then the NT use may seem strange or may not properly be understood.

3. How is the OT quotation or source handled in the literature of Second Temple Judaism or (more broadly yet) of early Judaism? The reasons for asking this question and the possible answers that might be advanced are many. It is not that either Jewish or Christian authorities judge, say, Jubilees or 4 Ezra to be as authoritative as Genesis or Isaiah. But attentiveness to these and many other important Jewish sources may provide several different kinds of help. (1) They may show us how the OT texts were understood by sources roughly contemporaneous with the NT. In a few cases, a trajectory of understanding can be traced out, whether the NT documents belong to that trajectory or not. (2) They sometimes show that Jewish authorities were themselves divided as to how certain OT passages should be interpreted. Sometimes the difference is determined in part by literary genre: Wisdom literature does not handle some themes the way apocalyptic sources do, for instance. Wherever it is possible to trace out the reasoning, that reasoning reveals important insights into how the Scriptures were being read. (3) In some instances, the readings of early Judaism provide a foil for early Christian readings. The differences then demand hermeneutical and exegetical explanations; for instance, if two groups understand the same texts in decidedly different ways, what accounts for the differences in interpretation? Exegetical technique? Hermeneutical assumptions? Literary genres? Different opponents? Differing pastoral responsibilities? (4) Even where there is no direct literary dependence, sometimes the language of early Judaism provides close parallels to the language of the NT writers simply because of the chronological and cultural proximity. (5) In a handful of cases, NT writers apparently display direct dependence on sources belonging to early Judaism and their handling of the OT (e.g., Jude). What is to be inferred from such dependence?

4. What textual factors must be borne in mind as one seeks to understand a particular use of the OT? Is the NT citing the MT or the LXX or a Targum? Or is there a mixed citation, or perhaps dependence on memory or on some form of text that has not come down to us? Is there significance in tiny changes? Are there textual variants within the Hebrew tradition, within the tradition of the Greek OT, or within the Greek NT textual tradition? Do such variants have any direct bearing on our understanding of how the NT is citing or alluding to the OT?

5. Once this groundwork has been laid, it becomes important to try to understand how the NT is using or appealing to the OT. What is the nature of the connection as the NT writer sees it? Is this merely a connection of language? One of the editors had a father who was much given to communicating in brief biblical quotations. His mind was so steeped in Scripture that Scripture provided the linguistic patterns that were the first recourse of his speech. If one of his children was complaining about the weather, he would quietly

say (quoting, in those days, the KJV), "This is the day the Lord hath made; let us rejoice and be glad in it." In fact, he knew his Bible well enough that he was fully aware that the original context was not talking about the weather and our response to it. He knew that the verse occurs in one of the crucial "rejected stone" passages, and the "day" over which the psalmist rejoices is the day when the "stone" is vindicated (Ps. 118:22–24; note v. 24 in the TNIV: "The Lord has done it this very day; let us rejoice today and be glad."). Nevertheless the passage provided the verbal fodder for him to express what he wanted to say, and granted what the Bible does actually say elsewhere about God's goodness and providence, he was accurately summarizing a biblical idea even though the biblical words he was citing did not, in their original context, articulate that idea. Are there instances, then, when the NT writers use biblical language simply because their minds are so steeped in Scripture that such verbal patterns provide the linguistic frameworks in which they think?

On the other hand, are there occasions when a NT writer uses an expression that crops up in many OT passages (such as, say, "day of the Lord," especially common in the prophets), not thinking of any one OT text but nevertheless using the expression to reflect the rich mix of promised blessing and promised judgment that characterizes the particular instantiations of the OT occurrences? In this case, the NT writer may be very faithful to OT usage at the generic level, even while not thinking of any particular passage, that is, individual OT occurrences may envisage particular visitations by God, while the generic pattern combines judgment and blessing, and the NT use may pick up on the generic pattern while applying it to yet another visitation by God.

Alternatively, NT writers may be establishing some sort of analogy in order to draw a moral lesson. Just as the ancient Israelites were saved out of slavery in Egypt but most of the adult generation did not make it into the promised land because they did not persevere in faith and obedience, so believers contemporary with Paul and with the writer to the Hebrews need to persevere if they are to be saved at the last (1 Cor. 10:1–13; Heb. 3:7–19). But when is such a formal analogy better thought of as a typology, that is, a pattern established by a succession of similar events over time?

Or again, is the NT writer claiming that some event or other is the fulfillment of an OT prophecy—a bold "this is what was spoken by the prophet" (e.g., Acts 2:16) sort of declaration? Soon, however, it becomes clear that the "fulfillment" category is remarkably flexible. An event may "fulfill" a specific verbal prediction, but in biblical usage an event may be said to "fulfill" not only a verbal prediction but also another event or, at least, a pattern of events. This is commonly labeled typological fulfillment. In that case, of course, a further question arises. Are the NT writers coming to their conclusion that this fulfillment has taken place to fulfill antecedent events simply out of their confidence in the sovereign God's ordering of all things, such that he has established patterns that, rightly read, anticipate a recurrence of God's actions? Or are they claiming, in some instances, that the OT texts themselves point forward in some way to the future?

More generally, do the NT writers appeal to the OT using exactly the same sorts of exegetical techniques and hermeneutical assumptions that their unconverted Jewish contemporaries display—one or more of the classic lists of middoth, the "rules" of interpretive procedure? The most common answer to this question is a decided "Yes," but the affirmation fails to explain why the two sets of interpreters emerge with some very different readings. One must conclude that either the exegetical techniques and hermeneutical assumptions do not determine very much after all or else that there are additional factors that need careful probing if we are to explain why, say, Hillel and Paul read the Hebrew Scriptures (or their Greek translations) so differently.

6. To what theological use does the NT writer put the OT quotation or allusion? In one sense, this question is wrapped up in all the others, but it is worth asking separately as it highlights things that may otherwise be overlooked. For instance, it is very common for NT writers to apply an OT passage that refers to YHWH (commonly rendered "Lord" in English Bibles) to Jesus. This arises from the theological conviction that it is entirely appropriate to do so since, granted Jesus' identity, what is predicated of God can be predicated no less of him. In other passages,

however, God sends the Messiah or the Davidic king, and Jesus himself is that Davidic king, thus establishing a distinction between God and Jesus. The subtleties of these diverse uses of OT texts meld with the complexities of NT Christology to constitute the essential building blocks of what would in time come to be called the doctrine of the Trinity. Other theological alignments abound, a few of which are mentioned below. Sometimes, more simply, it is worth drawing attention to the way a theological theme grounded in the citation of an OT text is aligned with a major theological theme in the NT that is treated on its own without reference to any OT text.

These, then, are the six questions that largely control the commentary in the following pages. Most of the contributors have handled these questions separately for each quotation and for the clearest allusions. Less obvious allusions have sometimes been treated in more generic discussions, though even here the answers to these six questions usually surface somewhere. Moreover, the editors have allowed adequate flexibility in presentation. Two or three contributors wrote in more discursive fashion, meaning they kept these questions in mind, but their presentations did not separate the questions and the answers they called forth.

Five further reflections may help to orientate the reader to this commentary.

First, one of the reasons for maintaining flexibility in approach is the astonishing variety of ways in which the various NT authors make reference to the OT. Matthew, for instance, is given to explicit quotations, sometimes with impressive formulaic introductions. By contrast, Colossians and Revelation avoid unambiguous and extensive citations but pack many, many OT allusions into their texts. Some NT writers return again and again to a handful of OT chapters; others make more expansive references. To this must be added the complications generated by NT books that are literarily dependent on other NT books or are, at very least, very similar to others (e.g., 2 Peter and Jude, the Synoptic Gospels, Ephesians and Colossians). The contributors have handled such diversity in a variety of ways.

Second, in addition to the obvious ease with which NT writers (as we have seen) apply to Jesus a variety of OT texts that refer to YHWH, so also

a number of other associations that are initially startling become commonplace with repetition. NT writers happily apply to the church, that is, to the new covenant people of God, many texts that originally referred to the Israelites, the old covenant people of God. In another mutation, Jesus himself becomes the eschatological locus of Israel—an identification sometimes effected by appealing to OT texts (e.g., "Out of Egypt I called my son," Matt. 2:15; Hos. 11:1) and sometimes by symbol-laden events in Jesus' life that call to mind antecedent events in the life of Israel, for example, Jesus being tempted in the wilderness for forty days and forty nights, Matt. 4/Luke 4, closely connected with Deut. 8 and the forty years of Israel's wilderness wanderings. This example overlaps with another pregnant set of associations bound up with the "son" language that abounds in both Testaments. In fact, it is likely because of conceiving Jesus as representing true Israel that NT writers began to conceive of the church this way as well, since Christ corporately represents the church, and what he is in so many ways is likewise true of the church.

Third, one of the distinctive differences one sometimes finds between the way NT writers read the OT and the way that their non-Christian Jewish contemporaries read it is the salvation-historical grid that is often adopted by the former. Some kind of historical sequence under the providence of a sovereign God is necessary for almost any kind of typological hermeneutic, of course, but there is something more. In Galatians 3, for instance, Paul modifies the commonly accepted significance of the law by the simple expedient of locating it after the Abrahamic promise, which had already established the importance of justification by faith and which had already promised blessing to the Gentiles. Thus instead of asking an atemporal question such as, "How does one please God?" and replying, "By obeying the law," Paul instead insists on reading the turning points of OT history in their chronological sequence and learning some interpretive lessons from that sequence. That sort of dependence on salvation history surfaces elsewhere in the NT (e.g., Rom. 4), and not only in Paul (e.g., Heb. 4:1–13; 7). Thus, eschatological fulfillment has begun with Christ's first advent and will be consummated at his last coming. Ostensible parallels in Jewish literature preserve (especially at Qumran) a sense of what might be called "inaugurated eschatology" (several texts insist that the Teacher of Righteousness brings in the last times), but that is something differentiable from this sense of historical sequencing within the Hebrew Scriptures being itself a crucial interpretive key to the faithful reading of those Scriptures.

Fourth, here and there within the pages of this commentary one finds brief discussion as to whether a NT writer is drawing out a teaching from the OT—i.e., basing the structure of his thought on the exegesis of the OT text—or appealing to an OT passage to confirm or justify what has in fact been established by the Christian's experience of Christ and his death and resurrection. This distinction is a more nuanced one than what was mentioned earlier, viz., the distinction between those who think that the citations bring with them the OT context and those who think that the NT writers resort to prooftexting. For the evidence is really quite striking that the first disciples are not presented as those who instantly understood what the Lord Jesus was teaching them or as those who even anticipated all that he would say because of their own insightful interpretations of the Hebrew Scriptures. To the contrary, they are constantly presented as, on the one hand, being attached to Jesus yet, on the other, being very slow to come to terms with the fact that the promised messianic king would also be the Suffering Servant, the atoning lamb of God, that he would be crucified, rejected by so many of his own people, and would rise again utterly vindicated by God. Nevertheless, once they have come to accept this synthesis, they also insist, in the strongest terms, that this is what the OT Scriptures actually teach. They do not say, in effect, "Oh, if only you could experience Jesus Christ the way we do, you would then enjoy a different set of lenses that would enable you to read the Bible differently." Rather, they keep trying to prove from the Scriptures themselves that this Jesus of Nazareth really does fulfill the ancient texts even while they are forced to acknowledge that they themselves did not read the biblical texts this way until after the resurrection, Pentecost, and the gradual increase in understanding that came to them, however mediated by the Spirit, as the result of the expansion of the church, not least in Gentile circles. This tension between what they insist is actually there in the Scriptures and what they are forced to admit they did not see until fairly late in their experience forces them to think about the concept of "mystery"—revelation that is in some sense "there" in the Scriptures but hidden until the time of God-appointed disclosure.

In other words, the same gospel that is sometimes presented as that which has been prophesied and is now fulfilled is at other times presented as that which has been hidden and is now revealed. This running tension is a lot more common in the NT than might be indicated by the small number—twenty-seven or twenty-eight—of occurrences of the Greek word *mystērion*. Galatians and John, for example, are replete with the theological notion of "mystery" without the word "mystery" being present. Transparently, this complex issue is tightly bound up with the ways in which the NT writers actually quote or allude to the OT—in particular, what they think they are proving or establishing or confirming. Nowhere is there a hint that these writers are trying to diminish the authority of what we now refer to as the OT Scriptures. After a while the alert reader starts stumbling over many instances of this complex phenomenon and tries to synthesize the various pieces. A favorite illustration of some in explaining this phenomenon is the picture of a seed. An apple seed contains everything that will organically grow from it. No examination by the naked eye can distinguish what will grow from the seed, but once the seed has grown into the full apple tree, the eye can then see how the seed has been "fulfilled." It is something like that with the way OT passages are developed in the NT. There are "organic links" to one degree or another, but those links may not have been clearly discernible to the eye of the OT author or reader. Accordingly, there is sometimes a creative development or extension of the meaning of the OT text that is still in some way anchored to that text. But it would take another sort of book to gather all the exegetical evidence gathered in this commentary and whip it into the kind of biblical-theological shape that might address these sorts of questions more acutely.

Fifth, contributors have been encouraged to deploy an eclectic grammatical-historical literary method in their attempts to relate the NT's reading of the OT. But it would not be amiss to point out (1) that such an approach is fairly "traditional" or "classical"; (2) that such an approach overlaps substantially with some recent postcritical methods that tend to read OT books as whole literary units and that take seriously such concepts as canon, Scripture, and salvation history (concepts that would not be entirely alien to the authors of the NT), though it allows for more extratextual referentiality than do most postcritical methods; and (3) that we sometimes need reminding that the NT authors would not have understood the OT in terms of any of the dominant historical-critical orthodoxies of the last century and a half.

Without further reflection, then, we devote this commentary to the study of the NT text as it quotes and alludes to the OT text.

MATTHEW

CRAIG L. BLOMBERG

Introduction

The Hebrew Scriptures—or Christian Old Testament—permeate Matthew's Gospel. Approximately fifty-five references prove close enough in wording for commentators typically to label them "quotations," compared to about sixty-five for the other three canonical Gospels put together. About twenty of these texts are unique to Matthew. Twelve times Matthew speaks explicitly of a passage or theme of Scripture being "fulfilled." In addition to explicit quotations, numerous allusions and echoes of Scripture may be discerned in every part of this Gospel, roughly twice as often as in Mark, Luke, or John. Virtually every major theological emphasis of Matthew is reinforced with Old Testament support, often by the addition of segments of texts to the sources Matthew employed, most notably Mark.

The reasons for the pervasiveness of the Jewish Bible in Matthew do not take long to discover. According to uniform early church tradition, the author of this Gospel was Levi, also known as Matthew, a member of Jesus' band of twelve apostles and a converted tax collector (cf. Matt. 9:9–13; 10:3; Mark 2:13–17). Because of his profession, Levi most likely featured among the minority of the populace that was literate. Even though he had gone to work, indirectly at least, for the occupying Roman forces, he remained Jewish. His

elementary school education and subsequent synagogue attendance, even if abandoned at some point in his adult life, would have steeped him in the contents and interpretation of the Hebrew Scriptures. All of these features combine with the potentially autobiographical reference in Matt. 13:52 to lead some scholars to suspect that his role as one of Jesus' followers may have resembled that of a Christian scribe.

Most likely Matthew's audience was also predominantly Jewish Christian, living perhaps in and around Syrian Antioch, about one-seventh of which was comprised of Jews. Although many possible relationships between Matthew's addressees and other local Jews have been suggested, a slight majority would favor the hypothesis of a fairly recent break from the synagogue. This best accounts for the seemingly anti-Jewish polemic in places (culminating in Matt. 21:43; 23:1–39; 27:25), where wounds may still have been raw due to eviction from mainstream Judaism. At the same time, Jewish Christians remained passionately concerned to continue trying to convince their unconverted family members and close friends that Jesus was the Jewish Messiah and that following him was the way to constitute the new true—or freed—Israel. Thus Matthew could simultaneously emphasize the uniquely Jewish stages of Christ's mission (10:5–6; 15:24), depict

1

all the links with the Jewish Scriptures, and highlight distinctively Jewish theological categories in his redactional emphases, including Jesus as the Son of David and messianic king and discipleship as practicing righteous living as the fulfillment of the Law.

Even Matthew's canonical placement highlights his links with Jewish Scriptures. Although one persistent early church tradition argues that Matthew wrote something, probably a collection of sayings of Jesus in Hebrew or Aramaic, most scholars agree that Mark's finished Gospel predated Matthew's. Some patristic testimony hints at this conclusion as well. Why then was Matthew put first when the canonical sequence of the four Gospels, and eventually of the entire New Testament, was crystallized? Doubtless, one answer is because of Matthew's clearest and most frequent links back to the Old Testament. A collection of books believed to reflect similarly inspired and authoritative Scripture to accompany God's new covenant would naturally begin best with the accounts of its inaugurator, Jesus of Nazareth. Of the four, Matthew helped form the transition between old and new most smoothly.

Sometimes one hears an eager apologist cite the more than two hundred Old Testament prophecies that the New Testament teaches were fulfilled in Jesus. Then some miniscule mathematical probability of all of these events randomly coalescing in the same person is used to "prove" the messiahship and deity of Jesus. The problem is that only a small handful of these Old Testament references were predictive in their original contexts. Micah 5:2 (cited in Matt. 2:6) does indeed prophesy that the Messiah would be born in Bethlehem, a prediction that excludes most self-styled messianic claimants a priori. But Hos. 11:1 (cited in Matt. 2:15) does not even contain future-tense verbs; it declares a past event—"Out of Egypt I called my son." In context, the prophet is referring to Israel collectively as God's son and recalling the exodus event. But, as the text-by-text commentary below will elucidate, Matthew is following standard (indeed, fairly conservative) forms of Jewish "typology" in interpreting the Scriptures here. Key patterns of activity ascribed to God recur in striking, discernible patterns such that the believer can only affirm the same hand of God at work in both events. The apologetic is more

subtle than with directly predictive prophecy but no less persuasive.

Some portions of the New Testament quote the Old primarily or exclusively by way of the Septuagint, the Greek translation of the Hebrew Scriptures stemming from approximately two hundred years before Christ. On many occasions Matthew does as well, particularly when he is largely following his sources—Mark and Q (material found in both Matthew and Luke but not in Mark). But at least as frequently he goes his separate way at key junctures, reflecting a more literal translation from the Hebrew text or adopting a Hebrew or Aramaic variant that had developed in Jewish tradition. If and when these come from written sources or oral tradition as opposed to Matthew's own translation de novo is often difficult to determine. But the variations in form do suggest that he is not merely dependent on his *Greek*-language predecessors. Given that already by around AD 60, the earliest probable date for the finished form of Matthew, Christianity around the empire had come to be more Gentile than Jewish, such consistent traces of Hebrew origins can only inspire confidence that Matthew was relying on either accurate information or very early Christian interpretation.

With these introductory comments we proceed to the commentary proper. Segments of text without explicit quotations of the Old Testament will be mined for the most probable allusions or echoes, which will be briefly presented. When clearer quotations emerge, we will slow down and adopt the six-part format of analysis: New Testament context, Old Testament context, use in Jewish sources, textual background, hermeneutic employed, and theological use.

Matthew 1:1–17

The very first verse of this Gospel leads the reader to suspect that the OT will play an important role in it: "A book of the genesis of Jesus Christ, son of David, son of Abraham" (1:1). The phrase *biblos geneseōs* may echo the Greek name for the first book of the Bible (Genesis) or be translated "genealogy," introducing 1:2–17 and reflecting the frequent scriptural use of records of ancestors to demonstrate one's pedigree (for the identical phrase, see Gen. 2:4; 5:1 in the LXX). More likely still, it can be rendered "origins" and refer to all of

Matt. 1–2 (cf., Gen. 5:1a as the introduction to 5:1–9:29). That Jesus is the Christ identifies him as the Jewish Messiah, the longed-for Savior of Israel. Even the name "Jesus" is a Grecized form of the Hebrew "Joshua," recalling the successor of Moses and liberator of God's people. As a descendant of David, Jesus comes as an Israelite king (see esp. 2 Sam. 7:11b–16; *Pss. Sol.* 17:21–18:7); as a descendant of Abraham, he will bless all the nations of the earth (Gen. 12:1–3). For more discussion of the segments of Matthew in which the OT is not explicitly quoted, see Blomberg 1992 and other standard commentaries.

Jesus' genealogy selects just enough ancestors ("begat" can mean "was the ancestor of") to create three series of fourteen names, probably employing *gematria* (the numerical value of the sum of the Hebrew consonants of a given word) on the name דוד ("David"), which equaled fourteen (ד = 4, ו = 6, ד = 4). The first series climaxes with David, the second with the deportation to Bablyon, a momentous turning point in Israelite history (2 Kings 25). All the names from "Abraham" to "Zerubbabel" appear in the OT. The patriarchs Abraham, Isaac, Jacob, and Judah figure prominently in Gen. 12–50. The other male names in 1:2–6a all correspond to 1 Chron. 2:3–15. "Solomon" through "Josiah" (1:6b–11) all appear in 1 Chron. 3:10–14, once we recognize that Azariah and Uzziah were the same person (cf. 2 Kings 15:1–2 with 2 Chron. 26:3). "Jeconiah" (1:12) is a variant form of "Jehoiachin," who with Shealtiel and Zerubbabel are mentioned in 1 Chron. 3:17–19. The rest of the names (from "Abiud" to "Jacob") are otherwise unknown. For the fullest study of the Gospels' genealogies, also supportive of their historical accuracy, see Masson 1982.

More interesting than the men are the women in Jesus' genealogy. Tamar, Rahab, Ruth, and Bathsheba ("Uriah's wife" [1:6]) were Gentiles but also women who were under suspicion, rightly or wrongly, of illicit sexual relations (see, respectively, Gen. 38; Josh. 2; Ruth 3; 2 Sam. 11). Mary was not a Gentile, but she did experience the stigma of a conception out of wedlock, shrouded in suspicion among those who did not believe the story of a virgin birth. See further Blomberg 1991a.

Matthew 1:18–25

Matthew 1:18–2:23 comprises Matthew's infancy narrative, which is constructed around five OT texts. The choice of material in this section is entirely dictated by these quotations. In this first paragraph this even extends to the wording of 1:18 ("having in her womb"), 1:20 ("behold"), and 1:21 ("she will give birth to a son"), all taken directly from the Isa. 7:14 quotation in 1:23 (cf. similar promises in Gen. 16:11; 17:19). Matthew also may intend that readers recall the childless matriarchs whose wombs God opened, most notably Sarah (Gen. 21:1–7), Rachel (Gen. 30:22–24), and Hannah (1 Sam. 1:20). Angelic announcements, of course, have numerous OT precedents (e.g., Gen. 16:11–12; Judg. 13:3–7), as do revelatory dreams (see esp. Gen. 37; 40; Dan. 2; 7; see also Gnuse 1990). The angel's words to Joseph remind us that he too was a descendant of David (1:20); Jesus would be eligible to be the Messiah through both his human mother, Mary, and his adoptive father, Joseph. The references to a righteous man, the language of the birth announcement, and the command in a dream not to fear also echo God's promises to Abraham about his son Isaac (see esp. Gen. 17:19; see also Erickson 2000). And, as noted above, the name "Jesus" (1:21) is merely the Greek equivalent of "Joshua," a common Jewish appellation, resulting no doubt from the heroics of Moses' successor by that same name.

1:23

A. NT Context. Joseph is engaged to Mary, but before the marriage and its sexual consummation, he discovers that she is pregnant. No doubt greatly upset, he nevertheless wants to minimize her shame and so plans a quiet divorce, the method of formally ending a Jewish betrothal. God's angel, however, appears to him in a dream, explaining that the child was conceived by means of the Holy Spirit and instructing him to continue plans for the marriage. He commands them to name the child "Jesus" ("Yahweh is salvation"), explaining that he will be a savior of his people, not from the physical oppression of the Roman occupying forces but from the spiritual enslavement of their sins. Joseph obeys, and the passage ends with Matthew reinforcing the supernatural nature of this conception, as the young couple refrains from sexual relations not only until after their marriage, but also after Jesus' birth.

In these remarkable events Matthew sees the fulfillment of prophecy about what is commonly referred to as the virgin birth (Isa. 7:14), bolstered by references to the child as "Immanuel," meaning "God with us" (Isa. 8:8, 10).

B. OT Context. The Lord is speaking to King Ahaz of Judah, challenging him to ask for a sign to confirm God's promise that he would destroy the two kings from the lands to the north that were currently threatening Judah (Isa. 7:10–11), Rezin in Aram and Pekah in Israel (see 7:1). Ahaz protests that he will not test the Lord (7:12), but Isaiah, speaking for God, berates Ahaz for trying God's patience with his reply, probably recognizing his insincerity (7:13). Then comes the famous prophecy of the imminent birth of a child to a young woman of marriageable age (Heb. 'almâ). It is widely agreed that the Hebrew word, in and of itself, need carry no more than this meaning (see, e.g., Walton 1997; cf. NRSV), a child who will be God's sign (7:14). Before the child is old enough to know the difference between right and wrong, the lands of the dreaded kings will be laid waste (7:15–16). But before that can be interpreted as very good news, the prophet adds that they will be replaced by an even worse invader: Assyria (7:17).

Who is this special child? Although a handful of very conservative scholars insist on seeing solely a messianic prophecy here (e.g., Motyer 1993: 84–86; Reymond 1989), most recognize that there is at least a provisional fulfillment in Isaiah's day, given the explicit statements of 7:15–16. Many have suggested Ahaz's royal son, King Hezekiah, or some anonymous prophet, or a collective remnant in Israel (for a thorough survey of these and related exegetical options, see Willis 1980: 157–69), but the most probable interpretation is that Isaiah's prophecy refers to his own son Maher-Shalal-Hash-Baz (e.g., Oswalt 1986–1998: 1:213). Isaiah 8:3, introducing this son, echoes the language of 7:14 as Isaiah goes to his wife, and she conceives and then gives birth to the child with this symbolic name ("quick to the plunder, swift to the spoil" [NIV mg.]). The next verse repeats the sense of 7:15, describing how the wealth of Damascus (in Aram) and Samaria (in Israel) will be plundered before the child can say

"My father" or "My mother" (8:4). This same son is called "Immanuel" in 8:8, which is explained in 8:10 as "God with us," accounting for Matthew's linking the two portions of Isaiah together. In 8:18 Isaiah describes his two sons, Maher-Shalal-Hash-Baz and Shear-Jashub (cf. 7:3), as "signs and symbols in Israel," which description ties back in with the sign God promised in 7:11, 14. But in 9:1–7 the more distant future is in view, as exiles are once again restored to Galilee. Here, in 9:6, another description of the birth of a wonderful child appears, one who can be called "Almighty God," "Eternal Father," and "Prince of Peace," who will rule from David's throne and establish universal justice forever—prophecies that scarcely could have been fulfilled in a mere earthly king.

C. Use in Jewish Sources. Unfortunately, there are no demonstrably pre-Christian Jewish texts that reflect on the meaning of Isa. 7:14. However, the LXX translated 'almâ with parthenos, a Greek term that more consistently meant "virgin." This would suggest that already before the NT age at least some Jews had come to link the passages in Isa. 7–9 together and to deduce that there would be an additional, longer-term fulfillment of the birth of a messianic king, portended by a more supernatural conception (Hindson 1978: 67–70; see also Hagner 1993: 20). Post-Christian Jewish sources would at times link this text with Hezekiah, who was also viewed as a type of the Messiah (e.g., *Num. Rab.* on Isa. 7:48; see Davies and Allison 1988–1997: 1:213), and it is not likely that a messianic interpretation was first suggested in an era when Christians were already known to use this text in their apologetic. But we must confess that we have no certain knowledge of Jewish interpretation during the pre-Christian period.

D. Textual Background. The MT matches the LXX and Matthew for the first clause, "the virgin shall conceive and bear a son." Then the MT reads, "she will call him," whereas the LXX has, "you will call him," and Matthew writes, "they will call him." LXX ℵ also contains the third-person plural, so Matthew may have been following a variant form of the LXX (Menken 2004a: 117–31). Or he could have been writing in a Semitized form of Greek in which the third-person plural is somewhat equivalent to a passive form such as "his name will be called" (Archer and Chirichigno 1983: 95). Perhaps more likely still, because the "they" in Matthew clearly refers back to the people whose sins Jesus will forgive (1:21), the change may simply reflect Matthew's paraphrase to make the quotation better fit his context. Brown (1993: 152) notes that this is the most commonly accepted explanation.

E. Hermeneutic Employed. As noted above, some conservatives treat this as direct, predictive prophecy. The majority of scholars deny any predictive element (for a representative treatment, see J. D. W. Watts 1985: 98–104). Better than both of these approaches, however, is the concept of double fulfillment (for the hermeneutic in general, see Blomberg 2002b; for this specific passage, see Gundry 1994: 25). Matthew recognized that Isaiah's son fulfilled the dimension of the prophecy that required a child to be born in the immediate future. But the larger, eschatological context, especially of Isa. 9:1–7, depicted a son, never clearly distinguished from Isaiah's, who would be a divine, messianic king. That dimension was fulfilled in Jesus (similarly, Schibler 1995: 103–4), who was unequivocally born to a young woman of marriageable age, but to a woman who also was a virgin at the time of the conception. Whether or not Matthew was aware of any previous interpretation of Isa. 7:14 as referring to a sexually chaste woman, the "coincidence" of Jesus being born of a virgin was too striking not to be divinely intended. Matthew could indeed speak of Isaiah's prophecy as fulfilled in Christ. The canonical form of Isaiah was already pointing in this twofold direction (Williamson 1998).

F. Theological Use. Matthew's primary doctrinal intent is, of course, christological. Conceived of a virgin, Jesus is a messianic king but also the embodiment of divine presence among his people. Both themes are important for Matthew's Gospel, the first especially in these infancy stories and the passion narratives (see Nolan 1979), and the second as an *inclusio* around Matthew's entire narrative (cf. Matt. 28:18–20; see Kupp 1996). Soteriology lies close at hand too, with the promise of salvation from sin. Given first-century Jewish experience of Roman imperialism, this redefinition of the true slave-master proves all the more poignant (see Carter 2000). The larger contexts in both Isaiah and Matthew remind us that the flip sides of these offers of salvation involve judgment on those who reject it (Watts 2004).

Matthew 2:1–12

From Jesus' supernatural conception, Matthew turns to the story of the magi. Jewish readers would know, of course, that Bethlehem was the birthplace of David, the ancestor of the messianic king (1 Sam. 16:4). The star that guided the magi might have called to mind Num. 24:17, a messianic text in Jewish apocalyptic thought, in which a metaphorical star would come from Jacob or a scepter from Israel (see Viviano 1996). In this event, the magi may replace Balaam as unlikely Gentile witnesses to God's redemption (Davies and Allison 1988–1997: 1:231). "All Jerusalem" becoming troubled (2:3) may echo 2 Sam. 4:1. Verse 11 probably alludes to Ps. 72:10–11, 15, in which the kings of distant lands bring gifts and tribute to the ruler of Israel, and/or Isa. 60:6, in which Shebans will come to Israel in the age to come bearing gold and incense (Brown 1993: 187–88). Davies and Allison (1988–1997: 1:250–51) find a possible Jesus/Solomon typology here too, in part because gold and frankincense were firmly associated with the temple that Solomon built (1 Kings 10:2, 25; 1 Chron. 9:29; 2 Chron. 9:24; Neh. 13:5, 9). In the OT, faithful Israelites prove superior to foreign magicians (Gen. 41; Exod. 7–10; Dan. 2), but here in Matt. 2 the tables are turned.

2:6

A. NT Context. The explicit OT quotation in this section deals with Jesus' birthplace. Matthew 2:1–12 is unified in focusing on the events surrounding Bethlehem. The supernatural star guides the magi to the nearby capital city of Jerusalem (2:1–3). Herod, after consulting his priestly and scribal advisors, learns that the Messiah was to be born in the adjacent village (2:4–6). He insists that the magi go and report back to him what they discover there, but they are warned in a dream, presumably by an angel, not to do so (2:7–12).

B. OT Context. Micah prophesied in the eighth century BC, warning both Israel and Judah of impending judgment. As so often happens with the OT prophets, short- and long-range prophecies are starkly juxtaposed. Micah 4:6–13 alternates between predictions of the more distant return from exile (4:6–8, 13) and of more imminent judgment (4:9–12). Micah 5 begins with this latter theme (v. 1), but the rest of the chapter returns to the more distant future, promising a ruler who will shepherd his flock in the Lord's strength and majesty and bring peace to the land (vv. 2–5a). Indeed, a complete cadre of rulers will one day destroy Assyria (5:5b–6), leaving the remnant of Israel triumphant (5:7–9) and purged of their past idolatry (5:10–15). In this context 5:2 is most naturally taken as messianic. Micah consciously predicted that the tiny city of Bethlehem would produce an Israelite king "whose goings out are from aforetime, from ancient times [or, 'from days of eternity']." Though not as clear as Isa. 9:6, this final clause suggests a king who is more than a mere human (see McComiskey 1985: 427). Some scholars have seen Mic. 5:3 as then consciously alluding to Isa. 7:14: the woman who gives birth, ending the time of Israel's abandonment, is the virgin who will supernaturally conceive (e.g., L. C. Allen 1976: 345). But the common prophetic motif of messianic birth pangs is applied to the *corporate* sufferings of Israel often enough to make such an allusion by no means secure.

C. Use in Jewish Sources. The Targum of the Minor Prophets very explicitly takes this text as messianic: "And you, O Bethlehem Ephrathah, *you who were too small to be numbered among the thousands of the house* of Judah, from you shall come forth *before me the anointed One, to exercise dominion* over Israel, *he whose name was mentioned* from of old, from ancient times." (All translations from Targumim of various minor prophets are taken from Cathcart and Gordon 1989. The italicized material reflects changes from the MT here and throughout quotations from the Targumim of all the OT books.) The title "the anointed One" denotes the messianic king, but the addition of "he whose name was mentioned" deflects interpreters from assuming the Messiah to be divine and thus compromising Jewish monotheism. Other post-Christian rabbinic literature recognized that the Messiah was to be born in Bethlehem (e.g., *Tg. Ps.-J.* Gen. 35:21), so there is no reason to reject the claim of the Gospels that this information was recognized already in the first century. Matthew 2:5 claims that Herod received this information from the Jewish leaders of whom he inquired, while John 7:42 depicts some of Jesus' Jerusalem audience as unwilling to think of him as the Messiah because they believed that he was born in Galilee, not in

Bethlehem as "Scripture says." *Sibylline Oracles* 8:479 also affirms that "Bethlehem was said to be the divinely named homeland of the Word" (Charlesworth 1983–1985: 1:428). This is clearly a Christian interpolation, but like the evidence from Matthew and John, it reflects the conviction that Jews already agreed on the birthplace of the Messiah.

D. Textual Background. A literal translation of Mic. 5:1 MT (5:2 ET) reads, "And you Bethlehem Ephrathah, little [or, 'insignificant'] among the thousands [or, 'clans'] of Judah, from you to me will go forth to be a ruler in Israel...." Micah 5:1 LXX (5:2 ET) translates the Hebrew quite literally, but adds "house of" before "Ephrathah" and changes "thousands" to "rulers of thousands." Matthew follows the LXX verbatim for "and you Bethlehem," replaces "(house of) Ephrathah" with "land of Judah," adds "by no means" before "little," changes the adjective to the superlative form "least," replaces "rulers of thousands" with "governors," omits "to me," but then reproduces "out of you will go forth" using LXX wording. The final clause in Matt. 2:6, perhaps inspired by the theme of Mic. 5:4 (Keener 1999: 103n87), picks up the language of 2 Sam. 5:2: "you will shepherd my people Israel," with the final five Greek words following the LXX verbatim. There may be an allusion to the almost identical statement in 1 Chron. 11:2 as well.

Matthew's text form resembles targumic and midrashic approaches that often reproduce some words of the MT verbatim, paraphrase others, insert additional texts, and add interpretive commentary (an observation overly played down in Heater 1983 and exaggerated in Petrotta 1985; 1990). There is not enough verbal parallelism to prove dependence on the LXX. "Land of Judah" could have been substituted for "Ephrathah" to clarify for Matthew's audience that it was the Bethlehem five miles south of Jerusalem, not the one in Galilee (see Josh. 19:15) that was meant (Archer and Chirichigno 1983: 157). The addition of "by no means" creates a formal but not a material contradiction (Carson 1984: 88). Bethlehem was insignificant by worldly standards, but once it was graced with the birth of the Messiah, it was no longer insignificant, at least not by God's standards. The rest of Matthew's differences from the LXX do not alter the essential meaning and could well have resulted from his independent translation of the MT, stressing the Davidic, regal nature of this figure (Gundry 1994: 29; Menken 2004a: 255–63 argues for Matthew's use of a special M source).

E. Hermeneutic Employed. This is the only OT text in Matt. 1–2 not explicitly described as "fulfilling" prophecy. If 2:6 is the continuation of the Jewish leaders' words, it could be that Matthew was "unwilling to attribute the fulfillment formula to the hostile high priests and scribes" (Luz 1989: 130). This is also the only text of the five in the infancy narrative that can be viewed via a very straightforward scheme of prediction and fulfillment, with no multiple or deeper levels of meaning or use of typology. Micah prophesied that the Messiah would be born in Bethlehem, and now it has happened (see Hagner 1993: 29–30; Lust 1997: 82).

F. Theological Use. The four OT quotations in Matt. 2 focus on key locations that played a significant role in Christ's birth and infancy: Bethlehem, Egypt, Ramah, and Nazareth (Stendahl 1960). Matthew's christological focus here is on Jesus as the messianic shepherd (cf. Ezek. 34). Matthew 2:1–12 as a whole contrasts Jesus' legitimate kingship and sovereignty with the illegitimate roles of Herod and the Jewish leaders in Jerusalem, many of whom he had appointed (Blomberg 1991a). To the extent that the Messiah ushers in the age of salvation for God's people, there are soteriological implications here too, but they are not as explicit as in 1:18–25.

Matthew 2:13–15

The entire contents of this short paragraph are dictated by the need to explain the fulfillment of Hosea's "prophecy." Like Moses rescued from the edict to kill the Israelites' baby boys (Exod. 1:15–2:10), Jesus is spared from the slaughter of the "innocents" in Bethlehem. Was 1 Kings 11:40 also in Matthew's mind as he phrased this brief narrative in this fashion?

2:15

A. NT Context. The third of the five OT quotations that govern Matt. 1:18–2:23 relates to the holy family's flight to and return from Egypt. The Lord's angel warns Joseph that Herod will look for baby Jesus in order to kill him, so they must leave the country. They obey and stay away until Herod has died (2:13–15a). Matthew will not narrate the family's return to Israel until 2:19–23, because another event intervenes in which he sees prophecy fulfilled: the massacre of the babies in and around Bethlehem (2:16–18). But he inserts the reference to the prophecy about coming out of Egypt already here in order to create five discrete pericopes concerning five fulfillments of prophecy. Thus we must supply what is only implicit: it is baby Jesus' return from Egypt, after their original flight from Herod, that matches Hosea's declaration that God's son has been called out of Egypt.

B. OT Context. Hosea 11:1 is a reference to the exodus, pure and simple. Hosea 10 has already described the earlier glory days of Israel that have been supplanted by the wickedness of the current nation. Hosea 11 repeats this pattern. Hosea 11:1 reflects synonymous parallelism: "When Israel was a youth, I loved him, and from Egypt I called my son." Israel is the son; God's love is demonstrated by rescuing Israel from slavery in Egypt. But 11:2–7 goes on to lament how Israel has wandered increasingly further astray from the Lord and to predict their future return to enslavement—that is, exile—in Egypt (11:5). As consistently happens in the prophets, though, God's final word is one of restoration. Verses 8–11 poignantly describe how God can never fully give his people up and will one day bring them back from exile.

C. Use in Jewish Sources. The exodus event was regularly seen in the rabbinic literature as a type of the salvation of the messianic age to come (see Str-B 1:85–88). However, there are no extant Jewish uses, before or after the first century, that explicitly link Hos. 11:1 with this typology or suggest that it was ever understood as explicitly messianic.

D. Textual Background. The LXX uses a compound verb, *metakaleō* ("summon"), while Matthew uses the simple *kaleō* ("call"). The LXX changes the Hebrew "my son" to "his children," perhaps because 11:2 proceeds to refer to Israel with the third-person plural pronoun "they." Matthew restores "my son" in his translation. Both changes could be viewed as modifying the LXX to bring it more in line with the MT, but the quotation is too short to prove literary dependence (*contra* Menken 2004a: 133–42). Matthew may well have been creating his own independent, literal translation of the Hebrew.

E. Hermeneutic Employed. Occasionally, attempts have been made to argue that "son" in Hosea is messianic, as in various other parts of the OT (e.g., Ps. 2:7; 89:26–27; 2 Sam. 7:14; and esp. Num. 24:7–8 LXX, in which the messianic star or scepter as an individual, not the Israelites as a people [as in the MT], is brought out of Egypt; see Kaiser 1985: 49). But none of the other five uses of "son" in Hosea suggests this at all. The term is used merely to refer to literal, biological offspring (1:1 [2x], 3, 8) and to compare Ephraim to an unwise child (13:13). It has also been suggested that Hosea consciously employed a messianic reading of the exodus narrative (Sailhamer 2001), but the connections postulated seem overly subtle (McCartney and Enns 2001). It is, however, plausible to suggest that Num. 24:8 LXX combined with the history of Jesus to lead Matthew to Hos. 11:1 (Davies and Allison 1988–1997: 1:262).

It is better, though, to understand Matthew's actual use of Hos. 11:1 as a classic example of pure typology: "the recognition of a correspondence between New and Old Testament events, based on a conviction of the unchanging character of the principles of God's working" (France 1985: 40; see also Goppelt 1982). The original event need not have been intentionally viewed as forward-looking by the OT author; for believing Jews, merely to discern striking parallels between God's actions in history, especially in decisive moments of revelation and redemption, could convince them of divinely intended "coincidence." Because the concept of typology has been abused in the history of interpretation, some writers prefer to speak of "correspondence in history" or "analogical correspondence," but the meaning is essentially the same (see, respectively, Snodgrass 2001: 215; Howard 1986). That Israel had been delivered from Egypt, that Israel would again be exiled there but again restored, and that the child believed to be the Messiah also had to return to Israel from Egypt formed too striking a set of parallels for Matthew to attribute them to chance. God clearly was at work orchestrating the entire series of events (see Garrett 1997: 220–22; cf. Hagner 1993: 36). The logic is not identical to the classic "proof from prophecy" arguments of much of church history, but, given the theistic worldview that it presupposes, it was every bit as compelling in first-century Judaism.

F. Theological Use. "Out of Egypt" is the first of several parallels in Matthew's infancy narrative to events from the life of Moses, leading some to speak of a christological portrait of Jesus as a "new Moses" (on this theme in Matthew more generally, see Allison 1993; Aus 2004). This motif is clearer elsewhere, however; here the parallel is more directly with Israel as a people. Clearly, though, a "new exodus" motif is present (France 1981). Moreover, Jesus will prove faithful where the nation had been faithless; in numerous respects he recapitulates the history of Israel as a whole (see Kynes 1991). Clearer still is Matthew's conviction that Jesus is God's divine Son, both as regal Messiah and as uniquely intimate with his Father. Luz (1989: 146) observes that "son" is the only christological title in all of Matt. 2, making it that much more important. On the close link between "Son of God" and "Messiah" in Matthew, see Kingsbury 1975, but note also the important qualifications in Verseput 1987. More generally, the passage also demonstrates God's providential care for his people.

Matthew 2:16–18

The fourth OT passage in which Matthew finds a parallel to the events surrounding Jesus' birth accounts for the contents of this small paragraph. The massacre of the infants calls to mind Pharaoh's orders to the Hebrew midwives to kill all the baby boys they delivered (Exod. 1:15–16, 22).

2:18

A. NT Context. For the first time, Matthew specifies the prophet whom he is citing, in this case, Jeremiah. When Herod recognizes that the magi have left without reporting back to him, he decides to kill all the baby boys in Bethlehem and its environs up through two years of age, "according to the time he carefully ascertained from the magi" (2:16). This suggests that it may now be nearly two years since Jesus' birth. This horrible slaughter would, of course, bring immense grief to the mothers who lost their children (2:17–18).

B. OT Context. Almost all of Jer. 31 describes the future days of God's new covenant with his people, when he will restore them to their land, forgive their sins, and bless them with peace and prosperity. Verses 1–14 and 16–20 enunciate all of these themes. Verses 21–22 call Israel to return to their land and faith on the basis of God's promises that Jeremiah has just announced. Verses 23–30 again employ the form of future predictions, leading to the passage that explicitly anticipates a "new covenant" (31:31–35), a passage quoted at length in Heb. 8:8–12 as having been fulfilled in Jesus (cf. also Heb. 10:16–17). Jesus himself alluded to this new covenant in his words about the bread and cup at his final supper (Luke 22:20; 1 Cor. 11:25), as did Paul in contrasting the periods of time before and after the coming of Christ (2 Cor. 3:6).

Tucked into these wonderful promises is Jer. 31:15, the lone verse in this chapter that reflects the current grief surrounding the Assyrian and Babylonian exiles. Jewish mothers have watched their sons go off to battle, some to die and others to be carried away captive to distant lands. Still more were forcibly evicted from Israel to ensure that the nation would not pose a military threat in the future. Ramah was six miles north of Jerusalem; departing captives from Judah's capital had to go through it on the road to the lands of the northern invaders (Jer. 40:1). Ramah was thus about the same distance north of Jerusalem as Bethlehem was south, along the same road. Rachel is said to have been buried on the way to Bethlehem (Gen. 35:19–20), and more explicitly near the border of Benjamin (1 Sam. 10:2), which would have been very close to Ramah. Thus it was natural to personify the grieving mothers in Israel as "Rachel weeping for her children." Keown, Scalise, and Smothers (1995: 119) note how Rachel was uniquely qualified to be personified in this fashion: she died "on the way" to the promised land (Gen. 35:19), her last words expressed her sorrow (Gen. 35:18), death in childbirth proved the extent of her motherly love, and as mother of Israel, she does not forget her children (Isa. 49:15). That Rachel's children, along with the other sons of Jacob, also had to leave the promised land (Gen. 42–50) adds to the appropriateness of this personification, although Rachel herself had died by that time. Harrison (1973: 136), however, thinks that Rachel's ghost is depicted as mourning the exile from the afterlife, in which case she could have mourned her family's flight from Canaan

as well. Further links between Jacob's family and Jeremiah's words appear when Jacob refuses to be comforted at the initial loss of Joseph (Gen. 37:35), and when Joseph is described as no longer existing (esp. Gen. 37:30; 42:32, 36). "Things may look hopeless . . . but God has a plan" (Brown-Gutoff 1991: 185).

C. Use in Jewish Sources. The Targum on Jer. 31:15 reads, "Thus says the Lord: 'The voice has been heard *in the height of the world, the house of Israel who weep* and lament *after Jeremiah the prophet, when Nebuzaradan, the chief of the killers, sent him from Ramah,* with a dirge; *and those who* weep *for* the bitterness *of Jerusalem,* as she weeps for her children, refusing to be comforted for her children, because they *have gone into exile.*'" (All translations from the Jeremiah Targum are taken from Hayward 1986.) The personification of Rachel is replaced with the literal referent "the house of Israel," her children are explicitly identified as Jeremiah the prophet and others from Jerusalem, and the cryptic Hebrew "because they are not" is explained as the people's departure into exile. There also seems to be a desire to clarify why Ramah appeared in the original OT text, hence the allusion to Nebuzaradan's action (see Jer. 40:1). All of these explanations elaborate on the natural meaning of the more poetic MT and fit an understanding of the passage that Matthew could have presupposed. In later rabbinic literature, Rachel becomes a consummate mourner (Whitters 2006: 236–37). But there is nothing here or in other ancient Jewish literature to suggest that anyone specifically looked for a similar event to recur in the context of the birth of the Messiah.

D. Textual Background. The MT reads literally, "A voice in Ramah is heard, a lamentation, weeping and bitterness, Rachel weeping for her children. She refuses to be comforted for her children because he is not" (thus *BHS*, but all the ancient versions read, "because they are not," which may well reflect the original Hebrew). The LXX (Jer. 38:15) offers a reasonably literal translation throughout, except that it omits the first "for her children," which is redundant anyway. Matthew uses the identical wording as the LXX for the first clause, omits the first of the three terms for "crying," puts the remaining two in the smoother nominative case (vs. the LXX's genitive), adds the adjective *polys* ("great" crying—a reasonable interpretation), changes the compound middle participle for "weeping" to a simple active form (a stylistic improvement), restores the MT's first use of "for her children" (and deletes the second where the LXX had preserved it), and uses a more literal Greek verb to translate "comforted." The ten Greek words exactly paralleled in the LXX could suggest literary dependence, combined with revisions to create a smoother but also more literal rendering of the Hebrew. But the words repeated verbatim are natural choices for translation, and the fact that Matthew has chosen to delete the first of the MT's "for her children" rather than the second could suggest independent translation from the Hebrew. Soarés Prabhu (1976: 253) adopts a mediating perspective: "We have here a targumic translation from the Hebrew, with perhaps some reminiscence of the LXX."

E. Hermeneutic Employed. Matthew is employing a very similar kind of typology to what we saw in 2:15 with Hos. 11:1. The text in Jeremiah is not a prediction, nor does it even use the future tense. But the parallel of mothers near Ramah bemoaning the loss of their children is too striking for the believing Jew to see it as a coincidence; it must be divinely intended. That Ramah evokes memories of Rachel's tomb and of the departure of her children centuries earlier makes the choice of OT quotation for Matthew that much more appropriate. Davies and Allison (1988–1997: 1:269) note that two other OT prophecies involve Ramah, both with a reference to a disaster (Isa. 10:29; Hos. 5:8), so that "Ramah might be regarded as a city of sadness *par excellence.*" Keener (1999: 111) notes that "some later rabbis even said that Jacob buried Rachel in Bethlehem so that she could pray for the exiles when they later passed that way." Jeremiah has already employed the Genesis material somewhat typologically in the new context of exile to Babylon; how much more appropriate for Matthew to do so in the context of the Messiah's birth, especially since virtually all of the rest of Jer. 31 speaks explicitly of the coming new age. Matthew could well have intended for the astute Jewish listener to hear an echo of Jer. 31:16 as well, as God immediately calls on the mothers in Israel to restrain their weeping because their work will be rewarded, and their children will one day return from exile. Moreover,

the events of Matt. 2:13–18 belong together. It was danger from Herod that caused Joseph and his family to flee to Egypt; but they will return, like the exiles of old, as the last fulfillment quotation in Matt. 2 will clarify (see Becking 1994).

F. Theological Use. Matthew continues to point out key geographical locations surrounding the fulfillment of prophecy in the events of Christ's infancy (see above, p. 7). As just noted, there might be implicit eschatology in the echo of return from exile. There may well be "new Moses" typology in baby Jesus, like baby Moses, being preserved from the threat of death ordered by a wicked ruler for the baby boys around him. And this, of course, reminds us of the nature of God's sovereignty and providence. God is not beyond permitting terrible evil in this world, even to comparatively innocent people (see Knowles 1993: 52). This occurs throughout both Testaments as an explicit legacy of the fall (Gen. 3:14–19; Rom. 8:20–23). But Matthew's recognition of divine intention in all of this, even if only indirect, also reminds us, as Paul said, that God is working for good in all things for those who love him (Rom. 8:28). God has spared the Messiah from Herod's massacre so that Jesus can live to complete all of God's will for his life, including the atonement for the sins of humanity (recall Matt. 1:21; cf. 27:25) and the conquest of the very evil that has caused this current "injustice" (see Erickson 1996). "Again, in Matthew's perspective Jesus is understood as summarizing the whole experience of Israel as well as bringing it to fulfillment" (Hagner 1993: 38). And if Matthew presupposed the Targum's reading cited above, he may also see Jesus as a new and greater Jeremiah (i.e., a suffering prophet, who also spent time in Egypt [Jer. 43–44]; see Menken 1984).

Matthew 2:19–23

An angel appearing to Joseph in a dream in 2:19 creates a literary *inclusio* with 1:20 (for OT background, see comments there). Verse 20b alludes to Exod. 4:19, with verbal parallelism for most of the clause, "for those seeking (your/the child's) life have died." But whereas in Exodus God told Moses to go back to Egypt, here he instructs Joseph to leave Egypt. The paragraph as a whole sets the stage for the final fulfillment quotation of Matt. 1–2: "He shall be called a Nazarene" (2:23).

This text is introduced very similarly to the other four explicit OT quotations in Matthew's infancy narrative. But no OT text ever declares that anyone will be called a Nazarene! Nor does any known apocryphal or pseudepigraphal text include such a statement. How, then, can Matthew think that prophecy is fulfilled? Three main explanations have been suggested. First, he may be making a play on words, noting the similarity between "Nazarene" and the Hebrew *nēṣer* ("branch"), especially in light of the use of this term as a messianic title in Isa. 11:1 (see Hagner 1993: 41–42; Pesch 1994: 174). Second, he may be using "Nazarene" as a derogatory slang term for someone from the insignificant little town of Nazareth in Galilee—the same attitude that seems to be reflected by Nathanael in John 1:46: "Can any good thing be from Nazareth?" Isaiah 53:2, a text that Christians would come to associate with Jesus in his role as Suffering Servant, and that spoke of one who grew up like a tender shoot but had no beauty or majesty to make him humanly attractive, could tie in with this view of Nazarenes as "backwoodsmen" or "country bumpkins" (see France 1985: 88–89). Third, perhaps Matthew is alluding to Judg. 13:7, in which God tells Samson's mother that her son will be a Nazirite, especially since this verse also includes a promise that the woman will conceive and bear a son, similar to Matt. 1:21 (see Menken 2004a: 161–77). Although Jesus was not a literal Nazirite (refraining from strong drink and haircuts), he could be seen as a charismatic individual empowered by the Spirit just as Samson had been (Berger 1996; J. A. Sanders 1994). Alternatively, "Nazirite" could mean "holy," and Matthew could be referring to Isa. 4:3 by substituting the former word for the latter (Brown 1993: 223–25; Soarés Prabhu 1976: 215).

The fact that this is the only place in the entire Gospel where Matthew makes reference to "prophets" in the plural (rather than a singular "prophet") as the source of an OT reference suggests that he knows that he is not quoting one text directly but rather is summing up a theme found in several prophetic texts. Davies and Allison (1988–1997: 1:275) note that John 7:38; Rom. 11:8; and James 4:5 attribute to Scripture sentences that at best paraphrase the substance of several OT passages; there is also a rabbinic example in *b. Ketub.* 111a. Indeed, perhaps more than one of the above passages is in view. It is interesting that Isa. 11:1 and 53:2 both refer to a "shoot," although they do not use the identical words in the Hebrew. Perhaps Matthew intended both of the first two meanings proposed above. Orthographically, it is harder to derive "Nazirite" from the Greek of Matt. 2:23 (*Nazōraios*) than "Nazarene," since the long *o/a* interchange is attested elsewhere in Galilean Aramaic, but not *o/i* (Ruger 1981). It is also difficult to imagine Matthew thinking of Jesus as a Nazirite even figuratively, since his ministry was otherwise so far removed from the asceticism of the literal Nazirites.

Whatever the precise origin of the quotation (better understood as an allusion), Matthew continues his interest in geographical locations of divinely intended significance surrounding Jesus' early years. Depending on the specifics of the allusion, he may be furthering his interest in presenting Jesus as regal prince or hinting at his roles as Suffering Servant or Spirit-anointed holy man.

Matthew 3:1–17

Matthew now jumps ahead to the events that would inaugurate Jesus' public ministry as an adult. As in the other three Gospels, this means introducing John the Baptist. The only explicit OT quotation in all of Matt. 3 comes near the beginning (v. 3), but the entire chapter demonstrates how John fulfills this prophecy, preparing the way of the Lord. That preparation involves calling Israel to repentance, a standard OT prophetic theme, which is symbolized by baptism, the hallmark of John's ministry (3:1–12). It will culminate in John's baptism of Jesus himself (3:13–17). On the John the Baptist material in the Gospels more generally, see Webb 1991.

3:1–12

The Judean wilderness (3:1) will make Jewish readers think of Moses leading the Israelites into and out of the wilderness (see esp. Numbers). The imminence of the kingdom of heaven (3:2) may call to mind various texts, from the messianic psalms to Daniel, that look forward to God's kingly reign being more perfectly established in the future. John's attire is intentionally that of a prophet (3:4), modeled after Elijah (2 Kings 1:8; cf. Zech. 13:4). His diet was that of a desert ascetic (Exod. 16:31; for locusts as food, see Lev. 11:22). Fleeing from God's wrath (3:7) may echo language like that of Zech. 14:5. The idea that one's nationality guaranteed one's spiritual safety (3:9) harked back to Israel's elect status as the sole nation of the world with whom God had made his covenant (see esp. Deuteronomy), but the cycles of judgment and redemption throughout the OT should have made it obvious that such complacency was unjustified. The metaphor of the axe laid at the root of the trees (3:10) may echo Isa. 10:34 (Bauckham 1995). Eschatological fire appears paradigmatically in Isa. 66:24. That non-Jews can be blessed through Abraham reflects God's promise to the patriarch as early as Gen. 12:1–3. The "one coming after me" in 3:11 probably should be understood as a messianic title, alluding to Ps. 118:26 and perhaps echoing Ps. 40:7 (see Kirchevel 1994). Water baptism would call to mind the spiritual cleansing predicted in texts such as Ezek. 36:25–27. Spirit and fire are linked in Isa. 4:4 and 30:27–28 (Davies and Allison 1988–1997: 1:317).

3:3

A. NT Context. Once again, Matthew uses the formula "this is the thing having been spoken through . . . the prophet," and, as in 2:17, he names the prophet, this time Isaiah. This introduction closely follows the model of those in Matt. 1–2, except that the actual word for "fulfillment" is lacking. Gundry (1994: 44) thinks that Matthew consciously reserves the verb "fulfill" for texts referring to Jesus. This is also the first of Matthew's OT quotations in which he is following Mark, and the only one paralleled in Mark in which he uses such an elaborate formulaic introduction. The Greek of the quotation in Matt. 3:3 exactly matches its counterpart in Mark 1:3. Mark has a longer, composite quotation, however, incorporating elements of Mal. 3:1 as well, which Matthew will use in a later context (Matt. 11:10). John 1:23 has a shorter excerpt of Isa. 40:3, attributed directly to the Baptist, with slightly different wording that may reflect independent tradition. All three Gospels apply the text to the preaching of John the Baptist. Apparently interpreting "in the wilderness" as referring to the location

in which the voice cries out, Matthew sees the fulfillment of Isaiah's prophecy in the preaching of John in the Judean desert (3:1). His message of repentance (3:2), symbolized by the ritual of baptism (3:6) and summarized by the concepts of fleeing from God's wrath (3:7) and of bearing fruit (3:8), corresponds to Isaiah's call to "prepare the way of the LORD, make straight his paths" (40:3). John goes on to explain that the moral cleansing of the nation for which he calls does indeed precede the ministry of a much greater individual who will baptize with the Spirit and with fire, providing the promised salvation and judgment of the Lord (3:11–12).

B. OT Context. Isaiah 40:3 comes virtually at the very beginning of the second part of Isaiah (Isa. 40–66), in which the prophecy shifts abruptly from present judgment to future restoration after both the Assyrian and the Babylonian captivities. Motyer (1993: 300) takes a minority view that sees Isaiah speaking only of God coming to his people and not also of the exiles returning from Babylon, but Isa. 35:8–10 makes this difficult to sustain. Chapter 40 begins this part of the book with the proclamation of comfort and tender speech to Jerusalem, whose sins, God assures, have been forgiven (vv. 1–2). Isaiah 40:3 harks back to the imagery of 26:7 with its teaching about God making the ways or paths of the righteous smooth. But even the land and its topography are metaphorically changing, as 40:4 describes the leveling of the mountains, the elevation of the valleys, and the smoothing out of rugged places. Then the Lord's glory will be revealed and all humanity will see it (40:5). Nothing in the immediate context of Isa. 40 suggests that Isaiah is referring to anyone other than Yahweh himself returning to Israel as king (Goldingay 2005: 5–7), but the references to special sons in Isa. 7–9 and to the messianic branch in Isa. 11, along with the Servant Songs yet to come (beginning in Isa. 42), do indicate God revealing himself through a specially anointed agent. The "shepherding" imagery of a text as close to ours as 40:11 also dovetails with other prophecies in which a messianic figure is likened to a shepherd (esp. Ezek. 34).

C. Use in Jewish Sources. The most significant pre-Christian Jewish uses of Isa. 40:3 appear in the Dead Sea Scrolls. The *Rule of the Community* declares,

And when these have become a community in Israel in compliance with these arrangements they are to be segregated from within the dwelling of the men of sin to walk to the desert in order to open there His path. As it is written: "In the desert, prepare the way of [YHWH], straighten in the steppe a roadway for our God." This is the study of the law wh[i]ch he commanded through the hand of Moses, in order to act in compliance with all that has been revealed from age to age, and according to what the prophets have revealed through his holy spirit. (1QS VIII, 12–16) (All quotations from the Dead Sea Scrolls are from García Martínez and Tigchelaar 1997.)

In short, the Essenes at Qumran viewed their monastic community as the fulfillment of Isa. 40:3. This same interpretation is reflected in an allusion to this Scripture in 1QS IX, 19–20. An allusion in 1QS IV, 1–2 applies the metaphor of making straight paths to the establishment of justice, truth, and the respect for the precepts of God. An even longer explicit quotation of Isa. 40:1–5 appears in a fragment of another Qumran scroll (4Q176 1–2 I, 4–9), but not enough context has been preserved for us to know how it was used.

From a very different, Pharisaic branch of Judaism, *Pss. Sol.* 8:17 seems to allude to this text when it refers to the Jewish leaders' (probably literal) grading of rough roads to Jerusalem to prepare the way for the conquering Roman general Pompey to enter the city. This part of the welcome was appropriate for a king, albeit ironic because the king was a foreign invader. Other texts, especially apocalyptic ones, allude to Isa. 40:4–5 with its topographical transformations and its expectations of seeing the Lord's glory in the context of a coming new age (esp. *1 En.* 1:6; Bar. 5:7; *As. Mos.* 10:4; see Brooke 1994: 130–31). *Targum Isaiah* at this point appears to change the focus from Yahweh's coming to the people's return (Snodgrass 1980: 27).

D. Textual Background. The MT begins, "A voice crying in the wilderness prepare the way of the LORD," which the LXX essentially translates literally (changing only the participle to the genitive: "of one crying"). Matthew, like Mark, follows the LXX verbatim. But the parallelism within the OT verse would seem to require that "in the wilderness" modifies "prepare the way" (just as it does in the next line with "make smooth") rather than "a voice crying," as in the Gospels. The MT

thus continues, "make smooth in the desert a highway for our God," which the LXX renders as "make straight the paths of our God," omitting the redundant "in the desert." Matthew and Mark again follow the LXX verbatim, except that they change "of our God" to "his," which scarcely alters the meaning.

E. Hermeneutic Employed. The difference between "a voice crying in the wilderness" and a call to "prepare a way in the wilderness" has often been exaggerated. Both in fact fit John the Baptist's ministry; he (or the Synoptic writers) could easily have seen a double meaning in the position of the phrase in the Hebrew text, as rabbis often did in their exegeses. But the Hebrew also allows for such a double meaning to have been originally intended (Taylor 1997: 25–29).

Originally, Isaiah had in mind a preliminary fulfillment in the return of the Jewish exiles from distant lands to Israel. But his language already reuses "exodus" imagery, making it natural for the evangelists to reapply this imagery in the greater restoration from (spiritual) exile inaugurated by the ministry of Jesus to which John's preaching pointed (see Childs 2001: 299). And given that no return from Babylon (or Persia or Greece or Rome) ever came anywhere close to fully ending Israel's hard service, paying for its sins, or leveling (even metaphorically) all its rugged places, and certainly no event prior to Christ's coming ever revealed the glory of the Lord to all humanity, it seems reasonable to suggest that Isaiah had a more distant, grander fulfillment in mind as well. Hagner (1993: 48) comments, "The words of Isaiah occur in a context of comfort and deliverance from the exile, but they also allude to Messianic fulfillment." At the very least, that is how a group such as the one at Qumran would have taken it, so that they could apply it to themselves, demonstrating that the NT's hermeneutic was not a novel appropriation of the text.

F. Theological Use. For Matthew and Mark, now that Jesus had come and was believed to be the Messiah, it was natural to associate his forerunner, John the Baptist, with OT prophecies referring to one who would prepare for the coming messianic age. Thus the "Lord" in this quotation is not simply Yahweh, but Jesus as God's self-revelation. The burden of the quotation, however, is not so much christological but ethical: people must repent and show the actions befitting repentance to be able to welcome the coming king properly. Additionally, "John's location symbolizes the coming of a new exodus, the final time of salvation, and the price a true prophet of God must be willing to pay for his or her call: total exclusion from all that society values—its comforts, status symbols and even basic necessities" (Keener 1999: 118).

3:13–17

There are two important allusions to the OT in the account of Jesus' baptism, both audible in the words of the heavenly voice (3:17). The voice alludes first to Ps. 2:7, especially in its older, Markan form ("You are my Son" [1:11]). France (1985: 95) suspects that Matthew has assimilated his wording to that of the divine voice at Jesus' transfiguration, in which even Mark has "This is my beloved son" (9:7), and then to Isa. 42:1 ("my beloved, in whom I am well pleased"). The conjunction of the two allusions is especially significant inasmuch as at least a segment of pre-Christian Judaism apparently took both as messianic (cf. 4Q174 1 I, 10–14 with *Tg. Isa.* 42:1). Together they reflect the heavenly Father's understanding of Jesus' dual role: one day a kingly messiah, but for now a Suffering Servant—both appropriate to his unique identity as the divine son. For additional possible echoes of Isa. 63:7–64:12 and Ps. 74:19–20, see Capes 1999: 37–49. More distant echoes may be heard of the creation out of a watery chaos (Gen. 1:3) and the adoption of Israel as God's son at the exodus, including the crossing of the Red Sea (recall Hos. 11:1; see Davies and Allison 1988–1997: 1:328). The dove likewise may allude to the Spirit "brooding" over God's original creation; in Christ, God is fashioning a new creation (Allison 1992). Gibbs (2002: 511–26) thinks Jer. 38:20 LXX (= 31:20 MT), rather than Ps. 2:7, accounts for the sonship language so that Matthew here as elsewhere sees Jesus successfully recapitulating Israel's role, particularly where it had failed. The two options, however, scarcely prove mutually exclusive.

Matthew 4:1–11

Mosaic typology continues. Just as Moses had to lead the Israelites during forty years of wandering in the Sinai wilderness as punishment for their sin (Deut. 8:2–3), so Jesus is driven by the Spirit into the Judean wilderness for forty days to be tempted by the devil (4:1–2). The exact phrase "forty days and nights" may allude to the period of time Moses spent fasting on Mount Sinai to prepare to confirm God's covenant with his people (Exod. 24:18; Deut. 9:9). The temptation to turn stones into bread might also echo Moses' rebellion in striking the stone to make it bring forth water (Num. 20:1–13). But where in both instances Israel as a people or Moses as a leader failed the test, Jesus passes his. In fact, in each of the three specific temptations that Matthew depicts (this time paralleled in Luke 4:1–13), Jesus confounds the devil by citing Scripture. In one case he does so in response to a verse that Satan himself has quoted (on the temptation narratives in general, see Gibson 1995).

4:4

A. NT Context. The four Scripture quotations in Matt. 4 are different from any of the quotations surveyed thus far. Instead of representing Matthew's observations as narrator, three appear on the lips of Jesus, while the fourth is attributed to the devil. All begin with the simple introduction "it stands written." None of the four has anything to do with prophecy, literal or typological; instead, they reflect the use of the OT to support or refute certain forms of behavior. The first comprises Jesus' response to his temptation by the devil to end his fast (4:2) and turn stones into bread (4:3). The clause "if you are the Son of God" (4:3, 6) is in Greek a first-class condition and does not suggest that the devil doubts Jesus' sonship; rather, he wants to find out what kind of Son Jesus will be. In each instance the devil tempts Jesus to bypass the suffering that God has marked out for him and to use his power in a triumphalist, self-glorifying fashion (see Blomberg 1988). To this first temptation Jesus replies, in essence, that the satisfaction of physical hunger is not as significant for human sustenance as the satisfaction of spiritual hunger that the word of God provides. The Lukan parallel cites only the first half of the couplet (4:4).

B. OT Context. Somewhat ironically, in Deut. 8:3 Moses is recalling the period of the Israelites' wandering in the wilderness (8:2), during which God supernaturally provided them manna to eat in order to teach the principle that people do not live by bread alone! The point, of course, is that the Israelites were unable to provide for themselves in their own strength, so God had to intervene miraculously. Likewise, their clothes did not wear out or their feet swell for forty years (8:4). God did not prevent them from meeting their physical needs, but he provided for them in a way that dramatically reminded them of their need to depend entirely on him. Tigay (1996: 92) comments, "Man does not live on natural foods alone, but on whatever God decrees to be nourishing." The wilderness wanderings provide the paradigm for God's experience with Israel thus far (cf. 29:4–5; Nelson 2002: 107) and reverse the testing of Yahweh by the people at Massah (6:16; McConville 2002: 169).

C. Use in Jewish Sources. *Targum Pseudo-Jonathan* on Deuteronomy here reads, "Not by bread alone does man live but by everything that *is created by the Memra of* the Lord does man live." (All translations of this Targum are from Clarke 1998.) *Targum Neofiti* and *Targum Onqelos* speak of everything that comes from the mouth of the decree of the Memra. Since it is words that often come out of people's mouths, the references to the personified Memra (Aram. for "word") and its decree prove understandable. The rest of the extant references to this text, apart from later rabbinic sources, all come in Philo. In *Alleg. Interp.* 3.174 God's stripping his people of all their pleasantries was actually a sign of being propitious to them. *Allegorical Interpretation* 3.175 contrasts the spiritual hunger that proceeds from virtue with that which comes from vice, while 3.176 stresses that the perfect person must be nourished by all of God's word. *On the Preliminary Studies* 170–174 contains a more elaborate exposition, noting that God brings only good things on his people, so that his affliction instructs and corrects and is balanced by his gracious provision of manna. And in *Spec. Laws* 2.199 Philo encourages his readers to take heart from the fact that God is always able to nourish and preserve his people as he did the Israelites in the wilderness.

D. Textual Background. Matthew cites the LXX verbatim, probably following Q, with the omission of a superfluous dative definite article before the participle "coming out of." The LXX in turn translates the MT quite literally, except that it specifies "everything" that comes from the

mouth of God as "every word." There could be literary dependence on the targumic rendering (or vice versa), but the change is natural enough that it could have arisen independently in the two traditions.

E. Hermeneutic Employed. Jesus is distilling the timeless spiritual or moral principle contained in the text of Deuteronomy and applying it to his temptation. One might imagine the devil retorting, "But the context of Deuteronomy is precisely that of the very kind of miraculous provision of food I am asking you to replicate!" The point, however, is that the devil is asking Jesus to do it in a context that would break his fast, use his divine power for solely self-serving ends, and demonstrate his unwillingness to depend on his heavenly Father for the strength he needs. In the Israelites' wilderness wanderings, the provision of manna created precisely that kind of dependence because the people on their own could not provide for themselves.

F. Theological Use. Both Christ and his followers must rely entirely on God for sustenance. Thus the doctrine of providence is clearly addressed (Weinfeld 1991: 389). In normal situations this does not preclude the ordinary means of gathering food, but in every situation, normal or abnormal, spiritual nourishment takes priority over physical sustenance. One will die physically without food and water, but one will die spiritually and be lost for all eternity without salvation. The unique lesson of all three temptations for Jesus is that he cannot bypass the road of suffering that eventually will lead to the cross. Jesus relives the experience of the Israelites, but he succeeds where they failed (Hagner 1993: 65). Not all Christians will follow him in martyrdom, but all must be prepared to do so if called on. Mark 8:31–38 pars. form an apt commentary on these themes.

4:6

A. NT Context. In the second temptation the devil himself quotes Scripture. Because Jesus is the Son of God, the devil says, he should throw himself off the temple (4:6a). After all, the psalmist promised that angels would take charge over God's faithful people to keep them from harm (4:6b). Luke places this temptation third rather than second, probably because he is arranging the temptations thematically rather than chronologically and wants them to culminate with Jesus' temptation in the temple (Luke 4:9–12; see Carson 1984: 411; Marshall 1978: 167).

B. OT Context. Psalm 91 is one of many psalms that appears to promise the faithful believer complete freedom from harm. Here the promises appear to apply to "a monarch or a daring man of war who has just escaped violent death and is still exposed to future danger" (Terrien 2003: 652). No one psalm is a compendium of all theological truth, however, and balancing passages make it clear that many times the righteous do suffer. Also, there was more of a theology of "blessing for obedience" under the Mosaic covenant, but this reflected God's unique arrangements with Israel, which do not carry over to the new covenant. For key texts from Psalms on both sides and an application to the related topic of material blessings, see Blomberg 1999: 60–62. At any rate, even within the context of the psalms' worldview, there is no justification for provoking God by deliberately putting oneself in harm's way, demanding that he come to rescue. Verses 11–12 speak of protection against accidental stumbling, not intervention to prevent suicide (Nolland 1989: 181; France 1985: 99)!

C. Use in Jewish Sources. Even the late rabbinic literature only rarely cites these verses, and it sheds no light on their original meaning (Str-B 1:151–52). In pre-Christian Jewish texts, only 1QH^a IX, 11 makes a possible allusion to this protective angelic function, but it does not illuminate the OT and NT texts in question either.

D. Textual Background. The MT reads, "For his angels he will give charge over you to protect you in all your ways; on their hands they will bear you up lest you dash your foot against a stone." The LXX (Ps. 90:11) offers a reasonably literal translation into Greek with "command" for "give charge" and "stumble" for "dash," both possible translations of the Hebrew anyway. Matthew follows the LXX verbatim, except that he omits "to protect you in all your ways," replacing this phrase with an "and." Interestingly, the Lukan parallel preserves "to protect you" but still omits "in all your ways" (Luke 4:10–11). Given that this is a Q passage, it may be that Matthew has simply abbreviated his source more than Luke did.

E. Hermeneutic Employed. This is the lone instance in Matthew of the devil quoting Scripture, so we scarcely need to be concerned to justify his

hermeneutic! In fact, he distorts the meaning of the text in its context, which should not surprise us. He is trying to entice Jesus to sin.

F. Theological Use. If the devil can manipulate Scripture, we can understand how cults and false religions will distort it too (see Sire 1980). More specifically, it is wrong to test God by demanding that he rescue us or provide for us in ways that we stipulate. God is sovereign and omniscient and knows when it is best to allow us to go through difficult experiences and when it is better to keep us from them. In this light, the "health and wealth" gospel (or "name it and claim it" approach to prayer) errs almost as much as Satan did! "The security which God brings is something to be accepted in humble trust, not something to be used for personal aggrandizement" (Davidson 1998: 305).

4:7

A. NT Context. Jesus replies to the devil's misapplication of Scripture by quoting Scripture himself, as he did in response to the first temptation. He recognizes that to deliberately jump off the temple and insist that God rescue him would be to violate the command not to test God.

B. OT Context. The context of Deut. 6:16 begins with the reaffirmation by Moses of some of the most fundamental commands of God from the covenant at Sinai. As the Israelites finally get ready to take possession of the promised land, they must recall their most central obligations to Yahweh (6:1–3). These include recognizing him alone as God and loving him with all their beings (6:4–5). Their clothing and conversation must regularly remind them of his precepts (6:6–9). They must not forget the Lord once they settle into their new homeland and experience his blessing (6:10–12). And they dare not run after the gods of the nations that they dispossess (6:13–15). It is precisely in this context that Moses reminds the Israelites that they should not put God to the kind of test (or trial, temptation) that they did at Massah (6:16). The allusion is to Exod. 17:7 and the incident of the people demanding that Moses provide them with drink when they did not believe that God would care for them (see Tigay 1996: 81). In contrast to the skepticism that makes inappropriate demands, Merrill (1994: 172) speaks of "demands or requirements that are inappropriate either to [God's] nature and character or to the circumstances." Deut. 6 continues by enjoining obedience to God's laws, doing what is right and good so that the people may flourish in Canaan (6:17–19).

C. Use in Jewish Sources. The late rabbinic literature specifies various ways in which one should not test God (e.g., by not tithing) and stresses that many of its precautionary demands are to prevent people from testing God (Str-B 1:152–53). The earlier Targumim refer to ten key tests (*Pseudo-Jonathan*), add "the glory of the shekinah [the divine presence]" before "the Lord your God" (*Neofiti*), or substitute "Nisetha" for "Massah" (*Onqelos*). But none of these uses clearly illuminates our text.

D. Textual Background. The LXX is a literal translation of the MT, except that it turns the plural "you" of the imperative into a singular "you." Matthew quotes the LXX verbatim, probably via Q; the singular is, of course, appropriate when Jesus applies the command to himself. Luke 4:12 presents the identical excerpt from the LXX Q.

E. Hermeneutic Employed. As with his counter to Satan's first ruse, Jesus applies a central, timeless moral principle to the situation at hand. One must never test God in the sense of telling him what he must do. Weinfeld (1991: 356) observes, "Deuteronomy 6:10–19, which demands complete devotion to YHWH alone, and which forbids one to follow foreign gods or to put YHWH to the test, is then most appropriate for such a polemic against Belial as is told in the NT passages."

F. Theological Use. One might be tempted to think that Jesus, being both God and a human being, was telling the devil not to tempt him, since he was God, and one should not tempt God! But temptation is different from testing. Humans can choose to test God, even if they should not. They cannot entice God to sin (the meaning of "tempt" [James 1:13]). And the whole point of the temptations of Jesus Christ is that they were addressed to his completely temptable human nature, not his untemptable divine nature. Thus it is better to see Jesus applying the principle of Deuteronomy to his own behavior as an obedient human, not to Satan's actions. As with the first temptation, Jesus responds in accordance with his Father's will in an area that the Israelites of old had not. And again he cites Deuteronomy's reference to a time of Israelite rebellion against God in the desert to make this point clear.

4:10

A. NT Context. This final temptation offers Jesus all the kingdoms of the world if he will worship Satan (Matt. 4:8–9). After Jesus resists this enticement to so heinous a sin, the devil leaves him, and angels come to minister to him (4:10–11). Once he has passed his tests without relying on supernatural help, he is permitted to receive it to help him recover from his ordeal.

B. OT Context. The overall context for Deut. 6:13 is identical to that described above for 6:16. The most immediate context sandwiches 6:13 between reminders not to forget God, who brought Israel out of Egypt (6:12), as they did when they fashioned the golden calf, and not to follow the gods of the Canaanites and their neighbors (6:14). Verse 16, like chapter 6 more generally, is one of the classic OT affirmations of Jewish monotheism. One must reverence only Yahweh. Verse 13 itself sets up a sharp contrast with the Israelites' previous bondage in Egypt, with its use of the identical term for "service" as throughout Exodus (Christensen 2001: 147).

C. Use in Jewish Sources. Targum Onqelos adds a second verb to this half-verse, so that its readers are called explicitly to worship before Yahweh and not merely to fear or reverence him. Jesus' use of this text fits this expansion very nicely. Philo expounds the need to swear by God's name in the second half of this verse (*Alleg. Interp.* 3.208), while the *Apocalypse of Adam* (1:11–12) speaks of serving God in fear and subjection after the fall, but these texts do not appear very relevant to ours.

D. Textual Background. The MT reads, "Yahweh your God you shall fear, and him you shall serve and in his name you shall swear [i.e., take oaths]." The LXX adds a third clause after the first two, "and to him you shall cleave," but otherwise translates the verse literally. Matthew and Luke (4:8) substitute "worship" for "fear" and add "only" between "him" and "you shall serve." The "only" could be an echo of "serve him only" in 1 Sam. 7:3 (see Gundry 1994: 58). Both changes simply emphasize what is already implicit in the original Hebrew in its Deuteronomic context, although "worship" is the natural word to use since that is what the devil has just asked Jesus to do.

E. Hermeneutic Employed. As with his responses to the first two temptations, Jesus employs a timeless theological and moral principle to defeat the devil. If it was wrong for the Israelites to worship pagan gods rather than Yahweh, it would be abominable to worship Satan, no matter what the reward! Gerhardsson (1966) thinks that the three Matthean temptations link with the exhortation in Deut. 6:5 to love God with all one's heart, soul, and might, respectively, but the connections seem too vague to be convincing.

F. Theological Use. The main point in both Testaments is that fear, reverence, worship, and all related activities may properly be directed only to the God of Israel. Christians would come to worship Jesus within that monotheistic framework, but in this context we see Jesus the man, obeying God's law, without inappropriately relying on his divine nature, and thereby thwarting the devil, as Israel in the wilderness centuries earlier should have done but did not (see Davies and Allison 1988–1997: 1:373). Derivatively, we learn that Satan still has access to the kingdoms of this world, but only to the extent that God in his sovereignty permits. God remains the master of all creation and of all creatures, and so he alone merits worship.

Matthew 4:12–16

4:15–16

A. NT Context. This is the last passage in Matthew's overall introduction to the ministry of Jesus. The main body of the Gospel begins in 4:17 as Jesus "from that time on began to teach" his message of the kingdom throughout Galilee (see Kingsbury 1975; Bauer 1989). The final event of Jesus' preparation for ministry that Matthew finds significant enough to narrate is his move from Nazareth to Capernaum as his Galilean residence (4:13). Matthew sees in this move an explicit fulfillment of the prophecy of Isaiah, who is again mentioned by name (4:14). Mark and Luke acknowledge this move (Mark 1:21; Luke 4:31), but only Matthew describes the change of residence and refers to it as fulfilling Scripture. Zebulon and Naphtali were the OT territories closest to first-century Galilee. Jesus obviously is the light dawning on the peoples of those regions, presumably including Gentiles as well as Jews.

B. OT Context. Isaiah 9:1–2 (8:23–9:1 MT/LXX) reflects the shift from the immediate future to beyond the exile, described in conjunction with the use of Isa. 7:14 in Matt. 1:23 above. These two verses form part of the subsection of chapter 9 (vv. 1–5) that immediately precedes the promise of a child who will become Wonderful Counselor, Almighty God, Everlasting Father, and Prince of Peace, ushering in an age of permanent justice emanating from David's throne (vv. 6–7)—obviously no mere mortal. Verse 1 contrasts the past humbling of the northern territories of Israel by the divine judgment meted out via the Assyrian deportation (Cole 1994) with their coming honor via restoration from exile. Already in the eighth century BC enough foreigners would invade the north of Israel that the region could be called "Galilee of the Gentiles" (Oswalt 1986–1998: 2:237). "The road to the sea, beyond the Jordan" referred to the highway running from Damascus in Syria in a southwesterly direction, alongside the Jordan River, through Capernaum and part of the rest of the province of Galilee, and eventually cutting diagonally across to Caesarea on the Mediterranean (see Hagner 1993: 73). This is the road that the returning exiles would have followed, at least part way, to their various hometowns in Israel (Davies and Allison 1988–1997: 1:383). The light dawning on them in darkness and in the land of the shadow of death would thus refer initially to their return from exile. The perfect tenses should be taken as prophetic: "have seen" and "has dawned" mean "will see" and "will dawn." On the predictive role of this passage more generally, see Wegner 1992, but given the larger messianic context, it could also have been intended to refer to the even greater deliverance that the Messiah would bring. Childs (2001: 80–81) recognizes this for the "canonical" form of Isaiah—i.e., the time at which the book was completed. He adds that 9:6 "makes it absolutely clear that (the child's) role is Messianic" (see also Goldingay 2001: 70). It is not clear whether Isaiah thought only of Jews benefiting from the original return from exile, but previous Scriptures more generally, beginning with Gen. 12:1–3, certainly would have made him envisage Gentile blessings in the longer-term fulfillment (cf. the climax of this theme in Isa. 66:8; see Motyer 1993: 100).

C. Use in Jewish Sources. *Targum Isaiah* makes it explicit that the passage is describing the exile and adds that the Israelites did not remember the miracles of the exodus and conquest or past wars with Gentiles. It explicitly refers to the people who are transformed from darkness into light as the house of Israel. But in 9:6 the remarkable child to be born is explicitly equated with the Messiah, "in whose days peace will increase upon us." So presumably the targumist had a double fulfillment in view, too. *Second Enoch* 46:3 alludes to Isa. 9:1–2 by speaking of the Lord sending out his great light, while also sending judgment in the darkness, but the text is too mutilated to know what the immediate context of this prophecy is. The author of 1QS XI, 10, presumably the Teacher of Righteousness, contemporizes Isaiah's passage by admitting that evil humanity, including himself, belongs "to the assembly of worms and of those who walk in darkness." Neither of these latter two texts proves very helpful for our purposes.

D. Textual Background. The relevant portion of the MT can be translated, "In former times, the land of Zebulon and the land of Naphtali were brought into contempt, but in the latter times he will glorify the way of the sea beyond the Jordan, Galilee of the Gentiles. The people walking in darkness saw a great light. A light shines on the ones dwelling in the land of the death-shadow." The LXX is unusually free in its translation. It places "the way of the sea" immediately after the references to "the region of Zebulon" and "the land of Naphtali" but then adds "and the rest of those dwelling nearby." After "Galilee of the Gentiles" the LXX inserts, seemingly gratuitously, "the regions of the Jews." Conversely, it altogether omits the Hebrew clause "but in the latter times he will glorify." The past-tense verbs are translated into present or future to clarify the prophetic sense, and one of them is turned into an imperative ("See!").

Matthew can be understood as following the LXX but improving its translation at several points to bring it more in line with the Hebrew. He restores the parallelism of using "land" both times before "Zebulon" and "Naphtali." He leaves out the clause that the LXX had added to the MT after "the way of the sea." He restores the past-tense indicative verbs, "have seen" and "has dawned," and uses a more literal translation for

the latter. On the other hand, he substitutes the verb "sitting" for both "walking" and "dwelling," perhaps echoing either Ps. 107:10 or Isa. 42:7. Enough words remain identical to the LXX to suggest literary dependence; however, no distinctive of the LXX over against the MT remains, so it is just barely possible that Matthew arrived at the same translation of the Hebrew independently. The expressions in which Matthew and the LXX match exactly are a series of short phrases in which the translations employed are the obvious ones. Stendahl (1954: 104) likewise notes signs of both dependence and possible independence (see also Gundry 1967: 108).

E. Hermeneutic Employed. As with the previous two uses of Isaiah in Matthew, it seems best here to speak of double fulfillment. Matthew recognized a short-term fulfillment during OT times but also saw a longer-term fulfillment in the coming of Jesus the Messiah. What began as physical liberation from the exile culminates in spiritual liberation in the messianic age. Luz (1989: 196) speaks more cautiously but agrees that Isa. 9:6 was never fulfilled by any Davidic king, concluding that "there is in our prediction from the beginning an openness which is never historically closed." Whether or not Gentiles received any offshoot blessings when the Jews returned from Assyria, they certainly do through the ministry of Jesus.

F. Theological Use. As with four of the five prophecies in the infancy narratives, Matthew again wants to link a specific geographical location with OT prophecy: Capernaum, near the Jordan River, by the Sea of Galilee, in a province populated with even more Gentiles in the first century than in Isaiah's day. He also recognizes the Messiah's ministry as shining spiritual light into the dark corners of both Jewish and Gentile religion, a theme that frequently reappears in John and in the later rabbis. By following Christ, people of either background can experience spiritual life rather than death. Menken (2004a: 15–33) thinks that Matthew's form of the quotation stresses more the plight of the people and the beginning of salvation, but this may be overly subtle.

Matthew 4:17–5:20

Matthew's introduction (1:1–4:16) has barraged the reader with OT quotations to show that

Jesus is indeed the Jewish Messiah, prophesied directly, indirectly, and typologically in numerous passages of the Hebrew Scriptures. As the body of the Gospel unfolds, the frequency of explicit quotations of the OT tails off dramatically; indeed, the only quotations in the first main subsection of the body (4:17–7:29) are ethical commands that appear only to show how radically Jesus differs from them, or at least from their conventional interpretation (5:21–48). Perhaps this offers a clue as to Matthew's strategy. Having established Jesus' Jewish credentials, he is now more interested in showing how Jesus differed from Judaism. Far from establishing a new law, Jesus came to fulfill and thus transcend the Mosaic covenant (see Moo 1984).

Nevertheless, one may detect allusions and echoes to the OT in the intervening material. In calling his first disciples (Matt. 4:18–22), Jesus' directness and the immediacy of response may be modeled on Elijah's call to Elisha in 1 Kings 19:19–21. In the summary of Christ's ministering throughout Galilee (Matt. 4:23–25), the references to his healing many diseases call to mind the healings associated with the messianic age, especially in Isa. 35:5–6. The Sermon on the Mount (chaps. 5–7) is the first of five major blocks of sermonic material that distinctively punctuate Matthew's narrative (along with chaps. 10; 13; 18; 23–25). These discourses have often been likened to the five books of Torah (Genesis–Deuteronomy; beginning esp. with Bacon 1918). "Jesus on the mountain" is likewise a more common theme in Matthew than elsewhere, including here with the Sermon on the Mount (Matt. 5:1). This motif calls to mind Moses receiving the law on Mount Sinai (see esp. Donaldson 1985). But labels of Jesus as a "new Moses" must be at least as sensitive to the discontinuities between the two covenant makers as to the continuities. Helpful in this respect are Meier 1976 and Banks 1974. The critical consensus wrongly sees Matthew's Gospel as promoting a much more law-observant form of Christianity than his canonical companions (see Overman 1990; Saldarini 1994).

The Beatitudes, with which Jesus' great sermon begins (5:3–12), contain several key allusions to the OT. The "poor in spirit" (5:3) probably alludes to the *ănāwîm*, the materially impoverished who recognize God as their only hope, who appear in so many prophetic and wisdom passages and especially in Isa. 61:1 (Schweizer 1975: 86; Carson 1984: 131; Bruner 1987: 135). There the Spirit-anointed prophet preaches to them good news, just as here Jesus declares them blessed. Isaiah 61:2 is almost certainly alluded to in the second beatitude (Matt. 5:4), as it seeks "to comfort all who mourn." Again we should think of both spiritual and social causes. Matthew 5:5 alludes to Ps. 37:11. The pious Israelites who inherit the land have become the meek followers of Jesus who inherit the whole earth (the poor mourners of Isa. 61:1–2 also are described as inheriting the earth in 61:7, at least in the LXX). Verse 6 may echo Isa. 55:1–3 with its call for the spiritually hungry and thirsty to come to the Lord to eat and drink. Verse 7 calls to mind Exod. 34:6 with its famous self-revelation of God's nature, highlighting his mercy. Psalm 24:3–5 may underlie 5:8 with its call for clean hands and a pure heart as a requirement for those who would come into God's presence and receive his blessings. Psalm 34:14 sounds a note that echoes in the blessing of peacemakers in 5:9. The final verse of this section (5:12) alludes to the persecution of the prophets, described in both the OT (most notably Jeremiah) and intertestamental literature (most notably *Ascension of Isaiah* [= *Martyrdom and Ascension of Isaiah 6–11*]).

The metaphors of salt and light (5:13–16) reflect common Jewish imagery but do not point obviously to any particular OT texts. Matthew 5:17–20 forms the thesis paragraph of the Sermon on the Mount and the key to understanding Matthew's presentation of the relationship between Jesus' teaching and the law (or the OT more generally). Jesus neither abolishes the Hebrew Scriptures nor preserves them without changing the way many portions apply to his followers. The key to the relationship again is "fulfillment"—bringing to completion everything that was originally intended by God. The sacrifices will clearly be abolished, fulfilled once and for all in Christ's death (see Hebrews throughout), while many moral principles will equally clearly remain unchanged. In most cases, however, one will have to pass specific OT commands through a grid or filter of NT teaching to see the ways in which they apply to Christians today (see Klein, Blomberg, and Hubbard 2004: 344–50; Dorsey 1991; Hagner 1997).

Matthew 5:21–48

Six times in these so-called antitheses Jesus begins, "You have heard it said of old [or, 'to the ancients']" or, with an abbreviated form of this introduction, "You have heard it said" or "it was said" (5:21, 27, 31, 33, 38, 43). In five cases Jesus then proceeds to quote a fundamental OT law. In the sixth case (5:43) he quotes what appears to be a two-part law, but only the first part is an OT quotation. As a result, most interpreters think that Jesus is contrasting traditional, unwritten interpretations of the laws in question (hence, "you have heard") with his own interpretations (representative, and particularly useful, is Westerholm 1978, esp. p. 113). On the other hand, 5:43b can be viewed as an allusion to the OT (see below, p. 27), and even written Scripture was normally read aloud, so it is hard to be sure that Jesus' complaints are only with unwritten tradition (see Luz 1989: 247–49).

A range of approaches has tried to see a uniform methodology in Jesus' sixfold quotation of the law. In some cases Jesus seems to make his demands stricter (murder, adultery, divorce). In other cases his teaching seems to supersede the law (oaths, retaliation). In every instance, however, what stands out is his claim to act as the law's authoritative interpreter, illustrating the "greater righteousness" demanded of his followers, than that exhibited by many Jewish leaders (5:20). The crowds pick up on this, marveling at the kind of authority he displays (7:28–29). For a succinct exposition along these lines, see Moo 1992. All six antitheses also implicitly contrast hate and love, broken and whole relationships (see H. D. Betz 1995: 204–5).

5:21

A. NT Context. The first antithesis (5:21–26) deals with the commandment from the Decalogue prohibiting murder. Here Jesus radically internalizes the command by stressing that the person who is inappropriately angry with another, or who speaks spitefully or slanderously of another, is likewise guilty of sin (5:22). "Raca" was a quasi-expletive in Aramaic, while "fool" (Gk. *mōros*) could connote an immoral or godless person as well as an "idiot" (see Sorg 1975–1985). A strong manuscript tradition adds the phrase "without cause" following the word "brother";

this may reflect a later textual variant, but the interpretation is almost certainly implied in the original, since Jesus himself demonstrates righteous anger in "cleansing" the temple later in this same Gospel (Matt. 21:12–13). Therefore, people should take decisive action, however drastic, to initiate reconciliation with their adversaries, lest God inflict on them severe judgment (5:23–26). Ruzer (1996) thinks that the second part of 5:21, on whoever murders being subject to judgment, reflects traditional interpretation, as in *Tg. Ps.-J.* Gen. 9:6.

B. OT Context. The Ten Commandments are given to the Israelites twice in the OT: in Exod. 20:1–17, after Moses descends from Mount Sinai, and in Deut. 5:1–21, as he repeats the law in preparation for their entry into the promised land. The first four commandments reflect a right relationship with God, while the last six deal with interpersonal relationships. The proscription against murder, the sixth commandment, obviously falls into the latter category. Cassuto (1967) observes that the sixth through eighth commandments are found in every civilized society yet are unusual here because of their absolute, unqualified form as abstract, eternal principles. "Murder" is a better translation in this context than "kill" for the verb *rāṣaḥ,* because the law does allow for killing people in prescribed cases of capital punishment, self-defense, and war (Kaiser 1983: 90; Sarna 1991: 113). The underlying principle, however (which also allows these exceptions), is the general sanctity of life (cf. Gen. 9:6; see Childs 1974: 419). "Whoever murders will be liable to judgment" (Matt. 5:21) "is a fair summary of the legislation set forth in Exod. 21:12" and elsewhere (Davies and Allison 1988–1997: 1:511).

C. Use in Jewish Sources. The *Fragmentary Targum* on Exod. 20:13 begins to generalize some by declaring that the Israelites should not be murderers, or friends or partners of murderers, or seen in the assembly of murderers, lest they teach their children to imitate such violence. *Targum Pseudo-Jonathan* and *Targum Neofiti* on both the Exodus and Deuteronomy passages have very comparable additions. But the generalization is more guilt by association than internalization of the basic command. Philo and Pseudo-Philo have numerous references to the prohibition of murder, discussing its meaning and purpose, while the rabbinic literature contains a large number of discussions of the situations in which the prohibition applies and the nature of punishment for violating the command, but virtually nothing appears to parallel Jesus' internalization (despite over twenty pages of small-print references in Str-B 1:254–75!). Pseudo-Phocylides warns against devising treachery (3:21), a command that begins to focus on mental attitudes. Perhaps the most significant parallel is Philo's observation that this second of the brief commandments "is that under which are implied all of those necessary and most advantageous laws, relating to acts of violence, to insults, to assaults, to wounds, to mutilation" (*Decalogue* 170). (All quotations from Philo are from Yonge 1993.) At least "insults" suggests something along the lines of Jesus' commentary. But this is not conventional Jewish elaboration. On the other hand, one can find separate commandments prohibiting profanity, blasphemy, cursing, defiling and abusive language, and swearing falsely (see Childs 1974: 412).

D. Textual Background. The Exodus and Deuteronomy texts are identical in the Hebrew, and the LXX translates them literally. Matthew, in turn, matches the wording of the LXX.

E. Hermeneutic Employed. As noted above (p. 21), Jesus takes a commandment about external behavior and internalizes it. He also applies it to additional interpersonal contexts, thus strengthening the original command or making it stricter.

F. Theological Use. Although we should not interpret the Sermon on the Mount in light of later Pauline thought, there is a parallel of sorts here to Paul's logic that the law demonstrates the sinfulness of humanity (e.g., Gal. 3:19–25). Those who may think that they have not violated the sixth commandment, since they have not literally murdered anyone, have almost certainly harbored wrongful anger and done violence to others with their speech. Jesus is not abolishing the law, but rather is fulfilling it (Matt. 5:17), which in this instance means applying the spirit of the Decalogue to a wide variety of hateful thoughts and actions. The Sermon on the Mount is a kingdom manifesto with high ideals.

5:27

A. NT Context. The second antithesis (5:27–30) deals with adultery almost exactly as the first one did with murder. Again Jesus speaks of internal thoughts and not just outward actions. Anyone "who looks at a woman with the intention of committing adultery" (Bratcher 1981: 47) or, possibly, "who looks at a woman for the purpose of getting her to lust after him" (see Haacker 1977) is also guilty of sin. People should metaphorically mutilate themselves (i.e., take drastic action) to avoid these sins lest God judge them eternally (5:29–30). Obviously, gouging out one's eyes or cutting off one's hands is not to be taken literally; after all, one can still lust even if blind or maimed!

B. OT Context. The command against adultery is the seventh of the Ten Commandments. The context is identical to that of the sixth command, described above (p. 21). For definitions of the concept, see Meyers 2005. Although technically involving at least one married person having sexual relations with someone other than his or her spouse, Stuart (2006: 463–64) thinks other instances of sex outside of marriage are condemned "by implication."

C. Use in Jewish Sources. The same Targumim that amplified the sixth commandment do so again with the seventh, forbidding friendship, partnership, and association in the assembly with adulterers. Philo and Pseudo-Philo contain the greatest number of oldest traditions, while the rabbinic texts exercise extensive casuistry to define what is and is not meant by adultery and when and how it should be punished. Philo goes on at great length to defend the notion that adultery is the worst of all violations of the law and to refute arguments in favor of the practice (*Decalogue* 121–131). Although the OT does not elsewhere proscribe lust per se, the later rabbinic traditions frequently do so, but again not necessarily in the context of expounding the seventh commandment (Str-B 1:298–301). Earlier parallels include *T. Iss.* 7:2; *T. Isaac* 4:53 and *Jub.* 20:4 (Davies and Allison 1988–1997: 1:522). The closest potentially pre-Christian Jewish parallel may be *T. Benj.* 8:2: "For the person with a mind that is pure with love does not look on a woman for the purpose of having sexual relations" (Charlesworth 1983–1985: 1:827). Jesus' teaching here is not nearly as countercultural as in the first antithesis (Luz 1989: 295). Gundry (1994: 88) adds Job 31:1; Sir. 23:4–6; 26:9–11; and *Pss. Sol.* 4:4–5.

Nevertheless, rabbinic traditions often expected women to wear head coverings to prevent men from lusting after them, whereas Jesus places the responsibility squarely on the person doing the lusting (Keener 1999: 187).

D. Textual Background. Again the Hebrew is identical in Exodus and Deuteronomy. The LXX translates literally, and Matthew matches the LXX.

E. Hermeneutic Employed. As with the first antithesis, we see internalization and intensification. Jesus fulfills this law exactly as he did the commandment against murder.

F. Theological Use. As in Matt. 5:21–26, Jesus broadens the application of the prohibition to a wide variety of interpersonal relationships and even imaginary interpersonal relationships. One may not have committed physical adultery, but one has almost certainly committed mental adultery, and perhaps frequently. The strong idealism of the Sermon on the Mount continues.

5:31

A. NT Context. The third antithesis (5:31–32) follows naturally after the second. Except for adultery, Jesus accepts no excuse for divorce. The introductory formulas have grown successively shorter, each one presupposing the fuller, previous introduction. The first three antitheses also form a unit, in that in each case Jesus internalizes or intensifies a law in a way that differs somewhat from his approach in the second three (5:33–48). Jesus expands on his teaching on divorce and remarriage in Matt. 19:1–12, where the same "exception clause" appears: no divorce "except for sexual immorality" (*porneia*). These teachings should be compared and contrasted with the parallel to Matt. 19:1–12, Mark 10:1–11, in which no exception clause appears at all, and with 1 Cor. 7:10–16, in which Paul introduces a second exception: desertion by an unbeliever. For a detailed exegesis of each of these passages and a response to these apparent contradictions, see Blomberg 1990b; for an excellent book-length treatment, see Keener 1991.

B. OT Context. Deuteronomy 24:1 forms only a small portion of a lengthy conditional sentence that does not end until midway through 24:4. Contrary to what one might imagine just from the excerpt that Jesus cites, it does not command divorce per se; rather, it states that *if* a man finds something "indecent" about his wife and issues her a certificate of divorce, and *if* she marries a new husband who then legally divorces her (or dies), *then* the woman may not remarry her first husband. It is possible that the original motive behind this law was to protect the woman from having to provide the same man with two dowries (Westbrook 1986), and support for this interpretation might appear in *Targum Neofiti*, which elaborates, "if a man takes a wife and endows her" (referring to her dowry). Note also D. Instone-Brewer 1998: in light of ancient Near Eastern parallels, the use of the marriage certificate in Israelite society actually made divorce easier. Philo (*Spec. Laws* 3:31) proposes a quite different rationale: the man remarrying a former wife who herself had remarried lays himself open to the charges of effeminacy! It is not at all clear, though, why this should be the case. The original meaning of indecency could not have been limited to infidelity, since the provision of the Mosaic law for adultery was death (Lev. 20:10). But other forms of seriously immoral or indecent sexual behavior could well be in view (C. J. H. Wright 1996). The larger context of Deuteronomy is a fairly loosely organized collection of miscellaneous laws, although 24:5 also deals with marriage: a newlywed man must not be sent to war or have other duties laid on him for his first year of marriage, so that he is free to bring happiness to his wife.

C. Use in Jewish Sources. There appear to be no demonstrably pre-Christian Jewish sources that shed further light on the meaning or application of Deut. 24:1. But an important mishnaic debate may well go back to Jesus' day, since it is attributed to the rival first-century Pharisees Hillel and Shammai, both some twenty years older than Jesus. In the tractate *Gittin* (9:10), Hillel and Shammai derive opposite conclusions from the phrase in Deuteronomy "something indecent" (Heb. *'erwat dābār*) by stressing opposite words. The typically more conservative Shammai takes "indecent" in a sexual sense and thus permits divorce only in the case of infidelity (capital punishment laws for adultery had already been substantially relaxed). The typically more liberal Hillel takes "something" (lit., "a thing") in the sense of "anything" inappropriate and allows for divorce in a wide variety of circumstances, including spoiling the cooking! Palestinian Jewish husbands could divorce for virtually any reason (Josephus, *Ant.* 4.253), explicitly including their wives' disobedience (Sir. 25–26; *'Abot R. Nat.* 1a; Josephus, *Life* 426, the latter apparently including something beyond her control; see Keener 1999: 192). Jesus appears to side with Shammai in this instance, though elsewhere he can be closer to Hillel. But Jewish law *required* divorce in the case of adultery (*m. Yebam.* 2:8; *m. Soṭah* 5:1), whereas Jesus only permits it. Jesus is thus actually more conservative even than Shammai. His ideal clearly is lifelong allegiance, as God had originally created the institution of marriage to represent (Matt. 19:5).

D. Textual Background. The LXX translates Deut. 24:1 reasonably literally. Jesus' words in Matthew, however, form more of a paraphrasing summary of the relevant portions of this verse. "Whoever divorces" does not actually appear in the OT text, but the conditional clause, "if a man . . . finds something indecent . . . and gives her a certificate of divorce," obviously is talking about the legal dissolution of a marriage. "Wife" and "her" are the only words repeated verbatim from the LXX, though "give" and "certificate of divorce" appear in only slightly different syntactical forms. Thus it is possible that we should call this an allusion rather than a quotation (Stendahl 1954: 137). But ancient Jewish interpretation did not always distinguish clearly between a quotation and a summary of a quotation (H. D. Betz 1995: 244).

E. Hermeneutic Employed. It is not clear whether Jesus is deliberately turning Deuteronomy's "if clause" into a command to reflect a distorted use of the text by certain Jewish leaders in his day. Implicit in Deut. 24:1–4 is that issuing a certificate of divorce is the appropriate procedure for establishing a legal divorce. Even if Jesus wants merely to contrast Jewish leniency on the topic with God's original intentions for marriage, Matt. 5:31 is appropriately worded (see Gundry 1994: 89–90; Guelich 1982: 243). Here one should not speak of the internalization of God's will so much as its intensification (cf. the disciples' response in 19:10!). Divorce is not God's design for marriage. Even when it is permitted, in the case of infidelity, this is only because the sexual exclusivity of the covenant has already been breached. A formal divorce declares de jure nothing more than what de facto is already the case. The same

is true with desertion, as in 1 Cor. 7:13–16 (see Atkinson 1981).

F. Theological Use. Jesus continues to show how the law is fulfilled in him (5:17). The greater righteousness with which he empowers his followers enables them to preserve marriages that others might choose to end. Adultery occurs not only when a spouse is unfaithful to a current marriage but also when he or she wrongly marries another. Given that Jesus speaks of a wrongful divorce making the partner who did not initiate it "commit adultery" (5:32), and given that not all divorcées remarried (though most in Jesus' world did), he may also be referring to divorce itself as a metaphorical kind of adultery (see Luck 1987: 247–51). Clearly the OT frequently uses adultery as a metaphor for unfaithfulness, especially between Israel and Yahweh (see Ortlund 1996).

5:33

Given the lack of verbal parallelism between the OT passages and Matthew, one might refer to this as an allusion rather than a quotation. However, since Jesus continues his series of comparisons with OT texts and themes in this fourth of his six antitheses, the text merits the same kind of treatment devoted to the first three. After all, free quotations and allusions in antiquity were at times indistinguishable.

A. NT Context. The second triad of antitheses begins again with the fuller introductory formula, "You have heard it said of old [or, 'to the ancients']." These last three antitheses (5:33–48) differ in at least two main ways from the first three. First, although there is a sense in which one can speak of an intensification of the law, it is not as easy to refer to these as internalizations; rather, in each case a specific part of Torah seems actually to be superseded (see Carson 1984: 154–56). Oaths were permitted in the OT, hence the legislation to insist on keeping one's oaths quoted here. Now Jesus seems to be excluding them altogether. But, second, there are other NT texts that call into question an approach that would absolutize Jesus' words to the same degree as in the first set of antitheses (see the chart in Blomberg 1997: 252). Paul twice invokes God's name to assure the truth of his claims (Gal. 1:20; 2 Cor. 1:23), while Heb. 6:13–14 refers to God himself "swearing" in his own name. In Matt. 26:63–64, Jesus will reply to the high priest's question "under oath." The context in Matthew (5:34–36) explains the kind of swearing that Jesus is prohibiting: that in which at least some of the Jewish leaders were caught up, establishing an elaborate casuistry of which kinds of oaths were binding and which were not, so that it became difficult ever to take certain people at their word. The goal for believers is to be so trustworthy in keeping their promises that oaths prove unnecessary (5:37). France (1985: 124) explains, "An oath is needed only if a person's word alone is unreliable; it is an admission of failure in truthfulness." Jesus expands on several of these sentiments in Matt. 23:16–22. James 5:12 either alludes to or actually quotes Matt. 5:37.

B. OT Context. Leviticus 19:12 declares, "Do not swear in my name with falsehood and profane the name of your God. I am the LORD." The context is the Holiness Code of Leviticus (chaps. 17–26). Leviticus 19 alone intermingles fundamental ethical principles with seemingly minor civil or ceremonial responsibilities. The injunctions immediately surrounding 19:12 also proscribe deceit (19:11, 13–16). Numbers 30:2 likewise requires those who make a vow or oath not to break their promises, but to keep their word. This command comes near the beginning of an entire chapter on vows. One could imagine that Jesus also had Deut. 23:21 in mind, which commands those who make vows not to be slow in paying them, since God will hold them accountable. Keener (1999: 1993n100) thinks that Matthew has conflated Lev. 19:12 with Deut. 23:21 in targumic fashion. Gundry (1994: 92) thinks that Matt. 5:33b is drawing on Ps. 50:14 (49:14 LXX), but the only word in common here is an alternate inflectional form of the verb for "pay back." Guelich (1982: 212) drastically exaggerates by calling these two texts "almost verbatim parallel." Davies and Allison (1988–1997: 1:533–34) add Exod. 20:7; Zech. 8:17; 11Q19 LIII–LIV; *T. Ash.* 2:6; *Sib. Or.* 2:68; Ps.-Phoc. 16 as texts that Jesus could be summarizing. Verses 34–35 also contain OT allusions: to "heaven and earth [as] my footstool" (Isa. 66:1) and to "the city of the great King" (Ps. 48:2).

C. Use in Jewish Sources. The closest intertestamental parallel seems to be Sir. 23:11: "The one who swears many oaths is full of iniquity, and the scourge will not leave his house. If he swears in error, his sin remains on him, and if he disregards it he sins doubly; if he swears a false oath, he will not be justified, for his house will be filled with calamities." (All translations from the Apocrypha are taken from Metzger and Murphy 1991.) *Second Enoch* 49:1–2 twice swears that it is good not to have to swear! Josephus (*J.W.* 2.135) contends that the Essenes avoid oaths and that what they say is firmer than an oath, but we have no such command from the Dead Sea literature itself. Philo (*Decalogue* 86) explains that an oath calls on God to give testimony concerning matters that are in doubt; thus, it is most impious to invoke God to be a witness to a lie (cf. the almost identical comment in *Spec. Laws* 2.10). In another context, Philo quotes Deut. 23:21, followed by an exhortation not to delay in performing that which one vows to God (*Sacrifices* 54; cf. *Spec. Laws* 2.38). The entire mishnaic tractate Šebu'ot is given over to detailed casuistic legislation on making and keeping oaths, while the tractate *Nedarim* devotes extensive attention to vows. Josephus at an earlier date demonstrates that oath-taking in general was seen as valid in typical Jewish life (e.g., *Ant.* 15.370; 17.42; *J.W.* 2.451). Numerous Jewish texts, before and after the first century, treat perjury, false witness, profaning God's name, and the like, but no one seems ever to have made as sweeping a command as does Jesus, even given its contextual limitations (Luz [1989: 315] concludes, "Jesus thus stands completely in the tendency of Jewish parenesis but goes beyond it by categorically prohibiting oaths"; cf. H. D. Betz 1995: 263).

D. Textual Background. The text of Matthew shares only minor elements of verbal parallelism with either Lev. 19:12 or Num. 30:2, and the LXX is a reasonably accurate translation of the MT in each instance. Only "do not" appears in both OT texts and in Matthew. Matthew shares "the Lord" with Lev. 19:12 and "swear" with Num. 30:2. Whether free quotation or allusion, Matthew's text does not contain enough signs of literary dependence to make the question of text form a meaningful one. There is actually a higher degree of verbal parallelism in the allusions to Isa. 66:1 and Ps. 48:2 (47:3 LXX), but even then not enough to speak with confidence of literary dependence. Ruzer (1996) sees the influence of *Targum Pseudo-Jonathan* on Exod. 20:7 in the background: the combination of the command not to swear falsely with the modifier "by the name of the Memra of the Lord your God."

E. Hermeneutic Employed. Despite the differences with the first three antitheses noted above, Jesus continues to be the law's sovereign interpreter. He also opposes a system of legal interpretation that introduces loopholes or exceptions into moral commands that vitiate the original intent of those commands. At the same time, he is not replacing one law with another; contemporary application will have to be sensitive to each individual context (cf. the approach reflected in Horsley 1986).

F. Theological Use. The prohibition of oaths, therefore, probably does not prevent Christians today from swearing "to tell the truth, the whole truth, and nothing but the truth" in a court of law or from occasionally inserting in their speech to emphasize the complete veracity of a pronouncement a statement such as "as God is my witness" or "I swear to God." Nonetheless, the seriousness of such statements should lead to their very judicious use, and only in contexts in which people are absolutely sure of the truthfulness of what they utter. For a similar approach from within the Mennonite tradition, despite this tradition's frequent absolutizing of the prohibition against oath-taking, see Zook 1999. Nor does the NT encourage the practice of vows, especially those that appear to negotiate with God—"If only you will grant my prayer, I will do such-and-such"—though it does carry over the vestiges of vows from an OT context in settings that do not give us enough specific information to know all of what was involved (see esp. Acts 18:18; 21:23). The ideal is to arrive at a state in one's behavior and speech whereby one's word can be trusted without special promises or asseverations attached, and in which one's faith in God is strong enough that one does his will irrespective of his apparent response.

5:38

A. NT Context. Here Jesus even more clearly sets aside a fundamental Mosaic law. The legal "tit-for-tat" system of justice reflected in this law was not merely permitted, but explicitly required. Jesus obviously changes the focus to nonretaliation, but the specific illustrations that he provides are contextually limited in application. The word for "resist" in 5:39a (*anthistēmi*) was often used in legal contexts (cf. Isa. 50:8), and in light of 5:40

it is probably to be taken that way here (Davies and Allison 1988–1997: 1:540; Guelich 1982: 220). "Turning the other cheek" in 5:39b suggests a backhanded slap from, typically, a right-handed aggressor and was a characteristic Jewish form of insult (Hagner 1993: 131). Verse 40 refers to collateral that could or could not be required in a court of law (cf. Exod. 22:26–27). Sabourin (1978: 71) plausibly sees Lam. 3:30 behind 5:39b, and Exod. 22:25–26 behind 5:40. "Going the extra mile" involved the Roman conscription of private citizens to help carry military equipment for soldiers as they traveled (5:41). And giving to those who ask is not the same as giving everything that is requested, as Augustine (*Serm. Dom.* 67) noted long ago. It can be argued from all of these illustrations, therefore, that Jesus is not challenging the Jewish legal system, but rather is prescribing new attitudes and behaviors among individuals and communities that wish to follow him (see Blomberg 1997: 252; Horsley 1986; Tannehill 1970). The shift from retaliation to nonresistance nevertheless remains striking (on which, see Stassen 1992, esp. 33–52; Wink 1998). Jesus is stressing the need to break decisively the natural chain of evil action and reaction that characterizes human relationships. Nolland (1989: 294–304) includes excellent comparative ethical material and incisive analysis.

B. OT Context. The three occurrences of the identical phrase "an eye for an eye and a tooth for a tooth" occur in (1) a section of Mosaic legislation on the punishments for personal injuries (Exod. 21:12–36); (2) a series of laws surrounding the stoning of a blasphemer (Lev. 24:10–13); (3) legislation involving the witnesses needed to convict an accused person of a crime (Deut. 19:15–21). In each passage there are additional examples of the *lex talionis* ("hand for hand, foot for foot" in Exod. 21:24; "fracture for fracture" in Lev. 24:20; "life for life" in Deut. 19:21 and elsewhere). Indeed, the principle of "measure for measure," illustrated with numerous body parts, permeates all portions of the OT (see the catalog in Shemesh 2005) but J. F. Davis (2005) disputes this. It is important, however, to recognize that the original purpose of this Hebrew legislation probably was to limit the amount of revenge that could be exacted for an offense and to limit the location of that exaction to a court of law (Childs 1974: 472; see

Josephus, *Ant.* 4.35). Many other ancient Near Eastern cultures were often not even this humane (see C. J. H. Wright 1983: 166).

C. Use in Jewish Sources. It is impossible to determine how literally the *lex talionis* was implemented in first-century Jewish law. At least by the time of one of the Targumim, it is clear that monetary compensation was required rather than a literal body part: *Targum Pseudo-Jonathan* for each of the three OT texts rewrites, "*the value of* an eye for an eye, *the value of* a tooth for a tooth," and so on. It may well be that the text was interpreted in this more lenient sense from early on (see Sarna 1991: 127). Sarna also notes that only "a life for a life" cannot be implemented by means of monetary substitution. Philo expounds the law as "the interpreter and teacher of equality," commanding "that offenders should undergo a punishment similar to the offence which they have committed" (*Spec. Laws* 3.182; see also 3.195). *Jubilees* 4:32 describes the rationale for Cain's death as his being killed by stones that fell from his house as a righteous judgment for his having killed Abel with a stone. In a discussion of the *lex talionis*, Broer (1994) argues that Wis. 25:21–22 and *Jos. Asen.* 28:14 provide the key to understanding pre-Christian Jewish interpretation. However, these two texts speak of feeding one's enemy and not returning evil for evil, which seem more apt as parallels to the final antithesis in Jesus' sermon than to this one. The "measure for measure" principle more generally pervades rabbinic literature, but applications—for both rewards and punishments—often go beyond the natural limitations suggested by the principle (Phillips 2004).

D. Textual Background. All three OT texts are translated literally and identically by the LXX. It is this translation that Matthew reproduces exactly.

E. Hermeneutic Employed. At first glance, it seems that Jesus has abolished this OT law (*contra* Matt. 5:17). However, if he recognized that its original purpose was to restrict the severity of punishment, and if it had already been mitigated further by subsequent Jewish tradition, he may have had that same ameliorating purpose behind what seems to be a formal annulment. If he was focusing exclusively on his followers and their communities and not on governmental legisla-

tion, one can see how he could have believed that he was fulfilling and not abolishing the spirit of the original law. Verses 39–42 can be spoken of as a "focal instance" in ethical discourse—extreme commands that attract our attention to a key ethical principle that must variously be applied as circumstances change (Tannehill 1970; see, more generally, Harvey 1990). But Jesus' distinctive authority as the law's sovereign interpreter certainly continues.

F. Theological Use. Another key OT principle, that vengeance is reserved for God alone, points to a central theological application of Jesus' teaching here. On the one hand, it is crucial to observe that "a willingness to forgo one's personal rights and to allow oneself to be insulted and imposed upon is not incompatible with a firm stand for matters of principle and for the rights of others" (France 1985: 126; cf. Paul's attitude in Acts 16:37; 22:25; 25:8–12). On the other hand, even the best systems of human justice all too frequently fail to provide it—for ourselves or for others. Knowing that there is an omnipotent, omniscient God who will one day mete out absolutely fair judgment upon all humanity (and wonderfully gracious judgment on his followers) gives us the strength to endure injustice perpetrated on ourselves and others that might otherwise lead us to despair or to personal revenge.

5:43

A. NT Context. The unique feature of this "quotation," among the antitheses, is that only half of it appears to correspond to any OT text. "You shall love your neighbor" clearly comes from Lev. 19:18 ("you shall love your neighbor as yourself"), but no canonical Hebrew passage ever commands, "You shall hate your enemy." For this reason, commentators have often assumed Jesus was not necessarily quoting one written text, but rather was referring to an oral interpretive tradition of various texts (hence, "you have heard it *said* of old"). This certainly is possible, but it is equally possible that Jesus is summarizing in the second clause of his "quotation" a very natural inference that could be drawn from the original meaning of various OT passages (e.g., Deut. 23:3–6; 25:17–19; Ps. 139:21; Mounce [1991: 50] adds Deut. 7:2; 20:16).

In either case, Jesus continues the sharp contrasts that characterize Matt. 5:21–48. Perhaps this "antithesis" is the most radical of all: "Love your enemies and pray for those who persecute you" (5:44). Only in this way will Jesus' followers distinguish themselves against the common human trait of loving only those who treat one kindly (5:45–47). Whatever emotions may be involved, "love" here refers primarily to "generous, warm, costly self-sacrifice for another's good" (Carson 1984: 158). Not surprisingly, this section of the Sermon on the Mount ends with a statement that aptly summarizes this paragraph, the antitheses in general, and the thrust of Jesus' message thus far: "You therefore be perfect [or, 'mature'] as your heavenly Father is perfect [or, 'mature']" (5:48)—a command perhaps deliberately modeled on the structure of Lev. 19:1 ("Be holy, for I the LORD your God am holy"). On Jesus' exacting demands in general and on the particular command to love one's enemies, see Luz 1989: 349–51. Jesus will appeal to Lev. 19:18 again in Matt. 19:19 and 22:39 and parallels in discussions on the most important commandments, and in Luke 10:27 immediately prior to the parable of the Good Samaritan. "You shall love your neighbor as yourself" is likewise quoted as a central moral obligation for Christians in Gal. 5:14 and James 2:8.

B. OT Context. As noted previously, Lev. 19 forms part of that book's Holiness Code. The opening two verses call on Moses to tell Israel to be holy because the Lord their God is holy—phraseology that may have inspired Matt. 5:48. There does not seem to be any overarching structure to the chapter, which intermingles very sweeping commands, paralleled in the Decalogue (e.g., 19:3–4, 11–13), with other seemingly minor issues (e.g., 19:19, 27–28; but see Rooker 2004). The command to love one's neighbor as oneself clearly falls into the former category and forms the theological zenith of the chapter. It appears as the second, contrasting clause in a sentence that begins, "You shall not take vengeance or bear a grudge against the children of your people" (19:18). This contrast would naturally lead to the interpretation that the "neighbor" whom one is to love is also a member of one's own people, so that one would not naturally think of including enemies as neighbors. That the resident alien is listed separately in 19:34 seems to confirm this suspicion (Milgrom 2000: 1654).

C. Use in Jewish Sources. The most intriguing pre-Christian Jewish uses of Lev. 19:18 appear in the Dead Sea Scrolls. CD-A IX, 2–5 quotes this text and then continues, "Everyone of those who entered the covenant who brings an accusation against his fellow, unless it is with reproach before witnesses, or who brings it when he is angry, or he tells it to his elders so that they despise him, he is 'the one who avenges himself and bears resentments.'" After a lacuna in the manuscript, we read, "Is it not perhaps written that only 'he [God] avenges himself and bears resentment against his enemies' [Nah. 1:2]?" The juxtaposition of loving one's neighbor and avenging and resenting one's enemy, even if only God is supposed to do the latter, could have led to the type of misinterpretation that Jesus "quotes." CD-A VI, 20 has already presented the need for each one to love a spiritual "brother," and CD-A VII, 2 has introduced the concept of not bearing resentment against the same (cf. 1QS VII, 8–9). The *Rule of the Community* likewise refers to judgment belonging to God (1QS X, 18), and the writer (the Teacher of Righteousness?) quickly avers, "I shall not be involved at all in any dispute of the men of the pit until the day of vengeance" (1QS X, 19). But he also adds, "However, I shall not remove my anger from wicked men, nor shall I be appeased until he carries out his judgment" (1QS X, 20). This could easily be interpreted as "hate your enemy," even if only in attitude and not in action. In 1:4 the faithful community member is "to detest all the sons of darkness, each one in accordance with his guilt" (cf. Josephus, *J.W.* 2.139). Even in the immediate context of 6:21 ("I shall not comfort the oppressed until their path is perfect"), one may hear a distorted echo of Matt. 5:48.

In striking contrast, Exod. 23:4–5 commands helping an enemy's ox or donkey, but we do not find in the OT any command to love one's enemies in general (for partial anticipation of this teaching in the OT, see the list of texts cited in Hagner 1993: 134; cf. the elaboration in Piper 1979: 27–35). One must show concern for the resident alien living in one's midst (e.g., Lev. 19:34), and God certainly demonstrates concern for Gentile nations in various contexts (most notably Gen. 12:1–3; also throughout Jonah). But that is still a far cry from a command to love all people or peoples indiscriminately. The rabbinic literature likewise expands on the positive models of Exodus and other Hebrew Scriptures. Hillel summarizes the law as a kind of a negative Golden Rule: "What is hateful to you, do not do to your neighbor; that is the whole Torah, while the rest is commentary" (*b. Šabb.* 31a; on which, see Stern 1966). But the rabbis never formulate as sweeping and positive a love-command with respect to one's enemies as Jesus does (Str-B 1:368). It is particularly telling, given the hundreds of early Tannaitic parables, and given the fact that almost all of Jesus' stories find at least a partial parallel within the rabbinic haggadah, that no parallel of any kind to the parable of the Good Samaritan (Luke 10:30–37) appears, with its dynamic of being treated lovingly by one's most hated enemy. For the full collection of these parables, see Johnston 1978; for a more accessible representative sampling, see Johnston and McArthur 1989.

D. Textual Background. The relevant portion of Lev. 19:18 is translated literally from the MT in the LXX, and wherever the text is excerpted in the NT, it follows the LXX verbatim. Interestingly, after "you shall love your neighbor" *Targum Pseudo-Jonathan* on Lev. 19:18 adds "so that what is hateful to you, you shall not do to him," a negative equivalent to Jesus' "Golden Rule" that will also feature prominently in this sermon, at the conclusion to its body and as a summary of all "the law and the prophets" (Matt. 7:12).

E. Hermeneutic Employed. If Jesus is not formally setting aside a portion of written Torah, he is at the very least heralding an era in which nationalist ethics are giving way to universalistic ones. We should not be surprised that the NT nowhere endorses the holy wars of the OT, that Jew and Gentile are throughout put on an equal footing, and that God's love is clearly said to extend to all peoples. Jesus is requiring a "greater righteousness" (recall 5:20) than Jew or Gentile have thus far displayed with any regularity. He is the law's sovereign interpreter, at times appearing even to transcend it.

F. Theological Use. The Good Samaritan aptly illustrates what Jesus is teaching here in a nutshell. But in our world of naming hospitals and awards after the Good Samaritan, we must remind ourselves that the entire radical thrust of that parable lay in its point that even one's enemy was one's neighbor (see Blomberg 1990a: 233). As through-

out the Sermon on the Mount, Jesus' ethics do not necessarily dictate what responsibilities governments have to protect their citizens; one cannot articulate a full-orbed biblical understanding of war and peace from this one message. Nonethless, for God's people, living in community, Jesus' message is clear. We must reach out with every kind of humanitarian aid at our disposal, even to people in nations with whom our governments may be at war, and even to people in our own countries who otherwise despise and mistreat the church. Only then will people see any difference in us that makes our more overtly evangelistic appeals to them compelling (cf. Reiser 2001 and J. L. Bailey 1993).

Matthew 6:1–7:28

The rest of the Sermon on the Mount contains no formal quotations of the OT, although parallels to other Jewish literature abound (see Stoutenburg 1996). Almsgiving (Matt. 6:2) played a fundamental role in Judaism from at least the time of Deut. 15:11 onward. There are verbal echoes to the OT in Matt. 6:6 (to Isa. 26:20 and 2 Kings 4:33 on entering a room with a closed door and on entering a room to pray, respectively), but the larger contexts make it doubtful that Jesus was actually calling these texts to mind. Matthew 6:8 possibly echoes Isa. 65:24 on God answering people even before they call on him. It has long been noted that almost every clause in the Lord's Prayer bears some resemblance to the Jewish Qaddish prayers (on which, see Petuchowski and Brocke 1978). A probable echo of Ezek. 36:23 may be heard in Matt. 6:9, with its concern that the name of the Lord be made holy. The petition that God's kingdom come and his will be done (6:10) may have Nebuchadnezzar's judgment and prayer in its background (cf. Dan. 4:32, 35, esp. Θ; see Philonenko 1992). The pleas for daily bread and lack of temptation (6:11–12) may echo Prov. 30:7–9 (Byargeon 1998). The later scribal additions to the Lord's Prayer (6:13) seem to be based on 1 Chron. 29:11–13. Matthew 6:16–17 may echo Isa. 58:5 on the true fast that God desires, involving moral more than ritual purity.

As for the rest of the Sermon on the Mount, 6:26 must be read against the backdrop of Prov. 6:6–8 and taken not as a call to inaction, but as one to trust in God's providence as one works hard (Healey 1989). Matthew 6:29 alludes to Solomon's fabled wealth (on which, see 1 Kings 4:20–34; 7:1–51; 10:14–29). For dogs as a metaphor for wicked people who attack God's anointed (Matt. 7:6), see Ps. 22:16. We have already examined one extrabiblical parallel to 7:12 (see above, p. 29), to which many others could be added, but none appears in the Hebrew OT. The Sermon on the Mount concludes with three illustrations in the Jewish "Two Ways" genre, already modeled in Deut. 30:15–20. The right path that leads to life (7:14) may echo Ps. 16:11; the proper gate may hark back to Ps. 118:19–20 (Davies and Allison 1988–1997: 1:699). For backgrounds on discerning false prophets (7:15–20), see especially Deut. 13:1–5; 18:20–22. The lament "Did we not prophesy in your name?" (7:22) alludes to language of texts such as Jer. 14:14; 27:15. Jesus' banishing reply (7:23) may allude to Ps. 6:9 LXX (6:8 ET): "Away from me, all you workers of lawlessness" (Davies and Allison 1988–1997: 1:719).

Matthew 8:1–17

Matthew 8–9 comprises the first large narrative section within the body of this Gospel. Thematically, it is unified by a series of ten miracles, mostly of healing. The first healing, of a leper (8:1–4), relies on the provisions of Lev. 13 for its background. The leper's audacity to mingle with the crowd in search of Jesus, contrary to the prohibition in Lev. 13:46, is matched by Jesus' willingness to heal with a touch. Holiness, not impurity, here proves contagious (despite Lev. 5:3; see Borg 1984). The leper's confidence in Jesus' ability to heal him in the first place may have derived from the story of Elisha and Naaman in 2 Kings 5. Jesus, in sending the man to the priest, obeys the laws of Lev. 14:1–32, but his main purpose may be disclosed in the final phrase of Matt. 8:4 ("as a testimony to [or, perhaps 'against'] them"; see Ridderbos 1987: 160).

The clearest allusion in the next account, that of the healing of the centurion's servant (8:5–13), comes in v. 11. "From the east and west" probably alludes to Ps. 107:3, in which those whom God redeems from the enemy are "those he gathered from the lands, from east and west, from north and south." In the psalm it is not clear that Gentiles are necessarily in view, but in Jesus' usage they most certainly are. The combination of "gnashing" with "teeth" (8:12), frequent throughout Matthew in references to hell (cf. 13:42, 50; 22:13; 24:51; 25:30), appears already in Job 16:9; Ps. 35:16; 37:12; 112:10; and Lam. 2:16 (Davies and Allison 1988–1997: 2:31).

8:17

A. NT Context. After one more miracle story, that of the healing of Simon Peter's mother-in-law of a fever (8:14–15), Matthew generalizes and speaks of a larger healing service after sundown in which Jesus also exorcises the demon-possessed (8:16). All three of the miracle stories of 8:1–15 are paralleled in either Mark or Luke or both, but only Matthew sees in Jesus' healing ministry a fulfillment of prophecy (8:17).

The context in Matthew is clearly one of physical healings. Charismatic exegetes have regularly picked up on this observation, combined it with the observation that Isa. 52:13–53:12 is about the atonement provided by God's Suffering Servant, and thus stressed that there is physical healing in the atonement. If by this they mean that God sometimes does still miraculously heal people today of physical afflictions on the basis of Christ's work on the cross, they are absolutely correct; but if by this they promise anyone such healing, based only on sufficient faith, they fly in the face of numerous NT texts to the contrary, most notably Jesus' prayer in the Garden of Gethsemane (Mark 14:36 pars.) and the Lord's response to Paul's prayer concerning his "thorn in the flesh" (2 Cor. 12:9). Noncharismatics, often recoiling from such abuse of Matt. 8:17, sometimes deny that Matthew had anything but spiritual healing in mind, on the basis of the context of Isa. 53:4. If that is so, however, it then makes no sense for him to have put this text at the end of a section on physical healing. For a balanced assessment of physical and spiritual dimensions of the atonement see Moo 1988 (see also Carson 1984: 207).

It is possible that both sides in the debate have missed Matthew's original thrust, which may have been to focus primarily on *ritual* purity and impurity (Patte 1987: 117). The three individuals physically healed would have also been considered ritually unclean (or at least "second-class"

citizens) for additional reasons: the uniquely defiling nature of the disease of leprosy, the Gentile
background of the centurion's servant, and the
gender of Peter's mother-in-law. France (1985:
157) speaks of a series of three "excluded" people
who are healed. For non-life-threatening injuries,
the social stigma and ostracism attached to ritual
impurity often caused graver suffering than the
physical maladies themselves (although 8:6 suggests that at least one of these three sick people
suffered in both respects). Whether or not this
emphasis was explicitly intended here, it certainly
had become clear by Matthew's day that in Christ
there no longer existed categories such as ritually
pure and impure (see esp. Acts 10:1–11:18).

B. OT Context. As already noted, this verse
appears as part of the last of four Servant Songs in
Isaiah (the first three are 42:1–4; 49:1–6; 50:4–9).
Both within and in between these four passages,
Isaiah explicitly equates the servant with Israel
(41:8–10; 44:1–2; 45:4; 49:3). Thus, as with the
Isaianic prophecy of a young woman's conception
(7:14), it is natural to look for a "near-fulfillment"
of this prophecy within OT times: in some sense
Israel suffered vicariously on behalf of humanity.
These explicit identifications of the servant with
Israel also make it difficult to adopt the view that
the near-fulfillment of these prophecies lay with
some anonymous individual within ancient Israel
(as in, e.g., Ceresko 1994; Bergey 1997).

Of course, it is not necessary for each of the Servant Songs to have the identical referent in view,
but there is enough recurring imagery throughout
them to make this assumption natural: one who is
God's chosen (42:1; 49:1), who will bring justice
(42:1, 4; 53:11) and blessing (49:3–5; 53:10–12),
even for Gentiles (42:1, 4; 49:6; 52:15), despite
appearing not to triumph at first because he does
not speak out or quarrel (42:2–3; 50:5–7; 53:7)
and because he is mocked, despised, and rejected
(49:7; 50:6; 53:3). Yet in the end he will be vindicated (42:4; 50:8–9; 53:10–12; see further
Blomberg 2002b).

At the same time, there is a progression of revelation from one text to the next. Isaiah 42:1–4
could be speaking of an individual, but it makes
sense taken strictly as Israel, too. Isaiah 49:1–6,
while again calling Israel the servant, pushes the
boundaries of a collective interpretation, for how
can Israel restore Israel (v. 6)? A separate person

seems to be required to fit the description of one
"who was despised and abhorred by the nation"
(49:7). In 50:4–9 the description of the servant's
rejection becomes more detailed and explicit:
mocked, beaten, spat upon—language that most
readily suggests the treatment of an individual but
could still be a striking metaphor for a nation. By
the time we come to 52:13–53:12, there is nothing that requires Israel as a nation to be in view at
all, even though parts of this text could fit such an
interpretation. But only an individual fits those
verses that speak of substitutionary sacrifice for
the nation, including 53:4. Likewise, the servant's
disfigured appearance (52:14; 53:2), his label as "a
man of sorrows" (53:3), and his death and vindication (53:8–9, 11) prove far more intelligible when
taken of a specific person within Israel, a specific
person who had not yet lived before the coming
of Christ. For the need to see an individual here,
see Blocher 1975: 67 and Blenkinsopp 2002: 351.
For the presence of substitutionary sacrifice, see
Oswalt 1986–1998: 2:377. It seems appropriate,
therefore, to speak of Isaiah envisaging two levels
of fulfillment: one in the restored, partially obedient, postexilic Israel, and a much grander, complete fulfillment in the Messiah, whom Matthew
would recognize as Jesus (see esp. Smillie 2005;
cf. Gundry 1967: 230; Childs 2001: 422–23, at
least at the level of canonical Isaiah; and Hugenberger 1995).

A second kind of double-entendre seems present in the ailments described in 53:4. "Infirmities"
naturally suggest physical illnesses or injuries, but
"sorrows" could include emotional discouragement or mental pain as well (see BDB s.v. *ḥālî*
and *mak'ōb*, respectively; see also *TWOT* 1:287,
425). The next verse will refer to "transgressions"
and "iniquities" (53:5). Thus it is not clear that
we have to choose among the various things that
make us unwell. The servant will bring healing for
all of them; the "peace" (*šālôm*) that he brings is
holistic, restoring body and soul alike. Other texts
in Isaiah that demonstrate physical as well as spiritual well-being characterizing the messianic age
include 29:18; 32:3–4; and 35:5–6 (see further
Gundry 1994: 150).

C. Use in Jewish Sources. Isaiah 53:4 is not itself cited or alluded to in any extant, unambiguously pre-Christian Jewish source. Many scholars
believe that the entire fourth Servant Song finds

no messianic interpretation prior to Jesus and/or the NT. While Isa. 53:4 is not cited elsewhere in the NT either, the song itself is: in two quotations ascribed to Jesus in Luke 22:37 (of Isa. 53:12) and John 12:38 (of Isa. 53:1) and in three epistolary contexts (Rom. 10:16; 15:21; 1 Pet. 2:22); see also Acts 8:32–33. On the probability of this early Christian interpretation actually originating with Jesus, see O. Betz 1998. For Mark 10:45 pars. containing a probable allusion to the fourth Servant Song by the historical Jesus, see R. E. Watts 1998. France (1971: 110–32) deals thoroughly with Jesus' own use of Isa. 53 and adds as one more clear allusion Mark 14:24 pars. and as probable allusions Mark 9:12; Matt. 3:15; and Luke 11:22. However, a credible case can be made that hints remain of such an interpretation, at least among certain branches of early Judaism. The translation of the terms for "root" and "child" in the LXX of Isa. 53:2 match those used of the Messiah in 11:1 and 9:6, respectively (Page 1985: 486). The variant Isaiah scroll found at Qumran (1QIsaᵃ) reads a little more clearly as a reference to an individual, especially with its unique addition to 53:11, "out of the suffering of his soul he will see light" (Abegg, Flint, and Ulrich 1999: 360; see their notes on p. 358). Other fragmentary materials from Qumran include 4Q491c (frg. 1), which seems to allude to Isa. 52–53 in the context of a description of the Messiah, and 4Q541, which twice refers to a messianic-like figure as suffering (frgs. 2–3) and once as providing atonement (frg. 9). *Testament of Levi* 2:10–11 predicts figures like Levi and Judah (priest and king) who will redeem Israel and save the whole race of humanity, while *T. Benj.* 3:8 in its shorter Armenian form speaks of one who will fulfill the heavenly prophecy concerning a spotless person defiled by the lawless, a sinless human dying for the sake of impious people (for details with respect to all of these references, see Hengel 2005). These last two texts, however, are usually taken to be the product of later Christian interpolations into the *Testaments of the Twelve Patriarchs*.

Whatever one makes of all these hints, if indeed they are even that, a clear messianic interpretation of Isa. 52:13–53:12 appears in the post-Christian *Targum Isaiah* (see explicitly in 52:13; 53:10). On the one hand, it is important to stress that the Targum so rewords the text that this messiah no longer suffers or dies, but instead destroys and reigns over his various enemies (rightly Syrén 1989). On the other hand, it is difficult to imagine *any* kind of messianic interpretation arising for the first time in Jewish circles once it became widely known that Christians used this text to support their identification of the crucified Jesus as the Messiah (rightly Jeremias 1967). By the time of the Babylonian Talmud, the messianic interpretation was well entrenched (as one of three main Jewish approaches, alongside interpretation that saw the servant either as all Israel or as the righteous within Israel). Evidence from Justin Martyr suggests it was already well established in the mid-second century. The most balanced conclusion seems to be that although there is no unambiguous pre-Christian evidence for a messianic perspective on the Servant Songs, and especially for a suffering messiah, "there is good reason to think that some initial steps had been taken in that direction" (Page 1985: 493). For the texts from the rabbinic period, see Page 1985: 491–92; and Str-B 1:481–85; both sources also note probable allusions to this Servant Song in *1 Enoch*, which is increasingly being viewed, even in its "Parables" section, as stemming from a pre-Christian milieu.

D. Textual Background. Matthew's rendering seems much closer to the MT than to the LXX. The Hebrew can be translated, "He himself has borne our illnesses, and as for our sufferings, he has loaded himself with them," while the LXX reads, "This man bears our sins and suffers anguish for our sake" (Archer and Chirichigno 1983: 121). The MT obviously fits Matthew's context of physical healings much better than does the LXX. Nothing in Matthew's translation requires dependence on the LXX (*contra* Menken 2004a: 35–49); he may have created his own, comparatively literal, fresh rendering into Greek from the original Hebrew. Stendahl (1954: 106–7) speaks of Matthew functioning as his own "targumist" here.

E. Hermeneutic Employed. As with Matthew's previous uses of Isaiah, double fulfillment would appear to be the best label for the hermeneutic at work here. Isaiah explicitly identified the servant in earlier Servant Songs as Israel but increasingly used imagery that was impossible for a nation to fulfill. Matthew recognized this, may have known of an already existing messianic interpretation of what remained unfulfilled, and drew on the holistic understanding of affliction and redemption throughout Isaiah to introduce one of his distinctive and characteristic fulfillment formulas here. Referring to the prophet by name may have encouraged listeners to consider other teachings of that same prophet relevant to the material at hand. Gundry (1994: 150) observes that Matthew's "quotations from Isaiah all occur in summaries of Jesus' salvific work," in contrast with, say, the "doleful quotations" of Jeremiah.

F. Theological Use. At the very least, Matthew is showing that Jesus' ministry of healing was prophesied as part of his messianic role. The question of Jesus' identity must thus again come to the fore. Thus Vledder (1997: 185–86) speaks of Matthew legitimizing Jesus' deeds: they are not merely the sensational workings of an extraordinary man, but rather the exhibitions of God's almighty will. Hagner (1993: 211) comments, "The point of the healings is not so much to be found in the events themselves but in their witness to the person of Jesus; i.e., they are basically Christological in character." To the extent that Matthew can expect his readers to know more of his quotation's Isaianic context, he may well be dropping hints, which will become clearer as Jesus' crucifixion draws nearer, that Jesus is the Suffering Servant in other respects as well, most notably in suffering vicariously for the sins of humanity. Knowing that Jesus himself had already used Isaiah 53 in a messianic fashion would have given Matthew considerable confidence to develop this theme further. This use of Isaiah, like Matthew's next (Isa. 42:1–4), quoted in Matt. 12:18–21, brings balance to his messianic portrait. The same Messiah who will return as the fearful, majestic, transcendent Son of Man to judge the world is also the sympathetic, kindly Savior, who experiences sorrow and is acquainted with grief (Davies and Allison 1988–1997: 2:59).

Matthew 8:18–9:13

The next several Matthean pericopes contain no OT quotations. Matthew 8:20 introduces the essential title "Son of Man," which is Jesus' preferred self-designation in all four Gospels. A number of scholars have argued that in at least these "earthly Son of Man sayings," if not in all of Jesus' uses of this title, the background throughout Ezekiel of God calling the prophet "son of man" as a reference to a mere mortal is all that is in view (see also Ps. 8:4). This view then subdivides into seeing "son of man" as equivalent simply to "a man" (e.g., Casey 1979), as a circumlocution for "I" (e.g., Vermes 1973), or as referring to "a man like me" or "a man in my position" (e.g., Lindars 1983). It is increasingly recognized, however, that Dan. 7:13–14 forms the more important OT background, in which a human being is ushered into the very presence of the "Ancient of Days" (i.e., God) and given universal dominion over the kingdoms of the earth (S. Kim 1985; Caragounis 1986; Collins 1992; Slater 1995; Burkett 1999). Even in a text such as Matt. 8:20, the poignancy arises from one who was the exalted, heavenly Son of Man living in human ignominy, with no regular place to sleep during his itinerant ministry.

Jesus' dialogue in Matt. 8:21–22 with the man who wants to first go and bury his father reminds the reader of Elisha's request of Elijah in 1 Kings 19:19–21. There, Elisha's request to kiss his parents good-bye is granted; for Jesus, however, discipleship is so urgent that the request is denied (the man may be asking of Jesus considerably more time than at first seems apparent; see McCane 1990). The stilling of the storm in 8:23–27 demonstrates that Jesus has the identical sovereignty over wind and waves attributed to Yahweh in the OT (see Jon. 1–2; Ps. 104:6–7; 107:23–32). In the OT, the ability to sleep untroubled is "a sign of faith in the protective power of God (Lev 26.6; Job 11.18–9; Ps 3.5; 4.8; Prov 3.23–4). Furthermore, there were moments of disaster or peril when it seemed as though God were asleep, and his people sought to wake him up (Ps 35.23; 44.23–4; 59.4; Isa 51.9)" (Davies and Allison 1988–1997: 2:72). The threatening question posed by the Gadarene demoniac of Christ in 8:29 may allude to the misguided rebuke of Elijah by the Zarephath widow in 1 Kings 17:18. Jesus' claim to forgive sins in 9:2 elicits charges of blasphemy (9:3) because of texts such as Isa. 43:25, which were understood to ascribe that privilege to God alone.

9:13

A. NT Context. In his version of his own call to discipleship (Matt. 9:9–13), Matthew uniquely adds a reference to Jesus telling his critics, "Go and learn what this is: 'I wish for mercy and not sacrifice'" (9:13). Matthew is described as a tax collector who immediately follows Jesus when called (9:9). Jesus subsequently celebrates a festive meal with Matthew and other social outcasts at his house, which triggers Pharisaic criticism (9:10–11). Table fellowship in ancient Israel was reserved for intimate friends and usually implied an endorsement of the practices of those with whom one associated. Tax collectors were notorious for raking in more than Rome demanded; the occupation was traitorous enough even when they did not charge excessive fees to line their own pockets (see Donahue 1971). Jesus replies with the proverb that it is not the healthy but the sick who need a doctor (9:12), and then, at least in Matthew, he adds the reference to Hos. 6:6. "Sacrifice," by synecdoche, probably stands for "strict obedience to the commandments of God" (Hagner 1993: 239). As in its original OT context, the "not x but y" form of seemingly absolute comparison probably meant "y much more than x" (G. I. Davies 1992: 170). Jesus never abolishes any of the written Torah (Matt. 5:17), and even the dramatic changes that he does introduce come fully into play only after his death and resurrection. By Matthew's time, it will be recognized that the system of sacrifices in the Jewish temple has been superseded by Christ's once-for-all sacrifice, but, if Jesus is hinting at that here, it is not likely that he was yet understood so radically. In this context, the only unambiguous point of the OT quotation is to justify Jesus' celebration with repentant sinners. The passage will appear again in 12:7.

B. OT Context. Hosea 6:1–3 describes what at first glance looks like genuine repentance on the part of Israel in response to Hosea's prophecy. Verses 4–10, however, demonstrate that the repentance is merely feigned. God alternately laments and threatens, but it is clear his people's periodic good behavior is too short-lived (6:4b). Verse 6a thus repeats the theme of 1 Sam. 15:22, that obedience, in this case by means of mercy, is better than sacrifice (cf. also in the LXX: Ps. 39:7; Prov. 16:7). With synonymous parallelism, the second half of the verse repeats the concept: "the knowledge of God rather than burnt offerings" (6:6b). As in Matthew's context,

Hosea is not abolishing the sacrificial system, but rather is declaring its meaninglessness apart from heartfelt repentance demonstrated through consistently changed behavior (Andersen and Freedman 1980: 430; *contra* Macintosh [1997: 234], who thinks that "Hosea repudiates radically the whole sacrificial cult with its licentious feasting").

C. Use in Jewish Sources. The relative rather than absolute contrast implied in Hos. 6:6 is made clear in the Targum on Hosea, which here reads, "For those who do acts of kindness are more desirable before me than he that sacrifices, and those who carry out the law of the Lord more than those that offer up burnt offerings." The *Sibylline Oracles* twice alludes to this teaching in its more absolute form (2:80–83; 8:334), but at least the latter text appears in a clearly Christian interpolation, so it is hard to know how much weight to give either reference. After the destruction of the temple in AD 70, of course, texts such as Hosea's would take on great significance in answering for the rabbis the question of how one could be made right with God apart from actual animal sacrifices (see, e.g., the texts cited in Str-B 1:500).

D. Textual Background. The five Greek words that Matthew cites represent verbatim LXX material (unless one follows LXX B, in which case "rather than" appears for "and not"; Matthew then could be seen as bringing his translation into even closer line with the MT [see further Hill 1977]), which in turn comprises a reasonably literal translation of the MT. "The only comment needed here is that חָפֵץ means 'take pleasure in—delight in' [the probable meaning here, according to BDB 342b], whereas θέλειν = 'wish, desire.' But θέλειν is quite often used for חָפֵץ in the LXX" (Archer and Chirichigno 1983: 145).

E. Hermeneutic Employed. Jesus here is following good rabbinic form in citing Scripture to justify seemingly novel behavior. His introduction, "Go and learn what this is," corresponds to a standard later rabbinic introductory formula (see the references in Str-B 1:499). Jesus never informs the Jewish leaders of principles that they do not already know; instead, he calls them to "ponder a creative reinterpretation of their tradition . . . to push their thoughts beyond conventional interpretations" (Davies and Allison

1988–1997: 2:104; cf. Cope [1976: 68]: "Where Torah-piety and the interests of mercy conflict, mercy should prevail"). This is not a text about the fulfillment of Scripture so much as the application of a fundamental moral principle of the OT that continues throughout the new age that Jesus is inaugurating.

F. Theological Use. If God desired mercy more than sacrifice even during the era of the Mosaic covenant, when animal sacrifices were required for the forgiveness of sins, much more then does he uphold that principle in the new age in which ritual concerns increasingly give way to moral ones. "Cultic observance without inner faith and heartfelt covenant loyalty is vain" (Davies and Allison 1988–1997: 2:105). Jesus' audience should be delighted rather than upset that the "riff-raff" of society are repenting. In eating with them, Jesus does not incur uncleanness, but rather acknowledges their newly found purity. To contemporize Jesus' principles for our day, we might affirm in God's name, "I desire devotion and not hymn-singing, service and not sermons" (Garrett 1997: 161)!

Matthew 9:14–38

Other possible allusions to the OT in Matt. 9 include v. 15, given that a bridegroom was a common Jewish metaphor for God (see esp. Hos. 2:16–23). The proverb in v. 17 may reflect the same features of new wine and old wineskins depicted in Josh. 9:13 and Job 32:19. The ritual impurity of the woman with the flow of blood, presupposed in 9:20–22, depends on Lev. 15:19–33. The edge of Jesus' cloak (9:20) probably refers to the fringes or tassels of a prayer shawl (cf. Num. 15:38–39 with Deut. 22:12). The resurrection of the synagogue leader's daughter (9:23–26) calls to mind the resurrections performed by Elijah and Elisha and seems to echo 1 Kings 17:19 or 2 Kings 4:33 with its commands to exclude the public (Theissen 1983: 61). The reference to those who are like sheep without a shepherd (9:36) almost certainly alludes to Ezek. 34:5. Numerous other OT texts develop this theme, too, most notably Num. 27:17; 1 Kings 22:17; 2 Chron. 18:16; and Zech. 10:2.

Matthew 10:1–42

Chapter 10 begins with the list of the twelve apostles whom Jesus chose (vv. 1–4), undoubtedly based on the number of tribes of Israel in OT times (cf. 19:28). Jesus is reconstituting God's covenant community among his followers. The rest of the chapter contains his instructions to the Twelve, both for their first short-term mission (10:5–16) and for the rest of the "church age" (10:17–42). The reference to the lost sheep of Israel's house (10:6) may allude to Jer. 50:6 (see also Isa. 53:6; Ezek. 34). The disciples are charged to proclaim the same message of the kingdom that John and Jesus preached (on which see above, pp. 11–12, 18). Their miracle-working ministry (10:8) will rely on the same texts as Jesus' ministry, too (esp. Isa. 35:5–6). The reference to Sodom and Gomorrah (10:15) recalls the events of Gen. 18:20–19:28. The overthrow of these cities had become proverbial already in OT times (Isa. 1:9; 13:19; Jer. 23:14; 50:40; Amos 4:11; see Davies and Allison 1988–1997: 2:179). "Shrewd" is a natural characteristic to attribute to serpents (10:16), in light of the description of the serpent in the garden (Gen. 3:1).

In the second half of the chapter (10:17–42), the family strife predicted in 10:21 echoes Mic. 7:6 and foreshadows 10:35, which will quote this text explicitly. Verse 30 seems to echo 1 Sam. 14:45, on not allowing a hair of Jonathan's head to fall to the ground. Verse 37 contains an echo of Deut. 33:9, in which Levi says that he had no regard for his parents, he did not recognize his brothers, and he did not acknowledge his own children but watched over God's word and guarded his covenant. "Receiving a prophet" in 10:41 may hark back to the stories about the reception of Elijah by the widow of Zarephath (1 Kings 17:9–24) and of Elisha by the Shunammite woman (2 Kings 4:8–37). "Little ones" as a designation for the disciples (10:42) may have been borrowed from a text such as Zech. 13:7, which Matthew will more explicitly cite later (26:31) (Davies and Allison 1988–1997: 2:229).

10:35

A. NT Context. A central theme in Matt. 10:17–42 is the coming hostility that the disciples would experience after Christ's death and resurrection, reflected in part in the persecutions described in

Acts, the epistles, and Revelation. In this context, Jesus reminds his followers that he did not come to bring peace, in the sense of absence of external strife, in this life (10:34a). Schweizer (1975: 251) observes: "God's kingdom has never been the peace of the false prophets who cry, 'Peace, peace!' while avarice and meanness lay waste the earth and transform God's good creation into its opposite (Jer. 6:14; etc.); neither, however, is it the 'holy war' of the devout who take the field to conquer their oppressors with the mighty support of God." Quite the contrary, at times his ministry would create conflict, as people became polarized in their responses to his message and missionaries (10:34b). Thus Jesus can declare, "I came to turn a man against his father, and a daughter against her mother, a daughter-in-law against her mother-in-law, and the enemies of a person will be household members" (10:35–36). For the first time thus far, Matthew gives no introduction to show that Scripture is being quoted, but lack of such a formula was common enough in ancient Judaism.

The quotation does not apply in the same way to households that are entirely Christian; Jesus is thinking primarily of the competing allegiances of believers and unbelievers. However, even in the best of families one person's desires may go against God's will, in which case loyalty to God must clearly take precedence over even the closest of human ties (10:37). Such loyalty may lead to cross-bearing, literally or metaphorically (10:38), but those who lose their physical lives for Christ will gain eternal life (10:39). The context makes it clear that Jesus is not directly initiating warfare within families, but he is talking about the frequent response of those who reject him. Knowing that this would happen and yet carrying forward with his mission, Jesus can indirectly claim to be causing the hostility. France (1985: 188) concludes, "Jesus calls not for an unloving attitude, but for a willingness to put him first in the concrete situation where the call of Jesus and of family conflicts." The same saying appears in expanded form in Luke 12:53. If this was a Q logion, neither Matthew nor Luke has followed it all that closely, but presumably Matthew has preserved the more original form (see Heil 1997).

B. OT Context. Micah 7 describes the godlessness in Israel prior to its defeat by Assyria in 722 BC. Sins include murder (7:2b), bribery and injustice (7:3), and betrayal, even of one's most intimate friends (7:5). The list of examples of enemies within one's own household (7:6) follows naturally. Wolff (1990: 210) sees this as the intensification of the provisional hostility already described. All males (including adults) in a household were under the authority of the patriarch; all females (including sons' wives and male children) were under that of the matriarch. Hence, the examples provided cover all possible breaches (Andersen and Freedman 2000: 573). Finally, Micah contrasts his attitude: watching expectantly for the Lord and waiting for God his Savior to hear him (7:7). The main difference from the context in which Jesus employs these words is that Micah apparently envisions no innocent victims—the righteous for whom the unrighteous cause trouble—since he has already declared that the godly have been swept from the land and that no one upright remains (7:2a)!

C. Use in Jewish Sources. Micah 7:1–5 in the Targum continues to describe the godlessness in Micah's day, but 7:6 shifts abruptly to the future tense: "For *in that time* son shall spurn father, a daughter shall quarrel with her mother, a daughter-in-law *shall treat* her mother-in-law *with contempt*; a man's own household shall be his enemies." If the Targum understood this verse as a prophecy of something beyond just that which occurred in the eighth century BC, and if Jesus knew this interpretive tradition, then it would have been very natural for him to reapply the verse to the hostility that he knew his followers would face. From texts such as these and others cited below, Hagner (1993: 292) thinks that the Micah passage itself originally referred "to a time of trouble before eschatological deliverance." Interestingly, 7:7 in the Targum continues, "But I will *rejoice in the Memra of* the Lord, I will *exult in* the God *who accomplishes* my salvation; my God will hear *my prayer*," while 7:8 explicitly identifies the time of fulfillment as that of the Roman oppression by adding, "Do not rejoice over me, *O Rome* my enemy."

Otherwise, there are no explicit, demonstrably pre-Christian Jewish quotations of Mic. 7:6. Possible allusions include *Ahiqar* 139: "My distress is my own fault, before whom will I be found innocent? My own sons spied out my house, what shall I say to strangers?" (and cf. line 140 with its reference to a poisoner from one's own house); *3 Bar.* 4:17: "Brother does not show mercy to brother, nor father to son, nor son to father," speaking of those who do evil via drunkenness (cf. also 5:17); *1 En.* 56:7: "A man shall not recognize his brother, nor a son his mother, until there shall be a (significant) number of corpses from among them," speaking of when the city of "my righteous ones" shall become an obstacle to Israel's enemies (cf., more vaguely, 99:5; 100:2); *Sib. Or.* 8:84–85: "Neither will parents be friendly to children nor children to parents because of impiety and affliction beyond hope," speaking of a future time of confusion throughout the earth when the universal ruler comes and judges all humanity. The last of these references is perhaps the most interesting parallel to Matt. 10:35–36 but also the most likely post-Christian reference. Park (1995: 154) finds parallel ideas in 4Q175 14–20, but the parallels do not seem nearly as close as in the passages cited here. Still, there were enough general scenes of households at war in earlier Jewish apocalyptic to make Jesus' application of this text to his context natural (L. C. Allen 1976: 389). Much later rabbinic literature would specifically apply Mic. 7:6 to the days of the Messiah (see esp. *b. Sanh.* 97a; cf. *m. Soṭah* 9:15; *b. Soṭah* 49b, *Midr. Song* 2:13; on which, see Grelot 1986).

D. Textual Background. The MT reads literally, "For a son treats as a fool the father; a daughter rises up against a mother, a daughter-in-law against her husband's mother; the enemies of a man [are] the men of his house." The LXX translates "treats as a fool" as "dishonors" but otherwise renders the Hebrew quite literally into Greek, supplying appropriate possessive pronouns and the necessary verb in the final clause. Matthew replaces "son" with "man," omits the first verb (since Jesus has already used one) but appropriately, on the basis of its later usage in the verse, inserts "against," omits the second verb, and paraphrases or abbreviates the final clause by reading simply "the enemies of a man are his householders." It is difficult to demonstrate dependence exclusively on either the MT or the LXX, but the sense of both is clearly retained.

E. Hermeneutic Employed. Because neither Matthew nor Jesus introduces this quotation with any formula, it is quite possible that neither

of them thought of this as any kind of fulfillment of prophecy. The hermeneutic employed is to cite biblical language that is appropriate to a specific context that contains certain parallels to its original context, just as we might today try to encourage an oppressed fellow-Christian by saying, "The first shall be last and the last shall be first" (a saying that itself was used in several different NT contexts). Indeed, it could be argued that "this is not a quotation, but only allusive language derived from an OT verse dealing with tensions in the home during the reign of Ahaz, which was an age of sagging morality, presenting a pattern of apostasy which Micah had to denounce" (Archer and Chirichigno 1983: 159). Given the amount of parallelism, however, it is perhaps better to call it a quotation but not try to categorize it as a particular scheme of prophecy and fulfillment. Jesus is speaking of what he came to do and simply lapses into biblical language because of the parallels in the two situations. At the same time, especially if the rendering of the Targum were already known, one could envisage this as a form of typology easily enough: a recurring pattern of hostility on the part of God's opponents at key junctures in the history of his people.

F. Theological Use. Whether or not deliberately employing typology, Jesus, as reported by Matthew, is using biblical language solemnly to underline his prediction of future opposition to his followers, even from among their own relatives. (Nolland [2005: 441] thinks the direction of hostility—from the younger generation to the older—is meant to point out disobedience to the command to honor parents.) Unlike all the passages treated thus far, the focal point of the quotation is neither Jesus himself, nor John as forerunner, nor some abiding moral principle, but rather the future persecution of Jesus' followers. Still, Jesus and Matthew, like ancient Jews more generally, believed that Scripture spoke relevantly and comprehensively to all situations, hence the appropriateness of couching these predictions in biblical terminology. If either envisaged some in his audience recalling the next verse in Micah as well (7:7), he could have hoped that they would infer that the salvation that Micah waited for was now provided in Christ (see Waltke 1993: 749).

Matthew 11:1–30

Here begins Matthew's second major block of narrative material in the body of his Gospel (chaps. 11–12). Matthew 11:1–19 deals with Jesus and John the Baptist. On the question about Jesus as the "coming one" (11:3), see above (p. 2). Verse 4 refers again to specific healing miracles as having messianic significance, as already in the LXX of Isa. 29:18–19; 35:5–6; and 61:1. Verse 5 may allude to Isa. 42:18, with its call to the deaf to hear and to the blind to see. Verse 13 refers to the entirety of the Hebrew Scriptures with the expression "the prophets and the law." A clear allusion to Elijah preceding the day of the Lord (Mal. 4:5) appears in 11:14. The little parable of the children in the marketplace (11:16–19) may echo Deut. 29:6 in describing the Baptist's asceticism ("neither eating nor drinking") and Isa. 22:13 in describing Jesus' indulgence ("eating and drinking"). In striking contrast to the OT and Second-Temple Judaism, Jesus stresses how holiness can be more contagious in mixing with notorious sinners than impurity (Blomberg 2005).

The comparisons of Capernaum, Bethsaida, and Chorazin in Jesus' day to Tyre and Sidon in OT times (11:20–24) reflect the latter cities' role as paradigmatic enemies of Israel (see Isa. 23; Ezek. 26–28; Amos 1:9–10; Joel 3:4–8; Zech. 9:2–4). Sodom, like Gomorrah, typified the wickedness of Canaan before Israel conquered it (see esp. Gen. 18:16–19:29; see also above, p. 35). "Sackcloth and ashes" (11:21) were common public symbols of repentance in the ancient Near East (e.g., Esther 4:3; Jon. 3:6–9). Capernaum's attitude is even more specifically likened to the arrogance of the king of Babylon (Isa. 14:12–15), with Jesus promising it a similar fate (11:23). Here the text literally refers to Hades, the Greek rendering of Sheol, the shadowy underworld of OT times. In fact, the phrasing "Up to heaven will you be exalted? You will go down to Hades," could be viewed as an actual quotation of Isa. 14:13, 15 (thus the second edition [but not the third or fourth editions] of the United Bible Societies' *Greek New Testament* puts this text in boldface as an OT quotation). The MT reads here, respectively, "And you said in your heart 'to the heavens I will go up,'" and "But to Sheol you will go down." The LXX wording is somewhat different from Matthew's, with only "go down to Hades" preserved verbatim. Given

that Jesus employs no introductory formula and that he uses the language as a rhetorical question followed by its answer rather than as a pair of predictions as in Isaiah, it is perhaps better to see Jesus using deliberately allusive language in his condemnation of the three cities of his day that would make the astute listener think of Isaiah's similar judgment of notorious OT towns.

In 11:25–30 three final allusions to the OT in this chapter appear. In 11:25a Jesus praises God in wording reminiscent of Dan. 2:19–23. Verse 25b seems to allude to God hiding his wisdom from the wise in Isa. 29:14. And in 11:29 "you will find rest for your souls" alludes to Jer. 6:16. Charette (1992) surveys other texts as possible backgrounds for the themes of 11:28–30, esp. of "yoke" and "rest" (on the latter, see Laansma 1997). More generally, Jesus' appeal to the weary to find their rest in him resembles the appeals of Lady Wisdom in Proverbs and Sirach (see Deutsch 1987). Compare also Exod. 33:14. Davies and Allison (1988–1997: 2:283–86) also argue strongly for an influence of 33:12–13 on Matt. 11:25–30.

11:10

A. NT Context. Tucked into the discussion of John the Baptist is an intriguing composite OT quotation. The disciples of John have returned to their imprisoned master with Jesus' answer to their question about his identity (Matt. 11:2–6). Jesus takes this occasion to comment on John to the crowds (11:7–19). He dispels the notion that John was a weak or pampered figure (11:7–8), declaring instead that he was a genuine prophet, "and more than a prophet" (11:9). In language reminiscent of earlier testimony concerning John (recall 3:3), Jesus explains, "This is he of whom it stands written [a standard way of referring to Hebrew Scripture; see Davies and Allison 1988–1997: 2:249], 'Behold, I send my messenger before my face, who will prepare the way in front of me'" (11:10). The first clause quotes Exod. 23:20; the second, Mal. 3:1. Indeed, the two texts are combined by Mark in his parallel to the Matt. 3:3 passage (Mark 1:2) as an introduction to the quotation of Isa. 40:3. Matthew 11:10 reappears verbatim in Luke 7:27 (via Q?) minus the grammatically superfluous *egō* ("I").

Indeed, John is the greatest of all pre-kingdom humans ("those born among women"), but because of the greatness of the kingdom age, all of the kingdom's citizens will in some sense be greater even than John (11:11; cf. 11:13). Viviano (2000) thinks that "the least of human beings" echoes Daniel's "lowliest of human beings" theme in chapter 4, where Nebuchadnezzar is humbled. Verse 12 is a notorious interpretative crux, but probably it refers to the opposition that the kingdom has experienced thus far (including the hostility that led to John's imprisonment). For a full history of interpretation, see Cameron 1984; for the approach adopted here, cf. Barnett 1977 and Moore 1989. Finally, because Malachi appears to tie his prophecy in with his subsequent reference to the coming of Elijah (4:5), Jesus declares that John is the fulfillment of that prophecy, not in the literal sense of the ascended Elijah returned to earth, but metaphorically as the one who would come "in the spirit and power of Elijah" (thus Luke 1:17). Hence comes the concluding call to listen carefully (11:15), perhaps appealing to the crowds to discern the underlying significance of Malachi's words. John's and Jesus' ministries are then contrasted by means of a fascinating little parable (11:16–19).

B. OT Context. In context, Exod. 23:20 refers to God sending his angel to guard the Israelites, as they proceed from Mount Sinai, to prepare the way for them to take possession of the promised land. But in both Greek and Hebrew, the same words can mean either "angel" or "messenger" (and angels typically function as messengers), so an application to a human messenger in a different context follows naturally. The language of Exod. 23:20 recurs in Mal. 3:1, in two parts, with the intervening wording matching the second clause of Matt. 11:10. Malachi's prophecy may in fact deliberately allude to the Exodus text (Feinberg 1977: 260). This time, however, the messenger seems to refer to a human being who will prepare the way for the Lord to come suddenly to his temple, a messenger who in Mal. 4:5 (3:23–24 MT) is equated with Elijah and described as one who "will turn the fathers' hearts toward their children" (4:6), an example of the reconciliation that results from the kind of repentance for which John the Baptist had been calling. The connection of the messenger with Elijah is often denied or argued to have been made only with the canonical form of Malachi that combined otherwise unre-

lated pieces of tradition history. The connection, however, is the most natural way to take the text, and tradition-historical dissection fails to convince (see J. M. P. Smith 1912: 62–63; A. Cohen 1948: 349; D. Stuart 1998: 1352).

C. Use in Jewish Sources. Pre-Christian Jewish references to Exod. 23:20 seem to be limited to Philo, who quotes this text to illustrate God's role as shepherd (*Agriculture* 51) and the perfection of humanity as it follows the path of divine reason (*Migration* 174). Philo also allegorizes the text so that the angel becomes the "intellectual soul" or "holy mind" that ministers to various human needs (*QE* 2.13). But none of these uses seems relevant for our purposes. Malachi 4:5, of course, eventually became a fundamental part of Jewish eschatological expectation that the literal Elijah would return from heaven to prepare for the coming of the Messiah (for details, see Wiener 1978). The oldest known text to reflect this hope predates the Christian era by two centuries (Sir. 48:10), though no specific reference to the Messiah appears in this context. For the conviction that some pre-Christian precedent must have given rise to the linkage between Elijah and the Messiah, see Allison 1984. At least in the later rabbinic literature it is clear that Mal. 3:1 and 4:5 were connected, so that the messenger in the former text was equated with Elijah in the latter (e.g., *Tg. Ps.-J.* Num. 25:12). A late midrash also links Exod. 23:20 with Mal. 3:1 because of the similar language: God's pattern of sending special messengers recurs (*Exod. Rab.* 32.9; for a relatively full list of rabbinic texts relevant to the discussion, see Ginzberg 1976: 212n14). Jesus' combination of these two texts could suggest that the linkage was known already in his day (Stendahl 1954: 50), but the combination is natural enough for anyone familiar with the Scriptures, given the detailed parallelism of language.

D. Textual Background. The MT of Mal. 3:1 reads literally, "Behold me, the one sending my messenger, and he will make clear a way before my face." The MT of Exod. 23:20 reads literally, "Behold, I am sending an angel [or, 'messenger'] before your face in order to guard you in the way and to bring you to the place which I have prepared." The LXX of both passages is virtually identical and matches Matthew with respect to "Behold, I am sending my messenger," except that in Malachi the compounded form *exapostellō* appears for "I am sending," whereas in Exodus (as in Matthew) only *apostellō* is used. The phrase *pro prosōpou mou* ("before my face") appears only in Mal. 3:1, while Exod. 23:20 reads *pro prosōpou sou* ("before your face") and does not add any intervening words before this phrase, after "Behold, I send my messenger." On both these counts the theory of a composite quotation in Matthew thus remains best; otherwise one could have imagined Jesus relying wholly on Mal. 3:1. The part of Matthew demonstrably relying on Malachi ("who will prepare your way before your face") does not bear enough verbal similarity to the LXX, and the clause overall is too short to enable us to determine whether the Greek Scriptures were utilized or whether Matthew was translating independently from the Hebrew.

E. Hermeneutic Employed. To the extent that Jesus (or Matthew) has Exod. 23:20 in mind, we must speak of a typological use of the Scripture. God's pattern of sending a special messenger to prepare the way for a key event in the salvation history of his people is repeating itself. To the extent that Mal. 3:1 is in view, we may speak of a prediction-fulfillment scheme. Whether the prophesied forerunner of the day of the Lord is seen as a literal Elijah returned from heaven or as a new human messenger coming in Elijah's spirit and power, we have a future-oriented prediction. Jesus, according to Matthew, adopts the latter interpretation and believes that John has fulfilled the prediction. Whether one sees John as the *complete* fulfillment of the prediction depends in large part on one's understanding of the two witnesses in Rev. 11, depicted as mirroring the ministries of Moses and Elijah.

F. Theological Use. The primary function of the composite citation is to answer the question of John's identity. As in Matt. 3:3, he is viewed as a great prophet, preparing for the arrival of the messianic age. His ministry overlaps the beginning of the Messiah's ministry, but he will not live to be part of the new covenant inaugurated by Christ's death. But if the forerunner is here, then the Messiah must be near (see Hagner 1993: 308). Jesus' actual logic by which he came to these views, however, may have been the reverse. If he began with some Messianic self-understanding, seemingly evident at least from his baptism onward,

then his estimation of John could have developed from his assessment of his own identity: "If I am the Messiah, then Elijah must have come" (see further Blomberg 1987). And a Messiah who can so solemnly pronounce John the greatest of all mortals to date (11:11) sounds like someone who thinks that he is more than a mere mortal (see Witherington 1990: 34–53, esp. 45–46)! This suspicion is reinforced when we realize that Jesus is substituting his coming for the day of the Lord (i.e., the coming of Yahweh) in Mal. 4:5 (France 1985: 194). As the chapter began, so Matt. 11 continues to focus, if more indirectly here, on Jesus' identity as well as John's. And if both prophet and Messiah have appeared, then their joint call to repentance (recall 3:2; 4:17) must be urgently heeded by the crowds listening to Jesus talk about John. But whereas John's message seemed unremittingly austere, Jesus also preaches the joy of the kingdom (11:16–19).

Matthew 12:1–14

The controversy over plucking grain on the Sabbath (Matt. 12:1–8) relies heavily on the account of David's behavior at Nob in 1 Sam. 21:1–6. If under special circumstances Ahimelech allowed David and his companions to eat the sacred showbread despite the restrictions of Lev. 24:5–9 that only priests could eat this food, how much more appropriate it is for Jesus to determine when he and his disciples may pluck grain on a Sabbath (12:3–4). Jesus' second example appeals to Num. 28:9–10, which required priests to work by offering certain sacrifices on the Sabbath. Again Jesus argues that he should have that much more of a right to suspend certain Sabbath legislation (12:5). The rhetorical question, "Have you not read in the law?" recalls the numerous OT contexts in which the Scriptures were read aloud.

The second Sabbath controversy (12:9–14) contrasts strikingly with CD-A XI, 13–14, in which the Qumran sectarians did not allow even an animal to be rescued on the Sabbath. Keener (1999: 355) also cites Josephus, *Ant.* 12.4; 13.12–13; *Life* 159; 161; and *Ag. Ap.* 1.210–212, all suggesting that some such Sabbath laws were already in force in the first century. But this passage does not allude to the OT per se, unless we are meant to recall legislation about helping animals such as Deut. 22:4 or Jeroboam's temporarily withered hand healed by the prayer of an anonymous "man of God" in 1 Kings 13:1–10. In both Sabbath controversies, of course, Jesus' dispute is much more with the oral halakah of the Pharisees than with the OT. Something like the extensive casuistic Sabbath laws of the later Talmud (*b. Šabb.* 73b) seems to have already developed in intertestamental times (see esp. *Jub.* 50:12).

12:7

A. NT Context. Tucked into the first of these two controversy stories is Jesus' second reference to Hos. 6:6, again unique to Matthew's version of the account. The context this time is not that of table fellowship with notorious sinners (as in 9:13), but rather one of meeting basic human needs on the Sabbath. In each case Jesus is responding to Pharisaic criticism that misses fundamental features of God's will because of overly scrupulous legislation. "Sacrifice" again appears as a synecdoche for the entire ritual law. "Mercy," which allows Jesus' followers to reap a small crop to feed themselves, takes precedence over an interpretation of Sabbath work that would have stopped them (mercy resides at the center of God's will and unifies 12:3–7 here; see further Luz 2001: 182). After all, the Son of Man is someone "greater than the temple" (12:6); indeed, he is "Lord of the Sabbath" (12:8). Just as in 9:13 Jesus told the Jewish leaders to "go and learn" the meaning of Hos. 6:6, likewise here he laments that they have not learned what the text means (12:7). The repetition of the quotation reinforces that sad fact (see Gundry 1994: 224).

B. OT Context and Use in Jewish Sources. See above under Matt. 9:13.

C. Textual Background. Matthew employs the identical five-word excerpt as in 9:13. Thus again it matches the LXX verbatim, which in turn translates the MT literally.

D. Hermeneutic Employed. As before, Jesus puts fundamental morality above ritual law. As in the Sermon on the Mount, he claims the right to be the law's sovereign interpreter. More explicitly than in the context of 9:13, Jesus employs a "from the lesser to the greater" logic, common in Jewish hermeneutics, by claiming that "something" or "someone" greater than the temple is present (an indirect reference to his ministry and/or person). In the same way, Jesus is greater than the Sabbath

(and, from 12:4, one greater than David; cf. France 1985: 202–3). The logic in both instances seems to go beyond what would have necessarily been convincing by rabbinic standards (Cohn-Sherbok 1979; *contra* Levine 1976); Jesus is making a more sweeping claim about his personal authority. He does not have to persuade within conventional parameters of legal discussion.

E. Theological Use. The most obvious usage of the OT text is to justify the behavior of Jesus' disciples. Morality for Jesus' followers will be determined by God's fundamental attributes and priorities. But an important secondary theme is clearly Christology. Verseput (1986: 166–69) notes four major attempts to explain Matthew's use of Hosea here: a critique of the Pharisees' lovelessness, a justification of the disciples' behavior, a reflection on covenant loyalty as fundamentally Godward in direction, and, what Verseput believes is primary, a presentation of Jesus as a humble, merciful Savior offering relief from the burden of legalistic demand. Only a messiah who is the exalted, heavenly Son of Man can speak so authoritatively to articulate what does and does not fall into those fundamental categories. The will of God must be reinterpreted in the age of the kingdom. The Torah does not continue to apply without change; everything must be filtered through the grid of fulfillment in Christ (recall above on 5:17). Hagner (1993: 331) elaborates, "The Son of Man is with his people as sovereign Lord and Messianic king and acts as the final and infallible interpreter of the will of God as expressed in Torah and sabbath commandment."

For it to be lawful to do any kind of good on the Sabbath leaves the door wide open for a dramatically different approach to the seventh day of the week. Work of many kinds may indeed be required! The early church rightly recognized the Sabbath as an OT ritual that Christians did not literally observe, not even on Sunday, the new day of worship based on the day of Christ's resurrection. Only when Christianity was legalized would Sabbatarianism be reintroduced, with the notion that Christians had to cease from work one day out of seven. In striking contrast, Christians during the first three centuries condemned Sabbatarianism as a kind of Judaizing that reverted to a sub-Christian legalism (for an excellent analysis of Sabbath questions, exegetically and historically, see Carson 1982; cf. Blomberg 1991b). Those who object to this "liberty" today usually fail to grasp that "freedom from ritual commandment need not lead to moral chaos but within the Kingdom of God imposes a responsibility far greater than any law could demand" (Mounce 1991: 114). Despite many claims to the contrary, Matthew is most decidedly not trying to encourage his community to continue in a Torah-observant form of Jewish Christianity (rightly Lybaek 1997).

Matthew 12:15–21

12:18–21

A. NT Context. Jesus withdraws from the growing hostility generated by his controversial Sabbath behavior, but he continues to draw crowds and to heal many sick people (12:15). To avoid even more unwanted publicity that would fuel the opposition, he tells people to keep quiet about what he has done—the famous messianic secret motif (12:16; on which, see Dunn 1983). Matthew uniquely sees in all of this the fufillment of yet another prophecy of Isaiah, whom he again explicitly mentions (12:17). This is the longest sustained quotation of the OT in Matthew. The Messiah, whom God loves, whom God's Spirit anoints (recall the allusion to Isa. 42:1 by the heavenly voice at Jesus' baptism), will come in humility, neither fighting to get his way nor resisting his opposition, but gently and quietly carrying out his mission (12:18a, 19a, 20a). "No one will hear his voice in the streets" (12:19b) means that few will respond adequately, not that he never speaks publicly. Nevertheless, this Messiah's mission displays divine power and ultimately will lead to the universal triumph of God's kingdom (12:18b, 20b–21). Luz (2001: 196) notes that the story of Jesus, to the degree that we can understand it, "is the story of gentleness, of mercy, of nonviolence, and of love"; only in this way does God's judgment come to victory. The healings of 12:15 foreshadow this triumph; the next episode in Matthew will illustrate it even more forcefully as Jesus confronts the demonically possessed and demonstrates his power over the devil's domain (12:22–32). For further connections between 12:15–18 and Matt. 12 as a whole, see Neyrey 1982.

B. OT Context. Here appears the first of Isaiah's four Servant Songs (see above, p. 31). After threatening judgment throughout chapter 41, in chapter 42 Isaiah turns to the complementary theme of the coming salvation of God's people. The character of the "servant" is introduced somewhat abruptly, though 41:9 has already spoken of Israel as God's chosen servant. In light of 42:6–7, in which the prophet declares in God's name, "I will keep you and will make you to be a covenant for the people and a light for the Gentiles, to open eyes that are blind, to free captives from prison and to release from the dungeon those who sit in darkness" (NIV), it is natural to assume that the servant is still the entire nation of Israel in this chapter as well (so even Motyer 1999: 259). But, as noted above (p. 31), the more one progresses through the four Servant Songs, the more the servant looks like an individual, and it is plausible to imagine that Isaiah had both individual and corporate understandings in mind from the outset. The specific details of the servant's behavior, even in 42:1–4, read more naturally as the gentleness and humility (but also the triumph) of a messianic ruler within Israel, acting on behalf of the whole nation. Keener (1999: 360) concludes that the larger context of Isaiah compels this two-stage interpretation: "God's servant Israel failed in its mission (42:18–19), so God chose one person within Israel to restore the rest of his people (49:5–7); this one would bear the punishment (cf. 40:2) rightly due his people (52:13–53:12)." The Mosaic typology perceived by Baltzer (2001: 126) is less apparent. Goldingay (2005: 153) notes the threefold use of "justice" and finds this as the key theme here.

C. Use in Jewish Sources. Targum Isaiah 42:1–4 reads,

> Behold my servant, I *will bring* him *near*, my chosen in whom my *Memra is pleased*; I *will* put my *Holy* Spirit upon him, he will reveal *my* judgment to the *peoples*. He will not cry or *call* or *lift up* his voice outside. *The poor who are like* a bruised reed he will not break, and *the needy who are like* a dimly burning wick he will not quench; he will bring forth *judgment* for *his* truth. He will not *tire* or *be weary* till he has established *judgment* in the earth; and *islands* wait for his law. (All translations of *Targum Isaiah* are from Chilton 1987.)

In some editions "the messiah" is actually inserted after "my servant," in 42:1; even when it is omitted, the remaining changes in 42:1–4 from the MT suggest an individual and messianic interpretation (cf. the Targum on 43:10; 52:10, 13). This comports with one much later rabbinic interpretation, reflected in *Midr. Ps.* 2:9. As fundamental as these Servant Songs became for Christian messianic interpretation, it is difficult to imagine a Jewish messianic interpretation deriving solely from post-Christian times (see above, p. 32). Demonstrably pre-Christian Jewish allusions to these verses, however, remain inconclusive. *Psalms of Solomon* 12:6 and 17:21 speak explicity of the servant as Israel. A messianic interpretation seems to be favored in *2 Bar.* 70:10 (late first century): "All will be delivered into the hands of my Servant, the Anointed One." Unambiguously messianic is *1 En.* 39:6, but is "the Elect One" an adequate parallel in content to ensure a conscious allusion to Isa. 42? Similarly vague are the references in *Ascen. Isa.* 8:8 to "his Chosen One, whose name is unknown, and no heaven can learn his name" and in *T. Benj.* 11:2 to one who is "enlightening all the nations with new knowledge." Among the Dead Sea Scrolls, 1QS IX, 16 includes as a regulation for the instructor of the community: "He should not reproach or argue with the men of the pit." Despite the uncertainty, though, it seems probable that at least some pre-Christian strands of Judaism would have seen Isa. 42:1–4 as messianic.

D. Textual Background. The MT reads literally,

> Behold my servant whom I uphold, my chosen in whom my soul delights. I have given my spirit upon him. Justice to the Gentiles he will bring forth. He will not cry out, and he will not lift up and he will not make heard in the street his voice. A bruised reed he will not break and a dimly burning wick he will not quench. Truthfully he will bring forth justice. He will not fail and he will not be discouraged until he has established in the earth justice, and for his law the coastlands wait. (Each time "justice" appears in these translations, one could also render the Hebrew or Greek as "judgment"; but see Beaton 1999.)

The LXX begins the verse by interpreting the servant as the nation and translates, at times more paraphrastically than literally,

> Jacob, my servant, I will help him. Israel, my elect one, my soul has welcomed him. I gave my spirit upon him. He will lead out the nations

with justice. He will not cry out nor shout nor will his voice be heard outside. A broken reed he will not crush and a smoking wick he will not quench, but in truth he will bring forth justice. He will blaze forth and not be shattered, until he places justice on the earth. And upon his name the Gentiles will hope.

Matthew's Greek shares a couple of key words per line with the LXX, but in most instances these are the most natural Greek words that anyone would use to translate the Hebrew ("my servant," "my soul," "my spirit," "the nations with justice," "a reed," "quench," and "[upon] his name the Gentiles will hope"). For the rest of his text, Matthew seems independent of the LXX and provides a more literal rendering of the Hebrew than does the LXX. Verse 18a contains none of the LXX's interpretive insertions. Verse 18b uses the verb "announces," in contrast to both LXX and MT. Gundry (1994: 230) comments: "The persecuted Jesus does not seek justice by taking his cause to the public. Neither should his persecuted disciples. Like him, they are to proclaim justice, not seek it." Verses 19–20a follow the Hebrew tolerably well. Verse 20b then skips two full clauses (three in the LXX), adds "unto victory" to the next clause (unlike either MT or LXX). Archer and Chirichigno (1983: 114–15) nevertheless attempt to argue that "unto victory" brings out explicitly what was implicit in the original Hebrew. On the other hand, Hill (1972: 214) thinks that "until he brings justice to victory" was generated by Hab. 1:4, and concludes with the longest sustained set of verbal parallels to the LXX in this quotation in 12:21. "Matthew may well have formed the translation from sources available to him (e.g., Targumim) or produced his original translation (so Davies and Allison) in order to suit his own purposes" (Hagner 1993: 336; *contra* Menken 2004a: 67–88).

E. Hermeneutic Employed. As with our discussion of Isa. 53:4, indeed as with our discussion of all the Isaiah quotations employed by Matthew thus far, double fulfillment seems to be the best category to explain the hermeneutic involved (see esp. Beaton 2002). Matthew recognizes that Isaiah envisioned a servant role for Israel corporately throughout OT times and a later, greater messianic fulfillment. Grogan (1986: 254–55) declares, "There can be little doubt that we are intended to make the identification with Israel to begin with that we might be gently led to him who is the incarnation of God's mind for Israel (cf. Matt 12:15–21). The "bruised reed" and "smoldering wick" of Isa. 42:3 refer initially to the weakened and shattered Judeans, but more implicitly and ironically to Egypt and Babylon in Isaiah's larger context of assuring Israel of their ultimate consolation (H. C. P. Kim 1999). However, the future role of the Spirit coming on an anointed prophet (61:1) and the inability of Israel ever to bring justice to all the nations of the earth make it natural to look for a larger, more long-term fulfillment in an individual, a Davidic king or messiah (see Oswalt 1986–1998: 2:108–12).

F. Theological Use. Christologically, Matthew views Jesus as the ultimate fulfillment of the role of the Spirit-anointed, divinely chosen and beloved servant (Matt. 12:18). In the short term, through his ministry, Jesus will demonstrate not resistance to, but withdrawal from, hostility, until the appointed time comes for him to die. Then he will neither resist nor withdraw, but rather humbly submit to God's plan (12:19). Meanwhile, he treats the outcast and vulnerable with tenderness and gentleness (12:20). But also, through his resurrection and subsequent return from heaven, demonstrating his conquest of death, he will bring victory and justice for all the peoples of the world (12:21), which will entail salvation for those who acknowledge his lordship and condemnation for those who do not. Davies and Allison (1988–1997: 2:324) recognize that "all in all, the entirety of Mt 12.18–21 serves Matthean themes and interests very well. Nothing is superfluous; everything fits. Matthew has evidently latched onto Isa 42.1–4 because it serves so remarkably to illustrate the nature of Jesus' ministry in Israel. Jesus is the unobtrusive servant of the Lord. God's Spirit rests upon him. He does not wrangle or quarrel or continue useless strife. He seeks to avoid self-advertisement and to quiet the enthusiasm that his healings inevitably create. He has compassion upon all, especially upon the 'bruised reed' or 'smouldering wick'. And he brings salvation to the Gentiles." Beaton (2005) sees the twin themes of salvation and judgment highlighted were characteristic of Matthew's use of Isaiah more generally.

Matthew 12:22–50

The little parable about plundering the strong man's house (12:29) may allude to Isa. 49:24 ("Can plunder be taken from warriors or captives rescued from tyrants?"). The unforgivable sin, blasphemy against the Holy Spirit (12:32), parallels sins "with a high hand" in the OT (see esp. Num. 15:30–31). An unforgivable sin is also specified in 1 Sam. 3:14. The "evil and adulterous generation" (12:39) echoes descriptions of the Israelites in their wilderness wanderings (Deut. 1:35; 32:5). The reference to repentant Ninevites (12:41) is a historical allusion to the events depicted in Jon. 3:5–10; now, someone "greater than Jonah" has appeared. The reference to the queen of the South (i.e., Sheba) (12:42) alludes to the events described in 1 Kings 10:1–10; 2 Chron. 9:1–12. The queen learned firsthand of the fabled wisdom of Solomon, and now something "greater than Solomon" is present (on which, see L. Perkins 1998).

12:40

A. NT Context. Tucked into this discussion of one who is greater than both Jonah and Solomon (cf. 12:6 on one greater than the temple) is a quotation about Jonah's time in the belly of the great fish. Jesus is responding to his critics' demand for an unambiguous sign that will prove his identity (12:38). He replies that the only sign that God will give a wicked generation is the sign of Jonah (12:39). This sign is likened to Jonah's three days and nights in the fish: "so also the Son of Man will be in the heart of the earth three days and three nights" (12:40). Jesus then contrasts his opponents' skeptical response with the proper spiritual responses of both the Ninevites and the Queen of Sheba (12:41–42). With a spokesman for God greater than both Jonah and Solomon in their midst, these Jewish leaders should be that much quicker to repent! Jesus has now been shown to be greater than priest, prophet, and king—a comprehensive list of those to whom God's message came in OT times (France 1985: 214).

"Three days and three nights" reflects a Jewish idiom for any part of three consecutive twenty-four-hour periods of time, so there is no need to employ this verse to question the standard reconstruction of the events of Jesus' death and resurrection covering Friday, Saturday, and Sunday of

Passover week, probably in AD 30 (see further Gundry 1994: 244). The sign that Jesus has in mind is not the crucifixion per se, but rather the resurrection. Just as Jonah's time in the fish would have proved meaningless had he not been spit up onto the shore to continue his appointed ministry of preaching repentance to Nineveh, so also the crucifixion is not the decisive sign of who Jesus was, for his subsequent rescue from death is what vindicated his ministry and enabled his mission to go forward (cf. Bruckner 2004: 57). Because Jonah went on to preach repentance, it is sometimes said that the sign was not the resurrection but preaching, esp. in the slightly different parallel in Luke 11:29–32 (cf. also Mark 8:11–12), which lacks the OT quotation. However, Jesus has already been preaching for some time, so it is unlikely that more preaching would be a sign to authenticate his ministry, whereas the resurrection fits the bill well (see further Carson 1984: 295–96). The "contradiction" with Mark 8:12, which seems to rule out signs altogether, is merely apparent. Even a resurrection will not be so unambiguous that skeptics cannot reject it. Mark recognizes that Jesus has still not promised the specific kind of sign requested and so merely omits the exception clause from Jesus' words (see Swetnam 1985). The logic is very much that of Luke 16:31. Our text is also "the first prelude of the Matthean passion and the Easter story" and "a first response of Jesus to the decision of the Pharisees in 12:14" to kill him (Luz 2001: 218).

B. OT Context. The story of Jonah is one of conversion, first of the reluctant prophet, then of the Ninevites. The experience in the fish's belly forms the turning point for Jonah. Previously unwilling to preach to his nation's hated enemy, Assyria (1:1–16), he now prays to God a psalm-like thanksgiving for the fish that rescued him from certain drowning (chap. 2). After being vomited onto dry land, he is ready to obey God and proceed to Nineveh, which indeed does repent (chap. 3). Jonah's time under the sea afforded a close enough parallel to Jesus' burial in the earth to generate the analogy used in Matt. 12:40. "Three days and three nights" may be more symbolic than literal already in Jonah. L. C. Allen (1976: 213–14) thinks that the expression "emphasizes the great gulf between death and life and the difficulties God gloriously overcame in rescuing his

servant from his merited doom." However, this is based on a proposal that this period of time refers to the duration of a journey to the underworld and back, which may read in more than is implied (thus Alexander, Baker, and Waltke 1998: 112).

C. Use in Jewish Sources. In 3 Macc. 6:1–9 the priest Eleazar pleads to God to rescue his people Israel from their lawless Gentile overlords, based on his prior acts of salvation of his people from Pharaoh's armies, Sennacherib, and the Babylonians, and of Daniel from the lions and of Jonah from drowning. *Testament of Zebulun* 4:4 perhaps sees Jonah typology in Joseph's languishing in the well prior to his being sold to the Midianites, even claiming that it too lasted three days and three nights. Josephus summarizes the story of Jonah, as part of his recounting of OT history, and explicitly repeats the contents of Jon. 1:17 (*Ant.* 9.213). For Jewish tradition on Jonah more generally, see Chow 1995. But none of these early Jewish uses of Jonah sheds any further light on the meaning of the text itself.

D. Textual Background. The LXX translates this half-verse from the MT literally (which is numbered 2:1 in both versions). Matthew's excerpt matches the LXX verbatim. Since Luke has a close parallel to this text (Luke 11:29–32) minus the OT quotation, and since Matthew usually matches the LXX most closely when following his sources, one wonders if this quotation already appeared in Q, and Luke simply omitted it.

E. Hermeneutic Employed. Neither Jesus nor Matthew employs any introductory formula to signal that Scripture is being quoted. Jesus merely constructs a simple analogy based on the historical account of Jonah to illustrate what is going to happen to him. In doing so, he naturally adopts scriptural language, especially since the verse that he cites forms such an apt summary of what happened to Jonah. In the immediate context, the comparisons with the Ninevites and the Queen of Sheba (12:41–42) suggest that the logic employed is "from the lesser to the greater." This logic may extend to the fact that the Ninevites repented without having witnessed the sign of Jonah's "death and resurrection"; how much more, then, ought Jesus' audience to repent, given the miracles that they have already witnessed (Keener 1999: 367).

F. Theological Use. God never coerces belief. Jesus will not supply a sign so unambiguous that his opponents are compelled to follow him; that would override human freedom, which the Bible consistently stresses as something that God values highly. But for the person of faith, the resurrection should prove more than adequate. At the very least, Jesus is greater than Jonah or Solomon. And if foreigners, even hated enemies, believed in Yahweh in response to their ministries, how much more should Jesus' listeners, even his opponents, accept his message as heaven-sent. Hagner (1993: 355) clarifies: "There is in principle nothing wrong with the desire for a sign from God. The request for a sign only becomes unjustified and intrinsically wrong when one is already surrounded by good and sufficient evidence one chooses not to accept. In that case, unreceptivity and unbelief are the root problem, and it is unlikely that any sign would be sufficient to change such a person's mind."

Matthew 13:1–23

Matthew 13:1–52 comprises a collection of eight parables from Jesus. The form of a majority of Jesus' parables closely reflects that of the parable about the rich man and the poor man and their sheep, with which the prophet Nathan confronted King David (2 Sam. 12:1–10). Parables are otherwise rare in the OT but plentiful within the early rabbinic literature (see above, p. 29). The most important OT background for the parable of the Sower, which, with its interpretation, occupies most of Matt. 13:1–23, seems to be Isa. 55:10–11: God's promise that as the rain waters the earth to yield seed for sowers and bread to eat, so also God's word will not return empty, but rather will accomplish all his purposes (Evans 1985).

13:14–15

A. NT Context. After Jesus narrates the story of the sower (Matt. 13:3–9), the disciples ask him why he speaks to the crowds in parables (13:10). Jesus' reply appears to suggest that only "insiders" have been selected to understand the "mysteries" of God's kingdom, not "outsiders" (13:11–12). Jesus then buttresses this claim by quoting Isaiah, again by name. He alludes to the language of Isa. 6:9 in v. 13 and then formally quotes 6:9–10 in

vv. 14–15, employing the unique verb *anaplēroō* (rather than merely *plēroō*), meaning "to completely fulfill" the prophecy in question. Gundry (1994: 257) thinks that "completely fulfilled" implies human responsibility and that Matthew's overall introductory formula is phrased "to avoid any thought of divine causation that might be mistaken as a lessening of human responsibility." For those without ears to hear, parables seem to conceal more than they reveal, so that superficial hearing and seeing do not lead to true spiritual understanding or perception. Otherwise, these outsiders would repent and be saved. By way of contrast, Jesus blesses the disciples' eyes and ears because they do appropriately receive his word (13:16), as many in OT times longed to do (13:17); for both emphases, see Kingsbury 1975: 89–90. Verses 18–23 then proceed to give the explanation for the parable. This is the first explicit fulfillment of prophecy in Matthew that appears to focus more on Jesus' audiences than on Christ (or the Baptist) himself (but recall 10:35–36).

In the parallel account in Mark (4:12), only the first two and last lines of this lengthy quote appear, each in slightly different syntactical form, but the basic point is the same. Luke's parallel (8:10) also contains an abbreviated form of the quotation, excerpting only from Isa. 6:9, while in a quite different context, John (12:40) cites only Isa. 6:10. The full text of both verses reappears in Acts 28:26–27 to explain the Jewish rejection of the gospel with which that history of apostolic activity concludes.

B. OT Context. Isaiah 6 is, of course, best known for its description of Isaiah's vision of the Lord in his glory, which leads to Isaiah's commissioning as a prophet (6:1–8). The message that he is instructed to preach to his people is first of all one of judgment and is couched as a set of commands: "Hear and hear, but do not understand; see and see, but do not perceive. Make fat the heart of this people and make their ears heavy and their eyes shut, lest they see with their eyes and hear with their ears and understand with their hearts and they turn and be healed" (6:9–10). Beale (1991) observes that this language describes the rebellious Israelites as resembling the various idols that their rebellion led them to worship: blind, deaf, and heartless! Chapters 1–5 have made plain the sins of the people. This is not God's planning in advance to make Israel sin; instead, it is his confirming them in their repeated, freely chosen decisions to reject him (cf. Rom. 1:24, 26, 28). Childs (2001: 57) speaks of this as a turning point in God's dealings with Israel (see also Motyer 1993: 79). Nor need their disobedience prove permanent. Isaiah asks how long God's judgment will be in force (6:11a). God's first response is sufficiently discouraging: until the land is devastated, the people are exiled, and a remnant that survives is subsequently punished as well (6:11b–13a). However, the chapter ends with a message of hope. As trees when cut down leave stumps that can begin growing again, so also "the holy seed will be the stump in the land" (6:13b).

Taken as a whole, 6:9–13 suggest that the fulfillment of Isaiah's prophecy occurs over a continuous, prolonged period of time, beginning with the judgment that will befall his contemporaries (the Assyrian invasion and exile), continuing with later judgment still within OT times (the Babylonian invasion and exile), and not ending until a righteous people once again populate the land. Little wonder that Jesus and the apostles could continue to apply the text to responses to Jesus, since such a righteous remnant had yet to be fully established. W. C. Allen (1907: 145) also notes that the future tense (as in 6:13) in the LXX of Isaiah readily led to the use of the passage as a prediction of future events.

C. Use in Jewish Sources. There do not appear to be any extant pre-Christian Jewish quotations of Isa. 6:9–10. The allusions that appear do not shed any further light on the text (the clearest are *Sib. Or.* 1:360–61; Philo, *Joseph* 126; 1QS IV, 11). The other Isaiah scroll from Qumran, however, contains a dramatically reworded rendering: "Keep on listening, because you may understand. Keep on looking, because you may perceive. Make the heart of this people appalled. Stop its ears and turn away its eyes—lest it see with its eyes and hear with its ears. Let it understand in its heart and return and be healed" (1QIsaᵃ [quoted in Evans 1989: 55]).

The LXX, Peshitta, and later rabbinic literature to varying degrees likewise attempt to tone down the predestinarian theme of the original prophecy, though none does it as dramatically as in this Qumran scroll. Perhaps more significantly, at least by talmudic times, Isa. 6:13, the verse that

promises that a righteous remnant will survive the judgment on this current generation's stupor, was taken as referring to the "generation in which the Son of David will come"—that is, the messianic era (*b. Ketub.* 112b).

D. Textual Background. We have already seen a literal translation of the MT above. The infinitive absolute (yielding "hear and hear," "see and see") is an intensifier ("truly hear" or "surely see"; cf. NIV: "be ever hearing . . . be ever seeing"). The LXX translates literally by means of cognate datives, which carry the same intensifying force in the Greek. The three imperatives of 6:10 are apparently repointed by the LXX translators, thus yielding indicatives: "they became calloused," "they heard with heaviness," and "they closed their eyes." The final verb in the quotation, *iasomai* ("I will heal [them]"), is a more fluent expression than the impersonal Hebrew idiom, *rāpāʾ* ("[it] will be healed [to them]"; see Archer and Chirichigno 1983: 93–94). The imperatives of the MT are used to express a future certainty, so the LXX translation followed by Matthew is legitimate (Beare 1981: 295). Otherwise the LXX translates literally, and Matthew follows the LXX word for word, with the solitary omission of the superfluous "their" before "ears" in 6:15a. Matthew's close paralleling of the LXX is consistent with the occurrence of this same quotation, even if considerably abbreviated, in one of Matthew's sources, this time Mark, though a plausible case has also been made for Matthean priority for the overall passage containing the parable of the Sower and its interpretation (Wenham 1972).

More interesting than the differences between the MT and the LXX are the distinctives introduced in *Targum Isaiah* on these verses: "And he said, 'Go, and speak to this people *that* hear *indeed*, but do not understand, and see *indeed*, but do not perceive. Make the heart of this people *dull*, and their ears heavy and shut their eyes; lest *they* see with *their* eyes and hear with *their* ears, and understand with *their* hearts and repent and *it be forgiven them*.'" Both the statements that reflect the people's superficial hearing and seeing as present conditions and the change at the end to a verb describing spiritual forgiveness are paralleled in Mark 4:11–12. Did Jesus (or Mark) know and rely on this targumic tradition in his rendering of Isa. 6 (so esp. Chilton 1984: 90–98)? The question is less acute for an analysis of Matthew's Gospel, however, since he reverts to (or preserves?) the LXX without these distinctives.

E. Hermeneutic Employed. At first glance, Matthew's use of Isaiah here would seem to represent typology pure and simple. Jesus speaks in parables to confirm his opponents in their freely chosen rebellion, just as Isaiah had been sent to prophesy to reinforce his contemporaries' callous hard-heartedness (e.g., France 1971: 68). But in light of the comments above under "OT Context," it is perhaps better to classify this as "generic fulfillment"—a prediction that has come true repeatedly, almost continuously, from the time of its utterance to the time of Christ in the first century (for the category, see Beecher 1905: 130; the concept is regularly appealed to throughout Kaiser 1985). Obdurate hearts among God's people seem to characterize some in every generation. McLaughlin (1994) demonstrates the recurrence of this pattern in all three major parts of Isaiah (29:9–10; 44:18; 63:17). The chronological gaps between these passages support the idea that Isaiah understood an ongoing fulfillment to his prophecy concerning Israel's obduracy.

F. Theological Use. The complicated question of predestination confronts us here. It is often argued that Matthew has toned down Mark's emphasis on divine sovereignty by substituting *hoti* for *hina* in 13:13. Then one could translate "with the result that seeing they not see . . ." rather than "in order that seeing they might not see . . ." (as in Mark 4:12) (thus, e.g., Evans 1989: 107–13). However, Matthew has not edited predestination out of either 13:11 or 13:15 ("to you has been given . . ." and "lest they turn . . ."), so it is doubtful that so much can be inferred on the basis of an altered adverb (rightly Carson 1984: 309). Rather, the context in Isaiah is determinative for understanding Jesus' words, whether in their Matthean or Markan form. Concealing God's word from outsiders occurs only after they have freely and repeatedly rejected it, and it can always be disclosed again if they repent. Nothing in either Matthew or Isaiah suggests a predestination to eternal damnation. Furthermore, the kind of understanding that insiders retain and outsiders lack is not primarily cognitive. The disciples, after all, still need Jesus to explain this parable to them, while elsewhere even Jesus' most hostile opponents understand

cognitively the lessons of his parables (see esp. Mark 12:12 pars.). As throughout the Scriptures, the true understanding that outsiders lack is volitional. They are not prepared to commit themselves to Jesus, to follow him in discipleship and to learn further kingdom secrets. As throughout the Scriptures, divine sovereignty (Matt. 13:11–12) and human responsibility (13:13–15) are simultaneously affirmed, without any sense of contradiction (see Lambrecht 1992: 159). For more on the "Markan parable theory," see Blomberg 1990a: 39–41, 53–55, and the literature cited there.

Matthew 13:24–52

The parable of the Mustard Seed (13:31–32) alludes to Ezek. 17:23, in which the birds of the air nesting in the branches of the lofty cedar represent Gentiles (cf. Dan. 4:12; Menken [2004b: 65–66] thinks Ps. 104:12 is alluded to). This shrub, too, will grow enormously large for a mustard plant, just as one day God's kingdom will be universal in scope and ethnic membership. But, compared with the cedar, even an enormous mustard bush pales in comparison; perhaps there is a deliberate parody here (see Funk 1973). The parable of the Leaven (13:33) likewise teaches the surprising size to which the kingdom will grow, especially given its tiny beginnings. Here the most important OT background is not the well-known corrupting influence of leaven, but rather its positive use in texts such as Lev. 7:13–14; 23:17. In the interpretation of the parable of the Wheat and Tares, the Son of Man collects out of his kingdom every "stumbling block" (*skandalon*) and all "doers of wickedness" (13:41), perhaps borrowing the language of Ps. 139:6 LXX (Davies and Allison 1988–1997: 2:430). "All kinds of fish" in the parable of the dragnet (13:47) might allude to the eschatological abundance of fish in the river flowing from the new temple in Ezek. 47:10 (Derrett 1980, esp. 125–31).

13:35

A. NT Context. Matthew 13 forms the central pivot in this Gospel. After this chapter Jesus' ministry focuses increasingly on Gentiles and on his disciples, with fewer explicit appeals to the Jewish crowds or his opponents. Matthew 13:1–52 itself divides neatly into two sections (unlike the shorter parallels in Mark and Luke), as Jesus first addresses the crowds (13:1–33) and then the Twelve (13:36–52). At the dividing point, then, of this collection of parables Matthew inserts another fulfillment passage, ascribed to an unnamed "prophet" (a few early manuscripts insert "Isaiah" before "the prophet," but this reading is not likely original; for a dissenting viewpoint, believing that the quotation also alludes to texts in "Deutero-Isaiah" such as Isa. 40:5, see van Segbroeck 1965), in which Jesus' behavior is explained as reproducing a previously described pattern of figurative speech (13:34–35). For the probable chiastic structure of Matt. 13, see Wenham 1979.

B. OT Context. In its later superscription Ps. 78 (77 LXX) is ascribed to Asaph, who is elsewhere called a "seer" (i.e., prophet [e.g., 2 Chron. 29:30]). Here he composes a psalm that primarily recounts key events in Israel's history from the exodus to the time of King David. The Hebrew for "parable" (māšāl) has a broad semantic range, covering a wide variety of metaphorical forms of speech: "parable, similitude, allegory, fable, proverb, apocalyptic revelation, riddle, symbol, pseudonym, fictitious person, example, theme argument, apology, refutation, jest" (Jeremias 1972: 20). Here, "I will open my mouth in parables" (78:2a) is paralleled by "I will utter things having been hidden" (78:2b). Hossfeld and Zenger (2005: 294) identify their contents as "personal, wisdom-style instruction for life . . . couched in the verse style of 'similitudes' or 'sayings' and 'riddles.'" What is hidden from a new generation of Israelites must be disclosed so that they can learn from their history and in turn pass it on to generations to come (78:3–4). The psalmist's language may also suggest that he intends to disclose patterns in the events that he will narrate not always recognized even by those familiar with the stories themselves (Carson 1984: 321–23; Davidson 1998: 252). Still, Asaph's words clearly are intended to reveal and explain God's actions in Israel's history. Unlike the previous OT quotation in Matthew's parable chapter, the focus here is not on the cryptic nature or the concealing function of parabolic speech, but rather on its revelatory power. For the timeless principles that emerge, see McMillon 2001.

C. Use in Jewish Sources. The only clear pre-Christian Jewish allusion to this text is 1QS X, 23: "With hymns shall I open my mouth and my tongue will ever number the just acts of God and the treachery of men until their transgression is complete." A post-Christian midrash on this verse confirms that at least some rabbis much later found the concept of a "riddle" implied in the psalm (*Midr. Ps.* 78:2).

D. Textual Background. The Hebrew reads literally, "I will open my mouth in a parable. I will utter dark sayings from of old." The LXX turns the singular "parable" into a plural and renders "dark sayings" as *problēmata* ("something put forward as an excuse"?), but it otherwise translates literally. Matthew follows the LXX verbatim for the first of the two clauses in his quotation, but in the second clause the only word in Matthew that matches the LXX is "from." Matthew chooses a different but equally appropriate verb for "utter," uses *kekrymmena* ("things having been hidden") instead of *problēmata*, which seems to be a better translation of the MT, and renders "from of old" much more freely than the LXX's "from the beginning," substituting "from the foundation of the world." The genitive noun "of the world" is itself textually suspect, being absent from several older manuscripts. It is difficult to decide whether Matthew has begun with the LXX and revised it or has translated independently from the Hebrew. Either way, as regularly with his unparalleled quotes, Matthew shows more signs of not simply following the LXX than when he is taking over material from his sources (see Stendahl 1954: 116–17).

E. Hermeneutic Employed. This is a classic example of pure typology. Just as one of God's prophets spoke under inspiration to disclose narratives previously hidden from some of God's people in his day, so now the divinely inspired Jesus in his parables reveals previously hidden truth (particularly about the nature and timing of God's kingdom) to audiences in his day. Kidner (1975: 281) concludes that both Asaph and Jesus "make the past hold up a mirror to the present . . . for the true pattern of history is not self-evident." Since Matthew believed that Jesus recapitulated the history of Israel, and since Ps. 78 recounts a significant portion of that history, the typology becomes natural (Davies and Allison 1988–1997: 2:426).

F. Theological Use. Matthew wants to highlight how Jesus' ministry of speaking in parables was foreseen by Scripture, at least in the sense that patterns of speech from God's inspired spokesmen are recurring. This quotation nicely balances his earlier use of Isa. 6:9–10 to demonstrate that parables not only conceal but also reveal and that often they reveal that which was previously concealed. Matthew may also be implying that a new era of salvation history has arrived: the age of the inaugurated kingdom. The parables of Matt. 13, after all, are about precisely this inauguration, and the beginning of a new age is exactly the time one would expect God to disclose previously hidden information. Matthew 13:52 may allude back to 13:35, as the little parable of the scribe trained for the kingdom of heaven describes a household master bringing both old and new things out of his treasury.

Matthew 14:1–36

This chapter, part of Matthew's third large block of narrative material within the body of his Gospel, contains no OT quotations but a variety of allusions and echoes. When Antipas married his brother Philip's ex-wife, Herodias (14:3–4), he violated Lev. 18:16. That the dancing of Herodias's daughter pleased Herod may be worded so as to echo Esther 2:9, in which another young woman pleased a king famous for giving lavish banquets. The feeding of the five thousand (14:13–21), with Jesus supplying bread in the wilderness, again evokes the imagery of a new Moses (recall above, p. 8). For the provision of manna, see Exod. 16. The specific addition in 14:21 of "besides women and children" may reflect the language of Exod. 12:37. The promise of Ps. 132:15 and the somewhat parallel miracles by Elijah and Elisha (1 Kings 17:9–16; 2 Kings 4:42–44) also form important OT background. Though not involving bread, the miraculous gift of oil in 2 Kings 4:1–7 shows some similarity of language to Jesus' feeding miracle (see further Blomberg 1986: 337–40, and the literature there cited). In the account of Christ walking on water, the reference to a "ghost" (14:26) probably refers to a specter or apparition from the realm of the dead, as in 1 Sam. 28:8. Jesus' self-revelation to the disciples (14:27) can be translated "It is I," but literally it reads *egō eimi* ("I am"), a probable allusion to the divine name in Exod. 3:14 (see also Isa. 41:4; 43:10; 47:8, 10). In

demonstrating his mastery over wind and waves, Jesus clearly is exercising prerogatives previously reserved for Yahweh himself (cf. Job 9:8; Ps. 77:19; see further Blomberg 1986: 342–45, and the literature cited there). "It is God alone who can rescue from the sea. Note especially Exod 14.10–15.21; Ps 107.23–32; Jon 1.16" (Davies and Allison 1988–1997: 2:503). Peter's aborted attempt to follow his master (14:30) uses language and imagery reminiscent of Ps. 69:1–2.

Matthew 15:1–20

Conflict between Jesus and certain Jewish leaders resumes. The debate begins by focusing solely on the oral laws of the Pharisees (though couched in Mosaic language [e.g., Lev. 15:11, on handwashing]) but quickly affects the written Torah as well. Jesus' charge in 15:3 may echo Zechariah's prophecy in 2 Chron. 24:20. For OT background to keeping one's vows (15:5), see especially Num. 30:2–3; and Deut. 23:21–23. The imagery of 15:13 may originally have come from Isa. 60:21, on God's people as his planting. Jesus' illustrations of the evil thoughts that the heart produces (15:18) echo violations of the sixth through the ninth commandments of the Decalogue (on murder, adultery, stealing, and false witness), in sequence. Three very specific OT quotations must be considered in more detail. For a comprehensive study of Matt. 15:1–20, see Booth 1986.

15:4a

A. NT Context. Certain Jewish leaders have challenged the practice of Jesus' disciples because they do not follow Pharisaic halakah in washing their hands before eating (15:1–2). For later representative legislation, see the mishnaic tractate *Yadayim.* Jesus counters by asking why those same leaders break the written law of Moses on honoring their parents, when they abuse the practice of *qorbān*—devoting certain monies or properties to the temple upon their death (see throughout tractate *Nedarim,* esp. 1:2–4; 9:7) so that no one but themselves could benefit from them while they were still living (15:3–6). For an ancient ossuary inscription, found near Jerusalem, almost exactly paralleling the wording of 15:5b here, see Fitzmyer 1971a: 96; for the OT background and subsequent Jewish development of the theme of faithfulness to vows, see J. N. Bailey 2000. Matthew is largely following Mark (cf. Mark 7:10), but where Mark reads, "Moses [said]," Matthew substitutes "God." "Not merely human tradition is at stake here" (Hagner 1995: 431). The passage will be quoted again in Mark 10:19, with parallels in both Matthew and Luke.

B. OT Context. In both Exodus and Deuteronomy, honor for father and mother appears among the Ten Commandments. It is the first of six commandments dealing with interpersonal relationships, following the opening four, which deal with the relationship between humans and God. Paul later will stress the promise attached to this specific command (Eph. 6:2): living a long life in the promised land. In the OT this clearly is fulfilled corporately more than individually: to the extent that the Israelites as a whole prove more obedient than not, God blesses them with freedom and prosperity in their land. General rebellion and idolatry, on the other hand, regularly lead to national punishment.

C. Use in Jewish Sources. The *Fragmentary Targum* on Exod. 20:12 already begins to move in an individualizing direction by translating, "My people, my people, house of Israel, be careful about the honor of your father and about the honor of your mother; for whoever honors his father and his mother I will give him extended days and plentitude of years; because on account of the honoring of father and mother, I will cause him to inherit the world to come" (translation from M. L. Klein 1980). Not surprisingly, there are numerous references to this command, as one of Israel's ten central mandates, throughout both early and late Jewish literature, although most are not relevant for interpreting Matt. 15:4. We may observe, however, that Josephus notes that the law on honoring parents ranked second only to honoring God, and that if a son did not respond to the benefits that he received from his parents, he should be stoned (*Ag. Ap.* 2.27)! This certainly would support Jesus' understanding of the commandment as a very fundamental one.

Likewise, *Ahiqar* 138 declares, "Whoever takes no pride in his father's and mother's name, may Shama[sh] not shine [on him], for he is an evil man." Philo berates those who neglect their parents and enjoins them to "cover their faces from shame and reproach themselves for disregarding

those things which they ought to have cared for" (*Decalogue* 118). He elsewhere calls those who dishonor their parents disobedient and contentious (*Drunkenness* 17). In *Spec. Laws* 2.261 we find what may be Philo's most relevant comment: "Let not him who honors his parents dutifully seek for any further advantage, for if he considers the matter he will find his reward in his own conduct." Section 262 adds that a second reward, length of days, attaches to the commandment. Clearly, however, trying to gain additional financial reward in this life would destroy the spirit of the command. Pseudo-Phocylides 8 proclaims, "Honor God foremost and afterward your parents." The Jewish leaders' dishonoring of their parents was a grievous sin indeed.

D. Textual Background. The excerpted portion of Exod. 20:12 matches the comparable section of Deut. 5:16 exactly in the original Hebrew. The LXX translation is perfectly literal in Deuteronomy; in Exodus, the second, superfluous "your" is omitted. Mark follows the LXX (with both uses of "your") verbatim. Matthew, presumably following Mark, omits the "your" before both "father" and "mother," but the meaning remains unchanged.

E. Hermeneutic Employed. As with previous quotations of the Ten Commandments in Matthew, Jesus is employing a timeless moral truth in a new way to a situation that the Jewish leaders whom he is addressing have apparently neglected. Jesus himself radically relativizes some conventional interpretations of family obligations (see esp. Mark 3:31–35 pars.; Luke 14:26 par.), but he never overturns the fundamental mandate to honor one's parents. Also, as we have seen before, moral law takes precedence over civil or ceremonial law, and the written Torah carries an authority that the oral law ("the tradition of the elders" [Matt. 15:2]) never can.

F. Theological Use. Ritual handwashing is thus part of the unwritten ceremonial traditions that Jesus feels free to disregard. The Christology implied here is not necessarily as "high" as in other contexts where Jesus reinterprets the written law. Challenging the oral Torah does not elevate Jesus to a level higher than any of the other leadership sects in Israel that did not accept Pharisaic halakah. Even a Pharisaic teacher could have countered in the fashion that Jesus did in certain circumstances (see Keener 1999: 411). However, the passage is not yet concluded; more sweeping challenges, even to the written law, will yet emerge.

15:4b

A. NT Context. The context is identical to that of the Exod. 20:12 quotation treated above. This is simply a second quotation from the OT to underline the seriousness of honoring one's parents. The first commandment quoted above presented the obligation positively; this second one speaks negatively, warning against dishonor in the form of speaking evil of one's father or mother. This specific illustration of dishonoring parents prepares the way for Jesus' subsequent example of the abuse of *qorbān*, since that too involves saying something bad (15:5), namely, that particular material possessions are dedicated to God and thus are off limits as far as helping parents is concerned.

B. OT Context. Exodus 21:12–36 deals with personal injuries and their punishment or restitution. Verse 17 is unique in this context in that it refers not to an actual physical injury, but only to cursing, what we today would call verbal abuse. Nevertheless, such dishonor of parents was so serious as to require capital punishment. Presumably, some "egregious act of disrespect or repudiation" or "serious breach of filial duty" is in view (Enns 2000: 445). Meyers (2005: 192) observes that two contextual factors mitigate some of the apparent harshness of this law: (a) the children here are adults caring for elderly parents; and (b) the parents retain managerial authority requiring respect. An almost identical law appears in Lev. 20:9 in a context of punishments for various kinds of sin, most of them sexual. Verse 9b adds to the basic command and punishment found in Exodus the rationale that the curse has brought the blood of the offender onto his or her own head.

C. Use in Jewish Sources. The oldest existing Jewish use of these texts appears in Philo, *Spec. Laws* 2.248, which captures the narrative flow between Exod. 21:15 and 21:17: "And even if he has not laid hands upon his parents, but has only spoken ill of those whom he was bound to praise and bless, or if he has in other manner done anything which can tend to bring his parents into disrepute, still let him die." The rabbinic literature largely discussed under what circumstances someone had genuinely cursed parents, often limiting the application of the command to the explicit use

of certain divine names (Str-B 1:709–11). *Targum Pseudo-Jonathan* on Exod. 21:17 proves the most restrictive of all, limiting the kind of cursing subject to capital punishment to that which employed the holiest name for God, "Yahweh."

D. Textual Background. The MT of Exod. 21:17 reads, "The one cursing his father or his mother shall surely be put to death." The only difference in Lev. 20:9 is that the initial participle is replaced with the idiom "a person, a person who curses." The LXX (esp. B) for the Exodus text (numbered 21:16) is a sufficiently literal rendition of the Hebrew. Mark 7:10 deletes the two unnecessary personal pronouns and changes the imperatival use of the future indicative to an explicit third-person imperative. Matthew copies Mark word for word here.

E. Hermeneutic Employed. Jewish interpretation recognized Exod. 21:17 (or Lev. 20:9) as a specific application of the fourth commandment of the Decalogue (see, e.g., C. J. H. Wright [1983: 165–69], who also illustrates what we can learn and apply from the varying OT penalties to the NT age). Jesus believes that it remains wrong to speak evil of parents, even with all the other changes he is introducing into the law in the age of the new covenant. Indeed, by choosing a word that does not limit itself to "cursing" per se, Matthew, following Mark, recognizes a more widespread application of the principle than did the Jewish sources that were regularly seeking to narrow their focus. On the other hand, conspicuously absent from Jesus' teaching (and from the rest of the NT) are the specific OT sanctions for violating God's laws. Nowhere does the NT ever explicitly sanction capital punishment, and even those Christian traditions that believe it carries over into this age in limited contexts recognize that it is not appropriate for something as comparatively mild as verbal abuse. Sarna (1991: 123) calls it "a flagrant violation of the Decalogue's imperative in Exodus 20:12."

F. Theological Use. See under the "Theological Use" section, p. 51.

15:8–9

A. NT Context. The hypocrisy of certain Jewish leaders dishonoring their parents while claiming to set aside special gifts for God (15:5–6) leads Jesus to unleash the invective that spans 15:7–9. Once again quoting Isaiah by name and referring to his words as prophecy (15:7), Jesus cites a passage as applicable to his context as it was eight centuries earlier. Luz (2001: 332) observes, "As in 13:14–15 it is the biblical word that formulates the accusation. And, as there, the biblical word says more than the text: Not only Israel's leaders but 'this people' honors God only with the lips. In the context of Matthew 15 the accusation against the entire nation is still not justified; we have here a signal that points to the end of the Matthean Jesus' story." God's people honor him with their lips—they claim to be serving and worshiping Yahweh—but their heart attitudes do not match their outward professions (15:8). Thus their worship is futile (15:9a). Worse still, their proclamation involves the teaching of human tradition (the oral law), not the divinely inspired, written Torah (15:9b). From this accusation, Jesus turns to the more positive (and revolutionary) teaching that it is not what goes into people (such as food or drink) that defiles them, but rather what comes out of them (e.g., evil words and deeds). Poirier (2000) thinks that the reference to drawing near with their "mouths" in the Isaiah quotation formed the catchword for proceeding to discuss food—that which goes into one's mouth. By the end of this section (15:10–20), at least in Mark's parallel account, the evangelist will identify the principle that eventually would support the explicit annulment of the dietary laws (Mark 7:19b). Although it is often alleged that Matthew rejects such a radical departure from Torah and thus omits Mark's parenthetical aside, a consistent application of Matt. 15:11 by itself should lead to the declaration that all foods are clean (rightly W. C. Allen 1907: 166).

B. OT Context. As in numerous places in the prophets, God's people are berated for active participation in worship without the proper attitudes and/or behavior in their lives that make worship meaningful. The city of David (Jerusalem) goes on celebrating its many festivals (Isa. 29:1), but God promises only judgment (29:2–4). Israel's enemies will in turn be punished (29:5–8), but Isaiah's main point here is to stress the current sins of the nation. In language reminiscent of chapter 6 (recall the discussion under Matt. 13:13–15), Isaiah can even attribute the people's stupor to God's initiative (29:10), but only after it is clear that the Israelites have also blinded themselves

(29:9). Verses 11–12 describe the results of this blinding: inability to read God's words sealed in a scroll—a judgment that may well have led Jesus to apply the next verse (29:13) to the situation in his day (Booth 1986: 92). In the eighth century BC, 29:13 represents the official state cult "as driven by convention and routine, and not of a kind that might actually make a difference in the world of social and political realities" (Blenkinsopp 2000: 405–6). The rest of the chapter continues the alternation between the litany of Israel's sins and a description of their coming judgment (29:14–21), but 29:22–24 round out the chapter with a reminder of salvation after judgment.

C. Use in Jewish Sources. The only undeniably pre-Christian Jewish reference to this text is the allusion in *Pss. Sol.* 4:1, with its charge, "Why are you sitting in the council of the devout, you profaner? And your heart is far from the Lord, provoking the God of Israel by lawbreaking." *Targum Isaiah*, which at times preserves early tradition, reads at 29:13, "And the LORD said: 'Because this people *exalts itself* with *their* mouth and honour *before* me with their lips, while *their* heart is far from *my fear*, and their fear *before* me is *as* a commandment of men *who teach*, [then I will strike them . . . (29:14)].'" Unlike the Targum's rendering of 6:9–10, there appears to be no mitigation of the severity of God's language here. Even the Targum to 29:10 speaks of the Lord as casting a spirit of deception among the people. No other uses of this text appear in the later rabbinic literature, save for the very general reference to God looking on one's heart (*b. Sanh.* 106b; cf. 1 Sam. 16:7; see Str-B 1:716).

D. Textual Background. The MT reads literally, "And the LORD said, 'Because this people draws near with its mouth and with its lips honors me, and its heart is far from me, and fear of me is commandments of men taught. . . .'" Davies and Allison (1988–1997: 2:525) explain the meaning of the last clause as "their fear of me is [just] a human commandment which has been memorized." The LXX abbreviates slightly by leaving out "with its mouth," interprets "fear" as "worship," adds "in vain" as an appropriate explanatory clarification, and turns "commandments of men taught" into the more intelligible expression "teaching as commandments the teachings of men." There are just enough differences between the MT and the LXX for scholars to debate whether the LXX had a different Hebrew original in front of it, but it seems that all the changes can be accounted for as intelligible interpretations of the MT (for representative discussion, see Booth 1986: 38–39). Mark 7:6b–7 omits the first pronoun, changes the number of the verb "honor" back to the singular (more strictly grammatical than the LXX plural), puts "me" in a more natural position in the sentence, and improves the syntax of the last three words as well. Matthew puts "this" after (rather than before) "people" at the beginning of the quotation but otherwise follows Mark verbatim.

E. Hermeneutic Employed. The parallels between the setting in Isaiah's world and Jesus' context prove striking. "In both cases wrong teaching was based on a mishandling of God's true revelation, the sacrificial regulations and the Mosaic Law as a whole, respectively. In each case tradition allied to bad theology resulted in a mishandling of Scripture, and in each case the result was a self-justifying complacency in the presence of the most holy God" (Grogan 1986: 188). At the very least, we have a classic example of typology, with a striking recurrence of a deplorable pattern of behavior among God's people at crucial junctures in their history (thus, e.g., France 1971: 68–69). But the possible allusion to Isa. 6:9–10 in 29:9–10, the programmatic nature of chapter 6 for Isaiah more generally (on which, see Evans 1989: 52), and the concluding, hopeful ending of chapter 29 (also paralleled in the end of chap. 6) combine to suggest the interpretive framework of double (and perhaps even generic) fulfillment. Jesus and the Gospel writers who quote him recognize that the reaction of the Jewish leaders in their day was an additional stage of the fulfillment of Isaiah's description of his generation's sins, which would continue in various fashions until the fullness of the messianic age.

F. Theological Use. This quotation further reinforces the theology discussed above under Matt. 15:4. Ritual and ceremonial obedience, even fervent worship, sickens God when it is feigned, when it does not spring from a transformed heart (Mounce [1991: 149] comments, "When man-made rules are taught as the laws of God, all worship becomes useless"). At the very least, the reduction of the fear of the Lord "to a set of do's and don't's is to move one's faith from the center to the periphery of life" (Oswalt 1986–1998: 1:532). A sizable amount of research on first-century Judaism has demonstrated that it was not dominated by the stifling legalism that would characterize some later rabbinic discussions (so esp. E. P. Sanders 1977). However, there was sufficient legalism, including within the oral Torah that is rejected here as merely human tradition (see esp. Carson, O'Brien, and Seifrid 2001), to make Jesus' rebukes appropriate and to provoke even greater opposition among his contemporaries.

Matthew 15:21–18:14

Here appears the longest stretch of text in Matthew without any formal quotations of the OT. The woman whom Mark describes as a Syrophoenician (Mark 7:26) is in Matt. 15:22 identified as a Canaanite. No one in the first century used that term anymore; Matthew is deliberately conjuring up distasteful memories of the pagan Tyrians and Sidonians from OT times (see above on Matt. 11:22; see also Theissen 1991: 61–80). On the "lost sheep of the house of Israel" in 15:24, see the comments on 10:5–6 above. That the Gentiles should be blessed through the ministry of the Messiah, the seed of Abraham (recall 1:1), is a further fulfillment of Gen. 12:1–3. The feeding of the four thousand (15:29–39) evokes the same OT background discussed in conjunction with the feeding of the five thousand (14:13–21), but this time Jesus is ministering in Gentile territory (see Wefald 1995). Pairs of feeding miracles also occurred in the ministries of Moses (Exod. 16; Num. 11:4–9) and Elisha (2 Kings 4:1–7, 42–44). Matthew's version of Jesus' "withdrawal from Galilee" does not diminish but closely parallels Mark's emphasis in foreshadowing a more extensive Christian ministry to the Gentiles in the activity of Jesus. The categories of sick people and the healings performed in Matt. 15:30–31 again recall the prophecies of the miracles that would demonstrate the arrival of the messianic age (esp. Isa. 35:5–6).

Matthew 16:1–4 applies labels first used of the Israelites who wandered in the wilderness: "an evil and adulterous generation" (v. 4) harks back to the "evil generation" of Deut. 1:35 and the "crooked and perverse generation" of Deut. 32:5. Similar language frequently punctuates the

OT. The Pharisees and Sadducees are testing Jesus here (Matt. 16:1), just as the Israelites had often tested Yahweh in previous centuries (e.g., Exod. 17:1–7; Ps. 78:41, 56). Verse 5 reverts to the more common OT use of "yeast" as a metaphor for insidious evil, and hence to be purged from most meal offerings. For the requirement to eat bread without yeast during Passover, see already Exod. 12. Verse 14 recalls the common expectation of the return of Elijah prior to the messianic age, based on Mal. 4:5 (see above under Matt. 11:10). It also discloses that some expected a Jeremiah-like figure—an understandable notion in view of his unrelenting message combining warnings of severe judgment with explicit descriptions of the new covenant (see esp. Jer. 31; on the typology, see further Dahlberg 1975). Knowles (1993: 86–95) stresses the "rejected prophet" motif common to Jeremiah and Jesus. Various other comparisons between the coming Messiah and a prophet were inspired by Deut. 18:15–18.

The dialogue between Jesus and Peter (Matt. 16:16–20) contains numerous probable allusions to the OT, not to mention a Semitic style that points to authentic tradition and possibly even to Matthean priority, at least for this text (see Meyer 1979: 185–97; Maier 1985). "Son of the living God" (16:16) may allude to Hos. 2:1 LXX (=1:10 MT) and further the theme of Jesus doing right what Israel did wrong (Goodwin 2005). "Son of Jonah" (16:17) may be a typological comparison with the OT prophet Jonah, since Simon Peter was literally the son of John (John 1:42; 21:15; see Mounce 1991: 161). But *Bariōna* could also be a contraction of *bar Johanan* and thus in fact mean "son of John" (see Carson 1984: 375). Identifying Peter as a "rock," as the coming human foundation on which the church would be built (16:18a), could be meant to call to mind the famous cornerstone (or capstone) prophecy of Ps. 118:22 (see also Isa. 28:15–19), which will figure prominently later in Matthew (see below, pp. 73–74). There may also be an allusion to Isa. 51:1–2, to the rock from which Israel was hewn, making Peter a "founding father" of the new covenant community, just as Abraham was for Israel (see Davies and Allison 1988–1997: 2:624). The "gates of Hades" (16:18b) appears to allude to texts such as Job 38:17; and Isa. 38:10, while "the keys to the kingdom" (16:19) almost certainly

is based on the identical metaphor in Isa. 22:22. On the possible relationship between these two allusions, see Marcus 1988.

With 16:21, Matthew turns all attention toward Jesus' road to the cross. As Jesus begins to explain that he must suffer, he may have texts such as Isa. 52–53 and Dan. 7 in mind. Resurrection on the third day may have been suggested by Hos. 6:2. That Peter, the foundation stone, should so suddenly turn into a stumbling block (16:23) recalls God's role as "a stone of stumbling, a rock of offense" against wayward Israel in Isa. 8:14 (for a development of this contrast, see Wilcox 1975). Verse 26 may faintly echo Eccles. 1:3 on the ultimate futility of merely earthly labor (see also Ps. 49:7–9). The Son of Man coming in his Father's glory (16:27a) seems to allude to Zech. 14:5, in addition, of course, to its more direct allusion to Dan. 7:13–14. And Jesus' reference to judgment by works (16:27b) echoes the teaching of numerous OT texts (see esp. Ps. 28:4; 62:12; Prov. 24:12).

Matthew 17 begins with the account of Jesus' transfiguration (vv. 1–13). Here appears extensive, unambiguous Mosaic typology. The reference to six days (17:1) parallels Moses' six days of preparation on Mount Sinai before God revealed himself to him (Exod. 24:16). It is possible that we are also meant to recall Exod. 24:1, as Moses takes a special group of three companions with him (Davies and Allison 1988–1997: 2:694). Moses, with Elijah, is of course explicitly present for this theophany as well (17:3). The glorious transformation of Christ matches Moses' dazzling splendor as he descended from the mountain (Exod. 34:29–35). Peter's misguided suggestion that they erect shelters (17:4) is probably based on the pattern of living in tents as Moses led the Israelites in the desert and perhaps even alludes specifically to the Feast of Tabernacles (cf. Lev. 23; Deut. 16). The bright cloud (17:5a) makes one think of the cloud that enveloped the tabernacle when God's glory filled it (Exod. 40:34), along with the cloud that followed the Israelites by day throughout their wilderness wanderings (Exod. 40:36–38). As at Jesus' baptism (see Matt. 3:17), a heavenly voice refers to him by alluding to Ps. 2:7 and Isa. 42:1, combining allusions to his roles as messianic king and Suffering Servant (17:5b). The additional charge, "Listen to him," alludes to

Deut. 18:15 on heeding the prophet like Moses who would arise in later days. The disciples' fear in 17:6 matches that of those who saw Moses' face in Exod. 34:30.

Why Moses and Elijah were chosen to appear with Jesus is debated. Some have suggested they represented the law and the prophets, two key OT periods characterized by the miraculous, or two key messianic forerunners, at least typologically (in light of Deut. 18:15–18; Mal. 4:5). Some Jews believed that neither had physically died: the OT is explicit with respect to Elijah (2 Kings 2:1–12); intertestamental traditions made the same suggestion about Moses, since his body had never been found (see esp. *Assumption of Moses*). The disciples' response to the heavenly voice (17:6) may have been inspired by Dan. 10:15–19. The additional conversation about Elijah as Jesus, Peter, James, and John come down from the mountain (17:10–13) is natural enough, since Elijah has just appeared, and reflects the earlier discussion of Mal. 3:1 and 4:5 applied to John the Baptist (see above, pp. 38–39; for the fullest study of Matthew's version of the transfiguration, including discussion of these and other uses of the OT within it, see Moses 1996).

The rest of Matthew 17 relies on the OT considerably less. Jesus' lament in 17:17, "O unbelieving and crooked generation," again echoes regular OT charges (e.g., Deut. 32:5, 20). The remaining passion and resurrection predictions (here 17:22–23, but see also 20:18–19) may echo Isaiah's Servant Songs and perhaps even Dan. 7:25, especially since Dan. 12:2 goes on to supply the clearest OT reference to the resurrection of the saints (Schaberg 1985). The debate about the temple tax (Matt. 17:24–27) takes as its starting point the commands found in Exod. 30:13; 38:25–26. Brodie (1992) thinks that 17:24–27 combines allusions to the "fish-centered" list of animals in Deut. 14:1–21 and exhortation to pay the temple tithe in 14:22–27 with Matt. 18:15–35 alluding to commandments concerning sin, debt, and slaves in Deut. 15:1–5.

Matthew 18 forms another discourse of Christ. In 18:6 Jesus reuses the "stumbling block" imagery of Isa. 8:14. The parable of the lost sheep (18:10–14) calls to mind a variety of OT texts, including Ps. 23 (on Ps. 23 as background, see K. E. Bailey 1992: 194–212), but also the comparison

between Israel's false shepherds and the coming messianic shepherd in Ezek. 34 (W. G. Thompson 1970: 160). The psalmist in Ps. 119:176 can also speak of straying like a lost sheep. The concept of guardian angels, perhaps in view in 18:10, seems to have developed from Ps. 91:11. However, it is also possible that Jesus is alluding to the more collective concept of angels who watch over entire nations, as in Dan. 10:10–14 (for more details concerning possible Jewish background, see W. D. Davies 1964: 226–28). "Seeing God's face," also in Matt. 18:10, probably implies access to God and appears to be patterned after the similar expressions in 2 Sam. 14:24; and 1 Kings 10:8.

Matthew 18:15–35

No definite uses of the OT appear in this section of teaching, except for one explicit quotation.

18:16

A. NT Context. Matthew 18 forms the fourth of the five major blocks of sermonic material that this Gospel groups together (the others are chaps. 5–7; 10; 13; 23–25). Jesus is speaking privately to his disciples about the themes of humility and forgiveness. Matthew 18:15–18 forms the well-known passage on church discipline. Here a procedure is outlined not just for confronting flagrant sinners, but for dealing with any unresolved grievances. First, the offended Christian is to approach the offender privately to see if matters can be resolved at that level (18:15), perhaps in line with Lev. 19:17. If that does not work, the offended believer is to take one or two others along so that jointly there will be two or three witnesses to confirm what attempts were made to bring the offender to repent of sin (18:16). "Witness" here means not "witness to the original sin," but rather "witness to the attempts to show sinful persons their wrongs" (see Gundry 1994: 368). If that effort fails, then the matter is brought to the entire local congregation (18:17a), and if the sinner still refuses to change, then the church must proceed with putting that person out of the fellowship (18:17b). For excellent elaboration of this entire process, see Laney 1985. This punishment resembles the OT practice of cutting a person off from Israel's assembly (see, e.g., Gen. 17:14; Exod. 12:15, 19; 30:33, 38).

Verse 18 then explains that heaven is in accord with duly exercised church discipline (on which, see Porter 1988), while 18:19–20 promise God's presence during the process. On "binding and loosing," see above under 16:19. The "two or three" gathered in Jesus' name in 18:20 refer to the offended Christian plus the one or two witnesses of 18:16. Together, 18:15–20 provide an important contextual qualification, as do 18:23–35, to the apparently unlimited forgiveness that 18:21–22 enjoin. As the parallel in Luke 17:3–4 also demonstrates, that forgiveness is applicable only when genuine repentance has occurred. When it has, though, people truly forgiven by God *will* forgive others (see further Blomberg 2006). Deuteronomy 19:15 is cited again in 2 Cor. 13:1, alluded to in 1 Tim. 5:19, and its principle seems to lie behind the actions taken in Matt. 26:59–61; and John 8:17 (where this law appears to be paraphrased); Heb. 6:18; Rev. 11:3.

B. OT Context. Deuteronomy 19:15–21 is a short, self-contained section of the law dealing with the theme of witnesses. Verse 15a explains that one person's testimony is insufficient to convict another accused of a crime. Verses 16–21 explain what to do with a malicious or false witness. A more formal legal setting is in view here than in Matthew, because 19:17 refers to the judges who are in office at the time. In this context, 19:15b requires multiple witnesses "as a safeguard against dishonest or mistaken testimony" (Tigay 1996: 163). C. J. H. Wright (1996: 224) notes that this would be especially necessary when the accused was a weaker individual being confronted by a more powerful opponent. The principle has appeared already in Num. 35:30 and may lie behind Deut. 17:6.

C. Use in Jewish Sources. *Testament of Abraham* 13:8 explains how all creation must appear before Abel, Abraham, and God at the final judgment, so that a matter is established by three witnesses. Josephus proclaims, "Put not trust in a single witness, but let there be three or at least two, whose evidence shall be accredited by their past lives" (*Ant.* 4.219; see also *Life* 256). (All quotations from Josephus are taken from Whiston 1987.) He adds, however, "From women let no evidence be accepted because of the levity and temerity of their sex"—a restriction that Jesus nowhere endorses. Philo provides a mini-commentary on

the various reasons why a single witness may not prove trustworthy (*Spec. Laws* 4.53–54). The *Damascus Document* (CD-A IX, 16–23) deals with the need for at least two trustworthy witnesses in various community disputes at Qumran (see also 11Q19 LXI, 6–7; LXIV, 8). Perhaps the closest parallel to Jesus' procedure in Matthew appears in 1QS V, 25–VI, 1, where again emphasis is placed on resolving disputes privately; only then may they be brought to the congregation, with at least two witnesses (for a comparative study, see García Martínez 1989).

D. Textual Background. A woodenly literal rendering of the MT would read, "On the mouth of two witnesses [i.e., on the basis of their words] or on the mouth of three witnesses shall a word be established." The LXX renders the more idiomatic Hebrew in precisely such wooden fashion, changing only the "or" to an "and" and "a word" to "every word"—a contextually justifiable interpretation. Matthew's version abbreviates by deleting the redundant, second "on the mouth of" and "witnesses," changing the "and" back to the "or," and altering the future passive "shall be established" to the aorist passive "was established"—appropriate enough now that Jesus is looking back on the law. The fact that the interpretive "every" is retained suggests dependence on the LXX, despite the rest of the editorial changes to this half-verse (see Stendahl 1954: 139).

E. Hermeneutic Employed. This is not one of the scriptural quotations that is formally introduced; Jesus (or possibly Matthew) simply lapses into biblical language in pronouncing his injunction. This passage is not as obviously part of the fundamental moral law as, say, most of the Ten Commandments, and a rigid separation of moral from civil law might place it in the latter category. But this example is a good reminder of the fluid boundaries between such legal categories, categories that may not have been in the original authors' intent anyway. At any rate, the principle derives from the ninth commandment: do not bear false witness. Nothing in the new covenant that Jesus is inaugurating overturns the need for scrupulous truth-telling, so we should not be surprised to see Jesus and Matthew employing this principle to church discipline in their day.

F. Theological Use. Like the judicial system in the OT and like the disciplinary system at Qumran, Jesus and Matthew are concerned to protect their communities from the false charges or false testimony that one person, without any checks and balances, can so easily generate. In the cases of serious accusations, where reconciliation between believers has not come easily, one person's word against another seldom proves conclusive or even helpful. Two or three are needed to agree in public testimony as to what has already transpired. Although the context in Matthew is not nearly as formal as in Deuteronomy, the use of this principle elsewhere in Jewish and NT literature shows that it was understood to enshrine a more general principle with broad relevance (Davies and Allison 1988–1997: 2:784–85; *contra* Beare 1981).

Matthew 19:1–30

With this chapter, Jesus begins his final, fateful journey to Jerusalem (19:1–2). En route he dialogues with several people on a variety of issues central to discipleship. The first involves a Pharisaic "test," as certain leaders ask him about one of their own vexed controversies, divorce (19:3–12). Malachi 2:16, on how God hates divorce, provides important OT background. Next, Jesus will respond to little children brought to him (19:13–15) by laying hands on them and blessing them, asking for God's favor to rest on them (cf. Gen. 48:14–15). Finally, he will interact with the rich young ruler and then with the disciples about the cost of following him (19:16–30). In that passage, 19:17 alludes to Lev. 18:5 on living by keeping the commandments. Verse 22 may echo Ps. 62:10 on not setting one's heart on the increase of riches. For cross-references to the idea of all things being possible for God (19:26), see Gen. 18:14; Job 42:2; and Zech. 8:6 (LXX). The coming of the Son of Man in 19:28, with its specific reference to twelve thrones, clearly harks back not only to Dan. 7:13–14, as consistent with Jesus' use of "Son of Man," but also to the multiple thrones in heaven of Dan. 7:9–10. More explicit quotations of the OT in the first and last of the three main passages in Matt. 19 will introduce us to the remaining issues of this chapter. On the teaching of this chapter more generally, see Via 1985.

19:4

A. NT Context. We have already noted the intra-Pharisaic debate between the schools of Hillel and Shammai on the topic of divorce (see above, pp. 23–24). Verse 3 explicitly phrases the question posed of Jesus in light of that debate, as he is asked if divorce is acceptable "for every reason"—that is, for any kind of indecency, however minor. Jesus replies in good rabbinic fashion, answering a question with a question based on Scripture: "Have you never read that he who created from the beginning made them male and female?" (19:4) (recall the introductions to Jesus' two uses of Hos. 6:6). The rest of the dialogue will appear in our examination of the NT context of the subsequent two OT quotations, but even with this first citation of Scripture, Jesus' point begins to emerge. Man and woman were created to be with each other, not separated. W. C. Allen (1907: 203) reflects: "In 19:4 the idea seems to be that God created a single pair who were therefore destined for each other."

B. OT Context. Verse 27 forms a crucial part of the account of the six days of creation in Gen. 1. On the sixth day, God creates man and woman uniquely in his image (1:26, 27a), to have dominion—that is, to exercise good stewardship as God's vice-regents—over all the rest of creation (1:26, 28). However, God did not create an undifferentiated humanity; he established two genders to complement each other (1:27b; cf. 2:20–25). Throughout church history extensive discussion has gone on over the nature of the *imago Dei* and the role of the differentiation of the sexes in defining God's image. Suffice it to say here that although the two concepts are directly juxtaposed, neither here nor in any other Scripture is "male and female" called part of God's image. The *imago* is relational, but in no way does it require a person somehow to be linked to the opposite sex to reflect God's image fully (see further Wilson and Blomberg 1993, and the literature cited there.) He also established plants as food for both humans and animals (1:29–30), and he looked upon all these arrangements as "very good" (1:31). Genesis 5:2 repeats the relevant portion of 1:27 verbatim in recalling the creation of humanity at the beginning of the genealogical record of Adam's line down through Noah.

C. Use in Jewish Sources. Genesis 1:27 becomes a key text, frequently discussed in ancient Judaism. Most of the references have no bearing on Jesus' appeal to the passage here. Rabbi Eleazar, in the late third century, would reflect an opposite end of the spectrum from those who permitted easy divorce, declaring that the man without a wife was no true man (*b. Yebam.* 63a). Among pre-Christian sources, perhaps CD-A IV, 20–21 is most relevant, as it appeals to Gen. 1:27 to preclude second marriages (for a thorough treatment of perspectives at Qumran, see Mueller 1980). *Targum Neofiti* on this passage would later reflect the same perspective, reading, "male *and his partner* he created them" (translation taken from McNamara 1992). *Jubilees* reinforces the context of "male and female he created them" by repeating it in a discussion of God giving humanity dominion over the earth (2:14). Philo frequently refers to Gen. 1:27. In *Heir* 164 he stresses the equality of male and female in procreation despite their being "unequal in strength." In *QG* 2:56 that same equality is extended to their task of exercising dominion. None of Philo's treatments, however, sheds direct light on the topic of marriage and divorce.

D. Textual Background. The excerpt from Gen. 1:27 is rendered literally in the LXX. Matthew, in turn, follows the LXX verbatim, as did Mark 10:6 before him.

E. Hermeneutic Employed. This is the first instance in Matthew of what theologians have come to call a "creation ordinance"—an appeal to some facet of creation before the fall to support a NT speaker's or writer's perspective as equally appropriate in this new age. The statement of the biblical narrator is so important that it is directly attributed to God (Keener 1999: 465). Jesus' redemption begins the process of reversing the curse of God on all of creation. Human relationships thus should increasingly reflect God's original intentions in creation, irrespective of later OT concessions to fallen, human nature (see Farla 1989: 71). But Jesus' argument remains thoroughly Jewish: the more ancient the practice, the weightier it remains (Hill 1972: 279).

F. Theological Use. This verse thus forms the first plank in Jesus' platform from which he argues that marriage is intended to be permanent. Even though he will *allow* an exception (19:9) that seemingly parallels the perspective of Shammai, he will never *require* divorce, even in the case of marital unfaithfulness. Thus Jesus' overall approach to divorce and remarriage is even more conservative than any of the Jewish parties in his day. God intends marriage to be a lifelong commitment; those who enter it should reflect that commitment and then keep their promises of loyalty to each other (for further exegetical details relevant to this quotation and the next two in Matthew, see Blomberg 1990b).

19:5

A. NT Context. Not only did God create humanity male and female (19:4), but also he instituted heterosexual, monogamous marriage as the most intimate of interpersonal relationships and as the only relationship in which sexual union was appropriate. Jesus thus quotes a second OT text from the creation narrative that refers both to interpersonal allegiance and to sexual consummation between husband and wife (19:5). From this text he draws the conclusion that God is the one who joins marriages together. Humans therefore have no right to separate what God has united (19:6). The text does not say that marriages *cannot* be broken, but rather that they *should not* be broken. Marriage is not an indissoluble, mystical union; it is a covenant that, tragically, can, but ought not be, violated (see Atkinson 1981). For more contextual considerations, see the comments on the preceding and following OT quotations. The verse is quoted also in 1 Cor. 6:16; and Eph. 5:31.

B. OT Context. Genesis 2:24 forms the climax of the paragraph that begins with God observing that Adam had no suitable helper corresponding to him among the animals that he had just named (2:20). So God made the woman from the man's rib to provide him with that partner (2:21–22). Adam now recognizes one very much like himself, and the name that he gives her reflects that similarity (2:23). Verse 24 then provides an etiology—an explanation of how a particular custom or institution developed, in this case marriage. Waltke and Fredricks (2001: 90): "This aside by the narrator indicates the archetypal intent of the story. Every marriage is divinely ordained. The inspired explanation aims to correct cultures that give priority to the parental bonds over the marital bonds." Again, "God's intention that marriage be monogamous is implied by the complete unity and profound solidarity of the relationship." The loyalty and intimacy between husband and wife, at this juncture still untainted by sin, can explain how their nakedness does not cause shame (2:25).

C. Use in Jewish Sources. Again Philo is the most prolific Jewish writer to discuss this particular verse. He can at times completely allegorize the text (*Alleg. Interp.* 2.49), but on other occasions he supplies shrewd exegetical insights. The most relevant quotation appears in *QG* 1.29: "[God] here orders man to behave himself towards his wife with such excess of affection in their intercourse, that he is willing to leave his parents, not in order that by that means it may be more suitable, but as they should scarcely be a motive for his fidelity to his wife." Philo proceeds to give arguments as to why it is more appropriate for the man to leave his parents than for the woman to do so. With respect to the two becoming one flesh, he concludes, "Both man and woman may derive pleasure and pain from the same sources, and may feel the same; aye, and may still more think the same." *Jubilees* 3:7 recounts our text in abbreviated form, presupposing knowledge of the larger context (Davies and Allison 1988–1997: 3:11). Later rabbinic discussion seems to have focused primarily on what this principle meant in the context of extended families often living together (Str-B 1:802–3). This may also influence the rendering in some of the Targumim that speak merely of the man separating himself from the "couch," "bedroom," or "sleeping abode" of his parents, since often he would still live in the same house with them.

D. Textual Background. The MT reads, "For this reason a man shall leave his father and his mother and shall cleave to his wife, and they shall become one flesh." The LXX translates very literally, even to the point of rendering the Hebrew idiom *lĕbāśār* awkwardly as *eis sarka mian* (lit., "unto one flesh"), but substitutes "the two" for "they." Mark 10:7–8 follows the LXX verbatim, save for omitting the second, unnecessary "his." Matthew uses a slightly different form of the adverb, "for this reason," deletes the first "his," omits the superfluous prefix from the Greek for "cleave," and replaces the prepositional phrase "to his wife" with a simple indirect object.

E. Hermeneutic Employed. Again we may speak of a creation ordinance utilized here (see Farla 1989: 71–72). As the context of the next OT quotation will make clear, concessions to human hard-heartedness during the period of the Mosaic law do not nullify God's initial intentions for marriage and may no longer be used as an excuse for divorce (Matt. 19:7–8). The NT age begins the process of restoring God's original purposes in creation.

F. Theological Use. See the corresponding section under Matt. 19:4 above. This is the second plank in Jesus' platform of stressing marriage as a permanent, lifelong institution not to be ruptured.

19:7

A. NT Context. The Pharisees who had asked Jesus his views on divorce now counter by citing Deut. 24:1. If God's intention from creation was one man and one woman for life, then why did he make provisions for divorce in the Torah (19:7)? The Markan original presents this as a statement in answer to a question from Jesus (Mark 10:4). Davies and Allison (1988–1997: 3:13) posit that over against Mark, Matthew "stresses the Pharisees as opponents rather than Jesus as pedagogue." In Matthew it is Jesus who replies, explaining that this law was a concession to their hard-heartedness (19:8a). "But from the beginning it was not so" (19:8b). This restatement of God's creative purposes sets up Jesus' climactic pronouncement that except in the one case of sexual unfaithfulness, whoever divorces a spouse and marries another commits adultery (19:9) (recall 5:31–32; on this "exception clause," see Wiebe 1989). The disciples protest the severity of this charge (19:10); Jesus counters by explaining that God will give the ability to remain faithful to those who are meant to marry (19:11). To others who trust in him, he will give the gift of celibacy (19:12).

B. OT Context. See above under Matt. 5:31, which quotes the identical verse.

C. Use in Jewish Sources. Again, see above, pp. 23–24.

D. Textual Background. On the relationship between the MT and the LXX, see above, p. 24. Matthew here uses indirect discourse to lead into the quotation, without any precise introductory formula. The Pharisees' question is phrased simply as, "Why then did Moses command to give a bill of divorce and divorce her?" But it is clear from the words, "Moses commanded," and from the general parallelism of contents that the statement is intended as a free quotation of Deut. 24:1. The Greek for "bill of divorce" (*biblion apostasiou*) is taken exactly from the LXX (whereas in Matt. 5:31 the corresponding expression was simply *apostasion*). Matthew also contains a form of the same verb for "give" and uses a synonymous verb for "send away" that in fact often meant "divorce" (*apolyō* rather than *exapostellō*). He also reproduces the identical direct object *autēn* ("her").

E. Hermeneutic Employed. As with Jesus' reference to the traditional interpretation of Deut. 24:1 in Matt. 5:31, the Pharisees are assuming that what is technically a command about not remarrying a first spouse after already contracting a second marriage does in fact give permission to divorce under certain circumstances; otherwise, it would not have described the provisions for that divorce. Still, it is not quite accurate to say that Moses ever "commanded" anyone to divorce his wife, so we cannot altogether exclude an element of distortion in the Pharisees' interpretation. Warren (1998) argues that the Pharisees' interpretation is justified, but that they understand it as an obligation in certain circumstances, whereas Jesus takes it as mere permission.

F. Theological Use. Whatever the Pharisees' understanding of Mosaic provisions for divorce, Jesus radically relativizes them (Luz [2001: 491] observes that "the suspension of the law of Moses in our text is far removed from the mainstream of Jewish Torah interpretation"). Except in a situation in which the marriage vows have already been broken by adultery, Jesus does not countenance divorce. Paul later will add a second exception—abandonment by an unbeliever—but show no awareness of this first one (1 Cor. 7:15). From this it is possible to deduce that neither passage is intended to cover all possible scenarios. But if divorce is acceptable in any other situation, it would have to be an equally severe one (on the 1 Cor. 7 passage, see further Blomberg 1994: 132–44).

19:18–19

A. NT Context. A rich young man has come to Jesus and asked what he must do to have eternal life (19:16). Jesus gives a stock Jewish answer: "Keep the commandments" (19:17). We must resist the urge to speculate about the psychology behind Jesus' reply. Ridderbos (1987: 355) rightly observes, "Whoever fulfills the law's demands is blameless before God, and nothing prevents him

from entering eternal life. By adding the command to love one's neighbor to the end of his list, however, Jesus showed how deeply the commandments cut." But it is hard to know if this is reading later Pauline theology into a context in which it is not yet appropriate. Nevertheless, it is easy to imagine him setting up the young man for the kind of discussion found in the antitheses of the Sermon on the Mount (see above, on 5:21–48). Nor can we know for sure if the man's counter-question, "Which ones?" (19:18a), stems from the various rabbinic discussions about the weightier matters of the law (cf. 23:23) or about how to sum up the Torah in one or a few commandments. Jesus continues in a thoroughly conventional vein as he points to five of the Ten Commandments, along with the command to love one's neighbor—which are clearly fundamental Jewish obligations (19:18b–19). Still, the second table of the Decalogue and the command to love one's neighbor do remain a central part of God's will throughout the NT (on which, see Fuller 1989). The surprise twist in the story comes after the man claims to have kept all of these but still senses a lack (19:20). Mounce (1991: 184) thinks that the man's "uneasiness reveals an instinctive human awareness that legalism falls short of God's intention," but again it is hard to be sure. At this juncture Jesus tells him to sell his possessions, give the proceeds to the poor, and come and follow him in discipleship (19:21). Not surprisingly, the man refuses and goes away grieving (19:22). Leviticus 19:18 is the verse from the five books of Moses more often cited by the NT than any other (cf. Matt. 5:43; Mark 12:31 pars.; 12:33; Rom. 12:19; 13:9; Gal. 5:14; James 2:8).

B. OT Context. The sixth, seventh, eighth, ninth, and fifth commandments of the Decalogue appear in that order. All come from the section comprising the last six of the Ten Commandments, which deals with interpersonal relationships. On the context of Lev. 19:18, see under Matt. 5:43 above.

C. Use in Jewish Sources. Again, Lev. 19:18 is discussed above (see pp. 28–29). There our focus was on interpretations of "neighbor" and the issue of loving one's enemy. As a central expression of the command to love one's fellow humans more generally, one could compile a long list of Jewish texts. Davies and Allison (1988–1997: 3:44) include Sir. 13:15; *Jub.* 7:20; 20:2; 36:4, 8; 1QS V, 25; *T. Reub.* 6:9; *T. Iss.* 5:2; *T. Gad* 4:2; *T. Benj.* 3:3–4. The commandments to honor parents, not to murder, and not to commit adultery have also been treated already. The prohibitions against theft and false witness were equally fundamental, not merely for the written law, but also in subsequent halakah and midrash. Typical discussion dealt with the situations in which they did or did not apply and God's rationale in giving the commands in the first place. However, none of the later Jewish uses of these commands provides any further illumination of Jesus' meaning in Matthew.

D. Textual Background. The LXX renders the MT literally in each of these passages, though curiously in both Exodus and Deuteronomy it changes the order of commandments six through eight to create the sequence "do not commit adultery, do not steal, do not murder." Mark 10:19 restores the order of the MT and changes the imperatival futures of the LXX to aorist subjunctives used as prohibitions but utilizes the same verb roots. Mark also adds "do not defraud," perhaps reflecting the tenth commandment against coveting. Matthew reinstates the forms of the LXX but omits the "your" before "father and mother." He also deletes "do not defraud," perhaps desiring to conform Jesus' words more closely to the OT (Gundry 1994: 386). The "as yourself" of Lev. 19:18 is reproduced in both Matthew and Mark, following the LXX. The previous use of this text in Matt. 5:43 had quoted only "love your neighbor."

E. Hermeneutic Employed. As noted above, it is hard to be sure why Jesus points the young man to the law in the first place, unless he recognizes from the outset that it will serve as a foil to the real obstacle to the man entering the kingdom: his riches. But once he embarks on this path, the selection from the second table of the Decalogue and the commandment to love of neighbor are appropriate as fundamental illustrations of the core of the primary behavior that keeping the commandments would manifest. Perhaps the second table of the Decalogue was used because it is here that humans are most likely to fall (Sabourin 1978: 255); also possible is that Jesus is using sample commandments to represent the entire Decalogue (Davies and Allison 1988–1997: 3:45). One would have

found little disagreement among other Jewish teachers concerning Jesus' interaction with the young man thus far. The definite article *to* before the list of commands may reflect a catechetical use in which they had already been grouped together. Hill (1972: 283) compares Roman Catholic use in English of the expression "the Our Father" as a name for the Lord's Prayer.

F. Theological Use. As the conversation progresses, the most important theological use to which these commandments are put, however, is to demonstrate their inadequacy, at least in this case, to satisfy the man's question about what he needs to do to gain life. He apparently still senses a lack, even though he can claim to have obeyed everything that Jesus has set before him thus far. His possessions prove to be the real problem. It is interesting that this is the only person in all of Scripture whom God calls to sell all that he has, which should immediately answer the question that many sensitive Christians have raised: "Is Jesus calling all believers to do this?" Nevertheless, whatever prevents a person from entering the kingdom must be abandoned, and there have been a disproportionately large number of rich people throughout history who have thought that their wealth precluded their need for God. God may well require such people to give up a substantial portion of their riches if they are to come to him and demonstrate a truly altered allegiance (on a biblical theology of possessions more generally, see Blomberg 1999; on this passage in particular, see pp. 138–40).

Matthew 20:1–34

The vineyard is often a metaphor for Israel in the OT (see esp. Isa. 5:1–7). Matthew 21:33–46 will draw on this background explicitly; it may lie behind 20:1–16 as well. The grumbling workers echo the frequent complaints of Israel against God in Moses' day (e.g., Exod. 16:7–12; Num. 14:27; Deut. 1:27). The practice of paying workers at the end of each workday harks back to Deut. 24:15. On the final passion prediction (20:17–19), see above, p. 55. In the debate over positions of authority (20:20–28), one wonders if the appearance by the mother of James and John is described in language taken from 1 Kings 1:15–21 (Davies and Allison 1988–1997: 3:87).

The cup of suffering referred to in 20:22 clearly employs a common OT metaphor, frequently used for the outpouring of God's wrath (e.g., Ps. 75:8; Isa. 51:17). The ransom saying in 20:28 may echo Exod. 30:12 and/or Ps. 49:7–9 and probably alludes to the fourth Servant Song of Isaiah (see esp. Isa. 53:10–12; this has been hotly debated, but see O. Betz 1998). The healing of two blind men (20:29–34) does not utilize the OT, except for the obvious vocative "Son of David," on which, see under 1:1.

Matthew 21:1–11

From this chapter onward, Matthew begins to quote the OT explicitly with much greater frequency, reminiscent of the opening chapters of his Gospel. The events leading up to and including Jesus' passion, like those surrounding his birth, are seen as particularly replete with the fulfillment, both literal and typological, of OT prophecy. A more informal echo of Zech. 14:4, with its prophecy of a messianic appearance on the Mount of Olives, may be heard in Matt. 21:1. The "tied-up" donkey and its colt in 21:2 may allude to Gen. 49:11, which was interpreted messianically by some Jews of Jesus' day (Davies and Allison 1988–1997: 3:116).

21:5

A. NT Context. As Jesus approaches Jerusalem for the last time during his earthly life, he begins to act out the fulfillment of messianic prophecy. France (1985: 297) wonders if 21:1 contains an allusion to 2 Sam. 15:30 (David weeping as he went up the Mount of Olives) and to 16:1–12 (David saddling a string of donkeys with large provisions of food and wine). He instructs two disciples to bring him a mother donkey and her colt from Bethphage (perhaps from a family he already knew?), telling anyone who questioned them, "The Lord needs them" (21:1–3). The "lord" (*kyrios*) here need mean nothing more than the animals' owner, but Matthew undoubtedly sees a spiritual level of meaning as well. Jesus' divine authority makes him the true owner of anyone's property at any point in time. The disciples follow Jesus' instructions successfully, and he begins to ride on the younger animal, obviously old enough to hold him as he continues up the road (21:6–7).

Baldwin (1972: 166) notes that an "ass's colt" is attested at Mari as a purebred adult. Matthew, adding to the Markan account at this point (cf. Mark 11:1–11), sees the fulfillment of prophecy in this action. He uses the full introductory form, characteristic of several of his distinctive quotations, "This happened in order to fulfill the thing having been spoken by the prophet" (21:4). The quotation in fact appears to be composite, joining part of Isa. 62:11 to part of Zech. 9:9. The shorter excerpt from Isaiah, "Say to the daughter of Zion," probably was suggested because Zech. 9:9 itself used the expression "daughter of Zion" in its first clause with its call to Israel to rejoice. John 12:15, seemingly independently, cites a smaller section of this text.

B. OT Context. Isa. 62:11 appears in the closing chapters of a prophecy increasingly focusing on the glorious new age to come. The first ten verses of this chapter deal with Israel's restoration beyond both the Assyrian and Babylonian exiles. Verse 11 appears to be explicitly messianic: the Lord is proclaiming to his people ("the daughter of Zion") that their savior (or salvation) comes through a specific individual, who will lead to them being called the holy people, the Lord's redeemed, those sought after, and the city (Jerusalem) that is no longer deserted (62:12) (see R. L. Smith 1984: 256). Meyers and Meyers (1993: 123) observe that the king appears here in a context that is "unmistakably eschatological and which foreshadows the emergence of Messianic language in intertestamental literature and the New Testament."

Zechariah 9:9 likewise speaks of the salvation of Israel. It introduces a section describing the coming of Zion's king (9:9–13), heralding the appearance of the Lord, who will restore Israel's beauty and grandeur (9:14–17). Verse 9 itself speaks of that king—he who is righteous, bringing salvation, riding a donkey's colt. However, the context is one not of warfare, but of peace (see esp. Luz 2005: 7–8). God will remove the chariots and war horses from the land and proclaim peace to the nations (9:10). The blood of God's covenant will free prisoners from their waterless pit (9:11). Yet the section concludes with the hint of warfare's return (9:12), culminating in God's promise that Zion will triumph over Greece "like a warrior's sword" (9:13). The last half of v. 9 clearly employs synonymous parallelism: "riding on a donkey, and on a colt, the offspring of a donkey" (with two different words for "donkey" in the Hebrew). Zechariah is envisaging the king riding only one animal. For a direct link between donkeys (or mules), David, and David's son, see 2 Sam. 16:2 and 1 Kings 1:33, 38.

C. Use in Jewish Sources. Since Isa. 62:11 furnishes merely the wording for Matthew's introduction, its history of interpretation proves irrelevant for exegesis of the Gospels. Zechariah 9:9 seems not to have been quoted or alluded to in pre-Christian literature. There is an extensive quotation in *Sib. Or.* 8:324, but it is in a section that clearly is a Christian interpolation. In the rabbinic literature, however, Zech. 9:9 was frequently interpreted as messianic (see, e.g., *Gen. Rab.* 98.9; *b. Sanh.* 98a, 99a; *Eccles. Rab.* 1.9; see Lachs 1987: 344–45).

D. Textual Background. The three relevant Hebrew words quoted from Isa. 62:11 are translated literally in the LXX, which matches verbatim Matthew's Greek. The MT of the excerpt of Zech. 9:9 from which Matthew quotes literally reads, "Behold, your king comes to you, righteous and being saved [i.e., victorious], afflicted and riding on a donkey . . ." (see above for the rest of the quotation). The LXX renders "Behold, your king comes to you" perfectly literally, changes the grammatically passive form of "saving" to its active, functional equivalent, apparently reads the Hebrew *'ānî* ("afflicted") as *'ānāw* ("humble") (Archer and Chirichigno 1983: 131), continues to translate literally with "and riding on a donkey," but substitutes "a new colt" for "a colt, the offspring of a donkey." Matthew in turn follows the LXX verbatim for the first clause but omits "righteous and saving." "Humble and riding" follows the LXX exactly, but Matthew uses a more common, precise word for the first "donkey" (*onos* rather than *hypozygion*, which can mean just "beast of burden"). He also restores the literal meaning of the Hebrew by rendering "and on a colt, the offspring of a donkey" (though now using *hypozygion* for this second donkey). As frequently happens in his unparalleled fulfillment quotations, Matthew deviates from the LXX at least somewhat in the direction of a more literal translation of the MT. As consistently elsewhere, Menken (2004a: 105–6) thinks that all divergences from the LXX can be

accounted for by Matthew using different recensions of the Greek OT. Weren (1997: 132–33) thinks that influence from Gen. 49:8–12, 14–15, interpreted messianically, more likely accounts for the form of Matthew's text.

E. Hermeneutic Employed. Here one may speak of direct, literal prophecy and fulfillment, in the sense of forward-looking predictions of future events that now have taken place. Both Isa. 62:11 and Zech. 9:9 come in eschatological contexts where God is intervening in the coming messianic age to redeem his people. Although the OT does not supply every detail about this event, clearly it looks forward to a human agent acting on God's behalf coming to Jerusalem, riding on a donkey, to reign as king and establish peace. Rightly understood, Jesus fulfills every one of those elements with his so-called triumphal entry into Jerusalem.

Matthew is often accused of grossly misreading Zechariah's synonymous parallelism and turning one animal into two, even to the extent that Jesus is portrayed as straddling the two animals. Davies and Allison (1988–1997: 3:120–21) survey the various approaches to this text, give representative proponents, and note the improbability of Matthew misreading Zechariah this drastically, but see Instone-Brewer 2003! However, this accusation drastically underestimates Matthew's understanding of the OT and of the event in Jesus' life. Matthew has regularly seen fulfillment of prophecy where correspondence between OT and NT is not exact. Stendahl (1954: 200) deduces that "In breaking up the parallelism Matthew deviated from the common Messianic interpretation of the Rabbis. The only reason for such a treatment of the OT text must be that Matthew knew a tradition, which spoke about two asses." It is historically probable that a colt that had never previously been ridden (Mark 11:2) would need its mother present to calm it on an occasion such as this. "The sight of an unridden donkey colt accompanying its mother has remained common in Palestine up to modern times" (Gundry 1994: 409; see also Lindars 1961: 114). Hagner (1995: 594) thinks that Zech. 9:9 itself could refer to two animals. As for Matt. 21:7 ("They led the donkey and the colt and they placed on them garments, and he sat on them"), the nearest antecedent for the final "them" is "garments," which need not refer to the garments on more than one animal.

F. Theological Use. The central motif in this passage clearly is Jesus' deliberate symbolic claim to messiahship. Carson (1984: 437) concurs that riding on a colt was "a deliberate act of symbolic self-disclosure"; "secrecy was being lifted." This incident also has a high probability of authenticity (see, e.g., Witherington 1990: 490–93). But the subtleties in Zechariah's narrative, which juxtaposes peacemaking with triumphing over Israel's enemies, are lost on the crowds. Their response (see below, p. 74) suggests that they are looking only for a triumphant, nationalistic, even militaristic king, whereas Jesus, at least during this advent, enters Jerusalem entirely peacefully, humbly, and willing to submit even to crucifixion. The story, from Jesus' and Matthew's perspective, is more properly labeled the "atriumphal entry" (Kinman 1994; see also Duff 1992). Although Christ's death will make spiritual salvation available for any who come to him, that is not the kind of salvation that Jerusalem is seeking here. It is natural, therefore, for Matthew to omit "righteous and victorious" from his quotation, since he recognizes that earthly triumph and power will come only at Christ's second advent (Sabourin 1978: 269). Indeed, by the end of the week it will be clear that Jesus' coming to Jerusalem, despite leading to his own death, was actually God's coming to the city in judgment (cf. Matt. 23; 27:25)—condemning the counterfeit leaders spiritually even as he would judge the temple and city with physical destruction forty years later (cf. Matt. 24).

21:9

A. NT Context. As Jesus makes his way to Jerusalem astride the donkey, a large crowd spreads cloaks on the road and cuts nearby tree branches to help create the festal carpet as well (21:8). John's Gospel adds that they greeted him with palm branches (John 12:13), from which the church would develop the name "Palm Sunday" to commemorate this occasion.

As the multitudes continue to go before and behind Jesus, they shout, "Hosanna to the Son of David! Blessed is he who comes in the Lord's name! Hosanna in the highest!" (Matt. 21:9). "Hosanna" originally meant "God save us," but by the first century it probably was simply a cry of praise to Yahweh. It "became in common li-

turgical use a cry of jubilation, and in the present passage it amounts to 'God saves' . . . or more probably 'praise be' to the Messianic King" (Hagner 1995: 595; see further Fitzmyer 1987). "He who comes in the Lord's name" echoes John the Baptist's words about a "coming one," referring to the Messiah (see above on Matt. 3:11). On "Son of David," see above on Matt. 1:1.

Not surprisingly, when Jesus entered Jerusalem with this entourage, the people there marveled at the commotion and wondered who he really was (21:10a). One response from the accompanying crowd was to call him "the prophet" from Galilee (21:10b), a probable allusion to the eschatological messianic figure prophesied in Deut. 18:18. Though accurate, this title was inadequate in light of everything that the Gospel had disclosed about Jesus thus far. Jesus' well-wishers were still hoping for a conventional nationalistic or militaristic messiah. Like the prophets of old, he might speak in the name of God, but he would not be the uniquely divine Son of God, according to this popular line of thought.

B. OT Context. Psalm 118 is a psalm of thanksgiving. Its first and last verses are identical: "Thank the LORD, because he is good; his covenant love is forever" (118:1, 29). The unifying element for which the psalmist thanks God is deliverance. Because he cried to the Lord (118:5) and took refuge in him (118:8), he has triumphed over his enemies (118:7) and cut off the nations that surrounded him on every side (118:11). Verse 14 explicitly declares that Yahweh has become the psalmist's salvation. He will not die, but live (118:17), entering the Lord's gates of righteousness (118:19). In the immediate context of 118:26 appears a text that will be quoted later in Matt. 21: the stone that the builders rejected has become the head of the corner (118:22), which may have taken on a messianic sense by the first century (see below, p. 74).

By the time we come to the words that the crowds are quoting in Matt. 21:9, the psalmist appears to be praying for future deliverance, not yet realized. "Hosanna" in 118:25 is actually translated, not just transliterated, in many versions of the Bible, beginning already with the LXX, *ō kyrie sōson dē*, "O Lord, indeed save!" (Ps. 117:25 LXX). Verse 26 then speaks of someone other than Yahweh whom the psalmist equally blesses, including when he arrives in the temple ("the house of the LORD"). He calls on his listeners to join the festive parade with branches in hand and process toward the altar (118:27) and then concludes his petition with further thanks and praise (118:28). The entire picture parallels the victory parades that the Jewish people organized to welcome triumphant kings and generals returning to Jerusalem (cf. 2 Kings 9:13; 1 Macc. 13:51). The inclusion of this psalm in the Hallel psalms (Pss. 113–118) suggests that at least the psalm in general had come to be imbued with messianic import already during the period of the formation of the canonical collection of psalms (L. C. Allen 1983: 124–25). The exact phrase "Hosanna in the highest," with which Matt. 21:9 ends, does not appear in this psalm but may have been inspired by Ps. 148:1.

C. Use in Jewish Sources. Although "Hosanna" was a common Hebrew shout or prayer (see Str-B 1:845–49), the only extant pre-Christian allusion to blessing the one who comes in the name of the Lord appears in the Qumran hymns, with the affirmation, "In his assembly I shall bless your name" (1QHᵃ X, 30). Overall, Ps. 118 did come to be a significant text in the celebration of the Feast of Tabernacles, at least according to later rabbinic literature, in thanking God for the ancient Israelites' deliverance from Egypt (*m. Sukkah* 4:1, 8). If this use had begun already in Jesus' day, it may well have prepared the way for the crowd's application at Passover here (a use also attested in the later Mishnah; cf. *m. Pesaḥ.* 5:7; 8:3; 10:6; see Stendahl 1954: 66; Mays 1988: 300).

D. Textual Background. The Hebrew words *hōšî'â nā'*, as noted above, are translated in the LXX but only transliterated in the Gospels. Matthew follows his Markan parallel (Mark 11:9–10), except that he inserts "Son of David" (not found in the psalm) after the first "Hosanna" and omits "Blessed is the coming kingdom of our Father David" (also not found in the psalm). Perhaps his addition is an abbreviation of what he omitted. The words actually quoted from Ps. 118:26 follow the LXX verbatim, which in turn offers a literal rendering of the MT.

E. Hermeneutic Employed. This is not a fulfillment quotation per se. Matthew, following Mark, is simply recording the account of the crowds lauding Jesus with biblical language on his entry into Jerusalem. They cite the wording from the psalms as they might well have done on numerous previous occasions with celebrated guests. At the very least, this is vivid typology, reusing well-known language to thank God for his deliverance, often accomplished through human leaders. It is particularly appropriate given the fact that Jesus, like the psalmist, will head to the temple (Matt. 21:12–17), and given the parallels between the processions and the use of greenery in both OT and NT contexts. The crowds, of course, do not yet recognize that the kind of deliverance for which they are longing is not to be theirs at this time. If "the one coming in the Lord's name" had already taken on messianic significance, then obviously we may speak of more than mere typology but also a deliberate use of messianic terminology to acclaim Christ's entry, as he is seated on the very animal that Zechariah had prophesied that the Messiah would use (see above, p. 12).

F. Theological Use. How much theological freight we assign to Matthew here clearly depends on whether Ps. 118:22 was viewed as explicitly messianic by this time. At the very least, Jesus is portrayed as receiving acclaim as one through whom Yahweh is going to deliver his people. But probably Matthew also understands the acclaim as reinforcing Jesus' own messianic action in riding on the donkey (see J. A. Sanders 1987). The use of "Son of David" as part of the crowd's acclamation makes this latter interpretation preferable. But again, Jesus is no conventional messiah. In five short days some of these same people will be among the crowds calling for Jesus' crucifixion (Matt. 27:22–26). By then it will be painfully clear that Jesus does not view his mission as that of conquering the Romans.

Matthew 21:12–17

Jesus quotes three OT passages in Matthew's account of the temple clearing. Before the first of these, in the account of the temple's disruption, there appears a probable allusion to the variant rendering of Zech. 14:21: a day would come when no merchant would remain in the house of the Lord. The Jewish temple leadership may well have adopted the majority reading of "Canaanite" in the sense of "foreigner," whereas Jesus followed the minority reading of "trader" (Roth 1960). After the first quotation, another probable allusion reverses the situation described in 2 Sam. 5:8. In the OT the blind and lame were excluded from God's house; here they are healed in (or by) it (Matt. 21:14). Jesus countenances no second-class citizens in his kingdom (see Schweizer 1975: 408). There are also a variety of possible echoes to Mosaic traditions scattered about these verses (see Davies and Allison 1988–1997: 3:144); it is hard to be sure whether any of these are intentional.

21:13

A. NT Context. After entering Jerusalem, Jesus heads for the temple precincts, where he creates a disturbance by evicting the merchants and money changers and overturning the tables and chairs that they were using for hawking their wares (21:12). Justifying such inflammatory activity, he quotes Isaiah, using the simple introduction, "it stands written" (21:13). If rabbinic sources are to be trusted, Caiaphas, the high priest, had quite recently moved the trade of sacrificial animals from the Kidron Valley to the very court of the temple designed for God-fearing Gentiles to use in worshiping and praying to Yahweh, God of Israel (Eppstein 1964). Mark's version makes this location even clearer by including "for all the Gentiles" from the Isaiah quotation (Mark 11:17). Matthew, the more Jewish of the two Gospels, may have been more concerned that the court was unusable for prayer by anyone, Jews included, and thus omitted the focus on the Gentiles. Weren (1997: 140–41), however, thinks that by not reproducing "for all nations," Matthew was excluding the possibility of any reform of the current temple. Luke 19:46 replaces "shall be called" with "shall be" and moves the verb to the head of the clause.

B. OT Context. Isaiah 56 deals with both the restoration of Israel and the salvation of all peoples. Foreigners and eunuchs previously excluded from the assembly of Israel will now be treated as equal citizens in the community of God's faithful (56:3–6). Their sacrifices will be accepted alongside everyone else's on the altar in his temple (56:7a). "Verse 7 concludes with a summary that removes any doubt that God's purpose for his house is directed to all peoples without restriction" (Childs 2001: 459). The God who gathers the exiles of Israel back into their homeland will gather others—Gentiles, obviously—as well (56:8). The context is clearly eschatological,

if not explicitly messianic, and looks to a coming purity of worship in God's holy house, in which prayers are offered either "for" or "by" all the peoples of the world (or perhaps both). At this time, the temple will also be restored to its original purpose (cf. 1 Kings 8:27–30, 41–43; see Motyer 1993: 467).

C. Use in Jewish Sources. There appear to be no pre-Christian Jewish uses of this text that have survived. In the Talmud (and in an even later midrash), however, the temple's use as a house of prayer is associated with the coming of a Davidic messiah (*b. Meg.* 17b–18a; *Midr. Lam.* 1:2).

D. Textual Background. Matthew follows Mark word for word, except for, as noted above, the omission of "for the Gentiles." Mark in turn matches the LXX verbatim, which translates the MT literally at this point.

E. Hermeneutic Employed. One can readily speak of the fulfillment of direct predictive prophecy here. Christ "is implicitly claiming that his action is bringing into reality the eschatological blessings predicted in the Old Testament," especially given the additional allusion to Zech. 14:21 (France 1971: 94). The context in Isaiah is eschatological, looking to a future day when Jew and Gentile alike would more perfectly worship God than either had previously experienced. But even in Jesus' day, the actions of the Jewish leadership prevented more than a partial fulfillment of this text. Depending on how one understands Ezek. 40–48, Christians can still look forward in the age to come either to a new, glorious, and completely perfected literal temple or, more metaphorically, to the complete purification of all worship. But the equality of Jew and Gentile in that worship clearly began with Christ's first coming, as texts such as Rom. 9–11 and Eph. 2–3 make abundantly clear. This, then, is another kind of double fulfillment—not with one fulfillment in the OT age and another with the coming of Jesus, but with one fulfillment in Jesus' first coming and the other with his return (see Oswalt 1986–1998: 2:460–61; Keener 1999: 500).

F. Theological Use. The focus of this OT quotation is not as overtly christological as most in Matthew. Its primary use is obviously to justify Jesus' disruptive action as being necessary if the temple is to be restored to its God-ordained purpose. However, in coming chapters Matthew will portray Jesus leaving the temple, declaring it to be abandoned by God (23:38), and then announcing its coming physical destruction (24:1–20). In retrospect, even here in clearing the temple, Matthew probably understands Jesus to be foreshadowing the temple's destruction. His indignant outburst mirrors the prophetic object lessons of Isaiah (and other OT prophets) in centuries gone by. At this late date, Jesus recognizes that his protest will have no lasting effect, that those soon to call for his crucifixion will not repent, and that the current sacrificial system is therefore doomed (see E. P. Sanders 1985: 61–76; Neusner 1989). Though not as explicit as John 2:19, there is nevertheless implicit "new temple" theology here (recall 12:6 and cf. 26:61; see Knowles 1993: 174–75). Jesus in his coming death will replace the temple and its sacrifices as the locus of God's atoning activity for the sins of humanity. On the relationship between the Johannine and the Synoptic temple clearings, see Blomberg 2002a: 87–91.

21:13b

The fluctuation among successive editions of the United Bible Societies *Greek New Testament* in its use of boldface type demonstrates the fluid boundary between quotation and allusion. Only two Greek words are reproduced verbatim from the OT (*spēlaion lēstōn*, "cave of terrorists"), but there is no doubt that Jesus wants to cite Scripture. Therefore I will treat this as a quotation.

A. NT Context. Although the court of the Gentiles was designed to be a place of prayer, the introduction of the traders and money changers has corrupted the venue (Matt. 21:12–13a). Jesus therefore accuses the temple leadership of having transformed the court into what has traditionally been translated as "a den of robbers," and normally viewed, therefore, as simply protesting the exorbitant exchange rates and the high cost of sacrifices (e.g., Gundry 1994: 413). But *lēstēs* is more naturally taken as an "insurrectionist," or in today's popular parlance, a "terrorist" (this is precisely its meaning in Matt. 26:55; 27:38, 44), while *spēlaion* primarily means "cave"—hence my rendering "cave of terrorists." Of course, the temple was not a literal cave, nor were its leaders literal criminals. Jesus is employing a vivid metaphor, perhaps best captured in modern English by the rendering "nationalist stronghold" (Barrett 1978: 17). By preventing the Gentiles who fear

God from worshiping him in the place especially reserved for that purpose, the temple leadership represents ethnocentric prejudice and repression, analogous to literal, state-sponsored terrorism. "Not so much the brigands in the wilderness as the temple authorities are the real bandits" (Keener 1999: 501). Matthew is here following Mark, who reproduces the same expression (Mark 11:17). Luke also parallels Mark exactly at this point, while slightly altering the words of Jesus not taken from the OT (Luke 19:46).

B. OT Context. In Jer. 7:11 the Hebrew *mě'ārat pārisîm* similarly means "a cave of violent people." J. A. Thompson (1980: 281) retains the sense of "robbers" and thinks that Yahweh's people are fleeing to the temple for protection after having broken the law, just as robbers seek a secure hideout. McKane (1986: 163) takes "den of robbers" as pejorative for "places of asylum . . . frequently abused by knaves and scoundrels." Jeremiah 7 begins with the prophet lambasting Israel for trusting in participation in temple worship for their safety while committing all manner of injustice, immorality, and idolatry (vv. 1–10). Carroll (1986: 210) observes, "The holy place does not save people, but how they live outside the temple gives the holy place its real quality." Even more literally than in Jesus' day, the rhetorical question of Jeremiah's text ("Has my house, called by name upon it, become a cave of violent people?" [7:11]) accuses Israel's leaders of gross rebellion against the Lord. Holladay (1986: 246) suspects that Jeremiah's phrase "must have been even more shocking to his first hearers than was Jesus' adaptation in a later century." For example, actual murder seems to be implied in 7:6 with its reference to the shedding of innocent blood. Thus God promises that he will not respond to their pleas, but rather will pour out his wrath upon them and their supposedly holy house (7:12–20).

C. Use in Jewish Sources. The Targum dramatizes the significance of Jer. 7:11 by rewording it: "Was this house, upon which my Name is called, *like a house of an assembly of wicked* men in your eyes?" The Talmud describes four prominent Jews from post–New Testament times expelled from the forecourt of the temple for defiling it in various ways (*b. Pesaḥ.* 57a). However, there do not appear to be any certain pre-Christian Jewish uses of the text remaining.

D. Textual Background. The LXX translates the two relevant words from the MT literally, and Matthew records those exact two Greek words in his quotation of Jesus.

E. Hermeneutic Employed. Jesus may have envisioned his actual quotation of the OT, introduced with "it stands written," to include only Isa. 56:7, since he begins his next comment with his own words that set up the contrast ("but you are making it . . ."). He then simply reproduces a memorable scriptural phrase in order to liken the corruption of the temple in his day to that which Jeremiah attacked centuries earlier. This, therefore, is not any kind of fulfillment quotation or even formal typology, but rather merely the use of biblical language to describe a present phenomenon. In a looser sense, however, it resembles typology in that strikingly similar patterns of human behavior, and God's judgment on them, are recurring at crucial junctures in salvation history.

F. Theological Use. We may not infer that every sin attributed to those who found false security in the temple in Jeremiah's day was being replicated in the corruption of Jesus' day, though undoubtedly several of them were. The most direct parallel, of course, was the oppression of the foreigner (Jer. 7:6), mirrored in the corruption of the court of the Gentiles. Whatever the other specifics, Jesus is using biblical language to suggest God's impending judgment on the temple and its leadership, just as the first temple had been destroyed and its leaders exiled. In fact, numerous striking parallels exist between the Babylonian captivity in 586 BC and the Roman captivity of AD 70, most notably the invasion of Jerusalem, the destruction of the temple and of much of the city, and the exile of a large number of its townspeople, especially among the leadership. Jesus' words here form important evidence that he did obliquely threaten to destroy the temple, despite the garbled and thus false testimony at his trial (Matt. 26:61), and that Caiaphas's decision to destroy Jesus was not entirely groundless but was consistent with the high priest's fears that his leadership was under attack, though not in the way he imagined (see Evans 1993). Though Christology is not the primary focus in this passage, one may still speak legitimately here of Jesus as a prophet like Jeremiah, the most persecuted of all the OT spokespersons for God (Winkle 1986; cf. Knowles 1993: 176).

21:16

A. NT Context. After accusing the temple leaders of corrupting the court of the Gentiles (21:12–13), Jesus heals various blind and lame people who have come to him (21:14). Children repeat the refrain that the crowds had chanted as Jesus was traveling from Jericho to Jerusalem: "Hosanna to the Son of David." The miracles and acclamation combine to upset the chief priests and scribes further (21:15). They take particular offense at Jesus being praised as the Messiah, since they clearly believe that he is nothing of the sort (21:16a). Jesus replies by quoting a psalm that refers to children praising God himself (21:16b)! This can only have worsened matters, but Matthew is silent concerning the leaders' reaction. Not surprisingly, though, he does immediately say that Jesus left them and returned to Bethany, where he was lodging (21:17).

This portion of the temple-clearing episode (21:14–16) is unique to Matthew, including the Scripture quotation. As in 19:4, Jesus uses a very characteristic rabbinic introduction to his quotation, containing a mild rebuke: "Have you never read . . . ?" The quotation also harks back to the previous OT quotations in Matt. 21. The children's "Hosannas" match the crowd's acclamation in 21:9; the children's praise in the temple reflects the purpose of worship for which it was designed, which the commerce was interrupting (21:12–13).

B. OT Context. Psalm 8 is a majestic hymn of praise to the excellence of God. He who created the universe (8:1, 3) was also the one who created humanity a little "lower than the angels" or "lower than God" (8:4–5), commissioning them to have dominion over the rest of the created order (8:6–8). Little wonder that God has ordained that he receive praise even from very small children (8:2a). "Babes" or "sucklings" could at times describe children as old as three or four and thus quite capable of praising God (but the lack of a really close fit with Matthew's "children" ensures that the evangelist is not merely inventing the account based on the OT text. Keener (1999: 503) observes, "If God can speak through babies, from the lesser to the greater, how much more through children. And if children, by the same logic, how much more ought the religious leaders to join in." As paradigms of the helpless and often dispossessed, it is not surprising that they should praise him especially for avenging them against their enemies (8:2b). Kraus (1988: 182) adds that this verse shows "how the power of the enemies is broken by the voice of weak children," a striking parallel to what occurs in Matt. 21:14–16. As noted below, the MT literally speaks of their "strength," not "praise." Their "strength resides in the cry of one who has privileged access to one who embodies strength" (Broyles 1999: 71). Dahood (1965: 49) takes the text more metaphorically: "Before the majesty of God the psalmist can but babble like an infant." The LXX and the MT number the superscription as v. 1, so that all remaining verses are one number higher than in English translations.

C. Use in Jewish Sources. The Targum to Ps. 8:3 (8:2 ET) is noticeably expansive at this point, attaching "by the mouth of babes and infants" to the end of the previous sentence, "thou whose glory above the heavens is chanted" (8:2). Then it continues, "Thou hast founded a bulwark because of thy foes, *to destroy the author of enmity and the violent one*" (translation taken from Moloney 1981: 661). In the rest of the rabbinic literature various texts debated who the children were who were praising God (Str-B 1:854–55). The most interesting rabbinic reference contains a parable to explain why children were selected to praise God in the first place: they were the only ones whom God did not yet have something against (*Midr. Song* 1:4)! None of these references, however, sheds any direct light on Jesus' use of the psalm, nor do any come from pre-Christian times.

The early rabbinic midrash *Mekilta* (on Exod. 15:1), however, does connect Ps. 8:2 with Exod. 15:2 and its reference to praise as part of the Song of Moses and Miriam. This provided precedent for later rabbinic texts to bring these two passages together as well, supporting the belief that at the Red Sea children praised God (Davies and Allison 1988–1997: 3:142). We should not be surprised, therefore, to find the same two texts linked in the opposite direction, with the LXX inserting the "praise" from Exodus into its translation of the psalm. There is also a more general allusion to Ps. 8:2 in Wis. 10:21, with praise to God

"because wisdom opened the mouth of the dumb, and made the tongues of babes speak clearly."

D. Textual Background. Despite this quotation being found only in Matthew, it follows the LXX (8:3) verbatim. The LXX produces a quite literal translation of the MT, except, as noted above, for the final word. There the MT reads "strength," whereas the LXX renders "praise." One might also translate the Hebrew as "fortress" or "stronghold." One could surmise that the LXX paraphrased the text at this point to explain what the psalmist meant "by its unusual metaphor of an audible bulwark" (Kidner 1973: 67n1)!

E. Hermeneutic Employed. This would appear to be a fairly straightforward use of typology. God's acts in creation, his commissioning of humanity, and his deliverance of his people elicit praise, even (perhaps especially) from small children. God is bringing about a new creation, restoring humanity, and delivering his people again in the ministry and mission of Jesus. Moreover, Jesus' rebuke of the authorities "brought out the inherent contrast in the original Psalm; the children take the *name* [Son of David] upon their lips . . . but the authorities are intransigent and complain—in effect, they are the foes and the avengers of the Psalm. But, as in the Psalms, it is the children who have the truer perception, not the arrogant enemies" (Craigie 1983: 109–10).

F. Theological Use. At best, there is implicit Christology here. We cannot prove that Jesus' logic was this: (1) Ps. 8 praises God; (2) I am God; therefore (3) it is appropriate to praise me, as these little children are doing. The onlookers, whether the children here or the crowds during the "triumphal entry," almost certainly were praising Yahweh for what they believed he was doing in Jesus, not praising Jesus as God directly. The explicit theological teaching of the passage is that Yahweh is worthy of all praise and worship (thus the psalm), and now all the more because he has sent his Messiah (thus Matthew). Still, one cannot help but wonder if a more indirect claim of Jesus acting as God was not in mind at least by the time Matthew compiled his Gospel.

Matthew 21:18–32

There are no explicit quotations of the OT in this section, but Jesus' cursing of the fig tree is almost certainly an object lesson based on the frequent OT use of a fig tree or a fig tree as part of a vineyard that symbolizes Israel. Micah 7:1–6 and Jer. 8:13 both speak of the land producing no fig trees as part of God's judgment on his people. For a detailed list of symbolic texts in ancient Jewish literature involving fig trees, see Trautmann 1980: 335. The reference to "this mountain" in Matt. 21:21 refers to either the Mount of Olives or Mount Zion, depending on where Jesus and his disciples were as they journeyed from Bethany to Jerusalem. If Jesus pointed to the Mount of Olives, then the disciples may have been meant to recall Zech. 14:4, in which the Messiah's coming to that mountain triggers eschatological upheavals. If he was pointing to the temple mount, then he could have been prefiguring the destruction of that building and the entire sacrificial system for which it stood, central to the OT law though they were (see Telford 1980: 238–39). The debate about Jesus' authority (21:23–27) is significant precisely because Jesus does *not* appeal to the OT to defend himself, while the vineyard in the parable of the Two Sons may again allude to Isa. 5:1–7 and refer to Israel.

It is also possible that an even larger portion of Matthew here combines a string of sequential allusions to Jer. 7. The clearing of the temple leads Jesus to quote 7:11; the cursing of the fig tree could allude to 7:20 concerning God's wrath being poured out on the trees of the field. The rejection of John the Baptist's prophecy concerning Jesus mirrors Jeremiah's tirade about previous rejection of the prophets in 7:25, while the parallel of the two sons illustrates the rebellion described in 7:26 (Doeve 1955).

Matthew 21:33–46

The parable of the Wicked Tenants is clearly modeled on Isa. 5:1–7. The follow-up discussion utilizes other portions of the OT as well. In addition to explicit quotations, one should probably think of references to killing the prophets (e.g., 2 Chron. 24:21) behind 21:35 and to the plot to kill Joseph (Gen. 37:20) behind killing the son in 21:38. Verse 43, on the removal of the kingdom from the current Jewish leadership, may allude to 1 Sam. 15:28.

21:33

A. NT Context. The parable of the Wicked Tenants pursues the theme of Israel as a vineyard. The tenants who refuse to give their landlord his share in the harvest symbolize Israel's corrupt leadership. The stewardship of God's kingdom will pass from them to people of any ethnicity who follow Jesus (Matt. 21:43). For more detail on the parable in general, see Blomberg 1990a: 247–51. Mark and Matthew reproduce a fuller form of Jesus' parable than does Luke (cf. esp. Mark 12:1 with Luke 20:9). All three accounts speak of a man planting a vineyard, which alludes to Isa. 5:1. Matthew and Mark then proceed to cite the care that God lavished upon this vineyard by building a hedge around it, digging a winepress in it, and erecting a watchtower for it (cf. Isa. 5:2). These specific details should not be allegorized; they merely highlight God's love and concern for his people. The main lessons of the passage are clear enough without the material that Luke omits, but its inclusion, in quoting Isaiah's parable of the vineyard, makes it absolutely clear that Jesus is passing judgment on the Israel of his day and its leadership. It is questionable whether it is fruitful to pursue a significant distinction between the nation and its leadership in light of the frequent congruence throughout the OT, and the increasing congruence the farther one proceeds into Jesus' ministry, between the people in general and their leaders.

B. OT Context. The account in Isaiah is remarkably similar to Jesus' story. It is perhaps the next closest in form to Jesus' parables of any OT passage besides Nathan's parable about David in 2 Sam. 12:1–10. It is often called a "juridical parable" (see Blenkinsopp 2000: 206). Isaiah 5:1–7 is regularly called the "Song (or even, 'Parable') of the Vineyard." Verse 1 begins with the prophet announcing that he will sing about a vineyard of his beloved, thus referring to God. Verse 2 describes the beloved digging on the hillside, clearing the land of stones, planting choice vines, building a watchtower, and hewing out a winepress. The watchtower is perhaps the most unusual of these elements; a small hut was more typical (Wildberger 1991: 181). Thus these were the "first-class installations" of the day (J. D. W. Watts 1985: 55)! But when the farmer looked for a crop of good grapes, he found only bad fruit. Verse 3 calls on the people of Judah to judge this situation, while 5:4 forms a rhetorical question asking what more the owner could have done, implying that he had done his best to create a congenial climate for a harvest. Motyer (1993: 68) speaks of "leaving nothing undone." The point then is precisely to ask, "What can now be done for the people of God when a total work of grace has been lavished on them and yet they remain as if grace had never touched them?" Because of the failure of the vineyard, he will now bring judgment upon it. Its hedge will be destroyed. Its wall will be trampled down. The vineyard will become a wasteland instead of cultivated (5:5–6). The "song" closes with an unambiguous explanation of the imagery. The vineyard represents Israel and Judah; God looked for justice and righteousness but saw only bloodshed and cries of distress (5:7). The Hebrew creates a pair of wordplays here: "God looked for *mišpāṭ* ('justice'), behold *miśpāḥ* ('bloodshed'); for *ṣᵉdāqāh* ('righteousness'), behold *ṣᵉʿāqāh* ('iniquity')" Childs (2001: 45). The next section of Isa. 5 proceeds to enumerate Israel's sins, including those that involve literal plots of land: the rich accumulate property by unjust actions, exploiting the poor. As a result, their houses will become desolate and their vineyards nearly fruitless (5:8–13). The main message of the "song," therefore, is clearly about "Yahweh's frustrated expectations concerning Judah" (Williams 1985: 465).

C. Use in Jewish Sources. Targum Isaiah 5:1–7 explicitly refers to the watchtower and winepress as the sanctuary and altar of the Jerusalem temple, respectively. This can easily be seen as a post-Christian development in response to the literal destruction of the temple in AD 70 (Weren 1998), but one of the more recently discovered Dead Sea Scrolls fragments now demonstrates pre-Christian Jewish support for this interpretation. In 4Q500 there are allusions to a stone, a winepress, "branches of your delight," and a vineyard, again in the context of a critique of temple leadership and its corrupt offerings. All this makes it highly likely that the targumic interpretation was already known in Jesus' day and that Jesus consciously alluded to it as he told his parable in the temple precincts (see Brooke 1995). Some of Jesus' allusions are slightly clearer in Mark's account than in Matthew's, but Matthew in turn makes one notable addition (21:43) that seems to allude to *Targum Isa.* 5:5 with its verb "take away" (de Moor 1998: 69).

D. Textual Background. Again we observe the fluid boundary between quotation and allusion. There is no introductory formula to show that Jesus (or the evangelists) wanted to call attention to a direct citation of Scripture. Nevertheless, all eight key words—"planted, vineyard, laid, hedge, dug, winepress, built, tower"—are found in the LXX, if not in the identical form, at least employing the same root words. This amount of parallelism goes beyond that found in typical "allusions." Six of these eight words find close Hebrew equivalents in the MT, though not in the identical order. Missing is the imagery of setting a hedge as a fence; the Hebrew speaks instead of clearing the land of stones. Since Matthew is largely following Mark at this point, we are not surprised to find the quotation closer to the LXX than to the MT.

E. Hermeneutic Employed. This is no formal fulfillment quotation or even formal typology. Strictly speaking, all that Jesus is doing (and all that the evangelists are reporting) is reusing scriptural language in creating a new parable. However, the parallels are so complete that obviously we are meant to infer that Israel's leaders, and more specifically the temple leadership, have become as corrupt as those whom Isaiah condemned. This, then, is informal typology. The rest of the parable of Jesus promises judgment and destruction just as decisively as the rest of Isaiah's vineyard song does.

F. Theological Use. At the very least, Jesus is speaking as a prophet like Isaiah, explaining God's great love for his people, the seriousness of their disobedience, and the resulting wrath that God must bring upon them. But by the end of the parable it will be clear that Jesus himself plays a role in the story as the landlord's beloved son whom the wicked tenants kill and cast out of the vineyard (Matt. 21:37–39). Jesus will again quote the OT and make a more direct messianic claim thereby (21:42). For more on both of these points, see the section on this verse immediately below. In retrospect, then, it will be plain that Jesus speaks already at the beginning of his parable as more than a prophet. He is in fact a messianic claimant, one who is so close to God that he can speak from God's very heart. The best full-length treatment of this parable, including its hermeneutics and theology, is Snodgrass 1983.

21:42

A. NT Context. The narrative portion of the parable of the Wicked Tenants ends with the execution of the son (21:39). Jesus then addresses the crowds with the rhetorical question about what the landlord will do to his traitorous tenants (21:40). Answering his own question, Jesus predicts a horrible fate for them and the leasing of the vineyard to new tenants (21:41). At this point he quotes Ps. 118, which speaks of the rejected stone that becomes a cornerstone in a building project (21:42). As in Matt. 19:4 and 21:16, Jesus uses the characteristic rabbinic introduction and rebuke, "Have you never read . . . ?" to introduce this particular "scripture."

It is not at all clear at first glance what this quotation implies in this context. Once one knows the story of the coming crucifixion of Jesus, however, one suspects that the stone is a person, rejected by some but valued by others (or at least by God). The underlying Hebrew and/or Aramaic suggests a play on words that would link the rejected stone with the rejected son of 21:38–39: *bēn* (= son) and *'eben* (= stone) (see Black 1971: 13; against the charge that this "pun" could work in Hebrew but not in Aramaic, see Brooke 1995: 287–88). This figure apparently has something to do, then, with the transfer of the vineyard to new tenants. In a verse unique to Matthew's account of the parable, 21:43 proceeds to speak explicitly of the transfer of leadership in God's kingdom from the Israel of that day to a new "people" (*ethnos*), presumably the multiethnic community of Jesus' followers. That something along these lines was understood even by Jesus' opponents seems clear from the response of the Jewish leaders: their anger leads them to plot his arrest (21:45). Verse 44, also unique to Matthew (21:44 is also textually uncertain, but the external evidence seems strong enough to support its inclusion; the verse additionally appears to combine allusions to Isa. 8:14–15; Dan. 2:34–35), creates an interpretive ambiguity with respect to the stone. People can fall on it, suggesting a stone laid on the ground like a "cornerstone," but it can also fall on people, suggesting the "capstone" placed at the center of an archway to complete the structure.

Matthew's comparatively lengthy OT quotation follows Mark's account word for word (cf. Mark 12:10–11). Luke's parallel presents a shorter excerpt (Luke 20:17), still following Mark verbatim, which in turn matches exactly the portion of the text cited in 1 Pet. 2:7. Acts 4:11 contains an abbreviated allusion to the cornerstone motif.

B. OT Context. We have already looked at the overall contents of Ps. 118 in conjunction with Matthew's quotation of vv. 25–26 in Matt. 21:9. The psalmist is giving thanks for deliverance from danger (118:1–21) and is getting ready to appeal for further rescue (118:25), which will in turn trigger further thanksgiving and praise (118:26–29). Apparently as part of that initial deliverance, the Lord has done a marvelous work worthy of exultation (118:23–24). This good deed is obliquely described as taking a stone that certain builders have rejected and turning it into a cornerstone (118:22). The verse is obviously metaphorical, almost forming a small parable in itself. It describes how "something or someone, rejected as useless, comes to be accepted as essential" (Davidson 1998: 386). Given the importance of building correctly, the decision to use a stone deemed inappropriate by the construction workers causes considerable surprise.

There has been extensive debate, with both the OT and NT usages of this motif, as to whether one should translate the Hebrew and Greek as "cornerstone" or "capstone." The Hebrew calls it a *rōš pinnâ*, literally a "head of a corner." Still, there is ambiguity, since "head" suggests "top" and hence a capstone, while "corner" suggests a cornerstone. But *rōš* can also mean "chief," so perhaps "cornerstone" is somewhat preferable. Dahood (1970: 159) notes that the translation "cornerstone" finds further support in partial parallels in Jer. 51:26; and Job 38:6; for "capstone," see Cahill 1995.

Without further contextual clues in the psalm, it is easy to imagine that the cornerstone is a metaphor for the psalmist himself. Since he has vanquished his enemies in battle with the help of the Lord (118:10–14), it is natural to imagine the speaker to be a Davidic king. Then the rejected-but-now-honored stone would represent how close the king had come to death, followed by God's salvation in making him victorious (118:15–18). Kraus (1989: 400) sums up: "One who was despised has been brought to honor. One who was consigned to death is allowed to see life" (118:17a). Less likely is the view that the stone was Israel considered collectively, deemed unimportant by the great empires of its day but receiving an honored place in the building of Yahweh's kingdom (so Dahood 1970: 159). As a later application of the psalm, however, this interpretation is perfectly intelligible (Mays 1994: 305–6).

C. Use in Jewish Sources. For Ps. 118 more generally, see above (p. 55). The *Testament of Solomon* seems to have understood the stone in 118:22 as a cornerstone. In *T. Sol.* 23:1–4, Solomon asks a wind demon to move an unspecified stone and place it into the corner of the building at the entrance of the temple, and then he quotes this OT verse (see also 22:6–8). In the Cairo Geniza *Songs of David* A 18, Ps. 118:22 is quoted and applied to David, suggesting an emerging pre-Christian messianic interpretation. The Targum to this verse renders "stone" as "child," probably also alluding to David and adopting a messianic perspective (for both of these points, see de Moor 1998: 77–78). The Targum to Zech. 4:7 takes the cornerstone in that passage as explicitly referring to the Messiah. Given Jesus' (and Matthew's) use of Zechariah throughout this last week of his life, it is quite possible that Jesus and his first followers were aware of this interpretive tradition (S. Kim 1987).

At Qumran, on the other hand, the Dead Sea sect interpreted the passage metaphorically to refer to the entire community. It would be "the tested rampart, the precious cornerstone . . . the most holy dwelling for Aaron with eternal knowledge of the covenant of justice . . . a house of protection and truth in Israel" (1QS VIII, 7–9). One recalls Qumran's communal interpretation of Isa 40:3 (see above, pp. 12–13), which both the original OT and subsequent NT usage took in an individual sense. In the later rabbinic literature, the text came to be used as thanksgiving for the Israelites' deliverance from Egypt (Davidson 1998: 387). Individualistic interpretations continued, however, focused on David (and hence the Messiah) and also at times on Abraham (e.g., *Pirqe R. El.* 24; see Lane 1974: 420).

D. Textual Background. All the NT quotations of these verses follow the LXX (which numbers Ps. 118 as 117) exactly. The LXX in turn is a highly literal translation of the MT throughout all of 21:22–23.

E. Hermeneutic Employed. Here is classic Davidic typology or, if one thinks the psalm originally referred to Israel as a nation, one may see the continuance of Matthew's theme of Jesus recapitulating the experience of Israel (so, e.g., France 1971: 58). A passage, presumably originally reflecting the thanksgiving for physical rescue by David or one of his successors, is applied already in pre-Christian times to the coming Davidic messiah, whom God will lead in an even greater victory over Israel's enemies. But whereas conventional Jewish messianic hope often focused on national deliverance, Jesus applies the passage to himself as Messiah, but as one bringing spiritual salvation. The text, even in its OT context, has an "individual-transcending, archetypal proclaiming power" (Kraus 1989: 401). Following closely on the heels of his "triumphal entry," Jesus is again consciously playing the part of the king of Israel in an enthronement ceremony. No wonder the response was so explosive, leading to imminent arrest and execution (see J. A. Sanders 1987).

F. Theological Use. Like his use of the figure of the son in the parable proper, Jesus employs the metaphor of the stone to draw attention to his coming fate, but also to his subsequent exaltation. We may speak of implicit Christology here. These are not the explicit predictions of his death and resurrection scattered throughout Mark 8–10 pars. They may not even have been perceived by all his listeners, which also makes their authenticity more probable. In any event, Jesus is alluding both to his identity, as Messiah and divine Son, and to his mission—soon to be rejected and crucified but then to be restored to a position of power through his victory over death. Those who opposed him will then be judged (cf. Dillon 1966). In Matthew's larger context the story of the wicked tenants functions as the second of three parables that sequentially depict Israel's indictment (21:28–32), sentence (21:33–46), and execution (22:1–4) (Schweizer 1975: 402; cf. Horne 1998).

Matthew 22:1–22

The imagery of the wedding feast in the eschatological parable spanning Matt. 22:1–14 probably alludes to the messianic banquet of Isa. 25:6–9. The motif of a king destroying a city of reb[...]ous citizens echoes typical OT and intertesta[...]ental depictions of the ravages of war as part of G[...]'s judgment (see esp. Judg. 1:8; Isa. 5:24–25; 1 Macc. 5:28). Several of Matthew's distinctives may be viewed as inspired by Zeph. 1:7–10 (Olson 2005). The question about paying taxes to Rome in Matt. 22:15–22 must not be confused with the earlier discussion of the temple tax (see above, p. 56) and does not obviously draw on any OT background.

Matthew 22:23–33

As Jesus is teaching in the temple for the last time, during the last week of his life, representatives of the Sadducees take their turn as part of a series of people who ask Jesus hard questions, hoping to trap him in his words. Two key OT quotations appear in this material.

22:24

A. NT Context. The Sadducees were well known for not believing in the bodily resurrection of God's people at the end of time. Their hermeneutic required points of doctrine to be established from one or more texts of the Torah—that is, the five books of Moses (Josephus, *J.W.* 2.162–166). Daniel 12:2 is the clearest OT text that teaches the resurrection of good and bad alike at the final judgment, but of course it is not found in the law. There is no text in the Torah proper that addresses the question of resurrection directly.

Certain Sadducees, therefore, come to Jesus not to ask a genuine theological question, but to ridicule the notion of resurrection (22:23). They create an improbable case study in which a woman has married seven brothers, following the levirate laws that required the brother of a deceased man who had left a childless widow behind to marry the woman to try to produce offspring for the family line. None of the marriages has produced a child, each husband has died while the same woman lives on, and thus the situation results of a woman who has been married seven times (22:24–27). The Sadducees now challenge Jesus to determine who will be the woman's husband in the life to come (22:28). The question, of course, arises even for someone who has been married twice, but by sketching an extremely improbable scenario, Jesus' interrogators hope to create a farci-

cal situation. The plot may have been borrowed from the fictitious but well-known folk-tale reflected in Tob. 3:8 (see Bolt 1994).

Jesus replies at two levels. He charges his questioners with knowing neither the Scriptures nor God's power (22:29). He then unpacks these charges in the reverse sequence. In the resurrection life God's power is so great that he can re-create life, including humanity, so that we will not experience marriage as we know it now (22:30). Technically, all that Jesus denies is that people will no longer give others or be given in marriage, as when a father gives his daughter to her groom at their wedding (22:30a), but that in itself would not answer the Sadducees' question. Presumably, Jesus' point is that when interpersonal relationships are perfected among the company of the redeemed, all human interaction will be as loving and rewarding as the best of human marriages in this life, so that it will no longer be necessary or appropriate to speak of any believer as being uniquely married to one other person. This would seem to be implied by the comparison of resurrected humanity to the angelic world (22:30b); no text of Scripture ever hints at angels being married. Later rabbinic tradition explicitly affirms that (good) angels do not engage in sexual relations or procreate, but it would also suggest that demons (fallen angels) can (see esp. *b. Ḥag.* 16a)! According to Acts 23:8, the Sadducees do not believe in angels, so Jesus may be deliberately inserting this jibe as well.

As for deriving doctrine from the Pentateuch, Jesus believes that he can support the notion of bodily resurrection by citing Exod. 3:6 (cf. vv. 15–16). Further discussion of that passage will appear in the section below (pp. 77–78).

Matthew is again following Mark, but not nearly as slavishly as usual (cf. Mark 12:19). Mark himself has rendered the OT rather paraphrastically, and Matthew omits or rewords the loosest portions of Mark's quotation to bring it somewhat more in line with the OT. Luke 20:28 contains yet a third rendering of the Sadducees' question. All three accounts are much more closely parallel for the second half of the verse, when Gen. 38:8 is exclusively in view, than in the first half, where elements of Deut. 25:5 and Gen. 38:8 are combined. Stendahl (1954: 71) notes that *epigambreuō* ("to marry one's next of kin") occurs in Lucian's version of Gen. 38:8 LXX, but he also observes that it was a technical term known in the Palestinian Greek tradition, which "opens up the possibility of explaining Matthew's text without assuming the influence of the parallel passage in Genesis." However, the rest of Matthew's wording seems too close to Gen. 38:8 to render this hypothesis very probable.

B. OT Context. The Sadducees phrase their question in such a way as to combine the wording of two different texts of Torah. "If someone dies not having children" seems to paraphrase Deut. 25:5, which literally reads, "If brothers dwell together and one of them dies and a child there is not to him, there shall not be the wife of the dead outside [the family] to a strange person. Her husband's brother shall go in to her and take her as his wife and perform the duty of a husband's brother to her." The Sadducees' example appears to begin by borrowing the language of the first part of this verse: "If . . . one of them dies and a child [*bēn*] there is not to him . . ." Tigay (1996: 231) thinks that the original legislation understood *bēn* exclusively as a "son" but concedes that both the LXX and later rabbinic legislation took it inclusively as "son or daughter."

Deuteronomy 25:5 is tucked into a long section of fairly miscellaneous laws spanning 23:15–25:19. The immediately preceding verse is unrelated to the laws of levirate marriage, as it cautions about not muzzling an ox while it treads out grain (25:4). Verses 6–10 continue to outline details about the levirate practice, particularly if the nearest male relative does not wish to perform the duty of marrying the widow in question. Subsequent verses, however, then move again in unrelated directions.

The clearer direct quotation of the OT appears with the use of Gen. 38:8. Here we see an instance of the levirate law in practice before it actually became codified in the laws of Moses. Levirate laws were found in many ancient societies, so this should not be surprising (see Manor 1984). The patriarch Judah has seen his firstborn son, Er, die as part of God's judgment on his wickedness (38:6–7). He then commands his next son, Onan: "Lie with your brother's wife and fulfill your duty to her as a brother-in-law to produce offspring for your brother" (38:8). Onan pretends to do this but spills his seed on the ground to ensure that the process will fail (38:9). This wickedness

leads God to take Onan's life as well (38:10). The rest of Gen. 38 is about the successful ploy of this mistreated woman, Tamar, to become pregnant by disguising herself as a prostitute and having relations with her father-in-law, Judah. From this, in part, Coats (1972) argues that the levirate laws did not necessarily require remarriage, but only conception. If this was true and was still the case in Jesus' day, then the Sadducees went beyond the formal stipulations of the law in the way they presented their case. But even if Coats is right about the original practice, it could well have developed to the point where marriage was required in Jesus' time, given the high view of marriage within Judaism more generally.

The levirate laws seemed to have had three main purposes. First, they provided security for the widow during her bereavement and mitigated the stigma attached to her barrenness. Second, they prevented the loss of the deceased husband's property to the larger family or clan. Third, they ensured that the dead man's name would be preserved for posterity within the family (C. J. H. Wright 1996: 266).

C. Use in Jewish Sources. The most famous application of the levirate laws in later OT literature appears in the wonderful short story of Ruth. Boaz must make sure that a nearer kinsman to Ruth does not want to marry her, so that he can have that privilege (Ruth 4:1–12 [on which, see Hubbard 1988: 230–62]).

In intertestamental Judaism the book of *Jubilees* recounts the story of Gen. 38 in abbreviated form (*Jub.* 41:1–22). *Jubilees* 41:4 repeats Judah's command to Onan, "Go to your brother's wife and act as levirate and raise up seed for your brother." The *Testament of Judah* (10:1–6) alludes to this story as well, adding certain embellishments, most notably that Er disliked Tamar because she was not from Canaan (10:2), and that Onan's disobedience was part of "his mother's treacherous scheme" (10:3). But the understanding of the actual practice of levirate marriage appears unchanged.

After the time of Christ, *Targum Pseudo-Jonathan* to Deut. 25:5 uniquely begins, "When brothers *from the (same) father* sojourn *in this world at the same time and claim the (same) inheritance.* . . ." It then proceeds to follow the MT, including, "the wife of the dead one shall not be free. . . ." Interestingly, the early rabbinic midrash

Sipre Deuteronomy presents an extensive passage discussing the very problems that could arise if the levirate marriage laws were enforced for more than a pair of brothers. These rabbis concluded that a woman who had married two brothers who both had died without enabling her to conceive *would* be free from the levirate law that had previously required her to keep marrying brothers from the same family (*Sipre Deut.* 25:5). Other rabbinic legislation appears scattered throughout the Mishnah's and Tosefta's tractate *Yebamot* (on the mishnaic foundations for the various rabbinic discussions, see Weisberg 1998).

D. Textual Background. As noted above, the text form in the Gospels of Deut. 25:5 reads more like an abbreviated paraphrase than a direct quotation. In Matthew's account "if" and "dies" match the LXX exactly, "a brother" has been turned into "someone," and "not having children" is the semantic equivalent to "there is no seed for him." Gundry (1967: 45) thinks that the use of *teknon* by the Synoptists avoids the inexact *sperma* of the LXX and correctly renders the Hebrew *bēn*. The translation of the MT by the LXX here is reasonably literal. The Gospels' use of Gen. 38:8 is more straightforward. All of Matthew's words find an equivalent in the LXX, either verbatim or via a different form of the same lexical root or part of speech. And here the LXX is a highly literal translation of the MT. Archer and Chirichigno (1983: 47) conclude for Deut. 25:5 that "none of the evangelists has borrowed directly from the LXX, and all have abbreviated or paraphrased slightly the Heb. text." This seems to be accurate. But how they can then claim that "as far as Gen 38:8 is concerned, it has no verbal resemblance to the NT quotation" is mystifying. That statement is simply incorrect.

E. Hermeneutic Employed. Without the formal introduction, "Moses said," in 22:24, we could easily label these two references to the OT as allusions rather than quotations. Well-known scriptural language and principles are being used simply to create a new case study, which the Sadducees hope will lead Jesus to say something with which they can find fault. But the introductory words do suggest that the Sadducees were at least paraphrasing specific Scriptures that they believed generated their almost absurd illustration. "Moses," of course, stands for the five books

of Torah. The Sadducees think that there is no way Jesus can wriggle out of the application of the principles of these texts that render the doctrine of resurrection ludicrous. As throughout his ministry, however, Jesus surprises his opponents, avoids their traps, and utters profound truths on the topic at hand.

F. Theological Use. There is little to say here that has not already been discussed above. The Sadducees do not believe in a bodily resurrection. They think that the levirate law renders such a doctrine unintelligible. One can say that the dead live on in their children—precisely one of the points of the levirate practice—but not in any literal fashion (Davies and Allison 1988–1997: 3:224). Thus these Sadducees present an extreme example of the contradictions that they believe the levirate laws present for the idea of resurrection. And Jesus proceeds to refute them.

22:32

A. NT Context. After dealing with the Sadducees' specific question about what happens in the resurrection life for a person who had more than one spouse in this life (22:23–30), Jesus turns to the underlying hermeneutical issue. Childs (1974: 81) observes that by combining two arguments, one scriptural and one based on the power of God, Jesus is not limiting himself to an artificial reading of a written text apart from its substance. If doctrine must be demonstrated on the basis of Torah, then he must find a text in the five books of Moses that teaches about resurrection. Since there is no obvious text, in good rabbinic fashion Jesus must derive the notion from a less obvious passage. For a full listing of other texts in the Torah from which various rabbis derived a resurrection, see Cohn-Sherbok 1981. The passage that he chooses is Exod. 3:6. Because God identifies himself to Moses as currently the God of the patriarchs ("I *am* the God of Abraham . . ."), Jesus infers that they must still be living; but since they have physically died by the time of Moses, their life must be a new resurrection life (Matt. 22:31–32). Whatever the Sadducees may have thought of this conclusion, Matthew reports that the temple crowds listening in were astonished (22:33). Jesus has successfully extricated himself from yet another seemingly unavoidable exegetical trap. Kilgallen (1986: 487) summarizes the point of Jesus' argument as claiming that the Sadducees misunderstood "what it is that makes this life without end a certainty."

As in 19:4, 21:16, and 21:42, Jesus uses the characteristic rabbinic introduction, "Have you not/never read . . . ?" to introduce the Scripture that he cites. For the first time, however, instead of citing "the prophet," with or without his name, he speaks of "that which was spoken to you by God." Clearly, Jesus follows the Jewish belief of his day that Scripture was inspired by God. Perhaps because of the controversy at hand, he wants to make his point that much more forcefully here by stressing God as the very author of the position that he is defending. Matthew is still following Mark, abbreviating his longer introduction, "Have you not read in the book of Moses, in the passage about the bush, how God said to him . . . ?" (Mark 12:26). Matthew then reproduces exactly Jesus' citation of Exodus, except that he reinstates the verb "am" (eimi) from the LXX, which Mark had omitted (a natural omission because the Greek frequently left out a form of the verb "to be" when it was clearly understood from the context and the present tense would be assumed [see Stendahl 1954: 21]). Acts 3:13 quotes the same text from Exodus in a different context and picks up the expression "the God of our fathers" from Exod. 3:15 as well.

B. OT Context. Exodus 3 recounts the dialogue between God and Moses at the site near Mount Horeb where God revealed himself in a burning bush that was not consumed (3:1–3). In the course of the encounter God commissions Moses to liberate his people from Pharaoh's oppression (3:7–22). Before giving this commission, God discloses himself as the same God who had revealed himself to the patriarchs Abraham, Isaac, and Jacob (3:4–6). He will later identify himself with the more enigmatic, "I am who I am" (or, "I will be who I will be") in 3:14, after which the identical triad, "God of Abraham, (God of) Isaac, and (God of) Jacob," appears twice more (3:15, 16). This form of referring to Yahweh recurs frequently throughout the OT to tie in later revelation with the initial events in which God selected one man and his descendants to be the founding fathers of an elect people. In the rest of the ancient Near East similarly "solemn, self-identifying" modes of address frequently introduced royal proclamations

and gave an authoritative air to their announcements (Sarna 1991: 15).

C. Use in Jewish Sources. Intertestamental Judaism continued from time to time to refer to Yahweh with this tripartite formula. Ezekiel the Tragedian (104–5), as part of a poetic retelling of the Exod. 3 narrative, declares in Yahweh's name, "God am I of those, your fathers three, of Abram, Isaac, Jacob, I am He." Philo reflects on the various virtues of the three patriarchs in his discussion of Exod. 3:6 (*Abraham* 51–52). Elsewhere he discusses why God might have chosen to reveal himself by this triadic name. The Lord God has three natures, "of instruction, and of holiness, and of the practice of virtue; of which Abraham, and Isaac, and Jacob are recorded as the symbols" (*Names* 12). Verse 1 of the *Prayer of Manasseh* demonstrates how formulaic this triad had become, as it begins, "O LORD, God of our fathers, God of Abraham, and of Isaac, and of Jacob, and of their righteous offspring . . ." (here Exod. 3:15 rather than 3:6 seems most directly in view).

The only intertestamental reference directly relevant to understanding Jesus' use of Exod. 3 in the Gospels is 4 Macc. 16:24–25. Near the end of the famous story of the woman and her seven sons who all faced martyrdom rather than transgress God's commandments, she exhorts them all to stand fast and die because "they knew full well themselves that those who die for the sake of God live unto God, as do Abraham and Isaac and Jacob and all the patriarchs." Life after death, in other words, will far more than compensate for a life prematurely ended in this world. And the hope of that life is modeled on the belief that the founding fathers of the Jewish nation likewise lived on.

The rabbinic literature continued to propound the idea that God has a relationship with his people after they die and to defend and discuss the resurrection on the basis of both individual OT verses and larger OT resurrection narratives (see Str-B 1:892–97). The most significant of these post-Christian Jewish texts is *b. Sanh.* 90b. An identical hermeneutic seems to be at work as in the Gospels, as the Talmud derives the notion of resurrection from Num. 18:28. This text of Torah commands the Levites, once they are in the promised land, to tithe from the offerings that they receive to Aaron the priest, as if he were still alive. And that is precisely the conclusion that the Talmud draws from this text: he does indeed live. Whatever we may think of the logic today, it probably was well understood in Jesus' world and may have persuaded many in his original audience (recall Matt. 22:33).

D. Textual Background. Matthew follows the LXX verbatim (as did Mark), except for inserting the definite article before the second two occurrences of "God" and leaving out the redundant "of your Father, the God" between "I am the God" and "of Abraham." Minor textual variants harmonistically omit the articles; in Mark 12:26 the omissions are much better attested though perhaps still not original. The LXX translates the MT literally here.

E. Hermeneutic Employed. Jesus is appealing to a text of Torah to teach a timeless theological principle. The closest parallels to this that we have seen in Matthew involved his replies to Satan during the temptations (4:1–11), his appeal to the principle of two or three witnesses in the context of church discipline (18:15–18), and his use of "creation ordinances" in teaching about marriage (19:1–12). In none of those texts, however, did we sense so "strained" an interpretation of an OT passage, apparently turning on the tense of a single verb ("I am"), as we do here. From our modern perspective, "I am the God of Abraham, Isaac, and Jacob" need mean nothing more than "I am the same God as the God who disclosed himself to the patriarchs"—that is, even though the patriarchs are now dead. It does not seem to imply anything about the existence or nonexistence of resurrection life. For a contrary view, defending the idea that Jesus displays the "deepest sensitivity to the context in which Ex. 3.6 originally occurs," namely, as a response of hope in the face of death, see Janzen 1985.

Seven major options have been put forward for understanding Jesus' hermeneutic: (1) Jesus is simply contrasting the present tense with what otherwise would have been the expected past tense ("I was the God . . . ," not "I am the God . . ."); (2) the Sadducees' objection involved cases of sterility, so Jesus is pointing out how God overcame sterility among the patriarchs and matriarchs and thus how he can bring life from death; (3) God's covenant promises to the patriarchs were not entirely fulfilled in this life, demonstrating that their complete fulfillment

must be in a life to come; (4) it is absurd for the immortal to define himself in terms of the mortal, therefore the patriarchs are not dead; (5) the text assumes that the three patriarchs are now dead, but because of God's covenant with them, their resurrection is assured; (6) the consonants of the Hebrew word for "Yahweh" should be repointed to create the verb "to be," showing that God makes Abraham to exist; (7) Jesus has adopted an argument somewhat parallel to Philo's in which the patriarchs stood for imperishable virtues (Davies and Allison 1988–1997: 3:231–32).

None of these approaches, even in various combinations, seems entirely satisfactory. But there are other examples of ad hoc or ad hominem arguments in Scripture, which seem designed simply to apply the logic of a person or group with which the inspired author disagrees in order to make a point that is convincing by that very logic, even though the logic itself may be flawed (e.g., the appeal to Ps. 82:6 in John 10:34; see Longenecker 1999: 53–54). One thinks especially of Jesus' reply to those Jewish leaders who accused him of drawing on satanic power for his exorcisms (Matt. 12:25–27) and of Paul's argument for the resurrection based on experiences of the Corinthians and from his own ministry that were never intended to be normative (1 Cor. 15:29–32). So perhaps that is all that we are meant to understand Jesus doing here—he is speaking in an ad hoc or ad hominem fashion. The close parallel in the Talmud cited above (p. 78), combined with the other Jewish texts that demonstrate a widespread conviction that the patriarchs were not dead (on which, see Charlesworth 1985: 78–79), seems to have provided a model for Jesus to make his point convincingly at least in the context in which he had been challenged.

F. Theological Use. Strictly speaking, one could argue that even by the logic discussed above, all that Jesus has demonstrated is immortality of some kind, not actual bodily resurrection. However, since the Sadducees appeared to be relatively alone among segments of Judaism in disbelieving the bodily resurrection, again, *in this specific context*, Jesus can assume that the only debate is between bodily resurrection and cessation of all existence. In another context Paul will have to argue for resurrection against the standard Greek view of disembodied immortality of the soul (1 Cor. 15). For exceptions to the stereo-typical generalizations about both the Jewish and the Greco-Roman beliefs, see Porter 1999. It is not clear, however, that Porter has amassed enough evidence to overturn the generalizations altogether. One might also allege that arguing for the resurrection of the patriarchs does not accomplish as much as arguing for the resurrection of all people (or even of all believers). But again, in the context of the intra-Jewish debate, other parties accepted Dan. 12:2, which clearly did teach the bodily resurrection of just and unjust alike at the end of the age. A cardinal Jewish tenet was that the resurrection of one person demonstrated the beginning of the general resurrection of all people (a point stressed esp. by N. T. Wright throughout his writings [see, e.g., 1997: 141]), so Jesus does not have to present as much evidence as others would in different contexts (again cf. Paul using the identical "firstfruits" argument more explicitly in 1 Cor. 15:20–28).

Matthew 22:34–39

22:37

A. NT Context. After the Sadducees leave, a Pharisaic lawyer attempts to trap Jesus in his words (Matt. 22:34–35). He raises a question that the rabbis debated extensively in ancient Judaism: "What is the greatest commandment in the law?" (22:36). For the most relevant sources, see Hagner 1995: 646. Apparently unwilling to select only one law, Jesus replies by quoting the two commandments about loving God and neighbor (22:37–39). These vertical (Godward) and horizontal (humanward) relationships sum up not just the Torah, or five books of Moses, but the whole of the Hebrew Scriptures ("the law and prophets" [22:40]). Jesus made a similar comment about the "Golden Rule" in Matt. 7:12. Unlike the other controversies surrounding Jesus' teaching in the temple, his response here should have satisfied most of the listeners in his audience (cf. Mark 12:32–33). On the other hand, Matthew omits this reasonably positive conclusion, leading Furnish (1972: 30) to argue that Matthew depicts the controversy as unresolved, with Jesus' refusal to accept all of Torah as equally important as setting him over against the rest of Judaism in his day. This probably goes well beyond what we

can reasonably infer from an omission that could have been prompted merely by the abbreviating tendencies of the oral tradition!

The command to love God with all one's heart, soul, and mind does not divide the human person into three parts. The Bible consistently recognizes only a material and immaterial dimension to humanity, if one must speak of dividing the person at all. Rather, as with similar formulations elsewhere (e.g., 1 Thess. 5:23; Heb. 4:12), the listing of various aspects of the human person makes the point vividly and emphatically that one's whole being must be involved. Davies and Allison (1988–1997: 3:241) paraphrase the three prepositional phrases as "with every globule of one's being" (cf. Merrill 1994: 163). Matthew is following Mark at this juncture, but whereas Mark presents four elements with which one must love God (heart, soul, mind, strength [Mark 12:30]), Matthew mentions only the first three. Luke quotes Jesus citing the same verse in a different context when he replies to another lawyer who would go on to ask him to define who one's neighbor is. Luke has the same four elements as Mark but reverses the order of the last two (Luke 10:27). The fact that love can be commanded demonstrates that it is primarily attitudes and behavior God desires, not emotions (R. A. Wright 2001).

B. OT Context. Deuteronomy 6:5 appears immediately after the Shema, the call to Israel to affirm monotheism as the central doctrine of Jewish theology (6:4). Deuteronomy 6 represents Moses' recounting and summary of the law as the Israelites get ready to enter the promised land (vv. 1–3). After enunciating the command to love God with all that one has, Moses instructs the people to take these laws to heart, impress them on their children, and live by them in everything they do (6:6–9). Again, we see three parts of the human being explicitly mentioned (heart, soul, strength) as a powerful rhetorical device for speaking about the whole person. The "heart" in the OT is actually the seat of the intellect, will, and intentions. The "soul" is the entire inner self with all its emotions, desires, and personal characteristics that make each human unique. "Strength" actually translates a word that normally means "greatly" or "exceedingly." One might thus render the entire verse, "'Love the Lord your God with total commitment (heart), with your total self (soul), to total excess.' Loving God should be 'over the top'!" (C. J. H. Wright 1996: 98–99).

Joshua repeats the contents of Deut. 6:5 after the first phase of the conquest of the promised land (Josh. 22:5). Second Kings 23:25 describes how Josiah turned to the Lord "with all his heart and with all his soul and with all his strength, in accordance with all the law of Moses." Not surprisingly, the commandment would continue to play a central role in subsequent Jewish life.

C. Use in Jewish Sources. Philo offers precedent for adding "mind" or "understanding" to the Deuteronomic triad of heart, soul, and strength by alluding to Deut. 6:5 and enjoining, "Let us rather, with our mind and reason, and with all our strength, gird ourselves up vigorously and energetically in the service of that Being who is uncreated and everlasting" (*Decalogue* 64). The Qumran sectarians required those who entered the council of the community to "swear with a binding oath to revert to the Law of Moses, according to all that he commanded, with whole heart and whole soul" (1QS V, 8–9), which of course is not necessarily the same as loving *God* with all one's being (this quotation refers only to heart and soul, but 11Q5 XXII, 1 adds a reference to loving Zion with all one's "powers," an apparent equivalent to the third element of "strength" from loving God in Deut. 6:5). *Testament of Dan* 5:3 describes the patriarch Dan commanding his children to love the Lord throughout their whole lives and one another with a true heart. If this language predates the Christian revision of the *Testaments of the Twelve Patriarchs*, it shows another Jewish combination of the two love commands (but the current phrasing may well be Christian in origin; see Gundry 1994: 449). Otherwise, it is Philo, in *Spec. Laws* 2.15, who provides the closest unambiguously non-Christian Jewish precedent for combining the two:

> And there are, as we may say, two most especially important heads of all the innumerable particular lessons and doctrines: the regulating of one's conduct towards God by the rules of piety and holiness, and of one's conduct towards men by the rules of humanity and justice; each of which is subdivided into a great number of subordinate ideas, all praiseworthy.

For additional partial parallels to this combination, see Bruner 1990: 794; for definitely pre-

Christian Jewish texts, see Keener 1999: 531; for exposition, see P. Perkins 1982: 12–21. In post-Christian rabbinic literature, including the Targumim, "strength" was sometimes replaced with "possessions" or "goods." The rabbis also discussed the differences between loving and fearing God in the context of references to Deut. 6:5 (see further Str-B 1:905–7).

D. Textual Background. The LXX translates the MT of Deut. 6:5 literally. As noted above, Mark follows the LXX verbatim for loving God with heart and soul, adds "and with all your understanding," and closes by using a different Greek word (*ischys* rather than *dynamis*) for "strength" (Mark 12:30). Matthew deletes Mark's last phrase ("with all your strength") but preserves his addition of "understanding" (*dianoia*). Matthew changes the awkward preposition of the LXX and Mark from *ex* to *en* throughout, thus reverting to the triadic form (but not the contents) of the OT text. Given that *dianoia* was a frequent Greek rendering of the Hebrew for "heart," the meaning of the original Deuteronomic text is scarcely altered by any of these changes (Foster 2003: 333). Bascom (1996) argues that the expanded Synoptic forms actually better bring out in Greek the meaning of the Hebrew original.

E. Hermeneutic Employed. Jesus' use of the OT proves straightforward here. He has been asked to identify the greatest commandment in the law. He replies by citing two fundamental moral principles that encapsulate the original meaning of the Torah as well as any that he could have chosen. God gave his law because he loved his people, had already rescued them from Egypt, and wanted them to live by the principles of love, both with him and with each other (see Craigie 1976: 169–70). Jesus' ethic likewise has regularly and correctly been summarized by one or both of these passages, beginning already within the NT (cf. Rom. 13:9; Gal. 5:14; James 2:8). Timeless theological truth appears in each of the two commands. As elsewhere, it is interesting to observe that Jesus does not formally distinguish the moral from the civil or ceremonial law (see Stern 1966).

F. Theological Use. As just noted, love is the heart of both the law and the gospel, despite other important differences between them. Jesus has answered his questioners with as profound a reply as anyone could have given. His summary "permits of no fulfillment of the Law, which is not, in its very core, obedience to God and service to one's neighbor" (Hill 1972: 306). Here is no situation ethic; but neither is this obedience mere legalism divorced from internalized love.

22:39

A. NT Context. See above under Matt. 22:37. Jesus is asked to summarize the law in a single command, but he cannot refrain from quoting two laws. Verse 38 appears to say that Deut. 6:5 is the single law that summarizes the whole of Torah, but 22:39 adds "a second is like it," probably meaning that this commandment is of equal importance (see Gerhardsson 1976). See also the discussions under Matt. 5:43 and 19:18–19 (for a full exposition in this context, see Brooks 1998).

B. OT Context. See above under Matt. 5:43 and 19:18–19.

C. Use in Jewish Sources. Again, see above under Matt. 5:43; 19:18–19. For a history of postbiblical Jewish exegesis of this text, see Neudecker 1992.

D. Textual Background. The LXX translates the MT literally. Mark changes the imperative "you shall love" into the infinitive "to love" to fit it more smoothly into his sentence structure (Mark 12:33). He also deletes the "your" before "neighbor." Matthew restores the exact form of the LXX: "You shall love your neighbor as yourself."

E. Hermeneutic Employed. See also above under Matt. 22:37. This is another timeless theological absolute that captures the interpersonal heart of the law, just as Deut. 6:5 summed up the relationship between humans and God. Both remain as crucial in the NT age as they were in the OT. The formal rabbinic technique that Jesus adopts here is "*gezera shavah* . . . the association of scripture passages on the basis of a common word," in this context, "love" (Hagner 1995: 647).

F. Theological Use. Love for neighbor is commanded to be like love for oneself. Pathological aberrations are not in view here! This is not a formal law to love self, as has often been alleged, but rather the observation that healthy individuals care deeply about their own well-being. Jesus wants to ensure that their care for others runs at least as deep. Paul will make an even more challenging statement along these lines in Phil. 2:4. With the parable of the Good Samaritan, Jesus will demonstrate that even one's enemy is one's

neighbor (Luke 10:25–37), contrasting dramatically with conventional Jewish interpretations (see above, pp. 28–29; and Luz 2005: 83–84). Finally, if love is the heart of the law, then obedience to God and friendship with fellow humans may fairly be said to flow out of love as the primary motivation. Particularly after the atoning death of Christ, believers naturally live lives that please God and care for others out of a profound sense of gratitude for what he has done for them that they could never have done for themselves (observations that have considerable implications for our understanding of NT ethics more generally [on which, see Verhey 1984; White 1979]).

Matthew 22:41–46

22:44

A. NT Context. After successfully avoiding all the traps set for him, Jesus now turns the tables on his audience by asking them a difficult question (22:41). He sets the question up with a far easier, noncontroversial inquiry: What will be the human ancestry of the Messiah (22:42a)? The answer is uncontested. The Messiah will be a descendant of David (22:42b). But then comes the hard question. Jewish tradition, based on the psalms' superscriptions, attributed Ps. 110:1 to David and, as part of Scripture, to the Holy Spirit, who was inspiring him (22:43). But this inspired remark of Israel's king refers to two different individuals "above" him, both called "Lord" (Gk. *kyrios*). Hagner (1995: 651) remarks, "It is astonishing that David should call his son 'my lord'; by Jewish standards of familial respect, it is rather the son who might refer to his father as 'my lord.'" The first is clearly Yahweh, but who is the second? Moreover, this second lord sits at God's right hand and has all his enemies placed under his feet (22:44). "If David therefore calls him 'Lord,' how is he his son?" (22:45). This question cannot mean that Jesus is now denying Davidic ancestry to the Messiah; that much has just been clearly established. Instead, we must understand him to be asking, "How can the Messiah be *merely* a human descendant of Israel's great king?" Plummer (1909: 310) concurs: "Christ's argument is seriously misunderstood if seen as challenging the Davidic lineage of the Messiah. Rather, Jesus is criticizing this view as by itself inadequate" (see also Hill 1972: 307). Despite what seems to have been the majority perspective in first-century Judaism, Jesus affirms that the Messiah must be more than a mere mortal. In the words of W. C. Allen (1907: 242): "The solution suggested, though not expressed, is that the Messiah is not only Son of David but Son of God." Tellingly, no one in Jesus' audience was able to answer the question; the logic seemed irrefutable (22:46a). Nor did anyone dare to ask him any further questions (22:46b).

As throughout this series of controversy stories during Jesus' last day of public teaching in the temple, Matthew is following Mark (12:36). Both excerpt the identical portion of Ps. 110:1 with the identical words. Luke likewise follows Mark, changing only the word for "under" (Luke 20:42–43). Because of the compelling nature of Jesus' argument, early Christian preaching would reuse portions of this text to make similar points (esp. Acts 2:34–35; Heb. 1:13).

B. OT Context. Most modern commentators deny the accuracy of the ascription of this psalm to David, merely on the grounds that the superscriptions were later additions to the text of the original psalms. For a variety of perspectives, given this general denial, see L. C. Allen 1983: 86–87; Davidson 1998: 367; Dahood 1970: 114. Then the writer is viewed as some anonymous person ascribing praise to and praying for the king of Israel. However, this interpretation requires the rest of the psalm to be employing an unprecedented degree of literary hyperbole. Kidner (1975: 392): "Those who deny David's authorship of the psalm on the ground that the psalm reads like an enthronement oracle curiously miss the point. It is just such an oracle. What is unique is the royal speaker, addressing this more-than-royal person." No king of Israel was ever so close to God that he could normally be described, even metaphorically, as sitting at God's right hand. Terrien (2003: 752) terms this "stupendous for the Hebrew mind," suggesting an "exceptional degree of intimacy between God and the new monarch." The triumph over the king's enemies as he is arrayed in holy majesty (110:2–3) can possibly be taken of an earthly Davidic king, but 110:4 returns to language that seems highly inappropriate even for one as exalted as David (so also Carson 1984: 467). This "king" embodies an eternal priesthood (110:4), whereas legitimate Israelite kings in the line of David came from the tribe of Judah, not the tribe of Levi, from whom priests had to descend. And in 110:5 Yahweh is said to be at this king's right hand, rather than vice versa, as if God and king were interchangeable! Finally, this monarch will do what God alone is described elsewhere as doing: judging the nations and crushing the rulers of the whole earth (110:6). For all these reasons, B. C. Davis (2000) concludes that the psalm is purely messianic.

C. Use in Jewish Sources. Pre-Christian Jewish interpretation seems at times to have taken this psalm as messianic, though not necessarily understood as speaking of a divine messiah. The LXX of Ps. 110:3 (109:3 LXX), however, "distinctively describes the birth of a divine child" (Hay 1973: 21). *Testament of Job* 33:3, on the other hand, depicts Job speaking of an eternal kingdom for himself in alluding to this text. First Maccabees 14:41 describes Simon, brother of Judas Maccabeus, as an eternal high priest in his irregular role as both political leader and priest. *Assumption of Moses* 6:1 calls the Hasmonean kings those who speak of themselves as "priests of the most high God" (see also *T. Levi* 8:3). The Qumran writings do not unambiguously cite Ps. 110:1, but the figure of Melchizedek, to whom this king's eternal priesthood is likened in v. 4, plays a prominent role in this literature. One entire document, *11QMelchizedek*, is given over to a description of Melchizedek in angelic, even quasi-divine, terms. For pre-Christian Jewish expectation regarding the Son of David more generally, see Fitzmyer 1971b.

Post-Christian Jewish interpretation developed an unambiguously messianic interpretation of Ps. 110:2 (see esp. *Gen. Rab.* 85:9; *Num. Rab.* 18:23; see also the Targum to Ps. 110), suggesting that v. 1 would have been seen in the same light (Davies and Allison 1988–1997: 3:254n23). The earliest rabbinic reference, in the name of Rabbi Ishmael (ca. AD 100) applies the psalm to Abraham. However, Ishmael was an anti-Christian zealot who probably introduced this distinctive interpretation to counter Christian use of the text (see Hengel 1995: 178–79). The older, messianic interpretation, hinted at in pre-Christian texts, became dominant again after AD 250. It almost certainly would not have been invented at that late date, given the then-regnant Christian interpretation (France 1971: 164–65).

D. Textual Background. The LXX, which numbers this psalm as 109, provides a reasonably literal translation of the MT. The best-attested version of Mark, followed by Matthew, deletes the definite article before the first "Lord" and substitutes *hypokatō* ("under") for *hypopodion* ("underfoot"), thus avoiding the redundancy of the LXX: *hypopodion tōn podōn sou* ("underfoot of your feet"). More speculatively, Davies and Allison (1988–1997: 3:253) think that this change is a borrowing from Ps. 8:7 LXX, the psalm that is cited in Matt. 21:16 in connection with the Son of David and that had a messianic meaning in the Targum.

E. Hermeneutic Employed. Despite many who would disagree, this seems to be a case of straightforward prediction and fulfillment. Again, see B. C. Davis (2000), moving beyond the earlier impasse in the debate between Johnson 1992 (arguing for a directly predictive role on the basis of the analogy of faith) and Bateman 1992 (arguing for a "typological-prophetic" hermeneutic on the supposition that David originally was addressing Solomon). From an older era of scholarship, see Delitzsch 1984: 3:185–86. God speaks to the Messiah, telling him to remain in the honored position of presence at his right hand until some future date when all his enemies will be destroyed. The rest of the psalm unpacks the events that will surround this coming ultimate vengeance. Jesus fulfilled part of God's promises with his first advent as the legitimate Messiah, coming from and returning to Yahweh's right hand. He will fulfill the rest of God's promises when he returns and institutes the final judgment of all the earth's inhabitants.

F. Theological Use. Clearly, Christology is central. The Messiah is no mere mortal, not even the most exalted of human kings. He is divine. God in his sovereignty has planned things this way. God's plan also includes the future implementation of perfect justice throughout the universe, at the end of time, through this Messiah, who is both priest and king. Then God's enemies will be destroyed and God's people rewarded. The rest of the NT likewise speaks of God putting his enemies under *Jesus'* feet (1 Cor. 15:25–28; Eph. 1:22; Heb. 10:13).

Matthew 23:1–36

The final extended discourse segment of Matthew's Gospel spans chapters 23–25. In this section's denunciation of the hypocrisy of various scribes and Pharisees, Jesus frequently alludes to or echoes the OT but never quotes it outright. Matthew 23:2, with its reference to Moses' seat, may echo Deut. 17:10, in which the people of Israel are directed to act according to the decisions of the priests, Levites, and judges of Israel and to obey everything that they are commanded to do. For further insight on this difficult verse, see Powell 1995. Verse 3 may echo Mal. 2:7–8, which describe how the lips of priests should preserve knowledge and how people should seek instruction from them, in sharp contrast with the disobedience of the Jewish leaders in Malachi's day. For OT background to the wearing of phylacteries and tassels on one's garment (23:5), see Exod. 13:2–16; Deut. 6:4–9; and 11:13–21. The wearing of the phylactery boxes probably developed as an overly literal application of Deut. 6:8; and 11:18, while Num. 15:38–39 provides further precedent for the tassels.

The abolition of ranks among God's people (Matt. 23:8–11) echoes one of the promises concerning Jeremiah's new covenant (Jer. 31:33–34). The one teacher of v. 8 may echo Isa. 54:13 (see further Derrett 1981). The one heavenly Father probably alludes to the one God of Deut. 6:4. Exalting the humble and humbling the proud (23:12) find OT parallels in Job 22:29; Prov. 29:23; Isa. 10:33; and Ezek. 21:26. The woes against the Jewish leaders, beginning in 23:13, may echo Zech. 11:17. On the holiness of the altar and anything that touches it (23:19), see Exod. 29:37. On the magnificence of the temple, consult 1 Kings 8:13, and for the house in which God's glory or presence dwells, compare Pss. 26:8 and 135:21. Each of these texts helps to illuminate Matt. 23:21. For heaven as God's throne, see above under Matt. 5:34 and, again, compare especially Isa. 66:1. The laws of tithing (23:23) rely particularly on Lev. 27:30 (see also Num. 18:21–32; Deut. 14:22–29; 26:12–15). Later OT references to tithing, like the subsequent oral Torah, build on these texts. The specific mention of justice, mercy, and faithfulness alludes to Mic. 6:8, with faithfulness equivalent to walking humbly with one's God. Jesus could have had Zech. 7:9 in mind here as well. A variety of possible texts might be echoed in 23:24–30 (Derrett 1986), but it is hard to be confident about any of them. The most striking parallel, perhaps, is Ps. 5:9, comparing wicked people to open graves (cf. Matt. 23:27).

The reference to Abel in Matt. 23:35 corresponds to Gen. 4:8. Most commentators, assuming the sequence of the Hebrew OT canon, take the Zechariah in this verse in Matthew to refer to the son of Jehoiada, murdered in the temple, as described in the last book of the Jewish Scriptures (2 Chron. 24:20–21). But this would make Christ's reference to "Zechariah son of Berekiah" a mistake. Later rabbinic traditions believed that the prophet Zechariah son of Berekiah, who is depicted in the OT book that bears his name, was also killed in the temple (e.g., Tg. to Lam. 2:20; *Midr. Eccles.* 3:16). For a full presentation of varying rabbinic approaches, see Blank 1937–1938; for the range of interpretive options for Matthew's reference, see Gundry 1967: 86–88. So perhaps Jesus is referring to the first and last OT martyrs chronologically rather than canonically, in which case no specific OT text would be in view.

Matthew 23:37–39

The imagery of 23:37, in which Jesus longs to have gathered Jerusalem's children together as a hen gathers her chicks under her wings, echoes the imagery of, for example, Deut. 32:11; Ps. 36:7; Ruth 2:12; Isa. 31:5 (for a full list of references, see Marshall 1978: 575). That the Jews' house—that is, the temple—is being left to them abandoned (23:38) alludes to the dramatic scene of Ezek. 10–11, in which the glory of the Lord departs from the temple (see France 1971: 332). Previous threats by God to leave his house desolate include 1 Kings 9:7–8; Jer. 12:7; and 22:5.

23:39

A. NT Context. The unrelenting thrust of Matt. 23 thus far has been one of judgment. The Jewish leaders have been berated for their hypocrisy (vv. 1–36), and Jesus has just pronounced God's condemnation on their most sacred building (v. 38). But 23:37 discloses Christ's tender side, as he laments how often he wanted to comfort and nurture these people, but it was their unwillingness that prevented him. There is a ray of hope in

23:39, as Jesus concludes his words in the temple with the promise that they will not see him again until they say, "Blessed is the one coming in the name of the Lord." Hagner (1995: 679) calls Matthew's last word in this chapter a positive note of grace and thus of hope. A majority of commentators see only forced worship here, comparable to Isa. 45:23 (see esp. Garland 1979: 208), but the straightforward interpretation of this acclamation is that of genuine belief. Although the crowds misunderstood the true import of Jesus' "Palm Sunday" entrance into Jerusalem, their acclaim there, employing this identical verse, was nevertheless a heartfelt, positive response and scarcely coerced. Thus there may be a hint here of something like Rom. 11:25–27, which depicts a great outpouring of faith in Jesus among ethnic Jews at the end of the church age. The people on Palm Sunday acclaimed Jesus sincerely but without full understanding; one day they will acclaim him even more sincerely and with full understanding (see Allison 1983, noting intertestamental and rabbinic sources that hint at a similar interpretation and pointing out parallels in, e.g., Matt. 5:26; 15:59; 18:30 to contingent *heōs* clauses).

B. OT Context. See above under Matt. 21:9.

C. Use in Jewish Sources. See above under Matt. 21:9.

D. Textual Background. Despite the fact that this verse forms part of Matthew's unique material, he follows the LXX of Ps. 118:26 (117:26 LXX) exactly, as he did in Matt. 21:9, where he was following Mark. And, as noted above, the LXX is a literal translation of the MT.

E. Hermeneutic Employed. Most of what was said above under Matt. 21:9 proves relevant here as well. This is not an OT text introduced with any kind of reference to Scripture or its fulfillment. Just as the crowds acclaimed Jesus on "Palm Sunday," one day they will do so again with fuller understanding, yet still using the language of the psalmist. As we noted above, at the very least this is vivid typology. But, to the extent that "the coming one" had become an expression referring to the Messiah, then we can see a second stage of a more direct prediction-fulfillment scheme with Christ's return. This kind of "double fulfillment" does not refer to one short-term OT-era fulfillment followed by a fuller fulfillment in the life of Jesus, as with so many of Matthew's uses of Isaiah, but rather to one partial fulfillment at Christ's first advent and a second, more complete fulfillment yet to come at his second advent (see Gundry 1994: 474).

F. Theological Use. Again, the amount of Christology present depends on whether "coming one" was used as a messianic title. If it was, then we can use this text for further support that Jesus was the Messiah. More so than with most messianic Christology in Matthew, however, there is explicit reference to Christ's second coming, so that the passage is also important for understanding the evangelist's eschatology. Whether that eschatology included a special place for a repentant Israel, one day acknowledging Jesus as the Messiah and thus receiving salvation, obviously depends on the interpretation of the acclamation here. If salvation is not in view, then the passage at least speaks about God's sovereignty and self-disclosure in Jesus. One day his identity will be so plain that no one will be able to deny it, whether or not they have voluntarily made him their Lord and joined the company of his true followers.

Matthew 24:1–31

Jesus' pronouncement that God is abandoning the temple leads naturally to his prediction of its literal destruction (24:1–2). The disciples, equally naturally, question Jesus about this (24:3); the eschatological Olivet Discourse forms his response (24:4–25:46). Daniel, like the disciples, had asked about the timing of the end (Dan. 12:6). The Mount of Olives is a theologically appropriate place for Jesus' address, given the upheavals that it was to experience when the Messiah came to judge his enemies (Zech. 14:4). The warfare that "must take place" (Matt. 24:6) may echo a similar phrase used of God's eschatological kingdom in Dan. 2:45 Θ. For people rising up against people (24:7a), compare 2 Chron. 15:6; for kingdom versus kingdom (24:7b), see Isa. 19:2; and Dan. 7:23–24. For the persecution of God's people (24:9), compare Dan. 7:25. The necessary endurance (24:13) may echo Dan. 12:12 Θ.

The "desolating sacrilege" in 24:15 clearly alludes to the horror prophesied in Dan. 9:27 and repeated in 11:31; and 12:11, with Jesus explicitly mentioning the prophet's name. In the OT it occurs first in the context of Daniel's famous

but notoriously difficult prophecy about seventy "weeks of years" (i.e., 490 years [9:24–27]). Seven times seven times ten almost certainly represents a symbolic number for a perfect period of time, and the abomination is related to something "set up on a wing," presumably of the temple, since Jerusalem and its sanctuary are said to be destroyed (Dan. 9:26; for the meaning of this text, see Baldwin 1978: 168–72). First Maccabees 1:54 understood this prophecy to have been fulfilled in the desecration of the temple sanctuary by Antiochus Epiphanes, the Seleucid ruler who sacrificed swine on the Jewish altar and ransacked the capital city, leading to the Maccabean revolt of 167–164 BC. Jesus is envisioning a similarly horrifying event accompanying the destruction of the temple in the first century; indeed, Roman troops did again desecrate the building as they virtually razed it to the ground in AD 70 (cf. Luke 21:20). The disciples comment on the temple that they can see from the Mount of Olives. Jesus then predicts *its* destruction. Luke explicitly takes it this way. Nothing in the context supports the notion that a temple rebuilt centuries later, only to be destroyed again, is in view. The disciples would have naturally associated the destruction of the temple with "the end of the age" (24:3), even if Jesus goes on to separate the two in his sermon (see Carson 1984: 488–95). Foretelling the destruction of the temple, of course, places Jesus in a long line of prophets (cf. Mic. 3:12; Jer. 7:8–15; 9:10–11; 26:6, 18; see Davies and Allison 1988–1997: 3:335).

The language of the flight from Jerusalem described in 24:16–18 may echo the description of the flight of Lot's family from Sodom and Gomorrah (Gen. 19:17), especially with its reference to not turning back. The horrors of life in a city under siege (24:21) prove graphic and gruesome, as Deut. 28:53–57 illustrates. Verse 21 also alludes to Dan. 12:1, referring to a kind of distress or tribulation that has not happened "from the beginning of nations" until that time. For the rise of false prophets, compare Deut. 13:1–3, and for the imagery of the Lord appearing with his arrow flashing like the lightning, see Zech. 9:14; echoes of these two texts may be heard in Matt. 24:24, and 27, respectively.

The four indented lines in the United Bible Societies *Greek New Testament* of 24:29 poetically allude to Isa. 13:10, with echoes of 34:4. The former passage literally reads, "For the stars of the heavens and their constellations will not give their light; the sun will be dark at its rising [or, 'while going forth'], and the moon will not shed its light." The closest thing to an actual quotation that we find in Matthew is "the moon will not give its light," with a different Greek word used for "light" than in the LXX. It is Isa. 34:4, though, that actually has the stars being dissolved and falling. Ezekiel 32:7 likewise declares, "When I snuff you out, I will cover the heavens and darken their stars. I will cover the sun with a cloud, and the moon will not give its light." Joel 2:10, 31; and 3:15 refer to the sun and moon turning dark or no longer giving their light or to stars no longer shining. And convulsion of the heavens was standard in Jewish eschatology; compare further Ezek. 32:7–8; 2 Esd. 5:4; *1 En.* 80:4; and *As. Mos.* 10:5 (W. C. Allen 1907: 258). It is therefore difficult to agree with the NIV's use of quotation marks here. A constellation of allusions rather than an actual quotation seems to be a more accurate description of Matthew's form.

Verse 30 contains possible references to the OT before the one actual quotation in this chapter. The sign of the Son of Man in heaven may hark back to the banner (or ensign) raised for the nations that gathers the exiles in Isa. 11:12, though we do better to speak of a conceptual parallel than even a formal echo, much less an allusion (cf. Isa. 18:3; see Glasson 1964). The middle of 24:30 seems to allude to Zech. 12:10, borrowing the words in the LXX for "they will weep" and "all the tribes." After the formal quotation in the latter part of 24:30, further uses of the OT in this chapter include an echo of Isa. 27:13 with its trumpet sounding on the day of deliverance (24:31a), an allusion to the ingathering of Israel in Deut. 30:4; Zech. 2:6 (24:31b), and a recollection of the story of Noah and the flood in Gen. 6:13–7:24 (24:37). See also Gen. 9:29 for "the days of Noah" here and in 24:38; for a comprehensive discussion of possible OT backgrounds to details in all three Synoptic versions of Jesus' eschatological discourse, see Evans 1992. That the day of the Lord was near (24:33) was of course a commonplace of OT prophecy (on which, see Bauckham 1980).

24:30

A. NT Context. Matthew 24 contains numerous exegetical cruxes and has spawned as many interpretations as there are understandings of biblical eschatology more generally (for a good survey of evangelical options, see Turner 1989). The main debate involves the question of how many of the details of Jesus' prediction concern first-century events, how many deal with still future events, and how many treat both. Most interpreters today, as throughout church history, have agreed nevertheless that with 24:29–31 we have reached a description of Jesus' public return at the end of human history as we know it. Matthew's use in 24:29 of "immediately after the tribulation of those days" has, however, led some interpreters to take 24:29–31 as speaking of first-century events, especially if the tribulation of 24:15–27 is understood as the suffering surrounding the destruction of the temple in AD 70. Most notable is the proposal that the coming of the Son of Man in 24:30 is Jesus' invisible coming in judgment on the nation of Israel with the Roman invasion of Jerusalem in AD 70. It is further argued that the Son of Man's coming on the clouds in Dan. 7:13, quoted here, describes his private travel to the throne room of God, not his public descent to earth (e.g., France 1985: 343–44; N. T. Wright 1996: 360–65; see also below, p. 93).

On the other hand, 24:23–27 have warned at some length against interpreting Christ's parousia as anything other than an event as visible from the earth as the lightning flashing from east to west in the sky (24:27). Verse 29 describes cosmic upheavals, and v. 30 speaks of the Son of Man's sign in the sky causing people of every tribe on earth to weep. No doubt these are metaphorical prophecies, but they combine to suggest changes more cataclysmic than the ravages of merely human warfare (against N. T. Wright's version of this interpretation, see several of the contributions to Newman 1999, esp. Allison 1999). Jesus will shortly quote this passage from Daniel again, adding the phrase about "seated at the right hand of power" (i.e., God), in a different position than in the OT text, so that Christ is *first* in God's presence and *then* coming on the clouds, presumably therefore coming from heaven to earth. The picture is one of a theophany, "which is always from heaven to the world of humankind" (Beasley-Murray 1993: 430;

cf. Davies and Allison 1988–1997: 3:351–52). It makes most sense to assume that he has the same idea in mind here, too. At that time the angels will gather together all the company of the redeemed already in heaven to meet Jesus and join him as he returns to this earth and to his people still alive on it (24:31). On Jesus' use of the title "Son of Man" more generally and its background, see above, p. 33.

The "immediately" in 24:29 thus suggests that the "great tribulation" of which Jesus speaks begins with the events of AD 70 and continues until Christ's public return at the end of the age. It forms, in other words, the entire interadvent period. After all, if the "great tribulation" were only a few-year period of intense suffering just before the parousia, it would be so trite as to be pointless to say that such distress would never again be equaled (24:21); of course it would never again be equaled, because Christ's return will put an end to such a possibility! But if the tribulation refers to events that began in AD 70, then the comment carries great significance and poignancy. Neither before nor after the destruction of Jerusalem has "so high a percentage of a great city's population [been] so thoroughly and painfully exterminated and enslaved" (Carson 1984: 501). This is not to say that all portions of the church age have been equally full of suffering for Christians, nor to rule out a particularly intense period of suffering at the end of this longer period of tribulation (on which Revelation will focus and also call "great tribulation"); rather, it is to concur with 2 Tim. 3:12 that "all who want to live godly lives in Christ will be persecuted."

The somewhat cryptic 24:32–36 reinforce these conclusions. Signs can suggest the end is near (24:32–33), but they will never enable us to calculate the time of its arrival (24:36). The generation that Jesus addressed will not pass away before all the preliminary events that must precede the *parousia* have occurred (24:34). That "all these things" in 24:34 do not include Christ's return itself is made plain by 24:33, which likewise refers to "all these things." But those things are that which enables one to recognize that the end is near, that "it [or, 'he'] is at the doors." It would make no sense to say, "When you see that Christ has returned, know that he is near." So the "these things" must refer to the preliminary events of 24:4–28 preceding the cosmic upheavals that usher in his return in 24:29–31. In short, once the temple was destroyed, everything was in place for Christ to come back (see Ridderbos 1987: 449; Cranfield 1977: 408–9; Gundry 1993: 746). However, he has not done so yet, so we cannot predict when it will happen except to say that it will catch many by surprise (24:37–42), and the rest of Jesus' sermon stresses faithful living so that Christians are ready whenever it takes place (24:43–25:46).

Matthew is generally following Mark at this point. Mark 13:26 contains the same quotation, minus the "of heaven" after "the clouds." Luke 21:27 reproduces Mark's slightly shorter citation. The quotation will recur in the context of Jesus' hearing before the Jewish high priest Caiaphas (Mark 14:62; Matt. 26:64; Luke 22:69). In none of the texts does a formal introduction or any explicit reference to Scripture appear; rather, Jesus simply promises his audiences that "you will see" and then proceeds with the excerpt from Dan. 7:13.

B. OT Context. Daniel 7 depicts the prophet's bizarre dream about four beasts, each representing successive empires and culminating in the awful "end-times" empire at the end of human history. This final empire is the most destructive, the most opposed to God and his people, and the one that God will ultimately most condemn. Within this overall picture appear several glimpses of heaven that remind Daniel of God's sovereignty and judgment despite the manifestations of godless terror on earth. In 7:9–10, "thrones were set in place" (using a dual Hebrew form that led to much Jewish speculation about who could sit on a heavenly throne in judgment next to Yahweh). Recent studies suggest this was a crucial text for creating a flexibility within monotheism that allowed Jesus to be viewed as fully God within *Jewish* Christianity (see Hurtado 1988, esp. pp. 71–92). God is depicted as "the Ancient of Days," like a judge in his court, opening the books that presumably contained a comprehensive record of human behavior. In 7:13 Daniel sees "one like a son of man"—that is, appearing to be human—who comes on the clouds of heaven and is led into the very presence of the Ancient of Days. This is quite some special man! Moreover, he receives authority, glory, and sovereignty over all the people

of the earth, an everlasting dominion and an inde-
structible kingdom (7:14). It is difficult to see how
anything but the most exalted of men, depicted
in language otherwise reserved for God himself,
could be in view here. Longman (1999: 186–88)
notes parallels both inside and outside the OT to
the "divine cloud-rider"—language consistently
used for deity itself. Likewise, S. Kim (1985: 69)
sees both Daniel and Jesus depicting a divine Son
in the use of this text.

It is true that when Daniel asks for the vision
to be interpreted, he is told "that the saints of the
Most High will receive the kingdom and possess
it forever" (7:18; cf. 7:22), an explanation that in
Daniel's day would have referred to faithful Israel.
This is the view that has come to dominate critical
scholarship (see, e.g., Porteous 1979: 111; Seow
2003: 108–9). Lacocque (1979: 146) decides that
"the 'son of man' is the personification of the righteous people, the perfect image of the righteous
individual." Perhaps the next most popular view is
that an archangel, such as Michael, is in view (see,
e.g., Goldingay 1989: 169–72). However, eternal
reception and possession of God's kingly reign are
not the same as universal sovereignty and dominion over every person on earth. Verse 27 speaks of
the grandeur of *other* kingdoms being handed over
to these same saints, but worship and obedience
are nevertheless reserved for God. The picture
in 7:13–14 is still best taken of an individual—a
divine, messianic ruler of God's people establishing his kingdom in all its fullness, for the sake of
his saints, on this earth (so, e.g., Young 1949: 154;
now defended again in Miller 1994: 207–9).

C. Use in Jewish Sources. Debates still rage
about the pre-Christian understanding of Dan.
7 and the Son of Man. In *1 Enoch* the Son of Man
is clearly a heavenly, messianic, elect individual—
especially in 46:1–3; 48:5–7; 62:6–8—but these
passages appear in a section of the book (the Similitudes) that may be post-Christian (as reflected
in the absence of this section of *1 Enoch* from the
indisputably pre-Christian Enoch manuscripts
found at Qumran). *Fourth Ezra* 12:31–33; and
13:1–3 reflect a similar perspective but were
almost certainly written in the wake of AD 70.
Both 11Q13 II, 18 and Ezekiel the Tragedian are
demonstrably pre-Christian and also attest a messianic interpretation, though the latter is quoted
only secondhand by the Christian historian Euse-

bius. The texts of *Sib. Or.* 5, the Targum to Ps. 80,
and Num. 24:7 LXX may point to a pre-Christian
messianic Son of Man (Horbury 1985), but there
are problems of either dating or interpretation (or
both) in each case.

On the other hand, the individual messianic
view of Dan. 7:13–14 prevails throughout early
rabbinic literature (see esp. *b. Sanh.* 98a, in which
if Israel is worthy, the Messiah will come on the
clouds; if not, humble and riding on a donkey).
This view is not likely to have been invented after
Christianity's clear appropriation of this imagery
for Jesus. Indeed, it is the majority perspective in
Judaism well into the medieval period. The "collective interpretation," in which the Son of Man
is merely Israel, is not clearly attested in Judaism
until the Middle Ages; earlier proponents, beginning with Ephrem the Syrian in the fourth century
AD, were actually Christian (for this history, see
Collins 1993).

D. Textual Background. Matthew has reproduced the LXX even more closely than his
Markan source did. Mark 13:26 reads literally,
"in clouds," whereas Matthew and the LXX have
"on the clouds." And, as noted above, Matthew
preserves the "of heaven" that Mark does not. The
LXX, however, has the two parts of the quotation
in the reverse order: "on the clouds of heaven, as
a son of man he was coming." Matthew has also
slightly altered this second clause to "the son of
man coming."

E. Hermeneutic Employed. Because no formal introduction alerts the reader to a specific
use of Scripture, we may speak simply of Jesus
using scriptural language to describe his return.
On the other hand, the context of Dan. 7:13 is
clearly that of prophecy. Daniel was given a dream
or vision of the future and a partial explanation of
it after he awoke. Nothing remotely like this has
occurred, even to this day, that could be said even
to partially fulfill Daniel's prophecy. Therefore,
it seems appropriate to speak of direct predictive
prophecy, fulfilled only when the future events
that Jesus describes come to pass. When he returns, he will come on the clouds of heaven as
the messianic Son of Man, arriving to reign over
the whole earth. However, to the extent that Dan.
7:13 depicts an invisible scene in God's throne
room, we may speak of typology between that
portrait and Christ's. And the allusion to Zech.

12:10 earlier in 24:30 sets up an a fortiori relationship between the OT and NT uses (Carson 1984: 505), so perhaps a similar relationship is implied with Dan. 7:13. The Son of Man's return may be even more glorious than his original ascent to his Father.

F. Theological Use. Christology and eschatology come together in this radiant portrait. Jesus is the exalted, even divine Son of Man and Messiah, who will one day return from heaven just as he would soon ascend into heaven (cf. Acts 1:1–11). When that happens, the chain of events culminating in Jesus officiating at the final judgment of all the peoples of the earth will have been set inexorably into motion. Then all will weep—his people with joy, and his enemies with sorrow because they will now recognize that their fate is sealed (see Hagner 1995: 714). Despite numerous false prophets throughout the history of the church, whom Jesus himself predicted (Matt. 24:23–24), no one can ever know when that time will be, so all must be prepared. It could come at any time!

Matthew 25:1–46

God is already depicted as a bridegroom, as in the parable of the Ten Bridesmaids (Matt. 25:1–13), in OT texts such as Isa. 54:4–6; Ezek. 16:8, 45; and Hos. 2:19. We may speak of this as a stock metaphor, as Jesus frequently drew on for his parables (see Blomberg 1990b: 37). The motif of the delay of the end was one that Jews had wrestled with since the eighth-century BC, as numerous writing prophets had declared the day of the Lord to be at hand (see Bauckham 1980). The parable of the Talents (25:14–30) may faintly echo Prov. 9:9, esp. in 25:29, on the wise gaining more wisdom. The story of the sheep and the goats (25:31–46) may allude in 25:31 to Deut. 33:2 LXX, which speaks of the Lord shining forth with angels with him at his right hand. Or perhaps Zech. 14:5 is in mind, in which the Lord comes with all the holy ones accompanying him. The separation of sheep from goats in 25:32 may allude to Ezek. 34:17–19. Verses 35–36 probably allude to Isa. 58:7, with its reference to the kind of fast that the Lord has chosen: to share food with the hungry, to provide the wanderer with shelter, and to clothe the naked. The departure of the people of the nations at the final judgment into eternal punishment or eternal life (25:46) builds on the conceptual background of the resurrection of just and unjust to everlasting life and everlasting contempt, respectively, in Dan. 12:2.

Matthew 26:1–30

We come next to the account of Jesus' final supper with his disciples (on which, see Marshall 1980). For the institution of the Passover see Exod. 12 (for additional, related laws, see Lev. 23:4, 8; Num. 9:1–14; Deut. 16:1–8). Jesus' words in response to those who criticized the woman who anointed him with a lavish amount of perfume (26:11) clearly allude to Deut. 15:11a. The poor will indeed always be with us, but the rest of the verse in Deuteronomy goes on to command God's people to be open-handed toward their fellow believers and other needy persons in their land. The point of Jesus' comment, therefore, is not to discourage charity, but rather to remind his disciples that they can and must regularly help the poor, but here is a one-time special opportunity to minister to him before he dies (see further Sugirtharajah 1990). Matthew later will see a typological fulfillment of prophecy with the thirty pieces of silver mentioned in 26:15 (see 27:9–10, quoting Zech. 11:12). It may be merely coincidental that thirty shekels of silver is also the price that an owner of a bull must pay to the master of a slave gored to death by that bull (Exod. 21:32). For the origin of the use of unleavened bread in the Passover ceremony (26:17), see Exod. 12:14–20. Although there is no verbal parallelism, 26:23 seems to echo Ps. 41:9: "Even my close friend, whom I trusted, who shared my bread, has lifted up his heel against me."

Events turning against the Son of Man, "as it has been written concerning him" (Matt. 26:24), may allude to the Servant Songs of Isa. 42–53, now that the servant and Son of Man have been linked together. One thinks especially of Isa. 53:9, but also of Ps. 22:7, 8, 16–18, especially since this psalm will be exploited typologically several times in Matthew's crucifixion narrative (see below, pp. 97–100). "The blood of the covenant" in 26:28 continues important Passover allusions (esp. Exod. 24:8), as well as alluding to Jeremiah's "new covenant" (Jer. 31:31). Ham (2000) believes that Isa. 53:11–12 and Jer. 3:31–34 were the two key generative texts behind Jesus' unique Passover celebration. Zechariah 9:11 also refers to "the blood of my covenant with you." The actual Passover service revolved around the four promises of Exod. 6:6–7a, each one coming to be associated with the drinking of one of four cups of wine. The cup of 26:27 appears to have been the third one, the one drunk just after the supper in conjunction with God's promise to redeem his people. The hymns sung just before leaving for the Mount of Olives (26:30) appear to have been a fixed part of the Passover tradition already and would have corresponded to our Pss. 113–118 (or perhaps Pss. 113–114 were sung earlier and 115–118 at this juncture). On the primary sources for the Passover haggadah or liturgy, see Bahr 1970. For a recent reassessment of what is attributable to the first century and for the relationship of the accounts in Mark and Matthew to this reconstruction, see Theiss 1994.

Matthew 26:31–35

26:31

A. NT Context. After celebrating the Last Supper, Jesus predicts that all of the Twelve will be "scandalized," or take offense at him, that very evening (26:31a). This apparently involves their scattering—that is, fleeing from him, like sheep without a shepherd (26:31b), but Jesus promises to meet up with them again after his resurrection (26:32). Peter protests that even if all the rest flee, he will take no offense at Christ and (presumably) will stand by him (26:33). Jesus, however, knows better and takes this opportunity to predict Peter's threefold denial (26:34). The Twelve, with one voice, insist that they could never do this (26:35), but subsequent events will completely vindicate Jesus' take on things. After Jesus is arrested in the Garden of Gethsemane, all the disciples desert him and run away (26:56). Matthew is again following Mark here, who includes the identical quotation in slightly different form (Mark 14:27). Both writers explicitly introduce the citation with the formula "it stands written," a clear testimony to the fact that they know they are citing Scripture.

B. OT Context: Zechariah 9–14 forms the most overtly apocalyptic section of this prophetic work. In chapter 11 Zechariah himself is portrayed as a symbolic shepherd, "pastoring" the flock that is

God's people. Because of their rebellion, God predicts the dissolution of the unity between north and south, Israel and Judah (11:14). Matthew 27:9–10 will cite verses from the immediately preceding context (Zech. 11:12–13) and typologically apply them to Jesus and the events of his betrayal. In Zech. 12, however, the prophet looks beyond the judgment of his people to the coming destruction of their enemies. At that time they will mourn in repentance (12:10)—the very imagery that Jesus has recently utilized in the Olivet Discourse (Matt. 24:30). Zechariah 13 begins with explicit references to "that day"—the eschatological future or messianic age. The house of David is at that time cleansed from sin and impurity (13:1). Idols are purged from the land along with all the idolatrous prophets (13:2–6). Even then, further judgment is necessary: two-thirds of the people must perish in order to leave a purified remnant (13:7–9). The survivors, however, will know God and follow him, and the Lord will come and directly reign in their midst (chap. 14).

Who, then, is the shepherd whose sheep are scattered? The critical consensus agrees that he is one of the Judaic kings in the line of David whose rule comes to a violent end in the sixth century BC (Meyers and Meyers 1993: 385–87). Then the purified remnant can be seen as the Jewish nation restored to their land after exile. But if 12:10 informs our interpretation of chapter 13, the shepherd struck down is "one they have pierced," which is a more apt description of Jesus' crucifixion than of the demise of any previous Jewish king (McComiskey 1998: 1214, 1223). Moreover, "the man who is close to me" in 13:7 more naturally suggests someone on God's side, not a wicked king about to be punished (Keil 1984: 397). R. L. Smith (1984: 283) summarizes, "The day is coming when God's appointed leader in Israel will be cut off and the people will be scattered." Ezekiel 34, with its references to a messianic shepherd, probably also informs a valid interpretation of Zechariah. Thus both the historical and literary contexts, as well as the actual imagery employed in the passage itself, suggest that this is a messianic prophecy. Cook (1993) postulates a prior tradition history in which chapters 11 and 13 originally had different meanings but believes that at least in the finished, canonical form of Zechariah their placement implies that they belong together referring to the Messiah.

C. Use in Jewish Sources. Zechariah 13:7 appears explicitly in only one demonstrably pre-Christian Jewish source, but there it is given a seemingly messianic interpretation. France (1971: 177), however, thinks that this refers to the persecution of the Teacher of Righteousness, separate from the coming of the two messiahs. From Qumran, CD-B XIX, 7–11 reads,

> "Wake up, sword, against my shepherd, and against the male who is my companion—oracle of God—wound the shepherd and scatter the flock and I shall return my hand upon the little ones." Those who are faithful to him are the poor ones of the flock. These shall escape in the age of the visitation; but those that remain shall be delivered up to the sword when there comes the messiah of Aaron and Israel.

The association of the shepherd motif with a messianic interpretation is strengthened by 4Q521 because, on at least one key interpretation of this short fragment, it predicts that God's Messiah will "shepherd" the Qumran sectarians in the latter days (Davies and Allison 1988–1997: 3:486).

From post-Christian Jewish literature, the Targum to Zech. 13:7 more unambiguously takes the shepherd as a Davidide, but without the positive relationship between God and king suggested in Zechariah itself: "O sword, *be revealed* against *the king* and against the *prince his* companion *who is his equal, who is like him*, says the Lord of hosts; slay the *king* and the *princes* shall be scattered and I will bring back *a mighty stroke* upon the *underlings*." Not until the Talmud do we find an unambiguously messianic interpretation, at least of the pierced one of Zech. 12:10, who presumably is the same individual referred to again in Zech. 13:7 (*b. Sukkah* 52a). Still later, ibn-Ezra will refer to the shepherd of Zech. 13:7 in similar terms and identify him as Messiah ben Joseph (R. L. Smith 1984: 283–84).

D. Textual Background. The MT reads literally, "you [sg.] strike the shepherd and the sheep will be scattered." The LXX changes three key words: the command becomes plural ("you [pl.] strike"), the direct object becomes plural ("the shepherds"), and the prediction becomes a command ("you [pl.] scatter"). Somewhat unusually, Mark (rather than Matthew) restores two of the three original Hebrew forms ("shepherd" and "will be scattered"), but he also changes the first command to a first-person singular future ("I will strike"). This may be a legitimate inference from Zech. 13:7b–9, however, that God's coming punishment in some sense involves him striking the shepherd as well as the wayward sheep. Archer and Chirichigno (1983: 163–64) comment: "Those who earlier in the verse are bidden to smite are to do so only as God's agents in carrying out His plan." Matthew follows Mark but puts "scattered" before "the sheep" (as in both the MT and the LXX) and adds "of the flock" after "the sheep," perhaps to stress that Israel is still in view. Davies and Allison (1988–1997: 3:485), however, think that Matthew is simply following LXX A for this change.

E. Hermeneutic Employed. If we could be confident that Zechariah was referring only to a Davidic king in OT times, then we would have another example of typology. However, to the extent that the shepherd and smitten one of chapters 11–12 informs our understanding of chapter 13, and given the eschatological context of chapters 12–14, it is hard to maintain that Zech. 13:7 was fulfilled, even partially, in any pre-Christian figure. Conversely, the cumulative portrait of chapters 11–13 goes far beyond either Zechariah himself or any merely human king, coalescing instead around the figure of Jesus as crucified Messiah. This is precisely the context in which Jesus refers to this Scripture, as he looks ahead to the scattering of the disciples when he is arrested—the first of the ineluctable succession of events that will lead to his execution. It would appear that direct, predictive prophecy has been fulfilled in a straightforward fashion. At the very least, Qumran testifies to "a broader eschatological reading in Matthew's day of which he could make apologetic use" (Keener 1999: 635). The twist in the NT is that the good shepherd who is rejected ultimately takes the punishment the bad shepherd deserves in order to bring about the eschatological transformation depicted throughout Zech. 9–14 (Boda 2004: 515).

F. Theological Use. Jesus is thus the Good Shepherd, not merely as the pastor of his flock, but as the ruler of his people. He is the messianic King who one day will avenge God's enemies and his own executioners, but for now he goes voluntarily to his death, a death that Matthew recognizes is a substitutionary atonement for the sins of the world (see esp. 20:28; 26:28). As a fulfillment of Scripture, though, it remains part of God's plan all along (Ham 2005: 83). In the process Israel is being purified, being transformed from a literal, largely monolithic ethnic group into the metaphorical, multicultural "Israel" that is the church (recall Matt. 21:43).

Matthew 26:36–56

This portion of Matt. 26 narrates events in the Garden of Gethsemane. As Jesus prays (26:38), the triple refrain of Ps. 42:5, 11; 43:5 appears to lie in the background: "Why are you downcast, O my soul? Why are you so disturbed within me? Put your hope in God, for I will yet praise him, my Savior and my God." A fainter echo of Jon. 4:9 may also be present. Yet another text that may have generated Jesus' wording is Ps. 116:4, with the psalmist's blunt call to God to save him from death (so Kiley [1986], who, however, attributes this link to the early church and not to Jesus himself). On submitting to God's will (26:39), compare the psalmist's will in Ps. 40:8; 143:10. Jesus' willing spirit may echo yet another psalm (51:12). Verse 42 may allude to Isa. 51:21–23, in which God finally takes away his cup of wrath from Israel (Davies and Allison 1988–1997: 3:499).

As the events are set in motion leading to Jesus' arrest, Judas' traitorous kiss (26:49) illustrates Prov. 27:6. Behind Jesus' remark that those who live by the sword will die by the sword (26:52) lies the principle of a life for a life, enunciated foundationally in Gen. 9:6. Jesus' language here may even more directly allude to Jer. 15:2, alluded to also in Rev. 13:10. On the possibility of Jesus calling on twelve legions of angels to help him (26:53), compare and contrast 2 Kings 6:17, in which Elijah told the kings to look and see the hills full of horses and chariots of fire all around them. The general reference to the fulfillment of the writings of the prophets in 26:56 suggests that Jesus has in mind a general theme found in several prophetic texts (as in Matt. 2:23). Most directly, the various Servant Songs come to mind, culminating with the servant's suffering depicted in Isa. 52:13–53:12.

Matthew 26:57–75

The closing verses of Matt. 26 contrast Jesus' hearing before the Sanhedrin (vv. 57–68) with Peter's denial (vv. 69–75). The false witnesses of 26:59 resemble those who attacked David in Ps. 27:12. Jesus' initial silence (26:63) may echo David's in Ps. 39:9. The Sanhedrin's verdict (26:65) is couched in language reminiscent of the Jewish leaders' outcry against Jeremiah in Jer. 26:7–11. Jesus' beating typologically alludes to Isa. 50:6. Peter's bitter weeping after his denials (26:75) may echo texts such as Isa. 22:4; 33:7 (Davies and Allison 1988–1997: 3:550).

26:64

A. NT Context. After Jesus' arrest in the Garden of Gethsemane, he is brought to Caiaphas, the high priest, for interrogation (26:57–62). Because Jesus remains silent while he is accosted with false accusations, Caiaphas finally charges him directly, under oath, to declare if he is the Christ, the Son of God (26:63). Jesus replies, "You said [it]"—a response that most likely was a veiled affirmative, somewhat equivalent to "That is your way of putting it" (see Catchpole 1970–1971). Jesus was the messianic Son of God, but not the kind of messiah that most of the Jews were looking for. But he continues his reply by quoting and combining portions of Dan. 7:13 and Ps. 110:1 in sandwich fashion (26:64). "The Son of Man" and "coming on the clouds of heaven" stem from the Daniel text. In between, Jesus inserts "seated at the right hand of power" from the psalm. This "Son of Man" saying, rather than the claim that he was some kind of messiah, is what would have led the high priest to tear his garments and proclaim that Jesus had blasphemed (26:65). Alleging messiahship was no capital offense; otherwise, the Jews could never have received a messiah! But claiming to be the exalted, heavenly Son of Man, one who was Lord and next to the Father himself in heaven, transgressed the boundaries of what most of the Jewish leaders deemed permissible for mere mortals (see Bock 1998). So the Sanhedrin condemned Jesus to die (26:66). Matthew is following Mark closely at this point (cf. Mark 14:62). Luke again abbreviates (Luke 22:69).

B. OT Context. For Dan. 7:13, see above under Matt. 24:30; for Ps. 110:1, under Matt. 22:44.

C. Use in Jewish Sources. Again, see above under Matt. 24:30; 22:44.

D. Textual Background. Matthew's translation of Jesus' words uses the identical excerpt of Dan. 7:13 ("the Son of Man . . . coming on the clouds of heaven") as in Matt. 24:30, despite the two parts of the quotation being separated by the insertion from Ps. 110:1. So again, see above under Matt. 24:30 for the textual background comparing this excerpt with the LXX and the MT. As there, Matthew has modified his Markan source slightly to conform more closely to the LXX. Specifically he has changed "with [*meta*] the clouds" to "on [*epi*] the clouds."

The use of Ps. 110:1 resides on the border between quotation and allusion. Given Jesus' use of the text as recently as Matt. 22:44, it is clear that he has this OT reference in mind with his expression "seated at the right hand of power." Matthew preserves the same five Greek words that Mark does but changes the order from *ek dexiōn kathēmenōn tēs dynameōs* to *kathēmenōn ek dexiōn tēs dynameōs*, a more natural word order in Greek (and one that corresponds to standard English word order as well). The LXX, like the MT, reads simply, "Sit at my right hand." The change in grammatical forms is necessitated by the context into which Jesus inserts the quotation. When the Jewish leaders see Christ coming on the clouds, he will already have been seated at God's right hand, in fulfillment of Yahweh's command to his Messiah in the psalm to sit in that honored location.

E. Hermeneutic Employed. As with the two previous uses of these Scriptures by themselves in Matthew, it appears here too that we can speak of direct predictive prophecy and its fulfillment. Jesus does not introduce his quotations with a formula that demonstrates that he is citing Scripture, but Matthew's readers will recognize these previously used references. The Sanhedrin, steeped in the Hebrew Scriptures, unquestionably would have recognized them. Jesus refers to a literal future time when the Jewish leaders will see him in his role as exalted, heavenly Son of Man. He will first be seated at the right hand of the Father and then come back to earth on the clouds at the end of the age. In the previous use of Ps. 110:1, Jesus asked how the Christ could be merely David's human descendant when David called him "Lord." There the focus was on the two "Lords"

in the declaration, "The Lord said to my Lord, 'Sit at my right hand . . .'" (Matt. 22:44). Here the focus is on the fact that the second Lord, the Messiah, does indeed sit next to God himself in his heavenly glory. Hagner (1995: 801) clarifies: "If not precisely claiming deity . . . Jesus was at least ranking himself with God in a unique status." Neither part of the verse, however, had been fulfilled, even partially, until Jesus was resurrected, ascended, and returned to his prior position of heavenly glory. In the previous use of Dan. 7:13, Jesus was referring to his parousia (Matt. 24:30), exactly as he is here. That event has not yet occurred even today.

F. Theological Use. Christology and eschatology continue to dominate. Jesus is the divine Son of Man, just as he is the divine Lord. Both concepts supplement and do not eradicate his messianic role. In conventional Jewish thinking, being a messiah did not necessarily mean that one was anything more than a great human king or military general. Even "son of God" in some texts was merely a synonym for "messiah" (see now esp. 4Q246 from the more recently translated Dead Sea Scrolls). Jesus adds a great deal more to the picture, and he does so by taking two OT texts that he considers to have overtones of exaltation and divinity and associates them with the role of messiah. As we have seen previously (p. 89), it is hard to know how much of this linkage may have already been made in certain strands of pre-Christian Jewish expectation and how much was created by Jesus. On either score, however, there is enough chutzpah in Jesus' pronouncements to explain his condemnation and crucifixion by those unprepared to believe his claims (see Linton 1961).

What is more, Jesus will return again, this time not to be judged but to judge, and to avenge all the injustices of history and vanquish his enemies. The idea that his parousia is Christ's invisible coming in judgment on Jerusalem in AD 70 is even less convincing here than it was with Matt. 24:30, since he is seated at the right hand of the Father *before* he comes on the clouds of heaven (or perhaps we are meant to see Jesus sitting and moving at the same time, if he is being pictured as coming in the divine "chariot"—akin to Ezekiel's vision of God in Ezek. 1 [see Evans 2001: 452]). He is not going into the presence of the Ancient of Days, as the Son of Man did in Dan. 7:13; rather, he is leaving God to return to earth. For Jesus to say, "from now on [*ap' arti*], you will see . . ." does not refer to one continuous vision from the time of his interrogation forward, but rather means simply "in the future" (Davies and Allison 1988–1997: 3:530–31). At the same time, the trial initiates decisive events of eschatological significance, and Jesus' exaltation will continue throughout the church age (Sabourin 1978: 359).

Matthew 27:1–10

After Jesus is delivered to Pilate (27:1–2), Judas regrets having betrayed his master (27:3–10).

27:9–10

A. NT Context. Perhaps the strangest fulfillment quotation in all of Matthew is this last one. Judas has just betrayed Jesus to the chief priests and elders in Jerusalem. He has suffered some kind of remorse but has not truly repented (the word in 27:3 is not the normal Greek word for "repentance" [*metanoeō*], but rather a milder verb meaning "to change one's mind, to feel regret" [*metamelomai*]). As a result, he returns to the temple, gives back the money he had been paid for his treachery, goes out, and hangs himself (27:3–5). He may have been following the model of Ahithophel in 2 Sam. 17:23. The Jewish leaders, according to their traditions, cannot put the thirty shekels back into their treasury, so they take the money to buy a nearby potter's field to use for burying foreigners (27:6–8). In this action, Matthew sees a fulfillment of Scripture, which he attributes to the prophet Jeremiah (27:9a).

The closest verbal parallels to the Scripture cited in 27:9b–10, however, appear in Zech. 11:12–13, with its references to thirty pieces of silver thrown to the potter in the house of the Lord. On the other hand, many commentators point to the fact that Jer. 32:6–9 describes Jeremiah buying a field, which he sells for seventeen shekels of silver. Rabbis at times would create a composite quotation of more than one Scripture but refer to only one of their sources by name, often the more obscure one (though sometimes also the more important one) to ensure that others would pick up the reference. So there is no problem by the standards of the day for Matthew to

refer to two texts like this and name only the more obscure prophetic source. In fact, this is precisely what Mark does in Mark 1:2, as he combines parts of Isa. 40:3 and Mal. 3:1 but cites only Isaiah by name (Davies and Allison 1988–1997: 3:569; for conflated quotations in the OT, see Gundry 1994: 557). But is Jer. 32 the passage (or the only passage) that Matthew has in mind? It may be that Jer. 19 offers a better cluster of images that Matthew may be citing, especially with its references to "the blood of the innocents" (27:4), the "potter" (27:1, 11), the renaming of a place in the Valley of Hinnom (27:6 [the traditional site of the Potter's Field]), violence (27:11), and the judgment and burial of the Jewish leaders by God (27:11) (see Moo 1983b; Conrad 1991; see also Brown 1994: 651). References to the house of the potter also appear in Jer. 18:2–3.

B. OT Context. Zechariah 11:4–17 begins with God calling the prophet to shepherd the flock marked out for slaughter (11:4–6). Zechariah does this, caring particularly for the oppressed of the flock (11:7) and getting rid of evil shepherds (11:8a). But the flock detests him, Zechariah grows weary of the opposition, and he finally decides to leave them to die. He breaks the two staffs that represented the covenant he had made with the people and the brotherhood between Israel and Judah (11:8b–11, 14). Verse 12 is thus dripping with irony when Zechariah tells his people to pay him if they think it best; but if not, they should just keep the money. They do pay him his wages, but 11:13 simply adds to the irony as Zechariah refers to the thirty shekels that he has received as a "handsome price," when in fact it was a comparatively paltry sum for the work he had done (McComiskey 1998: 1200). Although equivalent to the price of a slave in Exod. 21:32, as remuneration for a spiritual leader, thirty shekels was an insultingly low wage (Petersen 1995: 97). So Zechariah throws the pieces of silver back into the temple "to the potter." The potter may originally have been a temple functionary who dealt with donations of precious metal (Meyers and Meyers 1993: 276). The Lord then promises to raise up a new, wicked shepherd to give the ungrateful flock what they deserve (11:15–17).

Jeremiah 32 is the chapter in which Jeremiah buys a field near Jerusalem, despite the imminent destruction of the city and exile of the people, as a dramatic object lesson that one day the people of Israel will be restored to their land, making property deeds again valid and meaningful. This context seems more remote from the context in Matthew than either Zech. 11 or Jer. 19. Jeremiah 19 finds the Lord commanding the prophet to buy a clay jar from a potter and then to smash it, as a dramatic object lesson of the nation's coming judgment. This theme fits much better with Matthew's emphasis, especially as Jesus' crucifixion draws near, that the Jewish leaders who resist and condemn him are actually bringing God's judgment down on themselves and on their land.

C. Use in Jewish Sources. Neither the clusters of allusions in Jeremiah nor the more specific reference in Zechariah is discussed in extant pre-Christian Jewish sources. Later rabbis debated at length an allegorical interpretation of Zechariah's thirty pieces of silver, frequently suggesting that they stood for thirty righteous Jews or thirty commandments for Gentiles (Str-B 1:1030–31), but this discussion sheds no light on Matthew's use of the text.

D. Textual Background. The MT of Zech. 11:12–13 reads literally, "And I said to them, 'If [it is] good in your eyes, give my wages, and, if not, keep them.' And they weighed out my wages, thirty [shekels] of silver. And Yahweh said to me, 'Cast it to the potter, the lordly price at which I was paid off by them.' So I took the thirty [shekels] of silver and cast them in the house of Yahweh to the potter." A variant reading substitutes "treasury" for "potter." If Matthew knew this, it would afford another link with the events of Judas' betrayal, since the Jewish leaders refused to put the returned money into the treasury (see Hagner 1995: 813–14). The LXX translates 27:12 and 13b fairly literally but is more paraphrastic with 27:13a, notably substituting the potter's kiln for the potter himself. Matthew verbally parallels the LXX only for his first clause, "I took the thirty pieces of silver." Matthew's next clause, "the honorable price with which the sons of Israel valued me," is a summarizing paraphrase of 27:13b, closer to the Hebrew than to the LXX. Matthew's wording about giving the money for the field of the potter more resembles the imagery found in Jeremiah, as an allusion rather than a quotation, than anything in Zechariah. And it is possible that Matthew's final clause, "as the Lord commanded me," picks up language from Exod. 9:12 LXX (see further Archer and Chirichigno 1983: 161, 163).

E. Hermeneutic Employed. Clearly, Matthew is employing typology here rather than any kind of single or double fulfillment of actual predictive prophecy. The very fact that even after he has combined quotations and allusions to two or more OT texts, the fit with the actions of Judas and the Jewish leaders is still quite loose demonstrates that he is not inventing history to match prophecy. But there is enough "analogical correspondence" (recall above, p. 8) for him to be convinced that God is in fact sovereignly at work, even in the tragic events of Jesus' betrayal and Judas' death, just as he had been in the highly symbolic ministries of the prophets Zechariah and Jeremiah. No directly messianic motifs appear in either Zech. 11 or Jer. 19, but the quality of Israel's leadership, both good and bad, provides a unifying theme (R. L. Smith 1984: 272). If we combine that theme with the cluster of verbal parallels already discussed and Matthew's conviction that key events in salvation history all happen under the guiding hand of God's providence, we can understand why he uses the language of fulfillment here (see Carson [1984: 564], who finds the cluster of parallels "stunning"). Whitters (2006: 238) prefers to speak of Matthew's theological source rather than his literary one. Moreover, the language of the "potter" in Zechariah, the closer parallel to Matthew, undoubtedly brought to mind the more distant parallels in Jeremiah's texts that refer to potters—an example of the rabbinic practice of *gezerah shavah*, linking texts via common words (see Hagner 1995: 813).

F. Theological Use. Like the Jews who rejected Jeremiah's and Zechariah's prophecies, Judas and the temple establishment find themselves opposing God and under his judgment. Like Jeremiah and Zechariah, Jesus attempts to lead his people with a prophetic and pastoral ministry, but instead he ends up suffering innocently at their hands. Baldwin (1972: 184) summarizes the theology of Zechariah's text with words that could apply without a single change to the passage in Matthew: "Responsibility for human chaos lies squarely on human shoulders. God has offered men His shepherd, but they have rejected Him, to their own irreparable loss." But Ham (2005: 69) adds that the combination of words from Jeremiah and

Zechariah "attest that even the betrayal of Jesus by Judas and the rejection of Jesus by Israel's religious leaders take place according to the divine purpose." It is interesting that the noticeably different account of Judas' death in Acts 1:18–19 is nevertheless also interpreted as the typological fulfillment of prophecy, this time with reference to two psalms believed to be by David, who is describing his archenemies (Acts 1:20, citing Ps. 69:25; 109:8). Because money is paid to secure Jesus' death, Matthew may also be suggesting what Matt. 20:28 states more clearly: Jesus' death is a ransom, the price paid to secure a slave's freedom. That this "blood money" was subsequently used to buy a burial ground for foreigners may hint at what Matthew will explicitly highlight in his closing verses: Jesus' death makes salvation possible for all the peoples of the world, including the Gentiles, to whom the disciples are commanded to go and preach (28:18–20).

Matthew 27:11–44

Like the infancy narrative, Matthew's passion narrative contains an unusually intense cluster of uses of the OT. For a detailed list of possibilities for all four evangelists, of which only the most secure in Matthew are mentioned here, see Marcus 1995; for a full exegetical discussion, see Moo 1983a. But, whereas in chapters 1–2 there were five explicit fulfillment quotations, chapters 26–27 contain only one, and that describing Judas' (not Jesus') fate (Matt. 27:9–10). We have also seen one quotation introduced with "it stands written" (26:31), along with the composite quotation used by Jesus to reply to Caiaphas, without any introductory formula (26:64). Matthew 27 will include one more explicit quotation of the OT in v. 46, but it contains numerous allusions in which brief phrases verbally parallel the OT but not to the extent that we can confidently label them actual citations (on which, see Senior 1997). The boundaries between quotations and allusions, of course, were much more fluid in the ancient world, as we have already seen at numerous points in Matthew's Gospel, so there is a certain amount of arbitrariness in the assigning of various texts to the two different categories. What is consistently highlighted is Matthew's theme of God's

judgment on Israel, even as Israel thinks that it is judging Jesus (Knowles 1993: 52–81).

Jesus' silence when accused by the Jewish leaders (Matt. 27:12) and again when interrogated by Pilate (27:14) alludes to the behavior of the Suffering Servant in Isa. 53:7, who "did not open his mouth" but kept "silent" when oppressed, afflicted, and led to his slaughter (on which, see further under 12:17–21 above). Pilate probably was not conscious of imitating the OT in washing his hands to declare himself innocent of Jesus' blood, but Matthew may well have written his narrative in such a way as to allude to the psalmist's similar declaration in Ps. 26:6 and perhaps to echo the legislation of Deut. 21:6–9. The Jewish crowd's willingness to assume the responsibility for Christ's death (27:25), however, may well have consciously alluded to the Mosaic legislation that spoke of someone's blood being on a person's head (repeatedly in Lev. 20:9–16; cf. Ezek. 33:5; see Lovsky 1987).

Jesus' flogging (27:26) and subsequent physical abuse (27:29–30) surely alludes to Isaiah's Suffering Servant once more (see Isa. 50:6, in which the servant offers his back to be beaten and his face to be spat upon in a context of mockery). The wine mixed with gall that Jesus is offered to drink (27:34) almost certainly alludes to Ps. 69:21a ("they put gall in my food"), especially since Matt. 27:48 will allude to the second half of this verse. The practice of giving strong drink to the dying is in turn indebted to Prov. 31:6. Matthew 27:35 could almost be viewed as a quotation, since the Greek words for "they divided," "garments," and "lot" match the LXX of Ps. 21:19 (22:19 MT; 22:18 ET) exactly. At the very least, it is a clear allusion to a psalm about David's suffering almost to the point of death, which will be reused several more times in this chapter. Clearly, David is a natural OT figure to study for typological parallels to events in the life of Jesus, the Davidic messiah. John 19:24 describes the division of Jesus' clothes among the soldiers with a more detailed, explicit quotation of this same verse from the psalms. These apparently independent uses of the same text, coupled with this psalm's repeated use throughout the various Gospel passion narratives, could suggest the use of a collection of OT prooftexts by early Christians to explain Jesus' crucifixion (see Bruce 1983: 369).

Matthew may well have seen Jesus' death on a cross between two crucified insurrectionists as a typological equivalent to Isa. 53:12, in which the servant pours out his life even to death and is numbered among transgressors (Matt. 27:38). The bystanders' mockery as they "wag their heads" (27:39) employs the same Greek words for "wag" and "head" in different forms that are found in Ps. 21:8 LXX (22:8 MT; 22:7 ET), which again is about the mockery and insulting of David by his enemies. Psalm 109:25 and Lam. 2:15 use the same kind of expression in similar contexts. The same Greek words for "rescue" and "delight" appear in Ps. 21:9 LXX (22:9 MT; 22:8 ET) as in Matt. 27:43. Here, Jesus' taunters do seem to be quoting the psalm that many would have known well: "He had confidence in God; let him now rescue him if he delights in him." However, Matthew's Greek wording is not close enough to either the LXX or the MT to call it a true quotation. Still, it is more than allusion; perhaps "paraphrase" does best justice to the phenomenon. In any event, Matthew's typological use of Ps. 22 (21 LXX) clearly continues. Schweizer (1975: 511–12) notes that Matthew throughout his passion narrative depicts the crucifixion primarily in terms of mockery.

Matthew 27:45–66

The rest of Matt. 27 describes Jesus' death and burial. The preternatural darkness that envelopes Jesus' crucifixion (Matt. 27:45) reminds the reader of the plagues and apocalyptic portents in texts such as Exod. 10:22; Joel 2:10; Amos 8:9 (esp. with its reference to the sun going down at noon, precisely the "sixth hour" referred to here). The one direct quotation of the OT in this chapter comes in 27:46, on which, see below. The vinegar offered to Jesus in 27:48 alludes to Ps. 69:21b, just as the gall alluded to the first half of this verse. The rending of the temple veil (27:51) refers to one of two temple curtains that were modeled after the pattern of the tabernacle in Exod. 26:31–35 (for a survey of various early Christian interpretations, see de Jonge 1986). The resurrection of certain "saints" in 27:51–53 is clearly the oddest part of this chapter, but it builds on OT belief in the general resurrection of all people when the Messiah comes (see esp. Dan. 12:2; cf. Ezek. 37:12). Recall

also Zech. 14:4–5 with its great earthquake. What was unexpected was the death and resurrection of the Messiah in advance of the general resurrection and final judgment, but perhaps this handful of additional faithful people coming back to life was meant to further guarantee that Jesus' resurrection did in fact function as the "firstfruits" of many more to come (cf. 1 Cor. 15:20–22; see further Senior 1976).

Joseph of Arimathea's desire to bury Christ's body quickly (27:57–58) was based on the Mosaic legislation that the corpse of a capital offender hung on a tree should not be left there overnight lest it defile the land (Deut. 21:22–23). By Jesus' day, crucifixion—suspending a person from a wooden cross—was deemed equivalent to hanging on a tree, so the same legislation applied. This same Deuteronomic text also explains the scandal of the cross (cf. 1 Cor. 1:18); orthodox Jews would understand the crucifixion as demonstrating that Jesus was cursed by God (but see Gal. 3:13). Probably nothing short of bodily resurrection could have convinced Jewish followers of Jesus that this curse had been overcome! The wealthy Joseph's burial of Jesus' body in his own unused tomb provides one final allusion to the fate of Isaiah's Suffering Servant, who similarly was assigned a place "with the rich" (Isa. 53:9).

27:46

A. NT Context. As Jesus nears his death, suffering in physical agony on the cross (27:45–49), he apparently senses the spiritual absence of his heavenly Father as well. The only statement from the cross that Matthew records, out of seven found in the four canonical Gospels, is this loud cry. Jesus would have uttered it in Aramaic, and apparently it became significant enough in the history of the early church for Matthew to have preserved it and reported it in Greek transliteration before offering his actual translation. Jesus' undoubtedly slurred, stammering speech, due to his intense suffering, made some in the crowd watching think he was calling for "Elijah," whose name would have been pronounced very similar to *Ēli* ("my God"). Thus they wonder if Elijah, in his role as messianic precursor (recall Mal. 4:5), will come at the last second to rescue Jesus before he dies. But of course, Elijah does not come, because the crowd has not understood Jesus' cry. Matthew is following Mark throughout this section (for the parallel to the quotation, see Mark 15:34; Mark's *Elōi* transliterates the Hebrew, perhaps conforming more to the psalm itself; Matthew's *Ēli* follows the Aramaic that Jesus may have actually spoken).

B. OT Context. This verse appears at the beginning of Psalm 22 (21 LXX), which is attributed to David in its superscription. The first eighteen verses depict a plight so dire (22:1–13) that the psalmist despairs of life itself (22:14–15); an unidentified group of enemies has surrounded him and attacked him (22:16–18). As a devout believer in God, the writer "is someone being torn apart because he cannot deny the reality of faith, nor can he reconcile it with the savage reality of life as he now experiences" it (Davidson 1998: 79). Weiser (1962: 221) adds that this is not a reproach leveled at God, but rather "the psalmist is terrified when he becomes conscious of the agonizing mystery of the hidden God which presents itself to him." He thus appeals to Yahweh to deliver him (22:19–21) and, in anticipation of that deliverance, promises to proclaim God's mighty acts in the congregation of his people when he is restored to them (22:22–25). Indeed, so great will be this deliverance that all the earth will turn to the Lord and worship him (22:27–31).

Arguably, this remarkable psalm could simply reflect the hyperbolic language of David in dire straits. However, it contains an astonishing number of close parallels to the events of Jesus' crucifixion: a cry of abandonment (22:1–2), despising and mocking (22:6–7), the taunt that the Lord should deliver the one who trusts in him (22:8), a near-death experience described as being poured out like water with all his bones out of joint, his heart melted like wax, and his strength dissipated (22:14–15). Furthermore, he is surrounded by wicked onlookers (22:16a) who pierce his hands and feet (22:16b) and divide his garments by lot (22:18). Not surprisingly, commentators throughout church history have wondered whether a larger, messianic meaning was intended by the psalmist from the outset. The end of the psalm scarcely alleviates this tension, since the universal response and acclamation of Yahweh that results far exceeds that experienced by any Davidic king. Kidner (1973: 105) comments: "No incident recorded of David can begin to account for this. . . . Whatever the initial stimulus, the language

of the psalm defies a naturalistic explanation; the best account is in the terms used by Peter" in Acts 2:30–31. For rich theological reflection on Ps. 22 overall, see esp. Goldingay 2006: 340–43.

C. Use in Jewish Sources. The only extant pre-Christian Jewish reference to Ps. 22:1 appears to be the allusion in *T. Sol.* 6:8, in which Satan says, "If anyone adjures me with the oath (called) 'the Elo-i,' a great name for [God's] power, I disappear." The much later Targum to Ps. 22:1, of course, uses the Aramaic, and thus it matches Matthew's *Ēli* for "my God," rather than Mark's Hebrew *Elōi*. But, as noted above, this may reflect Jesus' actual wording; it is impossible to know whether Jesus would have quoted the verse in the Hebrew form of the Jewish Scriptures or in the Aramaic vernacular of common speech. Much later, in medieval Judaism, the *Midrash Teḥillim* makes the cry of Ps. 22:1 a central prayer of Esther, showing how a different speaker or narrator could reappropriate the text in a new but equally fitting context (Menn 2000).

D. Textual Background. The MT reads, "My God, my God, why have you forsaken me?" The LXX translates this literally, but adds "you protected me" after the invocation and before the psalmist's question. Mark includes only the portion of the text found in the MT, transliterates an Aramaic paraphrase, but follows the LXX verbatim for the Greek translation of Jesus' words, except for a slight alteration in the expression for "why." Matthew mostly follows Mark but changes the spelling of "my God" in transliteration and changes the Greek translation of the same expression from the nominative used for direct address to the actual vocative (*thee* rather than *ho theos*).

E. Hermeneutic Employed. There is no formal introduction to this quotation. We need speak only of a typological use of Scripture by Jesus (and Matthew), but the psalm does seem to transcend a naturalistic explanation. Just as Jesus would have learned to pray and sing many of the psalms in his private and corporate devotional life, so also it is natural for him to quote one here in a situation so parallel to that of his kingly ancestor. What is more controversial is the question of whether Jesus, in uttering this cry of dereliction (or Matthew in recording it), was thereby alluding to the entire psalm, following the common rabbinic practice of citing just the beginning of a given text when a larger, entire passage was in view. This would enable one to interpret Jesus' words as anticipating the same victory described in 27:19–31 even as he uttered his cry of abandonment (so, cautiously, Hill 1972: 355; Keener 1999: 685). However, neither Jesus nor Matthew seems to have employed this technique elsewhere, and nothing in the immediate context of Matt. 27 suggests it (though of course Jesus elsewhere repeatedly predicted his resurrection, which in fact does occur). So it is probably safer not to assume that Jesus' cry of abandonment was simultaneously a cry of faith. Jesus really did sense the absence of his Father, and this is precisely the moment when we should expect him, in his humanity, to be *least* confident of his future (see Davies and Allison 1988–1997: 3:624–25). Readers of the Gospels who cannot accept this concept probably reflect an unwitting Docetism—the heresy that Christ was not fully human. Indeed, if one wants to do more with Matt. 27:46 than hear a cry of derelictions, one is better off looking to other uses of Ps. 22:27–31 in the Gospels as a sign of God's judgment (see Schmidt 1994).

F. Theological Use. Throughout church history, Jesus' cry of derelictions has been identified as the moment of divine abandonment. Jesus, who died to atone vicariously for the sins of humanity, recognized at this point in his suffering that he no longer was experiencing the communion with his heavenly Father that had characterized his life. Understandably, theologians have debated all kinds of questions that arise from this affirmation, involving the relationship between Father and Son and between Christ's divine and human natures, but this is about as far as the text of Matthew by itself can take us. For helpful theological reflections on the theme of Jesus' abandonment by God within the context of Matthew, see Gerhardsson 1969; the rest of the NT presents numerous passages that arguably reflect on this moment in Christ's agony (e.g., Rom. 3:25; 2 Cor. 5:21; Col. 1:20; Heb. 5:7–10; 7:27; 9:11–14). Jesus, as the sin-bearing sacrifice, must endure the temporary abandonment of the Father. Separation from God is horrible enough for any creature; "when it concerns one who is uniquely the Son of God . . . , it is impossible to assess what this may have meant to Jesus. This is one of the most impenetrable mysteries of the entire Gospel narrative" (Hagner 1995: 844–45). At the same time, Jesus still cries out to

the one he no longer senses. In our worst moments of feeling abandoned by God we can do no less (Luz 2005: 551).

Matthew 28:1–20

The concept of bodily resurrection draws its clearest OT background from Dan. 12:2. As already noted, though, what was distinctive about Jesus' resurrection was that it occurred apart from the general resurrection of all people at the end of human history (see above, p. 80). Davies and Allison (1988–1997: 3:666) note of Matt. 28:3, "The description of the angel's garment draws upon the theophany of Dan 7.9 . . . , and Dan 10.6 could be the source of the description of the angel's countenance." The angelophany of 28:4 creates trembling, possibly echoing Dan. 10:7.

Jesus' closing "Great Commission" of his apostles seems to allude to Dan. 7:14. Jesus, whose favorite title for himself throughout the Gospel has been "Son of Man," is given all authority on heaven and earth (Matt. 28:18), just as the Son of Man in Daniel's vision received an identical universal authority. It is even possible that the trinitarian formula in 28:19 reflects a modification of the triad of Ancient of Days (God the Father), Son of Man (God the Son), and angels as God's spiritual servants as the implied agents of the Son of Man being led into God's presence (and thus functionally analogous to the Holy Spirit), also found in Dan. 7:13–14 (see Viviano 1998). The climax of Matthew's Gospel may also conclude his Mosaic typology. Both Jesus and Moses end their lives on mountains. God also commissions Joshua, through Moses, just as Jesus commissions the apostles here (see Deut. 31:14–15, 23; cf. Josh. 1:1–9; see Davies and Allison 1988–1997: 3:679–80, 686). The language of "everything I have commanded you" occurs frequently in the OT (see esp. Exod. 7:2; Deut. 1:3; Josh. 22:2; Judg. 13:14; Jer. 1:7). The Messiah, whom Matthew introduces as the son of Abraham and David (1:1), is also a new Moses. But more importantly, in a way true of no OT character save Yahweh himself, he is God with us (28:20). Matthew's presentation of Jesus is appropriately completed.

Bibliography

Abegg, M., Jr., P. Flint, and E. Ulrich, trans. 1999. *The Dead Sea Scrolls Bible.* San Francisco: HarperSanFrancisco.

Alexander, T. D., D. W. Baker, and B. K. Waltke. 1988. *Obadiah, Jonah, Micah.* TOTC. Downers Grove, IL: InterVarsity.

Allen, L. C. 1976. *The Books of Joel, Obadiah, Jonah, and Micah.* NICOT. Grand Rapids: Eerdmans.

———. 1983. *Psalms 101–150.* WBC 21. Waco: Word.

Allen, W. C. 1907. *A Critical and Exegetical Commentary on the Gospel according to St. Matthew.* ICC. Edinburgh: T&T Clark.

Allison, D. C., Jr. 1983. "Matt. 23:39 = Luke 13:35b as a Conditional Prophecy." *JSNT* 18: 75–84.

———. 1984. "Elijah Must Come First." *JBL* 103: 257.

———. 1992. "The Baptism of Jesus and a New Dead Sea Scroll." *BAR* 18 (2): 58–60.

———. 1993. *The New Moses: A Matthean Typology.* Minneapolis: Fortress.

———. 1999. "Jesus and the Victory of Apocalyptic." Pages 126–41 in *Jesus and the Restoration of Israel: A Critical Assessment of N. T. Wright's "Jesus and the Victory of God."* Edited by C. C. Newman. Downers Grove, IL: InterVarsity.

Andersen, F. I., and D. N. Freedman. 1980. *Hosea.* AB 24. Garden City, NY: Doubleday.

———. 2000. *Micah.* AB 24E. New York: Doubleday.

Archer, G. L., and G. C. Chirichigno. 1983. *Old Testament Quotations in the New Testament.* Chicago: Moody.

Atkinson, D. 1981. *To Have and to Hold: The Marriage Covenant and the Discipline of Divorce.* Grand Rapids: Eerdmans.

Aus, R. D. 2004. *Matthew 1–2 and the Virginal Conception.* Lanham, MD: University Press of America.

Bacon, B. W. 1918. "The Five Books of Matthew against the Jews." *The Expositor* 15: 56–66.

Bahr, G. J. 1970. "The Seder of Passover and the Eucharistic Words." *NovT* 12: 181–202.

Bailey, J. L. 1993. "Sermon on the Mount: Model for Community." *Currents in Theology and Mission* 20: 85–94.

Bailey, J. N. 2000. "Vowing Away the Fifth Commandment: Matthew 15:3–6 // Mark 7:9–13." *ResQ* 42: 193–209.

Bailey, K. E. 1992. *Finding the Lost: Cultural Keys to Luke 15.* St. Louis: Concordia.

Baldwin, J. G. 1972. *Haggai, Zechariah, Malachi.* TOTC. Downers Grove, IL: InterVarsity.

———. 1978. *Daniel.* TOTC. Downers Grove, IL: InterVarsity.

Baltzer, K. 2001. *Deutero-Isaiah: A Commentary on Isaiah 40–55.* Translated by M. Kohl. Hermeneia. Philadelphia: Fortress.

Banks, R. 1974. "Matthew's Understanding of the Law: Authenticity and Interpretation in Matthew 5:17–20." *JBL* 93: 226–42.

Barnett, P. W. 1977. "Who Were the 'Biastai' (Matthew 11:12–13)?" *RTR* 36: 65–70.

Barrett, C. K. 1978. "The House of Prayer and the Den of Thieves." Pages 13–20 in *Jesus und Paulus: Festschrift für Werner Georg Kümmel zum 70. Geburtstag.* Edited by E. E. Ellis and E. Grässer. Göttingen: Vandenhoeck & Ruprecht.

Bascom, R. A. 1996. "Adaptable for Translation: Deuteronomy 6:5 in the Synoptic Gospels and Beyond." Pages 166–83 in *A Gift of God in Due Season: Essays on Scripture and Community in Honor of James A. Sanders.* Edited by R. D. Weis and D. M. Carr. JSOTSup 225. Sheffield: Sheffield Academic Press.

Bateman, H. W., IV. 1992. "Psalm 110:1 and the New Testament." *BSac* 149: 438–53.

Bauckham, R. 1980. "The Delay of the Parousia." *TynBul* 31: 3–36.

———. 1995. "The Messianic Interpretation of Isa. 10:34 in the Dead Sea Scrolls, 2 Baruch and the Preaching of John the Baptist." *DSD* 2: 202–16.

Bauer, D. R. 1989. *The Structure of Matthew's Gospel: A Study in Literary Design.* JSNTSup 31. Sheffield: Almond.

Beale, G. K. 1991. "Isaiah vi 9–13: A Retributive Taunt against Idolatry." *VT* 41: 257–78.

Beare, F. W. 1981. *The Gospel according to Matthew.* San Francisco: Harper & Row.

Beasley-Murray, G. R. 1993. *Jesus and the Last Days: The Interpretation of the Olivet Discourse.* Peabody, MA: Hendrickson.

Beaton, R. 1999. "Messiah and Justice: A Key to Matthew's Use of Isaiah 42.1–4?" *JSNT* 75: 5–23.

———. 2002. *Isaiah's Christ in Matthew's Gospel.* SNTSMS 123. Cambridge: Cambridge University Press.

———. 2005. "Isaiah in Matthew's Gospel." Pages 63–78 in *Isaiah in the New Testament.* Edited by S. Moyise and M. J. J. Menken. London: T&T Clark.

Becking, B. 1994. "'A Voice Was Heard [sic] in Ramah': Some Remarks on Structure and Meaning of Jeremiah 31,15–17." *BZ* 38: 229–42.

Beecher, W. J. 1905. *The Prophets and the Promise.* New York: Crowell.

Berger, K. 1996. "Jesus als Nasoräer/Naziräer." *NovT* 38: 323–35.

Bergey, R. L. 1997. "The Rhetorical Role of Reiteration in the Suffering Servant Poem (Isa 52:13–53:12)." *JETS* 40: 177–88.

Betz, H. D. 1995. *The Sermon on the Mount: A Commentary on the Sermon on the Mount, Including the Sermon on the Plain (Matthew 5:3–7:27 and Luke 6:20–49).* Hermeneia. Minneapolis: Fortress.

Betz, O. 1998. "Jesus and Isaiah 53." Pages 70–87 in *Jesus and the Suffering Servant: Isaiah 53 and Christian Origins.* Edited by W. H. Bellinger Jr. and W. R. Farmer. Harrisburg, PA: Trinity Press International.

Black, M. 1971. "The Christological Use of the Old Testament in the New Testament." *NTS* 18: 1–14.

Blank, S. H. 1937–1938. "The Death of Zechariah in Rabbinic Literature." *HUCA* 12–13: 327–46.

Blenkinsopp, J. 2000. *Isaiah 1–39.* AB 19. New York: Doubleday.

———. 2002. *Isaiah 40–55.* AB 19a. New York: Doubleday.

Blocher, H. 1975. *Songs of the Servant.* London: Inter-Varsity.

Blomberg, C. L. 1986. "The Miracles as Parables." Pages 327–60 in *The Miracles of Jesus.* Vol. 6 of *Gospel Perspectives.* Edited by D. Wenham and C. Blomberg. Sheffield: JSOT Press.

———. 1987. "Elijah, Election, and the Use of Malachi in the New Testament." *CTR* 2 (1): 104.

———. 1988. "The Temptations of Jesus." *ISBE* 4:784–86.

———. 1990a. *Interpreting the Parables.* Downers Grove, IL: InterVarsity.

———. 1990b. "Marriage, Divorce, Remarriage and Celibacy: An Exegesis of Matthew 19:3–12." *TJ* 11: 161–96.

———. 1991a. "The Liberation of Illegitimacy: Women and Rulers in Matthew 1–2." *BTB* 21: 145–50.

———. 1991b. "The Sabbath as Fulfilled in Christ: A Response to S. Bacchiocchi and J. Primus." Pages 122–28 in *The Sabbath in Jewish and Christian Traditions.* Edited by T. C. Eskenazi, D. Harrington, and W. Shea. New York: Crossroad.

———. 1992. *Matthew.* NAC 22. Nashville: Broadman.

———. 1994. *1 Corinthians.* NIVAC. Grand Rapids: Zondervan.

———. 1997. *Jesus and the Gospels: An Introduction and Survey.* Nashville: Broadman & Holman.

———. 1999. *Neither Poverty nor Riches: A Biblical Theology of Possessions.* NSBT 7. Leicester: Inter-Varsity.

———. 2002a. *The Historical Reliability of John's Gospel: Issues and Commentary.* Downers Grove, IL: InterVarsity.

———. 2002b. "Interpreting Old Testament Prophetic Literature in Matthew: Double Fulfillment." *TJ* 23: 17–33.

———. 2003. "Messiah in the New Testament." Pages 111–41 in *Israel's Messiah in the Bible and the Dead Sea Scrolls.* Edited by R. S. Hess and M. D. Carroll. Grand Rapids: Baker Academic.

———. 2005. *Contagious Holiness: Jesus' Meals with Sinners.* NSBT 13. Leicester: Inter-Varsity.

———. 2006. "On Building and Breaking Barriers: Forgiveness, Salvation and Christian Counseling with Special Reference to Matthew 18:15–35." *JPC* 25: 137–54.

Bock, D. L. 1998. *Blasphemy and Exaltation in Judaism: A Philological-Historical Study of the Key Jewish Themes Impacting Mark 14:61–64.* WUNT 2/106. Tübingen: Mohr Siebeck.

Boda, M. J. 2004. *Haggai, Zechariah.* NIVAC. Grand Rapids: Zondervan.

Bolt, P. G. 1994. "What Were the Sadducees Reading? An Enquiry into the Literary Background of Mark 12:18–23." *TynBul* 45: 369–94.

Booth, R. P. 1986. *Jesus and the Laws of Purity: Tradition History and Legal History in Mark 7.* JSNTSup 13. Sheffield: JSOT Press.

Borg, M. 1984. *Conflict, Holiness, and Politics in the Teaching of Jesus.* SBEC 5. New York: Mellen.

Bratcher, R. G. 1981. *A Translator's Guide to the Gospel of Matthew.* HT. New York: United Bible Societies.

Brodie, T. 1992. "Fish, Temple Tithe, and Remission: The God-Based Generosity of Deuteronomy 14–15 as One Component of Matt 17:22–18:35." *RB* 99: 697–718.

Broer, I. 1994. "Das Ius Talionis im Neuen Testament." *NTS* 40: 1–21.

Brooke, G. J. 1994. "Isaiah 40:3 and the Wilderness Community." Pages 117–32 in *New Qumran Texts and Studies: Proceedings of the First Meeting of the International Organization for Qumran Studies, Paris, 1992.* Edited by G. J. Brooke and F. García Martínez. STDJ 15. Leiden: Brill.

———. 1995. "4Q500 1 and the Use of Scripture in the Parable of the Vineyard." *DSD* 2: 268–94.

Brooks, O. S. 1998. "The Function of the Double Love Command in Matthew 22:34–40." *AUSS* 36: 7–22.

Brown, R. E. 1993. *The Birth of the Messiah: A Commentary on the Gospels of Matthew and Luke.* Rev. ed. ABRL. New York: Doubleday.

———. 1994. *The Death of the Messiah: From Gethsemane to the Grave; A Commentary on the Passion Narratives in the Four Gospels.* 2 vols. ABRL. New York: Doubleday, 1994.

Brown-Gutoff, S. E. 1991. "The Voice of Rachel in Jeremiah 31: A Calling to 'Something New.'" *USQR* 45: 185.

Broyles, C. C. 1999. *Psalms.* NIBCOT 11. Peabody, MA: Hendrickson.

Bruce, F. F. 1983. *The Gospel of John.* Grand Rapids: Eerdmans.

Bruckner, J. K. 2004. *Jonah, Nahum, Habakkuk, Zephaniah.* NIVAC. Grand Rapids: Zondervan.

Bruner, F. D. 1987. *The Christbook: Matthew 1–12.* Waco: Word.

———. 1990. *The Churchbook: Matthew 13–28.* Dallas: Word.

Burkett, D. 1999. *The Son of Man Debate: A History and Evaluation.* SNTSMS 107. Cambridge: Cambridge University Press.

Byargeon, R. W. 1998. "Echoes of Wisdom in the Lord's Prayer (Matt 6:9–13)." *JETS* 41: 353–65.

Cahill, M. 1995. "Not a 'Cornerstone': Translating Ps 118,22 in the Jewish and Christian Scriptures." *RB* 106: 345–57.

Cameron, P. S. 1984. *Violence and the Kingdom: The Interpretation of Matthew 11:12.* ANTJ 5. Frankfurt: Peter Lang.

Capes, D. B. 1999. "Intertextual Echoes in the Matthean Baptismal Narrative." *BBR* 9: 37–49.

Caragounis, C. C. 1986. *The Son of Man: Vision and Interpretation.* WUNT 38. Tübingen: Mohr Siebeck.

Carroll, R. P. 1986. *Jeremiah.* OTL. Philadelphia: Westminster.

Carson, D. A., ed. 1982. *From Sabbath to Lord's Day: A Biblical, Historical, and Theological Investigation.* Grand Rapids: Zondervan.

———. 1984. "Matthew." Pages 3–599 in vol. 8 of *The Expositor's Bible Commentary.* Edited by F. E. Gaebelein. Grand Rapids: Zondervan.

Carson, D. A., P. T. O'Brien, and M. A. Seifrid, eds. 2001. *The Complexities of Second Temple Judaism.* Vol. 1 of *Justification and Variegated Nomism: A Fresh Appraisal of Paul and Second Temple Judaism.* WUNT 2/140. Tübingen: Mohr Siebeck.

Carter, W. 2000. "Evoking Isaiah: Matthean Soteriology and an Intertextual Reading of Isaiah 7–9 and Matthew 1:23 and 4:15–16." *JBL* 119: 503–20.

Casey, M. 1979. *Son of Man: The Interpretation and Influence of Daniel 7.* London: SPCK.

Cassuto, U. 1967. *A Commentary on the Book of Exodus.* Translated by I. Abrahams. Jerusalem: Magnes.

Catchpole, D. R. 1970–1971. "The Answer of Jesus to Caiaphas (Matt. XXVI.64)." *NTS* 17: 213–26.

Cathcart, K. J., and R. P. Gordon, trans. and eds. 1989. *The Targum of the Minor Prophets.* ArBib 14. Wilmington, DE: Glazier.

Ceresko, A. R. 1994. "The Rhetorical Strategy of the Fourth Servant Song (Isaiah 52:13–53:12): Poetry and the Exodus–New Exodus." *CBQ* 56: 42–55.

Charette, B. 1992. "'To Proclaim Liberty to the Captives': Matthew 11.28–30 in the Light of Old Testament Prophetic Expectation." *NTS* 38: 290–97.

Charlesworth, J. H., ed. 1983–1985. *The Old Testament Pseudepigrapha.* 2 vols. Garden City, NY: Doubleday.

———. 1985. *The Old Testament Pseudepigrapha and the New Testament: Prolegomena for the Study of Christian Origins.* SNTSMS 54. Cambridge: Cambridge University Press.

Childs, B. S. 1974. *The Book of Exodus.* OTL. Philadelphia: Westminster.

———. 2001. *Isaiah.* OTL. Louisville: Westminster John Knox.

Chilton, B. D. 1984. *A Galilean Rabbi and His Bible: Jesus' Use of the Interpreted Scripture of His Time.* GNS 8. Wilmington, DE: Glazier.

———, trans. and ed. 1987. *The Isaiah Targum.* ArBib 11. Wilmington, DE: Glazier.

Chow, S. 1995. *The Sign of Jonah Reconsidered: A Study of Its Meaning in the Gospel Traditions.* ConBNT 27. Stockholm: Almqvist & Wiksell.

Christensen, D. L. 2001. *Deuteronomy 1–21:9.* Rev. ed. WBC 6a. Nashville: Nelson.

Clarke, E. G., trans. and ed. 1998. *Targum Pseudo-Jonathan: Deuteronomy.* ArBib 5B. Collegeville, MN: Liturgical Press.

Coats, G. W. 1972. "Widows' Rights: A Crux in the Structure of Genesis 38." *CBQ* 34: 461–66.

Cohen, A., ed. 1948. *The Twelve Prophets.* London: Soncino.

Cohn-Sherbok, D. M. 1979. "An Analysis of Jesus' Arguments concerning the Plucking of Grain on the Sabbath." *JSNT* 2: 31–41.

———. 1981. "Jesus' Defence of the Resurrection of the Dead." *JSNT* 11: 64–73.

Cole, D. P. 1994. "Archaeology and the Messiah Oracles of Isaiah 9–11." Pages 53–69 in *Scripture and Other Artifacts: Essays on the Bible and Archaeology in Honor of Philip J. King*. Edited by M. D. Coogan, J. C. Exum, and L. E. Stager. Louisville: Westminster John Knox.

Collins, J. J. 1992. "The Son of Man in First-Century Judaism." *NTS* 38: 448–66.

———. 1993. *Daniel*. Hermeneia. Minneapolis: Fortress.

Conrad, A. 1991. "The Fate of Judas: Matthew 27:3–10." *TJT* 7: 158–68.

Cook, S. L. 1993. "The Metamorphosis of a Shepherd: The Tradition-History of Zechariah 11:17 and 13:7–9." *CBQ* 55: 453–66.

Cope, O. L. 1976. *A Scribe Trained for the Kingdom of Heaven*. CBQMS 5. Washington: Catholic Biblical Association of America.

Craigie, P. C. 1976. *The Book of Deuteronomy*. NICOT. Grand Rapids: Eerdmans.

———. 1983. *Psalms 1–50*. WBC 19. Waco: Word.

Cranfield, C. E. B. 1977. *The Gospel according to St Mark*. CGTC. Rev. ed. Cambridge: Cambridge University Press.

Dahlberg, B. T. 1975. "The Typological Use of Jeremiah 1:4–19 in Matthew 16:13–23." *JBL* 94: 73–80.

Dahood, M. 1965. *Psalms 1–50*. AB 16. Garden City, NY: Doubleday.

———. 1970. *Psalms 101–150, with an Appendix, "The Grammar of the Psalms."* AB 17A. Garden City, NY: Doubleday.

Davidson, R. 1998. *The Vitality of Worship: A Commentary on the Book of Psalms*. Grand Rapids: Eerdmans.

Davies, G. I. 1992. *Hosea*. NCBC. Grand Rapids: Eerdmans.

Davies, W. D. 1964. *The Setting of the Sermon on the Mount*. Cambridge: Cambridge University Press.

Davies, W. D., and D. C. Allison Jr. 1988–1997. *A Critical and Exegetical Commentary on the Gospel according to Saint Matthew*. 3 vols. ICC. Edinburgh: T&T Clark.

Davis, B. C. 2000. "Is Psalm 110 a Messianic Psalm?" *BSac* 157: 160–73.

Davis, J. F. 2005. *Lex Talionis in Early Judaism and the Exhortation of Jesus in Matthew 5.38–12*. JSNTSup 281. London and New York: T&T Clark.

de Jonge, M. 1986. "Matthew 27:51 in Early Christian Exegesis." *HTR* 79: 67–79.

de Moor, J. C. 1998. "The Targumic Background of Mark 12:1–12: The Parable of the Wicked Tenants." *JSJ* 29: 63–80.

Delitzsch, F. 1984. *Psalms*. Translated by J. Martin. 3 vols. in 1. Grand Rapids: Eerdmans.

Derrett, J. D. M. 1980. "ἮΣΑΝ ΓΑΡ ἈΛΙΕΙΣ (Mk 1.16): Jesus' Fishermen and the Parable of the Net." *NovT* 22: 125–31.

———. 1981. "Mt 23,8–10 a Midrash on Is 54,13 and Jer 31,33–34." *Bib* 62: 372–86.

———. 1986. "Receptacles and Tombs (Mt 23,24–30)." *ZNW* 77: 255–66.

Deutsch, C. 1987. *Hidden Wisdom and the Easy Yoke: Wisdom, Torah and Discipleship in Matthew 11.25–30*. JSNTSup 18. Sheffield: JSOT Press.

Dillon, R. J. 1966. "Towards a Tradition-History of the Parables of the True Israel (Matthew 21:33–22:14)." *Bib* 47: 1–42.

Doeve, J. W. 1955. "Purification du temple et desséchement du figuier." *NTS* 1: 297–308.

Donahue, J. R. 1971. "Tax Collectors and Sinners." *CBQ* 33: 39–61.

Donaldson, T. L. 1985. *Jesus on the Mountain: A Study in Matthean Theology*. JSNTSup 8. Sheffield: JSOT Press.

Dorsey, D. 1991. "The Law of Moses and the Christian: A Compromise." *JETS* 34: 321–34.

Duff, P. B. 1992. "The March of the Divine Warrior and the Advent of the Greco-Roman King." *JBL* 111: 55–71.

Dunn, J. D. G. 1983. "The Messianic Secret in Mark." Pages 116–31 in *The Messianic Secret*. Edited by C. M. Tuckett. IRT 1. Philadelphia: Fortress.

Enns, P. 2000. *Exodus*. NIVAC. Grand Rapids: Zondervan.

Eppstein, V. 1964. "The Historicity of the Gospel Account of the Cleansing of the Temple." *ZNW* 55: 42–58.

Erickson, R. J. 1996. "Divine Injustice? Matthew's Narrative Strategy and the Slaughter of the Innocents (Matthew 2.13–23)." *JSNT* 64: 5–27.

———. 2000. "Joseph and the Birth of Isaac in Matthew 1." *BBR* 10: 35–51.

Evans, C. A. 1985. "On the Isaianic Background of the Sower Parable." *CBQ* 47: 464–68.

———. 1989. *To See and Not Perceive: Isaiah 6.9–10 in Early Jewish and Christian Interpretation*. JSOTSup 64. Sheffield: JSOT Press.

———. 1992. "Predictions of the Destruction of the Herodian Temple in the Pseudepigrapha, Qumran Scrolls, and Related Texts." *JSP* 10: 105–17.

———. 1993. "Jesus and the 'Cave of Robbers': Toward a Jewish Context for the Temple Action." *BBR* 3: 93–110.

———. 2001. *Mark 8:27–16:20*. WBC 34B. Nashville: Nelson.

Farla, P. 1989. "'The Two Shall Become One Flesh': Gen. 1.27 and 2.24 in the New Testament Marriage Texts." Pages 67–82 in *Intertextuality in Biblical Writings: Essays in Honour of Bas van Iersel*. Edited by S. Draisma. Kampen: Kok.

Feinberg, C. L. 1977. *The Twelve Minor Prophets*. Chicago: Moody.

Fitzmyer, J. A. 1971a. "The Aramaic Qorban Inscription from Jebel Hallet et-Turi and Mk 7:11/Mt 15:5." Pages 93–100 in *Essays on the Semitic Background of the New Testament*. London: Chapman.

———. 1971b. "The Son of David Tradition and Mt. 22.41–46 and Parallels." Pages 113–26 in *Essays on the Semitic Background of the New Testament*. London: Chapman.

———. 1987. "Aramaic Evidence Affecting the Interpretation of Hosanna in the New Testament." Pages 110–18 in *Tradition and Interpretation in the New Testament: Essays in Honor of E. Earle Ellis for His 60th Birthday*. Edited by G. F. Hawthorne and O. Betz. Grand Rapids: Eerdmans.

Foster, P. 2003. "Why Did Matthew Get the *Shema* Wrong? A Study of Matthew 22:37." *JBL* 122: 309–22.

France, R. T. 1971. *Jesus and the Old Testament: His Application of Old Testament Passages to Himself and His Mission*. London: Tyndale.

———. 1981. "The Formula-Quotations of Matthew 2 and the Problem of Communication." *NTS* 27: 243–44.

———. 1985. *The Gospel according to Matthew*. TNTC. Grand Rapids: Eerdmans.

Fuller, R. H. 1989. "The Decalogue in the New Testament." *Int* 43: 243–55.

Funk, R. W. 1973. "The Looking-Glass Tree Is for the Birds: Ezekiel 17:22–24; Mark 4:30–32." *Int* 27: 3–9.

Furnish, V. P. 1972. *The Love Command in the New Testament.* Nashville: Abingdon.

García Martínez, F. 1989. "La reprensión fraterna en Qumrán y Mt 18,15–17." *FN* 2: 23–40.

García Martínez, F., and E. J. C. Tigchelaar, eds. 1997. *The Dead Sea Scrolls Study Edition.* 2 vols. Grand Rapids: Eerdmans.

Garland, D. E. 1979. *The Intention of Matthew 23.* NovTSup 52. Leiden: Brill.

Garrett, D. A. 1997. *Hosea, Joel.* NAC 19A. Nashville: Broadman & Holman.

Gerhardsson, B. 1966. *The Testing of God's Son (Matt. 4:1–11 & Par.): An Analysis of an Early Christian Midrash.* ConBNT 2. Lund: Gleerup.

———. 1969. "Jésus livré et abandonné d'après la passion selon Saint Matthieu." *RB* 76: 206–27.

———. 1976. "The Hermeneutic Program in Matthew 22:37–40." Pages 129–50 in *Jews, Greeks, and Christians: Religious Cultures in Late Antiquity: Essays in Honor of William David Davies.* Edited by R. Hamerton-Kelly and R. Scroggs. SJLA 21. Leiden: Brill.

Gibbs, J. A. 2002. "Israel Standing with Israel: The Baptism of Jesus in Matthew's Gospel (Matt 3:13–17)." *CBQ* 64:511–26.

Gibson, J. B. 1995. *The Temptations of Jesus in Early Christianity.* JSNTSup 112. Sheffield: Sheffield Academic Press.

Ginzberg, L. 1976. *An Unknown Jewish Sect.* Moreshet 1. New York: Jewish Theological Seminary.

Glasson, T. F. 1964. "The Ensign of the Son of Man (Matt. XXIV.30)." *JTS* 15: 299–300.

Gnuse, R. 1990. "Dream Genre in the Matthean Infancy Narratives." *NovT* 32: 97–120.

Goldingay, J. 1989. *Daniel.* WBC 30. Dallas: Word.

———. 2001. *Isaiah.* NIBCOT 3. Peabody, MA: Hendrickson.

———. 2005. *The Message of Isaiah 40–55: A Literary and Theological Commentary.* London and New York: T&T Clark.

———. 2006. *Psalms 1–41.* BCOTWP. Grand Rapids: Baker Academic.

Goodwin, M. J. 2005. "Hosea and 'the Son of the Living God' in Matthew 16:16b." *CBQ* 67: 265–83.

Goppelt, L. 1982. *Typos: The Typological Interpretation of the Old Testament in the New.* Translated by D. H. Madvig. Grand Rapids: Eerdmans.

Grelot, P. 1986. "Michée 7:6 dans les évangiles et dans la littérature rabbinique." *Bib* 67: 363–77.

Grogan, G. 1986. "Isaiah." Pages 1–354 in vol. 6 of *The Expositor's Bible Commentary.* Edited by F. E. Gaebelein. Grand Rapids: Zondervan.

Guelich, R. 1982. *The Sermon on the Mount: A Foundation for Understanding.* Waco: Word.

Gundry, R. H. 1967. *The Use of the Old Testament in St. Matthew's Gospel: With Special Reference to the Messianic Hope.* NovTSup 18. Leiden: Brill.

———. 1993. *Mark: A Commentary on His Apology for the Cross.* Grand Rapids: Eerdmans.

———. 1994. *Matthew: A Commentary on His Handbook for a Mixed Church under Persecution.* Rev. ed. Grand Rapids: Eerdmans.

Haacker, K. 1977. "Der Rechtsatz Jesu zum Thema Ehebruch." *BZ* 21: 113–16.

Hagner, D. A. 1993. *Matthew 1–13.* WBC 33A. Dallas: Word.

———. 1995. *Matthew 14–28.* WBC 33B. Dallas: Word.

———. 1997. "Balancing the Old and the New: The Law of Moses in Matthew and Paul." *Int* 51: 20–30.

Ham, C. 2000. "The Last Supper in Matthew." *BBR* 10: 53–69.

———. 2005. *The Coming King and the Rejected Shepherd: Matthew's Reading of Zechariah's Messianic Hope.* Sheffield: Sheffield Phoenix.

Harrison, R. K. 1973. *Jeremiah and Lamentations.* TOTC. London: Tyndale.

Harvey, A. E. 1990. *Strenuous Commands: The Ethic of Jesus.* Philadelphia: Trinity Press International.

Hay, D. M. 1973. *Glory at the Right Hand: Psalm 110 in Early Christianity.* SBLMS 18. Nashville: Abingdon.

Hayward, R., trans. and ed. 1986. *The Targum of Jeremiah.* ArBib 12. Wilmington, DE: Glazier.

Healey, J. F. 1989. "Models of Behavior: Matt 6:26 (// Luke 12:24) and Prov. 6:6–8." *JBL* 108: 497–98.

Heater, H., Jr. 1983. "Matthew 2:6 and Its OT Sources." *JETS* 26: 395–97.

Heil, C. 1997. "Die Rezeption Micha 7,6 LXX in Q und Lukas." *ZNW* 88: 212–22.

Hengel, M. 1995. *Studies in Early Christology.* Edinburgh: T&T Clark.

———. 2005. "The Effective History of Isaiah 53 in the Pre-Christian Period." Pages 75–146 in *The Suffering Servant: Isaiah 53 in Jewish and Christian Sources.* Translated by D. P. Bailey. Edited by B. Janowski and P. Stuhlmacher. Grand Rapids: Eerdmans.

Hill, D. 1972. *The Gospel of Matthew.* NCB. London: Oliphants.

———. 1977. "On the Use and Meaning of Hosea VI.6 in Matthew's Gospel." *NTS* 24: 107–19.

Hindson, E. E. 1978. *Isaiah's Immanuel: A Sign of His Times or the Sign of the Ages?* ILPTBTS. Philadelphia: Presbyterian & Reformed.

Holladay, W. L. 1986. *Jeremiah 1–25.* Hermeneia. Philadelphia: Fortress.

Horbury, W. 1985. "The Messianic Associations of 'The Son of Man.'" *JTS* 36: 34–55.

Horne, E. H. 1998. "The Parable of the Tenants as Indictment." *JSNT* 71: 111–16.

Horsley, R. A. 1986. "Ethics and Exegesis: 'Love Your Enemies' and the Doctrine of Non-Violence." *JAAR* 54: 3–31.

Hossfeld, F.-L. and E. Zenger. 2005. *Psalms 2.* Hermeneia. Translated by L. M. Maloney. Minneapolis: Fortress.

Howard, T. L. 1986. "The Use of Hosea 11:1 in Matthew 2:15: An Alternative Solution." *BSac* 143: 314–28.

Hubbard, R. L., Jr. 1988. *The Book of Ruth.* NICOT. Grand Rapids: Eerdmans.

Hugenberger, G. P. 1995. "The Servant of the Lord in the 'Servant Songs' of Isaiah: A Second Moses Figure." Pages 105–40 in *The Lord's Anointed: Interpretation of Old Testament Messianic Texts.* Edited by P. E. Satterthwaite, R. S. Hess, and G. J. Wenham. THS. Grand Rapids: Baker Academic.

Hurtado, L. 1988. *One God, One Lord: Early Christian Devotion and Ancient Jewish Monotheism.* Philadelphia: Fortress.

Instone-Brewer, D. 1998. "Deuteronomy 24:1–4 and the Origin of the Jewish Divorce Certificate." *JJS* 49: 230–43.

———. 2003. "The Two Asses of Zechariah 9:9 in Matthew 21." *TynBul* 54: 87–98.

Janzen, J. G. 1985. "Resurrection and Hermeneutics: On Exodus 3.6 in Mark 12.26." *JSNT* 23: 43–58.

Jeremias, J. 1967. "Παῖς θεοῦ." *TDNT* 5:697–98.

———. 1972. *The Parables of Jesus*. Third ed. Translated by S. H. Hooke. Philadelphia: Westminster.

Johnson, E. E. 1992. "Hermeneutical Principles and the Interpretation of Psalm 110." *BSac* 149: 428–37.

Johnston, R. M. 1978. "Parabolic Interpretations Attributed to Tannaim." PhD diss., Hartford Seminary.

Johnston, R. M., and H. K. McArthur. 1989. *They Also Taught in Parables: Rabbinic Parables from the First Centuries of the Christian Era*. Grand Rapids: Academie Books.

Kaiser, W. C., Jr. 1983. *Toward Old Testament Ethics*. Grand Rapids: Zondervan.

———. 1985. *The Uses of the Old Testament in the New Testament*. Chicago: Moody.

Keener, C. S. 1991. *And Marries Another: Divorce and Remarriage in the Teaching of the New Testament*. Peabody, MA: Hendrickson.

———. 1999. *Commentary on the Gospel of Matthew*. Grand Rapids: Eerdmans.

Keil, C. F. 1984. "Zechariah." Pages 217–421 in vol. 2 of *The Minor Prophets*. Translated by J. Martin. Grand Rapids: Eerdmans.

Keown, G. L., P. J. Scalise, and T. G. Smothers. 1995. *Jeremiah 26–52*. WBC 27. Dallas: Word.

Kidner, D. 1973. *Psalms 1–72: An Introduction and Commentary on Books I and II of the Psalms*. TOTC. London: Inter-Varsity.

———. 1975. *Psalms 73–150: A Commentary on Books III–V of the Psalms*. TOTC. London: Inter-Varsity.

Kiley, M. 1986. "'Lord, Save My Life' (Ps. 116:4 as Generative Text for Jesus' Gethsemane Prayer [Mark 14:36a])." *CBQ* 48: 655–59.

Kilgallen, J. J. 1986. "The Sadducees and Resurrection from the Dead: Luke 20:27–40." *Bib* 67: 478–95.

Kim, H. C. P. 1999. "An Intertextual Reading of 'A Crushed Reed' and 'A Dim Wick' in Isaiah 42.3." *JSOT* 83: 113–24.

Kim, S. 1985. *The "Son of Man" as the Son of God*. Grand Rapids: Eerdmans.

———. 1987. "Jesus—The Son of God, the Stone, Son of Man, and the Servant: The Role of Zechariah in the Self-Identification of Jesus." Pages 138–40 in *Tradition and Interpretation in the New Testament: Essays in Honor of E. Earle Ellis for His 60th Birthday*. Edited by G. F. Hawthorne and O. Betz. Grand Rapids: Eerdmans.

Kingsbury, J. D. 1975. *Matthew: Structure, Christology, Kingdom*. Philadelphia: Fortress.

Kinman, B. 1994. "Jesus' 'Triumphal Entry' in the Light of Pilate's." *NTS* 40: 442–48.

Kirchevel, G. D. 1994. "He That Cometh in Mark 1:7 and Matthew 24:30." *BBR* 4: 105–11.

Klein, M. L., trans. and ed. 1980. *The Fragment-Targums of the Pentateuch according to Their Extant Sources*. Vol. 2. AnBib 76. Rome: Biblical Institute Press.

Klein, W. W., C. L. Blomberg, and R. L. Hubbard Jr. 2004. Rev. ed. *Introduction to Biblical Interpretation*. Dallas: Word.

Knowles, M. 1993. *Jeremiah in Matthew's Gospel: Rejected Prophet Motif in Matthean Redaction*. JSOTSup 68. Sheffield: JSOT Press.

Kraus, H.-J. 1988. *Psalms 1–59*. Translated by H. C. Oswald. CC. Philadelphia: Fortress.

———. 1989. *Psalms 60–150*. Translated by H. C. Oswald. CC. Philadelphia: Fortress.

Kupp, D. D. 1996. *Matthew's Emmanuel: Divine Presence and God's People in the First Gospel*. SNTSMS 90. Cambridge: Cambridge University Press.

Kynes, W. 1991. *A Christology of Solidarity: Jesus as the Representative of His People in Matthew*. Lanham, MD: University Press of America.

Laansma, J. 1997. *"I Will Give You Rest": The "Rest" Motif in the New Testament with Special Reference to Mt 11 and Heb 3–4*. WUNT 2/98. Tübingen: Mohr Siebeck.

Lachs, S. T. 1987. *A Rabbinic Commentary on the New Testament: The Gospels of Matthew, Mark and Luke*. Hoboken, NJ: KTAV.

Lacocque, A. 1979. *The Book of Daniel*. Translated by D. Pellauer. Atlanta: John Knox.

Lambrecht, J. 1992. *Out of the Treasure: The Parables in the Gospel of Matthew*. LTPM 10. Leuven: Leuven University Press.

Lane, W. L. 1974. *The Gospel according to Mark*. NICNT. Grand Rapids: Eerdmans.

Laney, J. C. 1985. *A Guide to Church Discipline*. Minneapolis: Bethany.

Levine, E. 1976. "The Sabbath Controversy according to Matthew." *NTS* 22: 480–83.

Lindars, B. 1961. *New Testament Apologetic: The Doctrinal Significance of the Old Testament Quotations*. Philadelphia: Westminster.

———. 1983. *Jesus, Son of Man: A Fresh Examination of the Son of Man Sayings in the Gospels in the Light of Recent Research*. Grand Rapids: Eerdmans.

Linton, O. 1961. "The Trial of Jesus and the Interpretation of Psalm 110." *NTS* 7: 258–62.

Longenecker, R. N. 1999. *Biblical Exegesis in the Apostolic Period*. Rev. ed. Grand Rapids: Eerdmans.

Longman, T. 1999. *Daniel*. NIVAC. Grand Rapids: Zondervan.

Lovsky, F. 1987. "Comment comprend 'Son sang sur nous et nos enfants'?" *ETR* 62: 343–62.

Luck, W. F. 1987. *Divorce and Remarriage: Recovering the Biblical View*. San Francisco: Harper & Row.

Lust, J. 1997. "Mic 5,1–3 in Qumran and in the New Testament and Messianism in the Septuagint." Pages 65–88 in *The Scriptures in the Gospels*. Edited by C. M. Tuckett. BETL 131. Leuven: Leuven University Press.

Luz, U. 1989. *Matthew 1–7: A Commentary*. Translated by W. C. Linss. Minneapolis: Augsburg.

———. 2001. *Matthew 8–20*. Translated by H. Koester. Hermeneia. Minneapolis: Fortress.

———. 2005. *Matthew 21–28*. Translated by J. E. Crouch. Hermeneia. Minneapolis: Fortress.

Lybaek, L. 1997. "Matthew's Use of Hosea 6,6 in the Context of the Sabbath Controversies." Pages 491–99 in *The Scriptures in the Gospels*. Edited by C. M. Tuckett. BETL 131. Leuven: Leuven University Press.

Macintosh, A. A. 1997. *A Critical and Exegetical Commentary on Hosea*. ICC. Edinburgh: T&T Clark.

Maier, G. 1985. "The Church in the Gospel of Matthew: Hermeneutical Analysis of the Current Debate." Pages 45–63 in *Biblical Interpretation and the Church: The Problem of Contextualization*. Edited by D. A. Carson. Nashville: Nelson.

Manor, D. W. 1984. "A Brief History of Levirate Marriage as It Relates to the Bible." *ResQ* 27: 129–42.

Marcus, J. 1988. "The Gates of Hades and the Keys of the Kingdom (Matt 16:18–19)." *CBQ* 50: 443–55.

———. 1995. "The Old Testament and the Death of Jesus: The Role of Scripture in the Gospel Passion Narratives." Pages 205–33 in *The Death of Jesus in Early Christianity*. Edited by J. T. Carroll and J. B. Green. Peabody, MA: Hendrickson.

Marshall, I. H. 1978. *The Gospel of Luke*. NIGTC. Grand Rapids: Eerdmans.

———. 1980. *Last Supper and Lord's Supper*. Grand Rapids: Eerdmans.

Masson, J. 1982. *Jésus, fils de David, dans les genealogies de saint Matthieu et de saint Luc*. Paris: Tequi.

Mays, J. L. 1988. "Psalm 118 in the Light of Canonical Analysis." Pages 299–311 in *Canon, Theology and Old Testament Interpretation: Essays in Honor of Brevard S. Childs*. Edited by G. M. Tucker, D. L. Petersen, and R. R. Wilson. Philadelphia: Fortress.

———. 1994. *Psalms*. IBC. Louisville: John Knox.

McCane, B. R. 1990. "'Let the Dead Bury Their Own Dead': Secondary Burial and Matt 8:21–22." *HTR* 83: 31–43.

McCartney, D., and P. Enns. 2001. "Matthew and Hosea: A Response to John Sailhamer." *WTJ* 63: 97–105.

McComiskey, T. E. 1985. "Micah." Pages 393–445 in vol. 7 of *The Expositor's Bible Commentary*. Edited by F. E. Gaebelein. Grand Rapids: Zondervan.

———. 1998. "Zechariah." Pages 1003–1244 in vol. 3 of *The Minor Prophets: An Exegetical and Expository Commentary*. Edited by T. E. McComiskey. Grand Rapids: Baker Academic.

McConville, J. G. 2002. *Deuteronomy*. ApOTC. Leicester: Apollos.

McKane, W. 1986. *A Critical and Exegetical Commentary on Jeremiah 1–25*. ICC. Edinburgh: T&T Clark.

McLaughlin, J. L. 1994. "Their Hearts Were Hardened: The Use of Isaiah 6,9–10 in the Book of Isaiah." *Bib* 75: 1–25.

McMillion, P. 2001. "Psalm 78: Teaching the Next Generation." *ResQ* 43: 219–28.

McNamara, M., trans. and ed. 1992. *Targum Neofiti 1: Genesis*. ArBib 1A. Collegeville, MN: Liturgical Press.

Meier, J. P. 1976. *Law and History in Matthew's Gospel: A Redactional Study of Mt. 5:17–48*. AnBib 71. Rome: Biblical Institute Press.

Menken, M. J. J. 1984. "The References to Jeremiah in the Gospel according to Matthew." *ETL* 60: 5–24.

———. 2004a. *Matthew's Bible: The Old Testament Text of the Evangelist*. BETL 173. Leuven: Leuven University Press.

———. 2004b. "The Psalms in Matthew's Gospel." Pages 61–82 in *The Psalms in the New Testament*. Edited by Steve Moyise and Maarten J. J. Menken. London and New York: T&T Clark.

Menn, E. M. 2000. "No Ordinary Lament: Relecture and the Identity of the Distressed in Psalm 22." *HTR* 93: 301–41.

Merrill, E. H. 1994. *Deuteronomy*. NAC 4. Nashville: Broadman & Holman.

Metzger, B. M., and R. E. Murphy, eds. 1991. *The New Oxford Annotated Bible, with the Apocryphal/Deuterocanonical Books*. New York: Oxford University Press.

Meyer, B. F. 1979. *The Aims of Jesus*. London: SCM.

Meyers, C. L. 2005. *Exodus*. NCBC. Cambridge: Cambridge University Press.

Meyers, C. L., and E. M. Meyers. 1993. *Zechariah 9–14*. AB 25C. New York: Doubleday.

Milgrom, J. 2000. *Leviticus 17–22*. AB 3A. New York: Doubleday.

Miller, S. R. 1994. *Daniel*. NAC 18. Nashville: Broadman & Holman.

Moloney, F. J. 1981. "The Re-interpretation of Psalm VIII and the Son of Man Debate." *NTS* 27: 656–72.

Moo, D. J. 1983a. *The Old Testament in the Gospel Passion Narratives*. Sheffield: Almond.

———. 1983b. "Tradition and Old Testament in Matt. 27:3–10." Pages 157–75 in *Studies in Midrash and Historiography*. Vol. 3 of *Gospel Perspectives*. Edited by R. T. France and D. Wenham. Sheffield: JSOT Press.

———. 1984. "Jesus and the Authority of the Mosaic Law." *JSNT* 20: 3–49.

———. 1988. "Divine Healing in the Health and Wealth Gospel." *TJ* 9: 191–209.

———. 1992. "Law." *DJG*: 450–61.

Moore, W. E. 1989. "Violence to the Kingdom: Josephus and the Syrian Churches." *ExpTim* 100: 174–77.

Moses, A. D. A. 1996. *Matthew's Transfiguration Story and Jewish-Christian Controversy*. JSOTSup 122. Sheffield: Sheffield Academic Press.

Motyer, J. A. 1993. *The Prophecy of Isaiah*. Leicester: Inter-Varsity.

———. 1999. *Isaiah*. TOTC 18. Downers Grove, IL: InterVarsity.

Mounce, R. H. 1991. *Matthew*. NIBCNT. Peabody, MA: Hendrickson.

Mueller, J. B. 1980. "The Temple Scroll and the Gospel Divorce Texts." *RevQ* 10: 247–56.

Nelson, R. D. 2002. *Deuteronomy*. OTL. Louisville: Westminster John Knox.

Neudecker, R. 1992. "'And You Shall Love Your Neighbor as Yourself—I Am the Lord' (Lev. 19:18) in Jewish Interpretation." *Bib* 73: 496–517.

Neusner, J. 1989. "Money-Changers in the Temple: The Mishnah's Explanation." *NTS* 35: 287–90.

Newman, C. C., ed. 1999. *Jesus and the Restoration of Israel: A Critical Assessment of N. T. Wright's Jesus and the Victory of God*. Downers Grove, IL: InterVarsity.

Neyrey, J. H. 1982. "The Thematic Use of Isaiah 42,1–4 in Matthew 12." *Bib* 63: 457–73.

Nolan, B. M. 1979. *The Royal Son of God: The Christology of Matthew 1–2 in the Setting of the Gospel*. OBO 23. Fribourg: Éditions Universitaires.

Nolland, J. 1989. *Luke 1–9:20*. WBC 35A. Dallas: Word.

———. 2005. *The Gospel of Matthew*. NIGTC. Grand Rapids: Eerdmans.

Olson, D. C. 2005. "Matthew 22:1–14 as Midrash." *CBQ* 67:435–53.

Ortlund, R. C., Jr. 1996. *Whoredom: God's Unfaithful Wife in Biblical Theology*. NSBT 2. Leicester: Apollos.

Oswalt, J. N. 1986–1998. *The Book of Isaiah*. 2 vols. NICOT. Grand Rapids: Eerdmans.

Overman, J. A. 1990. *Matthew's Gospel and Formative Judaism: The Social World of the Matthean Community*. Minneapolis: Fortress.

Page, S. H. T. 1985. "The Suffering Servant between the Testaments." *NTS* 31: 481–97.

Park, E. C. 1995. *The Mission Discourse in Matthew's Interpretation*. WUNT 81. Tübingen: Mohr Siebeck.

Patte, D. 1987. *The Gospel according to Matthew: A Structural Commentary*. Philadelphia: Fortress.

Perkins, L. 1998. "'Greater than Solomon'/Matt 12:42." *TJ* 19: 207–17.

Perkins, P. 1982. *Love Commands in the New Testament*. New York: Paulist Press.

Pesch, R. 1994. "'He Will Be Called a Nazorean': Messianic Exegesis in Matthew 1–2." Pages 129–78 in *The Gospels and the Scriptures of Israel*. Edited by C. A. Evans and W. R. Stegner. JSNTSup 104. Sheffield: Sheffield Academic Press.

Petersen, D. L. 1995. *Zechariah 9–14 and Malachi*. OTL. Louisville: Westminster John Knox.

Petrotta, A. J. 1985. "A Closer Look at Matthew 2:6 and OT Sources." *JETS* 28: 47–52.

———. 1990. "An Even Closer Look at Matthew 2:6 and Its OT Sources." *JETS* 33: 311–15.

Petuchowski, J., and M. Brocke, eds. 1978. *The Lord's Prayer and Jewish Liturgy*. London: Burns & Oates.

Phillips, E. A. 2004. "The Tilted Balance: Early Rabbinic Perceptions of God's Justice." *BBR* 14: 223–40.

Philonenko, M. 1992. "La troisième demande du 'Notre Père' et l'hymne de Nabuchodonoser." *RHPR* 72: 23–31.

Piper, John. 1979. *"Love Your Enemies": Jesus' Love Command in the Synoptic Gospels and in Early Christian Paraenesis; A History of the Tradition and Interpretation of Its Uses*. SNTSMS 38. Cambridge: Cambridge University Press.

Plummer, A. 1909. *An Exegetical Commentary on the Gospel according to St. Matthew*. London: Stock.

Poirier, J. C. 2000. "The Interiority of True Religion in Mark 7,6–8: With a Note in Pap. Egerton 2." *ZNW* 91: 180–91.

Porteous, N. 1979. *Daniel*. OTL. Philadelphia: Westminster.

Porter, S. E. 1988. "Vague Verbs, Periphrastics, and Matt 16:19." *FN* 1: 155–73.

———. 1999. "Resurrection, the Greeks and the New Testament." Pages 52–81 in *Resurrection*. Edited by S. E. Porter, M. A. Hayes, and D. Tombs. JSNTSup 186. Sheffield: Sheffield Academic Press.

Powell, M. A. 1995. "Do and Keep What Moses Says." *JBL* 114: 419–35.

Reiser, M. 2001. "Love of Enemies in the Context of Antiquity." *NTS* 47: 411–27.

Reymond, R. L. 1989. "Who Is the ʿLMH of Isaiah 7:14?" *Presbyterion* 15: 1–15.

Ridderbos, H. N. 1987. *Matthew*. Translated by R. Togtman. Bible Student's Commentary. Grand Rapids: Zondervan.

Rooker, M. F. 2004. "The Best-Known Verse in Leviticus." *Faith and Mission* 21(2): 3–16.

Roth, C. 1960. "The Cleansing of the Temple and Zechariah XIV 21." *NovT* 4: 174–81.

Ruger, H. P. 1981. "ΝΑΖΑΡΕΘ/ΝΑΖΑΡΑ ΝΑΖΑΡΗΝΟΣ/ΝΑΖΩ-ΡΑΙΟΣ." *ZNW* 72: 257–63.

Ruzer, S. 1996. "The Technique of Composite Citation in the Sermon on the Mount (Matt 5:21–22, 33–37)." *RB* 103: 65–76.

Sabourin, L. 1978. *L'Évangile selon Saint Matthieu et ses principaux parallèles*. Rome: Biblical Institute Press.

Sailhamer, J. H. 2001. "Hosea 11:1 and Matthew 2:15." *WTJ* 63: 87–96.

Saldarini, A. J. 1994. *Matthew's Christian-Jewish Community*. CSHJ. Chicago: University of Chicago Press.

Sanders, E. P. 1977. *Paul and Palestinian Judaism*. Philadelphia: Fortress.

———. 1985. *Jesus and Judaism*. Philadelphia: Fortress.

Sanders, J. A. 1987. "A New Testament Hermeneutic Fabric: Psalm 118 in the Entrance Narrative." Pages 177–90 in *Early Jewish and Christian Exegesis: Studies in Memory of William Hugh Brownlee*. Edited by C. A. Evans and W. F. Stinespring. Homage 10. Atlanta: Scholars Press.

———. 1994. "Ναζωραῖος in Matthew 2.23." Pages 116–28 in *The Gospels and the Scriptures of Israel*. Edited by C. A. Evans and W. R. Stegner. JSNTSup 104. Sheffield: Sheffield Academic Press.

Sarna, N. 1991. *Exodus*. JPSTC. Philadelphia: Jewish Publication Society.

Schaberg, J. 1985. "Daniel 7,12 and the New Testament Passion-Resurrection Predictions." *NTS* 31: 208–22.

Schibler, D. 1995. "Messianism and Messianic Prophecy in Isaiah 1–12 and 28–33." Pages 87–104 in *The Lord's Anointed: Interpretation of Old Testament Messianic Texts*. Edited by P. E. Satterthwaite, R. S. Hess, and G. J. Wenham. THS. Grand Rapids: Baker Academic.

Schmidt, T. E. 1994. "Cry of Dereliction or Cry of Judgment? Mark 15:34 in Context." *BBR* 4: 145–53.

Schweizer, E. 1975. *The Good News according to Matthew*. Translated by D. E. Green. Richmond: John Knox.

Senior, D. 1976. "The Death of Jesus and the Resurrection of the Holy Ones (Mt 27:51–53)." *CBQ* 38: 312–29.

———. 1997. "The Lure of the Formula Quotations: Re-assessing Matthew's Use of the Old Testament with the Passion Narrative as Test Case." Pages 89–115 in *The Scriptures in the Gospels*. Edited by C. M. Tuckett. BETL 131. Leuven: Leuven University Press.

Seow, C. L. 2003. *Daniel*. WestBC. Louisville: Westminster John Knox.

Shemesh, Y. 2005. "Punishment of the Offending Organ in Biblical Literature." *VT* 55: 343–65.

Sire, J. W. 1980. *Scripture Twisting: 20 Ways the Cults Misread the Bible*. Downers Grove, IL: InterVarsity.

Slater, T. B. 1995. "One Like a Son of Man in First-Century CE Judaism." *NTS* 41: 183–98.

Smillie, G. R. 2005. "Isaiah 42:1–4 in Its Rhetorical Context." *BSac* 162: 50–65.

Smith, J. M. P. 1912. *A Critical and Exegetical Commentary on the Book of Malachi*. ICC. Edinburgh: T&T Clark.

Smith, R. L. 1984. *Micah–Malachi*. WBC 32. Waco: Word.

Snodgrass, K. 1980. "Streams of Tradition Emerging from Isaiah 40:1–5 and Their Adaptation in the New Testament." *JSNT* 8: 24–45.

———. 1983. *The Parable of the Wicked Tenants: An Inquiry into Parable Interpretation*. WUNT 27. Tübingen: Mohr Siebeck.

———. 2001. "The Use of the Old Testament in the New." Pages 209–29 in *Interpreting the New Testament: Essays on Methods and Issues*. Edited by D. A. Black and D. S. Dockery. Nashville: Broadman & Holman.

Soarés Prabhu, G. M. 1976. *The Formula Quotations in the Infancy Narrative of Matthew: An Enquiry into the Tradition History of Mt 1–2*. AnBib 63. Rome: Biblical Institute Press.

Sorg, T. 1975. "ῥακά." *NIDNTT* 1:417–18.

Stassen, G. 1992. *Just Peacemaking: Transforming Initiatives for Justice and Peace*. Louisville: Westminster John Knox.

Stendahl, K. 1954. *The School of St. Matthew and Its Use of the Old Testament*. ASNU 20. Lund: Gleerup.

———. 1960. "Quis et Unde: An Analysis of Matthew 1–2." Pages 94–105 in *Judentum, Urchristentum, Kirche: Festschrift für Joachim Jeremias*. Edited by W. Eltester. BZNW 26. Berlin: Töpelman.

Stern, J. B. 1966. "Jesus' Citation of Dt 6,5 and Lev 19,18 in the Light of Jewish Tradition." *CBQ* 28: 312–16.

Stoutenburg, D. 1996. *With One Voice/B'qol Echad: The Sermon on the Mount and Rabbinic Literature*. San Francisco: International Scholars Publications.

Stuart, D. 1998. "Malachi." Pages 1245–1396 in vol. 3 of *The Minor Prophets: An Exegetical and Expository Commentary*. Edited by T. E. McComiskey. Grand Rapids: Baker Academic.

———. 2006. *Exodus*. NAC 2. Nashville: Broadman and Holman.

Sugirtharajah, R. S. 1990. "'For You Always Have the Poor with You': An Example of Hermeneutics of Suspicion." *AJT* 4: 102–7.

Swetnam, J. 1985. "No Sign of Jonah." *Bib* 66: 126–30.

Syrén, R. 1989. "Targum Isaiah 52:13–53:12 and Christian Interpretation." *JJS* 40: 201–12.

Tannehill, R. C. 1970. "The 'Focal Instance' as a Form of New Testament Speech: A Study of Matthew 5:39b–42." *JR* 50: 372–85.

Taylor, J. E. 1997. *The Immerser: John the Baptist within Second Temple Judaism*. SHJ. Grand Rapids: Eerdmans.

Telford, W. R. 1980. *The Barren Temple and the Withered Fig Tree: A Redaction-Critical Analysis of the Cursing of the Fig-Tree Pericope in Mark's Gospel and Its Relation to the Cleansing of the Temple Tradition*. JSNTSup 1. Sheffield: JSOT Press.

Terrien, S. L. 2003. *The Psalms: Strophic Structure and Theological Commentary*. ECC. Grand Rapids: Eerdmans.

Theiss, N. 1994. "The Passover Feast of the New Covenant." *Int* 48: 17–35.

Theissen, G. 1983. *The Miracle Stories of the Early Christian Tradition*. Translated by F. McDonagh. Edited by J. Riches. Philadelphia: Fortress.

———. 1991. *The Gospels in Context: Social and Political History in the Synoptic Tradition*. Translated by L. M. Maloney. Minneapolis: Fortress.

Thompson, J. A. 1980. *The Book of Jeremiah*. NICOT. Grand Rapids: Eerdmans.

Thompson, W. G. 1970. *Matthew's Advice to a Divided Community: Mt. 17, 22–18, 35*. AnBib 44. Rome: Biblical Institute Press.

Tigay, J. H. 1996. *Deuteronomy*. JPSTC. Philadelphia: Jewish Publication Society.

Trautmann, M. 1980. *Zeichenhafte Handlungen Jesu: Ein Beitrag zur Frage nach dem geschichtlichen Jesus*. FB 37. Würzburg: Echter.

Turner, D. L. 1989. "The Structure and Sequence of Matthew 24:1–21: Interaction with Evangelical Treatments." *GTJ* 10: 3–27.

van Segbroeck, F. 1965. "Le scandale de l'incroyance: La signification de Mt. xiii, 35." *ETL* 41: 344–72.

Verhey, A. 1984. *The Great Reversal: Ethics and the New Testament*. Grand Rapids: Eerdmans.

Vermes, G. 1973. *Jesus the Jew: A Historian's Reading of the Gospels*. London: Collins.

Verseput, D. 1986. *The Rejection of the Humble Messianic King: A Study of the Composition of Matthew 11–12*. EUS 23/291. Frankfurt: Peter Lang.

———. 1987. "The Role and Meaning of the 'Son of God' Title in Matthew's Gospel." *NovT* 33: 532–56.

Via, D. O. 1985. *The Ethics of Mark's Gospel: In the Middle of Time*. Philadelphia: Fortress.

Viviano, B. T. 1996. "The Movement of the Star, Matt 2:9 and Num 9:17." *RB* 103: 58–64.

———. 1998. "The Trinity in the Old Testament: From Daniel 7:13–14 to Matthew 28:19." *TZ* 54: 193–209.

———. 2000. "The Least in the Kingdom: Matthew 11:11, Its Parallel in Luke 7:28 (Q), and Daniel 4:14." *CBQ* 62: 41–54.

Vledder, E.-J. 1997. *Conflict in the Miracle Stories: A Socio-Exegetical Study of Matthew 8 and 9*. JSNTSup 152. Sheffield: Sheffield Academic Press.

Waltke, B. K. 1993. "Micah." Pages 591–764 in vol. 2 of *The Minor Prophets: An Exegetical and Expository Commentary*. Edited by T. E. McComiskey. Grand Rapids: Baker Academic.

Waltke, B. K., with C. J. Fredricks. 2001. *Genesis*. Grand Rapids: Zondervan.

Walton, J. 1997. "עֹלָמִים." *NIDOTTE* 3:415–19.

Warren, A. 1998. "Did Moses Permit Divorce? Modal *wĕqāṭal* as Key to NT Readings of Deuteronomy 24:1–4." *TynBul* 49: 39–56.

Watts, J. D. W. 1985. *Isaiah 1–33*. WBC 24. Waco: Word.

Watts, R. E. 1998. "Jesus' Death, Isaiah 53, and Mark 10:45: A Crux Revisited." Pages 125–51 in *Jesus and the Suffering Servant: Isaiah 53 and Christian Origins*. Edited by W. H. Bellinger and W. R. Farmer. Harrisburg, PA: Trinity Press International.

———. 2004. "Immanuel: Virgin Birth Proof Text or Programmatic Warning of Things to Come (Isa. 7:14 in Matt. 1:23)?" Pages 92–113 in *From Prophecy to Testament: The Function of the Old Testament in the New*. Edited by C. A. Evans. Peabody, MA: Hendrickson.

Webb, R. L. 1991. *John the Baptizer and Prophet: A Socio-Historical Study*. JSNTSup 62. Sheffield: JSOT Press.

Wefald, E. K. 1995. "The Separate Gentile Mission in Mark." *JSNT* 60: 3–26.

Wegner, P. D. 1992. "A Re-examination of Isaiah IX 1–6." *VT* 42: 103–12.

Weinfeld, M. 1991. *Deuteronomy 1–11*. AB 5. New York: Doubleday.

Weisberg, D. E. 1998. "Levirate Marriage and Halitzah in the Mishnah." *ARJ* 1: 37–69.

Weiser, A. 1962. *The Psalms: A Commentary*. Translated by H. Heartwell. OTL. Philadelphia: Westminster.

Wenham, D. 1972. "The Synoptic Problem Revisited: Some New Suggestions about the Composition of Mark 4:1–34." *TynBul* 23: 3–38.

———. 1979. "The Structure of Matthew XIII." *NTS* 25: 517–18.

Weren, W. J. C. 1997. "Jesus' Entry into Jerusalem: Mt 21,1–17 in the Light of the Hebrew Bible and the Septuagint." Pages 117–41 in *The Scriptures in the Gospels*. BETL 131. Edited by C. M. Tuckett. Leuven: Leuven University Press.

———. 1998. "The Use of Isaiah 5,1–7 in the Parable of the Tenants (Mark 12,1–12; Matthew 21,33–46)." *Bib* 79: 1–26.

Westbrook, R. 1986. "The Prohibition on Restoration of Marriage in Deuteronomy 24:1–4." Pages 387–405 in *Studies in the Bible, 1986*. Edited by S. Japhet. ScrHier 31. Jerusalem: Magnes.

Westerholm, S. 1978. *Jesus and Scribal Authority*. ConBNT 10. Lund: Gleerup.

Whiston, W., trans. 1987. *The Works of Josephus*. Peabody, MA: Hendrickson.

White, R. E. O. 1979. *Biblical Ethics*. CCCE 1. Exeter: Paternoster.

Whitters, M. F. 2006. "Jesus in the Footsteps of Jeremiah." *CBQ* 68: 229–47.

Wiebe, P. H. 1989. "Jesus' Divorce Exception." *JETS* 32: 227–33.

Wiener, A. 1978. *The Prophet Elijah in the Development of Judaism: A Depth-Psychological Study*. LLJC. London: Routledge & Kegan Paul.

Wilcox, M. 1975. "Peter and the Rock: A Fresh Look at Matthew XVI:17–19." *NTS* 22: 73–88.

Wildberger, H. 1991. *Isaiah 1–12*. Translated by T. H. Trapp. CC. Minneapolis: Fortress.

Williams, G. R. 1985. "Frustrated Expectations in Isaiah V 1–7: A Literary Interpretation." *VT* 35: 459–65.

Williamson, H. G. M. 1998. "The Messianic Texts in Isaiah 1–39." Pages 238–70 in *King and Messiah in Israel and the Ancient Near East: Proceedings of the Oxford Old Testament Seminar*. Edited by J. Day. JSOTSup 270. Sheffield: Sheffield Academic Press.

Willis, J. T. 1980. *Isaiah.* LWCOT 12. Austin: Sweet.

Wilson, R. W., and C. L. Blomberg. 1993. "The Image of God in Humanity: A Biblical-Psychological Perspective." *Themelios* 18 (3): 8–15.

Wink, W. 1998. *The Powers That Be: Theology for a New Millennium.* New York: Doubleday.

Winkle, R. E. 1986. "The Jeremiah Model for Jesus in the Temple." *AUSS* 24: 155–72.

Witherington, B. 1990. *The Christology of Jesus.* Philadelphia: Fortress.

Wolff, H. W. *Micah.* 1990. CC. Translated by G. Stansell. Minneapolis: Augsburg.

Wright, C. J. H. 1983. *An Eye for an Eye: The Place of Old Testament Ethics Today.* Downers Grove, IL: InterVarsity.

———. 1996. *Deuteronomy.* NIBCOT 4. Peabody, MA: Hendrickson.

Wright, N. T. 1996. *Jesus and the Victory of God.* Minneapolis: Fortress.

———. 1997. *What St. Paul Really Said: Was Paul of Tarsus the Real Founder of Christianity?* Grand Rapids: Eerdmans.

Wright, R. A. 2001. "The Impossible Commandment." *ATR* 83: 579–84.

Yonge, C. D., trans. 1993. *The Works of Philo.* Peabody, MA: Hendrickson.

Young, E. J. 1949. *The Prophecy of Daniel.* Grand Rapids: Eerdmans.

Zook, D. 1999. "Matthew 5:38–48 and Mennonite Confessional Statements." MA thesis, Denver Seminary.

MARK

RIKK E. WATTS

Introduction

Due to space limitations this study is confined to citations of and close allusions to particular OT texts. While most are widely acknowledged, it is inevitable that some readers might feel that a given text ought to have been included or omitted. I offer my apologies in advance. Echoes or fulfillments of OT events (e.g., Jesus' healings and feedings) or motifs (e.g., gospel, kingdom of God) have perforce been excluded, although many are briefly noted where appropriate. Since the references are often combined (up to four in one place) and are not of equal weight or narrative importance, caution should be exercised in drawing all but the most general conclusions from the following raw data.

Of the sixty-nine OT references noted, six occur in two locations within the prologue (1:1–13/15) and the rest are distributed as follows: seventeen occur in thirteen locations in the first section (1:14/16–8:21/26), twenty-two occur in twelve locations in the second section (8:22/27–10:45/52), and twenty-four occur in fifteen locations in the third section (10:45/11:1–16:8). The occurrence of the OT references approximately doubles in the last eight chapters, that is, "on the way" to and within Jerusalem. Over half are from the prophets (37 [54%]), including Daniel (9 [13%]). Isaiah is particularly influen-

tial (19, [28%]), especially chapters 40–66 (14 [20%]), and alone equals references to Torah (19 [28%]). Apart from one historical book (1%), the rest are from Psalms (12 [17%]) with all but one having Davidic connections and these mostly messianic/prophetic (7 [10%]). Each of the three larger groups is evenly represented except for Psalms, which is absent from the first main section. Granted the inevitable overlap and the generalizations inherent in categorizing, the great majority of the OT references concern Jesus' identity and mission (36 [52%]), then points of law (16 [23%]), threats of judgment (10 [15%]), and warnings concerning discipleship (7 [10%]).

This study has taken the OT context seriously even though this approach may be controversial. Seen by some as assuming what one seeks to argue (Hatina 2002) or as being obviated by a citation's rhetorical nature (cf. Stanley 1999), this approach is born of the well-attested principle of explanatory power: that doing so brings new light and coherence to Mark and strongly suggests he was thinking along similar lines. As will be seen, this approach is also supported by various Jewish interpretative traditions.

In considering Jewish backgrounds I have attempted to be exhaustive, though undoubtedly some potential parallels have escaped my notice. Dating these materials, particularly the rabbinica, is highly problematic, not least when there is the possibility of a late document reflecting an early tradition. Given this uncertainty and the more difficult question of how aware Mark or his Jesus might have been of these traditions, I have considered all of the clearer connections, leaving it to the reader to decide whether or not individual parallels are more or less likely. The awareness of Mark's diverse readership is yet more contentious. It is likely that at least part of his Hellenistic readership was nurtured in the synagogue with some being well trained in the Scriptures (Acts 18:24), able and willing to search them (Acts 17:11) and presumably knowing at least some interpretative traditions associated therewith. Whatever the precise details, it seems dubious to assume that their knowledge of Israel's Scriptures did not exceed that of most modern NT scholars, let alone the average lay person.

As will be clear, Mark and his Jesus share most of the hermeneutical assumptions and methods of their contemporaries. Allegory, however, while present in Mark (e.g., 4:3–8) and picked up from the OT (e.g., Isa. 5:1–4 in Mark 12:1–9), is never used to interpret the Scriptures. Common practice in bringing out what the interpreter held to be the true meaning of the text (Stanley 1992), partial, exegetically and contextually modified, and combined forms (e.g., 1:2–3, 11; 8:17–18), is similarly found in Mark, with combined forms appearing particularly at key narrative junctures (Kee 1975). In engaging his critics on legal matters, Mark's Jesus largely assumes the priority of Torah (10:6–8 on divorce) and David's exemplary status (2:23–25 on Sabbath). His arguments are contextually aware and relatively straightforward (cf. Instone-Brewer 1992).

On the other hand, Jesus' invocation of prophetic texts is often considered to reflect a significantly different mindset (Mead 1994). In fact, his understanding of, for example, Isaiah's future salvation and the messianic psalms generally coheres with the broad consensus, even occasionally reflecting similar text combinations. Where Jesus differs is in his particular identifications of the various players within that consensus. But even this is not unusually idiosyncratic. Like many in his day, Mark's Jesus knows that not all Israel is Israel (Elliott 2000). Mark's Jesus sees himself as inaugurating the climax of Israel's history, embodying in his own person the nation's identity, and not unlike Qumran, Israel's promises must necessarily find their fulfillment in him and his followers. Similarly, to reject him is to invite the same judgments as pronounced on past and future idolaters, whether apostate Jews (e.g., Isa. 6:9–10 and Jer. 7:11 in Mark 4:12 and 11:17) or rebellious Gentiles (e.g., the Isaianic oracles against Babylon, 13:10, and Edom, 34:4, which now fall on Jerusalem, Mark 13:24–25). As this study reveals, Mark and his Jesus seem remarkably consistent in this contextual reading of their Scriptures.

All this reflects the conviction of Scripture's abiding authority but always through the even greater hermeneutical authority of Jesus. Thus, while Mark's Jesus holds his opponents to the Torah, he not only considers his authority greater than Moses' (Hooker 1988) but also magisterially opens up new understandings by means of his own unique combinations of previously unrelated texts (e.g., the classic and debated combination of Dan. 7 with Isa. 53; see also Jer. 7:11 and Isa. 56:7).

In terms of the narrative, Mark's prologue introduces two clusters of prophetic references, both laden with indications of Jesus' identity and mission. Come to effect Isaiah's long-awaited new exodus (1:2–3), he is not only Israel's Davidic and Isaianic servant Messiah who embodies all that Israel was called to be (1:10–11) but also as Mark's opening sentence implies in some mysterious way the very presence of God himself (1:2–3). Since both are fundamentally concerned with the purity of Jerusalem and the temple, Mark's climactic confrontation in Jerusalem is hardly unexpected. Indeed, the references to Malachi's and Exodus's messenger (1:2) and Isaiah's rent heavens (1:10) intimate an element of threat should an unrepentant nation be unprepared for Yahweh's coming.

The first section's initial emphasis thus concerns Jesus' staggering—even divine—authority as the Son of Man to grant forgiveness (2:7), effect deliverance (3:27), and pronounce on (2:23–25) and even embody Torah (3:5). The subsequent hostility sees the OT citations shift toward threats of prophetic judgments against a resistant leadership (3:29; 4:12; 7:6, 10), including a final transitioning pericope directed at the similarly uncomprehending disciples (8:17–18).

The great majority of "the way" section's references focus on Jesus' rejection, suffering, and final vindication wherein his summons to cross-bearing discipleship crystallizes the true nature of holiness. The few OT warnings exclusively address his disciples. Strikingly, Jesus' words, and not Torah citations per se, primarily define discipleship. The only two OT clusters that concern points of law are initially directed at outsiders.

In Jerusalem, Jesus' mission and identity is fittingly expressed primarily through three Davidic psalms, two of which are messianic. This includes—at the high point of the temple confrontation—the Ps. 110 conundrum that, as did Mark's opening sentence, enigmatically points beyond Jesus being merely the Messiah to David's Lord (12:36). While the few references involving points of law are again directed to outsiders, there is a more than two-fold increase in OT prophetic judgment on Jerusalem and its temple. Two texts combine to explain the significance of Jesus' death (14:24), and while one warns of the disciples' future scattering (14:27), several others reiterate the messianic Son of Man's certain vindication over his enemies. Finally, the three non-messianic psalm references, all from Psalm 22, close out the narrative, but I would argue again with the implication of vindication and Gentile inclusion.

In conclusion, eschatology clearly matters to Mark: Israel's calling and the nations' hopes find their fulfillment in Jesus. Christology is thus the fundamental issue. But Jesus is no mere teacher, prophet, or even Messiah. There is a greater secret to be penetrated. While John's Gospel might at times be more explicit, in keeping with a consistent undercurrent of hints that begins with Mark's opening sentence, he alone has Jesus exercise Yahweh's judicial and creational prerogatives in forgiving sins and twice commanding the sea. Only in a crucified Jesus does the true holiness to which Torah points find its origin, fulfillment, and embodiment. Ecclesiologically, Israel itself is consequently redefined: only in Jesus do God's people, Jew and Gentile together, find their true identity.

1:2–3

A. NT Context: Introducing Mark's Gospel. In keeping with ancient practice, Mark's opening sentence in 1:1–3 (see Guelich 1982) establishes the horizons for his life of Jesus (R. E. Watts 2000: 53–90; cf. Earl 1972; D. E. Smith 1990). Although the word *euangelion* had political over-

tones for Mark's Greco-Roman audience (C. A. Evans 2001b: lxxxi–xciii), his "As it is written in the prophet Isaiah . . ." (1:2a) indicates that the primary horizon is Israel's narrative and in particular Isaiah's prophetic hopes of restoration (cf. 1:4b; *Pss. Sol.* 11; Isa. 40:9; 52:7; 60:6; 61:1; see Stuhlmacher 1968; R. E. Watts 2000: 96–99). For Mark, God has "come in strength" to deliver his people (cf. 1:7; *Tg. Isa.* 40:10; see Chilton 1979: 81–95; Schneck 1994: 38).

The second half of the citation (1:3) is therefore an almost verbatim quote from Isa. 40:3 LXX, except that Mark substitutes *autou* for *tou theou hēmōn.* Perhaps merely a simplifying substitution of a single pronoun for a noun phrase, it nevertheless shifts the focus to "of the Lord," already a common designation for Jesus, thereby identifying him with "our God" (on an early and high Christology in the first decades of the church, see Hurtado 2003). The LXX follows the MT closely but omits *bāʾărābâ,* thereby losing some of the parallelism with "in the desert," which then modifies the "voice" instead of "the way." This leads some authors to suggest that Mark deliberately chose the LXX because John was preaching in the desert (see discussion in R. E. Watts 2000: 62–63). Be that as it may, Jewish tradition fully understood that the emphasis lay on "the way" being God's, not where the announcement took place.

The first half of the citation (1:2b) is more complex. Traditionally, Mal. 3:1 LXX (which accurately renders the MT) is rightly regarded as the primary source. Mark is interested in its eschatological orientation and promise of "preparation," although he (1) uses *apostellō,* his usual form of the word, (2) omits the emphatic *egō,* and (3) in converting the paratactic *kai* into the relative *hos,* substitutes *kataskeuasei tēn hodon sou* for Mal. 3:1's *kai epiblepsetai hodon.* On the other hand, Mark 1:2b's *apostellō,* with its modifying *pro prosōpou sou,* is found only in the messenger text of Exod. 23:20 LXX (Mal. 3:1's *pro prosōpou mou* has a first-person possessive and belongs to the second clause), and, more importantly perhaps, Mal. 3:1 is itself a close reworking of the Exodus text (Glazier-McDonald 1987: 130; see also below). This is consistent with a typical first-century exegetically modified conflation (Stanley 1992: 342–47), and as such, both Exodus and Malachi are in view, with the latter providing the center of gravity.

This naturally raises questions about Mark's attribution. Sometimes regarded as having made a mistake (e.g., Jerome, CorpCh 78.452; and hence the *v.l.* "in the prophets"), Mark is either (1) using a now-lost *testimonium* (recently, Donahue and Harrington 2002: 35), (2) following common Jewish practice in citing only one author when using composite texts (Gundry 1967: 125), or (3) following a version of (2) but using his characteristic sandwich structure, whereby the Malachi/Exodus reference is intended to modify the Isaiah material that frames it (R. E. Watts 2000: 88–90; cf. Edwards 1989: 216). As we will see, this combination, although apparently lacking a direct precedent, reflects a certain logic implied in the texts themselves. Malachi 3:1 appears already to be a reworking of Exod. 23:20, but at the same time in its appeal to an eschatological messenger and the preparation of Yahweh's way (*pnh-drk*), it echoes key ideas found in Isa. 40:3.

B. The Composite Citation. 1. Isa. 40:3 in Context. The book of Isaiah usually is divided into three sections, with chapters 40–55 dealing with the end of the Babylonian exile. Mark's text is taken from the prologue, 40:1–11 (C. R. Seitz 1990), which introduces the themes of the following chapters (Spykerboer 1978: 183–85; Kiesow 1979: 23–66). Although commonly understood to be a call narrative, the text is more concerned with the message than the identity of the messenger.

The dual pronouncement of comfort (40:1) answers the double punishment (40:2) and announces Yahweh's plan for Jerusalem/Zion (49:14–26; 50:1–3; 51:9–52:12; 54) (see Mettinger 1983: 26; Wilcox and Paton-Williams 1988: 82–85). Employing imagery that subverts the ceremonial parades of Babylonian deities (Stummer 1926), 40:3–5 more importantly evokes the exodus (cf. Exod. 3:18; 13:21; 23:20; Deut. 1:31, 33; see, e.g., Isa. 41:17–20; see Oswalt 1998: 52). These verses call for the preparation of the way for Yahweh's return to his people (cf. Ezek. 10–11; see Goldingay 2001: 224; see, e.g., Isa. 43:19–20; also 42:8–16; 43:7; 48:11) so that all flesh might know his glory—the real presence of the invisible God (cf. 1 Sam. 4:21–22; 1 Kings 8:11; Ezek. 43:1–5; 44:4; see Blenkinsopp 2000–2003: 2:183).

A declaration of the word of God's supremacy over the passing pretensions of Babylon and its idols (40:6–8; cf. 42:21; 44:26–28; 45:23; 46:10–11; 48:14; 55:10–13) results in another summons, this time to Jerusalem (chap. 52; cf. 49:14–18) to announce the good news of warrior-shepherd King Yahweh's coming in strength (LXX: *meta ischyos*) to deliver his people (40:9–11). The preparation of the *derek/měsillâ/hodos* for Yahweh's royal *parousia* (40:3–4) naturally implies the same for his redeemed peoples' return to Zion (40:9–11; 42:16; cf. 35:8) (see Blenkinsopp 2000–2003: 2:181).

Isaiah 40–55's message draws extensively from Israel's first exodus (see B. W. Anderson, 1962; Stuhlmueller 1970: 59–98). As Israel's front and rear guard (52:12; cf. Exod. 13:21–22; 14:19–20), Yahweh will lead his "blind" people along a way that they do not know (40:10–11; 42:7, 16; 49:10; cf. 35:5–7). As they pass through the waters (43:1–3; 51:9–10) and the desert (41:17–20; 43:19–20), he will turn darkness into light before them (42:16). As their compassionate shepherd (40:11; cf. Exod. 15:13; Ps. 77:20; 78:52–53), he will provide food and water (43:19–20; 49:9–10; cf. 48:21; Exod. 16:31–35; 17:6–7) as he leads his people back to a gloriously restored Jerusalem, where again he will be enthroned (40:9; 44:26; 45:13; 52:6; 54:11–17) (Preuß 1976: 45; Schoors 1973: 243). He will pour out his Spirit upon Jacob's offspring (44:3–5), and they will glory in him (45:24–25), being both taught (54:13) and owned (44:5) by him—all to his renown among the nations (40:5; cf. 52:10) (Elliger 1978: 20–23).

The original exodus pattern—deliverance from Egypt, journey through the desert, and arrival in the promised land—is transformed into the hope of a grander new exodus: deliverance of the exiles from the power of Babylon and its idols, Yahweh's leading of and provision for his blind people along the "way," and his arrival and enthronement in a gloriously restored Zion. But Isa. 40:3 is key: without Yahweh's presence (cf. Isa. 40:5, 9, 10, 11) there can be no salvation. It is his advent as a mighty warrior that is the sine qua non of Israel's deliverance (40:10–12; 51:9–11; 52:10–12).

However, as evident in Malachi and Isa. 56–66 (see below), these great hopes did not fully eventuate (see N. T. Wright 1992: 268–69; C. A.

Evans 1999; cf. Churgin 1944). I have argued elsewhere that Isa. 40–55 is therefore an explanation for the return's failure to live up to these expectations—a failure directly due to blind and deaf Israel's refusal to accept Yahweh's methods or Cyrus his agent (e.g., 42:18–20; 48:1, 8) (R. E. Watts 1990a). Consequently, the new exodus was delayed until finally effected through the enigmatic and future "messianic servant" (49:1–6[or 7]; 52:11–53:12) (R. E. Watts 1990a: 49–59; Clifford 1984: 181).

2. Isa. 40:3 in Judaism. Few chapters play as important a role in Israel's future hope as Isa. 40 (Snodgrass 1980). For the Community of the Rule, even as the rest of the world remains in exile (cf. CD-A IV, II–V, 15a; see Campbell 1995: 149–50), Isa. 40:3 encapsulates their self-understanding as they heed the call for repentance by preparing the "way" for God's return through pursuing holiness and studying Torah in the wilderness (cf. 1QS VIII, 12b–16a; IX, 17b–20a; CD-B XIX, 16; 1QM I, 3; see also 4Q161 2–6 II, 14; see Starkova 1992; cf. O. Seitz 1963; Charlesworth 1997). In 4Q176, which describes God's intervention to reverse the calamity of his people, there is a series of Isaianic consolations, with Isa. 40:1–3 occupying first place.

Baruch's Consolation Poem (5:5–7) is replete with Isaianic images (Burke 1982: 247–55). Jerusalem is directed to watch from a high place (5:5; cf. Isa. 40:9; 49:18) as Yahweh restores the exiles (5:6; cf. 2:34; Isa. 40:11; 49:22; 60:4) and levels the terrain (5:7; cf. Isa. 40:4; 42:16) so that "Israel may go safely in the glory of God" (5:7b; cf. Isa. 40:5). Although Isa. 40 is not cited, this emphasis on Yahweh himself bringing the exiles home is also found in, for example, Tob. 14:5a; *Jub.* 1:15; 11Q19 LIX, 11–12, and later in, for example, *Exod. Rab.* 29:6 (of the messianic era citing Isa. 52:12). Sirach 48:24–25 sees in Isaiah's prophecies comfort to Zion's mourners (cf. Isa. 40:1–2; 49:8–13; 61:1–3; see Skehan and Di Lella 1987: 539), while *T. Mos.* 10:1–5 employs Isa. 40:4 to describe the advent of the kingdom of God (cf. *1 En.* 1:6).

The vision in *Pss. Sol.* 11 of the exiles' return and the restoration of Jerusalem is replete with allusions to Isaiah (Schüpphaus 1977: 56). A signal trumpet in the sanctuary (on the importance of the temple for *Psalms of Solomon* generally, see

Embry 2002) announces "good news" summoning Jerusalem to observe the exiles' return (11:1–2a; cf. Isa. 40:1–2, 9; 43:25; 44:23; 52:7) from the four corners of the earth (11:2b–3; cf. Isa. 42:5; 43:5–6; 49:18–26; 54:1–3). Mountains are leveled and fragrant trees spring up before the glory of the returnees (11:4–6; cf. Isa. 35:10; 40:2–4; 41:15; 42:15; 45:2; 49:7, 10–11; 66:19–20) as Jerusalem is commanded to ready itself (11:7–8; cf. Isa. 52:1–12). In *Pss. Sol.* 17, the Isaianic agent of the return (see Isa. 49:6; 52:1; 55:5 in, respectively, 17:28; 17:27–28, 30; 17:30–31) is a Davidide, described in terms of Ps. 2 (17:23) and Isa. 11 (17:36–37).

The targumic addition in 40:3—"the way *before the people* of the Lord . . . *the congregation* of our God"—highlights the close connection between Yahweh's coming and the exiles' return.

In subsequent rabbinic literature, Isaiah is the prophet of salvation par excellence (*Pesiq. Rab.* 29/30A:5; 32–37; cf. Isa. 54:11; 51:12; 60:1–2; 61:10), and 40:1–9 is the classic statement of God's eschatological comfort of Israel (*Pesiq. Rab.* 29/30A; 29/30B; 30; 33; *Tanh. Gen.* 6:16 associates Isa. 40:9 with the Messiah; *Gen. Rab.* 100:9; *Lev. Rab.* 10:2; 21:7; *Lam. Rab.* 1:2.23 [reversing Jeremiah's lament in Lam. 1:4]; 1:22.57; *Midr. Ps.* 4:8; 22:27; 23:7; cf. *Lev. Rab.* 1:14; *Deut. Rab.* 4:11). On the first Sabbath after the fast commemorating the destruction of the temple, Isa. 40:3 was the haftarah reading.

Isaiah 40:1–11 may thus be regarded as the *locus classicus* of Isaianic new-exodus salvation, particularly linking Yahweh's coming with the end of exile. But at the same time, explicitly at least in 1QS and implied in *Psalms of Solomon*, this salvation entails preparatory repentance. With this in mind, we return to the first half of the citation.

3. Exod. 23:20 in Context. Central to Israel's founding moment, the Book of the Covenant in Exodus (20:22–23:33) serves as the nation's constitutive document. Bracketed by cultic material (20:24–26; 23:14–19), it encapsulates what it means for Israel to be God's son (4:22) and his holy people (22:31; cf. 19:4–6) (Childs 2001: 456). Yahweh's name must not be reviled (22:28), his offerings not withheld (22:29), immorality and idolatry eschewed (20:26; 22:19), and the weak must be protected (22:22–27) and justice upheld (23:2, 8). The book's epilogue (23:20–33) emphasizes Israel's relationship to Yahweh himself and, in the section from which Mark's text is taken (23:20–21), his agent. Previously, Israel had been led by the cloud and fire, but now Yahweh's messenger would guide, instruct, and preserve them "in the way" (LXX: *en tē hodō*) (Durham 1987: 335). If the messenger's nature is debated—is he human or angelic? (see Sarna 1991: 114)—even more so is his relationship to Yahweh (see *TDOT* 8:315–24). He is closely identified with Yahweh's presence (see R. North 1967)—for Israel to rebel against the messenger is to reject Yahweh and thus invite judgment, since "my name is in him" (23:21)—yet not completely, since Israel's rebellion in worshiping the golden calf means that although the messenger goes with them, Yahweh's presence will not (cf. 33:2–3). But two points are clear: disobeying the messenger results in judgment, and his very presence is a result of Israel's rebellion.

The second section deals with Yahweh's promise to drive out the nations (23:22–23, 27–31) and Israel's obligation to avoid idolatry (23:24, 32–33a), with attendant blessings for obedience (23:25–26) and a warning against disobedience (23:33b–c). Israel's possession of the land is dependent on their continued covenant loyalty.

4. Exod. 23:20 in Judaism. Probably because of the close link between Yahweh and his messenger, Exod. 23:20 features prominently in speculation concerning Yahweh's heavenly chief servant (see Hurtado 1988). *Apocalypse of Abraham* 10:1–14 speaks of the angel Yahoel, "in whom God's name dwells," who is to consecrate and strengthen Abraham (10:5–6), to bless him and the land (10:13), and, in a direct allusion to Exod. 23:20, to show him the way to the land (10:14). Philo identifies the angel of Exod. 23:20, who bears the name of God, with the Logos or "right reason" (*QE* 2.13; cf. *Agriculture* 51 ["God's son"]; *Migration* 174). In the much later *3 Enoch* the angel Metatron, "the Angel of the Divine presence" (cf. Isa. 63:9), is strikingly described as "the lesser YHWH . . . as it is written, 'My name is in him'" (*3 En.* 12:5, citing Exod. 23:21). Even so, in refutation of a Minim this is no reason to worship him, since he is not to be confused with God (*b. Sanh.* 38b, citing Exod. 33:15).

Targum Neofiti, recognizing that even the giving of a messenger is a gracious act, glosses "angel" with "of mercy," and *Targum Pseudo-Jonathan*, perhaps echoing the concern for Yahweh's presence, understands the prepared place to be the dwelling of the Shekinah (cf. the tradition that identifies the angel with the ark [Ginzberg 2003: 1:644]). Other later texts focus on the reasons for Yahweh's sending of his messenger. Positively, the messenger mediated Yahweh's guiding, protecting, and delivering presence (*Exod. Rab.* 32:6, citing Ps. 34:8; 68:18; 91:7, 11; cf. *S. Eli. Rab.* 22[20]) and hence he appeared to Joshua (*Tanḥ. Exod.* 6:10). His protective presence becomes a model for the rewards of studying Torah (*S. Eli. Rab.* 18, [30]28) and the paradigm for future redemption where the coming of a messenger presages eschatological salvation (*Exod. Rab.* 32:6, 9, citing Mal. 3:1; cf. *Midr. Ps.* 90:9; *Deut. Rab.* 11:9; see Steichele 1980: 65).

There is, however, a dark side. Just as several OT passages recall Israel's rebellion (e.g., Ps. 106:19–23; Neh. 9:9–25; Isa. 63:8–10), so there are frequent admissions that it was the nation's idolatry that occasioned the provision of a messenger: "God said to Israel: 'Had you merited it, I Myself would have become your messenger, just as I was in the wilderness, as it says, *And the Lord went before them by day* [Exod 13:21]; but now that you have not merited this, I am entrusting you into the hands of a messenger'" (*Exod. Rab.* 32:2; cf. *Tanḥ. Exod.* 6:10; *Midr. Ps.* 17:3). Whereas even a harlot is grateful for her hire, Israel was not, and this despite God's mighty deeds on her behalf (*Exod. Rab.* 32:5, citing Jer. 2:6). For *Exod. Rab.* 32:1, this moment sets the tone for Israel's history—"Had Israel waited for Moses and not perpetrated that act, there would have been no exile"—and hence becomes the basis for the utter destruction of idolaters (*y. Ber.* 9:1 [XVI.A]).

5. Mal. 3:1 in Context. Malachi addresses the disappointment attending the apparent failure of Isaiah's new exodus, Ezekiel's temple vision, the promised prosperity of Haggai, and the restorationist hopes of Zechariah (Verhoef 1987: 284, 294; Glazier-McDonald 1987: 17). Quite different from the vision of the nations streaming to Jerusalem, the struggling city remained under Persian sway (1:8), the land was ravaged by locusts and drought (3:11), and the wicked flourished while the righteous suffered (2:17; 3:14–15). This gave rise to a crisis of faith, with doubts about

Yahweh's faithfulness openly expressed (1:2, 13; 2:17; 3:14).

In a series of polemical speeches Malachi ("my messenger") defends Yahweh's integrity and commitment to Israel (1:2–5), declaring instead that the present misfortune is the result of the faithlessness of priesthood (1:6–2:9) and people (2:10–16). An affirmation of the certainty of Yahweh's coming (2:17–3:5) is followed by a summons to repentance (3:6–12) and a final warning (3:13–4:4). An epilogue repeats the demand for reformation and announces that the day of Yahweh will be preceded by the coming of Elijah lest the people be unprepared (4:5–6).

Mark's text belongs to 2:17–3:5, which is in direct response to the cynical question of the whereabouts of "the God of justice" (2:17b). Speaking for God, the prophet declares, "I will send my messenger [mal'ākî] to prepare my way before me, and the Lord [hā'ādôn] whom you seek will suddenly come to his temple! And the messenger of the covenant [mal'ak habběrît] in whom you delight? Oh yes, he is already coming!" (3:1). When "he" does come, he will deal with the priests (3:3), and then "I" will deal with the wicked, including those who oppress widows (3:5) (in 3:1 "suddenly" means "surprisingly," and in the prophets this has an ominous tone [A. E. Hill 1998: 267]).

The problem, however, concerns the various designations. The issues are complex. If "Lord" indicates the messenger's superiority, then given the common term "messenger," all three refer to one figure: a prophetic forerunner of Yahweh (France 1982: 91n31).

But since it is to "his" temple that "the Lord" ('ādôn) comes, it is difficult to see "the Lord" as anyone other than Yahweh (cf. Zech. 4:14; 6:5) ("Lord" with the definite article is always paired with Yahweh [A. E. Hill 1998: 268], mostly in terms of God's powerful presence [see Isa. 1:24; 3:1; 10:16, 33; 19:4; see also Ps. 114:7; cf. Mal. 3:2c]).

And who is this "messenger of the covenant"? The appellation "messenger" suggests that he is the same as "my messenger." But if so, why the additional "of the covenant"? And what about the parallels between (1) the "messenger of the covenant" who "comes" (bā') and the Lord who will come (yābô'), (2) the messenger of the covenant

"(in) whom you delight" and the Lord "whom you seek," and (3) the "day of his coming" (presumably the messenger of the covenant [3:2]) and the "day of the Lord" (4:5)? Combined with the lexical similarity of the "messenger of the covenant" to the "messenger of the Lord" (as in Exod. 23:20), understood to be Yahweh in representative form (Driver 1906: 318; R. L. Smith 1984: 328; Verhoef 1987: 289; Glazier-McDonald 1987: 133), these suggest that "my messenger"/"messenger of the covenant" is none other than the mal'āk-yhwh and so to be identified with Yahweh himself (so, e.g., R. North 1967). But this too is problematic, not least because in Exodus a similar situation of rebellion caused Yahweh's presence and the angel to be distinguished (Exod. 33:2–3).

It is probably best, then, to read the parallels not as a single event, but instead as correlating two separate ones (a-b-a'-b'). Malachi 3:1a–b outlines the basic sequence where (a) "my messenger" prepares (v. 1a) for (b) Yahweh's (= the Lord's) coming to his temple (v. 1b). Mal. 3:1c–4 then details (a') the preparatory actions of the messenger who is to purify the Levitical priesthood before (b') returning Yahweh acts against evildoers (3:5). On this reading, "my messenger" and the "messenger of the covenant" are one and the same (pace A. E. Hill 1998: 288). Malachi 4:5 then identifies him as Elijah, who is sent before that great and terrible day of the Lord to reconcile the people to one another (4:6a) lest Yahweh in his coming smite the land and, implicitly, the people with a curse (4:6b) (cf. Isa. 11:4; Jer. 43:11).

If so, we have a call for the God of justice to return to his temple (see A. E. Hill 1998: 384). But the presence of a corrupt priesthood would result only in judgment, so Yahweh mercifully promises to send his messenger to purify them before he comes to deal with evildoers.

The second major feature is the engagement with Isaianic and Exodus traditions. In terms of Isaiah, Mal. 3:1's "(he will) prepare the way" (pinnâ-derek) closely resembles Isa. 40:3's "prepare the way" (pannû derek), which language is also repeated in the "postexilic" Isa. 57:14; 62:10 (Elliger 1982: 206; Glazier-McDonald 1987: 136–38). Moreover, there are numerous parallels between Malachi and Isa. 55–66. The latter also begins with a warning concerning Yahweh's coming (56:1), false leaders are prominent

(56:9–12; cf. chap. 65), and there is distress over the apparent delay of the new exodus (64:1, 6–7, 12), which delay is also explained in terms of covenant unfaithfulness (59:1–2; chaps. 58–59, esp. 58:13–14; 59:9–13) (R. E. Watts 1990a); there is a concern for right worship (56:1–7; 58; 66:3 [see below; also Dumbrell 1984; 1985]) and covenant faithfulness (59:21; 61:6, 8); Mal. 2:17's opening charge of "wearying" Yahweh is reminiscent of Isa. 43:24 (Mason 1990: 249); and finally, in keeping with Malachi's use of Exod. 23:20, Isaiah sees in Yahweh's coming a threat against his own sinful people (65:1–7, 11–15) (McKenzie and Wallace 1983: 554). Malachi and Isa. 56–66 thus share the same concern over Yahweh's delayed second-exodus coming and, because of Israel's parlous condition, the threat inherent in that coming.

Numerous commentators have also observed that the similarity between Mal. 3:1 (*hnny šlḥ ml'ky pnh-drk lpny*) and Exod. 23:20 (*hnh 'nky šlḥ ml'k lpnyk lšmrk bdrk*) is so strong as to suggest that the former is a deliberate reworking of the latter (Glazier-McDonald 1987: 130; Petersen: 1977: 43–44). Again there are significant contextual parallels. The sins described in Mal. 3:5 are in breach either of the Decalogue or the Book of the Covenant (cf. Deut. 5:1–21; Lev. 19:13; Exod. 22:18, 22–24; see R. L. Smith 1984: 330), the fate of crops in Mal. 3:11–12 and the idolatrous worship in Mal. 2:10–12 echo the blessings and warnings of Exod. 23:24–25, 32–33, and the primary concern of the epilogue to the Book of the Covenant is the integrity of Israel's relationship to Yahweh, which is precisely the issue here.

6. Malachi's Use of Exod. 23:20; Isa. 40:3. All this suggests that Malachi sees the delayed second exodus as an ironic recapitulation of the first. Whereas in the first exodus Yahweh sent his messenger to prepare Israel's way by destroying the idolatrous nations (Exod. 23:22–23), now the messenger prepares Yahweh's way, and it is faithless Israel who, having become like those nations, is under threat (Mal. 4:5–6; cf. 2:3) (McKenzie and Wallace 1983: 554; Glazier-McDonald 1987: 130–33). The problem for Malachi is not Yahweh's tardiness, but rather Israel's all-too-familiar disobedience. Echoing Exod. 23:20, he warns that Yahweh will send his messenger, "Elijah," to prepare Isa. 40:3's delayed new-exodus way by purifying Israel's priestly leaders and reconciling his faithless people to "the fathers." But they must obey him lest Yahweh, when he comes, smite the land with a curse (Mal. 4:6).

7. Mal. 3:1 in Judaism. Since Mal. 3:1 uses the language of Exod. 23:20, it is hardly surprising that the two were connected in later Jewish traditions—evidence, perhaps, of such associations in the first century. *Seder* 61a has Mal. 3:1–8 as the haftarah for Exod. 23:20 (J. Mann 1940: 1:479), and as we noted, *Exod. Rab.* 32:9 invokes Exod. 23:20 as the paradigm for the future deliverance citing Mal. 3:1 (cf. *Num. Rab.* 16:11 below; *Deut. Rab.* 11:9). *Exodus Rabbah* 3:4 does likewise and explicitly connects it with the sending of Elijah, citing Mal. 4:6. According to *Tanḥ. Exod.* 6:12, whereas in this world God sent an angel to destroy the nations (citing Exod. 23:23), in the world to come he will send Elijah to restore Israel (Mal. 4:5).

Because Moses' writing of the second set of tablets testifies to his reconciling intervention, Yahweh will send him along with Elijah in the time to come (Mal. 4:4–6; *Deut. Rab.* 3:17; cf. Mark 9:4; *Sipre Deut.* 342; also the extended identification of the two in *Pesiq. Rab.* 4:2), again linking the exodus with Malachi's delayed Isaianic salvation.

Malachi 4:5's identification of 3:1's messenger as "Elijah" (3:22 LXX: *ton Thesbitēn*, "the Tishbite") gave rise to lively speculation about his future role. Ushering in the last days, he will calm God's wrath and restore the tribes of Israel (Sir. 48:9–10; cf. *4 Ezra* 6:26; 4Q521 2 III, 1; 4Q558 1 II, 4). According to later rabbinic tradition, he will bring three signs on earth (the last apparently being the resurrection of the dead [see *Sib. Or.* 2:187–89; cf. *Did.* 16:6]; *m. Soṭah* 9:15; cf. *Song Rab.* 1:6 §9; *L.A.B.* 23:13), effect peace by restoring families unjustly expelled from the congregation (*m. 'Ed.* 8:7 [cf. *Song Rab.* 4:12 §5]), overthrow the foundations of the heathen (*Gen. Rab.* 71:9), effect the true repentance of Israel (*Pirqe R. El.* 43), and resolve theological, genealogical, and legal disputes (e.g., *m. B. Meṣi'a* 1:8; 3:4; *b. Ber.* 35b; see also further *Mek. Exod.* 16:33; *Tg. Ps.-J.* Deut. 30:4; *Pesiq. Rab.* 35:4; *Sipre Deut.* 41:4 [3.C]; *S. Eli. Zut.* 1).

Evidence in pre-Christian tradition for Elijah's and thus perhaps Mal. 3:1's association with the messianic age is thin (cf. *b. 'Erub.* 43b; see R. E.

Watts 2000: 75), though not in later rabbinic materials (cf., e.g., *m. 'Ed.* 8:7; *Tg. Ps.-J.* Deut. 30:4; *b. Sukkah* 52b; *Deut. Rab.* 4:11 combines Mal. 4:5–6 with Zech. 9:9; *Deut. Rab.* 6:7; *Midr. Ps.* 3:7; 42/43:5 links the first and second redeemers: Elijah in Mal. 4:5 [cf. *Pesiq. Rab.* 4:2; 33:8] and the servant Messiah in Isa. 42:1; *Midr. Prov.* 19 identifies Elijah of Mal. 4:5 with the Messiah). But if the messianic age was in some way connected with the day of Yahweh/last days (cf. *Pss. Sol.* 17:26–27, 30, 36 with Mal. 3:2–5; 4Q174 1 I, 10–13, 18–19; *T. Levi* 18:1–9; *T. Jud.* 24:1–6), having Elijah precede the Messiah makes sense.

The key point is that Mal. 3 makes no mention of a messianic figure. Instead, the focus is on Yahweh's new-exodus coming and the threat that this means to Israel. Thus in Sir. 48:10 Elijah is "to calm God's wrath before it breaks out in fury, by turning the heart of the father to the son and by restoring the tribes of Jacob" (see *Liv. Pro.* 21:3). CD-B XX, 16–21, employing the language of Mal. 3:16–18, sees the names of the righteous being recorded in heaven in anticipation of the time when God will "distinguish again between the just and the wicked" in Israel (cf. the later *Lev. Rab.* 34:8). *Pirqe Rabbi Eliezer* 43 admits that Israel repents only because of distress, suggesting that even this is only partial because "Israel does not repent quite sincerely until Elijah comes" (citing Mal. 4:5–6).

C. Mark's Use of the Composite Citation. For many commentators, Mark's opening citation simply introduces the Baptist (e.g., Lohmeyer 1953: 9; Gundry 1993: 31). After all, the LXX, unlike the MT, locates the voice in the wilderness. However, the dual mention of preparation (*kataskeuasei* and *hetoimasate*) and the focus of John's proclamation of the coming "Stronger One," both of which only reinforce John's subordinate role (Robinson 1957: 24–25; Ambrozic 1972: 19–20), along with the use of these texts in Judaism clearly place the emphasis on the one being heralded. Granted that John is authorized to communicate God's word of repentance and to perform it (hence his baptism [see *TDOT* 8:317]), Mark makes it clear that he is but a preparatory figure who is heralding and clearing the way for no one less than "strong" Yahweh himself (1:7) (this a key motif already in Isa. 40–55 [Zimmerli 1963] and an emphasis in some sections of Judaism; cf. *Pesiq. Rab.* 36,

where God himself will go ahead of Israel at their return, though not necessarily to the exclusion of an agent [Horbury 1998: 78–83]).

What these texts lead us to expect is Israel's warrior-shepherd himself coming to effect the nation's salvation (see Marcus 1992: 12–47; Donahue and Harrington 2002: 67–68). Substituting *autou*, referring to Jesus, for Isa. 40:3's *tou theou hēmōn* (but see 1QS VIII, 13: *drk h'wh'*), Mark makes the forthright claim that Israel's new-exodus hopes have been inaugurated in Jesus: he is the one through whom Yahweh's delivering personal presence and kingly reign is manifest (1:15).

But the Malachi-Exodus combination allows no doubt as to the seriousness of Israel's position: there would be no need for a messenger were it not for Israel's faithless condition. Elijah might have been expected to destroy the Gentiles, but Malachi warns that it is Israel who is at risk (on the idea in the intertestamental period of judgment on faithless Israel, see Elliott 2000). For Mark, because John clearly functions as Malachi's Elijah (1:6; 9:11–13; cf. 2 Kings 1:8; 2:8, 13–14 LXX; *Tg. Ps.-J.* 2 Kings 2:8; Zech. 13:4; see Marcus 1999: 156–57), Israel must listen to him if they are to avoid the curse that Yahweh's coming might occasion.

In keeping with the role of opening sentences in literary antiquity (see above), Mark's Gospel unfolds within this tension: Jesus, whom John heralds, is the one who inaugurates Israel's longed-for salvation (Isa. 40:3), but there is the danger that Yahweh's offered salvation will become a curse (Exod. 23:20/Mal. 3:1).

Thus for Mark, the reign of God that Jesus announces (1:14–15) is none other than Yahweh's kingly intervention as it is written in Isaiah (1:1–3). Just as Yahweh had promised to deliver Israel from the strong man Babylon (Isa. 49:24–25), to lead his blind people along a path that they did not know (Isa. 42:16), and to return them finally through the suffering of his servant to Jerusalem (Isa. 52–54), so too Mark's new-exodus macro-structure presents Jesus delivering Israel from the strong man Beelzebul (1:16–8:21/26; where 21/26 indicates a hinge pericope, i.e., vv. 22–26; see Stock 1987), leading his blind followers along a way (i.e., of cross-bearing discipleship) that they do not understand (8:22/27–10:45/52), and ar-

119

riving finally in Jerusalem (10:46/11:1–16:8) (R. E. Watts 2000; cf. Marcus 1992).

Tragically, official Israel's refusal to submit to John (1:14a; cf. 11:27–33) means that Jerusalem, instead of sounding the joyful trumpet and summoning the cities of Judah to do likewise (cf. Isa. 40:9), spurns the invitation, coming on the scene only to censure (3:22; 7:1–5; cf. 11:18). Yahweh's coming in Jesus results in a curse (11:13–14, 20–21; cf. Mal. 4:5–6) and the temple's destruction (chap. 13). Nevertheless, God's new-exodus plan will not be thwarted. He will build a new people-temple around Jesus (12:10–11), including both faithful Jews and later believing Gentiles from all four corners of the earth (11:17b; 13:27; 15:39).

D. Theological Use. Christologically speaking, the striking identification of Jesus (1:1) with Yahweh's coming (1:2–3) can hardly be missed (see Horbury 1998: 78–83). Key here, especially given present debates concerning the influence of exalted mediatorial angelic or patriarchal figures on NT Christology, is that two of Mark's texts, Mal. 3:1 and Exod. 23:20, explicitly contrast such figures with the very presence of Yahweh himself. Whatever else, for Mark Israel's Lord is, in some mysterious and unparalleled sense, present in Jesus.

As such, eschatologically, in Jesus Isaiah's long-delayed new-exodus deliverance of Israel has begun in Malachi's great and terrible day of the Lord (Mal. 4:5). The Isaianic *euangelion* of God's inbreaking kingdom is identified with the good news "of Jesus" (Mark 1:1a, 15 [perhaps an intentionally ambiguous choice of the genitive where Jesus is both the agent and content]; cf. *Pss. Sol.* 11:1). Jesus is Israel's compassionate shepherd (6:34) and warrior-deliverer—though now from the power of the demons who ultimately stand behind the nations and their idols (1:24; 3:27; cf. Isa. 49:24–26 [see below])—who provides food in the desert (6:42; 8:8), heals the blind, deaf, mute, and lame (2:12; 7:37; 8:35; cf. Isa. 35:5–7; 42:18), and instructs his people in the "way" they should go (8:31–10:45).

Ecclesiologically, heeding John and thus following Jesus are the marks of faithful Israel. To refuse to do so is to reject the possibility of living in Yahweh's presence in a restored Zion.

1:10

A. NT Context: The Torn Heavens. After establishing his new-exodus setting and John's role as a new Elijah calling Israel to repentance, Mark focuses on Jesus. John's baptism has been variously understood. It could allude to proselyte baptism, if such was practiced at this time (e.g., France 2002: 66), but it seems more likely to be a reenactment of the exodus sea crossing (cf. Isa. 63:11–64:1; see below). Either one implies Israel's apostasy and need of repentance.

In terms of John's baptism of Jesus, Mark's rending of the heavens is regarded either as stock imagery for apocalyptic revelation (e.g., Ezek. 1:1; Rev. 11:19; 19:11; *T. Ab.* [A] 7:3; *2 Bar.* 22:1 [but see Gundry 1993: 50]) or as divine eschatological intervention (e.g., Isa. 64:1; Job 14:12 LXX; Hag. 2:6, 21; 2 Pet. 3:10; cf. Rev. 6:14; *Sib. Or.* 3:82). However, Mark's thoroughgoing Isaianic framework and the descent of the Spirit (cf. Isa. 63:14 LXX: *katebē pneuma* [*katabainō* + *pneuma* is used in the NT only of Jesus' baptism]) through the "rent" heavens (instead of the more usual "opened" heavens of apocalyptic revelation; *schizō*, not *anoigō*, best renders *qr'* [cf. Isa. 36:22; 37:1]) as Jesus passes through the water (cf. Isa. 63:11, 13) and that prior to a forty-day journey into the wilderness (1:10, 13) strongly suggest that Isa. 64:1, connected as it is with the delayed new exodus, is in view (R. E. Watts 2000: 102–8; Marcus 1992: 58; Buse 1956).

This has been questioned, however, since in Mark it is not God who descends, nor is judgment of the wicked in view (Lentzen-Deis 1970: 99–107). But in Isa. 63 (vv. 8–10) the Spirit is intimately linked with Yahweh's own saving presence (see Hanson 1979: 90), and in Mark Israel's demonic enemies "tremble" (see below) as do Yahweh's adversaries (1:23–24; 3:11; 5:7; Isa. 64:2) and, be it noted, his own people (e.g., 1:27; 2:12; 4:41; 5:15; Isa. 64:3).

B. Isa. 64:1 in Context. Isaiah 56–66 usually is understood within a postexilic context (e.g., Williamson 1994: 19–20; Elliger 1933; cf. the parallels with Malachi cited above). Located near the end of this section, Isa. 63:7–64:12 is the final lament and petition (Bautch 2003: 29–63) over Israel's condition in the aftermath of a meager return (cf., e.g., 59:8–14; see Banwell 1965). Immediately following a divine-warrior hymn

(63:1–6) in which the prophet envisages Yahweh himself responding to his people's cries (63:5–6; cf. 62:6–9), he turns to the foundational memory of the exodus, where Yahweh had first bared his mighty arm in response to Israel's suffering.

The opening (63:7–14) recalls when Yahweh earlier became Israel's savior (63:8: *yāšaʿ*, used of Yahweh in the exodus account only in Exod. 14:30 [Motyer 1993: 513]). The *malʾak pānāyw* ("the angel of his presence") of 63:9, understood in the LXX as "no angel or messenger but Yahweh himself" (cf. Exod. 33:14–15; 2 Sam. 17:11 [on this, see Blenkinsopp 2000–2003: 3:260–61]), had led Israel through the waters and sent his Holy Spirit among them (63:11). However, just as Israel earlier had grieved his Spirit and he had become their enemy (63:10), so also now in this new exodus: their idolatrous refusal to accept Yahweh's announcement of salvation had again made him their enemy, hence their present parlous condition (63:15–19a; cf. 42:18–20; 48:1–8; see R. E. Watts 1990a).

In direct contrast to Yahweh's "Holy Spirit" (in the OT only here and in Ps. 51:11 [51:13 MT]), the prophet grieves over Israel's uncleanness (64:6–7) and yearns for Yahweh's compassion (63:15b). Couching his presentation in terms of ancient divine-warrior hymns (64:1–3; cf. 59:15b–20; 63:1–6; and especially of God's descent on Sinai; see Hanson 1979: 87; Cross 1973), the prophet recollects Yahweh's mighty deeds of the exodus, urging him to break his silence (64:12), to again split the heavens, and to come down (64:1; cf. Exod. 19:18–20) and do awesome things (64:2; cf. Exod. 19:16; 23:27) (see Sarna 1991: 114).

C. Isa. 64:1 in Judaism. There are few explicit references to this text in Jewish literature. It is appealed to in describing the descent of the glory on Mount Sinai (*Mek. Exod.* 19:20), in recalling the crossing of the sea (*ʾAbot R. Nat.* 33 [at which time, according to *Mek. Exod.* 14:26–31, the Holy Spirit rested on Israel]), and paradigmatically of the new exodus, where it provides grounds for Israel's rejoicing in its likewise miraculous future redemption and abundance (*S. Eli. Rab.* [30]28; [22]20).

Testament of Levi 18:6–7, although possibly the subject of heavy Christian reworking (de Jonge 1960, but see *OTP* 1:777–78; Schürer 1973–

1986: 3.2:767–70), offers an interesting parallel: the heavens open, and a glorious spirit of sanctification and understanding (cf. Isa. 11:2) descends on an eschatological kingly (18:3) priest (18:2) "in the water." Given that Israel was called to be a kingdom of priests (Exod. 19:6) and that Yahweh had sent his Spirit upon them as he brought them through the midst of the waters (Isa. 63:11–14 [see *Mek. Exod.* 14:13 below]), it is possible that *T. Levi* 18 represents an eschatological reenactment of Israel's exodus experience, but now upon a representative deliverer figure. The text goes on (18:9, 12) to say that Beliar will be bound by him, and the nations will be enlightened (cf. Isa. 49:6) and "multiplied in knowledge" (cf. Isa. 42:4; 51:4–5). *Testament of Judah* 24:2 speaks of the heavens opened over and the Spirit poured out upon the gentle "Shoot of God Most High" (the Davidic messianic king [cf. Isa. 11:1]), of whom God is the Holy Father (cf. Ps. 2:7?). The "scepter of my kingdom" will be illumined and Israel restored, and through him will come the rod of righteousness for the nations (24:3–6).

Although the symbolism of the dove is far more difficult and the manifold options impossible to canvass here (see Davies and Allison 1988–1997: 1:331–33), we may at least note that in 4Q521 2 II, 6 the Spirit will hover (cf. Gen. 1:1; *b. Ḥag.* 15a) over the poor in the time of eschatological salvation (cf. 1QHᵃ IV, 26; VI, 13; VIII, 16–17; XVII, 32; XX, 12, where the presence of the Spirit marks out the "Teacher of Righteousness"). In *Mekilta Exodus* 14:13 the Spirit rests on Israel during the Red Sea crossing (cf. Isa. 63:11–14), and Israel is granted a heavenly vision (cf. *Seder Eliyahu Rabbah* 4, citing Isa. 63:11, where the presence of the Spirit is attested in the one who truly has the Torah within him, who agonizes over the profanation of the glory of God and Israel, and who longs for the restoration of the glory of Jerusalem and the temple).

D. The Use of Isa. 64:1 in Mark. Given the opening mixed citation, the rent heavens and descent of the Spirit can hardly be anything but the sign that God himself has now come in power to rescue his people. The long-awaited new exodus has begun, and in keeping with the prophet's request and later Jewish understanding (cf. *S. Eli. Rab.* [30]28), Mark repeatedly emphasizes the fear and amazement that Jesus' unexpected mighty deeds occasioned (see Isa. 64:2; cf. Mark 1:22, 27; 2:12; 4:41; 5:15, 20, 33, 42; 6:2, 50, 51; 7:37; 16:8; see C. D. Marshall 1989: 70–71).

Jesus' coming up out of the water and going into the desert for forty days also suggest a recapitulation of Israel's exodus experience, with Jesus either equivalent to or representative of Israel (as per Isa. 63 and *Mek. Exod.* 14:13; see Buse 1956; Lentzen-Deis 1970: 102; Bretscher 1968; see commentary on Mark 1:11 below).

But who are Yahweh's adversaries? At the very least they are the demonic forces, which for Mark ultimately stand behind the idolatrous nations (see commentary on Mark 3:27 below) and whom Mark's Jesus engages in eschatological conflict (1:21–28, 34, 39; 3:10–11, 15, 22–27; 5:1–20; 6:7, 13; 7:24–30; 9:12–29; cf. 4Q174; see Kee 1967: 243; R. E. Watts 2000: 144–64). Interestingly, Mark's emphasis lies on the unclean nature of these spirits (1:23; 5:2; 7:25; 9:25 [see Pimental 1988]), which is precisely Israel's condition in the Isaianic lament (Isa. 64:6). And in both cases this is over against, respectively, Jesus as the Holy One of God (Mark 1:24) and Yahweh's Holy Spirit (Isa. 63:10) (see commentary on Mark 3:29 below). As we will see, holiness, or purity, is a major concern for Mark (Neyrey 1986; cf. Stettler 2004).

But in Isaiah and Malachi, Yahweh's advent also meant judgment on Israel's apostate leaders and temple dignitaries (65:1–15; 66:3–6, 14b–17, 24; cf. Mal. 3:1–4; see E. Achtemeier 1982: 128–29). So too in Mark, Jesus' conflict with these groups is an early and thoroughgoing motif (e.g., 2:7–3:6, 20; 7:1; 11:12–25; 12:1–12; 13). John's prophesied "Stronger One" has indeed come (1:7; cf. Isa. 40:10; *Tg. Isa.* 40:10; also Mark 3:27; Isa. 49:24).

E. Theological Use. Because Mark's story concerns Isaiah's delayed new exodus, with John the Baptist as Malachi's preparatory Elijah, the rending of the heavens at Jesus' baptism constitutes Yahweh's long-awaited response. Isaiah's final lament has been answered: God has come down to deliver his people, baring his mighty arm to do "awesome things that we did not expect." Christologically, just as Isa. 40 and Mal. 3 anticipated the coming not of a messianic figure, but of God himself, so too Isa. 64. Jesus is identified not merely as Yahweh's agent, but in some mysterious way with Yahweh's very presence, whose

coming, eschatologically, inaugurates that great and terrible day of the Lord (Mal. 4:5) and the beginnings of the new heaven and the new earth (Isa. 65:17–25; 66:10–14, 18–24). At the same time, ecclesiologically, the parallels with the Spirit coming upon Israel during the crossing of the sea identify Jesus in some sense as the true Israel.

1:11

A. NT Context: The Voice from Heaven. Climaxing Mark's introduction, a voice—surely that of God—speaks from the rent heavens in divine approbation of Jesus. Although some commentators find the statement too allusive to indicate clear dependence on any particular OT text (Hooker 1959: 68–73; Suhl 1965: 97–104; Ruckstuhl 1983: 208–9), most see allusions to several OT passages. The primary contenders are (1) Ps. 2:7 (Vielhauer 1965: 205–6; Lindars 1961: 140n2; Gnilka 1978–1979: 1:53 [cf., e.g., the reading of Codex D in Luke 3:22; Justin, *Dial.* 88; 103; Clement of Alexandria, *Paed.* 1.6.25]), (2) Isa. 42:1 (Jeremias 1971b: 53–55; Maurer 1953: 31–32; Fuller 1954: 55; Pesch 1976–1977: 1:92), (3) Gen. 22:2, 12, 16 (Best 1990: 169–72; Vermes 1961: 222–23; Daly 1977: 68–70; Wood 1968), (4) Exod. 4:22–23 (Bretscher 1968; Feuillet 1959), (5) a combination of the first three (I. H. Marshall 1968–1969; Guelich 1989: 33–34; Gundry 1993: 49; Schneck 1994: 55–68; R. E. Watts 2000: 108–18; Marcus 1999: 162; France 2002: 80–82).

A combined approach is most likely correct. Granted that Mark's emphatic first-person address reflects a more natural order (3:11; 8:29; 14:61; 15:2), *sy ei ho huios mou* almost certainly alludes to Ps. 2:7 (*huios mou ei sy*). For the second phrase, even though Mark's *en soi eudokēsa* differs from *prosedexato auton* of Isa. 42:1 LXX, it is the natural and most common rendering of *rṣh [b]* in the LXX and is found in Theodotion and Symmachus (I. H. Marshall 1968–1969: 335, also citing Aquila; cf. *Tg. Isa.* 41:8–9; 44:1–2; 43:10; see Chilton 1984: 129–30). This, together with the descent of the Spirit and the present Isaianic new-exodus context, serves to make an allusion to Isa. 42:1 almost certain.

More difficult is *ho agapētos.* Although occasionally it is attributed to an evocation of the sacrificial elements of Gen. 22, the absence of any explicit Jesus-Isaac typology or *aqedah* theology in Mark and the NT suggests otherwise (Davies and Chilton 1978). Similarly, seeing here an additional allusion to Isa. 42:1 (cf. Matt 12:18; "Jacob my servant" in Isa. 44:2; *Tg. Isa.* 42:1; see Gundry 1967: 30–31; Schneck 1994: 53–55) is problematic because *agapētos* is never used to render *bāḥîr* in the LXX, and the syntax suggests that it should be taken with *huios* to mean "beloved" (Turner 1926). The adjective "beloved" is used of Israel (LXX: Ps. 59:7 [60:5 ET]; 107:7 [108:6 ET]; 126:2 [127:2 ET]; 67:13?; 4Q522 9 II, 8; 4Q462 1, 11; *m. 'Abot* 3:15), of Abraham (4Q252 II, 8), Levi (4Q379 1, 2), Benjamin (4Q174 8, 3), of the Teacher of Righteousness (CD-B XX, 1, 14), the righteous (4Q177 IV, 14), and David, significantly, in *Targum Ps.* 2:7. In two nearby "servant Israel" passages in the LXX (Isa. 41:8–9; 44:2) *agapaō* is used of Israel (Gundry 1967: 31).

Although a clear-cut decision may not be possible or even desirable because Israel, the Davidic king, and presumably the servant are all Yahweh's "beloved sons," that *agapētos* seems syntactically connected with the Ps. 2 allusion suggests that the Psalms targumic tradition, of which Mark might well reflect an earlier form, is probably in view (but see Davies and Allison 1988–1997: 1:337, for whom *'itrĕ'ĕ* from *Targum Isa.* 42:1 is best rendered "beloved"). Jesus is Yahweh's beloved messianic son.

B. The Combined Citation/Allusion. 1. Ps. 2:7 in Context. Almost certainly reflecting 2 Sam. 7:14's statement of God's promise to David (cf. Ps. 89:26), Ps. 2 is commonly classified as an enthronement psalm written to celebrate the accession of the Davidic scion (Kraus 1986: 111–22). Such transitions, when the new king was relatively weak, often were ideal times for rebellion. On the other hand, rebellions were hardly confined to these occasions, and the Lord's speech to the king seems to imply that the enthronement is a past event—"I will tell of the decree the LORD *said* to me" (2:7a)—as do the events that the psalm envisages (Willis 1990: 36). Perhaps it is wiser to take the opening stanza (2:1–3) at face value and see the psalm as a response to the nations gathered in revolt against the Lord's universal kingship expressed on earth through his messianic regent, *mĕšîḥô* (Willis 1990: 44).

Initially incredulous at their folly, the psalmist records the Lord's mocking response, which soon turns to anger because God himself has set "my king on Zion, my holy mountain" (2:4–6). The divine commitment is then reiterated, but now by the Davidic scion, who recounts the prophetic word that the Lord decreed concerning David's offspring: "You are my son; this day I have begotten you" (2:7 [cf. 2 Sam. 7:14]). "Sonship," of course, is the language of covenantal relationship (e.g., Exod. 4:22; 2 Kings 11:12). That Pss. 1 and 2 were combined in some traditions (*y. Ber.* 4:3 [I.B]; *y. Ta'an.* 2:2 [II.C]; *b. Ber.* 9b–10b) suggests that as Yahweh's son, in keeping with the wisdom tradition, the Davidic king must accept Yahweh's instruction (Ps. 1:2; Deut. 17:18–20; cf. 2 Sam. 7:14b; see Brownlee 1971). Obviously, a "son" who delights in Yahweh's instruction (*torah* [again Ps. 1:2]) will enjoy prosperity, while those who rebel perish (Ps. 1:4, 6b; 2:2, 9, 12a).

The king continues with Yahweh's promise that he will inherit the nations (2:8), ruling them with a rod of iron and shattering their idolatrous rebellion (2:9). Because the Lord's decisive intervention is imminent (2:12 [see Kraus 1988–1989: 1:129]), the psalmist concludes with a warning: serve the Lord and give due homage to his anointed (2:11–12).

2. Ps. 2:7 in Judaism. Although the Davidic kingship lapsed with the Babylonian exile, this and other royal psalms were retained in Israel's Psalter probably because the Davidic covenant was eternal (e.g., 2 Sam. 7:16; 22:51; 23:5; cf. Isa. 55:3–5), thereby giving them an eschatological focus (H. Klein 1979: 68; A. A. Anderson 1972: 1:40; on the ongoing interest in a Davidic messiah during the exilic period, see Horbury 1998).

Psalms of Solomon 17 is virtually a commentary on Ps. 2, beginning with the confident declaration that the "kingdom of our God is forever over the nations in judgment" (v. 3 [cf. Mark 1:15]), and continuing especially in vv. 21–25, 30–32. Hostile rulers are destroyed (17:22–25), and the nations are subjugated to the Messiah (17:29–31), whose reign, as in the psalm, is both subordinate to and an extension of Yahweh's own kingship (17:1–4). However, because of Israel's rebellion, the land and Jerusalem are presently under foreign oppression (17:5–20). The later poet anticipates the day when a messianic Davidic king will purify God's city, and particularly the temple, (Embry 2002) of his enemies both inside and out (17:22, 30,

36). More generally, *Psalms of Solomon* combines the hope of Isa. 40's new exodus (*Pss. Sol.* 11 [see §B.2 of commentary on Mark 1:2–3 above; also Isa. 52:1 in *Pss. Sol.* 17:27–29; Isa. 55:5 in 17:31; Isa. 40:5 in 17:35]) with that of a Davidic messiah who is to rule over "my servant Israel," an expression largely confined to Isaiah's new-exodus prophecies (e.g., Isa. 41:8; 44:1, 21; 45:4; 49:3).

In 4Q174 1, I, 10–19, Ps. 2:1 relates to the "end of days." Establishing the "branch of David," to whom "I will be a father . . . and he will be a son" (1, I, 11, citing 2 Sam. 7:14 [cf. Ps. 2:7; Heb. 1:5]), the Lord through his Davidic agent will destroy the sons of Belial (1, I, 7–8; cf. Bons 1992, who links Ps. 2:2 and CD-A II, 7), raise up the fallen "hut of David" to restore Israel (1, I, 12–13, citing Amos 9:11), and establish his temple (1 I, 3–6 [cf. 2 Sam. 7:12–14]). 1Q28a II, 11–12 appropriately describes this future salvation as the time "when God begets the Messiah." Although subject to debate, if 4Q246's powerful "son of God" and "son of the Most High" who will rule nations (4Q246 II) is a messianic figure, then this too could be an echo of Ps. 2.

1 Enoch 48:10 (cf. 46:4) also appears to allude to Ps. 2:2 when stating that the kings and the mighty who have "denied the Lord of the Spirits and his Messiah" will fall before "that [previously referred to] Son of Man," the Elect One, the Messiah (VanderKam 1992: 171). For some, *4 Ezra* 13's account of "my son" who standing on a reconstituted Mount Zion destroys the nations assembled against him (13:32–38) amounts to an eschatological commentary on Ps. 2 (Knibb 1979: 169; Box 1912: lvi–vii).

As we noted, in the later Targum the Davidic son is "beloved" of God (2:7). But Yahweh is also described as terrifying the rebels by speaking to them "in his strength" (2:5). In 2:6, "I have anointed by my king and set him over my sanctuary," the Targum goes beyond Ps. 2 in making explicit the king's responsibility to safeguard the sanctity of the temple (cf. 4Q174). The final warning now becomes an admonition to the rebels "to accept instruction" (cf. the later *Midr. Ps.* 2:9, where the Messiah's victory is because he occupies himself with Torah, reflecting the close link between Pss. 1 and 2).

Similar themes emerge in the frequent citation of Ps. 2:1–4 in rabbinic literature, most often in the Messiah's eschatological defeat of Gog and Magog (cf. *Mek. Exod.* 15:9–10; *Lev. Rab.* 27:11; *Midr. Ps.* 2:3, 9, 10; *Pirqe R. El.* 18; 28; *Tanḥ. Gen.* 2:24; *Tanḥ. Lev.* 8:18; *b. Sukkah* 52a; see Signer 1983: 274) and Israel's victory over idolaters (e.g., *b. Ber.* 7b). Several texts relate this victory to the Yahweh-Warrior of Isa. 42:13 (*Exod. Rab.* 1:1; *Midr. Ps.* 2:2, 4; *Pesiq. Rab Kah.* 9:11). In *Pesiq. Rab Kah.* S 2:2, Ps. 2:2 warns Israel to expect future conflict prior to final victory, and in *S. Eli. Rab.* 18 the nations are given to the Sages because they studied Torah (Ps. 2:7–8; cf. the Torah-studying Messiah in *Midr. Ps.* 2:9).

Of particular interest is *Midr. Ps.* 2:9 (on Ps. 2:7), where the decree to David prompts a threefold recitation of Yahweh's decreed sonship of Israel, citing first Exod. 4:22 (the Law), then the exaltation of Isaiah's servant in Isa. 42:1; 52:13 (the Prophets), and finally Ps. 110:1; Dan. 7:13–14 (the Writings). Apparently, David's sonship is inseparable from Israel's, perhaps because he is seen as Israel's representative head. At the very least it indicates that in this tradition these five texts are central to Israel's identity.

3. Isa. 42:1 in Context. After the prologue's joyful announcement of warrior-shepherd Yahweh's coming in strength to save his exiled people (40:1–11), the prophet addresses fearful and unbelieving Israel on two fronts. First, in a lengthy disputation (40:12–31) he challenges Israel's questioning of Yahweh's ability and wisdom by extolling his incomparable supremacy over creation (40:12–26), which supremacy is now focused in his care for his people (40:27–31). Second, this compassion comes to concrete expression in his raising of Cyrus (41:1–7) to aid his servant Israel (41:8–20), against whom the idols and those who worship them are helpless (41:21–29) (see Brueggemann 1998: 22, 28–29). In a sense, then, Isa. 42:1–7(9), which consists of two distinct but clearly related parts, comes as something of a climax. In the first stanza Yahweh presents his servant whom he has chosen and in whom he delights (42:1–4), and in the second stanza Yahweh directly addresses the servant (42:5–7 [42:8–9 is addressed to "you" plural]).

The timeless difficulty is the identity of this enigmatic figure. There are several contributing factors. First, although the four "Servant Songs" identified by Bernhard Duhm exhibit a similar character (their extent and number is debated [see C. R. North 1948; Mettinger 1983]), the fact that ancient interpreters saw them describing different figures suggests caution in using these poems to interpret either each other or without regard to their immediate context.

Second, the term "servant" has a broad usage, including individual and corporate senses. In the singular, and almost always in apposition, it designates most commonly David (e.g., 2 Sam. 7:5–8; 1 Kings 3:6; 2 Kings 8:19; Ps. 78:70; 89:3; Isa. 37:35; Jer. 33:21; Ezek. 34:23) and members of the Davidic dynasty (2 Sam. 3:18; 1 Kings 8:24–26; 2 Kings 19:34 [cf. Jer. 33:21–22, 26]), including the future scion (Zech. 3:8), then Moses (e.g., Deut. 34:5; Josh. 1:2; 9:24), as well as Abraham (Gen. 26:24; Deut. 9:27 [with Isaac and Jacob]), the nation of Israel/Jacob (e.g., Jer. 30:10; Ezek. 28:25), Job (Job 1:8), Caleb (Num. 14:24), Zerubbabel (Hag. 2:23), and even Nebuchadnezzar (Jer. 25:9). When "servant" is combined with "chosen" (Isa. 42:1), the range is reduced to David (Ps. 78:70; 89:3 [see Rowe 2002: 50–51]), Zerubbabel (Hag. 2:23), and perhaps Moses (Ps. 106:23; cf. 105:26). In Isaiah, "servant" in this individual sense is used of Isaiah himself (20:3), Eliakim (22:20), David (37:35), and perhaps an unnamed prophet (44:26). (In the plural it is also used of the prophets [2 Kings 9:7; 17:13, 23; 21:10; 24:2; cf. Jer. 7:25; 25:4; 26:5; Amos 3:7], and in Isaiah of the righteous [54:17; 56:6; 63:17; 65:8–9, 13–15; 66:14].)

In the immediate context, however, "chosen servant" (sg.) is used repeatedly of collective Jacob-Israel (Isa. 41:8–9; 42:1; 44:1–2; 45:4 [but of the pl. "witnesses" in 43:10; cf. 1 Chron. 16:13; Ps. 105:6, 43; 136:22; Isa. 65:9, 13–15; see Blenkinsopp 1997]), who is also "upheld" (41:10). The parallelism between 41:1–20 and 41:21–42:17 overall, and particularly 41:8–16 and this passage, suggests that the servant is Jacob-Israel (Clifford 1984: 89; cf. Goldingay 1979).

However, there are well-known problems. The servant of this poem—the one on whom Yahweh's spirit rests, who accepts Yahweh's purposes (cf. 40:13; see Goldingay 2001: 239), is concerned for justice and yet gentle to the bruised, exhibits steadfast faithfulness, and for whose *tôrâ* the nations wait—stands in marked contrast to Jacob-Israel, who is already despondent, aggrieved (40:27),

and fearful (41:10–14), and later appears as blind and deaf (42:18–25; 43:8) and hostile (45:9–10; 46:8; 48:1–8) (see R. E. Watts 1990a). Moreover, the justice that the servant effects—kindness and gentleness to the bruised and fading—is counter to Jacob-Israel's expectations (Beuken 1972). Consequently, 42:1–7(9) seems to describe both what Yahweh intended his servant Jacob-Israel to be but is now in no state to realize—a light to the nations (see Goldingay 1979: 292)—and the means by which Israel, now become like those nations, will also itself be delivered (42:6b–7). This might explain why, although the prophet elsewhere describes Jacob-Israel as Yahweh's servant, he is strangely silent here (cf. 49:3, where in another similar installation oracle, although Israel is mentioned, the characteristically paired "Jacob" element is surprisingly absent). If 49:5–6 describes the same figure as does 42:1–7(9), then the former's having a responsibility to Israel also supports this distinction between the servant and Jacob-Israel, though now magnified because of Jacob-Israel's intervening recalcitrance (48:1–8) (see Goldingay 2001: 281–82).

In terms of characteristics, however, while Isa. 42's servant resembles aspects of the prophets (particularly if 49:1–6[7] describes the same servant as does 42:1), the concern for justice (42:1, 3–4 [Beuken 1972]) and the formal similarities with a kingly installation (1 Sam. 9:15–17; 16:12–13; Zech. 3:8; 6:12 [Beuken 1972]) implies royalty (Kaiser 1962; Dijkstra 1978).

Although this figure sometimes is understood to be Cyrus (also called in righteousness [41:2] and taken by the hand [45:1]; cf. 42:6 [Blenkinsopp 2000–2003: 2:211]), the cluster of Judean royal cult motifs in the surrounding context more strongly suggests a Davidic figure (Wilson 1986: 24–62, citing, e.g., Pss. 2; 46; 48; 72; 89; 132; Isa. 9; cf. Sommer 1998: 84–85 on Isa. 11 parallels; Schultz 1995; cf. Williamson 1998, 117–20, who sees here the transfer of the Davidides' task to servant Israel), who, as we noted, also happens to be the individual most commonly designated as the Lord's chosen servant (2 Sam. 6:21; 1 Kings 8:16; 11:34; 2 Chron. 6:6; Ps. 78:70; 89:3). Given that the focus of Isaiah as a whole is the restoration of Zion (Dumbrell 1985; C. R. Seitz 1991), it is noteworthy that Yahweh's rescue and protection of Zion is commonly on behalf of "my servant

David" (Isa. 37:35; cf. 2 Kings 19:34; 20:6; Ps. 132:10; 144:10), and it is the covenant mercies extended to him that are connected with the restoration of Zion in Isa. 55:3–5 (cf. R. E. Watts 2004a, 503). If so, the Targum's messianic interpretation of this passage makes sense (see below). Nevertheless, it is significant that the prophet again stops short of an explicit identification, perhaps because of the utter failure of the Davidic line earlier in the book and/or because he wants to emphasize Yahweh's supreme kingship (see Eissfeldt 1962: 203–5; Mettinger 1997; Schultz 1995: 158–59).

At the same time, however, a case can be made for parallels with Moses (especially if the four so-called songs are read together), the second most frequently designated "servant," not least because of the combination of prophetic and new-exodus motifs (Hugenberger 1995).

The nature of the servant's task is clearer and is probably the main point of the oracle. As we noted, the key theme throughout is justice. It is through Yahweh's servant that his merciful new-exodus justice will be extended in gentleness and persistence to the bruised, the fading, the blind and imprisoned, though apparently it will not resemble the usual exercise of kingly power (Beuken 1972; in contrast to the conqueror from the north [Childs 2001: 325]). Here too there is ambiguity (see Blenkinsopp 2000–2003: 2:212). On the one hand, the recipients resemble exiled Jacob-Israel—note the particular focus on blindness (42:7 [cf. the Targum]; also the promise to lead the blind along a path that they do not know [42:16]), a condition almost characteristic of Jacob-Israel in these chapters (42:18–19; 43:8)—yet on the other hand, the idolatrous nations are also blind (44:18) and are described as demoralized "survivors" (45:20; cf. 41:11), and they too eagerly await (*yḥl* [42:4b]) and will benefit from the servant's *tôrâ* (van Winkle 1985; Beuken 1972; cf. R. E. Watts 2004a).

The unique expression *librît 'ām* in 42:6 is likewise ambiguous and could refer to a covenant people or, more likely, in a metonymic sense to one who will establish a covenant for the people. But who is/are the "people"? The language is ambiguous (see Oswalt 1998: 117–20; Blenkinsopp 2000–2003: 2:212). But whether understood as "blind" Jacob-Israel (recalling that it was really

only under the covenant made with David and his son Solomon that Israel became—even if only momentarily—"a light to the nations," Watts 2004a: 501–5) and/or the nations, the climactic second synonymous expression envisages the servant as a light to the nations, probably related to their awaiting his *tôrâ* and perhaps reflecting the Abrahamic covenant, through which Abraham would become the father of many nations (Goldingay 2001: 241; again Watts 2004a: 501–5). Finally, that the servant will not grow faint or be crushed (42:4) suggests not only that his task will require some effort, but also that he will face resistance (J. L. McKenzie 1968: 38; Westermann 1964b: 96).

What are we to make of all this? Many commentators seem to feel the pressure to choose between a collective interpretation and an individual one. Perhaps the choice is a false one. On the one hand, it is clear that the "servant" is somehow Israel; on the other hand, if Israel was to play a part in God's plan for the nations, then his people would need some kind of leader, as the Targum quite naturally understood.

Since the leader-representatives were to embody Israel's call, it is not unreasonable that the prophet blurs the distinction between leaders and people, hence his vision of a restored Israel comprised of many servants (54:17 [see Beuken 1990]) upon whom the Davidic blessings devolve (55:3 [see Williamson 1978]). If so, it might be that in light of Israel's past (Abraham, exodus/ conquest, David/Solomon), the prophet knows what God's servant Israel is called to be, and thus 42:1–7(9) could be an invitational restatement of that call. On the other hand, he understands that Jacob-Israel is hardly living up to that call. He also knows that in the past God raised up individual servants (e.g., David, Moses) who also have some kind of representative role vis-à-vis the nation (see Rogerson 1970) to lead and save his people and therefore *tôrâ* knows the kind of servant that Yahweh must and will provide to effect his purposes. If so, then 42:1–7(9) describes all that Israel was called to be and at the same time the nation's concomitant representative leader. As the latter, the servant, in combining various facets of former deliverers (e.g., David and Moses), not only embodies all that Israel was meant to be, but also acts on Israel's behalf. It is through him that other previously blind and deaf Jacob-Israelites will truly become Yahweh's servants.

The enigma of the servant is thus perhaps due to the tension between the ideal and the reality, combined with the very close identification of Israel and its leaders. The servant in 42:1–7(9) seems, then, to reflect what Israel was meant to be as well as characteristics of the nation's representative deliverer, through whom that ideal will be attained. Ultimately, however, the enigma remains, perhaps intentionally, and dogmatism is best avoided (see Childs 2001: 326; Goldingay 2001: 239).

4. Isa. 42:1 in Judaism. One of the earliest interpretations is the Old Greek, which, in keeping with the surrounding "servant" passages (41:8; 43:10), identifies the servant with Jacob-Israel by inserting "Jacob" in the first verset and "Israel" in the second. In terms of the Dead Sea Scrolls, it has been suggested that 42:1–6 lies behind the declaration by the Teacher of Righteousness in 1QH[a] XII, 12:5–6, "You have brightened my face with your covenant . . . you have revealed yourself to me with your light" (Brooke 1997: 615), but the connections are faint.

On the other hand, the messianic Son of Man in the largely first-century Similitudes of Enoch (*1 En.* 37–71) is described as the Chosen One (39:6), who will be a light to the nations (48:4) and bring forth justice (46:4–5; 49:2), which combination around a Spirit-anointed figure suggests the influence of at least the Isaianic servant as described in Isa. 42:1–7(9) (cf. 49:6; 40:5). The picture in *Pss. Sol.* 17:29, 31, 35 of the nations streaming to Jerusalem to receive justice from a messianic king upon whom the spirit rests resembles Isa. 42:3b, 4, 6b, but dependence is not explicit.

Similarly, in *Tg. Isa.* 42:7 the servant is to open "the eyes of the house of Israel who are as blind to the law" (cf. *S. Eli. Rab.* 18[16]; cf. [14]15, citing Isa. 42:16, 18) and "to bring out their exiles . . . from among the Gentiles," which activities are elsewhere attributed to the Messiah (cf. *Tg. Isa.* 10:27; 14:29; 16:1, 53; see Chilton 1987: 81). This is perhaps why several of that Targum's manuscript traditions of 42:1 have "my servant, the Messiah" (cf. 43:10: "my servant the Messiah with whom I am well pleased"; see Chilton 1987: 80, xxxi).

Testament of Judah 24:1–6, mentioned earlier in the context of the opened heavens, describes the messianic king as one who will enable Israel to be true sons through his teaching, who is a fountain of life for all humanity (cf. 1QH[a] XXIII, 10; 4Q431 I, 5), and who will "illumine the scepter of my kingdom" and be a "rod of righteousness for the nations" (24:3–6). This cluster of ideas—restoration of Israel, life and righteousness for the nations, and in the context of illumination—are close to those found in Isa. 42. Again, this could be a later Christian interpolation, though not as clearly so as in other parts of the *Testaments of the Twelve Patriarchs* (see §C of commentary on Mark 1:10 above).

There are a number of allusions to elements of Isa. 42 in the Talmud (42:3 in *b. Ber.* 56b; *b. Yebam.* 93b; 42:5 in *b. Ber.* 52b), but they, strikingly enough, are concerned with matters such as dream interpretation. Only slightly more relevant is *b. Ketub.* 111a, where Yahweh's giving of breath/ spirit to the people upon the earth (Isa. 42:5) is interpreted to mean the resurrection of those who lived specifically in the land of Israel, suggesting an eschatological orientation (*Pesiq. Rab Kah.* 22:5a reads likewise, but specifically in terms of Israel's vindication).

The later *Midr. Ps.* 2:9 on Ps. 2:7 (already alluded to in the voice from heaven) sees Isa. 42:1 and 52:13 as referring to Israel, though in a messianic setting that links David's and Israel's sonship. *Midrash Psalms* 42:5 (6), on the other hand, speaks of two redeemers, Elijah in Mal. 3:1 and the servant in Isa. 42:1. Describing the former as light and the latter as the truth, namely, the Messiah the son of David, it reads Isa. 42:1 messianically, concluding with a prayer that God send forth both. *Pesiqta Rabbati* 36:1 likewise applies Isa. 42:1 to noble Israel during the messianic time.

Consequently, when it actually touches on the identity of the "servant," Jewish tradition is divided between Israel and an individual, though there is something of a representational dynamic present in *Midr. Ps.* 2:9. However, in each case where an individual is understood, he is always Israel's messianic deliverer.

C. Ps. 2:7; Isa. 42:1 in Mark. Mark's opening mixed citation and the Spirit's descent through the rent heavens have already announced Yahweh's new-exodus eschatological intervention on behalf of his people. And as in the psalm, God in heaven declares that Jesus is his Davidic messianic agent (cf. 10:47; 11:10; also Ps. 110:1 in 12:36; 1Q28a), his obedient and beloved Son (e.g., 3:29; 9:7; 12:28–34), whose first public action is to announce the inbreaking new-exodus reign of God (1:14–15).

But there are some further implications. Psalm 2, as does Isaiah's rending of the heavens (see above), envisages resistance from the hostile idolatrous nations (cf. *Pss. Sol.* 17; 4Q174; also various rabbinic materials noted above). This too is picked up in Mark. On the one hand, the designation of Jesus as "son of God" collides with Roman imperial claims (cf. the centurion's confession in 15:39; see C. A. Evans 2000), as did Moses' similar designation of Israel in the first exodus challenge those of Pharaoh (Exod. 4:22). On the other hand, as we noted earlier (see commentary on Mark 1:10 above), the nations' hostility translates in Mark primarily into Jesus' conflict with the demons (who stand behind the nations' idols). And just as in the later Targum God's intervention was characterized by strong and terrifying speech, so too Jesus' strong word provokes terror in the demons (1:23–27; 5:7–13; cf. 1:7). Finally, as Davidic authority extended over the nations, so also in Mark there are intimations of his messianic son's rule likewise extending beyond Israel's heartland (5:1–20 [on the military overtones of this text, see Derrett 1984b]; cf. 7:24–8:10).

But at the same time, as the Dead Sea Scrolls and *Psalms of Solomon* imply, opposition to the messianic rule also comes from the apostate within Israel. This again is echoed in Mark where Israel's leadership (2:6, 16, 18, 24; 3:2, 6) and particularly the Jerusalem authorities (3:22; 7:1; 11:18, 27; 12:12–13) quickly align themselves against Jesus (1:22, 27; 2:10; 3:15; 11:28; 12:35–40) (see Kingsbury 1989). Finally, just as the interpretations of Ps. 2 in 4Q174 and *Psalms of Solomon* focused on the temple and the purging of Jerusalem, so also in Mark. This time, however, the intercalated cursing of the fig tree and demonstration in the temple (11:12–14, 17b, 20–21) are followed by the announcement of the latter's impending destruction and apparent replacement with another built around Jesus (13:2; 12:10; cf. CD-A I, 4–5; 1QS VIII, 7–14; see commentary on Mark 12:10–11 below). Consequently, just as

Ps. 2:12 urges the rebels to submit to the son or, with the later Targum, to "accept instruction," so in Mark Jesus' instruction becomes definitive of authentic Israel (3:28–35; cf. the builders metaphor again in 12:10–11).

As will be developed later at various points, this invocation of Ps. 2 also prepares for Mark's later appeal to other royal psalms: Pss. 118 (11:9–10; 12:10–11 [celebration of the victory anticipated in Ps. 2]); 110 (12:36; 14:62); 22 (Mark 15:24, 34 [exaltation, after tribulation, over the nations]).

Turning to Isa. 42:1, we note that its being linked with Ps. 2:7 resolves much of the ambiguity that otherwise surrounds the Isaianic "servant" and also integrates the psalm's messianic hopes within Mark's overarching Isaianic new-exodus horizon—a pattern consistent with the Targum, which sees the Davidic messiah as the agent of God's vindication of Israel (cf. *Midr. Ps.* 2:9; see Chilton 1987: xvii). For Mark, in keeping with (1) the royal motifs both within and around the "song," (2) the most common use of "servant" terminology in connection with Zion/Jerusalem (cf. Ps. 2:6: "my holy hill"), and (3) those Jewish traditions wherein the addressee is held to be an individual, Isaiah's Spirit-anointed (cf. Mark 1:10) "servant" is also Israel's Davidic messianic deliverer.

As with Ps. 2, Isa. 42 recognizes that Yahweh's agent can expect resistance. And just as Mark subsequently appeals to other royal psalms to develop this Ps. 2 theme, so too his accounts of Jesus' passion predictions will draw on elements of Isaianic anticipation of opposition and suffering (see commentary on Isa. 50; 53 in Mark 9:12b; 10:33–34; 14:61, 65 below).

However, whereas Ps. 2 took a threatening stance toward the rebellious nations and, in several Jewish traditions, the faithless in Israel, Isa. 42 presents the positive alternative. Although he will face opposition (see commentary on Mark 8:31; 9:31; 10:33–34, 45 below), Jesus will restore exiled blind and deaf Jacob-Israel (see commentary on Mark 8:18, 22–26; 11:46–52 below), upon whom the Davidic blessings will devolve, and be a light to the nations, whose survivors will benefit from his Torah (see commentary on Isa. 56:7 in Mark 11:17 and on Deut. 6:4; Lev. 19:8 in Mark 12:29–31 below) and the covenant that he establishes (see commentary on Exod. 24:8 in

Mark 14:24 below). In this sense, the observation by E. Lohmeyer (1953: 24) that the *eudok-* word group reflects appointment for an eschatological task is correct. Here again we find the two alternatives implied in Mark's opening mixed citation: salvation for those who submit to Yahweh's agent, judgment on those who do not.

At the same time, just as Isaiah's enigmatic "servant" was also understood in some sense to be faithful Israel, so Jesus' "Son of God" designation, his passing through the water, and his forty-day desert sojourn identify him with Israel's past (Exod. 4:22; cf. Jer. 38:20 LXX [31:20 ET]; see Bretscher 1968; Hooker 1991: 47): as Yahweh's Davidic messianic servant deliverer, he is also true and faithful Israel.

Interestingly, Mark's combination of texts here (Ps. 2:7; Isa. 42:1; Exod. 4:22 [see below]) and more broadly his presentation of Jesus as Dan. 7:13's son of man (see commentary on Mark 2:10 below) in combination with Ps. 110 (Mark 12:36; 14:62 [both Pss. 2 and 110 being linked with first-century "son of man" speculation; again see commentary on Mark 2:10 below]) and allusions to the Isaianic servant (see below) are entirely consistent with the later *Midr. Ps.* 2:9, which not only integrates corporate and individual sonship, but also does so in terms of exaltation and vindication.

D. Theological Use. The allusions to Ps. 2 and Isa. 42 continue the eschatological fulfillment focus of Mark's narrative, since both were understood in various ways to refer to Israel's final deliverance. However, their primary contribution is to Mark's Christology. Whereas Mark's opening mixed citation identified Jesus with Yahweh's very presence, here he invokes two figures from Israel's Scriptures. Jesus is David's messianic heir who will finally prevail over the enemies of God's people and who, in several Jewish traditions, is expected to restore the purity of the temple (Ps. 2). He is also Yahweh's Spirit-anointed "servant" who will both deliver servant Israel's blind and deaf captives and bring justice to the nations (Isa. 42). In both instances, however, serious opposition and, in the case of Isaiah, deep suffering are expected. At the same time, reflecting something of the ambiguity surrounding Isaiah's "servant," Jesus is also the one who realizes Israel's call to sonship.

1:44–45

A. NT Context. NA[27] identifies Jesus' command to the healed man in 1:44 as an allusion to Lev. 13:49; 14:2–4, but more likely it reflects a general influence of the Levitical instructions for sufferers who have recovered from the disease. The account in 1:40–45 of the healing of the "leper" (or one suffering "scale disease" [so Milgrom 1991–2001: 768, in order to distinguish the ailment from modern leprosy]) concludes Mark's opening presentation of Jesus' mighty words and deeds (1:16–45). Whereas Jesus' casting out an unclean spirit (1:21–28) and his healing of Peter's mother-in-law (1:29–31) serve as specific examples of the exorcisms and healings that characterize Mark's summation of Jesus' ministry (1:34a, 34b), this somewhat "isolated" event seems to have a significance all its own (cf. Kertelge 1970: 70–71; Marcus 1999: 178). In another display of his authority to remove impurity, and either motivated by compassion (reading, with most manuscripts, *splanchnizomai*) or enraged (*orgizomai*, the minority reading) at the unclean spirit causing the disease (Hooker 1991: 80; see §C below), Jesus heals the sufferer. In compliance with the law given to Moses (Lev. 14:1), he charges the newly restored man to show himself to the priest (*deixon tō hierei* [cf. Lev. 13:49]).

B. Lev. 13:49; 14:2–4 in Context. Leviticus 13:49 and 14:2–4 belong to the major biblical treatment of "leprosy," found in Lev. 13–14. "Scale disease" constituted a grave threat against Israel's cultic purity (Lev. 5:3). Its contamination was likened to that contracted in touching a corpse (Num. 12:12). Sufferers were regarded as the living dead (Num. 12:12; 2 Kings 5:7; Job 18:13; cf. rending the clothes in Gen. 37:34; 2 Sam. 1:11, and covering the upper lip in Ezek. 24:17, 22 [see Wenham 1979: 200–201]) and were excluded from the camp (Lev. 13:45–46). In several high-profile cases leprosy is seen as judgment on particularly egregious sins (e.g., Num. 12:10; 2 Kings 5:27; 15:5; 2 Chron. 26:21; cf. 2 Sam. 3:29). A cure lay solely in Yahweh's purview, the rare healings occurring only through his agents calling on his name (Num. 12; cf. 2 Kings 5:1–14). In Leviticus, the priest merely responds to circumstances in order to safeguard the sanctity of Yahweh's people and dwelling place (Lev. 14:1–7; cf. *m. Neg.* 3:1). The prophets offer no explicit eschatological hope for the restoration of those having the affliction, but there is the general promise of the removal of all uncleanness (note in the LXX *akathartos* in Isa. 35:8; 64:5 [64:6 ET]; cf. *akatharsia* in Ezek. 36:25–29; see also Isa. 52:1, 11; Ezek. 14:11; 43:7; Zech. 13:2).

C. Lev. 13:49 in Judaism. Later Jewish tradition reflected in the Dead Sea Scrolls, the rabbis, and the Targumim contain numerous discussions of and allusions to purity issues surrounding "lepers" (see the examples in Milgrom 1991–2001: 768–901; cf. Neyrey 1986). Those afflicted with the malady continue to be regarded as a grave threat to purity (Josephus, *Ag. Ap.* 1.281), likened to a corpse in terms of uncleanness (11Q19 XLV, 17–18), and excluded from the community (1Q28a II, 3b–7; Josephus, *Ant.* 3.261; *Ag. Ap.* 1.281). In the Dead Sea Scrolls, with their clear division between the righteous/pure and the wicked/impure (e.g., 1QS V), and in spite of the hope of eschatological purification (1QS IV, 18–23), there seems to be some expectation of lepers remaining in the messianic age, since they were to be excluded from the eschatological messianic feast (1Q28a II, 6) and the new temple (11Q19 XLV, 17–18; 11Q20 XII, 10).

For the rabbis, the defilement of leprosy was of particular concern (occupying an entire tractate, *m. Nega'im*). Sometimes attributed to demons (*b. Hor.* 10a), leprosy was regarded as judgment on particularly wicked sins (e.g., *Lev. Rab.* 16:1; 17:3) and seen as God's way of exiling the wicked (*Lev. Rab.* 18:5). In *Pesiq. Rab Kah.* 7:10, leprosy of the skin (after first afflicting the stones of the house, then the house, garment, etc. [see *Tanh. Lev.* 4:14; 5:7, 12]) is the last stage of God's warning to an unrepentant sinner before that person is finally excluded from the camp. As such, it becomes a precursor to national exile (*Tanh. Lev.* 5:12; cf. *Pesiq. Rab.* 33:13). Curing leprosy was equivalent to raising the dead (cf. *b. Ned.* 64b; *b. Sanh.* 47a; *b. Hul.* 7b; cf. 2 Kings 5:7). The removal of leprosy might have been seen as part of the messianic age (if included in general healing [cf. 1QS IV, 6; 4Q427 7 II, 6; *Jub.* 23:26–30; *1 En.* 96:3; *2 Bar.* 73:2; *4 Ezra* 8:53; *Gen. Rab.* 20:5]; the evidence of oft-cited Str-B 1:594–95 is at best indirect, applying only if the healing of Isa. 35:5 in *Pesiq. Rab.* 15:22 is assumed to include leprosy [cf. *Tanh. Exod.* 5:13; *Mek. Exod.* 20:18; *b. Sanh.* 91b; *Sipre*

Num. 1:10 (2:2); *Lev. Rab.* 18:3–4; *Num. Rab.* 7:1; *Pesiq. Rab.* 7:7; also Matt. 11:5/Luke 7:22]). In the Dead Sea Scrolls and for the rabbis, the ailment seems to have been attributed to evil spirits (cf. *b. Ketub.* 61b; 4Q272 1 II, 2; see Baumgarten 1990; 1999).

D. Lev. 13:49 in Mark. Mark's account highlights a number of issues. Most significantly, and in keeping with the opening sentence, Jesus does what only Yahweh can do (cf. *ean thelēs* and *dynasai* in 1:40b with Wis. 12:18; see Davies and Allison 1988–1997: 2:12). Jesus did not pursue his own glory (1:44a), and we learn why he was no longer able to go about openly in the towns (1:45). Although Jesus' command (1:44b) echoes most closely Lev. 13:49 LXX, which concerns infected clothing, it nevertheless presupposes priestly primacy in matters of cultic purity. As the immediate context for the following five controversy stories in 2:1–3:6 (see Dewey 1977), the account also serves to undercut the various charges of "lawbreaking" contained therein (Hooker 1988: 225–26).

Mark's "witness" demonstrates that Jesus' basic orientation toward both the law and the priesthood was one of compliance (1:44b, echoing Leviticus [see Milgrom 1991–2001: 776–77]) and that he cured the man. In regard to the latter, whereas Moses had to cry out to God (cf. Hanina ben Dosa in *b. Ber.* 34b), Elisha refrained from physical contact with Naaman, and the priest could only pronounce on the cure, Jesus by his own word and touch effects it, thereby transcending Moses the lawgiver, Elijah the prophet, and the priesthood (see commentary on Deut. 30:15 in Mark 3:4 and on Ps. 110 in Mark 12:36 below).

11Q19 LVIII, 15–21 emphasizes the dependence of the king on the high priest's guidance before waging holy war. Here it follows Num. 27:21, where Joshua's authority is explicitly stated to be less than Moses' and thus subordinated to the high priest, whom the king must consult before engaging in his liberation of Israel (see Milgrom 1989: 186). In Mark, however, for Jesus to have already begun his campaign while only subsequently sending the man to the priests, and that to notify them, not to seek their approval, further intimates his greater authority.

E. Theological Use. If the baptism, echoing Israel's exodus experience, designated Jesus as God's son, then this passage demonstrates that he is indeed an obedient son (see commentary on Ps. 2 in Mark 1:11 above). Not only does the healing itself reinforce the claim that God's victorious intervention on behalf of his people has begun, but also the fact that Jesus commands rather than requests the cure underlines the implication of Mark's opening mixed citation that in some mysterious way God himself has come among us. Whereas the law could declare the man clean only after the fact, Jesus, by his personal authority, effects the purification. Jesus not only conforms to Moses' requirement on purity, but also, in his power to effect that very purity and grant access to God's presence, transcends both Moses and the priesthood. Furthermore, to the extent that leprosy was linked to exile (*Tanh. Lev.* 5:12) and its removal to Israel's restoration, the healing suggests that the age to come has broken in. Here is the one who can purify not only the unclean within Israel but also unclean Israel itself.

2:7

A. NT Context. If 1:16–45 lays out in a few brief but powerful vignettes the inauguration of Yahweh's Isaianic new-exodus intervention through Jesus' mighty words and deeds, then 2:1–3:6 presents the negative response. Already intimated in Mark's opening appeal to Mal. 3:1 (1:2–3) and his linking of John's imprisonment with the beginning of Jesus' proclamation (1:14), official Israel's "idolatrous" unpreparedness (see commentary on Mark 4:12 below) now comes to the fore. Although Mark has just shown that Jesus does not take a cavalier approach to Moses or the priestly task of regulating Israel's purity (1:39–45), the account of the healing of the paralytic (2:1–12) is the first in a series of five increasingly hostile controversies (Gundry 1993: 109) in which Jesus is compelled to respond to precisely such criticisms (Dewey 1977: 52–55, 181–97; Kingsbury 1989: 67–69; Hooker 1991: 83–84; Marcus 1999: 212–13) and which culminate in a plot against his life (3:6).

The central issue is Jesus' forgiveness of the paralytic's sins (2:5). Appearing here for the first time, Mark's scribes have no firsthand experience of Jesus' authority, and their initial encounter is with his audacious words (only later, when his powerful deeds are undeniable, will questions concerning their origins emerge [3:22]). The scribes regard Jesus' words as blasphemous, and their indignant response, with its Shema-like syntax

in 2:7b (Marcus 1999: 222; Donahue and Harrington 2002: 95), reflects the thoroughgoing conviction that there is only one who forgives sin: God (see, e.g., Exod. 34:9; Num. 14:18–19; Ps. 25:18; 32:5; 103:3; 130:4; Isa. 55:7). Since they do not say "only priests can forgive sins" (nor be it noted, "only wisdom") nor express concern about the location—"sins can only be forgiven in the temple"—it seems clear that their primary concern is Jesus' assuming authority that belongs to God alone. There are, however, only two texts where Yahweh's self-identification—an emphasis suggested by the allusion to the Shema (cf. Deut. 6:4 with Mark 2:7b)—is explicitly predicated on such a declaration. They occur in the contexts of the first exodus (Exod. 34:6–7) and the Isaianic new exodus (Isa. 43:25; cf. 44:22–24). Mark's opening sentence and the unique Isaianic association of the lame and forgiveness of sins in the eschatological time (cf. Isa. 33:23–24; 35:6; see R. E. Watts 2000: 172–74) suggest that if any echo is in view, it is of the latter (Grimm 1981: 135–37; van Iersel 1988: 62; Schneck 1994: 70–73).

B. Isa. 43:25. Yahweh's declaration—"I, I am he who, for my own sake, wipes away your transgressions and who remembers your transgressions no more"—occurs in the midst of a confrontation with Jacob-Israel in 43:22–28 (Schoors 1973: 190–93). Accused of abandoning his people (43:28), Yahweh responds by pointing to the nature of Israel's past worship (43:23–24b [so Westermann 1969; Schoors 1973; Oswalt 1998; Blenkinsopp 2000–2003]) or, perhaps less likely, more recent complaints (40:27 [so Delitzsch 1973; Goldingay 2001]). The fact is, however, that Israel, despite its profuse religious observances, had abandoned Yahweh (43:24b).

Then, in stark contrast and echoing the opening new-exodus declaration of forgiveness in the prologue (40:1–2), 40:25 recalls Yahweh's response to Jacob-Israel's idolatry in the first exodus: although punishing when he must (40:28), his very identity is predicated on forgiving sins (Exod. 34:5–9). It is time, therefore, for Jacob-Israel to forget the past and accept the new thing (43:19) that Yahweh, for his own glory and to extend his light to the nations, was doing: forgiving their transgressions and coming to effect their deliverance (40:2) (see Westermann 1964b: 133; cf. Blenkinsopp 2000–2003: 2:232).

C. Isa. 43:25 in Judaism. In the Targum, Isaiah's charges against Israel's cultic aberration are amplified to include its teachers' rebellion against Yahweh's Memra (43:27), meaning both Torah and the prophetic word (Chilton 1987: xv).

The conviction that it is God alone who forgives sin is present in several texts (Sir. 2:11; *Midr. Ps.* 17:3; cf. CD-A III, 18; 1QS XI, 14; 1QHᵃ XII, 37). Although it is sometimes claimed that the eschatological priest (*T. Levi* 18:9) or the Messiah (*Tg. Isa.* 53:4; *Pesiq. Rab.* 37:2) also can do so, in fact the former merely announces and the latter only intercedes for God's forgiveness (Guelich 1989: 87; Marcus 1999: 217). The situation is clearer in the oft-cited *Prayer of Nabonidus*, where the supplicant appears to claim that a Jewish exorcist "forgave my sins" (4Q242 1–3 4). However, apart from the translational uncertainties (Blackburn 1991: 139), given the overwhelming preponderance of Jewish tradition explicitly to the contrary, its solitary nature and that this assessment is put in the mouth of a Babylonian suggest caution (Green 1997: 241n52). It is difficult to see Mark's scribes (or the Jewish exorcist himself) affirming this evaluation carte blanche.

Yet sin and sickness were closely related in Jewish thinking (Deut. 28:27; 2 Sam. 12:13; Ps. 41:4; 107:17–18; *b. Šabb.* 55a [see commentary on leprosy above]), as were healing and forgiveness (2 Sam. 12:13; 2 Chron. 7:14; Ps. 103:3; Isa. 38:17; 57:18–19; James 5:15; *b. Ned.* 41a) (see C. D. Marshall 1989: 88n2). On this basis, a healed individual might subsequently consider his or her sins to have been forgiven. Significantly, initiating a healing with a pronouncement of forgiveness is unattested.

Of particular interest, given Mark's account of Jesus granting forgiveness apart from cultic activity, is *Tanh. Lev.* 3:6. After a discussion of Lev. 9:2's requirements for sin offerings, the section concludes with a statement of the Holy One, based on Isa. 43:25, that whereas in this world forgiveness of sins requires sacrifice, in the world to come "I will wipe away their sins without an offering."

D. Isa. 43:25 in Mark. Jesus' forgiveness of the paralytic's sin is, as we will see, the other side of the coin of his extraordinary cure of the leper—a connection strengthened if the scribes are primarily of priestly origin (note the absence of any reference to Pharisees [see Marcus 1999: 519–24]). Jesus' question here, "Which is easier to say . . . ?" is really about "whom," not "which" (cf. "who" in 2:7b), since although anyone can "say" (2:9) anything, the real issue is whether what is said actually transpires. Thus the answer is, "Neither one" (Hooker 1967: 88; Hofius [1983], who also rejects any notion of a putative priestly absolution being in view). For humans, both things are equally impossible, and for God, neither is harder because "healing" comprised restoration of the whole person, including the person's relationship with him (Brown 1995: 28–31). The point at issue, then, seems to be not only Jesus' initiation of a healing with a declaration of forgiveness (2:5b) but also his blasphemously autonomous manner in doing so. Hence comes Jesus' subsequent remark on the authority given to the Son of Man (see below).

This healing thus constitutes a characteristic sign of Isaiah's new exodus (Isa. 35:6a; cf. the later *Pesiq. Rab Kah.* 106b; *Mek. Exod.* 20:18), where the lame walking (and the blind seeing, deaf hearing, etc.) reverses the idolater's curse: "Their idols . . . have feet but they do not walk, . . . those who make them are like them" (Ps. 115:4–8; 135:15–18; cf. Isa. 6:10–12; see Beale 1991). There is, however, one significant difference. The language of Isa. 35 is most probably metaphorical, as it is in Isa. 6 (and from which it derives) and as several earlier Jewish traditions apparently understood (see, e.g., *Tg. Isa.* 35; CD-A I, 9; II, 14–16; 1QS IV, 6b–11a; 4Q434 1, I, 3–4; 4Q504 1–2, II, 12–16). Here it is concrete. To the extent that Yahweh's granting of forgiveness was the sine qua non of Israel's release from exile (Isa. 43:25; cf. 40:1–2; 44:22), Jesus' pronouncement is fully consistent with Mark's assertion that the new exodus has begun with him (Grimm 1981: 135–37; Klauck 1981: 236–37) and that God himself is specially present in him (Blackburn 1991: 139). This identification with Yahweh is further reinforced both by the Markan scribes' allusion to the Shema—the recitation of which was a central feature of worship in the synagogue—and Jesus' knowledge of their thoughts (cf., e.g., Ps. 139:23; Prov. 24:12; see Marcus 1999: 222).

Given the close connection between healing and forgiveness in Jesus' ministry (C. D. Marshall 1989: 89), one wonders why this is the only instance in Mark where forgiveness is explicitly linked with healing, and that specifically of a lame man. Interestingly, in Israel's Scriptures a similar combination is found only in Isa. 33:23–24. There, the time of Yahweh's eschatological reign through his messianic king (33:22; cf. 32:1; see Childs 2001: 248; Goldingay 2001: 190) and the consequent restoration of David's city, Zion (33:20 [see commentary on Mark 1:11 above]), result in both the absence of illness and the forgiveness of sins (33:24), such that even the lame would participate in the victory (33:23). If this background is in view, then Jesus' healing/forgiveness of the lame man is yet another indication that Israel's new-exodus restoration has begun.

It is striking, at this first explicit mention of official criticism of Jesus, that we find this particular allusion to Isa. 43. There, Yahweh's self-declaration was in response to exiled Jacob-Israel's criticism of his announcement of Isaianic new-exodus salvation (R. E. Watts 1990a), glossed in the Targum particularly to include Israel's rebel teachers. The same pattern emerges as Jesus' announcement of salvation is likewise met with criticism from Israel's teachers (see Schneck 1994: 71–72), which criticism, though understandable, must submit to the reality that Jesus is no ordinary figure.

E. Theological Use. Once again, consistent with Mark's fundamental framework, we are reminded that Jesus is indeed the one who inaugurates Israel's eschatological return from exile: sins are forgiven, and the lame walk—the particular combination itself being peculiarly Isaianic. And since for Mark, Israel's healing necessarily included "spiritual" and "physical" aspects in the one continuum, Jesus' forgiveness/healing of the lame man is simply the correlate of his cleansing of the leper. If the tradition contained in *Tanḥ. Lev.* 3:6 goes back to the first century, then for Jesus to wipe away sins apart from sacrifice indicates that the world to come is even now breaking in (cf. Mark 1:14–15). Christologically, this is no mere question of Jesus operating outside official cultic channels. As the scribes well realize, only God can so authoritatively pronounce forgiveness, and, as Jesus presses home, only God can then heal to prove it (see Blackburn 1991: 139).

Finally, this first explicit moment of official opposition hints that the lines around which Israel is organized are about to change. Ecclesiologically, because the priests can only recognize the cleansing of a leper while Jesus effects it, and the scribes can only debate forgiveness while Jesus actually forgives and heals, he is emerging as the new center around which Israel and its relationship to God is to be reconstituted. Israel's response to him is increasingly becoming of vital importance.

2:10

A. NT Context: The Son of Man. The reason for the raising of the paralytic, in this first occurrence of Jesus' favorite self-designation recorded in Mark (fourteen times), is now given here: "so that you might know that the Son of Man has authority upon the earth to forgive sin." Largely absent from the first half of Mark's account (only here and in 2:28), this purportedly awkward Greek expression *ho huios tou anthrōpou* (though no more cumbersome than the common *ho huios tou theou* [see Moule 1995]), lacking any exact Aramaic or Hebrew counterpart and found in the canonical Gospels almost entirely and consistently on the lips of Jesus as a self-designation, has generated several small libraries of discussion. Alas, no resolution is in sight (see, e.g., Hare 1990; Burkett 1999; C. A. Evans 2001b: lxxiii–lxxx; Dunn 2003: 724–37).

Important, though mentioned here only briefly because it lies outside the OT's direct influence, is the view that the Aramaic underlying the Gospels' *ho huios tou anthrōpou* is an idiomatic form of self-reference, whether as a circumlocution for "I" (Vermes 1967; Bauckham 1985) or generically of a group of people among whom the speaker is included (Casey 1987; 2002). However, since P. Owen and D. Shepherd (2001) have raised strong doubts about this suggestion, and since our business is with the Markan Jesus, whose usage of "Son of Man" in 8:38; 13:26; 14:62 echoes Dan. 7:13 (e.g., Tuckett 1982: 60; cf. Dunn [2003: 760], who sees a combination of an Aramaic self-reference and "at least some reference" to Dan. 7:13), and assuming that Mark's articular usage implies a consistent sense (Moule 1977: 11–22), we now turn to the OT background.

B. "Son of Man" in the OT. One of the few areas of agreement is that the language derives from a Jewish milieu. The nonspecific form "son of man" (*ben-ʾādām/ben-ʾĕnôš*) characteristically occurs as the second element in poetic synonymous parallelism and means "human being" (e.g., Num. 23:19; Ps. 8:4 [8:5 MT]; 144:3; Isa. 51:12; Jer. 50:40; cf. in the LXX: Jdt. 8:16; Job 16:21; Sir. 17:30).

A rare exception to this poetic use occurs in Ps. 80:17 (80:18 MT), this psalm being a lament possibly from either the exilic or the postexilic period (see Tate 1990: 311–12). The psalmist beseeches God to let his hand be upon the man of his right hand, the "son of man" whom he made strong for himself (the LXX reinforces the connection by substituting *huiou anthrōpou* for *bēn* in 80:16b [80:15b ET]; cf. Peshitta). The expression could refer to Israel, who is Yahweh's vine (80:8–15 [cf. Isa. 5:1–7; Ezek. 15:1–8]), and who, although ravaged by wild beasts (80:13 [cf. *Midr. Ps.* 80:5–6, which interprets this in the light of Dan. 7's four beasts]), is the "son [*bēn*] you made strong for yourself" (80:16b MT [cf. Exod. 4:22–23; Hos. 11:1]). Alternatively, it could refer to the "strengthened" Davidic king who sits at God's right hand (Ps. 110:1; cf. the vine/king allegory of Ezek. 17 and the later *Tg. Ps.* 80:16b, 18a, where the branch is interpreted to be the "King Messiah . . . the son of man you made mighty for yourself"; see D. Hill 1973; Beyerlin 1973: 13; Kraus 1986: 110). Or, given the confluence of nation and king in the ancient Near East (see Dan. 7:16–17, 23), both might be in view whereby the Davidic king functions as Israel's representative as Yahweh protects both from the beastly nations. Here the idea seems to be that Israel, under its representative Davidic king, is Yahweh's new Adam-humanity (cf., e.g., Ps. 8; see Wifall 1974: 103–7; Bentzen 1970: 39–44; cf. Kraus 1988–1989: 2:143).

Unique among the prophets, Ezekiel is addressed as "son of man" ninety-three times (ninety-four in the LXX [see 17:12]), emphasizing either his humanity over against the divine word that he bears or his lofty status as *the* human being chosen by God to communicate his message (Nickelsburg 1992: 137). More than any other prophet, he is concerned with the temple, first announcing its destruction because of the idolatries practiced within (Ezek. 8–11) but then offering hope of a glorious renewal (chaps. 40–48) in a restored nation, under a Davidic figure (37:15–28), and culminating in the return of Yahweh's presence (48:35). However, "son of man" is always a voca-

tive used *of* him (LXX: *huie anthrōpou*) and is never a self-designation.

The classic crux is Dan. 7:13, where "one like a human being" (Aram. *bar ʾĕnāš*) is vindicated over against the beastlike kings/kingdoms, especially the terrifying fourth beast with its arrogant little horn who uniquely makes war on the "holy ones 'of' the Most High" (7:21–22), and is given, along with the "holy ones," an everlasting kingdom (7:14, 18).

The identity of this figure is hotly contested. The language of 7:13a typically describes God, who appears on the clouds of heaven (see Ps. 68:4; 104:3; Isa. 19:1; cf. Deut. 33:26; see Emerton 1958; Goldingay 1989: 171) and in human form. Daniel 7:13 then describes some kind of divine hypostatization (cf. Ezek. 1:26; 8:2; see Procksch 1920; Feuillet 1953). However, Daniel's humanlike being seems both subordinate to the Ancient of Days and paired with the beastlike kings/kingdoms; and "clouds," though sometimes theophanic, can be modes of transport to indicate vindication (e.g., the two prophets in the later Rev. 11:12; Jesus [Acts 1:9; *T. Ab.* 10:1]; Moses [Josephus, *Ant.* 4.326; cf. *b. Yoma* 4a; *Pesiq. Rab.* 20:4]; Israel [*Tg. Neof.* and *Tg. Ps.-J.* on Exod. 19:4]; perhaps Elijah [2 Kings 2:11]).

Failing this, the question devolves into a series of dichotomies—is the figure concrete or symbolic, celestial or human, individual or corporate?—with answers reflecting almost every combination thereof.

One place to start is with the "holy ones" (*qaddîšîn* [7:21]; the "holy ones 'of' the Most High," *qaddîšê ʿelyônîn* [7:18, 22, 25]; "the people 'of' the holy ones," *ʿam qaddîšê ʿelyônîn* [7:27]) with whom the human figure is in some way connected. Although clearly the beasts are symbolic (of both kings and kingdoms [7:4, 8, 17, 23]), the "holy ones" appear not to be, and so the options are three: God's people (e.g., Charles 1929: 19; Brekelmans 1965; Poythress 1976), angelic beings (esp. J. J. Collins 1993: 313–17), or both (Goldingay 1989: 178; cf. J. J. Collins 1993: 315).

The angelic case is argued because (1) Daniel elsewhere understands the conflict in terms of angelic representatives (e.g., 10:13), and (2) the substantival "holy ones" (*qadîšîn/qĕdôšîm*) elsewhere in Daniel, as almost universally in the OT and commonly in later literature, refers to heavenly beings (e.g., in the MT: Dan. 4:10, 14, 20 [4:13, 17, 23 ET]; 8:13; note esp. J. J. Collins [1993: 313–17], for whom the "stars" of Dan. 8:10 are angelic). If so, then because (1) of the numerous occasions where angelic beings appear in human form, and (2) the humanlike figure, like the "holy ones," is not explained (Rowland 1982: 180), the one like a son of man is understood also to be a real heavenly figure who participates in God's authority (e.g., S. Kim 1983; Caragounis 1986: 73–81; Slater 1995), perhaps the archangel Michael (J. J. Collins 1993: 310–19), and who represents Israel in heaven (Völter 1902). Naturally, it is still Israel who is ultimately vindicated, since peoples represented by angels share in their victories (7:27; note the exaltation of Michael's kingdom and thus of Israel in 1QM XVII, 5–8 [see J. J. Collins 1993: 318]; Dan. 10:20–21; 12:1; Deut. 32:8 LXX; cf. Matt. 18:10 [see Lacocque 1979: 130–34, 153]; note Dan. 8:10, where "stars" can also include people, as with the intermingling of angels and faithful Israelites in 1QM X–XII; see also Matt. 13:43).

Nevertheless, there are problems. If Israel's angelic prince is in view, then why are the nations in Dan. 7 not also represented by their celestial princes (cf. Dan. 10:13, 20–21), and why the reluctance to name Michael, given his prominence later? Even though angels often appear in human form, it does not follow that everything so likened is angelic (Casey 1979: 32), and the fact that angels are never described, even elsewhere in Daniel, using the precise expression "son of man" suggests that the human element in Dan. 7 is nonnegotiable. Likewise, even if most uses of the substantival "holy ones" (qadîšîn/qĕdôšîm) refer to heavenly beings (though the exact phrase "holy ones of the Most High" occurs nowhere else in the OT and might indicate, as with "stars" in Dan. 12:3, an extension of "holy ones" to faithful Israelites), the fact remains that some usages do refer to Israel (admittedly rare, but see Ps. 34:9 [34:10 MT], strikingly a psalm of Davidic deliverance; cf. Lev. 19:2; Num. 16:3; perhaps 1QM III, 5; X, 10; also later in Tob. 12:15; 1 En. 39:4–5; 93:6; 100:5; T. Levi 18:11; T. Iss. 5:4; cf. also the "stars" in Dan. 8:10, which seem to be understood as persecuted Israelites in 8:11, 24 LXX/Theodotion; perhaps also Gen. 22:17). Isaiah 4:3 also notes that those left in Jerusalem after God's purifying work will be called "holy." In other words, the internal logic of Dan. 7, not statistics, must be determinative. Nor is the absence of any explanation of the humanlike figure decisive, since it might be for other reasons (e.g., the author either did not know or felt it unnecessary [see below]). And since unlike the "Ancient of Days," both the beasts (7:4, 8) and the "son of man" are preceded by the preposition "like," one is inclined also to read the latter along with the beasts as a symbol (Casey 1979: 27–28; pace Slater 1995: 188).

Moreover, contextually speaking, if Dan. 2 (where angels are not mentioned) and Dan. 7 are intended as chiastic reflections of the same concern (so, e.g., Lenglet 1972; Goldingay 1989: 158; N. T. Wright 1992: 291–96, the caveats of J. J. Collins [1993: 34] notwithstanding), with Dan. 3 and Dan. 6 exemplifying the testing and vindication of God's people Israel (and with one of their oppressors actually becoming "beastlike" [Dan. 4]), then we would expect the "holy ones" who are tested and vindicated in Dan. 7 to be at least Israel. After all, the point of the human/beast contrast concerns whether a nation exalts God or itself (Dan. 4; cf. Ps. 49:20; 68:30; 73:21–22; Jer. 4:7; Ezek. 29:3–4; see Hooker 1967: 17). Finally, the idea of judgment being made in favor of angelic beings seems odd (unless Dan. 10:13, 21 refer to a legal battle), as does the notion of their receiving the kingdom—where were they ever promised such (see Hare 1990: 11; although J. J. Collins 1974: 63, cites 1QM XVII 6–8, cf. XII 7, the angelic host is present to aid Israel, not receive the kingdom)? On the other hand, in Dan. 3 and 6 faithful Israelites have suffered under Gentile tribunals, and the promised dominion over the nations of a restored Israel under a Davidic king is common enough. All this suggests that the holy ones are at least faithful Israel awaiting and receiving vindication.

Similarly, because the humanlike figure stands with the saints, again at least Israel, over against the Gentile beasts who are also kings, one of which in 7:4 is given the mind of a man (see Hooker 1967: 15; cf. Dan. 4), he has traditionally been seen as Israel's future messianic king, distinct from the saints (Rowe 1982: 95–96; the Tg. on 1 Sam. 2:10, in the context of a four-nation schema, sees God's agent of deliverance in messianic terms;

135

see the survey in Casey 1979: 30–35; see also below).

But here too there are questions. A Davidic messianic hope is hardly central to Daniel, and according to J. J. Collins (1995: 22–48), messianic hope was largely absent during the period 500–200 BC. Furthermore, and as we noted above, the preposition "like" suggests that he is not actually a "son of man," but rather a symbol—in this case, for the saints, faithful Israel (Hooker 1967: 29; Casey 1979: 25–28; N. T. Wright 1992: 291–97). However, not only is Collins' argument contested by W. Horbury, who cites evidence to the contrary (1998: 36–63), but also in, for example, Isa. 55:3–4, in an exilic setting and also lacking an explicit messianism, the nations are nevertheless subject to a Davidic nāgîd (cf. Dan. 9:25's "anointed nāgîd," a term most commonly connected in the Former Prophets and the Writings with the Davidic king, who is cut off; see the later 4 Ezra 7:29).

But perhaps the "Israel or messianic" choice is in any case a false one and historically implausible. Although modern Westerners naturally conceive of states existing in their own right, it seems anachronistic, given ancient Near Eastern views of kingship, to import this into Daniel, where the beastly nations are primarily conceived of in terms of their kings (hence the king/kingdom pairing [7:17, 23] and the book's emphasis on Nebuchadnezzar, Belshazzar, and Darius), and where Israel's vindication necessarily involves kingship (7:14, 27). What other kingship could there be if not that of a Davidic messiah (see Horbury 1998: 64–77; pace Casey 1979: 30)? And to whom else are the nations to be subject if not to David, not least since this subjection is a staple element of that hope (Ps. 2:8–9; 110:1–2, 5–6; 118:10–11; cf. 4Q174 1 I, 18; Pss. Sol. 17:21–35)? Finally, the only kingdom that God promises to be everlasting is David's (2 Sam. 7:16; 22:51; 1 Kings 9:5; 2 Chron. 13:5 [cf. 1 Kings 2:33, 45; Ps. 18:50; 4Q174 1 I, 10–11; 4Q252 V, 4]; Isa. 55:3; Ezek. 37:25).

A Davidic messianic component to the vindication of the saints is further supported by the following: (1) the many thematic correlations between Daniel and the psalms (Heaton 1956; Hooker 1967: 23), and especially the accounts of the nations and their kings rebelling against

Yahweh and his agent in Pss. 2; 110 (Goldingay 1989: 149); (2) already in Ps. 110 a passive human figure, the Davidic king, sits at God's right hand, sharing in his authority as the hostile nations are destroyed (see commentary on Ps. 110 in Mark 12:36 below; cf. the exaltation of the servant in Isa. 52:13 with 6:1; 14:13–14; 33:10); and (3) Ps. 80 uniquely combines Israel's oppression by beasts, "son of man" terminology, and the latter's sharing God's authority by sitting at his right hand in a lament concerning the vindication of Israel under a "strengthened" Davidic king.

Thus the highly exalted status of "the son of man" is merely an extension of the psalms, wherein the Davidic king's victories are already only a participation in and extension of God's power over creation (cf. the exodus motif in Ps. 89; see Roberts 2002), which creation theme is echoed in Dan. 7 (Lacocque 2001). The idea of the nations bowing before Israel is found in the prophets (particularly in the insistently monotheistic Isa. 45:14; 49:7, 23; also 60:14, which undermines the argument of Caragounis [1986: 72] that such action signifies Dan. 7's son of man's participation in deity) and in subsequent literature (notably, given the scroll's occasional use of "holy ones" to refer to Israel, 1QM XII, 14–16 [cf. I, 5]). This would cohere with an otherwise consistent OT eschatology that knows only Israel under Davidic kingship—there is no mention of angels per se—having a great kingdom.

Consequently, the dichotomy between symbolic and messianic readings probably is a false one. The "one like a son of man"/"holy ones" pairing, when understood over against the beastlike kings/kingdoms, represents Israel and speaks of its vindication over its oppressors. However, the logic of ancient Near Eastern kingship, the emphasis on individual kings as embodiments of their kingdoms, and the special congruence of the Davidic promises with this material naturally suggest an Israel under a Davidic messianic king upon and in whom God's authority especially devolves and resides, as both Jewish and Christian tradition have long and almost unanimously understood (see below).

As such, Dan. 7, like Ps. 80 (cf. Pss. 2; 110), envisages the exaltation of the messianic king and his people Israel as a new Adam/humanity, which exercises authority over the rebellious beast-nations

(7:18, 27; cf. Ps. 8:6–8; 73:22; see Hooker 1967: 15–21) as the summit of God's creational activity (Lacocque 2001). Not unexpectedly, given Daniel's narrative setting is that of the exile, this victory echoes the symbolism of the exodus and Isaiah's new-exodus, new-creational redemption, where the clouds of heaven (e.g., Exod. 13; 14; 19; 24; Num. 9–10; Isa. 4; Ezek. 30:3; cf. 1 Cor. 10:1–2) stand over against the sea (e.g., Isa. 17:12–13; Jer. 46:7–8) in order to indicate the respective origins, character, and destiny of the nations and of Israel (Hooker 1967: 24–30). In this case, it seems more likely that Pss. 8 and 80 and Dan. 7 lie along the same trajectory (and thus ought not be played off against one another [*contra*, e.g., Goulder 2002]). The vindication of Israel under its messianic king is therefore its new-creational new exodus from bondage to the nations.

Finally, if there is already a trend toward the supreme exaltation of the faithful Davidic king (Ps. 110) and true servant Israel (Isa. 52:13; cf. 6:1; 14:13–14; 33:10, of which I suspect the "heavenly" savior figures of *1 Enoch* and *4 Ezra* are merely stronger manifestations), then it is not so big a step, especially given the nature of apocalyptic hyperbole, to use "celestial" language of an Israel/messianic-Davidic-king symbol (see Black 1975; Horbury 1998: 89–104). In other words, the rigid distinction between a human and a heavenly figure along either/or lines appears to misunderstand the more integrative and multifaceted trajectory evident in the texts themselves (see Riesenfeld 1947: 62–65).

C. *"Son of Man" in Judaism.* Although not yet a formal title for a recognizable figure (Casey 1979), Daniel's son of man is picked up in several later Jewish sources (on the influence of Dan. 7 generally on Judaism, see France 1982: 179–83, 185–88). The Similitudes of *1 Enoch* (probably first-century [see Horbury 1998: 13–63; Dunn 2003: 619–22]; also probably pre-Christian [see Collins 1998: 177–78; Elliott 2000: 491–92]) have the most extensive reflection of Dan. 7:13's implied messianism, interpreting the "son of man" (about sixteen times, though employing three different expressions, with half the occurrences following Dan. 7:13) as a messianic figure (48:10; 52:4) who also exhibits numerous features of the Isaianic "servant" (VanderKam 1992: 189–90). He is a righteous (53:6) and anointed (48:10;

52:4 [cf. Ps. 2:2]) individual who is hidden but will be revealed to the elect (62:7), be seated on a throne of glory (61:8; 62:5 [cf. Ps. 110:1]), open all the hidden storerooms (46:3), dethrone kings and the mighty and strong ones (46:4–5), crush the teeth of sinners (46:4), be a light to the Gentiles and the hope of those sick in heart (48:4), judge sinners (62:2), cause confusion and panic among oppressors who as they recognize, worship, and beg for mercy (62:3–10) will nevertheless be shamed as they are driven out from his presence (63:11), and with whom the righteous will eat, rest forever (62:14), and rejoice while sinners are destroyed (69:26–28).

Similarly interpreted is the figure who rises from the sea and rides on the clouds of heaven in *4 Ezra* 13:2–3. Later called "my son" (13:32, 37, 52 [cf. Ps. 2:7; see Hare 1990: 12]) and standing on Mount Zion (13:35 [cf. Ps. 2:6; 110:2–3]), a mountain not carved out by human hands (cf. Dan. 2:34), he defeats the rebellious nations (cf. Ps. 110:5–6) that have gathered against him (13:8–9a [cf. Ps. 2:1–3]), not by using sword or spear, but with the fiery word of his mouth (13:9b–11, 33–38 [cf. Isa. 11:4]), and presides over the new-exodus return of the exiles (13:12–13, 39–47). So too the blessed man from heaven in *Sib. Or.* 5:414–33 (cf. Trypho on Dan. 7 in Justin, *Dial.* 32).

Interestingly, in each of these independent cases Dan. 7:13 has been combined with Isa. 11:2–4 and Pss. 2; 110 (Horbury 1985). Regardless of whether the son of man was a recognized eschatological figure, a messianic reading of Dan. 7 was apparent to three different traditions in the first century—four, if we include Mark (who also invokes Pss. 2; 110)—and apparently with no hint of exegetical violence. So too the emphasis on his heavenly, exalted authority (perhaps under the influence of Ps. 110 [Hengel 1995: 180–84]). However, this messianic reading ought not be seen, as it is by some (e.g., J. J. Collins 1993), to contradict a symbolic reading; rather, it naturally focuses on a key aspect of the Israel/messianic-king combination.

In rabbinic and later materials (Vermes 1973: 170–77; Casey 1979: 80–92; Segal 1977: 33–59) the messianic interpretation is also predominant (e.g., Tg. on 1 Chron. 3:24; *Tanḥ. Gen.* 6:20; *b. Sanh.* 98a; probably *b. Ḥag.* 14a and *b. Sanh.* 38b, where Rabbi Akiba sees two thrones in Dan. 7:9, one of which is for David [cf. *Pesiq. Rab.* 36:1]; *Midr. Ps.* 2:7–9, which also invokes in close association with Israel Ps. 110:1; Isa. 42:1; 52:13; *Num. Rab.* 13:14, combining Dan. 7:13–14 with Dan. 2:35; *'Ag. Ber.* 14:3; 23:1; see further C. A. Evans 2001a: 507–9). Not surprisingly, given the multifaceted nature of Dan. 7, there is also perhaps some suggestion of corporate (*Midr. Ps.* 21:5) and "divine" interpretations (*Mek. R. Sim.* 15; perhaps *Mek. Exod.* 20:2).

D. Dan. 7:13 in Mark. The form of the Greek expression *ho huios tou anthrōpou* and its limitation to Jesus—used only by him of himself—almost requires that it functions as at least a semititle for Mark (see Lindars 1983: 102; *pace* C. A. Evans 2001b: lxxv) and presumably for most of his first readers (Gathercole 2004: 367) (accordingly, I will capitalize it here). And if we can assume a unitary Markan approach, the clear Danielic overtones of 8:38; 13:26; 14:62 (e.g., Casey 1979: 163; Tuckett 1982: 60; also C. A. Evans 2001a, on various Danielic themes in Jesus' preaching; *pace* Goulder 2002; Kirchevel 1999; although, insofar as Dan. 7's Israel/king figure is intended to be truly human, Ps. 8 is indirectly relevant, as is a "new Adam" typology [see Marcus 2003a; 2003b]) imply that the same applies here. The Greek article *ho*, at least in Mark, may well be demonstrative, indicating "*that* Son of Man," the one mentioned in Dan. 7 (see Moule 1995: 278; Davies and Allison 1988–1997: 1:47–50; Gathercole 2004). But why introduce Son of Man at all?

Given that Jesus' impressive authority has already been noted without "Son of Man" at 1:17, "authority" alone cannot explain its introduction here in 2:10 (Hare 1990: 190), the absence of a self-referential statement in 1:17 notwithstanding. Instead, it must be the kind of authority in question, namely, that of forgiving sins (*pace* Tuckett 1982: 62), which provokes the lawyers' response and clearly exceeds that of 1:17.

This explains the modifier "on earth," presumably over against "in heaven." Since nowhere in Jewish apocalyptic literature do we find any mention of the Son of Man's authority encompassing forgiving sins in heaven—characteristically he is God's agent of judgment upon the earth (Tuckett 1982: 64; Casey 1991: 29n1; *pace* Hooker 1967: 93, it is not obvious that eschatological figures

typically overcome evil by forgiving sins)—this cannot represent a relocation of this role (Hare 1990: 187; cf. Casey 1979: 160). On the other hand, there is no question of who forgives sins or of where such a one dwells, as the scribes well know. But Mark has already implied that Jesus is more than a Davidic messianic figure (on the spiritual aspects of messianism, see Horbury 1998: 86–104), and if, as M. D. Hooker (1967: 178–82) suggests, the issue at the heart of Mark's Son of Man language is Jesus' authority, then it is not just an impressive authority (1:17), but rather one that equals God's (see commentary on Ps. 110 in Mark 12:36 and on Dan. 7 in Mark 14:62 below) here in the present on earth (see Hooker 1991: 87–88). In this respect, Jesus' authority to forgive sins on earth is inherent in his task of inaugurating Israel's new exodus, where forgiveness is precisely what Yahweh announces to Israel (Isa. 40:2) (see commentary on Mark 2:7 above).

Because one cannot fundamentally separate Messiah and Son of Man in Mark (Hengel 1995: 69), this Gospel lies along the characteristic Jewish trajectory of an implicit messianism in Dan. 7:13 but both surpasses and modifies *1 Enoch* and *4 Ezra* by having Jesus, in forgiving rather than judging sins, do what only Yahweh can do. Just as the leper was sent "as a witness" to the priests (1:44), Jesus' forgiveness of the lame man testifies to the scribes that a new era is dawning wherein the old priesthood and its cultus are replaced (cf. Ps. 110:4's promise of priesthood "after the order of Melchizedek" and the "rejected stone" saying in Mark 12:10).

For Mark, Jesus is not only Israel's Davidic messiah and Isaianic servant, but also Daniel's messianic Son of Man. But the wine of Jesus cannot be contained by such wineskins (Mark 2:22), because his messianic Son of Man authority on earth is nothing other than that of God himself (Dan. 7:14).

E. Theological Use. Christologically speaking, in drawing on the exalted humanlike figure who in Dan. 7 participates in God's authority, Mark's Jesus likewise claims exactly that to which the scribes have objected: he not only has but also will exercise Yahweh's authority "upon the earth." Where he is, God is. In Dan. 7 and in the Similitudes of *1 Enoch* this authority meant judgment on the nations and sinners (presumably faithless

Israelites), whom "I shall destroy . . . from the face of the earth" (*1 En.* 45:6), where the strong "shall have no hope to rise from their beds" (46:4–6 [and further, e.g., 50:2, 4; 53:2]), and all this "by the authority of his Messiah so that he may give orders and be praised upon the earth" (52:4). At the outset of Mark, Jesus' exercise of the Son of Man's authority means, instead, forgiveness and healing. Consequently and ecclesiologically, in a startling reversal this authority means that the lame, excluded from the Dead Sea Scrolls' messianic feast (1Q28a II, 3–11; cf. 4Q266 8 I, 8–9, presumably as sinners [see Olyan 2001]), will in this new exodus walk into the new Jerusalem (Isa. 33:23–24; cf. the newly seeing Bartimaeus rejoicing on the way in the Messiah's train in Mark 10:46–52; R. E. Watts 2000: 309).

Finally, just as Mark's narrative linked the first allusion to the Davidic messiah with Isaiah's enigmatic servant (1:10), so this first mention of the Danielic messianic Son of Man is connected with Isaiah's new exodus in the allusion to Yahweh's extension of forgiveness to idolatrous and lame Israel. As we will see, Mark will continue to develop this nexus.

2:23–25

A. NT Context.
In the fourth and next-to-last controversy, Jesus is criticized by the Pharisees because they hold him responsible for his disciples' actions (Daube 1972–1973), namely, plucking ears of grain (cf. Philo, *Moses* 2.22; *m. Šabb.* 7:2; *t. Šabb.* 9:17), which they regard as a breaking of Sabbath, the ultimate breach of covenant loyalty (*Jub.* 2:25–33; CD-A X, 14–XI, 23) (see Schürer 1973–1986: 2:467–75; Borg 1988: 156–73; Dunn 2003: 281–86, and for a better understanding of the gravity, Elliott 2000) and punishable by death (*Jub.* 50:8–13; *m. Sanh.* 7:4.). For a well-known teacher to take Sabbath lightly threatened both Jewish community life and vocation (Pawlikowski 1970: 425). Jesus counters with the example of David, who, he says, during the time of Abiathar ate bread reserved for the priests and shared it with his compatriots. Jesus then insists that Sabbath was created for people, not people for Sabbath, concluding therefore that the Son of Man is also Lord of the Sabbath.

Several questions arise: (1) Jesus' account of David's action contains various elements that are not immediately clear in, or seem at variance with,

the OT version; (2) the links between David and Jesus and his disciples, and Jesus' declarations on the humanitarian nature of Sabbath and his own authority, are not immediately clear; and (3) what does it mean for the Son of Man to be Lord of the Sabbath?

B. 1 Sam. 21:1–7 in Context.
David, Israel's anointed king, flees from a murderous Saul and, though claiming to go to one House of Bread (= Bethlehem [20:6]), goes instead to another, the shrine at Nob (Fokkelman 1986: 352). In need of provisions, he tells an uneasy Ahimelech, who might have heard of the tense events at Naioth (19:19–24; cf. *ḥrd* in 16:4; 21:1; see Bergen 1996: 221), that he is alone because he is on a secret mission, presumably related to holy war (21:2; cf. Josh. 3:5; Deut. 23:9–14; 2 Sam. 11:11–12), and has stationed his men nearby. The priest has nothing at hand except the consecrated bread, which he gives to David and his men on the proviso that they have maintained sexual purity. He also supplies David with Goliath's matchless sword.

For many scholars, David's story appears to be a fabrication. We hear nothing elsewhere of this secret mission, though it is possible that the task was already on the agenda—perhaps a regular clandestine raid on the Philistines—and David uses the opportunity to find refuge instead (21:11). But if so, David's lack of sword or spear sounds incredible, as does Ahimelech's happy acceptance of David's seemingly "lame" excuse. Was such a situation not unknown, or was Ahimelech simply naive or wisely politic when caught between the bizarre circumstances and Israel's preeminent hero? Although the fleeing David might have collected from among his cohort some allies who were also increasingly disaffected with Saul (cf. 22:1–2), we hear nothing of them elsewhere either. Alternatively, David's apparently less-than-honest account might have been an attempt to protect Ahimelech from charges of complicity (M. J. Evans 2000: 97).

Our difficulty arises from a terse narrative that omits key details—for example, Ahimelech's inquiry of the Lord for David, which, although a central matter in the priest's indictment, is entirely absent from the encounter itself (cf. 22:10, 13, 15; see Hertzberg 1964: 178). Even David's oft-noted "admission" of guilt (22:22) puts the blame more on Doeg's treachery and perhaps his failure to kill him (Bergen 1996: 231) than on any dissembling on David's part. Furthermore, there is far more going on than mere recollection (Fokkelman 1986: 355). As 1 Sam. 20 already made abundantly clear, the unspecified "king" who "sent out" David (21:2) is none other than Yahweh, God and king of Israel (20:22 [cf. 20:12, 13, 14, 15, 16, 23, 42]). His "secret mission" and "his men" are likewise subsequently revealed to have a double meaning.

Central to the narrative is both the sense of urgency, haste, and danger around Israel's anointed yet fugitive king (Brueggemann 1990: 155) acting under Yahweh's orders and Ahimelech's judgment that David's need during his holy-war mission takes precedence over Levitical law (Lev. 24:9). Ahimelech's assistance constitutes an implicit affirmation of the future king (R. W. Klein 1983: 214; McCarter 1980: 350), and David's taking of the holy bread and Goliath's sword is also a double blow to Saul's prestige (Fokkelman 1986: 353), made more telling when soon after, Abiathar, Ahimelech's son, serves as David's priest (22:20–23).

C. 1 Sam. 21:1–7 in Judaism. Strikingly, most references ignore David, remarking instead on the implied miracle where it is supposed that the bread was miraculously fresh (e.g., *y. Šeqal.* 6:3 [I.C]; *b. Yoma* 21a–b; *b. Ḥag.* 26b; *b. Menaḥ.* 29a). Those that do comment on David nowhere suggest any dishonesty on his part, although *b. Sanh.* 95a holds him responsible for the slaughter at Nob, Doeg's condemnation (cf. *b. Sanh.* 90a), and the death of Saul and his three sons on Mount Gilboa. Given the seriousness of David's action, most seek to justify him by postulating that the bread was baked on a weekday and thus was common (*b. Menaḥ.* 95b; *Yal.* 130), or his life was at stake (*b. Menaḥ.* 96a [though it is not obvious how being hungry is life-threatening]), or Jonathan's failure to provide for him was the catalyst for the ensuing woes (*b. Sanh.* 103b). Based on David's "how much more today," Rabbi Simeon held that it happened on the Sabbath (cf. *b. Menaḥ.* 95b; *Yal.* 130; see France 2002: 145).

In regard to the issue at hand, it seems certain that the Sabbath command of Exod. 34:21 (cf. Exod. 20:8–11; 31:14–15; 35:2; Deut. 5:12–15) was held by all to be binding and of increasing importance in the construction of Jewish iden-

tity. Nevertheless, it seems equally true that its vagueness left considerable room for interpretation (cf. the lengthy tractate in Mishnah), including nonobservance of Torah in exceptional cases because, in a phraseology close to that of Jesus, "The Sabbath is handed over to you, not you to it" (*Mek. Exod.* 31:13–14; *b. Yoma* 85b; *b. Yebam.* 90b [though the context assumes that Sabbath is to be kept]) (see Hultgren 1979: 140n62). The question then becomes not only what constitutes a legitimate exception, but also whose interpretation is authoritative.

D. 1 Sam. 21:1–7 in Mark. Mark's Jesus does not debate what constitutes work or Sabbath, nor does he address any distinction between the Pharisees' oral tradition and Torah. Instead, even if not as precise as later rabbinic criteria demanded (see Cohn-Sherbok 1979; Daube 1956: 71), his argument focuses on a more foundational issue, the relationship between Torah and the Son of Man: if regulations to protect the holy could be set aside for great David and those with him (Hooker 1967: 99), then how much more so for those with Daniel's messianic Son of Man, who has supreme authority over the Sabbath, which in any case was created for humanity. The issue is not Sabbath, but Christology (Moloney 2002: 69).

Whether Jesus' version of the story means effacing David's lie (so Marcus 1999: 240) depends on certainty about the original narrative, which, as we have noted, is not as clear as is sometimes supposed, and further presupposes that first-century interpreters likewise regarded David as dishonest, which seems not to be the case. If so, then the additional details in Jesus' version—David was hungry, entered the house of God, ate the bread, and shared it with his companions (see Gundry 1993: 141)—are not especially problematic, being legitimate inferences from the narrative.

From a legal perspective, Mark's Jesus follows Ahimelech more closely than the rabbis and their exceptions (*pace* Cohn-Sherbok 1979). Because of the gravity of their mission, Ahimelech responds only to the need of David and his companions. He has no idea about nor makes mention of any threat to David's life or of the bread being common. And if, in Ahimelech's mind, David and his men, who out of either carelessness or the turmoil of their departure had not made provision yet were not required to fast, then why should Jesus' disciples do so (*pace* Rordorf 1968: 61–62)? That Ahimelech was priest and therefore ultimately responsible for interpreting the law would be even more significant if the Pharisees themselves were concerned with maintaining an intensified form of priestly purity (Neusner 1973; cf. the admittedly late *b. Ḥul.* 106a; see N. T. Wright 1992: 187; Marcus 1999: 522).

However, the analogy works only if Jesus' mission and personal authority are at least equal to David's, hence Mark's emphasis on David's role rather than Ahimelech's decision. This coheres with his overall presentation of Jesus as Israel's Davidic messiah (Ps. 2 in Mark 1:11; 9:7; cf. 8:29; 10:47–48), who has at least the same authority (*pace* Cranfield 1959: 115; cf. Matt. 12:5–6; see also Banks 1975: 116; Gnilka 1978–1979: 1:122; Guelich 1989: 123; Hooker [1988: 225] argues that the analogy works only if Jesus is comparable to David, although the rabbinic attempts to justify David's action suggest that his status does not obviate his need to obey Torah).

In later traditions David's piety and importance as the one who molded Israel and planned its temple were of increasing significance (Ginzberg 1925). Mark's Jesus also molds Israel, is concerned with the temple (cf., e.g., Ps. 118 in Mark 11:9–10; 12:10–11), and engaged in holy war (R. E. Watts 2000: 140–69; Betz 1958; Stevens 1987; Borg 1988: 165; see commentary on Mark 3:23–27 below). These royal parallels could explain Mark's odd expression "to make a road" (*hodon poiein* [2:23]), which, at a stretch, might allude to the king's right (cf. *m. Sanh.* 2:4; see Derrett 1977b: 85–95) while also perhaps echoing Mark's new-exodus motif in 1:2–3 (Hooker 1991: 102; Marcus 1999: 239). It could also be a (thickly) veiled allusion to Jesus also having been sent "on the way" in a mysterious mission by "the king" (so Fokkelman 1986) to bring Israel into its longed-for Sabbath rest (cf. *4 Ezra* 6:35–59; see Hooker 1967: 100–102; Marcus 1999: 239).

Consequently, Mark's Jesus finally grounds his authority in the Danielic Son of Man (2:28). If the Sabbath was created for humanity ("the Sabbath is delivered to you . . ." [*Mek. Exod.* 31:14]), in this case Israel (cf. Dan. 7's "humanlike" figure; *Jub.* 2:30–31; *b. Sanh.* 58b; see Manson 1947), then how much more (*hōste*) is Daniel's messianic Son of Man its Lord, who is none other than

true-humanity Israel's cloud-borne representative (Hooker 1967: 95–96) now on earth (2:10) and with God's authority effecting Israel's new-exodus deliverance in his own holy war?

At the same time, that this so closely follows 2:10—the only other appeal to Son of Man in this first section (1:1–8:21/26)—suggests that the issue is again Jesus' uniquely divine authority and his right to give the final word on the meaning of this "his" Sabbath (on Sabbath belonging to Yahweh, cf. Exod. 16:25; 20:10; 31:13; Ezek. 20:12–13; see France 2002: 148). Why link a forgiveness/healing account with a legal pronouncement on Sabbath? According to the later *Pesiq. Rab Kah.* 106b, because God would not give the perfect Torah to an imperfect people, his healing power ensured that there were no blind, lame, or deaf among Israel at the exodus, and since the end time corresponds to that of Moses, one could expect healing again (*Mek. Exod.* 20:18). From this perspective, in Mark's new exodus Jesus' healing through forgiving sins is integral to his lordship as the one who brings a new law (see commentary on the transfiguration in Mark 9:7 below).

Ominously, the Nob incident is also significant because it becomes the catalyst for the decisive shift of Yahweh from Saul to David (in the form of the ephod). Thus, although the Markan Jesus' referencing of Abiathar instead of Ahimelech might simply be substituting the more important for the less (Hooker 1991: 103), Abiathar's later role is worth noting. If the point is to establish an authoritative precedent, then the actions of Abiathar, as Ahimelech's son, in taking the ephod to David to become his chief priest and subsequent blessing underscore God's affirmation of Ahimelech's decision, his presence with David, and his abandonment of David's opponent Saul. Not only are Jesus' disciples justified, but also to oppose them (and, of course, Jesus) is to oppose both "David" and ultimately God, who vindicated him and who will also vindicate Jesus.

E. Theological Use. The analogical use of 1 Sam. 21 by Mark's Jesus initially articulates the right relationship of Torah to people, but in appealing to David, it also functions christologically to establish Jesus as one who, likewise engaged in holy war (in Mark's case, Jesus' expulsion of demons), has at least David's authority. However, just as Mark's Jesus later will press the point of

David addressing the Christ as his Lord (12:36), so here his authority goes even further. This same Son of Man who has authority on earth to forgive sins is therefore also Lord of "his" Sabbath.

3:4

A. NT Context: Do Good or Do Evil? In language reminiscent of the first controversy (Dewey 1977: 100–101), this fifth, last, and in many ways climactic confrontation also involves a mighty deed, the healing of a man with a withered hand (3:1–6). "Withered," occurring more frequently in Mark than in the other Gospels, describes the dry plants in the parable of the Soils (4:6) and the Cursed Fig Tree (11:20–21), and elsewhere refers to loss of power (*T. Sim.* 2:12–13), those without offspring (Isa. 56:3) or on the threshold of death (Job 14:11; 18:16; Ps. 22:15; 102:4, 11), God's judgment (of Jeroboam [1 Kings 13:4]; of the wicked shepherd [Zech. 11:17]; of Israel [Lam. 4:8; Ezek. 17:9–10; 19:12; Hos. 9:16; Joel 1:12, 20]; of the land because of wickedness [Jer. 12:4; 23:10]; of the nations [Isa. 37:27]), Israel in exile (Ezek. 37:2, 4, 11), and the wicked and godless (Job 8:12–13; 18:16; Sir. 6:3; 40:13).

The contention again concerns the Sabbath (cf. 2:23–27), but for the first time in the series the setting is the synagogue. The issue for Mark is much more than whether healing constitutes Sabbath-breaking work or whether the situation was life-threatening (e.g., *m. Yoma* 8:6; *m. Šabb.* 14:3–4; *t. Šabb.* 12:8–14; *b. Šabb.* 12a; cf., perhaps, CD-A XI, 9–10). The preceding presentation of Jesus as the one who delivers (1:21–26), heals (1:29–34), cleanses (1:40–44), forgives sins (2:1–12), reconciles (2:13–17), inaugurates Yahweh's new-exodus marriage of his people (2:18–22), and, as the authoritative and messianic Son of Man, is Lord of the Sabbath (2:23–28), puts his mission and identity squarely in the center (see Guelich 1989: 140).

The opening words of Jesus' question in 3:4, "Is it lawful . . . ," presuppose that his action is about the law, while the completion of it, " . . . to do good or to do evil, to save life or to kill?" closely echoes the very choice that the law itself offers, particularly as expressed in Deut. 30:15 LXX (cf. 30:19; see Derrett 1984a; Gundry 1993: 153; France 2002: 150).

Although the MT pairs the positives "life and good" and the negatives "death and evil" and then in the final restatement pairs the contrasting "life and death" and "blessing and curse" (30:19), the LXX shifts this around somewhat, with 30:15 reflecting the paired contrasts of the MT's 30:19 and reading instead "life and death" and "good and evil," which order Mark's text more closely resembles. Sirach 33:14 employs the same antitheses but also with its own twist, reversing the words in each pair (Gundry 1993: 153). The freedom displayed in Mark's version is thus consistent with this interpretive tradition, but strikingly, Jesus' question turns the paired oppositions into actions, with Jesus clearly being the implied agent. That being so, at issue is the heart of Torah and Jesus' relationship to it.

B. Deut. 30:15 in Context. Deuteronomy 29:1–30:20 is the third and final Mosaic speech, which recapitulates and summarizes much of the foregoing material as it appeals for covenant faithfulness and calls for decision (C. J. H. Wright 1996: 284). The opening historical review (29:1–15) reminds all Israel, both those present and those generations yet to come (29:13–14), that although they had witnessed Yahweh's mighty deeds in delivering them from Egypt, they had until this day neither heart to understand nor eyes to see (29:4). But through the long provision in the wilderness God had brought them to this point where they finally understand (i.e., "given them a heart") that "I am Yahweh, your God" (29:6), trust his power (see Tigay 1966: 278), and realize that diligent covenant observance is the key to prosperity (29:9). Recalling the curses of chapter 28, Israel is then warned in the present (29:16–21) and from the perspective of the future exile (29:22–28) of the dire consequences of turning away from their new understanding to "walk" in "stubbornness of heart" (29:19): God would not pardon such a deliberate offense (29:20).

The section from which our verse is taken (30:1–20) assumes the gloomy outcome of the exile (cf. 30:1; 28:64–68; see McConville 2002: 423). Nevertheless, if in their distress Israel turns to God with all their hearts, he will have compassion on them and bring them back (30:3). God would reconstitute (see Thompson 1974: 285) and enable them to love him with all their hearts and souls (30:6; cf. Jer. 31:31–34; Ezek. 36:26–27), blessing them abundantly (30:9; cf. 28:3–6). Then, 30:11–14 reminds Israel that the terms of the covenant are neither too difficult to understand nor inaccessible, but rather are capable of being memorized in the heart and repeated by the mouth (30:14; cf. 31:19, 21; Josh. 1:8)—an echo of the instruction following the Shema in 6:6–7a (Merrill 1994: 391)—and are as present as hearing and sight (Thompson 1974: 286; cf. God's nearness in 4:7 [see C. J. H. Wright 1996: 291]).

Now that everything has been plainly laid out, Moses concludes on a climactic note (30:15–20), perhaps the high point of Deuteronomy (Lenchak 1993: 113). Echoing the initial speech that sets up the whole work (cf. 1:21; see C. J. H. Wright 1996: 291), and based on the preceding account of all that Yahweh has done (see McConville 2002: 430), the final solemn invocation (note the summoning of heaven and earth as witnesses in 30:19) addresses Israel in intensely personal second-singular forms. Two simple alternatives are offered—God sets before Israel this day a choice: life, good, and blessing, or death, evil, and cursing—which constitute the main themes of the paragraph (life, four times; to live, twice; death, thrice), with life and death forming an inclusio (Lenchak 1993: 179). The summons, then, is not to accept the covenant—that is already assumed—but rather to obey. To "love the LORD your God"—again echoing the Shema (Merrill 1994: 392)—and obey him means blessing and long life in the land (30:20). Apostasy means death. If anything captures the heart of Deuteronomy, this is it; Israel's fate lies in its own hands.

C. Deut. 30:15 in Judaism. Not surprisingly, the pithy and starkly presented alternatives of Deut. 30:15 (cf. Lev. 26:3–45) became a thoroughgoing motif recapitulated in, for example, Josh. 24:15; Jer. 21:8–14 (in the context of the coming Babylonian destruction of Jerusalem and again with numerous references to "walking" in "stubbornness of heart" [e.g., 7:24; 9:14; 11:8]); Isa. 65 (in the eschatological division of Israel in a text whose "Deuteronomic" flavor is widely noted [e.g., Westermann 1969: 401–2, 405; Blenkinsopp 2000–2003: 3:270, 275, 281]); 2 Esd. 7:59[129], and expanded in the intertestamental literature on the "two ways" with frequent emphasis on individual responsibility before the covenant as to whether one inherited life or death in this life and the next (e.g., Sir. 15:11–20, where the reader is told to "stretch out your hand" and

choose one or the other [see Derrett 1984a: 177]; *1 En.* 94–107; 1QS I, 3–15; CD-A III, 13–20; 4Q473; *T. Ash.* 1:3–5:4; 6, including also a prophecy of the coming exile; *T. Ab.* 11–12; *1 En.* 91:18; 94:1; *4 Ezra* 7:1–25, 116–31; Philo, *Planting* 37; *Sib. Or.* 8:399; see also *Pss. Sol.* 9:4–5; 14:1–2; *2 En.* 30:15, where the two ways were pointed out to Adam; *T. Levi* 19:1; *T. Mos.* 3:12; 12:10–11; *2 Bar.* 19:1; 84:2–4; see also Brock 1990).

Of particular interest in this list are 1QS I, 3–15; III, 13–IV, 26; and CD-A 3:13–20, both of which documents, as we have seen (see commentary on Mark 1:2–3 above), define the community in terms of Isa. 40:3 and, echoing Deut. 29:19, repeatedly warn against "stubbornness of heart," the hallmark of those who have broken the covenant (cf., e.g., 1QS I, 6; II, 14, 26; III, 3; V, 4; VII, 19, 24; IX, 10; CD-A II, 17; III, 5, 11–12; CD-B XIX, 20) and thus remain in exile (see Campbell 1995: 149–50).

For Philo, Moses' offer stands over against the actions of impious Cain and means to love the living God (*Posterity* 12; 69). It lies within humans to choose good or evil (*Unchangeable* 50), so that the great soul may rise above creation and, cleaving only to the uncreated God (*Prelim. Studies* 134), find life (*Flight* 58). The Mishnah sees here a defense of free will (*m. 'Abot* 3:15), while *Targum Neofiti* (mg.) takes on an eschatological aspect when it glosses "life" as that "of the world to come and the blessing of the Garden of Eden," and "death" as "the evil state of Gehinnom" (cf. *b. Ber.* 28b).

The "two ways" doctrine is continued in the rabbinic writings (e.g., the extended discussion in *Pirqe R. El.* 25; *m. 'Abot* 2:12–13; *Gen. Rab.* 21:5, where for Rabbi Akiba the words are also addressed to Adam; *Deut. Rab.* 4:3; 8:4; *Sipre Deut.* 53; *b. Ber.* 28b; *b. Yoma* 38b), with Elijah sometimes stationed between them (*Pirqe R. El.* 15), and where the blessing of Deut. 30:15–20 is coupled with a love of Torah (*b. Ber.* 16b; 55a; 61b; *b. Šabb.* 13a; *b. Ketub.* 111b; *b. Ned.* 62a; *b. Qidd.* 40a; cf. *b. Pesaḥ.* 49b; *b. Sukkah* 46b; *Deut. Rab.* 4:3; *S. Eli. Rab.* [5]6; *S. Eli. Zut.* 1; at length, *Sipre Deut.* 53–54). The theme of free will is likewise continued (e.g., *m. 'Abot* 3:15). It also exercised considerable influence, at least in part through Jesus (cf. Matt. 7:13–14), on later Christian teaching (e.g., *Did.* 1–6; *Barn.* 19–20; cf. Gal. 5:16–6:8;

Rom. 6–8), but this lies outside our purview (see commentary on Mark 10:19 below).

D. The Use of Deut. 30:15 in Mark. Mark again presents Jesus as upholding the law (see commentary on Mark 1:44–45 above). J. D. M. Derrett (1984a), on the basis of several shared terms, sees here a threefold midrash on Deut. 30:15, the reversal of the covenantal curses of the powerless "hand" in Deut. 28:20, 32 (cf. *T. Sim.* 2:12–13), and the promises in Isa. 56:3–5 to the Sabbath-observing and covenant-keeping eunuch ("hand" being a euphemism for male genitalia [Song 5:4; Isa. 57:8]) who is not to see himself as a "dry" tree, but rather will be given "a hand" in God's house and within God's walls. One also notes the later tradition that since handicapped persons could not keep Torah, all Israelites were miraculously made whole at the giving of the law at Sinai (*Tanh. Exod.* 5:13; *Mek. Exod.* 20:18; *b. Sanh.* 91b; *Sipre Num.* I:X [2:2]; *Lev. Rab.* 18:3–4; *Num. Rab.* 7:1; *Pesiq. Rab.* 7:7). Granted that the man whom Jesus heals is not a eunuch (though his "hand" is withered), the combination is intriguing. If something like this is in view, then in "stretching out his hand" (cf. Sir. 15:16) in response to the Torah embodied in Jesus, the curse of powerlessness (Deut. 28:20, 32) is reversed and the man finds life (Deut. 30:15, 19) as a new hand is given to him in the house of the Lord in fulfillment of Isaiah's new exodus (Isa. 56:4–5).

Be that as it may, this climactic controversy scene, echoing the Shema, as did the first of the five controversies, summarizes in Jesus' question the core of his ministry and its relationship to Torah. In doing good (reversing the man's adversity) and saving life, Jesus acts "for the glory of God and the benefit of man," and thus he embodies the law (cf. Mark 12:29–31; see Hooker 1991: 107; though Marcus [1999: 252] sees in "to save life or to kill" an apocalyptic intensification consistent with eschatological holy war). Here, then, in this new exodus and after an awesome display of mighty deeds and authoritative words, Jesus' question, like that of Moses, calls for a decision. To this point in Mark there is no hint that Jesus' teachings or actions have been either aloof or esoteric. Like the terms of the covenant, they are clear enough—sometimes too clear (2:7). Now Israel must choose.

But just as Israel in Moses' day had been blind and deaf, likewise are Jesus' critics in this new exodus hard-hearted (3:5; cf. 2:6, 8; also Isa. 6:9–10 in 4:12), in spite of all the mighty deeds that Jesus had done (cf. Deuteronomy). The Torah, which offered life and good, is perverted to keep a man crippled, to turn the synagogue into a house of bondage, and so it makes them mortal foes of the one who himself gives the life and does the good that the Torah promised. This hard-heartedness is exactly what Deut. 29:19 warned against (cf. also Jeremiah, 1QS, and CD above) and caused God to become Israel's enemy (Isa. 63:10–19). Thus, to reject Jesus is to reject the heart of Torah and to choose death. It is no small irony that over against the wonder that greeted Jesus' first mighty deed (1:27) his critics seek to work his death, and that on the Sabbath, a day in which life and the God who gives it were to be celebrated.

E. Theological Use. The high point of the first exodus was Yahweh's self-revelation through his word (Deut. 30:11–14), near enough for all Israel to hear and see (Deut. 29:29). Christologically, for Mark, God's presence and his Torah are now embodied in Jesus (as John 1:14 will later so memorably put it, "the Word become flesh"). In Deuteronomy, Jeremiah, and Isaiah, stubbornness of heart meant rejecting God for idols, while in, for example, Qumran's second exodus (Isa. 40:3) it was a failure to live according to the sectarians' understanding of Torah. But here the focal point is the action of Jesus, the Son of God, who not only upholds the heart of the Torah but also surpasses it, since in this new exodus he does that to which the Torah could only point and that which only Yahweh himself could do (1:40–44; 2:1–12; 3:10–11). Whereas sin is a transgression of God's will as expressed in Torah, now it is to reject Jesus, in whom God's will is fully expressed.

Not only so, but also the deliberate echoes of the Shema in the first and last encounters suggest that in Jesus is also present the one true God. And just as the first controversy begins with a charge of blasphemy (2:7), and the last one concludes with his condemnation (3:6), the two finally come together in 14:64 (F. Lang 1977: 11). To reject Jesus, as Mark will soon clarify, is to reject God's Holy Spirit (3:29) and to come under Isaiah's terrifying implementation of the idolaters' curse (see commentary on Isa. 6:9–10 in Mark 4:12 below). In this sense, sin too is being redefined.

Ecclesiologically, Israel is now to be reconstituted around Jesus (3:13–19). To do God's will is to listen to him in "his" house (3:35). Thus "today" (cf. Deut. 30:15, 16, 18, 19; see Derrett 1984a: 176) Israel must choose. Mark began his story with an allusion to Mal. 3:1 and its associated hope that Elijah would restore the postexilic generation to Torah faithfulness. However, in rejecting John (1:14; 11:31–33), not unexpectedly they reject true Torah-obedience as embodied in Jesus.

3:27

A. NT Context: Binding the Strong Man. Following the last (3:1–6) of the five controversies (2:1–3:6), in which the Pharisees finally decide to do away with Jesus (3:6), Mark first summarizes Jesus' continuing popularity and powerful ministry among the masses (3:7–12) and then relates his reconstitution of Israel around himself through the institution of the Twelve (3:13–19; cf. 1QS VIII, 1; 4Q164 on Isa. 54:11–12; see Marcus 1999: 267; Hooker 1991: 111). The stage now set, Mark returns to and heightens the theme of opposition in the climactic Beelzebul confrontation.

Nearly every major player in Mark's account to date is present either in person or by name: Jesus, the Twelve, the wider group of disciples, the crowds, the demons, and the Spirit, as well as, for the first time, both Jesus' family and religious authorities ominously from Jerusalem (3:22). The issue again is Jesus' manifest authority, but this time over the demons (Hooker 1991: 114; R. E. Watts 2000: 152–56). Characteristic for Mark of Jesus' power (Kallas 1961: 78–79; Kertelge 1970: 56–57; Iwe 1999), exorcisms are mentioned far more often than any other type of mighty deed (1:21–28; 5:1–20; 7:24–30; 9:14–29) and are singled out in the summaries (1:34, 39; 3:10–11) and commissionings (3:15; 6:7–13) (see R. E. Watts 2000: 156). Furthermore, this is the only occasion when the Markan Jesus hints at the meaning of his exorcisms (Hoskyns and Davey 1947: 170–71; Kee 1983: 160–62).

The whole is a nested chiasm arranged around the scribes' potentially capital charge of collusion with Beelzebul, the Prince of Demons (3:22; cf. T. Sol. 2:9–3:6; 1QS III, 20–21; see J. Becker 1964: 209–10), and Jesus' response.

a The crowds come to Jesus (3:20)
  b Jesus' family thinks that he is beside himself (3:21)
    c The scribes' accusation (3:22)
      d Jesus' response (3:23–29)
    c′ The scribes' accusation restated (3:30)
  b′ Jesus' family comes to take charge (3:31–33)
a′ The crowds sit around Jesus as his new family (3:34–35)

The exact meaning of "Beelzebul" is unclear, perhaps "lord of the flies" (cf. 2 Kings 1:2–3, 6, 16; Josephus, *Ant.* 9.19; see MacLaurin 1978; Marcus 1999: 272). Another possibility, "lord of the house" (*zĕbûl* = "dwelling"), would resonate with Jesus' use of *oikia* in 3:25, 27 (see Oakman 1988): the house of the strong "lord of the house" is being plundered by the stronger one (1:7) who is truly the Lord of the House (meaning the temple [1 Kings 8:13; Isa. 63:15] or heaven [Hab. 3:11] or Sheol [Ps. 49:14] [so Gaston 1962] or all creation [Philo, *Spec. Laws* 1.66]). For the rabbis, the householder was most commonly Yahweh (cf., e.g., *m. 'Abot* 2:15; *b. Ber.* 50a; *Midr. Ps.* 3:3; see Flusser 1981: 32, 109n8 [cited in Marcus 1999: 274]). Given that for Mark, the demons are nothing if not unclean (*akathartos* [1:23, 26–27; 3:11; cf. 5:2, 8, 13; 6:7; 7:25; 9:25]), he might be alluding to Mal. 3:1, where the Lord whom Israel seeks will suddenly come to his temple/house to purify it (*katharizō* [Mal. 3:3]; see §B.5 of commentary on Mark 1:2–3 above, and commentary on Jesus' action in the temple below).

Jesus' response, clearly the all-important center and significantly for the first time in parables (3:22 [see commentary on Mark 4:12 below]), is in three parts. First, he shows the fallaciousness of the charge: if it were true, then Satan's divided house would have fallen already, and there would be no conflict with the demons to be had (3:23–26). Then he gives the reason why he is able to plunder Satan's house (on *to skeuos* as someone occupied by Satan, see *T. Naph.* 8:6): he has already bound the strong man (3:27). Whether this is once and for all during the temptation (Best 1990: 18–20) or on the occasion of each individual exorcism (Leivestad 1954: 46–47 [on the binding of demons, see Tob. 3:17; 8:3; *Jub.* 5:6; 10:7–11; *1 En.* 10:4; 13:1]) is debated. Nevertheless, Jesus, for Mark, is clearly the Stronger One (*ischyroteros* [cf. 1:7; see Lane 1974: 143]).

Although Jesus' words are not a direct citation, many commentators see here an allusion to Isa. 49:24, noting the conceptual parallels of (1) "strong man" (*ischyros/gigas*, the former term apparently replacing the latter in the NT period [R. E. Watts 2000: 148n57]), and (2) "taking/plundering" in the context of (3) the eschatological deliverance of Israel (Grimm 1981: 88–92; so, e.g., Cranfield 1959; Lane 1974; Nineham 1963; Barrett 1970: 70–72; Gnilka 1978–1979; Hooker 1959; Pesch 1976–1977; Best 1990: 12–13; Marcus 1999; cf. Davies and Allison 1988–1997: 2:342). The larger context of Mark's Isaianic horizons strengthens this identification.

Additionally, the seizing of the strong man's vessels (*ta skeuē autou diarpasai*) has suggested to some an allusion to Isa. 53:12, where the enigmatic servant divides the spoils of the strong (*skyla tōn ischyrōn*), apparently envisaging the plunder of Israel's defeated foes (e.g., *TDNT* 3:400–401; Fuller 1963: 72; Legasse 1962; Cranfield 1959). Mark may indeed have something like this in view, given that (1) Matt. 8:17 sees in Jesus' mighty deeds the fulfillment of Isa. 53:4, and that prior to any suffering, (2) the final victory and deliverance from exile envisaged in Isa. 53, especially as glossed in the Targum, where the Messiah delivers his people from the nations and their kings (53:10–12), is also an expression of the Yahweh-Warrior's acts on behalf of his people ("I will allot . . ." [53:12]), and (3) Isa. 53:12 is the only parallel with this imagery in an eschatological setting, particularly when it is noted that Mark's *skeuē* seems to have largely replaced the LXX's *skyla* by the NT period (but see the single exception in Luke's account of the Beelzebul controversy [11:22], where he seems to have Isa. 53:12 in mind [Legasse 1962]).

B. Isa. 49:24 in Context. Isaiah 49 represents a turning point in chapters 40–55 (Blenkinsopp 2000–2003: 2:71–72; Goldingay 2001: 280; cf. Melugin 1976: 85). Whereas Isa. 40–48 concerns Jacob-Israel's failure to respond positively to the news of Yahweh's choice of Cyrus and the humiliation of daughter Babylon (e.g., 48:1–20), the future-oriented promises in Isa. 49–55 (R. E. Watts 1990a: 56–57) focus on the suffering and vindication of the enigmatic servant who will facilitate the deliverance of daughter Jerusalem-Zion

(Mettinger 1983: 26; cf. Ceresko 1994: 53–54). Pivotal here is the installation in 49:1–6(7) (Melugin 1976: 70–71; Williamson 1989) of a new servant Israel who will both restore Jacob-Israel and be the light to the nations that Jacob-Israel was not (49:6; cf. Ps. 2?; see R. E. Watts 1990a: 54; Childs 2001: 384–85). This occasions two proclamations of new-exodus salvation in 49:(6) 7–13, 14–26 (Westermann 1964a: 366–68; 1964b: 121, 132–33; cf. Schoors 1973: 106).

Our text occurs in the second proclamation. Here Yahweh responds to bereaved Zion-Jerusalem's complaint that he has forgotten her (49:14). He confirms his unfailing love (49:15–16) and his commitment to rebuild her walls and to fill her to overflowing with her returning children (i.e., exiles [49:19–21] and perhaps survivors of the nations [49:20–23]), promising their exaltation such that kings and queens will be their foster parents (49:22–23).

Given the might of Israel's oppressors, however, the task seems hopeless. So Yahweh, demonstrating his incomparability (Kuntz 1997) and again employing military language (cf. 49:2; see Blenkinsopp 2000–2003: 2:300), returns to the promise of 49:9 and asks another rhetorical question on Zion's behalf (cf. 49:15): "Can the prey be taken from a strong man or the captive of a righteous one [*ṣaddîq*] be seized?" (49:24).

Here *ṣaddîq* could refer to Yahweh (cf. *Pss. Sol.* 5:3), or a righteous person (*Tg. Isa.* 49:24), or Babylon as the agent of Yahweh's righteous judgment (Goldingay [2001: 288] suggests also Persia, which has captured Babylon). Its presence explains the LXX's odd attempt at clarification: "If one takes a captive unjustly [*adikōs*], will he be saved?" Alternatively, 1QIsa[a] reads "captive of a tyrant" (*ʿryṣ* [cf. Syriac; Vulgate]), which could indicate Israel's arrogant enemy Babylon (chap. 48 [e.g., Blenkinsopp 2000–2003: 2:315]; cf. Ezek. 28:7; 30:11; Ps. 54:3; 86:14), or even perhaps Yahweh, elsewhere described because of his righteousness as a "dread" (*ʿārîṣ*) warrior on his servant's behalf (Jer. 20:11–12).

The content of the following "Thus says Yahweh" in 49:25 is also problematic: does *gam* mean a definite "surely"—"No matter how strong Israel's captors, Yahweh will rescue his people"—or a doubtful "even if"—"Even if one could take prey from the mighty, no one will take Yahweh's people from him" (cf. 49:15b: "Even if these forget, I will not forget you"; see Schoors 1973: 115)? Although "righteous" is more difficult, the vast majority of modern commentators affirm the traditional reading: regardless of the strength of Israel's captors, mighty Yahweh himself will surely deliver his people (cf. *Tg. Isa.* 49:25).

In a string of increasingly emphatic self-declarations Yahweh continues, "I myself" (*'ānōkî*) will "enter the lists on your behalf" (Blenkinsopp 2000–2003: 2:315), and "I myself" will save (49:25b). Israel's enemies will slide into internecine warfare (49:26a), with the result that all flesh will know that "I am Yahweh"—a standard form of self-presentation (Schoors 1973: 113; Zimmerli 1963)—"your Savior and your Redeemer, the Mighty One of Jacob" (49:26b). Here again is Isa. 40–66's emphasis on Yahweh-Warrior's very own saving presence (see 40:3), though its clear connection with the newly appointed servant (49:3) suggests that Yahweh himself will be especially present through his agent (49:5d, where Yahweh is the servant's "strength" [*ischys*]).

All this echoes the prologue's presentation of Yahweh, who comes "in strength" (40:10 LXX: *meta ischyos*; cf. the increased emphasis on Yahweh's might in *Tg. Isa.* 40:10; 49:22; 51:5; 53:1) with his arm ruling for him (40:10a; cf. 42:13), whose people are his booty (*sēkārô . . . ûpĕ'ullātô* [40:10b]; cf. Ezek. 29:18–20; see Begrich 1969: 59; Whybray 1975: 52), so that all his glory might be known to all flesh (40:5). Whereas in chapters 1–39 the Lord of Hosts (*sĕbā'ôt*) had fought against Israel (e.g., 1:7–9, 24–25; 2:12; 3:1; 10:23) with "outstretched arm" (5:25b; 9:12b, 17b, 21), in chapters 40–55 this title occurs primarily in new-exodus salvation oracles as God now fights on Israel's behalf (45:13; 47:4; 51:15; 54:5; cf. 40:26).

The overarching importance of the Yahweh-Warrior motif is evident later when the oracles concerning Jerusalem's final restoration (Isa. 60–62), which constitute the heart of Isa. 56–66 (Dumbrell 1985; Rendtorff 1984), are bracketed with two "Warrior" passages wherein Yahweh, again coming *meta ischyos* (63:1), declares that he himself will wage war for his people (59:15b–20; 63:1–6) (see Hanson 1979: 124–26, 203–5; Polan 1985).

Finally, we note that although Yahweh's judgments are executed against the nations—primarily Babylon, but also others (43:14; 47:1–47; 48:14; and 41:11–12; 49:26; 51:7–8, 22–23)—his warrior activities are directed primarily against the gods who epitomize their wealth and power, whether in anti-idol polemics (40:18–20; 44:9–20; 46:5–7) or the trials against the nations (41:1–5, 21–29; 43:8–13; 44:6–8; 45:18–25). Yahweh's sole control over history dethrones the idols and thus effects Israel's deliverance (Clifford 1980; J. C. Kim 1962; Preuß 1971: 208–15).

C. Isa. 49:24 in Judaism. The closest parallel to Isa. 49:24 is a proverbial saying in *Pss. Sol.* 5:3: "No one takes plunder from the strong man." Being either directly dependent on or sharing a common source with Isa. 49 (Ryle and James 1891: 54), it provides the basis on which the writer concludes, "Who can take anything from what you [Lord God] have done?" Here Yahweh is the strong man, and the emphasis lies—to use Mark's language—on the inviolability of his house. But for Mark, who heightens the correlation between Jesus' casting out of demons and the plundering (*diarpasei* [cf. LXX: *lēmpsetai*]) of Satan's house, the point lies in the opposite direction: no strong man's house can resist Yahweh.

Also, whereas in Isa. 40–55 Israel was understood to be in bondage to the nations and especially their idols, during the intertestamental period the belief emerged that behind the idols stand the demons (cf., e.g., Ps. 95:5 LXX [96:5 ET]; Isa. 65:3, 11 LXX; *Tg. Isa.* 65:3, 11; *1 En.* 19:1; 99:7; *Jub.* 1:11; 11:4; 22:17; 1 Cor. 10:20; Rev. 9:20; see Theissen 1983: 255–56; Annen 1976: 181–82). The binding of the demons is thus a common theme in various Jewish eschatological traditions (e.g., *1 En.* 10:11–12; 54:3–5; 69:28; cf. Isa. 24:21–22; Rev. 20:1–3; see also *1 En.* 10:4–5; 21:1–6; *Jub.* 10:7–9; see Hiers 1985: 235–37). According to *T. Levi* 18:12, in the time of deliverance "Beliar shall be bound by him" (perhaps referring to a priestly Messiah [18:2–3]), and in *T. Zeb.* 9:8 (b, d, g) "the Lord himself . . . will liberate all the prisoners of Belial" (cf. *T. Sim.* 6:6; *T. Dan* 5:10–13; *T. Zeb.* 9:8).

Likewise, in 1QM XII, 10–14; XIX, 2–8 Yahweh is depicted in the end time as a warrior taking his plunder (Ringgren 1963: 152–66; van der Ostern-Sacken 1969). In 11Q13 when the warrior Melchizedek, usually understood to be a heavenly figure but perhaps a human messiah (Rainbow 1997), executes the judgments of God in accordance with the reign of God in Isa. 52:7 and the restoration of Zion in Isa. 61:2–3 (de Jonge and van der Woude 1965–1966), he does so by delivering Israel from the hand of Belial and all his spirits. In the Dead Sea Scrolls this is largely understood in terms of purification from defilement (Pimental 1988).

Similar conceptions, often expressed in terms of Isaianic imagery, are found elsewhere, whether of Yahweh (Wis. 5:16–23; Sir. 35:22–36:17; *T. Mos.* 10:2–6) or his messianic agent (*Pss. Sol.* 17:23–39; *2 Bar.* 39–42; 72–74; *1 En.* 37–71; *4 Ezra* 12:31–34; 13; Philo, *Rewards* 91–97; cf. 1Q28b V, 27; 1Q28a II, 11–12; 4Q161) who will set free those under Satan's power. *Pesiqta de Rab Kahana* 17:4–5, citing Zion's lament (Isa. 49:14) in the context of Dan. 7's four beasts, correlates Rome and Babylon and has Daniel ask how long God's right hand of power will be bound, to which query God responds, "When I deliver my children, I will deliver my right hand."

D. The Use of Isa. 49:24 in Mark. In this climatic confrontation we have Mark's clearest statement that Jesus' authority over the demons constitutes the inbreaking of God's reign, heralding and effecting the demise of Satan's dominion over humanity (in *Jub.* 10:6–7 the binding of evil spirits prevents them from having power over humanity [see Kee 1967: 245]). In view of several of the Dead Sea Scrolls that looked forward to a final purification from all defilement, Mark's previously noted emphasis on Jesus' power over the "unclean" spirits (see commentary on Mark 1:10 above) underlines the point.

However, Mark's Isaianic horizon suggests that we can be more specific: the Yahweh-Warrior himself, having rent the heavens and come down in the person of Jesus (cf. Isa. 63:5–6; also Isa. 64:1 in Mark 1:10), is now effecting the long-awaited new-exodus deliverance of his people from their bondage (R. E. Watts 2000: 149–50). At the same time, however, just as in Isaiah Yahweh's personal deliverance of Israel nevertheless included his newly designated servant Israel (49:1–6[7]), who would both fulfill the nation's calling (42:1–7[9]) and deliver blind and deaf Jacob-Israel from imprisonment (49:5–6a, 9; cf. 42:7, 22), so in Mark

Israel's deliverance from the strong man Satan (Isa. 49:24 in Mark 3:27) is through Jesus, who at his baptism and under the rent heavens was designated true servant Israel (Isa. 42:1 in Mark 1:11).

Furthermore, Mark's emphasis on Jesus' constitution of a new family around himself (Kee 1977: 109; van Iersel 1999; cf. Lambrecht 1974) might also take on added significance. Isaiah 49–66 focuses, as do various traditions attending Ps. 2, especially on Yahweh's deliverance of Zion. This, as we noted, was the special concern of Isa. 49:18–21, which immediately precedes our text, and wherein Zion is exhorted to lift up her eyes and see her children restored to her (cf. 60:4; see Marcus 1999: 286). In Mark it is around Jesus that Zion's new family is gathered, over against the delegation of scribes, who are, for the first time in Mark, from Jerusalem. Ironically, instead of embracing Jerusalem's call to announce the good news of deliverance to the people of Judah (Isa. 40:9), they seek to marginalize Jesus by leveling a potentially capital accusation against him (Malina and Rohrbaugh 1992: 200–201).

E. Theological Use. Mark continues to build his case that in Jesus Israel's long-awaited eschatological new exodus from exile has begun. In keeping with the intertestamental shift, however, the enemy is no longer Babylon or Rome and their idols, but rather the demons. Christologically, this is no garden-variety exorcist. Jesus' casting out of demons, unlike those of his contemporaries (cf. Matt. 12:27//Luke 11:19), is uniquely identified with both the inbreaking and the powerful kingly rule of Isaiah's Yahweh-Warrior himself and his true-Israel servant. Equally strongly, the opposition of official Jerusalem continues Mark's Malachi theme: unprepared Israel could well come under Yahweh's curse.

3:29

A. NT Context: Blasphemy against the Holy Spirit. It is of this potential curse that Mark's Jesus now warns. Immediately following his explanation of the significance of his exorcisms, Jesus formally pronounces (*amēn legō hymin* [here too for the first time in Mark]) an authoritative and sober warning: such blasphemies against the Spirit have no forgiveness.

For Mark, the association of Jesus with the Holy Spirit is continued in his being both the Davidic messiah and Yahweh's Isaianic servant, both of whom are anointed by the Spirit, and in Mark's programmatic first mighty deed Jesus is identified as the "Holy One of God" (1:24). However, given the prominence of the theme of opposition, it is significant that the only place where Jesus himself makes this connection is here in the Beelzebul controversy (see Fitzer 1957: 173–74).

As C. K. Barrett (1970: 104–5) ventured some time ago, the closest, if not only, conceptual parallel in Israel's Scriptures is Isa. 63:10: "But they grieved his Holy Spirit, and he turned against them to become their enemy, fighting against them" (cf. Lövestam 1968: 30–34). The text is striking for its emphasis, without parallel in Israel's Scriptures, on Yahweh's "Holy Spirit" (63:10–11; cf. 63:14; Ps. 51:11), which Spirit, though also infrequent in Mark, nevertheless occurs in his opening chapters only in connection with Jesus' baptism (1:10–12) —already seen by Mark as Yahweh's response to Isa. 63's lament—and here where it concerns the origin of Jesus' undoubted authority.

B. Isa. 63:10 in Context. Since this text was discussed earlier (see §B of commentary on Mark 1:10 above), only those aspects relevant to the present setting are discussed here. Echoing the language of the covenantal self-revelation in Exod. 34:6–7 (cf. Ps. 145), the prophet begins by recalling Yahweh's loving-kindness (*ḥesed*), his great goodness (*rab-ṭûb*), and his mercy (*raḥămîm*) toward his people (63:7). Trusting that his son Israel (Exod. 4:22) would not deal falsely, the Lord himself became their savior (63:8), personally entering into their distress and redeeming them (63:9 [on the difficulty of this verse, see Blenkinsopp 2000–2003: 3:260]; cf. 63:1–6). Yet as Israel well knew, this extraordinary grace was met with rebellion (cf. Ps. 78:40; 106:33, 43), and in grieving God's Holy Spirit, they made him their enemy (63:10 [see Lövestam 1968]). This is precisely what Exod. 23:21 had warned against: God's name was in his messenger, and he would not forgive their rebellion.

For the prophet, then, as it was in the first exodus, so also in the second. Yahweh had again heard Jacob-Israel's cry and come to save them from exile (40:1–11). But they had rebelled, questioning his power (e.g., 41:1–5, 21–29; 43:8–13; 44:6–8; 45:18–25), his love for them (42:18–25; 43:22–28; 50:1–3), and above all his choice of

agent (44:24–28; 45:1–4, 9–13; 46:5–11) (see R. E. Watts 1990a). Against such faithless "sons" (48:1, 8 [see Beuken 1983: 277]) Yahweh had again become an enemy and subsequently hardened their hearts (63:17), just as he had done to Pharaoh (but cf. 42:18–25; 46:8–12; 48:1–5, 8; also Ps. 95:8, where Israel, as did Pharaoh, harden their own hearts; see R. E. Watts 1990a). In contrast to his servants, they will find no peace, their name will become a curse, and they will be put to death (cf., e.g., 48:22; 63:17; 65:11–15; 66:24; see Childs 2001: 379).

C. Isa. 63:10 in Judaism. Numerous texts address the question of blasphemy—slandering God, his deeds, his people, or his temple—mostly done by Gentiles (e.g., 2 Kings 19:4–6, 22; 1 Macc. 2:6; 2 Macc. 15:24; on account of Israel's exile: Isa. 52:5 LXX; 4Q372 I, 11–13; also Josephus, *Ag. Ap.* 1.59, 223; 2.143; *Ant.* 3.307), but also by faithless Israelites (Isa. 66:3 LXX; Sir. 3:16; CD-A V, 11b–12, which speaks of those who defile their holy spirits with a blaspheming tongue; 4Q396 III, 10; *Sipre Num.* 112; *b. Pesaḥ.* 93b). Others discuss those sins for which there is no repentance (e.g., *Sipre Deut.* 328: "The Holy One, blessed be he, pardons everything else, but on the profanation of the Name he takes vengeance immediately" [but see *Mek. Exod.* 20:7]; according to *m. ʾAbot* 5:18, a person who leads many to sin will be given "no means for repentance").

There was also a fairly widespread awareness that not all Israel was faithful and that God's coming would see the judgment of those who had rejected his covenant (cf., e.g., 1QS V, 10–13; CD-A VII, 9–VIII, 3; 1QHᵃ VII, 18–23; 4Q386; *1 En.* 5:4–8; 79–82; 83–90; *Jub.* 23:8–22; 30:13–23; *4 Ezra* 7:1–25; 8:14–18; *2 Bar.* 54:22; see Elliot 2000), perhaps involving internecine warfare among them (4Q385a 41).

In terms of Isa. 63:10 specifically, the Targum renders the rebellion as being against the "Memra of his holy prophets." What is significant here is that "Memra," which cannot even be approximately rendered in English, stands at the nexus of God's personal and present response to Israel and Israel's response to God and thus focuses not on a static concept, but rather on the relation between God and Israel (Chilton 1987: xv–xvi). Thus for *Tanḥ. Lev.* 10:2, Israel's idolatry (2 Kings 17:9) caused God to change from being merciful and gracious toward them (Exod. 34:6) to becoming an enemy (Isa. 63:10) and rejecting them (Hos. 9:17). Interpreting Eccles. 3:1–8 in terms of Israel, *Eccles. Rab.* 3:10 sees in Isa. 63:10 a time for war when "He . . . himself fought against them." Of particular interest are some later traditions that, in comparing *lex talionis* Israel's punishment ("an eye for an eye") to the nation's sin, state, "They sinned against the one known as 'He,' for it is written: *They have belied the Lord, and said: 'It is not He'* [Jer. 5:12]; and they were smitten by the one known as 'He,'" before citing in full Isa. 63:10 (*Pesiq. Rab.* 33:13 [also *Lam. Rab.* 1:57; *Pesiq. Rab Kah.* 16:11]).

D. The Use of Isa. 63:10 in Mark. For Mark's Jesus, his casting out of demons is nothing if not the work of Yahweh's Holy Spirit (cf. the Targum's "holy prophets"). And given the Targum's Memra, where the concern is Israel's response to God's action, to attribute Jesus' authority to Satan is effectively to "belie the Lord" by saying, "It is not He" (e.g., *Pesiq. Rab.* 33:13), and thus to make an enemy of God. The Isaianic correlation is again all too clear: this new descent of the Spirit "was greeted in precisely the same way as the old," and since "this is God's final, eschatological, deed of salvation, those who utterly reject it can, in the nature of the case, find no salvation" (Barrett 1970: 105). We are reminded also of Exod. 23 (see Grundmann 1959: 112), upon which Isa. 63 is at least partly based and to which Mark alludes at the outset of his Gospel (1:2). There Israel was warned of rebellion against Yahweh's messenger, in whom was his name, because he would not forgive their transgression (Exod. 23:21). Here in this new-exodus, rebellion against Jesus, in whom, as God's Son (e.g., 1:11; 3:11) and bearer of his Spirit, is also God's name, and in whom, for Mark, in some mysterious way God himself is present among his people, would not be forgiven (3:29).

E. Theological Use. It is difficult to overestimate the significance of the Beelzebul controversy in Mark. At two crucial moments in Jesus' career, his baptism and here, the one place where he hints at the meaning of his most characteristic expression of his authority, Isaiah's last great lament plays a central role. At the baptism the lament is answered as Yahweh's (Holy) Spirit descends upon Jesus to do awesome things in effecting Israel's deliverance. In the Beelzebul controversy

that awesome deliverance has again been met with rebellion. Thus, while many commentators have noted that to reject Jesus, God's agent of eschatological salvation, is in the nature of the case to cut oneself off from the possibility of forgiveness (e.g., Lövestam 1968: 62), the OT backgrounds suggest a sharper edge. In grieving God's Holy Spirit by rejecting his messenger who bears his name, Jerusalem's officialdom is in grave danger of making God himself their enemy.

The tragic and profound irony is that when the bona fide Lord of the House casts out unclean spirits, they confess him to be the Holy One/Son of God, but those responsible for the purity of Israel and the house of God instead accuse him of having an unclean spirit (3:30). In light of the fact that internecine warfare among Israel's enemies will attend Yahweh's deliverance of his people from the strong man (Isa. 49:26), and since Jesus has just declared that a "house" divided against itself will surely fall, his family's and the leaders' division over against him hardly bodes well either for the "house" of Israel or for the "house" of God that they superintend (cf. Mark 13).

Christology and ecclesiology are fully integrated here. The Markan Jesus' self-identification with the Holy Spirit only continues the theme that Israel's God is himself in some mysterious way specially present in him. But this again means that to reject Jesus is to exclude oneself from God's servant community.

4:12

A. NT Context: The Purpose of the Parables. Having just mentioned for the first time Jesus' use of parables in the climactic Beelzebul controversy (3:23), Mark now turns to an extensive explanation of their role in Jesus' teaching that many see as playing a crucial role in summarizing Mark's narrative plot (see Keegan 1994: 507). Setting Jesus' teaching beside the sea, which perhaps evokes the fulfillment of Isaianic prophecies (so Derrett 2001b), he begins with the paradigmatic parable of the Soils (4:2–9) and its emphasis on the response of the hearers, reflected in the repeated injunctions to listen carefully (4:3, 9, 23–24). Central to the presentation is Jesus' perplexing use of Isa. 6:9–10, a text of considerable importance to Mark's entire work (Beavis 1989). He appears to state that the parables serve to exclude and harden outsiders. The literature on the nature of parables, the setting, redaction, and structure of Mark 4, and so on is massive, but the present discussion will necessarily focus on the role of Isa. 6.

The citation is obviously periphrastic. Mark's Jesus (1) omits all but the last colon of Isa. 6:10, either to emphasize the "so that"/"lest" coordination and/or because 3:1–6 has already raised the issue of stubbornness/hardness of heart (but cf. Theodoret's citation of Symmachus, which also omits Isa. 6:10), (2) reverses the "seeing" and "hearing" clauses, perhaps due to Mark's interest in seeing (note the two healing-of-sight mighty deeds that begin and conclude his "way" section [8:22–26; 10:46–52]), given that "seeing" is also the center of the concentric pattern in Isa. 6:9–10 (Landy 1999: 71), and (3) not unexpectedly converts the second-person forms to third person under the influence of the narrative (but perhaps following the Targum [see Chilton 1984: 91–98]). More importantly, Mark's substitution of *aphethē* for the MT's *rāpāʾ* (LXX: *iasomai*) both explains the meaning of the MT's "healing" (cf. the Targum: *šbq*) and significantly links the purpose of the parables directly to the threat in the immediately preceding Beelzebul controversy (*ouk echei aphesin* [3:29]) (see Coutts 1964).

A crucial question concerns the sense of Mark's *hina* clause (see C. A. Evans 1989b: 92–99). Many commentators accept the more difficult but usual telic sense (e.g., Marcus 1986: 119–21; C. A. Evans 1989b: 95–106; Räisänen 1990: 83; Gundry 1993: 202), whereby the parables serve to harden "outsiders"—why else would Matthew and Luke seek to "soften" it? Others, finding this unacceptably harsh and difficult to reconcile with the several injunctions to listen and in the light of Mark's omission of the central "fattening of the heart" clause (Isa. 6:10a), propose a considerable range of alternatives—for example, shorthand for *hina plērōthē* (Lagrange 1947; Jeremias 1963: 17); a mistranslation of the Aramaic relative particle (Manson 1948: 76–77); causal, with *mēpote* as "perhaps" (Burkill 1963: 112–13; Moule 1969); consecutive (= result), with *mēpote* as "unless" (Chilton 1984: 91–98; Peisker 1968); imperatival (Cadoux 1941); and prophetic irony in that Jesus' apparent failure was foretold (Hurtado 1983).

B. Isa. 6:9–10 in Context. Whether Isa. 6:1–13 is understood as a call (Clements 1980a;

Sweeney 1988: 136) or as a commissioning narrative (Steck 1972; Vermeylen 1977: 191–92; Goldingay 2001)—and both too strictly conceived are problematic (Childs 2001: 53; Landy 1999: 59n6)—its unusual setting six chapters in suggests that the preceding material is essential to its interpretation (Liebreich 1954; cf. Sonnet 1992: 231–33).

Chapter 1 of Isaiah is generally understood as the introduction to both the book as a whole and chapters 1–12 in particular (Clements 1980a: 28–29; Sweeney 1988: 120–23). Here, in language evoking the Deuteronomic code (e.g., 1:2–3; cf. Deut. 30:19; 32:1; but also throughout [Rignell 1957; Roberts 1982; Niditch 1981]), Yahweh initiates legal proceedings against his rebellious "sons" (1:2b [see Nielsen 1979; Niditch 1981]) who refuse to understand (1:3; a major motif throughout [Vriezen 1962]). They apparently are convinced that intensification of religious observance (1:10–15) will deliver them from their wounds and desolation (1:5–9). But Yahweh instead requires justice (1:16–17; cf. 5:7–24). In rejecting his offer of salvation (1:18–19)—repent and eat the fat of the land—they will be devoured by the sword (1:20) as Yahweh purges the city (1:24–28). Like the withered terebinths in which they worship, idolaters and their works will burn together (1:29–31 [see Wildberger 1972–1982: 78]; cf. 6:13a: "burned again" [see Beale 1991: 260–65]).

Consequently, apart from the occasional moment of hope (e.g., 2:1–4; 4:2–6), chapters 2–5 constitute a sustained determination of judgment. Two themes emerge. First, there is an emphasis on idolatry and illicit cultic practice (2:6–8, 18–20; 3:3), which is considerably expanded in the Targum (cf., e.g., 1:29; 2:6; 8:19 [2]; see Smolar and Auerbach 1983: 150–52), as the cause of Jerusalem's destruction (Clements 1980b: 425–29). Second, the primary responsibility rests with the Jerusalem leadership, whose self-reliant wisdom causes them to reject Yahweh's instruction (cf. 1:10, 23–26; 3:12b–15; 5:18–24; see Schreiner 1967: 149; Sweeney 1988: 38–39; Jensen 1973: 65–104; R. E. Watts 1990a).

The so-called Song of the Vineyard (5:1–7) has the people condemn themselves, and following a final comment on the leaders' repudiation of Yahweh's instruction (5:24) that suggests that a complete break has occurred (Wildberger 1991: 213), the last of the six woes resembles a war oracle but, ironically, with an invading army serving as God's instrument of judgment (5:25–30) (see Gitay 1991: 116).

Given the foregoing, Isaiah's commission, as he sees and hears (6:1, 3, 5, 8) what the nation does not, marks the beginning of the implementation of Yahweh's *lex talionis* (see Goldingay 2001: 60; Childs 2001: 57; on this principle in regard to Isa. 63:10, as discussed above, see, e.g., *Pesiq. Rab.* 33:13; also *Lam. Rab.* 1:57; *Pesiq. Rab Kah.* 16:11, where Israel's sinning with the eye is met with blindness, citing Isa. 3:16; 29:10; see commentary on Mark 7:6 below). Idolatrous Israel has rejected the Lord's instruction and refused to understand (cf. 6:9 and 6:10a LXX: "For the heart of this people has become heavy . . . and their eyes they have closed"). Enthroned in his temple as Zion's great king (see Liebreich 1954; Dumbrell 1984), Yahweh as judge ratifies their choice, sentencing them (cf. *b. Roš Haš.* 34b; on the numerous parallels between Isa. 1 and 6, see Beuken 2004) to a hardening of heart (not unlike Pharaoh) and confirming them through the prophet's word in the blind and deaf image of the gods that they have chosen (Beale 1991, citing Ps. 115:4–8; 135:15–18: "All who trust them [idols] shall become like them"; cf. Goldingay 2001: 61). Confident in their self-reliant and idolatrous wisdom, Judah's leaders, like their sightless and deaf gods, will continue to "see" but not understand, "hear" but not comprehend, until the cities lie waste (6:12; cf. Deut. 28:28; see further R. E. Watts 2000: 188–93). This continuing condition seems to be the basis of the lament in Isa. 63:17–64:10, where, given that the cities already lie desolate (64:10), the prophet wonders why Yahweh has not yet relented from hardening the people's hearts (63:17).

Reflecting the emphasis on the leadership's responsibility, the immediately following narrative of Ahaz's "pious" demurral of Yahweh's invitation (chap. 7) simply realizes Isaiah's commission (Liebreich 1954; Steck 1972; Childs 2001: 59). Although there is no reason to doubt the sincerity of Yahweh's offer, Ahaz remains steadfast. It is not that he does not understand. The message is clear enough. He simply refuses to believe that it could conceivably be true, and hence, presumably,

the wise ones' opposition (cf. 5:19; see Fichtner 1951; Jensen 1973: 53–58; R. E. Watts 1990a). His self-reliant rejection of the first parable-name of salvation (7:3–9) and the subsequent offer of a sign (7:10–11) results in two further parable-names now announcing judgment and the destruction of the land (7:13–8:8) (see R. E. Watts 2004b: 93–102).

In sum, Isa. 6:9–13 is Yahweh's judicial response, effected through the parabolic proclamation of his prophet, to an idolatrous Judah, whose protestations of faithfulness are belied by the leaders' rejection of Yahweh's instruction.

C. Isa. 6:9–10 in Judaism. The theme of Israel's obduracy (i.e., blindness and deafness) not only continues throughout Isaiah (e.g., 29:9–10; 42:18–20; 43:8; 44:18; 63:17), but also is a long-standing characteristic found throughout Israel's Scriptures all the way back to the exodus traditions (e.g., Exod. 32:9; 33:3–5; 1 Sam. 15:23; 2 Kings 17:14; Neh. 9:16–29; Ps. 78; Jer. 5:21–23; Ezek. 12:2–3; Zech. 7:11–12), being especially important in Deuteronomy (e.g., 9:6–27; 28:28; 29:1–4; 31:27), a text, as we noted, of some significance in Isaiah's opening lawsuit. (As such, the metaphorical language of sensory function/malfunction is part of a larger biblical-theological theme related to anti-idolatry polemic inherent in the Genesis "image of God" motif [see R. E. Watts 2002].)

Of particular interest is the way in which later textual traditions of Isa. 6 handled the issue of divine hardening (C. A. Evans 1989b: 53–80). The LXX, by changing the imperatives ("see . . . , hear . . . , make fat") to future indicatives ("you will see, . . . hear . . ." [6:9]) and an aorist passive ("has grown fat" [6:10a]), and by introducing the latter with an explanatory "for" ("for the heart of this people has grown fat"), puts the emphasis on the people's prior condition, and so "lest" expresses the people's desire, not Yahweh's. Rather than necessarily lessening the judgmental aspect, as is sometimes claimed, the LXX clarifies the reasons for God's judgment that are already present in the MT.

On the other hand, in 1QIsaᵃ 6:9 *ʾ* becomes *ʾ* ("because"), the final *n* of 6:10's *hšmn* is omitted to read "make appalled," and the copula form *wlbbw* has been replaced with *blbbw*, "let it understand" (C. A. Evans 1989b: 55–56, following Brownlee

1964: 186). Although regarded by some as scribal error (e.g., Abegg, Flint, and Ulrich 1999), the combination suggests intentional changes reflecting the conviction that over against those in Israel who are already blind and walk in the stubbornness of their hearts (see §C of commentary on Mark 3:4 above), those of the Qumran community are "the holy seed" (6:13). Since this is the first time in Mark that blindness and deafness terminology appears, it is noteworthy that according to CD-A I, 9–11 the "exiled" faithful were also as the blind who grope for a path (cf. Isa. 59:10). But God, seeing their undivided hearts, provided a Teacher of Righteousness, and now having gone into the wilderness to prepare the way of the Lord (citing Isa. 40:30 in 1QS VIII 12b–16a; see on 1:2–3 section B.2 above), they are exhorted to hear so that their eyes being opened they might walk perfectly on all his paths (CD-A II, 112b–16; cf. 4Q166 I, 8; CD XVI, 1–3 [= 4Q271 4 II, 3–5]). Thus Isa. 6, read now as a word to them, is reinterpreted as an exhortation to "keep listening because you may understand . . . make the heart of this people (those who join the holy seed) appalled (at evil), stop its ears (from evil) . . . let it understand . . . and be healed." But one might ask whether the community saw any possibility of the already blind escaping judgment, and if not, then in this respect they too adhere to the MT's declaration of irrevocable doom for rebels (cf. those who secretly entertain the idols of their hearts, *glwly lbw*) and are cursed (1QS II 11–14).

The Targum introduces the relative particle "who" (*dšmm'n*: "to this people *who* hear but . . ." [6:9]) and so, like the LXX, presents the blindness as a prior condition of the people. However, in retaining the causative "make dull the heart," it provides a clearer explanatory link between the preceding rebellion and Yahweh's judgment—it is because they hear but refuse to understand that their hearts are to be dulled—which might also explain the previously noted expansions articulating Judah's idolatry. As we observed earlier, the MT's "healed" is rendered "forgiven." But the sense of the Targum's *dlm'* (6:10b [MT: *pen*]) is uncertain. If it is telic ("lest"), then the Targum adheres to the causative sense of the MT. If it is conditional, which possibly is implied by *Tg. Isa.* 8:18, where if they see and repent, the decree to go into exile will be void (cf. *Tg. Isa.* 42:19; 57:18–19), then the

hardening will apply only if they do not repent—a significant change from the MT and the LXX. As in 1QIsa[a], the "holy seed" is then interpreted as those who are gathered from the exile. Finally, the Peshitta, of uncertain provenance, in resembling the MT in 6:9, the LXX in 6:10, and the Targum in reading "forgiven" (6:10d), has overall the same sense as the LXX: it is the people's obduracy that leads to the prophetic pronouncement.

Thus the general trend, apart from 1QIsa[a], whose concern is instead the righteous, is not so much to soften the impact of the MT as to clarify the reasons already inherent in it as to Yahweh's hardening of Judah's heart.

Outside of these textual traditions appeals to Isa. 6:9–10 are relatively rare, but in each case the focus is not on the threat of hardening, but rather on the promise of forgiveness (for the following, see C. A. Evans 1989b: 137–40). *Mekilta Exodus* 19:2 cites Isa. 6:10 alongside Ps. 78:36–38's account of God's willingness to forgive Israel's unfaithfulness so that, 6:10's "lest" omitted, the fattening of the heart effects repentance and thus healing. Rabbi Johanan (*b. Roš Haš.* 17b) apparently took 6:10 conditionally (cf. the Targum's possible "unless"), implying that if repentance came in the interval between the announcement and the judgment, forgiveness would be given—there is no hint of intentional hardening in order to prevent repentance. Similarly, in *b. Meg.* 17b the Amidah's sequence of the fourth ("You grant understanding") and fifth ("Bring us back, Father") benedictions is justified on the basis of Isa. 6:10's order "lest they, understanding with their heart, return and be healed," which assumes that judgment should lead to repentance (cf. *y. Ber.* 2:3 [V.F.]). In the same section, after a citation of Ps. 103:3–4 to show that healing and redemption follow forgiveness, Isa. 6:10 is invoked with the explanation that the healing in view is that of forgiveness (cf. the Targum). According to *S. Eli. Rab.* 3, the idea that God would seek to prevent repentance is folly. Instead, since Isaiah knew the prophecies of restoration (i.e., Zech. 2:8–9; 8:4) the statement, sarcasm pure and simple, is designed to get Israel to repent.

Finally, although it makes no reference to Isa. 6, the beginning of the fourth vision of *4 Ezra* (9:26–37) speaks of God sowing the law in the hearts of Israel during the first exodus (9:31). Although the fathers received it, in keeping with the book's overriding theme of the irreversibility of the wicked in Israel's judgment (Elliott 2000: 99–107), they did not keep it and were destroyed (9:34).

D. The Use of Isa. 6:9–10 in Mark. Although often missed, striking parallels exist between the setting of Isa. 6 and Mark's presentation (see R. E. Watts 2000: 184–210; also Gnilka 1961: 205; Schneck 1994: 125–27). In Isa. 6 the fundamental datum is Yahweh's kingship; in Mark's Gospel Jesus inaugurates the kingdom of God (mentioned three times in the parables material [4:11, 26, 30]), and the Beelzebul debate concerns the clash of kingdoms (3:24). In both cases God's proffered salvation is met with rebellion cloaked in piety, especially on the part of the nation's wise leaders (on the proverbial wisdom of the Jerusalemites, cf. *Lam. Rab.* 1:1; see Gundry 1993: 357).

Thus, in spite of his mighty inauguration of Isaiah's long-awaited new exodus, Mark's Jesus is confronted with a consistent pattern of hostility and rejection (2:1–3:6) resulting in a secret plot against his life by the Pharisees and Herodians (3:6) and, in the first appearance of leaders from Jerusalem, a public denunciation of him as an agent of Satan (3:22), again with potentially lethal consequences. Jesus' subsequent warning against blasphemy (3:29), with its allusion to Isa. 63:10 (note also the prophet's reference to subsequent hardening just a few verses later in 63:17), indicates that a line has been crossed (3:30). In Isaianic terms, blind and deaf to Jesus' embodiment of Torah's goodness and life (see commentary on Deut. 30:15 in Mark 3:4 above), they have made Yahweh an enemy. Consequently, as in Isaiah, Jesus responds in parables (3:23), which likewise confirm "those on the outside" in their prior rebellion and ultimate judgment (4:12; 12:8–12). In this sense, Mark reflects the understanding in the MT as clarified in the LXX, the Targum, and the Peshitta: it is the prior stubborn rebellion of the nation that leads to its judgment. Recalling the language of CD-A and 1QS, their hearts are not undivided (cf. Mark's soils) and thus they still grope along as the blind. The obvious implication is that sight and hearing come from being instructed in ways of the Lord and his Torah, not by the Teacher of Righteousness or the scribes, but by Jesus who mysteriously (4:11) is the very

presence of the one (the Lord) and therefore fully embodies the other (the Torah). It is no surprise that Jesus concludes his first parable by saying, "Whoever has ears to hear, let him hear!" as it is evident that some do not (on the OT backgrounds to this combination, see Derrett 2001a).

Nevertheless, there are obvious differences and ambiguities (R. E. Watts 2000: 199–205). Whereas in Isaiah both people and leaders—Judah and Jerusalem—have made their decision, in Mark this clearly is not yet so. Jesus' family members, in keeping their concerns private and not denouncing him, are hardly in the same boat as the Jerusalem scribes. Although for Mark, until they make a conscious choice for Jesus, they too will remain on the outside (3:31–32), familial ties notwithstanding (R. E. Watts 2000: 202). The great crowd (4:1) is apparently as yet undecided, hence the repeated summons to listen carefully. And of course, many have responded in faith. Hence, in the parable of the Soils the responses vary. But in the end—and this is Mark's primary concern—it all boils down to producing a harvest or not, to being on the inside or the outside, which is the point that the Isaiah citation addresses.

Everything, as in Isaiah (e.g., Isa. 7:9b), centers on hearing in faith and repentance (cf. 1:14–15; see C. D. Marshall 1989). Those who do so are healed and saved (2:5; 5:34–36; 9:24; 10:52). However, for those who refuse, who remain on the outside, Jesus' parables of both word and deed (cf. "everything" [4:11]; see Blomberg 1986; Guelich 1989: 213; and note the preceding division over Jesus' exorcisms) merely confirm them, as in Isaiah's day, in their unbelief (cf. 3:22; 12:12).

Mark's Jesus, in perhaps a deliberate echo of the Shema of Deut. 6:4–5 (Gerhardsson 1968) and thus the final conflict over Sabbath activity (see commentary on Mark 3:4 above), therefore warns his hearers to "hear" carefully and teaches them as "they are able to hear" (4:33). Now, however, it is Jesus who embodies that to which Torah pointed, and his teaching, not Torah itself, stands at the center. His proclamation in word and deed of the kingdom of God will reveal as clearly as a lamp on a stand (4:21–23) and as surely as the planted seed grows (4:26–29) the state of his hearers' hearts and thus their destinies. If they do not respond to the good that he does and the life that he gives with repentance and faith, then even the little that they have will be taken away (4:24–25; cf. *b. Ber.* 40a, which expresses a similar idea; contrast Bartimaeus, who, although *para tēn hodon* [10:46; cf. 4:4], responds in faith and receives sight and salvation). Just as in *4 Ezra 9* where Israel's failure to respond to the sowed Torah in the first exodus led to the nation's condemnation, so now failure to respond to the sowed word of Jesus in the second likewise results in judgment.

E. Theological Use. Jesus' message to Israel was unexpected and thus mysterious (4:11; cf. 1QpHab VII, 8, 14; see Beale 1998: 215–55; *TDNT* 4:822), as was Isaiah's to Judah. And it occasioned, as crystallized in the stubbornness seen in the final synagogue confrontation (3:1–6) and the climactic Beelzebul controversy, the same rejection (as also in Isa. 40–55 [see R. E. Watts 1990a]). Soteriologically, in this respect the parables are neither esoteric nor rigidly predestinarian, but rather are revelatory of the kingdom and of the hearers' hearts. They are the judicial response from the one who inaugurates God's kingly reign to stubbornness of heart and blasphemous rebellion. As such, they are also a warning to those who, perhaps like Jesus' family, are less hostile but nevertheless still on the outside. Ecclesiologically, those who are confident in their own wisdom reject the word and work of the Holy One of God (1:24; cf. Isaiah's characteristic "Holy One of Israel") and despise the instruction of Yahweh-Warrior (cf. "Lord of Hosts" [Isa. 5:24b]). In contrast to those who "do the will of God" (3:35), they will find that "their root will become rotten and their blossom like dust" (Isa. 5:24a [cf. Mark 4:3–6]).

Christologically, Mark is increasingly clear that something special has happened in Jesus. Yahweh has at last responded to long-exiled Israel's lament and come down in him. Tragically, however, as was so often the case in the nation's history, many have hardened their hearts. To reject Jesus is to reject Yahweh himself, to cut oneself off from the faithful in Israel, to choose death, and so to face judgment (11:13–14, 20–23; 12:9; 13). But for those who will listen carefully, this need not be the result. Taken together, the Beelzebul controversy and the material on the parables indicate that the eschatological division of Israel has begun, and it all turns on one's response to Jesus (3:24–25; 4:11; cf. Isa. 65:1–13; see also §B of commentary on Mark 3:29; see especially Elliott [2000: 263–73], who notes the importance in various intertestamental sources for an appropriate individual response).

4:32

A. NT Context: Birds of the Air. The fourth and final parable in Mark's parables section, 4:30–32, is the second kingdom simile and the third involving seed. Granted that the orchid seed is smaller (Trever 1962), the minuteness of the mustard seed was proverbial (see *m. Nid.* 5:2; *m. Ṭehar.* 8:8; *b. Ber.* 31a; *Midr. Lev.* 24:2) and thus better served the more obvious point of the story: although the kingdom that Jesus inaugurates appears inconsequential at present, inevitably it will become the greatest of all shrubs, so that "the birds of the air can make their nests in its shade" (4:32). This imagery is widely recognized as echoing the representation common in the ancient Near East of great kingdoms as cosmic trees (Zimmerli 1983: 146–47) with the "birds of the heaven"—the nations—finding shelter in their branches (e.g., Guelich 1989: 251; Gundry 1993: 230; Marcus 1999: 324, 330). It is picked up particularly in Ezek. 17:23 (of the renewed Davidic kingdom), 31:3–18 (of Assyria and Pharaoh), and Dan. 4:11–12, 21 (of Nebuchadnezzar). Of these, only Ezek. 17:23 describes the unexpected exaltation from humble beginnings of the Davidic messianic kingdom, through which God exercises his sovereign reign (cf. Pss. 1; 2; see also the discussion of Ps. 2 in Mark 1:11 above).

B. Ezek. 17:23 in Context. Ezekiel 17, one of the judgment oracles against Judah (Ezek. 4–24) and situated in a section focusing particularly on the folly of Jerusalem (Ezek. 16–20) (see Clements 1996: 67), is a wisdom-flavored riddling parable or fable (Hals 1989: 115). It rebukes Judah's King Zedekiah for breaking covenant with the king of Babylon by plotting with Egypt (cf. Isa. 30:1–5; 31:1–3) and thereby dishonoring Yahweh, in whose name he earlier swore allegiance (see Zimmerli 1979: 366; Zedekiah's Babylonian-bestowed name means "Righteousness of Yahweh" [Brownlee 1986: 271]). The fable (17:1–10) tells of a finely plumaged eagle, *nešer* (the king of Babylon), removing the topmost shoot (Jehoiachin) from the cedar in Lebanon (Jerusalem) and transplanting it to the city of merchants (Babylon). He then planted a seed (Jehoiachin's uncle, Zedekiah, and therefore not a shoot from the cedar) in a fertile field beside a river (probably a reference to the latter's alliance with Babylon on the Euphrates) so that it should become a fast-growing vine whose branches were turned toward him. However, because the vine instead spread its roots and branches toward a second eagle (Pharaoh), it would be uprooted and destroyed. The parable is followed by the interpretation (17:11–15) and two words of judgment that focus on Zedekiah's disloyalty first to the covenant's human partner (17:16–18) and then especially toward Yahweh, whose name he has sullied (17:19–21; cf. Exod. 20:7; Lev. 19:2; Matt. 6:9).

Our text comes from the concluding salvation oracle (17:22–24). Recalling his actions through his agent Nebuchadnezzar (Allen 1994: 260), Yahweh himself will also take a young sprig from the cedar, but he will transplant it instead to a high and lofty mountain so that all the "trees of the forest might know" that he alone exalts and lays low (17:24; cf. 1 Sam. 2:7; Ps. 18:27; 75:7; 147:6; Isa. 2:2–17; 57:15). The picture combines (1) the Edenic imagery of the cosmic divine tree (cf. Hos. 14:5–7 [note Ezek. 17:23; cedars do not bear fruit]; see Allen 1994: 261) and (2) the mountain of Yahweh—Zion—with its implied focus on the sanctuary (Ezek. 20:40; 40:2; cf. 28:11–14; Ps. 48:1–2; Isa. 2:2; Zech. 14:10; see Eichrodt 1970: 228; Brownlee 1986: 273) with (3) that of the messianic promise (Ezek. 34:23–24; 37:24–25) concerning the tender shoot/branch ($ḥṭr/ṣmḥ$) of the Davidic house (cf. Isa. 4:2; 11:1; Jer. 23:5; 33:15; Zech. 3:8; 6:12; see Zimmerli 1979: 367; nobility, status, being set on a high mountain, and the birds resting under and residing in the shade of a tree are royal topoi [Metzger 1991: 215–16, 200–203]).

That there is no mention of the earlier "vine" imagery and that language of humiliation and exaltation is found elsewhere in Ezekiel only in the scathing attack on Zedekiah (21:30–32) suggest that there is also a polemic against the present Judahite leadership (Zimmerli 1979: 368), and that this promise of astonishing reversal and universal prominence is only for the rightful heir (21:32). With the coming of that heir, the Davidic shoot would become Yahweh's great cosmic tree planted on his holy mountain, and it would "produce boughs" in the shade of which "every

kind of bird" (i.e., all the nations [cf. 31:1–9; Dan. 4:11–12, 21]) would find rest (17:23).

The main point, then, concerns the faithless attempt of Judah's leaders to extricate themselves from the justice of God's exilic judgment. God will direct Zedekiah's wicked folly back upon his own head (Hals 1989: 117). At the same time, in God's own good time will he plant his choice messianic shoot such that it becomes a great tree so that all will know that it is he alone who exalts or humbles.

C. Ezek. 17:23 in Judaism. The image of the tree is picked up in several ways in the Dead Sea Scrolls. Noah is portrayed as "a great cedar . . . standing . . . on the top of the mountains" (1QapGen ar XIV, 9–17; cf. XIX, 14–20, where Abraham is likened to a cedar; according to Philo [*Sobriety* 65–66], Shem is the root of Abraham), and, following scriptural tradition, the various nations are also seen as trees (4Q552 1 II; cf. 4Q553 6 II). Of particular interest are 1QHᵃ XIV, 14–17 and XVI, 5–9, where Israel is described as a stand of various trees. Of these, only some—the trees of life that are hidden among the others and that represent the community of the righteous—take advantage of the nearby spring (cf. Ps. 1; *Pss. Sol.* 14:3–4; Ps. 92:12; Isa. 61:3). It is among these that a sheltered and hidden shoot (*nēṣer* [Isa. 11:1]) grows to become a great tree whose shade spreads over all the earth and in whose branches all the birds roost. At this point the tree image is combined with fire and light (perhaps under the influence of the narrative about the burning bush?), which fire burns the wicked, including those in Israel who have turned aside from righteousness (14:18–19).

1 Enoch 10:16 anticipates the appearance of the plant of righteousness and truth, after which all the nations will worship God, and pollution, sin, plague, and suffering will be removed from the earth. The imagery of the forest/tree and vine is modified in *4 Ezra*, where Israel is the one vine chosen from all the forests upon the earth (5:23), although of this again only the eschatological remnant will remain (9:21). A similar treatment is found in *2 Baruch*. Over against a great forest stands a vine (cf. Ezek. 17:6–7; Ps. 80:8–17) from under whose roots flows a fountain that, on meeting the forest, becomes a flood that destroys all but a single great cedar that eventually is burnt, leaving the vine alone to fill the plain (36:1–37:1). In the subsequent interpretation the trees of the forest represent various nations, the final cedar a fourth and more evil kingdom (Rome [cf. Dan. 2; 7]), and the vine and fountain Yahweh's anointed one (39:6–40:5). But here too the blessing applies only to the faithful remnant of Israel (42:2; cf. 40:2; see Elliot 2000: 343–44).

The Targum is more explicit in regard to the shoot's messianic identity ("a child from the kingdom of the house of David" [17:22]) and understands the greatness of the tree in blatantly militaristic terms: "He shall gather together armies and build fortresses and become a mighty king" (17:23a). The mountain height of Israel becomes the temple mount (17:23a; cf. *y. Sanh.* 11:3 [I.A], which argues that therefore the temple can be built only on the highest point in the world), and the birds and winged creatures that find shelter in his shade are "the righteous . . . and the humble" (17:23b).

As in Ezekiel, the birds of heaven represent Gentile nations (*1 En.* 90:30; *Midr. Ps.* 104:10–13). The notion of dwelling (*kataskēnoun* [Mark 4:32b]) is used of the eschatological ingathering of the nations under Israel (Zech. 2:15 LXX; some manuscripts of *Jos. Asen.* 15:6; see Marcus 1999: 324).

D. The Use of Ezek. 17:23 in Mark. The parable and its Markan context exhibit several parallels with Ezek. 17, not least of which is a shared genre. Mark's opening sentence sets all within the framework of God's response to the nation's Babylonian exile. The voice from heaven designates Jesus as the Davidic messiah (cf. the messianic connotations of Dan. 7:13's Son of Man in Mark 2:10, and the appeal in Mark 2:23–25 to David's action 1 Sam. 21:1–7), who then announces the inauguration of God's kingdom, the mystery of which is precisely the subject of this very parable (4:30; cf. 4:13 and the Markan parables generally [see Hooker 2000]). And only Ezek. 17:22–23 combines small beginnings, eventual greatness, and an emphasis on boughs and shade for the birds of the air (cf. 17:23 LXX's *hypo tēn skian autou*) in the context of God's activity. Given the various traditions discussed above that were associated with such imagery and the characteristic royal connotations of language involving tree, great size, bird, and bough (Metzger 1991), it seems reasonable to assume that there is more here than a simple contrast. The kingdom that Jesus announces is also Yahweh's timely planting of the shoot of the Davidic cedar. And if the traditions relating the mountain to the temple are in view, it will be intimately connected with the temple and Jerusalem (see commentary on Ps. 2 in Mark 1:11 above), which only increases the gravity of the tensions between Jesus and the Jerusalem authorities.

However, there are, as we have come to expect with Mark, significant variations. Ezekiel's shoot comes from the exalted crown of the great cedar. Mark's Jesus speaks of a tiny and lowly mustard seed that, naturally enough, grows not into a mighty tree, but rather a shrub. And not only are mustard shrubs short-lived annuals, but also they generally do not provide nesting places. Although these differences might merely be the allowable consequence of hyperbole (see Huffman 1978: 211–12), they also might indicate an explicitly ironic fulfillment of Ezek. 17. In keeping with the mystery of the kingdom, and in stark contrast to the grandeur of the trees of Ezekiel and later Jewish interpretation, the great cosmic cedar, comparable to others of its kind (e.g., of Pharaoh, as noted above) and planted on Yahweh's cosmic mountain, is instead only the greatest of all shrubs (see Funk 1973; Scott 1981: 71–73). Unlike the Targum, where the Davidic king establishes military forces, Mark's Jesus takes up a cross. Thus his kingdom is "great" only in terms of the crucified Messiah, not the rulers of this world, and hence it offers genuine protection from the lust for power of the great ones (8:31–38; 9:35–37; 10:35–45) both at home and among the nations to which this gospel of the kingdom will go (13:10). And as the Targum interpreted the birds as the righteous and humble, in Mark the righteous who will find shelter are those who do the will of the father by hearing Jesus' teaching (3:34–35; 4:9).

Finally, each of the parables in this chapter contains some element of warning—not surprisingly given their immediate occasion (3:20–34). The paradigmatic parable of the Soils articulates the consequences of not hearing aright. That of the lamp warns about the revelatory power of Jesus' teaching and the danger of losing what little one has (cf., 1QH^a XIV, 18–19, where the tree becomes a revealing light and a consuming flame over against the nations and faithless Israel). Given the Markan context to this point and the thrust of judgment so central to the Ezekiel original, it seems reasonable to suppose that implication here. The rapidly growing mustard seed illustrates not only mysterious growth but also the sudden certainty of the irrevocable and speedily approaching sickle of God (Joel 3:13; Rev. 14:14–19) in the eschatological harvest (e.g., *4 Ezra* 4:36–37; 4:40–43; *2 Bar.* 22:5–6; cf. Mark 13:14–23). It is the Lord alone who exalts and demotes, withers and causes to flourish (Ezek. 17:24), and he sets his face against those who impugn his name by faithlessly disregarding his ways.

E. Theological Use. Brief though this parable is, its importance as the last in the series ought not to be overlooked, especially when read in light of all that has preceded. The parables material itself emerged out of the increasing alignment of the various authorities over against Jesus: the Pharisees, the Herodians, the experts in the law from Jerusalem, and, yes, even his family. Even if Mark makes no explicit mention of Israel's messianic expectations to this point, neither Mark's Jesus nor his movement looks very messianic. Nevertheless, to dismiss Jesus' message would be to make a serious mistake. In the end this is the seed that God has planted and in whose eschatological shade the nations will find succor and rest. And since the Son of Man came not to be served but to serve (10:45), the great Davidic cedar of OT hope becomes in Jesus' hands the greatest of all shrubs. Ecclesiologically, as evident in various later traditions, Yahweh's tree/shrub represents faithful Israel over against the apostate. Furthermore, those who seek their own liberation by faithlessly impugning Yahweh's name or, presumably, who resist Yahweh's exaltation of his chosen one—for Mark, those who do not listen receptively—will be brought low.

6:34

A. NT Context: Like Sheep without a Shepherd. Corresponding to the four parables (4:1–34), the following four "amazing" parable-deeds (4:41; 5:15, 33, 42; cf. Isa. 64:3) further identify Jesus with Yahweh-Warrior, who inaugurates Israel's Isaianic new exodus (4:35–5:43; cf. Isa. 3:11–13; 64:5–7; 65:1–7, 19–20; see R. E. Watts 2000: 157–66; 2004c). But then it is Jesus' turn to be amazed, though now at his home town's lack of faith, failure to offer prophetic honor, and umbra-

geous rejection of him (6:1–6a). This final scene both concludes the preceding material—rejected for the first time by an entire Jewish Galilean community, Jesus is finally able to do little for them (see Marcus 1999: 380)—and sets the scene for (1) the sending of the Twelve to the nation at large (6:6b–13) and (2) Herod's paradigmatic rejection and execution of the prophet John (6:14–29). Over against the corrupt and failed "kingship" of Herod, who feasts in his palace and is concerned only for his status and the great ones of Galilee, stands Jesus. He withdraws privately with his disciples to a desert place (6:30–31; cf. 1:3, 12–13), the crowds inevitably gather, and he has compassion on them and teaches them because they were "like sheep without a shepherd" (6:32–34). The latter phrase is a close rendition of Num. 27:17 (cf. 1 Kings 22:17; 2 Chron. 18:16), with the immediately following event of Jesus feeding the crowds in the wilderness (6:35–44) contributing to the exodus/new-exodus setting.

B. Num. 27:17 in Context. Belonging to a larger section concerned with the conquest generation (26:1–36:13), Num. 27:12–23 deals with the succession of Moses (Milgrom 1989: 172). That is, the preceding materials having dealt with the issues of succession in inheritance (26:1–27:11), the question naturally arises as to the succession in leadership as the people enter that inheritance (cf. *Num. Rab.* 21:13).

In 27:12–14, after Moses is reminded that his disobedience at Meribah has disqualified him from leading Israel into the land, he asks the Lord to appoint a successor who, in military idiom, "shall go out before them . . . take them out and bring them in" lest they be "like sheep without a shepherd" (27:17; cf. Josh. 14:11; 1 Sam. 18:13, 16; 29:6; *Tg. Onq.*; *Tg. Ps.-J.*; *Sipre Num.* 139; see Plöger 1967: 178–81). Joshua, in whom is spirit (27:18; "spirit" is indefinite [cf. the Targum: "the spirit of prophecy"]), is then selected, although it is made clear that he is not Moses' equal. Full of a spirit of wisdom (see Deut. 34:9), Joshua nevertheless partakes only some of Moses' *hôd* ("majesty, authority"), and unlike Moses, he does not receive divine guidance directly but instead must stand before the priest who by means of the Urim will communicate Yahweh's decision in regard to holy war (27:21; cf. 11Q19 LVIII, 15–21). So while on the one hand, Moses' disobedience means that he cannot lead the people into their inheritance, on the other hand, Israel will indeed inherit, but will do so under the warrior Joshua, who nevertheless is clearly Moses' subordinate.

C. Num. 27:17 in Judaism. Already an ancient image for the gods' and therefore the kings' justice and kindness in caring for their peoples (Vancil 1992), shepherding is likewise a common metaphor in the OT and later Jewish literature for both God's (e.g., Gen. 48:15; 49:24; Ps. 23:3; cf. Ps. 80:1; Jer. 13:17; Mic. 7:14; *Num. Rab.* 23:2) and human leaders' care for Israel (e.g., 2 Sam. 5:2; Jer. 2:8 LXX; 3:15; 10:21; 23:1–8; 25:34–38; Ezek. 34:23; 37:24; Mic. 5:4–5; Zech. 11:4–17; CD-A XIII, 9; *2 Bar.* 77:13–15; *Exod. Rab.* 41:7). On a cosmic scale, for Philo, God shepherds the created order through his own right reason, his firstborn son (*Agriculture* 51), and this, says Philo, citing Num. 27:17, is especially so for humanity (*Posterity* 67–68), for whom right reason is the law. For the rabbis, Joseph shepherds the world by his provision during the great famine of Gen. 41–47 (*Gen. Rab.* 91:5).

The metaphor is employed especially in the exodus led by Yahweh (Ps. 78:52–55, 70–72; cf. Exod. 15:13, 17) and his agents Moses and Aaron (Ps. 77:20; Isa. 63:11), and consequently it becomes a key image in Isaiah's new exodus. In Isaiah's programmatic prologue the mighty Yahweh-Warrior is presented as a tender shepherd gently escorting his flock home (40:11 [see §B.1 of commentary on Mark 1:2–3 above]). Although Cyrus is designated as Yahweh's shepherd (44:28), it is through his newly appointed true servant Israel (49:1–6[7]; on servant-Moses typology, see Hugenberger 1995; Baltzer 1999: 19–22), who will reenact Joshua's distribution of the land (49:8d; cf. the Davidic messiah in *Pss. Sol.* 17:28; see Blenkinsopp 2000–2003: 2:306), that Yahweh's flock will be compassionately pastured on the heights (49:9b–10) in fulfillment of the Warrior's promised deliverance (49:14–26 [see §B of commentary on Mark 3:27 above]). It is perhaps on this basis that Isa. 40:11's picture of the shepherd Yahweh-Warrior is applied to the Teacher of Righteousness (4Q165 1–2, 2–3).

In later rabbinic tradition Moses was first proven as a shepherd of sheep before he was allowed to shepherd God's people (Philo, *Moses* 1.60–62; *Exod. Rab.* 2:2), and according to *Exod. Rab.*

3:6 (cf. 2:2), it was Moses' concern for afflicted Israel that demonstrated his worthiness. Thus as a faithful shepherd who stood in the breach on Israel's behalf (*Esther Rab.* 7:13), he led Israel away from sin (*Exod. Rab.* 24:3), though it was the one shepherd Yahweh who gave Israel the oral and written Torah (*b. Ḥag.* 3b; *Num. Rab.* 13:15–16; 14:4; *Eccles. Rab.* 12:10) and who performed mighty deeds on their behalf (*Num. Rab.* 23:2 on Ps. 77:21).

In terms of Num. 27:17 in particular, the only other biblical use of the idiom "to lead out and bring in" (Hiphil forms [Num. 27:17b]) is to establish David's royal credentials (2 Sam. 5:2; cf. 1 Chron. 11:2). In leading Israel's armies, he did that for which Saul was chosen but ultimately failed to do (cf. 1 Sam. 8:20; see Grønbæk 1971: 249). As the one who effectively concludes the conquest, David is presented as Moses' true successor (see Milgrom 1989: 185). The connection is strengthened by the fact that both were tested as literal shepherds before being given their metaphorical vocation over Israel (see *Exod. Rab.* 2:2–3). With this view of kingship in mind, when Israel's kings failed to live up to their covenantal obligations, the people became what Moses had feared, "sheep without a shepherd," which, given the original conquest context, occurs naturally enough only in settings of military defeat (1 Kings 22:17 = 2 Chron. 18:6; Jer. 50:6–7; Jdt. 11:19; cf. Ezek. 34:5).

The twin motifs of David's and Yahweh's exodus/new-exodus shepherding are combined in Ps. 78 and Ezek. 34. The former, in the context of remembering Yahweh's control over the sea and his provision for his people in the wilderness (78:12–20), celebrates his taking David from tending "nursing ewes" to be Israel's shepherd (78:70–72; cf. "nursing ewes" imagery in Isa. 40:11). The latter is an extended account of the nation's suffering under oppressive preexilic kings (34:1–10; cf. 19:1–14; 21:25; Jer. 10:21; 12:10; 23:1–2). Because the flock was Yahweh's (34:6) and its shepherds were by his appointment (34:8), he will punish the wicked royal shepherds and, as in Isa. 40:11, will himself rescue his scattered exiled people, cause them to rest in the rich pasture of the hills of Israel (34:11–16; cf. Mark 6:34), and appoint over them one shepherd, his servant

David (34:23–24; cf. 17:22–24; see commentary on Mark 4:32 above).

These hopes are reflected in *Pss. Sol.* 17, where, in combination with language taken from Ps. 2 (see commentary on Mark 1:11 above), the Davidic king will, in the time of Jerusalem's restoration, expose officials, drive out sinners, be powerful in the Holy Spirit, wise, and "mighty in his actions," and compassionately shepherd the Lord's flock, allowing none to stumble (17:36–42; cf. Isa. 40:11).

Among the Dead Sea Scrolls, 11Q5 has a psalm in which David rejoices that he was made shepherd over the flock of Israel in spite of his lowly station (XXVIII, 3–4). Not unlike Isa. 63, 4Q504 is a confession of sin in the context of an exilic commemoration of Yahweh's mighty exodus deeds on Israel's behalf. Recalling when God chose David to shepherd his people (1–2 IV, 6–7), it then goes on to implore the Lord, who does wonders from all eternity, to withdraw his wrath and free his people from exile (1–2 VI, 10–13). The first three and most likely ancient benedictions of the *Birkat ha-Mazon* invoke God as the shepherd of Israel, celebrate his compassion, and pray for his mercy on "the kingdom of the house of David your anointed" (Millgram 1971: 292–94, cited in Marcus 1999: 409; cf. *b. Ber.* 48b; cf. *Sipre Deut.* 41). The fragmentary *Apoc. Ezek.* 5 explicitly recalls Yahweh's promise of Ezek. 34:14–16 to bind up the lame, heal the troubled, return those who stray, and feed and shepherd them on his holy mountain.

Finally, in later rabbinic literature, for *Sipre Deut.* 305, Moses' words in Num. 27:17 anticipate the time when Israel will lack a wise and understanding leader and be subject to the four beasts (of Dan. 7), recalling the days of Ahab and Jehoshaphat when the nation was scattered like sheep without a shepherd upon the mountains (citing 1 Kings 22:17 and again Num. 27:17). *Genesis Rabbah* 33:1 cites Ezek. 34:14 to describe the dwelling of the righteous, and in *Exod. Rab.* 34:3, citing Ezek. 34:31, the building of the tabernacle is likened to providing a lodge for shepherd Yahweh. The latter Ezekiel text is cited over a score of times as testimony to Yahweh's choice of Israel as his flock (e.g., *Gen. Rab.* 33:1; *Exod. Rab.* 24:3; *Song Rab.* 3:21; *Eccles. Rab.* 3:21). At the same time, however, God also shepherds David

because David too is Israel's shepherd (*Gen. Rab.* 59:5), proving his righteousness in shepherding his flock (*Exod. Rab.* 2:2). During a famine in his days he asks God to show compassion by shepherding (feeding) the people as Joseph did (*Gen. Rab.* 91:5).

In sum, Israel's understanding of Yahweh as the compassionate yet strong shepherd springs from the first exodus, when the Lord provided for them, performed mighty deeds on their behalf, gave them Torah, and led them through his servant Moses. Likewise in the new exodus, the compassionate Yahweh-Warrior will again shepherd his people through his new servant. Although in Num. 27 Joshua succeeds Moses to lead the people into their inheritance, it is Yahweh's servant David who eventually becomes Israel's paradigmatic shepherd—probably because he effectively completes the conquest and begins the process of establishing Yahweh's dwelling on his holy mountain, Zion—and is therefore the focus of Israel's eschatological shepherd hope.

D. The Use of Num. 27:17 in Mark. Caught between the hostility of the religious authorities toward Jesus and Herod's venal murder of John, Israel is like sheep without a shepherd (Donahue and Harrington 2002: 209). Against such false shepherds Mark invokes what seems to be a straightforward Jesus-as-the-new-shepherd-Moses motif (Marcus 1999: 406). Here is the leader Israel needs. In a desert place, Jesus' teaching about the kingdom echoes Israel's instruction in Torah and its organization (6:40; cf. Exod. 18:21; see Hooker 1991: 167) and feeding during the exodus (R. E. Watts 2000: 178–79; Marcus 1999: 408–10, 418–21).

But there might be more. As we noted, the phrase "sheep without a shepherd" occurs in contexts of military leadership, and in Num. 27 it specifically concerns the conquest that Moses himself was not permitted to lead. If Mark intends a clear allusion to Num. 27, then the implication is that it is Jesus—*Iēsous* being Greek for "Joshua," and like Joshua, Jesus is a man of S/spirit (1:10; 3:29)—who will lead God's flock in a new conquest (e.g., his casting out of demons, especially his defeat of Legion [5:9, 15]).

Mark's contrasting Jesus with the false shepherds, his interest in Jesus' Davidic features (e.g., Ps. 2 in 1:11; see further on Pss. 118; 110 below, particularly in association with Jerusalem/Zion in the light of, e.g., *Pss. Sol.* 17; 4Q504), and what I have argued is the Davidic messianic coloring of both the Isaianic servant (see commentary on Isa. 42 in Mark 1:11 above) and Daniel's Son of Man (see commentary on Mark 2:10 above) suggest that we should see the "shepherd" metaphor in a Davidic light as well (so, e.g., Guelich 1989: 340; see also Ezek. 34; *Pss. Sol.* 17). Here, then, is the rejected lowly shepherd (6:1–6a; cf. 11Q5), compassionate (6:34; cf. *Pss. Sol.* 17:34; *Gen. Rab.* 91:5) though powerful in spirit and mighty in action (6:14; cf. *Pss. Sol.* 17:37, 40), through whom God will expose wicked shepherds (*Pss. Sol.* 17:36) and faithfully shepherd his flock in their pasture (6:39; cf. *Pss. Sol.* 17:40). Interestingly, just as Ps. 78 links God's care for Israel in his power over the sea and provision of food in the exodus (78:12–20) with his appointment of David to shepherd them (78:70–72), so too Mark presents Jesus as Israel's shepherd in the context of a feeding followed by a demonstration of his power over the sea on behalf of the Twelve, the Israel that he has reconstituted around himself (see 6:51–52, where Mark links the significance of both events).

In this respect, Jesus' "Son of Man" self-designation also suggests an interesting correlation with the later *Sipre Deut.* 305. There, Moses' concern anticipated the time when the scattered sheep of Israel would be subject to Dan. 7's four beasts. In Dan. 7, of course, it is one like a Son of Man who is vindicated over against them. From this perspective, Jesus, in exercising this messianic leadership—twice already he has spoken of his authority as the Son of Man—could be understood as inaugurating the end of Israel's leaderless oppression (see commentary on Mark 14:62 below).

But as his feeding of the crowds and power over the sea suggest, however much Jesus may be a new Moses/Joshua/David, these comparisons pale alongside his Isaianic new-exodus Yahweh-Warrior activities (already Isa. 49:24 in Mark 3:27), which are further articulated, for example, just prior to this chapter when he calms the sea and then drowns Israel's demonic enemy hosts therein before healing the unclean woman and raising a dead girl (4:35–5:43; cf., respectively, Isa. 63:11–13; 64:5–6; 65:1–7, 19–20; see R. E.

Watts 2004c). That Mark combines "shepherd" and "warrior" imagery sits well with an Isaianic horizon wherein Yahweh himself is so described (cf. Isa. 40:10–11; see Schneck 1994: 157–58) and who characteristically in Israel's Scriptures has compassion on his people, especially in his returning them from exile (e.g., Exod. 33:19; Deut. 30:3; Isa. 14:1; 49:10, 13, 15; 54:8; 55:7; 60:10; Jer. 12:15; 30:18; 33:26; 42:12; Ezek. 39:25; Hos. 1:6–7; 2:23). As we have already noted on several occasions, there is little question that for Mark, in some mysterious way the great shepherd Yahweh is himself present in Jesus. At the same time, in light of the "servant" imagery at the baptism and Jesus' recent rejection by his own (6:1–6a), the crowds coming from all the towns around, the desert hills, and the green grass are intriguingly suggestive of Isa. 49:9's "new exodus" imagery of God's people from all over pasturing on the bare heights under the auspices of the Isaianic servant, who likewise had only recently experienced a lack of success (Isa. 49:4) and who is also Israel's teacher (R. E. Watts 2000: 252–56).

E. Theological Use. Once again, Mark's motif of the fulfillment of return from exile and his high Christology are in view. Not only are the shepherding hopes of a new Moses, a new Joshua, a new David, and perhaps the Isaianic servant fulfilled in Jesus, but also again, in some mysterious way, Yahweh himself has uniquely come among his people.

7:6–7

A. NT Context: Tension over Purity. As we come to this story about Jesus' disciples eating with unwashed hands, its topic (purity), extent, fieriness, and hitherto unmatched concentration of some weighty OT texts should alert us to its importance. Israel was defined by the command "Be holy, for I am holy" (Lev. 11:44) and was in exile for failing to be so. It has been on the agenda from the moment John the Baptist appeared to prepare for holy Yahweh's coming and Jesus' first mighty deed in casting out an unclean spirit (cf. 1:13, 26–27; 3:11; 5:2, 8, 13; 6:7; also healings: 1:41; 2:5, 11–12, 17; 5:28–29, 41–42; see Neyrey 1986).

Following the feeding of the five thousand (6:32–44) and a second demonstration of Jesus' power over the sea (6:45–52)—both having obvious exodus/new-exodus overtones (see, e.g.,

Neh. 9:11–15; Ps. 78:12–20; cf. Job 9:8; *Tg. Zech.* 10:11; see R. E. Watts 2000: 160–63, 177–79)—Mark offers his final summary statement concerning Jesus' popularity (6:53–56). Although chapter 7 is regarded as the midpoint of the larger section 6:6b–8:21 (e.g., Donahue and Harrington 2002: 226), it is near universally understood to break with the preceding narrative (e.g., Lane 1974; Gundry 1993; Hooker 1988; Gnilka 1978–1979; Moloney 2002). However, the occurrence of the rare "marketplace" (*agora*) for the first time in Mark in 6:56 (*en tais agorais*) and then soon after in 7:4 (*ap'agoras* [elsewhere only in 12:38]), where both are editorial, strongly suggests otherwise. The motif of "touching," whether conveying restoration (6:56) or impurity (7:1–5), similarly unites the two accounts. Instead of breaking the flow, this final summary allows Mark to juxtapose Jesus' healings in the marketplace with Jerusalem's antagonism over purity laws.

The appearance, then, in 7:1 of Pharisees and some scribes signals a return to the pattern of official opposition not seen since the pivotal Beelzebul controversy (3:19b–35). (As in several previous incidents, it is the disciples' behavior, not that of Jesus, that provokes the clash [cf. 2:18, 23–24]). The leaders "gathering to him" recalls the last of Mark's first five controversy stories (the Sabbath healing in 3:1–6) and similarly suggests hostile intent (cf. 7:5 with 2:16, 18, 24). J. Marcus (1997: 192n 44) detects here an echo of the coalition against the Lord's anointed in Ps. 2:2—a text already of some importance for Mark and whose interpretation in Jewish tradition concentrated on the eschatological purification of Jerusalem (see above and note the origin here of Jesus' opponents)—and also of the wicked against the righteous (Ps. 30:14 LXX [31:13 ET]; 34:15 LXX [35:15 ET]).

But whereas in the past Mark's Jesus responded by asking questions (2:8–9, 19, 25; 3:4, 23–26), delivering aphorisms (2:17, 27; 3:27), or issuing warnings (3:28–30), here for the first time, ominously, he employs an Isaianic judgment text in a scathing denunciation of the Jerusalem authorities' criticism as a faithless abandonment of God's will for the sake of merely human tradition (7:6–8; see Isa. 29:13).

Several points are worth noting. First, Jesus has already been shown to be Israel's Davidic/Yahweh shepherd. Thus, in the context of shepherding Israel (6:34) Mark's emphasis on Jesus' "tassel" (6:56) suggests, in addition to Jesus' Torah-observant practice (Rudolph 2002: 299), his kingly and priestly authority (see Milgrom 1983; Waldman 1989; Matthews and Benjamin 1993: 147). As such, he has been dispensing to the common folk in the villages, cities, farms, and marketplaces of the entire region (6:55–56) nothing less than new-exodus healings—what else could they be, given Mark's overarching new-exodus horizon and the immediately preceding feeding and power over the sea stories (cf. Ps. 78:12–20, 70–72, again linking Yahweh and David)? Since sin, sickness, healing, and forgiveness, and therefore wholeness and purity, were closely connected in much Jewish tradition (cf., e.g., Ps. 107:17; Isa. 33:24; Mark 2:1–12; John 9:2; James 5:14–15; *b. Šabb.* 55a, citing Ezek. 18:20; Ps. 89:32), these new-exodus healings necessarily restore holiness and purity (see Phelan 1990). Thus, in contrast to the scribes who see the marketplace as a source of impurity from which they must outwardly wash their hands (even if inwardly they love the honorific greetings received therein [12:38]), Mark's Jesus, already declared to be the Holy One of God in Mark's first mighty deed (1:24) and having cleansed lepers (1:40–42), forgiven sins (2:1–12), restored the impure woman (5:29–34), raised the unclean corpse (5:41–42), and cast out unclean spirits (1:23–27; 3:11; 5:2–13; 6:7), not only sees no threat but also recognizes an opportunity to extend purity to others (see Neyrey 1986: 105–22; Bockmuehl 2000: 11).

Jesus' opponents did not see things this way. That they are "from Jerusalem," said for only the second time in Mark, not only highlights their special authority but also links them with the earlier, crucial Beelzebul confrontation (3:22). In that clash the Jerusalem scribes attributed Jesus' power to Satan, and nothing here suggests that they have changed their minds. On that occasion Mark's Jesus regarded their assessment as blasphemy against the Holy (= pure) Spirit, which, in making God their enemy, led directly to the implementation of Isa. 6's judgment through the parables. This second encounter again results in an extended citation, again from Isaiah (also for only the second time), but now from Isa. 29, which also echoes Isa. 6.

Textually, Jesus' initial response is a close citation of Isa. 29:13. The several variants in both the Hebrew (including 1QIsaᵃ; cf. the Targum) and Greek traditions suggest some form of early corruption (J. D. W. Watts 1985: 384; Stendahl 1968: 56–58; Gundry 1967: 14). The LXX differs from the MT in (1) omitting the opening causal particles (*ya'an kî*) and sometimes *bĕpîyw* ("with its mouth" [as in א, A, Q]), (2) apparently reading *wĕtōhû* (LXX: *matēn*, "in vain") over against *wattĕhî* ("it is"), (3) using a predicate instead of a nominal phrase when reading *sebontai* ("they worship me") for the MT's *yir'ātām 'otî* ("their fear of me" [1QIsaᵃ drops the suffix]), (4) doubly translating the singular *miṣwat* (1QIsaᵃ and the Targum add the smoothing preposition *k*) with the pluralized *entalmata . . . kai didaskalias*, and (5) reading Piel masculine plural *mĕlammĕdîm* ("teaching" [so too the Targum]) instead of the MT's Pual feminine singular *mĕlummādâ* ("that is taught"), thereby possibly suggesting a causal clause.

Though dropping the LXX's and MT's "draw near," Jesus' citation generally follows the tradition contained in the LXX. The minor variations include (1) transposing the demonstrative *houtos* to the emphatic position, (2) employing the singular verb *tima*, in keeping with the singular subject (and the MT), and omitting the possessive, whether the LXX's third-person plural or the MT's singular, (3) moving the subject "me" to before the verb sarcastically to emphasize the contrast with "this people," (4) omitting *kai* (with the MT), and (5) advancing *didaskalias* to create a double accusative. These variations, mostly for emphasis and consistent with first-century conventions (Stanley 1992), make no impact on the overall sense.

B. Isa. 29:13 in Context. Our text belongs to that series of woe oracles (Isa. 28–31) that, in building on the earlier polemics against idolatrous wisdom (see Petersen 1979), constitute Isaiah's most sustained attack on the nation's rulers (Sweeney 1988: 56–58; Vriezen 1962: 134n9). Although Isa. 28 opens with a declaration of coming judgment against the proud garland of Ephraim's drunken and corrupt princes (28:1–4), the overall thrust is clearly against the Jerusalemite leaders who have rejected the prophet's message (28:14) (see Exum 1979: 124; Wildberger 1972–1982:

1044; cf. Clements 1980a: 229). The setting is Judah's abortive participation in a rebel coalition with Egypt against Assyria, but the issues remain largely unchanged from those earlier in the work (Jensen 1973: 115–18; Goldingay 2001: 151; Beuken 1992a [see commentary on Mark 4:12 above]). Those purported to be "wise" are in fact nothing more than "obstinate children" (30:1, 9; cf. 1:2 [see the discussion below on children honoring parents]) who reject Yahweh's instruction (30:9–11), relying instead on their own clever strategies (28:15; 30:1–5, 6–7; 31:1–3). But Yahweh's purging purpose will stand (28:2–3, 18–20; cf. 6:10–13), and the policies of Judah's blind and deaf leaders will lead irrevocably to the land's devastation and the nation's exile (30:1–5, 12–17; 31:1–3; cf. 6:11–13).

Chapter 29 begins with yet another woe oracle, which captures the essence of Yahweh's "strange plan." On the one hand, it announces that Yahweh himself will lay siege to Jerusalem (29:1–4) but then unexpectedly envisages the "sudden" (*lĕpeta'*) theophanic visitation of the Lord of Hosts to deliver his city (29:5–8). But that lies in the future. In the meantime, 29:9–14, a chiastic formulation in which each stanza is a variation on the theme of incomprehension (Exum 1981: 347), forms a derisive indictment of Jerusalem's blind and deaf leaders. Here too, although 29:13 has "this people," the nation's leadership is clearly the primary target (cf. 29:10, 14b; see McKane 1965: 70–71; Jensen 1973: 51, 55–56; Clements 1980a: 236).

Although difficult in some respects, the point of 29:9 is clear enough: those leaders who ought to have known Yahweh's will but have rejected it are mockingly likened to staggering drunkards upon whom the Lord has poured out a spirit of deep sleep (cf. 28:7). The fact that this insensible condition is Yahweh's doing (29:10), in combination with the unique expression *hišta'aš'û wāšō'û* ("blind yourselves and be blind" [29:9a]), the reference to shutting the eyes (*way'aṣṣēm 'et-'ênêkem*, "he has shut your eyes" [29:10b]), and the twice-occurring "this people" (29:13–14), strongly suggests that this is a continuation of the trajectory initiated with Isaiah's earlier commission in 6:10–13 to close the eyes (*wĕ'ênāyw hāša'*) of "this people" until the whole land lies desolate (J. D. W. Watts 1985: 385; cf. Clements 1980a: 238; McLaughlin 1994 [although lacking the reference to blinding in 29:9a, the LXX does have *kammysei* in 29:10]). As a result, Judah's head and eyes—its prophets and seers—are now so incapable of comprehending Yahweh's prophetic "plan" that it has become as doubly impenetrable as a sealed book to an illiterate (29:12).

Nevertheless, and just as in the events preceding Isaiah's commissioning (cf. 1:10–15), leaders and people together persist in earnest prayers and performance of religious duties even as they pursue strategies that are directly at odds with Yahweh's word (29:13; see Clements 1980a: 238–39; Dietrich 1976: 173–75; Wildberger 1972–1982: 1120; cf. Hos. 7:14; 10:1–2; Mic. 3:11; 6:6–8). And again Yahweh indignantly rejects this "honor" as worthless lip service and empty adherence not even to his word, but rather, adding insult to injury, to merely human requirements (whether cultic regulations [Wildberger 1972–1982: 1121–22] or the wisdom tradition [Jensen 1973: 67]). Deliberately employing language evoking his past saving acts, especially in the exodus/conquest (forms of *pl'* occur three times in 29:14; cf., e.g., Josh. 3:5; Ps. 78:12; 98:1), Yahweh declares that he will again do amazing things. This time, however, his own people will feel the strength of his mighty arm as he demolishes both the oppressive wisdom of the self-reliant wise and the nation—a theme that pervades these chapters (29:14, 20; cf. 28:1–4, 13–22; 29:1–4; 30:1–5, 12–15; Clements 1980a: 239; Exum 1981: 348; McKane 1965: 70–71).

In responding to rebellious Israel, Isa. 29:13 thus describes a national leadership already under the judicial blinding of Isa. 6 now further given over to their own foolish wisdom and hence destruction, even as they continue to profess loyalty to Yahweh by their adherence to what he dismisses as merely human tradition.

C. Isa. 29:13 in Judaism. Several intertestamental texts envision an eschatological Jewish apostasy in the substitution of human commandments for the divine Mosaic law (Berger 1972: 489–90, citing CD-A IV–V; *Jub.* 23:21; *T. Ash.* 7:5; *T. Levi* 14:4; 16:2). Of these, CD-A V, 20 speaks of the "Boundary Shifters"—an unidentified group of Israelites, perhaps priests or scribes who from the sectarians' point of view misinterpreted the law (cf. CD-A VIII, 3 with CD-B XIX, 15–16)—who revile the statutes of the covenant,

claiming that they are not well-founded. A people without insight (CD-A V, 16, citing Isa. 27:11), they led Israel astray by inciting rebellion against the law of Moses (CD-A V, 20–21). We also know that the sectarians denounced the "seekers of smooth things" (or "flatterers" [probably the Pharisees]) for being hypocrites (e.g., 1QH[a] XI, 28; XII, 13; XV, 34) who meddled with Torah, presumably substituting their own human traditions for God's (e.g., CD-A I, 18; 1QH[a] XII, 10, 13; 4Q163 23 II, 10–15, citing Isa. 30:19–21; 4Q169 3–4 II, 2–5). The fragmentary Isaiah commentary 4Q163, although having a lacuna at precisely this point, apparently sees Isa. 29–30 as describing God's eschatological judgment on the "congregation of those looking for easy interpretations who are in Jerusalem," which might refer to the same group (4Q163 23 II, 10–11; cf. 1QS XI, 1, which might allude to Isa. 29:14; see Ploch 1993: 222–23).

The patriarch Asher attributes the desolation of the land, the destruction of the sanctuary, and Israel's exile to the Sodom-like behavior of his children, "corrupted by evil, heeding not the Law of God but human commandments" (*T. Ash.* 7:5). More extensively, Levi complains of the future impiety of his priestly offspring in the last days (*T. Levi* 14:1). Inflated with pride on account of their priesthood, they will bring a curse upon the nation because, having abandoned God's requirements for purity, they will teach commandments that are opposed to his just ordinances (14:4–8). Through their wicked perversity they will set aside the law, nullify the words of the prophets, and persecute the righteous (16:2), resulting in God's severe judgment and the temple's destruction (15:1) (on the issue of Christian reworking of this material, see §C of commentary on Mark 1:10 above).

The Targum introduces two significant changes. The addressees, "the seers and the prophets," reflecting the later setting of the Targum, become "the prophets and the scribes and the teachers who were teaching the teaching of the law" (29:10). More importantly, whereas in Isaiah these blinded rebels were responsible for Jerusalem's destruction, the Targum not only absolves them but also rehabilitates them. The vision is no longer hidden from these teachers. Instead, as bearers of God's word, they are hidden from the people. The people, on the other hand, are censured because of their insincere fear of the Lord, regarding God's word as no more than a merely human commandment (29:14).

In rabbinic tradition, in a discussion on Torah regulations, Deut. 28:59 (the Lord will make thy plagues wonderful) is interpreted by Isa. 29:14, and it is said that God's amazing and wonderful work means that Torah will be forgotten in Israel (the wisdom of the wise will perish) and no one will be able to tell the clean from the unclean (*b. Šabb.* 138b). Elsewhere, Isa. 29 explains God's severe judgment on arrogant and idolatrous Pharaoh and his advisors (*Exod. Rab.* 5:14), whose willful hard-heartedness is the cause for God's *lex talionis* or hard judgment (*Midr. Prov.* 27). Similarly, the smearing of the eyes in Isa. 29:10 is the *lex talionis* judgment on Israel's sinning with the eye (*Pesiq. Rab.* 33:13, citing Isa. 3:16; cf. Isa. 6:10).

Seder Eliyahu Rabbah (26)24, in the context of discussing the commandment to honor one's father and mother (Exod. 20:12), cites Isa. 29:13–14 as evidence of God's harsh decrees against those who in the name of doing the will of God forgo honoring their parents by not providing for them.

In these various traditions, some earlier than others, there is then a clear awareness that (1) unscrupulous leaders or teachers could and did employ merely human tradition to subvert the law's true intent and that doing so would invite God's severe judgment; (2) some of God's people, both leaders and the rank and file, took his word no more seriously than merely human commandments; and (3) judgment on the self-reliant wise was seen to find its greatest expression in God's response to Pharaoh's hard-heartedness during the exodus.

D. The Use of Isa. 29:13 in Mark.

It is often claimed that the Markan Jesus' argument depends particularly on the LXX's attack on the "teachings of men" because the MT and the Targum are concerned instead with deficient worship "commanded by men and learned by rote" (e.g., Schweizer 1971: 145; Nineham 1963: 194–95; Booth 1986: 91; Poirier 2000). However, there is in fact no substantive difference between them, since in each case the fundamental issue is Yahweh's refusal to accept worship when the worshipers themselves are actively disregarding him (e.g., Banks 1975: 134–35; Guelich 1989: 367; Gundry 1993: 351; Schneck 1994: 171; France 2002: 284–85). In this respect, adherence to "the traditions of men" is only a symptom of this deeper issue (as is evident in the perspective of the Dead Sea Scrolls and the Targum on those who set aside God's law for their own). Obviously, such worship is "empty," as the LXX pointedly notes.

Likewise, although it is often remarked that Mark's Jesus alters the addressees from the entire nation, "this people" (Isa. 29:13), to the Jerusalemite authorities, "Pharisees and scribes" (e.g., Gundry 1993: 351), his emphasis accurately reflects not only the original context, as we noted above, but also the targumic gloss in Isa. 29:10, "the scribes and the teachers who were teaching the teaching of the law" (although obviously, in retaining the original force, Jesus rejects the Targum's absolution).

Whatever the status and nature of handwashing practice at the time (see Booth 1986: 23–144; Gundry 1993: 358–60; Gnilka 1978–1979: 1:279–80; Poirier 1996; France 2002: 280–82; Marcus 1999: 440–42), the only scriptural requirement for this kind of ritual purity concerned the priests prior to offering sacrifice (Exod. 30:18–21; 40:30–32), or an Israelite having a discharge (Lev. 15:11), or the elders after the special sacrifice of the heifer (Deut. 21:6). As *b. Ber.* 52b recognizes when it states that the washing of hands for secular food is not from the Torah, the Pharisees' implicit demand is based merely on human tradition.

The question for Mark's Jesus is not whether Torah required reinterpreting due to changing historical circumstances. As in Isaiah, he was concerned with the hypocrisy inherent in the leaders' professed devotion to God expressed in their excessive concern for ritual purity alongside their employment of that merely human tradition to reject the sanctifying new-exodus work that God was accomplishing through Jesus before their very eyes (see Marcus 1997: 192). Hence Jesus' use of "hypocrite," which denotes "the wicked man who has alienated himself from God by his acts" (*TDNT* 8:564; cf. Suhl 1965: 81). (Since it is unlikely that Jesus would have judged Isaiah to have prophesied "badly" about the Pharisees, we probably should see in his statement not a conviction that Isaiah had them in mind, but rather that his prophetic words are particularly apt.)

In this case, unlike the probable relaxation of Torah's purity requirements against which the Dead Sea Scrolls, *Testament of Asher*, and *Testament of Levi* fulminate, the issue is the reverse. They have gone beyond what God required, and though seemingly a pious act, it still placed human commands ahead of God's (see Rudolph 2002: 296). The commandment that they have laid aside (Mark 7:8) is most likely the much more limited Mosaic injunctions concerning washing listed above, though the reference to "heart" could also indicate a more fundamental breach of the great commandment to love God with all one's heart (cf. Deut. 6:4–5; see Pesch 1976–1977: 1:373). For the Pharisees and scribes, their attempts at heightened holiness were a sign of commitment, but for Jesus, their polemical intent and the ultimately marginalizing impact of their traditions both on the common people, whom they were meant to shepherd, and himself, Israel's holy (e.g., 1:11, 24; 3:29) and true shepherd, rendered such "worship" utterly vain.

Moreover, if Isa. 29 describes the outcome of Isa. 6, then its application here is even more appropriate. Only those whose soil/heart is hard (Mark 4:5 and Isa. 6:9–10; cf. Mark 3:5) and far from God (Mark 7:6) could continue to attack this good news. For the first time since the Isa. 6 warning concerning the parables, we meet those on the outside who, blinded by an idolatrous commitment to human regulations, truly do not and cannot see or understand that in Jesus Isaiah's long-awaited new exodus has begun. Ironically, in the language of *b. Šabb.* 138b, the true understanding of Torah has indeed perished, and they cannot tell pure from impure. For the first time, they too, like idolatrous and hard-hearted Pharaoh, come under the "hard" judgment of Jesus' first denunciation (as per *Exod. Rab.* 5:14; *Midr. Prov.* 27; cf. the Pharisees' hard-heartedness in Mark 3:5).

But as J. Marcus (1999: 450) correctly observes, the same charge could, with some justification, be laid against Jesus: is not his teaching merely human precepts? Therein lies the rub. As I have argued throughout, for Mark, Jesus is no mere teacher or even a great prophet. Something much more is going on in this one in whom Yahweh himself seems present (Hooker [1988: 227–28]

notes that Jesus, at one and the same time, upholds the law and exercises a greater authority than Moses). To reject him is to reject God (see Marcus 1999: 450).

E. Theological Use. That this is the only explicit reference to Isaiah outside Mark's opening sentences should highlight, even if the extent of the material did not, the significance of this encounter. Eschatologically, in keeping with Malachi's warning, it indicates the unpreparedness of Jerusalem's Pharisaic and scribal authorities and, insofar as Isa. 29 can be seen as the fulfillment of Isa. 6, the beginning of the end for that self-reliant and blind leadership. Hence comes Jesus' first explicit and public denunciation. If the traditional interpretations of Isa. 29 are anything to go by, such hard-hearted and idolatrous hypocrisy will lead to a new exile, which, for Mark, will mean the transfer of the vineyard (12:1–9; cf. *T. Ash.* 7) and destruction of the temple (13; cf. *T. Levi* 14–16). Correspondingly, if purity delimits the community, then the confrontation here turns on the question of who has the authority to define what constitutes the boundaries of Israel. In terms of ecclesiology, not only does that authority clearly lie with Jesus, around whom Israel is being reconstituted, but also the Jerusalem leadership is now disqualified because of its hypocrisy.

It is in respect of this last point that Mark's high Christology is seen yet again. Implicit in all of this is the unmatched authority inherent in the person of Jesus. He not only effects Israel's purification but also speaks authoritatively as to what true Torah purity entails.

7:10

A. NT Context: Neglecting the Command of God. Mark's Jesus now moves from the general to the particular (7:9–13), raising the question of which God values most: the ritual purity that his opponents have emphasized or the ethical purity of one's responsibilities to others (see Rudolph 2002). He begins by citing (7:10), positively, the command to honor one's parents (Exod. 20:12/ Deut. 5:16) and, negatively, the judgment on those who do not (Exod. 21:17; cf. Lev. 20:9). He then highlights the tension between the two commandments and his critics' practice of *corban* as typical of their hypocritical demand for stricter adherence in one area while aiding and abetting circumvention in another when their own interests are at risk (7:11–13). Following the pattern established in chapter 4, he next turns to the crowds and tells a parable whose implications are even more controversial than his teaching on Sabbath (7:14–16 [see France 2002: 276]), which he then privately explains to his uncomprehending disciples (7:17–23).

The first OT citation, Exod. 20:12/Deut. 5:16, is directly from the LXX, which is a straight translation from the MT. The second, Exod. 21:17, follows Exod. 21:16 LXX (21:17 MT), though omitting both second-person possessive pronouns and, altering the future *teleutēsei* to the imperative *teleutatō* (cf. A, F, Lucian; see Gundry 1967: 13), reversing the *teleutēsei thanatō* pairing in the LXX (Codex B) to *thanatō teleutatō*.

B. The Double Citation. 1. Exod. 20:12 in Context. The fifth commandment is found identically in both sets of the commandments, whether given at Sinai or on the Plains of Moab. Although many readers are familiar with the Decalogue, the contexts of the two sets are rarely appreciated.

The most important thing about the Decalogue in Exodus is its setting. Located in a narrative that more than any other in the OT is focused on Yahweh's awesome personal presence and by beginning with his priority over all creation and humanity, the Ten Words intimately and uniquely bind Israel, waiting at the "perimeter of holiness," to him and ground their identity in his (Durham 1987: 278). Because "I AM" (20:2) has given himself to Israel, Israel must now move toward "becoming" his holy people (see Childs 1974: 397).

In establishing in this founding moment how Israel is to relate to Yahweh, the first commandment and the following three that extend it lay the foundation for the final six, which concern how his people are to relate to one another and the world. Thus they open with "the Lord your God" and conclude with "your neighbor" (Sarna 1991: 80). Equally importantly, there is no distinction between the cultic and the social/ethical; they are simply fused (see Childs 1974: 396). And as Yahweh as the source of life must be honored in his priority, it is right and good that the first relationship among humans likewise recognizes the priority of parents as fundamental to the existence of both the individual and society (Durham 1987: 290). Near the heart of this command was a concern that parents not be abused or driven out

when they were no longer able to work (Childs 1974: 418, citing Exod. 21:15–17 [see below]; Lev. 20:9; Deut. 21:18–21; 27:16; cf. Tigay 1966: 72; Albertz 1978).

Significantly granting equal status to father and mother (cf. the reversed order in Lev. 19:3), the honor due them goes beyond mere obedience or polite respect to loving them and honoring their role as Yahweh's proxies in giving their children life (cf. "revere" in Lev. 19:3, where this command is both first among the laws of holiness and connected with the Sabbath command, suggesting that honoring parents is a counterpart to honoring Yahweh [Tigay 1966: 72]). Primarily directed at adults—who else could enter into the terms of the covenant? (see Harrelson 1980: 92–95)—this is the only commandment that comes with a specific promise: "that you might live long in the land."

2. Deut. 5:16 in Context. The setting in Deuteronomy likewise stresses the centrality of the Decalogue. Exodus has the Ten Words immediately following Yahweh's descent on Sinai, stressing his immediate presence. Here, their placement at the very beginning of the second and by far longest discourse (on the covenant at Moab, see 4:44–28:68) stresses Moses' mediatorial role (5:4–5 [see Tigay 1966: 61]) and makes them the foundation on which Israel's life in the land is to be conceived (Craigie 1976: 149). Hence to the prolongation of days is added "that it may go well with you in the land" (*Targum Pseudo-Jonathan*: "that he [the Lord] do good to you"); failure to honor parents results in a national loss of inheritance—that is, the promised land (Tigay 1966: 72). This connection between obedience and the land is made repeatedly throughout (e.g., 4:1, 5, 21, 40; 6:18; 8:1). In a sense, the Ten Words provide the introductory basis for, and Deut. 29–30 (see commentary on Mark 3:4 above) the recapitulating appeal to observe, the intervening body of law.

3. Exod. 20:12/Deut. 5:16 in Judaism. The fundamental identity of the two texts as coming from the one law code justified their often being treated as the one command, and I will follow suit. Given the fifth commandment's importance, it is not unexpected that even excluding recitations of the Decalogue itself, it figures prominently in Jewish traditions (see further the extensive survey in Gamberoni 1964; Phillips 1970: 80–82; Blidstein

1975). Within the OT its influence is pervasive (Exod. 21:15, 17; Lev. 20:9; Deut. 21:18–21; 27:16) especially in the Wisdom literature (e.g., throughout Prov. 1–9, but esp. 20:20; 30:11, 17; cf. 15:20; Sir. 30:1–13), and it is used metaphorically of Yahweh and Israel (e.g., Deut. 32:6–12; Isa. 1:2, 4; 30:1, 9; 57:3–4; 63:8; Jer. 3:14, 22; 4:22; Hos. 1:10b; Mal. 1:6; 3:17).

Sirach expends considerable effort discussing and amplifying the command (3:1–16) and urges children to serve their parents as masters (3:7). Fulfillment of this command atones for sins (3:3, 14, 15), is like laying up treasure (3:4), facilitates heard prayers (3:5), and leads to long life (3:6). It is to be fulfilled with the whole heart (7:27), especially in caring for one's parents in their old age (3:12–15).

For Philo, since parents in begetting are to children as God is to the world (*Spec. Laws* 2.2, 225), he exhorts his readers to honor them accordingly by taking care of them, not least since what the children have they in any case owe them, and especially by seeking above all virtue (*Decalogue* 117–118, 165–167; *Spec. Laws* 2.234–236; *Drunkenness* 5.17; *Good Person* 87). In *Let. Aris.* 228 honoring parents is of first importance (cf. 238; *Sib. Or.* 3:594; Ps.-Phoc. 180; *L.A.B.* 44:7), and in *Jub.* 7:20 Noah's enjoining it of his sons establishes it as an important theme throughout the rest of the work (e.g., 25:3–5; 29:20; 35:10–11; 37:5, 11–13). Obedient sons serve as role models (*T. Jud.* 1:4–5; *T. Ab.* 3:7–5:6) and can anticipate great blessing (see esp. the expanded version in *L.A.B.* 11:9).

Among the Dead Sea Scrolls, 4Q416 2 III, 16–19 advises the poor man to honor his parents even in his poverty, first because they are the "oven of your origin" and thus as God is to a man so too are they in dominion over him, and second so that he might be blessed with life and length of days (cf. 4Q418 9–10; 4Q158 7–8, 1). Only loyalty to God takes precedence, and thus in the reconstructed text of 4Q174 6–7 3–5 Levi is honored with the priesthood for putting his fidelity to Yahweh above that owed his parents (cf. 4 Macc. 2:10; Josephus, *Ag. Ap.* 2.206; Ps.-Phoc. 8; see also *Syr. Men.* 2:94–98).

Given such importance, there is considerable reflection in the rabbinic tradition as to what degree and at what expense one ought to give that honor, particularly in caring for parents in old age. According to *Mek. Exod.* 20:12–14, one should honor them with one's substance as one honors God (Prov. 3:9) and fear them as one fears God (Lev. 19:3; cf. Deut. 6:13). The rewards are likewise equal, and one will live long in the land—here, interestingly enough, the *Mekilta* cites Mal. 3:20, a text already connected with Israel's eschatological hope of restoration through Elijah.

Likewise among the later rabbis, honoring parents was the weightiest of the commandments. Since they participated in one's creation (*b. Qidd.* 30b; *Pesiq. Rab.* 23/24:2), honoring them was again likened to honoring God (*y. Pe'ah* 1:1 [X.C]; *Num. Rab.* 8:4; cf. *b. Qidd.* 31a; *Pesiq. Rab.* 23/24:1), and this included feeding, clothing, washing, and taking in and out at their whim (e.g., *y. Pe'ah* 1:1 [X.I]; *t. Qidd.* 1:11B; *y. Qidd.* 1:7 [VIII.A–K]). Those who did so were similarly promised blessing (*Gen. Rab.* 36:6) and a long life in this world (*y. Pe'ah* 1:1 [X]; *Tg. Ps.-J.* Exod. 20:12; *b. Qidd.* 30b, 31a; *b. B. Meṣi'a* 32a–b; *Deut. Rab.* 6:2; cf. *Pesiq. Rab.* 20:4; also the several meritorious examples in 23/24) and in the world to come (*'Abot R. Nat.* 40A; *m. Pe'ah* 1:1; *Sipre Deut.* 336; cf. *b. Qidd.* 39b; *b. Ḥul.* 142a; even if there was a question concerning this promise in Exod. 20:12, it was understood from Deut. 5:16; *b. B. Qam.* 54b–55a).

There was some debate over whether it should be the son's or the father's substance from which one drew, and the general opinion was that it should be the son's no matter what the cost, even if it entailed begging (*y. Qidd.* 1:7 [VIII.K]; *y. Pe'ah* 1:1 [X.L–M]; *Pesiq. Rab.* 23/24:2; *b. Qidd.* 32a; *S. Eli. Rab.* [26]24; see the extended discussion in *Pesiq. Rab.* 23/24). Moreover, because through poverty one might be excused from various offerings but never from one's obligations to provide for parents, it was thought that in this respect one honors one's parents even above God (*y. Qidd.* 1:7 [VIII.F–J]; *b. Qidd.* 31b–32b). This particularly high view might help explain the opinion that because the Sabbath command and this one were placed alongside each other, neither profanation of Sabbath nor any other sin would befall him who honored his parents, since for keeping the latter, he would be forgiven the former (*S. Eli. Rab.* [26]24, citing Isa. 56:2 and taking "this" to refer to honoring parents).

4. Exod. 21:17 in Context. Immediately following the Decalogue is the "Book of the Covenant" (20:22–23:33), a collection of laws whose primary unifying principle is that they explicate in various ways the fundamental requirements of being peculiarly Yahweh's holy people (19:4–6) (see Durham 1987: 318). Dominated by second-person singular imperatives (Childs 1974: 455), it begins and ends with the command that Israel is to have no other God than the one whose very presence has come among them and spoken to them (20:23; 23:32–33). And as the various references to God throughout suggest, it is not simply that he has given the law, but that he is intimately concerned with the ongoing life of the community: regardless of the legal authorities' decision, he will not acquit the wicked (23:7) (see Fretheim 1991: 245, 249).

In the MT, 21:17 names the second of two capital offenses involving parents (see 21:15 [the LXX reverses the order of the MT's vv. 16 and 17 so that the two offenses involving parents are in direct sequence]). The first addresses striking a parent, and our text addresses "cursing" (*qll*, "repudiate" [see Brichto 1963: 132–35]; this often is the antonym of *brk*, "bless" [Gen. 27:12; Deut. 11:26–28; 23:5; 30:1; Ps. 37:22; 62:4; Prov. 30:11], and *kbd*, "honor" [1 Sam. 2:30; Isa. 9:1] [see Sarna 1991: 92]). It is an action done in blatant repudiation of Exod. 20:17, with the punishment's severity reflecting the gravity attributed to the fifth commandment and its vision of the centrality of the family: to curse your parents is to curse God, who gave you life through them (cf. Lev. 24:16).

Finally, it is of some interest, given the opening verses of Mark's Gospel, that the whole Book of the Covenant concludes (23:20–33) with God's promise to send ahead of Israel his messenger, in whom is his name, and with the warning that they must obey him because he will not let their transgressions pass (23:20–21). However, if they listen carefully to him and utterly reject the nations' idolatry, God himself will remove sickness from their midst, they will enjoy the full measure of their days, and their enemies will be overcome (23:25–27).

5. Exod. 21:17 in Judaism. Given the importance of the positive command (Exod. 20:12), it is not surprising that the negative (Exod. 21:17) is repeated closely in the OT (e.g., Lev. 20:9; Deut.

21:18–21; 27:16). It underlies God's dealings with his faithless children Israel, who refuse to honor him, and frequently involves the threat of exile and death (e.g., the contexts of Deut. 32:6–12; Isa. 1:2, 4; 30:1, 9; 57:3–4; 63:8; Jer. 3:14, 22; 4:22; Hos. 1:10b; Mal. 1:6; 3:17).

According to Sirach, the failure to honor one's parents brings dishonor upon oneself (3:10–11), and one who forsakes them is like a blasphemer (3:16). Various authors warn of divine judgment against children who act dishonorably by failing to repay or abandoning aged parents (*Syr. Men.* 20–24; *Sib. Or.* 1:74–75; 2:273–76 [eternal punishment]; cf. *b. Ḥul.* 110b, where judgment lay in God's hands).

Among the Dead Sea Scrolls, in citation of Deut. 21:18–21, it is affirmed that rebellious sons are to be stoned (11Q19 LXIV, 1–6; cf. 4Q524 14, 5–6), as occurs in Josephus to the son who ignores his debt to his parents by failing to provide for them (*Ag. Ap.* 2.206). For Philo, children who do not attempt to care for their parents are less than beasts (*Decalogue* 112–118).

In the rabbis, in citation of Lev. 24:15, to curse one's parents is to curse God (*Mek. Exod.* 20:12–14; *y. Pe'ah* 1:1 [X.D]; *y. Qidd.* 1:7 [VII.F]; *Pesiq. Rab.* 23/24:2), and according to *t. Šeb.* 3:6, one does not dishonor parents unless one has already dishonored God. Viewing words as more serious than actions, *t. 'Arakin* stipulates a harsher death penalty for cursing one's parents than for smiting them (cf. *b. Sanh.* 85b; *m. Sanh.* 7:4). This led to some debate over what constituted a curse—for some, if the divine name was used; for others, if a euphemism was used (*y. Sanh.* 7:11; *m. Sanh.* 7.8; *Tg. Ps.-J.* Exod. 21:17; *b. Šebu.* 35a)—and whether it involved one or both parents (*b. Ḥul.* 78b; *b. Šebu.* 27a–b; *b. Sanh.* 66a; *b. B. Meṣi'a* 94b–95a).

Several traditions appear to link exile with the negation of living long in the land. According to *Gen. Rab.* 36:6, Ham's dishonoring of Noah led to the Assyrian exile of captive Egyptians and Ethiopians (citing Isa. 20:4), and Israel's failure to honor parents was one of the primary reasons for Jeremiah's message of doom (*Pesiq. Rab Kah.* 13:8). *Seder Eliyahu Rabbah* (26)24–(27)25 warns that harsh decrees befall the one who does not truly honor father and mother by providing for them, even to the point of begging if need be. Intriguingly, given Mark's account, it then cites Isa. 29:13. In keeping with the sentiments expressed above, claiming to honor God while not truly honoring parents was in fact to keep one's heart far from God and subject to severe judgment, per Isa. 29:14: "Therefore I shall further shock this people with shock upon shock."

C. The Use of Exod. 20:12/Deut. 5:16; Exod. 21:17 in Mark.

Here again as Jesus appeals to a point of law in the context of a debate, he upholds it and calls others to obedience. The details of the practice of *corban* to which Mark's Jesus next refers (7:11–12) need not detain us here, except to note that it was professedly for God's glory (see Derrett 1977a: 112–17; Wilcox 1984; Bailey 2000). In effect, it meant conniving to withhold support from one's parents, in violation of the weightiest of commandments governing human relationships. Practioners had exerted themselves not to provide for their parents, but rather to defraud them. Though not an explicit curse of one's parents, it did, for Jesus, amount to the same thing because both things effectively repudiated the parent-child relationship. And since dishonoring parents was equivalent to dishonoring God, the avoidance of this most fundamental obligation in his name is blasphemous (Sir. 3:16). For Jesus, such hearts are far from God. Given the already central place of Isa. 6 in his early confrontation with these "outsiders," Jesus' invocation of Isa. 29:13 is doubly appropriate (it too was addressed to obstinate children [Isa. 30:1, 9] and later was applied in *S. Eli. Rab.* [26]24–[27]25 to those who dishonor parents).

At issue, then, are not ritual purity codes per se. It is instead the hypocrisy of worship (whether involving Sabbath or purity) that meticulously observes human regulations but hard-heartedly ignores God's requirements for the welfare of people (cf. 3:5; 6:56), not least in circumventing his clear command concerning parents in order to protect personal interests, and that aggressively denies the Torah's core orientation to glorify God by doing good and bringing life (cf. Deut. 30:15 in Mark 3:1–6 with the outcome that Jesus' opponents plot against his life). In the light of the traditional linkage of keeping Sabbath and honoring parents, the correlation between the two in Mark is striking (Pharisees appear in 2:23–28; 3:1–6; here in 7:1).

There are broader parallels. What are we to make of Mark's inclusion just before this confrontation of two exodus-evoking narratives—Jesus' feeding of the crowd and his control over the sea (6:32–52)—both of which preceded the giving of the Ten Words (cf. Exod. 14:21–31; 16:13–36)? In this, combined with the shepherd imagery (6:34), might we not see a recapitulation of Isaiah's account of Israel being kept through the depths and desert and given rest (Isa. 63:11–14a)? In addition, in earlier evoking that passage's account of Israel's first-exodus grieving of God's Holy Spirit (Isa. 63:10), Mark strongly implied a tragic repetition by leaders from Jerusalem in this new exodus (Mark 3:29). Is this dishonoring of parents similarly the counterpart of a first-exodus breach of covenant again in the very midst of a new-exodus deliverance? This strong exodus hue would also add extra weight to the Pharaoh/Pharisee parallel suggested by the Isa. 29:13 citation and its implicit warning of exile (see above).

Furthermore, just as the order of the commandments in mirroring the larger Sinai narrative emphasized the centrality of Yahweh's relationship with his people, so one early Jewish tradition understood that one dishonors parents only when one has already dishonored God (*t. Šeb.* 3:6; cf. Sir. 3:16). Since for Mark, Yahweh himself is uniquely present in Jesus, we should not be surprised that he too is dishonored. Similarly, just as the conclusion of the Book of the Covenant contained Yahweh's promises to remove sickness from Israel's midst and to give them their full days in the land (Exod. 23:25–26), so it was Jesus' healings in the midst of Israel's marketplaces that occasioned the present confrontation (6:1 [on restoring full days, see 5:35–42; cf. Isa. 65:19–20; see R. E. Watts 2004c: 21–22; on Jesus' casting out of demons as Yahweh's driving out their enemies, see 1:24; cf. Exod. 23:27]). Is it any wonder that those who dishonor their parents dishonor Jesus?

As was well understood, this alone of the Ten Words came with an explicit promise and also an implicit warning. To fail to honor parents risked not only God's "harsh" judgment (again esp. *S. Eli. Rab.* [26]24–[27]25, citing Isa. 29:13) but also disinheritance from the land, as several traditions noted (esp. *Pesiq. Rab.* 13:8's understanding of Jeremiah's preaching, which also figures prominently in Jesus' words against the temple [see commentary on Mark 11:17; 13:14 below]). The same applied to Israel as God's rebellious children (see §B–C.5 above) and underlay Mal. 4:5–6, where Yahweh's messenger Elijah, responding to the false teaching of Israel's religious authorities "who displayed partiality in their teaching" (Mal. 2:1–9), was sent to reconcile children and parents "lest I come and strike the land with a curse."

All this suggests that there is more to Jesus' singling out the practice of *corban* than meets the eye. In the midst of an intensive conflict over the nature of holiness, his opponents' hard-heartedness on this particular point of Torah more clearly than most invokes the threat of God's exilic censure.

D. Theological Use. Jesus' scathing response, his use of Isa. 29 (given Isa. 6 earlier), and the focus on honoring parents—with its impressively weighty tradition—constitutes a watershed. Eschatologically, it increasingly confirms the sense of foreboding that Israel's leadership cannot escape God's judgment of which Malachi warned. Ecclesiologically, it finally and completely discredits the authorities from Jerusalem who, already guilty of grieving the Spirit, are revealed to be rebellious and self-serving children. We will not see them again until the climactic confrontation. Instead, christologically, Jesus is Israel's true teacher, who as a compassionate shepherd both upholds Torah and yet transcends Moses' mediatorial role (see Hooker 1988: 228), and around whom reconstituted Israel must gather. And even allowing for the enigmatic character of his statement concerning what defiles, it is clear that his Torah's holiness/purity is centered on doing good to others and bringing life, even if this means, as Mark will later show, a cross-bearing laying down of one's own life.

8:18

A. NT Context: Uncomprehending Disciples.
In contrast to the tension over purity in Jewish territory, Jesus now takes his "purifying" ministry into Gentile regions, where very similar activities (healings [7:24–37], in fulfillment of Isaianic hopes [cf. Isa. 35:6; 29:18–19], and a feeding [8:1–10] [see R. E. Watts 2000: 175–77, 172–73, respectively]) elicit a vastly different response. Whereas Isaiah prophesied "well" (*kalōs*) of the Pharisees' hypocrisy (7:6), the crowds laud Jesus as having done all things "well" (*kalōs* [7:37]). But the local Pharisees return to argue yet again (8:11–13; cf. Israel's first-

exodus questioning of their deliverer [Exod. 17:2; Num. 14:10–23; cf. Deut. 32:5–6]). Refusing their request for a "sign"—have not enough been given?—Jesus "departs," leaving "this generation" behind.

The subsequent boat scene (8:14–21) functions as a transitional passage. It draws the preceding material to a close by bringing together various figures, events, and motifs, such as Herod (6:14–29) and the Pharisees (7:1–13; 8:11–13; cf. 3:6), the feedings (6:30–44; 8:1–10), and the disciples' incomprehension (combining terms from 6:52 and 7:18) and hard-heartedness (6:52) (see Hawkin 1972: 495; Heil 1981: 131–44; Guelich 1989: 419). The intensity of Jesus' questioning also creates a sense of climax that prepares the reader for the following "way" section (R. E. Watts 2000: 221–57).

The disciples' forgetting to bring bread sets up their misconstrual of Jesus' warning (*blepete* [8:15]) concerning the leaven of Herod and the Pharisees as a rebuke for forgetting bread. Leaven already had negative connotations (forbidden in offerings [Lev. 2:11]; symbol of pride and sensual pleasure [Philo, *QE* 1.15; 2.14]; evil instinct [*b. Ber.* 17a]), and since it was avoided in the first exodus, presumably it ought also be so here.

Surprisingly, Jesus' response—"Do you still not perceive or understand? Are your hearts hardened? Do you have eyes, and fail to see? Do you have ears, and fail to hear? And do you not remember?" (8:18 NRSV)—is strongly reminiscent of the purpose of the parables (4:12) and recalls the disciples' failure to understand them (4:13; 7:18) (see Beavis 1989: 158; Lemcio 1978; cf. also *blepete*, which occurs previously only in 4:24). It also recalls Moses' words to Israel where God's long provision in the wilderness was to enable them finally to understand, see, and hear (Deut. 29:3–4) as he sets before them the two ways (see commentary on Mark 3:4 above)—an interesting echo as Mark is about to lay out his "way" of life, his new Torah, the way of the cross. But what is it that the disciples do not understand, and why is their incomprehension particularly connected with the loaves? If previous instances are anything to go by, the OT contexts of these allusions will offer some help.

Mark 8:18 has provided a point of some debate in the past (see Schneck 1994: 204–20), but most recent commentators see here a combination primarily of Jer. 5:21 and secondarily of Ezek. 12:2 (Moloney 2002: 161), though with clear echoes of Isa. 6:9–10 (Gundry 1993: 415; Hooker 1991: 196; Donahue and Harrington 2002: 254; Marcus [1999: 511–13], citing Myers 1988: 225, suggests Deut. 29:2–4 as well). Although none is exact, the parallel with Jeremiah, whose LXX text accurately renders the MT, is initially the clearest. Mark's "eyes/ears," the idea of personal attribution, and verbs of sensory malfunction maintain both the order and the content, though the indicatives become interrogatives, "eyes" (*ophthalmoi*) become direct objects (*ophthalmous*), the possessive pronouns (*lāhem/autois*) are idiomatically rendered as participles (*echontes*), and the address shifts from third person to second person.

An allusion to Ezek. 12, though it more easily explains the verbal stem *ech-* and the accusative case of "eyes/ears," also requires changing the finite verb to a participle, reversing the verb-noun sequence, and omitting the leading relative pronoun and the secondary articular infinitive with its notion of purpose (i.e., to see/hear). Further muddying the waters is the fact that Mark's preceding "direct object-verb" sequence and the *ech-* stem ("to have") in 8:16b, 17b, d (partial) could suffice to explain the form of 8:18 without having to appeal to Ezekiel.

In the final analysis it seems that the Jer. 5 option, with its minimal changes and high degree of preservation of both order and content, is preferable. If so, would the shift from nominative to accusative and from pronoun to *echontes* be sufficiently marked to alert the reader to a second allusion to Ezek. 12? On the other hand, a reader might think first of Ezek. 12. Numerous commentators have noted both options, and it is difficult to decide. Both contexts require consideration.

At the same time, as we noted above and as nearly all commentators remark, this language is typically used in Mark of those who, in rejecting the Holy Spirit's work, have placed themselves "outside" and under God's judgment (3:5; 4:12). In this respect, if 8:18a alludes to Jeremiah/Ezekiel, then 8:17b alludes to the unquoted part of Isa. 6:9–10 in Mark 4, since neither the cognitive language (*noeō, syniēmi*) nor the hard-heartedness (*epachyvthē* [Isa. 6:10]; *pepōrōmenēn* [Mark 8:17]) is found in either Jer. 5 or Ezek. 12 (Beavis 1989:

114; see also Gundry 1993: 415; Schneck 1994: 218; cf. Suhl 1965: 152; on this rabbinical technique, see Cranfield 1955: 59; Jeremias 1967: 701; Marcus 1992: 200; cf. Dodd 1952: 126–27.) It appears that at this pivotal moment, just before Peter's climactic confession, we encounter a multiple allusion, just as we did in Mark's opening sentence.

Given the larger new-exodus setting, others have also seen echoes of Israel's incomprehension in the first exodus (Deut. 29:4) and in the second exodus (Isa. 40:18–20) (see Marcus 1999: 508). Although there is probably something to this, at least at the more general thematic level, the textual connections are less obvious, and so, due to space limitations, we will consider these possibilities in §D below.

B. The Composite Citation. 1. Jer. 5:21 in Context. The overall literary and hence thematic structure of both the long and the short version of Jeremiah continue to be the subject of debate, not least because the book(s) seem organized along very general thematic lines. The context of our section consists of God's complaint that his people, although professing loyalty (5:2), have hardened their faces like rock against his correction (5:3). His rebellious children have become like any other nation (5:9, 29 [see McConville 1993: 46]) and therefore are consigned to judgment (5:7–9) at the hands of Babylon (5:15–19).

Jeremiah 5:20–31 is generally understood to consist of three units, vv. 20/21–25, 26–29, and 30–31, united around the theme of "the people" (*'am*) (Craigie, Kelley, and Drinkard 1991: 93). Our text is from the first unit. Yahweh, employing metaphors that in the Israelite wisdom tradition connote idolatrous rebellion (see Jer. 6:10; 10:1–16; see also commentary on Mark 4:12 above; Holladay 1986: 195), contends with his foolish and senseless people, who, though having eyes and ears, neither see nor hear (5:21). Since the beginning of wisdom is the fear of the Lord (Prov. 1:7), he asks, with some annoyance, how it could possibly be that they neither fear him— the "him" occupying the emphatic first position in the Hebrew (Thompson 1980: 248)—nor tremble in his furious presence (Holladay 1986: 195–96). Evoking Israel's most potent image of chaos, he sets out what ought equally to be the most convincing evidence of his authority and power: he alone controls the unruly and roaring sea (5:22b–d; cf. the divine-warrior hymns celebrating Yahweh's control over the sea [Exod. 15; 18:8–16; 104:7; Isa. 51:9–11; 63:12–13; cf. Ps. 76:5–6; 89:9–15; 107:24–30]; see Cross 1973: 91–144; Hanson 1979: 299–316). As the sole Lord of creation, he, not Baal, provided the rains (5:24a) and thus Israel's bread as celebrated with the first sheaf at Passover and another seven weeks later at the Feast of Weeks (5:24b) (see Thompson 1980: 248–49).

Unfortunately, their stubborn and rebellious hearts (5:23a, 24a; in direct contrast to Deut. 6:4–5; cf. 21:18–20; see Brueggemann 1988: 64) prevent them from recognizing even this most obvious and overwhelming of truths (5:23).

The second poem, consisting of material that foreshadows the famous Temple Sermon (Bright 1965: 42), then rebukes wicked people who "grow fat" (the verb *šmn* is used elsewhere only in Deut. 32:15; Isa. 6:10; Neh. 9:25, always of rebellious Israel; see Schneck 1994: 209) and rich on other people's property, especially of the weak and the vulnerable. The third poem announces God's vengeance on lying prophets (the LXX has them making unjust prophecies; cf. 23:9–32) and venal priests who rule "on their own authority" (so Craigie, Kelley, and Drinkard 1991: 94; the verb that governs the phrase "upon their hands" is uncertain, and the LXX has the priests applauding—either way, the priests are at least accessories to the fact).

2. Jer. 5:21 in Judaism. Obduracy in terms of failing to see and hear, and hardness of heart along with the folly of self-reliant wisdom are key themes in Isaiah, but are also relatively common throughout the OT and the literature of later Judaism (see §C of commentary on Mark 4:12 above). However, although there are no specific citations of Jer. 5:21 in later Jewish literature of which I am aware, there are several occasions where 5:22 is invoked to declare Yahweh's control over the sea (*b. B. Bat.* 73b; *Gen. Rab.* 8:7; *Exod. Rab.* 15:22). In *Exod. Rab.* 21:6 Moses queries whether it is right for him to divide the sea, given God's statute (Jer. 5:22), and though the sea initially refuses to obey Moses, it does respond to the presence of God's hand (Isa. 63:12). On several occasions the creation account is read in terms of Yahweh treading the restive sea into submission and confining it within its

bounds (Jer. 5:22 in *Num. Rab.* [18:22 with Amos 4:13]; *Midr. Ps.* 93:5; cf. *Exod. Rab.* 15:22 with Job 28:8). For *Lev. Rab.* 35:4 the statutes wherein Israel should walk (Torah) carry the same weight as Yahweh's commands at creation (Jer. 5:22). Finally, Jer. 5:23 also features in *Eccles. Rab.* 1:36's reflections on a rebellious heart.

3. Ezek. 12:2 in Context. Apart from the larger structural units of oracles of judgment against God's people (chaps. 1–14), oracles against the nations (chaps. 25–32), oracles of restoration (chaps. 33–48), and some of the divisions between smaller units, the more detailed literary arrangement of Ezekiel is debated. For our purposes, 12:1–20 marks the beginning of a collection of woe oracles addressed to the exiles concerning the sins of Judah and Jerusalem (12:1–24:27). It consists of Yahweh's declaration of Israel's continuing rebellious nature (12:1–2) followed by two acted prophecies (12:3–16, 17–20; cf. chaps. 4–5). The first, consisting of Yahweh's instructions (12:3–6) followed by his interpretation (12:7–16), presages the fall of Jerusalem and the subsequent exile of its population. The second describes the profound state of anxiety of the surviving remnant (12:17–20) (see Block 1997: 364–65).

The opening address is to "a rebellious house" (12:1–2 [this is Ezekiel's unique descriptor; cf. Jer. 5:23; see Allen 1994: 178]), who has eyes and ears but neither sees nor hears (perhaps borrowed from Jer. 5:21b [Block 1997: 368]). Astonishingly, the exiles whom he addresses seem to have learned nothing from their experience. Thus, whereas Isaiah was called to harden further the hearts of his hearers, Ezekiel presupposes it (Eichrodt 1970: 149; cf. 2:3–8). Whereas Jer. 5 focused on the heart (5:23–24), Ezekiel's emphasis is now on Israel's outright rebellion (12:2–3, 9) (see Zimmerli 1979: 269). Yahweh's "perhaps" seems, therefore, more a sign of resignation than of hope. Even so, as was Jeremiah, Ezekiel is concerned with helping "blind" Israel see the obvious. Hence his enacted prophecy is to be done in broad daylight (*yômām* [12:3, 4, 7]) and in the clear sight of all (*lĕʿênêhem* [12:3, 4, 5, 6, 7]) in the hope that his sign might succeed where others have failed (12:3).

Ironically, however, the sign that is offered, Ezekiel himself, is one of impending judgment and exile: as he does, so will it be done to them, and especially their leader, from whose throne all supports will be removed (12:10–14). Their city will be destroyed (12:20), and their land lost. And it will happen in their time (12:25).

4. Ezek. 12:2 in Judaism. As with Jer. 5:21, although the larger themes are common, Ezek. 12:2 itself appears not to have figured in later Jewish literature. On the other hand, Ezek. 12:27's word of impending doom is cited, always in the context of God's judgment on the scoffing wicked who thought that Yahweh and his day of reckoning were far off and failed to see that Ezekiel's very prophetic acts signified their imminent demise and loss of the land (*Lam. Rab.* Prol. 12; cf. *Lam. Rab.* 8:11).

5. Isa. 6:9–10 in Context and in Judaism. See commentary on Mark 4:12 above.

C. The Use of Jer. 5:21; Ezek. 12:2; Isa. 6:9–10 in Mark. The key to the disciples' failure to understand turns on two questions. First, what is the meaning of the leaven of Herod and the Pharisees (already in 3:6; cf. 12:13; see Marcus 1999: 507, 510; cf. *Tg. Esth. II* 3:8, where it is applied to an evil ruler)? Second, why link the loaves with the disciples' incomprehension and hardened hearts?

Scholarly discussion has been considerable (see surveys in Quesnell 1969: 1–28; Boucher 1977: 69–80; Gibson 1986). First, however, it seems certain that the fundamental question upon which all understanding in Mark depends is that of Jesus' identity. Clearly, neither Herod, who, in misreading Jesus' powers, thinks that he is a resurrected John (6:14), nor the Pharisees and Jerusalem scribes, for whom, also misreading Jesus' powers, he is a lawbreaking agent of Satan and a purveyor of uncleanness (3:1–6, 30; 7:5), understand who Jesus is. Whatever it is that underlies these mistaken perceptions—the soon-to-emerge and thereafter controlling theme of cross-bearing suggests that it ultimately concerns self-preservation, whether expressed in the lust for power (9:33–37; 10:35–45) or religious exclusivity (9:38–41)—the disciples must at all costs avoid such heart-defiling "leaven" (7:21–23) (see Marcus 1999: 510).

Second, Jesus' linking the disciples' incomprehension with the feedings harks back to 6:51–52, when they are beside themselves with fear (cf. *exestē* [3:21]), and their failure to grasp the significance of Jesus' treading the terrifying sea underfoot is explained by their earlier failure to comprehend the meaning of the feedings and by the hardness of their hearts (6:51–52; *pōroō* [only here and in 8:17]). Underlying both events is, again, the issue of Jesus' identity.

In this respect, all three allusions are appropriate. In Jer. 5 and later Jewish tradition the salient characteristic of Yahweh's unmatched and sole authority as Lord of creation is his power over the sea—he sets its bounds and tramples it into submission. By the same token, God alone provided Israel's bread. But if the disciples did not understand the feedings—in contrast to nearly every other mighty deed, there is in both instances almost no reaction (Schneck 1994: 207)—how could they grasp the meaning of Jesus' walking on the water? They are not alone. Herod and the Pharisees, against whose leaven the disciples are warned, sound remarkably like the scoundrels of Jer. 5:26–28, whose houses are full of treachery (so Herod [6:17–28]), who have taken over the goods of others and grown fat and sleek (the Pharisees [7:11–13]), and who do not judge with justice (both Herod and the Pharisees).

And as in Ezek. 12, while Herod, in executing Malachi's Elijah, is clearly a rebel, so too are Mark's Pharisees and scribes from Jerusalem (3:5, 29–30; 7:6), who, in spite of even Jesus' most obvious and amazing acts performed before all in broad daylight (e.g., 2:1–12; 3:1–6), have no understanding and still demand a sign (8:11). As Ezekiel's signs declared imminent exile to the rebellious house of his day, so too Jesus' casting out of demons, because of his opponents' antagonistic response, implied that Israel's divided house would not stand (3:24–25) and his vindication would mean their destruction (14:62). This is precisely the dangerous condition of which Isa. 6 (and Isa. 29) spoke and under which judgment Jesus' opponents now stand.

Jesus' questions—and because they are questions, not statements, the situation is significantly different from Mark 4:12—serve to warn the disciples that if they are to avoid being like Herod and the Pharisees, they must think more carefully about the meaning of the feedings and, by implication, his walking on the sea. Like Deuteronomy's Israel in the exodus and Isaiah's Israel in exile, they have seen many things but have not understood (Deut. 29:4; Isa. 40:21, 28; 42:18–20). However, they have one thing in their favor: unlike those whose hearts are truly hardened, the Twelve, even if they do not understand, still follow. That is no small thing.

In this context, then, while the disciples are warned against becoming like rebellious and hence culpably blind Israel in Isaiah's new exodus (Isa. 40:21, 28; cf. 42:18–20; 48; see Marcus 1999: 508), they are closer to Israel in Deut. 29, who are being brought to the point of greater understanding (as per Jesus' "not yet" [8:17, 21]; see Guelich 1989: 420; Marcus 1999: 513; on Deut. 29, see commentary on Mark 3:4 above; see also Myers 1988: 225, though he reads this more negatively than is warranted; *pace* also Weeden 1971; Kelber 1979: 41). The point in Deut. 29 (and in Jer. 5)—that Israel might know that "I am the LORD your God"—is close to Mark's heart; his readers need to understand that Jesus is indeed the Son of God, Yahweh himself mysteriously among us. And hence Mark's Jesus, having already restored a deaf man (7:31–37), will now lead his "blind" disciples along a new-exodus way that they do not know (cf. Isa. 42:16), which appropriately enough begins and ends with the granting of sight to the blind (8:22–26; 10:46–52) (for an extended discussion of this theme in Isa. 40–55 and Mark's "way" section, see R. E. Watts 2000: 170–73, 239–52).

D. Theological Use. Soteriologically, because of their "idolatrous" commitments, whether to power or to their own wisdom's understanding of holiness, neither Herod nor the Pharisees, like those in Jer. 5, Ezek. 12, and Isa. 6, can comprehend the nature of God's works in Jesus. But, christologically, for Mark there is only one who feeds God's people in the desert and treads the waters into submission. That being so, his "statutes" carry equal weight (cf. *Lev. Rab.* 35:4). Eschatologically, all three texts describe a rebellious Israel careening headlong toward judgment. In this new exodus, to refuse to see or believe (Isa. 42:18–20; 48) can mean only the same thing (cf., e.g., Isa. 66:24 in Mark 9:48; Mark 13). The disciples' lack of perception has them teetering in that direction. On the other hand, ecclesiologically speaking, if, akin to Israel in Deut. 29, the disciples continue to follow in Jesus' ways, they will participate in God's restoration of his people.

8:31

A. NT Context: The Rejected Son of Man. The disciples' journey toward understanding begins inauspiciously. As many commentators recognize, the preceding two-stage healing of the blind man (8:22–26) prepares for the inadequacy of Peter's confession (see, e.g., Matera 1989). The man's "I see people as trees walking" declaration, though a beginning—Jesus is indeed Israel's Messiah—requires a "second touch" (Hooker 1991: 198; Guelich 1989: 430). Hence, Jesus begins to lead them in the new-exodus way, which they do not yet understand, by immediately following Peter's statement with the first of his three passion predictions (each followed by misunderstanding and subsequent teaching), by which, in combination with his two healing-of-sight stories, Mark structures this whole section (Perrin 1971; R. E. Watts 2000: 124, 221–57). On the earlier assumption that for Mark, "Son of Man" has a consistent content, then, as I have argued above, he is thinking of Daniel's "one like a son of man" figure (see commentary on Mark 2:10 above; C. A. Evans 2001b: 16). Although Mark's *dei* (8:31a; cf. Dan. 2:28–29 in conjunction with *mystēria*; see Mark 4:11) does not explicitly invoke scriptural warrant, its use later in 9:11 suggests as much (Matera 1982: 117), though in a mysterious way (cf. 14:49; see Beale 1998: 270–72; cf. Fascher 1954). Furthermore, Mark's Jesus characteristically has particular texts, rather than merely general themes, in view. The question involves which OT texts he has in mind here.

One option is Dan. 7 itself. Even if understood as a messianic figure, the son of man stands for and with Israel, and since faithful Israel ("the holy ones") suffers, this implies a suffering "son of man," (Hooker 1967: 27–30, 108–14; Barrett 1959: 13–14; Gundry 1993: 446). The whole book, after all, concerns God's vindication of his suffering but faithful people (which is consistent with the Davidic messianic cast, since David himself suffers and is vindicated [see commentary on Pss. 22; 118 below]). The wrinkle in this neat solution is that while the "holy ones" suffer (7:21, 25) before gaining the kingdom (7:22, 27), Dan. 7 speaks only of the exaltation of the son of man (7:13–14). This is perhaps why no ancient interpretation makes any mention of a suffering son of man (Casey 1979: 24–27, 39–42)—"he" is singularly a figure of Israel's future glory best embodied in the nation's messianic king (see France 1982: 128–29). Clearly, this does not mean that Dan. 7 thereby excludes any possibility of a suffering son of man—it might even be implied. We should note, however, that the vision seems deliberately centered on his exaltation, and hence there are no linguistic contacts between the "suffering" language of Mark 8:31 and either the LXX or later Greek versions of Dan. 7. That being so, the primary impetus for the Markan Jesus' understanding of the suffering that the Son of Man "must" undergo apparently derives from elsewhere.

Beginning with *apodokimazō*, we note that it occurs only ten times in the LXX, one of which is Ps. 117:22 (118:22 MT/ET), the only possible eschatological candidate. Consistent with a Davidic messianic interpretation of Dan. 7 (see commentary on Mark 2:10 above) and the baptism's use of Ps. 2 with which Ps. 118 was apparently already associated (see below), Ps. 118 explicitly describes attacks by human opponents upon the Davidic king and his final vindication, and it is prominent in two key Markan scenes (11:1–10; 12:1–12).

But what about the first part of the expression, *polla pathein*, which has no linguistic ties at all to Dan. 7 or any of the potential psalms (e.g., 22 [21 LXX]; 118 [117 LXX]; 119 [118 LXX]; see Watts 2000: 260–62)? Part of the problem is that although *paschō*, "to experience" (e.g., Gal. 3:4), and thus also "to suffer," is common in the first century, it occurs rarely and late in the LXX (it is apparently beginning to absorb a range of other Greek words [see R. E. Watts 2000: 263]). However, on the one occasion when it expresses suffering (Amos 6:6), the underlying Hebrew is *ḥālâ*, "to grow weak, feel pain, be exhausted, be overcome with sickness."

Again, neither this word, nor its nominal forms, nor any of the Greek translational options appear in any of the above candidate texts, whether in Hebrew, the LXX, or later Greek versions. However, it does appear three times in a unique concentration in Isa. 53 (in v. 10 as a Hiphil, and in vv. 3, 4 as a substantive [see R. E. Watts 2000: 263–65]). And just as Daniel's son of man is implicitly identified with Israel, so too the Isaianic servant, who is also true Israel. But there is more to the Isa. 53 parallel. Whereas in Dan. 7 the son of man is, at

most only by implication, Israel's representative sharing in the nation's suffering, in Isa. 53 the servant's suffering is, as in Mark, distinct from any that watching Israel might be experiencing and uniquely on their behalf (see below; see also France 1982: 129).

Other factors point toward an Isaianic origin (*pace* Hooker 1959: 92–97; Barrett 1959): (1) Isa. 53 is the only explicitly eschatological text in the OT that contains not only the suffering and vindication, but also the death (see below) of Yahweh's agent; (2) Isa. 53 is the linchpin of Isaiah's new-exodus hope (see below), which itself is central to Mark's understanding of Jesus; (3) Isa. 53:10's explicit statement of the divine will explains Mark 8:31a's *dei*; (4) the servant will be vindicated and highly exalted (*yārûm wĕniśśā'* [Isa. 52:13–15; 53:11–12]; cf. *rām wĕniśśā'* in Isa. 6:1b), not unlike Dan. 7's son of man; (5) since both Isa. 53 and Dan. 7 address the issue of Israel's restoration from exile, their association here, though novel, is not incongruent. Furthermore, of the four so-called Servant Songs, only Isa. 53 and 42 appear to have been interpreted messianically, and Jesus' baptism has already described him in terms of the latter (see commentary on Mark 1:11 above). Subsequent evidence likewise points to Isa. 53 (see 9:12, 31; 10:33–34, 45).

The *apokteinō* would thus be explained on this basis too (cf. Isa. 53:8–9, 12; see also 53:7 [see below]; Zech. 12:10 is far from clear, Dan. 7 makes no explicit mention of the death of the son of man or the saints, and in none of the various candidate "righteous sufferer" psalms does the individual actually die).

For the "after three days" there are two options—Dan. 7:25's "time, times, and half a time" (Schaberg 1985; McKnight 2005) and Hos. 6:1–2 (McArthur 1971–1972; Jeremias 1971a; C. A. Evans 2001b: 17)—both of which concern eschatological salvation after a period of suffering (in Dan. 7's case, at least, for the saints). For J. Schaberg, Daniel's expression can mean "half a week" (9:27)—hence Mark's "after three days" (though "over" and "in" in Mark 14:58; 15:29 caution against being too precise)—and a subsequent resurrection is implied by 12:2 (Dan. 3; 6 also resemble resurrections). The fundamental difficulty here is that Daniel's phrase simply does not mean "three and half times," but rather refers to a period that looks like a series of doubled times (1, 2, 4 = 7 times—i.e., reaching out "forever") but which is suddenly cut short (Goldingay 1989: 181). Consequently, given the context of already sixty-two weeks of years derived from Jeremiah's seventy years, one cannot assume that 9:27's half week (lit., "in the middle of") means the same thing as 7:25 (as J. J. Collins [1993: 357] does, without argument). And in any case, if it does lie behind, for example, 9:27, it is consistently taken to mean not three and a half days, but rather three and a half years, and hence 1,260 days or forty-two months (cf. 12:11–12; Rev. 12:6, 14). Neither does Dan. 7 mention resurrection.

Hosea 6:2, on the other hand, specifically mentions "days," employs the ordinal "third" and the temporal prepositions "after/on" (in Jewish usage "after" in the temporal sense can mean "on" [Josephus, *Ant.* 7.280–281; 8.214, 218; cf. Mark 14:58; 15:29; see France 2002: 337]), follows suffering (*ḥālyô* [5:13]), and is fundamentally concerned with resurrection (*anistēmi* [cf. the Targum]). In light of Isa. 53, Hosea too speaks of suffering and wounds (5:13; cf. Isa. 53:3–10) and of Yahweh's healing (5:13; 6:1; cf. Isa. 53:4–5; Ps. 103:3), and that in response to obedience (6:3; cf. Isa. 53:11; 50:4–5, 7–10) (see R. E. Watts 2000: 253–54). It is objected that Hos. 6:1–2 appears nowhere in early Christian exegesis (McKnight 2005: 234). However, the Targum sees it as referring to the final resurrection, and the later church fathers saw it as pointing to Christ's resurrection (Wijngaards 1967: 226), whereas, as far as I know, Dan. 7:25 is not invoked for either. Finally, to exclude Hosea because it refers to national restoration and not physical resurrection (but then, neither does Dan. 7 or Isa. 53 explicitly speak of physical resurrection) is precisely to miss the point of Jesus' identification in his person of the Son of Man and the servant with Israel.

In sum, Mark 8:31's predication of suffering, while not inconsistent with Dan. 7, draws primarily on Isa. 53:4–10, Ps. 118:22, and probably Hos. 6:2.

B. The Composite Allusion. 1. Isa. 52:13–53:12 in Context. After the appointment of a new servant (49:1–6[7]), the focus in the second half of this larger section (49:1–55:13) shifts toward the future and increasingly to Yahweh's promised restoration of Zion (R. E. Watts 1990a). Recalling the first exodus, when Yahweh bared his mighty arm (51:5, 9–10; 52:10; cf. 40:10; 48:14), and echoing the introductory announcement of comfort (51:12–16; cf. 40:1–11), the prophet calls daughter Zion to prepare for her redemption (51:11, 17). The subsequent extended summons to depart from captivity (52:1–12), along with our passage (52:13–53:12; cf. the second Servant Song, which also follows a summons to depart [48:20–22]; see Blenkinsopp 2000–2003: 2:349), and the final celebration of restored Zion (chap. 54) together form the climactic vision of chapters 40–55.

The fourth Servant Song is generally understood to consist of three units: a confession on the unexpected meaning of the servant's suffering (53:1–11a), which is bracketed by two statements by Yahweh (52:13–15; 53:11b–12). The textual and exegetical problems are too numerous to canvass, let alone discuss; even the sometimes stuttering syntax seems to be a deliberate attempt to communicate confused astonishment. Nevertheless, even if the details are unclear, the general sense, no matter how surprising, is not. Set between the summons (52:1–12) and celebration of restoration (54:1–17), the song declares that Yahweh's mighty arm (53:1) of new-exodus deliverance is revealed in none other than his Suffering Servant (see R. E. Watts 2000: 115n135 and literature cited there).

The first section's opening "Behold my servant" (52:13) picks up the earlier call (42:1), but as the identity of that individual was enigmatic, so too here (see Clines 1976). The important thing is what he does and how it happens, and here the attention focuses on his trials (cf. 49:5–6; 50:7–9). Two contrasts dominate: one between the servant's humiliation and exaltation, and one between the people's initial assessment and the reality of Yahweh's intention (Raabe 1984). Setting the tone for the entire poem is the declaration that he will prosper, in the sense of being wise according to God's ways (cf. Josh. 1:7–8; 1 Sam. 18:14; Jer. 23:5), and will be exalted, surprisingly, as highly as God himself (see Isa. 6:1; 33:10; 57:15; cf. Ps. 110:1; Dan. 7:14)—this in stark opposition to the humiliating judgment under which many held him to be (*šmm* [52:14]; cf. the word in Lev. 26:32; 1 Kings 9:8; Isa. 54:1; Jer. 49:20; 50:13 [because of the wounds, *makkôt*, that Yahweh inflicted; cf. *mūkkēh* in Isa. 53:4]; Mic. 6:13; see Westermann

1969: 259). Even kings and nations, awaiting God's justice (42:6; 49:6–7), will fall silent in submission because of this staggeringly unexpected event (52:15; cf., e.g., Pss. 2; 18; 33:10; 46:10; 47; 110; see R. E. Watts 1990b).

In response, the largest section is a confession offered presumably by a newly repentant Israel or more probably by a group within Israel ("we" is characteristically used of God's people [Isa. 16:6; 42:24; cf. Jer. 3:22b–24; Dan. 9:5–19; Hos. 6:1–3; see Oswalt 1998: 381; Childs 2001: 413]). In taking the literary perspective of looking back on the event, it affirms the efficacy of God's action in his servant. Whereas the problem all along has been that God's people were blind and deaf to his purposes (e.g., Isa. 42:18–25; 48:8), because of this extraordinary act they finally see, hear, and understand the new thing that God was doing (53:1; cf. 42:6–7; 48:6–8; 49:5–6). Although initially he was held to be of no account and people recoiled from his suffering (53:2–3, cf. Ps. 22:6–7; 88:8), a new realization has dawned.

In a series of contrasts (53:4–6) the speakers relate their startling reversal of conventional opinion. Far from his wounds and suffering being a punishment for his own rebellion, they now understand that he was bearing in himself Deut. 28:59–61's exilic affliction that they themselves deserved (cf. *mūkkēh* in 53:4 with *tūkkû* in 1:5, and *ḥabbûrâ* in 53:5 and 1:6; see Ceresko 1994) and thus brought the peace that they did not (cf. 48:22; see Goldingay 2001: 305). Even more amazing (53:7–9), given his innocence and in stark contrast to guilty Israel's response to perceived wrongs, was his quiet and uncomplaining submission in the face of genuine injustice, even when it led to his brutal death (also 53:12; cf. LXX's "stricken to death"; see Blenkinsopp 2000–2003: 2:353; Childs 2001: 416; *pace* Whybray 1978; Orlinsky 1977). But most surprising is that even though it was Jacob-Israel who rejected him (50:6–9), this was God's doing (53:10–11a). It was God who accepted his servant's suffering as compensation for Israel's wrong (53:10a [see commentary on Mark 10:45 below]). Because of this his days will be prolonged (the prophet says nothing about what this means or how, given the servant's death, this is to happen), and in fulfillment of his mission he will see "offspring"—that is, more righteous servants (cf., e.g., 54:17; see

Beuken 1990)—thus prospering the Lord's good pleasure (*ḥēpeṣ* [53:10b]; cf. 42:1).

The song closes with a second speech from Yahweh, which takes up the theme of vindication (53:11b–12). Recapping the reason for these unexpected events—my servant, in bearing their punishment, will make many righteous—and the servant's subsequent vindication, God declares that his servant will share the spoil with a mightily reconstituted Israel (see 60:22; cf. 9:3).

Fundamental to all of this is the question of Yahweh's justice (see Beuken 1972). Failing to understand that they are suffering because of their own iniquities, Jacob-Israel complained in chapters 40–48 that Yahweh had neglected their *mišpāṭ*. But it is precisely because of their continuing idolatrous rebellion (48:1–8 [see R. E. Watts 1990a]), expressed finally in their hostility toward Yahweh's servant (50:6–9), that this justice cannot be what they expect: their simple exaltation over the nations (cf. Malachi's warning about the threat inherent to a sinful Israel in Yahweh's coming). Yes, Yahweh will keep his covenant promises; however, because faithless Jacob-Israel stands even now condemned, deliverance can come only through the atoning suffering of the servant who not only will bear blind and deaf Israel's iniquities (see commentary on Mark 10:45 below) but also will transform Israel itself (Childs 2001: 418) and, in doing so, be a light to the nations.

2. Isa. 52:13–53:12 in Judaism. The material here is substantial, diverse, and often problematic because rarely does the date of a given document necessarily determine the age of the tradition that it contains. Numerous commentators detect varying degrees of influence of Isa. 53 in (1) the pierced one of Zech. 12:10–14; (2) the cleansing of sin in the days of the smitten shepherd and scattered sheep of Zech. 13:1, 7–9 (cf. Isa. 53:4, 6; Zech. 11:4–17); (3) the wise who fall, possibly, to refine many (Dan. 11:35; Isa. 52:13; 53:12); (4) the downcast faces of the kings before the Son of Man (*1 En.* 62:3–7; Isa. 52:13, 15). But the parallels are either too limited (*1 Enoch*), are based on uncertain exegesis (Dan. 11), or lack specificity (Zech. 12, where the emphasis is, in any case, on mourning) or genuine thematic coherence (it is not clear that Zech. 13's smiting of the shepherd is a positive act, let alone the means of forgiveness) to confirm direct dependence.

Sometimes cited as evidence of one person dying for another (e.g., Davies and Allison 1988–1997: 3:98–99), the following differ from Isa. 53 in that (1) the forgiveness extended in 11Q10 is extended not because of Job's suffering, but because of his righteousness; (2) although in *L.A.E.* 3 Eve requests that Adam kill her to avert the divine wrath, she is hardly righteous; (3) the offering of humility and contrition in place of the now discontinued sacrifices in the Pr. Azar. 15–17 (Dan. 3:38–40 LXX) is of and for the righteous, not for the wicked.

In terms of Isa. 53 itself, the LXX offers a number of translational variations, but the most interesting is 53:10, where the Lord no longer inflicts the servant, but rathers cleanses him from his wound, and, in spite of his bearing their sins (53:4), the congregation is required to make a sin offering so that they might join in the servant's salvation. Apparently, the servant dies not for the Gentiles, the rich, the wicked, and the mighty who are to be judged (52:15; 53:9, 12), but rather for straying Israel.

Among the Dead Sea Scrolls, the fragmentary 4Q541 has Jacob presumably speaking to Levi of a "smitten" (4 II + 6) eschatological high-priestly figure who will atone for his generation (apparently in a rebuilt temple), whose word is like the word of heaven, before whom darkness will vanish (cf. "he will see light" [1QIsa^(a/b) 53:11]), and who is slandered with every kind of disparagement by an evil generation (9 I, 2–6). If this reflects Isa. 53, then the servant is seen as a priest who is rejected by his own but whose suffering is not vicarious (Hengel and Bailey 2004: 117–18). 1QS might offer a collective eschatological interpretation of Isa. 53 whereby the suffering of the righteous in the midst of wickedness atones for the land (V, 6; VIII, 3–7, 10; IX, 4; cf. 1Q28a I, 1–3; see Black 1953: 7–8; Marcus 1992: 191–92).

In the book of Wisdom the response of the unrighteous persecutors who are "amazed" and admit their own sinfulness at the vindication of the slandered righteous sufferer resembles the reaction to the servant (Isa. 52:13 in Wis. 2:13; 52:15 in 5:2; 53:2–4 in 5:3–4; 53:3 in 4:20; 53:6 in 5:6–7; 53:7–8 in 2:19–20; 53:10–12 in 5:15–16; 53:11 in 2:13; 53:12 in 5:5 [Jeremias 1967: 684]). From the other side, the Maccabean martyrs ask that their righteous deaths be a ransom (*antipsy-chos*) for Israel (4 Macc. 6:27–29; 17:22; 18:4; cf. 2 Macc. 7:37–38; 4 Macc. 1:11; see de Jonge 1988), Isaac's willing death results in the election of Israel (*L.A.B.* 18:3), and in *1 En.* 47:1–4 the blood of the righteous apparently functions in the same way such that when the "number" is offered, in an allusion to Dan. 7:9–10, the books are opened before the "Ancient One" and judgment is given.

In a close parallel to Isa. 53:5b, 9b, the Armenian version of *T. Benj.* 3:8 relates a prophecy to be fulfilled in Joseph (and hence unlikely to be a Christian interpolation, though it is difficult to tell [cf. the Greek text]), that the spotless one will be defiled by the lawless and will die for the sake of the impious; however, the subject is unclear (Hengel and Bailey 2004: 138–39).

The Targum, on the other hand, reflects a consistent theological perspective (Ådna 2004). Because the exalted "servant" of 52:13a could be only the Messiah, the suffering must apply to Israel, or the Gentiles, or the wicked (Betz 1996: 202). Thus it is long-awaiting Israel whose appearance was dark (52:14), whereas the Messiah's holy brilliance not only demands respect (53:2) but also will cause the glory of the nations to cease, like those acquainted with sorrows (53:3). Rather than the servant being crushed, it is the temple that is profaned for Israel's sins and "made whole" through rebuilding (53:5a), while Israel will be forgiven, and peace and prosperity will be enjoyed to the extent that they obey the Messiah's teaching of the law (53:5b, 11–12). Instead of suffering for Israel, it is a smitten and exiled Israel for whom he intercedes and gains forgiveness (53:7a; also 53:4b, 6, 12b), and the unimagined future is now the great wonders amid which he returns the exiles (53:8a). Instead of his life, the nations' rule over Israel is taken away, and upon them Israel's sins are visited (53:8b). Their strong ones are handed over like a lamb for sacrifice (53:7b), and instead the wicked see Gehenna (53:9). God's will is not to crush him, but rather to purify the remnant of Israel so that they will see his kingdom, increase through sons and daughters, and, in doing Torah, prolong their days (53:10). The Gentiles will receive retribution, and Israel will enjoy the plunder of kings, which the Messiah will divide among them (53:11–12a). And all this is because he, like Moses, was willing to risk his life in intercession for rebellious Israel (53:12b) (see Ådna 2004: 221).

Among the rabbinic writings, *y. Sanh.* 11:5 [IV.R] declares that the blood of the stricken prophet (1 Kings 20:37) atoned for all Israel, and *y. Šeqal.* 5:1 [II.A–B] assigns Rabbi Akiba a place with the many (Isa. 53:12) because of his role as a preeminent teacher (cf. the role of Torah in the Targum). *Tanḥuma Genesis* 6:20 cites Isa. 52:13 in explaining why Zech. 4:7's exalted mountain is the Messiah. On the other hand, *b. Sanh.* 98b, based on Isa. 53:4, famously names the Messiah as the Leprous One or the Sick One. Appealing to Isa. 53:10a, *b. Ber.* 5a argues that God chastises all whom he loves, and if accepted with consent (as a trespass offering must be bought with consent [53:10b]), he rewards with children, long life (53:10c), and advancement in the study of Torah (= the will of the Lord) (53:10d; cf. *S. Eli. Rab.* [6]7, which argues similarly in explaining Lev. 7:1's guilt offering). In *b. Soṭah* 14a Moses, anxious about being unable to fulfill those precepts of the law that pertain only to life in the land, is nevertheless promised by God that they will be accounted to him as fulfilled (citing Isa. 53:12). Moses will share the spoil with Abraham, Isaac, and Jacob, who were "strong" in Torah, because he surrendered himself to die (Exod. 32:32), bore the sins of many in making atonement for the golden calf, and made intercession for the transgressors by praying for mercy for the sinners in Israel (cf. *Mek. Exod.* 12:1, which teaches that the patriarchs offered their lives for Israel, but without any reference to Isa. 53, which suggests that its use in the Talmud is a later development).

According to *Sipre Deut.* 333 on Deut. 32:43, while the deaths of Israelites slain by the nations will be their own expiation (citing Ps. 79:1–3), the descent of the wicked into Gehenna suffices for the entire nation (Isa. 43:3–4), and merely dwelling in the land of Israel might also atone for one's sin (Isa. 33:24). For *Sipre Num.* 131, Phinehas, in Num. 25:13, is an example of one who, "for the sake of his ministry," risks his life (Isa. 53:12). *Midrash Psalms* 2:9 on Ps. 2:7 sees Isa. 52:13 and 42:1 as referring to Israel, though in a messianic setting that links David's and Israel's sonship. *Ruth Rabbah* 5:6 sees in Isa. 53:5 the sufferings of the Messiah for Israel's transgressions, though without explanation, whereas in *Num. Rab.* 13:2 it is

Israel in exile who bears its soul even to death (Isa. 53:12). In *S. Eli. Rab.* (27)25, Isa. 53:11 describes those who, in anguish over their generation's wickedness, teach Torah to Israel (cf. [14]15).

In summary, the materials focus on either exaltation or suffering. In terms of exaltation, a few texts offer an individual messianic interpretation emphasizing judgment on the nations and refocusing the suffering on Israel (Targum, *Midrash Psalms*; cf. the LXX), while one exalts Rabbi Akiba as a preeminent teacher (*y. Šeqal.*). Most focus on the suffering described in Isa. 53. Although a few late texts attribute nonvicarious sickness or suffering to the Messiah (*Ruth Rabbah*, *b. Sanhedrin*), the majority apply it to Israel (LXX, *Sipre Deuteronomy*, Targum, *Numbers Rabbah*) or the righteous (*Sipre Numbers*, *S. Eli. Rab.* [27]25) who are either oppressed by the wicked (Wisdom; 4Q541) or disciplined by God (*b. Berakot*, *S. Eli. Rab.* [6]). In some cases, the suffering expiates the sufferer's own sin (Israel [*Sipre Deuteronomy*]), and in others it is vicarious, whether in the past (Moses [*Mekilta*, *b. Soṭah*]) or, in a few early texts, the present (Qumran: 1QS; Maccabean martyrs: 4 Maccabees), or the eschaton through an indistinct figure (*Testament of Benjamin*).

3. Ps. 118:22 in Context and in Judaism. Because this psalm figures so prominently later in Mark, including a citation of the "rejected [*apodokimazō*] stone" verse in its entirety, I will leave a fuller treatment until then. Briefly, Ps. 118 is essentially a thanksgiving temple introitus celebrating Yahweh's victory against great odds (as promised in Ps. 2) on behalf of his Davidic king. Verse 22 then comes as something of a surprise within the larger context of rejoicing. But it reminds the celebrants that in spite of David's initial rejection, God had become his salvation, hence this great victory for Israel. Emphatically connected with David in the Targum, particularly with respect to 118:22, the psalm figured prominently in later Jewish eschatological new-exodus reflection, being especially associated with Ps. 2 and the messianic defeat of enemies and restoration of Jerusalem.

4. Hos. 6:2 in Context. For Hosea, a resurgent Assyria's building of pressure on an increasingly desperate Israel—Judah and Ephraim—is the divine fulfillment of the covenant curses (Deut. 28–32; Lev. 26). Israel and their leaders are unjust and idolatrous fools who have no understanding and whose chasing of foreign alliances is pursuing the wind (4:1, 6, 14; 12:1 [see Seow 1982]). Although God loves his people (2:16–23; 11:8–9), in keeping with the general historical construct of Deut. 4:20–31, the looming exile is inevitable, and only after that discipline will a repentant remnant experience blessing (6:1–2, 11; 14:4–7 [see Stuart 1987: 7–8]). Consequently, references and allusions to the exodus permeate the work (e.g., 1:9; 2:14–15; 9:10; 11:1; 12:9, 13; 13:4), but Israel would now experience it in reverse (8:13; 9:3, 17; 11:5) (see S. McKenzie 1979).

Chapters 1–3 begin with the famous metaphor of Israel as Yahweh's promiscuous wife, who must first be sent away before being reunited with him in new-exodus fidelity (2:14–15). Chapters 4–13 are largely concerned with judgment occasionally interspersed with subsequent promise, the latter being the focus of the concluding chapter 14 and its final call to fidelity. Beyond this, the delineation of a more detailed structure, the limits of pericopae, and even particular historical settings are much more subjective.

Our text, 6:1–3, comes in response to Israel's attempts to find "healing" from the king of Assyria (5:12–13). Echoing the covenant curses of Deut. 28:21–22, 27, 35, 59–61 (Stuart 1987: 105), the imagery is graphic: sick and wounded Israel is afflicted with pus and rotten infection (cf. Isa. 1:5–6; on parallels with Isa. 40–55, see van der Merwe 1966). And since this is Yahweh's discipline, only he can restore.

The opening verses recognize that Israel's condition is not something that Yahweh has merely allowed; it is punishment directly from him. But if they return to him, by the same Deuteronomic token—"I put to death and bring to life, I wound and I heal" (Deut. 32:39 [see Mays 1969: 95])—he will heal (rāpā') what he himself has torn and bind what he has smitten (nākâ [cf. Isa. 53:4; also Hos. 5:2: mûsar). Verse 2 is a chiasm—(a) bring to life (b) two days (b') third day (a') raise us up—where the "two/two-plus-one" pair means neither "soon" nor "in a couple of days," but that Yahweh would not forget them, and after a fixed time they would be restored (Stuart 1987: 108; but see Zakovitch 1977: 1–37, cited in Cogan and Tadmor 1988: 254 on 2 Kings 20:5, where "after three days" especially in prose tales means "after a short span of time").

Whether Hosea is thinking in terms of resurrection (cf. Aquila: anazōōsei; see F. I. Andersen 1980: 419–21, noting 2:5; 5:14; 6:5), Ezek. 37's vision of a nation dead in exile (Stuart 1987: 108) or simply rising from a sickbed (cf. Origen: hygiasei; see Wolff 1974: 117) is made moot by the Deut. 32 allusion. God can do either. But he requires faithfulness, hence the summons: "Let us know and press on to know the LORD" (6:3). However, given Israel's rapidly evaporating love (6:4), the promise can hardly be realized until after the exile.

5. Hos. 6:2 in Judaism. 3 Enoch 28:10 cites Hos. 6:2 to describe the purgatorial punishments undergone in the first three days of death to fit one for God's presence. In the Targum "after the second day" is changed to "in the days of consolations that will come," and "on the third day" becomes "on the day of the resurrection of the dead," which idea is thoroughgoing in the rabbis (Pirqe R. El. 51; y. Ber. 5:2 [I.A–B]; y. Sanh. 11:6 [I.O–Q]; b. Roš Haš. 31a and b. Sanh. 97a with Ps. 90:4; Gen. Rab. 56:1; Deut. Rab. 7:6; Esther Rab. 9:2). "After three days" is the time of deliverance, since God never leaves the righteous in distress for more than that time (Gen. Rab. 91:7; Midr. Ps. 22:5). In S. Eli. Rab. (5)6 the "first day" refers to life in this world, and the "second day" to the time of the Messiah and being raised in the world to come. Such a broad consensus suggests that this interpretation is quite early (I suspect it was not used in the early church because they were concerned not with the promise of a resurrection, as is the issue for the rabbis, but with what Jesus' resurrection said about his identity). Hosea 6:3's pursuit of knowing Yahweh equates with eagerness to know Torah (b. Ber. 6b; S. Eli. Zut. 13).

C. The Use of Isa. 53:3, 6, 10; Ps. 118:22; Hos. 6:2 in Mark. In conjoining these various texts with his "Son of Man" self-designation, Mark's Jesus engages in what appears to be an unprecedented interpretive act and the disciples are as astonished as the witnesses in Isaiah. In response to Peter's pivotal "messianic" confession, Jesus' use of the to-date rarely invoked "Son of Man" self-designation (only twice in the first half of the book) makes sense given Dan. 7:13's messianic connotations. And even his conjoining it with Isaianic servant texts is in principle not necessarily novel (VanderKam 1992: 189–90, on 1 Enoch), since some of those may well have been regarded messianically at this time (cf. *Tg. Isa.* 42; 53). On the other hand, although the suffering element of Isa. 53 was widely ascribed, sometimes vicariously to Moses (*Mekilta, b. Soṭah*) and possibly to an eschatological figure (*Testament of Benjamin*), this did not extend to either Daniel's son of man or the Messiah, who evoked instead glory and vindication. Jesus' predicating his messianic Son of Man identity with Isa. 53's suffering was apparently utterly unexpected, as was the consequent notion that Israel's peace would come through his bearing, even to death, the Deuteronomic wounds and sicknesses of idolatrous Israel's exilic judgment. (Ironically, if Jesus does see himself and his followers as a substitute temple, then, as in the Targum, the true temple is also profaned [see commentary on Mark 12:10–11 below].)

Isaiah 53 also speaks of Jesus' final vindication (Targum, *Midrash Psalms*), and that is apparently the point of the short but pregnant allusion to Ps. 118. For although he would be rejected, the larger setting of this Davidic messianic psalm, also concerned with the new exodus, is overwhelmingly focused on inexorable vindication and a celebratory procession into Yahweh's temple. And hence finally the reference to Hosea's "resurrection," without which there would be no such celebration (cf. Mark 14:58). Jesus, in taking God's wounding and bruising of Israel (Hos. 5:12–13; Isa. 53) and undergoing their exile and death (again the Deuteronomic curses), entrusts himself to the one who can both heal and make alive (Deut. 32:39 [see commentary on Deut. 30:15 in Mark 3:4 above]), citing what, if it was not already so, will soon become one of the great texts of eschatological vindication through resurrection.

In a sense, the later Targum was right to see the Messiah in Isa. 53. What it had not understood was that he was present in all of it, including the suffering. In this respect, Ps. 118:17 is correct. Jesus is punished severely (albeit with Israel's discipline [cf. Isa. 53; Hos. 6]), but he will not, in the final analysis, be given over to death. Is it too much, then, to suggest that after offering this faithful confession, Jesus "presses on" that the Twelve might also see, understand, and know the Lord (Hos. 6:3) by leading them in the way of the new Torah of a crucified Messiah (see commentary on Mark 9:7 below; on the cross as a unifying theme in Mark, see Bolt 2004)?

D. Theological Use. Clearly, Mark 8:31 is a major turning point in the narrative. Declared "Messiah" for the first time, Jesus responds swiftly. Soteriologically, Isaiah's new-exodus redemption comes only through the messianic Son of Man's taking upon himself the law's curse. Having already embodied the law in doing good and giving life by healing on the Sabbath (3:1–6; Deut. 30:15), Jesus now, in "embodying" the law's exilic judgment, will through his vindication bring life and healing to all. Ecclesiologically, this time the nation/beast opposing the Son of Man is none other than Israel's leadership. Even more sobering is that the kind of nationalistic messianic expectation expressed in the Targum, to which Peter and presumably the others adhere, is rebuked as satanic (8:32–33; *epitimaō*, used also to rebuke the demons and the sea [see Kee 1967])—a leaven that, if not removed, defiles and excludes from this new exodus. Living among an adulterous and sinful generation, and not unlike blind and deaf Israel in Isa. 40–55, they need a second touch in order "to see" and understand God's "new thing" (Isa. 48:6–8).

8:37

A. NT Context: In Exchange for One's Life. The
Markan Jesus' penetrating questions about the disciples' lack of understanding, his declaration of suffering as the path to the Son of Man's vindication, and his startlingly strong denunciation of Peter's rejection of a suffering Messiah bring Israel's moment of decision to a head. Summoning the crowd with the disciples, Jesus lays out the choice in the starkest possible terms: Israel either follows him, losing its life in a self-renouncing and cross-bearing discipleship for the sake of Jesus and his gospel (8:34), or, since there is nothing that either Israel or anyone can give as an exchange (*antallagma*) to ransom their lives (8:37), in seeking to save themselves they will lose everything (8:38). (C. A. Evans [2001b: 26] omits "for me" in 8:35 as a later interpolation that takes the focus off the good news of the kingdom. This omission, however, seems artificially to separate teacher and teaching, and the king and his kingdom. It is Jesus, Israel's messianic Son of Man, in whom God is present, who is followed [8:34], and it is he, not his gospel, who comes on the clouds of heaven [8:38] [cf. 10:29; 13:9–10].)

Although to some extent the idea of the value of life is proverbial (e.g., *2 Bar.* 51:15; *Syr. Men.* 843; cf. Sir. 24:14), this is not the point here. Instead, Jesus' "exchange" statement closely echoes Ps. 49:7–9 (Dautzenberg 1966: 71–75; cf. C. A. Evans 2001b: 26; Hooker 1991: 209). Both texts share similar language and concepts ("ransom/exchange" [LXX: *lytroō, lytrōsis/antallagma*] [cf. in the LXX: *lytroō/antallagma* in Ps. 54:19–20; *antallassō/lytron* in Prov. 6:35; *antallagma/lytroō* in Jer. 15:13, 21], "man," "to give," "abundant wealth/the whole world," and "God" [implicit in Mark]), and both are concerned with the inability of human beings to ransom their own lives from death. However, there is more here.

B. Ps. 49:7–9 in Context. Psalm 49 (48 LXX) is a somewhat unusual wisdom psalm in that it deals with only a single enigma or riddle. Structurally, after an opening exposition (49:1–4), generally agreed upon by interpreters, there is no consensus on the remaining material, though fortunately this does not impact the basic message (e.g., 49:5–12, 13–20 [Craigie 1982]; 49:5–19, 20 [Witte 2004]). The psalmist, speaking essentially for the poor and the disenfranchised who can only cast themselves on Yahweh, poses a single question to humanity: Should I be afraid when in evil days I am surrounded by the treachery of powerful and wicked foes (49:5–6 [see Kraus 1988–1989: 1:481])? The answer: I should not and will not. For all their riches they cannot offer a ransom (*exilasma/lytrōsis*) to redeem (*lytroō*) their lives from God's power and the fate that he has allotted to all humanity (49:7–11).

Such people, seduced by visions of self-reliant wealth and confirmed in them by the applause of those who come after (49:10 is difficult [see Craigie 1982: 357])—itself an ironic comment on their fleeting existence—do not realize that it is precisely this folly (49:13) that inexorably leads to being consumed in Sheol (49:14a). In the end, far from their riches protecting them against death, death separates them from their riches. They are like sheep, but their shepherd will be Death (49:14b). True wisdom is to know that humanity's one hope is in God, who alone can redeem from the pit (49:15 [see Witte 2004]; whether this means resurrection or not, and in what ways, cannot be answered [see Kraus 1988–1989: 1:48]). The psalm concludes with a repetition of injunctions not to fear the pompous and oppressive rich, for in their folly they fail to understand that they will not abide.

C. Ps. 49:7–9 in Judaism. Pseudo-Phocylides 109–13 reflects similar sentiments, exhorting the rich to be generous, since they will die like everyone else. In *'Abot R. Nat.* B §35, the way to save one's life is to preserve one thing of Torah, whereas losing one thing of Torah forfeits one's life (cf. Matt. 5:19). According to the *Mek. Exod.* 21:28–30, the nations have no redemption because the price is impossible (cf. Ps. 49:7–8), but Israel does because they, being beloved of God, have been given the nations as their ransom (cf. Isa. 43:3–4).

The Targum, emphasizing the wickedness of those who love riches, more fully develops the contrast between them and the righteous. For example, 49:7–9 (note that there is considerable variation in the traditions at this point) states that the wicked man will not use his riches to redeem his captive brother, but if he does, he will live again for eternal life and avoid Gehenna. Righteously using one's wealth earns favor with God, who then can grant eternal life. The mortals who abide in pomp are now clearly the wicked who die like beasts and are worthless (49:12, 20). They are destined to decay in Gehenna because they have destroyed both the temple and the Torah-serving righteous like sheep (49:14; "sheep" is a common metaphor for the righteous poor under abusive leadership [e.g., Ezek. 34]). But as David prophesied, God redeems the souls of the righteous, teaches them Torah, and, in some editions, guides them to the world to come (49:15).

Similar ideas are found in *Gen. Rab.* 26:2 and *b. Roš Haš.* 17a, where Ps. 49:14 is applied to the particularly wicked who stretched out their hand against the temple. *Roš Haššanah* also includes those who lead the masses astray or abandon Israel, citing also Isa. 66:24 (see commentary on Mark 9:48 below). According to *Pirqe. R. El.* 25 (on the sin of Sodom), the wicked's trust in wealth thrusts aside the fear of heaven (citing Ps. 49:6; cf. *b. Šabb.* 31b on Ps. 49:13). *Pirqe Rabbi Eliezer* 34 tells of a dying man (= days of evil [Ps. 49:5]) whom neither his sons (Ps. 49:7–8) nor his money can save, but his charity (Prov. 11:4) and his righteousness (Isa. 58:8) will go before him.

D. The Use of Ps. 49:7–9 in Mark. As in the psalm and the widely held interpretive tradition, Jesus and his followers find themselves to be outcasts, without property (10:28), in the midst of an adulterous and sinful generation, in an evil and eschatologically climactic day, confronted by powerful and wealthy enemies: Herod, who has just executed John (Malachi's Elijah), and Jerusalem's religious elite, who are on track to do the same to Jesus (see commentary on Mark 9:11 below). In this context Jesus sets out the two paths open to Israel. One is the path taken by his powerful opponents who, confident in their resources (whether wealth or righteousness), seek to secure their own existence, and to which path the leaven-infected disciples contending for greatness still seem attracted (9:34; 10:37–41). But as the psalmist realizes, such people, in spite of their pomp, are fools, for there is no exchange (*antallagma*) that they can make to ransom (*lytroō*) themselves from death. The other path—the one that Jesus himself exemplifies, wherein all such claims are renounced even to the point of laying down one's life if need be, and wherein one trusts solely in God, who alone can raise the dead—paradoxically leads to life.

In contrast to the traditions in *'Abot de Rabbi Nathan* and *Pirqe Rabbi Eliezer*, the key is neither preserving Torah nor one's charity or righteousness, but rather adhering to Jesus and his gospel. Nor, by the time Mark writes, is participation in eschatological redemption a question of whether one is a Gentile or an Israelite, where the former are given for the latter (cf. *Mekilta*). Instead, what matters is whether one follows Jesus as the suffering-servant Son of Man, who "gives" his life (*psychē*) for Israel (Isa. 53:12; cf. Hos. 6:2; see commentary on Mark 10:45 below; on Isa. 55's closing invitation to Jerusalem to partake of this wisdom without price and without which there is no life, see Spykerboer 1989; Blenkinsopp 2000–2003: 2:369).

In the Targum the wicked oppress God's Torah-observant sheep (cf. Isa. 40:11; Mark 6:34) and destroy the temple (cf. *Gen. Rab.* 26:2; *b. Roš Haš.* 17a). Ironically, since to listen to Jesus is to do God's will (3:34–35), it is Herod and the Pharisees who oppress God's sheep (see commentary on Mark 6:34 above) and whose rejection of Jesus will inevitably lead to the destruction of the temple.

E. Theological Use. No doubt shocking in the first-century world, cross-bearing is now the "boundary marker" of reconstituted Israel (8:35) and will become its basic covenantal sign (see commentary on Mark 14:22–25 below). So fundamental is this dual act of self-renunciation and trust in God, that if need be, even life itself must be let go. As Rome's ultimate symbol of degradation, it directly repudiates Israel's nationalistic messianic hopes and first-century Graeco-Roman conceptions of power and status, whether expressed through the all-pervasive patron/client structure or in the embodiment of that structure's pinnacle, divine Caesar, who presided over all as the great surrogate priest and father. Here Mark presents a king and a good-news message with a very different vision of what it meant to be the son of g/God, whether from a Roman perspective (as in Caesar's deity) or a Jewish one (cf. Exod. 4:22) (see commentary on Mark 1:11 above), and therefore what it meant for humanity to be created in God's image (cf. 1 Cor. 1:18–25). For the millions who groaned under the weight of a status-seeking, wealthy elite, the invitation to renounce that entire mindset was good news. This was the beginning of a new creation and a new humanity, built first and foremost on trust in God, not one's own wealth and station.

8:38

A. NT Context: The Son of Man on the Clouds. On these terms, then, to fail to give absolute allegiance in the present to Jesus and his announcement of God's kingdom will result in eschatological ruin (cf. "shame" in Ps. 119:6; Isa. 1:24) when the Son of Man comes in the glory of the Father with his holy messengers/angels. The combination of the "coming of the Son of Man," the glory (Dan. 7:14) of the Father (cf. "Ancient of Days," "Most High" [Dan. 7:9, 13, 22, 25]), and the holy "angels" (cf. the hosts of Dan. 7:10, and the "holy ones" of Dan. 7:22, 25, 27; cf. Zech. 14:5) is generally agreed upon to point to Dan. 7 (in spite of some demurrals because of the third-person reference, which in Mark's usage obviously refers to Jesus).

B. Dan. 7:13 in Context and in Judaism. Having discussed Daniel's son of man earlier (see commentary on Mark 2:10 above), here I will keep to a few salient points. Regardless of the particular direction of travel, to heaven or earth (see Goldingay 1989: 167; J. J. Collins 1993: 311), the primary thrust of Dan. 7's son of man "coming on the clouds" to the Ancient of Days is the striking reversal of Israel's fortunes through his exaltation over the beastly kings/nations (7:11–12, 26). Invested as king (Goldingay 1989: 168), to him and his holy ones will be given an everlasting dominion over all nations (7:14, 27).

This central message of Dan. 7 is echoed in *1 Enoch*, where one of the chief characteristics of the glorious son of man (i.e., seated on a throne of glory [45:3; 55:4; 61:8; 62:5; 69:29]) is that he dethrones kings and the mighty (46:4–5) and discomforts, shames, and destroys sinners (46:4; 62:2–10; 63:11; 69:26–28). Likewise, in *4 Ezra* he defeats the rebellious nations (13:8–11). The Targum to 1 Sam. 2, working with a four-nation schema, anticipates God giving power to his king and magnifying the kingdom of his anointed one (cf. *Frg. Tg.* Exod. 12:42).

In the rabbinic writings, for example, the Messiah who comes riding on the clouds of heaven (*Tanḥ. Gen.* 6:20; on the clouds if Israel is meritorious, on a donkey if not [*b. Sanh.* 98a; cf. Mark 11:7–8]) subjugates the nations (Isa. 49:7; *b. Sanh.* 98a). *Num. Rab.* 13:14 cites Dan. 7:14; 2:35 in support of the Messiah's worldwide dominion (cf. *Midr. Ps.* 2:7–9; 21:5; 93:1).

Finally, it is worth noting that in *1 Enoch* and *4 Ezra* the exaltation of the messianic Son of Man does not mean the vindication of all Israel any more than does the Davidic messiah in the Dead Sea Scrolls or *Psalms of Solomon*. In *1 En.* 62:13–14 the righteous and elect are saved (cf. 38:2; 39:6; 48:7; 50:1–5; 53:6–7; 62:7–8), and *4 Ezra* 13:13, 26, 48–49 seem to envisage the salvation of a righteous remnant. The Davidic messiah in the Dead Sea Scrolls is the prince for the exclusive holy community, (1Q28b V, 20; CD-A VII, 20; 1QM V, 1; 4Q376 1 III, 1), and in *Psalms of Solomon* he similarly distinguishes between faithful and unrighteous in Israel (17:3–9, 27, 36; cf. *Tg. Isa.* 28). His exaltation is always only for the elect, however they might be defined (cf., e.g., Isa. 65:8–16; see Elliott 2000: 472–514).

C. The Use of Dan. 7:13 in Mark. Even though Jesus has stunned his followers with his declaration that the vindication of the Son of Man comes only after suffering, and that at the hands of Israel's leadership, vindication it will indeed be. The reference to "my Father," here for the first time since Jesus' baptism, anticipates the transfiguration and implies that Jesus is indeed the true servant Israel, David's messianic son, and Son of God. Thus the messianic Son of Man is not merely a symbol for Israel; he is also Israel's messianic king. And as with other messianisms, far from Israel taking its election for granted, anyone from "this adulterous and sinful generation" who would join in his vindication must join in his suffering, even unto death. And as we will see, this applies even if they are like the rich man who is Torah-observant and whose wealth in those terms shows that he is blessed by God (10:17–22). With the coming of God's Christ, even this righteousness is no exchange for his soul.

D. Theological Use. Whatever the various positions taken within Israel over whether all Israel or, if not, who within Israel and on whose interpretation of Torah would participate in the coming reign of God, Jesus makes his position abundantly clear. Participation in the messianic Son of Man's eschatological vindication required unashamedly identifying with him (and his gospel) as the suffering Messiah and, over against the powerful and self-sufficient, following his footsteps through cross-bearing self-renunciation and utter trust in God. To be scandalized by these words or, for fear of the powerful wicked, to refuse to imitate Jesus' "way" by daily living as though dead to their self-sufficient world and their threats (8:34) will only mean eschatological repudiation when, as in Malachi's day of the Lord, the Son of Man comes with his messengers/angels in glory and exercises his authority over the beasts (8:38). On the other hand, accepting shame in this fleeting present life, whose brevity we cannot escape, will lead to eternal glory. As in Ps. 49:15, the same God who will vindicate Jesus by raising him from the dead will likewise vindicate and raise his followers.

Once again, Mark's Jesus stands at the very center of eschatology, soteriology, and ecclesiology: God's kingdom and Israel's vindication have arrived in him, the long-awaited salvation has come through his death, and membership in the people of God is through cruciform discipleship. And it is this that God himself soon will affirm.

9:7

A. NT Context: A New Sinai, a New Torah? Immediately after Jesus' disturbing explanation of what genuine discipleship entails, Mark relates the extraordinary event of the transfiguration. Various interpretations have been offered (see Donaldson 1985), but the most significant factor seems to be the number of well-recognized echoes of Israel's Sinai experience: the mountain setting (Exod. 24:12–15), the unusual Markan mention of six days (Exod. 24:16), Moses and Jesus both taking three individuals along (Exod. 24:1–9 [though Moses also takes seventy unnamed elders, and only Joshua ascends the mountain with him]), Moses' shining face and Jesus' dazzling clothes (Exod. 34:29–35 [cf. *T. Levi* 4:3, 5; *T. Jud.* 24:1; *T. Zeb.* 9:8, where the Messiah will radiate like the sun and be called "son and light of righteousness"), Peter's odd remark about building *skēna*, the disciples' fearful response (Exod. 34:30), a voice (God's) from the overshadowing cloud on the seventh day (Exod. 24:16; cf. 40:35), the subsequent descent to encounter a *genea apistos* (Mark 9:19; Deut. 32:20 LXX [see Ziesler 1970; Mauser 1963: 111–18; Swartley 1994: 102–4]; cf. *L.A.B.* 11–12, which intermingles elements from Exod. 20; 24; 32; 34), and finally, the fact that the only mountain on which God spoke from a cloud that involved either Moses or Elijah was Sinai. Of course, the parallels are not exact, any more than Jesus' feedings or control of the sea corresponds perfectly to particular exodus events. These are paradigmatic moments, not precisely constructed replicas. But given Mark's thoroughgoing OT intertextuality, and when taken together and in context, these echoes obviously served his purpose in alerting readers to the frame in which to understand the transfiguration, as Matthew and Luke demonstrate (*pace* Gundry 1993: 475–78). If, as I have argued, Mark is describing a new exodus, then this is its new Sinai.

For only the second time in Mark there is the voice of divine attestation, and here using words almost identical to those at Jesus' baptism: "This is my beloved Son." Reflecting Mark's new-exodus schema, if the first attestation occurred during a new Red Sea crossing (see commentary on Mark 1:11 above), the second takes place on a new Mount Sinai.

Again allowing for the more natural mode of address and the change from *sy* to *houtos* as here the disciples are addressed by the voice, we see that Mark 9:7, like Mark 1:11, carries an allusion to Ps. 2:7 (complete with targumic expansion).

B. Ps. 2:7 in Context and in Judaism. See commentary on Mark 1:11 above.

C. The Use of Ps. 2:7 in Mark. Since the disciples were not present at Jesus' baptism, this is their first and only experience of the divine affirmation. The use of the messianically laden Ps. 2 is God's confirmation of Peter's confession (8:29): Jesus is the Lord's Messiah. And the resemblance between Dan. 7:9's Ancient of Days, whose "clothing was as white as snow" and to whom the son of man comes on the clouds, and, in the context of the overshadowing cloud, Jesus' clothing, which is "dazzling white," confirms Jesus' self-designation that he is the glorious Son of Man (8:31) (see C. A. Evans 2001b: 36).

At the baptism the one voice connected the messianic Ps. 2 with Isa. 42. Here two voices, Jesus' and God's, but speaking as one through the conjoined passion prediction and transfiguration scenes, connect it with Isa. 53. Significantly, these are the only two Isaianic "Servant Songs" that were at some point interpreted messianically. Following the Isaianic trajectory, the baptism's declaration introduced Jesus as taking up Israel's calling (Isa. 42:1), and here in response to official Israel's hostile sightlessness he is also Isa. 53's Suffering Servant. This means that the traditional hopes that had attached to Ps. 2 of a restored Jerusalem in which a victorious king-messiah drives out the unclean and purifies the temple (*Pss. Sol.* 17; 4Q174; cf. *Tg. Ps.* 2:6) must undergo radical transformation. These things Jesus will do, even to becoming the "keystone" of a new temple (Ps. 118:22 in Mark 12:10), but his wielding a rod of iron and shattering the nations like pots (Ps. 2:9) will come through the power of redeeming death and resurrection. Consequently, just as the Targum, which also shares the "beloved" expansion, concludes with a call to "worship in the presence of the Lord with fear, and pray with trembling" and an admonition "to accept instruction" (2:11–12), so too the terrified disciples (Mark 9:6b) are enjoined lest they be accounted rebels: "Listen to him!" (9:7b). And this means not just Jesus' teaching in general, but particularly the preceding passion prediction and the nonnegotiable summons to cross-bearing discipleship.

But what has this to do with Moses and Elijah (the significance of the order "Elijah with Moses" is debated and turns on the meaning of *syn* [see Heil 1999])? Their pairing makes sense in that both faced rejection at the hands of their people and were vindicated, both met and spoke with God on Sinai (Horeb [1 Kings 19; Sir. 45:5; 48:7]), both were regarded as not having died (Moses according to some traditions: Josephus, *Ant.* 4.326; *Assumption of Moses*; *b. Soṭah* 13b; cf. the long list of comparisons in *Pesiq. Rab.* 4:2; see Basser 1998), and more importantly, in later Jewish eschatological tradition, Moses, because of his reconciling role at Sinai, was permitted to return with Elijah (e.g., *Deut. Rab.* 3:17; *Sipre* 342), though Elijah clearly played the more significant role (see commentary on Mark 1:2–3 above)—hence the disciples' question in Mark 9:11 (see Kee 1972: 144–46). Thus the presence of Elijah and Moses strongly suggests that Israel's end-time salvation has begun (cf. the restoration of "all things" in 9:12; see Schweizer 1971: 183).

But Elijah and Moses have already been mentioned side by side, and this in just one place in Israel's Scriptures. At the conclusion of Malachi—a text already of some importance for Mark—and perhaps of the whole prophetic corpus, both men appear as ideal figures joined by their mutual association with Horeb and Yahweh's glory (4:4b), and both are to be obeyed in preparation for the long-awaited new exodus, the great and terrible day of the Lord (4:4–5). The one recalls the beginning of Israel's story when he prepared for Yahweh's coming in glory upon his tabernacle, and the other anticipates its consummation by preparing for Yahweh's glorious return to and permanent residence in his temple. Together, they connect the preexilic and postexilic communities (A. E. Hill 1998: 366, 387–88).

As the glory descends on Jesus, "my servant" Moses, whose statutes given at Horeb were to be remembered (Mal. 4:4), bears witness that Jesus fulfills the heart of Torah by doing good and bringing life (e.g., Deut. 30:15 in Mark 3:1–3; also 7:6–10). Elijah, whose task was to prepare the way of the Lord by reconciling the faithless postexilic generation to that Mosaic covenant of their forefathers (Mal. 4:5–6), testifies to Jesus doing precisely this in his concern for the first commandment accompanied by a promise (Mark 7:10–13; cf. Exod. 20:12/Deut. 5:16; see Hooker 1987: 68). Counter, then, to common scholarly opinion, the traditional view that Moses represents the law and Elijah the prophets is essentially correct because in Malachi, Elijah the representative prophet will call the people back to the law of Moses (A. E. Hill 1998: 384, 387–88).

In *Midr. Ps.* 2:9 the Messiah, "my son," is victorious because he occupied himself with Torah. The surprising thing here in Mark is that there is no divine self-identification of the Lord who brought them out of Egypt, nor is the voice's declaration followed by a repetition of the Decalogue. There is but one command, "Listen to him!" and it follows God's identification of the glorified Son of Man, Jesus, as his messianic and new-exodus-inaugurating son. Moses and Elijah are the only OT figures to converse with God on Sinai, but strikingly, they now converse with Jesus. Thus, although the "Listen to him" might indicate that Jesus is Deut. 18:15's "a prophet like me" (Marcus 1992: 80–92), clearly he is much more.

The voice, then, confirms that Jesus is truly Israel's long-awaited Messiah, who will lead "this generation" out of exile (Lövestam 1995). The presence of Moses and Elijah testify to the in-breaking of the great and terrible day of the Lord, and that Jesus, who alone of the three is clothed in glory and whose word is identified with God's, is mysteriously the Lord whom Israel seeks and who will indeed come suddenly to his temple (Mal. 3:1).

D. Theological Use. Together with the first passion prediction and Jesus' word on cross-bearing discipleship, the transfiguration confirms the transition from the previous stories of Jesus' Yahweh-like mighty deeds of deliverance, the official opposition, and the growing incomprehension of the disciples to Mark's new-exodus "way" section, with its greater focus on private instruction of the "blind" disciples in regard to the meaning of Jesus' reconstituted vision of messiahship, Torah, and therefore Israel (Best 1970; R. E. Watts 2000: 221–57).

Christologically, as in the water so now on the mountain, Jesus, attested by Elijah and Moses at the climax of Israel's soteriological hopes, is declared to be God's messianic Son of Man, through whose suffering and vindication Jerusalem will be purified and the temple restored. Beyond both

Moses the lawgiver and Elijah the paradigmatic prophet, Jesus is the living, embodied word of a newly reconstituted Torah (see Standhartinger 2003) around whom a reconstituted people of God gather in the new exodus. Ecclesiologically, for this restored Israel, "son of God" (Exod. 4:22) and called to "be holy as I am holy" (Lev. 11:44), Jesus' teaching in general, and his word of cross-bearing discipleship in particular, are the essence of the Torah that defines them. Not only is Jesus its supreme interpreter (see U. Becker 2001), but also his words carry the authority of the one who gave it. As shocking as this might seem, it ought not to surprise. All along, Mark has built his case that Jesus is not merely a reforming rabbi, a great prophet, or even the Messiah (let alone personified wisdom). There is only one who forgives sins, and who commands the sea and treads it underfoot. And his words are now identified with the words of Jesus (cf. Mark 3:34–35).

9:11–13

A. NT Context: Elijah Has Come, and the Son of Man Must Suffer.
As they descend the mountain, Jesus instructs his disciples to say nothing of what they have witnessed until after his resurrection. Having just seen Elijah and puzzling over the meaning of his reference to being raised from the dead, the three disciples ask Jesus why it is that the scribes say that Elijah must come first (9:11). Jesus replies with his own question: given that Elijah was indeed to restore "all things," how can it be written that the Son of Man "should suffer many things" and "be treated contemptibly [*exoudenēthē*]" (9:12)? He then states that Elijah has indeed come, but again as it is written, they have treated him as they wished. The question and the first part of its enigmatic reply presuppose Mal. 4:5–6, and the suffering of the Son of Man repeats the previously noted allusion to Isa. 53 (see commentary on Mark 8:31 above). The two questions, then, concern (1) *exoudenēthē*, which "replaces" the previously used *apodokimazō*, and (2) where it is written concerning Elijah that he would be so treated.

In regard to *exoudenēthē*, although Acts 4:11's citation of Ps. 118:22 has *exouthenētheis*, indicating an accepted translational variation, it seems unlikely that here Mark would intend an allusion to Ps. 118 but then employ *apodokimazō* when he actually cites it (12:10). Several other

psalms also use either the verb or its cognates to describe the unhappy condition from which the petitioner seeks deliverance (e.g., 22:6 [21:7 LXX]; 89:38 [88:39 LXX]; 123:3–4 [122:3–4 LXX]; cf. 78:59 [77:59 LXX]). However, since Mark cites or alludes to Ps. 22 several times in his passion narrative, Ps. 22:6 [21:7 LXX] seems the best option here (cf., e.g., 15:24, 29, 30–32, 34; see Hooker 1991: 220; A. Y. Collins 1997: 234; also see below).

Alternatively, in view of the translational variations already noted concerning Ps. 118:22, the importance of Isaiah for Mark as a whole, and the likely Isaianic background to *polla pathē*, it is significant that Aquila (once), Symmachus (twice), and Theodotion (twice), in a remarkable display of unanimity, reject the LXX's *atimon* and translate Isa. 53:3's *bāzâ* (2x) with *exoudenōmenos* (France 1982: 123–24; cf. Moo 1983: 89–91). The latter is the standard LXX rendering (dos Santos 1973: 23; Hooker 1959: 94), which again suggests either a process of semantic change or a rejection of the Isaiah translator's choice as idiosyncratic (which the objection by Gundry [1993: 485] that these are post-Christian does not address).

The predominance of Isaianic imagery to date, that Isa. 53 is already an eschatological text, and the word occurring twice in that text favor an Isa. 53 allusion. On the other hand, given the single-minded focus on suffering—unlike 8:38, there is no reference to resurrection—it could be that Mark's Jesus, wanting to retain a Davidic element, substituted an allusion to Ps. 22 because of its greater emphasis on suffering; a reader already familiar with Mark's passion narrative might spot the shift (as do various commentators). On the other hand, if one is already thinking of Isa. 53, then that would suffice (again as it does for other commentators). Finally, it is not impossible that the word might have been chosen precisely because it echoes both Isa. 53 and Ps. 22. Either way, the options are probably just these two texts, and as the background to Isa. 53 has already been covered under Mark 8:38 above, and Ps. 22 will be discussed under Mark 15:23 below. We will concentrate here only on Mal. 4:4–5.

B. Mal. 4:4–5 in Context.
The overall structure and themes of Malachi and many of the key issues relating to Elijah were dealt with earlier (see commentary on Mark 1:2–3; 9:7 above). In sum-

mary, Mal. 4:4–6 forms a kind of double appendix to the book. The appeal to Moses looks back to remind the nation that it is still under the law, thus linking the prophets to the ancient tradition, and the reference to Elijah, by looking forward, anticipates Yahweh's future return (Childs 1978; Petersen 1995: 232–33).

Elijah (cf. the LXX's *ton Thesbitēn*), widely understood to be an identification of the (covenant) messenger of 3:1, is to prepare the nation for "the great and terrible day of the LORD." The expression is found in Joel 2:11, 31 and reflects a similar interest in postexilic writings (cf., e.g., the parallel expressions in Zech. 2:11; 3:9; 9:16; 14:1, 4; see A. E. Hill 1998: 376). In Mal. 1:14, in response to being dishonored by a cheating Israel's defective offerings, outraged Yahweh describes himself as "great" and "terrible," setting the threatening tenor for the rest of the book (e.g., 2:3, 9; 3:2, 5; 4:1, 3).

Elijah's task—"to turn [*šwb*] the hearts of the parents to their children" and vice versa—though sometimes taken to mean righting the family dislocations of 2:10–16, seems best understood in the light of the immediately preceding reference to Moses as the restoration of the postexilic faithless generation to the covenant loyalty of the ancient forefathers (Verhoef 1987: 342; A. E. Hill 1998: 387–88; cf. Jer. 6:16's exhortation to return to the ancient paths, and Isa. 63:16, where "Abraham does not know us"), which was a primary concern behind the fifth commandment (Phillips 1970: 81).

The whole work finishes on a disturbing note: the possibility that Elijah will not succeed, that Israel will not return to true obedience of Torah, and consequently that Yahweh will "strike the land with a curse" (4:6). In light of the covenant language throughout (e.g., 2:4–5, 10; 3:1) and the proximity of a reference to the statutes of Moses, the verb *nākāh* ("strike") recalls the exodus (Exod. 3:20; 9:15; 12:12) and the Deuteronomic curses (Deut. 28:22, 27, 28, 35) (see A. E. Hill 1998: 389)—the same word is used of the servant's wounds as he bears exiled Israel's covenant curses (Isa. 53:4). In combination with *'ereṣ* it includes not just the land, but especially the people (Isa. 11:4; Jer. 43:11; cf. Judg. 19:30; Isa. 66:8). The noun *ḥērem* likewise recalls the stipulations of Deuteronomy (e.g., 20:17 [*ḥāram*]), suggesting

that if Israel continues to behave like the surrounding nations, it will come under the same exterminating judgment (e.g., Isa. 34:2; cf. 66:24).

On this basis, *pen* ("lest") does not refer to whether Yahweh will come—that much is certain. The only question is Israel's fate when he does, and that depends entirely on their response to Elijah (Verhoef 1987: 343–45; A. E. Hill 1998: 390).

C. Mal. 4:5–6 in Judaism. The problematic nature of the last verse (4:6), with its threat of curse, probably led the LXX to rearrange the verses so as to finish instead on the positive note of remembering the law of Moses (4:4). The same shift of emphasis continued into later Jewish tradition where Elijah, seen as the great reconciler, would calm God's wrath by effecting the genuine repentance of Israel and thus oversee the restoration of the twelve tribes. Only CD-B XX, 16–21 suggests the possibility that not all in Israel would respond. (See also commentary on Mark 1:2–3 above.)

D. The Use of Mal. 4:5–6 in Mark. The disciples' question is best understood as a shorthand reference to the suffering and death of Jesus, with which they are still wrestling (cf. their continuing discussions about greatness [9:33–34; 10:35–37, 41]). Having just seen Elijah (with Moses), presumably they assumed that the eschatological reconciliation of Israel had begun (Gundry 1993: 483). How is it, then, that Jesus can still speak of his resurrection and, necessarily thereby, his rejection and death? Does not Elijah restore all things?

Jesus responds in the affirmative (*pace* Marcus [1992: 99], who follows Wellhausen's suggestion that 9:12a is a question), but, invoking Isa. 53 (*exoudenēthē* [and perhaps Ps. 22]), he highlights the tension between the scribal expectation of reconciliation and the prophecies of a suffering messianic deliverer. Since Scripture itself teaches that the messianic servant-Son of Man would be rejected, surely it must presuppose the same of Elijah, since "they" could not reject Jesus without first rejecting him. Malachi 4:4–6 was not, after all, a blanket promise of restoration as the scribes and the disciples seem to have thought (and apparently most commentators [e.g., Gundry 1993: 465; Marcus 1992: 100–107; France 2002: 358]); rather, it was a final, disturbing warning, as CD-B XX understood.

In other words, the rejection of John, who for Mark's Jesus was Malachi's Elijah, his imprisonment in 1:14, which was the catalyst for Jesus' inaugurating proclamation of the kingdom, and subsequent death in 6:17–29, "was written"—not in a direct prophecy, but nevertheless necessarily in the Isaianic predictions of the suffering Son of Man. Yes, Elijah-John's coming did initiate the eschatological restoration of all things (this before, not after, Jesus' passion [*pace* Gundry 1993: 464]), and for Jesus, this is being fulfilled in him (as both messianic Son of Man and Yahweh's personal presence, and hence the applicability of Mal. 3:1 etc.). But the Scriptures also understood that only the faithful remnant of historically rebellious Israel would participate (see, e.g., Isa. 6 and 29 in Mark 4 and 7, respectively; cf. 48:8, 17–22; 65:1–16; 66:24). And this, for Mark, is the restored Israel (cf. Sir. 48:10), beginning with the Twelve (Mark 3:13–19), which gathers around Jesus (3:31–35).

E. Theological Use. Eschatologically, Jesus' identification of John with Malachi's promised Elijah further confirms that this is the great and terrible day of the Lord, and that Jesus himself is necessarily specially identified with Yahweh's personal presence (e.g., 2:1–12; 4:35–41; 6:47–52). Since Jesus' opponents have rejected Elijah-John, who was to purify the Levitical priesthood and call them back to Torah and covenantal faithfulness, it is little wonder that they clash with Jesus on precisely these issues (2:1–3:6; 7:1–23). In other words, Jesus is again the one who truly represents the core of Torah. Ecclesiologically, it also means that official Israel ("they"), in rejecting John and consequently Jesus by choosing Jesus' death rather than the life that he offered (Deut. 30:15 in Mark 3:4–6), had put themselves under the covenant curse. The scene is now set for the confrontation when the Lord whom they sought suddenly comes to his temple.

9:31

A. NT Context: More on the Suffering Son of Man. Immediately following the descent from the mountain and the failure of the disciples to deliver the demonized boy, Jesus makes his second passion pronouncement. This time he states that the Son of Man "will be given over into the hands of men" and twice mentions his death. Since we have examined most of the material earlier (see

commentary on Mark 8:31; 9:12 above), here we will consider only these newer elements.

In terms of the main textual contenders (as per previous discussions), the verb *paradidōmi* is found in Ps. 118:121 LXX (119:121 ET), but used in a prayer that such handing over might not happen. Daniel 7:25 LXX has both the verb and the modifying prepositional phrase when it speaks of "all things" being "given over into the hands" of the fourth beast (Theodotion has *dothēsetai*, whose implied subject seems to be the times [Goldingay 1989: 146]). Since "all things" arguably (but see below) includes the saints, Mark's Jesus might have been identifying the Son of Man with them in his being given over *eis cheiras anthrōpōn* (cf. the stone "uncut by [human] hands" in Dan. 2:34). At the same time, Isa. 53, already the weightiest influence in 8:31, twice explicitly speaks of the servant being given over for/because of Israel's sins (53:6, 12), though significantly the modifying prepositional phrase is not present (Gundry 1993: 506). Mark's dual mention of death (i.e., *apokteinō*), again only explicitly found in Isa. 53:8–9, 12 (LXX: *thonatos*), further strengthens the connection.

On this basis, and given the larger contextual and thematic parallels, it seems best again to see Isa. 53 as the main source, but with the additional influence of Dan. 7:25.

B. Isa. 52:13–53:12 in Context and in Judaism. See commentary on Mark 8:31 above.

1. Dan. 7:25 in Context. Daniel 7:25 belongs to the interpretation of the vision (7:15–27), specifically as it relates to the significantly different and therefore more important fourth beast (7:23–26). Here the brief account of the beast in the vision (7:7–8) is expanded, emphasizing its terrifying brutality and willful, godless destructiveness and focusing on the climactic confrontation between the fourth beast and the "holy ones" (see commentary on Mark 2:10 above).

Although the meaning of many of the details is problematic, and the beast itself is unidentified (see J. J. Collins 1993: 320–22; Goldingay 1989: 179–81), the focus is on the emergent but similarly unidentified little horn. He makes war against and oppresses the "holy ones" (who, I argued earlier, are at least faithful Israel), speaks arrogantly against God, and seeks to usurp God's control over history, which for a "time, times, and half a time" is "given into his hand" (7:21, 25). The antecedent of the unexpressed subject of "given" seems to be "times and law," not the holy ones, but, as we noted earlier, much depends on what the LXX's *panta* includes. But after a fixed time (see commentary on Mark 8:31 above) he will suddenly be cut short, and his authority will be utterly and permanently destroyed (7:26).

2. Dan. 7:25 in Judaism. In Judaism the fourth beast was widely identified as Edom/Rome ("Edom" being code for "Rome"; see, e.g., Josephus, *Ant.* 10.203–210; *Mek. Exod.* 20:15–19; *Tg. Neof.* Gen. 15:12–17; *Tg. Ps.-J.* Gen. 15:12–17; Lev. 26:44; Deut. 32:24; *Gen. Rab.* 44:17; 76:6; *Exod. Rab.* 15:6; 25:8; 35:5; 51:7; *Pirqe R. El.* 28; *Midr. Ps.* 80:5–6; *b. Šeb.* 6b; *b. ʿAbod. Zar.* 2b; *Pesiq. Rab Kah.* 4:9; *Pesiq. Rab.* 14:15), from whom the Messiah would deliver Israel (*4 Ezra* 12:10–34; *2 Bar.* 39:1–8; *Targum of the Prophets* on Hab. 3:17–18; *Lev. Rab.* 13:5; cf. *T. Mos.* 10:8; *Gen. Rab.* 99:2). Daniel's "time, times, and half a time" was variously interpreted as referring to Israel's Babylonian exile (*b. Sanh.* 97b), or the interval before Israel's final redemption (*b. Sanh.* 97b–98a), or a general period of testing (*Midr. Ps.* 10:1). (See also commentary on Mark 2:10; 8:31 above.)

C. The Use of Isa. 52:13–53:12; Dan. 7:25 in Mark. The second passion prediction highlights again the fundamentally different nature of Jesus' messianic self-understanding and, by implication, what this means for genuine discipleship. However, in a new development, perhaps adumbrated by the previous allusion to Ps. 49 and its polemic against the wealthy, beastlike wicked, the Dan. 7 phraseology "be given into the hands of" could intimate a subtle recasting of Israel's authorities in the role of the idolatrous fourth beast and its blasphemous little horn. If so, then the shift, although initially shocking, is not unwarranted. They too have spoken against Jesus, in whom, for Mark, God himself is especially present, and in rejecting his claim that his expulsion of demons signals the inauguration of God's royal new-exodus intervention, they have blasphemed the Holy Spirit (3:29). In resisting Jesus' mission and message they are, like the little horn, seeking to wrest control of history from God.

Why Mark has included the prediction at this point is less obvious. Most commentators see him simply resuming his narrative, but there might be more to it.

In between the descent from the mountain and this second passion prediction is the account of the demonized boy (9:14–29). For some, the crowd's unexpected "amazed" response can be explained only by Jesus' appearance displaying, Moses-like, residual effects of the transfiguration in a continuation of the new Sinai theme (Hooker 1991: 222–23; Marcus 1992: 82–83; cf. Gundry 1993: 487–88). However, there are other noteworthy features: (1) it is the only encounter with an unclean spirit outside of Mark's first main section; (2) it is the only mighty deed in Mark when all seven possible dramatis personae are present, which suggests that it is of some significance (C. D. Marshall 1989: 113); (3) it is the only detailed account that we have of the disciples' direct involvement in a healing; (4) it is the only time they fail (cf. the successes in 6:13, 30); and (5) in combination with the two healings of the "blind" (the only other "mighty deed" stories in Mark's "way" section), the restoration of a "deaf-mute" intriguingly echoes the idolatry metaphors of 8:17–18; cf. 4:10. As most commentators agree, the question is this: why this story, with these unique particulars, in this setting?

Since both healing-of-sight stories have a larger theological function—signifying the leading of blind Israel along Isaiah's new-exodus way (R. E. Watts 2000: 236–57)—and the transfiguration likewise represents a new Sinai, perhaps the disciples' failure to expel a "deaf-mute" unclean spirit has a deeper significance as well. Several commentators have already extended the Sinai parallel such that Jesus' descent from the glory of the mountain to encounter failure below echoes Moses' descent in Exod. 32 (Farrer 1951: 110; Hobbs 1958: 45–46; Swartley 1994: 103). This would cohere with the content of Jesus' rebuke where (1) *genea apistos* (9:19a) recalls God's complaint against Israel's long-standing fondness for idolatry (cf. Deut. 32:20 LXX; see Gnilka 1978–1979: 1:47; Hooker 1991: 223), and (2) *anechomai* (9:19b) is used both of Yahweh's frustration with Israel's idolatrous worship (Isa. 1:13) and in his promise to blind and deaf Israel, in the middle of an Isaianic new-exodus anti-idol polemic, that as he bore them from birth, so he will continue if they will but trust him (Isa. 46:4) (see Tödt 1965: 179; Martin 1972: 109). The sequence would also naturally fit the new-exodus setting overall, the journey section in particular, and the nexus between idolatry, unclean spirits, and literal and metaphorical sensory malfunction (see R. E. Watts 2000: 157; see also commentary on Mark 4:12; 8:18 above).

Obviously, once again the parallels are not exact. Nonetheless, they are strikingly congruent and suggest that the disciples' inability to deal with the "deaf-mute" unclean spirit is related both to their own idolatrous, blind and deaf condition (8:14–33) and to the fact that this kind of thing is driven out only by prayer. Intriguingly, the only other time Jesus mentions prayer to his disciples is in 11:22–25, where he assures them that having the "faith of God" (cf. *genea apistos*) will be sufficient to cast idolatrous Mount Zion, no longer fit to be a place of prayer (C. A. Evans 2001b: 195), into the sea (Telford 1980: 119).

In this respect, the location of the second passion prediction suggests that effective prayer against the unclean and idolatrous is predicated on "seeing" and "understanding" that the faithfulness which God seeks is expressed in imitating Jesus in cross-bearing discipleship (hence the later injunction that whenever praying, one should forgive others [11:25]).

D. Theological Use. On the assumption that the points made in 8:31 as to the unexpected means by which the messianic servant Son of Man will effect Israel's new exodus, the subtle shift in Jesus' language toward the human-beast kingdoms of Dan. 7 makes the widening gap between him and his opponents even more serious. Ecclesiologically, in resisting him they are siding with Rome, and the vindication of the Son of Man, when he comes with the clouds, will mean their utter loss of authority and final destruction.

9:48

A. NT Context: The Undying Worm. After the second passion prediction comes the most extensive body of teaching in Mark (France 1980), which in the context of a new Sinai suggests that it constitutes Jesus' new Torah for a new people of God. It begins with a series of stories that explain what it means for cruciform discipleship to be free of the unclean and idolatrous "leaven" of Herod, who executed John, and of the Pharisees, who reject God's holiness for their own. Greatness in God's kingdom means to be last and servant of all, to be concerned not with how one is

received, but with how one receives the lowliest (9:33–37 [in *m. 'Abot* 3:11 children's talk is likened to drinking wine at midday and consorting with the ignorant]). Competition and rivalry between camps is now excluded (9:38–40), and even the most humble act of kindness will receive its reward (9:41). The seriousness of this is underlined in the aphoristic warnings about stumbling and causing others to stumble (9:42–50): better to enter life maimed than to be cast into Gehenna, "where their worm does not die, and the fire is not quenched" (9:48). This is a close citation of Isa. 66:24, the changes being that for the two verbs, the MT's imperfects and LXX's futures become presents, and the LXX's second *autōn* ("their") is not present.

B. Isa. 66:24 in Context. As we noted earlier, Isa. 56–66 reflects the postexilic tension between, on the one hand, a continuing hope in the delayed new-exodus promises of Yahweh's glorious return (59:15b–20), the extension of the servant's ministry to his offspring servants (56:6; 65:13–15 [see Beuken 1990]), the restoration of Jerusalem (60:10–22; 62) in a new heaven and a new earth (65:17; 66:22), and the coming of the nations to its light (60:3; 62:2; 66:18–20), and, on the other hand, the continuing rebellious resistance of some within Israel to God's inbreaking rule (57:3–13; 59:1–8; 65:1–7, often drawing on the language of, e.g., chaps. 1; 28–30 to demonstrate their theological continuity with the preexilic nation [see Childs 2001: 446–48]).

Chapters 65–66 are designed to conclude not only the larger unit but also the entire book (Liebreich 1955–1957; Steck 1987; Tomasino 1993; Beuken 1991). Although the internal structure is problematic, the themes are relatively clear (see Childs 2001: 532–34). Whereas previously promises or curses fell on the nation as a whole, these chapters, drawing heavily on the lawsuit language of Deuteronomy (cf. Isa. 1; see Westermann 1969: 401–2; Blenkinsopp 2000–2003: 3:270, 275, 281), introduce a strong contrast between Yahweh's blessing on the humble and contrite offspring of the servant of Isa. 40–55 (65:8–26; 66:1–3, 10–14, 18–21) and his fiery judgment on the arrogant rebels, with their elitist pseudoholiness, who refuse his summons, neglect Torah, and seek to control their own destinies (65:1–7,

11–15; 66:3–4, 6, 15–16, 24) (see Goldingay 2001: 367; Blenkinsopp 2000–2003: 3:275).

The final three verses, 66:22–24, employing the language and imagery of chapters 1–2, unite and succinctly summarize the eschatological vision of the entire work (Blenkinsopp 2000–2003: 3:316–17; Childs 2001: 542). By way of invitation, they lay out two eternal destinies: participation in the expansive vision of all flesh coming to worship Yahweh (66:23; cf. 2:1–5) over against, not unlike Mal. 4:4–6, a final, chilling picture of the corpses of the rebels, "whose worm will not die, and whose fire will not be quenched" (66:24; cf. 1:2, 27–31; Jer. 4:4; 7:20; 2 Chron. 34:25). The imagery probably reflects the garbage dump in the Hinnom Valley (2 Kings 23:10) just outside Jerusalem, which eventually will become a metaphor for Gehenna (Oswalt 1998: 692–93). In the end, as Isaiah warned, "there is no peace for the wicked" (57:21).

C. Isa. 66:24 in Judaism. In Jdt. 16:17 the nations that rise against Israel will be given over to worms and fire, and in Sir. 7:17 the wise son is warned to humble himself greatly, "for the punishment of the ungodly is fire and worms." Similar language occurs frequently in accounts of the judgment of the wicked (e.g., *1 En.* 10:13; 26–27; 48:8–10; 1QH^a IV, 1–13; *4 Ezra* 7:36, 65–67; *2 Bar.* 59:10; 85:13; *Gk. Apoc. Ezra* 1:24; 4:19; *Sib. Or.* 1:103; 2:291; 4:186).

In the targumic and rabbinic traditions, Isa. 66:24 is associated with Gehenna (*Midr. Ps.* 12:5 [cf. *Tg. Isa.* 66:24]; *m. 'Abot* 5:20; *b. Sanh.* 100b; *Lev. Rab.* 32:1; *Num. Rab.* 23:5; *Lam. Rab.* 1:40; *Eccles. Rab.* 7:23), to which, according to one tradition and based on the participial form of "rebel," only persistent transgressors are assigned (*Midr. Ps.* 1:22; *b. 'Erub.* 19a). Because it is held that every prophet ends with words of peace to Israel, Isa. 66:24 must be directed, as in Jdt. 16, against the nations (*Pesiq. Rab Kah.* 13:14; *Midr. Ps.* 4:12; *Lev. Rab.* 32:1; *S. Eli. Rab.* 17; *S. Eli. Zut.* 12). In this respect, *Midr. Ps.* 149:6 on Ps. 149:7 also combines Isa. 66:24 with Mal. 4:1, noting these are nations, particularly Babylon, that have oppressed Israel. In likewise assigning the nations to Gehinnom (Isa. 66:24) because they toss up all kinds of wickedness (Isa. 57:20) to which the righteous are exposed, *Tanḥ. Lev.* 1:18 distinguishes between sins that are under human control (in-

volving mouth, hands, and feet) and those that are not (of eyes, ears, and nose).

But as Sir. 7 warned, faithless Israelites are also in danger, as noted above (8:38) in *b. Roš Haš.* 17a, where, also citing Isa. 66:24 of Gehinnom, Ps. 49:15 MT (49:14 ET) was applied to the particularly wicked—those who had led the masses astray, abandoned Israel, or stretched out their hand against the temple. Thus, before citing Isa. 66:24 in respect to sinners in Zion (Isa. 33:14), *Pesiq. Rab Kah.* 28:3 (= *Pesiq. Rab.* 52:3) contains a discussion of various means of averting judgment, including prayer, charity, turning to God in repentance, fasting, and a change of name, conduct, or residence.

D. The Use of Isa. 66:24 in Mark. Given Mark's Isaianic new-exodus schema, the Isaiah citation is not inappropriate. Like the rebels of Isa. 65–66, the Pharisees, with their elitist pseudopurity that falsely separates themselves from others (2:16–17; 7:1–2) and in fact rejects Torah (3:4–6; 7:6–13), along with Herod have rejected God's call (cf. Isa. 65:1–3, 4b), seeking instead to secure their own futures. But Jesus, already Isaiah's Suffering Servant, leads his "offspring servants" along the path of humility and contrition (neither themselves stumbling nor causing others to do so) that they must take if they are to continue his work of being a light to the nations (cf. Mark 10:42–44; Acts 13:47).

But unlike Isaiah, who addressed Israel, or the later tradition that applied Isa. 66:24 to the nations, Jesus addresses the warning to his newly reconstituted community, still struggling with its own "idolatrous" conceptions of being Israel (8:17–21; 9:14–29). Nor is the object of abuse the Torah, the temple, or the masses as in some traditions on Ps. 49:15 (see commentary on Mark 8:37 above), but rather one of the little ones who believes in Jesus (e.g., the solitary exorcist [9:38]) or oneself (cf. Jesus' warning to the Jerusalem scribes whose public denunciation of him threatens to stumble the crowds [see C. A. Evans 2001b: 72]). And unlike *Tanḥuma*, Jesus makes no distinction between foot, hand, and eye. Everything must be done (see C. A. Evans 2001b: 71, on 2 Macc. 7:4) to ensure the purge of "idolatrous leaven" lest it lead to the abuse of one's brother or sister, no matter his or her status.

E. Theological Use. The same themes continue to emerge. Eschatologically, Jesus' warning coheres with the coming of the new-exodus new heavens and new earth. Ecclesiologically, the much narrowed focus of Jesus' address suggests that the makings of a renewed Israel are found "in his name" (cf. 9:38), and increasingly his words constitute the new Torah. By the same token, merely following Jesus to Jerusalem is not enough. His "offspring servants" must follow his cruciform and servanthood manner of life, abandoning the idolatry of elitist self-sufficiency, whether of power or holiness, in which others are marginalized or devalued. Already he had warned against the abuse of Torah, reminding his opponents that Sabbath was made for people, not people for Sabbath (2:27), and that genuine Torah-observance was about doing good and bringing life (3:4). The same thought continues here: genuine purity is focused on how one treats the least.

9:49

A. NT Context: Salted with Fire. Directly following this warning, Jesus makes the profoundly enigmatic pronouncement, "Everyone will be salted with fire," which is commonly seen as an allusion to Lev. 2:13.

B. Lev. 2:13 in Context. Belonging to the opening unit (chaps. 1–3) of the first section of the book (chaps. 1–7), Lev. 2 describes the second of the three principal types of sacrifices regularly offered in Israel (cf. 2:3; see Levine 1989: 3). Although here a specially prepared grain offering, *minḥâ* in its original sense referred to tribute or a gift to show reverence (1 Sam. 10:27), homage (Gen. 32:14 [32:13 ET]), political friendship (2 Kings 20:12), or political submission (Judg. 3:15, 17), both to secure or retain good will (Milgrom 1991–2001: 196) and to bind the offerer to the recipient in an act of covenant solidarity (Hartley 1992: 33). If, as is likely, that idea was transferred across, then the offering expressed not only the subservient status of the worshiper but also that Yahweh as his treaty-suzerain was responsible for his well-being and protection (Wenham 1979: 69–70). Beyond this, partly because of its ubiquity, the precise purpose of the *minḥâ* is unclear, though it seems that the burnt element functioned as a memorial so that God might remember and thus bless the offerer (Hartley 1992: 32). Unlike blood sacrifices, it did not require

a priesthood or temple (Milgrom 1991–2001: 199–200, citing Jer. 41:5; *T. Levi* 3:6).

This "most holy" offering always included "the covenant of salt" (Lev. 2:13). Various proposals are made as to the meaning of this expression and why salt was used. For example, as a symbol of permanence, salt bespoke a binding covenant (Num. 18:19; 2 Chron. 13:5), or it was associated with solemn covenant-sealing meals (cf. Ezra 4:14; as in, e.g., Gen. 26:28–31; 31:54; Exod. 24:11, though salt is not mentioned; see Milgrom 1991–2001: 191; for the counterview, see Levine 1993: 449). In addition, its savory quality might also have played a part (cf. Job 6:6; Col. 4:6).

C. Lev. 2:13 in Judaism. Although according to Leviticus salting was specifically required only of cereal offerings, it seems to have been extended to burnt offerings (Ezek. 43:24; cf. Ezra 6:9; *Jub.* 21:11; 11Q19 XX, 13–14; Josephus, *Ant.* 12.140; *T. Levi* 9:14; *m. Mid.* 5:3; *Ord. Levi* 29, 37, 52; *b. Soṭah* 15a; *b. B. Qam.* 10b; *b. Zebaḥ.* 108a). According to the tradition in *Midr. Ps.* 20:8, this would cause God to remember them as one remembers a tasty meal. *Mek. Exod.* 12:1 states that before Aaron and David were specially chosen for the priesthood and kingship all Israelites were qualified, but afterward all others were eliminated citing as evidence the eternal covenant of salt in Num. 18:19 and 2 Chron. 13:15 respectively (both regarded as unconditional in *Midr. Ps.* 132:1, 3; cf. *b. Ḥul.* 133b). This suggests that "salt" marked not only permanency but special status before God (cf. *T. Sol.* A 18:34, where salt and olive oil drives out a demon).

Philo (*Spec. Laws* 1.271) and rabbinic tradition regarded the cereal offering as the poor person's burnt offering (*Lev. Rab.* 8:4; cf. *m. Menaḥ.* 13:11; *b. Menaḥ.* 110a; 104b; see Milgrom 1991–2001: 195–96), the point being that God graciously accepts any offering, no matter how humble, if given in love.

In a discussion on why God allows the righteous to suffer, *b. Ber.* 5a, having cited the obedient suffering of Isa. 53:10 (see commentary on Mark 8:31 above), argues that because covenant is connected both with salt (Lev. 2:13) and with Israel's sufferings (Deut. 28, esp. v. 69), then just as the salt savors the meat, so also suffering washes away sins.

D. The Use of Lev. 2:13 in Mark. Understandably, the precise meaning of Jesus' statement has proven elusive. In view of the warnings, it has been taken to refer to purification whereby just as every sacrifice needed salt to be acceptable, so too the disciples must be purified if they are to enter the kingdom (Hooker 1991: 233; C. A. Evans 2001b: 73), or to the sacrificial character of discipleship (France 2002: 384), not unlike *b. Ber.* 5a, where suffering is the covenant salt that purifies.

The significance of the fire is likewise unclear, and Mark nowhere else offers a comparable reference to fire to guide us (see the survey in Gundry 1993: 526–27). Among more recent serious contenders, it has been understood as (1) a metaphor for purifying suffering (Lane 1974: 349; France 2002: 384, given Jesus' passion predictions and the severity of the measures to be taken in 9:43–47; again cf. *b. Ber.* 5a); (2) a testing fire that will purify genuine disciples and consume apostates (Gundry 1993: 515; cf. Hooker 1991: 233); (3) the purifying eschatological fire of Mal. 3:2–3 (though on my reading, this describes John's activity, not that of Jesus) over against Gehenna's consuming fire (C. A. Evans 2001b: 73). The sense, then, would concern the purifying fiery cost of following Jesus (France 2002: 383) in which either these lessons will be learned or one will perish. This seems to be a valid perspective based on the use of salt in the first century.

The difficulty with these purification options, if an allusion to Leviticus is assumed, is that the *minḥâ* salt apparently does not signify purification, and in Leviticus it was applied only to the "most holy" *minḥâ* (which would rule out "salting" any but a disciple as well as the idea of sacrifice in general). Perhaps the point, then, is not what the salt does, but what its presence signifies: every cross-bearing and disenfranchised disciple (8:34–38 with Ps. 49), even the little one, is regarded by God as a *minḥâ*. He or she is a most holy offering to God, the embodiment of utter dependence on (again 8:34–38 with Ps. 49) and covenant loyalty to him (cf. Rom. 12:1). Consequently, anyone who defiles (stumbles) such a one would face severe judgment, and hence the preceding severe warnings (Jesus' use of Isa. 53, with its *'āšām* [53:10], already moves in this direction). This would be consistent with the general trend of the preceding material, where the focus of holiness

shifted from keeping Torah or temple (cf. 12:10, where the temple seems to be replaced by God's new people) to not abusing even the least of Jesus' disciples. "Least" would make the *minḥâ* allusion particularly appropriate, since it was commonly the burnt offering of the least—that is, the poor (cf. commentary on Ps. 49 in Mark 8:37 above). It would also stand in appropriate contrast to Jesus' warning against the "leaven" of Herod and the Pharisees, especially since in Lev. 2:11 leaven was expressly forbidden in these "most holy" grain offerings.

What of the "fire" with which every disciple will be salted? It could indeed refer to fiery testing or trials that everyone who embraces following Christ must endure (1 Pet. 4:12; 2 Tim. 3:12). In other words, the disciples' dealing with these issues is what it means to be God's most holy offerings. On the other hand, to complicate things further, why must fire signify testing? Although not explicitly described with the metaphor of fire in Mark, the promised Holy Spirit, associated with Jesus' coming (1:8), his mastery over unclean idolatrous spirits (3:29; cf. the disciples' failures in 8:17–18; 9:18), and presumably his embrace of suffering messiahship, is often connected with fire (Matt. 3:11; Luke 3:16; cf. Acts 2:3–4). From this perspective, Jesus' words might not so much constitute a warning as provide the positive rationale for the preceding: every cross-bearing disciple is a living "most holy" sacrifice soon to be irrevocably and exclusively "salted" to God by the fiery presence of the Holy Spirit (over against the fire of Gehenna) and therefore to be treated with the utmost care.

Given the enigmatic nature of Jesus' statement, the idea of humans having the Holy Spirit might even be an allusion to their restoration in God's image—in accordance with the pervasive Markan themes of sight, hearing, speech, and so forth (see Beale 1991; R. E. Watts 2002)—since one of the hallmarks of the animation of the deity's image was the indwelling of his fiery breath (Clines 1968: 81; Hart 1999: 322). If so, this would only heighten the seriousness of stumbling or causing another to stumble, an act of the worst sacrilege, and hence the severe measures taken to avoid this (9:43–47). On this view, then, Jesus declares that even the least disciple is God's most holy sacrifice (cf. Rom. 12:1; 1 Pet. 2:5), and each one will be salted by either the fiery purifying ordeal of cross-bearing discipleship or the fiery sanctifying presence of the Holy Spirit.

In the end, however, much has to be assumed (which is probably why Matthew and Luke omitted the saying altogether [note also the several textual variants]), given the evocative mix of metaphors and the apparently intentional ambiguity of the statement.

As most commentators agree, the salt metaphor shifts in 9:50. How could a fiery test lose its saltiness, and what would it mean to encourage the disciples to have fiery tests among themselves? It might, though, refer now to the raison d'être of the cross-bearing disciple: to savor or "cure" their relationships, so bringing peace (unlike the oppressive and leaven-ridden Herod and Pharisees).

E. Theological Use. If "salt," over against leaven, was intended to evoke the idea of the *minḥâ*, then it might imply a shift in the locus of reconstituted Israel's worship. Just as purity was more a matter of the person's heart than the food ingested (Mark 7), so here the emphasis moves from the *minḥâ* symbolizing dependence on God to the disciples' lives embodying it (see Rom. 12:1; cf. 1 Cor. 3:16; 5:6–7; 6:19). If so, then this marks the beginning of a move to a time when the defining characteristics of God's Spirit-indwelt people would not be temple, sacrifice, food laws, or Torah-observance, but rather the quality of their lives and relationships (cf. John 13:35).

10:6–8

A. NT Context: On Marriage and Divorce. Jesus' beginning to teach "beyond Jordan" suggests to some a new giving of the law by a new Moses in a new exodus (cf. Deut. 4:26; 8:8–11; see Farrer 1951: 113–14; Hobbs 1958: 45–46; Swartley 1994: 102–6). The Pharisees test Jesus by inquiring whether it is lawful for a man to divorce his wife (10:2). He asks them what Moses says (10:3), to which they respond, summarizing Deut. 24:1–4, that he allowed them to write a bill of dismissal and then send her away (10:4). Jesus challenges this understanding by appealing to a combination of Gen. 1:27/5:2 and 2:24, declaring publicly that no man can put asunder what God has joined (10:9) and then, privately to his disciples (cf. 4:10; 7:17), that divorcing one person and marrying another is adultery (10:11). Apart from the possible addition of the variant *autou*

(10:7a), and even with the textual uncertainty of *kai proskollēthēsetai pros tēn gynaika* (10:7b), all three Genesis texts are identical to the LXX, which, apart from the addition of *hoi dyo* for the unexpressed subject (10:8a), is identical to the MT.

B. The Composite Citation. 1. Deut. 24:1–4 in Context. After the prologue and preamble of Moses' second speech (Deut. 5–11), chapters 12–26 outline various laws given in Moab as Israel is about to cross the Jordan into the land (11:31–12:1) (see Tigay 1966: 117). Our passage belongs to a series of miscellaneous civil and domestic regulations (21:10–25:19). It is concerned not with divorce laws per se, which the Torah nowhere fully explicates but rather assumes (Craigie 1976: 305), but instead with a supplementary prohibition against a man remarrying his former wife if she was married to another man in the interval. The validity of the bill of divorce is assumed and, in a sense, incidental to the process, as are the grounds "if she displeases him." The following clause, "because he finds something obnoxious [*'erwat dābār*] about her," seems less a restriction than the most common example of "displeasure" and probably refers to offensive conduct (Tigay 1966: 222). It does, however, raise the question of how serious this displeasure could have been if he then remarries her. In any case, there is nothing to suggest that the grounds of the divorce are improper, since no financial restitution is involved (McConville 2002: 358). The reason for the law is not stated but might reflect a concern that if this practice were permitted, adultery might begin to appear less wicked (Tigay 1966: 222), or, perhaps preferably, it sought to prevent the woman from being treated as an object in subordination to the man's interests (see McConville 2002: 359–60).

2. Deut. 24:1–4 in Judaism. The only OT instance where this principle is clearly invoked is in Jer. 3:1, but here it is the husband, Yahweh, who is being abused (Craigie, Kelley, and Drinkard 1991: 51–52). In view of Deut. 24:1–4, Yahweh asks, how is it that his adulterous wife, Israel, incredibly taking his forgiving love for granted and yet abandoning him for prolific fornication, could possibly be restored?

Beyond this, two separate issues emerge. The implicit and broader matter concerns divorce in general, the validity of which Deut. 24 assumes, for which various parameters apparently existed, though only a few are mentioned in the Torah (elsewhere Exod. 21:10–11; Deut. 21:14; 22:19, 29), and which God himself had initiated without fault because of the prodigious promiscuity of his people (Hos. 1–3; Jer. 3; Ezek. 16, 23) (see Instone-Brewer 2002: 35–54; but see also Hugenberger 1994: 231–34). This is in keeping with Mal. 2:14–16, where God's hatred is directed not at divorce per se, but rather at unfaithfulness to one's marriage vows (Hugenberger 1994: 48–83).

The Dead Sea Scrolls are less clear but seem also to allow divorce (11Q19 XLIV, 4–5; LXVI, 8–11; despite 11Q19 LVII, 17–19; CD-A IV, 20–21) (see Instone-Brewer 2002: 65–72; *pace* Gundry 1993: 537; C. A. Evans 2001b: 81), as do Sir. 25:24–26, Philo, Josephus (see below), and the rabbis (who also discuss other aspects, such as the meaning of "write," what constitutes a "bill," whether witnesses are required, and whether the divorce can have conditions [e.g., *b. 'Erub.* 13b; 15b; *b. Sukkah* 24b; *b. Ned.* 5b; *b. Soṭah* 2b; *Sipre Deut.* 269], but these do not directly concern us). The woman could initiate, though not enact, the process (*m. Yebam.* 14:1; *t. Ketub.* 12:3; Josephus, *Ant.* 15.259 [see Gundry 1993: 543]). Generally regarded as "undesirable but sometimes necessary," the Hillelite "any matter" divorce very quickly became the most common procedure (Instone-Brewer 2002: 85–132).

The second and more immediate issue concerns the grounds for divorce based on Deut. 24:1's "indecent thing" (*'erwat dābār*). Neither the Dead Sea Scrolls nor other intertestamental writings say anything about this, but the tractate *Giṭṭin* exemplifies the rabbis' wrestling with the issue (see also, e.g., *b. Yebam.* 11b; 44b; 52b; 55b; 69a). Although there was general agreement on matters such as infertility, unfaithfulness, and neglect (material and emotional [cf. Exod. 21:10–11]), "no fault" divorces were the center of contention. Josephus (*Life* 426–427; *Ant.* 4.253), Philo (*Spec. Laws* 3.30), the school of Hillel, and Akiba took the law to mean "indecency" or "any matter" (treating *'erwat dābār* as two distinct items, with the latter including the wife ruining dinner or the husband finding a more attractive woman), while for the Shammaites, whose minority view eventually lost out, it concerned only "indecency" (*Sipre Deut.*

269; *m. Giṭ.* 9:10; *b. Giṭ.* 90a; *Num. Rab.* 9:30) (see Instone-Brewer 2002: 91–132). Both recognized that remarriage after a valid divorce was appropriate (Mur 20; *m. Giṭ.* 9:3).

3. Gen. 1:27/5:2; 2:24 in Context. Coming on the climactic sixth day of God's creational activity (as indicated by its extent, special affirmation, and the definite article marking the day number [*haššiššî*]), Gen. 1:27 accords the creation of humanity a special status (as indicated by being last in the ascending order, the exceptional divine jussive "let us," and the threefold use of *bārā'* [Sarna 1989: 11]). That only humans are designated "male and female" indicates that both genders are included in the image of God, and both are essential to fully articulate our humanity—hence the twofold blessing-instruction to be fruitful and multiply, to fill the earth and rule (1:28 [see Hamilton 1990: 139]). Genderedness is God's good gift, and its abuse is a serious affront to the holiness of God, whose image humanity, as male and female, bears. That the statement is repeated in 5:2 at the head of the great genealogy indicates its importance and fulfillment.

In between these two texts is the passage to which 2:24 belongs: the more focused account of the creation of humanity (2:4–25) and of woman (2:18–24). Two features stand out. Man is a social being and, as indicated by the story of the rib and that her name is a phonetic play on the one that he for the first time gives himself, needs woman to complete him (Sarna 1989: 23). To this creational reality is traced the institution of marriage as its sole appropriate expression (2:24). Since honoring parents is next to honoring God (see commentary on Mark 7:10 above), for a man to forsake them and cling (which is covenantal language [Deut. 4:4; 10:20; 30:20], as is also "flesh of my flesh" [Brueggemann 1970]) to his wife stresses the supreme sanctity of marriage (see Wenham 1987: 71). In other words, this is not merely descriptive, but rather, in the context of Torah, constitutes a divine decree.

4. Gen. 1:27/5:2; 2:24 in Judaism. The significance of marriage (e.g., Prov. 5:18–20; 31:10–31; Eccles. 9:9) is indicated by its use as a common metaphor for God's relationship to Israel (e.g., Isa. 61:10; 62:5; Jer. 3:1–3; 31:32; Ezek. 16:8; Hos. 2:14–23). Malachi 2:14–16's reprimand might be an allusion to Gen. 2:24 (Hugenberger 1994:

125–67), Tobit 8:5–6 looks to Gen. 2:18 for its understanding of marriage, as does, from a less happy aspect, Sir. 25:24–26, while 1 Esd. 4:20–25 testifies to the strength of the marital bond.

Especially noteworthy is the addition of *hoi dyo* in Gen. 2:24 LXX, which reflects a gloss widely attested across the ancient versions and suggests that marriage was increasingly seen as monogamous. In the Dead Sea Scrolls, Gen. 1:27 is invoked to argue just this (CD-A IV, 21), with Gen. 2:24 being the basis for marriage (4Q416 2 IV, 1; 4Q418 10, 5).

Among the rabbis, Gen. 1:27 is invoked in a discussion of human nature (e.g., *Gen. Rab.* 17:4). The apparent contradiction between the initial decision to make man (one) and the subsequent creation of male and female (two) generated various resolutions (e.g., *b. Ketub.* 8a; cf. *Tg. Ps.-J.* Gen. 1.27; *Gen. Rab.* 8:1; *b. Ber.* 61a; *b. 'Erub.* 18a; *Midr. Ps.* 139:5).

More commonly, Gen. 1:27 and 2:24 are cited separately or often together in support of marriage (*b. Mo'ed Qat.* 7b; 8b; 18b; 23a; *b. Git.* 43b) and procreation as a requirement thereof (e.g., *m. Yebam.* 6:6; *b. Mo'ed Qat.* 8b; 23a; *b. Yebam.* 61b). According to *b. Yebam.* 63a, a man who has no wife is incomplete, and in *Gen. Rab.* 17:2, to lack a wife is to be without goodness, joy, blessing, atonement, well-being, or a full life and reduces the representation of the divine image (cf. *Gen. Rab.* 18:1). Genesis 2:24 is cited also on matters of appropriate sexual relations (*y. Qidd.* 1:1 [IV.Y]; *Gen. Rab.* 16:6), questions concerning various aspects of adultery or improper marriages (*b. Qidd.* 13b; *b. Sanh.* 58a; *Gen. Rab.* 18:5), and issues of inheritance (*b. B. Bat.* 113a). On the other hand, reflecting an unhappy reality, *Gen. Rab.* 17:4 explains that God did not create woman from the beginning because he knew that man would bring charges against her, and so he waited until expressly asked.

C. The Use of Deut. 24:1–4; Gen. 1:27/5:2; 2:24 in Mark. One difficulty here is that Mark does not explain the potential dilemma that the Pharisees' test presupposed. It is unlikely that they knew Jesus' views when even his closest followers did not (10:10; cf. 4:10; 7:17, both of which evoke the idea of idolatrous hard-heartedness [cf. 10:5]). The Pharisees might be attempting to ensnare him politically in light of recent high-profile divorces (perhaps assuming that he held a view similar to John's [France 2002: 390]; note also the question about the coin [12:13–17]), to gather further evidence of his unorthodox views, and/or to marginalize him socially by getting him to defy popular opinion.

In the first century the primary question surrounding divorce in the public mind concerned what constituted valid grounds. Since it would make little sense to ask Jesus if divorce itself was lawful when everyone assumed that it was, the Pharisees' question is almost certainly truncated, the intent of it being this: is it lawful to divorce for any matter (the view that was dominant and considered more righteous) or only for indecency (for this and the following, see Instone-Brewer 2002: 133–67)? Jesus' response, even in its obviously abbreviated and minimal form, can hardly be what they expected.

When Jesus asks what Moses commanded, there is of course only Deut. 24. But for Jesus, Deut. 24 itself would not exist were it not for Israel's *sklērokardia* ("hard-heartedness" [10:5]). This particular word occurs only twice in the LXX, both regarding Israel (Deut. 10:16; Jer. 4:4; cf. Ps. 95:8 [94:8 LXX]; Ezek. 3:7]). Both texts involve idolatry, with Jer. 4 particularly addressed to Israel's prolific adulteries (see Ortlund 1996). For Jesus, the problem underlying people's divorcing of one another was their idolatrous adultery against God (France 2002: 391).

Then, turning to the two verses that played a central role in arguments for monogamous marriage (10:6–7), and which point Jesus underlines by emphasizing the *oi dyo* gloss (10:8a), he reads them in an entirely unexpected way: God intended marriage to be lifelong. Again he shifts the emphasis: since (the holy) *God* put the two together, let no (hard-hearted and adulterous) *human* separate them (which includes not only the immediate issue of formalizing divorce but also the prior faithlessness that occasioned it). And in citing God, he trumps their misconstrued appeal to Moses (cf. the debate on the appropriate number of children, which the Hillelites won for this very reason [cf., e.g., *t. Yebam.* 8:4; see Instone-Brewer 2002: 139]). In other words, a proper understanding of God's prior intention in Gen. 1–2 should have alerted them to the fact that the later Deut. 24 was not about what constituted a pious divorce, but rather about regulating the unacceptable problem that occasioned it in the first place (cf. Deut. 23:17–18 with Jer. 5:7; Prov. 6:26). Jesus' position, then, is that there are no "no-fault" divorces (10:9).

Jesus' private explanation to his disciples (10:11) reflects the expected outcome in a tradition that regards marriage as the preferred estate: subsequent remarriage. But because Jesus sees "no-fault" divorce as invalid and God's plan is for monogamy, then not only the woman but also, amazingly, the man, commits adultery against the spouse when remarrying.

As in previous debates on a point of law, Jesus' exegesis, even if novel, is straightforward. The law is upheld, and his opponents are challenged to adhere.

Two final comments are in order. First, if Jesus' final declaration (10:9) is taken to mean "no divorce" under any circumstances, then he is at odds not just with Moses, but with God, who himself was obliged to divorce Israel (i.e., the northern kingdom) at one point (Jer. 3:8). The fact that Jesus says nothing about non-"no-fault" divorces is probably best understood as an acceptance of those grounds as outlined in Exod. 21:10–11 (hence Matt. 19:9's exception and Paul's instructions in 1 Cor. 7:10–16). But, second, following Yahweh's example, divorce even in these situations is not mandatory, and reconciliation and forgiveness are much to be preferred.

D. Theological Use. Several unifying themes point to Mark's intentional placement of this account. First, no relationship is more susceptible to causing either oneself or a little one to stumble than marriage. For Jesus' cross-bearing disciples, the goal was no longer a righteous divorce, but rather the imitation of God's grace. Second, if my suggestion that "salting with fire" reflects the restoration of the image of God is heading in the right direction, then Jesus' appeal to texts that link genderedness with marriage and being made in God's image carries that theological fundamental into perhaps its most important concrete expression.

Given Mark's interest in Malachi's threat and John as Elijah, it might be, in view of the breach of marriage vows that the Pharisees' understanding of Deut. 24 aided and abetted, that he has included Jesus' criticism as a further indictment

on the very issue for which John was imprisoned (Mal. 2:14–16). From a new-exodus perspective, christologically, Jesus, the new Mosaic-Isaianic servant-teacher, continues to instruct his reconstituted Israel in the ways of the "new" Torah, focused on a self-renouncing, humble dependence on God (see Hugenberger 1995; R. E. Watts 2000: 252–57).

10:19

A. NT Context: The Ten Words and Eternal Life. If the story of Jesus and the children returns to the question of greatness and status in God's kingdom, but from the side of those who have none and can only accept it without question (10:13–16), the account of the rich would-be disciple addresses it from the other side. Jesus' redirection of the man's unparalleled use of "good" teacher (but cf. the later tradition in *b. Ta'an.* 24b) serves as a reminder that God's opinion is the only one that counts, and hence he points to the Torah (Hooker 1991: 241).

The list of commandments comes from the second, interpersonal half of the Decalogue (cf. Philo, *Decalogue* 121) and is given in the Hebrew order, employing *mē* plus the subjunctive (as opposed, generally speaking, to the LXX's order and *ou* plus the indicative). But Jesus transposes the command to honor parents to last place, perhaps so that its unusual position will attract attention, emphasizing its importance (see commentary on Mark 7:10 above) with its promise of life and thereby returning in part to the man's question (Gundry 1993: 561). Jesus also replaces "covet" with "defraud," perhaps because the man, being wealthy, might have defrauded his workers (cf. *apostrephō* in Mal. 3:5; Sir. 4:1; 34:22 [34:26 ET]), or perhaps emphasizing the need to care for one's wife (cf. Exod. 21:10; recall the question about marriage and divorce in Mark 10:1–9; see C. A. Evans 2001b: 96–7).

B. Exod. 20:12–16; Deut. 5:16–20 in Context. See commentary on Mark 7:10 above, where although the focus is on the fifth commandment, the overall significance of the Decalogue and its setting in both Exodus and Deuteronomy is discussed. As we noted there, covenantal love of Yahweh necessarily leads through honoring parents to love of neighbor, the basics of which the last five commandments articulate.

C. Exod. 20:12–16; Deut. 5:16–20 in Judaism. The Decalogue is, of course, central to Judaism, and an examination of the individual roles of each of the six commandments listed by Jesus is far beyond the scope of this study. But as Moses' final summons in his third and final speech in Deut. 30 makes clear, observing Torah was the path to life, good, and blessing (30:15–20). The equation of the Torah and the good is found in, for example, Amos 5:14; Mic. 6:8; and in *m. 'Abot* 6:3, which states, "Good is nothing else but the Law" (see also *b. Ber.* 28b).

In addition to the texts on the "two ways" (see commentary on Mark 3:4 above), the idea of finding life in Torah permeates the OT (e.g., Lev. 18:5; 25:18–19; 26:3–5; Deut. 5:33; 6:2; 11:8–9; 1 Kings 3:14; Neh. 9:29; Ps. 16:11; 91; 119; Prov. 6:23; Isa. 1:19; Ezek. 3:21; 18:5–9; 20:11; Amos 5:4–6; Mal. 2:4–5) and is echoed in the Apocrypha (e.g., 2 Esd. 7:17–21, 59[129]; Sir. 1:12, 20; Bar. 3:9; 4:1), Philo (e.g., *Prelim. Studies* 86–87), Josephus (e.g., *Ant.* 3.88; 6.336; 7.153), the Dead Sea Scrolls (e.g., 4Q185 1–2 II, 11–12; 11Q19 LI, 15), the Pseudepigrapha (e.g., *4 Ezra* 14:30), and the rabbinic writings, in which it is the presupposition (e.g., *m. 'Abot* 2:7; *b. Ber.* 56b; 61b; *b. Šabb.* 13a; *b. 'Erub.* 54a; *b. Yoma* 85b; *b. Mak.* 23b; *b. 'Arak.* 15b; *Exod. Rab.* 30:22; *Num. Rab.* 18:15, 16), and wherein it applies even to Gentiles (*b. B. Qam.* 38a; *b. 'Abod. Zar.* 3a; *Midr. Ps.* 1:18). Of particular interest is Philo's comment that abiding by the law of firstfruits (e.g., Exod. 23:16, 19; 34:26) results in abundance and a refined and luxurious life (*Spec. Laws* 1.153)—witness Mark's rich man—as opposed to Hanina ben Dosa's self-imposed poverty (*b. Ta'an.* 24b–25a).

Once the idea of the resurrection develops, that too is included in the rewards of keeping Torah (e.g., CD-A III, 15–20; VII, 4–6; CD-B XIX, 1; 1QS IV, 7; 1QH[a] IV, 15; 4Q181 1 II, 4; Wis. 5:15; 2 Macc. 7:9; 4 Macc. 17:9–18; *Pss. Sol.* 3:12; 9:5; 13:11; 14:2–3, 10; *1 En.* 3:8 [Greek]; 25:6; *Sib. Or.* 4:187; 5:503; *T. Levi* 18:11; Philo, *Decalogue* 49–50; *m. 'Abot* 2:7; *b. Ber.* 21a), and so both *Targum Onqelos* and *Targum Pseudo-Jonathan* on Lev. 18:5 take "life" to mean "eternal life."

Of course, this raises the question of what law was meant to be kept and how, and hence the debates among the various religious factions of Jesus' day.

D. The Use of Exod. 20:12–16; Deut. 5:16–20 in Mark. Given the diversity within first-century Israel of what constituted Torah-obedience and Jesus' burgeoning reputation as a teacher with unique authority (e.g., 1:28, 45; 3:7, 22), the rich man's pursuit of a ruling from him is understandable. Jesus' articulation of only the interpersonal elements of the Decalogue is consistent with his thoroughgoing concern that Torah is not just about loving God but also about doing good to all, even the little ones.

In stark contrast to the wicked wealthy of Ps. 49 who oppress the righteous (Mark 8:36–37), and in spite of the questions of some commentators, here is a man whose righteousness is attested by his scrupulous Torah-observance, which Jesus nowhere questions (on the possibility of such observance, see Phil. 3:6; *b. Yoma* 38b; *b. Šabb.* 55a; *Gen. Rab.* 22:6), his subsequent abundant blessing (cf. Philo, *Spec. Laws* 1.153; Sir. 31:8; *b. Ned.* 38a), and Jesus' love for him (France 2002: 403). He is, in effect, the archetype of Jewish righteousness. In the light of the inaugurated kingdom, however, everything has been realigned. If he wishes to gain eternal life, all his wealth, which was both the reward and the sign of his righteousness, must be relinquished to the poor (counter to later rabbinic teaching [*b. Ketub.* 50a]), whereby he would store up treasure in heaven (cf. Tob. 4:8–9; Sir. 29:10–12; *Pss. Sol.* 9:5; *2 Bar.* 24:1). And his obedience must now center not on Torah, but rather on the person and teaching of Jesus, who embodies that Torah (Mark 3:1–6; 9:7; cf. 10:28–30) and thus himself now binds Israel to Yahweh and gives Israel its identity (see commentary on Exod. 20:12 in Mark 7:10 above). Not surprisingly, then, Jesus here again upholds the Torah, only to place his person and authority above it (Hooker 1988: 223).

Mark's "he was dismayed" in 10:22 employs a rare word, *stygnazō*, all three occurrences of which in the LXX belong to laments over the utterly unexpected fall of the paragons of power and wealth as a result of God's judgment on their self-reliance (Tyre and its prince [Ezek. 27:35; 28:19]; Pharaoh [Ezek. 32:10]). Tragically, even this righteous man proves, in the end, to have been leavened by wealth's illusions (10:23–24; cf. Matt. 6:24). Although first in Torah and wealth, he is unable to place himself in utter dependence upon the

God who is present in Jesus, and so he finally will lose his soul and be last (10:31; cf. 8:35–37; see Hooker 1991: 243). On the other hand, for those who do leave all behind, there is, albeit with persecutions, the abundance of the new community, where even the least are well-received in this life, and eternal life in the world to come (10:28–30; cf. Bartimaeus who although a beggar abandons even his cloak, 10:50; and Deut. 24:13).

E. Theological Use. Christologically, having begun by reminding the rich man that only God can speak to the good and thus eternal life, in keeping with the transfiguration as a new Sinai and his words as the new Torah, Jesus' summons to leave Torah's blessings and follow him again puts himself at the center of reconstituted Israel. The nexus of righteousness is no longer Torah, but rather Jesus. Not only does he do what Yahweh alone does, but also his words are now the authoritative revelation of God's will, and obeying them and following him are now the path to the eternal life of Israel's long-awaited eschatological redemption.

10:33–34

A. NT Context: Mocked, Spat Upon, and Beaten.

After Jesus' response to the rich man's sorrowful departure (10:23–31), the scene changes. Mark returns to the new-exodus journey motif (*en tē hodō* [10:32a]) with Jesus walking on ahead to Jerusalem, but now with an increasing sense of foreboding among the disciples (*ethambounto, ephobounto* [10:32a]). Jesus next makes his third and final passion prediction (10:32b–34), considerably expanding on his suffering (for the other elements see 8:31; 9:31; cf. 9:12) and declaring that the Son of Man will be condemned to death (*katakrinō thanatō*), mocked (*empaizō*), spat upon (*emptyō*), scourged (*mastigoō*), and handed over to the nations (the latter being a common enough outcome of God's judgment and, although not echoing any particular text, suggesting that Jesus is undergoing Israel's exilic judgment on the nation's behalf [Bolt 2004: 56–58]).

While Ps. 21:16 LXX (22:15 ET) has *eis choun thanatou katēgages me*, and Ps. 117:18 LXX (118:18 ET) has *tō thanatō ou paredōken me*, Isa. 53 LXX has a far greater emphasis on the servant's death (53:8–9, 12), and that due to judgment (cf. *katakrinousin* in Mark 10:33), which occurs explicitly only in 53:8 (*krisis*).

None of the remaining three terms is found in any of the OT texts previously considered in the two earlier predictions (but cf. *ekmyktērizō* in Ps. 21:8 LXX [22:7 ET]), except for the last two, which occur only in the third Servant Song, in Isa. 50:6 LXX, where they describe the servant's affliction (*mastix, emptysma*) (see Moo 1983: 88–89; Marcus 1992: 186–90; the LXX omits the "cheeks" phrase). That neither the verb *mastigoō* nor its cognate noun is used in the passion narrative further supports an Isa. 50:3 allusion (why else include it?), as again do the larger Isaianic new-exodus setting and the already established links with Isa. 53's Suffering Servant (*pace* Gundry [1993: 576], who objects because of the absence of Isa. 50:6's *rhapisma*; it occurs, however, in Mark 14:65).

Interestingly, *katakrinō*, though common in the NT, occurs only rarely (five times) and late in the LXX, where it renders only one Hebrew word, the equally rare Niphal of *gzr* ("to be cut off from life" or, once, "to be decided by legal action"). Of the proposed "suffering" texts, this Hebrew form occurs only in Isa. 53:8 (*nigzar*), which makes *katakrinō* a reasonable allusion (the LXX has *airetai* [cf. John 17:15; Acts 8:33]).

B. Isa. 50:6 in Context. After the pivotal appointment of a new servant Israel (49:1–6[7]), and even with its two successive proclamations of new-exodus salvation (49:[6]7–13, 14–26)—the latter, in response to Zion's complaint (49:14), declaring the Yahweh-Warrior's commitment to deliver his people from the strong man Babylon (49:24–25; see commentary on Mark 3:27 above)—divorced Israel (see commentary on Mark 10:6–8 above) remains unrepentant (50:1–3) (see Oswalt 1998: 318). The exodus imagery ominously turns threatening, but now against God's recalcitrant people (50:2–3 [see Childs 2001: 394]), in contrast to whom stands the new faithful servant (50:4–9[11]). Whereas in 49:2 his mouth was a sharp sword, now he teaches words of comfort to the faithful because each morning his ear, unlike deaf Israel, is open to Yahweh's instruction (50:4). This instruction includes his obedient suffering (Oswalt 1998: 325) as Israel's previously confessed resistance to his message (49:4) breaks out, in 53:6, into the ugly violence of beatings (*mastix*; Heb. *nch* [cf.

Isa. 53:4]) and spitting (*emptysma*) (see Childs 2001: 394–95).

Nevertheless, setting his face like flint and trusting in God's sure vindication (cf. 52:13–53:12), in 50:8–9 he utters three defiant rhetorical questions replete with courtroom language (see Blenkinsopp 2000–2003: 2:321–22)—who dares contend with me, who dares accuse me, and who dares find me guilty?—the first of which ironically takes up the language of the Yahweh-Warrior's judgment on Babylon (49:25b) and employs it against the servant's opponents in Israel. Because God is his helper, they will be worn out and consumed (50:9). Then, 50:10–11 distinguishes between those who, still trusting Yahweh, walk in the fear and confusion of darkness and those who rely on their own wisdom, which ultimately will destroy them (Westermann 1969: 235; Childs 2001: 396).

C. Isa. 50:6 in Judaism. The Targum interprets the song as a reference to the prophets whom Yahweh raises early to send so that Israel might listen (50:5) and to teach the righteous who thirst for Torah (50:4), contrasting those who obey in spite of the darkness (50:10) and those who "grasp a sword" (50:11), apparently a reference to those who resort to violence.

Among the rabbinic writings, *t. B. Qam.* 9:31 G cites Isa. 50:6 as an example of extreme humiliation, while another tradition associates the verse with Isaiah's willingness to suffer and thus his great prophetic gift (*Tanḥ. Lev.* 4:13; *Lev. Rab.* 10:2; *Pesiq. Rab.* 29/30A:5; *Pesiq. Rab Kah.* 16:4; *Pesiq. Rab.* 33:3).

In *Midr. Ps.* 60:1 Torah is the one who is near to justify (cf. Isa. 50:8), and on its testimony (citing various promises) David dispossessed the nations. Similarly, for *S. Eli. Rab.* 18, Isa. 50:4–7 refers to one's dedication to study Torah.

D. Isa. 50:6 in Mark. With this third and final passion prediction, the new-exodus way of a suffering Messiah and cruciform discipleship approaches its conclusion. It balances the promises of 10:28–31 ("with persecutions") and stands in contrast to the following last grasp at power by James and John, which introduces the famous "ransom" saying. But why allude to Isa. 50:6 and the third Servant Song in particular? There are a number of parallels. First, this section in Mark is dominated by Jesus' teaching of his followers—a

Jesus who also communes early with the Father (1:35)—though in this case it is not Torah (cf. the Targum; see also *S. Eli. Rab.* 18), but rather his words that are the focus, and these likewise over against those who would use the sword (14:47). The third Servant Song most emphasizes the servant's role as teacher, and in the face of violent opposition, to the faithful within Israel and particularly over against those who rely on their own wisdom (in the Targum, those who grasp the sword). And just as the faithful in Isa. 50:10–11 do not understand and walk in darkness, so too the disciples (10:32b; cf. 10:26)

Jesus' astounding determination and assurance (10:32a) also parallels Isa. 50:4–9[11], the one song where the servant, confronted with violent opposition, most strongly expresses his confidence and comforts his disciples with his conviction of final vindication. And if in *Midr. Ps.* 60:1 God's word supported David in his conquests, so here great David's greater son (Mark 10:47 and Mark's use of Pss. 2; 110; 118) will dispossess the nations, though the focus is now on rebellious Israel (see commentary on Mark 9:31 above and Mark 14:62 below). If later tradition, referring to Isa. 50:6, considered Isaiah the greatest of all prophets because of his suffering, then so also Jesus.

It is interesting, too, since this is the first explicit mention of Jerusalem as the goal of the journey, that Isaiah's third Servant Song is immediately preceded by Yahweh's retort that Zion's unfaithfulness was what forced him to divorce her and that even now she has failed to respond. This too has been Jesus' experience (cf. the Jerusalem authorities in 3:22; 7:1; cf. 12:9).

E. Theological Use. Eschatologically, Jesus is again presented as Isaiah's servant, whose rejection is integral to God's new-exodus redemption of his people. Ecclesiologically, Jesus' disciples are therefore the faithful in Israel to whom God's ways again seem dark. Although not specifically mentioned here in Mark, this third song contains the strongest denunciation of those who reject the servant's instruction in favor of their own wisdom. Accordingly, both the rich man, as in the traditional interpretations of Ps. 49, and the chief priests and scribes will wear away and be consumed (Isa. 50:9).

10:45

A. NT Context: A Ransom for Many. Reflecting for the final time Mark's triadic pattern of prediction, misunderstanding, and teaching (see 8:31 above), James' and John's underhanded grab for greatness (10:35–40) and the rest of the Twelve's outraged response (10:41) are countered by Jesus' teaching on the servant nature of leadership in God's kingdom (10:42–44). His concluding statement, "The Son of Man came not to be served but to serve and to give his life a ransom for many" (10:45), encapsulates the wisdom of the new-exodus way, contrasting the sight provided by Jesus' salty new Torah over against the leaven that blinds Herod and the Pharisees, with which the journey began.

Because, for example, *diakonēsai* describes the servant's call, *dounai tēn psychēn autou* closely resembles Isa. 53:12's *he'ĕrâ lammāwet napšô* (LXX: *paredothē eis thanaton hē psychē autou* [cf. 53:10: *tāśîm 'āšām napšô*]), *lytron anti* and *'āšām* express the same fundamental idea, *psychē* is repeated three times (53:10–12 LXX), and *anti pollōn* is a particular feature of Isa. 53:11–12 (*lārabbîm, bārabbîm, rabbîm*; LXX: *pollois, pollous, pollōn*), it was in the past almost universally assumed that 10:45 derived from the suffering of the servant in Isa. 53:10–12.

But in the second half of the last century, under the critical analysis of M. D. Hooker and C. K. Barrett, that consensus largely collapsed (the following represents a summary of a more detailed assessment, R. E. Watts 1998; also, earlier, France 1982: 116–21; Moo 1983: 122–27). Taking the verse in two halves, interpreters objected that (1) the key word *diakoneō* is not found in Isa. 53; (2) in the NT it means "domestic service"; (3) the servant serves God, not people; (4) *diakoneō* is best explained by a contrast with Dan. 7's ruling son of man (Hooker 1959: 74–75; Barrett 1959: 4).

However, the problems that these objections raise are more apparent than real. In regard to objection 1: (a) although *diakoneō* is popular in the NT, it occurs only rarely and late in the OT—it is not found in the proposed Dan. 7 alternative either—which suggests this is yet another example of semantic change; (b) the range of Greek terms used to translate the Hebrew idea of service (cf. Symmachus's *latreuō* in Isa. 53:11) suggests that a rigid approach is mistaken; (c) that Isa. 53's *douleuō*

cannot form the passive, which is essential to Jesus' rhetorical contrast, requires the substitution of a word that can; (d) Mark's Jesus has already signaled in the parallelism of 10:43 (*diakonos*) and 10:44 (*doulos*) that for him, the two terms are synonymous. This last point largely invalidates objection 2. Nevertheless, in regard to objections 2 and 3: (a) that Paul's use of *diakoneō* cannot be understood apart from his being Christ's *doulos* indicates that the God/people dichotomy is a false one, as it is in Isa. 53:11, where the servant also serves the many (LXX: *eu douleuonta pollois*); (b) on the contrary, Paul's use of *diakoneō* when focusing on those who benefit from his being Christ's *doulos* suggests that it is a perfectly appropriate first-century choice to emphasize the servant's action when it benefits others. Finally, in regard to objection 4: granted that the serving Son of Man stands in clear contrast to the ruling figure in Dan. 7, this hardly tells against the use of Isa. 53 to explain how it is that the Son of Man comes to rule—that is, in Jesus' own creative exegesis, through his suffering service for others.

In regard to the second part of 10:45, *kai dounai tēn psychēn autou lytron anti pollōn*, even critics recognize that it is difficult to deny some parallelism with Isa. 53:12. Indeed, the idea's very uniqueness in the OT only strengthens the link with Mark 10:45. Nonetheless, it was objected that (1) *lytron* does not correspond to Isa. 53:10's *'āšām*; (2) although the *lytroō/lytron* group is central to Isa. 40–55's new-exodus redemption (*gā'al/gĕ'ullâ* in 41:14; 43:1, 14; 44:22–24; 52:3; cf. *pādāh* in 51:11), it is not connected to the servant (Barrett 1959: 5–6; Hooker 1967: 144; 1959: 76–78); (3) in any case, because (a) *anti pollōn* does not render either *lrbym* or *brbym* (Isa. 53:11–12), (b) *dounai tēn psychēn* better reflects *ntn npš*, and *lytron anti* likewise *kpr tḥt*, and (c) Mark's *dounai* (active) differs from the LXX's *paredothē* (passive), the closest parallel is instead Isa. 43:3–4, where Yahweh gives the (many) nations as Israel's ransom (Grimm 1981: 231–77; but see the criticisms of Vieweger and Böckler 1996).

Again these objections fail. In not distinguishing the means from the result, objections 1 and 2 miss the larger picture, in which it is precisely through the servant's becoming an *'āšām* (53:10) that Israel's new-exodus redemption is effected. In regard to objection 3: W. Grimm is right to note the link between *kōper* and *lytron*, but (a) *anti pollōn* is a perfectly acceptable interpretive rendering of how the servant benefits "the many" whose place he takes (as Grimm states, *pollōn* alone is sufficient to evoke Isa. 53); (b) Mark's active *dounai* versus the LXX's passive *paradothē* merely reflects the MT, where the servant actively pours out his life (53:12b). However, even if the concept, if not the language, of exchange is present in both passages, Isa. 43, which seems to reflect the handing over of these nations to Cyrus, contains no hint of self-giving service or of death, and in the overall context of Isa. 40–55 it is surely Isa. 53, not Isa. 43, that inaugurates Israel's new exodus. Focusing on Isa. 43 also misses the link between Israel's redemption/ransom and the servant as Israel's *ʾāšām*.

In other words, the two fundamental problems with these criticisms are that they, first, downplay or ignore the larger Markan context and, second, fail to recognize that 10:45 is not a translation of Isa. 53:10–12, but rather is Jesus' own interpretative summary statement thereof as it concerns his mission (France 2002: 421). Thus, although Mark's presentation of Jesus has drawn on several OT figures, the combination of his overall Isaianic new-exodus schema, the exclusive role in Isaiah of the servant's suffering in facilitating that new exodus, and the primary influence of that servant's suffering (Isa. 50; 53) in shaping the language of Jesus' two previous passion predictions constitutes a formidable prima facie case that his serving by giving his life to ransom many also derives from Isa. 53. Add to this the unique combination of conceptual parallels between Mark 10:45 and Isa. 53, and it is quite difficult to avoid the conclusion that Isa. 53 is here yet again the fundamental influence (see C. A. Evans 2001b: 120–21).

B. Isa. 53:10–12 in Context. Having discussed this earlier (see commentary on Mark 8:31 above), I will concentrate here on Isa. 53:10–12, and particularly the connection between Israel's redemption and the servant's being made an *ʾāšām* (53:10). Whatever iniquities the servant bears, they cannot be preexilic, since those have already been dealt with (cf. Isa. 40:2; see Childs 2001: 297; Blenkinsopp 2000–2003: 2:180; Baltzer 1999: 52). Even so, it is abundantly clear from the increasing conflict between Yahweh and his rebellious and "idolatrous" blind and deaf ser-

vant Jacob-Israel that little has changed (see R. E. Watts 1990a). The crisis erupts in the series of disputations that conclude the first section, Isa. 48 (see Schoors 1973: 283–94). Yahweh accuses Jacob-Israel, who has seen many things but not responded and who has treated his Torah with contempt (e.g., 42:18–25; 46:12; 48:4, 6–8), of high-handed rebellion and swearing falsely in his name (48:1–2 [see Oswalt 1998: 261]; 45:23). This has caused Yahweh's name to be profaned, and it would have led to Israel's destruction, had he not shown mercy (48:9–11; cf. Ezek. 17 [see commentary on Mark 4:32 above]; see Blenkinsopp 2000–2003: 2:290). So serious is this breach that in spite of the continuing offer of redemption (48:20–21), the reality is that "there is no peace for the wicked" (48:22), and thus Yahweh appoints a new servant (49:1–6[7]) (see Childs 2001: 382–84).

How does this relate to the servant's being an *ʾāšām*? Although as yet imperfectly understood, not least due to the variation in meaning in Israel's scriptures (see Kellermann, *TDOT*, 1:429–37), when considered in the light of the above context there are two basic options (Blenkinsopp 2000–2003: 2:354). First, the *ʾāšām* was, among other things, involved in the ritual purification of the leper, reintegrating him into the community from which he had been exiled (Lev. 14:1–32). Its gravity is evident in that even though the burnt and sin offerings are reduced for the poor person, the guilt offering remains a lamb. The references in Isa. 53:3–5 to the servant's diseases and appalling disfigurement as he bears Israel's exilic curse (cf. Lev. 26:14–45; Deut. 28:59–61; see Ceresko 1994), understood in later tradition as leprosy (note Aquila's *haphēmenon*; Vulgate: *quasi leprosum*; *b. Sanh.* 98a, b; see Jeremias 1967: 690), might indicate that his lamb-like death effects "leprous" Jacob-Israel's purification and recall from exile (also *NIDOTTE* 1:563).

Alternatively, the *ʾāšām* also atoned for the desecration of *sancta*, including the violation of Yahweh's holiness by deliberately swearing falsely in his name and thereby making him an accomplice to the fraudulent behavior (cf. Ezek. 17:18–20; cf. Philo, *Spec. Laws*, 1.255; 4.31–32; *m. B. Meṣiʿa.* 4:8)—for example, in a court of law or preeminently by engaging in idolatry, which constitutes rebellion (cf. 46:8; 48:8; see Milgrom

1991–2001: 1:347–49; 365–73). This is equally, if not more, appropriate because Jacob-Israel, called to be Yahweh's witness (e.g., 43:10–12; 44:8), had not, because of their idolatrous "blind and deaf" condition (note 48:4's "neck of iron" and "forehead of brass"; see Beale 1991; see also commentary on Mark 4:12 above), borne true testimony, even while invoking Yahweh's name (42:18–25; 48:6–7). In such a case, the individual concerned had to bring an 'āšām and to verbalize remorse (cf. Philo, *Spec. Laws* 1.235–238; *b. Ketub.* 42a; see Milgrom 1991–2001: 1:365). In Isa. 53 this action is bifurcated: since rebellious Jacob-Israel is in no position to make restitution for their guilt, God both occasions and accepts true servant Israel's obedient suffering instead (cf. Janowski 2004: Oswalt 1998: 402) while the repentant within Israel do the one thing they can, voice their remorse (53:4–6), thus laying claim to the 'āšām for themselves (see Childs 2001: 418).

In Isa. 52 Yahweh declared that Israel would not be redeemed with money, and that in response to his name being despised on account of Israel's captivity, he would have mercy on Zion by baring his arm in the sight of the nations (52:3–10). This is precisely what follows in the fourth Servant Song where Yahweh's arm is revealed. In this "new thing" (48:6), this unprecedented act of mercy, Yahweh accepts his new servant's faithful and obedient submission to Jacob-Israel's abuse, even "unto death," both as bearing Israel's exilic curses and as an acceptable 'āšām for their high-handed infidelity. The demands of justice are met. The way is opened for blind and deaf Israel's new-exodus redemption, which Yahweh, for the sake of his honor (42:8; 43:20; 48:11), has continually promised (e.g., 41:14; 43:1, 14; 44:6). It is this extraordinary turn of events to which the speakers in Isa. 53:1–11a bear confessional witness—to whom has the arm of the Lord been revealed?—and that leads to the emergence of more servants (54:17) (see Beuken 1990). This, then, is finally the way of the Lord (40:3), the way of his unexpected justice (40:14), a way that blind and deaf Israel did not know (42:16), but in which way Yahweh will teach them to go (48:17).

The next question concerns the identity of "the many" who benefit from the servant's suffering (53:11–12). In the psalms "many" usually refers to those who observe the suffering petitioner

(cf., e.g., Ps. 3:1–2; 4:6; 31:13; see Childs 2001: 413), and so too here. The "many" first appear as onlookers in 52:14a and then again in 52:15a, though now as "many nations" (cf. 42:1; 49:7; see Blenkinsopp 2000–2003: 2:349). On the other hand, the speakers of 53:1 must at least include Israelites, who also looked on (53:4b). Consequently, since 53:12–13 follows the servant's being made an 'āšām, then "the many" seems to refer to all those, whether from Jacob-Israel or the nations, who in making the necessary confession of sin are then included among the offspring of the servant (e.g., 54:1, 17; see commentary on Isa. 56:7 in Mark 11:17 below). As it was in the first exodus, where both Israelites and a mixed multitude were redeemed, so here in the second.

C. Isa. 53:10–12 in Judaism. See commentary on Mark 8:31 above. A similar use of "many" recurs for the righteous (and the wicked) in Dan. 11:34; 12:2–4, 10 and might reflect Isaiah (Ginsberg 1953; J. J. Collins 1993: 393; Lucas 2002: 295). The Qumran sectarians also designate themselves as "the Many" (cf., e.g., CD-A XIII, 7; XIV, 7–12; 1QS VI–VII; 1Q28b IV, 27; 1QH[a] VII, 14; XII, 27–28; see Werner 1981), but even with their self-defining use of Isa. 40:3, an Isaianic background is uncertain. The reaction of the kings (Isa. 52:15) might find an echo in the reaction of the oppressors to the vindication of the righteous in Wis. 5:2 and in the revelation of the messianic Son of Man in *1 En.* 62:3–5. Finally, *y. Šeqal.* 5:1 [II.A–B] assigns Rabbi Akiba a place among the righteous many of Isa. 53:11, apparently on the basis of his fidelity to Torah.

D. The Use of Isa. 53:10–12 in Mark. Although expressing some general thematic commonalities, the differences between Jewish tradition and the Markan Jesus' language suggest that his reflection on Isa. 53 is largely his own. The parallels between Israel in Isa. 40–55 and in Mark are clear. In Mark, although professing to be loyal to Yahweh and his Torah, Israel's blind and deaf (4:12), hypocritical (7:6–13), and impure (8:15 [leavened]) leadership has both grieved the Holy Spirit (3:29), making Yahweh their enemy, and resolved to do violence to his servant (e.g., 3:6; 8:31). Even Jesus' disciples are infected (8:17–18; 9:19): following a soon-to-be crucified Messiah, they squabble over preeminence (9:34). As in Isaiah, Israel's new-exodus redemption can come only through Yahweh's utterly unexpected "way" of a suffering servant. Jesus' statement, appropriately at the conclusion of Mark's "way" section with its three passion predictions, is simply a concise summary of how his death as Isaiah's servant effects Israel's redemption. The purification of Israel that contemporary interpretations of Ps. 2 anticipated (see commentary on Mark 1:11 above) will come about through Jesus' bearing of Israel's guilt. As in 8:35–36, alluding to Ps. 49:7–9, where regardless of wealth or power one could not ransom one's life (*lytrōsis tēs psychēs*), cross-bearing discipleship is the way that reconstituted Israel must take if they are to live (8:34).

Already the Son of Man, anticipated as the eschatological messianic ruler and judge whom all will serve, had unexpectedly exercised God's authority on earth to forgive sins (2:1–12). Now he subversively exercises the same authority by serving in the climactic laying down of his life as a ransom for many, and he bids his disciples to exercise their leadership likewise (10:42–44).

Finally, the inherent logic of Jesus' interpretation of Isa. 53's *'āšām* is that participation in the many is determined not by conformity to a particular version of Torah-observance (as per, e.g., Daniel, Qumran, Rabbi Akiba), but rather by confession of the significance of Jesus' death.

E. Theological Use. Soteriologically, Mark's Jesus declares that he dies for Israel's sins (cf. 1 Cor. 15:3), as indeed is effectively the case in Isa. 53:4–6. Eschatologically, by bearing in his body the guilt offering owed because of the sins of God's fraudulent and impure people, Jesus in his death marks the inauguration of Israel's return from exile. All that is needed, as Mark's opening summary of Jesus' message declares, is to repent and believe (1:14–15; cf. Rom. 10:9). The new Torah of self-giving cruciform love, toward both God and neighbor (12:29–31), stands at the heart of this new people of God. Not only is it a repudiation of the leaven of self-reliance, whether of power or wisdom (cf. 1 Cor. 1:18–25), but also it embraces the utterly unexpected "new way" of God's extraordinary and entirely undeserved grace (cf. Eph. 2:8; 2 Tim. 1:9), which God has shown for his own name's sake and for which justice the nations long (cf. 2 Cor. 4:15; Phil. 2:11; Col. 1:27). In such ways reconstituted Israel's new

leaders must walk (cf. Mark 12:9; also, e.g., 1 Cor. 4:1–13; Phil. 2:6–11; 1 Pet. 5:1–6).

11:9–10

A. NT Context: The One Who Comes. As Mark's new-exodus "way" began with a healing-of-sight story, so likewise it concludes (10:46–52). Absent the need for a second touch, the story is awash with echoes of Isa. 35:3–10 as Jesus, now-seeing Bartimaeus, and the rejoicing crowds fulfill the new-exodus return of Yahweh and his healed people to Zion (R. E. Watts 2000: 309). Looking back, in combining the "Son of David" acclamation with the beggar's request "to see," the story stands in poignant contrast to Peter's initial "leavened" messianic confession and presumption "to see" better than Jesus (8:14–33), to James' and John's equally "leavened" request for status at the end (10:35–40), and to the rich man who departed sorrowing (10:22). The former need to be less concerned with status and instead, like the former "son of uncleanness," to ask for mercy and the sight to walk in Yahweh's holy way and so become "sons of honor" (the name "Bartimaeus" can mean both [Just 1998; cf. Gundry 1993: 599]). The latter needs to be willing to leave his wealth as Bartimaeus the beggar left his cloak (10:50).

Looking ahead, this first public "Son of David" confession prepares for a return in the "triumphal entry" to the more explicit Davidic themes evoked earlier by Ps. 2 at Jesus' baptism and transfiguration (see S. H. Smith 1996; Matera 1982; Catchpole 1984). Although Jesus' entry into Jerusalem has echoes of formal entries of the ancient world (Catchpole 1984; Duff 1992), our interest is in scriptural influences, and while the emphasis on the colt evokes various royal, messianic, and even divine entry motifs (cf., e.g., 1 Kings 1; Zech. 9:9–10; 2 Sam. 6; see Kinman 1995; on Gen. 49:11, see Blenkinsopp 1961), Mark does not pursue them. His first clear OT reference is instead also his first explicit citation of a psalm. As the exultant pilgrim crowd escorts Jesus toward Jerusalem (11:8–10), the opening lines of their salutation come from Ps. 118 [117 LXX]. "Hosanna," a transliteration of the Hebrew "save now" (*hôšî'â nā'*), reflects 118:25's "Please, Yahweh, save now; please, Yahweh, grant success now," and the first "Blessed . . ." is a direct quotation from the first half of 117:26 LXX, which accurately translates the Hebrew. But whereas 118:26b MT reads,

"We bless you [LXX: 'have blessed you'] from the house of the LORD," Mark's crowd blesses the coming Davidic kingdom.

B. Ps. 118:25–26 in Context. As part of the fifth and final book (Pss. 107–150), Ps. 118 concludes the Hallel collection (Pss. 113–118). The psalm itself appears to have been composed as a "royal song of thanksgiving for military victory" that later was incorporated into a processional liturgy (e.g., 118:1–4, 29; cf. *Tg. Ps.* 118, *b. Pesaḥ.* 119a; see Allen 1983: 122, 124). The singer is unidentified, but the fact that he leads the community in thankful celebration for his triumph over the encircling hostile nations (118:10–12) strongly suggests that he is a Davidic king. Reciting how he was threatened on all sides (cf. Ps. 2:1–3) and employing the exodus imagery of Yahweh's mighty right hand, the king rejoices in the Lord's intervention on his behalf (118:14–18; cf. Exod. 15:2, 6; see Dahood 1970: 155). Surrounded now by glad victory songs from the righteous (118:15–16), he approaches the temple and requests entrance from the gatekeepers (118:19) who readily admit him to the place where "conformity to the covenant is enshrined" since covenant blessing so clearly rests upon him (118:20) (see Allen 1983: 125).

Once he is inside the temple, his thanksgiving (118:21) is joined by the congregation (118:22–25), to whom a group of priests respond by blessing, "from within the house of the LORD," the king who comes in his name (118:26; cf. Ps. 2:8), directing the procession to the altar (118:27). The whole concludes with a final declaration by the king (118:28) and a communal rejoinder (118:29). If Ps. 2 celebrates the promise given to the Davidic king in the face of the threatening nations, then Ps. 118 is its victorious realization.

C. Ps. 118:25–26 in Judaism. Although the evidence is late, its widespread nature suggests that Ps. 118 was sung during the Second Temple era on Passover Eve (*m. Pesaḥ.* 10:6) and subsequently integrated into other feasts in which 118:25 in particular was recited (*b. 'Arak.* 10a; e.g., Tabernacles: *m. Sukkah* 3:9, 11; 4:5; *y. Ber.* 8:8 [II.H]; *y. Sukkah* 3:8 [H]; 4:3 [D]; *b. Sukkah* 37b–39a; 45a; 45b; *Pesiq. Rab Kah.* 27:5; 51:7; *Midr. Ps.* 17:5). The Passover connection reflects the exodus theology that dominates the collection,

hence the title "the Egyptian Hallel" (*b. Ber.* 56a; *b. Pesaḥ.* 117a; cf. *Mek. Exod.* 13:1–4; *Midr. Ps.* 118:9). Consequently, Ps. 118, with its focus on the temple and Zion as the goal of the new exodus (Zenger 1998: 91–92; Schröten 1995), became a communal anticipation of Israel's eschatological redemption under a royal Davidide, as indicated by the Targum's numerous expansions (118:26, 28; cf. 118:22–25).

In a parallel to the crowd's salutation, 4Q252 V, 3–4 speaks of the "coming" of the Branch of David. In the Targum (see further commentary on Mark 12:10–11 below) 118:19's "gates of righteousness" become the gates of the righteous city, which stand in parallel to the gates of the sanctuary and indicate the close link between city and temple.

"Our father David" is also found in various rabbinic traditions where David is honored along with the patriarchs (*Der. Er. Zut.* 1; *b. Mo'ed Qat.* 16b; *Midr. Ps.* 18:8; cf. Acts 2:29; see C. A. Evans 2001b: 145–46). In this literature two further themes emerge. The fourfold recitation of Yahweh's steadfast love (118:1–4) occasioned considerable exposition noting that praise was all that Israel could offer in view of God's wonderful acts and bountiful mercy (*Midr. Ps.* 118:3–6; *b. Sukkah* 88b). The Hallel psalms also continued to play a significant role in eschatological expectation, with Ps. 118 being associated with the last judgment (*Midr. Ps.* 118:10) and, as was Ps. 2, the final war against Gog and Magog (*y. Ber.* 2:3 [IV.I]; *Midr. Ps.* 118:12; 26:6; *Pesiq. Rab.* 51:7), messianic salvation (*y. Ber.* 2:3 [IV.J]; *b. Pesaḥ.* 119a; *Pesiq. Rab.* 36:1; *Midr. Ps.* 118:22 [cf. 118:24]), the joyful restoration of Jerusalem (*Pesiq. Rab Kah.* 17:5; *Lev. Rab.* 37:4 [cf. 30:5]), the rebuilding of the temple (*y. Ber.* 2:3 [V.C]), and the world to come (*Pesiq. Rab Kah.* 27:5; *Midr. Ps.* 26:6) (see Jeremias 1977: 256n3; Berder 1996: 170–241).

Granted that most of these references are late (Fitzmyer 1987), their widespread occurrence, the pervasive new-exodus aura of the Hallel in general, that the central individual in Ps. 118 is almost certainly a Davidic figure, and Mark's unselfconscious messianic application within a new-exodus framework nevertheless suggest that the eschatological perspective was an early one (see Wagner 1997).

D. The Use of Ps. 118:25–26 in Mark. The various themes of Mark's narrative now begin to come together, particularly around the temple, the goal of Isa. 40 and Mal. 3, and beginning with Ps. 118 and continuing all the way to Jesus' death (15:29–30, 38) (see Juel 1977: 127–39). Mark's thoroughgoing integration of new-exodus and Davidic themes makes entirely understandable the crowd's blessing of "the coming kingdom of our father David" (Ps. 118:25). The Hallel's larger new-exodus associations are only heightened by the Passover setting, the very feast on which messianic new-exodus deliverance was anticipated (*Mek. Exod.* 12:42; cf. *Tg. Ps.-J.* Exod. 21:42; *Frg. Tg.* Exod. 15:18; later, *Exod. Rab.* 18:12 on 12:24; also the messianic interpretations of Isa. 42; 53, as above).

As we have noted, Jesus' exorcisms (especially his drowning of the demonic legion in the sea in 5:1–20 [see Derrett 1984b]), forgiveness of sins, healings of the lame, deaf, mute, and blind, feedings of the crowds, and control over the sea testify to the victorious inauguration of Isaiah's new exodus (see Catchpole 1984: 322–24)—exactly the kinds of wonders and merciful acts for which, in the rabbinic tradition on Ps. 118, the nation could only give thanks as do the joyful pilgrims ("Hosanna" is as much a thankful salutation as a plea). At the same time, Jesus, as the authoritative Son of Man, is also Israel's Messiah. But then, as in the psalms, the Davidic king's victories are only a participation in and an extension of God's power over creation (cf. the exodus in Ps. 89; see Roberts 2002). And just as Ps. 2 promised the defeat of the nations (see commentary on Mark 1:11 above), so too does Isaiah's new exodus. Reflecting Davidic theology (Wilson 1986: 48–60), Yahweh's superiority over the nations and their idols is evident in his supreme authority over creation, demonstrated notably at the exodus (cf., e.g., Isa. 43:14–17; see R. E. Watts 2000: 160).

If at the outset of Mark, Ps. 2 designated Jesus as the agent of God's promised victorious intervention (1:11), which in later tradition focused on the restoration of Jerusalem and the temple (see commentary on Mark 1:11 above), then here Ps. 118 fittingly applies to this victorious Davidic messianic S/son of God coming in splendid joyful procession to the temple. Simultaneously, it is also the climax of "the march of the divine warrior," the coming of Yahweh himself to a restored and glorious Jerusalem, which Mark's opening citation of Isa. 40:3 and Mal. 3:1 heralded (cf. esp. the Yahweh-Warrior's intervention on behalf of restored Zion in Isa. 59:15b–21 and 63:1–6, which form an inclusio around chs. 60–62; see R. E. Watts 2000: 296–304; cf. Duff 1992). On this Passover, God indeed has acted mercifully to save.

There is, however, also a profound irony. Unlike Ps. 118, Jerusalem's response is bitterly divided. Ominously, having consistently opposed Jesus (e.g., 3:22; 7:5) and therefore being under God's severe judgment, which in the past meant laying waste the city (Isa. 6:9–11; 29:13–14 [cf. 29:1–4]), the temple hierarchs and the Jerusalem leadership offer no welcome, nor does any blessing come from the house of the Lord (cf. Ps. 118:26b). From the perspective of 4Q174 and *Pss. Sol.* 17 (see commentary on Ps. 2 in Mark 1:11 above), the defiling elements from which Jerusalem and the temple must be cleansed are primarily Israel's rebellious leadership (the Maccabean entries to cleanse and rededicate the temple were also accompanied by branch-bearing followers [see R. E. Watts 2000: 330–31]). Nevertheless, in keeping with Ps. 118 and the formal entry pattern, Jesus enters the temple. However, having surveyed it all, most likely in preparation for his action there the next day, Israel's unwelcome messianic king returns to Bethany (11:11).

E. Theological Use. Christology, eschatology, and ecclesiology are again intertwined. Psalm 118 presents Jesus as Israel's Davidic messiah, in whom Yahweh's authority is uniquely invested, returning victoriously from defeating the nation's oppressors, in this case the demonic. Eschatologically, this signals the climax of Israel's hopes of messianic restoration, and in particular, that of the temple. Ecclesiologically, to reject Jesus is to be an enemy of the Lord's anointed and therefore equally liable to the wrath of the Lord, who enthroned him as his Son.

11:17

A. NT Context: The Cursed Temple. The juxtaposition of Jesus' identity and his rejection by the Jerusalem authorities almost certainly explains Mark's nested chiastic structure (see commentary on Mark 4:12 above), with its interleaving of Davidic, cursed fig tree, and temple motifs:

Jesus, "triumphant" Davidic king (Ps. 118:25–26) (11:1–11)
    Cursing of the fig tree (11:12–14)
        Jesus' temple demonstration (Isa. 56:7/Jer. 7:11) (11:15–19)
    Withered fig tree, and mountain-moving (11:20–25)
Jesus, rejected but vindicated Davidic king (Ps. 118:22–23) (11:27–12:12)

The cursing of the fig tree has long been recognized as a prophetic act (cultic aberration issues in judgment against fig and vine [cf., e.g., Jer. 5:17; Hos. 2:12; 9:16; Amos 4:9; see Telford 1980: 132–63]). Flourishing in appearance but lacking even a single bud (cf. Mic. 7:1; see Gundry 1993: 636; C. A. Evans 2001b: 155; in *Exod. Rab.* 1:36 putting forth figs is a metaphor for repentance), it symbolizes both the hollow reality behind the imposing religious structure and, as in the prophets, to the extent that the temple represents unrepentant Israel, the nation itself (see Gnilka 1978–1979: 2:124; Hooker 1991: 262; *pace* Geddert [1989: 122–24], who because of Mark 12:1–12 limits the curse only to the hierarchs, whereas, e.g., in Mark 4 all those who reject Jesus' word face judgment). Malachi's Lord whom they had long sought had come, unexpectedly, to his temple (Mal. 3:1). But having rejected Malachi's "Elijah," who was to refine the Levites (Mal. 3:3–4; cf. Mark 11:27–33; see R. E. Watts 2000: 338–39), the authorities are not only unprepared, but also hostile, and the "land" is cursed (Mal. 4:6b; see commentary on Mark 9:13 above; cf. Mark 13:14–20; see Telford 1980: 163; R. E. Watts 2000: 311–18).

This private act is then writ large in Jesus' public "demonstration" in the temple. Disrupting commercial activity and preventing transit (11:15–16 [although not developed by Mark, this recalls Zech. 14:21; see Grant 1948; Roth 1960]), Jesus justifies his action with a combined citation of Isa. 56:7, which, along with the kinds of activity mentioned, almost guarantees that the court of the Gentiles is in view, and an allusion to Jer. 7:11. Mark's texts agree with both the LXX and the MT, the former being in both instances a literal rendition of the latter.

B. The Composite Citation. 1. Isa. 56:7 in Context. The final third of Isaiah, chapters 56–66, although much debated, confronts two issues from an eschatological standpoint: a call to live in anticipation of the delayed new exodus and, over against the rebels, the consequent situation of Yahweh's servants (see Beuken 1990). Isaiah 56:1–8 introduces these themes (cf. Isa. 66; see Blenkinsopp 2000–2003: 3:312).

The oracle begins with two concerns. The first, in 56:1–2, is a summons to the justice and righteousness of a Torah-observance marked by loyalty to Yahweh and right relationships (Childs 2001: 455–56). This is not a legalistic attempt to manipulate Yahweh's coming, but rather, as in Malachi, is a preparatory response to his imminent salvation (see commentary on Mark 1:2–3 above). The second concern, in 56:3, is an encouragement to foreigners and eunuchs who have embraced Yahweh. Although already integral to Israel's past (see R. E. Watts 2004a), the inclusion of proselytes from the ends of the earth (e.g., 45:22; 49:6; 52:10) in a restored Zion will be a central feature of the new thing that Yahweh was doing (56:4–7; 60–62; cf. 42:1–6; 49:1, 6; 52:15; also 14:1; 19:19–25; see Childs 2001: 458). At issue, then, is what distinguishes God's servants from the rebels both within and without Israel. No longer ethnicity, it is instead a love for God, a desire to minister to him and to be his servant, and a willingness to keep Torah (56:6; as per Deuteronomy [see Childs 2001: 459]). Thus even some proselytes will become priests and Levites (cf. 66:21; see Blenkinsopp 2000–2003: 3:140; Childs 2001: 542). For the sake of his glory, Yahweh will bring such ones to his holy mountain, for it is his intention that his house be a house of prayer for all peoples, universal and without restriction (cf. Isa. 2:1–4; note also the language of Solomon's prayer in 1 Kings 8:41–43, which seems to be used here). The Isaianic oracle concludes with another solemn if enigmatic declaration: the Lord, who gathers the outcasts of Israel (into a newly restored people), will gather others, presumably both Israelites and foreigners, to those already gathered (56:8).

It says something about the conflict that the very next oracle (56:9–57:13) is directed against corrupt leaders. In a manner anticipating Mark's Jesus and to set them in the "sharpest possible contrast" with the foregoing, these verses devastatingly employ stereotypical images from the preexilic period combined with those applied to exilic Jacob-Israel to reveal fully the nature of the leaders' rebellion (Childs 2001: 463). Denounced as blind shepherds who neither care for the flock nor understand (56:10–11), they are treacherous rebels (57:4) and nothing more than idolatrous adulterers (57:6–8).

2. Isa. 56:7 in Judaism. In contrast to the egalitarian attitude of Isa. 56:7, in CD-A XIV, 4–6 proselytes rank behind priests, Levites, and Israelites, and in 1 Macc. 7:37 the temple as the "house of prayer" is explicitly delimited as being for God's people Israel. On the other hand, *Mek. Exod.* 20:23 cites Isa. 56:6–7 to prove God's love for "strangers" in that he speaks of them as he does Israelites. In the Targum of Isa. 56:3–9 the foreigner is explicitly a son of the Gentiles who will go up "for my pleasure," but the focus is still on the returning exiles and Jerusalem's victory over the Gentile kings who will become food for the beasts of the field (cf. *b. Šabb.* 118b, where because Israel's failure to keep the first Sabbath allowed the nations to have dominion over them, keeping two Sabbaths would redeem them [cf. Isa. 56:4, 7]). *Psalms of Solomon* 17:30–31 seems to reflect a similar idea where, after the defeat of the Gentile kings and unrighteous rulers (17:22–25), the nations will come from the ends of the earth to a purged Jerusalem to see God's glory.

Among the later rabbinic writings, *y. Ber.* 2:3 [V.C] cites Isa. 56:7 in connection with the rebuilding of the temple, which it associates with the Hallel, Ps. 118:27–28, and the messianic triumph. Likewise, for *b. Meg.* 18a, when David comes, God will bring the children of Israel to his holy mountain to worship in a rebuilt temple (Isa. 56:7; cf. *Lam. Rab.* I.2.23). With more emphasis on the marginalized but absent the proselyte, *Pesiq. Rab Kah.* 10:10 states that if Israel will bless all those in their households, whether family, Levite, or the stranger, fatherless, and widow, then God will bring blessing and joy into his house, the temple in Jerusalem (citing Isa. 56:7). Still, in *Num. Rab.* 8:2 proselytes are indeed beloved of God (see Isa. 56:6; cf. *S. Eli. Rab.* [29]27).

In general, Isa. 56:7, not surprisingly, was read eschatologically, and even though in some traditions proselytes are clearly understood to be included, the emphasis is firmly on Israel's blessing with, occasionally, Gentile judgment.

3. Jer. 7:11 in Context. Coming not long after Jeremiah's denunciation of blind and deaf Israel in 5:21 (see commentary on Mark 8:18 above), his famous Temple Sermon (7:1–15), given at its "righteous gates" (cf. Ps. 118:19–20) and probably during one of the three annual pilgrimage feasts, reflects somewhat ironically a typical entrance liturgy (7:1–2) (see Holladay 1986: 244; Jones 1992: 146; cf. the Targum of 7:4). An indignant Yahweh declares that if his people want him to dwell among them (7:3, 7), they must abandon the self-deception of the temple's inviolability (mentioned three times [7:4, 8, 14]), amend their ways, and keep covenant by acting justly toward one another (7:4–5). Rehearsing a litany of crimes directly reflecting the Decalogue, he asks whether the entering throngs are really so foolish as to think that they can steal, shed innocent blood, commit adultery, swear falsely, engage in idolatry, oppress the widow (7:6, 9), then, having committed all these abominations (7:10, cf. 8:12; see Mark 13:14), "flee" to the temple like murderous brigands to their cave, confident in escaping judgment simply because of their cultic largesse (Bright 1965: 56; McKane 1986: 163; cf. LXX 7:10b, which instead has the people claim they have in fact refrained from "all these abominations").

But if they have "seen" the temple as a "den of robbers" (LXX: *spēlaion lēstōn*), the true owner of the temple, has also "seen it" (7:11). Because they have persisted in their rebellious ways, disdaining his warnings and refusing to respond when he called (7:13, 24–26), their overflowing sacrifices might as well be domestic meals (7:21 [see Carroll 1986: 215]) and are rejected forthwith (Thompson 1980: 287). Judgment is irrevocable, and the Lord's anger will be poured out on the land, including the trees and fruit (7:13–20; cf. 7:27; also 8:13, where the fig will not bear fruit). Shiloh was not immune, and neither is the temple. God's presence will depart, his house destroyed, and his people cast out of his sight (7:14; cf. 1 Sam. 4).

4. Jer. 7:11 in Judaism. The fragmentary 4Q182, apparently citing Jer. 5:7, seems to expect a repetition of Jeremiah's judgment on faithless Israelites in the last days, as apparently does Jesus son of Ananias, who prophesied doom to Jerusalem prior to the revolt and whose words against "bride and bridegroom" could be an echo of Jer. 7:34

(Josephus, *J.W.* 6.301; cf. *b. Naz.* 32b, where the threefold "temple" of Jer. 7:4 anticipated the destruction of both the first and the second temple). *Psalms of Solomon* 2:4 recalls that Israel was cast into captivity (Jer. 7:15) because the sons of Jerusalem defiled the temple of the Lord by profaning the offerings with lawless acts (Embry 2002)—a situation that the coming Davidic messiah was to remedy (*Pss. Sol.* 17:21–46).

The Targum explicitly mentions the three pilgrimage feasts (7:4), interestingly adds proselytes to those who are oppressed (7:6), interprets the deceptive words as those of false prophets (7:8), and glosses God's speaking to Judah with "my servants the prophets whom you did not receive" (7:13 [cf., within Jesus' parable of the Vineyard, Mark 12:2–5]). *Pesiqta Rabbati* 27:4 recognizes that Jer. 7:9 reflects the Ten Words of Exod. 20:13, arguing in 33:4 that God could not have given Judah more warning (Jer. 7:13), and thus *Tanḥ. Lev.* 1:15 exhorts Israel not to be like that generation (Jer. 7:9).

C. The Use of Isa. 56:7; Jer. 7:11 in Mark. Set at the center of Mark's double intercalation to indicate its gravity, Jesus' combined citation encapsulates the contradiction between what the postexilic temple was meant to be and what it had in fact become, thereby sealing its fate should Yahweh return (R. E. Watts 2000: 310–37). Whatever the other reasons that might have led to Jesus' action, for Mark, the combined citation is key.

The texts raise two major concerns. First, in direct contravention of God's intention in Isa. 56 that his temple become a house of prayer for all nations, the location of these business and transport activities (not necessarily the acts in themselves) display an utter disregard for the Gentile court and any prayers that might have been offered therein (see France 2002: 445). As in many of the later traditions on Isa. 56:7, and in spite of some later texts welcoming proselytes, the primary focus was firmly on the temple as *Israel's* house of prayer, and thus the "no entry on pain of death" warning on the temple's *soreg* ensured that the court primarily signified separation not invitation (cf. Josephus, *J.W.* 5.194; 6.124–125; see Gaston 1970: 87).

Second, it is obvious from Mark's narrative that Israel's leaders had rejected the summons to do justice and righteousness (Isa. 56:1–2; e.g., Mark 3:1–6; 7:10–13; 12:41–44). As did Isa. 56–66,

Mark's Jesus characterizes them in preexilic and exilic terms as idolatrously blind rebels who lack understanding and do not shepherd the flock (see commentary on Mark 6:34 above). In terms of Jer. 7, aside from the possibility of unscrupulous business practices, of which nothing is said, it is interesting that (1) the breaches of the Decalogue have Markan counterparts—Israel's religious leaders have stolen (from their parents [7:10–12]), conspired, or will conspire, to shed innocent blood (3:6; 11:18), committed adultery via their lax divorce laws (10:2–12), sworn falsely by professing a love of God and yet avoiding his most important commands (7:6–9), are idolaters (of heart, and hence are blind and deaf [3:29; 4:12; 7:6–7]), and oppress widows (12:41–44) (see also Geddert 1989: 124–25)—and (2) Jesus has had a particular interest in the interpersonal half of the Ten Words throughout Mark's story (e.g., 3:1–6; 7:10; 10:19). Whether these are specifically in view or indicative of a more general failure (as per Isa. 56 [on the numerous complaints against the priesthood, see C. A. Evans 1989a]), Jesus' criticism is that far from becoming a house of prayer for all, the temple had reverted to being a preexilic refuge for brigands (cf. the warning in *Tanḥ. Lev.* 1:15) who not only failed to provide the requisite fruits of justice and mercy but also abused God's vineyard for their own advantage (12:1–12). In this respect, and because of their lethal hostility toward Jesus, who is the temple's rightful Lord and Israel's messianic Son of Man, the contemporary insurrectionist meaning of Jeremiah's *lēstēs* is appropriate (cf. 15:27; see Bauckham 1988).

Jesus, earlier rejected at the gates of what, according to *Tg. Ps.* 118:19, was meant to be the righteous city, now stands, as it were, at the gates of the sanctuary (*Tg. Ps.* 118:20; cf. Jer. 26:2) also during the annual Passover pilgrimage feast to announce a repetition of Jer. 7's judgment (cf. 4Q182). Whereas in Jer. 8:13 the fig tree's fruitlessness was a sign of God's judgment, here it is the cause (cf. Mal. 4:6; Micah 7:1), and both are thus withered. So serious was Israel's calling to be a light to the nations that the same Jesus who allowed the destruction of the swine (5:1–20) declares God's judgment on a faithless temple. Or, in the language of the later *Pesiq. Rab Kah.* 10:10 on Isa. 56:7, if they would not in their houses bless their families, the "stranger" (cf. *Mek. Exod.*

22:20–33, also citing Isa. 56:7), or the widow (cf. Mark 12:41–44), neither would Yahweh bless them in his "house."

Hence, then, Jesus' linkage of the withered fig tree with "this" mountain, meaning Zion (11:20–25; cf. 9:2, 9; Exod. 15:17; Ps. 78:54; Isa. 2:2; Ezek. 17:22–23; and the temple [*b. Pesaḥ.* 87b; *b. Giṭ.* 56b; *Tg. Isa.* 5:1–2], whose imagery is echoed in the parable of the Wicked Tenants; see Telford 1980; R. E. Watts 2000: 332–39; *pace* France [2002: 448–49], if the fig tree represents Israel, why could the mountain not represent the temple?). In the language of Isa. 40:3–5 it is this one mountain that had consistently resisted the way of the Lord, and it too would be leveled and cast, like the demonized pigs, into the sea as the glory of the Lord and his vindicated Son of Man are revealed (esp. Zech. 4:7, where the great mountain is laid low in the context of completing the temple; see Ps. 118:22–23 in Mark 12:10–11; Bar. 5:7; *Pss. Sol.* 11:4; cf. Mark 13:26–27; 14:62; great Torah scholars were also called "uprooters of mountains" [*b. Ber.* 64a; *b. Sanh.* 24a], as were kings [*b. B. Bat.* 3b]).

Thus, as reflected in some later traditions on Isa. 56:7, Israel's messianic shepherd had come as in Ps. 118 (cf. *y. Ber.* 2:3 [V.C]; *b. Meg.* 18a). But since he was rejected, and also he is the temple's Lord (Mal. 3:1), the present corrupt temple would be destroyed (Mark 13; as was implied by the opening imprisonment of John [1:14] and Jesus' use of Isa. 6:10–11 in Mark 4 and Isa. 29:13–14 in Mark 7). Consequently, another would be raised in its place (Hooker 1991: 268; see commentary on Mark 12:10–11 below) wherein the prayers of faithful, "Torah-abiding" (as defined by Jesus) Gentile converts from "the ends of the earth" would be heard, and their offerers would experience joy (cf. *Pss. Sol.* 17:30–31; Isa. 45:22; 52:10).

D. Theological Use. Eschatologically and christologically, in Jesus Israel's long-awaited Davidic messiah and Lord of the temple has unexpectedly come. But, ecclesiologically, because of its corruption and failure to be a light to the nations (cf. Rom. 2:24), the temple would be destroyed and replaced by a new one, as we will see in the next appeal to Ps. 118.

12:10–11

A. NT Context: The Rejected Stone. After teaching on the withered tree and "this mountain" (11:20–25), Jesus returns to the temple to be confronted by a delegation of the chief priests, the scribes, and the elders (11:27–33), here together for the first time in Mark and whom Jesus predicted would seek his death (8:31). As we have already noted, the thrust of this exchange is that if John was Malachi's Elijah, then not only have they rejected his preparatory call to repentance and are therefore under Yahweh's curse, but also, in rejecting Jesus, they have opposed the Lord's Messiah and the Lord of the temple himself.

As on previous occasions, Jesus responds with a parable, this time about insurrectionist tenants (12:1–12). Employing traditional Jewish metaphors (cf., e.g., *Sipre Deut.* 312; the vineyard parables in *Tanh. Lev.* 7:6, interestingly in the context of David and keeping God's commandments; *Pesiq. Rab Kah.* 16:9; *Gen. Rab.* 42:3; *Exod. Rab.* 30:17; *Midr. Prov.* 19:21; see Kowalski 1994; C. A. Evans 2001b: 220–21) and particularly Isa. 5:1–7's juridical parable (see C. A. Evans 2001b: 224–28), which contrasts Yahweh's care with his people's rebellion (though in Mark the issue is not the quality of the fruit and the vineyard's destruction, but rather the leaders' rejection of the owner's son and their demise), Jesus' story is a searing condemnation of his interrogators (cf. 12:12; see R. E. Watts 2000: 339–46; Weren 1998; cf. Jer. 2:21; Ezek. 19:10; Hos. 10:1; also Jer. 7:25; 25:4; Amos 3:7; Zech. 1:6).

The fenced vineyard with vat and tower is Zion with its altar and sanctuary (cf., e.g., 4Q500 1, 3–7; *t. Meʾil.* 1:16 and *t. Sukkah* 3:15, citing Isa. 5:1–2; see esp. *Tg. Isa.* 5:1–7; *1 En.* 89:56, 67, 72–73; see R. E. Watts 2000: 342), the owner is God, the vine is his people, the tenants are Israel's present leadership (cf. 4Q162, which reads Isa. 5 eschatologically and is directed against "the men of mockery in Jerusalem" who "have rejected the law of the Lord and cast off the word of Israel's Holy One" [cf. Mark 1:24]), the servants are the prophets, and the owner's "beloved" son is Jesus. That the son is sent last simply reflects the eschatologically climactic tenor of Mark's entire story.

"Beloved" occurs elsewhere in Mark only at Jesus' baptism and transfiguration (1:11; 9:7). Both are allusions to Ps. 2, wherein in the face of insurrection God affirms his messianic son's inheritance (*klēronomia* [Ps. 2:8]), which is the focus of the parable in Mark (*klēronomos, klēronomia* [12:7]). As that psalm warned and its intertestamental interpreters understood, those who rebel against God's rule through his Messiah, in this case the insurrectionist tenants, would be destroyed (Ps. 2:12; cf. Mark 12:9; see commentary on Mark 1:11 above), and so in the parable the superintendence of God's people-vineyard is transferred (12:9). Jesus concludes with an almost sarcastic question: can it be that they have not read this scripture, again citing Ps. 118, but this time from earlier in the poem (118:22–23): "The stone which the builders rejected has become the head of the corner. This is from the Lord, and it is wonderful in our eyes" (12:10–11)? The citation is identical to the LXX, which accurately renders the Hebrew (adding only a *kai* to aid the syntax).

B. Ps. 118:22–23 in Context and in Judaism. See commentary on Mark 11:9–10 above. In addition to the more common Davidic interpretation, the "stone" was understood also as Abraham, Jacob, Joseph, and Israel (*Midr. Ps.* 118:20; see survey in Berder 1996: 170–241), and "builders" is often used of "scholars" or "religious leaders" (CD-A IV, 19–20; VIII, 12, 18; CD-B XIX, 31; *b. Šabb.* 114a; *b. Ber.* 64a; *Midr. Song* 1:5; cf. Acts 4:11; 1 Cor. 3:10; see Derrett 1978). Psalm 118:22 is alluded to in *T. Sol.* 22:3 and cited in *T. Sol.* 24:3 where it literally describes the stone that completes Solomon's temple. There is also a tradition that associated the dwelling of the divine presence with a stone named "Foundation," upon which the ark sat, so called because the world was founded upon and centered on it (*t. Yoma* 3:6 [2:14]; *y. Yoma* 5:4 [42c]; *b. Yoma* 54b; *Num. Rab.* 12:4; *Tanḥ. Lev.* 6:4; 7:10).

Of particular interest is the Targum's explicit and thoroughgoing identification of the rejected stone with David (cf. *Tg. Zech.* 10:4, where this is associated with return from exile; *b. Pesaḥ.* 119a; *Exod. Rab.* 37:1). In 118:22 "the stone" becomes "the child" who "was among the sons of Jesse" and who "was worthy to be appointed king and ruler." Additional references to Jesse, his family, David, and even Samuel and his sacrifice (118:23–29) suggest that the Targum interpreted the second half of the psalm in light of 1 Sam. 16:1–13, where David, although initially rejected, is ultimately appointed king first over the tribes of Judah (2 Sam. 2:1–4 [*Tg. Ps.* 118:27b]) and then Israel (2 Sam. 5:1–9 [*Tg. Ps.* 118:29]). Psalm 118 thus becomes a celebration of David's inexorable accession to the throne, and that with prophetic attestation (cf. the "servants" in Jesus' parable).

Similarly, in the context of Zech. 4's oracle concerning the building of the temple, in which a "foolish kingdom"-mountain "becomes" a plain, *Tg. Zech.* 4:7 translates the top-stone (*hā'eben hārō'ša*) as "his [the Lord's] anointed one," probably due to a messianic interpretation of Ps. 118 (cf. *Tg. Isa.* 28:16). In *Tg. Zech.* 6:12–13a it is the Messiah who rebuilds the temple (cf. *Tg. Isa.* 53:5). In *Tanḥ. Gen.* 6:20, the stone of Zech. 4:7 is Dan. 2:34–35's stone that smites the image to become a great mountain. This stone in linked in *Esther Rab.* 7:10 with Ps. 118:22's rejected stone and in *Num. Rab.* 13:14 with the one like a son of man, Dan. 7:13 (C. A. Evans 2001a: 507–10). Several Jewish traditions anticipated the Messiah's rebuilding of the temple (Zech. 6:12; cf. *Tg. Zech.* 6:12).

A second feature in the Targum of Ps. 118 is the repeated references to "the builders" who, having earlier rejected the child, now confess that this is from "the presence" of the Lord, and that the day is God's doing, and who now anticipate the Lord's deliverance and bless the one who comes in his name (118:22–26).

C. The Use of Ps. 118:22–23 in Mark. Even if the well-noted Hebrew wordplay between "son" (*bēn*) and "stone" (*'eben*) (cf. Exod. 28:9–12, 21; 39:6–7, 14; Lam. 4:1–2; Zech. 9:16) does not translate into Greek, the point is abundantly clear. In contrast to the later Targum's expectation, the builders' rejection of the stone reflects the temple authorities' rejection of Jesus (Snodgrass 1983: 96). Occurring in Mark only here and in 8:31, the verb *apodokimazō* recalls Jesus' first passion prediction, where he is "rejected" by the elders, chief priests, and scribes. The latter follows immediately after the first messianic confession (8:29), which, when repeated publicly by Bartimaeus and then the crowds, sets the stage for the present confrontation. The tenants' murder of the beloved son (1:11; 9:7) is simply that which the passion predictions anticipated: the rejection of the messianic son-stone by Israel's teacher-builders (cf. *Tg. Ps.* 2:12). But again in keeping with predictions of vindication, the citation affirms that God will reverse their decision. In this respect, the oft-cited "incredible naïveté" of both the owner and the tenants merely reflects the tension in the prophets between God's extraordinary patience and the breathtaking folly of Israel's persistently rebellious leaders who seek to take advantage of it. Although perhaps heightened, the parable's dynamics are nevertheless true to form. But as Mark's opening allusion to Mal. 3 warned, the long-threatened judgment that marked the end of God's long-suffering has arrived: he will accomplish his purposes (see Blomberg 1990: 247–51).

But what of the traditions surrounding Ps. 118 (and Isa. 56) that anticipated the rebuilding of the temple? The resolution apparently lies with the "stone" metaphor. Resuming the architectural imagery of "vat" and "tower," it provides the only hint of rebuilding by implying that Jesus will become the most important "stone" of a new temple (probably a highly placed crowning-stone [Cahill 1999]; cf. *T. Sol.* 23:4, citing Ps. 118:22). Although still a matter of debate (Kampen 1999), and even though the Qumran community seems to expect an eschatological physical temple (4Q174 1 I, 1–7; perhaps 11Q19 XXIX, 8–10), 1QS VIII, 5–14 reflects a similar understanding when it describes the congregation as "the foundation of the holy of holies . . . the precious cornerstone . . . the most holy dwelling" (cf. CD-A III, 19–IV, 6; see Brooke 1999), and this to fulfill Isa. 40:3 by studying and observing Torah (cf. 4Q174; see de Roo 1999: 50–51).

If so, then the "restoration" of the temple envisaged by contemporary messianic interpretations of Ps. 2 (4Q174; *Pss. Sol.* 17; cf. *Jub.* 1:17, where God builds his sanctuary; *1 En.* 90:28–29; 91:13b; and *Tg. Isa.* 53:5, where it is rebuilt by the messianic servant; see Ådna 2000: 40–89) and celebrated by the new-exodus traditions associated with Ps. 118 is fulfilled by Jesus, and the newly reconstituted Israel is gathered around him (cf. *Tanḥ. Lev.* 6:4; 7:10, where Zion is the foundation stone of the world). And perhaps in this new temple the only sacrifices will be those of Jesus (see commentary on Isa. 53 in Mark 10:45 above; Ådna 2000: 419–30; see also commentary on Exod. 24:8 in Mark 14:24 below ["blood of the covenant], and note that Jesus' execution occurs at the same time as the offering of the *tamid,* namely,

the third hour [15:25]) and his disciples (see commentary on Lev. 2:13 in Mark 9:49 above; further, Lohmeyer 1962). This is clearly so in 1 Pet. 2:4–7, where, citing Ps. 118, the author shows that Jesus, the rejected stone, is the foundation of a spiritual temple in which spiritual sacrifices are offered (cf. Juel 1977: 205).

Although the primary focus of the parable concerns the authorities, the vineyard, in contrast to Isa. 5, is not destroyed, as most commentators note. However, from the Markan perspective, the vineyard can only be the obedient reconstituted Israel gathered around Jesus (cf. 3:31–35). Tragically, and as Jesus has repeatedly implied, for those who refuse his message there is only judgment (e.g., 3:29; 4:1–17; 7:6–13; 8:11–13, 35–38). The "others" into whose care it is given are the Twelve, whose servant leadership must reflect the pattern of Jesus' self-giving (10:42–45).

In Mark's new exodus, then, it is the rejected Davidic son-stone Jesus who through his resurrection becomes the preeminent stone of a new people-temple (14:58; cf. 1 Pet. 2:4–7; note also "stone," "building," and "wonder" in Mark 13:1–2; see Marcus 1992: 119–25). This would indeed be "the Lord's doing" and "wonderful in our eyes" (12:11), which language of seeing Yahweh's wonderful deeds originates in delivering and vindicating his people with the defeat of Egypt at the exodus (Exod. 15:11; 34:10), is echoed in the celebration of King Yahweh's worldwide victory over the nations in general (Ps. 97:1–2 LXX [98:1–2 ET]), and provides the basis of their eschatological defeat in Micah's vision of the new exodus (Mic. 7:15–20 LXX). At the same time, in Ezekiel the new exodus was also understood as a "resurrection" (37:1–14) in which a Davidic king would oversee a reconstituted people and a new sanctuary (37:15–28).

D. Theological Use. In addition to the points already noted on Ps. 118 above (e.g., Jesus is the Davidic messiah), this particular citation not only emphasizes the motif of vindication in the face of rejection but also, by invoking architectural imagery, speaks to ecclesiology. Jesus is the basis of the reconstituted vineyard of Israel (cf. Gal. 6:16), which via the implied temple imagery is also the eschatological temple (cf. John 2:21; 1 Cor. 3:16; 2 Cor. 6:16; Eph. 2:21; Rev. 21:2).

12:26

A. NT Context: Knowing Not the Power of God.
After the consortium of temple authorities is seen off, each of the remaining power groupings in the city attempts to discredit Jesus in a series of confrontations not unlike those in 2:1–3:6 (Dewey 1977: 156–63). Here, the Sadducees (12:18–27), employing a serial-marriage story, invoke the law of levirate marriage (Deut. 25:5–10; cf. Gen. 38; Josephus, *Ant.* 4.254–56; 4Q524 15–22, 7–8; the rabbis discussed levirate marriage at length in the *Yebamot* tractates and elsewhere) to demonstrate the absurdity of the notion of resurrection (perhaps because it is implied in 12:10–11?). The dilemma requires the dual assumption that the Torah, the one authority that they recognize, and human relations continue unchanged in the putative world to come.

Their error, Jesus responds, arises because they know neither the Torah (like the earlier temple delegation) nor the power of God. First, he dismisses the marriage problem by declaring that human relations do not continue unchanged, since after being raised (by God's power), people will in this respect be like the angels, neither giving nor taking in marriage (12:25; cf. 1Q28b IV, 24–25; *b. Ber.* 17a; *1 En.* 104:4–6; *2 Bar.* 51:5–10; see Davies and Allison 1988–1997: 3:227–28). Second, he criticizes their failure to comprehend God's power, and turning to the Scriptures, he cites God's self-designation from Exod. 3:6 (repeated in 3:15–16). Whereas LXX B follows the MT slavishly, Mark's version follows LXX A, which introduces an article before *theos Abraam*.

B. Exod. 3:6 in Context.
Exodus 3:1–12, which is the moment when God inaugurates his self-revelatory redemption of his people and is the beginning of the larger narrative of Moses' commissioning in 3:1–4:17 (Sarna 1991: 12), consists of a combined theophany and call. As such, it sets up the presence-response pattern that is so fundamental not only to Israel's defining Sinai encounter but also to the nation's entire history (Durham 1987: 30). Three elements are central to this defining encounter: (1) a God who speaks (cf. 20:1–17); (2) God's holiness, the approaching of which must be closely controlled (cf. 40:34–35); and (3) God's self-identification—"the God of Abraham, the God of Isaac, and the God of Jacob"—as the one who, over the unbroken generations, is faithful to his covenant with the fathers (cf. 6:1–8; 34:6–7) (see Sarna 1991: 13).

Because of the latter, God has heard his people's outcry and come down, baring his mighty arm, to deliver them from bondage and set them in a bountiful land (3:7–8; theologically, a new Eden [see Fretheim 1991: 59]). In a brilliantly conceived passage constructed of emphatic pronouns and the verb *hyh* ("to be"), from which the name of self-sustaining and life-giving Yahweh is derived, Moses' complaints of "Who am I . . . that I . . . ?" (3:11) are met with the divine self-predication "I AM with you" (3:12a [see Durham 1987: 33]). The point, well recognized, is not who Moses is, but rather the character of the one who is with Moses and thus the revelation of the name (3:13–22). Yahweh offers an authenticating sign: Israel as a people will encounter I AM and enter into the covenant of life with him at Sinai (3:12b). Because of I AM, Israel will come to be.

The ensuing exchange between Yahweh and the still-doubting Moses makes precisely this point (4:1–11). The serpent being a symbol of resurrection in Egypt, Moses' serpent-staff demonstrates that he, as Yahweh's agent, now exercises over Egypt the power of life and death, of order and chaos (see Currid 1977: 88–94). So also does the power over "leprosy," the living death (cf. Num. 12:12; 2 Kings 5:7) that Yahweh alone can cure, and the turning of water into blood, where both are essential to and representative of life. This in part explains the Lord's anger when he finally demands, using the imagery of the opening-of-the-mouth ritual associated with the enlivening of the images of the gods (Lorton 1999), that Moses tell him who it is that gives speech and hearing and sight, which are so characteristic of humanity. Everything in this passage presupposes Yahweh's utterly sovereign control over every aspect of human existence and even existence itself (cf. Deut. 32:39).

C. Exod. 3:6 in Judaism.
There is remarkably little explicit reference to this part of Exod. 3:6. Ezekiel the Tragedian 105 simply recalls it as part of relating the exodus. Among the rabbinic writings, *Pesiq. Rab.* 33:8 argues that the special form *ʾānōkî* connotes affection, citing, among a number of divine self-references, Exod. 3:6, and *Tanḥ. Gen.* 8:27 relates that after Jacob, God never again joined his name to a human.

The threefold "ancestor" formula itself (apart from any explicit link with Exod. 3) occurs on numerous occasions to express God's faithfulness to deliver from Egypt (Gen. 50:24; Exod. 2:24; 3:15–16; 6:8; Deut. 1:8; 6:10; cf. 2 Kings 13:23; Sir. 51:12 [Hebrew]; 2 Macc. 1:2), from exile (Lev. 26:42; Jer. 33:26; Bar. 2:34; *T. Mos.* 3:9; *4 Bar.* 6:21), and from death because the faithful will live to God as do Abraham, Isaac, and Jacob (4 Macc. 7:18–19; 16:25 [cf. 13:17]; *T. Levi* 15:4; 18:11–14; *T. Jud.* 25:1; cf. *y. Ber.* 2:2 [IX.G], where Deut. 34:4 is cited in support of the righteous being called living even though dead; *b. Ber.* 18a). Philo, in *Abraham* 50–55, speaks of God attaching his immortal name to Abraham, Isaac, and Jacob, but by this he means their virtues, not their mortal humanity. Though not explicitly mentioning their names, *b. Sanh.* 90b appeals to God's covenant promise in Exod. 6:4 to give "them" (the patriarchs) the land, which, if it is to be fulfilled, demands their resurrection.

D. The Use of Exod. 3:6 in Mark. Presumably in order to make a compelling case to the Sadducees, Mark's Jesus appeals to the Torah (cf. Gamaliel in *b. Sanh.* 90b). Whether or not he strictly adheres to the rules of rabbinic argument (Cohn-Sherbok 1981 [but see Downing 1982]), Jesus' cryptic response is not dissimilar in that it forces the reader to probe more deeply in an attempt to follow the rationale (see Juel 1988: 43–45; for the range of alternatives, see Davies and Allison 1988–1997: 3:231–33).

Although, as we have seen, the ancestor formula was long associated with God's faithful promise to deliver (cf., e.g., Exod. 2:24; Lev. 26:42; see Dreyfus 1959), Jesus' reference to Exod. 3:6 uniquely grounds his argument not only in Torah but also in the one place where God himself uttered this self-designation, and that in the context of his powerful exodus redemption of Israel. At issue, then, is not the phrase itself, but rather the nature of God, who uttered it. And in the context of Exod. 3 this means the character and power of the self-sustaining I AM, who is the source of creation's order and life, the pinnacle of which is humanity made in his image (the genealogy itself testifies to God's power to bring life out of Abraham's and Sarah's "dead" bodies; see Gen. 17:1–21; cf. Rom. 4:19; Heb. 11:11–12; see Janzen 1985). Since God has faithfully exercised this

matchless power in order to keep the covenant, it is inconceivable that those with whom he chooses to identify would not also participate in that life. In terms of the Sadducees' question, this can mean nothing else but resurrection (in contrast to Philo, whose sole concern was the disembodied rational soul [see Dreyfus 1959]). To deny this is to deny God his very name and identity, and perhaps this is what prompts Jesus' curt rejoinder, "You are much mistaken" (cf. God's impatience with Moses). And of course, disbelief in the resurrection offers no comfort to wicked tenants: God not only can but will raise his Son.

E. Theological Use. Not uncharacteristically, Jesus' concern is the text's underlying significance in terms of God's character and his dealings with his people. In this case, because God is characterized by life, so finally will be all of those who put their trust in him. Soteriologically, Jesus affirms that the Lord is indeed "for the body" (cf. 1 Cor. 6:13b–14) and that resurrection is an integral part of his people's eschatological hope (cf. 1 Cor. 15).

12:29–31

A. NT Context: The Great Commandment. Overhearing the dispute and impressed with Jesus' answer, one of the scribes engages him. Mark says nothing about his motivation, but the absence of a respectful address (cf. 10:17) and the final "no one dared ask," coupled with the glowing compliment, suggest that he moves from initial questioning to outright admiration. Reflecting a long tradition in Judaism that sought to encapsulate the Torah, he asks, "Which commandment is first of all?" (12:28; see esp. Mic. 6:8; also Isa. 66:2; Jer. 22:3; Zech. 8:16–17; Pss. 15; 24; *Mek. Exod.* 15:26; *b. Ber.* 63a; *b. Šabb.* 31a; *b. Mak.* 23b; *Tanḥ. Deut.* 5:10).

Jesus responds, but with two commandments. The first, "Love the Lord your God . . ." (12:29–30), is, strictly speaking, an injunction. The beginning of the Shema (see Deut. 6:4–9; 11:13–21; cf. Num. 15:37–41; see Sanders 1992: 195–96), it largely follows Deut. 6:4–5 LXX (itself having a range of variants [see Gundry 1967: 22–24]) but adds *kai ex holēs tēs dianoias sou* after the second modifier (perhaps reflecting the scribe's intellectual concerns [Gundry 1993: 711]) and replaces the LXX's final *dynameōs* with *ischyos.* The second commandment follows the MT/LXX of Lev. 19:18b exactly.

B. The Double Citation. 1. Deut. 6:4–5 in Context. After looking back on the Decalogue as given on Horeb (5:1–21) and Moses' mediatorial role therein (5:22–33), his second discourse transitions through 6:1–3's introduction—"This is the command"—to the heart of his exhortation, the covenant, and the book. Consisting of three sections, 6:4–19 begins with a succinct sermonic paraphrase of the first commandment urging this and future generations to keep faith (6:4–9 [see Tigay 1966: 78]; cf. "Hear, O Israel" in 5:1), develops into a warning that having enjoyed Yahweh's blessing, they must not forget him (6:10–15), and concludes, echoing 5:32–33, with a reminder of their obligation to keep all of Yahweh's commandments (6:16–19) (see McConville 2002: 139).

Deuteronomy 6:4 contains the familiar Shema, and although the following declaration is well known, the exact nuances of the pithy Hebrew— *yhwh 'ĕlōhênû yhwh 'eḥād*—are difficult to capture (Weinfeld 1991: 337–38). Clearly, it means that Israel is to worship only Yahweh (our God), but at the same time it points to Yahweh's "uniqueness" (he is not like other gods [C. J. H. Wright 1996: 96]) and his "unity" or "integrity" (he alone delivered Israel, he alone can bless them, and he alone is entitled to their obedience [Tigay 1966: 78; McConville 2002: 141]). Thus, echoing the language of both covenant loyalty and the father-son relationship (Craigie 1976: 170), Deuteronomy is the first book of the Torah to call Israel to love Yahweh with their whole being unreservedly and exceedingly, even to the death (6:5 [see Weinfeld 1991: 351–52]). This means that they must safeguard these words (i.e., Moses' entire teaching) in their hearts (6:6), in the very fabric of their conversation and life so that they might be passed on to their children (6:7; cf. Ps. 119:13, 46; Prov. 6:21–22), and keep them in symbolic form always before their eyes (6:8–9).

Maintaining this loyalty is especially important when they are enjoying the blessing of the land that Yahweh has given them. They must revere, serve, and swear by Yahweh alone (6:13–15; cf. Yahweh's complaint against Israel's swearing falsely in Isa. 48:1 and the servant's being made an *'āšām*; see commentary on Mark 10:45 above). Capturing Deuteronomy's thoroughgoing integration of

righteousness and the good, Moses instructs them that if they do what is "right and good" (6:18; cf. Deut. 30:15), all will go well (6:24–25). But it can take place only in the context of the steadfast loyalty of covenant love toward God, which, in keeping his commandments, issues forth in embodying his benevolence by acting lovingly toward one's neighbor (see Moberly 1999: 138–40; Tigay 1966: 79).

2. Deut. 6:4–5 in Judaism. Although not citing Deut. 6, Josephus, in discussing Jewish precepts and law, observes that the first command, which leads all the others, concerns God (*Ag. Ap.* 2.190). In the Second Temple period it was liturgical custom to recite the Decalogue, the Shema, and the prayer of *'Emet wĕyaṣṣib* (*m. Tamid* 5:1; *m. Ber.* 2:2), in part because the Shema was believed to embody the Ten Words (*y. Ber.* 1:4 [II]; cf. *m. 'Abot* 2:13) and expressed Israel's unique relationship with Yahweh (*Mek. Exod.* 23:13–18; *b. Ḥag.* 3a; *Pirqe R. El.* 4; *S. Eli. Rab.* [28]26; *S. Eli. Zut.* 21).

For the rabbis (taking the more significant from the scores of references especially in the tractate *Berakot*), the love of God was considered more durable than fear of him (*Sipre Deut.* 32; *b. Soṭah* 31a; cf. *y. Soṭah* 5:5 [I.A]). To recite the Shema was to take upon oneself the yoke of the kingdom of heaven (*m. Ber.* 2:2; *t. Pesaḥ.* 3[2]:19; *y. Ber.* 2:1 [II.G–H]; *b. Pesaḥ.* 56a; cf. *Tanḥ. Gen.* 12:1, 9), but to do so without wearing phylacteries was like giving false testimony (*b. Ber.* 14b).

Recognizing that Deut. 6:5 required action, they glossed the three phrases with specific behaviors (*m. Ber.* 9:5; *Sipre Deut.* 32 [cf. 41]; *Tg. Ps.-J.*; *b. Pesaḥ.* 25a; *b. Yoma* 82a [cf. 86a]; *b. Sanh.* 74a): "all your heart" refers to the human inclination both to good and to evil, "all your soul" means even at the cost of one's life (*y. Ber.* 9:7, 14b; *b. Ber.* 61b), and "all your strength" means all of one's property (attested earlier in Sir. [Heb.] 7:30–31; 1QS I, 11–12; CD-A 12:10; cf. *Tg. Onq.*; *Tg. Neof.*; see also *Tg. Ezek.* 11:19–20; Acts 5:1–11).

Although not directly part of our paragraph, it is worth noting, given the role of unclean spirits in Mark, the caution in the immediately following 6:10–19 against forgetting the Lord and pursuing other gods, which actions were understood in the Second Temple period to be motivated by Satan/Beliar and to involve worship of him (cf., e.g., 1QS I, 16–18; *Ascen. Isa.* 2:2; Matt. 4:1–11/ Luke 4:1–13; see Weinfeld 1991: 355–56; Urbach 1979: 472–75).

3. Lev. 19:18b in Context. Part of a larger unit addressing covenant renewal (Lev. 17–26), this speech (19:1–37) is concerned that Israel's life mirror Yahweh's holiness (19:1). Lacking an immediately identifiable structure, it is unified by its emphasis on holiness, its exposition of the Decalogue, and the principle of loving others as oneself (Hartley 1992: 310–12). The first set of laws (19:3–18) opens with several paradigmatic commandments reflecting the foundations of Israel's social and spiritual life (19:3–8 [see Hartley 1992: 312–13]) before moving on to our paragraph, a series of five statutes governing relationships with "neighbors" (19:9–18).

It covers a range of social concerns, including prohibitions against swearing falsely in Yahweh's name and thereby demeaning his honor before others, perverting justice in the courts, and conspiracy to murder. Although 19:16a is normally translated as describing "slander," the phrase in question can literally mean "to act like a trader/ merchant," indicating that one should not act solely for profit or commit corruption and betrayal (Jer. 6:28; Ezek. 22:9; cf. *Sipra* 89a; see Levine 1989: 98). However, the rhetorical device of increasing the number of references to others (associate, friend, people, brother, compatriot) focuses attention on the climactic final couplet (19:17–18 [see Wenham 1979: 267]). In the interests of justice and functioning relationships, Israelites are forbidden to hate one another in their hearts, but rather must argue cases publicly to determine if any given complaint is just (19:17 [see Hartley 1992: 316]). Seeking vengeance and "nurturing a grudge" are likewise forbidden; instead, shifting to the positive, one is to love and help (cf. 2 Chron. 19:2 [see Malamat 1990]) any Israelite or resident alien (19:34) with whom one has contact as if that person were oneself. Just as one's own will is naturally centered on self-beneficence, it must now look outward to extend that concern to others.

Finally, that the speech freely intermingles "cultic" and "ethical" requirements demonstrates the holistic manner in which every aspect of Israel's life must conform to Yahweh's holy character.

4. Lev. 19:18b in Judaism. Ezekiel 22:6–12's condemnation of Israel and the nation's princes draws heavily on Lev. 19 (Levine 1989: 95), and the later rabbis saw therein an exposition of the Decalogue from which most of the essential laws of Torah could be derived (*Lev. Rab.* 24). Love of neighbor became a key part of Jewish summaries of the law well before the first century (cf., e.g., *Jub.* 7:20; 36:7–8; CD-A VI, 20–21; 1QS I, 9–10; Philo, *Spec. Laws* 2.53; *Virtues* 15; *Abraham* 208; *T. Reub.* 6:9; *T. Jud.* 18:3; *T. Iss.* 5:2; 7:6; *T. Zeb.* 5:3; *T. Dan* 5:3; see Berger 1972: 143–68; see also the references below). Rabbi Akiba claimed that Lev. 19:18 encompassed the whole law (*Sipra* 200), and similarly, Rabbi Hillel's golden rule states, "Whatever is hateful to you, do not to your neighbor" (*b. Šabb.* 31a; cf. *t. Pe'ah* 4:19; *Gen. Rab.* 24:7; interestingly, it also occurs frequently in moderating death penalties [e.g., *b. Pesaḥ.* 75a; *b. Ketub.* 37b; *b. Soṭah* 8b], though it should not exclude the idolater from a penalty [*Sipre Deut.* 89]). Failure to love one's neighbor will eventually lead to murder (*Sipre Deut.* 186/7; 235).

But who was the "neighbor"? Although Lev. 19:18 originally had Israelites and resident aliens in mind (*T. Gad* 6:1), some drew the lines more tightly around the edges of group loyalties (e.g., CD-A VI, 20–21; 1QS I, 9–10; cf. 1QS II, 24; V, 25; 1QM I, 1), while others included all people (*Let. Aris.* 131; 228; Tob. 4:15a; Philo, *Hypothetica* 7.6; *T. Iss.* 5:2; *Mek. Exod.* 15:22–26; *T. Zeb.* 5:1).

Finally, given the conflict in Mark, it is noteworthy that 1QS V, 24–VI, 1, reflecting the concerns of Lev. 19:17–18, requires that disputes be conducted in truth, humility, and loving consideration. Court action must be preceded by an official reproach of the offender (CD-A IX, 2–8 [see Kugel 1987]), and bringing a charge without witnesses, in anger or resentment or in order to defame, is to act in vengeance and resentment and thus be in breach of Lev. 19:18 (4Q270 6 III, 17–18).

5. The Combination of Deut. 6:4–5 and Lev. 19:18b in Judaism. Even if not explicitly connected, the prominence of the Shema and of the command to love one's neighbor effectively makes that connection, and hence the combination of love of God and of others—the two commands could be seen as a summary of the two "tables" of the law (Lohmeyer 1953: 258)—is found in several places, though without scriptural citation and sometimes as part of a longer list—for example, in Philo's thought, where to love only God or human beings is to attain only half-virtue (*Decalogue* 109–110; *Spec. Laws* 1.299–300, 324; 2.63; *Abraham* 208; *Virtues* 15), the Pseudepigrapha (*Jub.* 36:7–8; *T. Iss.* 7:6; *T. Dan* 5:3; *T. Benj.* 3:3–5), and the rabbis (*Sipre Deut.* 323; *Sipra* 89b). *Seder Eliyahu Rabbah* (28)26, although not explicitly citing Lev. 19, perceptively interprets Deut. 6:5 to mean that Israel should "cause (Yahweh) to be loved" (by humanity) due to their loving attitude toward others in life (*b. Yoma* 86a).

C. The Use of Deut. 6:4; Lev. 19:18b in Mark.
Although the Markan Jesus' explicit combination of these two central texts appears to be unique, the dual emphasis—undivided loyalty and devotion to the one true God and love of neighbor—is not. Jesus' answer and its hearty affirmation by a Jerusalem scribe demonstrate that he stands with the best of his generation in understanding the central concerns of Torah. From the perspective of Jesus' baptism, this is the Torah of the gentle servant, the light, for which the nations wait (see commentary on Isa. 42:1 in Mark 1:11 above).

Coming at the conclusion of the Jerusalem controversies and as part of Jesus' final public teaching in the capital, it also functions as something of a climax. Just as later he will speak of his messianic identity (14:64), here for the first time Jesus, the beloved messianic Son of God who is responsible for the purity of Israel's worship and temple and to whom the disciples "must listen" (9:7), authoritatively summarizes the heart of the Torah, by which he has lived (e.g., 1:40–44; 3:1–6; 7:1–23). In respect of Deut. 6, Jesus' own life adumbrates the later rabbinic rendering of the three aspects into actions (e.g., *m. Ber.* 9:5). He has likewise exhorted his disciples, for the sake of God's kingdom, to deal with their human inclinations (9:42–48), to lay down their lives for his and for his gospel's sake (8:34–35), and to put following him above all their material goods (10:17–31). In making himself the focus, Jesus claims a loyalty that later tradition offered only to God. In respect of Lev. 19:18, he has sought the well-being of all who came to him, including Gentiles (even if on occasion they have to pass the test of faith [7:24–30]; see Marcus 1999: 468–69), even if it meant trans-

gressing a religious requirement or tradition (e.g., 3:1–6; cf. 7:1–4). So too the disciples, who were warned against stumbling the little ones or rejecting any who bear Jesus' name.

The scribe's surprising additional commentary echoes this concern by referring to the important scriptural theme that genuine and wholehearted love of the one true God (cf. Deut. 4:35) and love of neighbor far surpasses any amount of sacrifice (e.g., 1 Sam. 15:22; Hos. 6:6; cf. Ps. 40:6; 51:16; Isa. 1:10–17; Jer. 6:19–20; 7:22–23; Amos 5:22; Mic. 6:6–8; *'Abot R. Nat.* 4:2; *b. Sukkah* 49b; *Deut. Rab.* 5:15). This possibly is what underlies the Qumran community's conviction that it will atone for sin better than burnt offerings and sacrifices through its perfect embodiment of the divine will (1QS IX, 3–4; so also the Messiah in 4Q226 10 I, 13 [so Baumgarten 1990; 1999]). Granted that these various summations of Torah were never understood to render sacrifice irrelevant (as per *m. 'Abot* 1:2's comment that the world rests on three things: the law, sacrificial worship, and expressions of love; cf. *b. Sukkah* 49b), in the context of Mark the scribe's response underlines those hints in Jesus' teaching that the temple cultus might be approaching its end (see C. A. Evans 2001b: 262).

The larger hostile context of this pericope highlights other, less pleasant dynamics. Insofar as Jesus speaks for God, the leaders' hostility toward him means that they do not love God (cf. John 5:42–43; 8:42). Concluding with Jesus' criticism of the scribes and the tragic situation of the widow, this section constitutes a final indictment on the "leafy tree" in that they have not loved their neighbor either (12:38–40).

In Deut. 6:13 Israel in the land was warned that they must swear by Yahweh alone, and that faithfully. But as blind and deaf Israel swore falsely in the pivotal Isa. 48:1–2, so also in Mark (e.g., 3:29; 7:6–8; 9:12–13; 11:17), and hence Jesus' warning about their blaspheming the Spirit (in doubting him, are they aligning themselves with Beliar?) and his understanding of his death as an *'āšām* (10:45). Moreover, in direct breach of Lev. 19:17–18's call to imitate God's holiness, Israel's leaders have continued to harbor hatred in their hearts and to conspire against Jesus, even though in open dispute he has time and again shown himself to be innocent of their reproaches.

While this solitary scribe represents for Mark how Israel's teachers ought to have responded, the lines instead are increasingly hardened. Having been challenged about his authority to announce the temple's destruction, Jesus is shown to be not only orthodox but also superior in his orthodoxy (Gundry 1993: 713). His credentials as a teacher of Israel are impeccable.

D. Theological Use. Christologically, in these two commands Jesus sums up the Torah, which he embodies in his life and death. Further, if the later rabbinic threefold actions reflect early traditions, then in retrospect Jesus' demands of his disciples seemingly imply a status equal to God. Ecclesiologically, these commands are also the new Torah by which his cross-bearing followers must live (cf. Matt. 7:12; 1 Cor. 16:22; Gal. 5:14).

12:36

A. NT Context: David's Son, David's Lord. Having seen off the opposition and won glowing approval, Jesus goes on the offensive with his own enigmatic and open-ended question. With his words chiastically arranged around a citation of Ps. 110:1 (109:1 LXX) (Marcus 1992: 130), and assuming David to be speaking prophetically (*nĕ'um* is characteristic of prophetic utterances; cf. 2 Sam. 23:2; 11Q5 XXVII, 4–11; *b. Sukkah* 25a; also Acts 1:16), he challenges the adequacy of the scribes' conception of the Messiah. Apart from replacing the LXX's "footstool of" with "under" and omitting the article before the first *kyrios*, the citation follows the LXX. Although the LXX uses *kyrios* of both speaker and addressee (Heb. uses *yhwh* and *'ādôn*), the syntax comfortably preserves the distinction.

B. Ps. 110:1 in Context. Concluding the short collection ascribed to David (Pss. 108–10) found in the fifth book, Ps. 110 (109 LXX) is a royal psalm (see Allen 1983: 83–83; Kraus 1986: 111). Most modern scholars take the addressee to be either David or his royal descendents, possibly at enthronement. The setting and the content suggest that Ps. 110 is a new interpretation of Ps. 2 (Zenger 1998: 90). Both describe the nations' subjugation (2:1–3, 8–12; 110:1–2), a shattering of Israel's enemies (2:9; 110:5–6), and Yahweh's anger against rebellious kings (2:5a; 110:5). Victory is certain in both because the Davidic king shares in, and is yet subordinate to, Yahweh's cosmic kingship, whether as "son" (2:7; cf. 109:3

LXX: *exegennēsa se*) or as one who sits at Yahweh's right hand (110:1; cf. *Midr. Ps.* 2:7).

Psalm 110, however, amplifies several core ideas. More explicit than Ps. 2:7's "son," the king's sitting at Yahweh's right hand implies the highest possible authority and honor short of usurpation (cf., e.g., 1 Chron. 28:5; 29:23; 2 Chron. 9:8), and thus blessing (cf. Gen. 48:13–14) and participation in his power (Exod. 15:6; Ps. 80:17; 98:1) and righteousness (Ps. 48:10). In Ps. 2 the nations take counsel against the Lord's anointed, while in Ps. 110 they surround him ("in the midst of your enemies" [110:2]). In Ps. 2 Yahweh invites the king to ask for the nations as his inheritance (2:8), while in Ps. 110 the king sits while the Lord fights for him (110:1; cf. 110:5–6). The latter is a common enough holy-war motif (e.g., Exod. 14:13; 2 Chron. 20:17; cf. Isa. 7:4–9) and a staple of David's victories (2 Sam. 5:10, 17–25; 8:6, 14). Ominously, Ps. 2's warning to the nations to submit has apparently been ignored, hence in Ps. 110:5–6 the grotesque outcome of Yahweh's intervention: shattered heads and a corpse-filled earth (cf. the finale of Isa. 66:24).

A striking addition is Ps. 110:4's unique designation of the Davidic king as a priest after, or "on account of," Melchizedek (*'al-dibrātî* is particularly difficult; cf. LXX: *kata tēn taxin*). Mentioned elsewhere in the OT only in Gen. 14:18–20 (cf. Josephus, *Ant.* 1.180; Philo, *Alleg. Interp.* 3.79–82), Melchizedek was a priest of "God Most High" whose superiority Abram recognized in being blessed by and tithing to him. In supplanting the Jebusite priest-king, the Davidic kings engaged in various priestly activities (Rooke 1998; Day 1998: 73–75). For example, David, clad in a priestly linen ephod, took the ark to Jerusalem (2 Sam. 6:14–15) and offered sacrifice (2 Sam. 6:13, 17–18; 24:25; cf. Solomon [e.g., 1 Kings 3:4, 15; 8:5, 62–64; 9:25]), and his sin, like that of the high priest, brought guilt on the whole people (2 Sam. 24; cf. Lev. 4:3). The promise recalls this divinely appointed inheritance and declares its restoration (cf. Jer. 30:21; see Jones 1992: 381–83).

C. Ps. 110:1 in Judaism. Psalm 110's unique understanding of exaltation probably informed two other passages, both of which, as we have already seen, were read eschatologically: (1) the exaltation of Isa. 52:13's obedient yet Suffering

Servant, understood in the Targum messianically but not as suffering, who will be "high and lifted up," and which elsewhere in Isaiah is appropriate only of God (e.g., 6:1; 14:13–14; 33:10); and (2) the exaltation of Dan. 7:13's son of man, who, together with the "holy ones," will enjoy eternal dominion and glory, which again is normally reserved for Yahweh (Ezek. Trag. 68–69 has Moses on an exalted throne, but independently of Ps. 110; see Hay 1973: 26; Hengel 1995: 180–84).

Probably because of its staggering claim concerning the sharing of God's throne, Ps. 110 is rare in intertestamental literature (Hengel 1995: 179; Hay 1973). Its royal-priestly combination might lie behind the attempts of the militarily successful priestly Hasmoneans' attempts to legitimate their fusing of priestly and royal roles (e.g., 1 Macc. 14:41; *T. Mos.* 6:1; *Jub.* 32:1; cf. Ps. 110:4; *T. Levi* 8:3, 14; see Hay 1973: 25).

Among the Dead Sea Scrolls, 11Q13 describes Melchizedek's return at the end of days (II, 4) to preside over Israel's new-exodus liberation (Isa. 61:1). Atoning for the congregation, he will release them from their sins (II, 6–8), effect God's vengeance on Belial and his spirits (II, 13), free his captives, inaugurate God's kingly reign (Isa. 52:7 in II, 16, 24), and be exalted to God's presence (II, 9–11). Commonly regarded as an angelic being, he is possibly a human messianic figure (Rainbow 1997). Although debated, the influence of Ps. 110 seems likely (Rainbow 1997: 184; Marcus 1992: 133). Similarly, 4Q491c 1, 11 apparently draws on Ps. 110 in describing a figure who, after victory and the vindication of the priestly community in the eschatological battle, is enthroned among the gods.

The apparently first-century Similitudes of *1 Enoch* (chaps. 37–71) also reflects the influence of Ps. 110 when the "Chosen One," also described in language derived from the Isaianic servant and the Danielic son of man, sits on God's throne at the end of days (51:3; 55:4; 61:8; 62:2 [see Black 1992; VanderKam 1992]). Not much later, Rabbi Akiba is rebuked for profaning the divine presence because he saw in Dan. 7:9's two thrones one for God and one for David (*b. Ḥag.* 14a; *b. Sanh.* 38b; cf. also *Hekhalot Rabbati*, where David is given a radiate crown and throne of fire beside God's [Hengel 1995: 195]), again probably under the

influence of Ps. 110 (but cf. *Midr. Ps.* 18:29; see Juel 1988: 138).

Testament of Job 33:3 alludes to Ps. 110:1 when righteous but suffering Job vindicates himself by pointing to his throne at the right hand of God. *Testament of Levi* describes a new priest who will understand the word of the Lord (18:2), whose star will rise in the heaven like a king (18:3; cf. Ps. 110:3), who will have no successor (18:8; cf. Ps. 110:4), and who will bind Beliar and grant to his children authority to trample wicked spirits (18:12; cf. Ps. 110:1; with nearby Christian interpolations, 18:6–7, 9). *Mekilta Exodus* 15:7–8 cites Ps. 110:1–4 to describe Yahweh's rising up against his enemies.

The Targum interprets the psalm eschatologically, with David appointed as the leader of the age to come because of his meritorious righteousness (110:4). In later rabbinic materials God defeats the kings, echoing Gen. 14, while Abraham sits at his right hand (*b. Sanh.* 108b; cf. *Midr. Ps.* 110:4; *Tanḥ. Gen.* 3:17; 4:3), and in *b. Sukkah* 52b Melchizedek returns in the messianic age.

In *Midr. Ps.* 18:29 the Messiah sits at God's right hand, with Abraham relegated to his left (citing Ps. 110:1, 5; cf. 110:2 which in *Gen. Rab.* 85:9 and *Num. Rab.* 18:23 refers to the Messiah). *Midrash Psalms* 2:9 (on Ps. 2:7), citing Ps. 110:1 along with Isa. 52:13; Dan. 7:13–14, states that the children of Israel are sons. Because of his many good deeds David is seated at the right hand of the presence (*S. Eli. Rab.* 18).

In summary, Ps. 110 seems to have informed two streams of speculation: the combination of priestly and royal roles (Hasmoneans; 11Q13) and the idea of supreme eschatological exaltation, particularly of a messianic/son-of-man figure and often after tribulation over God's and his opponents (cf., e.g., Isa. 52; Dan. 7).

D. The Use of Ps. 110:1 in Mark. It has been suggested that Jesus repudiates the popular assumption that the Christ would be a son of David (e.g., P. J. Achtemeier 1978; cf. Chilton 1982). However, Mark's use of various OT messianic texts thus far and his unqualified recording of Davidic-messiah affirmations clustered conspicuously around Jesus' arrival in Jerusalem (10:47–48; 11:10) make this improbable (Marcus 1992: 151–52; C. A. Evans 2001b: 274–75). Nor is the point merely that the Markan Jesus' vision of messiahship is different from Israel's. That much is already abundantly clear. Instead, his question is whether the scribes are justified in calling the Messiah "merely" "the son of David" (cf. *Pss. Sol.* 17:21; *b. Sanh.* 98a), when David himself, speaking by the Spirit, calls him "lord" (C. A. Evans 2001b: 274–75; *pothen* does not necessarily imply negation and is often used of an unsettling or surprising fact that requires explanation [R. E. Watts 2000: 287]).

While there is the formal element—the Scriptures nowhere use "Son of David" of the Messiah, whereas in Ps. 2, understood messianically, God calls him "my son" (cf. Gundry 1993: 723)—the real point of the question is, What does it mean for the Messiah to be David's Lord? And for Mark, given the use of Ps. 2 in Jesus' baptism and transfiguration and the previously noted parallels between Ps. 2 and Ps. 110, what does it mean for Jesus to be "son" (of God)?

Just as Isa. 52:13–53:12, Dan. 7:9–14, 11Q13, *1 Enoch*, and Rabbi Akiba suggest a trajectory of exaltation based on Ps. 110, there is, as we have seen, much in Mark to indicate that Jesus is indeed far more than David's human son (Marcus 1988: 136–37). Mark's Jesus has already identified himself with the exalted figures of Dan. 7 and Isa. 52–53 (e.g., 2:10, 28; 8:38; 10:45; 14:62), both texts being linked in the tradition to Ps. 110. But Mark's Jesus transcends even the intertestamental heavenly figures. The Gospel's new-exodus opening mixed citation points not to a messianic figure, but rather to the mysterious presence of God himself. Thus Jesus exercises divine prerogatives in pronouncing forgiveness of sin (2:5–7), rebuking and then walking on the sea (4:39–41; 6:49–52), and commanding healings rather than requesting them; small wonder, then, that the subjugated demons' cries of recognition suggest more than a merely human messiah (cf. 11Q13; *T. Levi* 18). As the scribe affirmed in the preceding pericope, there is only one God (and one power in heaven) (cf. the use of Deut. 6:4 in the synagogue [Segal 1977: 139; Marcus 1992: 145]). What is striking is that Jesus has just responded to the good scribe by declaring the Lord our God, the Lord is one (12:29). What then might it mean for Mark's Jesus himself immediately thereafter to draw attention to David's calling the Messiah "Lord"?

Likewise, Jesus' actions and teaching of Torah in the temple display his ultimate authority over the purity of Israel's worship. If so, then the citation implies not just Jesus' priestly authority, but also that this authority, by virtue of its Melchizedekian character, supersedes that of the present temple authorities (cf. *T. Levi* 18; Heb. 7).

Finally, if the question concerned only the nature of Jesus' messianic identity, then the first strophe of Ps. 110:1 would have sufficed. However, the addition of Yahweh's promise to make his enemies his footstool adds yet again a darker note, the most explicit to date: Jesus' enemies are God's enemies, and they are destined for destruction.

For Mark, Ps. 118 in Jesus' entry into Jerusalem celebrates in part his victories over the demonic hosts (cf. 11Q13 II, 13). As Ps. 2 warned, the Lord has sent forth his mighty scepter from Zion (Ps. 110:2), but, ironically, against those in Zion through Jesus' powerful silencing of Israel's authorities (12:34b) (see Marcus 1992: 135). Portentously, this part of Ps. 110 reinforces the point of the parable of the Wicked Tenants: those who refused to bless Jesus from the house of the Lord and instead plotted his death will be shattered and placed under his feet by Yahweh himself.

At his baptism and transfiguration Mark's Jesus was privately designated as Son of God. But just as Ps. 110 and its trajectories represent a heightening of Ps. 2, so too, as Mark's narrative nears its zenith, his Jesus publicly discomfits the scribes with the inadequacy of their messianic expectations. Jesus cannot be merely David's messianic son; he is also David's exalted Lord, Son of God, who, as Mark's unfolding portrayal of his extraordinary and superhuman authority suggests, uniquely sits at God's right hand, sharing in his blessing, authority, and righteousness. Furthermore, God will see to it that he rules in the midst of his enemies, shattering kings in the day of his wrath and, if need be, their temple "safe-house" (ch. 13; cf. Jer. 7:11 in Mark 11:17b). Just what this means will soon be revealed when at the final moment of confrontation Mark's Jesus again appeals to Ps. 110:1.

E. Theological Use. The primary focus here is Christology. Whatever else, Jesus cannot be merely a human messiah. Nor are his actions throughout Mark's Gospel merely those of an exalted angelic being—only Yahweh forgives sins and controls the sea. Ecclesiologically, in assuming the formation of a reconstituted Israel around Jesus, the most explicit warning to date adumbrates, eschatologically, God's coming judgment on an unrepentant nation and its leadership.

13:14

A. NT Context: The Abomination of Desolation.
Hard on the heels of the climactic series of confrontations, Jesus' pronouncements against the temple are now made explicit. Often characterized as apocalyptic, Jesus' language in Mark 13 stands firmly in the prophetic tradition as he announces the building's destruction "before this generation has passed" (13:30). Because the insurrectionist authorities have rejected God's "stone," not one stone of the present temple will remain atop another (13:2). Although the speech's extent reflects the gravity of the matter—not surprising, given the temple's central place in Israel's Scriptures and identity—Jesus' primary concern is with the preparation and "nondestruction" of his followers. (This chapter is brimming with OT echoes [see Hartman 1966: 156–57; Dyer 1998: 101–15; N. T. Wright 1996: 339–65]. Due to space limitations, I confine the discussion to citations and some of the more obvious allusions.)

Initially ignoring the disciples' question as to when this will happen, Jesus warns of coming deception and persecution (3:3–13). These, however, are but the precursor to the great tribulation, which itself heralds the temple's calamitous end (13:14–23). In my view, these verses describe the horrors immediately preceding that destruction during the first revolt in AD 70 (France 2002: 519; N. T. Wright 1996: 339–65; but see Beasley-Murray 1993: 407–8). Key to escaping the conflagration will be recognizing "the abomination of desolation" standing where "it/he" ought not be (13:14). The precise expression, *to bdelygma tēs erēmōseōs*, is found in Dan. 12:11 LXX, while *bdelygma erēmōseōs* occurs in 11:31 (also 12:11 Theodotion), and *bdelygma tōn erēmōseōn* occurs in 9:27 (LXX; Theodotion; cf. *hē hamartia erēmōseōs* [8:13 LXX; Theodotion]). All render the Hebrew *šiqqûṣ šōmēm*: "a 'detested thing [normally used of idols] which desolates,' or perhaps 'appals' [sic]" (France 2002: 523), though Mark's context suggests the former.

B. The Abomination of Desolation in the OT.
It is generally agreed that all four Danielic references (including 8:13) concern the actions of the "little horn" (8:9), Antiochus Epiphanes, who in 167 BC "threw truth to the ground" in destroying Torah scrolls (8:12), abolished the daily sacrifice, and established "an abomination of desolation" (cf. 1 Macc. 1:54; 6:7; 2 Macc. 6:1–5). The expression is thought to be a derogatory pun on "Lord of Heaven" (*ba'al šōmēm*), the Syrian counterpart of Zeus Olympius, to whom the Seleucids dedicated the temple (2 Macc. 6:2 [see Goldingay 1989: 212]), but the actual referent is uncertain, being an image (cf. 1 Macc. 1:54; see Lacocque 1979: 199), or an altar for pagan sacrifice (Josephus, *Ant.* 12.253; cf. 2 Macc. 6:5; 1 Macc. 1:59), or the sacrifices themselves (Lust 2001), or sacred stones (cf. 1 Macc. 4:43). In any case, it left an indelible mark on Jewish consciousness, and the expression "came to symbolize an unspeakable affront to the sanctity of God's house and to God himself" (C. A. Evans 2001b: 318).

An important exegetical question concerns Dan. 8:12, where this desolation occurs "in or because of rebellion" (*bĕpāša'*). J. Goldingay and J. J. Collins read "in (an act of) rebellion" (i.e., Antiochus') because Daniel nowhere explicitly attributes the present distress to Israel's transgressions. Strangely, although both authors draw heavily on 1–2 Maccabees, neither one mentions at this point 1 Macc. 1:11–15, 43, and Collins merely footnotes 2 Macc. 7:18 (but not 7:32), all of which states Israel's idolatrous culpability in no uncertain terms. Furthermore, Dan. 9:20–27 ("rebellion" [9:24]; cf. Lev. 26:27–45); 11:30–35; and 12:10 indicate that Israel's sin was indeed a factor (cf. *Tanḥ. Gen.* 1:23), even if Daniel's primary focus is Antiochus' wickedness (Porteous 1965: 141; Fishbane 1988: 487–90; Lucas 2002: 241–42, 250–52).

In this respect, the combination of these two word groups (*šqṣ/bdelygma* and *šmm/erēmōsis*) and related concepts was already well established (see Ford 1979: 155–56). In the epilogue to the Holiness Code, Lev. 26:30–33, to which Dan. 9 alludes (Fishbane 1988: 487–90), warns that Israel's land and sanctuaries would become desolate if Israel broke covenant and engaged in idolatry. In Jeremiah's famous Temple Sermon Israel's idolatrous abominations pollute Yahweh's very house, causing it, as happened to Shiloh, to be laid waste (7:30–34; cf. 9:10–14; 13:24–27).

Ezekiel similarly sees Israel's abominable idolatries as defiling the sanctuary and leading to the land's desolation (5:9–14; 6:4–14; 33:27–29). Hence the sad conclusion of 2 Chronicles: in spite of Yahweh's compassion in continually sending his prophets (cf. Mark 12:1–9), all the leading priests and the people persisted in their abominations, polluting his house and ensuring the destruction of the temple and the devastation of the land (2 Chron. 36:14–21; cf. 2 Kings 21:2–13).

C. The Abomination of Desolation in Judaism. As we noted above, 1 Macc. 1:54's account of the cessation of the daily sacrifice understands the abomination as an altar (1:59). For *Tanḥ. Gen.* 1:23, the "desolation" of Dan. 8:13 is because of Israel's sins, and in *b. Taʿan.* 28b, Dan. 12:11's "detestable thing that caused to be appalled" consisted of two idols (cf. *m. Taʿan.* 4:6; see Gaston 1970: 24).

D. The Use of the Abomination of Desolation in Mark. All agree that Jesus warns of a Daniel-like sacrilege in the temple that signals the disciples' last chance to flee. Exactly what that sacrilege is, is far less clear. Numerous solutions have been proposed (e.g., imperial standards, Caligula's image, the Zealots' unqualified high priest, Titus's entry, a pagan statue, a deified human, imperial coins [cf. 2 Thess. 2:3–4]). All these suggestions fail because the events did not take place, or were too soon or too late, and/or did not result in the temple's desolation (e.g., C. A. Evans 2001b: 318–19).

But perhaps the attempt at an overly precise identification is misguided. Mark 13, although clearly referring to a historical event, does so using prophetic topoi. As with all such prophetic language, the concern is the significance of the event, not an exact description (N. T. Wright 1996: 339–65; *pace*, e.g., Gundry 1993: 754–800; C. A. Evans [2001b: 320], whose overly concrete reading leads him to suggest that the prophecy is as yet unfulfilled). Furthermore, Mark's "let the reader understand," his only such instruction, and the odd combination of the masculine participle *hestēkota* with the neuter *to bdelygma* indicate that some subtlety is involved, especially if the "abomination" expression is also a topos. Thus, while perhaps envisaging a single act or person, it could (as in the above OT usages) refer to a series of related, idolatrous events involving several persons and actions that effectively amounted to

Daniel's "abomination," though not necessarily identical in all respects.

Second, in Mark, as in the prophets, it is Israel's rebellion, epitomized in the leadership and described using metaphors for idolatry (e.g., blindness, deafness [4:12]), that culminates finally in Jesus' announcement of the temple's destruction (11:17). Not surprisingly, Jesus cites Jeremiah's Temple Sermon, which explicitly links the sanctuary's looming desolation (Jer. 7:32–34; cf. Mark 13:17–19) with Israel's abominations. The Daniel connection arises through an act of reinterpretation (see Daube 1956: 325–29, 418–37). This time it is not Antiochus, but, ironically, Israel's insurrectionist leaders (whether high priests, elders, and/or Zealots), whose idolatrous blindness leads them to "make war" on God's people and kill the Son of Man, and whose actions are therefore shockingly likened to the "little horn's" abominations (cf. Prov. 21:27). That is, the nation's leaders, in rejecting Jesus, unwittingly set the whole sorry affair in motion (cf. the ironic comment in John 11:48).

On this reading, the "abomination" of which Jesus warns is probably that which, beginning with the abuses and rebellion that he saw in his own day (see Jer. 7:11, cf. 7:10; 8:12 in Mark 11:17 above), reached its apostate and sacrilegious culmination in the Zealot takeover of the temple and its subsequent horrors (cf. Josephus, *J.W.* 4.150–167, 196–207, 388; see Lane 1974: 469; France 2002: 525; perhaps Mark uses the masculine participle to indicate the personal nature of the profanation but refrains from pluralizing the expression to maintain the Daniel link).

There might also be more lying beneath the surface. If Jesus is himself the keystone of God's new temple, then to crucify him is surely the supreme act of temple profanation (Mark 14:58). Perhaps, then, the tearing of the veil at Jesus' death is the prophetic sign that the temple is also effectively "dead." Because they have expelled God's presence in Jesus, God signifies that he has likewise abandoned his house and Jerusalem, which, for those with eyes to see, will be abundantly clear with what turns out to be the Zealot occupation of the temple.

E. Theological Use. Eschatologically, in a shocking reversal Jesus announces that instead of Isaiah's glorious hope, Jerusalem faces a future more grim than even the dark days of the "little horn." Equally if not more shocking, Israel's rebellious leaders have brought this on themselves. For Jesus, their defiling abominations are one with the worst in Israel's history: Antiochus' idolatrous pollution of the temple. Such categorizations, though appearing extreme, are in fact the flipside of Mark's high Christology. How else could one describe the outcome of those who kill Dan. 7's Son of Man, in whom Yahweh himself is present?

13:24–25

A. NT Context: The End of the Era. Having described the terrible suffering that precedes it, Jesus finally comes to the destruction of the temple (*pace* Gundry 1993: 754). As befits the awesome significance of this event, his account consists of multiple allusions cast again in the prophetic topoi of Israel's Scriptures. Because of the ubiquity of the imagery, 13:24b echoes a number of texts (Ezek. 32:7; Joel 2:10, 31; 3:15; Amos 8:9), but its closest parallel is Isa. 13:10 LXX. The antecedent of 13:25a is less clear but is generally traced to Isa. 34:4 LXX, which is the only OT text that speaks of stars falling in the context of judgment.

B. The Composite Citation. 1. Isa. 13:10 in Context. The collection of "oracles concerning the nations" is intended not so much to speak against the nations or to affirm Israel's salvation as to explain to Israel the meaning of various events as evidence of Yahweh's sovereign control over world affairs (Childs 2001: 114) and in particular human pretensions (C. R. Seitz 1993: 122). Although the details of its historical setting are debated (see Erlandsson 1970; C. R. Seitz 1993: 115–38), the extensive lead oracle, Isa. 13:1–14:32, which provides the lens through which the remaining oracles should be read, is composed primarily of two large units, one focusing on the destruction of Babylon presented as the pretentious world city (13:2–22), the other being a dirge sung over Babylon's king (14:4b–21).

After the superscription (13:1), the oracle proper begins with Yahweh as the Divine Warrior (Miller 1986) summoning "from a distant land and the extremities of the heavens" his terrifying and tumultuous war host whom he has "consecrated" to execute his anger and to devastate "all the earth" (*kol-hāʾāreṣ* [13:2–5]). Jesus' words come from the next section (13:6–16). Partly echoing a lament (13:6–8 [see Wolff 1964: 55]),

they describe the baleful eschatological "day of the Lord" as God comes to desolate the earth and destroy sinners from it (13:9b; cf. Amos 5:18–20; Zeph. 1:16–18). The pride of the arrogant and the insolence of tyrants will be laid low (13:11b), and the judgment from which there is no hope of escape will be so severe that humanity will barely survive (13:12). The seismic theological significance of this event is expressed through the metaphors of cosmic disorder. Earthquakes, shaken heavens (13:13), and, in a reversal of Gen. 1:14–18, the dimming of the sun, moon, and stars, which normally mark the seasons, all testify to the extent of Babylon's wickedness and the depth of Yahweh's indignation.

But the two judgments are linked by 14:1–4a. Yahweh has a purpose in the destruction of Babylon and its king: Israel's restoration from exile and, in a foreshadowing of both chapters 40–55 and the central concern of chapters 56–66, the inclusion of foreigners among his people (14:1 [see Childs 2001: 126]; see commentary on Isa. 56:7 in Mark 12:17 above; note also 14:2b, which speaks of Israel taking captive their captors, in the light of Jesus' binding of Satan [see commentary on Mark 3:27 above]).

2. Isa. 13:10 in Judaism. Isaiah 13:10 is applied to several significant events. It is used of the exodus and the drowning of Pharaoh's army (*Mek. Exod.* 15:5–6), of the fall and Adam's loss of status (*Tanḥ. Gen.* 1:18), of the day when the rebuilding of the temple was hindered (*Song Rab.* 5:5), and of the end of the age (*Sib. Or.* 8:233). The preceding verse, 13:9, is applied to the plagues (*Mek. Exod.* 12:11–14, 21–24), and in contrast to Israel's deliverance, which is far off, it teaches that the destruction of the heathen nations is at hand (*Pesiq. Rab.* 41:3).

In terms of the general motif, in the OT, because God's word underlies the good order of creation and its times and seasons (Gen. 1; Jer. 33:25–26; cf. the exodus plagues), the withdrawal of that order, expressed in part through the cessation of the heavenly lights, is God's judgment on idolatrous nations (Isa. 24:23; Ezek. 30:3–4, 18; 32:6–8; Joel 3:15) and Israel (Isa. 5:25, 30; Jer. 4:23–28; 15:9; Joel 2:10, 30–31; Amos 8:7–10), and often in contexts where God uses one nation to carry out his judgment on another (Isa. 13:10–13; 34:4; Ezek. 32:6–8; cf. Hab 3:6–11).

Similarly, in intertestamental literature the failing of the sun and moon attends God's judgment of humanity (*T. Levi* 4:1; *T. Mos.* 10:5; *4 Ezra* 7:39–40). In later Jewish tradition, because Torah was God's agent at creation and sustains it (e.g., *Exod. Rab.* 47:4; *Lev. Rab.* 35:4; *Num. Rab.* 10:1; *b. Pesaḥ.* 68b; *Midr. Ps.* 6:1; *S. Eli. Rab.* 18; cf. *b. Šabb.* 88a; 137b; *b. Meg.* 31b; *b. Ned.* 31b–32a), and because creation was made for Israel (*4 Ezra* 6:55; *2 Bar.* 14:17–19; *T. Mos.* 1:12), Israel's failure to accept or keep Torah results in the failure of the lights of heaven (e.g., *b. ʾAbod. Zar.* 3a; *Exod. Rab.* 47:5; cf. *Midr. Ps.* 20:3). Hence, eclipses are bad omens prefiguring suffering (*b. Sukkah* 29a). Israel's unique status means that its destruction at the hands of the nations would also lead to the dissolution of the heavens and earth (*Esther Rab.* 7:11; *Exod. Rab.* 15:6).

3. Isa. 34:4 in Context. Isa. 34 belongs to the larger unit of chapters 28–35, of which the first section (chaps. 28–33) is largely characterized by woe oracles concerning Assyria's earlier attack on Jerusalem, while the second section (chaps. 34–35) forms a bridge between the divine judgment on the nations' arrogance in chapters 13–23 (chap. 34) and the new-exodus return from exile, which dominates the second half of the book (chap. 35) (see Beuken 1992b). Whereas Babylon had earlier been the archetypal enemy, that dubious honor now shifts to Edom, the nation most vilified by the prophets (possibly because of this "brother's" involvement in Nebuchadnezzar's sack of Jerusalem [cf., e.g., Ps. 137:7; Ezek. 35:15; Obad. 8–14; cf. Isa. 63:1–6; Jer. 49:7–22; Ezek. 25:12–14; 35; Amos 1:11–12] see Cresson 1972; Bartlett 1989: 184–86).

The opening unit (34:1–4) summons the nations to God's court to hear the sentence of their coming dreadful slaughter epitomized in Edom's fate. Our text, 34:4, portrays its cosmic scale through the description of heavenly disintegration as the stars rot away and the skies roll up like shrunken parchment. As terrible as this is, it is only the curtain-raiser. The carnage soon moves to earth. The remainder of the oracle presents the disturbing (though restrained compared to some ancient Near Eastern analogues) image of Yahweh's blood-soaked sword slaughtering Edom's leaders and people in an unparalleled glut of sacrifice (34:5–7 [see Sweeney 1996: 439]) and, in

a change of metaphor, rendering it, like Sodom (34:9–10), an eternal pre-creation chaos (34:10, 11b, 17 [see Goldingay 2001: 195]) depopulated and inherited only by wild animals (cf. Babylon in 13:21–22).

But as in chapters 13–14, and employing imagery that could hardly be more comprehensive in contrast, representative Edom's demise is the necessary complement of the vision of Israel's salvation (Gosse 1990; Dicou 1991) wherein Yahweh leads his once blind, deaf, mute, and lame but now healed people in glorious procession through a new creational blossoming desert to Zion (chap. 35). For C. R. Seitz (1993: 238–39), the key to the linkage of the two chapters lies in the parallels between 35:1–2 and 27:6's new Song of the Vineyard: Edom's wilderness desolation is the destiny of any nation that tampers with Yahweh's vineyard.

4. Isa. 34:4 in Judaism. LXX B reflects the tradition that associates stars with *hai dynameis* (cf. *Song Rab.* 8:14, where they are identified as evil angels who represent Edom) and in which their falling from heaven signifies the end of the age (*Sib. Or.* 3:82; 8:233), as does other irregular behavior (*1 En.* 80:4–7; *4 Ezra* 4:4–5; *Sib. Or.* 3:75–90).

In rabbinic literature Isa. 34:4 applies to the replacement of the old creation with the new, the resurrection, citing Hos. 6:2 (*Pirqe R. El.* 51; see commentary on Mark 8:31 above), and the eschatological judgment of the wicked (*Pesiq. Rab Kah.* S. 2:1). Edom, blamed in 1 Esd. 4:45 for the burning of the temple during the Babylonian invasion, later becomes in the rabbinic writings a standard reference to Rome (e.g., *Tg. Isa.* 34:9; *Gen. Rab.* 42:2; 44:15; *Midr. Ps.* 68:15; 97:1; *b. Yoma* 10a; *b. Sanh.* 12a; *b. Giṭ.* 56a; *b. Pesaḥ.* 118b; *b. Meg.* 6a; *Exod. Rab.* 23:11; *Pesiq. Rab Kah.* 4:1), also understood to be the fourth beast (e.g., *Gen. Rab.* 44:18; *Exod. Rab.* 23:11; 25:8; *Lev. Rab.* 13:5; 29:10; *Num. Rab.* 10:2), which would be especially harshly judged for its razing of the temple (e.g., *b. Giṭ.* 57b; *Exod. Rab.* 35:5; cf. *Midr. Ps.* 97:1). Ultimately Edom/Rome would be destroyed by the Messiah (*Pirqe. R. El.* 44), its requital signaling the rebuilding of the temple (*Pesiq. Rab Kah.* S. 5:3).

C. The Use of Isa. 13:10; 34:4 in Mark. Jesus' concern here is again not photorealism, but rather the significance of the event (*pace* Allison [1998: 160–62], who with admirable tenacity refuses to recognize prophetic hyperbole). More than simply describing the demise of the city, which it surely does (Hatina 1996), the cosmic language is consistent with the widely held Jewish belief that the temple stood at the center of creation, which originated from Zion (Levenson 1984). Furthermore, as early as Amos, cosmic chaos was seen to be the consequence of Israel's failure to obey Torah. As we have seen, many of Jesus' most pungent criticisms of Israel's leadership concerned exactly this. Consequently, and consistent with later Jewish tradition concerning Isa. 13, Jesus indicates that this event is of the same order as the fall, the destruction of Pharaoh's army in the sea, interfering with the temple's rebuilding, and the end of days. The world as it was is coming to an end (Moloney 2002: 266).

More shocking is his scandalous application to Israel of oracles directed against the two nations that epitomize idolatrous and arrogant hostility toward God (France 2002: 533). For Jesus, Israel's "Antiochan" leaders, in hijacking God's vineyard, have perverted Jerusalem's role (e.g., Isa. 2:2–5; Ezek. 5:5; *Tanḥ. Lev.* 7:10), transforming it into an Edom-like traitor and a Babylon-like world city seeking to challenge God's sovereignty, both nations having participated in the temple's destruction. As such, Jerusalem itself comes under similar judgment (*pace* Verheyden 1997, Jesus thus retains the original sense of both texts). Even more ironic, whereas later tradition singles out Edom, a cipher for Rome, for special retribution because it razed the temple, on Jesus' use of Isa. 13 the Roman armies are now God's consecrated ones called to judge Edom-Jerusalem. The hyperbolic horrors and depopulation of the "great tribulation" of Mark 13:14–23 are also entirely in keeping with the topoi of the two Isaiah oracles and yet retain the link with Daniel via 13:19's echo of Dan. 12:1 (Hooker 1991: 315–16).

Finally, in both instances God's judgment was closely connected with Israel's new-exodus redemption—a key theme in Mark's Gospel. Isaiah 13–14 anticipates the inclusion of aliens (14:1; cf. Isa. 56:7 in Mark 11:17), and Isa. 34–35's combination of vineyard imagery (C. R. Seitz 1993) and the return in Yahweh's train of those newly healed to Zion is echoed in Jesus' vineyard parable

and the healing of Bartimaeus (see commentary on Mark 11:9–10 above).

D. Theological Use. The central theological point of Jesus' use of these two passages is ecclesiological. Hostile Jerusalem has joined the arrogant and idolatrous world cities, and its fate will be no different from all other such tyrants. Its demise marks God's eschatological cosmic intervention against "the earth" and the beginning of the new creation with a newly restored temple-people with whom he will dwell, constituting its new center.

13:26–27

A. NT Context: On the Clouds of Heaven. Then, Jesus says, the disciples will see "the Son of Man coming in the clouds" with great power and "glory" as he sends out his angels to gather his elect from the four winds (13:26–27). The first part of the statement is universally understood to be a close allusion to Dan. 7:13–14, and the second part to be a combined allusion to Zech. 2:6 (2:10 LXX) (*ek tōn tessarōn anemōn tou ouranou synaxō*) and Deut. 30:4 (*ap' akrou tou ouranou heōs akrou tou ouranou ekeithen synaxei*), changing the main verb to *episynagō* and the first *tou ouranou* to *gēs*.

B. The Composite Allusion. 1. Dan. 7:13–14 in Context and in Judaism. See commentary on Mark 2:10; 8:38 above. By way of reminder here, we note that the messianic Son of Man's exaltation means that he exercises great power in judgment over the rebellious nations and in providing salvation for the elect.

2. Zech. 2:6 in Context. The primary concern of the first eight chapters of Zechariah is the postexilic restoration. After a series of oracles exhorting the returning exiles not to imitate their fathers (1:1–6) and announcing the return of Yahweh to Zion (1:7–17), the end of foreign domination (1:18–21), and Jerusalem's future posterity (2:1–5), 2:6–13 exhorts the exiles to return home. Probably inspired by the refounding of the temple and drawing heavily on Isaiah (Sweeney 1989: 588), it is the climactic commentary on the previous visions (Meyers and Meyers 1988–1993: 1:176–77).

The opening dual interjections, *hôy hôy/ō ō*, normally imply a sense of threat if the subsequent instruction was not obeyed (Redditt 1989: 59). Here it conveys at least urgency (Meyers and Meyers 1988–1993: 1:162). The exiles, here called "Zion" (2:7a [LXX: *eis Ziōn*]; cf. Isa. 52:1–12) and whom Yahweh had earlier scattered to the four winds of heaven, are to flee from their captivity in the land of the north, Babylon (2:7b; cf. Jer. 1:13–14; 6:22). Yahweh is about to break Babylon's power (1:18–21), for in striking his people, they have struck the very apple of his eye (cf. Deut. 32:10 [the pupil is most sensitive]), and now he will raise his hand (cf. Isa. 11:15; 19:16) against them as they themselves become plunder (2:8–9; cf. Exod. 12:35–36). Then, in 2:10–11 the prophet exhorts his hearers to rejoice, declaring, in a close echo of Isa. 56:3–8, that many nations will join themselves to the Lord and become his people (cf. Isa. 2:2–4; 66:18–24; see Petersen 1984: 181), probably in covenant (cf. Isa. 42:6; 56:3–8; Jer. 50:5), when Yahweh, having again chosen Jerusalem (2:12), is enthroned in his renewed temple (2:13; cf. Hag. 2:20–23).

3. Zech. 2:6 in Judaism. The Targum glosses "Zion" with "the congregation of" (2:7, 10), exchanges the "hand" of 2:9 for a "mighty scourge," has the people inheriting the land (2:16), and expands 2:13 to state that all the wicked will perish. Zechariah 2:6 occurs only rarely in the rabbinic writings, where it is used to argue that just as the world could not exist without winds, neither could it exist without Israel, but in scattering Israel, God actually protected his creation (*b. Ta'an.* 3b; *b. 'Abod. Zar.* 10b).

4. Deut. 30:4 in Context. For the larger setting, see §B of the commentary on Mark 3:4 above. Following a Sodom-like description of the cursed land (29:20–28), our text comes from the first section, 30:1–10, of the concluding unit (30:1–20), which, assuming the exile, offers hope to that future generation. Yahweh promises that when they remember and return to him with all their hearts and souls (30:2), which, as prisoners of foreign powers, is all they can do (Craigie 1976: 363), he will have compassion on them. He will turn their fortunes (cf. Jer. 30:18; 33:26) and gather them even if exiled to the very ends of the heavens (30:4), and they, outnumbering their ancestors, will again possess the land (30:5). Unlike 10:16, where the people of Israel were summoned to circumcise their own hearts, here Yahweh himself will do it (30:6; cf. Jer. 31:31–34; Ezek. 36:24–32; see McConville 2002: 427). They will love him with all their hearts and souls and so live prosperously (30:6, 9), observing all his commandments

(30:8), while he will turn the covenant curses back on their oppressors (30:7). Of particular interest is the emphasis on turning to, loving, and obeying God with all their hearts and souls (30:2, 6, 10) by observing the commandments (30:8, 10)—recurrent themes in Deuteronomy (Tigay 1966: 285).

5. Deut. 30:4 in Judaism. Deuteronomy 30:4 appears only in the rabbinic writings. In *Mek. Exod.* 12:37–42, Deut. 30:3 is evidence that the Shekinah will return, and in *Num. Rab.* 23:14, citing Isa. 11:12; 35:10, Deut. 30:4 is fulfilled in the time to come (cf. *Tanḥ. Num.* 10.10.III, which adds Isa. 51:3).

The four winds (in this spatial sense) and the corners of the heavens and earth refer to the entire known world (e.g., Jer. 49:36; Zech. 6:5; Josephus, *Ant.* 8.80; *J.W.* 4.262; Philo, *Cherubim*, 99; *Migration*, 181; *4 Ezra* 13:5; *T. Ash.* 7:3). Human arrogance seeks to control it (Dan. 8:8; 11:4), but when Yahweh acts, the ends of the earth know (Ps. 22:27; 59:13; 95:3; Isa. 52:10), hence the prayer in fulfillment of his promise (Ps. 2:8) that the rule of his Davidic king will similarly extend (Ps. 72:8). Having scattered the exiles to the four corners of the earth, Yahweh can, of course, restore them (Isa. 11:12; 41:9; 43:6; Ezek. 39:27–28; Zech. 10:6–11), hence the later idea of the Messiah gathering the exiles (e.g., *Pss. Sol.* 8:28; 11:1–4; 17:21–28; *Tg. Isa.* 53:8; *Tg. Hos.* 14:8; *Tg. Mic.* 5:1–3).

C. The Use of Dan. 7:13–14; Zech. 2:6; Deut. 30:4 in Mark. Jesus now returns to the earlier warning of 8:38. Jerusalem, the idolatrous world-city (Babylon-Edom), having rejected his words, is "ashamed" and is replaced with God's kingdom (cf. 1:14–15), ruled by the enthroned messianic Son of Man. His "power" and "glory" (Dan. 7:14), as were David's, are an extension of God's (cf. Ps. 63:2; 1 Chron. 29:11; see Roberts 2002) as the presumably resurrected and ascended Jesus effects the deliverance "through his angels" of the elect from the beastly nations. In terms of ancient entry patterns (see Catchpole 1984), this is indeed a parousia, and Jesus' second one, but only to Jerusalem, not to the rest of the world (hence, perhaps, Mark's avoidance of the term). Having been rejected on his first, peaceful entry, this time he comes in power to own his royal claim, and as with other such second comings of the day, it results in the destruction of the recalcitrant city (cf. Alexander and Tyre [Duff 1992: 61–62]), hence the two Isaianic texts in 13:24–25.

Nevertheless, the Son of Man's coming does fulfill God's promise to rescue his people (Zech. 2:6; Deut. 30:4). For Mark, the new exodus has already begun in Jesus, but here it expands to include those outside the land of Israel who are yet to hear the good news of Yahweh's return to Zion (Mark 1:14–15; 13:9–11). But as ought to be clear by now, this, for Mark, means newly reconstituted Israel—including foreigners as the Son of Man now holds sway over "all peoples, nations, and languages" (Dan. 7:14; cf. Isa. 56:7 in Mark 11:17) who do God's will by listening to Jesus (cf. 3:32–35; 8:34–38). (As other Jewish traditions well understood, the rebels in Israel will be judged along with the nations [Elliott 2000; cf. France 2002: 534].)

On this view, the gathering refers to God's claiming for himself a people, whether Jewish or Gentile, from among the nations through faith in his Christ (see, e.g., Acts 15). The gathering, however, is not to present Jerusalem, which is to be destroyed (cf. Ps. 147:2), but rather to the new temple, of which Jesus is the keystone. On this reading, the destruction of the temple and the inauguration of the prophetic vision for a people of God from among the nations are the twin signs testifying to Jesus' vindication (France 2002: 535).

There are other synchronicities. As in Zechariah, this return from exile happens even as "Babylon"—here Jerusalem—comes under judgment (cf. *Tg. Zech.* 2:13's gloss on the destruction of the wicked), because to harm Yahweh's "son" Israel is to harm him (cf. Mark 12:8–9). The redeemed are in both cases warned to flee. In Zechariah God's people are addressed as "Zion," among whom Yahweh dwells in his restored temple, while in Mark Jesus is the beginning of a new spiritual temple-people (cf. Isa. 54:1 in Gal. 4:26–27; Rev. 21). And as Zechariah envisaged many nations joining themselves to the Lord, so the Son of Man gathers his elect from the entire world.

Deuteronomy's vision of the return emphasized the need to obey Torah with all one's heart and soul. This has been a fundamental concern of Jesus as well (e.g., 3:1–6; 12:28–34). For Mark, God has, in Jesus, acted in merciful compassion to re-store his people (e.g., 1:41; 5:19; 6:34; 8:2; 9:22; 10:47–48). In one later Jewish tradition Deut. 30 promised the return of the Shekinah as Isa. 35:10's ransomed returned with joy to Zion. Mark too is aware that uniquely in Jesus God's presence has returned to his people, hence the account of the now-seeing Bartimaeus joyfully returning in Jesus' retinue to Jerusalem.

D. Theological Use. Much of the preceding theology continues. Christologically, Jesus is the enthroned Son of Man, through whom, eschatologically speaking, Yahweh's cosmic rule over the beastly nations—now including apostate Jerusalem—will be exercised. Ecclesiologically, Jesus and his people, comprised of faithful Israelites and many from the nations, now make up the Israel of God (cf. Gal. 6:16).

14:24

A. NT Context: The Blood of the Covenant.
Given Mark's new-exodus theme, the culmination of his Gospel fittingly takes place on Passover. Whatever the exact nature of the meal might be (see, e.g., McKnight 2005: 243–73), for Mark, this is a Passover (14:12–16). After breaking the bread, Jesus took the cup, declaring it to be "my blood of the covenant which is poured out for many" (14:24). Characteristically, the Markan Jesus combines two texts. The first part, *to haima mou tēs diathēkēs*, which explains the significance of his blood, echoes Exod. 24:8 LXX, with *touto estin* instead of *idou/hinnēh* and the interposition of *mou* (less so, Zech. 9:11, itself a shorthand allusion to Exod. 24).

The second part, *to ekchynnomenon hyper pollōn*, which describes how this covenant is to be effected and on whose behalf, is often seen as yet another interpretative allusion to Isa. 53:12. It is sometimes objected that the pouring out of blood connotes merely violent and unjust death (e.g., Gen. 9:6; Deut. 19:10; 2 Kings 21:16; Ps. 106:38; Isa. 59:7), and that in the LXX *ekxeō* (cf. Mark's *ekchynnō*, which does not occur in the LXX) is never used of Isa. 53:12's *'ārâ* (Hooker 1959: 82; Pesch 1976–1977: 2:358–59). Nevertheless, Mark's *ekchynnō* is a perfectly acceptable rendering (France 1982: 122; Moo 1983: 131; Gundry 1967: 59). "Pouring out of blood" is also used in various sacrificial contexts, including sanctification and atonement (Exod. 29:12; Lev. 4:7, 18, 25, 30, 34; 8:15; cf. Ps. 106:38), and the servant's death has both violent and sacrificial elements (the blood of the 'āšām is also "dashed" on the altar [Lev. 5:6–7, 15–19; 7:1–6]). Moreover, the thoroughgoing influence of Isa. 53 on the Markan Jesus' understanding of his death, especially in 10:45, which already has "many," strongly suggests that *hyper pollōn* derives from Isa. 53:12 (France 1982: 122; Grimm 1981: 832; Pesch 1976–1977: 2:538; Gundry 1993: 832; Marcus 1992: 187). If so, it seems atomistic to deny that the whole clause does so as well (see R. E. Watts 2000: 356–62).

Finally, some see an allusion to *diathēkēn kainēn*, "new covenant," in Jer. 38:31 LXX (31:31 ET) (e.g., C. A. Evans 2001b: 392), but since Mark lacks the distinctive "new," it is impossible to be certain (cf. Luke 22:20).

B. The Composite Citation. 1. Exod. 24:8 in Context. In fulfillment of the promissory sign upon which Moses' call was validated (3:12 [see Schenker 1994: 491]), Exod. 19:1–24:18 describes Yahweh's coming to his people at Sinai. Following the warning to obey the messenger of the covenant (23:32–33 [see commentary on Mark 1:2–3 above]), the moment of formal covenant commitment arrives (24:1–18).

The people agree (24:3, 7; cf. 19:8) to abide by all of Yahweh's words (i.e., the Decalogue [20:1–17] and the Book of the Covenant [20:22–23:33], itself predicated on the Decalogue [see Durham 1987: 337]), which Moses inscribes (24:4a). Moses next sets up twelve witness pillars (24:4b) and offers sacrifices, probably signifying atonement/consecration and the resulting well-being (cf. 24:8 in Targumim *Pseudo-Jonathan* and *Onqelos*; see Sarna 1991: 117). Then, in one of the formative moments of the biblical narrative, he dashes half of the sacrificial blood upon the altar of the presence (24:6) and, after reading from the book of the covenant (24:7), dashes the other half upon the people (24:8), thus eternally binding Israel to Yahweh (cf. Gen. 15:9–21; Jer. 34:18–19; see Sarna 1991: 117).

Several ideas are expressed. Symbolizing life, the blood on the altar witnesses to life being God's gift, and that on the people marks them as dependent participants in that gift (Fretheim 1991: 258–59). In addition, the ritual not only cements Israel's election—the nation is already God's son (cf. 4:22)—but also now articulates the nation's vocation as Yahweh's "kingdom of priests and a holy nation" (19:6; cf. Lev. 8:23–24; see Nicholson 1982: 86; Fretheim 1991: 258–59), which itself presupposes God's covenant with Abraham and his purposes for the nations (Gen. 26:4–5).

As with the whole exodus event, this covenant, in which worship and obedience cannot be separated (24:1b, 3b, 7, 9–11), is Yahweh's initiative (24:8) and it is Yahweh's presence that stands at the center (Durham 1987: 348). Consequently, immediately following the covenant ratification meal on the mountain of God (24:9–11) and the giving of the tablets (24:12–18), the remaining third of the book largely concerns preparations for the tabernacle whereby God can dwell among his people (25:1–31:17; 35:1–40:38).

2. Exod. 24:8 in Judaism. The only other place in Israel's Scriptures where blood and covenant are associated is Zech. 9:11. A shortened form of Exod. 24:8, it provides the basis, by analogy with Israel's past redemption, for a future new-exodus restoration of the land (9:1–8), the future king (9:9–10), and deliverance of the captive (9:11–17; cf. Exod. 5:1–2; see Meyers and Meyers 1988–1993: 139, 175). Possibly in reaction to the Christian abrogation of the circumcision, a number of rabbinic references apply Exod. 24:8 to the rite on the basis of its frequent connection with covenant (e.g., *b. Ned.* 31b; *b. Šabb.* 134a; 135b; 137b; cf. *b. Yebam.* 46b). In an extensive discussion *Lev. Rab.* 6:5 understands the blood to indicate the penalty for covenant transgression, and thus in *Num. Rab.* 9:47 it is the oath by which the suspected woman swears. Remembering Exod. 24:5–8's blood of the covenant is understood to activate the promise of Zech. 9:11 (*Lev. Rab.* 6:5; 19:6).

On the other hand, that the immediately preceding 24:7—Israel promises obedience, and that to Torah—occurs throughout rabbinic literature emphasizes the indissoluble link between obedience and covenant, though often in terms of Israel's failure (e.g., *Sipre Deut.* 306; 319; *b. Šabb.* 88a; *Exod. Rab.* 1:36; *Lev. Rab.* 1:1; *Midr. Ps.* 1:20; 75:1; *Tanḥ. Gen.* 3:21). In practical shorthand, to keep Torah is to keep covenant.

3. Isa. 53:11–12 in Context and in Judaism. See commentary on Mark 8:31; 10:45 above.

C. The Use of Exod. 24:8; Isa. 53:11–12 in Mark. Mark's Jesus, in his characteristically enigmatic and shorthand manner, innovatively adds two otherwise distinct interpretive traditions to the meaning of his death: Passover and Exod. 24 (McKnight [2005: 306–8] correctly notes this distinctiveness, but then, in an apparent non sequitur, uses it to deny that Jesus could have integrated the two, because no one else had). Initially the allusion to Isa. 53 recalls Mark 10:45, where Jesus' death as the Isaianic 'āšām was linked to Israel's new-exodus redemption. Consistent with that conviction, he now astoundingly makes himself the focal point of Israel's great memorial meal, shifting its focus from the past to the future in anticipation of his coming death (later Jewish tradition also saw in the Passover an anticipation of the future deliverance [*Mek. Exod.* 12:42; *Tg. Ps.-J.* Exod. 21:42; *Frg. Tg.* Exod. 15:18; cf. 12:42; *Exod. Rab.* 18:12; 51:1; see Jeremias 1977: 207). Henceforth it will be his sacrifice, his blood "poured out," that is remembered as effecting the Passover of Israel's eschatological redemption (cf. the Targumim, which understood the Exod. 24 sacrifice also as atonement; see C. A. Evans 2001b: 388). If there is an allusion to Zech. 9:11, it will now look to this blood of the covenant.

Passover, however, was never an end in itself. The goal to which it pointed was the Exod. 24 covenant, which vocationally bound the nation to Yahweh as his kingdom of priests. By uniquely combining the two, Jesus not only compresses and references the whole of Israel's founding moment, but also, in the context of a new exodus and a reconstituted Israel, reconfigures it around himself (see C. S. Mann 1986: 575).

The implications, when teased out, are breathtaking. Completely ignoring the deaths of all the righteous martyrs before him (see commentary on Mark 8:31 above), Jesus claims that his death alone is efficacious in bearing Israel's punishment (cf. Isa. 53:5–6). Not content with remembering the Passover, he supplants it—and if this feast, what about the others?—integrating it with the inaugural covenant meal of Exod. 24, the only place where covenant blood and a formal meal are combined (see Aalen 1963). Moreover, in distinguishing his Passover and his sacrifice from what goes on in the temple, he supplants that institution, at least implicitly, as well (see McKnight 2005: 326). But this too is in keeping with his being the keystone of a new people-temple. Fur-

thermore, the Sinai covenant, as Moses made clear, was Yahweh's doing (Exod. 24:8), but here Jesus initiates it. There, the representatives of Israel ratified the covenant with a celebratory meal in the presence of God; here, the Twelve, representatives of the restored tribes (e.g., Jer. 31:27–28; 50:4; Ezek. 34:11–24; cf. Matt. 19:28/Luke 22:30), do so with Jesus (14:16–17; cf. 3:13–19) (see Myhre 1985). This is hardly less provocative than his action in the temple. One surely has to ask, By what authority? The disciples' question after the first stilling of a storm likewise comes to mind: Who is this? But then, Mark has consistently nudged his audience in this direction all along.

In later Jewish tradition Exod. 24 functioned primarily in two ways. First, it provided an interpretative framework for the blood of circumcision. On Mark's reading, circumcision as a mark of entry into covenant must now be related to Jesus. Second, and more commonly, Exod. 24 necessarily meant Torah-obedience (24:7)—understandably so, as this was Israel's fundamental covenant obligation (oddly, McKnight [2005: 308–9] affirms Jesus' concern for the one, Torah, while denying his interest in the other, covenant). That Mark's succinct account mentions no stipulations needs to be balanced with Jesus' eminent concern for Torah throughout and the fact that Mark begins his story with Malachi's messenger of the covenant. Consequently, Israel's "kingdom of priests" vocation, expressed in terms of Isa. 40–66's vision of including Gentiles and hence "the many" (see, e.g., commentary on Isa. 56:7 in Mark 11:17 above), can be fulfilled only in relation to Jesus and an equally exclusive commitment to him (see Dodd 1971: 108–9) and his "cross-bearing" Torah (see France 2002: 570).

Finally, we should note that even if Mark does not explicitly say so, this converges with the work of the servant whom Yahweh twice declares is appointed as a "covenant for the people," which probably means for the faithful within Israel and the survivors of the nations who turn to him (cf. Isa. 42:6; 49:6–8; see van Winkle 1985).

D. Theological Use. On the more immediate level, Jesus' use of Exod. 24 continues Mark's ecclesiological argument that the people of God find their vocational identity as his kingdom of priests in loyalty to Jesus, his messianic Son (cf. 1 Pet. 2:9; Rev. 1:6; 5:10). Soteriologically and eschatologically, Exod. 24 indicates that Jesus' death constitutes both the new Passover and the atoning/purificatory sacrifice of Exod. 24 (cf. Rom. 3:25; 1 Cor. 5:7; 11:25; Eph. 1:7; Heb. 9; 1 Pet. 1:18–19; Rev. 5:6).

At a deeper level it also speaks of God himself. At this new-covenant meal reconstituted Israel, like Israel of old, sees something of the face of God, who in Jesus lays down his life for his enemies (as John's Gospel strives to demonstrate [see Bauckham 1998]).

14:27

A. NT Context: The Smitten Shepherd. Hard on the heels of the meal, the Markan Jesus, citing Zech. 13:7, informs the Twelve that they will "fall away." Mark's form is closer to the MT, the LXX being something of a bird's nest of textual issues (Gundry 1967: 25–27). The shift from an imperative to a future first-person singular, *pataxō*, merely expresses the original sense more economically (cf. Isa. 53:10; see France 2002: 575).

B. Zech. 13:7 in Context. Zechariah 13:7–9 belongs to the more enigmatic and difficult half of the book (chaps. 9–14), in particular the final unit (chaps. 12–14), which is characterized by the eschatological refrain "on that day" (16x). The focus is still the return of Yahweh to his temple (9:1–8) and the future of Jerusalem as the world center (14:16–21), though now from the perspective of the disappointment of the return (see Childs 1979: 483). After a word on Jerusalem (12:1–9), attention shifts to the restored house of David (12:10–13:1) and the cessation of prophecy (13:2–6), and then comes the perplexing 13:7–9, which resumes the earlier "shepherd" theme (10:1–3; 11:4–17; cf. Jer. 23; Ezek. 34; 37).

Yahweh summons his sword to strike "my shepherd," his "strong associate" (*geber 'ămîtî*; cf. Lev. 6:2 [5:21 MT]; 18:20, where *'ămît* refers to a near neighbor), scattering the flock as he turns his hand against the "little ones" (13:7b; cf. Jer. 49:20; 50:45). Only a remnant of the land will survive (cf. 12:1–2; see Conrad 1999: 189), but after being refined by Yahweh (cf. Mal. 3:2–3), they will call on him, and he will own them in a reconstitution of covenant. If this much is clear, the rest is not: who is the shepherd (which depends in part on his relationship to the shepherd

of 11:17, and to the pierced one of 12:10), why is he struck, and when?

The literature is vast. For some, he is the worthless shepherd who betrays his calling and against whom the sword was already summoned (11:17; cf. Jer. 25:34–38, the only other occasion where a sword is invoked against shepherds and they are wicked; see Person 1993: 134; Conrad 1999: 189–90; Redditt 1989; Mason 2003: 130). For others, he is a deliberately enigmatic but presumably righteous future leader who, like Isa. 53's servant, is struck by Yahweh in order to purify his people (Baldwin 1972: 198; cf. Larkin 1994: 177). For yet others, since "shepherd" and "associate" best describe a Davidic figure, and because of the parallels with 12:10, he is that same messianic figure whose suffering leads to Israel's final restoration (Lamarche 1961: 138–47; France 1982: 108; Moo 1983: 176–78; Cook 1993; Duguid 1995: 274–76). Similarly, because scattering is connected in Jer. 23:1–6 and Ezek. 34 with hopes of a Davidic shepherd-king and *geber* (never used of a prophet, once used of David [2 Sam. 23:1]), he is indeed a Davidide but a preexilic figure who, because of his sin, comes to a violent end, thus explaining the present difficulties of the scattered sheep (cf. Jer. 21:5–7; see Meyers and Meyers 1988–1993: 2:385–88). Others simply note that he is a leader (R. L. Smith 1984: 283), perhaps a prophet (O'Brien 2004: 270), or even the Persian monarch (Sweeney 1989: 696; cf. the "shepherd" Cyrus in Isa. 44:24–28; 45:1–19).

The problem is that Zechariah is not clear, and perhaps deliberately so. We must admit that we know only that the shepherd is a strong leader, that his being struck probably happens after the return when the nation is afflicted with corrupt leadership (chaps. 11–12), and that it results in the scattering of the flock with a view to producing a purified remnant that is truly dependent on Yahweh and so facilitates the eschatological renewal of the covenant.

C. Zech. 13:7 in Judaism. CD-B XIX, 6–14 interprets Zech. 13:7 eschatologically as a time of distress when God visits the earth. The shepherd might be the Teacher of Righteousness, though he could be a wicked leader—the text, like Zechariah's, is not explicit. The "little ones" are those who have entered covenant (XIX, 16), being the community, or Israel, or even both (see Elliott 2000:

60–64). The nation's apostate leaders are faithless (XIX, 15). But, in keeping with the bifurcation in Zech. 3:8–9, these leaders, along with the wicked, will be destroyed by the Messiah (XIX, 10b, 13), while the "poor of the flock," the suffering community who keep covenant, will escape (XIX, 9b–10a). If *Sib. Or.* 3:544; 5:103 allude to Zech. 13:8, then they too read it eschatologically.

Consistent with its practice elsewhere, the Targum translates "the shepherd" as "the king" (e.g., 10:2; 11:3; 13:7)—the associate is his prince—whose death scatters the princes as the Lord smites the underlings. But this translation is used of both good and bad shepherds (cf. 10:2–4), and, as in Zechariah, no further identification is offered.

Although there is no clear reference to our verse in the later rabbinic writings, several traditions read Zech. 13:8–9 eschatologically. The "two-thirds" refers to the large numbers of idolaters (*Tanḥ. Deut.* 5:8) going to perdition (*b. Sanh.* 111a), with the purified "one-third" being Israel (*Tanḥ. Deut.* 5:10; *Tanḥ. Lev.* 2:4, citing Isa. 19:24; cf. *Tanḥ. Num.* 3:16; *Num. Rab.* 15:14; *Deut. Rab.* 2:33) or the penitent (*Song Rab.* 1:22; cf. *b. Roš Haš.* 17a).

D. The Use of Zech. 13:7 in Mark. Following a meal that cements covenantal loyalty, Jesus' statement is bracing. But Zechariah foresaw that a postexilic Israel led by corrupt shepherds would require drastic action if Jerusalem and God's people were to attain their calling. For Mark's Jesus, that drastic action was unfolding in his death (see C. A. Evans 2001b: 403; Marcus 1992: 159).

As the first-person "I will strike" indicates, Jesus' suffering "is necessary" (8:31), since ultimately God is behind it (cf. Isa. 53:10; see Hooker 1991: 344; *pace* Gundry 1993: 847, who else could "I" be?). Jesus knows what will happen. But the primary focus, as in Zechariah, is on the disciples' scattering (cf. 14:26–31, 66–72; see Wilcox 1970–1971). For all their self-confident grasping for greatness (9:33–34; 10:35–37) and desire to "shepherd" others (9:38; 10:42–44), the Twelve will finally be forced to admit that they too are only "little ones" (Zech. 13:7b; cf. Mark 9:42–48) who themselves will stumble (14:31, 50).

The smiting of the shepherd, probably encompassing the entire passion (Moo 1983: 186), will ultimately mean devastation for the faithless, in Mark's case Jerusalem (chap. 13), and hence the future lies in Galilee, where it all began (16:7). But as in Zechariah and CD-B, God's purpose will stand, and, in a twist unforeseen by Zechariah, this shepherd will be resurrected to go ahead of his purified remnant (see France 2002: 577).

E. Theological Use. Given Mark's new-exodus perspective, and in keeping with several Jewish traditions, his Jesus interprets Zech. 13 eschatologically. Through his suffering a purified remnant will emerge, and the nations will be gathered to worship (13:27). Ecclesiologically, Jesus too sees Israel as the remnant, but, as we would expect, it is the Israel gathered around and in covenant with him, not Torah or the *Damascus Document*'s community rule (see Bruce 1961: 344; Marcus 1992: 159). Christologically, whereas in Zechariah, the *Damascus Document*, and the Targum the shepherd's identity was unclear, here in Mark he is revealed to be the messianic servant Son of Man. And whereas in Zechariah the purified remnant called on God's name, here in Mark it is Jesus whom they will see in Galilee.

14:62

A. NT Context: Sitting at the Right Hand. In what is probably a preliminary hearing to finalize charges against him, Jesus' confrontation with official Israel comes to a head (14:53–65; cf. 8:31; 11:27–28). In the christological pinnacle of the Gospel, Jesus for the first time publicly declares his messianic Son of Man status.

Mark's recording of the accusation that Jesus declared that he would destroy the temple (*naos*) "made by hands"—already offensive because *cheiropoiētos* implies idolatry (LXX: Lev. 26:1, 30; Isa. 2:18; 10:11; Dan. 5:4, 23; 6:28), especially if later rabbinic tradition that God established the temple was already held (cf. *Mek. Exod.* 5:17–21; see C. A. Evans 2001b: 446)—and replace it in three days with a different one (*allon*) of divine origin (cf. *2 Bar.* 4:3) is fully consistent with his earlier presentation. Whatever the significance of Jesus' refusal to answer might be, the reference to the *naos* is important for Mark (cf. 15:29, 38) and coheres with Jesus' action in the temple, his appeal to Ps. 118's rejected stone, Ps. 110's exalted combination of royal and priestly prerogatives, and the Olivet Discourse.

The pivotal moment, however, is the high priest's question concerning Jesus' messianic identity. Given their response to the parable of the Wicked Tenants, it is unlikely that Israel's educated elite would have missed the implications of Jesus' approach to Jerusalem, his use of Jer. 7 in the temple demonstration, or his earlier jibe based on Ps. 110. Mark's high priest, apparently seeing a direct question as the best way to force the issue, asks contemptuously, "Are *you* the Messiah, the Son of the Blessed One?" (the two expressions have one and the same referent [*pace* Marcus 1988]). His response to Jesus' reply suggests that he got everything he hoped for, and more.

The debate over what actually constitutes blasphemy is too extensive to canvass here (see Bock 2000). In my view, it is not so much Jesus' affirmation as what is implied by his scriptural addition, a characteristically combined allusion, this time to Dan. 7:13 and Ps. 110:1 (109:1 LXX). Mark's participle *erchomenon* and preposition *meta* are closer to Theodotion's text of Dan. 7:13, the wording is changed to emphasize Mark's customary definite "the Son of Man," and the whole is arranged chiastically around the Ps. 110 allusion but without any significant change in meaning. In terms of Ps. 110, Jesus' first-person usage explains the shift from the LXX's second-person imperative "sit" and first-person possessive pronoun "my," while his substitution of the present participle "sitting" envisages the realization of the promise. The circumlocution "the power" emphasizes at whose right hand he sits (cf. *1 En.* 62:7; *'Abot R. Nat.* [A] 37:12; *Sipre Num.* 112), and its setting within the Daniel allusion seems designed to stress Jesus' close relationship with God (Gundry 1993: 886). It might also be a deliberate echo of God's "powerful" scepter wielded on behalf of his king in the day of his "power," so as to stress what is at stake (*dynamis* [Ps. 109:2–3 LXX]). The combination of Dan. 7 and Ps. 110 is not surprising, since the latter probably influenced the former and is found in several first-century traditions concerning the Son of Man (e.g., *1 Enoch*, *4 Ezra*; cf. the later *Midr. Ps.* 2:9; see commentary on Mark 2:10; 12:36 above).

B. The Composite Citation/Allusion. 1. Dan. 7:13 in Context and in Judaism. See commentary on Mark 2:10; 8:38; 13:26–27 above.

2. Ps. 110:1 in Context and in Judaism. See commentary on Mark 12:36 above.

C. The Use of Dan. 7:13; Ps. 110:1 in Mark. In combining Dan. 7 and Ps. 110, Mark's Jesus

reflects his consistently messianic Son of Man self-understanding. However, since Jesus is already under suspicion of speaking against the temple, an act that itself apparently could warrant execution (see Josephus, *J.W.* 6.300–309; if Gentiles' defiling presence in the temple warranted death to the Jew responsible for bringing them there [Acts 21:27–36], what of a Jew whose language implied worse? [see C. A. Evans 2001b: 446]), several factors make his doing so here particularly offensive. Although Ps. 110 and Dan. 7 anticipate that in the day of Israel's redemption God would endow his chosen agent with extraordinary status, for Jesus as a mere human to assert that he will sit at God's right hand, thereby arrogating God's prerogatives to himself, is quite another matter (Bock 2000: 202–6). To do so at his own trial by citing Dan. 7, which itself presupposes a courtroom confrontation wherein the cloud-riding son of man is vindicated over the beastlike and idolatrous nations, is incendiary (cf. *T. Job* 33:3, where the righteous but suffering Job vindicates himself by pointing to his throne at the right hand of God).

Add to this Ps. 110's Melchizedekian promise, with its change of polity and thus the ousting of the present temple leadership along with Yahweh's crushing of the Messiah's enemies (again the temple authorities), and the implications could hardly be plainer. Mark's Jesus not only claims the highest possible status for himself but also casts his opponents both as Yahweh's enemies (cf. 11Q13, where Melchizedek's enemy is Belial; *T. Levi* 18) and, more particularly, as Dan. 7's defiling and murderous fourth beast, with the further implication that the high priest is the blasphemous little horn who wages vicious war against the saints (see N. T. Wright 1996: 524–28). The affront would hardly be lessened if, as in widespread later tradition, the fourth beast was already identified with Edom/Rome. The response of the high priest, himself anointed, comes as no surprise.

Psalm 2's warning (Mark 1:11; cf. Ps. 2:10–11), underlined by Ps. 118's motifs of victory and reversal (Mark 11:9–10; 12:10–11) and breaking the surface in Ps. 110:1 in Mark 12:36, now culminates in a devastating denunciation of Israel's faithless shepherds. Furthermore, Jesus' introductory "you will see," as opposed to Daniel's seeing in his vision, is consistent with Jesus' "this generation" in 13:30 (cf. 9:1). The high priest and his associates will witness the truth of Jesus' claims in their own lifetimes (see France 2002: 611). From Jesus' point of view, the trajectory of abomination that is already implicit in his second prediction (9:31) and that eventually will lead in his second parousia to the insurrectionist city's desolation is already well under way (see commentary on Mark 13:26–27 above).

D. Theological Use. Eschatologically, Jesus' appeal to these two texts suggests that the crisis moment in Israel's history has come. The christological implications are the same: from early on in Mark's Gospel Jesus' astounding authority has been clear. Here, in another climactic moment, he is faithful Israel's representative messianic Son of Man sharing God's authority. By the same token, ecclesiologically, those who follow him constitute the authentic remnant Israel, and the temple authorities, in opposing him, have ironically put themselves in the same category as Daniel's fourth beast and little horn.

15:24, 29, 34

A. NT Context: The Righteous Sufferer. Mark's passion narrative is replete with echoes of the "righteous sufferer" psalms (see Marcus 1992: 172–84; Moo 1983: 264–83; A. Y. Collins 1997). Mark's portrayal of the authorities who plan to take Jesus "by guile to kill him" (14:1; cf. Ps. 10:7–8) corresponds to the psalmist's enemies who operate with guile, slander, and false witness as they plot the innocent's demise (Kraus 1986: 130). Other resonances with these psalms abound: betrayal by "one who eats with me" (14:18; Ps. 41:9), Jesus' soul being "deeply saddened" (14:34; Ps. 42:5, 11; 43:5), his being "delivered" into the "hands" of sinners (14:41; Ps. 36:11; 71:4; 82:4; 140:4–8), enemies seeking testimony to justify his death (14:55; Ps. 37:32; 54:3), false witnesses (14:57; Ps. 27:12; 35:11), Jesus' silence (14:61; 15:4–5; Ps. 38:13–15; cf. Isa. 53:7), the offer of vinegar (15:36; Ps. 69:21), and friends observing from a distance (15:40; Ps. 38:11). Not all are uniformly obvious or necessarily intentional, but the overall effect strongly suggests that Mark interprets Jesus' suffering through this genre. (On the possible allusions to Isa. 53 in Mark 14:61, 65, in keeping with its influence on the passion predictions and 10:45, see R. E. Watts 2000: 362–65.)

Our concern, however, is with the clear and pervasive presence of Ps. 22 (21 LXX) in the crucifixion narrative: the division of Jesus' garments (15:24; cf. Ps. 22:18), mockery and head shaking by onlookers (15:29; cf. Ps. 22:7), and Jesus' cry of dereliction (15:34; cf. Ps. 22:1) (see France 2002: 640; on further possible echoes, see Marcus 1992: 175).

B. Ps. 22:1, 7, 18 in Context. Part of the first book of the Psalter (Pss. 1–41), Ps. 22 is attributed to David (whose authorship I will assume, in keeping with the Markan Jesus' first-century understanding). An unusual combination of lament, prayer, and praise, the psalm uniquely progresses from the deepest distress and suffering (22:1–21) to the most expansive praise and thanksgiving for deliverance (22:22–31) (see Craigie 1982: 198). Given David's representative role, its liturgical elements naturally express the corporate implications of Yahweh's salvation (22:23, 26, 27–31).

The opening verses present the singularly terrifying situation—the overwhelming sense of God-forsakenness (22:1–2)—and in stark contrast a vision of God's holiness (22:3), his enthronement in Zion (cf. Ps. 99:1–2; Isa. 57:15; see Kraus 1988–1989: 1:295), and his past faithfulness in delivering those who trusted in him (22:4–5).

David, however, has been reduced to scorn, and his trust is being parodied in the derision of his enemies (22:6–8). For these threatening foes from whom he cannot escape (22:12–13, 16), his dehumanizing and extreme suffering (22:14–15, 17) demonstrate God's utter abandonment (22:7–8) (see Davis 1992: 97). They divide his last shreds of human dignity as though he is already deceased (22:18 [see Matthews and Benjamin 1993: 147, 203]). Nevertheless, David persists in crying out for divine intervention (22:11, 19–21).

Then, in a remarkable reversal, he suddenly declares, "You have answered me!" (22:21b [22:22b MT]). Celebrating Yahweh's salvation, David summons his hearers to join an ever-widening circle of praise so that not only the ends of the earth, but even the dead and generations yet unborn, will recognize Yahweh's cosmic dominion over the nations (22:27–31 [see Davis 1992: 101]). In keeping with the Zion traditions of Yahweh's universal kingship (Kraus 1988–1989: 1:300), the entire earth is to know that "he has done it" (22:31) so that they might worship him.

C. Ps. 22:1, 7, 18 in Judaism. Although containing no direct citations of the "righteous sufferer" psalms, including Ps. 22, the Qumran hymns (1QH[a]) utilize their imagery (Moo 1983: 230n3; Steichele 1980: 246; that 1QH[a] XIII, 31 intentionally alludes to Ps. 22:15 is doubtful [*pace* Marcus 1992: 178]). The community apparently saw in them their own eschatological vindication over Belial and his agents. The same hermeneutic appears to inform 4Q88. Beginning with Ps. 22:15–17, it concludes with a series of eschatological hymns anticipating, first, a victorious Zion whose enemies are quelled and whose praise is heard throughout the whole world (VIII, 6–8; cf. Ps. 22:27–28), second, the renewed bounty of the earth such that "the poor will eat" (IX, 14; cf. Ps. 22:26), and third, a joyful Judah exultant at the enemy's demise, and all to Yahweh's eternal glory (X, 7–14; cf. Ps. 22:29–31). Here too, Ps. 22's suffering is the prelude to the community's eschatological vindication (see Marcus 1992: 178).

The motif of the vindication of the "righteous sufferer" is found also in various intertestamental writings (e.g., Wis. 2:12–24; 5:1–8; *2 Bar.* 15:7–8; 48:49–50), though again there are no clear citations or undisputed allusions to Ps. 22.

The Targum naturally assumes that David's enemies are Gentile kings (22:12–13, 16, 20–21). In keeping with the conviction of Yahweh's universal kingship that underlies the psalm's initial appeal and its conclusion, there is an eschatological element to the nations' coming to worship (2:27; cf. Isa. 2).

Nevertheless, in spite of these several eschatological interpretations, there is as yet no firm evidence that Ps. 22 was understood messianically. Perhaps although such utter abandonment and profound suffering was applicable to Israel (cf. *Midr. Ps.* 22:7, where David is understood to have prophesied concerning Queen Esther), it was inconceivable of the Messiah (cf. Mark 8:31–32; see also *Tg. Isa.* 52:13–53:12, where although Israel and the nations suffer, the Messiah knows only triumph).

D. The Use of Ps. 22:1, 7, 18 in Mark. Mark's deliberate application of Ps. 22 to Jesus, the messianic Son of Man, is unparalleled in any of the traditions to which we have access. But Ps. 2 had already been radically re-read at the transfiguration: the restoration of the temple and God's people would come now through the suffering servant death of his messianic son. And in view of the repeated passion predictions, there is every reason why Ps. 22 can describe not just Israel or Zion, but great David's greater eschatological son. The crucial question is whether Mark expects his readers to "fill in the gaps" and so anticipate Jesus' vindication. Everything in the tradition, whether concerning the righteous sufferer in general (Wisdom, *2 Baruch*) or Ps. 22 in particular (4Q88, Targum), and certainly Mark's narrative suggest that they should do so (*pace* France 2002: 652–53, there is no reason why both suffering and vindication cannot be held together even as they are in the psalm).

As we noted previously, the various contemporary perspectives on Pss. 2; 118; 110 all testify to Yahweh's eschatological upholding of his messianic king—a conviction explicit in the "resurrection after three days" element of the passion predictions and implied by the "son-stone" saying (Mark 12:10–11). Psalm 22 likewise assumes Yahweh's able protection of his own. Consequently, while not detracting from Jesus' suffering, it is hard to understand why Mark would work so hard at evoking Ps. 22 if he did not also expect his informed readers to know exactly what was coming next: a startling reversal and deliverance. And as J. Marcus notes (1992: 182), this is precisely what they get. In keeping with the conclusion of Ps. 22, a representative of the Gentiles confesses Jesus to be the Son of God (15:39; cf. Ps. 22:27), reference is made to God's dominion (15:43; cf. Ps. 22:28), life is regained (16:6; cf. Ps. 22:29), and proclamation is encouraged (16:7; cf. Ps. 22:30–31) (see Marcus 1992: 182). Furthermore, far from Mark's silence on the deliverance section denying this expectation, the rhetorical gapping combined with the tension created by reversing the progression through the psalm (22:18, 7, 1) in the climactic searing cry can only heighten it, especially when Mark's original audience already knows the outcome.

The same apparently applies to the response of those gathered around the cross (15:35–36). Although frequently said to be a misunderstanding of *elōi*, it indicates exactly the opposite. As we noted earlier, Elijah was widely held to be the agent of Israel's deliverance (whether eschatological [see commentary on Mark 1:2–3 above] or of individuals in times of distress [*b. 'Abod. Zar.* 17b; *b. Ta'an.* 21a]). It is precisely because they too hear in Jesus' cry the expectation of deliverance that the crowd waits to see if Elijah will come (see C. A. Evans 2001b: 508–9). Their basic instinct is correct even though the delayed deliverance is far more amazing than they might have thought and is effected not by Elijah, but God himself. Likewise, the centurion's confession makes more sense if Jesus' "loud shout" is exultant rather than a despairing cry of final anguish (see France 2002: 655).

On the other hand, as CD-B apparently anticipated in Ps. 22 the demise of the wicked, so too at Jesus' death the curtain of the temple (*naos*) is torn (15:38; cf. the torn heaven in 1:10; the suggestive contention by Ulansey [1991], citing Josephus, *J.W.* 5.214, that it was the outer "heavenly" curtain cannot be substantiated). A powerful riposte to the mockery of 15:29–30, it signifies and perhaps initiates the present temple's coming destruction (cf. chap. 13; *Liv. Pro.* 12:11–12; *T. Levi* 10:3; also the portents in Josephus, *J.W.* 6.288–315; *y. Soṭah* 6:3; *b. Yoma* 39b; *b. Giṭ.* 56a), Jesus' future vindication, and the constitution of a new temple.

Finally, as a correlate of Peter's confession, the centurion's affirmation of Jesus as *huios theou*, for the first time in the Gospel, from a Gentile, and that unbidden (cf. Ps. 22:27), suggests the beginning of the ingathering of the nations to which various OT texts throughout Mark have pointed (e.g., Isa. 56:7 in Mark 11:17).

E. Theological Use. Not unexpectedly, the same themes continue. Although Ps. 22 might not have been read as a direct messianic prophecy, the character of God, who stands behind it, is unchanged. What he did for David, he surely will do for great David's greater son. Christologically, then, Jesus is the Davidic messiah, whose suffering leads to the worldwide proclamation of Yahweh's name. Ecclesiologically and eschatologically, the confession by the centurion foreshadows the fulfillment of the prophetic hope of the nations coming to worship. The resurrection of Jesus will indeed be proclaimed throughout the world.

We have come full circle. In the baptism scene, God declared through Ps. 2 that Jesus was his messianic Son. He is the one who will purify his people, Jerusalem, and the temple, inherit the nations, and rule to the ends of the earth. Here, at Jesus' death and in keeping with the "suffering" element introduced by the transfiguration's integration of Ps. 2 with the first passion prediction, the fulfillment of that promise makes its own mustard seed beginning. As the curtain in the old temple is torn, Isaiah's new exodus hopes of Israel being a light to the nations find their firstfruits in the Roman centurion, who, over against the imperial cult, joins with the two earlier divine attestations and declares Jesus to be the Son of God. Here then, in spite of official Israel's lack of preparedness, is the beginning of a new, purified, and "restored" temple for all nations in which God's presence dwells (Isa. 56:7).

Finally, Mark maintains his Gospel's enigmatic character to the very end. As he began by casting his story within the schema of Isaiah's new exodus hopes, he does so also at his conclusion. In Isaiah the prophet's hearers had been encouraged time and again not to fear (Isa. 40:9; 41:10, 13, 14; 43:1, 5; 44:2, 8; cf. 51:7, 13; 54:4, 14; R. E. Watts 1990a: 35–49). If the glory of God was to go out among the nations such that their survivors would turn to him and be saved (45:22), much depended on his servant people bearing faithful testimony (cf. 40:9; 52:7–9). Similarly, Mark's account concludes with the unresolved tension between the worldwide proclamation of the good news (8:35; 13:10) and the fearful silence of the women (16:8). Is this an implicit warning? If the nations are to hear and more Gentiles to join in the centurion's confession, Mark's audience must also resist their fear and, bearing faithful servant witness, proclaim the good news. But perhaps the very fact of Mark's existence offers its own obvious and encouraging resolution: someone had courageously broken the silence. Mark's readers need to continue in that good work.

Bibliography

Aalen, S. 1963. "Das Abendmahl als Opfermahl." *NovT* 6: 128–52.

Abegg, M., Jr., P. Flint, and E. Ulrich. 1999. *The Dead Sea Scrolls Bible.* New York: HarperSanFrancisco.

Achtemeier, E. 1982. *The Community and Message of Isaiah 56–66: A Theological Commentary.* Minneapolis: Augsburg.

Achtemeier, P. J. 1978. "'And He Followed Him': Miracles and Discipleship in Mark 10:46–52." *Semeia* 11: 115–45.

Ådna, J. 2000. *Jesu Stellung zum Tempel: Die Tempelaktion und das Tempelwort als Ausdruck seiner messianischen Sendung.* WUNT 2/119. Tübingen: Mohr Siebeck.

———. 2004. "The Servant of Isaiah 53 as Triumphant and Interceding Messiah: The Reception of Isaiah 52:13–53:12 in the

Targum of Isaiah with Special Attention to the Concept of Messiah." Pages 189–224 in *The Suffering Servant: Isaiah 53 in Jewish and Christian Sources*. Edited by B. Janowski and P. Stuhlmacher. Translated by D. P. Bailey. Grand Rapids: Eerdmans.

Albertz, R. 1978. "Hintergrund und Bedeutung des Elterngebots im Dekalog." *ZAW* 90: 384–74.

Allen, L. C. 1983. *Psalms 101–150*. WBC 21. Waco: Word.

———. 1994. *Ezekiel 1–19*. WBC 28. Dallas: Word.

Allison, D. C. 1998. *Jesus of Nazareth: Millenarian Prophet*. Minneapolis: Fortress.

Ambrozic, A. M. 1972. *The Hidden Kingdom: A Redaction-Critical Study of the References to the Kingdom of God in Mark's Gospel*. CBQMS 2. Washington, DC: Catholic Biblical Society of America.

Andersen, F. I. 1980. *Hosea*. AB 24. New York: Doubleday.

Anderson, A. A. 1972. *The Book of Psalms*. 2 vols. NCB. London: Oliphants.

Anderson, B. W. 1962. "Exodus Typology in Second Isaiah." Pages 177–95 in *Israel's Prophetic Heritage*. Edited by B. W. Anderson and W. Harrelson. New York: Harper.

Anderson, D. R. 2001. *The King-Priest of Psalm 110 in Hebrews*. SBL 21. New York: Lang.

Annen, F. 1976. *Heil für die Heiden: Zur Bedeutung und Geschichte der Tradition vom besessenen Gerasener (Mk 5,1–20 parr.)*. FTS 20. Frankfurt: Knecht.

Bailey, J. N. 2000. "Vowing Away the Fifth Commandment: Matthew 15:3–6/Mark 7:9–13." *ResQ* 42: 193–209.

Baldwin, J. G. 1972. *Haggai, Zechariah, Malachi*. TOTC 24. London: Tyndale.

Baltzer, K. 1999. *Deutero-Isaiah: A Commentary on Isaiah 40–55*. Translated by M. Kohl. Hermeneia. Minneapolis: Fortress.

Banks, R. 1975. *Jesus and the Law in the Synoptic Tradition*. SNTSMS 28. Cambridge: Cambridge University Press.

Banwell, B. O. 1965. "A Suggested Analysis of Isaiah xl–lxvi." *ExpTim* 76: 166.

Barrett, C. K. 1959. "The Background of Mark 10:45." Pages 1–18 in *New Testament Essays: Studies in Memory of T. W. Manson*. Edited by A. J. B. Higgins. Manchester: Manchester University Press.

———. 1970. *The Holy Spirit and the Gospel Tradition*. London: SPCK.

Bartlett, J. R. 1989. *Edom and the Edomites*. JSOTSup 77. Sheffield: JSOT Press.

Basser, H. W. 1998. "The Jewish Roots of the Transfiguration." *BRev* 14: 30–35.

Bauckham, R. 1985. "The Son of Man: 'A Man in My Position' or 'Someone'?" *JSNT* 23: 23–33.

———. 1988. "Jesus' Demonstration in the Temple." Pages 72–89 in *Law and Religion: Essays on the Place of the Law in Israel and Early Christianity*. Edited by B. Lindars. Cambridge: Clarke.

———. 1998. *God Crucified: Monotheism and Christology in the New Testament*. Grand Rapids: Eerdmans.

Baumgarten, J. M. 1990. "The 4Q Zadokite Fragments on Skin Disease." *JJS* 41: 54–56.

———. 1999. "Messianic Forgiveness of Sin in CD 14:19 (4Q266 10 I 12–13)." Pages 537–44 in *The Provo International Conference on the Dead Sea Scrolls: Technological Innovations, New Texts, and Reformulated Issues*. Edited by D. W. Parry and E. Ulrich. STDJ 30. Leiden: Brill.

Bautch, R. J. 2003. *Developments in Genre between Post-exilic Penitential Prayers and the Psalms of Communal Lament*. SBLAB 7. Atlanta: Society of Biblical Literature.

Beale, G. 1991. "Isaiah vi 9–13: A Retributive Taunt against Idolatry." *VT* 41: 257–78.

———. 1998. *John's Use of the Old Testament in Revelation*. JSNTSup 166. Sheffield: Sheffield Academic Press.

Beasley-Murray, G. R. 1993. *Jesus and the Last Days: The Interpretation of the Olivet Discourse*. Peabody, MA: Hendrickson.

Beavis, M. A. 1989. *Mark's Audience: The Literary and Social Setting of Mark 4.11–12*. JSNTSup 33. Sheffield: JSOT Press.

Becker, J. 1964. *Das Heil Gottes: Heils- und Sündenbegriffe in den Qumrantexten und im Neuen Testament*. SUNT 3. Göttingen: Vandenhoeck & Ruprecht.

Becker, U. 2001. "Elia, Mose und Jesus: Zur Bedeutung von Mk 9,2–10." *BN* 110: 5–11.

Begrich, J. 1969. *Studien zu Deuterojesaja*. TB 20. Munich: Kaiser.

Bentzen, A. 1970. *King and Messiah*. Edited by G. W. Anderson. 2nd ed. Oxford: Blackwell.

Berder, M. 1996. *"La pierre rejetée par les bâtisseurs": Psaume 118,22–23 et son emploi dans les traditions juives et dans le Nouveau Testament*. EBib 31. Paris: Gabalda.

Bergen, R. D. 1996. *1, 2 Samuel*. NAC 7. Nashville: Broadman & Holman.

Berger, K. 1972. *Die Gesetzesauslegung Jesu: Ihr historischer Hintergrund im Judentum und im Alten Testament; Teil I, Markus und Parallelen*. WMANT 40. Neukirchen-Vluyn: Neukirchener Verlag.

Best, E. 1970. "Discipleship in Mark: Mark viii.22–x.52." *SJT* 23: 323–37.

———. 1978. "The Miracles in Mark." *RevExp* 75: 539–54.

———. 1990. *The Temptation and the Passion: The Markan Soteriology*. SNTSMS 2. Cambridge: Cambridge University Press.

Betz, O. 1958. "Jesu heiliger Krieg." *NovT* 2: 116–37.

———. 1996. "Die Übersetzung von Jes 53 (LXX, Targum) und die Theologia Crucis des Paulus." Pages 197–216 in *Jesus, der Herr der Kirche: Aufsätze zur biblischen Theologie II*. WUNT 52. Tübingen: Mohr Siebeck.

Beuken, W. A. M. 1972. *"MIŠPĀ : The First Servant Song and Its Context."* *VT* 22: 1–30.

———. 1983. *Jesaja*. Vol. 2. POuT. Nijkerk: Callenbach.

———. 1990. "The Main Theme of Trito-Isaiah: 'The Servants of Yahweh.'" *JSOT* 47: 67–87.

———. 1991. "Isaiah Chapters LXV–LXVI: Trito-Isaiah and the Closure of the Book of Isaiah." Pages 204–21 in *Congress Volume: Leuven 1989*. VTSup 43. Leiden: Brill.

———. 1992a. "Isa 29,15–24: Perversion Reverted." Pages 43–64 in *The Scriptures and the Scrolls: Studies in Honour of A. S. van der Woude on the Occasion of His 65th Birthday*. Edited by F. García Martínez, A. Hilhorst, and C. J. Labuschagne. VTSup 49. Leiden: Brill.

———. 1992b. "Isaiah 34: Lament in Isaianic Context." *OTE* 5: 78–102.

———. 2004. "The Manifestation of Yahweh and the Commission of Isaiah: Isaiah 6 Read against the Background of Isaiah 1." *CTJ* 39: 72–87.

Beyerlin, W. 1973. "Schichten im 80. Psalm." Pages 9–24 in *Das Wort und die Wörter: Festschrift Gerhard Friedrich zum 65. Geburtstag*. Edited by H. Balz and S. Schulz. Stuttgart: Kohlhammer.

Black, M. 1953. "The Servant of the Lord and Son of Man." *SJT* 6: 4–8.

———. 1975. "Die Apotheose Israels: Eine neue Interpretation des danielischen 'Menschensohns.'" Pages 92–99 in *Jesus und der Menschensohn: Für Anton Vögtle.* Edited by R. Pesch and R. Schnackenburg. Freiburg: Herder.

———. 1992. "The Messianism of the Parables of Enoch." Pages 145–68 in *The Messiah: Developments in Earliest Judaism and Christianity.* Edited by J. H. Charlesworth. Minneapolis: Fortress.

Blackburn, B. 1991. *Theios Aner and the Markan Miracle Traditions.* WUNT 2/40. Tübingen: Mohr Siebeck.

Blenkinsopp, J. 1961. "The Oracle of Judah and the Messianic Entry." *JBL* 80: 55–64.

———. 1997. "The Servant and the Servants in Isaiah and the Formation of the Book." Pages 155–74 in vol. 1 of *Writing and Reading the Scroll of Isaiah: Studies of an Interpretive Tradition.* Edited by C. C. Broyles and C. A. Evans. VTSup 70/1. Leiden: Brill.

———. 2000–2003. *Isaiah.* 3 vols. AB 19, 19A, 19B. New York: Doubleday.

Blidstein, G. J. 1975. *Honor Thy Father and Mother: Filial Responsibility in Jewish Law and Ethics.* New York: KTAV.

Block, D. I. 1997. *The Book of Ezekiel: 1–24.* NICOT. Grand Rapids: Eerdmans.

Blomberg, C. L. 1986. "The Miracles as Parables." Pages 327–59 in *The Miracles of Jesus.* Vol. 6 of *Gospel Perspectives.* Edited by D. Wenham and C. Blomberg. Sheffield: JSOT Press.

———. 1990. *Interpreting the Parables.* Downers Grove, IL: InterVarsity.

Bock, D. L. 2000. *Blasphemy and Exaltation in Judaism: The Charge against Jesus in Mark 14:53–65.* Grand Rapids: Baker Academic.

Bockmuehl, M. 2000. *Jewish Law in Gentile Churches: Halakhah and the Beginning of Christian Public Ethics.* Edinburgh: T&T Clark.

Bolt, P. G. 2004. *The Cross from a Distance: Atonement in Mark's Gospel.* NSBT 18. Downers Grove, IL: InterVarsity.

Bons, E. 1992. "Zu jsd *II* 'beratschlagen' (Ps 2,2; 31,14; CD2,7)." *Zeitschrift für Althebraistik* 5: 209–17.

Booth, R. P. 1986. *Jesus and the Laws of Purity: Tradition History and Legal History in Mark 7.* JSNTSup 13. Sheffield: JSOT Press.

Borg, M. J. 1988. *Conflict, Holiness, and Politics in the Teachings of Jesus.* Harrisburg, PA: Trinity Press International.

Boucher, M. 1977. *The Mysterious Parable: A Literary Study.* CBQMS 6. Washington, DC: Catholic Biblical Commission.

Bousset, W. 1926. *Kyrios Christos: Geschichte des Christusglaubens von den Anfängen des Christentums bis Irenaeus.* 3rd ed. Göttingen: Vandenhoeck & Ruprecht.

Box, G. H. 1912. *The Ezra-Apocalypse, Being Chapters 3–14 of the Book Commonly Known as 4 Ezra (or II Esdras).* London: Pitman.

Brekelmans, C. H. W. 1965. "The Saints of the Most High and Their Kingdom." *OTS* 14: 305–29.

Bretscher, P. G. 1968. "Exodus 4:22–23 and the Voice from Heaven." *JBL* 87: 301–11.

Brewer, David Instone. 1992. *Techniques and Assumptions in Jewish Exegesis before 70 CE.* TSAJ 30. Tübingen: Mohr Siebeck.

Brichto, H. C. 1963. *The Problem of "Curse" in the Hebrew Bible.* JBLMS. 13. Philadelphia: Society of Biblical Literature.

Bright, J. 1965. *Jeremiah.* AB 21. New York: Doubleday.

Brock, S. 1990. "The Two Ways and the Palestinian Targum." Pages 139–52 in *A Tribute to Geza Vermes: Essays on Jewish and Christian Literature and History.* Edited by P. R. Davies and R. T. White. JSOTSup 100. Sheffield: JSOT Press.

Brooke, G. J. 1997. "Isaiah in the Pesharim and Other Qumran Texts." Pages 609–32 in vol. 2 of *Writing and Reading the Scroll of Isaiah: Studies of an Interpretive Tradition.* Edited by C. C. Broyles and C. A. Evans. VTSup 70/2. Leiden: Brill.

———. 1999. "Miqdash Adam, Eden and the Qumran Community." Pages 285–301 in *Gemeinde ohne Tempel/Community without Temple: Zur Substituierung und Transformation des Jerusalemer Tempels und seines Kults im Alten Testament, antiken Judentum und frühen Christentum.* Edited by E. Beate, A. Lange, and P. Pilhofer. WUNT 118. Tübingen: Mohr Siebeck.

Brown, M. L. 1995. *Israel's Divine Healer.* SOTBT. Grand Rapids: Zondervan.

Brownlee, W. H. 1964. *The Meaning of the Qumrân Scrolls for the Bible: With Special Reference to the Book of Isaiah.* New York: Oxford University Press.

———. 1971. "Psalms 1–2 as a Coronation Liturgy." *Bib* 57: 321–36.

———. 1986. *Ezekiel 1–19.* WBC 28. Waco: Word.

Bruce, F. F. 1961. "The Book of Zechariah and the Passion Narrative." *BJRL* 43: 342–45.

Brueggemann, W. 1970. "Of the Same Flesh and Bone (Gn 2,23a)." *CBQ* 32: 532–42.

———. 1988. *To Pluck Up, to Tear Down: A Commentary on the Book of Jeremiah 1–25.* ITC. Grand Rapids: Eerdmans.

———. 1990. *First and Second Samuel.* IBC. Louisville: John Knox.

———. 1998. *Isaiah 40–66.* WestBC. Louisville: Westminster John Knox.

Burke, D. G. 1982. *The Poetry of Baruch: A Reconstruction and Analysis of the Original Hebrew Text of Baruch 3:9–5:9.* SBLSCS 10. Chico, CA: Scholars Press.

Burkett, D. 1999. *The Son of Man Debate: A History and Evaluation.* SNTSMS 107. Cambridge: Cambridge University Press.

Burkill, T. A. 1963. *Mysterious Revelation: An Examination of the Philosophy of St. Mark's Gospel.* Ithaca, NY: Cornell University Press.

Buse, I. 1956. "The Markan Account of the Baptism of Jesus and Isaiah LXIII." *JTS* 7: 74–75.

Cadoux, C. J. 1941. "The Imperative Use of *dei* in the New Testament." *JTS* 42: 165–73.

Cahill, M. 1999. "Not a Cornerstone! Translating Ps 118,22 in the Jewish and Christian Scriptures." *RB* 106: 345–57.

Campbell, J. G. 1995. "Essene-Qumran Origins in the Exile: A Scriptural Basis." *JJS* 46: 143–56.

Caragounis, C. C. 1986. *The Son of Man: Vision and Interpretation.* WUNT 38. Tübingen: Mohr Siebeck.

Carmignac, J. 1965. "Les citations de l'Ancien Testament dans 'La guerre des fils de lumière contre les fils de ténèbres.'" *RB* 63: 234–60, 375–90.

Carroll, R. P. 1986. *Jeremiah.* OTL. London: SCM.

Casey, M. 1979. *Son of Man: The Interpretation and Influence of Daniel 7.* London: SPCK.

———. 1987. "General, Generic and Indefinite: The Use of the Term 'Son of Man' in Aramaic Sources and in the Teaching of Jesus." *JSNT* 29: 21–56.

———. 1991. "Method in Our Madness, and Madness in Their Methods: Some Approaches to the Son of Man Problem in Recent Scholarship." *JSNT* 42: 17–43.

———. 2002. "Aramaic Idiom and the Son of Man Problem: A Response to Owen and Shepherd." *JSNT* 25: 3–32.

Catchpole, D. R. 1984. "The 'Triumphal' Entry." Pages 319–34 in *Jesus and the Politics of His Day*. Edited by E. Bammel and C. F. D. Moule. Cambridge: Cambridge University Press.

Ceresko, A. R. 1994. "The Rhetorical Strategy of the Fourth Servant Song (Isaiah 52:13–53:12): Poetry and the Exodus-New Exodus." *CBQ* 56: 42–55.

Charles, R. H. 1929. *A Critical and Exegetical Commentary on the Book of Daniel*. Oxford: Clarendon.

Charlesworth, J. H. 1997. "Intertextuality: Isaiah 40:3 and the Serek Ha-Yahad." Pages 197–224 in *The Quest for Context and Meaning: Studies in Biblical Intertextuality in Honor of James A. Sanders*. Edited by C. A. Evans and S. Talmon. BIS 28. Leiden: Brill.

Childs, B. S. 1974. *Exodus*. OTL. London: SCM.

———. 1978. "The Canonical Shape of the Prophetic Literature." *Int* 32: 46–55.

———. 1979. *Introduction to the Old Testament as Scripture*. Philadelphia: Fortress.

———. 2001. *Isaiah*. OTL. Louisville: Westminster John Knox.

Chilton, B. D. 1979. *God in Strength: Jesus' Announcement of the Kingdom*. SNTSU B/1. Freistadt: Plöchl.

———. 1982. "Jesus ben David: Reflections on the Davidssohnfrage." *JSNT* 14: 88–112.

———. 1984. *A Galilean Rabbi and His Bible: Jesus' Own Interpretation of Isaiah*. London: SPCK.

———, trans. and ed. 1987. *The Isaiah Targum*. ArBib 11. Wilmington, DE: Glazier.

———. 1994. "The Kingdom of God in Recent Discussion." Pages 255–80 in *Studying the Historical Jesus: Evaluations of the State of Current Research*. Edited by B. D. Chilton and C. A. Evans. NTTS 19. Leiden: Brill.

Churgin, P. 1944. "The Period of the Second Temple: A Period of Exile." *Horeb* 8: 1–66.

Clements, R. E. 1980a. *Isaiah 1–39*. NCBC. London: Marshall, Morgan & Scott.

———. 1980b. "The Prophecies of Isaiah and the Fall of Jerusalem in 587 B.C." *VT* 30: 421–36.

———. 1996. *Ezekiel*. WestBC. Louisville: Westminster John Knox.

Clifford, R. J. 1980. "The Function of Idol Passages in Second Isaiah." *CBQ* 42: 450–64.

———. 1984. *Fair Spoken and Persuading: An Interpretation of Second Isaiah*. TI. New York: Paulist Press.

Clines, D. J. A. 1968. "The Image of God in Man." *TynBul* 19: 53–103.

———. 1976. *I, He, We, and They—A Literary Approach to Isaiah 53*. JSOTSup 3. Sheffield: JSOT Press.

Cogan, M., and H. Tadmor. 1988. *II Kings*. AB 11. New York: Doubleday.

Cohn-Sherbok, D. M. 1979. "An Analysis of Jesus' Arguments concerning the Plucking of Grain on the Sabbath." *JSNT* 2: 31–41.

———. 1981. "Jesus' Defense of the Resurrection of the Dead." *JSNT* 11: 64–73.

Collins, A. Y. 1997. "The Appropriation of the Psalms of Individual Lament by Mark." Pages 223–41 in *The Scriptures in the Gospels*. Edited by C. M. Tuckett. BETL 131. Leuven: Leuven University Press.

Collins, J. J. 1974. "The Son of Man and the Saints of the Most High in the Book of Daniel." *JBL* 93: 50–66.

———. 1992. "The Son of Man in First-Century Judaism." *NTS* 38: 448–66.

———. 1993. *Daniel*. Hermeneia. Minneapolis: Fortress.

———. 1995. *The Scepter and the Star: The Messiahs of the Dead Sea Scrolls and Other Ancient Literature*. ABRL. New York: Doubleday.

———. 1998. *The Apocalyptic Imagination: An Introduction to Jewish Apocalyptic Literature*. 2nd ed. Grand Rapids: Eerdmans.

Conrad, E. W. 1999. *Zechariah*. RNBC. Sheffield: Sheffield Academic Press.

Cook, S. L. 1993. "The Metamorphosis of a Shepherd: The Tradition History of Zechariah 11:17 + 13:7–9." *CBQ* 55: 453–66.

Coutts, J. 1964. "'Those Outside' (Mark 4, 10–12)." *SE II*: 155–57.

Craigie, P. C. 1976. *The Book of Deuteronomy*. NICOT. Grand Rapids: Eerdmans.

———. 1982. *Psalms 1–50*. WBC 19. Waco: Word.

Craigie, P. C., P. H. Kelley, and J. F. Drinkard Jr. 1991. *Jeremiah 1–25*. WBC 26. Waco: Word.

Cranfield, C. E. B. 1955. "A Study of St. Mark 1.9–11." *SJT* 8: 55–63.

———. 1959. *The Gospel according to St. Mark*. CGTC. Cambridge: Cambridge University Press.

Cresson, B. C. 1972. "The Condemnation of the Edomites in Post-Exilic Judaism." Pages 125–48 in *The Use of the Old Testament in the New and Other Essays: Studies in Honor of William Franklin Stinespring*. Edited by J. M. Efird. Durham, NC: Duke University Press.

Cross, F. M. 1973. *Canaanite Myth and Hebrew Epic: Essays in the History of the Religion of Israel*. Cambridge, MA: Harvard University Press.

Cullmann, O. 1950. *Baptism in the New Testament*. Translated by J. K. S. Reid. SBT 1. London: SCM.

Currid, J. D. 1977. *Ancient Egypt and the Old Testament*. Grand Rapids: Baker Academic.

Dahood, M. 1970. *Psalms III, 101–150*. AB 17A. New York: Doubleday.

Dalman, G. H. 1902. *The Words of Jesus: Considered in the Light of Post-biblical Jewish Writings and the Aramaic Language*. Translated by D. M. Kay. Edinburgh: T&T Clark.

Daly, R. 1977. "The Soteriological Significance of the Sacrifice of Isaac." *CBQ* 39: 45–75.

Daube, D. 1956. *The New Testament and Rabbinic Judaism*. London: Athlone.

———. 1972–1973. "Responsibilities of Master and Disciples in the Gospels." *NTS* 19: 1–15.

Dautzenberg, G. 1966. *Sein Leben bewahren: Ψυχή in den Herrenworten der Evangelien*. SANT 14. Munich: Kösel.

Davies, W. and D. C. Allison Jr. 1988–1997. *A Critical and Exegetical Commentary on the Gospel according to Saint Matthew*. 3 vols. ICC. Edinburgh: T&T Clark.

Davies, W. D., and B. D. Chilton. 1978. "The Aqedah: A Revised Tradition History." *CBQ* 40: 514–46.

Davis, E. F. 1992. "Exploding the Limits: Form and Function in Psalm 22." *JSOT* 53: 93–105.

Day, J. 1998. "The Canaanite Inheritance of the Israelite Monarchy." Pages 72–90 in *King and Messiah in Israel and the Ancient Near East: Proceedings of the Oxford Old Testament Seminar*. Edited by J. Day. JSOTSup 270. Sheffield: Sheffield Academic Press.

de Jonge, M. 1960. "Christian Influences on the Testament of the Twelve Patriarchs." *NovT* 4: 99–117.

———. 1988. "Jesus' Death for Others and the Death of the Maccabean Martyrs." Pages 142–51 in *Text and Testimony: Essays on*

New Testament and Apocryphal Literature in Honour of A. F. J. Klijn. Edited by T. J. Baarda et al. Kampen: Kok.

de Jonge, M., and A. S. van der Woude. 1965–1966. "11Q Melchizedek and the New Testament." *NTS* 12: 301–26.

de Roo, J. C. R. 1999. "David's Deeds in the Dead Sea Scrolls." *DSD* 6: 44–65.

Delitzsch, F. 1973. *Isaiah*. Vol. 7 of *Commentary on the Old Testament*. Translated by J. Martin. Grand Rapids: Eerdmans.

Derrett, J. D. M. 1977a. *Glimpses of the Legal and Social Presuppositions of the Authors*. Vol. 1 of *Studies in the New Testament*. Leiden: Brill.

———. 1977b. "Judaica in St. Mark." Pages 85–100 in *Glimpses of the Legal and Social Presuppositions of the Authors*. Vol. 1 of *Studies in the New Testament*. Leiden: Brill.

———. 1978. "'The Stone That the Builders Rejected.'" Pages 60–67 in *Midrash in Action and as a Literary Device*. Vol. 2 of *Studies in the New Testament*. Leiden: Brill.

———. 1984a. "Christ and the Power of Choice (Mark 3:1–6)." *Bib* 65: 168–88.

———. 1984b. "Contributions to the Study of the Gerasene Demoniac." *JSNT* 3: 2–17.

———. 2001a. "He Who Has Ears to Hear, Let Him Hear (Mark 4:9 and Parallels)." *DRev* 119: 255–68.

———. 2001b. "Preaching to the Coast (Mark 4:1)." *EvQ* 73: 195–203.

Dewey, J. 1977. *Markan Public Debate: Literary Technique, Concentric Structure, and Theology in Mark 2:1–3:6*. SBLDS 48. Chico, CA: Scholars Press.

Dicou, B. 1991. "Literary Function and Literary History of Isaiah 34." *BN* 58: 30–45.

Dietrich, W. 1976. *Jesaja und die Politik*. BEvT 74. Munich: Kaiser.

Dijkstra, M. 1978. "De koniklijke Knecht: Voorstelling en investituur van de Kneckt des Heren in Jesaja 42." Pages 41–52 in *De Knecht: Studies rondom Deutero-Jesaja; door collega's en oud-leerlingen aangeboden aan J. L. Koole*. Edited by H. H. Grosheide et al. Kampen: Kok.

Dodd, C. H. 1952. *According to the Scriptures: The Sub-structure of New Testament Theology*. London: Nisbet.

———. 1971. *The Founder of Christianity*. London: Collins.

Donahue, J. R. 1986. "Recent Studies on the Origin of the 'Son of Man' in the Gospels." *CBQ* 48: 484–98.

Donahue, J. R., and D. J. Harrington. 2002. *The Gospel of Mark*. SP 2. Collegeville, MN: Liturgical Press.

Donaldson, T. L. 1985. *Jesus on the Mountain: A Study in Matthean Theology*. JSNTSup 8. Sheffield: JSOT Press.

Dormeyer, D. 1997. "Mk 1,1–15 als Prolog des ersten idealbiographischen Evangeliums von Jesus Christus." *BibInt* 5: 181–211.

dos Santos, E. C. 1973. *An Expanded Index for the Hatch-Redpath Concordance to the Septuagint*. Jerusalem: Dugith.

Downing, F. G. 1982. "The Resurrection of the Dead: Jesus and Philo." *JSNT* 15: 42–50.

Dreyfus, F.-P. 1959. "L'argument scripturaire de Jesus en faveur de la resurrection des morts (Marc, XII,26,27)." *RB* 66: 213–25.

Driver, S. R. 1906. *The Minor Prophets*. Edinburgh: Jack.

Duff, P. B. 1992. "The March of the Divine Warrior and the Advent of the Greco-Roman King: Mark's Account of Jesus' Entry into Jerusalem." *JBL* 111: 55–71.

Duguid, I. 1995. "Messianic Themes in Zechariah 9–14." Pages 265–80 in *The Lord's Anointed: Interpretation of Old Testament*

Messianic Texts. Edited by P. E. Satterthwaite, R. S. Hess, and G. J. Wenham. THS. Grand Rapids: Baker Academic.

Dumbrell, W. J. 1984. "Worship in Isaiah 6." *RTR* 43: 1–8.

———. 1985. "The Purpose of the Book of Isaiah." *TynBul* 36: 111–28.

Dunn, J. D. G. 2003. *Jesus Remembered*. CM 1. Grand Rapids: Eerdmans.

Durham, J. I. 1987. *Exodus*. WBC 3. Waco: Word.

Dyer, K. D. 1998. *The Prophecy on the Mount: Mark 13 and the Gathering of the New Community*. ITS 2. Bern: Lang.

Earl, D. C. 1972. "Prologue-Form in Ancient Historiography." *ANRW* I.2:842–56.

Edwards, J. R. 1989. "Markan Sandwiches: The Significance of Interpolations in Markan Narratives." *NovT* 31: 193–216.

Eichrodt, W. 1970. *Ezekiel*. OTL. Translated by C. Quin. Philadelphia: Westminster.

Eissfeldt, O. 1962. "The Promises of Grace to David in Isaiah 55:1–5." Pages 196–207 in *Israel's Prophetic Heritage*. Edited by B. W. Anderson and W. Harrelson. New York: Harper.

Elliger, K. 1933. *Deuterojesaja in seinem Verhältnis zu Tritojesaja*. BWANT 63. Stuttgart: Kohlhammer.

———. 1978. *Deuterojesaja*. BKAT 11/1. Neukirchen-Vluyn: Neukirchener Verlag.

———. 1982. *Das Buch der zwölf kleinen Propheten II: Die Propheten Nahum, Habakuk, Zephanja, Haggai, Sacharja, Maleachi*. ATD 25/2. Göttingen: Vandenhoeck & Ruprecht.

Elliott, M. A. 2000. *The Survivors of Israel: A Reconsideration of the Theology of Pre-Christian Judaism*. Grand Rapids: Eerdmans.

Embry, B. 2002. "The *Psalms of Solomon* and the New Testament: Intertextuality and the Need for a Re-evaluation." *JSP* 13: 99–136.

Emerton, J. A. 1958. "The Origin of the Son of Man Imagery." *JTS* 9: 225–42.

Erlandsson, S. 1970. *The Burden of Babylon: A Study of Isaiah 13:2–14:23*. ConBOT 4. Lund: Gleerup.

Evans, C. A. 1989a. "Jesus' Action in the Temple: Cleansing or Portent of Destruction?" *CBQ* 51: 237–70.

———. 1989b. *To See and Not Perceive: Isaiah 6.9–10 in Early Jewish and Christian Interpretation*. JSOTSup 64. Sheffield: JSOT Press.

———. 1999. "Jesus and the Continuing Exile of Israel." Pages 77–100 in *Jesus and the Restoration of Israel: A Critical Assessment of N. T. Wright's Jesus and the Victory of God*. Edited by C. C. Newman. Downers Grove, IL: InterVarsity.

———. 2000. "Mark's Incipit and the Pirene Calender Inscription: From Jewish Gospel to Greco-Roman Gospel." *JGCJ* 1: 67–81.

———. 2001a. "Daniel in the New Testament: Visions of God's Kingdom." Pages 490–527 in vol. 2 of *The Book of Daniel: Composition and Reception*. Edited by J. J. Collins and P. W. Flint. VTSup 83/2. Leiden: Brill.

———. 2001b. *Mark 8:27–16:20*. WBC 34B. Nashville: Nelson.

———. 2003. "Defeating Satan and Liberating Israel: Jesus and Daniel's Visions." *JSHJ* 1: 161–70.

Evans, M. J. 2000. *1 and 2 Samuel*. NIBCOT 6. Peabody, MA: Hendrickson.

Exum, J. C. 1979. "Isaiah 28–32: A Literary Approach." *SBLSP* 16–17: 2:123–51.

———. 1981. "Of Broken Pots, Fluttering Birds, and Visions in the Night: Extended Simile and Poetic Technique in Isaiah." *CBQ* 43: 331–52.

Farrer, A. M. 1951. *A Study in St. Mark*. London: Dacre Press.

Fascher, A. 1954. "Theologische Beobachtungen zu *dei.*" Pages 228–54 in *Neutestamentliche Studien für Rudolf Bultmann: Zu seinem siebzigsten Geburtstag am 20. August 1954.* Edited by W. Eltester. BZNW 21. Berlin: Töpelmann.

Feuillet, A. 1953. "Le fils de l'homme de Daniel et la tradition biblique." *RB* 60: 170–202, 321–46.

———. 1959. "Le baptême de Jésus d'après l'Évangile selon Saint Marc (1,9–11)." *CBQ* 21: 468–90.

Fichtner, J. 1951. "Jahves Plan in der Botschaft des Jesaja." *ZAW* 63: 16–33.

Fishbane, M. 1988. *Biblical Interpretation in Ancient Israel.* Oxford: Clarendon.

Fitzer, G. 1957. "Die Sünde wider der Heiligen Geist." *TZ* 13: 161–82.

Fitzmyer, J. A. 1987. "Aramaic Evidence Affecting the Interpretation of Hosanna in the New Testament." Pages 110–18 in *Tradition and Interpretation in the New Testament: Essays in Honor of E. Earle Ellis for His 60th Birthday.* Edited by G. F. Hawthorne and O. Betz. Grand Rapids: Eerdmans.

Flusser, D. 1981. *Die rabbinischen Gleichnisse und der Gleichniserzähler Jesus.* JC 4. Bern: Lang.

Fokkelman, J. P. 1986. *The Crossing Fates (I Sam. 13–31 and II Sam. 1).* Vol. 2 of *Narrative Art and Poetry in the Books of Samuel: A Full Interpretation Based on Stylistic and Structural Analyses.* SSN 23. Assen: Van Gorcum.

Ford, D. 1979. *The Abomination of Desolation in Biblical Eschatology.* Washington, DC: University Press of America.

France, R. T. 1980. "Mark and the Teaching of Jesus." Pages 101–36 in *Studies of History and Tradition in the Four Gospels.* Vol. 1 of *Gospel Perspectives.* Edited by R. T. France and D. Wenham. Sheffield: JSOT Press.

———. 1982. *Jesus and the Old Testament: His Application of Old Testament Passages to Himself and His Mission.* Grand Rapids: Baker Academic.

———. 2002. *The Gospel of Mark.* NIGTC. Grand Rapids: Eerdmans.

Fretheim, T. E. 1991. *Exodus.* IBC. Louisville: John Knox.

Fuller, R. H. 1954. *The Mission and Achievement of Jesus: An Examination of the Presuppositions of New Testament Theology.* SBT 12. London: SCM.

———. 1963. *Interpreting the Miracles.* Philadelphia: Westminster.

Funk, R. W. 1973. "The Looking-Glass Tree Is for the Birds." *Int* 27: 3–9.

Gamberoni, J. 1964. "Das Elterngebot im Alten Testament." *BZ* 8: 161–90.

Gaston, L. 1962. "Beelzebul." *TZ* 18: 247–55.

———. 1970. *No Stone upon Another: Studies in the Significance of the Fall of Jerusalem in the Synoptic Gospels.* NovTSup 23. Leiden: Brill.

Gathercole, S. 2004. "The Son of Man in Mark's Gospel." *ExpTim* 11: 366–72.

Geddert, T. J. 1989. *Watchwords: Mark 13 in Markan Eschatology.* JSNTSup 26. Sheffield: JSOT Press.

Gerhardsson, B. 1968. "The Parable of the Sower and Its Interpretation." *NTS* 14: 165–93.

Gibson, J. B. 1986. "The Rebuke of the Disciples in Mark 8.14–21." *JSNT* 27: 31–47.

Ginsberg, H. L. 1953. "The Oldest Interpretation of the Suffering Servant." *VT* 3: 400–404.

Ginzberg, L. 1925. "David in the Rabbinical Literature." *JE* 4:453–57.

———. 2003. *Legends of the Jews.* Translated by H. Szold and P. Radin. 2nd ed. 2 vols. Skokie, IL: Varda.

Gitay, Y. 1991. *Isaiah and His Audience: The Structure and Meaning of Isaiah 1–12.* SSN 30. Assen: Van Gorcum.

Glazier-McDonald, B. 1987. *Malachi, the Divine Messenger.* SBLDS 98. Atlanta: Scholars Press.

Gnilka, J. 1961. *Der Verstockung Israels: Isaias 6,9–10 in der Theologie der Synoptiker.* SANT 3. Munich: Kösel.

———. 1978–1979. *Das Evangelium nach Markus.* 2 vols. EKKNT 2. Zürich: Benziger.

Goldingay, J. 1979. "The Arrangement of Isaiah XLI–XLV." *VT* 29: 289–99.

———. 1989. *Daniel.* WBC 30. Waco: Word.

———. 2001. *Isaiah.* Peabody, MA: Hendrickson.

Gosse, B. 1990. "Oracles contre les nations et structures comparées des livres d'Isaïe et d'Ezéchiel." *BN* 54: 19–21.

Goulder, M. 2002. "Psalm 8 and the Son of Man." *NTS* 40: 18–29.

Grant, R. M. 1948. "The Coming of the Kingdom." *JBL* 67: 297–303.

Green, J. B. 1997. *The Gospel of Luke.* NICNT. Grand Rapids: Eerdmans.

Grimm, W. 1981. *Weil ich dich liebe: Die Verkündigen Jesu und Deuterojesaja.* ANTJ 1. Bern: Lang.

Grønbæk, J. H. 1971. *Die Geschichte vom Aufstieg Davids (1 Sam. 15–2 Sam. 5): Tradition und Komposition.* Translated by H. Leisterer. ATDan 10. Copenhagen: Prostant Apud Munksgaard.

Grundmann, W. 1959. *Das Evangelium nach Markus.* THKNT 2. Berlin: Evangelische Verlaganstalt.

Guelich, R. A. 1982. "'The Beginning of the Gospel': Mark 1:1–15." *BR* 27: 5–15.

———. 1989. *Mark.* WBC 34a. Waco: Word.

Gundry, R. H. 1967. *The Use of the Old Testament in St. Matthew's Gospel: With Special Reference to the Messianic Hope.* NovTSup 18. Leiden: Brill.

———. 1993. *Mark: A Commentary on His Apology for the Cross.* Grand Rapids: Eerdmans.

Hals, R. M. 1989. *Ezekiel.* FOTL 19. Grand Rapids: Eerdmans.

Hamilton, V. P. 1990. *Genesis 1–17.* NICOT. Grand Rapids: Eerdmans.

Hanson, P. D. 1979. *The Dawn of Apocalyptic: The Historical and Sociological Roots of Jewish Apocalyptic Eschatology.* Rev. ed. Philadelphia: Fortress.

Hare, D. R. A. 1990. *The Son of Man Tradition.* Minneapolis: Fortress.

Harrelson, W. 1980. *The Ten Commandments and Human Rights.* OBT 8. Philadelphia: Fortress.

Hart, I. 1999. "Genesis 1:1–2:3 as a Prologue to the Book of Genesis." *TynBul* 49: 315–36.

Hartley, J. E. 1992. *Leviticus.* WBC 4. Waco: Word.

Hartman, L. 1966. *Prophecy Interpreted: The Formation of Some Jewish Apocalyptic Texts and of the Eschatological Discourse Mark 13 par.* Translated by N. Tomkinson and J. Gray. ConBNT 1. Uppsala: Gleerup.

Hatina, T. R. 1996. "The Focus of Mark 13:24–27: The Parousia or the Destruction of the Temple?" *BBR* 6: 43–66.

———. 2002. *In Search of a Context: The Function of Scripture in Mark's Narrative.* London: Sheffield Academic Press.

Hawkin, D. J. 1972. "The Incomprehension of the Disciples." *JBL* 91: 491–500.

Hay, D. M. 1973. *Glory at the Right Hand: Psalm 110 in Early Christianity.* SBLMS 18. Nashville: Abingdon.

Heaton, E. W. 1956. *The Book of Daniel.* TBC. London: SCM.

Heil, J. P. 1981. *Jesus Walking on the Sea: Meaning and Gospel Functions of Matt 14:22–33, Mark 6:45–52 and John 6:15b–21.* AnBib 87. Rome: Pontifical Biblical Institute.

———. 1999. "A Note on 'Elijah with Moses' in Mark 9,4." *Bib* 80: 115.

Hengel, M. 1995. *Studies in Early Christology.* Edinburgh: T&T Clark.

Hengel, M., and D. P. Bailey. 2004. "The Effective History of Isaiah 53 in the Pre-Christian Period." Pages 75–146 in *The Suffering Servant: Isaiah 53 in Jewish and Christian Sources.* Edited by B. Janowski and P. Stuhlmacher. Translated by D. P. Bailey. Grand Rapids: Eerdmans.

Hertzberg, H. W. 1964. *I & II Samuel.* OTL. Philadelphia: Westminster.

Hiers, R. H. 1985. "'Binding' and 'Loosing': The Matthean Authorizations." *JBL* 104: 233–50.

Hill, A. E. 1998. *Malachi.* AB 25D. New York: Doubleday.

Hill, D. 1973. "'The Son of Man' in Psalm 80 v. 17." *NovT* 15: 261–69.

Hobbs, E. C. 1958. "The Gospel of Mark and the Exodus." PhD diss., University of Chicago.

Hofius, O. 1983. "Vergebungszuspruch und Vollmachtsfrage." Pages 114–27 in *"Wenn nicht jetzt, wann dann?" Aufsätze für Hans-Joachim Kraus zum 65. Geburtstag.* Edited by H.-G. Geyer et al. Neukirchen-Vluyn: Neukirchener Verlag.

Holladay, W. L. 1986. *Jeremiah 1: A Commentary on the Book of the Prophet Jeremiah, Chapters 1–25.* Hermeneia. Philadelphia: Fortress.

Hooker, M. D. 1959. *Jesus and the Servant: The Influence of the Servant Concept of Deutero-Isaiah in the New Testament.* London: SPCK.

———. 1967. *The Son of Man in Mark: A Study of the Background of the Term "Son of Man" and Its Use in St. Mark's Gospel.* London: SPCK.

———. 1987. "What Doest Thou Here, Elijah?" Pages 59–70 in *The Glory of Christ in the New Testament: Studies in Christology in Memory of George Bradford Caird.* Edited by L. D. Hurst and N. T. Wright. Oxford: Clarendon.

———. 1988. "Mark." Pages 220–30 in *It Is Written: Scripture Citing Scripture; Essays in Honour of Barnabas Lindars, SSF.* Edited by D. A. Carson and H. G. M. Williamson. Cambridge: Cambridge University Press.

———. 1991. *The Gospel according to St. Mark.* BNTC. London: SPCK.

———. 2000. "Mark's Parables of the Kingdom (Mark 4:1–34)." Pages 79–101 in *The Challenge of Jesus' Parables.* Edited by R. N. Longenecker. MNTS. Grand Rapids: Eerdmans.

Horbury, W. 1985. "The Messianic Association of 'The Son of Man.'" *JTS* 36: 34–55.

———. 1998. *Jewish Messianism and the Cult of Christ.* London: SCM.

Hoskyns, E. C., and N. Davey. 1947. *The Riddle of the New Testament.* London: Faber & Faber.

Huffman, N. A. 1978. "Atypical Features in the Parables of Jesus." *JBL* 97: 207–20.

Hugenberger, G. P. 1994. *Marriage as a Covenant: A Study of Biblical Law and Ethics Governing Marriage, Developed from the Perspective of Malachi.* VTSup 52. Leiden: Brill.

———. 1995. "The Servant of the Lord in the 'Servant Songs' of Isaiah: A Second Moses Figure." Pages 105–40 in *The Lord's Anointed: Interpretation of Old Testament Messianic Texts.* Edited by P. E. Satterthwaite, R. S. Hess, and G. J. Wenham. THS. Grand Rapids: Baker Academic.

Hultgren, A. J. 1979. *Jesus and His Adversaries: The Form and Function of the Conflict Stories in the Synoptic Tradition.* Minneapolis: Augsburg.

Hurtado, L. W. 1983. *Mark.* GNC. New York: Harper & Row.

———. 1988. *One God, One Lord: Early Christian Devotion and Ancient Jewish Monotheism.* London: SCM.

———. 2003. *Lord Jesus Christ: Devotion to Jesus in Earliest Christianity.* Grand Rapids: Eerdmans.

Instone-Brewer, D. 2002. *Divorce and Remarriage in the Bible: The Social and Literary Context.* Grand Rapids: Eerdmans.

Iwe, J. C. 1999. *Jesus in the Synagogue of Capernaum: The Pericope and Its Programmatic Character for the Gospel of Mark; An Exegetico-Theological Study of Mark 1:21–28.* TGST 57. Rome: Editrice Pontifica Università Gregoriana.

Janowski, B. 2004. "He Bore Our Sins: Isaiah 53 and the Drama of Taking Another's Place." Pages 48–74 in *The Suffering Servant: Isaiah 53 in Jewish and Christian Sources.* Edited by B. Janowski and P. Stuhlmacher. Translated by D. P. Bailey. Grand Rapids: Eerdmans.

Janzen, J. G. 1985. "Resurrection and Hermeneutics: On Exodus 3.6 in Mark 12.26." *JSNT* 23: 43–58.

Jensen, J. 1973. *The Use of* tôrâ *by Isaiah: His Debate with the Wisdom Tradition.* CBQMS 3. Washington, DC: Catholic Biblical Association of America.

———. 1986. "Yahweh's Plan in Isaiah and in the Rest of the Old Testament." *CBQ* 48: 443–55.

Jeremias, J. 1963. *The Parables of Jesus.* London: SCM.

———. 1967. "Παῖς θεου." *TDNT* 5:654–717.

———. 1971a. "Die Drei-Tage-Worte der Evangelien." Pages 221–29 in *Tradition und Glaube: Das frühe Christentum in seiner Umwelt; Festgabe für Karl Georg Kuhn zum 65. Geburtstag.* Edited by G. Jeremias, H.-W. Kuhn, and H. Stegemann. Göttingen: Vandenhoeck & Ruprecht.

———. 1971b. *New Testament Theology, Part I: The Proclamation of Jesus.* Translated by J. Bowden. New York: Scribner.

———. 1977. *The Eucharistic Words of Jesus.* Translated by N. Perrin. Philadelphia: Fortress.

Jones, D. R. 1992. *Jeremiah.* NCBC. Grand Rapids: Eerdmans.

Juel, D. 1977. *Messiah and Temple: The Trial of Jesus in the Gospel of Mark.* SBLDS 31. Missoula, MT: Scholars Press.

———. 1988. *Messianic Exegesis: Christological Interpretation of the Old Testament in Early Christianity.* Philadelphia: Fortress.

Just, F. 1998. "Was Blind Bartimaeus a 'Son of Impurity'?" Paper presented at the annual meeting of the Society of Biblical Literature, Orlando, FL, 22 November 1998.

Kaiser, O. 1962. *Die königliche Knecht: Eine traditionsgeschichtlich-exegetische Studie über die Ebed-Jahwe-Lieder bei Deuterojesaja.* FRLANT 70. Göttingen: Vandenhoeck & Ruprecht.

Kallas, J. 1961. *The Significance of Miracles in the Synoptic Gospels.* London: SPCK.

Kampen, J. I. 1999. "The Significance of the Temple in the Manuscripts of the Damascus Document." Pages 185–97 in *The Dead Sea Scrolls at Fifty: Proceedings of the 1997 Society of Biblical Literature Qumran Section Meetings.* Edited by R. A. Kugler and E. M. Schuller. SBLEJL 15. Atlanta: Society of Biblical Literature.

Käsemann, E. 1969. *Jesus Means Freedom.* Philadelphia: Fortress.

Keck, L. E. 1966. "The Introduction to Mark's Gospel." *NTS* 12: 352–70.

Kee, H. C. 1967. "The Terminology of Mark's Exorcism Stories." *NTS* 14: 232–46.

———. 1972. "The Transfiguration in Mark: Epiphany or Apocalyptic Vision?" Pages 137–52 in *Understanding the Sacred Text: Essays in Honor of Morton S. Enslin on the Hebrew Bible and Christian Beginnings.* Edited by J. Reumann. Valley Forge, PA: Judson.

———. 1975. "The Function of Scriptural Quotations and Allusions in Mark 11–16." Pages 165–85 in *Jesus und Paulus.* Edited by E. Earle Ellis and E. Grässer. Göttingen: Vandenhoeck & Ruprecht.

———. 1977. *Community of the New Age: Studies in Mark's Gospel.* Philadelphia: Westminster.

———. 1983. *Miracle in the Early Christian World: A Study in Sociohistorical Method.* New Haven: Yale University Press.

Keegan, T. J. 1994. "The Parable of the Sower and Mark's Jewish Leaders." *CBQ* 56: 501–18.

Kelber, W. H. 1979. *Mark's Story of Jesus.* Philadelphia: Fortress.

Kertelge, K. 1970. *Die Wunder Jesu im Markusevangelium: Eine redaktionsgeschichtliche Untersuchung.* SANT 23. Munich: Kösel.

Kiesow, K. 1979. *Exodustexte im Jesajabuch: Literarkritische und motivgeschichtliche Analysen.* OBO 24. Göttingen: Vandenhoeck & Ruprecht.

Kim, J. C. 1962. "Verhältnis Jahwes zu den anderen Göttern in Deuterojesaja." PhD diss., University of Heidelberg.

Kim, S. 1983. *"The 'Son of Man'" as the Son of God.* WUNT 30. Tübingen: Mohr Siebeck.

Kingsbury, J. D. 1989. *Conflict in Mark: Jesus, Authorities, Disciples.* Minneapolis: Fortress.

Kinman, B. 1995. *Jesus' Entry into Jerusalem: In the Context of Lukan Theology and the Politics of His Day.* AGJU 28. Leiden: Brill.

Kirchevel, G. D. 1999. "The 'Son of Man' Passages in Mark." *BBR* 9: 181–87.

Klauck, H.-J. 1981. "Die Frage der Sündenvergebung in der Perikope von der Heilung des Gelähmten." *BZ* 25: 223–48.

Klein, H. 1979. "Zur Auslegung von Psalm 2: Ein Beitrag zum Thema: Gewalt und Gewaltlosigkeit." *TBei* 10: 63–71.

Klein, R. W. 1983. *1 Samuel.* WBC 10. Waco: Word.

Knibb, M. A. 1979. "Commentary on 2 Esdras." Pages 76–307 in *The First and Second Books of Esdras.* By R. J. Coggins and M. A. Knibb. CBC. Cambridge: Cambridge University Press.

Knierim, R. 1968. "The Vocation of Isaiah." *VT* 18: 47–68.

Kowalski, B. 1994. "Die Wertung von Versagen und Unheil in der Geschichte." *Judaica* 50: 18–33.

Kraus, H.-J. 1986. *Theology of the Psalms.* Translated by K. Crim. Minneapolis: Augsburg.

———. 1988–1989. *Psalms.* Translated by H. C. Oswald. 2 vols. Minneapolis: Augsburg.

Kruse, H. 1977. "Das Reich Satans." *Bib* 58: 29–61.

Kugel, J. L. 1987. "On Hidden Hatred and Open Reproach: Early Exegesis of Leviticus 19:17." *HTR* 80: 43–61.

Kuntz, J. 1997. "The Form, Location and Function of Rhetorical Questions in the Book of Isaiah." Pages 121–41 in vol. 1 of *Writing and Reading the Scroll of Isaiah: Studies of an Interpretive Tradition.* Edited by C. C. Broyles and C. A. Evans. VTSup 70/1. Leiden: Brill.

Lacocque, A. 1979. *The Book of Daniel.* Translated by D. Pellauer. London: SPCK.

———. 2001. "Allusions to Creation in Daniel 7." Pages 114–31 in vol. 1 of *The Book of Daniel: Composition and Reception.* VTSup 83/1. Edited by J. J. Collins and P. W. Flint. Leiden: Brill.

Lagrange, M.-J. 1947. *Évangile selon Saint Marc.* Rev. ed. EBib. Paris: Gabalda.

Lamarche, P. 1961. *Zacharie IX–XIV: Structure littéraires et messianisme.* EBib. Paris: Gabala.

Lambrecht, J. 1974. "The Relatives of Jesus in Mark." *NovT* 16: 241–58.

Landy, F. 1999. "Strategies of Concentration and Diffusion in Isaiah 6." *BibInt* 7: 58–86.

Lane, W. L. 1974. *The Gospel of Mark.* NICNT 2. Grand Rapids: Eerdmans.

Lang, B. 1978. *Kein Aufstand in Jerusalem: Die Politik des Propheten Ezechiel.* SBB. Stuttgart: Katholisches Bibelwerk.

Lang, F. 1977. "Kompositionsanalyse des Markusevangeliums." *ZTK* 74: 1–24.

Larkin, K. 1994. *The Eschatology of Second Zechariah: A Study of the Formation of a Mantalogical Wisdom Anthology.* CBET 6. Kampen: Kok Pharos.

Legasse, S. 1962. "'L'homme fort' de Luc. xi 21–22." *NovT* 5: 5–9.

Leivestad, R. 1954. *Christ the Conqueror: Ideas of Conflict and Victory in the New Testament.* London: SPCK.

Lemcio, E. E. 1978. "External Evidence for the Structure and Function of Mark iv. 1–20, vii. 14–23 and viii. 14–21." *JTS* 29: 323–38.

Lenchak, T. 1993. *"Choose Life": A Rhetorical-Critical Investigation of Deut 28,69–30,20.* AnBib 129. Rome: Pontifical Biblical Institute.

Lenglet, A. 1972. "La structure littéraire de Daniel 2–7." *Bib* 53: 169–90.

Lentzen-Deis, F. 1970. *Die Taufe Jesu nach den Synoptikern: Literarkritische und gattungsgeschichtliche Untersuchungen.* FTS 4. Frankfurt: Knecht.

Levenson, J. D. 1984. "The Temple and the World." *JR* 64: 275–98.

Levine, B. A. 1989. *Leviticus.* JPSTC. Philadelphia: Jewish Publication Society.

———. 1993. *Numbers 1–20.* AB 4A. New York: Doubleday.

Liebreich, L. J. 1954. "The Position of Chapter Six in the Book of Isaiah." *HUCA* 25: 37–40.

———. 1955–1957. "The Compilation of the Book of Isaiah." *JQR* 46: 259–77; 47: 114–38.

Lindars, B. 1961. *New Testament Apologetic: The Doctrinal Significance of the Old Testament Quotations.* London: SCM.

———. 1983. *Jesus Son of Man: A Fresh Examination of the Son of Man Sayings in the Gospels.* London: SPCK.

Lohmeyer, E. 1953. *Das Evangelium des Markus.* 12th ed. KEK 1/2. Göttingen: Vandenhoeck & Ruprecht.

———. 1962. *Lord of the Temple: A Study of the Relation between Cult and Gospel.* Translated by S. Todd. Edinburgh: Oliver & Boyd.

Lorton, D. 1999. "The Theology of Cult Statues in Ancient Egypt." Pages 123–210 in *Born in Heaven, Made on Earth: The Making of the Cult Image in the Ancient Near East.* Edited by M. B. Dick. Winona Lake, IN: Eisenbrauns.

Lövestam, E. 1968. *Spiritus Blasphemia: Eine Studie zu Mk 3,28f par Mt 12,31f, Lk 12,10.* ScrM 1. Lund: Gleerup.

———. 1995. *Jesus and "This Generation": A New Testament Study.* Translated by M. Linnarud. ConBNT 25. Stockholm: Almqvist & Wiksell.

Lucas, E. 2002. *Daniel*. ApOTC 20. Leicester: Apollos.

Lust, J. 2001. "Daniel in the New Testament: Visions of God's Kingdom." Pages 671–88 in vol. 2 of *The Book of Daniel: Composition and Reception*. Edited by J. J. Collins and P. W. Flint. VTSup 83/2. Leiden: Brill.

MacLaurin, E. C. B. 1978. "Beelzeboul." *NovT* 20: 156–60.

Malamat, A. 1990. "'Love Your Neighbor as Yourself': What It Really Means." *BAR* 16: 50–51.

Malina, B. J., and R. L. Rohrbaugh. 1992. *Social Science Commentary on the Synoptic Gospels*. Minneapolis: Fortress.

Mann, C. S. 1986. *Mark*. AB 27. New York: Doubleday.

Mann, J. 1940. *The Bible as Read and Preached in the Old Synagogue*. 2 vols. Cincinnati: Jewish Publication Society.

Manson, T. W. 1947. "Mark II.27f." Pages 138–46 in *Coniectanea neotestamentica XI: In honorem Antonii Fridrichsen sexagenarii edenda curavit Seminarum Neotestamenticum Upsaliense*. ConBNT 11. Lund: Gleerup.

———. 1948. *The Teaching of Jesus: Studies of Its Form and Content*. Cambridge: Cambridge University Press.

Marcus, J. 1986. *The Mystery of the Kingdom of God*. SBLDS 90: Atlanta: Scholars Press.

———. 1988. "Mark 14:61: 'Are You the Messiah-Son-of-God?'" *NovT* 31: 125–41.

———. 1992. *The Way of the Lord: Christological Exegesis of the Old Testament in the Gospel of Mark*. Louisville: Westminster John Knox.

———. 1997. "Scripture and Tradition in Mark 7." Pages 177–95 in *The Scriptures in the Gospels*. Edited by C. M. Tuckett. BETL 131. Leuven: Leuven University Press.

———. 1999. *Mark 1–8*. AB 27A. New York: Doubleday.

———. 2003a. "Son of Man as Son of Adam." *RevB* 110: 38–61.

———. 2003b. "Son of Man as Son of Adam, Part II: Exegesis." *RevB* 110: 370–86.

Marshall, C. D. 1989. *Faith as a Theme in Mark's Narrative*. SNTSMS 64. Cambridge: Cambridge University Press.

Marshall, I. H. 1968–1969. "Son of God or Servant of Yahweh? A Reconsideration of Mark 1:11." *NTS* 15: 326–36.

Martin, R. P. 1972. *Mark: Evangelist and Theologian*. Grand Rapids: Zondervan.

Mason, R. 1990. *Preaching the Tradition: Homily and Hermeneutics after the Exile*. Cambridge: Cambridge University Press.

———. 2003. "The Use of Earlier Biblical Material in Zechariah 9–14: A Study in Inner Biblical Exegesis: Zechariah 13.7–9." Pages 117–30 in *Bringing Out the Treasure: Inner Biblical Allusion in Zechariah 9–14*. Edited by M. J. Boda and M. H. Floyd, with R. Mason. JSOTSup 370. Sheffield: Sheffield Academic Press.

Matera, F. J. 1982. *The Kingship of Jesus: Composition and Theology in Mark 15*. SBLDS 66. Chico, CA: Scholars Press.

———. 1989. "The Incomprehension of the Disciples and Peter's Confession (Mark 6,14–8,30)." *Bib* 70: 153–72.

Matthews, V. C., and D. C. Benjamin. 1993. *Social World of Ancient Israel 1250–587 BCE*. Peabody, MA: Hendrickson.

Maurer, C. 1953. "Knecht Gottes und Sohn Gottes im Passionsbericht des Markusevangeliums." *ZTK* 50: 1–38.

Mauser, U. 1963. *Christ in the Wilderness: The Wilderness Theme in the Second Gospel and Its Basis in the Biblical Tradition*. SBT 39. London: SCM.

Mays, J. L. 1969. *Hosea*. OTL. Philadelphia: Westminster.

McArthur, H. K. 1971–1972. "On the Third Day." *NTS* 18: 81–86.

McCarter, P. K., Jr. 1980. *I Samuel*. AB 8. Garden City, NY: Doubleday.

McConville, J. G. 1993. *Judgement and Promise: An Interpretaton of the Book of Jeremiah*. Leicester: Apollos.

———. 2002. *Deuteronomy*. ApOTC. Leicester: Apollos.

McKane, W. 1965. *Prophets and Wise Men*. SBT 44. London: SCM.

———. 1986. *Jeremiah*. Vol. 1. ICC. Edinburgh: T&T Clark.

McKenzie, J. L. 1968. *Second Isaiah*. AB 20. Garden City, NY: Doubleday.

McKenzie, S. 1979. "Exodus Typology in Hosea." *ResQ* 22: 100–108.

McKenzie, S. K., and H. N. Wallace. 1983. "Covenant Themes in Malachi." *CBQ* 45: 549–63.

McKnight, S. 2005. *Jesus and His Death: Historiography, the Historical Jesus, and Atonement Theory*. Waco: Baylor University Press.

McLaughlin, J. J. 1994. "Their Hearts Were Hardened: The Use of Isaiah 6,9–10 in the Book of Isaiah." *Bib* 75: 1–25.

Mead, Richard T. 1964. "A Dissenting Opinion about Respect for Context in Old Testament Quotations." *NTS* 10: 279–89.

Melugin, R. F. 1976. *The Formation of Isaiah 40–55*. BZAW 141. Berlin: de Gruyter.

———. 1991. "The Servant, God's Call, and the Structure of Isaiah 40–48." *SBLSP* 30: 21–30.

Merrill, E. 1994. *Deuteronomy*. NAC 4. Nashville: Broadman & Holman.

Mettinger, T. N. D. 1983. *A Farewell to the Servant Songs: A Critical Examination of an Exegetical Axiom*. ScrM 3. Lund: Gleerup.

———. 1997. "In Search of the Hidden Structure: YHWH as King in Isaiah 40–55." Pages 143–54 in vol. 1 of *Writing and Reading the Scroll of Isaiah: Studies of an Interpretive Tradition*. Edited by C. C. Broyles and C. A. Evans. VTSup 70/1. Leiden: Brill.

Metzger, M. 1991. "Zeder, Weinstock und Weltenbaum." Pages 198–229 in *Ernten, was man sät: Festschrift für Klaus Koch zu seinem 65. Geburtstag*. Edited by D. R. Daniels, U. Glessmer, and M. Rösel. Neukirchen-Vluyn: Neukirchener Verlag.

Meyers, C. L., and E. M. Meyers. 1988–1993. *Zechariah*. 2 vols. AB 25B, 25C. New York: Doubleday.

Milgrom, J. 1983. "Of Hems and Tassels." *BAR* 9: 61–65.

———. 1989. *Numbers*. JPSTC. Philadelphia: Jewish Publication Society.

———. 1991–2001. *Leviticus*. 3 vols. AB 3, 3A, 3B. New York: Doubleday.

Miller, P. D. 1986. "The Divine Council and the Prophetic Call to War." *VT* 18: 100–107.

Millgram, A. E. 1971. *Jewish Worship*. Philadelphia: Jewish Publication Society.

Moberly, R. W. L. 1999. "Toward an Interpretation of the Shema." Pages 124–44 in *Theological Exegesis: Essays in Honor of Brevard S. Childs*. Edited by C. Seitz and K. Greene-McCreight. Grand Rapids: Eerdmans.

Moloney, F. J. 2002. *The Gospel of Mark*. Peabody, MA: Hendrickson.

Moo, D. J. 1983. *The Old Testament in the Gospel Passion Narratives*. Sheffield: Almond Press.

Motyer, A. 1993. *The Prophecy of Isaiah*. Leicester: Inter-Varsity.

Moule, C. F. D. 1969. "Mark 4:1–20 Yet Once More." Pages 95–113 in *Neotestamentica et Semitica: Studies in Honour of Matthew Black*. Edited by E. Ellis and M. Wilcox. Edinburgh: T&T Clark.

———. 1977. *The Origin of Christology*. Cambridge: Cambridge University Press.

———. 1995. "'The Son of Man': Some of the Facts." *NTS* 41: 277–79.

Myers, C. 1988. *Binding the Strong Man: A Political Reading of Mark's Story of Jesus*. Maryknoll, NY: Orbis.

Myhre, K. 1985. "'Paktens blod' i vinordet: En undersøkelse av henspillingen på Ex 24,8 i Mark 14,24/Matt 26,28." *TTKi* 55: 271–86.

Neusner, J. 1973. *The Idea of Purity in Ancient Judaism*. SJLA 1. Leiden: Brill.

Neyrey, J. H. 1986. "The Idea of Purity in Mark's Gospel." *Semeia* 35: 91–128.

Nicholson, E. W. 1982. "The Covenant Ritual in Exodus XXIV 3–8." *VT* 32: 74–86.

Nickelsburg, G. W. E. 1992. "Son of Man." *ABD* 6:137–50.

Niditch, S. 1981. "The Composition of Isaiah 1." *Bib* 61: 509–29.

Nielsen, K. 1979. "Das Bild des Gerichts (*rib*-pattern) in Jes. i–xii." *VT* 29: 309–24.

Nineham, D. E. 1963. *The Gospel according to St. Mark*. PGC. London: Black.

North, C. R. 1948. *The Suffering Servant in Deutero-Isaiah: An Historical and Critical Study*. London: Oxford University Press.

North, R. 1967. "Separated Spiritual Substances in the Old Testament." *CBQ* 29: 419–49.

Oakman, D. E. 1988. "Rulers' Houses, Thieves, and Usurpers." *Forum* 4: 109–23.

O'Brien, J. M. 2004. *Nahum, Habakkuk, Zephaniah, Haggai, Zechariah, Malachi*. AOTC. Nashville: Abingdon.

Olyan, S. M. 2001. "The Exegetical Dimensions of Restrictions on the Blind and Lame in Texts from Qumran." *DSD* 8: 38–50.

Orlinsky, H. M. 1977. "The So-Called 'Servant of the Lord' and 'Suffering Servant.'" Pages 1–133 in *Studies on the Second Part of the Book of Isaiah*. By N. H. Snaith and H. M. Orlinsky. VTSup 14. Leiden: Brill.

Ortlund, R. C. 1996. *Whoredom: God's Unfaithful Wife in Biblical Theology*. Leicester: Apollos.

Oswalt, J. N. 1998. *The Book of Isaiah, Chapters 40–66*. NICOT. Grand Rapids: Eerdmans.

Owen, P., and D. Shepherd. 2001. "Speaking Up for Qumran, Dalman and the Son of Man: Was *Bar Enasha* a Common Term for 'Man' in the Time of Jesus?" *JSNT* 81: 81–121.

Painter, J. 1997. *Mark's Gospel: Worlds in Conflict*. NTR. London: Routledge.

Pawlikowski, J. T. 1970. "On Renewing the Revolution of the Pharisees: A New Approach to Theology and Politics." *Cross Currents* 20: 415–34.

Peisker, C. H. 1968. "Konsekutives ἵνα in Markus 4:12." *ZNW* 59: 126–27.

Perrin, N. 1971. "The Christology of Mark: A Study in Methodology." *JR* 51: 173–87.

Person, R. F. 1993. *Second Zechariah and the Deuteronomic School*. JSOTSup 167. Sheffield: Sheffield Academic Press.

Pesch, R. 1976–1977. *Das Markusevangelium*. 2 vols. HTKNT 2. Freiburg: Herder.

Petersen, D. L. 1977. *Late Israelite Prophecy: Studies in Deutero-Prophetic Literature and in Chronicles*. SBLMS 23. Missoula, MT: Scholars Press.

———. 1979. "Isaiah 28: A Redaction Critical Study." *SBLSP* 2:27–45.

———. 1984. *Haggai and Zechariah 1–8*. OTL. Philadelphia: Westminster.

———. 1995. *Zechariah 9–14 and Malachi*. OTL. London: SCM.

Phelan, J. E., Jr. 1990. "The Function of Mark's Miracles." *CovQ* 48: 3–14.

Phillips, A. 1970. *Ancient Israel's Criminal Law: A New Approach to the Decalogue*. New York: Schocken.

Pimental, P. 1988. "The 'Unclean Spirits' of St. Mark's Gospel." *ExpTim* 99: 173–75.

Ploch, W. 1993. *Jesaja-Worte in der synoptischen Evangelientradition*. St. Ottilien: EOS Verlag.

Plöger, J. G. 1967. *Literarkritische, formgeschichtliche und stilkritische Untersuchungen zum Deuteronomium*. BBB 26. Bonn: Hanstein.

Poirier, J. C. 1996. "Why Did the Pharisees Wash Their Hands?" *JJS* 47: 217–33.

———. 2000. "The Interiority of True Religion in Mark 7,6–8." *ZNW* 91: 180–91.

Polan, G. J. 1985. "Salvation in the Midst of Struggle." *TBT* 23: 90–97.

Porteous, N. 1965. *Daniel*. OTL. London: SCM.

Poythress, V. 1976. "The Holy Ones of the Most High in Daniel VII." *VT* 26: 208–13.

Preuß, H. D. 1971. *Verspottung fremder Religionen im Alten Testament*. BWANT 92. Stuttgart: Kohlhammer.

———. 1976. *Deuterojesaja: Eine Einführung in seine Botschaft*. Neukirchen-Vluyn: Neukirchener Verlag.

Procksch, O. 1920. "Die Berufungsvision Hesekiels." Pages 141–49 in *Beiträge zur alttestamentlichen Wissenschaft: Karl Budde zum siebzigsten Geburtstag am 13. April 1920*. Edited by K. Marti. BZAW 34. Giessen: Töpelmann.

Quesnell, Q. 1969. *The Mind of St. Mark: Interpretation and Method through the Exegesis of Mark 6.52*. AnBib 38. Rome: Pontifical Biblical Institute.

Raabe, P. 1984. "The Effect of Repetition in the Suffering Servant Song." *JBL* 103: 77–81.

Rainbow, P. 1997. "Melchizedek as a Messiah at Qumran." *BBR* 7: 179–94.

Räisänen, H. 1990. *The "Messianic Secret" in Mark*. Translated by C. Tuckett. SNTW. Edinburgh: T&T Clark.

Redditt, P. 1989. "Israel's Shepherds: Hope and Pessimism in Zechariah 9–14." *CBQ* 51: 631–42.

Rendtorff, R. 1984. "Zur Komposition des Buches Jesaja." *VT* 34: 295–320.

Riesenfeld, H. 1947. *Jésus transfiguré: L'arrière-plan du récit évangélique de la transfiguration de Notre-Seigneur*. ASNU 16. Copenhagen: Munksgaard.

Rignell, L. G. 1957. "Isaiah Chapter 1: Some Exegetical Remarks with Special Reference to the Relationship between the Text and the Book of Deuteronomy." *ST* 11: 140–58.

Ringgren, H. 1963. *The Faith of Qumran: Theology of the Dead Sea Scrolls*. Translated by E. T. Sander. Philadelphia: Fortress.

Roberts, J. J. M. 1982. "Isaiah in Old Testament Theology." *Int* 36: 130–43.

———. 2002. "The Enthronement of Yhwh and David: The Abiding Theological Significance of the Kingship Language of the Psalms." *CBQ* 64: 679–86.

Robinson, J. M. 1957. *The Problem of History in Mark*. SBT 21. London: SCM.

Rogerson, J. A. 1970. "The Hebrew Conception of the Corporate Personality: A Re-examination." *JTS* 21: 1–16.

Rooke, D. W. 1998. "Kingship as Priesthood: The Relationship between the High Priesthood and the Monarchy." Pages 187–208 in *King and Messiah in Israel and the Ancient Near East: Proceedings of the Oxford Old Testament Seminar.* Edited by J. Day. JSOTSup 270. Sheffield: Sheffield Academic Press.

Rooker, M. 1990. *Biblical Hebrew in Transition: The Language of the Book of Ezekiel.* JSOTSup 90. Sheffield: JSOT Press.

Rordorf, W. 1968. *Sunday: The History of the Day of Rest and Worship in the Earliest Centuries of the Christian Church.* Translated by A. A. K. Graham. London: SCM.

Roth, C. 1960. "The Cleansing of the Temple according to Zechariah xiv 21." *NovT* 4: 297–303.

Rowe, R. D. 1982. "Is Daniel's 'Son of Man' Messianic?" Pages 71–96 in *Christ the Lord: Studies in Christology Presented to Donald Guthrie.* Edited by H. H. Rowdon. Downers Grove, IL: InterVarsity.

———. 2002. *God's Kingdom and God's Son: The Background to Mark's Christology from Concepts of Kingship in the Psalms.* AGJU 50. Leiden: Brill.

Rowland, C. 1982. *The Open Heaven.* London: SCM.

Ruckstuhl, E. 1983. "Jesus als Gottessohn im Spiegel des markinischen Taufberichts." Pages 193–220 in *Die Mitte des Neuen Testaments: Einheit und Vielfalt neutestamentlicher Theologie; Festschrift für Eduard Schweizer zum siebzigsten Geburtstag.* Edited by U. Luz and H. Weder. Göttingen: Vandenhoeck & Ruprecht.

Rudolph, D. J. 2002. "Jesus and the Food Laws: A Reassessment of Mark 7:19b." *EvQ* 74: 291–311.

Ryle, E. H., and M. R. James. 1891. *Psalms of the Pharisees, Commonly Called the Psalms of Solomon.* Cambridge: Cambridge University Press.

Sanders, E. P. 1992. *Judaism: Practice and Belief 63 BCE–66 CE.* London: SCM.

Sarna, N. M. 1989. *Genesis.* JPSTC. Philadelphia: Jewish Publication Society.

———. 1991. *Exodus.* JPSTC. Philadelphia: Jewish Publication Society.

Sawyer, J. F. A. 1977. *From Moses to Patmos: New Perspectives in Old Testament Study.* London: SPCK.

Schaberg, J. 1985. "Daniel 7, 12 and the New Testament Passion-Resurrection Predictions." *NTS* 31: 208–22.

Schenker, A. 1994. "Les sacrifices d'alliance, Ex XXIV,3–8, dans leur portée narrative et religieuse: Contribution à l'étude de la berit dans l'Ancien Testament." *RB* 101: 481–94.

Schneck, R. 1994. *Isaiah in the Gospel of Mark I–VIII.* BDS 1. Vallejo, CA: BIBAL Press.

Schoors, A. 1973. *I Am God Your Saviour: A Form-Critical Study of the Main Genres in Is. XL–LV.* VTSup 24. Leiden: Brill.

Schreiner, J. 1967. "Das Buch jesajanischer Schule." Pages 142–62 in *Wort und Botschaft: Eine theologische und kritische Einführung in die Probleme des Alten Testaments.* Edited by J. Schreiner. Würzburg: Echter.

Schröten, J. 1995. *Entstehung, Komposition und Wirkungsgeschichte des 118. Psalms.* BBB 95. Weinheim: Beltz Athenäum.

Schultz, R. 1995. "The King in the Book of Isaiah." Pages 141–65 in *The Lord's Anointed: Interpretation of Old Testament Messianic Texts.* Edited by P. E. Satterthwaite, R. S. Hess, and G. J. Wenham. THS. Grand Rapids: Baker Academic.

Schüpphaus, J. 1977. *Die Psalmen Salomos: Ein Zeugnis Jerusalemer Theologie und Frömmigkeit in der Mitte des vorchristlichen Jahrhunderts.* ALGHJ 7. Leiden: Brill.

Schürer, E. 1973–1986. *The History of the Jewish People in the Age of Jesus Christ (175 B.C.–A.D. 135).* Edited by G. Vermes et al. 3 vols. Edinburgh: T&T Clark.

Schwager, R. 1985. "Christ's Death and the Prophetic Critique of Sacrifice." *Semeia* 33: 109–23.

Schweizer, E. 1971. *The Good News according to Mark.* Translated by D. H. Madvig. London: SPCK.

Scott, B. B. 1981. *Jesus, Symbol-Maker of the Kingdom.* Philadelphia: Fortress.

Segal, A. 1977. *Two Powers in Heaven: Early Rabbinic Reports about Christianity and Gnosticism.* SJLA 25. Leiden: Brill.

Seitz, C. R. 1990. "The Divine Council: Temporal Transition and New Prophecy in the Book of Isaiah." *JBL* 109: 229–47.

———. 1991. *Zion's Final Destiny: The Development of the Book of Isaiah; a Reassessment of Isaiah 36–39.* Minneapolis: Fortress.

———. 1993. *Isaiah 1–39.* IBC. Louisville: John Knox.

Seitz, O. 1963. "Praeparatio Evangelica in the Markan Prologue." *JBL* 82: 201–6.

Seow, C. L. 1982. "Hosea 14:10 and the Foolish People Motif." *CBQ* 44: 212–24.

Signer, M. A. 1983. "King/Messiah: Rashi's Exegesis of Psalm 2." *Prooftexts* 3: 273–78.

Skehan, P. W., and A. A. Di Lella. 1987. *The Wisdom of Ben Sira.* AB 39. Garden City, NY: Doubleday.

Slater, T. B. 1995. "One Like a Son of Man in First-Century CE Judaism." *NTS* 41: 183–98.

Smith, D. E. 1990. "Narrative Beginnings in Ancient Literature and Theory." *Semeia* 52: 1–9.

Smith, J. M. P. 1951. *Haggai, Zechariah, Malachi and Jonah.* ICC. Edinburgh: T&T Clark.

Smith, R. L. 1984. *Micah–Malachi.* WBC 32. Waco: Word.

Smith, S. H. 1996. "The Function of the Son of David Tradition in Mark's Gospel." *NTS* 42: 523–29.

Smolar, L., and M. Auerbach. 1983. *Studies in Targum Jonathan to the Prophets.* LBS. New York: KTAV.

Snodgrass, K. 1980. "Streams of Tradition Emerging from Isaiah 40:1–5 and Their Adaptation in the New Testament." *JSNT* 8: 24–45.

———. 1983. *The Parable of the Wicked Tenants: An Inquiry into Parable Interpretation.* WUNT 27. Tübingen: Mohr Siebeck.

Sommer, B. 1998. *A Prophet Reads Scripture: Allusion in Isaiah 40–66.* Stanford, CA: Stanford University Press.

Sonnet, J.-P. 1992. "Le motif de l'endurcissement (Is 6,9–10) et la lecture d'Isaïe." *Bib* 73: 208–39.

Spykerboer, H. C. 1978. "The Structure and Composition of Deutero-Isaiah." PhD diss., University of Grönigen.

———. 1989. "Isaiah 55:1–5: The Climax of Deutero-Isaiah; an Invitation to Come to the New Jerusalem." Pages 357–59 in *The Book of Isaiah/Le livre d'Isaïe: Les oracles et leurs relectures; unité et complexité de l'ouvrage.* Edited by J. Vermeylen. BETL 81. Leuven: Leuven University Press.

Standhartinger, A. 2003. "Jesus, Elija und Mose auf dem Berg: Traditionsgeschichtliche Überlegungen zur Verklärungsgeschichte (Mk 9,2–8)." *BZ* 47: 66–85.

Stanley, C. D. 1992. *Paul and the Language of Scripture: Citation Technique in the Pauline Epistles and Contemporary Literature.* SNTSMS 74. Cambridge: Cambridge University Press.

———. 1999. " 'Pearls before Swine': Did Paul's Audiences Understand His Biblical Quotations?" *NovT* 41: 124–44.

Starkova, K. B. 1992. "The Ideas of Second and Third Isaiah as Reflected in the Qumran Literature." *QC* 2: 51–62.

Steck, O. H. 1972. "Bemerkungen zu Jesaja 6." *BZ* 16: 188–206.

———. 1987. "Beobachtungen zur Anlage von Jes 65–66." *BN* 38/39: 103–16.

Steichele, H.-J. 1980. *Der leidende Sohn Gottes: Eine Untersuchung einiger alttestamentlicher Motive in der Christologie des Markusevangeliums; zugleich ein Beitrag zur Erhellung des überlieferungsgeschichtlichen Zusammenhangs zwischen Altem und Neuem Testament.* BU 14. Regensburg: Pustet.

Stendahl, K. 1968. *The School of St. Matthew and Its Use of the Old Testament.* 2nd ed. ASNU 20. Lund: Gleerup.

Stettler, A. 2004. "Sanctification in the Jesus Tradition." *Bib* 85: 153–78.

Stevens, B. A. 1987. "Divine Warrior in Mark." *BZ* 31: 101–9.

Stock, A. 1987. "Hinge Transitions in Mark's Gospel." *BTB* 15: 27–31.

Stuart, D. 1987. *Hosea-Jonah, Word Biblical Commentary*, v. 31. Waco: Word Books.

Stuhlmacher, P. 1968. *Das paulinische Evangelium: Vorgeschichte.* FRLANT 95. Göttingen: Vandenhoeck & Ruprecht.

Stuhlmueller, C. 1970. *Creative Redemption in Deutero-Isaiah.* AnBib 43. Rome: Pontifical Biblical Institute.

Stummer, F. 1926. "Einige keilschriftliche Parallelen zu Jes 40–66." *JBL* 45: 171–89.

Suhl, A. 1965. *Die Funktion der alttestamentlichen Zitate und Anspielungen im Markusevangelium.* Gütersloh: Mohn.

Swartley, W. M. 1994. *Israel's Scripture Traditions and the Synoptic Gospels.* Peabody, MA: Hendrickson.

Sweeney, M. A. 1988. *Isaiah 1–4 and the Post-Exilic Understanding of the Isaianic Tradition.* BZAW 171. Berlin: de Gruyter.

———. 1989. *Micah, Nahum, Habakkuk, Zephaniah, Haggai, Zechariah, Malachi.* Vol. 2 of *The Twelve Prophets.* Berit Olam. Collegeville, MN: Liturgical Press.

———. 1996. *Isaiah 1–39: With an Introduction to Prophetic Literature.* FOTL 16. Grand Rapids: Eerdmans.

Tate, M. E. 1990. *Psalms 51–100.* WBC 20. Waco: Word.

Telford, W. R. 1980. *The Barren Temple and the Withered Tree: A Redaction-Critical Analysis of the Cursing of the Fig-Tree Pericope in Mark's Gospel and Its Relation to the Cleansing of the Temple Tradition.* JSNTSup 1. Sheffield: JSOT Press.

Theissen, G. 1983. *The Miracle Stories of the Early Christian Tradition.* Translated by F. McDonagh. SNTW. Philadelphia: Fortress.

Thompson, J. A. 1974. *Deuteronomy.* TOTC 5. Leicester: Inter-Varsity.

———. 1980. *The Book of Jeremiah.* NICOT. Grand Rapids: Eerdmans.

Tigay, J. H. 1966. *Deuteronomy.* JPSTC. Philadelphia: Jewish Publication Society.

Tödt, H. E. 1965. *The Son of Man in the Synoptic Tradition.* Translated by D. M. Barton. London: SCM.

Tomasino, A. 1993. "Isaiah 1.1–2.4 and 63–66, and the Composition of the Isaianic Corpus." *JSOT* 57: 81–98.

Trever, J. C. 1962. "Mustard." *IBD* 3:476–77.

Tuckett, C. 1982. "The Present Son of Man." *JSNT* 14: 58–81.

Turner, C. H. 1926. "O UIOS MOU O AGAPHTOS." *JTS* 27: 113–29.

Ulansey, D. 1991. "The Heavenly Veil Torn: Mark's Cosmic Inclusio." *JBL* 110: 123–25.

Urbach, E. E. 1979. *The Sages: Their Concepts and Beliefs.* Translated by I. Abrahams. 2nd ed. Jerusalem: Magnes.

Vancil, J. M. 1992. "Sheep, Shepherd." *ABD* 5:1187–90.

VanderKam, J. 1992. "Righteous One, Messiah, Chosen One, and Son of Man in 1 Enoch 37–71." Pages 169–91 in *The Messiah: Developments in Earliest Judaism and Christianity.* Edited by J. H. Charlesworth. Minneapolis: Fortress.

van der Merwe, B. J. 1966. "Echoes from the Teaching of Hosea in Isa. 40–55." *OTWSA* 7: 20–29.

van der Ostern-Sacken, P. 1969. *Gott und Belial: Traditionsgeschichtliche Untersuchungen zum Dualismus in den Texten aus Qumran.* SUNT 6. Göttingen: Vandenhoeck & Ruprecht.

van Iersel, B. M. F. 1988. *Reading Mark.* Collegeville, MN: Liturgical Press.

———. 1999. "A Dissident of Stature: The Jesus of Mark 3.20–35." *Concilium* 2: 65–72.

van Winkle, D. W. 1985. "The Relationship of the Nations to Yahweh and to Israel in Isaiah XL–LV." *VT* 35: 446–58.

Verheyden, J. 1997. "Describing the Parousia: The Cosmic Phenomena in Mk 13.24–25." Pages 525–50 in *The Scriptures in the Gospels.* Edited by C. M. Tuckett. BETL 131. Leuven: Leuven University Press.

Verhoef, P. A. 1987. *The Books of Haggai and Malachi.* NICOT. Grand Rapids: Eerdmans.

Vermes, G. 1961. *Scripture and Tradition in Judaism: Haggadic Studies.* StPB 4. Leiden: Brill.

———. 1967. "The Use of *bar nash/bar nasha* in Jewish Aramaic." Pages 310–28 in *An Aramaic Approach to the Gospels and Acts.* Edited by M. Black. Oxford: Clarendon.

———. 1973. *Jesus the Jew: A Historian's Reading of the Gospels.* London: SCM.

Vermeylen, J. 1977. *Du prophète Isaïe à l'apocalyptique: Isaïe I–XXXV, miroir d'un demi-millénaire d'expérience religieuse en Israël.* Vol. 1. EBib. Paris: Gabalda.

Vielhauer, P. 1965. *Aufsätze zum Neuen Testament.* TB 31. Munich: Kaiser.

Vieweger, D., and A. Böckler. 1996. "'Ich gebe Ägypten als Lösegeld für dich': Mk 10,45 und die jüdische Tradition zu Jes 43,3b.4." *ZAW* 108: 594–607.

Völter, D. 1902. "Der Menschensohn in Dan 7,13." *ZNW* 3: 173–74.

Vriezen, T. C. 1962. "Essentials of the Theology of Isaiah." Pages 126–46 in *Israel's Prophetic Heritage: Essays in Honor of James Muilenburg.* Edited by B. W. Anderson and W. Harrelson. New York: Harper.

Wagner, R. J. 1997. "Psalm 118 in Luke-Acts: Tracing a Narrative Thread." Pages 154–78 in *Early Christian Interpretation of the Scriptures of Israel: Investigations and Proposals.* Edited by C. A. Evans and J. A. Sanders. JSNTSup 148. Sheffield: Sheffield Academic Press.

Waldman, N. M. 1989. "The Imagery of Clothing, Covering, and Over-Powering." *JANESCU* 19: 161–70.

Walker, W. O. 1983. "The Son of Man: Some Recent Developments." *CBQ* 45: 584–607.

Watts, J. D. W. 1985. *Isaiah 1–33.* WBC 24. Waco: Word.

Watts, R. E. 1990a. "Consolation or Confrontation? Isaiah 40–55 and the Delay of the New Exodus." *TynBul* 41: 31–59.

———. 1990b. "The Meaning of *'ālāw yiqpĕṣû mĕlākîm pîhem* in Isaiah lii 15." *VT* 40: 327–35.

———. 1998. "Jesus' Death, Isaiah 53, and Mark 10:45: A Crux Revisited." Pages 125–51 in *Jesus and the Suffering Servant: Isaiah 53 and Christian Origins.* Edited by W. H. Bellinger Jr. and W. R. Farmer. Harrisburg, PA: Trinity Press International.

———. 2000. *Isaiah's New Exodus in Mark.* BSL. Grand Rapids: Baker Academic.

———. 2002. "The New Exodus/New Creational Restoration of the Image of God." Pages 15–41 in *What Does It Mean to Be Saved? Broadening Evangelical Horizons of Salvation*. Edited by J. J. Stackhouse Jr. Grand Rapids: Baker Academic.

———. 2004a. "Echoes from the Past: Israel's Ancient Traditions and the Role of the Nations in Isa 40–55." *JSOT* 28: 481–504.

———. 2004b. "Immanuel: Virgin Birth Proof-Text or Programmatic Warning of Things to Come? The Old Testament in Matthew." Pages 95–117 in *From Prophecy to Testament: The Function of the Old Testament in the New*. Edited by C. A. Evans. Peabody, MA: Hendrickson.

———. 2004c. "Jesus and the New Exodus Restoration of Daughter Zion: Mark 5:21–43 in Context." Pages 13–29 in *The New Testament in Its First Century Setting: Essays on Context and Background in Honour of B. W. Winter on His 65th Birthday*. Edited by P. J. Williams et al. Grand Rapids: Eerdmans.

Webster, E. C. 1990. "The Rhetoric of Isaiah 63–65." *JSOT* 47: 89–102.

Weeden, T. J. 1971. *Mark: Traditions in Conflict*. Philadelphia: Fortress.

Weinfeld, M. 1991. *Deuteronomy 1–11*. AB 5. New York: Doubleday.

Wenham, G. J. 1979. *The Book of Leviticus*. NICOT. Grand Rapids: Eerdmans.

———. 1987. *Genesis 1–15*. WBC 1. Waco: Word.

Weren, W. J. C. 1998. "The Use of Isaiah 5,1–7 in the Parable of the Tenants (Mark 12,1–12; Matthew 21,33–46)." *Bib* 79: 1–26.

Werner, F. 1981. "'Theologie' und 'Philologies': Zur Frage der Überseztung von Mk 14, 24 'für die Vielen' oder 'für Alle'?" *BL* 54: 228–30.

Westermann, C. 1964a. "Das Heilswort bei Deuterojesaja." *EvT* 24: 355–73.

———. 1964b. "Sprache und Struktur der Prophetie Deuterojesajas." Pages 92–170 in *Forschung am Alten Testament*. TB 24. Munich: Kaiser.

———. 1969. *Isaiah 40–66*. Translated by D. M. G. Stalker. OTL. London: SCM.

Whybray, R. N. 1975. *Isaiah 40–55*. NCB. London: Oliphants.

———. 1978. *Thanksgiving for a Liberated Prophet: An Interpretation of Isaiah Chapter 53*. JSOTSup 4. Sheffield: JSOT Press.

Wifall, W. 1974. "David—Prototype of Israel's Future?" *BTB* 4: 94–107.

Wijngaards, J. 1967. "Death and Resurrection in Covenantal Context (Hos. vi. 2)." *VT* 17: 226–39.

Wilcox, M. 1970–1971. "The Denial-Sequence in Mark XIV.26–31, 66–72." *NTS* 17: 426–36.

———. 1984. *Semitismus in the New Testament*. ANRW II.25.2:978–1029.

Wilcox, P., and D. Paton-Williams. 1988. "The Servant Songs in Deutero-Isaiah." *JSOT* 42: 79–102.

Wildberger, H. 1972–1982. *Jesaja*. 3 vols. BKAT 10. Neukirchen-Vluyn: Neukirchener Verlag.

———. 1991. *Isaiah 1–12*. Translated by T. H. Trapp. CC. Minneapolis: Fortress.

Williamson, H. G. M. 1978. "'The Sure Mercies of David': Subjective or Objective Genitive?" *JSS* 23:31–49.

———. 1989. "The Concept of Israel in Transition." Pages 141–61 in *The World of Ancient Israel: Essays by Members of the Society for Old Testament Study*. Edited by R. E. Clements. Cambridge: Cambridge University Press.

———. 1994. *The Book Called Isaiah: Deutero-Isaiah's Role in Composition and Redaction*. Oxford: Clarendon.

———. 1998. *Variations on a Theme: King, Messiah and Servant in the Book of Isaiah*. The Didsbury Lecture Series. Carlisle: Paternoster.

Willis, J. T. 1990. "A Cry of Defiance—Psalm 2." *JSOT* 47: 33–50.

Wilson, A. 1986. *The Nations in Deutero-Isaiah: A Study in Composition and Structure*. ANETSt 1. Lewiston, NY: Mellen.

Witte, M. 2004. "'Aber Gott wird meine Seele erlösen'—Tod und Leben nach Psalm XLIX." *VT* 50: 540–60.

Wolff, H. W. 1964. "Der Aufruf zur Volksklage." *ZAW* 76: 48–56.

———. 1974. *Hosea*. Edited by P. D. Hanson. Translated by G. Stansell. Hermeneia. Philadelphia: Fortress.

Wood, J. E. 1968. "Isaac Typology in the New Testament." *NTS* 14: 583–89.

Wright, C. J. H. 1996. *Deuteronomy*. NIBCOT. Peabody, MA: Hendrickson.

Wright, N. T. 1992. *The New Testament and the People of God*. Minneapolis: Fortress.

———. 1996. *Jesus and the Victory of God*. Minneapolis: Fortress.

Zakovitch, Y. 1977. "The Pattern of the Numerical Sequence Three-Four in the Bible." PhD diss., Hebrew University.

Zenger, E. 1998. "The Composition and Theology of the Fifth Book of Psalms: Psalms 107–145." *JSOT* 80: 77–102.

Ziesler, J. A. 1970. "The Transfiguration Story and the Markan Soteriology." *ExpTim* 81: 263–68.

Zimmerli, W. 1963. "Ich bin Jahwe." Pages 11–40 in *Gottes Offenbarung*. TB 19. Munich: Kaiser.

———. 1979. *Ezekiel 1–24*. Translated by R. E. Clements. Hermeneia. Philadelphia: Fortress.

———. 1983. *Ezekiel 25–48*. Translated by J. D. Martin. Hermeneia. Philadelphia: Fortress.

LUKE

David W. Pao and Eckhard J. Schnabel

Introduction: Luke's Use of Scripture

The evidence of Luke's use of scriptural quotations in his Gospel can be summarized as follows (see Fitzmyer 1998; Rusam 2003: 4–7, 492–96; Powery 1999: 239–47).

1. Luke does not cite extended passages from the OT, but cites only a verse or two (the one exception is Acts 2:17–21). In contrast to the *Reflexionszitate* in Matthew, in Luke's Gospel all except the first three quotations (2:23, 24; 3:4–6) are found in the narration of direct speech—that of Jesus (4:4, 8, 12, 18–19; 7:27; 18:20; 19:46; 20:17, 37, 42–43; 22:37), of the devil (4:10–11), of a scribe (10:27), and of the Sadducees (20:28).

Luke evidently was familiar with the tripartite canon of the Hebrew Scriptures: note particularly 24:44: "the law of Moses, the prophets, and the psalms" (cf. 16:16: "the law and the prophets"; 16:29, 31: "Moses and the prophets"). Luke quotes from the Pentateuch (10x), from the prophets (7x), and from the psalms (7x). It is striking that he does not quote from the Historical Books (which is also true for Acts), despite Luke's program of writing the history of Jesus and his disciples imitating the biblical narratives of the OT Scriptures (see Fitzmyer 1998: 303).

2. The fact that Luke uses fewer explicit quotations in his Gospel (twenty-five [see Fitzmyer 1998: 297, 311n5]) than Matthew does in his (thirty-eight) must not be misread to suggest that Luke was less interested in intertextual links with Israel's Scriptures. Luke's allusions to OT material need to be taken into account as well: C. A. Kimball (1994b: 206–12) finds 439 OT allusions in the Gospel of Luke (note that Kimball [1994b: 204–5] finds thirty-three OT quotations in Luke). It is not helpful to argue that "Jesus rarely appropriates scripture to talk about himself specifically," interpreting Luke's use of explicit quotations as "a conservative portrayal" on the basis of eliminating allusions to and echoes of OT passages (Powery 1999: 243). In the first-century Jewish context it does not seem to have made much difference whether a passage of Scripture is explicitly quoted or alluded to. Luke's references to the law of Moses, the prophets, and the psalms clearly express his conviction that the person and ministry of Jesus, as well as the Christian communities and their message, are based on the Jewish Scriptures. In Luke's presentation in his Gospel, as well as in the book of Acts, "the community of followers of Jesus, the Messiah, is to be understood in the perspective of the ongoing history of Israel" (Tomson 2002: 180).

3. Luke explicitly quotes seven OT passages in Luke-Acts: (1) the allusion to Ps. 2:7 LXX in Luke 3:22 is quoted explicitly in Acts 13:33; (2) the allusion to Isa. 61:1–2 in Luke 7:22 is quoted

explicitly in Luke 4:18–19; (3) the allusion to Isa. 61:1–2 in Acts 10:34–38 is quoted explicitly in Luke 4:18–19; (4) the allusion to Isa. 6:9 in Luke 8:10 is quoted explicitly in Acts 28:26; (5) the allusion to Ps. 68:26 LXX in Luke 13:35 is quoted explicitly in Acts 1:20; (6) the allusion to Ps. 118:22 in Acts 4:11 is quoted explicitly in Luke 20:17; (7) the allusion to Exod. 3:6 in Acts 3:13 is quoted explicitly in Luke 20:37; Acts 7:32. When OT passages are both quoted and alluded to, the allusion always comes before the quotation (with the exception of Ps. 118:22, which is first quoted in Luke 20:17 and then alluded to in Acts 4:11). This suggests that Luke could assume a high level of biblical literary competence among his readers.

The introductory formulas do not follow a uniform scheme. It is evident, however, that Luke often is interested in marking the location of the quotation in a manner that is as precise as possible. Note 20:42, "for David himself says in the book of Psalms" (*autos gar Dauid legei en biblō psalmōn*), compared with the parallel passage Mark 12:36, "David himself said in the Holy Spirit" (*autos Dauid eipen en tō pneumati tō hagiō*); Luke 3:4: "as it is written in the book of the words of Isaiah the prophet" (*hōs gegraptai en biblō logōn Ēsaiou tou prophētou*).

4. The discussion about the source(s) of Luke's OT quotations continues. Whereas some scholars assume that Luke used both the LXX and *testimonia*, which are collections of OT passages devoted to specific themes, particularly texts regarded as messianic prophecies (Harris 1916; Albl 1999), other scholars argue that Luke used only the LXX (Rese 1969: 222–23; Gundry 1967: 165–66), never the Hebrew or Aramaic text (Holtz 1968: 12; Fitzmyer 1998: 305–6), or both the LXX and the Hebrew and Aramaic texts (Bock 1987: 271).

5. Luke's exegetical methods are evaluated differently by different scholars. Some argue that in some passages—for example, Luke 1–2—Luke composed a midrash based on OT texts (Laurentin 1964; R. E. Brown 1993), while other scholars reject this analysis (Fitzmyer 1981–1985: 308; cf. Bock 1987: 55, 292 with note 2). Most scholars agree that Luke employs various methods of contemporary Jewish exegesis (see Ellis 1991:

91–101; Kimball 1994b: 199–200; Bock 1987: 272).

6. Luke understands Scripture (*hē graphē*) as normatively directing the actions of people (2:23–24; 4:8, 10, 12; 10:25–37; 18:18–25; 19:46; cf. 20:37). It should be noted that most of the quotations that Luke uses come from the Pentateuch. Jesus' life and ministry was, from the beginning, a history that fulfilled the *nomos kyriou*, the "law of the Lord" (2:23–24; cf. 4:8, 10, 12; 19:46). The question "What must I do to inherit eternal life?" is answered with scriptural quotations (10:27; 18:20), demonstrating that the function of Scripture is to show the path to eternal life (Rusam 2003: 127, 492–93).

7. Luke's use of OT Scripture underlines his conviction that Scripture prophetically announced Jesus' life and ministry (18:31–33; 24:26–27, 44–47), and that Scripture illustrates the story of Jesus' ministry, rejection, and death (4:24; 11:47–51; 13:31–35; cf. the end of Luke–Acts in Acts 28:25–28). For Luke, both the fact that Jesus' life and ministry can be illustrated by allusions to the OT Scriptures and the fact that some OT passages announced events in Jesus' life prove that Jesus' ministry was divinely ordained. It is significant that this prophetic use of Scripture is derived from Jesus himself (Luke 18:31–33; 24:26–27, 44–47). Luke will show in his second volume that it is this "prophetic interpretation of Scripture"—that is, the application of certain OT texts to Jesus—that separates unbelieving Jews from the followers of Jesus (Rusam 2003: 493–96).

While many scholars argue that Luke's use of the OT should be understood in terms of a prophecy-and-fulfillment pattern or in terms of proof-from-prophecy concerns (Conzelmann, Lohse, Schubert, Fitzmyer), some argue that there is no linear-temporal movement from promise to fulfillment, since Luke uses the OT simply as an explanation of events without the notion of prophecy being present (Rese). The evidence of Luke's Gospel, as well as advances in hermeneutical method, render the latter view implausible and suggest a modification of the former view because Luke's use of the OT is not primarily defensive in terms of a polemical apologetic. We may describe Luke's use of the OT, particularly as it concerns Christology, in terms of "proclamation from prophecy and pattern" because "Luke sees the Scripture fulfilled in Jesus in terms of the fulfillment of OT prophecy and in terms of the re-introduction and fulfillment of OT patterns that point to the presence of God's saving work" (Bock 1987: 274–77). Luke repeatedly emphasizes in his Gospel that the OT Scriptures are "fulfilled" in Jesus (4:18–19; 18:31; 24:44). This does not mean, however, that for Luke "Scripture is fundamentally [verbal] prediction" (P.-G. Müller 1984: 324). Rather, for Luke, Scripture is the means to comprehend God's acts of salvation in the past, in the present, and in the future (Rese 1969: 209) and is also a means of demonstrating the fulfillment of God's promises given to the people of Israel in the person of Jesus and of underscoring the presence of God's salvation in the ministry of Jesus (Bock).

8. Jesus' explicit use of Scripture in the Gospel of Luke increases markedly in Jerusalem: of the twelve quotations of scriptural passages in this Gospel, five are linked with Jesus' stay in Jerusalem at the end of his ministry—19:46 (Isa. 56:7); 20:17 (Ps. 118:22); 20:37 (Exod. 3:15); 20:42–43 (Ps. 110:1); 22:37 (Isa. 53:12)—with three important programmatic statements about Scripture in 24:27, 32, 44–45 in the final chapter of the Gospel. Jesus' use of Scripture in chapters 19–22 coincides with the growing tension in the narrative caused by Jesus' presence in Jerusalem: note the constant presence of Jewish leaders in the context of Jesus' use of Scripture, and note the focus on important Jewish symbols and concepts (temple, resurrection, messiah) in the context of the scriptural quotations (Powery 1999: 239–40). This "christological" use of the OT can be traced back to Jesus himself (Bock 1987: 273–74).

9. Luke begins his narrative of Jesus' activities with the scene of Jesus in the Jerusalem temple discussing matters of Scripture containing the first explicit words of Jesus (2:41–50) and with the scene of Jesus in his hometown synagogue reading and interpreting Scripture (4:16–30), and he ends the first volume of his narrative with the scene of the risen Jesus interpreting Scripture (24:44–47) (see Powery 1999: 242).

10. Jesus' programmatic statements on Scripture, particularly in 24:27, 32, 44–45, emphasize that the Christians' belief in Jesus as the risen Lord is essential for understanding Scripture: "For

Luke, the use and persuasiveness of scripture is more about power and revelation than logic. Or, the logic of scripture is discovered in the power and revelation of the resurrected Lord" (Powery 1999: 245). As Luke clearly was concerned to show through his OT quotations and allusions how the story of Jesus fitted into the history of God's dealings with his people in the Scriptures, "he, too, wrote biblical history" (Fitzmyer 1998: 309).

Luke 1:5–2:52

The elegant and balanced Greek sentence in 1:1–4 is followed by a long section that provides an introduction to the public ministry of Jesus in chapter 3. Not only is the Greek of this section strikingly different from the Lukan prologue (and the rest of Luke-Acts), but also allusions to the OT occur throughout this section. A survey of patterns of OT echoes and allusions is necessary before examining them in detail.

Language and Genre

Discussions of the language of Luke 1–2 involve the nature of the Greek in this section, the sources behind the text, and the purpose of using this writing style. Terms such as "Semitism," "Hebraism," and "Aramaism" have been used especially by those who argue for the presence of written Semitic sources behind individual sections of Luke 1–2 (see Burrows 1940: 6–39; Winter 1954). Although individual examples of Semitism can be cited, this source-critical solution fails to account for the unity of style throughout this section. Equally important is the consistent presence of the Lukan hand in this section (Hawkins 1899: 13–23). Although not denying the presence of Semitic sources behind the text, others (N. Turner 1955; Fitzmyer 1981: 114–25, 312) have provided strong arguments for the use of the term "Septuagintism" instead for this section with the assumption that Luke imitates the style of the Greek OT (while acknowledging that the distinction between translation and imitation Greek may be hard to discern [see Farris 1981]). The strengths of this position lie in the distinction between Septuagintism and Semitism, and in the emphasis on Luke's intentionality in his use of language. The significant presence of the

LXX in the rest of the Lukan writings also lends support to this hypothesis, although evidence of "translation Greek" cannot be discounted (see Farris 1985: 50–62). The purpose of such imitation (or retention of the style of Semitic sources) has been attributed to the emphasis on the Palestinian context of the events (Plummer 1896: xlix; Moulton 1929: 7–8), the concern to situate the text within the beginning of the apostolic age (Plümacher 1972: 72–78), and the evocation of the mighty acts of God in Israel's past (Ó Fearghail 1991: 127–28). With the absence of explicit OT quotations in this section (with the exception of the parenthetical note in Luke 2:23–24), these allusions may also serve as an indication of Luke's intention to write "biblical history" as he highlights the continuation of God's work in history.

In light of the saturation of OT language, concepts, and allusions, the label "midrash" has been used for this section. The validity of the application of this label depends on one's precise definition of this term. On the level of hermeneutical foundation, the term is useful in highlighting the affirmation of the transcendent authority of the ancient text as well as the belief of the one God behind salvation-historical events (see Kugel 1983). As a literary technique, implicit midrash rightly focuses on the significance of scriptural language in ancient theological discourse (Ellis 1991: 91–101). As a label for the genre of this section (Gertner 1962: 273–82; Goulder 1974: 457–71), however, this term fails to account for the literary and historical nature of the text. First, explicit OT quotations that play a critical part in midrashic literature do not play the same role in this text. Second, the focus of the story is on the events surrounding the birth of John the Baptist and Jesus and not on the explication of the OT text. Third, the creation of a series of events apart from the temporal framework of the ancient text is not a characteristic of midrashic literature. Moreover, the sustained interest in situating the events within their proper historical framework throughout the Lukan writings also argues against midrashic creativity in this section. On the exegetical utility of this label, Hays (1989: 14) rightly notes that "the label *midrash* tends to bring the interpretive process to a halt, as though it had explained everything." In recognizing the significant presence of scriptural language in this

tense, "imitative historiography" (Burrows 1940: 1–3) draws attention to the literary relationships to ancient texts, while "confessional history" (Schneider 1992: 77–78; Bock 1994–1996: 71) points to the nature of such imitative acts.

Continuity of Salvation History

The use of biblical language is complemented by the textual links between the time of Jesus and the history of Israel. The temple scene begins this section with references to the priesthood and to Aaron himself (1:5). Zechariah serves "according to the custom of the priesthood" as he enters "the sanctuary of the Lord and offer(s) sacrifice" (1:9), and it is in this setting that the announcement of the birth of John was made. The birth narrative ends with a temple scene (2:21–24), while the entire infancy narrative also ends with the appearance of Jesus in the temple at the age of twelve (2:41–52). Since Jerusalem was understood as the center of Israel, the prophets were looking forward to the reappearance of God's mighty acts in that city (see Isa. 40:1–2; 52:1; 56:7; Jer. 31:38–40). The significance of the temple in the Lukan infancy narrative reflects an awareness of such beliefs, as people "were looking for the redemption of Jerusalem" (2:38).

Within the context of the cultic life of Israel, the piety and faithfulness of the main characters are highlighted. Zechariah and Elizabeth are described as "righteous before God, living blamelessly according to all the commandments and regulations of the Lord" (1:6), and Joseph and Mary acted "according to what is stated in the law of the Lord" (2:24). Simeon was "righteous and devout" (2:25), and Anna "never left the temple, but worshiped there with fasting and prayer night and day" (2:37).

Perhaps the strongest link between the ministry of Jesus and the OT lies in the character of John the Baptist. In the step parallelism developed between Jesus and John, the connection between the two eras is emphasized. As the eschatological Elijah, John will "turn the hearts of parents to their children . . . to make ready a people prepared for the Lord" (1:17; cf. 1:76). With allusions to Mal. 3:22–24 LXX (4:4–6 ET; cf. Sir. 48:10) and Isa. 40:3, John was portrayed as the eschatological Elijah who points back to God's work in history while looking forward to the fulfillment of prophetic promises. With John as the eschatological prophet, a radical discontinuity is also emphasized, when salvation history is to be brought to its climax. John can be understood as being among "the holy prophets from of old" (1:70), but Jesus is the "Savior, who is the Messiah, the Lord" (2:11). With the ambiguous symbol of John, one therefore finds both continuity and discontinuity with Israel's past.

Dawn of the Eschatological Era

As the appearance of John the Baptist signifies the renewal of prophecy and the salvific acts of God in history (see 1 Macc. 9:27; 14:41; *b. Yoma* 9b), this section highlights the dawn of the eschatological era. The intensity of the presence of the Holy Spirit highlights this point: Elizabeth "was filled with the Holy Spirit" (1:41), and so was Zechariah (1:67). The ministry of John the Baptist is characterized as that of the Spirit (1:15). Simeon, who looks forward to the consolation of Israel (cf. Isa. 40:1), receives the Spirit (2:25) and the revelation "by the Holy Spirit that he would not see death before he had seen the Lord's Messiah" (2:26). Although the presence of the Spirit can be found in the accounts of OT characters (e.g., Joshua [Num. 27:18], Samson [Judg. 13:25], David [1 Sam. 16:13]), this intensity can be paralleled only by the Pentecost event in Luke's second volume (Acts 2), where the promises uttered by John (Luke 3:16) and Jesus (Luke 11:13; 12:12; Acts 1:8) are fulfilled (Ravens 1995: 26). These events point to the fulfillment of ancient promises that speak of the role of the Spirit at the end of times (see esp. Isa. 32:14–17 [cf. Luke 24:49; Acts 1:8]; Joel 2:28–32 [cf. Acts 2:17–21]), when God restores his people for his glory (Acts 3:19–20) (see Pao 2000: 131–35).

Most significant of all is the role of the Holy Spirit in the conception of Jesus, as expressed in the words addressed to Mary: "The Holy Spirit will come upon you, and the power of the Most High will overshadow you; therefore the child to be born will be holy; he will be called Son of God" (1:35). Parallels have been sought in texts that refer to the creation of the world (Gen. 1:2; Ps. 33:6) or individuals (Job 33:4; Ps. 104:30; Jdt. 16:14; *2 Bar.* 21:4) (see Strauss 1995: 91), but the unique role of the Spirit in the conception of Jesus is unparalleled.

Within this eschatological setting one finds the identification of the angel as Gabriel (1:19, 26). The revelatory role of Gabriel in Dan. 8–10 should not be missed. Not only are there references to the name "Gabriel" (Dan. 8:16; 9:21), but also wider parallels between Dan. 8–10 and Luke 1–2 can be further identified: prayer (1:13; Dan. 9:23), sacrifice (1:9–10; Dan. 9:20–21), vision (1:22; Dan. 8:17), favor of God (1:28; Dan 9:23), fear (1:12; Dan. 8:17; 10:8–9, 12, 19), and speech impediment (1:20; Dan. 10:15) (Laurentin 1964: 45–46; Goulder 1989: 1:211; R. E. Brown 1993: 270–71; Ravens 1995: 30). As the one who acts on behalf of God (cf. *1 En.* 40:9; 54:6; *T. Sol.* 18:6), Gabriel, in both Daniel and Luke, symbolizes the renewal of God's involvement among his people.

The eschatological content of this section is reinforced by the form in which much of the material is presented. Since hymns typically were composed by prophets (e.g., Exod. 15:20; Judg. 4:4), the prophetic and hymnic nature in Luke 1–2 falls within Israel's tradition. Especially important is Exod. 15, where the paradigmatic mighty acts of God are depicted in hymnic language. With the decline of classical prophecy in Second Temple Jewish literature, biblical hymns were reused (e.g., Exod. 15 in Jdt. 16; Deut. 32 in Tob. 13), and poetry became the primary medium through which eschatological hope was expressed (see Horgan and Kobelski 1989; Weitzman 1997: 65–70). The Qumran *Thanksgiving Hymns* (1QH^a), for example, provide a parallel to the Lukan hymns, where one finds similar themes (praise of the redemptive acts of God, humility, salvation, the fulfillment of eschatological hopes) together with a saturation of biblical language. The Lukan hymns therefore reflect not only the classical hymns of Israel's history but also the modes of eschatological discourse in first-century Palestinian Judaism (Cross 1958: 166).

Barren Women and the Redemption of Israel

The birth stories of John and Jesus belong to the long tradition of birth stories in the OT and in Jewish literature (see Callaway 1986: 13–72). Prominent among these stories is the motif of barrenness. This appears in the stories of Sarah (Gen. 18), Rebekah (Gen. 25), Rachel (Gen. 30), the mother of Samson (Judg. 13), and Hannah (1 Sam. 1–2). Not only are these stories concerned with the reversal of the fortune of the individual barren women, but also the births of the heroes are linked with the fulfillment of God's covenantal promises to Israel. The presence of God for his people is therefore the underlying theme behind these narratives.

Already in the OT the barren women came to be understood as representing Israel. In the Song of Hannah the subject moves from "the barren" (1 Sam. 2:5) to "his [God's] faithful ones" (2:9) and finally to "his king" and "his anointed" (2:10). Hannah therefore serves also as a symbol of a suffering Israel (Callaway 1986: 54). Moving to the prophets, we see Isaiah using the barren woman to symbolize the scattered people of God (Isa. 49:20–21), whose fortune will be reversed when their enemies "bow down" to them (49:23). This is explicitly stated in Isa. 54:1: "Sing, O barren one who did not bear; burst into song and shout, you who have not been in labor!" Not only does this symbolic usage survive in later Jewish literature, but also the various barren women in the historical material were linked together with the Isaianic symbol of suffering Israel (cf. *Pesiq. Rab Kah.* 20:2, which includes citations of Gen. 21:7; 30:11; 1 Sam. 1:2; 2:21; Isa. 49:21; 54:1; Jer. 30:17; see Callaway 1986: 122). In the Magnificat (Luke 1:46–55) the shift from Mary's own self ("He has looked with favor on the lowliness of his servant" [1:48]) to the people of God ("He has helped his servant Israel, in remembrance of his mercy" [1:54]) fits well within the Jewish usage of the OT motif of barren women. What is unique in the Lukan account is the lack of hints of competition between John and Jesus, as both participated in the fulfillment of ancient promises (see Brenner 1986: 269–70).

Amid the numerous allusions made to the various birth stories in the OT, two stand out as the primary reference for reading the Lukan birth narrative. Allusions to the story of Sarah have frequently been noted (see commentary below), but Green (1994) has shown that Luke consistently alludes in Luke 1–2 to the wider story of Abraham in Gen. 11–21 while explicitly naming Abraham in 1:55 as the patriarch of "our ancestors." These allusions do not make strict typological connections between individual characters, however,

since the allusions are related in a complex way among the various characters. The interest lies, therefore, not primarily in the individual characters, but rather in the Abrahamic covenant, which finds its climax in the story of Luke. This interest of Luke in the Abrahamic promises is not limited to the birth narrative (note, e.g., the role of Abraham in Stephen's speech in Acts 7:2–8; see Dahl 1966; Siker 1991: 103–27; Lampe 1993), but the intensity of the Abrahamic references in Luke 1–2 highlights the significance of this series of events as the fulfillment of "the oath that he swore to our ancestor Abraham" (1:73).

The second focus in the use of OT birth stories is found in the story of Hannah at the beginning of 1 Samuel. The Lukan use of the Hannah story is found in the introduction to the Lukan birth narrative (1:5; cf. 1 Sam. 1:1–2), the Nazirite framework (1:15; cf. 1 Sam. 1:11), allusions to the Song of Hannah (1 Sam. 2:1–10) in the Magnificat (1:46–55), the presentation of Jesus in the temple (2:21–24; cf. 1 Sam. 1:24–28), and the summary statements in 1:80; 2:40, 52 (cf. 1 Sam. 2:21, 26). While falling within the paradigm of barren women, the allusions to Hannah in Luke 1–2 point in particular to the role of Samuel in the introduction and installation of King David (Rusam 2003: 41). This connection is explicitly made in Acts, where the anointing of King David is located during the time of "Samuel the prophet" (Acts 13:20–22). As the Abrahamic covenant finds its expression in the Davidic covenant, the fulfillment of God's promises to Israel also points back to the Davidic era. This is confirmed by the numerous references to the Davidic sonship in this section, the most explicit found in Luke 1:32–33 ("He will be great, and will be called the Son of the Most High, and the Lord God will give to him the throne of his ancestor David"), a passage that alludes to 2 Sam. 7 and also to the royal psalm in Ps. 87 (see Strauss 1995: 87–88).

People of God

In this introductory section Luke also draws attention to the ecclesiological impact in depicting the climax of salvation history. Using biblical language, Luke describes the ministry of John as one that is addressed to Israel: "He will turn many of the people of Israel to the Lord their God" (1:16; cf. Deut. 30:2; Hos. 3:5; 7:10; see

Bock 1994–1996: 87). The ministry of Jesus is likewise described as a mission for Israel (1:54) in the context of the ancient promises (1:55; cf. 1:72). Drawing out the original intent of the Abrahamic promises (1:55, 73), Israel will also serve as an instrument of God's blessings for the nations. In Isaianic terms, the Messiah will serve as "a light for revelation to the Gentiles" (2:32; cf. Isa. 42:6; 49:6), although the full effect can be felt only in Luke's second volume, where one finds an explicit reference to Isa. 49:6 (Acts 13:47). Isaiah had been widely used in Jewish material in depicting the redemption of Israel, but the emphasis on the mission to the Gentiles represents a major transformation of Second Temple Jewish eschatological hope (see Pao 2000: 217–48).

1:5

The division of priests into classes can be traced back to the time of David (1 Chron. 28:13), and contemporary Jewish writers testify to the use of a similar system in the first century (Josephus, *Ant.* 7.363–367; see Creed 1930: 8). The style and vocabulary call to mind Judg. 13:2 and 1 Sam. 1:1, but the general introduction that provides the essential biographical data frequently appears in prophetic literature (e.g., Jer. 1:1–3; Amos 1:1; Mic. 1:1; Zeph. 1:1; Zech. 1:1). Moreover, the opening formula using the word *egeneto* is found at the beginning of a number of Jewish works (Joshua, Judges, Ruth, 2 Samuel, Judith, 1 Maccabees, *Jubilees, Joseph and Aseneth*). The cultic context evoked by references to the priests, priesthood, and Aaron is enhanced by the name "Elizabeth," the name of the wife of Aaron (Exod. 6:23).

1:6

The phrase "commandments and regulations" (*entolais kai dikaiōmasin*) reflects biblical expressions (Gen. 26:5; Num. 36:13; Deut. 4:40; cf. 1 Kings 8:61).

1:8–10

The word *naos* refers to the place outside the holy of holies. Exodus 30:7–8 provides the regulations for the offering of the morning and evening incense sacrifice (cf. *m. Tamid* 6–7). With the presence of the crowd and the possible parallel with Dan. 9:21, the evening sacrifice may be the intended reference here (Schneider 1992: 45; Fitzmyer

1981–1985: 325; Bock 1994–1996: 80). The casting of lots would determine who among the large group of priests would be chosen for this task (cf. *m. Tamid* 5:2–6:3). The offering of prayer during the sacrifice is also well attested (Ezra 9:5–15; Dan. 9:21; Jdt. 9:1–14; Sir. 50:12–21; see Green 1997: 71).

1:11

The "angel of the Lord" often represents God himself (cf. Gen. 16:7–13; Exod. 3:2–4; 14:19; 23:20; Num. 20:16; Judg. 6:11–22; Isa. 63:9; Hos. 12:4–5; see Juncker 2001: 34). The interchangeability of the two can explain the appearances of angels in the announcements of the births of Ishmael, Isaac, and Samson (cf. Gen. 16:10–12; 18:9–15; Judg. 13:3–21), while other birth announcements point directly to the presence of God himself (Gen. 17:15–19; 25:22–23).

1:12–13

Fear is the expected response to the presence of God or his messengers (Exod. 15:16; Judg. 6:22–23; 13:6, 22; 2 Sam. 6:9; Isa. 6:5; Dan. 8:16–17; 10:10–11; see Bock 1994–1996: 81). The command "Do not be afraid" (1:13) is found in OT birth announcements (Gen. 21:17; 35:17; 1 Sam. 4:20), and it often also appears in divine war narratives (Num. 14:9; Deut. 1:20–21; 20:3–4; Josh. 8:1–2; 2 Kings 6:15–19; Isa. 41:10). The appearance of this formula in other "unconventional" military settings suggests that it should be understood in its wider covenantal context—the focus of which is the act of God on behalf of his people (cf. Gen. 15:1–2; 21:17–18; 26:24; 46:3–4; Exod. 14:13–14; see Conrad 1985: 124–45). The naming of the child by the angel confirms the significance of that person in the covenantal plan of God (cf. "You shall name him Isaac. I will establish my covenant with him as an everlasting covenant for his offspring after him" [Gen. 17:19; cf. Isa. 7:14]).

1:15

The phrase "from his mother's womb" (*ek koilias mētros autou*) can mean "from birth" (cf. Ps. 22:10 [21:11 LXX]), but in light of 1:41 it has to refer to "before birth" (cf. Judg. 13:7; Isa. 44:2; 49:1; Gal. 1:15). The prohibition against "wine or strong drink" (*oinon kai sikera*) suggests to some that Luke considers John to be a Nazirite (cf. Judg. 13; see

Fitzmyer 1981–1985: 326; R. E. Brown 1993: 268). The lack of reference to the cutting of hair has led others to describe him simply as an ascetic prophet (cf. Luke 7:25–33; see Bock 1994–1996: 85). The appearance of the exact phrase *oinon kai sikera* in the commandments delivered to Aaron in Lev. 10:9 has further encouraged some to highlight the priestly context here (Bovon 2002: 36). In light of the portrayal of Samuel as one who is to avoid wine and strong drinks (cf. 1 Sam. 1:11 LXX and the identification of him as a Nazirite in 1 Sam. 1:22 in 4Q51) and the parallel between the Magnificat and the Song of Hannah (1 Sam. 2:1–10), the audience is encouraged to see 1 Sam. 1–2 behind this verse as well. The absence of the prohibition against the cutting of hair may be explained by the Lukan emphasis on John as one who devotes himself entirely to the Lord (cf. Eph. 5:18) and not on his formal status as a Nazirite. This reading would therefore also acknowledge the significance of Lev. 10:9 and the cultic setting in both Luke 1 and 1 Sam. 1–2.

1:16

The language of "turning" or "returning" to God is used in the OT for the repentance of God's people (Deut. 30:2; 1 Sam. 7:3; Hos. 3:5; 7:10; cf. Acts 15:19). An allusion to Mal. 2:6 (*pollous epestrepsen*) in particular is probable in light of the words *pollous . . . epistrepsei* ("he will turn many") and the role of Malachi in Mal. 2:7 (cf. Luke 1:17; see Fitzmyer 1981–1985: 326; Bock 1994–1996: 87).

1:17

"To turn the hearts of parents to their children" (*epistrepsai kardias paterōn epi tekna*) clearly alludes to Mal. 4:6 (3:24 MT; 3:23 LXX), although the wordings are not exact. The MT provides a close conceptual parallel, but the LXX uses a different verb (*apokatastēsei*) with the singular *patros* and a different word for "son" (*huion*). A closer parallel in wording is found in Sir. 48:10, where the same verb is used (*epistrepsai kardian patros pros huion*). The Sirach passage clearly is based on Malachi, and in both one finds references to Elijah and his role in the eschatological reconciliation between God and his people. Sirach makes it explicit with reference to the restoration of Israel (*katastēssai phylas Iakōb*), and this restoration theme plays an important role in the Lukan account of John's ministries (see M. Turner 1996: 151).

The phrase "before him" (*enōpion autou*) may point back to *pro prosōpou mou* ("before me") in Mal. 3:1 (see Creed 1930: 11). The Malachi passage in turn draws on Isa. 40:3 ("prepare the way of the LORD," *hetoimasate tēn hodon kyriou*), a text that has a history of its own in Jewish exegetical traditions (see Luke 3:4–6 below). Although the expression "prepared people" may recall other passages (e.g., 2 Sam. 7:24; Isa. 43:7; see Fitzmyer 1981–1985: 321), the Elijah framework urges a focus on the Malachi passages.

These references to the role of Elijah in Malachi raise questions concerning Luke's view of the relationship between Elijah and John the Baptist. R. E. Brown sees an explicit identification of John with the eschatological Elijah here (R. E. Brown 1993: 276–77), while others limit the parallel to the prophetic ministries of the two (see Marshall 1978: 59). The fact that Jesus was also portrayed within this Elijah paradigm (cf. 4:25; 7:16) highlights the wider context in which the Elijah reference should be understood (Brodie 1987). Instead of insisting on the connection between Elijah and John, this verse points to the arrival of the eschatological era wherein one encounters the prophetic activities that reflect the renewal of God's mighty acts among his people. The specific reference to Mal. 4:6 serves to highlight the reconciliatory role of John as he prepares God's people for this great day.

The context of Mal. 4 also focuses on the sinful condition of Israel. The remaining phrase in this verse, "the disobedient to the wisdom of the righteous" (*apeitheis en phronēsei dikaiōn*) may likewise reflect the juxtaposition of "the righteous" and "the wicked" in Mal. 3:18 (cf. 2:6; see Green 1997: 77). The parallelism developed in this verse (parents/children, disobedience/righteous) may be a loose one pointing to the general theme of reconciliation (Marshall 1978: 59; Johnson 1991: 33). In light of the significance of Mal. 4:6, however, the Lukan phrase "the disobedient to the wisdom of the righteous" may also parallel the implied act of repentance that will lead to God's promise not to "strike the land with a curse" (Mal. 4:6).

1:18

Zechariah's response, "How do I know that this is so?" (*kata ti gnōsomai touto*), is almost identical to

Abraham's reaction to the promise of God (Gen. 15:8), while the second half of the verse parallels Gen. 18:11 (cf. 17:17).

1:19–20, 22

See discussion above (on 1:5–2:52) for the parallels with Dan. 8–10. The verb *euangelizomai* ("to bring good news") evokes the Isaianic promises (Isa. 40:9; 52:7) where the new exodus is in view (Stuhlmacher 1968: 109–79, 218–25). This word group also appears in Roman imperial propaganda (see Priene Inscription [*OGIS* #458]), and Luke's use of this verb may carry a secondary significance in reaction to such propaganda.

1:23–24

The note on returning home and conception parallels Elkanah and Hannah, who "went home," and "in due time Hannah conceived" (1 Sam. 1:19–20).

1:25

The mentioning of the deliverance from disgrace recalls the words of Rachel ("God has taken away my reproach" [Gen. 30:23; cf. 21:6]), although Rachel's reaction came after the birth of her son and not immediately after conception (see Creed 1930: 13; *contra* R. E. Brown 1993: 281). The statement that precedes, while belonging to the same tradition (cf. Gen. 30:22), further describes the gracious acts of God for the lowly ones: "This is what the Lord has done for me when he looked [*epeiden*] favorably on me" (cf. Ps. 138:6 [137:6 LXX]; see Bovon 2002: 40).

Luke 1:26–38

The focus of this annunciation scene finds its parallel in other OT birth announcements (Gen. 17; Judg. 13:1–23), but the form resembles that of a commission story (see Ó Fearghail 1993): introduction (1:26–27), confrontation (1:28–30), the call (1:31–33), reservations (1:34), reassurance (1:35), sign (1:36–37), and conclusion (1:38). Here Mary is called to participate in the unfolding of salvation history by being the mother of Jesus.

1:27

The status of Mary as a virgin (*parthenos*) is mentioned twice in this verse. Many see the word *par-*

thenos as intended to evoke Isa. 7:14 (Schürmann 1990–1994: 1:46; Schneider 1992: 49; Marshall 1978: 66; M. Turner 1996: 154), while others remain skeptical (R. E. Brown 1993: 299–300; Fitzmyer 1981–1985: 336; Bock 1987: 61–62; 1994–1996: 108; Rusam 2003: 47). To support such a connection, the verbal connection between Luke 1:31 (*kai idou syllēmpsē en gastri kai texē huion kai kaleseis to onoma autou Iēsoun*, "And now, you will conceive in your womb and bear a son, and you will name him Jesus") and Isa. 7:14 (*idou hē parthenos en gastri hexei kai texetai huion, kai kaleseis to onoma autou Emmanouēl*, "Look, the virgin [LXX] is with child and shall bear a son, and shall name him Immanuel") has been noted. The references to the "house of David" in their immediate contexts (Luke 1:27; Isa. 7:13) together with the unique references to *parthenos* further highlight the significance of this Isaianic parallel as compared to other annunciation-type scenes in the OT (cf. Gen. 16:11; Judg. 13:5). Other parallels between Luke 1:26–38 and Isa. 7:1–10 further point to the role of Isa. 7:14 behind this verse (see Fitzmyer 1981–1985: 336). Although it is true that the tradition concerning Mary's virginity can be traced beyond the use of Isa. 7, this intertextual connection would at least exist in the mind of the Gospel's audience. The strong emphasis on the Davidic promise in the immediate context (1:32–33) and throughout Luke 1–2 (see commentary on 1:5–2:52 above) makes it likely that the author also recognizes the hermeneutical significance of Isa. 7–9 in explaining the role and identity of Jesus.

1:28

Instead of taking it as a word of greeting, some (e.g., Lyonnet 1939) have understood *chaire* as meaning "rejoice." This reading in turn is understood as pointing back to Zeph. 3:14–17, where eschatological joy is in sight (cf. Joel 2:21; Zech. 9:9). In light of 1:29, however, nothing more than a simple word of greeting seems to be implied (R. E. Brown 1993: 324; Bock 1994–1996: 109; Bovon 2002: 50). On the other hand, the statement "the Lord is with you" does point to Mary's special role in salvation history (cf. Gen. 26:24; 28:15; Exod. 3:12; Judg. 6:12; Jer. 1:8; Acts 18:9–10; see Creed 1930: 17–18; Green 1997: 87).

1:30

For the "do not fear" formula, see 1:12–13 above.

1:31

See 1:27 above.

1:32–33

These verses unmistakably point back to OT expectations of the renewal of the Davidic dynasty. Although numerous passages may have contributed to these verses (Laurentin 1964: 72), significant conceptual parallels exist between these verses and 2 Sam. 7:8–16 (cf. 1 Chron. 17:13–14): Davidic descent (7:8), promise of greatness (7:9), "throne" of David (7:13), divine sonship of the Davidic king (7:14), and perpetual nature of his kingdom (7:16). A similar conglomeration of ideas that appears in Ps. 89 reflects the continued expectation of a Davidic son in the OT (Ps. 2:7; Isa. 7–9; Jer. 23:5–8; 33:14–26; Ezek. 37:24–28; Zech. 3:8–10; 12:7–9) and in Jewish traditions (*T. Sim.* 7; *T. Jud.* 24:1–6; *T. Naph.* 5:1–3; 8:2–3) (see Mitchell 1997; cf. Juel 1988: 87–88). Of particular importance are 4Q174 1 I, 11–14, a pesher of 2 Sam. 7:10–14, which focuses on one ultimate Davidic king, and *Pss. Sol.* 17, which provides an elaborate account of the activities of this Davidic messiah. In the NT the significance of the Davidic paradigm is reflected in Matt. 1:1–17; 22:41–42; Mark 12:35–36; John 7:42; Acts 13:22–23; Rom. 1:3; Rev. 22:16. In Luke 1–2 the Davidic continues to play a significant role (1:69; 2:4, 11) (see Strauss 1995: 76–125).

1:35

The expression "Holy Spirit" (*pneuma hagion*) appears in Ps. 51:11 (50:13 LXX) and Isa. 63:10–11. The latter depicts the redeeming activity of God, although a clear connection with Luke 1:35 cannot be established, as this expression appears frequently in early Christian traditions (*contra* Plymale 1994: 29). More probable is an allusion to Isa. 32:15, which contains similar wording: "until a spirit from on high is poured out on us" (*heōs an epelthē eph' hymas pneuma aph' hypsēlou*). As in Isaiah, Luke speaks of the renewal of Israel as God brings about the new exodus event (M. Turner 1996: 159). Significantly, Isa. 32:15 also plays an important role in other Lukan passages (cf. 24:49; Acts 1:8; 3:20; see Pao 2000: 92, 131–35). The

use of OT language can also be identified in the use of the verb *episkiazō* ("to overshadow"), where the glorious presence of God is in view (cf. Exod. 40:35; Luke 9:34; see Marshall 1978: 70; Fitzmyer 1981–1985: 351). In light of 1:32–33, the "Son of God" reference should likewise be understood with reference to 2 Sam. 7:14, where the divine sonship of the Davidic king is affirmed.

1:37

The assertion of the power of God is found throughout the OT (cf. Job 10:13 [LXX]; 42:2; Jer. 32:17, 27; Zech. 8:6), but the significance of this theme in the foundation story of Abraham and Sarah should be recognized (cf. Gen. 18:14; see Brueggemann 1982). The presence of numerous allusions to Gen. 18 in Luke 1–2 make it probable that Gen. 18:14 is behind the formulation of this verse.

1:41

The movement of the fetus finds its precedent in Gen. 25:22–28, although it is doubtful that the struggle between Jacob and Esau is in view here (Bock 1994–1996: 135; Nolland 1989–1993: 66; cf. Fitzmyer 1981–1985: 358). More relevant is the reference to the expressions of eschatological joy in Mal. 4:2 (3:20 LXX) (see Schürmann 1990–1994: 1:66–67; Bovon 2002: 58).

1:42

"Blessed are you among women" echoes similar words of blessing in Judg. 5:24; Jdt. 13:18, and "blessed is the fruit of your womb" echoes the Mosaic blessing promised to the obedient ones in Deut. 28:1, 4. These echoes suggest that the concern was not simply with Mary as an individual, but with God's people as a whole (R. E. Brown 1993: 342). This concern is also reflected in the close parallel in the prayer of Baruch: "Blessed is my mother among those who bear, and praised among women is she who bore me. For I shall not be silent in honoring the Mighty One but with the voice of glory I shall narrate his marvelous works" (*2 Bar.* 54:11). It seems that both Luke and the author of *2 Baruch* draw on the same tradition in their descriptions of the mighty acts of God.

1:43

The expression "my Lord" (*tou kyriou mou*) echoes the language of Ps. 110:1 (cf. Luke 20:41–44;

Acts 2:34) and therefore points to the messianic status of Jesus. The verse also echoes 2 Sam. 6:9, although the understanding of Mary as the ark is less than apparent (R. E. Brown 1993: 344; *contra* Laurentin 1964: 91–94).

Luke 1:46–55

The Magnificat belongs to the tradition of Jewish hymns in the Second Temple period where both the form and content draw on a variety of OT hymns. Schürmann (1990–1994: 1:71) considers this a combination of an eschatological hymn and a personal thanksgiving psalm, but such a distinction dissolves in postexilic material. In terms of content, the closest parallel probably is in the Song of Hannah in 1 Sam. 2:1–10 (see Haupt 1904), where one finds the theme of deliverance as the Holy God of Israel looks upon the humble state of his maidservant. In both texts this personal concern is transformed into the general theme of reversal as God lifts up the poor and humbles the powerful ones. Others have pointed to the significance of a number of psalms behind this song (cf. Pss. 34; 35; 89; 103; see Goulder 1989: 1:228). The *Psalms of Solomon* provides a later parallel where one finds the appearance of nearly every phrase in the Magnificat. Instead of hypothesizing a common Pharisaic source (Bovon 2002: 56), however, it seems best to see both as reflecting the tendency to compose hymnic material using the language of Israel's Scripture (cf. Qumran *Hodayot*).

1:46–47

The language is reminiscent of that of the psalmist (esp. Ps. 34:1–3 [33:2–4 LXX]), although the parallelism between "soul" (*psychē*) and "spirit" (*pneuma*) appears frequently only in later material (cf. Isa. 26:9; Job 12:10; Dan. 3:39, 86 [LXX]; Wis. 15:11; see D. R. Jones 1968: 20). The response of Mary also recalls the response of Hannah in 1 Sam. 2:1. The statement "and my spirit rejoices in God my Savior" (*kai ēgalliasen to pneuma mou epi tō theō tō sōtēri mou*) uses liturgical language as found in Hab. 3:18: "Yet I will rejoice in the LORD; I will exult in the God of my salvation" (*egō de en tō kyriō agalliasomai, charēsomai epi tō theō tō sōtēri mou*) (see Creed 1930: 303).

1:48

The reference to "lowliness" (*tapeinōsis*) has been taken as a reference to the humiliation suffered by the betrothed virgin who became pregnant (cf. Deut. 22:23–24; see Schaberg 1987: 100; Robbins 1994: 183–84), but neither the context nor its wider parallels with OT birth accounts support this reading. A closer parallel is found in 1 Sam. 1:11, where the term appears in reference to the reversal of the fortunes of Hannah in her pregnancy. As in the Song of Hannah in 1 Sam. 2:1–10, however, *tapeinōsis* can also refer to the humiliation of the oppressed people of God (Deut. 26:7; 1 Sam. 9:16; 1 Macc. 3:51; 3 Macc. 2:12; see Green 1992: 470). This connection between the fortunes of the individual and the fate of God's people is best expressed in *4 Ezra* 9:45, where the blessings bestowed upon the barren Zion are taken as a sign of God's care for Israel's "low estate" (*tapeinōsis*). The appearance of the title "the Mighty One" (*ho dynatos*) in the very next verse in both works (Luke 1:49; *4 Ezra* 9:46) points to the relevance of this context for understanding the use of the term *tapeinōsis* here. Not to be missed is the significance of the reversal of the fortunes of "the poor" (*ptōchos*) throughout this Gospel (cf. Luke 4:18; 6:20–22; 7:22; 14:13, 21; 16:20–22).

1:49

In the OT, the "Mighty One" (*ho dynatos*) is used to refer to God the warrior (cf. Zeph. 3:17; see D. R. Jones 1968: 23), and "great things" (*megala*) recalls the mighty deeds of God during the exodus event (Deut. 10:21). References to the "holy" (*hagion*) name of God also appear most often in the depiction of God's work in the new-exodus event (cf. Isa. 47:4; 57:15; Ezek. 36:22–25; Mal. 1:11; Wis. 10:20).

1:50

The expression "his mercy" (*to eleos autou*) presupposes the covenantal relationship between God and his people, and the affirmation that "his mercy is for those who fear him" belongs to the language of Israel's liturgical traditions (cf. Ps. 103:17 [102:17 LXX]; *Pss. Sol.* 2:33).

1:51

In both the exodus (Exod. 6:1, 6; Deut. 3:24; 7:19) and new-exodus traditions (Isa. 51:5, 9; 53:1; cf.

30:30) one finds the use of the imagery of the arm/hand of God in reference to the power of God (see Seely 1990). In this case, a closer allusion can be identified in Ps. 88:11 LXX, a verse that departs from the MT: "You brought down the proud as one that is slain, and with the arm of your power you scattered your enemies" (*sy etapeinōsas hōs traumatian hyperēphanon kai en tō brachioni tēs dynameōs sou dieskorpisas tous echthrous sou*). This allusion may be significant in light of the royal messianic interpretation of this psalm in Jewish traditions (*b. Sanh.* 97a; *Gen. Rab.* 22:11; *Exod. Rab.* 13:1; *Tg. Ps.* 89:51–52; see Juel 1988: 104–5). The use of the aorist tense here (and elsewhere in the Magnificat) can be taken as an affirmation of the certainty of God's eschatological acts (Farris: 1985: 114–16; Bock 1994–1996: 155), especially when the perfective (rather than the temporal) aspect of the aorist is recognized (cf. Porter [1993: 132–33], who nonetheless sees the past as providing the basis for 1:51–53).

1:52

In its setting as a response to God's blessings in relation to the gift of a child, this verse easily reminds one of the Song of Hannah (esp. 1 Sam. 2:7–8). Nevertheless, the theme of reversal is found throughout the OT to the extent that the expression *hypsōsen tapeinous* ("he lifted up the lowly") "may be said to be a stylized, conventional expression (cf. [LXX] Ezek. 21:26; Esth. 1:1; Job 5:11; Ps. 87[88]:15; Isa. 2:22; 10:33)" (D. R. Jones 1968: 25). This reversal motif survives in postbiblical Jewish traditions (*Sib. Or.* 13:3; *Ahiqar* 150). The adjective *tapeinous* ("the lowly") is not simply a socioeconomic status label, but is one that refers to the oppressed people of God (cf. 1:48). This text does not, however, support a narrower reference to the *Anawim* of the Qumran community (see 1QM XIV, 10–11) (*contra* R. E. Brown 1993: 350–55, 359).

1:53

General OT conceptual parallels can be found for the filling of the hungry with good things (cf. 1 Sam. 2:5; Ps. 107:9; 146:7) and the sending of the rich away empty (cf. 1 Sam. 2:5; Job 15:29; Jer. 17:11) (see Bock 1994–1996: 157), but precise allusions cannot be identified.

1:54–55

Three specific OT passages provide the context for this conclusion to the Magnificat: Isa. 41:8–9; Ps. 98:3 (97:3 LXX); Mic. 7:20. All three make the connection between the Abrahamic promises and God's redemptive act for his people (see Lampe 1993: 76–77). Isaiah 41:8–9 stands out with an explicit reference to Israel as "my servant" (*pais mou*) (cf. Isa. 42:1; 44:1–2, 21; 45:4; 48:20; 49:3) together with the use of the same verb as in Luke 1:54, *antilambanomai* ("to help"). In its Isaianic context this oracle sees the eschatological role of Israel as that which will fulfill the original call to Abraham. The psalmist contributes to the expression "in remembrance of his mercy" (*mnēsthēnai eleous*; cf. *emnēsthē tou eleous autou* [Ps. 97:3 LXX]) in a similar setting where the victorious God of Israel will reveal himself in fulfillment of "his steadfast love and faithfulness to the house of Israel" (Ps. 97:3a LXX). A similar set of ideas (mercy, promise/oath to our ancestors, Abraham) is found also in the final verse of Micah (7:20), which points to the eschatological hope of God's final delivery of Jacob/Israel.

The reference to Abraham in this verse paves the way for the role of Abraham in Luke-Acts. This symbol is used not only in reference to the promises of old (cf. Luke 1:72–73; Acts 3:13) but also in the redefinition of God's people whereby through the use of the reversal motif the people of God are no longer defined on the basis of physical descent (cf. Luke 3:8–9; 13:28; 16:19–30; 19:9–10; Acts 3:25).

1:57–58

The expression "the time came for Elizabeth to give birth" (*ho chronos tou tekein autēn*) echoes the birth of Esau and Jacob in Gen. 25:24: "her [Rebekah's] time to give birth was at hand" (*eplērōthēsan hai hēmerai tou tekein autēn*), and the theme of rejoicing also finds its parallel in OT birth accounts (cf. Gen. 21:6; see R. E. Brown 1993: 375). The theme of mercy connects this birth account with God's wider expression of mercy toward Israel (1:50, 54).

1:59

According to the OT, the rite of circumcision was to take place on the eighth day after birth (Gen. 17:12; 21:4; Lev. 12:3). Whereas the naming of a child usually takes place during the time of birth

(Gen. 25:24–26; 29:31–35), Abram received his name "Abraham" when he was circumcised as an adult (Gen. 17:5, 23). In light of the significance of circumcision as a sign of the Abrahamic covenant, it is tempting to see John's (and Jesus' [cf. 2:21]) reception of name during the rite of circumcision as an attempt to make a connection between Abraham and the fulfillment of the Abrahamic promises (cf. 1:55). The Lukan use of the expression "covenant of circumcision" (Acts 7:8) may lend support to this reading. This verse does not, however, explicitly affirm that the naming of the child on the eighth day was the widely accepted practice of first-century Palestinian Jews.

1:66

Hebraic expressions were used in the phrases *ethento . . . en tē kardia autōn* ("placed . . . in their hearts"; see 1 Sam. 21:12 [21:13 LXX]; 2 Sam. 13:20; Mal. 2:2; cf. Luke 2:19, 51) and *cheir kyriou* ("the hand of the Lord"; see Deut. 2:15 [*cheir theou*, "hand of God"]; Ezek. 8:1; 37:1; cf. Acts 11:21; 13:11) (see Creed 1930: 25; Bock 1994–1996: 170).

1:67

The filling with "the Holy Spirit" and the appearance of "prophecy" point to the arrival of a significant period of salvation history when the mighty acts of God are evident to all (cf. Isa. 32:14–17; 44:1–4). The Lukan commentary on such prophetic activities is provided in Acts 2, where the quotation from Joel 2:28–32 is used to describe the arrival of the eschatological era. God's people in this era will experience the power of the Spirit, and thus they will be described as the "sons of the prophets" (Acts 3:24–25) (see comments on 1:5–2:52 above).

Luke 1:68–79

As words of prophecy, the Benedictus focuses not on John the individual, but on God and his mighty acts on behalf of his people. In this portrayal of the work of God, the promises to David and Abraham are again evoked. When the role of John is addressed (1:76–79), it is his relation with Jesus that is noted. In this section, Isaiah provides the language through which the ministries of John and Jesus are articulated.

1:68

The opening blessing resembles the blessing formula found in the Psalter, where it ends three of the books (Ps. 41:13; 72:18; 106:48). The location of the formula at the beginning of a hymn is characteristic of the postbiblical hymnic tradition in Qumran (cf. 1QH[a] XIII, 20; XVIII, 14; XIX, 27, 29, 32; XXII *bottom*, 15; see D. R. Jones 1968: 28). The expression "blessed be the Lord God of Israel" (*eulogētos kyrios ho theos tou Israēl*) is almost identical to 1 Kings 1:48: "Blessed be the Lord, the God of Israel" (*eulogētos kyrios ho theos Israēl*). Significantly, this occurs in the context of the discussion of the Davidic heir (cf. 1 Kings 8:15; see Bock 1994: 70–71; Strauss 1995: 98–99). The connection to the house of David reappears in the final part of this verse ("he brought redemption for his people," *epoiēsen lytrōsin tō laō autou*) if Ps. 111:9 [110:9 LXX] ("he sent redemption to his people," *lytrōsin apesteile tō laō autou*) can be identified as the Scripture context behind it (see Creed 1930: 305; Ravens 1995: 38). This paves the way for 1:69, where the Davidic connection will be made explicit.

The verb *episkeptomai* ("visit") or its cognate noun is used in the OT to refer to God's presence in judgment (Ps. 89:32 [88:33 LXX]; Sir. 2:14) and in redemptive acts that evoke the exodus event (Exod. 3:16; 4:31; 13:19; 30:12; Isa. 23:17; Ps. 80:14 [79:15 LXX]; 106:4 [105:4 LXX]). In postbiblical material this terminology came to signify the eschatological "visit" of God (Wis. 3:7; *Pss. Sol.* 3:11; 10:4; 11:6; 15:12) (see Bovon 2002: 72). In Luke's Gospel this vocabulary is used in reference to the arrival of the eschatological era when God delivers Israel (Luke 1:78; 7:16; 19:44) while providing a redefinition for his own people (Acts 15:14).

1:69

The "horn" is a symbol of might (Deut. 33:17), and the expression "horn of salvation" (*keras sōtērias*), as understood in the context of the Davidic promises, finds its closest parallel in *keras sōtērias mou* ("horn of my salvation") as it appears in 2 Sam. 22:3; Ps. 18:2 (17:3 LXX). Significantly, both texts are attributed to David. Similar phrases that may have contributed to the use of this expression here includes *keras christou autou* ("horn of his anointed" [1 Sam. 2:10]); *keras tō Dauid* ("horn for David" [Ps. 132:17 (131:17 LXX)]);

keras panti tō oikō Israēl ("horn for the entire whole of Israel" [Ezek. 29:21]) (see Ravens 1995: 37; Strauss 1995: 99–100). This language survived in Jewish liturgical tradition, as is evident in the Babylonian version of the fifteenth benediction in the *Shemoneh Esreh*: "May he spring up quickly the Branch of David and exalt his horn for your salvation. Blessed are you, Lord, you who spring up the horn of salvation" (see Manns 1992).

In the OT David is almost never called a *pais*, "servant" (but see 1 Chron. 17:4 LXX A: *dauid ton paida* [B: *doulon*] *mou*, "David my servant"; cf. 1 Macc. 4:30). In light of 1:54, where the term *pais* is used to describe Israel, "David" could be understood as a symbol for Israel, which awaits the fulfillment of its eschatological hope, via Jesus the *pais* (cf. Acts 3:13, 26; 4:27). In Acts 4:25 the same label is likewise used for David in the context of prayer.

1:71

The language of the deliverance from "our enemies" and "those who hate us" belongs to the Psalter, where the fate of the individual merges with the fate of God's people (cf. Ps. 18:17; 106:10). In the evoking of these psalms, the deliverance of Israel is connected with the hope that rests on the house of David (cf. 2 Sam. 22:18). A similar articulation of the hope of Israel is found in 4Q174 1 I (see McNicol 1998: 30–32), but they diverge on the identity of the "enemies" of Israel and the goal of such an eschatological program. For Luke, instead of the temple cult, the enemies are those who opposed the "way" of the Lord as embodied in the life and ministry of Jesus. Instead of simply replacing the temple cult with the "house" of the Lord, Jesus' suffering and exaltation leads to the availability of salvation for all who accept him.

1:72

Covenantal language serves to bring the Davidic hope and the Abrahamic promise together (cf. 1:78), but the fulfillment of the Abrahamic promises by a future Davidic king is not without OT precedents (cf. Ps. 72:17; see Clements 1967: 47–60). The first part, "He has shown the mercy [*eleos*] promised to our ancestors," echoes Mic. 7:20, "You will show faithfulness to Jacob and unswerving loyalty [*eleos*] to Abraham, as you have sworn to our ancestors from the days of old," although the promise of "mercy" is not

limited to this passage (cf. Gen. 24:12; Judg. 1:24; 8:35; Ruth 1:8; 1 Sam. 20:8; see Schürmann 1990–1994: 1:88; Bovon 2002: 74). This final section of Micah is particularly important, however, as it provides the conceptual framework for the various elements in the immediate context of 1:72. These include the preceding note on the victory over God's enemies (1:71; Mic. 7:8–10) and the explicit mentioning of Abraham that follows (1:72; Mic. 7:20). These parallels show the widespread availability of such a complex of ideas (cf. *Apoc. Zeph.* 11:1–4; *T. Levi* 15:4; *T. Ash.* 7:7; see Lampe 1993: 85).

The second part, "and has remembered his holy covenant," recalls the mighty acts of God during the exodus event: "God remembered his covenant with Abraham, Isaac, and Jacob" (Exod. 2:24; cf. Ps. 105:8–9; 106:45). Significantly, it is within the expectation of the new exodus that the Abrahamic and Davidic covenants find their fulfillment (Acts 7:5; 13:34).

1:73

The "oath" sworn to Abraham may allude to the original promise in Gen. 22:16–17; 26:3. Nevertheless, this promise and its later renderings focus largely on the promise of the land (Gen. 50:24; Exod. 13:5, 11; 33:1; Num. 11:12; 14:16; Ps. 105:9–11; Jer. 11:5), although variations can be found where the land does not play such a central role (Deut. 4:31; 7:8; 8:18; 13:17; 28:9; 29:13) (see Creed 1930: 26, 305; Lampe 1993: 84). The verses that follow (1:74–79; cf. Acts 7:5–7) would provide a reappropriation of these traditions.

1:74–75

Deliverance from the hands of the enemies is a theme that was introduced earlier (see 1:71; cf. Ps. 18:17; 106:10). The purpose of divine deliverance is formulated with exodus language ("Let my people go, so that they may worship me in the wilderness" [Exod. 7:16; cf. Josh. 24:14]) together with a possible allusion to the Davidic promise: "If you will walk before me, as David your father walked, with integrity of heart and uprightness [*en hosiotēti kardias kai en euthytēti*] . . . then I will establish your royal throne over Israel forever, as I promised your father David, saying, 'There shall not fail you a successor on the throne of Israel'" (1 Kings 9:4–5) (see R. E. Brown 1993: 388).

1:76

With this verse, the attention now turns to the role of John the Baptist. This verse recalls 1:17, where one also finds allusions to Mal. 3:1 and Isa. 40:3. It also paves the way for 3:4–6 with the lengthy quotation from Isa. 40. In light of 1:16–17, the "Lord" (*kyrios*) is most likely a reference to God himself. The giving of a meaningful name or title also characterizes the prophecies of Isaiah (cf. 1:26; 57:4; 58:12; 60:14; see D. R. Jones 1968: 35). The title "prophet of the Most High" appears in *T. Levi* 8:15 (R. E. Brown 1993: 372), but Christian influence on this text cannot be ruled out.

1:78

The exact phrase "tender mercy of our God" (*splanchna eleous theou hēmōn*) does not appear in the LXX, but the idea of the deliverance of God as an act of his covenantal faithfulness is rooted in OT thought (cf. Ps. 89:28; 130:7–8; Isa. 54:7–8). Similar ideas can be found in Jewish traditions (cf. *T. Zeb.* 8:2; see R. E. Brown 1993: 388).

The word *anatolē* in the LXX had been used to translate the Hebrew *ṣemaḥ*, "sprout" or "branch" (Ezek. 16:7; Zech. 6:12), a word that appears in the context of the hope for the Davidic heir (Jer. 23:5; Zech. 3:8; 6:12; cf. Jer. 33:15; Isa. 11:1–10). This usage survives in Jewish traditions (cf. 4Q174; 4Q252; see Fitzmyer 1981–1985: 387). In the LXX the cognate verb *anatellō* is also used to refer to sunrise or the imagery of light (Num. 24:17; Mal. 3:20 [4:2 ET]). This "light" imagery seems to fit the Lukan context better. First, the phrase "from on high" (*ex hypsous*) fits well with the imagery of the rising sun. Second, the theme of light and darkness in its immediate context (1:79) also favors this reading. Third, in Isaiah the verb *anatellō* frequently appears in contexts of God's eschatological restoration (Isa. 42:9; 43:19; 44:4, 26; 45:8; 60:1; 61:11; 66:14; cf. 2 Pet. 1:19; see Ravens 1995: 39), and this may have also contributed to the use of this imagery of dawn here. This "light" imagery also survives in Jewish traditions that point to the eschatological hope of Israel (see Schlier 1964: 353; Bock 1994–1996: 192). Although this "light" imagery may be prominent behind the word *anatolē*, in light of the strong Davidic messianic reference and the probable connections between the "light/star" and "branch" imageries in early Christian traditions (the use

of *anatolē* may point to *testimonia* traditions [see esp. Gen. 49:10–11; Num. 24:17; Isa. 11:1, 10], see Albl 1999: 208–16), one cannot rule out a secondary reference in the use of this word.

1:79

The wording of the first part of the verse, "to give light to those who sit in darkness and in the shadow of death" (*epiphanai tois en skotei kai skia thanatou kathēmenois*), echoes Ps. 106:10 LXX: "sitting in darkness and in the shadow of death" (*kathēmenous en skotei kai skia thanatou*). In terms of context, however, Isa. 9:2 provides a better parallel: "The people who walked in darkness have seen a great light; those who lived in a land of deep darkness—on them light has shined" (see Creed 1930: 306; D. R. Jones 1968: 39). The idea of guidance in the second half of the verse is further paralleled by Isa. 42:6–7: "I have given you as . . . a light to the nations, to open the eyes that are blind, to bring out the prisoners from the dungeon, from the prison those who sit in darkness." This is consistent with the reading of 1:78 that portrays the *anatolē* as one who provides light for those in darkness (see Strauss 1995: 104–5).

The characterization of the way as one of "peace" (*eirēnē*) introduces a significant Lukan theme. This word occurs fourteen times in Luke, the majority of which are in uniquely Lukan passages (1:79; 2:14, 29; 7:50; 10:5–6; 14:32; 19:42; 24:36). In passages with Synoptic parallels, the word also appears only in Luke (11:21 [Matt. 12:29; Mark 3:27]; 19:38 [Matt. 21:9; Mark 11:10]) (see Swartley 1983: 25–26). In the OT the concept of peace (*šālôm*) is not limited to the social and political realms; it is used also to symbolize the arrival of the eschatological era. S. Talmon (1997: 114) rightly notes that "the apex of biblical Israel's hope for peace is reached in prophetic visions which transcend the horizon of human experience." This is best expressed in the work of Isaiah (e.g., Isa. 11:6–9; 65:17–25; cf. "the way of peace" in Isa. 59:8). In light of the Lukan uses of the peace motif, the meaning of the word here should not be limited to the realm of interpersonal relationship. As the conclusion of the Benedictus, the word evokes the prophetic hopes for the eschatological era, the presence of which affects the entirety of humanity.

1:80

As the birth announcements model the birth accounts of OT heroes, this verse likewise uses OT language to describe the growth of John the Baptist and Jesus (2:40, 52; cf. Gen. 21:8 [Isaac]; Judg. 13:24 [Samson]; 1 Sam. 2:21, 26 [Samuel]).

2:1

Some (Nestle 1910; R. E. Brown 1993: 417–18; Bovon 2002: 83) have detected an allusion to Ps. 87:6 (86:6 LXX), where the targumic version points to the raising up of a king, and the Quinta Greek version explicitly mentions the census context: "In the census of the peoples, this one will be born there" (cf. Eusebius, *Commentary on the Psalms* [PG 23:1052C]). It is doubtful, however, that Luke was aware of the Quinta traditions and the even later targumic text.

2:3

The phrase *hekastos eis tēn heautou polin* ("each one to his own town") recalls a similar phrase in Lev. 25:10: *hekastos eis tēn patrian autou* ("each one to his own family"), especially when the word *patria* ("family") also appears in 2:4 (see Kilpatrick 1989). An allusion to the Jubilee context is possible especially in light of Luke 4:16–30, where both the Jubilee and the references to one's own "native land" (*patris* [4:23–24]) are found. Nevertheless, the historical practice of returning to one's hometown in the Roman imperial period is sufficient in explaining the appearance of this note in this context (cf. P.Lond. 904; see McRay 1991: 155).

2:4, 11

In the OT the label "city of David" normally is used in reference to Jerusalem (e.g., 2 Sam. 5:7, 9; 6:10, 12, 16; 1 Chron. 11:5–7). The closest parallel in the LXX is in 1 Sam. 20:6, where Bethlehem is referred to as "his city." In light of Mic. 5:1–2 (4:14–5:1 MT), where the connection between Bethlehem and the coming Davidic ruler is made, one can agree with Strauss (1995: 110) that this is a "descriptive phrase" that aims at emphasizing the "Davidic connection to Bethlehem."

2:6

As in 1:57 above, the wording echoes Gen. 25:24.

2:7

In early Christian traditions *prōtotokos* ("firstborn") became a christological title in reference to Christ's redemptive role in salvation history (cf. Rom. 8:29; Col. 1:15, 18; Heb. 1:6; Rev. 1:5). In this context, however, this word may simply recall the stories of the patriarchs (e.g., Gen. 25:25; 27:19, 32; 35:23; 38:6–7; 41:51; 46:8; 48:18), although the focus on the right of inheritance is implicit in this emphasis on birth order (cf. Exod. 13:12; Deut. 21:15–17). In any case, the use of this term here seems to describe the unique status and role of Jesus and not his relative position in relation to his younger brothers and sisters (*contra* Bock 1987: 76).

It is unclear whether the reference to *phatnē* ("manger") alludes to Isa. 1:3 ("The ox knows its owner, and the donkey its master's crib [*phatnē*]; but Israel does not know, my people do not understand"), but this reading can already be found in early Christian works (e.g., *Sib. Or.* 8:477). If this Isaianic reference can be established, then the eschatological era is portrayed as one in which God's people will turn to their Lord. The exact identity of this people will be further defined in Luke's two-volume work.

In light of the emphasis on the Davidic dynasty in Luke 1–2, it is tempting to follow J. W. Olley (1992) in seeing an allusion to 2 Sam. 7:6 LXX, "I have not lived in a house since the day I brought up the people of Israel from Egypt to this day, but I have been moving about in a lodge [*katalyma*] and a tent" (cf. 1 Chron. 17:5), in the use of the word *katalyma* ("inn"). This would fit quite well in this Lukan context where one finds references to "the city of David" and "the house and family of David" (Luke 2:4). Nevertheless, this word alone is insufficient to establish this connection, since it also appears in the LXX in various contexts unrelated to the Davidic promises (cf. Exod. 4:24; 15:13; 1 Sam. 1:18; 9:22; Jer. 14:8; 40:12 [33:12 MT]; Ezek. 23:21).

Luke 2:8–14

Individual elements in this passage find their parallels in Isa. 9:2–7 (9:1–6 LXX/MT): light in the midst of darkness (2:8–9; Isa. 9:2); joy (2:10; Isa. 9:3); birth of a child (2:11; Isa. 9:6); Davidic messiah (2:11; Isa. 9:7); eschatological era of peace (2:14; Isa. 9:6–7) (see Meyer 1964: 42; Westermann 1971: 320; Doble 1996: 28–29). To this list one could add that this eschatological era will involve the nations/Gentiles, as they too will witness the glory of the Lord (2:10; Isa. 9:1). Significantly, this message of the birth of a mighty ruler that ushers in an era of peace is situated in a chapter that opens with the mention of "Emperor Augustus" (2:1).

2:8

Many have pointed to the "tower of the flock" in Mic. 4:8 as providing the context for understanding the reference to shepherds here. This phrase appears also in Gen. 35:21, and in the contexts of both texts one finds references to Bethlehem (Gen. 35:19; Mic. 5:2) (see Creed 1930: 31–32; Meyer 1964: 42; R. E. Brown 1993: 420). The *Targum of Pseudo-Jonathan* on Gen. 35:21 provides an explicit messianic reference that strengthens the relevance of these texts: "And Jacob proceeded and spread his tent beyond the tower of flocks, the place from whence it is to be that the king Meshiha will be revealed at the end of the days." Bock's (1987: 76–77; 1994–1996: 226) objection to this reading, based on the fact that these texts seem to refer primarily to Jerusalem, fails because of the close connection between Jerusalem and Bethlehem in Mic. 4–5. Moreover, one wonders if the connection between Micah and Luke 2 has to rest primarily on the reference to the "tower of the flock." The imagery of shepherding (Mic. 5:4) together with the reference to Bethlehem in the context of the promises of the "ruler over Israel" (Mic. 5:2) evokes the memory of King David, who "tend[s] his father's sheep at Bethlehem" (1 Sam. 17:15). It is quite appropriate, therefore, to find the Davidic messiah portrayed "as a ruler born in shepherd-country" (Fitzmyer 1981–1985: 395; cf. Ravens 1995: 42–43). The critical departure in Luke 2, in which Jesus is portrayed not as a shepherd but as one visited by the shepherds, should deter one from arguing for more specific connections between the two texts. The significance of Mic. 5 in the portrayal of the birth of Jesus in early Christian traditions is further affirmed by the explicit use of Mic. 5:2 in Matt. 2:6.

2:9

For the "angel of the Lord," see 1:11 above. The "glory of the Lord" signifies the presence of God

himself (e.g., Exod. 16:10; 24:16–17; 29:43; 40:34–35; Lev. 9:6; Num. 14:10; 16:19, 42; 20:6; 1 Kings 8:11; Ps. 138:5; Isa. 58:8; Ezek. 1:28; Tob. 12:15). Fear is the typical response in the presence of the divine (see 1:12 above).

2:10

As in 1:12–13, the angelic message begins with a "fear not" formula, and also the verb *euangelizomai* recalls 1:19.

2:11

In 1:47, in the liturgical language of Hab. 3:18, the title *sōtēr* ("savior") is applied to God. Luke here introduces Christ as the *sōtēr* in the context of his presentation as the Davidic messiah. In the LXX the title is applied to Israel's deliverer (Judg. 3:9, 15; 12:3; Neh. 9:27), but most often it points to God himself (Deut. 32:15; Ps. 23:5 [24:5 MT]; 24:5 [25:5 MT]; Isa. 12:2; 17:10; 45:15, 21) (see Bock 1994–1996: 217). As in the case of *euangelizomai*, Luke's use of this title may also be a reaction to the imperial propaganda that labels Augustus as the *sōtēr* of the world (see Priene Inscription [*OGIS* #458]).

The exact combination of the two titles *christos kyrios* ("Messiah, the Lord") without a conjunction is unusual. It appears nowhere else in the NT, and in the LXX it appears only in some Greek translations of Lam. 4:20 as a mistranslation of the Hebrew *měšîaḥ YHWH* ("the LORD's messiah"). The Greek word *christos*, together with its Hebrew equivalent *měšîaḥ*, refers to "the anointed one." In the OT one finds the anointing of Israel's kings (1 Sam. 9:16; 24:6), but the title also appears in priestly (Lev. 4:3, 5, 16) and prophetic (1 Kings 19:16; Ps. 105:15; Isa. 61:1) contexts. The royal messianic figure is described in detail in *Pss. Sol.* 17, a chapter where one also finds the combination title *christos kyrios* (*Pss. Sol.* 17:32; cf. 18:7). Although *christos* came to be used as a proper name, especially in the second volume of Luke's writings (e.g., Acts 2:38; 3:6; 4:10), the immediate context clearly points to a Davidic messianic reading of this title.

Prior to this verse in Luke, the word *kyrios* is most often used to refer to God himself (e.g., Luke 1:6, 9, 11, 15, 16, 17, 28, 32, 46, 76), although in 1:43 Mary is called "the mother of my Lord." This early Christian use of *kyrios* to refer to God can be traced back to the LXX (Cullmann 1963:

200–201), and there is evidence for the use of this term in pre-Christian Palestinian Judaism (see Fitzmyer 1975). In early Christian circles the Hellenistic context may also have contributed to the popularity of this title (cf. Acts 25:26). In Luke 1–2, however, the Jewish usage dominates as Luke highlights the authority of Jesus as one that equals that of God. The use of the three titles "Savior, Messiah, Lord" brought out both the active and the passive connotations of Jesus' authority: the Savior and Messiah is one who delivers God's people, while the Lord is one who is to be obeyed and honored (Marshall 1988: 145).

2:14

Unlike "glory of the Lord" in 2:9, the ascription of glory to God here belongs to the liturgical language of postbiblical times (cf. 1 Esd. 9:8; Bar. 2:17–18; 4 Macc. 1:12; see Fitzmyer 1981–1985: 410). Peace, on the other hand, is a typical Lukan theme that draws on the OT (cf. 1:79). The combination of the utterance of praise and the concern for the well-being of God's people within the expression of divine favor can already be found in the eschatological poem of *Pss. Sol.* 8:33–34.

2:19

In exploring the significance of Mary's treasuring and pondering the words of the angel (through the mouths of the shepherds), attempts have been made to identify the conceptual precedence of this verse: apocalyptic (cf. Dan. 4:28 LXX; 7:28 Θ; *L.A.E.* Apocalypse 3:3; see Neirynck 1960: 51–57), prophetic (cf. Gen. 37:11; see Meyer 1964: 43), and wisdom (cf. Ps. 119:11; Prov. 3:1; Sir. 13:12–13; 39:1–3; see R. E. Brown 1993: 430). The wording, especially in the version of Luke 2:51 (*hē mētēr autou dietērei panta ta rhēmata*, "his mother treasured all these things"), closely resembles that of Gen. 37:11 (*ho de patēr autou dietērēsen to rhēma*, "his father kept [or treasured] the matter"). In both, the parent awaits the unfolding of God's work in the child. Nevertheless, the fact that the two Lukan verses (2:19, 51) differ in form may imply that Luke did not have one particular text in mind. The various other conceptual contexts suggested also point to the wide availability of similar ideas and formulations.

Luke 2:21–40

The presentation of Jesus in the temple on the eighth day after his birth echoes the presentation of Samuel "to the house of the LORD at Shiloh" when "the child was young" (1 Sam. 1:24) (see R. E. Brown 1993: 450–51; Plymale 1994: 28). The phrase "to present him to the Lord" (2:22) recalls a similar note in 1 Sam. 1:22, and the aged Simeon brings to mind the figure of Eli. The rite outlined in 2:22–24 may also echo the tradition that identifies Samuel as a Nazirite (see comments below). The summary statement that concludes this chapter ("And Jesus increased in wisdom and in years, and in divine and human favor") likewise draws on 1 Sam. 2:26: "Now the boy Samuel continued to grow both in stature and in favor with the LORD and with the people." As pointed out earlier (see introductory comments for 1:5–2:52), parallels with the Samuel narrative serve to draw attention to the Davidic royal traditions as Jesus is presented as the Davidic messiah, who will bring deliverance to God's people.

2:21

As in the case of John the Baptist, Jesus was circumcised on the eighth day according to OT customs (see comments on 1:59).

2:22–23

These verses are significant because they contain numerous references to the law of Moses together with the account of Jesus' first visit to the Jerusalem temple. A quotation formula appears twice, but an explicit, direct quotation is found only in the next verse (2:24).

Verse 22 begins with the phrase "when the time came for their purification." The description of this rite will continue in v. 24, but what attracts attention here is the use of the third-person plural pronoun *autōn* ("their"). In Lev. 12 only the mother who had recently given birth is required to go through the rite of purification. This reading is supported by the best witnesses (א A B et al.). A number of manuscripts have omitted the pronoun (435 bo[pt] Ir[lat]). Codex D and some other versions have the masculine pronoun *autou* ("his"), while the reading in it[pt] and vg could be read as either a masculine or feminine singular pronoun. The weight of the external evidence makes the *lectio difficilior, autōn,* the most probable reading. This plural pronoun could refer to Jesus and Mary, as suggested already by Origen, and Creed (1930: 38–39) supports this reading by suggesting that Luke might have misunderstood the stipulations of Exod. 13:1–2, where the sanctification of the firstborn is to be accomplished by the rite of purification in Lev. 12. The second part of the verse strongly argues against this, however, since the implied plural subject has to be Joseph and Mary: "they brought him up to Jerusalem" (cf. 2:27, 33, 34, 39; see Robert 1990). The possible reason for Joseph's inclusion can be understood within the development of the Levitical rite.

Immediately after the introduction of the rite of purification, Luke turns his attention to the dedication of the firstborn (2:23). Luke begins with a quotation formula, "as it is written in the law of the Lord" (*kathōs gegraptai en nomō kyriou*), but what follows is not a direct quotation from the OT: "Every firstborn male shall be designated as holy to the Lord." Conceptual parallels can be identified in Exod. 13:2, 12, 15, although these wordings are quite different: the key term *prōtotokos* ("firstborn") that these Exodus passages share does not appear in this Lukan passage, whereas the Lukan *hagion . . . klēthēsetai* ("shall be called holy") finds no parallel in these three verses. Against the conclusion that this verse has "a non-Hellenistic origin" (Bock 1994–1996: 237), it seems that it is not Luke's intention to provide an exact rendering of the OT text.

Exodus 13 lays out the requirements for all firstborn sons of Israel to be consecrated to the Lord as a response to the sparing of the lives of the firstborn Israelite males during the Passover event. This legislation is further developed in Num. 18, where the Levites will serve on behalf of the firstborn sons. The parents of these firstborns must in turn redeem them by paying "five shekels of silver" (Num. 18:16).

The mention of these two rites together has led many to conclude that Luke "seems to have confused them" (R. E. Brown 1993: 447). More likely, however, is that Luke is simply providing a summarized representation of these rites (see Schürmann 1990–1994: 121–22) while focusing on Jesus' (and his parents') obedience to the law. First, the thrice-mentioned *nomos* in these verses serves to highlight Luke's intention in describing the observances of these rites. Second, the lack of

mention of the five-shekels redemption price also shows that the detailed portrayal of these rites is not Luke's primary intention. Moreover, this omission also points to the focus on Jesus as the one wholly devoted to God. The use of the term *hagion* ("holy") in describing Jesus further fulfills the promises to Mary concerning him in 1:35: "The child to be born will be holy; he will be called Son of God." This interpretation of Exod. 13 in terms of one's total devotion to God is not foreign to Hellenistic Jewish exegetical traditions (e.g., Philo, *Sacrifices* 97; *Spec. Laws* 1.248). The presentation to the Lord during the rite of purification (2:22) is thus connected to the rite of consecration, when Jesus' lifelong dedication to God is emphasized (2:23).

Luke 2:24

This verse deserves separate treatment because it represents the first explicit OT quotation in Luke's writings.

A. NT Context: Dedication to God. As noted above in the discussion of 2:22–23, this verse belongs to a summary paragraph that highlights Jesus' (and his parents') fulfillment of the requirements of the law. The precise combination of the two rites in these verses also serves to focus on the characterization of Jesus' life and ministry as that which is entirely devoted to carrying out the plan of God. The rite of purification noted in 2:22 finds its completion in this verse, although this verse also may carry a secondary sense as it alludes to yet another rite of dedication. In the wider context 2:22–24 provide the context for the Nunc Dimittis (2:29–32), which outlines the significance of Jesus' ministry in Isaianic terms.

B. Lev. 12:8 in Context. Leviticus 12 belongs to a wider section (Lev. 11–16) that deals with the issue of impurity. This chapter follows the rules of animal purities (chap. 11) and is related to the later discussion of genital discharges (chap. 15). Leviticus 12 in particular deals with impurity after childbirth. The birth of a son renders the mother unclean for seven days, and then she would go through a period of thirty-three days of blood purification. If she gives birth to a daughter, the time of uncleanness and blood purification is doubled. After this period of blood purification is completed, the mother is to present a lamb in its first year for a burnt offering and a pigeon or a turtledove for a sin offering. If she cannot afford a lamb, "she shall take two turtledoves or two pigeons, one for a burnt offering and the other for a sin offering" (12:8). This set of offerings is required before the mother can return to the state of being "clean."

C. Lev. 12:8 in Judaism. One of the earliest explicit comments on Lev. 12 is in *Jub.* 3:8–14 (see Schearing 2003: 431–32). In this text the origin of this stipulation is hypothesized in an attempt to explain the lengthier period of uncleanness and blood purification that a mother had to go through after giving birth to daughters rather than sons. In seeing the Garden of Eden as an archetypal temple, the author of *Jubilees* suggests that since Eve was created after Adam, and her entrance into the garden (i.e., temple) followed that of Adam, giving birth to a daughter would render a woman unclean (i.e., not being able to enter a sanctuary) for a longer period of time.

This concern to explain the differences in the lengths of the period of uncleanness and blood purification survives in other texts. In 4Q265 and 4Q266 the same solution is provided for this problem. Significantly, the implications of the *Jubilees* text is clearer here: Adam and Eve were rendered unclean through childbirth even though there is no mother present in this case. In a sense, then, those associated with the childbirth are also rendered unclean (see Baumgarten 1994: 5–6; Kugler 2003: 355–56). This would provide support for understanding the plural pronoun *autōn* in 2:22 as referring to Jesus and his mother, although the context makes it implausible (see comments on 2:22). One wonders if this can be extended to include the husband, who may be considered involved in the process of childbirth.

In rabbinic literature the discussion of this aspect of the stipulation continues. In addition, other details were discussed and debated. These include the exact nature of the "sin" that led to the requirement of a sin offering (cf. *b. Nid.* 31b) and the related question of the extent of the requirement of sexual abstinence after childbirth (cf. *b. Ketub.* 61b; see Schearing 2003: 435).

D. Textual Matters. The precise wording of this offering, *zeugos trygonōn ē dyo nossous peristerōn* ("a pair of doves or two young pigeons"), deviates slightly from that of LXX Lev. 12:8, *dyo trygonas*

ē dyo neossous peristerōn ("two doves or two young pigeons"), although the meaning is identical (as in the MT: *šĕtê tōrîm 'ô šĕnê bĕnê yônâ*). A closer verbal parallel can be identified in the description of the sin offering (of the poor) in Lev. 5:11 LXX: *zeugos trygonōn ē dyo neossous peristerōn* ("a pair of doves or two young pigeons"), although an earlier reference within the same chapter (5:7) is identical to Lev. 12:8 in wording. In terms of context where the rite of purification is concerned, Luke is most certainly quoting from Lev. 12:8. Nevertheless, Luke may also have Lev. 5:11 in mind, as sin offering is part of the rite of purification.

E. The Use of Lev. 12:8 in Luke 2:24. As in 2:22–23, the evocation of this Mosaic stipulation clearly points to Jesus' (and his parents') faithfulness to the observance of the law. The reason for the listing of the content of this offering is debated, however. First, the mention of "a pair of turtledoves or two young pigeons" may have been evoked because this serves as an alternative for those who "cannot afford a sheep" (Lev. 12:8a). Thus the emphasis is on the economic status of Jesus' family. In light of the development of the narrative, many would also see this as reflecting Luke's interest in the poor as he uses the reversal motif to describe the effect of the dawn of the eschatological era (see O'Toole 1983: 11; Barrett 1988: 235). Luke's interest in the poor cannot be denied, but this emphasis does not exhaust the reason for the inclusion of this quotation in this context.

Noting that one of the "two turtledoves or two pigeons" is for a "sin offering" (Lev. 12:8), some have pointed to the need for Mary to be cleansed of her "sins" as one of the focuses of this text (see Schearing 2003: 400). Although this may have contributed to the later debate concerning the dogma of Mary's "immaculate conception," this text focuses rather on the faithfulness of Mary. The performance of the rite of purification draws attention to the fulfillment of the requirements of the law and not to the prior state of uncleanness.

More fruitful is the approach that sees this note on the content of the offering as echoing a similar rite for a Nazirite in the case of defilement. In this rite the defiled one "shall bring two turtledoves or two young pigeons to the priest at the entrance of the tent of meeting" (Num. 6:10). Given that

Samuel himself is a Nazirite (1 Sam. 1:11), this offering may carry added significance: the dedication of the firstborn to the Lord's service in the model of Samuel (cf. 1 Sam. 1–2; see Marshall 1978: 117; Schürmann 1990–1994: 1:121–22; Bock 1994–1996: 234; Bovon 2002: 99). First, the parallels between the dedications of Samuel and Jesus have already been noted (see comments on 2:21–40 above), and the parallels between the two are extended to the entire Lukan birth narrative (Luke 1–2). As in the case of Samuel, the dedication of Jesus focuses not only on purity issues related to childbirth but also on the definition of his life and mission. Second, the model of Samuel's dedication will be able to bring together the two rites mentioned above: dedication of the firstborn and the rite of purification after childbirth. The Nazirite rite fulfills the intent of the stipulation concerning the dedication of the firstborn, and the rite of purification draws attention to the sanctity required for service in the presence of God. After all, at stake is not Mary's state of purity, but rather the mission of Jesus.

F. Theological Use. In ecclesiological terms this quotation draws attention to the continuity of salvation history. In fulfilling the requirements of the law, Jesus fulfills the past by bringing it to its climax. The thrice-repeated mention of the Torah in the context of the Jerusalem cult provides the setting in which the way to know the perfect will of God and the means through which one can approach him can be introduced. Situated squarely within the traditions of Israel, the significance of Jesus is not limited to the Israel of flesh, however. The connection between this passage and the Nunc Dimittis, which follows, is most striking when the mission to the Gentiles is announced through the promises of Isaiah.

Christologically, this passage introduces Jesus not simply as a firstborn, but rather as the "holy one" whose life fulfills those of all the firstborn of Israel in his dedication to the service and plan of God. The rest of the narrative will make this point abundantly clear.

2:25

In the LXX the expression "consolation of Israel" (*paraklēsis tou Israēl*) is found in the prophetic literature in reference to the promise of Israel's restoration (cf. Jer. 38:9 LXX [31:9 MT]). In the writings of Luke a more specific context can be identified. The word *paraklēsis* appears most often in Isaiah, where it becomes a symbol for the arrival of the eschatological era when God fulfills his promises to Israel (Isa. 28:29; 30:7; 57:18; 66:11). Significantly, the verbal form, *parakaleō*, appears more than twenty-five times in Isaiah. Isaiah 40:1–11 can be considered as a summary of this message of consolation when the eschatological second exodus is expressed through the several appearances of *parakaleō* (40:1, 2, 11). Similarly, the reiteration of this message in Isa. 61:1–2 is also formulated with this key term. While Isa. 40 is evoked in the block quotation in Luke 3:4–6, Isa. 61 forms the basis of Jesus' sermon in Nazareth in Luke 4:18–19. In its immediate context, 2:25 also paves the way for the fuller expression of the Isaianic program in the Nunc Dimittis.

2:27

The expression "the Lord's Messiah" (*ho christos kyriou*) is an idiom used in the LXX (cf. 1 Sam. 24:7, 11 [24:6, 10 ET]; 26:9, 11, 16; see Bovon 2002: 101). It is not to be confused with a similar expression in 2:11 (*christos kyrios*), where the two stand in appositional relationship.

Luke 2:29–32

The Nunc Dimittis is formulated with language borrowed from Isaiah. These allusions point to the universal significance of God's salvific plan for his own people. Christologically, the mission of Jesus is portrayed in the model of the Isaianic Suffering Servant.

2:29

The closest parallel to this verse is found in Gen. 15:15, *sy de apeleusē pros tous pateras sou met' eirēnēs* ("you shall go to your ancestors in peace"), but the general sense is found elsewhere (cf. Num. 20:29; Tob. 3:6; 2 Macc. 7:9; see Creed 1930: 41; D. R. Jones 1968: 40). In light of the significance of the Lukan theme of peace that was introduced in 1:79 and 2:14, this "peace" should not be limited to an individualistic sense, as it is also "associated with the fulfillment of Israel's messianic hopes" (Swartley 1983: 27). The eschatological tone of this statement also reflects the sentiments of *Pss. Sol.* 17:44: "Blessed are those born in those days to see the good fortune of Israel which God will bring to pass in the assembly of the tribes."

2:30

In this verse, Luke uses the neuter *sōtērion* ("salvation") instead of the feminine form, *sōtēria*, which he usually prefers (1:69, 71, 77; 19:9; Acts 4:12; 7:25; 13:26, 47; 16:17; 27:34). J. T. Carroll (1988: 47) suggests that since "salvation" is applied to "the child" (*to paidion*) of 2:27, the neuter form was used. A better solution is available when the other two instances of the neuter form are identified in the Lukan writings. The next appearance of this neuter noun comes in the quotation of Isa. 40:5 in Luke 3:6; its only other occurrence in the Lukan writings is in Acts 28:28, where Luke probably also had Isa. 40:5 in mind (see Pao 2000: 108). A reasonable assumption is that in 2:30 Luke is also alluding to Isa. 40:5, as it appears in Luke 3:6, a verse that also adopts the metaphor of vision: "and all flesh shall see the salvation of God" (*opsetai pasa sarx to sōtērion tou theou*). Other Isaianic parallels in 2:31–32 confirm this reading. In Jewish traditions conceptual parallels can be identified in Bar. 4:24 [cf. Isa. 52:10] and CD-B XX, 34 (D. R. Jones 1968: 41; Nolland 1989–1993: 120; R. E. Brown 1993: 458).

2:31

As in 2:30, the preparation of "salvation" may also be an allusion to the Isaianic quotation that appears in Luke 3, where both the verb *hetoimazō* ("prepare") and the noun *sōtērion* ("salvation") appear: "Prepare the way of the Lord" (*hetoimasate tēn hodon kyriou* [3:4]) ... "and all flesh shall see the salvation of God" (*opsetai pasa sarx to sōtērion tou theou* [3:4, 6; cf. Isa. 40:3, 5]). This Isaianic allusion also affects how the second part of this verse is read: "in the presence of all peoples" (*prosōpon pantōn tōn laōn*). Although the singular *laos* ("people") is a term most often applied to Israel in the LXX (translating the Heb. *'am*; see *NIDNTT* 2:796), in this verse the qualifying *pantōn* ("all") with the plural *laōn* in the context where Isa. 40:5 is in view encourages readers to see the word as inclusive of Gentiles (cf. Isa. 52:10 without the use of *laos*). This "people" therefore includes both "Gentiles" (2:32a) and "Israel" (2:32b). The inclusion of the Gentiles within God's elected ones is made explicit in Acts 15:14, where the singular *laos* is now applied to the Gentiles: "Simeon has

related how God first looked favorably on the Gentiles, to take from among them a people [*laon*] for his name."

2:32

The first part of the verse focuses on the significance of the dawn of salvation for the Gentiles: "a light for revelation to the Gentiles" (*phōs eis apokalypsin ethnōn*). The imagery of light echoes Isa. 49:6 LXX (*idou tetheika se ... eis phōs ethnōn tou einai se eis sōtērian heōs eschatou tēs gēs*, "I set you ... as a light to the nations, that you may bring salvation to the end of the earth" [cf. Isa. 42:6]), a verse quoted in Acts 13:47. The phrase "for revelation" (*eis apokalypsin*) may in turn echo Isa. 52:10 (*kai apokalypsei kyrios ton brachiona autou ton hagion enōpion pantōn tōn ethnōn*, "And the LORD shall reveal his holy arm before the eyes of all the nations") and 56:1b ("soon my salvation will come, and my mercy be revealed," *to sōtērion mou paraginesthai kai to eleos mou apokalyphthēnai*); this concept of the final revelation of God survives in Jewish traditions (cf. *3 Bar.* 1–2; 4:13–14; 11:7; 17:4; see Bovon 2002: 103).

The texts behind the second part of the verse ("glory to your people Israel," *doxan laou sou Israēl*) are more difficult to identify, although conceptual parallels can be found in texts such as Isa. 60:1–2: "Arise, shine; for your light [*phōs*] has come, and the glory [*doxa*] of the LORD has risen upon you.... the LORD will arise upon you, and his glory [*doxa*] will appear over you." Drawing on Isaianic passages, Bar. 4:24 reflects a similar thought pattern in which the metaphor of vision appears together with the bestowal of glory upon God's people: "For as the neighbors of Zion have now seen your capture, so they soon will see your salvation by God, which will come to you with great glory and with the splendor of the Everlasting."

These OT and Jewish texts provide a way to understand the two parts of the verse. Some commentators see "revelation" and "glory" as in apposition to "light" (see Fitzmyer 1981–1985: 428; Tiede 1988a: 327–41; Bock 1994–1996: 244), while others see "light" and "glory" as parallel with both in apposition to "salvation" in 2:30 (D. R. Jones 1968: 42; Schürmann 1990–1994: 1:126; Bovon 2002: 103; Kilgallen 1994: 307). In light of Isa. 49:6, which is quoted in Acts 13:47, salvation does seem to be presented as a light to the Gentiles in particular. As in Bar. 4:24, the arrival of this age of salvation will also be for the glory of Israel. The parallelism between light and glory found in Isa. 60:1–2 is therefore likely to be reflected here. This parallelism makes a striking point anticipated by the previous reference to "all peoples" (2:31): with the arrival of Israel's deliverer, Gentiles will be able to participate in the people of God. One has to wait for Luke's second volume for the unpacking of this point.

2:34

The imagery used here draws on Isa. 8:14–15, where God is portrayed as setting up a stone that Israel will stumble over, while the act of "rising" points to Isa. 28:16 ("See, I am laying in Zion a foundation stone, a tested stone, a precious cornerstone, a sure foundation"). The connection between these two Isaianic passages appears also in other early Christian texts (e.g., Rom. 9:33; 1 Pet. 2:7–8). Psalm 118:22 (117:22 LXX), "The stone that the builders rejected has become the capstone," also would not be far from Luke's mind, especially when the quotation of this verse in Luke 20:17 is also combined with the imagery of falling in 20:18 (see R. E. Brown 1993: 461). The use of this psalm elsewhere in Luke (cf. 13:35; 19:38; Acts 4:11) further supports this connection.

The identification of scriptural passages behind the "stone" imagery does not resolve the issue of the identity of the groups referred to in the metaphor of "falling" and "rising." For some, this verse refers to the schism within Israel (as in Acts 28:24; see Nolland 1989–1993: 121; Bovon 2002: 104), while for others, it refers to the sequential falling and rising of God's people as in Isa. 51:17–23 (see Caird 1963: 64; Koet 1992). The third possibility is to read this verse in light of the parable of the Wicked Tenants (Luke 20:9–19), where one finds the fall of God's people and the rise of those who were excluded. This third option is unlikely in light of the phrase "in Israel" in 2:34, although the theme of Israel's persistent rejection in this parable is relevant in this discussion. In view of the prominence of the theme of division (cf. Luke 12:53) within Israel and the reference to the sword in the verse that follows, the first option is to be preferred. Moreover, the way the "stone" imagery functions in Luke 20:17 also rules out the sequential view.

Finally, the "sign" (*sēmeion*) imagery also has OT parallels. As the "stone" imagery is drawn from Isa. 8, Isa. 8:18 may be relevant here because the prophets were considered to be "signs [*sēmeia*] and portents [*terata*] in the house of Israel from the LORD of hosts." Jesus therefore becomes a prophetic sign through which the message of God is revealed (see Bovon 2002: 104). This prophetic sign is not unlike the *sēmeion* of Jonah in Luke 11:29–32, where prophetic judgment is pronounced. Ironically, the sign that is spoken against became the sign of judgment for those who spoke against it.

2:35

Numerous suggestions have been offered for this imagery of the sword (see surveys in Fitzmyer 1981–1985: 429–30; Bock 1994–1996: 248–49). The two most plausible readings see this as (1) a reference to the sorrow that Jesus would cause his mother; and (2) a sword that separates the people of God. The first option rightly takes note of the phrase "your own soul" (*sou [de] autēs tēn psychēn*), which points to the personal nature of this statement. The second fits well in its wider context, where the theme of judgment is clearly expressed. This view is also supported by the possible allusion to Ezek. 14:17, where the sword is the instrument of judgment and discrimination. As in the case of the prophetic *sēmeion* ("sign") in 2:34, both views may be embedded in this symbol: the path to the cross creates intense personal pain for Jesus' mother, and it is this journey that serves as an instrument through which God's people are judged. The reading would fit well with the Lukan portrayal of Jesus' prophetic journey to Jerusalem in particular (see comments on Luke 9:51–19:44 below).

2:36

Recent years have witnessed a renewed interest in the person of Anna and the rhetorical role that she has in the Lukan narrative (age, marital status, parallels with OT and postbiblical Jewish figures, prophetic role, practices of piety, etc.; see Elliott 1988; Wilcox 1992; Bauckham 1997; Thurston 2001). In this verse she is explicitly identified as one from the "tribe of Asher." Asher, one of the northern tribes, was never considered a noteworthy tribe. In the book of Judges the Asherites were remembered as living "among the Canaanites, the inhabitants of the land; for they did not drive them out" (Judg. 1:32). Nevertheless, after the fall of Samaria, Asher was numbered among a few tribes that were willing to participate in the Passover feast in Jerusalem (2 Chron. 30:10–11). The name of Anna's father, "Phanuel," reflects his origin, pointing back to the city of Penuel, a city mentioned together with Shechem in 1 Kings 12:25. D. Ravens (1995: 47) suggests that this minor northern tribe serves as a symbol of the northern kingdom, and Anna's worshiping in the Jerusalem temple is taken as an indication of the expectation of the entire people of God for the arrival of Israel's deliverer. Her recognition of Jesus as the bearer of Israel's redemption points forward to Luke's second volume, where the Samaritans join the Judeans in acknowledging the mighty acts of God in Jesus the Messiah (Acts 8:1–25). Rather than "add[ing] little to the story" (Bock 1994–1996: 251), Anna's ancestry and tribal affiliation may have been intended to pave the way for the development of Luke's account of the unfolding of salvation history.

2:38

"Redemption of Jerusalem" (*lytrōsin Ierousalēm*) echoes Isa. 52:8–10 (cf. Ps. 130:5–8; see Green 1997: 152), although verbal parallels in the LXX are lacking. This focus on Jerusalem as the center of God's eschatological salvation is also the emphasis of Isa. 40:1–11, a passage evoked repeatedly in the early chapters of Luke (cf. 1:17, 19, 76; 2:25, 30–31; 3:4–6).

2:40

Besides the parallels identified in our earlier discussion of the growth statement of John the Baptist in 1:80, this verse draws attention to the "wisdom" of Jesus. Moving beyond the study by H. J. de Jonge (1978: 348–49) that identifies the presence of wisdom motifs in texts that portray the eschatological deliverers (e.g., *Pss. Sol.* 17:37; *1 En.* 49:3; *T. Levi* 18:7), Strauss (1995: 122–23) draws attention to Isa. 11:1–3 as a source for many of these later texts. He also argues that Isa. 11:1–3 provides the conceptual context for the second half of this summary statement: *plēroumenon sophia, kai charis theou ēn ep' auto* ("filled with wisdom, and the favor of God was upon him"). In both, one finds the wisdom motif (*sophia*), the reference to God's bestowing of favor/the Spirit "on

him" (*ep' auto/n*), and a verb of "filling" (*emplēsei* [Isa. 11:3]; *plēroumenon* [Luke 2:40]). If so, this summary moves beyond that of John the Baptist (1:80) in identifying Jesus as the Davidic figure of Isa. 11. This is not inconsistent with the christological presentation of Luke 1–2, where Jesus is portrayed as the Davidic messiah, who is filled with the wisdom of the Spirit (2:41–52).

Luke 2:41–52

Rather than being a secondary insertion to the Lukan birth narrative (see R. E. Brown 1993: 480, 489), this story illustrates the wisdom of Jesus, as is noted in the summary statement of 2:40 (see H. J. de Jonge 1978: 322; M. Turner 1996: 161). In the LXX and in Jewish traditions several heroes were remembered as possessors of extraordinary wisdom: Solomon (1 Kings 3:5–14; 4:29), Samuel (Josephus, *Ant.* 5.348), and Daniel (Dan. 2:13, 48). In Jewish traditions the Messiah is also portrayed as one endowed with divine wisdom (see comments on 2:40). This manifestation of wisdom in Jesus' knowledge of the law (2:46–47) may also reflect Jewish wisdom traditions that see a connection between wisdom and Torah (cf. Sir. 1:25–27; 6:37; 15:1; 19:20; 24:23; 33:2–3; Bar. 4:1; see Witherington 1994: 115). In the narrative development of Luke's story this account points forward to Jesus' (polemical) interaction with Jewish leadership in the second half of Luke's Gospel (see Doble 2000: 187–88).

2:41

For the Feast of Passover, see comments on 22:1.

2:49

The elliptical expression *tois tou patros mou* has been understood as referring to either "my Father's business" (NKJV) or "my Father's house" (NIV, NRSV, et al.). It is possible that the ambiguity is intentional, since Jesus points both to his Father's "matters" and more specifically to his Father's "house" (Weinert 1983). In any case, the focus is on God as Jesus' Father. "Father/son" language appears in the OT (Exod. 4:22; Isa. 63:16; Jer. 3:4) and Jewish traditions (Wis. 2:16, 18; Sir. 4:10; 23:1; 51:10) (see Schürmann 1990–1994: 1:137) to express the covenantal relationship between God and his people. In this verse the special relationship between Jesus and his "Father" is introduced as the Jesus-God relationship symbolizes the perfection of the covenantal relationship between God and his people. With the juxtaposition of the earthly "father" (2:48) and the heavenly one (2:49), Luke points to the primary frame of reference in which the ministry of Jesus is to be understood. Throughout Luke's writings God continues to be portrayed as the Father of Jesus (Luke 9:26; 10:21–22; 22:29, 42; 23:34, 46; 24:49; Acts 1:4, 7), and Jesus is expected to do the will of this Father (Luke 22:42).

2:51

See comments on 2:19 above.

2:52

In addition to Jesus receiving divine favor as in 2:40 (see comments above), this verse also makes note of "human" (*para . . . anthrōpois*) favor. This additional element may point to Jesus' obedience to his parents in 2:51 (cf. Prov. 3:1–14; see R. E. Brown 1993: 495). It is more likely, however, that this verse has a wider reference, as it points to the impression that Jesus left on the Jewish teachers in the temple (2:47). The early chapters of 1 Samuel, evoked numerous times in Luke 1–2, provide yet another parallel to this verse, as the focus on both divine and human favor finds its precedence in 1 Sam. 3:19–20: "As Samuel grew up, the Lord was with him and let none of his words fall to the ground. And all Israel from Dan to Beer-sheba knew that Samuel was a trustworthy prophet of the Lord."

3:1–2

The appearance of "the word of God" (*rhema theou*) with a complete synchronism noting the political and religious contexts of the time echoes language of Israel's prophets (cf. Jer. 1:1–3). This explicit appearance of the prophetic word is noteworthy. Some commentators have pointed to prophetic activities in the Second Temple period (see Aune 1983: 103–6; Webb 1991: 317–42), but the intensity of prophetic activities in Luke 1–2 points to the realization that God is acting in history in a new way (cf. Luke 1:42–45, 46–55, 68–79; 2:29–32, 36–38). These voices materialize with the explicit portrayal of the arrival of the word of God in the ministries of John the Baptist in this new era.

3:3

Various attempts have been made to identify the background of the baptism of John. The OT ritual of cleansing provides an obvious candidate, but it is neither related to acts of repentance nor a one-time act. In the early Christian centuries proselyte baptism was practiced, but evidence for this is too late for John's practice, and conversion accounts of early postbiblical Jewish literature fail to mention such baptism (cf. Josephus, *Ant.* 20.38–48, 137–140; *Jos. Asen.* 10–18; see D. C. Smith 1982). The parallels between John's ministry and the Qumran community provide an alternative: use of Isa. 40:3, similar ascetic practices, attitudes toward the temple and "mainstream" Jewish groups, eschatological emphasis, and geographical locations. The ritual washing that might have been practiced at Qumran (see 1QS V, 13) is similar to that of John's, as both carry a moral message and eschatological urgency (cf. 1QS I, 24–II, 1; IX, 9–11; CD-A XV, 4; see Robinson 1957). Although Qumran ritual washing does provide a helpful parallel, unlike John's baptism, it too is an act that needs to be repeated. Moreover, a closer examination of the evidence casts doubt on the significance of the apparent parallels between the two groups (see Taylor 1997: 15–48). Without arguing that John's baptism is entirely "unique and new" (see Schürmann 1990–1994: 1:156–57), we do best to see the various "baptisms" as drawing from the symbolism embedded in OT ritual cleansing (cf. the eschatological interpretation in *Sib. Or.* 4:165) while developing separately within their own contexts and communities. John's baptism falls within the prophetic traditions where external acts actualize mental decisions. In the context of John's preaching this baptism is also a preparatory act for the arrival of God's salvation.

Luke 3:4–6

A. NT Context: New Act of God. With this passage one finds the appearance of the first lengthy OT quotation in Luke's writings. The quotation of Isa. 40:3–5 should not be considered as an isolated quotation from Isaiah introducing the ministry of John the Baptist; rather, it is one that is significant for establishing the foundation for the rest of Luke's narrative (see Pao 2000: 37–69). This point is well established by the fact that Luke's quotation extends beyond Mark's use of Isa. 40:3, which can possibly be interpreted primarily in terms of John's own preparatory ministry (see Stendahl 1968: 48; but cf. R. E. Watts 1997: 86–88). In Luke 3 the quotation climaxes in a note that emphasizes the universal significance of this dawn of salvation: "and all flesh shall see the salvation of God" (*kai opsetai pasa sarx to sōtērion tou theou* [3:6]). On the assumption that Luke is using Mark here (see Dunn 1994; although other traditions may be available to him [Bovon 2002: 117–19]), Luke's inclusion of this longer quotation shifts the focus from John the Baptist to the entire early Christian movement. This insertion not only highlights the importance of the mission to the Gentiles but also points to the unity of Luke's two volumes through this scriptural citation. The history of the early church therefore becomes an extension of the ministry of Jesus himself.

B. Isa. 40:3–5 in Context. The length of this Isaianic quotation points to the significance of its wider context for the narrative of Luke. Isaiah 40:1–11 serves as the prologue to Isa. 40–55, and together with 55:1–13 it provides unity to the diverse themes developed in the intervening chapters. Although Isa. 40–55 has often been understood as quite distinct from the pessimistic tone of Isa. 1–39, Isa. 40–55 should be seen as the announcement of the ultimate fulfillment of the salvific message that has already been hinted at earlier (e.g., Isa. 2:1–4; 4:2–6; 32:15–20). Isaiah 40:1–11 consists of four subsections (vv. 1–2, 3–5, 6–8, 9–11) that provide an introduction to the themes of Isa. 40–55 (see Westermann 1969: 32–46; Kratz 1993). Isaiah 40:1–2 begins with the language of consolation in portraying the arrival of God's deliverance. This note of consolation embodies the promise to restore God's people (cf. 51:3; 52:9). Isaiah 40:3–5 functions as a response to 40:1–2 in its calls for the transformation of the wilderness in the preparation for the Lord's return. The speaker seems to be the prophet himself, although direct discourse from his mouth is unusual in Isaiah. The universalistic note in 40:5 forms the "centerpiece" of this prologue (see Freedman

1987: 160), as it paves the way for the distinct Isaianic universal vision (cf. 42:4, 10–13; 49:6; 51:4–6; 52:10). Isaiah 40:6–8 focuses on the power of the word of God (cf. 45:23; 55:10–11) in contrast with the frailty of the nations and their "idols" (40:18–20; 41:5–7; 44:9–20; 46:5–7). The conclusion of this prologue (40:9–11) again focuses on the restoration of God's people while highlighting the place of Jerusalem/Zion in the fulfillment of the eschatological program.

As a prologue to Isa. 40–55, this passage also introduces the second-exodus program. The "way" (*derek*) motif (40:3) in particular evokes the "way" through which God delivers his people from Egypt (cf. Exod. 13:21–22; 23:20; Isa. 43:16–19; 44:26–27; 52:10). The fact that this "way" signifies the salvific act of God on behalf of his people is further explicated by the fact that this "way" is prepared for both God (40:3) and his people (42:16; 43:16–19; 49:11–12). As in the first exodus, this new exodus will reveal the glory of God (40:5; cf. 52:7–12). As an eschatological event, this new exodus also symbolizes a new creative act of God (40:12–31; 42:5; 44:24; 45:9–18; 48:12–13; 51:12–16) whereby the national story is transformed into a cosmological one. It is precisely within this cosmological vision that "all people" will be able to witness God's mighty acts in history (40:5; cf. 49:6).

C. Isa. 40:3–5 in Judaism. This section within the prologue has a long history in Jewish exegetical traditions (see Snodgrass 1980; Bascom 1988: 221–46; Davis 1996: 61–102). Already in the LXX the phrase *to sōtērion tou theou* ("the salvation of God") had been inserted in 40:5 to define further the object of the sight of all people. This might have served to establish this text as an icon signifying the coming salvation of God. Within the OT, Mal. 3:1 provides an interpretation of Isa. 40:3 in an explicit eschatological context (cf. Mal. 3:2). Instead of the joyous tone of Isa. 40:3, the element of judgment is present in this Malachi passage, which moves away from a reference to the physical return of the exiles from Babylon.

The expectation of the literal return of the exiles survives in references to Isa. 40:3 in postbiblical material (e.g., Bar. 5:6–9; *Pss. Sol.* 11:4, 6). With such uses, one also finds the ironic use of Isa. 40:3 where Pompey becomes the one whose arrival the people are anticipating (*Pss. Sol.* 8:17).

The eschatological reading of Isa. 40:3–5 dominates in apocalyptic literature (*T. Mos.* 10:1; *1 En.* 1:6–7), but it is found also in rabbinic literature (e.g., *Pesiq. Rab.* 20.30A). This eschatological interpretation finds its concrete manifestation in the Qumran documents where a separate eschatological community is envisioned. Isaiah 40:3 is explicitly noted in 1QS VIII, 13–16; IX, 16–21; 4Q176. More importantly, the self-designation *derek* ("Way") appears in various contexts (1QS IX, 9, 16–21; X, 21; 1QH[a] IX, 36) and apparently is derived from an eschatological reading of Isa. 40:3. The wilderness locality further reflects this connection with the Isaianic passage (see Charlesworth 1997). Finally, the composite quotation of Isa. 40:3 together with Exod. 23:20 and Mal. 3:1 in Mark 1:2–3 provides the programmatic statement for the eschatological new-exodus program for the entire Gospel (see R. E. Watts 1997: 96–121). The mediation of Mark in Luke's use of this Isaianic quotation cannot be doubted, although the striking extension of this quotation highlights the unique role that it plays in Luke's two-volume work.

D. Textual Matters. Luke follows the LXX over against the MT, and this is reflected in his preference for the reading *phōnē boōntos en tē erēmō* ("a voice crying in the wilderness") rather than having "in the desert" modifying "prepare," although the LXX reading may reflect an earlier Hebrew tradition, especially in light of significant agreements between the LXX and 1QIsa[a] against the MT's text of Isaiah (see Gundry 1967: 10). Luke's dependence on the LXX is also reflected in the omission of the MT's *bā'ǎrābâ* ("in the desert") in 40:3b and in the insertion of the phrase *to sōtērion tou theou* ("the salvation of God") in 40:5. Four changes from the LXX, however, can be identified. First, as in Mark and Matthew's citation, Luke has *autou* ("his") instead of *tou theou hēmōn* ("our God"). This change probably is an attempt to apply the passage to Jesus himself. Second, Luke omits *panta* ("all") before *ta skolia* ("the crooked"), but the omission is found also in certain LXX traditions (A, V). Since the MT does not contain the equivalent of *panta*, these LXX traditions (perhaps even Luke himself) may have attempted to conform to the Hebrew reading. The third change is similar in this respect, as Luke uses the plural *hai tracheiai* ("the rough ways") instead of the LXX's singular *hē tracheia* ("the rough way"). The plural is also attested in some LXX traditions that attempt to conform to the Hebrew text (see Ziegler 1983: 267). Finally, Luke omits *kai ophthēsetai hē doxa kyriou* ("and the glory of the LORD shall appear") of Isa. 40:5. The omission may be due to the presence of a similar phrase that contains a central idea in Luke's writings: *kai opsetai pasa sarx to sōtērion tou theou* ("and all flesh shall see the salvation of God"). In any case, the omission is not theologically significant.

E. The Use of Isa. 40:3–5 in Luke 3:4–6. The appearance of this quotation is anticipated by Luke 2:30, where one finds the neuter *sōtērion* ("salvation") in Simeon's statement: *eidon hoi ophthalmoi mou to sōtērion sou* ("my eyes have seen your salvation"). The appearance of *paraklēsis* in 2:25 and the concept of "preparation" found in 1:17, 76 also pave the way for this block quotation. These earlier references to the prologue of Isa. 40:1–11 challenge the reading of this Isaianic quotation simply as a "prooftext" that is tied solely to the ministry of John the Baptist. The importance of this citation beyond its immediate context is also reflected in its deviation from the Markan usage. In Mark 1:2 the Isaianic quotation is preceded by a quotation of Mal. 3:1. Luke's (and probably Q's) separation of the two, by moving this quotation to Luke 7:27, encourages one to look beyond John the Baptist for the significance of this Isaianic text.

As noted above, this quotation serves to connect the ministry of the apostles with that of Jesus. The themes introduced in the prologue of Isa. 40:1–11 contribute to the structure of Luke's theology: restoration of Israel, mission to the Gentiles, power of the word of God, and the frailty of the enemies of God's people (see Pao 2000: 111–249). This quotation, appearing at the very beginning of Jesus' ministry, therefore serves as the hermeneutical framework within which the ministry and significance of Jesus' ministry can be understood. The connection between this quotation and Luke's second volume is further established by the verbal link between the *hodos* ("way") terminology in Isa. 40:3 and the designation of the early Christian movement as *hē hodos* ("the Way") in Acts 9:2; 19:9, 23; 22:4; 24:14, 22. This use of the "way" terminology as self-designation is found also in the Qumran literature, where the word *derek*, used as an identity marker (see discussion above), is also derived from Isa. 40:3.

Finally, the connection between this quotation and the one quoted at the end of the Lukan narrative (Isa. 6:9–10 in Acts 28:26–27) further sheds light on the significance of Luke's use of Isa. 40:3–5. In its wider context Isa. 40:1–11 is considered a "remarkable parallel to Isaiah 6:1–12" (Cross 1973: 188; cf. Fisher 1974). In both, one finds the cries of heavenly beings, the protest of weakness and unworthiness, a commissioning account, and the use of a vision metaphor. Moreover, both are pivotal for their respective sections of the book (Isa. 1–39; 40–55). The striking difference between the two is that whereas Isa. 6 announces the message of doom, Isa. 40 proclaims the arrival of God's salvation. In the Lukan writings, however, this judgment-salvation reversal has again been turned around. Whereas Luke 3 uses Isa. 40 to announce the arrival of God's salvation, Acts 28 ends the narrative on a pessimistic note with the citation of Isa. 6:9–10. The joyous note that all will "see" the salvation of God (Luke 3:6; Isa. 40:5) turns out to be a note of judgment for God's people, as "they have shut their eyes" (Acts 28:27; Isa. 6:10). The fact that the next occurrence of the neuter *sōtērion* ("salvation") after Luke 3:6 (Isa. 40:5) appears in Acts 28:28 further confirms that Isa. 40:3–5 is in Luke's mind as he concludes his work with yet another quotation from Isaiah. Accordingly, the intervening material in Luke-Acts has to be read in light of the dramatic tension created by the placement of these two Isaianic quotations.

F. Theological Use. In salvation-historical terms, this quotation links Jesus' ministry with the prophetic promises of Israel of the past and the apostolic ministry of the future. In its immediate context this quotation situates the ministry of John the Baptist within the unfolding plan of God. In the emphasis on the continuity with the past, the evocation of this Isaianic text also points to the realization of God's promise to accomplish a "new thing" in history (Isa. 43:19) as John prepares the people for the salvation that is brought about by the life and ministry of Jesus. In ecclesiological terms, this lengthy quotation ends with a note that "all flesh shall see the salvation of God" (Luke 3:6; cf. Isa. 40:5). With the arrival of the climax of God's covenantal relationship

with his people, Gentiles will be able to witness the salvation of God. Luke's second volume will make it clear that the Gentiles are not simply observers from a distance; rather, together with Israel they will become part of God's people. The theme of Gentile inclusion is accompanied by the portrayal of Israel's obduracy. As in the prophetic traditions of Israel, the note of judgment does not shut the door on Israel but serves as a call for Israel to repent.

3:7

The word *echidna* ("viper") does not appear in the LXX, but it does appear as a variant reading to *aspis* ("viper") in Isa. 59:5 (Aquila), a verse whose context is particularly important for this passage. While Isa. 59:5 mentions the evildoers hatching out "vipers," 3:7–8 describe their evil deeds with language reminiscent of Isa. 40:3: "The way [*hodon*] of peace they do not know, and there is no justice in their paths [*hodois*]. Their roads [*triboi*] they have made crooked; no one who walks in them knows peace" (59:8). The call to "prepare the way [*hodon*] of the LORD, make his paths [*tribous*] straight" (Luke 3:4; Isa. 40:3) is answered by the vipers who aim at destroying the work of God. The connection may have already appeared in Q (cf. Matt. 3:7), and the author of this source may be aware of this variant tradition.

Hē mellousē orgē ("the wrath to come") finds its roots in prophetic traditions (cf. Isa. 13:9; 30:27; Zeph. 2:2; see Creed 1930: 51). The manifestation of the wrath of God on those who oppose him is well illustrated in Mal. 3:2; 4:1, where one finds imagery of destructive fire. The relevance of these passages is affirmed in light of the significance of Mal. 3–4 for the portrayal of John the Baptist.

3:8

Abrahamic ancestry was frequently evoked in Judaism (cf. 2 Esd. 6:56–58; Josephus, *Ant.* 3.87–88; *Pss. Sol.* 9:9; *Jub.* 22:10–24; see Bock 1994–1996: 305). The mention of the "stones" (*lithōn*) may reflect pagan worship (cf. Acts 17:29; see Bovon 2002: 123), or it could be an Aramaic wordplay on *běnayyā'* ("children") and *'abnayyā'* ("stones") (see Creed 1930: 51). A clear OT parallel can be identified in Isa. 51, where Abraham is compared to the rock from which God's people are hewn (Lampe 1993: 130):

Look to the rock from which you were
  hewn,
  and to the quarry from which you were
  dug.
Look to Abraham your father
  and to Sarah who bore you;
for he was but one when I called him,
  but I blessed him and made him many.
    (51:1b–2)

This use of the "rock/stone" imagery with the figure of Abraham is unique in the OT. This Isaianic promise focuses on God's blessings on the descendants of Abraham, and the link between Abraham and the concept of "fruitfulness" is made explicit in the 1QIsaᵃ text of Isa. 51:2. A similar point is made with the use of the "rock/stone" imagery in *Tg. Neof.* Deut. 33:15, which speaks of the production of "good fruits by the merits of our fathers—who are like the rocks, Abraham, Isaac, and Jacob" (Allison 2000a: 104). In Luke (and Q) this imagery is strikingly used in a way to suggest that Abrahamic ancestry alone will not secure one's position among God's people.

3:9

In the OT Israel is frequently compared to a fruitless vine (Ps. 80:8; Isa. 5:2; Jer. 2:21; Ezek. 15:6; 17:6; 19:10; Hos. 10:1). Images of fire and judgment may again evoke Mal. 3–4, but the use of an ax in the act of destruction points specifically to Isa. 10:33–34, where the judgment of the Assyrians is announced. The judgment on Israel's enemies will fall upon those within God's people who refuse to repent. In Jewish traditions (*2 Bar.* 36–40; 4Q161 8–10; 4Q285 5) Isa. 10:33–34 receives a messianic interpretation and is connected with Isa. 11:1–5 (Bauckham 1995). The preaching of John may reflect an awareness of these traditions.

3:16

The description of the Messiah as the one who "comes" (*erchetai*) alludes to the eschatological figure of Mal. 3:1 ("he is coming," *erchetai*) and the royal messianic figure of Ps. 118:26 [117:26 LXX] ("Blessed is the one who comes in the name of the LORD," *eulogēmenos ho erchomenos en onomati kyriou*) (see Dunn 1994: 51). The adjective *ischyros* ("strong") has been applied to God (Deut. 10:17; Isa. 28:2), but the nominal *ischys* ("strength") also appears in Isa. 11:2, where the

spirit of counsel and strength" (*pneuma boulēs kai ischyos*) is promised to the coming royal figure.

The baptism "with the Holy Spirit and fire" (*en pneumati hagiō kai pyri*) should be regarded as referring to one baptism, as both terms are governed by one preposition (*en*, "with"), and the address is directed to one group (*hymas*, "you"). In the OT the Spirit (*rûaḥ/pneuma*) is associated with judgment (Isa. 4:4; 40:24; 41:16; Jer. 4:11–16; 23:19; 30:23; Ezek. 13:11–13), as is fire (Isa. 66:24; Joel 2:30; Mal. 4:1) (see Davies and Allison 1988–1997: 1:310–17). The combination of the symbols of spirit and fire with the imagery of water is found in Isa. 30:27–28, where one also finds the expectation of the discriminating judgment of God (Dunn 1994: 51). Together with Isa. 32:15, which informs other Lukan passages such as Luke 24:49; Acts 1:8; 3:19–20, these Isaianic oracles provide the language for John's message.

3:17

The presence of eschatological fire that will burn up the chaff in the context of the judgment of Israel brings to mind Mal. 4:1a: "See, the day is coming, burning like an oven, when all the arrogant and all evildoers will be stubble." The presence of this echo behind 3:17 is plausible in light of the portrayal of John the Baptist, which is couched in language reminiscent of the Elijah figure of Mal. 3–4 in 3:7–17 and elsewhere in Luke (1:17, 76; 7:27) (see Trumbower 1994). Nevertheless, the comparison of the judgment of the wicked to chaff burning in fire is not unique to Malachi (cf. Ps. 83:13–14; Isa. 29:5–6; Obad. 18; see Allison 2000a: 123), and our discussion above, especially on 3:16, has shown how various OT passages have also contributed to John's message. The reference to *pyri asbestō* ("unquenchable fire"), for example, finds its parallels in other passages where the punishment of the wicked is described: "for their worm shall not die, their fire shall not be quenched [*kai to pyr autōn ou sbesthēsetai*], and they shall be an abhorrence to all flesh" (Isa. 66:24b; cf. 34:8–10; Jer. 17:27).

3:21–22

On the assumption that Luke is using Mark in his account of Jesus' baptism (Nolland 1989–1993: 159–60; Lambrecht 1992), his departure from Mark here is striking. Instead of Mark's focus on Jesus' water baptism (Mark 1:9–11), Luke focuses on the opening of the heaven that leads to the descent of the Spirit and the deliverance of the heavenly voice. The actual water baptism of Jesus is relegated to the background by the adverbial participle *baptisthentos* ("when [Jesus] was baptized"). Unlike Mark's *eis auton* ("on him" [1:10]), in Luke the descent of the Spirit upon (*epi*) Jesus anticipates the citation of Isa. 61:1–2 ("the Spirit of the LORD is upon [*ep'*] me. . . .") in 4:18. This focus on the descent of the Spirit points to the arrival of the eschatological era, when the Spirit is with God's people (cf. Acts 2:17–21; Joel 2:28–32). Jesus' anointment by the Spirit provides further definition to the title "messiah" as it appeared in 2:11. Although anointment can be applied to prophetic and priest figures (see comments on 2:11), the portrayal of the future Davidic figure as one anointed by the Spirit should not be ignored: "A shoot shall come out from the stump of Jesse, and a branch shall grow out of his roots. The spirit of the LORD shall rest on [*ep'*] him" (Isa. 11:1–2a) (see Strauss 1995: 203). The repeated echoes of Isa. 11 (Luke 1:78; 2:40; 3:9, 16) encourage one to see a reference to Davidic messiahship behind Jesus' anointment by the Spirit.

The opening of heaven belongs to apocalyptic traditions with the focus being placed on the revelatory motif (cf. Ezek. 1:1; *2 Bar.* 22:2; *T. Levi* 2:6; John 1:51; Acts 7:56; 10:11; see Nolland 1989–1993: 160). Many scholars readily admit that the meaning behind the symbolism of the dove cannot be determined with any degree of certainty (see survey in Davies and Allison 1988–1997: 1:331–34). Noting the comparison between the deliverance of Noah and baptism in 1 Pet. 3:20–21, some have maintained that the dove sent out by Noah (Gen. 8:8–12) is behind this symbolism (see Dunn 1970: 27). More probable is the allusion to Gen. 1, where one finds the appearance of the Spirit as signaling the beginning of a new creative act of God. Allison (1992) has pointed to a possible parallel in the recently published *Messianic Vision Fragment* (I 6), where one finds a similar use of Gen. 1:2 in describing the eschatological future where the Spirit will hover over the saints.

Concerning the voice from heaven, a major textual variant needs to be noted. Instead of *sy ei ho huios mou ho agapētos, en soi eudokēsa* ("You are my Son, the Beloved; with you I am well pleased"),

some Western manuscripts and patristic witnesses (D it Ju [Cl] Meth Hil Aug) have the LXX text of Ps. 2:7: *huios mou ei sy, egō sēmeron gegennēka se* ("You are my son, today I have begotten you"). This Western reading has been adopted by some (e.g., Rese 1969: 193–96; Vigne 1992: 20–21) because the non-Western reading could be explained by its assimilation to the Markan source. A number of factors argue against this conclusion, however. First, this reading is supported by only one major Greek manuscript. Second, other similar examples of assimilation to the LXX can be identified in the Western text (e.g., Acts 7:37; 13:33). Third, composite citations are known to have been reduced to one OT text (see Bovon 2002: 129). Fourth, a harmonization with Matthew would be more likely than with Mark. Fifth, a later scribe might have harmonized this citation with the one in Acts 13:33.

Psalm 2:7 is likely to have contributed to the direct address and the words *sy ei huios mou* ("you are my Son"). Luke's awareness of this psalm is illustrated by the explicit quotation of its first two verses in the believers' prayer in Acts 4:25–26. In Paul's speech in Pisidian Antioch this verse of the psalm is also quoted together with several other texts of the Davidic traditions (Acts 13:32–37; cf. Ps. 2:7; Isa. 55:3; Ps. 16:10). This royal messianic text is also prepared for by passages in Luke 1–2, where one finds the anticipation of the promised Davidic figure (1:32–33, 68–79; 2:11). Moreover, the use of the term *huios* ("son") in a royal messianic sense can be detected also in 4:41; 9:35; 18:38–39; 20:41, 44 (cf. 8:28; 10:22; 22:70; Acts 9:20). Thus the "foundational" nature of Ps. 2:7 should be recognized (Rusam 2003: 168). This Lukan usage is fully established even when the messianic use of the title "Son of God" cannot be securely grounded in Second Temple Jewish traditions (Fitzmyer 1981–1985: 485; but cf. 4QFlor 1 I, 21, 2.10–14; 1Q28a II, 11–12; 4Q246; see Green 1997: 186).

The final clause of the quotation, *en soi eudokēsa* ("with you I am well pleased"), may allude to Isa. 42:1, although verbal parallels are not obvious: *prosedexato auton hē psychē mou* ("my soul has accepted him"). A number of Greek versions (Theodotion) resemble the MT in having *eudokēsa* ("pleased"), and the existence of different versions of this text is also evident in Matthew's quotation of Isa. 42:1–4 in 12:18–21 (see Gundry 1967: 110, 112–13). Nevertheless, one cannot rule out that Luke himself is aware of the Hebrew text: *rāṣĕtâ napĕšî* ("in whom my soul delights"). In any case, Luke's awareness of Isa. 42:1 is indicated by his redaction of Mark's *agapētos* ("beloved") into *eklelegmenos* ("chosen") in 9:35. The allusion to Isa. 42:1 fits well within the Lukan context here, which mentions the bestowal of the Spirit (3:22; cf. "I will put my Spirit upon him") with a view to the Gentiles (3:4–6, 8–9; cf. "he will bring forth justice to the nations"). Christologically, this allusion links the royal messianic status of Jesus with that of the Isaianic Servant of Yahweh as he participates in the unfolding of the eschatological program as indicated in 3:4–6. Moreover, this points forward to Jesus' Nazareth sermon (4:18–19), where the anointment of the Spirit is again explicated by two Isaianic passages (Isa. 58:6; 61:1–2).

What is unclear in this verse is the OT context behind the expression *ho agapētos* ("the Beloved"). In light of the fact that in 9:35 Luke changes Mark's *agapētos* to align with Isa. 42:1, the expression *ho agapētos* could be taken together with *en soi eudokēsa* as "a relatively free rendering of Isa. 42:1b altered to a second-person address" (M. Turner 1996: 198). This phrase could also be related to Ps. 2:7, in which case it is meant to modify *huios* ("son") and not be taken as a separate title (cf. Tg. to Ps. 2:7; see Marshall 1978: 146). For those who would look elsewhere for its OT context, Gen. 22:2, 12, 16, where the word *agapētos* is used, offer a possible parallel. More importantly, in *Jub.* 17:16, where one finds the use of the Isaac tradition, the formulation provides a close parallel for the entire verse: "Behold, Abraham loves Isaac, his son. And he is more pleased with him than everything" (see Stegner 1989: 19–20). Isaac typology may be working here, but the parallel is limited to the unique relationship between the father and his son. Moreover, this parallel is to be qualified by clear allusions to the expected Davidic and servant figure (*contra* Daly 1977; Stegner 1989: 28). Finally, some have pointed to Exod. 4:22–23 and thus the existence of Israel typology here (Bretscher 1968). Nevertheless, the use of *prōtotokos* instead of *agapētos* weakens the force of this parallel. Of the foregoing options, Gen. 22:2, 12, 16 provide clear verbal parallels, while

Isa. 42:1 itself may also be sufficient to explain this additional expression, especially with reference to the idea of election. With both, one finds the emphasis on the special relationship between Jesus and his Father. For the exact models through which Jesus is presented in this heavenly utterance, one has to be content with the clear allusions to the Davidic messianic and servant paradigms.

Luke 3:23–38

Our discussion of the use of the OT in Luke's genealogy of Jesus affects our understanding of this genealogy in various ways: its placement, form, source, and function within Luke's narrative. Unlike Matthew, who places Jesus' genealogy at the very beginning of his narrative (1:1–17), Luke places it between Jesus' baptism and his temptation. Luke may have followed Moses' genealogy in Exod. 6, where it appears after the account of his call in Exod. 3 (see Kurz 1993: 24). It is not necessary, however, to look beyond Luke to discern the reason for this specific placement of the genealogy. Since the genealogy immediately follows the heavenly voice that provides the identity of Jesus, the genealogy performs a similar function in pointing to Jesus' messianic status.

Although no particular genealogy in the OT can be identified as the model for Luke's genealogy, its length may point to its connection with its OT precedents (Aune 1987: 121). Comparable to Hellenistic genealogies, however, is its order, which starts with the main character, and its emphasis on divine ancestry (cf. Diogenes Laertius, *Life of Plato* 3.1–2; Plutarch, *Alex.* 2.1; see Johnson 1991: 72). This ordering is found also in biblical genealogies (cf. Ezra 7:1–5), and Jesus' divine ancestry is likewise an emphasis already found in Luke 1–2. Thus the form of Luke's style in this section can be attributed to "the function of the genealogy in this context, rather than an allegiance to the Hellenistic practice" (Lampe 1993: 138).

This genealogy may have drawn from the LXX rather than the MT because of the LXX form of many of the names and the lack of a Hebrew equivalent for the name *Kainan* ("Cainan") in 3:36 (cf. in the LXX: Gen. 10:24; 11:12; 1 Chron. 1:18 [A]). Many of the names are absent from the OT, both LXX and MT (Jannai [3:24], Esli [3:25], Semein [3:26], Josech [3:26], Rhesa [3:27], Cosam [3:28], Melea [3:31], Menna [3:31]), however, and therefore Luke perhaps had other sources for this genealogy. Some would argue that an existing genealogy is available to Luke (see Schürmann 1990–1994: 203; Fitzmyer 1981–1985: 491; Strauss 1995: 210–12), which would explain its difference from Matthew's genealogy (see the survey of solutions in Marshall 1978: 158–59). In this genealogy one can detect the presence of seventy-seven names grouped into groups of sevens, with notable figures such as Enoch, Abraham, David, and Joseph ending some of the groups. Luke's apparent ignorance of (or lack of emphasis on) this numbering further reflects his use of an existing genealogy (Marshall 1978: 160–61). Finally, the presence of non-LXX forms of some of the names (e.g., *Iōrim* [3:29], *Iōbēd* [3:32], *Kainam* [3:36–37]) further confirms this conclusion (see Bauckham 1991).

Several proposals have been offered to identify the function of Luke's genealogy. The reference all the way back to Adam may point to an Adam typology wherein Jesus is presented as the one who fulfills the intended destiny of the first Adam (Marshall 1978: 161), but an explicit Adam typology is not developed elsewhere in Luke. It could also point to the universal significance of Jesus' life and ministry (Schürmann 1990–1994: 1:202; Nolland 1989–1993: 173; Bock 1994–1996: 360). References to Abraham and David may also be important in light of Luke's narrative, but these names were not highlighted in the genealogy. Finally, the note on divine ancestry may be important (Fitzmyer 1981–1985: 498, 501; Johnson 1991: 72), but it is difficult to imagine Luke emphasizing Jesus' divinity through human mediation (see Marshall 1978: 161). In tracing the line from God through Adam all the way to Jesus, Luke may be indicating that Jesus' humanity (and therefore his universal significance) is at issue.

In the following discussion only names that are identifiable in the OT will be briefly noted.

3:27

Zerubbabel is the first person in the genealogy who can be clearly identified in the OT. He often is identified as the son of Shealtiel (Ezra 3:2, 8; 5:2; Neh. 12:1; Hag. 1:1, 12, 14; 2:2, 23; 1 Chron. 3:19 LXX) and therefore the grandson of King Jehoiachin. Zerubbabel served as the governor

of Jerusalem when some of the Jews returned in 538 BC.

3:31

Instead of tracing the line through Solomon the son of David, Luke (probably following his source) traces the line through Nathan the third son of David (3:31; cf. 2 Sam. 5:14; 1 Chron. 3:5; 14:4). This may be due to his knowledge of Jeremiah's prophecies against Jehoiakim (Jer. 36:30) and Jechoniah (Jer. 22:24–30) of the line of Solomon that their descendant will not inherit the throne of David (Strauss 1995: 215). Also plausible is the influence of a reading of Mic. 5:1–2 MT, where the promised ruler is to be derived from the line of David but not necessarily through the Davidic dynasty that follows (Böhler 1998). The exact rationale behind this shift remains unclear.

The mentioning of the name of David is significant, and its appearance immediately links this genealogy with the allusion to Ps. 2:7 in 3:22. The Lukan birth narrative has already pointed to Jesus' Davidic connection (1:32–33, 68–79; 2:11). Beginning with David, one finds OT parallels with the genealogy in 1 Chron. 1:34–2:15.

3:32

Jesse is the father of David, the Bethlehemite who belongs to the tribe of Judah (1 Sam. 16:1). Particularly important in this context is the Isaianic identification of the future messianic king as "from the stump of Jesse" (Isa. 11:1) and "the root of Jesse" (Isa. 11:10). Obed, Boaz, Sala (or Salmon), and Nahshon all appear in the genealogy in 1 Chron. 2:10–12.

3:33

Amminadab and Hezron appear in 1 Chron. 2:9–10, but the names that come between them in Luke 3:33 ("Admin" and "Arni") do not appear in 1 Chron. 2, although the name "Aram" that appears in some manuscripts (A D 33 565 1079) possibly appears in 1 Chron. 2:10 in the form of the Hebrew name Ram. The existence of "a bewildering variety of readings" (Metzger 1994: 113) renders the search for the original text quite difficult. Perez and Judah appear in 1 Chron. 2:4, and Judah is the fourth son of Jacob, whose name represents one of the twelve tribes of Israel (Gen. 35:23). A hint of the promised messiah who is to come from this tribe can be found already in Gen. 49:8–12.

3:34

Isaac, Jacob, and Abraham receive brief mention, but together they point to the Abrahamic covenant and the continuation of the Abrahamic line (cf. Gen. 50:24; Exod. 2:24; 6:8; Num. 32:11; Deut. 6:10; Jer. 33:26). Moving beyond Abraham, this genealogy draws on Gen. 5:1–32; 11:10–26; 1 Chron. 1:24–27. Terah is the father of Abraham (Gen. 11:26; 1 Chron. 1:26), and Nahor, Abraham's grandfather (Gen. 11:22–25; 1 Chron. 1:26).

3:35–38

The list from Serug to Arphaxad appears in the genealogies in Gen. 11 and 1 Chron. 1. Cainan (3:36) appears in the LXX of Gen. 11:12 and 1 Chron. 1:18 (A) without a Hebrew equivalent. The list from Shem (the eldest son of Noah) to Seth (the third son of Adam and Eve, but listed as the firstborn of Adam in Gen. 5:3–8; 1 Chron. 1:1) is found in the genealogies of Gen. 5 and 1 Chron. 1. The genealogy of Gen. 5 begins with this note in v. 1: "When God created man [*'ādām*], he made him in the likeness of God" (NIV). This may have contributed to Luke's description of Adam as *tou theou* ("the [son] of God"). An exact parallel to this description of Adam cannot be identified in Jewish traditions (cf. Philo, *Virtues* 37.204–205; see Bock 1994–1996: 360).

Luke 4:1–13

Three interweaving traditions can be identified in this account of Jesus' temptation: Israel's wilderness experience, Deut. 6–8, and Ps. 91:11–12 (90:11–12 LXX). Because of the interconnectedness of these elements, these citations will be considered together with the narrative framework in which they are placed.

A. NT Context: Jesus the Faithful Son. Luke's account of Jesus' temptation follows the baptismal narrative and the lengthy genealogy. Anointed with the Spirit (3:22), Jesus is now "full of the Holy Spirit" and "led by the Spirit in the wilderness" (4:1). After proving to be faithful to God, Jesus was again "filled with the power of the Spirit," and this focus on the Spirit leads directly

to the Isaianic quotation in 4:18–19 that explains the significance of Jesus' anointment. The issue of Jesus' status as the Son of God (3:22) resurfaces in this temptation account (4:3; cf. 3:38) when the content of this recognition is clarified through Jesus' refusal to yield to the plan of Satan. Its connection with the genealogy is evident also through Jesus' identification with Israel (and maybe even Adam) in his use of Scripture in this account. Situated in this context, this story is no longer one that is concerned with the private life of an individual.

The narrative introduction of this temptation account resembles Mark's summary statement (Mark 1:12–13): the temptation of Jesus in the wilderness for forty days. The conversation between Jesus and Satan is found only in Matthew and Luke. Many would conclude that Luke is using Q as his source, without ruling out the accessibility of Mark (Schürmann 1990–1994: 1:218–20). The apparently minor and theologically insignificant differences between Matthew and Luke may also point to the use of different versions of Q (see Bock 1994–1996: 365). On the assumption that they share the same source, the different ordering of the temptation events is noteworthy. Most would affirm that Matthew's order reflects the ordering in Q (Fitzmyer 1981–1985: 507–8; Nolland 1989–1993: 177) and that the redactional change in Luke is intended to make the temple scene the climax of the temptations. Others see Luke's redaction as highlighting Jesus' final statement in 4:12, which could provide a fitting conclusion for the series of challenges: "Do not put the Lord your God to the test" (see Goulder 1989: 1:294).

B. Deut. 6:13, 16; 8:3; Ps. 91:11–12 in Context. The three responses of Jesus come from Deut. 6–8. These chapters belong to the wider section that starts in 4:44, where one finds the stipulations of the covenant made between God and Israel his covenant partner. The opening section of Deut. 6–8, which focuses on the call to Israel to be faithful and obedient, contains the Shema: "Hear, O Israel: The LORD is our God, the LORD alone. You shall love the LORD your God with all your heart, and with all your soul, and with all your might" (6:4–5). The remaining material in this chapter is framed by references to the exodus events, in which God delivered his people from slavery (6:10–12, 20–25). Significantly, this section contains a note that mentions Israel's testing of God in the wilderness (6:16). Chapter 7 again focuses on God's faithfulness in the past and the promise of his continued love and mercy to those who are faithful to him. Chapter 8 points again to God's work among Israel and how God had disciplined his people as "a parent disciplines a child" (v. 5). This chapter continues the call to Israel to be faithful to their deliverer and concludes with a curse: "Like the nations that the LORD is destroying before you, so shall you perish, because you would not obey the voice of the LORD your God" (8:20). A cursory survey of this section shows that the call to be God's faithful partner is grounded in their interaction during the exodus event: while the exodus experience reminds one of God's faithfulness, it also points to Israel's disobedience. Echoes of the book of Exodus in particular confirm this observation (13:9–16 [Deut. 6:6, 20–21]; 16:1–36 [Deut. 8:3]; 17:1–7 [Deut. 6:16; 8:15]; 23:20–33 [Deut. 7:12–26]).

The chapters that follow also highlight the theme of faithfulness (or the lack of it) within the context structured by the exodus events. Chapters 9–10, which echo the narrative about the golden calf in Exod. 32–34, provide the prime example of Israel's disobedience. Themes of apostasy, self-sufficiency, and disobedience found in the preceding material (see McConville 2002: 173) crystallize in this narrative when forgetfulness expresses itself in acts of idolatry. Situated within this wider context, the individual verses that Jesus cites draw on the force of this entire section. Jesus' response to Satan's first temptation comes from Deut. 8:3 (Luke 4:4), a verse that points to complete reliance on God and his promises. The responses to the second and third temptations are drawn from the same section in Deut. 6 where the Shema is explicated. The call to worship and serve YHWH alone (6:13; Luke 4:8) becomes Jesus' response to the temptation to receive "the kingdoms of the world" (Luke 4:5) from the hands of Satan, and Israel's testing of God at Massah/Meribah (6:16; Luke 4:12) is evoked in Jesus' rebuke of Satan for his testing of God. The account to which Deut. 6:16 is alluding ends with the question that the Israelites raised in their testing of God: "Is the LORD among us or not?" (Exod. 17:7). It is this questioning of the sovereignty of God and his Messiah that is at the heart of Satan's three attempts to challenge Jesus.

Psalm 91 (90 LXX), the psalm that Satan uses in his third temptation in Luke, is called in the LXX "Praise, a Song of David" (*ainos ōdēs tō Dauid*), although its connection to David is not obvious. This psalm serves as a response to Ps. 90, which begins with the affirmation of God as "our dwelling place in all generations" (v. 1) and ends with a call for God's protection and presence: "Let the favor of the LORD our God be upon us" (v. 17). Using traditional language, Ps. 91 affirms God's protection by calling him "my refuge" (*maḥĕsî* [v. 2; cf. 14:6; 46:1; 62:7–8; 71:7; 142:5]) and stating that his people will be found under "his wings" (*kĕnāpāyw* [v. 4; cf. 17:8; 36:7; 57:1; 61:4; 63:7]). The concluding divine oracle likewise focuses on the assurance of divine protection: "Those who love me I will deliver; I will protect those who know my name" (91:14). Many would see this as a liturgical psalm that anticipates God's protection in the temple worship (Tate 1990: 450–51), and it is this theme of protection that emerges in Satan's testing of Jesus (91:11–12; Luke 4:10–11).

As in Deut. 6–8, the exodus journey may have also provided the context for this psalm (Mitchell 1997: 277–78). The "thousand" who "fall at your side" (91:7) may be an allusion to the generation that died in the desert, and the promise of protection from the dashing of one's foot "against a stone" (91:12) and from "the lion and the adder" (91:13) may likewise assume a wilderness environment. Parallels with Deut. 32, a passage that is closely tied with Deut. 8 in particular, further strengthen this connection. References to "pinions" (*'ebrâ*) and "wings" (*kĕnāpāyw*) in the same context are found only in Ps. 91:4 and Deut. 32:11. Divine protection against "pestilence/destruction" (*qeṭeb*) in Ps. 91:6 also echoes the "pestilence/destruction" of Deut. 32:24. Finally, the "punishment/vengeance" (*šillūmâ*) that the wicked will go through in Ps. 91:8 is also the fate of those in Deut. 32:35, 41 (*šillēm*). If the wilderness setting of this psalm is established, then Satan's use of Ps. 91 in the context of Jesus' use of Deut. 6–8 in the wilderness setting becomes all the more significant.

C. Deut. 6:13, 16; 8:3; Ps. 91:11–12 in Judaism. The significance of Deut. 6:4–9, with its focus on the worship of one God, finds its echoes throughout the later writings (cf. Deut. 32:39; 2 Sam. 7:22; 1 Chron. 17:20; Ps. 86:10; Isa. 43:10; 44:6; 45:18), and this focus of the section dominates later Jewish traditions especially when the Shema is recited (cf. Josephus, *Ant.* 4.13; *m. Ber.* 2:2; *m. Meg.* 4:3; *m. Tamid* 5:1). Deuteronomy 6:13 continues with this theme and is evoked when the worship of the one God is noted (cf. *Apoc. Adam* 1:12; Philo, *Alleg. Interp.* 3.208). Deuteronomy 8:3 evokes another set of concerns, where the contrast between bread and the word of God can be found. Although the text in its context focuses on the contrast between self-reliance and total dependence on God, it often is evoked to highlight the contrast between material and spiritual nourishment. This is best illustrated in the writings of Philo where, on the basis of this verse, one is called to flee one's passion (*Alleg. Interp.* 3.174) and to seek divine laws (*Decalogue* 13), wisdom (*Prelim. Studies.* 170–173), and spiritual nourishment (*Alleg. Interp.* 3.176).

Deuteronomy 6:16 deserves special treatment because it explicitly highlights the prohibition against testing God. This verse alludes to Exod. 17:1–7 (cf. Num. 20:1–13), where one finds the narrative that gave rise to the legend of the well that follows Israel in the wilderness (cf. *L.A.B.* 10:7; 11:15; *Num. Rab.* 19:26; *Tg. Ps.-J.* Num. 21; *t. Sukkah* 3.11–13; cf. 1 Cor. 10:4; see Ellis 1981: 67–68). It is the negative tradition of Israel's distrusting their God, however, that contributes to the understanding of Luke 4. Israel's testing of their deliverer at Massah/Meribah becomes one of the prime examples of disobedience in the wilderness in the later narrative in Deuteronomy (9:22; 32:51; 33:8) and beyond (Ps. 81:7; 95:8; 106:32; cf. Ps. 78:56). This narrative also contributes to the tradition of Israel's murmuring, which extends beyond the canonical text (cf. CD-A III, 8; Philo, *Moses* 1.181; *T. Mos.* 7:7; *4 Ezra* 1:15–16; see Bauckham 1983: 98). Thus the evocation of Deut. 6:16 in Luke 4 points beyond one historical event to Israel's long history of being an unfaithful partner to their God.

Moving to Ps. 91, we see that the theme of divine protection in the wilderness context continues in the Jewish traditions where the foundation story of Israel is transformed into one in which the personal protection against demons becomes

the focus of Jewish exegetical traditions (Hugger 1971: 331–33; van der Ploeg 1971: 128–39; Mitchell 1997: 279–81). Already in the LXX the protection from noonday (sunshine) is interpreted as protection from *daimoniou mesēmbrinou* ("noonday demon" [91:6]), and similar interpretive renderings of this verse can be found in the Peshitta and the Targum (Allison 2000a: 159). In 11Q11, with three other noncanonical psalms, Ps. 91 is understood as a text to be used in exorcistic liturgy. The allusion to this psalm later in Luke 10:19, where Jesus empowers his apostles to subdue the evil powers, fits well within this interpretive tradition. Thus the use of this psalm by Satan in the temptation narrative is striking because the divine power offered to Jesus is actually one to be used against the evil one.

D. Textual Matters. The first quotation of the temptation narrative, in Luke 4:4, is taken verbatim from Deut. 8:3 LXX, which faithfully renders the Hebrew text, and it is identical to Matthew's quotation, which includes the clause *all' epi panti rhēmati ekporeuomenō dia stomatos theou* ("but by every word that comes from the mouth of God" [Matt. 4:4]). This clause is included also in some manuscripts of Luke 4:4, but they are likely secondary, reflecting an attempt to assimilate to the Matthean or septuagintal reading (Holtz 1968: 61; Metzger 1994: 113). The second quotation, in Luke 4:8, is identical to Matthew's reading (4:10), and they are identical to LXX A of Deut. 6:13, while LXX B (which reflects the Hebrew of the MT) has *phobēthēsē* ("fear") instead of *proskynēseis* ("worship"), and the word *monō* ("only") is omitted. T. Holtz (1968: 62–63) argues for Q's use of LXX A, but others (e.g., New 1993: 58; Kimball 1994b: 85–86) see the reading in LXX A as an assimilation to Q or the NT text. Either influenced by LXX A or as an intentional redactional move, the use of the verb *proskyneō* ("worship") in 4:8 corresponds to Satan's use of the same verb in 4:7. Jesus' third quotation, in Luke 4:12, is identical to both Matt. 4:7 and Deut. 6:16 LXX, which has a singular *ouk ekpeiraseis* ("do not test") rather than the plural *lō těnassû* ("do not test") of the MT.

Satan's quotation in Luke 4:10–11 is identical to Ps. 90:11–12 LXX (which accurately translates Ps. 91:11–12 MT) but omits the phrase *en pasais tais hodois sou* ("in all your ways"). Luke's citation is identical to Matt. 4:6, although Matthew's citation is further abbreviated by the omission of the words *tou diaphylaxai se* ("to protect you"). If these words were not in Q, their inclusion may reflect Luke's attempt to include them to complete the verb *enteleitai* ("he will command") (see New 1993: 56).

E. The Use of Deut. 6:13, 16; 8:3; Ps. 91:11–12 in Luke 3:4–6. Before examining the role of the citations in Luke 3, we should explore both the setting and the combination of the three "tests" in light of the exodus context as evoked by the explicit quotations themselves. It has been noted that the temptation narrative is framed by allusions to Israel's wilderness experience (see Gerhardsson 1966: 42–44). The reference to "forty days" may evoke Israel's forty-year journey (cf. Exod. 16:35; Num. 32:13; Deut. 2:7; Josh. 5:6; Neh. 9:21; Ps. 95:10; Amos 2:10), as "forty days" has already come to symbolize the forty-year journey in the OT, especially when the temporal reference applies to an individual rather than a nation (cf., e.g., Num. 14:34; Ezek. 4:5–6; see Gibson 1995: 83; Allison 2000a: 26). Luke's interest in Israel's forty-year wilderness wanderings is reflected in its reference in Acts 7:30, 36, 42; 13:18. Closer to Deut. 6–8, one also finds reference to Moses' forty-day fast on Mount Horeb: "I remained on the mountain forty days and forty nights; I neither ate bread nor drank water" (Deut. 9:9 [see also Exod. 34:28]; cf. Matt. 4:2: "forty days and forty nights"). These references make it unlikely that "forty" is simply used as "a round figure" (cf. Gen. 7:4, 12; 1 Kings 19:8; see Creed 1930: 62).

Equally important is the "wilderness" (*erēmos*) setting of Jesus' temptation. In the OT the wilderness journey brings to mind divine revelation as well as Israel's disobedience, but S. Talmon (1993: 236) has shown that the motif of disobedience and punishment dominates the later references to the wilderness period (with the clear exception of Isa. 40–55). It is this aspect of the wilderness motif that is critical to this temptation narrative, as the disobedience of Israel is evoked to highlight the perfect obedience of Jesus as God's faithful Son. The numerous details that reflect the wilderness context therefore acquire added significance (Dupont 1957). The "wilderness" is closely tied with the symbol "forty" in the memory of Israel (cf. Num. 32:13; Deut. 2:7; 29:5; Neh. 9:21; Amos 5:25), and the phrase "forty years in

the wilderness" appears in a context resembling that in which the quotation of Luke 4:4 appears: "Remember the long way that the LORD your God has led you these forty years in the wilderness, in order to humble you, testing you to know what was in your heart, whether or not you would keep his commandments" (Deut. 8:2). These textual indicators lead the reader to see the testing of Jesus in light of the testing of Israel in the wilderness journey.

Not only does the setting evoke memories of the history of Israel, but also the three "temptations" may reflect Jewish interpretive traditions. In the psalms one already finds a listing of Israel's disobedient acts in the wilderness. In Ps. 106, for example, there are references to the sin of "wanton craving" (vv. 14–15; cf. Exod. 16:1–12; Num. 11:1–6), idolatry (vv. 19–23; cf. Exod. 32:1–15), and the "testing" of God at Massah/Meribah (vv. 32–33; cf. Exod. 17:1–7; Num. 20:1–13). These traditions seem to lie behind Jesus' three temptations, as they involve the craving of food, worshiping of a false god, and testing of God. Moreover, in Jewish traditions one can also find the listing of three particular sins to characterize Israel's disobedience in the wilderness, although the sins listed may not be the same in the different lists (cf. *Tg. Neof.*; *Frg. Tg.*; *Deut. Rab.* 1:2; see Stegner 1990: 14).

In light of the allusions to the OT behind the various elements of this narrative, the point of the entire narrative is clear: unlike the Israelites who failed in the wilderness, Jesus is the faithful Son of God. Therefore, the three individual citations from Deut. 6–8 should be read together as establishing this point. With the first temptation, Jesus quotes from Deut. 8:3 to point to his total reliance on God. With the second, Jesus reaffirms the central point of Deut. 6, which emphasizes the need to worship God only. With the third, the use of Deut. 6:16 makes it clear that the point is the refusal to force God to provide a sign of his presence, since God is the one to be trusted. In all three, then, the focus is on the faithful obedience to the one God of Israel. In their context, however, all three temptations also point to the nature of Jesus' messianic ministry. The use of divine power, the means to accomplish the plan of God, and the way the dawn of the eschatological era is to be manifested are issues that this narrative introduces, and they will be further developed in Luke's narrative.

Most would agree that the missing phrase "in all your ways" should not be considered as the key to Satan's use of Ps. 91:11–12 (see Bock 1994–1996: 381; Bovon 2002: 144). On a rhetorical level, it is ironic to have Satan using a psalm that had been understood as an excorcistic text (Allison 2000a: 159). In light of the wilderness context of this psalm, one also can see how Satan is using Scripture to tempt Jesus to test the presence of God as Israel did in the times of old. The possible connection between the *pterygion* ("pinnacle" [Luke 4:9]) of the temple and the *pterygas* ("wings" [Ps. 90:4 LXX]) of God's protection further confirms this point, as it is the way that God's presence is to be experienced that is at issue (Brawley 1992: 428–29).

F. Theological Use. With the use of Scripture, an Israel typology is clearly developed. Unlike Israel, which failed in the wilderness, Jesus has proven to be the faithful Son of God. In Luke's narrative the story of Israel's failure continues to be documented in accounts of their refusal to respond to the gospel (cf. Acts 13:46; 18:6; 28:28), and this failure is explicitly linked with Israel's rebellious acts in the wilderness (cf. Acts 7:35–42, 51–53). In ecclesiological terms, Jesus also "fulfills" the destiny of Israel as he accomplishes what Israel was called to perform as God's son (cf. Deut. 8:5). When the foundation story of Israel is evoked, Jesus does not simply embody Israel, but rather becomes the foundation of God's people in the eschatological era. As he did in the past, God is once again calling a "people [*laon*] for his name" (Acts 15:14).

Building on the significance of the wilderness context, some have further argued for a Mosaic Christology behind this text. This view would be strengthened if the use of Deut. 34:1–4 could be established in Luke's account of Jesus' second temptation when the devil "showed him in an instant all the kingdoms of the world" (4:5) (see Stegner 1990: 9). Luke's further portrayal of Jesus as the prophet like Moses (Acts 3:22; 7:37) would also be consistent with this view. Nevertheless, it is difficult to see how Deut. 34:1–4 contributes to the main point of the second temptation. More importantly, the focus throughout the narrative is on Jesus as the true Israel, and there is no explicit

attempt to portray Jesus as the new Moses in this account.

Equally questionable is the presence of an explicit Adam typology in this text (see Schürmann 1990–1994: 1:214). Although the testing of Adam in the Garden of Eden would provide an attractive parallel, the use of Deut. 6–8 strongly links this testing with Israel's wilderness experience. Nevertheless, Luke's genealogy, which ends with Adam as the son of God immediately before the temptation narrative, argues for the presence of thematic links on some levels, and clearly the creation story often was linked with the exodus story (cf. Exod. 15; Deut. 32:7–14; Ps. 74:12–17; 77:12–20; 89:5–37; 114), especially when the new creative act of God is expected (cf. Isa. 43:15–21; 45:9–18; 51:12–16).

Luke 4:18–19

A. NT Context: Definition of Jesus' Ministry. The Nazareth sermon scene follows the introduction of Jesus' identity through the heavenly voice in the baptismal scene, his genealogy, and his temptation in the wilderness. This passage continues to clarify the significance of Jesus' ministry by situating it within its wider context in salvation history. As in Luke 3:4–6, Jesus' ministry is further explicated by a block quotation from the text of Isaiah (see Pao 2000: 70–84). Some commentators (see Miesner 1978: 223–24; Tiede 1980: 103–7) have pointed to a chiastic structure in Luke 4:16–21: the synagogue setting (4:16, 20), Jesus' standing and sitting down (4:16, 20), Jesus' being given the book (4:17, 20), and the opening and closing of the book (4:17, 20). At the center is the reading of Isa. 61:1–2; 58:6.

Following Bultmann (1963: 31–32, 386–87), many identify Mark as the source for this Lukan scene. Both accounts contain a question concerning Jesus' origin and a proverb within a Nazareth synagogue setting. Beyond this framework, however, much of the material in Luke is without Markan parallel. Some have pointed to the use of Q (Tuckett 1982: 347–48), but the availability of other traditional material cannot be ruled out (Chilton 1981: 164). The source-critical question should not be allowed to undermine Luke's role in highlighting the programmatic nature of this scene for his story of Jesus and his apostles.

B. Isa. 61:1–2; 58:6 in Context. Isaiah 61 begins with a renewed focus on the prophet and his message. The good news announced in Isa. 61 is anticipated by the message in chapters 58–60, where the call to repentance accompanies the promise of God's salvation. Chapter 61 stands out, however, in that the proclamation is to be performed by an individual who receives the special anointment of the Spirit. This individual has parallels in the servant figure of Isa. 40–55. The anointment of the Spirit recalls 42:1, and his being "sent" by the Lord with his Spirit points back to 48:16. The description of the mission of the prophet of Isa. 61:1–2 also reflects the first Servant Song, in which the servant is sent "to open the eyes that are blind, to bring out the prisoners from the dungeon" (42:7). Moreover, the idea of "the year of the LORD's favor" (61:2) parallels the "time of favor" of 49:8. Thus Beuken (1989) is correct in understanding Isa. 61 as an "interpretation" of Isa. 40–55.

This context also contributes to our understanding of the specific goals of the prophet's ministry: to bring good news to the poor, to proclaim release to the captives, to restore sight to the blind, and to proclaim the year of the Lord's favor. In light of Isa. 40–55, these individual elements point to the same reality: the reversal of the fortunes of God's oppressed people (see M. Turner 1996: 250). Metaphors from the economic, political, physical, and social realms were used to express the expectation of the total reversal of the fate of Israel with the arrival of the eschatological era. Isa. 61:1–2, therefore, does not provide a detailed agenda of the prophet's ministry; it does echo Isa. 40:1–11 in proclaiming consolation to Israel when God lifts up his humiliated people.

Isaiah 58:6 should likewise be understood within this wider context where the infinitive clause "to set the oppressed free" contributes to the constellation of metaphors in describing the good news. As in Isa. 40–55, where the justice of God is to be manifested (cf. 51:1–6), God's people are also called to act justly in Isa. 58. Although Israel may be able to perform certain religious rituals, the prophet here points to the way in which the righteousness of God can be acted out (58:6–9). Read together with Isa. 61:1–2, the call to Israel "to set the oppressed free" in 58:6 becomes the promise of the anointed prophet who points to the realization of Israel's call.

C. Isa. 61:1–2; 58:6 in Judaism. Isaiah 61 plays an important role in the Qumran documents. There are texts where Isa. 61:1–2 is used to refer to the prophets within the community (cf. CD-A II, 12; XIII, 10; 1QM XI, 7; see Nolland 1989–1993: 196), but other texts point to the eschatological understanding of these verses. In 11Q13 phrases from Isa. 61:1–2 are linked with Lev. 25:13; Deut. 15:2; Ps. 7:8–9; 82:1–2; Isa. 52:7 to portray the expectation of the eschatological Jubilee (M. P. Miller 1969; J. A. Sanders 1975: 85). Other texts, such as 4Q521, reflect a similar eschatological reading of Isa. 61 without connecting it with the Jubilee setting of Lev. 25 (Collins [1997] further suggests that 4Q521 reflects a nonsectarian reading of Isa. 61). Thus the Jubilee setting is not necessarily tied to an eschatological interpretation of Isa. 61:1–2 (cf. *Midr. Lam.* 3:50 [73a]; *Tg. Ps.-J.* Num. 25:12; see J. A. Sanders 1975: 86–88).

The prophetic nature of the text is affirmed by the Targum of Isa. 61:1–2, where the speaker is explicitly identified as the prophet. This is consistent with the portrayal of Isaiah in *Lev. Rab.* 10:2, where the themes from Isa. 40–55 are combined with that of Isa. 61:1–2 in the explication of the mission of the anointed prophet (Crockett 1966b: 276). The messianic use of the text also appears in 4Q521, where one finds a similar combination of Isa. 61:1–2 and 58:6 in depicting the ministry of the "Messiah" (cf. CD-A XIII). This paves the way for Jesus' combination of the two texts in describing his prophetic and messianic role.

D. Textual Matters. This quotation (Isa. 61:1–2 with 58:6) is likely to have been drawn from the LXX, which accurately reflects the sense of the MT except for the infinitive clause *liqrō'… wĕla'ăsûrîm pĕqaḥ-qôaḥ* ("to proclaim…release for the prisoners"), which was translated as *kēryxai… typhlois anablepsin* ("to proclaim … sight to the blind ones"). The interchangeability of these ideas may support the interpretation of these infinitive clauses that use different metaphors to refer to the same reality: the reversal of the fortune of Israel. In any case, the exact sense of the Hebrew text is uncertain, and the LXX may have provided a legitimate rendering of the clause (see Kimball 1994b: 100).

Luke's quotation follows the LXX, with four changes: (1) the clause *iasasthai tous syntetrimmenous tē kardia* ("to heal the brokenhearted" [Isa. 61:1c]) is omitted; (2) a clause from Isa. 58:6 is inserted in Luke 4:18: *aposteilai tethrausmenous en aphesei* ("to let the oppressed go free"), and the LXX of Isa. 58:6 has *apostelle* instead of *aposteilai*; (3) Luke 4:19 has *kēruxai* ("to proclaim") instead of *kalesai* ("to declare") of Isa. 61:2; and (4) the Isaianic quotation in Luke 4:19 stops with the phrase *eniauton kyriou dekton* ("a year of the Lord's favor") without including the final part of Isa. 61:2.

The inclusion of the clause *iasasthai tous syntetrimmenous tē kardia* ("to heal the brokenhearted" [Isa. 61:1c]) in the Lukan citation in some manuscripts (e.g., A Θ Ψ 0102 f^1 𝔐) seems to be an attempt to assimilate the quotation with the LXX reading. Its omission can be attributed to Luke's use of a traditional source (Chilton 1984: 181) or to his use of a defective copy of Isaiah (Holtz 1968: 125). Rese's (1969: 145) suggestion that Luke intentionally leaves out the phrase to avoid emphasizing the healing ministry of Jesus is unlikely in light of the Lukan context (4:23, 27). One can only tentatively conclude that the omission is not theologically motivated.

The inclusion of a phrase from Isa. 58:6 may be motivated by the presence of *aphesis* ("release") in both Isa. 58:6 and 61:1 (Koet 1989: 30). This would serve as an example of what is later known as *gezerah shavah*. The significance of *aphesis* in the sense of "forgiveness" in Luke's writings (Luke 1:77; 3:3; 24:47; Acts 2:38; 5:31; 10:43; 13:38; 26:18) supports this reading. It should be noted, however, that Isa. 61:1 and 58:6 are already connected in documents such as 4Q521 (see above). F. Bovon (2002: 153) has further pointed to the connection between Isa. 57:15–58:14 and 61:1–11 in texts associated with the celebration of Yom Kippur.

Luke's use of *kēryxai* ("to proclaim") instead of *kalesai* ("to declare") may again reflect the significance of the term *kēryssō* in Luke's vocabulary (cf. Luke 3:3; 4:44; 8:1, 39; 9:2; 12:3; 24:47; Acts 8:5; 9:20; 10:37, 42; 15:21; 19:13; 20:25; 28:31). Although Luke may be following the MT here, the semantic fields of these two Greek words are too close to establish this point.

Finally, the omission of Isa. 61:2b probably is motivated by Luke's intention to highlight *dekton* ("favor") as the final word of his scriptural quotation. This is confirmed by the function of *dektos* in the discussion that follows (4:24). The suggestion (Fitzmyer 1981–1985: 533) that 61:2b is omitted because Luke wanted to downplay the theme of judgment is unlikely in light of its appearance already in 2:34–35; 3:7–17.

E. The Use of Isa. 61:1–2; 58:6 in Luke 4:18–19. The significance of the Nazareth synagogue scene is indicated by Luke's placement of it at the beginning of Jesus' ministry. The fulfillment of the eschatological program of Isaiah is indicated by Jesus' statement after his reading of the scriptural passages: *sēmeron peplērōtai hē graphē hautē en tois ōsin hymōn* ("Today this Scripture has been fulfilled in your hearing").

The foregoing discussion of Isa. 61:1–2 has shown that the different metaphors used in this passage all point to the oppressed condition of Israel. In light of Luke 7:22, however, a literal reading cannot be ruled out, since the metaphors become actualized in the ministry of Jesus himself. The "poor," then, symbolize not only Israel in suffering (6:20), but also those who are without means and the outcasts in general (11:41; 12:33; 14:13). The "blind" likewise can be used in a symbolic way to describe those without salvation (1:78–79; 2:29–32; 3:6), but it also refers to those who are physically impaired (18:35–43; Acts 9:18–19). The "release" can also refer to the freedom from the power of Satan (13:10–17; Acts 10:38) or the literal release from debts (11:4) (see Green 1997: 211).

The hermeneutical significance of Isa. 61:1–2 for the ministry of Jesus is indicated by its allusion in Luke 7:22 in response to a question raised concerning the nature and meaning of his ministry. The allusion to Isa. 61:1–2 and the Nazareth sermon scene in Acts 10:35–38 further confirms the programmatic nature of Luke 4:18–19 (see Turner 1981: 22–23). As in the case of Luke 3:4–6 (Isa. 40:3–5), the ministry of Jesus is to be understood in light of the program outlined in Isaiah.

In light of the way Isa. 61 is used in 11Q13 (see above), one has to consider whether Luke intends to evoke the Jubilee theology with this Isaianic citation. Some commentators (see Sloan 1997; Prior 1995) have argued for the presence of a full-blown theology in the use of this quotation, but other Jewish documents (e.g., 4Q521) have shown that the phrase "the year of the Lord's favor" does not necessarily point to the Jubilee paradigm. Moreover, as O'Brien (2001: 438–39) has pointed out, distinct Jubilee themes and references are entirely absent in the Lukan writings, and there is no evidence that Luke was aware of the Jubilee interpretation in his use of Isa. 61:1–2. Nevertheless, one can concede that the Jubilee connection does highlight the social, economic, and political impact of the arrival of the eschatological era. As in Isa. 61 (and 40–55), this Jubilee theme is one among many that contribute to the wider prophetic paradigm of the second exodus. It is this paradigm that finds repeated emphasis in Luke's writings.

While Isa. 61:1–2; 58:6 provide the content of the proclamation of God's salvific acts, the Lukan context in which it is placed provides significant qualification to this jubilant note. First, the comment on how the prophet is not welcome (*dektos*) in his own land in 4:24 not only identifies Jesus as prophet but also indicates that his ministry is to be characterized by rejection. Despite the actualization of the promises of eschatological salvation, Israel fails to accept God's messenger. Second, the contrast between native and foreign land in 4:23–24 is illustrated by the examples of Elijah and Elisha in 4:25–27, where the mission to the Gentiles is at least implied. Without arguing for a cause-and-effect relationship, Luke's story of the early Christian movement is characterized by the rejection of the Jews and the inclusion of the Gentiles.

F. Theological Use. As noted above, the relationship between Isa. 61:1–2 and 40–55 highlights the role of the prophet and the servant in the eschatological new exodus. Jesus' self-identification as a prophet in 4:24 and the use of the examples of Elijah and Elisha in 4:25–27 give further support to this reading. Moreover, in Luke 7, where one finds another evocation of Isa. 61 (v. 22), Jesus is identified as *prophētēs megas* ("a great prophet" [v. 16]).

Whether a messianic reference is intended with the use of Isa. 61:1–2 is subject to debate, however. J. A. Fitzmyer (1981–1985: 529–30) argues for an exclusive prophetic reading of the text, but the reference to "anointment" may also

have messianic connotations. First, the Isaianic servant figure already displays both prophetic and messianic characteristics (Strauss 1995: 244–49). Second, a messianic reading of Isa. 61:1–2 can already be identified in 11Q13 and 4Q521. Third, in 3:22 the phrase *sy ei huios mou* ("you are my Son") clearly points to the messianic Ps. 2:7. Together with *en soi eudokēsa* ("with you I am well pleased"), which alludes to Isa. 42:1, this again produces the combination of servant and messianic texts to identify Jesus. Finally, the "anointment" motif is most often applied to royal figures. In short, a clear distinction between the prophetic and the messianic character of Isa. 61:1–2 should not be made, and the remaining narrative in Luke's Gospel will point to both Jesus' prophetic and messianic roles.

Finally, the theological significance of this passage is not limited to Luke's Gospel. Themes such as the rejection of the Jews in a synagogue setting, inclusion of the Gentiles, the role of the Spirit, and the powerful nature of the *logos* ("word") in 4:16–31 point to the significance of this passage for Luke's narrative in Acts. Thus the ministry of Jesus is again connected with the ministry of the apostles in a setting containing a lengthy Isaianic quotation.

4:25–27

The story of Elijah in 4:25–26 is taken from 1 Kings 17:8–24, where Elijah is sent to Zarephath of Sidon after warning Ahab of God's judgment (4:1). Elijah's leaving for Zarephath can be understood as a reaction to Ahab's persecution (cf. 4:3). The ironic point is that while he was rejected by a Jewish king, he was welcomed by a Gentile (see C. A. Evans 1993a: 74). In Luke, Jesus is likewise rejected by the Jews while turning to those outside of God's community. The story of Elisha in 4:27 alludes to Elisha's healing of Naaman in 2 Kings 5:1–19. After his healing, Naaman, a commander of the army of the Syrian king of Aram (5:1), acknowledges the God of Israel: "Now I know that there is no God in all the earth except in Israel" (5:15). In the words of Elisha, the visit of Naaman is to show those outside of Israel that "there is a prophet in Israel" (5:8). Luke's use of this story points to the recognition of Jesus as the prophet of Israel as well as the concern for those outside the covenant community. The use of the stories of Elijah and Elisha may also reflect the eschatological use of these traditions to point to the prophetic ministries of the one to come (see Crockett 1966b: 248–76).

As these stories follow the proverb concerning the rejection of Jesus as a prophet (4:24), they point to Israel's history of rejecting God's messengers. Moreover, references to the widow of Zarephath and Naaman point to a turn to the Gentiles. What is not clear, however, is the exact relationship between the themes of Jewish rejection and Gentile inclusion. A strict cause-and-effect relationship cannot be established in light of the prophetic nature of this warning that aims at calling Israel to repent. Moreover, the mission to the Jews continues to the end of Luke's narrative (and beyond). Nevertheless, although the Gentile mission is not brought about by Israel's rejection of their Messiah, the two events are at least mentioned together to highlight the consequences of Israel's disobedience. In the wider context, where Isa. 61:1–2; 58:6 are used (4:18–19), these stories serve as qualifications to the jubilant note that points to the dawn of Israel's salvation. The response to this act of God remains to be seen in the remaining narrative of Luke.

4:34

Variations of the title *ho hagios tou theou* ("the Holy One of God") have been applied to Aaron (Ps. 106:16 [105:16 LXX]), Samson (Judg. 13:7; 16:7 [LXX B]), and Elisha (2 Kings 4:9). In light of these references, some have hypothesized a priestly, Naziritic, or prophetic context behind the Lukan use of the title here (see Hahn 1969: 231–35). In 1:35 the term *hagios* ("holy") is applied to Jesus in a context where he is presented as the royal Messiah, and in Acts 4:27, 30 the term is used with the noun *pais* ("servant") in describing Jesus. From these different uses, it becomes apparent that the title should not be limited to one conceptual framework. In 4:34 the title points to Jesus' special status as one who is able to overpower the unclean spirits, and thus it is used as a way to denote "the sphere of the divine" (Twelftree 1993: 67). Elsewhere in Luke, Jesus' identity as messiah, prophet, and servant explains the unique presence of this power in him.

4:43

The concept of the Davidic kingdom is already introduced in 1:32–33, and in this verse the expression *hē basileia tou theou* ("the kingdom of God") finds its first appearance in the Lukan writings. In the OT the reign of God is expressed primarily through the covenant framework, but the reign of Yahweh is often noted (1 Chron. 17:14; 28:5; 29:11; Ps. 103:19; 145:11–13; Dan. 4:3, 34; 7:27), while the title *melek* ("king") is also applied to Yahweh himself (cf., e.g., 1 Sam. 12:12; Ps. 5:3 [5:2 ET]; 10:16; 29:10; 44:5 [44:4 ET]; 47:3, 7–8 [47:2, 6–8 ET]; 74:12; 145:1; 149:2; Isa. 6:5; 41:21; 43:15; Jer. 10:7; 48:15; 51:57; Zech. 14:9, 16–17; Mal. 1:14; see Patrick 1987: 72). The focus of these passages, however, is on the sovereignty of God and his control over his creation. Some texts do point to the renewal of God's kingdom (cf. Isa. 33:22; 52:7; Zeph. 3:15), and also relevant are the traditions that point to the reestablishment of the Davidic kingdom (cf. Isa. 7–9; Jer. 23:5–8; 33:14–26; Ezek. 37:24–28; Zech. 3:8–10; 12:7–9).

In Jewish traditions one finds a variety of images attached to this symbol of God's sovereignty. It could point to the establishment of God's political kingdom on earth (*Pss. Sol.* 17) or the eschatological/messianic kingdom (*T. Mos.* 10; *1 En.* 37–71; *4 Ezra* 7:28–30). The expectation of the restoration of God's sovereignty continues to appear in Jewish liturgical traditions, as expressed in Benediction 11 of the *Shemoneh Esreh*. Popular messianic movements of the Second Temple period also testify to the continuation of the hope of the realization of God's promises on earth (cf. Josephus, *Ant.* 17.271–285; *J.W.* 2.71–75, 422–442; see Horsley and Hanson 1985: 110–27; Collins 1987; M. de Jonge 1988: 156–58).

In the Lukan writings the "kingdom of God" evokes a number of images. First, the Davidic kingdom as introduced in 1:32–33 and emphasized throughout the Lukan writings provides continuity with Jewish expectation. This kingdom, however, is not to be portrayed primarily in political terms, since kingdom language in Luke points further to the physical (cf. 9:2) and spiritual renewal of God's people (cf. 12:31–34). Second, the cosmic significance of the arrival of God's kingdom is illustrated in 11:18–20 with the reference to the fall of Satan. The onset of God's kingdom is therefore considered as a challenge to Satan's power and control. Third, the emphasis on the presence of God's kingdom is balanced by the expectation of the consummation of God's kingdom (see 11:1–4). These two aspects also characterize Luke's kingdom parables (13:18–21). Finally, the preaching of God's kingdom also provides a link between Jesus and his apostles (Acts 1:3; 8:12; 19:8; 28:23, 31). This is particularly important in light of the fact that Luke's work concludes with a note about Paul preaching the kingdom in Rome, the center of the Roman Empire. The story of the spread of the gospel becomes one that reflects the sovereignty of God and Jesus, his exalted Messiah (cf. Acts 2:33–36; 4:24–30).

Luke 5:1–11

Despite the similarities between Luke 5:1–11 and John 21:1–9, significant differences between the two texts suggest that the account of the call of the first disciples here should be analyzed on its own terms (Abogunrin 1985: 592–93). A number of elements recall similar OT call accounts (Exod. 3:1–22; Josh. 1:1–9; Isa. 6:1–10; Jer. 1:4–10): divine initiative (5:4), Simon's protest (5:8) and reaction (5:9), divine reassurance (5:10b) and commission (5:10c) (see Polich 1991: 138–39). In terms of form, Isa. 6:1–10 provides the closest parallel, as the actual commissioning is the final element of the account (Green 1997: 233). Other themes in the story may also reflect Elijah's call of Elisha in 1 Kings 19:19–21, especially since the calling took place when the disciples were fishing, just as Elisha was plowing (Aus 2000: 92–104, 124).

5:10

Conceptual parallels to "fishers of men" can be found in Jer. 16:16; Amos 4:2; Hab. 1:17. Instead of seeing this as a metaphor for hunting and killing, some have suggested that the use of the word *zōgrōn* ("taking alive") emphasizes the instilling of new lives (see Wuellner 1967: 237–38).

5:14

The instruction to the healed leper, "Go and show yourself to the priest," reflects Lev. 13:49; 14:1–32 (cf. Luke 17:14). The continued relevance of this Mosaic regulation in the time of Jesus is reflected in 11Q19 XLVIII, 17–XLIX, 4 and in the later Mishnah (cf. *Ṭeharot* and *Nega'im*; see Fitzmyer 1981–1985: 575; Bock 1994–1996: 476). In the context of OT ritual laws this Mosaic regulation points to a rite of passage where the celebrant moves from the realm of impurity and is restored into the worshiping community of Israel (Milgrom 1991–2001: 887–89).

5:21

The charge of blasphemy is directed against Jesus, who proclaimed forgiveness apart from the Jerusalem cult (cf. Lev. 4:22–5:16; 16:15–16; see Chilton 1992: 133). The theological basis for this cultic practice is that Yahweh is the God of Israel (Exod. 29:46), and that forgiveness belongs to God alone (Ps. 130:4; Isa. 43:25; Mic. 7:18). To proclaim forgiveness to the paralyzed man, therefore, is to make a theological statement that challenges the Pharisees and the teachers of the law.

5:24

The origin and significance of the expression *ho huios tou anthrōpou* ("Son of Man") has been widely debated. This expression appears eighty-two times in the Gospels, always used by Jesus as a self-reference (with the exception in John 12:34). Parallels from the OT for this expression can be identified in three contexts: (1) in the psalms it is used as a generic reference to human beings in general (Ps. 8:4; 144:3) and to Israel in particular (Ps. 80:17); (2) in Ezekiel it is used when God addresses the prophets (e.g., 2:1; 3:3; 4:1); and (3) in Dan. 7:13–14 it appears in an apocalyptic context where one like a Son of Man "came to the Ancient One" and "was given dominion and glory and kingship." When we come to the time of Jesus, the meaning of the phrase in Aramaic has generated another set of debates. G. Vermes (1967), for example, argues that the phrase could be used as a circumlocution in an exclusive sense, while others question this conclusion (Fitzmyer 1979a).

The generic reference of this phrase receives substantial support in biblical and Aramaic sources, but the use of the expression in apocalyptic material demands further attention. Drawn from Dan. 7:13–14, the expression is used in *1 En.* 37–71 and *4 Ezra* 13. According to J. J. Collins (1992), the independent traditions in the Similitudes of *1 Enoch* and *4 Ezra* point to the common first-century understanding of Dan. 7: (1) the use of the expression as a reference to an individual; (2) the works of the individual can be compared to that of the expected Messiah; (3) the individual acquires some divine attributes such as preexistence; and (4) moving beyond Dan. 7, this figure takes on a more explicit destructive role. Although "Son of Man" is not yet a title in these documents, one can speak of a formulaic expression deriving from the readings of Dan. 7.

The exact significance of the expression can be determined primarily by its use in the NT contexts. The use of the expression in the later portions of Luke (cf. 21:27, 36; 22:69) clearly points to the apocalyptic figure that one finds in exegetical traditions deriving from Dan. 7:13, but earlier references seem to be used in a more ambiguous way. Even in these references, however, one may detect that the circumlocution is functioning in a "quasi-titular" manner (Marshall 1990: 113), the full significance of which is made clear only at the end of Luke's narrative. The authority of Jesus the Son of Man to forgive sins in 5:24 fits well with this reading, where the ambiguity is at least partly clarified by references to Jesus' authority.

5:30

The use of *egongyzon* ("were complaining") here in describing the Pharisees and the teachers of the law is significant. In the LXX this word group (*gongyzō, diagongyzō, gongysmos*) is often used to describe the "murmuring" of Israel in their wilderness journey (Exod. 15:24; 16:7–12; 17:3; Num. 11:1; 14:2, 27–29, 36; 16:11, 41; 17:5, 10). In later writings Israel's rebellion against God is described with the use of the same word group (Ps. 59:15 [58:16 LXX]; Ps. 106:25 [105:25 LXX]; Sir. 46:7; 1 Cor. 10:10). In Luke's Gospel the rebellious nature of Israel has already been hinted at with the evocation of Deut. 6–8 in Jesus' response to Satan in 4:1–13. Here, in opposing the faithful Son of God, the Pharisees and the scribes are following the rebellious ways of their ancestors. In 15:2; 19:7 the verb *diagongyzō* is similarly used in describing the Jewish leadership's misunderstanding of the mission of Jesus.

5:33–35

In the OT fasting was practiced when individuals (2 Sam. 12:16–23; 1 Kings 21:27; Ps. 35:13; 69:10; 109:24) or the people of God (Judg. 20:26; 2 Chron. 20:3; Ezra 8:21–23; Neh. 1:4; Esther 4:3, 16) were in a time of crisis. Fasting was also frequently the response of sinners in their acts of confession (1 Sam. 7:6; Joel 1:14; 2:12–15; Jon. 3:5). Particularly relevant for our purposes is the connection between fasting and mourning (1 Sam. 31:13; 2 Sam. 1:12; 1 Chron. 10:12). Of the Jewish feasts, fasting is required only on the Day of Atonement (Lev. 23:26–32; Num. 29:7–11), but during the time of Jesus days of fasting were observed regularly, and this emphasis on fasting had even attracted the attention of the pagans (cf. Suetonius, *Aug.* 76.2; see Diamond 2004: 95–98, 181). The Pharisaic practice of fasting is noted elsewhere in Luke (cf. 18:12), and later rabbinic sources confirm the continuation of this emphasis (Str-B 2:241–44). The discussion between Jesus and the Pharisees in 5:33–35 is probably not primarily intended to be a discussion of the validity of the Mosaic law in general, but rather a discussion of the lesser rituals practiced by the Pharisees and their scribes (E. P. Sanders 1985: 207). In the OT fasting as a religious ritual had already been an object of prophetic critique (Isa. 58:3–6; Jer. 14:12). Jesus further points to the connection between fasting and grieving, however, in making his point. On the surface, therefore, Jesus notes the arrival of a new era that calls for rejoicing instead of mourning. Implicit is a critique of the fasting of the Pharisees and the scribes who care more about external observances than the will of God.

The metaphor of the bridegroom is applied to God in the OT (cf. Isa. 54:5–8; 62:4–5; Jer. 2:2; Ezek. 16; Hos. 2:18, 21), and it is only in later traditions that this metaphor is applied to the Messiah (cf. 2 Cor. 11:2; Eph. 5:25–27; Rev. 19:7–10; 21:2; *Pirqe R. El.* 4; *Pesiq. Rab.* 149a; see O'Neill 1988: 485; Bock 1994–1996: 516). In rabbinic traditions there is a list of days on which fasting is forbidden (cf. *Megillah Ta'anit*; see Bovon 2002: 191), and the day of the wedding is one of them. Jesus may be aware of similar traditions when he addresses the arrival of times of eschatological joy.

6:1–5

A number of elements in this text presuppose a knowledge of relevant OT and Jewish traditions: plucking of grains in the fields, Sabbath regulations, and the story of David in the "house of God." First, the disciples' plucking of heads of grain in the field reflects the regulations for gleaning in Lev. 19:9–10: "When you reap the harvest of your land, you shall not reap to the very edges of your field, or gather the gleanings of your harvest. . . . you shall leave them for the poor and the alien: I am the LORD your God" (cf. Lev. 23:22; Deut. 24:21; Ruth 2:1–23). The disciples may be considered as the poor ones, although in the rabbinic traditions a traveler can be considered among the "poor" who are allowed to glean from the field: "[As regards] a householder who is traveling from one place to another, and [because he has no money] he needs to collect gleanings, forgotten sheaves, *peah* or poor man's tithe, let him collect [what he needs]" (*m. Pe'ah* 5:4 [Neusner 1988: 24]).

Under debate, however, is not the act of gleaning itself, but rather the act as practiced on a Sabbath. The complex set of Sabbath regulations grows out of the basic command to "rest" found in the Ten Commandments (Exod. 20:8–11; Deut. 5:12–15). In Exod. 34:21 a further emphasis is added: "even in plowing time and in harvest time you shall rest." Further explication of the Sabbath regulation is found in later writings, especially when the Jews were living among the Gentiles (cf. Neh. 13:15–22). As a "sign" between God and his covenant partner (Ezek. 20:12), the Sabbath became one of the distinctive markers of Israel (cf. 1 Macc. 2:27–41; Josephus, *J.W.* 1.157–160). Building on Exod. 34:21, further development of Sabbath regulations concerning the works of the field is found in rabbinic traditions where plowing, reaping, threshing, winnowing, sorting through produce or crops, and other works of the field are prohibited (cf. *m. Šabb.* 7:2), although common agreement as to exactly what is prohibited may be lacking in the time of Jesus. It is also unclear whether "plucking" is commonly considered to be an unacceptable act on a Sabbath.

The story of David is taken from 1 Sam. 21:1–6, where the "shewbread," or "bread of the Presence," was offered to David and his companions when he came to the priest Ahimelech at the sanctuary in Nob. The main point of comparison between the disciples' plucking of grain and the story of David and his companions is debated. To some, the obvious point of comparison is that "ceremonial restrictions of law are to give way to human need" (Bock 1994–1996: 525). While even in Jewish discussions the overriding of Sabbath regulations is permitted in cases of urgent need (cf.

Mek. Exod. 21:12–17; see Casey 1988: 15), the lack of emphasis on the "need" of Jesus' disciples forces one to look for stronger parallels between the two.

The second point of comparison is between David and Jesus himself, as the connection between them has already been established in the earlier chapters (1:32–33, 68–79; 2:11; 3:22, 31). The point is that "David had the authority to act as he did, and that Jesus has the same right, but in a higher degree, to reinterpret the law" (Marshall 1978: 228). The Lukan omission of Mark's comment on the intent of the law may heighten the significance of this christological point, although it is Matthew who explicitly notes Jesus saying that "something greater than the temple is here" (Matt. 12:6). Nevertheless, the explicit mentioning of David's entering "the house of God" (Luke 6:4) may presuppose an understanding similar to that of Matthew's when Jesus is compared with the temple, where the presence of God is found. To further suggest that a eucharistic context is presupposed in this text is to move beyond the evidence of the text (*contra* Grassi 1964).

The third point builds on the Jewish interpretation of 1 Sam. 21:1–6. In 6:4 Jesus himself stated that only the priests could eat the bread of the Presence; this exceptional clause, though absent in 1 Sam. 21, is present in texts such as Lev. 24:8–9, where the priests are allowed to eat the bread when it was changed on a Sabbath day. Jesus' mentioning of this priestly right may therefore reflect the Jewish traditions that connect the story of David in 1 Sam. 21:1–6 with the Sabbath context. M. Casey (1988: 10–12) rightly points to the explicit location of 1 Sam. 21:1–6 within a Sabbath context in rabbinic traditions (cf. *Yalquṭ Shim'oni* 2:30; *y. Yoma* 8:5; *b. Menaḥ.* 95b). If Luke was aware of this connection, then Jesus may be using the Pharisaic traditions to argue against their interpretation of the law.

6:9

On the fulfillment of human needs on the Sabbath, see discussion on 6:1–5 above.

6:12–16

Some commentators (see, e.g., Schürmann 1990–1994: 1:313) have detected an exodus allusion here, as Jesus' act of establishing the Twelve brings to mind what Moses did on his way to the mountain as "he set up twelve pillars, corresponding to the twelve tribes of Israel" (Exod. 24:4). F. Bovon (2002: 208) points further to postbiblical traditions where motifs of mountain and prayer are connected with the renewal of Israel (cf. *L.A.B.* 11–15). In light of the significance of the prayer motif in Luke's Gospel (cf. 3:21; 9:18, 28; 11:1–13; 18:1–8; 22:31–32, 40, 46), Jesus' praying on the mountain in this context (cf. 9:28) is not unexpected. Nevertheless, the call of the Twelve does bring to mind the foundational event of Israel. The connection between the twelve disciples and the twelve tribes of Israel is made explicit in 22:28–30.

Luke 6:20–26

In the OT two broad types of beatitudes can be identified. The first type focuses on the ethical conduct that is to be imitated, and blessings are promised for such behavior (Ps. 84:12; Prov. 3:13; 8:34). The second type aims at describing the life of a person as a blessing of God (Ps. 144:12–15). Applied to the community of God's people, these beatitudes often are framed by the covenantal concerns whereby Israel is blessed precisely because they are God's chosen people (Deut. 33:29; Ps. 33:12; 146:5; Isa. 56:2) (see Catchpole 1986: 299; Thompson 1999: 111). It is within this covenantal framework that the woes also find their place (Isa. 5:8–25; 31:1; Jer. 13:27; 22:13–14; Amos 6:1; Hab. 2:12–17), although they are also used against those opposing God and his people (Num. 21:29; Isa. 10:5; Jer. 48:1, 46).

In apocalyptic literature the promised blessings often point to the eschatological era (Dan. 12:12). This eschatological focus characterizes many of the beatitudes in Jewish traditions (Tob. 13:16; *1 En.* 58:2), although those that point to the blessings in this present age can still be found (4Q525). In terms of form, the list in Sir. 25:1–10 resembles the ones in Matt. 5 and Luke 6, but the content of Sir. 25 is distinctly sapiential, as the focus there is on present living. Closer to Jesus' Beatitudes is the list in the late first-century AD *2 En.* 42:6–12 (Bovon 2002: 222), although the motif of eschatological reversal is noticeably missing in this list.

In terms of function, the apocalyptic framework of Jesus' Beatitudes shows that they were

not to be taken as "entrance requirements" (see Guelich 1973). The earlier proclamation of the dawn of the eschatological era (cf. 4:16–30) together with the narrative framework of the Gospel, which climaxes in the events of Jesus' crucifixion and resurrection, should prevent this from being understood simply in an ethical sense. The prophetic call to repentance is implicit, however, especially in light of the woes that follow (Green 1997: 265).

The allusions to the OT belong to this discussion of the form and function of the Beatitudes. The influence of Isa. 61:1–2 in particular has been recognized by many (Dupont 1973: 92–99; Neirynck 1997). The *ptōchoi* ("poor") in 6:20 in particular reflects the *ptōchoi* of Isa. 61:1. Although Luke may be drawing on Q for his version of the Beatitudes, the quotation of Isa. 61:1 already in 4:18 shows Luke's familiarity with this passage. The second beatitude in Matthew, which uses the words *hoi penthountes* ("those who mourn" [5:4]) and *paraklēthēsontai* ("they will be comforted"), further evokes Isa. 61:2 (*parakalesai pantas tous penthountas*, "to comfort all who mourn"), but their absence in the Lukan version has prompted H. D. Betz (1995: 578), among others, to conclude that Isa. 61:1–2 should not be identified as the source behind the Lukan beatitudes. Nevertheless, the appearance of both verbs in the Lukan woes (6:24, 25) seems to reflect Luke's awareness of the significance of the Isaianic allusion here. Moreover, Luke's use of *hoi klaiontes* ("those who weep") and *gelasete* ("you will laugh") could be seen as variations of the Isaianic *parakalesai pantas tous penthountas* ("to comfort all who mourn"). D. C. Allison (2000a: 104–6) has suggested that the indirect way in which Luke 6:20–23 uses Isa. 61:1–2 found its "near parallel" in 1QH[a] XXIII *top*, 12–15 (cf. 11Q13 II, 4, 6, 9, 13, 17, 18, 20). He further notes that the appearance of Isa. 61:1–2 in Luke 7:22, which is immediately followed by a blessing formula (7:23), may provide a significant parallel within the Lukan text to the connection between Isa. 61:1–2 and the form of the Beatitudes.

6:20, 24

While Isa. 61:1–2 provides the context for the Lukan beatitudes and woes, other OT texts may also have contributed to the individual verses. The reference to the poor recalls other Lukan passages that draw attention to the poor ones (1:48; 4:18; 7:22; 14:13, 21; 16:20–22), and the juxtaposition of the "rich" and the "poor" is not foreign to the prophetic traditions of Israel (cf. Isa. 29:19; 57:15; Jer. 5:28; 12:1). As in Isa. 61:1, the "poor" should not be defined primarily in material terms (see 4:18 above). The numerous parallels in the psalms (Ps. 34:6 [LXX 33:7]; 37:14 [36:14 LXX]; 69:32 [LXX 68:33]; 86:1 [85:1 LXX]; 109:22 [108:22 LXX]) and in the Qumran documents (1QM XI, 9; XIV, 6–7; 1QS IV, 3; 1QH^a XIII, 22) (see Carson 1984: 131) not only confirm this reading but also show how the Matthean *hoi ptōchoi tō pneumati* ("poor in spirit" [5:3]) is entirely consistent with Luke's unqualified use of the term.

6:21, 25

The contrast between hunger and being satisfied appears often in the OT (Ps. 107:5–9, 36, 41; 146:7; Isa. 32:6–7; 58:6–10; 65:13), and the eschatological promise is often symbolized by the messianic banquet, developed in texts such as Isa. 25:6. The significance of the Lukan banquet motif may have found its origin in this tradition (cf. 9:10–17; 11:37–54; 14:8–24; 15:23–24; 22:7–30; D. E. Smith 1987).

The contrast between weeping/mourning and laughing/rejoicing is likewise one that is familiar to the OT context (Esther 9:22; Jer. 31:13, 16; Lam. 5:15; Amos 8:10), although in the LXX the verb *gelaō* ("laugh") is often used in a negative sense to denote mockery or laughter of derision (see *TDNT* 1:660). The theme of rejoicing echoes earlier references to eschatological joy in Luke (1:41; 2:10) as Luke draws on the OT traditions in which the arrival of the era of salvation will be characterized by that of rejoicing (Isa. 9:3; Joel 2:21; Zeph. 3:14–17; Zech. 9:9). In light of the use of Isa. 61:1–2 in the formulations of the Beatitudes, Isa. 61:3 may also have influenced the construction of this contrast when the anointed one receives the divine promise "to provide for those who mourn in Zion—to give them a garland instead of ashes, the oil of gladness instead of mourning, the mantle of praise instead of a faint spirit."

6:22–23, 26

The theme of end-time rejoicing follows this note on persecution. The phrase *ho misthos hymōn polys en tō ouranō* ("your reward is great in heaven") may recall a similar phrase in Gen. 15:1 LXX, *ho misthos sou polys estai sphodra* ("your reward shall be very great"). To further support this connection, D. C. Allison (2000a: 76) has further pointed to the eschatological interpretation of Gen. 15:1 in *Targum Neofiti* and *Targum Pseudo-Jonathan*. The verbal link between the two fails to establish a sure connection, however, and the immediate context of this verse does not explicitly support an allusion to the Abrahamic promises.

References to the persecution of the prophets of old are found throughout the OT (cf. 1 Kings 18:4, 13; 19:10, 14; 22:27; 2 Chron. 16:10; 24:21; Neh. 9:26; Jer. 2:30; 11:18–21; 20:2; 26:8–11, 20–23; 37:15–16; see *TDNT* 6:834; Bock 1994–1996: 582). Similar sentiment is expressed in the rhetorical question posed by Stephen: "Was there ever a prophet your fathers did not persecute?" (Acts 7:52). The motif of the rejected prophet manifests itself in the Jewish rejection of Jesus (Luke 4:24, 29; 11:47–51; 13:33–35; 23:18) and his apostles (cf. Acts 13:46; 18:6; 28:28). Corresponding to Israel's rejection of the messengers of God is their fond reception of false prophets (Isa. 9:14–15; Jer. 2:8; 5:30–31; 14:13–16; 23:16–17; Ezek. 22:28; Mic. 3:5). The Lukan parallels to these false messengers are not easily identifiable, however (see Schürmann 1990–1994: 1:338–39).

Luke 6:27–45

The significance of Lev. 19:2 ("Be holy, because I the LORD your God am holy") behind 6:36 ("Be merciful, just as your Father is merciful") has long been recognized (see discussion below), but many have attempted to show the wider influence of Lev. 19 for this section. D. R. Catchpole (1986: 316), for example, sees 6:27–35 interacting with Lev. 19:18, while 6:37–45 reflects the concerns of Lev. 19:17. D. C. Allison (2000a: 33) further suggests that the two passages share a set of related themes: *imitatio Dei*, question of judgment, the Golden Rule, love, and fraternal relations. Read against the context of Lev. 19, the distinct emphases of Jesus are easily identifiable: the call to be merciful, the love of one's enemies, and the command to extend the act of mercy to those outside one's community. The dichotomy between "holiness" and "mercy" (cf. Borg 1984) cannot be maintained, however, since the issue at hand is the way God's holiness is to be manifested (cf. 6:46–49).

6:27

The teaching on nonretaliation finds parallels in Greco-Roman (Plato, *Crito* 47c–49d; *Resp.* 1.331e–336a; Diogenes Laertius 8.1, 23) and Jewish (Prov. 24:17; 25:21–22; *T. Benj.* 4:3; *T. Jos.* 18:2) traditions (see Fitzmyer 1981–1985: 637–38; Gill 1991), but the emphasis on loving one's enemies goes beyond these traditions. "Enemies" are often defined in ethnic terms in Leviticus (e.g., 26:6–46) and elsewhere in the OT (Exod. 23:22; Num. 25:17; Deut. 28:7; 1 Kings 8:44; Isa. 29:5; 59:18; Ezek. 16:27). In light of this background, Jesus' teaching should not be limited to an individualistic sense, since the challenge to the Jewish ethnic theology of the Second Temple period may also be implied here. This interpretation is further supported by the possible rephrasing of the command "Love your neighbor" (Lev. 19:18) into "Love your enemies."

6:29

Differing from the parallel in Matthew (5:40), Luke ignores the legal context and mentions *himation* ("the cloak/coat") before *chitōna* ("the tunic/shirt"). In the OT the cloak is an "inalienable possession" (cf. Exod. 22:26–27; Deut. 24:10–13; see Carson 1984: 156). Apart from a legal context, the act of beating accompanied by the removal of one's clothing may echo Song 5:7: "The sentinels found me; they beat me, they wounded me, they took away my mantle." In rabbinic traditions slapping a person and pulling off his mantle are considered among the most serious acts of insult (cf. *B. Qam.* 8:6; see Catchpole 1986: 306).

6:30

The command "Give to everyone who begs from you" appears to be a general saying, but if the Matthean parallel (5:42; cf. Luke 6:35) is to be considered, it appears to be an extension of the Mosaic regulations against usury (Exod. 22:25; Lev. 25:36–37; Deut. 23:19–20; cf. Ezek. 18:8). The intent of these regulations is further expressed by an additional mandate in Luke, "If anyone takes away your goods, do not ask for them again" (cf. Deut. 15:8; Ps. 37:21, 26; Prov. 22:7).

6:31

Many have identified Greco-Roman (Herodotus 3.142; Seneca, *Ben.* 2.1.1) and Jewish (Sir. 31:15; Tob. 4:15; *2 En.* 61:2; *b. Šabb.* 31a) parallels to the Golden Rule (see Bock 1994–1996: 596–97), but its connection with Lev. 19 should be emphasized. The connection between Lev. 19:18 and the Golden Rule is made in *Did.* 1:2; *Let. Aris.* 207 (Allison 2000a: 31), although it generalizes the commandment to love one's "neighbor" (cf. *Tg. Ps.-J.* Lev. 19:18). In its context this rule should not be understood as advocating a "reciprocal ethic" wherein one's acts are determined by the acts of others (see Ricoeur 1990; Kirk 2003). The commandment to love one's "enemies" (6:27, 35) and the examples that follow, which climax in the *imitatio Dei* principle, provide the necessary basis for understanding this well-known saying of Christ.

6:34

What is implied in 6:30 is made explicit here when the Mosaic regulations concerning borrowing and lending are evoked. In Deut. 23:19–20 the distinction between Israelites and foreigners is made, as Israelites are not allowed to charge interest on a loan given to fellow Israelites, but they are allowed to charge interest to foreigners. Although it is unclear what the lender in this example is hoping to receive *ta isa* ("as much" [see the options in Bovon 2002: 237–38]), the main point is clear: Jesus is pointing beyond the distinction in Deut. 23 in affirming that self-interest should not be the guide of one's action. Nevertheless, the distinction of Deut. 23 may be important in the use of the Lukan term *hamartōloi* ("sinners"), since elsewhere in Luke the term is often applied to outcasts (5:30; 7:34; 13:2; 15:1–2; 18:13; 19:7). A subpoint of this passage could be identified in that those who fail to forsake their self-interest are ironically comparable to those to whom they can charge interest. The understanding of "enemies" (6:35) in an ethnocentric sense may support this reading (see 6:27 above), but this ethnic reading certainly does not exhaust the meaning and significance of this verse. Moreover, stronger verbal links between 6:34 and Deut. 23 are necessary to secure this connection.

6:35

In the OT the description of God's people as his *huioi* ("sons/children") belongs to the covenant language of Israel (Deut. 14:1; Hos. 1:10; 11:1). In Luke this usage appears when God's people are redefined according to one's response to Jesus himself (12:32), and in Luke's second volume Jews and Gentiles will worship the one God as *adelphoi* ("brothers") (Acts 15:22, 36).

6:36

In terms of the form of this verse, commentators have pointed to Lev. 19:2 as a close parallel: *hagioi esesthe hoti egō hagios kyrios ho theos hymōn* ("Be holy, because I the LORD your God am holy") (see Fitzmyer 1981–1985: 641). In Jewish traditions this call to imitate God's holiness has been used together with the various attributes of God (see Allison 2000a: 30–31; Bovon 2002: 241). In an allusion to Lev. 19:2 in *Lev. Rab.* 24:4, one finds the call to be pure, and in *b. Šabb.* 133b and *Tg. Ps.-J.* Lev. 22:28 the focus is on being compassionate. The use of this form in relation to the different divine attributes may explain the different saying in Matt. 5:48. As in the case of *eleos* ("kindness"), *oiktirmos* ("mercy") applied to God often appears in covenantal contexts (1 Chron. 21:13; 2 Chron. 30:9; Neh. 9:19, 27, 28, 31; Ps. 25:6 [24:6 LXX]; 51:1 [50:3 LXX]; 69:16 [68:17 LXX]; 79:8 [78:8 LXX]; 119:77 [118:77 LXX]; Isa. 63:15; Dan. 9:9, 18 [Θ]; Hos. 2:19 [2:21 LXX]; Zech. 1:16). Thus the command here to imitate the merciful God should be understood not simply as an ethical precept, but as a call to be a faithful partner in the covenant relationship.

6:39

The imagery of the *bothynon* ("pit") alludes to the Hebrew proverb that depicts the judgment of God (cf. Isa. 24:17–18; Jer. 48:43–44 [31:43–44 LXX]; see Bovon 2002: 249).

6:41–42

The vivid imagery in these verses serves to explicate the command not to judge in 6:37. An allusion to and a clarification of Lev. 19:17 may be present, especially in light of the significance of Lev. 19 throughout this section (Allison 2000a: 32–33). In addition to discussion on the judicial aspects of this issue of reproach (see CD-A IX, 2–8), one finds a similar focus on moral issues springing from the injunction in Lev. 19:17 (cf. Sir. 19:13–17; 20:2; *T. Gad* 6:3–4; see Kugel 1987: 57–58). Nevertheless, the emphasis here is not on reproach, but on hypocrisy. A closer parallel to Lev. 19:17 can be identified in 17:3–4 (cf. Matt. 18:15–20).

6:43–45

In the OT "fruit" imagery can be applied to the physical labor of an individual (Ps. 109:11; 128:2), but most often it is applied to moral acts (Prov. 1:31; 11:30; Isa. 3:10; 32:16–17; Jer. 6:19) and speech (Prov. 12:14; 13:2; 18:21; Hos. 14:2). Two related traditions may also have contributed to the use of this imagery here. First, the reference to "grapes" may evoke the OT description of Israel as a vineyard (Isa. 5:1–7; Jer. 12:10; cf. Luke 13:6–9; 20:9–18). Second, the theme of judgment is already present in the "vineyard" imagery in Isa. 5:1–7, and it can be found also in other passages where the "fruit" imagery is used in a judgment context (cf. Ezek. 17:9). These two themes seem to have played a role in Matt. 7:16–21, but neither dominates in this Lukan passage, as the focus here is primarily on the issue of hypocrisy.

6:46–49

The parable of the Wise and the Foolish Builders concludes this long discourse by presenting a choice to the readers. Its function is comparable to the conclusion of the Holiness Code (Lev. 26) and the covenant discourse in Deut. 28 (see Catchpole 1986: 298), where warning is issued to those who do not act within the covenantal boundary.

7:1–10

While Jesus' summary of his own ministry in his response to the messengers of John in 7:22 connects this section to the Isaianic quotation in chapter 4, the two healing stories in this chapter may also recall the stories of Elijah and Elisha evoked in 4:25–27 (for other possible parallels between chaps. 4 and 7, see Ringe 1981: 173–74). In 7:1–10 is the story illustrating the faith of a centurion. If Matt. 8:5–13 serves as a parallel to this healing account, then the Lukan emphasis is easily identifiable. These include the worthiness of the centurion (7:2, 4), the use of intermediaries (7:3, 6), and the omission of the meeting between Jesus and the centurion. Although numerous OT parallels have been suggested (see Derrett 1970:

161–62), the connections with Elisha's healing of Naaman in 2 Kings 5:1–16 seem evident, especially in light of the use of this story already in 4:27 (see Crockett 1969: 18; Ravens 1995: 130; cf. Brodie 1992). Like the centurion in Luke 7:1–10, Naaman is described as a respected Gentile military officer (2 Kings 5:1). Also, without meeting Elisha in person, he only received instructions from the prophet through an intermediary (2 Kings 5:10). Moreover, the healing resulted in the recognition of the power of the prophet of Israel and the God whom he represents (2 Kings 5:8, 15; cf. Luke 7:16).

The conclusion of Luke's account (7:9) highlights the response of one who does not belong to Israel. Unlike Matt. 8:13, which explicitly notes Jesus' words of healing, the Lukan account draws attention not to the healing miracle, but rather to the worthiness of a Gentile to receive divine blessings (see Achtemeier 1978: 155–56). This emphasis on the conversion of a Gentile also paves the way for the conversion account of Cornelius in Acts 10, where again a respected military officer communicates with the messenger of God through an intermediary. If Acts 10 serves as the culmination of the narrative sequence that begins in Luke 4:16–30, then 7:1–10 serves as a bridge between the two texts as Jesus' mission paves the way for the Gentile mission of his apostles.

Luke 7:11–17

As 7:1–10 finds its possible parallel in 2 Kings 5:1–16, so 7:11–17 may recall Elijah's raising of the widow's son in 1 Kings 17:17–24, as already noted in 4:25–26. C. A. Evans (1993a: 76–77) and T. L. Brodie (1987: 134–53) list the following parallels: a widow as the main character (7:12; 1 Kings 17:9, 17), the death of her son (7:12; 1 Kings 17:17), the meeting of the widow at the "gate of the city" (7:12; 1 Kings 17:10), and the clause *edōken auton tē mētri autou*, "he gave him to his mother" (7:15; 1 Kings 17:23). Moreover, the acclamation "A great prophet has arisen among us" (7:16) resembles the targumic reading of 1 Kings 17:24: "You are the prophet of the LORD." A similar account of the raising of a woman's son is found in 2 Kings 4:32–37, where Elisha carries on the ministry of his predecessor. It is also important to note how this narrative surpasses the Elijah account in that Jesus is able to speak directly to the dead son and resuscitate him. Thus Jesus is to be viewed as *ho kyrios* ("the Lord" [7:13]), not merely as a prophet of old (see Bovon 2002: 268; Green 1997: 290).

7:16

The visitation of God and the raising up of God's messenger recall 1:68–69, where God's visitation is manifested by the appearance of a Davidic figure. Although the prophetic ministry of Jesus is connected with that of Elijah and Elisha in 4:25–27, the title *prophētēs* ("prophet") should not be limited to the Elijah parallel of this story, but rather is to be understood in the wider sense whereby Jesus is portrayed as the prophet like Moses (Deut. 18:15; cf. Acts 3:22; 7:37). Nevertheless, the title itself is insufficient to explain the significance of Jesus and his ministry (9:19–20; cf. John 7:40–44).

7:19

The reference to *ho erchomenos* ("the coming one") recalls the earlier reference in 3:16, where one detects an allusion to passages such as Mal. 3:1; Ps. 118:26 [117:26 LXX].

7:22

The response of Jesus draws on a number of Isaianic passages, the most prominent being Isa. 35:3–4 (the blind see, the lame walk, the deaf hear) and 61:1–2 (the blind see, the poor receive good news). Other texts from Isaiah that may have played a role include 29:18–19; 42:7, 18; and especially 26:19, with its reference to the raising of the dead. Only the healing of the leper is missing in these Isaianic passages, although some have suggested that both the healing of the leper and the raising of the dead allude to the stories of Elijah (1 Kings 17:17–24) and Elisha (2 Kings 5:1–16) that appear earlier in 4:25–27 and 7:1–17 (see Tuckett 1982: 353; Neirynck 1997: 50). It should be noted that the inclusion of the raising of the dead in this Isaianic list can already be found in the list in 4Q521, where the Messiah is introduced (2 II, 1), and he is the one who will revive the dead and proclaim good news to the humbled ones (2 II, 12). The connection between the Isaianic list and the ministries of Elijah and Elisha is again present here as the Messiah is portrayed as an Elijah-type figure. Collins (1994: 112) may be right in concluding that "there is good reason to think that actions described in Isaiah 61, with the addition of the raising of the dead, were already viewed as 'works of the messiah' in some Jewish circles before the career of Jesus" (cf. Tabor and Wise 1992). Further support is needed, however, to substantiate the suggestion that "it is quite possible that the author of the Sayings source knew 4Q521" (Collins 1994: 107).

The text of 4Q521 is important also for our discussion on the issue of judgment. This fragment confirms that the lack of explicit mention of judgment and vindication in the list should not lead to the conclusion that the omission is intentional, since the judgment theme is emphasized in the context of this list. In a similar manner, the absence of the judgment theme in Luke 7:22 should not prevent one from noticing the presence of this theme in Isa. 26; 35; 61. The verse that follows ("Blessed is anyone who does not fall away on account of me") should then be considered as a warning to those who consider the delay of God's judgment to be an excuse for the rejection of Jesus' messianic ministry.

7:27

A. NT Context: Role of John the Baptist. With 7:24, Jesus speaks directly about the role and ministry of John the Baptist. The Matthean parallel (11:2–19) combines the two discrete Lukan passages (7:18–23; 16:16), and together they constitute the second block of Q material on John the Baptist. This passage is set within the wider context where the identity of Jesus himself is questioned (7:18–23). After situating his own ministry within the Isaianic program of the new exodus as laid out in 4:16–30, Jesus provides a definition of John's significance in relation to his own ministry. The OT quotation is preceded by Jesus' declaration of John as one who is "more than a prophet" (7:26). The "greatness" of John is emphasized again after the citation, but it is followed by the enigmatic saying "Yet the one who is least in the kingdom of God is greater than he" (7:28). J. P. Meier (1994: 142–44) calls this "dialectical negation," as the eschatological turning point initiated by Jesus surpasses everything that precedes this moment in salvation history.

The presence of this quotation is important because it is a mixed quotation drawing on Exod. 23:20; Mal. 3:1. At this point, it is sufficient to note that both OT texts are connected with the Isaianic program as outlined in Isa. 40:3 (cf. Mark 1:2–3). The relationship between 7:18–23 and this passage becomes apparent as the significance of John and Jesus are explained within the wider Isaianic program of the new exodus.

B. Exod. 23:20; Mal. 3:1 in Context. Exodus 23 belongs to the Book of the Covenant (20:22–23:33), where the statutes and ordinances for the covenantal relationship are laid out, and these regulations can be considered as an explication of the Decalogue, which precedes them (20:1–17). The conclusion (23:20–33), to which our text belongs, is of a hortatory nature and forms an appropriate conclusion to this book. Connected with the previous section (23:14–19), this conclusion focuses on the land and thus can be considered as "a homily on the proper use of the land" (Childs 1974: 461). These opening verses (23:20–23) of the epilogue are characterized by the conditional nature of the covenant, where one finds a clear articulation of the warning to Israel against any rebellious act against their God (23:21–22) framed by the references to God's messenger who guards the way as God's people approach the promised land (23:20, 23).

The relationship between the *mal'āk* ("messenger") and God himself is less than clear in these verses (cf. Exod. 3:2; 14:19). In 23:22 the equation of following "his voice" and "do all that I say" seems to identify Yahweh with his own messenger. J. I. Durham (1987: 335) considers the messenger an "extension" of Yahweh, while others prefer to see the angel as the manifestation of God's presence (cf. 23:21; see Juncker 2001: 94–95). It is precisely this ambiguity that provides a fertile field of exegetical work.

Although Exod. 23 supplies the language for part of the quotation in Luke 7:22, it is Mal. 3:1 that directly contributes to this quotation. Malachi begins with the failure of God's people and their leaders to live faithfully as God's covenant partners (1:6–2:16). The section culminates in their questioning of the one who judges: "Where is the God of justice?" (2:17), a verse that starts off the fourth prophetic oracle (2:17–3:5). Malachi 3:1 provides a response to the rebellious acts of God's people as it points to the presence of God through his *mal'āk* ("messenger"). Unlike the messenger in Exod. 23, however, this messenger is directly related to the arrival of God's judgment: "But who can endure the day of his coming, and who can stand when he appears?" (3:2). The theme of judgment dominates the rest of this book, where the wicked (3:7–15) are separated from the righteous (3:16–18).

Unlike the preceding material, this oracle (2:17–3:5) is characterized by its eschatological focus. The image of the messenger draws on Exod. 23:20, while the role of this messenger as one who is to "prepare the way before me" also builds on Isa. 40:3. Unlike Isa. 40:3, where the clearing of the way points primarily to the deliverance of God's people from the hands of their enemies, in this prophetic oracle the clearing of the way points to the purification that is accompanied by the presence of God. More perplexing is the relationship between "my messenger," "the messenger of the covenant," and "the LORD of hosts" in this oracle. Most would affirm that "the LORD of hosts" refers to Yahweh, the God of Israel. Unlike Exod. 23:20, however, the separation between "my messenger" and Yahweh is clearer. What remains unclear is the relationship between "my messenger" and "the messenger of the covenant." In the context of Malachi the two may be separate beings that represent God (see Hill 1998: 286–89), although the distinction between "the messenger of the covenant" and "the LORD of hosts" is more difficult to discern. Those who advocate the two-character approach have provided a strong case for identifying "the messenger of the covenant" with God himself (cf. Exod. 3:6; 14:19; see Glazier-McDonald 1987: 128–42). In light of 4:5–6 [3:23–24 MT], "my messenger" may be identified with the Elijah figure who prepares the way by proclaiming a message of repentance (Stuart 1998: 1393–96). It is this reading that dominates the Jewish and early Christian interpretation of Mal. 3:1.

As Mal. 3:1 draws on Exod. 23:20, the two also share in their concern with covenantal faithfulness. While Exod. 23:20–33 concludes the Book of Covenant with a word of warning, Mal. 3:1 uses a phrase unattested elsewhere in the Hebrew Bible, *mal'ak habbĕrît* ("messenger of the covenant"), in highlighting the covenantal framework within which the acts of purification should be understood. The use of Isa. 40:3 (cf. 57:14; 62:10) also locates the eschatological hope within a context of the new exodus wherein God would act as he did in the days of old. The connections between judgment and salvation in Mal. 3:1–5 qualify the jubilant note of Isa. 40:3, however, as the presence of God also brings judgment to his own people.

C. Exod. 23:20; Mal. 3:1 in Judaism. The precise identity of the messenger of Exod. 23:20 naturally attracts the attention of Jewish exegetes. In the LXX, for example, one finds a separation of the messenger and Yahweh by omitting the references to the pardoning of sins and by identifying the voice as "his [messenger's] voice" instead of the voice of the God who speaks in Exod. 23:21 (Wevers 1990: 370). In Philo this messenger becomes the agent through which God controls the universe (*Agriculture* 51), but it could also serve as the divine reason for the guidance of one's life (*Migration* 174). Elsewhere, Philo also points to the messenger as the prophetic voice coming from the mouth of God (*QE* 2.13). In *3 En.* 10:5 the messenger becomes the "Prince of Wisdom" and the "Prince of Understanding." Further speculation concerning the "name" of God as it relates to divine beings may also reflect an influence of Exod. 23:20–21 (cf. *1 En.* 48:2–3; *Apoc. Ab.* 10:3–8; see Juncker 2001: 253, 262).

In *Exod. Rab.* 32:9 there is an allusion to this verse (together with Mal. 3:10) in the discussion of the theme of divine deliverance. Equally important is the fact that the sending of the messenger in this passage is considered to be a consequence of Israel's faithlessness (Mann 1940: 479; R. E. Watts 1997: 66). It is the presence of both aspects that affects the reading of this verse in later literature.

The significance of Mal. 3:1 in Jewish literature needs to be discussed in relation to its connection with other passages. As noted above, its connection with Exod. 23:20 is reflected in *Exod. Rab.* 32:9, where one finds the theme of deliverance. More importantly, situated within the trajectory emanating from Isa. 40:3, this text points to the eschatologization of the "way" motif in the expectation of God's deliverance (*T. Mos.* 10:1; *1 En.* 1:6–7; *Pesiq. Rab.* 20:30A). Finally, the connection between 3:1 and 4:5–6 (3:23–24 MT) has given rise to a long tradition of Elijah redivivus (cf. Sir. 48:10–11; *1 En.* 89:52; 90:31; *4 Ezra* 6:26; 4Q521; 4Q558; *Sop.* 19:9; *Tg. Ps.-J.* Exod. 40:10; *Tg. Ps.-J.* Deut. 30:4; *Tg. Lam.* 4:22; *m. Soṭah* 9; *Pesiq. Rab Kah.* 76a; see *TDNT* 2:931–34; Collins 1995: 119–22). Consensus is lacking in Jewish literature, however, as far as the role of this Elijah figure is concerned. He may be a priestly figure who takes on a messianic role (4Q541), but whether there is a widespread belief in Elijah as a precursor of the Messiah is debatable (Taylor 1997: 285). One can, however, point to the existence of a certain prophetic figure who would prepare for the work of the Messiah (cf. 1QS IX, 10–11; 4Q175; 11Q13 II, 18–20; see Bovon 2002: 283).

D. Textual Matters. The first part of the verse, *idou apostellō ton angelon mou pro prosōpou sou* ("See, I am sending my messenger ahead of you"), reproduces the first half of Exod. 23:20 LXX, with the omission of the first-person pronoun *egō*, which is present in both its Matthean parallel (11:10) and Exod. 23:20. Other than the addition of *mou* ("my"), the LXX accurately reflects the Hebrew text of Exod. 23:20. Although the primacy of Mal. 3:1 behind this verse is to be affirmed (Fitzmyer 1981–1985: 674), the influence of Exod. 23:20 on the wording of this citation cannot be denied, especially since it also contributed to the formulation in Mal. 3:1 (see Gundry 1967: 11–12).

The second half of the verse, *hos kataskeuasei tēn hodon sou emprosthen sou* ("who will prepare your way before you"), is identical to its Matthean parallel, but it departs significantly from both Exod. 23:20b LXX (*hina phylaxē se en tē hodō*, "that he may guard you in the way") and Mal. 3:1b LXX (*kai epiblepsetai hodon pro prosōpou mou*, "and he will survey the way before me"). It does represent the Hebrew text of Mal. 3:1, *ûpinnâ-derek lĕpānāy* ("to prepare the way before me"), with the change of the first-person pronoun into second person probably because of the context. K. Stendahl (1968: 51–54) suggests that *kataskeuasei* ("[who] will prepare") in the citation assumes that the MT reads *pnh* in the *pi'el*, but the LXX reads it as a *qal*. Theologically, one may also argue that by using *epiblepsetai* ("he will survey"), the LXX intentionally downplays the role of this messenger in the eschatological age (Hill 1988: 266). With the use of *epiblepsetai* ("he will survey"), the failure of the LXX to recognize the connection between Mal. 3:1 and Isa. 40:3 (*hetoimasate*, "prepare") is also evident.

The connection and conflation of Exod. 23:20 and Mal. 3:1 could be made on the level of the

LXX with the appearance of the phrase *ton angelon mou* ("my messenger") in both verses. On the other hand, Luke's (or Q's) apparent dependence on the MT for Mal. 3:1 and the fact that the two are already connected in rabbinic traditions (e.g., *Exod. Rab.* 32:9) point to the possibility that the two verses were connected on the level of the Hebrew text, where both begin with the participle *šōlēaḥ* ("sending") with a first-person singular construction (Exod. 23:20, *hinnēh 'ānōkî*; Mal. 3:1, *hinĕnî*) (see France 1971: 242–43).

E. The Use of Exod. 23:20; Mal. 3:1 in Luke 7:27. In context, the use of these two texts aim primarily at defining the role of John the Baptist in salvation history. The fact that two distinct passages are used further enriches the portrayal of John's ministry. The use of Exod. 23:20 evokes the foundation story of Israel as it locates the ministries of Jesus and John the Baptist within the framework of the new exodus, which depicts God's creation of a true Israel at the end of times. The use of Mal. 3:1 points directly to the preparatory role of John the Baptist as he prepares for the climactic moment in history. It clarifies the picture presented in 1:76 as John is here further identified with the Elijah figure through the connection of Mal. 3:1 and 4:5 (3:23 MT). This unique role of John the Baptist explains Jesus' statements that he is "more than a prophet" (7:26) and that "among those born of women no one is greater than John" (7:28).

Moving beyond the focus on John as an individual, we need to note the covenantal framework in which Exod. 23:20 and Mal. 3:1 are situated. In both passages the call is on Israel to be faithful to their covenantal partner, and judgment is promised to those who rebel against their God (Exod. 23:21; Mal. 3:2–3). In context, this quotation links the presence of John the forerunner and the divine judgment that follows. The Lukan note concerning the rejection of God's purpose by the Pharisees and the lawyers in 7:30 together with the discourse on *tous anthrōpous tēs geneas tautēs* ("the people of this generation") in 7:31–35 (cf. Matt. 11:16–19), a phrase that recalls the rebellious generation in the wilderness (see 7:31 below), clearly shows that the significance of the citations is not limited to John the Baptist.

The shift from the first person of Mal. 3:1 to the second in 7:27 requires further discussion.

The change of person can be attributed to the context, as Jesus is now addressing his audience. This change may then reflect "a shift of emphasis from John as going before the Lord to John preparing the people before the Lord comes" (Bock 1987: 113). This reading draws on Isa. 40:3–5 (cf. Luke 3:4–6), with its prophetic call to the people to be prepared for the coming of the Lord. On the other hand, this change of person may be intended to establish a further christological point. When the citation is taken as an independent unit, the change of person "has the effect of making Yahweh address Messiah" (Carson 1984: 264; cf. S. Brown 1969: 132). This is significant in that the role played by "the messenger of the covenant" in Mal. 4:1 is now played by the Messiah. In the Gospel context this Messiah is Jesus himself. With this reading, not only is the relative position between John and Jesus clarified, but also the functional identity between Jesus and God himself is implied. This reading is further supported by the singular form of the second-person pronoun and by the lack of reference to the role of the people in Mal. 4:1 itself.

F. Theological Use. The significance of Mal. 3:1 for the portrayal of John the Baptist has already been hinted at in 1:17, where he is portrayed as one with "the spirit and power of Elijah" who will "go before" and "make ready a people" for the Lord. In 1:76 it is again noted that he "will go before the Lord to prepare his ways." It is in 7:27, however, that the relationship between John, Jesus, and the Lord is made explicit. It is not surprising, therefore, that the clarification of Jesus' role and ministry in 7:22 is immediately followed by a discussion of John's role and ministry. Jesus takes on the role of the "messenger of the covenant" in Mal. 3:1, and the significance of John's position is derived from the eschatological significance of Jesus himself.

While the clarification of Jesus' ministry is immediately followed by a word of warning (situated within a beatitude formula) in 7:23, the discussion of John's ministry is also followed by a word of judgment (7:29–30). This aspect of the ministry of John is clarified through the transformation of the tradition of Isa. 40:3 in Mal. 3. In Isa. 40:3 the idea of preparation is primarily one that points to the joyous anticipation of the dawn of salvation. With the delay of the fulfillment of such promises, Mal. 3 points to another aspect of preparation where the call to repentance is issued to God's people. While Mal. 3:1 builds on the failure of Israel to be cultically pure, 4:5–6 (3:23–24 MT) concludes with the moral and social transformation that will be accompanied by the turning of "the hearts" (4:6 [3:24 MT]). In the Lukan context the same dual emphases can be found in that while Isa. 40:3–5 appears in 3:4–6 with the announcement of the good news, the use of Mal. 3:1 (together with Exod. 23:20) in 7:27 clarifies the repentance that is required with the presence of God's Messiah. The prophetic call to repentance dominates the central section of Luke (9:51–19:44), which is preceded by the transfiguration narrative (9:28–36), where again Jesus is in the company of Moses and Elijah.

7:31–35

Several phrases reflect the use of biblical language in Jesus' comments on the reception of his and John's ministries. First, the use of the expression *hē genea hautē* ("this generation") in this parable (cf. Matt. 11:16–19) recalls other similar formulations in the context of the proclamation of judgment (cf. 9:40–41 [Matt. 17:16–17]; 11:29–32 [Matt. 12:38–42]; 11:49–51 [Matt. 23:34–36]; 17:22–37 [Matt. 24:26–28, 37–39]; Acts 2:40). Pejorative adjectives found in some of these passages clarify the way this expression is used: *genea apistos kai diestrammenē* ("faithless and perverse generation" [9:41; cf. Matt. 17:17]); *genea ponēra* ("evil generation" [11:29; cf. Matt. 12:39]); *tēs geneas tēs skolias tautēs* ("this corrupt generation" [Acts 2:40]). E. O. Lövestam (1968: 8, 14–15) has shown that these expressions find their roots in Deut. 32:4b–5 ("A faithful God, without deceit, just and upright is he; yet his degenerate children have dealt falsely with him, a perverse and crooked generation [*genea skolia kai diestrammenē*]") and 32:20 ("He said, 'I will hide my face from them, I will see what their end will be; for they are a perverse generation [*genea exestrammenē*], children in whom there is no faithfulness [*pistis*]'"). These passages clearly refer to the wilderness generation, which rebelled against their God after experiencing his acts of deliverance. In the prophetic traditions the same term is used in describing God's disobedient people: "for the LORD has rejected and forsaken the generation [*tēn genean*] that provoked his wrath" (Jer. 7:29). In this Lukan context "this generation" likewise rejected God's messengers after witnessing God's acts through them. The description of the Pharisees and the lawyers as those who "rejected God's purpose for themselves" (7:30) therefore links them with their ancestors who had rejected their God.

The phrase *anthrōpos phagos kai oinopotēs* ("a glutton and a drunkard" [7:34]) may be an echo of Deut. 21:20. Although the exact meaning of the MT's *zôlēl* ("profligate") is unclear, the Targumim *Pseudo-Jonathan*, *Onqelos*, and *Neofiti* understand the term to refer to gluttony. The tradition behind Luke's expression may thus reflect the influence of the Targumim, especially when the wording departs from the LXX's *symbolokopōn oinophlygei*, "he is given to feasting and drunkenness" (see Allison 2000a: 40). In Deut. 21:20–21 the son who is described as a "glutton and a drunkard" is the rebellious one who is to be stoned to death. In Luke's context the use of this phrase not only points to Jesus' refusal to conform to the expectation of the Jewish leaders but also reflects his readiness to suffer under their hands (see Kee 2002: 329).

The final saying of this pericope, *edikaiōthē hē sophia apo pantōn tōn teknōn autēs* ("wisdom is vindicated by all her children" [7:35]), is difficult, especially when the identity of the *teknōn* ("children") is unclear. D. P. Moessner (1989: 103–4) represents many by arguing for the connection between vv. 29 and 35, concluding therefore that those who accept John and Jesus in general, and the tax collectors in particular, are the intended references behind *teknōn*. In light of the flow of the narrative, however, an equally strong case can be made that the *teknōn* refers primarily to Jesus and John the Baptist (see Carson 1994b). The Matthean parallel, *ta erga* ("the deeds" [11:19]), refers then to the works of John and Jesus. The Lukan inclusion of the term *pantōn* ("all") may widen the intended references to include John, Jesus, and their disciples (Fitzmyer 1981–1985: 679). For our purposes, it is sufficient to note that an explicit wisdom Christology cannot be detected in Matt. 11:19 (*contra* Witherington 1994: 145, 227) and especially in this Lukan parallel in light of *pantōn* ("all") and the plural *teknōn* ("children"). Moreover, although early Jewish wisdom texts (cf. Prov. 8:32–33; Sir. 4:11; see Schürmann 1990–1994: 1:427) do provide a general context

for this saying, parallels are lacking in which these "children" provide justification for wisdom.

7:42–43

J. A. Sanders (1993b: 87) has argued for the presence of an allusion to the Jubilee legislation (Deut. 15:1–3; Lev. 25) with the use of the analogy of the cancellation of debts. This is questionable in light of the use of the verb *charizomai* instead of *aphiemi* in reference to the "canceling/releasing" of debts. In light of 7:21, which has the only other occurrence of the verb *charizomai* in this Gospel, however, the connection with the wider Isaianic program as represented in Isa. 35:3–4; 61:1–2 is possible, where the gracious acts of God are promised to be revealed. The appropriateness of this analogy can thus be affirmed even without the presence of an explicit Jubilee reference.

7:48–49

For the issue of divine forgiveness, see 5:21 above.

7:50

The expression *poreuou eis eirēnēn* ("go in peace") finds its LXX parallels in 1 Sam. 1:17; 20:42, where divine approval is expressed. This sense fits well in this context, where the woman receives divine forgiveness. Other related formulations point to a request granted (cf. *anabēthi eis eirēnēn* [1 Sam. 25:35]; *badize eis eirēnēn* [2 Sam. 15:9]; *deuro eis eirēnēn* [2 Kings 5:19]). Both senses are present in 8:48, where the same phrase occurs with the clause *hē pistis sou sesōken se* ("your faith has saved you") in the context of Jesus' healing of the hemorrhaging woman.

8:10

A. NT Context: Responses to the Word. The parable of the Sower follows a summary statement of Jesus' preaching of the good news (8:1) and healing of those who are plagued by "evil spirits and infirmities" (8:2). This parable focuses on the different responses to the ministries of Jesus, and the Isaianic quotation in 8:10 focuses squarely on this issue of response. Echoes from the OT provide structure for this parable. Metaphors of sowing can be found in Jer. 31:27; Ezek. 36:9; Hos. 2:23 (see Bock 1994–1996: 723), while Jer. 4:3 in particular should be highlighted in light of its reference to the sowing "among thorns" (Gertner 1962: 272).

In light of the focus on the "word of God" (8:11), further parallels with Isa. 55:10–11 should not be overlooked (see C. A. Evans 1985). It is in this Isaianic passage that one finds the "seed" and the "sower" together in the context of the portrayal of the powerful "word of God": "For as the rain and the snow come down from heaven, and do not return there until they have watered the earth, making it bring forth and sprout, giving seed to the sower and bread to the eater, so shall my word be that goes out from my mouth. . . ."

On the assumption that Luke has Mark as his source for this parable (see Fitzmyer 1981–1985: 700–702), several Lukan emphases can be detected. First, the focus on the seed (8:5; cf. Mark 4:3) draws attention to the word of God itself (8:11; cf. Mark 4:14). The explicit mentioning of the sower who "called out" (8:8; cf. Mark 4:9) may reflect the same emphasis. Second, unlike Mark, who highlights the separation between the crowd and the disciples (Mark 4:10) and therefore sees this parable as an introduction to the teachings to the disciples, Luke uses this parable to emphasize the general response that the gospel demands. The omission of the disciples' lack of understanding (Mark 4:13) confirms this point.

Although the Markan separation between the crowd and the disciples is not maintained in Luke, the distinction between them is retained. Immediately preceding the allusion to Isa. 6:9–10, it is said that while outsiders will encounter parables, Jesus' disciples will receive *ta mystēria* ("the mysteries" [8:10]) of the kingdom of God. The *mystērion* of the Hellenistic mystery cults is quite foreign to the way this term is used here. R. E. Brown (1968) and others (Tuckett 1988: 15; Bockmuehl 1990: 24–126) have convincingly pointed to the Semitic background where *mystērion* refers to the eschatological acts of God to be revealed to the elect. Daniel 2 in particular provides a conceptual parallel where *rāz* refers to the eschatological plan of God that is yet to be revealed (cf. *mystērion* in Dan. 2:18, 19, 27, 28, 29, 30, 47). In the context of this parable the mysteries refer to God's eschatological plan, but they also point to the specific role that Jesus is playing in such unfolding of salvation history.

B. Isa. 6:9–10 in Context. The proclamation of judgment in Isa. 6 is anticipated by the previous chapters with the listing of Israel's sins. Isaiah 1 opens with the accusation against Israel, who had "rebelled" against their God (1:2). Their leaders are accused of misleading and confusing them (cf. 3:12–16), and together with the people they will be judged: "Therefore Sheol has enlarged its appetite and opened its mouth beyond measure; the nobility of Jerusalem and her multitude go down, her throng and all who exult in her" (5:14). In the midst of chaos, Isa. 6 begins with a vision of the holy God who sits on the throne (vv. 1–4). This is followed by the prophetic call account proper, which contains an admission of human frailty (6:5), divine affirmation (6:6–7), and the response to the divine call (6:8). This is followed by the message that Isaiah is called to proclaim (6:9–13).

Three related elements in this prophetic message are emphasized throughout Isaiah. First, the obduracy theme is developed with the one of Israel's rebellion against their God, and it is one found beyond Isa. 6 (cf. 29:9–10; 42:18–20; 43:8; 44:18; 63:17; see C. A. Evans 1989: 43–46). The repeated references to this theme in Isaiah show that it is as much an indictment as it is a diagnosis of Israel's condition in the presence of their covenant partner.

Second, the connection between sin and exile reflected in 6:11–12 ("Until cities lie waste without inhabitant, and houses without people, and the land is utterly desolate; until the LORD sends everyone far away, and vast is the emptiness in the midst of the land") is already noted in 5:13. This connection can also be found in 27:8–13; 49:20–21. The "sin" of Israel is one that is characterized by idolatry, and this charge of idolatry is paved by 2:5–8, 18–22, which depicts the sins of Judah. G. K. Beale (1991) has shown that the language used in 6:9 in particular ("listening, but do not comprehend . . . looking, but do not understand") reflects the language used to describe the idols themselves as in Ps. 135:16–17 (cf. 115:5–6). The ironic point established by the use of these metaphors of sight and audition is that Israel has turned into the idols that they had worshiped. Extensive anti-idol polemic occurs in Isa. 42:16–20; 43:8–12; 44:8–20; 47:5–11, where a similar use of this set of metaphors is found in speeches against the idols of the pagans.

Third, a "faint, but sure, ray of hope" (Oswalt 1986–1998: 1:190) may be present in 6:13b in the statement "The holy seed is its stump." The precise interpretation of this phrase is subject to debate (see J. D. W. Watts 1985–1987: 1:76), but the presence of a hopeful note within the gloomy message is found elsewhere in Isa. 1–39 (cf. 2:2–4; 9:2–7; 11:1–3, 10–16; 25:6–10; 32:14–20; 35). Particularly important is Isa. 40:1–11, which serves as a striking reversal of this passage (see Fisher 1974). In both, one finds a commissioning scene and the use of the metaphor for sight. Unlike Isa. 6, however, Isa. 40 proclaims the arrival of the eschatological era, in which God will reverse his indictment by providing salvation for his own people. Isa. 6, therefore, should not be considered as the final statement on the relationship between God and his people.

Together, these elements serve to unpack the nature and function of Isa. 6. The reality of God's judgment is to be affirmed, but so is the promised redemption. In terms of function, the prophetic nature of this section likewise points to the emphasis on both the predictive element, which reveals the consequence of Israel's pattern of disobedience, and the hortatory nature of the call to respond to the one and the only living God. The ambiguity and the creative tension created by these considerations have led to the various uses of this passage in the different conceptual frameworks apart from the constraints of the Isaianic context.

C. Isa. 6:9–10 in Judaism. One of the earliest interpretations of Isa. 6:9–10 is in the LXX, on the assumption that the MT reflects the original Hebrew text. The toning down of the hardening process is reflected in the following changes from the MT. First, the future indicatives *akousete* ("you will hear") and *blepsete* ("you will see") replace the Hebrew imperatives *šimʿû* ("hear") and *rěʾû* ("see"). Second, the aorist passive *epachynthē* ("has grown dull") is used instead of the Hebrew imperative *hašmēn* ("make dull") and thereby tones down the role of God as an active agent. The *hipʿil* imperatives *hakbēd* ("stop") and *hāšaʿ* ("shut") are likewise translated by the indicatives *[bareōs] ēkousan* ("hard of hearing") and *ekammysan* ("they have shut"). Moreover, the insertion of *gar* ("for") at the beginning of 6:10 also shifts the focus away from the role of God.

These concerns of the LXX translators represent the general areas of interest of the interpretive traditions deriving from these verses (C. A. Evans 1989: 51–60, 69–80). In the 1QIsaᵃ 6:9–10, for example, the negative particle *ʾal* ("not") is strikingly replaced by *ʿal* ("because"), and thus the negative statement becomes a causal one: "Keep listening, because you may understand; keep looking, because you may perceive." Moreover, the negative conclusion is turned into a positive one: "Let it understand...." These changes turned this passage into one that is "to warn and aid the elect in protecting themselves from evil" (C. A. Evans 1989: 56).

The Targumic reading (cf. *Tg. Isa.* 6:9–10) reflects similar concerns. The command to the prophet is transformed into a description of the rebellious nature of God's people. While the negative tone of these verses is downplayed, emphasis is placed on 6:13b, where one finds further development of the idea of the "holy seed." The Peshitta reflects the influence of both the LXX and the Targumim, as it emphasizes the stubbornness of the people and downplays the agency of God.

Beyond these attempts to soften the harshness of the prophetic message, this text is evoked in various other ways. In Philo, for example, the anti-idol language is overlooked, and the contrasts between listening and comprehending, and looking and understanding, are used to illustrate the lack of ability to discern true reality as in the state of dreams (*Joseph* 126). Closer to the early Christian uses of this text is *Sib. Or.* 1:360–364, a text that betrays Christian influences, where the ethnic focus is evident: "And then, Israel, intoxicated, will not perceive nor yet will she hear, afflicted with weak ears. But when the raging wrath of the Most High comes upon the Hebrews, it will also take faith away from them, because they did harm to the son of the heavenly God."

D. Textual Matters. Unlike Matthew, who includes an explicit quotation of Isa. 6:9–10 in the discussion that follows the parable of the Sower (Matt. 13:14–15), Luke moves it to the end of his work (Acts 28:26–27). The fact that Luke is aware of the textual tradition behind Matthew's quotation is indicated by the omission of *autōn* ("their") after *ōsin* ("ears") in his quotation in Acts 28:27 (cf. Matt. 13:15). Instead of the explicit quotation, Luke retains the Markan allusion to the Isaianic text, with two major changes. First, like Matthew, Luke simplifies the Markan compound clauses (*hina blepontes blepōsin kai mē idōsin, kai akouontes akouōsin kai mē syniōsin*, "in order that they may indeed look, but not perceive, and may indeed listen, but not understand" [Mark 4:12a]), although Luke and Matthew seem to be working independently in this case (*hina blepontes mē blepōsin kai akouontes mē syniōsin*, "in order that looking they may not perceive, and listening they may not understand" [Luke 8:10; cf. Matt. 13:13: *hoti blepontes ou blepousin kai akouontes ouk akouousin oude syniousin*, "that seeing they do not perceive, and hearing they do not listen, nor do they understand"]).

Second, and more importantly, Luke omits Mark's further allusion to the final words of Isa. 6:10, *mēpote epistrepsōsin kai aphethē autois* ("so that they may not turn again and be forgiven" [Mark 4:12; cf. Matt. 13:15]). Rather than seeing this omission as an intentional softening of Jesus' "arbitrary exclusion of some from forgiveness" (Stagg 1997: 218), it seems that Luke has reserved this final word of judgment for the very end of his work (cf. Acts 28:27; see Pao 2000: 104–9).

E. The Use of Isa. 6:9–10 in Luke 8:10. Unlike Mark and Matthew, in Luke this Isaianic quotation appears in the response of Jesus concerning not the purpose of using parables in general, but rather the precise meaning of this parable about the sower (8:9; cf. Mark 4:10; Matt. 13:10). This could be interpreted as an intentional narrowing of the application of this Isaianic text, but equally plausible is that Luke considers this parable to be the key to understanding the rest of Jesus' teaching. This reading is affirmed by the summary statement that precedes, which points to Jesus *kēryssōn kai euangelizomenos tēn basileian tou theou* ("proclaiming and bringing the good news of the kingdom of God" [8:1]). Moreover, the use of this citation in this context provides a link to Luke's central section (9:51–19:44), where the Jewish rejection of the gospel is repeatedly noted.

The telic force of *hina* ("in order that") in Mark 4:12 is retained in 8:10, and the difficulty of this saying should not be resolved by the softening of the force of the *hina* clause (Fitzmyer 1981–1985: 708–9; cf. Nolland 1989–1993: 380). This *hina* clause has to be understood in its wider literary and theological contexts, however. First, the note on the sovereignty of God in general, and the evocation of the *mystēria* ("mysteries") of the kingdom

of God in particular, point to the unfolding of the salvation plan of God. Therefore, the telic force of the *hina* clause should not be limited to the statement on the use of parables. Second, in the context of Isaiah, 6:9–10 serves as a prophetic word of judgment. The pattern of the rejection of God's plan by his people is highlighted, but the failure of the people to respond does not reflect on the efficacy of God's word. In Luke, the rejection of the prophetic message is a theme that was already introduced at the beginning of Jesus' ministry (4:16–30), but the implicit call to repentance can still be detected behind this prophetic word of judgment. This "both-and" aspect of prophetic ministry is well illustrated in Luke's second volume, where the claim to turn away from the Jews (Acts 13:46–47; 18:6) nonetheless does not signify the end of Paul's ministries to the Jews. Moreover, the prophetic call in 8:8 ("Let anyone with ears to hear listen!") reflects this continued call to repentance.

Although Luke omits the *mēpote* clause of Mark 4:12 (see discussion above), he does insert a similar phrase within the parable itself: "The devil comes and takes away the word from their hearts, so that they may not [*hina mē*] believe and be saved" (8:12). Some commentators (see C. A. Evans 1989: 117) see this as Luke's attempt to soften the Isaianic saying by shifting the focus from Jesus to Satan as the one who promotes human obduracy. This is insufficient for two reasons. First, the *mēpote* clause does appear at the end of Luke's narrative (Acts 28:27), and it is clear that the finality of this word of judgment is not suppressed but is reserved for that significant narratological position. Second, to align human rejection of the gospel with the will of Satan highlights the rejection of the messianic ministry as an act of active rebellion against God and his plan of salvation. This is consistent with the description of the Jewish leadership as those who "rejected God's purpose [*tēn boulē tou theou*] for themselves" (7:30).

Finally, as Isa. 6:9–10 uses anti-idol language to depict the failure of Israel to respond to their God, similar use of anti-idol polemic is found in Luke's second volume. In Acts 7:48, for example, the temple that is supposed to be used as the place where the creator God is worshiped is described as *cheiropoiētois* ("made with human hands"), a word that is always used in connection with acts of idolatry in the LXX (Lev. 26:1, 30; Isa. 10:11; 16:12; 19:1; 21:9; 31:7; 46:6; cf. *tois ergois tōn cheirōn autōn*, "works of their hands" [Acts 7:41]). In this context the pattern of Israel's rejection of the plan of God is again noted: "You stiff-necked people, uncircumcised in heart and ears, you are forever opposing the Holy Spirit, just as your ancestors used to do" (Acts 7:51). The pattern of Jewish rejection of God's plan is therefore established, and, as in Luke 8, Israel is described as a people who fail to hear and therefore have aligned themselves with the enemy of God.

F. Theological Use. From the foregoing discussion, it is clear that the use of Isa. 6:9–10 is not limited to the explication of Jesus' use of parables. It also serves as an indictment against Israel for repeatedly failing to respond to their God. In light of Acts 28:26–27, the focus on the application of this citation on Israel is made explicit (see Longenecker [2000: 136], who downplays this emphasis by noting Luke's primary interest in his Gentile audience). The Jewish leaders at the time of Jesus in particular are to be blamed, as were the leaders of Israel at the time of Isaiah (Isa. 3:12–16). In the Lukan context the call of repentance to the people at large is still available (10:1–16; 13:1–9; 14:15–24; 15:1–32; 17:26–37; 19:1–10), even though the Jewish leaders were already discussing "what they might do to Jesus" (6:11).

While the Israel of Jesus' time is typologically connected with the Israel that rejected the plan of God, the prophet Isaiah also provides the framework to understand Jesus' own ministry. As Isa. 6 points to rejection as part of Isaiah's vocation (see McLaughlin 1994: 24), Luke 8:10 confirms the words in Jesus' inaugural speech, which note that "no prophet is accepted in the prophet's hometown" (4:24). Significantly, the reappearance of Isa. 6 at the end of Acts 28 connects the ministry of Jesus with that of the apostles. Thus the persecution and suffering that characterize the ministries of the apostles are not to be interpreted as signs of failure.

8:22–25

R. D. Aus (2000: 11–55) has provided extensive discussion of the parallels between the account of Jesus' calming the storm and Jon. 1, especially in light of the embellishment of the story in various recensions of *Midrash Jonah* (*Pirqe R. El.* 10; *Tanḥ.*

Viyiqra' 8; *Yal. Shem'oni Jonah* 549–51). Many of the parallels noted (e.g., the presence of other boats, the crossing over, the role of the sailors, the presence of the storm, the danger of sinking, the ceasing of the storm) are, however, naturally present in any account of a storm story. Moreover, the fact that Aus (2000: 56–70) further argues for the influence of the account of Julius Caesar's attempt to cross the Adriatic Sea during a winter storm in 48 BC shows that some of the details in the Gospel account of Jesus' calming the storm naturally belong to any historical account of sea travel.

What is certain, however, is the presence of a significant OT motif that focuses on the power of God. The mastery of Yahweh manifested in his ability to control the waters/seas is considered "the basic idea of Israelite religion" (Kaufmann 1972: 60; cf. Levenson 1988: 3), and the presence of this idea is most apparent in the liturgical traditions of Israel (Ps. 24:1–2; 29:3–4; 32:6–7; 33:6–7; 46:1–3; 65:5–8; 69:13–15; 77:16–20; 93:3–4; 104:7–9; 124:1–5). In the historical memory of Israel the foundational event of God's deliverance of Israel from the hands of their enemies is captured in the scene in Exod. 14, where God divides the sea and brings his people out of Egypt (cf. Ps. 66:6; 74:13–15; Isa. 43:2, 16–19; 44:26–27; 51:9–11). The connection between God's ability to calm a storm in times of distress and the paradigmatic exodus event is made in Ps. 107:23–32, where "individual salvation and corporate salvation are held together as the wonderful work of the LORD's *hesed*" (Mays 1994: 347). As in the exodus event, Jesus' calming of the storm provides yet another historical manifestation of God's power and control. What is striking in this instance is that Jesus is the one who is able to calm the waters. This miracle, therefore, makes a clear christological claim as Jesus is again recognized to be working as his Father is.

8:26–39

For the Jewish audience of first-century Palestine, the account of the Gerasene demoniac who lived in the graves naturally involves issues of purity and impurity, since touching a corpse rendered a person unclean (Lev. 11:24–28; Num. 19:11, 14–16). For the description of the demoniac, some commentators (Schürmann 1990–1994: 1:480; Bovon 2002: 327) also point to Isa. 65

LXX, where the connection between idols and demons is made (*autoi thysiazousin en tois kēpois kai thymiōsin epi tais plinthois tois daimoniois ha ouk estin,* "they offer sacrifices in the gardens and burn incense on bricks to the demons, which do not exist" [65:3]) in a context where pagan cults are described in terms of worshiping inside the tombs and eating the flesh of swine (65:4). Both passages do contain a similar conglomeration of ideas, but the connection between impurity and pagan/demonic worship of the idols of the Gentiles is common in prophetic traditions (Ezek. 36:25; Hos. 8:5; Zech. 13:2; cf. Ps. 24:4). Thus it is best to see 8:26–39 as reflecting the general pagan context in which this event is situated.

The word *abyssos* ("abyss" [8:31]) is an adjective ("bottomless") that came to be used as a noun meaning "bottomless pit." It is used in reference to deep places (Gen. 1:2; Deut. 33:13; Job 28:14; Ps. 42:7 [41:8 LXX]) in general, and deep waters (Gen. 7:11; 8:2; Deut. 8:7; Ps. 33:7 [32:7 LXX]; 77:16 [76:17 LXX]; 148:7) in particular. It also came to be used to refer to the realm of the dead (Ps. 71:20 [70:20 LXX]), and in Jewish literature this usage is extended to refer to the place for the fallen spirits (*1 En.* 10:4–6; 18:11–16; *Jub.* 5:6–7) (see *NIDNTT* 2:205). In this context it refers to the deep waters that are considered to be the place for demons.

8:43–48

Again the issue of purity forms the background of this pericope. Leviticus 15:19–30 provides the basic regulations on menstrual bleeding, and this Levitical passage is evoked through the expression *rhysis haimatos* ("flow of blood"), which appears in both Luke 8:43 and Lev. 15:25. In Lev. 15 a woman with "regular discharge" is impure for seven days (v. 19), and "if a woman has a discharge of blood for many days, not at the time of her impurity, or if she has a discharge beyond the time of her impurity, all the days of the discharge she shall continue in uncleanness" (v. 25). The threat of death is present for those unclean who approach the tabernacle (15:31). Detailed regulations are developed in later rabbinic material (cf. *m. Zabim* 2:14; *m. Nid.* 3:2; see Weissenrieder 2002: 220n4), but it is not clear how widespread was the observance of such complex regulations in the first century.

Jesus' interaction with the hemorrhaging woman and his allowing her to touch his cloak seem to have violated the "Pharisees' core value of maintaining holiness (Lev. 11:44)" and challenged "their exclusive strategy" (Love 2002: 97). Moreover, since purity is primarily a cultic issue, Jesus' act of healing takes on added significance. It is not surprising, therefore, that Jesus' final words to her are identical to those he uttered to the woman whose sins he had declared forgiven: *hē pistis sou sesōken se, poreuou eis eirēnēn* ("Your faith has saved you; go in peace" [7:50; 8:48]). Not only is her health restored, but also the healed woman regains the right to be part of the worshiping community. It is in this sense that both the authority of Jesus and the cultic community that centers on him are established through this healing miracle.

9:1–6

As in 6:12–16, this passage focuses on the Twelve. This commissioning account may remind the readers of Num. 13, where the twelve spies represent the twelve tribes of Israel (Num. 13:2; cf. Luke 22:28–30). Significant verbal parallels are missing, however, and the purposes of the two commissioning reports are quite different (see Bovon 2002: 344). In the Lukan context the Twelve represent Jesus in the proclamation of "the kingdom of God" (9:2). As in the mission of Jesus (4:24), the rejection of the Twelve is also to be expected (9:5).

9:8

Three possibilities are available for understanding the reference to Elijah in this verse. First, there may be an allusion to 2 Kings 2:1–12 whereby the return of Elijah is expected in the person of Jesus. Second, building on 2 Kings 2:1–2, the eschatological traditions in Mal. 4:5 point to an eschatological Elijah figure who is sent "before the great and terrible day of the Lord comes." Third, Elijah might be considered simply as a prophet of old who is able to perform great miracles. In light of the reference to the response of "others" who suggest later in this verse that in Jesus "one of the ancient prophets had arisen," the third option seems the least likely. The first option, which suggests the unmediated connection between this verse and 2 Kings 2:1–2, is also unlikely in light of Luke's awareness of the Malachi traditions and the long exegetical tradition that builds on Mal. 3–4 (see 7:27 above). The reference to an eschatological figure is therefore probable, especially in light of the allusion to Mal. 3:1 in 7:27. Two distinct but related aspects of the eschatological Elijah of Mal. 3–4 are developed in Jewish exegetical traditions. First, this prophetic figure is to prepare the people for the coming of Yahweh (cf. Sir. 48:10). Second, the presence of this figure (*Tg. Ps.-J.* Exod. 40:10; *Tg. Ps.-J.* Deut. 30:4) signifies the presence of the eschatological era, as the manifestation of divine power and authority are witnessed through the ministry of this figure. This may explain how both John the Baptist and Jesus could be connected with this Elijah tradition in Luke. John the Baptist fulfills the role as the precursor of God (and his Messiah), while Jesus signifies the presence of divine power and authority. The application of the Elijah paradigm in the explication of the ministry of Jesus in 4:25–26, together with the mention of Elijah in the transfiguration account (9:30), fit well with this reading. The inadequacy of this identification should also be noted, however, and this is implied in the observations by Herod in 9:7–9 and by the crowd in 9:19.

9:10–17

Two OT events are often noted as providing the proper framework in which to understand Jesus' feeding of the five thousand. First, the short account of Elisha's feeding of a hundred men in 2 Kings 4:42–44 provides a number of structural parallels (Bovon 1993: 28): the presentation of the bread to the prophet (9:13; 2 Kings 4:42), the prophet's order for the people to be fed (9:13; 2 Kings 4:42), the reaction of the prophet's followers (9:13; 2 Kings 4:43), the new order from the prophet (9:14; 2 Kings 4:43), the distribution and eating of the bread (9:16; 2 Kings 4:44), and the note concerning the leftovers (9:17; 2 Kings 4:44).

As the Elisha story builds on the feeding of the Israelites in the wilderness (Exod. 16–18), so may the setting in the account of Jesus' feeding of the five thousand evoke the same event (9:12; Exod. 16:1–3). Moreover, the connection between fish and quail is already made in Num. 11:22, 31, and thus the "five loaves and two fish" may be a reference to the manna and quail that God had provided for his people during the wilderness journey (see Stegner 1989: 59). Others have further traced this connection between birds and fish through

Second Temple and rabbinic literature (cf. Wis. 19:10–12; *b. Ḥul.* 27b; see van Cangh 1971).

Before suggesting that a tight Moses or Elijah/Elisha typology is developed through these allusions, we should note a few points. First, in its Lukan context this story is framed by two passages that highlight the inadequacy of the Elijah and prophetic paradigms for understanding the significance of Jesus' ministry (cf. 9:7–8, 19). It is only with the confession of Peter and Jesus' discussion of his own fate (9:20, 22–27) that the mission of Jesus is properly presented. Second, the general theme of God's provision for his people can be detected, and the Moses and Elisha miracles should also be considered as individual manifestations of God's provision. This theme of God's faithfulness culminates in the eschatological banquet tradition, which utilizes the "meal" imagery to portray the satisfaction that God's people would experience at the end of times (Isa. 25:6; cf. 55:2; Ezek. 34:14). Third, although the manna tradition did merge with that of the eschatological banquet, no texts provide a convincing parallel for the pairing of manna and fish (or even Leviathan) within the context of the eschatological banquet. It seems best to conclude that the "inclusion of fish is probably due to the proximity of the Feeding Miracle to the Sea of Galilee" (Wong 1998: 180).

With these qualifications noted, it still seems probable that the feeding of God's people in the wilderness in the time of Moses does provide one viable framework to appreciate the significance of the feeding act by Jesus. The transfiguration narrative that follows (9:28–36) likewise situates Jesus within the trajectory of the Moses traditions. Perhaps it is best to recognize both the continuity and discontinuity of Jesus' ministry with the ancient prophetic traditions. It is this tension that seems to have dominated this entire chapter, where the presentation of the identity and function of Jesus the Messiah is constantly framed with, but not limited by, traditional paradigms.

9:18–20

Peter's confession serves as a response to Herod's earlier question concerning the identity of Jesus (9:7–9). Unlike Matthew, who included Jeremiah in the list (Matt. 16:14), Luke's account of how others understood Jesus includes the same list as the one in 9:7–8: John (the Baptist), Elijah, and "one of the ancient prophets." The *christos*

("Christ/Messiah") of Peter's response is a title that first appears in the Lukan birth narrative (see 2:11), and the title is consistently used to refer to the expected royal Davidic figure. The title is absent from the central section of Luke, and its next appearance, in 20:41, followed by the quotation of Ps. 110:1, explicitly relates Jesus' messianic status to the Davidic expectation.

9:21–22

The expression *ho huios tou anthrōpou* ("Son of Man") first appears in 5:24. Here it is used to explicate the messianic ministry of Jesus (cf. 17:24–25). This suffering Son of Man serves to qualify the Jewish expectation of a messiah who is defined by political power and might (cf. *Pss. Sol.* 17). Jesus' rejection has been noted (cf. 4:24; 7:31–35), but this is the first explicit note that he would suffer death as the Messiah of God (cf. 9:43b–45; 18:31–34). The precise background for this combination of ideas and titles is unclear. The "Son of Man" title, of course, recalls Dan. 7:13–14, but the connection between suffering and this Son of Man is weak in its context. A more likely candidate is Isa. 53, where one finds the combination of "the motifs of prophetic necessity and the Isaianic NE [new exodus]" (R. E. Watts 1998: 132). The absence of a clear Jewish precedent for the connection between the Messiah and the Suffering Servant of Isa. 53 (see Fitzmyer 1981–1985: 780) is not a critical argument against the existence of this connection in the NT. Finally, the use of the word *apodokimasthēnai* ("be rejected") in 9:22 (cf. Mark 8:31) may have been taken from Ps. 118:22 (117:22 LXX): *lithon ho apedokimasan hoi oikodomountes* ("the stone that the builders rejected"). Noting that almost all of the other occurrences of this verb in the NT can be found in allusions or quotations of Ps. 118 (Mark 8:31; Luke 17:25; 1 Pet. 2:4, 7), Wagner (1997: 162) concludes that this "strongly suggests that the verb in Lk. 9.22 should be understood as a reference to Ps. 118.22." In light of the significance of both Isa. 53 and Ps. 118 in the Lukan writings, to have to choose between the two seems arbitrary.

9:26

The description of *ho huios tou anthrōpou* ("the Son of Man") who *elthē en tē doxē* ("comes in glory") may recall the Danielic figure *hōs huios anthrōpou erchomenos* ("coming as the Son of Man"), the

one who was given *hē archē kai hē timē kai hē basileia* ("dominion and glory and kingship") (Dan. 7:13–14 Θ). Rather than suppressing the reference to the Danielic figure (see Juel 1998: 160), Matthew, in explicitly identifying this figure with Jesus himself (Matt. 10:32–33), reflects what is implied in the Markan (8:38) and Lukan texts.

Luke 9:28–36

Allusions to a number of OT texts can be identified in the Lukan transfiguration narrative, and together they provide a picture of Jesus' identity and the mission he will accomplish. Allusions to the exodus context have been noted by many (see Liefeld 1974; Moessner 1989: 60–62; Strauss 1995: 268–72). Two texts are particularly relevant for this account: Exod. 24:9–18; 34:29–35. First, the mountain as a place of revelation parallels the Sinai setting of Exod. 24. Second, the presence of the cloud may recall God's guidance of his people by the cloud (Exod. 13:21–22; 14:19–20, 24; 16:10; 19:9, 16), but the voice coming from the cloud finds its possible parallel in the later passages where Moses is said to have "entered the cloud" (Exod. 24:15–18) and received divine revelation (Exod. 25–31). These paradigmatic events may have contributed to the later uses of the "cloud" imagery as signifying God's eschatological presence (Isa. 4:5; 14:14; 19:1; Ezek. 10:3–4; Dan. 7:13–14). Third, Luke's *to eidos tou prosōpou autou heteron* ("the appearance of his face changed" [9:29]) may echo *to de eidos tēs doxēs kyriou* ("the appearance of the glory of the Lord" [Exod. 24:17]) and/or *dedoxastai hē opsis tou chrōmatos tou prosōpou autou* ("the appearance of the skin of his face shone" [Exod. 34:29]). Fourth, the unique Lukan note on the conversation among Jesus, Moses, and Elijah is particularly relevant with the appearance of the phrase *tēn exodon autou* ("his exodus/departure" [9:31]). In context, it is clear that Luke considers Jesus' death and resurrection/ascension to be an exodus (cf. Luke 9:31; see Garrett 1990). Moreover, this term has been used to refer to the death of an individual (Philo, *Virtues* 77; Josephus, *Ant.* 4.189; 2 Pet. 1:15). A secondary reference might be present, however, in light of the frequent usage of this term in the LXX in reference to the historical exodus event when God saved his people from bondage (Exod. 19:1; Num.

33:38; 1 Kings 6:1; Ps. 105:38 [104:38 LXX]; 114:1 [113:1 LXX]). P. Doble (1996: 211) has highlighted the significance of Wis. 3:1–3 for this discussion, with its reference to the death and vindication of the righteous individual in a context where the historical paradigm of the exodus event best illustrates God's role in such acts of vindication (Wis. 8–19). This double reference in Wis. 3:1–3 may also be present in Luke's transfiguration narrative, where the foundational event of Israel is connected with the life of an individual. Fifth, a typological reference to Moses is present in the command *autou akouete* ("listen to him" [9:35]; cf. *akouete autou* [Mark 9:7; Matt. 17:5]). The Lukan word order makes it clear that it should be taken as an allusion to Deut. 18:15: *autou akousesthe* ("you shall listen to him"). Finally, the mention of the *skēnas* ("booths" [9:33]) may again be a reference to the extensive discussion of *to paradeigma tēs skēnēs* ("the model of the tent/ sanctuary" [Exod. 25:9]) in Exod. 25–28 (Stegner 1989: 88) and possibly also to the Feast of Tabernacles (Lev. 23:43), which came to be understood as a reference to God's eschatological presence (*Jub.* 32:27–29; *Tg. Neof.* Lev. 23:42–43). Admittedly, not all of these allusions are of equal strength, but together they are sufficient to show the relevance of the Moses/exodus framework for this narrative. The presence of Moses himself in 9:33 secures this connection, and this is consistent with the Lukan portrayal of Jesus as the Mosaic prophetic figure (Acts 3:19–24; cf. 7:37).

With this evocation of the Moses/exodus paradigm, the presence of other paradigms that clarify the significance of this event also needs to be noted. First, the presence of Elijah recalls 4:25–26; 9:8, 19. While the ministries of both John the Baptist and Jesus are related to the prophecies of Mal. 3–4, John fulfills the role of Elijah as the precursor of God (and his Messiah), as Jesus fulfills the eschatological hope embedded in this prophecy and brings in the eschatological era. The appearance of Moses and Elijah may draw attention to a number of parallels between these two OT figures: their unusual departure (Deut. 34:6; 2 Kings 2:11), their experience of God's glory (Exod. 25–31; 1 Kings 19:8–18), their pivotal prophetic status, and their possible representation of the law and the prophets (Schürmann 1990–1994: 1:557–58; Carson 1984: 385).

The expectation of their appearance together at the end of times is also attested in rabbinic traditions: "Moses, I swear to you, as you devoted your life to their service in this world, so too in the time to come when I bring Elijah the prophet to them, the two of you shall come together" (*Deut. Rab.* 3:17 [on 10:1]; cf. *b. Soṭah* 13b; see C. A. Evans 1993a: 81n47).

Second, the address of Jesus as *ho eklelegmenos* ("the chosen" [9:35]) by the heavenly voice is likely an allusion to Isa. 42:1 ("Here is my servant, whom I uphold, my chosen [*ho eklektos mou*], in whom my soul delights"), especially in light of the allusion to the same verse in the heavenly voice of the baptismal account: *en soi eudokēsa* ("with you I am well pleased" [3:22]). As in the qualification to Peter's confession where the suffering of the Messiah is explicitly noted (9:22), this glorious experience on the mountain is also qualified by the mission of the Suffering Servant, who will be rejected.

Third, as *ho eklelegmenos* ("the chosen") points back to Jesus' baptismal experience, so the phrase *ho huios mou* ("my son" [9:35]) is identical to *ho huios mou* of 3:22, where one finds the allusion to the Davidic psalm of Ps. 2:7. As in that context, here the royal messianic sense is clear. This use of the "Son" terminology is found elsewhere in the Lukan writings (4:41; 18:38–39; 20:41, 44 [cf. 8:28; 10:22; 22:70; Acts 9:20]).

With these allusions appearing in one context, a Mosaic figure emerges who is also the Suffering Servant and the Davidic royal figure appearing at the end of times. These paradigms help to clarify the mission of Jesus, even though by themselves they are inadequate to explicate fully his significance.

9:41

The expression *genea apistos kai diestrammenē* ("faithless and perverse generation") again alludes to the wilderness generation of old (see discussion on 7:31–35).

9:44

It is tempting to see the use of the verb *paradidosthai* ("to be betrayed") as alluding to Isa. 53:6b, *kai kyrios paredōken auton tais hamartiais hēmōn* ("and the LORD handed him over for our sins"). The context would support this connection, although the use of this verb in the LXX is not limited to this context.

9:49–50

For the significance of this dialogue between John and Jesus, some commentators (see Bovon 2002: 396) have pointed to the relevance of the story of Eldad and Medad in Num. 11:24–30, where Joshua tried to stop these two from prophesying because they were not part of the seventy who received the Spirit. Moses, however, said, "Would that all the LORD's people were prophets, and that the LORD would put his spirit on them" (Num. 11:29). A similar concern is expressed in this short dialogue, and Jesus' response likewise prevents John from stopping those who are not within the inner circle from carrying out their work.

Luke 9:51–19:44

At 9:51 we come to the central section of Luke, which deserves an extended introduction. Unlike Mark (10:1–52) and Matthew (19:1–20:34), Luke includes an extensive travel narrative that spans a third of his Gospel. Most would agree that 9:51 signals the beginning of Luke's journey report, but consensus is lacking as to the location of the end of this section. Suggestions range from 18:14 to 19:48 (see Bock 1994–1996: 957), but the explicit note of Jesus' entry into Jerusalem (and its temple) is found only in 19:45 with travel notes of his approach to the city leading right up to this point (cf. 9:51, 53; 13:22, 33; 17:11; 18:31; 19:11, 28, 41). Moreover, a significant shift of focus comes in 19:45, where Jesus enters the temple, and his daily teaching there culminates in the passion account.

Although notes of Jesus approaching Jerusalem are found throughout this section, detailed temporal and geographical references that characterize typical journey narratives (such as those in Acts 12:25–21:16; 27:1–28:16) are noticeably absent in this lengthy account of Jesus' journey to Jerusalem. This well-known discrepancy between the "form" and the "content" of Luke's central section has led to numerous proposals concerning its theological purpose. These include christological (Conzelmann 1960), ecclesiological (Miyoshi 1974), catechetical (Gill 1970), and representation of Jewish rejection (Egelkraut 1976). One's view of the theological purpose of this collection of material is affected by one's view of the role that scriptural paradigms play in this section.

On the formal level, C. F. Evans (1955) has provided the first sustained attempt to argue for the significance of Deuteronomy for Luke's central section. According to Evans, not only are there a significant number of allusions to Deuteronomy in Luke's central section, but also the ordering of the events in this section resembles that in Deut. 1–26. These parallels include the journeying motif (10:1–3, 17–20; Deut. 1); the sending of messengers (10:4–16; Deut. 2:1–3:22); the Shema (10:25–27; Deut. 5–6); foreigners (10:29–37; Deut. 7); on serving God alone (11:27–36; Deut. 10:12–11:32); laws on clean and unclean (11:37–12:12; Deut. 12:1–16); wealth (12:13–34; Deut. 12:17–32); communal judgment (12:54–13:5; Deut. 13:12–18); restoration and loss (15; Deut. 21:15–22:4); and the poor and the oppressed (16:19–18:8; Deut. 24:6–25:3). J. Drury (1976: 138–64) follows Evans in labeling this Lukan section as a "Christian Deuteronomy," but many have suggested that the parallels listed by Evans are too vague to be convincing, and parallels to major portions of Deuteronomy are missing in Luke (cf., e.g., Deut. 14; 19; 21:1–14; 22:5–23:14; 25:4–19; see Blomberg 1983: 217–28).

In response to these criticisms, others have provided further refinements of this Deuteronomy hypothesis. In particular, C. A. Evans (1993b) has provided clearer definitions and qualifications for this hypothesis. First, "neither the evangelist Luke nor earlier Christian tradents composed the contents of the central section as homilies (or midrashim) on the parallel passages from Deuteronomy" (p. 130). Second, although Luke is responsible for arranging the material in the order of Deut. 1–26, "the redaction is infrequent and slight" (p. 132). Third, not all parallels are equally clear, and it is "in the most general sense" that one can claim that Luke is writing a commentary on Deuteronomy (p. 133). Finally, a full-blown Deuteronomy hypothesis can be established only when individual parallels are evaluated with the criteria of dictional, thematic, and exegetical coherence (pp. 137–38). While C. A. Evans aims at defending the Deuteronomy hypothesis, his conclusion is strikingly similar to Blomberg's in that the significant presence of Deuteronomy in selected passages of Luke's central section cannot be denied (cf., e.g., 14:15–24, 28–33; 15:1–7, 11–32; 16:1–18; see Blomberg 1983: 227–28). The critical issue is whether the agreement of order between the two works can be established. In this sense, C. A. Evans's work actually prepares for studies that focus primarily on thematic parallels without the corresponding emphasis on the ordering of passages.

D. P. Moessner's (1989: 91–206) detailed analysis of Luke's central section represents the best example of this thematic approach. Instead of focusing on the formal elements and the ordering of the events, Moessner focuses on the Deuteronomic view of history and how this influences Luke 9:1–50 and Luke's entire travel narrative. According to the delineation of Deuteronomic themes done by O. H. Steck (1967), four themes are repeatedly emphasized by Luke: (1) like their ancestors, this generation is a faithless and rebellious generation (11:14–54; 12:54–13:9; 17:20–37); (2) God sent his prophet to reveal his will and to call his people to repent (10:1–16; 11:14–54; 12:54–13:9; 13:22–35; 14:15–24; 15; 17:22–37; 19:1–27); (3) but Israel rejects his prophets (9:52–58; 10:25–37; 11:37–54; 12:35–53; 13:22–35); and (4) as a result, Israel will be judged (11:31–32, 50–51; 12:57–59; 13:24–30, 35; 14:24; 17:26–30; 19:27, 41–44). Ecclesiologically, the rejection of the Jews is considered to be the focus of this section, and christologically, Jesus is portrayed as belonging to a long line of rejected prophets. Moessner's work is successful in highlighting the role of Deuteronomy in Luke's central section without imposing arbitrary labels on Lukan passages to establish the parallelism with the Deuteronomic ordering of subjects. Moreover, these themes do highlight major concerns of Luke in this lengthy narrative. Two issues remain, however. First, even if these themes accurately summarize Luke's concern in his central section, it is questionable whether they accurately represent what is known as Deuteronomic theology (Denaux 1997: 285). Second, one wonders if this Deuteronomic theology is sufficient in explaining the theology of Luke's central section.

The question of the sufficiency of the Deuteronomic framework and of the Mosaic prophetic Christology is addressed in the work of M. L. Strauss (1995: 294–96), which highlights both the significance of the Isaianic new exodus and the centrality of the Davidic royal messianic paradigm in Luke's Christology of the central section. The link between the Isaianic new exodus and the Davidic expectations is already found in Isa. 11, and the explicit mentioning of the "sure love for David" in Isa. 55:3 confirms the significance of David for Isa. 40–55. Later uses of the Isaianic new exodus also include the Davidic figure playing a major role in it (cf. *Pss. Sol.* 11:2–5; *4 Ezra* 13; *Tg. Lam.* 2:22). The Lukan journey that ends in Jerusalem may also reflect the goal of Isaiah's journey of the new exodus in Jerusalem, where the promise of the revelation of God's glory is to be fulfilled (Isa. 40:5; 52:10). Strauss's work supplements Moessner's in showing the complexity of Luke's Christology, a complexity already found in the figure of the Suffering Servant, who reflects both Mosaic and Davidic traits (see Hugenburger 1995). Moreover, the significance of the paradigm of the new exodus in the Lukan writings merits emphasis.

A few points are sufficient to conclude this survey. First, the significance of Deuteronomy can no longer be denied, although one might want to point further to the wider exodus paradigm (Mánek 1957). Second, the rejection of the prophet is indeed a central concern of this section, and this concern is to be situated within the allusions to Israel's wilderness experience (Mayer 1996: 134–73). Third, our discussion has shown that Luke's central section represents the meeting point of a number of scriptural traditions. Beyond Deuteronomy and Isaiah, the significance of the Elijah/Elisha narrative for this section also should be recognized (Brodie 1987; C. A. Evans 1993a). This search for a proper scriptural context should resist becoming a reductionistic one, and the complexity of how these traditions work in Luke's arrangement of the historical events of the life of Christ should be recognized. Finally, the parallelism between the journey narrative in Luke and the one in Acts also should be considered when the role of Scripture is discussed (Pao 2000: 150–67). The interpretation of one necessarily affects our understanding of the other.

9:51

This verse introduces the Lukan central section with a note that points to Jerusalem as the destination of Jesus' journey. As 4:16–30 introduces Jesus' Galilean ministry with an emphasis on his rejection, so also 9:51–56 introduces a major section with that same theme. In this verse the phrase *tas hēmeras tēs analēmpseōs autou* ("the days of his being taken up") may be a reference to his death, but the use of the verbal cognate *analambanō* ("take up") in Acts 1:11, 22 points to the inclusion of the resurrection/ascension events in this expression (Green 1997: 403). In light of the influence of the Elijah traditions in 9:51–56, an allusion to the translation of Elijah is possible (cf. 2 Kings 2:10–11).

The expression *autos to prosōpon estērisen* ("he set his face") may reflect Jesus' determination to move forward (cf. Gen. 31:21; Dan. 11:17–18; see Bock 1994–1996: 968), but C. A. Evans (1982; 1987) has suggested that a sense of judgment is often implied in the use of this expression in the prophets (Isa. 50:7; Jer. 3:12; 21:10) and in Ezekiel in particular (6:2; 13:17; 20:46 [21:2 LXX]; 21:2 [21:7 LXX]). Evans points to Ezek. 21:2–6 as providing contextual parallels to this verse. In both texts one finds this expression together with references to Jerusalem. Furthermore, Luke's awareness of the wider section of Ezek. 20:45–21:7 is reflected in 23:31. Moreover, Jesus' weeping over and words of judgment on Jerusalem (19:41–44) may also bring to mind Ezek. 21:2–6. This theme of judgment fits well with the wider concerns of Luke in this central section.

9:52–53

With these verses, the term "Samaritans" makes its first appearance in the Lukan writings. In tracing the history of the Samaritans, 2 Kings 17 has often been mentioned. That chapter does contribute to our understanding of the residents of Samaria in the eighth century BC, but these "Samarians" are not to be equated with the "Samaritans" of the NT, Josephus, and rabbinic literature. Syncretistic practices as noted in that chapter should not be considered as the only factor that contributes to the "Samaritan schism." From the writings of Hosea and Jeremiah it is clear that syncretism is not a label that could be attached to the northern kingdom alone. Moreover, the continued interaction between Judah and Israel after 722 BC (cf. 2 Chron. 30:25; 34:9) shows that 2 Kings 17 is not the pivotal point in the development of Samaritanism.

The time of Ezra and Nehemiah points to increased tension between the two people groups. Some would see this as yet another critical point in the process that defines them and their relationship with each other (Coggins 1975: 35). The Samaritans of the north were called the "adversaries of Judah and Benjamin" (Ezra 4:1), and Nehemiah called them people "of foreign descent" (Neh. 13:3; cf. 13:30). There is no doubt that the building of the temple on Mount Gerizim after the rebuilding of the Jerusalem temple further signaled the rivalry between the two groups. The animosity between the two groups culminated in the destruction of Shechem and the Gerizim temple by John Hyrcanus in the second century BC. The existence of these two distinct groups with their distinct identities is symbolized by the development of the Samaritan Pentateuch, "through which the cultic traditions of Jerusalem were declared illegitimate" (Purvis 1986: 86). Thus the Samaritans whom we encounter in the NT are a people whose identity was formed through a long process of interaction and conflict with the Judeans. It is in this light that the Samaritans' refusal to receive Jesus in Luke 9:52–53 is to be understood. The reason for such refusal is "because his face was set toward Jerusalem." The issue centers on the existence of competing cultic centers, and this would explain the Samaritans' resentment of Jewish pilgrims who pass through their land on the way to the Jerusalem temple (Hamm 1994: 276).

Luke's interest in the Samaritans is further reflected by their repeated appearances in the narrative (9:52; 10:33; 17:16), which climaxes in the reconciliation between the two groups in Acts 8 when the Jerusalem apostles testify to the fact that "Samaria had accepted the word of God" (v. 14). Not only are the Samaritans symbols of the outcast in Luke's theology, but also they represent Luke's wider salvation-historical concerns, which point to the restoration of God's people at the end of times. Jesus' refusal to follow his disciples in condemning the Samaritans should therefore be understood within this wider perspective.

9:54

Clear allusions to the Elijah narrative can be detected in this verse. In 2 Kings 1:1–17 fire came down twice at Elijah's request to kill the messengers of Ahaziah, king of Samaria, who rejected the God of Israel by turning to Baal-zebub, the god of Ekron. The fact that early Christians were fully able to recognize this connection with the Elijah story is evidenced in the scribal insertion of the phrase *hōs kai Ēlias epoiēsen* ("as also Elijah did") in a number of manuscripts (A C D W Θ Ψ *f*[1.13]). Jesus' rebuke of the disciples' request to destroy the Samaritans who reject Jesus is therefore unexpected in light of the scriptural precedent. It does, however, point to the arrival of a new era when God will act in a new way. The theme of reversal should not be missed when Jesus travels to Jerusalem to proclaim judgment on God's people while he apparently refuses to condemn the "foreigners" or "outcasts."

9:58

In comparing *ho huios tou anthrōpou* ("the Son of Man") to *ta peteina tou ouranou* ("birds of the air"), there is a possible allusion to Ps. 8, where in one context one also finds *huios anthrōpou* ("son of man" [8:5 LXX]) and *ta peteina tou ouranou* ("birds of the air" [8:9 LXX]) (see Allison 2000a: 160). However, the focus of the second half of this psalm (8:5–8 [8:6–9 LXX]) is on the dominion of human beings over the creation, including animals and birds, whereas in this saying of Jesus the point is that the condition of the Son of Man is worse than that of the birds because he "has nowhere to lay his head." Psalm 8 is not foreign to early Christian writers (1 Cor. 15:25–28; Eph. 1:22; Heb. 2:5–9), who use this psalm for the exaltation of Jesus, but D. C. Allison (2000a: 160–61) has suggested that these verses are closer to another exegetical tradition that "disparage(s) Adam, Israel, or humanity" (*Midr. Tehillim* Ps. 8:5; *t. Sotah* 6:4–5; *b. Sanh.* 38b; cf. Job. 7:17–18; Ps. 144:3). The focus on the mortality of human beings in v. 4 (v. 5 LXX) should also be noted, wherein created beings are compared to the Creator, and the implicit identity of Jesus with the vulnerable ones may also be detected in the use of this psalm.

9:59–61

In these verses many commentators have again detected the presence of Elijah traditions (see Brodie 1987: 216–26; Bovon 1991–2001: 2:33–34). Verse 59 echoes the story of 1 Kings 19:19–21, where Elijah allowed Elisha to bid farewell to his family before following him. The significance of

this passage is further supported by the wording in 9:61–62, where the phrase *akolouthēsō soi* ("I will follow you" [9:61; cf. 1 Kings 19:20]) appears with *arotron* ("plow" [9:62; cf. *ērotria*, "he was plowing," in 1 Kings 19:19]). The contrast between Jesus and Elijah not only highlights the unique authority of Jesus but also points to the eschatological urgency present in Jesus' ministry.

M. Bockmuehl (1998: 564) further suggests that Jesus' demand not to bury one's father aims at symbolizing the impending judgment on Israel (cf. Jer. 16:5–9; Ezek. 24:16–24). Nevertheless, the historical practice of secondary burial that requires the dead to be reburied after one year may be sufficient in explaining the urgency of Jesus' note (McCane 1990). The theme of judgment cannot be denied, however, in light of the immediate context of this section (10:1–16) and of the wider emphasis in Luke's central section.

Finally, the act of looking back in 9:62 may also be an allusion to the story of Lot's wife, who "looked back" and "became a pillar of salt" (Gen. 19:26) (see Allison 2000a: 79). In both texts verbs of looking (*blepōn* [9:62]; *epeblepsen* [Gen. 19:26]) appear with the phrase *eis ta opisō* ("to the back" [9:62; Gen. 19:26]). The use of the Sodom story in its Lukan context (10:12) further supports the presence of this allusion in 9:62. Again, one finds the presence of the theme of urgency in the context of divine judgment.

10:1

The textual problem surrounding the numbers "seventy" and "seventy-two" in this verse (and in 10:17) is well known. The inclusion of *dyo* ("two") is supported by major Alexandrian and Western witnesses (𝔓[75] B D), but its omission is also attested by significant manuscripts (ℵ A C L W Θ Ξ Ψ *f*[1.13]). Two major conceptual parallels have been suggested, but neither one settles this textual issue. First, in light of the possible allusion to Num. 11 in 9:49–50, also conceivable is an allusion to Num. 11:16–30, where Moses is told to choose seventy (or seventy-two if Eldad and Medad are included) elders "so that they shall bear the burden of the people along with [Moses]" (11:17). This interpretation is strengthened by Luke's portrayal of Jesus as the prophet like Moses elsewhere (9:35; Acts 3:22; 7:37). S. R. Garrett (1989: 47) further sees the bestowal of the Spirit in Num. 11:17, 25 as foreshadowing the ministry of the apostles as they are filled with the Spirit in Acts.

The second possible allusion is to the list of nations in Gen. 10–11, where the Hebrew text has seventy while the LXX has seventy-two. For those who see Gen. 10–11 as the framework for the interpretation of Jesus' commissioning of the seventy(-two), the foreshadowing of the coming mission of the Gentiles is the primary point of Luke 10 (see Parsons 1998: 163). The reference to seventy-two princes in the world in *3 En.* (17:8; 18:2–3; 30:2) and the seventy-two translators of the LXX for the pagan world (*Let. Aris.* 35–51) (see Green 1997: 412) may likewise reflect the use of this number as a reference to the Gentile world. Both Num. 11 and Gen. 10–11 point to the significance of 10:1–16 for Luke's second volume, while various other possible allusions behind the number seventy(-two) could be further identified (Metzger 1959).

10:3

Reading the metaphor of *arnas en mesō lykōn* ("lambs in the midst of wolves") in its wider context, where the eschatological significance of this commissioning is noted (cf. 10:17–20), suggests an allusion to Isa. 11:6: *symboskēthēsetai lykos meta arnos* ("the wolf shall feed with the lamb") (cf. Isa. 65:25; see Bovon 1991–2001: 2:55). In the immediate context, however, divine protection in the midst of hostility and rejection seems to be the focus, and the use of this "lamb/sheep" imagery is found already in the prophetic literature (Isa. 40:11; 53:7; Jer. 50:6–7; Ezek. 34; Mic. 2:12). The use of this metaphor for the theme of divine protection together with the mentioning of the seventy nations is found later in *Midr. Tanhuma Toldos* 5 (see *TDNT* 1:340): "There is something great about the sheep [Israel] that can persist among 70 wolves [the nations]. He replied: Great is the Shepherd who delivers it and watches over it and destroys them [the wolves] before them [Israel]."

10:4

The command neither to carry sandals (*hypodēmata*) nor to greet (*aspasēsthe*) anyone may allude to both the Mosaic and the Elisha tradition, where the theme of urgency appears (see Allison 2000a: 41–42, 145). In Exod. 12:11 the Israelites were commanded to eat their first Passover with

their *hypodēmata* ("sandals") on their feet, and in 2 Kings 4:29 Elisha sent Gehazi on his way with this command: "If you meet anyone, *ouk eulogēseis auton* ['give him no greeting']." These traditions highlight the point of Jesus' commands, as the eschatological urgency of his ministry surpasses that of the first Passover, and the command not to offer greetings reflects the same concerns. Verbal connection is not exact, however, and Jesus may be using general expressions rather than appealing to specific texts.

10:12

The evocation of Sodom in this context points to the inhospitality that the city had shown to the messengers of God in Gen. 19. Three sets of related texts may have contributed to the use of this symbol here. First, the theme of sin and judgment is inextricably tied with this symbol (cf. Deut. 29:23; 32:32; Isa. 13:19; Jer. 49:18; 50:40; Amos 4:11; Zeph. 2:9; *Jub.* 20:6; *T. Naph.* 3:4; *T. Ash.* 7:1; *T. Benj.* 9:1; *L.A.B.* 45:2; see Bovon 1991–2001: 2:58). Second, the specific sin that Sodom is often remembered to have committed is inhospitality and the rejection of God's messengers (cf. Ezek. 16:49–50; Wis. 19:13–14; Josephus, *Ant.* 1.194; *Sipre Deut.* 11:13–17 (43); *b. Sanh.* 109a–b; *Pirqe R. El.* 25; see Allison 2000a: 81–82), and it is precisely this aspect that may have prompted Jesus to use this symbol here (cf. 10:10–11). Third, the comparison of Jerusalem/Israel with Sodom appears often in prophetic literature (Isa. 1:9–10; 3:9; Jer. 23:14; Lam. 4:6; Ezek. 16:43–58), as it does in this verse. It is this aspect that leads to the further pronouncements of judgment in 10:13–14.

10:13–14

In the OT Tyre and Sidon came to be cities condemned for their worship of foreign gods (Isa. 23; Ezek. 26–28; Joel 3:4–8; Amos 1:9–10). Their arrogance is best captured in Ezek. 28:2, where Tyre is described as claiming, "I am a god; I sit in the seat of the gods, in the heart of the seas." It may be no coincidence that the following verse, concerning Capernaum (Luke 10:15), also focuses on the issue of pride. Beyond the focus on the sin of inhospitality in the previous verses, this section further illustrates the consequence of Israel's failure to repent and respond to Jesus' ministries.

"Sackcloth and ashes" are often mentioned in contexts of mourning (Esther 4:1, 3; Jer. 6:26) and petition (Isa. 58:5; Dan. 9:3). This expression survives in Jewish traditions (cf. 1 Macc. 3:47; Josephus, *Ant.* 11.221; 20.123; *Jos. Asen.* 13:2; *T. Jos.* 15:2; see Allison 2000a: 124), although in the NT it appears only in this passage (and its parallel, Matt. 11:21).

10:15

The evocation of OT symbols of judgment and destruction continue with this verse, which contains an allusion to Isa. 14:13–15 in the prophetic oracle against Babylon: "You said in your heart, 'I will ascend to heaven; I will raise my throne above the stars of God . . . I will ascend to the tops of the clouds, I will make myself like the Most High.' But you are brought down to Sheol, to the depths of the pit." A similar pattern of thought is found in Ezek. 28:2–10. In Acts 12:22–23 the fall of King Herod is described in similar terms (see Pao 2000: 199–201). What is striking is that warnings once directed against Israel's neighbors are now applied to Israel as they too refuse to acknowledge their God.

10:18

As does 10:15, the description of the fall of Satan draws on Isa. 14. The phrase *ek tou ouranou pesonta* ("fall from heaven") in particular echoes *exepesen ek tou ouranou* ("has fallen from heaven") in Isa. 14:12. The application of this verse to the fall of Satan in this context is particularly appropriate. First, Isa. 14:12 seems to have used ancient Near Eastern mythic language in portraying the downfall of Babylon (Marx 2000), and Jesus' use of similar language (assuming that Jesus is the subject of the verb *etheōroun*, "I/they saw" [see Hills 1992]) to apply to Satan may recall the background behind Isaiah's language. Second, Jewish interpretive traditions also apply Isa. 14:12 to the fall of Satan/Lucifer (*2 En.* 29:3; *L.A.E.* 12:1). Third, as in the Qumran documents where the fall of the evil one is accompanied by the exaltation of the righteous in cosmic battles (cf. 11Q13; see Garrett 1989: 51), this fall of Satan may also point forward to the exaltation of Jesus.

10:19

The pairing of *opheōn kai skorpiōn* ("snakes and scorpions") may allude to *ophis daknōn kai skor-* *pios* ("biting snakes and scorpions") in Deut. 8:15, where God's protection of Israel in the wilderness is noted. The imagery of treading may be a reference back to Ps. 91:13 [90:13 LXX], where this imagery is applied to *leonta kai drakonta* ("lion and serpent"). Commentators have debated as to which imagery dominates (see Fitzmyer 1981–1985: 863; Bock 1994–1996: 1008), but choosing between the two may be unnecessary. First, Deut. 8 and Ps. 91 have already appeared together in the Lukan temptation narrative (4:4, 11–12, see above). More importantly, D. C. Mitchell (1997: 277–78) has shown that Ps. 91 draws on Deut. 6–8 and the wilderness traditions, and this would explain the conceptual parallels between the two. In 10:19 Luke may have alluded to both texts in reference to the promise of divine protection. In light of the possible use of Ps. 91 in Jewish traditions as an exorcistic psalm (see 4:1–13), the continuation of the theme of victory over Satan in the previous verse may also be present.

10:20

The presence of the "book of life" is assumed here (cf. Exod. 32:32–33; Ps. 69:28; Isa. 4:3; Dan. 7:10; 12:1; Mal. 3:16–17; *1 En.* 47:3; 104:1; 108:7; *Jub.* 5:13–14; 23:32; 30:19–23; 1QM XII, 1–3; Rev. 3:5; 20:12, 15; 21:27; see Creed 1930: 147; Bock 1994–1996: 1008). This book, which is not explicitly mentioned, is not the focus of this verse, however. In 10:17 the submission of the demons is tied with the use of the name of Jesus. In 10:20 both ideas are present again, and the emphasis is on the disciples being counted as belonging to Jesus, who will be exalted in heaven.

10:21–22

In the LXX the verb *exomologeomai* ("I confess/ thank") could be used for the confession of sins (e.g., Dan. 9:4, 20), but it is most often used in the sense of praise and thanksgiving. This use of the verb *exomologeomai* could be explained by the fact that *eucharisteō* ("I thank") is rarely used before the second century BC. The interchangeability of the two verbs in the first century is reflected in the writings of Philo, who frequently replaces *exomologeomai* of the LXX with *eucharisteō* (Audet 1959: 654). The content of this thanksgiving prayer of Jesus falls within OT prayers of praise and thanksgiving where the focus is on the mighty acts of God (cf. Exod. 18:8–11; Pss. 77; 136; Isa. 12:4–5).

In its Lukan context this prayer constitutes the climax of Israel's long tradition of thanksgiving psalms and prayers as it points to the fulfillment of the eschatological promises in the person of Jesus.

D. C. Allison (2000a: 43–51) has provided detailed arguments for reading this focus on Jesus as the exclusive recipient and revealer of divine knowledge in light of Exod. 33:11–23, where the unique role of Moses as the mediator of God's revelation is noted (cf. Num. 12:6–8; Deut. 34:10). This connection is supported by the Moses/exodus connection elsewhere in Luke. Nevertheless, clear verbal links are missing, and one wonders if the emphasis on the unique and exclusive nature of Jesus' role could be explained primarily by references to the Mosaic paradigm that was considered inadequate earlier in Luke's narrative (cf. 9:8, 19). The authority of Jesus as emphasized in his ability to choose to whom divine revelation is to be delivered further moves beyond the Mosaic paradigm. More importantly, the father-son relationship also points beyond the Mosaic traditions, as it draws on the Davidic messianic expectations in explicating the distinct relationship between Jesus and God (see 3:21–22 above). Perhaps Jesus' transcendence over both the Mosaic and the Davidic paradigms is the point, and this would explain Jesus' statement in 10:24, where it is said that his presence will reveal more than what *polloi prophētai kai basileis* ("many prophets and kings") had seen.

10:23–24

The use of the verbs *blepō* ("see"), *horaō* ("see"), and *akouō* ("hear") in one context brings to mind Isa. 6:9–10, where those three verbs are used (Allison 2000a: 115). Luke's awareness of this passage (8:10; Acts 28:26–27) cannot be doubted, but the reversal of Isa. 6:9–10 is found already in Isaiah where metaphors of sight and vision are used to describe the arrival of God's salvation (cf. Isa. 18:3; 29:18; 32:3; 42:18–19; 52:15). Isaiah 52:15, of the fourth Servant Song, in particular provides a closer conceptual parallel, where the uniqueness of God's eschatological acts through his servant would surprise even *basileis* ("kings"): *hoti hois ouk anēngelē peri autou opsontai, kai hoi ouk akēkoasin synēsousin* ("For what they were not told, they will see, and what they have not heard, they will understand" [cf. Rom. 15:21]).

10:27

A. NT Context: Definition of One's Neighbor.
The quotations of Deut. 6:5 and Lev. 19:18 appear in the dialogue between Jesus and the expert of the law concerning the way to "inherit eternal life" (10:25). In its Lukan context this dialogue focuses on the definition of one's neighbor as the dialogue continues in Jesus' parable of the Good Samaritan (10:30–37). Some (Marshall 1978: 450; Kodell 1987: 419) further suggest that the pericope of Mary and Martha (10:38–42) is meant to complement this discussion on loving others by focusing on the love of God.

Reviewing the Lukan context of this dialogue, one cannot avoid noting its relationship with its conceptual parallels in Mark 12:28–31; Matt. 22:34–40, especially when the same two OT texts appear together when Jesus is questioned by Jewish scribal leadership. Significant differences between Luke's text and its Markan and Matthean parallels are equally noteworthy, however. First, unlike Luke, who places this dialogue earlier in Jesus' ministry, Mark and Matthew place this passage in the final days of Jesus' earthly ministry. Second, the question that Jesus is addressing in Mark and Matthew centers on the "greatest command," while the way to inherit eternal life is the topic in Luke. Third, Jesus is the one citing the OT in Mark and Matthew, while the lawyer cites the two OT texts in Luke. Finally, the parable of the Good Samaritan, which follows in Luke, is missing in Mark and Matthew. Therefore, it seems best not to consider Mark as the source for Luke 10:25–28 (Marshall 1978: 441; Barrett 1988: 232; Kimball 1994b: 119–20).

B. Deut. 6:5; Lev. 19:18 in Context.
Deuteronomy 6 belongs to a wider section that contains "the stipulations, decrees, and laws that Moses gave them [the Israelites] when they came out of Egypt" (4:45). This verse serves as a response to the first line of the Shema, which points to the pillar of Israel's faith: "The LORD our God, the LORD is one" (6:4). In response, Israel is called to "love" (*ʾāhēb*) their God (6:5). This "love" must be interpreted within its covenantal context, where faithfulness and loyalty are to characterize the life of Israel as God's covenant partner (see Moran 1963). Both the focus on the exclusive devotion to the one true God and the command to love

this God of Israel rest on God's faithful acts on behalf of his people:

> It was because the LORD loved you and kept the oath he swore to your forefathers that he brought you out with a mighty hand and redeemed you from the land of slavery.... Know therefore that the LORD your God is God; he is the faithful God, keeping his covenant of love to a thousand generations of those who love him and keep his commands. (Deut. 7:8–9)

These two aspects form the foundation of the rest of the detailed commandments and stipulations. The way the material is presented reflects covenant formulations that aim at clarifying the relationship between the suzerain and the vassals. As J. D. Levenson (1985: 84) rightly notes, "One must first accept the suzerainty of the great king, the fact of covenant; only then can he embrace the particulars which the new lord enjoins upon them, the stipulations."

The total dedication required for Israel the covenant partner is expressed by the references to one's *lēbāb* ("heart"), *nepeš* ("soul"), and *mĕʾōd* ("strength"). Similar expressions are found throughout Deuteronomy (4:29; 6:5; 10:12; 11:13; 13:3; 26:16; 30:2, 6, 10). It is well known that in the Hebrew mindset *lēbāb* ("heart") points to one's will or intellect, and together with one's life and physical abilities, this combination of terms refers to the totality of one's personhood.

The command to love one's *rēaʿ* ("neighbor") is found within the Holiness Code (Lev. 17–26), where the focus is on the holy living of individual Israelites. A strict separation from the previous chapters cannot be maintained, however, since cultic concerns that dominate chapters 1–16 are found also in this section (e.g., 17:1–9; 19:5–8; 23:4–43). Moreover, recent scholarship has cast doubt on the hypothesis that posits an independent existence of a holiness code (see G. J. Wenham 1979: 240–41; Hartley 1992: 251–60). In terms of theological coherence, the center of this section is in 19:2, which forms the basis for the covenantal relationship between the one God of all and Israel, his chosen people: "You shall be holy, for I the LORD your God am holy." The call to love one's neighbor in 19:18 builds on this *imitatio Dei* command while summarizing the concern of a subsection (19:11–18) that focuses

on the Israelites' relationship with and responsibilities to their fellow citizens.

The meaning of the word *rēaʿ* ("neighbor") has to be understood within this context in Leviticus. The wider literary context, which focuses on cultic concerns, shows that this section is addressed primarily to the people of Israel, and the phrase "one of your people" in the first part of this verse confirms this observation. The existence of a separate provision concerning the "aliens" in 19:34–35 complicates the picture, however. Although this provision does confirm that the primary reference behind the word *rēaʿ* ("neighbor") is the fellow Israelites, these verses require that the Israelites also extend the mandate of 19:18 to aliens: "The alien who resides with you shall be to you as the citizen among you; you shall love the alien as yourself." It is precisely this perceived ambiguity that forms the center of Jesus' dialogue with the expert of the law in Luke 10:25–37.

C. Deut. 6:5; Lev. 19:18 in Judaism. As part of the Shema, Deut. 6:5 belongs to Israel's confessional statement, which was recited twice daily (see *m. Ber.* 1:1–4), and allusions to this verse are found in Hellenistic and Palestinian Jewish traditions where the worship of the one true God is affirmed (see Philo, *Decalogue* 64; 1QS V, 9; *Sib. Or.* 8:482; *T. Dan* 5:3). Rabbinic traditions make it clear that the affirmation of the one God in 6:5 is to be understood as the basis of all commandments (*m. Ber.* 2:2), and to recite the Shema is to affirm the sovereignty of God (*m. Ber.* 2:5) (see Levenson 1985: 84–85).

The call to love one's neighbor is likewise repeatedly made (CD-A VI, 20–21; 1QS VII, 8–9; *Sib. Or.* 8:481; cf. Rom. 13:9; Gal. 5:14; James 2:8). In rabbinic traditions this command is also considered to be the foundation of the whole Torah (*b. Šabb.* 31a; cf. *t. Peʾah* 4.19; see E. P. Sanders 1992: 258). In these traditions the definition of one's *rēaʿ* ("neighbor") receives further attention. Most rabbinic interpreters see the word as referring to fellow Israelites, while the foreigners and the Samaritans are explicitly excluded (*Mek. Exod.* 21:35), although full proselytes are included in this category (cf. *Sipra Qed.* 8; see *TDNT* 6:135; Neudecker 1992: 499).

The combination of the commands to worship one God and to love one's neighbor can be identified in Jewish traditions (cf. *T. Iss.* 5:2; 7:6; *T. Dan*

5:3; Philo, *Spec. Laws* 2.63; see Creed 1930: 152; Bovon 1991–2001: 2:86), although they did not appear as explicit quotations/allusions to Deut. 6:5; Lev. 19:18. The difficulties in determining a date for the *Testament of the Twelve Patriarchs* make it hard to conclude whether these traditions predate the time of Jesus.

D. Textual Matters. In describing the total devotion demanded of one who belongs to the covenant community, the list in Deut. 6:5 LXX, which accurately reflects the MT, has three items, *kardia* ("heart"), *psychē* ("soul"), and *dynamis* ("power"), while Luke has four, *kardia* ("heart"), *psychē* ("soul"), *ischys* ("strength"), and *dianoia* ("mind"). Although Luke has followed the LXX's order, *dynamis* is replaced by the rough synonym *ischys* along with the insertion of *dianoia* ("mind") to the list. Regardless of their literary relationships, the fact that Mark 12:30 also has four identical items (though in different order) may suggest that the insertion of *dianoia* to the list did not originate with Luke, and Matt. 22:37 confirms this observation, since it also contains *dianoia* (but without *ischys*). In terms of structure, Luke is closest to the LXX, where *kai en holē tē dianoia sou* ("and with all your mind") is inserted at the end of the LXX list, and this (probably pre-Lukan) insertion may be motivated by the clarification of the sense of the word *kardia* ("heart"), which is to be understood as referring primarily to the intellect rather than to emotions. In terms of wording, however, Mark is closer to the LXX in the use of *ek* in all four phrases, while Luke has *ek* in the first and *en* in the final three, and Matthew uses only *en*.

Luke's citation of the second half of Lev. 19:18 follows the LXX verbatim, which in turn is an accurate translation of the MT. Its connection with Deut. 6:5 may reflect the use of *gezerah shavah* through *agapēseis/'āhabĕt'ā*, "you shall love" (see Kimball 1994b: 129). Nevertheless, the obvious conceptual connections between the two, and the appearance of these two commands together in Jewish traditions apart from an explicit evocation of these two texts, render the appeal to *gezerah shavah* unnecessary.

E. The Use of Deut. 6:5; Lev. 19:18 in Luke 10:27. Unlike Mark 12:29–31; Matt. 22:37–40, where Deut. 6:5 and Lev. 19:18 are separately listed as the *prōtē* ("first") and the *deutera* ("second") of the greatest commandments, the two are

merged into one in Luke in Jesus' dialogue with the expert of the law. The contexts of both passages are also alluded to in Luke's account. First, these two passages appear in a dialogue concerning the inheritance of eternal life: *ti poiēsas zōēn aiōnion klēronomēsō* ("What must I do to inherit eternal life?"). An allusion to the wider context of Deut. 6 can be detected in that the observance of these commandments is required for the inheritance of the land: "Do what is right and good in the sight of the LORD, so that it may go well with you, and so that you may go in and inherit [*klēronomēsēs*] the good land that the LORD swore to your ancestors to give you" (Deut. 6:18; cf. 6:1). In addition, the reference to *zōēn aiōnion* ("eternal life") may also be an allusion to Deut. 6:24: "the LORD commanded us to observe all these statutes . . . so that we may live [*zōmen*]." A Mosaic typology might be detected behind these allusions (see Wall 1989: 21–22), and the attainment of salvation is understood in light of the ancient promises to Israel.

An allusion to the wider context of Lev. 19:18 can also be identified in the verse that follows Luke's citation of the OT texts: *touto poiei kai zēsē* ("do this, and you will live"). This verse brings to mind Deut. 6:24, but its affinity with Lev. 18:5 is to be noted with the use of *poieō* ("do") and *zaō* ("live"): "You shall keep all my commandments, and all my judgments, and do [*poiēsete*] them; and if a person does [*poiēsas*] so, he shall live [*zēsetai*] by them" (see Verhoef 1997; Noël 1997).

In the Lukan context the focus is on the definition of one's "neighbor," as illustrated by the parable of the Good Samaritan. Two specific OT passages may have further contributed to this parable. First, the story of the compassionate Samaritans in 2 Chron. 28:8–15 provides a conceptual parallel to Jesus' parable (Furness 1969; Spencer 1984). Second, Hos. 6:6 may also have played a part, where one finds the discussion of mercy (or love) in the context of the cultic practices of Israel (Bock 1994–1996: 1029). To appreciate the power of this parable, the listing of priest, Levite, and Samaritan should be further explored. M. Gourgues (1998) has shown that forms of the trilogy "priests, Levites, and people" are common in postexilic texts (1 Chron. 28:21; 2 Chron. 34:30; 35:2–3, 8, 18; Ezra 2:70; 7:7, 13; 8:15; 9:1; 10:5, 18–22, 25–43; Neh. 7:73; 8:13; 9:38;

10:28; 11:3, 20; cf. 1QS II, 11, 19–21), and this is what first-century Jews would have expected. The appearance of the Samaritan instead of a lay Judean is therefore striking, and this directly challenges the Jewish interpretation of the "neighbor" of Lev. 19:18.

F. Theological Use. Luke's concern for the redefinition of God's people resurfaces here in Jesus' dialogue with the expert of the law. The clarification of the range of application of Lev. 19:18 challenges the exclusivist theology reflected in Jewish interpretive traditions. This is particularly significant when the pillar of Jewish election theology is evoked with the use of Deut. 6:5 in this interchange. The term "Samaritans," as introduced in 9:52–53, becomes a symbol for those who would be able to participate in God's people. The fact that the Samaritan is able to prove himself to be a neighbor when the priest and the Levite fail may also reflect the Lukan theme of reversal, where the failure of Jewish leadership is highlighted through acts of mercy performed by an outcast.

In christological terms, Jesus is presented as one who has the authority to interpret the law. With this parable, the implicit challenge to the scribal leadership is accompanied by the critique of the Jerusalem cult. Some commentators (see Graves 1997) have further suggested that the beaten man symbolizes Jesus, who is the rejected one left to die by Jewish leaders. This would fit well with the theme of Luke's central section, but this christological theme is not further developed in this passage.

10:38–42

Although it has no clearly identifiable allusions to the OT, the story of Mary and Martha has been seen by some as an illustration of Deut. 6:5, as the parable of the Good Samaritan is for Lev. 19:18 (see 10:27 above). Others have pointed to the emphasis on the obedience to the word of God in Deut. 8:1–3 as providing the framework for this passage (see Wall 1989). It is clear that this story operates within the thought world of the OT, but further verbal links are required to establish the influence of texts beyond the explicit citations found in 10:27.

11:1–4

Numerous parallels to the Lord's Prayer have been identified in Jewish prayer traditions, and two in particular stand out. First, the kiddush that focuses on the name of God and his kingdom provides a striking parallel to the first part of the Lord's Prayer. It is unclear, however, whether this prayer was widely circulated in the first century. Second, the *Shemoneh Esreh*, or Eighteen Benedictions, provides parallels to the second half of the Lord's Prayer, where one finds the focus on divine forgiveness and provision. In light of these prayers, the uniqueness of the Lord's Prayer clearly stands out (Davies and Allison 1988–1997: 1:595): (1) simple and intimate address, (2) brevity, and (3) eschatological orientation.

Although the father-son relationship has been applied to God and his people in the OT (cf. Exod. 4:22; Deut. 32:6; Isa. 63:16; Jer. 3:4; 31:9) and in other Jewish literature (Tob. 13:4; Wis. 2:16; 3 Macc. 5:7; *Jub.* 1:28; Josephus, *Ant.* 7:380), "nowhere in the entire wealth of devotional literature produced by ancient Judaism do we find *'abbā'* being used as a way of addressing God" (*NIDNTT* 1:614). In the Gospels Jesus often addresses or refers to God as "father" (cf. Matt. 11:27; 20:23; 25:34; 26:29, 39, 42, 53; Mark 8:38; 14:36; Luke 2:49; 10:22; 22:29; 24:49; John 2:16; 5:17, 43; 6:40), and this practice is followed by early Christian authors (Rom. 8:15; Gal. 4:6). The use of the "father" imagery in the Lord's Prayer is consistent with these usages, as they draw attention to the reality of the eschatological era that is brought about by the life and ministry of Jesus. The relationship between God and his people is thereby defined in light of this event.

The petition on the sanctification of God's name is not an appeal to God to sanctify himself, but rather one to God to act in his people so that his name would not be profaned by them. Ezekiel 36 provides a clear conceptual background, where God's condemnation of Israel's profaning *to onoma mou to hagion* ("my holy name" [v. 22]) is followed by this promise: "I will sanctify my great name [*hagiasō to onoma mou to mega*], which has been profaned among the nations, and which you have profaned among them; and the nations shall know that I am the LORD ... when through you I display my holiness before their eyes" (v. 23). The petition for God's name to be sanctified is therefore a call to fulfill his own promises.

This call for God to act is more explicitly noted in the petition concerning the arrival of God's kingdom. It is well known that in the Synoptics the kingdom of God is portrayed as being present (cf. Matt. 12:28–29; Mark 1:15; Luke 11:20; 17:20), although its consummation lies in the future (cf. Matt. 6:10; 25:1–13; Mark 10:17–31; Luke 19:11). This petition presupposes this tension and points forward to the fulfillment of God's salvation program, which is inaugurated by Jesus himself.

The meaning and significance of the petition for bread is complicated by the difficulties surrounding the understanding of the term *epiousios*. Intense debate on this term has failed to produce a consensus as to whether it should be understood in an eschatological sense (see Hultgren 1990: 41–42; Boismard 1995). Regardless of the reading adopted, the theme of divine provision is clearly present (cf. Ps. 145:15–16; 146:5–7). This general theme finds its roots in the manna tradition of Israel, where God's faithfulness to his people in the wilderness provides the foundation for Israel's trust in their God. Exodus 16:5, in particular, may provide the language for Luke's *to kath' hēmeran* ("daily") (see Allison 2000a: 51), and they both address the manifestation of God's faithfulness. The eschatologization of the manna tradition (cf. *1 En.* 10; *2 Bar.* 29:5) may also be relevant if *ton arton* ("the bread") of this petition is further identified with the *arton* ("bread") of 14:15 that one partakes *en tē basileia tou theou* ("in the kingdom of God").

The appeal to divine forgiveness is not foreign to OT liturgical traditions (cf. Exod. 32:32; 34:9; 1 Kings 8:33–34, 46–53; Ps. 19:12; 25:11; 32:1; 65:3; 78:38; 79:9), but the correspondence between human and divine forgiveness is not emphasized in ways that it is in this Gospel (cf. 6:37–38; 23:34). In the OT the appeal to divine forgiveness is instead often grounded in God's own previous acts of kindness (cf. Num. 14:19: "Forgive the iniquity of this people according to the greatness of your steadfast love, just as you have pardoned this people, from Egypt even until now").

The final petition, on *peirasmos* ("trial/testing"), recalls the beginning of this prayer, where God's holiness is noted. The role of God in the

testing of Israel is frequently noted in the OT (cf. Exod. 16:4; 20:20; Deut. 8:2, 16; 13:3; 33:8; Judg. 2:22; see Fitzmyer 1981–1985: 906). Many have attempted to address the apparent theological problems raised by this petition (see Porter 1990), but in its context this petition primarily serves to reaffirm the sovereignty of God while acknowledging the way his people can participate in the unfolding of his plan of salvation.

11:13

The Holy Spirit has already been introduced in Luke's birth narrative (1:15, 35, 41, 67; 2:25–27), and in this verse the bestowal of the Spirit is promised as a response to prayer. This connection is rooted in the OT (Num. 11:29; Ps. 51:11), and it is an emphasis found elsewhere in Luke (3:21–22; Acts 1:14–2:4; 4:31; 8:15; 9:11, 17) (see Shepherd 1994: 143).

11:20

In the LXX *daktylos theou* ("the finger of God") points to the presence of God and his involvement in history (Exod. 8:15 LXX [8:19 ET]; 31:18; Deut. 9:10; see Klingbeil 2000). While these passages assume an exodus setting, Exod. 8:15 LXX (8:19 ET), which recounts the contest between Moses and the Egyptian magicians, is particularly relevant, as Moses was able to prove that the power of the one true God was on his side. In Luke's context Jesus likewise affirms the presence of divine power when he is challenged by his competitors (see Garrett 1989: 132–33).

Some commentators (see Fitzmyer 1981–1985: 918) would assume that Luke's version is original here because it is difficult to imagine Luke changing Matthew's *en pneumati theou* ("by the Spirit of God" [Matt. 12:28]), while others (see M. Turner 1996: 259) point to Luke's interest in the exodus typology as the reason behind his preference for the reference to "the finger of God." In any case, it should be noted that in the OT both "the finger/hand of God" and the "Spirit of God" are used to refer to the same reality (cf. Ps. 8:3; 33:6; Ezek. 3:14; 8:1–3; 37:1; see Davies and Allison 1988–1997: 2:340).

11:21–22

The parable of the Strong Man finds its conceptual parallels in two Isaianic passages. The overcoming of the strong man echoes Isa. 49:25,

"Even the captives of the mighty shall be taken," while the dividing of the spoils brings to mind Isa. 53:12, "I will allot him a portion with the great, and he shall divide the spoil with the strong" (see Garrett 1989: 45). It is unclear, however, whether the wider biblical context is also evoked with the use of such language.

11:23

With this verse, the imagery shifts to one of shepherding. This imagery has been used in the OT and subsequent Jewish traditions for the ingathering of God's scattered people (cf. Isa. 11:12; 40:11; Ezek. 5:12; 34:13, 21; Zech. 11:16; Tob. 3:4; *T. Naph.* 8:3; *T. Benj.* 10:11; *Pss. Sol.* 8:28; 11:2; see Bovon 2002: 165; Green 1997: 458).

11:29–30, 32

The different emphases of the Lukan (11:29–30) and Matthean (12:38–41) use of the sign of Jonah have often been noted (see Swetnam 1987; Rusam 2003: 219). In Matthew there is an explicit reference to Jesus' death and resurrection (12:40), while in Luke the focus appears to be on the prophetic ministry of Jesus that culminates in the judgment of Israel. Nevertheless, the Matthean emphasis on the resurrection is located in the context of judgment, while the Lukan discussion of the sign presupposes the vindication of Jesus the prophet. To clarify the function of the "Jonah" imagery in this Lukan passage, two aspects should be highlighted. First, implicit in the reference to the future (cf. *estai*, "will be" [11:30]) act of the Son of Man as a sign is a reference to the death and resurrection of Jesus, which are yet to come. Jesus' preaching, therefore, should not be considered as the primary reference of this symbol. Second, moving beyond the vindication of the righteous, this symbol also focuses on the judgment of Israel. The significance of the expression *genea ponēra* ("evil generation" [11:29]) has already been noted (cf. 7:31–35), and here it is again used to compare Jesus' contemporaries with the rebellious wilderness generation of old. The theme of judgment continues in 11:31–32, where condemnation is promised to those who fail to recognize the presence of this greater sign.

Both uses of the Jonah symbol can be identified in Jewish interpretive traditions (see Chow 1995: 27–44). In some texts the deliverance of Jonah comes to symbolize God's deliverance of his own

people (3 Macc. 6:8; *De Jona* 69–99a; *m. Taʿan.* 2:4). In other texts Jonah becomes a symbol of God's judgment for those who are disobedient to his will (Josephus, *Ant.* 9.214; *Tg. Neof.* Deut. 30:12–13). Particularly relevant are those passages that see Jonah as a symbol of judgment for Jerusalem (*Liv. Pro.* 10:10; *Pirqe R. El.* 10). Although many of these texts cannot be dated to the first century AD, one can at least detect the presence of the different uses of the symbol of Jonah. In Jesus' reference to the sign of Jonah both aspects are present: his death and resurrection point to God's vindication, and this vindication demands a proper response, without which judgment will be delivered.

11:31

This verse alludes to the visit of the Queen of Sheba with Solomon (1 Kings 10:1–13; 2 Chron. 9:1–12). As in the case of the Ninevites, a pagan approaches the messenger of God and listens to him. Implicit is the judgment on God's own people, who are characterized as the "evil generation" that rejects the mighty acts of God.

11:37–41

In Jesus' dialogue with the Pharisees the issue of cleanliness is raised. Jesus' comments on the concerns of the Pharisees may reflect the dominance of the Shammaite opinion in the time of Jesus that the cleanliness of the outside of a cup does not affect the cleanliness of the inside (see Neusner 1976). Jesus' statement on the inner impurities of the Pharisees should therefore be seen as a critique of this distinction.

11:42

In the OT Israelites were required to tithe for the priests, the Levites, the poor, and the support of Jerusalem and its cult (Lev. 27:30–32; Num. 18:21–32; Deut. 14:22–27), and these regulations receive extensive treatment in rabbinic literature as they are developed into a twelve tithe system (cf. *m. Maʿaś.*; *m. Maʿaś. Š.*; see E. P. Sanders 1992: 147–50). Jesus' comments may be directed against those who focus on these detailed systems of regulations instead of the intent of the law. Jesus' accusation of the Pharisees for their neglect of *tēn krisin* ("justice") and *tēn agapēn tou theou* ("the love of God") may further echo the discussion of the commandments to love God and one's neighbors in 10:27 (cf. Deut. 6:5; Lev. 19:18), although similar sentiments are common in prophetic traditions (cf. Hos. 12:6; Amos 5:15; Mic. 6:8; Zech. 7:9).

11:44

Jesus' comparison of the Pharisees to unmarked graves assumes a knowledge of OT purity laws concerning contacts with corpses (Lev. 21:11; Num. 6:5–8; 9:6–7; 19:11–16). The irony of Jesus' statement cannot be missed (see Gowler 1994: 234): the Pharisees' zealous concerns to maintain boundaries of purity (11:38) fail to protect them from being impure in the eyes of God. In neglecting justice and the love of God, they became the impure objects with which they so zealously avoid contact. Moreover, everyone interacting with them is also rendered impure.

11:49–51

While the identity of Abel is clear (cf. Gen. 4), the identity of Zechariah is subject to debate. In spite of some who would point to an unknown figure (Ross 1987), most identify this figure with the Zechariah of 2 Chron. 24:20–25, who was killed in the temple court (see Schürmann 1990–1994: 2:325). The identification of Zechariah as representing the last of the martyrs may reflect the MT order of the canonical list, which concludes with Chronicles. Allison (2000a: 149–51) has noted additional parallels with 2 Chron. 24:17–25: the sending of the prophets (11:49; 2 Chron. 24:19), the blood of Zechariah (11:51; 2 Chron. 24:25), and the reference to the temple precinct (11:51; 2 Chron. 24:21). These parallels further support the identification of the Zechariah of 11:49 with the one in 2 Chron. 24.

The reference to *hē sophia tou theou* ("the wisdom of God" [11:49]) is unusual. The understanding of wisdom as an extension of God's will is common in Jewish traditions (cf. Prov. 8; Job 28; Sir. 1; 4; 14–15; Bar. 3–4; Wis. 6–11), and the rejection of Wisdom's envoy is also a recurring motif (e.g., Sir. 24; Bar. 3:9–4:4; *1 En.* 42). In light of the Matthean parallel (23:34) and early Christian identification of Jesus as God's wisdom (cf. 1 Cor. 1:24, 30), it is possible to see this expression as referring to Jesus himself, especially in his identification with the role of his Father. Nevertheless, in the Lukan context it is also possible to see this as a general reference to the divine wisdom that speaks without explicitly emphasizing the identification of Jesus as the personified Wisdom (see Marshall 1978: 502–4).

12:1

Jesus' warning here to "beware of the leaven of the Pharisees" has been interpreted against the background of the Mosaic instruction not to allow leaven (*zymē*) in the Passover bread (Exod. 12:14–20) (see Danker 1988: 244; Bock 1994–1996: 1133; Bovon 1989–2001: 2:248). However, the only connection between Exod. 12:14–20 and Luke 12:1 is the term "leaven." Neither Israel's history in general nor the Passover festival in particular is alluded to in the context of 12:1. The "leaven/yeast" metaphor was a familiar figure of speech (cf. Plutarch, *Quaest. rom.* 109; Aulus Gellius, *Noct. att.* 10.15, 19) suggesting, according to J. B. Green (1997: 480), corrupting influence and the capacity to penetrate in a concealed fashion, connotations that are absent from the Passover tradition. While it may be debated in the case of the parallel passage in Mark 8:15 whether "leaven" has a neutral meaning ("influence") or a negative one ("corrupting influence"), the sense in Luke 12:1 is clearly negative, as Luke interprets "leaven" in terms of the *hybris* of the Pharisees.

12:2

Jesus' saying about the futility of hypocrisy in 12:2, "Nothing is covered up that will not be revealed [*apokalyphthēsetai*], and hidden [*krypton*] that will not be known," may echo Eccles. 10:20, "Do not curse the king, even in your thoughts, or curse the rich, even in your bedroom; for a bird of the air may carry your voice, or some winged creature tell the matter." There are no verbal parallels, and since the wisdom is proverbial, it is uncertain whether Jesus, or Luke, wants to point the listener to this passage. There are similar passages in rabbinic literature: *Tg. Qoh.* 12:13, "In the end every thing in this world which is done in secret will be publicized and made known to mankind, and for this reason, fear the Lord"; *m. 'Abot* 4:4, "R. Johanan b. Beroqa says: Anyone who profanes the name of Heaven in secret, they exact the penalty from him openly" (see Lachs 1987: 185). Note also Sir. 1:30: "The Lord will reveal your secrets [*apokalypsei kyrios ta krypta sou*] and cast you down in the midst of the congregation, because you did not come in the fear of the Lord, and your heart was full of deceit" (cf. *2 Bar.* 83:3). In the context of Luke 12 Jesus asserts not only that what is hidden inside a person's heart will be manifest, but also that the true identity of his followers will come to light as they experience persecution and that secret (i.e., private) conversations will become public at the eschaton (Green 1997: 481).

12:5–7

Verses 4–5 belong to Jesus' exhortation to bold confession in vv. 2–9, encouraging and warning the disciples to be fearless in times of persecution, even in martyrdom. After the announcement that all deeds that are done in secret will be exposed (12:2–3), Jesus calls on his followers to fear God and not human beings (12:4–7), and to confess Jesus and not to disown him (12:8–9). The call to fear God and not human beings consists of two parts.

First, Jesus challenges his disciples to fear the one who has the authority not only to cause physical death but also to hurl into Gehenna (12:4–5). The statement in 12:5, "Fear him who after he kills has authority to cast into Gehenna [*meta to apokteinai echonta exousian embalein eis tēn geennan*]," echoes three OT passages that refer to Yahweh's authority over life and death: Deut. 32:39, "See now that I, even I, am he; there is no god besides me. I kill and I make alive [*egō apoktenō kai zēn poiēsō*]; I wound and I heal; and no one can deliver from my hand"; 2 Kings 5:7, "When the king of Israel read the letter, he tore his clothes and said, 'Am I God, to give death or life [*mē theos egō tou thanatōsai kai zōopoiēsai*], that this man sends word to me to cure a man of his leprosy? Just look and see how he is trying to pick a quarrel with me'" (see also Job 1–2); 1 Sam. 2:6, "The LORD kills and brings to life; he brings down to Sheol and raises up" (*kyrios thanatoi kai zōogonei katagei eis hadou kai anagei*), which is the closest echo. Note the reference to God's authority to kill and the reference to Gehenna/Hades in 12:5 and in 1 Sam. 2:6. In Hannah's prayer Yahweh is praised as the "God of knowledge" who weighs the actions of every human being (1 Sam. 2:3) and who reverses the fate of the mighty and of the feeble, of the wealthy and of the hungry, of the barren and of the women with children (2:4–5), of the living and of the dead (2:6), of the poor and of the rich (2:7–8), of the faithful and of the wicked (2:9). This section in Hannah's prayer does not

praise the righteousness of Yahweh, who makes all people equal; rather, it praises God for his "lordly might which is exercised in a mercy which condescends to the needy" (Hertzberg 1964: 30). Luke, who employs the reversal theme in 12:3, emphasizes in 12:4–5 that "disciples are not to fear loss of physical life at the hands of other human beings; they should rather fear the consequences of apostasy" (Fitzmyer 1981–1985: 957). Fear of those who may persecute Jesus' disciples should be replaced by the fear of God (Marshall 1978: 513), who oversees events not only in this world but also in the world to come.

The term *geenna* is the Grecized form of the Heb. *gêy(ʾ) hinnōm* (Aram. *gêhinnām* [see BDF §39.8]), "valley of (the son[s] of) Hinnom," a phrase translated in the LXX as *pharanx Onom* (Josh. 15:8), *pharanx huiou Ennom* (2 Kings 23:10; Jer. 7:31–32; 39:35), *napē Onnam* (Josh. 18:16), *Gaibenenom* (2 Chron. 28:3), and *Gaienna* (Josh. 18:16 [in Codex B], written by a Christian scribe and thus possibly influenced by the NT spelling of *geenna*; Codex A reads *epi gai onnom*; see Fitzmyer 1981–1985: 959; *EDNT* 1:239–40). The Valley of the Sons of Hinnom is a ravine (Wadi er-Rababi) at the western edge of Jerusalem that runs north-south before entering the Kidron Valley. The traditional view that the valley was the place where Jerusalem's citizens burned their garbage and that the rising smoke and the stench of corruption connoted the fiery punishment and torment of the damned could be correct, but it cannot be supported from ancient sources (Davies and Allison 1988–1997: 1:515). In OT times, during the reigns of Ahaz and Manasseh, the valley was the site of a high place where Judeans sacrificed children as burnt offerings to Baal-Molech (2 Kings 16:3; 21:6; 23:10; 2 Chron. 28:3; 33:6; Jer. 32:34–35) and was associated with judgment in the prophets (Jer. 7:32; 19:4–6) (see *ThWAT* 8:744–46). In the OT, Sheol, the dwelling place of the dead, was associated with fire (Deut. 32:22) (see *NIDOTTE* 4:6–7). In Jewish traditions the abode of the sinners after death is described as a lake or abyss of fire in which the wicked are punished (Jdt. 16:17; *1 En.* 10:13; 18:11–16; 26:4; 27:1–3; 54:16; 90:26; *Jub.* 9:15; cf. 1QH^a XI, 29–36). Several Jewish texts refer to the "hell of fire" as *gehinnom* or *ge hinnam*, without reference to the topography of Jerusalem (cf.

4 Ezra 7:36; *2 Bar.* 59:10; 85:13; *Sib. Or.* 1:103; 2:292; see *EDNT* 1:239).

In the Gospels *geenna* is used as a term that stands for "the place of punishment in the next life, *hell*" (BDAG 191), as in Matt. 5:22, 29, 30; 10:28; 18:9; 23:15, 33; Mark 9:43, 45, 47; Luke 12:5 (cf. James 3:6), the state that John calls "the second death" (Rev. 2:11; 20:6, 14; 21:8). Jesus states in 12:5 that God will judge human beings after death, and he asserts that disciples should fear God, the judge who punishes the wicked, rather than their persecutors, who have no real authority (see *TDNT* 2:566–67).

Second, Jesus challenges the disciples to understand that God cares for them, as his providence knows no limits (12:6–7). Five sparrows cost only two *assaria* (one *assarion* [Lat. *assarius*], a Roman copper coin, which was worth about one-sixteenth of a denarius, one day's wages for a laborer)—that is, only about one hour's worth of work. Sparrows (*strouthion*, used in the LXX to translate Heb. *ṣippôr*), the cheapest of the birds, were part of the diet of the poor. The privileged status of sparrows that Jesus refers to echoes Ps. 84:3: "Even a bird finds a home, and a swallow a nest for herself, where she can put her young near your altars, O Yahweh Sabaoth." The birds that nest in the temple precinct near the altars "are truly blessed, for they have found a safe residence in the house of the living God" (Tate 1990: 358). Here, Yahweh's holy temple is "the epitome of the undisturbed, fulfilled life" (Kraus 1993: 2:168).

Some commentators find in 12:6 an allusion to Amos 3:5, "Does a bird fall in a snare on the earth, when there is no trap for it? Does a snare spring up from the ground, when it has taken nothing?" (LXX: "Will a bird fall on the earth without a fowler?" *ei peseitai orneon epi tēn gēn aneu ixeutou* [the parallel Matt. 10:29 reads, *hen ex autōn ou peseitai epi tēn gēn aneu tou patros hymōn*, "Yet not one of them will fall to the ground apart from your Father"]). If Jesus' audience was familiar with the reading of Amos 3:5 that speaks of a "fowler" (LXX, Targum, Peshitta), then the replacement of the fowler by God ("Yet not one of them is forgotten in God's sight") would make Jesus' assertion more forceful and memorable (Allison 2000a: 130).

Jesus' *qol vayomer* argument that no disciple will ever be forgotten by God, who takes notice even of sparrows (12:6), has been compared with a similar argument in Isa. 49:15: "Can a woman forget her nursing child, or show no compassion for the child of her womb? Even these may forget, yet I will not forget you." In the context of Isa. 40–49 the assurance that Yahweh has neither deserted nor forgotten Jerusalem refers specifically to his commitment that the city would be rebuilt (cf. Isa. 49:14; see Blenkinsopp 2000–2003: 2:310). It is impossible to say with any degree of certainty whether Jesus wants to direct his audience to Isa. 49:15. A closer parallel is found in the later rabbinic text *y. Šeb.* 9:1, 38d (22): "No bird perishes without God, how much less a man" (cf. *Gen. Rab.* 79:6; *Pesiq. Rab Kah.* 10 [88b]; *Midr. Ps.* 17:13 [27b]; *Esther Rab.* 1:9; *Eccles. Rab.* 10:9; see Str-B 1:582–83; Lachs 1987: 185; Marshall 1978: 514; Bock 1994–1996: 1138).

The assertion in 12:7 that "even the hairs of your head are all numbered" takes up an Israelite idiom that spoke of not having a single hair fall from one's head as a metaphor for "total deliverance in a situation of potential danger" (Nolland 1989–1993: 678; cf. Fitzmyer 1981–1985: 960). Note 1 Sam. 14:45, "As the LORD lives, not one hair of his [Jonathan's] head shall fall to the ground; for he has worked with God today"; 2 Sam. 14:11, "As the LORD lives, not one hair of your son shall fall to the ground"; and 1 Kings 1:52, "If he [Adonijah] proves to be a worthy man, not one of his hairs shall fall to the ground; but if wickedness is found in him, he shall die." Other scholars emphasize that the context focuses less on divine protection than on divine knowledge that surpasses all human knowledge and thus on the fact that God's purposes cannot be fully grasped even by his followers. This focus echoes Job 38:37: "Who has the wisdom to number the clouds? Or who can tilt the waterskins of the heavens?" If Jesus wants to point his listeners to this text, he asserts that God numbers not only the clouds, but also the hairs on people's heads, emphasizing God's infinite knowledge of even the minutest details of human existence, including the lives of his followers, even when they are persecuted (Allison 1989–1990, with further reference to Sir. 1:2; *4 Ezra* 4:7; *1 En.* 93:14; see Green 1997: 483). This proverbial statement is repeated in Jesus' admonitions about the coming persecution that his followers will face (21:18).

The assertions that God does not forget even a single sparrow (12:6) and that he knows the number of hairs on a person's head (12:7) do not state, in the present context of persecution, that the disciples will be protected from or kept safe in dangerous situations. Rather, Jesus asserts that as God cares for the most insignificant creatures and counts what human beings cannot count, his sovereign design cannot be fully grasped by human beings, and his knowledge surpasses any human knowledge. This means that the followers of Jesus should understand that "the mystery of God's incomparable wisdom makes evil endurable" because "God is not absent from or unaware of persecution" (Green 1997: 483). They are not spared persecution or martyrdom, but they have little reason to fear their persecutors, because God in his limitless providence takes care of them and because their names are already written in heaven (10:20).

12:8–9

This "Son of Man" saying in 12:8–9, "And I tell you, everyone who acknowledges me before others, the Son of Man also will acknowledge before the angels of God; but whoever denies me before others will be denied before the angels of God," has been interpreted as an allusion to Dan. 7:13–14. Both texts concern the last judgment, speak of the Son of Man as the central figure, describe this Son of Man as being "before" (enōpion [12:9; Dan. 7:13 Θ]) the divine court, refer to the angels, and refer to a situation of persecution (Allison 2000a: 130–31). Luke describes Jesus as God's appointed eschatological agent asserting a role for himself at God's side on the day of judgment (Bock 1994–1996: 1139).

Others suggest that the juxtaposition of acknowledging or denying the Son of Man alludes to the two ways of life and death, prosperity and adversity, blessing and judgment, that Moses places before Israel (cf. Deut. 30:15–20; see Bovon 1989–2001: 2:257). If Jesus' saying is indeed a deliberate allusion to Deut. 30 and thus to one of the most fundamental covenantal passages in the OT, then Jesus defines loyalty to the covenant in terms of loyalty to himself, implying possibly the notion that the promised new covenant has been inaugurated. As the decision that Israel faced in the plains of Moab involved not only an affirmation of loyalty to covenant and the law but

also an entire way of life based upon that decision (Craigie 1983: 366), so loyalty to Jesus determines his followers' entire life.

12:10

The saying about forgiveness in 12:10 is best regarded as addressed to opponents, warning against blaspheming against the Holy Spirit, whereas the preceding saying in 12:8–9 is addressed to the disciples, warning against denying Jesus in times of persecution (Marshall 1978: 519). The phrase "who blasphemes the Holy Spirit" (to hagion pneuma blasphēmeō) echoes OT passages that link Moses' successors who share in his possession of God's Spirit, who is eventually grieved by the people of Israel in the desert (cf. Num. 11:17; 27:18; Deut. 34:9; Ps. 106:32–33; Isa. 63:7–14; on blasphemy, cf. Lev. 24:11–23; Num. 15:30–31; see Lövestam 1968: 7–57; Fitzmyer 1981–1985: 966). The closest parallel is Isa. 63:10: "But they rebelled and grieved his Holy Spirit; therefore he became their enemy; he himself fought against them." This verse belongs to the first part of the communal complaint in Isa. 63:7–64:11, in which the prophet recounts Israel's praise of God for past mercies (63:7–14). Isaiah 63:10 introduces the theme of Israel's rebellion and of God's judgment that followed. The description of Israel's disobedience to God in terms of grieving (LXX: paroxynomai) the Holy Spirit (rûaḥ qodšô; LXX: to pneuma to hagion) is rare in the OT (cf. Ps. 51:11: "Do not cast me away from your presence, and do not take your Holy Spirit from me"). The "Spirit" is "the holy presence of Yahweh, which is a form of his outward manifestation to Israel theologically retrojected to the period of the nation's inception" (Childs 2001: 524). The prophet describes the Israelites' rebellion against God's saving revelation at the time of the exodus as grieving God's Spirit.

In 12:10 the phrase to hagion pneuma blasphēmeō, then, describes not simply blasphemous speech but "the denial or rejection of the manifest saving intervention of God on behalf of his People" (Nolland 1989–1993: 679). The rejection of the Son of Man—that is, the rejection of Jesus during his earthly ministry—can be forgiven, whereas the rejection of the Holy Spirit cannot be forgiven, as persistent and obdurate opposition to the influence of the Spirit is opposition to God himself and rejection of his saving power (Marshall 1978:

517; Fitzmyer 1981–1985: 964–65). At the same time, the saying is linked with Jesus' proclamation of the good news and the call to repentance: the radical proclamation of the criteria of God's future judgment aims to challenge the audience to repent and find salvation through acceptance of God's gracious revelatory presence (see Lövestam 1968: 67–68).

12:12

The saying in 12:12, "The Holy Spirit will teach you in that hour what is necessary to say," provides the reason for Jesus' instruction to his disciples not to worry about how to defend themselves when they are brought before Jewish and Gentile authorities (12:11; cf. 21:14–15). This logion that promises the help of the Holy Spirit (12:12) follows after the saying about speaking against the Holy Spirit (12:10). Verse 12 possibly echoes Yahweh's words to Moses in Exod. 4:12, "Now go, and I will be with your mouth and teach you what you are to say." Although there are no direct verbal connections between the two passages—Exod. 4:12 LXX has *symbibazō* ("instruct, teach, advise," for Heb. *yārâh* [*hip'îl*], which the LXX translates five times with *symbibazō* and eight times with *didaskō*) and *ho melleis lalēsai* ("what you will speak"), while 12:12 has *didaskō* ("instruct, teach") and *ha dei eipein* ("what is necessary to say")—both passages promise the leader(s) of God's people divine inspiration and guidance on what to say in potentially dangerous situations. Similarly, Yahweh promises the reluctant prophet Jeremiah that he will give him words to speak: "Then the LORD put out his hand and touched my mouth; and the LORD said to me, 'Now, I have put my words in your mouth'" (Jer. 1:9; note the context in 12:6–10). If the echoes of Exod. 4:12 and Jer. 1:9 are intentional, then Jesus promises his followers the same kind of divine assistance in critical situations that the prophets since Moses experienced (see also Ps. 119:41–46). Note also Philo's paraphrase of Num. 22:32–35 in *Moses* 1.274, where the angel says to Balaam: "I shall prompt the words you need without your mind's consent, and direct the organs of your speech as justice and convenience may require. I shall guide the reins of your speech, and, though you understand it not, use your tongue for each prophetic utterance" (Fitzmyer 1981–1985: 966).

12:14–15

Jesus' answer to an unnamed man who asks Jesus to settle quarrels between him and his brother over an inheritance (12:13) in 12:14, "Man, who appointed me to be a judge or arbitrator over you?" (*tis me katestēsen kritēn ē meristēn eph' hymas*), reflects the phraseology of Exod. 2:14 LXX: "Who made you a ruler and judge over us?" (*tis se katestēsen archonta kai dikastēn eph' hēmōn*). The variant reading in some manuscripts reflects the influence of Exod. 2:14 (or of Acts 7:27, 35, which quotes the OT passage), replacing *kritēn* with *dikastēn* (e.g., A Q W Θ Ψ 28 𝔐 [see Metzger 1994: 135]). In Exod. 2 the statement is uttered by two Israelites, living in Egypt, quarreling with each other who are confronted by Moses, who attempts to stop the fight. In Luke 12 Jesus refuses to be recruited as the arbitrator in a dispute over the division of family holdings, "addressing instead the dispositions out of which he apparently perceives the man's dispute to have arisen" (Green 1997: 488). The similarity of language does not seem to be intentional. (For the OT laws of inheritance, see Num. 27:1–11; 36:7–9; Deut. 21:16–17.)

Jesus' admonition in 12:15, "Take care! Be on your guard against all kinds of greed; for one's life does not consist in the abundance of possessions," provides a commentary on the previously narrated request for arbitration, warning against the danger of the possession of material wealth, even when it is inherited. Life is defined not by objects, "but by relationships, especially to God and his will" (Bock 1994–1996: 1150). Several OT passages state the same perspective: Job 31:24–25; Ps. 49; Eccles. 2:1–11 (cf. Sir. 11:18–19; *T. Jud.* 18–19; *1 En.* 97:8–10; see Manson 1949: 271).

12:20

In the parable of the Rich Fool (12:16–21), which illustrates Jesus' teaching about greed, 12:20 narrates God's reaction to the rich landowner who arranges for sufficient storage space for his crops, which he does not want to lose, and who concludes that he can henceforth live in leisure and self-indulgence: "You fool! This very night your life [lit., 'soul'] is being demanded of you. And the things you have prepared, whose will they be?" The word for "fool" (*aphrōn*) in the OT refers to a person who acts without God or without wisdom concerning the possibility of destruction (cf.

Job 34:36–37; Ps. 14:1 [13:1 LXX]; 53:1 [52:2 LXX]; Eccles. 2:1–17; see Bock 1994–1996: 1153; see also Donald 1963). The note that "they" will demand his soul from him may refer to "angels" of death (cf. Job 33:23 LXX; Heb. 2:14; cf. Grundmann 1978: 258; Marshall 1978: 524) or, more likely, reflects a Semitic circumlocution for God (cf. Job 4:19; 6:2; Prov. 9:11; see Fitzmyer 1981–1985: 974; Bock 1994–1996: 1153).

The final (rhetorical) question underlines that the pursuit of possessions is futile in view of one's ultimate priorities and the real meaning of life. Some OT passages that convey similar notions are Job 27:16–22; Ps. 39:6; 49:6; 90:10; 103:15–16; Eccles. 2:18–23 (see Plummer 1896: 325; Bock 1994–1996: 1154).

12:22–34

In the passage about Jesus' call to avoid anxiety, Jesus challenges the disciples in 12:24: "Consider the ravens: they neither sow nor reap, they have neither storehouse nor barn, and yet God feeds them. Of how much more value are you than the birds!" The reference to the ravens recalls Ps. 147:9 [146:9 LXX]; Job 38:41, where ravens are mentioned as crying for food, and Lev. 11:15; Deut. 14:14, where they are declared as forbidden food for Israelites. Jesus' saying underscores that if God cares even for unclean animals, surely he will care for the disciples. Some scholars see an echo of Prov. 6:6–11, which also appeals to nature: "Go to the ant, you lazybones; consider its ways, and be wise. . . . it prepares its food in summer, and gathers its sustenance in harvest," to which the LXX adds another illustration: "Or go to the bee, and learn how diligent it is, and how earnestly it is engaged in its work, whose labors kings and private citizens use for health, and it is desired and respected by all; although weak in body, it is advanced by honoring wisdom" (Healey [1989] points out that Luke 12:24/Matt. 6:26 and Prov. 6:7 LXX, "without having any cultivated land," *ekeinō gar geōrgiou mē hyparchontos*, are the only passages that make the striking assertion that the animals do not harvest. If we follow the lead of Cyril of Alexandria (in Aquinas, *Catena aurea* on Luke 12:24–26), we may see Luke 22:22–31 as an allusion to Prov. 6:6–11, with Jesus turning the moral of the Proverbs passage ironically upside down; whereas Prov. 6:6–11 points to the ant and the bee in order to promote work, Jesus points to the ravens and the lilies in order to emphasize the providential benevolence of God, who supports creatures that do not work for food and clothing (Allison 2000a: 173–74).

The reference to Solomon's glory in 12:27 echoes OT passages that describe King Solomon's proverbial wealth (1 Kings 10:4–23; 2 Chron. 9:13–21). The following verbal connections can be detailed (for these, see Allison 2000a: 153–54). The word *doxa* often was associated with Solomon's reign (1 Kings 3:13; 1 Chron. 29:25; 2 Chron. 1:12; *T. Sol.* 5:5; Josephus, *Ant.* 8.190). Over half of the occurrences of the word *krinon* ("lily") in the LXX are used in connection with Solomon, particularly with the temple that he built (e.g., 1 Kings 7:8, 12 [MT 7:19, 22, 24, 26]; 2 Chron. 4:5), and the traditional ascribed author of Song of Songs, Solomon, is described as "a lily of the valleys" (Song 2:1). In the LXX the verb *kopiaō* ("toil") is connected with traditions about Solomon as well (cf., e.g., Eccles. 1:3, 8 [Aquila]; 2:18 [B]; 2:24; 4:6 [Symmachus]; Ps. 126:1 [127:1 MT]; Prov. 4:12; cf. Wis. 3:11). The reference to anxiety concerning food, drink, and clothing in 12:22–31 recalls Solomon's sumptuous food, drink, and clothing (1 Kings 4:20, 22; 10:5; 2 Chron. 9:4) as well as the information that Solomon received all this from God because he sought wisdom and knowledge (1 Kings 3:11–13; 2 Chron. 1:11–12; cf. Wis. 7:10–11). In 12:22–31 Jesus similarly asserts that those who seek the kingdom of God will have their physical needs met.

The *a minori ad maius* argument in 12:28, which stresses God's providence even for grass, "which is alive today and tomorrow is thrown into the oven," echoes OT descriptions of the transitory and passing nature of grass (cf. Ps. 37:2; 90:5–6; 102:11; 103:15; Isa. 37:27; see Fitzmyer 1981–1985: 979).

The description of his disciples as "little flock" in 12:32 echoes OT passages that use the figure of the "flock" for God's people, who are fragile yet cared for by God (cf. Ps. 23:1; 28:9; 74:1; 77:20; Isa. 40:11; Jer. 13:17; Zech. 11:11; 13:7; see Ellis 1974: 179; Bock 1994–1996: 1165). The statement "Do not be afraid, little flock, for it is your Father's good pleasure to give you the kingdom" has been interpreted as a possible allusion to Isa. 41:14 LXX, "Jacob, smallest of Israel, I shall help you," emphasizing that Jesus promises to his followers, a small community, God's greatest gift (Fitzmyer 1981–1985: 980). We should note, however, that the term "flock" is not used in Isa. 41:14.

12:35–46

Jesus' sayings about vigilance and faithfulness in 12:35–36 contain several allusions to OT passages. In 12:35 the phrase "let your loins be girded" (*estōsan hymōn hai osphyes periezōsmenai*) may be an allusion to God's instruction given to the Israelites in directing them to be ready for a hasty departure from Egypt (Exod. 12:11: *hai osphyes hymōn periezōsmenai*). In other OT texts the phrase is used as an expression for readiness or service (cf. 1 Kings 18:46; 2 Kings 4:29; 9:1; Job 38:3; 40:7; cf. 1QM XV, 14; 11Q10 XXX, 1; XXXIV, 2–3; Philo, *Sacrifices* 63; see Fitzmyer 1981–1985: 987–88; Green 1997: 500). The addition "and your lamps burning" also emphasizes watchfulness (cf. Exod. 27:20; Lev. 24:2). Whether the allusion to Exod. 12:11 suggests a connection between Exod. 12:8, where the Israelites are directed to eat the Passover lamb with unleavened bread, and Jesus' warning of the "leaven of the Pharisees" in 12:1, suggesting that he teaches that the Pharisaic mind-set that must be avoided is a lack of watchfulness with regard to Yahweh's eschatological coming (Green 1997: 500), seems less plausible; note that 12:1 is too far removed from 12:35–46. But the allusion to Exod. 12:11 is clearly more than decoration: it expresses the conviction that the last redemption will be reminiscent of the redemption of the exodus (Allison 2000a: 60; cf. Bovon 1989–2001: 2:325–26; the suggestion that this probably reflects the belief that the Messiah will return on Passover night agrees with *Mek. Exod.* 12:42; *Frg. Tg. P* Exod. 15:18; *Frg. Tg. V* Exod. 12:42; *Targum Neofiti*, but it overinterprets the allusion in 12:35).

The theme of watchfulness, related to the eschatological day of Yahweh, which is the emphasis of the parable of the Waiting Servants (12:35–38) and the parable of the Unexpected Thief (12:39–40), echoes several OT passages (cf. Isa. 13:6; Ezek. 30:3; Joel 1:15; 2:1; Amos 5:18; Obad. 15; Zeph. 1:14–18; Mal. 4:5–6; see Fitzmyer 1981–1985: 987).

The parable of the Faithful and Prudent Manager in 12:42–46 possibly alludes to Gen. 39:4–5:

"So Joseph found favor in his sight and attended him; he made him overseer of his house [*katestēsen auton epi tou oikou autou*] and put him in charge of all that he had. From the time that he made him overseer in his house [*meta to katastathēnai auton epi tou oikou autou*] and over all that he had, the LORD blessed the Egyptian's house for Joseph's sake; the blessing of the LORD was on all that he had, in house and field." Note the opening rhetorical question of Jesus' parable in 12:42: "Who then is the faithful and prudent manager whom his master will put in charge of his servants [*hon katastēsei ho kyrios epi tēs therapeias autou*], to give them their allowance of food [grain] at the proper time?" (Allison 2000a: 87–92; C. F. Evans 1990: 336; cf. Bovon 1989–2001: 2:334). The words of 12:42 are often quoted in Jewish writings about Joseph (Allison [2000a: 88] refers to *Jub.* 39:3; 40:7; Philo, *Joseph* 37, 38, 117; *T. Jos.* 2:1; 11:6; *Jos. Asen.* 4:7; 20:9; Josephus, *Ant.* 2.39; see also Acts 7:9–10). Key words of 12:42 are prominent in the traditions about Joseph: *ho kyrios*, "the master" (e.g., Gen. 39:3–4); *phronimos*, "prudent" (cf. Gen. 41:33, 39; cf. Ps. 104:21 LXX [105:21 MT]); *doulos*, "servant" (cf. Gen. 39:17, 19; 41:12, but using the term *pais*; note that *T. Jos.* 1:5; 11:2, 3; 13:6, 7, 8; 15:2, 3 use *doulos* for Joseph), grain (*to sitometrion*, "measured allowance of grain," is a Lukan *hapax legomenon*, but *sitos*, "grain," is a key term in the Joseph narrative; see the LXX of Gen. 41:35, 49; 42:2–3, 25–26; 43:2; 44:2; 47:12–14). Jesus' declaration in 12:44, "Truly I tell you, he will put that one in charge of all his possessions [*epi pasin tois hyparchousin autou*]" is a variation of the original declaration, "Who then is the faithful and prudent manager whom his master will put in charge of his servants, to give them their allowance of food at the proper time?" The same kind of variation is found in Gen. 39: after the twice-repeated statement that the master appointed Joseph over his household (39:4–5a), another declaration follows: "The blessing of the LORD was on all that he had [*en pasin tois hyparchousin autō*], in house and field" (39:5b [this phrase occurs only one other time in the LXX, at Jdt. 8:10; see Allison 2000a: 91]). Biblically informed readers of Luke's Gospel would find in Joseph an example of a faithful servant who is eventually rewarded, the antithesis of the servant in the parable who reasons that since his master is delayed in coming, he can begin "to beat the other slaves, men and women, and to eat and drink and get drunk" (see Allison 2000a: 91–92).

The reference to the delay of the return of the master possibly echoes Hab. 2:3: note 12:43, "blessed is that slave whom his master will find at work when he arrives [*elthōn*]"; 12:45, "if that slave says to himself, 'My master is delayed in coming [*chronizei ho kyrios mou erchesthai*]'"; 12:46, "the master of that slave will come [*hēxei*] on a day when he does not expect him." Habakkuk 2:3 raises the delay of eschatological salvation as a possibility: "For still the vision awaits its time; it hastens to the end—it will not lie. If it seems slow, wait for it; it will surely come [*erchomenos hēxei*], it will not delay [*ou mē chronisē*]." The interpretation in *Targum of the Prophets on Hab.* 2:3 is clearly eschatological: "For the prophecy is ready for a time and the end is fixed, nor will it fail; if there is delay in the matter wait for it, for it will come in its time and will not be deferred." The allusion is established through (1) the verbs *erchomenos/elthōn*, *hēxei/hēxei*, and *chronisē/chronizei*, (2) the juxtaposition of a servant who is "faithful" (*pistos*) and one who is "faithless" (*apistōn*) in vv. 42–44/45–47 and the juxtaposition of people who "live by faith" (*ex pisteōs*) and people whose "spirit is not right in them" in Hab. 2:4, and (3) the statement in Hab. 2:5 that wine is treacherous (MT and Targum, not the LXX) and the description of the faithless servant in 12:45 who drinks and gets drunk (Allison 2000a: 132). If Jesus' disciples noticed this allusion, they would have been comforted by the notion that the delay of the day of judgment was part of prophecy and thus "nothing to be surprised or too anxious about" (Allison 2000a: 132).

The parable-like saying in 12:47–48 contrasts a disobedient servant who knows his master's wishes and one who is ignorant and does something that deserves punishment. This contrast is based on the OT distinction between deliberate sins—sins committed with a "high hand"—and sins done in ignorance, as is described in Num. 15:27–30 (cf. Wis. 6:6–8; 1QS V, 11–12; 4Q83 3–10 IV, 15; CD-A VIII, 8; 10:3; *m. Šabb.* 7:1; *b. B. Bat.* 60b; see Manson 1949: 119; Fitzmyer 1981–1985: 992; Bock 1994–1996: 1184).

12:49–59

Jesus' sayings about the coming crisis contain several OT allusions. Verse 49, "I came to bring fire to the earth, and how I wish it were already kindled!" echoes OT passages that speak of fire as a figure of judgment (Jer. 43:12; Ezek. 15:7; Hos. 8:14; Amos 1:4–14; 2:2, 5; Nah. 3:13; Zech. 13:9; Mal. 3:2–3; cf. *1 En.* 18:15; 102:1; *2 Bar.* 37:1; 48:39; *4 Ezra* 13:10–11; *Pss. Sol.* 15:4–5; *Jub.* 9:15; 36:10; 1QH[a] XVI, 20; see Bock 1994–1996: 1192n6).

In 12:50 the "baptism" with which Jesus has to be baptized has been interpreted in terms of the "inundation of the waters of divine judgment" against the background of the metaphorical sense of being overwhelmed by catastrophe (see *TDNT* 1:538–39; Marshall 1978: 547) and the OT imagery of floods for persecution or judgment (cf. Ps. 18:4, 16; 42:7; 69:1–2; Isa. 8:7–8; 30:27–28; Jon. 2:3–6; see Bayer 1986: 81): Jesus announces that he will be "uniquely inundated with God's judgment, an allusion to rejection and persecution" (Bock 1994–1996: 1194; cf. Green 1997: 509). In Ps. 11:6 the image of God raining fire upon the wicked is combined with the image of a scorching wind as the content of the "cup" that the wicked have to drink. If this passage is echoed in 12:50, then the "baptism" that Jesus refers to "may have the sense of deluging someone from above with fire" (Marshall 1978: 547, referring to Delling 1970a: 248). Some scholars derive the notion of a "baptism of death" from Isa. 53:10, "yet it was the will of the LORD to crush him with pain," translated in the LXX as "and he will cleanse [*katharisai*] him from the wound," while the Targum writes that "before the Lord it was a pleasure to refine and to cleanse the remnant of his people, in order to purify their souls from sins." If this is correct, then Jesus possibly combined the two meanings of the Hebrew verb *dikkāʾ*, "crush" and "cleanse, purify," in the image of the "baptism," which signifies death, asserting that it is the will of God to "crush" his servant so that "the many" will be "cleansed" on account of the vicarious death of the righteous servant (O. Betz 1996; 1998: 84–85).

Jesus' assertion in 12:51–53 interprets (12:52) and alludes to (12:53) Mic. 7:6: "For the son treats the father with contempt, the daughter rises up against her mother, the daughter-in-law against her mother-in-law; your enemies are members of your own household." The breakdown of the solidarity of society in general and of the members of households in particular that the prophet laments is interpreted as the result of Jesus' message and ministry (see Manson 1949: 121; Kessler 1999: 292; cf. also *Jub.* 23:16, 19; *4 Ezra* 6:24; *m. Soṭah* 9:15). As Luke formulates three pairs of comparisons (father against son, mother against daughter, mother-in-law against daughter-in-law), which are in each case reversed (son against father, etc.), the effect is heightened (Ernst 1977: 414–15; Bock 1994–1996: 1196). Jewish texts apply Mic. 7:6 to the messianic days (cf. *Jub.* 23:19; *1 En.* 99:5; 100:1–2; *2 Bar.* 70:6; 1Q14; see Ellis 1974: 183). Jesus links the time of his mission with discord rather than with peace and emphasizes with the allusion to Mic. 7:6 that the new age that the prophets predicted has not yet come and that it does not come without tribulation (Allison 2000a: 133).

13:2–3

In the passage about tragedy and the need to repent (13:1–5), Jesus asks the rhetorical question whether people "think that because these Galileans suffered in this way they were worse sinners than all other Galileans" (13:2). The notion that calamity, including illness, is the result of sin echoes several OT passages (cf. Exod. 20:5; Job 4:7–8; 8:4, 20; 22:5; Prov. 10:24–25; cf. 1QapGen ar XX, 16–29; John 9:1–3; see Plummer 1896: 338; Fitzmyer 1981–1985: 1007). Jesus does not endorse this conviction, but rather calls his audience to repentance.

Jesus' plea to repent is substantiated in 13:3 by the warning "Unless you repent, you will all perish as they did." He argues that repentance is the only way to avoid eternal death, a fate that will fall upon everyone who does persist in sin. This echoes Jer. 12:17, "But if any nation will not listen, then I will completely uproot it and destroy it, says the LORD," and Ps. 7:11–16 (Fitzmyer 1981–1985: 1008).

13:6

Jesus' parable of the Barren Fig Tree (13:6–9), directed at his Palestinian contemporaries whom he calls to repentance after learning about the incident in which Pilate had killed Galileans in Jerusalem (13:1–5), uses a familiar metaphor. Since fig trees are among the most common fruit trees in Palestine, a comment on fruit bearing and fruitlessness would naturally use the symbol of a fig tree, whether it is a common OT symbol for Judah or Israel (cf. Jer. 8:13; 24:1–10; Hos. 9:10; Mic. 7:1; see Fitzmyer 1981–1985: 1008; C. A. Evans 1990: 206; Stein 1992: 370; Bock 1994–1996: 1208 with note 12) or not (Marshall 1978: 555; Nolland 1989–1993: 718). For fruit trees planted in vineyards, see Deut. 22:9; 1 Kings 4:25; 2 Kings 18:31; Mic. 4:4. The fact that the fig tree is situated in a vineyard may suggest that Jesus wanted his listeners to think of Isa. 5:1–7, in which the prophet compares the inhabitants of Jerusalem and the people of Judah with a vineyard that yields only wild grapes. If this is correct, then the vineyard stands for Israel, and the fig tree represents Israel's barren leadership (cautiously, Green 1997: 515n126). Jesus challenges his listeners not to delay repentance and to live fruitful lives, as God, who mercifully holds back judgment at the present time, will not spare those who refuse to orient their heart and life around God's purposes (Green 1997: 515n126).

13:14–17

In the miracle story that narrates the healing of a crippled woman on the Sabbath (13:10–17), the leader of the synagogue, eager to uphold and enforce proper legal observance of the Torah, reminds the people who are present, "There are six days on which work ought to be done; come on those days and be cured, and not on the Sabbath day" (13:14). This statement alludes to the Mosaic legislation prohibiting work on the seventh day (Exod. 20:9; Deut. 5:13). The synagogue ruler does not argue for a particular interpretation of the Sabbath law, but rather implies that this position represents the self-evident will of God (Green 1997: 523): the woman had suffered from her illness for eighteen years, her condition is not life-threatening, and she could easily wait one day for her cure.

Jesus responds in 13:15 by questioning the synagogue ruler's interpretation of the law, reminding him that the Sabbath legislation applies not only to human beings but also to oxen and donkeys (Deut. 5:14), arguing that if this is the case, then people should not be allowed to untie their animals, and animals should not be allowed to walk to a trough for water. Jesus' reference to "ox or donkey" in his reply echoes OT passages that mention the same pair of household animals: ox/cow (*ho/hē bous*) and ass/donkey (*ho/hē onos*). We should note, however, that the LXX uses the terms *bous* and *onos* only in Isa. 32:20, "Happy will you be who sow beside every stream, who let the ox and the donkey [*bous kai onos*] range freely," and in the narrative texts Gen. 32:5; 34:28. The legal texts that form the general background for Luke 13:15 translate with *hypozygion* ("donkey, ass" [Deut. 5:14]) and *moschos* ("calf, ox" [Deut. 22:4]). The *Damascus Document* limits the provision of pasture and water to animals on the Sabbath to a distance of two thousand cubits for members of the Essene communities (CD-A XI, 5–6). For rabbinic texts about the care of animals, particularly on the Sabbath, see *m. Šabb.* 5:1–4; 2:2; 15:1–2; *b. Šabb.* 113a; *m. ʿErub.* 2.1–4; *b. ʿErub.* 20b–21a (see Lachs 1987: 298; Marshall 1978: 558–59). Jesus argues in 13:15–16 that what is permissible for cattle is all the more permissible for a human being, and he calls his critics "hypocrites" for not understanding God's purpose and for not understanding the meaning of the Scriptures (Green 1997: 524).

The comment in 13:17, "all his opponents were put to shame" (*kateschynonto pantes hoi antikeimenoi autō*), echoes Isa. 45:16, which speaks of the shame (*aischynthēsontai*) of opponents (*oi antikeimenoi autō*) in the context of producers of idols, which are contrasted with Israel's God, who saves with an everlasting salvation (Isa. 45:15, 17). The description of the crowd that rejoiced "at all the wonderful things [*epi pasin tois endoxois*] that he was doing" echoes OT language, particularly Exod. 34:10, "Before all your people I will perform marvels [*poiēsō endoxa*] such as have not been performed in all the earth or in any nation; and all the people among whom you live shall see the work of the LORD; for it is an awesome thing that I will do with you," stressing that the miraculous deeds of Jesus are the work of God (Marshall 1978: 559; Bock [1994–1996: 1219] also refers to Deut. 10:21; Job 5:9; 9:10).

13:19

The parable of the Mustard Seed, in which the seed grows into a tree (*dendron*) in whose branches (*en tois kladois autou*) "the birds of the air" (*ta peteina tou ouranou*) make nests (*kateskēnōsen*) alludes to Dan. 4 LXX and Ezek. 17:22–24. In Dan. 4 LXX,

note the following verbal links: *basileia* (13:4, 27, 30, 31, 32, 36, 37); *dendron* (13:10, 20, 22, 23, 26); *ta peteina tou ouranou* (13:12, 21); *kladoi* (13:12, 17). In Ezek. 17:22–24, note *pan peteinon hypo tēn skian* and *ta klēmata* (13:23); the tree is specifically a cedar (see also Ezek. 31:5–6). In Dan. 4 the tree represents Nebuchadnezzar and his kingdom; it is eventually cut down. In Ezek. 17 the parable about the cedar implicitly depicts the kingdom of Israel, which will replace pagan kingdoms, and communicates the messianic promise of a Davidic king whom Yahweh will grant growth and comprehensive rule under which people will find peace and refuge (Zimmerli 1969: 389–90). The Targum interprets the text as expressing the hope for the restoration of the Davidic dynasty. Jesus' parable of the Mustard Seed, by alluding to Dan. 4 and Ezek. 17, not only implies scriptural authority but at the same time reaffirms the expectation of the arrival of the restoration of Israel, when God establishes his kingdom, which Jesus proclaims (Allison 2000a: 136; cf. Kogler 1988: 149–62; Reinhardt 1995: 120–23). Thus it is not surprising that Jesus begins the parable by pointing out that it illustrates the kingdom of God (13:18). The allusion to Ezek. 17:23 provides the parable with a messianic nuance, implying the claim that Jesus' messianic ministry inaugurates the kingdom of God (Kogler 1988: 166; Reinhardt 1995: 123). The fact that the parable does not speak of the growth of a mighty cedar tree, as Ezek. 17:23 does, illustrates the "dissonance" of Jesus' message: the kingdom of God that he proclaims is established not through bullying power but through developments that initially seem inconsequential (Green 1997: 526).

Some scholars suggest that the verb *kateskēnōsen* ("made nests") alludes to the OT traditions of the pilgrimage of the nations to Zion, particularly to Zech. 2:11 (2:15 LXX), "Many nations shall join themselves to the LORD on that day, and shall be my people; and I will dwell in your midst. And you shall know that the LORD of hosts has sent me to you," a text that combines the motif of the pilgrimage of the nations with the promise of a continuous sojourn (*kataskēnōsousin*) of the nations in the midst of Israel (Jeremias 1971: 146–49; Reinhardt 1995: 123–25). This suggestion has not convinced every scholar (see Kogler 1988: 169;

cf. Fitzmyer [1981–1985: 1017], who points out that Luke does not add his favorite word "all").

13:27–29

In his discussion of the question of how many will share in the salvation promised in the kingdom (13:22–30), Jesus asserts that entry into the kingdom depends on the master of the house, who is indirectly identified in 13:26 as Jesus himself (Fitzmyer 1981–1985: 1022). The question in 13:23 has no parallel in the OT but was often addressed in Second Temple Judaism; note *4 Ezra* 8:1: "The Most High made this world for the sake of many, but the world to come for the sake of few" (see also *4 Ezra* 7:47; 9:15). Isaiah 37:32, a text that is sometimes referred to in this context, speaks of a "remnant" and a "band of survivors" who shall go out from Jerusalem, but the context in Isa. 37 is limited to a temporary restoration of fortunes for Jerusalem.

The assertion in 13:27, an answer given to those who stand outside the door appealing to the householder as contemporaries who shared food with him and who listened to his teaching, has two parts, both containing OT allusions. The statement in 13:27a, "I do not know where you come from," recalls OT passages that speak of people being known by God (Jer. 1:5; Hos. 5:3; 13:5; Amos 3:2)—that is, people who are chosen by God (cf. Ps. 138:6; see Fitzmyer 1981–1985: 1022).

The second part of 13:27, "Depart from me, all doers of evil" (*apostēte ap' emou pantes ergatai adikias*), alludes to Ps. 6:8 (6:9 LXX), "Depart from me, all you workers of evil, for the LORD has heard the sound of my weeping," to emphasize not only that Jesus does not know them, but also that he positively excludes them (Marshall 1978: 567; Fitzmyer 1981–1985: 1025–26; Allison [2000a: 166] and Bovon [1989–2001: 2:435] speak of a [unmarked] quotation). Luke's text agrees exactly with the first four words of Ps. 6:9 LXX (*apostēte ap' emou pantes hoi ergazomenoi tēn anomian*). He changes the second part of the quotation in accordance with his style: he exchanges the nominalized participle *hoi ergazomenoi*, which he never uses, for the noun *ergatai* (cf. Luke 10:2a, 2b, 7), and he replaces the noun *anomia*, which he never employs, with *adikia* (cf. Luke 16:8–9; 18:6; Acts 1:18; 8:23; note Holtz [1968: 159], who surmises, unconvincingly, that Luke did not recognize that

his source was quoting from Ps. 6:9). Unless Jesus uses the words of Ps. 6:8 only to add solemnity, we note that in Ps. 6 the speaker is someone who suffers and is subsequently vindicated by God, and that in 13:27–28 he refers to weeping and to the gnashing of teeth. This suggests that Jesus may have used the language of Ps. 6:8 in order to describe himself as the one who has suffered at the hands of hostile opponents and will pronounce judgment against those who heard but opposed his message to be excluded from the heavenly banquet (Green 1997: 531; cf. Allison 2000a: 166).

In 13:28–29 the image of the joyous banquet of the kingdom echoes OT passages that describe, first, a gathering of Israel from all corners of the earth (Ps. 107:2–3; Isa. 43:5–6; 49:12; Zech. 2:10 LXX [on the textual problem in Ps. 107:3, see Allison 2000a: 168]); second, the worship of Yahweh by the Gentiles (Isa. 45:6; 59:19; Mal. 1:11); third, the eschaton as a great banquet (Isa. 25:6–8; 55:1–2; 65:13–14; Zeph. 1:7; *1 En.* 62:14; *2 Bar.* 29:4) (see Crockett 1966b: 294–95; France 1971: 63; Fitzmyer 1981–1985: 1026). The "gnashing of teeth" (*brychō* ["gnash"] + *odous* ["tooth"]) appears in the LXX as an expression of hatred (Job 16:9; Ps. 34:16; 36:12; 112:10; Lam. 2:16), with 13:29 resembling Ps. 112:10 (111:10 LXX) more closely: "The wicked see it and are angry; they gnash their teeth and melt away; the desire of the wicked comes to nothing." Since both of these texts depict the judgment of sinners, since both use a future tense, and since the gnashing of teeth is linked in both texts with the sinners seeing the good fortune of the righteous, 13:29 most probably should be regarded as an allusion to Ps. 112:10, although it is possible that the motif of "gnashing of teeth" is merely an eschatological topos (cf. *Sib. Or.* 2:205–206; 8:104–5, 231, 350; see Allison 2000a: 169). The weeping of those who are barred from access to the heavenly banquet of God's kingdom is contrasted with the joy of those who have entered through the "narrow door" (13:24)—that is, those who have gained entry into the banquet hall of the kingdom of God (Green 1997: 532).

13:31–35

In 13:31–35 Luke reports Jesus' fourth announcement of his violent death (after 9:22, 44; 12:50), following a warning from sympathetic Pharisees that Herod Antipas plans to kill him. Jesus comments that he will continue his ministry of casting out demons and healing the sick for as long as it was intended and that he will then go to Jerusalem, where he will be killed. Jesus implies that his fate is determined not by Herod's plot, but by the will of God, to which he submits (Bovon 1989–2001: 2:449). The passage ends with Jesus' lament over Jerusalem (13:34–35).

Jesus' assertion in 13:33, "It is impossible for a prophet to be killed outside of Jerusalem," echoes several OT texts. Jeremiah 26:20–23 narrates the killing of the prophet Uriah in Jerusalem by King Jehoiakim. During the reign of King Joash, Zechariah the son of Jehoiada was killed in Jerusalem (2 Chron. 24:20–22). Zechariah was a priest rather than a prophet, but he is mentioned in Luke 11:51, together with Abel, as prophets whose blood has been spilled (Stein [1992: 343] comments that Luke designates both Abel and Zechariah son of Jehoiada as prophets because he regards the entire OT as prophecy). According to Jer. 38:4–6, an attempt was made on Jeremiah's life in Jerusalem. The comment in 2 Kings 21:16 that King Manasseh "shed very much innocent blood, until he had filled Jerusalem from one end to another" was understood in Jewish tradition to refer to all righteous Jews, including the prophets: "He spared not even the prophets, some of whom he slaughtered daily, so that Jerusalem ran with blood" (Josephus, *Ant.* 10.38). Later traditions claim that the prophet Isaiah was killed in Jerusalem (*Mart. Isa.* 5:1–14; Justin, *Dial.* 120.14–15). Other OT passages and Jewish tradition refer to the murder of prophets more generically (cf. 1 Kings 18:4, 13; 19:10, 14; Neh. 9:26; Jer. 2:30; *Jub.* 1:12; Acts 7:52; note Tan [1997: 75–76], who points out that with the exception of Jer. 26:20–23 and Josephus, *Ant.* 10.38, the OT and Jewish traditions assert only that the *nation* killed the prophets). Stoning was the most common form of execution, used in, for example, cases involving blasphemy (Lev. 24:14, 16, 23) and apostasy (Lev. 20:2; Deut. 13:10). Since stoning was a standard punishment for other crimes as well, this OT background cannot be taken to signify that Jerusalem attributes blasphemy or apostasy to those whom God has sent (so Green 1997: 538). Jesus' statement does not quote an existing proverb, but asserts the appropriateness of death in Jerusalem: since Jerusalem kills prophets

(13:34), "it is appropriate that Jesus as a prophet should die there too" (Marshall 1978: 573; cf. Fitzmyer 1981–1985: 1032).

Jesus' statement in 13:34, "How often have I desired to gather your children together as a hen gathers her brood under her wings, and you were not willing!" recalls several OT passages that use illustrations from nature to describe Yahweh's care for Israel: "Like an eagle stirs up its nest, and hovers over its young, spreading out its wings, catching them, bearing them aloft on its pinions . . ." (Deut. 32:11); "Hide me in the shadow of your wings" (Ps. 17:8); "All people may take refuge in the shadow of your wings" (Ps. 36:7); "In the shadow of your wings I will take refuge" (Ps. 57:1); "And under his wings you will find refuge" (Ps. 91:4); "May you have a full reward from the LORD, the God of Israel, under whose wings you have come for refuge" (Ruth 2:12) (see also *4 Ezra* 1:30; *2 Bar.* 41:3–4; *1 En.* 39:7; *Sipre Deut.* 296:3; 306:4; 314:1; *b. Soṭah* 13b; *Pesiq. Rab Kah.* 16:1; *Pesiq. Rab.* 4:1). Rabbinic texts use the image of finding refuge under wings for proselytes who come under the wings of the Shekinah (cf. *'Abot R. Nat.* 12a; *Sipra Qed.* pq. 8:205; *Sipre Num.* 80:1; *Sipre Deut.* 32:2; *b. 'Abod. Zar.* 13b; *b. Šabb.* 31a; *Gen. Rab.* 47:10; *Pesiq. Rab.* 14:2). As this figure speaks of care and protection, Jesus, the preacher of the dawn of God's kingdom, describes his mission in terms of bringing the Jewish people "into the care which he was sent to manifest as the new herald of God's salvific kingdom" (Fitzmyer 1981–1985: 1036). The OT background of the figure suggests that Jesus identifies with God's care for his people.

In 13:35a the threat of eventual judgment on Jerusalem is formulated with the phrase "See, your house is left to you" (*idou aphietai hymin ho oikos hymōn*). This phrase recalls the language and the images of Jer. 12:7, "I have forsaken my house, I have abandoned my heritage" (*enkataleloipa ton oikon mou aphēka tēn klēronomian mou*), and Jer. 22:5, "This house shall become a desolation" (*eis erēmōsin estai ho oikos houtos*) (see also Ps. 69:25; Ezek. 8:6; 11:23). The term "house" refers not to the temple alone, but to the "household" of Jerusalem—that is, Jerusalem, the center of Israel, as God's people who are opposed to God's will (see Tan 1997: 114–15; Green 1997: 539). While Jer. 22 speaks of the possibility of exile for the nation if the people continue to oppose the will of God, Jesus announces that a time of abandonment has come: "Rather than being gathered under God's wings, their house is left empty and exposed" (Bock 1994–1996: 1250). An allusion to Jer. 12:7, which recalls the martyred prophet Jeremiah, serves to reinforce the declaration of Luke 11:49–51 that Jerusalem has often rejected prophets, implying that Jesus is like Jeremiah, who met hostility in Jerusalem (Allison 2000a: 127–28). It should be noted that 13:34–35a are linked with Jer. 12:7 via the words *aphiēmi* ("let go, abandon") and *oikos* ("house"), and via the word *oikos* with 2 Chron. 24:17–25 (alluded to in 13:33; Jer. 12:7 and 2 Chron. 24:17–25 also share the word *enkataleipō* ["forsake"]) and Ps. 118:26 (quoted in 13:35b), illustrating the hermeneutical principle of *gezerah shavah* (Allison 2000a: 128).

The phrase "you will not see me" in 13:35b probably recalls OT and Jewish traditions of figures who were translated to heaven and expected to play a future eschatological role, particularly the translation of Elijah in 2 Kings 2:11–12 (cf. *4 Ezra* 6:26; see Zeller 1985: 515–16). If this is the background of Jesus' statement, then he asserts that he will depart (through death) and go to heaven until the time comes in which he will fulfill his eschatological role (Nolland 1989–1993: 742).

13:35

A. NT Context: Lament over Jerusalem. In

13:35b Jesus announces that the people of Jerusalem will not see him until the time comes when they say, "Blessed is the one who comes in the name of the Lord," an allusion to Ps. 118:26 (Marshall 1978: 577; Fitzmyer 1981–1985: 1037; Bock 1994–1996: 1250). It is unlikely that Luke did not recognize these words as a quotation from Ps. 118 (so Holtz 1968: 160).

B. Ps. 118:26 in context. Psalm 118 (117

LXX) has the form of an individual thanksgiving, with a summons to praise Yahweh in 13:1–4, 29, and with communal praise for the main speaker's thanksgiving in 13:22–25, 27, whose adversity from which he has been rescued is the subject of 13:5–18. There is no consensus who the main speaker is: some suggest a liturgy for the circumcision of a proselyte, some argue that the "I" stands for the people and that the psalm is a communal thanksgiving, while others suggest that the psalm

celebrates the military victory of a king that was celebrated at the autumn festival (Dahood 1966–1970: 3:155; Allen 1983: 123). As a result of the last suggestion, many scholars classify Ps. 118 as a royal psalm. Many scholars think that Ps. 118 was used in the annual rite of reenthronement of the king. Interpreted against this background, "the psalm speaks to the saving acts of Yahweh, but also recognizes the place of humiliation and rejection in the divine plan" (Green 1997: 709). (On Ps. 118, see P. Constant [2001: 27–187], who argues for a messianic understanding in an OT canonical context, with reference to Pss. 18; 132; Exod. 15; Isa. 8; 12.)

C. Ps. 118:26 in Judaism. Several scholars

claim that Ps. 118, and indeed the entire body of Hallel psalms, had eschatological and messianic connotations, at least toward the end of the Second Temple Period (see Jeremias 1966: 255–61; Lindars 1961: 173; Kraus 1986: 193; Lachs 1987: 345; Allison 2000a: 163). Some NT scholars accept these claims (see Bock 1987: 118; Kimball 1994b: 159; Kinman 1995: 57), but others point out that texts that are quoted in support of a messianic interpretation of Ps. 118 or of the entire body of Hallel psalms—for example, *b. Pesaḥ* 118b (Ps. 118:1); *b. Pesaḥ* 118a (Ps. 115:1); *y. Ber.* 4d [2:4] (Ps. 118:27–28); *Midr. Ps.* 36 [6] (Ps. 118:27); *Pesiq. Rab Kah.* 17:5 (Ps. 118:15)—cite rabbinic authorities that date to the late second century AD at the earliest, while midrashic eschatological interpretations (*Midr. Ps.* 26 [6]; 27 [1]; 36 [6]; 118 [8, 12–14, 22]) have no attributions and date not earlier than the third century (Wagner 1997: 158–59). There seem to be no quotations of Ps. 118 in Second Temple literature.

On the other hand, the canonical form of the Psalter suggests to some scholars that the royal psalms were interpreted in the context of the messianic hope of Israel, since the postexilic editors' arrangement of the psalms is "highly eschatological in nature": at a time when the institution of Israelite kingship belonged to the distant past, the earthly king of the psalms would have evoked God's Messiah (Childs 1977: 516, 518; cf. Wagner 1997: 159). Also, the use of Ps. 118 in Jewish liturgy may have suggested an eschatological interpretation: Ps. 118 was sung as part of the Hallel at the Feasts of Tabernacles (*m. Sukkah* 3:9; 4:1–8), Hanukkah (*m. Ta'an.* 4:4–5), and

Passover—both at the sacrificing of the lambs and at the meal—(*m. Pesaḥ.* 5:7; 10:5–7; *t. Pesaḥ.* 10:8–9; cf. Mark 14:26; Matt. 26:30), and on the first day of the Feast of Weeks (*t. Sukkah* 3:2). The association of Ps. 118 with the divine deliverance that was celebrated at these festivals may have suggested "readings of the psalm that focused on the hope of God's future deliverance of Israel through the agency of his Anointed One" (Wagner 1997: 160). These lines of evidence establish the possibility of an interpretation of Ps. 118 in terms of the royal Messiah, but due to the lack of specific evidence there can be no certainty. The argument that the widespread use of Ps. 118 suggests that the messianic interpretation predates the writing of the Gospels (Wagner 1997: 161, with the NT references listed in nn. 24–25) is plausible, especially if we allow for the possibility that this interpretation goes back to Jesus.

D. Textual Matters. The quotation from Ps. 118:26 in 13:35: "Blessed is the one who comes in the name of the Lord" (*eulogēmenos ho erchomenos en onomati kyriou*) reproduces verbatim the LXX text (117:26), which accurately translates the MT's *bārûk habbā' bĕšem Yahweh.*

E. The Use of Ps. 118:26 in Luke 13:35. The first explicit quotation of Ps. 118 in Luke's work (see also 19:38; 20:17; Acts 4:11) belongs to a context in which Jesus responds to the Pharisees' warning that King Herod is actively involved in a plot to kill him (13:31). This may remind the readers of the Gospel of the first allusion to Ps. 118, in the context of John the Baptist's imprisonment by Herod (7:19, with the term *ho erchomenos,* "the coming one"). Since John was executed by Herod, the Pharisees' warning carries weight, prompting Jesus to assert that it is not fitting for a prophet to die outside Jerusalem and to lament Jerusalem's violent resistance against God's messengers (Wagner 1997: 163).

There are several different answers to the question concerning the intended reference of the quotation from Ps. 118:26. First, Jesus' OT quotation refers to the parousia, the return of the Messiah, a time when Jerusalem would respond with the words of Ps. 118:26, positively recognizing Jesus as Messiah (Zahn 1988: 543; Strauss 1995: 315–17; Constant 2001: 279–80; Bovon 1989–2001: 2:458–59; Bock 1987: 117–21; 1994–1996: 1251, with reference to Luke 21:24;

Rom. 11:11–32). In the context of Jesus' lament over Jerusalem in Matt. 23:37–39, introducing the eschatological discourse in Matt. 24, the reference of Jesus' quotation of Ps. 118:26 to the parousia is much more explicit. Luke placed Jesus' lament and the quotation of Ps. 118:26 before Jesus' entry into Jerusalem, however, which makes this interpretation less obvious.

Second, since the same words from Ps. 118:26 are cited in 19:38, and since Luke places Jesus' lament and the quotation in the context of the travel narrative, the reference in 13:35 is to Jesus' anticipated arrival in Jerusalem (Danker 1988: 162; Fitzmyer 1981–1985: 1037; Lindars 1961: 172; Wagner 1997: 163; Döpp 1998: 41; Rusam 2003: 224). If this was Luke's intention, the words of Ps. 118:26 would have a heavily ironical meaning. We should note also that Ps. 118:26 is not quoted exactly at 19:38, and there it is spoken not by Jesus, but by the people of Jerusalem (Marshall 1978: 577).

Third, Jesus' assertion in 13:35b, taking the form of a conditional promise, means that if Jerusalem repents from its refusal to acknowledge God's messenger, and if the people receive "the one who comes in the name of the Lord" with blessing, then disaster and judgment will be averted and Israel will experience the coming of salvation (Green 1997: 538; Allison 1983; Kinman 1995: 97; cf. Wagner 1997: 163–64). It should be noted that the second and third explanations are not mutually exclusive, but rather complementary.

F. Theological Use. The quotation of Ps. 118:26 creates dramatic tension as Luke evokes images of opposition and hostility awaiting Jesus in Jerusalem and builds suspense with the suggestion that Jerusalem will receive Jesus as King (and Messiah) once he arrives in the city. This possibility contrasts with Jesus' repeated prediction of his rejection and death (Wagner 1997: 163–64). The words of the psalm about worshipers blessing the one who comes in the name of the Lord and about a blessing that comes from the house of the Lord (i.e., the temple) are consistently interpreted in 13:34–35 as a prophecy concerning the "forsaken" house—that is, presumably both the temple and Jerusalem: since Jerusalem and the temple have opposed God's messengers and fallen into sin, they are headed for disaster and judgment, which means that the temple and the city (which at present refuse to bless the one who comes as the Son of Man) can no longer be the source of God's blessing (Allison 2000a: 163–64).

Luke 14:10–11

In 14:1–24 Luke depicts Jesus' enjoying the hospitality of a leader of the Pharisees following a synagogue service on the Sabbath (14:1). Given, first, the importance of social status as determined by the perception of one's contemporaries, and, second, the importance of the reciprocity of gift and obligation in ancient society, Jesus' assertions on meal etiquette undermine the values and expectations that his meal companions would have taken for granted, constructing a new vision of life and community (Green 1997: 550–51). In 14:8–10 Jesus advises against taking the "first seats," which are more honorable, because if one's claim to honor is not acknowledged by the host, then humiliation in front of the other guests will follow. Jesus asserts that it is better to sit at a less honorable place and be promoted by the host to a more lofty seat assignment.

Verse 10, "When you are invited, go and sit down at the lowest place, so that when your host comes, he may say to you, 'Friend, move up higher'; then you will be honored in the presence of all who sit at the table with you," is a wisdom saying that echoes Prov. 25:6–7, "Do not put yourself forward in the king's presence or stand in the place of the great; for it is better to be told, 'Come up here,' than to be put lower in the presence of a noble," adapting sapiential advice for court etiquette to a banquet setting (Fitzmyer 1981–1985: 1047). Jesus insists that honor must be given, not taken. The analogous advice in Sir. 3:17–20 is also related to a more general setting: "My child, perform your tasks with humility; then you will be loved by those whom God accepts. The greater you are, the more you must humble yourself; so you will find favor in the sight of the Lord. For great is the might of the Lord; but by the humble he is glorified." A later rabbinic passage resembles Luke 14:10 much more closely when Rabbi Simeon b. Azzai asserts, "Stay two or three seats below your place [i.e., where you felt you should sit], and sit there until they say to you, 'Come up!' Do not begin by going up because they may say to you, 'Go down!' It is better that they say to you, 'Go up,'

than that they say to you, 'Go down!' (*Lev. Rab.* 1:5; cf., similarly, *'Abot R. Nat.* 25; see Lachs 1987: 303; Fitzmyer [1981–1985: 1047] surmises that this rabbinic tradition may have been influenced by the early Christian tradition).

Verse 11 demonstrates that Jesus does more than acknowledge the honor system of the Greco-Roman world, suggesting a clever approach to securing one's prestige that results in even greater honor. The statement "All who exalt themselves will be humbled, and those who humble themselves will be exalted" (*pas ho hypsōn heauton tapeinōthēsetai, kai ho tapeinōn heauton hypsōthēsetai*) recasts the values of contemporary society: God acknowledges the "humble," and he judges those who seek honorable status. Jesus' aphorism alludes to Ezek. 21:26 ("Exalt that which is low, abase that which is high" = 21:31 LXX: *etapeinōsas to hypsēlon kai to tapeinon hypsōsas*; cf. Ezek. 17:24; see Fitzmyer 1981–1985: 1047; Bock 1994–1996: 1265), a text in which Yahweh castigates the "wicked prince of Israel" whose time of final punishment has come (21:25), who is asked to take off his crown (21:26a) because all is ruin "until he comes whose right it is; to him I will give it" (21:27). Also note Sir. 3:19: "Many are lofty and renowned, but to the humble he reveals his secrets." A similar passage is found in *Let. Aris.* 263, which answers the king's question of how one can avoid being arrogant: "By maintaining impartiality, and by reminding himself in the case of each individual that he is a ruler of men and still a man himself. Moreover, God destroys the proud, and exalts the gentle and humble." The allusion to these OT and Jewish texts in Luke 14:11 indicates that the assertion in v. 10 needs to be seen in a larger, eschatological perspective. The source of honor (*doxa* [14:10]) in God's kingdom is derived not from the social order described by affluent friends, siblings, relatives, or rich neighbors (cf. 14:12), but from the judgment of God (note the *passivum divinum* of *hypsōthēsetai* in 14:11; see Fitzmyer 1981–1985: 1045), who loves the poor, the crippled, the lame, and the blind (cf. 14:13). Jesus emphasizes that God implements new values in his kingdom, values that differ from those that control the contemporary social world. The text asserts that "the only commendation one needs comes from God who is unimpressed with such social credentials as govern social relations in Luke's world" (Green

1997: 552). God acknowledges as guests in his kingdom only those who acknowledge their own poverty.

14:15–24

The parable of the Great Supper (14:15–24) contains several OT allusions that Jesus' audience would easily have noticed. It has been suggested that the excuses of the invited guests as described in 14:18–20 allude to Deut. 20, which lists various reasons that provide legitimate excuses for not joining an army at war (Derrett 1970: 126–55). It is argued that there is a close relationship between the notion of preparation for holy war and the preparation to enter the great banquet that is celebrated when the kingdom of God arrives (J. A. Sanders 1974: 257–58; C. A. Evans 1990: 225). This is not very likely, since the features of war and king are absent from the parable (Marshall 1978: 586, 588; Fitzmyer 1981–1985: 1056; Nolland 1989–1993: 756; Bovon 1989–2001: 2:509–10). Jesus does not refer to "fighting" for the kingdom of God. The excuse of the third invited guest in 14:20, "I have just married," has been said to recall Deut. 20:5–7; 24:5 (cf. *m. Soṭah* 8:1–6), recognizing the status of newlyweds (Fitzmyer 1981–1985: 1056). On the other hand, he was invited to a banquet that would separate him from his new wife only for several hours. The dominant factor in this excuse is either the obligation to conceive a child or the weakness of the excuse (Marshall 1978: 589). The suggested links with Deut. 20 depend in a large measure on the question whether Luke's central section corresponds to the contents and themes of Deut. 1–26. If this is indeed the case, then the parable of the Great Supper can be interpreted in terms of protesting and challenging abuses of Deuteronomy's theology and ethic of election—that is, the assumption that the blessings and the curses of Deuteronomy are reflected in people's health and wealth or, respectively, their sickness and poverty, signaling either the righteousness or the sinfulness of individuals (J. A. Sanders 1974, followed by C. A. Evans 1990: 223–26).

Another question relates to "the poor, the crippled, the blind, and the lame" (14:21) who are invited instead of the original, evidently wealthy and respectable, guests. Some have suggested a link with Lev. 21:17–23, where such people are described as being unqualified for and therefore excluded from priestly service, even if they were Levites (J. A. Sanders [1974: 262] points out that this list in Lev. 21 inspired the stipulations in 1QM VII, 4–6; 1Q28a II, 3–22, texts that exclude such "defective" persons from participation in the eschatological holy war and from the feast). Possibly these were "popular" views (so C. A. Evans 1990: 225) that Jesus rejects with his parable, but this cannot be demonstrated. Some commentators relate the list of the disadvantaged to the OT tradition of Yahweh's mercy for the downtrodden, the oppressed, the ill, and the weak (Bovon 1989–2001: 2:512, with reference to Isa. 35:5–6a: "Then the eyes of the blind shall be opened, and the ears of the deaf unstopped; then the lame shall leap like a deer, and the tongue of the speechless sing for joy").

Whether Jesus (or Luke) intended to see a reference to the Gentiles in the third series of invitees (14:23), who live in "the roads and lanes" on the edge of the town, continues to be debated. Luke does not provide any hints in the parable concerning socioreligious identifications. Traditions in the OT of the eschatological banquet help us to understand the parable. Note, for example, Isa. 25:6–10:

> On this mountain the LORD of hosts will make for all peoples a feast of rich food, a feast of well-aged wines, of rich food filled with marrow, of well-aged wines strained clear. And he will destroy on this mountain the shroud that is cast over all peoples, the sheet that is spread over all nations; he will swallow up death forever. Then the LORD God will wipe away the tears from all faces, and the disgrace of his people he will take away from all the earth, for the LORD has spoken.

Granted that the OT tradition of the eschatological banquet scene reverberates through the parable, one cannot preclude the possibility that Gentiles might be included (Green 1997: 561).

14:26

In the context of a passage on the conditions of discipleship (14:25–33), Jesus asserts in 14:26, "Whoever comes to me and does not hate father and mother, wife and children, brothers and sisters, yes, and even life itself, cannot be my disciple." The first part of this stipulation alludes to the commandment "Honor your father and mother"

(Exod. 20:12; Deut. 5:16). Some scholars argue that 14:26 constitutes the annulment of the fourth commandment of the Decalogue (Hengel 1981: 13), while others point out that this is unlikely in the light of 16:17 and that the rabbis were well aware of the fact that the Torah sometimes presented conflicting claims, a situation that did *not* entail a "deconstruction of Torah but the subordination of one commandment to another" (Allison 2000a: 63, with reference to *m. Yoma* 8:6; *b. Yebam.* 5b; 90b). Jesus' requirement has been explained as echoing Deut. 33:9, where Levi's devotion to the Torah is highlighted (Marshall 1978: 592; Fitzmyer 1981–1985: 1063; Bovon 1989–2001: 2:533). Levi is reported to have said of his father and mother, "I regard them not," because "he ignored his kin, and did not acknowledge his children; for they observed your word, and kept your covenant." The fact that Deut. 33:9 is quoted in Jewish texts suggests that Jesus' stipulation does not contradict Torah (Allison 2000a: 64, referring to 4Q175 14–20; Philo, *Alleg. Interp.* 2.51; *Worse* 67; *Drunkenness* 72; *b. Yoma* 66b; *Num. Rab.* 1:121; *Eccles. Rab.* 4:8).

Luke 15:1–32

The unit of three parables in chapter 15—the Lost Sheep (15:4–7), the Lost Coin (15:8–10), and the Lost Son (15:11–32)—has been explained as an allusion to Jer. 31:10–20, a text in which Yahweh is a shepherd who gathers his flock (31:10–14), Rachel weeps for her children (31:15–17), and Ephraim is the son of Joseph who repents and receives God's mercy (31:18–20) (Kossen 1956; for a critique, see Marshall 1978: 598; Fitzmyer 1981–1985: 1072). Although this suggestion is plausible for the parable of the Lost Son, there are no clearly discernible echoes of Jer. 31 in the first two parables, which makes rather unlikely the view that Jer. 31 explains or dictates the composition of Luke 15.

The view that interprets Luke's central section against the background of Deut. 1–26 links chapter 15, particularly the parable of the Lost Son, with Deut. 21:15–22:4 (C. F. Evans 1955: 48; C. A. Evans 1990: 234). The parallels are as follows. Deuteronomy 21:15–17 deals with the status of a firstborn son, who will be honored over a second son even if the father loves the second

son more than the firstborn; the firstborn son will receive a "double portion" of the father's inheritance (21:17). Deuteronomy 21:18–21 deals with an obstinate son who does not obey his father and is "a glutton and a drunkard"; such a son will be taken out of the city and stoned. Jesus' parable stands in stark contrast to this part of Deuteronomistic legislation: the wayward son is not expelled and stoned; rather, the father receives him back into the family (C. A. Evans [1990: 234] points out that Deut. 21 formulates civil law and does not intend to exclude the possibility of repentance, forgiveness, and restoration).

15:4

In the parable of the Lost Sheep (15:4–7) the description of the shepherd who goes after the one lost sheep (15:4) echoes Ezek. 34:11–12, 16:

> For thus says the LORD God: I myself will search for my sheep, and will seek them out. As shepherds seek out their flocks when they are among their scattered sheep, so I will seek out my sheep. I will rescue them from all the places to which they have been scattered on a day of clouds and thick darkness. . . . I will seek the lost, and I will bring back the strayed, and I will bind up the injured, and I will strengthen the weak.

Jesus asserts that he does the work of God, whose love and mercy for sinful and weak people is reflected in Jesus' calling tax collectors and sinners (15:1) to repentance. As Jesus' audience consists of the Pharisees and scribes who complain about Jesus welcoming and eating with sinners (15:2), he challenges them to understand themselves as shepherds. The Pharisees' and scribes' lack of concern and mercy for sinners echoes Ezek. 34, in which Yahweh directs the prophet to speak against the leaders of the nation who neglect their duties and leave Israel scattered "like sheep without a shepherd," announcing that Yahweh himself will seek out, rescue, and care for the sheep. Jesus' parable indicts the scribes and Pharisees for their failure to be the faithful shepherds of Yahweh's flock and implies that Jesus' love and mercy for the sinners is consistent with Yahweh's mercy and care for his sheep (Green 1997: 574–75). The emphasis on joy in heaven over the repentance of one sinner in 15:7 may echo Ezek. 18:23: "Have I any pleasure in the death of the wicked, says the LORD God, and not rather that they should turn from their ways and live?" (see Fitzmyer 1981–1985: 1078).

15:11–32

In the parable of the Lost Son (15:11–32) the younger son asks the father to give him the share of the property that will fall to him (*dos moi to epiballon meros tēs ousias* [15:12]). Since, according to Deut. 21:17, the firstborn son was to receive twice the amount that a father would give to each of the other sons, the younger of the two sons in Jesus' parable would receive one-third of the property on his father's death. The legal situation presupposed by the father's actions in the parable raises several problems.

(1) A father could dispose of his property in two ways: either by a will (Gk. *diathēkē*) that is executed after his death or as a gift during his lifetime (Gk. *dōrēma*; Lat. *donatio inter vivos*). In OT law the disposal of property upon the death of a father is regulated in Num. 27:8–11; 36:7–9. The possibility of a father disposing of part of his estate by gift during his lifetime is not addressed in OT law, although it is possible that Abraham's behavior reported in Gen. 25:5–6 ("Abraham gave all he had to Isaac. But to the sons of his concubines Abraham gave gifts, while he was still living") survived in Jewish society and "allowed for a settlement upon younger sons, leaving the main estate intact for the eldest son" (Nolland 1989–1993: 782; Daube 1955: 330–33). Sirach 33:20–24 warns fathers against passing on their property to their children during their lifetime:

> To son or wife, to brother or friend, do not give power over yourself, as long as you live; and do not give your property to another, in case you change your mind and must ask for it. While you are still alive and have breath in you, do not let anyone take your place. For it is better that your children should ask from you than that you should look to the hand of your children. Excel in all that you do; bring no stain upon your honor. At the time when you end the days of your life, in the hour of death, distribute your inheritance.

Sirach's warning confirms that this custom existed in Jewish society of the Second Temple period (see Fitzmyer 1981–1985: 1087; see also Tob. 8:21; *b. B. Meṣiʿa* 75b, which is also critical). It seems plausible to assume that a Jewish father who (par-

tially) disposes of his estate in his lifetime would follow the stipulation of Deut. 21:17 and give a double share to the firstborn son. Some scholars suggest that the younger son would have received less than one-third, possibly two-ninths (Derrett 1970: 100–125).

(2) It was presumably highly irregular, and certainly strikingly presumptuous, for the younger son to initiate the settlement of his father's estate and to request his father to dispose of (at least part of) his property. Nothing in the parable hints at plausible reasons for the younger son's action, such as the prospect of an imminent marriage (cf. *m. B. Bat.* 8:7) or plans to emigrate with the goal of improving his life situation (see Jeremias 1971: 129). The parable does not explain why the father acquiesced to the wishes of his younger son, whose request signifies his rejection of his family (Green 1997: 580). The father characterizes the son, at the end of the story, as dead and lost (15:24, 32).

(3) The disposition of the father's property during his lifetime, giving his younger son the portion that was his due, would not have required the father to dispose of his entire estate and give two-thirds to his elder son. However, this apparently is what happened: 15:12 asserts that the father "divided his property between them," and in 15:31 the father emphasizes in his conversation with the elder son that "all that is mine is yours." The continuation of the parable suggests, on the other hand, that the elder son does not exercise the main control over the estate: in 15:22–24 it is the father who commands the servants, slaughters the fatted calf, and organizes the feast (Nolland 1989–1993: 782). Perhaps the father had merely assigned capital goods to the elder son rather than the claim of their produce during his lifetime, thus allowing him to retain an interest in the property until his death (cf. *m. B. Bat.* 8:7; see Nolland 1989–1993: 782).

(4) On the assumption that the father had given property to his younger son, 15:13, "after not many days the younger son gathered together all he had," seems to imply that the latter liquidated his portion of the inheritance and turned it into cash. The available evidence concerning the legal situation suggests that "if the son sold the property, the purchaser would take possession of it only at the death of the father. In doing so, the younger

son would have no further claim on the property, either capital or usufruct" (Fitzmyer 1981–1985: 1087). The younger son acknowledges this when he repents and returns to the father (15:19). If this is indeed the legal scenario, then the father would not have been in a position to reinstate the younger son without infringing on the property rights that he had signed over to the elder son.

(5) Thus the scope of the younger son's reinstatement is disputed (see below on 15:20–24). If the son is restored to the status of son, then the emphasis may be solely on the father's surprising forgiveness and compassion, which fly in the face of accepted social custom, and on the honor that the undeserving but repentant son receives (Nolland 1989–1993; Green 1997). If the son is indeed reinstated "with full privileges" (Bock 1994–1996: 1314), then the emphasis is on the authority, possessions, and freedom that the repentant son is given by his compassionate father. In this case, the dramatic setting of the parable simply does not raise the question of the legal status and the further inheritance of the restored son (Marshall 1978: 607).

The reference to "pigs" (Gk. *choiros*) in 15:15–16 echoes the OT legislation that declared pigs as "unclean" and forbidden as food for Israel (Lev. 11:7; Deut. 14:8; cf. Isa. 65:4). Rabbinic tradition formulates the dictum "Cursed is the man who rears swine" (*b. B. Qam.* 82b; cf. *y. Ter.* 8:46b [62]; *Gen. Rab.* 63:8; see Lachs 1987: 308).

The scene of reconciliation of father and prodigal son in 15:20–24—the embrace, the kiss, and the gifts of robe, ring, and sandals—underlines the restoration of the son to the father and to the family that he had rebuffed. The gift of a robe and of a ring is interpreted by some scholars in the light of Gen. 41:42, where Pharaoh makes Joseph his plenipotentiary, and Esther 8:2, where Mordecai is honored with a ring (see Jeremias 1971: 130; Marshall 1978: 610–11). Others argue that there is no clear evidence in the text that the younger son is invested with his father's authority: the ring is not identified as a signet ring, and the robe might simply have been a basic necessity, given the destitute state of the son (15:15–16), rather than a dress code symbolizing social status. If the latter interpretation is followed, then the symbolic actions in 15:20–24 simply "signify the restoration of the younger son's honor as son" (C. A.

Evans 1990: 583; cf. Nolland 1989–1993: 785, with reference to Esther 6:11 for a comparable concern with honor).

16:9–13

The application of the parable of the Shrewd Manager (16:1–9) in 16:9, "And I tell you, make friends for yourselves by means of mammon so that when it is gone, they may welcome you into the eternal tents [*aiōniai skēnai*]," possibly echoes the exodus tradition, as it refers to the "tent" (*skēnē*) or tabernacle of God's presence (see *TDNT* 7:378–79; Bovon 1989–2001: 3:81; Bock [1994–1996: 1333n20] sees an allusion to the Feast of Tabernacles [*heortē skēnōn*], which celebrates the exodus [Lev. 23:34]). The adjective "eternal" clarifies that Jesus refers not to temporary dwellings, but rather to the permanent place where God's presence dwells (Marshall 1978: 621).

Jesus' sayings in 16:10–13 about stewardship and wealth draw lessons from the parable of the Shrewd Manager (16:1–9), describing "a form of stewardship that is firmly rooted in the OT understanding of Yahweh as the true owner and conferrer of all land and property" with the corollary that since property and land are given to God's people to manage in the horizon of their accountability before God, they are to be used for the good of all, including the poor (Green 1997: 597, with reference to Gen. 12:7; Exod. 3:8; 32:13; Lev. 20:45; 25; Deut. 7:13).

16:15

Verse 15 belongs to the sayings that Luke appends to the parable of the Shrewd Manager (16:1–9), while the reference to the Pharisees in 16:14 strengthens the link between 15:1–32 and 16:1–31, reporting the Pharisees' negative response to the teaching of the parable (16:1–8) and to Jesus' assertions about God and mammon (16:9–13). Verse 15 states that money may help a person to secure an image of uprightness in the eyes of fellow citizens, but that this means nothing to God, who knows the depths and desires of the human heart, and who alone establishes the value of human beings (see Fitzmyer 1981–1985: 1112). The statement in 16:15 "God knows your hearts"—that is, the seat of human desire and volition, reaction and emotion—echoes OT passages such as Deut. 8:2; 1 Sam. 16:7; 1 Kings 8:39; 1 Chron. 28:9; Ps. 7:10; 44:21; Prov. 21:2;

24:12; Jer. 11:20; 17:9–10 (cf. Acts 1:24; 15:8). The notion that God knows the innermost being of people affirms God's omniscience. As for the Pharisees, as "lovers of money" who seek to bolster their own righteousness before others, Jesus condemns both their inner disposition and their outer behavior (Green 1997: 602).

The assertion in 16:15b, "What is prized [*hypsēlon*] by human beings is an abomination [*bdelygma*] in the sight of God," echoes OT passages that use the term "abomination" (*bdelygma*, translating Heb. *šeqqûṣ* and *tôʿēbāh*), meaning generally "unclean" (e.g., Gen. 43:32; 46:34; Exod. 8:26 [8:22 MT/LXX]), and more specifically "idolatry" (e.g., Deut. 7:25; 12:31; 1 Kings 11:5; cf. Dan. 9:27; 11:31; 12:11). Several OT passages affirm that God rejects self-adoration; note, for example, Prov. 16:5: "All those who are arrogant [*hypsēlokardios*] are an abomination to the LORD [*akathartos para theō*]; be assured, they will not go unpunished"; Isa. 2:9–11: "And so people are humbled, and everyone is brought low—do not forgive them! Enter into the rock, and hide in the dust from the terror of the LORD, and from the glory of his majesty. The haughty eyes of people shall be brought low, and the pride of everyone shall be humbled; and the LORD alone will be exalted on that day." Other OT passages also link pride with idolatry (cf. 1 Kings 11:5; Dan. 11:31; see Lachs 1987: 311). A later rabbinic text closely parallels Luke 16:15b: "All who are lofty of heart are called an abomination, as it is said, 'Everyone who is lofty of heart is an abomination to the Lord' [Prov. 16:5]. Idolatry is called 'abomination,' as it is said, 'And thou shalt not bring an abomination into thine house' [Deut. 7:26]. As idolatry pollutes the land and causes the Shekhinah to withdraw from it, so also does pride" (*Mekilta de Rabbi Ishmael Baḥodesh* 9 on Exod. 20:21).

16:16–17

The statement in 16:16a, "The law and the prophets were in effect until John came," should not be taken to mean that Luke sees the law as no longer having any validity. Luke's narrative shows that this is not the case (Powery 1999: 197–98): the law continues (cf. 2:23–24) to play an important role after 16:16 (cf. 23:56; 24:44), Paul is presented as respecting the law (cf. Acts 21:20, 24; 24:14; 25:8), and in 16:17 Luke reports Jesus' assertion "It is easier for heaven and earth to pass away than for one stroke of a letter in the law to be dropped." The reference to the temporary nature of the original creation in 16:17 echoes Job 14:12; Ps. 102:25–27; Isa. 51:6; Jer. 4:23–26; Amos 9:8 (cf. *1 En.* 72:1; 91:16; *Tg. Ps.* 102:27; 2 Pet. 3:10; Rev. 21:1; see Fitzmyer 1981–1985: 1118).

16:18

Jesus' stipulation concerning divorce and remarriage in 16:18, "Anyone who divorces his wife and marries another commits adultery, and whoever marries a woman divorced from her husband commits adultery," would have been heard against the background of the Mosaic legislation concerning divorce in Deut. 24:1–4, one of the rare cases where the subject matter alone was sufficient to recall a specific OT text (Allison 2000a: 65). Jesus proclaims monogamy and prohibits successive polygamy that divorce makes possible (Fitzmyer 1981–1985: 1121). Jesus' fundamental assertion in 16:17 about the inviolable validity of the law indicates that his prohibition of divorce is not understood as an abrogation of the law. Yahweh's declaration in Mal. 2:16, "I hate divorce," has a similar ring to Jesus' words (note that whereas Mal. 2:16 may be interpreted in terms of spiritual unfaithfulness, *b. Giṭ.* 90b and the LXX interpret the passage as opposing divorce; see Allison 2000a: 65). This verse shows that "Jesus' affirmation of the authority of the law is qualified by his (implicit) insistence that the law does not speak for itself and is susceptible to erroneous appropriation" (Green 1997: 604).

Jesus' prohibition of divorce has been explained against the background of arguably similar stipulations in the Qumran community (cf. 11Q19 LVII, 17–19; CD-A IV, 19–21) and in terms of the members of priestly families serving in the temple: "They shall not marry a prostitute or a woman who has been defiled; neither shall they marry a woman divorced from her husband. For they are holy to their God" (Isaksson 1965: 147; Fitzmyer 1981–1995: 1121). Jesus' high standards concerning marriage can be understood as reflecting the fact that his followers have an even higher calling than the priests have, which means that their standards cannot be any lower (C. A. Evans 1990: 247; note Instone-Brewer [2002: 159–60, 166], who argues that Luke presents an abbreviated version of Jesus' saying).

16:19–31

The parable of the Rich Man and Lazarus contains several OT allusions and echoes. Commentators point out that the parable alludes to the injunctions regarding the treatment of the poor and needy in Deut. 24:7–15 (C. F. Evans 1955: 49; C. A. Evans 1990: 250; cf. Marshall 1978: 632). The clothing of the rich man is described in 16:19, "dressed in purple and fine linen," in OT terms reminiscent of Prov. 31:22, suggesting that he lived like a king (Fitzmyer 1981–1985: 1130). The name "Lazarus" (16:20), which corresponds to the Hebrew name "Eliezer" ("God helps"), has sometimes been taken to allude to Abraham's trusted servant of the same name (Gen. 15:1–2), due to the presence of Abraham in the story (Derrett 1970: 86–87): Eliezer came close to becoming Abraham's heir (Gen. 15:2–4), and he was afraid that he might not be welcome before he met Rebekah at the well (Gen. 24:10–12) (see the critique in Bovon 1989–2001: 3:120). The reference to the dogs who came and licked Lazarus's sores (16:21) echoes OT passages in which dogs consume the dead (cf. 1 Kings 14:11; 16:4; 21:24; Ps. 22:15–16; Jer. 15:3; see Hultgren 2000: 112). The statement in 16:22 that Lazarus was "carried away by the angels to be with Abraham" has been interpreted as alluding to Enoch, who was taken to heaven by God (Gen. 5:24), and to Elijah, who was taken to heaven in a whirlwind (2 Kings 2:11) (see Hultgren 2000: 113). This is unlikely, however, because these heroes of the OT were extricated from death (Bovon 1989–2001: 3:120–21). The notion of flames (16:24)—that is, fire—in Hades probably echoes Isa. 66:24, "And they shall go out and look at the dead bodies of the people who have rebelled against me; for their worm shall not die, their fire shall not be quenched, and they shall be an abhorrence to all flesh" (cf. Sir. 21:9–10; *1 En.* 10:13; 63:10; Rev. 20:14–15; see Fitzmyer 1981–1985: 1133). Several OT passages refer to thirst as an image of divine judgment (cf. Isa. 5:13; 50:2; 65:13; Hos. 2:3 [2:5 MT]; 2 Esd. 8:59; *1 En.* 22:9; see *TDNT* 2:228–29; Bock 1994–1996: 1371). The notion that the dead can contact the living, especially through dreams (16:27–28, 30), echoes 1 Sam. 28:6–19; 2 Kings 21:6; Isa. 8:19 (there are also Greek parallels [see Fitzmyer 1981–1985: 1134]). Abraham's reply to the rich man who wants to have his brothers warned so that they may avoid his fate by repenting—probably from indulging in the same hard-hearted lifestyle—in 16:27, "They have Moses and the prophets; they should listen to them," echoes numerous OT passages that teach how fellow human beings should be treated, especially the poor (cf. Deut. 14:28–29; 15:1–3, 7–12; 22:1–2; 23:19; 24:7–15, 19–21; 25:13–14; Isa. 3:14–15; 5:7–8; 10:1–3; 32:6–7; 58:3, 6–10; Jer. 5:26–28; 7:5–6; Ezek. 18:12–18; 33:15; Amos 2:6–8; 5:11–12; 8:4–6; Mic. 2:1–2; 3:1–3; 6:10–11; Zech. 7:9–10; Mal. 3:5; see Bock 1994–1996: 1375).

17:3–4

Jesus' statement about forgiveness in 17:3–4, "If your brother sins [*ean hamartē ho adelphos sou*], you must rebuke [*epitimēson*] the offender, and if there is repentance, you must forgive. And if he sins [*hamartēsē*] against you seven times a day, and turns back to you seven times and says, 'I repent,' you must forgive," alludes to Lev. 19:17, "You shall not hate your brother [*ton adelphon sou*] in your heart, but you shall reprove [*elegmō elenxeis*] your neighbor, lest you bear sin [*hamartian*] because of him," as the verbal and particularly the material parallels indicate (the parallel in Matt. 18:15 has *elenxon*, a Matthean *hapax legomenon*, which corresponds to Lev. 19:17 LXX more closely; see Allison 2000a: 65–66; Plummer 1896: 400; the NRSV translation of Lev. 19:17, "You shall not hate in your heart anyone of your kin," and of Luke 17:3, "if another disciple sins," obscures the parallels). The exhortation in Lev. 19:17a indicates that "hate is not just emotion, but implies a mental activity, namely, plotting countermeasures," while 19:17b "provides the answer to the prohibition against harboring hatred" (Milgrom 1991–2001: 1646, 1647). The wisdom tradition interprets the outlawed hatred "in the heart" in Lev. 19:17a as covered under a veil of hypocrisy (cf. Prov. 10:18; 26:24–25; cf. Zech. 8:17). In Jewish tradition Lev. 19:17 was interpreted in two ways: (1) in a moral sense, that the unoffended person shall not reproach the offending person so insistently that the offender is moved to swear (cf. *T. Gad* 6:3–4); (2) in a legal sense, that the reproach of the offender by the offended person is a necessary step in the judicial process, which, if the matter is not resolved, takes the offender to court (CD-A IX, 2–8; 1QS V, 23–VI, 1) (see Kugel 1987: 49–54,

57–58; Hartley 1992: 317). Jesus' stipulation in 17:3 agrees with Lev. 19:17, which demands that one reprove a brother, while 17:4 emphasizes the need to forgive once the person who has been rebuked repents, even if forgiveness might need to be extended seven times a day—that is, again and again and again. As much as Jesus is interested in correction, he is more interested in forgiveness, which knows no limits.

The demand to forgive seven times a day probably represents a deliberate reversal of a Jewish exegetical tradition concerning the phrase "you shall reprove [*hôkēaḥ tôkîaḥ*] your neighbor" (Allison 2000a: 67–68). The rabbinic text *Sipra* 200 on Lev. 19:17 says, "And how do we know that if one has rebuked him four or five times, he should still go and rebuke him again? Scripture says, 'Reproving you will reprove [*hôkēaḥ tôkîaḥ*] your neighbor.' Should one suppose that this is to be done even if his countenance blanches when he is rebuked? Scripture says, 'Or you will incur guilt yourself.'" A similar interpretation is given in *b. B. Meṣiʿa* 31a: "One of the rabbis said to Raba: [You will not hate your brother in your heart but] *hôkēaḥ tôkîaḥ* [you will surely reprove] your neighbor. Perhaps *hôkēaḥ* means once, *tôkîaḥ* twice? He replied, *hôkēaḥ* implies even a hundred times." If this exegetical tradition lies behind the interpretation of Lev. 19:17 in the first century, Jesus challenges it: "What he demands is not repeated rebukes but repeated acts of forgiveness" (Allison 2000a: 67). Another Jewish text is closer to Jesus' saying, *T. Gad* 6:3, 7: "Love one another from the heart, therefore, and if anyone sins against you, speak to him in peace. Expel the venom of hatred, and do not harbor deceit in your heart. If anyone confesses and repents, forgive him. . . . But even if he is devoid of shame and persists in his wickedness, forgive him from the heart and leave vengeance to God" (Kugel 1987; Allison 2000a: 67; Bock 1994–1996: 1389).

17:11–19

The story of the grateful Samaritan leper evokes the OT story of the healing of Naaman, a foreigner who likewise had suffered from leprosy (2 Kings 5:1–19). Some scholars suggest that Luke's story is a retelling of the Naaman story, investing Jesus with prophetic characteristics and making him greater than Elisha (Bruners 1977: 103–18; for a critique, see H. D. Betz 1981: 339), while others deny any connection with 2 Kings 5 (Glöckner 1983: 131–39). Most scholars take a mediating position, acknowledging allusions to the Naaman account (e.g., Nolland 1989–1993: 844). The allusion is established by several elements: the characterization of Naaman and the Samaritan as lepers and as foreigners, the Samaritan location, the communication from a distance, the delayed cleansing (after leaving the healer), the return of the healed leper, praise from the healed leper, and thanksgiving. The point of the allusion is both christological and theological: the story underscores again the connection between Jesus and God's prophets in the Scriptures, and it emphasizes that not only do Israelites receive the benefits of salvation, but foreigners do as well (Green 1997: 620).

Jesus' command in 17:14, "Go and show yourselves to the priests" (*epideixate heautous tois hiereusin*), alludes to Lev. 13:49: "If the disease shows greenish or reddish in the garment, whether in warp or woof or in skin or in anything made of skin, it is a leprous disease and shall be shown to the priest [*deixei tō hierei*]" (cf. Lev. 14:2–4). A priest was required to assess whether the skin disease had cleared up before the leper could be readmitted into society. The action of the Samaritan in 17:15 is startling: when he realizes on the way to the temple (on Mount Gerizim?) that he is healed, he evidently does not continue on his journey, but rather returns to Jesus, acknowledging that God's healing power is present in Jesus (Green 1997: 621).

17:21

Jesus' declaration that the kingdom of God cannot be determined through scientific analysis, and that it cannot be localized in a particular place or nation (Green 1997: 629), because "in fact, the kingdom of God is among you," possibly echoes Isa. 45:14, "God is among you," if Jesus indeed emphasizes that the kingdom of God is closely related to his person, message, and activity (see Bock 1994–1996: 1416).

17:24–25

Jesus compares the coming of the Son of Man with the flashing of lightning, which lights up the sky (17:24), echoing OT passages in which the image of lightning is tied to theophanies, suggesting that the return of the Son of Man involves God acting on behalf of his people (cf. Exod. 19:16–20; 20:18–20; Ps. 97:2–4; Ezek. 1:4, 13; see Bock 1994–1996: 1429). In Jesus' fifth passion prediction, in Luke in 17:25 (see 9:22, 44; 12:50; 13:32–33; cf. 18:32–33), the use of the verb *paradidōmi* is probably an allusion to the Suffering Servant in Isa. 53, since "here, as nowhere else in the Old Testament, are the sufferings of the (Messianic) figure explicitly and consistently attributed to the activity of Yahweh" (Moo 1983: 95–96; cf. Lindars 1961: 80–81; Strauss 1995: 328; differently, France 1971: 126; Hooker 1998: 94). The verb *apodokimasthēnai* may echo the "rejected stone" of Ps. 118:22 (117:22 LXX) (Constant 2001: 282–83).

17:26–37

In 17:26–37 Jesus describes the "days of the Son of Man" (17:22–25) and compares them with "the days of Noah" (17:26–27) and with "the days of Lot" (17:28–29), warning against the indifference and nonchalance of "this generation," which will face judgment on the day of the Son of Man (17:30–35).

The reference to the "days of Noah" in 17:26–27 alludes to Gen. 6–7; the reference to Noah entering the ark (*eisēlthen . . . eis tēn kibōton*) alludes to Gen. 7:7, "And Noah with his sons and his wife and his sons' wives went into the ark [*eisēlthen . . . eis tēn kibōton*] to escape the waters of the flood"; the reference to the "flood" (*kataklysmos* [only here in Luke-Acts]) alludes to Gen. 6:17; 7:6, 7, 10, 17; and the reference to the destruction of humankind alludes to Gen. 7:21–23, "And all flesh died that moved on the earth . . . everything on dry land in whose nostrils was the breath of life died. He blotted out every living thing that was on the face of the ground, human beings and animals and creeping things and birds of the air; they were blotted out from the earth." One commentator has called Luke's text "a composite Genesis commentary" (Stendahl 1968: 93).

Luke's typological appeal to the flood in the "days of Noah," which he compares to the "days of the Son of Man," has roots in the Jewish tradition that uses the flood as a prototype of the last judgment or of the end of the world (cf. Isa. 24:18; 3 Macc. 2:4; *Jub.* 20:5–6; *1 En.* 1–16; 67:10; 93:4; *L.A.B.* 3:1–3, 9–10; 49:3; Josephus, *Ant.* 1.72–76; see also 2 Pet. 2:5; 3:6–7; *2 En.* [J] 70:10; *Apoc. Adam* 3:3; *3 En.* 45:3; *Mek. Exod.* 18:1; *b. Sanh.*

108a; see Lewis 1968: 10–100; Schlosser 1973; Allison 2000a: 93). Jesus does not focus on the sins of Noah's contemporaries, as the rabbis did (cf. *m. Sanh.* 10:1; see Str-B 1:961–64), nor on Noah's righteousness, but rather on the unexpectedness of the cataclysm (cf. Jesus' statements in 17:22–24, 28). Interpreted against the background of Jewish traditions about Noah, the text's emphasis is not on the impossibility of knowing the day on which the last judgment will arrive, but rather on the unwillingness of Jesus' contemporaries to reckon with the possibility and prospect of divine judgment (Nolland 1989–1993: 860).

Several explanations have been given for the fact that Luke uses neutral terms to describe the "days of Noah" (17:26) as monopolized by people who were "eating and drinking, and marrying and being given in marriage, until the day Noah entered the ark," when "the flood came and destroyed all of them" (17:27). First, it can be argued that Luke uses neutral or indifferent activities to connote the "wickedness of humanity" and the "evil inclination" of people's hearts (Gen. 6:5) and the "corruption" and "violence" (Gen. 6:11) of Noah's generation (Fitzmyer 1981–1985: 1170; Bock 1994–1996: 1432). Second, it has been suggested that the list of everyday activities describes people then and now as unsuspecting and unprepared for the judgment that God announced (Zahn 1988: 602; Marshall 1978: 663; Stein 1992: 439). Third, it can be argued that Luke lists activities, not inherently bad, that can prove to be potentially disastrous distractions from the necessity of recognizing and obeying God's purposes (Green 1997: 635). Fourth, read against the background of the description of Noah's contemporaries in Gen. 6, "eating and drinking" might have been understood in terms of pejorative connotations, and "marrying and being given in marriage" may have recalled the giants of Gen. 6:1–4 and their intercourse with human women (Allison 2000a: 94). These interpretations are not mutually exclusive: although it is indisputable that the list of everyday "neutral" activities underlines the unpreparedness of the generation of Noah's contemporaries, and that eating and drinking can distract from the much more serious question of God's revealed purposes, it is equally evident that they were destroyed in the flood not because they were distracted or unprepared, but because they deserved God's judgment. This is confirmed by the Jewish traditions that allude to the flood, emphasizing the certainty of judgment rather than the suddenness of its arrival (see Schlosser 1973; Nolland 1989–1993: 860).

The opening words of 17:26, "just as it was in the days of Noah," may also allude to Isa. 54:9–10, which begins with the words "this is like the days of Noah to me" (thus the reading in 1QIsaᵃ and the reading presupposed by Symmachus, Theodotion, the Peshitta, the Targum, and the Vulgate; cf. NRSV, NIV; MT has *kî-mê noaḥ*, and LXX translates *apo tou hydatos epi Noē*; see Allison 2000a: 118; Oswalt 1986–1998: 2:413n14). Isaiah 54:9–10 continues, "For this is like the days of Noah to me: as I swore that the waters of Noah should no more go over the earth, so I have sworn that I will not be angry with you and will not rebuke you. For the mountains may depart and the hills be removed, but my steadfast love shall not depart from you, and my covenant of peace shall not be removed, says the LORD, who has compassion on you." Whereas Isaiah recalls the days of Noah in order to emphasize God's compassion, Jesus offers no reassurances and announces judgment. It is possible, although this cannot be demonstrated, that Jesus changes the tone vis-à-vis Isaiah (so Allison 2000a: 118).

The reference to the "days of Lot" (17:28) alludes to the people who lived in "the cities of the plain," particularly of Sodom, where Lot lived after his separation from Abraham (Gen. 13:12–13; 19:1–11). While Gen. 13:13 describes the people of Sodom as "wicked, great sinners against the LORD," Luke's reference to Sodom's people as "eating and drinking, buying and selling, planting and building" (17:28), again, does not explicate the sinfulness of these people. It is not clear whether the fact that some of these activities are referred to by Luke as "distractions from what human existence should be about" (Fitzmyer [1981–1985: 1171], who refers to 14:18–19 for buying, to 12:18–19 for eating, drinking, and building, and to 19:45 for selling; cf. Schneider 1992: 356–57; Green 1997: 635) is relevant for the interpretation of 17:28, characterizing their existence as culpable nonchalance. We should note that Luke does not indicate that these activities can be distractions. Nor does the list of activities by itself suggest the activity of immoral

people (so Bock [1994–1996: 1433], who refers to Deut. 32:32–33; Isa. 1:10; Jer. 23:14; Lam. 4:6; Ezek. 16:46–52). The activities of the people of Sodom are listed as normal rhythms of everyday life (Nolland 1989–1993: 860). They underline the unexpectedness of God's judgment.

The reference to Lot leaving Sodom (17:29a) alludes to Gen. 19:16–17, omitting the note that Lot "lingered" in the city before the angels forced him to leave. The statement that "it rained fire and sulfur from heaven" (*ebrexen pyr kai theion ap' ouranou* [17:29b]) alludes to Gen. 19:24 (*ebrexen . . . theion kai pyr para kyriou ek tou ouranou*). Fire and sulfur, signifying volcanic eruptions, occur elsewhere in the OT as references to divine judgment of the land or of apostates and sinners (cf. Deut. 29:23; Job 18:15; Ps. 11:6; Isa. 30:33; Ezek. 38:22; cf. 3 Macc. 2:5; Philo, *Moses* 2.10; cf. also Rev. 9:17–18; 14:10; 19:20; 20:10; 21:8; see Bock 1994–1996: 1433–34; Fitzmyer 1981–1985: 1171).

In order to reinforce his emphasis in 17:31 on the necessity to act decisively in view of the approaching catastrophe, to flee without stopping to collect personal possessions and without looking back to house and home in order not to be swallowed up by the coming judgment, Luke reminds his readers in 17:32 of Lot's wife ("Remember Lot's wife!"). Genesis 19:26 describes Lot's wife as "looking back" (*epeblepsen . . . eis ta opisō*), a phrase that is perhaps echoed in 17:31, where Jesus warns against "looking back" (*mē epistrepsatō eis ta opisō*). Jesus does not mention the OT statement that she became a "pillar of salt," as he could assume his listeners' familiarity with this story and its tradition. Note that Josephus claims that he has seen this pillar (Josephus, *Ant.* 1.203). In Wis. 10:7 Lot's wife is described as "a monument to an unbelieving soul." Jesus' reference to Lot's wife may be interpreted, similarly, as a general warning to his unbelieving contemporaries to accept and heed his announcement of the impending divine judgment (Stein 1992: 440); or, it may be interpreted as a warning to his followers that belonging to the rescued group does not absolve them from taking decisive, radical action, particularly renouncing personal possessions and pursuits (Marshall 1978: 665; Nolland 1989–1993: 861).

The statement in 17:34–35 possibly also alludes to the Noah narrative: despite the wickedness of the era preceding the flood, there was Enoch, who "walked with God" (Gen. 5:21–24), and whom "God took" (Gen. 5:24), a phrase that was understood to mean that Enoch was transported to heaven (Sir. 49:14; *1 En.* 14:8; 70:1–3; *Jub.* 4:23; 10:17; Philo, *Names* 38; *L.A.B.* 1:15–16; cf. Heb. 11:5; *Ascen. Isa.* 9:9 [Ethiopic]; *Tg. Ps.-J.* Gen. 5:24). Readers who had just been reminded of the flood at the time of Noah might draw the conclusion that just as Enoch the righteous was snatched by God from the midst of a wicked generation, so also the righteous will be "taken" in the last days when the final cataclysm destroys the world (Allison 2000a: 94–95).

18:1–8

In the parable of the Widow and the Unjust Judge (18:2–5), the characterization of the judge in 18:2 evokes OT passages against the background of which he appears as a negative character. The statement that he does not fear God possibly echoes 2 Chron. 19:7, where King Jehoshaphat appoints judges in Judah, charging them, "Let the fear of the LORD be upon you; take care what you do, for there is no perversion of justice with the LORD our God, or partiality, or taking of bribes." Despite the emphasis on impartiality in 2 Chron. 19, the OT repeatedly speaks of the obligation to show special regard for the alien, the orphan, and the widow (see Lev. 19:9–10; 23:22; Deut. 14:28–29; 24:19–22; 26:12; cf. James 1:27; on widows, see also Exod. 22:22–24; Deut. 10:16–18; 24:17; Ps. 68:5; Isa. 1:16–17; 54:4; Lam. 1:1; Mal. 3:5) (see Green 1997: 639).

In Jesus' comments on the parable in 18:7, after directing the disciples to learn from the judge's behavior that God, who *is* just, surely will respond to the persistent prayer of his people (18:6), Jesus asserts with a rhetorical question that "God will vindicate his chosen ones" who cry to him day and night. The term "the chosen ones" (*hoi eklektoi*), used in Luke-Acts only here, echoes texts such as Isa. 42:1; 43:20; 65:9, 15, 22; Ps. 105:6, 43 (cf. Sir. 47:22), which use the term "chosen" in a context that emphasizes election to serve Yahweh (see Delling 1970b: 215–16; Fitzmyer 1981–1985: 1180; Green [1997: 642] also refers to Deut. 4:37; 7:7; 1 Chron. 16:13; Ps. 77:31; 88:3). The widow in the parable represents God's elect, who are thus characterized as people who persevere in faith and prayer (18:1, 8) in the midst of hostilities

during the time in which they wait for the visible consummation of the kingdom of God (note the context in 17:22–37).

18:9–14

In the parable of the Pharisee and the Tax Collector, Jesus uses the subject of prayer in order to continue to explain the character and the behavior that are demonstrated in people who are fit for the kingdom of God (Green 1997: 644). Jesus contrasts a Pharisee and a tax collector in stark terms with the intention of prompting the audience to identify with the tax collector as the (paradoxical) positive model. The text contains several OT allusions (for an interpretation against the background of Deut. 26, see C. A. Evans 1994).

In 18:9 Luke records that Jesus told this parable "to some who trusted in themselves that they were righteous [*tous pepoithotas eph' heautois hoti eisin dikaioi*] and regarded others with contempt." This situational comment echoes Ezek. 33:13, a text in which the prophet had criticized his contemporaries for trusting in their own righteousness: "Though I say to the righteous [*tō dikaiō*] that they shall surely live, yet if they trust in their righteousness [*pepoithen epi tē dikaiosynē autou*] and commit iniquity, none of their righteous deeds shall be remembered; but in the iniquity that they have committed they shall die" (see Fitzmyer 1981–1985: 1185). The pride of self-righteousness is condemned in several Jewish texts (cf. 1QS XI, 1–2; 1QHª XV, 34; Josephus, *J.W.* 1.110; *m. 'Abot* 2:4–5; *b. Ber.* 28b; *b. Sanh.* 101a; *b. Sukkah* 45b; note also *t. Ber.* 6:18, where a male Jew thanks God that he is not a Gentile, a boor, or a woman; see Jeremias 1971: 142–43; Bock 1994–1996: 1161).

In the prayer of the Pharisee in 18:11 the reference to "thieves, rogues, adulterers" echoes the seventh and eighth commandments of the Decalogue (Exod. 20:14–15; Deut. 5:18–19), with the middle term, "rogues" (*adikoi,* "unrighteous" or "evildoers"), being a generic reference to lawlessness.

The reference to fasting in 18:12 echoes the stipulation to fast on the Day of Atonement (Lev. 16:29, 31; 23:27, 29, 32; Num. 29:7), during Purim (Esther 9:31), and during further annual days of fasting (Zech. 7:3, 5; 8:19), as well as OT passages that report fasting by individuals as an expression of mourning (2 Sam. 12:21), penance

(1 Kings 21:27; Ezra 10:6), and supplication (Neh. 1:4; Dan. 9:3) (see Fitzmyer 1981–1985: 1187; Nolland 1989–1993: 876). Verse 12 is the earliest text that attests the Jewish custom of fasting twice a week (according to *b. Taʿan.* 12a, on Mondays and Thursdays; cf. *y. Pesaḥ* 4:1). Fasting involved eating only bread and drinking only water. The reference to tithing recalls Lev. 27:30–32; Num. 18:21–24; Deut. 14:22–27.

The tax collector's reticence to "look up to heaven" (18:13a) echoes Ezra's prayer upon hearing of the numerous mixed marriages in Jerusalem: "O my God, I am too ashamed and embarrassed to lift my face to you, my God, for our iniquities have risen higher than our heads, and our guilt has mounted up to the heavens" (Ezra 9:6) (see Nolland [1989–1993: 877], who also refers to Josephus, *Ant.* 11.143). Both of the situational comments in 18:13a—the downward gaze and the breast-beating—speak of a deep sense of unworthiness and embarrassment.

The tax collector's prayer in 18:13b, "God, be merciful to me, a sinner!" (*ho theos hilasthēti moi tō hamartōlō*), echoes Ps. 51:1, 3 (50:3, 5 LXX), "Have mercy on me, O God. . . . For I know my transgressions, and my sin is ever before me" (50:3, 5 LXX: *eleēson me ho theos . . . kai hē hamartia mou enōpion mou estin dia pantos*) (see Marshall 1978: 680; cf. Fitzmyer [1981–1985: 1188], who for the spirit of the prayer refers to 1QS XI, 3–5, 9–12; 1QHᵃ XIX, 15–22). The verb *hilaskomai* occurs only here in Luke-Acts, in the sense "be merciful/gracious," which is found also in Add. Esth. 4:17h (13:17 NRSV), "Hear my prayer, and have mercy upon your inheritance"; Lam. 3:42, "We have transgressed and rebelled, and you have not forgiven"; Dan. 9:19 (Θ; NRSV), "O LORD, hear; O LORD, forgive; O LORD, listen and act and do not delay! For your own sake, O my God, because your city and your people bear your name!"

Jesus' declaration in 18:14, "For all who exalt themselves will be humbled, but all who humble themselves will be exalted" (*pas ho hypsōn heauton tapeinōthēsetai, ho de tapeinōn heauton hypsōthēsetai*), echoes Ezek. 21:26: "Exalt that which is low, and abase that which is high" (21:31 LXX: *etapeinōsas to hypsēlon kai to tapeinon hypsōsas*) (see Fitzmyer 1981–1985: 1189). The suggestion that this conclusion of the parable parallels the confession of Deut. 26:5–10, in which the father tells his family

of Israel's disgrace and eventual glory (C. A. Evans 1994: 351), has no linguistic basis in the text, and the material parallels are remote.

18:18–20

A. NT Context of Exod. 20:12–16; Deut. 5:17–20: The Question about Eternal Life.

Near the end of Jesus' journey from Galilee to Jerusalem, Luke recounts an encounter with a magistrate who asks Jesus how he can inherit eternal life (18:18–23). This encounter follows after the parable of the Pharisee and the Tax Collector (18:9–14), which highlights the attitude of humility that God commends in order to be justified and God's openness to sinners who contritely appeal for mercy, and after Jesus' calling little children (18:15–17), which emphasizes the notion of complete trust as a precondition for receiving the kingdom of God. The question of the magistrate, "What must I do to inherit eternal life?" (18:18), is identical with the question asked in 10:25 by a scribe who, unlike the magistrate in Luke 18, seeks to "test" Jesus. The notions of "being justified" (18:14), "receiving the kingdom" (18:17), and "inheriting eternal life" (18:18) are related in Luke-Acts (Nolland 1989–1993: 884).

The expression "eternal life" (*zōē aiōnios* [18:18]) occurs for the first time in Dan. 12:2 in the context of Daniel's prophecy of the final deliverance of Israel, in the days when "Michael, the great prince, the protector of your people" will arise, days of anguish "such as has never occurred since nations first came into existence" (12:1). At that time, "Many of those who sleep in the dust of the earth shall awake, some to everlasting life [*hayyê ʿôlām*; LXX: *zōē aiōnios*], and some to shame and everlasting contempt" (12:2). Daniel 12:2 predicts a bodily life on earth, while v. 3 speaks of the wise teachers and of those who lead others to righteousness as being exalted to the heavenly realm and shining "like the brightness of the firmament" and "like the stars forever and ever." Many see this as an allusion to the scenario in Isa. 65:17–25, which speaks of the creation of a "new heavens and a new earth" and of days when the righteous will live long lives in the new Jerusalem. In texts of the Second Temple period the phrase "eternal life" becomes increasingly frequent (cf. 2 Macc. 7:9; *Pss. Sol.* 3:12; *1 En.* 37:4; 40:9; 58:3; 4 Macc. 15:3; in the Qumran literature, see 4Q181 1 II, 4; CD-A III, 20; for belief in eternal life, see also 1QS IV, 6–8; 1QHᵃ XI, 19–23; XIX, 10–14).

Jesus' answer, "Why do you call me good? No one is good but God alone" (18:19), echoes the OT theme of the goodness of Yahweh (cf. 1 Chron. 16:34; 2 Chron. 5:13; Ps. 25:8; 34:8; 100:5; 106:1; 118:1, 29; 136:1; Nah. 1:7), combined with an allusion to the monotheistic belief in the oneness of God in the OT (cf. Deut. 6:4). The emphasis that true goodness belongs to God implies neither that Jesus asserts his divinity nor that he acknowledges his sinfulness; rather, it finds fault with the notion that Jesus is a teacher, even a "good" teacher, but nothing more (Marshall 1978: 684). Jesus' answer perhaps also suggests that Jesus rejects the word game rooted in contemporary traditional concerns with status that the ruler plays by commending Jesus as "good," refusing to be defined by the standard values of society by expressing a similar commendation in return (Green 1997: 655).

In contrast to Luke 10:25–28, where the discussion about eternal life quotes from Deut. 6:5 and Lev. 19:18, which focus on loving Yahweh and on loving one's neighbor as oneself, Jesus quotes in Luke 18:20 five commandments from the Decalogue: "You know the commandments: 'You shall not commit adultery; You shall not murder; You shall not steal; You shall not bear false witness; Honor your father and mother'" (Exod. 20:12–16; Deut. 5:16–20; for the commandment to honor father and mother, see also Lev. 19:3). These are commandments seven, six, eight, nine, and five from the second part of the Decalogue. The commandment "You shall not bear false witness" [*mē pseudomartyrēsēs*] abbreviates the longer commandment "You shall not bear false witness [*ou pseudomartyrēseis . . . martyrian pseudē*] against your neighbor" (Deut. 5:20). The reduced form brings the citation formally into line with the other commands (see Nolland 1989–1993: 886). This is the only explicit OT quotation by Jesus that Luke includes in the central section of his Gospel.

B. Exod. 20:12–16; Deut. 5:17–20 in Context. In Exodus the Decalogue in 20:1–17 follows Moses' encounter with Yahweh on Sinai (19:1–13) and the consecration of Israel for the nation's encounter with God at the foot of the mountain on which Yahweh's presence was revealed (19:14–25;

cf. 20:18–21). The Decalogue is followed by an exposition of Yahweh's laws (20:22–23:33) and the confirmation of Yahweh's covenant that he had made with Abraham, Isaac, and Jacob (24:1–18; cf. 2:24; 6:2–5; 19:5). The Decalogue is understood as an "essential segment of the account of Yahweh's presentation of himself to Israel" (Durham 1987: 278). In Deuteronomy the Decalogue is repeated in 5:6–21 in the context of the second major section of Moses' address to Israel on the plain of Moab in 4:44–26:19, after the historical prologue in 1:6–4:43. After a brief introduction to the declaration of the law (4:44–49), Moses' exposition and exhortation of the basic commandments follow (5:1–11:32): the summons to obey the law (5:1–5) is followed by the Decalogue (5:6–21), followed by an explanation of Moses' mediatory role at Horeb (5:22–33). In Deuteronomy the Decalogue is again presented as the foundation of the covenant relationship that Yahweh has granted to Israel: it is legally binding as an expression of Israel's response of love for Yahweh (6:4–5), who saved the nation from slavery in Egypt (7:6) (see Craigie 1976: 149–50). Apart from Exod. 20 and Deut. 5, the commandments of the Decalogue are rarely cited in the OT, but note the reflection of the Ten Commandments in Exod. 34:17–26; Lev. 19:1–4, 11–19, 26–37; Deut. 27:15–26; Ps. 15:2–5; Jer. 7:9; Ezek. 18:5–9; Hos. 4:1–2 (see Durham 1987: 280–81).

C. Exod. 20:12–16; Deut. 5:17–20 in Judaism. There is ample evidence that the Decalogue was a central piece of Jewish tradition in the Second Temple period: the Nash Papyrus and the tefillin found at Qumran suggest a liturgical significance of the Ten Commandments, and the evidence of early rabbinic texts indicates that the recitation of the Decalogue was an integral part of the daily temple service (cf. *m. Tamid* 5:1; see *ABD* 6:386). In contrast to later Christian commentators, the rabbis never isolated the Decalogue from the rest of the Torah. However, the fact that some sources classify the 613 commandments of the Torah under the ten headings of the commandments of the Decalogue underscores the foundational significance of these commandments (cf. Philo, *Decalogue*; *Num. Rab.* 13:15–16).

D. Textual Matters. Luke's list of the commandments of the Decalogue is remarkable for two reasons. First, the form of the commandments uses *mē* and the aorist subjunctive (as in Mark 10:19), while the LXX uses *ou* with future indicative in both Exod. 20 and Deut. 5 (as in Matt. 19:18–19). This indicates that "Luke is here dependent on the tradition followed by Mk" (Marshall 1978: 685; differently, Kimball 1994b: 135–36). Second, Luke inverts the order of the first two commandments quoted by Mark and omits "You shall not defraud," which is not among the Ten Commandments (also omitted by Matthew, who, however, follows the order of commandments in Mark). While Mark and Matthew preserve the order of the first four commandments in the MT and in LXX Codex A of Exod. 20:12–16 and Deut. 5:17–18, Luke preserves the order of the first four commandments as found in LXX Codex B of Deut. 5:17–18; Nash Papyrus lines 18–19; Philo, *Decalogue* 51 (cf. Rom. 13:9; James 2:11). Many scholars explain this divergence of order from the MT (which is followed in the parallel texts in Mark and Matthew) in terms of Luke following a catechetical pattern that was in use in the early church (Stendahl 1968: 62; Gundry 1967: 17–19; Holtz 1968: 81–82; Thomas 1975–1976; Marshall 1978: 685; Fitzmyer 1981–1985: 1199; Kimball 1994b: 139; Powery 1999: 222; Albl 1999: 191).

E. The Use of Exod. 20:12–16; Deut. 5:16–20 in Luke 18:20. Jesus quotes in 18:20 the seventh, sixth, eighth, ninth, and fifth commandments from the second part of the Decalogue, answering the magistrate's question concerning the requirements for being granted eternal life. After accepting the magistrate's response that he keeps the law (18:21), Jesus asserts that what he lacks is selling his possessions, giving the proceeds to the poor, and following him (18:22). Jesus thus emphasizes that keeping the law and maintaining covenant loyalty to Yahweh is no longer sufficient for entering eternal life: it is now necessary to be loyal to him, to acknowledge the significance of his person and message for God's covenant with Israel, to recognize the authority of Yahweh in his ministry and thus to be willing, if summoned, to sell all possessions, trusting God to supply all needs in the following of Jesus. Obedience to God's revelation in the covenant and in the Mosaic Torah is no longer sufficient to inherit eternal life; such obedience must be coupled with obedience to Jesus. Jesus' initial answer to the magistrate

confirms "the validity and continuing life-giving significance of the OT commandments of God" (Nolland 1989–1993: 886; cf. Powery 1999: 223). In the next verses Luke contrasts the reaction of the magistrate (18:23) with the disciples who have left everything to follow Jesus (18:24–30).

Jesus' assertion in 18:19 that "no one is good but God alone" echoes texts such as 1 Chron. 16:34; 2 Chron. 5:13; Ps. 34:8; 118:1, 29; Nah. 1:7 (cf. Philo, *Alleg. Interp.* 1.14; *Dreams* 1.23). Jesus directs the ruler's attention to God and to the will of God as the source of everything that is good—that is, of what pleases God (Fitzmyer 1981–1985: 1199). This means that since nobody is "good" as a result of personal behavior and achievements, nobody can be saved and inherit eternal life as the result of religious and moral achievements: only God can save and grant entrance into the kingdom of God (18:25–27).

F. Theological Use. Jesus' quotation of the commandments of the Decalogue (18:20) is not meant as a provocation for the Jewish leader who had asked him about the entrance requirements for eternal life, suggesting that if the leader thinks that he has indeed obeyed these commandments—which he does (18:21)—he is misguided. Jesus' directive that the *archōn* sell all possessions and follow him (18:22) is not a test to establish whether he has kept the law only "externally" or whether he truly loves God and neighbor (cf. 10:27); rather, Jesus makes it clear that to obtain eternal life now requires more than obedience to God's revelation in the law: it requires following Jesus (18:20), linked with the recognition that it is Jesus who provides entrance into the kingdom of God (18:24, 29). Thus Jesus' reference to the Decalogue and his directive to sell all possessions and follow him aim not at demonstrating the necessity of repentance (so Rusam 2003: 122), but rather at establishing for the Jewish leader the connection between himself and the kingdom of God and thus of his authority to ask what only God can ask (selling all possessions).

The OT quotation in 18:20 is therefore intended to show the way to eternal life: the keeping of the commandments of the Torah needs to be linked with following Jesus—that is, with the active recognition that Jesus embodies and inaugurates the kingdom of God, that Jesus has divine authority and can expect full obedience even in matters such as personal possessions.

18:24, 27

Jesus' statement that it is "hard for those who have wealth to enter the kingdom of God!" in 18:24 echoes OT passages that warn not to think of wealth as an automatic sign of blessing (cf. Prov. 28:6; 30:7–9; Jer. 5:27–28; Amos 8:4–8; Mic. 2:1–5; cf. Sir. 10:22–23; for OT passages that could be appealed to for such a notion, see Deut. 8:1–10; 26:1–9; 28:12–14; Prov. 6:6–11; 10:4; 28:19; see Bock 1994–1996: 1484–85). On the background of the pervasiveness of a theology that linked divine blessing and wealth and that attributed poverty to laziness and wickedness, Jesus emphasizes that in the new world order of the kingdom of God, status distinctions based on wealth—used by leaders such as the magistrate who had asked Jesus the question about entry into eternal life (18:18), people who generally were in charge of the interpretation of Scripture, as a source of legitimation—have become irrelevant and certainly do not determine one's standing before God (Green 1997: 657–58).

Jesus' reply to his disciples' astonished reaction in 18:27, "What is impossible for mortals is possible for God" (*ta adynata para anthrōpois dynata para tō theō estin*) echoes Gen. 18:14 LXX (*mē adynatei para tō theō*, "nothing is impossible before God"), in a passage in which Yahweh assures Abraham that his promise that he will have a child through Sarah will certainly come to pass despite the fact that she is too old to have children. Since God can work the impossible, he can break the spell that wealth and possessions hold on people (see Bock [1994–1996: 1487], who also refers to Jer. 32:17; Zech. 8:6).

18:31–32

Jesus' declaration to his disciples in 18:31, "See, we are going up to Jerusalem, and everything that is written about the Son of Man by the prophets will be fulfilled," sets the stage for scriptural prophecies concerning Israel's promised savior to "play a major role in the unfolding of events" (Wagner 1997: 165). If the reference to the Son of Man is understood as a reference to the messianic figure who suffers, then both Isa. 53 and Dan. 7:13 may be in view (Nolland [1989–1993: 895] points out that the book of Daniel is not among the prophets

in the Masoretic divisions of the Hebrew Bible, which may suggest that Jesus has a broader scope of texts in mind, cf. Bock 1994–1996: 1496). Jesus' declaration alerts Luke's readers to expect allusions to Scripture in the passion narrative that follows. It is thus plausible to argue at least for the possibility that the use of the verb *paradidōmi* in 18:32 represents (as in 17:25) an allusion to the Suffering Servant in Isa. 53 (Lindars 1961: 80–81; Moo 1983: 92–96; Strauss 1995: 328).

18:38–39

The blind beggar in Jericho who was healed by Jesus (18:35–43) addresses Jesus as "Son of David" (*huie Dauid* [cf. 1:27, 32; 2:4])—the first public declaration that Jesus is the long-awaited Son of David—a royal messianic designation that alludes to 2 Sam. 7:12–16, a text in which Yahweh promises David a descendant whose throne would be established forever and who would be Yahweh's son (cf. Ps. 89:3–4; *Pss. Sol.* 17–18; 1QM XI, 1–18; 4Q174 I, 10–13; 4Q161 8–10 III, 18–21; 4Q175 9–13; 2 Esd. 12:31–32; see Green 1997: 663). The expectation of a healing miracle that would allow the blind man to regain his eyesight is derived from the expectation of the servant of God who would give sight to the blind (Isa. 61:1; note the link that Jesus establishes between Isa. 61:1 and his ministry of restoration and healing). The blind man evidently inferred from the reports about Jesus' miracle-working activity that he possessed divine authorization to wield divine power and that his mission could, or should, be understood in messianic terms—the mighty works of Jesus legitimate him as the Son of David, who does the work of Yahweh's servant (see Marshall 1978: 693; Green 1997: 665). Some scholars interpret the blind man's cry for mercy as an echo of David's plea in the penitential lament of Ps. 51:1 (cf. Ps. 6:2; 9:13; 41:4, 10; 123:3; see Bock 1994–1996: 1508; Ernst 1977: 510).

19:1–10

Zacchaeus's declaration in 19:8, "If I have defrauded anyone of anything, I will pay back four times as much," alludes to Exod. 22:1, "four sheep for a [stolen] sheep," and 2 Sam. 12:6, "he shall restore the lamb fourfold." The LXX of 2 Sam. 12:6 has "sevenfold" (cf. Josephus, *Ant.* 16.3): rustlers were required to repay the amount plus a threefold penalty. Since the legal restitution for monetary extortion was the amount plus twenty percent (Lev. 5:16; Num. 5:7), Zacchaeus's resolve is an expression not only of his willingness to restore the damage that he has caused but also of his inward transformation resulting from his encounter with Jesus (Nolland 1989–1993: 907; for a critique of Fitzmyer 1981–1985: 1225, cf. C. A. Evans [1990: 280] and Green [1997: 671–72], who argue that Zacchaeus describes in 19:8 his regular practice and not his postconversion intention; see also Nolland 1989–1993: 907; Bock 1994–1996: 1519–20; Bovon 1989–2001: 3:275).

The assertion in 19:10, "for the Son of Man came to seek out and to save the lost [*zētēsai kai sōsai to apolōlos*]," concludes the Zacchaeus story and sums up the soteriological message of Luke's central section: Jesus has come to seek and save the lost. This formulation echoes Yahweh's self-description in Ezek. 34:16 as the true shepherd who will seek and save the lost sheep of Israel: "I will seek the lost [*to apolōlos zētēsō*], and I will bring back the strayed, and I will bind up the injured, and I will strengthen the weak" (see France 1971: 96; Fitzmyer 1981–1985: 1222; Bovon 1989–2001: 2:277). Jesus describes his mission in terms of the will of Yahweh, who seeks out the lost in Israel, healing and restoring the people who have been mistreated by Israel's leaders.

19:23

In the parable of the Ten Pounds (19:11–27), the master's question, "Why then did you not put my money into the bank? Then when I returned, I could have collected it with interest" (19:23), echoes Exod. 22:25; Lev. 25:36–37; Deut. 23:19–20, passages that prohibit Israelites from charging and collecting interest (from Israelites). Perhaps the parable implies that even lending the money to non-Jews would have been better than inaction (Fitzmyer 1981–1985: 1237).

Luke 19:28–40

Luke's narrative of Jesus' royal entry into Jerusalem contains several allusions to and echoes of OT passages.

The geographical reference not only to Bethphage and Bethany but also to the "Mount of Olives" in 19:29 has been treated as a possible allusion to Zech. 14:4 as the place where the Messiah will show himself; according to Zech. 14:4, "On that day his feet shall stand on the Mount of Olives, which lies before Jerusalem on the east; and the Mount of Olives shall be split in two from east to west by a very wide valley; so that one half of the Mount shall withdraw northward, and the other half southward" (see Rusam 2003: 225). However, since there are no verbal parallels besides the reference to the Mount of Olives, and since the messianic implications of Jesus' entry into Jerusalem surface only later in the narrative, it is more plausible to assert that Luke makes nothing of this point (Bock 1994–1996: 1553).

The reference to the "colt" (*pōlos* [19:30, 33, 35]) that had never been ridden (19:30), and the use of the verbs *epibibazō* ("to cause someone to mount, to put on" [19:35]) and *chairō* ("rejoice" [19:37]), suggest an allusion to Zech. 9:9 LXX, "Rejoice greatly, O daughter Zion . . . your king comes to you . . . riding on a new donkey" (*chaire . . . epibebēkōs epi hypozygion kai pōlon neon*), a text that speaks of a humble and gentle king who is victorious because God has delivered him and who brings peace and prosperity (see France 1971: 105; Bock 1994–1996: 1556; Green 1997: 685; Wagner 1997: 165; Tan 1997: 150–51; differently, Fitzmyer 1981–1985: 1244; Kinman 1995: 109–15). Zechariah 9 begins with a judgment oracle against Israel's enemies (vv. 1–8) to the northwest, west, and southwest of Jerusalem, ending with the promise that Yahweh will establish a garrison in Jerusalem that will guarantee the city protection. The following oracle begins with the announcement that Zion's king is coming to the city (for potential links of Zech. 9:9–10 with the narrative of Solomon coming to Zion in 1 Kings 1, see Kinman 1995: 54–56). As Luke brings out this allusion more clearly than Mark, he emphasizes (again) the nature of Jesus' messiahship: Jesus arrives in Jerusalem not as a conquering warrior, but riding on a colt—that is, as the triumphant yet humble king (Strauss 1995: 314). Some scholars refer to Jacob's blessing of Judah in Gen. 49:11 for the association of a colt with the Messiah (Wagner 1997: 166, with reference to Blenkinsopp 1961; Green 1997: 684).

Other scholars refer to the account in 1 Kings 1:28–53, depicting Solomon riding on David's mule (*hēmionos*), which was symbolically significant for the new king's claims to be David's legitimate successor (Fernández-Marcos 1987; Kinman 1995: 49–54, 91–94, 109–13). If the narrative of Jesus' entry into Jerusalem alludes to Solomon, then Luke may want to reinforce the idea that even though Jesus' royal credentials are authentic, "he will not usurp political power but, like Solomon before him, will wait to receive it at the appropriate time" (Kinman 1995: 112–13). Since both the verbal and the material links with Zech. 9:9 are stronger, the parallels with 1 Kings 1 appear to be reflections of royal motifs. Note that although in 1 Kings 1 the motif of an orchestrated welcome is significant, the motif of entry is not: Solomon moves from the city to the spring of Gihon in the Kidron Valley and back to the city, movements that are mentioned only in passing; also, the animal on which he rides is not described as a *pōlos*.

Some suggest an allusion to Isa. 1:3, "The ox knows its owner, and the donkey its master's crib; but Israel does not know, my people do not understand," with the argument that the context of Isa. 1 accounts for Luke's inclusion of the Pharisees' criticism of the excited crowds in 19:39 and of Jesus' lament over Jerusalem's ignorance (Danker 1988: 312). This interpretation may be too subtle. If Zech. 9:9 is taken as the most plausible background, then Jesus' symbolic action of riding on a donkey implies the claim that he is the viceroy of Yahweh who fulfills the promises of the restoration of Jerusalem (Tan 1997: 151; cf. J. A. Sanders 1993a: 179).

The assertion in 19:36 that people were "spreading their cloaks on the road" (*hypestrōnnyon ta himatia autōn en tē hodō*) has been interpreted as an echo of the homage paid to the newly anointed King Jehu in 2 Kings 9:13 LXX (Fitzmyer 1981–1985: 1250; Green 1997: 685; Kinman 1995: 95; Rusam 2003: 227; cf. Lachs [1987: 344], who points to *Yal. Exodus* 168 and *b. Ketub.* 66b for parallel practices reported in later rabbinic literature).

The reference to the Mount of Olives in 19:37 is probably not an allusion to Zech. 14:4, one of two OT texts (cf. also 2 Sam. 15:30) that mention the Mount of Olives. Zechariah states that "on that day" Yahweh (Bock [1994–1996: 1553] speaks of the Messiah) "shall stand on the Mount of Olives, which lies before Jerusalem on the east; and the Mount of Olives shall be split in two from

east to west by a very wide valley." Luke makes nothing of the passage in the context of Jesus' entry into Jerusalem (Kinman 1995: 95).

The greeting in 19:38a, "Blessed is the king who comes in the name of the Lord!" (*eulogēmenos ho erchomenos ho basileus en onomati kyriou*), is an allusion to Ps. 118:26 (117:26 LXX: *eulogēmenos ho erchomenos en onomati kyriou*). The acclamation corresponds formally to acclamations of kings in the OT (cf. 1 Sam. 10:24; 1 Kings 1:34, 39; 2 Kings 11:12; see Kinman 1995: 96; Rusam 2003: 226). The addition of "the king" may reflect a reference to the historical context of Ps. 118, which perhaps was originally addressed to the king (see Weiser 1962: 724–27); or, the term *ho basileus* was added in order to emphasize Jesus' royal status more clearly than Mark does. If Luke generally follows the text of Mark in this passage, then he has omitted the Grecized Aramaism *hōsanna* (Mark 11:9), either because he follows the wording of Ps. 118:26 (117:26 LXX) or—the Hebrew *hôšî'â nā'* (transliterated in Greek as *hōsanna*) occurs in Ps. 118:25, where the LXX translates it as *sōson dē* ("save indeed")—due to his custom of eliminating Semitic words or phrases (Zahn 1988: 12n20; Fitzmyer 1981–1985: 58, 1250; for other connections between 19:38 and Ps. 118, see Constant 2001: 289–91). The addition of "the king" may also reinforce the allusion to Zech. 9:9: "Rejoice greatly, O daughter Zion! Shout aloud, O daughter Jerusalem! Lo, your king comes to you [*ho basileus sou erchetai soi*]; triumphant and victorious is he, humble and riding on a donkey, on a colt, the foal of a donkey" (see Rusam 2003: 227). Interpreted in the context of the first quotation of Ps. 118:26 in Luke 13:35, where the positive reception of the king in Jerusalem was at least a possibility, it is significant that here it is "the whole multitude of the disciples" (19:37) who welcome Jesus with the words of the psalm, indicating that "Jerusalem" has *not* received Jesus as king-messiah (see Wagner 1997: 167; Kinman 1995: 98). The fact that Jesus planned the event of his entry into Jerusalem (19:28–32) "suggests his awareness and promotion of its messianic connotations" (Kinman 1995: 97).

The shout in 19:38c, "Peace in heaven, and glory in the highest heaven!" (*doxa en hypsistois*), echoes Ps. 148:1, "Praise the LORD! Praise the LORD from the heavens; praise him in the heights!" (LXX: *aineite ton kyrion ek tōn ouranōn, aineite auton en tois hypsistois*). In *Tg. Ps.* 148:1 the heavenly beings and the hosts of angels are called upon to praise God (Lachs 1987: 345). The phrase "peace in heaven" suggests that the messianic peace that Luke connects with Jesus is realized now only in heaven; since the Jerusalem leadership rejects the "peace on earth" (2:14) of the kingdom of God (19:42), it must await the parousia to be realized. Although Jesus is indeed the king of Zech. 9:9 and Ps. 118:26 who brings peace to Jerusalem, "this peace is presently available only in the spiritual realm" (Strauss 1995: 315, with reference to Luke's other citation of Ps. 118:26 in 13:35).

In 19:40 Jesus' response to the Pharisees' request for the disciples to stop the celebrating crowd, "I tell you, if these were silent, the stones would shout out" (*hoi lithoi kraxousin*), possibly alludes to Hab. 2:11, "for the stone will cry out from the wall" (LXX: *dioti lithos ek toixou boēsetai*), in a passage in which the prophet levels charges against the Chaldeans and predicts their eventual destruction, calling in v. 11 inanimate objects to witness the divine judgment (Ellis 1974: 226; Fitzmyer 1981–1985: 1252). If Hab. 2:11 is in view, then Jesus' reply may imply a comparison of Habakkuk's Chaldeans with the citizens of Jerusalem, expressing the notion that Jesus regards the Jerusalemites' failure to welcome him as more heinous than the sins of the Chaldeans (cf. 10:12–14), or it may be a veiled threat of the future destruction of the city (see Kinman 1995: 99). The later rabbis used Hab. 2:11 similarly (cf. *Midr. Ps.* 73:4 (108a); *b. Ḥag.* 16a; *b. Taʾan.* 11a; see Lachs 1987: 346). Some commentators have argued that in 19:40 the stones of the temple are in view (cf. Ps. 118:26: "We bless you from the house of the LORD"), advancing three reasons for this interpretation: (1) there is a wordplay on "stone" in the temple scenes in 19:44; 20:6, 17–18; 21:5–6; (2) after his arrival, Jesus immediately enters the temple (19:45–46); (3) in his references to Ps. 118:22 Luke contrasts the stones of the temple with Jesus as the divinely chosen cornerstone (J. A. Sanders 1993a: 150; Wagner 1997: 168). Others see Jesus' reply as a straightforward metaphor, similar to OT texts that speak of creation responding with joy to the coming of God (Ps. 96:11–13; Isa. 55:12). These scholars

suggest that the responses of Jesus' disciples and the response of the stones are equivalent: "This moment is of such importance that it must find a response—if not a human one, then another" (Kinman [1995: 100], who points to Cicero, *Pis.* 52, as a non-Semitic parallel; cf. *TDNT* 4:270; Green 1997: 688n27).

19:41–44

In the Lukan narrative of Jesus' lament over Jerusalem in 19:41–44, several OT allusions have been identified.

In 19:41 Jesus' weeping at the sight of the city is a prophetic sign for the destruction of Jerusalem, which is predicted in the following verses. Weeping as a prophetic sign has parallels in 2 Kings 8:11; Jer. 9:1 (8:23 MT). In 2 Kings 8:11 Elisha weeps in the presence of Hazael and explains that he knows the evil that Hazael will do to the people of Israel; note 8:12: "You will set their fortresses on fire, you will kill their young men with the sword, dash in pieces their little ones, and rip up their pregnant women." In Jer. 9:1 (8:23 MT) the prophet cries out: "O that my head were a spring of water, and my eyes a fountain of tears, so that I might weep day and night for the slain of my poor people!" Note Jer. 14:17: "Let my eyes run down with tears night and day, and let them not cease, for the virgin daughter—my people—is struck down with a crushing blow, with a very grievous wound" (see Fitzmyer 1981–1985: 1258; Bock 1994–1996: 1560).

The five descriptions of hostile activity against Jerusalem in 19:43–44 echo several OT passages. First, "your enemies will set up ramparts around you" (*parembalousin hoi echthroi sou charaka soi* [19:43]) echoes Isa. 29:3: "And I will encamp against you round about [*balō peri se charaka*]; I will besiege you with towers and raise siegeworks against you" (cf. Isa. 37:33; Jer. 6:6–21; Ezek. 4:1–3; see Fitzmyer 1981–1985: 1258). Second, "your enemies will . . . surround you" (*perikyklōsousin se* [19:43]) echoes 2 Kings 6:14: "So he sent horses and chariots there and a great army; they came by night, and surrounded the city." Third, "your enemies will . . . hem you in on every side" (*synexousin se pantothen* [19:43]) echoes Jer. 52:5; Ezek. 4:2; 21:22. Fourth, "they will crush you to the ground, you and your children within you" (*edaphiousin se kai ta tekna sou en soi* [19:44]) echoes the taunt addressed to the "daughter of Babylon" in Ps. 137:9, "Happy shall they be who take your little ones and dash them against the rock!" (136:9 LXX: *hos kratēsei kai edapiei ta nēpia sou pros tēn petran*), and also 2 Kings 8:12; Hos. 10:14; Nah. 3:10 (Fitzmyer 1981–1985: 1258; Neyrey 1985: 116). Fifth, "they will not leave within you one stone upon another" (*ouk aphēsousin lithon epi lithon en soi* [19:44]) echoes the prophecy of Mic. 3:12: "Jerusalem shall become a heap of ruins." These several OT echoes suggest that Luke portrays Jerusalem's rejection of Jesus as reminiscent of Israel's betrayal of the covenant that caused the first destruction of Jerusalem and the exile (Green 1997: 691).

The concluding statement in 19:44, "because you did not recognize the time of your visitation [*episkopē*] from God," probably refers, positively, to the coming of God's grace and power, echoing LXX texts such as Gen. 50:24–25; Exod. 3:7, 16; Job 10:12; 29:4 (cf. Wis. 2:20; 3:13; see Marshall 1978: 719; Bock 1994–1996: 1563). If "visitation" is understood negatively in terms of divine judgment, then appeal is made to the LXX texts Isa. 10:3; Jer. 6:15; 10:15. The "visitation" that was intended to bring salvation for the nation, as proclaimed by Jesus, now becomes the basis for divine judgment in the future (Marshall 1978: 719).

19:45–46

A. NT Context: The Messiah and the Temple.
After recounting Jesus' royal entry into Jerusalem (19:28–40) and his lament over the city (19:41–44), Luke narrates Jesus' arrival in the precinct of the temple (19:45). Before the note that Jesus taught in the temple precinct (*to hieron*) "daily" (*kath' hēmeran* [19:47]), Luke includes the episode of Jesus' "cleansing of the temple," as the episode is traditionally referred to. The purpose of this episode has traditionally been linked with Jesus' action: he begins to "drive out" (*ekballō*) the vendors who sold animals for the various sacrifices (oxen, sheep, pigeons [cf. John 2:14]) and other forms of offerings (19:45) (Luke omits from Mark references to the buyers, the money changers, and the dove sellers [cf. Mark 11:15]). The focus on Jesus' action prompts scholars to interpret it as a prophetic act that purges the temple of those who profane it by corrupt commercial activity (see Nolland 1989–1993: 938). It seems preferable,

however, to interpret the purpose of Jesus' action in connection with his accompanying teaching.

Luke summarizes Jesus' teaching on this occasion with an OT quotation from Isa. 56:7 and with an allusion to Jer. 7:11 (and perhaps echoing Zech. 14:21; Mal. 3:1): "It is written, 'My house shall be a house of prayer'; but you have made it a 'den of robbers'" (19:46). Interpreted in the context of these OT texts, Jesus—standing in the court of the Gentiles, in which the temple authorities tolerated the commercial activities—proclaims the holiness of the entire temple area and thus announces the beginning of the (messianic) transformation of the temple and of its role, and, indeed, the destruction of the temple.

B. Isa. 56:7; Jer. 7:11 in Context.
The text from Isa. 56:7 belongs to a larger context in which Yahweh announces that his salvation will come soon and his deliverance will be revealed (56:1). This will be a time in which foreigners and eunuchs, people who had been excluded (for eunuchs, see Lev. 21:20; Deut. 23:1; cf. Josephus, *Ant.* 4.290–291; for foreigners, see Exod. 12:43; Lev. 22:25; Deut. 23:3–7; Ezra 9–10; Neh. 13:1–3, 23–31; Ezek. 44:9), will no longer be separated from God's people (56:3). Some scholars caution that since our knowledge of postexilic Jewish history is limited, there is insufficient evidence to warrant the conclusion that the measures against the proselytes against which Isa. 56:1–8 protests (56:6 implies that the foreigners who keep Yahweh's covenant are proselytes) were those of the reforms of Ezra and Nehemiah. Rather, the text may address a movement that demanded the exclusion of proselytes (Van Winkle 1997). In 56:4–7 Yahweh addresses in two parallel sections the eunuchs (56:4–5) and the foreigners (56:6–7), each of which begins with a threefold characterization of these groups of people. They have in common that they keep the Sabbath and Yahweh's covenant (56:4, 6). God promises the eunuchs who keep his covenant "in my house and within my walls" both "a monument" and "an everlasting name that shall not be cut off" (56:5). And God promises the foreigners who come to love his name and hold fast his covenant that he will bring them "to my holy mountain, and make them joyful in my house of prayer; their burnt offerings and their sacrifices will be accepted on my altar; for my house shall be called a house of prayer for all peoples" (*ho gar oikos*

mou oikos proseuchēs klēthēsetai pasin tois ethnesin [56:7]). In other words, the foreigners/proselytes are promised full access to and participation in the cult in the Jerusalem temple. The Lord "who gathers the outcasts of Israel" promises that he will "gather others to them besides those already gathered" (56:8); in other words, non-Israelites, non-Jews will be added to God's people to enjoy his salvific presence, extending God's promise of integration into his people beyond the proselytes to "all nations." In the context of 2:2–4; 60:1–9, 14; 62:2; 66:18–21, the promise in 56:7 receives an eschatological-messianic dimension: a time will come in which Gentiles will be allowed to worship in the temple, and when they even will be involved in priestly ministry (66:21). B. F. Meyer summarizes the eschatological perspective regarding the temple in the book of Isaiah: "The temple, then, would have a role not only in Israel and for history but for the whole world at time's end in the reign of God (Isa. 2:2–4; 56:1–8). This would be the last and eternal—the eschatological—temple, located on a Zion (Isa. 2:2–4; 28:16) rebuilt in carnelians and sapphires (Isa. 54:11). . . . This temple no one could build but God himself—or the Messiah transcendently enthroned at his right hand" (Meyer 1979: 184). Understood in this context, Isa. 56:7 promises the Gentiles, together with Israel, participation in Yahweh's eschatological salvation in the eschatological temple.

The second part of Jesus' teaching focused on Jer. 7:11—linked with Isa. 56:7 by the reference to "this/my house"—a text that belongs to the larger context of Jer. 7:1–20, in which the word of the Lord, proclaimed by the prophet Jeremiah, standing in the gate of the temple, warned the people of Judah that if they continue to desecrate the temple through lawlessness and idolatry (7:6, 9), they should not trust in the fact that this is the temple of the Lord (7:4) as a guarantee of their safety (7:10). The prophet asks, accusingly, in the name of Yahweh, "Has this house, which is called by my name, become a den [cave] of robbers [*hamĕʿārat pāriṣîm*; LXX: *spēlaion lēstōn*] in your sight?" (7:11). He challenges the Judeans to remember the destruction of Shiloh—Yahweh's dwelling place after Israel entered the promised land (7:12; cf. Judg. 18:31; 1 Sam. 1:3; 3:21; 4:3–4)—a fate that will fall on Jerusalem as its people refuse to listen to God's message (7:13–15;

cf. 7:20). From a form-critical perspective, Jer. 7:1–15 is a sermon exhorting the nation to repent, but the content, particularly the conclusion of the sermon, implies that judgment and destruction are inevitable (von Rad 2001: 2:197–98). The repentance and change that would procure Yahweh's salvation and the Judeans' continued existence in the land (7:7) are opportunities that have been forfeited. Jeremiah unmasks the false sense of security of the Judeans who believe that their misdeeds cannot rob them of the protection that the existence of the temple in Jerusalem provides, guaranteeing the presence of Yahweh. Jeremiah is told to proclaim a message of destruction, even though the Judeans will neither listen nor obey (7:27–28): the city, the temple, and the land will be laid waste (7:34). Jeremiah will announce in a later message that Yahweh will leave his "house" (Jer. 12:7).

C. Isa. 56:7; Jer. 7:11 in Judaism. The prophecy of Isa. 56:7 was understood to refer to the eschatological temple, expecting an influx of Gentiles to Zion to worship Yahweh in this temple (Tan 1997: 188–89, with reference to Ps. 22:27; Isa. 2:2–3; Zeph. 3:9–10; Tob. 13:11; *Pss. Sol.* 17:31, 34; *Sib. Or.* 3:702–718, 772–76; *T. Benj.* 9:2). A different tendency can be observed in *Tg. Isa.* 56:1–12, which emphasizes the return of the "outcasts of Israel," who are identified with the "exiles" (56:8), and the victory of "Jerusalem" over the Gentile "kings of the peoples" (56:9), placing Isa. 56:7 in a nationalistic rather than universalistic context (see Str-B 1:852–53; *TDNT* 5:121).

The Targum interprets "den of robbers" as an assembly of the ungodly. The translation of the LXX renders the Hebrew literally. The prophet Jesus ben Ananias used Jer. 7 to prophecy doom against Jerusalem and against the temple in AD 62–69 (Josephus, *J.W.* 6.300–309). He does not call the temple a "cave of robbers," but he does refer to the "voice of the bridegroom and the voice of the bride," quoting Jer. 7:34 (for the parallels between Jesus of Nazareth and Jesus ben Ananias, see C. A. Evans 2001: 177).

D. Textual Matters. Whereas Mark 11:17 quotes Isa. 56:7 verbatim, Luke has altered the wording, replacing *klēthēsetai* ("will be called") with *kai estai* ("and will be"). The term *klēthēsetai* is the variant reading in C[2] 1241 1424 e r[1] Epiph, probably a harmonization with the wording of

Matthew or Mark, or of Isa. 56:7 LXX. Luke may follow a pre-Markan tradition of Jesus' words, as suggested by the phrase *kai estai*, which may suggest a Semitic background (Holtz 1968: 164). Further, Luke omits the phrase *pasin tois ethnesin*, "for all nations" (see discussion below).

E. The Use of Isa. 56:7; Jer. 7:11 in Luke 19:46. Jesus' teaching, occurring in the court of the Gentiles and referring to Isa. 56:7, advocates the holiness of the entire temple precinct, the possibility that Yahweh may be worshiped by the Gentiles, who were allowed to stand here and who were expected to come to Zion in the last days. Note that Jesus does not disturb the sacrifices in the interior temple courts, which did not depend upon the sale of sacrificial animals in the court of the Gentiles, nor does he advocate for a cult without sacrifices.

Why, given his interest in the Gentile mission, does Luke omit the phrase *pasin tois ethnesin* ("for all nations")? Some suggest that since by the time of Luke's writing of the Gospel the temple had been destroyed and had in fact not become a house of prayer for the nations, Luke altered the citation because the temple no longer had any significance after the destruction of Jerusalem (Ploch 1993: 134), perhaps to save Jesus from uttering a false prophecy (Marshall 1978: 721; Danker 1988: 315). This interpretation presumes, however, that Luke did not understand Jesus' words in an eschatological sense, which the juxtaposition of Isa. 56:7 with Jer. 7:11 clearly presupposes. More plausible is the suggestion that Luke reports Jesus as being more focused on the fulfillment of the promises for Israel/Zion than for the Gentiles (Tan 1997: 191; Ådna 2000: 286).

We should note that the text does not criticize the sacrificial cult of the temple, which makes it difficult to imagine that Jesus' concern focused solely on the sale of sacrificial animals (and on the changing of money, mentioned in Mark 11:15; Matt. 21:12). The sale of sacrificial animals took place in the outer temple precinct, more specifically in the monumental Royal Portico (*stoa basileios* [see Josephus, *Ant.* 15.411–416]), located on the south side of the *temenos*. This colonnaded hall was eight hundred feet long and had three rows of columns, each twenty-seven feet high, constructed as a basilica that functioned as a market hall (see Ådna 1999). In other words,

Jesus' action took place in the court of the Gentiles—that is, *not* in the area in which sacrifices and prayers were offered. The activities of selling sacrificial animals and changing money were necessary for worshipers who came from cities outside Judea (see E. P. Sanders 1985: 61–65; Ådna 2000: 247–56; see also Green 1997: 693; Bock 1994–1996: 1572n2). Since the Jewish leadership does not respect the temple as a "house of prayer" characterized by the acceptance and the teaching of God's revelation, resulting in their not recognizing the time of God's visitation (19:44), and since the Jewish leadership does not respect the temple as a "house of prayer" characterized by humble openness to God, resulting in their failure to understand the nature of the inbreaking of God's kingdom, Jesus "stops short of embracing the role of the temple as a house of prayer *for all people*" (Green 1997: 694; cf. ibid., 693, with reference to Luke 3:21–22; 4:42–44; 9:18–20; 10:21–24, on prayer and divine revelation, and to 18:1–8, 9–14, on the character of prayer). In Jesus' vision as recounted by Luke, Gentiles would not come to the temple to find Yahweh; rather, the Lord goes to the Gentiles as the apostles go from Jerusalem to the ends of the earth.

Characterizing the temple as a "den of robbers," thereby referring to Jeremiah's temple sermon in Jer. 7:1–15, Jesus denounces the persistent disobedience of the nation and announces the destruction of the temple, since the people and their leaders refuse to listen to God's message and obey his word. It seems too narrow to interpret the phrase "den of robbers" merely in terms of an assertion by Jesus that "the righteous do not reside at the temple; rather the unrighteous do" (Bock 1994–1996: 1579). In light of Jesus' teaching concerning Jeremiah's prophecy in Jer. 7, Jesus' action can be interpreted as an enacted parable that predicts the imminent destruction of the temple (see E. P. Sanders 1985: 61–76). We should note that Jeremiah's temple sermon does not merely emphasize the necessity of repentance (Jer. 7:3, 5–7), implying the possibility of a purification of the temple; it also announces the destruction of the city and of the temple (7:7–15), since God has spoken persistently, but the Judeans have not listened and responded (7:13). This focus on judgment is supported by the context in which Luke has placed the temple episode. It follows right after

Jesus' lament over Jerusalem (19:41–44), with its prediction of judgment. Jesus' next statement involving the temple announces its destruction (21:20–24). The "city that kills the prophets and stones those who are sent to it" (13:34) is the city that will be overtaken by the horrors of war. Jesus' action in the temple symbolically expresses his conviction, expounded in his teaching based on Jer. 7, that the present "visitation" of God (19:44) no longer needs the temple, whose destruction is announced. Jesus' accusation that the managers of the temple cult have turned the temple into a "den of robbers" indicts them for assuming that the temple guarantees their safety despite their sinfulness, which includes their unwillingness to heed God's revelation in his messianic ministry that ushers in the kingdom of God (see Ådna 2000: 267–75, 381–87).

F. Theological Use. The point of Jesus' action is intended neither to purge the temple in order to prepare it for his subsequent teaching nor to eliminate all mercantile activities as violating the purpose of the temple, as some scholars suggest (see C. A. Evans 1990: 291). Rather, Jesus' action "symbolized his belief that, in returning to Zion, Yahweh would not after all take up residence in the Temple, legitimating its present administration and its place and function within the first-century Jewish symbolic world" (Wright 1996: 423). Interpreted in the context of Jesus' reference to Jeremiah's temple sermon in Jer. 7, warning his listeners in the outer temple court of impending judgment and destruction, his quotation of Isa. 56:7 points to an alternative that would follow from the conversion of Israel that Jesus still hopes for: the fulfillment of the eschatological promise of the conversion of the nations on the occasion of the restoration of Israel (Ådna 2000: 283–84). In the context of his message of the dawn of God's kingdom, Jesus' action in the temple was a challenge to Israel's leadership in Jerusalem not to continue the sacrificial cult in the face of God's new revelation, but to prepare, in the temple, for the time of the eschatological, new worship of God (Stuhlmacher 1992: 84).

20:9–19

After Jesus' encounter in the temple with the chief priests, legal experts, and elders, representative of the Jerusalem Sanhedrin, who seek to shame Jesus publicly by casting doubt on his authority

(20:1–8), following Jesus' demonstration ("cleansing") in the temple (19:45–48), Luke recounts Jesus' teaching to the people in the form of the parable of the Vineyard Tenants (20:9–19). Although Jesus refused to reveal the nature and source of his authority to the Jerusalem leadership in 20:1–8, he does so now, in parabolic form, in his teaching to the people (20:9), with the high priests and scribes in attendance (20:19). The parable draws its meaning from two contexts: the designation of Jesus as God's "beloved son" and the OT background of Isa. 5:1–7 (Green 1997: 704–5; cf. Brawley 1995: 27–41).

First, the larger Lukan narrative indicates that the designation of the son of the owner of the vineyard as "my beloved son" (20:13) reminds the reader of God's affirmation of Jesus (3:22). The desire of the tenants of the vineyard to kill the son (20:14, 19) reminds the audience of the desire of the Jerusalem leaders to kill Jesus (19:47). The designation of Jesus as (corner)stone (20:17–18) reminds the reader of Jesus' prediction of the destruction of Jerusalem (19:44). The details of the parable are recognized by the people and by the Jerusalem leadership as having "literal" significance in the real world (20:16, 19). Jesus thus uses this parable to teach the people about his rejection and death as "son," about the judgment that will fall upon those who reject God's envoy(s), and about the transfer of authority to "others."

Second, the intertextual relationship with Isa. 5:1–7, the Song of the Vineyard, informs the meaning of the parable. Several verbal associations establish this link: the vineyard owner's statement "I will send my beloved son [*ton huion mou ton agapēton*]" (20:13) echoes the beginning of the Song of the Vineyard in Isa. 5:1–7, with its repeated references to Israel as God's "beloved" (*tō ēgapēmenō . . . tou agapētou . . . tō ēgapēmenō* [Isa. 5:1]). The deliberative question "What will the owner of the vineyard do?" (*ti oun poiēsei . . .* [20:15]) may echo the question "What more was there to do (for my vineyard)" (*ti poiēsō . . .* [Isa. 5:4]). The phrase "the owner of the vineyard" (*ho kyrios tou ampelōnos* [20:15]) echoes the phrase "the vineyard of the LORD" (*ho ampelōn tou kyriou* [Isa. 5:7]). Other links with Isa. 5, which are included in the Markan version of the parable in Mark 12, such as the fence around the vineyard, the pit for the winepress, and the watchtower

(Mark 12:1; Isa. 5:2), are omitted by Luke, not because he wanted to eliminate allegorizing motifs (Schneider 1992: 398), but because the allusion to Isa. 5 was clear enough (Rusam 2003: 230; on the issue of allegory in this passage, see Kimball 1994b: 148–52), or because he wanted to abbreviate unessential details (Snodgrass 1983: 47–48).

In its OT context, Isa. 5:1–7 is a juridical parable in allegorical form (Willis 1977; Yee 1981; Childs 2001: 46; for the following exposition, see Childs 2001: 45–46). The opening lines of Isa. 5:1–7 suggest to the reader, or listener, that the text is a song of a beloved one concerning the vineyard that he has planted, sung by another person (v. 1: "I will sing for my beloved"). Verses 1–2 recount that the beloved had a vineyard on a fertile hillside; he prepared the ground, planted the choicest vines, constructed a watchtower, and built a winepress in expectation of the harvest. However, the vineyard yielded only bitter grapes, which could not be used for the production of wine. The last line of 5:2 thus indicates that the content of the song is a complaint. In 5:3 the owner of the vineyard, the beloved of 5:1, takes over and speaks in the first person: he wants to know what more he could have done (5:4) and asks the audience—the inhabitants of Jerusalem and the people of Judah—to adjudicate between himself and his vineyard (5:3b). Before the audience comes forward with an opinion or a verdict, the owner announces in 5:5–6 his decision, which is formulated as a judgment oracle: "I will remove its hedge, and it shall be devoured; I will break down its wall, and it shall be trampled down. I will make it a waste; it shall not be pruned or hoed, and it shall be overgrown with briers and thorns." The final threat, in 5:6, reveals the identity of the speaker: "I will also command the clouds that they rain no rain upon it." The speaker is the owner of the vineyard, which means that the song about the beloved is a parable about the failure of the people of God to meet God's expectations. The last verse of the song/parable leaves no doubt that this is the prophet's message: "For the vineyard of the LORD of hosts is the house of Israel, and the people of Judah are his pleasant planting; he expected justice, but saw bloodshed; righteousness, but heard a cry!" (5:7). As the song turns out to be a juridical parable in which the prophet indicts the nation for its sin against God, the subtle introduction of the audience in 5:3 is significant: the audience is the nation that God addresses through the prophet as his spokesman; that is, God challenges the people to abandon their neutral stance, forcing them unknowingly to pass judgment on themselves. Other passages that use the metaphor of the vineyard as a symbol for Israel include Ps. 80:8–13; Isa. 27:2; Jer. 2:21; Ezek. 19:10–14; Hos. 10:1. The representation of prophets as God's "servants" evokes texts such as 1 Kings 14:18; 15:29; 2 Kings 9:7, 36; 10:10; 14:25; 17:13, 23; 21:10; 24:2; Ezra 9:11; Isa. 20:3; 44:26; 50:10; Jer. 7:25; 25:4; 26:5; 29:19; 35:15; 44:4; Ezek. 38:17; Dan. 9:6, 10; Amos 3:7; Zech. 1:6 (Kimball 1994b: 156).

The Song of the Vineyard in Isa. 5:1–7 has echoes in Isaiah's prophecies. He prophesies that on the coming day of ultimate salvation, when God judges Leviathan and the dragon in the sea (27:1), a "new song" of the vineyard will be heard: "On that day: A pleasant vineyard, sing about it!" (27:2). God assures Israel that he continues to be the "keeper" of his vineyard: "Every moment I water it. I guard it night and day so that no one can harm it" (27:3). He will burn up all thorns and briers (27:4), and when they will cling to him for protection, when they make peace with him (27:5) "in days to come," then "Jacob shall take root, Israel shall blossom and put forth shoots, and fill the whole world with fruit" (27:6). This theme continues in the context of the Servant of Yahweh passages. In Isa. 42, when God will cause "new things" to come to pass (v. 9), when he will judge the earth (vv. 13–15) and initiate a new exodus (v. 16), a "new song" will be heard: "Sing to the LORD a new song, his praise from the end of the earth! Let the sea roar and all that fills it, the coastlands and their inhabitants" (v. 10); this new song will be heard in the desert and in the villages of Kedar, in Edom, and in the coastlands (vv. 11–12). This "new song" theme entered Israel's liturgy and became a continuous motif of expectation and hope (cf. Ps. 96:1; 98:1; 144:9; 149:1; see Childs 2001: 46).

Rabbinic interpretations of Isa. 5 understood Isaiah's Song of the Vineyard as a prophecy of the destruction of the temple in 586 BCE by Nebuchadnezzar, equating the watchtower with the temple and the winepress with the altar (cf.

t. Sukkah 3:15; see C. A. Evans 1990: 302). In the later Isaiah Targum, the judgment that God sends on "Israel . . . the seed of Abraham" (*Tg. Isa.* 5:1) includes the removal of the Shekinah, the destruction of "their sanctuaries" (5:5)—presumably a reference to synagogues (Chilton 1987: 11), although the context would suggest that the temple is meant (in 5:2 the watchtower of Isa. 5:2 is interpreted in terms of the Jerusalem temple)—and the cessation of prophecy (5:6). If Jesus' audience understood his parable of the Vineyard Tenants as an allusion to Isa. 5:1–7, then probably they understood its imagery in terms of the interpretation in the Targum, grasping the fact that Jesus speaks about God's judgment against the temple leadership (Chilton 1984: 111–14).

Isaiah 5:1–7, when read in the light of the OT Scriptures, reflects the notion of Israel as God's special possession (cf. Exod. 19:3–6; Deut. 7:6–11; 14:2; Ps. 44:3). This concept of divine election expressed the significance of belonging to the people of God. Since no other nation had been chosen by God as Israel had been chosen (Deut. 10:14–15), it is utterly "foolish, even suicidal, to renounce one's obligations to the relationship"; and it is thus not surprising that "virtually every passage in Deuteronomy which speaks of Yahweh's choice of Israel is juxtaposed to admonitions to obey him" (*ABD* 2:436, 438, with reference to Deut. 7:6–11; 10:12–20; 14:1–2; 28:1; cf. also Isa. 41:8–9; 42:24; Amos 3:1–2).

The intertextual connection between Isa. 5:1–7 and Jesus' parable of the Vineyard Tenants marks the parable as a short version of God's dealings with Israel, the climax of which Luke narrates in his Gospel, beginning with the owner's decision to send his "beloved son" and ending with the tenants decision to kill the son. Luke will narrate the transfer of authority from the tenants to the son (and his envoys) in the second volume of his work, the book of Acts. The OT background underlines the legitimacy of God's claims on his people, from whom he can rightfully expect righteousness, which includes obedience to his messengers and their message. The form and function of Jesus' parable corresponds to that of Isaiah's song: both Isaiah and Jesus "invite the hearers to pass judgment upon themselves" (C. A. Evans 1990: 302).

We need to note two important ways in which Jesus' parable departs from Isaiah's song. First, in Isa. 5 the vineyard produces sour grapes, whereas in Jesus' parable there is no indication that the vineyard does not produce a good harvest or that the tenants have not cared for the vineyard. On the contrary, the fact that they are unwilling to share the profits with the owner suggests that their work in the vineyard was very successful (Marshall 1978: 726). This suggests that the focus is not on "works" (the fruit or harvest of the vineyard), but rather on the authority of the owner: it is the insubordination of the tenants that leads to their dismissal and eviction. Second, in Isa. 5 the owner of the vineyard pronounces judgment on the vineyard for producing wild grapes (Isa. 5:5–6). Jesus, on the other hand, announces that judgment would fall on the tenants and that the vineyard would be given to others (Luke 20:16). This indicates that for Luke, the destruction of Jerusalem (cf. 19:41–44) does not signify the destruction of Israel, as the destruction of the tenants does not signify the demolition of the vineyard (Kimball 1994b: 158; Brawley 1995: 38–41; C. A. Evans 1990: 298; Green 1997: 705).

20:17–18

A. NT Context of Ps. 118:22; Isa. 8:14–15; Dan. 2:34, 44–45. Luke interrupts the parable of the Vineyard Tenants (20:9–19) in 20:15 to note Jesus asking the audience their opinion concerning the fate of the tenants, providing his own answer in 20:16a: "He will come and destroy those tenants and give the vineyard to others." After noting the horrified reaction of the crowd (20:16b), Jesus quotes Ps. 118:22 and alludes to Isa. 8:14–15 and Dan. 2:34, 44–45, introduced by a phrase that suggests that the answer to the question of what should happen to the insubordinate tenants is self-evident (20:17a: "What then does this text mean?"), since Scripture speaks of God's judgment on the builders of the house of Israel. Luke suggests that the scribes and the chief priests clearly understood both Jesus' parable of the Vineyard Tenants and his interpretation of OT Scripture concerning the fate of the insubordinate tenants as referring to themselves, as they wanted to arrest Jesus on the spot (20:19).

Luke quotes Ps. 118:22 with echoes of the reference to the stone of stumbling in Isa. 8:14–15, while the second part of the image derives from the stone in Dan. 2:34, the stone cut, not by human hands, from a mountain, which is later identified as an everlasting kingdom that crushes all other kingdoms (Dan. 2:44–45) (see *TDNT* 4:280–81; Lindars 1961: 183–86; France 1971: 98–99; Snodgrass 1983: 68; Albl 1999: 270; Marshall 1978: 732; Fitzmyer 1981–1985: 1286). Some see also an allusion to Ps. 110:5–6 (Wagner 1997: 171), while others doubt that Luke intends an allusion to Dan. 2 (Blomberg 1990: 251) or to Isa. 8:14 (Johnson 1991: 309; cf. Holtz 1968: 161n6). The uncertainty concerning the specific OT background of 20:18 has sometimes been said to be an extreme example of Luke's "freedom" in his use of OT texts (Rese 1969: 173; cf. Rusam 2003: 232), while others are content to observe, if not a verbal connection, a conceptual allusion (Bock 1994–1996: 1605).

B. Ps. 118:22; Isa. 8:14–15; Dan. 2:34, 44–45 in Context. For Ps. 118, see the commentary on Luke 13:35. In Isa. 8 the nation is threatened with invasion by Syria and northern Israel, a crisis that prompts Isaiah to challenge the people to fear not conspiracy and invasion, but Yahweh. In 8:14–15 the prophet announces that Yahweh will be a sanctuary for those who fear him, but for those who do not fear Yahweh in Israel he will be a rock on which they will stumble and be broken.

Daniel 2 is concerned with the significance of a dream of Nebuchadnezzar, king of Babylon. The first scene relates the failure of the king's diviners to interpret the dreams (2:2–12). The second scene recounts Daniel's involvement in the matter and the divine communication of the king's dream, which is, however, not revealed at this point (2:13–23). The third scene (2:24–30) further delays the resolution, until Daniel recounts the dream and its prophetic meaning in the fourth scene (2:31–45). The king saw in his dream a huge statue made of gold, silver, bronze, and iron, which was destroyed by a rock because the statue's feet were made partly of iron and partly of clay. Daniel interprets the dream in terms of world history, the golden splendor of the head representing Nebuchadnezzar's empire. The following regimes that replace each other are not identified. The fourth empire will be destroyed as a result of God's sovereign act (2:34–35, 40) at the time when God will establish a new kingdom (2:44). When God's time comes, "his kingdom requires the destruction of earthly kingdoms . . . when his moment arrives, his kingdom comes by catastrophe, not by development" (Goldingay 1989: 59).

C. Ps. 118:22; Isa. 8:14–15; Dan. 2:34, 44–45 in Judaism. In the later rabbinic text *Esther Rab.* 7:10 (on Esther 3:6), which is evidently messianic (Lachs 1987: 355), the author cites Ps. 118:22 along with a saying that corresponds to Luke's saying in 20:18: "(The Israelites) are compared to stones, as it says, 'From thence the shepherd of the stone (i.e., the Messiah) of Israel' (Gen. 49:24); 'The stone which the builders rejected' (Ps. 118:22). But the other nations are likened to potsherds, as it says, 'And he shall break it as a potter's vessel is broken' (Isa. 30:14). If a stone falls on a pot, woe to the pot! If a pot falls on a stone, woe to the pot! In either case, woe to the pot! So whoever ventures to attack [the Israelites] receives his desserts on their account" (Str-B 1:877; C. A. Evans 1990: 303). Strikingly, this midrash also quotes Dan. 2:34.

D. Textual Matters. T. Holtz suggests that Luke's omission of Ps. 118:23 ("This is the Lord's doing; it is marvelous in our eyes," quoted in Mark 12:10; Matt. 21:42) has theological reasons: the triumph of the crucified Jesus Christ was regarded as "marvelous" during the initial period of the early church, whereas later Christians were no longer surprised about Jesus' vindication, but rather about the Jews not recognizing Jesus as God's revelation (Holtz 1968: 161, with reference to John 9:30). It is preferable, however, to note that the omission enables Luke to establish a closer link with the following explanation of the "stone" imagery in 20:18 (Marshall 1978: 732).

E. The Use of Ps. 118:22; Isa. 8:14–15; Dan. 2:34, 44–45 in Luke 20:17–18. Jesus explains his exposition of Isa. 5:1–2, a text that he interpreted with the parable of the Vineyard Tenants (20:9, 10–16), with a quotation from Ps. 118:22, whose "rejected stone" he links with the "stumbling stone" of Isa. 8:14–15 and with the "crushing stone" of Dan. 2:34, 44–45.

Some scholars argue that Jesus' parable of the Vineyard Tenants in 20:9–19 is an example of a "proem midrash" (Ellis 1978: 251–52; 1991: 98, 134–35; Blomberg 1990: 251; Kimball 1994b: 162–63; 1993: 91; on the proem midrash, see Ellis 1991: 96–97). The proem midrash has these elements: (1) the biblical text; (2) a second text, the proem or "opening" for the discourse; (3) exposition, with supplementary quotations, parables, and other commentary, with verbal links to the initial and final texts; (4) a final text, repeating or alluding to the initial biblical text, sometimes with a concluding application. Applied to 20:9–19, the OT quotation and allusions fit this midrash pattern as follows: (1) The initial biblical text is provided in 20:9a, reduced to an allusion (Isa. 5:1–2). (2) A second text is omitted; the initial biblical text serves as the opening. (3) The exposition of Isa. 5:1–2 is provided by means of the parable of the Vineyard Tenants in 20:9b–15, linked to the initial text by the catchword "vineyard" (*ampelōn* [20:9, 10, 13, 15]). (4) The application in 20:16–18 is linked with the initial text and with the parabolic exposition by the catchword *ampelōn* (20:16) and applies the exposition further in 20:17–18 with several concluding texts: Ps. 118:22; Isa. 8:14–15; Dan. 2:34, 44–45; these latter texts are connected by the catchword "stone" (*lithos*). It should be noted that in Luke's version of Jesus' exposition of Isa. 5:1–2, there is no link between the "stone" texts and the "vineyard" text. (In Matt. 21:33–46 the link is not very strong either, provided by the reference to the building of the watchtower in Isa. 5:2, implying that the "building" [*oikodomeō*] was done with stones. As we have noted, Luke omits the reference to the watchtower; the suggested link via the catchword *sāqal* ["to clear of stones"] assumes use of the Hebrew text of Isa. 5.)

Scholars suggest that Jesus' parable of the Vineyard Tenants is related to Ps. 118:22 through a wordplay involving "son" (Heb. *bēn*) and "stone" (Heb. *'eben*). For this wordplay, see Exod. 28:9–29; 39:6–14; Josh. 4:6–21; 1 Kings 18:31; Isa. 54:11–13; Lam. 4:1–2; Zech. 9:16 (Kimball [1994b: 161], who also lists early Jewish and rabbinic texts). Such a wordplay is probably behind the Targum of Ps. 118:22, which reads "the son which the builders rejected" (Snodgrass 1983: 63–65, 113–18; C. A. Evans 1990: 303). Each text that Jesus (and Luke) alludes to serves a distinct function in the context of his interpretation of Isa. 5:1–2.

The quotation of Ps. 118:22 in 20:17 is about a stone that the "builders" rejected as useless but that was destined to become the "cornerstone." It continues to be debated whether the "corner-stone" or "keystone" is a capstone (see *TDNT* 4:268–80, esp. 275–76; Derrett 1978: 60–67) or a foundation stone (see BDAG, s.v. *kephalē* 2b; Snodgrass 1983: 102–3). The latter view is shared by a majority of contemporary scholars (see Fitzmyer 1981–1985: 1282, 1285; Bock 1994–1996: 1603; Green 1997: 709n43). It should be noted, however, that the position of this "keystone" is not significant for understanding Jesus' exposition of Isa. 5:1–2 with the quotation of Ps. 118:22. As God's vineyard failed to yield a harvest in the OT text, and as the tenants of the vineyard rejected the owner's son in Jesus' parable, and as the stone—the king—was rejected by the builders in another OT text, so Jesus is rejected by the Jewish leaders. But as the stone that was rejected became a cornerstone, so Jesus will be ultimately vindicated. Jesus uses the quotation of Ps. 118:22 with the following perspectives (Green 1997: 709; Constant 2001: 308–12): (1) to provide scriptural warrant for the sequence of events in the parable, implying the divine necessity of these events, including the violent death of the owner's son; (2) to indicate that the death of the son is not the end of the story, but will be followed by the son's exaltation (cf. Acts 4:11; 5:30–31); (3) to explain the announcement of judgment of the insubordinate tenants; (4) to suggest to the people that they should distance themselves from the tenants in order not to be implicated in the death of the owner's son—the crowd's shocked reaction in 20:16 indicates that they recognize that Jesus places Israel's leaders and thus, potentially, the entire nation in opposition to God (see Bock 1994–1996: 1603); (5) to vindicate the son in the eyes of his detractors and to emphasize his significance as a "stone" for Israel, the messianic Son of God (Kimball 1994b: 161); (6) the conclusion of the parable suggests, in the context of the reference to builders and a new foundation stone, an ecclesiological perspective as well: the rejected Messiah will build a new house, a new "temple."

Since the "stone" was a messianic image in contemporary Judaism, Jesus draws on Isa. 8:14–15 and Dan. 2:34, 44–45 to further explain the devastating consequences of rejecting the Messiah (see Bock [1994–1996: 1603n10], who also refers to Isa. 28:16; Gen. 28:17–19; Zech. 4:8–10; 3:8–9; *Tg. Ps.* 118:24; *Tg. Isa.* 28:16).

The allusion to Isa. 8:14–15 in v. 18a explains that the "stone" will bring disaster to the people who stumble over it and thus emphasizes the inevitability of judgment. As Yahweh had warned that while he is a "sanctuary" for the people, he has become to the two houses of Israel "a stone of stumbling and a rock of offense" on which they will stumble and be broken. The allusion implies that Jesus is a sanctuary for those who trust in him and a stone of stumbling for those who do not trust in him, and the latter group will suffer the consequences for their refusal to believe.

The allusion to Dan. 2:34, 44–45 in v. 18b explains a second function of the "stone": it will bring disaster on the people on whom it will fall in judgment (Fitzmyer 1981–1985: 1286). As the stone in Dan. 2 crushed the statue of gold, silver, bronze, iron, and clay in Nebuchadnezzar's vision, so those who oppose Jesus will be crushed. The "stone" that is rejected but vindicated brings judgment (Green 1997: 709; Snodgrass 1983: 105–6).

F. Theological Use. The OT quotation in 20:17 and the allusions in 20:18 serve to establish the legitimacy of Jesus' assertion that God's judgment will fall on Israel and its leaders. Jesus' coming death is explained by a word of Scripture—that is, in a salvation-historical sense (Rusam 2003: 233). As Jesus tells the parable of the Vineyard Tenants in Jerusalem (note "the people" as the audience in 20:9), the "stone" passages in Ps. 118:22; Isa. 8:14; Dan. 2:34; 44–45 focus the meaning of the parable in terms of a warning to the citizens of Jerusalem to beware of the impending divine judgment, thus challenging the Jewish people to accept the one who is rejected by the Jewish leaders (Green 1997: 709). The "stone" passages that Jesus quotes in his interpretation of the parable of the Vineyard Tenants explain the parable as an accusation and a threat against the Jewish leaders, and at the same time they communicate a veiled claim of Jesus to be God's authoritative and decisive representative (Snodgrass 1983: 109).

There is evidence for a written collection of *testimonia* of the early Christians that focused on "stone" texts and was used in five traditions in the NT: (1) the interpretation of Jesus as the rejected cornerstone (Matt. 21:33–46; Mark 12:1–11; Luke 20:9–19); (2) the portraits of Jesus and the "stone" *testimonia* in the Gospels (Mark 14:58; 15:29; John 2:19–21; Acts 6:14); (3) the metaphor of the stumbling stone set in Zion (Rom. 9:33; 1 Pet. 2:6–8); (4) the stone metaphor for the Christian community and the temple (2 Cor. 6:14–7:1; Eph. 2:20–22); (5) the designation of Peter as the rock and foundation stone (Matt. 16:18). Four passages are central for the stone *testimonia* tradition: Isa. 8:14; 28:16; Ps. 118:22; Dan. 2:34, 44–45 (Albl 1999: 265–85). It appears that the early church adopted Ps. 118:22 as a "resurrection apologetic" because Jesus had used this text in an important parable (Snodgrass 1983: 109–10).

20:25

The controversy dialogue about paying taxes to Caesar (20:20–26) contains several OT allusions. Jesus' pronouncement in 20:25, "Give to the emperor the things that are the emperor's, and to God the things that are God's," has been interpreted in terms of two kingdoms, his own kingdom and Caesar's kingdom, which are not in rivalry with each other. The kingdom of God, which has been inaugurated through Jesus' ministry, does not suppress or supplant the political kingdoms of the present age (for a list of interpreters who hold this influential view, see Fitzmyer 1981–1985: 1292). This view, which assumes that Jesus not only recommends that Jews should pay the Roman tax but also seeks to inculcate respect for the political authorities, can refer to Jewish ideas derived from OT passages such as Dan. 2:21, 37–38 ("He changes times and seasons, deposes kings and sets up kings; he gives wisdom to the wise and knowledge to those who have understanding. . . . You, O king, the king of kings, to whom the God of heaven has given the kingdom, the power, the might, and the glory, into whose hand he has given human beings, wherever they live, the wild animals of the field, and the birds of the air, and whom he has established as ruler over them all—you are the head of gold") and Prov. 8:15–16 ("By me kings reign, and rulers decree what is just; by me rulers rule, and nobles, all who govern rightly" [cf. Wis. 6:1–11]). However, this interpretation needs to be linked with the entrapment that the Jewish leaders seek to achieve with their question in 20:22 of whether it is lawful to pay taxes to the emperor in Rome (for a critique of the two-kingdoms view, see Marshall 1978: 736; Fitzmyer 1981–1985: 1292–93). Some scholars suggest that interpreted in the political context of first-century Judea, Jesus' reply has to be related not only to the emperor's image on the coin (presumably the image of Tiberius) but also to the inscription on the coin ("Tiberius Caesar, son of the divine Augustus, Augustus"), and that Jesus' reply echoes Isa. 44:5 ("This one will say, 'I am the Lᴏʀᴅ's,' another will be called by the name of Jacob, yet another will write on the hand, 'The Lᴏʀᴅ's,' and adopt the name of Israel"), a passage in which Isaiah describes serving God in terms of writing "I belong to God" (LXX: *tou theou eimi*) on one's hand (Giblin 1971: 520–25). This interpretation probably is too subtle (Marshall [1978: 736] calls it "a (correct) theological deduction from the saying [rather] than an inherent element in the argument"). A similar caveat applies to the suggestion that Jesus' reply echoes passages that are concerned with the inscription of God's law on the human person (cf. Exod. 13:9; Prov. 7:3; Jer. 31:33; so Green 1997: 716, with reference to Giblin 1971: 521–23; Owen-Ball 1993: 10–11).

Since Jesus' pronouncement implies a comparison between the coin that bears the emperor's image and the Jews (and/or people in general) who bear God's image, and Jesus often focuses his answers on fundamental theological and scriptural truths, 20:25 may echo Gen. 1:26–27, with its emphasis on human beings being created in the image of God (Green 1997: 715–16; Fitzmyer 1981–1985: 1293). If Jesus indeed aims at this basic OT text, he emphasizes that since human beings belong to God, whose image they bear, they are obliged to recognize and acknowledge his lordship as they experience the fullness of life not in allegiance to political authorities, but in obedience to God, the Creator of life (see Fitzmyer 1981–1985: 1293).

Luke 20:28

A. NT Context: The Discussion about the Resurrection of the Dead. The quotation in 20:28 belongs to a controversy dialogue (20:27–40) in which the Sadducees attempt to destroy Jesus' credibility by raising the question of who interprets Moses faithfully, as they seek to demonstrate the alleged unreasonableness of faith in the resurrection of the dead, which Jesus shares. This is the first reference to the Sadducees in the Gospel of Luke, which is not surprising: consider the fact that the Sadducees exercised their aristocratic influence in the city of Jerusalem, and note that Luke focuses his narrative on Jesus' Galilean ministry. In 20:27 Luke characterizes the Sadducees as people who teach that there is no resurrection of the dead (cf. Josephus, *Ant.* 18.16; *J.W.* 2.165), a point that influences much of Luke's reference to the Sadducees in the book of Acts as well (cf. Acts 4:1–2; 23:6–8).

The starting point of the discussion is Moses' stipulation concerning levirate marriage (Deut. 25:5–10; cf. the examples of Judah and Tamar in Gen. 38:6–11, and of Ruth and Boaz in Ruth 3:9–4:10). The Mosaic provision required a widow whose husband had died childless to be married by one of the brothers of the deceased husband—that is, one of her brothers-in-law. The purpose of the levirate marriage legislation was to continue the name of the deceased husband and to give him an "afterlife" through the children that his wife and his brother would conceive. The term "levirate" is derived from the Latin *levir* (*laevus vir*), "husband's brother, brother-in-law."

B. Deut. 25:5 in Context. Among the miscellaneous laws listed in Deut. 25:1–19, the third piece of legislation concerns levirate marriage (25:5–10). The law of levirate marriage, which had parallels in other ancient Near Eastern cultures (see *ANET* 182), stipulated that a man should marry his deceased brother's childless widow, provided that he and his brother had been living together, and provided that the widow was childless in the sense that she had not given birth to a son. The firstborn son from this levirate marriage would represent his dead brother's name; that is, he would be the legal equivalent to the son of the deceased (Craigie 1983: 314; cf. Schwankl 1987: 340–42).

C. Deut. 25:5 in Judaism. On the levirate marriage in rabbinic texts, see *Sipre Deut.* 237, 288; *Meg. Ta'an.* 4; *m. Yebam.* 12:6; *b. Ketub.* 46a. A woman who had been widowed repeatedly was considered to be dangerous. Rabbi Judah ha-Nasi argued that twice sufficed to establish the presumption that she had killed her husband, while Rabbi Simeon ben Gamaliel argued that three dead husbands established the presumption, prohibiting a fourth marriage (cf. *t. Šabb.* 15:8;

b. Yebam. 64b; see Lachs 1987: 361). The term *ateknos* ("childless") is attested in several Jewish-Greek inscriptions from Tell el Yehudie (Lietzmann 1923; cf. *CIJ* 1461, 1500, 1511).

D. Textual Matters. Luke narrates the question of the Sadducean representatives as a generic allusion to the Torah that conflates Deut. 25:5 and Gen. 38:8, giving the substance of the Mosaic provision of levirate marriage. Luke 20:28 reads, "Teacher, Moses wrote for us that if someone's brother dies [*ean tinos adelphos apothanē*], and he has a wife but is childless [*echōn gynaika kai houtos ateknos ē*], then his brother must take the woman [*hina labē ho adelphos autou tēn gynaika*] and raise up offspring for his brother [*kai exanastēsē sperma tō adelphō autou*]." This sentence abridges Deut. 25:5–10 and paraphrases Deut. 25:5 LXX, which reads: "If brothers dwell together [*ean de katoikōsin adelphoi epi to auto*], and one of them dies [*kai apothanē heis ex autōn*] and he has no offspring [*sperma de mē ē auto*], the wife of the dead man will not become (a wife) to an outsider not related [*ouk estai hē gynē tou tethnēkotos exō andri mē engizonti*]. The brother of her husband will go into her [*ho adelphos tou andros autēs eiseleusetai pros autēn*] and will take her to himself (as) a wife [*kai lēmpsetai autēn heautō gynaika*] and will live with her [*kai synoikei autē*]" (see Fitzmyer 1981–1985: 1304). The last clause of Luke's allusion depends on Gen. 38:8 LXX: *kai anastēson sperma to adelphō sou* ("and raise up offspring for your brother").

Luke is dependent not on Deut. 25:5 directly, but rather on Mark 12:19 or on an earlier source on which both authors depend. He follows Mark's wording, the construction of which is difficult, with slight stylistic modifications (Holtz 1968: 69; cf. Schwankl 1987: 443–61; Rusam 2003: 101–4): (1) he omits the conjunction *hoti*, which is unnecessary before the following *hina*; (2) he eliminates Mark's parataxis (*kai katalipē gynaika kai mē aphē teknon*) by formulating with a participle (*echōn gynaika*); (3) he avoids the uncommon use of the verb *aphiēmi* (see BDAG, s.v. *aphiēmi* 4) and replaces it with the *hapax legomenon ateknos*, "childless" (Holtz 1968: 68–70; Marshall 1978: 739). He has not changed Mark's formulation with *hina*, which is grammatically difficult (it probably should be interpreted as an imperative; see BDF §470.1; Matthew replaced the awkward

hina labē with *epigambreusei*; cf. Deut. 25:5 [Aquila]; Gen. 38:8 LXX v. l.)

E. The Use of Deut. 25:5 in Luke 20:28. The focus on the resurrection from the dead in Jesus' controversy dialogue with the Sadducees (20:27, 33, 35, 36, 37, 38) raises the more basic question of the nature of Jesus' authority and the relationship of his authority with the authority of Scripture and its faithful interpretation (Green 1997: 718). The Sadducees argue that if one takes the levirate marriage legislation seriously, it is obvious that the belief in a future resurrection of the dead is farcical because the reality of levirate marriage potentially leads to a complex web of familial relationships that would be impossible to sustain in the life to come. In other words, since rules such as levirate marriage exist for the present life, it is logically impossible that life goes on after death through resurrection (Nolland 1989–1993: 968). Jesus tells the Sadducees that people who quote Moses—in this case, the legislation concerning levirate marriage in Deut. 25—should also listen to Moses, about, for example, resurrection (Fitzmyer 1981–1985: 1301; cf. Schwankl 1987: 338–44).

F. Theological Use. The scene of Jesus' debate with the Sadducees about levirate marriage and the resurrection has been characterized as a "battle over the Scriptures" (Green 1997: 718). In regard to the question of the resurrection of the dead, Jesus argues that the Sadducees' focus on (levirate) marriage was bound up with a focus on the social conditions of the present world (20:34), whereas entirely different conditions govern the life of those who are deemed worthy of the resurrection (20:35a), conditions that are no longer dependent upon marriage (20:35b) because the new mode of existence of the "children of God" no longer depends upon procreation, but rather corresponds to that of the angels (20:36). This argument does not mean that Jesus holds the view that the meaning of Scripture is not self-evident, but rather that it must be grasped in the context of an eschatological perspective (so Green 1997: 718). Jesus' assertion in 20:37 demonstrates that this interpretation misses the point of Jesus' scriptural argument, which implies that the truth of belief in the resurrection of the dead can be ascertained in the plain meaning of the text of Gen. 38:8.

20:35–36

Jesus' assertion that "those who are considered worthy of a place in that age and in the resurrection from the dead neither marry nor are given in marriage" in 20:35 is similar to a statement in *b. Ber.* 17a: "In the world-to-come there is no eating and drinking, or procreation and childbearing, or trade or business, or enmity and strife, but the righteous sit with crowns on their heads and enjoy the radiance of the Shekinah" (cf. *'Abot R. Nat.* 1; see Lachs 1987: 361).

The statement "they are like angels" (*isangeloi* [20:36]) finds parallels in several early Jewish texts. In *1 En.* 104:6 we read, "For you shall become companions of the hosts of heaven," and in *2 Bar.* 51:4, "They shall respectively be transformed, the latter into the splendor of the angels, and the former shall yet more waste away" (cf. *Gen. Rab.* 8:11; *Num. Rab.* 21; *b. Ḥag.* 16a; *Pesiq. Rab.* 43 [179a]; 16 [80a]; *Pesiq. Rab Kah.* 6 [57a]; see Lachs 1987: 361). Jesus asserts that those who attain resurrection life are "sons of God" and "sons of the resurrection" (20:34): as "sons of God," they are "like angels" (for the "sons of God" as angels, see Job 1:6; 38:7; Ps. 29:1; 89:6 [89:7 MT]). Thus, as "sons of the resurrection," they are like angels, and angels neither need food nor marry (cf. *1 En.* 15:6; 51:4; 104:4–6; Wis. 5:5, 15–16; *2 Bar.* 51:10; 1QHᵃ XI, 21–23; XIV, 13; 1Q28b IV, 24–28), which proves that relationships in the age of the resurrection are different from contemporary human relationships, and which means that the dilemma of multiple husbands that the Sadducees had construed disappears (Bock 1994–1996: 1623–24).

20:37–38

A. NT Context. Jesus supports his belief in the resurrection of the dead by referring to the "story about the bush" (NRSV), which recounts Moses' encounter with the Lord in Exod. 3:1–4:17. Jesus' statement that Moses "speaks of the Lord as the God of Abraham, the God of Isaac, and the God of Jacob" (*hōs legei kyrion ton theon Abraam kai theon Isaak kai theon Iakōb* [20:37]) is a quotation of Exod. 3:6 (*egō eimi ho theos tou patros sou theos Abraam kai theos Isaak kai theos Iakōb*). Jesus' reference to Moses in 20:37 harks back to the quotation formula used by the Sadducees in 20:28, and it underlines the common basis of the conversation (Rusam 2003: 105).

B. Exod. 3:6 in Context. The pericope of Moses at the burning bush (Exod. 3:1–4:17) recounts one of the most basic events in the history of Israel: Yahweh's self-identification at Mount Horeb, "the mountain of God" (3:1), and Moses' call to return to Egypt and lead the people of Israel out of bondage. The passage combines three traditions that define Israel: the patriarchs, the exodus, and Sinai. The first section of this passage, Exod. 3:1–22, is a theophany account. After God told Moses to come no closer (3:5), he reveals himself with the words "I am the God of your father, the God of Abraham, the God of Isaac, and the God of Jacob" (3:6). The phrase "the God of your father" affirms "that God enters into a personal commitment to individuals" and reminds Israel that their God not only is the mighty and awesome Creator and Lord but also is intimately involved with people (Goldingay 2003: 245). The fact that God describes himself in his revelation to Moses as "the God of Abraham, the God of Isaac, and the God of Jacob" indicates that as God was bound to Israel as a fact of the past, he reaffirms his covenant commitments of long ago in the present, giving the Israelites hope for both the present and the future (see Goldingay 2003: 303). The self-identification as "Yahweh" underscores this reality as well: God promises that he will be there for Moses and for Israel in different situations, but always active and sufficient. Moses' encounter with Yahweh in the desert initiated the exodus, Israel's defining experience of salvation (see Goldingay 2003: 337). The self-identification of Yahweh occurs at the moment when he explains to Moses why Israel should respond with faith to the exhortation to leave Egypt: "To mention Yahweh's name is to move Israel to the greatest trust; because of Him their freedom will be assured" (Kilgallen 1986: 488).

C. Exod. 3:6 in Judaism. The formula "I am the God of Abraham, the God of Isaac, and the God of Jacob," with all three elements—self-identification of God, reference to the three patriarchs, and correlation of the three patriarchs to God—is not attested in other OT passages or in early Jewish texts. The phrase "the God of Abraham, the God of Isaac, and the God of Jacob" (without self-identification) occurs in Exod. 3:15, 16; 4:5, while the phrase "the God of Abraham, Isaac, and Israel" occurs in 1 Kings 18:36; 1 Chron. 29:18;

2 Chron. 30:6 (Schwankl 1987: 397). The first of the Eighteen Benedictions of the *Shemoneh Esreh*, the main prayer of Judaism that was recited three times daily and constituted the central prayer of the synagogue service, begins with the words "Blessed art thou, Lord our God and God of our fathers, God of Abraham, God of Isaac, and God of Jacob, great, mighty, and fearful God, most high God," while the second benediction begins with the words "Lord, thou art almighty forever, who makest the dead alive. Thou art mighty to help, thou who sustainest the living out of grace, makest the dead alive out of great mercy." The *Shemoneh Esreh* thus links the names of the three patriarchs with the hope of the resurrection of the dead. The litany-type text Sir. 51:12 (Heb. text) includes the lines "Give thanks to the shield of Abraham, for his mercy endures forever. Give thanks to the rock of Isaac, for his mercy endures forever. Give thanks to the mighty one of Jacob, for his mercy endures forever." Notable is Jacob's prayer before his death in *Jub.* 45:3: "And now let the Lord, the God of Israel, be blessed, the God of Abraham and the God of Isaac, who did not withhold his mercy and his kindness from his servant Jacob." The Prayer of Manasseh begins with the words "O Lord, God of our fathers, God of Abraham, Isaac, Jacob, and their glorious offspring." Several Jewish texts speak of the resurrection of the patriarchs (cf. *T. Jud.* 25:1; *T. Benj.* 10:6), or express the conviction that the deceased patriarchs are in God's presence (cf. *Apoc. Zeph.* 13:5; 14:3–4; 17:3), or voice the hope that the pious will be united with the fathers after death (cf. *T. Isaac* 1:4–5; 4 Macc. 5:37; 13:17; 18:23). In 4 Macc. 7:19; 16:25 the postmortem life of the patriarchs is directly linked with God (16:25: "Those who die for the sake of God live unto God, as do Abraham and Isaac and Jacob and all the patriarchs"). Other texts of the Second Temple period also express belief in survival beyond death (see Wis. 1:15; 3:4; 8:13; 15:3). The Pharisees believed in the immortality of the soul—at least that is how Josephus describes their beliefs (*J.W.* 2.163; 3.374).

Philo comments on Exod. 3:6, 15 that as God's name was linked with the names of the patriarchs, he "integrally joins his name with" the human race (*Abraham* 51). We should note, however, that Philo interprets the patriarchs not as human figures, but as virtues, asserting that "for the nature of man is perishable, but that of virtue is imperishable" (*Abraham* 55), since it is more reasonable that the name of the eternal God is conjoined with what is immortal than with what is mortal (see Downing 1982).

Rabbinic arguments for the resurrection of the dead appeal to Exod. 6:4; 15:1; Num. 15:31; 18:28; Deut. 4:4; 11:9; 31:16; 32:1, 39; 33:6; Josh. 8:30; Job 19:26; Ps. 16:9, 11; 50:4; 84:5; Song 7:10; Isa. 26:19; Ezek. 37:9; Dan. 12:2; see, for example, *b. Sanh.* 90b (baraita); 91b (baraita); 92a; *Sipre Num.* 15:31 (112); *Sipre Deut.* 32:2 (306) (see Str-B 1:893–95; *TDNT* 1:368–72).

D. Textual Matters. Some suggest that the quotation in 20:38 is closer to Exod. 3:15 (*eipen ho theos . . . kyrios ho theos tōn paterōn hymōn theos Abraam kai theos Isaak kai theos Iakōb*) than the Markan parallel (Kilgallen 1986: 488; Nolland 1989–1993: 966). Some assume a paraphrase rather than a quotation; they suggest that since Luke uses an "implicit" rather than an explicit reference to Scripture, he downplays the issue (Powery 1999: 235). This view is unconvincing: if Luke wanted to downplay belief in the resurrection, he could have simply omitted the story. Some have argued that the unique citation formula in 20:37, which uses *mēnyō* ("inform, give information, make known"), indicates that Luke deliberately distinguishes pre-Easter arguments for the resurrection and post-Easter arguments, the latter being tied to Jesus' resurrection (Rusam 2003: 107, with reference to Luke 24:44–48; Acts 2:24–32; 3:15; 5:31; 13:32–39; 26:23). However, this interpretation reads too much into the text.

E. The Use of Exod. 3:6 in Luke 20:38. Luke adapts the quotation to his narrative context by formulating Yahweh's self-identification in the accusative, with the result that Moses himself says that Yahweh is the God of Abraham, the God of Isaac, and the God of Jacob (differently, Mark 12:26, where Moses is said to describe his encounter with God at the bush when God said to him, "I am the God of Abraham [etc.]"). This means that "Jesus is made to appeal more directly to the authority of Moses" (Marshall 1978: 742). The authority of Moses, to which Jesus appeals for the belief in the resurrection, is underlined by the present tense of *legei*. The omission of the phrase "(I am) the God of your father" places the focus entirely on the patriarchs, avoiding an interpretation that might see Moses as the only addressee of Yahweh's words (Schwankl 1987: 385n180).

Jesus argues by quoting Exod. 3:6, 15, that since Yahweh's self-identification to Israel challenged Israel to respond with faith and trust, Yahweh's name implies the reason for the certainty that the dead will rise: the words of this text assert the fidelity of Israel's covenant God, who committed himself to Abraham and the other patriarchs, expressing a love of God for Abraham "which can only mean that Abraham will be forever with God" (Kilgallen 1986: 488). As "Yahweh" is the name that assures Israel of the love and faithfulness of their God—the name and the covenantal love that constitute the foundation of Israel and of the exodus—Jesus reminds the Sadducees of the absolute confidence that Yahweh expects Israel to have. Jesus asserts that Yahweh's love that caused the exodus from Egypt also guarantees the resurrection of the dead (see Kilgallen 1986: 489).

Jesus interprets the quotation from Exod. 3:6, 15 with the statement "He is God not of the dead, but of the living; for to him they are all alive" (20:38). The last phrase, "for to him they are all alive" (*pantes gar autō zōsin*), is similar to the Jewish text 4 Macc. 7:19 (cf. 16:25), which asserts concerning the martyrs who imitate Eleazar that "they believe that they, like our patriarchs Abraham and Isaac and Jacob, do not die to God, but live unto God [*alla zōsin tō theō*]" (Fitzmyer 1981–1985: 1307; Green 1997: 722). Jesus argues that since Moses designates God as God of Abraham, Isaac, and Jacob, at a time when they had died long ago, they are alive, since "only living people can have a God, and therefore God's promise to the patriarchs that he is/will be their God requires that he maintain them in life" (Marshall 1978: 743; cf. Rusam 2003: 106).

Jesus' interpretation agrees in a fundamental sense with the original meaning of Exod. 3:6: since God's promise to the patriarchs is not a singular but a typical reality, since God's commitment to Abraham and Isaac and Jacob defines Israel as a people of hope, since God's promise to Israel has not been completely realized in the history of the patriarchs but became a reality again at the time of Moses in the exodus and will become a reality also in the future, since the formula "I am the God of your father, the God of Abraham, the God of Isaac, and the God of Jacob," which stands at the

beginning of the exodus events, "works" not only in the past and in the present but also in the future, since Yahweh's covenant commitment is the constant while the specific historical situation is the variable, Yahweh's revelatory self-identification assures Israel of his active salvific presence in the past, present, and future. Although Exod. 3:6 says nothing about resurrection, Jesus' use of this text as proof for the reality of the resurrection fully and completely grasps its meaning as "transfer" from the past and present into the future (Schwankl 1987: 392–95).

Jesus' argument on the basis of Exod. 3:6, that if God has confirmed his covenant relationship with the dead patriarchs, he will therefore resurrect not only the patriarchs but all the dead who have the same covenant relationship with him, employs Hillel's third hermeneutical rule about deriving a general principle from one verse (*binyan 'ab mikatub 'ehad*) (see Ellis 1991: 89, 131). The meaning of the phrase "to him they are all alive" in 20:38 is best understood in terms of the assertion that although the patriarchs and indeed all people die from a human point of view, they are not dead, but alive "so far as God is concerned and because God gives them life" (Marshall 1978: 743).

The comment in 20:40 that "they"—presumably both the Sadducees and the scribes—"no longer dared to ask him another question" suggests that this controversy dialogue should be linked with Jesus' third and final temptation in 4:9–12, where the devil uses a quotation from Scripture to test Jesus. We should note, however, that Jesus' use of Scripture in 20:38 differs from 4:12: whereas he refers the devil to a divine commandment (normative use), he points the Sadducees to Exod. 3:6, 15 as an illustration of the reality of the resurrection (Rusam 2003: 104, 107–8).

F. Theological Use. The quotation of Exod. 3:6, 15 makes at least the following points in the discussion about the resurrection of the dead (Green 1997: 722). First, Jesus argues that when Yahweh was speaking to Moses at the burning bush, he was still the God of the patriarchs who had long been dead. Second, Jesus infers that the suggestion that God would assert a covenant relationship with people who had died long ago is absurd. Third, Jesus concludes that the patriarchs must therefore still be alive in some sense, and/ or can be expected to be raised from the dead.

Fourth, Jesus deduces that Moses, in relating the passage of the burning bush, attests to the belief in the resurrection of the dead.

The question has been raised whether Jesus uses the quotation to argue that the patriarchs are still alive, an argument that presupposes either their immortality (perhaps implying the notion of the afterlife conceived in terms of Greek dualism) or their continued existence in Sheol. However, it seems most plausible to assume that Jesus' argument "is not concerned with the niceties of Sheol, immortality and resurrection, but simply asserts that God will raise the dead because he cannot fail to keep his promises to them that he will be their God" (Marshall 1978: 743; cf. Ellis 1974: 235–36).

20:42–43

A. NT Context: The Question about the Son of David. In 20:41–44 Jesus initiates a discussion on a text of Scripture for the first and only time in the Gospel. After the discussion about the resurrection (20:27–39), no one dared to ask Jesus another question (20:40). When Jesus initiates the next round of discussion with "them" (*autous* [20:41]), he presumably addresses the scribes (20:39, 45) and the Sadducees (20:27–38) as well as the crowds in the temple (20:45) who had been following the previous discussion. Jesus asks a twofold question: "How can they say that the Messiah is David's son? For David himself says in the book of Psalms, 'The Lord said to my lord, "Sit at my right hand, until I make your enemies your footstool."'" The implication of the second question, which quotes Ps. 110:1, answers the first question: David, the author of Ps. 110, can indeed be the father of the Messiah, whom he himself calls "lord" because the messianic king is not only David's son but also indeed David's lord.

B. Ps. 110:1 in Context. Psalm 110 is classified with the royal psalms (on the objections of France [1971: 166], see Bock 1994–1996: 1637). The scholarly discussion suggests that any reconstruction of its historical setting and original meaning can only be tentative (Allen 1983: 86; for the following remarks, see ibid., 85–86). The psalm can be interpreted as celebrating David's conquest of Jerusalem and his accession to the throne, highlighting the implication of these events as divine pledges of universal dominion. Scholars debate whether subsequently the psalm was used by succeeding kings in a context of national enthronement. The psalm consists of two parts. The first part is an invitation from Yahweh to the king to take up a seat of honor beside him, emphasizing the fact that Yahweh is the real king: David rules "not in his own right but as co-regent and representative, deriving his authority from his divine counterpart." Yahweh, who is called "Lord" in the LXX, addresses the king (Heb. *nĕ'ūm yhwh*; LXX [109:1]: *eipen ho kyrios*), who is called "my lord" (Heb. *'adōnî*; LXX [109:1]: *kyriō mou*), telling him to ascend the throne and sit at his "right hand." Yahweh will make the enemies of the king a footstool for his feet; in other words, the king is promised military victory (Kraus 1993: 2:346–47). As the psalm expresses much of the "high theology" of Israelite and Judean kingship, the eclipse of the Davidic dynasty resulted in the fact that "the psalm lived on as an expression of faith in God's ultimate fulfillment of his king-centered purposes for his people" (Allen 1983: 87). (On the "son of David" traditions, see Fitzmyer 1997: 115–25.)

C. Ps. 110:1 in Judaism. Some scholars point out that neither the LXX nor the echo of the psalm in 1 Macc. 14:41; *T. Job* 33:3; *T. Levi* 8:3; 18:1–3, 8, 12 reflects a messianic understanding of Ps. 110 (Hay 1973: 19–33; Albl 1999: 221–22; Fitzmyer 1981–1985: 1311). There is evidence for the messianic interpretation of the psalm in rabbinic literature, but not before the second half of the third century AD (see Str-B 4:452–65). Assuming that Second Temple Judaism did not interpret Ps. 110 messianically, some argue that if this episode relates an authentic event in Jesus' ministry, "then the messianic interpretation may have begun with Jesus" (Fitzmyer 1981–1985: 1311).

Other scholars suggest that Ps. 110 was understood in Second Temple Judaism in terms of the enthronement of the expected Messiah (France 1971: 166; Larkin 1974: 402–4; Ellis 1974: 237–38), surmising that the nonmessianic interpretations—for example, among the Tannaitic rabbis—may have an anti-Christian tendency (see Callan 1982; Hengel 1995: 178–79). The interpretation of the enthronement of the son of man/messiah in the Similitudes of *1 Enoch*, which is dependent upon Ps. 110:1, is an important piece of evidence (*1 En.* 51:3; 55:4; 61:8; 62:2), regardless of the precise date of the composition of the

Similitudes, written by a non-Jewish-Christian group that was not later than early Christianity (see Hengel 1995: 185–86). Furthermore, it has been argued that the messianic interpretation of the royal psalms seems to be presupposed by the redaction of the Psalter: note that the relevant texts have been placed at the beginning of a Davidic Psalter (Pss. 2; 107) or at the end of a Davidic Psalter (Pss. 72; 110), which suggests that "for those who composed the collection of psalms in the post-exilic period these psalms apparently had programmatic character, and that can only be a messianic one" (K. Koch [quoted in Hengel 1995: 179]). The Targum of the psalms preserves developed paraphrases of Ps. 110:1 that do not help our understanding of the interpretation of the psalm in the first century. It should be noted, however, that the Targum interprets Ps. 110 in terms of the Davidic (royal) messiah (C. A. Evans 2004: 85–86).

D. Textual Matters. The quotation of Ps. 110:1 follows the LXX, except for the lack of the definite article before *kyrios* (B D; in Mark 12:36 the article is missing in B D, and in Matt. 22:44 in ℵ B D Z). The fact that most NT manuscripts read *eipen ho kyrios* (ℵ A L R W Θ Ψ 0117 $f^{1.13}$ 33 𝔐) is explained by most scholars as harmonization with the LXX tradition (Holtz 1968: 51; Fitzmyer 1981–1985: 1315). The meaning of the quotation is unaffected by this variant. The parallel texts Mark 12:36 and Matt. 22:44 read *hypokatō* ("under, below") instead of *hypopodion* ("footstool" [read in Mark 12:36 by ℵ A L Θ Ψ 087 $f^{1.13}$ 33 2427 𝔐 lat sy$^{p.h}$, and in Matt. 22:44 by W 0102 0161 0281 f^1 33 𝔐 lat mae]), which Luke prefers, following the LXX (*hypokatō* appears only in D it sy$^{c.p}$ in Luke 20:43).

E. The Use of Ps. 110:1 in Luke 20:42–43. The quotation of Ps. 110:1 (109:1 LXX) in 20:42 retains the pun of the Greek text: *eipen ho kyrios tō kyriō mou* ("The Lord said to my lord"). The Hebrew text does not have the pun: *nĕ'ūm yhwh l'adonî* ("oracle of Yahweh to my lord"). If Jesus quoted the Hebrew text, the pun would have been introduced into the tradition of Jesus' sayings at a later stage. Since Jesus probably spoke Aramaic, he could easily have quoted Ps. 110:1 with the pun that we find in the (later) Greek version: *'ămar māryā lĕmār'î* (Fitzmyer 1979b: 90; 1981–1985: 1312). Jesus asks how it can be possible for the

Messiah to be regarded as the son of David (as Jewish tradition does) in view of the fact that Ps. 110:1 states that the Messiah is the lord of David. He assumes with regard to the text of Ps. 110:1 that the "Lord" (*kyrios*) is Yahweh and that "my lord" (*kyrios mou*) is the Messiah, and he assumes that David is the author of the psalm and that a son is not superior to his father (France 1971: 163–69; Kimball 1994b: 182).

The conviction in many Jewish circles that the Messiah would be a "son of David" is based on passages such as 2 Sam. 7:14–17; 23:1–7; Ps. 89:29–37; Isa. 9:6–7; 11:1–10; Jer. 23:5–8; 30:9; 33:14–18; Ezek. 34:23–24; Dan. 9:25; Mic. 5:2 (cf. *Pss. Sol.* 17:23, 36; 18:6, 8; 4Q174 I, 11–13; *4 Ezra* 12:32; *Shemoneh Esreh* 14; *b. Sanh.* 98a; see *TDNT* 7:480–82; Fitzmyer 1974: 113–26; more generally, Charlesworth 1992).

Jesus points to an apparent contradiction between these biblical texts and Jewish convictions that assert that the Messiah is the son of David and the assertion of Ps. 110:1 that the Messiah is David's lord (Juel 1998: 142–43). This contradiction is implicit in Jesus' first question, and it is made explicit in the citation of Ps. 110:1 and Jesus' second question (Marshall 1978: 747; Kimball 1994b: 181). Jesus' hermeneutical question addresses the connection between the Davidic descent of the Messiah and the authority or status of the Messiah as lord (France 1971: 101–2; Fitzmyer 1981–1985: 1313; Bock 1994–1996: 1640). Jesus argues that the title "son of David" is neither the ultimate nor the only category for understanding the Messiah, since he is David's "lord" (see Bock 1987: 132). Jesus is not concerned to dispute the traditional idea that the Messiah is of Davidic descent; rather, he is concerned "to overturn its controlling influence on people's messianic understanding" (Nolland 1989–1993: 974). Jesus does not answer the question that he poses, and Luke records no answer of the scribes. His exposition of Ps. 110:1 argues that "the implication of the second question answers the first. It is not a matter of either/or, but of both/and: Yes, the Messiah is David's son, but he is more: He is indeed David's lord" (Fitzmyer 1981–1985: 1310). The text leaves open the further question of how the Messiah/lord sits at God's "right hand" (20:42), or whether Jesus' enemies, particularly the Jewish leadership linked with the Jerusalem temple (note the hostile co-text of chap. 20), are in some way related to the enemies mentioned in the psalm (20:43).

Some scholars argue that Jesus' initiation of a discussion about the identity of the Messiah and quotation of Ps. 110:1 do not make an implicit messianic claim. Some argue that Jesus' provocative remark was "designed to open up the question of the nature of the hoped-for ultimate intervention of God in the affairs of his People" (Nolland 1989–1993: 972). On the assumption that Jesus' teaching in the temple (20:1, 9, 21, 45) was connected with his message of the dawn of the kingdom of God, and given that Jesus linked the kingdom of God with his own person (11:20), Jesus' remarks about the identity and authority of the Messiah suggest, however, that he implicitly raised the question of the character of his own authority.

Psalm 110:1 is the scriptural passage most often quoted or alluded to in the NT, referring to Jesus' exaltation or vindication after his death, associated with his resurrection, ascension, and parousia, and the subjection of the heavenly powers to him (Hay [1973: 15, 163–66] finds thirty-three NT quotations and allusions; Albl [1999: 217–18] lists twenty-two NT passages). Some scholars suggest that several of the allusions to Ps. 110:1 derive from confessions or hymns of the early church (Hay 1973: 38–43). Others argue that even the confessional or hymnic use of Ps. 110:1 in the earliest Christian circles presupposes prior exegetical activity in which the messianic interpretation of Ps. 110:1 and its significance for explaining Jesus were established in connection with texts such as Dan. 7:13; Ps. 8:6, suggesting that it formed part of two advent collections and of specific *testimonia* collections (Albl 1999: 216–36).

F. Theological Use. Interpreted in the historical context of Jesus' teaching in the temple in Jerusalem in the days immediately before his arrest, trial, and execution, the discussion about the person of the Messiah, initiated by Jesus, who quotes Ps. 110:1, indicates that he hinted at his messianic dignity without explicitly affirming this claim at this point (Fitzmyer 1981–1985: 1313). Since Jesus provides no answer to the question that he posed, and since he does not clarify his dignity as "Lord," the implicit claim to be "Messiah" as "Lord" remains enigmatic. As Luke quotes Ps.

110:1 again on the occasion of Peter's sermon at the Feast of Pentecost, in the context of an emphasis on Davidic sonship (Acts 2:25–36) and of specific reference to David (Acts 2:25, introducing the quotation of Ps. 16:8–11; 2:34–35, introducing the quotation of Ps. 110:1), he implies that "the full understanding of Jesus' relation to David and of the nature of his lordship" comes only with Jesus' resurrection and with the disciples' faith in the risen Jesus (Fitzmyer 1981–1985: 1313). Jesus' exaltation to the right hand of God and his authority as "Lord" are linked with his resurrection and ascension and with his provision of the divine Spirit (see Green 1997: 724).

20:47

Jesus' denouncement of the scribes as "devouring widows' houses," interpreted as a prophetic generalization, echoes OT passages about the plight of the widows: Isa. 1:23; 10:2; Jer. 22:3–5; Ezek. 22:7, 29; Zech. 7:10–14; Mal. 3:5 (cf. Deut. 10:18; 24:17; 27:19; Job 22:9; 24:3; Ps. 68:5; see *TDNT* 9:449; Danker 1988: 327; Bock 1994–1996: 1643). If these echoes are intentional, this invests Jesus' denouncement with prophetic authority, resuming and applying the prophets' oracles against the rich and influential who oppress the widows. The text does not specify the trouble that the scribes caused. Perhaps they cheated the widows of what was rightly theirs acting as guardians appointed by the deceased husband's will to care for the widow's estate (Derrett 1977: 118–28; Fitzmyer 1981–1985: 1318). A later rabbinic text complains against lawyers who manage a widow's estate and extract excessive fees (*b. Giṭ.* 52a–b).

21:6

The discourse about the last days (21:5–38) begins with people commenting on the beauty of the temple and with Jesus' prediction of the destruction of the temple in 21:6: "As for these things that you see, the days will come when not one stone will be left upon another; all will be thrown down." In regard to the beauty of the temple, note Josephus's description of one of the temple gates that was completely overlaid with gold (*J.W.* 5.210–212; *Ant.* 15.395). In view of Jesus' reference to Jeremiah's temple sermon, in which the prophet announces the destruction of the temple (Jer. 7:1–14; cf. 22:5) in the context of his teaching in the temple (Luke 19:46), the announcement in 21:6 clearly alludes to these oracles of the prophet that were fulfilled in the first destruction of Jerusalem in July 587 BC (cf. the description in Jer. 52:12–13; 2 Kings 25:1–21). It has been suggested that first-century Jews believed that the exile had not yet ended and that they prayed and hoped for divine liberation from oppression and for the restoration of the land (Wright 1992: 268–71, 299–301). Whether Jews believed that the exile had ended yet or not, Jesus' prediction of total annihilation certainly must have been stunning, both with regard to the monumental architecture of the Herodian temple and with regard to religious, social, and political significance of the temple as the center of the Jewish universe (Green 1997: 733).

21:8–11

In the first section of his answer to the question concerning the time in which the temple would be destroyed, Jesus predicts false prophets (21:8), wars and rebellions (21:9–10), earthquakes, plagues, famines, and portents in the sky (21:11). Jesus' prophecy evokes several prophetic oracles of the OT, implying that Israel's history will repeat itself as a result of the nation's disobedience, and warns his followers so that they will not be surprised when "these things" (21:9) happen.

Jesus' brief description of the false prophets' proclamation with the phrase "The time is near!" (*ho kairos ēngiken* [21:8]) possibly echoes Dan. 7:22, a text that belongs to the interpretation of the vision of the four great beasts (Dan. 7:1–28) that signify four great kings who will arise from the earth (7:17). The interpretation of the fourth beast with ten horns (7:9–14) in 7:21–22 underscores its wickedness: "This horn made war with the holy ones and was prevailing over them, until the Ancient One came; then judgment was given for the holy ones of the Most High, and the time arrived when the holy ones gained possession of the kingdom." The phrase "the time arrived" (LXX: *ho kairos edothē*; Theodotion: *ho kairos ephthasen*) does not use the same verb as in 21:8, but the apocalyptic context is similar: expressing Jesus' words with echoes of Dan. 7 sharpens Jesus' denial in 21:9b ("the end will not follow immediately"): his followers must not trust these false prophets (Fitzmyer 1981–1985: 1336).

The assertion in 21:9 that this "must happen first" (*dei gar tauta genesthai prōton*) but that "the

end will not follow immediately" (*all' ouk eutheōs to telos*) echoes Dan. 2:28, where Daniel says to King Nebuchadnezzar, "There is a God in heaven who reveals mysteries, and he has disclosed to King Nebuchadnezzar what will happen at the end of days [*ha dei genesthai ep' eschatōn tōn hēmerōn*]." This link with Dan. 2:28 highlights the notion that Jesus speaks about events that mark the "last days."

The description of apocalyptic wars in 21:9–10 alludes to 2 Chron. 15:6; Isa. 19:2 (Fitzmyer 1981–1985: 1335; Nolland 1989–1993: 992). The prophet states in his oracle against Egypt (Isa. 19:1–17) that Yahweh "will stir up Egyptians against Egyptians, and they will fight, one against the other, neighbor against neighbor, city against city, kingdom against kingdom" (19:2). As Egyptians are "stirred up" (*epegerthēsontai*) against Egyptians, so "nations will rise up against nations" (*egerthēsontai ethnos ep' ethnos* [Luke 21:10]). The "wars and insurrections" (*polemoi kai akatastasiai*) of Luke 21:9 echo Isaiah's prophecy that the Egyptians "will fight [*polemēsei*] one against the other, neighbor against neighbor, city against city." The war of "kingdom against kingdom" (*basileia epi basileian* [Luke 21:10]) echoes Isaiah's prediction of the fight of "kingdom against kingdom" (*mamlākâh bĕmamlākâh*; LXX: *nomos epi nomon*, where *nomos* refers to the "districts" or nomes of Egypt [see LEH 2:318]).

It is less obvious that 21:10 echoes the prophet Azariah's description in 2 Chron. 15:6 of the "great disturbances" that "afflicted all the inhabitants of the lands" (15:5) when Yahweh had punished Israel in the past when the nation was "without the true God" (15:3). The prophet reminds King Asa that "they were broken in pieces, nation against nation and city against city, for God troubled them with every sort of distress" (15:6; LXX: *kai polemēsei ethnos pros ethnos*, "and nation will fight against nation"). Although the verb *polemeō* and the phrase *ethnos epi/pros ethnos* occur in both passages, the context of 2 Chron. 15:6 is not apocalyptic (*pace* Fitzmyer [1981–1985: 1335], who links the "end" in Luke 21:9 with the destruction of Jerusalem and the temple in AD 70, citing Josephus's description in *Ant.* 6.274, 285, 288–289, although he acknowledges the presence of apocalyptic language in Luke 21:8–11).

Both earlier and later apocalyptic and rabbinic texts consider international conflicts and wars as a sign that the end is approaching: "When you see the kingdoms fighting against one another, look and expect the foot of the Messiah" (*Gen. Rab.* 42:4; cf. *Sib. Or.* 3:538, 635–651, 660; 5:361–385; *4 Ezra* 13:29–31; *b. Sanh.* 97a; see Lachs 1987: 379–80).

The description of cosmic cataclysms, which include earthquakes, plagues, famines, and terrifying portents in the sky, reads, "There will be great earthquakes [*seismoi te megaloi*], and in various places famines and plagues; and there will be dreadful portents and great signs from heaven" (21:11). This is an echo of and possibly an allusion to Ezek. 38:19–22 (Fitzmyer 1981–1985: 1335, 1337). In Ezekiel's oracle against Gog of the land of Magog (38:17–39:6), Yahweh declares, "On that day there shall be a great shaking in the land of Israel [*estai seismos megas epi gēs Israēl*]; the fish of the sea, and the birds of the air, and the animals of the field, and all creeping things that creep on the ground, and all human beings that are on the face of the earth, shall quake at my presence, and the mountains shall be thrown down, and the cliffs shall fall, and every wall shall tumble to the ground. I will summon the sword against Gog in all my mountains, says the LORD God; the swords of all will be against their comrades" (38:19–21). Similar apocalyptic announcements are found in Isa. 5:13–14 (hunger); 8:21 (hunger); 13:13 (earthquake); 14:30 (famine); Hag. 2:6 (earthquake) (cf. *2 Bar.* 2:3; *Jub.* 23:13).

21:12–19

The reference in 21:16 to close relatives becoming persecutors ("You will be betrayed even by parents and brothers, by relatives and friends; and they will put some of you to death") and the prediction of receiving hatred in 21:17 ("You will be hated by all because of my name") echo several OT passages and early Jewish and rabbinic traditions that speak of the breakdown of family solidarity in the last days, particularly Mic. 7:2, 6; Zech. 13:3 (cf. *Jub.* 23:19; *1 En.* 100:1–2; *4 Ezra* 5:9; 6:24; *2 Bar.* 70:3; *m. Soṭah* 9:5; *b. Sanh.* 97a; see Lachs 1987: 381). Several authors argue that the allusion to Mic. 7:6, "For the son treats the father with contempt, the daughter rises up against her mother, the daughter-in-law against her mother-in-law; your enemies are members of your own

household," in the parallel text Mark 13:12, "Brother will betray brother to death, and a father his child, and children will rise against parents and have them put to death," has been removed by Luke (Fitzmyer 1981–1985: 1340; Nolland 1989–1993: 997). Indeed, unlike Mark, Luke does not list pairs (brother betraying brother, father betraying child, etc.), but rather provides a list of unfaithful relatives and friends. Even though Luke's list in 21:16 is more general than Micah's (and Mark's) list, there is no reason to deny that 21:16–17 echo Mic. 7:6, as well as Zech. 13:3: "And if any prophets appear again, their fathers and mothers who bore them will say to them, 'You shall not live, for you speak lies in the name of the LORD'; and their fathers and their mothers who bore them shall pierce them through when they prophesy."

The proverbial assertion in 21:18, "Not a hair of your head will perish," echoes 1 Sam. 14:45; 2 Sam. 14:11; 1 Kings 1:52 and occurred in Jesus' exhortation to fearless confession in Luke 12:7 (see commentary there). Read in the light of 21:16, which announces the execution of some of Jesus' followers, this proverbial expression does not promise complete physical safety, but rather asserts that nothing will happen to the disciples apart from God's sovereign will. And, read in the context of 21:17, the proverbial expression implies a promise that "persecution, even death, does not spell the end of life for the faithful" (Green 1997: 738).

The statement in 21:19, "By your endurance [*en tē hypomonē hymōn*] you will gain your souls," perhaps reminds the reader of Mic. 7:7, "But as for me, I will look to the LORD, I will wait for the God [LXX: *hypomenō epi tō theō*] of my salvation"; Dan. 11:32, 35, "The people who are loyal to their God shall stand firm and take action. . . . Some of the wise shall fall, so that they may be refined, purified, and cleansed, until the time of the end, for there is still an interval until the time appointed"; Dan. 12:1, 12, "There shall be a time of anguish, such as has never occurred since nations first came into existence. But at that time your people shall be delivered, everyone who is found written in the book. . . . Happy are those who persevere [*makarios ho hypomenōn*] and attain the thousand three hundred thirty-five days." For the motif of endurance in an apocalyptic or eschatological context, see also *4 Ezra* 6:18; 13:16; *2 Bar.* 25:1–7; *Lam. Rab.* 2:13 (100b); *b. Sanh.* 97b (Lachs 1987: 382).

21:20–24

In the section about the destruction of Jerusalem, the reference in 21:20 to the "desolation" (*erēmōsis*) echoes the phrase "abomination of desolation" of Dan. 12:11 LXX (*bdelygma tēs erēmōseōs* [quoted verbatim in Mark 13:14; cf. Dan. 9:27; 11:31]), which translates the Hebrew *šiqqûṣ šōmēm* ("desolating abomination")—that is, the detestable thing that causes the desolation, or desecration, of the Jerusalem temple (Fitzmyer 1981–1985: 1345). In 1 Macc. 1:54 the phrase *bdelygma erēmōseōs* is used for the "desolating sacrilege" that the people of Antiochus IV Epiphanes erected on the altar of burnt offering. Luke does not specify what will cause the "desolation"—the encircling armies do not constitute the "desolation" itself but merely signal that it has "come near," which suggests that for Luke the *erēmōsis* is the destruction of the city and the temple. Many scholars refer to Josephus's description of the destruction of Jerusalem in AD 70 (*J.W.* 5.47–97; 6.93, 149–156, 201–211, 271–273, 420; 7.112–115, 118, 138, 154) as the basis for Luke's account (see Fitzmyer 1981–1985: 1343), while others point to OT descriptions of earlier threats to Jerusalem (Isa. 29:3; Jer. 34:1; 44:6, 22; cf. 2 Kings 6:24–31) (see Nolland 1989–1993: 1000).

In 21:21a the call to flee to the mountains is a common OT and apocalyptic image (cf. Gen. 19:17, 19; Judg. 1:34; 6:2; 1 Sam. 23:19; 26:1; 1 Kings 22:17; Isa. 15:5; Jer. 16:16; 49:8; 50:6; Lam. 4:19; Ezek. 7:16; Amos 5:19–20; Nah. 3:18; Zech. 14:5; cf. 1 Macc. 2:28; 2 Macc. 5:27; *T. Moses* 9:6; see Marshall 1978: 772; Bock 1994–1996: 1677; Nolland 1989–1993: 1001). The second and third clauses of Jesus' counsel in 21:21b–c, "Those inside the city must leave it, and those out in the country must not enter it," focusing strictly on events in Jerusalem, are perhaps an allusion to Jer. 51:45: "Come out of her, my people! Save your lives, each of you, from the fierce anger of the LORD!" Note also Jeremiah's advice to the doomed inhabitants of Jerusalem in Jer. 21:8–10. The Babylonian siege of Jerusalem, which occasionally provided opportunities for slipping out of the city after an initial encirclement, provides a historical precedent for this kind of behavior (cf.

Jer. 34:21; 37:11; 52:7; see Nolland 1989–1993: 1001).

In 21:22 the assertion that "these are the days of vengeance" (*hēmerai ekdikēseōs hautai eisin*) is an allusion to Hos. 9:7 LXX, which announces that "the days of vengeance have come" (*hēkasin hai hēmerai tēs ekdikēseōs*, accurately translating Heb. *bāʾû yĕmê happĕqûddāh*). This announcement belongs to Hosea's accusation that Israel has rejected Yahweh and rebuffed his prophet, the basis for his prophecy that God will punish the nation (see Neyrey 1985: 118). Luke's phrase may also echo Jer. 51:6 [28:6 LXX], in which the prophet calls Israel and Judah to "flee from the midst of Babylon" in order not to perish, "for this is the time of the LORD's vengeance" (*kairos ekdikēseōs autēs estin para kyriō*). Even though the context is Babylon's judgment, the fact that Hebrew *nĕqāmāh* is closer to the Greek *ekdikēsis* than Hebrew *šillūm* in Hos. 9:7 and the fact that it follows a reference to fleeing from a doomed city (as in Luke 21:22) suggest to some scholars that an allusion to Jer. 51:6 is more likely: this OT background would prepare for "the move from judgment upon Jerusalem by the Gentiles to judgment in turn upon the Gentiles" (cf. 21:24, 25–26), as Jer. 51:6 predicts that God will inflict upon Babylon what the Babylonians had earlier inflicted upon Jerusalem (Nolland 1989–1993: 1001). Luke is the only Gospel writer who includes this reference to God's vengeance, although he does not explain in what sense the "desolation" of Jerusalem is "vengeance" (Fitzmyer [1981–1985: 1345], who refers to Deut. 32:35; Jer. 46:10 [26:10 LXX] for similar expressions of God's vengeance).

The reference to the coming days of vengeance as a "fulfillment of all that is written" (*tou plēsthēnai panta ta gegrammena*) not only refers to Deut. 28:64; Jer. 20:4–6; Zech. 12:3, which are alluded to in 21:24, but also echoes other OT oracles that announce punishment for Israel as a result of covenantal unfaithfulness (cf. Lev. 26:31–33; Deut. 28:49–57; 32:35; 1 Kings 9:6–9; Isa. 34:8; Jer. 5:29; 6:1–8; 7:8–15; 26:1–9; 46:10; 50:27; 51:6; Dan. 9:26; Hos. 9:7; Mic. 3:12; Zech. 11:6; cf. 8:1–8; see Bock 1994–1996: 1678).

In 21:23b the announcement that "there will be great distress on the earth [*anankē megalē epi tēs gēs*] and wrath against this people [*orgē tō laō toutō*]" conceptually recalls Deut. 28:58–68, a passage that announces plagues, diseases, illnesses, disasters, destruction, exile, anxious minds, weariness, despairing hearts, dread, and terror for God's people if they do not carefully follow all the words of God's law (Bock [1994–1996: 1679n31], who further refers to Isa. 9:12; Jer. 4:4; Ezek. 5:13; 30:3; 32:9). The term *anankē* ("distress") stands for the term *thlipsis* ("tribulation"), used in the parallel text of Mark 13:19, which frequently occurs in apocalyptic contexts (Dan. 12:1; Hab. 3:16; Zeph. 1:15; cf. *2 Bar.* 15:8; 48:50; *4 Ezra* 7:89; 1QM I, 12; 1QHᵃ X, 6–12).

The prophecy of 21:24, that the inhabitants of Jerusalem "will fall by the edge of the sword [*kai pesountai stomati machairēs*] and be taken away as captives among all nations [*aichmalōtisthēsontai eis ta ethnē panta*], and Jerusalem will be trampled on by the Gentiles [*Ierousalēm estai patoumenē hypo ethnōn*], until the times of the Gentiles are fulfilled," recalls several OT predictions of God's judgment upon Jerusalem. For OT descriptions of the destruction of Jerusalem, see Jer. 20:4–6; 39:1–10; 52:5–10. For prophecies of judgment upon Jerusalem and/or Israel/Judah, see Isa. 10; Jer. 50–52 (see Nolland 1989–1993: 1004). For the concept of being "trampled" by hostile armies, see Isa. 28:3; 41:25; Ezek. 26:11 (see Neyrey 1985: 118).

The first part of the prediction echoes Jer. 20:4, "They shall fall by the sword of their enemies. . . . He [the king of Babylon] shall kill them with the sword [*pesountai en machaira echtrōn autōn*]," a passage that predicts the destruction of Jerusalem following Jeremiah's symbolic action of smashing a potter's jar to pieces (Jer. 19:1–15).

The second phrase of Jesus' prophecy alludes to Deut. 28:64 LXX, "The Lᴏʀᴅ your God will scatter you among all peoples [*diasperei se kyrios ho theos sou eis panta ta ethnē*], from one end of the earth to the other," a text that records Moses' explanation of the curses that will bring Yahweh's judgment upon disobedient Israel in Deut. 27. The assertion that in Luke's context the captivity would refer to that of the Romans (Fitzmyer 1981–1985: 1346) must not be misinterpreted. It is certainly true that the reference is to the events of AD 66–70 when a Roman army besieged and destroyed Jerusalem and carried thousands of Jews into captivity. We should note, however, that we do not know how many of the ninety-seven thou-

sand Jews taken prisoner during this entire period (Josephus, *J.W.* 6.420) were sold into slavery and forced to leave Judea. Furthermore, not all of these Jewish slaves were taken to Rome and Italy: at one point during the war, Vespasian transported six thousand Jewish prisoners to Corinth to work on Nero's canal through the isthmus there (Josephus, *J.W.* 3.539).

The third part of Jesus' prediction is an allusion to Zech. 12:3 LXX: "And it will come to pass on that day that I shall make Jerusalem a stone trampled upon by all the nations [*thēsomai Ierousalēm lithon katapatoumenon pasin tois ethnesin*]; all who lift it shall grievously hurt themselves. And all the nations of the earth shall come together against it." This is a paraphrase of the Hebrew text of Zech. 12:3, which reads, "On that day I will make Jerusalem a heavy stone for all the peoples." This text belongs to Zechariah's oracle against Jerusalem, whose citizens are summoned to repent of sin and infidelity.

In regard to the fourth and final phrase in 21:24, "until the times of the Gentiles are fulfilled" (*achri hou plērōthōsin kairoi ethnōn*), the notion of a limit to apocalyptic sufferings recalls Dan. 8:13–14; 12:5–13 (cf. 1QS IV, 18), while the idea of a fixed period of rule echoes Jer. 27:7: "All the nations shall serve him and his son and his grandson, until the time of his own land comes." The language of the phrase is similar to Tob. 14:5, "God will bring them back into the land of Israel; and they will rebuild the temple of God, but not like the first one, until the period when the times of fulfillment shall come [B: *heōs plērōthōsin kairoi tou aiōnos*]," part of Tobit's last words before he dies, reassuring the reader that the word of God spoken through the prophets will come to pass, as God will bring them back from exile into the land of Israel (see Marshall 1978: 773). The suggestion that the phrase "times of the Gentiles" refers to the period of the Gentile mission in which Gentiles are converted (see Bock 1994–1996: 1680–81, with reference to Rom. 11:25–26)—a thought that is found in Tob. 14:6 (see also Zech. 8:12–14) and may recall the explicit reference to the preaching of the gospel to "all the nations" before the end comes in Mark 13:10—is possible, although other scholars interpret the "times of the nations" in terms of "the time for a turn of judgment for each one of the nations" (Nolland 1989–1993: 1004).

Luke 21:25–28

The description of the future coming of the Son of Man—the fourth sign saying in the Lukan eschatological discourse, following those about messianic pretenders, wars, and catastrophes (21:8–11), about the persecution of Jesus' followers (21:12–19), and about the destruction of Jerusalem (21:20–24)—contains several allusions to and echoes of OT passages that prophetically describe future events of final judgment and deliverance.

In 21:25a the "signs in the sun, the moon, and the stars" (*sēmeia en hēliō kai selēnē kai astrois*) alludes to Joel 2:30–31: "I will show portents in the heavens and on the earth, blood and fire and columns of smoke. The sun shall be turned to darkness, and the moon to blood, before the great and terrible day of the LORD comes" (3:3–4 LXX: *terata en to ouranō . . . ho hēlios metastraphēsetai . . . hē selēnē eis haima*). Note that similar cosmic signs are linked with the appearance of Yahweh in Isa. 13:10; 24:23; 34:4; Ezek. 32:7; Amos 8:9; Hag. 2:6, 21; cf. *4 Ezra* 5:4; 13:30–32; *1 En.* 80:4–7; *T. Levi* 4:1; *As. Mos.* 10:5; *Sib. Or.* 3:796–803; *b. Sanh.* 91b; *b. Pesaḥ.* 68a; *b. Sukkah* 29a (Lachs 1987: 385–86; Kimball 1994b: 192).

The reference to the distress of the nations in 21:25b, "on the earth distress among nations in their perplexity" (*epi tēs gēs synochē ethnōn en aporia*), may allude to Isa. 24:19 ("The earth is utterly broken, the earth is torn asunder, the earth is violently shaken" [LXX: *tarachē tarachthēsetai hē gē kai aporia aporēthēsetai hē gē*]). See also Isa. 8:22; 13:4; Ps. 65:8 (Fitzmyer 1981–1985: 1349).

The reference to the roaring of the sea in 21:25c, "by the roaring of the sea and the waves" (*ēchous thalassēs kai salou*), possibly alludes to Ps. 46:3: "Though its waters roar and foam, though the mountains tremble with its tumult" (45:4 LXX: *ēchēsan kai etarachthēsan ta hydata autōn etarachthēsan ta orē en tē krataiotēti autou*). See also Ps. 89:9 (88:10 LXX); Isa. 5:30; 17:12.

In 21:26a the reference to the fear of the people is based on Isa. 13:6–11 (cf. Ps. 65:8 [64:9 LXX]). The statement in 21:26b, "the powers of the heavens will be shaken" (*dynameis tōn ouranōn saleuthēsontai*), is an allusion to Isa. 34:4: "All the host of heaven shall fade away, and the skies roll up like a scroll" (*heligēsetai ho ouranos hōs biblion kai panta ta astra peseitai*, "the heaven will be rolled up like a scroll, and all the stars will fall"; Codex B and Lucian: *takēsontai pasai hai dynameis tōn ouranōn*, "all the powers of heaven will be dissolved"). In Isa. 34 the prophet describes the terrifying end of God's enemies, symbolically depicted as the hosts of heaven; Luke uses the passage to emphasize the "reversal of the created order and the return to chaos" (Fitzmyer 1981–1985: 1350).

The reference in 21:27 to "the Son of Man coming in a cloud" is an allusion to Dan. 7:13, used to refer to the appearance of the risen Jesus as the Son of Man who returns in judgment (cf. 22:67–69; see Albl 1999: 230; Fitzmyer 1981–1985: 1350; some prefer to speak of a quotation [see Kimball 1994b: 190]). The exalted Son of Man who appears in heavenly glory brings both judgment (21:25–26) and redemption (21:28), with the emphasis on the latter function. The coming of the Son of Man with the clouds in Dan. 7:13 is reminiscent of the coming of God to earth in Ps. 18:10–13; Isa. 19:1 (Goldingay 1989: 167). The coming with clouds is a divine attribute (cf. Exod. 13:21–22; 19:9, 16; 34:5; Num. 10:34; 11:25; Ps. 97:2; 104:3; Ezek. 1:4–6; see Kimball 1994b: 193).

Since Luke's account makes perfect sense without a reference to "seeing" (*opsontai*) the Son of Man, and since there is evidence for a widespread early Christian reading of Zech. 12:10, "And I will pour out a spirit of compassion and supplication on the house of David and the inhabitants of Jerusalem, so that, when they look on [*epiblepsontai*] the one whom they have pierced [*katōrchēsanto*], they shall mourn [*kopsontai*] for him, as one mourns for an only child, and weep bitterly over him, as one weeps over a firstborn," with *opsontai* ("they see") instead of *epiblepsontai* (see Lindars 1961: 124), many scholars argue that the use of the term *opsontai* suggests an allusion to Zech. 12:10 (Marshall 1978: 775–76; Perrin 1967: 180–85; Albl 1999: 257–58; see the discussion in D. Wenham 1979: 315–18). In regard to the early Christian reading of Zech. 12:10 with *opsontai*, we should note not only the wordplay with *kopsontai* at the beginning of Zech. 12:10b but also the early Christian tradition that uses the verb *horaō* for the witnessing of Jesus Christ's parousia (cf. Mark 9:1 pars.; 13:26 pars.; Matt. 5:8; Luke 3:6; 13:28; 17:22; Heb. 9:28; 12:14; 1 John 3:2; Rev. 22:4; see Menken 1993: 501–2). The Zechariah passage belongs to a context that describes the mourning of Jerusalem and the mourning of the land for the one who has been pierced (Zech. 12:10–14). The Masoretic vocalization of Zech. 12:10 suggests, taking 'ēt as *nota accusativi*, that the one who is pierced and God are identified, while the following statements suggest that the pierced one is a human being, distinct from God (for the textual problem see Sæbø 1969: 97–102). The LXX translated the difficult Hebrew text as *kai epiblepsontai pros me anth' hōn katōrchēsanto*, "and they shall look at me because they have danced," reading the Hebrew as *rāqādû* ("they have danced") instead of *dāqārû* ("they have pierced"), transposing the letters *dalet* and *resh* not only because they look similar but also because the interchange of similar consonants was an accepted exegetical device (Menken 1993: 499–500; for the following comments, see ibid., 500–501). Aquila translated *syn hō exekentēsan*, "with the one whom they have pierced," solving the problem of the identity of God and the pierced one differently; in Theodotion's translation the problem of the anthropomorphism remains: he translates *kai epiblepsontai pros me hon exekentēsan*, "and they shall look on me whom they have pierced" (MS 86; so also the Vulgate), or *kai epiblepsontai pros me eis hon exekentēsan*, "and they shall look on me, to whom they have pierced" (Syro-Hexapla; so also the Peshitta). The Targum interprets "looking" as "praying," and "piercing" as "exiling" ("and they shall pray before me for those who were exiled"). It should be noted, however, that the motif of "seeing" is already present in Dan. 7:13 (*etheōroun*) (see Marshall 1978: 776).

21:29–33

In the parable of the Fig Tree, Luke adds the phrase "and all the trees" to the reference to the fig tree (21:29), implying that any tree could reveal the lesson of leaves being the sign of the proximity of the summer. If the parable utilizes the play on the Hebrew words *qēṣ* ("end") and *qayiṣ* ("summer [fruit]"), it should be noted that the same pun is present in Amos 8:1–2 (Lachs 1987: 386, with further reference to Mic. 7:1; 2 Sam. 16:1; Isa. 28:4). Some suggest that Luke mentions the fig tree along with "all the trees" to avoid a limited association with Israel, whose judgment is sometimes associated with the fig tree (cf. Jer. 8:13; Mic. 7:1; see Danker 1988: 337).

The reference to the temporary nature of the original creation in 21:33a, "heaven and earth will pass away," echoes Ps. 102:25–26; Isa. 51:6; Jer. 4:23–26; cf. Amos 9:8 (cf. *1 En.* 72:1; 91:16; *Tg. Ps.* 102:27; 2 Pet. 3:10; Rev. 21:1; see Bock 1994–1996: 1692). The assertion in 21:33b that "my words will not pass away" echoes several OT passages that stress the immutability of Yahweh's words, such as Ps. 119:89, 160; Isa. 40:8; 55:10–11 (cf. Wis. 18:4; Bar. 4:1; *4 Ezra* 9:36–37). Jesus uses language that echoes OT assurances of the certainty and permanence of the word of Israel's covenant God in order to affirm the certainty and permanence of his own prophetic instruction (Green 1997: 742). This entails the claim that he is divine Lord. Jesus assures the disciples that no matter how long the interval and how distressing the tribulations of the last days will be, they will never lose confidence in his words, since the end will certainly come.

21:34–35

The phrase in 21:34a, "lest your hearts be weighed down" (*barēthōsin hymōn hai kardiai*), corresponds to the idiom used in the LXX to describe the hardening of Pharaoh's heart (Exod. 7:14: *bebarētai hē kardia pharaō*; 8:28 [8:32 ET]: *ebarunen pharaō tēn kardian autou*). It should be noted, however, that Jesus' exhortation links the phrase with "dissipation and drunkenness" (*en kraipalē kai methē*) and thus corresponds to the idiom "to be heavy with wine," an expression often used in Greek literature (Homer, *Od.* 3.139: *oinō bebarēotes*; cf. 19.122; see G. Schwartz 1979: 40), suggesting that a failure to be alert is in view rather than hard-heartedness. Quite possibly the exhortation in 21:34b, "Be on guard so that your hearts are not weighed down with dissipation and drunkenness," is reminiscent of the language of Isa. 24:20 ("The earth staggers like a drunkard, it sways like a hut; its transgression lies heavy upon it, and it falls, and will not rise again"), where the LXX has the same juxtaposition of "dissipation" and "drunkenness" (*hōs ho methyōn kai kraipalōn*). The exhortation includes a warning against literal drunkenness, but the primary sense is metaphorical, "warning disciples against succumbing to the intoxicating attractions of the sinful world" (Marshall 1978: 782; note also Rev. 14:8).

In 21:34 the phrase "like a trap" (*hōs pagis*) forms the end of the preceding clause, "[be on guard so that] that day does not catch you unexpectedly like a trap," if we follow those manuscripts that place *gar* after the verb *epeiseleusetai* (ℵ* B D 070 it co) (see Fitzmyer 1994–1996: 1356; Nolland 1989–1993: 1012). If we follow the manuscripts that place *gar* before *epeiseleusetai* (A C W Θ Ψ *f*¹.¹³ 33 𝔐 lat sy), then the phrase "like a trap" (*hōs pagis*) belongs at the beginning of the following clause, "[that day] will come like a trap upon all who live on the face of the whole earth" (*hōs pagis epeiseleusetai gar epi pantas tous kathēmenous epi prosōpon pasēs tēs gēs*) (see Zahn 1988: 659–60n7; Bock 1994–1996: 1694). The latter reading may have been influenced by the allusion to Isa. 24:17: *phobos kai bothynos kai pagis eph' hymas tous enoikountas epi tēs gēs* (see Metzger 1994: 147). If Luke indeed alludes to Isa. 24:17, a text that is part of Isaiah's oracle about the desolation of the earth, then he formulates Jesus' prophecy of universal judgment in terms of the fulfillment of OT prophecy and warns the disciples (21:34) that they will escape the judgment of the day of the Lord, which will affect all the inhabitants of the earth, only if they are "on guard."

22:1

The reference to the "Feast of Unleavened Bread [*hē heortē tōn azymōn*], which is called the Passover [*pascha*]" recalls the yearly feast instituted at the time of Israel's exodus from Egypt (Exod. 12:3–14; Num. 9:1–14; Deut. 16:1–8). The Feast of Passover (Heb. *pesaḥ*, Aram. *pashā'* or *pishā'*; in the LXX transliterated as *to pascha* [cf. Exod. 12:11, 21, 27, 43, 48], sometimes as *phasek* or *phasech* [cf. 2 Chron. 30:1, 2, 5; 35:1, 6, 7]) was prepared for by the slaughter of the lamb in the late hours of 14 Nisan and celebrated by the family after sundown—that is, on 15 Nisan (Lev. 23:6). Everything that had been prepared with yeast (leaven) had to be removed from the house before the Passover lamb was killed (Deut. 16:4; cf. *m. Pesaḥ.* 1:1–4), and unleavened bread continued to be eaten for seven days (Exod. 12:17–20; 23:15; 34:18). It was this seven-day period that was referred to as the "Feast of Unleavened Bread" (Heb. *ḥag hamaṣṣôt*), but already in the OT the term "Passover" was used for all seven or eight days (Deut. 16:1–4; Ezek. 45:21–25; cf. Josephus, *Ant.* 6.423; 20.106). Sometimes the term "Feast of Unleavened Bread" was used for the whole festive period (cf. Josephus, *J.W.* 2.280; *Ant.* 17.213), as

Luke does (22:1, 7). According to Exod. 34:23; Deut. 16:16 (cf. Exod. 23:15), all male Israelites were to appear before the Lord with an offering, a requirement that defined Passover, or the Feast of Unleavened Bread, as one of the pilgrim festivals when male Jews from other parts of Palestine or the Diaspora were expected to come to Jerusalem (see Fitzmyer 1981–1985: 1:439–40; for the connection between Passover and Jesus' last meal with his disciples, see Routledge 2002). The celebration of the Passover in Jewish Palestine had a twofold dimension. First, the Passover meal represented the historical exodus of the people of Israel during the time of Moses, emphasizing the deliverance from bondage in Egypt by a recitation of the Passover liturgy based on Exod. 12. Second, the Passover meal anticipated the messianic deliverance of the last days that the prophets had announced and that Israel continued to hope for, expressed by the singing of the second part of the Hallel, particularly Ps. 118:26: "Blessed is the one who comes in the name of the LORD. We bless you from the house of the Lord" (see Fitzmyer 1981–1985: 1390).

The setting of Jesus' passion in the context of the Feast of Passover needs to be seen in the context of Jesus' fusing of the horizons between Passover and the kingdom of God (22:5–6, 15–16, 18–19, 29–30). Two questions arise: What kind of kingdom does Jesus assert that he ushers in? What is the connection between his suffering, death, and resurrection and the kingdom of God as it is related to Israel's self-identity before Yahweh in the exodus tradition? The juxtaposition of the passion narrative, which begins in 22:1, and the Passover (i.e., the exodus tradition) underscores the importance of sacrifice in relation to deliverance, the importance of acknowledging the gracious sovereignty of Israel's God as Israel's king, and the expectation of the new covenant that God had promised through Israel's prophets, brought to completion through Jesus' death (see Green 1997: 750–51; see also commentary below on 22:16).

22:10

In the context of Luke's narrative of the preparation for the Passover meal (22:7–14), Jesus' instructions to the disciples in 22:10–12 have been understood by some scholars to echo Samuel's instructions to Saul just after his anointment as king. The words "When you have entered the city [a man carrying a jar of water] will meet you" (*eiselthontōn hymōn eis tēn polin synantēsei...*) have verbal parallels with 1 Sam. 10:5 ("There, as you come to the town, you will meet [*eiselthēte ekei eis tēn polin kai apantēseis*] a band of prophets coming down from the shrine"). The fact that both narratives deal with signs delivered by a prophet and that both mention a man carrying a vessel as part of the sign suggests to some scholars that the verbal parallels represent a deliberate allusion (Boismard 1972: 2:377). However, in view of the fact that the phrase *eiserchomai eis tēn polin* occurs fourteen times in the LXX, and in view of the fact that Luke's wording destroys the syntax of 1 Sam. 10:5 LXX, it is unlikely that Luke alludes here to the OT (Schürmann 1953: 93–94; Larkin 1974: 108–9).

22:14–16

The reference to the "hour" (22:14) in which Jesus sat down with his disciples to eat the Passover meal (22:15) alludes to a stipulation in Exod. 12:8: "They shall eat the lamb that same night; they shall eat it roasted over the fire with unleavened bread and bitter herbs" (see Schürmann 1953: 105). Whereas this allusion is historical and social in nature, Jesus' assertion in 22:16 that he will not eat the Passover meal again "until it is fulfilled in the kingdom of God" makes a theological point: Jesus fuses the Jewish hopes for a "new exodus" in the future messianic deliverance with his message of the dawn of the kingdom of God in the present, which will be consummated in the future (Fitzmyer 1981–1985: 1397; Green 1997: 759–60). Jesus' pronouncement concerning the "fulfillment" of the Passover "in the kingdom of God" refers either to the parousia and the messianic banquet (Jeremias 1966: 122–25; *TDNT* 5:900–904; Ellis 1974: 253; Stein 1992: 541; Green 1997: 760) or to the new age that Jesus' death inaugurates, specifically to Jesus' presence with his disciples in the Lord's Supper (Marshall 1978: 797, as a possibility). If the former view is indeed more likely (for a critique of the latter view, see Nolland 1989–1993: 1050; Bock 1994–1996: 1720–21), then the anticipated messianic banquet is interpreted as a Passover meal, celebrating God's mighty acts of deliverance that established the covenant at Mount Sinai as well

as the new covenant (cf. 22:20) inaugurated on Mount Zion.

Luke 22:17–20

Jesus' interpretation of the Passover meal in 22:19–20 (for the text-critical problem concerning 22:19b–20, and arguments for the authenticity of the longer text, see Larkin 1974: 137–43; Metzger 1994: 148–50; Fitzmyer 1981–1985: 1387–88) and in 22:19d, "This is my body, which is given for you [*to hyper hymōn didomenon*]," echoes the tradition of the Servant of Yahweh in Isa. 53 LXX. In Isa. 53 the Servant of Yahweh "gives" himself (53:10 LXX: "if you give [*dōte*] your life for sin"), and at the same time he is "given" by Yahweh (53:6 LXX: "and the LORD has laid [*paredōken*] on him our sins"; 53:12 LXX: "he was delivered [*paredothē*] to death"). The texts are linked through the verb *didōmi*, which can be used with reference to sacrifice (cf. Exod. 30:14; Lev. 22:14) and to martyrdom (Isa. 53:10), which holds true for the preposition *hyper* as well. Some suggest that both the sacrificial and the martyrological motifs are present (Marshall 1978: 803), while others focus on the sacrificial concepts (Schürmann 1955: 20, 28, 116–17; Fitzmyer [1981–1985: 1401] acknowledges that the text affirms the vicarious aspect of Jesus' life and death, but he does not see a connection with the Servant of Yahweh tradition).

The formula "for you" (*hyper hymōn*) is best understood not in terms of the death of the Jewish martyrs (cf. 2 Macc. 7:9; 8:21; 4 Macc. 1:8–11; 6:29–30; 17:21–22), but in terms of the guilt offering and/or sin offering (cf. Lev. 5:7; 6:23; Ezek. 43:21; see Schürmann 1955: 22–23, 101–2).

The sentence in 22:19e, "Do this in remembrance of me" (*touto poieite eis tēn emēn anamnēsin*), echoes statements in the Passover narrative that this feast was to be celebrated by Israel's future generation in remembrance of God's deliverance of his people from slavery in Egypt (Exod. 12:14, 25–27; 13:3, 9, 14; Deut. 16:3). Both meals commemorate a saving act of God, the Lord's Supper replacing the Passover as the new covenant replaces the old covenant. The interpretation of this phrase as meaning "Do this so that God may remember me" (Jeremias 1966: 237–55) is implausible (see Larkin 1974: 163–64).

In 22:20 Luke formulates the saying about the cup thus: "This cup [*touto to potērion*] that is poured out for you is the new covenant in my blood [*hē kainē diathēkē en tō haimati mou*]." This wording removes Mark's more explicit reference to Exod. 24:8: "Moses took the blood and dashed it on the people, and said, 'See the blood of the covenant [*idou to haima tēs diathēkēs*] that the LORD has made with you in accordance with all these words'" (Mark 14:24 and Matt. 26:28 read, "This is my blood of the covenant [*touto estin to haima mou tēs diathēkēs*], which is poured out for many"). Luke introduces the term "new" (*kainē*) and places the term "blood" (*haima*) in a prepositional phrase. Whereas Mark relates *touto* to the wine in the cup, which represents the blood of Jesus, interpreted as the blood that inaugurates a (new) covenant, Luke (and Paul) relates *touto* to the cup that is, together with its contents, the symbol of the new covenant, which the blood of Jesus inaugurated (Marshall 1978: 805–6).

The OT background of the phrase in 22:20, "in my blood which is poured out for you" (*en tō haimati mou to hyper hymōn ekchynnomenon*), is less clear. Scholars see (1) a material allusion to the sacrificed paschal lamb, with its redemptive shedding of blood, thus to Exod. 12:6–7, 13 (Larkin 1974: 157); (2) a material allusion to the bloody sacrifice that established the Mosaic covenant, thus to Exod. 24:8; Zech. 9:11 (Moo 1983: 302; Green 1997: 763 with note 74); (3) a verbal allusion to the Hebrew text of Isa. 53:12 (Marshall 1978: 807); (4) a phrase that simply expresses violent death (Fitzmyer 1981–1985: 1403; Green 1997: 762).

First, since the context of Jer. 31:31–34 contrasts the new covenant with the covenant made at the time of the exodus without referring specifically to Exod. 24, some scholars conclude that the phrases that follow the reference to the "new covenant" allude to the blood of the Passover lamb and not to the blood of the covenant at Sinai. The advantage of seeing the phrase "the new covenant in my blood which is poured out for you" as based in the narrative of the exodus Passover is "that the blood at the Passover functions to bring salvation, protection from the wrath of God, just as now Jesus' poured blood on their behalf will bring them salvation" (Larkin 1974:

158). We should note, however, that the blood of the Passover lamb is never described, in its original context, as the blood of a covenant, which creates a difficulty for identifying in 22:20 an allusion to Exod. 12:6–7, 13.

Second, in regard to a possible allusion to Exod. 24:8, it can be argued that the controlling factor in the formation of Luke's "liturgical formula" was not the desire to allude verbally to the OT, since the words of institution "probably derive their syntactical form from the ritual of Passover haggadah" (Larkin 1974: 152). Since Exod. 24:8 does not view the blood of the covenant ceremony as atoning sacrifice, some scholars suggest that we need to look elsewhere for the notion that the pouring out of blood has redemptive significance for the many. It should be noted that in *Targum Onqelos* and *Targum Pseudo-Jonathan* the sacrifice of Exod. 24:8 is regarded as making atonement for the people, which may suggest that this sacrifice was interpreted in contemporary Judaism as having atoning significance (Larkin 1974: 158n2). In regard to Matthew's inclusion of the phrase "for the forgiveness of sins" (*eis aphesin hamartiōn*), which recalls Jer. 31:34 (38:34 LXX), and in regard to his inclusion of the phrase "blood of the covenant," which recalls Exod. 24:8, it has been argued that both allusions may have originally existed side by side, and that the Gospel tradition emphasized one or the other of the allusions (France 1971: 94; Larkin 1974: 153). Several scholars advance the same argument for Luke's explanation of the cup, assuming an allusion both to Exod. 24:8, with a focus on the covenant sacrifice, and to Jer. 31:31, with an emphasis on the new covenant, which reflects the "old covenant" and is established by the blood of Jesus (Fitzmyer 1981–1985: 1402; Nolland 1989–1993: 1054; Green 1997: 763). In the Targum the covenant sacrifice of Exod. 24:8 is interpreted as an atoning sacrifice that effected Yahweh's covenant with the people of Israel. The allusion of the cup saying to Exod. 24:8 establishes a typological relationship between the covenant sacrifice at Sinai and Jesus' death on the cross, expressing the conviction that Jesus' death atones for the sins of the people, enabling them to become part of the new covenant with God that had been anticipated for the messianic last days (Green 1997: 763). If Jesus alludes to Exod. 24:8, then an allusion to Zech. 9:11 ("As for you also, because of the blood of my covenant [*en haima diathēkēs*] with you, I will set your prisoners free from the waterless pit") may be present as well. In Zech. 9:11 the phrase "in the blood of the covenant" refers to the future release of captives, and thus it is reminiscent of the bloody sacrifice of the Passover lamb on the occasion of the exodus. Similarly, the Targum of Zech 9:11 associates this new redemption of the release of Israel's captives with the exodus.

Third, several scholars suggest that the phrase "the blood . . . poured out for many" in the saying about the cup alludes to the Hebrew text of Isa. 53:12: "He poured out himself to death, and was numbered with the transgressors; yet he bore the sin of many, and made intercession for the transgressors" (see France 1971: 122; Leske 1995: 262; Marshall 1978: 807). The parallels in Mark 14:14; Matt. 26:28 with Isa. 53:12 are more readily discernible, particularly in the phrase *hyper pollōn* ("for the many"), where Luke 22:20 has *hyper hymōn* ("for you"). This change has been explained either as a result of the adaptation of the tradition to the use in the liturgy of the early church (*TDNT* 6:543) or as a clarification for Gentile Christians who may understand *polloi* ("the many") in an exclusive sense instead of the inclusive sense of Hebrew *rabîm* (Maurer 1953: 18). This change does not eliminate the material allusion to Isa. 53:12, which is the only OT passage in which a person chosen by God pours out his life for "the many" (Wolff 1952: 65–66; Larkin 1974: 160). If *hyper hymōn* is accepted as a material allusion to Isa. 53:12, then it provides an important link between the death of Jesus and the salvation of the "new covenant," explaining how Jesus' death can be redemptive (Lindars 1961: 78; for a discussion whether Jewish martyrological thinking provides a more plausible background, see Larkin 1974: 173–80).

The reference to "blood" in 22:20 possibly has another OT connotation, as Jesus asserts that his life is involved, alluding to Lev. 17:11: "For the life of the flesh is in the blood; and I have given it to you for making atonement for your lives on the altar; for, as life, it is the blood that makes atonement" (cf. Lev. 17:14: "For the life of all flesh is its blood"). If Jesus intended his disciples to think

of this text, then the emphasis is on the cultic and vicarious significance of his death (see Fitzmyer 1981–1985: 1402; Bock 1994–1996: 1727).

Luke's emphasis of the "new covenant" theme, with its reference to the eschatological vision of Jer. 31:31, highlights, in the context of the Passover meal that Jesus celebrated with his disciples, the contrast between God's redemptive action in the exodus and his new redemptive act in Jesus' death, fulfilling the Sinaitic "old" covenant and inaugurating the new covenant. A typological interpretation of Exod. 24:8 can include such a future reference as well; Jer. 31:31 refers to this future aspect more explicitly. In Jer. 31 the "new covenant" is established by God, who puts his law in the minds and hearts of his people who have continuously broken his (old) covenant, declaring himself to be their God, and declaring the people of Israel and Judah to be his people, as he forgives their sins. In Luke 22:15–20 God establishes the new covenant through Jesus' death, as he pours out his blood for his followers.

Jesus explains that his mission, soon to be accomplished in his death, inaugurates the new covenant by drawing on Isa. 53; Exod. 24:8; Jer. 31:31–34. This mission can be achieved only by fulfilling the role of the Isaianic Servant of Yahweh in his vicarious death (France 1971: 123).

22:21–23

Jesus' prediction of his betrayal by one of his disciples in 22:21, "But see, the one who betrays me is with me, and his hand is on the table," possibly echoes Ps. 41:9 (40:10 LXX): "Even my bosom friend in whom I trusted, who ate of my bread, has lifted the heel against me." There are no verbal parallels, but the possibility cannot be excluded that Jesus points to the suffering of the righteous person in Ps. 41, who was betrayed by a table companion, in order to emphasize both the insidious nature of Judas's betrayal and the notion that he suffers innocently (Green [1997: 764–65] speaks of "reverberations"). Note that Jesus refers in 22:22 to the will of God (for the phrase "as it has been determined" [*kata to hōrismenon*], see Acts 2:23; 10:42; 11:29; 17:26, 31; see also Fitzmyer 1981–1985: 1409–10). The use of the verb *paradidōmi* is probably again (as in 17:25; 18:32) an allusion to the Suffering Servant of Isa. 53 (Lindars 1961: 80–81; Moo 1983: 92–96; Strauss 1995: 328).

Luke 22:24–38

Jesus' remarks about greatness in the kingdom of God (22:24–30) contains several OT allusions. The statement in 22:27, "I am among you as one who serves [*ho diakonōn*]," summing up Jesus' life and ministry, has been regarded by some scholars as a material allusion to Isa. 53:12, building on the correspondence between the service of the Servant of Yahweh for "the many" and Jesus' service in and through his ministry (Lindars 1961: 78n1; Rese 1969: 164). Luke's characterization of Jesus' service emphasizes his relationship to people. This represents, perhaps, a reinterpretation of the service of the Servant of Yahweh, emphasizing that Jesus' obedience in his saving action is a service for "the many." This suggestion has convinced few interpreters, however, since the service that Jesus commends to his disciples is humility, an image derived from table-serving (Fitzmyer 1981–1985: 1418), while the "saving" work of the Servant of Yahweh in Isa. 53 is primarily described in terms of his relationship with and obedience to God (Larkin 1974: 215; cf. Leske 1995: 261).

In 22:30b, "You will sit on thrones judging the twelve tribes of Israel" recalls the imagery of Israel's tribes and of thrones in Ps. 122:4–5: "To it the tribes go up, the tribes of the LORD, as was decreed for Israel, to give thanks to the name of the LORD. For there the thrones for judgment were set up, the thrones of the house of David." It should be noted that in Luke's context the "thrones" are kingly thrones for ruling and are not restricted to judging (Fitzmyer 1981–1985: 1418). Even though Luke does not make the reference to the OT passage explicit, he may have formulated Jesus' promise as an allusion to Ps. 121 to underline the authority of the promise, perhaps hinting at the continuity with the OT promises (Larkin 1974: 218). Psalm 121 itself is not a prophetic text: it praises Jerusalem and mentions the conditions at the time when the kingdom of the Davidic messiah arrives. Rather than focusing on the specific content of the psalm, Luke's allusion, if present and when seen in the larger context of his Gospel, forms part of his presentation of Jesus as the Davidic messiah (Larkin 1974: 218). Jesus' statement may also allude to Dan. 7:9–18, a text that describes the bestowal of the kingdom upon the Son of Man and the "saints of the Most High" (Dupont 1964: 380; Marshall 1978: 818; Allison

2000a: 138–39). This is the only text in the OT that speaks of a group of judges at the last judgment (Reiser 1997: 262). The allusion to Dan. 7 confirms that Jesus' prophecy is the prophecy of Scripture: when the disciples "rule" God's people, they bring to realization Israel's hopes as expressed in Daniel (Allison 2000a: 139).

22:31–34

According to the Gospel of Mark, Jesus announced on the way to Gethsemane that all the disciples would be scandalized because of him (Mark 14:27), an announcement that is confirmed as the plan of God by the quotation of Zech. 13:7. Since this is the only explicit OT quotation in Mark's passion narrative, we need to understand why—on the assumption that Luke followed Mark—Luke omitted it (for the following material, see Larkin 1974: 238–41). First, on compositional grounds, we note that Luke's account is placed in the context of the Last Supper and presented as a farewell discourse. The focus is on Jesus, much less on interaction between Peter and Jesus, which explains why Luke does not follow Mark at this point. Second, a theological reason may be Luke's theme of the solidarity of Jesus with his disciples, a major theme in the discourse during the Last Supper (Luke 22:11, 15, 28, 33; cf. 22:40, 46), which prompted him to remove any suggestion that Jesus was forsaken by his followers.

In 22:31–32, "Simon, Simon, listen! Satan has demanded to sift all of you like wheat, but I have prayed for you that your own faith may not fail; and you, when once you have turned back, strengthen your brothers," Luke explains Peter's denial with an allusion to Job 1:6–12 (Larkin 1974: 241–43; Marshall 1978: 820; Fitzmyer 1981–1985: 1424). Job 1:6–12 is the only OT passage where "Satan" (a term not used in Job 1) demands in God's presence that a righteous person be exposed to trials that test his faithfulness to God. The formulation of Satan's intention ("to sift all of you like wheat") echoes Amos 9:9: "For lo, I will command, and shake the house of Israel among all the nations as one shakes with a sieve." The prophet uses the image of winnowing in his message that God will preserve Israel, the "good grain." In 22:31 it is Satan, not God, who sifts the disciples, and Satan's purpose is to preserve not the good grain, but rather the "chaff," which their abandonment of Jesus represents and which serves as evidence in Satan's case as accuser of the disciples before God (cf. Zech. 3:1). Despite these and other (linguistic) differences, the thought is similar (Fitzmyer 1981–1985: 1424; differently, Larkin [1974: 243], who sees not an allusion to Amos 9:9 but the use of an OT metaphor for judgment).

It is debated whether Jesus' prediction of Peter's "turning back" (*kai sy epistrephas*) in 22:32b echoes 2 Sam. 15:20: "Go back, and take your brethren with you" (*epistrepsou kai epistrepson tous adelphous sou*). Since the verb *epistrephō* in the latter passage is used in a geographical sense, while Peter's "turning" is moral or religious, this is an unlikely possibility (see Fitzmyer 1981–1985: 1425).

22:37

A. NT Context: New Instructions for the Impending Crisis.

The conclusion of Jesus' farewell discourse at the Last Supper in 22:35–38 is peculiar to the Gospel of Luke. In view of the impending crisis, Jesus modifies advice that he had given to the disciples at an earlier time (10:3–12). After quotations from the book of Isaiah in 3:4–6 (Isa. 40:3–5) and in 4:18–19 (Isa. 61:1–2), the final citation from Isaiah is found in 22:37, quoting Isa. 53:12. This is the only text in the Gospel tradition that explicitly quotes from Isaiah's fourth Servant Song (see Fitzmyer 1981–1985: 1432; Stendahl 1968: 94; France [1971: 114–16], who defends the authenticity of the saying; Dunn [2003: 809–17] remains skeptical). The narrative of Jesus' final supper with his disciples points forward to Jesus' imminent passion: Jesus describes this meal to be the last Passover meal before his suffering (22:15–18). He refers to his imminent death (22:19–20); he emphasizes servant leadership with reference to his own example (22:24–27); he promises his disciples a share in the kingly reign that God has given to him (22:28–30); he emphasizes that the coming events in which he will be involved represent the fulfillment of Scripture, quoting Isa. 53:12 (22:37). Placing the quotation from Isa. 53 at the beginning of his passion narrative, and prefacing the quotation by a long and emphatic introductory formula ("For I tell you, this scripture must be fulfilled in me"), Luke wants his readers to understand Isaiah's fourth Servant Song as the hermeneutical key to the narrative of Jesus' suffering and death (Schwemer 1998: 18–19; cf. Larkin

1974: 329–35; Moo 1983: 132–33; Strauss 1995: 326; Green 1990; Neagoe 2002: 80; on Isaiah's Suffering Servant in the Gospels, see France 1971: 110–32).

The recent suggestion that the word about the swords in 22:36–37 echoes the OT tradition of Yahweh as "divine warrior" (cf. Exod. 15:3; Deut. 32:40–43; Ps. 24:8; Isa. 27:1; 42:13; 51:19; 59:17; 66:16; Ezek. 21:3–5; see Kruger 1997) is implausible, since it ignores the context of the OT quotation in 22:36–38.

B. Isa. 53 in Context.

Isaiah 53:12 belongs to the fourth Servant Song (52:13–53:12), which answers the open question of the third Servant Song in 50:4–9 of whether the Suffering Servant, whose future was entirely in Yahweh's hands, failed totally in the eyes of Israel and in the eyes of the nations (Janowski 1996: 36). The fourth Servant Song shows, first, that the consequences of the sins of the people, which the people would not and could not carry, are placed upon the Suffering Servant: Yahweh, who takes the initiative (53:6, 10), directs the nexus of sin and judgment not against Israel, but against the Suffering Servant, who perishes while the people are saved. Second, as the "we" recognize these events, they acknowledge the guilt that the Suffering Servant carried as their own guilt: the confession of guilt and sin in 53:4–6 is the presupposition for Israel's future and the presupposition for the forgiveness of sin and for the transformation of Israel, since only the repentant and transformed "offspring" of the Suffering Servant will return into fellowship with Yahweh (Janowski 1996: 44).

The statement in 53:12 forms the second of four statements that conclude the prophet's account of the suffering of a human agent whose death atones for the sins of "the many." The first two statements describe the servant's suffering from an objective perspective: (1) "he poured out his soul to death" (LXX: "his soul was handed over to death"); (2) "he was numbered with the transgressors." The next two statements describe the theological significance of the servant's suffering: (3) "he bore the sin of many"; (4) "he made intercession for the transgressors" (LXX: "he was handed over because of theirs sins"). The Hebrew verb *mânâh* ("to count, number") is translated in the LXX with *logizomai*, which normally translates *ḥâšab* ("to think, account, esteem, reckon"), perhaps "as an attempt to interpret the summary phrase in the light of that earlier description of the people's low estimation of the suffering Servant" (Larkin 1974: 273, with reference to Isa. 53:3, 4). While the Hebrew verb *mânâh* emphasizes the classification to which the Suffering Servant has been assigned, the Greek verb *logizomai* introduces inferences about the character of the act of evaluation (cf. P.Lond. 328:8, which states that a camel's colt that is fully grown may be "classified" with the mature camels), possibly including the notion of subjective prejudice (Larkin 1974: 273; for the following discussion, see ibid., 273ff). The class of persons to whom the Suffering Servant is assigned is described with the term *pōšě'îm*, translated into Greek with the term *anomōn*, which is used in the LXX to describe people who are fundamentally irreligious or disloyal to God, as demonstrated in, for example, rebelliousness and disobedience to the law (cf. Ps. 50:15 [51:13 ET]; Prov. 28:10), sometimes designating pagans as "sinners" pure and simple (cf. Esther 4:17).

In the context of the fourth Servant Song, to be "reckoned with transgressors" means to experience rejection, distress, ill-treatment (Isa. 53:3, 4), to be regarded by people as someone whom God has smitten (53:4), since God brings judgment upon evildoers (cf. 1 Kings 8:32; 2 Chron. 6:23; Job 19:29; 34:17; Ps. 37:28). As the larger context of the Servant Song indicates that the servant was innocent, the prophet asserts that he was smitten for the sins of the people (Isa. 53:8, 12). This point of theological explanation is present not so much in the statement itself, but rather in the passive voice of the (Greek) verb, implying divine activity that is emphasized by the fact that the fourth Servant Song begins with God's perspective (52:13) and ends with God's perspective (53:11–12) (see Janowski 1996: 36–37).

C. Isa. 53 in Judaism. The changes in the Isaiah scroll 1QIsa^a compared with 1QIsa^b also suggest that the text Isa. 52:13–53:12 was of greater importance for the Qumran community than many scholars are prepared to argue (see Hengel 1996: 66–69). For example, the word *mišḥat* or *mašḥēt* ("devastation") in 52:14, a difficult *hapax legomenon*, is changed by the addition of a final *yod* to *māšaḥtî* ("I have anointed"), and the noun *'ādām* is provided with an article, so that the text reads, "In accordance with the fact that many were

horrified about you, I have anointed his countenance, in contrast to any [other] human being and his form in contrast to the sons of man [or Adam]." This "priestly" anointing would help to explain the first line of 52:15: the Suffering Servant sprinkles (cf. Aquila: *rhantisei*) "many nations" in order to purify them from their sins (see Hengel 1996: 68; for a possible messianic interpretation of 52:13–53:12 in the LXX, see ibid. 75–85).

The publication of 4Q541 and 4Q491 has demonstrated that earlier claims that Isa. 53 was not a significant text in Second Temple Judaism were misguided (see Zimmermann 1998: 247–77, 285–310, 475). In 4Q541, an Aramaic text that displays similarities with *Testament of Levi*, frg. 9 seems to represent an interpretation of Yahweh's Suffering Servant in Isa. 53 in terms of a priestly figure: note the atoning activity of the servant (frg. 9 I, 2; cf. Isa. 53:10); the references to "his generation" (frg. 9 I, 1, 2, 6; cf. Isa. 53:8), to pain (frg. 6 I, 3; frg. 2 II, 3; cf. Isa. 53:3–4), to mocking, lies, and verbal attacks (frg. 9 I, 5–7; cf. Isa. 53:2–10), and to physical violence (frg. 9 I, 7; cf. Isa. 53:9). A comparison of 4Q541 with Isa. 53 MT/LXX and the Targum shows that *Tg. Isa.* 53 avoids all statements that point to the suffering of the servant (who is interpreted as the "king messiah" who teaches the law, rebuilds the temple, and forgives sin through intercessory prayer; see Ådna 1996: 145–58). The relevant phrases of Isa. 53 MT are not eliminated altogether, but they appear in a modified form. The Messiah "will build the sanctuary which was profaned for our sins" (*Tg. Isa.* 53:5). He will intercede for Israel's iniquities, which will be forgiven for his sake (*Tg. Isa.* 53:4). And "by his teaching his peace will increase upon us" (*Tg. Isa.* 53:5). 4Q541 stands between this version of the Targum and Isa. 53 MT: at least the extant fragments no longer speak of vicarious suffering, but the figure whose actions are described will bring about atonement for sins, and like the Targum, the text emphasizes the significance of the servant's teaching (Zimmermann 1998: 270). It is possible that 4Q541 is an early individualistic interpretation of the Servant Song in Isa. 53 that aims in a cultic direction, portraying the Messiah not as a king (as the later Targum), but as a priestly figure (Brooke 1993). The actions of the priest appear to reflect the actions of the Suffering Servant of Isa. 53, evident in the references to his mission, to light, to slander, to suffering/sacrifice, and to his ministry benefiting others. The Davidic-messianic interpretation of the later rabbis, attested in the Targum, may have displaced an older interpretation that focused on an eschatological priest whose sapiential and didactic characteristics were retained, as was the motif of an action for the sake of, and benefiting, sinners (Zimmermann 1998: 271; cf. Brooke 1993: 100; Hengel 1996: 74–75). Some suggest that he is the eschatological high priest (e.g., Zimmermann 1998: 308, 310), while others suggest a messianic figure (e.g., Hengel 1996: 88–90). Since there is no consensus concerning the identification of the speaker of 4Q491, the significance of the connection with Isa. 53 (for details, see Zimmermann 1998: 306) is not entirely clear. The speaker is a person whom God has given a throne in the heavenly assembly of the angels, and who evidently interprets his status and his history with the tradition of the Servant of Yahweh of Isa. 50:4–9; 52:13–53:12.

In regard to the interpretation of Isa. 53 in the LXX, it has been repeatedly noted that the Greek translation reflects the statements of the Hebrew text that the Suffering Servant bore the sins and weaknesses of the many, and that he was reckoned among the sinners even though he was innocent, but the translators did not view the actions of the servant as constituting an atoning sacrificial death (cf. Isa. 53:9a, 10–11b LXX; see Sapp 1998).

There was no unified interpretation of the Servant Songs in general and of Isa. 53 in particular in Second Temple Judaism to which Luke's quotation could appeal. One Jewish tradition identifies the Servant of Yahweh with the "righteous one," interpreting his suffering as the lot of the righteous (Wis. 2:20; 5:1). Another tradition identifies the servant as the Messiah (*Tg. Isa.* 52:13–53:12), relating his suffering to Israel (*Tg. Isa.* 52:14; 53:4, 10), to the nations that oppress Israel (*Tg. Isa.* 53:3, 8), or to the wicked (*Tg. Isa.* 53:9), since the Messiah, understood as a zealous victor, cannot suffer (Chilton 1987: 103, 105).

D. Textual Matters. The text of the quotation from Isa. 53:12 in Luke 22:37—Luke reads *kai meta anomōn elogisthē* ("And he was counted with lawless people")—diverges from the LXX, which has *kai en tois anomois elogisthē* (quoted in

Justin, *Dial.* 13.7; 89.3; *1 Apol.* 50.2 reads *meta tōn anomōn elogisthē* and *kai tois anomois exilasetai*). Whereas no LXX manuscript supports Luke's text, the latter is paralleled in the variant reading in Mark 15:28: *kai eplērōthē hē graphē hē legousa: kai meta anomōn elogisthē* ("And the Scripture was fulfilled which says: 'And he was counted with lawless people'" [L Θ 083 0250 *f* [1.13] 33 𝔐 lat sy[p.h] Eus]). This variant reading at Mark 15:28 is generally reckoned to be derived from Luke 22:37 (see C. A. Evans 2001: 497). Whereas the quotation from Isa. 53:12 is used in Luke 22:37 to describe Jesus' awareness that what is about to happen is the fulfillment of what Isaiah had written in Scripture about the fate of the Servant of Yahweh, the quotation in Mark 15:28, which is inserted after the comment that two thieves were crucified together with Jesus (15:27), is included as scriptural fulfillment of (merely) the circumstances of Jesus' death (Holtz 1968: 41n5). The MT reads *wĕʾet pōšĕʿîm nimnâ* ("and with transgressors he was counted"), which is reflected in Luke's quotation (Wolff 1952: 57; Stendahl 1968: 94; Rese [1969: 154] traces the quotation to the MT; Larkin [1974: 259–62] thinks that the quotation was originally based on the MT and was later assimilated to the LXX; others argue for a derivation from the LXX: Holtz [1968: 42–43] points to the fact that both Luke and the LXX text use the verb *logizomai*, a translation that the LXX uses for the Hebrew verb *mânâh* only in Isa. 53:12; 2 Chron. 5:6; note that Aquila and Symmachus translate in Isa. 53:12 with *ērithmēthē*). The substitution of the preposition *en* by *meta* is probably due to stylistic considerations and does not imply a particular theological nuance.

E. The Use of Isa. 53:12 in Luke 22:37. The verbs used in the introductory formula in Luke 22:37 (*dei telesthēnai*) characterize Luke's hermeneutical approach in this passage in terms of the scheme of promise and fulfillment, where the promise of Scripture becomes the promise of Jesus. Jesus' quotation of Isa. 53:12 underlines his claim to fulfill the role of the Servant of Yahweh, of whom the prophet had written, "Therefore I will allot him a portion with the great, and he shall divide the spoil with the strong; because he poured out himself to death, and was numbered with the transgressors; yet he bore the sin of many, and made intercession for the transgressors." Some argue that the fact that Jesus quotes from Isa. 53 at the beginning of the passion demonstrates that he understood his approaching death in the light of the fate of Isaiah's Suffering Servant: "If Jesus saw these words as destined to be fulfilled in him, and as written about him, it is hard to avoid the conclusion that he identified himself with the one of whom they were written, the Servant of Yahweh" (France 1971: 116; see also Bock 1987: 138; cf. Grundmann 1978: 409). Luke was familiar with the Christian interpretation of Isa. 53 in terms of Jesus and with the text of Isa. 53 itself, as Acts 8:32–33 demonstrates (Wolff 1952: 91; Holtz 1968: 42; Ploch 1993: 188–89).

In addition to this function as a prophetic promise, the quotation from Isa. 53:12 has another function: it provides the reason why the disciples need to make provisions for their own support and defense (Larkin 1974: 277). The relationship of these two functions has been a matter of debate. Some suggest that the quotation is introduced by Luke in order to clarify, for the disciples, a possible misunderstanding of the use of swords, interpreting the instruction to buy a sword by the explanation that Jesus does not fight but is willing to be treated as a transgressor (Conzelmann 1960: 83). It may be argued that the "explanation function" and the "fulfillment function" of the quotation should each be allowed to exist independently: the disciples, who are not personally involved in the fulfillment of Isa. 53:12, are asked to take precautions because the situation in which they will find themselves is analogous to the situation that Jesus experiences in his fulfillment of Isa. 53:12. Luke argues on the basis of the disciples' identity with Jesus, reversing the terms of the *a maiori ad minus* argument: the followers of Jesus should not expect to be treated differently than their master, and since the master, by divine necessity, must be reckoned with the transgressors, the disciples should expect no better lot. The causal relationship between Jesus' fulfillment of Isa. 53:12 and the disciples' situation in which they need to take precautions is not contingent upon Jesus' fulfillment of prophecy but rather exists on account of the disciples' solidarity with Jesus (Larkin 1974: 278).

Since Luke's only other use of the term *anomos* in the Gospel and Acts (Acts 2:23) may refer to "pagans" in a pejorative sense (differently, Conzelmann 1960: 91), some scholars suggest that Luke may want to emphasize that Jesus was unjustly crucified by godless pagans. It is impossible, however, to draw such a far-reaching conclusion from such scarce evidence. It is preferable to assume in 22:37 either the more general meaning of "lawless transgressor" or the more specialized meaning of "criminal" (assuming that Jesus asks the disciples to defend against being treated as outlaws or enemies of society), or both (Larkin 1974: 275–76).

What is the occasion at which Isa. 53:12 is fulfilled? Scholars suggest several places in the passion narrative as constituting the fulfillment of this prophecy: (1) Jesus' arrest (Zahn 1988: 685); (2) the exchange of Jesus for Barabbas (D. G. Miller 1960: 163); (3) Jesus' crucifixion between two criminals (Rese 1969: 156; Bock 1987: 138; 1994–1996: 1748); (4) the disciples with their reliance on swords (Minear 1964–1965; Tannehill 1986–1990: 1:265–68; Rusam 2003: 246–52). The lack of clear verbal parallels between Luke's narration of Jesus' arrest and of his exchange for Barabbas makes the first two suggestions unlikely. The third suggestion is supported by the fact that only Luke describes the two criminals as *kakourgoi* (22:32) and that Jesus' crucifixion between two criminals literally fulfills his being numbered with transgressors. However, the lack of verbal agreement and the lack of editorial comment concerning the fulfillment of Scripture suggests again that Luke does not see Isa. 53:12 fulfilled in this specific incident. As for the fourth suggestion, it is unlikely that Jesus would label his disciples as "lawless," despite their failure to remain faithful. Thus it appears that Luke has the whole course of events of Jesus' passion in view, which is plausible because Luke quotes Isa. 53:12 at the end of Jesus' interpretation of his suffering and at the beginning of the events of Jesus' passion (Larkin 1974: 279–83). The quotation in 22:37 thus represents "the objective basis for the soteriological significance of the death of Jesus" (Larkin 1974: 294).

F. Theological Use of Isa. 53:12 in Luke 22. Luke quotes Isa. 53:12 to show that Jesus' ignominious death, as seen in his being treated as a transgressor, was destined by God's will as prophesied in Scripture (Larkin 1974: 283–87). This can be understood christologically in terms of martyrdom. More likely, however, it can be understood soteriologically, analogous to the main thrust of Isa. 53, in terms of vicarious atonement: as the suffering of the innocent servant is explained in Isa. 53:12 with reference to the servant's vicarious atonement for the sins of the many, so Luke explains Jesus' suffering as the innocent righteous one, condemned as a transgressor, with reference to God's will as expressed in Isaiah's prophecy, prompting his readers to reflect on the explanation for these events that God has ordained.

22:38

Some scholars suggest that Jesus' response to the disciples' statement in 22:38, that they have two swords, with the words "It is enough" (*hikanon estin*) is an allusion to 1 Kings 19:4, in a text in which Elijah asks God that he might die: "It is enough [*hikanousthō*]; now, O LORD, take away my life, for I am no better than my ancestors" (see Crockett 1966b: 318). However, the mere similarity of the Greek term used cannot establish an allusion to Elijah and his resigned and misguided desire to die in the desert.

22:39–46

Some scholars suggest that since there were no eyewitnesses to Jesus' agony in the Garden of Gethsemane, as the disciples had fallen asleep, the scene has been created from OT passages. Some scholars point to similarities with Job 42:2; Ps. 88:9, while others find OT allusions in Jesus' agony and sweat (22:44), identifying Jesus with Adam (Gen. 3:19), the Suffering Servant (Isa. 53:3, 10), or the suffering Righteous One (Ps. 22:2, 3, 15) (see Selwyn 1912: 367; Baldwin 1920: 431; Loisy 1924: 528; cf. Green 1986: 41–43). Apart from the fact that 22:43–44 may be secondary (omitted in $\mathfrak{P}^{69vid}$ $\mathfrak{P}^{75}$ $\aleph^1$ A B N T W 579 1071*; see Fitzmyer 1981–1985: 1443–44; Nolland 1989–1993: 1080; but see also R. E. Brown [1994: 180–86], who defends the originality of the verses), none of these passages "explains" Luke's text. This does not negate the fact that several OT allusions are present in this passage.

Jesus' prayer in 22:42 that God the Father might, if it is his will, remove "this cup" (*touto to potērion*) from Jesus echoes OT passages that link the metaphor of the "cup" to divine eschatological judgment (which is, however, not the final judgment) (cf. Isa. 51:17, 22; Jer. 25:15, 17, 28; Ezek. 23:31–34; Zech. 12:2). Luke reports Jesus asserting on the Mount of Olives that the eschatological judgment is about to begin. The fact that Jesus addresses God as "Father" may suggest that Jesus, who believes that God is able to remove the cup at any time, is convinced that even "while he is judged as the unrighteous, he is vindicated as the righteous one" (Bayer 1986: 77, with reference to Ps. 11:6–7).

The angel's intervention in 22:43 has been treated as an allusion to Elijah (1 Kings 19:5–6), or Dan. 3:28; 10:17–18 (Grundmann 1978: 412), or Ps. 91:11 (Loisy 1924: 528) (see also Marshall 1978: 832; Bock 1994–1996: 1760, referring to all three passages). The strongest case can be made for the first suggestion: both Jesus and Elijah face death, and in both cases an angel provides strength. However, since both the attitude of the two prophets and the purpose of the angel's intervention are different, it is unlikely that Luke wants his readers to see an allusion here (see Larkin 1974: 313–19). It is fair to say, however, that Luke's assertion that God confirms to Jesus by an angel that he must perform his will, taking the cup that God has ordained for him and being numbered with the transgressors, echoes in general terms the role of angels in the OT as God's messengers proclaiming God's will to human beings (see Larkin 1974: 326–29, with reference to Gen. 16:7–12; Exod. 3:2–12; Judg. 6:11–18).

22:47–53

Judas Iscariot's approach to Jesus in order to kiss him (22:47–48), the disciples' question (22:49), and the severing of the high priest's slave's ear (22:50–51) have been explained in terms of OT allusions. Before we look at these suggestions, we should note that Mark's reference to the fulfillment of Scripture in his account of Jesus' arrest (Mark 14:49: "Day after day I was with you in the temple teaching, and you did not arrest me. But let the scriptures be fulfilled") has been omitted in Luke 22:53 ("When I was with you day after day in the temple, you did not lay hands on me. But this is your hour, and the power of darkness!"). Some scholars explain this omission by appealing to Luke's perspective of wanting his readers to relive the events of salvation history that he narrates, limiting explicit references to fulfillment to the context of predictions that are made (22:22, 37), and to Luke's emphasis on the voluntary nature of Jesus' suffering (Larkin 1974: 336–40).

Judas's intention to kiss Jesus in 22:47–48 has been interpreted as an allusion to Joab's kiss of treachery (2 Sam. 20:9). Others compare the text with Prov. 27:6, which warns of the kisses of enemies (see Bultmann 1963: 281). We should note, however, that Luke does not explain the significance of Judas's kiss as a sign of identification and thus of betrayal (contrast this with Mark 14:44), and so the kiss may be nothing more than the traditional mode of greeting. Joab's kiss involved treachery, but Joab, the king's faithful general, does not betray David, prompting a typological reenactment of a detail in David's life in the life of Jesus, but rather Amasa, who is rebelling against David. The general maxim of Prov. 27:6 does not display sufficient material parallelism with Luke 22:47–48 to justify the identification of an allusion (Larkin 1974: 340).

Some suggest that the text represents a midrash that combined vv. 8, 5–6, 13 of Ps. 91 with Amos 3:12 as the source of Luke's new material (Doeve 1954, 168–74). This is said to account for the disciples' question in 22:49, "Lord, should we strike with the sword?" (cf. Ps. 91:8: "You will only look with your eyes and see the punishment of the wicked"), Jesus' words about the hour and the power of darkness in 22:53, "When I was with you day after day in the temple, you did not lay hands on me. But this is your hour, and the power of darkness!" (cf. Ps. 91:5–6: "You will not fear the terror of the night, or the arrow that flies by day, or the pestilence that stalks in darkness, or the destruction that wastes at noonday"), and the theme of nonretribution (Ps. 91:13, developed with the help of Amos 3:12 into the detail of the healing of the servant's ear, the word "lion" linking the two passages). These suggested links are unconvincing (Larkin 1974: 343–44).

22:63–65

Luke places the taunting of Jesus with the elements of mocking, beating, and blindfolding before the trial, presenting it as unprovoked and undeserved, underlining the theme of Jesus' innocence, which is part of Luke's emphasis on the fulfillment of Isa. 53:12 (cf. Luke 22:37). In contrast to Mark, Luke does not relate Jesus' mistreatment as having included being spat upon, an echo of the mistreatment of the Suffering Servant (Isa. 50:6 LXX: *emptysmatōn*) in Mark 14:65, where the verb *emptyō* is used.

The reference to Jesus being blindfolded (22:64) has been taken as an allusion to Isa. 53:3. We should note, however, that there is no verbal parallelism: 22:64 has *perikalypsantes*, while Isa. 53:3 has *apestraptai*. And the material parallelism is forced: in 22:64 the blindfolding serves the purpose of taunting Jesus to prophesy who struck him in the face, while the covering of the face of the servant in Isa. 53 is prompted by the disfigurement of the servant's face due to his suffering. While Isa. 53:3 may have "served as a control on what details were remembered," Luke's narrative is based on the historical recollection of his sources, accompanied by his understanding of prophetic fulfillment (Larkin 1974: 379). The blindfolding game may have been inspired by talk about Jesus as a prophet (cf. Luke 7:39; 9:7–8, 18–19), or by an existing game such as the *kollabismos*, in which a player with his eyes covered has to guess whether another player has struck him with his left or with his right hand, or the *chalkē miya*, in which a blindfolded player has to find other players who strike him with papyrus husks (see Nolland 1989–1993: 1099).

Rather than alluding to the specific experiences of the Suffering Servant (Isa. 50:5; 53:3) as Mark does, or to specific terms in the Suffering Servant texts, Luke's narration of Jesus' abuse (22:63: *empaizō, derō*; 22:64: *perikalyptō, paiō*; 22:65: *blasphemeō*) focuses on the theme of unprovoked unjust treatment, as suggested by the setting and the content of the passage (Larkin 1974: 379–83; for the following comments, see ibid., 83–84; Green 1997: 789). Luke's narrative of Jesus' mistreatment may remind readers of the figure of the martyr and of the righteous person who suffer abuse unjustly (see Bock [1994–1996: 1790], who points to Isa. 50:6; 53:3; Ps. 69:7–13), a motif sometimes linked with taunts suggesting the impotence of God, in whom they trust (cf. Ps. 22:8; Wis. 2:13, 17; 2 Macc. 7:16). In 22:64 the taunt is directed against Jesus as a prophet, which significantly agrees with the fact that Luke consistently compares Jesus' mission and fate with the rejection, suffering, and death that Israel's prophets had to endure (Luke 4:24, 27; 6:22–23; 11:47–51; 13:33–35; 20:9–18; cf. Acts 7:37–40; see 1 Kings 22:24–28; Jer. 28:10–16). Also, note that Luke, in the passion narrative, consistently presents Jesus as a prophet who knows what is going to happen (Luke 22:10, 21–22, 31–34, 35–38, 61; cf. Jesus' anticipation of his abuse in 18:32; 20:10–11).

22:66–71

In Luke's narrative of the (Saturday) morning session of Jesus' trial before the Sanhedrin, the detail of the false witnesses (Mark 15:55–60) has been omitted. The reason for Luke's omission of this detail may be "Luke's desire to work out the innocence portion of his theme concerning the Passion as the fulfillment of Luke 22:37/Isa. 55:12" (Larkin 1974: 395–96). Despite some verbal parallels between 22:67b–68 and Isa. 41:28; Hab. 1:5; Jer. 38:15 (45:15 LXX), there are no OT allusions here (Larkin 1974: 397–99).

Jesus' response to the Sanhedrin's demand in 22:67a, "If you are the Messiah, tell us," reads, "If I tell you, you will not believe; and if I question you, you will not answer. But from now on the Son of Man shall be seated at the right hand of the power of God" (22:67b–69). The second sentence combines an allusion to Dan. 7:13, "As I watched in the night visions, I saw one like a son of man coming with the clouds of heaven," with an allusion to Ps. 110:1, "The LORD says to my lord, 'Sit at my right hand until I make your enemies your footstool'" (Fitzmyer 1981–1985: 1462, 1467; Marshall [1978: 850], Bock [1994–1996: 1800], and others think that Luke omits the reference to Dan. 7:13).

The verbal agreement between 22:69 and Ps. 110:1 is not exact. Verse 69 reads *ho huios tou anthrōpou kathēmenos ek dexiōn tēs dynameōs tou theou*, while Ps. 110:1 (109:1 LXX) reads *eipen ho kyrios tō kyriō mou, kathou ek dexiōn mou*. It should not be doubted, however, that Jesus' statement alludes both to Ps. 110:1 and to Dan. 7:13. We should note that Ps. 110:1 is the only OT passage in which a human figure is directed to sit at God's right hand. Also, the phrase belongs to a prophetic prediction (cf. Luke 22:28–30), and it is introduced by *apo to nyn* ("from now on"), a time marker that points to future fulfillment—facts that confirm that 22:69 should be understood as an OT allusion (France 1971: 103; Larkin 1974: 399–400). (On Ps. 110, see above on 20:42–43.) Jesus draws on the enthronement language of Ps. 110:1 to announce his reign at God's right hand, associating himself with divine power (which he had exercised during his ministry [see Green

1997: 796]) and asserting that he, not the council of the Sanhedrin, is judge.

Is the allusion to Ps. 110:1 also an allusion to Dan. 7:13 (*epi tōn nephelōn tou ouranou hōs huios anthrōpou ērcheto*), which is clearly present in the parallel account in Matt. 26:64; Mark 14:62: "You will see the Son of Man seated at the right hand of the Power, and coming with the clouds of heaven" (*ton huion tou anthrōpou ... erchomenon epi/meta tōn nephelōn tou ouranou*) (see Albl 1999: 229–30)? Luke, who omits the clause about the "clouds of heaven," reduces the verbal parallelism to the phrase "Son of Man," but several material parallels seem to warrant the assumption of an allusion in 22:69 not only to Ps. 110:1 but also to Dan. 7:13. The locus of the Son of Man's action is heaven: Dan. 7:13 mentions "heaven" (*ouranos*) explicitly. Although 22:69 speaks less specifically of "the right hand of the power of God," the reaction of the Sanhedrin in v. 70, "Are you, then, the Son of God?" suggests that Luke intends his readers to recognize an abbreviated allusion to both Dan. 7:13 and Ps. 110:1 (Larkin 1974: 412–13). The fact that the context of Dan. 7:13 does not identify the Son of Man with the Messiah and does not describe him as being seated on a throne (in Dan. 7:9–10, 22, 26, it is the Ancient of Days and the heavenly court who sit on thrones) does not negate the possibility of an allusion. Note that according to Dan. 7:14, the Son of Man is given dominion, which implies the right to sit on a throne (cf. *1 En.* 62:5, which has the Son of Man "sitting on the throne of his glory"; see also 69:26–29). Note, further, that some Jewish circles may have interpreted Daniel's Son of Man figure messianically in the first century AD (see Horbury 1985, with reference to *1 En.* 37–71; *4 Ezra* 13; Ezek. Trag. 67–89; for later evidence, see *b. Sanh.* 38b; *b. Ḥag.* 14a; see also Juel 1998: 162–64; R. E. Brown 1994: 509–12; Collins 1995: 143, 173–94). Finally, it should be noted that Ps. 110:1 and Dan. 7:13 are linked in (later) Jewish exegesis as well (cf. *Midr. Ps.* 2:9 on Ps. 2:7). Why did Luke omit a more explicit reference to Dan. 7:13, which speaks of the return to earth of the Son of Man? The suggestion that Luke's eschatology deemphasizes the imminent parousia, accepting the delay of Christ's return as a given fact (Conzelmann 1960: 84), is unconvincing because Mark 14:62 does not imply that the parousia of the Son of Man will follow immediately upon his exaltation, nor does Luke eliminate the possibility of an imminent parousia (cf. Luke 12:40; 17:24–30; 18:8; 21:36). Rather, any reference to the coming of the Son of Man is, in this context, by default a declaration of coming judgment: note that the coming of the Son of Man signifies both judgment (9:26; 12:8–10; 21:36) and salvation (21:27–28, 36), and note the Jewish leaders' unbelief expressed in the text. W. J. Larkin comments, "Luke avoids this in order to promote his theme of Jesus' innocence in two ways. It removes any hint of vindictiveness in Jesus' speech.... Positively, Jesus in his earthly ministry even on the cross is constantly portrayed as the one who seeks to save the lost (19:10; 23:34, 43). The best way Jesus could continue to offer salvation in this situation was to attempt to correct their view that a suffering, humiliated, defenseless prisoner could not be the victorious Messiah. He does so by bearing witness to the fact that God's plan of salvation will be fulfilled" (Larkin 1974: 414–15). (For arguments in support of the authenticity of Jesus' use of Ps. 110:1 and Dan. 7:13, see Bock 1998: 220–24.)

The allusion to Ps. 110:1 and Dan. 7:13 has several functions in the context of 22:69 (see France 1971: 103; Larkin 1974: 404–10; Strauss 1995: 320–21). First, although Jesus does not give a direct answer to the authorities' question of whether he is the Messiah (22:67), the allusion to Ps. 110:1 expresses his assertion that he is indeed destined for the messianic throne. Second, Jesus clarifies for the Sanhedrin the nature of his messiahship, placing it into the transcendent sphere of God's presence by removing it from historical/political misunderstanding. Third, Jesus provides an explanation for his present humiliation, which should not be misunderstood in terms of negating his messianic claims. Fourth, Jesus predicts his destiny: *from now on* he will enjoy heavenly, divine glory.

In 22:70 the council responds to Jesus' assertion by asking, "Are you, then, the Son of God?" (*sy oun ei ho hyios tou theou*). The Jewish leaders take up Jesus' royal enthronement language from Ps. 110 and link it with Ps. 2:6–7, a passage in which Yahweh's anointed is enthroned on Zion and designated "son of God"; they ask Jesus if he is claim-ing the intimacy of divine sonship expressed in Ps. 2:7 (Green 1997: 791; Strauss 1995: 321).

23:2

The formal charge against Jesus that the Sanhedrin takes to Pilate in 23:2, "We found this man perverting our nation," has been interpreted as echoing Deut. 13, implying that Jesus was accused of being a false prophet by the Jewish leadership, although the formulation of the charge would have been interpreted by Pilate in terms of instigation to rebellion and civil unrest (Green 1997: 800). However, the specification of the charge in terms of obstructing the payment of taxes to the emperor and in terms of claiming to be an anointed king do not conform to a charge of being a false prophet.

23:9–11

Luke interrupts the trial of Jesus before Pilate in 23:6–12, narrating Jesus' appearance before Herod Antipas. Some scholars have suggested that Ps. 2:1–2, "Why do the nations conspire, and the peoples plot in vain? The kings of the earth set themselves, and the rulers take counsel together, against the LORD and his anointed," was regarded by the early church as having been fulfilled in Jesus' trial before Herod and Pilate in 23:6–12, as evidenced by the quotation in Acts 4:24–30. Some scholars claim that 23:6–12 is a Lukan creation on the basis of Ps. 2:1–2 (Dibelius 1953; Bultmann 1963: 273; Loisy 1924: 544–45). The arguments adduced for this theory are unconvincing (see Hoehner 1972: 224–50; R. E. Brown 1994: 779–82; Fitzmyer 1981–1985: 1497). The focus of 23:6–12 is not the opposition of Herod and Pilate to Jesus, but rather Herod's testimony that he cannot find anything in Jesus deserving punishment (Fitzmyer 1981–1985: 1480). Others suggest Deut. 19:15 as background for a Christian apologetic: Pilate and Herod—that is, "two witnesses"—have testified to Jesus' innocence (Fitzmyer 1981–1985: 1488). Since Luke does not describe either of the two men as a "witness," it remains hypothetical whether Luke's readers would have perceived such a reference.

Jesus' silence in 23:9 has been interpreted as an allusion to Isa. 53:7–8 (*TDNT* 5:713; Grundmann 1978: 425; Moo 1983: 148–51; Nolland 1989–1993: 1123; Green 1997: 805; cf. Marshall 1978: 856; Bock 1994–1996: 1819). Several factors suggest, however, that Luke does not intend his audience to see an allusion to Isa. 53 at this point. First, there is no verbal parallelism between Luke 23:9 (*ouden apekrinato autō*) and Isa. 53:7 (*ouk anoigei to stoma . . . ouk anoigei to stoma autou*). Second, there is no material parallelism: the statement in Isa. 53:7 is related to physical violence to which the servant is subjected, not to his accusers. Although the picture of the Suffering Servant silently accepting his violent fate provides, perhaps, the general hermeneutical background for Jesus' refusal to defend himself, it is preferable not to link Jesus' silence during his cross-examination in the trial with Isa. 53:7, as Luke (and the other Gospel writers) does not make such an allusion explicit (Schnabel 1999: 241–45). Suggestions that Jesus' silence alludes to Ps. 22:15, or echoes the silence of the suffering righteous person (Ps. 38:14–16; 39:9) or the silence of the teacher of wisdom (Job 13:5; Prov. 11:13; 15:23; 20:19; 23:9; 30:32–33; Eccles. 3:7b; cf. Sir. 20:1–8) likewise are unconvincing (see Schnabel 1999: 245–48).

Verse 11a, "Even Herod with his soldiers treated him with contempt [*exouthenēsas*] and mocked [*empaixas*] him," possibly echoes 2 Chron. 36:16a: "They kept mocking the messengers of God, despising his words [*exoudenountes*], and scoffing [*empaizontes*] at his prophets." There is indeed some verbal and material parallelism here, which may suggest that Luke echoes this passage in order to underline, again, his portrayal of Jesus' suffering "in the context of the rejected prophet" (Larkin 1974: 457).

23:18, 25

It has been suggested that the crowd's response to Pilate's suggestion of releasing Jesus in 23:18, "Away with this fellow [*aire touton*]!" is an allusion to Isa. 53:8 LXX: "For he was cut off [*airetai*] from the earth" (Larkin 1974: 464–65; Marshall 1978: 860; Green 1997: 809). The notice in 23:25 that Jesus was "handed over" (*paredōken*) while the criminal Barabbas was released is possibly an allusion to Isa. 53:6, 12 LXX: "He handed him over [*paredōken*] for our sin . . . because he handed over [*paredothē*] his life to death" (Larkin 1974: 465–66; cf. Marshall 1978: 861). The OT background of these verbs in 23:18, 25 in Isa. 53 is interpreted by some in terms of "the theological theme of an innocent Jesus who receives an un-

just punishment" (Larkin 1974: 469). This OT background underlines Luke's concern to portray Jesus as the innocent servant who fulfills Yahweh's will. Note that passages such as Ps. 27:12; 41:2; 74:19; 118:18; 140:9 assert that righteous people neither desire nor deserve to be "given over" into the power of enemies. Several OT passages state that when God "hands over" the people of Israel, it is as punishment for their sins (cf. 1 Kings 8:46; 14:16; 2 Chron. 25:20; 4 Ezra 9:7). If we interpret 23:25 on this background, then Luke may be preparing his readers for a soteriological interpretation of the death of Jesus, who experiences the fate appropriate for those who have sinned and who therefore are handed over to their enemies (Larkin 1974: 471–73).

23:27–31

As Jesus walks to the place of his execution (23:27), he is accompanied by "a great number of the people" and by "women who were beating their breasts and wailing for him." The latter clause has been interpreted as an allusion to Zech. 12:10–14 (Fitzmyer 1981–1985: 1497; Green 1997: 815; Bock 1994–1996: 1845), while others argue that there is insufficient evidence to support this view (Moo 1983: 221).

The phrase "daughters of Jerusalem" in 23:28 is used in the OT (cf. Song 2:7; 5:16; 8:4 ["daughters"]; Isa. 37:22; Zeph. 3:14; Zech. 9:9 ["daughter"]). This address is occasioned by the women who accompany Jesus, and it is prompted by Isaiah's messages concerning the sinful daughters of Zion (Isa. 3:16–17; 4:4). The "daughters of Jerusalem" stand for the inhabitants of Jerusalem who reject Jesus and who thus face the danger of God's severe judgment, as Jesus notes with sadness (Larkin 1974: 493–94; cf. Fitzmyer 1981–1985: 1498).

Jesus' directive to weep in 23:28, "Weep for yourselves and for your children," possibly echoes Jer. 9:19 ("For a sound of wailing is heard from Zion: 'How we are ruined! We are utterly shamed, because we have left the land, because they have cast down our dwellings'"), in a passage in which the prophet summons his listeners, after an oracle of judgment (9:12–15), to weep and mourn (9:16–21) (Rusam 2003: 234; cf. Bock 1994–1996: 1846).

The introductory phrase in 23:29, "For behold, days are coming" (*hoti idou erchetai hēmerai*), echoes

393

prophetic texts that introduce oracles of judgment and restoration with this or similar phrases (see 1 Sam. 2:31; 2 Kings 20:17; Isa. 13:9; Jer. 7:32; 16:14; 19:6; 31:31 [38:31 LXX]; 51:52 [LXX 28:52]; Amos 4:2; Zech. 14:1; Mal. 4:1 [3:19 LXX]). As Luke uses this phrase to introduce references to the eschatological judgment of the last days (Luke 5:35; 17:22–31; 19:43; 21:6, 22–23), Jesus' statement to the women alerts them "to the decisive eschatological finality of the approaching judgment" (Larkin 1974: 495).

The beatitude of 23:29, "Blessed are the barren, the wombs that have never given birth, and the breasts that have never given suck," is an echo of Isa. 54:1: "Sing, O barren one, who did not bear; burst into song and shout, you who have not been in labor! For the children of the desolate woman will be more than the children of her that is married, says the LORD" (Käser 1963; Ploch 1993: 109–11; Rusam 2003: 234; Fitzmyer 1981–1985: 1498). On the assumption that 23:29 indeed alludes to Isa. 54:1, Jesus uses this OT passage to emphasize the terrible nature of the coming judgment upon Jerusalem. Whereas the context of Isa. 54 was the promised new beginning after the catastrophe, announcing that "the desolate woman" (*hē erēmos* [54:1]) will have more children than the woman who is married, Jesus' words do not seem to leave room for the hope of a new beginning. The coming catastrophe will be so devastating that the childless women, who cannot lose any children, will be better off than women who have children (Rusam 2003: 234). Other scholars argue that the images are too different to warrant the identification of an echo or allusion. In Isa. 54:1b the barren woman is promised a child; she is declared fortunate because her barrenness will be taken away. In Luke 23:29 the reason for the beatitude, which involves both irony and the motif of paradoxical reversal, is the fact that barren and childless women have less to worry about in the dreadful days that lie ahead, since they will be spared the grief of seeing their babies being put to death (Marshall 1978: 864; Nolland 1989–1993: 1137; Bock 1994–1996: 1846n6; R. E. Brown 1994: 923). When Paul quotes Isa. 54:1 LXX in Gal. 4:27, he preserves the original eschatological context of Isaiah's prophecy. A better analogy for Luke 23:29 is Lam. 4:4, where the author describes suckling babies who cry for food at the time of

Jerusalem's fall to the Babylonian army, when nobody is there to feed them. It can be argued, however, that the context in Luke 23:27–31 gives a new meaning to Isa. 54:1–10 (Rusam 2003: 234). Other prophets who witnessed the fall of Jerusalem also proclaim that childlessness is preferable to having children (cf. Jer. 16:2; Lam. 2:20; 4:3; see Larkin 1974: 496).

The proverb in 23:31, "For if they do this when the wood is green, what will happen when it is dry?" is best explained in terms of the green wood representing Jesus and the dry wood standing for the Jews. The basic idea is that dry wood burns more easily than green wood. The background of this proverb is the OT use of "fire" as a metaphor of God's consuming judgment (cf. Jer. 11:16; Ezek. 21:31), particularly passages that compare God's judgment of Israel with fire that consumes a tree (Isa. 10:16–19; Jer. 5:14; 7:20; Ezek. 15:1–8; Joel 1:19). Several OT passages compare faithful Israel with a green and fruitful plant (Isa. 5:1; Jer. 11:16; Hos. 10:1), as lush greenness sometimes stands for righteousness (cf. Ps. 1; Prov. 11:30; Jer. 11:19; Hos. 14:8), while unfaithful Israel is described as dry and unfruitful (Isa. 37:27; Hos. 9:16; Joel 1:12; Nah. 1:10). Note Joel 1:10–20; Amos 1:2, where dryness is the result of God's judgment on sin. Interpreted against this background of OT ideas, the metaphor of the dry wood that burns quickly "intensifies the terribleness of the prospective judgment" and "also points out the moral and theological basis for the judgment" (Larkin 1974: 498). If God allows Jesus, who is innocent, the "green wood," to suffer the fate that Jerusalem is preparing for him, what will be the fate of Jerusalem, the "dry wood" (Fitzmyer 1981–1985: 1498)?

23:30

A. NT Context: On the Way to Crucifixion.
Jesus' instruction to the wailing women who follow him on his way to the place of execution in 23:28, "Weep for yourselves," is given a threefold explanation, each one heightening the severity of the conditions that are described. The first two explanations form a contrasting couplet, describing the "coming days" as a period in which people will prefer nonexistence to life, praising the barren woman (23:29) and voicing the desire to die (23:30). The third explanation links Jesus' present experience with the future knowl-

edge of the crowd that accompanies him (23:31). The allusion to Isa. 54:1 and the quotation from Hos. 10:8 in 23:30 ("Then they will begin to say to the mountains, 'Fall on us,' and to the hills, 'Cover us'") constitute the second explanation, describing the people in the last days as blessed if they have no children and as calling on God to destroy them so that they would not have to face his wrath. The quotation is part of a series of prophecies concerning the future judgment on Jerusalem (Luke 13:34–35; 19:41–44; 21:20–24; cf. 21:23/23:29) (see Larkin [1974: 483], who argues [pp. 488–92] that there is no clear evidence that the passage has been written against the background of Zech. 12:10; 2 Chron. 35:24; 2 Kings 23:25). The possible allusion to Isa. 54:1 and other allusions to OT texts in 23:27–31 will be discussed in the next section.

B. Hos. 10:8 in Context. In Hos. 10 Israel is described as a "luxuriant vine" that yields fruit, but also as having "altars" and "pillars" that will be broken down and destroyed by Yahweh (vv. 1–2). Israel is a nation that does not fear the Lord, makes covenants with empty oaths, and engages liberally in litigation (10:3–4), with the result that Yahweh will bring destruction on Samaria and Ephraim, leading their people into captivity (10:5–7) because Israel has sinned (10:9). Verse 8 speaks of God's judgment on the idolaters, portraying them as rebels who seek refuge from divine wrath in mountains and rocks. The call "to the mountains, 'Cover us,' and to the hills, 'Fall on us'" probably expresses a desire for relief through death from the terrible suffering caused by God's judgment (Nolland 1989–1993: 1137). Similar imagery is used in Jer. 4:29: "At the noise of horseman and archer every city takes to flight; they enter thickets; they climb among rocks; all the cities are forsaken, and no man dwells in them." Some scholars interpret these references as an allusion to Gen. 3:8, according to which Adam and Eve "hid from the presence of the LORD God" (Beale [1999: 400] describes the underlying presupposition "that God has determined that sinful history must end in the same way that it began").

C. Textual Matters. Verse 30, "Then they will begin to say to the mountains, 'Fall on us,' and to the hills, 'Cover us'" (*legein tois oresin: pesete eph' hēmas, kai tois bounois: kalypsate hēmas*), quotes from Hos. 10:8 LXX: *erousin tois oresin: pesete eph'*

hēmas, kai tois bounois: kalypsate hēmas (A 106). Other LXX traditions change the sequence of the verbs *pesete* and *kalypsate*, following the MT, which first has *kāssûnû* ("cover us") and then *nipĕlû* ("fall upon us"). Although it is possible that the reading of Codex A is an adaptation of the Christian scribe of the manuscript to Luke 23:30, one should note that Rev. 6:16 alludes to Hos. 10:8, also in a form that has the same sequence of the verbs (although with more variations from the LXX text). This suggests that the reading of Codex A is an original form of the LXX text that existed besides other LXX traditions as early as the first century (Holtz [1968: 28], who concludes from the evidence of Luke-Acts that Luke used a text of the Minor Prophets that was close to the text-type represented by Codex Alexandrinus; see ibid., 5–29; Larkin 1974: 482; Nolland 1989–1993: 1137).

D. The Use of Hos. 10:8 in Luke 23:30. The quotation from Hos. 10 provides "a link with the apostasy and subsequent exile of Israel" (Nolland 1989–1993: 1138). The words of the quotation form part of Jesus' prophecy of future events affecting Jerusalem (note in 23:28 the "daughters of Jerusalem"). The quotation expresses the intense suffering that Jesus predicts. The severity and the finality of the divine judgment are illustrated by the desire of those who experience divine judgment, realizing that their lives might come to an end. As Jesus quotes Hos. 10:8, he appropriates the Hosea passage into his own prophetic statements, claiming that the events that he prophesies are "the proper context of fulfilment for OT prophetic predictions" (Larkin 1974: 481). "Jerusalem" (23:28) is seen as the representative of sinful Israel, the city that rejects Jesus as it has rejected the prophets whom God had sent to it (Luke 13:33–34; 18:31; 19:41–44)—a fact that results in Jerusalem becoming a place of judgment.

E. Theological Use. The quotation of Hos. 10:8 reminds the audience of Hosea's words of judgment and thus represents a final appeal to the inhabitants to repent, reminding them of Israel's substitution of faithfulness to Yahweh with idolatry, leading to judgment and exile, and anticipating a time when "those who have rejected God's salvific purpose by rejecting Jesus and his divinely ordained mission will articulate a similar death wish" (Green 1997: 816). Israel's idolatry (Hos. 10:1–5) corresponds to Jesus' crucifixion: both are punished in God's severe judgment (Rusam 2003: 234–35). At the same time, Luke is convinced that while the people of Israel deserve divine judgment, Jesus was innocent, thus taking upon himself the judgment that Israel's sinners deserve.

23:32–43

The narration of Jesus' crucifixion (23:32–43) focuses on the immediate aftermath of the crucifixion, detailing the mockery by the Jewish leaders, by the Roman soldiers, and by one of the two criminals. At the same time, Luke highlights the fact that, from his perspective, confirming again Jesus' suffering as that of a righteous person by an allusion to Ps. 22 in 23:34–35, the crucifixion "seals the identity of Jesus as the Messiah and king who accomplishes the divine purpose precisely as the suffering one" (Green 1997: 819). Many Alexandrian and Western manuscripts omit Jesus' prayer in 23:34 ($\mathfrak{P}^{75}$ $\aleph^1$ B D* W Θ 070 579 1241 a sy^s sa bo^{pt}); the prayer is included in $\aleph^{*.2}$ (A) C D^2 L Ψ 0250 $f^{1.(13)}$ 33 $\mathfrak{M}$ lat sy$^{c.p.h}$ (bo^{pt}), but internal factors favor the inclusion of 23:34 as original (see the discussion in R. E. Brown 1994: 975–81; note, arguing for authenticity, Marshall 1978: 867–68; Bock 1994–1996: 1867–68; Nolland 1989–1993: 1141, 1144).

The crucifixion of two criminals with Jesus (23:33) should not be considered an allusion to Isa. 53:12 (Larkin 1974: 280, 508; *contra* Grundmann 1978: 432). There are no verbal connections, and this detail follows naturally in the normal progression of Luke's narrative.

Jesus' intercession for the two criminals in 23:34a ("Father, forgive them," *patēr, aphes autois*) possibly echoes Isa. 53:12 MT: *wělapoš'îm yapgia'* ("he made intercession for the transgressors"). The LXX translates *dia tas hamartias autōn paredothē*, "he was handed over because of their sins," changing "transgressors" into "their sins," and "to intercede" into "to be handed over." Even though there are no verbal parallels, because of the conceptual links both Jesus and the early church may have understood Jesus' prayer on the cross as a fulfillment of Isaiah's prophecy (so Wolff 1952: 76–77; *TDNT* 5:713 with note 455; Larkin 1974: 509; Bock 1994–1996: 1849).

The reference to Jesus' garments being divided in 23:34b, "And they cast lots to divide his cloth-

ing" (*diamerizomenoi de ta himatia autou ebalon klērous*), is an allusion to Ps. 22:18 (21:19 LXX): "They divide my clothes among themselves, and for my clothing they cast lots" (21:19 LXX: *diemerisanto ta himatia mou heautois kai epi ton himatismon mou ebalon klēron*). Even though Luke includes no hints in the context that mark this phrase as an OT allusion, three things suggest that we should see 23:34b as such: the verbal parallels, the fact that the suffering of a righteous person is described this way only in Ps. 22:18, and the fact that this detail is not essential for the progress of the narrative (Larkin 1974: 510–11; cf. Fitzmyer 1981–1985: 1504; Green 1997: 820). Psalm 22 consists of lament (vv. 1–21) and thanksgiving (vv. 22–32). Whereas this psalm eventually was used in the corporate worship of Israel (cf. vv. 23–24), it narrates the experience of an individual who endures physical, emotional, and spiritual suffering as the public suffering of a righteous person. The image of the sufferer's enemies casting lots and distributing his clothes (22:19) anticipates his death and underlines the hopelessness of his situation (Weiser 1962: 224). The fact that the psalm ends with an expectant declaration of the universal rule of Yahweh (22:27–31) allows a messianic interpretation of Ps. 22. Verses 27–31 are interpreted as describing the messianic last days in general (*Tg. Ps.* 22:27–32; *y. Šeb.* 4, 35c [31]; *Midr. Ps.* 22, 32 [99a]; *b. Sanh.* 110b; see Str-B 2:574–75). The suffering of the righteous person in the first part of the psalm is interpreted messianically in late midrashic homilies (*Pesiq. Rab.* 36 [162a]; 37 [163a]; see Str-B 2:579–80). The view that the phrase *eis to telos* in the LXX superscription indicates that contemporary Jewish exegesis understood Ps. 22 messianically (Bornhäuser 1947: 191) is unwarranted, as the lack of external evidence and the inconsistent meaning of the phrase *eis to telos* indicate. The echo of Ps. 22:18 in 23:34 presupposes a typological and prophetic interpretation of the psalm: Jesus, who is mocked, is the model of the suffering righteous one (Bock 1994–1996: 1850; see also Larkin [1974: 512–22], who argues that the source of the allusion rests probably in the exegesis of the early church).

Luke's formulation of the Jewish leaders' mockery of Jesus in 23:35, "He saved others; let him save himself if he is the Messiah of God, his chosen one!" is an allusion to Ps. 22:7–8 (21:8–9 LXX) (Larkin 1974: 522–30; Brawley 1995: 55; Fitzmyer 1994–1996: 1504; Green 1997: 821). The verbal parallels focus on *theōreō, ekmyktērizō,* and *sōzō*: 23:35, "And the people stood by, watching [*theōrōn*]; but the leaders scoffed [*exemyktērizon*] at him, saying, 'He saved others; let him save [*sōsatō*] himself if he is the Messiah of God, his chosen one!'"; Ps. 22:7–8, "All who see [*theōrountes*] me mock [*exemyktērisan*] at me, they make mouths at me, they shake their heads; 'Commit your cause to the LORD; let him deliver, let him rescue [*sōsatō*] the one in whom he delights!'" The verbs *theōreō* and *ekmyktērizō* occur in the same immediate context only in Ps. 21:8 LXX, and Luke uses *ekmyktērizō* only in Luke 16:14; 23:35. Luke, in linking the "watching" crowd and the "scoffing" leaders in 23:35a with the mocking of the righteous sufferer in Ps. 22, suggests that he does not absolve the people of their mockery of Jesus: Jesus' crucifixion is witnessed by the Jewish people (Marshall 1978: 868–69). The sufferer in Ps. 22 refers to himself as a "worm" who is "not human, scorned by others, and despised by the people" (22:6), which corresponds to the picture that Luke paints of Jesus.

It is unclear whether these allusions to Ps. 22 are meant to point to the second part of the psalm, which emphasizes Yahweh's universal salvation, implying that the allusion shows the scriptural and thus divine necessity of the pattern of messianic suffering and glory (Larkin [1974: 526] does not find such a connection). But perhaps no allusions to the second half of Ps. 22 are needed for readers of Luke's Gospel to understand the situation that he portrays: the Jewish leaders refer to Jesus correctly as "the Messiah of God, his chosen one," but they think that Jesus has to save himself in order to prove the genuineness of his claims and of his message, without recognizing the fact that "the psalm on which their behavior is modeled recognizes God as the one who delivers" (Green 1997: 821).

The Jewish leaders refer to Jesus, sarcastically, in 23:35 as "God's Messiah, the chosen one" (*ho christos tou theou ho eklektos*), reformulating Mark 15:32: "the Messiah, the King of Israel" (*ho christos ho basileus Israēl*). Some manuscripts link *tou theou* ("God's") with "the chosen one" (A C³ Γ Δ Θ 𝔐: *ho tou theou eklektos*; C* ff²: *ho eklektos tou theou*;

ℵ*: *ho tou theou ho eklektos*; 𝔓⁷⁵ [0124] *f*¹³ Eus: *ho huios tou theou ho eklektos*; the NA²⁷ text is supported by ℵᶜ B [D] L W *f*¹). Grammatically, *tou theou* probably goes with *ho christos*, but it can be linked with both nouns in terms of the meaning of the formulation (Marshall 1978: 869). The title "the chosen one" (*ho eklektos*) in 23:35 possibly echoes Isa. 42:1 LXX, where the expression is used to describe the Servant of Yahweh (Ploch 1993: 108; Fitzmyer 1981–1985: 803; Green 1997: 821) (cf. Luke 9:35, which has *ho eklelegmenos*). This passage was interpreted messianically (cf. *1 En.* 39:6–8; 40:5; 45:3–5; 48:6–10; 49:2, 4; 51:52; 61:5, 8, 10; 62:1; *Apoc. Ab.* 30–31; see *TDNT* 4:184–85). The Jewish leaders taunt Jesus, ironically using an expression from one of Isaiah's Servant Songs that was used of the Messiah and that describes the identity of Jesus as Yahweh's servant and as the Messiah, "language that leaves the door open for the identification of a Messiah who suffers" (Green 1997: 821; cf. Strauss 1995: 266–67). Luke includes the allusion to Isa. 42:1 to emphasize that Jesus is the Messiah chosen by God in view of his suffering (Marshall 1978: 869). Less likely is an allusion to Wis. 3:9; 4:15, where the language of election (*hoi eklektoi*) is used in connection with the righteous who are persecuted by the wicked (so Nolland 1989–1993: 1147).

The offer of "sour wine" (*oxos*) in 23:36 is reminiscent of Ps. 69:21 (68:22 LXX), where the gift of "sour wine" or "vinegar" is an act of mockery and insult. The soldiers join the mockery of Jesus by offering him the cheap wine that was popular among the lower ranks of society, insulting the "king" whom they have crucified (R. E. Brown 1994: 997; Green 1997: 821). The allusion, if intended (Brawley [1995: 54] is skeptical), explains another detail of Jesus' crucifixion against the background of another psalm that describes the treatment of a righteous sufferer by his enemies, highlighting both Jesus' suffering in being mocked and the fulfillment of Scripture in what Jesus had to endure at the cross (Larkin 1974: 530–34).

In 23:42 the penitent criminal's request, "Jesus, remember me when you come in[to] your kingdom," echoes texts such as Ps. 115:12; Judg. 16:28; 1 Sam. 1:11, 19, where Yahweh's "remembrance" is a source of divine blessing in keeping with his covenant (Green 1997: 822; cf. Larkin 1974: 553–55).

Jesus' reply in 23:43 promises fellowship with him "in paradise" (*en tō paradeisō*), a term that the LXX uses to translate the Hebrew *gan*, "garden" (Gen. 2:8: "a garden in Eden" [LXX: *paradeison en Edem*]; Gen. 13:10: "the garden of God" [*ho paradeisos tou theou*]; for *paradeisos* in Gen. 2–3 LXX, see Gen. 2:8, 9, 10, 15, 16; 3:1, 2, 3, 8, 10, 23, 24). The term "paradise" also echoes texts such as Isa. 51:3; Ezek. 28:13; 31:8–9 (cf. *T. Levi* 18:10–11; *T. Dan* 5:12; *Pss. Sol.* 14:3; *1 En.* 17–19; 32:3; 60:8; 61:12; cf. 2 Cor. 12:4; Rev. 2:7), in which *paradeisos* is understood as an eschatological image of new creation, a place of expected bliss, the abode of the righteous after death (see *TDNT* 5:765–73; Fitzmyer 1981–1985: 1510–11; Bock 1994–1996: 1857). Jesus asserts, in other words, that he has the key to paradise—a reality implied in his statements that the kingdom of God is present in him (11:20; 19:9) and that he will pour out God's Spirit on his followers (Luke 24:49; Acts 1:4–5; cf. Acts 2:16–21). Jesus' remark to the criminal on the cross can thus be understood as "a juridical pronouncement by Jesus the Judge of the living and the dead," and it characterizes him as the "new Adam," who inaugurates a new period of salvation (Neyrey 1985: 182, 183, with reference to Acts 10:42; 17:31; *T. Levi* 18:10–12).

23:44

The darkness that "came over the whole land" (23:44) echoes OT texts that describe the same cosmic phenomenon in connection with the coming of the day of the Lord (cf. Joel 2:10, 30–31; 3:15; Amos 8:9; Zeph. 1:15; see Larkin 1974: 602–3; Rese 1969: 54; Fitzmyer 1981–1985: 1517). Whether taken as a reference to a literal event (which is more likely) or as a symbolic comment on Jesus' death, this OT background underscores the significance of Jesus' death, both in terms of the cosmic stage on which the final hours of Jesus' life are played out and in terms of the arrival of the "last days" for which God's presence and judgment were prophesied (see Bock 1994–1996: 1858; Green 1997: 824–25).

23:46

A. NT Context of Ps. 31:5. Luke's description of Jesus' death in 23:44–49 presents Jesus' last words on the cross as a quotation from Ps. 31:5 (30:6

LXX): "Father, into your hands I commend my spirit" (in contrast to Mark 15:34, where a first cry of Jesus quotes the words of Ps. 22:2; see Larkin [1974: 572–77], who argues that Luke omitted this quotation for theological reasons, focusing on the innocence of Jesus, who is consistently obedient to the will of God—an emphasis that the cry of despair in Ps. 22:2 would interrupt; see also Matera 1985). Verses 44–49 form the final climax of three units that describe Jesus' crucifixion: the account of the crucifixion (23:33–38), the two criminals who were crucified together with Jesus (23:39–43), and the account of Jesus' death (23:44–49).

B. Ps. 31:5 in Context. In Ps. 31, commonly designated an individual lament, David prays for deliverance from enemies who threaten to put him to shame (v. 1), who attack him (vv. 2–3), who seek to trap him (v. 4), who cause distress, grief, and sorrow (vv. 9–10), who have made him "a horror to my neighbors, an object of dread to my acquaintances" (v. 11), who scheme to take his life (v. 13), who have made him "like a broken vessel" (v. 12). In the face of his enemies, the psalmist expresses his confidence in Yahweh: he seeks refuge in the Lord (31:1–2, 4). He appeals to God's righteousness (31:1), to his willingness and ability to hear, see, and help (31:2, 7, 22), to his name (31:3; cf. 31:14, 17), to his redemption and faithfulness (31:5), to his steadfast love (31:7, 16, 21), and to his grace (31:9). In Ps. 31 the righteous sufferer prays that God might deliver him from his enemies, while expressing his confidence that his fate is in God's hands, a confidence based on his previous experience of God's deliverance (v. 5). The psalm ends with thanksgiving and praise (31:20–25), words of absolute confidence "as if the actual deliverance had already been experienced" (Craigie 1983: 262).

C. Ps. 31:5 in Judaism. In later rabbinic tradition Ps. 31:5 was used as part of the evening prayer: pious Jews ask God to care for them and protect them during sleep in the descending night (cf. *b. Ber.* 5a; see Fitzmyer 1981–1985: 1519). As this prayer fits the evening before sleep, it fits the evening of life before death, as sleep was regarded as the threshold of death (Marshall 1978: 876). There is no evidence in Jewish texts that Ps. 31 was interpreted messianically.

D. Textual Matters. Luke (*pater, eis cheiras sou paratithemai to pneuma mou*) follows the LXX (*eis cheiras sou parathēsomai to pneuma mou*) with minor changes: he inserts the term "father" and changes the future tense *parathēsomai* to the present tense *paratithemai* (the future tense is retained in the reading of L 0117 0135 *f*¹³ 𝔐), which adapts the quotation to the occasion (Holtz 1968: 58; France 1971: 241). The Hebrew text has the singular "hand" in *bĕyādĕkâ*. It has been argued that the OT influenced the preservation of Ps. 31:5 as words that the dying Jesus spoke on the cross rather than being the source of their creation, while the historical event controlled its text-form in Luke 23:46 (Larkin 1974: 591–92).

E. The Use of Ps. 31:5 in Luke 23:46. Where the psalmist entrusts himself to God as he is surrounded by enemies, Jesus entrusts himself to God in the face of imminent death, expressing his submission to God's will and his confidence that God will deliver him—that is, bring him back from the dead (note Jesus' predictions of his resurrection in Luke 9:22; 18:33; 22:69; 23:43; see Bock 1994–1996: 1862; Larkin 1974: 583–90). The appropriation of Ps. 31:5 in v. 46 does not violate the original context and meaning in the psalm, but extends the sphere of God's protection of the righteous sufferer from a dangerous situation in the life of a righteous person to death, heightening the strength of the psalmist's profession of faith (Larkin 1974: 588).

The comparison of the Suffering Servant's vicarious death in Isa. 53 with a lamb going to the altar to be killed as a sacrificial victim may have been understood by Luke as a prophecy of Jesus' voluntary death: note that Luke quotes Isa. 53:12 in 22:37 as the hermeneutical key of the passion narrative. In Ps. 31 David refers to himself as God's "servant" (*doulos* [v. 16]) and as "righteous" (*dikaios* [v. 18]). Jesus' loud cry (*megalē phōnē*) at the cross was heard as a cry of distress, but the words that Jesus quotes from Ps. 31 do not express the alarm, distress, and lament that are also present in the psalm, but rather focus on the element of confidence and trust in God. Jesus' death, accompanied by the words of the psalmist, "Father, into your hands I commend my spirit," is portrayed as a proactive event, as a gesture of confidence (Schwemer 1998: 20; for the following comment, see ibid. 20–21). The voluntary

nature of sacrifices, which included the notion that the sacrificial animal agrees with the sacrificial act, was an important presupposition of the sacrificial system in Greece (cf. Plutarch, *Quaest. conv.* 8.8.3 [729f]: "People are very careful not to kill the animal till a drink-offering is poured over him and he shakes his head in assent") as well as in ancient Judaism (cf. *m. Tamid* 3:4; *Num. Rab.* 23:9; however, there is no OT evidence for this view). Since Luke places the passion narrative in 22:37 into the horizon of Isa. 53, the voluntary nature of Jesus' death is thus emphasized by the quotation of Ps. 31:5: as the vicarious death of the Suffering Servant in Isa. 53 was compared with the lamb that goes to the altar to be killed as sacrificial victim, so Jesus went to his death voluntarily. On the relationship between Jesus' death and the death of the sacrificial lamb in the OT cult, see Heb. 9:11–14.

F. Theological Use. Jesus' final words on the cross demonstrate that Jesus' death fulfills God's purposes: in the midst of darkness (23:44–45) God is still present, as the tearing of the temple curtain signifies (23:45), and the words "Into your hands I commend my spirit" emphasize not only that God continues to be Jesus' Father, but also that he will rescue him from his enemies and raise him from the dead. The consistent faith in the face of enemies and the confident hope for deliverance that Ps. 31 expresses, focused in the words "Into your hands I commend my spirit," are used by Jesus to assert that God will protect him in death, thus fulfilling his merciful purposes. Jesus' final words before his death in the Gospel of Luke, "Father, into your hands I commend my spirit," explain why Jesus died the most shameful death: Jesus' prayer with the words of Ps. 31:5 points to God's plan of salvation and to Jesus' acceptance of God's salvific plan as announced in the Scriptures, and it underscores the voluntary nature of his death (cf. Luke 24:25–26, 44–49). The voluntary nature of Jesus' vicarious death is established by Isa. 53, but the quotation from Scripture is taken from Ps. 31 (Schwemer 1998: 22).

23:47–49

Several details of Luke's description of the various responses to Jesus' death in 23:47–49 have been explained as OT allusions.

The centurion's declaration that Jesus was "innocent" (*dikaios*) in 23:47 has been interpreted as echoing OT passages about the suffering righteous one (Ps. 22; 31:18; cf. Wis 2:12–20; 5:1–7), the Servant of Yahweh (Isa. 53:11), and OT passages that describe the expected Davidic king as *dikaios* (Jer. 23:5; Zech. 9:9; cf. *Pss. Sol.* 17:32). On the historical level, the Gentile centurion would have attested Jesus' innocence (*dikaios* means "innocent" in Prov. 6:17; Joel 3:19 [4:19 LXX]; Jon. 1:14; see Bock 1994–1996: 1864). It is debated whether he also "recognizes the salvific hand of God at work in Jesus" (Green 1997: 827), or whether the latter is Luke's interpretation of the term *dikaios* (Larkin 1974: 611–15; R. E. Brown 1994: 1163–67; Fitzmyer 1981–1985: 1520).

The description of the crowd's reaction in 23:48 ("they returned home, beating their breasts") has been interpreted as an allusion to Zech. 12:10: "And I will pour out a spirit of compassion and supplication on the house of David and the inhabitants of Jerusalem, so that, when they look on the one whom they have pierced, they shall mourn for him, as one mourns for an only child, and weep bitterly over him, as one weeps over a firstborn" (see Loisy 1924: 562). Since there are no verbal parallels, and since the material parallel depends on whether the crowd's reaction signifies mourning over Jesus' death—that is, admission of guilt and repentance, which may or may not be present—the evidence for such an allusion is not very strong (Larkin 1974: 594–95).

The same holds true concerning the suggestion that the reference to Jesus' "acquaintances" who "stood at a distance" (23:49) echoes Ps. 38:11 and/or Ps. 88:8 (Loisy 1924: 563; Creed 1930: 288). The "standing at a distance" in these psalm passages has a negative significance, whereas Luke's portrayal of the reactions after Jesus' death is positive (R. E. Brown 1994: 1171; cf. Brawley 1995: 54). Others seek to establish Ps. 31:11 [30:12 LXX] as an allusion for 23:48–49, after the quotation of Ps. 31:5 in 23:46 (Larkin 1974: 595–99). This is unlikely because of the intervening reference to the centurion in 23:47.

23:56

Luke's comment on the behavior of the Galilean women who witnessed Jesus' burial and then returned to Jerusalem to prepare spices and ointments in 23:56, stating that "on the Sabbath they rested according to the commandment," refers the reader to the Mosaic legislation of the Sabbath in Exod. 20:8–11; Deut. 5:12–15. Luke's comment, beyond narrating historical events that involved Torah-observant women, suggests that Luke was convinced that "the new form of God's salvation comes with obedience to his law" (Fitzmyer 1981–1985: 421; Powery 1999: 197).

24:13–35

The narrative of Jesus' appearance to two disciples on the road to Emmaus contains several terms that speak of scriptural interpretation: *syzēteō* (24:15), *dianoigō* (24:31–32), *diermēneuō* (24:27), and perhaps *homileō* (24:14–15), characterizing Jesus as teacher and Jesus' followers as interpreters of OT Scripture (Koet 1989: 56–72).

Jesus' exclamation in 24:25, "Oh, how foolish you are, and how slow of heart to believe all that the prophets have declared!" is not followed by an enumeration of OT prophetic passages that predicted the Messiah's death and resurrection. Later Christians understood Jesus' statement as a model for the "global reading of the OT as *praeparatio evangelica*" (Fitzmyer 1981–1985: 1565).

The rhetorical question in 24:26, "Was it not necessary that the Messiah should suffer these things and then enter into his glory?" recalls the earlier passion predictions in 9:22, 44; 12:50; 13:32–33; 17:25; 18:32–33, applying the suffering of the Son of Man to the Messiah. This shift is "without direct and explicit precedent in the OT, for which 'a suffering Messiah' would be an oxymoron" (Green [1997: 848], whose suggestion that the text implies that it does not matter which texts Jesus explains to the two disciples has no basis in the text).

When the reference to "Moses and all the prophets" in 24:27 ("Then beginning with Moses and all the prophets, he interpreted to them the things about himself in all the scriptures") is factored in, the logic of Jesus' exposition is perhaps based on a correlation of the destiny of the prophets who were rejected, who suffered, and who were often killed with his fate as the Messiah, asserting that the Scriptures "presage the eschatological king who would suffer before entering his glory" (Green 1997: 849; cf. Strauss 1995: 257). At the same time, 24:27 highlights Luke's emphasis on continuity with the Jewish Scriptures (Tomson 2002: 168).

24:44–49

The narrative of Jesus' appearance to his followers in Jerusalem in 24:33–49 includes a passage in which Jesus explains, from Scripture, his death and resurrection. Jesus "opened their minds to understand the scriptures" (24:45) so that they would grasp "that everything written about me in the law of Moses, the prophets, and the psalms must be fulfilled" (24:44). This explanation focused particularly on the notion "that the Messiah is to suffer and to rise from the dead on the third day, and that repentance and forgiveness of sins is to be proclaimed in his name to all nations, beginning from Jerusalem" (24:46–47). Verse 44 is prime evidence for the early existence of the tripartite "canon" of Law, Prophets, and Writings, paralleled in 4Q397 14–21; 4Q398 14–17 I, 3–4. Jesus' reference to the law of Moses, the prophets, and the psalms establishes not only a general continuity with the Jewish Scriptures, but also, and more importantly, a continuity between the past reality of divine salvation in Israel's history and the present reality of the events that had just transpired in the Holy City (see Tomson 2002: 169).

Some scholars suggest that Luke demonstrates with this passage that the resurrection itself does not appear to be adequate for belief (see Powery 1999: 242). This is true only insofar as the significance of Jesus' resurrection and the meaning of his suffering and death are concerned. Note that Jesus argued in 16:31 that if God's revelation in Scripture is unconvincing, neither will a resurrected person be able to convince sinners to repent. If in 16:31 the Scriptures are more persuasive than a resurrection, in 24:44–47 the Scriptures themselves are misunderstood without belief in Jesus' resurrection. In other words, Jesus' death and resurrection are what give proper meaning to the Scriptures.

The statement in 24:46, that Jesus' death fulfills Scripture, is supported by references to OT passages in other parts of the Gospel of Luke; see the references to Ps. 118:22 (Luke 20:17), Isa. 53:12 (Luke 22:37), Ps. 31:5 (Luke 23:46), and Ps. 22:7, 18; 69:21 (Luke 23:34–36). See also the references in the book of Acts, where Jesus' death is interpreted with reference to Ps. 118:22 (Acts 4:11), Ps. 2:1–2 (Acts 4:25–26), and Isa. 53:7–8 (Acts 8:32–33); note also the reference to Ps. 16:8–11 (Acts 2:25–28; 13:35) and Isa.

55:3 (Acts 13:34) to explain Jesus' resurrection, presupposing his death (Tannehill 1986–1990: 1:285; Pao 2000: 85 with note 86).

Verse 47, "and that repentance and forgiveness of sins is to be proclaimed in his name to all nations [*eis panta ta ethnē*], beginning from Jerusalem," formulates Jesus' final commission to the disciples in this Gospel. This statement should be read in the light of Jesus' final commission in the book of Acts in Acts 1:8b, "You will be my witnesses in Jerusalem, in all Judea and Samaria, and to the ends of the earth [*heōs eschatou tēs gēs*]," a text that alludes to Isa. 49:6: "I will give you [Yahweh's Servant] as a light to the nations, that my salvation may reach to the end of the earth [*eis sōtērian heōs eschatou tēs gēs*]." Note that Isa. 49:6 is alluded to in Luke 2:32, quoted in Acts 13:47, and echoed in Acts 1:8 (Green 1997: 857). Granted that the connection between the programmatic statements in 24:47 and in Acts 1:8 is deliberate, 24:47 may be regarded as an allusion to Isa. 49:6 and thus as a reference to the Isaianic new-exodus program as announced in Luke 4:16–30, pushed forward with the introduction of the Gentiles (Pao 2000: 84–91; cf. Dupont 1974: 136–38). The allusion to Isa. 49:6 "provides continuity with the past history of the people of God while at the same time justifying the move to the Gentiles and the eventual redefinition of the people of God" (Pao 2000: 91).

The notion that the beginning of the messianic age will be noticeable first in Jerusalem, where the good news of repentance and the forgiveness of sins is first proclaimed (24:47), indicates a reversal of the direction assumed by the OT promises concerning the conversion of the Gentiles in the last days (Isa. 2:2–5 [Mic. 4:1–4]; 14:2; 45:14; 49:22–23; 55:5; 66:20; Jer. 16:19–21; Zeph. 3:9–10; Zech. 8:20–23; 14:16–19). Whereas the Jews expected the nations to come from "outside" to Jerusalem as the center of the world, Jesus tells his disciples that they will begin in Jerusalem and then move out to the nations. Note also, however, several rabbinic texts—for example, *Lev. Rab.* 24: "R. Levi said: All goodness and blessings and consolation which the Holy One, blessed be He, will give to Israel comes only from Zion"; see also *Pesiq. Rab.* 41 (173b); *Midr. Ps.* 14 (57a); 20 (88b); *b. Yoma* 54b; *'Ag. Ber.* 53 (Lachs 1987: 444). The conversion of the Gentiles and their integration into the people of God as converted *Gentiles* belongs to the "mystery" to which Paul repeatedly refers (cf. Rom. 16:25–27; Col. 1:25–27; Eph. 3:5; see Carson 2004; Schnabel 2004: 441–42).

The designation of God's Spirit in 24:49 as "power from on high" (*ex hypsous dynamin*), applying the "language of promise" to God's Spirit (Nolland 1989–1993: 1220), echoes texts such as Isa. 32:15; 44:3; Ezek. 39:29; Joel 2:28. Note Isa. 32:15: "until a spirit from on high [*rûaḥ mimmārôm*; LXX: *pneuma aph'hypsēlou*] is poured out on us, and the wilderness becomes a fruitful field, and the fruitful field is deemed a forest." The Targum renders the phrase "spirit from on high" as "Spirit from his Shekhinah in the heavens of the height."

24:50–51

Jesus' final act in 24:50 before his ascension, "lifting up his hands, he blessed them," has been interpreted as an allusion to the priestly blessing in Lev. 9:22, "Aaron lifted his hands toward the people and blessed them; and he came down after sacrificing the sin offering, the burnt offering, and the offering of well-being" (cf. Sir. 50:20–22), linked with the suggestion that Luke closes his Gospel with a reference to Jesus as priest (Lohfink 1971: 169ff; Grundmann 1978: 453–54; Ernst 1977: 672; cf. Nolland [1989–1993: 1227], who refers also to Gen. 49; Deut. 33). It should be noted, however, that Luke in his Gospel shows no interest in depicting Jesus as a priest (Marshall 1978: 909; Fitzmyer 1981–1985: 1590; Bock 1994–1996: 1946).

Luke's statement in 24:51 that Jesus "was carried up into heaven" recalls several OT texts that describe the departure of supernatural figures (Gen. 17:22; 35:13; Judg. 6:21; 13:20; cf. Tob. 12:20–21; 2 Macc. 3:34), especially Gen. 5:24, which relates the translation of Enoch (cf. Sir. 44:16; 49:14; Heb. 11:5). Luke's description of Jesus' ascension in Acts 1:9–11 displays links with the translation of Elijah (2 Kings 2; cf. Sir. 48:9; 1 Macc. 2:58) (Marshall 1978: 909; Nolland 1989–1993: 1228; cf. Lohfink [1971: 170–71], who points out that Luke often describes the departure of supernatural visitors [see Luke 1:38; 2:15; 9:33; 24:31; Acts 10:7; 12:10]).

Bibliography

Abogunrin, S. O. 1985. "The Three Variant Accounts of Peter's Call: A Critical and Theological Examination of the Texts." *NTS* 31: 587–602.

Achtemeier, P. J. 1978. "The Lukan Perspective on the Miracles of Jesus." Pages 153–67 in *Perspectives on Luke-Acts*. Edited by C. H. Talbert. Danville, VA: Association of Baptist Professors of Religion.

Ådna, J. 1996. "Der Gottesknecht als triumphierender und interzessorischer Messias: Die Rezeption von Jes 53 im Targum Jonathan untersucht mit besonderer Berücksichtigung des Messiasbildes." Pages 129–58 in *Der leidende Gottesknecht: Jesaja 53 und seine Wirkungsgeschichte*. Edited by B. Janowski and P. Stuhlmacher. FAT 14. Tübingen: Mohr Siebeck.

———. 1999. *Jerusalemer Tempel und Tempelmarkt im 1. Jahrhundert n. Chr.* ADP 25. Wiesbaden: Harrassowitz.

———. 2000. *Jesu Stellung zum Tempel: Die Tempelaktion und das Tempelwort als Ausdruck seiner messianischen Sendung.* WUNT 2/119. Tübingen: Mohr Siebeck.

Albl, M. C. 1999. *"And Scripture Cannot Be Broken": The Form and Function of the Early Christian Testimonia Collections.* NovTSup 96. Leiden: Brill.

Aletti, J.-N. 1985. "Jésus à Nazareth (Lc 4, 16–30): Prophétie écriture et typologie." Pages 431–51 in *À cause de l'Évangile: Études sur les Synoptiques et les Actes, offertes au P. Jacques Dupont O.S.B. à l'occasion de son 70e anniversaire.* Paris: Cerf.

Allen, L. C. 1983. *Psalms 101–150.* WBC 21. Dallas: Word.

Allison, D. C. 1983. "Matt. 23:39 = Luke 13:35b as a Conditional Prophecy." *JSNT* 18: 75–84.

———. 1989–1990. "'The Hairs of Your Head Are All Numbered.'" *ExpTim* 101: 334–36.

———. 1992. "The Baptism of Jesus and a New Dead Sea Scroll." *BAR* 18: 58–60.

———. 1993. *The New Moses: A Matthean Typology.* Minneapolis: Fortress.

———. 2000a. *The Intertextual Jesus: Scripture in Q.* Harrisburg, PA: Trinity Press International.

———. 2000b. *Scriptural Allusions in the New Testament: Light from the Dead Sea Scrolls.* DSSCOL 5. North Richland Hills, TX: BIBAL Press.

Audet, J. P. 1959. "Literary Forms and Contents of a Normal Εὐχαριστία in the First Century." *SE* I: 643–62.

Aune, D. E. 1983. *Prophecy in Early Christianity and the Ancient Mediterranean World.* Grand Rapids: Eerdmans.

———. 1987. *The New Testament in Its Literary Environment.* LEC 8. Philadelphia: Westminster.

Aus, R. D. 2000. *The Stilling of the Storm: Studies in Early Palestinian Judaic Traditions.* Binghamton, NY: Global Publications.

Baldwin, E. 1920. "Gethsemane: The Fulfillment of Prophecy." *BSac* 77: 429–36.

Baltzer, K. 1965. "The Meaning of the Temple in the Lukan Writings." *HTR* 58: 263–77.

Barrett, C. K. 1988. "Luke/Acts." Pages 231–44 in *It Is Written: Scripture Citing Scripture; Essays in Honour of Barnabas Lindars, SSF.* Edited by D. A. Carson and H. G. M. Williamson. Cambridge: Cambridge University Press.

———. 1996. "The First New Testament." *NovT* 38: 94–104.

Bascom, R. A. 1988. "Preparing the Way—Midrash in the Bible." Pages 221–46 in *Issues in Bible Translation.* Edited by P. C. Stine. UBSMS 3. London: United Bible Societies.

———. 1996. "Adaptable for Translation: Deuteronomy 6.5 in the Synoptic Gospels and Beyond." Pages 166–83 in *A Gift of God in Due Season: Essays on Scripture and Community in Honor of James A. Sanders.* Edited by R. D. Weis and D. M. Carr. JSOTSup 225. Sheffield: Sheffield Academic Press.

Bauckham, R. J. 1983. *Jude, 2 Peter.* WBC 50. Waco: Word.

———. 1991. "More on Kainam the Son of Arpachshad in Luke's Genealogy." *ETL* 67: 95–103.

———. 1995. "The Messianic Interpretation of Isa. 10:34 in the Dead Sea Scrolls, 2 Baruch and the Preaching of John the Baptist." *DSD* 2: 202–16.

———. 1997. "Anna of the Tribe of Asher (Luke 2:36–38)." *RB* 104: 161–91.

Baumgarten, J. M. 1994. "Purification after Childbirth and the Sacred Garden in 4Q265 and Jubilees." Pages 3–10 in *New Qumran Texts and Studies: Proceedings of the First Meeting of the International Organization for Qumran Studies, Paris 1992.* Edited by G. J. Brooke. STDJ 15. Leiden: Brill.

Bayer, H. F. 1986. *Jesus' Predictions of Vindication and Resurrection: The Provenance, Meaning and Correlation of the Synoptic Predictions.* WUNT 2/20. Tübingen: Mohr Siebeck.

Beale, G. K. 1991. "Isaiah 6:9–13: A Retributive Taunt against Idolatry." *VT* 41: 257–78.

———. 1999. *The Book of Revelation: A Commentary on the Greek Text.* NIGTC. Grand Rapids: Eerdmans.

Betz, H. D. 1981. "Review of *Die Reinigung der zehn Aussätzigen und die Heilung des Samariters* by W. Bruners." *TLZ* 106:338–39.

———. 1995. *The Sermon on the Mount: A Commentary on the Sermon on the Mount, Including the Sermon on the Plain (Matthew 5:3–7:27 and Luke 6:20–49).* Hermeneia. Minneapolis: Fortress.

Betz, O. 1996. "Jesus und Jesaja 53." Pages 3–19 in *Frühes Christentum.* Vol. 3 of *Geschichte, Tradition, Reflexion: Festschrift für Martin Hengel zum 70. Geburtstag.* Edited by H. Lichtenberger. Tübingen: Mohr Siebeck.

———. 1998. "Jesus and Isaiah 53." Pages 70–87 in *Jesus and the Suffering Servant: Isaiah 53 and Christian Origins.* Edited by W. H. Bellinger and W. R. Farmer. Harrisburg, PA: Trinity Press International.

Beuken, W. A. M. 1972. "Mispat: The First Servant Song and Its Context." *VT* 22: 1–30.

———. 1986. "An Example of the Isaianic Legacy of Trito-Isaiah." Pages 48–64 in *Tradition and Re-interpretation in Jewish and Early Christian Literature: Essays in Honour of Jurgen C. H. Lebram.* Edited by J. W. Van Henton et al. StPB 36. Leiden: Brill.

———. 1989. "Servant and Herald of Good Tidings: Isaiah 61 as an Interpretation of Isaiah 40–55." Pages 411–12 in *The Book of Isaiah—Le livre d'Isaïe: Les oracles et leurs relectures; Unité et complexité de l'ouvrage.* Edited by J. Vermeylen. BETL 81. Leuven: Leuven University Press.

Blenkinsopp, J. 1961. "The Oracle of Judah and the Messianic Entry." *JBL* 80: 55–64.

———. 2000–2003. *Isaiah.* 3 vols. AB 19, 19A, 19B. New York: Doubleday.

Blomberg, C. L. 1983. "Midrash, Chiasmus, and the Outline of Luke's Central Section." Pages 217–59 in *Studies in Midrash and Historiography.* Vol. 3 of *Gospel Perspectives.* Edited by R. T. France and D. Wenham. Sheffield: JSOT Press.

———. 1990. *Interpreting the Parables.* Leicester: Inter-Varsity.

Bock, D. L. 1986. "Jesus as Lord in Acts and in the Gospel Message." *BSac* 143: 146–54.

———. 1987. *Proclamation from Prophecy and Pattern: Lucan Old Testament Christology.* JSNTSup 12. Sheffield: JSOT Press.

———. 1990. "The Use of the Old Testament in Luke-Acts: Christology and Mission." *SBLSP* 29: 494–511.

———. 1994. "Proclamation from Prophecy and Pattern: Luke's Use of the Old Testament for Christology and Mission." Pages 280–307 in *The Gospels and the Scriptures of Israel.* Edited by C. A. Evans and W. R. Stegner. JSNTSup 104. Sheffield: Sheffield Academic Press.

———. 1994–1996. *Luke.* 2 vols. BECNT. Grand Rapids: Baker Academic.

———. 1998. *Blasphemy and Exaltation in Judaism and the Final Examination of Jesus.* WUNT 2/106. Tübingen: Mohr Siebeck.

Bockmuehl, M. 1990. *Revelation and Mystery in Ancient Judaism and Pauline Christianity.* WUNT 2/36. Tübingen: Mohr Siebeck.

———. 1998. "'Let the Dead Bury Their Dead' (Matt 8:22/Luke 9:60): Jesus and the Halakhah." *JTS* 49: 553–81.

Böhler, D. 1998. "Jesus als Davidssohn bei Lukas und Micha." *Bib* 79: 532–38.

Boismard, M. E. 1972. *Synopse des quatre Évangiles en Français: Avec parallèles des Apocryphes et des Pères.* 2nd ed. 2 vols. Paris: Cerf.

———. 1995. "'Notre pain quotidien' (Mt 6, 11)." *RB* 102: 371–78.

Borg, M. 1984. *Conflict, Holiness, and Politics in the Teachings of Jesus.* SBEC 5. New York: Mellen.

Bornhäuser, K. 1947. *Die Leidens- und Auferstehungsgeschichte Jesu.* Gütersloh: Bertelsmann.

Bovon, F. 1978. "La figure de Moïse dans l'œuvre de Luc." Pages 47–65 in *La Figure de Moïse: Écriture et relectures.* Edited by R. Martin-Archard et al. Publications de la Faculté de théologie de l'Université de Genève 17. Geneva: Labor et Fides.

———. 1989–2001. *Das Evangelium nach Lukas.* 3 vols. EKKNT 3. Zürich: Benziger; Neukirchen-Vluyn: Neukirchener Verlag.

———. 1991–2001. *L'Évangile selon Saint Luc.* 3 vols. CNT 3A, 3B, 3C. Geneva: Labor et Fides.

———. 1993. "The Role of the Scriptures in the Composition of the Gospel Accounts: The Temptations of Jesus (Lk 4:1–13 par.) and the Multiplication of the Loaves (Lk 9:10–17 par.)." Pages 26–31 in *Luke and Acts.* Edited by G. O'Collins and G. Marconi. New York: Paulist Press.

———. 2002. *Luke 1: A Commentary on the Gospel of Luke 1:1–9:50.* Translated by C. M. Thomas. Hermeneia. Philadelphia: Fortress.

Bratcher, R. G. 1982. *A Translator's Guide to the Gospel of Luke.* HT. New York: United Bible Societies.

Brawley, R. L. 1987. *Luke-Acts and the Jews: Conflict, Apology, and Conciliation.* SBLMS 33. Atlanta: Scholars Press.

———. 1990. *Centering on God: Method and Message in Luke-Acts.* Louisville: Westminster John Knox.

———. 1992. "Canon and Community: Intertextuality, Canon, Interpretation, Christology, Theology, and Persuasive Rhetoric in Luke 4:1–13." *SBLSP* 31: 419–34.

———. 1995. *Text to Text Pours Forth Speech: Voices of Scripture in Luke–Acts.* ISBL. Bloomington: Indiana University Press.

Brenner, A. 1986. "Female Social Behavior: Two Descriptive Patterns within the 'Birth of the Hero' Paradigm." *VT* 36: 257–73.

Bretscher, P. G. 1968. "Exodus 4.22–23 and the Voice from Heaven." *JBL* 87: 301–11.

Brodie, T. L. 1987. *Luke the Literary Interpreter: Luke-Acts as a Systematic Rewriting and Updating of the Elijah-Elisha Narrative.* Rome: Pontifical University of St. Thomas Aquinas.

———. 1989. "The Departure for Jerusalem (Luke 9:51–56) and a Rhetorical Imitation of Elijah's Departure for the Jordan (2 Kings 1:1–2:6)." *Bib* 70: 96–109.

———. 1990. "Luke-Acts as an Imitation and Emulation of the Elijah-Elisha Narrative." Pages 78–85 in *New Views on Luke and Acts*. Edited by E. Richard. Collegeville, MN: Liturgical Press.

———. 1992. "Not Q but Elijah: The Saving of the Centurion's Servant (Luke 7:1–10) as an Internalization of the Saving of the Widow and Her Child (1 Kings 17:1–16)." *IBS* 14: 54–71.

Brooke, G. H. 1993. "4QTestament of Leviᵃ (?) and the Messianic Servant High Priest." Pages 83–100 in *From Jesus to John: Essays on Jesus and New Testament Christology in Honour of Marinus de Jonge*. JSNTSup 84. Edited by M. C. de Boer. Sheffield: JSOT Press.

Brown, R. E. 1968. *The Semitic Background of the Term "Mystery" in the New Testament*. FBBS 21. Philadelphia: Fortress.

———. 1993. *The Birth of the Messiah: A Commentary on the Infancy Narratives in the Gospels of Matthew and Luke*. Rev. ed. ABRL. New York: Doubleday.

———. 1994. *The Death of the Messiah: From Gethsemane to the Grave; A Commentary on the Passion Narratives in the Four Gospels*. 2 vols. ABRL. New York: Doubleday.

Brown, S. 1969. *Apostasy and Perseverance in the Theology of Luke*. AnBib 36. Rome: Pontifical Biblical Institute.

Brueggemann, W. 1982. "'Impossibility' and Epistemology in the Faith Tradition of Abraham and Sarah (Gen 18:1–15)." *ZAW* 94: 615–34.

Bruners, W. 1977. *Die Reinigung der zehn Aussätzigen und die Heilung des Samariters, Lk 17,11–19: Ein Beitrag zur lukanischen Interpretation der Reinigung von Aussätzigen*. FB 23. Stuttgart: Kohlhammer.

Buckwalter, H. D. 1996. *The Character and Purpose of Luke's Christology*. SNTSMS 89. Cambridge: Cambridge University Press.

Bultmann, R. 1963. *The History of the Synoptic Tradition*. Oxford: Blackwell; New York: Harper & Row.

Burrows, E. 1940. *The Gospel of the Infancy and Other Biblical Essays*. Edited by E. F. Sutcliffe. Bellarmine 6. London: Burns, Oates & Washbourne.

Cadbury, H. J. 1958. *The Making of Luke-Acts*. London: SPCK.

Caird, G. B. 1963. *Gospel of Saint Luke*. PNTC. Hammondsworth: Penguin.

Callan, T. 1982. "Psalm 110:1 and the Origin of the Expectation that Jesus Will Come Again." *CBQ* 44: 622–35.

Callaway, M. 1986. *Sing, O Barren One: A Study in Comparative Midrash*. SBLDS 91. Atlanta: Scholars Press.

Carroll, J. T. 1988. *Response to the End of History: Eschatology and Situation in Luke-Acts*. SBLDS 92. Atlanta: Scholars Press.

Carson, D. A. 1984. "Matthew." Pages 3–599 in vol. 8 of *The Expositor's Bible Commentary*. Edited by F. E. Gaebelein. Grand Rapids: Zondervan.

———. 1994a. "Do the Prophets and the Law Quit Prophesying before John? A Note on Matthew 11.13." Pages 179–94 in *The Gospels and the Scriptures of Israel*. Edited by C. A. Evans and W. R. Stegner. JSNTSup 104. Sheffield: Sheffield Academic Press.

———. 1994b. "Matthew 11:19b/Luke 7:35: A Test Case for the Bearing of Q Christology on the Synoptic Problem." Pages 128–46 in *Jesus of Nazareth: Lord and Christ; Essays on the Historical Jesus and New Testament Christology*. Edited by J. B. Green and M. Turner. Grand Rapids: Eerdmans.

———. 2004. "Mystery and Fulfillment: Toward a More Comprehensive Paradigm of Paul's Understanding of the Old and the New." Pages 393–436 in *The Paradoxes of Paul*. Vol. 2 of *Justification and Variegated Nomism: A Fresh Appraisal of Paul and Second*

Temple Judaism. WUNT 2/181. Edited by D. A. Carson, P. T. O'Brien, and M. A. Seifrid. Tübingen: Mohr Siebeck.

Casey, M. 1988. "Culture and Historicity: The Plucking of the Grain (Mark 2.23–28)." *NTS* 34: 1–23.

Catchpole, D. R. 1986. "Jesus and the Community of Israel—The Inaugural Discourse in Q." *BJRL* 68: 296–316.

Chance, J. B. 1988. *Jerusalem, the Temple, and the New Age in Luke-Acts*. Macon, GA: Mercer University Press.

Charlesworth, J. H., ed. 1992. *The Messiah: Developments in Earliest Judaism and Christianity*. Minneapolis: Fortress.

———. 1997. "Intertextuality: Isaiah 40:3 and the Serek ha-Yahad." Pages 197–224 in *The Quest for Context and Meaning: Studies in Biblical Intertextuality in Honor of James A. Sanders*. Edited by C. A. Evans and S. Talmon. BIS 28. Leiden: Brill.

———. 2000. "The Qumran Beatitudes (4Q525) and the New Testament (Mt 5:3–11, Lk 6:20–26)." *RHPR* 80: 13–35.

Childs, B. S. 1974. *The Book of Exodus*. OTL. Louisville: Westminster.

———. 1977. *Introduction to the Old Testament as Scripture*. Philadelphia: Fortress.

———. 2001. *Isaiah*. OTL. Louisville: Westminster John Knox.

Chilton, B. D. 1981. "Announcement in Nazara." Pages 147–72 in *Studies in History and Tradition in the Four Gospels*. Vol. 2 of *Gospel Perspectives*. Edited by R. T. France and D. Wenham. Sheffield: JSOT Press.

———. 1984. *A Galilean Rabbi and His Bible: Jesus' Use of the Interpreted Scripture of His Time*. GNS 8. Wilmington, DE: Glazier.

———, trans. and ed. 1987. *The Isaiah Targum*. ArBib 11. Wilmington, DE: Glazier.

———. 1992. *The Temple of Jesus: His Sacrificial Program within a Cultural History of Sacrifice*. University Park: Pennsylvania State University Press.

Chow, S. 1995. *The Sign of Jonah Reconsidered: A Study of Its Meaning in the Gospel Traditions*. ConBNT 27. Stockholm: Almqvist & Wiksell.

Clements, R. E. 1967. *Abraham and David: Genesis XV and Its Meaning for Israelite Tradition*. SBT 2/5. London: SCM.

Coggins, R. J. 1975. *Samaritans and Jews: The Origins of Samaritanism Reconsidered*. Oxford: Blackwell.

Collins, J. J. 1987. "The Kingdom of God in the Apocrypha and Pseudepigrapha." Pages 81–95 in *The Kingdom of God in 20th-Century Interpretation*. Edited by W. Willis. Peabody, MA: Hendrickson.

———. 1992. "The Son of Man in First-Century Judaism." *NTS* 3: 448–66.

———. 1994. "The Works of the Messiah." *DSD* 1: 98–112.

———. 1995. *The Scepter and the Star: The Messiahs of the Dead Sea Scrolls and Other Ancient Literature*. ABRL. New York: Doubleday.

———. 1997. "A Herald of Good Tidings: Isaiah 61:1–3 and Its Actualization in the Dead Sea Scrolls." Pages 225–40 in *The Quest for Context and Meaning: Studies in Biblical Intertextuality in Honor of James A. Sanders*. Edited by C. A. Evans and S. Talmon. BIS 28. Leiden: Brill.

Conrad, E. W. 1985. *Fear Not Warrior: A Study of 'al tîra' Pericopes in the Hebrew Scriptures*. BJS 75. Chico, CA: Scholars Press.

Constant, P. 2001. "Psaume 118 et son emploi christologique dans Luc et Actes: Une étude exégétique, littéraire et herméneutique." PhD diss., Trinity Evangelical Divinity School.

Conzelmann, H. 1960. *The Theology of St. Luke*. 2nd ed. New York: Harper & Brothers.

Cosgrove, C. H. 1984. "The Divine ΔEI in Luke-Acts: Investigations into the Lukan Understanding of God's Providence." *NovT* 26: 168–90.

Craigie, P. C. 1976. *The Book of Deuteronomy*. NICOT. Grand Rapids: Eerdmans.

———. 1983. *Psalms 1–50*. WBC 19. Dallas: Word.

Creed, J. M. 1930. *The Gospel according to St. Luke*. London: Macmillan.

Crockett, L. C. 1966a. "Luke iv 16–30 and the Jewish Lectionary Cycle: A Word of Caution." *JJS* 17: 13–46.

———. 1966b. "The Old Testament in the Gospel of Luke: With Emphasis on the Interpretation of Isaiah 61:1–2." PhD diss., Brown University.

———. 1969. "Luke 4:25–27 and Jewish-Gentile Relations in Luke-Acts." *JBL* 88: 177–83.

Cross, F. M. 1958. *The Ancient Library of Qumran and Modern Biblical Studies*. Garden City, NY: Doubleday.

———. 1973. *Canaanite Myth and Hebrew Epic: Essays in the History of the Religion of Israel*. Cambridge, MA: Harvard University Press.

Crump, D. 1992. *Jesus the Intercessor: Prayer and Christology in Luke-Acts*. WUNT 2/49. Tübingen: Mohr Siebeck.

Cullmann, O. 1963. *The Christology of the New Testament*. Translated by S. C. Guthrie and C. A. M. Hall. Rev. ed. Philadelphia: Westminster.

Culpepper, R. A. 1995. "Luke." Pages 1–49 in vol. 9 of *The New Interpreter's Bible*. Nashville: Abingdon.

Dahl, N. A. 1966. "The Story of Abraham in Luke-Acts." Pages 139–59 in *Studies in Luke-Acts: Essays Presented in Honor of Paul Schubert*. Edited by L. E. Keck and J. L. Martyn. Nashville: Abingdon.

Dahood, M. 1966–1970. *Psalms*. 3 vols. AB 16, 17, 17A. Garden City, NY: Doubleday.

Daly, R. J. 1977. "The Soteriological Significance of the Sacrifice of Isaac." *CBQ* 39: 45–75.

Danker, F. W. 1988. *Jesus and the New Age: A Commentary on St. Luke's Gospel*. Rev. ed. Philadelphia: Fortress.

Daube, D. 1955. "Inheritance in Two Lukan Pericopes." *Zeitschrift der Savigny Stiftung für Rechtsgeschichte* 72: 326–34.

Davies, W. D., and D. C. Allison Jr. 1988–1997. *A Critical and Exegetical Commentary on the Gospel according to Saint Matthew*. 3 vols. ICC. Edinburgh: T&T Clark.

Davis, C. J. 1996. *The Name and Way of the Lord: Old Testament Themes, New Testament Christology*. JSNTSup 129. Sheffield: Sheffield Academic Press.

de Jonge, H. J. 1978. "Sonship, Wisdom, Infancy: Luke II.41–51a." *NTS* 24: 317–54.

de Jonge, M. 1988. *Christology in Context: The Earliest Christian Response to Jesus*. Philadelphia: Westminster.

Delling, G. 1970a. "Βάπτισμα, Βαπτισθῆναι." Pages 236–56 in *Studien zum Neuen Testament und zum hellenistischen Judentum: Gesammelte Aufsätze 1950–1968*. Edited by F. Hahn. Göttingen: Vandenhoeck & Ruprecht.

———. 1970b. "Das Gleichnis vom gottlosen Richter." Pages 203–25 in *Studien zum Neuen Testament und zum hellenistischen Judentum: Gesammelte Aufsätze 1950–1968*. Edited by F. Hahn. Göttingen: Vandenhoeck & Ruprecht.

Denaux, A. 1997. "Old Testament Models for the Lukan Travel Narrative: A Critical Survey." Pages 271–305 in *The Scriptures in the Gospels*. Edited by C. M. Tuckett. BETL 131. Leuven: Leuven University Press.

Denova, R. I. 1997. *The Things Accomplished among Us: Prophetic Tradition in the Structural Pattern of Luke-Acts*. JSNTSup 141. Sheffield: Sheffield Academic Press.

Derrett, J. D. M. 1970. *Law in the New Testament*. London: Darton, Longman & Todd.

———. 1973. "Law in the New Testament: The Syro-Phoenician Woman and the Centurion of Capernaum." *NovT* 15: 161–86.

———. 1975. "Further Light on the Narratives of the Nativity." *NovT* 17: 81–108.

———. 1977. *Glimpses of the Legal and Social Presuppositions of the Authors*. Vol. 1 of *Studies in the New Testament*. Leiden: Brill.

———. 1978. *Midrash in Action and as a Literary Device*. Vol. 2 of *Studies in the New Testament*. Leiden: Brill.

———. 1983. "Luke's Perspective on Tribute to Caesar." Pages 38–48 in *Political Issues in Luke-Acts*. Edited by R. J. Cassidy and P. J. Scharper. Maryknoll, NY: Orbis.

———. 1999. "Luke 2.7 Again." *NTS* 45: 263.

DeYoung, J. B. 1994. "The Function of Malachi 3.1 in Matthew 11.10: Kingdom Reality as the Hermeneutic of Jesus." Pages 66–91 in *The Gospels and the Scriptures of Israel*. Edited by C. A. Evans and W. R. Stegner. JSNTSup 104. Sheffield: Sheffield Academic Press.

Diamond, E. 2004. *Holy Men and Hunger Artists: Fasting and Asceticism in Rabbinic Culture*. New York: Oxford University Press.

Dibelius, M. 1953. "Herodes und Pilatus." Pages 278–92 in *Zur Evangelienforschung*. Vol. 1 of *Botschaft und Geschichte: Gesammelte Aufsätze*. Edited by G. Bornkamm. Tübingen: Mohr Siebeck.

Doble, P. 1996. *The Paradox of Salvation: Luke's Theology of the Cross*. SNTSMS 87. Cambridge: Cambridge University Press.

———. 2000. "Something Greater than Solomon: An Approach to Stephen's Speech." Pages 181–207 in *The Old Testament in the New Testament: Essays in Honor of J. L. North*. Edited by S. Moyise. JSNTSup 189. Sheffield: Sheffield Academic Press.

Dodd, C. H. 1952. *According to the Scriptures: The Sub-structure of New Testament Theology*. London: Nisbet.

Doeve, J. W. 1954. *Jewish Hermeneutics in the Synoptic Gospels and Acts*. Assen: Van Gorcum.

Donald, T. 1963. "The Semantic Field of 'Folly' in Proverbs, Job, Psalms, and Ecclesiastes." *VT* 13: 285–92.

Döpp, H.-M. 1998. *Die Deutung der Zerstörung Jerusalems und des Zweiten Tempels im Jahre 70 in den ersten drei Jahrhunderten n. Chr.* TANZ 24. Tübingen: Francke.

Downing, F. G. 1982. "The Resurrection of the Dead: Jesus and Philo." *JSNT* 15: 42–50.

Drury, J. 1976. *Tradition and Design in Luke's Gospel: A Study of Early Christian Historiography*. Atlanta: John Knox.

Dunn, J. D. G. 1970. *Baptism in the Holy Spirit: A Re-examination of the New Testament Teaching on the Gift of the Spirit in Relation to Pentecostalism Today*. SBT 2/15. London: SCM.

———. 1994. "John the Baptist's Use of Scripture." Pages 42–54 in *The Gospels and the Scriptures of Israel*. Edited by C. A. Evans and W. R. Stegner. JSNTSup 104. Sheffield: Sheffield Academic Press.

———. 2003. *Jesus Remembered*. Christianity in the Making 1. Grand Rapids: Eerdmans.

Dupont, J. 1957. "L'arrière-fond biblique du récit des tentations des Jésus." *NTS* 3: 287–304.

———. 1964. "La logion des douze trônes." *Bib* 45: 355–92.

———. 1973. *La bonne nouvelle*. Vol. 2 of *Les béatitudes*. EBib. Paris: Gabalda.

———. 1974. "La portée christologique de l'évangélisation des nations d'après Lc 24,47." Pages 125–43 in *Neues Testament und Kirche: Für Rudolf Schnackenburg zum 60. Geburtstag am 5. Jan. 1974 von Freunden und Kollegen gewidmet*. Edited by J. Gnilka. Freiburg: Herder.

———. 1985. "Un peuple d'entre les nations (Actes 15.14)." *NTS* 31: 321–35.

Durham, J. I. 1987. *Exodus*. WBC 3. Waco: Word.

Egelkraut, H. L. 1976. *Jesus' Mission to Jerusalem: A Redaction-Critical Study of the Travel Narrative in the Gospel of Luke, Lk. 9:51–19:48*. EUS 23/80. Frankfurt: Peter Lang.

Elliott, J. K. 1988. "Anna's Age (Luke 2:36–37)." *NovT* 30: 100–102.

Ellis, E. E. 1974. *The Gospel of Luke*. NCBC. Grand Rapids: Eerdmans.

———. 1978. *Prophecy and Hermeneutic in Early Christianity: New Testament Essays*. WUNT 18. Tübingen: Mohr Siebeck.

———. 1981. *Paul's Use of the Old Testament*. Grand Rapids: Baker Academic.

———. 1991. *The Old Testament in Early Christianity: Canon and Interpretation in the Light of Modern Research*. WUNT 54. Tübingen: Mohr Siebeck.

Ernst, J. 1977. *Das Evangelium nach Lukas*. RNT. Regensburg: Pustet.

Evans, C. A. 1982. "'He Set His Face': A Note on Luke 9,51." *Bib* 63: 545–48.

———. 1985. "On the Isaianic Background of the Sower Parable." *CBQ* 47: 464–68.

———. 1987. "'He Set His Face': Luke 9,51 Once Again." *Bib* 68: 80–84.

———. 1989. *To See and Not Perceive: Isaiah 6.9–10 in Early Jewish and Christian Interpretation*. JSOTSup 64. Sheffield: JSOT Press.

———. 1990. *Luke*. NIBCNT 3. Peabody, MA: Hendrickson.

———. 1993a. "The Function of the Elijah/Elisha Narratives in Luke's Ethic of Election." Pages 70–83 in *Luke and Scripture: The Function of Sacred Tradition in Luke-Acts*. Edited by C. A. Evans and J. A. Sanders. Minneapolis: Fortress.

———. 1993b. "Luke 16:1–18 and the Deuteronomy Hypothesis." Pages 121–39 in *Luke and Scripture: The Function of Sacred Tradition in Luke-Acts*. Edited by C. A. Evans and J. A. Sanders. Minneapolis: Fortress.

———. 1994. "The Pharisee and the Publican (Lk 18:9–14 and Deuteronomy 26)." Pages 342–55 in *The Gospels and the Scriptures of Israel*. Edited by C. A. Evans and W. R. Stegner. JSNTSup 104. Sheffield: Sheffield Academic Press.

———. 2001. *Mark 8:27–16:20*. WBC 34B. Nashville: Nelson.

———. 2004. "The Aramaic Psalter and the New Testament: Praising the Lord in History and Prophecy." Pages 44–91 in *From Prophecy to Testament: The Function of the Old Testament in the New*. Edited by C. A. Evans. Peabody, MA: Hendrickson.

Evans, C. A., and J. A. Sanders, eds. 1993. *Luke and Scripture: The Function of Sacred Tradition in Luke-Acts*. Minneapolis: Fortress.

Evans, C. F. 1955. "The Central Section of St. Luke's Gospel." Pages 37–53 in *Studies in the Gospels: Essays in Honour of R. H. Lightfoot*. Edited by D. E. Nineham. Oxford: Blackwell.

———. 1990. *Saint Luke*. TPINTC. Philadelphia: Trinity Press International.

Farris, S. 1981. "On Discerning Semitic Sources in Luke 1–2." Pages 201–37 in *Studies in History and Tradition in the Four Gospels*. Vol. 2 of *Gospel Perspectives*. Edited by R. T. France and D. Wenham. Sheffield: JSOT Press.

———. 1985. *The Hymns of Luke's Infancy Narratives: Their Origin, Meaning and Significance*. JSNTSup 9. Sheffield: JSOT Press.

Feiler, P. F. 1986. "Jesus the Prophet: The Lucan Portrayal of Jesus as the Prophet like Moses." PhD diss., Princeton Theological Seminary.

Fernández-Marcos, N. 1987. "La unción de Salomón y la entrada de Jesús en Jerusalén: 1 Re 1,33–40/Lc 19,35–40." *Bib* 68: 89–97.

Finkel, A. 1994. "Jesus' Preaching in the Synagogue on the Sabbath (Lk 4.16–28)." Pages 325–41 in *The Gospels and the Scriptures of Israel*. Edited by C. A. Evans and W. R. Stegner. JSNTSup 104. Sheffield: Sheffield Academic Press.

Fisher, R. W. 1974. "The Herald of Good News in Second Isaiah." Pages 117–32 in *Rhetorical Criticism: Essays in Honor of James Muilenburg*. Edited by J. J. Jackson and M. Kessler. PTMS 1. Pittsburg: Pickwick.

Fitzmyer, J. A. 1974. *Essays on the Semitic Background of the New Testament*. SBS 5. Missoula, MT: Scholars Press.

———. 1975. "Der semitische Hintergrund des neutestamentlichen Kyriostitels." Pages 267–98 in *Jesus Christus in Historie und Theologie: Neutestamentliche Festschrift für Hans Conzelmann zum 60. Geburtstag*. Edited by G. Strecker. Tübingen: Mohr Siebeck.

———. 1978. "The Composition of Luke, Chapter 9." Pages 139–52 in *Perspectives on Luke-Acts*. Edited by C. H. Talbert. Danville, VA: Association of Baptist Professors of Religion.

———. 1979a. "Another View of the 'Son of Man' Debate." *JSNT* 4: 58–68.

———. 1979b. *A Wandering Aramean: Collected Aramaic Essays*. SBLMS 25. Missoula, MT: Scholars Press.

———. 1981–1985. *The Gospel according to Luke*. 2 vols. AB 28, 28A. Garden City, NY: Doubleday.

———. 1997. "The Son of David Tradition and Mt 22:41–46 and Parallels." Pages 113–26 in *The Semitic Background of the New Testament*. Combined ed. BRS. Grand Rapids: Eerdmans.

———. 1998. "The Use of the Old Testament in Luke-Acts." Pages 295–313 in *To Advance the Gospel: New Testament Studies*. 2nd ed. BRS. Grand Rapids: Eerdmans.

Ford, J. M. 1983. "Reconciliation and Forgiveness in Luke's Gospel." Pages 80–98 in *Political Issues in Luke-Acts*. Edited by R. J. Cassidy and P. J. Scharper. Maryknoll, NY: Orbis.

France, R. T. 1971. *Jesus and the Old Testament: His Application of Old Testament Passages to Himself and His Mission*. London: Tyndale.

Freedman, D. N. 1987. "The Structure of Isaiah 40:1–11." Pages 167–93 in *Perspectives on Language and Text: Essays and Poems in Honor of Francis I. Andersen's Sixtieth Birthday*. Edited by E. W. Conrad and E. G. Newing. Winona Lake, IN: Eisenbrauns.

Frein, B. C. 1994. "Narrative Predictions, Old Testament Prophecies and Luke's Sense of Fulfillment." *NTS* 40: 22–37.

Furness, J. M. 1969. "Fresh Light on Luke 10:25–37." *ExpTim* 80: 182.

Gagnon, R. A. J. 1994. "Luke's Motives for Redaction in the Account of the Double Delegation in Luke 7:1–10." *NovT* 36: 122–45.

Garrett, S. R. 1989. *The Demise of the Devil: Magic and the Demonic in Luke's Writings*. Minneapolis: Fortress.

———. 1990. "Exodus from Bondage: Luke 9:31 and Acts 12:1–24." *CBQ* 52: 656–80.

———. 1998. *The Temptation of Jesus in Mark's Gospel*. Grand Rapids: Eerdmans.

Geldenhuys, N. 1977. *The Gospel of Luke*. 10th ed. NICNT. Grand Rapids: Eerdmans.

Gerhardsson, B. 1966. *The Testing of God's Son (Matt. 4:1-11 & Par.): An Analysis of an Early Christian Midrash.* ConBNT 2. Lund: Gleerup.

Gertner, M. 1962. "Midrashim in the New Testament." *JSS* 7: 267–92.

Giblin, C. H. 1971. "'The Things of God' in the Question concerning Tribute to Caesar (Lk 20:25; Mk 12:17; Mt 22:21)." *CBQ* 33: 510–27.

Gibson, J. B. 1995. *The Temptations of Jesus in Early Christianity.* JSNTSup 112. Sheffield: Sheffield Academic Press.

Gill, D. H. 1970. "Observations on the Lukan Travel Narrative and Some Related Passages." *HTR* 63: 199–221.

———. 1991. "Socrates and Jesus on Non-retaliation and Love of Enemies." *Hor* 18: 246–62.

Glazier-McDonald, B. 1987. *Malachi: The Divine Messenger.* SBLDS 98. Atlanta: Scholars Press.

Glöckner, R. 1983. *Neutestamentliche Wundergeschichten und das Lob der Wundertaten Gottes in den Psalmen: Studien zur sprachlichen und theologischen Verwandtschaft zwischen neutestamentlichen Wundergeschichten und Psalmen.* Walberger Studien der Albertus-Magnus-Akademie, Theologische Reihe 13. Mainz: Grünewald.

Gnilka, J. 1961. *Der Verstockung Israels: Isaias 6,9–10 in der Theologie der Synoptiker.* SANT 3. Munich: Kösel.

Gnuse, R. 1998. "The Temple Theophanies of Jaddus, Hyrcanus, and Zechariah." *Bib* 79: 457–72.

Goldingay, J. E. 1989. *Daniel.* WBC 30. Dallas: Word.

———. 2003. *Israel's Gospel.* Vol. 1 of *Old Testament Theology.* Downers Grove, IL: InterVarsity.

Goulder, M. D. 1974. *Midrash and Lection in Matthew.* London: SPCK.

———. 1989. *Luke: A New Paradigm.* 2 vols. JSNTSup 20. Sheffield: JSOT Press.

Gourgues, M. 1998. "The Priest, the Levite, and the Samaritan Revisited: A Critical Note on Luke 10:31–35." *JBL* 117: 709–13.

Gowler, D. B. 1994. "Hospitality and Characterization in Luke 11:37–54: A Socio-Narratological Approach." *Semeia* 64: 213–51.

Grassi, J. A. 1964. "The Five Loaves of the High Priest (Mt xii, 1–8; Mk ii, 23–28; Lk vi, 1–5; 1 Sam xxi, 1–6)." *NovT* 7: 119–22.

Graves, M. 1997. "Luke 10:25–37: The Moral of the 'Good Samaritan.'" *RevExp* 94: 269–75.

Grayston, K. 1993. "The Decline of Temptation—and the Lord's Prayer." *SJT* 46: 279–95.

Green, J. B. 1986. "Jesus on the Mount of Olives (Luke 22.39–46): Tradition and Theology." *JSNT* 26: 29–48.

———. 1990. "The Death of Jesus, God's Servant." Pages 1–28 in *Reimaging the Death of the Lukan Jesus.* BBB 73. Edited by D. D. Sylva. Frankfurt: Hain.

———. 1992. "The Social Status of Mary in Luke 1,5–2,52: A Plea for Methodological Integration." *Bib* 73: 457–72.

———. 1994. "The Problem of a Beginning: Israel's Scriptures in Luke 1–2." *BBR* 4: 61–85.

———. 1997. *The Gospel of Luke.* NICNT. Grand Rapids: Eerdmans.

Grogan, G. W. 1982. "The Light and the Stone: A Christological Study in Luke and Isaiah." Pages 151–67 in *Christ the Lord: Studies in Christology Presented to Donald Guthrie.* Edited by H. H. Rowdon. Leicester: Inter-Varsity.

Grundmann, W. 1978. *Das Evangelium nach Lukas.* 8th ed. THKNT 3. Berlin: Evangelische Verlagsanstalt.

Guelich, R. A. 1973. "The Matthean Beatitudes: 'Entrance-Requirements' or Eschatological Blessings?" *JBL* 95: 415–34.

Gundry, R. H. 1967. *The Use of the Old Testament in St. Matthew's Gospel: With Special Reference to the Messianic Hope.* NovTSup 18. Leiden: Brill.

Hahn, F. 1969. *The Titles of Jesus in Christology: Their History in Early Christianity.* Translated by H. Knight and G. Ogg. London: Lutterworth.

Hamm, D. 1994. "What the Samaritan Leper Sees: The Narrative Christology of Luke 17:11–19." *CBQ* 56: 273–87.

Harrington, D. J. 1989. "Birth Narratives in Pseudo-Philo's Biblical Antiquities and the Gospels." Pages 316–24 in *To Touch the Text: Biblical and Related Studies in Honor of Joseph A. Fitzmyer, S.J.* Edited by M. P. Horgan and P. J. Kobelski. New York: Crossroad.

Harris, J. R. 1916. *Testimonies.* 2 vols. Cambridge: Cambridge University Press.

Hartley, J. E. 1992. *Leviticus.* WBC 4. Dallas: Word.

Haupt, P. 1904. "The Prototype of the Magnificat." *ZDMG* 58: 617–32.

Hawkins, J. C. 1899. *Horae Synopticae: Contributions to the Study of the Synoptic Problem.* Oxford: Clarendon.

Hay, D. M. 1973. *Glory at the Right Hand: Psalm 110 in Early Christianity.* SBLMS 18. Nashville: Abingdon.

Hays, R. B. 1989. *Echoes of Scripture in the Letters of Paul.* New Haven: Yale University Press.

Healey, J. H. 1989. "Models of Behavior: Matt 6:26 (// Luke 12:24) and Prov 6:6–8." *JBL* 108: 497–98.

Hengel, M. 1981. *The Charismatic Leader and His Followers.* Translated by J. Greig. New York: Crossroad.

———. 1995. *Studies in Early Christology.* Edinburgh: T&T Clark.

———. 1996. "Zur Wirkungsgeschichte von Jes 53 in vorchristlicher Zeit." Pages 49–91 in *Der leidende Gottesknecht: Jesaja 53 und seine Wirkungsgeschichte.* FAT 14. Edited by B. Janowski and P. Stuhlmacher. Tübingen: Mohr Siebeck.

Hertzberg, H. W. 1964. *I & II Samuel.* OTL. Philadelphia: Westminster.

Hilhorst, A. 1994. "Deuteronomy's Monotheism and the Christians: The Case of Deut 6:13 and 10:20." Pages 83–91 in *Studies in Deuteronomy: In Honour of C. J. Labuschagne on the Occasion of His 65th Birthday.* Edited by F. García Martínez et al. VTSup 53. Leiden: Brill.

Hill, A. E. 1998. *Malachi.* AB 25D. New York: Doubleday.

Hills, J. V. 1992. "Luke 10.18—Who Saw Satan Fall?" *JSNT* 46: 25–40.

Hoehner, H. W. 1972. *Herod Antipas.* SNTSMS 17. Cambridge: Cambridge University Press.

Holtz, T. 1968. *Untersuchungen über die alttestamentlichen Zitate bei Lukas.* TUGAL 104. Berlin: Akademie-Verlag.

Hooker, M. D. 1998. "Did the Use of Isaiah 53 to Interpret His Mission Begin with Jesus?" Pages 88–103 in *Jesus and the Suffering Servant: Isaiah 53 and Christian Origins.* Edited by W. H. Bellinger and W. R. Farmer. Harrisburg, PA: Trinity Press International.

Horbury, W. 1985. "The Messianic Association of 'The Son of Man.'" *JTS* 36: 34–55.

Horgan, M. P., and P. J. Kobelski. 1989. "The Hodayot (1QH) and New Testament Poetry." Pages 179–93 in *To Touch the Text: Biblical and Related Studies in Honor of Joseph A. Fitzmyer, S.J.* Edited by M. P. Horgan and P. J. Kobelski. New York: Crossroad.

Horsley, R. A., and J. S. Hanson. 1985. *Bandits, Prophets, and Messiahs: Popular Movements at the Time of Jesus*. San Francisco: Harper & Row.

Horton, F. L. 1978. "Reflections on the Semitisms of Luke-Acts." Pages 1–23 in *Perspectives on Luke-Acts*. Edited by C. H. Talbert. Danville, VA: Association of Baptist Professors of Religion.

Hugenberger, G. P. 1995. "The Servant of the Lord in the 'Servant Songs' of Isaiah: A Second Moses Figure." Pages 105–40 in *The Lord's Anointed: Interpretation of Old Testament Messianic Texts*. Edited by P. E. Satterthwaite, R. S. Hess, and G. J. Wenham. THS. Grand Rapids: Baker Academic.

Hugger, P. 1971. *Jahwe meine Zuflucht: Gestalt und Theologie des 91. Psalms*. Münsterschwarzach: Vier-Türme.

Hultgren, A. J. 1990. "The Bread Petition of the Lord's Prayer." Pages 41–54 in *Christ and His Communities: Essays in Honor of Reginald H. Fuller*. Edited by A. J. Hultgren and B. Hall. Cincinnati: Forward Movement Publications.

———. 2000. *The Parables of Jesus: A Commentary*. Grand Rapids: Eerdmans.

Instone-Brewer, David. 2002. *Divorce and Remarriage in the Bible*. Grand Rapids: Eerdmans.

Isaksson, A. 1965. *Marriage and Ministry in the New Temple: A Study with Special Reference to Mt. 19.13–12 [sic] and 1. Cor. 11.3–16*. ASNU 24. Lund: Gleerup.

Janowski, B. 1996. "Er trug unsere Sünden: Jes 53 und die Dramatik der Stellvertretung." Pages 27–48 in *Der leidende Gottesknecht: Jesaja 53 und seine Wirkungsgeschichte*. Edited by B. Janowski and P. Stuhlmacher. FAT 14. Tübingen: Mohr Siebeck.

Janzen, A. 2002. *Der Friede im lukanischen Doppelwerk vor dem Hintergrund der Pax Romana*. EUS 23/752. Frankfurt am Main: Peter Lang.

Jeremias, J. 1966. *The Eucharistic Words of Jesus*. Translated by N. Perrin. London: SCM.

———. 1971. *The Parables of Jesus*. Translated by S. H. Hooke. London: SCM.

Jervell, J. 1972. *Luke and the People of God*. Minneapolis: Augsburg.

Johnson, L. T. 1977. *The Literary Function of Possessions in Luke-Acts*. SBLDS 39. Missoula, MT: Scholars Press.

———. 1989. "The New Testament's Anti-Jewish Slander and the Conventions of Ancient Polemic." *JBL* 108: 419–41.

———. 1991. *The Gospel of Luke*. SP 3. Collegeville, MN: Liturgical Press.

Jones, D. R. 1968. "Background and Character of the Lukan Psalms." *JTS* 19: 19–50.

Jones, J. N. 1995. "'Think of the Lilies' and Prov 6:6–11." *HTR* 88: 175–77.

Judge, P. J. 1989. "Luke 7,1–10: Sources and Redaction." Pages 473–89 in *L'Évangile de Luc—The Gospel of Luke*. Edited by F. Neirynck. 2nd ed. BETL 32. Leuven: Leuven University Press.

Juel, D. H. 1988. *Messianic Exegesis: Christological Interpretation of the Old Testament in Early Christianity*. Philadelphia: Fortress.

Juncker, G. H. 2001. "Jesus and the Angel of the Lord: An Old Testament Paradigm for New Testament Christology." PhD diss., Trinity Evangelical Divinity School.

Kähler, C. 1994. "Satanischer Schriftgebrauch: Zur Hermeneutik von Mt 4,1–11/Lk 4,1–13." *TLZ* 119: 857–68.

Käser, W. 1963. "Exegetische und theologische Erwägungen zur Seligpreisung der Kinderlosen, Lc 23,29b." *ZNW* 54: 240–54.

Kaufmann, Y. 1972. *The Religion of Israel*. New York: Schocken.

Kazmierski, C. R. 1987. "The Stones of Abraham: John the Baptist and the End of Torah (Matt 3,7–10 par. Luke 3,7–9)." *Bib* 68: 22–40.

Kee, H. C. 2002. "Jesus: A Glutton and Drunkard." Pages 311–32 in *Authenticating the Words of Jesus*. Edited by B. Chilton and C. A. Evans. Boston: Brill Academic.

Keener, C. S. 1993. *The IVP Bible Background Commentary: New Testament*. Downers Grove, IL: InterVarsity.

Kelhoffer, J. A. 2003. "'Locusts and Wild Honey' (Mk 1.6c and Mt. 3.4c): The *Status Quaestionis* concerning the Diet of John the Baptist." *CBR* 2: 104–27.

Kessler, R. 1999. *Micha*. HTKAT. Freiburg: Herder.

Kilgallen, J. J. 1986. "The Sadducees and Resurrection from the Dead: Luke 20:27–40." *Bib* 67: 478–95.

———. 1994. "Jesus, Savior, the Glory of Your People Israel." *Bib* 75: 305–28.

———. 1997. "The Conception of Jesus (Luke 1,35)." *Bib* 78: 225–46.

Kilpatrick, G. D. 1989: "Luke 2,4–5 and Leviticus 25,10." *ZNW* 80: 264–65.

Kimball, C. A. 1993. "Jesus' Exposition of Scripture in Luke 20:9–19: An Inquiry in Light of Jewish Hermeneutics." *BBR* 3: 77–92.

———. 1994a. "Jesus' Exposition of Scripture in Luke 4:6–30: An Inquiry in Light of Jewish Hermeneutics." *PRSt* 21: 179–202.

———. 1994b. *Jesus' Exposition of the Old Testament in Luke's Gospel*. JSNTSup 94. Sheffield: Sheffield Academic Press.

Kingsbury, J. D. 1992. "The Pharisees in Luke-Acts." Pages 1497–1512 in vol. 2 of *The Four Gospels: Festschrift Frans Neirynck*. Edited by F. van Segbroeck et al. BETL 100. Leuven: Leuven University Press.

Kinman, B. R. 1995. *Jesus' Entry into Jerusalem: In the Context of Lukan Theology and the Politics of His Day*. AGJU 28. Leiden: Brill.

Kirk, A. 2003. "'Love Your Enemies,' The Golden Rule, and Ancient Reciprocity (Luke 6:27–35)." *JBL* 122: 667–86.

Klingbeil, G. A. 2000. "The *Finger of God* in the Old Testament." *ZAW* 112: 409–15.

Kodell, J. 1987. "Luke and the Children: The Beginning and End of the Great Interpolation (Luke 9:46–56; 18:9–23)." *CBQ* 49: 415–30.

Koet, B. J. 1989. *Five Studies on Interpretation of Scripture in Luke-Acts*. SNTA 14. Leuven: Leuven University Press.

———. 1992. "Simeons Worte (Lk 2,29–32, 34c-35) und Israels Geschick." Pages 1149–69 in vol. 2 of *The Four Gospels: Festschrift Frans Neirynck*. Edited by F. van Segbroeck et al. BETL 100. Leuven: Leuven University Press.

———. 2000. "Purity and Impurity of the Body in Luke-Acts." Pages 93–106 in *Purity and Holiness: The Heritage of Leviticus*. Edited by M. J. H. M. Poorthuis and J. Schwartz. JCPS 2. Leiden: Brill.

Kogler, F. 1988. *Das Doppelgleichnis vom Senfkorn und vom Sauerteig in seiner traditionsgeschichtlichen Entwicklung*. FB 59. Würzburg: Echter.

Kossen, H. B. 1956. "Quelques remarques sur l'ordre des paraboles dans Luc XV et sur la structure de Matthieu XVIII,8–14." *NovT* 1: 75–80.

Kratz, R. G. 1993. "Der Anfang des Zweiten Jesaja in Jes 40,1f. und seine literarischen Horizonte." *ZAW* 105: 400–419.

Kraus, H.-J. 1986. *Theology of the Psalms*. Translated by K. Crim. Minneapolis: Augsburg.

———. 1993. *Psalms*. Translated by H. C. Oswald. 2 vols. Minneapolis: Fortress.

Kremer, J. 1992. *Lukasevangelium*. 2nd ed. NEchtB 3. Würzburg: Echter.

Kruger, H. A. J. 1997. "A Sword over His Head or in His Hand? Luke 22:35–38." Pages 597–604 in *The Scriptures in the Gospels*. Edited by C. M. Tuckett. BETL 131. Leuven: Leuven University Press.

Kugel, J. L. 1983. "Two Introductions to Midrash." *Prooftexts* 3: 131–55.

———. 1987. "On Hidden Hatred and Open Reproach: Early Exegesis of Leviticus 19:17." *HTR* 80: 43–61.

Kugler, R. A. 2003. "Rethinking the Notion of 'Scripture' in the Dead Sea Scrolls: Leviticus as a Test Case." Pages 342–57 in *The Book of Leviticus: Composition and Reception*. Edited by R. Rendtorff and R. A. Kugler. VTSup 93. Leiden: Brill.

Kurz, W. S. 1993. *Reading Luke-Acts: Dynamics of Biblical Narrative*. Louisville: Westminster John Knox.

———. 1994. "Intertextual Use of Sirach 48.1–16 in Plotting Luke-Acts." Pages 308–24 in *The Gospels and the Scriptures of Israel*. Edited by C. A. Evans and W. R. Stegner. JSNTSup 104. Sheffield: Sheffield Academic Press.

———. 1999. "Promise and Fulfillment in Hellenistic Jewish Narratives and in Luke and Acts." Pages 147–70 in *Jesus and the Heritage of Israel: Luke's Narrative Claim upon Israel's Legacy*. Edited by D. P. Moessner. Harrisburg, PA: Trinity Press International.

Lachs, S. T. 1987. *A Rabbinic Commentary on the New Testament: The Gospels of Matthew, Mark, and Luke*. Hoboken, NJ: KTAV.

Lambrecht, J. 1992. "John the Baptist and Jesus in Mark 1:1–15: Markan Redaction of Q?" *NTS* 38: 357–82.

Lampe, S. J. 1993. *Abraham in Luke-Acts: An Appropriation of Lucan Theology through Old Testament Figures*. Rome: Pontificia Universitas Gregoriana.

Landy, F. 1999. "Strategies of Concentration and Diffusion in Isaiah 6." *BibInt* 7: 58–86.

Landry, D. T. 1995. "Narrative Logic in the Annunciation to Mary (Luke 1:26–38)." *JBL* 114: 65–79.

Larkin, W. J. 1974. "Luke's Use of the Old Testament in Luke 22–23." PhD diss., University of Durham.

Laurentin, R. 1964. *Structure et théologie de Luc I–II*. EBib. Paris: Gabalda.

Leske, A. M. 1995. "The Influence of Isaiah on Christology in the Gospels of Matthew and Luke." Pages 241–69 in *Crisis in Christology: Essays in Quest of Resolution*. Edited by W. R. Farmer. Livonia, MI: Dove.

Levenson, J. D. 1985. *Sinai and Zion: An Entry into the Jewish Bible*. NVBS. Minneapolis: Winston.

———. 1988. *Creation and the Persistence of Evil: The Jewish Drama of Divine Omnipotence*. New York: Harper & Row.

Lewis, J. P. 1968. *A Study of the Interpretation of Noah and the Flood in Jewish and Christian Literature*. Leiden: Brill.

Liefeld, W. L. 1974. "Theological Motifs in the Transfiguration Narrative." Pages 162–79 in *New Dimensions in New Testament Study*. Edited by R. N. Longenecker and M. C. Tenney. Grand Rapids: Zondervan.

Lietzmann, H. 1923. "Jüdisch-griechische Inschriften aus Tell el Yehudijeh." *ZNW* 22: 280–86.

Lindars, B. 1961. *New Testament Apologetic: The Doctrinal Significance of the Old Testament Quotations*. Philadelphia: Westminster.

Linnemann, E. 1970. *Studien zur Passionsgeschichte*. FRLANT 102. Göttingen: Vandenhoeck & Ruprecht.

Linton, O. 1976. "The Parable of the Children's Game." *NTS* 22: 159–79.

Litke, W. D. 1993. "Luke's Knowledge of the Septuagint: A Study of the Citations in Luke-Acts." PhD diss., McMaster University.

Lohfink, G. 1971. *Die Himmelfahrt Jesu: Untersuchungen zu den Himmelfahrts- und Erhöhungstexten bei Lukas*. SANT 26. Munich: Kösel.

Lohse, E. 1954. "Lukas als Theologe der Heilsgeschichte." *EvT* 14: 256–75.

Loisy, A. F. 1924. *L'Évangile selon Luc*. Paris: Nourry.

Longenecker, R. N. 2000. "Luke's Parables of the Kingdom (Luke 8:4–15; 13:18–21)." Pages 125–47 in *The Challenges of Jesus' Parables*. Edited by R. N. Longenecker. MNTS. Grand Rapids: Eerdmans.

Love, S. L. 2002. "Jesus Heals the Hemorrhaging Woman." Pages 85–101 in *The Social Setting of Jesus and the Gospels*. Edited by W. Stegemann, B. J. Malina, and G. Theissen. Minneapolis: Fortress.

Lövestam, E. O. 1968. *Spiritus Blasphemia: Eine Studie zu Mk 3,28f par Mt 12,31f, Lk 12,10*. ScrM 1. Lund: Gleerup.

———. 1995. *Jesus and "This Generation": A New Testament Study*. ConBNT 25. Stockholm: Almqvist & Wiksell.

Lyonnet, S. 1939. "Χαῖρε κεχαριτωμένη." *Bib* 20: 131–41.

Malamat, A. 1990. "'You Shall Love Your Neighbor as Yourself': A Case of Misinterpretation." Pages 111–15 in *Hebräische Bibel und ihre zweifache Nachgeschichte: Feschrift für Rolf Rendtorff zum 65. Geburtstag*. Edited by E. Blum. Neukirchen-Vluyn: Neukirchener Verlag.

Mánek, J. 1957. "The New Exodus in the Books of Luke." *NovT* 2: 8–23.

Mann, J. 1940. *The Bible as Read and Preached in the Old Synagogue*. Vol. 1. New York: KTAV.

Manns, F. 1992. "Une prière juive reprise en Luc 1,68–69." *EL* 106: 162–66.

Manson, T. W. 1949. *The Sayings of Jesus as Recorded in the Gospels according to St. Matthew and St. Luke*. London: SCM.

Marshall, I. H. 1978. *The Gospel of Luke: A Commentary on the Greek Text*. NIGTC. Grand Rapids: Eerdmans.

———. 1988. "Jesus as Lord: The Development of the Concept." Pages 129–45 in *Eschatology and the New Testament: Essays in Honor of George Raymond Beasley-Murray*. Edited by W. H. Gloer. Peabody, MA: Hendrickson.

———. 1990. *Jesus the Saviour: Studies in New Testament Theology*. Downers Grove, IL: InterVarsity.

Marx, A. 2000. "La chute de 'Lucifer' (*Esaïe* 14, 12–15; *Luc* 10, 18). Préhistoire d'un mythe." *RHPR* 80: 171–85.

Matera, F. J. 1985. "The Death of Jesus according to Luke: A Question of Sources." *CBQ* 47: 469–85.

———. 1993. "Jesus' Journey to Jerusalem (Luke 9:51–19:46): A Conflict with Israel." *JSNT* 51: 57–77.

Maurer, C. 1953. "Knecht Gottes und Sohn Gottes im Passionsbericht des Markusevangeliums." *ZTK* 50: 1–38.

Mayer, E. 1996. *Die Reiseerzählung des Lukas (Lk 9,51–19,10): Entscheidung in der Wüste*. EUS 23/554. Frankfurt: Peter Lang.

Mays, J. L. 1994. *Psalms*. IBC. Louisville: John Knox.

McCane, B. R. 1990. "'Let the Dead Bury Their Own Dead': Secondary Burial and Matt 8:21–22." *HTR* 83: 31–43.

McConville, J. G. 2002. *Deuteronomy*. ApOTC 5. Leicester: Apollos.

McLaughlin, J. L. 1994. "Their Hearts Were Hardened: The Use of Isaiah 6,9–10 in the Book of Isaiah." *Bib* 75: 1–25.

McNicol, A. J. 1998. "Rebuilding the House of David: The Function of the Benedictus in Luke-Acts." *ResQ* 40: 25–38.

McRay, J. 1991. *Archaeology and the New Testament*. Grand Rapids: Baker Academic.

Meier, J. P. 1994. *Mentor, Message, and Miracles*. Vol. 2 of *A Marginal Jew: Rethinking the Historical Jesus*. ABRL. New York: Doubleday.

Menken, M. J. J. 1993. "The Textual Form and the Meaning of the Quotation from Zech 12:10 in John 19:37." *CBQ* 55: 494–511.

Metzger, B. M. 1959. "Seventy or Seventy-Two Disciples?" *NTS* 5: 299–306.

———. 1994. *A Textual Commentary on the Greek New Testament*. 2nd ed. Stuttgart: Deutsche Bibelgesellschaft and United Bible Societies.

Metzler, N. 2002. "The Lord's Prayer: Second Thoughts on the First Petition." Pages 187–202 in *Authenticating the Words of Jesus*. Edited by B. Chilton and C. A. Evans. Boston: Brill Academic.

Meyer, B. F. 1964. "'But Mary Kept All These Things . . .' (Lk 2, 19.51)." *CBQ* 26: 31–49.

———. 1979. *The Aims of Jesus*. London: SCM.

Meynet, R. 1988. *L'Évangile selon Saint Luc: Analyse rhétorique*. 2 vols. Paris: Cerf.

Miesner, D. R. 1978. "The Circumferential Speeches of Luke-Acts." *SBLSP* 14: 2:223–37.

Milgrom, J. 1991–2001. *Leviticus*. 3 vols. AB 3, 3A, 3B. New York: Doubleday.

Miller, D. G. 1960. *Saint Luke*. The Laymen's Bible Commentary. London: SCM.

Miller, M. P. 1969. "The Function of Isa 61:1–2 in 11Q Melchizedek." *JBL* 88: 467–69.

Minear, P. S. 1964–1965. "A Note on Luke xxii 36." *NovT* 7: 128–34.

———. 1994. *Christians and the New Creation: Genesis Motifs in the New Testament*. Louisville: Westminster John Knox.

Mitchell, D. C. 1997. *The Message of the Psalter: An Eschatological Programme in the Book of Psalms*. JSOTSup 252. Sheffield: Sheffield Academic Press.

Mittmann-Richert, U. 1996. *Magnifikat und Benediktus: Die ältesten Zeugnisse der judenchristlichen Tradition von der Geburt des Messias*. WUNT 90. Tübingen: Mohr Siebeck.

Miyoshi, M. 1974. *Der Anfang des Reiseberichts Lk 9,51–10,24: Eine redaktionsgeschichtliche Untersuchung*. AnBib 60. Rome: Biblical Institute Press.

Moessner, D. P. 1983. "Luke 9:1–50: Luke's Preview of the Journey of the Prophet like Moses of Deuteronomy." *JBL* 102: 575–605.

———. 1989. *Lord of the Banquet: The Literary and Theological Significance of the Lukan Travel Narrative*. Minneapolis: Fortress.

———. 1999. "The Appeal and Power of Poetics (Luke 1:1–4): Luke's Superior Credentials (παρηκολουθηκότι), Narrative Sequence (καθεξῆς), and Firmness of Understanding (ἡ ἀσφάλεια) for the Reader." Pages 84–123 in *Jesus and the Heritage of Israel: Luke's Narrative Claim upon Israel's Legacy*. Edited by D. P. Moessner. Harrisburg, PA: Trinity Press International.

Moessner, D. P., and D. L. Tiede. 1999. "Two Books but One Story?" Pages 1–4 in *Jesus and the Heritage of Israel: Luke's Narrative Claim upon Israel's Legacy*. Edited by D. P. Moessner. Harrisburg, PA: Trinity Press International.

Moo, D. J. 1983. *The Old Testament in the Gospel Passion Narratives*. Sheffield: Almond.

Moran, W. L. 1963. "The Ancient Near Eastern Background of the Love of God in Deuteronomy." *CBQ* 25: 78–82.

Morris, L. 1988. *Luke*. Rev. ed. TNTC 3. Leicester: Inter-Varsity.

Moulton, J. H. 1929. *A Grammar of New Testament Greek*. Vol. 2. Edinburgh: T&T Clark.

Müller, M. 2001. "The Reception of the Old Testament in Matthew and Luke-Acts: From Interpretation to Proof from Scripture." *NovT* 53: 315–30.

Müller, P.-G. 1984. *Lukas-Evangelium*. SKKNT 3. Stuttgart: Katholisches Bibelwerk.

Neagoe, A. 2002. *The Trial of the Gospel: An Apologetic Reading of Luke's Trial Narratives*. SNTSMS 116. Cambridge: Cambridge University Press.

Neirynck, F. 1960. *L'evangile de Noël selon S. Luc*. ERel 749. Brussels: La Pensée Catholique.

———. 1997. "Q 6,20b–21; 7,22 and Isaiah 61." Pages 27–64 in *The Scriptures in the Gospels*. Edited by C. M. Tuckett. BETL 131. Leuven: Leuven University Press.

Nestle, E. 1910. "Die Schätzung in Lukas 2 und Psalm 87(86), 6." *ZNW* 11: 87.

Neudecker, R. 1992. "'And You Shall Love Your Neighbor as Yourself—I Am the Lord' (Lev 19,18) in Jewish Interpretation." *Bib* 73: 496–517.

Neusner, J. 1976. "First Cleanse the Inside: The 'Halakhic' Background of a Controversy-Saying." *NTS* 22: 486–95.

———. 1988. *The Mishnah: A New Translation*. New Haven: Yale University Press.

New, D. S. 1993. *Old Testament Quotations in the Synoptic Gospels, and the Two-Document Hypothesis*. SBLSCS 37. Atlanta: Scholars Press.

Neyrey, J. H. 1985. *The Passion according to Luke: A Redaction Study of Luke's Soteriology*. Theological Inquiries. New York: Paulist Press.

Nielsen, A. E. 2000. *Until It Is Fulfilled: Lukan Eschatology according to Luke 22 and Acts 20*. WUNT 2/126. Tübingen: Mohr Siebeck.

Noël, F. 1997. "The Double Commandment of Love in Lk 10,27: A Deuteronomistic Pillar or Lukan Redaction of Mk 12,29–33?" Pages 559–70 in *The Scriptures in the Gospels*. Edited by C. M. Tuckett. BETL 131. Leuven: Leuven University Press.

Nolland, J. 1979. "Classical and Rabbinic Parallels to 'Physician, Heal Yourself' (Lk. IV.2)." *NovT* 21: 193–209.

———. 1984. "Words of Grace (Luke 4:22)." *Bib* 84: 44–60.

———. 1989–1993. *Luke*. 3 vols. WBC 35A, 35B, 35C. Dallas: Word.

Ó Fearghail, F. 1991. *The Introduction to Luke-Acts: A Study of the Role of Lk 1,1–4,44 in the Composition of Luke's Two-volume Work*. AnBib 126. Rome: Pontifical Biblical Institute.

———. 1993. "Announcement or Call? Literary Form and Purpose in Luke 1:26–38." *PIBA* 16: 20–35.

Oakman, D. E. 2002. "The Lord's Prayer in Social Perspective." Pages 137–86 in *Authenticating the Words of Jesus*. Edited by B. Chilton and C. A. Evans. Boston: Brill Academic.

O'Brien, D. P. 2001. "A Comparison between Early Jewish and Early Christian Interpretations of the Jubilee Year." Pages 436–42 in *Historica, Biblica, Theologica et Philosophica*. Vol. 1 of *Papers Presented at the Thirteenth International Conference on Patristic Studies Held in Oxford, 1999*. Edited by M. F. Wiles, E. Yarnold, and P. M. Parvis. StPatr 34. Leuven: Peeters.

O'Connell, R. H. 1990. "Deuteronomy VIII 1–20: Asymmetrical Concentricity and the Rhetoric of Providence." *VT* 40: 437–52.

Olley, J. W. 1992. "God on the Move—A Further Look at Kataluma in Luke." *ExpTim* 103: 300–301.

O'Neill, J. C. 1988. "The Source of the Parables of the Bridegroom and the Wicked Husbandmen." *JTS* 39: 485–89.

Oswalt, J. N. 1986–1998. *The Book of Isaiah.* 2 vols. NICOT. Grand Rapids: Eerdmans.

O'Toole, R. F. 1983. "Luke's Position on Politics and Society in Luke-Acts." Pages 1–17 in *Political Issues in Luke-Acts.* Edited by R. J. Cassidy and P. J. Scharper. Maryknoll, NY: Orbis.

Owen-Ball, D. T. 1993. "Rabbinic Rhetoric and the Tribute Passage (Mt. 22:15–22; Mk. 12:13–17; Lk. 20:20–26)." *NovT* 35: 1–14.

Pao, D. 2000. *Acts and the Isaianic New Exodus.* WUNT 2/130. Tübingen: Mohr Siebeck.

Parsons, M. C. 1998. "The Place of Jerusalem on the Lukan Landscape: An Exercise in Symbolic Cartography." Pages 155–71 in *Literary Studies in Luke-Acts: Essays in Honor of Joseph B. Tyson.* Edited by R. P. Thompson and T. E. Phillips. Macon, GA: Mercer University Press.

Patrick, D. A. 1987. "The Kingdom of God in the Old Testament." Pages 67–79 in *The Kingdom of God in 20th-Century Interpretation.* Edited by W. Willis. Peabody, MA: Hendrickson.

Perrin, N. 1967. *Rediscovering the Teaching of Jesus.* New York: Harper & Row.

Petzke, G. 1990. *Das Sondergut des Evangeliums nach Lukas.* ZWB. Zürich: Theologischer Verlag.

Ploch, W. 1993. *Jesaja-Worte in der synoptischen Evangelientradition.* Dissertationen: Theologische Reihe 64. St. Ottilien: EOS Verlag.

Plümacher, E. 1972. *Lukas als hellenistischer Schriftsteller: Studien zur Apostelgeschichte.* SUNT 9. Göttingen: Vandenhoeck & Ruprecht.

Plummer, A. 1896. *A Critical and Exegetical Commentary on the Gospel according to St. Luke.* ICC. Edinburgh: T&T Clark.

Plymale, S. F. 1994. "The Prayer of Simeon (Luke 2:29–32)." Pages 28–38 in *The Lord's Prayer and Other Prayer Texts from the Greco-Roman Era.* Edited by J. H. Charlesworth et al. Valley Forge, PA: Trinity Press International.

Polich, J. C. 1991. "The Call of the First Disciples: A Literary and Redactional Study of Luke 5:1–11." PhD diss., Fordham University.

Porter, S. E. 1990. "Mt 6:13 and Lk 11:4: 'Lead Us Not into Temptation.'" *ExpTim* 101: 359–62.

———. 1993. *Verbal Aspect in the Greek of the New Testament, with Reference to Tense and Mood.* SBG 1. New York: Peter Lang.

Powery, E. B. 1999. *Jesus Reads Scripture: The Function of Jesus' Use of Scripture in the Synoptic Gospels.* BIS 63. Leiden: Brill.

Prior, M. 1995. *Jesus the Liberator: Nazareth Liberation Theology (Luke 4:16–30).* BSem 26. Sheffield: Sheffield Academic Press.

Purvis, J. D. 1986. "The Samaritans and Judaism." Pages 81–98 in *Early Judaism and Its Modern Interpreters.* Edited by R. Kraft and G. W. E. Nickelsburg. BMI 2. Atlanta: Scholars Press.

Ravens, D. 1995. *Luke and the Restoration of Israel.* JSNTSup 119. Sheffield: Sheffield Academic Press.

Reinhardt, W. 1995. *Das Wachstum des Gottesvolkes: Untersuchungen zum Gemeindewachstum im lukanischen Doppelwerk auf dem Hintergrund des Alten Testaments.* Göttingen: Vandenhoeck & Ruprecht.

Reiser, M. 1997. *Jesus and Judgment: The Eschatological Proclamation in Its Jewish Context.* Minneapolis: Fortress.

Rese, M. 1969. *Alttestamentliche Motive in der Christologie des Lukas.* SNT 1. Gütersloh: Mohn.

Richert-Mittmann, U. 1996. *Magnifikat und Benediktus: Die frühesten Zeugen für die judenchristliche Tradition von der Geburt des Messias.* WUNT 2/90. Tübingen: Mohr Siebeck.

Ricoeur, P. 1990. "The Golden Rule: Exegetical and Theological Perplexities." *NTS* 36: 392–97.

Ringe, S. H. 1981. "The Jubilee Proclamation in the Ministry and Teaching of Jesus: A Tradition-Critical Study in the Synoptic Gospels and Acts." PhD diss., Union Theological Seminary.

Ringgren, H. 1986. "Luke's Use of the Old Testament." *HTR* 79: 227–35.

Robbins, V. K. 1994. "Socio-Rhetorical Criticism: Mary, Elizabeth and the Magnificat as a Test Case." Pages 164–209 in *The New Literary Criticism and the New Testament.* Edited by E. S. Malbon and E. V. McKnight. JSNTSup 109. Sheffield: Sheffield Academic Press.

Robert, R. 1990. "Comment comprendre 'leur purification' en Luc II, 22?" *RThom* 90: 449–55.

Robinson, J. A. T. 1957. "The Baptism of John and the Qumran Community: Testing a Hypothesis." *HTR* 50: 175–91.

Robinson, W. C. 1960. "The Theological Context for Interpreting Luke's Travel Narrative (9:51ff)." *JBL* 79: 20–31.

———. 1960. "The Way of the Lord: A Study of History and Eschatology in the Gospel of Luke." ThD diss., University of Basel.

Ross, J. M. 1987. "Which Zechariah?" *IBS* 9: 70–73.

Routledge, R. 2002. "Passover and Last Supper." *TynBul* 53: 203–21.

Rusam, D. 2003. *Das Alte Testament bei Lukas.* BZNW 112. Berlin: de Gruyter.

Sabourin, L. 1992. *L'Évangile de Luc: Introduction et commentaire.* Rome: Gregorian University Press.

Sæbø, M. 1969. *Sacharja 9–14: Untersuchungen von Text und Form.* WMANT 34. Neukirchen-Vluyn: Neukirchener Verlag.

Sanders, E. P. 1985. *Jesus and Judaism.* Philadelphia: Fortress.

———. 1992. *Judaism: Practice and Belief, 63 BCE–66 CE.* Philadelphia: Trinity Press International.

Sanders, J. A. 1974. "The Ethic of Election in Luke's Great Banquet Parable." Pages 247–71 in *Essays in Old Testament Ethics: J. Philip Hyatt, in Memoriam.* Edited by J. L. Crenshaw and J. T. Willis. New York: KTAV.

———. 1975. "From Isaiah 61 to Luke 4." Pages 75–106 in vol. 1 of *Christianity, Judaism and Other Greco-Roman Cults: Studies for Morton Smith at Sixty.* Edited by J. Neusner. SJLA 12. Leiden: Brill.

———. 1982. "Isaiah in Luke." *Int* 36: 144–55.

———. 1993a. "A Hermeneutic Fabric: Psalm 118 in Luke's Entrance Narrative." Pages 140–53 in *Luke and Scripture: The Function of Sacred Tradition in Luke-Acts.* Edited by C. A. Evans and J. A. Sanders. Minneapolis: Fortress.

———. 1993b. "Sins, Debts, and Jubilee Release." Pages 84–92 in *Luke and Scripture: The Function of Sacred Tradition in Luke-Acts.* Edited by C. A. Evans and J. A. Sanders. Minneapolis: Fortress.

Sapp, D. A. 1998. "The LXX, 1QIsa, and MT Versions of Isaiah 53 and the Christian Doctrine of Atonement." Pages 170–92 in *Jesus and the Suffering Servant: Isaiah 53 and Christian Origins.* Edited by W. H. Bellinger and W. R. Farmer. Harrisburg, PA: Trinity Press International.

Schaberg, J. 1987. *The Illegitimacy of Jesus: A Feminist Theological Interpretation of the Infancy Narratives.* San Francisco: Harper & Row.

Schearing, L. S. 2003. "Double Time . . . Double Trouble? Gender, Sin, and Leviticus 12." Pages 429–500 in *The Book of Leviticus:*

Composition and Reception. Edited by R. Rendtorff and R. A. Kugler. VTSup 93. Leiden: Brill.

Schlatter, A. 1960. *Das Evangelium des Lukas: Aus seinen Quellen erklärt.* 2nd ed. Stuttgart: Calwer.

Schlier, H. 1964. "ἀνατέλλω, ἀνατολή." *TDNT* 1:351–53.

Schlosser, J. 1973: "Les jours de Noé et de Lot: À propos de Luc, xvii, 26–30." *RB* 80: 13–36.

Schnabel, E. J. 1999. "The Silence of Jesus: The Galilean Rabbi Who Was More Than a Prophet." Pages 203–57 in *Authenticating the Words of Jesus.* Edited by B. Chilton and C. A. Evans. NTTS 28/1. Leiden: Brill.

———. 2004. *Early Christian Mission.* 2 vols. Downers Grove, IL: InterVarsity.

Schneider, G. 1992. *Das Evangelium nach Lukas.* 3rd ed. ÖTK 3. Gütersloh: Mohn; Würzburg: Echter.

Schreck, C. J. 1989. "The Nazareth Pericope: Luke 4:16–30 in Recent Study." Pages 399–471 in *L'Évangile de Luc—The Gospel of Luke.* Edited by F. Neirynck. 2nd ed. BETL 32. Leuven: Leuven University Press.

Schubert, P. 1954. "The Structure and Significance of Luke 24." Pages 165–86 in *Neutestamentliche Studien für Rudolf Bultmann zu seinem 70. Geburtstag am 20. August 1954.* Edited by W. Eltester. BZNW 21. Berlin: Töpelmann.

Schürmann, H. 1953. *Eine quellenkritische Untersuchung des Lukanischen Abendmahlsberichtes Lk 22,7–38: I. Teil. Der Paschamahlbericht Lk 22,(7–14),15–18.* NTA 19/5. Münster: Aschendorff.

———. 1955. *Eine quellenkritische Untersuchung des Lukanischen Abendmahlsberichtes Lk 22,7–38: II. Teil. Der Einsetzungsbericht Lk 22,19–20.* NTAbh 20/4. Münster: Aschendorff.

———. 1990–1994 [1990 = 4th ed.]. *Das Lukasevangelium.* 2 vols. HTKNT 3. Freiburg: Herder.

Schwankl, O. 1987. *Die Sadduzäerfrage (Mk 12.18–27 parr): Eine exegetisch-theologische Studie zur Auferstehungserwartung.* BBB 66. Frankfurt: Athenäum.

Schwarz, G. 1979. "μήποτε βαρηοῶσιν ὑμῶν αἱ καρδίαι." *BN* 10: 40.

Schweizer, E. 1984. *The Good News according to Luke.* Translated by D. E. Green. Atlanta: John Knox.

Schwemer, A. 1998. "Jesu letzte Worte am Kreuz (Mk 15,34; Lk 23,46; Joh 19,28ff)." *TBei* 29: 5–29.

Seccombe, D. 1994. "Luke and Isaiah." Pages 248–56 in *The Right Doctrine from the Wrong Texts? Essays on the Use of the Old Testament in the New.* Edited by G. K. Beale. Grand Rapids: Baker Academic.

Seely, D. R. 1990. "The Image of the Hand of God in the Exodus Traditions." PhD diss., University of Michigan.

Selwyn, E. C. 1912. *The Oracles in the New Testament.* London: Hodder & Stoughton.

Shepherd, W. H., Jr. 1994. *The Narrative Function of the Holy Spirit as a Character in Luke-Acts.* SBLDS 43. Atlanta: Scholars Press.

Siker, J. S. 1991. *Disinheriting the Jews: Abraham in Early Christian Controversy.* Louisville: Westminster John Knox.

Sloan, R. B., Jr. 1977. *The Favorable Year of the Lord: A Study of Jubilary Theology in the Gospel of Luke.* Austin: Schola Press.

Smith, D. C. 1982. "Jewish Proselyte Baptism and the Baptism of John." *ResQ* 25: 13–32.

Smith, D. E. 1987. "Table Fellowship as a Literary Motif in the Gospel of Luke." *JBL* 106: 613–28.

Snodgrass, K. 1980. "Streams of Tradition Emerging from Isaiah 40:1–5 and Their Adaptation in the New Testament." *JSNT* 8: 24–45.

———. 1983. *The Parable of the Wicked Tenants: An Inquiry into Parable Interpretation.* WUNT 27. Tübingen: Mohr Siebeck.

Spencer, F. S. 1984. "2 Chronicles 28:5–15 and the Parable of the Good Samaritan." *WTJ* 46: 317–49.

Stagg, F. 1997. "Luke's Theological Use of Parables." *RevExp* 94: 215–29.

Steck, O. H. 1967. *Israel und das gewaltsame Geschick der Propheten: Untersuchungen zur Überlieferung des deuteronomistischen Geschichtsbildes im Alten Testament, Spätjudentum und Urchristentum.* WMANT 23. Neukirchen-Vluyn: Neukirchener Verlag.

Stegner, W. R. 1989. *Narrative Theology in Early Jewish Christianity.* Louisville: Westminster John Knox.

———. 1990. "The Temptation Narrative: A Study in the Use of Scripture by Early Jewish Christians." *BR* 35: 5–17.

Stein, R. H. 1992. *Luke.* NAC 24. Nashville: Broadman.

Stendahl, K. 1968. *The School of St. Matthew and Its Use of the Old Testament.* 2nd ed. ASNU 20. Lund: Gleerup.

Sterling, G. E. 1993. "Jesus as Exorcist: An Analysis of Matthew 17:14–20; Mark 9:14–29; Luke 9:37–43a." *CBQ* 55: 467–93.

Strauss, M. L. 1995. *The Davidic Messiah in Luke-Acts: The Promise and Its Fulfilment in Lukan Christology.* JSNTSup 110. Sheffield: Sheffield Academic Press.

Stuart, D. 1998. "Malachi." Pages 1245–1396 in vol. 3 of *The Minor Prophets: An Exegetical and Expository Commentary.* Edited by T. E. McComiskey. Grand Rapids: Baker Academic.

Stuhlmacher, P. 1968. *Das paulinische Evangelium: Vorgeschichte.* FRLANT 95. Göttingen: Vandenhoeck & Ruprecht.

———. 1992. *Grundlegung von Jesus zu Paulus.* Vol. 1 of *Biblische Theologie des Neuen Testaments.* Göttingen: Vandenhoeck & Ruprecht.

Swartley, W. M. 1983. "Politics and Peace (*Eirene*) in Luke's Gospel." Pages 18–37 in *Political Issues in Luke-Acts.* Edited by R. J. Cassidy and P. J. Scharper. Maryknoll, NY: Orbis.

Swetnam, J. 1987. "Some Signs of Jonah." *Bib* 68: 74–79.

Tabor, J. D., and M. W. Wise. 1992. "4Q521 'On Resurrection' and the Synoptic Gospel Tradition: A Preliminary Study." *JSP* 10: 149–62.

Talmon, S. 1993. *Literary Studies in the Hebrew Bible: Form and Content; Collected Studies.* Jerusalem: Magnes; Leiden: Brill.

———. 1997. "The Signification of שלום and Its Semantic Field in the Hebrew Bible." Pages 75–115 in *The Quest for Context and Meaning: Studies in Biblical Intertextuality in Honor of James A. Sanders.* Edited by C. A. Evans and S. Talmon. BIS 28. Leiden: Brill.

Tan, K. H. 1997. *The Zion Traditions and the Aims of Jesus.* SNTSMS 91. Cambridge: Cambridge University Press.

Tannehill, R. C. 1986–1990. *The Narrative Unity of Luke-Acts: A Literary Interpretation.* 2 vols. FF. Philadelphia: Fortress.

Tate, M. E. 1990. *Psalms 51–100.* WBC 20. Dallas: Word.

Taylor, J. E. 1997. *The Immerser: John the Baptist within Second Temple Judaism.* SHJ. Grand Rapids: Eerdmans.

Thomas, K. J. 1975–1976. "Liturgical Citations in the Synoptics." *NTS* 22: 205–14.

Thompson, J. W. 1999. "The Background and Function of the Beatitudes in Matthew and Luke." *ResQ* 41: 109–16.

Thurston, B. 2001. "Who Was Anna? Luke 2:36–38." *PRSt* 28: 47–55.

Tiede, D. L. 1980. *Prophecy and History in Luke-Acts.* Philadelphia: Fortress.

———. 1988a. "Glory to Thy People Israel." Pages 327–41 in *The Social World of Formative Christianity and Judaism: Essays in*

Tribute to Howard Clark Kee. Edited by J. Neusner et al. Philadelphia: Fortress.

———. 1988b. *Luke*. ACNT. Minneapolis: Augsburg.

Tomson, P. 2002. "Luke-Acts and the Jewish Scriptures." *Analecta Bruxellensia* 7: 164–83.

Trumbower, J. A. 1994. "The Role of Malachi in the Career of John the Baptist." Pages 28–41 in *The Gospels and the Scriptures of Israel*. Edited by C. A. Evans and W. R. Stegner. JSNTSup 104. Sheffield: Sheffield Academic Press.

Tuckett, C. M. 1982. "Luke 4,16–30, Isaiah and Q." Pages 343–54 in *Logia: Les paroles de Jésus—The Sayings of Jesus; Mémorial Joseph Coppens*. Edited by J. Delobel. BETL 59. Leuven: Leuven University Press.

———. 1988. "Mark's Concerns in the Parables Chapter (Mark 4,1–34)." *Bib* 69: 1–26.

———. 1993. "Mark and Q." Pages 149–75 in *The Synoptic Gospels: Source Criticism and the New Literary Criticism*. Edited by C. Focant and F. Neirynck. BETL 110. Leuven: Peeters.

Turner, M. M. 1981. "Jesus and the Spirit in Lucan Perspective." *TynBul* 32: 3–42.

———. 1996. *Power from on High: The Spirit in Israel's Restoration and Witness in Luke-Acts*. JPTSup 9. Sheffield: Sheffield Academic Press.

Turner, N. 1955. "The Relation of Luke i and ii to Hebraic Sources and to the Rest of Luke-Acts." *NTS* 2: 100–109.

Twelftree, G. H. 1993. *Jesus the Exorcist: A Contribution to the Study of the Historical Jesus*. WUNT 2/54. Tübingen: Mohr Siebeck.

Tyson, J. B. 1990. "The Birth Narratives and the Beginning of Luke's Gospel." *Semeia* 52: 103–20.

van Cangh, J.-M. 1971. "Le thème des poissons dans les récits évangéliques de la multiplication des pains." *RB* 78: 76–80.

van der Ploeg, J. P. M. 1971. "Un petit rouleau des psaumes apocryphes (11QPsApᵃ)." Pages 128–39 in *Tradition und Glaube: Das frühe Christentum in seiner Umwelt; Festgabe für Karl Georg Kuhn zum 65. Geburtstag*. Edited by G. Jeremias, H.-W. Kuhn, and H. Stegemann. Göttingen: Vandenhoeck & Ruprecht.

Van Leeuwen, R. C. 1985. "What Comes Out of God's Mouth: Theological Wordplay in Deuteronomy 8." *CBQ* 47: 55–57.

Van Winkle, D. W. 1997. "Isaiah LVI 1–8." *SBLSP* 36: 234–52.

Verhoef, E. 1997. "(Eternal) Life and Following the Commandments: Lev 18,5 and Luke 10,28." Pages 571–77 in *The Scriptures in the Gospels*. Edited by C. M. Tuckett. BETL 131. Leuven: Leuven University Press.

Vermes, G. 1967. "The Use of *bar nash/bar nasha* in Jewish Aramaic." Pages 310–28 (appendix E) in M. Black, *An Aramaic Approach to the Gospels and Acts*. 3rd ed. Oxford: Clarendon.

Vigne, D. 1992. *Christ au Jourdain: Le baptême de Jésus dans la tradition judéo-chrétienne*. EBib 16. Paris: Gabalda.

von Rad, G. 2001. *Old Testament Theology*. Translated by D. M. G. Stalker. 2 vols. Repr., Louisville: Westminster John Knox.

Wagner, J. R. 1997. "Psalm 118 in Luke-Acts: Tracing a Narrative Thread." Pages 154–78 in *Early Christian Interpretation of the Scriptures of Israel: Investigations and Proposals*. Edited by C. A. Evans and J. A. Sanders. JSNTSup 148. Sheffield: Sheffield Academic Press.

Wall, R. W. 1989. "Martha and Mary (Luke 10.38–42) in the Context of a Christian Deuteronomy." *JSNT* 35: 19–35.

Walton, J. H. 2003. "The Imagery of the Substitute King Ritual in Isaiah's Fourth Servant Song." *JBL* 122: 734–43.

Watts, J. D. W. 1985–1987. *Isaiah*. 2 vols. WBC 24, 25. Waco: Word.

Watts, R. E. 1997. *Isaiah's New Exodus and Mark*. WUNT 2/88. Tübingen: Mohr Siebeck.

———. 1998. "Jesus' Death, Isaiah 53, and Mark 10:45: A Crux Revisited." Pages 121–51 in *Jesus and the Suffering Servant: Isaiah 53 and Christian Origins*. Edited by W. H. Bellinger and W. R. Farmer. Harrisburgh, PA: Trinity Press International.

Webb, R. L. 1991. *John the Baptizer and Prophet: A Socio-Historical Study*. JSNTSup 62. Sheffield: JSOT Press.

Weinert, F. D. 1983. "The Multiple Meanings of Luke 2:49 and Their Significance." *BTB* 13: 19–22.

Weiser, A. 1962. *The Psalms: A Commentary*. Translated by H. Hartwell. Philadelphia: Westminster.

Weissenrieder, A. 2002. "The Plague of Uncleanness? The Ancient Illness Construct 'Issue of Blood.'" Pages 207–22 in *The Social Setting of Jesus and the Gospels*. Edited by W. Stegemann, B. J. Malina, and G. Theissen. Minneapolis: Fortress.

Weitzman, S. 1997. *Song and Story in Biblical Narrative: The History of a Literary Convention in Ancient Israel*. ISBL. Bloomington: Indiana University Press.

Wenham, D. 1984. *The Rediscovery of Jesus' Eschatological Discourse*. Vol. 6 of *Gospel Perspectives*. Edited by D. Wenham and C. Blomberg. Sheffield: JSOT Press.

Wenham, G. J. 1979. *The Book of Leviticus*. NICOT. Grand Rapids: Eerdmans.

Westermann, C. 1969. *Isaiah 40–66*. OTL. Philadelphia: Westminster.

———. 1971. "Alttestamentliche Elemente in Lukas 2,1–20." Pages 317–27 in *Tradition und Glaube: Das frühe Christentum in seiner Umwelt; Festgabe für Karl Georg Kuhn zum 65. Geburtstag*. Edited by G. Jeremias, H.-W. Kuhn, and H. Stegemann. Göttingen: Vandenhoeck & Ruprecht.

Wevers, J. W. 1990. *Notes on the Greek Text of Exodus*. SBLSCS 30. Atlanta: Scholars Press.

Wiefel, W. 1988. *Das Evangelium nach Lukas*. THKNT 3. Berlin: Evangelische Verlagsanstalt.

Wilcox, M. 1992. "Luke 2.36–38 'Anna bat Phanuel, of the tribe of Asher, a prophetess . . .': A Study in Midrash Special to Luke." Pages 1571–79 in vol. 2 of *The Four Gospels: Festschrift Frans Neirynck*. Edited by F. van Segbroeck et al. BETL 100. Leuven: Leuven University Press.

Willis, J. T. 1977. "The Genre of Isaiah 5:1–7." *JBL* 96: 337–62.

Winter, P. 1954. "Some Observations on the Language in the Birth and Infancy Stories of the Third Gospel." *NTS* 1: 111–21.

Witherington, B. 1994. *Jesus the Sage: The Pilgrimage of Wisdom*. Minneapolis: Fortress.

Wolff, H. W. 1952. *Jesaja 53 im Urchristentum*. 3rd ed. Berlin: Evangelische Verlagsanstalt.

Wong, F.-K. 1998. "Manna Revisited: A Study of the Mythological and Interpretative Contexts of Manna." ThD diss., Harvard Divinity School.

Wright, N. T. 1992. *The New Testament and the People of God*. Minneapolis: Fortress.

———. 1996. *Jesus and the Victory of God*. Minneapolis: Fortress.

Wuellner, W. H. 1967. *The Meaning of "Fishers of Men."* NTL. Philadelphia: Westminster.

Yee, G. A. 1981. "The Form Critical Study of Isaiah 5:1–7 as a Song and as a Juridical Parable." *CBQ* 43: 30–40.

Zahn, T. 1988. *Das Evangelium des Lucas*. 4th ed. KNT. Repr., Wuppertal: Brockhaus.

Zeller, D. 1985. "Entrückung zur Ankunft als Menschensohn (Lk 13,34f.; 11,29f.)." Pages 513–30 in *À cause de l'Évangile: Études sur les Synoptiques et les Actes, offertes au P. Jacques Dupont O.S.B.*

à l'occasion de son 70e anniversaire. Edited by F. Refoulé. LD 123. Paris: Cerf.

Ziegler, J. 1983. *Isaias*. 3rd ed. Septuaginta 14. Göttingen: Vandenhoeck & Ruprecht.

Zimmerli, W. 1969. *Ezechiel*. 2 vols. BKAT 13. Neukirchen-Vluyn: Neukirchener Verlag.

Zimmermann, J. 1998. *Messianische Texte aus Qumran: Königliche, priesterliche und prophetische Messiasvorstellungen in den Schriftenfunden von Qumran*. WUNT 2/104. Tübingen: Mohr Siebeck.

JOHN

ANDREAS J. KÖSTENBERGER

Introduction

Although it is the Gospel of Matthew that is widely known to focus on Jesus' fulfillment of OT messianic expectations, John's Gospel, too, roots Jesus' mission firmly in OT conceptualities and specific texts. From the very beginning and throughout the prologue of his book, the Fourth Evangelist operates within a scriptural, salvation-historical framework (Pryor 1992). In his references to the OT John spans the entire range from explicit quotations to verifiable allusions and thematic connections. In keeping with John's purpose statement, Jesus is identified as the Christ and Son of God and is set in relation to the major figures in Israel's history, whether Abraham, Jacob, or Moses, as well as the Prophet, by citations of or allusions to Scripture.

The following essay first takes inventory of the explicit OT quotations in John's Gospel (for monograph-length studies see Freed 1965; Reim 1974; Schuchard 1992; and esp. Menken [1996a], who interacts extensively with these and other earlier works). This includes a survey of John's use of introductory formulas; a comparison between John's explicit OT citations and the rest of the NT; a survey of the alignment of John's explicit OT references with the LXX, the MT, or other texts; the attribution of OT quotations in John to specific persons, be it Jesus, the evangelist, or others; a list of OT quotations in John's Gospel in OT order (including book of the Psalter and author attribution, as appropriate); a list of OT allusions and verbal parallels in John's Gospel; and a chart of Dead Sea Scrolls parallels to John's OT usage. Following this introductory material, the study treats all explicit OT quotations as well as allusive and thematic OT material in the order they appear in John's Gospel.

Explicit Old Testament Quotations in John's Gospel

There are fourteen explicit OT quotations in John's Gospel, nine in the first part (chaps. 1–12), five in the second part (chaps. 13–21) (Carson 1988: 246–51). The citation format changes from the first part to the second, the latter featuring a series of "fulfillment quotations" (see chart below). Structurally, the most significant OT quotations are found at the end of the first part in 12:38, 40. Many of the numerous allusions and a considerable amount of the OT symbolism relate in one way or another to various Jewish religious festivals. In terms of distribution, seven quotations (or 50 percent) are from Psalms; four from Isaiah; two from Zechariah; one from the Pentateuch.

The overall purpose of the use of the OT in John's Gospel, as evidenced by the formal quotations, is to show that both Jesus' public ministry and his cross-death fulfilled scriptural patterns and prophecies (Porter 1994: 401, citing Evans 1993: 174). The clustering of explicit quotations around the motifs of Jewish obduracy (12:38, 40) and Jesus' passion (19:24, 28, 36–37) suggests that a major burden informing John's use of explicit OT quotations is to provide his readers with a biblical rationale for the rejection of Jesus as Messiah (cf. 20:30–31). The Suffering Servant of Isaiah 53 underlies John's portrayal of Jesus especially in chapter 12. Davidic typology is present in 2:17; 15:25; 19:24, 28; and several other texts.

Introductory Formulas in John's Gospel

The following is a survey of introductory formulas used for each of the explicit OT quotations in John's Gospel, followed by a brief general overview. For more detailed discussions, see the treatment of the specific quotations below. An asterisk marks passages where no OT text is cited or identifiable.

John	Introductory Formula	Translation
1:23	*Ephē*	he said
2:17	*hoti gegrammenon estin*	that it is written
6:31	*kathōs estin gegrammenon*	as it is written
6:45	*estin gegrammenon en tois prophētais*	it is written in the prophets
7:38*	*kathōs eipen hē graphē*	as Scripture said
7:42*	*ouch hē graphē eipen*	has not Scripture said
10:34	*ouk estin gegrammenon en tō nomō hymōn*	is it not written in your law
12:13	—	—
12:14	*kathōs estin gegrammenon*	as it is written
12:38	*hina ho logos Ēsaiou tou prophētou plērōthē hon eipen*	in order that the word of Isaiah the prophet might be fulfilled which he spoke
12:39	*hoti palin eipen Ēsaias*	for again Isaiah said
13:18	*all' hina hē graphē plērōthē*	but in order that Scripture might be fulfilled
15:25	*all' hina plērōthē ho logos ho en tō nomō autōn gegrammenos hoti*	but in order that the word may be fulfilled that is written in the law
17:12*	*hina hē graphē plērōthē*	in order that Scripture might be fulfilled
19:24	*hina hē graphē plērōthē [hē legousa]*	in order that Scripture might be fulfilled [which says]
19:28*	*hina teleiōthē hē graphē*	in order that Scripture might be fulfilled

John	Introductory Formula	Translation
19:36	*hina hē graphē plērōthē*	in order that Scripture might be fulfilled
19:37	*kai palin hetera graphē legei*	and again another Scripture says

The seven OT quotations in 1:1–12:36a are somewhat sporadic (chaps. 3–5, 8–9, and 11 do not feature any formal OT citations) and characterized by a certain degree of variety, though the phrase *estin gegrammenon* or *gegrammenon estin* ("it is written") constitutes a common denominator (2:17; 6:31, 45; 10:34; 12:14; the only exceptions are citations attributed to the Baptist in 1:23 and to the crowd in 12:13).

A marked shift takes place at 12:38, the evangelist's concluding verdict on the Jews, which features the first of a string of seven fulfillment quotations (12:38; 13:18; 15:25; 17:12; 19:24, 28, 36, 37 [the two follow-up quotations in 12:39 and 19:37 are no real exceptions]). The phrase *hina hē graphē plērōthē* ("in order that Scripture might be fulfilled") is found in 13:18; 17:12; 19:24, 36.

Although the purposes of the formal OT citations in the first half of John's Gospel are varied, in the second half of his Gospel the evangelist consistently seeks to emphasize the fulfillment of Scripture with regard to Jesus' passion and the obduracy motif associated with it (Carson 1988: 248, with reference to Evans 1982a). The closer the narrative approaches the cross, the more forcefully John stresses that even Jesus' rejection by the Jews fulfills Scripture.

Old Testament Quotations in John and the Rest of the New Testament

The following chart, organized by type of introductory formula and in chronological order, provides a comparison between the explicit OT quotations in John's Gospel and the OT usage found in the rest of the NT. Again, a brief overview commentary is provided immediately following this chart. An asterisk indicates either the presence of a different introductory formula or the lack of one.

John	Old Testament	Rest of the New Testament
"It is written":		
1:23*	Isa. 40:3	Matt. 3:3; Mark 1:3; Luke 3:4; cf. Luke 1:76

John	Old Testament	Rest of the New Tesament
2:17	Ps. 69:9a	—
6:31	Ps. 78:24b	cf. 1 Cor. 10:3; Rev. 2:17
6:45	Isa. 54:13a	—
10:34	Ps. 82:6a	—
12:13*	Ps. 118:26a	Matt. 21:9; Mark 11:9–10
12:15	Zech. 9:9	Matt. 21:5

"In order that Scripture might be fulfilled":

12:38	Isa. 53:1	Rom. 10:16
12:40	Isa. 6:10	Matt. 13:15; Mark 4:12; Acts 28:27
13:18	Ps. 41:9b	cf. Matt. 26:23; Mark 14:18; Luke 22:21; John 17:12; Acts 1:16
15:25	Ps. 35:19; 69:4	—
19:24	Ps. 22:18	see Ps. 22:1 quotation in Matt. 27:46; Mark 15:34; cf. Mark 9:12; Luke 24:26
19:36	Exod. 12:46; Num. 9:12; Ps. 34:20	—
19:37	Zech. 12:10	Matt. 24:30; Rev. 1:7

John's use of the OT, as well as Jesus' use of the OT according to John, are generally in keeping with that found in the other canonical Gospels, in the book of Acts, the letter to the Romans, and the book of Revelation. The Baptist's reference to Isa. 40:3 occurs also in the Synoptics (though only in John is the passage found on the Baptist's lips). References to Ps. 118:25–26 and Zech. 9:9 are present also in Matthew, and the quotation of Ps. 118 is also in Mark. The citations of Isa. 53:1 and 6:10 are paralleled in Romans and Matthew, Mark and Acts respectively. The reference to Ps. 22:18 is corroborated by the specific quotations of Ps. 22:1 in Matthew and Mark and possible allusions to the psalm in Mark and Luke. Finally, the citation of Zech. 12:10 finds parallels in Matt. 24:30; Rev. 1:7.

Interestingly, both of Jesus' appeals to OT Scripture in the first half of this Gospel (6:45; 10:34) are unique to John, as is Jesus' OT reference in 15:25. This may suggest that John is seeking to supplement the Synoptic Gospels and, in any case, attests to John's independence in writing his Gospel. As M. Daly-Denton (2004: 121) notes, John's use of the psalms, too, while generally congruent with the Synoptics, evidences a certain form of independence—a feature highlighted further by John's penchant for formal citation. Daly-Denton also notes that John's use of the psalms is spread throughout the entire Gospel rather than being concentrated on the passion narrative, as is the case in the Synoptics.

Alignment of Old Testament Quotations in John's Gospel with the Masoretic Text or the Septuagint

The text form underlying the various explicit OT quotations in John's Gospel has been the subject of considerable debate (see esp. Menken 1996a). The following chart provides an initial survey. More detailed treatments are provided in the discussions of specific passages below.

John	Old Testament	Relationship with [proto-] Masoretic Text, Septuagint
1:23	Isa. 40:3	LXX? Change from *hetoimasate … eutheias* to *euthynate*
2:17	Ps. 69:9a	LXX? Change from *katephagen* to *kataphagetai*
6:31	Ps. 78:24b	LXX? *Phagein* at end rather than beginning; *ek tou* added
6:45	Isa. 54:13a	LXX? As in MT, *pantes* nom. rather than acc. (as in LXX); as in LXX, *theou* rather than *kyriou*; "your sons" omitted
10:34	Ps. 82:6a	Same as LXX = MT
12:13	Ps. 118:26a	Same as LXX = MT (adds *kai ho basileus tou Israēl*)
12:15	Zech. 9:9	Independent adaptation of LXX/MT: "do not fear" added (Isa. 40:9?); *sou* omitted; "sitting," not "mounting"; "colt of a donkey" (Gen. 49:11?)
12:38	Isa. 53:1	Same as LXX = MT
12:40	Isa. 6:10	Independent adaption of LXX/MT: "hearing" omitted; concentric structure changed to parallel one; etc.
13:18	Ps. 41:9b	Seems independent of LXX; own translation from Hebrew?
15:25	Ps. 35:19 or 69:4	LXX? Accurately reflects both MT and LXX
19:24	Ps. 22:18	Same as LXX = MT
19:36	Exod. 12:46 or Num. 9:12; Ps. 34:20	LXX? Combination of Exod. 12:46/Num. 9:12; Ps. 34:20
19:37	Zech. 12:10	Close to Hebrew; LXX misreads the Hebrew; *testimonium*?

Overall, as the detailed discussions below will demonstrate, John seems to exhibit a pattern of closeness to the OT text in the Hebrew and as reflected in the LXX. John's default version seems to have been the LXX, but in no way does he use it slavishly, and throughout he exhibits a highly intelligent and discerning mode of OT usage. In four passages his Greek is identical to the LXX wording (10:34; 12:13, 38; 19:24). In several other passages John likely adapts the LXX rendering by making minor changes to suit his context (1:23; 2:17; 6:31, 45; 15:25; 19:36). In four cases John seems to be independent of the LXX (12:15, 40; 13:18; 19:37), whereby 12:15, 40 represent independent adaptations of the relevant texts; 13:18 may feature John's own translation from the Hebrew; 19:37 may draw on a Christian *testimonium* (in this final case the LXX is unsuitable because it misconstrues the Hebrew). It therefore appears that John was familiar with both the Hebrew text and the LXX (as well as with Jesus' own use and earlier Christian quotation practices) and thus was able to cite the Scriptures either in the exact or slightly adapted LXX version or to draw on the Hebrew where this suited his purposes or seemed necessary for some reason or another. Finally, in keeping with Jewish exegetical practice, John at times clusters two OT texts (12:13, 15; 12:38, 40; 19:36, 37) or combines interrelated texts (e.g., Zech. 9:9; Isa. 40:9; Gen. 49:11 LXX in 12:15; Exod. 12:46/Num. 9:12; Ps. 34:20 in 19:36; see also 7:38) (see Menken 1996a: 52–53, 159–60).

Attribution of Old Testament Quotations in John's Gospel and Old Testament Passages Cited

Yet another way to categorize the explicit OT quotations in John's Gospel is by way of attribution to specific Johannine characters. The chart below is followed by a brief summary discussion.

John	Attribution	Old Testament Passage
1:23	John the Baptist	Isa. 40:3
2:17	disciples/evangelist	Ps. 69:9a (David)
6:31	crowd	Ps. 78:24b (Asaph)
6:45	Jesus	Isa. 54:13a
10:34	Jesus	Ps. 82:6a (Asaph)
12:13	crowd	Ps. 118:26a (none)
12:15	evangelist	Zech. 9:9
12:38	evangelist	Isa. 53:1
12:40	evangelist	Isa. 6:10
13:18	Jesus	Ps. 41:9b (David)
15:25	Jesus	Ps. 35:19 or 69:4 (David)
19:24	evangelist	Ps. 22:18 (David)

John	Attribution	Old Testament Passage
19:36	evangelist	Exod. 12:46/Num. 9:12; Ps. 34:20
19:37	evangelist	Zech. 12:10

Four OT quotations in John's Gospel are attributed to Jesus (6:45; 10:34; 13:18; 15:25), seven to the evangelist (2:17; 12:15, 38, 40; 19:24, 36, 37), one to the Baptist (1:23), and two to the crowd (6:31; 12:13). Three of Jesus' four OT references are to the psalms, and one is to the book of Isaiah. References to Isaiah are also attributed to the Baptist and the evangelist. Both quotations of Zechariah are the work of the evangelist. Overall, the evangelist's use of the OT is varied, featuring two references each to Psalms, Isaiah, and Zechariah and one to the Pentateuch. Interestingly, references to Davidic psalms are limited to Jesus' interaction with, or perception of, the disciples (2:17; 13:18; 15:25; 19:24).

Regardless of the person to whom the respective quotes are attributed, ultimately all references have Jesus and his messianic identity in view (Carson 1988: 246). John 1:23 defines the Baptist's role, over against that of Jesus, as a voice preparing the way for the coming king. John 2:17 and 12:15 align Jesus' actions with those anticipated in OT messianic passages. John 6:31 and 12:13 likewise relate Jesus to messianic expectations rooted in the Hebrew Scriptures. Opposition to Jesus fulfills the pattern established in the OT (12:38–40; 13:18; 15:25), as do various details of Jesus' death (19:24, 36, 37; see also 19:28). Jesus is the Son of God (10:34), and all of God's true sons will be taught by Yahweh through him (6:45).

Old Testament Quotations in John's Gospel in Old Testament Order

In addition to the listing of explicit OT quotations in John's Gospel, it may be helpful to provide a chronological chart of these references in OT order. In the case of Psalms references, the book of the Psalter and any author attribution in the title (where available) are provided as well. An asterisk marks Psalms quotations proposed by Daly-Denton (2004).

Old Testament	John
Exod. 12:46/Num. 9:12	19:36
Ps. 22:18 (David; Book 1)	19:24

Old Testament	John
Ps. 34:20 (David; Book 1)	19:36*
Ps. 35:19 (David; Book 1)	15:25
Ps. 41:9b (David; Book 1)	13:18
Ps. 69:4 (David; Book 2)	15:25
Ps. 69:9a (David; Book 2)	2:17
Ps. 69:21 (David, Book 2)	19:28*
Ps. 78:15, 20 (Asaph; Book 3)	7:38*
Ps. 78:24b (Asaph; Book 3)	6:31
Ps. 82:6a (Asaph; Book 3)	10:34
Ps. 118:26a (none; Book 5)	12:13
Isa. 6:10	12:40
Isa. 40:3	1:23
Isa. 53:1	12:38
Isa. 54:13a	6:45
Zech. 9:9	12:15
Zech. 12:10	19:37

The direct OT quotations in John are concentrated on a select few portions of the canon. The OT theological center, at least as far as explicit OT quotations are concerned, is clearly the Psalter (Daly-Denton 2000; 2004; cf. Wifall 1974). References to the psalms are spread fairly evenly throughout the entire Gospel, through both the first part (2:17; 6:31; 10:34; 12:13) and the second part (13:18; 15:25; 19:28; cf. 19:28, 36). Both the quantity and the consistent distribution of references to the Psalter in John's Gospel are truly impressive and attest to the significance of the psalms in John's theology and Jesus' self-understanding and to the connection between Jesus' messianic claims and identity and the person and kingship of David (Menken 1996a: 44).

The other important OT portion for the theology of John is the second part of Isaiah, which, in terms of explicit quotations, is represented in the Fourth Gospel at the beginning (1:23), the middle (6:45), and the end (12:40) of the first part (F. W. Young 1955; Evans 1987; Janowski and Stuhlmacher 2004). The Baptist, Jesus, and the Fourth Evangelist, respectively, draw on passages found in the second part of Isaiah to establish (1) the identity of the Baptist as one who prepares the way for the coming of Jesus, the royal Messiah; (2) the fact that it is through Jesus' teaching ministry that God's people are taught in the eschatological age inaugurated by Jesus the Messiah; (3) the notion that the rejection of Jesus by the Jewish nation fulfills the OT characterization of the Jews as resisting God's message as delivered through his appointed spokesmen.

Last but not least, Zechariah is represented significantly in John's Gospel as well with two major references at the end of the first and second parts respectively (Bruce 1960–1961; France 1971: 103–10, 148–50, 208–9). Both references are decidedly christological in focus, the first depicting Jerusalem's visitation by the Messiah, a humble servant-king who enters the city mounted on a donkey, the second shifting the point of application from Yahweh to Jesus as the object of the people's looking "on the one they have pierced" (see further commentary at 19:37 below).

Old Testament Allusions and Verbal Parallels in John's Gospel

The penultimate survey chart lists verifiable OT allusions and verbal parallels in John's Gospel. A more detailed discussion is provided in the following commentary. It is often precarious to identify OT allusions, especially in light of the standard applied in the present study: authorial intention as expressed in the text. For this reason the following chart remains, of necessity, tentative. The list below is conservative; only those passages have been included that can be determined with a reasonable degree of confidence to have been intended by the Fourth Evangelist as allusions or verbal parallels to specific OT texts. Beyond this, the reader is referred to the discussion in the following commentary, which includes references to a variety of other echoes and relevant OT background passages. In order to provide a full view of OT references for the reader, explicit quotations are included in square brackets.

John	Old Testament
1:1	Gen. 1:1
1:14	Exod. 34:6
1:17	Exod. 34:6
1:18	Exod. 33:20
1:21	Deut. 18:15, 18
[1:23	Isa. 40:3]
1:29, 36	Isa. 53:6–7
1:45	Deut. 18:15, 18
1:49	Ps. 2:7; 2 Sam. 7:14; Zeph. 3:15
1:51	Gen. 28:12
2:5	Gen. 41:55
[2:17	Ps. 69:9a]
3:5	Ezek. 36:25–27
3:8	Eccles. 11:5

John	Old Testament
3:13	Prov. 30:4?
3:14	Num. 21:9; Isa. 52:13
3:16	Gen. 22:2, 12, 16
3:28	Mal. 3:1
4:5	Gen. 33:19; 48:22; Exod. 13:19; Josh. 24:32
4:10	Num. 20:8–11; cf. 21:16–18
4:14	Isa. 12:3; Jer. 2:13
4:20	Deut. 11:29; 12:5–14; 27:12; Josh. 8:33; Ps. 122:1–5
4:22	Isa. 2:3?
4:36	Amos 9:13?
4:37	Mic. 6:15?
5:27	Dan. 7:13
5:29	Dan. 12:2
5:45	Deut. 31:26–27
5:46	Deut. 18:15, 18
6:14	Deut. 18:15, 18
6:29	Mal. 3:1
[6:31	Ps. 78:24b]
[6:45	Isa. 54:13a]
7:22	Gen. 17:10–13; Lev. 12:3
7:24	Lev. 19:15
7:38	Neh. 9:15, 19–20; cf. Num. 20:11 et al.; Ps. 77:16, 20 LXX; Isa. 58:11; Zech. 14:8
7:40	Deut. 18:15, 18
7:42	2 Sam. 7:12; Ps. 89:3–4; Mic. 5:2
7:51	Deut. 1:16–17; 17:4; 19:18
8:12	Isa. 9:1–2; cf. 49:6
8:15	1 Sam. 16:7
8:17	Deut. 17:6; 19:15
8:28	Isa. 52:13
8:35	Gen. 21:1–21
8:44	Gen. 3:4 (cf. 2:17); Isa. 14:12?
9:2	Exod. 20:5; Ezek. 18:20
9:5 [= 8:12]	Isa. 9:1–2; cf. 49:6
9:24	Josh. 7:19
9:34	Ps. 51:5
10:3–4	Num. 27:15–18
10:8	Jer. 23:1–2; Ezek. 34:2–3
10:16	Isa. 56:8; Ezek. 34:23; 37:24
10:33	Lev. 24:16
[10:34	Ps. 82:6a]
12:8	Deut. 15:11
[12:13	Ps. 118:26a]
[12:15	Zech. 9:9]
12:27	Ps. 6:3; 42:5, 11
12:32	Isa. 52:13
12:34	Ps. 89:4, 36–37?
[12:38	Isa. 53:1]
[12:40	Isa. 6:10]
12:41	Isa. 6:1
[13:18	Ps. 41:9b]
15:1	Isa. 5:1–7; cf. Jer. 2:21
[15:25	Ps. 35:19; 69:4]
16:22	Isa. 66:14

John	Old Testament
16:32	Zech. 13:7
17:12	Ps. 41:9
19:7	Lev. 24:16
19:18	Isa. 22:16; cf. 52:13
[19:24	Ps. 22:18]
19:28–29	Ps. 69:21 (cf. 22:15)
19:31	Deut. 21:22–23
[19:36	Exod. 12:46; Num. 9:12; Ps. 34:20]
[19:37	Zech. 12:10]
19:38	Isa. 53:9
20:22	Gen. 2:7
20:23	Isa. 22:22?

Apart from the fourteen direct OT quotations listed above, John's Gospel features numerous OT allusions and verbal parallels with the OT (Carson 1988: 251–53). The range of allusions spans virtually the entire OT. Particularly frequent are allusions to the Pentateuch, Psalms, and OT prophetic literature, particularly Isaiah (see also Ezekiel and Zechariah). In some cases, a given Johannine reference presupposes a foundational passage in the OT (e.g., 19:31 with reference to Deut. 21:22–23). At times, reference is made to a particular OT event (e.g., 3:14; 6:32; 7:22–23). In yet other instances, a given statement in John's Gospel employs OT language (e.g., 16:22 with reference to Isa. 66:14).

More significant still are verifiable OT allusions and verbal parallels that draw on the theology of a particular OT passage (e.g., 10:16 with reference to Isa. 56:8; Ezek. 34:23; 37:24). Together with the direct OT quotations and references to broader OT themes (including the Johannine replacement motif [see Carson 1988: 253–56]), the OT allusions found in John's Gospel create a web of intertextuality that grounds the theology of the Fourth Gospel profoundly in the Hebrew Scriptures, particularly with regard to the person and teaching of Jesus (Carson [1988: 246] cites the following passages "where 'the Scripture' or some OT person or persons are said to speak or write of Jesus or of some aspect of his teaching or mission": 1:45; 2:22; 3:10; 5:39, 45–46; 12:34; 20:9).

The discussion below of OT-related material in John focuses on verifiable OT allusions (or "higher-volume echoes," per Hays 1989: 24) and thematic interconnections. To the extent that it can be determined with reasonable confidence, Johannine authorial attention will be considered to be the primary criterion for treatment or non-treatment of a given OT text. This procedure is in keeping with the acknowledgment by R. B. Hays (1989: 29) that the "concept of allusion depends . . . on the notion of authorial intention" and observes the distinction between echoes and allusions drawn by J. Hollander (1981: 64), who notes that "echo is a metaphor of, and for, alluding" that "does not depend on conscious intention," while striking a more conservative note than both of these authors.

Old Testament Quotations in John and the Dead Sea Scrolls

Finally, it is interesting to compare John's OT quotations with references to the Hebrew Scriptures in the Dead Sea Scrolls. Only citations in community documents are listed below.

John	Old Testament	Dead Sea Scrolls
1:23	Isa. 40:3	1QS VIII, 14; 4Q176 1–2 I, 6–7; 4Q259 III, 4–5
6:45	Isa. 54:13	CD-B XX, 4?
10:34	Ps. 82:6a	cf. use of Ps. 82:1–2 in 11Q13 II, 10–11
12:15	Zech. 9:9	1QM XII, 13?

Most notable are three references to Isa. 40:3 in 1QS; 4Q176; 4Q259, underscoring the prominence of this OT prophetic passage in the Dead Sea community, especially with regard to its self-understanding (Charlesworth 1997; Brooke 1994; see also Metso 1998; VanderKam 1999). Also worthy of comment are the use of Ps. 82:1–2 in 11Q13 II, 10–11 and the possible references to Isa. 54:13 in CD-B XX, 4 (Menken 1996a: 68) and to Zech. 9:9 in 1QM XII, 13. Beyond this, most of the OT passages cited in John's Gospel are attested in the biblical documents found at Qumran, which indicates that the Dead Sea community was familiar with these passages and used them in worship and their study of Scripture.

The Prologue (1:1–18)

The prologue's opening words, "In the beginning was the Word" (1:1), echo the opening phrase of the Hebrew Bible, "In the beginning God created the heavens and the earth" (Gen. 1:1), and, in an effect similar to Luke's use of septuagintal language in the first two chapters of his Gospel, establish a canonical link between the first words of the OT Scriptures and John's Gospel (Schwarz 1982). Yet instead of "In the beginning God created," John has "In the beginning [i.e., prior to creation] was the Word." This locates Jesus' existence in eternity past with God and sets the stage for John's lofty Christology, which is unmatched by any of the other canonical Gospels.

The term "the Word" conveys the notion of divine self-expression or speech (cf. Ps. 19:1–4). The Genesis creation account provides ample testimony to the effectiveness of God's word: he speaks, and things come into being (Gen. 1:3, 9; cf. 1:11, 15, 24, 29–30). Both psalmists and prophets portray God's word in close-to-personified terms (Ps. 33:6; 107:20; 147:15, 18; Isa. 55:10–11), but only John claims that this word has appeared in space-time history as an actual person, Jesus Christ (1:14, 17).

Most critical in this regard is Isaiah's depiction of God's word as going out from his mouth and not returning to him empty, but as accomplishing what he desires and achieving the purpose for which he sent it (Isa. 55:11; cf. 40:8). In this passage Isaiah provides the framework for John's "sending" Christology, which presents Jesus as the Word sent by God the Father who pursues and accomplishes his mission in obedience to the one who sent him. This sender-sent relationship, in turn, provides the paradigm for Jesus' relationship with his followers (cf. esp. 17:18; 20:21–23; see Köstenberger 1998b).

In the following verses of the prologue, the evangelist, after explicitly referring to the Word's instrumentality in creation (1:3), continues to draw on Genesis motifs, particularly the contrast between light and darkness (1:4–5, 7–9; cf. Gen. 1:3–5, 14–18) and the notion of life (1:4; cf. Gen. 1:20–31; 2:7; 3:20). Significantly, "light" symbolism is also found in later OT prophetic, including messianic, passages (e.g., Isa. 9:2; 42:6–7; 49:6; 60:1–5; Mal. 4:2; cf. Luke 1:78–79; see already Num. 24:17; cf. 4Q175 9–13).

The reference to believers' right to become "children of God" in 1:12 clearly builds on the OT characterization of Israel as God's children (Deut. 14:1; see also the reference to Israel as God's son and firstborn in Exod. 4:22; cf. 1 John 3:1–2). On the heels of the oblique reference to the rejection of the Word by "his own" (i.e., the Jews) in 1:11, however, the reference to children of God "born not of natural descent . . . but born of God" in 1:13 distinguishes between an illegitimate, presumptuous claim of divine sonship based on physical descent and true divine sonship based on faith in the name of God's Messiah (1:12; cf. 8:41–47; 11:51–52).

Later in the prologue one finds allusions to God's presence among Israel during the exodus (1:14: *eskēnōsen*, "he pitched his tent"; cf. Exod. 25:8–9; 33:7; 2 Sam. 7:6; Ps. 15:1; 26:8; 27:4–6; 43:3; 74:7; 84:1; Ezek. 37:27–28) and to God's giving of the law through Moses (1:17; cf. Exod. 31:18; 34:28). In both cases John's purpose of adducing these OT antecedent passages is to locate Jesus at the climactic end of the spectrum of God's self-disclosure to his people. In the past God was present among his people in the tabernacle (e.g., Exod. 33:9; 40:34–35) and the temple (e.g., 1 Kings 8:10–11) (for a discussion of God's "dwelling" [*šākan*] among his people in the OT, see Carson 1991: 127–28), but now he has taken up residence among his people in the person of Jesus Christ (1:14). In the past God made himself known through the law, but now he revealed himself definitively in and through Jesus Christ (1:16–17) (for the interpretive issues surrounding the phrase "grace [in return] for grace" in 1:16 and the explication of this phrase in 1:17, see Köstenberger 2004: 46–48 and also here below).

The reference in 1:14 to Jesus taking up residence among God's people resulting in the revelation of God's glory (the first occurrence of the term *doxa* in this Gospel) also harks back to OT references to the manifestation of the presence and glory (*kābôd*) of God, be it in theophanies, the tabernacle, or the temple (cf., e.g., Exod. 33:22; Num. 14:10; Deut. 5:24; Ps. 26:8; 102:15 [102:16 MT]; Jer. 17:12; Ezek. 10:4; see Köstenberger 1997: 230). Whereas the Second Temple period was marked by the relative paucity of God's revelation because of Israel's apostasy, John makes clear that now, in Jesus, God's glory has taken up residence in the midst of his people once again. To bring glory to God is said to be Jesus' overriding purpose in John's Gospel (9:3; 11:4, 40). As he brings glory to God, glory also comes to Jesus. This continues what was true of Jesus already prior to his coming, since glory characterized Jesus' eternal relation-

ship with God (17:5) as well as his preincarnate state (12:41). While on earth, Jesus' glory is manifested to his first followers particularly through his "signs" (cf. 2:11; see Carson 1991: 128). As the obedient, dependent Son, Jesus brings glory to God the Father throughout his entire ministry. However, this he does supremely by submitting to the cross, which for John is the place of God's—and Jesus'—ultimate glorification (cf. 12:23–33; 13:31–32; 14:13; 17:1, 4–5). The themes of light and life, likewise, culminate in the person of Jesus Christ, in whom these divine realities and gifts find fulfillment (1:4–5, 7–9).

Another significant and verifiable OT allusion is present in the Johannine depiction of Jesus as "full of grace and truth" (1:14, 17), which in all probability harks back to the phrase "lovingkindness [*ḥesed*] and truth [*ĕmet*]" in Exod. 34:6 (cf. 33:18–19; see Mowvley 1984: 137; Kuyper 1964: 3–13; cf. Ps. 25:10; 26:3; 40:10; Prov. 16:6; see also Ps. 83:12 LXX [84:11 ET]). In its original context this joint expression refers to God's covenant faithfulness to his people Israel. John's message is that this covenant faithfulness found ultimate expression in the sending of God's one-of-a-kind Son (1:14, 18) (on the expression *monogenēs*, see esp. Pendrick 1995; Winter 1953: 336; cf. Schlatter 1948: 25; see also Moody 1953; *contra* Dahms 1983).

The predominant sense of the term *monogenēs* in the OT and the Apocrypha is "only child" (e.g., Judg. 11:34; Tob. 3:15; 8:17). Being an only child, and thus irreplaceable, makes a child of special value to the parents (cf. Luke 7:12; 8:42; 9:38; see Pendrick 1995: 593–94). Hence the LXX often uses *agapētos* ("beloved") in the place of *monogenēs* (Gen. 22:2, 12, 16; Amos 8:10; Jer. 6:26; Zech. 12:10; cf. Prov. 4:3; in Judg. 11:34 both terms are used). The seminal event in OT history in this regard is Abraham's offering of Isaac, who in Genesis 22:2, 12, 16 is called Abraham's "one-of-a-kind" (*yāḥîd*) son (note the probable allusion to this text in John 3:16), even though the patriarch had earlier fathered Ishmael (cf. Heb. 11:17; Josephus, *Ant.* 1.22: *monogenēs*; see *EDNT* 2:440; Winter 1953: 337–40; Moody 1953, esp. 217). Thus *monogenēs* means not "only begotten," but "one-of-a-kind" son (in Isaac's case, "son of promise"; according to Heb. 11:17, Isaac is a *typos* of

Christ; see Pendrick 1995; Moody 1953; W. O. Walker 1994: 41n37).

In both OT and Second Temple literature the Son of David and Israel are called God's "firstborn" or even "only" son (cf. Ps. 89:27; *4 Ezra* 6:58; *Pss. Sol.* 18:4; *Jub.* 18:2, 11, 15). In a decisive step further, John applies the designation *monogenēs* to God's "one-of-a-kind" Son par excellence, Jesus (cf. 1:18; 3:16, 18; 1 John 4:9). This is similar to the designation of Jesus as God's "beloved son," which surfaces in the Synoptics in the voice from heaven at Jesus' baptism and transfiguration and in the parable of the Wicked Tenants (esp. Mark 1:11; 9:7; 12:6; cf. Luke 20:13; see Pendrick 1995: 595n42).

In keeping with the Isaac narrative and the parable of the Wicked Tenants, the term *monogenēs* in the present passage thus contains a significant soteriological dimension, culminating in John's assertion in 3:16 that "God so loved the world that he sent his one-of-a-kind Son" (cf. 3:18). This designation also provides the basis for Jesus' claim that no one can come to the Father except through him (14:6). Moreover, it is likely that "one of a kind" in John's context refers to Jesus' uniqueness in that "he is *both* the *human* Son of Joseph *and* the *divine* Son of God" (W. O. Walker 1994: 41n37).

Also important for understanding the larger framework of John's use of the OT is the implicit contrast between God's giving of the law through Moses (cf. Exod. 31:18; 34:28) and the appearing of grace and truth through Jesus Christ in 1:17 (cf. 1:16; see also the brief comments on this passage above). As the Fourth Evangelist notes, "True grace—that is, final, eschatological grace—came through Jesus Christ" (Köstenberger 2004: 47; cf. Edwards 1988: 11, following Brown 1966–1970: 16). Rather than drawing a sharp contrast between God's giving of the law at Sinai and the grace and truth brought by Jesus (note the absence of the word "but" between the two phrases in 1:17), John in essence presents Jesus as the climactic eschatological revelation of God's covenant love and faithfulness (thus there is no real tension with texts such as Matt. 5:18 or Rom. 10:4; on the former text, see esp. Carson 1984: 140–47). As the ensuing narrative will develop in greater detail, Jesus' ministry is superior to Moses (5:46–47; cf.

9:28), just as he is superior to Jacob (4:12) and Abraham (8:53).

The Book of Signs (1:19–12:50)

The first half of John's Gospel is given primarily to a narration of seven of Jesus' signs addressed specifically to the Jews (Köstenberger 1995). There are two major OT antecedents for Jesus' signs: (1) the signs and wonders performed by Moses at the exodus; (2) prophetic symbolic acts denoting future judgment (e.g., Isa. 20:3). Many of these signs proceed against the backdrop of the OT. The first sign, Jesus' turning of water into wine at the wedding of Cana (2:1–11), contrasts the barrenness of first-century Judaism with the end-time messianic joy inaugurated by Jesus the Messiah. In the second possible sign, Jesus performs the prophetic act of clearing the temple (2:13–22), symbolically conveying future judgment on the Jewish nation. At the occasion of the third sign, the long-distance healing of the royal official's son (4:46–54), Jesus excoriates the people for being dependent on "signs and wonders"—the only instance of this expression in the Gospel.

Chapters 5–10, which are characterized by mounting controversy between Jesus and his Jewish opponents, feature the second set of three of Jesus' signs: the healing of the man who had been lame for thirty-eight years and the subsequent Sabbath controversy, in which Jesus claims that his work is congruent with, and continuous of, the creative activity of God (chap. 5); the feeding of the multitude plus the ensuing "bread of life" discourse (chap. 6), which presents the experience of wilderness Israel under Moses, particularly God's provision of "bread from heaven," as the backdrop for Jesus' messianic activity; and the healing of the man born blind (chap. 9), which represents an acted parable of the blind receiving sight by the ministry of the Messiah and of those who claim to see being made blind by their rejection of the Messiah.

The final and climactic Johaninne sign, Jesus' raising of Lazarus from the dead, is part of the transition section in chapters 11–12, which show the ultimate hardening of the Jews against Jesus and the revelation of God in his signs, works, and words and thus set the stage for chapters 13–21, which narrate Jesus' formation of the new messianic community in and through his inner circle, the Twelve (minus Judas). Healing the lame, feeding the hungry, giving sight to the blind, and raising the dead, according to the OT, are activities characteristic of the ministry of the Messiah, as is made clear by Jesus' response to the messengers sent by John the Baptist in the words of the prophet Isaiah: "Go back and report to John what you hear and see: the blind receive sight, the lame walk, those who have leprosy are cured, the deaf hear, the dead are raised, and the good news is preached to the poor. Blessed is the man who does not fall away on account of me" (Matt. 11:4–6; cf. Isa. 35:5–6; 42:18; 61:1).

Hence John's purpose statement, made explicit in 20:30–31, of demonstrating that the Christ, the Son of God, is Jesus, is fulfilled in the first half of his Gospel. The overarching vindication of God's righteousness in and through Jesus (theodicy) makes clear that the Jews' rejection of the Messiah took place in the face of the ever-increasing revelation of God's character and of his divine nature through the Messiah; and Jesus is shown to engage in a ministry of ever-escalating, continually startling expressions of his divinely inspired mission in fulfillment of a variety of OT texts and typological patterns pointing forward to the coming of the Messiah. While therefore the number of specific OT quotations is relatively small, the OT serves as a continual backdrop to the Johannine narrative. It remains to trace the unfolding of John's story with special attention to OT quotations, allusions, and thematic OT connections in greater detail below.

John the Baptist and the Inception of Jesus' Ministry (1:19–51)

SURVEY

This section, which narrates John the Baptist's witness to the Jews and concerning Jesus (1:19–28, 29–34) and the results of the Baptist's witness at the inception of Jesus' ministry (1:35–51), features one explicit OT quotation (1:23) and several likely OT allusions (1:21, 29, 36, 45, 49, 51). It is significant that the first explicit OT quotation in this Gospel is attributed to John the Baptist, Jesus' forerunner, clarifying his status and at the same time pointing to Jesus as Israel's Messiah. The OT allusions in chapter 1, likewise, relate in one way or another to the Baptist's or Jesus' identity: in 1:21

the Baptist denies being the Prophet spoken of by Moses; in 1:45 it is Philip's testimony that the one of whom Moses wrote in the law and of whom the prophets wrote as well is Jesus. The complex OT background to the Baptist's reference to Jesus as "the lamb of God" in 1:29 is discussed in some detail below. Nathanael's address of Jesus as "Son of God" and "King of Israel" (1:49) also speaks of Jesus in OT terms. The final verse of the chapter, 1:51, unmistakably alludes to the narrative involving Jacob and Bethel in Gen. 28:12.

DISCUSSION

When queried by the Jerusalem delegation, the Baptist denies being the Christ, Elijah, or the Prophet (1:19–21). Within the literary structure of the Fourth Gospel, the Baptist's threefold denial at the very outset of the Johannine narrative provides the positive equivalent of Peter's later denial of Jesus prior to Jesus' passion (18:15–18, 25–27). The Baptist's first denial—he is not the Christ—reiterates what the reader of John's Gospel already knows: the Baptist is not the expected deliverer or Messiah (1:15; see also 1:8: "not the light"; 3:28). The Greek term *christos*, like its Hebrew counterpart, *māšiaḥ*, means "anointed one." The term was applied in the OT to a variety of men who were set apart and anointed to serve God and his people in a special capacity (such as priest or king), but OT predictive prophecy gave rise to the expectation that there would be a future figure, *the* Anointed One, sent by God to deliver and rule his people (see Horbury 1998).

Messianic hopes were widespread in early first-century Palestine (Horsley 1992). Many Jews waited for the greater Son of David predicted to be coming in the OT (see 2 Sam. 7:11b–16; Hos. 3:5; cf. Matt. 1:1, 6, 17; Luke 3:31; Rom. 1:3). However, people were not necessarily united in their expectations, nor were these necessarily in keeping with scriptural predictions. The Fourth Evangelist gathers several messianic expectations current in Jesus' day in chapter 7 of his Gospel.

With regard to the Baptist's second denial, the people's question of whether or not John was Elijah certainly was appropriate: not only did the Baptist display the demeanor of a prophet, but also he resembled Elijah in his rugged lifestyle (Matt. 3:4; cf. 2 Kings 1:8) and powerful message of judgment (Matt. 3:7–12; Luke 3:7–17) (see Morris 1995: 119). Yet John nonetheless denied being Elijah (cf. 5:35), the figure whose arrival many first-century Jews expected in addition to that of the Messiah (Matt. 16:14 pars.; 17:3–4, 10 pars.; Matt. 27:47, 49 par.; Sir. 48:10; *m. Šeqal.* 2:5; *m. Soṭah* 9:15; *m. B. Meṣi'a* 1:8; *m. 'Ed.* 8:7; probably also 1QS IX, 11). According to Mal. 4:5, Elijah, who had never died (2 Kings 2:11), was to come "before that great and dreadful day of the LORD" (see Morris 1995: 118). Some expected him to settle rabbinic disputes; others thought that he would perform great miracles or introduce the Messiah (e.g., *4 Ezra* 6:26–27; Justin, *1 Apol.* 35.1; see Beasley-Murray 1999: 24). In any case, he would "restore all things" (Matt. 17:11), turning the hearts of the fathers to their children and vice versa (Mal. 4:6; cf. Sir. 48:10; Luke 1:17).

Although John denied literally being the returning prophet Elijah, according to the Synoptics, Jesus clearly stated that the Baptist "was Elijah" (Matt. 11:14; 17:12; Mark 9:13), since his ministry constituted the typological fulfillment of the prophecy of Mal. 4:5 (cf. Luke 1:17; see Schnackenburg 1990: 1:289). Even before the Baptist's birth, an angel prophesied to his father, Zechariah, that John would "go on before the Lord in the spirit and power of Elijah" (Luke 1:17; see also Mark's conflation of Mal. 3:1 ["I will send my messenger"] and Isa. 40:3 [also found in John 1:23 and Synoptic parallels] in Mark 1:2–3; Carson [1991: 143] also notes that false prophets often dressed in a manner similar to Elijah [Zech. 13:4]). Did John perhaps not realize that he really *was* "Elijah"? Or do John and the Synoptics contradict each other? More likely, the Baptist denied being "Elijah" to counter the expectation (current in his day) that the same Elijah who escaped death in a fiery chariot would return in like spectacular manner.

The Baptist's third denial pertained to the so-called Prophet. The coming of this Prophet, mentioned in 1:21 and repeatedly later in John's Gospel (6:14; 7:40), was predicted by Moses in Deut. 18:15, 18 (see Acts 3:22; 7:37; cf. 1 Macc. 4:46; 14:41; *T. Benj.* 9:2). Hence the Jews, the Samaritans (Macdonald 1964: 197–98, 362–71, 443; Carson 1991: 143), and the Qumran community were waiting for the coming of the Prophet. The Qumran covenanters, for their part, waited not only "until the prophet comes," but also for "the Messiahs of Aaron and Israel" (1QS IX, 11; see

also the collection of messianic passages in 4Q175 5–8 citing Deut. 18:18–19).

The Baptist's threefold denial is followed by a positive self-identification in 1:23.

1:23

A. NT Context: The Identity of John the Baptist.

In the prologue the Fourth Evangelist presented John as "a man sent from God" to "bear witness concerning the light" (i.e., Jesus): "He was not the light, but came to bear witness concerning the light" (1:6–8; see also 1:15; and later 5:33). This opening characterization sets the stage for the narration of John's ministry in 1:19–34. John's identity is further probed when he is called to account by a delegation sent by the Jewish leaders in Jerusalem. Three times John denies being a particular end-time figure: the Christ (1:20; cf. 1:8, 15); Elijah (1:21a [see Köstenberger 2004: 60–61]); the Prophet (1:21b; cf. 6:14; 7:40; cf. Deut. 18:15, 18).

After thus affirming three times who he is *not*, John in the present passage, at long last, is telling his interrogators who he *is*. Even though he is none of the scriptural figures expected to make their appearance in Israel in the last days, John does respond in terms of a figure spoken of in Scripture. He is "the voice of one crying out in the wilderness, 'Make straight the way of the Lord'" featured in Isa. 40:3. In this characterization of John, the Fourth Evangelist coheres fully with the Synoptic portrayal of the Baptist (cf. Matt. 3:3; Mark 1:3; Luke 3:4). According to the Fourth Evangelist, John's witness centered on Jesus' role in the divine plan of salvation as the "Lamb of God who takes away the sin of the world" (1:29, 36). At its very heart, the purpose of John's baptism and ministry is described as being bound up with revealing Jesus' true identity to Israel (1:31).

B. The OT Context of Isa. 40:3.

Isaiah 40:3 constitutes the opening of the second of four well-defined speeches in Isa. 40:1–9 that comprises 40:3–5. The entire passage serves as a prologue that sets the tone for Isa. 40–48 (Blenkinsopp 2002: 179), and indeed for the rest of the book, by announcing the intentions of Yahweh (Watts 1985–1987: 2:79; Oswalt 1986–1998: 2:49). After all the judgment and condemnation sounded in Isa. 1–39, the opening of chapter 40 marks a major shift in orientation, introducing the theme of comfort that represents the leitmotiv for the remainder of the book.

The precise identity of the calling voice is unspecified, but the context makes clear that reference is made to a creature, a human messenger (Young 1972: 26). In light of the fact that several elements of Isa. 40:1–11 are reminiscent of Isa. 6:1–13, it is likely that the present passage describes not a "new call of a new person," but rather "an expansion and adaptation of the single Isaiah's original call" (Oswalt 1986–1998: 2:48). The lack of specification of the identity of the messenger focuses attention on the substance of the message (this is well captured by the Baptist's insistent words in 3:30, "He must increase, but I must decrease" [see Oswalt 1986–1998: 2:51]).

The Hebrew allows for the readings "a voice crying" or "the voice of one crying"; the LXX, followed by the NT writers, adopted the latter version. Also, the Hebrew has, "A voice crying, '*In the wilderness* prepare the way of the LORD,'" while the LXX, followed by the NT writers, reads, "A voice crying *in the wilderness*, 'Prepare the way of the LORD'" (Snodgrass 1980). In the original, taking "in the wilderness" with what follows preserves the parallelism; in the NT, reading "in the wilderness" in conjunction with the "voice crying" adapts Isaiah's message to the person of John the Baptist. It is not clear that the LXX and the NT writers here change the meaning of the original Hebrew, however. If the way for Yahweh is to be prepared in the wilderness, it makes perfect sense for the voice to cry in the wilderness to call for such preparations.

Another important part of the voice's message is that Yahweh will come to his people through the wilderness. It is possible that this notion is grounded in Sinai traditions (cf. Hab. 3:3; see Oswalt 1986–1998: 2:52). The desert is also a fitting figure for the desolate condition of God's people (Young 1972: 29n15).

Just as the calling voice is not identified, no addressees of the voice in 40:3 are explicitly stated. Most likely these are the "my people" mentioned in 40:1, namely, Jacob/Israel of the captivity (cf. Isa. 40:12–44:12; see Watts 1985–1987: 2:79). No longer is Israel referred to as "this people" (Isa. 6:9; 8:6); once again the language used is that of the covenant (cf., e.g., Exod. 6:7; 19:5; Lev. 26:12; Deut. 26:17–18; see Oswalt 1986–1998: 2:49).

The message to God's people is that they are to prepare Yahweh's way in the wilderness and make straight in the desert a highway for their God. This would be in keeping with normal procedure for preparing for a visiting dignitary (J. A. Motyer 1993: 300). The prophet Ezekiel had depicted Yahweh as abandoning Jerusalem (Ezek. 9–11); now Yahweh will return to take up residence in his city once again, which calls for "monstrous preparation, including a *highway*" (Watts 1985–1987: 2:79; see Isa. 35:8–10; cf. 35:1).

How are God's people to prepare the way for his return? While, again, not explicitly stated, the probable answer is "by way of repentance" (Young 1972: 28). If Yahweh is to return, his people must prepare the way by repenting of the sins that caused them to be led into exile. This is borne out clearly by the Baptist's own message: "Bear fruit in keeping with repentance" (Matt. 3:8). As Isa. 40:1–2 makes clear, God's ultimate purpose for his people is not judgment but salvation, life rather than death (cf. the Fourth Evangelist's words in John 3:17–18; and Jesus' words in John 12:47). All is forgiven.

Yet comfort for God's people is grounded not in anything they do, but solely in "the activity of the Lord, his coming into the sphere of human activity . . . the revelation of him in human sight" (Oswalt 1986–1998: 2:50). The purpose for these preparations is the revelation of God's glory (one of the "ruling concepts" of all Isaiah [Oswalt 1986–1998: 2:52]), not merely to Israel and Judah, but to all of humanity (Isa. 40:5; cf. 60:1–3). This harks back to the exodus, where God's glory was revealed as well (Exod. 16:10; 24:16–18; 33:18; 40:34). That all humanity will witness Yahweh's triumphant return to his lowly people is part of the prophetic defiance of political realities (cf. Isa. 49:26; 66:16, 23–24; see Blenkinsopp 2002: 183).

Later, Isaiah also speaks of the coming "Servant" (esp. Isa. 52:13–53:12), who will provide an even greater deliverance (Oswalt 1986–1998: 2:51), which is consummated in the new heaven and new earth (Isa. 65–66). Similar to other OT prophetic writings, Isaiah's vision draws heavily on exodus typology (e.g., Jer. 2:6–7; 7:22, 25; 11:4, 7; Hos. 2:14–15; 11:1; 12:9, 13; 13:4–5; Amos 2:9–10; 3:1–2; 9:7; Mic. 6:4; see also Isa. 10:24, 26; 11:15–16). In fact, "the intensity and fullness of Exodus symbolism in Isa. 40–55 is unique" (Watts 1985–1987: 2:81). The Messiah and his redemption will bring about a new exodus in which God's glory will be revealed (Young 1972: 30n18).

C. Isaiah 40:3 in Judaism. Interestingly, the Qumran community applied the same passage in Isaiah to itself, specifically to the role of the community council and the interpreter in the study of the law of Moses (Burrows 1974: 246). Both 1QS VIII, 14 and 4Q259 III, 4–5 envision a time when the community is "to be segregated from the dwelling of the men of sin to walk to the desert in order to prepare the path of truth," citing Isa. 40:3. Yet while these covenanters understood the passage as a call to dwell in the desert and to devote themselves to the study of God's word, the Baptist recognized it as a call to prepare the people of Israel for the coming Messiah (Morris 1995: 121).

Isaiah 40:1–5 is invoked also at the outset of another Qumran document, 4Q176 (Isa. 40:3 is cited in 4Q176 1–2 I, 6–7), as part of a prayer for God to restore Jerusalem and the temple. This is important because it shows that in the century preceding the appearance of John the Baptist there were at least segments in (sectarian) Judaism that expected God to liberate his holy city and holy place from pagan rule and corruption and that did so on the basis of Isa. 40 and other passages later in the book (4Q176 also cites Isa. 48:1–9; 49:13–17; 52:1–3). The Dead Sea community was right in anticipating God's future restoration of Jerusalem and the temple, but it was wrong about the means and way in which God would do so. Yet, importantly, as is evident at the temple clearing (John 2:14–23), Jesus shared the Qumran community's criticism of the corruption surrounding the temple and called the Jewish leaders to account for their abuse of power (e.g., John 10).

D. Textual Matters. The quotation from Isa. 40:3 follows the LXX (Beasley-Murray 1999: 20 note b), except that the evangelist uses *euthynate* instead of *hetoimasate* (Barrett 1978: 173). This may be because John (1) translated straight from the Hebrew; (2) was influenced by the later instance of *eutheias* in the LXX and conflated the LXX rendering from *hetoimasate . . . eutheias* to *euthynate*; or, least likely, (3) took his cue from the use of *euthynō* with *hodos* in Sir. 2:6; 37:15; 49:9.

The second option seems most probable. Beyond this, M. J. J. Menken (1985: 202–4) contends that the change is motivated by the Fourth Evangelist's desire "to make John the Baptist not so much the precursor of Jesus as a witness contemporaneous with Jesus."

E. The Use of Isa. 40:3 in John 1:23. As Isa. 40:3, in the context of the entire book of Isaiah, has made clear, God's people, conceived more broadly than OT Israel, would be called to prepare for Yahweh's coming by a prophetic voice. According to John the Baptist, and the Fourth Evangelist, the Baptist is that voice. Several elements of the original context of Isa. 40:3 resonate with the passage's use in John 1:23: (1) the wilderness as the site of prophetic activity (Köstenberger 2004: 62–63); (2) the focus away from the messenger and onto the message; (3) the coming revelation of God's glory through his visible coming and bringing of salvation, not merely to Israel, but to all humanity; (4) the need for repentance to prepare the way. Isaiah 40:3, in turn, invokes the larger exodus motif, which also entails the themes of salvation and God's glory. The use of Isa. 40:3 in John 1:23 suggests therefore that the Baptist's salvation-historical role is that of "the herald of a new exodus, announcing that God is about to redeem his people from captivity, as he had in the days of Moses" (Keener 1993: 266), and to do so through the instrumentality of John the Baptist, who served as the Isaianic "voice in the wilderness." In accordance with Isaiah's prophecy, the Baptist calls God's people to repentance in preparation for the coming Servant (Carson 1991: 144).

F. Theological Use. Working from the hermeneutical axiom that Jesus is the Messiah, the Fourth Evangelist presents John the Baptist in fairly straightforward terms as the fulfillment of the predicted end-time figure of a "voice of one crying out in the wilderness, 'Make straight the way of the Lord.'" The multiple attestation of this reference strongly suggests the historicity of this claim by the Baptist himself. When asked about his role, he must give an answer, not merely in his own terms, but in scriptural terms. As in the other canonical Gospels, the use of Isa. 40:3 with reference to the Baptist is thus foundational to the gospel story, signaling the impending epochal intervention of God in and through his Messiah, Jesus.

Subsequently, the flow of the narrative moves from clarifying the identity of John as a witness to Jesus to the content of John's witness regarding Jesus. The Baptist's reference to Jesus as "the Lamb of God who takes away the sin of the world" in 1:29 (cf. 1:36) likely involves multiple levels of meaning. Very possibly, the Baptist here speaks better than he knows, thinking primarily of the lamb led to the slaughter referred to in Isa. 53:7 (LXX: *amnos*; elsewhere in the NT only in Acts 8:32, citing Isa. 53:7 LXX, and 1 Pet. 1:19: cf. 2:21–25), which contemporary Judaism interpreted not with reference to a dying messiah, but as conveying the notion of substitutionary suffering for sin that fell short of actual death (cf. Matt. 11:2–3; Luke 7:18–20).

It is also possible that the Baptist may have proclaimed Jesus as the apocalyptic warrior-lamb who would bring judgment (cf., e.g., *1 En.* 90:9–12; *T. Jos.* 19:8; *T. Benj.* 3:8; Rev. 5:6, 12; 7:17; see Brown 1966–1970: 59, citing esp. Luke 3:17; Carson 1991: 150; Beasley-Murray 1999: 24–25; Schlatter [1948: 46–47] refers to both; for the Baptist's message of judgment, see esp. Matt. 3:7–12; Luke 3:7–17; Carson [1991: 149] notes also the doubts expressed by the Baptist in Matt. 11:2–3). Some who hold this view would also say that the Fourth Evangelist thinks that the Baptist is speaking better than he knows—much as Caiaphas does in 11:49–52 (Carson 1991: 150–51). If so, this would mean that while the Baptist thinks that Jesus "takes away" the sin of the world in his capacity as the warrior-lamb, the evangelist knows that, whatever truth there is in this perspective, he also "takes away" the sin of the world by means of the cross (cf. the melding together of the Lamb who was slain and of the triumphant Lion of Judah in Rev. 5:5–6, 12–13).

Another possible association is the lamb provided by God for Abraham when he was ready to offer up his son of promise, Isaac, in obedience to the divine command (Gen. 22:8, 13–14) (for a discussion of additional alternatives, see Morris 1995: 127–29; cf. Barrett 1978: 176; Ridderbos 1997: 73–74). This is especially suggestive because John 3:16 probably alludes to this scene, highlighting one important difference: what Abraham was spared from doing at the last min-

ute, God actually did—he gave his one and only Son (cf. Rom. 8:32).

Less likely options are the gentle lamb of Jer. 11:19 (no overtones of bearing sin); the scapegoat that symbolically bore the sins of the people and was banished to the desert in Lev. 16 (a goat, not a lamb); and the guilt offering sacrificed to deal with sin in Lev. 14; Num. 6 (involving bulls and goats, not lambs).

The Fourth Evangelist, for his part, places the Baptist's declaration into the wider context of his passion narrative, where Jesus is shown to be the ultimate fulfillment of the yearly Passover lamb (see Exod. 12), whose bones must not be broken (John 19:36; cf. Exod. 12:46; Num. 9:12; Ps. 34:20 and commentary below; cf. also 19:14; see Burge 2000: 73–74; Barrett 1978: 176; cf. 1 Cor. 5:7).

This "lamb of God" will take away sin, presumably by means of a sacrificial, substitutionary death (Morris 1995: 130). According to the pattern set by the OT sacrificial system, the shed blood of the substitute covered the sins of others and appeased the divine wrath by way of atonement (cf. 1 John 2:2; 4:10). As the book of Hebrews makes clear, however, the entire OT sacrificial system was merely provisional until the coming of Christ.

Moreover, as God's lamb, Jesus takes upon himself the sin, not merely of Israel, but of the entire world (cf. 1:10). The idea that the Messiah would suffer for the sins of the world (rather than merely for Israel) was foreign to first-century Jewish ears; John, however, makes clear that Jesus came to save the entire world (John 3:17; 1 John 2:2), and that he is the Savior of the world, not merely Israel (4:42; 1 John 4:14). The NT's depiction of Jesus as "God's lamb" culminates in Revelation, where Jesus is the "lamb who was slain" who returns in universal triumph (see Rev. 5:6, 8–9, 12; 7:17; 12:11; 13:8; 17:14; 19:7, 9; 21:22–23; 22:1–3).

John's teaching on Jesus' substitutionary atonement builds on the evangelist's earlier reflection on Jesus' incarnation. For it is in the flesh that Christ suffered vicariously; his humanity was an indispensable prerequisite for his cross-work on behalf of others. In fact, the atonement theme, far from being absent, is part of the warp and woof of John's Gospel: Jesus is the Bread of Life, who will give his flesh for the life of the world (6:51; cf. 6:32–33, 53–58); he is the Good Shepherd, who lays down his life for his sheep (10:15; cf. 10:17–18); and his sacrifice fulfills Passover symbolism (e.g., 19:14, 31).

Subsequent to John's witness to Jesus as "God's lamb" in 1:29, 36, the narrative moves further still to reactions regarding Jesus by his first followers, several of whom previously had been followers of the Baptist. The statement in 1:45, "about whom Moses wrote in the law," most likely alludes to predictions of a coming prophet in Deut. 18:15, 18 (see at 1:21 above). The fact that Philip refers to Jesus as "the one Moses wrote about in the law, and about whom the prophets also wrote" indicates that Philip had come to believe that Jesus was the Messiah foretold in the Scriptures, both in the law (Deut. 18:15, 18) and in the prophets (cf., e.g., Isa. 9:1–7; 11:1–5, 10–12; 52:13–53:12; see Carson 1991: 159). The expression "the law and the prophets" was a common Jewish designation for the Hebrew Scriptures in their entirety (cf. Matt. 5:17; 7:12; 11:13; 22:40; Luke 16:16; 24:44; Acts 13:15; 24:14; 28:23; Rom. 3:21).

Moving on to 1:49, Nathanael's confession of Jesus, we note that the designations "Son of God" and "King of Israel" are messianic titles roughly equivalent in nature (Barrett 1978: 186; cf. Ridderbos 1997: 91). By attaching to Jesus the label "Son of God," Nathanael identifies him as the Messiah predicted in the OT (2 Sam. 7:14; Ps. 2:7; cf. 1 Sam. 26:17, 21, 25; see at 1:41 above; 20:31 below); the term "Son [of God]" was also a current messianic title in Jesus' day (cf. 1Q28a II, 11–12; 4 Ezra 7:28–29; but see 4Q246 II, 1; see Collins 1993; Köstenberger 1998b: 48–49n17). "King of Israel," likewise, is a common designation for the Messiah (e.g., Zeph. 3:15; cf. John 12:13, an inclusio; note also the phrase "King of the Jews" in John 18–19). Because of the expression's political overtones, however, Jesus was reluctant to identify himself in such terms (note the possible correction provided by Jesus in the present context in 1:50–51; see also 6:15; 18:36; see Painter 1977: 360–61; Ridderbos 1997: 91). The terminologies converge in Jewish literature where the Davidic king is described as God's son (cf. 4QFlor 1:6–7; 1Q28a II, 11–12; 1 En. 105:2; 4 Ezra 7:28–29; 13:52; 14:9; see Carson 1991: 162; "Messiah" and "King of Israel" are juxtaposed in Mark 15:32/ Matt. 27:42).

Jesus' response in 1:51, finally, contains an allusion to the story of Jacob in Gen. 28 (see esp. Gen. 28:12; on Jacob traditions in nonbiblical Jewish sources, see Neyrey 1982; Rowland 1984). In 1:51 Nathanael, who stepped out in faith on the basis of Jesus' display of supernatural knowledge (1:48–49), and the other disciples (note the Greek plurals hymin ["to you"] and opsesthe ["you will see"]) are told that they will see the greatness of the Son of Man, far surpassing the vision of Jacob the patriarch (this is part of the "greater than Jacob" motif in John's Gospel; cf. 4:5–6, 11–12). Jesus is the "new Israel" (Carson 1991: 164).

To see "heaven open," which was every Jewish apocalyptist's dream, is to receive a vision of otherworldly realities (Acts 10:11; Rev. 4:1; 19:11). The yearning for a glimpse of heaven spawned an entire genre of literature in the Second Temple period wherein enigmatic figures such as Enoch (who, according to Gen. 5:24, was translated to heaven without dying) are depicted as traversing heaven and reporting what they see. In 3:13, however, Jesus affirms the impossibility of anyone other than the Danielic "Son of Man" gaining access to heaven (Dan. 7:13; cf. Matt. 26:64; Acts 7:56).

The picture of "heaven open and God's angels ascending and descending" in the present context is drawn from Jacob's vision of the ladder "resting on the earth, with its top reaching to heaven, and the angels of God were ascending and descending on it [or, 'him'—i.e., Jacob]" (Gen. 28:12; see the rabbinic disputes on this point: Gen. Rab. 68:18; 69:7; see the discussion in Carson 1991: 163). Especially if the proper rendering is "on him," the parallel is clear: as the angels ascended and descended on Jacob (who was later renamed "Israel")—a sign of God's revelation and reaffirmation of faithfulness to his promises made to Abraham (Ridderbos 1997: 93)—so the angels will ascend and descend on the Son of Man (Jesus).

A further parallel relates to the respective place of worship and of the revelation of God. When Jacob awoke from his dream, he exclaimed, "How awesome is this place! This is none other than the house of God; this is the gate of heaven" (Gen. 28:17); and he called that place "Bethel," which means "house of God." Correspondingly, Jesus' message to Nathanael and the other disciples is that he himself will be the place of much greater divine revelation than that given at previous occasions (cf. Heb. 1:1–3). Jesus will mediate greater revelation than Abraham (8:58), Jacob (cf. 4:12–14), Moses (1:17–18; 5:45–47; 9:28–29), and Isaiah (12:37–41).

Jesus is the "new Bethel," the place where God is revealed, where heaven and earth, God and humanity, meet (Carson 1991: 163–64; Witherington 1995: 72; cf. Burge 2000: 79; Borchert 1996–2002: 1:149; Schnackenburg 1990: 1:320), just as he is the new temple (2:19–22) and the new proper place of worship (4:20–24). In fact, Jesus is the very culmination of all of God's revelatory expressions (1:14–18; Heb. 1:1–3), providing a fullness of divine self-disclosure of which even Jacob (Israel) could only dream; and these disciples, who as of yet know little of what awaits them, will soon be witnesses of revelation far exceeding that received by any Israelite in previous history (Ridderbos 1997: 93–94).

Moreover, the expression "heaven open and God's angels ascending and descending" also seems to convey an image of the "uninterrupted communion between Jesus and the Father" (cf. 8:16, 29; 10:30; 16:32), presenting the ensuing "signs" as manifestations of this communion (Bultmann 1971: 105–6). With respect to the present passage, note especially Jesus' statement in response to large-scale defection later in this Gospel: "Does this offend you? What if you see the Son of Man ascend to where he was before?" (6:61b–62). In this related verse the Son of Man's ascent clearly implies descent ("where he was before") in the context of preexistence (cf. 1:1–2; see Ham 1998: 89n67; *contra* Pryor 1991: 342).

Jesus' self-designation "Son of Man," which clearly harks back to the Danielic passage concerning "one like a son of man" (Dan. 7:13–14), blends together the mysterious figure from the book of Daniel with the Suffering Servant, featured in the book of Isaiah, a theme culminating in the so-called Servant Songs of Isa. 42–53. Unlike "King of Israel" and "King of the Jews," both of which have nationalistic or political overtones, the expression "Son of Man," while scriptural, was sufficiently malleable to allow Jesus to define its content in christological terms. According to Jesus, that "Son of Man" would be subject to crucifixion as a mode of exaltation (3:14; 8:28);

he was to provide divine revelation (6:27, 53); and he would act with eschatological authority (5:27; 9:39).

What, then, is the point of reference at which the disciples will "see heaven open, and the angels of God ascending and descending on the Son of Man" (1:51)? In the Synoptics, Jesus' statement to the Jewish high priest in Matt. 26:64, "In the future you will see the Son of Man sitting at the right hand of the Mighty One and coming on the clouds of heaven" (cf. Mark 14:62; Luke 22:69), places this event in the future, subsequent to Jesus' cross-death. In the context of John's realized/inaugurated eschatology, however, it is already in the here and now—in Jesus' signs (e.g., 2:11; 9:3; 11:40), in his entire ministry in both word and deed (14:9–11), and supremely in his crucifixion itself (3:14; 8:28; 12:23–24, 32–34)—that the glory of the Son of Man is revealed (Beasley-Murray 1999: 28).

The Cana Cycle (2:1–4:54)

SURVEY

The Cana cycle, which spans Jesus' "first" (2:11) and "second" (4:54) messianic signs in Cana of Galilee, contains only one explicit OT quotation, found in 2:17. The focus of the first explicit OT quotation, in 1:23, was on the role of John the Baptist in the salvation-historical plan of God. The focus of the second quotation is squarely on Jesus and his all-consuming zeal for God as displayed at the temple clearing and as perceived and related to OT Scripture by his disciples.

The only likely OT allusion in John 2 is found in 2:5, which may establish a link between Jesus and the patriarch Joseph. The range of OT allusions in John 3 spans from the Pentateuch (3:14 alluding to Num. 21:9; 3:16 alluding to Gen. 22:2, 12, 16) to wisdom (3:8 possibly alluding to Eccles. 11:5; 3:13 possibly alluding to Prov. 30:4) and prophetic literature (3:5 possibly alluding to Ezek. 36:25–27 and similar passages; 3:14 alluding to Isa. 52:13; 3:28 possibly alluding to Mal. 3:1).

Jesus' conversation with the Samaritan woman features several OT allusions as well, such as to Jacob's giving of a field to Joseph (4:5; cf. Gen. 33:19; 48:22; Exod. 13:19; Josh. 24:32); to God's giving of "living water" to the Israelites in the desert (4:10; cf. Num. 20:8–11; cf. 21:16–18); Jesus' references to his gift of "living water" as "welling up" in a person (4:14; cf. Isa. 12:3; Jer. 2:13), to Jerusalem being the proper place of worship (4:20; cf. Deut. 11:29; 12:5–14; 27:12; Josh. 8:33; Ps. 122:1–5), and to salvation being from the Jews (4:22; cf. Isa. 2:3?).

Finally, the sayings invoked by Jesus when instructing his followers that "even now the reaper draws his wages ... so that the sower and the reaper may be glad together" in 4:36, and that "one sows and another reaps" in 4:37, echo the language of Amos 9:13 and Mic. 6:15, respectively.

THE CHANGING OF WATER INTO WINE: THE FIRST SIGN IN CANA (2:1–11)

At the Cana wedding Jesus is shown to be the bringer of messianic joy who fills up the depleted resources of Judaism (cf. esp. the reference to the six stone water jars used by the Jews for ceremonial washing in 2:6; see Köstenberger 2004: 96–97 and further below). In Jewish thought wine is a symbol of joy and celebration: "There is no rejoicing save with wine" (*b. Pesah.* 109a; on wine in biblical times, see *DJG* 870–73). The running out of wine at the Cana wedding may be symbolic of the barrenness of Judaism. Prophetic expectation cast the messianic age as a time when wine would flow freely (see Isa. 25:6; Jer. 31:12–14; Hos. 14:7; Joel 3:18; Amos 9:13–14; *2 Bar.* 29:5; *1 En.* 10:19; cf. Matt. 22:1–14 par.; 25:1–13; see also Gen. 49:11).

The language of 2:4, "Why do you involve me?" is reminiscent of OT parallels that convey distance between two parties and frequently carries a reproachful connotation (cf., e.g., Judg. 11:12; 2 Sam. 16:10; 1 Kings 17:18; 2 Kings 3:13; 2 Chron. 35:21; see Maccini 1996: 100–102; Keener 2003: 505–6; see further Köstenberger 2004: 95). The only possible OT allusion in this pericope is found in Jesus' mother's words in 2:5 ("Do whatever he tells you"), which represent a close verbal parallel to Pharaoh's words in Gen. 41:55 instructing the people to do whatever Joseph tells them. Just as Joseph had provided famine relief, so Jesus would be able to find a way out of the present dilemma. Jesus' mother thus takes what sounded like a stern reprimand as an indication that Jesus is ready to help. Her instructions to the servants in 2:5 express complete confidence.

As we noted, the reference to the Jewish purification ritual in 2:6 in conjunction with the mention of the wedding party's running out of wine conveys the notion of the barrenness of first-century Judaism. Jesus' production of a very large quantity of wine, together with the remark in 2:7 that he filled the water jars "to the brim," points to the abundance of Jesus' messianic provision (so, e.g., Ridderbos 1997: 107; Morris 1995: 162; Carson 1991: 174; see OT references to the abundance of wine in the new age listed above). In the following chapter Jesus is likewise shown to be the one who mediates the abundant provision of the Spirit (3:34; cf. 7:37–38; 20:21–22; see Keener 2003: 512). The reference to Jesus' revelation of God's glory at his first sign in Cana in 2:11 harks back to the testimony borne in the prologue: "We have seen his glory, glory as that of the one-of-a-kind Son from the Father" (1:14 [see commentary there]).

THE CLEARING OF THE TEMPLE: A POSSIBLE SECOND SIGN (2:12–22)

The Jerusalem temple was a symbol of Jewish national and religious identity (see the sidebar in Köstenberger 2002b: 30). The original Solomonic temple was destroyed by the Babylonians and later rebuilt by Zerubbabel. It was renovated by Herod just prior to Jesus' coming. Both OT and Second Temple literature express the expectation of the establishment of a new temple for the messianic age (Ezek. 40–44; *1 En.* 90:28–36; *Pss. Sol.* 17:30; 4QFlor 1:1–13). It is against this backdrop that Jesus' rather striking action of clearing the temple must be understood. What may at first appear to be an impetuous outburst of uncontrolled anger is cast by John as an outflow of genuine spiritual zeal. Thus Jesus is shown to typify the pronouncement of Ps. 69:9: "Zeal for your house will consume me."

2:17

A. The NT Context: Jesus' Zeal for His "Father's House." Jesus' early ministry in John's Gospel commences with Jesus calling his first disciples (1:35–51) and has as its first exclamation point the turning of water into wine, Jesus' "first sign" (2:11). After a brief stay in Capernaum, Jesus travels to Jerusalem for the Passover (2:12–13). Upon his arrival, he is dismayed to find the temple as a place of commerce rather than worship. He drives out the money changers, overturns their tables, and removes from the temple area the sacrificial animals being sold there. According to the Fourth

Evangelist, Jesus' clearing of the temple stirred in his disciples the memory of the righteous sufferer of Ps. 69:9 (note the verbal parallel between 2:16, "my Father's house," and Ps. 69:9, "zeal for your house"; note also Ps. 118:139 LXX [119:139 MT]: "Zeal *for your house* [italicized words not in MT] consumed me [*exetēxen me ho zēlos tou oikou sou*], because my foes forget your words").

The fact that in the inaugural scenes of the Gospel Jesus is referred to as the "Messiah" (1:41), the "Son of God" (1:49; cf. 2 Sam. 7:14; Ps. 2:7; cf. Ps. 89:26–29), and the "King of Israel" (1:49; see at 12:13 below) makes it plausible that observing Jesus' clearing of the temple would invoke in his disciples the memory of David's words in Ps. 69:9. This, in turn, is in keeping with Jewish expectations, current in the first century, that the Messiah would purge and reconstitute the temple (*Pss. Sol.* 17:21–22, 36; cf. Mark 14:57–61; see Daly-Denton 2004: 123). This would follow, and transcend, the pattern of great national deliverance last experienced by the Jews when Judas Maccabeus rededicated the temple in December of 165 BC, after it had been desecrated by Antiochus Epiphanes IV (cf. 10:22–39; see also Jesus' discussion of true freedom from sin in 8:31–38).

B. The OT Context of Ps. 69:9. Psalm 69 (which is quoted here and in 15:25; see also 19:28) and Ps. 22 (quoted in 19:24) share Davidic typology and the theme of the righteous sufferer (Tate 1990: 196; Mays 1994: 229). Psalm 69, attributed to David, is part of Book 2 of the Psalter, a collection titled "The Prayers of David the Son of Jesse" (Ps. 72:20). The psalm presents the psalmist as one who has borne reproach for God's sake (69:7): "For zeal for your house has consumed me, and the reproaches of those who reproach you have fallen on me" (69:9). Verse 9 is part of the psalmist's plea in 69:7–12, with 69:7–8 and 9–12 as subunits (note the use of *kî*, "for," in 69:7, 9). Verse 8, the text immediately preceding the verse quoted here, says, "I have become a stranger to my brothers, an alien to my mother's sons," which underscores the psalmist's alienation even from his own kin. This is in addition to the numerous and vicious enemies who are mentioned in 69:4 (quoted in 15:25; see commentary there).

The precise nature of the psalmist's zeal for God's "house" is not made clear in the passage. There may be a royal as well as a prophetic component: as a king, he may have devoted attention to the upkeep and protection of the temple; as a prophetic figure, he may have advocated the importance of proper conduct within the confines of the temple area (Tate 1990: 196). For someone living subsequent to the fall of Jerusalem (69:35–36), zeal for God's house would connote a desire to see the temple rebuilt (Rogerson and McKay 1977: 96). Beyond this, concern for God's "house" may extend also to God's "household" more broadly conceived—that is, the condition of God's people (cf. Jer. 12:7–9; Tate 1990: 196), extending the scope of the passage to "not only the tabernacle, but the congregation that used to assemble there" (Tholuck 1858: 290). The nature of any zealous action on the psalmist's part is left unspecified, but in context a contrast seems to be drawn between some in the community who act as the psalmist's and God's enemies and the psalmist himself. In fact, the suppliant has engaged in fasting and praying out of concern over the situation (69:10–11).

The psalmist is "consumed" (69:9a), both literally, in that he is at the point of death, and figuratively, in that he is passionate about God's house and his people (Dahood [1968: 158] suggests that the image conveyed by *'ākal*, "consume," is that of "a devouring flame," and by *nāpal*, "fall," of "burning coals" falling on someone; cf. Ps. 120:3–4). The psalmist's passionate concern for God's people is all the more striking as it is these same people who mock and humiliate him (69:10–12). In all his righteous suffering, the psalmist prays to the Lord and in faith looks to him for help and deliverance (69:13–18). In the end it is the psalmist's firm hope and assurance that "God will save Zion" and that "those who love his name shall dwell in it" (69:35–36).

Historically, the characterization of one consumed by zeal for God's "house" does fit King David, whose son Solomon built the temple. Destroyed by the Babylonians and rebuilt subsequent to the exile, the temple served as the center of Israelite worship, as the place where God had taken up residence among his people. The characterization of the righteous sufferer in Ps. 69:9 and the designation of the psalmist as God's "servant" in v. 17 (cf. 2 Sam. 7:5) are also congruent with the depiction of Yahweh's faithful servant in Isaiah (cf. esp. Isa. 50:4–9; 52:13; 53:12; see Tate

1990: 197; see also commentary at 12:38 below). Further possible associations are Elijah (1 Kings 19:10; cf. Sir. 48:2) and the flames consuming the victim acceptable to God in the OT sacrificial system (Daly-Denton 2004: 122).

C. Ps. 69:9 in Judaism. No explicit reference to Ps. 69:9 in ancient Judaism has been identified. However, religious zeal was an important part of Jewish piety (Köstenberger 2001: 32). In the OT Phinehas is promised a covenant of a lasting priesthood "because he was zealous for honor of his God" (Num. 25:13), and God himself is shown to be zealous for his holy name (Ezek. 39:25; cf. Exod. 34:14). In the second century BC the Maccabees revived Jewish nationalistic fervor, while the Qumran community as well as the Pharisees were concerned for the religious state of Judaism. First-century Palestine was rife with religious as well as nationalistic zeal (Heard 1992; Hengel 1988). The Pharisees sought to practice righteousness in everyday life, while the Zealots played an important part in the rebellion against Rome in AD 66–70. Particularly notorious were the Sicarii (from Lat. *sica*, "dagger"), religious terrorists who murdered people in broad daylight in an effort to destabilize the political situation in Roman-occupied Palestine (Schürer 1973–1979: 2:598–606).

D. Textual Matters. The LXX has the aorist *katephagen*, "has consumed me" (Moloney 1998: 77); in John's quotation the verb is the future deponent middle *kataphagetai*, "will consume me," which may represent an interpretation of the Hebrew as a prophetic perfect (Archer and Chirichigno 1983: 73; Menken 1996a: 40). The change of verb tense most likely serves to shine the spotlight prophetically on Jesus' cross-death as it is narrated later in the Gospel (Daly-Denton 2004: 122; Menken 1996a: 40–41). Otherwise, the quotation in John is identical in wording to the LXX, which in turn closely corresponds to the MT.

E. The Use of Ps. 69:9 in John 2:17. This is the only reference to Ps. 69:9a in the NT (though see the quotation of Ps. 69:4 in 15:25 and the possible allusion to Ps. 69:21 in 19:28 below). The introductory formula is characteristic of John's usage in the first part of the Gospel: "that it is written" (*hoti gegrammenon estin*). The function of the quotation of Ps. 69:9a in John's account of the temple clearing is to characterize Jesus' action and to do so in scriptural terms by linking Jesus with the righteous sufferer of this Davidic psalm. Jesus' zeal, righteous rather than blindly nationalistic (compare the Zealots [see above]), was so great that it would "consume" him. In the context of the subsequent narrative this refers to his death, which would bring life to the world (Ridderbos 1997: 117; Schnackenburg 1990: 1:347). At the very outset of his ministry, then, John portrays Jesus as one who was consumed with passion for God's glory and driven by a desire to remove from his people any obstacles to proper worship. What is more, as 2:17 makes clear, Jesus' disciples, upon seeing Jesus clear the temple, realize that the words of Ps. 69:9a applied to Jesus, the Son of David, the Messiah, who would be involved in a fatal conflict (Menken 1996a: 44).

Yet the present reference to Jesus in terms of Ps. 69 is not limited to the characterization of Jesus as one who is consumed by zeal for God's "house." Jesus also fits the larger pattern of the righteous sufferer who has an abundance of enemies who plot his downfall (e.g., 5:18; 11:53) and who is alienated even from his own brothers and the members of his own household (7:1–9; see also 4:44; cf. Ps. 69:8). What is more, according to the Fourth Evangelist, Jesus' zeal for God is not limited to zeal for the temple, but rather encompasses active concern for the Jewish nation on a comprehensive scale. In his own person Jesus is said to restore, renew, replace, and/or fulfill the symbolism inherent in the Feast of Tabernacles and Passover, and to reconstitute God's people as a new messianic community as "one flock" comprising believing Jews as well as Gentiles (e.g., 10:16; 11:51–52). In this, Jesus fulfills Davidic and "Suffering Servant" typologies and shows himself to be the Messiah predicted in various OT passages.

In view of John's emphasis on the commerce proceeding in the temple courts (2:14–16), one further dimension of his portrayal of Jesus at the temple clearing may be that he wants his readers to view Jesus as the one who inaugurated the great "day of the Lord," on which there would no longer be a merchant (or Canaanite—one morally or spiritually unclean) in the house of the Lord (Zech. 14:21). No longer would there be a need for special ritual arrangements to be made, but rather access to participation in the worship of God and membership among God's people would be available to all in and through Jesus and the new "temple of his body" (2:21) (see Daly-Denton 2004: 123, citing Moloney 1990; Schuchard 1992: 17–32; Menken 1996a: 37–45; Obermann 1996: 114–28; Derrett 1997; Daly-Denton 2000: 118–31). Jesus' action also calls to mind the words of Mal. 3:1, 3, that on the coming day of judgment "suddenly the LORD . . . will come to the temple," so that people may once again offer acceptable sacrifices to the Lord (Carson 1991: 179; Hiers 1971: 86–89). These connections, in turn, tie in with the Johannine temple motif (P. W. L. Walker 1996, esp. 161–200; Coloe 2001; Kerr 2002; Busse 2002: 323–66; Beale 2004, esp. 192–200; Köstenberger 2005a).

F. Theological Use. The Fourth Evangelist's practice of invoking Ps. 69:9a in connection with Jesus' temple action represents an instance of typology in which the pattern of the righteous sufferer is found to be present in Jesus. As throughout John's Gospel, this presupposes the hermeneutical axiom that Jesus is the messianic Son of God. The use of Ps. 69:9a in the present passage also reflects Jesus' messianic consciousness at the inception of his ministry. It is part of a larger pattern, both in Jesus' understanding and in the Fourth Evangelist's presentation, of aligning Jesus and his ministry with the experience of a king and/or prophet who is zealous for God and as a result suffers humiliation by God's own people—a pattern that encompasses the use of Ps. 69 both here and in 15:25 and extends also to the use of Ps. 22 in 19:24 and the possible allusion to Ps. 69:21 in 19:28–30 (see also Paul's use of Ps. 69:9b in Rom. 15:3). The mention of Jesus' brothers immediately prior to the present pericope in 2:12 (cf. 2:1–2) in conjunction with the reference to their unbelief in 7:5 may further accentuate the evangelist's depiction of Jesus in terms of the psalmist's lament that he has become a stranger to his brothers (cf. Ps. 69:8; see Daly-Denton 2004: 122).

Finally, if "zeal for God's house" also extends to a desire to see the temple rebuilt, this would invoke the motif of the exile and raise the vision of the restoration of God's people to proper worship (cf. 4:21–24). Significantly, in the present passage reference is made not to the future construction of a literal, physical temple, but to a restoration of worship centered on the "temple" of Jesus' body (2:21). This, in turn, is part of John's inaugurated eschatology, according to which "the time is coming, and has now come, when the true worshipers will worship the Father in spirit and truth" (4:23) by believing in the Messiah (4:26).

JESUS' FURTHER MINISTRY IN JERUSALEM AND SAMARIA (2:23–4:42)

The subsequent pericopes revolve around two interchanges, one between Jesus and Nicodemus, and one between Jesus and the Samaritan woman.

Jesus and Nicodemus, and John the Baptist's Testimony (2:23–3:36)

The references to the kingdom of God in 3:3, 5 are significant in that they constitute the only instance of this terminology in the entire Gospel (contrast the frequent use of this expression in the Synoptics; in 18:36, a possible *inclusio*, Jesus twice refers to "my kingdom" vis-à-vis Pilate). The Hebrew Scriptures make clear that "the Lord is king" and that his sovereign reign extends to every creature (e.g., Exod. 15:18; Ps. 93:1; 103:19). The Jews expected a future kingdom ruled by the Son of David (Isa. 9:1–7; 11:1–5, 10–11; Ezek. 34:23–24; Zech. 9:9–10), the Lord's Servant (Isa. 42:1–7; 49:1–7), indeed, the Lord himself (Ezek. 34:11–16; 36:22–32; Zech. 14:9). Although not everyone was to be included in this kingdom, Jews in Jesus' day generally believed that all Israelites would have a share in the world to come, with the exception of those guilty of apostasy or some other blatant sin (*m. Sanh.* 10:1). Hence it is all the more remarkable that Jesus' stipulation that those who would enter God's kingdom must be "born of water and the spirit" excludes Nicodemus and his fellow Sanhedrin members.

The first significant portion featuring an allusion to OT material in 2:23–4:42 involves the reference to being "born again/from above" in 3:3, explicated in 3:5 as being "born of water and spirit" (Louw 1986: 9–10; *contra* NIV/TNIV: "water and the Spirit"; rightly Carson 1991: 195). Most likely this passage constitutes an allusion to Ezek. 36:25–27, which presages God's cleansing of human hearts with water and their inner transformation by his Spirit (cf. also Isa. 44:3–5; *Jub.* 1:23–25; see Schlatter 1948: 89; Carson 1991: 191–96, esp. 194–95; McCabe 1999; Cotterell 1985: 241; Kynes 1992, esp. 575). The notion of a new beginning and a decisive inner transformation of a person's life is found in other OT prophetic passages (e.g., Jer. 31:33–34; Ezek. 11:19–20). It is this spiritual reality of which Nicodemus, Israel's teacher, ought to have been aware but which he (and, one may assume, his fellow Sanhedrin members—the personal pronouns in Jesus' statements "You must be born again" [3:7] and "You [people] do not accept our testimony" [3:11] are plural in the Greek) personally lacked.

Jesus illustrates his pronouncement in 3:5–7 with an analogy between the wind and the person born of spirit. "Wind"—a common image for the Spirit (Ridderbos 1997: 129)—and "spirit" translate the same Greek and Hebrew words (Gk. *pneuma*; Heb. *rûaḥ*). Both OT and Jewish literature contain numerous references to the mystery of the wind's origin (see esp. Eccles. 8:8; 11:5; see also *1 En.* 41:3; 60:12; *2 Bar.* 48:3–4). In the present instance the point of Jesus' analogy is that both wind and spiritual birth are mysterious in origin and movement—wind goes sovereignly where it pleases—yet although the wind's origin is invisible, its effects can be observed; it is the same with the Spirit (Ridderbos 1997: 129; Carson 1991: 197). Despite its inscrutability, spiritual birth is nonetheless real, as real as the mysterious movements of the wind. Moreover, just as the wind blows "where it pleases," so the Spirit's operation is not subject to human control, eluding all efforts at manipulation (Moloney 1998: 93).

Jesus' statement in 3:13, "No one has ascended into heaven except he who descended from heaven, the Son of Man" (the phrase "who is in heaven," added in several manuscripts, is an interpretive gloss reflecting later christological developments; see Köstenberger 2004: 132, following Carson 1991: 203; *contra* Barrett 1978: 213; Black 1984), may allude to Prov. 30:4a ("Who has ascended to heaven and come down?"). The OT identifies heaven as the place where God dwells (cf., e.g., Ps. 14:2; 33:14; 103:19; see Schoonhoven 1979–1988; Reddish 1992). John's Gospel refers several times to a descent *from* heaven, be it of the Spirit (1:32–33), angels (1:51), the Son of Man (3:13), or the "Bread of Life" (6:33, 38, 41, 42, 50, 51, 58). However, this is one of only three instances where it speaks of an ascent *into* heaven (angels [1:51]; the Son of Man [3:13]; the risen Lord [20:17]). Jesus here contrasts himself, the

"Son of Man" (cf. Dan. 7:13), with other human figures who allegedly entered heaven, such as Enoch (Gen. 5:24; cf. Heb. 11:5), Elijah (2 Kings 2:1–12; cf. 2 Chron. 21:12–15), Moses (Exod. 24:9–11; 34:29–30), Isaiah (Isa. 6:1–3), and Ezekiel (Ezek. 1; 10). An entire cottage industry of Second Temple literature revolved around such figures and their heavenly exploits (e.g., *1 Enoch*; see Tabor 1992; Borgen 1977). Although believers will join Christ in heaven in the future (cf. 14:1–3; 17:24), only Jesus both descended from heaven and ascended back up to heaven (cf. Luke 24:51; Acts 1:9; although note the similar ascent-descent pattern by angels in John 1:51, on which, see commentary above).

The allusion to Moses lifting up the serpent in the wilderness in 3:14 is plainly to Num. 21:8–9, where God is shown to send poisonous snakes to judge rebellious Israel. When Moses intercedes for his people, God provides a way of salvation in the form of a raised bronze serpent, so that "when anyone was bitten by a snake and looked at the bronze snake, he lived." But the primary analogy established in the present passage is not that of the raised bronze serpent and the lifted-up Son of Man; rather, Jesus likens the restoration of the people's physical lives as a result of looking at the bronze serpent to the people's reception of eternal life as a result of "looking" in faith at the Son of Man (cf. 3:15–18; see Barrett 1978: 214; cf. Carson 1991: 202). Yet, as in the case of wilderness Israel, it is ultimately not a person's faith, but rather the God in whom the faith is placed, that is the source of salvation (cf. Wis. 16:6–7).

There is a second, slightly more subtle, connection between the source account in Numbers and Nicodemus. Just as the sin, failure, and murmuring of the Israelites in the wilderness and their standing in judgment of God and his revelation were deserving of divine judgment and death and requiring salvation by way of looking at God's means of deliverance, so also Nicodemus was in danger of duplicating the same stance toward God's revelation in Jesus and of repeating the pattern of sin, failure, and murmuring in his own day and situation. Hence it is not only the looking in faith at the God-appointed means of salvation that constitutes a parallel but also the predicament leading to the divine remedy in the first place. Thus Nicodemus and his fellow Sanhedrin members, as well as the other Jews and all readers of John's Gospel, are not in the position of objective, neutral judges of the merits or shortcomings of Jesus' claims as they might deem themselves; rather, they themselves are called to render a verdict that will either allow them to pass from death to life (5:24) and from God's wrath to God's favor (3:36) or confirm the verdict of death upon their lives (3:19–21).

Yet another important connection between the Johannine source text in the book of Numbers and its appropriation in the context of Jesus' conversation with Nicodemus in John 3 represents the theme of life—new physical life in the case of the original wilderness incident, new spiritual life in the case of believers in the crucified Jesus. Significantly, the affirmation in 3:15 that "everyone who believes may in him [Jesus] have eternal life" (*contra* the NIV's "everyone who believes in him") constitutes the first reference to "eternal life" in this Gospel (see later 3:16, 36; 4:14, 36; 5:24, 39; 6:27, 40, 47, 54, 68; 10:28; 12:25, 50; 17:2–3; and the reference to "life in his name" in 20:31, which, in turn, by way of *inclusio*, corresponds to 1:12). The probable meaning of the expression "eternal life" is "the life of the age to come"—that is, resurrection life, which, according to John, can to some extent already be experienced in the here and now (e.g., 5:24; 10:10). That life, however, is found only "in him" (3:15, explicating and harking back to the prologue, 1:4). Hence the eternal life entered into by the new, spiritual birth is none other than the eternal life of the preexistent Word-become-flesh in Jesus, who has life in himself (5:26) and is himself the resurrection and the life (11:25) (see Carson 1991: 202–3). In the flow of the discourse Jesus moves from a reference to being born from above by water and spirit in terms of Ezekiel (John 3:5) to an OT narrative passage, the account of the bronze snake in the wilderness (Num. 21:4–9), which served as the divinely appointed means of new physical life to the people of Israel. Correspondingly, Jesus presents himself as the means of new spiritual life—eternal life—for those who become children of God by looking at the lifted-up Savior in faith (3:14–15; cf. 1:12).

Just as the new birth, the entrance into eternal life, is grounded in the "lifting up" of God's Son (3:14–15), so the "lifting up" is in turn grounded in God's love (3:16) (see Carson 1991: 204). In theological adaption of the *hypsōthēsetai* language

of Isa. 52:13 LXX (see, e.g., Dodd 1953: 247), the expression "lifted up" (*hypsōthēnai*) has a double meaning here (3:14) and elsewhere in John's Gospel (cf. 8:28; 12:32, 34; see further below), referring (1) to the lifting up of the bronze snake in the wilderness and to Jesus' lifting up on the cross, and (2) figuratively to the exaltation that Jesus will receive from God as a result of his obedient submission to God's will in the pursuit of his mission all the way to the cross (see Ridderbos 1997: 136–37; note esp. the *inclusio* between 4:34 and 17:4 and Jesus' final cry on the cross, "It is finished!" in 19:30). In addition, John may have drawn the connection between the term *hypsoō* and crucifixion on the basis of the Aramaic term z-q-p, "to lift up, to crucify" (Carson 1991: 201, citing Bertram 1972: 610, who in turn cites 1QS VII, 11).

What is more, not only is John's use of the verb *hypsoō* in a dual sense not original with the evangelist, but also it draws on Isaianic terminology; it is not only in John, but already in Isaiah, that the theme of "lifting up" is linked with the theme of "being glorified," and, a further element of crucial significance, this in the context of the figure of the Suffering Servant of the Lord (cf. Isa. 52:13–53:12; esp. 52:13 LXX; see Carson 1991: 201). What John discerns in this source text, and draws out by appropriating Isaianic theology, is that in truth Jesus' crucifixion and exaltation are not distinct steps that are realized successively (as one might surmise from reading the Synoptics); rather, it is precisely Jesus' crucifixion itself that constitutes, at the same time, his exaltation in that it marks the culmination of his messianic mission as the heaven-sent Word and the obedient Son of the Father. Hence, according to the Fourth Evangelist, Jesus' death is not a moment of ignominy and shame, but rather a glorious event that not only brings glory to God, Jesus' sender (12:28; 17:1, 4), and accrues glory to the Son owing to his obedience to the Father's will (12:23; 17:1), but also becomes the way by which Jesus returns to the glory that he had with the Father before the world began (17:5; cf. 17:24; see also 13:1; 16:28).

Although the dual meaning of the term "lifted up" was clearly veiled to Jesus' original audience, Nicodemus, and although the double entendre is likely to escape even John's first-time readers, the reference to Jesus being "lifted up" is gradually illumined in the further course of the Johannine narrative (cf. the other Johannine "lifted up sayings" in 8:28; 12:32, 34; see Nicholson 1983: 75–144; Köstenberger 1998b: 126–30). In effect, therefore, John's use of *hypsoō* here and throughout his narrative is similar to the Synoptic parables in that the term, at one and the same time, "both intimates and also obscures what is to come" (Bertram 1972: 610). Nevertheless, Nicodemus, on the basis of the analogy of Num. 21, was called "to turn to Jesus for new birth in much the same way as the ancient Israelites were commanded to turn to the bronze snake for new life. Only when Nicodemus saw Jesus on the cross, or perhaps only in still later reflection on the cross, would it become clear that the 'lifting up'/exaltation of Jesus" served as the life-giving analogue of the raised-up serpent in the wilderness (Carson 1991: 202). Thus there is an aspect of Jesus' saying that calls for Nicodemus's immediate action and attention while a fuller appreciation of Jesus' message awaits a later time at which Jesus' prophetic words have been realized and his words can be interpreted with the benefit of hindsight.

In addition, in light of the fact that the double meaning of "lifted up" is not original to Jesus or John but is found already in Isaiah, it would, and perhaps should, have been possible for Nicodemus at least to have the categories in place to understand Jesus' pronouncement regarding his being "lifted up"—that is, physically elevated as well as spiritually exalted—without, of course, necessarily being able to discern that Jesus' physical "lifting up" would take place on a cross, a truth that was veiled even to Jesus' closest followers (cf. Mark 8:31–33; 9:30–32; 10:32–45 pars.; see also John 6:60, 66; 12:23–26, 33).

Finally, Jesus' adduction of the account of Num. 21 and John's inclusion of this instance of Jesus' use of Scripture in his Gospel are part of a very broad exodus typology or Moses/exodus typology that pervades much of the Gospel. This typology includes Jesus' "signs" (see commentary above), which to a significant extent hark back to Moses' performance of "signs and wonders" at the exodus. It also includes the references to the Prophet envisaged in Deut. 18 in 1:45; 6:14; 7:40; the references to Moses writing about Jesus and testifying about him in 5:45–47; and the entire Johannine

Farewell Discourse (chaps. 13–17), which is patterned after Moses' final words to the Israelites in the book of Deuteronomy. Jesus is also set in relation to Moses, and the giving of the law, in the opening prologue (1:17; cf. 9:28). Yet another important part of the Moses/exodus typology in John's Gospel is the feeding of the multitude (chap. 6), which includes Jesus' correction that it is not Moses, but God, who has given the Israelites the bread from heaven (6:32), and which presents Jesus as the "bread from heaven" as the typological fulfillment of the manna provided by God for Israel in the wilderness (6:30–58).

The next possible allusion in the narrative comes as part of the Baptist's statement in 3:28 that he has been "sent before" the Messiah. This may allude to Mal. 3:1: "Behold, I send my messenger, and he will prepare the way before me" (quoted with reference to the Baptist in Matt. 11:10; Mark 1:2; Luke 7:27; cf. Luke 1:17, 76). The phrase "sent ahead" (an intensive perfect [Wallace 1996: 574–75]) is used in the OT for messengers sent ahead of a given person (e.g., Gen. 24:7; 32:3; 45:5; 46:28; cf. Ps. 105:17). The Baptist's words in 3:29, which liken him to the friend of the bridegroom, cast John's relationship to Jesus in terms of a "best man" standing ready to do the bridegroom's bidding at his wedding (cf. *m. Sanh.* 3:5; *m. B. Bat.* 9:4; note that Jesus calls himself "the bridegroom" in Matt. 9:15 pars.). In light of the OT background where Israel is depicted as "the bride of Yahweh" (cf., e.g., Isa. 62:4–5; Jer. 2:2; Hos. 2:16–20; see Morris 1995: 213–14; Carson 1991: 211), the Baptist is suggesting that Jesus is Israel's awaited king and Messiah (Carson 1991: 211; Brown 1966–1970: 156; Barrett 1978: 223). The "bride" imagery is further applied to the church in NT theology (e.g., 2 Cor. 11:2; Eph. 5:25–27; Rev. 21:2, 9; 22:17).

Jesus and the Samaritan Woman (4:1–42)

The setting of Jesus' encounter with the Samaritan woman is replete with history: they are by Jacob's well, with Mount Gerizim (the referent of "this mountain" in 4:20–21) in the background in plain view. Mount Gerizim, of course, was the OT setting for the Deuteronomic blessings (Deut. 11:29; 27:12) and near Mount Ebal, the mountain on which Moses commanded an altar to be built (Deut. 27:4–6). The references to Jacob's well and Mount Gerizim place Jesus' encounter with the

Samaritan woman in the framework of "holy geography" (Davies 1994: 288–355, esp. 298–302), which Jesus is shown to transcend: he is greater than Jacob (cf. 1:51 and commentary above), and the divine worship that he makes possible is not limited to physical structures or locations (4:23–24) (see Köstenberger 2004: 155–58).

Another pertinent geographical site mentioned in the OT is involved in the evangelist's reference to "the field that Jacob had given to his son Joseph" in 4:5. The reference reflects the customary inference from Gen. 48:21–22 and Josh. 24:32 that Jacob gave his son Joseph the land at Shechem that he had bought from the sons of Hamor (Gen. 33:18–19) and which later served as Joseph's burial place (cf. Exod. 13:19; Josh. 24:32; see Neyrey 1979; Dalman 1935: 212–16).

The evangelist's aside in 4:9, "For Jews do not associate with Samaritans," masks a long history of strained relations between Samaritans and Jews. The Samaritans had built a temple on Mount Gerizim about 400 BC, which was destroyed about 128 BC by the Jews, who claimed that proper worship must be rendered in Jerusalem. Religiously, the Samaritan Scriptures consisted only of the Pentateuch; the Jewish canon also included the Writings and the Prophets. Socially, Jews in Jesus' day generally would have avoided contact with Samaritans, especially Samaritan women, although there would have been a spectrum of behavior depending on locale, class, education, and other factors (Maccini 1996: 131–44).

On the whole, the scope of the phrase "do not associate" in 4:9 is probably broader than merely the sharing of drinking vessels (Ridderbos 1997: 154; Beasley-Murray 1999: 58 note ff; contra, e.g., Daube 1956: 375–82). Some Jews were willing to eat with Samaritans (*m. Ber.* 7:1; 8:8), but many were not, fearing ritual defilement. Samaritans were thought to convey uncleanness by what they lay, sat, or rode on, as well as by their saliva and urine. Samaritan women, like Gentiles, were considered to be in a continual state of ritual uncleanness (cf. *m. Nid.* 4:1; see Danby 1933: 803; Daube 1950; 1956: 373–82; Derrett 1988). Apart from these ethnic sensibilities, men generally would not want to discuss theological issues with women. All of this puts Jesus' dealings with the Samaritan woman into proper context and underscores how Jesus was not afraid to break social barriers in the pursuit of his mission.

The references to Jesus as the giver of living water in 4:10–15 involve double entendre. On a physical level, "living water" refers to the highly sought-after fresh spring water as opposed to stagnant water (Gen. 26:19; Lev. 14:6; Jer. 2:13); on a spiritual level, it was God who was known to be the source and giver of life (Gen. 1:11–12, 20–31; 2:7; Job 33:4; Isa. 42:5). (On water symbolism in John's Gospel, see Ng 2001.) In Num. 20:8–11, an incident to which Jesus may allude in the present passage, water gushes out of the rock, supplying the Israelites with badly needed refreshment (see also Num. 21:16–18). In Jer. 2:13 God laments that his people have forsaken him, "the spring of living water." In Isa. 12:3 the prophet envisions the joy with which people "will draw water from the wells of salvation" in the last days. Rabbinic thought associated the provision of water with the coming of the Messiah (*Eccles. Rab.* 1:9; see also the reference to Exod. 17:6 in 1 Cor. 10:4).

In John's Gospel Jesus is identified explicitly with the Creator and Life-giver (5:26), and he dispenses the gift of "living water," later unveiled as the Holy Spirit (7:37–39). This end-time blessing, bestowed subsequent to Jesus' exaltation, transcends John's water baptism (1:26, 33), Jewish ceremonial purification (2:6; 3:25), proselyte baptism (cf. 3:5), and the torch-lighting and water-pouring symbolism of the Feast of Tabernacles (chaps. 7–8). It also supersedes nurturing or healing waters such as Jacob's well (chap. 4) and the pools of Bethesda and Siloam (chaps. 5; 9). In fulfillment of the OT prophetic vision (Zech. 14:8; Ezek. 47:9), Jesus inaugurated the age of God's abundance. Jesus' offer of living water signals the reversal of the curse and the barrenness that are characteristic of the old fallen world (Beale 1997: 29). Jesus' inauguration of the age of a new creation marks the fulfillment of the vision of texts such as Isa. 35.

The phrase "will in him become a supply of water welling up to eternal life" in 4:14 is reminiscent of Isaiah's vision of people joyfully "drawing . . . water from the wells of salvation" in the last days (Isa. 12:3). In the future age envisioned by the prophet, people "will neither hunger nor thirst" (Isa. 49:10; cf. 44:3), and Yahweh will make "an everlasting covenant" with all those—Jews as well as believing representatives of "the nations who do not know you" (Isa. 55:4–5)—who follow his invitation, "Come, all you who are thirsty, come to the waters . . . that your soul may live" (Isa. 55:1–3a; cf. Sir. 24:21; *1 En.* 48:1; *Tg. Neof.* of Gen. 28:10 referring to the well at Haran; see Díaz 1963: 76–77). If people forsake their wicked ways, God in his mercy "will freely pardon" (Isa. 55:6–7). Indeed, Jesus will in short order turn the conversation to the woman's immoral lifestyle and confront her with her sin (4:16–18).

As D. A. Carson (1991: 220) aptly notes, Samaritans, whose canon was limited to the Pentateuch, may not have appreciated such allusions to the Prophets, although John's Jewish readers would have done so. What is more, even in the Samaritans' own liturgy it is said regarding the Taheb (the Samaritan equivalent to the Messiah) that "water shall flow from his buckets" (cf. Num. 24:7; see Bruce 1983: 105). Later in John's Gospel "living water" terminology is applied to the Spirit, who would be given to believers in Jesus subsequent to his glorification (7:38–39). The term "well up" (*allomai*) in 4:14 is used in Isa. 35:6 with reference to a lame person leaping up like a deer; the same sense is present in the term's other two NT references, Acts 3:8; 14:10. This intriguing connection links the new life brought by the Messiah with Jesus' (and the apostles') healing ministry, which resulted in the restoration of physical life to those suffering from a variety of ailments.

The "ancestors" who "worshiped on this mountain" (4:20) include Abraham (Gen. 12:7) and Jacob (Gen. 33:20), who built altars in this region. The woman's reference to "this mountain" (Mount Gerizim) in 4:20 harks back to texts such as Deut. 11:29; 12:5–14; 27:12; Josh. 8:33. The Samaritans held that many other significant events during the patriarchal period were associated with Mount Gerizim (Macdonald 1964: 327–33). According to Samaritan tradition, a temple was built in that location in the fifth century BC. It was razed by John Hyrcanus and the Jews in 120 BC (Josephus, *Ant.* 13.254–256). Thus the dispute between Jews and Samaritans regarding the proper place of worship had been raging for centuries when the Samaritan woman broached the subject with Jesus.

Jesus' response in 4:22 that "salvation [*sōtēria*] is from the Jews" (the only reference to *sōtēria* in this Gospel) does not imply the salvation of all Jews, nor is its primary point of reference that the coming Messiah (or Taheb) will be Jewish (though this is, of course, the case, and indicated by both the Hebrew Bible and the Samaritan Pentateuch; see esp. Gen. 49:10). Rather, as D. A. Carson (1991: 225) points out, "The idea is that, just as the Jews stand within the stream of God's saving revelation, so also can it be said that they are the vehicle of that revelation, the historical matrix out of which that revelation emerges. 'In Judah God is known; his name is great in Israel' (Ps. 76:1)." Jesus' statement here may also echo Isa. 2:3 ("For out of Zion shall go the law, and the word of the LORD from Jerusalem"). Jesus here contrasts the Samaritans' religious ignorance ("You [Samaritans] worship what you do not know" [4:22]) with the Jews' status as God's chosen people and as the instrument through which God's redemption was to be mediated to others. Nevertheless, although Jesus freely acknowledges Jewish salvation-historical preeminence, he does not allow it to become a barrier keeping others from benefiting from divine salvation blessings. What is more, not only is Samaritan worship on Mount Gerizim declared obsolete, but also Jewish worship in the Jerusalem temple is pronounced superseded in Jesus ("neither on this mountain nor in Jerusalem" [4:21; cf. 2:17–22 and commentary above]). Coming from Jesus, a Jew, and one who affirmed that "salvation is from the Jews," this is truly a revolutionary statement.

In elaborating on the true nature of God-pleasing worship, Jesus affirms that "God is spirit" (4:24; cf. the affirmation that God is light and love in 1 John 1:5; 4:8). The term "spirit" here does not refer to the Holy Spirit, but rather designates an attribute of God (see Köstenberger 2004: 156–57). God is a spiritual rather than material being (a qualitative reference "stressing the nature or essence of God" [Wallace 1996: 270]; cf. the similar phrase in 3:6; cf. also 3:8; see Barrett 1978: 238). The spiritual nature of God is taught clearly in the OT (cf. Isa. 31:3; Ezek. 11:19–20; 36:26–27). Because God is spirit, the Israelites were not to make idols "in the form of anything" as did the surrounding nations (Exod. 20:4). Jesus' point here is that since God is spirit, proper worship of him is also a matter of spirit rather than physical location (Jerusalem versus Mount Gerizim) (*contra* Keener 2003: 617–19).

In response, the woman affirms her belief that the "Messiah is coming" and that he will explain everything (4:25), issuing in Jesus' self-identification as just that Messiah (4:26). Although the woman here refers to a coming "messiah," the Samaritans did not regularly use this term until the sixteenth century (Kippenberg 1971: 303n216), preferring terms such as "Taheb" or "Restorer." The figure of the Taheb, in turn, apparently originated independently of Deut. 18:15–18 and was only later identified with the "prophet like Moses" (see Bammel 1957; Boring, Berger, and Colpe 1995: 264–65; Kippenberg 1971: 276–327). The woman's affirmation, "He will explain everything to us," is consistent with the fact that Samaritans, rather than looking for the royal Messiah from the house of David (as did the Jews), apparently expected a "teaching" messiah (Bowman 1958: 298–308). This is where the conversation ends, being interrupted by the return of Jesus' disciples from the nearby village.

The two final possible OT allusions in the present unit are found in Jesus saying, "Even now the reaper draws his wages, even now he harvests the crop for eternal life, so that the sower and the reaper may be glad together" (4:36), and, "One sows and another reaps" (4:37). The former saying is reminiscent of the eschatological passage in Amos 9:13: "'The days are coming,' declares the LORD, 'when the reaper will be overtaken by the plowman, and the planter by the one treading grapes.'" This image paints a picture of the abundance and prosperity of the new age. Thus Jesus' message is that this age has dawned in and through his ministry, in which sowing and reaping coincide. The immediate application in John's narrative, of course, is the approaching Samaritans (4:39–42).

The latter saying, cited in 4:37, may allude to Mic. 6:15: "You shall sow, but not reap." If so, important differences would apply, however, for in Micah the saying is part of a word of judgment, while Jesus appears to refer to a general saying that seems devoid of connotations of judgment. Again, the immediate application is to Jesus' ministry among the Samaritans and his commissioning of his disciples to enter into his work. Others—Jesus

and his predecessors, most immediately John the Baptist, the final prophet associated with the OT era (Köstenberger 1998b: 180–84; cf. Carson 1991: 231; Morris 1995: 249)—have done the hard work; Jesus' followers are the beneficiaries of these preceding labors and will bring in the harvest.

THE HEALING OF THE ROYAL OFFICIAL'S SON: THE SECOND SIGN IN CANA (4:43–54)

The pericope narrating Jesus' healing of the royal official's son in 4:43–54 is relatively free from OT allusions. The connection established by the evangelist between 4:46 and 2:1–11 may convey the message that the one who turned water into wine, eclipsing Jewish ceremonial washings and anticipating the impending joy of the messianic banquet, is here shown to continue his messianic mission, administering healing to a life close to death (cf. Isa. 35:5–6; 53:4a [cited in Matt. 8:16–17]; 61:1; see Carson 1991: 238). Jesus' denunciation of the people's dependence on "signs and wonders" in 4:48 may hark back to the "signs and wonders" performed by Moses at the exodus (see Köstenberger 1998a: 58–59, esp. n43; and commentary above). Tellingly, the phrase occurs elsewhere in the Gospels only in Jesus' eschatological discourse (Matt. 24:24 par.; cf. 2 Thess. 2:9), where Jesus warns that false messiahs and prophets will perform "signs and wonders" in an attempt to deceive the elect.

The Festival Cycle (5:1–10:42)

SURVEY

The "festival cycle," which revolves around Jesus' attendance of various Jewish religious feasts, features three additional messianic "signs" by Jesus: the healing of the lame man (chap. 5); the feeding of the multitudes (chap. 6); the opening of the eyes of the blind man (chap. 9). If this were the Synoptic Gospels, the miracles themselves would be sufficient to demonstrate Jesus' authority over sickness (cf. Mark 2:1–12) or his fulfillment of the messianic mission envisioned by Isaiah (cf. Matt. 8:17; 12:18–21; Luke 4:18–19). In John's Gospel, however, the miracles are transmuted into "signs" (e.g., 7:21–24), acts with inherent christological symbolism.

The "festival cycle" includes three specific OT quotations, in 6:31, 45 (both in the context of Jesus' "bread of life" discourse at the Galilean Passover [6:4]); 10:34 (Jesus at the Feast of Dedication [10:22]; see also the scriptural references in 7:38, 42 at the occasion of Jesus' attendance at the Feast of Tabernacles in Jerusalem). The first reference is attributed to the Jews, while the second and third form part of Jesus' teaching. All three quotations are introduced by a formula including the phrase *estin gegrammenon*, "it is written" (cf. 2:17; 12:14).

The OT reference in 6:31, "He gave them bread from heaven to eat," links Jesus' ministry to the Jews with Moses' leadership of Israel during the exodus and establishes the superiority of Jesus' person and work over this revered figure in Jewish history (on Moses in the Fourth Gospel, see Glasson 1963; Meeks 1967; Boismard 1993: 1–68; Harstine 2002). The discussion surrounding this passage also clarifies how it would be that Jesus' zeal for God would "consume" him (the message of the last explicit OT quotation in 2:17). In the context of this discussion, Jesus maintains that in his ministry the prophetic vision is fulfilled when in the last days all God's people would be taught by God (6:45; cf. Isa. 54:13).

The next explicit and identifiable OT quotation, also by Jesus, in 10:34, is given in support of Jesus' claim to be the Son of God. In an argument from the lesser to the greater, Jesus argues that even mere mortals are called "sons of God" in OT Scripture, and so people should not take exception to his claim of being the Son of God. Possible OT allusions in John 5–10 include those found in 5:27, 29, 45, 46; 6:14, 29; 7:22, 24, 38, 40, 42, 51; 8:12, 15, 17, 28, 35, 44; 9:2, 5, 24, 34; 10:3–4, 8, 16, 33 (see discussion below).

The Healing of the Lame Man and the Sabbath Controversy (5:1–47)

In the aftermath of Jesus' healing of the lame man, the Jews object, in a petty display of religious legalism, to the man's picking up of his mat on the Sabbath (5:10). Although the Jewish leaders may have thought of passages such as Exod. 31:12–17; Jer. 17:21–27; Neh. 13:15, 19, the man did not actually break any biblical Sabbath regulations. According to Jewish tradition, however, the man was violating a code that prohibited the carrying of an object "from one domain into another" (*m. Šabb.* 7:2)—in the present instance, his mat. Apparently, it was permissible to carry a bed with a person lying on it, but not one that was empty (*m. Šabb.* 10:5). At this point Jesus is accused not of violating the law himself, but of enticing someone else to sin by issuing a command that would have caused that person to break the law.

In the ensuing "Sabbath controversy" (5:16–47) Jesus aligns his messianic activity with the work of his divine Father, which did not cease at creation. Jesus' address for God as "my Father" in 5:17 and elsewhere has few OT precedents (though see Jer. 3:4, 19; Ps. 89:26). The Jews were committed monotheists, believing in only one God (cf. Num. 15:37–41; Deut. 6:4; 11:13–21; see Schürer 1973–1979: 2:454–55; Hurtado 1998). Indeed, the Hebrew Scriptures make clear that God is incomparable and without equal (e.g., Isa. 40:18, 25), and that those who "make themselves" like God, such as Pharaoh (Ezek. 29:3), Joash (2 Chron. 24:24), Hiram (Ezek. 28:2), and Nebuchadnezzar (Isa. 14:14; Dan. 4), are subject to severe judgment. The Jewish belief in only one God became an important distinguishing characteristic of Jewish religion in a polytheistic environment (see Tacitus, *Hist.* 5.5; Cohon 1955). Jesus' claim of a unique relationship with God seemed to compromise this belief by elevating Jesus to the same level as the Creator as a second God (5:18; 8:58–59; 10:30–31). The same charge will later lead to the crucifixion (19:7).

Although Gen. 2:2–3 teaches that God rested (*šābat*) on the seventh day of creation, Jewish rabbis agreed that God does indeed work constantly, without breaking the Sabbath (*Exod. Rab.* 30:9; cf. *Gen. Rab.* 11:10). After all, the whole world is God's domain (Isa. 6:3), and God fills the entire universe (Jer. 23:24). Just as the Father continues to be active, Jesus claimed to colabor with him (5:17; cf. 4:34). As to healing on the Sabbath, the one who created the Sabbath has authority over it, determining its purpose, use, and limitations. In fact, even the Jews made exceptions to the rule of refraining from work on the Sabbath, most notably in the case of circumcision (see 7:23; cf. *m. Šabb.* 18:3; 19:2–3). If God is therefore above Sabbath regulations, so is Jesus (cf. Matt. 12:1–14 pars.; see Brown 1966–1970: 217; Barrett 1978: 256; Carson 1991: 247–49).

The remaining interchange features several possible OT allusions and frequently invokes important OT themes. Jesus' claim in 5:19 that "the Son can do nothing by himself" echoes Moses' affirmation in Num. 16:28 that "the LORD has sent me to do all these things, and it was not my own idea" (Brown 1966–1970: 214). An even more significant OT theme resonates in the background of Jesus' statement in 5:21 that the Son gives life to whom he is pleased to give it, just as the Father raises the dead and gives them life. The OT and Second Temple literature concur that raising the dead and giving life are the sole prerogatives of God (cf. Deut. 32:39; 1 Sam. 2:6; 2 Kings 5:7; Tob. 13:2; Wis. 16:13). Jesus' contemporaries therefore did not believe that the Messiah would be given authority to raise the dead (see references in Köstenberger 2004: 187n61). This renders Jesus' claim of being able to raise the dead and to give them life at will even more striking. Although Elijah sometimes was considered to be an exception because he was used by God to raise the dead, Jesus' claim is much bolder in that he claimed not merely to be God's instrument in raising other people, but to give life himself *to whom he is pleased to give it.*

The statement in 5:22 that the Father judges no one but has entrusted all judgment to the Son is remarkable as well, since according to the Hebrew Scriptures, judgment likewise is the exclusive prerogative of God (e.g., Gen. 18:25; cf. Judg. 11:27; though see Ps. 2:2). In Second Temple literature, too, the Messiah remains very much in the background as far as judgment is concerned, apart from carrying out God's judgment on his enemies, in keeping with Jewish nationalistic expectations (e.g., *Pss. Sol.* 17:21–27). Rabbinic writings also ascribe the role of judging the world to God alone.

Jesus' self-characterization as his sender's authorized messenger in the present passage is in keeping with God's dealings with his people in OT times, where Moses and the prophets were considered to be God's agents and mouthpieces who acted and spoke on God's behalf. Consequently, the Jewish fundamental affirmation regarding a messenger (*šālîaḥ*) was that "a man's agent is like the man himself" (e.g., *m. Ber.* 5:5). The purpose statement in 5:23, "that all may honor the Son just as they honor the Father," in effect establishes Jesus' right to be worshiped (Carson 1991: 255) and amounts to a claim to deity (Morris 1995: 279). Because of Jesus' unique relationship to the Father, God's glory, which God vowed not to give to another (Isa. 42:8; 48:11), is neither lessened nor compromised by honor being given to the Son. Those prior to Jesus' coming were able to worship only God, but now that Jesus the Word has been made flesh, those who want to honor God must also honor his Son, or by failing to honor the Son they also fail to honor the Father.

Jesus' words in 5:25, "The dead will hear the voice of the Son of God, and those who have heard it will live," are reminiscent of Ezekiel's vision of the valley of dry bones (Ezek. 37; cf. Rom. 4:17; Eph. 2:1–5). This is one of several instances in this Gospel where the book of Ezekiel looms in the background (cf. chap. 10, esp. 10:16; see Deeley 1997; Vawter 1964; Bullock 1982).

Yet another startling pronouncement is found in 5:26, where Jesus asserts that just as the Father has life in himself, so he has given the Son to have life in himself (cf. 5:21). The OT states repeatedly that God grants life to others (e.g., Gen. 2:7; Job 10:12; 33:4; Ps. 36:9). Here, however, Jesus claims that God granted him life *in himself,* a divine attribute. The phrase rendered "he is the Son of Man" in 5:27 reads more literally "he is Son of Man"— the only instance of this christological title without articles before both "Son" and "Man" in the entire NT. This may indicate an allusion to Dan. 7:13 LXX, where the expression "son of man" likewise lacks articles (cf. Rev. 1:13; 14:14; see Carson [1991: 257–59], who also notes Colwell's Rule; Ridderbos 1997: 200; Brown 1966–1970: 215; Moloney 1998: 183; and commentary here at 1:51). In his humanity the heaven-sent Son of Man is given authority to judge. As elsewhere in John's Gospel, revelation and judgment go hand in hand (3:19; 8:16; 12:31).

Jesus' reference to the resurrection in 5:29 ("those who have done what is good to the resurrection of life, and those who have done evil to the resurrection of judgment") may hark back to Dan. 12:2 ("some to everlasting life, and some to shame and everlasting contempt"). A glimpse of the future resurrection was given moments after Jesus died on the cross (Matt. 27:52–53). The statement in 5:31, "If I testify about myself, my testimony is not valid," is in keeping with the scriptural teaching regarding the need for multiple witnesses (Deut. 17:6; 19:15; cf. Num. 35:30), which was reaffirmed by Jewish tradition (*m. Ketub.* 2:9; *m. Roš Haš.* 3:1; cf. Josephus, *Ant.* 4.219; see also John 8:13–18; 2 Cor. 13:1 [citing Deut. 19:15]; 1 John 5:7; Rev. 11:3).

In 5:35 Jesus calls John the Baptist "a lamp that burned and gave light," a description that seems to echo Ps. 131:17 LXX (132:17 MT), where it is said that God will "set up a lamp" (*lychnos*) for his "anointed one" (*christos*) (see Carson 1991: 261; Morris 1995: 289n100; Barrett 1978: 265; note the presence of the Greek article in conjunction with the word "lamp" in 5:35, which indicates a known person or phenomenon). Inherent in the designation of the Baptist as a "lamp" is the recognition that his witness was small (albeit important) and of a temporary nature (cf. the similar portrayal of Elijah in Sir. 48:1). According to 1:7–9, he was a lamp that exuded light, but he was not the light itself (see Carson 1991: 261). Thus Jesus' reference to John as a "lamp" keeps the roles of the Baptist and of Jesus in God's salvation-historical plan in proper balance and perspective.

Jesus' statement in 5:37 that people "have never heard his [God's] voice nor seen his form" (cf. 1:18) seems to allude to the experience of wilderness Israel, which received the law at Mount Sinai without hearing God's voice or seeing his form through Moses as a mediator. Many of Israel's leaders in OT times did in fact hear God's voice (Gen. 7:1–4; 12:1–3; Exod. 3:4–4:17; 19:3–6, 9–13; 33:11; 1 Sam. 3:4, 6, 8, 11–14; 1 Kings 19:13, 15–18) or "see" God in one sense or another (e.g., Gen. 18:1–2; 32:24–30; Exod. 33:11; Isa. 6:1–5). In 5:38 Jesus' words "nor does his [God's] word dwell in you" hark back to the OT depiction of a God-fearing person within whose heart dwells the word of God (e.g., Josh. 1:8–9; Ps. 119:11; cf. Col. 3:16).

Jesus' assertion in 5:39 that the Scriptures testify to him is one of five instances in this Gospel where Scripture or a given OT writer is said to refer to Christ although no specific passage is adduced (cf. 1:45; 2:22; 5:45–46; 20:9). D. A. Carson (1991: 263) rightly contends that what is at issue here is that Scripture is presented as providing "a comprehensive hermeneutical key": "By predictive prophecy, by type, by revelatory

event and by anticipatory statute, what we call the Old Testament is understood to point to Christ, his ministry, his teaching, his death and resurrection."

The closing appeal to Moses in 5:45–47 prepares the way for chapter 6, where Jesus is presented as the new Moses providing God's people with the new "bread from heaven" (Keener 2003: 662). Jesus' reference to Moses as a witness against the Jews in 5:45 may allude to Deut. 31:26–27, where the Mosaic law is invoked as a witness against the Israelites. Indeed, Jewish hopes were set on Moses (cf. 9:28–29), and in OT history Moses frequently served as Israel's intercessor (e.g., Exod. 32:11–14, 30–32; Num. 12:13; 14:19–20; 21:7; Deut. 9:18–20, 25–29). In Jesus' day many Jews, in keeping with the portrayal of Moses in OT and Second Temple literature (*As. Mos.* 11:17; 12:6; *Jub.* 1:19–21), saw Moses' role as that of continuing mediator and advocate. Yet, ironically, according to Jesus, it was precisely the one on whom the Jews had set their hopes who was going to serve as their accuser (Deut. 31:19, 21, 26; cf. Rom. 3:19).

The reference in 5:46 to Moses writing about Jesus may allude to the first five books of the OT (attributed to Moses) or to the prediction of a "prophet like Moses" in Deut. 18:15 (cf. John 1:21; 6:14; 7:40), or both. Alternatively, the reference is not to the Pentateuch or to the "prophet like Moses," but to "a certain *way* of reading the books of Moses" (Carson 1991: 266). The reason that Moses, as the lawgiver, would accuse the Jews was that he, as the lawgiver, knew the law's true purpose. Rather than being an end in itself, the law served to point to Christ (cf. Matt. 5:17–20; see Carson 1991: 266).

The Feeding of the Multitude and the Bread of Life Discourse (6:1–71)

Chapter 6 is replete with OT allusive material. Jesus' question in 6:5 to Philip, "Where shall we buy bread for these people to eat?" echoes Moses' similar question to God in the wilderness, "Where can I get meat for all these people?" (Num. 11:13). This is one of several parallels between John 6 and Num. 11. Other parallels include the grumbling of the people (Num. 11:1; John 6:41, 43); the description of the manna (Num. 11:7–9; John 6:31); the reference to the eating of meat/flesh (Num.

11:13; John 6:51); and the striking disproportion between the existing need and the available resources (Num. 11:22; John 6:7–9).

In 6:9 mention is made of a boy who has five barley loaves and two fish. In a similar account in 2 Kings 4:42–44, Elisha fed one hundred men with twenty barley loaves and some ears of grain (see Ridderbos 1997: 211–12; Barrett 1978: 275). The use of the word *paidarion* ("boy") both in 6:9, which is its only NT occurrence, and several times in the LXX of the 2 Kings passage (there referring to Elisha's servant [2 Kings 4:38, 41]) is one major verbal connection between these two narratives. Other links include the mention of barley and the overall mode of narration, including a question of disbelief, the command to distribute the loaves, and the fact that all ate with food left to spare.

The reference in 6:10 to the abundance of grass in that place may constitute an allusion to the messianic age (cf. Ps. 23:2; John 10:9–10; see Schnackenburg 1990: 2:16). The bountiful meal evokes OT messianic prophecy (cf. Isa. 25:6–8; 49:9–11; also Matt. 22:1–14; Luke 22:15–30; see Ridderbos 1997: 213). Jesus' words to his disciples in 6:12, "Gather the leftover pieces, so that nothing may perish," echo those of the narrative in Ruth 2:14, "She ate all she wanted and had some left over" (see Daube 1956: 46–51). It was customary at Jewish meals to collect what was left over. Pieces of bread were not to be thrown away (*b. Ber.* 50b), and any food the size of an olive or larger was to be picked up (*b. Ber.* 52b). The expression "so that nothing may perish" is also documented in rabbinic literature with reference to food (*y. Sanh.* 6:6; *y. Ḥag.* 2:2). "Twelve" baskets perhaps alludes to Jesus' restoration of Israel (the twelve tribes) by calling twelve disciples to form the core of his new messianic community (Carson 1991: 271).

When people saw the "sign" that Jesus had performed, they asked whether Jesus was "the prophet who is to come into the world" (6:14), a clear allusion to Deut. 18:15, 18 (see 7:40 below and commentary at 1:21 above). This passage featured significantly in the messianic expectations at Qumran (cf. 4Q175 5–8; 1QS IX, 11; see Anderson 1996: 174–77) and presumably in other circles in first-century Judaism. Later, in the third century, Rabbi Isaac held that "as the former redeemer caused manna to descend . . . so will the

latter Redeemer cause manna to descend" (*Eccles. Rab.* on Eccles. 1:9; see commentary at 6:31). As we noted, Jesus' multiplication of barley loaves is reminiscent of the miracle performed by Elijah's follower Elisha (2 Kings 4:42–44). In 1 Kings 19 a parallel is drawn between Elijah and Moses (e.g., 19:8; cf. Exod. 24:18; 34:28). The popular expectation expressed in John 6:14 may represent an amalgamation of the two figures (Brown 1966–1970: 234–35). In Jesus' day the notion of the "prophet" apparently merged with that of "king" (6:15). Indeed, "The step from a prophet like Moses (6:14), the first Redeemer and worker of miracles, to a messianic deliverer was a short one for enthusiasts in contemporary Israel to make" (Beasley-Murray 1999: 88; cf. Horsley 1984). The figure also featured prominently in early Christian preaching (Acts 3:23; 7:37).

The Johannine account of Jesus' walking on the water in 6:16–24 may hark back to the OT in the description of Jesus "walking" across the sea, which may echo Job 9:8 LXX, where God is said to walk on the waters (note also the parallel wording in Mark 6:48 ["passing by"]; cf. Job 9:11; see Keener 2003: 673). Jesus' words to the disciples in 6:20, "It is I; do not be afraid," likewise suggest an OT background. Apart from the plain meaning of the words "It is I" (*egō eimi*) as conveying Jesus' self-identification, there may be overtones of epiphany ("I Am" is God's name in the OT [see Exod. 3:14]), especially in light of Jesus' walking on water. The statement may allude to Ps. 77:16, 19, describing God's manifestation to Israel during the exodus (Beasley-Murray 1999: 89–90). "Do not be afraid" was frequently God's message to his people in the OT (e.g., Gen. 26:24; Deut. 1:21, 29; 20:1, 3; Josh. 1:9). The reference to the boat reaching the shore at once in 6:21 may allude to Ps. 107:23–32, especially vv. 29–30: "He [the Lord] stilled the storm to a whisper . . . and he guided them to their desired haven" (Carson 1991: 276).

The people's and Jesus' references to "works of God" in 6:28–29 draw on a common Semitic expression (cf. Matt. 26:10 par.; John 9:4; Acts 13:41 [quoting Hab. 1:5]; 1 Cor. 16:10). In Jewish literature this phrase, which may reflect Zealot parlance (Schlatter 1948: 171), refers normally to works done by God, not those required by him (cf. John 3:21; 9:3–4; for similar terminology in the Dead Sea Scrolls, see CD-A II, 14–15; cf. 1QS IV, 4; 1QH[a] XIII, 36; CD-A I, 1–2; XIII, 7–8). In the present instance the people's response seems to reflect a misunderstanding of Jesus' words in 6:27, where he speaks of "working not for food that spoils, but for food that endures to eternal life." What Jesus intended as a reference to the people's proper pursuit, the crowd took as an invitation to literally "work the works of God." In light of the Jewish emphasis on "works of the law" (see Rom. 3:20, 27–28; Gal. 2:16; 3:2, 5, 10; cf. Phil. 3:6, 9; see Carson 1991: 285; Carson, O'Brien, and Seifrid 2004), Jesus' answer is nothing less than stunning: God's requirement is summed up as believing in "the one he has sent" (the language may reflect Mal. 3:1)—that is, the Messiah. This contrasts with the people's apparent confidence that they are able to meet the demands of God (Carson 1991: 285; Morris 1995: 319; Barrett 1978: 287).

Another misunderstanding between Jesus and the Jews is evident in 6:30, hinging on two different senses of the word "sign." The Jews demand further evidence for Jesus' claims; the evangelist presents as "signs" works of Jesus that are christologically significant (Ridderbos 1997: 226). In the people's thinking, if Jesus was the prophet like Moses (6:14), he could be expected to perform further signs (Carson 1991: 285; Beasley-Murray 1991: 91; Barrett 1978: 288; Brown 1966–1970: 265; Moloney 1998: 212). The people's question in 6:30, "What are you going to perform?" represents a common OT expression of incredulity (cf. Job 9:12; Eccles. 8:4; Isa. 45:9; see Derrett 1993). The irony, of course, is that while the people are asking for a "sign," they have just witnessed it in the form of Jesus' miraculous feeding of the multitude. Thus their demand for a "sign" reveals their unbelieving attitude and failure to discern in Jesus' actions the work of God. This obduracy will, in short order, lead to the departure of even many of Jesus' disciples (6:60–66) and eventuate in the evangelist's indictment of Jewish unbelief at the close of Jesus' public ministry in terms of Isa. 53:1 and especially Isa. 6:10 (12:37–40; see commentary there).

Undaunted, the Jews invoke the OT Scriptures concerning their ancestors' eating the manna in the wilderness.

6:31

A. NT Context: Jesus as the End-Time Manna.
Jesus' feeding of the multitude (6:1–15), which is recorded in all four Gospels and is one of the Johannine "signs" (6:26, 30), provides the occasion for his extended interchange with the crowds (6:25–58), which at some point transitions into Jesus' instruction in the synagogue at Capernaum (see 6:59). The people's immediate reaction to the miraculous multiplication of the loaves and fishes was to recognize Jesus as the Prophet spoken of by Moses (6:14; cf. Deut. 18:15, 18) and to attempt to make him king by force (6:15). Jesus withdraws, but eventually he is found by the crowds (6:25), who engage him in further conversation.

Jesus chides people for their failure to look beyond the miracle to its "signs" character as pointing to Jesus' messianic identity (6:26–27; cf. 20:30–31). When they ask Jesus what works God requires (6:28), he responds that the only work needed is for them to believe in "the one whom God has sent" (6:29). The crowd promptly asks for a sign from Jesus that would warrant such belief, oblivious to the fact that he had just supplied such proof in the multiplication of the loaves (6:30). At this point people invoke the experience of Israel's wilderness generation at the exodus: "Our ancestors ate the manna in the wilderness; as it is written, 'He gave them bread from heaven to eat'" (6:31; see Ps. 78:24b; cf. Num. 11:7–9).

B. The OT Context of Ps. 78:24b.
The reference "He gave them bread from heaven to eat" seems to be derived from several OT passages (cf. esp. Exod. 16:4, 15; Ps. 78:23–24; 105:40; see Carson 1991: 286; Gunkel 1968: 344; Schlatter [1948: 172–73] also cites Neh. 9:15). Perhaps most relevant as a potential background for John 6:31 is the reference to the giving of manna in Ps. 78:23–24 (Menken 1996a: 47–54), where it is part of a recital of wilderness events during Israel's exodus (vv. 12–39). Verses 12–16 speak of God's gracious and wondrous deeds, while vv. 17–20 recount Israel's rebellion, balanced in ten statements each (Tate 1990: 290, citing Campbell). Verses 21–22 describe God's wrath kindled by the Israelites' lack of trust in his saving power.

Nevertheless, as 78:23–31 proceed to narrate, God still "rained" (78:24, 27) down manna, "the grain of heaven," as well as meat on the Israelites. Interestingly, in this section God's gracious provision is intermingled with his judgment on the unbelieving Israelites (Tate 1990: 291). Because the wilderness generation improperly "tested God" (78:18, 41, 56), provoking him and rebelling against him, God struck them at the very moment when they were feeding on the food they had craved (78:29–31; cf. Num. 11:33–34). This draws a stark contrast between the goodness and long-suffering nature of God and the ingratitude and sinful unbelief of his chosen people. Psalm 78 continues to recount subsequent events in Israel's history and concludes with a reference to David, the shepherd and servant of God and of his people.

C. God's Provision of Manna in Judaism. The divine provision of manna for wilderness Israel is celebrated in later OT passages. Besides Ps. 78:24, other important references include Ps. 105:40 ("gave them bread from heaven in abundance") and Neh. 9:15 ("You gave them bread from heaven for their hunger"). Beyond this, Second Temple literature looked forward to a time when God would again provide manna for his people (Wis. 16:20; cf. Philo, *Alleg. Interp.* 3.169–176; *Worse* 118; *Heir* 79, 191; *Names* 259–260; see Menken 1988).

Sibylline Oracles states that "those who honor the true eternal God inherit life . . . feasting on sweet bread from starry heaven" (Frg. 3:46–49 [second century BC?]). Another work expresses the expectation of an end-time recurrence of God's provision of manna: "And it will happen at that time that the treasury of manna will come down again from on high, and they will eat of it in those years because these are they who will have arrived at the consummation of time" (*2 Bar.* 29:8 [ca. AD 100]; cf. Rev. 2:17).

The same expectation is found in later rabbinic tradition. Thus Rabbi Berechiah (ca. AD 340) said in the name of Rabbi Isaac (ca. AD 300), "As the first Redeemer was, so shall the latter Redeemer be. . . . As the former Redeemer [i.e., Moses] caused manna to descend [citing Exod. 16:4], so will the latter Redeemer cause manna to descend" (*Eccles. Rab.* 1:9). Similarly, "R. Eleazar Hisma [ca. AD 120] says: You will not find it [the manna] in this world but you will find it in the world to come" (*Mek. Exod.* 16:25) (see Köstenberger 2002b: 68–69).

D. Textual Matters. The reference to Ps. 78:24b in John 6:31 is aligned quite closely with the LXX, except that the word *phagein* ("to eat") is found at the end rather than the beginning of the line, and the phrase *ek tou* ("from the") is added in John, the latter most likely owing to the influence of Exod. 16:4 (see the discussions in Daly-Denton 2004: 134; Menken 1996a: 52–54). The reason for the addition of *ek tou* probably is christological: for John, Jesus is not merely the "bread *of* heaven," but rather the "bread *from* heaven," accentuating more keenly Jesus' provenance from God (cf. John 8:42, 47: *ek tou theou*; also, e.g., 3:13, 31; see Menken 1996a: 53).

E. The Use of Texts on God's Provision of Manna in John 6:31. The crowd's citation of Ps. 78:24b, or a similar OT reference to that effect, that God "gave them bread from heaven to eat" is part of the Johannine "misunderstanding" theme. Jesus had just performed an amazing miracle, the feeding of the multitude (6:1–15), but the crowd is asking for the kind of evidence of Jesus' messianic calling that he had just provided. Hence the crowd had failed to discern the true significance of this Johannine "sign," as is duly noted by Jesus (6:26). In this way these Jews were unwittingly perpetrating the wilderness generation's pattern of unbelief in the face of miraculous "signs" performed by God's servants.

One further element of misunderstanding centers on the reference to "he" in the quotation in 6:31. The crowd attributes the provision of manna in the original instance to Moses. Their confidence and trust in Moses is ironic because the Israelites in Moses' day in fact did not follow Moses' leadership. What is more, as Jesus proceeds to point out, the "he" providing the manna in the wilderness was not Moses, but God (6:32), the very God who had now sent Jesus as "the bread of God . . . who comes down from heaven and gives life to the world" (6:33) (see the discussion in Menken 1996a: 55–65). In the ensuing interchange the connection between Jesus' present-day Jewish interrogators and the unbelieving wilderness generation is developed yet further (see, e.g., 6:41, 44, 61).

F. Theological Use. Three factors link the present chapter with the exodus account: (1) the Passover motif; (2) Jesus as the prophet like Moses; (3) the expectation that God would again provide manna in the messianic age (Ridderbos 1997: 226; Morris 1995: 321; Beasley-Murray 1999: 91). The implicit contrast is between Moses and Jesus (Ridderbos 1997: 226–27). Continuity is present between the wilderness generation and the Jews in Jesus' day.

As in 3:14, an event from Israel's wilderness wanderings during the exodus is shown to anticipate typologically God's provision of salvation in and through Jesus (Barrett 1978: 290). Also as in 3:14, the typology entails an element of escalation: whereas the manna in the wilderness had Israel as its recipient, God's gift of Jesus is universal in scope and extends beyond believing Israelites also to believing Gentiles (cf., e.g., 10:16; 11:51–52; 12:32; see Carson 1991: 287).

An "I am" saying, a "sign," and two OT quotations (see further below) combine to highlight Israel's obduracy at this juncture of Jesus' ministry at the end of the first half of the first half of John's Gospel (see esp. 6:60–71). The feeding of the multitude is presented as one of Jesus' messianic "signs" that typologically fulfills, in an escalated manner, God's "signs and wonders" performed through Moses and meets with rejection just as Moses did (see commentary at 12:38–40 below).

Jesus' words in 6:32, "Not Moses . . . but my Father," exhort the Jews to see, behind Moses, God as the true provider of the heavenly bread, whereby "bread from heaven/of God" in 6:32–33 points to Jesus' heavenly origin (cf. 3:13, 31; see Ridderbos 1997: 228). With regard to the phrase "gives life to the world" in 6:33, it is interesting to note that in rabbinic teaching the giving of the law at Sinai was described in similar terms: "The earth trembled when he gave life to the world" (*Exod. Rab.* 29:9). In the present passage the same function is said to be fulfilled by Jesus (cf. 5:39).

While the crowd interprets Jesus' words impersonally (6:34), the personal sense gradually builds throughout the discourse (Brown 1966–1970: 263). Throughout the dialogue the Jews see Jesus in light of their preconceived notions and are entirely motivated by physical concerns (Ridderbos 1997: 229). By claiming "Whoever comes to me will never go hungry, and whoever believes in me will never, ever thirst" (6:35), Jesus plainly claims to fulfill OT messianic expectations in keeping with prophetic passages that speak of the opera-

tion of God's word in the provision of eschatological salvation (cf. esp. Isa. 55:1; see Carson 1991: 289; cf. also Isa. 49:10, cited in Rev. 7:16).

The expressions "eternal life" in 6:40 and "raise up" in 6:39–40 continue the theme of life sounded in 6:33, 35, underscoring the permanence of life made available in and through Jesus in contrast to the temporary nature of God's provision of manna to wilderness Israel (Ridderbos 1997: 231).

The Jews' murmuring against Jesus in 6:41, as we noted, parallels the Israelites' murmuring against Moses in the wilderness (cf., e.g., Exod. 17:3; Num. 11:1; 14:27, 29). There are obvious parallels between Jesus' Jewish opponents and wilderness Israel (cf. Exod. 16:2, 8–9; Num. 11:4–23). Just as the Israelites grumbled about the first giver of bread, Moses, likewise they grumbled about the second, Jesus (cf. 1 Cor. 10:10), and just as in the wilderness, the Jews' grumbling here is ultimately directed against God himself (Moloney 1998: 217). By linking the response of the Jews in Jesus' day to the Israelites' response to Moses in the wilderness, the Fourth Evangelist establishes a typology that associates Jesus' opponents with a trajectory of unbelief that sets up both the Jews' rejection of Jesus as the Messiah in the passion narrative and the evangelist's concluding indictment of the Jews at the end of chapter 12 (see commentary at 12:38, 40 below).

Jesus' statements in 6:37, 44, "Everyone the Father has given me will come to me" and "No one can come to me unless the Father who sent me draws him," are part of the Johannine twin motifs of predestination and election. John 6:37 encapsulates the Gospel's "universalism" (better, "universal scope"), "individualism," and "predestinarianism" (Barrett 1978: 294). On the basis of the Father's prevenient work, Jesus will receive the ones who come to him. What he *will not* do is fail to recognize these individuals as his own and eject them from his fellowship (Ridderbos 1997: 231n123); what he *will* do is keep and preserve them (Carson 1991: 290). These motifs culminate in the Good Shepherd Discourse (cf. esp. 10:28–29; see Schnackenburg 1990: 2:47) and continue through Jesus' final prayer (cf. esp. 17:6, 9, 11–12; cf. also 18:9) and his concluding commissioning of Peter and the "disciple whom Jesus loved" (chap. 21) (the idea of accepting someone called by God into the community and not rejecting him is also found in the Qumran literature: e.g., 1QS VI, 16, 19, 22; IX, 15–16; XI, 13–14). Although the focus in 6:37 is on the Father's "giving" of the people to Jesus and on Jesus' receptive attitude, it remains true that persons must "come" to him (cf. 6:44). This underscores the need for a positive human response to the divine initiative (Borchert 1996–2002: 1:265). Still, there is no indication here or elsewhere in this Gospel that God's predestinatory purposes ever fail (*contra* Witherington 1995: 158).

In 6:44 Jesus proceeds to underscore the human inability to gain salvation apart from divine assistance. People can come to Jesus only if the Father who sent him draws them. Ultimately, therefore, salvation depends not on human believing, but on the "drawing" action of the Father (presumably by the Holy Spirit) by which God moves a person to faith in Christ (see 12:32; cf. Jer. 31:3; Hos. 11:4; see Ridderbos 1997: 232). In the rabbinic sources, Rabbi Hillel (first century AD) uses the expression "to bring near to the Torah" with reference to conversion (*m. 'Abot* 1:12) (see Moloney 1998: 220). There is a certain affinity between John's teaching on predestination and the Qumran doctrine of the "two spirits" (1QS III, 14–IV, 6). The rabbinic view is summed up by the saying attributed to Rabbi Akiba (ca. AD 135): "All is foreseen, but freedom of choice is given" (*m. 'Abot* 3:16; cf. Josephus, *Ant.* 18.13, 16, 18; *J.W.* 2.162–165; see the excursus in Schnackenburg 1990: 2:265–70).

In the present instance Jesus' point is not merely general, but rather specific and salvation-historical. Because the Jews are refusing to come to God in his prescribed manner—that is, through faith in the Messiah—they cannot receive eternal life. Jewish obduracy constitutes the focus of the "paternity dispute" in chapter 8, the healing of the blind man in chapter 9, the Good Shepherd Discourse in chapter 10, and the events surrounding the raising of Lazarus in chapters 11–12. The Pharisee-led plot against Jesus that surfaces intermittently in the narrative (esp. during the "festival cycle" in chaps. 5–10) is motivated by the Jews' unwillingness to come to God on his terms.

6:45

A. The NT Context: Believers in Jesus as End-Time Disciples of Yahweh. Later in the same interchange that featured the previous OT quotation by the crowd in 6:31, Jesus makes reference to the OT as part of his teaching. In response to the Jews' demand for Jesus to produce something akin to Moses' giving of the manna to the Israelites in the wilderness, Jesus went beyond these expectations, not only by demonstrating his ability to accomplish a similar feat (the feeding of the multitude) but also by arguing that this event merely constituted a "sign" pointing beyond what Jesus *did* to who he *was*. Jesus claimed not only to be able to *give* the bread from heaven but also, in his very own person, to *be* that bread (6:33, 35, 38).

At this the Jews "grumbled" (*gongyzō*), in keeping with the Israelites' response to Moses in the wilderness (6:41, 43, 61; cf. Exod. 17:3; Num. 11:1; 14:27, 29), pointing to Jesus' obvious humanity as evidence against his divine origin (6:42).

Jesus, in response, acknowledged that only those whom the Father who sent him would draw to him would be able to "come" to him (a Johannine synonym for "believing" in Jesus). In this way, Jesus asserted, people would witness at the present time the fulfillment of the prophetic vision that all would be taught by God (6:45; cf. Isa. 54:13a; see also Jer. 31:34; Joel 3:1–2; 1 Cor. 2:13; 1 Thess. 4:9; 1 John 2:20; *Barn.* 21:6). According to Jesus, the scope of "all" included those who proved receptive to his teaching (6:45). While the Jews prided themselves on being students of Scripture (e.g., 5:39; 9:29), Jesus here alleges that they refuse to "come to him" (i.e., believe in him as the Messiah) because they are unwilling to learn from God.

B. The OT context of Isa. 54:13. The present passage has links with Isa. 40:1–3 (Isa. 40:3 is cited in John 1:23; see commentary there), where the prophet is urged to speak words of comfort to the woman Jerusalem. In the present chapter Yahweh, again through the prophet, is speaking just such words of comfort to Jerusalem, laying out a grand vision of her restoration, including the notion that all her children will be taught by Yahweh (Isa. 54:13; cf. Jer. 31:31–34). This is set in the context of the reference to Jerusalem as a "barren woman, who has borne no child" and the prospect that "the children of the wife that was abandoned will outnumber those of the wife with a husband" in the opening verse of the chapter (Isa. 54:1).

The words of assurance in 54:4 convey "the pathos of the situation in which a woman deprived of the protection of a husband, or unable to bear children, would have found herself" (Blenkinsopp 2002: 362). The greatest spiritual wealth that Isaiah is able to imagine for God's people is that all their children "will be taught by [lit., 'become disciples of'] the LORD." In this way the inner glory of Zion's sons will correspond to its external beauty (cf. Isa. 54:11–12; see Young 1972: 370). Notably, in Isa. 50:4 the same word twice refers to the Servant being "taught" by God. Hence, "the ideal represented by the Servant is now represented in the individual members of the new Jerusalem" (Oswalt 1986–1998: 2:428n67, citing Skinner). Significantly, this promise follows on the heels of the reference to the Servant of Yahweh and his substitutionary suffering in Isa. 53 (e.g., Isa. 53:5).

The present passage also significantly harks back to Isa. 50:4, where, in the context of contrasting portraits of Israel's sin and the Servant's obedience, the same word, "taught" (*lmd*), is used twice with reference to the Servant of Yahweh: "The Lord GOD has given me the tongue of those who are taught, that I may know to sustain with a word him who is weary. Morning by morning he awakens; he awakens my ear to hear as those who are taught." This is the same Servant who gives his back to those who strike it, turns the other cheek, and is the object of extensive abuse (50:6), yet who professes his innocence (50:9) and is confident of his vindication by God (50:8).

The section concludes with the question "Who among you fears the LORD and obeys the voice of his servant?" followed by the exhortation "Let him who walks in darkness and has no light trust in the name of the LORD and rely on his God" (50:10). In the chapters leading up to Isa. 54:13, therefore, the Servant of Yahweh is identified as one who himself has both an "ear to hear as those who are taught" and "the tongue of those who are taught" by God and who can therefore command the obedience of those who would trust in the name of the Lord. It is that Servant, then, who, as God's paradigmatic disciple, is the instrument chosen by Yahweh to accomplish the prophetic end-time vision of calling those who "walk in darkness and have no light" to trust in the name of the Lord so that "all will be taught by God."

In this characteristic of openness to divine revelation, and subsequent mission of teaching God's words to others, the Servant stands in stark contrast to the people of Israel, who are hardened to the prophetic message in their dullness of hearing, spiritual blindness, and intransigence to the things of God (see esp. Isa. 6:9–10, quoted in John 12:40; see also Isa. 53:1, quoted in John 12:38). These people honor God with their lips, but their hearts are far from him, substituting humanly devised commandments for the fear of God (Isa. 29:13; cited by Jesus in Matt. 15:8–9; Mark 7:6–7). As the prophet laments, Israel, "the servant of the LORD," "sees many things, but does not observe them; his ears are open, but he does not hear" (Isa. 42:19–20).

Yet God longs for "the people who are blind, yet have eyes, who are deaf, yet have ears" (Isa. 43:8) to be gathered and to be part of a "new thing" God is about to do (Isa. 43:9, 19). A day will come when a king will reign in righteousness, and "the eyes of those who see will not be closed, and the ears of those who hear will give attention" (Isa. 32:3). The ransomed will return and see the glory of the Lord, and then "the eyes of the blind shall be opened, and the ears of the deaf unstopped" (Isa. 35:5; cf. vv. 1–2). Hence, both positively (the Servant's obedience and the future gathering of a believing remnant from all nations) and negatively (Israel's present sin, disobedience, and obduracy toward God's revelation and the prophetic message), Isa. 54:13 forms an integral part of the theology of Isaiah.

C. Isaiah 54:13 in Judaism. The expression "disciples of God" or "the ones taught by God" is found also in the Qumran writings (CD-B XX, 4; 1QHᵃ X, 39; XV, 10 [possibly alluding to Isa. 50:4]; cf. XV, 14). A messianic reference involving the phrase "taught by God" occurs in *Pss. Sol.* 17:32: "And he will be a righteous king over them, taught by God . . . and their king shall be the Lord Messiah" (prior to AD 70; cf. Isa. 32:1, 3). It was commonly believed in Judaism that to learn the Torah was to be taught by God himself (Schnackenburg 1990: 2:51). In a talmudic reference (*b. Ber.* 64a) Isa. 54:13 is invoked in support of the notion that those who study the Torah are taught by God (see Borgen 1965: 150). The Jews believed that God's presence would rest on those who sit and work hard on the Torah (*m. ʾAbot* 3:6). Those who say that the Torah does not come from God, on the other hand, will have no portion in the world to come (*m. Sanh.* 10:1).

D. Textual Matters. In favor of a Hebrew *Vorlage* is the fact that John features *pantes* ("all") as well as *didaktoi* ("taught") in the nominative (as in the MT) rather than the accusative case (so the LXX). In favor of a dependence on the LXX is that John, like the LXX, has *theou* rather than *kyriou* (MT: "Yahweh"). Moreover, *didaktos* is used in the LXX only in Isa. 54:13; 1 Macc. 4:7; *Pss. Sol.* 17:32. The reference to "your sons," found in both the MT and the LXX, is omitted from the quotation in John's Gospel, presumably in order to accommodate the notion that not only Israelites but also Gentiles will be included in the orbit of God's salvation provided by Jesus (e.g., 10:16; 11:51–52; cf. Isa. 54:15; see Menken 1996a: 76). While the use of *pantes* and *didaktoi* in the nominative rather than accusative case could indicate John's use of the MT, it is equally possible that the evangelist is dependent on the LXX and that the change of case is an inconsequential change necessitated by the Johannine sentence structure (Menken 1996a: 73–75). If so, John dropped the LXX's *thēsō* in Isa. 54:12, inserted the verb *esontai*, and changed the accusative to the nominative.

E. The Use of Isa. 54:13 in John 6:45. In light of the Jews' largely negative response to his message, Jesus points out that while his ministry in fact fulfills the prophetic vision that one day—which has now arrived—all people will be taught by God, this applies only to those who are drawn by the Father, the sender of Jesus (6:44), and who subsequently come to believe in him as the Messiah. This explains Jewish unbelief in Jesus (which is the subject of further OT substantiation in 12:38–41) and at the same time affirms God's hand upon Jesus and his mission.

Beyond this, P. Borgen (1965: 150) contends that the exposition of Isa. 54:13 in John 6:45b–46 also harks back to the theophany at Sinai by invoking two of its central features: positively, hearing (6:45), and negatively, seeing (6:46). While "hearing" is an important aspect of Sinai (e.g., Deut. 4:12; 5:24; 18:16; Sir. 17:13; 45:5; *Mek. Exod.* 19:2), "seeing" is not; for no human being can see [God] and live (Exod. 33:20). John 6:46, in turn, harks back to John 1:18, which is part of John 1:14–18, which interprets the theophany at Sinai

narrated in Exod. 33–34 (Köstenberger 1999: 52; see also John 5:37 in the context of 5:37–47; cf. Borgen 1965: 151–54).

F. Theological Use. In the present passage Jesus sees a prophetic portion of Scripture fulfilled in and through his ministry, appropriating Scripture in a midrash/pesher-type format. There seems to be a difficulty with Jesus' use of Isa. 54:13 in a context that implies that not all Jews will be saved when this passage seems to speak of a time when all Israel will be taught by Yahweh (Ridderbos 1997: 233). The resolution of this apparent problem is provided by the realization that not every Jew will be taught by God, but only "all" those who are truly receptive to divine revelation (6:44; cf. 10:16; 11:51–52; 12:32). In accounting for massive Jewish unbelief and opposition to Jesus' ministry and message, the present passage is similar in function to the Synoptic parable of the Sower (Matt. 13:1–23; Mark 4:1–20; Luke 8:4–15).

In 6:49–50 the previously introduced contrast between the OT manna and Jesus the bread from heaven is taken to a new level. Although the manna was heaven-sent, as well as nurturing and sustaining of life, the argument goes, it was unable to impart life that is eternal. After all, all those in the wilderness who ate the manna eventually died. By contrast, anyone who "eats this bread" (i.e., appropriates the salvation offered by Jesus through faith) will live forever and not die (spiritually speaking). Jesus' assertion in 6:51 that the bread is his flesh, which he will "give for the life of the world" (cf. 1:29, 36; paralleled later in 10:11, 15; see also 11:51–52; 15:13; 17:19; 18:14), evokes the memory of the Isaianic Suffering Servant, who "poured out his life unto death" and "bore the sins of many" (Isa. 53:12; cf. 52:13–53:12; note the citation of Isa. 54:13 in John 6:45). Just as the scope of Isaiah's Suffering Servant is universal (Isa. 49:6), likewise Jesus will give his life not merely for Israel, but for the world (cf. 12:20–36, esp. 12:32).

The Jews' fighting among themselves (6:52) resembles their striving with Moses and God during the exodus (cf. Exod. 17:2; Num. 20:3; see Beasley-Murray 1999: 94; Borchert 1996–2002: 1:271; Schnackenburg 1990: 2:60). Although later rabbinic teaching in fact speaks (figuratively) of "eating the Messiah" (cf. *b. Sanh.* 99a; see

Talbert 1992: 138), Jesus' repeated references to people "eating" his flesh and "drinking" his blood in 6:50–51, 53–58 militate against the people's scruples against the drinking of blood and the eating of meat containing blood, both of which were proscribed by the Hebrew Scriptures, in particular the Mosaic law (cf. Gen. 9:4; Lev. 17:10–14; Deut. 12:16; see Koester 2003: 102–4). "Flesh and blood" is a Hebrew idiom referring to the whole person (cf. Matt. 16:17; 1 Cor. 15:50; Gal. 1:16; Eph. 6:12; Heb. 2:14). Jesus' insistence in 6:55, harking back to 6:27, 32, that his flesh and blood are real—that is, spiritual—food and drink carries the connotation of eschatological, typological fulfillment in relation to OT precursors. (Regarding the reference to Jesus' ascension in 6:62, see commentary at 1:51; 3:14; 8:28.)

Jesus' affirmation in 6:63 that "the Spirit is the one who gives life" (cf. Isa. 40:6–8) resembles his earlier pronouncement to Nicodemus in 3:6 (see also 5:21). Jesus' point here seems to be that human reason unaided by the Spirit is unable to discern what is spiritual (Ridderbos 1997: 246; Morris 1995: 340). According to the Hebrew Scriptures, life was created through God's word (Gen. 1:2; cf. 2:7). Later, Moses instructed his fellow Israelites, "People do not live on bread alone, but on every word that comes from the mouth of the Lord" (Deut. 8:3). Ezekiel memorably depicts the Spirit as life-giving (e.g., 37:1–14, esp. v. 5), and Jeremiah exemplifies receptivity to God's word (Jer. 15:16; cf. Ezek. 2:8–3:3) (see Carson 1991: 302; Barrett 1978: 305). Both Testaments view God's word as fully efficacious (Isa. 55:11; Jer. 23:29; Heb. 4:12). Here it is stated that it is *Jesus'* words (*rhēmata*) that are spirit and life (cf. 5:24, 40, 46–47; 6:68), which is in keeping with God's nature as spirit (4:24) (see Schlatter [1948]: 182], who also cites 1:1) and contrasts with the Jewish belief that life is found in the words of the law (5:39; cf. *Mek. Exod.* 15:26, citing Prov. 4:22; *m. 'Abot* 6:7).

Peter's confession of Jesus as "the Holy One of God" in 6:69 (the reading is clearly original [see Köstenberger 2004: 223]) anticipates later references to Jesus being set apart for God in 10:36; 17:19. Although there is no evidence that the expression functioned as a messianic title in Judaism (but cf. Ps. 16:10, applied to Jesus in Acts 2:27; 13:35), clearly it does so here. In the Synoptic equivalent Peter confesses Jesus as "the Christ, the Son of the living God" (Matt. 16:16; Mark 8:29: "the Christ"; Luke 9:20: "the Christ of God"). This rare expression, "the Holy One of God," occurs elsewhere in the NT only in Mark 1:24 (cf. Luke 4:34), there uttered by a demon (though see Luke 1:35; Acts 3:14 [cf. Ps. 16:10]; 4:27; 1 John 2:20; Rev. 3:7; the term is also seldom used in the OT, occasionally occurring with regard to men consecrated to God: see the LXX of Judg. 13:7; 16:17; Ps. 105:16 [cf. 106:16 MT]).

Jesus' question in 6:70, "Have I not chosen you, the Twelve?" harks back to the OT designation of Israel as God's "chosen people" (Deut. 10:15; 1 Sam. 12:22). In the NT this designation is transferred to the community of believers in Jesus (e.g., Eph. 1:4; Col. 3:12; 1 Pet. 1:1–2; 2:9). Jesus' choice of *twelve* disciples likely was intended to correspond to the number of tribes of Israel (Ridderbos 1997: 250).

Jesus at the Feast of Tabernacles (7:1–8:59)

Chapters 7–8 do not include any "sign" by Jesus, featuring instead two cycles of Jesus' teaching at the Feast of Tabernacles (7:1–52; 8:12–59; regarding the noninclusion of 7:53–8:11, see the excursus in Köstenberger 2004: 245–49). This is now the third (and as it turns out, final) trip of Jesus to Jerusalem (cf. 2:13; 5:1), which finds Jesus spending two months in the Jewish capital from the Feast of Tabernacles to the Feast of Dedication (10:22). At this stage of Jesus' ministry he is increasingly viewed within the matrix of messianic expectations. Was the Coming One to emerge from secret, mysterious beginnings (7:4, 10, 27), or was he a known figure of Davidic descent (7:41–42)? Did Jesus' miracles identify him as the Messiah (7:21, 31)?

In chapters 7–8 the evangelist addresses these issues by showing Jesus' fulfillment of symbolism surrounding the Feast of Tabernacles and by dealing with representative questions regarding Jesus' identity (Köstenberger 1998b: 94–96). The narrative depicting Jesus' first teaching cycle in chapter 7 builds toward the climax of 7:37b–38, where Jesus issues the invitation to all who are thirsty to come to him and drink, so that believers would, once the Spirit had been given, become sources of "streams of living water" (see further below). Thus, in keeping with the theme of Tabernacles,

"With joy you will draw water from the wells of salvation" (Isa. 12:3), the prophetic vision of Isa. 58:11 would be fulfilled.

Tabernacles was celebrated from 15 to 21 Tishri, which fell in September or October, after the grape harvest and two months prior to Dedication (cf. Lev. 23:33–43; Num. 29:12–39; Neh. 8:13–18; Hos. 12:9; Zech. 14:16–19; *m. Sukkah* 5:2–4; see Avi-Yonah 1964: 144). The feast followed shortly after the Day of Atonement and marked the conclusion of the annual cycle of religious festivals that began with Passover and Unleavened Bread six months earlier. Originally a harvest festival, Tabernacles (or Booths) recalled God's provision for his people during the wilderness wanderings (Lev. 23:42–43; cf. Matt. 17:4 pars.). Festivities lasted seven days, culminating in an eighth day of special celebration and festive assembly. Owing to the daily solemn outpouring of water during the festival (Num. 28:7; cf. Isa. 12:3), Tabernacles came to be associated with eschatological hopes (Zech. 14:16–19). Immensely popular, it was simply called "the Feast" by the Jews (e.g., 1 Kings 8:2, 65; 12:32; 2 Chron. 5:3; 7:8; Neh. 8:14, 18; Ps. 81:3; Ezek. 45:25). Josephus (*Ant.* 8.100) called it "the greatest and holiest feast of the Jews."

Jesus' brothers' advice in 7:3–4 that Jesus go and display his miracle-working abilities to the large Jerusalem crowd at the festival is shown to be unsound and to stem from their unbelief (7:5). In essence, Jesus' brothers duplicate Satan's temptation of Jesus at the beginning of his ministry by interpreting Jesus' messianic calling in self-seeking terms (cf. Matt. 4:5–7 par.; see Brown 1966–1970: 306–8; Borchert 1996–2002: 1:280–81). This reveals a fundamental misunderstanding of the nature of Jesus' messianic identity. Jesus' cautious response that his time had not yet come (7:6–9) is well in keeping with Jewish wisdom that there was a proper time for everything (Eccles. 3:1; cf. *Eccles. Rab.* 3:1 and the rabbinic and Qumran material cited in Köstenberger 2002b: 73). In the face of mounting persecution, Jesus chooses a more gradual, judicious approach, traveling to the feast in private at a later time (the probable sense of the most likely variant in 7:8; see Köstenberger 2004: 230–31, 244). As at 2:4, Jesus will not be pressured to act before his time (cf. Mark 9:30; 10:1; John 6:1–4).

The comment by some at the feast in Jerusalem that Jesus deceived the people (7:12) probably traces its background to the stipulation in Deut. 13:1–11 that a false prophet must die "because he . . . has tried to turn you from the way the LORD your God commanded you to follow." A similar charge is recorded by Matthew (27:63; cf. Luke 23:2; see Brown 1966–1970: 307). Jesus is labeled as a deceiver in later Jewish literature (*b. Sanh.* 43a; cf. *b. Soṭah* 47a). According to Jewish law, the punishment for leading people astray was stoning, further distinguishing between those who mislead an individual and those who lead an entire town astray (*m. Sanh.* 7:4, 10). Josephus names several first-century deceivers (see the list in Köstenberger 2002b: 74; for a general survey, see Heard 1992).

The Jews' reference in 7:14 to Jesus' lack of formal rabbinic training sought to disqualify him from assuming the posture of a religious teacher. The rabbis of Jesus' day typically taught by referring to the rulings of other, well-known rabbis. By contrast, Jesus prefaced his pronouncements by asserting his unique authority: "You have heard that it was said . . . , but I tell you"; "I tell you the truth"; "Truly, truly, I say to you" (Riesner 1981: 97–245). At the same time, Jesus did acknowledge that his teaching was not his own (7:16). Yet, rather than referring to the rulings of other rabbis, he claimed direct knowledge from the Father (8:28) (see Carson 1991: 312; Morris 1995: 359–60). Underlying the maxims stated by Jesus in 7:18–20 seems to be the contrast established in Deut. 18:9–22 between a false prophet, who deserves to be executed, and Jesus, the Son of God, who must be followed.

The question "Has not Moses given you the law?" (7:19) refers to the great event in Israel's history subsequent to the exodus: God constituted Israel as a nation by giving them the law. Later in the Fourth Gospel the Pharisees call themselves "disciples of Moses" (9:28), and yet Jesus' contemporaries are trying to kill him (7:19); this hardly is in keeping with the Mosaic law that proscribed murder (Exod. 20:13). The reference in 7:22 to circumcision being given by Moses, yet ultimately by the patriarchs, harks back to Gen. 17:9–14 (Abraham) and to Exod. 12:44, 48–49; Lev. 12:3 (Moses). In the ensuing argument from the lesser to the greater (cf. 5:47), common among the rabbis, Jesus points to the commonly acknowledged dilemma that arose when the Sabbath commandment conflicted with the stipulation, also in the law, that a boy must be circumcised on the eighth day (7:21–23).

If circumcision was judged important enough to override the Sabbath, Jesus maintained, what about healing a person? This would seem to be at least as significant an act as circumcision and worthy of being considered to override the Sabbath commandment. In fact, later rabbinic teaching sides with Jesus, holding that, granted the lesser premise that circumcision (which "perfects" but one member of the human body) supersedes the Sabbath commandment, the saving of the entire body transcends it all the more (see the material cited in Köstenberger 2002b: 76; Keener 2003: 717).

Jesus' stinging rebuke in 7:24, "Do not judge by appearances, but judge with right judgment," may allude to Lev. 19:15 (see also Deut. 16:18–19; Isa. 11:3–4; Zech. 7:9; cf. John 5:30). His Jewish contemporaries fundamentally misread the scriptural matrix of passages pertaining to the Messiah and hence judged Jesus on the basis of external, superficial criteria rather than being grounded in a sound spiritual and theological appreciation of the messianic teachings of Scripture. Jesus exhorts them to exercise proper judgment in evaluating his claims and in perceiving his actions.

The next three smaller scenes (7:25–31, 32–36, 37–44) center on the critical question, "Is Jesus the Christ?" The first messianic expectation is given expression in 7:27: "When the Christ comes, no one will know where he is from" (for OT information regarding the origins of the Messiah, see esp. Mic. 5:2; Dan. 7:13; for apocalyptic references, see *1 En.* 48:6; 2 Esd. [*4 Ezra*] 13:51–52 [these may be post-Christian]). According to rabbinic teaching, some believed that the Messiah would be born of flesh and blood yet be wholly unknown until he set out to procure Israel's redemption (Carson 1991: 317–18). Yet, as Jesus proceeds to note, the real question is whether his authority is merely of human derivation or whether he has been divinely commissioned (7:28–29). The second messianic expectation is voiced in 7:31: "The Christ, when he comes, will not perform more signs than he has done, will he?" There is little direct evidence in the OT that miracles were expected of the Mes-

siah, though this may be implied from the fact that Jews expected a prophet like Moses (Deut. 18:15, 18), who performed miraculous signs at the exodus (Exod. 7–11). In any case, it would have been natural for people, upon witnessing Jesus' miracles, to wonder whether he might be the Messiah (see Mark 13:22; cf. Deut. 13:1–3; see Meeks 1967: 162–64).

John 7:37–39 finds Jesus at the last and greatest day of the festival (cf. 7:14: "halfway through the feast"). Every day during Tabernacles priests would march in solemn procession from the Pool of Siloam to the temple and pour out water at the base of the altar. The seventh day of the festival, the last day proper (Lev. 23:34, 41–42), was marked by a special water-pouring rite and lights ceremony (*m. Sukkah* 4:1, 9–10). This was to be followed by a sacred assembly on the eighth day, which was set apart for sacrifices, the joyful dismantling of the booths, and repeated singing of the Hallel (Pss. 113–118; cf. Lev. 23:36; Num. 29:35; Neh. 8:18). Hence, by the first century many Jews had come to think of the Feast of Tabernacles as an eight-day event (Josephus, *Ant.* 13.245; *b. Sukkah* 48b; *m. Sukkah* 5:6; 2 Macc. 10:6).

Whether Jesus' words in 7:37–38 and 8:12 were uttered on the climactic seventh day, with its water-pouring and torch-lighting ceremonies (Brown 1966–1970: 320; Bultmann 1971: 302n5; Schnackenburg 1990: 2:152; Ridderbos 1997: 272; Burge 2000: 227), or on the eighth day of joyful assembly and celebration (Carson 1991: 321; Morris 1995: 383, esp. note 79; Barrett 1978: 326; Moloney 1998: 256; Schlatter 1948: 199), they would have had a tremendous impact on the pilgrims (on the water-drawing ceremony, see Keener 2003: 722–24). Just when the events of Tabernacles—and their attendant symbolism—were beginning to sink into the people's memories, Jesus' words promised a continuous supply of water and light, perhaps also alluding to the supply of water from the rock in the wilderness.

Jesus' invitation in 7:37, "If anyone is thirsty, let him come to me and drink" (NIV), harks back to OT prophetic passages such as Isa. 55:1 (see also Pss. 42–43; Matt. 5:6; John 4:10–14; 6:35; Rev. 22:1–2, 17; Sir. 24:19–21; 51:23–24). Tabernacles was associated with adequate rainfall (cf. Zech. 14:16–17, a text that was read on the first day of the feast, according to the liturgy in *b. Meg.*

31a). Another OT passage associated with this feast is Isa. 12:3: "With joy you will draw water from the wells of salvation." This water rite, although not prescribed in the OT, was firmly in place well before the first century AD (perhaps indicated by 1 Sam. 7:6; rabbinic sources that may or may not reach back to the first century are *Pesiq. Rab.* 52:3–6; *t. Sukkah* 3:3–12 [see Grigsby 1986]). The festival seems to speak of the joyful restoration of Israel and the ingathering of the nations. Here Jesus presents himself as God's agent to make these end-time events a reality.

The following reference to Scripture by Jesus creates difficulty in that it does not seem to conform precisely to any one OT passage: "Whoever believes in me, as the scripture has said, streams of living water will flow from within him" (7:38 NIV). Possible scriptural allusions include those promising spiritual blessings (Isa. 58:11; cf. Prov. 4:23; 5:15; Zech. 14:8; see Menken [1996a: 187–203; 1996b], who favors Ps. 77:16, 20 LXX [78:16, 20 MT], with the epithet "living" coming from Zech. 14:8; cf. Daly-Denton 2004: 134), including blessings related to the outpouring of water (Isa. 12:3; 44:3; 49:10; Ezek. 36:25–27; 47:1; Joel 3:18; Amos 9:11–15; Zech. 13:1; an allusion to Ezek. 47:1–11 is favored by Hodges 1979: 243–48; Knapp 1997: 116–17), in line with the feast itself (Neh. 9:15, 19–20; cf. Exod. 17:6; Ps. 105:41; Prov. 18:4; Isa. 43:19–20; 48:21; 55:1; Jer. 2:13; 17:13; see also 1QH^a XVI, 4–40). Clearly, however, it is not any one of those passages by itself that is in view, but rather the entire matrix of scriptural expectations associated with the eschatological abundance presaged by the Feast of Tabernacles, as is reflected in the references to the feast in Neh. 9 and in this chapter's references to the provision of water from the rock during Israel's wilderness wanderings (see the detailed treatment in Carson 1991: 326–28).

There is some question as to whether the phrase "whoever believes in me" in 7:38 is to be read with what follows, which is the traditional interpretation (so all modern critical editions of the Greek NT, virtually all the Greek fathers, and the vast majority of English translations [but not the NRSV]), or with the preceding 7:37, which is the christological interpretation (on this issue, see Carson 1991: 323). Most likely, the syntax is to be construed with the phrase "from within him"

at the end of 7:38, referring to the one who believes in Jesus the Messiah (the traditional view), with the first clause of 7:38 ("whoever believes in me") functioning as a pendant subject (Ridderbos 1997: 273; Carson 1991: 323–25; Barrett 1978: 326–27; Lindars 1972: 300–301; cf. Wallace 1996: 52, 654; Carson also notes that John frequently begins a sentence with a substantival participle). The phrase *touto de eipen* ("and he said this") customarily refers to the words of Jesus in John (Carson 1991: 324–25, citing Fee 1978). If this is the case here, then 7:38 contains the words of Jesus, not the evangelist, and thus "from within him" would be parallel to "whoever believes in him" (other instances of the pendant nominative in John are 1:12; 6:39; 15:2; 17:2 [Hodges 1979: 241, citing Cortés 1967: 79]), and the source of the rivers of living water, albeit not in an ultimate sense (see the qualifications in Carson 1991: 323–24), is the person who believes in Jesus.

Less likely, the focus of the passage is christological, and Jesus is here presented as the source of "rivers of living water" (a view held by a sizable contingent of commentators [e.g., Brown 1966–1970: 320; Beasley-Murray 1999: 115; Schnackenburg 1990: 2:154; Menken 1996b: 165–66; Burge 1987: 88–93; 2000: 228]—although on any reading this is true in an ultimate sense). In any case, Jewish parallels abound (see Köstenberger 2002b: 78–79; Grigsby 1986). According to certain traditions (*b. Sanh.* 37a; Ezek. 5:5; 38:12; *Jub.* 8:19), Jerusalem was situated in the "navel" of the earth, so that John may be using "belly" as a synonym for "Jerusalem" (Abrahams 1917: 1:11, referring to Zech. 14:8; cf. Köstenberger 2002b: 79; Marcus 1998; Schnackenburg [1990: 2:156] connects *ek tēs koilias autou* ["from within him"] with the water flowing from Jesus' side at 19:34).

In a characteristic aside (cf. 2:11, 21–22; 12:16, 33; 21:19, 23), the evangelist in 7:39 notes that by this statement Jesus was referring to the Spirit, whom those who believed in Jesus were later to receive (cf. 20:22; see commentary there). He further adds that up to that time the Spirit had not yet been given, since Jesus had not yet been glorified. As in other instances (e.g., cf. 2:17 with 2:22), this admirably preserves the precrucifixion vantage point of the present narrative. Occasionally in the OT water is used as a symbol for the

Holy Spirit (cf. Isa. 44:3; Ezek. 36:25–27; Joel 2:28). Manna/water and the gift of the Spirit are linked in Neh. 9:20 (cf. 9:13, 15; see Carson 1991: 326–28; Shidemantle 2001). In John, this motif dovetails with 5:46 and the portrayal of Jesus as the true bread of heaven in chapter 6 (cf. 6:35; for rabbinic and Qumran parallels, see Köstenberger 2002b: 79). Yet the giving of the Spirit, evoked by Jewish Tabernacles traditions, was contingent on Jesus being "glorified" (Ridderbos 1997: 275)—a Johannine euphemism for the cluster of events centering on the crucifixion. The present statement thus anticipates the Farewell Discourse and the commissioning scene in 20:22.

John 7:40 features another reference to "the Prophet" of Deut. 18:15–18 (so Carson 1991: 329; *contra* Ridderbos 1997: 276–77; see commentary at 6:14 above). The previous reference in 6:14 was evoked by Jesus' feeding of the multitudes against the backdrop of Moses' provision of manna; in the present instance Moses may have come to mind again because of Jesus' reference to the "streams of living water," harking back to Moses' provision of water from the rock (cf. Num. 20:11; 24:7; 1 Cor. 10:4). As John 1:19–21 illustrates, in first-century thinking the Prophet and the Messiah often were viewed as two separate personages (however, for the view that the roles of Prophet and Messiah were interwined in the minds of many, see Meeks 1967; Martyn 1979: 113–14). The Qumran community looked forward to the coming of the Prophet and the Anointed Ones of Aaron and Israel (1QS IX, 11), whereby the Prophet was held to be different from the priestly and royal messiahs. Concerning the eschatological successor to Moses, *Eccles. Rab.* 1:9 states, "As the former redeemer made a well to rise [Num. 21:17–18], so will the latter Redeemer bring up water [Joel 4:18]" (see commentary at 4:10; 6:31).

Some said that Jesus was the Prophet (7:40), while others said that he was the Christ (7:41) (see commentary at 1:41). Yet others objected, "Does the Christ come from Galilee? Does not Scripture say that the Christ will come from the seed of David and from Bethlehem, the village where David was?" (7:42). This is now the third public conjecture highlighted in this section (cf. 7:27, 31 above). There was ample scriptural support for the people's contention that the Messiah would come from David's family and from Bethlehem (see 2 Sam. 7:12–16; Ps. 89:3–4, 35–37; Isa. 9:7; 11:1; 55:3; and esp. Mic. 5:2), a village (*kōmē*, elsewhere in John applied only to Bethany [11:1, 30]) located south of Jerusalem in the heart of Judea. Bethlehem is implied as David's city in texts such as 1 Sam. 16:1, 4; 20:6. Matthew 2:5–6 confirms that at least by the beginning of the first century AD, Jewish scholars generally expected the Messiah to be born in Bethlehem (cf. Luke 2:1–20). No comparable evidence existed for a Galilean origin (cf. 7:52).

Again, one cannot help but note the irony (Carson 1991: 330; Morris 1995: 380; *contra* Ridderbos 1997: 278). For while people erroneously thought that Jesus hailed from Galilee, John's readers clearly are expected to know that Jesus had in fact been born in Bethlehem, thus fulfilling messianic prophecy (cf. Matt. 2:5–6; Luke 2:4, 15). Jesus' interrogators are unmasked as ignorant (cf. 7:52, where Jesus' Pharisaic opposition is shown to be in error). The apparent difficulty of Jesus' supposed Galilean origin was one with which Christian apologists (including John) had to deal already in the first century. The division (*schisma*) that arose in the crowd indicates, historically, that there was a diversity of opinion regarding Jesus' legitimacy during his earthly ministry.

Following Jesus' appearance at the Feast of Tabernacles, the evangelist narrates a Sanhedrin meeting at which the Pharisees heap abuse on the temple guards for failing to arrest Jesus and contemptuously speak of the crowds as "this crowd that does not know the law—they are accursed" (7:45–49). The Pharisees' condemnation alludes to the Deuteronomic curses that are pronounced on those who fail to observe the Mosaic law (see Deut. 27:26; 28:15; cf. Ps. 119:20–21; see Brown 1966–1970: 325; Ridderbos 1997: 279–80; Carson 1991: 331–32). More accurately, it was not that people were entirely unfamiliar with what the law said, but they did not observe the Pharisaic traditions as scrupulously as the Pharisees did (Morris 1995: 383).

By way of caution, care must be taken not to identify the crowd in the present instance with the "people of the land" (Heb. *'am hā'āreṣ*) in later rabbinic literature. As J. P. Meier (2001: 28–29) notes, first, the reference here is not necessarily to common people in general, but specifically to the crowd of pilgrims who are in Jerusalem for the Feast of Tabernacles; second, the dispute here concerns not rules of purity and tithing in the Mosaic law (the context in which later rabbinic literature refers to ordinary Jews as "people of the land" with a pejorative connotation) but the proper identification of Jesus; third, the crowd acts here (as throughout much of John 7) as the evangelist's sounding board for the christological revelation of Jesus (see further Meier 2001: 38–39n36).

Nicodemus's question in 7:51, "Does our law judge a man without first giving him a hearing and learning what he does?" harks back to texts such as Deut. 1:16–17; 17:4; 19:18, which charge judges to investigate accusations against a person fairly and thoroughly. The supreme irony in the present instance is that the appointed guardians of the law themselves fail to keep the law in the way they deal with Jesus (Morris 1995: 384; Köstenberger 2005b). What is more, in light of the fact that Nicodemus's fellow Sanhedrin members have just expressed contempt toward the masses who are ignorant of the law, the evangelist surely sees irony in Nicodemus's calling them to task on a point of simple Jewish—indeed, universal—legal procedure (see Josephus, *Ant.* 14.167; *J.W.* 1.209; cf. *m. Sanh.* 5:4; *Exod. Rab.* 21:3).

In 7:52 the Fourth Evangelist proceeds to recount another dubious claim made by Nicodemus's colleagues: "You are not from Galilee as well, are you? Look, and you will see that no prophet arises from Galilee" (note that the text may say either "a prophet" or, more likely, "the prophet" [see Köstenberger 2004: 244]). Yet, contrary to these confident assertions, prophets had indeed come out of Galilee in the past, including Jonah (2 Kings 14:25) and possibly Elijah (1 Kings 17:1) and Nahum (Nah. 1:1) (see the rabbinic literature cited in Köstenberger 2002b: 81; for another doubtful assertion, see 8:33).

After the material in 7:53–8:11, which, in the judgment of the vast majority of commentators, was inserted at a later time (see Köstenberger 2004: 245–49), 8:12–59 records the second teaching cycle of Jesus at the Feast of Tabernacles. In 8:12 Jesus launches a major discourse, commencing with the startling claim "I am the light of the world." The term "light" (*phōs*) spans the entire first half of John's Gospel, from the prologue (1:4, 5, 7, 8–9) to the concluding section (12:35–36, 46), in each of which it occurs six times. The word is absent from the second half of John's Gospel, which suggests that it is part of the evangelist's presentation of Jesus' entrance into the world and ministry to the Jews in chapters 1–12.

The motif of light and darkness (sounded in 8:12) ties in several thematic strands in the Gospel: (1) the Word's participation in creation (1:3); (2) the moral contrast between spiritual life and spiritual death (12:35–36); (3) Jesus' fulfillment of Tabernacles symbolism (chap. 7; 8:12); and (4) Jesus' healing of the man born blind (9:4–5), which becomes a parable of the Pharisees' spiritual blindness in contrast to the man's newly found vision. The evangelist returns to the "light" motif at the raising of Lazarus (11:9–10) and Jesus' final indictment of Jewish unbelief (12:37–50).

The conjunction *oun* ("so") connects 8:12 with 7:52, indicating that the evangelist is going to show that the Messiah can indeed come from Galilee, based on the prophecy of Isa. 9:1–2 (cf. Matt. 4:16; see S. Motyer 1997: 155–56). Earlier in the Gospel the Word is called "the light of all people" (1:4), and Jesus' confrontation with his opponents is cast as a battle between light and darkness (1:5; 3:19–21; cf. 9:4–5; 12:35–36, 46). Together with the manna (chap. 6) and the rivers of living water (chap. 7), the reference to Jesus as "light" in chapter 8 may be part of a "wilderness theme," alluding to God's presence with the Israelites as a pillar of fire (Morris 1995: 388; Brown 1966–1970: 344; Burge 2000: 255; Moloney 1998: 268; Borchert 1996–2002: 1:295).

In the OT, God himself (Ps. 27:1; 36:9) and his word or law (Ps. 119:105; Prov. 6:23) are called a "light." Imagery of light is also applied to the end-time Servant of the Lord (Isa. 49:6; cf. 42:6) and to the Lord's own presence in the midst of his people in the last days (see Isa. 60:19–22; Zech. 14:5b–7, judged especially significant by Carson [1991: 338]; cf. Rev. 21:23–24). Contemporary Judaism applied the phrase "light of the world" not only to God but also to Israel, Jerusalem, the patriarchs, the Messiah, famous rabbis (e.g., Yohanan ben Zakkai), the Torah, the temple, and even Adam (Keener 1993: 285; see also Beasley-Murray 1999: 128; Brown 1966–1970: 344; Schnackenburg 1990: 2:190; Moloney 1998:

266). Here "light" terminology is applied to Tabernacles symbolism (cf. *m. Sukkah* 5:2–4; see Köstenberger 2002b: 82).

The entire earthly sphere (controlled by the "ruler of this world," Satan) is in darkness, but Jesus has come as "the light of the world." Thus those who follow him will never "walk in darkness, but will have the light of life" (8:12). The "following" motif is also found in the exodus narrative, with the Israelites following the pillar of fire (Beasley-Murray 1999: 128–29; for Qumran and Second Temple parallels, see Köstenberger 2002b: 82). "Light of life" language is found in the OT as well as in other Jewish literature (cf. Ps. 36:9; 56:13; *Pss. Sol.* 3:12 [cf. *4 Bar.* 9:3]; 1QS III, 7; *1 En.* 58:3 [cf. 58:4–6; 92:4]). In the present context "light of life" could have several specific nuances, such as "gives life," "is life," "springs from life," or "illuminates life" (Morris 1995: 389n10; Laney 1992: 159).

The Pharisees' challenge to the validity of Jesus' testimony and Jesus' response in 8:13–14 picks up where 5:31–47 left off (for similarities and differences and a detailed commentary on the present passage, see Köstenberger 2004: 254–55). Again, stipulations in the Mosaic law are clearly in view (cf. Deut. 17:6; 19:15; *m. Ketub.* 2:9). Jesus' statement in 8:15, "You judge according to the flesh; I judge no one" (cf. 7:24), may echo 1 Sam. 16:7 (see also Isa. 53:2–3; cf. 2 Cor. 5:16). People rejected Jesus as the Messiah at least in part because he did not come with regal fanfare or bring political liberation to Israel as they expected (cf. 6:15; 18:36). Yet, as Jesus intimates, appearances can be deceiving.

The reference in 8:17 to the requirement of two witnesses in the law is to Deut. 17:6; 19:15 (cf. John 8:13). There may be a hint of deity in Jesus' "I am" statements in 8:24, 28 (see Köstenberger 1999: 261), recalling passages such as Isa. 43:10 (Morris 1995: 393n25; Ball 1996: 186). The OT background of Jesus' statement "If you don't believe that I am [the one I claim to be]" in 8:24 (cf. 8:28, 58) appears to be Exod. 3:13–14 via Isa. 40–55 (so Carson 1991: 343–44; Beasley-Murray 1999: 130–31; Schnackenburg 1990: 2:200; see esp. Isa. 41:4; 43:10, 13, 25; 46:4; 48:12; cf. Deut. 32:39). Anyone other than God who appropriated this designation was guilty of blasphemy and subject to God's wrath (Isa. 47:8–9; Zeph. 2:15).

The expression "lifted up" (*hypsōsēte*, in the active voice [cf. 3:14b]) in 8:28 most likely harks back to the Suffering Servant of Isaiah, who "will be raised and lifted up and highly exalted" (Isa. 52:13). John is the only NT writer to use the term "lifted up" in a dual sense with reference both to Jesus' crucifixion (his literal "lifting up") and to his exaltation (metaphorical use [for NT instances of the latter usage, see, e.g., Matt. 23:12 = Luke 14:11 = 18:14; Luke 1:52; Acts 2:33; 5:31]). There is great irony in the fact that the Jews, by having Jesus crucified, are actually "lifting" Jesus up (Bultmann 1971: 350, followed by Witherington 1995: 176). Jesus' reference to his dependence on the Father in 8:28 once again invokes the Jewish notion of the *šālîaḥ* (see commentary at 5:22 above).

The Jews' proud claim in 8:33 that they are Abraham's descendants has its basis in several OT passages that extol the blessings of descent from Abraham (e.g., Ps. 105:6; Isa. 41:8). Abraham was considered to be the founder of Jewish worship; he recognized the Creator and served him faithfully (see the references to Philo cited in Köstenberger 2004: 262n56). The contrast between the son and the slave in 8:35 may allude to Abraham's respective sons through Sarah and Hagar in Gen. 21:1–21 (see also Exod. 21:2; Hanson [1994: 366] contends that Isaac is a type of Christ). With regard to Jesus' statement in 8:37–38, it should be noted that even in the OT physical descent from Abraham was insufficient to establish lineage (e.g., Jer. 9:25–26); this is often noted by Paul (e.g., Rom. 2:28–29; 9:7; Gal. 4:21–31); by contrast, Jesus' paternity is secure.

Jesus' exhortation to his Jewish contemporaries in 8:39, "If you were children of Abraham, you would do the works of Abraham," may hark back to passages such as Gen. 18:1–8, where Abraham welcomed divine messengers with eager hospitality (Witherington 1995: 177; Brown 1966–1970: 357). Other acts of obedience on the part of Abraham include those recounted in Gen. 12:1–9; 15:1–6; 22:1–19 (though less noble instances are recorded as well). The rabbis frequently upheld Abraham as a moral example to be emulated by the Jews (*m. 'Abot* 5:19; *b. Beṣah* 32b, where reference is made to the "works of Abraham") and distinguished between people who acted like Abraham and those who acted like Balaam (*m. 'Abot* 5:19; cf. *Jub.* 23:10). Abraham was believed to have fulfilled the whole Torah even before it was given.

In the dynamic of the argument, the Jews' thinking seems to be that even if Jesus is unwilling to grant their true descent from Abraham, surely he cannot dispute their claim to be children of God (cf. 8:41; see Carson 1991: 352). To be sure, OT teaching clearly affirms that Yahweh is the only true God, and the people of Israel are his children (Exod. 4:22; Deut. 14:1–2; 32:6; Isa. 63:16; 64:8; Jer. 31:9; Mal. 2:10). In the context of John's Gospel, however, the Jews' claim to be born from God is ironic; the perceptive reader understands that those who lack the Spirit have not been born from God (cf. 1:12–13; 3:3–8; see Keener 2003: 759). Later on, Jesus will affirm that his opponents are not his "sheep" (10:26) and that he, not Israel, is the "true vine" (15:1).

Jesus' reference to the devil as "the father of lies" in 8:44 may hark back to the fall narrative in Gen. 3:4, where the devil blatantly contradicted God's word (cf. Gen. 2:17; so Morris 1995: 411; Ridderbos 1997: 315; Carson 1991: 353; Barrett 1978: 349; Beasley-Murray 1999: 135). It was commonly recognized in Second Temple literature that death was the result of Satan's initiative (Wis. 2:23–24; Sir. 25:24; cf. Rom. 5:12). On a secondary level, the passage may allude to Cain, the murderer of Abel (cf. 1 John 3:15, the only other reference featuring the term "murderer"; see Brown 1966–1970: 358). If so, then Jesus' comment may imply that the devil is the father of "the Jews" because they would kill Jesus, their fellow Jew, just as Cain had killed his brother Abel (Díaz 1963; Dahl 1963). Antiochus Epiphanes IV is called a "murderer and blasphemer" in 2 Macc. 9:28.

The phrase "not holding to the truth" in 8:44 (cf. 8:31–32) may allude to the fall of Satan (Isa. 14:12?), which preceded the fall narrative in Gen. 3. Genesis 3, in turn, makes clear that Satan flatly contradicted the truthfulness of God's word (Gen. 3:3–4; cf. 2:17). Parallels to the notion of not holding to the truth are present in the Dead Sea Scrolls (1QS VIII, 5–6; 1QHᵃ XII, 14).

In the present passage Jesus and the devil are pitted against each other as complete opposites, with Jesus as the life-giver and truthful witness and the devil as the quintessential murderer and liar (Witherington 1995: 178). This characterization,

too, is paralleled by the contrast in the Dead Sea Scrolls between the "Teacher of Righteousness" and the "Man of Lies" (1QpHab II, 1–2; V, 11; CD-B XX, 15), with the Teacher saying of the people who want to divert him from his path, "They are sowers of deceit and seers of fraud, they have plotted evil against me … and are not firmly based in your truth" (1QHᵃ XII, 9–10, 14).

Jesus' challenge in 8:46, "Who among you can convict me of sin?" (stated positively in 8:29) coheres with the affirmation in Isa. 53:9 that there was no deceit in the mouth of the Suffering Servant. Alluding to this passage, *Testament of Judah* speaks of the "Star from Jacob," in whom "will be found no sin" (24:1 [Christian interpolation?]). Jesus' calm, nonretaliatory response in 8:49 to the Jewish charge of demon possession, "I honor my Father, and you dishonor me," likewise evokes reminiscences of Isaiah's Suffering Servant (cf. 1 Pet. 2:23, alluding to Isa. 53:7). Jesus' charge in 8:55 that his opponents do not (truly) know God stands in continuity with the message of some of the OT prophets (e.g., Hos. 4:1; 6:6); later prophetic passages predict a time when people will indeed know God (cf., e.g., Isa. 11:9; Jer. 31:31–34; Hab. 2:14; see Carson 1991: 356). Nonetheless, even the prophets could not profess to be free from sin or to know God as Jesus did.

Jesus' statement in 8:56, "Your father Abraham rejoiced at the thought of seeing my day; he saw it and was glad," refers to Abraham's joyful anticipation of the coming of the Messiah. Jewish tradition took Abraham's rejoicing to refer to his laughter at the prospect (or actual birth) of his son Isaac. This interpretation was based partly on Gen. 17:17 (seen as joy, not scorn, as in Philo, *Names* 154–169; see Moloney 1998: 286; Brown 1966–1970: 360) and partly on Gen. 21:6 (cf. *Jub.* 15:17; 16:19–29; see further references in Köstenberger 2004: 272n100). Hence what may be at work here is a typology that extends from Abraham's son of promise, Isaac, to Jesus the Messiah (cf. Gal. 3; Rom. 4). The Jews' objection does not arise from the notion of Abraham foreseeing the messianic age; rather, the point of contention is Jesus' claim that the messianic age is "his day," in direct spiritual lineage from Abraham (cf. Gal. 3:16). Yet, according to Jesus, Abraham did indeed understand, however imperfectly, that the covenant promise that in him all the nations of the earth would be blessed (e.g., Gen. 12:1–3) involved God's future provision of a redeemer.

The claim in 8:58, "Before Abraham came into being, I am" (cf. Ps. 90:2), contrasts an allusion to Abraham's birth with a reference to Jesus' eternal existence, focused on his incarnation (Ridderbos 1997: 322–23). Jesus' language here echoes God's self-identification to Moses in Exod. 3:14 (cf. Isa. 43:10, 13; see Ball 1996: 195–96; Schnackenburg 1990: 2:224; Burge 2000: 263). Thus Jesus claims not merely preexistence—in that case, he could have said, "before Abraham was born, I was"—but deity (note the reaction to Jesus' claim in 8:59; see S. Motyer 1997: 159). The present instance of "I am" startlingly culminates earlier occurrences of this expression in this chapter (cf. 8:24, 28; see Freed 1983b).

Upon hearing Jesus say this, they took up stones to throw at him (cf. 10:31–33; 11:8). Stoning was the prescribed punishment for blasphemy (cf. Lev. 24:16; cf. Deut. 13:6–11; *m. Sanh.* 7:4; see Carson 1991: 358). However, such punishment was to be the result of righteous judgment, not mob violence (cf. Deut. 17:2–7; see Daube 1956: 306). People in OT times considered stoning righteous men such as Moses (Exod. 17:4), Joshua and Caleb (Num. 14:10), and David (1 Sam. 30:6). Stephen, the church's first martyr, was stoned on account of alleged blasphemy (Acts 7:57–60). Paul too was stoned, although he escaped with his life (Acts 14:19; 2 Cor. 11:25), as were other Christian saints (Heb. 11:37).

As at previous occasions, Jesus eludes arrest (8:59; cf. 7:30, 44; 8:20). In the present instance Jesus hides himself and slips away from the temple grounds, similar to God's *Shekinah* glory departing from the temple. As the evangelist has previously made clear, Jesus himself has now "pitched his tent" among God's people (1:14), and his body (to be destroyed and raised again in three days) is the new temple (2:19–21). In the OT, God dwelt (*šākan*) in the midst of his people Israel (e.g., Exod. 25:8; 29:46; Zech. 2:14–15 [2:10–11 ET]), and his glory filled both the tabernacle (Exod. 40:34–35) and later the temple (1 Kings 8:10–11). The withdrawal of Jesus' presence from the Jews in the present passage strikes an ominous note of judgment similar to the removal of God's favor from King Saul (1 Sam. 15:23) or David's

fear that God would take his Holy Spirit away from him (Ps. 51:11).

The Healing of the Blind Man (9:1–41)

The healing of the man born blind, narrated in chapter 9, is the sixth sign by Jesus narrated in the Gospel, chosen by the evangelist to demonstrate Jesus' messiahship. There are numerous parallels and contrasts between the present sign and Jesus' healing of the lame man in chapter 5 at the beginning of the larger unit of which the pericope is a part, 5:1–10:42 (Malina and Rohrbaugh 1998: 109; Culpepper 1983: 139 [cited in Witherington 1995: 194–95]; Köstenberger 2004: 277). The sites for both healings are pools (5:2; 9:7); both healings take place on a Sabbath (5:9; 9:14); in both cases the healing is made difficult by the attending circumstances (5:5: lameness for thirty-eight years; 9:1: blindness from birth); and in both instances Jesus' chosen method of healing is unconventional (5:8–9; 9:6–7). However, the healed men's responses could not be more different (Carson 1991: 366; Brown 1966–1970: 377; *contra* Beck 1997: 86–90; Thomas 1995: 18).

Restoring sight to the blind is considered to be a messianic activity in the OT (Isa. 29:18; 35:5; 42:7). Both Matthew and Luke set Jesus' healing of the blind in the context of the ministry of Isaiah's Servant of the Lord (Luke 4:18–19; Matt. 11:5/Luke 7:21–22; Matt. 15:30–31; 21:14; cf. Isa. 35:4–6; 61:1–2; see also Isa. 29:18; 42:7). John too patterns Jesus' ministry to a significant extent after Isaiah's portrait of the Servant of the Lord (see esp. 12:38–41; see also the commentary at 8:46, 49 above). In the context of this Gospel, the healing is cast in terms of "light/darkness" imagery. Just as Jesus is the light of the world by fulfilling Tabernacles symbolism (see 8:12), so also he shows himself to be the light of the world by giving sight to the blind man. The world, and the Jews with it, lies in darkness; whoever wants to walk in the light must come to Jesus.

This contrast between light and darkness is illustrated by the two main characters (Lee 1994: 162). While the blind man progresses from calling Jesus a prophet (9:17) to defending him against the Pharisees' charges (9:25), inviting them to become Jesus' disciples (9:27), correcting their doctrine (9:34), and confessing Jesus as Lord and worshiping him (9:38), the Pharisees, in a display of Johannine irony, are oblivious to their spiritual blindness (Talbert 1992: 158). Thus the Pharisees' guilt remains, while the man walks home not only with his physical sight restored but also spiritually changed—a believer and worshiper of Jesus (the paradoxical reversal between the blind seeing and the seeing being blind is in keeping with the dynamic unleashed by Jesus' ministry elsewhere, seen especially in the Synoptic parables; see also Matt. 9:12–13 pars.). Jesus, the one supposedly under investigation, has the last word in a scathing pronouncement that exposes the Pharisees' spiritual blindness. More than a mere miracle, this sign represents a highly symbolic display of Jesus' ability to cure spiritual blindness. As the present story makes clear, the only sin against which there is no remedy is spiritual pride that claims to see while in fact being blind.

The disciples' question in 9:2, "Who sinned, he or his parents, so that he was born blind?" (cf. 9:34), seems to reveal the customary direct cause-and-effect relationship established between suffering and sin in ancient Judaism (see the book of Job [e.g., 4:7]; *b. Šabb.* 55a, citing Ezek. 18:20). Underlying the disciples' question is the (well-intentioned) concern not to charge God with perpetrating evil on innocent people (cf. Exod. 20:5; Num. 14:18; Deut. 5:9). Although several passages in the OT and Second Temple literature strongly challenge the notion that children suffer for their parents' sin (e.g., Jer. 31:29–30; Ezek. 18; cf. Tob. 3:3), rabbinic speculation often took its starting point in OT texts such as Gen. 25:22 (the struggle of Jacob and Esau in their mother's womb; cf. *Gen. Rab.* 63:6) or Deut. 21:18–20 (*Tg. Ps.-J.* Deut. 21:20; cf. *Song Rab.* 1.6 §3; *Ruth Rab.* 6:4). Both Jesus and Paul, however, while acknowledging that suffering may be the result of sin (e.g., John 5:14; Rom. 1:18–32; 1 Cor. 11:30), denied that such was invariably the case (cf. Luke 13:2–3a; 2 Cor. 12:7; Gal. 4:13; see Carson 1991: 361). In the present instance Jesus maintains, in 9:3, that the purpose of the man's blindness was the manifestation of the work of God (cf. 11:4, 40, referring to seeing the "glory of God"; see Duke 1985: 118–19). Viewed from a spiritual vantage point, even evil can ultimately contribute to the greater glory of God (the most important example is the crucifixion [cf. 12:28, 37–41; 17:1, 5]).

Jesus' pronouncement in 9:4, "We must accomplish the works of the one who sent me as long as it is day," has several rabbinic parallels (cf. *m. 'Abot* 2:15; *b. Šabb.* 151b). Jesus' announcement that his earthly role would be limited in time (9:4–5; cf. 7:33–36; 12:35–36; 13:33) was contrary to the popular notion that the Messiah and the messianic age would last forever (cf. 12:34). The statement in 9:5, "I am the light of the world," links the present incident with the Feast of Tabernacles (see commentary at 8:12). The anointing of the blind man's eyes with mud in 9:6 may involve an allusion to Isa. 6:10; 29:9 (Derrett 1994: 251–54). Jesus' sending the man to wash in the Pool of Siloam in 9:7 (for ancient Jewish references, see Köstenberger 2004: 283–84) is reminiscent of Elijah's sending Naaman to wash in the Jordan (2 Kings 5:10–13). In mentioning Siloam (= Heb. Shiloah) in 9:7, the evangelist provides an aside, "which translated means 'Sent,'" which may invoke Gen. 49:10, "The scepter will not depart from Judah until Shiloh comes," a text that was interpreted messianically by both Jewish and Christian interpreters (see references in Köstenberger 2004: 284n30; and commentary at 12:15 below). As the Jews in Isa. 8:6 rejected Shiloah, so here they reject Jesus, the paradigmatic "Sent One" (cf. 20:21; for further background, see Carson 1991: 364–65; Köstenberger 2004: 283–84). After 9:7, Jesus is not heard from again until 9:35.

The (belated) mention of the Sabbath as the day on which the healing had taken place in 9:14 brings into play Jewish Sabbath regulations. According to the Pharisees, Jesus may have "broken" the Sabbath in the following ways: (1) since this was not a life-or-death situation, Jesus should have waited until the next day to heal the man; (2) Jesus kneaded the clay with his saliva to make mud, and kneading (dough, and by analogy, clay) was among the thirty-nine classes of work forbidden on the Sabbath (*m. Šabb.* 7:2; cf. 8:1; 24:3); (3) later Jewish tradition stipulated that it was not permitted to anoint eyes on the Sabbath, although opinion seems to have been divided (*b. 'Abod. Zar.* 28b) (Carson 1991: 367).

The division apparent in 9:16—"So some of the Pharisees were saying, 'This man is not from God, because he does not keep the Sabbath.' But others were saying, 'How can a sinful man perform such signs?'"—roughly follows the differing ways of reasoning followed by the schools of Shammai and Hillel (Carson 1991: 367). The former based its argument on foundational theological principles ("Anyone who breaks the law is a sinner"), while the latter argued from the established facts of the case ("Jesus has performed a good work") (Schlatter 1948: 227). Already in OT times the Israelites were warned against the appearance of a prophet or dreamer who would perform "a miraculous sign or wonder" to lead people astray (Deut. 13:1–5).

The Pharisees' exhortation to the formerly blind man in 9:24, "Give glory to God," constitutes a solemn warning to tell the truth (Conway [1999: 131] suggests "Tell us the truth" as a suitable idiomatic translation) and to make a confession, with the implication that the person so exhorted has done something wrong. The Pharisees' words echo Joshua's exhortation to Achan to confess his wrong in Josh. 7:19 (see also 2 Chron. 30:8 LXX; Jer. 13:16; 1 Esd. 9:8; *m. Sanh.* 6:2). The Pharisees' claim in 9:28 to be disciples of Moses is belied by their failure to listen to the one of whom Moses wrote (cf. 5:45–47; see further Köstenberger 2004: 291n59). The Pharisees' claim in 9:29, "We know that God spoke to Moses," harks back to the establishment of Israel as a nation through the giving of the Mosaic covenant at Sinai, where "the LORD would speak to Moses face to face, as a man speaks with his friend" (Exod. 33:11; cf. Num. 12:2–8; see Ridderbos 1997: 345; Carson 1991: 373).

The formerly blind man's major premise in 9:31–33, that God does not listen to sinners but rather to those who fear him and do his will, has ample OT substantiation. The Hebrew Scriptures establish a clear link between a person's righteousness and God's responsiveness to that person's prayers (Job 27:9; Ps. 34:15; 66:18; 109:7; 145:19; Prov. 15:8, 29; 21:27; 28:9; Isa. 1:15; cf. John 14:13–14; 16:23–27; 1 Pet. 3:7; 1 John 3:21–22). Later rabbis shuddered at the thought of God listening to sinners (cf. *b. Sanh.* 90a; *b. Ber.* 58a; see Barrett 1978: 363) and affirmed God's responsiveness to the prayers of those who fear God (cf. *b. Ber.* 6b; *Exod. Rab.* 21:3; see also Isa. 65:24).

The formerly blind man is also correct in his minor premise in 9:32, that the opening of the eyes of a person born blind was unprecedented.

In the OT the opening of the eyes of the blind was limited to unusual circumstances (e.g., 2 Kings 6:8–23), and instances of blind persons being healed in Jewish tradition were extremely rare (Tob. 11:10–14; cf. 2:10). Yet there is no evidence for the healing of a person born blind (Carson 1991: 374; Morris 1995: 422). The man's conclusion in 9:33, "If this man were not from God, he could do nothing" (cf. 3:2), likewise is firmly in keeping with Judaism at large, which regarded miracles as answers to prayer (see Brown 1966–1970: 375).

The fact that the opening of the eyes of the blind was to be one of the characteristics of the messianic age casts the Pharisees' opposition in the present passage as a failure to recall the prophetic promises to that effect (see Carson 1991: 375; Morris 1995: 422). Indeed, both giving sight to the blind (Ps. 146:8; Isa. 29:18; 35:5; 42:7, 18) and the blinding of those who see (Isa. 6:10; 42:19; Jer. 5:21; cf. Matt. 13:13–15 pars.; John 12:40) are common OT themes. This twin theme provides the framework for Jesus' concluding pronouncement on the Pharisees in 9:39–41 (see further the commentary at 12:40 below). The Pharisees' charge in 9:34, that the formerly blind man was born in sin, may allude to Ps. 51:5 (Köstenberger 2004: 293). The reference to Jesus as the "Son of Man" in 9:35, in light of its proximity to the reference to judgment in 9:39, in the context of John's Gospel harks back particularly to 5:27 (see commentary there).

The Good Shepherd Discourse and Jesus at the Feast of Dedication (10:1–42)

The Good Shepherd Discourse of 10:1–21 follows chapter 9 (which concludes with Jesus' indictment of the Pharisees' spiritual blindness in 9:39–41) without transition (note that the double *amēn* never begins a discourse in John; see also the *inclusio* in 10:21), which suggests that the audience remains the same (Ridderbos 1997: 352–53). The Pharisees' expulsion of the formerly blind man from the synagogue because of his faith in Jesus as the Messiah (9:34; cf. 9:22) places them within the trajectory of Jewish leaders who resisted the will and revelation of God in times past (cf. Zech. 11:17; 12:10 [cited in John 19:37]; 13:7 [alluded to in John 16:32]). Thus the dark backdrop of Jesus' Good Shepherd Discourse is the glaring irresponsibility of the Jewish religious leaders (see esp. France 1971: 104; Köstenberger 1998b: 133–38).

The present discourse bears a certain resemblance to Synoptic-style parables (see Schweizer 1996; both Greek words *parabolē* and *paroimia* render the Hebrew term *māšāl*; see Carson 1991: 383; Borchert 1996–2002: 1:329; Köstenberger 2004: 302n17; and commentary below) but is best classified as a "symbolic discourse" (Barrett 1978: 367, 370; Moloney [1998: 303, 309], citing K. Berger, calls it an "image field"), in which a given metaphor—here, shepherding (on the imagery of sheep and shepherd, see Keener 2003: 799–802)—provides the backdrop for extended reflection (see Köstenberger 2002a: 72–75; note the occurrence of the term *paroimia*, "illustration," in 10:6 [with reference to 10:1–5] and 16:25, 29 [referring to 16:21–24]). The discourse contains a whole web of OT allusions and echoes, with those to Ezek. 34 and 37 being particularly pronounced (Köstenberger 2002a; Deeley 1997; cf. esp. 10:8, 9, 11, 16, 33; see commentary below).

The metaphor of the "flock," an everyday feature of Jewish life, pervades the OT (see commentary below; on shepherding imagery in the OT and John, see Nielsen 1999: 76–80). God himself was known as Israel's Shepherd (e.g., Gen. 48:15; 49:24; Ps. 23:1; 28:9; 77:20; 78:52; 80:1; Isa. 40:11; Jer. 31:9; Ezek. 34:11–31; see Thomson 1955), and his people are the "sheep of his pasture" (e.g., Ps. 74:1; 78:52; 79:13; 95:7; 100:3; Ezek. 34:31). Part of this imagery was also the notion of chief shepherd and assistant shepherds and of hired hands. David, who was a shepherd before he became king, became a prototype of God's shepherd. Jesus saw himself as embodying the characteristics and expectations attached to this salvation-historical biblical figure as the Good Shepherd par excellence.

The references in 10:3–4 to the shepherd leading out his sheep until he has brought out all his own, and to him going on ahead of his sheep, may involve an allusion to Num. 27:15–18 (see esp. Num. 27:17; see also Ps. 80:1; Ezek. 34:13), a possible typological passage alluding to Christ (Carson 1991: 383; cf. Barrett 1978: 369; *contra* Schnackenburg 1990: 2:293; Moloney 1998: 308). In that passage Moses prays for a future figure who will lead God's people and bring them in, "so the

LORD's people will not be like sheep without a shepherd" (Num. 27:17; applied to Jesus in Matt. 9:36). The following verse mentions Joshua (Gk. *Iēsous*, "Jesus") as that successor (Num. 27:18; cf. Heb. 4:8–10). In addition, Israel's exodus from Egypt is occasionally portrayed in terms of a flock being led by its shepherd (i.e., God, by the hand of Moses and Aaron [Ps. 77:20; Isa. 63:11, 14; cf. Ps. 78:52]). OT prophetic literature holds out similar visions of end-time deliverance for God's people (e.g., Mic. 2:12–13).

Jesus' reference to himself as "the gate for the sheep" in 10:7, 9 may hark back to messianic readings of passages such as Ps. 118:20: "This is the gate of the LORD through which the righteous may enter" (note that this psalm is used in 12:13). Jesus' pronouncement in 10:8 (cf. 10:1, 10), "All who have come before me were thieves and robbers," takes its point of departure from the OT prophet Ezekiel referring to the "shepherds of Israel who only take care of themselves" but "do not take care of the flock" (Ezek. 34:2–4; see the entire chapter; see also Jer. 23:1–2).

Jesus' language in 10:9, "will go in and out," a Semitism, echoes covenant terminology, especially Deuteronomic blessings for obedience (see Deut. 28:6; cf. Ps. 121:8). It is also reminiscent of Moses' description of Joshua (LXX: *Iēsous*), who led Israel into the promised land (Num. 27:16–18). "Find pasture" (*nomē* [only here in John]) is a common OT expression (e.g., 1 Chron. 4:40). The psalmist basked in the assurance of God's provision (Ps. 23:2), and God's people are frequently called "the sheep of his pasture" (e.g., Ps. 74:1; 79:13; 100:3; cf. Lam. 1:6). The imagery is found also in OT references to Israel's final restoration (Isa. 49:9–10) and deliverance from the nations (Ezek. 34:12–15; note also the messianic reference in *Pss. Sol.* 17:40). The reference to the abundant life brought by Jesus harks back to OT prophetic passages, particularly in the prophet Ezekiel, who envisions pasture and abundant life for God's people (Ezek. 34:12–15, 25–31). As the Good Shepherd, Jesus gives his sheep not merely enough, but more than plenty (cf. Ps. 23; Ezek. 34; see Ridderbos 1997: 359; and commentary below).

In 10:11 Jesus says, "I am the good shepherd." In the OT, God as the true shepherd is repeatedly contrasted with unfaithful shepherds who are subject to divine judgment (Jer. 23:1–4; cf. 3:15; Ezek. 34; Zech. 11:4–17). David (or the Davidic messiah) is spoken of frequently as a (good) shepherd (2 Sam. 5:2; Ps. 78:70–72; Ezek. 37:24; Mic. 5:4; cf. *Pss. Sol.* 17:40–41; *Midr. Rab.* 2:2 on Exod. 3:1). Moses likewise is portrayed as the "shepherd of his flock" (Isa. 63:11; cf. Ps. 77:20; *Midr. Rab.* 2:2 on Exod. 3:1). Philo speaks of a "good" (*agathos*) shepherd (*Agriculture* 44, 49) and applies "shepherd" terminology not only to kings and sages but also to both God and his firstborn Son or Word (*Agriculture* 50–54; *Posterity* 67–68).

Jesus elaborates that the good shepherd lays down his life for the sheep (10:11). Young David, first shepherd, then king, literally risked his life for his sheep (1 Sam. 17:34–37; cf. Sir. 47:3). The phrase "to lay down one's life" is rare in Greek and may reflect the Hebrew idiom "to hand over one's life" (possible parallels include Judg. 12:3; 1 Sam. 19:5; 28:21; Job 13:14; Ps. 119:109). Several OT passages hint at the Messiah's self-sacrifice (see esp. Isa. 53:12). In a cluster of messianic references, Zechariah refers to a figure who is "pierced" and for whom people mourn, a shepherd who is put to death and whose death brings about a turning point (Zech. 12:10; 13:7–9; cf. Mark 14:27; John 19:37; Rev. 1:7).

The "hired hand" (10:12), in contrast to the shepherd, will abandon the flock in times of danger, putting self-interest first. This renders the flock an easy prey for those (like wolves) who would attack it. Both OT and later Jewish literature are replete with references to leaders who fail to perform their God-given responsibilities and as a result render their charge vulnerable to attack (e.g., Jer. 10:21; 12:10; 23:1–4; Ezek. 34; Zeph. 3:3; Zech. 10:2–3; 11:4–17; *1 En.* 89:12–76; 90:22–31; *T. Gad* 1:2–4). Shockingly, the shepherds themselves had turned into wolves (Ezek. 22:27). The "hired hands" of Israel (whose function is temporary) are contrasted with those who hold a permanent shepherding office: God and his Messiah, whose role is patterned after God's "good shepherd" par excellence, David (1 Sam. 17:34–36). The figure of the hired hand who abandons his sheep in times of adversity was wellworn in Jesus' day (e.g., *4 Ezra* 5:18).

In 10:16 Jesus says, "And I have other sheep that are not from this sheep pen; I must bring them also" (cf. 11:52; 17:20; see Köstenberger

2002a). In light of OT expectations of the incorporation of the Gentiles among God's people, the "other sheep that are not from this sheep pen" probably are Gentiles (see esp. Isa. 56:8; for Jewish material indicating that the Messiah would gather the Gentiles, see Hofius 1967). The present passage clearly indicates that Jesus envisioned a full-fledged Gentile mission subsequent to his cross-death (Köstenberger 1998b; Köstenberger and O'Brien 2001: 73–127, 203–26). Although this mission is to be carried out through his followers, the pronoun "I" makes clear that Jesus will be involved from his exalted position with the Father (cf. Matt. 28:18–20; Acts 1:1).

Jesus' statement "There will be one flock, one shepherd" represents an allusion to Ezek. 34:23; 37:24. The notion of one flock being led by one shepherd as a metaphor for God's providential care for his united people is firmly rooted in OT prophetic literature (Jer. 3:15; 23:4–6; Ezek. 34:23–24; 37:15–28; Mic. 2:12; 5:3–5) and continued in later Jewish writings (see *Pss. Sol.* 17:40; *2 Bar.* 77:13–17; CD-A XIII, 7–9). Yet whereas the OT envisions primarily the gathering of the dispersed sheep of Israel, the present passage refers to the gathering of Jews and Gentiles into one messianic community (cf. Eph. 2:11–22; 4:3–6; see Lindars 1972: 363). Though hinted at in certain later OT prophetic passages (e.g., Isa. 56:6–8; Ezek. 37:15–28; Mic. 2:12), the full revelation of this truth awaited the NT era.

The reference to "this command I received" in 10:18 invokes covenantal language, relating Jesus' relationship with his disciples to God's relationship with OT Israel (Köstenberger 1998b: 162n83, citing Pryor 1992). The references to division among the Jews "again" in 10:19 (cf. 9:16) and to the opening of the eyes of the blind in 10:21 (cf. chap. 9) constitute *inclusios* linking the Good Shepherd Discourse in 10:1–21 with the healing of the blind man in the preceding chapter (see commentary on 9:1–41 above). The charge against Jesus of demon possession, which harks back to similar charges earlier in the Gospel (cf. 7:20; 8:48, 52), and insanity is contradicted by the OT teaching that it is the Lord who gives sight to the blind (Ps. 146:8; cf. Exod. 4:11).

The Feast of Dedication, which is the occasion of Jesus' follow-up discourse and encounter with the Jews in 10:22–39, was not established in OT times but celebrates the rededication of the Jewish temple in December 164 BC after its desecration by the Seleucid ruler Antiochus Epiphanes (1 Macc. 1:59; Josephus, *Ant.* 12.320–321). The Jews' demand in 10:24, "If you are the Christ, tell us plainly," seems disingenuous: if they had not understood him to claim to be the Messiah, why did they repeatedly try to kill him (5:18; 7:25; 8:59; cf. 10:33 below; see Carson 1991: 392)? Indeed, Jesus replies that he did make this claim (10:25). The references to those who are and are not Jesus' "sheep" in 10:26–29 build on the Good Shepherd Discourse in 10:1–21 (on which, see commentary above).

Jesus' claim in 10:30, "I and the Father are one [entity]" (cf. 5:17–18; 10:33–38), echoes the basic confession of Judaism, "Hear, O Israel: The LORD our God, the LORD is one" (Deut. 6:4; the term "one" is neuter rather than masculine; Morris [1995: 464] suggests the rendering "one thing"). For Jesus to be one with the Father yet distinct from him amounts to a claim to deity (cf. 1:1–2). To be sure, the emphasis here is on the unity of their works (Ridderbos 1997: 371), yet an ontological (not just functional) unity between Jesus and the Father seems presupposed (see Carson 1991: 394–95). While this statement does not affirm complete identity, clearly there is more in view than a mere oneness of will between Jesus and the Father.

Consequently, Jesus' assertion of oneness with the Father challenged narrow Jewish notions of monotheism, even though there are already hints in the OT of a plurality within the Godhead, some of which Jesus was careful to expose (e.g., Matt. 22:41–46 pars.). Jesus' present pronouncement constitutes the first major climax in John's Gospel (the penultimate high point being 8:58; see Carson 1991: 395). The second, no less important, climax in 19:30 has Jesus cry from the cross, "It is finished" (see Hengel 1999: 319). Jesus' unity with the Father later constitutes the basis on which Jesus prays that his followers will likewise be unified (17:22; note again the neuter *hen*, "one").

The Jews' charge against Jesus in 10:33 appears to be grounded in Lev. 24:16, which says, "Anyone who blasphemes the name of the LORD must be put to death. The entire assembly must stone him" (see also Num. 15:30–31; Deut. 21:22). The present passage represents an *inclusio* with 5:18, which, together with 7:25, 8:59, and the present passage, punctuates the current section (chaps. 5–10) as part of an escalating pattern of controversy between Jesus and the Jews. Jesus' rebuttal in 10:34–38 involves an explicit quotation of Ps. 82:6.

10:34

A. The NT Context: Is Jesus the Son of God? The present scriptural quote, following on the heels of the Good Shepherd Discourse (10:1–18, 25–30), occurs in the context of a trial scene that focuses, seriatim, on the dual question of whether Jesus is the Christ (10:24) and the Son of God (10:33). In both cases the Jews mount an initial charge (10:24, 33) that is rebutted by Jesus (10:25–30, 34–38) but is rejected by the Jews, who unsuccessfully attempt to stone or arrest him (10:31, 39). With its dual focus on the question of whether Jesus is the Christ, the Son of God, the present scene anticipates Martha's confession in the following chapter (11:27) and the Johannine purpose statement in 20:30–31 (Daly-Denton 2004: 123).

A similar line of investigation is found in the Synoptic portraits of Jesus' Jewish trial before the Sanhedrin (Mark 14:62; Luke 22:67, 70). However, in contrast to the Synoptic Gospels, which locate Jesus' trial at the end of his ministry, John's Gospel has Jesus on trial throughout his entire ministry (see commentary on the temple clearing at 2:17 above). What is more, John's "trial motif" turns the notion of trial on its head by focusing not on Jesus' guilt, but on the Jews' culpability in rejecting their Messiah despite ample evidence to the contrary (esp. 12:37–41, on which, see below; see Lincoln 2000; Daly-Denton 2004: 124; Köstenberger 2005b).

After a heated dispute about the true spiritual origins of Jesus and the Jewish leaders, respectively, in chapter 8, and Jesus' indictment of the Pharisees subsequent to his healing of the blind man in chapters 9–10 (see esp. 9:39–10:21) and Jesus' claim to be one with God the Father (10:30), the Jews are once again ready to stone him (10:31). In response, Jesus asks for which good work they intend to stone him, exploiting a division within their own ranks (cf. 10:19–21). The Jews answer that it is not for any good work that they want to stone Jesus, but rather for blasphemy, "because you, being a man, make yourself God" (10:33).

It is in response to this charge of blasphemy that Jesus cites OT Scripture: "Is it not written in your law, 'I have said, "You are gods"'? If it [i.e., the law; see Köstenberger 2004: 314] called those 'gods' to whom the word of God came…'" (10:34). The quotation is from Ps. 82:6, which in its entirety reads, "I said, 'You are gods, and all of you are sons of the Most High,'" the only reference to Ps. 82 in the NT. In context, Jesus' purpose in adducing this particular OT passage in response to the Jews' charge of blasphemy "is an appeal to Scripture to justify His claim to be *one with the Father*, and to be His Son (cf. vv. 25, 29–30)" (Johnson 1980: 28). In essence, Jesus is saying that there is OT precedent for referring to humans as "gods."

In what follows Jesus adduces his works as evidence for his claim of divine sonship (10:37–39). It is his hope that when people see the kinds of works that he does—works that stand in continuity with those done by God the Father—they will recognize that Jesus does in fact stand in perfect communion with the Father and that he therefore rightfully claims to be God's Son. The present passage builds on previous similar encounters between Jesus and his Jewish opponents, most importantly the aftermath of Jesus' healing of the lame man in chapter 5. There Jesus, when accused of breaking the Sabbath, claimed to do his work in continuity with the Father, and he was promptly charged with blasphemy (see 5:18–21).

B. The OT Context of Ps. 82:6. The subject addressed in Ps. 82 is the judgment of unjust judges or rulers (Leupold 1959: 592, cited in Johnson 1980: 29). This psalm, attributed to Asaph, consists of an indictment (82:1–5), a verdict (82:6–7), and a plea (82:8) (Leupold 1959: 594–96, cited in Johnson 1980: 29). The statement "I said, 'You are gods'" is part of the section containing the verdict. God has put judges (or Israel) in an exalted position (82:6), but they will die an ordinary death because they failed to administer justice (82:7; cf. 82:2–5; cf. the references to Samson in Judg. 16:7, 17). The words uttered in Ps. 82:6 may be either those of the psalmist, who "had been under the impression that the pagan deities were of some importance, but now realizes that they are nothing, because they are quite incapable of defending the poor and rescuing the downtrodden" (Dahood 1968: 270), or those of God, who may recall a previous decree (Tate 1990: 330, 337–38).

C. Psalm 82:6 in Judaism. A reference to Ps. 82:1–2 is found in 11Q13 II, 10–11 in the context of Melchizedek freeing the sons of God from the hands of Belial. Hence the term *ĕlōhîm* is taken in this document as a reference to (evil) angels rather than human judges or OT Israel (cf. Johnson 1980: 31; see further §E below). Rabbinic tradition regards the psalm as being addressed to Israel or part of Israel (cf. the citation of Ps. 82:1 in *m. ʾAbot* 3:6; see Johnson 1980: 31–32).

D. Textual Matters. The quotation here is identical with the LXX, which is an exact equivalent of the Hebrew text.

E. The Use of Ps. 82:6 in John 10:34. The preceding Good Shepherd Discourse (10:1–18, 25–30), with its allusions to Yahweh's end-time Davidic shepherd envisaged by the prophet Ezekiel (e.g., 10:16 alluding to Ezek. 34:23; 37:24; see further below), provides the context for John's account of Jesus' reference to Ps. 82 in the present scene. The royal Solomonic-Davidic motif is underscored also by the external surroundings of the portico named after David's son Solomon (10:23) and Jesus' quotation of a psalm (albeit not attributed to David). Both the book of Psalms and the OT prophets can speak of Israel's king in highly exalted terms (cf., e.g., Ps. 45:7; Isa. 9:6; Zech. 12:8; see Daly-Denton 2004: 125).

Jesus' argument, in typical rabbinic fashion, is from the lesser to the greater (cf., e.g., 5:47; see Brown 1966–1970: 410; Morris 1995: 469; Schnackenburg 1990: 2:310; Moloney 1998: 316; *contra* Ridderbos 1997: 374). His practice of posing a question that proves too difficult for his opponents to answer is attested repeatedly in the Synoptics (e.g., Matt. 22:41–46 pars.; see Borchert 1996–2002: 1:343). Jesus' point is that if Israel can in some sense be called "god" in the Scriptures, how much more appropriate this designation is for him, "whom the Father consecrated and sent into the world" (10:36) and who truly is the Son of God (on the charge of blasphemy against Jesus, see Hurtado 1999: 35–58, esp. 36–37).

Jesus' commentary on the scriptural passage that he adduces commences, "If he called them 'gods' to whom the word of God came" (10:35). In the OT the phrase "to whom the word of God came" often is used with reference to those who speak or act in God's name. The expression "the word of the LORD that came" is found at the opening of the prophetic books of Jeremiah, Hosea, Joel, Micah, and Zephaniah (see also Luke 3:2). The phrase is used also with reference to David (1 Chron. 22:8) and Solomon (1 Kings 6:11) (see Daly-Denton 2004: 125). Fittingly, the backdrop for the present use of Scripture is the Feast of Dedication and a portico named for David's son Solomon (10:22–23).

In the original context the designation "gods" may have referred to, in order of likelihood, the following (see the survey in Schuchard 1992: 62–63): (1) Israel's corrupt judges who were called "gods" because the administration of justice was a divine prerogative delegated to a few select individuals (Exod. 21:6 [NIV]; 22:8–9, 28; Deut. 1:17; 1 Chron. 29:23; 2 Chron. 19:6–7; cf. Ps. 82:1–4; see Jungkuntz 1964; Johnson 1980: 29; Schnackenburg 1990: 2:311; Morris 1995: 467; Beasley-Murray 1999: 176–77); (2) Israel at the time of the giving of the law (cf. b. 'Abod. Zar. 5a; see Hanson 1964–1965; 1967; Ackerman 1966: 186–88; Ridderbos 1997: 373; Carson 1991: 398; Barrett 1978: 384; Schnackenburg 1990: 2:311); (3) angelic powers who abused the authority that God had given to them over the nations (Emerton 1960; 1966; this is unlikely in light of the scarcity of references to angels in John; cf. Tg. Ps. 82:6, cited in Johnson 1980: 30–31, with reference to Freed 1965: 63).

We may highlight several aspects of Jesus' argument from Ps. 82:6 in the present passage. First, there is a polemic point made (note the reference to "your" law in 10:34; cf. 15:25). Jesus' Jewish opponents, though willing to admit that corrupt human judges may be called "gods," were unwilling to accept, and in fact could not endure, that Jesus, sanctified and sent into the world by the Father, called himself "Son of God" (Johnson 1980: 33, citing Warfield 1948: 32). Thus Jesus' use of the OT in the present instance is aimed at pointing to an inherent inconsistency in the Jews' stance toward OT representatives of God and Jesus.

Second, Jesus' a fortiori argument follows the lines of a syllogism that may be expressed as follows (Johnson 1980: 33, citing Lenski 1942: 765): *major premise:* Scripture cannot be broken; *minor premise:* Scripture calls human beings to whom God's word came "gods"; *conclusion:* there is nothing inherently blasphemous in Jesus referring to himself as "Son of God."

Third, and most important, Jesus' argument at one and the same time breaks down the strict dichotomy erected between God and humans upheld by his contemporaries and on this basis claims divine sonship in a sense that represents a major escalation over the sense in which humans in OT times were referred to as "gods." OT history witnesses to a series of individuals who served as God's representatives, including judges, prophets, priests, and kings. God filled these individuals with his Spirit in order to enable them to accomplish a particular task or gave them his word, which they were to proclaim to his people. In these individuals, therefore, we find a paradigm of a union between the divine and the human, no matter how qualified or limited it may have been.

On the basis of this contention—the possibility of a union between the human and the divine—Jesus proceeds to assert that this type of union is realized in himself, and this in a sense is infinitely greater than had been done previously (Johnson 1980: 33, citing Bernard 1928: 2:368). Hence Jesus used the reference to certain Israelites in Ps. 82:6 as the substructure for his theology (to appropriate C. H. Dodd's terminology) of divine sonship, which is presented within the framework of John's "sending" Christology. As S. L. Johnson rightly points out, the incarnation is thus shown not to be alien to the spirit of the OT Scriptures and not standing in necessary conflict with the notion of monotheism, rightly understood. To the contrary, it is found in the OT in "typical anticipations" (Johnson 1980: 34).

F. Theological Use. Jesus' argument here may seem peculiar to our ears, but it is best understood as limited to the following point. For argument's sake, Jesus says that his claim of divine sonship does not necessarily involve blasphemy, since in the Hebrew Scriptures there are places where humans are called *ĕlōhîm* ("gods"). Psalm 82:6 is a case in point. Hence it is wrong for his opponents to consider him guilty and stone him for blasphemy merely because he claimed equality with the Father (10:30). Once again, Jesus proceeds to offer his works as evidence for the truthfulness of his claim of divine sonship (10:37–38; cf. 10:32).

This does not mean that Jesus' claim to a unique relationship with God fails to involve a claim to deity, for it does, as the Johannine prologue makes abundantly clear. It does mean, however, that Jesus' opponents must carefully investigate the nature of his claims rather than react to what they perceive to be a claim that conflicts with their notion of monotheism. Jesus' argument is of the rabbinic kind that rests theological weight on a particular word or phrasing of an OT passage (cf. Gal. 3:16). In the present instance the scriptural passage cited by Jesus provides common ground for further argumentation with his rabbinic counterparts.

For this reason it is best to understand Jesus' use of Scripture here in terms of analogy rather than typical fulfillment (*contra* Johnson 1980: 34). The analogy here extends to one point, and one point only: just as certain individuals in the OT Scriptures could legitimately be called "gods," so also can Jesus, without necessarily involving them or him in blasphemy and violation of monotheism. Of course, any analogy stretched beyond its limit breaks down. In the present case the limit constitutes the sense in which the term "god" could be applied to the referents of *ĕlōhîm* in Ps. 82:6 and to Jesus.

Jesus' statement in 10:35 that the Scripture cannot be broken is evidence for his belief in the inviolability of God's written word (in this case, the Hebrew Scriptures). Elsewhere, Jesus contended that "until heaven and earth disappear, not the smallest letter, not the least stroke of a pen, will by any means disappear from the law until everything is accomplished" (Matt. 5:18). In this belief, Jesus knew himself to be united with his Jewish contemporaries (Matt. 5:20; cf. 2 Tim. 3:16; 2 Pet. 1:20–21). In the present instance Jesus affirms, over against his opponents' claim that they alone upheld the authority of God's word, that he too has a high view of Scripture. By his statement, Jesus emphatically pits his Jewish opponents against the word of God and the inviolability of Scripture (Ridderbos 1997: 374).

Jesus' assertion that he was set apart and sent into the world by the Father harks back to passages in the OT and Second Temple literature where the term "set apart" referred to those appointed to fulfill an important task or office, be it Moses the lawgiver (Sir. 45:4), Jeremiah the prophet (Jer. 1:5), or the Aaronic priests (see Exod. 28:41; 40:13; Lev. 8:30; 2 Chron. 5:11; 26:18). Not only did Jesus replace previous sanctuaries (1:14; 2:21),

the Sabbath (chaps. 5; 9), the manna (chap. 6), and the light and water at the Feast of Tabernacles (chaps. 7–9), but also the present reference to Jesus' setting apart may recall the event behind the celebration of the Feast of Dedication: the consecration of the altar that replaced "the abomination of desolation" erected by Antiochus Epiphanes IV (see Carson 1991: 399).

Bridge: The Climactic Sign and Closing Indictment (11:1–12:50)

SURVEY

The present unit features Jesus' final visit to Jerusalem at the Passover and his performance of the climactic sign in this Gospel, the raising of Lazarus. Mary's anointing of Jesus for burial in chapter 12 becomes the occasion for Judas's antagonism to be revealed, which is given further expression at the supper in chapter 13. There are four explicit OT quotations in this unit, which are concentrated in two sections, 12:13, 15 and 12:38, 40.

The first cluster of OT references, taken from Psalms and Zechariah, identifies Jesus as the messianic king making his entry into the holy city, Jerusalem.

The second set of quotations, both from Isaiah, are adduced to account for Jewish unbelief in Jesus. OT allusions or echoes in chapter 12 possibly include a reference to Deut. 15:11 in John 12:8; echoes of the language of Psalms in John 12:27 (Ps. 6:3; 42:5, 11); allusions to the "lifting up" of Jesus in John 12:32 (cf. Isa. 52:13) and to the eternal origins of the Christ and Son of Man in John 12:34 (Ps. 89:4, 36; 110:4; Isa. 9:7; Dan. 7:14); and a possible allusion to Isa. 6:1 in John 12:41.

THE RAISING OF LAZARUS (11:1–57)

The raising of Lazarus constitutes the seventh and climactic sign of Jesus in this Gospel. Raising the dead is rare in the OT, occurring only four times: Elijah's raising of the widow's son (1 Kings 17:17–24); Elisha's raising of the son of the Shunammite woman (2 Kings 4:32–37); Elisha's "posthumous" raising of a dead man (2 Kings 13:21); and the witch of Endor's illicit bringing Samuel back out of the grave at King Saul's request (1 Sam. 28) (see also Ezekiel's vision of the valley of dry bones in Ezek. 37:1–14). Raisings of the dead generally were viewed in light of the final resurrection and as an expression of God's power to bring it about. The raising of Lazarus is one of only three such events in the Gospels.

As part of the climactic Johannine sign, the death and raising of Lazarus serves as a type for Jesus' own death and raising later in the narrative (see also 2:20–22). In the context of the narrative the raising of Lazarus triggers the Jewish leaders' resolve to have Jesus arrested and tried for blasphemy (11:45–57), so that John 11 serves a crucial bridge function between the narration of Jesus' ministry to the Jews in chapters 1–10 and the narrative of his passion in chapters 13–20 (Ridderbos 1997: 381). Significantly, the raising of Lazarus is more than a mere miracle; it is a "sign," a demonstration of Jesus' true identity as the Christ and Son of God (cf. 20:30–31). In addition, the Jews' opposition to Jesus' raising of Lazarus puts the last nail in the coffin, as it were, of the Jewish leaders and serves as the final damning piece of evidence against Jesus' opponents. A more powerful sign of Jesus' messianic identity could not be given.

By coming to comfort Martha and Mary after their brother Lazarus's death (11:17), Jesus fulfills one of the most essential obligations in the Jewish culture of his day. Martha's affirmation of end-time resurrection in 11:24 was in keeping with Pharisaic beliefs (cf. Acts 23:8; Josephus, *J.W.* 2.163; see Barrett 1978: 395) and those of the majority of first-century Jews (Bauckham 1998) as well as Jesus' own teaching on the subject (cf. 5:21, 25–29; 6:39–44, 54). The resurrection of the dead was the subject of lively debate between the Pharisees and their opponents (e.g., *b. Sanh.* 90b, referring to Deut. 31:16; Isa. 26:19; Song 7:9). Mishnaic passages likewise denounce those who refuse to affirm the resurrection of the dead (*m. Sanh.* 10:1; cf. *m. Ber.* 9:5).

Belief in the resurrection is also evident from the second of the Eighteen Benedictions: "Lord, you are almighty forever, who makes the dead alive. . . . Blessed are you, Lord, who makes the dead alive" (cf. *m. Ber.* 5:2; *m. Soṭah* 9:15; see Schürer 1973–1979: 2:456). The Sadducees (as well as the Samaritans), in contrast to the Pharisees, flatly denied the future reality of resurrection (cf. Matt. 22:23–33 pars.; Acts 23:8; Josephus, *J.W.* 2.165; *Ant.* 18.16; see Oepke 1964: 370; Meyer 1971:

46–47). The concept of Jewish corporate personality, wherein one continued to exist only in the lives of one's descendants, hardly provided satisfactory hope for many pious Jews in Jesus' day. Yet Jesus' message went far beyond what Martha had in mind; he himself was the resurrection and the life (11:25 [see commentary at 1:4: "in him was life"]).

Martha's reference to "the one who is coming into the world" in 11:27 takes up the messianic expression derived from Ps. 118:26 (Beasley-Murray 1999: 192), which is applied to Jesus by others in the Gospels (see esp. Matt. 11:3 par.; John 12:13 pars.).

Jesus' prayer at the outset of the raising of Lazarus in 11:41–42 (for a commentary on the various aspects of the prayer, see Köstenberger 2004: 344–45) finds an OT antecedent in the prayer of Elijah, "Answer me, O Lord, answer me, so these people will know that you, O Lord, are God" (1 Kings 18:37; cf. Ps. 118:21; 121:1; 123:1). A. T. Hanson (1973: 254) and M. Wilcox (1977: 130) contend that 11:41 is actually a quotation of Ps. 118:21a MT (see the discussion in Hunter 1979: 68), and Wilcox (1977: 131) further argues that Ps. 118:22 also resonates in the present passage via the "stone" motif (cf. the citation of Ps. 118:25–26 in 12:13, on which, see the commentary below; see also the possible allusion to Ps. 118:26 in 11:27 above).

The Jews' fear is that if they allow Jesus to go on like this, the Romans will come and take away their "place" (TNIV: "temple") and their nation (11:48; cf. 12:19; 2 Macc. 5:19). In Jewish literature "the place" (Heb. *māqôm*) may refer metaphorically to the Lord (e.g., *Gen. Rab.* 68:9; *b. 'Abod. Zar.* 40b), the promised land (2 Macc. 1:29), Jerusalem (*m. Bik.* 2:2), or the temple (2 Esdr. 14:7 LXX). Of these, the temple is the most concrete and climactic referent because it is located in Jerusalem, the capital city of the promised land, and the place where God himself dwells (Ridderbos 1997: 408; Carson 1991: 420). Importantly, the temple assumes a central role in God's judgment of Israel (Jer. 7:14; cf. 1 Kings 9:7).

Apparently, the Jews' repeated, traumatic (albeit temporary) loss of land and temple elicited the fear (at least on the part of its leaders) that God would once again visit the nation in judgment and allow them to be exiled and the temple to be destroyed if

Israel was disobedient to God. This concern resurfaces in another, later Sanhedrin meeting, when false witnesses testify that Stephen "never stops speaking against this holy place," predicting that Jesus would "destroy this place" (Acts 6:13–14). Later, Paul likewise is charged with teaching "all men everywhere against our people and our law and this place," as well as with defiling "this holy place" by bringing Greeks into the inner temple area (Acts 21:28).

The pronouncement by the Jewish high priest Caiaphas in 11:50, that it was better for one man to die for the nation than for the whole nation to perish, is firmly rooted in Jewish thought. Discussions frequently turned to 2 Sam. 20, where Sheba is slain while the city of Abel is spared, the argument being made that a person should be handed over rather than all people being killed only if such an individual is specifically identified by name (*Gen. Rab.* 94:9; cf. *t. Ter.* 7:20; for further references, see Köstenberger 2004: 352n142). In Jesus' case, of course, Caiaphas's words prophetically anticipated the substitutionary atonement that Jesus was to render, without thereby excusing Jewish (or Gentile) unbelief (11:51–52) (on the OT background for prophetic abilities of the high priest, see Köstenberger 2004: 352–53).

The reference to the "scattered children of God" in 11:52, in context, plainly refers to the Gentiles. Although Israel's end-time hopes were tied to the expectation that the "scattered children of God" (i.e., Jews in the Diaspora) would be regathered in the promised land by the Messiah (or Messiahs [cf. 1QS IX, 11]) to share in God's kingdom (Ps. 106:47; 107:2–3; Isa. 11:12; 43:5–7; 49:5; Jer. 23:3; 31:8–14, Ezek. 34:11–16; 36:24–38; 37:21–28; Mic. 2:12; cf. James 1:1), OT prophetic literature also includes frequent depictions of the Gentiles as streaming toward the mountain of the Lord (Isa. 2:2–3; 56:6–8; 60:6; Zech. 14:16; cf. 1 Pet. 1:1), and the Jerusalem temple is characterized as "a house of prayer for all nations" (Isa. 56:7; cited in Mark 11:17). Thus Jesus is here shown to anticipate the Gentile mission (cf. esp. 10:16; see also 12:20–21, 32).

The reference to ceremonial cleansing before the Passover in 11:55 is rooted in OT injunctions concerning ritual purity. Individual purification was necessary because ceremonial uncleanness

prevented a person from celebrating the Passover (see Num. 9:6; 2 Chron. 30:17–18; John 18:28; cf. *m. Pesaḥ.* 9:1). This need arose particularly for those who lived in contact with Gentiles, since the latter frequently buried their dead near their houses, which would make their Jewish neighbors subject to the purification commanded by the law (Num. 19:11–12). An OT law still operative in Jesus' day stipulated the need for ceremonial cleansing before the Passover for anyone who had become defiled, such as by touching a corpse (Num. 9:6–14). The appropriate purification rites might last as long as one week (Num. 19:12), so that many traveled to Jerusalem early, especially in light of the large numbers involved (Josephus, *J.W.* 1.229; *m. Pesaḥ.* 9:1).

The Anointing at Bethany (12:1–11)

The first scene in chapter 12 features the familiar characters of Martha, Mary, and Lazarus, joined with Jesus at a festive dinner in Jesus' honor (12:1–11). Mary's act of devotion briefly captures the spotlight (12:3), but the evangelist uses the anointing of Jesus for burial primarily as an occasion to reveal Judas's antagonism toward Jesus (12:4–8) (see Köstenberger 2001: 49–63). The time reference "six days before the Passover" in 12:1 (cf. 11:55) significantly places Jesus' ensuing passion within the context of that important festival (Barrett 1978: 410), which may intend to remind the reader that Jesus is the paradigmatic sacrificial lamb (Carson 1991: 427).

The response to Judas's objection by Jesus in 12:8, "For you will always have the poor among you, but you will not always have me," probably involves an allusion to Deut. 15:11: "There will always be poor people in the land." Jesus' point is that under normal circumstances concern for the poor has its place, but these are not normal circumstances. The Messiah is about to die, and Mary, in a gesture rich with prophetic symbolism, has met the need of the moment by anointing Jesus for burial. Hence faith and devoted discipleship triumph over religious observance and works. The Fourth Evangelist has sprinkled references to Jesus' coming "hour" throughout his narrative up to this point; now this "hour" is close at hand (cf. 12:23).

Jesus' Triumphal Entry into Jerusalem (12:12–19)

The second scene in chapter 12 is Jesus' triumphal entry into Jerusalem (12:12–19), at which Jesus is hailed by the people as the coming messianic king in the terms of two OT passages, Ps. 118:26 and Zech. 9:9. The people's waving of palm branches may signal nationalistic hopes that in Jesus a messianic liberator had arrived (cf. John 6:14–15; for a discussion of the history and symbolism of palm trees in ancient Judaism, see Köstenberger 2004: 369). In light of the disciples' failure to understand the significance of Jesus' actions at the time (12:16), it appears that both the crowds (which, as mentioned, cherished false nationalistic notions of the Messiah) and the disciples misunderstood Jesus' true identity at the triumphal entry.

12:13

A. The NT Context: The Triumphal Entry.
Jesus' triumphal entry into Jerusalem as told by the Fourth Evangelist is interwoven with Jesus' climactic "sign," the raising of Lazarus, which is narrated in 11:1–44, with the festive dinner and Mary's anointing of Jesus in 12:1–8 as a sequel. Immediately prior to the account of the triumphal entry the reader is told that the large crowd came not only to see Jesus but also to see Lazarus (12:9). John also reports a plot by the chief priests to put Lazarus to death as well (12:10–11). Following the account of the triumphal entry, the raising of Lazarus is mentioned once again (12:17–18).

The present citation of Scripture is the only one in this Gospel not preceded by a quotation formula. John's presentation here coheres quite closely with that of the Synoptic writers (cf. esp. Matt. 21:4–9; Freed [1961] maintains that the OT quotations in John 12:13–15 demonstrate Johannine literary dependence on the Synoptics, but see the rebuttal by D. M. Smith [1963]). At the onset of passion week Jesus enters Jerusalem in messianic fashion, mounted on a donkey, and is greeted by the crowd with the words of Ps. 118:26: "Hosanna! Blessed is the one who comes in the name of the Lord!" "The one who comes" was technical language for the Messiah or the end-time Prophet.

Although Jesus had frustrated earlier efforts by some of his followers to "take him by force to make

him king" (6:15), he now rides into the Jewish capital mounted on a donkey, in keeping with OT messianic prophecy. The reference to the people's waving of palm branches, which is unique to John's Gospel, while evocative of Feast of Tabernacles liturgy, may also suggest the people's nationalistic conception of Jesus' kingship (cf. 1 Macc. 13:51; 2 Macc. 10:7; see Daly-Denton 2004: 126–27). As is indicated by coins minted during the Jewish revolts of AD 66–70 and 135, the palm tree served as a national symbol in Second Temple Judaism.

B. The OT Context of Ps. 118:26. Psalm 118 appears to have been a royal processional psalm, perhaps sung in the temple during an autumn festival, begun outside the temple and continued inside (cf. Ps. 100:4). The psalm celebrates the king's vice-regency within the context of Yahweh's ultimate kingly reign. After the opening thanksgiving liturgy (118:1–4), the king is depicted as surrounded by his enemies but as eventually delivered by the power of Yahweh. In its original context Ps. 118 conferred a blessing on the pilgrim headed for Jerusalem (Brown 1966–1970: 457), with possible reference to the Davidic king (Carson 1991: 432). Verse 22, with its reference to "the stone that the builders rejected" that "has become the cornerstone," is quoted or alluded to repeatedly in the NT (Matt. 21:42; Mark 12:10–11; Luke 20:17; Acts 4:11; Eph. 2:20; 1 Pet. 2:4–7; see also Isa. 28:16).

The change of subject from the first-person singular to the first-person plural in 118:22–27 marks out this section as containing the congregation's exultation. Since the king was considered to be the Davidic representative, and the pattern of David's rule was seen as revived in the person of the actual king (Ps. 18), the application of the illustration of the chief cornerstone—rejected by the original builders, but chosen and precious in the sight of God—stands squarely in the line of messianic scriptural interpretation. Hence the people marvel at God's reversal of the fortunes of that "stone" (118:23) and exult that "*this* is the day that the LORD has made; let us rejoice and be glad in it" (118:24). The "day of the LORD" is therefore the day of God's deliverance and exaltation of the Davidic king from the "builders" who "rejected" him.

This deliverance of the Davidic king, in turn, corresponds to the personal experience of the psalmist (possibly the king himself or the priestly leader of the congregation speaking on its behalf), whose anguished prayers in distress were answered by the Lord's salvation (118:5–21) and issue in his closing prayer of thanksgiving (118:28–29). The speakers in 118:26–27 most likely are the priests who pronounce a blessing on the worshipers approaching the "house of the LORD." The first part of the blessing probably is addressed to the king and the second part to the festive congregation. Later, the phrase "he who comes" became a messianic designation (e.g., Matt. 11:3; Luke 19:38). The words in 118:27, "The LORD is God, and he has made his light shine upon us," are patterned after the Aaronic benediction in Num. 6:24–26 and may reflect a reference to the Sinai theophany (Weiser 1962: 728–29).

C. Ps. 118:26 in Judaism. Psalm 118 was well known in late Second Temple Judaism because of its association with the Feast of Tabernacles and as the final psalm of the Hallel, sung annually at the Passover. Later rabbinic commentary interpreted this psalm messianically (*Midr. Ps.* on Ps. 118:24; note also the interesting connection between a donkey and the "ruler from Judah" in Gen. 49:11; see further at 12:15 below). The term "hosanna," originally a transliteration of the identical Hebrew expression (lit., "give salvation now," "O save!"; cf. 2 Sam. 14:4; 2 Kings 6:26), had become a general expression of (festal) acclamation or praise (cf. Matt. 21:9; Mark 11:9–10).

Most familiar was the term's occurrence in the Hallel (Pss. 113–118), a psalm sung each morning by the temple choir during various Jewish festivals (cf. *m. Pesaḥ* 5:7; 9:3; 10:7). At such occasions every man and boy would wave their *lulab*, a bouquet of willow, myrtle, and palm branches (*b. Sukkah* 37b; cf. Josephus, *Ant.* 3.245), when the choir reached the "Hosanna!" in Ps. 118:25 (*m. Sukkah* 3:9). Some have suggested that the psalm took on eschatological significance in the postexilic period as it was recited as part of the Hallel during various Jewish feasts, with people anticipating a new exodus at which Yahweh would deliver his people through his Messiah (Brunson 2003: chap. 2, following Wright).

D. Textual Matters. The quotation in John is identical with the LXX and MT, except that the phrase *kai ho basileus tou Israēl* ("even the king of Israel") is added at the end (cf. 1:49; see also 18:37; 19:19). The phrase, recorded only in John, may have been added by the people to the Psalms passage (if so, it may constitute a second acclamation [and others], "The king of Israel!" [Coakley 1995: 477]) or represent an interpretive gloss by the evangelist, with "king of Israel" epexegetically defining "the one who comes in the name of the Lord" (Ridderbos 1997: 423; Barrett 1978: 418; Morris 1995: 520). The expression is in keeping with the emphasis on Jesus' royalty in this Gospel (especially in the passion narrative).

E. The Use of Ps. 118:26 in John 12:13. As we noted, Jesus' raising of Lazarus serves as a literary framing device for John's account of Jesus' triumphal entry into Jerusalem. In light of the fact that Jesus' "signs" are adduced by the Fourth Evangelist as proof that Jesus is in fact the Messiah and Son of God (12:37; 20:30–31), this places the account of Jesus' triumphal entry squarely within the framework of Jesus' messianic identity at the very outset. It is this very Messiah who had performed a series of christologically significant "signs" who now enters the holy city in messianic fashion as the paradigmatic "Sent One" of God (Brunson 2003: chaps. 5–7).

The Synoptics appropriate Ps. 118 by identifying Jesus as the Davidic king, speaking of "the Son of David" (Matt. 21:9; cf. 23:39; Luke 13:35), "the coming kingdom of our father David" (Mark 11:10), and "the King" (Luke 19:38); John's subsumes the psalm under his divine Christology (Brunson 2003: chap. 3). Together with the depiction in 12:15 of Jesus as the humble shepherd-king mounted on a donkey in terms of Zech. 9:9, this underscores the nature of Jesus' kingship, in contrast to both Jewish nationalistic and worldly conceptions (cf. 1:49?; 6:15; 18:36–37; and the references to Jesus as "king of the Jews" in the passion narrative).

F. Theological Use. Jesus is here presented as the prototypical, paradigmatic worshiper who comes to Jerusalem to render proper worship and who in turn is hailed by worshipers as Jerusalem's king. In the context of Ps. 118:22 and its NT usage (Lindars 1961: 169–85), John here appropriates Ps. 118:26 on the basis of his hermeneutical axiom that Jesus is the messianic king and Son of David who fulfills OT prophecy. Possibly, the new exodus and replacement themes are at work as well (Brunson 2003: chap. 4). A. C. Brunson (2003:

chap. 10) suggests other possible allusions to Ps. 118 elsewhere in John's Gospel (8:56; 10:7–10, 24–25; 11:41–42).

12:15

A. NT Context: The Humble King. Immediately following the crowd's citation of Ps. 118:26 with reference to Jesus in John 12:13, the evangelist narrates that Jesus found a young donkey and sat upon it (for a fuller description of how Jesus "found" the donkey, see Matt. 21:1–3 pars.; note the harmonization proposed in Carson 1991: 433; Morris 1995: 520–21). Jesus' choice of a donkey invokes prophetic imagery of a king coming in peace (Zech. 9:9–10), which contrasts sharply with notions of a political warrior-messiah (cf. 1 Kings 4:26; Isa. 31:1–3; *contra* Brunson [2003: chaps. 5–7], who believes that Jesus presented himself as a victorious warlord who had conquered death by raising Lazarus and stood ready to do so decisively by his own death and resurrection). By riding on a donkey, Jesus expresses his willingness to become the king of Israel (Ridderbos 1997: 424), though in more humble terms than the prevailing nationalism of the day. The evangelist duly notes that the disciples did not understand the significance of this event at first, but later they realized that what had happened fulfilled Scripture (12:16).

B. The OT Context of Zech. 9:9. Zechariah 9:9, "the prophet's vision of peace under the rule of a new David in Jerusalem" (R. L. Smith 1984: 255), starts a unit in the book that depicts the coming king of Zion and urges the "daughter Zion" (a common way of referring to Jerusalem and its inhabitants; the words are in apposition rather than in a construct relation) to respond by rejoicing greatly and by shouting aloud (the different meter in 9:9–10 marks the climactic nature of these verses [R. L. Smith 1984: 255]). This harks back to the reference earlier in the book, "Sing and rejoice, O daughter of Zion, for behold, I come and I will dwell in your midst, declares the LORD" (Zech. 2:10 [2:14 MT]; cf. Zeph. 3:14–15).

The king is described as "righteous" (cf. 2 Sam. 23:3–4; Ps. 72:1–3; Isa. 9:7; 11:4–5; 32:1; 53:11; Jer. 23:5; 33:15) and as "having salvation" (cf. Isa. 45:8; 46:13) or "saved" in the sense of "dependent on divine action" (cf. Ps. 33:16; see R. L. Smith 1984: 256; Meyers and Meyers 1993: 127), as well as "humble" (cf. Zeph. 3:12, where "humble"

is a corporate reference; contrast Absalom's action in 2 Sam. 15:1; see also Isa. 53:2–3; cf. Matt. 11:29) and as mounted on a donkey (Baldwin 1972: 165–66; cf. Gen. 49:10–11, where an early messianic prophecy speaks of a ruler from Judah who will command the obedience of the nations and who rides on a donkey; *contra* Leske [2000: 672–73], who disputes the messianic connection, claiming instead that the reference is to "the faithful people of Judah" [p. 677]). "Righteous" may include the notion of "rightful" or "legitimate"; "saved" may indicate that the king will not be empowered to rule without divine help; "humble" may suggest that the king will not benefit economically or socially by his position (Meyers and Meyers 1993: 126, 128). "Humble" may also be connected with Moses' meekness (Num. 12:3) and the Isaianic Suffering Servant (Isa. 53:4) (see R. L. Smith 1984: 256).

The donkey "stands out in this text as a deliberate rejection of this symbol of arrogant trust in human might"—that is, instruments of war (McComiskey 1998: 1166). In OT times donkeys were used by the sons of judges (Judg. 5:10; 10:4; 12:14), by Bathsheba's grandfather Ahithophel, a wise and respected counselor (2 Sam. 17:23), and by Mephibosheth, Saul's son, on the occasion of his visit to Jerusalem to meet David (2 Sam. 19:26). Indeed, Absalom's rebellion against David and David's return to Jerusalem subsequent to Absalom's death may constitute part of the background of the present passage (Jones 1962: 256–59, cited in R. L. Smith 1984: 256).

The primary emphasis in the present passage is on the dual nature of God's kingdom as one of peace (cf. Isa. 2:4; Mic. 4:3) and of universal scope (cf. Ps. 72:8) (see Petersen 1995: 56; R. L. Smith 1984: 257). Conversely, chariots, war horses, and battle bows will be cut off (cf. Zech. 4:6; Mic. 5:10–15). This marks a decisive rejection of a politics of violence and of the nations' practice of warfare in order to enlarge their territories.

C. Zech. 9:9 in Judaism. In keeping with notions prevailing in ancient Israel, two associations with the donkey were dominant in first-century Palestine: humility and peace. In contrast to the war horse (cf. Zech. 9:10), the donkey was a lowly beast of burden: "Fodder and a stick and burdens for a donkey" (Sir. 33:24; cf. Prov. 26:3). Donkeys were known also as animals ridden in pursuit of peace, be it by ordinary folk, priests, merchants, or persons of importance (Judg. 5:10; 2 Sam. 16:2).

A possible reference to Zech. 9:9 is found in 1QM XII, 13 (Baldwin 1972: 164n2). Rabbinic literature unanimously applies Zech. 9:9 to the coming of the Messiah (see the survey in France 1971: 188–89). Authorities cited in this regard are "the Rabbis" (including Rabbis Judah and Nehemiah, ca. AD 150; *Gen. Rab.* 75:6; 98:9), Rabbis Samuel (d. AD 254) and Joshua ben Levi (ca. AD 250; *b. Sanh.* 98a), Rabbi Levi (ca. AD 300; *Midr. Sam.* 14:9 [45b]), Rabbi Isaac (ca. AD 300; *Eccles. Rab.* 1:9 §1; *Gen. Rab.* 56:2), and Rabbi Joseph (d. AD 333; *b. Sanh.* 99a).

The rabbis had difficulty reconciling the humble notion of the Messiah riding on a donkey with that of the Danielic Son of Man "coming on the clouds of heaven" (*b. Sanh.* 98a). Riding on a donkey is one of the three signs of the Messiah in *Eccles. Rab.* 1:9, where the redeemer in Zech. 9:9 is the counterpart to Moses in Exod. 4:20. Two passages connect Zech. 9:9 with the messianic reference in Gen. 49:10–11 (*Gen. Rab.* 98:9; 99:8). In most cases the stress lies on the humble nature of the coming of the royal Messiah, the son of David.

D. Textual Matters. The introductory formula *kathōs estin gegrammenon* ("just as it is written") is Johannine, occurring elsewhere in the NT only in 6:31 (Menken 1996a: 81). The quotation does not agree precisely with either the MT or the LXX. At least four peculiarities of John's citation are noteworthy (Menken 1996a: 79–80):

(1) The phrase "fear not" is not found in the Hebrew or other versions of Zech. 9:9, replacing the expression "rejoice greatly." It may be taken from Isa. 40:9, where it is addressed to the one who brings good tidings to Zion (Carson 1991: 433; cf. Barrett 1978: 418; *contra* Morris 1995: 521n48; see also Isa. 35:4; 41:10; 44:2; Brown [1966–1970: 1:458] points to Zeph. 3:16; Menken [1996a: 84] thinks that both Isa. 40:9 and Zeph. 3:16 are in view). This sort of conflation of OT quotations is not uncommon in the NT (e.g., Matt. 27:9–10; Mark 1:2–3).

(2) John omits the characterization of the king riding on a donkey as "righteous and having salvation, humble" (cf. Matt. 21:5, where "humble" is included), including reference only to "your

king is coming [here omitting the phrase "to you," which is included in Matt. 21:5, perhaps since Jesus came not merely to Jerusalem but to the world; see Menken 1996a: 90–91], sitting on a donkey's colt."

(3) John 12:15c has "sitting" (*kathēmenos*) rather than "mounting" (*epibebēkōs* [Matt. 21:5]), perhaps to emphasize Jesus' royal dignity (Menken 1996a: 92–94, citing possible Davidic parallels).

(4) The final words of the quotation, *pōlon onou*, do not precisely agree with the Hebrew or any known Greek versions. Most likely this was taken from Gen. 49:11 LXX (Menken 1996a: 95; Schuchard 1992: 82–83; Freed 1965: 79).

Overall, it appears that the quotation is shortened in John to include only what is relevant to the actual context (Jesus' arrival as a king mounted on a donkey). Some think that the Hebrew text is used, especially at the end of the quotation; others believe that the Fourth Evangelist used the LXX or Matthew (21:5), or that he quoted from memory (see references in Menken 1996a: 81). There is little evidence for the direct use of Matthew, but it is hard to decide between the other possibilities, especially since in the relevant cited portions the LXX essentially coheres with the Hebrew text. The phrase "do not fear," as we noted, may derive from Isa. 40:9, added perhaps owing to John's drawing of a connection between the triumphal entry and the raising of Lazarus (Menken 1996a: 85–88); the expressions "sitting" and "colt of a donkey" do not conform to any known version and may have been used to emphasize Jesus' regal dignity in allusion to messianic passages such as Gen. 49:11.

E. The Use of Zech. 9:9 in John 12:15. In conjunction with the crowd's acclamation of Jesus as the one "who comes in the name of the Lord, even the King of Israel" (12:13), the evangelist's reference to Zech. 9:9, "Fear not, daughter Zion; look, your king is coming, sitting on a donkey's colt," designates Jesus as the humble shepherd-king entering the Holy City to assume his rightful place. His subsequent rejection by the Jewish people will result in his crucifixion and have important salvation-historical implications for the way in which God's future work is centered on a new messianic community made up of believing Jews and Gentiles (e.g., 10:16). Beyond this, John may conceive of Jesus' visitation of the Holy City in terms of Zechariah's "day of the Lord," when "living water will flow out from Jerusalem," the "LORD will be king over the whole earth" (Zech. 14:8–9; cf. 13:1), and a great Feast of Tabernacles will be celebrated by all the nations (Zech. 14:16) (see Daly-Denton 2004: 127).

It is unclear why John does not include the characterization of Jesus as "righteous and having salvation, humble" (by comparison, Matthew does include "humble" but not "righteous and having salvation"; see further in §D above). Nevertheless, this characterization still seems implied in John's appropriation of Zech. 9:9 and the depiction of Jesus as "sitting on a donkey's colt." Jesus certainly fulfills the imagery of a righteous and humble king who is dependent upon God's saving action for his rule, in keeping with the meaning of these descriptions in the original context of Zech. 9:9 (see at §B above): he is both righteous and the rightful and legitimate heir to the OT messianic and Davidic line of prophecy; he does not act independently, but rather stresses consistently his dependence on God the Father throughout his ministry; and he is humble—that is, he does not stand to profit politically or socially from assuming his reign.

Positively, the notion of Jesus' kingship conveyed by his triumphal entry into Jerusalem coheres with his depiction as the "good shepherd" in John 10. Negatively, it contrasts with Jewish nationalistic conceptions (1:49?; 6:15) and a worldly understanding of rule primarily in terms of power (18:36–37). In Jesus' case the medium is the message; the character of the king is indicative of the nature of his kingship, which stands in sharp contrast to both Jewish and non-Jewish notions of dominion. Because Jesus is rejected as king (12:36–50; chaps. 18–19), however, he constitutes, instructs (chaps. 13–17), and commissions the representatives of his new messianic community to spread his message of forgiveness in the power of the Holy Spirit (20:21–22).

F. Theological Use. In the present passage the Fourth Evangelist appropriates messianic prophecy and applies it to Jesus, designating him as the Messiah and the king of Israel. In the context of this Gospel this comes on the heels of Jesus' performance of a series of seven striking "signs" of his messianic power and is followed by the advance of Greeks/Gentiles in 12:20–36a and the evangelist's

concluding indictment of Jewish obduracy to end the first part of the Gospel in 12:36b–50. The fact that the evangelist quotes Zech. 9:9 but not v. 10 may indicate an awareness that the present fulfillment of the passage is only partial and that Jerusalem's disarmament and the proclamation of peace among the nations still await future realization (Baldwin 1972: 164).

THE DAWNING AGE OF THE GENTILES (12:20–36)

The third scene in the present chapter finds Greeks approaching Philip at the festival asking to see Jesus, followed by Jesus' response (12:20–36). Rather than granting these Gentiles an audience, Jesus, startlingly, announces that "the time has come for the Son of Man to be glorified" (12:23; cf. 1:51; 3:14; 8:28; 12:32–34). This striking statement may well hark back to Isa. 52:13, where it is said that the Servant of the Lord "will be raised and lifted up and highly exalted [*doxasthēsetai*]" (Carson 1991: 437–38). In pre-Christian usage the glory of the Son of Man and his function of uniting heaven and earth are conceived in primarily apocalyptic terms (Dan. 7:13; cf. *1 En.* 45–57, esp. 46, 48 [first century AD?]).

Jesus' expression of anguish in 12:27 (cf. 11:33; 13:21; see also 14:1, 27) may invoke texts in Davidic psalms such as Ps. 6:3 or Ps. 42:5, 11 (see the interchange between Beutler 1979 [modifying Freed 1965: 117–30] and Freed 1983a). This depiction of Jesus in Davidic terms, too, involves Davidic typology and adds to the presentation of Jesus in terms thoroughly prepared by OT messianic passages. The heavenly voice responding to Jesus' utterance in 12:28 (one of only three such incidents recorded in the NT; cf. Matt. 3:17 pars.; 17:5 pars.) likewise is not without OT precedents (see 1 Sam. 3:4, 6, 8; 1 Kings 19:13; Dan. 4:31–32; for references in Second Temple and NT literature, see Köstenberger 2004: 381–82n29). In particular, one notes an affinity between the present incident and Isa. 52–53 (see Evans 1981; for a comparison and contrast between the heavenly voice and the rabbinic concept of *bat qōl* [lit., "daughter of a voice"], see Köstenberger 2004: 382).

God's revelation in the context of thunder and through angels is well documented in the Hebrew Scriptures. Thunder was perceived to speak of the power and awesomeness of God (1 Sam. 12:18;

2 Sam. 22:14; Job 37:5). Perhaps most significantly, thunder was part of the theophany at Mount Sinai (Exod. 19:16, 19). God's intervention on behalf of his people is portrayed as a fierce thunderstorm sweeping down on his enemies (Ps. 18:7–15). In such instances the power of the Creator is tied to that of Israel's redeemer (Exod. 9:28; 1 Sam. 7:10; Ps. 29:3; cf. Sir. 46:16–17). The manifestations of God's power also highlight the contrast between his omnipotence and the idols' powerlessness (Jer. 10:13 = 51:16). Angels (or the angel of the Lord) spoke to Hagar (Gen. 21:17), Abraham (Gen. 22:11), Moses (Acts 7:38), Elijah (2 Kings 1:15), and Daniel (Dan. 10:4–11). Elsewhere, in the NT, angels are said to minister to Jesus (Matt. 4:11; Luke 22:43; cf. Matt. 26:53).

Anticipating his substitutionary cross-death, Jesus says in 12:32 that he, "when lifted up from the earth, will draw all kinds of people" to himself (that "lifting up" refers to Jesus' crucifixion is made clear by the evangelist's explanatory aside in 12:33). This third and most explicit "lifted up" saying in this Gospel in 12:32 (cf. 12:28) completes the earlier references in 3:14 and 8:28 (see commentary there) and, like these, draws on the terminology and theology of Isa. 52:13, particularly in linking the notions of glory and exaltation (Brown 1966–1970: 146, 478; Carson 1991: 444). The reference to "all kinds of people" in 12:32 (on the text-critical issue in this verse, see Köstenberger 2004: 388) at long last answers the Greeks' question at the outset of the present pericope: it is only subsequent to his cross-death that Jesus will draw "all kinds of people," Gentiles as well as Jews, to himself (cf. 10:16; 11:51–52; see commentary above).

Yet what is good news for the Gentiles is bad news for the Jews (cf. the reference to "many Gentiles" in Isa. 52:15 and the quotation of Isa. 53:1 in 12:38 below). The anticipation of the inclusion of the Gentiles in the orbit of salvation also indicates that the Jewish rejection of the Messiah has all but reached its full measure. The crowd's final messianic misunderstanding, involving the law's portrayal of the Messiah as eternal (12:34; see further below), is met with merely a faint exhortation on Jesus' part for them to "believe in the light" while they have it in order that they may become "sons of light" (12:36).

The people's reference in 12:34 to the Christ remaining forever finds its basis in texts such as Ps. 89:4, 36 (in turn grounded in 2 Sam. 7:12–16 [see commentary at 7:42 above]); 110:1; Isa. 9:7; Dan. 7:14. Palestinian Judaism in Jesus' day generally thought of the Messiah as triumphant and frequently envisioned his future reign to be without end. Such hopes were rooted in the Son of David, of whom it was said that God would "establish the throne of his kingdom forever" (2 Sam. 7:13; cf. 12:16). This prospect was nurtured in both the psalms (e.g., 61:6–7; 72:17; 89:3–4, 35–37) and the prophetic literature (Isa. 9:7; Ezek. 37:25; cf. Dan. 2:44; 7:13–14). It was affirmed also in Second Temple literature (*Pss. Sol.* 17:4; *Sib. Or.* 3:49–50; *1 En.* 49:1; 62:14; *4 Ezra* 7:28–29) and at the outset of Luke's Gospel (1:33).

Perhaps the closest parallel to the present passage is Ps. 89:37, where David's seed is said to "remain forever" (88:37 LXX: *eis ton aiōna menei*) (see Schnackenburg 1990: 2:395; for a summary and bibliographic references, see Köstenberger 1998b: 95n180). Notably, this psalm is interpreted messianically in both the NT (Acts 13:22; Rev. 1:5) and rabbinic sources (*Gen. Rab.* 97, linking Gen. 49:10; 2 Sam. 7:16; Ps. 89:29), but probably reference is made here not so much to any one passage as to the general thrust of OT messianic teaching (Barrett 1978: 427). Elsewhere in John people express the expectation of a Davidic messiah born at Bethlehem (7:42) and of a hidden messiah to be revealed at the proper time (7:27; cf. 1:26). As to the juxtaposition of the terms "Christ" and "Son of Man," it is unclear whether Palestinian Jews in Jesus' day, whose concept of the Messiah was bound up largely with the expectation of the Davidic king, also linked the Coming One with the apocalyptic figure of the Son of Man (cf. Dan. 7:13–14; see de Jonge 1974).

The people's question in 12:34, "Who is this 'Son of Man'?" (cf. 1:51; 9:35–36), may pertain to the nature of the Son of Man (i.e., "What kind of Son of Man are you speaking of?") rather than his identity (Ridderbos 1997: 441). L. Morris (1995: 532) thinks the crowd asks what the function of the Son of Man is and whether he is one and the same as the Messiah. D. A. Carson (1991: 445) observes that although four months earlier the Jewish authorities were unclear whether Jesus used the "Son of Man" title messianically, the less knowledgeable crowd, already ripe with messianic expectations, made the "Son of Man = Messiah" connection. Yet, if taken at face value, the crowd's question reveals not understanding, but misunderstanding, even ignorance, or at least confusion (rightly Morris 1995: 533).

In response to the people's messianic speculation, Jesus urges that this is the time for action, not idle conjecture. For people will have the light with them for just "a little while" longer (cf. 7:33; 16:16–19). Although Jesus does not answer the crowd's question directly, the discerning reader of the Gospel understands that he already has: his eternality is a function of his impending glorification (Carson 1991: 446). R. E. Brown (1966–1970: 1:479) rightly notes that the people's need was not so much to come to terms with the exact nature of the Son of Man as to face up to the judgment associated with him. Thus Jesus, in a way, really does address the crowd's deeper need at that hour: in light of the brevity of time, they must believe while this is still possible; messianic speculation will soon give way to the harsh realities of crucifixion and judgment. To be sure, the Messiah remains forever, "but it is only the incarnation of the Word and the descent of the Son of man in and from which the Messiah's 'remaining forever' can be known and understood" (Ridderbos 1997: 442).

The reference to "the light" in 12:35–36 harks back particularly to 9:4; 11:10 and provides an *inclusio* with the references to Jesus as the light in the prologue. The term "move about" or "walk" (*peripateō*), which is used by Jesus in 12:35, frequently occurs in John's Gospel in a figurative sense in conjunction with light and darkness (see 8:12; 11:9–10; cf. 1 John 1:6–7; 2:11; see also 1:4–5, 7–9; 3:19–21; 9:4). Similar terminology is found in the Qumran literature (1QS III, 20–21; cf. IV, 11).

The notion of "walking in the light/darkness" in John resembles the thought in the Dead Sea Scrolls that these are the two ways in which people may walk. Probably both John and the Dead Sea Scrolls hark back independently to OT terminology, especially Isaiah (e.g., 50:10 [see Morris 1995: 533]; 9:2, quoted in Matt. 4:16). The important difference between John and the Dead Sea Scrolls is that the former calls people to "believe in the light," while the latter assume that the members

of the community are already "sons of light" (see Morris 1995: 534).

"Son of . . ." reflects a Hebrew idiom; the expression "sons of light," however, is unattested in rabbinic literature. A "son of light" displays the moral qualities of "light" and has become a follower of the "light" (cf. Luke 16:8; Eph. 5:8; 1 Thess. 5:5). This expression is also common in the Dead Sea Scrolls, where it designates members of the Qumran community (e.g., 1QS I, 9; II, 16; III, 13, 20–21, 24–25; 1QM I, 1, 3, 9, 11, 13). "Born of light" occurs in *1 Enoch* (108:11; see also *T. Naph.* 2:10).

After this, Jesus left and hid himself from them (12:36; see commentary at 8:59; see also 7:4, 10; 18:20). The present passage constitutes a dramatic illustration of the passing of the light (Brown 1966–1970: 479) and an acted parable of the judicial warning that Jesus had just pronounced (Carson 1991: 447). What had begun with Jesus' prophetic visitation of the temple, where the temple area was cleared in a predictive display of divine judgment, now closes with an ominous reference to Jesus' self-concealment. Thus the incarnate Word, which had come into the world to give a full account of the Father (1:18), concludes its revelatory work. Thus the reference to Jesus' withdrawal serves as a climax to the series of preceding warnings and as a transition to the evangelist's theological reflections on unbelief that conclude the first major section of this Gospel (Carson 1991: 447).

THE SIGNS OF THE MESSIAH AND ISRAEL'S REJECTION (12:37–50)

The concluding section of chapter 12 provides the denouement of Jesus' public ministry to the Jews, consisting of the evangelist's placing the Jewish rejection of the Messiah in a scriptural context (12:37–43) and a summary of Jesus' message (12:44–50). The evangelist's indictment that "even though he [Jesus] had performed such great signs before them, they were not believing in him" establishes a link between the Jews' failure to believe during Jesus' day and the unbelief displayed by the wilderness generation. Just as that generation of Israelites had witnessed God's mighty acts of power (performed through Moses) at the exodus (Deut. 29:2–4; note the use of *sēmeia* in Exod. 10:1–2; Num. 14:11, 22; Deut. 4:34; 6:22; 29:3 [29:2 LXX]; 34:11; see Carson 1991:

447; Ridderbos 1997: 444; Brown 1966–1970: 485), so also the Jews in Jesus' day had witnessed a series of startling displays of Jesus' messianic identity (of which the Fourth Evangelist selects seven striking exemplars), culminating in the raising of Lazarus, which foreshadowed Jesus' own resurrection and presented Jesus in his very own person as the resurrection and the life. Yet, as John 6 demonstrates, like their Israelite counterparts in the wilderness, Jesus' Jewish contemporaries responded with "grumbling" (6:41, 61; cf. Exod. 17:3; Num. 11:1; 14:27, 29; 17:5, 10) and unbelief (12:39) rather than in faith (note the use of *pisteuō* in Isa. 53:1 and in John 12:37 and passim; see Schuchard 1992: 89).

12:38

In 12:38, 40 the texts of Isa. 53:1; 6:10 are brought together by the principle of *gezerah shavah*, "equivalence of expression" (Evans [1989: 132–34], who also notes the probable allusion to Isa. 6:9 in John 9:39). The internal logic connecting both passages is that the people's rejection of God's servant depicted in Isa. 53 is predicated upon their hardening mentioned in Isa. 6:10 (an instance of the scriptural "obduracy motif" [Evans 1987]). Both passages also share the themes of exaltation (*hypsēlos/hypsoō*) and glory (*doxa/doxazō*) (cf. Isa. 6:1, 3, 5, 7, 9; 52:12, 13, 15; see also *akoē* in 6:9; 53:1; see Carson 1988: 249, with reference to Evans 1987; Dodd 1953: 247; see also Evans 1989a: 133).

For this reason it is likely that John, by using a midrashic technique in chapter 12, identifies Jesus as the Isaianic Suffering Servant of the Lord (France 1971: 110–35; and several essays in Bellinger and Farmer 1998; *contra* Hooker 1959 and her essay in Bellinger and Farmer 1998: 88–103). In fact, as we noted, John 12:32 most likely alludes to the reference to the Suffering Servant being "lifted up" in Isa. 52:13, which brings into play the notion of Jesus being not merely crucified but also exalted and honored by God, which allows John to counteract the Jewish notion that crucifixion represents God's curse upon an individual.

Most likely, John's use of the OT in 12:38, 40 goes back to Jesus himself (Bellinger and Farmer 1998: 80–81; the classic study is Wolff 1984 [1942]; see the introduction by Stuhlmacher on pp. 7–11). Whereas 12:38 follows the LXX, 12:40 clearly does not. Whatever the reason, this hardly constitutes evidence for 12:40 having been added by an "ecclesiastical redactor" (so Bultmann 1971: 452–53; see further below). On the whole, the present passage is designed to show that it is precisely through the Servant's suffering and death that he (as the Danielic Son of Man) comes to be glorified. For John, Jesus' death is part and parcel of his glorification and exaltation as the obedient Son of the Father.

A. The NT Context: The Rejection of Jesus' Message by the Jews. At the end of his account of Jesus' public ministry to the Jews, the Fourth Evangelist notes in 12:36 that Jesus "departed and hid himself from them" (i.e., the Jews). This signifies a note of judgment, which is elaborated upon in the following fulfillment quotations from the book of Isaiah. Closing the book on Jesus' ministry to the Jews, the evangelist notes, "Though he had done so many signs before them, they still did not believe in him" (12:37; cf. 2:11, 18, 23; 4:45–48, 54; 6:14; 7:31; 8:30–31; 11:47; 12:11). This makes clear that the responsibility for the "failure" of Jesus' mission does not lie in Jesus' lack of revelation of God and of his own messianic power and mission; rather, it lies squarely in the people's obduracy, which is confirmed by their negative response to a series of "signs" climaxing in Jesus' raising of Lazarus, which anticipates Jesus' own resurrection.

While the evangelist's opening statement in 12:37 focuses on the Jews' continued unbelief, which confirms them in their obduracy, the following quotations from Isaiah make clear that behind their rejection of Jesus as the Messiah ultimately stands the judicial hardening of God, which in turn fulfills a pattern of scriptural prediction: "So that the word spoken by the prophet Isaiah might be fulfilled, 'Lord, who has believed what he heard from us, and to whom has the arm of the Lord been revealed?'" (12:38, quoting Isa. 53:1). This first instance of the phrase "this was to fulfill" (*hina plērōthē*) leads off a series of OT quotations that stress the fulfillment of prophecy in the events of Jesus' life, especially those surrounding his crucifixion (cf. 13:18; 15:25; 17:12; 19:24, 36; see Evans 1982a; 1987, esp. 225–26; cf. Matt. 1:22; 2:15, 17, 23; 4:14; 8:17; 12:17; 13:35; 21:4; 27:9).

B. The OT Context of Isa. 53:1. Isaiah 53:1 follows the reference to the Servant of the Lord, who was rejected by the people but exalted by God (cf. the prologue in 52:13–15). In the immediate context the verse harks back to 52:7, where reference is made to those who bring good news of peace and salvation and who say to Zion, "Your God reigns" (see the collocation of 52:7 and 53:1 in Rom. 10:15–16). In the context of the second major unit of Isaiah the passage ties in with the earlier reference to the messengers commissioned to say to the cities of Judah, "Behold your God!" in 40:9, a passage that, in turn, builds on the message of the "voice crying in the wilderness" cited in 40:3 (Watts 1985–1987: 2:226; see commentary at John 1:23 above).

Yet the prophetic message (cf. Isa. 28:9, 19) is not only of good news but also of impending suffering. The appearance of God's "servant" will be marred beyond recognition (52:14); he will "startle many nations" (52:15 NRSV; cf. LXX: *thaumasontai*; TNIV: "sprinkle"); people will despise and reject him, a man of sorrows and acquainted with grief (53:3). Yet he was wounded for our transgressions and crushed for our iniquities, and his chastisement brought us peace (53:5). He was taken away in judgment, cut off from the land of the living, and buried (53:8–9), all in accordance with God's will (53:10). In the end, however, the servant's days will be prolonged, and he will see his offspring and make many righteous (53:10–11).

The verse immediately preceding 53:1 (52:15) asserts that those who had not been told of the servant would see and understand that which they had not previously heard. Paul cites this passage as support for his belief that it was fulfilled in his apostolic preaching of the gospel to the Gentiles (Rom. 15:20–21). Hence, in the context of Isa. 53:1, the prophetic message and the revelation of God's power (in the OT, "arm/hand of the LORD" frequently serves as a figurative expression for God's power, including in the exodus narrative; see Exod. 6:1, 6; 15:16; 32:11; Deut. 3:24; 4:34; 5:15; 6:21; 7:8, 19; 9:26, 29; 11:2; 26:8; Isa. 40:10; 48:14; 51:5, 9; 52:10; 63:5; cf. Luke 1:51) clearly entail the vicarious sacrifice and subsequent exaltation of the Servant of the Lord (cf. esp. 52:13; see Oswalt 1986–1998: 1:381n85).

Yet implied in Isa. 53:1 is also the notion of the people's unbelief in the prophet's message of salvation in the Servant of the Lord. Not only

this, but unbelief is characteristic also of God's own people Israel (see the quotation of Isa. 65:2 in Rom. 10:21). As in the days of Moses, Israel fails to recognize the power of God when it is revealed to them. This will inexorably lead to judgment. In the preceding chapters (49–52) God has promised to deliver his people who are estranged from him so that they can fulfill their mission in and to the world. Now we are told how God will fulfill this promise. Despite the patent and persistent disobedience of his people, God will pursue his salvation purposes through the prophetic message and through the ministry and vicarious sacrifice of his Suffering Servant. It is in this Suffering Servant that God's salvific purposes are centered and fulfilled, and the Servant's rejection by God's own people is part of these purposes rather than something that thwarts them.

C. Isa. 53:1 in Judaism. *Targum Isaiah* 53:8 makes reference to miracles to be done in the messianic age (Bellinger and Farmer 1998: 80). *Targum Jonathan* interprets the Servant of the Lord of Isa. 53 not as a collective reference to true Israel, but messianically (Bellinger and Farmer 1998: 73).

D. Textual Matters. The quotation in John is identical to the LXX, which in turn matches the MT (Freed 1965: 85; Evans 1982a: 80). However, the MT lacks the Hebrew equivalent of *kyrie* (cf. Rom. 10:16). It is possible that John is dependent on a Hebrew *Vorlage* reflected in the LXX but not preserved in the MT. Alternatively, John here follows the LXX.

E. The Use of Isa. 53:1 in John 12:38. The Fourth Evangelist cites Isa. 53:1 as evidence for his contention that the Jewish rejection of Jesus is supported by, and in fact fulfills, Scripture rather than being in conflict with it. The hermeneutical axiom underlying John's appropriation of this passage is the conviction that Jesus is the Messiah, who in turn is identified with the Servant of the Lord, featured in the Isaianic Servant Songs. The typology extends not only to the linkage between Isaiah and his message, on the one hand, and Jesus and his message, on the other, but also to the rejection of Isaiah's message by his contemporaries and the rejection of Jesus' message and signs ("arm of the Lord") by the same trajectory of people. According to the Fourth Evangelist, Jewish rejection of God's words is nothing new: just as Isaiah's mission and message had been rejected, so also were Jesus and his ministry (Ridderbos 1997: 444).

F. Theological Use. The appropriation of Isa. 53:1 in John 12:38 serves the primary purpose of theodicy—that is, vindicating God's righteousness in condemning those who had rejected Jesus and his ministry. As we noted, underlying John's use of Isa. 53:1 in the present passage is the belief that Jesus was in fact the Messiah promised in the OT.

The Jews' failure to believe during Jesus' day is shown to be part of the trajectory of Jewish unbelief throughout Israel's history reaching back at least as far as to the unbelief of the wilderness generation, which had witnessed God's mighty acts of power (displayed through Moses) at the exodus (cf. Deut. 29:2–4; see Carson 1991: 447; Ridderbos 1997: 444; Brown 1966–1970: 485–86; see further below).

Interestingly, Paul cites Isa. 53:1 in Rom. 10:16 in the context of Jewish unbelief and the preaching of the gospel to the Gentiles (Bellinger and Farmer 1998: 75–76, 208–9). Hence the trajectory is further extended from Isaiah's prophetic ministry to Jesus' message to Paul's preaching. This is evidence that the early church, following Jesus, believed that the good news of salvation spoken of in Isa. 52:7; 53:1 was proclaimed by Jesus and the Christian gospel.

Another important NT passage utilizing Isa. 53 is 1 Pet. 2:22–25, which, in midrashic form, alludes to Isa. 53:4, 5, 6, 7, 9 (see also Rom. 4:25; 5:19; 1 Cor. 15:3; Gal. 1:4; 2:20; Phil. 2:7–9; Heb. 9:28). Isaiah 53 also played a significant role in the Jewish-Christian debate in the patristic period (*1 Clem.* 16, citing Isa. 53:1–12; Justin Martyr, *Dial.* 13, citing Isa. 52:10–54:6; *1 Apol.* 50–51, citing Isa. 52:13–53:12).

12:40

A. The NT Context: God's Judicial Blinding of the Jews to Jesus. The reference to Isa. 6:10 in John 12:40 is the second of two references to Isaiah by the Fourth Evangelist at the onset of the closing section of the first part of his Gospel. Hence Isaiah is called upon to pronounce the concluding verdict on the Jews' rejection of Jesus as the Christ and the Son of God. In both cases the Jews' conduct is shown to "fulfill" Scripture, commencing the series of OT quotations that stress the fulfillment of Scripture in and through the

ministry and death of Jesus. In the first instance Jewish unbelief in Jesus' message is shown to mirror typologically Jewish unbelief in the face of God's message through the prophet Isaiah. In the second instance Jewish unbelief and the Jews' rejection of Jesus are said even to be a consequence of God's judicial hardening of the Jews. As the evangelist states, "Therefore they could not believe" (12:39). This statement echoes Jesus' earlier pronouncement of judgment on the Jewish leaders on account of their spiritual blindness and pride (9:39–41) and his insistence that the Jewish leaders did not believe because they were not part of his flock (10:26). Isaiah 6:10 is cited by several other NT writers (cf. Matt. 13:13–15 pars.; Acts 28:26–27), which C. H. Dodd (1952: 38–39) takes as evidence that Isa. 6:10 served as a *testimonium* in the early church whose primary relevance was to provide a rationale for the Gentile mission (see also Michaels 1989: 233).

B. The OT Context of Isa. 6:10. It is important to locate Isa. 6:10 within the context of the entire chapter and within the structure of the book as a whole (see Evans 1989a: 17–52; Robinson 1998). Isaiah 6 begins a new scene, as is indicated by a chronological marker, a first-person reference (chap. 7 changes to the third person; cf. 1 Kings 22:17, 19–23; Amos 7:1–9; Zech. 1:8–6:8; and the visions of Jeremiah and of Ezekiel), and a monologue. The chapter opens with a throne-room scene (6:1–4), which is followed by an account of the purging of the prophet's sin (6:5–7), a delineation of the task for "this people" (6:8–10), the question, "How long, O LORD?" (6:11), and the follow-up question of the fate of any who survive and return (6:12–13; cf. Gen. 18:23–25).

Contrary to a commonly held view, Isa. 6 does not constitute a "call narrative" as does Ezek. 1—"send" is never used of a "call," but always of a specific mission or message (Wildberger 1991: 240, cited in Watts 1985–1987: 1:70)—but rather marks the conclusion of the unit on Uzziah (d. 740 BC) (see the connections between Isa. 1:2–9 and 6:9–10 adduced in Robinson 1998: 177). The chapter's purpose is to show that God's actions toward Israel and Judah will remain the same as they had been in the days of Uzziah until the eventual judgment strikes. Hence Isa. 6 "stands in a tradition in which God reveals (and in some measure defends) his decisions to bring judgment"

(Watts 1985–1987: 1:72; see the examples cited there).

In Isa. 6:9 God is shown to accept the volunteer's offer, "Here I am! Send me" (6:8), and to send him to "this people"—that is, his covenant people Israel (cf. Isa. 1:3; 2:6; 3:12, 15; 5:13, 25; 8:6, 11; contrast the more endearing phrase "my people" elsewhere in the Hebrew Scriptures; see Oswalt 1986–1998: 1:188). The MT makes clear that the people's hardening toward God's purposes is not merely the result of their own volition, but rather is brought about actively by the prophetic messenger. This is similar to the lying spirit's role in 1 Kings 22:20–23 and to the hardening of Pharaoh's heart in the exodus saga (cf., e.g., Exod. 8:32 with 9:12; see also Rom. 9:17–18).

Thus Isaiah's success is not determined by or dependent on a positive response on the part of the people, but rather by his faithfulness to his commission from God (Oswalt 1986–1998: 1:189–90, citing Jenni 1959: 338). Just as an obedient response by a receptive audience is success, so also is a rejection of the prophetic message with resulting judgment, if success is understood as fulfillment of God's purposes in and through his spokesperson (see the entire book of Jeremiah). Normally, however, revelation ought to lead to people not only seeing and hearing but also understanding and changing (or "turning") and being healed. This marks Israel's obduracy as irrational and culpably sinful.

Throughout the book of Isaiah the spiritual condition of the nation is depicted as one of deafness and blindness (e.g., 1:2–9; 6:9–10; 29:9–24; 42:18–20, 23; 44:6–28, esp. v. 18). Although God had delivered Ahaz, king of Judah, from the Syro-Ephraimite threat (Isa. 7–8 [732 BC]) and miraculously answered Hezekiah's prayer for deliverance from the Assyrian ruler Sennacherib (37:17), the Israelites failed to see God's hand of judgment in the Assyrian invasion and exile that the northern kingdom experienced in 722 BC. Thus Israel had proved to be unable to discern God's activity in both judgment and deliverance (Robinson 1998: 179–81) and so experienced a further hardening brought about ultimately by God himself.

C. Isa. 6:10 in Judaism. Isaiah 6:9–10 featured significantly in Qumran, the Septuagint, the Targum, the Peshitta, and the Rabbis (Evans

1989: chaps. 2, 3, 4, 5, 11). Isaiah 6:9–10 is referred to in 1QIsaᵃ col. VI: 2–5, where the thrust of the passage is altered from proclaiming a word of judgment to warning and aiding the elect in protecting themselves from evil (Evans 1989a: 56). Although the idea of obduracy is present in the Dead Sea Scrolls (Evans 1989a: 58–59), the Qumran community believes that their eyes and ears are open to spiritual truth and their hearts are attuned to God.

Isaiah 6:9–10 is represented also in *Targum Jonathan*, where the harshness of the Hebrew text is mitigated in several ways. First, the imperatives are converted into indicatives, with the result that what was to be brought about by the prophet is changed into a description of the hardened condition of the people. Second, the prophet is to harden the people's hearts only if they fail to repent. Third, obduracy is predicated merely of a limited group, in contrast to a believing remnant (Evans 1989a: 75–76).

Isaiah 6:9–10 is cited also in the rabbis (Evans 1989a: 138–42). The earliest reference is found in *Mekilta de Rabbi Ishmael*, which highlights the Israelite cycle of obduracy followed by forgiveness, taking its point of departure from Exod. 19:2a. The Babylonian Talmud includes two relevant references: in *b. Roš Haš.* 17b Rabbi Yohanan speaks of the "power of repentance that . . . rescinds a man's final sentence" of judgment; similarly, in *b. Meg.* 17b the rabbis speak of "the healing [power] of forgiveness."

D. Textual Matters. John's quotation of Isa. 6:10 does not perfectly match either the MT or the LXX (Freed 1965: 82–88; Evans 1982c; Tyler 1989; Schuchard 1992: 91–93; Menken 1996a: 99–122). C. Goodwin (1954 [cf. Schuchard 1992: 97, 106]) proposes that John may have cited the LXX from memory. E. D. Freed (1965: 85–87) suggests that John is dependent on the Hebrew but influenced by the LXX. Others believe that John's source was targumic (Barrett 1947: 167; Evans 1982b: 127–35; cf. Mark 4:10–12; John 12:41) or that John's wording may have been influenced by other similar Isaianic texts (cf., e.g., Isa. 29:10, 14; see Evans 1982c: 135). However, it is hard to settle this issue with any degree of certainty.

In the Hebrew original the prophet receives an order to dull the hearts of people. He is to tell the people, "Hear indeed [lit., "hear a hearing," adverbial use of infinitive; cf. Gen. 2:17], but do not understand; see indeed, but do not know"; and he is told, "Make the heart of this people fat; make its ears heavy and its eyes clouded, lest it should see with its eyes, and hear with its ears, and understand with its heart [note the chiasm: heart / ears / eyes / ears / heart], and turn and be healed."

By contrast, the LXX (quoted in Matt. 13:14–15; Acts 28:25–27) reads, "For the heart of this people became dull, and their ears heard heavily, and their eyes closed," placing the responsibility on the hearers rather than on God in an apparent effort to eliminate the theological problem presented by the MT of God's prophet being the agent of the people's hardening.

John, in keeping with the MT (and different from the LXX), retains the notion of God's judicial hardening of his people (it is difficult to decide between the textual variants *epērōsen*, "he maimed" [$\mathfrak{P}^{66.75}$ ℵ K W], which is the harder reading and has early attestation, and *epōrōsen*, "he hardened" [A B* L Θ Ψ f^{13} 33]; Menken [1996a: 101–4] prefers the former, but most commentators prefer the latter). At the same time, the Fourth Evangelist, in contrast to the MT (where, as we noted, the movement is from heart to ears to eyes and then back from sight to hearing to understanding), does not refer to hearing but focuses instead on sight (Lieu 1988), probably owing to his mention of Jesus' signs in 12:37 (Barrett 1978: 431; Keener 2003: 883) and perhaps also reflecting the fact that seeing represents the climactic element in the original chiasm (see Carson 1991: 449; cf. Barrett 1978: 431; for a helpful comparison and brief discussion of the MT, LXX, and Johannine forms of Isa. 6:10, see Brown 1966–1970: 486).

Replacing the concentric structure found in both the Hebrew and the LXX with a parallel arrangement, the Fourth Evangelist writes, "He has blinded their eyes and hardened [or 'maimed'] their heart, lest they should see with the eyes and understand with the heart." In the Johannine context, then, people saw the signs, but their seeing (with their eyes) was not met with believing (with their heart) (cf. 9:39). Hence John streamlines the source quotation, adapting both the MT and the LXX, in order to establish a direct correlation between seeing and believing.

E. The Use of Isa. 6:10 in John 12:40. In the context of the Johannine narrative, the reference to Isa. 6:10 in John 12:40 harks back to the healing of the man born blind in chapter 9 and Jesus' concluding indictment of the Jewish leaders for their spiritual blindness and rejection of divine revelation in 9:39–41 (see also 11:37). In the present instance the parabolic nature of this preceding narrative is set into the context of Isaiah's message denouncing the Jewish nation for turning a deaf ear to God's message of judgment and salvation (see §B above). Thus Isa. 6:10 is shown prophetically to include the Jews' reaction to Jesus' healing of the blind man in chapter 9 as well as their response to Jesus' other "signs" in their presence (12:37). Yet the prophet's vision of a future reversal of deafness and blindness (Isa. 29:17–21; 35:4–5; 43:8) will be realized in a believing remnant (John 20:30–31) (see Robinson 1998: 181–83).

Similar to the other evangelists, the Fourth Evangelist's primary apologetic task is to explain why the Messiah, predicted in the Hebrew Scriptures, was rejected by his own people, the Jews (though notice that whereas the Synoptics cite Isa. 6:9–10 to explain why the masses fail to understand Jesus' teaching in parables, John extends the scope of application to Jesus' entire ministry; see Michaels 1989: 231–32). In response, John points out that not only is the Messiah's suffering predicted in Scripture (see esp. John 19:24, 28, 36–37), but so also is his own people's rejection of him. What is more, according to John, this rejection is ultimately not the result of the people's hardening toward God's messenger and his message, but rather part of the actual plan and purpose of God's prophetic message (Menken 1996a: 109–10; *contra* Painter [1994], who says that the agent of the blinding is Satan). By their hardening, people therefore, far from resisting God's purposes in Christ, unwittingly collaborate with God's plan while at the same time remaining fully responsible for their actions (on theodicy, see Borchert 1996–2002: 2:63–65).

At the end of his narration of Jesus' public ministry to the Jews (cf. the possible *inclusio* with 1:11; see Keener 2003: 883), the Fourth Evangelist therefore establishes that despite the Jews' rejection of Jesus as the Messiah, everything is nonetheless proceeding according to plan: in accordance with the Scriptures, the Messiah will suffer (see commentary at chaps. 18–19 below), and the Jews' rejection of Jesus actually fulfills Scripture rather than being in conflict with it. Hence the evangelist's mission is accomplished: he has shown that the Scriptures predict and typologically foreshadow a crucified Messiah (see also the "lifted up" sayings in 3:14; 8:28; 12:32), and that the Jewish rejection of this Messiah does not represent the kind of problem that it was often made out to be by those who did not understand this part of the scriptural message.

What is more, Jesus' own mission to the Jews, as narrated in the first twelve chapters in John's Gospel, although appearing to end on a note of rejection and failure, in fact accomplishes God's purpose: God's glory has been revealed in and through Christ, in keeping with the Baptist's vision (1:23; cf. Isa. 40:3; see also John 1:32), both as a result of the Son's perfect submission and complete obedience to the Father (the Johannine "sending" theme) and through Jesus' messianic "signs" and fulfillment of the symbolism inherent in various Jewish festivals and institutions. Both Jesus and the evangelist perceive in the Jews' rejection the world's opposition and Satan's antagonism but look to God to glorify himself in and through, rather than apart from or in spite of, the cross (cf. 12:27–33).

As we noted briefly at 12:38 above, Isa. 6:10 in turn harks back to Israel's unbelief during the exodus (Evans 1989a: 134–35). Deuteronomy 29:2–4 is particularly instructive: "You have seen all that the LORD did before your eyes in the land of Egypt, to Pharaoh and to all his servants and to all his land, the great trials which your eyes saw, the signs, and those great wonders; but to this day the LORD has not given you a mind to understand, or eyes to see, or ears to hear." Thus John, by citing Isa. 6:10, does not refer merely to that passage, but rather taps into a trajectory that spans all the way from Israel's beginnings as a nation under Moses through the prophetic period to Jesus' day. The people's unbelieving response to the revelation of God mediated through Moses, Isaiah, and Jesus is part of a web of typology that links God's people throughout salvation history and presents human resistance to divine revelation in the face of God's provision of redemption in an escalating manner.

F. Theological Use. In the scriptural quotation faith (or lack thereof) and divine activity (the "arm of the Lord") are connected: "Even unbelief has some place in the purpose of God" (Morris 1995: 536). As we noted, John here accounts for the fact (surprising to some) that the Jews, God's chosen people of the old covenant, failed to accept their Messiah. His answer, far from implying that the Jews are not responsible for their refusal to believe (cf. 19:11–12, 15), shows that beneath the Jewish rejection of the Messiah lies God's judicial hardening of his people. While paradoxical on one level, John's theodicy places human choice under the larger rubric of God's sovereign salvation-historical purposes, carefully balancing the twin truths of divine sovereignty and human responsibility in a way that may be described as unambiguously predestinarian yet compatibilist (Carson 1991: 447–49; Ridderbos 1997: 444–45; Barrett 1978: 431).

But how could it be part of God's purpose to harden people so that they may not believe and be healed? No explicit rationale is provided, but we may infer that what is most important is the revelation of God's character and of the people's sinful condition in and through the public ministry and passion of Jesus Christ. Isaiah's faithful accomplishment of his mission, and Jesus' obedient submission to God's purposes (cf. the quotation of Isa. 53:1 in John 12:38), likewise contribute to the greater glory of God and show him to be true to himself and to his covenant purposes, and true even in judging human sin as it manifests itself in the revelation of himself in the person and work of Jesus Christ. In the context of the first part of John's Gospel, this revelation was pursued most markedly in Jesus' provision of (seven) messianic "signs."

In fact, it can be argued that God's plan must of necessity include the possibility of rejection of salvation. As J. N. Oswalt (1986–1998: 1:189n12) writes, "It is a fallacy to suppose that voluntary, loving trust can be compelled. It is either given freely or not at all." For this reason, although certainly it would be within God's power to compel belief in all his creatures, this would violate the principle of voluntary, intelligent submission and faith by responsible human agents and render the notion of any true human choice meaningless. Not that humans are "free" in an ultimate sense—

they are dependent creatures, and their choices are within parameters set by God. Nevertheless, the choices that they are called to make are real, and they will be held responsible for their decision of whether to accept Jesus' claims regarding himself and his relation to God.

In the wake of the two Isaianic quotes in 12:38, 40, the evangelist concludes that "he [Isaiah] saw his [Jesus'] glory" (12:41; cf. 8:56). In light of the preceding quotation of Isa. 6:10, the background for the present statement probably is the call narrative in Isa. 6 (Bultmann 452n4; Dodd 1952: 36). This is confirmed by the Targumim: *Targum Jonathan* to Isa. 6:1 changes "I saw the Lord" to "I saw *the glory* of the Lord," and the same Targum changes "the King, the Lord of hosts" in Isa. 6:5 to "*the glory of the shekinah of the eternal* King, the Lord of hosts" (Carson 1991: 449).

Yet while *autou* ("his") probably refers to Jesus (see Carson 1991: 449; Morris 1995: 538; Ridderbos 1997: 445; Brown 1966–1970: 484), the evangelist does not say that Isaiah saw Jesus himself, but rather that he saw Jesus' glory. Thus it is not necessary to conclude that the evangelist believed that Isaiah saw "the pre-existent Christ" (Schnackenburg 1990: 2:416; cf. Talbert 1992: 180; D. M. Smith 1999: 244) or that he saw Jesus "in some pre-incarnate fashion" (Carson 1991: 449), although the notion of a preexistent Christ who was present and active in the history of Israel is found elsewhere in the NT (1 Cor. 10:4; see also Philo, *Dreams* 1.229–230), and later interpreters speculated that the prophet looked into the future and saw the life and glory of Jesus (cf. Sir. 48:24–25; *Martyrdom and Ascension of Isaiah* [second century AD]; elsewhere the evangelist affirms the impossibility of a direct vision of God [cf. 1:18; 5:37; 6:46]).

Rather, Isaiah foresaw that God was pleased with a *Suffering* Servant who would be "raised and lifted up and highly exalted" (Isa. 52:13) yet who was "pierced for our transgressions" and "bore the sins of many" (Isa. 53:5, 12) (see Evans 1987). Hence Isaiah knew that God's glory would be revealed through a suffering Messiah, something deemed impossible by the crowds (John 12:34). Like Abraham, Isaiah saw Jesus' "day" (cf. John 8:58).

The final indictment of the Jews' unbelief in 12:37–43 is followed by a sort of epilogue (match-ing the prologue) that brings closure to the first major section of this Gospel and consists of a final appeal made by Jesus. In a somewhat stylized fashion the evangelist here provides "a deft summary of many strands in his [Jesus'] teaching" (Carson 1991: 451). The entire closing section presupposes Jewish teaching on representation, according to which the emissary represents the sender (cf. *m. Ber.* 5:5). Once again, too, Jesus claims to have come as light into the world, to deliver anyone who believes in him from darkness (see 1:4–5, 9; 3:19; 8:12; 9:5, 39).

Jesus' claim in 12:49 (cf. 5:19–47; 7:17; 10:18), that he did not speak of his own accord but took his cue from the Father who sent him, harks back to Deut. 18:18–19. Jesus' assertion that the Father's command is eternal life, too, is in keeping with the message of Deuteronomy, where God's commandments provide the framework within which Israel is to fulfill its calling as a people set apart for God (e.g., Deut. 8:3; 32:46–47). Yet now one greater than Moses is here: "For the law was given through Moses—true, ultimate grace came through Jesus Christ" (1:17). And with this, the Gospel has come full circle, and the stage is set for the narration of the outworking of the Jews' rejection of Jesus as the Messiah and of Jesus' preparation of his new messianic community for its mission to the world.

The Book of Glory (13:1–20:31)

There are two explicit OT quotations in Jesus' Farewell Discourse, found in 13:18; 15:25 (see also 17:12). The passion narrative features three quotations of the OT (19:24, 36, 37; see also 19:28). Possible OT allusions in the Farewell Discourse include the "vine" allegory in chapter 15; Jesus' illustration of a woman giving birth in 16:21–22 and his reference to the scattering of his disciples in 16:32; and his reference to Judas, the "son of destruction," in 17:12. Possible OT allusions in the passion narrative include 19:28–29, 31.

The Farewell Discourse (13–17)

INTRODUCTION

The Johannine Farewell Discourse, which spans chapters 13–17 (the discourse proper extends from 13:31 to 16:33), including a preamble

(13:1–30) and a concluding prayer (chap. 17), is patterned after Moses' farewell discourse in Deuteronomy (chaps. 31–33) and similar OT farewells (cf. Gen. 49; Josh. 23–24; 1 Sam. 12; 1 Kings 2:1–12; 1 Chron. 28–29). An entire genre of such works emerged during the Second Temple period (e.g., *Testaments of the Twelve Patriarchs*; *Assumption of Moses*; cf. *Jub.* 22:10–30; 1 Macc. 2:49–70; Josephus, *Ant.* 12.279–284). The standard pattern (though there are, of course, variations) of these farewells is as follows (Moloney 1998: 377–78):

1. Predictions of death and departure
2. Predictions of future challenges for the followers/sons of the dying man after his death
3. Arrangements regarding succession or continuation of the family line
4. Exhortations to moral behavior
5. Final commission
6. Affirmation and renewal of God's covenant promises
7. Closing doxology

John's presentation of Jesus' farewell discourse, of course, may not be consciously patterned after the Second Temple testament genre, but rather may build directly on the precedent of patriarchal deathbed blessings and/or Moses' final words in Deuteronomy. Present in the Johannine Farewell Discourse are (1) the familiar instruction to virtue (13:34; 15:17 ["love one another"]); (2) talk about Jesus' impending death or "departure" (13:33, 36; 14:5–6, 12, 28); (3) words of comfort to those about to be left behind (13:36; 14:1–3, 18, 27–28 [see Attridge 2002: 17]); and, (4) in keeping with the genre's concern for proper succession, an announcement of the coming of "another helping presence" (14:16; cf. 14:26; 15:26; 16:7) to ensure continuity between Jesus' ministry and that of his disciples (see esp. 15:26–27; 16:8–11).

However, important differences also apply (see Attridge [2002, esp. 9–10, 17–18], who speaks of John "bending the genre" here and elsewhere in the Gospel): (1) Jesus' farewell is but temporary (his followers will see him again in a "little while"), so that his final words focus on the future, whereas Jewish farewell discourses regularly consisted of extended rehearsals of the past; (2) extensive detailed predictions regarding the future, com-

mon in Second Temple testaments, are almost entirely absent; (3) the "vine" allegory in chapter 15 (where monologue replaces dialogue) is unprecedented in Jewish farewell discourses. In short, while the Johannine Farewell Discourse features Jesus' prediction of his absence, at the same time it promises his abiding presence, so that, in a "bending" of the testament genre, a focus on the past is transposed to a (more hopeful) portrayal of the inaugurated permanent relationship between the Father, Jesus, and his followers.

The parallels between the present discourse and "covenant language" in Moses' parting Deuteronomic instructions are further underscored by the preponderance of the five major verb themes of Exod. 33–34 and Deuteronomy ("love," "obey," "live," "know," "see") in John 14:15–24 (see Lacomara 1974; Pryor 1992, esp. 160, 166, 216n8, also citing Malatesta 1978: 42–77). The similarities between the Johannine and the Deuteronomic farewell discourses suggest that Jesus is cast in John's Gospel as the new Moses, who institutes a new covenant with his disciples (e.g., the "new commandment" in 13:34–35). Just as Moses was prevented by death from leading God's people into the promised land, so also Jesus will be separated, albeit only temporarily, from his followers. Yet in contrast to Moses, Jesus, as the new Joshua, entered heaven itself as our forerunner (cf. Heb. 4:8, 14; 12:2). Or, to use Johaninne terminology, Jesus will go to prepare a place for his disciples (14:2–3) and be glorified in the Father's presence with the glory that he had with him before the world began (17:5).

The Cleansing of the New Messianic Community: The Footwashing and Judas's Departure (13:1–30)

The Johannine Farewell Discourse's preamble, 13:1–30, revolves around the motif of cleansing. Jesus' inner circle is cleansed both physically (the footwashing in 13:1–17) and figuratively (the departure of the betrayer in 13:18–30) (see Westcott 1908: 2:159). Structurally, the cleansing motif in chapter 13 may correspond to that in chapter 2, both at the Cana wedding and at the clearing of the temple. Whereas in chapter 2 Jesus' attempt to cleanse corrupt Jewish custom and worship must be pronounced a failure in human terms (although both events serve as Johannine "signs" with messianic significance), chapter 13 witnesses his successful cleansing of the new messianic community. This cleansing, in turn, is necessary for the Farewell Discourse proper (13:31–16:33) to proceed.

The practice of footwashing has a long OT tradition (Hultgren 1982: 541–42; Keener 2003: 903–4). Customarily, footwashing was performed by slaves. In the present instance, however, Jesus, the Teacher, stoops to perform this role, not in order to institute a permanent rite, but rather to teach his followers the importance of humble, loving service (13:12–17; cf. Gal. 5:13; 6:2; Phil. 2:6–8; see Morris 1995: 544). The footwashing takes place at the outset of the Passover celebration (13:1; for the connection of Jesus' death with the Passover, see also 11:55; 12:1; 18:28, 39; 19:14). According to the Synoptics (Mark 14:12; Luke 22:15), Jesus and his disciples celebrated the Passover during the early hours of 15 Nisan (Thursday evening, with days beginning at sundown), preparations having been made earlier that day, 14 Nisan, the day on which the Passover lambs were slaughtered at the temple. The Johannine account coheres with this timeline (Köstenberger 2004: 400n1; 401–2; see also Carson 1984: 530–32; Blomberg 1987: 175–80).

The two major chronological markers running through John's Gospel, one referring to Jewish festivals (2:13, 23; 4:45; 5:1; 6:4; 7:2; 10:22; 11:55; 12:1), and one to Jesus' time (2:4; 7:30; 8:20; 12:23, 27; 16:32; 17:1), now converge: "the time had come" (13:1). "His own" (13:1) are now the Twelve, the representatives of the new messianic community, no longer the old covenant community, which had rejected Jesus as the Messiah (cf. 1:11; see also 10:3–4, 12; cf. 15:19). The reference to Jesus showing his disciples one final proof of his love in 13:1 may allude to Moses completing the inscription of the law (and his song) in Deut. 31:24, 30.

The image of Jesus' removing his outer clothing, wrapping a towel around his waist, and proceeding to wash his disciples' feet is stunning indeed. Jesus, the Teacher, here adopts the stance of a menial, even non-Jewish (*Mek. Exod.* 21:2) slave, a position looked down upon by Jews and Gentiles alike. Although other rabbis also stressed the virtue of humility, they did so within certain limitations (e.g., *y. Sanh.* 11:3 [cited in Keener 2003:

297]). Jesus, however, knew no such boundaries. The OT recounts several instances of footwashing as part of ancient hospitality (see Gen. 18:4; 19:2; 24:32; 43:24; Judg. 19:21; 1 Sam. 25:41; cf. *T. Abr.* 3:7–9; *Jos. Asen.* 7:1; also the Greco-Roman references cited in Thomas 1991: 35–40). Customarily, water was poured over the feet from one vessel and caught in another. Jesus' teaching style here follows the rabbinic pattern of "mystifying gesture–question–interpretation" (Köstenberger 1998a: 117), which served as a didactic tool designed to elicit questions and to facilitate learning.

13:18

A. The NT Context: The Treachery of Judas. As we noted, chapter 13 narrates the cleansing of the community, both physically (the footwashing in 13:1–17) and figuratively (the departure of the betrayer in 13:18–30). After instructing his followers about the significance of the footwashing and calling them to follow his example (13:12–17), Jesus makes clear that he is well aware that not all of them are truly chosen, and that a traitor is in their midst: "But in order that the Scripture might be fulfilled [one of only two fulfillment citations attributed to Jesus in this Gospel; cf. 15:25; cf. also 17:12; 19:24, 36], 'The one who is eating my bread has lifted up his heel against me.'"

Judas's treachery comes as no surprise to the reader; his act of betrayal had been signaled ahead of time in this Gospel: at the major watershed when many even of Jesus' disciples ceased following him in 6:60–71 (esp. 6:70–71); and at the anointing in 12:1–8 (see esp. 12:4). The emphasis in the present text is on Jesus' previous knowledge of Judas's defection. The text cited is Ps. 41:9 (41:10 MT; 40:10 LXX) (similar texts in Psalms include 31:9–13; 38:10–12; 55:13–14; see further below). The Fourth Evangelist's account here very likely reflects Jesus' messianic consciousness and placement of Judas's betrayal within a scriptural framework (cf. Mark 14:18; see France 1971: 57).

B. The OT Context of Ps. 41:9. The historical setting of Ps. 41 may well be Absalom's rebellion against King David, the "faithless friend" possibly being Ahithophel, whose counsels David considered on par with those "inquired of the word of God" (2 Sam. 16:23). Once Absalom, with Ahithophel's help, had stolen the hearts of

Israel, David (who had known about the rebellion but had done nothing about it) was forced to flee. Ahithophel's ignominious end—he later hanged himself—resembles the outcome of Judas's treachery (cf. Matt. 27:3–5).

This psalm of David, which concludes Book 1 of the Psalter (see 41:13), features the psalmist as a righteous sufferer facing opposition from malicious enemies who bring false charges against him (41:5–8). What is more, "Even my close friend [lit., 'man of my peace'] in whom I trusted, who ate my bread, has lifted his heel against me" (41:9; cf. Gen. 3:15; Ps. 55:12–14; the Hebrew word for "heel," *āqēb*, is related to the root '-q-b ["scheme"], from which the name "Jacob" is derived; see VanGemeren 1991: 328). Despite such opposition, the psalmist is confident of God's intervention on his behalf. Because of God's delight in him, God will graciously raise him up (41:10) and set him in his presence forever (41:11–12).

Verse 9 is part of a lament that spans 41:5–9 and is framed by the psalmist's prayer for deliverance in 41:4, 10 (Craigie 1983: 319). The psalmist expresses his assurance that God is his only source of help, while humans, friends (41:9) and foes (41:5) alike, have turned against him (Craigie 1983: 321). The treachery of David's "close friend" is presented as the action of one who "eats his bread" and enjoys the privilege of close personal fellowship (cf. 2 Sam. 9:10–13), but who rejected the privilege by kicking out like a beast.

C. Ps. 41:9 in Judaism. Rabbinic interpretation took Ps. 41:9 to refer to Ahithophel's conspiracy with Absalom against David (see *b. Sanh.* 106b; cf. 2 Sam. 15:12). In ancient Semitic cultures, eating bread at the table of a superior amounted to a pledge of loyalty (2 Sam. 9:7–13; 1 Kings 18:19; 2 Kings 25:29), and "to betray one with whom bread had been eaten . . . was a gross breach of the traditions of hospitality" (Bernard 1928: 2:467).

D. Textual Matters. John's quotation is closer to the MT than the LXX (rightly Johnson 1980: 74–75; see also Daly-Denton 2004: 128–29; Menken 1996a: 123–38). The differences in the texts include the following: (1) John's word for "eat" is *trōgō* rather than the LXX's *esthiō*, which harks back to the use of *trōgō* in Jesus' "bread of life" discourse in 6:54, 56, 57, 58 (elsewhere in the NT only in Matt. 24:38); (2) the possessive

pronoun *mou* in John precedes the object "bread" rather than following it as in the LXX; (3) "bread" in John is singular, as in the MT, while the LXX has the plural; the term "bread" harks back to previous references to bread at the feeding of the five thousand (6:11, 31); (4) John's rendering of the Hebrew word for "lifted up" is less literal than that in the LXX; (5) the phrase "his heel" in John (including the word for "heel") is different from both the LXX and the MT (although the LXX uses John's term elsewhere); (6) John does not cite the opening line of 13:9, "Even my close friend in whom I trusted."

Concerning (1), F. J. Moloney (1998: 384), on the strength of the evangelist's choice of the verb *trōgō* (used also in 6:54–58) in the place of the LXX's *esthiō*, postulates "eucharistic overtones" to the meal (on fulfillment quotations, see commentary at 12:38), though it is sufficient to understand the evangelist's choice of word as establishing a back reference to the feeding of the multitude without invoking the Eucharist. Regarding (2), the position of *mou* in John's text indicates emphasis, accentuating the severity of Judas's treachery. As to (3), John's agreement with the MT over against the LXX may indicate his knowledge of the Hebrew original and a desire to correct the LXX rendering, which departs from the Hebrew (see Menken [1990], who contends that the rendering of Ps. 41:9 in the present passage represents the evangelist's own translation from the Hebrew).

Regarding (4), John's rendering of "lifted up" may indicate a secondary dependence on Ps. 55:12–14 (55:13–15 MT), where the same Hebrew term for "lift up," *higdîl*, as in Ps. 41:9 (41:10 MT) is found. M. Daly-Denton (2004: 129) suggests that John links the two passages in keeping with the rabbinic device of *gezerah shavah*, an equivalence of expression (Menken [1996a: 133–36] posits a secondary influence by 2 Sam. 18:28, which in his view accounts for the two Johannine deviations from the Hebrew text: the use of *epēren*, and the addition of *autou*). In any case, John accurately gives the sense of the original passage. The same can be said in regard to (5), his choice of the word for "heel" (*pterna*), which is a cognate of the word chosen in the LXX (*pternismos*). As to (6), John's omission of the line "even my close friend in whom I trusted," this choice may reflect the Fourth Evangelist's desire to avoid any insinuation that Jesus was taken by surprise by Judas's betrayal. This is suggested by the fact that John repeatedly makes clear elsewhere that Jesus did not trust Judas and was always aware that Judas eventually would betray him (cf. 6:70–71; 13:10–11, 19; 17:12; see Tholuck 1858: 208).

Overall, then, this seems to be an instance where the Fourth Evangelist translated from the Hebrew, using appropriate means to adapt the passage to his present context. His nonuse of the LXX in the present case is noteworthy in light of his customary closeness to it, and this can be explained by the fact that its reference to the one who is betrayed having trusted in his close friend was judged christologically unsuitable by the Fourth Evangelist, who regularly affirms Jesus' full foreknowledge of events.

E. The Use of Ps. 41:9 in John 13:18. As we noted, the primary function of the OT quotation in the present passage is the assertion of Jesus' prior knowledge of Judas's treachery and the corresponding claim that the betrayal fulfilled OT Scripture. Whereas the Synoptic Gospels make general reference to Scripture being fulfilled (Matt. 26:24; Mark 14:21; Luke 22:22), John cites the specific passage being fulfilled (Daly-Denton 2004: 131). Here, then, is one passage where John complements and concretizes the other canonical Gospels.

In a Jewish context the expression "he who ate my bread" conveys the notion of close fellowship. The expression "lifted up his heel against me," while capable of several interpretations (see Köstenberger 2004: 411), brings out the "treacherous and faithless nature" of Judas's deed: he was about to betray the one in whose intimate company he had enjoyed fellowship (Ridderbos 1997: 467; cf. Matt. 26:50 and Psalms references cited in Köstenberger 2004 at 13:21; cf. Schlatter 1948: 285).

Not only do Jesus' foes plot against him, but even one of his inner circle cannot be trusted, and at his arrest all will desert him; yet the Father remains with him (16:32). By the time of Jesus, David had become a "type" or model of David's "greater Son," the coming Messiah, on the basis of passages such as 2 Sam. 7:12–16; Ps. 2. The reference to Ps. 41:9 in John 13:18 is further evidence of Jesus' self-consciousness of standing in

the messianic line of David and as fulfilling the pattern of the righteous sufferer who faced opposition from friend and foe alike (41:5–8) but who would be vindicated by God (41:10–12). Hence the reference to a Davidic psalm at the outset of Jesus' passion signals the fulfillment of Davidic typology in the ensuing narrative.

Predictably, it was not only the crucifixion of the Messiah but also his betrayal by one of his inner circle that required an apologetic by the early Christians. As in Jesus' case, the argument they advanced was that Judas's betrayal constituted a fulfillment of Scripture. This is not surprising, for one would expect that if the Messiah is prefigured in Scripture, so are his enemies (Johnson 1980: 77). It was believed that various aspects of the life of David, including the opposition against him, constituted a pattern that provided the framework for a similar type of opposition to the Messiah in his day. This use of typology also served as an important apologetic for Jesus' foreknowledge and God's sovereignty (cf. Acts 1:16; see Johnson 1980: 78).

F. Theological Use. The use of Ps. 41:9 in John 13:18 is part and parcel of the Fourth Gospel's presentation of Jesus as the righteous sufferer in fulfillment of Davidic typology (Johnson 1980: 69–79). In the Davidic psalms of the Psalter several aspects of David's life are presented that are given a messianic application here and elsewhere in John as well as in other NT passages. These include references to the psalmist's suffering, weakness, and betrayal (Carson 1991: 470; see especially the use of Ps. 22 in the Gospel passion narratives; the Davidic psalms listed in Köstenberger 2004 at 11:33; and commentary at 19:24, 36–37 below). What may appear to some as "paranoid imagination" (Craigie 1983: 321) in the original context is in Jesus' case the result of a genuine assessment of the spiritual forces amassed against him. Even the most treacherous act can, in God's hands and sovereign providence, become the occasion for trust in God and his powerful deliverance.

Jesus' statement in 13:19, "From now on, I am telling you before it happens, in order that you may believe when it does happen that I am [the one I claim to be]" (cf. 8:58), is one of several references to Jesus' prescience in this section (see 14:29; 16:1, 4, 32–33), which recall similar expressions referring to God in the OT (Ezek.

24:24; Isa. 43:10; cf. Isa. 41:26; 46:10; 48:3, 5–6; see Ridderbos 1997: 467). The evangelist here stresses that Jesus was not "the deceived and helpless victim of unsuspected treachery, but the One sent by God to effect the divine purpose going forward calm and unafraid" (Morris 1995: 553). The phrase "I am [the one I claim to be]" in 13:19, as in 8:24, 28, very likely has overtones of deity (Morris 1995: 553; Moloney 1998: 381; Köstenberger 1999: 261).

Jesus being "stirred up inside" (*tarassō*) at this occasion (13:21; cf. 11:33; 12:27) parallels the emotional state of David, who expressed extreme anguish over the betrayal of a close friend (Ps. 55:2–14; see also Ps. 31:9–10; 38:10). The supposition that Jesus may have sent Judas to give something to the poor (13:29) harks back to Judas's objection at Mary's anointing of Jesus, where he postured as a champion for the poor (12:5). Indeed, almsgiving was an important part of Jewish piety (cf. Matt. 6:2–4). As Rabbi Hillel used to say, "The more charity, the more peace" (*m. 'Abot* 2:7). For pilgrims traveling to Jerusalem, it was customary to give alms to the poor (Josephus, *Ant.* 4.227). On Passover night the temple gates were left open from midnight on, allowing beggars to congregate (cf. Josephus, *Ant.* 18.29–30; see Jeremias 1969: 54). In fact, almsgiving was regarded as particularly meritorious when done in Jerusalem. A talmudic maxim reflects a much older principle: "Even a poor man who himself lives from alms should give alms" (*b. Giṭ.* 7b; cf. Luke 21:1–4 par.). Nevertheless, in the present instance the disciples' guess, though reasonable, was wrong. Jesus did not send Judas on some harmless errand; he released him to betray the Son of Man into the hands of sinners.

THE FAREWELL DISCOURSE (13:31–16:33)

Jesus' Departure and the Sending of the Spirit (13:31–14:31)

Now that the new messianic community has been cleansed (13:1–30), the Farewell Discourse proper can proceed (13:31–16:33). As soon as Judas has slipped into the night, Jesus states, "Now has the Son of Man been glorified" (13:31). Outside of the NT the figure of the "Son of Man" is associated with glory (esp. Dan. 7:13–14; *1 En.* 37–71). In the Synoptics he is frequently associated with suffering. John brings these two

elements together in a striking fashion (Carson 1991: 482). The concept of "the glorification of the Son" (13:31–32; cf. 12:23, 28; 17:5), harking back to Isaianic passages such as 49:3, "You are my servant, Israel, in whom I will display my splendor," is a Johannine euphemism for the events related to Jesus' crucifixion. Fulfilling the "paschal role of head of the family" (Carson 1991: 483), Jesus here affectionately addresses his followers as his "dear children" (*teknia* [only here in John's Gospel]). The epithet is fitting in that farewell discourses often feature a dying father instructing his children (cf., e.g., *T. Reub.* 1:3; see Brown 1966–1970: 2:611).

Jesus' "new command" in 13:34–35, that his disciples love one another as he has loved them, takes its point of departure from the Mosaic commandments "Love the LORD your God with all your heart and with all your soul and with all your strength" (Deut. 6:5) and "Love your neighbor as yourself" (Lev. 19:18) (cf. Mark 12:28–33). It resembles, and yet transcends, the ethos of the Dead Sea community, which stressed love within the brotherhood but "everlasting hatred for the men of the pit" (1QS IX, 21–22; cf. 1QS I, 10; see also Josephus, *J.W.* 2.119; note also the neighbor love emphasized by the first-century rabbi Hillel [*m. 'Abot* 1:12] and several parallels in the *Testaments of the Twelve Patriarchs* [*T. Gad* 4:1–2; 6:1; *T. Zeb.* 5:1; 8:5; *T. Jos.* 17:1–2; *T. Iss.* 7:6–7; *T. Sim.* 4:7; *T. Reub.* 6:9]). Jesus, by contrast, preached love for one's enemies (Matt. 5:43–48), though this did not necessarily alter the world's negative stance toward him or his followers (cf. John 15:18–16:11; see Köstenberger 2004: 464n3). It is possible that "new commandment" also alludes to the new covenant established at the Last Supper that involved the people's inner transformation through the Spirit (see Jer. 31:29–34; Ezek. 36:24–26; see commentary at 3:3–8 above).

Jesus' encouragement to his followers in 14:1, that they not let their hearts be troubled, echoes repeated encouragements in the OT for God's chosen servants and his people Israel not to be afraid, such as when entering the promised land (Deut. 1:21, 29; 20:1, 3; Josh. 1:9) or when facing threats from their enemies (2 Kings 25:24; Isa. 10:24). The psalmist repeatedly affirms his unwavering trust in God (e.g., Ps. 27:1; 56:3–4). Isaac and Jeremiah likewise were encouraged not to be afraid (Gen. 26:24; Jer. 1:8). Jesus says, "Believe in God; believe also in me" (14:1). In the OT, too, God's people were called upon to trust in God and in his servants (e.g., Moses [Exod. 14:31]; the prophets [2 Chron. 20:20]; see Schlatter 1948: 291).

In Jesus' Father's house are many dwellings; he will go and prepare a place for his followers (14:2–3). In a pertinent Lukan parallel Jesus speaks of his disciples' being "welcomed into eternal dwellings" (Luke 16:9). Apocalyptic Second Temple literature provides descriptions of heavenly dwelling places for the saints (e.g., *1 En.* 39:4–5; 41:2; 71:16; *2 En.* 61:2–3). Philo regards heaven as a paternal house or city to which the soul returns after death (*Dreams* 1.256; see other references cited in Köstenberger 2004: 426n26). The rabbis believed that there were seven classes or departments, graded according to merit, in the heavenly Garden of Eden (*Midr. Ps.* 11 §6). John, however, is considerably more restrained than Jewish apocalyptic literature or Philo; the rabbinic notion of a compartmentalized heaven is likewise foreign to John.

In keeping with Jewish patriarchal culture, Jesus, the Son of the Father, is here shown as establishing his followers "as members of the Father's household" and as making "his home accessible to them as a final place of residence" (Schrenk 1967: 997), preparing a homecoming comparable to a son's return to his father's house (cf. Luke 15:11–32). Jesus' reassuring statement in 14:3, "I will come again and take you with me, so that where I am, you will be as well" (cf. 17:24), echoes the terminology found in Song 8:2a, where the bride says that she will bring her lover to her mother's house. Here Jesus, the messianic bridegroom (3:29), is said first to go to prepare a place for his own in his Father's house and then to come to take them home to be with him.

Jesus' claim of being "the way, the truth, and the life" (14:6) has a rich OT background. In the OT and in Second Temple literature "the way(s) of truth" is a life lived in conformity with the law (e.g., Ps. 119:30; Tob. 1:3; Wis. 5:6). "Way" and "life" are frequently combined in the OT Wisdom literature (e.g., Ps. 16:11; Prov. 15:24). In the Dead Sea Scrolls the ways of truth are contrasted with the ways of darkness and deceit, and the Qumran community considered itself to be

"the way" in absolute terms, perhaps on the basis of Isa. 40:3 (cited in John 1:23 with reference to the Baptist; cf. 1QS VIII, 12–16; IX, 17–20). In the OT people expressed their faith by keeping the law; now that Jesus has come, he is the way.

The emphasis in 14:7 on truly knowing Jesus and on knowing God the Father harks back to OT covenant language (e.g., Jer. 24:7; 31:34; Hos. 13:4). In the OT people are frequently exhorted to know God (e.g., Ps. 46:10; 100:3), with knowledge of God generally being anticipated as a future blessing (or being urged) rather than claimed as a present possession (but see Ps. 9:10; 36:10; Dan. 11:32). With Jesus' coming, however, the situation has changed (cf. 3:11; 4:22; 7:28 = 8:55; 8:14; 10:14, 27; 17:3). In response, Philip, in 14:8, apparently asks for some sort of theophany (Morris 1995: 571; cf. 14:5, 22). In the OT Moses asked for and was given a limited vision of God's glory (Exod. 33:18; cf. 24:10; see commentary at 1:14–18 above). Isaiah was granted a vision of "the LORD seated on a throne, high and exalted" (Isa. 6:1; see commentary at 12:41 above) and later predicted that in the day of the Messiah the glory of the Lord would be revealed (Isa. 40:5; see commentary at 1:23 above). In keeping with OT teaching, however, John repeatedly denies the possibility of a direct vision of God, unmediated by Jesus (1:18; 5:37; 6:46).

In response to Philip's request Jesus says, "Whoever has seen me has seen the Father" (14:9), again adducing the Jewish principle of representation (the *šālîaḥ*, "messenger"; cf. *m. Ber.* 5:5; see Barrett 1978: 459); yet John's Christology surely transcends such teaching by its unique "sonship" language (Carson 1991: 494). In Deut. 18:18 God says in regard to the prophet like Moses, "I will put my words in his mouth, and he will tell them everything I command him." In Deut. 34:10–12 Moses is said to have been sent by the Lord to perform signs and works. Similarly, Jesus offers his followers both his words and his works as evidence for his divine commission (14:10–11). As we noted, Jesus' words in 14:15 echo the demands of the Deuteronomic covenant (see Deut. 5:10; 6:5–6; 7:9; 10:12–13; 11:13, 22).

Jesus proceeds to promise his followers that after his departure he will send another "helping presence," *paraklētos* (14:16; cf. 14:26; 15:26; 16:7), who is "the Spirit of truth" (14:17; cf.

15:26; 16:13). The former term does not occur in the LXX (except for the plural form *paraklētoi* in Aquila's and Theodotion's versions of Job 16:2 per the Hexaplaric Apparatus), though both the noun *paraklēsis* and the verb *parakaleō* are used in the OT with regard to the "consoling" expected to occur during the messianic era (e.g., Isa. 40:1; cf. *b. Mak.* 5b; for a discussion of proposed backgrounds, see Köstenberger 2004: 435n67). The expression "spirit of truth" was current in Judaism (e.g., *T. Jud.* 20). The Qumran literature affirms that God placed within humankind "two spirits so that he would walk with them until the moment of his visitation; they are the spirits of truth and of deceit" (1QS III, 18; see also IV, 23–26; cf. 1 John 4:6; but see the cautions registered in Köstenberger 2004: 438). In the present instance the promise of the divine presence with Jesus' followers in 14:15–24 includes the Spirit (14:15–17), Jesus (14:18–21), and the Father (14:22–24).

Jesus' assurance in 14:18, "I will not leave you as orphans," is constrained by the farewell setting and evokes Moses' parting words to Israel: "The LORD . . . will never leave you nor forsake you" (Deut. 31:6; cf. Josh. 1:5). In OT times orphans needed someone to plead their case. Here, "orphan" is used in a metaphorical sense in connection with Jesus' departure and the resulting loss that will be experienced by his disciples. The expression "on that day" (14:20) frequently has end-time connotations and is commonly found in OT prophetic literature (e.g., Isa. 2:11; 3:7, 18; 4:1–2; cf. Matt. 24:36 par.). Most commentators take the present reference to be to Jesus' resurrection (e.g., Morris 1995: 579; Borchert 1996–2002: 2:126), though perhaps the more plausible view takes the statement as referring to Jesus' coming to his followers in the Spirit at Pentecost (see discussion in Köstenberger 2004: 439n80).

The phrase "whoever has my commands and keeps them" and the term "disclose" (*emphanizō*) in 14:21 hark back to the giving of the law at Mount Sinai (cf. 1:17) and to OT theophanies (see Exod. 33:13 and the reading of Codex B at Exod. 33:18), respectively. Jesus' reference to the Father's and his future indwelling of believers in 14:23 builds on OT references to God's dwelling among his people, first in the tabernacle (Exod. 25:8; 29:45; Lev. 26:11–12), then in the temple (1 Kings 8:10–11; cf. Acts 7:46–47). The book

of Revelation envisions the final state, wherein there will be no more temple, but rather "the Lord God Almighty and the Lamb" will be the temple (Rev. 21:22), and "the dwelling of God is with people, and he will live with them" (Rev. 21:3) (cf. 1 Kings 8:27; Ezek. 37:26–27; Zech. 2:10). Yet while John's Gospel does not deny the ultimate future consummation of God's salvation purposes, the focus here is plainly on believers' present experience of the indwelling presence of Father, Son, and Spirit (14:16–23).

Jesus' reference to "the helping presence, the Holy Spirit" in 14:26 features the only reference to the "Holy Spirit" in those terms in the Farewell Discourse (cf. 1:33; 20:22; for a listing of references in the other Gospels, see Köstenberger 2004: 441n89). The term rarely occurs in the OT (Ps. 51:11; Isa. 63:9–10). There are several references to the "Holy Spirit" in Second Temple literature (e.g., Wis. 9:17; *Pss. Sol.* 17:37; *Odes Sol.* 14:8). The Spirit's future ministry is described here in terms of teaching Jesus' followers (cf. 1 John 2:20, 27) and of reminding them of the things that Jesus taught them. "Teaching," in the sense of authentic exposition of Scripture, was a vital part of Judaism. "Remembering" was also an important part of the Jewish testament tradition (cf. *2 Bar.* 77:11; see Bammel 1993: 108). In Qumran the primary teaching office was occupied by the "Teacher of Righteousness," who interpreted the Hebrew Scriptures prophetically with reference to the Dead Sea community. However, whereas the Holy Spirit will guide people into truth definitively, the "Teacher of Righteousness" will be followed by another "teaching righteousness" at the end of time (CD-A VI, 11).

Following closely on Jesus' promise of the Spirit is his assurance of "peace" for his followers (14:27). Although this is also part of the term's range of meaning in Hebrew thought (e.g., Josh. 9:15; 1 Sam. 7:14; 1 Kings 2:5), the expression *shālôm* usually had much richer connotations, conveying the notion of positive blessing, especially that of a right relationship with God (Morris 1965: 237–44; Lindars 1972: 484). This is evident in the well-known blessing given by Moses and Aaron in Num. 6:24–26 (cf. Ps. 29:11; Hag. 2:9). The OT prophetic writings in particular look forward to a period of peace inaugurated by the coming of the Messiah. The "prince of peace" (Isa. 9:6) would "command peace to the nations" (Zech. 9:10; cf. 9:9), and there would be good tidings of peace and salvation (Isa. 52:7; cf. 54:13; 57:19). Through the royal messiah, God would make an everlasting "covenant of peace" with his people (Ezek. 37:26). Jesus' statement in 14:27, "Peace I leave with you," reflects the customary Jewish greeting and words of farewell, whereby "leave" (*aphiēmi*) probably has the sense of "bequeath" (cf. Ps. 17:14; Eccles. 2:18). Here, as at 16:33, the context of greeting is farewell; after the resurrection, it is welcome (20:19, 21, 26). By invoking "that day" anticipated by the prophets (14:20), Jesus places this period squarely in the context of OT expectation. On the merits of his substitutionary cross-death, the departing Lord bequeaths to his followers the permanent end-time blessing of a right relationship with God. Jesus' exhortation in 14:27, "Do not be afraid," evokes Moses' identical parting counsel in his farewell discourse (Deut. 31:6, 8).

Jesus the True Vine and the Disciples' Need to Remain in Him (15:1–17)

At the heart of the Johannine Farewell Discourse is the allegory depicting Jesus as the true vine in 15:1–17 (see Kellum 2004: 193–96, citing R. Longacre, who identifies 15:1–17 as the "peak" of the Farewell Discourse; on vine imagery in John's Gospel, see Nielsen 1999: 72–76). The OT frequently uses the vineyard or vine as a symbol for Israel, God's covenant people, especially in two "vineyard songs" found in Isaiah (Isa. 5:1–7; 27:2–6; cf. Ps. 80:8–16; Jer. 2:21; 6:9; 12:10–13; Ezek. 15:1–8; 17:5–10; 19:10–14; Hos. 10:1–2; 14:7; see also Sir. 24:17–23; 2 Esd. 5:23; an extensive allegorical depiction of Israel as a vine is also found in *Lev. Rab.* 36:2, with reference to Ps. 80:9). However, whereas the vine's purpose of existence is to bear fruit for its owner, references to Israel as God's vine regularly stress Israel's failure to produce good fruit, issuing in divine judgment (Carson 1991: 513). In contrast to Israel's failure, Jesus claims to be the "*true* vine," bringing forth the fruit Israel failed to produce. Thus Jesus, the Messiah and Son of God, fulfills Israel's destiny as the true vine of God (see esp. Ps. 80:14–17, cited by Carson 1991: 513–14; Sidebottom [1956–57: 234] draws parallels with Ezek. 17; see also Vawter 1964; Whitacre 1992).

As the paradigmatic vine, Jesus embodies God's true intentions for Israel: Jesus is the channel through whom God's blessings flow. Just as Jesus is the new temple and the fulfillment of Jewish festival symbolism (Carson 1991: 513), so also he is the new Israel, the *true* vine. Hence Jesus displaces Israel as the focus of God's plan of salvation, with the implication that faith in Jesus becomes the decisive characteristic for membership among God's people (Whitacre 1999: 372). Whereas OT Israel was ethnically constrained, the new messianic community, made up of believing Jews and Gentiles, is united by faith in Jesus the Messiah. Jews still have a place in God's family, but they must come to God on his terms rather than their own (Köstenberger 1998b: 166–67). A paradigm shift has taken place: faith in Jesus has replaced keeping the law as the primary point of reference (Köstenberger 1999: 159–60).

"I am the true vine" (15:1; cf. Jer. 2:21 LXX) is the last of John's seven "I am" sayings. "True" (*alēthinē*) vine contrasts Jesus with OT Israel in its lack of fruitfulness and spiritual degeneracy (Morris 1995: 593; Ridderbos 1997: 515; Beasley-Murray 1999: 272; Moloney 1998: 419). Joseph is called a "fruitful vine" in Gen. 49:22. Building on the OT depiction of Israel as a vine, later tradition employed the vine as a symbol for wisdom (Sir. 24:17), the dominion of the Messiah (*2 Bar.* 39:7), and the Judaism of Jesus' day (Barrett 1978: 472). The term *ampelos* ("vineyard") occurs elsewhere in the NT only in Matt. 26:29 pars.; James 3:12; Rev. 14:18–19. References to vines and vineyards occur frequently in Synoptic parables (Matt. 20:1–16; 21:28–32, 33–44 pars.; Luke 13:6–9).

Jesus' statement in 15:1 that his "Father is the vinedresser" harks back to Isaiah's first vineyard song, where God is depicted as spading, clearing, planting, and taking care of the vineyard, only to be rewarded with sour grapes (Isa. 5:1–7; cf. Ps. 80:8–9). According to 15:2, the vinedresser does two things to ensure maximum fruit production ("he removes . . . he prunes"; cf. Heb. 6:7–8): (1) in the winter he cuts off the dry and withered branches, which may involve pruning the vines to the extent that only the stalks remain (Engel 1948–1949); (2) later, when the vine has sprouted leaves, he removes the smaller shoots so that the main fruit-bearing branches receive adequate nourishment (Brown 1966–1970: 675; Schnackenburg 1990: 3:97).

The pruning activity of the divine vinedresser resembles that of his earthly counterpart. Since the term underlying *airō* in 15:2 can mean either "cut off" (negative purpose) or "prop up" (restorative purpose), some have suggested that the present reference should be understood in the latter sense. However, this is almost certainly erroneous (rightly Carson 1991: 518). More likely, the antithetical parallelism of the first part of each statement ("every branch in me that does not bear fruit"/"every branch in me that does bear fruit") is matched by corresponding divine action, be it judgment (negative [cf. 15:6]) or discipline (positive) (see Laney 1989, esp. 58–60). In the case of Jesus' followers, Judas was an example of the former, Peter of the latter. Pruning is also mentioned in prophetic texts such as Isa. 18:5; Jer. 5:10 (cf. Heb. 12:4–11).

The term *klēma*, "branch" (found in the NT only in John 15:2, 4–6), occurs in the LXX for the shoot of a vine (e.g., Num. 13:23; Ezek. 17:6), as distinct from the branch (*klados*) of other trees. The expression is used particularly of vine tendrils, although occasionally it refers to heavier branches as well. In 15:5 Jesus makes clear that the branches in the present symbolic discourse represent his followers. In the original instance "in me" (15:2) would include Judas (cf. 13:10–11; see Brown 1966–1970: 675–76). The reference in 15:6 to branches that do not remain in the vine being picked up and thrown into the fire and burned closely resembles the thought of Ezek. 15:1–8, where the prophet likewise warned that a vine failing to produce fruit would be good for nothing but a fire.

The repeated references "does not bear fruit … does bear fruit … bear even more fruit" (15:4, 5, 8) draw attention to the fact that the bearing of fruit is God's primary creative (Gen. 1:11–12, 22, 28) and redemptive purpose (cf. John 15:8, 16). The OT prophets envisioned a time when Israel would "bud and blossom and fill all the world with fruit" (Isa. 27:6; cf. Hos. 14:4–8). Indeed, the bearing of fruit is the essential purpose of a vineyard (Morris 1995: 594).

The "vine" metaphor illustrates the closely knit relationship that Jesus desires with his disciples. Even more than the "shepherd" imagery in chapter 10, which conveys the notion of the intimacy between Jesus and his "sheep," the illustration of a vine and its branches focuses on the organic, vital connection that Jesus has with his followers, a connection that will be made possible in the future (from the historical precrucifixion vantage point of Jesus and the disciples) through the indwelling presence of the Holy Spirit. As we noted, in a major paradigm shift, Jesus' presence among his disciples is about to be replaced by the Spirit's taking up residence in believers (cf. 14:16–18). This spiritual relationship must be nurtured if Jesus' followers are to remain connected to their exalted Lord (for a discussion of the Johannine references to *menō*, "remain," see Köstenberger 2004: 453).

The "in" terminology in chapter 15 harks back to OT covenant theology, including prophetic texts regarding a future new covenant (cf. Exod. 25:8; 29:45; Lev. 26:11–12; Ezek. 37:27–28; 43:9; see Carson 1991: 516; Malatesta 1978, esp. chap. 8; Pryor 1988: 49–50; Köstenberger 1999: 154–55). The imagery in 15:6 of a branch that is thrown away and withers and subsequently is picked up, thrown into the fire, and burned may hark back to the parallel in Ezek. 15:1–8, where a vine failing to produce fruit is said to be good for nothing but the fire (cf. Ezek. 19:12; see Carson 1991: 517). "Fire" (*pyr*, only here in John's Gospel) is a common Jewish and biblical symbol for divine judgment (e.g., Isa. 30:27; Matt. 3:12 par.; 5:22; 18:8; 25:41; Luke 12:49; Heb. 12:29; 2 Pet. 3:10; Jude 7, 23; Rev. 20:14).

Jesus, in order to forestall the notion that obedience is all gloom and doom (Carson 1991: 521), avers to the contrary that the goal of his instruction (telic *hina*; see Morris 1995: 598n27) is joy. Jesus' desire is that his joy may be in his followers and that their joy may be complete (15:11; cf. Ps. 19:8). In keeping with John's focus on believers' present experience of salvation blessings, he grounds their joy in OT prophetic notions of end-time rejoicing (e.g., Isa. 25:9; 35:10; 51:3; 61:10; 66:10; Zeph. 3:14–17; Zech. 9:9). In rabbinic thought joy was imperfect in the present age, marred by the certain prospect of death and the worries of this life (*Gen. Rab.* 42:3; attributed to *Rabbi Samuel ben Nahman* [ca. AD 260]). Only the age to come, the messianic era, would see perfect joy. Jesus' reference to "perfect joy" thus amounts to a claim to be the Messiah. (On Jesus' love commandment in 15:12–17 [cf. 15:9–10], see commentary at 13:34–35 above.)

In light of Jesus' statement that the greatest love is to lay down one's life for his friends (15:13), the question naturally arises, "Who are Jesus' friends?" Jesus' answer is, "You are my friends if you do what I command you." In the OT only Abraham (2 Chron. 20:7; Isa. 41:8) and, by implication, Moses (Exod. 33:11) are "friends of God." Other Jewish writings apply this designation to Abraham (*Jub.* 19:9; CD-A III, 2; *Apoc. Ab.* 9:6; 10:5; cf. James 2:23) and Moses (Philo, *Heir* 21; *Sacrifices* 130; *Cherubim* 49; *Moses* 1.156), and also to other OT figures, including Isaac, Jacob, and Levi (*Jub.* 30:20; CD-A III, 3–4), or even the Israelites (e.g., *Jub.* 30:21), holy souls (Wis. 7:27), and students of Torah (*m. 'Abot* 6:1). Here Jesus extends the same privilege of friendship to all believers, predicated on their obedience to his commands.

The disciples' status as Jesus' "friends" is not an idle privilege, but rather carries with it a solemn responsibility: "You did not choose me, but I chose you" (15:16). Election is hardly ever mentioned in the case of the OT "friends of God." Only once is it said of Abraham (Neh. 9:7) and Moses (Ps. 106:23) that they were chosen by God. The OT concept of election is primarily related to the king and Israel, God's "chosen people." Jesus here broke with contemporary custom, for it was common in first-century Palestine for disciples to attach themselves to a particular rabbi, not vice versa (*m. 'Abot* 1:6). The term for "appointed" (*tithēmi*) in 15:16 is probably a Semiticism; the same or a similar expression is used in the OT for God's appointment of Abraham as father of many nations (Gen. 17:5; cf. Rom. 4:17), the ordination of Levites (Num. 8:10), and Moses' commissioning of Joshua (Num. 27:18).

The Spirit and the Disciples' Witness to the World (15:18–16:33)

The next and final major unit in the Farewell Discourse deals with the world's hostility toward Jesus and his followers and with the future ministry of the Holy Spirit. The second first-class conditional sentence in 15:20, "If they kept my word, they will also keep yours," has several formal OT parallels linking the reception of a prophet's message with the people's stance toward God himself (e.g., 1 Sam. 8:7; Ezek. 3:7). Jesus' explanation in 15:21, "They will do this on account of my name," reflects OT terminology pertaining to God and his great name (cf. 1 Sam. 12:22; 2 Chron. 6:32; Jer. 14:21; see Brown 1966–1970: 687), though in the present context the expression is essentially synonymous with "me" (Carson 1991: 526; Moloney 1998: 433).

15:25

A. The NT Context: The Jews' Hatred of Jesus Fulfills Scripture. After instructing his disciples about various consequences related to his imminent departure, including the giving of the Holy Spirit (14:16–18, 25–26) and their need to remain in close spiritual union with him (15:1–17), Jesus turns his attention to the world's opposition, which in short order will shift from him to his followers, who remain in the world (15:18–16:4). According to Jesus, the world's opposition to him, like Judas's betrayal of him, is shown to fulfill OT Scripture. Five references to the world's hatred of both Jesus and his followers in 15:18–24 culminate in the scriptural citation in v. 25 (Daly-Denton 2004: 131).

The introductory formula here, "But in order that the word might be fulfilled that is written in their law . . . ," the longest in this Gospel if not the entire NT (Brown 1966–1970: 689; cf. Freed 1965: 94; Schnackenburg 1990: 3:117; on fulfillment quotations, see commentary at 12:38 above), is elliptical (so Ridderbos 1997: 525; Brown 1966–1970: 688; Morris 1995: 605; Barrett 1978: 482; Carson 1991: 527n2), the presumably required addition being "But *this happened* in order that . . ." (Ridderbos 1997: 525 and note 141, citing BDF §448.7). "Their law" (see 12:34; cf. 8:17; 10:34) ironically highlights the discrepancy between the law and the actions of the Jews (Carson 1991: 527; Morris 1995: 605), who are convicted by "their own law" (Barrett 1978: 482), whereby "law" means broadly "Scripture" (Ridderbos 1997: 525).

The citation here, "They hated me without a cause," is from Ps. 35:19 or 69:4, reflecting Davidic typology (Carson 1991: 527; note that the motif of groundless hatred is found also in Ps. 109:3; 119:161, though the wording is different). The latter passage is the more likely source of the present quotation, as Ps. 69 was widely regarded as messianic (so Ridderbos 1997: 525–26; Barrett

1978: 482; Carson 1991: 527; Beasley-Murray 1999: 276; Menken 1996a: 144–45; *contra* Moloney [1998: 434], who contends that "most" favor Ps. 35) and the evangelist previously cited Ps. 69:9 in 2:17 (see also Ps. 119:161; extrabiblical parallels include *Pss. Sol.* 7:1; *b. Yoma* 9b, cited in Köstenberger 2002b: 147; cf. Barrett 1978: 482; Brown 1966–1970: 689). Also, the parallelism between hate and persecution is found in Ps. 68:5a–b LXX (Menken 1996a: 144).

B. The OT Context of Ps. 69:4; 35:19. Psalm 69:9a is quoted in 2:17, and 19:28 may allude to Ps. 69:21 (see discussions above and below). This Davidic psalm presents the figure of a righteous sufferer who is zealous for God but is persecuted by God's enemies because of his zeal. The reference to "those who hate me without cause" in Ps. 69:4 is found at the beginning of a prayer for deliverance uttered by the psalmist, who is in dire distress in the face of the multitude of his enemies who actively plot to seek his downfall. In the same verse the psalmist elaborates that "mighty are those who would destroy me, those who attack me with lies." This points to the power of the psalmist's enemies and the falseness of their accusations against him. Beyond this, few details are given, which allows readers to fill in the specific situation out of their own imaginations (Tate 1990: 196).

The situation is similar in Ps. 35, also a psalm of David and a prayer for deliverance from enemies who pursue the righteous sufferer "without cause" (35:7, 19). There, too, the false charges of "malicious witnesses" (35:11, 21) and their deceitful words are highlighted (35:20). The righteous sufferer is called God's "servant" (35:27). Despite overwhelming opposition, the psalmist anticipates victory that will ensue when God rises up on his behalf (this assurance is sprinkled throughout the entire psalm, esp. 35:19–28; see Craigie 1983: 286). Beyond these two passages that talk specifically about the psalmist being "hated without a cause," there are numerous passages in Psalms that portray the psalmist as hated by those who hate God, particularly in psalms attributed to David (e.g., Ps. 9:13; 18:17–18; 25:19; 38:19; 41:7; 86:17; see also 44:7, 10; 118:7; see also Lam. 3:52).

C. Ps. 69:4; 35:19 in Judaism. The wording of *Pss. Sol.* 7:1 (written in Jerusalem prior to the end of the first century AD), "they who hated us without reason" (*hoi emisēsan hēmas dōrean*), suggests either Ps. 69:4 or Ps. 35:19 as the antecedent passage (see Menken 1996a: 142). The phrase occurs as part of the opening verse of a prayer, "Do not move away from us, O God, lest those who hate us without cause should attack us." The writer asks God to discipline his people as he wishes, but not to turn them over to the Gentiles (7:3). Hence there is precedent for Jesus' appropriation of Ps. 69:4/35:19 to himself in Jewish Second Temple literature.

D. Textual Matters. With regard to the introductory formula, the phrase *all' hina* occurs several times in this Gospel (1:8; 9:3; 11:52; 13:18; 14:31); *hina plērōthē ho logos* reflects Johannine style as well (12:38; 18:9, 32), as does the reference to "their law" (8:17; 10:34). John's quotation accurately reflects both the MT and the LXX, though in John the verb form is changed from the LXX's substantival participle "those who hate" (*hoi misountes*) to the finite verb "they hated" (*emisēsan*). In view of the translation of the adverb with *dōrean*, rather than with any of the available alternative renderings, the quotation most likely derives from the LXX (Menken 1996a: 142–43).

E. The Use of Ps. 69:4 and/or Ps. 35:19 in John 15:25. In 15:25, Jesus' appropriation from Ps. 69:4 or Ps. 35:19 of the phrase "they hated me without a cause" in the face of his imminent cross-death evokes the type of the righteous sufferer in these psalms (as well as Ps. 22 and other OT psalms), possibly including various entailments supplied by the context of the original passage. These include (1) the large number of the sufferer's enemies; (2) the great power of those enemies; (3) the false charges leveled by the enemies; (4) the righteous sufferer's prayerful trust in God. In his final instructions to his followers Jesus points out that the opposition against him is "without a cause"; that is, it is not based on rational argument or on legitimate grounds, but rather is a function of improper motives on the part of his pursuers. The Johannine account of Jesus' ministry to the Jews in 1:19–12:50 (including the opposition that he faced) and the passion narrative in chapters 18–19 provide ample documentation of this groundless hatred that motivated those who brought charges against Jesus and had him nailed to a cross.

F. Theological Use. As in 2:17, Jesus' and the evangelist's use of an OT psalm reflecting the experience of the righteous sufferer taps into the typological pattern of one who is zealous for God and his cause but is persecuted by his enemies as a result. In Jesus' case the pattern is one of both fulfillment of typology and of transformation of OT symbolism on a higher spiritual plane. Whereas the OT psalmist expected deliverance from his enemies and salvation from their wrath, in Jesus' case God's wrath was allowed to fall on him for the sake of the salvation of humankind. Rather than escape hatred, Jesus bore the full brunt of the world's hatred in order to provide deliverance for those who look to him in faith (cf. 3:14; see Craigie 1983: 288–89). Jesus found a precedent for this in the adversity and antagonism encountered by David, which in the ultimate analysis were no "strange misfortune," but rather David's "own predestined lot" (Kidner 1973: 144).

Concerning the references to the *paraklētos* and the "Spirit of truth" in 15:26, see commentary at 14:26 above. The call in 15:26–27 for Jesus' followers to serve as his witnesses in conjunction with the Holy Spirit is in keeping with OT prophetic literature (esp. Isaiah), where God's end-time people are called God's "witnesses" to the nations (e.g., Isa. 43:10–12; 44:8).

The expression "a time is coming" in 16:2 is reminiscent of prophetic or apocalyptic expressions such as "the days are coming" (e.g., Isa. 39:6; Jer. 7:32; 9:25; 16:14; 31:31, 38; Zech. 14:1; 2 Esd. 5:1; 13:29). The statement in 16:2, "Anyone who kills you will think he is rendering a service to God" (cf. Isa. 66:5), most likely refers to Jewish rather than Roman persecution (Brown 1966–1970: 691; Bultmann 1971: 556; *contra* Moloney 1998: 435). Some rabbinic authorities held that slaying heretics was an act of divine worship (*Num. Rab.* 21:3; cf. Num. 25:13; see Carson 1991: 531). However, these kinds of judgments rarely became public policy. For the most part, Jewish persecution of Christians was spontaneous, whereas seasoned voices counseled moderation (e.g., Acts 5:33–40; cf. *m. Sanh.* 9:6).

Jesus' reference to the sending of the *paraklētos* in 16:7 harks back to the anticipation of the pouring out of the Spirit and of the inauguration of the age of the kingdom in OT prophetic literature (e.g., Isa. 11:1–10; 32:14–18; 42:1–4; 44:1–5; Jer.

31:31–34; Ezek. 11:17–20; 36:24–27; 37:1–14; Joel 2:28–32; cf. John 7:37–39; 20:22). Jesus' words in 16:8–11 about the Spirit's work of convicting the world about sin, righteousness, and judgment most likely refer to the world's sin (expressed supremely in its hostility toward Jesus [15:18–25]), to Jesus' righteousness as the basis for the world's judgment (less likely, the world's *lack of* righteousness, per passages such as Isa. 64:6, is in view [so Carson 1979]), and to the resulting judgment of the world itself (cf. 16:33; see Köstenberger 2004: 471–73).

The Spirit's future "guidance in all truth," promised by Jesus in 16:13, entails providing entrance to the revelatory sphere of God's character and ways. In one very important sense, it is Jesus, as the eschatological Word, who has definitively explained the Father (1:18). In another sense, however, by salvation-historical necessity, it is the Spirit who guides his followers in "all" truth. Such divine guidance was already the psalmist's longing (Ps. 25:4–5; 43:3; 86:11; 143:10). The prophet Isaiah recounts how God led his people Israel in the wilderness by the Holy Spirit (Isa. 63:14) and predicts God's renewed guidance in the future (Isa. 43:19). Second Temple literature applies "guidance" terminology to the figure of divine Wisdom (Wis. 9:11; 10:10, 17; see also 1QS IV, 2; Philo, *Moses* 2.265; *Giants* 54–55).

Jesus' reference to the Spirit guiding Jesus' followers in all truth, speaking only what he hears and also telling Jesus' followers what is yet to come (16:13), may also contain an echo of OT terminology. The verb *anangellō* ("proclaim"), used twice in 16:14–15, occurs over forty times in the book of Isaiah (see Brown 1966–1970: 708, citing F. W. Young 1955: 224–26), where declaring things to come is the exclusive domain of Yahweh (Isa. 48:14). A close parallel to the present passage is Isa. 44:7, where Yahweh challenges anyone to declare the things to come (cf. Isa. 42:9; 46:10). Another striking parallel is found in Isa. 41:21–29 (esp. vv. 22–23; see also 45:19). The object of revelation, "what is yet to come" subsequent to the giving of the Spirit, cannot be the passion, but must be events following Pentecost. The emphasis may lie not so much on predictive prophecy (Schlatter 1948: 314), but rather on helping the believing community understand its present situation in light of Jesus' by-then-past revelation of

God. This entails both "a more profound penetration into the content of revelation" and "the application of that revelation to the behaviour of the community within the world" (Schnackenburg 1990: 3:135).

"A little while" (seven times in 16:16–19) harks back to previous instances of this expression (within the Farewell Discourse, see 13:33; see also 7:33; 12:35; 14:19). Similar terms are used by the OT prophets for announcing both God's judgment (Isa. 10:25; Jer. 51:33; Hos. 1:4; Hag. 2:6) and his salvation (Isa. 29:17). The repeated expression "then after a little while" is reminiscent of Isa. 26:20 (see also the reference to Isa. 26:17 in John 16:21, on which, see commentary below). In the present context the reference is plainly to the brief period between Jesus' crucifixion and resurrection in the first instance (the "little while" after Jesus' followers will no longer see him) and the resurrection appearances in the second (the "little while" after which the disciples will see Jesus again) (rightly Carson 1991: 543; cf. Morris 1995: 623; Burge 2000: 440).

Explaining his references to the "little while," Jesus predicts that his followers will weep and mourn, while the world will rejoice, but that his disciples' grief will turn to joy (16:20). In the OT Israel knew that it was God who could "turn their mourning into gladness" and give them "comfort and joy instead of sorrow" (Jer. 31:13; cf. Isa. 61:1–3; 2 Esd. 2:27; similar terminology for mourning is found in Jer. 22:10). The Jewish festival of Purim celebrates "the time when the Jews got relief from their enemies, and . . . when their sorrow was turned into joy and their mourning into a day of celebration" (Esther 9:22).

In the present instance Jesus illustrates this psychological dynamic by the experience of childbirth (16:21). The labor preceding birth is intense, but the moment the child is born, all anguish is forgotten out of joy that a new baby has been born. In the prophetic portions of the OT the image of a woman in labor is extremely common (see Isa. 13:8; 21:3; 26:16–21 [where the figure of a woman in labor, the phrase "a little while," and the promise of resurrection are found in combination]; 42:14; 66:7–13; Jer. 4:31; 6:24; 13:21; 22:23; 30:6; 49:22–24; 50:43; Mic. 4:9–10; cf. 2 Esd. 16:38) and frequently applies to the coming of end-time salvation through the Messiah.

The day of the Lord is regularly portrayed as "a time of distress" (Dan. 12:1; Zeph. 1:14–15). Second Temple Judaism coined the phrase "the birth pains of the Messiah" to refer to the period of tribulation that precedes the final consummation (e.g., 1QHᵃ XI, 8–12; cf. Rev. 12:2–5; see Brownlee 1956–1957, esp. 29). This terminology is also used in Jesus' teaching on the end times, in which he speaks of "the beginning of birth pains" and times of "great distress" (Matt. 24:8, 21, 29 pars.).

The phrase "a child [lit., 'a human being,' anthrōpos] is born into the world" (16:21) entails a certain amount of redundancy, since in rabbinic language "one born into the world" refers to a human being. The phrase "you [lit., 'your heart'] will rejoice" (16:22) duplicates the words of Isa. 66:14, where the Lord speaks words of comfort regarding Jerusalem (cf. Isa. 60:5; more generally, Ps. 33:21; see Menken 1996a: 14–15; Carson 1991: 545). The distinction in 16:25 between "illustrations" and "plain language" involves the use of paroimia (translating Heb. māšāl in the LXX). In biblical and extrabiblical literature this covers a wide range of parabolic and allegorical discourse (e.g., Sir. 39:3; 47:17; see commentary at 10:6 above).

The characterization in 16:28 of Jesus as having come from the Father and going back to the Father (cf. 8:14; 13:3), which sums up Jesus' entire mission, from his sending from the Father (3:16) through the incarnation (1:10–11, 14) to his departure from the world (14:19) and his return to the Father (the dominant theme of chaps. 14–17), develops the prophetic portrayal of the sent and returning Word of God in Isa. 55:10–11 (see commentary at 1:1 above; Brown 1966–1970: 735–36). Jesus' not needing anyone to ask him questions (16:30) should be understood in light of the Jewish notion that the ability to anticipate questions is a mark of divinity (e.g., Matt. 6:8; cf. Josephus, Ant. 6.230; also John 2:23–25; see Carson 1991: 548).

In 16:32 Jesus speaks prophetically of "a time that is coming" at which his followers "will be scattered," a probable allusion to Zech. 13:7 (quoted in Matt. 26:31 par.; cf. Matt. 26:56b; also 1 Kings 22:17; see Ridderbos 1997: 545). The image of shepherdless sheep and the scattering of God's flock is also the subject of other OT passages (e.g.,

Isa. 53:6; Jer. 23:1; 50:17; Ezek. 34:6, 12, 21; cf. John 10:12; 11:52). Yet in the present passage it is not that the disciples will be left without a shepherd, but rather that Jesus will be deserted by his sheep. As in 1 Kings 22:17, the scattering is linked with everyone "going to his own home" (*eis ta idia* [cf. John 19:27; Esther 5:10; 6:12; 3 Macc. 6:27; see Schnackenburg 1990: 3:165]). This probably refers to the disciples' temporary dwellings in Jerusalem rather than to their homes in Galilee.

The Farewell Discourse proper ends on a triumphant note, with Jesus anticipating his victory in the face of apparent defeat: "Take heart, I have triumphed over the world" (16:33). This is the only instance of the term *nikaō* ("triumph") in John's Gospel. The expression occurs several times in John's first letter (2:13, 14; 4:4; 5:4 [also has the related noun *nikē*, "victory"], 5) and well over a dozen times in the book of Revelation (esp. in the letters to the seven churches in chaps. 2–3) (see Schlatter 1948: 317). This verb occurs only rarely in the Greek of the canonical OT, with Ps. 50:6 LXX, for example, showing God as conqueror; it appears more often in the apocryphal and pseudepigraphical literature (e.g., Wis. 4:2; 16:10; 18:22; 1 Esd. 3:12).

Jesus' parting prayer in chapter 17 closes off the Johannine Farewell Discourse. The prayer culminates the Fourth Evangelist's portrayal of Jesus as the obedient, dependent Son of the Father, who, after completing his mission, is about to return to the one who sent him (cf. Isa. 55:10–11; see Ridderbos 1997: 547). Various elements of prayers are found in both Jewish and Hellenistic farewell discourses (e.g., Gen. 49; Deut. 32; *Jub.* 22:7–23). It is not uncommon for farewell discourses to conclude with a prayer (*Jub.* 22:28–30; Sir. 51:1–12, 29; cf. *Jub.* 1:19–21; *4 Ezra* 8:19b–36); some testaments conclude with a short prayer of praise (*T. Job* 43:4–17; *T. Isaac* 8:6–7; *T. Jac.* 8:6–9). Occasionally, prayers are used to link sections of an apocalypse (*4 Ezra* 8:20–36; *2 Bar.* 21; 34; 48:1–24). John 17 displays several thematic links with the Targumim to Exod. 19–20 (Marzotto 1977). Although the content of these prayers is markedly different from John 17, the form is present (see also Targumim on Deut. 32).

By lifting up his eyes toward heaven (17:1), Jesus strikes a customary posture in prayer (cf. Ps. 123:1; Mark 7:34; Luke 18:13). The first unit in this prayer is Jesus' intercession for himself (17:1–5). Jesus' opening petition, "Father, . . . Glorify your Son, in order that the Son may glorify you" (17:1), implies Jesus' claim to deity, as the OT affirms that God will not give his glory to another (e.g., Isa. 42:8; 48:11). God's granting of authority to Jesus (17:2; cf. 5:27) marks the inbreaking of a new era (cf. Isa. 9:6–7; Dan. 7:13–14; see also Matt. 11:27; 28:18; cf. also Wis. 10:2).

With regard to Jesus' statement in 17:2–3, the emphasis on the possession of eternal life in the here and now in John's Gospel differs from the perspective conveyed by the Synoptics, which, in keeping with the Jewish attitude prevalent at the time of Jesus, view eternal life primarily as a possession to be attained in "the age to come." But in John's Gospel the distinction between "the present age" and "the age to come" is collapsed; with Jesus, eternity has entered into human existence already in the present (Ladd 1993: 290–95). This realization is rooted in the knowledge that God is life itself, and that Jesus is the Son of God (cf. 1:4; 5:26; 20:31).

"Knowing" God (17:3) is not merely a function of cognitive knowledge (thus in his first epistle John disputes the communion with God falsely claimed by gnostic teachers); rather, it means living in fellowship with him (Carson 1991: 556; Barrett 1978: 504). This is in keeping with the Hebrew use of the term "to know," which encompasses even the most intimate human relationship, sexual intercourse (e.g., Gen. 4:1 LXX). Although God can be known to a limited extent through creation (Rom. 1:18–25), ultimately, as acknowledged also in Hellenistic Jewish literature (Wis. 15:3), knowledge of God is contingent upon salvation (Barrett 1978: 503). In the Dead Sea Scrolls "life" or "eternal life" and "eternal knowledge" are set in close parallelism (CD-A III, 20; 1QS II, 3; cf. 1QS IV, 22; XI, 3–4).

That God is the "only true God" (17:3) is affirmed supremely in the Shema: "Hear, O Israel: The LORD our God, the LORD is one" (Deut. 6:4; cf. John 5:44; 1 Thess. 1:9; 1 John 5:20; for additional references, see Köstenberger 2004: 488, esp. note 24). Jesus, in turn, is the exclusive agent, sole authorized representative of this one true God; he is the God-sent Messiah, God's Anointed One, the Christ. Just as there is only one true God, so also there is only one way to the Father: Jesus Christ

(17:3, forming an *inclusio* with 1:17; another *inclusio* is formed by the references to Jesus' "work," in the singular, in 17:4 and 4:34; regarding Jesus' self-reference in the third person, see Jackson 1999, esp. 24–31).

"And now, Father, glorify me in your presence with the glory I had with you before the world came into being" (17:5). The phrase "and now" is found also in the OT in Yahweh's instructions to Moses (Exod. 19:5) and in the conclusion of David's prayer (2 Sam. 7:25–26) with reference to a result that should follow on the basis of the truth of certain facts (Beasley-Murray 1999: 292 note c). Preexistence is ascribed also to wisdom in Second Temple literature (e.g., Wis. 7:25; 9:10–11) on the basis of its portrayal in the OT book of Proverbs (esp. 8:28, 30). In John's Gospel preexistence is ascribed to Jesus by the designation "the Word" (1:1, 14); the title "Son of Man" (3:13; 6:62); the reference to Jesus being the "I am" preceding Abraham (8:58); and the reference to Jesus as the one who came from the Father and who is about to return to him (16:28).

The next unit in Jesus' prayer contains his intercession for his disciples (17:6–19), which commences with a rehearsal of his own ministry to them (17:6–8). When Jesus speaks about revealing to his disciples God's "name" (17:6; cf. 17:11–12), this encompasses who God is in his character, his essential nature (cf. Exod. 3:13–15; see Carson 1991: 558). Because his name is glorious, God wants it to be made known (e.g., Ps. 22:22; Isa. 52:6; Ezek. 39:7). The notion that Jesus reveals the Father in his whole person, both works and words, is foundational to John's Gospel (e.g., 1:18; 8:19, 27; 10:38; 12:45; 14:9–11). In the OT God's name is put in the central sanctuary (Deut. 12:5, 11), and knowledge of his name implies life commitment (Ps. 9:10). In John's Gospel, likewise, Jesus' revelation of God's name must be met with obedience, and Jesus is shown to replace both tabernacle and temple, having become the "place" where God has put his name (see also Isa. 62:6; 65:15–16). The portrayal of Jesus in 17:7–8 is reminiscent of the description of the prophet like Moses in Deut. 18:18.

The following section contains Jesus' actual prayer on behalf of his followers (17:9–19). Jesus' petitions are for his disciples' protection (17:11–16) and for their consecration for ser-

vice in the truth (17:17–19). The conception underlying the address "Holy Father" in 17:11 goes back to Lev. 11:44 (cf. Ps. 71:22; 111:9; Isa. 6:3). Similar addresses appear in Jewish literature: "O holy Lord of all holiness" (2 Macc. 14:36); "O Holy One among the holy" (3 Macc. 2:2); "You are holy and your Name is awesome" (*Shemoneh Esreh* 3). Holiness is ascribed to God also in the book of Revelation (e.g., 4:8; 6:10). Importantly, in Jesus' case addressing God as "holy" does not create a distance between him and God.

Jesus' reference in 17:12 to "the son of destruction" (a Semitism; cf. Matt. 23:15; see also 1QS IX, 16; X, 19; CD-A VI, 15; cf. XIII, 14) could refer either to Judas's character (cf. Isa. 57:4 LXX; *Jub.* 10:3) or his destiny (Isa. 34:5 LXX). In keeping with Johannine theodicy (cf. 12:38–40), even Judas's betrayal is said to have occurred "in order for Scripture to be fulfilled." This does not alter the fact that Judas made his decision as a responsible agent (see Mark 14:21/Matt. 26:24). Yet God sovereignly overrode Judas's evil designs to bring about his own good purposes (cf. Gen. 50:20). The antecedent passage probably is Ps. 41:9 (applied to Judas in John 13:18; see commentary there). Other scriptures fulfilled through Judas are Ps. 69:25; 109:8 (cited in Acts 1:20).

In 17:18 Jesus anticipates the commissioning of the disciples in 20:21. Just as Jesus was "set apart" and sent into the world (Morris 1995: 647–48n56), so also the disciples are set apart in order to be sent into the world. Jesus' relationship with the Father serves as the pattern for the disciples' relationship to Jesus as their sender (Köstenberger 1998b). A partial OT parallel is the instruction to Moses, who himself had been consecrated by God (Sir. 45:4) in order to consecrate others so that they too may serve God as priests (Exod. 28:41). Jesus' self-sacrifice on behalf of others is also reminiscent of the OT notion of "setting apart" sacrificial animals (cf., e.g., Deut. 15:19; see Michaels 1989: 297).

Jesus does not stop at praying for himself and his disciples; his vision transcends the present, reaching beyond his immediate followers to those who will believe through their message (17:20–26; see the parallel in Deut. 29:14–15). Jesus' concern for unity (17:21–23) and love (17:26) among his followers is paralleled by exhortations to fraternal love and harmony in Jewish testamentary literature. This parting concern is attributed to Noah (*Jub.* 7:26), Rebecca (*Jub.* 35:20), Isaac (*Jub.* 36:4), Zebulon (*T. Zeb.* 8:5–9:4), Joseph (*T. Jos.* 17:2–3), and Dan (*T. Dan* 5:3). The Qumran covenanters, too, saw themselves as a *yaḥad* ("union") and displayed a keen consciousness of their election (for a discussion of Qumran parallels to the notion of unity in John 17, see Brown 1966–1970: 777). The vision of a unified people of God was expressed earlier in John's Gospel in 10:16 ("one flock and one shepherd," an allusion to Ezek. 34:23; 37:24) and 11:52 ("gathering of the scattered children of God into one"). In the present instance believers' unity results from being taken into the unity of God (cf. 10:38; 14:10–11, 20, 23; 15:4–5), and believers, once unified, will be able to bear witness to the true identity of Jesus as the Sent One of God.

The phrase "so that the world may believe/know that you sent me" (17:21, 23) is reminiscent of OT texts such as Zech. 2:9. The expression "before the beginning of the world" in 17:24 (an echo of 17:5) has frequent parallels in Judaism (e.g., *Gen. Rab.* 1:10; 2:5; *Lev. Rab.* 25:3; *Num. Rab.* 12:6; *Deut. Rab.* 10:2; *As. Mos.* 1:13–14; for further Jewish references, see Hauck 1965). A suggestive parallel is found in *Odes Sol.* 41:15, where the Messiah is said to have been "known before the foundations of the world, that he might give life to persons forever by the truth of his name."

The foundation for Jesus' following appeal is his recognition of God as the "righteous Father" (see commentary on 17:11). The OT commonly teaches that God is righteous and just (e.g., Ps. 116:5; 119:137; Jer. 12:1). With Jesus' betrayal and innocent suffering imminent, he affirms the righteousness of God his Father.

The words "I myself may be in them" in 17:26 are replete with covenantal overtones (cf. 14:20; 17:23). Subsequent to the giving of the law at Sinai, the glory of God displayed on the mountain (Exod. 24:16) came to dwell in the midst of Israel in the tabernacle (Exod. 40:34). As God's people moved toward the promised land, God frequently assured them that he was in their midst (Exod. 29:45–46; Deut. 7:21; 23:14). In John's prologue Jesus is said to have come to dwell (lit., "to tabernacle" [1:14]) among his people, and now Jesus' earthly presence is about to be transmuted into his spiritual presence in his followers, in keeping with

OT notions of a new covenant (see commentary at 17:6). This concludes Jesus' final instruction to his disciples prior to the events of his passion.

The Passion Narrative (18–19)

SURVEY

The use of the OT in John's Gospel climaxes in the three OT quotations related to Jesus' death in 19:24, 36, 37. The two final references to the OT in this Gospel, in 19:36–37, conclude the Johannine "fulfillment quotations" and culminate and complete the Passover theme in John's Gospel. Allusions to the OT are found in 19:18, 28–29, 31, 38. "Thus, in the death of Jesus, as climactically defined by the Old Testament quotations, the Old Testament fulfillment motif and the Passover theme converge" (Porter 1994: 401).

THE BETRAYAL AND ARREST OF JESUS, AND JESUS' JEWISH TRIAL (18:1–27)

The Johannine passion narrative commences with Jesus' arrest (18:1–11) and continues with him being questioned by the high priest and denied by Peter (18:12–27). This is followed by accounts of Jesus' Roman trial before Pilate (18:28–19:16a) and his crucifixion and burial (19:16b–42).

The Kidron Valley (18:1) is mentioned frequently in the LXX and Jewish intertestamental literature (though in the Gospels only in John; see, e.g., 2 Sam. 15:23; 1 Kings 2:37; 15:13; 2 Kings 23:4, 6, 12). Jesus' self-identification in 18:5, "I am," probably has connotations of deity (Ridderbos 1997: 576; see commentary at 8:24 above). This is strongly suggested by the soldiers' falling to the ground in 18:6, a common reaction to divine revelation (see Ezek. 1:28; 44:4; Dan. 2:46; 8:18; 10:9; Acts 9:4; 22:7; 26:14; Rev. 1:17; 19:10; 22:8). This falling of the soldiers is reminiscent of certain passages in Psalms (see Ps. 27:2; 35:4; cf. 56:9; see also Elijah's experience in 2 Kings 1:9–14). Jewish literature recounts the similar story of the attempted arrest of Simeon (*Gen. Rab.* 91:6). The reaction also highlights Jesus' messianic authority, in keeping with texts such as Isa. 11:4 (cf. 2 Esd. 13:3–4).

Jesus' statement in 18:8–9 summarizes 17:12, which in turn harks back to 6:39; 10:28 (Ridderbos 1997: 577). Jesus is portrayed as the good shepherd who voluntarily chooses death to save the lives of his sheep (cf. 10:11, 15, 17–18, 28). The reference to Jesus' "cup" climaxes the arrest narrative (Ridderbos 1997: 578). "Cup" serves here as a metaphor for death. In the OT the expression refers primarily to God's "cup of wrath," which evildoers will have to drink (e.g., Ps. 75:8; Isa. 51:17, 22; Jer. 25:15–17; Ezek. 23:31–34; Hab. 2:16). Similar terminology is found in later Jewish writings and in the NT (see 1QpHab XI, 10–15; Rev. 14:10; 16:19; 18:6). This imagery may have been transferred to the righteous, guiltless one taking upon himself God's judgment by way of substitutionary suffering (see Delling 1957, esp. 110–15).

Jesus' words "I spoke nothing in secret," spoken at the Jewish trial (18:20; cf. 7:26), echo the words of Yahweh in the book of Isaiah (cf., e.g., 45:19; 48:16; see Brown 1966–1970: 826; Schlatter 1948: 334). In the present instance Jesus' point is not that he never spoke in private with his disciples, but rather that his message was the same in private as in public; Jesus was not guilty of a sinister conspiracy (Morris 1995: 669; Carson 1991: 584; Borchert 1996–2002: 2:232). When challenged regarding his response to the high priest (18:21–22), Jesus alludes to the law of Exod. 22:28 ("Do not blaspheme God or curse the ruler of your people" [cf. Acts 23:5]) and denies having violated it.

Jesus' Roman Trial (18:28–19:16a)

The reference to the Passover in 18:28 may not merely be to Passover itself, but to the Feast of Unleavened Bread, which lasted seven days (note Luke 22:1: "the Feast of Unleavened Bread, called the Passover"), and in particular to the feast-offering (*hagigah*), which was brought on the morning of the first day of the festival (cf. Num. 28:18–19). "Eat the Passover" probably simply means "celebrate the feast" (cf. 2 Chron. 30:21; see Carson 1991: 590). Similarly, "at the Passover" in 18:39 refers to the entire festival (cf. Deut. 16:1–2; Ezek. 45:21; Luke 2:41; 22:1; John 2:13, 23; 6:4; 11:55; Acts 12:4; Josephus, *Ant.* 17.213).

The Jews' comment in 19:7, "We have a law, and according to that law he must die, because he claimed to be the Son of God," may refer to Lev. 24:16: "Anyone who blasphemes the name of the LORD must be put to death" (Carson 1991: 599; Barrett 1978: 541; Ridderbos 1997: 602). Yet in both the OT and other Jewish literature

the claim of being God's son need not be blasphemous and may refer to the anointed king of Israel (2 Sam. 7:14; Ps. 2:7; 89:26–27) or to the Messiah (4Q174; cf. John 1:49; see Michel 1975–1985: 637). Even Israel could be called God's "son" (Exod. 4:22; Hos. 11:1; cf. John 10:33–38 [see commentary there]). Jesus' silence before Pilate in 19:9 is reminiscent of Isa. 53:7 (cf. Mark 14:61; 15:5).

Some propose that *paraskeuē* in 19:14 refers to the day preceding Passover—that is, the day on which preparations for Passover were made (in the present case, Thursday morning). If so, John says that Jesus is executed at the time at which Passover lambs are slaughtered in the temple. The Synoptic writers, however, clearly have Jesus and his disciples celebrate Passover on the night prior to the crucifixion, and they use *paraskeuē* to refer to the day preceding the Sabbath (Matt. 27:62; Mark 15:42; Luke 23:54; cf. Josephus, *Ant.* 16.163–164). Hence the term most likely refers to the day of preparation for the Sabbath—that is, Friday (cf. *Did.* 8:1; *Mart. Pol.* 7:1)—and *tou pascha* in 19:14 means not "of the Passover," but "of Passover week" (so NIV; see Carson 1991: 604). Thus, all four canonical Gospels concur that Jesus' last supper was a Passover meal eaten on Thursday evening (by Jewish reckoning, the onset of Friday).

Jesus' Crucifixion and Burial (19:16b–42)

The final unit in John's passion narrative following Jesus' Roman trial recounts Jesus' crucifixion and burial (19:16b–42). "He went out" in 19:17 is in keeping with Jewish custom that prescribed that executions take place outside the camp or city (Lev. 24:14, 23; Num. 15:35–36; Deut. 17:5; 21:19–21; 22:24). The evangelist may find Jesus' crucifixion between two criminals (19:18) to be reminiscent of Ps. 22:16: "a band of evil men has encircled me." The passage may also echo Isa. 53:12: "he . . . was numbered with the transgressors" (Beasley-Murray 1999: 346; Bultmann 1971: 669n1; Brown 1966–1970: 900).

19:24

A. The NT Context: Dividing Jesus' Clothes. Jesus' trial before Pilate ends in Jesus being handed over to the Jews for crucifixion (19:16). Once Jesus had been crucified, four Roman soldiers took his clothes—presumably, his belt, sandals, head-covering, and outer garment (Carson 1991: 612)—and divided them into four shares, one for each of them. The outer garment, however, was in one piece, woven seamlessly from top to bottom. For this reason the soldiers decide not to divide it up, but rather to cast lots for it.

The Fourth Evangelist is quick to assert that this action by the soldiers, though resulting from their free decision, "happened in order that the Scripture might be fulfilled" (19:24). References to the OT become more frequent in this Gospel as Jesus' passion approaches, presumably because the evangelist's Jewish audience would have been particularly skeptical about a crucified Messiah (Carson 1991: 612; Witherington 1995: 308). The OT reference in view is clearly Ps. 22:18, a Davidic passage regarding the righteous sufferer, which the Fourth Evangelist sees fulfilled in Jesus.

According to the Synoptic Gospels, Jesus recited at least the opening line of Ps. 22, and perhaps the entire psalm, on the cross (Matt. 27:46/ Mark 15:34). This indicates Jesus' close identification with the righteous sufferer depicted in Ps. 22, expressing both his sense of God-forsakenness in his suffering and his trust in God for ultimate deliverance and vindication. Hence Jesus' messianic consciousness shows itself in his experience of the crucifixion in terms of the righteous Davidic sufferer (as well as the Isaianic Servant of the Lord).

Notably, however, whereas the Synoptic writers quote Jesus' citation of the opening line of the psalm, which expresses the psalmist's sense of being forsaken by God, and make reference to the psalm also by recording the words of the mocking bystanders, John cites v. 18 of Ps. 22, focusing attention on the fact that Jesus' garment remained untorn, in keeping with scriptural prediction. While drawing on the psalm's parallelism, John's use involves an element of midrash, whereby the second line elaborates on the first, and the lines are shown to be enacted by the soldiers.

M. Daly-Denton (2004: 132–33) provides an interesting survey of torn or untorn robes in Scripture that may have resonated in the evangelist's thinking. In one such incident the prophet Ahijah tears his new garment into twelve pieces, giving away ten to Jeroboam and keeping only two, an action symbolizing the division of Solomon's kingdom (1 Kings 11:29–31). The scene echoes David's tearing of Saul's cloak at En-Gedi, which presaged the impending loss of Saul's kingship and David's assumption of the throne (1 Sam. 24).

Yet another incident involves Samuel and Saul. When Samuel, after announcing the end of Saul's rule, turns to depart, Saul seizes his robe, and it tears. At this, Samuel utters the prophecy that just as his robe tore that day, so God would tear the kingdom away from Saul and give it to someone more worthy (1 Sam. 15:27–28). If these passages are relevant, John's reference to Jesus' untorn robe may symbolize the unity of his kingdom (10:16; 11:51–52; 12:32) and refer to God's keeping of his promises to David (2 Sam. 7:13) (see Daly-Denton 2004: 133).

B. The OT Context of Ps. 22:18. Psalm 22, the most frequently quoted psalm in the NT, is an individual lament psalm ascribed to David in which laments (vv. 1–2, 6–8, 12–18) are interspersed with expressions of the sufferer's confidence in Yahweh (vv. 3–5, 9–10) and his pleas for deliverance (vv. 1, 19–21). The psalm ends with an extended vow to praise Yahweh (22:22–31). The psalmist's predicament throws into ever starker relief the faithfulness of God and intensifies his resolve to trust in his only source of deliverance. The dynamic of the psalm moves from abject rejection through faithful suffering to praise of Yahweh.

The reference to the sufferer's executioners already dividing up his garments in 22:18 suggests that as far as his executioners are concerned, the sufferer is already dead (cf. Sir. 14:15). Also striking are the references in the original psalm to the sufferer's thirst (22:15; cf. John 19:28), to his "pierced . . . hands and feet" (22:16; cf. John 19:23, 34, 37; 20:25; Zech. 12:10), and to the preservation of all his bones (22:17; cf. John 19:33) in the immediate context of 22:18. Remarkably, all of these aspects of the psalmist's suffering are fulfilled in and through the crucifixion of Jesus (see the Johannine texts cited).

C. Ps. 22:18 in Judaism. Although the NT writers consistently interpret Ps. 22 as finding its fulfillment in Christ (Matt. 27:35–43; Mark 15:34; John 19:24; Heb. 2:12), there is no evidence for a messianic interpretation of Ps. 22 in ancient Judaism (see Str-B 2:574–80). Most interpret the psalm with reference to Israel or Esther (cf. *Midr. Ps.* 22 §7 [92b], cited in Str-B 2:579, where Ps. 22:19 is interpreted with reference to Esther 4:16).

D. Textual Matters. The quotation in John is the same as in the MT and the LXX.

E. The Use of Ps. 22:18 in John 19:24. The present reference is one of several to the OT as part of a pattern to portray Jesus' crucifixion as in keeping with the experience of the righteous sufferer in Psalms (cf. 19:28, 36, 37). According to the Fourth Evangelist, by dividing Jesus' garments among them and by casting lots for his robe, the Roman soldiers unwittingly fulfilled Scripture. The soldiers' reasoning was that they did not want to tear Jesus' tunic, which was woven as a single piece of cloth (19:23–24).

Moreover, "the Evangelist sees in the *entire* distribution of Jesus' clothes a fulfillment of *both* lines of Ps. 22:18, but mentions the peculiarity of the decision about the tunic because he was an eyewitness, and possibly because he saw something symbolic in the seamless garment" (Carson 1991: 614; see also Carson 1988: 249–50). In this, as well as in several other ways (see discussions above and below), Jesus' crucifixion conformed to the pattern of scriptural prophecy regarding the suffering of the Messiah (so also *Barn.* 6:6, citing Ps. 22:18 with reference to Jesus).

F. Theological Use. John's account of Jesus' crucifixion may be viewed in many ways as a midrash on Ps. 22:15–18 (cf. Matt. 27:35–43), which features the sufferer's thirst (v. 15), his "pierced . . . hands and feet" (v. 16), and the preservation of all his bones (v. 17). This may be intended to develop further the Synoptic references to Jesus' recitation of (the opening lines of) Ps. 22 (Matt. 27:46/Mark 15:34). This cluster of references strikes a strong note of fulfillment that is further underscored by the pattern of "fulfillment quotations" in the second half of John's Gospel, including the passion narrative (see commentary at 12:38).

The reference in 19:28 to Scripture being fulfilled builds on 19:24 (see above) and continues the evangelist's emphasis on Jesus' actively bringing about the respective events of his passion. John 19:28–29 most likely represents an allusion to Ps. 69:21: "They . . . gave me vinegar for my thirst" (cf. Matt. 27:34, 48; Ps. 69:21 is cited also in 1QH^a XII, 11; see Carson 1988: 252). The allu-

sion may involve the entire psalm in its portrayal of the righteous sufferer (Ridderbos 1997: 616; Carson 1991: 620). The choice of *teleiōthē* rather than *plērōthē* in 19:28 seems to be a function of the presence of *tetelestai* immediately preceding in 19:28 and following again in 19:30. John 19:28 constitutes "the final instance of Jesus' *active, self-conscious* fulfillment of Scripture" in this Gospel (Carson 1988: 252), and hence Jesus' cry there, "I thirst," fulfills the entire prophetic pattern of Scripture rather than merely matching an isolated trait of the psalmist's portrayal of the righteous sufferer (for a discussion of intertextuality in John 19:28–29, see Brawley [1993], who provides a positive assessment of the allusion to Ps. 69:21 in the present passage and yet notes the elusiveness of certainty because of the "absent complement").

Because the Jews did not want the bodies left on the crosses during the Sabbath, they asked Pilate to have the legs broken and the bodies taken down (19:31). The Jews' attitude was based on Deut. 21:22–23 (cf. Josh. 8:29), according to which bodies of hanged criminals must not defile the land by remaining on a tree overnight. There is also evidence that at times, especially during feast days, bodies were taken down and given to relatives (Philo, *Flacc.* 83–85). Josephus indicates that application of this passage was later extended to cover the crucified (*J.W.* 4.317; cf. Gal. 3:13).

When the soldiers came to Jesus and saw that he was already dead, they did not break his legs, but one of the soldiers pierced his side with a spear, and at once blood and water came out (19:34 [regarding Jesus' legs not being broken, see commentary on 19:36 below]). The flow of blood and water indicates that Jesus died as a fully human being (see *Lev. Rab.* 15:2 on Lev. 13:2; cf. 1 John 5:6–8). John may also be alluding to Exod. 17, especially v. 6: "Strike the rock, and water will come out of it for the people to drink" (cf. Num. 20:11; see Carson 1991: 624). An allusion to the Passover may also be in view (*m. Pesaḥ.* 5:5–8; cf. *m. 'Ohal.* 3:5), consisting of the hyssop (19:29), the unbroken bones (19:33, 36), and the mingled blood (19:34) (see Barrett 1978: 557; Burge 2000: 532). If so, John may witness to all three events that portray Jesus as the Passover lamb. Yet another scriptural fulfillment is noted by the evangelist in 19:37 (see commentary there).

19:36

A. The NT Context: The Preservation of Jesus' Bones. After 19:24, 28, this is now the third scriptural proof adduced by John that Jesus' death fulfills OT Scripture. Not only were Jesus' garments divided in fulfillment of Scripture (19:24) and did Jesus thirst on the cross (19:28), but also after Jesus had breathed his last, his legs were not broken, thus fulfilling OT Passover symbolism. Moreover, not only did Jesus escape the breaking of his legs (unlike those crucified with him), but also his body was pierced by a spear, again without sustaining bone damage.

Two sets of Scripture converge: (1) Ps. 34:20, depicting God's care for the righteous man: "He protects all his bones; not one of them will be broken"; (2) Exod. 12:46 and Num. 9:12, specifying that no bone of the Passover lamb may be broken (cf. 1 Cor. 5:7; 1 Pet. 1:19; see Brown 1966–1970: 952–53; Moloney 1998: 509). Apparently, "in Jewish thought disfiguration was an obstacle to resurrection," which may further explain why John takes pains to stress that no bone was broken (Daube 1956: 325–29; cf. Scheiber 1963).

B. The OT Context of Exod. 12:46; Num. 9:12; Ps. 34:20. The reference to bones not being broken in Exod. 12:46 comes in the context of requirements for Passover observance. No bone of the sacrificial animal may be broken, because, among other reasons, it is a symbol of the unity of the worshiping family and of the entire covenant community (Durham 1987: 173; Propp 1999: 418). This passage forms the conclusion of the exodus narrative, which began with references to the people's bondage in Egypt (chaps. 1–2) and to Moses' call (chaps. 3–4). The command of Exod. 12:46 is reiterated in Num. 9:12 (de Vaux 1964: 9–10, cited in Ashley 1993: 180n9). Psalm 34, a Davidic psalm, constitutes a (slightly irregular) acrostic poem centered on the assurance that the Lord will deliver the righteous (see esp. vv. 19–22).

C. Exod. 12:46; Num. 9:12; Ps. 34:20 in Judaism. The requirement that none of the bones of the Passover lamb be broken was observed in Judaism. Belief in God's protection of the righteous is amply attested in Jewish biblical and extrabiblical literature. The presupposed identification of the Passover lamb (Exod. 12:46; Num. 9:12) with the righteous sufferer (Ps. 34:20) is attested as well (see references in Menken 1996a: 160–64, with special attention to *Jub.* 49:13; see also Daube 1956: 309; Schuchard 1992: 139).

D. Textual Matters. The only difference between Exod. 12:46 and Num. 9:12 is that the verb in the former text is in the second-person plural (*syntripsete* [cf. Exod. 12:10 LXX]), while the latter has it in the third-person plural (*syntripsousin*). There are three differences between these texts and the citation in John 19:36: (1) the omission of the initial *kai*; (2) the omission of the preposition *apo* (Heb. 2; presumably owing to the influence of the psalm verse [Menken 1996a: 152]); (3) the verbal form, which is a third-person singular passive in John 19:36 rather than a second- or third-person plural active as in the Pentateuchal texts. In this regard, it is interesting to note that the Septuagint version of Ps. 34:20 (Ps. 33:21 LXX) features the exact same verb form as John 19:36: *syntribēsetai*. This makes it likely that Ps. 33:21 LXX is the source for the verbal form in John's quotation. Hence is it most likely that John's OT quotation represents a combination of Exod. 12:46/Num. 9:12 and Ps. 34:20.

E. The Use of Exod. 12:46; Num. 9:12; Ps. 34:20 in John 19:36. By this third of four fulfillment citations the Fourth Evangelist underscores the pattern of fulfillment characteristic of Jesus' death. This authenticates Jesus' claim of his messianic identity. In the present instance a powerful link is established between Jesus' sacrificial death and the Jewish Passover, which commemorated the deliverance of the Israelites from their bondage in Egypt (Exod. 12:46; Num. 9:12). This marks Jesus as the "lamb of God" who takes away the sins of the world (1:29, 36), in keeping with the Baptist's witness. This pattern of typology is also part and parcel of the Johannine replacement theme, according to which Jesus fulfills the symbolism inherent in a variety of Jewish festivals and institutions. Also, Jesus, in keeping with Davidic typology, is presented as a righteous man who is preserved by God in accordance with the assurance expressed by God's servants in the past (Ps. 34:20).

F. Theological Use. The present OT reference constitutes an instance of a typological use of Scripture whereby Jesus is shown to fulfill Passover symbolism. This taps into one of the most powerful symbols of Jewish national identity and connects Jesus' death with God's deliverance of his people from bondage in Egypt. According to the Fourth Evangelist, just as God effected deliverance from bondage for OT Israel through the exodus, so also he provided redemption from sin for the world through the vicarious death of Jesus. This Passover symbolism, in turn, is applied to God's preservation of the righteous sufferer, signaling that both motifs converge in Jesus, who was both God's perfect Passover lamb and the paradigmatic Davidic righteous sufferer.

19:37

A. The NT Context: Looking on the One Whom They Pierced. The present passage continues and completes the Fourth Evangelist's presentation of Jesus' crucifixion as conforming to the pattern laid out in the Hebrew Scriptures. The Roman soldiers' actions of dividing Jesus' clothes and casting lots for his garment (19:23–24), Jesus' indication of thirst (19:28–30), and the soldiers' not breaking Jesus' legs but piercing his side with a spear subsequent to the crucifixion (19:34–37) all proceed in keeping with biblical prophecy.

The present passage provides the second of two texts said to be fulfilled by the Romans' actions in 9:34, namely, Zech. 12:10: "They will look on the one they have pierced." The text is quoted also in Rev. 1:7; an earlier text in Zechariah, 9:9, is quoted in John 12:15 with reference to Jesus' kingship. The reference in John 16:32 to Jesus' followers being "scattered" may allude to the notion of the shepherd being stricken and the sheep being scattered in Zech. 13:7 (quoted by Jesus in Matt. 26:31/Mark 14:27).

B. The OT Context of Zech. 12:10. The text of Zech. 12:10 reads, "And I will pour out on the house of David and the inhabitants of Jerusalem a spirit of grace and pleas for mercy, so that, when they look on me, on him whom they have pierced, they shall mourn for him, as one mourns for an only child, and weep bitterly over him, as one weeps over a firstborn." This will result in great mourning in Jerusalem and by the family of the house of David (12:11–14).

Zechariah 12:9–10 is part of the second oracle, spanning 12:1–14:21, which concludes the book, focusing, by way of divine speech, on Yahweh's action against the nations. While 12:1–8 describes the external events to occur in Jerusalem "in that day," 12:9–14 depicts the internal condition of

God's people. Notably, Yahweh pouring out a spirit of grace (cf. Ezek. 36:25–26?) and supplication is connected to people looking on one whom they have pierced. An individual has been killed (a possible instance of a prophetic perfect), and this is followed by a period of profound mourning. In context (note the first-person references in 12:9, 10) the phrase "on me" can refer only to Yahweh himself (Keil 1889: 387; McComiskey 1998: 1214; the looking is more properly to be understood as looking "to" Yahweh in faith; see Num. 21:9; Isa. 45:22; cf. John 3:14–15; see Barker 1985: 683; Baldwin 1972: 190–91). Aided by the spirit of grace poured out on them, the people responsible for piercing the individual mentioned in 12:10 mourn and presumably ask God for forgiveness for what they have done, resulting in cleansing from sin (cf. 13:1–6; see McComiskey 1998: 1214–15).

Remarkably, it is not the nations that have pierced Yahweh, but rather "the house of David and the inhabitants of Jerusalem" (12:10). The piercing is in all likelihood literal, an actual killing (so McComiskey 1998: 1214; Keil 1889: 388), rather than figurative (as in being "pierced with sorrow"), since the Hebrew word *dāqar* in all its OT occurrences has a concrete sense ("spear": Num. 25:8; "sword": Judg. 9:54; 1 Sam. 31:4; 1 Chron. 10:4; Isa. 13:15; Lam. 4:9; cf. Zech. 13:7, where reference is made to the shepherd being struck by a sword; the figure of the "shepherd of the flock doomed to slaughter" in Zech. 11:4–14; and the instance of the word "pierce" in Zech. 13:3). The people's mourning "as one mourns for an only child" denotes extraordinary grief owing to the uniqueness of the individual (cf. Jer. 6:26; Amos 8:10).

The notion of the "piercing of Yahweh" in Zech. 12:10 suggests that suffering is not an unfamiliar experience to God, but that he knows it first hand. This clearly constitutes a mystery that can be understood more fully only in light of the incarnation and crucifixion of the Word-become-flesh, Jesus, who, as the God-man, was pierced for our transgressions as the messianic shepherd and the suffering servant in keeping with the pattern of OT prophecy regarding a suffering Savior (for an argument that Zech. 12:10 should be read against the backdrop of Isa. 53, see Deissler 1998).

C. Zech. 12:10 in Judaism. Later messianic interpretation developed the notion of one pierced into the belief that the Messiah ben Joseph, the precursor of the true Messiah, the Messiah ben David (the "royal messiah"), would be pierced by Israel's enemies, and people would look to Yahweh (Rabbi Dosa [ca. AD 90 or 180]; *b. Sukkah* 52a; see France 1971: 191n108; Bruce 1968: 112; Menken 1996a: 178–79). In this scenario the Messiah ben Joseph recaptures Jerusalem from the Romans. He is killed in a battle against the forces of Gog and Magog, and Israel escapes into the wilderness, until these nations are defeated and the Messiah ben David appears (France 1971: 191, citing Str-B 2:292–99).

D. Textual Matters. John's quotation here is close to the MT. Note, however, that both here and in Rev. 1:7 the original shift in Zech. 12:10 from the first to the third person ("on me," "for him") has become simply "on him." The LXX (which renders the phrase "because they have danced," misreading דקרו as רקדו, transposing the letters ד and ר) here misconstrues the Hebrew (Menken 1996a: 172–73; cf. McComiskey 1998: 1214; but see Aquila, Symmachus, and Theodotion, all of whom use *ekkenteō*; see Menken 1996a: 174), precluding John's use of it here (see further below). Another difference between the LXX and the citation of Zech. 12:10 in John 19:37 is that a different verb of seeing is used (*opsontai* rather than *epiblepsontai*). Whereas the Hebrew appears to refer to the piercing of Yahweh himself (see under §B above), John applies Zech. 12:10 to the piercing of Jesus. Although John normally seems to use the LXX, in the present instance this was not a valid option because the reference to the "piercing" is absent. For this reason it appears that John here presents an independent Greek translation of the Hebrew. In light of the preponderance of quotations of this passage in other Christian literature, it is possible (if not likely) that here John, rather than producing his own translation, drew on a Christian *testimonium* with which he was familiar (Menken 1996a: 185).

E. The Use of Zech. 12:10 in John 19:37. Together with the realization of other OT passages in conjunction with Jesus' cross-death, John saw the fulfillment of Zech. 12:10 at the crucifixion as confirmation that the Messiah was Jesus (cf. 20:31; see also the reference to the "smitten shepherd" in Zech. 13:7). Significantly, the fulfillment entails a reversal: it is as the one pierced that Jesus becomes the source of salvation for those who look on him in faith (cf. 3:14–15; 8:28; 12:32–33; see Menken 1996a: 180–81; see further below). In fact, all humanity will have to look at the pierced Messiah at the last judgment—to receive either final deliverance or final punishment (Ridderbos 1997: 623–24). Yet, in another important theological contribution, here the Fourth Evangelist does not place the "looking on" the Messiah in faith exclusively in the distant future (though he does that in 17:24; cf. 12:26; 14:3; cf. the use of Zech. 12:10 in Rev. 1:7), but rather, in keeping with his inaugurated-eschatological outlook, he projects a believing vision of the Messiah into the present and immediate future from a precrucifixion vantage point (see the verbs of "seeing" with Jesus as their object in 16:16–17, 19; 20:18, 20, 25, 29). If so, the evangelist himself is the first who has seen Jesus pierced and has believed (note in 19:35 the perfect-tense *heōrakōs*, "he has seen," so that "you too" may believe [see Menken 1996a: 184]). Finally, a related OT figure that may have been in John's mind is the Suffering Servant of Isa. 53:5, 10, who was "pierced for our transgressions" and "crushed" and "caused to suffer" (Bruce 1968: 112, citing Lamarche [1961: 136], who also adduces Ezek. 36:25–26, on which, see commentary at 3:5 above).

F. Theological Use. John's appropriation of Zech. 12:10 in the present passage operates on the basis of the hermeneutical axiom that Yahweh acts in the person of his authorized representative, the messianic shepherd, so that to strike and kill the shepherd, or to pierce him, is in a sense to pierce Yahweh himself. This is indicated in the original text by the shift from the first to the third person ("on me" [*ēlay*], "on him" [*ālāyw*]; see Keil 1889: 388); even though both John 19:37 and Rev. 1:7 simply read "on him," the presupposition seems nonetheless that Yahweh in the source text is represented by Jesus in their present context.

Not only this, but also it follows from the present text that people are looking at the same time at Yahweh and at the one whom they have pierced (cf. 3:14–15; see Meyers and Meyers 1993: 337). The mourning for the "only son" and "firstborn" described in Zech. 12:10, likewise, is taken up in Johannine theology with reference to Jesus, the "one-of-a-kind Son" of the Father (1:14, 18; 3:16, 18; cf. Gen. 22:2, 12, 16). In keeping with the prophecy of Zech. 12:11, Luke describes the mourning and remorse of the bystanders at the cross in Luke 23:48 and the subsequent repentance in response to the proclamation of the gospel in Acts 2:37–41.

John's account of Jesus' burial commences with Joseph of Arimathea, a wealthy member of the Sanhedrin (Matt. 27:57 pars.), asking Pilate for the body of Jesus (19:38). Joseph's intervention fulfilled another Scripture: "He was assigned a grave with the wicked, and with the rich in his death" (Isa. 53:9) (see Witherington 1995: 313). The number of aromatic spices brought by Joseph and Nicodemus was considerable (19:39–40), which has a precedent in King Asa's burial (2 Chron. 16:14). Burials in gardens are also recorded in the OT (Manasseh [2 Kings 21:18]; Amon [2 Kings 21:26]). According to Neh. 3:16 LXX (cf. Acts 2:29), the popular tomb of David was situated in a garden as well.

Jesus' Resurrection and the Gospel's Purpose (20:1–31) and the Epilogue (21:1–25)

Survey

John 20 provides the conclusion of the passion narrative and the penultimate conclusion of the entire Gospel, narrating Jesus' resurrection (though the actual resurrection is not recorded) and appearances to his disciples. At the heart of the chapter is the commissioning of Jesus' followers, encircled by narratives focusing on Mary Magdalene and Thomas, respectively. The chapter also continues the parallel feature of Peter and the Beloved Disciple in the second half of the Gospel, which is brought to final resolution in the epilogue in chapter 21.

The Empty Tomb, the Resurrection Appearances, and the Commissioning (20:1–31)

The evangelist's aside in 20:9 that Peter and "the other disciple" did not yet understand the Scripture—"that he [Jesus] must rise from the dead"—may point to a specific OT passage (suggestions include Ps. 16:10; Isa. 53:10–12; and

Hos. 6:2), although it is possible that the reference is to Scripture in its entirety (cf. Luke 24:25–27, 32, 44–47).

The common Jewish greeting "Peace be with you" (20:19, 21, 26; cf., e.g., 1 Sam. 25:6; see Morris 1995: 745), representing Hebrew *šālôm ʾălēkem*, is still used today. In Jesus' case "peace" was uniquely his gift to his followers by virtue of his vicarious sacrificial death on the cross (see commentary at 14:27; 16:33). The expression may also function as a formula of revelation (cf. Judg. 6:23; Dan. 10:19; see Borchert 1996–2002: 2:304–5). Jesus' greeting was to assuage any lingering fears that his followers may have had as a result of their deserting him prior to the crucifixion (cf. 16:32; see Morris 1995: 745). This pertains particularly to Peter, who doubtless was in their midst as well (see chap. 21; cf. Mark 16:7).

The disciples' commissioning in 20:21–23 climaxes the characterization of Jesus as the sent Son and shows Jesus' followers as drawn into the unity and mission of Father, Son, and Spirit (cf. 15:26–27; 17:21–26). Succession is important both in the OT and in Second Temple literature. In the Fourth Gospel Jesus succeeds the Baptist and is followed by both the Spirit and the Twelve (minus Judas), who serve as representatives of the new messianic community. OT narratives involving succession feature Joshua (following Moses) and Elisha (succeeding Elijah).

Jesus' act of breathing on his disciples and saying "Receive the Holy Spirit" in 20:22 is best understood as a symbolic promise of the impending gift of the Spirit, not the actual giving of it fifty days later at Pentecost (cf. Acts 2; see Carson 1991: 649–55; see the interaction with other views in Köstenberger 2004: 574n16). The theological antecedent clearly is Gen. 2:7, where the LXX has the exact same verb form as in John 20:22 (see also 1 Kings 17:21; Ezek. 37:9; Wis. 15:11). There in Genesis God breathes his Spirit into Adam at creation, constituting him as a living being. Analogously, in an instance of the "new creation" theme (Morris 1995: 747n58; Barrett 1978: 570; Brown 1966–1970: 1035, 1037; Keener 2003: 1204), Jesus' breathing on his disciples constitutes them as the new messianic community in anticipation of the outpouring of the Spirit subsequent to his ascension.

The reference to forgiveness or lack thereof in 20:23 may echo the reference to "the key to the house of David" in Isa. 22:22 (cf. Rev. 3:7; see Emerton 1962). If so, what is at stake is the authority to grant or deny access to God's kingdom. In a Jewish context "binding and loosing" described the activity of a judge who declared persons innocent or guilty and thus "bound" or "loosed" them from the charges made against them (see Schlatter 1959: 511).

The climactic christological confession, in an *inclusio* with 1:1, 18, is Thomas's confession of Jesus as his "Lord" and "God" in 20:28 (Harris 1992: 284–86; Ridderbos 1997: 648). In the OT these two expressions are frequently juxtaposed with reference to Yahweh (e.g., Ps. 35:23–24). The concluding statement in 20:30–31 finds literary parallels in several intertestamental Jewish writings (e.g., Sir. 43:27; 1 Macc. 9:22, cited in Köstenberger 2004: 581).

The Epilogue (21:1–25)

By taking the bread and giving it to his disciples, and doing likewise with the fish, Jesus performs the act of the Jewish host pronouncing the blessing at a meal (21:13; cf. 6:11, 23). Jesus' threefold command to Peter to tend his lambs and to shepherd his sheep (21:15–17) has ample precedents in the OT, which is pervaded by a yearning for shepherds who are devoted to God, to caring for his sheep, and to carrying out his will (Ezek. 34; Jer. 3:15; cf. Isa. 44:28; see commentary at chap. 10 above). The term "tend" (*boskō*) regularly occurs in the LXX for feeding sheep (e.g., Gen. 29:7; 37:12); the metaphorical sense is found already in Ezek. 34:2.

The ending of John's Gospel (21:25), hyperbolically asserting that the whole world could not contain the books that would be written if everything that Jesus did had been inscribed, stands firmly in literary conventions of the time in both Greco-Roman and Jewish literature. The OT book of Ecclesiastes says, "Of making many books there is no end" (12:12), and Rabbi *Yohanan ben Zakkai* (ca. AD 80) reportedly said, "If all the heavens were sheets, all the trees quills and all the seas ink, they would not suffice for recording my wisdom which I acquired from my masters" (*Sop.* 16:8 [see also the examples from Philo cited in Köstenberger 2002b: 195]).

Conclusion

The study of the use of the OT in John's Gospel impressively demonstrates that both on the level of Jesus and on that of the Fourth Evangelist, the OT provides the framework, the matrix of messianic expectations fulfilled in Jesus, the Christ and Son of God. This is true for John the Baptist, who prepared the way for the Messiah in keeping with the message of the second half of the book of Isaiah. It is true for Jesus, who validated his messianic claims with a series of powerful signs. It is true even for the Jewish people, despite their rejection of Jesus the Messiah.

As the one greater than Abraham, Jacob, and Moses, as the Isaianic Suffering Servant, and as the Danielic Son of Man, Jesus was the Word-become-flesh who took up residence among his people, the one who revealed to them God's glory and inspired faith in them, the one whose cross-death fit an entire mosaic of OT Scriptures and who, once resurrected, commissioned his new messianic community as his Spirit-filled representatives bringing his gospel of forgiveness and salvation to a dark and needy world.

"From the fullness of his grace we have all received grace for grace. For the law was given through Moses; grace and truth came through Jesus Christ. No one has ever seen God, but God the One and Only, who is at the Father's side, has made him known" (John 1:16–18).

Bibliography

Abrahams, I. 1917. *Studies in Pharisaism and the Gospels.* 2 vols. Cambridge: Cambridge University Press.

Ackerman, J. S. 1966. "The Rabbinic Interpretation of Psalm 82 and the Gospel of John." *HTR* 59: 186–91.

Anderson, P. N. 1996. *The Christology of the Fourth Gospel: Its Unity and Disunity in the Light of John 6.* WUNT 2/78. Tubingen: Mohr Siebeck.

Archer, G. L., and G. C. Chirichigno. 1983. *Old Testament Quotations in the New Testament: A Complete Survey.* Chicago: Moody.

Ashley, T. R. 1993. *The Book of Numbers.* NICOT. Grand Rapids: Eerdmans.

Attridge, H. W. 2002. "Genre-Bending in the Fourth Gospel." *JBL* 121: 3–21.

Avi-Yonah, M. 1964. *The World of the Bible: The New Testament.* Yonkers, NY: Educational Heritage.

Baldwin, J. G. 1972. *Haggai, Zechariah, Malachi.* TOTC. London: Inter-Varsity.

Ball, D. M. 1996. *"I Am" in John's Gospel: Literary Function, Background and Theological Implications*. JSNTSup 124. Sheffield: Sheffield Academic Press.

Bammel, E. 1957. "Zu 1QS 9:10f." *VT* 7: 381–85.

———. 1993. "The Farewell Discourse of the Evangelist John and Its Jewish Heritage." *TynBul* 44: 103–16.

Barker, K. L. 1985. "Zechariah." Pages 595–697 in vol. 7 of *The Expositor's Bible Commentary*. Edited by F. E. Gaebelein. Grand Rapids: Zondervan.

Barrett, C. K. 1947. "The Old Testament in the Fourth Gospel." *JTS* 48: 155–69.

———. 1978. *The Gospel according to St. John*. 2nd ed. Philadelphia: Westminster.

Bauckham, R. 1998. "Life, Death, and the Afterlife in Second Temple Judaism." Pages 80–95 in *Life in the Face of Death: The Resurrection Message of the New Testament*. Edited by R. N. Longenecker. Grand Rapids: Eerdmans.

Beale, G. K. 1997. "The Eschatological Conception of New Testament Theology." Pages 11–52 in *Eschatology in Bible and Theology*. Edited by Kent E. Brower and Mark W. Elliott. Downers Grove, IL: InterVarsity.

———. 2004. *The Temple and the Church's Mission: A Biblical Theology of the Dwelling Place of God*. NSBT 17. Downers Grove, IL: InterVarsity.

Beasley-Murray, G. R. 1999. *John*. 2nd ed. WBC 36. Waco: Word.

Beck, D. R. 1997. *The Discipleship Paradigm: Readers and Anonymous Characters in the Fourth Gospel*. BIS 27. Leiden: Brill.

Bellinger, W. H., Jr., and W. R. Farmer, eds. 1998. *Jesus and the Suffering Servant: Isaiah 53 and Christian Origins*. Harrisburg, PA: Trinity Press International.

Bernard, J. H. 1928. *A Critical and Exegetical Commentary on the Gospel of John*. 2 vols. ICC. Edinburgh: T&T Clark.

Bertram, G. 1972. "ὕψος, κτλ." *TDNT* 8:602–20.

Beutler, J. 1979. "Psalm 42/43 im Johannesevangelium." *NTS* 25: 33–57.

Black, D. A. 1984. "The Text of John 3:13." *GTJ* 6: 49–66.

Blenkinsopp, J. 2002. *Isaiah 40–55*. AB 19A. New York: Doubleday.

Blomberg, C. L. 1987. *The Historical Reliability of the Gospels*. Downers Grove, IL: InterVarsity.

Boismard, M.-É. 1993. *Moses or Jesus: An Essay in Johannine Christology*. Translated by B. T. Viviano. Minneapolis: Fortress.

Borchert, G. L. 1996–2002. *John*. 2 vols. NAC 25A, 25B. Nashville: Broadman & Holman.

Borgen, P. 1965. *Bread from Heaven: An Exegetical Study of the Concept of Manna in the Gospel of John and the Writings of Philo*. NovTSup 10. Leiden: Brill.

———. 1977. "Some Jewish Exegetical Traditions as Background for Son of Man Sayings in John's Gospel (Jn 3,13–14 and Context)." Pages 243–58 in *L'Évangile de Jean: Sources, rédaction, théologie*. Edited by M. de Jonge. BETL 44. Gembloux: Duculot.

Boring, M. E., K. Berger, and C. Colpe, eds. 1995. *Hellenistic Commentary to the New Testament*. Nashville: Abingdon.

Bowman, J. 1958. *Samaritan Studies*. Manchester: Manchester University Press.

Brawley, R. L. 1993. "An Absent Complement and Intertextuality in John 19:28–29." *JBL* 112: 427–43.

Brooke, G. J. 1994. "Isaiah 40:3 and the Wilderness Community." Pages 117–32 in *New Qumran Texts and Studies: Proceedings of the First Meeting of the International Organization for Qumran Studies, Paris, 1992*. Edited by G. J. Brooke and F. García Martínez. STDJ 15. Leiden: Brill.

Brown, R. E. 1966–1970. *The Gospel according to John*. 2 vols. AB 29A, 29B. Garden City, NY: Doubleday.

Brownlee, W. H. 1956–1957. "Messianic Motifs of Qumran and the New Testament." *NTS* 3: 12–30.

Bruce, F. F. 1960–1961. "The Book of Zechariah and the Passion Narrative." *BJRL* 43: 336–53.

———. 1968. *New Testament Development of Old Testament Themes*. Grand Rapids: Eerdmans.

———. 1983. *The Gospel of John*. Grand Rapids: Eerdmans.

Brunson, A. C. 2003. *Psalm 118 in the Gospel of John: An Intertextual Study of the New Exodus Pattern in the Theology of John*. WUNT 2/158. Tübingen: Mohr Siebeck.

Bullock, C. H. 1982. "Ezekiel, Bridge between the Testaments." *JETS* 25: 23–31.

Bultmann, R. 1971. *The Gospel of John*. Translated by G. R. Beasley-Murray. Oxford: Blackwell.

Burge, G. M. 1987. *The Anointed Community: The Holy Spirit in the Johannine Tradition*. Grand Rapids: Eerdmans.

———. 2000. *The Gospel of John*. NIVAC. Grand Rapids: Zondervan.

Burrows, E. W. 1974. "Did John the Baptist Call Jesus 'The Lamb of God'?" *ExpTim* 85: 245–49.

Busse, U. 2002. *Das Johannesevangelium: Bildlichkeit, Diskurs und Ritual*. BETL 162. Leuven: Leuven University Press.

Carson, D. A. *Matthew*. 1984. Pages 3–599 in vol. 8 of *The Expositor's Bible Commentary*. Edited by F. E. Gaebelein. Grand Rapids: Zondervan.

———. 1988. "John and the Johannine Epistles." Pages 245–64 in *It Is Written: Scripture Citing Scripture; Essays in Honour of Barnabas Lindars, SSF*. Edited by D. A. Carson and H. G. M. Williamson. Cambridge: Cambridge University Press.

———. 1991. *The Gospel according to John*. Grand Rapids: Eerdmans.

Carson, D.A., P. T. O'Brien, and M. A. Seifrid, eds. 2004. *The Paradoxes of Paul*. Vol. 2 of *Justification and Variegated Nomism: A Fresh Appraisal of Paul and Second Temple Judaism*. WUNT 2/181. Tübingen: Mohr Siebeck.

Charlesworth, J. H. 1997. "Intertextuality: Isaiah 40:3 and the Serek Ha-Yahad." Pages 197–224 in *The Quest for Context and Meaning: Studies in Biblical Intertextuality in Honor of James A. Sanders*. Edited by C. A. Evans and S. Talmon. BIS 28. Leiden: Brill.

Coakley, J. F. 1995. "Jesus' Messianic Entry into Jerusalem (John 12:12–19 par.)." *JTS* 46: 461–82.

Cohon, S. S. 1955. "The Unity of God: A Study in Hellenistic and Rabbinic Theology." *HUCA* 26: 425–79.

Collins, J. J. 1993. "The *Son of God* Text from Qumran." Pages 65–82 in *From Jesus to John: Essays on Jesus and New Testament Christology in Honour of Marinus de Jonge*. Edited by M. C. de Boer. JSNTSup 84. Sheffield: JSOT Press.

Coloe, M. L. 2001. *God Dwells with Us: Temple Symbolism in the Fourth Gospel*. Collegeville, MN: Liturgical Press.

Conway, C. M. 1999. *Men and Women in the Fourth Gospel: Gender and Johannine Characterization*. SBLDS 167. Atlanta: Scholars Press.

Cortés, J. B. 1967. "Yet Another Look at Jn 7, 37–38." *CBQ* 29: 75–86.

Cotterell, P. 1985. "The Nicodemus Conversation: A Fresh Appraisal." *ExpTim* 96: 237–42.

Craigie, P. C. 1983. *Psalms 1–50*. WBC 19. Dallas: Word.

Culpepper, R. A. 1983. *Anatomy of the Fourth Gospel: A Study in Literary Design.* FF. Philadelphia: Fortress.

Dahl, N. A. 1963. "The Murderer and His Father (John 8:44)." *NTT* 64: 129–62.

Dahms, J. V. 1983. "The Johannine Use of *Monogenēs* Reconsidered." *NTS* 29: 222–32.

Dahood, M. 1968. *Psalms II (51–100).* AB 17. Garden City, NY: Doubleday.

Dalman, G. 1935. *Sacred Sites and Ways.* London: SPCK.

Daly-Denton, M. 2000. *David in the Fourth Gospel: The Johannine Reception of the Psalms.* AGJU 47. Leiden: Brill.

———. 2004. "The Psalms in John's Gospel." Pages 119–37 in *The Psalms in the New Testament.* Edited by S. Moyise and M. J. J. Menken. NTSI. London: T&T Clark International.

Danby, H. 1933. *The Mishnah.* Oxford: Oxford University Press.

Daube, D. 1950. "Jesus and the Samaritan Woman: The Meaning of συγχράομαι." *JBL* 69: 137–47.

———. 1956. *The New Testament and Rabbinic Judaism.* London: Athlone.

Davies, W. D. 1994. *The Gospel and the Land: Early Christianity and Jewish Territorial Doctrine.* BibSem 25. Sheffield: JSOT Press.

de Jonge, M. 1974. "Messianic Ideas in Later Judaism." *TDNT* 9:509–17.

de Vaux, R. 1964. *Studies in Old Testament Sacrifice.* Translated by J. Bourke and R. Potter. Cardiff: University of Wales Press.

Deeley, M. K. 1997. "Ezekiel's Shepherd and John's Jesus: A Case Study in the Appropriation of Biblical Texts." Pages 252–64 in *Early Christian Interpretation of the Scriptures of Israel.* Edited by C. A. Evans and J. A. Sanders. JSNTSup 148. Sheffield: Sheffield Academic Press.

Deissler, A. 1998. "Sach 12,10—die grosse crux interpretum." Pages 49–60 in *Ich bewirke das Heil und erschaffe das Unheil (Jesaja 45:7): Studien zur Botschaft der Propheten; Festschrift für Lothar Ruppert zum 65. Geburtstag.* Edited by F. Diedrich and B. Willmes. FB 88. Würzburg: Echter.

Delling, G. 1957. "*Baptisma, Baptisthēnai.*" *NovT* 2: 92–115.

Derrett, J. D. M. 1988. "The Samaritan Woman's Purity (John 4.4–52 [*sic*])." *EvQ* 60: 291–98.

———. 1993. "*Ti ergaze?* (Jn 6, 30): An Unrecognized Allusion to Is 45, 9." *ZNW* 84: 142–44.

———. 1994. "John 9:6 Read with Isaiah 6:10; 20:9 [*sic.*]." *EvQ* 66: 251–54.

———. 1997. "The Zeal of the House and the Cleansing of the Temple." *DRev* 95: 79–94.

Díaz, J. R. 1963. "Palestinian Targum and New Testament." *NovT* 6: 75–80.

Dodd, C. H. 1952. *According to the Scriptures: The Substructure of New Testament Theology.* London: Nisbet.

———. 1953. *The Interpretation of the Fourth Gospel.* Cambridge: Cambridge University Press.

Duke, P. D. 1988. *Irony in the Fourth Gospel.* Atlanta: John Knox.

Durham, J. I. 1987. *Exodus.* WBC 3. Waco: Word.

Edwards, R. B. 1988. "Χαριν αντι χαριτος (John 1.16): Grace and the Law in the Johannine Prologue." *JSNT* 32: 3–15.

Emerton, J. A. 1960. "Interpretation of Psalm 82 in John 10." *JTS* 11: 329–32.

———. 1962. "Binding and Loosing—Forgiving and Retaining." *JTS* 13: 325–31.

———. 1966. "Melchizedek and the Gods: Fresh Evidence for the Jewish Background of John 10:34–36." *JTS* 17: 399–401.

Engel, F. G. 1948–1949. "The Ways of Vines." *ExpTim* 60: 111.

Evans, C. A. 1981. "The Voice from Heaven: A Note on John 12:28." *CBQ* 43: 405–8.

———. 1982a. "On the Quotation Formulas in the Fourth Gospel." *BZ* 26: 79–83.

———. 1982b. "The Function of Isaiah 6:9–10 in Mark and John." *NovT* 24: 124–38.

———. 1982c. "The Text of Isaiah 6:9–10." *ZAW* 92: 415–18.

———. 1987. "Obduracy and the Lord's Servant: Some Observations on the Use of the Old Testament in the Fourth Gospel." Pages 221–36 in *Early Jewish and Christian Exegesis: Studies in Memory of William Hugh Brownlee.* Edited by C. A. Evans and W. F. Stinespring. Homage 10. Atlanta: Scholars Press.

———. 1989a. *To See and Not Perceive: Isaiah 6.9–10 in Early Jewish and Christian Interpretation.* JSOTSup 64. Sheffield: JSOT Press.

———. 1989b. "Jesus' Action in the Temple: Cleansing or Portent of Destruction?" *CBQ* 51: 237–70.

———. 1993. *Word and Glory: On the Exegetical and Theological Background of John's Prologue.* JSNTSup 89. Sheffield: Sheffield Academic Press.

Fee, G. D. 1978. "Once More—John 7³⁷⁻³⁹." *ExpTim* 89: 116–18.

Fitzmyer, J. A. 1990–1993. "μονογενής." *EDNT* 2:439–40.

France, R. T. 1971. *Jesus and the Old Testament: His Application of Old Testament Passages to Himself and His Mission.* London: Tyndale.

Freed, E. D. 1961. "The Entry into Jerusalem in the Gospel of John." *JBL* 80: 329–38.

———. 1965. *Old Testament Quotations in the Gospel of John.* NovTSup 11. Leiden: Brill.

———. 1983a. "Psalm 42/43 in John's Gospel." *NTS* 29: 62–73.

———. 1983b. "Who or What Was before Abraham in John 8:58?" *JSNT* 17: 52–59.

Glasson, T. F. 1963. *Moses in the Fourth Gospel.* SBT 40. London: SCM.

Goodwin, C. 1954. "How Did John Treat His Sources?" *JBL* 73: 61–75.

Grigsby, B. H. 1986. "'If Any Man Thirsts . . .': Observations on the Rabbinic Background of John 7,37–39." *Bib* 67: 101–8.

Gunkel, H. 1968. *Die Psalmen.* 5th ed. Göttingen: Vandenhoeck & Ruprecht.

Ham, C. 1998. "The Title 'Son of Man' in the Gospel of John." *Stone-Campbell Journal* 1: 67–84.

Hanson, A. T. 1964–1965. "John's Interpretation of Psalm 82." *NTS* 11: 158–62.

———. 1967. "John's Interpretation of Psalm 82 Reconsidered." *NTS* 13: 363–67.

———. 1973. "The Old Testament Background to the Raising of Lazarus." *SE* VI: 252–55.

———. 1994. "John's Use of Scripture." Pages 358–79 in *The Gospels and the Scriptures of Israel.* Edited by C. A. Evans and W. R. Stegner. JSNTSup 104. Sheffield: Sheffield Academic Press.

Harris, M. J. 1992. *Jesus as God: The New Testament Use of Theos in Reference to Jesus.* Grand Rapids: Baker Academic.

Harstine, S. 2002. *Moses as a Character in the Fourth Gospel: A Study of Ancient Reading Techniques.* JSNTSup 229. Sheffield: Sheffield Academic Press.

Hauck, F. 1965. "καταβολή." *TDNT* 3:620–21.

Hays, R. B. 1989. *Echoes of Scripture in the Letters of Paul.* New Haven: Yale University Press.

Heard, W. J. 1992. "Revolutionary Movements." *DJG* 688–98.

Hengel, M. 1988. *The Zealots: Investigations into the Jewish Freedom Movement in the Period from Herod I until 70 A.D.* Translated by D. Smith. Edinburgh: T&T Clark.

———. 1999. "Das Johannes evangelium als Quelle für die freschichte des antiken Judentums." Pages 293–334 in *Judaica, Hellenistica of Christiana: Kleine Schriften III.* WUNT 109. Tübingen: Mohr Siebeck.

Hiers, R. H. 1971. "Purification of the Temple: Preparation for the Kingdom of God." *JBL* 90: 82–90.

Hodges, Z. 1979. "Problem Passages in the Gospel of John: Part 7: Rivers of Living Water—John 7:37–39." *BSac* 136: 239–48.

Hofius, O. 1967. "Die Sammlung der Heiden zur Herde Israels (Joh 10,16; 11,51f.)." *ZNW* 58: 289–91.

Hollander, J. 1981. *The Figure of Echo: A Mode of Allusion in Milton and After.* Berkeley: University of California Press.

Hooker, M. D. 1959. *Jesus and the Servant: The Influence of the Servant Concept of Deutero-Isaiah in the New Testament.* London: SPCK.

Horbury, W. 1998. *Jewish Messianism and the Cult of Christ.* London: SCM.

Horsley, R. A. 1984. "Popular Messianic Movements around the Time of Jesus." *CBQ* 46: 471–95.

———. 1992. "Messianic Movements in Judaism." *ABD* 4:791–97.

Hultgren, A. J. 1982. "The Johannine Footwashing (13:1-11) as Symbol of Eschatological Hospitality." *NTS* 28: 539–46.

Hunter, W. B. 1979. "The Prayers of Jesus in the Gospel of John." PhD diss., University of Aberdeen.

Hurtado, L. W. 1998. "First-Century Jewish Monotheism." *JSNT* 71: 3–26.

———. 1999. "Pre-70 C.E. Jewish Opposition to Christ Devotion." *JTS* 50: 35–58.

Jackson, H. M. 1999. "Ancient Self-Referential Conventions and Their Implications for the Authorship and Integrity of the Gospel of John." *JTS* 50: 1–34.

Janowski, B., and P. Stuhlmacher, eds. 2004. *The Suffering Servant: Isaiah 53 in Jewish and Christian Scriptures.* Grand Rapids: Eerdmans.

Jenni, E. 1959. "Jesajas Berufung in der neueren Forschung." *TZ* 15: 321–39.

Jeremias, J. 1969. *Jerusalem in the Time of Jesus.* London: SCM.

Johnson, S. L., Jr. 1980. *The Old Testament in the New: An Argument for Biblical Inspiration.* Grand Rapids: Zondervan.

Jones, D. R. 1962. "Fresh Interpretation of Zechariah 9–11." *VT* 12: 241–59.

Jungkuntz, R. 1964. "Approach to the Exegesis of John 10:34–36." *CTM* 35: 556–65.

Keener, C. S. 1993. *The IVP Bible Background Commentary: New Testament.* Downers Grove, IL: InterVarsity.

———. 2003. *The Gospel of John.* 2 vols. Peabody, MA: Hendrickson.

Keil, C. F. 1889. *The Twelve Minor Prophets.* Vol. 2. BCOT. Translated by J. Martin. Edinburgh: T&T Clark.

Kellum, L. S. 2004. *The Unity of the Farewell Discourse: The Literary Integrity of John 13:31–16:33.* JSNTSup 256. London: T&T Clark.

Kerr, A. R. 2002. *The Temple of Jesus' Body: The Temple Theme in the Gospel of John.* JSNTSup 220. London: Sheffield Academic Press.

Kidner, D. 1973. *Psalms 1–72.* TOTC. London: Inter-Varsity.

Kippenberg, H. G. 1971. *Garizim und Synagoge: Traditionsgeschichtliche Untersuchungen zur samaritanischen Religion der aramäischen Periode.* RVV 30. Berlin: de Gruyter.

Knapp, H. M. 1997. "The Messianic Water Which Gives Life to the World." *HBT* 19: 109–21.

Koester, C. R. 2003. *Symbolism in the Fourth Gospel: Meaning, Mystery, Community.* 2nd ed. Minneapolis: Fortress.

Köstenberger, A. J. 1995. "The Seventh Johannine Sign: A Study in John's Christology." *BBR* 5: 87–103.

———. 1997. "What Does It Mean to Be Filled with the Spirit?" *JETS* 40: 229–40.

———. 1998a. "Jesus as Rabbi in the Fourth Gospel." *BBR* 8: 97–128.

———. 1998b. *The Missions of Jesus and the Disciples according to the Fourth Gospel.* Grand Rapids: Eerdmans.

———. 1999. *Encountering John: The Gospel in Historical, Literary, and Theological Perspective.* EBS. Grand Rapids: Baker Academic.

———. 2001. *Studies in John and Gender: A Decade of Scholarship.* New York: Peter Lang.

———. 2002a. "Jesus the Good Shepherd Who Will Also Bring Other Sheep (John 10:16): The Old Testament Background of a Familiar Metaphor." *BBR* 12: 67–96.

———. 2002b. "John." Pages 1–216 in vol. 2 of *Zondervan Illustrated Bible Background Commentary: New Testament.* Edited by C. E. Arnold. Grand Rapids: Zondervan.

———. 2004. *John.* BECNT. Grand Rapids: Baker Academic.

———. 2005a. "The Destruction of the Second Temple and the Composition of the Fourth Gospel." *TJ* 26: 205–42.

———. 2005b. "'What Is Truth?' Pilate's Question in Its Johannine and Larger Biblical Context." *JETS* 48: 33–62.

Köstenberger, A. J., and P. T. O'Brien. 2001. *Salvation to the Ends of the Earth: A Biblical Theology of Mission.* NSBT 11. Downers Grove, IL: InterVarsity.

Kuyper, L. J. 1964. "Grace and Truth: An Old Testament Description of God and Its Use in the Johannine Gospel." *Int* 18: 3–19.

Kynes, W. L. 1992. "New Birth." *DJG* 574–76.

Lacomara, A. 1974. "Deuteronomy and the Farewell Discourse (Jn 13:31–16:33)." *CBQ* 36: 65–84.

Ladd, G. E. 1993. *A Theology of the New Testament.* 2nd ed. Grand Rapids: Eerdmans.

Lamarche, P. 1961. *Zacharie IX–XIV: Structure litteraire et messianisme.* EBib. Paris: Gabalda.

Laney, J. C. 1989. "Abiding Is Believing: The Analogy of the Vine in John 15:1–6." *BSac* 146: 55–66.

———. 1992. *John.* Moody Gospel Commentary. Chicago: Moody.

Lee, D. A. 1994. *The Symbolic Narratives of the Fourth Gospel: The Interplay of Form and Meaning.* JSNTSup 95. Sheffield: JSOT Press.

Lenski, R. C. J. 1942. *The Interpretation of St. John's Gospel.* Columbus, OH: Lutheran Book Concern.

Leske, A. M. 2000. "Context and Meaning of Zechariah 9:9." *CBQ* 62: 663–78.

Leupold, H. C. 1959. *Exposition of the Psalms.* Minneapolis: Wartburg.

Lieu, J. 1988. "Blindness in the Johannine Tradition." *NTS* 34: 83–95.

Lincoln, A. T. 2000. *Truth on Trial: The Lawsuit Motif in the Fourth Gospel.* Peabody, MA: Hendrickson.

Lindars, B. 1961. *New Testament Apologetic: The Doctrinal Significance of the Old Testament Quotations.* London: SCM.

———. 1972. *The Gospel of John.* NCB. Grand Rapids: Eerdmans; London: Marshall, Morgan & Scott.

Louw, J. P. 1986. "On Johannine Style." *Neot* 20: 5–12.

Maccini, R. G. 1996. *Her Testimony Is True: Women as Witnesses according to John.* JSNTSup 125. Sheffield: Sheffield Academic Press.

Macdonald, J. 1964. *The Theology of the Samaritans.* Philadelphia: Westminster.

Malatesta, E. J. 1978. *Interiority and Covenant: A Study of EINAI EN and MENEIN EN in the First Letter of Saint John.* AnBib 69. Rome: Biblical Institute Press.

Malina, B. J., and R. L. Rohrbaugh. 1998. *Social-Science Commentary on the Gospel of John.* Minneapolis: Fortress.

Marcus, J. 1998. "Rivers of Living Water from Jesus' Belly (John 7:38)." *JBL* 117: 328–30.

Martyn, J. L. 1979. *History and Theology in the Fourth Gospel.* 2nd ed. Nashville: Abingdon.

Marzotto, D. 1977. "Giovanni 17 e il Targum di Esodo 19–20." *RivB* 25: 375–88.

McCabe, R. V. 1999. "The Meaning of 'Born of Water and the Spirit' in John 3:5." *DBSJ* 4: 85–107.

McComiskey, T. E. 1998. "Zechariah." Pages 1003–1244 in vol. 3 of *The Minor Prophets: An Exegetical and Expository Commentary.* Edited by T. E. McComiskey. Grand Rapids: Baker Academic.

Meeks, W. A. 1967. *The Prophet-King: Moses Traditions and the Johannine Christology.* NovTSup 14. Leiden: Brill.

Meier, J. P. 2001. *Companions and Competitors.* Vol. 3 of *A Marginal Jew: Rethinking the Historical Jesus.* ABRL. New York: Doubleday.

Menken, M. J. J. 1985. "The Quotation from Isa 40,3 in John 1,23." *Bib* 66: 190–205.

———. 1988. "The Provenance and Meaning of the Old Testament Quotation in John 6:31." *NovT* 30: 39–56.

———. 1990. "The Translation of Psalm 41:10 in John 13:18." *JSNT* 40: 61–79.

———. 1996a. *Old Testament Quotations in the Fourth Gospel: Studies in Textual Form.* CBET 15. Kampen: Kok.

———. 1996b. "The Origin of the Old Testament Quotation in John 7:38." *NovT* 38: 160–75.

Metso, S. 1998. "The Use of Old Testament Quotations in the Qumran Community Rule." Pages 217–31 in *Qumran between the Old and the New Testaments.* Edited by F. H. Cryer and T. L. Thompson. JSOTSup 290. Sheffield: Sheffield Academic Press.

Meyer, R. 1971. "Σαδδoυκαῖoς." *TDNT* 7:35–54.

Meyers, C. L., and E. M. Meyers. 1993. *Zechariah 9–14.* AB 25C. New York: Doubleday.

Michaels, J. R. 1989. *John.* NIBCNT. Peabody, MA: Hendrickson.

Michel, O. 1975–1985. "υἱὸς τoῦ θεoῦ." *NIDNTT* 3:634–48.

Moloney, F. J. 1990. "Reading John 2:13–22: The Purification of the Temple." *RB* 97: 432–51.

———. 1998. *The Gospel of John.* Collegeville, MN: Liturgical Press.

Moody, D. 1953. "God's Only Son: The Translation of John 3:16 in the Revised Standard Version." *JBL* 72: 213–19.

Morris, L. 1995. *The Gospel according to John.* Rev. ed. NICNT. Grand Rapids: Eerdmans.

Motyer, J. A. 1993. *The Prophecy of Isaiah: An Introduction and Commentary.* Downers Grove, IL: InterVarsity.

Motyer, S. 1997. *Your Father the Devil? A New Approach to John and "the Jews."* PBTM. Carlisle: Paternoster.

Mowvley, H. 1984. "John 1[14–18] in the Light of Exodus 33[7]–34[35]." *ExpTim* 95: 135–37.

Neyrey, J. H. 1979. "Jacob Traditions and the Interpretation of John 4:10–26." *CBQ* 41: 419–37.

———. 1982. "The Jacob Allusions in John 1.51." *CBQ* 44: 586–605.

Ng, W.-Y. 2001. *Water Symbolism in John: An Eschatological Interpretation.* SBL 15. New York: Peter Lang.

Nicholson, G. C. 1983. *Death as Departure: The Johannine Descent-Ascent Schema.* SBLDS 63. Chico, CA: Scholars Press.

Nielsen, K. 1999. "Old Testament Imagery in John." Pages 66–82 in *New Readings in John: Literary and Theological Perspectives.* Edited by J. Nissen and S. Pedersen. JSNTSup 182. Sheffield: Sheffield Academic Press.

Obermann, A. 1996. *Die christologische Erfüllung der Schrift im Johannesevangelium: Eine Untersuchung zur johanneischen Hermeneutik anhand der Schriftzitate.* WUNT 2/83. Tübingen: Mohr Siebeck.

Oepke, A. 1964. "ἀνίστημι, κτλ." *TDNT* 1:368–72.

Oswalt, J. N. 1986–1998. *The Book of Isaiah.* 2 vols. NICOT. Grand Rapids: Eerdmans.

Painter, J. 1977. "Christ and the Church in John 1,45–51." Pages 359–62 in *L'Évangile de Jean: Sources, rédaction, théologie.* Edited by M. de Jonge. BETL 44. Gembloux: Duculot.

———. 1999. "The Quotation of Scripture and Unbelief in John 12:36b–43." Pages 429–58 in *The Gospels and the Scriptures of Israel.* Edited by C. A. Evans and W. R. Stegner. JSNTSup 104. Sheffield: Sheffield Academic Press.

Pancaro, S. 1975. *The Law in the Fourth Gospel.* NovTSup 42. Leiden: Brill.

Pendrick, G. 1995. "Μονογενής." *NTS* 41: 587–600.

Petersen, D. L. 1995. *Zechariah 9–14 and Malachi.* OTL. Louisville: Westminster John Knox.

Porter, S. J. 1994. "Can Traditional Exegesis Enlighten Literary Analysis of the Fourth Gospel? An Examination of the Old Testament Fulfilment Motif and the Passover Theme." Pages 396–428 in *The Gospels and the Scriptures of Israel.* Edited by C. A. Evans and W. R. Stegner. JSNTSup 104. Sheffield: Sheffield Academic Press.

Propp, W. H. C. 1999. *Exodus 1–18.* AB 2. New York: Doubleday.

Pryor, J. W. 1988. "Covenant and Community in John's Gospel." *RTR* 47: 44–51.

———. 1991. "The Johannine Son of Man and Descent-Ascent Motif." *JETS* 34: 341–51.

———. 1992. *John, Evangelist of the Covenant People: The Narrative and Themes of the Fourth Gospel.* Downers Grove, IL: InterVarsity.

Reddish, M. G. 1992. "Heaven." *ABD* 3:90–91.

Reim, G. 1974. *Studien zum alttestamentlichen Hintergrund des Johannesevangeliums.* SNTSMS 22. Cambridge: Cambridge University Press.

Ridderbos, H. N. 1997. *The Gospel of John.* Grand Rapids: Eerdmans.

Riesner, R. 1981. *Jesus als Lehrer: Eine Untersuchung zum Ursprung der Evangelien-Überlieferung.* WUNT 2/7. Tübingen: Mohr Siebeck.

Robinson, G. D. 1998. "The Motif of Deafness and Blindness in Isaiah 6:9–10: A Contextual, Literary, and Theological Analysis." *BBR* 8: 167–86.

Rogerson, J. W., and J. W. McKay. 1977. *Psalms 51–100*. CBC. Cambridge: Cambridge University Press.

Rowland, C. 1984. "John 1.51, Jewish Apocalyptic and Targumic Tradition." *NTS* 30: 498–507.

Scheiber, A. 1963. "'Ihr sollt kein Bein dran zerbrechen.'" *VT* 13: 95–97.

Schlatter, A. 1948. *Der Evangelist Johannes: Wie er spricht, denkt und glaubt; ein Kommentar zum vierten Evangelium*. 2nd ed. Stuttgart: Calwer.

———. 1959. *Der Evangelist Matthäus: Seine Sprache, sein Ziel, seine Selbständigkeit; ein Kommentar zum ersten Evangelium*. 5th ed. Stuttgart: Calwer.

Schnackenburg, R. 1990. *The Gospel according to St. John*. 3 vols. New York: Crossroad.

Schoonhoven, C. R. 1979–1988. "Heaven." *ISBE* 2:654–55.

Schrenk, G. 1967. "πατήρ, κτλ." *TDNT* 5:945–1022.

Schuchard, B. G. 1992. *Scripture within Scripture: The Interrelationship of Form and Function in the Explicit Old Testament Citations in the Gospel of John*. SBLDS 133. Atlanta: Scholars Press.

Schürer, E. 1973–1979. *The History of the Jewish People in the Age of Jesus Christ*. Revised and edited by G. Vermes et al. 4 vols. Edinburgh: T&T Clark.

Schwarz, G. 1982. "Gen 1:1, 2:2a und Joh 1:1a.3—ein Vergleich." *ZNW* 73: 136–37.

Schweizer, E. 1996. "What about the Johannine 'Parables'?" Pages 208–19 in *Exploring the Gospel of John: In Honor of D. Moody Smith*. Edited by R. A. Culpepper and C. C. Black. Louisville: Westminster John Knox.

Shidemantle, C. S. 2001. "Nehemiah 9 in John 7:37–39." PhD diss., Trinity Evangelical Divinity School.

Sidebottom, E. M. 1956–1957. "The Son of Man in the Fourth Gospel." *ExpTim* 68: 231–35.

Smith, D. M. 1963. "John 12:12ff and the Question of John's Use of the Synoptics." *JBL* 82: 58–64.

———. 1999. *John*. ANTC. Nashville: Abingdon.

Smith, R. L. 1984. *Micah–Malachi*. WBC 32. Waco: Word.

Snodgrass, K. 1980. "Streams of Tradition Emerging from Isaiah 40:1–5 and Their Adaptation in the New Testament." *JSNT* 8: 24–45.

Tabor, J. D. 1992. "Heaven, Ascent to." *ABD* 3:91–94.

Talbert, C. H. 1992. *Reading John*. Reading the New Testament. New York: Crossroad.

Tate, M. A. 1990. *Psalms 51–100*. WBC 20. Dallas: Word.

Tholuck, A. 1858. *A Translation and Commentary of the Book of Psalms for the Use of the Ministry and Laity of the Christian Church*. Translated by J. I. Mombert. Philadelphia: Martien.

Thomas, J. C. 1991. *Footwashing in John 13 and the Johannine Community*. JSNTSup 50. Sheffield: JSOT Press.

———. 1995. "'Stop Sinning Lest Something Worse Come upon You': The Man at the Pool in John 5." *JSNT* 59: 3–20.

Thomson, J. G. S. S. 1955. "The Shepherd-Ruler Concept in the Old Testament and Its Application in the New Testament." *SJT* 8: 406–18.

Tyler, R. L. 1989. "The Source and Function of Isaiah 6:9–10 in John 12:40." Pages 205–20 in *Johannine Studies: Essays in Honor of Frank Pack*. Edited by J. E. Priest. Malibu, CA: Pepperdine University Press.

VanderKam, J. C. 1999. "The Judean Desert and the Community of the Dead Sea Scrolls." Pages 159–71 in *Antikes Judentum und Frühes Christentum: Festschrift für Hartmut Stegemann zum 65. Geburtstag*. Edited by B. Kollmann, W. Reinbold, and A. Steudel. BZNW 97. Berlin: de Gruyter.

VanGemeren, W. 1991. "Psalms." Pages 3–880 in vol. 5 of *The Expositor's Bible Commentary*. Edited by F. E. Gaebelein. Grand Rapids: Zondervan.

Vawter, B. 1964. "Ezekiel and John." *CBQ* 26: 450–58.

Walker, P. W. L. 1996. *Jesus and the Holy City: New Testament Perspectives on Jerusalem*. Grand Rapids: Eerdmans.

Walker, W. O., Jr. 1994. "John 1.43–51 and 'the Son of Man' in the Fourth Gospel." *JSNT* 56: 31–42.

Wallace, D. B. 1996. *Greek Grammar beyond the Basics: An Exegetical Syntax of the New Testament*. Grand Rapids: Zondervan.

Warfield, B. B. 1948. "The Real Problem of Inspiration." Pages 201–8 in *The Inspiration and Authority of the Bible*. Edited by S. G. Craig. Philadelphia: Presbyterian & Reformed.

Watts, J. D. W. 1985–1987. *Isaiah*. 2 vols. WBC 24, 25. Waco: Word.

Weiser, A. 1962. *The Psalms: A Commentary*. Philadephia: Westminster.

Westcott, B. F. 1908. *The Gospel according to St. John: The Greek Text with Introduction and Notes*. 2 vols. London: Murray.

Whitacre, R. A. 1992. "Vine, Fruit of the Vine." *DJG* 867–68.

———. 1999. *John*. IVPNTC 4. Downers Grove, IL: InterVarsity.

Wifall, W. R. 1974. "David—Prototype of Israel's Future?" *BTB* 4: 94–107.

Wilcox, M. 1977. "The 'Prayer' of Jesus in John xi.41b–42." *NTS* 24: 128–32.

Wildberger, H. 1991. *Isaiah 1–12*. Translated by T. H. Trapp. CC. Minneapolis: Fortress.

Winter, P. 1953. "Μονογενὴς παρὰ Πατρός." *ZRGG* 5: 335–65.

Witherington, B., III. 1995. *John's Wisdom*. Louisville: Westminster John Knox.

Wolff, H. W. 1984 [1942]. *Jesaja im Urchristentum*. 4th ed. Berlin: Evangelische Verlagsanstalt.

Young, E. J. 1972. *The Book of Isaiah*. Vol. 3. NICOT. Grand Rapids: Eerdmans.

Young, F. W. 1955. "A Study of the Relation of Isaiah to the Fourth Gospel." *ZNW* 46: 215–33.

ACTS

I. Howard Marshall

Introduction

"The influence, whether literary or theological, of the Old Testament upon the Lucan writings ... is profound and pervasive" (Barrett 1988: 231). This is a verdict that probably nobody could dispute. An analytical count of the instances of the use of the OT in Acts is impossible because of the variety of types of usage and the difficulty of assigning uses to specific categories. However, we can gain some idea of the scale of the usage in Acts by observing that Steyn (1995: 26–31) lists twenty-five explicit quotations identified by the use of introductory formulas (actually twenty-seven, since two of these instances each cite two OT passages) and nine uses of direct phrases not introduced by formulas (cf. Longenecker 1999: 69–71). Alongside these there are a large number of uses of scriptural language, allusions, and uses of scriptural motifs.

Nevertheless, the relative distribution of the scriptural material in Acts is somewhat surprising. Formal citations are spread rather unevenly through the book, mainly in the first half. The texts that can be clearly identified as formal citations occur in chapters 1, 2, 3, 4, 7, 8, 13, 15, 23, 28; there are none in chapters 5, 6, 9–12, 14, 16–22, 24–27. The so-called speeches are naturally the main location for scriptural material in Acts, and all the quotations introduced by for-mulas occur in speeches addressed to Jewish (or Jewish-Christian) audiences (Steyn 1995: 230); contrast the lack of direct citation in the speeches in Lystra and Athens. Allusions are found much more widely (but are still sparse in the second half of Acts), and they are not confined to the speeches; the narrator can also use Scripture and is influenced by its wording (e.g., the Elijah/Elisha reminiscences in 1:1–11). The scriptural references are thus concentrated in the first half of the book in preaching and defensive speeches to Jews and proselytes, but they are surprisingly absent from Paul's defense speeches in the second half of Acts, even when these are directed to a predomi-nantly Jewish audience.

As with the rest of the NT, the use of the OT in Acts has been the subject of extensive investigation in recent scholarship. Detailed listings and texts of the scriptural sources for citations employed by Luke are given in Archer and Chirichigno 1983. The textual sources used by Luke have been in-vestigated at length in Clarke 1922; Holtz 1968. Introductory surveys of Luke's usage can be found in Barrett 1988; Fitzmyer 1998; Hanson 1983: 78–89; Longenecker 1999: 63–87; Moyise 2001: 45–62; Schneider 1980–1982: 1:232–38. The history of scholarship is surveyed in Bovon 2006: 87–121, 525–31; Steyn 1995: 1–21. Particular attention has been focused on the OT background to the Christology developed in Acts (Bock 1987; Rese 1969; Strauss 1995), but attention has begun to be directed also to the background to the ecclesiology (Dupont 1979, 1985; Pao 2000). Numerous studies examine specific passages and themes, including several significant contributions by Dupont. The most detailed recent study, but confined to the formal citations in the speeches of Peter and Paul, is Steyn 1995.

Luke's Perspective

We are fortunate that Luke has given us some insight into his approach. Two significant passages occur at the end of his Gospel. Jesus himself is represented as saying to the travelers to Emmaus,

> How foolish you are, and how slow of heart to believe everything that the prophets have said! Did not the Christ have to suffer these things and then enter his glory? (Luke 24:25–26)

Then Luke relates that

> beginning from Moses and all the prophets, he explained to them the things in all the Scriptures concerning himself. (Luke 24:27)

In the second passage we are told that Jesus

> opened their minds so that they could understand the Scriptures. He told them, "Thus it is written: The Christ will suffer and rise from the dead on the third day, and repentance leading to the forgiveness of sins will be preached in his name to all nations, beginning from Jerusalem. You are witnesses of these things." (Luke 24:45–48)

The effect of these two passages is to show that for Luke, the events in question were predescribed in Scripture and therefore necessarily had to take place, and that these events included not only the suffering and glorification of Jesus, but also the preaching to all nations. Luke's agenda in Acts picks up these two stages in the divine program. He frequently draws attention to the conformity of the career of Jesus to Scripture and also to the way in which the preaching of the gospel to all nations—and the consequent creation of a church composed of believing Jews and Gentiles—was what God had foretold and foreordained. The use of Scripture in Acts tends to revolve round these two related foci.

In both cases the use of Scripture has what we may call a broadly apologetic or forensic function. The argument is directed largely toward Jews, and it rests on what could be taken as common ground: the Scriptures accepted both by Jews (who did not yet accept Jesus as the Christ) and by Christians (whether believing Jews or Gentiles). The use made of Scripture elsewhere in the NT confirms Luke's picture of a constituency of Gentile Christians, many of whom had attended the synagogue (whether as proselytes or God-fearers), and others of whom had quickly accepted the Jewish Scriptures as their Scriptures. Both the identity of Jesus as the Christ and the admission of Gentiles to the people of God were contested issues, and the appeal to Scripture was central to the church's apologetic and evangelism and also to the establishment and confirmation of its own identity. In Acts there are general references to such an appeal in 17:2–3, 11; 18:28; 28:23, and Paul's activity in 9:22; 18:5 may be presumed to be the same. It is by appeal to the scriptural teaching about the Christ and then by showing that Jesus fits the picture that the conclusion can be drawn that he is the Christ (Albl 1999: 200–201).

At the same time, the appeal to Scripture serves to explain the significance of what is going on in Luke's story. It shows how the events are to be understood as the continuing work of God in accordance with his promises in Scripture and thus form part of the unfinished story of his judgments and saving acts. The use of Scripture thus also has what has been termed a "hermeneutical" or, better, "explanatory" function.

Luke's Sources and Methods

The questions of where Luke got his scriptural materials and how he used them can be posed at more than one level.

The upper level is concerned with whether the use of Scripture in Acts is essentially the work of Luke himself as a creative writer or of the historical characters whose words he reports. Most of the scriptural material occurs in the speeches attributed to the various principal actors, and it is common to attribute their composition to Luke himself with little if any source material on which to base them (e.g., Barrett 1994–98; Soards 1994). Other scholars attribute a greater role to possible sources, whether these were accounts of actual speeches given on the occasions described or were traditions of the kind of theology and preaching characteristic of the early missionaries (e.g., Bruce 1990; Larkin 1995; Witherington 1998).

The lower level is concerned with where Luke himself or his sources found the material that was used. Were the scriptural texts that were used taken from the Hebrew or the Greek texts of the OT (or possibly from other versions of the text, such as the version of the Pentateuch used by the Samaritan community)? And was there direct access to the texts or indirect access through such means as collections of *testimonia*? If versions of the Scriptures were directly used, were these reproduced from texts available to the writer (or the preacher), or were people reliant on memory?

But the question at this level is not simply about access to texts. There is, we may say, a tradition of how to understand and use the Scriptures from a Christian point of view. Where and when did this develop? No doubt it developed over time, but how much of it is due to Luke's own creativity, and how much is due to the scriptural activity of the early church? For example, is Peter's command of Scripture in Acts 1–2 credible within fifty days of the resurrection of Jesus?

Sources and Redaction

The question of sources (or tradition) and redaction (or creativity) is a tangled one. At one end of the spectrum we have the view that the account in Acts is fundamentally historical in the sense that it records events and teaching more or less exactly as things happened; the speeches in some cases may be abbreviated, but Luke is recording what Peter and the others said on the specific occasions that are described: "There is still no impediment to taking the speeches as containing in verbatim, précis or summary form the substance of what was said on the occasions cited" (Larkin 1995: 22–23). For upholders of this position, it is to be presumed that Luke got his information directly from people who were present at the time. At the opposite end of the spectrum we have the proposal that Luke is essentially a writer of fiction with very little regard for what actually happened, and it can be assumed that the speech material in particular is his own creation (Pervo 1987).

In between those views we find a variety of positions. Barrett, working as a critical historian who submits the material to a rigorous analysis, concludes that Luke was not always well or fully informed on what happened and did the best that he could with the available sources; the speeches are basically his own work. So with respect to Acts 2 he comments, "No one will maintain that this speech contains the very words used by Peter on a specific occasion in the life of the earliest church" (Barrett 1994–1998: 131) (nevertheless, Barrett [1994–1998: 334–40] does hold that there is a "Hellenist" sermon behind Acts 7, although this is not the same thing as saying that the actual defense of Stephen was the basis).

Others would emphasize more strongly that Luke was well informed for the most part, and that the speeches rest on a combination of early Christian traditions of the apostolic message and his own desire to express "the sentiments proper to the occasion, expressed as I [the speaker] thought would be likely to express them, while at the same time I endeavoured, as nearly as I could, to give the general purport of what was actually said"; these are the words not of Luke, but of the classical Greek historian Thucydides (1.22.1), with whom he has sometimes been compared (Bruce 1990: 34–40). Whether Thucydides actually followed the policy that he delineated here is, to be sure, a matter of debate.

The evidence is equivocal. With regard to the use of Scripture, the strongest argument for assigning Luke the major role in the composition is the fact that the material exhibits a considerable unity in that the same texts are cited or alluded to in more than one speech or by more than one speaker, and it is arguable that this harmony reflects the mind of a single author. The well-founded proposal that an Isaianic "new exodus" motif runs throughout Acts (see below) speaks for authorial shaping rather than piecemeal development by different Christians. The picture of Abraham found in various different speeches is a unified one (Dahl 1968). In some cases it is arguable that the complexity of the use of the OT appears to reflect careful thought and perhaps a lengthy development rather than the off-the-cuff remarks of a person suddenly summoned to address an occasion (Peter's speeches are presented as though they were unrehearsed, ad hoc treatments). In one or two cases it is claimed that the point being made must depend upon the use of a Greek version and could not have been made on the basis of the Hebrew MT (this point is made time and again with regard to James's use of Amos in Acts 15). There is some evidence for the use of *testimonia*, and if these were Christian compilations, they presumably took some time to be developed.

On the other side, stress must be placed on the fact that much of the material is not peculiar to Luke himself, but represents tendencies found elsewhere in early Christianity. There is material in common with Paul. The Isaianic motifs are shared with Mark and Paul. Although it must be admitted that the LXX on occasion is particularly congenial to the points being made, nevertheless in many cases the MT would still provide adequate support, and in other cases we certainly cannot rule out the use of a Greek version, particularly in a Hellenistic Jewish setting. In a number of cases it will be noted that Luke does not seem to recognize or draw out the implications in the texts that he cites, and this may mean that the material was originally framed by another hand.

In my opinion, the balance of probabilities tends to favor the kind of position proposed by Bruce (see Marshall 1980: 39–42; see further Witherington 1998: 46–49, 116–20). Justice must be done in recognizing both the use of source material by Luke and his own authorial shaping of the material, in which inevitably there is something of himself.

The Biblical Texts

Within Acts the main source for scriptural citation is the LXX rather than direct recourse to the Hebrew text. Following the research of Holtz, there is a consensus that the form of text used by Luke was close to that preserved for us in Codex Alexandrinus (A). Luke's variation from A is greatest in Psalms and to a lesser extent in the Pentateuch. Witherington (1998: 123–24, following Fitzmyer 1998: 304–6) identifies seven citations agreeing verbatim with the LXX, some fourteen in close agreement with the LXX, and two where there is little agreement with the LXX. The evidence suggests that Luke did not use the MT but on occasion may have used a Greek version other than the LXX or cited loosely from memory. Occasionally there are details that rest on extrabiblical sources (e.g., 13:21), and occa-

sionally Luke makes inferences from the text (e.g., 13:20). In a number of cases the citations are said to show an affinity to the Hebrew texts in the Dead Sea Scrolls (de Waard 1965: 78). What has been observed in the case of Acts is confirmed by the results of an examination of Luke's Gospel.

In any case, the citations from the LXX show numerous changes in wording. Holtz has claimed that where Luke is faithful to the LXX, this is evidence of his own activity, but where there are divergences, this indicates that he was using traditions; the weakness of this thesis and the failure to consider other explanations are explored by Bovon (2006: 110–14). Many of the divergences from the LXX are the result of working the citations into new syntactical contexts, but others entail modifications of content to bring out the significance that Luke saw in them. Rese (1969: 211–16) argues that Holtz has underestimated the extent and significance of these changes, but according to Bovon (2006: 116–17), Rese tends to exaggerate in the opposite direction.

Problems arise, as we have noted, where scholars have argued that a point made by Luke depends upon use of the LXX rather than the MT, especially where the LXX is probably to be deemed secondary to the MT in its wording. In some cases, it is argued, Luke is quoting speakers who probably were speaking Aramaic rather than Greek and are very unlikely to have based their arguments on a Greek translation of the Scriptures (this is frequently said about the speech attributed to James in 15:15–18, where, it is claimed, the point being made depends upon the Greek version, which [it is assumed] James himself would not have been using; however, see commentary on this passage below). Such cases will be noted as we proceed; at least in some examples it is arguable that essentially the same points could be established on the basis of the MT.

Controversy also surrounds the possible influence of the Samaritan Pentateuch. The Samaritan community had its own version of the Pentateuch, with a text that differs in points from the MT. Some scholars have argued for the influence of Samaritan theology and the Samaritan Pentateuch on Acts, specifically in Stephen's speech (Scharlemann 1968: 36–51; see the cautious discussion in Wilcox 1965). Opinion has continued to harden against this hypothesis that would include the use of this text of the Pentateuch (in addition to the references in Marshall 1980: 133n2, see Coggins 1982; Schneider 1980–1982: 1:448–50). Equally difficult to assess is whether Luke or his sources show any affinities to the Targumim (see Wilcox 1965 and the detailed critique in Emerton 1968).

From all this it is clear that for the most part Luke has followed the LXX, making appropriate changes to accommodate the material in his narrative and to bring out its significance more clearly, but also that there is some evidence of use of other textual traditions, whether by Luke himself or by the sources that he is using.*

Luke's "Canon"

Certain books are used more than others, particularly so far as the citations are concerned: Psalms (10x) and to a much lesser extent Exodus (5x), Isaiah (3x), and the Minor Prophets (4x). There are no citations from the Historical Books, Ezekiel, Daniel, and the Writings (other than Psalms; hence the limitation in Luke 24:44 to "the Law, the Prophets, and the Psalms" [not the Writings] is strictly correct). This fact led Holtz to the view that Luke had a limited collection of books at his disposal and was ignorant of some that he might have used. Holtz argued that Luke had access only to the Minor Prophets, Isaiah, and Psalms; he himself did not know the Pentateuch, although he could have taken over citations from his sources. In view of the virtual canonization of the OT as we know it by this time, this hypothesis was never a very likely one, and it is based on explicit citations without taking into account the wider field of allusions or echoes of Scripture and the usage in Luke's Gospel (see Steyn 1995: 230; Albl 1999: 190–91). For example, the full significance of Isaiah for Acts (formally cited just three times) emerges only when allusions and motifs are taken into account. There are also the passages where Luke refers generally to the Scriptures without specifying which passages he may have had in mind, leaving us the puzzle of trying to identify them (Acts 3:18, 24; 17:2, 11; 18:24,

28 [see also commentary on Acts 1:16 below]). In some places it has been suspected that a text may have influenced the composition, although it is not in Acts as we have it. See commentary on Acts 10:36 below, where there is a conjecture that Ps. 107:20 was originally in Peter's speech; similarly, it has been claimed that Luke sometimes abbreviated the citations, presumably because his space was limited (Dupont 1979: 151–52; see further below).

In one or two places we may suspect the presence of allusions made by the speakers in the narrative that Luke himself may not have observed (see commentary on Acts 2:32–33 below, where this may be the case, especially since the allusion is not based on the LXX; the typological possibilities in Stephen's speech in Acts 7 likewise do not seem to have been significant for Luke himself).

In any case, the wording and the formulation of the speeches strongly reflect the compositional skills of Luke himself, so that what he wrote was what he himself would have said in similar circumstances. Albl's work would imply that Luke (or his sources) may have taken some OT material not directly from the LXX but had access to it indirectly through collections of *testimonia*; this perhaps would cohere with Holtz's view that Luke used a limited set of OT books, but the latter does not stand or fall simply by this consideration.

An important fact confirmed by this analysis is that Jesus' statement that the Law, the Prophets, and the Writings bear witness to him is substantiated by the evidence of Acts. Pao (2000) has indicated how Isaiah in particular has shaped the understanding of the early Christian movement in Acts; but alongside Isaiah, we should also note how much has been contributed by Psalms.

Testimonia

Early in the twentieth century the hypothesis of a collection (or collections) of scriptural texts (*testimonia*) that were used by early Christians was popular, particularly with British NT scholars, of whom the best-known is perhaps J. R. Harris. The theory could appeal to material in the early church, but first-century evidence was lacking. The theory apparently was laid to rest by C. H. Dodd (1952), who offered in its place the proposal that early Christians drew their scriptural texts from a set of selected OT passages to which

---

*Decisions are sometimes difficult to reach because of the textual variants in both the LXX and Acts. Scribes often assimilated the texts of sources and citations to one another. No attempt has been made in the commentary to record minor variants, which in any case seldom affect the sense.

they repeatedly turned for appropriate support for their theological arguments. Thus there was a kind of canon within the canon that proved to be especially fruitful as a quarry for scriptural material, and with it there was developed a traditional method of interpreting the texts; it was known by oral tradition rather than being set down in writing, and it provided the basic starting point for early Christian use of the OT. Needless to say, individual writers, such as Paul, were not tied to it and ranged more widely. Dodd's hypothesis was criticized by A. C. Sundberg, but, in my opinion, unsuccessfully (Marshall 1988).

The *testimonia* hypothesis is still questioned (e.g., Steyn 1995: 232) but now has been given fresh life by Albl, who is able to adduce considerable evidence for similar collecting activity in the wider ancient world alongside the manifest examples of the genre found at Qumran (*4QTestimonia*; *4QFlorilegium*; *4QTanhumim*; *11QMelchizedek*) and the second-century Christian evidence. Albl argues that written activity goes back to the earliest stages of the church. He then argues along lines similar to earlier scholars for the existence and use of collections of *testimonia*, including materials used in Acts. The texts in Acts where such influence can be traced on this hypothesis are 1:20; 2:34; 3:22–25; 4:11, 25; 8:32; 13:16b–22 (Albl 1999: 198n145; 15:16–18 is said to be uncertain, but in favor of including it along with 7:42–43, see Stowasser 2001).

Albl claims that when Luke uses the texts cited in these passages, he can presume that his readers will regard the proofs as self-evident, and Albl contrasts the treatment in 2:25–28; 13:35, where Luke has to employ exegetical arguments to prove the applicability of the texts to Jesus. The implication of this hypothesis is that Scripture is used as "forensic proof" (Albl 1999: 200).

The significance of Albl's work is that, if sound, it enables us to relate much of the use of Scripture in Acts to the activity of other early Christians and makes it the more likely that what we have here is not Luke's own creation, but rather traditional usage. Clearly this does not rule out Luke's own hand in the composition, but it does make more probable that he was editing existing material.

Classification by Types of Formal Usage

There have been various attempts to analyze the different types of use that Luke makes of the OT. Three basic varieties of use are identified by Jervell (1996: 62):

1. *Summary references* to what the Scriptures as a whole say (Luke 24:26, 46; Acts 3:18, 24; 10:43; 17:3; 18:28; 24:14; 26:23). Luke is sometimes content simply to refer to the Scriptures for validation of a point without further development, leaving us to discover (not always successfully) which Scriptures he had in mind.

2. *Direct citations.*

3. *Reproductions and indirect citations* in historical summaries of the OT story (Acts 7; 13:17–25).

It is the merit of Jervell to have drawn attention to the significance of the summary references as an integral part of "Luke's *use* of the Old Testament." However, the material assigned to the other two categories needs a rather more detailed analysis. Formally, we can distinguish four categories:

1. *Actual citations.* A recognizable string of words from Scripture is quoted, with or without a formal indication that this is happening. On the use of formulas to introduce citations, see below. Sometimes it is disputed whether the term "citation" is appropriate when no formula is present (Rese 1969: 36), but this is pedantic and fails to recognize the fluidity of Luke's style.

2. *Allusions.* Sufficient words are used to make it certain that a specific passage is in the writer's mind. Included here are places where the writer refers to a specific passage (often a narrative) but does so quite loosely, paraphrasing the text.

Dupont (1979: 151–52) has argued that in a number of cases we gain the impression that Luke has cited only part of a passage that he has in mind, and the influence of the parts not cited may be present: a conclusion is being drawn from texts that had not been quoted or only partially quoted. See commentary on Acts 2:36; 4:11; 10:36; 13:34; 15:18 below.

3. *Echoes.* The language has been shaped by Scripture, sometimes by a form of words that is found more than once in Scripture. Sometimes the influence is purely literary, but at other times a theological nuance is given. Perhaps this feature should be labeled "imitation" (see Barrett 1994–1998: 551).

4. *Language.* A feature of Luke is the adoption of manners of expression that are typical of, and sometimes specific to, the "Semitic Greek" of the LXX; these are generally due to the attempt to devise equivalents of Hebrew idioms, and therefore it is not always clear with a NT writer whether they are due to translation (whether by the writer or an earlier source) from material in a Semitic language or simply to the effects of much exposure to the LXX. With Luke, it is likely that the latter is generally the case, although the former cannot be ruled out. Clarke (1922: 66–84) gives a detailed survey of the influence of LXX vocabulary and phraseology on Acts. The major part of the work of Wilcox (1965) is a discussion of this matter, arguing for the presence of Semitisms that are not septuagintalisms (see, however, the critique in Emerton 1968). Such features are on the fringe of "use of the Old Testament," and space limitations here allow only occasional mention of some of them. The boundaries between categories, especially between echoes and language, are fluid, and some of the phenomena may be more accurately regarded as "influences of the Old Testament on Luke" rather than "use of the Old Testament by Luke."

In his listing of types of usage, Steyn (1995: 26) offers a more nuanced classification:

1. citations with formulas
2. direct phrases without formulas
3. paraphrases—"free versions of a foreign text"
4. references—single formulations from a text that are integrated into the composition
5. allusions
6. scriptural terminology—concepts, technical terms, and the like
7. motifs—"the imitation of larger structural patterns"

This listing is helpful in specifically drawing attention to the use of motifs, such as where a narrative may show structure similar to a scriptural one or the broad use of a "new exodus" motif. Unfortunately, Steyn does not indicate the differences between "references" and "allusions," and his category of "scriptural terminology" is apparently restricted to specific terms such as "Passover" and "circumcision" and does not take account of the use of ordinary septuagintal language.

Combining these analyses and recognizing the danger of being overly precise, I suggest the following categorization:

1. summary references
2. citations with formulas
3. citations without formulas
4. paraphrases
5. allusions
6. echoes
7. scriptural terminology
8. language
9. motifs and structures

Classification by the Functions of the Scriptural Material

More important than the formal ways in which the wording is adopted, and not to be confused with it, is the problem of how it is used and interpreted.

1. *History.* In several passages the author is recounting a story (or part of one) from Scripture. The story may be given a "twist" or "spin" to bring out a specific point, but essentially it is a straightforward use (Longenecker 1999: 80–81). Dahl (1968: 142) notes that for Luke, Abraham is essentially a "historical person," an actor in history. In some cases Luke's version of what happened may differ from the OT account, sometimes in agreement with a variant version found in later Jewish sources.

2. *Promise and Fulfillment.* Here the accent may be varied. On the one hand, passages from the OT are understood as "history told in advance," in that the prophet is describing what was going to happen in the future. In such cases the prophet may not have been able to envisage how this would happen, but the early Christians could see that the description corresponded with what had happened in the life of Jesus or their own experience. In this case the emphasis may lie on the correspondence between prediction and event seen as a proof that the claims made by Christians concerning Jesus and themselves are valid. On the other hand, the emphasis may lie more on the fact that God has made promises to his people that are now being fulfilled, thus showing that God has been faithful and active in the course of history (see Schubert 1957). For "fulfillment" language in Acts, see 1:16; 3:18; 13:27 (*plēroō*); 13:29 (*teleō*); 13:33 (*ekplēroō*). This way of understanding his-

tory runs through the OT itself, the promises made to Abraham and the other "fathers" being partly fulfilled within the OT history itself and partly in the Christian history, and fresh promises continue to be made (Dahl 1968: 142–47).

3. *Pattern and Type*. In some cases the Scripture may establish a pattern that could recur but that fitted (supremely) the life of Jesus or the early church. This may be the case with the citations in Acts 1:20, which could be interpreted as examples of what should happen to the psalmist's enemies and therefore to Judas in particular rather than as specific predictions relating to Judas. Again, Deut. 18:15–22 may originally have had in mind a succession of prophets after Moses, and Christians saw in Jesus the last and greatest of the line, or they may have understood it as a specific prediction of Jesus (Acts 3:22–23).

Already in the OT later writers saw earlier patterns of events being repeated. The prime example of this is the way in which in Isa. 40–55 and elsewhere the exile to Babylon and the return of the people to Judea is seen to follow the pattern of the bondage of Jacob's descendants in Egypt and their subsequent journey through the desert to Judea—in both cases the deliverance brought about by God. The repetition of this pattern in the redemption of people from bondage in sin by Christ is a key feature in the NT and specifically in Acts (see Goppelt 1982: 121–24).

It is interesting that sometimes when Luke records texts that have typological possibilities, especially the material about Joseph and Moses in Acts 7, he does not draw attention to them, and they do not seem to be highly relevant to the main thrusts of the speech. The same may be true of the treatment of David (13:22). Acts 7 almost cries out for an understanding of the community of believers as the new temple, not made with hands, but Luke does not make the point explicitly. Again, there are hints of a typological relationship between the giving of the law at Sinai and the giving of the Spirit, but one might think that Luke was unaware of them.

The distinction between patterns and types is admittedly hard to define.

4. *Principles*. OT teaching, particularly about how God's people should live, is assumed to be still valid. Paul cites the civil law (Acts 23:5).

5. *Characterization*. Arnold (1996) uses this phrase when arguing that Luke uses OT quotations "for characterizing the main players in the narratives of Acts"—that is, for discerning the point of view of the character. The effect is that the characters, especially Peter and Stephen, are shown to stand within the OT tradition and to adopt an OT worldview, which sanctions them in Luke's eyes.

6. *Allegorization*. Allegorization should not be included in this list, since it is not characteristic of the usage in Acts. A comparison of the use of Amos in Acts 7:42–43; 15:16–17 with that in the Dead Sea Scrolls illustrates the point amply (see commentary on these passages below).

Jewish Models of Sermons

It is reasonable to assume that the early Christians used the OT in ways that were influenced by the practice of the Jews at the time. If you are a Christian missionary invited to speak in a synagogue service, it is highly likely that your manner of discourse will fit the customary pattern and style rather than being (for example) like a speech delivered by an actor in a play or a speech in a law court. An important attempt to understand how Luke has linked quotations and allusions together and used them in the construction of longer pieces has been made by Bowker (1967–1968), who looked for resemblances to synagogue sermons. The synagogue service was structured around prayers, readings from the Law and from the Prophets, and (if there was somebody present capable of giving one) a sermon. Synagogue sermons were essentially expositions of Scripture, based on the passages that had been read. Often they brought together citations from the different passages and let them throw light on one another. The meaning of a word in one passage might be fixed by citing its use elsewhere. The use of catchwords to link citations together and bind them into the discourse is noted by Bock (1987: 272).

Two types of sermon, which in fact scarcely differ in structure except in the manner of their opening, have been identified in Bowker's pioneering work. The *proem* homily was based upon an introductory text used as a bridge to link together the two readings, the seder from the Pentateuch and haftarah from the Prophets. So in

Acts 13, it is argued, Deut. 4:25–46 and 2 Sam. 7:6–16 are linked via 1 Sam. 13:14 (Targum). The *yelammedenu* homily begins with a practical (halakic) problem that is tackled scripturally. So in Acts 15, it is claimed, James, dealing with the practical problem of whether Gentiles should be circumcised, uses an argument that appeals to Amos 9:11–15. Other speeches that may be analyzed this way occur in Acts 2; 3; 7.

Some caution is called for in assessing this proposal. One problem lies in our uncertainty regarding the existence and contents of a synagogue lectionary at this time and as to whether such a lectionary would always have been determinative of local practice. There is no scholarly agreement in this area, and therefore we cannot build on it to develop a case for or against Bowker's hypothesis (see Rese 1979: 67–68; Fitzmyer 1998: 312n17).

The discussion in the commentary below will show that Bowker's proposals are largely impossible to confirm or refute. There is some inconsistency in the way in which in respect of one passage (Acts 13) he argues that verbal citation of the seder was avoided, but in others the seder is cited (Acts 3:13; 7:3).

It must be admitted that most of the rabbinic material dates from considerably later than the first century, and that the similarities are of a very general kind. It would seem to be going too far to speak of a particular structure (or structures) common to the Christian and the rabbinic sermons. That said, however, it should be observed that the very fact that both types of sermon contain scriptural exposition—more exclusively so in the case of the latter—is significant. Christian sermons presumably have their main precedent in synagogue sermons, and therefore it would be astonishing if they did not show similarities both in the kind of interpretation offered of the Scriptures and in the structural patterns. Furthermore, the general types of introduction, beginning from a scriptural text that is expounded and beginning from a question that concerned the audience, are very natural in a community where Scripture is regarded as the authoritative guide to religion and life. There is, accordingly, no likely "straitjacket" that shaped the early Christian sermons, but certainly they were molded by the kind of sermonizing that was familiar in the synagogues

and persisted into later rabbinic Judaism (see Barrett 1988: 241–42).

The value of Bowker's proposal is that it provides a setting in which some of the features of the use of Scripture in Acts are found to be at home and something of the rationale of a type of discourse whose logic may seem strange to us becomes apparent.

Jewish Exegetical Methods

The terms "midrash" and "pesher" regularly feature in discussions of the techniques employed by the NT authors when using the OT. The former term refers to the methods used in rabbinic texts to contemporize the meaning of Scripture. The latter term refers to one specific method employed at Qumran that used the phrase "its interpretation" (Heb. *pešer*) to explain the meaning and reference of items in an OT text with regard to the present time, understood as a period of eschatological fulfillment. Ellis (1978: 201) argues that in midrash simple contemporization takes place (he cites the change of "Damascus" to "Babylon" in Acts 7:43 as an example), whereas pesher is distinguished by the eschatological perspective. In both cases the procedures can involve the atomization of the text, so that each individual word or phrase can be considered separately and alterations in wording and plays on words used to obtain a new meaning. Examples of similar procedures are readily found in the NT and specifically in Acts. Ellis mentions the way in which the citation of Joel in Acts 2:17–21 contains interpretive variations from the LXX and then words from the text are used in the following exposition. But the actual "pesher" formula is not found, although we have phrases such as "This is that which was spoken" that move from the present event to the text (cf. Acts 4:10–11). A further step taken by Ellis (1978: 205–8), following Doeve (1954), is to argue that in some cases the presence of midrashic treatment of the same texts in more than one place in the NT may suggest that the midrashic interpretation was already developed and had become a part of Christian tradition before being utilized in Acts; the use of the "stone" imagery in 4:11 is a good example. See the discussion above on the question of the use of collections of *testimonia* with associated exegetical traditions by early Christian preachers and writers.

The Use of Citational Formulas

When Luke makes explicit citations, he does so by means of introductory formulas. "Formula," however, is too precise a term because it conveys the idea of a fixed and fairly formal introduction (like the stereotyped phraseology in, e.g., Matt. 1:22; 2:15, 17; 4:14; 8:17; 12:17), whereas Luke's usage is quite varied and the line between ordinary narrative and formula is hard to draw.

In Acts one group of introductions uses the verb "write," usually in the perfect-tense form "it has been written" (23:5), sometimes indicating the source (1:20; 7:42; 13:33; cf. 15:15). Similarly, Luke sometimes refers generally to "the things that have been written" (13:29; 24:14) without making an actual citation, but more commonly he uses the noun "Scriptures," *graphai* (17:2, 11; 18:24, 28). Probably the singular *graphē* in 1:16 refers to a single passage (cf. 8:35), and on one occasion "the Scripture" is used in an introductory formula (8:32).

Another group of citation formulas uses the verb "say" (both *legō* and *laleō* are found). General references are found in 3:21 ("all that God said by the prophets"); cf. 26:22 ("what the prophets and Moses said"). In citation formulas the subject of the verb may be God (3:25; 4:25; 7:6, 7; 13:22, 34, 35 [the Lord in 13:47]), the Holy Spirit (28:26), or the human author (David: 2:25, 31, 34; Moses: 3:22; the prophet [Isaiah]: 7:48; cf. 8:34; 26:22). Occasionally, "the Lord says" occurs in the heart of a quotation (2:17; 15:17; 7:49; cf. 7:7). The passive form "what has been said" is also found with an indication of the agent (Joel: 2:16; the prophets: 13:40) or possibly "Scripture" or indeterminate (13:35). Other appropriate verbs are also used (*epangellomai* [7:5]; *entellomai* [13:47]).

What is striking is that the closest parallels to the formulas used by Luke are found in the Qumran documents; the parallels in the later rabbinic writings are much less close (Fitzmyer 1998: 296–301). These formulas thus serve not only on occasion to identify broadly the source of the material, but also to indicate that God spoke in the past through the human authors and continues to speak to the contemporary generation. To be sure, God himself is usually named as the author only when specific statements made by him are cited (the exception is 4:25–26). The form "it has been written" can fairly be taken to imply the continu-ing authority of what was written in the past and still stands written. Nevertheless, in Acts Luke seems to prefer to mention the speaker rather than the fact of the writing (so Hübner 1990–1995: 3:121; Jervell 1996: 63).

From the above, we note that reference, often in broad terms, to the source of citations is quite common, with references to Moses (3:22; 7:37; cf. Luke 20:28), David (1:16; 2:25, 34; 4:25; cf. Luke 20:42), a psalm (13:33; cf. 13:35) or the book of Psalms (1:20; cf. Luke 20:42), Isaiah (8:30; 28:25; simply as "the prophet" in 7:48; 8:34; cf. Luke 3:4; 4:17), Joel (2:16), and the prophets (i.e., the collection of the Minor Prophets: 7:42; 13:40; 15:15).

The Theological Contexts for the Use of Scripture

We can now try to classify the areas where Luke uses Scripture in Acts.

A broad starting point is provided by Barrett (1988: 237–44), who categorizes the material under the three headings of preaching (12 references), prayer (1 reference), and direction for the church's life (6 references). This is helpful in noting the different types of context in the activity of the early church within which appeal is made to Scripture. However, it does not take us very far, since by far the largest amount of material occurs in "preaching," where its functions need to be defined more precisely.

We are taken further by Evans (1993b: 209–10), who lists the following five categories of use:

1. christological
2. soteriological—stressing universal salvation
3. apologetic—explaining Israel's lack of comprehension (Here the term is used in a narrower sense than in Barrett 1988: 237, where it is applied to the general use of the argument from prophecy.)
4. minatory—threats and warnings to Israel
5. critical—criticisms of past and present failings, but intended as warnings

This analysis is not wholly satisfactory because to some extent it is a mixture of doctrinal areas (christological and soteriological) and rhetorical functions (apologetic, minatory, and critical) that would be better separated. It inspired a fresh analysis by Bock (1998: 49):

1. covenant and promise
2. Christology
3. community mission or community guidance
4. commission to the Gentiles
5. challenge and warning to Israel

The effect of this analysis is to give a structure for the main lines of the theology that is found in Acts as a whole. Its broad framework is provided by the categories that Bock summarizes. First, the overarching theological structure is expressed in terms of covenant and promise: Luke is concerned with the activity throughout history of the God of Israel, who works through promise and fulfillment, who pledges himself to his people and provides for their welfare and salvation, who acts consistently throughout history, so that people can know what he is going to do. Second, God's activity is mediated through the agents through whom he speaks and acts: his prophets and the Messiah. So throughout Scripture runs the promise of the future deliverer, which is now fulfilled in the raising up of Jesus, and a major function of the use of Scripture is to demonstrate that the promised Messiah is Jesus and to make clear the nature of the deliverance brought by him. A third function of Scripture is to identify the continuing task of the followers of Jesus and to do so by giving them a role that is already provided for in Scripture. Fourth, the scope of the salvation to be announced by Jesus and his followers includes the Gentiles as well as the Jews, in accordance with the clear indications in the Scriptures that Israel had a mission outside its own people. And, fifth, it has to be made clear that the people of Israel must respond positively to the Messiah or else they forfeit the right to be the people of God; their history was one of repeated disobedience to the messengers of God, and they are called not to repeat the sins of their ancestors.

This summary demonstrates how the theology of Acts is based on Scripture and explicable in scriptural terms.

Scripture as Prophecy

How, then, does Scripture "work" to produce this effect? What is "Scripture"? Can we describe how it is used? Clearly there can be several aspects to this, and again we can attempt some analysis of the possibilities.

A simple but helpful twofold classification of the uses is provided by Steyn (1995: 233), who distinguishes the "informative" and "normative" modes. The former is where Luke picks up the story found in Scripture and uses scriptural language, whether in citation or paraphrase, to tell what happened. The latter is where Luke uses Scripture to show what God requires people to do; prophecies are presented that still have to be fulfilled.

However, we must attempt to go further than this. It is unclear whether Steyn thought that these two categories cover all possibilities or merely saw here two general characteristics of Luke's understanding of Scripture.

For Jervell (1996: 61–75), the OT is essentially the work of prophets, and all its authors, including Moses, are prophets. When Luke says "all the prophets," he means in fact the whole of the OT (Jervell 1983: 80; 1996: 62). The most important prophets are Moses and then David, who is specifically inspired by the Spirit. The whole of Scripture is authoritative and continues to be so (hence, for Jervell, the whole of the OT law still applies to all the people of God).

Jervell presents a refined version of a fairly common understanding of the nature of Scripture that can readily be attributed to Luke. It would seem that for Jervell's Luke, all of Scripture is understood to be predictive, with specific reference to the raising up of the Messiah and the church. The messages of the prophets are understood as finding their intended fulfillment in the events now taking place. There is a script written in advance that explains what is now happening, provided that there are interpreters (chiefly the apostles) who are able to recognize what is going on. So the primary way of understanding and using Scripture would seem to be in terms of prediction and fulfillment.

Such an understanding probably is simplistic, and it is open to misunderstanding. There is no indication in Acts that Luke favored the kind of interpretation found at Qumran whereby the whole of a text (Habakkuk) could be interpreted as finding fulfillment in the life of the sect by various ways of what we would call reinterpretation, as if the prophet had nothing to say to or about his own time. The use of Scripture is selective. And there is more than this one way of using it.

It is true, of course, that Scripture lays out what we might call the plot for the story, both by showing that what has happened (and is still in progress) is what God has promised to bring about, and by indicating the ways in which people must respond to God's requirements. Moessner (1996) argues that Scripture provides a "script" for what happens in Acts, a script that has been written out beforehand; in 1:15–26 Scripture functions to explain what has happened and to prescribe what needs to be done. There are three necessary "moments" in the plan: the suffering of the Messiah, his raising to the throne of God, and his preaching of light to Israel and the Gentiles. History proceeds in accordance with God's plan (13:36).

Rese (1969: 35–42) represents a reaction against seeing everything in terms of straight promise and fulfillment and wants to distinguish various types of usage. Of importance to him are the citations in which Scripture is used to explain what is happening rather than being seen as prophesying an event. He called this use "hermeneutical" and cited as typical examples of it 2:17–21; 3:22–23; 8:32–33. However, he does not deny that the category of prophecy and fulfillment is also present. In fact, he attempts to make a distinction within it. In one category it is the present event understood as fulfillment that makes the citation into a prophecy or prediction. In the other category the citation has the character of prediction from the outset, and the present event has the effect of bringing it to fulfillment; the present event is the future event that was predicted in the past. So the fact of the prediction indicates that the present event is God's action; this is evidence or confirmation from Scripture in the pattern of prediction and fulfillment. This is a helpful observation, indicating that sometimes a scriptural text is recognized to be prophetic only because it is seen in the light of what may plausibly be regarded as a fulfillment, just as a contemporary event is sometimes recognized to be a fulfillment only because a text has been found that appears to describe it in advance.

There has been some debate over the precise purpose of what we might call the argument from prophecy. The question has been raised whether the function of Scripture for Luke is better described as "proof from prophecy" or as "apologetic," but Barrett (1988: 237) rightly insists that these are essentially the same. There is no doubt that one important function of the appeal to Scripture in the evangelistic sermons in Acts and in the summaries of the evangelists' use of Scripture is to show from Scripture that Jesus is the Messiah, and this "proof from prophecy" manifestly has an apologetic function.

Prophecy and Pattern

Further precision has been brought by Bock, who recognized that there are occasions when Luke uses Scripture to explain current events without appealing to "straight-line promise and fulfillment" (cf. Soards 1994: 201). But he also argued that Rese had downplayed the element of promise and fulfillment. His own solution was to broaden the category of the appeal to prophecy. Luke, he argued, appealed to the fulfillment of prophecy and to the historic pattern of God's working demonstrated in the use of typology. Luke told the story in such a way as to indicate the typological and prophetic associations that lead one to see it in terms of fulfillment of God's plan. In so doing, he made use of texts that were seen in Judaism as looking forward to fulfillment.

"Luke sees the Scripture fulfilled in Jesus in terms of the fulfillment of OT prophecy and in terms of the reintroduction and fulfillment of the OT patterns that point to the presence of God's saving work" (Bock 1987: 274).

It must be emphasized that Bock offered this summary only in respect of Luke's christological use of the OT; the ecclesiological use was bracketed off for the purposes of his study. Bock notes that citational use of the OT for christological purposes ceases at the end of Acts 13 because by that point it has been made clear who Jesus is, and there is nothing more to be added. But the same might be said of the ecclesiastical use of the OT, in that by the end of Acts 15 the nature of the people of God has been fully clarified. (A further aspect of Bock's study that we need not take up here is that he traces a development from the presentation of Jesus as the Messiah-Servant in the Gospel to the understanding of him as Lord in Acts.)

Scripture Shaping the Narrative

A broader question of shaping in the light of the OT also arises. Brodie has proposed that Luke imitated Scripture in telling his story. In broad terms this is correct. Luke saw himself as continuing the story told in Scripture and to some extent adopted the style and diction of the LXX in so doing. More specifically, Brodie holds that to some extent Luke shaped his story on the Elijah/Elisha group of stories in the OT. There is no doubt that Luke did recognize the typological links between the mighty acts of God wrought by Elijah and Elisha and their counterparts in the stories of Jesus and his followers and included pointers to make this clear to his readers.

It appears, however, that Brodie wants to go further than this and see these stories as inspiring Luke in creative writing. Evans (1993c: 223–24) refers to the title of Brodie's *Luke the Literary Interpreter: Luke-Acts as a Systematic Rewriting and Updating of the Elijah-Elisha Narrative in 1 and 2 Kings.* He comments that this description of Luke's work is inappropriate. It is not that Luke rewrites the stories in 1–2 Kings and so creates dominical traditions, but rather that he "rewrites and updates the stories of Jesus and the early church in the light of 1–2 Kings (and other parts of the LXX)" (see Evans 1993a, esp. 70n4). Evans clearly gets the emphasis in the right place. Acts is not a midrash on the OT; rather, it is a telling of the story of the early church in the light of the OT that leads to a deeper understanding of what is going on.

In a vein similar to Brodie, Denova (1997: 155) holds that Luke's use of Scripture has so shaped his story that he has in fact constructed narrative events on the basis of scriptural oracles. So, for example, the rejection theme arises out of Scripture, and Stephen's polemic against the temple is likewise drawn out of Scripture. Even in the case of the inclusion of the Gentiles, "the underlying theme of prophetic fulfillment is what dictates their inclusion in this story" (Denova 1997: 186). This seems to me to be a total misunderstanding of what is going on in Acts, resting on a historical skepticism for which there is no justification. As in the case of the illumination of the passion narrative in the Gospels by evocation of scriptural parallels, so here too it is much more plausible that the narrator of Acts began with the histori-

cal events and added color to them in the light of Scripture.

An Overarching Biblical Pattern

The recognition that the first Christians were conscious of being involved in a new act of divine redemption comparable with the exodus from Egypt is well founded. There have been explorations of the way in which the shape and content of Deuteronomy may have influenced Luke's writings in particular, although these have usually been directed toward his Gospel (Moessner 1989).

But the new-exodus theme is already found in the OT itself, specifically in the book of Isaiah, and it is this formulation of it that has attracted the attention of Pao. He holds that the major theme running through Acts is that of the new exodus, in which the first exodus is seen through the lens of Isaiah: the new exodus foreseen in Isaiah takes place in the life of the church. Other scholars have noted the importance of Isaiah both for other NT authors (especially Matthew, Mark, and Paul) and for Luke-Acts (Denova; Garrett; D. E. Johnson; Sanders; Seccombe; Strauss; Turner), but Pao holds that none of them have sufficiently recognized the importance of Isaiah's use of the new-exodus theme particularly for the ecclesiology of Acts. "Isaiah is not used in a narrow christological sense. Instead, it serves to construct the identity of the early Christian movement" (Pao 2000: 100). The programmatic significance of Isaiah for Luke is seen in the full quotation of Isa. 40:3–5 in Luke 3:4–6. From this passage comes the concept of the "way," which becomes a self-designation and identity marker for the early church. Four other programmatic statements are identified, in all of which Isaiah occupies a significant role (Luke 24:44–49; Acts 1:8; 13:46–47; 28:25–28).

Pao identifies various subthemes in the Isaianic new-exodus program: the reconstitution of Israel; the ingathering of the exiles; the community of the Spirit; the rebuilding of the Davidic kingdom; repentance and turning to the Lord; the inclusion of the outcasts. He claims that these are significant in the first part of Acts. The hope of Israel is a key theme (Luke 1:54–55; 24:49; Acts 26:6–7; 28:20), and the various subthemes listed can be readily recognized. Doubtless these are themes that are not peculiar to the prophecy of Isaiah. The point of Pao's discussion is to show that they form a coherent unity in Isaiah that is then reproduced in Acts.

The role of the word of God in Acts is likewise to be understood within an Isaianic framework. The word goes out successfully from Jerusalem and could be said to be the main actor in the mission. We are reminded of Isa. 2:2–4 and the way in which the word is hypostatized as it goes out on its task of restoration and salvation (Isa. 9:7; 40:8; 55:10–11). The anti-idol polemic of Isaiah that continued to develop in Judaism (Pao 2000: 213–16) is also reflected in Acts, where God's victory over idols symbolizes the power of his people and his word over all competitors.

But Luke goes beyond Isaiah and transforms his vision in regard to the relationship of Jews and Gentiles. There is a tension between universalism and nationalism in Isaiah: even though there is salvation for the nations, they are subordinated to Israel. This tension is removed in Acts.

Pao observes that his work highlights several important features of the use of the OT in Acts: (1) Consideration must be given to the pattern of the narrative as well as to citations and allusions. "The scriptural traditions recalled in the use of certain key words may be more profound than the context explicitly noted in the scriptural quotations and allusions" (Pao 2000: 7n26). Nevertheless, all three may be evocative. (2) It may well be that the predominant use of Scripture in Acts is christological (Bovon 2006: 95), but this should not obscure the fact that ecclesiology as well as Christology is decisively shaped by the OT. Dupont in particular has studied in detail the scriptural basis for the mission. (3) Scripture has a hermeneutical function; there is more to Luke's usage than proof from prophecy. (4) Scripture has influenced the narrative as well as the speeches. (5) Luke has transformed the scriptural tradition by his fresh interpretation of it. (6) There may be a polemical function in the defense of the Christian interpretation of Scripture over against the usage and interpretation in other communities.

Pao's conclusions summarize a fresh understanding of Luke's use of the OT that is broadly convincing. One noteworthy consequence of it is to show that a fairly consistent Lukan purpose runs through the whole of the narrative, regardless of how far Luke's material is based on traditions.

Intertextuality

The term "intertextuality" has recently come into favor in discussions of the use of Scripture by other scriptural writers. According to Wall (2000: 542), it refers broadly

> to the various ways by which biblical writers presume the continuing authority of their Scripture that is cited or "echoed" (Hays) when it is exegeted to amplify the meaning of this sacred tradition (*traditium*) as the word of God (*traditio*) for new readers or auditors (Fishbane).

In effect, this is a recognition that texts are partially shaped by existing texts, sometimes finding fresh meaning or reference in them, or rather something that was not previously apparent. Since the texts in question are scriptural, it is open to the believing reader to claim that there is a fuller sense (*sensus plenior*) in them implanted there by divine inspiration.

In practice, recognition of the phenomenon has led to a realization of the significance of scriptural allusions and echoes alongside the more obviously recognizable citations, and the present enquiry continually takes these into account. Whether the new terminology actually covers significant phenomena that had not previously been detected remains to be seen. Wall, in his article on intertextuality, has an interesting discussion on the way in which Hab. 1:5 is used in Acts. He notes how the citation of that verse in 13:41 gives a new meaning to it that is not altogether removed from its original meaning and function. In fact "the intertextuality of Scripture presumes the interdependence of its theological subject matter" (Wall 2000: 548). This is perhaps simply a way of saying that the pattern of human events and God's response in the time of Habakkuk repeats itself in Paul's time: God can be expected to act in the same way as he has done in time past, and thus the threat voiced by Habakkuk can be seen as prophetic of God's action at this new stage in history. However, the "work" that God is going to do is now the fruitful mission to the Gentiles. Wall then goes on to note the way in which the citation may give fuller significance to the occurrences of "work" in 13:2; 14:26, where the mission of Barnabas and Paul is referred to as the "work"; he also notes possible resonances with the terms "wonder," "in your/ the last days" (2:17), and "believe" (13:38–39), so that these terms acquire a fuller biblical texture than they would otherwise have had. Nor is that all, for there is a further verbal link between the uses of "report" (ekdiēgeomai) in 13:41 and 15:3, which leads Wall to wonder whether the narrative is suggesting that the sin of the Jews at Antioch could repeat itself in the Christian church where there is failure to recognize the conversion of the Gentiles without the need for them to be circumcised as the work of God.

Thus the endeavor to read Acts intertextually has opened the commentator's eyes to possible resonances that might otherwise have been missed. This could be a fruitful approach, but it is disappointing that more is not made of it in Wall's fuller work in his commentary on Acts.

Scripture in Acts and the Gospel of Luke

The ways in which Scripture is used in the two parts of Luke's work are similar but not identical. In his Gospel there are some twenty-five citations or near-citations (3 by the narrator, 17 on the lips of Jesus, 5 by other people; of these, 7 are peculiar to Luke, 13 occur also in Mark, 5 are in Q). It is immediately apparent that nearly all of these are found on the lips of speakers (principally Jesus), just as in Acts, and that to a large extent they can be demonstrated to come from Luke's sources. Whatever the situation in Acts might be, here in his Gospel Luke certainly was constrained by his sources. Scripture provides the laws by which people must conduct themselves. It provides material that sets the role of Jesus and establishes that he is the fulfillment of prophecy. However, the detailed argumentation from prophecy found in Acts is absent until after the resurrection, when Jesus himself outlines to his disciples the way in which the course set for the Messiah and his followers is laid down in Scripture. Certain parts of the Gospel, principally the birth narratives, are filled with scriptural allusions and make use of scriptural language; the poetic "hymns" are especially soaked in Scripture, and there is nothing corresponding to them in Acts.

The way in which Scripture is used is thus somewhat different in Luke's Gospel. Nevertheless, the same broad understanding of Scripture is present. The new-exodus framework, with its appeal to Isaiah, is also to be found here, and the pattern for the use of Scripture in Acts is established in the postresurrection conversations. The question of a background in Deuteronomy for the theological story in the Gospel continues to exercise scholars, and although attempts have been made to trace it also in Acts (see esp. Moessner 1989), it can hardly be said to be prominent there.

Acts 1

1:1–11

The opening chapter of Acts describes the events surrounding the departure of Jesus, presented as the beginning of a new stage in God's activity of salvation. The departure of Jesus is paralleled with the ascent of Elijah and the empowerment of his successor. The promise of the Spirit and the summons to the disciples to be witnesses take up the pattern of the new exodus in Isaiah. The appointment of a replacement for Judas is seen as the appropriate action in the light of "cursing" texts from the psalms. Echoes of the OT are to be found throughout this narrative.

1:1–2

Luke refers back to his Gospel, summarizing its contents as "all that Jesus began to do and teach until the day when *he was taken up to heaven.*" The italicized phrase represents the one Greek verb anelēmphthē, from analambanō, a word not previously used by Luke (cf. the cognate noun analēmpsis [Luke 9:51]; in 24:51 Luke uses anapherō). It provides a link to the narrative in 2 Kings 2:11 (cf. 1 Macc. 2:58; Sir. 48:9 [Elijah]; Sir. 49:14 [Enoch]), where Elijah "went up to heaven in a whirlwind" in the sight of Elisha, his appointed successor, who proceeded to act as a prophet capable of mighty works in "the spirit of Elijah" (2 Kings 2:15). The term thus directs attention to the parallel between the departure of Elijah and his commissioning of his successor who acts in his spirit and the departure of Jesus after commissioning his followers to continue his work and promising them the gift of the Spirit. Thus, a single word alerts the observant reader (equipped with a good reference Bible!) to a narrative that shows interesting parallels to the present one and may be said to prefigure it. This raises the question how far Luke could presume that he had readers equipped to pick up his allusions. (For further possible Elijah/Elisha allusions, see Brodie 1983; 1986; 1987; 1990.)

1:8

The use of "comes upon you" (*eperchomai* [cf. Luke 1:35]) to describe the arrival of the Spirit on the disciples has a parallel in Isa. 32:15, "until the Spirit comes upon us from on high" (*erchomai*), in a passage that describes the promise of the transformation of the natural world and the inauguration of God's new era of justice, peace, and prosperity for his people. Other passages confirm that the gift of the Spirit is an indication of the arrival of the new era promised for the last days when God will establish his king who will reign in righteousness (Isa. 32:1; cf. Ezek. 39:29; Joel 2:28–29). The use of *(ep)erchomai* of the coming of the Spirit is sufficiently rare (Acts 19:6; cf. John 15:26; 16:7) for the coincidence in language with Isa. 32:15 to be striking. Pao (2000: 92) notes that the phrase "from on high" is not used here in Acts but does occur in the very similar statement in Luke 24:49 ("until you have been clothed with power from on high"). Since Luke is fond of literary variation, often using similar rather than identical wording to express the same thoughts, the evidence of this parallel materially strengthens the view that Isa. 32:15 lies behind Luke 24:49/Acts 1:8. The passage forms part of a web of allusions to the picture of the "new exodus" in Isaiah, which had considerable influence on the NT writers (Pao 2000: 91–96).

Confirmation of the point may come from another phrase in the same verse, in which the disciples were to be witnesses "to the ends of the earth" (*heōs eschatou tēs gēs*). The identical phrase occurs in Isa. 49:6, where the mission of the servant of Yahweh is to be "a light for the Gentiles, so that you may be for salvation to the end of the earth." This verse is quoted explicitly in Acts 13:47. The precise wording is actually found five times in the LXX and is not recorded elsewhere. This background is important, then, as confirming that the scope of the mission is to the Gentiles throughout the world, and not simply to the Jews (see Moore 1997; Pao 2000: 84–86). Although the phrase "end of the earth" is applied to Rome in *Pss. Sol.* 8:16, here it probably refers to the extremities of the known world, most probably Spain (Ellis 1991a; see, however, Barrett 1994–1998: 79–80).

In this context it then becomes likely that "you will be my witnesses" should be seen as echoing or paralleling the frequent references to Isaiah's hearers in their role as the Lord's servant acting as witnesses to him (Isa. 43:10, 12; 44:8). In Isaiah the role is a fairly general one of witness to God, his reality, power, and ability to announce beforehand what he is going to do; in Acts the witness is more specifically to the career of Jesus and in particular his resurrection (e.g., 2:32). The theme of witness is prominent throughout Acts, being applied to Peter and his colleagues and to Paul (cf. Clark 2001: 113).

The phrase "to the ends of the earth" comes at the end of a listing of the areas in which the apostles will bear their witness. The brief list is linked by Scott (1994: 522–44) to the Jewish tradition of a "table of the nations," which can be traced back to Gen. 10; 1 Chron. 1. In itself this verse shows little evidence of links to this tradition, but it is to be read in the light of Luke 24:46–47, with its reference to preaching to all the nations, and also of the rest of Acts (see further commentary on Acts 2:5–11 below). Scott proposes that Acts is structured geographically to give successive missions to the descendants of Shem (2:1–8:25), of Ham (8:26–40), and of Japheth (9:1–28:31).

1:9

Although a cloud accompanied the Israelites in the wilderness, it is unlikely that the cloud here is a symbol of God's presence (*pace* Wall 2002: 43).

1:10

L. T. Johnson (1992: 31) proposes that the two men represent Jesus' two predecessors, Moses and Elijah, who also ascended (cf. Luke 9:30–31; see also Wall 2002: 44). The fact that the disciples saw Jesus going up corresponds to the way in which Elisha saw Elijah ascending and thereby was assured that he would receive a double portion of his spirit (2 Kings 2:9–12).

1:15–26

1:15

The phrase *epi to auto* (1:15; 2:1, 44, 46 [D*], 47; 4:26; Matt. 22:34; Luke 17:35; 1 Cor. 7:5; 11:20; 14:23) raises an interesting point. It appears to mean "together," but in some occurrences it seems otiose. It occurs frequently (45x) in the LXX with the sense "together," "in the same place" (Heb.

yaḥad; yaḥdāw). This sense is found in the quotation of Ps. 2:2 cited in 4:26 and is also appropriate here (NRSV) and elsewhere, but other proposals have been made. The phrase is also found in Hellenistic Greek with the sense "in all, amounting to" (Barrett 1994–1998; 96) which could be appropriate here.

The peculiarity of the usage in 2:47 has led to further proposals for understanding. There we read that "the Lord added to their number daily those who were being saved." Black (1954: 246) noted the parallel in 1QS V, 7: "when they are enrolled in the community" (García Martínez 1996: 8). The evidence is discussed in detail by Wilcox (1965: 93–100), who develops the case that the Hebrew *lĕyāḥad* means "to the Congregation" and thus has what we might call a technical sense (for criticism of Wilcox, see Emerton 1968: 294). We might see a parallel in the way in which a phrase such as "in the house" used in the appropriate context in the United Kingdom becomes "in the House" (i.e., "in a meeting of the House of Commons"). In this way, what might at first seem to be no more than a septuagintalism in language takes on a specific nuance in both Qumran and the early church: "together in fellowship" (as Bruce [1990: 132] renders it). In one or two places the textual phenomena suggest that scribes found difficulty with the phrase and even added an explanation (so in Acts 2:47 Codex Bezae [D*] adds *en tē ekklēsia*). In 1 Corinthians, Paul uses the phrase similarly in 11:20, while in 14:23 it may signify fellowship together in a full assembly rather than in small house groups (see Bruce 1990: 108).

1:16

Peter takes the initiative in dealing with the problem caused by the reduction of the number of the apostles to eleven through the defection of Judas. He justifies his action by commenting that the Scripture had to be fulfilled that the Holy Spirit had spoken through the mouth of David. Similarly, in 4:25 God is said to have spoken by the Holy Spirit through the mouth of David (cf. the use of "David" to indicate the author of psalms in 2:25; 4:25; Luke 20:42 pars.; Rom. 4:6; Heb. 4:7; for "mouth" in this instrumental sense, see Luke 1:70; Acts 3:18, 21; 4:25; 15:7; Isa. 51:16; 59:21; Jer. 1:9; Zech. 8:9). This is a clear case of regarding a particular passage in Scripture as the utterance of the Holy Spirit through a human agent (cf.

4:25; 7:51; 28:25), and also as foretelling something that must be fulfilled. What is debatable is whether Peter is referring to some event that was bound to happen because God worked to bring it about or to some action that human beings must undertake (note the imperatives) because God had commanded it. The verb "fulfill" can be used in both ways.

But what Scripture is in mind here in 1:16? There are two possibilities. The first is that Peter is referring to a passage that foretold that Judas would betray Jesus, but that is not actually cited here. Some commentators (e.g., Barrett 1994–1998: 96–97) refer to Ps. 41:9 [40:10 LXX]: "Even the man of my peace, in whom I trusted, he who eats my bread, has lifted up his heel against me" (cited in John 13:18; for a possible echo, see Mark 14:18). However, there is no indication of such an allusion here, and there are no verbal contacts; moreover, the specific reference to David as the speaker makes it rather unlikely that Luke would not have included the actual citation. The second possibility, then, is preferable: Peter is looking forward to the citations that he will make in 1:20 (the gap between vv. 16 and 20 is lessened if vv. 18–19 are treated as a parenthesis inserted by the narrator in Peter's statement). What Peter is saying is that the commands in the psalms have to be carried out by the church so that the Scriptures are fulfilled.

Longenecker (1999: 81) argues that Peter is here using the principle of *qal waḥomer* ("light and heavy") to apply what is said of wrongdoers generally in the psalms to Judas specifically as the outstanding example of wickedness (see Bruce 1990: 110; Steyn 1995: 63). Others argue that Peter would have seen a specific prophecy regarding Judas in the psalms, since David was regarded as a prophet (cf. 2:30–31) and Jesus had already applied the psalms to himself (Larkin 1995: 46n).

1:18

Peter's account of the death of Judas describes how "he burst open in the middle and all his intestines spilled out [*ekcheō*]." The same motif occurs in the description of the death of Amasa (2 Sam. 20:10), but the suggestion that Peter's account is modeled on the latter (see Witherington 1998: 121) surely is remote. Clarke (1922: 77) found some influence from Wis. 4:19, where the term "swollen" (*prēnēs*) also occurs. The echo of the death of Antiochus (2 Macc. 9:1–12) perceived by Wall (2002: 50n74) is by no means as clear as he thinks.

1:20

The source of the citations is explicitly given (cf. Luke 20:42; 24:44; Acts 13:33). Psalm 69 is an "individual lament" in which the psalmist describes his plight of deep suffering, prays to God for deliverance, and calls upon God to exercise his wrath against the sufferer's foes. It was interpreted by early Christians as typifying Jesus in his suffering and death (John 2:17; 15:25; Rom. 15:3) and also as applying to those who rejected him (Rom. 11:9–10) (see Lindars 1961: 99–108); once this interpretation had been made, it was possible for the giving of wine (*oxos*) to Jesus on the cross to be seen as foreshadowed in Ps. 69:21. So the psalm could naturally be applied here in 1:20 to Judas: "Let their place be deserted; may there be no dweller in their tents" (Ps. 69:25 [68:26 LXX]).

Ps. 68:26 LXX [69:26 MT; 69:25 ET]	Acts 1:20a
genēthētō hē epaulis autōn erēmōmenē,	*genēthētō hē epaulis autou erēmos*
kai en tois skēnōmasin autōn	*kai mē estō ho katoikōn*
mē estō ho katoikōn;	*en autē,*

The citation follows the LXX with minor changes, the most important being the change from plural to singular so that the curse is directed against one individual, and the omission of "tents." The psalm can thus be regarded as a loose reference to the "field" purchased by Judas; the LXX's *epaulis* can refer to a dwelling, a fold, or a village (LEH 166). The whole statement is a poetic way of expressing a curse against a person, but it could be intended more literally: Matthew comments that the place bought with Judas's money was turned into a burial place (Matt. 27:7).

The use of Ps. 69 elsewhere in the NT (see references above and Eph. 4:8; for a possible allusion, see Acts 2:33; see also Lindars 1961: 99–110) suggests that Luke may have gotten it from tradition (Steyn 1995: 62), and that it may have figured in a collection of *testimonia* (so Albl 1999: 199).

The second citation, "May another take his place of leadership," is taken from the LXX (Ps. 108:8 [109:8 ET]).

Ps. 108:8b LXX [109:8b MT/ET]	Acts 1:20b
tēn episkopēn autou laboi heteros;	*tēn episkopēn autou labetō heteros;*

The change of mood from optative to imperative may be assimilation to the mood of the previous citation. This citation is from another individual lament in which the psalmist describes one of his foes in considerable detail and expresses a string of curses against him. The psalm is not cited elsewhere, but there are coincidences of language between 108:16 LXX and Acts 2:37 and between 108:25 LXX and Mark 15:29 (see Lindars 1961: 109–10); Hanson (1983: 83) finds an echo of 108:4–5 LXX in Matt. 5:43–44/Luke 6:27–28 (cf. 1 Cor. 4:12–13). Again, therefore, we may well have a psalm that was familiar to early Christians.

The interesting feature here is the term *episkopē*, translated as "place of leadership" and used in 1 Tim. 3:1 for the function exercised by an *episkopos*. The reference in the psalm is probably a general one to a role of leadership in the community. Peter himself refers to the role of Judas and his colleagues as one of service (*diakonia* [1:17]) and apostleship. (The term *klēros*, used here for Judas's share in the service, is also used in Num. 18:21–26, but the connection with that passage developed by L. T. Johnson [1992: 35] and Witherington [1998: 122] is unconvincing.) The task of church leaders was understood as one of oversight and pastoral care (in the manner of a shepherd) over the other members of the congregation (1 Pet. 5:2). This element in the work of the Twelve, who are otherwise seen preeminently as witnesses to Jesus, is significant. Since the appointment is to a place among the Twelve, the question arises whether the need to maintain twelve apostles to judge the tribes of Israel (cf. Luke 22:30) is in mind (see Evans 1993b: 185), but the stress seems to be principally, if not exclusively, on the tasks of service and witness.

Dodd (1952: 58n1) argues that the effect of the first citation is to show that Scripture allows for the creation of a vacancy in the apostolate caused by apostasy and not by death; contrast how there was no attempt to replace James when he was put to death (Acts 12:2). Note that the application could have been made on the basis of the MT, since the Hebrew root *pqd* is regularly translated by the Greek *episkept-*.

1:21

"Went in and went out" (cf. 9:28) is a septuagintalism for being active, often used of people in leadership roles (cf. Num. 27:17; Deut. 31:2; Josh. 24:11; 1 Sam. 18:16; 29:6; 2 Kings 19:27; Ps. 121:8 [120:8 LXX]; see Jervell 1998: 126–27).

1:25

Note a parallel in wording between Judas "turned aside from" (*parebē* with *apo*) and the use of the same verb in Deut. 9:16 (cf. 17:20), where the Israelites turned aside from the way that the Lord had commanded them; however, similar wording is found elsewhere (e.g., Exod. 32:8), indicating that we have nothing more than the use of biblical language.

1:26

Compare Prov. 16:33 for a recognition that God works through the casting of lots; there is no direct allusion to the assumption expressed here, although it clearly was the basis of the method chosen here. In any case, the point is made in the MT and not in the rather different rendering in the LXX. The casting of lots was a familiar OT procedure (Lev. 16:8; Num. 26:55), also used at Qumran (1QS V, 3; VI, 16).

Acts 2

In chapter 2, with its accounts of the descent of the Spirit upon the followers of Jesus, of Peter's speech to the people followed by their response, and of the nascent life of the early church, we have a number of scriptural points to observe. The first is the background to the event in the Feast of Pentecost and then possible models for the disciples' speaking in tongues. Second, Peter's speech makes a deliberate appeal to Scripture to show that the events are a fulfillment of prophecy and therefore are to be understood as the consequences of the exaltation of the Messiah, who is to be identified with Jesus. At the same time, the question of an implicit juxtaposition of the giving of the law to Moses and the giving of the Spirit to Jesus arises.

2:1–13

2:1

The occasion of the coming of the Spirit is the day of Pentecost, otherwise known as the Feast of Weeks (Exod. 23:16; 34:22; Lev. 23:15–21; Num. 28:26; Deut. 16:9–12). In the OT this feast was simply a celebration of the wheat harvest. By this time, however, the festival was associated with the renewal of the covenant made with Noah and then with Moses (*Jub.* 6:17–18), and in second-century Judaism it was regarded as the day when the law was given at Sinai.

2:2

The association of the coming of the Spirit with a noise like a powerful wind and with tongues like fire is no doubt to be understood primarily in the light of the prophecy by John the Baptist (Luke 3:16), but at a secondary level the imagery used is reminiscent of the descriptions of theophanies in the OT. God's coming is associated with mighty storms consisting of wind, thunder, and lightning (2 Sam. 22:16; Ps. 18:7–15; Ezek. 13:13). Denova (1997: 170) draws attention to the saving winds in Exod. 14:21; Num. 11:31, but these are more instrumental than revelatory. Fire accompanied the theophany at Sinai itself (Exod. 19:18). Johnson (1992: 46) argues for a Moses typology and holds that there is a deliberate allusion to the Sinai event. However, the imagery of "tongues" of fire is not found here in the OT (though cf. Isa. 5:24; 30:27–30; Beale 2005a: 84–87). The descent of the Spirit on the people and their consequent speech has a model in Num. 11:25, where the Lord came down in a cloud and took some of the Spirit that was on Moses and put it on seventy of the elders of Israel, causing them to prophesy. The common points are the reception of the Spirit and the subsequent verbal activity ("prophecy" is a term broad enough to include speaking in tongues). Whether Luke's readers were meant to make the association is not clear, since there are no clear verbal echoes. But the passage does go on to express the longing that all of the Lord's people would be prophets (Num. 11:29); it was understood in later Judaism as having an eschatological fulfillment and was linked with Joel, which was understood as its specific fulfillment (*Midr. Ps.* 14:6, cited in Evans 1993b: 187). "Filling" with the Spirit is mentioned with respect to Elisha in Sir. 48:12.

Another possible link is with Isa. 28:1–15, where there is an attack on priests and prophets who are intoxicated with wine and a prophecy that God will speak to his people with foreign lips and strange tongues (Betz 1968, cited in Evans 1993c: 215n8; Jervell 1998: 134–35). There is a citation from this passage in Paul's discussion of tongues in 1 Cor. 14:21 (Isa. 28:11), and the immediately following text about the precious cornerstone (Isa. 28:16) was also used by the early church. The verbal coincidences are noteworthy, but the thrust of the two passages is quite different.

2:5

The phrase "every nation under heaven" is paralleled in Deut. 2:25; 4:19. It is simply an example of biblical language. Similarly, "listen carefully" (*enōtizomai* [2:14]) uses a familiar LXX word for summoning the attention of the hearers (cf. Joel 1:2, perhaps an echo in light of the ensuing citation of Joel in Peter's sermon to the crowd; see Evans 1993c: 216n11).

2:9–11

More than one sermon has been preached on the multiplication of mutually unintelligible languages at Babel (Gen. 11:1–9) being undone at Pentecost, but there is no hard evidence in the text for seeing this interpretative nuance in Luke's story; the possibility of a verbal link in the use of the verb *syncheō* (2:6; cf. Gen. 11:7–9) is explored favorably by Barrett (1994–1998: 119): the crowd at Babel was confused by the multiplicity of languages, while the Pentecost crowd was confused by hearing their own languages. Nevertheless, the evidence is not strong. Even so, this may be a good example of how modern readers may helpfully read two narratives in the light of each other, even though there are no deliberate links from the later to the earlier.

The list of nations is unusual. It certainly is not derived from the OT, but it does stand in a line of "tables of the nations" exemplified in the OT (Gen. 10; 1 Chron. 1:1–2:2; cf. *Jub.* 8–9; 1QM II, 10–14; Josephus, *Ant.* 1.120–147; see Scott 1994: 527–30). P. S. Alexander (1992: 983) holds that the list here, though brief and selective, can be seen as an allusion to Gen. 10 if it is right to see in the Pentecost story a reversal of the confusion of languages reported in Gen. 11. Denova (1997: 173) and Pao (2000: 131) draw attention to Isa. 11:11, where the scattered exiles of Israel are to be brought home.

2:14–36

Peter's sermon begins with a text that not only very conveniently provides the scriptural explanation of the strange behavior of the believers, but also offers a golden opportunity to develop the theme of Jesus Christ thanks to its linking of the outpouring of the Spirit with the theme of salvation for those who call on the name of the Lord. The sermon thus becomes essentially an explanation of who this "Lord" is. Having noted that Jesus was attested by God through mighty works (echoing Joel 2:30, cited in v. 19), and having mitigated the opposing impression given by his death by insisting that it fell within the plan of God, Peter describes how God raised Jesus from the dead because he could not be held by it. What happened is interpreted by reference to Ps. 16 which, it is argued, cannot apply to David himself because he died (and did not rise); but God had promised a future ruler as a descendant of David (Ps. 132), and so Ps. 16 applies to this ruler. Now Jesus had been raised from the dead, and the Spirit had been poured out by him. It follows that he has been exalted to God's right hand, as prophesied in another psalm (Ps. 110), which again could not be applied to David himself. It follows also that Jesus is now the Lord who grants salvation to all who call upon him.

The argument from Scripture is not easy to follow. It demonstrates examples of so-called midrashic exegesis, with its catena of scriptural citations and allusions, the repetition of words from the citations in the accompanying exposition, and the use of changes in wording to bring out the significance the more clearly (e.g., 2:17, 30).

Bowker (1967–1968: 104–6) argues that this speech is "certainly" a proem homily with Joel 2:32 as the bridge text, Deut. 29:1–21 as the seder (reading from the Torah), and Isa. 63:9–19 as the haftarah (reading from the Prophets). The opening scriptural text is clear enough. Bowker finds allusions to Deut. 29 in 2:36 (call to all Israel to enter into the covenant [Deut. 29:10–11]) and in 2:39 (the covenant is with those present and absent [the unborn?] [Deut. 29:14]). The haftarah is identified on the grounds of linguistic parallels between Isa. 63:19 and Joel 2:32, and the use of "name" in 2:38 and Isa. 63:12 (not 63:13 [*pace* Bowker]), 16.

However, this explanation is less than convincing. One would expect the underlying texts to play some important role in a sermon that supposedly is based upon them, but there is not the faintest evidence that Isa. 63 in any way influenced the content of the sermon; at best it has some weak coincidences with Joel 2, which clearly is the decisive basis for the sermon. And equally there is no linguistic evidence that Deut. 29 has influenced the exposition. One might almost want to say that Peter had gone out of his way to disguise his sources!

2:17–21

Peter explains the events that have just been witnessed by the crowds by seeing in them the fulfillment of the prophecy in Joel 2:28–32 (3:1–5 LXX). The context of the prophecy is Joel's summons to the people to true repentance after they have been subjected to an invasion of locusts, a harbinger of worse things to come on "the day of the Lord." Yet the Lord promises to take pity on his people and to restore the land to its former prosperity. Then comes the prophecy of the outpouring of the Spirit as part of the events preceding the coming of the day of judgment. In the prophecy the coming of the Spirit is only a part of the event; it is accompanied by wonders in the sky and on the earth. And there will be the opportunity of deliverance for all who call on the name of the Lord before the judgment falls upon them. The judgment will be upon the nations that have oppressed God's people, whereas Israel will be saved. Within this set of events the outpouring of the Spirit will be upon "all people," and the effect will be that they will prophesy and see visions. The significance of this in its context is not immediately clear. The inspiration of prophets was a sign of the presence of the Spirit and thus of God's activity and presence with his people; visions were associated with prophecy, and here dreams are also included as the working of the Spirit.

The citation of the prophecy thus serves initially to explain the phenomenon of Spirit-possession and speaking in tongues, but the passage moves on to announce the closely related proclamation of salvation for those who call upon the Lord. This second theme becomes in fact the dominant one in Peter's speech with his identification of the risen and exalted Jesus as the Lord and Messiah through whom salvation is offered to his audi-

ence. Evans (1993c: 218–20) further notes how the prophecy foreshadows what happens later in Acts: the offer of salvation to all people (including Gentiles) and the consequent pouring out of the Spirit on all people (i.e., all who respond to the gospel), the performance of signs and wonders, the prophetic activity of women (21:9), and the experiencing of visions and dreams. Here and elsewhere in Acts "the prophetic Scripture is lived out in the experience of the believing community" (Evans 1993c: 221).

Rese's (1969: 46–55, 104) understanding of the citation as explaining what was happening by reference to Scripture and not in terms of fulfillment of a scriptural prediction is difficult to justify. When a passage of Scripture is explicitly in the future tense, announcing what God will do in the future, it is hard to understand the explanation of a contemporary event in terms of the passage as not conveying the implication that in this way a prophecy that was waiting to be fulfilled has now found its fulfillment (Bock 1987: 156–69).

2:17

The introduction to the citation "This is what was spoken by the prophet Joel" has been compared to the formula "Its interpretation refers to …" found in the pesharim in the Dead Sea Scrolls. But the formulations are quite different from each other, although their functions are similar: the goal is to identify some current event with something described in a prophecy. There is a dialectic here. On the one hand, the significance of a hitherto obscure prophecy (what is the prophet referring to?) is explained by seeing it fulfilled in a particular event. On the other hand, the significance of an event (what exactly is happening?) is illuminated by seeing it as the fulfillment of a prophecy. Thus the prophecy and the event shed light on one another. The assumption is that the correspondence between the scriptural description and the event will be self-evident or can be demonstrated fairly easily. Thus in the present case, if one rules out one possible explanation of the behavior of the disciples—drunkenness—by the reasonable argument that people normally do not become inebriated at that time of day, then the strange talk and exuberance can be seen to broadly match the description of prophecy in Joel; one would need to remember that in some cases prophecy involved people acting in strange and even bizarre ways (1 Sam. 10:5–6, 10–13; 19:20–24).

As is common when a citation is made, some of the wording is repeated in the surrounding material. Evans (1993c: 216–17) claims that some twenty words in Luke's narrative and the opening words of Peter's speech occur in Joel (whether in the passage cited or elsewhere in the prophecy). Some of these may be coincidental, but others may be significant. Note the use of "pour out" (2:17, 33) and "Lord" (2:21, 36).

Luke's wording in the citation is very close to the LXX, but there are a number of changes that Bock (1987: 156–87) and Turner (1996: 268–69) regard as pre-Lukan. Steyn (1995: 74–90) argues that a citation of such length probably was taken from a written text that differed in minor details from the LXX as we know it today and that Luke's changes tend to be theological rather than stylistic.

Joel 3:1–5 LXX [3:1–5 MT; 2:28–32 ET]	Acts 2:17–21
3:1 *kai estai meta tauta kai*	2:17 *kai estai en tais eschatais hēmerais,*
	legei ho theos,
ekcheō apo tou pneumatos mou	*ekcheō apo tou pneumatos mou*
epi pasan sarka,	*epi pasan sarka,*
kai prophēteusousin hoi huioi hymōn	*kai prophēteusousin hoi huioi hymōn*
kai hai thygateres hymōn,	*kai hai thygateres hymōn*
	kai hoi neaniskoi hymōn
	horaseis opsontai
kai hoi presbyteroi hymōn	*kai hoi presbyteroi hymōn*
enypnia enypniasthēsontai	*enypniois enypniasthēsontai;*
kai hoi neaniskoi hymōn	
horaseis opsontai;	
3:2 *kai epi tous doulous*	2:18 *kai ge epi tous doulous mou*
kai epi tas doulas	*kai epi tas doulas mou*
en tais hēmerais ekeinais	*en tais hēmerais ekeinais*
ekcheō apo tou pneumatos mou.	*ekcheō apo tou pneumatos mou, kai prophēteusousin.*
3:3 *kai dōsō terata en tō ouranō*	2:19 *kai dōsō terata en tō ouranō anō*
kai epi tēs gēs	*kai sēmeia epi tēs gēs katō,*
haima kai pyr kai atmida kapnou;	*haima kai pyr kai atmida kapnou.*
3:4 *ho hēlios metastraphēsetai eis skotos*	2:20 *ho hēlios metastraphēsetai eis skotos*
kai hē selēnē eis haima	*kai hē selēnē eis haima,*
prin elthein hēmeran kyriou	*prin elthein hēmeran kyriou*
tēn megalēn kai epiphanē.	*tēn megalēn kai epiphanē.*
3:5 *kai estai pas hos an epikalesētai to onoma kyriou sōthēsetai;*	2:21 *kai estai pas hos an epikalesētai to onoma kyriou sōthēsetai.*
hoti en tō orei Siōn kai en Ierousalēm estai anasōzomenos kathoti eipen kyrios	

Joel 3:1–5 LXX [3:1–5 MT; 2:28–32 ET]	Acts 2:17–21
kai euangelizomenoi hous kyrios proskeklētai.	

A major alteration is the replacement of the LXX's "afterwards" (*meta tauta*) with the phrase "in the last days" (*en tais eschatais hēmerais* [cf. Isa. 2:2]) in all manuscripts except B 076 (C *pc*) sa^[mss]. It is easier to explain the reading of the minority of manuscripts as assimilation to the text of Joel (Bock 1987: 160–61; Metzger 1994: 256) than to account for a change from the original text of Acts by later scribes (Haenchen 1971: 179; Holtz 1968: 7–8; Rese 1969: 51–52). Haenchen holds that Luke did not think that the last days were inaugurated by the time of Pentecost and therefore would not have made the replacement. This, however, is a dubious understanding of Lukan theology, and in any case it is arguable that both versions of the text have reference to the last days before the coming of the day of the Lord. Probably the intention of the change is to emphasize that the events of Pentecost do belong to the activity of God in the last days: a new age has arrived.

The insertion of "God says" (*legei ho theos*) conforms to typical prophetic style (cf. 7:6; see Rese 1969: 48–49). Turner (1996: 277–78) notes how it strengthens the contrast between God pouring out the Spirit and the Messiah doing so, thus emphasizing the significant position of the latter in taking over the divine function.

The order of the clauses about the young men and the old men is inverted compared with Joel. Luke inserts "my" with male and female slaves, emphasizing their role as God's agents rather than their social status. The effect is that the terms referring to literal slaves in Joel are now understood as a general description of God's servants (Holtz 1968: 10). At the end of 2:18 Luke inserts "and they will prophesy"; this repetition of the words from 2:17 makes the effect of the Spirit on the Lord's servants crystal clear. For Turner (1996: 270), this reinforces the presentation of the Spirit in Luke-Acts as the Spirit of prophecy.

2:18

Luke has *kai ge*, a reinforced form of Joel's *kai* ("and"), which raises the question of whether he was familiar with a trend to translate Hebrew *wĕgam* with *kai ge* and even with a hypothesized *kai ge* recension of the LXX (on this technical problem, see Jobes and Silva 2000: 171–73, 284–87).

2:19–20

The contrast of "above" and "below" and the addition of "signs" is Lukan. The last part of the passage (Joel 2:32b [3:5b LXX]) is not included, but it is partly cited in 2:39 (see commentary on Acts 2:39 below).

These changes exemplify the practice of Luke and other NT authors in formal citations. They feel quite free to make minor alterations that bring out the significance of the original more fully, or are purely stylistic, or are necessitated by the new context (whether in content or style).

The citation of the prophecy, then, has the effect of showing that what is happening is a fulfillment of prophecy and of explaining its character in the light of this divinely inspired commentary.

First, it was clear to the NT authors that a great deal of prophecy previously had gone unfulfilled or was only partially fulfilled, but now they recognized events taking place that were its fulfillment. It may well be that in many cases this was regarded as a simple matter for observation: once you compared the prophetic forecast with the actual event, the correspondences were obvious. At the same time, they probably believed that they were inspired by the Spirit to declare authoritatively, "This is what was spoken by the prophet" (2:16).

Second, the result of the identification was to see the true nature of the event. The fact of a large group of people (2:4 should almost certainly be taken to mean that the 120 rather than just the twelve were affected) praising God in different languages, evidently under some constraint to do so, provided an example of what the OT can broadly describe as "prophecy."

We should not expect a word-for-word fulfillment of every detail in the description. There will be dreams and visions later in Acts, but not necessarily confined to young and old respectively—early Christians could recognize poetry when they saw it! The reference to "women" chimes in with 1:14. Moessner (1998: 218–19) notes how the prophecy is fulfilled in the course of Acts.

But what about 2:19–20? Luke's addition of "signs" is doubtless fulfilled in the healing and other miracles in Acts. "Wonders in the heaven above," more closely defined as "blood and fire

and billows of smoke," are more puzzling; the next two clauses about the sun and the moon are a still closer definition. The language is that associated with theophany, especially with the judgment on the day of the Lord, and therefore precursors of that day probably are meant. It may well be that Peter quoted these verses simply because he had to use the last verse in the passage and did not feel that he could leave anything out. So 2:19–20 may be future from Peter's (and Luke's, and our) point of view; a readership familiar with Luke 21:25–28 would have had no difficulty making the leap. It is true that in 2:22 "miracles, wonders, and signs" were done by Jesus, but these hardly fit "wonders in the heaven above." Mention should be made of the hypothesis that the moon assumes a dull red color at the time of eclipse, and there was an eclipse visible in Jerusalem at Passover in AD 33, which is taken to be the year of the crucifixion (Humphreys and Waddington 1992). However, many scholars think that the crucifixion is more plausibly dated to AD 30, and the portents are more plausibly understood as direct precursors of the day of judgment.

A further point, however, is that the theophanic language is particularly associated with the description of the original giving of the law at Sinai, both in the OT and in later Jewish sources, including Philo, *Decalogue* 46 (see texts in Turner 1996: 283–84). So, although nothing is said at this juncture to point to a parallel with Sinai, and in fact the citation is from Joel with its future reference, there could be an implied secondary reference to what happened at Sinai, with the implication that God is now doing something similar but significantly different. The phenomena that accompanied the giving of the law now accompany the coming of the Spirit in the last days (Turner 1996: 279–89). Signs and wonders are especially associated with Moses and the exodus (Johnson 1992: 49–50). If so, this would be an example of OT language being used in a way that is evocative of another event when it is read in a wider context that recalls that event.

2:21

The final verse of the quotation was originally simply an offer of deliverance from the impending judgment. It retained this sense for Peter, but the reference to being "saved" broadened out in the early church to include all the present blessings experienced by those who were convinced that they would also be delivered from the final judgment and enter into the presence of God. From this passage developed the use of "call on" (*epikaleō*) as a term for seeking salvation; the same citation is made in Rom. 10:13, and the verb is found in Acts 9:14; 22:16; 1 Cor. 1:2; 2 Tim. 2:22; 1 Pet. 1:17. Interestingly, God "calls" (*kaleō*) people to salvation (e.g., Rom. 8:30), and people "call on" him to be saved. The full phrase used here, however, is "call on the name of the Lord" (cf. 9:14; 22:16; Rom. 10:13; 1 Cor. 1:2), which seems to be a Hebrew idiom that stresses the fact that this is not an unknown god, but rather the God whose character and reputation are known. In Joel (as elsewhere in the OT) "the Lord" is Yahweh. By 2:36, Peter has claimed that God has conferred the title "Lord" on Jesus (cf. 7:59; Rom. 10:12–14; 1 Cor. 1:2; but in 1 Pet. 1:17 it is the Father who is called upon).

It should not be overlooked that the verse constitutes an invitation and a promise of salvation to anyone who calls on the name of the Lord. Joel presumably was thinking only of Jews and tacitly excluded the Gentile nations (cf. Joel 3:1–2). Rese (1969: 50) and Turner (1996: 270) note that at this point Luke omits Joel 2:32b (3:5b LXX), which centers salvation on Jerusalem, although he cites the last few words in 2:39; Dupont (1979: 151) notes the literary skill evidenced in this way and concludes that the speech "is a product of conscious literary activity." At this stage Peter may have had only Jews (and proselytes) in his sights, but Paul uses the text as a prooftext for the universality of the offer of salvation to Jews and Gentiles (Rom. 10:12–13). "God admits all men to himself without exception . . . since no man is excluded from calling upon God, the gate of salvation is set open to all"—a sentiment that one might be tempted to ascribe to some Arminian theologian, but, no, this is Calvin (1965–1966: 1:62), rightly taking Scripture in its plain sense.

Here it may be convenient to note that the language of the citation also influences the very end of Peter's sermon (thus creating what is called an *inclusio*, whereby identical or similar material forms the framework for a passage). There, at 2:39, we find that the promise of the gospel is addressed to "all whom the Lord our God will call," which reflects Joel 3:5b LXX: "For on Mount Zion and Jerusalem will be one who is saved, as the Lord said, and those who preach good news to those whom the Lord has called." Doubtless, one could interpret 2:21 in the light of 2:39 to imply a limitation of the opportunity of calling upon the Lord to those whom the Lord has called, but it is sounder to interpret 2:39 in the light of 2:21. Luke has turned Joel's perfect "has called" (the MT has a present form, "is calling") into a statement of future intent and generalized it. It is incredible that the sermon could possibly have ended with a limiting statement that would have caused the hearers to ask, "But am I among those whom God is calling?" especially in the light of the first part of 2:39.

But we have gotten ahead of ourselves. Although Peter's citation has the immediate effect of offering an explanation of the odd behavior of the disciples in terms of the outpouring of the Spirit, it also has the very important function of drawing a link between this event and the offer of salvation to those who call on the name of the Lord (Rese 1969: 52–55). The next stage in Peter's argument, therefore, will be to identify the Lord as Jesus, or rather, to show that Jesus is the Lord.

2:23

Behind this reference to God's decreed plan and foreknowledge Allen (1970–1971) has traced the influence of the "decree" (*ḥōq*) made to David in Ps. 2:7, which is to be understood as a promise of what God will do. Allen argues that the same background lies behind 4:28; 10:42; 17:31, although, if this is the case, there is no evidence that the origin of the concept was in the mind of the author.

2:24–28

Having described the way in which God showed his approval of Jesus by giving him the ability to do mighty works and then deliberately let him be put to death, Peter states that God raised him from the dead. This simple statement (*anestēsen*) is then expanded by the phrase "freeing him from the agony of death"—literally, "by loosening the pangs of death" (*lysas tas ōdinas tou thanatou*). The word "pangs" normally refers literally to the pains of childbirth, which may seem to be a strange metaphor to use of death (even a death as painful as crucifixion), and the choice of verb also is unusual. There is a parallel phrase in Job

39:2 LXX: "Have you counted their months filled with bringing forth [i.e., until the time of gestation is complete], have you loosened their pangs?" The point seems to be that Job is unable to count up the days of gestation for mountain goats and then cause their birth pangs to start or act as midwife and bring their pangs to an end. The nineteenth-century scholar F. Field noted that the verb *lyō* can mean "to bring to an end." So the metaphor as used by Peter would refer to God bringing the pains of death to an end, but he uses it because out of the death comes a kind of rebirth to life for Jesus. Rese (1969: 105–7) is skeptical of this explanation because in his view there is no evidence for the concept of a birth out of death and for a corresponding interpretation of resurrection.

Luke has used an expression that occurs in the LXX, but without reference to the particular passage where it occurs. He may have been guided to it by the use of *ōdines* in Ps. 17:5–6 LXX (18:4–5 ET [cf. 2 Sam. 22:6]). There the MT has "cords" (cf. NIV, NRSV); an unvocalized Hebrew *ḥbl* could have been read in the LXX as *ḥēbel* ("pang") instead of as *ḥebel* ("cord, bond" [for this meaning, see 1QHᵃ XI, 28]). However, there is no need for the explanation given by some scholars that Luke was misled by this confusion, nor do we need the elaboration of this view by Lindars (1961: 39–40), that Ps. 18:4–5 has been reinterpreted in the light of Ps. 16:6 and then misunderstood by Luke. Barrett (1994–1998: 143–44) thinks that Luke followed Ps. 17:6 LXX (or Ps. 114:3 LXX [116:3 ET]), where, despite the use of "pangs," the verbs are appropriate for "cords," and this led Luke to use a verb appropriate for "cords." Hanson (1980: 150–55) argues that Luke used verbs that are more appropriate to cords than to pangs, and this indicates that underlying the Greek is a Semitic source that conceived of Christ being delivered from the realm of death by God. Bock (1987: 171–72) argues for the use of a mixed metaphor, with the elements of pain and distress associated with death encircling the psalmist already present in the MT, and the idea of travail leading to birth not being present. The Greek word *ōdin* has a broader meaning of pain in general (Exod. 15:14; Deut. 2:25; Job 21:17), but the Hebrew *ḥebel* is used only of travail.

In any case, Jesus could not be held captive by death for long. Why not? Peter answers by citing what David said about him. Again we have a lengthy quotation, from Ps. 16:8–11 (15:8–11 LXX), following the wording of the LXX precisely but omitting the last line of the psalm ("pleasures at your right hand forever"). But the LXX is not identical with the MT.

MT	LXX/Acts
I have set Yahweh before me continually;	I saw the Lord before me continually;
because he is at my right hand, I shall not be moved.	because he is at my right hand, so that I may not be moved.
Therefore my heart was glad, and my glory rejoiced;	Therefore my heart was glad, and my tongue rejoiced;
also my flesh will rest in confidence.	also my flesh will dwell in hope.
For you will not abandon my soul to Sheol,	For you will not abandon my soul to Hades,
you will not give your holy one to see the pit/destruction.	nor will you give your holy one to see corruption.
You will show me the path of life;	You have made known to me paths of life;
there is fullness of joy with your face,	you will fill me with joy with your face,
pleasures at your right hand forever.	pleasures in your right hand forever.

In the MT Ps. 16 (15 LXX) is ascribed to David. It is a prayer for help from God (16:1) that is based upon David's relationship with God and an affirmation of his commitment to God (16:2–6). This becomes a statement of praise to God and confidence in him (16:7–11), and it is this latter section that is cited here. The psalmist has placed Yahweh before himself; the LXX "I saw" (*proorōmēn*) is an interpretation of the Hebrew "I set." The implication is that he continually trusts in God and obeys him. With a shift of metaphor, he declares that Yahweh is at *his* right hand, the place where a helper would be (cf. expressions about God giving help with his right hand). (More commonly we hear of sitting at the right hand of Yahweh; the thought of the privileges enjoyed by a person sitting at the right hand of a king is used in 16:11b, but is not in mind at this point.) Consequently, he can be confident that he will not be affected by any opposition. According to the usual interpretation, David here is speaking not in his own person, but rather as the Messiah, who refers to the help that God will give him (throughout his life and not simply in relation to his death [see Pesch 1986: 1:122]). A different interpretation is offered by Moessner (1998: 223–29), who argues that the "Lord" who is at David's right hand to help him in his distress is none other than the Messiah. On this view, the citation is of David speaking in his own person (see further commentary on Acts 2:27 below).

Such a person can be glad and rejoice (16:9). Here the MT has "my glory" (*kĕbôdî*), a term that can be used for a person's inner being (cf. Ps. 7:5: "me" [NIV], "my soul" [NRSV]); consequently, the suggestion that originally the very similar "my liver" (*kĕbēdî*) may have stood here (cf. Lam. 2:11 MT; and see the LXX) is unnecessary. The NIV here follows the LXX's "my tongue" (*hē glōssa mou*) without indicating that this differs from the MT. In poetic parallelism David then declares that his body (lit., "flesh") will rest secure (note the change of tense). The Hebrew *lābeṭaḥ* is rendered "in hope" (*ep' elpidi*) in the LXX, but both forms may imply trust in Yahweh, who raises the dead (see Rese 1969: 56–57). David will not fear what can happen to him in the future.

By way of explication he adds that God will not abandon his life (*nepeš*) to Sheol; he will not let his faithful one (i.e., the psalmist) experience corruption (*šaḥat*; this normally means "grave, pit," but it also can have the abstract sense of "destruction"). Taken in its context, this need be no more than an expression of assurance that Yahweh will preserve him from dying, at least for the time being (the idea of never dying was not entertained). In the LXX "Sheol" is naturally rendered by *hadēs*, and *šaḥat* is rendered by *diaphthora*, "corruption" (Haenchen [1971: 182n1] unnecessarily claimed that the LXX misread Heb. *šaḥat* as *šiḥēt*). Hence it has been argued that whereas the MT refers only to deliverance from premature death, the LXX envisages deliverance from the corruption that follows death (Barrett 1994–1998: 147, following Benoit). Consequently, an interpretation in terms of resurrection is possible only on the basis of the LXX (and therefore could not have been made by Aramaic-speaking early believers [see Rese 1969: 57–58]). However, it may be fairer to say that this rendering simply made it marginally easier to interpret the psalm as referring to the actual destruction of the human body in the grave (see Bock 1987: 175–76).

Finally, Yahweh will make known to him a path that consists in life (16:11)—that is, fullness of life

and enjoyment (Bock [1987: 176–77] notes that the MT might be expected to mean the kind of life required by God that leads to eternal life). He will experience joy in the presence of Yahweh, and for the person at Yahweh's right hand there are pleasures forever. (This final clause is not included in the citation in Acts; Rese [1969: 55–56] accounts for this by suggesting that the Holy Spirit is one of the "pleasures," but it is poured out by Jesus rather than remaining at Yahweh's right hand!) All of this, then, can be understood to refer to a long life in which the psalmist experiences the goodness of God.

But let us see how the psalm is understood here. Peter starts from the acknowledged facts: (1) David did indeed die; (2) David knew that one of his descendants would be enthroned by God because God had sworn that this would happen (there is a clear verbal allusion to Ps. 132:11–12; cf. 2 Sam. 7:12–16; Ps. 89:3–4, 35–37). The fact that David had prophetic knowledge (Acts 2:30a) presumably applies not to his knowledge about his descendant (2:30b), but rather to his own statement about the Messiah (2:31). Therefore, Ps. 16 seems to be understood as a statement by this descendant that is voiced by David. Since David could not be talking about himself in these verses (because he himself died and suffered corruption), he must have been speaking prophetically in the first person on behalf of somebody else. Following Goppelt (1982: 122–23), Rese (1979: 76) holds that the usage is not so much prophetic (promise and fulfillment) as typological in that in what David says he is stating a pattern that is true in the case of the Messiah (although it was not true of himself); the psalm thus provides the authoritative language for explaining the life, death, and resurrection of Jesus. But is it appropriate to use the term "typological" of a statement that was not true of the "type" himself?

An alternative explanation is that the psalm is being understood of David speaking of himself and saying that the Lord (= the Messiah) is there to help him (2:25); he lives in hope because God will not abandon his soul to death (2:27a) nor let his Holy One (= the Messiah) suffer corruption (2:27b). David suffers in solidarity with the Messiah and rests his hopes on him (Moessner 1998: 226). This attractive proposal faces some problems. There is the question whether non-Greek-speaking Christians would have interpreted Yahweh as a reference to the Messiah (2:25): would this interpretation be possible only on the basis of the Greek text? And there is the difficulty that Hebrew poetic parallelism would strongly suggest that "my soul" and "your holy one" (2:27) must refer to the same person rather than to David and the Messiah respectively. Certainly by 2:31 it would seem that both parts of the verse are understood to refer to Jesus (as Moessner [1998: 228] agrees).

It is implicit in Peter's argument that when Jesus was seen by his followers as raised from the dead, it was his actual physical body that had been raised (so that his tomb was left empty) and exempted from physical decay. That is to say, what the psalm said is seen to fit what was known about Jesus by actual observation: he came alive after dying, and his body evidently had not decayed.

For what purpose has Peter used this psalm? One result is to explain why it was impossible for Jesus to be held prisoner by death. Jesus had the promise of God that he would not let his faithful one decay in the grave. But the other result, and the more significant one, is to claim that if what happened to Jesus fits what David prophesied in the psalm, then Jesus must be the Messiah. Dupont (1979: 109) expresses the point precisely:

> It is often asserted that Peter desires to prove that Jesus has really risen from the dead, but that is obviously inaccurate, for Peter presupposes the resurrection as a datum of faith. What Peter wishes to establish is rather the fact that Jesus, having really risen from the dead, is truly the Messiah of which the psalm speaks.... The resurrection owes its value as a sign precisely to the oracle of the psalm which announced that the Christ would rise.

The inevitable modern question is, Does this use of the psalm "work"? (1) So far as first-century people were concerned, the Davidic authorship of the psalm was unquestioned (cf. the psalm's heading: "A Miktam of David"). (2) The psalm appears to say "You will not let me die," but Peter takes it to mean something more like "You will not let me remain dead once I have died." The psalm is thus understood to refer to a person, once dead, not being left in death and suffering the consequent decay of the body. In favor of this interpretation is the way that the last verse of the psalm appears to refer to experiences in the presence of God that follow death, unless we take the reference to be a metaphorical one to the experience of joy in the period that follows deliverance from premature death. (3) The former interpretation of the psalm would be consistent with David's own experience. Only the latter requires that it be applied to somebody else who was resurrected. (4) The promises of an enthroned descendant of David appear to refer to one of his immediate offspring, Solomon, rather than to a distant descendant or ruler (the Davidic descent of Jesus is not in fact brought into the discussion here). However, it is obvious that Solomon and all David's subsequent descendants had died like David himself (2:29), so the argument about David's descendants is in fact concerned with the continuation of his line beyond his immediate descendants, and therefore Peter's interpretation in a wide sense in 2:30 is sufficiently plausible.

2:29

David is described as a "patriarch"; although the word *patriarchēs* is used in the LXX for the chief of a family or a tribe (1 Chron. 24:31) and is applied to Abraham, Isaac, and Jacob in 4 Macc. 7:19 (cf. Acts 7:8–9; Heb. 7:4; hence our familiar usage), it is not used elsewhere of David.

2:30

Here we have the only NT description of David as a "prophet," but the motif occurs in 11Q5 XXVII, 11 (García Martínez 1996: 309); Philo, *Agriculture* 50, and his prophetic speech is mentioned in Acts 1:16; Mark 12:36.

The language in 2:30 is generally thought to be based on Ps. 132:11 (131:11 LXX), paraphrased to fit the context: "The LORD swore truth to David and will not revoke it, 'I shall place [someone] from the fruit of your body on your throne.'"

Ps. 131:11 LXX [132:11 MT/ET]	Acts 2:30
ōmosen kyrios tō Dauid alētheian kai ou mē athetēsei autēn	*horkō ōmosen autō ho theos*
ek karpou tēs koilias sou	*ek karpou tēs osphyos autou*
thēsomai epi ton thronon sou;	*kathisai epi ton thronon autou,*

Where the psalm has simply *ōmosen* Luke adds the dative *horkō*, producing a Semitism (the noun is equivalent to the Heb. infinitive absolute) found in Exod. 13:19; Num. 30:3; Josh. 9:20; *T. Jud.*

22:3. The English "one of his descendants" paraphrases "from the fruit of his loins." Where the LXX has *ek karpou tēs koilias sou*, Luke has *ek karpou tēs osphyos autou*, using the more appropriate term for a male, *osphys* ("loin"; used euphemistically, as in 2 Chron. 6:9), and changing to the third person. *Kathisai* is based on the next verse, Ps. 131:12 LXX. Rese (1969: 107–9) at first expresses doubt whether a specific source can be found and holds that there is a multiplicity of passages that have influenced Luke: Ps. 131:11 LXX; 2 Chron. 6:9–10; Ps. 88:4–5 LXX (89:3–4 ET); 2 Sam. 7:12; but in the end he agrees that Ps. 131 is the main source, with some influence from 2 Chron. 6. However, he notes that in 2 Chron. 6 the promise of a son for David is assumed to be fulfilled in Solomon. In Ps. 131 the reference is to David's sons and grandsons sitting on the throne, but the promise is conditional on their obedience, and at a later stage a messianic reinterpretation took place. (Witherington [1998: 146] claims that this psalm was used at Qumran and cites 4Q174 1 I, 7–13; this seems to be a mistake.)

At this point there is an interesting reading in the Western Text of Acts yielding this result: "God had promised him that from the fruit of his heart *according to the flesh he would raise the Messiah and* seat him on his throne" (D*; other manuscripts, including the Majority Text, vary slightly). Black (1974: 121–23) defends this reading on the grounds of its good attestation (including 1739) and the consequent improvement to the syntax. It fits in with the Lukan use of *anistēmi* to refer to the raising up of Jesus from the dead, behind which may lie God's promise to raise up a scion of David onto the stage of history in 2 Sam. 7:12; there is similar material in 13:22–37 and also in Rom. 1:3. Black has not gained any supporters (see the critique in Bovon 2006: 107–8).

2:31

David is credited with "seeing what was to come." Thus the statement in the psalm is understood to be prophetic. But exactly what David foresaw is not stated. On the basis of this foreknowledge he spoke of the resurrection of "the Christ." This is the first use of the term in Acts, and here it is clearly a title signifying "the future ruler in the line of David who will reign in the kingdom of God." It is often said that although the concept of the Messiah/Christ is found in the OT, the

term itself is not found with this reference, and that this usage developed only later in Jewish literature. However, whereas the original reference in the relevant OT passages was to the reigning monarch (or an immediate successor), by the time the psalms were collected and effectively canonized (cf. Luke 24:44) the references in them were understood, where appropriate, as messianic (cf. Ps. 2:2; 18:50; 20:6; 28:8; 84:9; 89:38, 51; 105:15; 132:10, 17; see Mays 1994: 99–107). This is true of the Hebrew Psalter; it is all the more the case with the LXX version (Schaper 1995: 138–64). We can now see why it was appropriate to take Ps. 132:11–12 as a reference to the Messiah. The new element here, then, is not so much the recognition of the psalms as messianic as it is the claim that the fulfillment of the prophecy in Ps. 16 is resurrection. At this point the language of the citation is picked up and contextualized (third person instead of first person). An important verbal alteration in 2:31 is the replacement of "your Holy One" by "his flesh" (the parallelism of "soul" and "flesh" that could have resulted [cf. 2:27a/b] does not take place, since the former term is not repeated here). "Flesh" was used in the preceding verse of the psalm, so it is not an arbitrary insertion here, but it is the appropriate word for the human body in its character as corruptible material.

2:32–33

Having established what David said prophetically about the Messiah, Peter now repeats that God raised Jesus from the dead (cf. 2:24), a point that can be confirmed by the witness of the apostles.

This event is then understood as an exaltation by the right hand of God. The verb *hypsoō* is occasionally used for the resurrection and exaltation of Jesus (5:31; cf. John 3:14; 8:28; 12:32, 34; cf. *hyperhypsoō* in Phil. 2:9), and "the right hand of God" is a familiar OT expression for God acting in power. Dodd (1952: 99) proposed that behind the language here lies Ps. 117:16 LXX, "the right hand of the Lord has exalted me" (*dexia kyriou hypsōsen me* [= 118:16 MT, the text of which differs from the LXX]), and noted that the immediately following words are "I shall not die, but live." On this view, "the right hand of God" is understood instrumentally as the means of resurrection. In view of the not infrequent use of this psalm by Jesus and his followers, this proposal is quite plausible (see Brunson 2003; similarly, Dupont 1979: 124–26; Doble 2002a: 7).

However, Lindars (1961: 42–44) holds that the starting point for the phrase lay in the last clause of Ps. 15:11 LXX (not quoted by Peter), where "at [Gk. *en*] your right hand" expresses place. He then refers to Ps. 67:19 LXX (68:19 MT; 68:18 ET), *anebēs eis hypsos*, and finds here the source for the verb *hypsōsen*. Then *tē dexia tou theou* is to be taken locatively, as in Ps. 109:1 LXX (110:1 MT/ET), *ek dexiōn mou*, cited in 2:35 (similarly, Dupont 1973: 224; Pesch 1986: 1:124; Strauss 1995: 140n2; Turner 1996: 275n20).

Yet another proposal is that Ps. 139:8–10 (138:8–10 LXX) is relevant. There David speaks about his inability to escape from God's presence; whether he ascends (*anabainō*) to heaven or descends to Hades, God's right hand will hold him (Doble 2002b: 20).

In assessing these alternative solutions, we may find it unnecessary to choose between them, since scholars admit that more than one influence may be present; the wording was such that listeners or readers would be reminded of several OT passages. Nevertheless, the question as to which source is primary is a proper one.

So far as "the right hand of God" is concerned, the instrumental understanding is preferable. Acts 5:31 is ambiguous; the phrase used there is different from the locative one from Ps. 15:11 LXX used here in 2:34; and it can be argued that the phrase summarizes the action of God in 2:32 (Barrett 1994–1998: 149).

If, as is probable, Ps. 67:19 LXX lies behind the next part of the verse, this is a strong argument for seeing it as influencing the earlier part also. However, it can also be argued that the use of Ps. 117:16 LXX is primary, and that this then gave a verbal link to Ps. 67.

The next part of the verse introduces a fresh thought: Jesus "has received from the Father the promised Holy Spirit and has poured out what you now see and hear." "The promised Holy Spirit" is literally "the promise of the Holy Spirit" (so NRSV) and alludes back to Luke 24:49; "promise" is used for the content of the promise rather than (as more usually) for the action of promising. The reference to God as "the Father" echoes the same passage. But "has received" has another source.

Psalm 67:19 LXX (68:18 ET) states, "When you ascended on high, you took captivity captive, you received gifts [*domata*] among men [lit., 'in a man']." The psalm could be understood to refer to receiving gifts for men, and it was so understood in the Targum, where the words of the law were given to men: "You have ascended to heaven, that is, Moses the prophet; you have taken captivity captive, you have learnt the words of the Torah; you have given it as gifts to men" (cited in Lincoln 1990: 242–43). The verse is explicitly cited in Eph. 4:8, but with significant alterations: "he gave gifts to men." In this connection it may be significant that later Peter refers to "the gift [*dōrea*] of the Holy Spirit" (2:38; cf. 8:20; 10:45; 11:17); was it the influence of the psalm that led to the use of the term "gift" for the Spirit?

The verb "received" is seen by several scholars as evidence for the influence of the psalm (Lindars 1961: 51–59; Dupont 1973). The reference in 2:34 to David not ascending is strong confirmation for this. In rabbinic Judaism the giving of the law was associated with Pentecost. Hence there is a possibility that the early Christians saw a parallel (or contrast) between the giving of the law and the giving of the Spirit and took over Ps. 68 (67 LXX), which was interpreted of the giving of the law, and freshly understood it of the giving of the Spirit, and that this understanding lies behind not only Eph. 4:8, but also the present passage in Acts. A further link with the psalm was detected by W. L. Knox, who observed that the Targum of Ps. 68:34 described how God "with his word [*memra*] gave with his voice the Spirit of prophecy to the prophets" (cited in Barrett 1994–1998: 149).

In my commentary (Marshall 1980: 78–79) I expressed some doubt as to whether Luke himself saw this allusion. A significant difficulty is that the allusion rests upon the Jewish tradition, deposited in the Targum, and that there is no indication of its presence in the LXX, the Scripture that Luke was using. Bock (1987: 181–83) thinks that there is no influence by the psalm at all, on the grounds that all the elements in the verse can be traced to Luke himself. The only word in common with the psalm is "received," which Luke could not avoid using to describe the action between God and Jesus. Barrett (1994–1998: 149–50) thinks that the echoes are present but is doubtful that Luke's readers, and perhaps even Luke himself, would have picked them up. He notes, however, that if the allusion is present, it confirms the view that Jesus received the Spirit to confer on the church at his ascension, a different event from his own reception of the Spirit for his messianic ministry at his baptism (Luke 3:22; Acts 10:38). It remains possible that this exegesis of the psalm was known to Peter or to the tradition that Luke used, and that Luke therefore was influenced here by an interpretation that had become traditional in the church, although it was not reflected in his Scriptures (see Strauss 1995: 145–47). See further Beale 2005b: 69–72, who finds evidence here for understanding Pentecost as the descent of the latter-day temple of God's presence on his people.

The subsequent conferral of the Spirit is expressed by the verb "poured out" (*ekcheō*), which is derived from the quotation from Joel 3:1 LXX (2:28 ET) in 2:17.

2:34–35

Peter offers a further argument that it is indeed Jesus who ascended to heaven, not David, just as it was Jesus, not David, who was resurrected. Again the point is made by a citation of David's own words. The citation is the familiar Ps. 110:1 (109:1 LXX), quoted word-for-word from the LXX. As it stands, David himself said, "The Lord said to my lord: 'Sit at my right hand until I make your enemies a footstool for your feet.'" There is scope for ambiguity in the LXX, which has to use one Greek word, *kyrios*, for the two Hebrew words *yhwh* (the Tetragrammaton, whose original pronunciation probably was "Yahweh," and for which "Adonai" ["my Lord"] was substituted when the word was read aloud) and *'ādôn*. The former word refers to God, and the latter to the speaker's "lord." The invitation to "sit" is addressed to David's lord, not to David himself, and the one greater than David could only be the Messiah. The Hebrew for "at my right hand" (*lîmînî*) is translated by a plural in the LXX (*ek dexiōn mou*) (see Rese 1969: 59).

(This understanding presupposes that David is the implied author of the psalm; a common modern view is that the psalm was composed by a subject of David or a later king and said what Yahweh had promised to the subject's lord.)

There must also be some uncertainty about the interpretation of the oracle from Yahweh concerning the "lord." Clearly the language about the footstool is metaphorical for the subjugation of enemies (cf. Josh. 10:24; 1 Kings 5:3; Isa. 51:23), and the language about sitting at God's right hand could also be metaphorical for being given the authority and power of God to overcome the enemies. But Peter takes the latter phrase literally of the Messiah's ascent to heaven to sit beside God. It is understood likewise elsewhere in the NT (Luke 20:42–44 pars.; 22:69 pars.; Acts 7:55–56; Rom. 8:34; Eph. 1:20; Col. 3:1; Heb. 1:3, 13; 8:1; 10:12–13; 12:2; 1 Pet. 3:22; see Hay 1973; for the use of Ps. 110:1 as a *testimonium* elsewhere in the NT, see Albl 1999: 216–36). The phrase "at my right hand" echoes the usage from Ps. 16 earlier in Peter's speech (2:25), and it might be cited as an example of the Jewish practice of *gezerah shavah*, the linking together of two citations by their use of common expressions (Longenecker 1999: 81).

2:36

Hence this conclusion can be drawn: "all the house of Israel" (an OT expression [e.g., 1 Sam. 7:2; Ezek. 37:11] used frequently in Jewish prayers) can know for sure that Jesus, who had been crucified, has been made Lord and Messiah by God (for the association of Messiah and Lord, see *Pss. Sol.* 17:32). The argument here is not simply that the oracle in Ps. 110 applies to Jesus, but also that the title "lord," used in the psalm, must be applied to him; since it refers to a person of higher rank than David, it is a superlative title. The title "Messiah" is not actually used in any of the psalm citations, but we have seen that it is implicit in the context of some of these citations, notably Ps. 132:10 (131:10 LXX), which suggests to Dupont (1979: 150–53) that the author of the speech was taking note of the contexts. He concludes,

> Whoever composed the form of the speeches which has been transmitted to us clearly had at his disposal written sources: either collections of scriptural citations, or else earlier written versions of the speeches which cited more explicitly and at greater length the scriptural texts on which the speakers based their comments and arguments.

This observation might count as evidence that the written speeches in Acts are summaries of fuller oral proclamations.

Does this statement mean that Jesus was "made" Lord and Messiah only when he was exalted or that the exaltation proved that he already held this status? Certainly for Luke himself Jesus was already the Lord and Messiah before his crucifixion, and in the psalm the invitation to sit beside God is addressed to one who is already David's lord. Some think that Luke is recording an earlier tradition of how Christology was understood in the early church (Barrett 1994–1998: 151–52). But the force of the statement is more probably simply to contrast the attitude of those who crucified and rejected Jesus with God's confirmation of his real status by raising him from death and exalting him to his right hand (Rowe 2007). His baptism in the Gospel corresponds to his heavenly installation in Acts, both of them preceded by his birth as Son of God to rule over the house of Jacob forever (Luke 1:32–33).

2:37–41

2:37

The description of the response of the hearers to the speech is expressed in language paralleled in Ps. 108:16 LXX (109:16 ET), *katanenygmenon tē kardia* (*katanyssomai*, "to be pierced, stabbed" [cf. Gen. 34:7]); although the psalm was quoted previously in 1:20, it is unlikely that this led to the use of this phrase (*pace* Wilcox 1965: 61).

2:39

The width of the invitation to repent and be baptized is emphasized by a return to Joel 2:32 (3:5 LXX). The "promise" is, of course, the promise of the gift of the Spirit (cf. 2:33) made by Joel. "For you and your children" echoes OT language (Gen. 9:9; 13:15; 17:7–10; cf. Ps. 18:50). "For all who are far off" picks up a phrase from Isa. 57:19 that is also used in Eph. 2:13–17. The vision certainly includes Jews in succeeding generations and worldwide. Although some want to confine the scope to Jews (Denova 1997: 169–75; Wall 2002: 68n129), Barrett (1994–1998: 156–57) holds that potentially the message is also to other races (cf. the echo in 22:21; see Clark 2001: 113), and this is rightly confirmed by Pao (2000: 230–31). This interpretation can be justified by reference to one rabbinic interpretation of Isa. 57:19 that interpreted it of proselytes (*Num. Rab.* 8:4, cited in Lincoln 1990: 147) and by the Christian in-

terpretation in Eph. 2:13–17. Then comes the phrase from Joel "for all whom the Lord our God will call." Joel's plain relative clause (*hous kyrios proskeklētai*) is altered to an indefinite relative clause (*hosous an*) that implies indefinite extent and is plainly inclusive; true, the Lord may call only some, but no such implied horizon is in view, and the point of the clause is not to set limits, but rather to emphasize the gracious initiative of the Lord in announcing salvation. The omission of the latter part of Joel 2:32 LXX may also be significant as stressing the universalistic outlook here.

2:40

Peter urges his listeners, "Save yourselves from this corrupt generation." The implication is that the people are sinful and stand under God's judgment, but those who respond to Peter's words will escape from the judgment that is coming upon them. The term "generation" (*genea*), usually in the form "this generation" (contrast Phil. 2:15) and sometimes with an adjective (Luke 9:41; 11:29), is a pejorative term for the Jewish contemporaries of Jesus and his followers that reflects OT usage (Deut. 32:5, 20; Ps. 78:8 [77:8 LXX]; 95:10 [94:10 LXX]). Wilcox (1965: 30) suggests that a specific text, Ps. 12:7 (11:8 LXX), is reflected: "You, LORD, will guard us and preserve us from this generation and forever." However, the verb "save" is probably an echo of 2:21 (Barrett 1994–1998: 156), and the lack of verbal agreement with the psalm makes the hypothesis doubtful.

The use of "souls" (*psychai*) for "people" is common in Acts (e.g., 2:43; 7:14 [cf. Gen. 46:27 LXX]; 27:37; see also Rom. 13:1; 1 Pet. 3:20; cf. Acts 3:23) and reflects a septuagintalism for *nepeš*, although the idiom is also found in classical Greek (see *TDNT* 9:632).

On baptism in the name of Jesus, see commentary on Acts 3:6 below.

2:42–47

Any links with the OT in this section are confined to echoes in language. The "wonders and miraculous signs" performed by the apostles (2:43) echo the prophecy of Joel and the description of the activity of God through Jesus, thus implying that these occurrences also are wrought by God in fulfillment of prophecy and hence serve to accredit the apostles as his agents doing what was expected in the "last days." The coincidence between 2:46 and Eccles. 9:7 in regard to the motif of eating joyfully is insignificant.

On the community described in 2:44, 47, see commentary on Acts 1:15 above.

Acts 3

3:1–10

3:2

The phrase "from his mother's womb" (cf. 14:8) is found in the LXX (Judg. 16:17; Ps. 21:11 [22:10 ET]; 70:6 [71:6 ET]; Isa. 49:1). Wilcox (1965: 61–62) argues that the use of the phrase in passages well known to early Christians (cf. Luke 1:15; Gal. 1:15) could have suggested its use to the writer here.

3:6

We have here the first example of healing by the name of Jesus. Throughout Acts mighty works are done "in the name of Jesus" (3:6; 4:7, 10; 16:18; "by means of the name" in 4:30). Similarly, baptism takes place "in the name of Jesus" (2:38; 10:48; "into the name" in 19:5). Believers may witness "on behalf of" the name and suffer "on behalf of the name" (9:16; 21:13) and opponents act "against" it (26:9). Believers may speak openly "in" the name (9:27, 29). It would seem that a command to a demon uttered in the name of Jesus gains authority and power. Similarly, a command given to a disabled person confers the power to obey it. Such language is not in itself religious, but in the Jewish context it inescapably takes us back to the OT, where the name of God is of great importance; already in 2:21 (citing Joel 2:32) people call on the name of the Lord in order to be saved. In the OT action in the name of the Lord is action that claims his authority for what is said or done (Exod. 5:23; Deut. 18:19–21). Hence an idiom developed, and in early Christianity actions are done "in the name of Jesus" in a parallel way. This has profound christological implications (Buckwalter 1996: 182–84).

3:8

The healed lame man is twice said to jump (*exallomai, hallomai* [cf. 14:10]), which echoes Isa. 35:6 (*tote haleitai … ho chōlos* [the passage is already used

in Luke 7:22, but this particular verb is not used there]). Thus the healing is typical of the saving acts of God promised in the OT for the last days (Wall 2002: 77).

3:11–26

Peter's speech in Solomon's portico is also thought by Bowker (1967–1968: 106–7) to reflect the structure of a synagogue sermon. He proposes a seder of Exod. 3:1–21 and a haftarah of Isa. 52:7–15 with a proem text "such as" Nah. 1:15 (which was left out when the speech was included in Acts). This would account for the inclusion of 3:13 with its citation of Exod. 3:6 or Exod. 3:15 (see below) and the awkwardness of 3:16 (but Bowker's explanation of this is obscure). He holds that the speech was originally independent and was first given in Aramaic (see Wilcox 1965: 139–41). All this is conjectural, particularly when the sermon is not given in a synagogue setting against the background of set readings, but at least in this case the two passages are clearly alluded to in the speech.

3:12–13

When Peter comments on the healing, he attributes it not to the competence of the apostles in themselves, but to God; and his specific point is that it is the God of the Jews—that is, the God worshiped by his audience—who has acted to glorify his servant Jesus. God is faithful to the pattern of his care for his people in the OT, but now he does so through Jesus (see Bock 1987: 187–88; Wall 2002: 80). This point is achieved by describing God as "the God of Abraham, Isaac, and Jacob, the God of our fathers" (cf. 22:14).

There are a number of places where God refers to himself as the God of the ancestors or fathers (Gen. 26:24; 28:13; 31:42, 53; 32:9; Exod. 3:6, 15–16; 4:5; 1 Kings 18:36; 1 Chron. 29:18; 2 Chron. 30:6; Ps. 47:9). The closest parallels are to the statements by God to Moses in the incident of the burning bush in Exod. 3:6 LXX: "I am the God of your [sg.] father, God of Abraham, and God of Isaac, and God of Jacob"; Exod. 3:15 LXX: "[The] Lord, the God of your [pl.] fathers, God of Abraham and God of Isaac and God of Jacob, has sent me to you" (substantially repeated in 3:16). The use of the phrase "of your fathers" directly reflects the second of these two quotations. The same citation occurs in 7:32, and there is also an explicit allusion to Exod. 3:15 in Luke 20:37 pars. (there the inclusion of *kyrion* in Luke's text [absent from Matthew and Mark] confirms that Exod. 3:15 rather than Exod. 3:6 is in sight); the shorter description "the God of our/your fathers" recurs in 5:30; 22:14 (cf. 24:14). The same description of God is perpetuated in the first of the Eighteen Benedictions.

There is some uncertainty about the text in both occurrences. *Ho theos* is omitted in 3:13 in its usages before "Isaac" and "Jacob" by B 33 1739 𝔐 and in 7:32 by 𝔓⁷⁴ ℵ A B, against the LXX and the Gospels. UBS⁴ retained the words in brackets in 3:13 but rejected them in 7:32, where the weight of manuscripts for exclusion is stronger.

In the original context the words serve to identify the God who appears to Moses as indeed the God of his ancestors and therefore the God of the people of Israel. Moses and the people can therefore be assured of the identity of this God as their God, believe his promises, and fulfill his commands. Similarly here, it is important to underline that what has been happening is the work of the God of Israel, the God of Peter's audience, and therefore a direct line is drawn between the God who was active throughout the history of Israel and is now active in and through Jesus.

Peter goes on to affirm that this God "has glorified his servant Jesus" (*edoxasen ton paida autou Iēsoun*). The wording reflects Isa. 52:13, *ho pais mou . . . doxasthēsetai sphodra*, where the speaker is God. The use of the term *pais* for a servant of God is found with reference to a wide variety of people, including prophets, Abraham, Moses, and kings, especially David (cf. 4:25), and also it is a self-designation of the righteous sufferer in Wis. 2:13. It is used for Jesus also in 3:26; 4:30. The mention of David as God's servant in the same context (4:25) has raised the question of whether all that we have here is an application of David's title to Jesus. However, the combination with *doxazō* is found only in Isa. 52:13, and this must be regarded as decisive (the term "handed over" [*paredōkate*] is also used in Isa. 53:6, 12, but there it applies to Yahweh's action). The point is confirmed by the use of "servant" language elsewhere of Jesus (cf. the combination of suffering and glorification in Luke 24:26; see Wolff 1984: 88) and by the possible echo of Isa. 52:14 in 3:10

(Witherington 1998: 179–80; cf. Hooker 1959: 110; Bock 1987: 188).

The original context of the citation is, of course, the passage in Isa. 52:13–53:12, in which a person described as the Lord's servant is the object of great suffering and abuse, although in some way he is bearing the sins of others and suffering because of them; his role is upheld by God, and ultimately he will be glorified. The original significance is much discussed and disputed. It is perhaps impossible to discover what the prophet's hearers and readers would have made of the passage or what the prophet himself had in mind.

In the present context the language is used to establish who Jesus is and the fact of his glorification. This glorification may be seen in what has taken place—the resurrection and exaltation of Jesus (cf. Luke 24:26; see Rese 1969: 112–13)—or in Jesus acting powerfully in healing the lame man, or in a combination of these (Bock 1987: 189–90); Peter appears to be saying that it was because God had exalted Jesus that he now was able to do such a mighty work, so that the healing is evidence for the glorification. But the statement also serves to set the scene for the later use of a citation from Isa. 53 in 8:32–33. As it stands, the passage comes from a speech by Peter very early in the development of the church, and thus it would reflect a fairly rapid recognition that Jesus was the Servant of Yahweh. There are scholars who think that this aspect at least of the Christology in Acts is from a later date, reflecting perhaps the developments seen especially in 1 Peter, and chiming in with the use of similar motifs in the apostolic fathers (*Did.* 9:2–3; 10:2–3; *1 Clem.* 59:2–4; *Mart. Pol.* 14:1; 20:2; *Barn.* 6:1; 9:2 [so Barrett 1994–1998: 194]). However, the passages from the apostolic fathers show no links to Isaiah. In the *Didache* there is a David/Jesus typology; there is nothing Isaianic in *1 Clement* and the *Martyrdom of Polycarp*; only in *Barn.* 6:1 is there a citation of Isa. 50:8–9; the source of *Barn.* 9:2 is not identifiable. It is preferable to see here an earlier use of Isaiah through which perhaps the term "servant" found its way into Christology.

3:14

When Jesus is described as "holy and righteous," is this also an OT allusion? The phraseology is used of the Messiah in *1 En.* 38:2–3, but also of the group called "the holy, the righteous and the elect" (*1 En.* 38:4; 48:1; cf. 38:5; 48:7). But the Servant is described as righteous in Isa. 53:11. There is a righteous king in Zech. 9:9. Similarly, Jesus is "the righteous one" in Acts 7:52; 22:14, as if this were a self-evident way of referring to him. Jesus is "the holy one of God" in Luke 4:34/Mark 1:24; John 6:69 (cf. 1 John 2:20); cf. Rev. 3:7. He is God's "holy servant" in Acts 4:27, 30 (cf. the use of *hosios* in 2:27; 13:35 [citing Ps. 15:10 LXX]). It is perfectly possible that behind the use of *hagios* for Jesus lies the Hebrew equivalent for *hosios*. But it is all very loose. In the OT God himself is the Holy One, although agents of God may also be so designated. In Judg. 13:7 the boy Samson will be *hagion theou* (cf. 16:17, where it must mean "dedicated to God"; cf. Luke 1:35). Similar phraseology is used of Aaron (2 Kings 4:9; Ps. 106:16). Here the phrase basically means "belonging to God and authorized by God" (*NIDNTT* 1:228–29).

3:15

Jesus is referred to by the unusual phrase "the author [*archēgos*] of life"; similarly in 5:31 he is a "prince"; cf. in Hebrews "the author of their salvation" (2:10) and "the author of . . . our faith" (12:2). The term is found in classical Greek for the founder of a city, a chieftain, a first cause or originator of something (LSJ). But it also occurs in the LXX to refer to chiefs and rulers (Exod. 6:14; Judg. 11:6, 11 [of Jephthah]; Mic. 1:13 [of an "originator of sin"]; 1 Macc. 10:47 [of the first person to speak]). Here the meaning is something like "founder, originator," as in Hebrews (Barrett 1994–1998: 197–98), or perhaps "leader" (*EDNT* 1:163–64). However, although the same kind of usage is found in the LXX, it is unlikely that there is any specific OT influence here.

3:17–18

The speech proceeds to comment on the way in which the audience had acted in letting Jesus be put to death (rather than the murderer Barabbas) and so consented to the action of their leaders in doing so. Their action could be excused as resulting from ignorance of who Jesus really was. At the same time, it was in fulfillment of what God had announced beforehand "through the mouth of all his prophets." "Through the mouth of" (3:18, 21) is a septuagintalism (cf. 1 Kings 17:1; see Barrett 1994–1998: 202, 207). Luke is fond of "all" in what may sometimes be a rather hyperbolic

manner (e.g., Acts 1:1, 8, 19; 2:5, 14, 43), and so "all the prophets" may fall into this category (cf. Luke 24:27; Acts 3:24; 10:43). Acts 3:24 may in fact express something of a limitation.

This statement is often seen as puzzling because, it is alleged, the OT contains no statements about the suffering of the Christ, still less that *all* the prophets spoke about it. Concerning the first part of this statement: (1) we have noted earlier that the psalms were taken to contain references to the Messiah, and therefore it is probable that psalms such as Ps. 22; 69 were taken to be "fulfilled" in the case of Jesus; (2) if Jesus was identified as the Servant of Yahweh, who exalted him (3:13), then it was inevitable that he was also understood as the *Suffering* Servant; (3) isolated prophetic statements such as Zech. 12:10; 13:7 were understood to apply to the Messiah. If we include Jer. 11:19; Dan. 9:26 as passages that may have been understood similarly, then we have material from Psalms, Isaiah, Jeremiah, and the Minor Prophets (which were regarded as a single "book"). Material from all of these books and Ezekiel is cited in the NT as being fulfilled in "these days" (3:24).

3:19

But now that they knew who Jesus was, what could they do? If they were to repent of their sins, times of refreshing would come from the face of the Lord, and he would send them the one who had been chosen beforehand as the Christ, namely, Jesus. He had to remain in heaven until the fulfillment of all that God had spoken by his holy prophets from ages past. General statements like this one about the Scriptures are not unknown (Luke 18:31; 21:22; 24:27, 44, 45–47; Acts 13:29; 17:2, 11; 18:28; 24:14; 26:22; Rom. 1:2; 16:26; 1 Cor. 15:3–4). Clearly the reference is to the prophecies of what we might call the golden age to come that we find in the OT, but are there any specific details that would enable us to identify which particular prophecies were in mind? W. L. Lane (cited in Pao 2000: 131–35) has noted the use of the key term *anapsyxis* ("refreshing") in Symmachus's text of Isa. 32:15 (for the LXX's *pneuma*), and also the parallelism in structure between 3:19–20 and 2:38, which indicates that the period of refreshing is the time when the Holy Spirit is poured out. The use of "these days" confirms that it is the present age that is meant and not some future age (so, rightly, Barrett 1994–1998: 205). If so, then the "restoration of all things" can signify the process that goes on until the return of Jesus rather than the completion of the process.

3:22–23

Instead of pursuing this line further, however, Peter turns to one of those earlier prophets, Moses, and cites his statement in Deut. 18:15–20. The prophecy is cited selectively and loosely (cf. 7:37). Here is a translation of the LXX text with differences in its citation in Acts (variation: italicized text in braces; addition: plus sign [+] followed by italicized text in braces; omission: minus sign [−] followed by plain text in parentheses).

[15]The Lord your {*your* [pl.]} God will raise up for you {*you* [pl.]} a prophet like me from among your {*your* [pl.]} brothers; you shall listen to him, [16]according to everything that {+ *he says to you* [pl.]} (− you asked from the Lord your God at Horeb on the day of the assembly, saying, "We shall not listen again to the voice of the Lord our God, and we shall not see the great fire again, nor shall we certainly die." [17]And the Lord said to me, "They are right in all that they have said. [18]I shall raise up for them from among their brothers a prophet like you, and I shall put my word in his mouth, and he will speak to them according to whatever I instruct him. [19]And as for the man) {+ *But every soul* [Lev. 23:29]} who does not listen to (− all that) that prophet (− says in my name,) {+ *will be cut off from the people* [Lev. 23:29]} (− I will call him to account").

Deut. 18:15–19 [+ Lev. 23:29] LXX	Acts 3:22–23
[15]*prophētēn*	[22]*prophētēn*
ek tōn adelphōn sou hōs eme	
	hymin
anastēsei soi kyrios ho theos sou,	*anastēsei kyrios ho theos hymōn*
	ek tōn adelphōn hymōn hōs eme;
autou akousesthe	*autou akousesthe*
[16]*kata panta,*	*kata panta*
hosa ētēsō para kyriou tou theou sou en Chōrēb	
tē hēmera tēs ekklēsias legontes	
Ou prosthēsomen akousai tēn phōnēn	
kyriou tou theou hēmōn	
kai to pyr to mega touto	
ouk opsometha eti	
oude mē apothanōmen,	
[17]*kai eipen kyrios pros me*	
Orthōs panta, hosa elalēsan;	
[18]*prophētēn anastēsō autois*	

Deut. 18:15–19 [+ Lev. 23:29] LXX	Acts 3:22–23
ek tōn adelphōn autōn hōsper se	
kai dōsō to rhēma mou en tō stomati autou,	
kai lalēsei autois kathoti an enteilōmai autō;	
[19]*kai ho anthrōpos,*	
hos ean mē akousē	
hosa ean lalēsē	*hosa an lalēsē pros hymas.*
ho prophētēs epi tō onomati mou,	
egō ekdikēsō ex autou.	
[Lev. 23:29] *pasa psychē, hētis*	[23]*estai de pasa psychē hētis*
mē tapeinōthēsetai	
en autē tē hēmera tautē,	
	ean mē akousē
	tou prophētou ekeinou
exolethreuthēsetai ek tou laou autēs.	*exolethreuthēsetai ek tou laou.*

Essentially, the prophecy is abbreviated by the omission of Deut. 18:16b, 17, 18, 19a; the wording is altered accordingly, and in 3:23 Peter conflates wording from Lev. 23:29 (see Bock 1987: 191–92). Wilcox (1965: 33, 46) raises the question of whether Luke was using a text different from the LXX (cf. de Waard 1965: 21–24), but the argument does not seem compelling.

Albl (1999: 191–95) argues that the material is taken from a *testimonia* collection (for the possibility, cf. Barrett 1994–1998: 210) related to the Day of Atonement. He argues that (1) conflation of passages is typical of *testimonia* but not of Luke's own practice; (2) the passage was widely used by Jews and Christians (4Q175; Samaritan Pentateuch; Acts 7:37; cf. Mark 9:7; John 6:14); (3) here Moses is regarded as a prophet, whereas Luke usually distinguishes him from them.

Taking a suggestion from Bock (1987: 192–93), Albl further argues that the OT contexts of Gen. 22:18 (see commentary on Acts 3:25 below) and Lev. 23:29 are, respectively, the attempted offering of Isaac and the Day of Atonement, which are also linked in *Barn.* 7:3. On these grounds he postulates a *testimonia* source including the three passages cited. It saw Jesus as the prophet like Moses but interpreted this image against the background of the Day of Atonement and the Aqedah. Nevertheless, Luke made nothing of these associations but developed the application in other ways in terms of the typology between the people of Israel and their prophets and the Jews and the prophet Jesus.

This proposal may help us understand how the composite citation arose, but it sheds no light on the significance of the citation in its present context. Nor is it very likely in itself, for the following reasons: (1) composite passages are found elsewhere (Luke 4:18–19); (2) the evidence shows parallels for the use of Deut. 18, but not for this particular combination of passages; (3) the concept of Moses as a prophet arises out of the citation itself; (4) *Barn.* 7:3 does not allude to Deut. 18. The case for use of a *testimonia* passage is not persuasive.

In the original setting Moses is depicted as dealing with the situation that will arise when the Israelites have entered Canaan and are surrounded by other peoples whose practices are not in accord with the way of life laid down by Yahweh; Moses himself will not be there. But they will know what to do because God will raise up for them a prophet similar to Moses to act as intermediary between God and them. Since the people were fearful of direct communication with God, God promised that he would raise up one from among them to act as prophet and that he would put his own words into the mouth of the prophet. God would call to account anyone who disregarded the prophet. At the same time, the danger was recognized that a prophet might presume to utter words in the name of Yahweh that he had not commanded or even to speak in the name of another god. This leads to the question of how to discriminate between true and false prophets, which we do not need to pursue here. It is generally agreed that Moses' prophecy could well be fulfilled by a succession of prophets, and Deut. 18:19–22 presumes such a situation.

There is no significant difference between the MT and the LXX. The version in Acts severely abbreviates the text of Deuteronomy by removing all that refers to the request of the Israelites for an intermediary and by substituting a different expression from Lev. 23:29 for the judgment that will fall on those who do not listen to (i.e., obey) the prophet: the rather bare "I will call to account" is replaced by "will be completely cut off from among the people." Following Overbeck, Rese (1969: 67) notes that the insertion of the phrase *estai de* in 3:23 creates a parallel to 2:21, where it introduces a positive offer of salvation contrasting with the negative threat here. Obedience to the Messiah is the criterion by which people remain in the people of God or are removed from them. Thus the shift from the wording of Deuteronomy indicates as clearly as possible that continued membership in the people of God is dependent on a positive response to the Messiah.

The hope for such a prophet remained alive (1 Macc. 4:46; 14:41 may be relevant). The Qumran sect awaited a prophet and cited this passage (4Q175 I, 5–8; cf. 1QS IX, 11), and a firm expectation was held among the Samaritans (*Memar Marqah* 4:12). There were a number of "messianic prophets" in the first century—persons who claimed to be prophets and saw themselves as having a role to deliver Israel from its enemies (Evans 1993b: 190–92).

The prophet is raised up "from among your own people." Here, then, the focus is on Jesus as a Jewish man, which corresponds with the accent elsewhere on the identity of Jesus as a descendant of David (2:30).

3:24

Peter states that all the prophets from Samuel onward have prophesied these days. The reference to Samuel is unproblematic because the prophecy in 2 Sam. 7 is clearly in mind. The implication of the rest of the sentence is that reference is being made to all the prophets and not just to those whose books are preserved in the OT (see commentary on Acts 3:17–18 above). The form of the sentence is curious and seemingly tautologous because the concept of a prophet who did not speak is odd. Surprisingly, there are no efforts at scribal emendation.

3:25a

Peter continues with the statement that the hearers are children (Gk. "sons") of the prophets and of the covenant. The combination of the personal and the impersonal is surprising; in both cases, then, the usage is probably metaphorical, and the NIV tries to take account of this by translating "heirs." "Sons of the prophets" is not OT language, but it is found in a saying attributed to Hillel (*y. Šabb.* 19.17a4; Str-B 2:211). "Sons of the covenant" is found in Ezek. 30:5 LXX; *Pss. Sol.* 17:15.

3:25b

Now we come back to Abraham and his God (cf. 3:13). God made a promise to Abraham: "Through your offspring all peoples on earth will be blessed." This sentence recurs in the Abraham narrative.

In Gen. 12:3 God says to Abraham, "And in you all the tribes [*phylai*] of the earth will be blessed [*eneulogēthēsontai*]."

In Gen. 18:18 God soliloquizes and says, "And all the nations [*ethnē*] of the earth will be blessed in him."

In Gen. 22:18 this becomes part of a promise addressed to Abraham: "And all the nations will be blessed in your seed."

The promise is repeated in Gen. 26:4: "And all the nations of the earth will be blessed in your seed" (*kai eneulogēthēsontai en tōi spermati sou panta ta ethnē tēs gēs*).

The same promise is made to Jacob in Gen. 28:14: "And all the tribes of the earth will be blessed in you and in your seed."

The identification of the basic source is disputed (see Steyn [1995: 156], who asks whether it is a free citation from memory or a conflation). Rese (1969: 71–73) gives reasons for supposing that the basic source used here is Gen. 22:18. The LXX "all the nations," which for Jews would refer exclusively to Gentiles, is changed to "all tribes," so that the Jews are also included. Hanson (1983: 88), however, argues that in view of the uncertain basis of the citation, we cannot say categorically that Luke changed the wording deliberately to suit his own convenience.

The verb *eneulogēthēsontai* represents a Hebrew Niphal in Gen. 12:3; 18:18; 28:14, and a Hithpael in 22:18; 26:4, a difference reflected in the varying NRSV renderings, "shall be blessed in him" and "shall gain blessing for themselves." There is dispute as to whether the MT forms mean that the nations will be blessed through Abraham (i.e., a passive meaning), or that they will find blessing (i.e., a middle form [cf. NRSV]), or that they will bless themselves by Abraham (i.e., a reflexive meaning: the nations say something like "May God make us like Abraham and his descendants"; for this rendering, cf. Gen. 48:20). On this, see *NIDOTTE* 1:759–60; Wenham 1987: 277–78; 1994: 112. Wenham argues strongly that in the context in Gen. 12:3 a middle or passive sense is

more fitting than a reflexive. In any case, the LXX rendering is clearly passive.

In Acts the manuscripts vary in giving the verb as *eulogēthēsontai* (A* B 1739) or *eneulogēthēsontai* (𝔓⁷⁴ ℵ D 33 𝔐). The word order differs from all the Genesis texts in bringing forward "in your seed," presumably for emphasis. Acts also has *patria*, a word used frequently in the LXX for the Hebrew *mišpāḥâ* ("family, people") but not found in Genesis.

The citation takes us to God's repeated promise to Abraham to make his family into a great nation. Abraham would enjoy God's blessing—that is, God would make him prosper and would also favor those who favored Abraham; consequently, all the families of the earth would find blessing in Abraham. The LXX is perhaps even clearer that all the nations will be blessed in Abraham. Although this might be taken as a blanket declaration of something that will inevitably happen to everybody, it may be better to take it to mean that there will be universal possibilities of blessing through Abraham. Certainly the promise could be taken to mean that those who favor the Jews will enjoy God's favor (for the Jewish interpretation of the promise that saw other nations acquiring learning, knowledge, and religion from Abraham, see Evans 1993b: 192).

But what is Peter doing with the promise? This is not absolutely clear. It seems most likely (*pace* Barrett 1994–1998: 212–13) that Peter is identifying Jesus as the seed of Abraham through whom all peoples will be blessed by God. This is implicit in the "application" in 3:26, where God has sent his servant (whom we know from 3:13 to be Jesus) to bless "you."

The blessing is for "you." Now we may see why Peter used *patriai*, since *ethnē* could have been taken by a Jewish audience to mean "the [other] nations," and Peter's point is that God's blessing is for the Jews through Jesus. Thus Peter is in effect including the promise in Gen. 12:2 that God will bless the great nation that is descended from Abraham in the broader promise to all peoples expressed in Gen. 12:3 and its parallels.

The blessing is interpreted in a conditional manner by the insistence in 3:26 that it is conferred when the people turn away (= repent) from their wickednesses (Wolff [1984: 86] sees a rather vague link here with the mission of the Servant in

Isa. 53). Or does it mean that the blessing consists in enabling them to repent (Barrett 1994–1998: 214)? Such a spiritualization is not problematic.

There are some interesting links here between the exegeses of Peter and Paul.

First, the identification of Jesus as the seed of Abraham seems to be assumed without argument. This presumes that the seed is understood as a single person rather than collectively of Abraham's descendants. It appears to rest on the kind of argument that Paul develops in Gal. 3:8, where he refers to the same promise.

Second, although the reference in the citation is to the Gentile nations, Peter pays no attention to them here. Yet his "first to you" seems to imply that the gospel will come to them after it comes to the Jews; again the Pauline principle "to the Jew first and also to the Greek" may underlie what is going on here.

Acts 4

4:5–12

4:8

The arrest of the apostles is followed by their appearance before the Sanhedrin. It is natural that Peter addresses his audience as "rulers [*archontes*] ...of the people." However, the term plays a major role in the citation later in 4:26. It may also be significant that Ps. 118:9 (117:9 LXX) states, "It is better to take refuge in the LORD than to trust in princes [*archontes*]," and this psalm will be cited by Peter. Similarly, Ps. 146:3 (145:3 LXX) states, "Do not put your trust in princes," and this psalm is echoed later in 4:24.

4:11

Peter's speech has been described by Dupont (1979: 152) as "nothing but a paraphrase of Joel 3:5, though Joel is not explicitly cited in that context at all." This is an oversimplification, but it makes the valid point that the climactic reference in 4:12 to the "name" by which people are saved implicitly picks up on the verse already cited in 2:21.

In fact, the speech conforms to the general pattern of the speeches by Peter and others that are evangelistic or apologetic by including some appeal to Scripture. Although this speech is primarily a defense of the apostles in response to a request for a justification for their action (or an explanation of how they came to have the power to do it) and does not follow the typical pattern in every detail, it does contain an explicit appeal to Scripture: Jesus is declared to be (cf. 2:16 for this identification of a person or event with something prophesied in the OT) "the stone which the builders rejected—this has become the cornerstone" (Ps. 118:22 [117:22 LXX]).

Ps. 117:22 LXX [118:22 MT/ET]	Acts 4:11
lithon, hon apedokimasan hoi oikodomountes,	*ho lithos, ho exouthenētheis hyph' hymōn tōn oikodomōn,*
houtos egenēthē eis kephalēn gōnias;	*ho genomenos eis kephalēn gōnias.*

The citation is adapted to the context by changing the accusative *lithon* to the nominative *ho lithos*; the original relative clause is replaced by a participial phrase with a passive verb; the verb is changed to *exouthenētheis*, and the subject of the active verb naturally becomes the agent of the passive verb, *hyph' hymōn tōn oikodomōn*; introducing the quotation with "this is" (*houtos estin*) requires that the main verb "has become" be replaced by a participial phrase. The replacement of the original participle *oikodomountes* by the related noun does not affect the meaning; what is significant is the way in which Peter, having identified Jesus as the stone, inserts "you" (*hymōn*) into the quotation to identify his audience as the builders who rejected the stone; an original statement in the third person ("they rejected") is thus turned into a second-person accusation ("you rejected").

The text has three levels of meaning.

First, literally it describes how builders on a building site might reject a particular stone or building block as unsuitable for their purpose; someone else may come along and see that the stone has unrecognized potential, and instead of being, as it were, dishonored by being cast aside, the stone is now given pride of place. There is debate whether the description is that of a "cornerstone"—that is, a foundation stone at an angle in the building that sets the direction for the two walls that meet there (TNIV)—or a "coping stone" that completes the corner of a building (*TDNT* 1:791–93; 4:274; cf. NRSV mg.: "keystone"). Either way, the stone is the "most important" one (LEH 254).

Second, in the psalm the statement is used metaphorically. The king is pictured as going to the temple to give thanks to God for a military victory. It seems that there were people, possibly among his own nation, who doubted his ability to win the battle; however, he had won a splendid victory thanks to the help of the Lord.

Third, the psalm is quoted by Jesus at the conclusion of his parable about the vineyard, where it is used to make the same point about the Messiah, the descendant of the king of Israel in the psalm. There it refers to his own rejection by the rulers of the people (and, by extension, by the people themselves) and to his vindication by God, who raised him from the dead (Matt. 21:42; Mark 12:10–11; Luke 20:17). The same line of thought is found in 1 Pet. 2:6–8, where there is a combination of OT texts about stones: for believers, Jesus is understood to be the chosen, precious stone, laid by God himself, in whom they can safely put their trust, but unbelievers are like the builders who rejected the stone for their purpose, only to find that somebody else has stepped in and given the stone the honored position; consequently, the stone has become a stumbling block—that is, the means of their ruin because they have rejected it as the means of salvation provided by God.

This same line of thought lies behind the usage here. The two phrases in the psalm correspond to the two statements about Jesus made in the previous verse: "whom you crucified but whom God raised from the dead." The focus here is not so much on the condemnation of the rulers for what they did as on the fact that what they did (rejecting the stone) has been reversed by God (exalting the stone), and the stress lies on the fact that by raising Jesus from the dead, God has made him a savior—no, God has made him the only Savior.

In applying the psalm to the Messiah, Jesus and his followers were in line with the Jewish exegesis found in the Targum to the psalms, where the stone is identified as David. Psalm 118 was a fruitful source for early Christian messianic exegesis. Psalm 118:26 is cited in connection with Jesus' entry to Jerusalem (Luke 19:38 pars.; cf. Luke 13:35/Matt. 23:39), and 118:16 has been traced behind Acts 2:33; 5:31 (on which, see commentary above and below; see also commentary on Acts 13:27, 41 below; for detail on the use

of "stone" *testimonia* in the NT, see Albl 1999: 265–85).

The rewording of the verse here is basically motivated by the attempt to weave the application into the quotation by the insertion of "you." However, this does not explain the fact that the crucial verb *apodokimazō* ("to reject" [cf. Luke 20:17]) is replaced by *exoutheneō* ("to treat with contempt" [*exoudeneō* in Mark 9:12]). The latter verb is used in some Greek translations of Isa. 53:3 and also in the prediction of Jesus' rejection in Mark 9:12 (cf. *Barn.* 7:9). Luke himself uses the verb in narrative in Luke 18:9; 23:11 (the latter is a reference to Herod Antipas's ridiculing of Jesus). The reason for the change is not certain. Luke may simply have substituted a verb that was part of his own vocabulary. Hanson (1967: 78) thinks that Luke was using the Hebrew text rather than the LXX; Wilcox (1965: 51n2) mentions the proposal that Luke used a different Greek version (cf. Bock 1987: 199–200). Dupont (1967a: 261, 301) held that there was an allusion to Isa. 53:3 here (cf. Albl 1999: 271), as does Lindars (1961: 81–82, 170), who adds that Luke was influenced by the tradition found in the passion prediction; the weakness of this proposal is exposed by Rese (1969: 113–14), but he recognizes that certainty is not possible. Doble (2002a: 5n18) maintains that Luke is making a link with the action of the rulers referred to in 4:27 and described in Luke 23:11 (cf. also Luke 23:35–37).

4:12

The clause "salvation is found in no one else" has a parallel in Ps. 146:3 (145:3 LXX): "human beings, who cannot save [*ouk estin sōtēria*]." This might be nothing more than coincidence, but later in the chapter, in 4:24, there is a further echo (see commentary on Acts 4:24 below; also Doble 2002a: 4). Other uses of similar phraseology are more remote (Ps. 3:3 LXX [3:2 ET]; Isa. 47:15; 2 Macc. 14:3).

4:23–31

Here we have one of the rare examples of giving the actual wording when the church prays to God. Not surprisingly, the language reflects OT phraseology. There are some verbal links between the prayer and Hezekiah's prayer in Isa. 37:16–20 (cf. 2 Chron. 20:10–11): "truly" (4:27; Isa. 37:18);

"And now, Lord" (4:29; Isa. 37:20). The metaphor of God "stretching out his hand" (4:30) is common in the LXX. See Pao 2000: 211–12.

4:24

The opening address to God uses scriptural language. "Sovereign Lord" translates the one word *despotēs*, used of absolute rulers and the masters of slaves; it is used thirteen times of God in the OT, but, interestingly, not in Psalms; the title is linked with God's activity in creation in Wis. 13:3, 9, and it is used in prayer in Jer. 4:10; Dan. 9:8; Jdt. 9:12; 2 Macc. 15:22. In the NT the title is used of God (Luke 2:29; Rev. 6:10 [both times in prayer]) and of Christ (2 Pet. 2:1; Jude 4).

"You who made the heaven and the earth and the sea and everything in them" (repeated in 14:15; 17:24) corresponds exactly with Ps. 146:6 (145:6 LXX). The psalm contrasts the inability of human rulers with the power of God as creator of the universe; he is the God of Jacob, who reigns forever and cares for the needy. Similar phraseology is found in Exod. 20:11; Neh. 9:6 (2 Esd. 19:6 LXX); Isa. 42:5. The detailed description of God's mighty acts, similar to that in Luke 4:18–19 (cf. Isa. 61:1–2); 7:22 (cf. Isa. 35:5), would make Christians think of what God did through Christ. Here the focus is on the sovereign power of God to overcome opposition to his people and "frustrate the ways of the wicked" (Ps. 146:9).

4:25–26

The specific reference is to the opposition to the Lord's Messiah and his people; the condemnation of Jesus and the persecution of his followers are naturally seen as parts of the same process. Since Jesus is the Messiah, it is appropriate to go back to what God had promised in inspired prophecy concerning him. Accordingly, there is a specific quotation introduced by a statement of its divine origin. The statement is attributed to its human author, David, described as God's *pais*, "servant" (cf. 2 Sam. 3:18; 1 Kings 11:34; Ps. 89:3, 20; see also Luke 1:69), but at the same time it is communicated "by the Holy Spirit" (as in Acts 1:16); the Greek text here is notoriously confused, and the manuscripts vary considerably, but the general sense is clear.

The quotation is from Ps. 2:1–2 and follows the LXX exactly (which in turn reproduces the MT accurately). In general, the psalms can be inter-

preted on three levels: (1) the psalm as originally composed and used; (2) the psalm as forming part of the collection of psalms and interpreted within that context; (3) the psalm as understood in the context of its use by the early church. We take up each of these three in regard to the psalm in question here.

First, in its original context the psalm begins with a rhetorical question asking why the nations of the world and their rulers make a hopeless attack on the Lord and his anointed king. The situation is that they are subject to the Lord and his king and are trying in vain to gain independence. The psalmist comments that God reacts with scornful laughter to their puny efforts and with anger at their disobedience. It is he who has installed the king on Zion. The king himself cites the decree of God that established him as his son and promised him rule over the peoples of the world. The decree may perhaps be associated with 2 Sam. 7:14, as the only other OT text "in which God declares a king his son, thus legitimizing his position" (Weren 1989: 195). Finally, the rulers are admonished to serve the Lord and his son, lest they feel his wrath. The psalm is generally understood as an address to the king to reassure him in the face of enemy attack.

In the LXX it is easier to understand the psalm as spoken throughout by the king himself. This is because 2:6 says, "But I was installed by him on Zion his holy mountain," announcing the decree of the Lord. Then 2:10–12 becomes the king's own address to the people, and the last verse in particular replaces "kiss the Son, lest he be angry" with "accept correction, lest the Lord be angry." This certainly smooths out a difficult psalm with its sudden changes of speaker.

Second, nevertheless, the language is extravagant for an earthly king, although David and Solomon did rule over neighboring peoples. Consequently, by the time the psalms were gathered together as a collection, this and similar references to the "Anointed One" were seen as referring to the future ruler of Israel, the Messiah, and not to ordinary kings (cf. the use of language from this psalm in *Pss. Sol.* 17:26). The psalm is quoted in 4Q174 1 I, 18–19 in an eschatological context, but the interpretation is not clear (cf. Brooke 1985: 120–23; Evans 1993b: 192–94; 1993c: 220–21).

Third, in the NT the address of God to the Messiah is directed to Jesus at his baptism (Luke 3:22) and also cited in Acts 13:33; Heb. 1:5; 5:5 (for further allusions to the psalm, see Rev. 2:27; 11:18; 12:5; 19:15; Weren [1989: 200–202] finds implicit references to the psalm in Luke 22:66–71; 23:1–25, 32–42).

Here the point of the citation is to confirm from Scripture that when the rulers of the world rise up against the Lord and his Anointed One, their attacks are doomed to failure. Although the citation does not explicitly make this point, it is clearly implied by the rhetorical question, which might be paraphrased thus: "What was the point of rising up against the Lord, since it was bound to fail?" At the same time, the psalm is seen to foreshadow the unholy alliance made between the Gentiles and the Jews, personified by Pilate and Herod Antipas respectively (note the chiastic order in 4:27); thus the language of 4:27 is shaped by the psalm (Weren 1989: 197). Jesus is explicitly identified as the one anointed (*echrisas*) by God to be the Anointed One or Messiah (*Christos*) (for the use of "servant" [*pais*] of Jesus, see commentary on Acts 3:12–13 above). When Peter goes on to comment in 4:28 that the rulers conspired to do "what your power and will had foreordained to happen," presumably the psalm is seen to be foretelling what God had appointed to take place; the verb "gather together" (*synēchthēsan*) in 4:27 is picked up from the psalm and used of the conspiracy of Herod and Pilate as they "met together." The implication is that the conspiracy was defeated, and from this is drawn the confidence of the supplicants to ask the Lord to be aware of the threats against the followers of Christ; yet what they explicitly ask for is not that the threats will come to nothing or be defeated, but that they will be able to proclaim the word to the accompaniment of further signs and wonders performed by God himself.

In relation to the main thrust of the prayer, the motif of the conspiracy between Herod and Pilate is thus seen to be a minor theme. What is the point of it? The answer probably lies in the fact that the psalm refers to the "nations" (*ethnē*) and the "peoples" (*laoi*) in parallel; in the psalm this is most naturally understood as the typical parallelism of Hebrew poetry in which a thought can be repeated in different words to make a slightly different thought (here the development from

"raging" to the consequent "plotting"). But the word "people" is normally reserved for Israel, and the term "nations" for the Gentiles. Here, despite the plural form "peoples," the word is used for the Jewish people, with the result that the psalm can be seen to foreshadow the opposition to the Messiah not only from the Gentiles, but also from his own people, the Jews, and their rulers. In this context one might also perhaps connect the term "kings" with Herod, who was sometimes referred to as "king" (cf. Mark 6:14), and "rulers" with Pilate, the Roman governor, but "rulers" is elsewhere used quite generally for persons with authority, whether Jewish or Gentile.

Barrett (1994–1998: 243) holds that the prayer belongs to the usage of Luke's own time. The use of the citation here has been attributed to Luke himself by Lindars (1961: 143) in view of his belief that the psalm was originally understood in terms of Jesus being enthroned as Messiah at his resurrection and only secondarily understood of his appointment as Messiah at his baptism; he suggests that here the psalm has been fitted to Luke's own version of the passion narrative with its unique featuring of Herod Antipas. The case for Lukan creation, however, is carefully examined by Bock (1987: 203–5) and shown to be unconvincing.

4:27

The possibility that "whom you anointed" is an allusion to Isa. 61:1 (cited in Luke 4:18) is rightly dismissed by Rese (1969: 119–20); rather, the phrase serves to identify Jesus as the Christ mentioned in 4:26.

4:28

References to God's "hand" (cf. 4:30; 7:50; 11:21; 13:11) reflect anthropomorphic OT language (see the references in *TDNT* 9:427) and also the frequent metaphorical usage of the term to express agency ("by the hand of" [cf. 2:23]). The use here in which God's hand ("your power" [TNIV]) foreordains something is unusual; the accompanying "your plan" has dictated the choice of verb.

4:30

For God "stretching out his hand" (only here in the NT), see Exod. 6:8; Num. 14:30; Jer. 1:9; Zeph. 1:4. The purpose of healing is possibly reminiscent of the activity of the Servant (cf. Isa. 53:5; see Wolff 1984: 87).

4:32–36

4:32

The expression "one heart and soul" (*kardia kai psychē mia*) has been thought to echo Deut. 6:5, where the people of Israel are called to love God with all their heart (some manuscripts have *dianoia*, "understanding") and all their soul and all their might (*dynamis*). It is noted that in the next verse there is reference to the apostles giving their witness with great might, so that the three key terms occur together (B. Gerhardsson, cited in Barrett 1994–1998: 253–54). Thus two verses that seem to have different themes might be brought into a closer unity. However, the words are used rather differently here than in Deuteronomy, where they express total self-giving in love to God; here they express more the oneness between believers and the effectiveness of the apostles' preaching. If there is a Deuteronomic inspiration behind the wording, there has been some transmutation. The expression *psychē mia* occurs in 1 Chron. 12:38 (Johnson 1992: 86).

4:34

In "There were no needy persons among them" (*oude gar endeēs tis ēn autois*) there is an echo of Deut. 15:4, where it is prophesied that there will be no poor when the Israelites are settled in the land (*ouk estai en soi endeēs*), despite the rather more realistic depiction in 15:7–11. This could be part of a general typology that sees a correspondence between, on the one hand, the redemption of the Israelites from Egypt and their prosperous settlement in the land, and, on the other hand, the new redemption wrought by Christ and the setting up of the new community (see Barrett 1994–1998: 254).

Acts 5

5:1–11

The story of Ananias and Sapphira has a structural parallel with the story of Achan, who misappropriated what did not belong to him and suffered dire consequences. The verb *nosphizomai* (5:2) establishes a verbal link (Josh. 7:1; the verb

is found elsewhere in the LXX only in 2 Macc. 4:32). Otherwise, however, there are no specific links; note that the sin here is deceit rather than theft, and that Achan's wife is not expressly named as perishing along with him. Barrett (1994–1998: 262) notes the parallel with the judgment on Nadab and Abihu in Lev. 10; he picks up the suggestion that the story is of a "rule miracle" according to the definition by Theissen (1983: 106): "they justify rules, reward behaviour in accordance with the rules or punish behaviour contrary to the rules." The pattern is found in the OT passages noted (cf. also 1 Kings 14).

5:9

The sin of "testing" (*peirazō*) the Spirit of the Lord picks up the notion of testing the Lord, which was the sin of Israel in the wilderness (Exod. 17:2; Deut. 6:16; Ps. 78:18 [77:18 LXX]; cf. Luke 4:12/ Matt. 4:7). The culprit knows that God has issued some command and disobeys it to see if God was really serious about it and will react or not. Cf. 15:10.

5:17–42

5:19

The phrase "an angel of the Lord" for a heavenly messenger occurs several times in Acts (5:19; 7:30 [D 33 1739 𝔐]; 8:26; 12:7, 23; cf. 7:38; 12:11; cf. "angel of God" [10:3; 27:23]) and elsewhere in the NT. It reproduces the common OT designation for God's agents. In the OT, however, there is some reference to a specific figure, "the angel of the Lord," and it is a moot point whether this figure is intended here (Barrett 1994–1998: 284).

5:21

"They called together . . . the full assembly [*gerousia*] of the sons of Israel" is reminiscent of the formula used when the preparations are being made for the passover in Exod. 12:21 LXX: "Moses called the full assembly of the sons of Israel." The term *gerousia* is used of a council of elders and refers frequently in the Pentateuch to the ruling body of the Israelites; it then reappears in 1 Macc. 12:6 and Josephus to refer to the Sanhedrin. The similarity of the language to Exod. 12:21 LXX shows how steeped Luke was in the terminology of the LXX. If there is any significance in the use of LXX phraseology at this point, it presumably will be to underline the seriousness of the occasion in which the historic leadership of Israel must face up to the challenge of the church (cf. 7:51).

"People [lit., 'sons'] of Israel" is so common a designation in the OT that its use in the NT requires no explanation (Matt. 27:9; Luke 1:16; Acts 7:23, 37; 9:15; 10:36; Rom. 9:27; 2 Cor. 3:7, 13; Heb. 11:22; Rev. 2:14; 7:4; 21:12); here, however, it derives directly from Exod. 12:21 LXX.

5:30

For "the God of our fathers," see commentary on Acts 3:12–13 above. The phrase "hanging him on a tree" (*kremasantes epi xylou*) picks up on Deut. 21:22–23, which refers to the practice of exposing the body of an executed criminal; this public humiliation and shame corresponded to the fact that the person was cursed by God. The same allusion occurs in 10:39; Gal. 3:13; 1 Pet. 2:24 (cf. the use of *xylon* for the cross in 13:29, and for the stocks in 16:24). The theological significance of crucifixion, based on Deut. 21:23, is not explicit (Rese [1969: 116–17] strongly denies it, but against him see Bock 1987: 208–9), but the implication may well be: "You thought that by crucifying him you were putting him under God's curse, but in fact God exalted him."

5:31

God exalted Jesus "as Prince and Savior." The OT roots of the latter expression (*sōtēr* [cf. 13:23]) are obvious enough; the appellation is used both of God (Deut. 32:15) and of human deliverers (Judg. 3:9, 15), and it is used of God and of Jesus in the NT. Here the term is drawn from the common Christian vocabulary rather than directly from the OT. For "Prince" (*archēgos*), see 3:15; in the light of the usage there we might expect it to mean something like "originator" in that he is the source of repentance and forgiveness (see commentary on Acts 3:15 above). In the absence of a qualifying genitive here, however, the idea may be simply that of a leader or prince, with much the same meaning as "lord" (Barrett 1994–1998: 290). One might perhaps see a parallel with the judges (Judg. 11:6, 11). The term *archēgos*, however, is related to "ruler" (*archōn*), used of Moses in 7:35, and the similar structure of this verse raises the possibility that there is an implicit contrast between Moses and Jesus (Dupont 1973: 225–26). For the exaltation of Jesus to the right hand of God, see commentary on Acts 2:32–33 above.

Acts 6

6:1–7

6:3

NA²⁷ sees here a reference to Exod. 18:17–23, where Moses' father-in-law, Jethro, counsels him to choose godly men from all the people to take over the simpler judicial cases and leave him free to attend to more serious business. The linguistic parallels are not strong (cf. *episkeptomai* [6:3] with *skeptomai* [Exod. 18:21]; *kathistēmi* [6:3; Exod. 18:21]; and the listing of appropriate qualities). The echoes suggest that a divinely approved pattern is being followed. The expression "full of the Spirit" is also used of the artisan Bezalel in Exod. 31:3; 35:31, but its source here is surely early church language.

6:6

The use of the laying on of hands to confer authority goes back to the appointment of Joshua (Num. 27:18, 23; cf. also the use of *episkeptomai* in this context [Num. 27:16]). The OT parallel confirms that this is the conferral of authority on persons who already possess the Spirit (6:3, 5), not a conferral of the Spirit (though in Deut. 34:9 it is said that Joshua had the spirit of wisdom "because Moses had laid his hands on him").

6:7

The verbs "grew" (*auxanō*) and "multiplied" (*plēthynō*) are used in Acts 7:17 with the single subject of the people of Israel in Egypt, using wording based on Exod. 1:7 (cf. 1:20). In Acts 12:24 the same phrase is used with reference to the word of God in connection with the growth and spread of the Christian mission (cf. 19:20, where *ischyō* is used rather than *plēthynō*). Here the two verbs are given separate subjects: "the word of God grew and the number of disciples multiplied," and this indicates more clearly what Luke means in 12:24; 19:20. Thus there is some parallel between the growth of the people of God at the time of the exodus and the growth of the number of disciples at the time of the new exodus; the new factor in the latter case is the powerful effects of the preaching. The same entity apparently can be referred to both as the word and as the community, possibly because the people are the witnesses: "The community is the word as it testifies to the power and salvation of the God of Israel" (Pao 2000: 170 [see 167–71]). For the concept of the word as a powerful agent sent forth by God, see Ps. 147:15 (147:4 LXX); Hab. 3:5 LXX; Wis. 18:14–16 (Pao 2000: 177–79).

6:8–15

Brodie (1983) has argued that the OT account of the stoning of a good man, Naboth, as opposed to the legal texts and the accounts of the stoning of evil persons (Josh. 7:25; 1 Kings 12:18), has been used to provide the "underlying framework" of the story of Stephen's trial and death, "almost like a skeleton which, having lost its former body, is fleshed out once more until it supports a new body" (Brodie 1983: 421). Brodie claims that the parallels go beyond what would be expected in two accounts of stonings, and that no general pattern for such stories exists. The stories are both somewhat repetitive and show some parallelism in structure: the hostility against the victim, the setting up of false witnesses who make a twofold accusation, the manipulation of the people, the bringing of the accused person before them, the testimony of the false witnesses, and finally the stoning itself. At the same time, there are considerable differences because these are significantly different incidents. The Naboth story is incidental to the account of the conflict between Ahab and Jezebel and Elijah, whereas Stephen is a main character in the history of the early church. It is best to conclude that Luke has seen the similarities in the stories and that the echoes between them are used to confirm the way in which the persecution of the godly has been characteristic of the Jews throughout their history, as Stephen himself attempts to show in his speech with respect to the ongoing persecution of the prophets right through to Jesus himself.

6:13

The OT condemns the giving of false witness (Exod. 20:16; Prov. 14:5; 24:28) but also recognizes that the godly fall victim to it (Ps. 27:12).

6:15

Although there is no verbal link, it may be worth noting that the most famous example in Scripture of someone with a shining face is Moses (Exod. 34:29–35); but the comment by Wall (2002: 123) that this shows that Stephen, rather than the Sanhedrin, is the authorized interpreter of

Moses looks more like a point that could be made by an expositor rather than something that was necessarily in the mind of Luke.

Acts 7

7:2–53

Stephen's lengthy speech contains one of the most dense webs of OT material in the NT. The narration of the story of Israel from a particular angle is done by means of a considerable use of OT language. However, it is only at the end of the speech that there are recognizable citations formally introduced as such (7:42, 48); for most of the speech the OT account is simply picked up and incorporated in what Stephen says. It will be simplest to go through the story in detail first, and then try to assess what is going on.

Bowker (1967–1968: 107) again suggests that we have a proem type of homily, based on readings of Exod. 33:12–34:9 (for possible allusions, cf. 7:46, 51) and Isa. 65:22–66:5 (cited in 7:49–50) with Gen. 12:1 (cited in 7:3) as the proem text. This proposal is not impossible, but it would suggest that the original scene of the speech was a synagogue service rather than a trial before the Sanhedrin. Some similarities between the speech and Ezra's prayer-speech in Neh. 9:6–38 (2 Esd. 19:6–20:1 LXX) are tabulated by Soards (1994: 148–55).

Historical surveys are familiar in the OT and Judaism (Pesch [1986: 1:246] lists Deut. 6:20–24; 26:5–9; Josh. 24:2–13; Neh. 9:6–31; Jdt. 5:6–18; 1 Macc. 2:52–60; Pss. 78; 105; 106; 136; Wis. 10; Sir. 44–50; 3 Macc. 2:2–12; 4 Ezra 3:4–36; 14:19–31; CD II, 14–III, 9; Josephus, *Ant.* 3.84–88; 4.40–49).

7:2

The story begins with Abraham (see Dahl 1968), specifically God's appearance to him in Mesopotamia. The description "the God of glory" occurs only in Ps. 29:3 (28:3 LXX). No specific reason for the choice of the unusual phrase can be given except that it is majestic language. "Appeared" (*ōphthē*) occurs in Gen. 12:7. "Our father" is Stephen's description of him. "Mesopotamia" (i.e., "between the rivers") is the LXX equivalent of the Hebrew Aram Naharaim ("Aram of the Two Rivers"), used in Gen. 24:10 but not in the narrative that Stephen is following here, where it is called "the land of the Chaldeans" (Gen. 11:31; 15:7; the MT here has "Ur of the Chaldeans," but the LXX has *chōra*, translating Heb. *'ereṣ*). Haran was in the north of Mesopotamia. From the fourth century BC the use of "Mesopotamia" was extended to include the southern area nearer the Persian Gulf, where Ur was situated. Stephen follows this later usage (*NBD* 753). "Before he lived in Haran" refers to when Abraham lived in Ur. However, in Gen. 11:31–12:5 Abraham is already in Haran when he receives this revelation. One might assume from Gen. 15:7 and Neh. 9:7 that Abraham had a previous revelation with much the same content in Ur, and this appears to be the view of Philo, *Abraham* 71; Josephus, *Ant.* 7.1.

7:3

In any case, the wording of the divine message corresponds with that given in Haran according to Gen. 12:1: "Go out from your land and from your family . . . to the land which I shall show to you" (*exelthe ek tēs gēs sou kai ek tēs syngeneias sou . . . eis tēn gēn hēn an soi deixō*). The differences in wording are minor: the second use of "from" (*ek* [bracketed in NA]) is textually uncertain, and Stephen omits "and from your father's house" and inserts "and go" (*kai deuro*). This last phrase is not found in any of the Greek versions of the OT, but the equivalent does occur in *Targum Pseudo-Jonathan* (Wilcox 1965: 26–27; but the resemblance could be coincidental [Emerton 1968: 286]). The command is equally apt in Ur and Haran, since Abraham's family also traveled to Haran and settled there.

7:4

Although Mesopotamia included Haran (Gen. 24:10), Stephen here appears to regard Haran as being outside it; he is thinking of Mesopotamia as primarily the area around Ur. The story rests on Gen. 11:31. According to Stephen, Abraham left for Canaan after the death of his father (Gen. 12:4–5). Here again there is a problem in that Abraham was seventy-five at this point, but according to Gen. 11:26, 32, Terah was seventy when Abraham was born and died at the age of 205; on the basis of these figures, Abraham would have left Haran when Terah was 145—that is, sixty years *before* he died. Stephen's chronology can be supported by a combination of the statement by Philo (*Migration* 177) that Abra-

ham left Haran after Terah's death and the text of the Samaritan Pentateuch and the Pentateuch Targum, which give Terah's age at death as 145. This would suggest that there was a variant tradition from the MT that might have found its way into some Greek version (Wilcox 1965: 28–29; cf. Bruce 1988: 134n21). Another suggestion is made by Larkin (1995: 106n) that Gen. 11:26 does not name Terah's sons in chronological order but places Abram, the youngest, first because of his importance. However, Barrett (1994–1998: 342–43) holds that Stephen and Philo made the same simple mistake of reading the events in Gen. 11:32; 12:1 as being in the order in which they occurred.

7:5

Abraham was given no "inheritance" in Canaan, "not even a foot's length." The word *klēronomia* and its cognates frequently refer to the land that God promised to give to his people (Gen. 15:7; Exod. 6:8; 15:17; Josh. 11:23) and that was restored to them in the new exodus after the exile (Isa. 49:8) (see Pao 2000: 174–76). The phraseology of the second part of the statement is similar to Deut. 2:5, where God tells the Israelites that he will not give them any of the land of Edom, "not even enough to put your foot on." The first part, however, is not paralleled in the MT or LXX of the story in Genesis. The fact that the term "inheritance" is found in the Samaritan version of Deut. 2:5 (Scharlemann 1968: 38–39; Wilcox 1965: 27) may indicate the existence of a variant wording, but it must be remembered that Stephen is not actually quoting any specific text here. "Inheritance" (*klēronomia*) can refer to what is actually received during one's lifetime rather than something promised under a will. Yet God promises to Abraham that he will give the land to him and to his "seed" as a possession (Gen. 12:7; 13:15; 17:8; 48:4), and he does so even though at the time Abraham does not have a child. Thus there is a tension in the present verse that reflects the tension in Genesis. The land is given to Abraham, yet he does not own any of it but lives in a tent like a nomad. The fact that he specially purchases a piece of land as a burial ground (Gen. 23:1–20) indicates that he does not have a property of his own. The promise includes his descendants, and yet he has no child.

7:6–7

The story continues with a further divine message that combines Gen. 15:13–14 and Exod. 3:12. The introductory phrase, "God spoke to him in this way" (*elalēsen de houtōs ho theos hoti*), seems to be unparalleled. "In this way" does not suggest that God said something *like* this, but rather anticipates the quotation that follows.

Gen. 15:13–14 LXX	Acts 7:6–7
[13]*paroikon estai to sperma sou*	[6]*estai to sperma autou paroikon*
en gē ouk idiā	*in gē allotriā*
kai doulōsousin autous	*kai doulōsousin autous*
kai kakōsousin autous	*kai kakōsousin*
kai tapeinōsousin autous	
tetrakosia etē	*etē tetrakosia;*
[14]*to de ethnos*	[7]*kai to ethnos*
hō ean douleusōsin krinō egō	*hō ean douleusousin krinō egō (ho theos eipen),*
meta de tauta exeleusontai.	*kai meta tauta exeleusontai.*

The LXX of Gen. 15:13–14 has: (1) minor changes in word order; (2) change from direct speech (second person) to indirect speech (third person) (but TNIV has altered to direct speech); (3) substitution of *allotrios* for *ouk idios* (influence of Exod. 2:22; cf. 18:3); (4) omission of the repetitious *autous kai tapeinōsousin autous*; (5) inversion of order of *tetrakosia etē*; (6) two substitutions of *kai* for *de*; (7) substitution of Hellenistic future indicative *douleusousin* for classical aorist subjunctive *douleusōsin* in relative clause; (8) and the insertion of *ho theos eipen* (cf. the similar insertion in Acts 2:17). None of these changes affect the content of the statement. The changes show that Luke (or Stephen) was not tied to the wording of the LXX and was perhaps citing from memory rather than copying from a text.

The final clause, "and worship me in this place," is not found in the divine statement to Abraham but has a resemblance to Exod. 3:12: "and you will worship God on this mountain." There the reference is to Horeb, but here "this place" is Canaan, perhaps more specifically in Jerusalem (see Barrett 1994–1998: 345). The goal of the exodus is that the people worship God in the land promised to Abraham and his descendants (Dahl 1968: 144–45).

7:8a

The requirement of circumcision comes in Gen. 17:9–14, here summarized in God giving the covenant of circumcision. The idiom of "giving a covenant" is found rarely in the LXX (Num. 25:12; Sir. 47:11), but the phrase "covenant of circumcision" is unparalleled.

Jervell (1998: 354n458) comments that the purpose of historical surveys like this one in Acts is an unsolved problem. A possible answer is given by Dahl (1968: 144–47). The narrative stresses the promises of God to Abraham regarding the immediate history of his descendants and then goes on to describe how these promises were fulfilled. The effect is to show that God made promises that have been partially fulfilled in history and to encourage belief that his outstanding promises will be and are being fulfilled in the same way. More speculatively, Dahl suggests that the future worship "in this place" is a prophecy not of the temple in Jerusalem, but of "the re-erection of the 'tent of David'" (since God does not dwell in buildings made by human hands); God's purpose is true worship of him by his people (cf. Luke 1:72–75).

7:8b

"And so" (NRSV) Abraham fathered Isaac and circumcised him on the eighth day (Gen. 21:1–5); "so" means that Abraham acted in the light of God's messages that implied that he would have descendants who would be circumcised. The stories of Isaac and Jacob and the birth of Jacob's twelve sons (Gen. 25:19–26; 29:31–30:24; 35:16–18) are passed over rapidly. (The term "patriarchs" [cf. 2:29] used for the ancestors of Israel is not drawn from the OT, but rather represents later usage [4 Macc. 7:19; 16:25; *Testaments of the Twelve Patriarchs*].) Stephen is telling the story to people who already know it, and he can assume their general knowledge of it and stick on the whole to the parts that are significant for his purpose.

7:9–10

Similarly, the story of the enslavement of Joseph and his subsequent elevation is told with brevity. The summary reflects Gen. 37:11 (*ezēlōsan auton*); 37:28 (*apedonto*); 45:4 (*apedosthe eis Aigypton*); 39:2 (*kai ēn kyrios meta Iōsēph* [cf. 39:21]). "And rescued him from all his troubles" departs from the wording in Genesis; however, note that *exeilato*, from *exaireomai*, which means "choose" in classical Greek, here has its LXX sense "to rescue" and is actually used of Reuben's action in rescuing

Joseph from his brothers (Gen. 37:22); "trouble" (*thlipsis*) is used by the brothers when talking later about his sufferings (Gen. 42:21); for the whole phrase, cf. Ps. 34:4, 6 (33:5, 7 LXX). "He enabled him to win favor and to show wisdom when he stood before Pharaoh, king of Egypt" (NRSV) is a mixture of idioms that the NRSV and the NIV paraphrase in different ways. The noun "wisdom" (*sophia*) is not actually used of Joseph in Genesis (but see Ps. 105:22 [104:22 LXX]); rather, Pharaoh declares him to be more "discerning and wise" (*phronimōteros kai synetōteros*) than anybody else (Gen. 41:39). And when Stephen says that Joseph "won favor" with Pharaoh, this phrase that aptly sums up the situation is in fact used in Gen. 39:21 of the impression that Joseph made on the prison warden. "Pharaoh made him ruler over Egypt and all his palace" summarizes Gen. 41:41–43; 45:8 (but there it is God who appointed him as ruler; see Barrett 1994–1998: 348); cf. the brief account of Joseph's career in Ps. 105:16–22. The word for "ruler" (*hēgoumenos*) is not found here, but the verb *hēgeomai* is used of Joseph in Jacob's blessing in Gen. 49:26 LXX (cf. Sir. 49:15 LXX), albeit of his leadership over his brothers. Wilcox (1965: 27–28) notes that *Targum Pseudo-Jonathan* includes the word *sarkan* ("leader, officer"), the Aramaic equivalent for the Hebrew *nāgîd*, which is often translated by *hēgoumenos*; however, it is dubious whether this indicates that Luke was using a textual tradition akin to the Targum (Bovon 2006: 108).

7:11

The account of the famine is based on Gen. 41:54–57; 42:5. "Great suffering" is a phrase not used here in Genesis, but it aptly sums up the effects of the famine. "Our people/ancestors" (7:11, 12, 15, 19, 38, 39, 44, 45, 51, 52) is literally "our fathers" (cf. Ps. 106:7 [105:7 LXX]). "Food" (*chortasmata*) is specifically fodder for animals (Gen. 42:27; 43:24), but the related verb *chortazō* can be used to describe feeding people.

7:12–13

Stephen summarizes Gen. 42:1–2; interestingly, the minor differences from the LXX are removed by assimilation to it in some manuscripts. Thus Stephen uses *sitia* ("food") rather than the LXX's *sitos* ("corn"). For the "first visit," see Gen. 42:3–38,

and for the "second visit," see Gen. 43–45, especially 45:1, 2, 9, 13, 16.

7:14

"Seventy-five in all" reflects Gen. 46:27 LXX; Exod. 1:5 LXX; 4Q13; Philo, *Migration* 199. The MT here has "seventy" (cf. Deut. 10:22 MT and LXX), followed by *Jub.* 44; Josephus, *Ant.* 2.176–183, which list them by name, as in Gen. 46:8–27. Jacob went to Egypt with sixty-six members of his family. The smaller total of seventy is gained by adding in Jacob himself and Joseph and his two sons who were already there (*Targum Pseudo-Jonathan* includes Jochebed the daughter of Levi instead of Jacob himself). The larger number was reached by omitting Jacob and Joseph and including all nine of Joseph's sons (Gen. 46:27 LXX, where the MT mentions only the two named in 46:20). Despite the impression given by the text, the number recorded is thus not simply those who actually went with Jacob, but rather is the total number of Jacob's descendants when Joseph's offspring in Egypt were included. The problem is one for students of the LXX rather than of Acts, which has simply taken over the number in the LXX.

7:15

The account of Jacob's migration to Egypt summarizes Gen. 46:1–7, 28–47:12 (cf. Deut. 26:5); and his death is recounted in Gen. 49:33, but Stephen's summary is based on Exod. 1:6, which records the death of "Joseph and all his brothers." "Our ancestors" here must refer to the sons of Jacob.

7:16

"Their bodies" (lit., "they," referring to their bodies, which were embalmed) apparently includes both Jacob and his sons. "Were brought back," *metetethēsan*, is Stephen's own word for what happened.

Stephen has thus brought together the burials of Jacob and his sons, although the narrative does not require that they were buried simultaneously. This is possible, since the OT says nothing directly about the burial of the brothers. What the OT does record is the purchase of two sites and two burials.

First, Abraham bought a cave in the field of Machpelah to bury Sarah (Gen. 23), and he too was buried there (Gen. 27:8–10); also, Gen. 49:29–32; 50:12–14 state clearly that Jacob's sons buried Jacob there. The account in Genesis is purely of the burial of Jacob, and there is no mention anywhere of the burial of his sons (other than Joseph). According to *Jub.* 45:15; 46:9–10, Jacob and his sons (except Joseph) were buried "in the cave of Machpelah in the land of Hebron" (cf. Josephus [*Ant.* 1.237; 2.193–199], who simply calls the place "Hebron").

Second, according to Gen. 33:18–20, Jacob bought land at Shechem (in what was later to become Samaria) from the sons of Hamor, and Joseph was buried there after the conquest of Canaan (Josh. 24:32).

The purchase was made "from the sons of Hemmor." Genesis 33:19 LXX has "from Emmor," and Josh. 24:32 LXX has "from the Amorites," but in both places Aquila and Symmachus have "from the sons of Emmor," as here (the variant spellings "Hemmor" and "Emmor" are both equivalent to the Heb. "Hamor"). Wilcox (1965: 31) therefore argues that Luke follows a version other than the LXX here; Bovon (2006: 109), however, holds that Luke is not citing Scripture but rather is following a Jewish tradition.

Here in Acts it is said that Abraham (not Jacob) bought the land at Shechem from the sons of Hamor, and Shechem (not Machpelah/Hebron) is named as the site of the burial of Jacob. Thus there are two apparent differences from Genesis: (1) the attribution of the purchase of the tomb at Shechem from the sons of Hamor to Abraham instead of Jacob; (2) the burial of Jacob in the same tomb as his sons in Shechem rather than in the cave of Machpelah.

With regard to (1), most commentators think that a simple confusion in the names has been made by Stephen (or Luke). However, Bruce (1988: 134n16, 137n35) suggests that Stephen, who earlier ran together the two calls of Abraham in Ur and in Haran and two divine messages in 7:7, here runs together the two accounts of purchases of land in Canaan (it is unlikely that Stephen identified Shechem and Hebron, towns that were over thirty miles apart in separate territories). Stott (1990: 134) gives as one possibility that Jacob bought his property in the name of his father, Abraham, who was still alive at that point (although we might wonder how Stephen could

have known this). Larkin (1995: 110) proposes that Stephen followed a reliable oral tradition that originally Abraham bought land at Shechem (as well as the cave of Machpelah) but then forfeited his claim to it by his nomadic movements, and finally Jacob repurchased it. But how could an oral tradition to this effect persist until the time of Stephen? No solution offered thus far is entirely free from difficulty, but that of Bruce causes the fewest problems.

With regard to (2), it is possible, though unnatural, that "their bodies" refers solely to the sons of Jacob and that his burial is not in view (Barrett 1994–1998: 351). Alternatively, it may be that Stephen was more interested in Joseph than in Jacob, and it has been suggested that "he" in 7:15b is Joseph rather than Jacob.

There is said to have been a local tradition at Shechem that all twelve sons of Jacob were buried there (*TDNT* 8:463n427, following J. Jeremias, who cited Jerome, *Epist.* 57:10; 108:13). Barrett (1994–1998: 351) is skeptical of this and agrees with the simpler suggestion by Pesch (1986: 1:251) that Josh. 24:32 was read in the light of Exod. 1:6; 13:19 to imply that the bones of Joseph and his brothers were buried together. The alternative Jewish tradition that the brothers were buried with their father Jacob in the cave of Machpelah at Hebron is thus ignored.

In any case, the effect is that there is some emphasis on what God was doing in non-Jewish territory, speaking to Abraham in Mesopotamia, merely promising him a place in Judea, being with Joseph in Egypt, and letting the patriarchs be buried in Samaria and not in the promised land (see Wall 2002: 126).

7:17–18

Stephen reminds his listeners that all through this time there was still the promise that God had made to Abraham (cf. 7:5–7). Meanwhile, the people grew in number (*auxanō, plēthynō* [Exod. 1:7]; cf. Gen. 47:27; see commentary on Acts 6:7 above; cf. 12:24; 19:20). At last "a new king, to whom Joseph meant nothing, came to power in Egypt"; there are textual variants here, but the NA[27] text is identical with Exod. 1:8. The king dealt treacherously (*katasophizomai* [Exod. 1:10]) with the people and oppressed (*kakoō* [Exod. 1:11]) them, but whereas in Exod. 1:11 the verb *kakoō* refers to abusing the people at work, here it is used of forcing them to expose their infants (cf. Exod. 1:15–22). The phrase *poiein ta brephē ektheta* is not used in Exodus, which speaks of throwing the male children into the river rather than simply leaving them to die. "So that they would die" (*eis to mē zōogoneisthai*) is based on Exod. 1:18, where the midwives disobeyed orders and "preserved alive" the male children (cf., similarly, the female children in Exod. 1:22).

7:20

The narrative moves to the life of Moses (Lierman 2004). At his birth he was seen to be *asteios* (Exod. 2:2; also in Heb. 11:23). The word renders the Hebrew *ṭôb*, which has a wide range of meanings and here seems to mean "beautiful" in the way in which we would describe an attractive infant. However, Stephen adds the qualification *tō theō*, which rests on a Hebraism used to express superlative force; it is not used here in Exodus but is found in Jon. 3:3 to express the magnitude of Nineveh. Alternatively, the phrase simply means "fair in the sight of God" (TNIV mg.). Because he was such an outstanding child, his parents reared him for three months instead of exposing him (Acts has *anatrephō* rather than the LXX's *skepazō*).

7:21

Since the story was well known, Stephen could abbreviate considerably, and the description in Exodus of the making of the ark is summed up in the phrase "when he was placed outside" (for which, see Wis. 18:5). Two verbs describe the action of Pharaoh's daughter. She "took him up" (*aneilato auton*) could also mean that she "adopted" him (NRSV), but the literal meaning of *aneilato* is required in Exod. 2:5. She "brought him up" uses *anatrephō*, as in 7:20 (not used in the LXX here); "as her son" comes from Exod. 2:10.

7:22

The brief description of Moses' education is not found in the LXX, but the theme is developed at some length by Philo (*Moses* 1.21–24). Likewise, there is no reference to the proverbial wisdom of the Egyptians in Exodus, but see 1 Kings 4:30. Nor does Exodus tell us that Moses was "powerful in speech and action" (cf. Sir. 45:3), a phrase that echoes the description of Jesus in Luke 24:19; there is no real tension with the story in Exod. 4:10–16, which reflects Moses' self-depreciation at an early

point in his career. We see here examples of the way in which Christian reading of OT stories was shaped to some extent by the interpretations and developments in contemporary Judaism, in this case by eulogizing Moses.

7:23

The elaborate phrase simplified in the TNIV to "when Moses was forty years old" is not found in Exodus and reflects a division of his life into three periods of forty years that is found also in rabbinic sources (cf. 7:30). Exodus 2:11 has merely "after Moses had grown up." "He decided"—literally, "it went up into his heart"—is a Hebrew idiom (cf. Isa. 65:16–17; Jer. 3:16; see Wilcox 1965: 63). "To visit" expresses the idea of helping (Luke 1:68; 7:16). "His own people, the Israelites" is also taken from Exod. 2:11.

7:24

Stephen paraphrases Exod. 2:11b to produce a less clear text, in that he does not immediately identify the attacker and the attacked as Egyptian and Hebrew respectively. "Went to his defense and avenged him" is not in Exodus, but "by killing the Egyptian" is taken from there. Codex Bezae (D) adds from the LXX "and hid him in the sand"—a good illustration of the tendency of scribes to assimilate the text even more to the LXX.

7:25

This comment on Moses' thoughts and the response of the Israelites is not taken from Exodus. It is, therefore, perhaps especially significant for understanding the story that Stephen is telling on the basis of the OT. What is emerging at this point is a comparison between Moses as an offerer of salvation and Jesus as a savior (cf. Acts 4:12; 5:31) and between the incomprehension of the people toward Moses and toward Jesus (cf. Luke 2:50; 8:10; 18:34; Acts 28:26–27).

7:26–28

The comment is illustrated by the next incident, recounted in Exod. 2:13–14. "The next day" replaces the LXX's "the second day"; the TNIV "came upon" paraphrases Luke's favored verb "appeared to" (*ōphthē*), more usually applied to the appearances of supernatural figures, which displaces the LXX's "he saw" (which is closer to the MT's "and behold"). Perhaps the intention is to portray Moses as a divine messenger. Where the LXX has "two Hebrew men coming to blows" (*diaplēktizomai*, found only here in the LXX), Luke simply has "them fighting," which, unless we knew the story, we would assume to be the Israelites generally. He rightly interprets Moses' intervention to be an act of reconciliation (*synallassō*), and he gives his words differently: "Men, you are brothers; why do you want to hurt each other?" replaces "Why are you [sg.] beating your neighbor?" He then has to clarify the identity of the respondent as "the man who was mistreating the other," whereas Exodus can simply continue, "But he ..."; he also inserts that the man pushed Moses aside (*apōtheō* [cf. 7:39; 13:46]). There is, however, verbal agreement over what the man said. The reply implicitly denies Moses' divine appointment, which (it is assumed) the man should have recognized. The slaying of the Egyptian is seen as a threat rather than as a means of rescue. Thus the role of Moses as redeemer and reconciler is rejected; again a parallel with Jesus is implicit.

7:29

The account in Exod. 2:14–15 is simplified. There, Moses is struck with fear because the fact that it was he who had killed the Egyptian has leaked out, and the matter has come to the ears of Pharaoh, who naturally is anxious to take action against him; so Moses flees from Pharaoh and dwells in Midian, where later he comments, "I am an alien in a foreign land" (Exod. 2:22). Midian lay to the east of the Gulf of Aqabah and thus south of Edom. Here, Moses flees at the word of the Israelite and "settles as a foreigner" (*egeneto paroikos*) in Midian. Exodus 2:15–22 describes Moses' marriage and the birth of his son; later we learn that he had two sons (Exod. 18:3–4). Again Stephen abbreviates the story.

7:30

The mention of "forty years" is a deduction from Exod. 7:7 in the light of 7:23 above. Meanwhile, during Moses' stay in Midian Pharaoh died, the Israelites again cried out to God for help in their distress, and he responded to their cry. The first stage in the process of deliverance was to commission Moses. Moses had taken his father-in-law's flocks into the desert around the mountain called Horeb in Exod. 3:1 (also 17:6; 33:6; and else-

where, esp., e.g., Deut. 1:2, 6) but Sinai here (Acts 7:38; Gal. 4:24–25; Exod. 16:1; and frequently in Exodus, Leviticus, and Numbers). The two names may represent different traditions; the site is not known with certainty but is usually located in the south of the Sinai Peninsula, although this implies a very long journey by Moses from Midian. The rest of the verse is based on Exod. 3:2. For "angel of the Lord" Acts simply has "angel." "In the flames of a burning bush" (*en phlogi pyros batou*) is literally "in a flame of fire of a bush" and is based on the LXX's "in a fire of flame from the bush" (*en pyri phlogos ek tou batou*), but the manuscripts are divided between *phlogi pyros* and *pyri phlogos* in both the LXX and Acts.

7:31

That Moses was amazed is a natural deduction from the story. "He went over to get a closer look" again paraphrases Exod. 3:3–4. In both Exodus and Acts the angel is identified as the Lord himself.

7:32

The essential statement of the speaker's identity (postponing the command relating to the sanctity of the place) is given with minor verbal differences: "I [am] the God of your fathers, the God of Abraham, Isaac and Jacob" is based on the LXX's "I am the God of your father, the God of Abraham and the God of Isaac and the God of Jacob." The plural "fathers" (as in the repetition of the phrase in Exod. 3:15–16) is more appropriate (but Wilcox [1965: 29–30, 33–34] raises the question of a version closer to the Samaritan Pentateuch); some manuscripts insert "God of" before "Isaac and Jacob" here, as in 3:13. The description of Moses' fearful reaction is a paraphrase of Exod. 3:6b.

7:33

Stephen adapts the introductory formula "And the Lord said to Moses" from Exod. 3:7 LXX, but before going on to cite what the Lord says there, he interpolates the command to Moses to remove his sandals, which he had omitted in 7:32; there are trivial differences in the wording that are insufficient to suggest the use of a version other than the LXX (Barrett [1994–1998: 361] rightly against Wilcox [1965: 41–42]).

7:34

Now comes the statement of how the Lord has heard the "groaning" of his people (*stenagmos*, as in Exod. 2:24; 6:5, but Exod. 3:7 has *kraugē*, "cry"); Stephen omits the clause stating that the Lord knows their distress and goes directly to his statement that God has come down to rescue them. He omits the detailed expansion of what God is going to do and of his concern for the people in Exod. 3:8–9 and goes straight to the commission of Moses in Exod. 3:10, abbreviated to "Now come, I will send you back to Egypt" (LXX: "to Pharaoh king of Egypt, and you will lead my people, the children of Israel, from the land of Egypt").

7:35

Thus far the recounting of the story. Now Stephen pauses to comment on it, and the style becomes more allusive than citational. "This Moses" whom the Israelites had earlier rejected was the very person whom God had appointed as their leader; the repeated use of "this" perhaps derives from the citation that will follow in 7:40. "Reject" (*arneomai*) is not used in this context in the LXX (in fact, it is very rare); the wording of the rejection is repeated from 7:27 (Exod. 2:14). From it is taken the term "ruler" used here to describe the role assigned by God to Moses, although it is not elsewhere used for this purpose. Instead of repeating "judge," Stephen uses "deliverer" (*lytrōtēs*). This is the only use of this term in the NT; surprisingly, it is not used of Jesus (although "redeemer" became a familiar title for him later). In the OT it is used only twice, both times of God (Ps. 19:14 [18:15 LXX]; 78:35 [77:35 LXX]), and here it is ascribed to Moses as God's agent in delivering his people from bondage (Exod. 6:6, regarded by Barrett [1994–1998: 364] as the basis for Stephen's usage here). See Lierman 2004: 113–18. There is a typological pointer to Jesus waiting to be exploited, but it is not developed in any way. "Through the angel who appeared to him in the bush" reminds the readers of the occasion of the divine appointment. Again we note how it was an angel who spoke at the bush, although God spoke in the first person through the angel.

7:36

The speech proceeds with a further series of three "This is . . ." statements (7:36, 37, 38). The first tells how Moses "brought them out" of Egypt (Exod. 3:12, and very frequently, usually of God's own action) to the accompaniment of "wonders and miraculous signs" (e.g., Exod. 7:3, 9; 11:9–10; Deut. 4:34) in Egypt (Exod. 7:3), at the Red Sea (Ps. 106:22 [105:22 LXX]; Exod. 10:19), and in the wilderness. The "forty years" became proverbial, often as a period of Israel's disobedience and consequent punishment (Num. 14:33–34; Ps. 95:10 [94:10 LXX]), but also as a period when God graciously acted to sustain them (Exod. 16:35; Deut. 2:7). Again the statement is open to typological exploitation, and the reader of Acts has the resources to do so (Acts 2:22, 43).

7:37

The implicit typology is confirmed by the statement that it was Moses who prophesied to the children of Israel that "God will send you a prophet like me from your own people" (Deut. 18:15, cited with minor changes; *contra* Wilcox [1965: 33], who thinks that the wording is closer to Deut. 18:18, see Bock 1987: 218–19); this is a repetition of the same citation as in 3:22 but slightly abbreviated (see Rese [1969: 76–77], who notes that the citation of Ps. 16 in 13:35 is also abbreviated compared with that in 2:25–28). Again the identification of the fulfillment of the prophecy in Jesus is not made explicitly, but readers of 3:22 would pick it up, and by the end of Stephen's speech (7:52) it would have been clear enough to the hearers (Barrett 1994–1998: 365). Bock (1987: 219–20) observes that God is not given the fuller description "the Lord your God" here, in contrast to 3:22 (cf. 13:17), and thinks that this reflects the implication here in this speech that the nation's disobedience was disturbing that relationship.

7:38

The important role of Moses in the transmission of the law to the people is now developed. For the linking of Deut. 18 with the giving of the law, parallels may be found in the Samaritan Pentateuch (which conflates Exod. 20:21–22 with Deut. 18:18); 4Q175; 4Q158; *Mek. Exod.* 20:19 (Bock 1987: 220). Moses "was in the assembly in the desert." The use of *ekklēsia* specifically for the assembly of the people at Sinai is found in Deut. 18:16 (cf. 4:10; 9:10)—that is, in the context of Moses' statement just reported—and it coincides nicely with the preferred NT collective term for the followers of Jesus (e.g., Acts 5:11), thereby again suggesting a typological correspondence. However, this point is neither primary nor developed here, where the accent lies positively on what happened at Sinai. Here Moses was "with the angel who spoke to him on Mount Sinai" (for "angels," cf. 7:53), although Exodus mentions no angel mediating between God and Moses on this occasion. Where has this angel come from? In 7:53 we read of "angels" (plural) giving the law as commands. In the context, however, a reference to the angel who appeared to Moses at the bush near Mount Sinai (7:30, 35) is surely demanded. It would be natural to extend the activity of this angel to the subsequent revelation at Sinai (cf. *Jub.* 1:27, 29; 2:1). The continuing activity of the "angel of his presence" is mentioned in Isa. 63:9. Moses is "with the angel . . . and with our ancestors," a phrase that brings out his mediatorial role (but note Barrett 1994–1998: 365–66, against misreading the Greek text in the interests of this interpretation). From the angel Moses received "living words to pass on to us." The crucial point here is the description of the law (primarily the tables received at Sinai, but by extension the law as a whole) as "living oracles" (*logia zōnta*). This description of the law as divine oracles is found also in Rom. 3:2 (and of Christian teaching in Heb. 5:12; 1 Pet. 4:11). It is used for God's messages in Num. 24:4; Deut. 33:9 (where the Levites teach God's law to the people) and especially in Ps. 119. For the use of "living" with "oracles" there is no precedent, but Barrett (1994–1998: 366) draws attention to Ps. 119:50 (118:50 LXX). Here, therefore, is a positive evaluation of the law as the source of life (this is the probable force of "living"), and it is so for "us," which includes Stephen and his Jewish hearers. The point is that as God's covenant people, required to keep the law as the condition of remaining within the people, there is no life but only death for the disobedient (cf. Lev. 18:5; Deut. 30:15–20).

7:39

Disobedience, however, was what characterized the Israelites at this point (and subsequently). Exodus does not use the specific terms "disobey" and "reject" for their attitude toward Moses, but they are appropriate as a description of the mood in Num. 14:1–3. "Turned back" (*strephō*) echoes

apostrephō (Num. 14:3; Codex Bezae [D] assimilates to the LXX).

7:40

The specific example of disobedience comes from Exod. 32, where the Israelites grow tired of waiting for Moses to come down from Mount Sinai and ask Aaron to make gods to lead them on their journey. Their statement follows Exod. 32:1 (cf. 32:23) with minor alterations. Stephen omits the opening "Get up and" and abbreviates "this Moses, the man who led us" by omitting "the man," thereby making the phrase "even more contemptuous" (Barrett 1994–1998: 367). The LXX has "gods," correctly translating the Hebrew *ĕlōhîm* in a polytheistic sense, although the Hebrew can also be used of a single god (cf. NIV mg.).

7:41

So the idol was made. For the LXX "he made them [the items of jewelry] into a molten calf" (*epoiēsen . . . moschon*) Luke coins the word *emoschopoiēsan* (*moschopoieō*). Where the LXX has the singular form of the verb referring to Aaron, Acts uses the plural for the rebellious people of Israel who instigated his action. "That was the time" (lit., "in those days") is Luke's vague indicator of time. It probably is meant to stress that right from the time that the law was given the people had rebelled against God. Similarly, Acts has "they brought sacrifices" where Exod. 32:6 LXX has "he [MT: 'they'] offered burnt offerings and presented a fellowship offering"; Acts uses the synonym *anēgagon* (*anagō*, also found in Aquila and Symmachus), which is used (but rarely) elsewhere in the LXX, for *anebibazen . . . prosēnenken*. The statement that "the people sat down to eat and drink and rose to play" (Exod. 32:6, cited by Paul in 1 Cor. 10:7) is summarized in "reveled" (*euphrainō*); but the accent lies not so much on the impious revelry (on which, see 1 Cor. 10:7) but rather on the fact that it was directed to the idol "that their own hands had made." This is Stephen's homiletic interpretation of the passage where the man-made nature of the idol is not the point at issue; however, it agrees with the kind of teaching found in Deut. 4:28; Ps. 115:4; 135:15; Isa. 44:9–20; Jer. 1:16; Wis. 13:10, and picked up in Acts 17:29.

7:42–43

From this point onward Stephen begins to move away from the narrative in Exodus that he has been following, although it is not completely forgotten. He sums up the result of their idolatry not with the story of the punishment that followed in the wilderness, but with the general statement that "God turned away from them" (*strephō*). There is no LXX precedent for this usage, although Barrett (1994–1998: 368) cites the positive turning of God to his people in Ps. 6:4 (6:5 LXX). "He gave them over to the worship of the sun, moon, and stars" has its closest parallel in Paul's statements about God giving (*paradidōmi*) up the people to the consequences of their idolatry and sin in Rom. 1:24, 26, 28; less close are Deut. 4:19, and also Lev. 26:25; Ps. 106:41, where God gives up sinners to their enemies. "Sun, moon, and stars" (NIV) is literally "the host of heaven" (*hē stratia tou ouranou*), worship of which is condemned in Jer. 7:18 (LXX); 8:2; 19:13; Zeph. 1:5—not surprisingly, since God created it, according to the LXX addition to Hos. 13:4. The connection between idolatry in the wilderness and the later worship of false gods and the consequent judgment is brought out in the lengthy citation from Amos 5:25–27 that follows; its wording is already alluded to in the preceding verses (see Richard 1982: 43). The issues here are complex because of the variations between the three texts involved. Stephen attributes his citation to "the book of the prophets"—that is, the book containing the twelve so-called Minor Prophets (cf. 13:40, but in 2:16 Peter refers specifically to Joel as the author of the prophecy).

Stephen's quotation follows the LXX with minor variations. Here is the LXX text with a note of the variations in Acts:

Amos 5:25–27 LXX	Acts 7:42b–43
5:25 *mē sphagia kai thysias prosēnenkate moi*	7:42b *mē sphagia kai thysias prosēnenkate moi*
en tē erēmō tessarakonta etē, oikos Israēl?	*etē tessarakonta en tē erēmō, oikos Israēl?*
5:26 *kai anelabete tēn skēnēn tou Moloch*	7:43 *kai anelabete tēn skēnēn tou Moloch*
kai to astron tou theou hymōn Raiphan,	*kai to astron tou theou [hymōn] Raiphan,*
tous typous autōn, hous epoiēsate heautois.	*tous typous hous epoiēsate proskynein autois,*
5:27 *kai metoikiō hymas epekeina Damaskou,*	*kai metoikiō hymas epekeina Babylōnos.*

The only significant changes here are (1) the substitution of different forms for *Raiphan* in many manuscripts (including *Rompha* in B; *Rempha* in D); (2) the insertion of *proskynein*, which clarifies the sense; (3) the substitution of "Babylon" for "Damascus." From Jerusalem, Babylon certainly was "beyond Damascus." Where Amos was thinking of the Assyrian captivity of the northern kingdom of Israel, Stephen probably was thinking of the later, historically more significant exile of the southern kingdom of Judah in the more distant Babylon.

A literal translation of the MT is:

> Did you bring sacrifices and offering [sg.]
> to me
> in the wilderness for forty years, house of
> Israel?
> You shall take up Sikkuth your king
> and Kaiwan your images,
> the star of your god(s) which you made
> for yourselves;
> and I will take you into exile beyond
> Damascus.

The LXX (and Acts) differ from the MT in three ways: (1) There is a change of tense from "you shall take up" to "you took up." (2) The Hebrew *sikkût malkĕkem* is replaced by *sukkat mōlek*; the MT has the name of an Akkadian god, Sakkut (also called Ninurta; Adrammelech [2 Kings 17:31]), but the LXX has read a slightly different word meaning "tabernacle" followed by the name of a god. The god Moloch (Molech) is much better known in the OT (Lev. 18:21; 20:2–5; 1 Kings 11:7; 2 Kings 23:10; Jer. 32:35); however, the LXX did not always recognize it. (3) The MT has *kiyyûn ṣalmêkem kôkab*—literally, "Kiyyun [Akk. "Kaiwanu," another name for the god Ninurta], your images, star." The LXX may be an attempt to substitute the name of a better-known Egyptian god, Repa.

In its original context Amos's message was concerned with the contemporary idolatry of Israel. There was plenty of worship going on, but it was condemned by Amos both because it was contaminated with idolatry and because it was not accompanied by moral obedience to the commands of Yahweh. When Amos rhetorically asks whether the people brought sacrifices in the wilderness, the possible interpretations of his question are (1) the people did not bring sacrifices at all; (2) they brought obedience to God rather than sacrifice; (3) they brought obedience to God rather than merely sacrifices.

On Stephen's lips the opening question can be variously understood, but on any interpretation the expected answer is no. It could be heavily ironical, suggesting that Amos did not think that the people offered sacrifices in the wilderness (cf. how Jeremiah states that God, when he brought the people out of Egypt, required not sacrifices, but obedience to his commands [Jer. 7:21–26]). Alternatively, it could mean that they offered not only sacrifices, but also something else: heart-obedience. Or again, it could mean that the sacrifices were offered not to God ("to me"), but to other gods. In Stephen's speech the context supports the view that the people offered sacrifices not to Yahweh, but to idols like the calf (see Hübner 1990–1995: 3:149–50). Amos then describes how the people will continue their idolatry, and he pictures a procession in which religious objects were carried. Amos referred to an image of Sikkuth, usually identified as Sakkut, an Assyrian astral god of war, also known as Kaiwanu. In the LXX the Hebrew consonants were otherwise read to give the word for "tabernacle," which is also the reading of the citation in CD-A VII, 14–17 (on which, see de Waard 1965: 41–47; Evans 1993b: 196n98; Barrett 1994–1998: 370); presumably, some kind of portable shrine is meant. This reading enables a link with the "tent of testimony" in 7:44. It is not clear whether the star of Kaiwan is another image or whether there is poetic parallelism; it may be relevant that the Akkadian god or gods variously known as Ninib, Sakkut, and Kaiwan (or Kewan) were associated with the planet Saturn. The Hebrew of this line is notoriously difficult, and the text may well be corrupt. In any case, the statement that the people worshiped the host of heaven is substantiated by the prophecy. There is, however, no ambiguity about the last line. God threatens judgment upon his people by sending them into exile "beyond Damascus" (i.e., in Assyria), as duly happened (2 Kings 15:29). Stephen, with the advantage of hindsight, took the prophecy to include the definitive captivity of Judah in Babylon and paraphrased accordingly. (On this passage see Paulo 1985: 53–68.)

In CD-A VII the writer picks up the prophecy of judgment in Isa. 7:17 and applies it to those who despise God's word and commandments. Those who remained steadfast, however, are said to have escaped to the land of the north. Then Amos is quoted: "I will deport the Sikkut of your King and the Kiyyun of your images away from my tent to Damascus." This is followed by an explanation: "The books of the law are the Sukkat of the King, as he said, 'I will lift up the fallen Sukkat of David' [citing Amos 9:11]. The King is the assembly; and the plinths of the images and the Kiyyun of the images are the books of the prophets, whose words Israel despised" (García Martínez 1996: 37–38). It is noteworthy that CD-A links together citations from Amos 5 and 9 and that both citations are found in Acts, though in different contexts. The Qumran community thus understood the prophecy positively to refer to their own departure from the corrupt temple (the "tent") to their new habitat ("Damascus"); they take with them the law and the prophets and live under their authority. The allegorical character of this exegesis stands in contrast with the literal use here by Stephen, who sees in it a negative account of what happened in the history of Israel.

7:44

Despite the presence of the tabernacle of Moloch, however, the historical record tells how the people had "the tent of testimony" (NRSV) with them in the wilderness. This phrase (hē skēnē tou martyriou) is found in Exod. 27:21 and frequently thereafter in the Pentateuch, and occasionally in the Historical Books as the equivalent of Hebrew 'ōhel mô'ēd ("tent of meeting") and much less frequently of miškān hā'ēdūt (Exod. 38:21 [37:19 LXX]). In the latter case the LXX translation is accurate, since 'ēdūt does mean "testimony," but in the former case it is incorrect, since mô'ēd means "[place of] meeting, appointed time, feast"; it appears that the translator thought "that the Heb. term to be translated was in some way connected with 'ûd, 'ēd, which is not always true" (TDNT 4:482); thus the tent is connected with the witness or revelation of Yahweh to himself, which was concretized in the placing of the tables of the law in the ark that was kept in the tent (Exod. 25:21) (see TDNT 4:482–86). Hence the NIV paraphrase "the tabernacle of the covenant law" is not inappropriate. Nevertheless, Stephen's emphasis here is not so much on the law as on the tabernacle itself. The tabernacle was a tent that served as a portable temple and was used until Solomon built a more permanent structure in Jerusalem. It is this theme that Stephen now develops.

The Hebrew word *miškān* was used of tents and in particular of the so-called tabernacle, the portable place of worship that Moses was commanded to make in Exodus (e.g., Exod. 25:9).

Stephen continues: "just as the one who spoke to Moses commanded him to make it according to the pattern which he had seen." "The one who spoke to Moses" is a description based on the frequent phrase "And the LORD spoke to Moses" (e.g., Exod. 25:1). The rest of the verse reflects Exod. 25:40, "See that you make it according to the pattern shown to you on the mountain" (cf. Exod. 25:9), also cited in Heb. 8:5. Exodus records the instructions given to Moses on the mountain, but the impression given is that Moses also saw some kind of visual representation that the author of Hebrews understood to be a heavenly sanctuary (see also Rev. 15:5), of which the earthly one was to be a copy. The tabernacle was thus built by the express command of God.

7:45

The generation of Israelites who entered the land naturally took the appurtenances of their worship with them. Joshua 3:14 mentions that the priests took the ark of the covenant as they crossed the Jordan, and Josh. 18:1 notes that the tent of meeting was set up at Shiloh. "With Joshua" uses the Greek name *Iēsous*, but in the context there is no ambiguity, although there is the basis for a typological allusion to Jesus.

In the land "they took possession of the nations which the Lord thrust out from before the face of our fathers." The noun *kataschesis* is found frequently for the taking possession of Canaan (Gen. 17:8; 48:4; Lev. 25:24; Num. 13:2). To "take possession of the nations" here seems to refer to taking possession of the land that they inhabited by driving them out from it. The verb "drive out" (*exōtheō*) occurs in Deut. 13:6 LXX (13:5 ET) in a different context; the phraseology here is based on Josh. 23:9; 24:18, which describe how the Lord cast out and destroyed the nations from before the face of the Israelites. The thought is thus of the dispossession of the nations that previously inhabited the land, and a typological allusion to the church including the nations is not present—unless there is an anti-typology so that

the opposite is now happening! "Until the time of David" sums up the period of the judges and Saul and David, during which Israel ("our fathers" flexibly refers to the people of that time) completed the dispossession of its enemies and still had the tent of meeting—but only for a short time, since its replacement by the temple was impending.

7:46

That David "found favor in the sight of" God reflects a familiar form of words in the OT, used both of human relationships (Gen. 34:11; 1 Kings 11:19) and of relationships with God (Gen. 6:8; Exod. 33:12–17). The precise phrase is not used of David in the OT, but the very similar phrase "to find favor in the eyes of" is used of him (2 Sam. 15:25); Stephen is thus using LXX phraseology but not alluding to a specific text. However, David's request to God "to find a dwelling for the house of Jacob" (*heurein skēnōma tō oikō Iakōb*) is based on a specific text, Ps. 132:5 (131:5 LXX). In the psalm the Lord is besought to remember David and his hardships. Specifically, David made a vow to the God of Jacob, refusing to take any rest "until I find a place for the Lord, a dwelling for the God of Jacob" (*heōs hou heurō topon tō kyriō, skēnōma tō theō Iakōb*). The psalm as a whole is concerned with two interconnected issues. One is the Lord's vow to David that he would establish his descendants on the throne forever; the other is that he has chosen Zion to be his dwelling place. The psalmist calls on God to fulfill his promises, to be present in his dwelling place, the temple, and to bless priests and people alike. The verse cited is close to the MT, except that the MT has "the Mighty One of Jacob," while the LXX has "the God of Jacob." "To find" has the strong sense of actually providing a place for the Lord, acquiring the site, building the sanctuary, and so on. "Dwelling" (*skēnōma*) is related to the word "tent" (*skēnē*) and does not necessarily imply a permanent, built sanctuary. Evans (1993b: 197) notes that nothing is specifically said about David's wanting to "build" a temple for the Lord. The curious feature is the phrase "for the house [*oikō*] of Jacob" (𝔓⁷⁴ ℵ* B D sa^ms) against the variant "for the God [*theō*] of Jacob" (ℵ² A C 33 1739 𝔐). The former is clearly the harder reading, and the latter is an obvious correction by assimilation to the LXX. However, since "house" has been thought not to make sense in the context, it was suggested by Hort that it is a primitive corruption of an original *kyriō* (see Metzger 1994: 308–9). Barrett (1994–1998: 372) adopts "house" on the grounds that "a dwelling for the house of Jacob is a place that the house of Jacob may use as a temple, that is, it means a dwelling (for God) to be used as such by the house of Jacob."

The story of how God declined the request, not rejecting the idea of a dwelling but rejecting David as the person to carry it through (2 Sam. 7), is omitted but is to be inferred from the next statement.

7:47

Stephen sums up the building of the temple in a succinct statement: "But Solomon built a house for him" (echoing 1 Kings 6:2; 8:20; 1 Chron. 22:6). There are two contrasts. The first is the contrast between David, who wanted to provide a dwelling for God, and Solomon, who actually did so. The second is between the tent of meeting and the "house." In the light of 2 Sam. 7:6, it is clear that "house" means a permanent dwelling (even if it was only a wooden construction [2 Sam. 7:7]) as opposed to a portable tent that was moved from place to place. It is hard to tell whether the statement is critical and disapproving. Although God said that he had never asked for a house (2 Sam. 7:5–7), there is no indication in the OT that he did not go along with the proposal to build the temple, and indeed he committed the task to Solomon and approved the finished task (1 Kings 9:1–9). Furthermore, it is clear in the OT account that the temple was not a permanent dwelling for God, as if he could be confined to such a structure, but rather was a meeting place for the Israelites with the God who is so great that the heavens cannot contain him (1 Kings 8:27; 2 Chron. 6:18).

7:48

Now comes the surprise in the speech. "The Most High does not dwell in [buildings] made by human hands." The order of words lays emphasis on "the Most High" as compared with other deities worshiped in the ancient world. This title for God (used especially by Luke, but also in Mark 5:7; Heb. 7:1) reflects OT usage from Gen. 14:18 onward. The title is not used in this context in the OT, but it is appropriate in describing God, who is transcendent and cannot be confined to a human building. There is no special nuance in the term "dwell" (*katoikeō*), which can be used of permanent or transitory residence. "Made by human hands" (*cheiropoiētos*) is a term used in contrasts between the earthly temple and God's heavenly dwelling (Mark 14:58; Acts 17:24; Heb. 9:11, 24), and it is especially applied to idols (Lev. 26:1, 30; Isa. 46:6); in Isa. 16:12 LXX it is used of the temple of Moab where people pray to their god. The term is not used in connection with the dedication of the temple, but the idea is present in Solomon's description of "this temple which I have built" alongside the heavens that cannot suffice for God: how can he really dwell (*katoikeō*) with human beings (1 Kings 8:27)? Clearly, Solomon prays that God really will dwell with human beings, while recognizing that the temple is inadequate for the purpose, and that God hears prayer from the place where he does dwell: heaven (1 Kings 8:30). There is thus a paradoxical recognition that in one sense God comes to be with humanity in the temple and can even be said to dwell with them, but his real dwelling is in heaven, although even heaven is inadequate for him. This is what lies behind Stephen's statement, and therefore the text seems to suggest not that Solomon was wrong to build the temple (*contra* Marshall 1980: 146; see Evans 1993b: 197), but that those people are wrong who think that God dwells there and is confined to this one place. The use of "made with human hands" may suggest that the attitude of the people had become idolatrous (Pao 2000: 207).

For parallel material, see especially Evans (1993b: 198n107), who cites Philo, *Planting* 126; *Spec. Laws* 1.66–67; *Cherubim* 99–100; Josephus, *J.W.* 5.456–458; Bar. 3:24, and notes that the Qumran sect thought of itself as the true temple (1QS VIII, 8–9; 4Q174 1 I, 6).

7:49–50

Stephen's statement is not novel, but rather rests (not only on 1 Kings 8, but also) on a prophetic statement to the same effect in Isa. 66:1–2, which is cited fairly closely. The original has "The heaven is my throne, and the earth is the footstool for my feet; what house will you build for me? And what place for my resting place? For my hand created all these things and all these are mine, says the Lord."

Isa. 66:1–2 LXX	Acts 7:49–50
[1] ho ouranos mou thronos,	[49] ho ouranos moi thronos,
hē de gē hypopodion tōn podōn mou;	hē de gē hypopodion tōn podōn mou;
poion oikon oikodomēsete moi?	poion oikon oikodomēsete moi, legei kyrios,
ē poios topos tēs katapauseōs mou?	ē tis topos tēs katapauseōs mou?
[2] panta gar tauta epoiēsen hē cheir mou,	[50] ouchi hē cheir mou epoiēsen tauta panta?
kai estin ema panta tauta, legei kyrios.	

The changes made in Acts are (1) advancement of *legei kyrios*; (2) change of final statement into a rhetorical question: *ouchi* for *kai* and telescoping of clauses.

The prophecy is intended to make the same point as in 1 Kings 8. It does so in the context of stating that what God wants is humble obedience from his people rather than the building of an elaborate temple and the offering of sacrifices that are no better than the abominable practices of other people if unaccompanied by full obedience to him. It is thus not an absolute rejection of worship at the temple, although Hübner (1990–1995: 3:150–51) thinks that this is how Luke understood it.

The existence of passages such as this provides the basis for Stephen's accusation that the people of Israel have always been disobedient to God and assumed that they could domesticate him in their temple and enjoy his favor. He could have referred to Jeremiah's warning to people who kept repeating, "This is the temple of the LORD" (Jer. 7:4). Nevertheless, in the context of Acts as a whole it does not appear that the temple is entirely repudiated (see Barrett 1994–1998: 374).

7:51

Now at long last comes the accusation itself. The pejorative language is taken from the OT. "Stiff-necked" (*sklērotrachēlos*) is applied to the rebellious Israelites in the wilderness (Exod. 33:3, 5; 34:9; Deut. 9:6, 13; cf. Bar. 2:30). "Uncircumcised in heart and ears" reflects the OT usage of "uncircumcised" (*aperitmētos*) in a metaphorical sense to refer to the failure to expunge evil of which literal circumcision was intended to be symbolic. See Lev. 26:41; Jer. 9:26 (9:25 LXX); Ezek. 44:7, 9; cf. Jer. 4:4 ("circumcise your hard hearts"); "uncircumcised in ears" comes in Jer. 6:10. Stephen is thus using OT phraseology that was current

in Judaism (1QS V, 5; 1QpHab XI, 13; *Jub.* 1:7, 23). "You always resist the Holy Spirit" (*hymeis aei tō pneumati tō hagiō antipiptete*) is reminiscent of "they provoked his Holy Spirit" (*parōxynan to pneuma to hagion autou* [Isa. 63:10]), and the verb *antipiptō* is used in Num. 27:14 ("when the assembly rebelled"). Stephen picks up on the key theme in Isa. 63, where the prophet recounts the continuing mercies of God to his people, saving them through the angel of his presence; he records how the people remembered that he set his Holy Spirit among them in the days of Moses. Yet despite all this, they rebelled against him and provoked his Holy Spirit. Since this is the only OT passage (apart from Ps. 51:10–11) to refer to the Spirit as the "Holy Spirit," a deliberate allusion is certainly being made. The prophecy, with its comparison between the behavior of the Israelites in the wilderness and their contemporary behavior, justifies Stephen's statement that the present behavior of the Jews is of a piece with the continual (*aei*) behavior of *their* ancestors (the use of "their ancestors" rather than "our ancestors" is dictated by the form of the statement; nevertheless, it is significant that Stephen uses the term when it is the sins of the people that are the focus rather than the care of God for his people [see Pao 2000: 208]).

7:52

The indictment continues with a reference to the well-attested reputation that the people of Israel had by this time for persecuting and even killing the prophets (cf. 1 Kings 19:10, 14; 2 Chron. 36:16; Neh. 9:26; Jer. 26:20–24; Matt. 5:12/Luke 6:23; Matt. 23:29–36/Luke 11:47–51; Matt. 23:37/Luke 13:34; 1 Thess. 2:15; Heb. 11:36–38; see Str-B 1:943; Steck 1967). By the nature of their calling, prophets tended to be critical of the sins of the people and their leaders, and so Stephen's rather hyperbolical rhetorical question implying that no prophet was immune from opposition is broadly justified. However, the accusation takes on a distinctive nuance here. He singles out the actual slaying of the prophets who foretold the coming of the Righteous One. Since Isaiah was the prophet who was especially remembered as being murdered by Manasseh (see *Martyrdom and Ascension of Isaiah*), and since his book contained the account of the suffering of the righteous Servant (Isa. 53), it is he who is especially in mind (needless to say, modern doubts as to whether Isa. 53 actually came from the original Isaiah do not affect the issue). The execution of Jesus was of a piece with the past conduct of Israel.

7:53

Finally, Stephen reaches the climax of his speech; it is probably implied that he was cut short at this point by the furious audience, and therefore it is idle to speculate whether he would have said more. Although the law had been given centuries before, there was a solidarity between the original recipients and their descendants, so that "you received the law" is a justifiable statement. "You" in fact indicts the whole Jewish people throughout their history. The importance of the law is enhanced by the comment that it was received *eis diatagas angelōn*. The association of angels with the giving of the law is attested in Gal. 3:19; Heb. 2:2 (cf. Acts 7:38). The OT basis for this may lie in Deut. 33:2 LXX: "The Lord has come from Sinai and has appeared from Seir to us; and he hastened from the mountain of Paran with myriads of Kadesh, [and] on his right hand his angels were with him." The MT here is somewhat different; it has "he came from myriads of holy ones [*qōdeš*]" followed by a confused text; the LXX has vocalized *qōdeš* to give the place-name "Kadesh" and has interpreted the following phrase by parallelism with what preceded ("myriads of holy ones" would naturally be understood as angels) (Jobes and Silva 2000: 199–200). In any case, the presence of angels at Sinai became a fixed part of Jewish tradition (*Jub.* 1:29; *T. Dan* 6:2; cf. Josephus, *Ant.* 15.136, unless this refers to human messengers).

The Greek phrase here is odd; the usual explanation is that *eis* is equivalent to *en* used instrumentally: "by the commands of angels" who acted as God's intermediaries. Perhaps, however, it is used predicatively: "you received the law as the commands of angels" (cf. Acts 7:21 and examples in BDAG 291, s.v. *eis* 8b).

What are we to make of Stephen's speech in its relationship to the OT? The scene is set by the accusations in chapter 6 that Stephen speaks against the temple and the law, specifically stating that Jesus would destroy the temple and change the Jewish ancestral customs (i.e., the law) given by Moses. Essentially, Stephen is using the OT story to develop and defend his position. He does so by telling a story about the past that is rich in detail and whose thread is by no means easy to follow. The story has two aspects: one is a positive account of God's promises to his people, Israel, and his faithful fulfillment of them, and the other is an account of the continual opposition to God's message and messengers. As Evans (1993b: 194–99) notes, the first part of the story is essentially positive (except 7:9), but from 7:22 onward the motive of misunderstanding and rebellion develops.

The story is told selectively, at times following the OT closely, in some points citing the text fairly closely, in other points paraphrasing and summarizing it, and again moving silently over vast pieces of the story. The omissions are not surprising, given the brevity of Stephen's speech and the great length of the OT story. What is more surprising is the amount of detail given by Stephen on certain parts of the story and the presence of a fair amount of material whose relevance to the development of his main points is not obvious. Why, for example, are we told that Moses was educated in all the wisdom of Egypt? Is there an implicit comparison with Jesus (Luke 2:40, 52)?

The practice of telling a scriptural story with accompanying detail is traditional, and it adds to the interest of the story and perhaps makes it more effective than a straightforward argument or a recital of the bare facts could be. The same technique is found in Acts 13:16–25 (cf., e.g., Ps. 105; Heb. 11). There is the significant contrast, however, that whereas Acts 7 is predominantly negative in its evaluation of the history, Acts 13 is much more positive (Barrett 1988: 243).

1. The story is the story of God and his dealings with the people. It includes God's promise of the land to them and his care for them, and it reaches a climax with the establishment of the people in the land and the building of the temple. The subsequent history is omitted, since the goal of the account (see 7:7) has been reached.

2. But from the beginning there is opposition to God's appointed messengers and leaders of his people. Some of this comes from outsiders, the Egyptians (7:6, 18–19), but the main emphasis is on the Israelites themselves in their rejection of their leaders (7:9, 27–28, 35, 39) and their turning away from God himself (7:39–41, 52). This leads to punitive action by God (7:42).

3. It is possible for the reader to see where the characters in the story can be regarded as "types" (Goppelt 1982: 121–22), or perhaps we should say "prototypes" (Swartley 1997: 537), of Jesus (Joseph, Moses), but despite strong hints (e.g., God was "with" Joseph [7:9] and, later, "with" Jesus [10:38]; the description of Moses as a deliverer and the promise of a prophet like him), the possibility is not followed up. This might suggest that the scriptural material in the speech was used on various occasions, and that it was used in different ways. Bock (1987: 217–18) finds no use of a Joseph-typology here, since no "deliverance" terminology is present; Wall (2002: 126) proposes that Joseph typifies the prophets and their fate, including Jesus and now, in particular, Stephen. However, in the case of Moses there is the specific prophecy that the Lord will raise up a prophet "like me" (7:37), and this statement invites typological development, so that Bock (1987: 221) can speak of "typological-prophetic usage of the text."

4. Following on from a comment on the idolatry of the Israelites and God's giving them up to further idolatry and then condemning them to exile, Stephen develops the fact that the Israelites had the tabernacle in the wilderness, made according to God's direction, and used it until the time of David, who suggested a permanent dwelling place for God; this plan was put into action by Solomon.

5. Then the speech takes a surprising turn in that Stephen emphasizes that God does not live in a man-made house, as the OT itself clearly testifies. The unanswered question is, Where does God live?

Earlier, Stephen was assailed for saying that Jesus would destroy the temple. In the light of the undeveloped typology that we have already observed in this speech, it seems to me very probable that Stephen envisaged its replacement by the new house of God composed of his people. An alternative interpretation is that Stephen was merely emphasizing the transcendence of God (Sylva 1987).

Thus Stephen answers the accusation that Jesus would change the customs and law by pointing out that the Israelites themselves had been doing this all along by rejecting the law and acting idolatrously.

As for the charge that Jesus would destroy the temple, the answer may be that the temple is irrelevant because God transcends the temple (Sylva 1987). However, it is not clear how this constitutes an answer to the charge.

7:54–8:1a

7:54

The gnashing of teeth is a reaction of wicked opponents mentioned in the OT (Ps. 35:16; 37:12; 112:10; Lam. 2:16); it is also used metaphorically of God being thought to act like an enemy (Job 16:9). The references in the Gospels use the noun *brygmos* rather than the verb *brychō* used here. Presumably, even applied to human beings it is metaphorical rather than literal.

7:55

Looking up to heaven as the place from which succour comes is natural (cf. Eleazar in 4 Macc. 6:6), but to see the glory of God in such a context is unparalleled; the nearest approach is where people worshiping in the OT see the glory of God (Ps. 63:2; Isa. 6:1). The phrase probably is intended to be reminiscent of 7:2, so that the God who appeared to Abraham now appears to Stephen (Wall 2002: 131). Stephen sees Jesus standing at the right hand of God (cf. Acts 2:34), a motif based on Ps. 110:1, but there and elsewhere the victorious king sits, and there has been much debate as to why Jesus here stands. The OT does not throw any light on this, but presumably some kind of impending action is implied (for the possibilities, see Bock 1987: 222–25).

7:56

The opening of the heavens is a motif associated with the baptism of Jesus (Luke 3:21 pars.) and is a mode of revelation (Acts 10:11) or of entry into heaven (Rev. 4:1) or descent from it (John 1:51; Rev. 19:11). A cry to God to rend the heavens and come down is a call for divine help (Ps. 144:5; Isa. 64:1). Here, however, the traffic is in the other direction. Jesus is now identified, when Stephen sees him, as the Son of Man, which must be an identification of him with the exalted figure in Dan. 7:13–14.

7:57

The execution of Stephen takes place according to the pattern prescribed in the OT and adopted into Jewish law for blasphemers and idolaters; the victim was taken out of the inhabited area, in this case the town (but in the wilderness setting in Lev. 24:14 it is the camp; cf. Num. 15:35; Deut. 17:5; in Heb. 13:11–12, however, Jesus suffers outside the city by analogy with the disposal of sin offerings outside the camp). There he was stoned to death. In the OT the responsibility for carrying out the stoning lay with the witnesses who heard the blasphemy along with the people generally. Thus the protocol that identified a person as a condemned blasphemer and idolater was carried out exactly here.

7:59

The dying person's cry, "Receive my spirit," has its antecedent in Ps. 31:5 (30:6 LXX), "Into your hands I will commit my spirit," which is taken up fairly closely in the last words of Jesus in Luke's version, "Father, into your hands I commit my spirit"; here, however, words originally addressed to God the Father are now addressed to the Lord Jesus. Where the psalm has "I will commit" (*parathēsomai*), Stephen uses the imperative "receive" (*dexai*), but the force is much the same. In the psalm we have a statement by a person who is in distress through personal weakness, increasing age, and the attacks of enemies; however, he expresses his confidence that God will preserve and vindicate him. It has now become an affirmation that even though the person dies, God will still preserve and vindicate him. "Falling asleep" as a metaphor for dying is found in the OT (e.g., 1 Kings 2:10), but it is too widespread to be cast as characteristically OT language.

7:60

Commentators contrast the prayer for divine vengeance by the victim of murder in 2 Chron. 24:22 with Stephen's prayer for pardon for his murderers here (cf. Luke 23:34), but there is nothing to indicate that Luke deliberately intended the contrast.

Acts 8

8:4–25

In the first part of this chapter, depicting the mission to Samaria, there is very little that can be called "use" of the OT. Nevertheless, the inclusion

of Samaria within the Christian mission can be seen as an integral part of the restoration of Israel, which is forecast in 1:6–8 and is part of the Isaianic program (Pao 2000: 127–29).

8:10

LXX phraseology has affected the author's style in the phrase "from the greatest to the least" (cf., e.g., Gen. 19:11).

8:20

Peter's words to Simon offer a small cluster of texts reflecting scriptural phraseology. The curse "May your money perish with you" (*eiē eis apōleian*) is reminiscent of Dan. 2:5 Θ; 3:96 Θ (see further Pesch 1986: 1:276n26).

8:21

"You have no part or share" picks up the language of Deut. 12:12; 14:27, 29 (*meris oude klēros*), and "your heart is not right before God" echoes Ps. 78:37, "their heart was not right with him," as part of a general description of the corrupt wilderness generation.

8:22

The combination of "repent" and "from" (*metanoeō apo*, as in Jer. 8:6) is regarded as a Semitism by Wilcox (1965: 102–5), but the evidence is not compelling (see Barrett 1994–1998: 415).

8:23

Peter comments that Simon is "full of bitter poison, bound by unrighteousness" (Barrett 1994–1998: 417): *eis gar cholēn pikrias kai syndesmon adikias horō se onta*. *Cholē* is "gall," a juice renowned for its bitter taste (Prov. 5:4). The LXX has the hendiadys *en cholē kai pikria* (Deut. 29:18 [29:17 LXX]) to describe the result of idolatry for those who follow it (cf. Lam. 3:15). Although *cholē* can refer metaphorically to wrath and anger, this is inappropriate here, and the reference is rather to Simon's ungodliness as being like a bitter poison. The implication may be that he will experience the bitter results of his sinful attitude. The "bond of unrighteousness" (*syndesmos adikias*) is the evil desire that has taken Simon captive despite his initial belief and baptism. This expression appears in Isa. 58:6, where it refers to the bondage unjustly imposed upon people and from which they must be delivered; here, however, it is the wickedness that holds Simon firmly. Again, then, we simply have a use of biblical language, but it may be significant that it comes out of a tradition of opposition to idolatry that early Christians took over from the OT (Pao 2000: 197–99).

8:26–40

Hanson (1967: 109) notes the suggestion made by Clarke (1922: 101–3) that the story of Philip and the Ethiopian eunuch has been shaped so as to suggest that it is a fulfillment of Zeph. 2:4, 11–12; 3:4, 10, where there are references to Gaza, desert, midday, worship by all the nations, Ethiopians (but slain by the sword of the Lord), prophets borne by the wind (*pneumataphoroi* [3:4 LXX]), and from beyond the rivers of Ethiopia God's scattered people bringing sacrifices to him. This is an interesting set of coincidences running through the prophecy. It is the kind of material that might suggest to some scholars that the story in Acts was constructed as a midrash on elements in the prophecy, but it defies imagination to envisage how anyone might have done so. Nevertheless, the possibility remains that the story has been told in such a way as to suggest a reference to the fulfillment of the prophecy in Zeph. 3:10. However, there is also reference to worship by Ethiopia in Ps. 68:31 (67:32 LXX): "Ethiopia will stretch out its hand to God." Parsons (1998: 111) also draws attention to references to Ethiopia in Isa. 18:1; 45:14, which (together with 56:3–8 [see below]) would contribute to the eunuch's interest in reading Isaiah. More generally, we hear of foreigners coming from distant lands to pray in Solomon's temple and having their prayers answered (1 Kings 8:41–43), and promises of favor to foreigners and eunuchs in Isa. 56:3–8 (despite the prohibition against castrated men entering the tabernacle in Deut. 23:1; see also Jer. 41:19 LXX, *v.l.*). Although there is no allusion to these passages, we do have the phenomenon of echoes, intended or otherwise, that might be picked up by the alert reader; what is promised in the OT now finds fulfillment. Pao (2000: 140–42) claims that the primary concern of the narrative is not with the fact that the man is an Ethiopian, but rather that he is a eunuch in whom the promise of Isa. 56 finds fulfillment. It is part of the pattern of restoration in Isaiah that is picked up by Luke.

Yet another possibility is raised by Scott (1994: 533–38), who holds that this story is the section of Acts describing the mission to the second of the three geographic regions in the Jewish "table of the nations," and therefore the focus is on the conversion of an Ethiopian (i.e., a descendant of Cush [Gen. 10:6–8]). If this suggestion is accepted, it provides a plausible explanation for the inclusion of this brief narrative, which otherwise is not clearly integrated into the total story in Acts, except as a stage in the admission to the church of non-Jews. The story then gains in significance as the first extension of the gospel to the nations of Africa.

The initiation of the action by an "angel of the Lord" who spoke to Philip is a frequent motif in Acts and reflects a pattern in the OT (cf. Gen. 16:9; 2 Kings 1:3, 15). The phrase *kata mesēmbrian*, translated "toward the south" in the text of most recent versions, may also be rendered as "at noon" (so NJB), which would agree with Zeph. 2:4; this coincidence is hardly adequate reason for adopting this rendering, although it commends itself on other grounds (Marshall 1980: 161; Barrett 1994–1998: 422–23).

The centerpoint of the story is the reading of the OT. Here is a man who is actually using his Bible, or, more accurately, a specific scroll while he is sitting in his seat on the ancient equivalent of his private jet (though not as regards amenities and speed!). Coincidentally, or rather by divine providence, he is reading Isa. 53, and specifically 53:7–8:

MT	LXX/Acts
Like a lamb led to the slaughter,	Like a sheep, he was led to slaughter,
and like a sheep that before its shearers is dumb,	and like a lamb before its shearer is dumb,
he did not open his mouth.	so he does not open his mouth.
By oppression and judgment	In his humiliation his judgment
he was taken away;	was taken away;
and as for his generation,	who will explain his generation?
who considered that he was cut off	For his life is taken away
out of the land of the living?	from the earth.

The verbal agreement between Acts and the LXX is almost complete, and the differences are too minor for comment (though see Wilcox 1965: 31). The LXX here is for the most part sufficiently like the MT in sense. The main difference is the substitution of "in his humiliation his judgment was taken away" for the MT's "by oppression and judgment he was taken away." The judgment that the LXX version is easier to understand christologically may be accepted (Rese 1969: 97–98); in any case, it would have been the LXX that the Ethiopian and Philip were using rather than the MT.

In the Hebrew text of Isa. 52:13–53:12, which is far from easy to understand, we have a figure described as God's servant, who will be exalted and honored even by kings and yet is subjected to intense humiliation and suffering like a societal outcast. Yet he is said to bear this suffering on account of the sins of the people by the will of God, so that in effect he functions as a guilt offering; he suffers without complaint and is eventually killed and buried. Somehow, he will see the result of his suffering and will be vindicated by God. All this is tolerably clear despite difficulties in detail in the passage as a whole.

The passage is enigmatic, to say the least. How the prophet himself understood what he was saying and how his message was grasped by its original hearers and readers remains opaque. The problem is precisely that identified by the Ethiopian: what is the reference of the passage? Throughout this section of Isaiah (chaps. 40–55) there are numerous references to a person or persons who are servants of Yahweh. There is no reason why this common term used for all kinds of servants of God should necessarily always refer to the same person or persons in this section of the book. The earliest reference is 41:8–9, where the people of Israel collectively are God's servant, and in fact this usage predominates (43:10; 44:1–2, 21; 45:4; 48:20; 49:3). But God's messengers and prophets are also his servants (44:26 [pl. in MT; sg. in LXX]), and elsewhere rulers such as David are so termed (e.g., 37:35). When the term is used for someone who has a mission to Israel (49:5–7; 50:10), it is natural to think of a prophet, even the author of the prophecies himself. In some passages the description appears to be of an individual, conspicuously so in 42:1–7, and yet here the LXX inserts "Israel," as if the task described is that of the people as a whole. Later in the same chapter the servant who is God's messenger is chided for being blind, and it looks as though the people as a whole may be meant. One could be pardoned for being uncertain whether by the time we get

to chapter 53 the reference is to the people or to an individual messenger and servant of God, perhaps even the author himself, whose message was not always acceptable to his audience (cf. 50:10); in fact, the description in 50:4–9, with its account of rejection and scorn not unlike that in 52:13–53:12, could well reflect the prophet's own experiences.

The interpretation of the material in Judaism has been much discussed. According to Hengel (1996), Isa. 53 was read and interpreted messianically, although whether it was seen as expounding a vicarious atonement for sin is not altogether clear, and there was not necessarily one consistent line of interpretation.

In the present context the eunuch initiates the discussion simply by asking about whom the prophet is speaking, but one can naturally assume that this would open up the question of what was being said about the person. This was the kind of question asked at Qumran, where biblical prophecy was interpreted as referring to contemporary figures and events (Johnson 1992: 157, citing 4Q171 IV, 1–25; 1QpHab II, 1–15). As we have noted, the possibility that the prophet was speaking about himself was an obvious one. Somewhat similar material in Jer. 11:18–20 is autobiographical. For Philip, the answer is simply Jesus. This implies that even by this early date the recognition that the job description in Isa. 53 fit Jesus, and only Jesus, was current among Christians (unless, of course, the story is unhistorical at this point and reflects convictions that were arrived at later). This is probable for two reasons. First, the early Christians do appear to have studied the OT looking for material that applied to Jesus right from the start. It would be unfathomable if they had overlooked this chapter! Second, in this particular case there is evidence that Jesus himself directed their attention to the figure of the servant (France 1971: 110–35), although this has been disputed (Hooker 1959; 1998a). This is not the place to debate the issue, but I remain convinced that there is a good case for the influence of the "servant" concept on Jesus (see, e.g., Betz 1998; Watts 1998).

The section of the prophecy that is quoted is concerned with the injustice perpetrated on the Servant and with his patient acceptance of it without complaint. There is no explicit reference in this part of the text to the effects of the Servant's suffering. This omission is of a piece with the general tendency in Acts to ignore the significance of the death of Jesus as a vicarious sacrifice that opens up the possibility of forgiveness and salvation for repentant sinners (see, however, 20:28). However, the use made of the Scripture here is of a piece with the emphasis both in the Gospels and in the evangelistic and apologetic speeches in Acts of identifying Jesus as God's agent and accounting for the fact of his sufferings in terms of the divine necessity expressed in Scripture. It was important to establish that Jesus is the Messiah and that his suffering is not at odds with this but is rather an essential part of his vocation before going on to the question of the significance of his sufferings. Parsons (1998) suggests that the humiliation and rejection of Jesus are centered, since the point is that the eunuch can identify with Jesus. He builds on a hint by Johnson (1992: 156) and further suggests that the quotation stops where it does because "his life was taken from the earth" could be ambiguous and refer both to his death and to his exaltation (cf. the metaphor of "lifting up" in John's Gospel). A deliberate avoidance of the concept of atonement by Luke (so Rese 1969: 98–100) seems unlikely; more probably he is relating how the church at this early stage dealt with the offense of the crucifixion by emphasizing that it was willed by God. One might as well argue from the fact that the Servant's vindication is not mentioned here that Luke was not interested in it either!

Parsons (1998: 115–18) also notes that what Philip does here, "beginning from this scripture he preached the good news concerning Jesus to him," exemplifies the pattern established by Jesus in Luke 24:25–27, 44–46 (cf. esp. "beginning from Moses and all the prophets" [24:27]). What exactly he said in this exposition is not recorded, but we may presume that it covered the kind of things said in the earlier speeches in Acts and that it was of such a character as to lead the hearer to make a response that was expressed in the desire for baptism. This may suggest that Philip drew a line from Isa. 53 to the offer of forgiveness (so Parsons 1998 [pace Hooker 1998b]), but if so, Luke has not given any direct indication of how he may have done so.

The description of the baptism that relates how Philip and the eunuch went down into a stretch of water might suggest a faint parallel with the story of Elisha and Naaman; Naaman too was in danger of becoming a social reject by reason of his having contracted leprosy, but he came from a foreign land to Israel and was cured by washing (ebaptisato [2 Kings 5:14]) in the River Jordan (see Brodie 1986). The parallel is a faint one and does not add significantly to our understanding of the story.

8:39

The motif of a person being snatched away by the Spirit is found in 1 Kings 18:12; 2 Kings 2:16; Ezek. 3:14.

Acts 9

9:1–30

The account of Saul's conversion shows rather less contact with the OT than might have been expected. The story, relating a combination of a conversion and a call to missionary service, occurs three times in Acts, and in this version the element of conversion is predominant. Consequently, the understanding of the incident in the light of OT calls to a prophetic vocation (cf. Gal. 1:15 in the light of Isa. 49:1; Jer. 1:5) is muted here. There are some resemblances to the story of the attempt by Heliodorus to rob the temple treasury and his vision of a heavenly rider that caused him to fall unconscious to the ground; the high priest prayed for him to be restored and urged him to report the majestic power of God to all people (2 Macc. 3); however, as Barrett (1994–1998: 441) notes, these contacts, though real, are "relatively superficial."

9:2

The use of the term "way" for the Christian movement and the kind of life in accordance with God's will that was associated with it (19:9, 23; 22:4; 24:14, 22) has parallels in the language of the Qumran sect (e.g., 1QS IX:17, 19; X:21; XI:13; CD-A I:13; II:6). Behind it lie Old Testament references to the "way of the Lord." This phrase is perhaps best known from its occurrence in Isa. 40:3–4, but there the reference is to a way for the Lord to travel, not to the way in which his people must walk. Other passages speak of the way or ways of the Lord as the appointed way of life for his people (2 Sam. 22:22; Ps. 18:21; 138:5; Prov. 10:29; Jer. 5:4–5; Hos. 14:9. There are also frequent references to the Lord's way using the appropriate pronoun [my, your, his]; in Ezek. 18:25, 29; 33:17, 20 the reference is to the way that the Lord behaves). There are also broader references to the "way" that leads to life (Ps. 16:11, cited in Acts 2:28). See further Pao 2000, 59–68.

9:3–4

The appearance of Jesus to Saul is described in the same manner as theophanies in the OT. The shining light is a familiar feature in the OT and elsewhere (Exod. 19:16; 2 Sam. 22:13–15; Ezek. 1:13–14; Dan. 10:6), as is a heavenly voice (Exod. 3:1–6; Isa. 6:8). Falling to the ground is the appropriate human reaction to such manifestations (Ezek. 1:28; Dan. 8:17). No specific OT narratives are in the narrator's mind, unless the echoes of Exod. 3:1–6 can be taken to suggest that the story has been shaped in the light of the call of Moses (so Wall 2002: 151n366); rather, the incident that he is recording fits with an ongoing pattern. The difference here is that the appearance of Jesus is described in language that elsewhere describes a revelation of God.

For the use of the personal name of the one addressed by God, see Gen. 46:2; Exod. 3:4 (in each case the name is repeated, as here; contrast 1 Sam. 3:6; 1 Kings 19:9, 13).

9:7

The motif of the bystanders hearing the voice in a theophany but not seeing anything is found in Deut. 4:12; Dan. 10:7 (cf. Wis. 18:1).

9:9

Blindness is a judgment on God's enemies in 2 Kings 6:18; Acts 13:11 (see Denova 1997: 180), but it is unlikely that it is understood as such here (see Barrett 1994–1998: 452).

9:15

The phrase rendered "chosen instrument" (TNIV) or the like is literally "vessel of choice" (*skeuos eklogēs*) and is a Hebraism, reflecting the use of *kĕlî* (a utensil of any kind, such as a pot, tool, or weapon); the metaphorical use of human beings as instruments or tools that God can use is found in, for example, Jer. 22:28, but the usage

tends to be negative, of useless or broken clay pots, rather than positive, as here (cf. Jer. 18:1–10). The metaphor carries the nuance of the superiority of God over the instruments that he creates to carry out his purposes (see *TDNT* 7:358–67). The use of a defining genitive is also Hebraic, but there is no parallel to the wording here (*eklogē* is not used in the LXX except in *Pss. Sol.* 9:4; 18:5).

9:17

The verb "appear" (middle/passive of *horaō*) is used in the account of the appearance of God to Moses (Exod. 3:2, 16), but the verb is used so frequently of such events that a deliberate echo is improbable (see Clark 2001: 114, 205–8).

9:25

Although NA[27] gives a marginal reference to the letting down of the spies from a window in the city wall in Jericho (Josh. 2:15), an echo of this passage is most unlikely.

9:31–43

9:31

"The fear of the LORD" is a characteristic OT expression for the Jewish religion (e.g., Job 28:28; Ps. 111:10; Prov. 1:7; cf. Rom. 3:18), but this is the only instance in the NT describing the practice of the Christian religion. By this usage Luke indicates that the Christian religion is in continuity with OT religion; however, it may well be that the ambiguous "Lord" here refers to Jesus (cf. Acts 10:35).

9:32–43

The story of Peter's cure, or rather resuscitation, of Tabitha contains one or two similarities to the stories of Elijah and Elisha (1 Kings 17:17–24; 2 Kings 4:18–37); the same phenomenon can be observed in the narration of some of the healings wrought by Jesus (Luke 7:11–17), and it would be difficult to avoid the impression that the typology seen to exist between Elijah/Elisha and Jesus is now extended to cover the followers of Jesus who continue to do mighty works in the same way that he did (there are possible echoes here of the story of the raising of Jairus's daughter). (For an extended treatment of this matter, see Brodie 1987; cf. Pesch 1986: 1:322.) The general pattern of the stories is the same, since they belong to the same category of stories of miraculous healings.

More specifically, Tabitha's body is placed in an upper room (9:37), as in 1 Kings 17:19; 2 Kings 4:10, 21; this may be purely coincidental, since an upper room may have been the usual place for laying a corpse (see Barrett 1994–1998: 483). There is a verbal echo of Num. 22:16 in the phrase "do not delay to come to us" (9:38), but this is hardly significant. Peter's action in praying with no one else present corresponds to that of Elisha (2 Kings 4:33). The opening of the eyes is a sign of life restored (2 Kings 4:35).

Acts 10

The story of the conversion of Cornelius through the agency of Peter, which extends into chapter 11, is particularly significant because it is concerned with the problem of the OT law and its contemporary interpretation in Judaism. The present commentary is on the use of the OT by the NT writers rather than on the developing understanding of the OT in the early church, but the two issues cannot be sharply separated. An extended parallel between this story and that of Jonah is detected by Wall (2002: 160–61): both Peter and Jonah start from Joppa and go to the Gentiles, both protest against their commissions and need fresh revelations from God, and both have successful missions, the legitimacy of which is questioned.

10:2–10:28

10:2

The description of Cornelius as one who fears God, gives alms, and prays reflects the ideal of piety typified in Tob. 1:3; 12:8 and elsewhere. Almsgiving is not mentioned in the OT itself. However, the fear of God is a common OT motif (see commentary on Acts 9:31 above); there are references to fearers of the Lord in Ps. 115:11, 13; 118:4; 135:20. The LXX of 2 Chron. 5:6 inserts a mention of "fearers" (*phoboumenoi*), apparently referring to those distinct from the assembly of Israel itself who were present at the dedication of Solomon's temple (see *TDNT* 9:207).

10:3

Visions, dreams, and angelic messengers are media of divine revelation in the OT, and the reaction to an angelic visitor is normally fear. For the heavenly messenger addressing the person by name, see Gen. 31:11; 46:2. None of this is strictly use of the OT, but rather is part of the telling of a story that belongs in the same milieu.

10:4

The metaphor of prayers "going up" to God is a natural one, taken from the way in which the smoke of burning sacrifices ascended heavenwards. Prayer is compared with sacrifice in Ps. 141:2. "As a memorial offering before God" (*eis mnēmosynon emprosthen tou theou*) may reflect language used of sacrifices: part of the grain offering was designated "the memorial" and was burned on the altar (Lev. 2:2, 9, 16). However, a direct reference to Leviticus is unlikely here; the use of "memorial" in relation to God is found more broadly, and it is more likely that a common understanding of other religious acts functioning like sacrifice is present (cf. Sir. 50:15; Tob. 12:12; *1 En.* 99:3).

10:9

The flat roofs of houses and other buildings could be used as sites for worship and prayer (2 Kings 23:12; Jer. 19:13; Zeph. 1:5; cf. Tob. 3:10–17). Prayer at the sixth hour (noon) may imply adherence to the OT ideal of praying three times daily (Ps. 55:17; Dan. 6:10).

10:10

For the opening of heaven, see commentary on Acts 7:56 above.

10:12

The list of animals contains the three categories listed in Gen. 6:20; the list in Gen. 1:24 has a threefold division of land creatures, not including birds, and the list in Gen. 9:2 also includes fish. Thus the list here is meant to be inclusive of all kinds of creatures, with the implication that it was not confined to those animals that Jews were permitted to eat (*contra* Marshall 1980: 185, there may have been a mixture of clean and unclean animals).

10:13

Peter was commanded (still in the dream) to kill an animal and eat it; as in the similar phrase in Deut. 12:15, the verb *thyō* means "slaughter" rather than "sacrifice."

10:14

Peter's "Certainly not [*mēdamōs*], Lord!" is paralleled in Ezek. 21:5 LXX (which differs from 20:49 MT), but a closer parallel is in Ezek. 4:14, where Ezekiel was told to eat defiled food as a sign to the people of what would happen during the siege of Jerusalem, and he refused to do so. The parallel illustrates the strength of Jewish sentiment against doing what God had formerly forbidden, although the circumstances are quite different. In Ezekiel's case the food had been in contact with defilement, but here the point is that the animals themselves were defiled and unclean because God had declared that they must not be eaten. In Lev. 11 (cf. Deut. 14:3–20) there is a full list of animals deemed to be "unclean" (*akathartos*) and "abominable" (*bdelygma*); the term *koinos* ("impure"), also used here by Peter alongside *akathartos*, does not figure in the LXX vocabulary in this connection (except in 1 Macc. 1:47, 62; 4 Macc. 7:6 [*koinoō*]). On possible septuagintalisms in these verses, see Wilcox 1965: 72–73.

10:15

The heavenly voice tells Peter not to consider impure what God has cleansed. For *katharizō* in this sense of declaring something to be clean, see Lev. 13:13, where a priest declares a leper to be free of the disease.

With these words, says Hübner (1990–1995: 3:132), God himself annuls a considerable part of the Mosaic legislation, for which people were prepared to die (1–4 Macc.; cf. Dan. 1). Here, then, would appear to be a remarkable use of the OT. However, the matter is not quite so clear. In what follows Peter says that he has learned not to call any human being unclean (10:28), and this lesson is directly connected with the vision in 10:19–20. Consequently, there would appear to be an interpretation of the vision in which the application is to people rather than to foods. This application might be made by different routes. One is to argue allegorically from unclean foods to unclean people. Another is to argue that the implication of declaring foods clean is that the persons who might be held to defile them (cf. Mark 7, where the foods are unclean because they have been handled by unclean people) are also to be regarded as clean. Again, it could be that the vision is concerned purely with foods, and that the effect is to encourage Peter to go

to a Gentile home and eat whatever is set before him; against this is the unlikelihood that a person sensitive to Jewish susceptibilities, as Cornelius may very probably have been, would offer inappropriate food to Peter. The opposite position is taken by those who affirm that the vision is to be applied only to people and that the Jewish food laws were not rendered invalid by it (Jervell 1998: 306). (We should also ask whether there was a difference in principle between the animals that were declared unclean in the OT and the foods that were declared unclean in Pharisaic legislation by reason of having been handled by Gentiles. I suspect that the line between the two categories was hard to draw.) The difficulty in interpretation has led a number of commentators to argue for various forms of the hypothesis that the narrative is composite and that originally the vision and the visit to Cornelius were unconnected; even if that were the case, however, we would still have to ask how Luke saw the relationship between them. It is clear that the close link made in 10:19 requires that the effect of the vision is to enable Peter to visit Cornelius "making no distinctions" (this is the meaning of *mēden diakrinanta* in 11:12 and *outhen diekrinen* in 15:9, but the verb here is middle [*mēden diakrinomenos*] rather than active and is generally translated "without hesitation").

No solution is entirely free from difficulty. Certainly, as the vision stands, the effect is to state that God has cleansed certain foods and that Peter must no longer regard them as unclean. It seems to me, then, that Hübner's point stands (similarly, Pesch 1986: 1:339). Consequently, here we do have a case where implicitly a particular passage of Scripture is declared to be no longer authoritative as legislation; it had a role under the old covenant, but it no longer has this role under the new covenant.

10:28

The statement that it was "unlawful" for a Jew to associate with somebody of another race has no basis in the OT. It represents an interpretation of the law, the most likely one being that since contact with Gentiles conveyed uncleanness, from which a person required purification through the appropriate ritual, it was deemed right to avoid such contacts as far as possible (cf. *Jub.* 22:16).

10:34–43

Peter's speech to the household of Cornelius contains no formal citations of Scripture but does include significant wording that is dependent on the LXX. If the audience is regarded as non-Jewish and therefore likely to be ignorant of Scripture, this abstention might be regarded as fitting (cf. the speeches in chaps. 14; 17; see Rese 1969: 117); however, Barrett (1988: 240) rightly points out that Cornelius, as a God-fearing man, would have known the Scriptures well. It is more likely that on this occasion 10:43 summarizes what was said at greater length. Stanton (1974: 77) has shown that the account of Jesus' ministry here is based on scriptural phrases rather than being a Lukan summary of Luke's Gospel (as is sometimes argued).

10:34

Peter's opening words, *ep' alētheias katalambanomai hoti*, mean something like "In truth I realize that…" (cf. NRSV), but perhaps the force is as in the TNIV: "I now realize how true it is that…." The phrase closely resembles *ep' alētheias oida hoti* (Dan. 2:8), where the force is "I know for sure that…." Possibly there is an unconscious reminiscence of LXX diction.

The word *prosōpolēmptēs* ("respecter of persons") is not found in the LXX; rather, it is a formation based on the LXX expression *prosōpon lambanein*, which is an attempt to translate the Hebrew *nāśā' pānîm*, "lift the face [of someone]"— that is, to show someone favor, partiality. This is not how God behaves (Deut. 10:17: *ou thaumazei prosōpon*; cf. 2 Chron. 19:7; Wis. 6:7; Sir. 35:16 [35:13 LXX]), and he condemns those who do (Lev. 19:15; Deut. 28:50; Ps. 82:2). The word is found for the first time in the NT, and it is a good example of vocabulary formation based on the LXX (Jobes and Silva 2000: 108); it may have been current in Hellenistic Jewish Greek, but there is no direct evidence of this (see *TDNT* 6:779–80).

10:35

"Fear of God" is the basic attitude required in OT religion (cf. 9:31; Deut. 10:12; see Clements 1990). "Working righteousness" (*ergazomenos dikaiosynēn*) is paralleled in Ps. 15:2 (14:2 LXX), but references to "working iniquity" are much more common in Psalms.

10:36

God "sent [*apesteilen*] the word" (cf. 13:26, using *exapostellō*) again reflects OT phraseology (Ps. 107:20 [106:20 LXX]; 147:15, 18 [147:4, 7 LXX]). The OT passages are concerned with the powerful effects of God's commands, which achieve what he intends. That nuance may be somewhat muted here. "Proclaiming peace" (*euangelizomenos eirēnēn*) echoes Isa. 52:7 (*euangelizomenou akoēn eirēnēs*); Nah. 2:1 (1:15 LXX) (*euangelizomenou kai apangelontos eirēnēn*). Bock (1987: 233) is skeptical of a definite allusion and prefers to see the use of "scriptural language," as in Eph. 2:17; 6:15. However, a background in the proclamation of the Isaianic new exodus ties in with the use of this motif elsewhere in Acts. The same Isaianic passage is cited and linked to Isa. 61:2–3 in 11Q13 II, 15–25. There are a number of echoes of Luke 4:16–30, where Isa. 61:1–3 is being used (Turner 1996: 262; Pao 2000: 75n34). In 10:38 Peter alludes to Isa. 61:1b, but without using the hook word *euangelizomai*, which occurs in Isa. 61:1a and provides the link to Isa. 52:7 (Dupont 1979: 152).

Stanton (1974: 70–81) proposed that this speech originally had a citation of Ps. 107:20 (106:20 LXX) at this point and that it has been largely lost, leaving the present difficult construction. He notes that language from the psalm is used in 10:38 and also in Paul's speech in 13:26. Following Dupont (1979: 151–52), Stanton claimed that Luke tends to abbreviate his scriptural quotations and may have done so here (see commentary on Acts 2:36 above). The echo from Isa. 52:7 is used to explain the "word" in the psalm. Finally, Stanton suggested that Ps. 107:20 may have been a *testimonium* used to explain the significance of the ministry of Jesus (for the influence of the psalm here, see also Pesch 1986: 1:342–43). Bock (1987: 232) holds that all the echoes detected by Stanton are reflections of common themes in early Christian tradition, and that recourse to the psalm to explain their presence is superfluous. However, it is precisely the *combination* of themes that makes a reference to the psalm credible.

Perhaps the crucial statement in the verse (and the speech) is the statement of universal sovereignty and hence of universal ability to save, "he is Lord of all [people]." The concept of Yahweh as the creator of the heavens and the earth implies his sovereignty over all people (1 Chron. 29:12; Ps. 103:19), but there does not seem to be a precise equivalent to the phrase used here, except for a phrase such as "Lord of all the earth" (Ps. 97:5 [96:5 LXX]; cf. Ps. 113:4 [112:4 LXX]).

10:38

The description of Jesus as one whom God "anointed" reflects Luke 4:18, which in turn is based on Isa. 61:1. There the speaker declares that he has been anointed—that is, authorized and empowered—by God to proclaim good news. In its original context the speaker is most naturally understood to be the prophet himself, who is authorized by God to announce his message. But in so doing, he takes up the description of the Servant, on whom God's Spirit rests in Isa. 42:1 (cf. 49:1–6; 50:4–9). It was natural, therefore, for readers to combine these passages and to see in them the job description of the Lord's Servant, who would bring salvation, a figure combining traits of both prophet and king; we see this actually taking place in 11Q13 II, 15–25. The combination of anointing and the reception of the Holy Spirit is also found in the cases of Saul and David (1 Sam. 10:1, 6; 16:13), but the Isaianic background is much more probable here.

The linking of healing (*iaomai*) with "sending his word" is found in Ps. 107:20 (106:20 LXX), and the motif of God as a healer recurs in Psalms. Yet the effect here is to imply not that Jesus is divine, but rather that he is the agent of God, for God is with him (as in Isa. 58:11, where the Lord is with his faithful and obedient people, but also as in Gen. 39:21, echoed in Acts 7:9; cf. also Luke 1:28). This may be scriptural phraseology rather than a specific allusion (Bock 1987: 233–34).

10:39

The phrase "hanging on a tree" is repeated from 5:30 (cf. Deut. 21:22–23).

10:40

The frequent dating of the resurrection "on the third day" or "after three days" (e.g., Luke 9:22) rests on history, but the phraseology is similar to that in Hos. 6:2, where the repentant people of Israel who have been smitten by the Lord claim, "After two days he will heal us; on the third day we

shall rise, and we shall live before him." The language in Hosea probably is used metaphorically to indicate a very short time; if early Christians noted the phrase there (cf. how Matt. 2:15 cites Hos. 11:1 christologically), they may have been struck by the coincidence. (It hardly needs saying that suggestions that the ascription of the resurrection of Jesus to the third day arose out of use of this text are singularly unpersuasive, not least because the prophecy is about repentant Israelites, not about a specific individual.)

10:43

On "all the prophets," see commentary on Acts 3:17–18, 24 above. However, prophetic testimonies to the specific topic stated here are hard to find. The NA[27] margin suggests a reference to Isa. 33:24, speaking of future forgiveness, which is perhaps too general to apply here unless it was assumed that any references to the Lord as king and savior (Isa. 33:22) would be fulfilled in Christ (cf. also Isa. 55:7). Forgiveness is associated with the new covenant in Jer. 31:34.

10:45

The use of "poured out" makes the link not only with 2:17–18, 33, but also with the underlying Joel 2:28–29.

10:46

"Extolling [*megalynontōn*] God" uses language from the OT (e.g., Ps. 70:4 [69:5 LXX]) and so brings Cornelius and his friends into the community of the people of God.

Acts 11

11:1–18

The narrative here largely summarizes parts of the story in Acts 10 (on which, see commentary above).

11:3

"Uncircumcised" is literally "having foreskin," an idiom found in Gen. 34:14.

11:6

The list here has four categories of creatures, including wild animals (*thēria*), as in Gen. 1:24. See commentary on Acts 10:12 above.

11:8

The language here about nothing inappropriate entering Peter's mouth is close to Ezek. 4:14 ("has entered my mouth"). See commentary on Acts 10:14 above.

11:18

For God giving repentance, see Wis. 12:19.

11:19–30

11:21

The language here about "the hand of the Lord" (cf. Luke 1:66) is reminiscent of 1 Chron. 4:10; cf. Exod. 9:3; 2 Sam. 3:12 LXX. See commentary on Acts 4:28 above.

11:22

"Reached the ears" (*ēkousthē . . . eis ta ōta*) is curious Greek usage and is a septuagintalism (Isa. 5:9; cf. Gen. 20:8).

11:23

"With all their hearts" (TNIV) is literally "with purpose of heart" (*tē prothesei tēs kardias*), which has a parallel in Symmachus's text of Ps. 9:38 (10:17 ET); *prothesis* occurs also in 2 Macc. 3:8; 3 Macc. 1:22; the evidence is inadequate to suggest usage of the OT rather than Hellenistic Jewish vocabulary.

Acts 12

12:3

The stark Hebraism (*prostithēmi* + infinitive) seen in the phrase "proceeded to arrest" is common in the LXX (e.g., Gen. 4:2); elsewhere in the NT it is found only in Luke 19:11; 20:11–12. This is a clear example of adopting the style of the LXX. More broadly, Pao finds an evocation of Exodus traditions here with Pharaoh, the oppressor of God's people at the time of the Passover, who is destroyed by God (cf. Exod. 14–15; the implication is that Pharaoh perished along with his army [see Garrett 1990: 670–77; Pao 2000: 199–201, referring to the work of O. W. Allen]).

12:4

The faint verbal similarity to Jdt. 4:9 (prayer *en ekteneia megalē*) is surely coincidental. Similarly, there does not appear to be any echo in 12:7 of

the person (an angel in the MT, but not in the LXX) touching the sleeping Elijah in 1 Kings 19:5. Likewise, although there are parallels between 12:11 and the way in which God sent his angel and rescued the three young men from the furnace (Dan. 3:25) and later Daniel from the lions (Dan. 6:23 Θ [6:22 ET]), these are hardly intentional.

12:11

References to rescue are common in the OT, but the wording here is particularly close to Exod. 18:4, 10 LXX, where Moses' deliverance from Pharaoh is described (Garrett 1990: 675).

12:20

The supplying of foodstuffs from Judah to Tyre was long-standing and is mentioned in 1 Kings 5:9–12; Ezek. 27:17; however, there is no indication of any allusion to these texts here.

12:22

In Ezek. 28:2, 6, 9 the king of Tyre is accused of claiming to be a god. Here, however, the claim is made of the king of Judah, and the actual statement is made by the people, although he tacitly accepted it. A typology between the king of Tyre as the oppressor of Israel (Ezek. 26:2), bedizened in splendor on his throne (Ezek. 28:2, 13) and destroyed by God, and Herod is detected by Strom (1986).

12:23

For God striking down people, see 2 Kings 19:35 (cf. Sir. 48:21; 1 Macc. 7:41). The punishment of being eaten by worms appears in Isa. 51:8; Jdt. 16:17; 2 Macc. 9:9, and also in extrabiblical literature.

12:24

The LXX phrase "grew and multiplied" (*ēuxanen kai eplēthyneto*) originally applied to the people of Israel but now applies to the word of God, the preaching of which expands the number of believers (cf. 19:20). See commentary on Acts 6:7 above.

Acts 13

13:1–3

Various features of the narrative show that the early church lives in a context broadly shaped by

OT piety: the activity of prophets, the description of what went on in the congregational meeting as "service" (*leitourgeō* is used frequently in the LXX for the activity of the priests), and fasting as a religious practice. The laying on of hands as authorization for religious duties may echo Num. 8:11–12, where the motif of separation (*aphorizō*) for the work (*ergon*) of the Lord is also present (Daube 1956: 239–41).

13:10

"Full of deceit" is a current expression found in Jer. 5:27 LXX; Sir. 1:30; 19:26. The metaphor of perverting paths is found in Prov. 10:9, and the word "straight" (*euthys*) is used of God's paths in Hos. 14:9 (14:10 LXX). All of these are examples of septuagintal speech rather than conscious reminiscence (Barrett 1994–1998: 617). Pao (2000: 201–2) notes the contrast to Isa. 40:3 (cf. Luke 3:4).

13:11

For "the hand of the LORD" having negative effects, see Judg. 2:15; 1 Sam. 7:13; 12:15; Job 19:21 (see commentary on Acts 4:28 above). Pesch (1986: 2:25) cites Ezek. 13:9 as the most apt parallel. "Not seeing the sun" is language also found in Ps. 58:8. Deuteronomy 28:28–29 (Jervell 1998: 347n434) is less close (see commentary on Acts 22:11 below).

13:15

The reading of the law and the prophets corresponds with known synagogue practice. On the assumption that the sermon following was based on them (see introduction above), attempts have been made to identify the passages read on this occasion. Bowker (1967–1968: 101–4) suggests Deut. 4:25–46 and 2 Sam. 7:6–16, with Paul then using 1 Sam. 13:14 as a bridge between the readings; 13:17–21 functions as an introduction to the sermon in 13:22–41. Barrett (1994–1998: 624 [cf. 1988: 241–42]) recognizes the conjectural character of Bowker's reconstruction but does not dismiss it as totally unfounded. Pesch (1986: 2:32) takes the proposal seriously and on the basis of it argues that here Luke is editing source material rather than composing freely.

Admittedly, it is hard to see how 1 Sam. 13:14 joins together the alleged two readings or forms the center point of the sermon. Bowker himself admits that the link with Deut. 4 is unsure and can be only "a reasonable guess." For the identification of the haftarah, Bowker appeals to the work of Doeve (1954: 168–76), who pointed out several coincidences in expression between 13:17–36 and 2 Sam. 7:6–16, and especially notes the parallelism between 1 Sam. 13:14 and 2 Sam. 7:8. Dumais (1976: 67–114) holds that the sermon is based only on 2 Sam. 7 and not also on a seder. For a chart of the parallelism, see Strauss 1995: 154–55; this chart demonstrates the remarkable parallels in thought and structure to 2 Sam. 7 throughout the passage, but there is scarcely any direct use of its language.

Part of the problem is constituted by Bowker's observation that in rabbinic sermons the preacher aimed to allude to the set readings without actually quoting them. If so, it would seem that almost any tenuous coincidence in thought or expression could be used as a basis for assuming an underlying text. In favor of Bowker's proposal it can be said that if this was a normal synagogue service, there would have been readings from Scripture, and the preacher may well have had them in mind as he spoke; on that assumption, it could be argued that Bowker's identification of the passages is not altogether implausible and is superior to any other suggestions that have been offered (for which, see Bowker 1967–1968: 103n1).

For detailed study of the OT citations in 13:32–37, see Lövestam 1961.

A sermon based on Scripture is appropriately described as a message of "encouragement" (*paraklēsis*); cf. 1 Macc. 12:9; 2 Macc. 15:9 (Pesch 1986: 2:33).

13:17

Paul begins with God and his choice of Israel; *eklegomai* is used often from Deut. 4:37 onward. "Made great" (*hypsoō*; cf. Isa. 1:2) refers to the increase in population and in power while the Israelites were in Egypt; for the use of *paroikia* for the sojourn in Egypt, see Wis. 19:10. The TNIV's "with mighty power" conceals "with an uplifted arm," a metaphor found in this connection in Exod. 6:1, 6; 32:11; Ps. 136:12. "Brought them out" (*exagō*) is the appropriate verb used frequently (Deut. 4:37; 2 Sam. 7:6, however, has *anagō*).

13:18

The period of forty years was firmly embedded in tradition (Exod. 16:35; Num. 14:33–34; Ps. 95:10). The following verb is textually uncertain. *Tropophoreō*, "to put up with someone, endure someone's conduct" (NRSV text; TNIV text), is one Greek letter different from *trophophoreō*, "to care for [like a nurse with a child]" and has the better attestation. Both verbs are also found as variants in the text being alluded to, Deut. 1:31, which describes how the Lord "carried you, as a man carries his son"; the Hebrew verb *nāśāʾ* could be translated either way, but the thought of caring fits the context better. There is some evidence that the former reading in Acts could be a spelling variant for the latter. Barrett (1994–1998: 632) cautiously concludes that "care for" is contextually preferable in Acts, and I am inclined to agree. Gordon (1974) makes reference to targumic material that refers to God's care for Israel in the wilderness.

13:19

The expulsion of seven nations rests on Deut. 7:1, but "gave for a possession in the land of Canaan" derives from Josh. 14:1.

13:20

"About 450 years" is a puzzling figure not found in the OT and appears to be a deduction. The problem is exacerbated by some uncertainty as to what the period is meant to refer to. The dative form suggests the point of time at which the division of land was made, but it could refer to a period of time (see BDF §201), and the period may be a combination of four hundred years in Egypt, forty in the wilderness, and ten for the conquest of the land (Josh. 1–13). There is probably no connection with the figure in 1 Kings 6:1. "Gave" is a Semitism for "appointed" (cf. Exod. 31:6 MT/LXX), but Judg. 2:16 has "raised up" (*egeirō*) and 2 Sam. 7:11 has "appointed" (*tassō*). Samuel is identified as a prophet (1 Sam. 3:20) and ranked as the first of the prophets (Acts 3:24).

13:21

Paul summarizes the story in 1 Sam. 8–10. The identity of name with Saul of Tarsus, also a Benjaminite (Rom. 11:1; Phil. 3:5, but not mentioned in Acts), is purely coincidental and nothing is made of it. The "forty years" of his reign corresponds with Josephus, *Ant.* 6.378 (but *Ant.* 10.143 gives twenty years); the MT of 1 Sam. 13:1, which gives a reign of only two years, is corrupt, and the whole verse is lacking in the LXX.

13:22

The removal of Saul is described in 1 Sam. 15:23, 26; 16:1 as God's rejection of him and was followed by the anointing of David, but in fact Saul continued as king until his death, although this is not apparent from the way in which Acts summarizes a complicated story. In contrast to Saul, David is given a divine credential. The citation draws on a combination of passages (the parallel in 2 Sam. 7:8 is not especially close). In Ps. 89:20 (88:21 LXX) we read "I found David [*heuron Dauid*] my servant, with holy oil I anointed him." The psalm celebrates at length the divine covenant with David and his descendants and calls on God to honor it after his wrath has broken out against the dynasty and the land. It recounts how the dynasty was established. "Son of Jesse" is attached to David's name in 1 Chron. 10:14; 29:26; Ps. 72:20. "A man after my heart" is a lightly altered citation from God's words to Saul in 1 Sam. 13:14, where God announces that after Saul's disobedience at Gilgal he will "seek out" (the preliminary to "finding"?) "a man after his heart" (*anthrōpon kata tēn kardian autou*). For the combination of 1 Sam. 13:14 and Ps. 89:20, see *1 Clem.* 18:1. The words "who will do all my will [lit., 'wills']" actually agree with the description of Cyrus as the restorer of Jerusalem in Isa. 44:28 (*panta ta thelēmata mou poiēsei*). However, the Targum of 1 Sam. 13:14 paraphrases "a man after my heart" with "a man doing his will(s)," and knowledge of the targumic tradition may have exercised an influence here (Wilcox 1965: 21–24; Hanson 1983: 82; cf. Bock 1987: 243). Ellis (1978: 199) finds an allusion to Jer. 30:9 (37:9 LXX), but nothing in the context supports this supposition.

Various points lead Albl (1999: 195–98) to argue that a *testimonia* collection has been used here. The quotation is a complex one, and the historical details in 13:16–22 (especially the chronology in 13:20) do not seem to have any relevance for Luke's purpose. The use of the same material in *1 Clem.* 18:1, apparently independently of Acts, suggests the existence of a tradition (see Bock 1987: 243) in which there was a review of Israel's history under divine guidance leading up to the selection of David; this material was originally Jewish and was taken over by Christians who wanted to emphasize the superiority of Jesus to David. This explanation accounts for the material in Acts quite well.

The commendation of David may be meant to set up a typology with David's descendant, Christ, and to establish the credentials of the latter in view of his pedigree. However, it seems unlikely that Paul is saying, "Just as God replaced Saul by a king who was after his own heart, so also he has replaced David by a king who is even more after his own heart," which would seem to be the point if Bowker's analysis of the sermon as a homily on 1 Sam. 13:14 is correct.

This ends the brief account of Israel's history under the care and initiative of God, which culminates in the appointment of his agents as their rulers.

13:23

So God has brought to Israel a savior from the seed of David in accordance with his promise. The promise probably refers to 2 Sam. 7:12 (cf. 22:51; Ps. 89:29, 36–37; 132:11), now understood to include not merely the immediate continuation of the royal line through Solomon and later kings, but also the renewal of the line in the raising up of the Messiah. Although God is frequently designated as "Savior" in the OT, the Messiah is not; saving is a function of the Servant (Isa. 49:6, cited in 13:47), and it may be relevant that the judges were also so described (Judg. 3:9, 15).

13:24

The unusual phrase, *pro prosōpou tēs eisodou autou* (lit., "before the face of his coming"), is probably due to a Hebraism (*lipnê*), but it may be specifically an echo of Mal. 3:1–2, where *pro prosōpou mou* and *hēmeran eisodou autou* occur with reference to the eschatological messenger who prepares the way for the Lord (Stanton 1974: 83).

13:26

For the use of Ps. 107:20 (106:20 LXX) here as the source for "salvation . . . sent," see commentary on Acts 10:36 above (see Stanton 1974: 83).

13:27

The Jews and their rulers ignored the prophets, whom they heard read weekly in the synagogue,

and fulfilled (*plēroō*; cf. *teleō* [13:29]) their prophecies by condemning Jesus; we may surmise that texts such as Isa. 53:3 and Ps. 118:22 are in mind (Doble [2002b: 36–41] finds a "suppressed allusion" to Ps. 118:17 in 13:41). For Luke, Scripture was "fulfilled" (1:16; Luke 18:31; 22:37) by the rejection and execution of Jesus. Presumably, these references to the fulfillment of Scripture are intended to show how these actions of the Jews in rejecting Jesus were compatible with him being the Messiah.

13:29

This is another general reference, but this time not so much to "all the prophets" as to "all that had been prophesied with reference to Jesus," apparently up to the moment of his death (cf. Luke 22:37).

13:31

Bowker (1967–1968: 102) notes that "witnesses" also occurs in Deut. 4:26, but there it refers to heaven and earth functioning in a rather different manner.

13:32–33

The "promise" (i.e., the one in 13:23) was made to the fathers (Bowker finds an echo of Deut. 4:37–38) but has been fulfilled for their descendants. The raising up of Jesus is seen as fulfillment of Ps. 2:7.

This is the only instance in the NT where the precise location of an OT citation is given. Unfortunately, there is some textual uncertainty, as the vast majority of witnesses have "in the second psalm," but Codex Bezae (D) and some fathers have "in the first psalm," while the earliest witness, $\mathfrak{P}^{45}$, apparently has "in the psalms." The reading of $\mathfrak{P}^{45}$ is unlikely to be original, since it does not explain why virtually all scribes thought it necessary here (and here only) to be more specific. There is some evidence that in rabbinic and patristic sources the first two psalms were combined as one. The problem, then, is whether Luke himself knew the tradition found in the rabbinic sources or whether the substitution was made by a learned scribe. The latter possibility is the more probable (Bruce 1990: 309; Metzger 1994: 363–65).

The LXX is cited exactly: *huios mou ei sy; egō sēmeron gegennēka se*. In its original context the psalmist records a saying addressed to him by

God that serves to legitimate him as king, using the metaphor of a father assuring his son that he really is his father and that he will care for him. However, the interpretation is not easy. "Beget" strictly refers to the act of procreation, and therefore "today" addressed to the child is inappropriate; we should take it to mean something like "[I declare to you] today [that] I begat you." Such an oracle could be associated with an enthronement or a renewal of the divine promise to a monarch whose position is threatened (as is the case in the psalm). The psalm is seen as messianic in *Pss. Sol.* 17:26 (though this particular verse is not cited) and was cited previously in Acts 4:25–26 (cf. Luke 3:22; Heb. 1:5; 5:5). The thought is paralleled in 2 Sam. 7:14.

A number of scholars have argued that the text was originally applied to the resurrection of Jesus as the act in which God "begat" him in the sense that he bestowed new life on him and enthroned him and thereby gave him the status of Son (cf. the association of sonship with the resurrection in Rom. 1:3–4; Heb. 1:3–5; see Dupont 1979: 115–17). There is also a probable allusion to the text in the heavenly saying addressed to Jesus at his baptism (Luke 3:22 [cf. the variant reading in Codex Bezae and the Old Latin witnesses, which replicate Ps. 2:7 LXX exactly]), which has also suggested to some scholars that God "begat" or perhaps "adopted" Jesus at that point. Relevant to this problem is the question of how "raised" (*anastēsas*) is to be understood. In 13:34 the same verb is used unequivocally of the resurrection, but here in 13:33 the verb could also be translated "raised up" (TNIV), just as the synonym *egeirō* is used of making David king in 13:22 (cf. Luke 1:69; Acts 3:22).

Since, however, Paul has already referred to the resurrection in 13:30, many scholars think that this is in mind here (see Jervell 1998: 359; Anderson 2001: 245–47). Bock (1987: 244–45) maintains that the three elements in 13:32–33—the promise to the fathers, the fulfillment for their children, and the raising of Jesus—correspond to the three citations that follow: the promise to David in Ps. 2, the promise to "you" in Isa. 55:3, and the incorruptibility of the Holy One in Ps. 16; hence the "raising" of Jesus is his resurrection.

But whereas some of the defenders of this view tend to argue that it was through applying this verse to the risen Jesus that the early church came to believe that at the resurrection he gained the status of the Son of God (Schweizer 1968), it is much more likely that it was because he was already understood by early Christians to be the Son of God that they recognized a reference to him in this psalm and saw in the begetting a metaphor of God raising him from the dead.

Nevertheless, there are difficulties with this interpretation. Begetting is not an obvious metaphor for resurrection (against the attempt by Lövestam [1961: 37–49] to find a connection, see Bock 1987: 246–48), and it is also odd to beget somebody who is already God's son. We should note that 13:23–31 tells the story of Jesus, and then a fresh start is made with the good news that results from it in 13:32. Paul is talking about how God "raised up" Jesus (Rese 1969: 81–86; Barrett 1994–1998: 645–47). The resulting break allows Paul to go back to the beginning of the story in 13:32, and therefore 13:30 does not control the thought here. It is essential to interpret the verse in the context of Luke-Acts as a whole (a strategy demanded by Acts 1:1), in which case the reference may be to the raising up of Jesus (cf. Luke 1:69; see Bruce 1990: 309; *contra* Marshall 1980: 226–27) as Messiah at his birth, where the coming of the Spirit on Mary is tantamount to a divine begetting. See further the discussion by Strauss (1995: 162–66), who argues that the reference is to the whole Jesus event.

The significance of the citation is, accordingly, that a messianic psalm is applied to Jesus, who is given status as the Son of God. The promise made in the psalm is fulfilled in Jesus. Again we may have an example of *gezerah shavah* (cf. 2:34), here based on the expression "my son," which links this citation to 2 Sam. 7:6–16, alluded to earlier in the speech (13:23), although the key phrase is not actually cited there (Longenecker 1999: 82, following Doeve 1954: 172; Lövestam 1961: 6–15).

13:34

The thought then moves (note the *de* making a slight contrast) to the raising of Jesus from the dead, with the emphasis on the fact that Jesus will never return to the corrupting realm of the grave. The reference to corruption shows that Ps. 16:10 is already determining the direction of the discourse. The point at issue seems to be the eternal dominion of the Messiah, which qualifies him to continue in his function as Savior for all time. There is no significant problem with the second citation, but the interpretation of the first is problematic. The words "he has spoken thus" function as the introductory formula. The citation comes from Isa. 55:3 LXX: "And I shall make with you an eternal covenant, the sure, holy things of David" (*kai diathēsomai hymin diathēkēn aiōnion, ta hosia Dauid ta pista*). The verse is echoed in references to an eternal covenant in 1QS IV, 22; V, 5–6; 1Q28b I, 2–3; II, 25, evidently the covenant that God has made with the sect (Steyn 1995: 177). Dupont (1979: 145–46) raises the question of whether the speaker was directed to this verse because the immediate context refers to David as a witness to the nations (Isa. 55:4; cf. Acts 13:47).

For *diathēsomai* Acts substitutes "I shall give" (*dōsō* [probably under the influence of the use of the verb in the next quotation, thus making a link between them]) and omits reference to the covenant (cf. 13:47). Nothing in the argument depends upon the use of the LXX rather than the MT, which has "I shall make an everlasting covenant with you, the sure mercies of David." The text in Isaiah comes in the context of an invitation to the people to receive God's gifts and live. He promises that he will make an eternal covenant with them (it can be assumed that this is conditional on their continuing obedience), which is then defined as his acts of faithful love for David (*ḥasdê dāwid hanne'ĕmānîm*). This seems to indicate that God, having made promises to David, pledged himself to keep them, if not in David's lifetime, in the ongoing future of his people. The thought is present in 2 Sam. 7:15–16, but again the language is not taken from there. The Hebrew word *ḥasdê* (plural of *ḥesed*) means "acts of steadfast love." But what does the LXX mean? The word *hosios* means "holy, pious, devout," and this is its meaning in the citation in 13:35. In Wis. 6:10 the neuter plural may mean "holy things" or perhaps "divine decrees" (LEH 340). Perhaps the latter is the force here in Isa. 55, so that the "eternal covenant" is explained as the "sure divine decree made to David."

How, then, do we take it here? The promise is to "you" plural (*hymin*); therefore it is addressed to the hearers, not to the Messiah as an individual.

The close connection with the next citation, seen in the repetition of "give" and the word play on *hosia/hosios*, indicates that the promise must be associated with the fact that the Messiah will not see corruption. Thus we can conclude that the promise made to David in Ps. 16 has been transferred to "you" (Isa. 55) and therefore must refer not to him, but rather to the Messiah (BDAG 728). It is primarily a promise of resurrection from the dead and therefore of everlasting incorruption, but this is significant for "you" in that this implies the permanent dominion of the Messiah, which is made possible only by his resurrection (see Lövestam 1961: 48–81) and hence his ability to save and to forgive (13:38). So the verse is not saying that God will give to Jesus the promise of resurrection that was made to David—that would require that the "you" be singular, not plural; rather, the faithfulness of God to David will continue to be shown to a later generation by God's raising up of Jesus to be the author of forgiveness and justification (13:38). Thus there is a renewal of the covenantal promises to David through Jesus (Strauss 1995: 166–72).

The hypothesis that the "holy things" are in fact the Holy One (13:35), who rose from the dead and will not see corruption (whereas David did see corruption) (Hanson 1967: 144–45), is "impossible" (Barrett 1994–1998: 647). Likewise, the view that the "holy things" are the blessings that believers receive as a result of God's redemptive action (Dupont 1967e) probably should be rejected as the primary reference, but these are the blessings that flow from the resurrection of Jesus and are bound up with it (see Bock 1987: 252–54).

13:35

Again we have a citation of Ps. 16:10 (15:10 LXX), as in 2:27 (with *ou* appropriately replacing *oude* in the abbreviated form of the citation). The only problem is the connection with what precedes. The conjunction *dioti* can mean "because" (18:10) or "therefore" (20:26), here probably the latter, and the link is to 13:34a rather than 13:34b.

13:36

Now the argument is somewhat similar to that in 2:25–31. It is a historical fact that David did die and see corruption. His activity was confined to his own generation, and then he "fell asleep"

(2 Sam. 7:12; 1 Kings 2:10) and "was gathered to his ancestors" (Judg. 2:10; cf. 2 Sam. 7:12). But whereas in chapter 2 the use of the psalm is part of the argument regarding the exaltation of Jesus, here the stress is more on the continuing incorruptibility of the risen Jesus, so that he continues to be active as a savior (Bock 1987: 255).

13:39

From what could the law of Moses not justify? Paul's answer was "everything" (Rom. 3:20). Probably the same is meant here. Theoretically, the law could deal only with unwitting sins, those not committed deliberately, although the practical situation must have been different.

13:40

Since Jesus is thus the one through whom forgiveness and justification come, it is folly not to believe in him. Those who do so face the threat spoken "in the prophets," a phrase that may specify the book of the Minor Prophets.

13:41

The citation is from Hab. 1:5, which in the MT says, "Look at the nations, and see! Be astonished! Be amazed! For a work is being done in your days—you will not believe it when you are told." The LXX is essentially the same, but a slight variation in the text has produced "you scoffers" instead of "at the nations." The phrase *kai aphanisthēte* (lit., "and vanish away") appears to be a paraphrase of the repetitious "be amazed," possibly in the sense of hiding away in utter fear. (For the fragmentary text in 8*Hev*XII gr, see Steyn 1995: 188.)

Hab. 1:5 LXX	Acts 13:41
idete, hoi kataphronētai, kai epiblepsate	*idete, hoi kataphronētai,*
kai thaumasate thaumasia	*kai thaumasate*
kai aphanisthēte,	*kai aphanisthēte,*
dioti ergon egō ergazomai	*hoti ergon ergazomai egō*
en tais hēmerais hymōn,	*en tais hēmerais hymōn,*
ho ou mē pisteusēte ean tis ekdiēgētai.	*ergon ho ou mē pisteusēte ean tis ekdiēgētai hymin.*

Luke has abbreviated the wording and made one minor insertion (*ergon*).

The MT is a warning to the people in the prophet's own day that God is going to do something that they will find hard to believe: he will use the Chaldeans (i.e., Babylonians) to invade other countries to bring about his judgment. (Bowker [1967–1968: 102] holds that the same kind of point is made in Deut. 4:32.)

Although the citation of the text in 1QpHab II, 1–10 is fragmentary, it can be seen that the interpretation agreed with the LXX at this point, with *bôgĕdîm* ("traitors") suggesting that the LXX was following a variant form of the Hebrew (de Waard 1965: 17–19). In the Qumran commentary the passage was naturally interpreted of the apostates who refuse to heed the Teacher of Righteousness in his warnings against what is going to happen in the future; the Chaldeans are interpreted as the Kittim (see Evans 1993c: 221–22).

Here in Acts the warning is a vague one apparently directed against those who refuse to believe (cf. 13:39) the work that God is doing in their own days (cf. 2:17), in that he has raised Jesus from the dead (Anderson 2001: 258–59) and hence that he is the Savior. Alternatively, it is a warning of future judgment on those who scoff at the Christian message.

Luke thus regards the present situation as a repetition of what happened in Habakkuk's time, in which God again does a "work," and this is perhaps to be understood in the light of the use of *ergon* to refer to the apostolic mission referred to in the broader context (13:2; 14:26), which provokes unbelief among the Jews and renders them liable to God's judgment (Wall 2000: 549–50; Doble 2002b: 38). Wall also notes the references to "wonder" earlier in Acts (2:7; 3:12; 4:13) as expressive of an attitude that falls short of belief. Thus the language of the citation assembles a number of important themes in Acts and ties them together. Doble (2002b: 40–41) notes further echoes of Ps. 118:15–18, 22–24 and describes the phenomenon as a "suppressed intertextuality."

13:46–47

The refusal of the Jews to believe serves as permission for the apostles to go to the Gentiles, who are equally included in God's purpose of salvation. The apostles have fulfilled the obligation to go first to the Jews, and now they can take up the other part of the commission that has been laid down for them in Scripture. The Lord has given them his command (*entetaltai* is used appropriately as the introduction to the citation), which they find in the words of Isa. 49:6. In its original form this is part of a statement from Yahweh to his servant Israel, or, more precisely, to whoever has the task of restoring Israel, that the task of restoring Israel is too light an assignment: "I shall give you to be a light for the nations so that my salvation may be to the end of the earth" (MT). The LXX has "Behold, I have given you for a covenant of the nation, for a light to the Gentiles, so that you may be for salvation to the end of the earth." The addition of "for a covenant of the nation" (*eis diathēkēn genous*) is not found in any Hebrew version and appears to be simply a case of assimilation to Isa. 42:6. Acts omits "behold" and, more importantly, also omits "for a covenant of the nation," whether deliberately or because Luke was using a version of the text closer to the MT (note the similar omission in 13:34). Either way, the citation serves to motivate and legitimize the mission to the Gentiles as part of God's plan foretold in Scripture. "A light of the Gentiles" (*phōs ethnōn*) clearly means "a light for the Gentiles"; the rest of the clause expresses rather concisely that this will lead to (the bringing of) salvation to the end of the earth (echoing 1:8). But there is also an important echo of Luke 2:32, where similar language is used of Jesus. The mission of the Servant is undertaken both by Jesus (cf. 26:23) and by his followers (see Hanson 1983: 80–81). Here is the scriptural basis for the assertion in Luke 24:47 that the mission is a fulfillment of Scripture (see Pao 2000: 96–101). It is debated whether the speaker of the command here is to be understood as God (Dupont, as cited by Rese) or as Christ (Rese 1979: 77–79).

13:48

Behind the concept of being appointed for eternal life may lie the OT idea of being recorded in a book of God's people (Exod. 32:32–33; Ps. 69:28; Dan. 12:1), an idea developed later in Judaism (*Jub.* 30:18–23; *1 En.* 47:3; 104:1; 108:3). Cf. Rev. 13:8; 17:8.

Acts 14

14:10–14

NA[27] notes some coincidences of wording with the LXX in these verses, but nothing that could be characterized as use of the OT. Ezekiel 2:1 of-fers a verbal parallel to "Stand up on your feet" in 14:10, but there is a considerable difference between telling a person not to be afraid and healing a lame man. The expressions "tear one's clothes" (*diarrēgnymi ta himatia*) as a sign of emotion and "rush out" (*ekpēdaō*) in 14:14 also occur for different reasons in Jdt. 14:16–17.

14:15

For "of like passions" (*homoiopathēs*), see Wis. 7:3; 4 Macc. 12:13. "Vain things" (*mataios*) is a way of describing idols found in the OT (Lev. 17:7; 2 Chron. 11:15; Jer. 2:5); according to Barrett (1994–1998: 680), it is not found in this sense outside the LXX.

The description of God as "living" is common in the OT, especially when contrasting him with dead idols (Deut. 5:26; Josh. 3:10; 1 Sam. 17:26; 2 Kings 19:4, 16; Ps. 84:2; Hos. 1:10). Paul continues with an informal citation that Peter has already used in 4:24 and that will reappear in 17:24. The citation could be from Exod. 20:11 or Ps. 146:6 (145:6 LXX), since the wording is virtually identical.

14:16

The sovereignty of God over "all nations" has a parallel in Isa. 37:14–20 (Pao 2000: 204).

14:17

The description of God sending rain and causing harvests also has its basis in the OT passages that depict his care in providing food for human beings and animals (e.g., Gen. 8:22; Lev. 26:4; Ps. 145:15–16; 147:8–9; Jer. 5:24). However, there is no precise allusion here.

14:27

"What the Lord had done with them" (cf. 15:4; Luke 1:72; 10:37) has a verbal parallel in Jdt. 8:26, and the construction is common in the LXX; Wilcox (1965: 84–85) suggests that in Luke-Acts it may belong to early Christian vocabulary.

Acts 15

15:1–11

15:1

The "custom of [i.e., taught by] Moses" is another designation for the law of Moses (cf. 6:14) that was beginning to develop in Judaism (cf. Wis. 14:16), since it was the law that determined the characteristic manner of life.

Circumcision was inculcated by the story of Abraham and his family being circumcised in accordance with a direct divine command that was to continue to be obeyed in all future generations (Gen. 17:1–27; cf. 21:4); see Josh. 5:2–8. Somewhat surprisingly, circumcision does not figure elsewhere in the legislation in the last four books of the Pentateuch, except in Lev. 12:3 (where it is incidental to purification after childbirth) and in the Passover regulations for non-Israelites participating in the meal (Exod. 12:44, 48–49) and in metaphorical references (Lev. 19:23; 26:41; Deut. 10:16; 30:6 [cf. Jer. 4:4; 9:25–26]).

15:3

In pursuit of intratextual resonances, Wall (2000: 550) notes that "relate" (*ekdiēgeomai*) echoes the citation from Hab. 1:5 in Acts 13:41. But whereas the previous reference was to unbelief among the Jews, here the question is whether believing Jews will recognize what God has been doing through Paul.

15:10

For the motif of trying or testing God, see commentary on Acts 5:9 above.

15:12–21

Bowker (1967–1968: 107–9) has identified James's speech as falling into the pattern of the *yelammedenu* homily, in which a question of conduct (here posed in 15:5 by some believing Pharisees) is answered by reference to precedent and to Scripture. The precedent is the case of Peter's evangelism of Cornelius and his household, the Scripture is drawn from Amos 9, and James concludes with a strong recommendation that Bowker likens to a rabbinic *taqqanah*, in which the Torah is amended or alleviated. What is lacking is any evidence based on the Torah, without which an appeal to the prophets would have little force, and Bowker therefore has to postulate that what we have here is only a fragment of a longer discourse.

15:14

"To take from the nations a people for himself" (*labein ex ethnōn laon tō onomati autou*) has some

similarity to Deut. 14:2, where God "chose you to be a special people from all the nations on the face of the earth" (*laon periousion apo pantōn tōn ethnōn* [cf. Exod. 19:5; 23:22 LXX; Deut. 7:6; 26:18–19]), but whereas Deuteronomy refers to God selecting Israel to be his special people *separate from* the nations, James here appears to mean that God is now taking a group of people *out of the Gentile nations* to be a people for himself; James does not take up the question of the relationship between these believing Gentiles and the existing Jewish people. Maybe there is a deliberate use of the OT verse in a different sense from the original. The MT of Deut. 14:2 has the same Hebrew word (*'am*) that the LXX translates with two different words, so that Acts here reflects the LXX rendering. Moessner (1996: 241–42) traces the influence of Jer. 12:15–17, but although there is some similarity in motif, there are no decisive linguistic parallels. The combination "a people for his name" is not found in the LXX, but it is used in the Palestinian Targum as a paraphrase for "a people for the Lord" (Dahl 1957–1958). Dahl notes the relevance of Zech. 2:15 MT (2:11 ET; 2:15 LXX), "Many Gentiles will take refuge in the Lord in that day and will become his people," where the Targum has this phrase. See further Dupont (1985), who understands 18:10 similarly of a people that includes the Gentiles who have faith in God.

15:15–18

Although the quotation that follows 15:15 is essentially from Amos, James refers to "the words of the prophets." The phrase might refer to the book of the twelve so-called Minor Prophets (cf. 7:42), or James may have implied that other passages could have been cited also (cf., e.g., Zech. 2:11; see Dahl 1957–1958); however, the reference may take account of the fact that the quotation includes allusions to other passages (Bauckham 1996: 165).

The citation from Amos 9:11–12 is closer to the LXX than the MT, but with some differences in wording. It is difficult to compare the texts of Acts and the LXX because in both cases there are variants that make it difficult to be sure of the original wording.

Amos 9:11–12 LXX	Acts 15:16–18	
¹¹*en tē hēmera ekeinē*	¹⁶*meta tauta*	cf. Jer. 12:15
	anastrepsō	
anastēsō	*kai anoikodomēsō*	uses verb from omission below
tēn skēnēn Dauid	*tēn skēnēn Dauid*	
tēn peptōkuian	*tēn peptōkuian*	
kai anoikodomēsō		omission
ta peptōkota autēs		
kai ta kateskammena autēs	*kai ta katestrammena autēs*	shift of verb: "destroy/overturn"
anastēsō	*anoikodomēsō*	repeats verb used above
kai anoikodomēsō autēn	*kai anorthōsō autēn,*	change of verb
kathōs hai hēmerai tou aiōnos		omission
¹²*hopōs ekzētēsōsin*	¹⁷*hopōs an ekzētēsōsin*	adds *an*
hoi kataloipoi	*hoi kataloipoi*	
tōn anthrōpōn	*tōn anthrōpōn*	
	ton kyrion	addition
kai panta ta ethnē,	*kai panta ta ethnē*	
eph' hous epikeklētai	*eph' hous epikeklētai*	
to onoma mou ep' autous,	*to onoma mou ep' autous,*	
legei kyrios	*legei kyrios*	
ho theos		omission
ho poiōn tauta.	*poiōn tauta*	omits *ho*
	¹⁸*gnōsta ap' aiōnos.*	cf. Isa. 45:21?

Much more important are the differences between the MT and the LXX.

Amos 9:11–12 MT	Amos 9:11–12 LXX	
¹¹"In that day	¹¹*en tē hēmera ekeinē*	
I will raise up	*anastēsō*	
the booth of David	*tēn skēnēn Dauid*	("tent" or "tabernacle")
that is fallen	*tēn peptōkuian*	
and repair	*kai anoikodomēsō*	
their breaches,	*ta peptōkota autēs*	
and raise up his ruins,	*kai ta kateskammena autēs anastēsō*	
and rebuild it	*kai anoikodomēsō autēn*	
as in the days of old,	*kathōs hai hēmerai tou aiōnos,*	
¹²in order that they may possess	¹²*hopōs ekzētēsōsin*	
the remnant of Edom	*hoi kataloipoi tōn anthrōpōn*	object becomes subject: "Edom/Adam"
and all the nations	*kai panta ta ethnē,*	
who are called	*eph' hous epikeklētai*	the LXX represents the Hebrew
by my name,"	*to onoma mou ep' autous,*	relative construction overliterally

Amos 9:11–12 MT	Amos 9:11–12 LXX
says the LORD	*legei kyrios*
	ho theos
who does this.	*ho poiōn tauta.*

The MT citation comes from the last chapter of Amos, where the tone is more hopeful than in the earlier parts of the prophecy. Judgment has come upon the people, but there will be restoration, specifically of "the booth of David"; this odd phrase can hardly refer to the temple (which was not built by David) but could refer to the "house of David," the term "booth" signifying its weakness and temporariness until God sees fit to restore it "as in the days of old." Possessing the remnant of Edom implies the conquest of neighboring lands instead of the Israelites themselves being invaded and overcome. What nations are called by God's name? The answer seems to be the nations that are conquered by him (cf. 2 Sam. 12:28). So the passage envisages that God will bring about a change in Judah's fortunes expressed in the categories of the time.

In the LXX the first part of the prophecy is much the same. The claim that the text in Acts is closer to that in 4Q174 (de Waard 1965: 24–26; Wilcox 1965: 49; Hanson 1983: 17) is rightly rejected (Bruce 1990: 340; Barrett 1994–1998: 726; Stowasser 2001: 48–50). Nevertheless, some of the changes cause Ådna (2000: 136) to conclude that the citation is not dependent on the LXX.

In the second part, however, the LXX diverges from the MT. The object of "possess" in the MT has now become the subject, the new object is understood to be "me" (Bauckham 1996: 161–62), i.e., "the Lord" (supplied as *ton kyrion* in Acts 15:17), and the verb has changed from "possess" to "seek," a difference of one consonant in Hebrew (*yāraš/dāraš*). The remnant "of Edom" has become "the remainder of men," probably through reading the Hebrew consonants differently: *'ĕdôm/'ādām*. We can thus understand the LXX text as arising from a different version of the Hebrew text of Amos, with similar words being substituted for the original text. This type of change is known in rabbinic sources as *'al tiqrē'*. Bauckham (1996: 160–61) and Ådna (2000: 131) follow earlier scholars in assuming that this is what is happening here, but Barrett (1994–1998: 728) is skeptical of the possibility (though he does not offer an alternative explanation).

Which version is more likely to be original, the MT (which is followed by the Targum) or the Hebrew presupposed by the LXX? Evans (1993c: 222–23) notes that "Edom" was often understood as Rome in the Targumim, and therefore it is possible (though beyond proof) that an original "Adam" was repointed by the Masoretes as "Edom" to reflect Jewish hopes at this time, and consequential changes were made to the rest of the text ("they may possess" replacing "they may seek"). Archer and Chirichigno (1983: 155), followed by Larkin (1995: 223n), propose that the MT is corrupt and should be amended, but there is no adequate reason for doing so (Jobes and Silva 2000: 194–95).

Some light may be shed on the situation by the fact that there are two allusions to the text in the Dead Sea Scrolls, where the prophecy is applied to the current situation of the sect. In CD-A VII, 12–18 we read,

> When the two houses of Israel separated, Ephraim detached itself from Judah, and all the renegades were delivered up to the sword; but those who remained steadfast escaped to the land of the north. As he said, "I will deport the Sikkut of your King and the Kiyyun of your images away from my tent to Damascus" [Amos 5:26–27]. The books of the law are the Sukkat of the King, as he said, "I will lift up the fallen Sukkat of David" [Amos 9:11]. The King is the assembly; and the plinths of the images and the Kiyyun of the images are the books of the prophets, whose words Israel despised. (García Martínez 1996: 37–38)

It may be only coincidence that CD-A cites the same two texts from Amos that we find cited in Acts (7:43; 15:16–17). CD-A takes "Sikkut" in Amos 5 to refer to the Sukkat or tabernacles and then understands them as the book of the law. The "King" is understood as David in the light of Amos 9:11, but then the King is identified as the assembly or community itself. Once the Sikkut is understood as the books of the law, the Kiyyun could easily be understood as the companion books of the prophets. Evans (1993b: 207) takes the passage to mean that "Amos 9:11 was fulfilled when the Essenes restored the correct interpretation of the Law."

The other citation is in 4Q174 1 I, 10–13. Here we have a set of OT texts with a broadly messianic reference:

> And "YHWH declares to you that he will build you a house. I will raise up your seed after you and establish the throne of his kingdom for ever. I will be a father to him and he will be a son to me" [2 Sam. 7:12–14]. This refers to the "branch of David," who will arise with the interpreter of the law who will rise up in Zion in the last days, as it is written, "I will raise up the hut of David which has fallen" [Amos 9:11]. This refers to the "hut of David which has fallen," who will arise to save Israel. (García Martínez 1996: 136)

Here the messianic reference is maintained with the arising of "David" understood as the Messiah. Later rabbinic interpretation preserved this understanding in giving the name "Bar Naphle" ("Son of the fallen [tabernacle]") to the Messiah (b. Sanh. 96b–97a). (However, Qumran also has "the interpreter of the law," who is unknown to the early church, playing a role.) The Targum of Amos also interprets the passage in terms of the powerful restoration of the Davidic dynasty and empire (Evans 1993b: 207–8).

In the present context in Acts it seems that God is to restore the fallen dynasty of David and all that appertains to it, with the aim that the remainder of humankind will seek the Lord—that is, the nations over which God's name is called. The prophecy, however, has an addition at the beginning that appears to reflect Jer. 12:15 LXX: "And it will be after I have cast them out *I shall return* [*epistrepsō*] and have mercy on them, and I shall make them dwell each in their inheritance and each in their own land." "After these things" is a common enough phrase in prophecy (e.g., Joel 2:28 [3:1 LXX]; see commentary on Acts 2:17 above); here it may refer simply to the judgments described earlier in Amos (cf. Acts 7:42–43).

At the end of the citation James adds "known from of old," signifying that what God does is in accordance with his predetermined purpose; the words resemble Isa. 45:21 LXX (*tis akousta epoiēsen tauta ap' archēs*) and may be either a deliberate echo (Bauckham 1996: 164–65) or a coincidence (Barrett 1994–1998: 728). Dupont (1979: 145) notes that the rest of the passage is concerned with God's activity as Savior, issuing his appeal to the ends of the earth, which fits in nicely with the theme of James's speech.

The major discussion of the passage by Bauckham (1996: 156–70), closely followed by Ådna (2000: 126–42), makes the following points:

1. The avoidance of the use of *anastēsō* in Acts shows that the passage is not being interpreted of the resurrection of Jesus or of the restoration of the Davidic dynasty to the throne in the messianic rule of Jesus (Strauss 1995: 187–92), but rather of the restoration of a building: the temple of the messianic age (for *skēnē* in this sense, see Tob. 13:11 LXX [13:10 ET]). Bauckham argues that this could mean that God would build the eschatological temple through the agency of the Messiah. Here Bauckham differs from Barrett (1994–1998: 725–26), who suggests two possibilities: (a) the restoration of the kingdom is the appearing/resurrection of the Messiah, after which the way is open for Gentiles to enter the people of God; (b) the restoration of the kingdom is the conversion of Israel, only after which can the Gentiles enter. Barrett thinks that Luke would have held the former view, but the latter may have been held by some groups in the church. Stowasser (2001: 54) argues that the use of *anorthoō* reflects 2 Sam. 7:13; that is, the Amos prophecy is linked to the Nathan prophecy, just as in 4Q174 1 I, 10–12.

2. "I shall rebuild its fallen parts" is omitted because this could refer to the broken walls of a town rather than a temple; likewise, "as in the days of old" is omitted because the new temple will in fact be better than the old one.

3. The treatment of Amos 9:12 would not be strange for an exegete familiar with both the MT and the LXX versions. It is not possible to decide whether the differences between the texts are the result of accidental misreading or of deliberate interpretation, but Jewish exegetes of the time would "have welcomed the exegetical potential of the LXX text . . . as a legitimate way of reading the Hebrew text" (Bauckham 1996: 161).

4. The insertion of the object *ton kyrion* ("the Lord") rather than the expected *me* ("me") reflects influence from Zech. 8:22 LXX, which prophesies that "many peoples and many nations shall come to seek the face of the Lord Almighty in [the temple] in Jerusalem."

5. The opening "after these things" (*meta tauta*), instead of the LXX's "in that day" (*en tē hēmera ekeinē*), suggests that the fulfillment of this prophecy takes place after something else has happened: the turning away of God from judging Israel. Bauckham proposes that the phrase comes from Hos. 3:5, where the Israelites will "return" (*epistrephō* [used in Acts 15:19 of the Gentiles turning to God!]) and seek the Lord and David their king.

6. The "return" (*anastrepsō*) of the Lord reflects Jer. 12:15, which speaks of Yahweh's return to his people after judging them and goes on to refer to the Gentiles being built in the midst of God's people. A reference to Zech. 8:3 is possible but less likely. Hanson (1983: 85) notes that the LXX always uses *epistrephō* in this sense and concludes that a different Greek version is being used here.

7. The end of the citation includes words from Isa. 45:21, from yet another passage that refers to the nations drawing near to God and being saved.

8. All this makes it clear that the restored temple is in fact the Christian community. The hope of the Gentiles coming into the restored temple is widely attested in prophecy. But did this mean that they had to become Jews?

9. Finally, the phrase "all the nations over whom my name has been called" expresses God's ownership of the peoples; it is used frequently of Israel as God's special people (contrast Isa. 63:19, where the Gentiles are "those over whom your name has *not* been called"), and its use here indicates, remarkably, how the Gentiles are now understood as God's people, without any mention of the need for them to become Jews: "the nations *qua* Gentile nations belong to YHWH" (Bauckham 1996: 169). But this phrase is also used in James 2:7, probably with reference to Christian baptism; if so, Christian baptism suffices to recognize Gentiles as the people of God.

Opinions differ regarding the provenance of this citation. Barrett (1994–1998: 727–28) is typical of many scholars who hold that it was composed on the basis of the LXX by a Greek-speaking Christian and therefore cannot go back to James. Bauckham (1996: 182–84 [whose arguments evidently were unavailable to Barrett]) strongly disagrees and, in my opinion, has the better of the argument. Ådna (2000: 142–43) argues for the possibility that the citation is a Greek rendering of a Hebrew original independent of the LXX but, in my view, does not demonstrate this point sufficiently. The use of a collection of *testimonia* that included both this and the earlier citation of Amos in Acts 7 is defended by Stowasser (2001) on the grounds that both texts are cited in the Qumran texts and that there may be some signs of redaction of the quotation here at a pre-Lukan stage; the texts could well have been linked together by the catchword "tent" to describe judgment followed by restoration; the argument is delicate and, though falling short of proof, feasible.

The use of the citation establishes that "the Gentiles do not have to become Jews in order to join the eschatological people of God and to have access to God in the Temple of the messianic age" (Bauckham 1996: 178).

15:19–20

That, however, is not the end of the matter. The Gentiles are required to abstain from foods sacrificed to idols, sexual immorality, things strangled, and blood. Behind this list many scholars detect the influence of Lev. 17–18, which contains various regulations that are binding also on aliens "living among you" in Israel (Pesch 1986: 2:81; Jervell 1998: 397–98). In Leviticus only sacrifices offered at the tent of meeting are acceptable, with the implication that only the meat of these may be consumed; hence the text can be taken as indirectly forbidding the consumption of sacrificial meat offered to idols (Lev. 17:8–9). The consumption of blood is expressly forbidden (Lev. 17:10–12). The blood must be drained from any animal that is eaten; hence it can be argued that implicitly the eating of animals killed by strangulation (without draining off the blood) is forbidden (Lev. 17:13–14). Sexual immorality of all kinds is said to be forbidden in Lev. 18:26 (but the reference is to the preceding list of forbidden relationships, and prostitution is not mentioned). These four items occur in the same order in Acts 15:29 (though not in 15:20). In Leviticus these regulations are bound up with the fact that such actions pollute the land. The statement in Acts does not reflect specifically LXX phraseology at this point. The word *alisgēma* ("pollution") occurs in the Greek Bible only here in Acts 15:20

(although the cognate verb *alisgeō* occurs in Dan. 1:8; Mal. 1:7, 12; Sir. 40:29). The word *porneia* ("sexual immorality") is not used in Leviticus, but many examples of it are given. Bauckham (1996: 174–78) argues that the choice of these restrictions (excluding the Sabbath requirement on resident aliens in Exod. 20:10; Deut. 5:14) reflects the prophecies about the Gentiles joining the people of God and living "in the midst of them," specifically Jer. 12:16; Zech. 2:11. Only the pentateuchal rules for aliens "in the midst" are applied here to Gentiles in the new people of God. The *gezerah shavah* link (use of a common word creating a link) between the passages depends on the MT and not on the LXX. So Gentiles do not have to become Jews (i.e., proselytes) when they come into the new people of God, but they are required to keep the commandments that applied to Gentiles living in Israel. Thus certain aspects of the OT law were applied to Gentiles. Nevertheless, the prohibition of nonkosher food has been quietly dropped from most Christian practice. On this, see the comment by Calvin (Calvin 1965–1966: 2:51–52, cited in Barrett 1994–1998: 738).

This interpretation is not universally accepted. The proposal to find the origin of the requirements elsewhere, specifically in the "Noachian precepts" that developed in Judaism as God's law for all peoples (cf. Gen. 9:4–6; *Jub.* 7:20; see Str-B 3:37–38), is less convincing, but the broad similarities are not surprising. Barrett (1994–1998: 734–35) notes that Jews under persecution faced three issues on which compromise was impossible—idolatry, the shedding of blood, and incest—and thinks that these are the basis of the requirements here, but the parallel is much less close, and the rationale for the adoption of these points here is not clear. Turner (1982: 114–19) and Witherington (1998: 464–65) are skeptical of the appeal to Lev. 17–18. Turner argues that Luke did not expect believing Gentiles to keep the law and that Jewish law required more from the Gentiles than simply the four requirements listed; these are ad hoc requirements, the minimum needed to enable fellowship with scrupulous believing Jews. Witherington draws attention to the points where the requirements do not correspond very precisely with those in Leviticus and develops an alternative understanding of the passage as prohibiting the eating of sacrificial food in pagan temples. It can be seen that these regulations would in fact deal on a practical level with the problem of fellowship at the table in mixed churches (similarly, Blomberg 1984: 65–66).

15:21

The final comment by James refers to the way in which "from ancient times [the law of] Moses, being read, has people who proclaim it in every town in the synagogues each Sabbath." This refers to the continuing knowledge of the law among Jewish Christians and may confirm that the regulations are in fact drawn from Leviticus. Alternatively, it may be a way of saying, somewhat ironically perhaps, that if Gentiles want to find out more about the law of Moses, they know where to go (see Barrett 1994–1998: 737–38).

Acts 16

The only OT influence in this chapter comes in the form of some minor uses of biblical language.

16:14

The phrase "the Lord opened her heart" is reminiscent of 2 Macc. 1:4: "May he open your hearts to his law."

16:17

The slave girl can hardly be deliberately picking up the common LXX designation of God as the "Most High" (*hypsistos*); the term was also at home in Greek religion. Nevertheless, a knowledge of how Hellenistic Jews referred to their God could well have influenced the phraseology.

16:36

"Go in peace" is said to be "biblical Greek" (cf. Judg. 18:6; see BDF §4.3). Some commentators are skeptical as to whether a new convert could have picked up a Jewish Christian greeting quite so quickly as this.

Acts 17

17:2–3

Here Luke gives a succinct summary of how the missionaries regularly taught in a Jewish setting. There is insufficient evidence here to indicate which passages they may have used in arguing that the Messiah must suffer and rise from the dead (cf. Luke 24:26–27; see further commentary on Acts 26:22 below). Having developed the new conception of the Messiah from the Scriptures, they then claimed that Jesus (and Jesus only) fitted the job description.

17:22–23

Paul's reported speech in Athens is addressed to a non-Jewish audience and, like that in chapter 14, does not cite the OT but has a basis in it. The polemic against idols reflects an important OT motif that is particularly prominent in Isa. 40–55, where Pao (2000: 181–216) finds a pattern that has shaped the thought here.

The term "objects of worship" (*sebasma*) is also used in Wis. 14:20; 15:17; Bel 27 Θ in a pejorative sense. For worship of God as unknown, Barrett (1994–1998: 839) cites Isa. 45:15 LXX: "For you are God, and we did not know, the God of Israel, the Savior," a verse that Pesch (1986: 2:136) sees behind Paul's statement here.

17:24

The description of God as "the maker of the world [*kosmos*] and all that is in it" is based on the OT; although the term *kosmos* does not occur in the canonical LXX in this sense (there is no Hebrew equivalent), the language could be based on Isa. 42:5: "God, the LORD, who made the heaven and established it, who founded the earth and what is in it" (cf. Gen. 1:1; Exod. 20:11: "the LORD made the heaven and the earth and all that is in them"; Neh. 9:6; Ps. 146:6; Wis. 9:1, 9). For "Lord of heaven and earth," see Tob. 7:17 LXX.

That God does not dwell in temples made by hands is an OT motif repeated from 7:48.

17:25

God does not need to be served by human hands. The point is made in Ps. 50:7–15 (cf. 2 Macc. 14:35; 3 Macc. 2:9). For "serve" (*therapeuō*) used of service to God, see Isa. 54:17. There is no direct use of the OT here, but rather evidence of the theology of Hellenistic Judaism, which was based on the OT. Similar thoughts can also be found in Greek sources.

God is the source of life and breath in the creation story (Gen. 2:7; Isa. 42:5; 57:15–16; 2 Macc.

7:23). Again the language is Hellenistic, but the thought is fully in harmony with the OT.

17:26

Behind this statement lies the story of the creation of the one human being from whom all others are descended. "Made" (*poieō*) is used in the LXX for creation by God and is so used here (less likely is the meaning "caused . . . [to dwell]"). The reference to "every nation of human beings" or "the whole race of human beings" alludes to Gen. 10, with its "table of nations" that spread all over the earth after the flood (Scott 1994: 541–43). "The whole face of the earth" is LXX Greek (cf. Jer. 32:26 LXX [25:26 ET]). That God "appointed their times and places" could allude either to the seasons of the year (Ps. 74:17; cf. Acts 14:17) and to the natural boundaries between the land and the sea (Job 38:8–11; Ps. 104:5–9) or to the historical periods of the nations (cf. Dan. 2:36–45) and to the boundaries between them (Deut. 32:8). See also 1QM X, 12–16.

17:27

"Seeking God" is a familiar OT theme (Deut. 4:29; Ps. 14:2; Prov. 8:17; Isa. 51:1; 55:6; 65:1; Jer. 29:13; Amos 5:4; 9:12 LXX). The idea that God is near to his people is found in Ps. 145:18; Jer. 23:23–24, but here the thought is more that God is not far from all people. Barrett (1994–1998: 846) warns against making too sharp a distinction between the more intellectual seeking of Hellenistic thought and the OT's more existential seeking.

17:28

This verse is noteworthy for its quoting from nonbiblical sources. It establishes the kinship of God and human beings, which is expressed somewhat differently in the OT in the concept of creation in the image of God (Gen. 1:27).

17:29

The condemnation of belief that God resembles man-made images is common in the OT (e.g., Exod. 20:4; Deut. 5:8; Isa. 44:9–20; Wis. 13:10–19; 15; cf. Deut. 4:28) and Judaism but is found also in some Hellenistic philosophers. For the materials of which the idols are made, see Deut. 29:17 (Pao 2000: 195–96).

17:30

On human ignorance of God, see Wis. 14:22; 15:11, and for God's overlooking of human sin to give opportunity for repentance, see Wis. 11:23.

17:31

That God "will judge the world in righteousness" uses a phrase found in the psalms—for example, *krinei tēn oikoumenēn en dikaiosynē* (Ps. 9:9 LXX [9:8 ET]); similarly, Ps. 95:13 LXX (96:13 ET); 97:9 LXX (98:9 ET); the psalms are referring to a future occasion that was naturally identified subsequently as the last judgment.

The evidence shows how the OT is treated in a "third way" here. Instead of direct employment of biblical language (except in 17:31) or paraphrase, there is the expression of OT motifs in a recognizable way but using the language of the Hellenistic world in a clear attempt to accommodate to non-Jewish hearers.

Acts 18

18:6

Paul's action of shaking out his clothes may have a precedent in Neh. 5:13 where Nehemiah shakes his clothes as a prophetic sign of how God will "shake out" anyone who fails to keep the promise of obedience to him. Here the sign is one of abhorrence and a threat of judgment, and it may be intended to be understood in the same way as the shaking off of the dust from one's feet (cf. NRSV text) in 13:51. The motif of the messenger being free from guilt if the hearers do not accept the message is found in Ezek. 33:1–9: their blood is on their own heads (for this traditional expression, cf., e.g., 2 Sam. 1:16; see Wilcox 1965: 65; Jervell 1998: 459n304). The general motif is a natural one, but it has a firm basis in LXX diction.

18:9–10

For "Do not fear" with reference to opposing human beings, see Deut. 31:6; for "I am with you," see Exod. 3:12; Josh. 1:5; Jer. 1:19; for the combination of the two phrases, see Josh. 1:9; Isa. 41:10; 43:5; Jer. 1:8. Pesch (1986: 2:149) points out that this form of words is associated not with epiphanies, but rather with divine promises made to prophets and the Servant of Yahweh.

18:18

The vow (taken presumably by Paul, but syntactically it could be Aquila) is a Nazirite vow, following the procedure detailed in Num. 6; unfortunately, the details are left obscure here. The Nazirite abstained from alcohol and from cutting his hair for a period of time, the termination of which was marked by shaving the hair and offering a sacrifice. For another example later in Acts, see 21:21–26.

18:25–26

The "way of the Lord" is OT language for the kind of conduct that the Lord requires of his people and hence for the teaching that describes it (Exod. 32:8; Deut. 5:33). Cf. 9:2; 13:10.

18:28

For exposition on the basis of the Scriptures, see commentary on Acts 17:2–3 above.

Acts 19

19:9

The verb "became stubborn" (*sklērynō*) is used in Exod. 13:15 of the hardening of Pharaoh against the Israelites.

19:19

NA[27] suggests Deut. 18:10–14 as OT background for magical practices and the condemnation of them, but an allusion here is unlikely.

19:20

For the "growth" of the word (cf. Exod. 1:7, 20), see commentary on Acts 6:7; 12:24 above.

19:26

The Christian missionaries yet again take up the OT criticism of gods made by human hands (see commentary on Acts 17:29 above; Pao 2000: 205–6).

19:27

NA[27] gives Isa. 40:17; Wis. 3:17 as verbal parallels to the goddess being accounted as nothing, but there the reference is to the nations and adulterers respectively. The phraseology is not exclusive to the LXX.

19:28

For the acclamation "Great is . . . ," see Bel 18, 41. However, such an acclamation is attested in extrabiblical sources (BDAG, s.v. *megas*).

Acts 20

20:6

"After the days of unleavened bread" is a Jewish calendrical reference based on observing the feast, closely associated with the Passover, described in Exod. 12; 23:15; 28:16–25; Deut. 16:1–8. See also 27:9.

20:10

The description of the raising of Eutychus has echoes of the corresponding stories of Elijah and Elisha (1 Kings 17:17–24; 2 Kings 4:18–37); cf. the earlier echoes in stories of Jesus and Peter. The incident takes place in an upper room, where Eutychus, sitting in a window, falls asleep and tumbles out the window to his death; Paul lies on top of the boy, his life returns, and he is returned to his home. The typological resemblances between Elijah, Elisha, Jesus, Peter, and Paul give some unity to the story and emphasize how God works through each of them in similar ways.

20:22

Within Paul's address to the church we may expect to find some use of the OT. "And now" (*kai nyn idou* [cf. 13:11; 20:25]) is a septuagintalism.

20:26

"I am innocent of the blood of everybody" closely resembles Sus. 46 Θ and indicates that Paul has heeded Ezek. 3:18–21 (cf. 33:1–6).

20:28

The metaphor of shepherding the flock of God takes up a familiar OT picture of God's people under their rulers (Ps. 100:3; Isa. 40:11; Jer. 13:17; Ezek. 34) and applies it to the task of caring for and directing the church. Psalm 74:1–2 (73:1–2 LXX) brings together the motifs of the flock and God's acquiring of it (but there are no verbal links with the LXX, which has *ktaomai* and *lytroomai* rather than *peripoieomai* as here). In fact, the closer link is with Isa. 43:21, which has *peripoieomai* (cf. 31:5).

20:32

"An inheritance among all who are sanctified" (*klēronomian en tois hēgiasmenois pasin*; cf. the similar phrase [substituting *klēron*] in 26:18). The granting of an inheritance to God's people is found in Deut. 33:3–4 LXX, where there is reference to "all the sanctified ones under [God's] hands" and to "the law which Moses commanded us, an inheritance for the synagogues of Jacob." In Ps. 15:5 LXX (16:5 ET) the Lord is the share of the psalmist's "inheritance"; in Wis. 5:5 the just person "was reckoned among the sons of God, and in the holy ones is his lot [*klēros*]." See further 1QS XI, 7–8; 1QHᵃ XIX, 11–12. This seems to mean that the hearers are given a share in the blessings of God's salvation in and with the whole of God's new people. Pao (2000: 174–76) develops the link with the idea of the promised land as an inheritance (cf. Acts 7:5) in Gen. 15:7; Exod. 15:17; Josh. 11:23. Wilcox (1965: 35–37) thinks that Luke has used (here and elsewhere) a different version from the LXX, but this seems to be an unnecessary hypothesis.

20:33

There is something of a parallel here with the speech of Samuel in 1 Sam. 12:1–5, where he defends himself against possible accusations, but it is a fairly general one.

20:37

The tearful farewell and people "falling on Paul's neck" to kiss him goodbye resembles Gen. 33:4; 45:14–15; 46:29; Tob. 7:6; the cultural expression of grief at parting is shaped by the OT pattern.

Acts 21

21:10

Barrett (1994–1998: 986) refers to and rightly rejects A. Ehrhardt's hypothesis that Agabus follows Paul like Elisha follows Elijah while the latter predicts his imminent departure.

21:11

Agabus's prophetic signs have precedents in the narratives regarding OT prophets who acted symbolically (Jervell [1998: 520n699] lists 1 Kings 11:19–40; Isa. 8:1–4; 20:1–2; Jer. 13:1–11; 19:10–13; Ezek. 4–5), but there is no precise par-

allel to his specific action (the closest is Jeremiah wearing a yoke on his own neck to symbolize subjection to Nebuchadnezzar [Jer. 27]).

21:21

The complaints against Paul are reminiscent of those against Stephen, except that the critical matter of circumcision now comes to the fore.

21:24

The details of what happened and especially of Paul's part in them are obscure. However, the main background is the termination of what must be a Nazirite vow by the four men by the shaving of their heads and the offering of a substantial sacrifice (cf. Num. 6:13–21); Paul was invited to pay the costs. What is problematic is why Paul should have joined in the actual act of purification, and the OT sheds no light on this problem.

21:26

For "the fulfillment of the days of purification," see the similar phraseology in 1 Macc. 3:49.

12:28

Bringing uncircumcised foreigners into the temple was strictly forbidden in Ezek. 44:6–9.

Acts 22

22:9

NA²⁷ points to Wis. 18:1, where, in an account of the plagues in Egypt, it is reported that the enemies of God's people heard their voices but did not see their forms. This, however, is the reverse of what happened here—they saw but did not hear—and certainly no relationship exists between the two texts.

22:11

The description of the blinded Paul unable to find his own way at noon (22:6) has a parallel in the judgment of blindness on disobedient Israelites described in Deut. 28:28–29 (so NA²⁷ mg.), but there are no significant verbal links and nothing to suggest an allusion.

22:14

A Jew naturally refers to "the God of our fathers" (see commentary on Acts 3:12–13 above). For "the Righteous One," see commentary on Acts 3:14 above.

22:15

For the motif of witness, see commentary on Acts 1:8 above.

22:16

For "calling on his name," see commentary on Acts 2:21 above. The effect of the echoes is to tie in Paul with those who fulfilled Joel's prophecy by turning to the Lord at Pentecost.

22:22

The call "Take him from the earth" (*aire apo tēs gēs*)—that is, "Kill him"—reproduces the idiom in 8:33, where it occurs in the citation of Isa. 53:8 and is understood to refer to Jesus (cf. the use of the verb in Acts 21:36; Luke 23:18). It may therefore be an echo of this passage (Wilcox 1965: 67–68) and silently draw a parallel between the fates of Jesus and Paul.

Acts 23

23:3

The threat "God is going to strike [*typtein*] you" may be a prophecy, but this phrase is regarded as an adjuration written in the law in the Mishnah (*m. Šebu.* 4:13, cited in Str-B 2:766; Barrett 1994–1998: 1059). The law in question is possibly Deut. 28:22, 28 (*pataxai se kyrios*). Calling the high priest a "whitened wall" (cf. the whitewashed tombs in Matt. 23:27) may reflect the imagery in Ezek. 13:8–15 likening false prophets to rickety walls daubed with whitewash: they look solid, but the appearance is misleading. The high priest is accused of hypocrisy in that he is supposed to be a just judge and yet is acting contrary to the law in defiance of the requirement of justice in Lev. 19:15.

23:4–5

Paul himself cites the law that forbids the action of which he had been guilty. "You shall not speak evil of a ruler of the people," found in Exod. 22:28 (22:27 LXX), is one of a collection of miscellaneous laws. The quotation here differs slightly from the LXX, which has the plural "rulers" (but the text there is uncertain); the singular form identifies the high priest as the Jewish head of state. Paul here assumes that the law continues in force.

Acts 24

24:2

The similarity of "experiencing peace" (*eirēnēs tynchanontes*) to the phraseology in 2 Macc. 4:6, noted by NA[27], is coincidental.

24:5

Use of the word "plague" (*loimos*) to describe a person or group of people is paralleled in the LXX of 1 Sam. 1:16; 2:12; 25:25; Ps. 1:1; Prov. 22:10; 29:8 and so may be a septuagintalism, although it is also found elsewhere (see BDAG 602).

24:14

"The God of our ancestors" (lit., "the ancestral [*patrōos*] God") is a phrase found also in 4 Macc. 12:17, a Hellenistic Jewish variant on "the God of our fathers" (see commentary on Acts 3:12–13 above).

Paul here claims to believe everything that is "according to the law" and that is "written in the prophets." "*Behaving* according to the law" is a comprehensible phrase, but it is not so clear what "*believing* according to the law" signifies. Maybe it is a loose way of expressing the former idea and indicates that Paul claims to be a law-abiding Jew and to teach Jewish Christians accordingly, but there are indications in his letters that things were not quite so simple.

24:15

The resurrection of the righteous and the unrighteous is based on the prophecy of the end in Dan. 12:2–3, which indicates two groups of people, some being raised to eternal life and others to eternal reproach and shame, and then refers to the "righteous" (Θ) or to "righteousness" (MT). Clearly this passage lies behind Paul's statement, although the wording is different.

24:16

Hebrew has no equivalent for the word *syneidēsis* ("conscience"); what we have here is a rendering of the advice of father to son in Prov. 3:4, "Take thought for good deeds in the sight of the LORD and of human beings" (*pronoou kala enōpion kyriou kai anthrōpōn*), using the concept (*aproskopon syneidēsin echein pros ton theon kai tous anthrōpous).* This is a good example of a specific OT text being worked into discourse.

Acts 26

26:16

Although in the other accounts of his conversion (9:6; 22:10, 16) Paul is told in a conventional manner to "get up," here the wording "stand on your feet," followed by divine instructions, closely resembles the account of the call of Ezekiel (*stēthi epi tous podas sou*), whom Yahweh is sending (*exapostellō* [Acts has *apostellō*]) to Israel to speak to them (Ezek. 2:1–4). The call also echoes Jer. 1:7, which is a prophetic call similar to Ezekiel's.

26:17

The promise that the Lord will rescue (*exaireō*) Paul picks up the similar promise to Jeremiah in Jer. 1:8, 19; the prayer in 1 Chron. 16:35 ("Rescue us from the nations") may also be relevant because Paul is to be delivered from the people (Israel) and the nations (Gentiles).

26:18

To "open eyes [of the blind]" (some manuscripts of Acts supply *typhlōn* here) is based on the mission of the Servant in Isa. 42:7 (*anoixai ophthalmous typhlōn*); cf. 35:5 for this picture of the messianic age. In Isa. 42:16b God himself promises, "I will turn the darkness for them into light," so it is natural to make this part of the task of God's agent here. The rest of the language is more "Christian" (deliverance from Satan, forgiveness of sins; but cf. Isa. 61:1), but then we have a repetition of the OT motif of "a portion among those sanctified by faith in me" (cf. Wis. 5:5; see commentary on Acts 20:32 above). Again, then, the mission of Paul (and of the church) is understood in terms of the Isaianic Servant. Note, however, that the terminology was used more generally in the church (1 Pet. 2:9) and also in Hellenistic Judaism of conversion to Judaism (*T. Levi* 19:1; *Jos. Asen.* 8:9) (see Barrett 1994–1998: 1160).

26:22

Here is a further reminder that the Christian message is based on what the prophets and Moses had foretold. Now, however, this basis extends explic-itly to the suffering of the Messiah, and that as the first to rise from the dead, he would announce light to the people and the nations. Moses is witness to the coming of the prophet like himself (3:22–23). The evangelism of Jews and Gentiles accomplished by the Messiah through his followers is based on the mission of the Servant, as we have just noted (Isa. 42:6; 49:6; 60:1–3; cf. Acts 13:47). The suffering of the Messiah must depend on the identification of the Messiah with the Servant in Isa. 53, and presumably the resurrection of the Messiah was based on the same source (Isa. 53:10).

26:25

NA[27] suggests a reference to Jdt. 10:13, but the resemblance is indiscernible.

26:28

The suggested reference in NA[27] to 1 Kings 20:7 LXX (21:7 ET) is in regard to a possible parallel to the idiom *Christianon poiēsai*. It is not an example of use of the OT, but rather simply of a possible Greek usage.

Acts 27

27:9

The Jewish calendar is used (cf. 20:6). The "Fast" is a name for the annual Day of Atonement, whose ritual is laid down in Lev. 16. The ritual included fasting and general self-denial (Lev. 16:29, 31), but the term "Fast" for the festival is postbiblical (e.g., Philo, *Spec. Laws* 2.193).

27:18

The jettisoning of cargo is a well-attested procedure in such circumstances, and therefore the parallel in Jon. 1:5 is coincidental; a typological relationship between the two narratives is not intended.

Acts 28

28:23

Luke's final report on how early Christians, specifically Paul, did their evangelism ties in with earlier notices. The message is summed up as "the kingdom of God" (cf., e.g., 8:12), but in fact it appears to have been about "another king" (cf.

17:7). Since the OT uses the term "kingdom" with reference to God very rarely (but says a lot about God reigning), it is not surprising that it is rather Paul's preaching of Jesus that is based on both the law and the prophets (cf. 17:2–3; 18:5). The law specifically refers to the promise of a prophet like Moses (see commentary on Acts 26:22 above).

28:25–27

For the Holy Spirit as the inspirer of the prophets, see 1:16, and for naming Isaiah as the human source, see 8:28, 30. Similarly, in CD-A IV, 13–14 God speaks "by the hand of Isaiah."

The passage cited is Isa. 6:9–10, which appears also in Matt. 13:13–15 pars.; John 12:39–40; Rom. 11:8. However, whereas the prophecy is woven into the text in an abbreviated form in Mark 4:12; Luke 8:10, here it is cited in full, as in Matt. 13:13–15. Thus it gains significance as the final scriptural quotation in Luke-Acts (Pao 2000: 104–5).

Isa. 6:9–10 MT	Isa. 6:9–10 LXX	Acts 28:26–27
[9]Go and say to this people,	[9]poreuthēti kai eipon tō laō toutō,	[26]poreuthēti pros ton laon touton kai eipon,
"Hear continually, but do not understand;	akoē akousete kai ou mē sunēte	akoē akousete kai ou mē synēte
and see continually, but do not perceive."	kai blepontes blepsete kai ou mē idēte;	kai blepontes blepsete kai ou mē idēte;
[10]Make the heart of this people dull,	[10]epachynthē gar hē kardia tou laou toutou,	[27]epachynthē gar hē kardia tou laou toutou
and make their ears heavy,	kai tois ōsin autōn bareōs ēkousan	kai tois ōsin bareōs ēkousan
and shut their eyes;	kai tous ophthalmous autōn ekammysan,	kai tous ophthalmous autōn ekammysan;
lest they see with their eyes,	mēpote idōsin tois ophthalmois	mēpote idōsin tois ophthalmois
and hear with their ears,	kai tois ōsin akousōsin	kai tois ōsin akousōsin
and understand with their heart,	kai tē kardia synōsin	kai tē kardia synōsin
and turn again	kai epistrepsōsin	kai epistrepsōsin,
and be healed.	kai iasomai autous.	kai iasomai autous.

The significant differences between the MT and the LXX are these: (1) The ironic imperatives "hear continually, but do not understand" and "see continually, but do not perceive" are changed to emphatic future indicatives expressing what will happen. (2) The command to the prophet to make the people's heart dull and so on is changed to a statement that the people themselves have already done so. This "tones down the emphasis on God

as the agent" (Pao 2000: 102). (3) The passive "be healed" is changed to the future indicative "I will heal them," expressing more clearly that the healing is the work of God.

The variations between the LXX and Acts are trivial. Matthew's quotation is substantially the same as here, but only Acts has the introductory words "Go and say to this people." Mark and Luke weave words from the Isaiah text into *hina* clauses expressing the purpose or effect of the parabolic teaching, while Matthew precedes his quotation with something similar. John boldly says that God has blinded the people's eyes and hardened their heart so that they may not see with their eyes and perceive with their heart and turn and he would heal them. Paul weaves some of the wording into a composite quotation affirming that God has blinded and deafened the people.

In the MT the words come in the temple vision through which Isaiah receives a prophetic calling at a time of national apostasy. His mission is to tell the people ironically to go on behaving as they are, hearing God's word but neither receiving nor obeying it. He is told to make the people obdurate so that they will not hear and respond to God's word and then be healed. So great is their sin that there is for the time being no way that they can be allowed to repent and escape the judgment that must come upon them; only after judgment has run its course is there any hope of renewal (Isa. 9:11–13). How Isaiah is intended to make the people obdurate is not explained; maybe the point is simply that Isaiah is to go on calling them to repent and thereby give them further opportunities to reject God's message and reach the point where they are incapable of a positive response. Or it may be that his message is in effect a warning designed to encourage them to repent: if they go on disobeying God's word as they are doing, they are in danger that God will take away from them the ability to respond to it (see Goldingay 2001: 60–61).

In the LXX the prophecy sounds more like a firm statement of impending judgment rather than a warning. Even so, it is likely that it was meant to function as an appeal and not simply as a condemnation. Clearly, Isaiah expected that the people in general would continue in their sinful ways, but the possibility of response was not excluded.

In the present passage Paul's statement is emphatic (though the NIV translation "this final statement" is perhaps too strong). The words of Isaiah begin with a command to the prophet to deliver God's message to the people; the effect is that this command is now directed to Paul himself, so that he shares the prophet's mandate (Bovon 1984; Marguerat 2002: 225). The implication is that the mood of the people has not changed since Isaiah's time (cf. Rom. 11:8: "until this very day"). The "people" are clearly the Jews, in accordance with the normal reference of this word, in contrast to "the nations." They are accused of refusing to listen and respond to the preaching; this is said to be "lest they should hear and turn and be healed," as if the people's aim was to avoid being saved. The MT makes it clear that the prophet was told to make the people obtuse lest they should be saved when they deserved judgment; the purpose or aim is thus that of God himself. In the LXX and Acts the sense is the same: the purpose is not that of the people (*pace* Marshall 1980: 424–25), but rather of God himself, who brings inescapable judgment upon people who go on too long and too far in rejecting his message to them. Again, as in the original setting, it may confidently be assumed that this is not God's final word on the matter in the sense that from now on repentance is impossible for Jews; Luke would have agreed with what Paul says in Rom. 9–11 (see Koet 1989: 119–39; Larkin 1995: 390–91; Wall 2002: 361–64). However, several scholars think that the text stresses final rejection: "A future conversion of Israel of the kind in Romans 11 is excluded" (Jervell 1998: 628); others suggest that Luke may have allowed for the salvation of individual Jews (Schneider 1980–1982: 2:419; Pesch 1986: 2:310) or maintain that the situation should not be oversimplified (Barrett 1994–1998: 1246); Marguerat (2002: 221–30) argues that Luke is intentionally ambivalent. Pao (2000: 105–9) argues that Isaiah's order of judgment (chap. 6) followed by salvation (chap. 40) is reversed in Luke-Acts to stress the rejection of salvation by the Jews.

28:28

From this verdict Paul draws the consequence that salvation will be offered to the Gentiles and prophesies that they will accept it. This is to say nothing more than had already been apparent from earlier in the story where there was already a greater response from the Gentiles. The implication is that God will gather a people for himself regardless of the Jewish response. The phrase *tois ethnesin apestalē touto to sōtērion tou theou* may reflect Ps. 66:3 LXX (67:3 ET), where God is asked to pour out his blessing on Israel "to make known your way in the earth, your salvation among all the nations" (*tou gnōnai en tē gē tēn hodon sou, en pasin ethnesin to sōtērion sou*). The psalm is primarily concerned with God's blessing on Israel, and the purpose expressed might be simply that other nations would witness his goodness to Israel, but the rest of the psalm, with its references to the peoples of the earth rejoicing and experiencing the goodness of God, opens up the possibility that they too will share in salvation. Similar sentiments are found in Ps. 98:3, where again God has revealed his salvation in the sight of all the nations and "all the ends of the earth have known the salvation of our God" (see also Isa. 40:5). Again, therefore, the language implicitly picks up an OT theme.

Bibliography

Ådna, J. 2000. "James' Position at the Summit Meeting of the Apostles and Elders in Jerusalem (Acts 15)." Pages 125–61 in *The Mission of the Early Church to Jews and Gentiles*. Edited by J. Ådna and H. Kvalbein. WUNT 127. Tübingen: Mohr Siebeck. [Translation and revision of "Die Heilige Schrift als Zeuge der Heidenmission: Der Rezeption von Amos 9,11–12 in Apg 15,16–18." Pages 1–21 in *Evangelium, Schriftauslegung, Kirche: Festschrift für Peter Stuhlmacher zum 65. Geburtstag*. Edited by J. Ådna, S. J. Hafemann, and O. Hofius. Göttingen: Vandenhoeck & Ruprecht, 1997.]

Albl, M. C. 1999. *"And Scripture Cannot Be Broken": The Form and Function of the Early Christian* Testimonia *Collections*. NovTSup 96. Leiden: Brill.

Alexander, L. 2000. "L'intertextualité et la question des lecteurs: Réflexions de la Bible dans les Actes des Apôtres." Pages 201–14 in *Intertextualités: La Bible en échos*. Edited by D. Marguerat and A. Curtis. MdB 40. Geneva: Labor et Fides.

Alexander, P. S. 1992. "Geography and the Bible (Early Jewish Geography)." *ABD* 2:977–88.

Allen, L. C. 1970–1971. "The Old Testament Background of (ΠΡΟ) 'ΟΡΙΖΕΙΝ in the New Testament." *NTS* 17: 104–8.

Anderson, K. 2001. "The Resurrection of Jesus in Luke-Acts." PhD diss., London Bible College.

Archer, G. L., and G. C. Chirichigno. 1983. *Old Testament Quotations in the New Testament: A Complete Survey*. Chicago: Moody.

Arnold, B. T. 1996. "Luke's Characterizing Use of the Old Testament in the Book of Acts." Pages 300–323 in *History, Literature and Society in the Book of Acts*. Edited by B. Witherington III. Cambridge: Cambridge University Press.

Baasland, E. 1995. "Rhetorischer Kontext in Apg 15.13–21: Status-slehre und die Actareden." Pages 191–226 in *Texts and Contexts:*

Biblical Texts in Their Textual and Situational Contexts; Essays in Honor of Lars Hartman. Edited by T. Fornberg and D. Hellholm. Oslo: Scandinavian University Press.

Barrett, C. K. 1988. "Luke/Acts." Pages 231–44 in *It is Written: Scripture Citing Scripture; Essays in Honour of Barnabas Lindars, SSF.* Edited by D. A. Carson and H. G. M. Williamson. Cambridge: Cambridge University Press.

———. 1994–1998. *The Acts of the Apostles.* 2 vols. ICC. Edinburgh: T&T Clark.

Bauckham, R. 1995. "James and the Jerusalem Church." Pages 415–80 in *The Book of Acts in Its Palestinian Setting.* Edited by R. Bauckham. The Book of Acts in Its First-Century Setting 4. Grand Rapids: Eerdmans; Carlisle: Paternoster.

———. 1996. "James and the Gentiles (Acts 15.13–21)." Pages 154–84 in *History, Literature and Society in the Book of Acts.* Edited by B. Witherington III. Cambridge: Cambridge University Press.

Beale, G. K. 2004. *The Temple and the Church's Mission.* Leicester: InterVarsity.

———. 2005a. "The Descent of the Eschatological Temple in the Form of the Spirit at Pentecost. Part 1: The Clearest Evidence." *TynBul* 56 (1): 73–102.

———. 2005b. "The Descent of the Eschatological Temple in the Form of the Spirit at Pentecost. Part 2: Corroborating Evidence." *TynBul* 56 (2): 63–90.

Bellinger, W. H., Jr. 1990. "The Psalms and Acts: Reading and Rereading." Pages 127–43 in *With Steadfast Purpose: Essays on Acts in Honor of Henry Jackson Flanders Jr.* Edited by N. H. Keathley. Waco: Baylor University.

Bellinger, W. H., Jr., and W. R. Farmer, eds. 1998. *Jesus and the Suffering Servant: Isaiah 53 and Christian Origins.* Harrisburg, PA: Trinity Press International.

Betz, O. 1968. "Zungenreden und süsser Wein: Zur eschatologischen Exegese von Jesaja 28 in Qumran und im Neuen Testament." Pages 20–36 in *Bibel und Qumran: Beiträge zur Erforschung der Beziehungen zwischen Bibel- und Qumranwissenschaft.* Edited by S. Wagner. Berlin: Evangelische Haupt-Bibelgesellschaft.

———. 1998. "Jesus and Isaiah 53." Pages 70–87 in *Jesus and the Suffering Servant: Isaiah 53 and Christian Origins.* Edited by W. H. Bellinger Jr. and W. R. Farmer. Harrisburg, PA: Trinity Press International.

Black, M. 1954. *An Aramaic Approach to the Gospels and Acts.* 2nd edition. Oxford: Clarendon.

Black, M. 1974. "Notes on the Longer and the Shorter Text of Acts." Pages 119–31 in *On Language, Culture and Religion: In Honor of Eugene A. Nida.* Edited by M. Black and W. A. Smalley. ApSem 56. The Hague: Mouton.

Blomberg, C. L. 1984. "The Law in Luke-Acts." *JSNT* 22: 53–80.

Bock, D. L. 1987. *Proclamation from Prophecy and Pattern: Lucan Old Testament Christology.* Sheffield: JSOT Press.

———. 1997. "Old Testament in Acts." *DLNTD* 824–26.

———. 1998. "Scripture and the Realisation of God's Promises." Pages 41–62 in *Witness to the Gospel: The Theology of Acts.* Edited by I. H. Marshall and D. Peterson. Grand Rapids: Eerdmans.

Bovon, F. 1978. *Luc le Théologien: Vingt-cinq ans de recherches (1950–1975).* Neuchâtel: Delachaux & Niestlé.

———. 1984. "'Schon hat der heilige Geist durch den Propheten Jesaja zu euren Vätern gesprochen' (Acts 28.25)." *ZNW* 75: 226–32.

———. 2006. *Luke the Theologian: Fifty-five Years of Research (1950–2005).* 2nd revised edition. Waco: Baylor University Press.

Bowker, J. W. 1967–1968. "Speeches in Acts: A Study in Proem and Yelammedenu Form." *NTS* 14: 96–111.

Braun, M. A. 1977. "James' Use of Amos at the Jerusalem Council: Steps Toward a Possible Solution of the Textual and Theological Problems." *JETS* 20: 113–21.

Brawley, R. L. 1995. *Text to Text Pours Forth Speech: Voices of Scripture in Luke-Acts.* ISBL. Bloomington: Indiana University Press.

Brodie, T. L. 1983. "The Accusing and Stoning of Naboth (1 Kings 21:8–13) as One Component of the Stephen Text (Acts 6:9–14; 7:58a)." *CBQ* 45: 417–32.

———. 1986. "Towards Unravelling the Rhetorical Imitation of Sources in Acts: 2 Kings 5 as One Component of Acts 8,9–40." *Bib* 67: 41–67.

———. 1987. *Luke the Literary Interpreter: Luke-Acts as a Systematic Rewriting and Updating of the Elijah-Elisha Narrative in 1 and 2 Kings.* Rome: Pontifica Studiorum Universitas A.S. Thoma Aq. in Urbe.

———. 1990. "Luke-Acts as an Imitation and Emulation of the Elijah-Elisha Narrative." Pages 78–85 in *New Visions on Luke and Acts.* Edited by E. Richard. Collegeville, MN: Liturgical Press.

Brooke, G. J. 1985. *Exegesis at Qumran: 4QFlorilegium in Its Jewish Context.* JSOTSup 29. Sheffield: JSOT Press.

Bruce, F. F. 1987. "Paul's Use of the Old Testament in Acts." Pages 71–79 in *Tradition and Interpretation in the New Testament: Essays in Honor of E. Earle Ellis for His 60th Birthday.* Edited by G. F. Hawthorne and O. Betz. Grand Rapids: Eerdmans.

———. 1988. *The Book of the Acts.* Revised edition. Grand Rapids: Eerdmans.

———. 1990. *The Acts of the Apostles: Greek Text with Introduction and Commentary.* Third revised and enlarged edition. Grand Rapids: Eerdmans; Leicester: Apollos.

Brunson, A. 2003. *Psalm 118 in the Gospel of John: An Intertextual Study on the New Exodus Pattern in the Theology of John.* WUNT 2/158. Tübingen: Mohr Siebeck.

Buckwalter, H. D. 1996. *The Character and Purpose of Luke's Christology.* SNTSMS 89. Cambridge: Cambridge University Press.

Calvin, J. 1965–1966. *The Acts of the Apostles.* Translated by J. W. Fraser and W. J. G. McDonald. 2 vols. Edinburgh: Oliver & Boyd.

Carroll, J. T. 1990. "The Uses of Scripture in Acts." *SBLSP* 29: 512–28.

Carson, D. A., and H. G. M. Williamson, eds. 1988. *It Is Written: Scripture Citing Scripture; Essays in Honour of Barnabas Lindars, SSF.* Cambridge: Cambridge University Press.

Clark, A. C. 2001. *Parallel Lives: The Relation of Paul to the Apostles in the Lucan Perspective.* PBTM. Carlisle: Paternoster.

Clarke, W. K. L. 1922. "The Use of the Septuagint in Acts." Pages 66–105 in *The Beginnings of Christianity.* Part I, vol. 2. Edited by F. J. Foakes-Jackson and K. Lake. London: Macmillan.

Clements, R. E. 1990. "The Old Testament Background of Acts 10:34–35." Pages 203–16 in *With Steadfast Purpose: Essays on Acts in Honor of Henry Jackson Flanders Jr.* Edited by N. H. Keathley. Waco: Baylor University.

Coggins, R. J. 1982. "The Samaritans and Acts." *NTS* 28: 423–34.

Dahl, N. A. 1957–1958. "A People for His Name (Acts xv.14)." *NTS* 4: 319–27.

———. 1968. "The Story of Abraham in Luke-Acts." Pages 139–58 in *Studies in Luke-Acts: Essays Presented in Honour of P. Schubert.* Edited by L. E. Keck and J. L. Martyn. London: SPCK.

Daube, D. 1956. *The New Testament and Rabbinic Judaism.* London: Athlone.

Denova, R. I. 1997. *The Things Accomplished among Us: Prophetic Tradition in the Structural Pattern of Luke-Acts.* JSNTSup 141. Sheffield: Sheffield Academic Press.

deSilva, D. A. 1994. "Paul's Sermon in Antioch of Pisidia." *BSac* 151: 32–49.

de Waard, J. 1965. *A Comparative Study of the Old Testament Text in the Dead Sea Scrolls and in the New Testament.* STDJ 4. Leiden: Brill.

Doble, P. 2000. "Something Greater than Solomon: An Approach to Stephan's Speech." Pages 181–207 in *The Old Testament in the New Testament: Essays in Honour of J. L. North.* Edited by S. Moyise. JSNTSup. 189. Sheffield: Sheffield Academic Press.

———. 2002a. "The Stone-Saying and a Community Prayer: Acts 4.1–31." Unpublished paper.

———. 2002b. "Use of the Psalms in Luke-Acts: Towards Understanding Paul's Sermon at Pisidian Antioch." Unpublished paper.

———. 2004. "The Psalms in Luke-Acts." Pages 83–117 in *The Psalms in the New Testament.* Edited by S. Moyise and M. J. J. Menken. London: T&T Clark.

———. 2006a. "The Songs of God's Servant: David and His Psalms in Luke-Acts." *JSNT* 28 (3): 267–83.

———. 2006b. "Listening to a Prophet Like Moses (Acts 3.22–23)." Unpublished paper.

Dodd, C. H. 1952. *According to the Scriptures: The Sub-Structure of New Testament Theology.* London: Nisbet.

Doeve, J. W. 1954. *Jewish Hermeneutics in the Synoptic Gospels and Acts.* Assen: Van Gorcum.

Duling, D. C. 1973. "The Promises to David and Their Entrance into Christianity: Nailing Down a Likely Hypothesis." *NTS* 20: 55–77.

Dumais, M. 1976. *Le langage de l'évangélisation: L'annonce missionnaire en milieu juif, Actes 13,16–41.* Tournai: Desclée.

Dupont, J. 1948. "Filius meus es tu": L'interprétation de Ps. II, 7 dans le Nouveau Testament." *RSR* 35: 522–43.

———. 1967a. *Études sur les Actes des Apôtres.* LD 45. Paris: Cerf.

———. 1967b. "La destinée de Judas prophétisée par David." Pages 309–20 in *Études sur les Actes des Apôtres.* LD 45. Paris: Cerf.

———. 1967c. "L'Interpretation des psaumes dans les Actes des Apôtres." Pages 283–307 in *Études sur les Actes des Apôtres.* LD 45. Paris: Cerf. [Translated as "Messianic Interpretation of the Psalms in the Acts of the Apostles." Pages 103–28 in *The Salvation of the Gentiles: Essays on the Acts of the Apostles.* New York: Paulist Press, 1979.]

———. 1967d. "L'utilisation apologétique de l'Ancien Testament dans les discours des Actes." Pages 245–82 in *Études sur les Actes des Apôtres.* LD 45. Paris: Cerf. [Translated as "Apologetic Use of the Old Testament in the Speeches of Acts." Pages 129–59 in *The Salvation of the Gentiles: Essays on the Acts of the Apostles.* New York: Paulist Press, 1979.]

———. 1967e. "ΤΑ ʽΟΣΙΑ ΔΑΥΙΔ ΤΑ ΠΙΣΤΑ (Actes 13,34 = Isaïe 55,3)." Pages 337–59 in *Études sur les Actes des Apôtres.* LD 45. Paris: Cerf.

———. 1973. "Ascension du Christ et don de l'Esprit d'après Actes 2:33." Pages 219–28 in *Christ and Spirit in the New Testament: Essays in Honour of Charles Francis Digby Moule.* Edited by Barnabas Lindars and Stephen S. Smalley. Cambridge: Cambridge University Press.

———. 1979. *The Salvation of the Gentiles: Essays on the Acts of the Apostles.* New York: Paulist Press.

———. 1985. "Un Peuple d'entre les Nations (Actes 15.14)." *NTS* 31: 321–35.

Ellis, E. E. 1978. "Midrashic Features in the Speeches of Acts." Pages 198–208 in *Prophecy and Hermeneutic in Early Christianity.* Grand Rapids: Eerdmans.

———. 1991a. "'The End of the Earth' (Acts 1:8)." *BBR* 1: 123–32.

———. 1991b. *The Old Testament in Early Christianity: Canon and Interpretation in the Light of Modern Research.* WUNT 54. Tübingen: Mohr Siebeck.

Ellul, D. 1992. "Antioche de Pisidie: Une prédication … trois credos? (Actes 13,13–43)." *FN* 5: 3–14.

Emerton, J. A. 1968. Review of M. Wilcox, *The Semitisms of Acts.* *JSS* 13: 282–97.

Evans, C. A. 1993a. "The Function of the Elijah/Elisha Narratives in Luke's Ethic of Election." Pages 70–83 in *Luke and Scripture: The Function of Sacred Tradition in Luke-Acts.* By C. A. Evans and J. A. Sanders. Minneapolis: Fortress.

———. 1993b. "Prophecy and Polemic: Jews in Luke's Scriptural Apologetic." Pages 172–211 in *Luke and Scripture: The Function of Sacred Tradition in Luke-Acts.* By C. A. Evans and J. A. Sanders. Minneapolis: Fortress.

———. 1993c. "The Prophetic Setting of the Pentecost Sermon." Pages 213–25 in *Luke and Scripture: The Function of Sacred Tradition in Luke-Acts.* By C. A. Evans and J. A. Sanders. Minneapolis: Fortress.

Fitzmyer, J. A. 1998. "The Use of the Old Testament in Luke-Acts." Pages 295–313 in *To Advance the Gospel: New Testament Studies.* 2nd ed. BRS. Grand Rapids: Eerdmans; Livonia, MI: Dove.

France, R. T. 1971. *Jesus and the Old Testament: His Application of Old Testament Passages to Himself and His Mission.* London: Tyndale.

García Martínez, F., ed. 1996. *The Dead Sea Scrolls Translated: The Qumran Texts in English.* Translated by W. G. E. Watson. 2nd ed. Leiden: Brill; Grand Rapids: Eerdmans.

Garrett, S. R. 1990. "Exodus from Bondage: Luke 9:31 and Acts 12:1–24." *CBQ* 52: 656–80.

Goldingay, J. 2001. *Isaiah.* Peabody, MA: Hendrickson.

Goldsmith, D. 1968. "Acts 13:33–37: A Pesher on II Sam 7." *JBL* 87: 321–24.

Goppelt, L. 1982. *Typos: The Typological Interpretation of the Old Testament in the New.* Translated by D. H. Madvig. Grand Rapids: Eerdmans.

Gordon, R. P. 1974. "Targumic Parallels to Acts XIII 18 and Didache XIV 3." *NovT* 16: 285–89.

Gourges, M. 1978. *À la droite de Dieu: Résurrection de Jésus et actualisation du Psaume 110,1 dans le Nouveau Testament.* EBib. Paris: Gabalda.

Haenchen, E. 1971. *The Acts of the Apostles: A Commentary.* Translated by B. Noble and G. Shinn. Philadelphia: Westminster.

Hanson, A. T. 1980. *The New Testament Interpretation of Scripture.* London: SPCK.

———. 1983. *The Living Utterances of God: The New Testament Exegesis of the Old.* London: Darton, Longman & Todd.

Hanson, R. P. C. 1967. *The Acts in the Revised Standard Version.* New Clarendon Bible. Oxford: Clarendon.

Hay, D. M. 1973. *Glory at the Right Hand: Psalm 110 in Early Christianity.* SBLMS 18. Nashville: Abingdon.

Hengel, M. 1996. "Zur Wirkungsgeschichte von Jes. 53 in vorchristlicher Zeit." Pages 49–91 in *Der leidende Gottesknecht: Jesaja 53 und seine Wirkungsgeschichte.* Edited by B. Janowski and P. Stuhlmacher. FAT 14. Tübingen: Mohr Siebeck. [Cf. the brief summary in Bellinger and Farmer 1998: 256.]

Holtz, T. 1968. *Untersuchungen über die alttestamentliche Zitate bei Lukas.* TU 104. Berlin: Akademie.

———. 1997. "Geschichte und Verheissung: Auferstand nach der Schrift." *EvT* 57: 179–96.

Hooker, M. D. 1959. *Jesus and the Servant: The Influence of the Servant Concept of Deutero-Isaiah in the New Testament.* London: SPCK.

———. 1998a. "Did the Use of Isaiah 53 to Interpret His Mission Begin with Jesus?" Pages 88–103 in *Jesus and the Suffering Servant: Isaiah 53 and Christian Origins.* Edited by W. H. Bellinger Jr. and W. R. Farmer. Harrisburg, PA: Trinity Press International.

———. 1998b. "Response to Mikeal Parsons." Pages 120–24 in *Jesus and the Suffering Servant: Isaiah 53 and Christian Origins.* Edited by W. H. Bellinger Jr. and W. R. Farmer. Harrisburg, PA: Trinity Press International.

Hübner, H. 1990–1995. *Biblische Theologie des Neuen Testaments.* 3 vols. Göttingen: Vandenhoeck & Ruprecht.

Humphreys, C. J., and W. G. Waddington. 1992. "The Jewish Calendar, a Lunar Eclipse and the Date of Christ's Crucifixion." *TynBul* 43: 331–52.

Janowski, B., and P. Stuhlmacher, eds. 1996. *Der leidende Gottesknecht: Jesaja 53 und seine Wirkungsgeschichte.* FAT 14. Tübingen: Mohr Siebeck.

Jervell, J. 1983. "Die Mitte der Schrift: Zum lukanischen Verständnis des Alten Testaments." Pages 79–96 in *Die Mitte des Neuen Testaments: Einheit und Vielfalt neutestamentlicher Theologie; Festschrift für Eduard Schweizer zum siebzigsten Geburtstag.* Edited by U. Luz and H. Weder. Göttingen: Vandenhoeck & Ruprecht. [Largely reproduced in translation in Jervell 1996: 61–75.]

———. 1996. *The Theology of the Acts of the Apostles.* Cambridge: Cambridge University Press.

———. 1998. *Die Apostelgeschichte.* KEK. Göttingen: Vandenhoeck & Ruprecht.

Jobes, K. H., and M. Silva. 2000. *Invitation to the Septuagint.* Grand Rapids: Baker Academic.

Johnson, D. E. 1990. "Jesus against the Idols: The Use of Isaianic Servant Songs in the Missiology of Acts." *WJT* 52: 343–53.

Johnson, L. T. 1992. *The Acts of the Apostles.* SP 5. Collegeville, MN: Liturgical Press.

Johnston, P. S. 1995. "'Left in Hell'? Psalm 16, Sheol and the Holy One." Pages 213–22 in *The Lord's Anointed: Interpretation of the Old Testament Messianic Texts.* Edited by P. E. Satterthwaite, R. S. Hess, and G. J. Wenham. THS. Carlisle: Paternoster.

Juel, D. 1981. "Social Dimensions of Exegesis: The Use of Psalm 16 in Acts 2." *CBQ* 43: 543–54.

Kaiser, W. C. 1980. "The Promise to David in Psalm 16 and Its Application in Acts 2:25–33 and 13:32–37." *JETS* 23: 219–29.

Keathley, N. H., ed. 1990. *With Steadfast Purpose: Essays on Acts in Honor of Henry Jackson Flanders Jr.* Waco: Baylor University.

Keck, L. E., and J. L. Martyn, eds. 1968. *Studies in Luke-Acts: Essays Presented in Honour of P. Schubert.* London: SPCK.

Kilpatrick, G. D. 1978. "Some Quotations in Acts." Pages 81–97 in *Les Actes des Apôtres: Traditions, rédaction, théologie.* Edited by J. Kremer et al. BETL 48. Leuven: Leuven University Press.

Kimball, C. 1994. *Jesus' Exposition of the Old Testament in Luke's Gospel.* JSNTSup 94. Sheffield: JSOT Press.

Koet, B. J. 1989. *Five Studies on Interpretation of Scripture in Luke-Acts.* SNTA 14. Leuven: Leuven University Press.

———. 2005. "Isaiah in Luke-Acts." Pages 79–100 in *Isaiah and the New Testament.* Edited by S. Moyise and M. J. J. Menken. London: T&T Clark.

Larkin, W. J., Jr. 1995. *Acts.* IVPNTC 5. Downers Grove, IL: InterVarsity.

Lierman, J. 2004. *The New Testament Moses: Christian Perceptions of Moses and Israel in the Setting of Jewish Religion.* WUNT 2/173. Tübingen: Mohr Siebeck.

Lincoln, A. T. 1990. *Ephesians.* WBC 42. Dallas: Word.

Lindars, B. 1961. *New Testament Apologetic: The Doctrinal Significance of the Old Testament Quotations.* London: SCM.

Litwak, K. D. 2005. *Echoes of Scripture in Luke-Acts: Telling the History of God's People Intertextually.* JSNTSup. 282. London: T&T Clark.

Longenecker, R. N. 1999. *Biblical Exegesis in the Apostolic Period.* 2nd ed. Grand Rapids: Eerdmans; Vancouver: Regent College Publishing.

Lövestam, E. 1961. *Son and Saviour: A Study of Acts 13,32–37; with an Appendix, "Son of God" in the Synoptic Gospels.* Translated by M. J. Petry. ConBNT 18. Lund: Gleerup.

Marguerat, D. 2002. *The First Christian Historian: Writing the "Acts of the Apostles."* Translated by K. McKinney, G. J. Laughery, and R. Bauckham. SNTSMS 121. Cambridge: Cambridge University Press.

Marshall, I. H. 1980. *The Acts of the Apostles: An Introduction and Commentary.* Leicester: Inter-Varsity.

———. 1988. "An Assessment of Recent Developments." Pages 1–21 in *It Is Written: Scripture Citing Scripture; Essays in Honour of Barnabas Lindars, SSF.* Edited by D. A. Carson and H. G. M. Williamson. Cambridge: Cambridge University Press.

Marshall, I. H., and D. Peterson, eds. 1998. *Witness to the Gospel: The Theology of Acts.* Grand Rapids: Eerdmans.

Mays, J. L. 1994. *The Lord Reigns: A Theological Handbook to the Psalms.* Louisville: Westminster John Knox.

Metzger, B. M. 1994. *A Textual Commentary on the Greek New Testament.* 2nd ed. Stuttgart: Deutsche Bibelgesellschaft and United Bible Societies.

Mivra, Y. 2007. *David in Luke-Acts: His Portrayal in the Light of Early Judaism.* WUNT (forthcoming). Tübingen: Mohr Siebeck.

Moessner, D. P. 1989. *Lord of the Banquet: The Literary and Theological Significance of the Lukan Travel Narrative.* Minneapolis: Fortress.

———. 1996. "The 'Script' of the Scriptures in Acts: Suffering as God's 'Plan' (βουλή) for the World for the 'Release of Sins.'" Pages 218–50 in *History, Literature and Society in the Book of Acts.* Edited by B. Witherington III. Cambridge: Cambridge University Press.

———. 1998. "Two Lords 'at the Right Hand'? The Psalms and an Intertextual Reading of Peter's Pentecost Speech (Acts 2:14–36)." Pages 215–32 in *Literary Studies in Luke-Acts: Essays in Honor of Joseph B. Tyson.* Edited by R. P. Thompson and T. E. Phillips. Macon, GA: Mercer University Press.

———, ed. 1999. *Jesus and the Heritage of Israel: Luke's Narrative Claim upon Israel's Legacy.* Harrisburg, PA: Trinity Press International.

Moore, T. S. 1997. "'To the End of the Earth': The Geographical and Ethnic Universalism of Acts 1:8 in Light of Isaianic Influence on Luke." *JETS* 40: 389–99.

Moyise, S. 2001. *The Old Testament in the New: An Introduction.* CBSS. London: Continuum.

Nägele, S. 1995. *Laubhütte Davids und Wolkensohn: Eine auslegungsgeschichtliche Studie zu Amos 9,11 in der jüdischen und christlichen Exegese.* AGJU 24. Leiden: Brill.

Nellesen, E. 1975. "Tradition und Schrift in der Perikope von der Erwählung des Matthias." *BZ* 19: 205–18.

Nielsen, A. E. 2000. *Until It Is Fulfilled: Lukan Eschatology According to Luke 22 and Acts 20.* WUNT 2/126. Tübingen: Mohr Siebeck.

O'Toole, R. F. 1990. "The Parallels between Jesus and Moses." *BTB* 20: 22–29.

Pao, D. W. 2000. *Acts and the Isaianic New Exodus.* WUNT 2/130. Tübingen: Mohr Siebeck.

Parsons, M. 1998. "Isaiah 53 in Acts 8: A Reply to Professor Morna Hooker." Pages 104–19 in *Jesus and the Suffering Servant: Isaiah 53 and Christian Origins.* Edited by W. H. Bellinger Jr. and W. R. Farmer. Harrisburg, PA: Trinity Press International.

Paulo, P.-A. 1985. *Le problème ecclésial des Actes à la lumière de deux prophéties d'Amos.* Montreal: Bellarmin; Paris: Cerf.

Pervo, R. 1987. *Profit with Delight: The Literary Genre of the Acts of the Apostles.* Philadelphia: Fortress.

Pesch, R. 1986. *Die Apostelgeschichte.* 2 vols. EKKNT 5/1–2. Zürich: Benziger; Neukirchen-Vluyn: Neukirchener Verlag.

Rese, M. 1969. *Alttestamentliche Motive in der Christologie des Lukas.* SNT 1. Gütersloh: Mohn.

———. 1979. "Die Funktion der alttestamentlichen Zitate und Anspielungen in den Reden der Apostelgeschichte." Pages 61–79 in *Les Actes des Apôtres: Traditions, rédaction, théologie.* Edited by J. Kremer et al. BETL 48. Gembloux: Duculot; Leuven: Leuven University Press.

Richard, E. 1982. "The Creative Use of Amos by the Author of Acts." *NovT* 24: 37–53.

Riesner, R. 1994. "James's Speech (Acts 15:13–21), Simeon's Hymn (Luke 2:29–32), and Luke's Sources." Pages 263–78 in *Jesus of Nazareth Lord and Christ: Essays on the Historical Jesus and New Testament Christology.* Edited by J. B. Green and M. Turner. Grand Rapids: Eerdmans; Carlisle: Paternoster.

Rowe, C. K. 2007. "Acts 2.36 and the Continuity of Lukan Christology." *NTS* 53:37–56.

Rusam, D. 2003. *Das Alte Testament bei Lukas.* BZNW 112. Berlin: De Gruyter.

Schaper, J. 1995. *Eschatology in the Greek Psalter.* WUNT 2/76. Tübingen: Mohr Siebeck.

Scharlemann, M. H. 1968. *Stephen: A Singular Saint.* AnBib 34. Rome: Pontifical Biblical Institute.

Schmitt, A. 1973. "Ps 16,8–11 als Zeugnis der Auferstehung in der Apg." *BZ* 17: 229–48.

Schneider, G. 1980–1982. *Die Apostelgeschichte.* 2 vols. HTKNT. Freiburg: Herder.

Schubert, P. 1957. "The Structure and Significance of Luke 24." Pages 165–86 in *Neutestamentliche Studien für Rudolf Bultmann zu seinem 70. Geburtstag am 20. August 1954.* Edited by W. Eltester. BZNW 21. Berlin: Töpelmann.

Schweizer, E. 1968. "The Concept of the Davidic 'Son of God' in Acts and Its Old Testament Background." Pages 186–93 in *Studies in Luke-Acts: Essays Presented in Honour of P. Schubert.* Edited by L. E. Keck and J. L. Martyn. London: SPCK.

Scott, J. M. 1994. "Luke's Geographical Horizon." Pages 483–544 in *The Book of Acts in Its Graeco-Roman Setting.* Edited by D. W. J. Gill and C. Gempf. Grand Rapids: Eerdmans; Carlisle: Paternoster.

Seccombe, D. 1981. "Luke and Isaiah." *NTS* 27: 252–59.

Soards, M. L. 1994. *The Speeches of Acts: Their Contents, Context and Concerns.* Louisville: Westminster John Knox.

Stanton, G. N. 1974. *Jesus of Nazareth in New Testament Preaching.* SNTSMS 27. Cambridge: Cambridge University Press.

Steck, O. H. 1967. *Israel und das gewaltsame Geschick der Propheten: Untersuchungen zur Überlieferung des deuteronomistischen Ge-*

schichtsbildes im Alten Testament, Spätjudentum und Urchristentum. WMANT 23. Neukirchen-Vluyn: Neukirchener Verlag.

Steffer, E. 2001. "Luc-Actes et le'Ancien Testament." *FoiVie* 100 (4): 31–40.

Sterling, G. E. 1999. "'Opening the Scriptures': The Legitimation of the Jewish Diaspora and the Early Christian Mission." Pages 199–225 in *Jesus and the Heritage of Israel: Luke's Narrative Claim upon Israel's Legacy.* Edited by D. P. Moessner. Harrisburg, PA: Trinity Press International.

Steyn, G. J. 1995. *Septuagint Quotations in the Context of the Petrine and Pauline Speeches of the Acta Apostolorum.* CBET 12. Kampen: Kok Pharos.

Stott, J. R. W. 1990. *The Message of Acts.* Leicester: Inter-Varsity.

Strauss, M. L. 1995. *The Davidic Messiah in Luke-Acts: The Promise and Its Fulfillment in Lukan Christology.* JSNTSup 110. Sheffield: Sheffield Academic Press.

Strom, M. R. 1986. "An Old Testament Background to Acts 12.20–23." *NTS* 32: 289–92.

Stowasser, M. 2001. "Am 5,25–27; 9,11f. in der Qumranüberlieferung und in der Apostelgeschichte: Text- und traditionsgeschichtliche Überlegungen zu 4Q174 (Florilegium) III 12/CD VII 16/Apg 7,42b–43; 15,16–18." *ZNW* 92: 47–63.

Swartley, W. M. 1997. "Intertextuality in Early Christian Literature." *DLNTD* 536–42.

Sylva, D. D. 1987. "The Meaning and Function of Acts 7:46–50." *JBL* 106: 261–75.

Talbert, C. H. 1984. "Promise and Fulfilment in Lucan Theology." Pages 91–103 in *Luke-Acts: New Perspectives from the Society of Biblical Literature.* Edited by C. H. Talbert. New York: Crossroad.

Tasker, R. V. G. 1963. Pages 63–79 in *The Old Testament in the New Testament.* Grand Rapids: Eerdmans.

Theissen, G. 1983. *The Miracle Stories of the Early Christian Tradition.* Translated by F. McDonagh. SNTW. Edinburgh: T&T Clark.

Turner, M. 1982. "The Sabbath, Sunday, and the Law in Luke/Acts." Pages 99–157 in *From Sabbath to Lord's Day: A Biblical, Historical and Theological Investigation.* Edited by D. A. Carson. Grand Rapids: Zondervan.

———. 1996. *Power from on High: The Spirit in Israel's Restoration and Witness in Luke-Acts.* JPTSup 9. Sheffield: Sheffield Academic Press.

van de Sandt, H. 1991. "Why Is Amos 5.25–27 Quoted in Acts 7.42f.?" *ZNW* 82: 67–87.

———. 1992. "An Explanation of Acts 15.6–21 in the Light of Deuteronomy 4.29–35 (LXX)." *JSNT* 46: 73–97.

———. 1994. "The Quotations in Acts 13, 32–52 as a Reflection of Luke's LXX Interpretation." *Bib* 75: 26–58.

Wall, R. W. 2000. "Intertextuality, Biblical." *DNTB* 541–51.

———. 2002. "The Acts of the Apostles." Pages 1–368 in vol. 10 of *The New Interpreter's Bible.* Nashville: Abingdon.

Watts, R. E. 1998. "Jesus' Death, Isaiah 53, and Mark 10:45: A Crux Revisited." Pages 125–51 *Jesus and the Suffering Servant: Isaiah 53 and Christian Origins.* Edited by W. H. Bellinger Jr. and W. R. Farmer. Harrisburg, PA: Trinity Press International.

Weiser, A. 1981–1985. *Die Apostelgeschichte.* 2 vols. ÖTK 5. Gütersloh: Mohn; Würzburg: Echter.

Wenham, G. J. 1987. *Genesis 1–15.* WBC 1. Waco: Word.

———. 1994. *Genesis 16–50.* WBC 2. Dallas: Word.

Weren, W. J. C. 1989. "Psalm 2 in Luke-Acts: an Intertextual Study." Pages 189–203 in *Intertextuality in Biblical Writ-*

ings: *Essays in Honour of Bas van Iersel.* Edited by S. Draisma. Kampen: Kok.

Wilcox, M. 1965. *The Semitisms of Acts.* Oxford: Clarendon.

Witherington, B., III, ed. 1996. *History, Literature and Society in the Book of Acts.* Cambridge: Cambridge University Press.

———. 1998. *The Acts of the Apostles: A Socio-Rhetorical Commentary.* Grand Rapids: Eerdmans; Carlisle: Paternoster.

Wolff, H. W. 1984. *Jesaja 53 im Urchristentum.* 4th ed. MSt 233. Giessen: Brunnen.

ROMANS

MARK A. SEIFRID

Introduction

As Paul makes clear from the opening of the letter, his message to the church at Rome is nothing more than a proclamation of the Scriptures that have been fulfilled in the incarnate, crucified, and risen Christ. The roughly sixty citations of the Old Testament in Romans—more numerous and concentrated than any of Paul's other letters—are only a portion of the biblical witness upon which the letter rests. Much of the apostle's appeal to Scripture here appears in the form of allusions. The central theological vocabulary of the letter belongs to these allusions. Such terms as "gospel," "promise," "faith," "calling," "son of God," "holy Spirit" have their roots in the Hebrew Scriptures and implicitly recall the contexts from which they are drawn. The allusions extend to larger structures as well. The "fall" of idolatrous humanity (1:18–32), Adam and his transgression (5:12–21), and the human confrontation with the law of God (7:7–25) each in its own way recalls the narrative of Genesis 3 without citing that text. Paul's description of God's justifying work in Christ in 3:21–26, rich in its appeal to cultic texts and prophetic promises, cites no biblical text. Likewise, the apostolic appeal to the *Shemaʿ*, which serves a fundamental role in his argument through the end of Romans 11 and beyond, appears only in a suggestive allusion in 3:30.

The incarnate, crucified, and risen Christ is the center and end of Scripture. Paul's interpretation of Scripture arises from this confession. As the apostle makes clear at decisive points in his argument (1:1–7; 10:1–4; 15:4; 16:25–27), the letter is a lesson in hermeneutics for his readers. The "gospel of God, concerning his son" is the fulfillment of prophetic promise, and thereby of the message of the whole of Scripture (1:2; 16:25–27). The law along with the prophets bears witness to the righteousness of God manifest in Jesus Christ (3:21; see 10:4). This lesson is no mere intellectual exercise but a witness given for exhortation, comfort, and faith (see 1:12; 15:4, 14–15). The message of Scripture has been hidden in the past, not because it has not been announced, but because faith alone opens the Scripture to us (1:1–7). The once-hidden mystery of the Gospel now has been made known through the "prophetic scriptures" themselves for the "obedience which is faith" (*hypakoē pisteōs*; 16:25–26; see 1:5).

This hermeneutic shapes the terms by which Paul describes "Scripture." The message of Scripture is the "gospel" (1:1, 9, 15, 16; 2:16; 11:28; 15:16, 19, 20; 16:25). The Scriptures are no mere record of the past. They speak to the present, as do their human authors (4:3, 6; 9:15, 17, 26; 10:6, 8, 11, 16, 20, 21; 11:2, 4, 11; 15:12). The introductory formula "just as it is written" (*kathōs gegraptai*)

607

is a testimony to a present, eschatological reality and not a mere reminder of some past promise or demand (1:17; 2:24; 3:4, 10; 4:17; 8:36; 9:13, 33; 10:15; 11:8, 26; 12:19; 14:11; 15:3, 4, 9, 21).

God's righteousness revealed in the gospel overcomes the law, which works God's wrath (1:18, 32; 3:19–20; 4:15; 5:20; 7:7–25). The law, which also speaks in the present (3:19; 7:7; 10:5), pronounces not our salvation but our condemnation. The written demand of God ("letter"; *gramma*) addresses us from without, effecting guilt (2:27, 29; 7:6). Only the wonder of the gospel overcomes this condemnation worked by the law (3:21–26). The law is fulfilled outside itself in Christ, who is its goal (8:4; 10:1–4; 13:8–10). This uncompromising distinction between these two "words" is basic to Paul's interpretation of Scripture.

According to Paul, the voice of God in Scripture is an echo of the voice of the Creator in creation. The proclamation of the gospel retraces the proclamation of creation itself (10:18; Ps. 19:4). The apostle's paean in 11:33–36 offers the praise of the Creator that idolatrous humanity has refused to yield (1:8–32). The knowledge and praise of the Creator thus entails the confession of his unfathomable wisdom and ways. The dealings of God with Israel as recounted from Scripture in Romans 9–11 are not an appendix to the gospel but an elaboration of it. That which has been fulfilled in Christ must yet be fulfilled in humanity. Jew and Gentile, divided by the promise of God to Abraham, must be united in salvation by that same promise without the loss of their ethnic identities (4:9–11). Their final, common worship is a matter of unseen hope, grasped by faith alone (15:4–6). All hope is a hope against all outward appearance (4:18; 8:24). The same is true of the confession of the Creator in the face of human suffering. Creation "groans" together with believers, just as Israel once groaned in Egypt in anticipation of redemption (8:18–29). Paul takes up the lament of the psalmists, who do not attempt to explain present suffering but bring their complaint in the face of the unanswered promises of God (8:36; Ps. 44:22).

Consequently, although Paul's use of Scripture bears a salvation-historical dimension, it is fundamentally typological in nature. It is impossible to connect the lines or to obtain a bird's-eye view of the whole of God's plan. We grasp God's righ-

teousness only as it has been manifest in Jesus Christ (1:16–17). The Scriptures, according to Paul, are nothing other than God speaking to his people in the present through his words of judgment and salvation to Israel in the past.

The Opening of the Letter: The Apostle to the Gentiles to the Called Saints in Rome (1:1–15)

The Prayer-Report of Thanksgiving (1:8–12)

Here, as elsewhere, a prayer-report of thanksgiving reveals the apostle's perspective on the church and its needs in light of the Gospel.

The Self-Report (1:13–15)

Paul regularly reports his activities to his addressees before he turns to the subject of the letter (Schnider and Stenger 1987: 50–68). In this instance the section is exceedingly brief and closely tied to the report of prayer.

The Body of the Letter: God's Righteousness Revealed in the Gospel and Hidden in the Promise of Mercy for Israel (1:16–11:36)

The Revelation of God's Righteousness in the Gospel (1:16–3:26)

1:16–17

Following numerous allusions in 1:1–16, in 1:17b, for the first time in the letter, Paul cites Scripture directly. The revelation of God's saving righteousness has taken place in accord with the Scripture: "Just as it is written, 'The righteous one shall live by faith'" (Hab. 2:4b). In appealing to this text, Paul drops the pronominal ending attached to the Hebrew term *'ĕmûnâ* in Habakkuk. Coupled with this change is the shift in meaning entailed in his usage of *pistis*. Although the Greek word *pistis* may signify either "faithfulness" or "faith," Paul clearly uses the term in the latter sense: "the righteous person lives by faith." He thus varies from the Hebrew text, which speaks of the "faithfulness" (*'ĕmûnâ*) by which the righteous one lives. The placement of the prepositional phrase "by faith" after the noun next to the verb favors reading it adverbially (cf. Gal. 2:20), as with both the Hebrew text and the septuagintal readings.

Modern translations regularly read Paul's usage into the Hebrew text, so that 'ĕmûnâ is translated as "faith" in Hab. 2:4 (e.g., NRSV, NIV, NASB, ESV). But this rendering is illegitimate, as 'ĕmûnâ signifies fidelity, reliability, or faithfulness. Interpreters of Rom. 1:17b sometimes have moved in the opposite direction, suggesting that Paul has in view persistence or fidelity in believing when he cites Habakkuk (e.g., G. N. Davies 1990: 39–46; Fitzmyer 1993: 264; Silva 1993: 641; Garlington 1994: 49–50; Schreiner 1998: 74–75). Paul, too, it is thought, speaks of the righteous one living by faithfulness or "faithful believing." But in contrast with Jewish tradition (see below), Paul does not understand "faith" as a human quality or virtue. The context makes this clear. In proclamation ("from faith") God's saving righteousness is *revealed* and thus effects faith ("unto faith" [1:17a]). The righteousness of the one who believes (1:17b) is found in the righteousness of God revealed in the gospel (1:17a). Furthermore, as a citation of Hab. 2:4, it is clear that "living by faith" signifies "sharing in salvation," participating in the gospel, not merely the faithful living of an individual (or community).

The earliest septuagintal rendering of Hab. 2:4 differs from both the MT and Paul (Koch 1985). The righteous one is said to live "by my faithfulness" (*ek pisteōs mou*)—that is, the faithfulness of the Lord (cf. Heb. 10:38, *v.l.*). It is possible that we have here simply an alternative reading of the suffix attached to 'ĕmûnâ. In this period the Hebrew consonants *wāw* and *yôd* could be identical in appearance and might be confused at other points in Hab. 2:1–4 MT (Fitzmyer 1981: 236–41). One could read the ending as either "my faithfulness" or "his (or 'its') faithfulness." The latter reading appears in the Greek text of Habakkuk from *Naḥal Ḥever* (8ḤXIIgr 17:30) and in Aquila, Theodotion, and Symmachus.

On the other hand, the septuagintal reading could be interpretive, as are its other renderings in this context. For example, in Hab. 2:2–3 the LXX quite possibly reads the vision (*horasis*) messianically in terms of the "Coming One" (*erchomenos*) (cf. Heb. 10:37–38; see Strobel 1961: 47–56), a reading that resonates with the wider context of Romans: the "righteousness of God" is revealed in the good news of the crucified and risen Messiah (1:1–5; cf. 3:21–22; 10:3–4).

Targum of the Prophets on Habakkuk 2:4 anticipates Paul's interpretation of the text as a call to faith: "The wicked think that all these things are not so, but the righteous live by the truth of them" (Cathcart and Gordon 1989: 150–51). The antecedent to "all these things" appears to be "the prophecy written in the book of the Law" (*Tg. Hab.* 2:2–3). At the same time, other passages in *Targum of the Prophets* reflect the sort of tradition that we find in *Midr. Eccles.* 3:9: "The righteous shall live by their rectitude" (cf. Ezek. 18:9); the tradition of interpretation obviously was variegated.

The Qumran Habakkuk pesher reflects this alternative tradition, interpreting Hab. 2:4 as referring to "all those doing the Law in the house of Judah," whom God shall deliver on account of "their labor and their faithfulness to the Teacher of Righteousness" (1QpHab VIII, 1–3). Although the latter part of this text has been taken to speak of "faith in the Teacher of Righteousness," the context strongly suggests that the deeds of "the men of truth" are in view: 1QpHab VIII, 1–3 takes up the thought of 1QpHab VII, 10–12, which speaks of "men of truth who do the Law." According to the pesher, it is the "toil" of the "doers of the Law" that is 'ĕmûnâ. The "mysteries of the words of the prophets" revealed to the Teacher of Righteousness establish the proper observance of the law within the community (1QpHab VII, 4–5). Faithfulness to the revealed law brings life.

Habakkuk 2:4 also appears in later rabbinic tradition as the conclusion of a series of summaries of the requirements of the law that end in the single requirement of 'ĕmûnâ (*b. Mak.* 23; *Mek.* 14:15 [29b]; *Midr. Eccles.* 3:9; see Str-B 3:542–44). The roots of the tradition suggest that it represents the attempt to find a single overarching principle of all obedience in "faith(fulness)" and not a minimum requirement of the law, even if "faith(fulness)" sometimes could be treated in that way (*contra* Str-B 3:542–44; see Schlatter 1905: 17–86, 609–11). Here, "obedience" is identified with "faith" conceived as "fidelity" (or "faithful believing"), which consequently appears as a governing virtue.

Assuming that the third-person pronominal ending attached to 'ĕmûnâ is the original reading (as opposed to a first-person ending), we have good reasons for understanding it as referring not to the righteous one, but rather to the vision (ḥāzôn [2:2–3]) for which that one is to wait, or indeed, to Yahweh, who has given the vision. Habakkuk 2:2b–4 might be rendered as follows (see Janzen 1980; Haak 1992: 59; Seifrid 2004b: 112–13):

Write the vision and make it plain upon tablets,
so that the one who reads it may run.
For the vision is still for an appointed time,
and He [the vision/Yahweh] is a witness to the end and does not lie.
If He delays, wait for Him. For He shall surely come. He will not tarry.
Behold the proud one; with respect to the vision/Yahweh his spirit is not right.
But the righteous one shall live by the faithfulness of the vision/Yahweh.

The "faithfulness" of which Habakkuk writes is the faithfulness of the Lord to fulfill the promise of salvation given in the "vision" (3:1–15). To live by that faithfulness is to believe the astounding word of the Lord (1:5). To remain "puffed up" in pride will bring judgment and disaster (2:4–5). The LXX therefore preserves the sense of the Hebrew text, even if it reads the pronoun differently. On the assumption that as usual the LXX is the basis of Paul's citation, his omission of the first-person pronoun reflects the sense of its rendering, even if he shifts attention to the call to believe. To "live by *my* [i.e., the Lord's] faithfulness" is to live by faith.

There may also be a resonance between Habakkuk and the larger context in Romans. Habakkuk's complaint intimates the failure of the law to effect righteousness (Hab. 1:4). The vision that the prophet is instructed to "write on tablets" (cf. Exod. 24:12; Deut. 4:13) suggests that the saving judgment of God will inaugurate a new reality beyond Torah (cf. Jer. 31:31–34; see Watts 1999: 5–6).

Habakkuk has in view the immediate judgment coming upon Judah through the Babylonians, not the more distant judgment that later was to come on Babylon (*contra* Wright 2002: 425–26). Indeed, the pathos of the writing lies in Habakkuk's coming to terms with the Lord's announcement of this astonishing, destructive work (1:5–2:1; 3:16–19). Salvation comes only through delay and judgment ("the vision is for its appointed time" [2:3]). The narrative context of Rom. 1:17, which signals something of the structure of Paul's message in Romans, presupposes the impending hour of judgment, not the end of exile (see also 9:25–33; 10:19–21). The passage is simultaneously corporate and personal. These two dimensions of salvation are joined together in the unexpected ways in which God proves faithful to his promise.

The context of Hab. 2:4 also points to the link between "revelation of the righteousness of God" and the righteousness of "the one who lives by faith." Paul understands that the revelation of God's righteousness effects our justification. But how is this so? According to Paul's citation of Habakkuk, the righteousness of the one who believes has its basis in the promise of salvation. The revelation of God's righteousness is not merely an external event, but a word-event that includes the human being. The "revelation of God's righteousness" takes place "by faith and for faith" in the gospel. The righteousness of God thus comes to the human being by the word of promise, now fulfilled in Christ and proclaimed, but not yet visible in the world (see Rom. 1:1–4). Even in the fulfillment of the promise Paul presupposes the delay of salvation on which the call to faith in Hab. 2:4 is based. He thus stands in line with early Jewish interpretation (*contra* Strobel 1961: 175). In the present time the promise remains a promise that calls for faith even as it has come to fulfillment in Christ.

Paul introduces his following description of the wrath of God (1:18–32) as an explanation of 1:17. In some sense, the revelation of God's wrath from heaven explains the revelation of God's saving righteousness. Several considerations argue against assuming that in 1:18–32 Paul is simply describing the plight from which the gospel delivers us. If we take 1:18 as merely describing the human plight, we have to assume that it expresses the reason for Paul's announcement of the righteousness of God. It must then refer back to 1:15. Paul would be saying something like, "I am eager to proclaim the gospel to you in Rome [1:15].... Because God's wrath is revealed from heaven

[1:18]." According to this interpretation, then, he proclaims the gospel not only because it saves (1:16–17) but also because God's wrath is revealed (1:18). There are at least two problems with this reading. First, the explanatory conjunction that begins 1:18 (*gar*) is the fourth member of a string of these conjunctions that begins in 1:16a. It is unlikely that after providing three successively subordinated elaborations explaining his eagerness to preach the gospel, Paul, using the same conjunction, would jump back to the beginning to provide a second, new reason for proclamation. A reference to 1:15 that leaps over 1:16–17 without any formal signal or acknowledgment of the content of these verses would be more than unexpected and quite awkward. Second, this reading is unlikely because of the near parallelism between 1:17 and 1:18: just as the righteousness of God is revealed in the gospel, so the wrath of God is revealed from heaven. Paul's striking juxtaposition of these statements leaves little doubt that according to him, the revelation of God's wrath explains the revelation of God's saving righteousness.

But how can wrath explain salvation? The citation of Habakkuk together with crucial elements of Paul's language in 1:16–17 provides the essential clue: the promise to the prophet entails deliverance through judgment. Destruction must come in order for salvation to arrive. God's wrath sweeps away his enemies, in this way working salvation. As a result, the earth "will be filled with the knowledge of Yahweh, as the waters cover the sea" (Hab. 2:14). Paul later returns to this theme of "deliverance through destruction," which appears often in the prophets (Rom. 9:25–33; cf. Isa. 10:20–23; 28:14–29; Hos. 2; see Hofius 1989).

Paul sees the call of the Lord upon the prophet to "live" by the Lord's faithfulness in the face of the Babylonian invasion as a pattern of the Lord's saving work (or type) that has come to fulfillment in the gospel, which imparts faith in the face of the eschatological wrath of God, which is already present in the world.

The Revelation of God's Wrath from Heaven (1:18–2:16)

1:18–32

Although the various elements of Paul's announcement that "the wrath of God is revealed from heaven" obviously echo the Scriptures, the formulation itself is unique to Paul. It clearly is intended to reflect the preceding declaration concerning the righteousness of God, and thus it describes an eschatological reality (cf. 2:5) that is now present.

Paul's description of idolatry as "exchang(ing) the glory of God for the likeness of an image of a perishable human being and birds, and animals, and reptiles" (1:23) may echo various biblical texts. The "exchange of the glory of God" (1:23) is a pointed description of idolatry borrowed from biblical charges against Israel (Ps. 106:20; Jer. 2:11). But Paul does not here charge Israel with a present idolatry; rather, his language underscores that the rejection of the knowledge of God is inherent to idolatry.

2:1–16

Paul now shifts the object of his accusation. Not only the immoral idolater but also the moralist is guilty and condemned: "In that you judge another, you condemn yourself" (2:1). As in 1:18–23, the apostle announces his charge without elaboration: "For you who judge practice the same things" (2:1).

On the day of "revelation of righteous judgment" God "will recompense each one according to his works" (2:6). Aside from the introductory pronoun, this clause is a verbatim citation of Ps. 61:13 LXX (62:13 MT; 62:12 ET) and Prov. 24:12, where (varying) Hebrew generic singular forms ("human being" and "according to that one's work") are shifted to the distributive pronoun ("each one") and joined to a plural ("works"). Proverbs 24:11–12 warns against failure to intervene on behalf of the neighbor: the one who examines human hearts will bring recompense. In speaking of God's examining the heart, Ps. 62 MT anticipates Paul's following argument in 2:15–16, 29. Psalm 62:13 MT speaks of recompense positively, as the deliverance of the righteous. Paul's immediate reference in 2:7 to those who receive eternal life might suggest this passage.

Both Ps. 62:1–12 and Prov. 24:10–12 anticipate divine judgment within the context of human violence and oppression. The psalmist hopes for deliverance from God through judgment. The proverb issues the warning that human beings are responsible to intervene on behalf of others in need of such rescue; they are to do so in the knowledge that God will judge their deeds or their failure to act. In these texts Paul sees the pattern of divine judgment, which has taken place in many instances in the past, as anticipatory of the final judgment that is coming upon the world of human injustice and cruelty. The judgmental moralist also participates in that cruelty (see Rom. 3:10–18). The apostle's thought is based on the type or pattern of God's ways with human beings, which address us and call us to account.

Paul's shift to the singular form "(the patience of) a good work" (2:7) may recall the singular Hebrew forms in the passages that he echoes. Yet the characterization of the whole of life as a single (good) work is most likely unique to him. The expression anticipates his subsequent rejection of justification by "works of the law" (3:20): judgment includes the whole of one's life within its scope. A "work" is properly good only as the whole of the person and life are found in it (cf. Gal. 6:10; Phil. 1:6). Of course, Paul also speaks in terms of a plurality of good works (e.g., 2 Cor. 9:8; Eph. 2:10; 2 Thess. 2:17), as he has already done in 2:6 in reference to final judgment (cf. 2 Cor. 5:10). "Good works" appears in rabbinic literature alongside the more frequent term "commandments" as a broader category of deeds (including almsgiving) that please God (e.g., *Lev. Rab.* 30:12; see Str-B 4.1: 559–60). Here and elsewhere in Paul's letters the expression "work(s)" is larger, comprehending all works that are good. It thus bears a note of universalism.

The Law, Jewish Identity, and Jewish Advantage (2:17–3:20)

2:17–29

Paul's argument now moves to the question of Jewish identity. Over against the attempt to define that identity in terms of the possession of the law, he locates it in the keeping of the law, which the Spirit alone can effect. This "fulfilling the law" has its decisive locus in the human heart and therefore transcends the outward distinction between Jew and Gentile. Paul's concluding reference to God's knowledge of the heart recalls his announcement of God's final judgment of human secrets at the end of the preceding section (2:16, 29).

Paul's argument reaches a turning point in 2:23. As may be seen from his direct address to his imaginary interlocutor and from his following appeal to Scripture, he shifts away from rhetorical questions (2:21–22) to a charge: "You, the one who boasts in the law, through your transgression of the law you dishonor God" (2:23). "Boasting" in the law (2:23) is a false confidence (on boasting, see, e.g., Ps. 20:7; 49:6).

Paul supports his accusation by appeal to Scripture. He draws his second direct citation in the letter from Isa. 52:5 LXX. In this case the "introductory formula" ("just as it has been written") follows the citation: the emphasis lies on the way in which the text describes Israel.

In Isa. 52:5 MT the Lord's redemption of his people from exile stands at the center of attention. Israel's transgression, which brought it into exile, does not come into view (cf. 43:25; 44:22; 50:1). Both the sojourn in Egypt and the Assyrian invasion appear as examples of the kind of oppression that Israel has had to endure. The people have been taken away without cause (52:3, 5), so that the rulers of Israel wail (rightly RSV, ESV). "All day long" the name of the Lord "is despised" by foreign oppressors (52:5). As a result, the Lord will cause Israel to know his name; that is, he will fulfill his saving promises to them (52:6).

A similar passage, Ezek. 36:20–21, speaks of the presence of exiled Israel among the nations as the cause for blasphemy: "These are the people of the LORD, and yet they went forth from his land" (36:20).

Isaiah 52:5 LXX introduces a tension: Israel's sin now appears in the text. On the one hand, Israel has been sold and exiled without reason (*dōrean* [52:3, 5 LXX]); on the other hand, Israel is the cause for the blaspheming of God's name:

> My people have been taken away without cause.
> You marvel and cry out.
> And thus says the LORD:
> "On account of you, continually my name is blasphemed among the nations." (Isa. 52:5 LXX)

It is likely that in its interpretive rendering Isa. 52:5 LXX draws on the larger context of Isaiah, particularly 50:1–3. In this prior reference to the Lord's people being "sold" into exile (cf. 52:3), the Lord ascribes his judgment to "your sins, and the transgressions of your mother" (i.e., Jerusalem [50:1]). The phrase "on account of you" in Isa. 52:5 LXX recalls this prior context, supplementing and elaborating the opening statement by the Lord in 52:3: "You were sold without cause" (or "price," *dōrean* [cf. 50:1]). According to this rendering, there was a cause for the exile, after all: Israel's sins (see 53:5; 64:5–6, where the LXX likewise adds causal statements, ascribing judgment to Israel's sins).

Paul takes up the septuagintal reading of Isa. 52:5, shifting the divine address to Israel to a third-person accusation. He also emphatically fronts the reference to "God's name" in his citation: "The name of God is blasphemed. . . ." He also drops the septuagintal adverbial modifier "constantly" (*dia pantos*; MT: *tāmîd kol-hayôm*), almost certainly because he has in view individual self-examination, not a blanket condemnation of the Jewish people.

Thus, whereas the MT here sets aside the question of Israel's guilt, Paul, together with the LXX, speaks of Jewish transgressions as the cause of blasphemy, drawing on the larger Isaianic context. Insofar as Isa. 52:5 MT (cf. Ezek. 36:20) still resonates here for Paul and his readers, the sins of the people that brought about the exile by metonymy come to *be* the exile. In fact, Paul subsequently takes up the language of exile to describe the divine surrender of the human being to sin (3:9; 7:14). Israel's exile thus recapitulates humanity's fall and expulsion from the Garden of Eden and likewise anticipates the coming, final judgment.

As in his questioning, in this charge Paul continues to address his rhetorical dialogue partner in the singular: "you [singular] who boast in the Law, through your [singular] transgression of the Law you [singular] dishonor God" (2:23). The apostle is concerned first of all with individual guilt, even if he supposes that the conduct of many Diaspora Jews has caused the blasphemy of God's name among the Gentiles. It is, moreover, the present transgressions of those who call themselves Jews that dishonor God according to Paul's citation of Isaiah. The contemporary singular "you dishonor God" (2:23) is taken up within the following plural of the biblical text, "on account of you the name of God is blasphemed" (2:24). Otherwise Paul's appeal to Scripture makes no sense. A reference to Israel's past failures would fail to carry the argument. Had he charged that Diaspora Jews were responsible for the guilt of past generations, his rhetorical counterpart might well have responded with the words of Jeremiah or Ezekiel, "Everyone shall die for their own sins" (Jer. 31:27–30; Ezek. 18:1–32). Or perhaps he

would have cited Baruch: "We [in our exile] have put away from our hearts all the iniquity of our fathers who sinned against [the Lord]" (Bar. 3:6–7). Paul's appeal to Isaiah 52:5 is thus typical in nature. Israel's disobedience in the past has been repeated in the present. Just as Israel (according to Isa. 52:5 LXX) once brought shame upon God in its guilt and exile, so now Israel dishonors God by its disobedience. Paul's placement of the formula "just as it is written" after his citation text underscores the typical nature of his appeal. He does not provide a prooftext. Neither does his citation of Scripture build upon a common understanding of Israel's plight. The Isaianic text with its narrative of Israel's past reveals a reality of the present that otherwise would be hidden to Paul's contemporaries (*pace* Koch 1986: 260–61). As was true of Israel in the past, they themselves are in need of redemption by the true Servant of the Lord, whom Paul identifies as Jesus the Christ (Isa. 42:6; 49:5–7; 53:11; Rom. 5:19; 10:16; 15:21).

The rabbinic writings interpret Isa. 52:5 straightforwardly as a reference to the Babylonian exile (e.g., *b. Sukkah* 52b; *Midr. Ps.* 20 §1). The tenth-century *Midrash Tadshe* offers a parallel to Paul's use of Isa. 52:5 in that it charges Israel with a double sin, against both the Lord and the nations. Yet unlike Paul, it interprets the text simply in terms of the Babylonian exile (see Wilk 1998: 177–79). According to *T. Levi* 14:1–8, Israel's disobedience and exile bring a curse (probably from the nations) on Israel (rather than on the Lord).

This is not the only instance in which Paul appeals to Isa. 52 in Romans. He later takes up the promised announcement of good news to Israel (10:15; cf. Isa. 52:7) and finally returns to speak of the proclamation of the Messiah to the Gentiles (15:21; cf. Isa. 52:15). This awareness of the larger message of Isaiah indicates that even here Paul understands Israel's failure as the prelude to its salvation (Wagner 2002: 176–78). His following announcement of the arrival of the promised circumcision of the heart in 2:25–29 (cf. Deut. 30:6) shows that he ultimately has in view the fulfillment of the Lord's promise to his people.

The final verses of this subsection further unfold what Paul already has said, as is clear from the opening connective "for" (*gar* [2:25]). He now takes up the significance of circumcision, the prime mark of Jewish identity. In implicit agreement with his dialogue partner, Paul speaks of circumcision as a sign of commitment to keep the law (see Str-B 4.1:23–40). The mark of Jewish identity is hardly meant to exclude others; the task of the Jew is to impart knowledge of the law to the Gentile world! If, however, a person transgresses the law, circumcision is of no help. The sign is present, but the reality is lacking. Indeed, circumcision has then become uncircumcision (2:25). Paul draws this ironic image of reversal from Jer. 9:25–26, where the Lord threatens judgment not only on the nations neighboring his people but also on "the house of Israel" itself. Egypt, Edom, the Ammonites, and Moab are depicted as circumcised along with Judah, since they shave the hair from the temples of their heads. Yet just as these nations are not truly circumcised, neither is "the house of Israel," which remains uncircumcised in heart (cf. Jer. 4:4). The larger context speaks of the violence that takes place in Israel in much the same terms as Paul's subsequent reference to Isa. 59:7 in 3:15 (see Berkley 2000: 170–77). The text, despite its announcement of judgment, thus recalls the Deuteronomic promise of a circumcised heart (Deut. 30:6) and anticipates the announcement of a new covenant.

Paul further explains himself ("for," *gar* [2:28]) in the final verses of this subsection, recalling the Jeremianic charge that those who rebel against God are not truly circumcised, despite their outward circumcision. The apostle also has in view the promise of the new covenant in which the Deuteronomic promise of a circumcised heart comes to reality. From the perspective of this charge and this promise, circumcision and the enjoyment of God's favor as a Jew is not a matter of an outward mark or observable identity. Being a "Jew" is a hidden reality. Circumcision is a work of the Spirit of God in the heart. Paul thus differs from Philo, for whom the circumcision of the heart has its necessary counterpart in outward circumcision (e.g., *Spec. Laws* 1.304–305). Of course, Paul hardly excludes those outwardly circumcised as Jews; the promise to Abraham is theirs as well, provided that they follow him in faith (4:9–25). Furthermore, as he makes clear in chapters 9–11, he retains the hope that the promise of Deut. 30:6 will yet come to fulfillment for Israel.

3:1–20

The Jewish people have been entrusted with *logia theou*, the "utterances," or more properly, the "oracles of God" (NRSV, ESV, NASB). The term that Paul uses generally signifies "sayings," but in a number of contexts it refers more narrowly to revelatory speech—that is, oracles (e.g., Num. 24:4, 16 LXX; Philo, *Confusion* 166; *Joseph* 95; *Decalogue* 16). As Paul's following citations of Scripture show, that is the case here. He does not merely have divine promises in view, as some interpreters suggest. In his reference to God's "words" of judgment (*logoi* [3:4]) he recalls the "oracles" (*logia* [3:2]) entrusted to Israel. His focus rests on the divine charge against humanity that these oracles reveal (3:4, 10–18).

That is not to say that he does not have the promises of God in view at all. We have already noted how in 3:17–18 the revelation of God's righteousness is dependent upon the revelation of his wrath. Just as God's promises secure deliverance through judgment (not from it), so divine judgment is the vehicle by which his promises are secured. The failure of "some" to believe the divine oracles (and thus to believe the gospel) does not abrogate the faithfulness of God, but rather establishes it (3:3–4). The rhetorical question in 3:3, "Their unbelief does not abrogate the faithfulness of God, does it?" allows Paul to reframe the matter. Jewish unbelief does not raise a question, but rather confirms the "oracles of God." There is a contention between God and humanity as to who is speaking the truth. God's charge that human beings are "liars" is established in the unbelief of "some" within Israel.

Ultimately, God will overcome this unbelief as well; that is the theme of Rom. 9–11. Paul's immediate attention rests simply on the triumph of God. God's faithfulness (3:3; cf. Deut. 7:9; 32:4; Lam. 3:23)—that is, his being "true" (cf. in the LXX: Ps. 30:6; 70:22; 118:90; Isa. 65:16)—is not undermined by the unbelief of "some" Jews. On the contrary, Pauls says, "Let God be found true, and every human being a liar" (3:4). Verse 4 should be regarded not as a mere wish, but rather as an apostolic pronouncement. The language recalls not only the description of idolatry in 1:18–32 (see 1:18, 25; cf. 2:8) but also the contention between the Lord and the nations as it appears in Isa. 40–48, particularly the language of Isa. 41:26. The nations with their idols cannot bring forward anyone who announces salvation and brings it to fulfillment. They can offer no one to whom one must confess, "He is in the right [*saddîq*]" (Isa. 41:26 LXX: "It is true [*alēthē*]!" cf. 43:9; 47:10). It is the Lord alone who promises and fulfills and thus shows that he is the true God and Creator. Correspondingly, according to Paul, "Every human being is a liar." This second part of the pronouncement reflects Ps. 115:2 LXX (116:11 MT), which has in view the human attempt at self-preservation and justification. In affliction, the psalmist has come to trust in God (Ps. 115:1 LXX [116:10 MT]; cf. 2 Cor. 4:13). To say in this context that all are liars is to say that all are hypocrites, who may pretend to offer help but are unable to do so (cf. Ps. 118:6–9; 146:3; Rom. 2:17–29). Paul does not mount a theodicy here; he announces the triumph of God over the human lie.

The triumph of God necessarily takes place in the human lie (3:4). God is "true" in that his word, which announces human idolatry and unbelief, comes to fulfillment. Paul's opening declaration is thus rooted in Scripture, where the psalmist makes the startling confession to God that he sinned "in order that you might be justified in your words, and triumph when you judge" (Ps. 51:4 [51:6 MT; 50:6 LXX]). The citation begins with the purpose clause (*hopōs* [Heb. *lěma'an*]; cf. *b. Sanh.* 107a; *Midr. Ps.* 51:3), recalling, yet not citing, the confession "I have sinned," for which the apostolic pronouncement substitutes. Paul invites his readers to the same first-person confession.

God's justification is his triumph in judgment. As usual, Paul's citation corresponds to that of the LXX, altering the Hebrew *zakah* ("to be pure") to *nikaō* ("to triumph"). His use of the future indicative (*nikēseis*) instead of the LXX's aorist subjunctive (*nikēsēs*) is semantically insignificant. At most, Paul suggests the final judgment a bit more strongly than does the LXX. Both here and in the LXX the infinitive *krinesthai* is most likely a middle form, to be rendered actively: "to contend judicially" (cf. 1 Cor. 6:6; Isa. 50:8 LXX; Jer. 2:35; 32:31 LXX [25:31 MT]). The initiative rests with God, whose "oracles" bring the charge to which the human being must answer, either in confession and faith or in the persisting lie of unbelief.

Paul anticipates the human response ("I am speaking in human terms" [3:5]) to his affirmation of God's reign in human sin in two rhetorical questions. The first is universal in scope: "If our unrighteousness establishes God's righteousness, is the God who brings wrath unjust?" Paul dismisses this question with a simple appeal to the expectation—obviously shared by his dialogue partner—that God must yet judge the world (3:6). He then restates the question in different terms: "If the truth of God abounded in my lie for his glory, why am I still condemned as a sinner?" (3:7). As in the first instance, Paul brackets his response: it is blasphemy to suggest that evil deeds will not face judgment. He will not press beyond this truth with further questions. Here again God's righteousness is his truthfulness, his fidelity to his words (see 3:5). Paul uses a brief chiasm to point back to God's fidelity in Jewish unbelief (see 3:3). He likewise shifts from the universal to the personal: it is in *my* lie that the truth of God abounds; *I* am the one who is condemned as a sinner.

The conclusion likewise appears in the form of a response to a question: "What then? Do we make an excuse? Not at all." The preceding objections are excuse-making that must be rejected, "For we have already charged that both Jews and Greeks are under sin" (3:9). Paul now makes clear the thrust of his argument: the attack on idolatry and on moralism ultimately is an attack on the false ideals that hold Jews and Gentiles captive. The development of the argument from the address to mere "human beings" (1:18; 2:1) to the Jew (2:17) reflects the fallen state in which they are in common (3:23).

The charge is that both Jews and Greeks are "under sin" (3:9). The expression anticipates the expanded statement in 7:14, "I am fleshly, sold under sin," which reflects the language of Isa. 50:1 ("You were sold [into slavery and exile] on account of your sins"). Insofar as he recalls Isa. 52:5 LXX in 2:24, Paul already has used the image of the exile to describe human fallenness. Here the idea clearly shapes his language. It is, moreover, a *charge* that Paul brings against human beings. We are held accountable for our guilt. Yet, paradoxically, the charge is precisely that we are under sin; we have been given over by God to its power and are unable to free ourselves. The whole of

Paul's argument up to this point is summarized in *this* statement, in which our confession of guilt (1:18–2:29) confirms the word of God that has consigned us to sin (3:1–8).

The apostolic witness is only an echo of the voice of Scripture. Paul follows his charge with a chain citation, the lengthiest citation of Scripture in all of his letters. The apostle has spoken only that which has been written ("just as it is written" [3:10a]). The catena appears to be his own composition, since it has no parallels.

The citation falls into two parts. The first section speaks of human rejection of God, ending with a transitional statement on the failure of human beings to practice kindness toward one another (3:10b–12). The second section speaks of human violence toward others in word and deed, at the conclusion recurring to the theme of human rejection of God (3:13–18).

Paul's citation of Scripture in 3:10b–12 stands closer to Ps. 13:1–3 LXX (14:1–3 MT) than to the parallel Ps. 52:2–4 LXX (53:1–3 MT), but the transmission of Ps. 13 LXX has been influenced by the Romans text, so that the relationship remains uncertain. Paul's wording is sufficiently different from both that it is possible that he echoes the Hebrew text. The opening statement is a rephrasing of Ps. 13:1, 3 LXX, in which the charge that there is "no one who practices kindness, not even one" recurs. In place of "no one practices kindness," Paul substitutes "no one is righteous," perhaps drawing on Eccles. 7:20 ("There is no righteous person on earth"). Whereas Ps. 13 LXX here speaks of doing good to others, Paul shifts to the human-divine relation, in continuation of his argument concerning the justification of God. This move also accords with the thrust of the psalm, which announces the thought of the fool ("There is no God!" [cf. Rom. 1:21]), and its charge that "no one seeks God" (Ps. 13:2 LXX). Paul shortly takes up the human relations of which the psalm speaks. But his interpretive freedom in citation is obvious.

He omits the opening narrative statement of Ps. 13:2 LXX, that the Lord looks down from heaven on humanity "to see if there is someone who understands or seeks God." The inquiry thus becomes a declaration in 3:11: "There is no one who understands. There is no one who seeks God." Correspondingly, over against Ps. 13:2

LXX, the participles are articular. The wording in 3:12 follows Ps. 13:3 LXX, aside from the use of the article with the participle in 3:12c (*ho poiōn chrēstotēta* [but see the *v.l.*]):

a All have turned aside (cf., e.g., Deut. 29:17 [29:18 ET]; 31:29 LXX).
b Together they have been ruined.
c There is no one who does kindness.
d There is not even one.

The text juxtaposes acts of disobedience (3:3a, c) to passive experience (3:3b). The expression "doing kindness" may recall the kindness of God (2:4), which humanity has rejected.

The charge that humanity does not practice kindness, which rounds off the charge in Ps. 13:1–3 LXX in an *inclusio*, provides the transition to the "second table of the law." Paul's attention shifts to the wrongs done to the neighbor as he cites a series of eight brief pronouncements against enemies of the psalmists—and the Lord. The first four deal with human speech, the next pair deal with human conduct, and the final pair summarize the whole:

A 3:13a: An open grave (is) their throat (Ps. 5:10c LXX/MT [5:9c ET]).
B 3:13b: With their tongues they deceive (Ps. 5:10d LXX/MT [5:9c ET]).
A 3:13c: Venom of vipers (is) under their lips (Ps. 139:4b LXX [140:4b MT; 140:3b ET])
B 3:14a: Whose mouth of a curse and bitterness is full (Ps. 9:28 LXX [cf. Ps. 10:7 MT/ ET]).

The biblical language that Paul employs is typically concrete. His citation corresponds verbatim to the LXX in all but the last clause. There, the LXX differs from the MT ("a curse his mouth fills, and deceit and oppression") by opening with a relative pronoun, by adding the term "bitterness" (*pikria*), and by omitting the final term "oppression" ("of whom a curse his mouth fills, and bitterness and deceit"). In the LXX, over against the MT, the charge is thus more strictly limited to the speech of the opponent. This emphasis corresponds to that of Paul. He merely shifts to a plural form ("their mouth") in line with his preceding citations, drops the third element of the charge ("deceit"), avoiding repetition of the thought of 3:13b, and shifts the verb to final position, maintaining parallelism with 13b and an A-B-A-B structure of the whole. In their original contexts 3:13c and 3:14a are joined, front and back respectively, to clauses that speak of the "tongue." But the piling up of figures is typical of the psalms, so that one need not imagine that Paul is using keyword linkages to build his statement. He is simply choosing a full range of biblical imagery to make his point emphatically.

The human "lie" that denies God in unbelief finds its first expression in speech toward the neighbor: in death-dealing deceit, poison, cursing, and bitterness. The vice list in 1:29–31 is composed first and foremost of sins of the tongue. Paul here may recall something of the failure of the inward speech of the moralist (2:1–16) and the Jewish interlocutor (2:17–24). Now Paul names the organs of speech (throat, tongue, lips, mouth) as the fundamental locus of human fallenness. As in the psalms that he cites, human sinfulness is simultaneously rooted in the "being" of the fallen human ("their throat *is* an open grave") and expressed in culpable actions ("with their tongues *they* deceive").

In the final four clauses Paul turns to human "ways." The final pair of clauses summarizes the whole of the catena by returning to the theme of human refusal to acknowledge God:

A 3:15: Swift are their feet to shed blood (Isa. 59:7a–b; Prov. 1:16).
B 3:16: Destruction and distress (are) in their ways (Isa. 59:7d),
B 3:17: And the way of peace they have not known (Isa. 59:8a).
A 3:18: There is no fear of God before their eyes (Ps. 35:2 LXX [36:2 MT; 36:1 ET]).

In 3:15 Paul continues the pattern that he has already established, speaking first of the human "being"—that is, the fallen human pattern of existence. Now human "feet" are in view: they *are* swift to shed blood. The fronting of the adjective "swift" (cf. Amos 2:15) creates a measure of parallelism with 3:13a. As a result, Paul varies somewhat from the LXX, which itself differs from the Isa. 59:7a–b MT. The next clause in Romans describes the effect of human "ways": destruction and distress. Here Paul follows Isa. 59:7d LXX, which stands close to the MT. He omits Isa. 59:7c

("their thoughts are thoughts of wickedness"), which does not fit the theme of human conduct. Aside from a differing verb for "knowing" (*ginōskō* in place of *oida*), Paul reproduces the LXX reading of Isa. 59:8a in 3:17.

The words of Isa. 59:7–8 that Paul cites were originally directed against "the house of Jacob" (Isa. 58:1, 14); his citation therefore reflects the accusation that he has already brought: for those with ears to hear, Israel itself is included within the charge against the wicked. Paul's catena merges the prophetic charge against the people of God with the complaint of the psalmists against their enemies. Jesus Christ alone stands in the place of the innocent and righteous psalmist who complains to the Lord concerning the wickedness of his enemies (Bonhoeffer 1970: 17–21). Those who believe come to stand there as well (see Rom. 8:31–39).

Paul draws the final statement in the chain from Ps. 35:2 LXX (36:2 MT): "There is no fear of God before their eyes." The language in context is the psalmist's estimation of the "discourse" heart of the wicked, which comes to expression in the "words of their mouths" (Ps. 35:2–5 LXX; cf. Rom. 3:14). The catena thus implicitly returns to Ps. 13:1 LXX (14:1 MT), which likewise describes the inward thoughts of "the fool." In the "fear of God" the vertical and the horizontal meet. And the converse is true: violence toward the neighbor is the outworking of the rejection of God. The way of peace remains unknown to us. Only the gospel brings the reversal of this judgment, manifest in the praise of God through Jesus Christ with "one mouth" by Jew and Gentile (Rom. 15:13; see also 14:17, 19; 15:33).

Paul's summary in 3:19–20 is hermeneutical. The question as to how one is to read the law has been at stake throughout this section (2:17–3:20). The Jewish dialogue partner reads the law as the gift of the knowledge of God's will, with the underlying supposition that the human being (no doubt with divine aid) is able to put that knowledge into practice (2:17–24). Paul reads the law in a radically different way. As "letter"—that is, written demand addressed to the human being—it has a definite sphere of authority and power: those who hear the law are "in the law" (cf. 2:12). Within this sphere the law "speaks," announcing the tragic subjection of the human being to sin. It speaks in order that "every mouth might be shut" and all the world might be guilty (*hypodikos*) before God. The former phrase recalls Ps. 63:11, which announces the shutting of the mouth "of those who speak a lie" (62:12 LXX: "injustice"). The inner voice of conscience is insufficient. God's saving purpose requires the external voice of the law. It is not that Paul imagines that human beings are incapable of doing anything that the law demands. Obviously, those who possess the law are well able to accomplish the "works of the law," deeds of outward observance that mark a person as a Jew (cf. 4Q398 14–17, II, 3). Paul must speak to the false conclusion that has been drawn concerning these "works of the law." "No flesh" can be justified by these deeds before God. In this expression (*pasa sarx*) Paul alludes to Gen. 6:12: "all flesh has become corrupt." The divine contention that we are liars speaks to us as fallen persons—a reality that works cannot change. It is not justification that comes through the law, but rather "the knowledge of sin"—that is, the experience of sinning (see Rom. 7:7–13).

3:21–26

Although Paul does not cite the OT in this summary of his gospel, he alludes to it significantly. The revelation of the righteousness of God is a new, saving event, distinct from the law, which bears witness to it together with "the prophets" (3:21). This saving display of God's righteousness is his justification (cf. 3:4–5 and see below). In this context, "to bear witness" carries a forensic connotation (cf. Rom. 10:2; 1 Cor. 15:15). Paul's shift in wording from "reveal" (*apokalyptō*) in 1:17 to "manifest" (*phaneroō*) in 3:21 likewise indicates more of a visible and public idea, which implies a contrast with hiddenness, and which therefore frequently is bound up with faith and knowledge, especially in Paul's letters.

The righteousness of God is a saving righteousness, given "through the faith of Jesus Christ, to all who believe." It has been argued in recent debate that we should understand the genitive relation here as subjective ("Jesus' faith or faithfulness") rather than in the traditional, objective sense ("faith in Jesus"). There are good reasons, however, why we should read the semantically rich genitive in yet another way, as describing Jesus Christ as the definitive source of faith. In this case, the objective sense is presupposed (as it is

in any case in Paul's usage of "faith"), but the idea is larger. The "faith of Jesus Christ" (3:22) is the faith *given through* Jesus Christ. The expression describes not a pattern of obedience in which we participate, as R. Hays proposes (e.g., Hays 2000: 275–76), but rather the source of faith: God gives us faith as a gift through the crucified and risen Christ and the gospel that proclaims him (Seifrid 2000: 139–46).

The manifest righteousness of God is for all who believe, not merely for Jews (3:22). Paul's elaboration in 3:22b–23 takes up what he has argued already: "There is no distinction, for all have sinned and lack the glory of God" (3:23 [not, as in NIV and NRSV, "fall short of the glory of God," see Käsemann 1980: 94–95]). The two verbs in 3:23 are to be understood in conjunction. "All have sinned" is not a general statement. It describes the fundamental sin, the rejection of God, in which all human beings have participated and therefore lack God's glory. The wording not only recalls 1:23 ("they exchanged the glory of the incorruptible God"; cf. Ps. 106:20; Jer. 2:11), but also stands close to Jewish traditions that describe Adam's loss of divine glory (*Gen. Rab.* 11:2; *b. Sanh.* 38b; *L.A.E.* 20–21). Paul's language might recall more remotely the past experiences of Israel in which its disobedience led to the departure of the divine glory (1 Sam. 4:21; Ezek. 11:23), but these experiences, like the human fall into idolatry to which Paul primarily refers (1:23), are mere echoes of Adam's loss. The human being was created to participate in God's own glory (2:7). The gift of righteousness is the restoration of the glory of God to the human being, which is present already in the risen Christ, in whom we share (6:4; cf. 9:23).

The absence of distinction between Jew and Gentile also has a material implication that reappears in chapter 4. We are those who are justified freely by his grace—that is, without any advantage or quality that might commend us to God (3:24).

Our justification takes place through "the redemption which is in Christ Jesus" (3:24). At this juncture or in the following verse many commentators understand Paul to take up an early Christian confession, since the language is unusual for him. But one also has to reckon with the possibility that the apostle forms his own theological statement out of biblical or traditional language. There is no tradition in the NT that quite matches the thought and imagery of this passage. In any case, Paul returns to the theme of Israel's exile as an image of human bondage to sin, introducing the Isaianic theme of redemption in a new exodus and new creation (e.g., Isa. 43:14–21; 48:20–21; 52:1–12; cf. Ezek. 20:33–38; Hos. 2:14–23). The term "redemption" or "deliverance" (*apolytrōsis*) signifies the release of a slave or prisoner and therefore may also connote a price paid for that redemption (*EDNT* 1:138–40). The connotation is lacking in some contexts, however, including Rom. 8:23 (see also Dan. 4:34 LXX; Luke 21:28; Heb. 11:35). Here, the allusion to the Isaianic theme of redemption, as well as the usage in the later texts in Romans, shows that Paul's primary emphasis lies on liberation. The idea of "redemption by exchange" may nevertheless lie subtly in the background, since among the Isaianic passages substitutionary ideas do appear in Isa. 43:3–4 ("I give Egypt as your ransom") and the fourth Servant Song (Isa. 52:13–53:12). In the present context, moreover, deliverance (*apolytrōsis*) comes through the resurrection of the crucified Christ, who now is God's mercy seat (see below). The term *apolytrōsis* signifies "deliverance," but in this context it presupposes Christ's exclusive place-taking on our behalf.

Already in the book of Isaiah, Israel's exile and oppression are presented as the result of its sins, so that the liberation of the nation comes through forgiveness (Isa. 42:25; 44:22–23; 53:11). This imagery is now radicalized, so that Israel's exile becomes an image of human sin and alienation from God (cf. Rom. 2:24; 3:9). Redemption is nothing other than freedom from sin and death, the resurrection itself, which springs from God's forgiving favor in Christ. Paul has already spoken of the resurrection of Jesus as the Isaianic "good news of God" (1:1–4). Subsequently he speaks of union with Christ's resurrection as effecting liberation from sin (6:1–23). Just as Jesus' resurrection marked his instatement as "son" (1:4), the redemption "which is in Christ Jesus" (3:24) is nothing other than the arrival in hope of "the redemption of the body." It is the proleptic arrival of our own instatement as sons and daughters in Christ (8:23).

In 3:25 Paul's attention moves to Jesus himself: he is God's *hilastērion*. Modern translations have tended to render this word abstractly to indicate a means of atonement ("sacrifice of atonement" [NIV, NRSV]; cf., however, "place of atonement" [NRSV mg.]). But aside from one possible exception, this noun appears in only two uses (see Bailey 1999; Kraus 1991; Stuhlmacher 1986; 1992: 297–98): (1) as a description of a Hellenistic propitiatory gift (inscription, stele, or another object); (2) as the "mercy seat" in the tabernacle (e.g., Exod. 25:17–22; Lev. 16:2–15; Heb. 9:5) or a specific "place of atonement" (Ezek. 43:14, 17, 20; Amos 9:1). The exceptional use of the term in 4 Macc. 17:22 in reference to the death of the Jewish martyrs (A has the adjective *hilastērios*) may have been facilitated by an awareness of its significance ("an entity of propitiation"; *pace* Bailey [1999: 93–142], who establishes the substantival usage in S) and therefore might well involve allusion to the mercy seat ("place of propitiation/atonement"), even though the primary idea is that of a Hellenistic "propitiatory offering." Despite the Hellenistic flavor of 4 Maccabees, it is hard to imagine that its language is devoid of biblical overtones, given the fervent devotion to the law that it seeks to inculcate. The transposition of cultic realities to the ethical realm was common in Hellenistic Judaism. Fourth Maccabees transforms the "mercy seat" into a potentially repeatable act, presenting it as equivalent to a propitiatory offering or gift. That which is unique and particular to Israel is Hellenized and universalized.

Paul's thought moves in precisely the opposite direction. In all likelihood the term *hilastērion* in 3:25 describes Jesus as a "mercy seat." Yet the apostle's appeal to the text is not ethical, but rather eschatological. He retains the exclusivity of Lev. 16: God reveals himself savingly in a specific place to which access is restricted. A saving encounter with God is possible only through the means that God himself provides. Paul's anarthrous use of *hilastērion* is no obstacle to this reading; absence of the article may be due not only to the predicate position of the noun but also to the typological cast of the statement. To have said that Jesus is "*the* mercy seat" might have implied that the headpiece of the ark was illegitimate. In declaring Jesus to be God's "mercy seat," Paul announces him as the fulfillment of the promise that the original adumbrated. His thought comes intriguingly close to that of Hebrews, where the "once-and-for-all" of God's work in Jesus transcends the Day of Atonement (Kraus 1991: 257–59). Naturally, fulfillment implies the inefficacy of the original, but it does not call into question the legitimacy of the original as a promise.

Both "propitiation" (the aversion of God's punitive wrath) and "expiation" (the removal of sin) are in view in the term *hilastērion*. The Hellenistic usage ("propitiatory offering") almost certainly resonates here, despite the definite biblical reference. Furthermore, in the biblical context itself the divine instructions for approaching the mercy seat are given to avert God's wrath, as is clear from the opening reference to the deaths of Nadab and Abihu in Lev. 16:1–3, 6, 13. In providing the means of cleansing from sin, God's love overcomes God's wrath (cf. Lev. 17:11). The same dynamic appears in the present context in Romans. According to Paul, our sins themselves are an expression of the wrath of God on idolatry, a wrath that therefore cannot legitimately be reduced to an impersonal effect or natural result of a deed (1:18–32). Humanity has been subjected by God to the power of sin (3:9). The righteousness of God effects deliverance from the sin to which God's wrath delivered us (3:24; cf. 6:1–23, esp. 6:7). Expiation is thus contingent on propitiation. Propitiation effects expiation. Consequently, to render *hilastērion* either as "propitiation" or "expiation" cuts off one dimension of the sacrificial language or the other. Recent English translations have done well to translate *hilastērion* with the broader term "atonement," even if they have not yet come to terms with Paul's reference to the mercy seat.

The "tent of meeting" (or "encounter" with God), with its inner sanctuary, and especially the mercy seat, is the point of contact between the heavenly and earthly realms. The sins of the people defile not only them but also this holy place. The central rites on the Day of Atonement deal with both dimensions of defilement: one goat is sacrificed for the cleansing of the holy of holies, while another is sent away into the wilderness for the cleansing of the people. The two rites are presented as a single atoning event (cf. Lev. 16:20, 34; *contra* Kraus 1991: 45–59). Not only are the people brought to God through judgment and

death, but also their sins are carried away (qualification of Janowski 2000: 198–265). The laying on of hands in the scapegoat (elimination) rite may well convey, as usual, personal identification with the goat (Lev. 16:20–22). The carrying away of sins in this case includes the banishment of the sinful persons. The paired rituals may be regarded as complementary: sinful Israel is simultaneously banished from God's saving presence and carried into it through judgment and death.

According to the apostle, God is visibly present and savingly encounters us in the crucified and risen Jesus, as he once encountered Israel in the cloud on the mercy seat. Jesus transcends the sacrificial system in the same way in which the Day of Atonement transcends the regular sacrifices of Israel (Bailey 1999: 214). Just as "redemption" is solely "*in* Christ Jesus" (3:24b), we find a merciful God in him alone (3:25a). While 3:24b ("redemption") emphasizes the changed relation in which humanity stands to the world, sin, and death, 3:25a, with its image of Jesus as the mercy seat, emphasizes the changed relation in which humanity stands to God. Both verses underscore the idea that Jesus is the exclusive locus of God's saving work. Only in Jesus, the mercy seat, do the heavenly and the earthly savingly meet. Only in the crucified and risen Lord is God's glory present and promissorily restored to fallen humanity and the whole creation (cf. Exod. 40:34–35; 1 Kings 8:6–11; Ezek. 43:1–5). The eschatological sanctuary filled with divine glory has been consecrated in Jesus (cf. Ezek. 43:1–5; 44:4; see Kraus 1991: 159–67).

The translation of the finite verb *proetheto* in 3:25 is somewhat difficult. It might be rendered "set forward (as mercy seat)." Most of those who advocate reading *hilastērion* as "mercy seat" adopt this reading, pointing to the use of the cognate Greek noun *prothesis* to describe the setting out of the showbread. This ritual is distinct, however, from the annual appearance of the high priest before the mercy seat. Moreover, Paul already used this verb in the alternate sense of "to purpose" in 1:13 (cf. Eph. 1:9). His decided emphasis here on the distinction between the present moment of revelation and God's past hiddenness strongly suggests that we should understand Paul as saying that "God purposed Jesus as a mercy seat." The hour of fulfillment of the divine purpose has now arrived (Kraus 1991: 157–59).

Given the chain of three prepositional phrases in 3:25, it is likely that we should read each of them independently, not join the first two (i.e., not "faith in Jesus' blood"). The use of the prepositional phrase with "faith" would be unusual for Paul. He speaks rather of God's purposing Jesus as God's mercy seat, "through faith," "by his blood," and "for the demonstration of God's righteousness."

It is through faith that Jesus is God's mercy seat. Paul here again marks the saving event as universal. The note of exclusivity is likewise present: just as God was hidden in the darkness of the holy of holies, so also he is hidden in Christ (Janowski 2000: 362). Everything depends on whether we see the God made visible in the crucified and risen Jesus. Paul's reference to faith also underscores the idea of contemporaneity that runs through this passage: we are justified here and now in a living relationship with the risen Lord, who is the mercy seat. Yet it is not our decision that constitutes God's justifying work. That work is an extrinsic reality in Christ, behind and before our believing: Jesus is the mercy seat "by [or 'in'] his blood"—that is, by means of or on account of his death on the cross.

As in various sacrificial contexts, including the ritual of the Day of Atonement, "blood" here signifies a life offered up to God in death (Lev. 16:14–15; 17:11). The concept of "inclusive representation" is operative. Yet this identification of the sinner with the sacrifice entails the substitution of the sacrifice for the sinner (qualification of Gese 1981: 93–116; Janowski 2000: 198–265): it is not the offering that presents itself, but rather the sinful people who present the offering; nor is it the sinner who is slain in the sacrificial act, but rather the sacrificial animal. As we noted, the substitutionary rite of the "scapegoat" is integral to the Day of Atonement. In other NT references to Jesus' "blood" his vicarious suffering and death come into view (e.g., Rom. 5:9–10; 1 Cor. 11:25–26; Heb. 9:11–28). That we were included in that death does not in the least diminish the reality that we were also excluded as Jesus took our place. In this context, moreover, overtones of human violence remain subtly present. Paul has just spoken of the violence and murder of

fallen human beings in terms of (the shedding of) "blood." Jesus' life was taken away by those with "feet that are swift to shed blood" (cf. Rom. 3:15; Isa. 59:7a–b; Prov. 1:16). The violence of fallen humanity, itself the expression of divine wrath according to Rom. 1:18–32, took Jesus' life. The identification of the sacrifice with the sinner does not remove the distinction between the sinner who acts in violence and the victim who suffers violence. It is the *crucified* and risen Jesus who is God's mercy seat.

With the third prepositional phrase ("for the demonstration of his righteousness"), Paul brings his summary back to its opening theme, interpreting the appearance of God on the mercy seat as the manifestation of his righteousness. In 3:25 he changes his term for "revelation" yet again, now using language that in this context bears a distinct forensic edge, *endeixis* (cf. 2 Cor. 8:24; Phil. 1:28; cf. also *endeiknymi* in Rom. 9:17, 22). The use of the pronoun ("his" righteousness) and the alternate term for "revelation" (*endeixis*) remove the language one step from biblical allusion and suggest a return to the idea of God's triumph in contention that appears in 3:4–5.

The "demonstration of God's righteousness" has taken place "on account of the passing over of past sins in the forbearance of God" (3:25–26a). Despite debates on the meaning of this statement, it appears that Paul here recalls his earlier reference to God's present forbearance (2:4). The thought is proximate to that of 9:22, where Paul uses the verbal cognate of the noun *endeixis*. This time of God's patience recalls the annual period before each Day of Atonement (Kraus 1991: 92–157, esp. 148–49). The moment of revelation of God's righteousness is thus the final judgment brought into the present in Jesus Christ. The "passing over of sins" entails God's former bearing of reproach for apparently being unjust in dealing with the world. The patience of God once endured and still endures the injustice, oppression, and murder that now torment the creation (1:18–32). That violence reached its ultimate in Jesus' death on the cross. Here, unexpectedly, God was shown to be in the right in his charge against us in his "oracles" that we in word and deed are "liars." This "demonstration of God's righteousness" is not merely noetic, but effective. It "rights" the fallen world. Judgment on us and on the world has been executed in Jesus. God purposed him as "mercy seat [Paul's usage is anarthrous] . . . by his blood." In Jesus' death and resurrection for us, God has been vindicated as the Creator, who fulfills his promise to save, *through* human sin and rebellion.

As the mercy seat of God, then, Jesus is the vindication of God in his saving judgment. The cultic language serves to describe the revelation of God's saving righteousness, in which the condemnation and defeat of God's enemies works their justification. It informs Paul's description of God's justifying work at its most critical point, not only in its visible expression of representation and substitution, but also in its underlying conception of God's holiness—that is, his transcendent and numinous presence. In revealing his righteousness, God does not subject himself to human judgments and ideals. He conquers them and maintains his right as God. Even in its revelation, God's righteousness bears the depth of his untraceable ways. Sacrificial language and imagery communicate the meeting of judgment and salvation while leaving this meeting hidden in God.

As in 3:21–22, Paul doubles his reference to the revelation of God's righteousness, again defining it in terms of Jesus in the second member of the pair. God purposed Jesus as mercy seat "for the demonstration of his righteousness in the present time, so that he might be righteous and might justify the one who is of the faith of Jesus [i.e., the one who belongs to the faith that springs from Jesus]" (3:26). Paul now returns to underscore the present as the decisive hour in which God's righteousness has been revealed (cf. 3:21). God "is" righteous in that his righteousness has been demonstrated. He has condemned and defeated fallen humanity, with whom he contended, and he has fulfilled his saving word. The second affirmation, that "God is the justifier of the one of the faith of Jesus," is thus an extension of the first, and not a salvific counterpart to a notion of punitive justice. The first affirmation, "God is righteous," itself bears overtones of biblical "doxologies of judgment," in which the guilty human party gives God justice, confessing that God is in the right (e.g., Exod. 9:27; Lam. 1:18; Dan. 9:7). This confession of guilt, which bears a salvific dimension (see Isa. 45:20–25), has been given to us in the faith that springs from Jesus. "The faith of Jesus"—that is, the faith that comes from the crucified and risen

Lord—includes within itself confession of guilt and repentance (on the "faith of Jesus," see commentary above on 3:22).

The Righteousness of Faith as the Fulfillment of the Law and the Hope of Salvation (3:27–8:39)

In 3:27–31 there appears a triplet of questions concerning boasting (3:27a), God's saving lordship over the Gentiles (3:29), and the relation of faith to the law that guides the entire course of Paul's following argument. The matter of "boasting," which the apostle already has addressed in Romans 2:17–23, immediately reappears here (3:27). He treats this topic in Romans 4:1–8, again in Romans 5:1–11, and finally once more in Romans 8:12–39. The justification of the Gentiles (3:29) becomes the topic of Romans 4:9–12 and runs through the following chapters in transmuted form, i.e., the exclusivity of faith (e.g., 5:1–11) and the universalism of the gospel (e.g., 5:12–21). The final, fundamental question concerning the validity of the law (3:31) likewise continues through Romans 8, where Paul describes the fulfillment of its righteousness in God's work in Jesus Christ (vv. 1–11). In the conclusion of the argument, the opening triplet of questions concerning boasting, Gentiles, and the law are replaced by a triplet of affirmations concerning the hope of glory, the suffering elect, and the love of God in Christ (8:12–39).

THE JUSTIFICATION OF BELIEVING JEWS AND GENTILES BY THE ONE GOD IN FULFILLMENT OF THE LAW (3:27–31)

In this brief transitional statement Paul underscores the significance of his gospel (see 3:21–26) in relation to the law, which his readers were in danger of regarding as the basis of Jewish advantage (2:17–3:20). Yet these verses are not merely retrospective: Paul does not have merely a misunderstanding of the law in view. As his preceding summary in 3:19–20 makes clear, a proper understanding of the law is essential to his gospel.

ABRAHAM AS FATHER OF BELIEVING JEWS AND GENTILES (4:1–25)

4:1–8 (cf. 3:27–28)

Paul reads the story of Abraham in the light of Gen. 15:6, setting "boasting" in the context of the human relationship with God and inverting the early Jewish image of Abraham: "But with respect to God, Abraham has no boast" (4:2). The end of 4:2 is not a restrictive phrase, as if Abraham still might boast before human beings; such boasting cannot be separated from a boast before God, as is clear from 3:27–31. Paul, rather, introduces here the defining framework in which "boasting" is to be evaluated: the human relationship to God. One must listen to how the Scripture "speaks" (4:3): "Abraham believed God. And it was reckoned to him as righteousness." The citation corresponds closely to the LXX, which, aside from shifting "YHWH" (usually, *kyrios*) to "God" (*theos*), follows the MT. This reckoning of faith as righteousness does not involve God playing a sort of fictional game, counting faith as something that it is not; rather, it is, as the larger context shows, God's approval of the new reality created by the word of promise to Abraham (4:17; cf. Ps. 106:31; Gen. 1:31). As we will see, too, this "reckoning" is not a mere heavenly calculation; it is effective, granting and securing blessing. The gratuity of this reckoning is found in faith itself. To the one who works, recompense (*misthos*) is granted as an obligation (4:4). In contrast, faith is passive in both its origin and its exercise, dependent on the unconditioned favor (*charis*) of another (4:4). Abraham's faith thus had definite content and contours: he trusted in ("believed on") the one who justifies the ungodly (4:5). Paul's ensuing argument in 4:13–25 makes clear what it means to believe in *this One*. Early Judaism could use commercial imagery in relation to "works," but there is nothing as blatantly mercenary as we find in 4:4 (see 2:5). We must understand Paul here to be clarifying the unexamined implications of "boasting," the implications of its underlying assumption that works are a prerequisite to salvation, and the implications of the thought that human beings can secure or maintain God's favor by such works. In the realm of human relations and righteousness, recompense for works is to be expected. With God, however, matters are entirely different: he justifies the ungodly.

Although Paul's attention here is fixed on Gen. 15:6, he also has in view the narrative context in which this passage appears. His reference to reward (or recompense) undoubtedly recalls Abraham's vision in 15:1, in which God promises Abraham, "I am your shield. Your recompense [LXX: *misthos*] shall be very great." This "recompense" and its following elaborations reestablish the initial promise to Abraham that God would make him a great nation and a blessing to all the tribes of the earth (12:1–3). Paul's allusion to the context of Gen. 15:6 signals that he understands Abraham's faith in connection with the divine promise, a connection that becomes prominent in the final section of Rom. 4 (vv. 13–25). The divine "reckoning" (essentially, a declaration) by which Abraham was justified effects the blessing granted in the promise. It is, moreover, the theme of "blessing," with its concrete outworkings, with which Paul introduces the testimony of David (4:6). Paul understands Abraham's justification not as a bare declaration, but rather as the anticipatory enactment of the promise from which Abraham's faith arose. Abraham's justification is bound up concretely with God's promise to him and cannot rightly be abstracted from it. God's reckoning of Abraham as righteous is God's recognition of Abraham's answer to the promise of seed. The reality of that seed is already present for Abraham in the faith that the promise of God has created in him, as Paul will go on to explain (4:17).

Larger dimensions of the Genesis narrative come into play in Paul's appeal to Abraham. His characterization of Abraham's faith obviously implies that Abraham is ungodly—a shocking claim if one reads the narrative on the basis of Gen. 26:5. But Paul reads the Genesis story from the beginning, not from the end (see Rom. 2:26). Abraham appears in the narrative in the wake of the Lord's thwarting the plans of fallen humanity in the tower of Babel, dispersing humanity into many peoples and languages. He represents God's fresh beginning with the fallen world, the display of God's mercy in God's judgment. Abraham is one of the ungodly, whom God chose as a vehicle for his saving purpose—a solitary, weak, and defenseless individual, who is made so by the divine judgment on the united human race (Gen. 12:10–14:24). The childless, homeless, and wandering Abraham is the antithesis of Adam, who enjoyed the security and fruitfulness of the garden. In this fallen and frail figure, God the Creator takes up afresh his surprising work of blessing the world, which now stands under his curse (Gen. 3:14, 17). God by his promise alone will grant Abraham offspring and an inheritance, thus bringing Eden back into the fallen world. God alone justifies the ungodly—an act that he expressly forbids human beings (Exod. 23:7; Prov. 17:15; 24:24–25; Isa. 5:23; cf. Mark 2:7b: "Who can forgive sins but God alone?"). Yet, as God, he acts in this very manner, overcoming his own judgment, as is especially apparent in his dealings with his wayward people (e.g., cf. Hos. 2:14–3:5 with Deut. 22:22; cf. Hos. 11:8–9 with Deut. 21:18–21; see Hofius 1989: 131–47). Following the text of Genesis, the apostle views the Lord's dealings with Abraham (Gen. 12:1–14:24) as coming to a pivotal moment at the point of the divine word of promise given to Abraham in his despair over his childlessness. It is unclear what significance ought to be attached to the prior words of promise to Abraham or to Abraham's prior obedience and worship. In some sense, Abraham believes the prior words of promise. Yet, much like Peter's confession of Jesus as the Christ, the moment of response in Gen. 15:6 is decisive. Faith is never general or abstract, but always the response to a concrete word of promise. The decisive word of promise comes to Abraham at the point when its fulfillment seems impossible, but that is precisely when the God who promises is known as Creator.

Abraham's justification is equivalent to the experience of David, the most prominent of forgiven sinners in Scripture. David "speaks" as does the Scripture (4:6). Consequently, he serves as a second witness to justification apart from works. He speaks as a transgressor of the law; his witness to a righteousness apart from "works" introduces an ironic twist. With David, "works" are not deeds of obedience to the law, but rather "acts of lawlessness" and sins (4:7). Those who hope for a righteousness given through their works have misunderstood the law and its work of effecting sin and wrath (cf. 3:20; 4:15). A righteousness reckoned apart from "works" is nothing other than the forgiveness of sins, a not-taking-them-into-account. It is undeserved favor where there ought to be retribution and punishment.

In appealing to David, Paul follows Ps. 31:1–2 LXX (32:1–2 MT) without variation. With the LXX, Paul differs from the Hebrew Scriptures in shifting the singular forms in the first verse to a plural. The singular usage of the Hebrew psalm is paradigmatic in any case, and the psalm itself shifts to a plural in its final verse (32:11). The introduction of the plural into the first verse of the citation therefore makes the universality of the psalm explicit and invites the readers to find themselves in the experience of David. In contrast with many of the rabbinic references to Ps. 32, Paul makes no mention of the confession of sins, which is a central theme of the psalm (cf. Ps. 32:5; see Str-B 3:202–3). Confession is implicitly taken up in faith for Paul, in which sin that has overpowered our person is overcome: in faith we "give glory to God" (4:20; cf. 1:23; 3:26). As was the case with the story of Abraham, the broader context of the psalm makes clear that the "reckoning of righteousness" is no mere declaration, but rather an effective word. In the psalm the forgiveness of sins brings healing to both body and mind, deliverance in times of distress, and the guidance and loving care of the Lord (Ps. 32:3–11). Consequently, according to the apostle, the "reckoning of righteousness" is a blessing that (re)creates life. It is the forgiveness of sins, which effects all the benefits that Ps. 32 describes.

4:9–12 (cf. 3:29–30)

Again Paul makes his point from the story of Abraham in Genesis. God's reckoning of Abraham's faith as righteousness took place *before* Abraham was circumcised (4:9–10). For Paul, circumcision remains a sign of righteousness—not the "righteousness of the law," but rather "the righteousness of faith," a faith given to Abraham while he was still "in uncircumcision" (4:11). God acted in this way so that Abraham might become the father of all the uncircumcised who likewise believe. Righteousness is reckoned to them in the same way. Abraham is no mere model or example; he engenders his believing Gentile progeny by his faith.

He is also the "father of circumcision," but not to all the circumcised. He is father to those who "are not of circumcision alone, but also follow in (his) footsteps of faith" (4:12). As the context makes clear, faith is passive. Our acting in faith ultimately is a "being acted upon" by God (see 4:19–22). The word of promise performs its work in us. We merely receive what the promising and justifying God gives. Faith is therefore not a human "work," but rather a work of God in the human being. Faith is nevertheless obedience (cf. 1:5). Only those circumcised who follow "in the steps" of the faith of Abraham are his children (cf. 9:6–13). This metaphor for obedience almost certainly is derived from the biblical manner of describing conformity to one's father or mother (see 2 Cor. 12:18; 1 Pet. 2:21; Sir. 51:15; Philo, *Creation* 144; *Migration* 128; *Virtues* 64; cf. Judg. 2:17; 1 Kings 15:26; 22:43, 52; 2 Kings 21:21). Paul denies a presumption of benefits to ancestry. For him, ancestry becomes the basis of exhortation. Those who are Jews by birth are called by the promise to find salvation outside themselves in an "alien righteousness." Only in this way is Abraham truly their father (cf. John 8:39).

The promise of God to Abraham thus transcends the fallen world and the capacities of fallen human beings. It grants Abraham progeny among the Gentiles and brings judgment on Abraham's natural offspring. "For Paul salvation history is the history of the divine promise which runs contrary to earthly possibilities and expectations" (Käsemann 1980: 117). God's justifying work is nothing other than the establishment of his right as the Creator, who calls into being that which is not (4:17). By his word of promise, God the Creator effects faith, and with that faith he proleptically establishes the concrete earthly reality of that promise. The faith that grasps the promise justifies God, acknowledging him as the Creator, who forgives and redeems us, his fallen creatures.

4:13–25 (cf. 3:31)

In this final section Paul elaborates the faith of Abraham beginning in 4:13–15 by drawing on the context of Gen. 15:6, in which the Lord reaffirms the promise of "seed" and the "inheritance" of the land to Abraham (Gen. 15:3–5, 7; cf. 12:7; 13:14–17). These are not extraneous themes; Paul is laying bare the roots of Abraham's faith, found in the promise of God to him in all its particularity.

The promise is twofold; Abraham is given both "seed" and "inheritance." The "seed" to whom the promise belongs consists of believing Jews and Gentiles (4:16–17, 24). Yet Paul breaks off his subsequent narration of Abraham's faith at the point of Isaac's birth and figurative "resurrection" (4:25), speaking instead of the resurrection of "Jesus, our Lord." Implicitly Jesus himself is the promised seed of Abraham (4:24). Paul's argument here is therefore complementary to that in Galatians 3, where he expressly names Christ as

the promised seed (Gal. 3:16), and goes on to speak of those who share in Christ by faith as Abraham's seed (Gal. 3:29). The corporate reality in the risen Lord includes individual persons and their faith. Indeed, the term "seed" simultaneously bears individual and corporate significance (e.g., Gen. 15:4–5). The story of God's redeeming purpose in Abraham has its starting point in Babel, in the dispersion of humanity into many peoples and tongues (Gen. 11:1–9). Henceforth, community is the creation of God found outside our varied earthly identities in the promise of God fulfilled in Jesus Christ. Abraham is the father of us all (4:16), but this unity is a unity in difference (4:9–12). We meet one another *solely* in the mutual encouragement of faith (cf. Rom. 1:12; 15:5–6).

The "inheritance" here is elevated from "the land" (Gen. 12:7; 13:15; 15:18–19; 17:8; 24:7) to "the world" (4:13), as generally took place in early Judaism. The promise was interpreted and extended by the new horizons of Jewish life after the exile and transposed to the hope of the age to come (Sir. 44:21 [Hebrew, Syriac]; Jub. 19:21; 22:11–15; 32:19; *m. Sanh.* 10:1; *b. Sanh.* 110b; *Mek.* 14:31 [40ᵇ]; *Num. Rab.* 14 [173ᵃ]; *4 Ezra* 4:27; 7:50; 2 Bar. 14:13; Str-B 3:209; Davies 1994: 121–26, 370–71). Paul obviously shares this expectation: the promise is fulfilled in Jesus Christ, whom God raised from the dead (Rom. 4:17, 24–25).

The inheritance is given, Paul affirms, not through the law, but through the righteousness that comes from faith. If "those who are of the Law" were heirs of the world, faith would be empty and the promise void. This is so because, "the Law works wrath" (4:15a). In speaking of the Law "working wrath" Paul has in view God's surrender of idolatrous humanity to its desires, which he has characterized as the "revelation of God's wrath" (Rom. 1:18, 24, 26, 28; cf. 3:9). This reading of 4:15a is confirmed by Paul's continuing elaboration, "but where there is no Law, there is no transgression" (4:15b). Through the law, the wrath of God works transgression in fallen human beings. The full unpacking of this highly compressed and tantalizing statement comes later, in Romans 7:7–25 (see, however, Rom. 5:20; 6:14).

The promise to Abraham that Paul cites in 4:17, "I have appointed you father of many nations," is drawn from Gen. 17:5 LXX, which elaborates the promise given to Abraham in 15:5 (cf. 12:2). The unit in Genesis in which it appears (17:1–8) is juxtaposed to the covenant of circumcision (17:9–27). On first reading, one might suppose that the promise found in 17:5 would be fulfilled in "the circumcision" alone. In fact, in rabbinic tradition 17:5 was applied to proselytes (Str-B 1:211). Paul, however, sees the portent of something larger in these words. As his unelaborated introduction of the promise given to the "seed" of Abraham shows, he understands that promise to include both Jews and Gentiles (4:13, 16). Of course, the "seed" first given to Abraham was Isaac, his physical offspring, as were all the patriarchs to whom God granted the promise afresh. But, as Paul elsewhere takes pains to argue, Isaac was not a natural offspring of Abraham; he was born according to promise, not according to "the flesh" (Gal. 4:21–31). The promise thus transcends natural, ethnic lineage. As Paul has just indicated in his discussion of circumcision, being ethnically Jewish is insufficient; one must follow Abraham in faith. Conversely, Abraham is also the father of uncircumcised believers. Even more strikingly, Paul sees the fulfillment of the promise of the inheritance to Abraham's seed as being granted in the resurrection of Christ, in whom the distinction between Jew and Gentile is transcended (4:25; cf. Gal. 3:15–29). As we will see in Rom. 9–11, the apostle understands the ethnic dimension of God's promise to Abraham as bearing enduring validity. Its fulfillment comes, however, through a fresh act of God, the Creator and Redeemer of ethnic Israel (11:25–27). The apostle finds the signficance of the promise not in its intial recipients, but rather in its power as the word of the Creator, who fulfills his larger, saving purposes through that word. Consequently, Paul reads the promise of Gen. 15:5 in light of Gen. 17:5. But this reading merely sets the promise of 15:5 in its larger context. According to Genesis, the Lord's dealings with Abraham begin only in the wake of his thwarting the plan of rebellious humanity to build a common city and tower "with its top in the heavens" (11:1–9). After Babel, the Lord takes up his work as the saving Creator afresh in Abraham; from the very start, these dealings bear universal implications. The prior table of nations (10:1–32) likewise suggests something greater to come. The promise of the Lord to Abraham that he will make "nations of him" takes up this universal, saving concern of God. That this promise is juxtaposed to the promise of the land of Canaan to Abraham's seed (17:8) does nothing to diminish its significance. It is by this promise (17:5), not the promise of the land of Canaan (17:8), that Paul interprets the word of 15:5, "so shall your seed be." Contrary to convention (but according to God's ways), this promise is twice repeated to the younger offspring of the patriarchs, Israel and Ephraim (35:11; 48:19). Furthermore, the promise that Abraham would become the father of many nations remains open and unfulfilled in the narrative of the book of Genesis, since it is only the patriarchs who become numerous. Paul finds the fulfillment of the promise that Abraham would become "the father of many nations" only in the risen Jesus, God's beloved Son (see below). The nations come to believe in God through him.

The God in whose presence Abraham is "father of many nations" is "the one who gives life to the dead, and calls those things which are not as things which do exist" (4:17c). The confession of God as the one who "gives life to the dead" appears in the second blessing of the Eighteen Benedictions (an early Jewish synagogal prayer), elsewhere in early Jewish writings, and in the NT (e.g., *Jos. Asen.* 8:10–11; 20:7; *Test. Abr.* 18:11; 4Q521; *b. Ketub.* 8b; John 5:21; 2 Cor. 1:9; see Hofius 2002: 58–61). The language has its roots in biblical confessions of God as the one who "puts to death and raises to life" (Deut. 32:39; 1 Sam. 2:6; 2 Kings 5:7). Likewise the description of God as "the one who calls (for his purposes) that which is not, as if it exists" echoes the Isaianic message of the God who brings into existence and effects his purposes by his creative word alone (e.g., Isa. 42:5–9; 43:8–21; 45:1–7; 48:6–11; also Ps. 33:6; see Rom. 1:6, above). This theme was also taken up in early Jewish tradition (2 Macc. 7:28; 2 Bar. 21:4; 48:8; *Jos. Asen.* 12:2; Philo *Moses* 2 100:1; *Spec. Laws* 2 225:3; *Spec. Laws* 4 187:3). Paul stands especially close to Isaiah in that he understands "calling" (*verbum efficax*) as the creative act of God. As we have already observed with respect to Abraham's faith, this second characterization of God represents the foundation of the first: the "one who justifies the ungodly" does so in the effecting of his promise. Justifying faith is a vehicle by which the promise comes to reality among fallen human beings (4:13).

In 4:18–22 Paul presents the believing Abraham entirely in the light of God the Creator and his word of promise. Contrary to all outward appearances ("in hope against hope"), Abraham believed in order that he might become "the father of many nations," according to what had been spoken. And what was spoken? Paul returns to Gen. 15:5, "So shall your seed be," reading it in connection with Gen. 17:5, "'Abraham' shall be your name, for I have made you the father of many nations." The Lord's word of assurance to Abraham, that he himself is Abraham's "shield and reward," prompts the complaint from Abraham that the Lord has given him no offspring, no "seed," and that one of his servants will be his heir (Gen. 15:3). The Lord then speaks to him, promising Abraham that one who comes from his own body will be his heir. But that is not all. The remainder of the promise comes through a dramatic act. The Lord takes Abraham outside, out of his tent, and directs his gaze to the heavens. "Count the stars—if you can count them," Abraham is told. Then comes the word that Paul cites: "So shall your descendants be." The Lord is the Creator, who set the stars in the heavens, innumerable to Abraham and yet each counted, named and known by him alone (cf. Ps. 147:4; Isa. 40:26). As Paul later will remind his readers, the heavens declare the glory of their Creator: "Their line has gone out into all the world, and their words unto the ends of the earth." The apostolic proclamation retraces the course of the heavenly announcement of the Creator's glory, opening the ears of fallen human beings to the message to which their eyes are now blind (Rom. 10:18; Ps. 19:3–4; cf. Rom. 1:19–22). So also with Abraham, whose vision the Lord has directed to the countless stars. The Lord speaks to him the word of promise, opening his ears in order to open his eyes. God will act upon him as Creator, granting him countless "seed." The Lord's word of assurance to Abraham that he himself is Abraham's shield and reward continues in the Lord's response to Abraham's complaint. The Lord gives himself to Abraham as Creator. Abraham will know him thus. We must attend to the strong note of biblical individualism that Paul sounds here. The many "seed" from

Jews and Gentiles are in fact many "Abrahams" who believe the divine word of promise fulfilled in Jesus (Rom. 4:12, 23–25). They, too, come to know the Lord as their Creator in Christ.

As is implicit in the allusion to Gen. 17:5 and as Paul makes clear in 4:19–21, his attention has now shifted forward, for now Abraham is almost one hundred years old (Gen. 17:17), and Sarah's womb is "dead" (Gen. 18:11; cf. 17:17). Yet Paul has not lost sight of Gen. 15:6, which he cites again in 4:23–25, even while he alludes to the "binding of Isaac" (Gen. 22:1–19). The whole of God's dealings with Abraham are compressed into the moment of Abraham's believing in Gen. 15:6.

In returning to Gen. 15:6, Paul fashions an *inclusio*, rounding off his discussion: the whole of the chapter is concerned with Abraham's justifying faith. The words "it was reckoned to him" were not written solely on account of Abraham; this pronouncement was written also for "our" sake—that is, for those to whom righteousness was yet going to be reckoned (cf. Rom. 15:4). The word to Abraham was given for the effective strengthening and assurance of everyone who believes in God through Jesus. Paul understands the work of God in Christ as an outworking of the word of God to Abraham. It is given and rightly grasped only through that Scripture which affirms that Abraham believed God and "it was reckoned to him" as righteousness.

At the same time, the work of God in Christ brings the promise that created Abraham's faith to fulfillment. The word concerning Abraham's justification was written for us "who believe in the one who raised Jesus our Lord from the dead" (4:24). This third characterization of God completes the second: "the one who gives life to the dead" (4:17) has done so definitively in the resurrection of Jesus. Abraham's promised inheritance of the world is present in the risen Jesus, who is *our* Lord. That which was promised has arrived in him.

The Love of God in Christ and Hope in Tribulation (5:1–8:39)

Paul now expands his discussion of the themes of boasting, the Gentiles, and the law in light of God's justifying work in Christ. Before all else, in this section it becomes clear that the love of God in Christ toward sinners stands above the law and its demand and marks the place of the law. Larger realities than the law are at work. It is the triumph of Jesus Christ our Lord over the power of sin and death that secures our life and righteousness (4:24; 5:1, 11, 21; so also, decisively, 6:23; 7:25; 8:39). In this section direct citation of the OT recedes dramatically, although it does not disappear entirely (see esp. 7:1–6, 7–13 on the role and work of the law). Yet even as Paul develops the implications of the promise to Abraham, he shifts to new categories. He now describes eschatological realities that have entered the world through Christ, realities that are decisively new, no matter that they have been promised and foretold (1:17; 16:25–27). Aside from the entrance of death through Adam (5:12–21), the new realities in Christ transcend our present earthly life and thus remain without antecedent. It is only as Paul elaborates "the sufferings of the present time" that he returns to direct citation of the OT and more definite allusions to it (8:12–39, esp. 8:18). These sufferings, in which all believers participate, were also the experience of the people of God in the past, according to the witness of the Scriptures. The new life does not yet remove us from the old life of the fallen world; rather, it places us at the center of the battle between the two orders.

5:1–21

God's saving act of love in giving his Son over to death, which is simultaneously Christ's own act of self-surrender, now becomes the center of Paul's argument. Just as Paul describes the way in which the promise of God engendered Abraham's faith (4:16b–22), so he here presents Christ as the wellspring of life and righteousness. Behind and before our believing stands Christ, through whom God creates hope in our hearts and carries us into eternal life. At the conclusion of his discussion of Abraham, in his implicit identification of Jesus as Abraham's seed, Paul signals that those who believe in God through Jesus have been included in Jesus' death and resurrection. This theme, especially in relation to Jesus' death, now becomes Paul's explicit and primary topic. The apostle moves from speaking of Abraham and his justifying faith to Christ and his justifying death.

A. The Boast of Hope in God through Jesus Christ (5:1–11). The consecutive "therefore" (*oun*) provides the transition from the argument concerning faith to Christ, who is the basis and

origin of faith—a thought that Paul already hints at in 4:25. His opening statement signals the motif of the entire unit: to be justified by faith is to have peace with God *through* "our Lord, Jesus Christ" (5:1). In this case "through" (*dia*) very nearly means "by means of," since (as in the following verse) Paul has in view God's working "by" or "through" Christ (5:9, 11, 12, 17; also, e.g., 1:5; 2:16; 1 Cor. 8:6; 15:21, 57; 2 Cor. 1:5; 5:18; Gal. 1:1; 6:14). The phrase here does not express the means by which faith works, but rather the means by which God works (cf. 4:24–25). It clarifies the opening clause by describing salvation in the most fundamental way: being justified by faith is nothing other than having peace toward God, which he has effected through "our Lord, Jesus Christ." Paul here echoes the theme of Christ's lordship that he introduces in 4:24 and with which he twice brackets his discussion in chapter 5 (5:11, 21).

B. The Reign of Grace over Sin and Death through Jesus Christ (5:12–21). The reconciling work of God's love in Christ toward sinners (5:1–11) leads Paul to a summarizing contrast between Adam and Christ in 5:12 ("on account of this"). These two individuals ("through one human being") appear in terms of their single, decisive deeds: the transgression of the former and the death of the latter define the life and existence of all human beings. The entrance of the law significantly changes the situation of humanity, but it does not undo Adam's deed. Its role is entirely subordinate: in multiplying Adam's transgression (5:20), the law provides the "place" in which the grace of God in Christ may exercise its reign. It is not the law, nor is it ultimately Adam, but rather God in Christ whose work determines human destiny. Adam serves as a promissory pattern for Christ (*typos* [5:14]), whose death transcends and overcomes Adam's disobedience.

The typical relation between Adam and Christ also clarifies Abraham's place. Adam and his transgression, not Abraham and his faith, fill the opening, anticipatory (albeit negative) role in "the history of the promise." Christ likewise has priority over Abraham: in him the promise that created and carried Abraham's faith has come to fulfillment. Paul again answers his rhetorical question as to whether God's saving lordship extends to the Gentiles (3:29–30), from a yet broader perspective. Israel, with Abraham its "forefather according to the flesh" (4:1), takes a secondary, although necessary, place in the working out of God's saving purpose.

Early Jewish writings contain parallels to Paul's interpretation of Adam's fall, especially the apocalypses *4 Ezra* and *2 Baruch* (Lichtenberger 2004: 205–41; Levison 1988: 155–59; Oberhänsli-Widmer 1998: 128–47; Knittel 2002: 148–202). Paul's understanding of sin is more radical than theirs, however, with respect both to the origin of Adam's transgression and to its effect on the human race. Paul makes no attempt here to trace the origin of evil behind Adam's fall, as sometimes happens in early Jewish sources. In the *Apocalypse of Moses* (*Life of Adam and Eve*) the blame for the fall clearly rests with Eve, who appears weaker and more easily deceived than Adam (e.g., *L.A.E.* 9:2; 14:2; 21:2, 6; 24:1). Sirach 25:24 attributes the fall entirely to Eve: "From a woman sin had its beginning, and because of her we all die" (see also *2 En.* 31:1–8; *Gk. Apoc. Ezra* 2:16). In some measure these reflections on Eve's weakness represent an attempt to explain the origin of sin and thereby provide a way to avoid it. In a limited and secondary way, this thought appears in 2 Cor. 11:3; 1 Tim. 2:14. The same is obviously true of the texts that attribute the fall to Satan (e.g., Wis. 2:24; *3 Bar.* 4:8; *2 En.* 31:6). In *4 Ezra* the origin of sin is pushed back and in some measure relativized by the idea that an "evil heart" was already present within Adam when he fell into transgression. The law was given to conquer and control this "evil heart" (*4 Ezra* 3:20–27; 4:30–32); the idea is essentially the same as the later rabbinic concept *yēṣer hā-rāʿ*, "evil intent" (see W. D. Davies 1980: 31–35). Elsewhere, God himself is questioned about the reason for allowing evil into the human heart (*Apoc. Ab.* 23:14). In contrast with all such reflections, Paul here underscores the responsibility of the one human being for the entrance of sin into the "world" of human beings.

The tension between individual guilt and universal condemnation is especially prominent in *4 Ezra* and *2 Baruch*. Paul allows this tension to stand and finds in it an anticipation of Christ. These works present a solution to the difficulty in a two-age structure of the world within which they locate the gift of the law. As with Paul, death is decreed for all humanity through Adam's sin (*4 Ezra* 3:7–11; 7:118; *2 Bar.* 19:8;

23:4; 48:42–43). Nevertheless, the law provides a way to obedience that gives life in *the age to come* (*4 Ezra* 3:20). Human freedom to obey has not been lost, only diminished: "Adam therefore is not the cause, except for himself, but each of us has become our own Adam" (*2 Bar.* 54:19).

The tension between individual guilt and universal condemnation likewise appears in the rabbinic materials. There, however, no final resolution of the tension appears, but only the continuing debate over how to relate texts that speak of individual responsibility (e.g., Ezek. 18:20) with Gen. 3, and with passages that speak of a uniform destiny of human beings (e.g., Eccles. 9:2). Other texts, especially that of the translation of Elijah into heaven (2 Kings 2:1–11), also come into view (see Str-B 3:226–28).

Paul's contrast between Adam and Christ (5:12–21) serves to define and describe the grace of God. He thus takes up the theme of the love of God from the first part of the chapter (5:5–9) in the term "grace." Now he speaks concretely of God's free act of effecting salvation in the face of human sin (5:12, 13, 20; cf. 3:9, 20), which has brought death (5:12, 14, 17, 21; cf. 6:9, 7:10, 13; 8:38), and which has gained dominion over humanity through one human being and his transgression. Over against the power of sin and death stands the grace of God (5:15, 17, 20–21), which likewise gains dominion over all human beings through one human being, Jesus Christ. The deed of the one human being Adam is comprehended and overcome by the gracious deed of God in the one human being Jesus Christ (5:15, 17, 21).

This typological argument provides the larger structure in which the "location" of God's grace is marked out. This structure implies, first, that sin and death remain in God's hand: even Adam's transgression in a backward way serves the larger purpose of God. Second, by contrast, in his grace God comes to fallen humanity and acts directly in saving us. This immediacy of God's acting in grace results in a rich and profound description of the identity of God and Christ as well as the distinction between them (on divine identity, see Bauckham 1998). The grace of Christ—his undeserved favor toward us expressed in giving himself on the cross—coincides with the grace of God (5:15). Yet Christ's death is also an act of obedience toward God (5:19). It is by his death, moreover, that Christ comes into his saving lordship. As the larger context makes clear, Paul names Jesus as *our* Lord precisely with a view to his triumph over sin and death for us (6:9, 14, 23; 7:1, 25; 14:7–9). The grace of God rules through "our *Lord* Jesus Christ" (5:21). In this closing statement Paul brings to expression both the unity of God and Christ and the distinction between them. God in his saving grace acts immediately in and through the human Christ. The human Christ is none other than God acting in his grace, conquering our sin and death as our Lord.

The starting point for Paul's comparison is the entrance of sin into the "world" through "one human being," Adam (5:12). As the following context shows, "world" here signifies "the world of human beings" (5:13; see 1:8; 3:6, 19; 11:12, 15). Through the entrance of sin, death too entered the world, "passing through" sin to all human beings. The final, pivotal clause of 5:12, the meaning of which has been long debated, is best understood as a relative clause with the sense "under which circumstance all sinned" (Zahn 1925: 265–69, slightly modified; cf. 2 Cor. 5:4; Phil. 3:12; 4:10; see Fitzmyer 1993; Moo 1996). Paul acknowledges individual acts of sin in the time between Adam and Moses, but he regards them as subordinate to the reign of sin and death already introduced through Adam. As Paul will subsequently make clear, transgressions are likewise real but subordinate to the reign of God's grace in Christ (5:20–21). As 5:13 shows, Paul's point is that although sin was present in the world prior to the law, it was not "accounted"—that is, regarded (by God) as a matter of individual guilt. "Death" nevertheless (*alla* [5:14]) reigned over humanity "from Adam until Moses" even though human beings had not transgressed—that is, had not violated an external divine commandment as Adam had done.

In 5:15 Paul's comparison of Adam and Christ shifts to a contrast between Adam's deed and God's deed through Christ. Over against Adam's transgression stands "God's act of grace" (*charisma*) and "the gift which is by the grace of the one human being Jesus Christ." God's grace is found in Christ's grace and act of giving—that is, his willing death (5:15d). This gift has "much more abounded" for "the many," overcoming Adam's transgression by which "the many" (i.e., all humanity) died.

Whereas in the first comparison Paul presents Adam and God in Christ as acting persons, in the second comparison he treats Adam as merely a vehicle for the power of "death" (5:16–17). Over against Adam stands "the gift" (*to dōrēma*) of God (5:16a; in reference to 5:15d, *hē dōrea*). Paul first speaks simply of God's unexpected act of grace that reverses what took place through Adam (5:16; cf. 15a, b). He then expands the thought of 5:15 by describing the reversal effected by God's act of grace: whereas from the one transgression came (God's) act of judgment, which resulted in condemnation, from the many transgressions came (God's) act of grace (*charisma*), which brought the enactment of saving righteousness—that is, "justification" (*dikaiōma*; cf. "gift of righteousness" [5:17]). In speaking here of the "many transgressions" to which the gift of God responds, Paul anticipates his subsequent reference to the entrance of the law into the world (5:20–21; cf. 5:13–14). As in 5:14, here he points to God's ultimacy: behind sin and death and the transgessions effected by the law stands God's judgment, and beyond this judgment his unfathomable grace.

In 5:17 (which parallels 5:15c, d) Paul continues the comparison. Adam, in his transgression, became an instrument for the power of death, which through him has obtained its rule over humanity. By contrast, God's grace and "the [concrete] gift of righteousness" bring deliverance and freedom to humanity. Human beings, who passively receive this gift of God, have been delivered from the reign of death ("by much more" [5:17b]). In this passivity they actively "rule in life" through Jesus Christ, the one human being through whom this grace and gift are given. Like Adam, Jesus Christ thus also appears here as a vehicle: he is the vehicle of the power of God's grace. As Paul already has made clear, however, through this human being God in grace acts immediately (5:15) and thus delivers humanity from bondage to the power of death.

Paul finally contrasts the acts of the two human beings, Adam and Christ, in a third comparison (5:18–21). Christ is the human being in whom God is present and has savingly acted:

> Just as through one transgression condemnation came to all human beings, so also through one righteous deed [*dikaiōma*] the justification

which is life [*dikaiōsis zoēs*] came to all human beings. (5:18)

For just as through the disobedience of the one the many were instated [*kathistēmi*] as sinners, so also through the obedience of the one the many shall be instated as righteous ones. (5:19)

A pivot appears here in Paul's argument: he now speaks of the "righteous deed" of Christ (5:18b; *dikaiōma* [i.e., his willing death]) in place of his prior references to the gift of God (5:15a, 16a, 17a). His prior equation of God's grace with the gift given through Christ's grace has prepared the way for this shift (5:15c, d). Whereas in 5:16–17 Paul's attention was focused on Adam and Christ as vehicles of death and life, here he returns to their decisive acts (cf. 5:15).

The first two comparisons include defining affirmations that God's grace "much more" transcends sin and death. In this third comparison in 5:17–21 Paul expands his affirmation of the transcendent character of grace in narrative form. The law entered (into the world of human beings) in order that the transgression might increase (5:20a). As Paul later indicates, in the encounter between the fallen human being and the commandment of God, Adam's transgression is recapitulated in us (7:7–25). "Where" this happened, Paul goes on to say, grace "exceedingly" abounded (5:20b). In the larger purpose of God the law prepares for the work of grace. Finally, and before all else, it is God's will that his grace—his undeserved favor toward us—should reign over us, triumphing over our transgression, sin, and death. Redemption is thus a display of the ultimacy and power of God's grace, which is not hidden or remote, but rather has its concrete place in the world of fallen humanity in that it reigns through righteousness—that is, the saving death of Jesus, which took place in this fallen world (5:21). Grace reigns through Jesus Christ, the human being who is the risen Lord, in whom eternal life has entered the world (5:21). The failure of humanity in Adam is overcome by the triumph of God in the human Christ.

6:1–23

Paul now announces the implications of the grace of God in Christ for "the many" for whom Christ died and rose (Rom. 5:12–21). The larger unit of Rom. 6:1–8:39 bears an implicitly trinitarian

form. Paul speaks first of death to sin and life to God (6:1–23); he then speaks of death to the law and life to the risen Christ (7:1–25); finally he speaks of life in the spirit (8:1–30, 31–39). In each subsection, he first sets forth the gospel as participation in Christ's saving death and resurrection (6:1–14; 7:1–6; 8:1–11) and then moves to a description of the present situation of the human being in the light of faith (6:15–23; 7:7–25; 8:12–39). Each subsection concludes with a reference to the grace and love of God "in Christ Jesus our Lord" (6:23; 7:25; 8:39), pointing back to the one human being in whom God's grace and the gift of eternal life are present (5:12–21). In this first subsection (6:1–23), Paul presents the gospel afresh as a union with Christ in his death and resurrection that brings freedom from the reign of sin (6:1–14). In the second part of the chapter he describes the saving work of God on the human being from the perspective of faith: through the gospel God frees us from the slavery of sin and makes us slaves of righteousness (6:15–23).

7:1–25

Paul's lengthy elaboration of the purpose of the law in chapter 7 anchors his preceding presentation of the gospel in 6:15–23 within the larger purpose of God. In the presence of the commandment sin becomes transgression. Guilt and death thus become a reality within our person through the law, even if we cannot perceive the full dimensions of this reality apart from faith.

The apostle describes the work of the law in terms of the encounter with the prohibition against coveting, the wrongful desire to have that which belongs to another (7:7–11, esp. v. 7). He omits the various objects of coveting that are named in the elaborate and repeated prohibition in the Decalogue; variations in order and wording of the two forms of the commandment are not relevant to his usage (Exod. 20:17; Deut. 5:21). In citing the commandment in this way, he interprets it as a prohibition against coveting in all possible forms; he certainly cannot be supposed primarily to have in mind illegitimate sexual desires. The absolute prohibition of coveting, together with Paul's following characterization of the work of sin as deception (7:11), echoes the Genesis narrative of the temptation and fall of humanity. The Hebrew text of Gen. 3:6 describes Eve's attraction to the forbidden tree in terms for "desire" that correspond to the usage of the Decalogue (*ta'ăwâ*; *neḥmād* [cf. Deut. 5:21]; the LXX shifts to aesthetic language). Her outward action of taking and eating (and that of Adam as well) may be understood as already present within her very desire, especially the desire for the wisdom that promised to make her like God. As the connection with the Genesis narrative shows, coveting, and therefore all disobedience to the law, constitutes the rejection of God. It is the will that God not be God. There clearly exists, likewise, a fundamental connection between the idolatry of coveting (Rom. 1:21–23) and the failure to love one's neighbor (Rom. 13:9). Obviously, the prohibition against coveting cannot be fulfilled by any outward work.

The thought of Gen. 3 is deflected somewhat in the narrative of the fall that appears in *L. A. E.* 19:3. This text focuses on the "poison" of desire sprinkled on the fruit by the serpent. Nevertheless, coveting here, too, is named as the source of all sin (see also *m. 'Abot* 4:21). According *Lev. Rab.* 2:10, Joseph fulfilled this commandment in fleeing from Potiphar's wife.

Paul does not directly appeal to the story of humanity's fall in 7:7–12, but only alludes to the Genesis text, particularly the deception of Eve (7:11; cf. Gen. 3:13). He does, however, cite the law, which he expressly indicated earlier was not present at the fall but came only through Moses (5:14, 20). His position stands in contrast to *Tg. Neof.* 2:15; 3:22–24; *Frg. Tg.* 2:15; *Tg. Ps.-J.* 2:15; 3:24 as well as *Sipre* §41 and *Gen. Rab.* 16:6 (Lichtenberger 2004: 225–32). Paul sees in the human encounter with the commandment the recapitulation of Adam's transgression. Unlike the situation of the fall, sin is already present within the human being who hears the law: the commandment provides only the opportunity for sin to effect "all coveting" (7:8). Paul has already indicated that the law serves to "effect God's wrath" and to "increase [Adam's] transgression" (4:15; 5:14, 20). Here he describes the event itself, the encounter of the fallen human being with the law.

Paul's description of sin as "dead" and the human being as "alive" apart from the law arises from the anthropological framework of his argument. He speaks in absolute terms of "death" and "life" for the one who encounters the law because

in this passage he presents the human being solely in encounter with the law. Just as in 6:15–23 he considers human beings in themselves without bringing into view their union with Christ (yet, of course, under the power of the gospel), he here considers human beings in themselves without bringing into view their union with Adam (yet, of course, under the power of sin). Apart from the commandment, Paul was once "alive" insofar as he is viewed as an individual apart from his connection with Adam. Paul is not setting aside what he has announced concerning the reign of death through Adam, but only presenting the human being from the limited perspective of encounter with the commandment. Sin comes to "life" in the presence of the commandment in that through the commandment it comes to possess us in such a way that it cannot be separated from our person and identity. This tragic union of the human being with sin is the topic of 7:13–25.

Sanctions are attached to the commandment, and thus to the law as a whole. Paul's allusion to the Genesis narrative of the fall is built on this understanding: through the commandment sin works death. The deception of sin is the vain thought that transgression will *not* bring death (7:11; Gen. 2:17; 3:3). The context of the giving of the commandments in Exodus intimates death as the consequence of disobedience (Exod. 20:4–5, 19–21), but it is more likely that Paul draws on the book of Deuteronomy, especially the summary statement in Deuteronomy 30:15–20 (Deut. 30:19, "I have set before you life and death, blessings and curses"). Paul goes on to describe "the commandment as given "unto life" (7:10), a theme which appears in various other texts, including Leviticus 18:5, which Paul will later cite (Rom. 10:5; also, e.g., Deut. 6:24; Ezek. 18:17, 19; *Ps. Sol.* 14:2; Bar. 3:9; 4:1; *Exod. Rab.* 32:1; for rabbinic references see Str-B 3:237 and Avemarie 1996: 104–17, 376–99; on the Adamic commandment in early Jewish writings see Lichtenberger 2004: 205–40). When Paul expands his summary affirmation that "the Law is holy," he takes up language reminiscent of Deuteronomy: "and the commandment is holy, righteous, and good" (7:12). This characterization of the commandment carries overtones of the opening of Moses' address ("righteous statutes and judgments," Deut. 4:5–8) as well as the repeated refrain that "the commandment" (a collective singular, referring to the entire law) is for Israel's good (Deut. 4:40; 5:16, 29; 6:3, 18; 10:13; 12:25, 28; 22:7). Likewise, in the closing of Moses's address obedience is said to bring "life and good" (*hakhayim*; *hatob*; LXX: *hē zōē*; *to agathon*). For Paul, too, the "commandment unto life" (7:10) is "good" (7:12). His closing affirmation that the commandment is "good" reflects the law's offer of blessing, just as he elsewhere speaks of "the good" as that which is beneficial (e.g., Rom. 2:10; 12:2, 9, 21; 13:3–4; 14:16; 15:2; 16:19).

Consequently, when—nearly in the pattern of Romans 6 (cf. Rom. 6:15)—Paul raises a second question, "Did 'the good' become death for me?" (7:13), he is answering the potential charge that his gospel, and therewith his understanding of the law, is inconsistent or self-contradictory. It is absurd to say that "the good," i.e., that which is beneficial to me, brings my death! Paul's response is simple: the fatal outcome of the encounter between the human being and the law is due to the reality of sin, which he has already discussed. Indeed, the purpose of the law is to make manifest the reality of sin as it works "my" death. Through "the commandment sin becomes sinful beyond measure" (7:13b).

Paul's second elaboration of the goodness of the law is therefore nothing other than a fresh narration of his encounter with "the commandment." His affirmation of the opposition between the law and sin has not yet defined the "location" and character of sin. In exploring afresh his encounter with the commandment Paul marks that "location." Sin "dwells" in the human being (*oikein*; Rom. 7:17, 18; cf. Rom. 8:9, 11) and does so in such a way that it is inseparable from our person. While in the first narrative he describes the relation between the law and sin (7:7–12), in this second narrative he describes the relation between sin and self (7:13–25).

8:1–39

The section falls into two parts. The first focuses on God's work in Christ (8:1–11); the second centers on human beings as the recipients of that saving work (8:12–39).

The confessional question in 8:31, "What then shall we say to these things?" introduces Paul's summary of his entire exposition of the gospel in Romans (1:16–3:26; 3:27–8:39). The placement

of this question regarding suffering at the conclusion of the argument stands in contrast with the opening questions regarding sin (6:1) and the law (7:7) and underscores its fundamental character. The preceding argument that Paul takes up in his rhetorical question ("What then shall we say to these things?") already signals the nature of the response that Paul now voices for his readers. His treatment of God's righteousness (3:5) and Israel's failure to believe (9:30–33) is similar. In a highly concentrated manner, with the use of Isaianic themes, Paul recapitulates the gospel. As the structure of his argument shows, the gospel speaks especially to believers in their sufferings, which, Paul stresses, are inescapable for those who belong to Christ (5:3–5; 8:17–18). In the conclusion of this section, 8:35–39, Paul implicitly identifies Christ with God, anticipating his naming Christ as God in 9:5. He also breaks the silence of citation that has prevailed since 4:23–25 and appeals to the Scriptures in describing the sufferings of believers in the world (Ps. 43:23 LXX [44:23 MT; 44:22 ET]).

The apostle's reasoning concerning the present time (cf. 8:18) is grounded in the knowledge of God the Creator. Our hope as children and heirs of God is found in the One who has made himself known in Jesus Christ (8:17, 31–39). As his description of "the present time" as "creation awaiting its freedom" already indicates, the "what" question ("What shall we say?") in reality is a "who" question. Paul presents a series of four rhetorical "who" questions, which center on the identity of the Creator standing behind, yet in conflict with and triumphing over the powers of the creation under sin. The series echoes the third Servant Song of the book of Isaiah (Isa. 50:4–11), integrating into it the redeeming work of the Servant described in the fourth Servant Song (esp. Isa. 53:6, 11–12). In the descriptions Paul juxtaposes God and Christ in an ABBA pattern. The one who gave up his Son (and with him shall give us all things; 8:31–32) appears along with Christ Jesus, "the one who died, rather who was raised, who is at the right hand of God, who also intercedes for us" (8:34). Between the two descriptions, Paul raises questions concerning the adversaries of believers, who are real, yet unidentified and finally come to non-existence (Isa. 41:11–13, 21–24; 50:7–9; 51:4–8). The first member of the series introduces a question which leads to the identification of God ("If God is for us, who is against us?" 8:31); the fourth and final member of the series issues in an affirmation of Christ's identity ("Who shall separate us from the love of Christ?" 8:35).

The question in 8:31 ("If God is for us, who is against us?") is mildly reminiscent of the third Servant Song, especially Isaiah 50:9 ("Behold, the Lord God helps me, who is the one who condemns me?"; see also Isa. 50:7). As in the Isaianic context, Paul's opening question already presupposes the ultimate nothingness of the adversaries: by the power of the redeeming Creator, those who oppose the "chosen ones of God" are "nothings" (cf. Isa. 40:17; 41:24; 44:6–11; 45:21). The confidence of the psalmist ("What can human beings do to me?") now takes on even larger dimensions (Ps. 118:5–9; cf. Heb. 13:6).

This question is, of course, rhetorical. Paul here makes a fundamental affirmation about God in the context of trial. He answers his own question by raising a further question about God: "He who delivered up his Son . . . how shall he not also give us all things?" (8:32). The argument profoundly presupposes that the Son is above all (created) things. It is for this reason that the question "who is against us?" is ultimately a null set: if and only if the Creator has given himself to us in his Son, no created thing can be against us. God reveals himself as "for us" in his unreserved gift of himself in "his very own son" whom he "delivered up for all of us." With these words Paul echoes God's oath to Abraham upon Abraham's binding of Isaac (LXX Gen. 22:16; see discussion at Rom. 4:25). In the Genesis narrative of Abraham's testing, God remains the sole Giver, who provides the ram as a substitute (Gen. 22:9–14). Here, however, God's role as Giver transcends its former dimensions: God takes Abraham's place. The roles of the Aqedah have been reversed: God did not "spare," but "delivered up" his own Son. Now the surrender of the "beloved son" (Paul: *idios*; LXX: *agapētos*; MT *yahid*) is occasioned not by divine testing of faith, but by the unbelief, deceit, and violence of fallen humanity (see Rom. 3:10–18). The Isaianic contention between the Creator and the idols stands in the background to the entire passage. God the Creator gave over his Son to death at the hands of murderous creatures, in order to save those very murderers. In this way it is clear that

"God *is* for us" without reserve or qualification. Paul reminds his readers of God's unbounded and matchless love, in a manner quite similar to the reminders which appear in Isaiah (Isa. 40:1–11; 43:1–7; 49:14–23; 54:1–17). The description of God here not only echoes Genesis 22:16, but also the fourth Servant Song (Isa. 52:13–53:12). In its septuagintal form, that passage announces that "the Lord gave him [the Servant] over to our sins" (LXX Isa. 53:6) and "on account of our sins" (LXX Isa. 53:12; cf. Rom. 4:25). The Isaianic passage, which speaks of the Servant "led as a sheep to the slaughter" (Isa. 53:7a) may itself recall the Genesis text (Gen. 22:7, 8; however, "ram," Gen. 22:13, versus "ewe," Isa. 53:7b).

The opening question concerning God's help ("if God is for us . . . ?") is thus transformed into an affirmation of the identity of God the Creator ("how shall [God] not also with him [i.e., the Son] freely give to us all things?"). As the following context makes clear, it is the phrase "with him" that is operative: we are given "all things" with Jesus Christ. In and with him, in suffering, triumph, and finally possessing "all things" we come to know God as our loving Creator (Rom. 8:17). The "all things" should not be taken abstractly, but in a concrete sense that includes the dimension of their temporal reality (see 1 Cor. 3:21–23). Not only in the eschatological future, but throughout their existence, "all things," including trial and suffering, serve God's children (Rom. 8:18–21, 28).

The second question again recalls the third Servant Song, especially its first rhetorical question, "Who is the one who contends (*yarîb*) with me?" (Isa. 50:8); "Who will bring a charge against the chosen ones of God?" (8:33). The language of Paul's allusion (*egkalesei*: "bring a charge") comes closer to the Hebrew text than does the LXX (*ho krinomenos*: "one who condemns"). The description of believers as "chosen ones," implicitly identifies them with Christ, the Son (Rom. 8:17, 29) and with the figure of the Servant, which in the Servant Songs is simultaneously corporate and individual (e.g., Isa. 49:1–6: the figure recalls both Abraham and David, Isa. 51:1–3; 55:3–5; cf. 1 QH 2:13; 1QpHab 9:12; 4QFlor 1:19; 4QpIsa 1:19; 4 QpPs 2:5; 4Q534 1:10). The brief and immediate response: "God is the one who justifies" likewise echoes the Isaianic context ("My justifier/vindicator is near," Isa. 50:8; "the Lord God helps me," Isa. 50:9). In Romans, however, the affirmation follows the question, underscoring, perhaps, the contention into which "the chosen of God" have been thrust. As in Isaiah, the sufferings of God's people in the world come to a head in the conflict between the Lord and the idols. All else is secondary: the forces at work in the fallen creation, the idolatry and unbelief of Israel and the nations. All that matters is the call of the Creator, which renders everything—including sin itself—a tool of the Creator's good purpose. Yet that purpose has not yet come to fruition. The contention with the idols as to *who* is the true God remains. As the "chosen of God," believers in Christ, like the Isaianic Servant, are the objects of attack from the fallen world and its idols, an attack which takes the form of accusation. Consequently, Paul's affirmation, "the one who justifies is God," is not to be understood in the first instance as a justification before God, but as the justification of God and his chosen ones over against the idols and the world which worships and serves them. Here, too, "justification" is not merely a pronouncement, but includes the saving and vindicating action of God the Creator.

The third question ("Who is the one who condemns?"), which again constitutes an implicit affirmation, again takes up the language of Isaiah 50:9b. The allusion yet again more closely approximates the MT than the LXX, which focuses on the retributive dimension of the condemning verdict (*tis kakōsei me*; "Who shall harm me?"). Paul's usage of "condemnation" (*katakrima*) elsewhere bears this "executive" dimension (Rom. 5:16, 18; 8:1). It is entirely likely that the same is the case here. The language of "condemnation" like that of "justification" includes the performance of the verdict. The chosen ones of God shall not be put to shame (Isa. 50:7; 55:17). In this concrete sense, they shall not be condemned.

The chosen ones of God shall not be put to shame or condemned because of the One who has suffered death and has been raised in vindication for them. Christ here appears in the place of the anticipated reference to the justifying God: "Who is the one who condemns? The one who died, rather, who was raised is Christ Jesus" (8:34). Paul implicitly identifies the crucified and risen Christ with God, an identification which becomes evident in the following verses.

Paul here continues the thought of 8:32, where he describes the God who "delivered up" his "very own son." While there he speaks of Christ's death, here he lays emphasis on Christ's resurrection: "who died, rather, who was raised." In view of the other Isaianic allusions in this context, it is likely that Paul here echoes the fourth Servant Song, implicitly identifying Jesus with the Isaianic suffering Servant, who gave himself over to an unjust death and was vindicated, "justifying the many" (Isa. 52:13–53:12, MT Isa. 53:11).

Paul further expands his description of Christ with explicitly messianic language. The risen Christ is the one "who also is at the right hand of God, who also intercedes for us" (8:34b). Paul now identifies Christ with the priestly king to whom the promise is made, "Sit at my right hand, until I make your enemies a footstool for your feet" (Ps. 110:1). Earliest Christianity understood the exaltation of the risen Jesus in this way, most likely through Jesus's own interpretation of this messianic psalm (Mark 12:35–37 and par.; Mark 14:62 and par.; Acts 2:33; Eph. 1:20; Col. 3:1; Heb. 1:3; 8:1; 10:12; 12:2). "God's right hand" is a metaphor, drawn from the sphere of kingship and battle, for God's exercise of saving power (e.g., Exod. 15:6, 12; Pss. 16:8, 11; 17:7; 18:35; 20:6; 21:8; 44:3; 45:4; 48:10; 60:5; 63:8; 80:17; 108:6; 118:15; Isa. 41:10; 48:12–13; 1 Macc. 7:47). That Christ is at God's right hand implies, according to the allusion to the psalm, that all things are subject—or are being subjected—to him (cf. Mark 10:37; Matt. 20:21–23; 1 Cor. 15:24–25; Eph. 1:20–23). The triumph of the Chosen One, the messianic Servant, is the triumph of all God's chosen ones—those who share in him (Rom. 8:17, 33; cf. Eph. 1:20–23; Col. 3:1). At the same time, the distinction between Christ and believers is hardly obscured: he is there, we are here. Christ is present for us at God's right hand.

Paul develops this latter thought in a further description. Christ is the one "who also intercedes for us." The intercession of the Spirit for us in our hearts has its counterpart in the intercession of Christ for us at God's right hand. There may be a faint echo here again of the Hebrew text of the fourth Servant Song, which concludes by describing the Servant as one who "intercedes for transgressors" (Isa. 53:12; *yafgiʿa*; cf. Pss. 35:13; 109:4; LXX Isa. 53:12 "and on account of their sins, he was delivered up"). The Servant takes on the role of justifier, a role which belongs to the Lord alone (Isa. 53:11; cf. Isa. 43:8–13, 25–28; 45:20–25; 46:13; 51:4–8). That which the song ascribes to the Servant in his suffering, Paul now ascribes to the crucified and risen Christ. Perhaps, too, Paul presents Christ in the role of "priest according the order of Melchizedek" (Ps. 110:4; Hengel 1993; Stuhlmacher 2001). He concludes his description of Christ by returning to the opening affirmation concerning God: just as God is "for us," so the risen Christ lives and intercedes "for us" (see Heb. 7:25–26).

The question of 8:35, "Who shall separate us from the love of Christ?" with the concrete and extensive affirmation that follows it, draws together not only the entire series of questions but also the whole of the letter: here we have the *summa summarum*.

The language of separation (*chōrizō* [8:35, 39]) may recall the lament of abandonment of the psalmists (Ps. 43:2; 77:7; 88:5, 14) and of Israel in defeat and exile (Ps. 44:9, 23; 60:1; 108:11; Lam. 3:54). It also anticipates Paul's love for Israel as well as Israel's unbelief ("Would that I were anathema from Christ!" [Rom. 9:3]). Paul's summary of the gospel, including his sudden return to citation of Scripture, anticipates his affirmation of God's mercy in the face of Israel's unbelief.

The question, "Who shall separate us from the love of Christ?" implies that this love is universally present, all-pervading and all-encompassing, equal to the very presence of God of which the psalmist speaks (Ps. 139:7–12). This implicit affirmation that Christ's love is omnipresent arises from his confession that Christ is at God's right hand. The metaphorical image signifies not a limited location, but rather participation in the universal power and presence of God (cf. Eph. 4:10).

Paul now lists a catalog of troubles, closer to his own experience than to that of his addressees (cf. 2 Cor. 4:7–12; 11:23–27; 12:10). This form had Stoic parallels, which Paul clearly recalls (Ebner 1991: 365–86). The "sufferings of the present time" now receive seven names: "tribulation or distress, persecution or famine, nakedness or peril or sword" (8:35). The kind of troubles that Paul lists appear both ironically in the book of Job and straightforwardly in early Jewish writings as acts of divine vengeance reserved for the rebellious and disobedient (cf. Job 5:17–35; Sir. 39:28–31; *Pss. Sol.* 13:1–12; 15:1–13; *L.A.B.* 3:9; on this and the following observations, see Ebner 1991: 381–86). They also appear occasionally elsewhere as "seven" in number, obviously suggesting the punitive work of the Creator (Job 5:17–27; Sir. 40:8–11). In these early Jewish contexts the judgments once visited upon disobedient Israel become punishments reserved for the ungodly (Deut. 32:23–25; Isa. 51:19; Jer. 27:8; 38:2; Ezek. 5:17; 14:21). According to their trials, therefore, believers in Christ appear outwardly to be ungodly; the hidden Jew is the true Jew (Rom. 2:25–29). This is the only place in Paul's letters where "sword" (*machaira*), the final term in the series, appears in a hardship list. Probably it prepares for the following citation of Ps. 44 (43 LXX), which speaks of defeat in battle (the distinction between *machaira* ["short sword"] and *rhomphaia* ["scimitar"] is insignificant here). Very likely, too, it intimates execution—that is, persecution from the governing powers, despite Paul's later positive statements (cf. 13:4, which refers explicitly to the *ius gladii*). The list includes both the willful acts of human enemies of the gospel and the destructive forces of the fallen world. All such hardships are convulsions of the creation-rendered-futile. The question of "who" might separate us from Christ's love reverts momentarily to a "what" question. Yet Paul already has pictured the fallen creation as a living, conscious being (8:19–22). Behind such sufferings stand the powers of the fallen world (8:38–39).

Paul, in fact, immediately turns the question to God himself as it arises in a psalm of lament: "Just as it is written, 'On account of you we are slain all the day; we have been regarded as sheep for the slaughter'" (8:36, quoting Ps. 43:23 LXX [44:23 MT; 44:22 ET]). His quotation corresponds to the LXX, apart from his omission of the opening causal *hoti* ("because"; MT: *kî*), which implicitly resumes the psalmist's lament. The LXX follows the MT quite closely.

The psalmist grieves over the defeat and exile of the people of God. God has not gone forth with their army to battle (Ps. 43:10 LXX [44:10 ET]). "You have given us as sheep for slaughter [LXX: 'eating'] and have scattered us among the nations" (43:12 LXX [44:11 ET]). The people of God have been abandoned by God, their shepherd. God has sold them without price (43:13 LXX [44:12 ET]). God, who hides his face and forgets their affliction, is absent from them (43:25 LXX [Ps. 44:24 ET]). The setting of "exile" is indistinct, but clearly it is not the exile to Babylon that is in view. The lament is not accompanied by a confession of guilt (see also Ps. 89:38–52). Precisely the opposite: the psalmist protests the innocence of the people of God: "If we had forgotten the name of our God and lifted our hands to another God, would not God search this out? For he knows the secrets of the heart" (43:21–22 LXX [44:20–21 ET]). He questions in anguish, "Why do you hide your face? You forget our oppression and our affliction!" (43:25 LXX [44:24 ET]; cf. Ps. 74:10; 79:5; 89:47). The complaint that Paul cites from the psalm, "on account of you we are put to death all the day" (43:23 LXX [44:23 MT; 44:22 ET]), communicates the irreducibility of this experience of God's people under trial. There is no going behind it for an explanation or answer. The expression "all the day" is a typically concrete and vivid way of describing the unremitting suffering of the people of God (see Ps. 25:5; 38:6; 73:14; 74:22; 86:3; 102:8). Paul takes up the entire opening phrase in his citation. In context, it recalls Paul's earlier statement that "the creation was subjected to futility . . . on account of the one who subjected it, in hope" (8:20). As Paul stresses, the announcement of hope does not make visible the Creator's purpose (8:24–25). The second line of the psalm verse that Paul cites likewise attributes the condition of God's people to God: "we are reckoned as sheep for the slaughter." It is God who so "reckons," and in this effective reckoning God gives his people over to death. Here it is solely because of God, who hides himself, that his people suffer, and not because of their guilt. In taking up this lament, Paul suggests that believers share in Christ, the Suffering Servant, who likewise was led as a "sheep to slaughter" (Isa. 53:7; cf. Rom. 8:17, 32–34). The verse alludes to sacrifice, not only that of the Servant, but also perhaps the sacrifice of Isaac (Gen. 22:7–8). The "sufferings of the present time" are thus an "exile" without answer or evident basis for believers in Christ. They hear of God's love in Christ, as the apostle

will shortly remind them, but they do not yet see that love. Just as Israel knew the experience of God hiding his face, so now do believers. Christians in Rome generally were not experiencing troubles of the dimensions that Paul describes at the time of his writing. He reminds them of the lot of their brothers and sisters in the world and, without knowing it directly, prepares them for the sufferings that were to befall them within a few short years.

The very form of the psalm of lament, which remembers and anticipates the experience of God's goodness, signals that trial is not the end of the story (see Ps. 43:27 LXX [44:27 MT; 44:26 ET]). Paul likewise immediately points beyond present suffering to overwhelming triumph. Through "the one who loved us" we "super-triumph" (*hypernikōmen*). Paul's language almost certainly reflects the Stoic catalogs of troubles (especially by Epictetus), which take up athletic imagery to describe the tests in which those who are philosophically trained must triumph (*nikan*) in their confrontation with trials (*peristaseis*) that must become for them matters of indifference (*adiaphora*) (see Ebner 1991: 376–77). In these they triumph by maintaining their self-control and detachment. Paul offers a counter-image in at least three respects in regard to believers: (1) they encounter not matters of indifference, but rather real suffering and hardship in the fallen creation of the good Creator; (2) they triumph not only at the end of the trials but also here and now through Christ; (3) they do not merely triumph, but rather, as Paul announces with a neologism, they "super-triumph."

This "super-triumph" is ours through "the one who loved us" (8:37). Now Paul transposes the language of 8:28 ("those who love God"), revealing its foundation. His prior reference to the "love of Christ" (8:35) makes it clear that it is Christ to whom he refers as the "one who loved us." Moreover, just as it is clear in 8:32 that "the Son" whom God "delivered up" stands above all created things, so also here the love of Christ must be more than the mere love of a creature, since it is through this love that we "super-triumph" over the fallen creation. Paul goes on to make this matter explicit in 8:39: it is the love of *God* that is in Christ Jesus our Lord.

God's Righteousness and the Hidden Promise of Mercy for Israel (9:1–11:36)

THE WORD OF PROMISE AND THE UNBELIEF OF ISRAEL (9:1–29)

The second major movement of the letter opens with the apostle's lament over Israel's unbelief. Appearing abruptly without any connecting particle and standing in stark contrast to the soaring confession of God's unconquerable love in Christ, the lament constitutes a major caesura in Paul's argument. God's righteousness has been revealed in the gospel, yet it remains hidden and untraceable in the present outward course of events. It is the promise of Israel's salvation, not the visible evidence of it, that provokes Paul's lament here and that likewise elicits his closing hymn of praise in 11:33–36. The continuity between the gospel for Jew and Gentile and the salvation of Israel lies solely in Christ, who is both the proclaimed righteousness of God and the coming "Redeemer from Zion." In him both Israel and the nations encounter God as their Creator and Redeemer. The present proclamation, from which all but a remnant of Israel are estranged, will end in the coming of the "Redeemer," at which Israel will be forgiven for its unbelief and accepted by God, and the dead will be raised (11:12–15, 26–27).

The long drought of direct citation of the Scriptures in chapters 5–8, which Paul breaks in 8:36, is followed by a flood of citations in chapters 9–11. The "newness of life"—the entrance of the resurrection life into the world in Christ—has its precedent only in the counter-story of humanity's fall in Adam. Now Paul speaks of the ways of God within the present age, making the most extensive and concentrated use of Scripture in all his letters. Here again he takes up the question of Jewish advantage that he introduced in 3:1–8: the themes of God's word, glory, wrath, and righteousness reappear in chapters 9–11, as does the diatribal style.

Paul's opening lament provides the conceptual framework for the entire discourse, including the closing hymn of praise, which, according to the pattern of the psalms of lament, reaffirms the hope of the promises, contrary to all outward appearances (e.g., Pss. 10; 13; 22; 60; 102). The first section of Paul's discourse (9:1–29) here is oriented around lament, which appears at the opening and closing (9:1–5, 27–29). Paul's intervening instruc-

tion, which takes the form of diatribe, is essential to that lament, which otherwise would degenerate into unbelieving despair or a simplistic blaming of Israel. The lament arises from the unchanging gifts and calling of God upon Israel. Precisely in these gifts to which God has bound himself, God retains his freedom. The failure of Israel to believe the gospel consequently provokes contention with the fallen human being, who prefers a facile assignment of guilt to the acknowledgment of the Creator's freedom (9:14–29; cf. 3:4; 11:17–20). The lament thus stands alongside the word of God that provokes it in the face of outward circumstances (9:27–29).

In the second section of the discourse (9:30–10:21) Paul turns to Christ, the revealed and proclaimed righteousness of God in whom God's word has been savingly fulfilled. Upon this stone of offense Israel has stumbled. Here Paul elaborates his identification of Christ as God in 9:5. In him our Creator comes near, hears our petition, and richly saves us.

Finally, in the third section of the discourse (11:1–36) Paul's lament turns to praise as he affirms God's continuing faithfulness to Israel: God will yet be justified in the fulfillment of his promises to Israel through the coming Christ. The present "remnant" is a sign of the hope of Israel's final salvation, as "the Redeemer from Zion" comes to remove its ungodliness. Paul explicitly indicates in this final section that he is addressing his Gentile readers in Rome as he describes God's dealings with Israel (11:13). That is implicitly the case for the whole of his discourse. Yet he does not instruct merely Gentiles by Israel's example. For the sake of their own salvation, they must know that they possess no special quality or privilege. The end of God's purposes does not rest with them. The time of the gospel, the proclamation of Christ to "Jew and Greek," will come to an end. God finally will act in all particularity to save his people Israel. God, who created the distinction between Israel and the nations by his word, leads them by opposing paths in their rebellion and disobedience in order to bring them back to the knowledge of him as their Creator in Christ, who is both the proclaimed Lord and the coming Redeemer of Israel.

9:1–5

As the apostle to the Gentiles and for the Gentiles, Paul laments Israel's unbelief. Here he speaks to Gentile believers in a predominantly Gentile church (see 11:13; cf. 1:5–7). The constant grief and pain in his heart and his unfulfillable desire to be accursed, separated from Christ on behalf of his "brothers, his kinspeople according to the flesh," communicate his love for them and invite his Gentile readers to love them as well, or at the very least to reject all pride and boasting over against Israel (cf. 11:17–24). Paul takes much the same role as Moses, whose request is to be "blotted out of the book" of the Lord for the sake of Israel, whom the Lord rejects (see Exod. 32:30–34). Already here God's freedom and untraceable ways leave their mark. In the present Paul's grief finds no answer, just as there is presently no visible answer to the suffering of believers (8:35–36); therefore the lament.

9:6–13

Paul now instructs his primarily Gentile readers on the nature of his lament. Israel's failure is not the failure of the word of God. Scripture itself defines the children of Abraham and of Israel as those created by the word of promise. Paul's choice of the term "word [*logos*] of God" (not "promise") as a heading for the section recalls the theme of the triumph of God in his words (3:5; cf. Ps. 51:4). Here as well as in the earlier context, the "word of God" not only promises salvation but also brings the judgment through which salvation arrives (9:28). Thus the use of the broader term *logos* is understandable. Paul's opening words also echo Isa. 40:7–8 and anticipate the sharp distinction between "flesh" and the word of God that he sets forth: "It is not such a circumstance that the word of God has fallen" (9:6). It is, instead, "flesh"—that is, the fallen human being—that like grass and its flower withers and falls; the word of God stands forever.

Paul answers the implicit question of Israel's present failure in a simple assertion that already lies in the Isaianic text that he has echoed: "Not all those from Israel are Israel." Just as he redefines being a "Jew" in 2:17–29, so here he redefines "Israel" by appeal to Scripture, pointing to the pattern established by the word of promise given before the birth of Isaac and, later, before that of Jacob. The argument here has two brief movements: first the reminder of the story of Isaac's birth (9:6–9), then the story of Jacob and Esau (9:10–13).

Not all of Abraham's seed are "children"—that is, children of God; rather, according to the word to Abraham, "in Isaac your seed shall be called" (9:7–8). The brief citation of Gen. 21:12 in 9:7 follows the LXX, which does not vary from the MT. Paul here takes up the biblical language of "calling," in which naming determines the person and destiny of the recipient, as with the Lord's renaming of Abram and Jacob (Gen. 17:5; 35:10). The giving of a name thus communicates blessing, as in the case of Israel's blessing of Ephraim and Manasseh (Gen. 48:16). That Abraham's seed is called (or named) in Isaac makes Isaac and God's work in him constitutive. As recipients of blessing, the "children" and "seed" (or "descendants") must be children and seed not only of Abraham but also of God (9:8). The passage that Paul cites is God's word of instruction and comfort to Abraham in the face of Sarah's demand that Abraham expel Hagar and Ishmael. The word to Abraham excludes Ishmael, corresponding to Paul's use of it here. It is not Ishmael, nor the later sons of Keturah, but rather Isaac alone who bears God's blessing of Abraham (cf. Gen. 25:1–18). The "reckoning" (*logizetai*) of the children of promise as "seed" of Abraham is not hidden in the councils of God and remote, but rather is concrete and present in God's word (*logos*) to Abraham: "reckoning" (9:8) here refers to the event of "calling" (9:7). As elsewhere in Paul's usage, God's reckoning is effective: the children of promise *are* Abraham's seed. Paul finds in God's word to Abraham in Gen. 21:12 the pattern (or "type") of God's work: the word of promise always transcends human possibilities (9:9) and always entails the rejection of the capacities of fallen human beings in effecting blessing (9:8, 13).

Paul introduces the category of "promise" by pointing to God's announcement to Abraham that Sarah would give birth to a son (9:9). The language is nearly definitional in character: "This [word] is a word of promise." God alone promises and fulfills, contrary to all human abilities and expectations. The element of time, which Paul in fact fronts—"at this time I shall come"—is essential. There must be a time of waiting and faith before the promise is fulfilled. Perhaps the gift of a "son" to Sarah faintly anticipates the final redemption of Israel and all creation, in which its "sonship" is realized (8:22–23; 9:4; 11:26–27).

The citation does not precisely follow either Gen. 18:10 or 18:14, where the promise is pronounced and repeated. As we have noted, Paul fronts the reference to time and simplifies the expression over against both the LXX and the MT ("this time of season"). The simpler description of the time found in Gen. 18:10 serves as the starting point of the citation. Paul's use of the preposition *kata* follows the usage of the LXX. He omits some elements of the text. God's promise "I shall come *to you*" is shortened. He leaves out the exclamatory "*Behold,* there shall be a son" and likewise the reference to "Sarah, *your wife.*" Probably at this point he is recalling the briefer wording of Gen. 18:14. Early Jewish references to the wonder of Isaac's birth approximate Paul's use of the text in varying measures (*L.A.B.* 8:1–3; *Jub.* 16:1–4; *T. Ab.* [A] 8:6; *Gen. Rab.* 47:3–5; 48:16–20; 53:3–5; *b. B. Meṣiʿa* 87a). In defining "promise" by appeal to God's announcement to Abraham, Paul again discerns the pattern (or type) of God's saving dealings: in the face of human unbelief—Sarah's laughter—the word announces that which is humanly impossible and creates a faith that waits for the time of fulfillment.

What took place in the birth and divine choice of Isaac also took place in Rebecca, who, Paul takes care to note, was impregnated by one man, Isaac (9:6–13). Paul's naming of him as "our father" includes Gentile believers, recalling the earlier discussion of Abraham (4:13–25) and preparing for the following discussion (9:24–26, 30–33; 10:12–21). Yet it also underscores the continuation of the pattern established in Isaac. Again in the birth of Jacob and Esau God asserts his right to determine the recipients of blessing and to exclude the rest. Paul cites Gen. 25:23d only after a lengthy explanation, which he grammatically subordinates to the simple introduction, "It was said to her" (9:12). God's word came to Rebecca while the children were "not yet born and had not yet done anything good or evil" (9:11a). Neither Esau's exchange of his birthright nor Jacob's scheming (with Rebecca) comes into consideration. Nor does any working of the good come into view. Paul takes care to show that "the flesh" is entirely excluded from God's saving purpose: nei-

ther physical descent nor the doing of good plays a role. This took place so that "God's purpose, which accords with [God's] choice might abide, not according to works, but according to the one who calls" (9:11b–12a). "Election" (or "choice") is always "selection." Here again the context indicates that in speaking of "election" (*eklogē*), Paul has in view God's immediate choice of Jacob by his word, not a hidden divine purpose (so also 11:5, 7, 28). This choice of Jacob meant the rejection of Esau. Furthermore, as the translation above suggests, the prepositional phrases in 9:12a are best understood as adverbial modifiers: God's (effective) purpose abides, not by human works, but purely because of "the One who calls" (cf. *b. Nid.* 16b; see Str-B 3:266). In blessing and saving, God acts in freedom as Creator. Paul's appeal to God's work in Jacob and Esau is thus decisively contrary to the early Jewish construal of Esau's wickedness and Jacob's righteousness as the cause for the distinction between them (*b. Yoma* 38b; *b. Meg.* 6a; *Gen. Rab.* 63:8; *Jub.* 35:9–17; *L.A.B.* 32:5–6; cf. Heb. 11:20; 12:16–17; see Str-B 3:267–68).

Allusions to Isa. 40–55 continue to play subtly in the background. As we have noted, Paul's opening words in 9:5 recall that "the word of God abides [*menei*] forever" (Isa. 40:8 LXX). So also here, God's purpose abides apart from human works (9:11b–12a). Likewise in Isaiah, the Lord is the one who calls Israel and whose call effects and establishes his purpose (e.g., Isa. 40:26; 41:9; 43:1; 48:12). There, too, the choice of Israel means the rejection of other nations (Isa. 41:8–16; 43:1–7).

Paul's quotation of Gen. 25:23, which follows both the LXX and the MT, takes up only the second part of the oracle given to Rebecca, who "inquired of the Lord" because of the struggle between the twin children in her womb. The Lord first announces to her that she is going to give birth to two nations, two peoples who are going to be divided against each other; moreover, one will be stronger than the other (Gen. 25:23a–b). The final word, which Paul cites here, comes therefore as a surprising reversal, contrary to expectation and custom: "the greater shall serve the lesser." The one born first becomes subservient to the one born second. The Lord's choice of the later-born Jacob as "the beloved son" is part of the pattern of the story of Genesis, which has appeared already with Isaac, will appear again with Joseph, and yet again in the blessing of Ephraim and Manasseh (Levenson 1993). God's purpose is not only independent of human beings but also contrary to their expectations. This pattern of reversal has been repeated in Christ. The established tradition of Judaism does not count with God over against the fledging community of believing Jews and Gentiles. Nor do its considerable numbers outweigh the small and weak churches of Paul's day. In fact, these numbers, along with all things, are made to serve God's purpose of blessing those whom he calls (Rom. 9:22–29). Paul's language and thought here come close to that which we find in his recounting of the story of Hagar and Sarah (Gal. 4:21–31).

Yet that is not the end of the story. Paul concludes his "definition of Israel" with a second citation of Scripture, now with an introductory formula: "Just as it is written, 'Jacob I loved, but Esau I hated.'" The appeal to the words of Scripture as "having been written" signals that God's word to Rebecca already has come to fulfillment. The text that Paul cites is drawn from the opening of the book of Malachi (1:2b–3a). He follows the LXX (which follows the MT), apart from fronting the reference to Jacob in the first clause. The change obviously corresponds to his point. It is Jacob whom God has chosen, according to the word to Rebecca. In the context of Malachi, Israel lives under straitened conditions in the early Second Temple period, in which the Lord seems distant and indifferent to the conduct of his people (3:8–15). The opening words of the oracle thus constitute a rebuke to the nation: "'I have loved you,' says the LORD" (1:1). The Lord answers Israel's unbelieving response, "How have you loved us?" by pointing to Esau. Although Esau is Jacob's brother (and therefore in no way differs from him), the Lord has loved Jacob and hated Esau. As in Rom. 9, God's love is here defined by its freedom. The evidence for the Lord's love for Israel lies in the return from exile and the rebuilding that has already taken place. The Lord has brought Esau's land to ruin, as he has done with Israel. Yet no matter how resolutely Edom determines to rebuild its ruins, the Lord will tear them down (1:3–5). Matters are obviously different for God's people. Israel, blind to the evidence all about it of the Lord's love, seeing only

the unrequited conduct of the wicked and the righteous, lives in unthankfulness, indifference, and disobedience (e.g., 1:6–14). The prophetic announcement "Jacob I loved, but Esau I hated" is intended to open Israel's eyes. Paul's appeal to the text implies that the pattern has been repeated in his day. God in freedom has set his love on some within Israel, but not on others. And yet, faintly, the passage also brings a reminder of God's love for all Israel, which has its beginning in "Jacob" and the word spoken before his birth. Paul later names the nation according to its beginning as he speaks of its final salvation (Rom. 11:26–27). The reminder of God's love for Jacob casts a shadow, faint though it may be, of the salvation of Israel yet to come.

9:14–29

The question as to whether God is unrighteous in the freedom of his promises finds its answer in the pattern of God's promissory dealings itself. As in the opening lament, Paul's attention here is directed to the exodus event, in which Israel came into being as a nation. Here he turns to the Lord's response to Moses' petition to see the Lord's glory, a petition that the Lord did not grant, allowing Moses only to see his "back" (Exod. 33:23). In Exodus, the exchange between Moses and the Lord begins with Moses' complaint that the Lord has not made known to him whom the Lord will send with them (as their help) in their journey to the promised land (33:12). His statement of protest is essentially a parallel to his earlier question regarding the name of God that he should report to the Israelites as having sent him to them (3:13). Here, too, he makes a petition, which clearly represents an expansion of his complaint: Moses asks of the Lord, "Show me your ways" (33:13). In context, the petition is a request for a definite and final knowledge of the Lord, which would bind him and his favor to Moses and to Israel, the same demand that was implicit in Moses' earlier request to know the Lord's name. The Lord does not yield to this petition: he knows Moses by name (33:12, 17), but Moses is not permitted to know God by name. He knows him only by the name "Yahweh." This name, given in God's response to his earlier petition and which plays upon God's assertion of his freedom ("Tell them, 'I AM has sent me to you'"), was as much a refusal as it was a granting of Moses' request (3:13–15;

also 33:19). The Lord's response to Moses in the present context is much the same: he promises that his "face" (i.e., "presence") will go with him and that he will give him "rest" on the journey (33:14). The Lord deflects the petition, while yet granting saving help. Yet Moses positions himself for further negotiation by accepting this gift and extolling its benefits (33:15–16). The Lord simply confirms his promise in response to the petition that is implicitly present in Moses' praise: "I will do the thing that you have asked." The Lord's presence will go with Israel (33:17). Although he will not allow Moses to know his name or his ways in the manipulative manner that Moses has requested, in his freedom he promises the blessing of his presence. But Moses will not desist from his original complaint: "Show me your glory, I pray" (33:18). In his final response the Lord promises to cause all his goodness to pass before Moses and to pronounce his name before him, yet Moses must be content to see only God's back, not God's face, which "no one can see and live" (33:19–20). The word of the Lord to Moses that Paul cites in 9:15 represents a fresh assertion of the divine freedom: "I will have mercy on whom I will have mercy, and have compassion on whom I will have compassion" (33:19). The Lord's response again corresponds to his opening encounter with Moses (3:13–15) and with the tensile and inscrutable juxtaposition of the Lord's forgiving love and retributive judgment that Moses hears in the vision of God that follows (34:6–7). The Lord refuses to compromise his freedom. He yields no vision that defines him or his ways.

Moses' request was not at heart a longing to know the glory of God's character, but rather was an illegitimate desire to name and know God in a way that would obligate him to Israel. In Exod. 33:12–23 God's glory is not identified with God's freedom. Nor is the proclamation of God's name equivalent to a demonstration of divine glory (Exod. 34:5). God in his freedom refuses to yield his glory to Moses' complaint: the proclamation of his name is a reassertion of his freedom and a refusal of Moses' petition. Correspondingly, in Rom. 9:14–29 Paul's justification of God (9:14) does not rest in an appeal to the excellence of the divine being; rather, Paul asserts the freedom of the Creator in the face of human rebellion (9:20). Like God's righteousness, God's glory is salvific,

"poured out" on vessels of mercy that are now being prepared beforehand for that eschatological glory (9:23). God's glory is known only in his mercy, given freely, concretely, and particularly to fallen human beings. It is not found in abstract contemplation of the divine being.

As he frequently does in Rom. 9–11, Paul introduces the citation in the present tense. In this case he also emphasizes the direct address to Moses: "God *says* to Moses...." The address does not remain in the past, but rather continues into the present (cf. 4:3, 6). The citation corresponds verbatim to what we find in the LXX, which here, as often, legitimately renders the Hebrew *ḥānan* ("show favor" or "have mercy") with *eleeō* ("have mercy"), well within its range of meaning.

Paul's typical use of the citation corresponds very closely to its thrust in the exodus narrative described above. From the text he draws this conclusion: "So then, it [the obtaining of mercy and compassion] is not of the one who wills, nor of the one who runs, but of the mercy-showing God" (9:16). The abstract reference to "willing" reflects a Hellenistic conception of the human being that had already thoroughly penetrated early Jewish thought (Hengel 1981: 131–75; see Sir. 15:11–20, where instruction concerning the *yēṣer/diaboulion* ["will, inclination"] first appears; also *Pss. Sol.* 9:4–5, which uses the term *eklogē* ["choice"]). Paul's twofold presentation of the human being here as "willing" and "running" corresponds to the argument concerning "willing" and "doing" in 7:14–25. Here the "doing" is extended to "running" a course. The motif of a contest was commonly used in Hellenistic rhetoric and appears elsewhere in Paul's letters (1 Cor. 9:24–27; Gal. 2:2; 5:7; Phil. 3:12–14). The similar theme of running a path appears in biblical and early Jewish usage as well (e.g., Ps. 119:32; Isa. 40:31; Jer. 12:5; cf. Ps. 19:5; Sir. 19:17; 43:5). Paul shifts to this imagery here because the element of time is essential to the overarching theme of God giving and fulfilling his promises. The language of "pursuit" appears at the opening of the second section in this connection (9:30–33). The question at hand is whether the fulfillment of the promise depends on the course that human beings might run or on God alone. Paul has made clear in chapter 7 that "willing" to do good, in the ultimate and full sense, brings not the effecting of good, but rather its opposite. Yet there has been an intervening break in the argument of the letter. In the present context he reintroduces the possibility of the human being "doing good or evil" (9:11), a possibility not excluded by the argument of chapter 7 except in the absolute sense. Now Paul's topic is the freedom of the promising God, not the fallenness of the human being. Here, from a different angle, he revisits the question about the ability of human beings to contribute to salvation. From the divine word to Moses he draws the simple conclusion that God's mercy remains unconditioned by any human willing or striving to do good (MT Ps. 51:3 [Ps. 51:1 ET]; MT Hos. 2:25 [Hos. 2:23 ET]). Mercy rests solely in God, who determines to show mercy. Mercy remains mercy precisely because it is free.

Early Judaism had varied understandings of this description of God's mercy in Exod. 33:19. *Exodus Rabbah* 45:6 approximates Paul's description of the freedom of God's mercy; *b. Ber.* 7a reflects early debates on righteousness and reward; *Tg. Onq.* follows the MT; *Tg. Yer. I* binds mercy to human worthiness (cf. *Pss. Sol.* 2:35); CD-B XX, 21–25 interprets Exod. 34:6–7 as conditioned by human righteousness; 1QM XI, 4; 1QHª IX, 32; XIV, 9 appeal simply to God's mercy; *T. Jud.* 19:3 reflects the unqualified mercy of God that appears in this text. As we have noted, although Paul's argument touches early Jewish debates on the relationship between righteousness and reward, here he is not engaging them directly. If he were doing so, one might have expected a fuller integration of the arguments of chapters 7 and 9. His argument here is determined instead by his assertion of the freedom of God in giving and fulfilling his promises. The anthropological conclusion that Paul draws from the text ("It is not of the one who wills or runs" [9:16]) does not overturn the particularity of his argument. The Lord's refusal of Moses' request, which would have done away with the freedom of his mercy by binding it to Israel, remains constitutive of Israel's present. The response of the Lord to Moses at the birth of Israel as a nation is a word that he yet speaks and that yet determines the nation (9:15). Paul discerns in the divine word to Moses the pattern (type) of God's ways with all human beings, but not in abstraction from his dealings with Israel. The Lord does not address us as Israel, but in addressing Israel as his human

creature, he addresses us along with Israel (wording borrowed from Oswald Bayer).

An explanatory citation follows the first conclusion (9:17). Paul moves backward in the exodus narrative to the Lord's contention with Pharaoh, in the midst of the ten plagues that the Lord sent upon Egypt. Paul again introduces the text in the present tense as direct address, "For the Scripture says to Pharaoh..." (9:17). This address, too, continues in its relevance into the present. Yet here it is not "God" who speaks to Pharaoh, but rather "the Scripture." The shift is not derived from the Exodus passage. In personifying "Scripture," Paul most likely emphasizes that the divine word to Pharaoh (which otherwise might be regarded as entirely particular) bears divine instruction for believers in Christ. Pharaoh himself is determined and defined even into the present, not by his own plans and purpose, but rather by the divine word to him: "To this end I raised you up: that I might display in you my power, and that my name might be proclaimed in all the earth" (9:17). Paul takes up themes from this citation in his description of the present time (9:22). Paul's appeal to the figure of Pharaoh is thus simultaneously particular and universal: in God's word to Pharaoh the pattern (type) of his work with fallen humanity is manifest.

This citation of Exod. 9:16 appears to be basically independent of the LXX: Paul (1) renders the initial purpose clause more emphatically (*eis auto touto* versus *heneken toutou*); (2) remains closer to the Hebrew *heʾĕmadtîkā* ("I established you") with his *exēgeira se* ("I raised you up") than the LXX *dietērēthēs* ("you were kept"); (3) introduces the second purpose clause differently (*hopōs* versus *hina*); (4) renders the Hebrew *kōaḥ* as "power" (*dynamis*) rather than "strength" (*ischys*). The slight deviation from what we find in the MT, "raise up" instead of "establish," accentuates the divine triumph over Pharaoh, recalling perhaps the Lord's sovereign dealings with rulers (e.g., 1 Sam. 2:7; Ps. 75:7; Isa. 40:18–24; Dan. 2:21) and with the wicked (e.g., Ps. 73:18–20; 92:5–9). Early Jewish sources recount Pharaoh's wickedness and rebellion against the Lord (*b. Sanh.* 94b; *Exod. Rab.* 9:8; 11:6; 12:1; 19:8; Josephus, *Ant.* 2.281–348; Ezek. Trag. 149–151). According to *T. Sol.* 25:1–7, Pharaoh's heart was hardened by a demon. Passages in the Qumran writings describe Pharaoh's defeat as an adumbration of that of Rome and the nations (1QM XI, 9; 4Q374). Apparently, only Sir. 16:15 (preserved in the Hebrew, the Lucianic recension, and the Armenian version) parallels Paul, attributing Pharaoh's hardened heart to the Lord alone, "in order that his works might be known under heaven."

Contrary to outward appearance, but according to the Lord's word, Pharaoh is a mere tool in the hand of the Lord by which the Creator manifests his power and makes known his name. Paul returns to these themes shortly (9:22). His appeal to the figure of Pharaoh brings a reminder of human rebellion and fallenness to his argument. Pharaoh was hardly searching for mercy! Despite brief moments in which he yields to the Lord's will, he finally is set upon refusing the Lord's demand to let his people go. In fact, the "hardening" of Pharaoh's heart is at the center of the drama in the exodus narrative. At the outset of Moses' audiences with Pharaoh, the Lord announces to him that Pharaoh will not listen and that Israel will be delivered from Egypt "by mighty acts of judgment" (Exod. 7:4–5). Pharaoh's heart is "hardened" at their first meeting (7:14, 22). In the course of the contention he is said more than once to have "hardened his heart" (8:15, 32; 9:34). Yet it is not merely Pharaoh, but rather the Lord who "hardens" Pharaoh's heart, thus fulfilling his word and purpose (9:12; 10:1, 20; 14:8, 17–18). Paul draws his second conclusion directly from the narrative of Exodus: "So then, to whom he wills, he shows mercy, and whom he wills, he hardens" (9:18). "Hardening" thus signifies the encounter of the rebellious human being with the word of God in judgment.

The outcome of an encounter with the word of God, then, whether it is in mercy or in judgment and hardening, rests in God alone. The two outcomes are in fact bound together: the word of judgment on Pharaoh turns out at the same time to be mercy upon Israel. The hardening of Pharaoh effects Israel's exodus from Egypt. Paul recalls that in Pharaoh, God displayed his power as Creator and made known his name in all the earth (9:17). God's saving purpose for "all the earth" was already present in the act of judgment and mercy by which he created Israel. The act of hardening thus takes place within God's dealings with the world. Paul does not attempt to peer into the hidden purpose of God that stands behind this event.

The confessional form "What shall we say?" (9:14) gives way to the individual, diatribal style in 9:19: "You will say to me then, 'Why does he still accuse, for who resists what he has determined?'" As in 3:5, Paul voices the protest of the fallen human being to divine judgment. There the protest arises from the word of God that announces human guilt. Here it arises from the saving will of God announced in his word, by which in freedom he judges and shows mercy. God's right as Creator is at stake in both instances.

Here, however, Paul responds more sharply than in chapter 3, addressing the interlocutor in the same manner as he does the moralizer in 2:1: "O human being!" (9:20). Now the human question directly usurps the right of God, in the same manner as the presumption of the moralizing judge. It is, moreover, the individual human being, who contends with words and argument against the right of the Creator, whose power cannot be resisted. It is Pharaoh himself who contends with God here, not the community of Egyptians (even if the Lord hardens their hearts as well and they perish with him [Exod. 10:1]). The rhetorical question as to who is able to resist God's will or judgments has antecedents both in Scripture and in early Judaism, which recognize the right and power of the Creator (Job 9:19 LXX; Wis. 11:21; 12:12; 1QH V, 19–21; 1QH^a XVIII, 1–12; *Tg. Job* 9:12; see Str-B 3:269–70).

"But on the contrary," Paul asks, "who are you to debate [*antapokrinomai*] with God?" (9:20 [cf. the same verb in Job 32:12 LXX]). The creature is in no position to argue with the Creator. Paul immediately interprets his question in a near citation of Isa. 29:16b LXX, which carries over the interrogative from its opening clause: "The clay shall not be regarded as the potter, shall it? The thing shaped shall not say to the one who shaped it, 'You did not shape me,' shall it? Or that which is made to the one who makes it (shall not say, shall it), 'You made me without understanding'?" (cf. Isa. 29:16 MT). Paul shifts the question slightly, echoing Isa. 45:9b ("Does the clay say to the potter, 'What are you making?'"), thereby addressing the issue of God's freedom in mercy and judgment: "That which is formed will not say to the one who formed it, 'Why did you make me thus?' will it?"

A grudging acknowledgment of the impossibility of questioning the Creator appears in the complaint of Job. Yet upon his encounter with God, Job retracts this complaint, freely acknowledging the Creator's right (Job 9:1–10:22, esp. 9:12; cf. 42:1–6). Wisdom of Solomon 12:3–18 celebrates the right of the Creator to judge and destroy the inhabitants of Canaan (esp. 12:12). In Pseudo-Philo, Eli echoes Isa. 29:16 in acceptance of divine judgment on his house (*L.A.B.* 53:13). See also *Apoc. Sedr.* 3:8; *Sib. Or.* 8:444–445. The contrast between the creature of clay and the Creator appears thematically in the Qumran hymns (1QS XI, 20–22; 1QHᵃ IX, 21–23; XII, 28–29; XX, 28–36).

Although Paul shifts the challenge of the Creator that appears in Isaiah to a questioning of the Creator, the issue remains the same. In the broader Isaianic context the Lord asserts his right by questioning his rebellious people, charging them with inverting their true relation to him (Isa. 29:13–16) and condemning them in this contention (Isa. 45:9–13). In shifting the form of the citation, Paul borrows the divine rhetoric for his diatribe. The contention between the Lord and his rebellious people is nothing other than the contention between the Creator and the creature. The Lord's word to Israel in Isa. 29:14–16; 45:9–13 reveals the pattern (type) of this contention, which extends to every human being.

In 9:21 Paul himself reasserts the right of the Creator: "Does not the potter have authority over the clay to make from the same lump a vessel of honor and a vessel of dishonor?" The reference to the potter and clay recalls not only Isa. 29:16; 45:9, but also Jer. 18:1–12, where the Lord asserts his power to destroy or preserve "the house of Israel." As clay is in the hand of the potter, so is the nation in the hand of the Lord. Yet Paul has in view not the question of God's power that appears in Jeremiah, but rather the question of God's authority, God's right as Creator. Paul's prior citation of Isa. 29:16 LXX informs his appeal to the Jeremianic language. Furthermore, unlike the word of the Lord in Jeremiah that offers Israel the hope that the Lord will change his purpose if Israel repents, Paul speaks of determined destinies. This formation of "a vessel of honor" and "a vessel of

dishonor" out of the same lump of clay recalls the divine choice of Jacob over Esau mentioned by Paul in 9:10–13 (in connection with the potter, *skeuos* is best understood as "vessel," not "tool"). Paul here still has in view the divine choice within one people, Israel, yet the category of "Creator and creation" that he employs now broadens the scope of his statement. Furthermore, his interest remains fixed on the individual. His subsequent shift to the plural "vessels" (9:23) shows that his use of the singular in 9:21 is specific, not generic. As the following context indicates, "honor" and "dishonor" (or "infamy, shame") reflect, respectively, salvation and judgment (cf. 2 Tim. 2:19–21). The "vessels" correspond to, respectively, the experience of God's glory (9:23) and the destruction of Pharaoh (9:17, 22).

The structure of Paul's description of the work of the Creator comes intriguingly close to the description in the Wisdom of Solomon of the work of a potter, who can make both clean vessels and vessels that are "opposite"—that is, idols (Wis. 15:7–13; cf. Isa. 40:18–20; 41:6–7; 44:9–20; Jer. 10:1–5). Sirach 33:10–15 describes human beings as fashioned from dust and as clay in the hand of the Lord, the potter. Yet it is not clear that the language here is predestinarian, as it is with Paul (which would be exceptional for Sirach). Sirach singles out human "ways" and divine retribution as the essence of the Creator's work: "In this way [*houtōs*] human beings are in the hand of the one who made them" (Sir. 33:13 [the passage appears to be related to a similar tradition in *T. Naph.* 2:1–4]). The confession that the human being is mere clay appears regularly in the Qumran hymns (1QS XI, 22; 1QHᵃ IX, 21; XI, 21–23; XII, 29; XVIII, 3–4; XX, 26–27; XXII, 7, 11; XXIII *top*, 10b–12; cf. Job 4:19; 10:9; 33:6). According to *b. Ber.* 32a, Jer. 18:6, "Can I not do with you, house of Israel, as the potter has done?" explains the victory of Israel's enemies. In *Midr. Exod.* 46:4 the Lord responds in mercy to Israel's petitionary confession, "We are the clay, you are the potter" (Isa. 64:8). The same passage becomes the basis for appeal, since like the potter who leaves a pebble in the clay, God has left a defect in Israel, the "evil impulse" (*yēṣer hā-rāʾ*).

Verse 22 does not recall Jer. 27:25 LXX (50:25 MT/ET), despite the verbal similarity (nor the variant at Isa. 13:5 LXX [cf. 54:16–17 LXX]).

There the Lord brings forth from his storehouse "implements of his wrath" (*skeuē orgēs autou*) to be used against Babylon. Paul's thought here also differs from Wis. 12:10, 20–22, which interprets the divine patience as offering the opportunity of repentance (cf., however, Rom. 2:4–5).

As the image of the potter already indicates, Paul here speaks of "vessels of wrath"—that is, those who will experience divine wrath and destruction. His language in 9:22 recalls his citation of Exod. 9:16 in 9:17. The experience of Pharaoh is recapitulated in "the vessels of wrath, prepared for destruction." This preparation for destruction takes place in the present time, not in eternity past: just as the Lord raised up Pharaoh, so now he has prepared these vessels. Paul's thought thus stands close to wisdom psalms that reflect on God's dealings with the wicked (e.g., Pss. 37; 73). The present power and prosperity of the wicked merely prepare for destruction. Verses 14–23, moreover, speak of the human being, not Israel. Paul is not describing unbelieving Jews in this verse, although they are included in his description; rather, he is speaking about all human beings who oppose the gospel, recalling the opposition of the fallen creation to those who love God (see 8:31–39). Pharaoh, the former enemy of Israel, has his counterpart in the present enemies of those who believe. God's wrath is not abstract; it is directed against the human deceit, violence, and oppression that torment the present world (see 3:10–18). It is this reality that God presently bears with "great patience." Time—that is, the present time—is central to Paul's thought here. It is within time that God reveals his identity and makes himself known: the Creator who is sovereign and free in his freedom endures with patience "vessels of wrath." Here in v. 22 Paul has provided a second answer to the impertinent question of 9:19, one which emerges from his first response in 9:20–21.

Paul expands his response further: "And what if [he did so] in order to make known the riches of his glory on vessels of mercy, which he prepared beforehand for glory?" (9:23). As in 9:22, the preparation of these vessels takes place in the present time.

As in 8:29–30, the *pro*-compound (*proetoimazō*) is again prospective, anticipating the arrival of the eschaton, when God will glorify all his "sons"

(8:18, 30). Implicitly, the sufferings of the present time (8:18), inflicted in considerable measure by "vessels of wrath," prepare the "vessels of mercy" for glory (8:31–39; cf. 2 Cor. 4:16–18).

Paul's language here recalls Isaianic promises of the bestowal of divine glory, especially Isa. 60:1–3: God's glory is his saving presence. Paul again takes up a thematic thread that runs through his argument. The glory of the Creator, which fallen human beings have rejected, is restored to them in salvation (1:23; 3:23; 5:2; 6:4; 8:18). In fact, the participation in God's glory is the essence of salvation. Verses 23–24 echo Paul's description of hope in 8:18–39. The gift of God's glory to Israel (9:4) thus takes on added significance. The "riches of God's glory" are found in the mercy that he in freedom bestows on his people. Paul does not identify God with a hidden election of some to destruction and some to glory. Paul affirms that the Creator acts in sovereign freedom, but his response to the impertinent question of the human being does not rest with an abstract assertion of the Creator's right; rather, he bears witness to the promise of the gospel, that the Creator's purpose is the restoration of his glory to those whom he now is preparing.

In the following verse Paul identifies the recipients of mercy: "us, whom he called not only from among Jews, but also from among Gentiles" (9:24). God's calling of numerous Gentiles by the gospel, which Israel refuses to believe, forms the background of Paul's lament. "Calling" again signifies the effective and free word of the Creator, which is now visibly embodied in the calling of God's people not only from Jews but also from Gentiles. The people of God are thus a sort of *tertium quid*, distinct from earthly Israel and from the nations. Here Paul breaks the bounds of his previous argument that dealt with the definition of "Israel" within the context of earthly descent. Yet Paul's prior identification of "Israel" and "Abraham's children" as those created by the word of promise and not by physical descent already outlines a pattern with which God's calling of Gentiles through the gospel stands in continuity (see also 4:9–25, in which the promise to Abraham is foundational to God the Creator's saving work). The divine words of promise are definite, coming at distinct times, simultaneously hardening and granting mercy (cf. 9:6–13, 14–21). The same is true of the promise-come-to-fulfillment in the gospel. The Creator, who promises, remains free.

In 9:26–29 Paul in a remarkable way underscores the continuity between the present and the past word and work of God. For the first time since his reference to David (4:6) Paul names the locus of his citation ("in Hosea"), underscoring the pattern of salvation that is found in Israel's past and has been repeated in the present. The calling of a people from among both Jews and Gentiles corresponds to what God also says in Hosea:

> I shall call that which is not my people, "my people," and her who is not beloved, "beloved." (Hos. 2:25b MT/LXX [2:23b ET])

> And it shall be in the place where it was said to them, "You are not my people," there they shall be called "sons of the living God." (Hos. 2:1b MT/LXX [1:10b ET])

The passage understandably appears in rabbinic affirmation of God's mercy on Israel (esp. *b. Pesaḥ.* 87b; *Midr. Num.* 2:15, where Hos. 2:1 and 2:25 together appear) and in discussion about whether Israel remained God's sons even in disobedience (e.g., *b. Qidd.* 36a; see further Str-B 3:272–74). Paul's reference to Hosea is as much a summary of the message of the book as it is a citation. The wording represents a combination of Hosea 2:25b and 2:1b, in which Paul not only inverts the order of the excerpts but also alters the text significantly.

It is the first part of the reference (9:25) that shows the most significant variation from Hosea. (1) The promise of the Lord's mercy to *Lō'-rūḥāmâ* ("No-mercy") is omitted, perhaps because it is connected with the promise of being re-"sown" in the land (*pace* Wagner [2002: 81–82], who sees instead a reversal of order). (2) Rather than "saying" to *Lō'-'ammî* ("Not-my-people"), "You are my people," the Lord "calls" them his people. Paul thereby recalls the naming of Hosea's daughter (Hos. 1:6; cf. 1:4), underscoring the effective character of the Lord's word that makes Not-my-people the Lord's people. Paul thus links the text to God's calling of a people from Jews and Gentiles (9:24). (3) Paul omits the following response of *Lō'-'ammî* ("You are my God"), concentrating entirely on the work of God. (4) As something of a substitute for the opening promise of the Lord's

mercy on No-mercy, Paul adds a following word from the Lord: "And (I shall call) *her* who is not loved, beloved." In doing this, Paul effectively summarizes the following context, in which Hosea is called to embody the redeeming love of the Lord in again taking to himself his adulterous wife. In this reference to the adulterous wife Paul elaborates what it means to be called God's people: it is to be a harlot embraced and restored by God's love. Perhaps, too, Paul recalls restoration from the wilderness and exile, since that is God's way with his people, according to Hosea (2:14–20; cf. 11:1). Here it is given to a new people.

The second part of the reference (9:26) more closely follows Hos. 2:1b LXX (1:10b ET) and the Hebrew text itself. In the opening clause (9:26a) there is a difficult decision to be made on the variant "wherever they shall be called" instead of "where it was said." Despite the weight of 𝔓⁴⁶ as a witness to the former reading, the latter is to be preferred because (1) the indefinite temporal sense ("wherever") is unlikely here, given the emphatic *topos* and *ekei*; (2) the use of *hou (e)an* with the indicative mood is quite infrequent (six times in the LXX, never in the NT [cf. the subjunctive in 1 Cor. 16:6]); (3) "calling" in Pauline usage is consistently salvific, which it cannot be here; (4) the combination *ean klēthēsontai* could easily have been miscopied from the following *ekei klēthēsontai* (*pace* Wagner 2002: 84). In the final clause the LXX itself shifts the verb from "saying" to "calling" and changes the third-person plural active ("they shall say") to a divine passive ("they shall be called"). Here Paul follows the LXX, which fits his emphasis on the effective divine word. He also independently underscores "location," adding the emphatic adverb "there" (*ekei*) at the opening of the final clause: "in the place where it was said . . . *there* they shall be called. . . ."

The promise in the second part of Paul's citation (9:26b) appears in the wake of the announcement of divine judgment on Israel at the opening of Hosea. Paul omits this announcement, reserving the word of judgment for his following, closely related citation of Isa. 10:22 (cf. Hos. 2:1a MT [1:10a ET]). Yet the very wording of the text of Hos. 2:1b MT (1:10b ET) that Paul cites makes it clear that God's love and call follow rejection and judgment: it is the "Not-my-people" and the "Woman-not-loved" whom God again takes to himself. This note of saving reversal adds a profound turn to Paul's description of divine calling and rejection in the earlier part of the chapter. The rejected become the chosen. The citation thus anticipates Paul's closing summary of the unsearchable ways of God, who directs the destinies of Israel and the nations (see 11:28–36). Here, Paul's following citation of the divine words of judgment in Isaiah (9:27–29) already faintly suggests the restoration of Israel itself, the people whom Hosea addresses. Yet he primarily has in view here the call of a new people from Jews and Gentiles. The divine judgment announced in Hosea reduces Israel to the same status as the nations: they, too, are "Not-my-people." Paul implicitly picks up this thought (see 3:23; cf. Gal. 2:15–21; 3:10–14). The present call of a new people from both Jews and Gentiles is a fresh work of the Creator, who acts in freedom and in mercy; 9:24 is the concrete expression of the salvation that Paul describes in 9:22–23, and thereby it implies hardening and judgment.

Paul's emphatic reference to "place" ("in the place where it was said . . . *there* they shall be called . . .") recalls the desolation of the land and Israel's exile, which the Lord will finally follow with mercy (e.g., Hos. 2:14–15; 5:8–15; 11:8–11; 14:1–7). Implicitly, the present judgment on Israel will be followed by mercy. Already here Paul points to the final salvation of the nation. Yet "place," too, becomes level ground for the Gentiles: precisely in their place, there they shall be called "sons of the living God." The gospel must go forth to them, to the ends of the earth (cf. 10:18; 15:17–21; see Wagner 2002: 85). The theme of "sonship," which has become the primary category of Paul's description of salvation, appears as the closing word of his citation of Hosea (cf. 8:14, 19, 29; 9:9).

The pattern (type) of God's dealings with Israel in the past has been repeated in the present calling of Jews and Gentiles. Given that Paul in this very context presents Israel's unbelief as a new "exile" (9:27–29), it is unlikely that he regards Israel's exile as continuing from the time of the Assyrian invasion. He presupposes that the Hoseanic promise to Israel has come to fulfillment for Israel in its return to the land. Yet in more than one way the word of promise portends something larger. The pattern has been eschatologically repeated.

Through Jesus Christ, the Son of God (1:3), both Jews and Gentiles (9:24) have become "sons of the living God." As he did with Israel in the past, so now God calls those who were not his people, his people, both Jews and Gentiles (9:24). Paul arrives at the broadened, eschatological compass of the promise through his theology of the human being derived from that gospel. In God's judgment on Israel, which made it "Not-my-people" and scattered it in exile (9:26: "there"), Israel effectively came to be a Gentile nation. That is a fundamental point of Paul's appeal to the Hoseanic text. Likewise, in the present time the gospel makes clear that "there is no distinction between Jew and Greek" (10:12; cf. 3:23). The Hoseanic promise does not address Israel as Israel, but rather as an adulterous wife—that is, fallen and condemned human beings. One must not confuse "meaning" and "reference." Paul's appeal to Hosea can hardly be described as analogical. The inclusion of the Gentiles in the promise is direct, for they, too, are nothing other than fallen human beings. Yet Paul's appeal to the text is complex, not simple. Already here, in his omission of the word of judgment on Israel that he immediately takes up (see below), the apostle hints at the "mystery" of Israel's salvation that he will announce (11:25–27). The Hoseanic promise speaks not only of the new people of God created by the gospel but also of the final salvation of the nation of Israel. For this reason, we cannot properly speak of the fulfillment of the Scriptures in "the church" (so Moo 1996: 613). The Scriptures are fulfilled in Jesus Christ alone, who is both Israel's deliverer and the hope of the nations (11:25–27; 15:12).

The latent hope for the salvation of Israel in the Hosea citation becomes explicit in Paul's following quotation of Isaiah (9:27–28). Paul here brings into view the person of the prophet, who, like the apostle himself, cries out to God in lament and petition on behalf of Israel ("Isaiah cries out on behalf of Israel" [9:27]). The present tense (i.e., durative aspect) shows that Isaiah's lament bears continuing relevance. At the conclusion of his argument in this section, then, Paul returns to his opening lament. Both the apostle to the nations and the prophet to Israel cry out on behalf of Israel in the face of the unanswered promises of God:

Even if the number of the sons of Israel should be as the sand of the sea, (only) the remnant shall be saved. For the Lord shall perform a word final and decisive upon the earth. (9:27b–28)

Paul's citation of Isa. 10:22–23 clearly is interpretive. His "text" shows significant variations from the MT and in some measure from the LXX as well. First, whereas both the MT and the LXX of Isa. 10:22 have "if the people of Israel should be as the sand of the sea," Paul uses the language of Hos. 2:1a MT (1:10a ET), the part of the verse that he omitted in his immediately preceding citation: "if the number of the sons of Israel should be as the sand of the sea." In the Hoseanic context the language refers to the restoration of Israel after judgment; in the Isaianic setting it describes the nation, which, despite its numbers, will come under divine judgment. Paul here obviously speaks of Israel's present failure to believe and uses the text to characterize that failure as the effect of the divine word, which presently has brought judgment on Israel; thus he returns to his opening theme, that the word of God has not failed (9:6). At the same time, however, his use of the language of Hosea hints at a coming restoration of Israel to God. The reference to "the remnant" likewise implies the restoration of Israel (see discussion below). Paul develops the thought in 11:11–36. Paul's use of Isa. 10:22 is therefore typological. The pattern of divine judgment in the past has been repeated in the eschatological present. Just as past judgment portended salvation, so now God's rejection of Israel anticipates its salvation.

Second, both the LXX and Paul vary from the second clause of the MT of Isa. 10:22. Instead of "a remnant shall return with him [the Lord]," both the LXX and Paul have "a remnant shall be saved." Their terms for remnant vary only slightly (LXX: *kataleimma*; Paul: *hypoleimma*). For Paul, this interpretation of "restoration" as "salvation" shifts the center of the hope away from the possession of the land to faith and participation in Christ. This shift corresponds very closely with the Isaianic context, which promises that the remnant of Israel "truly will lean on the Lord, the Holy One of Israel," returning to God (Isa. 10:20–21). Consequently, without robbing Isaiah's lament of its significance in its own setting, the "word" that the Lord performs on the earth (9:28; Isa. 10:23) calls to mind nothing other than the gospel in Paul's context (see Rom. 11:28).

Third, the MT of Isa. 10:22 concludes by speaking of a "destruction decided, overflowing with righteousness," which the LXX takes up in its own way ("for it is a word final and decisive in righteousness"). In its context in the Hebrew Scriptures the statement undoubtedly promises the salvation of the remnant in the "righteous overflow" of destruction. The LXX probably reflects this salvific understanding (Wagner 2002: 103–4). Paul simply omits it.

Fourth, Paul does, however, take up the language of Isa. 10:23 in the pairing "(a word) final and decisive," which follows the MT more closely than the LXX ("God shall perform a decided word").

Fifth, for Paul it is "the Lord" who effects this word. Paul thus varies from the MT, which names "the Lord God of hosts," and from the LXX, which names "God." In Romans, aside from the possible exception of 4:8 (quoting Ps. 31:2 LXX [32:2 MT/ET]), Paul's usage of *kyrios* consistently refers to Christ, as is emphatically the case in the OT citations in 10:9–13. Given Paul's opening identification here of Christ as God (9:5), it is likely that he already suggests an identification of Christ with God in this citation.

Sixth, for Paul, the Lord performs his word "upon the earth," in contrast with the MT, which reads "in the midst of all the earth" (cf. LXX: "in all the inhabited earth [*oikoumenē*]"). The note of judgment is somewhat strengthened here by "upon" (cf. Isa. 28:22), and the locus of the deed is broadened.

Even though their number may be as "many as the sands of the sea" (cf. Gen. 22:17; Judg. 7:12; 1 Sam. 13:5; 2 Sam. 17:11; 1 Kings 4:20), the sons of Israel, by the word of the Lord, will be reduced to a remnant (cf. Isa. 48:19). This contrast elicits from Paul, in 9:29, a second citation of Isaiah. Just as in his initial citation of Isaiah in 9:27–28 Paul reintroduces the topic of the divine word, in his second citation of Isaiah in v. 29 he returns to the theme of the "seed." God now leaves for Israel "seed," not according to physical descent, but by his word of promise, a "seed" that adumbrates the final salvation of the nation (see 9:6–9). The introduction of the citation of Isa. 1:9 underscores the present relevance of the prophetic message, for Israel's present condition is just as "Isaiah said beforehand" (9:29). A Qumran pesher appears to interpret the text as referring to the coming last days, in which Israel will be reduced to a remnant, anticipating a future judgment of the nation (4Q163 4–6, II, 1–19).

Aside from one significant variation, which corresponds to the LXX, Paul's citation matches the MT of Isa. 1:9:

> Except that the Lord of hosts left for us a seed, we would have become as Sodom, and we would have been like Gomorrah. (9:29)

Where the MT has "the LORD of hosts left for us a few survivors [śārîd kim'āt]," both Paul and the LXX have "the Lord of hosts left for us a seed [sperma]." This rendering takes up the Isaianic theology of the remnant, which portends the restoration of the entire nation (cf., e.g., Isa. 6:13; 10:20–23; 11:11–16; 37:30–32; 49:5–6, 14–21; 51:1–3; see Wagner 2002: 111–16; Wilk 1998: 212–13). The text again hints at a coming restoration of the people of Israel to God. The "seed," moreover, is now God's work, and therefore in the proper sense it is "Abraham's seed." True to biblical form, the laments of both the apostle and the prophet recall the promise of salvation in the moment of failure, contrary to all human expectation. Paul finds in the Scripture the pattern (type) of God's eschatological dealings with his people. Despite Israel's unbelief, a remnant has believed in the Messiah—a harbinger of Israel's salvation.

THE FULFILLMENT OF PROMISE IN CHRIST (9:30–10:21)

"What, then, shall we say?" Paul's second confessional question brings a shift. He turns from the description of the effect of the fresh word of God's mercy and judgment upon Israel to Israel's response to that word (9:30–33). He then takes up the content of that word: Christ, the revealed and proclaimed righteousness of God, who is the goal of the law (10:1–13). Finally, he presents the proclamation of that word in the world as the fulfillment of promise (10:14–21). Only here in the argument of chapters 9–11 does Israel's particular guilt come into view: Israel has stumbled over the stone of stumbling, who is none other than Christ (9:30–10:21). The earlier identification of Christ as God in 9:5 now becomes central to Paul's argument. In Christ we meet our Creator, who has come near to us and saves all who call upon him.

9:30–33

The question of the human cause of Israel's failure naturally arises: "Why?" It is most natural to supply the verb and object from the preceding clause to Paul's abbreviated response in 9:32b: "Because Israel *pursued the law* not by faith, but as if *the law (and righteousness) were to be pursued* by works." The effective statement about the nature and function of the law could not be more significant. Paul develops it further in the following verses. Already his use of the image of a race indicates that the law plays a role in the course of God's dealings with humanity in his promises and is neither the end of God's purposes nor a static reality. Paul immediately underscores this subordination of the law to promise in his continuing explanation of Israel's failure in terms of "stumbling over the stone of stumbling" (9:32). The failure of Israel's pursuit of the law "not by faith, but as if by works" becomes visible in its stumbling. The opening explanation in 9:32a cannot be separated from its concrete expression in 9:32b–33 (note the lack of a connective particle). Israel's misunderstanding and misuse of the law become evident only in God's act of placing "in Zion" the stone of stumbling.

This stumbling took place, Paul indicates, "just as it has been written." Again he uses a mixed citation from Isaiah:

> Behold! I place in Zion a stone of stumbling and a rock which is a stumbling-block. And the one who believes upon it shall not be put to shame. (9:33)

The wording is drawn from Isa. 28:16, into which Paul inserts the language of Isa. 8:14. The opening words, "Behold! I place in Zion a stone," correspond to the opening of Isa. 28:16. Paul takes up the Hebrew *yissad* ("I lay a foundation") with the simple *tithēmi*, unlike the LXX (*egō embalō eis ta themelia*). His shift in terminology to "placing a stone" is likely due to his joining of Isa. 8:14 with this text (or just possibly represents an alternative LXX rendering: the verb *tithēmi* already appears in the context [Isa. 28:15, 17]). Isaiah 28:16 goes on to speak of the stone that the Lord sets as "a testing stone [for gold; or, perhaps, a 'tested stone'], a cornerstone, precious, a firm foundation" (cf. 1 Pet. 2:4, 6, 8; esp. v. 6). Paul draws his language instead from Isa. 8:14, which may be roughly rendered in the same manner as his citation: "a stone of stumbling and a rock which is a stumbling-block." His rendering stands closer to the MT than to the LXX, as does 1 Pet. 2:8 (see Koch 1986: 59–60). This shift, which appears at first to be an inversion of the figure of the "stone," in fact interlaces these two thematically related passages (see also Wilk 1998: 163). Isaiah 8:14 foretells the unbelief of "both houses of Israel" and "the inhabitants of Jerusalem," who will stumble and be destroyed in the judgment that the Lord brings. However, the larger Isaianic context is that of promise: the "Lord of hosts" himself will become "a sanctuary" for his people (8:13–14). It is not the temple that is the "holy place," but rather God himself, who in his saving intervention becomes a stumbling-stone to Israel. Only the prophet, who speaks the word of promise, and the "sons," whom the Lord gives him, await salvation through judgment: they hope in the Lord. This promissory dimension of Isa. 8:14 corresponds to the line from Isa. 28:16 that Paul omits. In fact, Isa. 8:14 LXX (likely borrowing from Isa. 28:16) makes the promissory dimension primary: "And if you [sg.] believe upon him, he shall be to you a sanctuary, and you shall not encounter him as a stone of stumbling or a rock of falling." In retaining the word of judgment, Paul remains closer to the Hebrew text.

Conversely, the promise of salvation that appears in Isa. 28:16 comes with judgment: the Lord is going to bring the destruction of the rulers in Jerusalem, sweeping away their scoffing and lying, their "covenant with death," and their false shelter. As in Isa. 8:14, the Lord alone will be the shelter of his people (cf. Isa. 4:6; 25:4). The imagery of temple replacement reappears (cf. Rom. 3:25): the Lord will lay a cornerstone, a sure foundation, so that "the one who believes shall not flee." Only the one who trusts will remain as the Lord performs his "strange" and "alien" work (Isa. 28:21). In citing Isa. 8:14 within Isa. 28:16, Paul underscores that the word of salvation arrives with judgment (Wilk 1998: 55–56). This double-edged character of the promise corresponds to the conjunction of election and rejection laid out by Paul in 9:6–29.

At the same time, Paul's insertion of the language of Isa. 8:14 into Isa. 28:16 bears subtle christological implications that he develops later (10:11–13). According to the former text, it is the

Lord himself who becomes the stone of stumbling for his people. According to the latter, primary citation text, the stone is placed by the Lord in Zion and thus is distinct from him. Paul clearly uses this text in 10:11 to refer to Jesus as the Lord, the one upon whom one believes (see 1 Pet. 2:6–8). The simultaneous identity of Jesus with God and distinction from God correspond to Paul's earlier use of the text in 9:33. Paul thus returns in 9:33 to his opening identification of Jesus as God in 9:5 and develops it throughout this section as he names Christ as God's righteousness and the one in whom the promise of salvation is fulfilled.

The Lord's promise to "place a stone in Zion" very likely is double-edged for Paul. In the first place, the wording localizes the moment of judgment and salvation at the very center of Israel. Judgment takes place in God's very dwelling place among his people. This localization also implies that the nations find their salvation only in Israel. This theme, which Paul sounds at the very opening of Romans, also runs like a thread through the book of Isaiah, which repeatedly announces the pilgrimage of the nations to Zion (e.g., Isa. 2:2–4; 25:6–10; 56:6–8; 60:1–22). At the same time, the theme of the replacement of the temple by the Lord himself, which appears in Isa. 8:14, probably also receives expression in the reference to Zion in the context of Romans. The "placing of a stumbling-stone in Zion" faintly suggests Christ's resurrection, since "Zion" for Paul takes on a heavenly dimension. In Rom. 11:26 Paul renders Isa. 59:20 interpretively as speaking of the Lord coming "from Zion"—that is, from the heavenly Zion, corresponding to his conception of the heavenly Jerusalem (see Gal. 4:26–27). Given the theme of temple replacement that is already present in Isa. 8:14, and Paul's use of "replacement" imagery in describing Jesus as God's mercy seat (Rom. 3:25), this allusion seems likely: the resurrected Jesus is installed as Lord in the heavenly Zion. Those who call on this exalted Lord are saved (Rom. 10:12–13). The imagery thus comes close to the Lord's vindication of the rejected cornerstone in Ps. 118:22–23.

In the second clause of his citation Paul returns to Isa. 28:16c: "the one who believes will not flee." Here, however, his reading corresponds to that of the LXX of Isa. 28:16c: "the one who believes on it shall not be put to shame" (although Paul has *ou kataischynthēsetai* rather than the LXX's emphatic double negative with the aorist passive subjunctive [*ou mē kataischynthē*]; cf. Isa. 8:14a LXX: "if you [sg.] believe on *him*"). The reference to faith creates a chiasm within 9:32–33: faith/stone/stone/faith (Wilk 1998: 32–33). In contrast with the Hebrew text, the object of trust appears—the cornerstone that the Lord lays in Zion—but this is entirely possible in a Jewish context (see below). The LXX renders the Hebrew *ḥûš*, "flee" or "make haste" (cf. Ps. 55:9 MT [54:9 LXX; 55:8 ET]), interpretively as "be put to shame," linking the promise to the larger theology of conflict and vindication in the book of Isaiah (see, e.g., Isa. 1:29; 20:4–5; 41:11; 42:17; 44:9–11; 45:16; 50:6–7; 54:4). Only those who believe the word of promise will be delivered (Isa. 7:9b; see also, e.g., Ps. 22:4–5; 31:1; 71:1). In the context of Romans the use of the language of shame recalls Paul's opening announcement of the gospel and later his assurance of hope (1:16; 5:5), the context of which is likewise the contention between God and the world. Not "being ashamed" again here is a "being vindicated," obtaining righteousness.

The individualizing language "the one who believes" and the moment of judgment within Israel that it represents again become for Paul an anticipation of the inclusion of the Gentiles. He cites this line to this effect in 10:11. God's act of judgment and promise within Israel simultaneously opens the door to those without (Wilk 1998: 89). Israel's stumbling here takes place not simply by its rejection of the crucified Jesus (to which Paul does not refer here), but by its failure to submit to the message of faith in the risen Lord (*contra* Wright 2002: 650; see Wilk 1998: 166).

Early Jewish tradition likewise related Isa. 8:14 and the stumbling-stone to the end time (*b. Sanh.* 38a; perhaps allusively, 1Q22 I, 5–11; 1QHᵃ X, 8–10). The Isaiah Targum anticipates LXX Isa. 8:14 in that it makes judgment contingent upon disobedience (see further Wilk 1998: 168–69; Str-B 3:276). The *Rule of the Community* identifies the community itself as the "precious cornerstone" of Isa. 28:16, a new temple, founded by God (1QS VIII, 1–10). The Isaiah Targum may interpret the "cornerstone" as the Roman emperor (Wagner 2002: 143, following Kaiser 1974: 174).

The joining of the two passages appears, however, to have been without precedent in early Judaism. It first appears in early Christianity and probably first with Paul. The two "stone" texts of Isa. 8:14 and Isa. 28:16 appear together in 1 Pet. 2:6–8, which combines them with Ps. 118:22–23 and employs them similarly to the way Paul does, probably under the influence of Romans and Gospel tradition. The distinct citation of the two texts, together with the variation in wording (1 Pet 2:6, like the LXX, has *kataischynthē*) and the addition of Ps. 118:22–23, suggests the influence of Paul and of gospel tradition rather than a common *testimonium* precursor. The common wording of the opening of Isa. 28:16 and of Isa. 8:14 may be due to this influence or, less likely, to a LXX tradition that stood close to the MT (*contra* Albl 1999: 271–75; Koch [1986: 69–71], who suggests oral tradition; rightly Wilk 1998: 31–34).

Again in Isa. 8:14 and Isa. 28:16 Paul finds in the pattern of God's dealings with Israel in judgment and salvation a pattern (type) that has come to fulfillment in his eschatological dealings with them in Christ.

10:1–13

This passage, which yet further elaborates 3:31, is hermeneutically the most significant of the entire letter (see also 3:19–20). In this text Paul builds upon his earlier arguments concerning the distinction between the law and faith (4:1–25) and the radical fallenness of the human being, whom God delivers from the law and death in Jesus Christ (7:1–25), in whom he has brought the law to fulfillment (8:1–4). Paul's argument, which here is both hermeneutical and "theological," cannot properly be isolated from what he has already said.

In the immediate context Paul has underscored Israel's particular failure as a misuse of the law in light of God's word of promise in Isaiah: human beings arrive at righteousness, and at the law itself, by faith, not by works. Israel's failure is a misunderstanding of Scripture and of the way Scripture is to be read. As the citation of Isa. 28:16 (and Isa. 8:14) in 9:33 already indicates, the goal of the law lies beyond the law. Paul now makes clear what is implicit there: Christ is the stumbling-stone whom God has set in Zion, the goal of the law. Christ brings righteousness to everyone who believes. Paul thus returns to his opening theme of the righteousness of God (1:16–17; 3:21–26) and to the related theme of the unique oneness of the God who saves (3:27–31). It is no accident that in this context, following his ascription of deity to Christ in 9:5, he applies to Christ Scriptures that speak of "the Lord." The proper knowledge of Scripture is bound up with the knowledge of God, who does not remain at a distance in the demand of the law. God in Christ comes near to all human beings by his word. Paul argues that Christ is the goal of the law by appealing to the pattern of God's dealing with his people in the gift of the law, a pattern that has come to fulfillment in the "word of faith." God's righteousness and God's name and identity are at stake in the question as to how the Scriptures speak to us.

The apostle's petition for Israel (10:1) again presupposes Israel's failure, which Paul here explains (*gar* [10:2, 3]) as a failure of knowledge, an ignorance of God's righteousness that has led to disobedience. In seeking to establish its own righteousness, Israel "did not submit to the righteousness of God." Israel's own righteousness would be a particular righteousness, of course, which set it apart from the nations. Yet neither ethnic particularity nor the self-righteousness bound up with it is Paul's concern at this moment, even though both fall within the scope of his following argument. The contrast here is between God's righteousness (which Paul underscores by fronting the genitive *tou theou* in 10:3a), and that which is Israel's own. Paul's language in 10:3 continues the thought of 9:31: "Seeking to establish their own righteousness, they did not submit to the righteousness of God." Israel did not attain to the law, nor did it establish its own righteousness. Above all else, Paul speaks of a failed and misdirected effort. He does not say anything of Israel's intent. That its quest led to a misguided ethnocentrism and a false pursuit of self-righteousness is a secondary phenomenon that we cannot properly read back into the mind of the nation. According to Paul, Israel's failure lies in its disobedience to the gospel and in the misunderstanding of Scripture that this disobedience reveals.

With respect to arriving at righteousness and salvation, therefore, believing and doing, faith and works, are distinct. Paul does not contemplate (nor could he conceive of) a "doing the law by faith," which some imagine to find in 9:30–33.

The word of promise demands that God alone "do" and that the human being only "believe" God, who promises and fulfills. This demand is clear not only from Paul's prior reference to the "stone of stumbling" but also from his following and corresponding description of Christ and of God's work in him (10:4–10). The distinction between the law and faith is likewise already clear in Paul's initial characterization of Israel's failure in 10:3: "Not knowing God's righteousness . . . they did not submit to the righteousness of God." God's righteousness is bound to the event in which his word is fulfilled, so that faith, which answers this act of revelation, cannot be regarded as a human disposition that in a generalized manner responds to the law. Earlier in the letter Paul made clear that God has manifested his righteousness "apart from the law," which both pronounces and effects human guilt (3:9–20, 21). The final and ultimate message of Scripture is not the law, but rather the revealed, saving righteousness of God. It is only with this righteousness that universal salvation arrives: the Gentiles have believed in the "stone of stumbling" (9:33). Christ, the goal of the law, brings righteousness to everyone who believes (10:4). The distinction between Jew and Gentile is overcome in this eschatological act, not in the prior gift of the law, which was distinct to Israel.

The righteousness of God is a gift that, precisely as a gift, brings its own particular demand. Paul's emphasis on the arrival of universal salvation makes it clear that God's righteousness is one in which human beings participate: Christ brings righteousness to all who believe (10:4). It is a righteousness of faith (10:6), which the Gentiles have obtained (9:30), and which is present in the heart of the human being (10:8–10). At the same time, this righteousness of God demands the faith of the human being. One must submit to it (10:3). The righteousness of faith warns against futile human speculation and effort (10:6–8). This aspect of demand makes it clear that Paul again understands God's righteousness to include the justification of God, the vindication of God, who promises and fulfills his word of judgment and salvation. The "righteousness of God" is thus an expression of the divine identity.

The explanation continues (*gar*): in 10:4 Paul identifies Christ as the goal (*telos*) of the law. He brings righteousness for all who believe. God's revealed righteousness is found in him and given through him. Paul's naming of Christ as the goal of the law obviously takes up his preceding image of running a course (9:30–31; cf. 9:16). It is thus Christ who is the cause of Israel's failure: he is the "stone of stumbling" that the Lord promised to place in Zion (9:30–33; Isa. 28:16 [with 8:14]). He has been set in the path of the false pursuit of the law, bringing both judgment and salvation. In a fresh act of salvation beyond the law, the Lord has set this stone in Zion. The path of Scripture, and indeed of the law itself, leads from Sinai to Zion and ends there. As the goal of the law, Christ is the message of Scripture.

The final element of the chain of explanatory statements is the lengthiest (10:5–9). In a sense it is also the most significant, since Paul here makes clear what he means by describing Christ as the goal of the law. Paul draws his explanation almost entirely from Scripture in direct citation of the biblical text. As he frequently does in this section of the letter, he introduces the text by identifying a biblical figure as the source of the utterance (cf. 9:27, 29; 10:19, 20; 11:9). Yet here the introduction takes an unusual turn: "the righteousness of faith" is now personified and speaks in Scripture alongside Moses (10:5–6).

The form of Paul's citation of Deut. 30:11–14 in 10:6–8 is likewise unusual. He excerpts three brief statements from this passage and follows them with the terse, interjected, equational statement "that is" joined to an interpretation of the Deuteronomic text in terms of God's work in Christ. The form has suggested early Jewish midrashic interpretive technique to some. Others have suggested that Paul engages in the sort of interpretation found in the Qumran pesher writings. Paul's style comes especially close to the latter form. It is quite possible that Paul intentionally recalls a pattern of early Jewish interpretation in his treatment of the text, expressing his Jewish identity at the most radical moment of his hermeneutic. However, certain factors caution against assigning too great a significance to similarities in form between Paul and midrashic interpretation or Qumran pesher. First, it is Paul's confession of Christ that determines his use of Scripture, not an interpretive technique (Hays 1989: 10–14). Second, material differences set him apart from

the pesher texts that the form of his citation here approximates. The Habakkuk pesher and other similar writings actualize the text by interpreting it in terms of contemporary persons and events. Paul differs in that he interprets scriptural texts as having reference to persons and events in the past. That is already clear from the broad sweep of his use of Scripture. Even in this context this perspective is apparent. Paul already has spoken of the "goal" of the law, introducing the category of time. He likewise introduces the message of "the righteousness of faith" with a telling adverb: it speaks "in this manner" (*houtōs*)—that is, in the same manner as Deuteronomy. The prior text retains a certain independence. In a related way, furthermore, unlike Qumran, Paul's interpretation is not so much contemporizing as it is eschatological. His purpose is to explain what Scripture is *finally* about, in the decisive context of God's saving work in Christ. Third, the explanatory expression "that is" was commonly used in Hellenistic rhetoric and in itself cannot be regarded as distinctively Jewish. Paul is writing primarily for Gentile readers, who would have had little problem recognizing his interpretation of the text.

Paul begins with the figure of Moses, who, as with the other persons to whom Paul refers in chapters 9–11, serves as a witness to God's word to Israel. Moses "writes the righteousness which is from the law" (10:5 [on the variant placement of the conjunction *hoti* and the associated changes of pronouns, see Metzger 1971: 524–25; the reading of UBS[4]/NA[27] is furthermore the *lectio difficilior* in that "law" replaces "righteousness" as the expected subject]). It is the righteousness *from the law itself* and not a misconceived "righteousness of works" which stands over against the righteousness of faith (10:6–8). The law that requires works has its goal beyond itself in Christ; for this reason Israel's pursuit of the law "as if by works" was misguided.

At least two features of this introduction are unique for Paul. It is the only instance in which he uses the present tense of the verb "write" (*graphō*) in reference to a human author of Scripture. It is likewise the only instance in which he describes the content of the citation (as he does there with the accusative noun group). Both features are significant. The "written" character of the righteousness of the law does not in the first instance signify normativity or fixedness. The "righteousness which is of faith" is also fixed and normative. It, too, presents an unchanging demand to which one must submit. It is rather the nature of this righteousness as the result of works that Paul underscores in describing it as "written." In other contexts Paul speaks of the law as addressing the human being, yet it does so with the demand to act in obedience. The law consequently speaks of the condemnation of the fallen human being (3:19; 7:7). As Paul expressly states here, the "righteousness from the law" is contingent on the action of the human being. It is not already present with the human being, but rather first arises through performance of its demand. Paul's reference to Moses' writing is thus related to his characterization of the law as "letter," which offers life and righteousness on the basis of the performance of its requirements (2:25–29; 7:6; 2 Cor. 3:3–11). Paul's striking use of the present tense, "Moses writes," expresses the continuing validity of this righteousness and of the demand of the law. His description of Lev. 18:5 as "the righteousness which is from the law" clearly represents a summary interpretation of the law as a whole. The law requires that the human being perform its demands as the condition of righteousness and life.

As Paul's statements elsewhere in Romans make clear, this demand is not abrogated, but rather is fulfilled in God's work in Christ. Only "the doers of the law" will be justified at the final judgment (2:13). Yet this fulfillment of the law is not found in the law or given through the law, but rather is worked by the Spirit apart from the law (2:25–29). Although those who believe in Christ are condemned as transgressors along with the rest of the world (3:19–20), and although this condemnation remains with them as long as they are in this body and life (7:7–25; 8:10), their condemnation has been effected without reserve upon another, Christ (8:3). As a result, for those who belong to Christ the new reality of the law's fulfillment, the life of the resurrection, which transcends the former subjection to sin and death, is present here and now (8:4). They will thus be carried through final judgment by the life-beyond-judgment given to them through the crucified and risen Christ.

Paul's citation of Lev. 18:5 differs slightly from both the LXX and the MT (10:5b [likewise Gal.

3:12]): "The one who does these things shall live by them." He omits the opening clause, in which the Lord enjoins his people, "You shall keep my statutes and judgments" (the LXX twice adds "all" [cf. Lev. 19:37; 20:22; 26:15–16]). The relative pronoun disappears; the object is now a demonstrative; the expression "the one who does *these things*" therefore has no definite antecedent. This generalizing of the text reflects Paul's interpretation of the passage as a summary of the entire law. Moreover, over against the LXX, Paul uses the definite article with the participle, so that the latter functions adjectivally: he speaks of the human being as a doer, "the person who does these things," unlike the LXX, in which the participle is adverbial ("doing which things, a person shall live"). The variation represents a return to the Hebrew text (MT: 'ăšer ya'ăśeh 'ōtām hā'ādām), but it also reflects theological intent. Paul contrasts "the doer" with the one who hears and believes (cf. 9:30–31). Furthermore, the concluding prepositional phrase is basically instrumental, yet with something of a local, exclusive sense: "(the one who does these things) shall live *by them*." The law requires that human beings secure their life by and in their deeds. Against those who wish to interpret Paul as referring to Christ as the one who lives by doing the law, it must be said that Paul nowhere speaks of Christ attaining life in this way, nor does Paul depict Christ's relation to the law in this manner: Christ has died to the law (7:1–6). It is even less satisfactory to imagine that Paul refers to Christians as those who live by doing the law, not only because of the recollection here of Israel's failure (9:31), but even more so in the light of the prohibition against coveting (7:7–13). Is there anyone who can remove covetousness from the heart and thus do the law (*contra* Wright 2002: 660)?

In Leviticus the injunction appears near the opening of the Holiness Code (Lev. 17–26). Israel is not to act as those do in Egypt, from which they have come, nor as in Canaan, where they are going. They are to follow not "their" statutes, but rather the statutes that the Lord gives them. If they do not, "the land will vomit them out" (18:25). The warning recurs sharply near the conclusion of the Holiness Code, in which the Lord threatens a series of punishments that, if Israel ignores the Lord's warning, will result in destruction and exile

(26:14–39). These threats take on the character of reality in the narrative as the conditional statements shift to a series of indicatives (26:27–39). The tradition continues into the postexilic life of Israel as a reminder of its failure (Neh. 9:29; Ezek. 20:11, 13, 21). Yet even in the original setting of this injunction hope remains for Israel. If, in exile, they confess their sin and repent, then the Lord will remember the land and the covenants that he made with the patriarchs (Lev. 26:40–43); moreover, even while they are in exile, the Lord will not forget them or destroy them utterly (26:44–45). The hope of "life in the land," an anticipation of a "resurrection from the dead," remains.

The starkly individualistic and universal nature of Lev. 18:5b stands out against the predominant background of warnings and threats directed to Israel as a whole in Leviticus. This aspect of the injunction is clearly related to the immediate contrast with the conduct of those in Egypt and in Canaan: the statutes and ordinances that the Lord gives particularly to Israel are of fundamental anthropological significance; they are good for all human beings. Paul's use of the text is similar: although the injunction and with it the law as a whole is addressed to Israel, not the nations, Paul understands that this injunction, and with it the law, addresses all human beings along with Israel (cf. Rom. 3:19–21).

The individualism of the injunction stands in a certain tension with the subsequent call to repent for the sins of the fathers (Lev. 26:40–45). The same tension is reflected thematically in the book of Ezekiel: in the face of Israel's cynical complaint of suffering for the sins of the fathers, the Lord emphatically binds the experience of life or death to the individual (Ezek. 18:1–32; 20:11, 13, 21; 33:10–20; cf. Neh. 9:29). Individual responsibility and corporate solidarity are not mutually exclusive, nor can they be played off against each other. The same is true for Paul, who goes on to speak of a different kind of righteousness given by God's work in Christ.

In rabbinic interpretation Lev. 18:5 was understood to speak not only of the present life but also of the life to come (*Sipre Lev.* 337a; *Tg. Onq.* Lev. 18:5; *Tg. Ps.-J.* Lev. 18:5; see Str-B 3:278). The purpose of the law to give life became the basis for the relaxing of prohibitions against idolatry or accepting help from a *min* ("heretic" [i.e., Christian])

under necessity or compulsion (*b. 'Abod. Zar.* 27b; 54a; *b. Yoma* 85b). The verse also announced the benefit of the commandments as a way of securing (eternal) life (*b. Mak.* 23b; *Midr. Exod.* 30:22). Consequently, according to the second-century rabbi Meir, "Even a Gentile who studies the Torah is equal to a high priest" (*b. 'Abod. Zar.* 3a [cf. *Midr. Num.* 13:15, 16]). Paul clearly shares this universalism but regards the requirement of "doing of the law" as entailing doing the whole of the law without reserve (cf. Lev. 18:5 LXX; Gal. 5:3). That is clear from his description of Israel's failed pursuit of the law and his charge that the circumcised also may be transgressors of the law (Rom. 9:31; 2:25–29). For the fallen human being, the "doing of the law" therefore never comes to reality (cf. Rom. 3:9–20; 7:7–13).

Over against "the righteousness from the law" that Moses *writes*, there is another righteousness of a different kind, "the righteousness from faith," which *speaks*. Strikingly, Paul finds the voice of this righteousness in the very words of Moses in Deuteronomy (Deut. 9:4; 30:11–14). He equates Moses' words, moreover, with God's work in Christ, interjecting statements concerning the incarnation, resurrection, and proclamation of Christ within his reading of the Deuteronomic text. At the same time, he marks the temporal distance between these words and God's work in Christ: the "righteousness of faith" speaks "in the same manner" (*houtōs*) as the Mosaic words. Moses, who "writes the righteousness from the law," was only a mediator of the law. He himself speaks within Deuteronomy of God's act of giving the law as a gift to Israel, an act that is prior to the law's demand and anticipates God's final act of giving in the crucified and risen Christ, in whom the law is brought to fulfillment.

It is the brief introductory admonition that Paul draws from Deut. 9:4 that lends the character of address to the whole of his interpretive citation: "Do not say in your heart..." (10:6). His wording matches that of the LXX, which itself does not vary from the Hebrew text. The words introduce a warning for Israel, whom the Lord addresses as a single person (as is the case elsewhere in Deuteronomy). In a sense, Paul's individualism corresponds to the Deuteronomic text. After coming into the land, Israel is not to imagine, "It is because of my righteousness that the Lord has brought me in to occupy this land" (Deut. 9:4). Not Israel's righteousness, but rather the "wickedness of these nations," caused the Lord to dispossess them (Deut. 9:4b–5). A lengthy reminder of Israel's stubbornness and rebellion follows the warning, culminating in a call for Israel to fear, love, and serve the Lord. The nation must "circumcise" its heart (Deut. 9:6–10:22).

At least three features of the passage stand out. The warning to Israel against relying on its righteousness corresponds closely with Paul's message. Israel did not submit to God's righteousness because it was "seeking to establish its own righteousness" (Rom. 10:3). The Deuteronomic context furthermore emphasizes that Israel is anything but obedient. It is rebellious and "stiffnecked." If it is to fear, love, and serve the Lord, it must change its heart. As the subsequent narrative of Deuteronomy shows—the very context from which Paul draws his main citation—it must be finally the Lord who "circumcises" Israel's heart (Deut. 30:6). The monitory language that Paul draws from Deut. 9:4 carries with it the reminder of Israel's rebellious heart and its need for a new, saving work of God. It is that saving work in Christ that Paul announces in Romans. Finally, the warning in Deuteronomy is a reminder to the people of Israel that the land that has been given to them is theirs because of the wickedness of those who preceded them. If they are to remain in the land, they must do what is right before the Lord, who executes justice impartially (Deut. 10:17–18). The law, therefore, is an essential gift to Israel, by which it can secure blessing and life in the land (e.g., Deut. 5:32–33; 6:16–25; 8:11–20; 11:8–32).

This is precisely the thrust of Deut. 30:11–14: God has conferred the law as a *gift* to Israel. The "commandment" (i.e., the whole of the law) is not beyond Israel's comprehension ("not too difficult, wonderful for you" [*niplē't*]). It is not beyond Israel's reach. They need not seek someone to attempt the impossible ascent into heaven to obtain and learn the law. Nor need they attempt what seemed to them the equally impossible task of crossing the Great Sea in order to obtain the law. Through Moses, the Lord had *given* them the law; it was now in their mouth and heart. Thus they were able to observe "the commandment"—even if in fact they never would do so.

Paul attaches the introductory warning from Deut. 9:4 to the first line of the superfluous question of Deut. 30:12: "Do not say in your heart, '*Who shall ascend into heaven?*'" (10:6b). He omits only the reference to benefit, "who shall ascend *for us*..." (see Deut. 30:12 MT/LXX), the plural form of which does not fit his focus upon the individual. "That is," declares Paul, "to bring Christ down" (10:6c). The gift of Torah has now been transcended by the gift of Christ. Paul in all probability speaks here of the incarnation (cf. Rom. 1:3; 8:3; 9:5). Just as it was not necessary for Israel to look beyond Moses for a superhuman to obtain and deliver the law, so God has sent his Son apart from any human work. The shift in imagery from a horizontal course that a human might run to an ascent to heaven in order to retrieve Christ underscores the inherent impotence of any human quest for righteousness (cf. Rom. 9:16, 30–33). God alone can traverse this gap between heaven and earth. This thought comes to expression in another way: the law was given through Moses the mediator (cf. Gal. 3:19–20). In Christ, God the Creator acts and meets humanity directly.

The second question, to which the warning remains implicitly attached, appears in altered form: "Or (do not say in your heart), '*Who shall descend into the abyss?*'" Paul changes the horizontal imagery of crossing the sea in Deuteronomy into the vertical one of descending into the realm of the dead (on this sense of *abyssos*, see in the LXX: Job 28:12–14; Ps. 70:20 [71:20 ET]; 106:26 [107:26 ET]; Ezek. 26:19–21). The perspective on the sea is now shifted, so that it is viewed as "the deep" and is associated with the netherworld and grave, as was not uncommon in early Judaism (see the preceding LXX references; frequent occurrences in rabbinic literature [e.g., *m. Pesaḥ.* 7:7; *m. Naz.* 9:2; *m. Parah* 3:2; *b. Pesaḥ.* 81a]; *Jub.* 24:31; *Tg. Neof.* Deut. 30:12–13 adds a reference to Jonah, who might "descend into the depths of the Great Sea and bring [Torah] up for us," likely associating the depths with the grave [cf. Jon. 2:1–10]). Paul's alteration of the imagery of the text very likely had precedents in early Jewish interpretation. Parallels appear in *b. Giṭ.* 84a and *b. B. Meṣi'a* 94a. Yet the change of the imagery is also theologically motivated. Again Paul boldly answers the false search for someone to descend to the grave and return: "That is to bring Christ up from the dead" (10:7). The Creator alone can perform such a work! God formerly gave the law through Moses, but now, apart from any mediator, God has raised Christ from the dead (cf. Rom. 1:4; 4:17, 24–25; 6:4; 7:4; 8:11).

There is a certain similarity between Paul's use of the imagery of height and depth, ascent and descent, and early Jewish traditions that identified the gift of "wisdom" with Torah. In varying degrees these Jewish traditions echo imagery of the Deuteronomic passage (Bar. 3:9–4:4, esp. 3:29–31; Sir. 1:1–10, esp. 1:3; 24:1–34, esp. 24:5–6; 4 Ezra 4:8; on the rabbinic literature, through which this theme runs, see Str-B 3:278–81; cf. Job 28:12–14; Prov. 30:1–4). "Wisdom" may appear here as a personified figure, which has suggested to interpreters proximity to Paul's connection of the text with Christ (e.g., Sir. 24:1–22). It is not unlikely that Paul's language might have recalled wisdom traditions for his Jewish-Christian readers. To the extent that this occurred, however, it is the contrast between Paul and broader Jewish tradition that would have stood out. Whereas Paul proceeds from the presence of Christ and the nearness of the "word," the wisdom traditions emphasize the inaccessibility of wisdom (e.g., Bar. 3:29–31). Likewise, the mediatorial figure of Moses, who has been replaced by God in Christ, is central to Paul's interpretation, whereas the role of the mediator generally is lacking in these wisdom traditions. There the question of who has discovered wisdom serves to underscore human inability. Obviously this emphasis parallels Paul's use of the text in a sense, but the apostle's attention is more narrowly focused on the work of God that transcends the role of Moses the mediator. Admittedly, Bar. 3:36 attributes the successful quest for knowledge to God, but God appears here only in the triumph of his own endeavor. Wisdom is mediated by the law. At this point Paul stands at odds with the wisdom traditions, which assert that the wisdom inaccessible to humanity has come to dwell in Israel in the gift of Torah (Sir. 24:8–12, 23; Bar. 3:35–36). Jewish tradition identified wisdom with the law. Paul announces that Christ transcends the gift of the law mediated by Moses. Precisely at the point at which these traditions become particular Paul asserts the universality of the gospel.

N. T. Wright (2002: 660–61) wishes to see the "end of exile" and eschatological blessing of Deut. 30 as it is taken up in *4QHalakhic Letter* as the background to Paul's appeal to the "nearness" of righteousness. Wright, however, fails to observe that in *4QHalakhic Letter* it is not only the blessings that will come at the "end of days," but also the curse (singular) (4Q398 14–17 I, 6–7). A "portion of the blessings and the curses" has come (4Q398 11–13, 3), but not all of them. The Qumran text proceeds from the emphatic prediction of Deuteronomy that *all* the blessings and curses will come upon Israel (Deut. 28:2, 15, 45; 29:21, 27). The defining pattern has been established in Solomon and Jeroboam, in whose days came, respectively, blessings and curses (1 Kings 3:10–14; 14:7–16). Curses were repeated in the exiles (plural) of Jerusalem and Zedekiah (4Q398 11–13, 1–2; 2 Kings 24:10–17, 18–20; 2 Chron. 36:5–21). In view of the impending end time, the letter correspondingly issues its warning and appeal for adherence to the law where obedience is lacking: "We have written to you a portion of the works of the law that we regard as good for you and your people. . . . so that you might rejoice in the last time when you find (this) portion of our words so" (4Q398 14–17 II, 2–6 [cf. Deut. 10:13]). The Qumran halakhic letter, like most early Jewish writings, sees the pattern of Scripture recapitulated in the end time. Final blessing, which has not yet arrived, is contingent on obedience. The suggested parallel is nonexistent.

The warning of the impossibility of a human pursuit of salvation and the vanity of seeking a human savior (a role that even Moses did not and cannot fill) issues nevertheless in a decisive word of assurance. The righteousness of faith says, "The word is near you, in your mouth and in your heart" (10:8ab; Deut. 30:14). In the context of Deuteronomy this affirmation is followed by the conclusion "so that you may do it." But the former giving of the law through Moses has now been transcended by the unmediated work and gift of God the Creator in Christ. No need or place therefore remains for the action or performance of the human being. Paul follows this final citation of Deut. 30 with a final bold affirmation: "That is the word of faith, which we preach" (10:8c). The word that demands our works has been transcended by the word that announces God's work. We must not imagine that righteousness is distant from us, that someone must yet obtain and bring it to us. The righteousness from faith announces that already it has been brought near to us in the "word of faith." It is already present within the heart of those who believe the apostolic preaching. Probably the septuagintal rendering of *dābār* as *rhēma*, which Paul takes up and uses, emphasizes the spoken character of this word. "The righteousness from faith" speaks in and through the apostles. The words of Moses that announce the law as God's gift to Israel come to fulfillment in the proclamation of Christ.

The remainder of the subsection (10:9–13) is an elaboration of the "word of faith" that Paul finds anticipated in the "near word" of Deut. 30:14. In 10:9 Paul articulates the content of this (spoken) word in a playful yet profound use of the words "mouth" and "heart" from the Deuteronomic text. The "word of faith" does not bring the demand of the law. Rather, it brings the work of God in Christ into the human mouth and heart. It is this message of faith that stands over against the "righteousness from the law" (10:5). At the same time, Paul's use of the wording of Deuteronomy underscores the way in which Christ is the goal of the law: through him God plants his word in the human mouth and heart in a way that the law could only anticipate (10:4). The "word of faith" thus announces both the event in which the righteousness of God is revealed and the manner in which it demands our submission (10:3).

Here Paul's delight in verbal detail and concreteness approximates forms of rabbinic interpretation and recalls his opening words in 9:4–5. It also recalls his earlier description of the fallen human being in the language of the psalms, which name the throat, tongue, lips, and mouth as fundamental places in which the fallenness of the human creature expresses itself (3:9–20, esp. 13–14). Paul's concreteness serves likewise as a reminder of universal human creatureliness. Salvation transforms us in the most radical and fundamental way: the human lie that denies the Creator, and that issues in cursing and bitterness, is now replaced by the confession of Christ as Lord and faith in God's work in him. The acts of "confessing" and "believing" arise from the "heart" and "mouth" in which the "word" is now present (cf. 3:12–14; 15:5–6).

Paul's play on words continues in a new string of explanatory statements in 10:10–13 (*gar* [5x]).

In 10:10 he expands the announcement of salvation (10:9) into a twofold form: "believing with the heart" brings "righteousness," and "confessing with the mouth" brings "salvation." This development of the wordplay makes it clear that Paul does not have different acts or results of actions in view; rather, he speaks perspectivally. "Confessing" and "believing" are inward and outward expressions of the one reality of the presence of the "word." Not only faith, but also "confession," is directed to God, as the acknowledgment of his right as God (14:11; 15:9; on the christological significance of this confession, see below). "Righteousness" and "salvation" likewise refer to the same event.

The twofold language leads finally in 10:11–13 to a twofold citation of Scripture by which Paul interprets his earlier citation of Isa. 28:16 LXX and thereby rounds off his discussion. The righteousness that comes from faith in the heart (10:10a) corresponds to the Isaianic promise that "the one who believes on him/it shall not be put to shame" (10:11). The individualism of the text bears an implicit universalism that Paul has already introduced: the work of the Creator in Christ comes by the word to the heart and mouth, which belong to every human creature (see 10:17). Paul now draws out that implicit universalism in the Isaianic text: "For the Scripture says, 'Everyone who believes in him shall not be put to shame.'" Paul adds the word "everyone" (*pas*) to Isa. 28:16b, reading the text interpretively (again varying from the LXX in his term for "being put to shame").

Again he understands the Isaianic text in a typological manner. The word of hope concerning faith in the Lord in the past, which came in the face of the judgment on Israel, is echoed in the present call to faith in Christ, in the face of the judgment coming on the world.

Paul follows the citation with an explanatory expansion, returning to the language of 3:22–24: "For there is no distinction between Jew and Greek" (10:12a)—a hermeneutical dimension of this earlier statement. He likewise takes up the language of 3:29–30: "The same Lord is (Lord) of all, bestowing riches [*ploutōn*] on all who call upon him." The one God is God of Jews and Gentiles. God's "oneness" is known in his saving action on behalf of all humanity: as in 9:23 (also 2:4; 11:33) the "riches" that God bestows are nothing other than the knowledge of God in his saving action.

Here Paul's language has shifted from "God" to "Lord," the proper name and identity of God in Scripture, now with christological overtones (on which, see below).

The explanatory expansion of Isa. 28:16b in 10:12 also serves as an introduction to one further citation of Scripture. Paul has not yet finished his intricate unfolding of the Deuteronomy text or his wordplay, which in these final citations of Isa. 28:16 and Joel 2:32 takes the form of a rabbinic *gezerah shavah* (interpretation by analogy). Just as in 10:11, where Paul cites the Isaianic promise that everyone who believes will not be put to shame, repeating the theme of righteousness by faith, so in 10:13 he takes up the outward, verbal expression of faith: "confession" now shifts to "calling upon the Lord," with precedent in biblical tradition (1 Chron. 16:8; Ps. 75:1; 105:1). The promise of Joel 2:32 (3:5 MT/LXX), "Everyone who calls on the name of the LORD shall be saved," confirms Paul's reading of Isa. 28:16b as a promise to "all," and it recalls the biblical tradition of "calling on the Lord" with universal overtones that extend beyond and behind the patriarchal narratives to the primal narrative of Genesis (Gen. 4:26; 12:8; 13:4; 21:33; 26:25; see also, e.g., 1 Kings 18:24; Ps. 99:6; Isa. 64:7). The two citations reflect the twofold form "mouth" and "heart" in Deut. 30:14, again presenting two perspectives on the believing human being. The promise from Joel again uses the language of "salvation," verbally completing the "exposition" of Deut. 30:14 that Paul began in 10:9 ("you shall be saved").

Paul's brief citation of the Joel text corresponds verbatim to the LXX (aside from the necessary explanatory particle *gar*), which in turn follows the Hebrew text closely. The recurrent theme of God's justifying work—deliverance through disaster and destruction—again stands in the background of the Joel text (Rom. 1:17 [Hab. 2:4]; 9:25–26 [Hos. 1:10; 2:23]; 9:27 [Isa. 10:20–23; 28:14–19]; 9:29 [Isa. 1:9]; 9:33 [Isa. 28:16; 8:14]). The advent of the "great and terrible day of the Lord" brings a crisis. The Lord enters into judgment on behalf of his people against the nations whom he has gathered together in the "valley of *Jehoshaphat*" (= "the LORD judges") (Joel 3:2 [4:2 MT/LXX]). The passage that Paul cites again has in view the salvation of a remnant, "survivors" from Jerusalem. Paul appropriates from the text the moment of judgment, with its sharp individualism of faith and prayer, as he also does with Isa. 28:16. In the reduction and reconstitution of Israel as those who believe and call upon the Lord, the ground is leveled between Israel and the nations (see discussion of 9:25–26 above). The moment of re-creation of Israel incipiently contains and anticipates the re-creation of all humanity.

10:14–21

The "righteousness from faith" speaks of the nearness of the "word of faith," which the apostles proclaim (10:8). The work of God in Christ includes proclamation within its scope, as Paul already makes clear in the letter opening (1:5–7). This section is likewise hermeneutical: the basis of the apostolic mission lies in Scripture itself and specifically in God's ways with his people in the past. In 10:9–13 Paul has unfolded the content of proclamation; in the present section he turns to the act of proclamation. The message itself demands its proclamation to all, the apostolic mission to the nations. Yet that mission must have its basis in a commission by God: only as God sends the apostles can they go. Again here Paul emphasizes the concrete realities associated with proclamation: God's word of promise not only creates salvation but also meets with rejection as it arrives (cf. 9:6–29). Paul's theology of mission is intrinsically and profoundly bound up with the temporary hardening of Israel for the sake of the Gentiles and their salvation.

As we noted, Paul's argument follows the word of Joel now fulfilled in Jesus (10:13; Joel 2:32 [3:5 MT/LXX]): people cannot call on the name of the Lord without believing, they cannot believe in someone of whom they have not heard, and they cannot hear without proclaimers, who cannot make proclamation unless they have been sent (10:14–15a). The sending of those who proclaim Jesus as Lord has taken place "just as it is written." The apostolic mission corresponds with Scripture, namely, Isa. 52:7: "How beautiful are the feet of the proclaimers of good news [*euangelizomenoi*] concerning good things" (10:15b). The divine announcement of the beauty of the feet that carry those who tell the good news implicitly affirms their having been sent.

Paul here takes up the second Isaianic promise of the return of the Lord to Zion after the Babylonian exile (Isa. 52:7; cf. 40:9), which itself is an echo of an oracle to Judah promising the defeat of Nineveh and the Assyrians (Nah. 1:15 [2:1 MT/LXX]). He varies from Isa. 52:7 LXX, which at a number of points diverges from the MT and bears its own text-critical questions (Ziegler 1939: 59–60, 318). The text of Isa. 52:6 LXX emphatically announces God's presence, to which the LXX attaches a series of comparative clauses ("as spring on the mountains, as feet of the one who announces good news of a report of peace, as one who announces good things"). Paul, probably following a differing septuagintal translation represented by the Lucianic recension (Wilk 1998: 24), retains the Hebrew exclamatory wording, "How beautiful . . . are the feet," which is central to his argument, omitting only the localizing phrase "upon the mountains." He changes the singular form of "messenger" to a plural, almost certainly in order to convey that the apostolic commission does not belong to him alone: "How beautiful are the feet of the proclaimers of good news." He supplies an object for the participle *euangelizomenoi* by skipping forward to the second use of the term in Isa. 52:7 (*ta agatha*, "good things"). F. Wilk (1998: 25) suspects haplography in the Greek version that Paul takes up, but it is more likely that Paul omits reference to "a report of peace" (*akoē eirēnēs*) in order to delay the use of the term "report" until 10:16. Along with his Greek text, he shifts the object of the proclamation to the plural "good things" (cf. MT: *mĕbaśśēr tôb*; probably, in variance from it, Paul includes the definite article *ta* with *agatha* [but see the *v.l.*]).

Paul's argument in Romans corresponds closely to the Isaianic context. There the Lord promises his exiled people that they will know his name. They will know "It is I. I am the one who is speaking. Behold, it is I" (Isa. 52:6). This very promise that God, through his word, would draw near to his people, and that they will then truly know his "name," has been fulfilled, according to Paul, in the incarnation, death, and resurrection of Jesus (10:6–13). The apostolic proclamation is not only for the nations but also for Israel, so that they, too, according to the word of Joel, might know, believe, and call on the name of the Lord (10:13). Paul has already cited Isa. 52:5 in 2:24, which describes the blasphemy of God's name among the Gentiles because of Israel's transgressions. However, Israel's transgression is not the end of the story, for God has acted savingly for Israel in Jesus.

Yet Paul's citation of Isa. 52:7 is also unmistakably universal in its scope. The proclamation of good news is for Jew and Greek, without distinction. In this respect, too, his use of the text corresponds with its context: the salvation that the Isaianic messenger is to announce of the "redemption of Jerusalem" is also for the nations; they, too, will see "the salvation of our God" (Isa. 52:10; cf. 40:5, 9). Paul later explicitly takes up this dimension of Isa. 52 in Rom. 15:21, where he goes on to cite Isa. 52:15: the nations will hear the announcement of the Lord's unheard of work in exalting his Servant. The promise of Jerusalem's redemption has been fulfilled in the resurrection of Jesus: in and through him salvation now comes to the Gentiles.

Furthermore, just as the "word of faith" brings the confession of the true God to the human mouth (cf. Rom. 3:13–14; Ps. 10:7), so also it creates the beautiful "feet" of its messengers, who now "run" to announce the good news, not to shed blood as Paul once did (cf. Rom. 3:15; Isa. 59:7; see Acts 22:19–21; *Lam. Rab.* 1:57 [147]). Redemption recaptures the human creature for the Creator.

Early Judaism also found in Isa. 52:7 the promise of eschatological salvation, particularly in the announcement of *shalom*, "peace" (e.g., *Lev. Rab.* 9:9 [119]; *Deut. Rab.* 5:15 [117]; see further references in Str-B 3:282–83; Stuhlmacher 1968: 148–50; Wilk 1998: 173–75).

The text appears prominently in *Pss. Sol.* 11, bracketing the entire psalm. The psalmist reads the passage in connection with Joel 2:1, 15 ("sound the trumpet in Zion") and Isa. 40:1–11; 43:5–7. Here it is not the "feet," but rather the "voice," of the herald of good tidings that the psalmist celebrates (cf. Isa. 40:3). The salvation of Israel is presented as a return from exile, as was common in early Judaism. It appears here as a fait accompli: God has been merciful; the children of Jerusalem have been led from exile and assembled (cf. Bar. 4:36–5:9, which may be dependent on this text). The trumpet is to be sounded, not for disaster, but for salvation. The psalmist calls Jerusalem to "put on the clothes" of its glory (cf. Isa. 61:10). God has "spoken" (i.e., promised) "good things" for Israel forever. The psalm returns to Isa. 52:7

at its close and ends with the petition that the Lord do what he has pronounced upon Israel and Jerusalem (11:7–9). The psalmist yet looks forward to redemption for Israel, as is clear from other psalms in the collection, especially *Pss. Sol.* 17–18. In these psalms the future hope appears as a heightened recapitulation of what God had accomplished already: the Lord has already brought judgment on the sinners who drove the pious into exile (17:1–10), and yet the psalmist hopes for a final judgment through the promised "son of David" (17:21–46). The pattern also appears in *Pss. Sol.* 9, which treats the exile as past and yet looks for final salvation. "Restoration from exile" appears not simply as a future hope but also as a past event, which adumbrates God's future dealings with Israel. Perhaps *Pss. Sol.* 11 conforms to this pattern, or perhaps it presents future salvation as a present reality according to the pattern of biblical hope.

In a number of instances of early Jewish use of Isa. 52:7 "the herald of good news" was identified with an eschatological figure, especially the Messiah (e.g., *Lev. Rab.* 9:9; *Song Rab.* 2:33), but also Elijah (e.g., *Pesiq. Rab.* 35:4), and even Israel collectively (*Midr. Ps.* 147 §2). In 11Q13 II, 15–18 the eschatological figure is identified as "the anointed of the Spirit" (cf. Isa. 61:1–3), who announces the saving figure of Melchizedek.

Clearly, Paul sees in Isa. 52:7 the promise of eschatological salvation, as did his contemporaries. Yet in this context it is the past event attested by Scripture that provides the warrant for the apostolic proclamation. Like *Psalms of Solomon*, Paul perceives a prophetic pattern of God's dealings in the Scripture. Unlike most early Jewish use of the text, his interest is not directed to the salvation announced, which he or (less likely) his Greek OT omits; rather, his focus is on the ones sent to announce it. Paul does not identify the figure of Isa. 52:7 with the Messiah; rather, it is the apostolic mission which is the counterpart to the prophetic mission. Paul again uses the text typologically, finding in it a pattern of the eschatological work of God.

The proclamation of good news meets with resistance, as has happened before: "but not all believed the gospel" (10:16). As the following corporate references to Israel show, Paul's language here is best understood as ironic and anticipatory of

Israel's final salvation. The apostle looks forward to a time when all Israel will believe (11:26).

In 10:16 Paul moves forward to cite Isa. 53:1, the opening of the fourth Servant Song (Isa. 52:13–53:12). The wording of the citation does not vary appreciably from the LXX or the MT. As he did in 9:25–29, Paul brings the person of the prophet into his introduction. Isaiah appears as a witness to the pattern of disobedience and unbelief that has now been repeated. Isaiah thus continues to speak in the present time: "But not all obeyed the gospel, for Isaiah says, 'Lord, who has believed our report [*akoē*]?'" As the broader context and the Isaianic citation make clear, the opening statement is a litotes: Israel as a whole has failed to believe (9:3; 11:5; cf. 3:3). Paul's attention remains fixed on the salvation of all Israel. Again here he characterizes Israel's refusal to believe the gospel as disobedience (10:3 [cf. 1:5; 16:26: "the obedience of faith"]). That disobedience corresponds typically to the past, when Israel disbelieved the "report" of the prophet; not only the aorist tense of the verb (*hypēkousan*) but also the repeated naming of Isaiah and Moses (with the temporal marker *prōtos*, "at the start" [10:19]) mark the event as lying in the past.

Both the prophet in the past and the apostle in the present bear "a report" (*akoē*), a message that is announced and proclaimed. The term also appears in Isa. 52:7 LXX ("good news of a report of peace"; the Hiphil *mašmîaʿ* is read as the noun *mišmaʿ*), which is thematically linked to Isa. 53:1 (see also 1 Thess. 2:13; Gal. 3:2, 5). In 10:17 Paul draws his point from the citation: "So then, faith comes by report"—that is, by a message announced and proclaimed. The sending of the prophet who was called to proclaim the message of coming salvation and judgment, and who met with unbelief from the nation as a whole, anticipated the sending of the apostle (see Isa. 6:6–13; cf. Gal. 1:15–16). Paul thus grounds his mission in the pattern of God's dealings with Israel in the past.

A report, however, must have content. "So then, faith comes by report, and the report by the word of Christ" (10:17). The statement is a summary. Paul returns to his description of the "word of faith," now underscoring its content: the resurrection of the incarnate and crucified Christ. The expressions "word of faith" and "word of Christ" are thus complementary descriptions of the gospel, the former underscoring the call to faith that is inherent to God's work in Christ, the latter underscoring the unchanging content of that address (see Hofius 1994: 153–54). Paul interweaves them in an inverted pattern in his argument, speaking of the "word of faith" where he describes the content of the gospel, and speaking of the "word of Christ" where he describes its proclamation. He thus conveys the understanding that the act of faith and the object of faith are inseparable. The apostolic mission to both Israel and the nations is ultimately grounded in the message of Christ, who is the promised righteousness of God and the goal of the law. There is a subtle play here upon the context of Isa. 53:1: Paul identifies the Suffering Servant, who is the content of Isaiah's message, with Jesus Christ.

In the remainder of this section (10:18–21) Paul voices and answers objections to his conclusion in 10:17 from Scripture. The first objection ("But, I say, they did not hear, did they?" [10:18a]) has in view the universal proclamation of Christ. Paul's preceding citations of Isaiah (Isa. 52:7; 53:1) have to do first with the prophetic announcement of good news for Israel. Here, however, Paul raises the objection that a proclamation to the nations is no fulfillment of Scripture, since it finds no precedent there. As becomes clear from the usage in context, Paul's attention remains focused on God's past dealings with humanity (10:19–21, esp. 19a). The objection, then, is that the nations have not heard, there has been no proclamation to them, no "word" has gone forth to them. Paul's answer ("on the contrary") is as profound as it is brief: "Into all the earth their sound has gone forth, and to the ends of the inhabited world their words (have gone forth)." Paul's citation of Ps. 19:4 (19:5 MT; 18:5 LXX) corresponds verbatim to the LXX. The LXX rendering of the Hebrew *qawwām* as *ho phthongos autōn* ("their sound") probably is right (over against "line" or "measure" or various conjectural readings that approximate this sense in any case); it best fits the context by far (Ps. 19:1–4: telling, proclaiming, speech, knowledge, words) and finds support elsewhere (Sir. 44:5; perhaps Isa. 28:10, 13). Likewise, the LXX renders the Hebrew *millâ* as *rhēma*, both of which suggest the idea of "spoken word." This rendering naturally

fits Paul's usage in context and is otherwise absent in his letters.

Psalm 19 celebrates the revelation of God's glory through the created order, especially the heavens (19:1–6), as a counterpart to its celebration of the revelation of the Lord's good will for the human being in the law (19:7–10). The third section of the psalm shifts attention to the inward life of the psalmist, especially the "mouth" and the "heart," for which, despite creation and the law, the psalmist appeals to the Lord for forgiveness and redemption. Then the psalmist will be able to join the heavens and the law in speaking and thinking rightly about the Lord (19:11–14). Paul's citation from the first section of the psalm may well carry with it echoes of the testimony of the law and the psalmist's petition for forgiveness. But these remain undeveloped. His attention is focused on the sound and words of the heavens, which, although they have no speech, words, or voice, nevertheless speak (19:3–4). The creation itself tells of the glory of the Creator.

Paul has already used visual imagery to express this same thought in 1:20: the unseen things of God are seen from the creation of the world, perceived through what has been made. It is for this reason that idolatrous humanity is without excuse. Furthermore, Paul has already shifted from the domain of sight to that of sound in 8:22, where he speaks of the "groaning" of creation. The sense of his appeal to Ps. 19:4 is clear: God the Creator has already been (and continues to be) proclaimed to the nations. According to Paul, "That which is known of God is manifest among them" (1:19). Paul has underscored, of course, that the idolatrous world has a "darkened heart" that no longer gives glory or thanks to the Creator (1:21). The problem, however, lies with the fallen creature, not with the creation, which continues to announce the Creator's glory according to the psalm. The apostolic proclamation thus has its anticipation in the creation itself and retraces its course to all the world (cf. 1:5; 15:19–21). As Paul's wording makes clear, the words of the heavens concerning the Creator anticipate the word of Christ (10:17–18). His identification of Christ as the one who descended from heaven to the depths of the grave and has been raised and exalted as Lord and God informs his appeal to Ps. 19. Christ, the righteousness of God, is identified as Creator, and the Creator thus is identified with Christ. The proclamation of Christ opens the closed ears of the fallen human being, bringing to us the knowledge of "the name of the Lord"—that is, to faith and petition (10:13–17). In and through Christ we begin again to call on the name of the Lord.

Paul voices a second objection, to which he provides a lengthier response, extending to the end of the section (10:19–21): "But, I say, Israel did not know, did it?" The nations have heard the message of the Creator, no matter that their ears have been deaf to the message. But did Israel know that a universal proclamation of the Lord's name would take place? Paul returns to his charge in 10:2–3: Israel's zeal is without knowledge. He has treated the question in terms of the content of the gospel, and now he deals with the proclamation of the gospel, immediately addressing the concrete result of the apostolic mission: Gentiles have obtained righteousness where Israel has stumbled—Christ, the righteousness of God and the goal of the law.

In accord with Scripture, Paul appeals to two witnesses, who as elsewhere in chapters 9–11 are marked by their names: "first" Moses, and then Isaiah (10:19–21 [cf. Deut. 19:15; 2 Cor. 13:1]). Paul opens with an appeal to the Song of Moses, where the Lord responds to Israel's rebellion and idolatry. Just as they have provoked him to jealousy with a "non-god," so he will provoke them to jealousy with a "non-people." He will make them angry with a "nation without understanding" (10:19b; Deut. 32:21b).

The citation again corresponds very closely to the LXX, which again diverges only slightly from the MT. The LXX rendering of *nābāl* ("foolish") as "without understanding" (*asynetos*) probably catches the sense of godlessness when read in a biblical context (cf. Ps. 91:7 LXX [92:7 MT; 92:6 ET]). The minor distinction that may exist between *'am* and *gōy* in the Hebrew text (in some contexts, "people" and "nation," respectively) is lost, since both terms are rendered as *ethnos*. There are some differences between Paul's citation and the LXX. Paul understandably drops the conjunction that joins his citation with the preceding line, so that unlike the MT and the LXX, he begins simply with the Lord's emphatic "I shall. . . ." He also sharpens the address, shifting from the third-person references to Israel to the second person: "I

shall provoke you to jealousy . . . I shall make you angry." The Lord now appears in direct contention with his people.

Paul's citation picks up a number of threads within his own argument and anticipates its further development as well. The provocation to jealousy does not signal a rejection of Israel on God's part, but rather anticipates Israel's salvation. God contends with wayward Israel, who set their affections on other gods: just as they have made him jealous, so he will make them jealous by causing another people to prevail over them (see Bell 1994: 81–106). Nevertheless, he will yet reclaim them as his own and save them (Deut. 32:26–43). The "anger" by which the Lord provokes his people is "jealousy": just as they gave their affection to other gods, so the Lord will give his affection to another people. In both Deuteronomy and in Romans God uses the "other nation" to punish his people: it is on account of the inclusion of the Gentiles that Israel remains in unbelief (see Rom. 11:28). In both instances this judgment turns to salvation by the coming of the Lord as deliverer (Deut. 32:36–43; Rom. 11:25–27). In Rom. 11:11–16 Paul returns to develop his appeal to the text more fully. The "non-people" by which God provokes Israel is not the Gentiles (who, of course, would be a plurality of nations [*pace* Wagner 2002: 202–3; Wilk 1998: 134–35; Bell 1994: 95–104]), but rather the eschatological people of promise, which consists of Jews and Gentiles. The language recalls Paul's earlier citation of Hos. 2:23 and 1:10 ("I shall call the 'Not-my-people,' 'My-people'" [admittedly, *laos* appears rather than *ethnos*]), where Paul has in view the new people called from Jews and Gentiles (Rom. 9:23–25). It also brings a reminder of God's promise to Abraham, which brings into being "the things which are not" and thus makes him the "father of many nations" (*ethnē*) (Rom. 4:17). Paul's use of the following clause of Deut. 32:21, "with a nation without understanding I shall anger you," underscores the fallen condition of both Jew and Gentile that he has set forth in his argument already (see Rom. 1:21, 31; 3:11 [Ps. 14:2]; cf. Deut. 32:28).

In its Deuteronomic setting the oracle in Deut. 32:21 foretells Israel's exile and destruction (32:22–33). The "no people" and "foolish nation" that is to provoke Israel is the unnamed enemy, whom the Lord will send against Israel. Yet the destruction is not final: the pride of the enemy will cause the Lord to turn against them and vindicate his people (32:26–27, 36–38, 43). Both Israel and the nations must yet learn that there is no god besides the Lord: "I put to death, and I make alive, I wound and I heal, and there is no one who can deliver from my hand" (32:39).

Paul already has used Israel's exile as an image of its present hardening and unbelief (9:27–29 [Hos. 1:10; Isa. 10:22; 28:22]; also 2:24 [Isa. 52:5]). He likewise has pictured the fallen human being in terms of Israel's exile as "sold under sin" (3:9; 7:14). His appeal to Deut. 32:21 follows this pattern. Here the emphasis lies on Israel's rebellion against the Lord. God has answered Israel's misguided pursuit of the law with a provocation to jealousy: he has called a new people from Jews and Gentiles. It is this "non-people" that serves as a basis of Paul's argument. In a pattern that transcends the Assyrians or the Babylonians, of whom the text originally spoke, God now provokes Israel with the gospel, which goes forth to the nations. This provocation was not unexpected. Israel, according to Paul, knew that it would come. The Lord's changing dealings with Israel and the nations in Deut. 32:19–43 anticipates his unfathomable dealings with them in Christ, as Paul will go on to elaborate (11:30–32). The provocation is not the end, just as in Deuteronomy the "jealousy" and "anger" with which Israel first provoked the Lord do not end the Lord's fatherly love and care for his children. For Paul as well as for Moses, a promise remains for the redemption of the nation. Nor is it only the redemption of Israel that comes into view in the Song of Moses. According to Paul, the very song that speaks of the destruction of the nations also speaks of their salvation: they are called to rejoice in the Lord with Israel (Deut. 32:32; Rom. 15:10 [see discussion there]).

Sirach 49:5 alludes to Deut. 32:21 ("They gave their horn to others, and their glory to an alien nation"). See also *Sipre* §320 (see further Str-B 3:284–85). Like Paul, *Tg. Neof.* Deut. 32:1 and *Midr. Deut.* 2:4 link the witness of Moses and Isaiah, in the former case at least because Deut. 32:1 and Isa. 1:2 have similar wording (Bell 1994: 244; for further early Jewish usage of Deut. 32, see Bell 1994: 217–50).

Isaiah, the second witness, bears two words, just as in 9:27–29. In chapter 10 Paul's citations come from two consecutive verses, Isa. 65:1–2. He again adds vividness to his introduction of the first citation, as he does in chapter 9: "Isaiah *is bold* and says . . ." (10:20). The apostle, who cites the book of Isaiah more than any other Scripture, has just appealed to the calling of the prophet Isaiah as anticipation of his own calling in 10:15–16. The expression of the prophet's emotion likely reflects Paul himself. The "boldness" that Paul attributes to Isaiah in all likelihood is the anticipation of the gospel, which the apostle finds in the prophetic words (Isa. 65:1). In this "boldness" the apostle imitates the prophet (see 15:14–16).

The wording of Paul's citation of Isa. 65:1 appears to follow the LXX, aside from the inversion of the verbal expressions that open the two lines of the verse. Paul writes, "*I was found* [*heurethēn*] among those who did not seek me. *I became manifest* [*emphanēs egenomēn*] to those who did not inquire after me," inverting the order of the LXX. The inversion does not essentially vary from the Hebrew text, where the verbs are nearly synonymous (*nidraštî, nimṣēʾtî*). Yet Paul is not following the Hebrew in any case. His alteration of the form found in the LXX likely derives from his linking this citation with the previous citation from Deut. 32:21. It is less likely that he follows an alternate septuagintal tradition (so Wagner 2002: 210–11; Wilk 1998: 34–35). The variant reading, "I was found *among* [*en*] those who did not seek me," which both the UBS[4] and the NA[27] retain despite the difficulty of the decision, may well be original (so also Wagner 2002: 206–7). If so, it allows for the translation above, which in turn links this citation with the previous citation of Deut. 32:21. The Lord provokes Israel with a "non-people," for the Lord is now found among those who did not seek him. Paul's inversion of the order of the verbs allows for this connection.

Paul's citations of Deut. 32:21 and Isa. 65:1 are closely connected in any case, since both implicitly speak of the eschatological people of God called from among Jews and Gentiles. Admittedly, Isa. 65:1 speaks in the first instance of Israel's disobedience, as the Lord's answer to the prophetic lament in Isa. 63:15–64:12: "Why do you cause us to stray from your ways and harden our heart so that we do not fear you?" (63:17). Israel has become like those not called by the Lord's name (63:19): the Lord has hidden his face, so that all Israel has become like one who is "unclean"; all its righteous deeds have become as a "menstruous rag" (64:6). Because the Lord has hidden his face, no one calls on his name or attempts to take hold of him (64:7). To these rebellious people the Lord causes himself to be discovered and found (65:1). In its context the verse bears a certain ambivalence that plays itself out in Paul's citation of the following verse, to which we will return shortly. Here it is sufficient to observe that according to the prophetic lament, through God's hiddenness and judgment Israel has become no different from the nations, who do not call on the Lord. The Lord is discovered and found precisely by such persons. In the Isaianic context, too, such persons include the Gentiles, to whom the Lord promises to send "survivors" (i.e., a remnant) to declare his glory. The nations will come, bringing the scattered people of Israel back to Jerusalem as an offering. The Lord will make "some" of the nations "priests and Levites" (66:18–21). God's giving of himself to those who do not seek or inquire after him is nothing other than his new-creation work, a work that embraces the nations (65:17–25).

Paul cites the text typologically in precisely this sense: God's dealings with Israel in the past have been recapitulated in the present. The apostle is still answering the objection that he introduced in 10:19, that Israel did not know of a universal proclamation of God's name, which anticipated the gospel. Isaiah serves as a second witness alongside Moses. Paul, too, most likely refers in the first instance to Israel as "those who do not seek or ask after God." It is Israel that has refused to submit to God's righteousness while insisting on its own. Yet Israel's failure to believe in Christ is nothing other than a manifestation of the fallenness of all humanity: "No one seeks after God" (3:11 [Ps. 14:3]). All human beings are idolaters, seeking their own things rather than God (1:21–23, 28; 2:7–8). Paul's citation of Isa. 65:1 implicitly encompasses the whole of humanity, as does the original text itself: the apostolic mission embraces not just Israel but the whole of the inhabited world (see 10:18). As his transposition of the lines of the verse indicates (see above), it is the eschatological people of Jews and Gentiles among whom God is found and to whom he has revealed himself.

To them God's righteousness has been revealed (1:17; 3:21–26; 10:3).

As we have noted, there is a certain ambiguity in Isa. 65:1 that plays itself out in Paul's citation of Isa. 65:2. The wording of Isa. 65:1 is most naturally taken to indicate an accomplished reality: the Lord has been sought and found by those who did not seek him. Yet the following statements, including Isa. 65:2, describe an invitation rejected: "I stretched out my hands all day to a rebellious people." The context obviously persuaded the RSV, the NRSV, and the ESV to take the Niphal forms as permissive: "I was ready to be sought . . . ready to be found." Yet the irony here makes the permissive sense unlikely (the Lord is sought by "those who did not seek" and found by "those who did not ask"). The usage more likely bears an effective sense, which nevertheless expresses an invitation (see, e.g., Isa. 55:6; Ezek. 36:37): "I have been sought . . . I have been found (therefore seek and find me)." The LXX renders the text with this effective sense (*emphanēs egenomēn . . . heurethēn*). In this reading, although Isa. 65:1 also invites, it stands apart from its immediate context, expressing the effective, saving work of the Lord. It thereby provides a bridge between the prophetic lament in Isa. 63:10–64:12, which describes the entire nation as "dissolved into the hand of its iniquity" (64:7), and the following promise that "the LORD's servants" will emerge as "survivors" from the destruction to come (65:8–16). Implicitly, the "LORD's servants" are those who did not seek him and yet found him. They represent the new creation, which is announced in the Isaianic context (65:17–25).

Paul's appeal to Isa. 65:1–2 corresponds remarkably to the text, despite its striking appearance. In citing Isa. 65:2, he takes up the theme of the Lord's rejected invitation of Israel, whom he now names as the object of the prophetic word: "And to Israel he says, 'All the day I have stretched out my hands to a people disobedient and contrary'" (10:21). The "splitting" of the two verses from Isa. 65 between universal scope and particular address does not finally stand at odds with the passage, which follows a similar pattern. The text speaks of a rejected invitation, as does the apostle. Yet in both cases, as the contexts make clear, this rejection is not the end of the story.

In 10:21 Paul follows the LXX in doubling the Hebrew description of Israel as "rebellious" (*sôrēr*): the people were "disobedient and contradictory" (*apeithounta kai antilegonta*). The LXX rendering may pick up the concrete expression of Israel's rebellion as it is portrayed in context, which includes dismissal of the "word of the Lord" (Isa. 65:3–7, 12; 66:3–5; also 59:1–15). In context, the Lord charges Israel with pursuing idolatrous sacrifices (Isa. 65:3–7). Paul's citation here may therefore very faintly anticipate 11:3, and perhaps also 11:9. Perhaps the LXX presents Israel as the antithesis of the Servant described in Isa. 50:5, where the terms "disobey" and "contradict" are also paired. Even in the LXX the pairing may be read as a hendiadys, which probably is the case in Romans as well. According to Paul, Israel's rebellion lies in its rejection of God's mercy (9:19–21, 31; 10:3). The nation refuses to "call on the name of the (risen) Lord" (10:3–4, 13)—the very charge that the Lord brings in Isaiah (Isa. 65:1b; cf. 64:7).

In contrast with the LXX, Paul fronts the adverbial expression "all the day," stressing God's abiding love for his people. The anthropomorphic language of Isaiah is dramatic and poignant, preparing Paul's readers for his following discussion of Israel's salvation: "All the day I have stretched out my hands. . . ." The expression indirectly also recalls the suffering to which believers in Christ are exposed according to Paul's citation of Ps. 44:22 in 8:36 ("On account of you, we are put to death all the day").

The references to the nations and Israel that bracket 10:18–21 are now complete. The present proclamation to the nations has its anticipation in the "word" of creation itself (10:18 [Ps. 19:4]). Yet the Lord also abidingly loves his people, as is evident in his former appeal to them (10:21). That love foreshadows their salvation.

The Unsearchable Ways of the Creator, Who Has Mercy on Israel and the Nations (11:1–36)

The final movement of Paul's argument places the gospel in the context of God's election and calling of Israel (11:28–29). According to human logic and perception, the freedom of the Creator in his effective word of promise and mercy (9:1–29) stands in irresolvable tension with the failure of Israel to believe in that word-come-to-fulfillment in Christ (9:30–10:21). These irreconcilables are located within the story of God's "unsearchable judgments" and "untraceable ways" (11:33). The Creator alone can fulfill Israel's calling *through* Israel's disobedience, and in so doing, wonderfully save the nations as well.

11:1–10

Paul again begins the fresh movement of his argument with first-person usage: "I say, then, God has not rejected his people, has he?" (11:1). In his introductory statement in 9:1–5 he stands alongside his kinspeople at a distance from his largely Gentile audience. His position shifts in 10:1, where he addresses his readers as *adelphoi*, brothers and sisters in the faith. Finally, in 11:1 Paul stands with his readers as he brings them to view Israel's future from his apostolic perspective. The rhetorical question that he raises is fully sympathetic to the hope of Israel's salvation that he has expressed implicitly at various points in his preceding argument, particularly in his preceding citation of Isa. 65:2, which describes God as constantly extending his hands to his people in invitation in the past. How could he reject them now? Paul summarily rejects the thought ("May it never be!") and explains his response by pointing to his Jewish identity: "I am an Israelite, of the seed of Abraham, of the tribe of Benjamin." He then rounds off the thought by asserting the answer to the very question he raised: "God has not rejected his people, whom he foreknew" (11:2a).

Yet how can the faith and salvation of a single individual answer the question about God's dealings with an entire people? Paul's opening question and closing affirmation allude to the words of Samuel upon Israel's repentance for having insisted on having a king ("For the Lord will not abandon his people, on account of his great name, for the Lord was pleased to make you a people for himself" [1 Sam. 12:22]). But his language also recalls the more numerous moments of divine hiddenness or judgment in which the biblical writers announce that the Lord had rejected his people (Judg. 6:13; 2 Kings 17:20; 21:14; 23:27; 2 Chron. 35:19–21; Ps. 60:1, 10; 108:11; Jer. 7:29; Lam. 2:7; 5:22; Hos. 9:17). God's promise to Israel triumphs only in the sheer wonder of divine mercy that comes through rejection and judgment. Paul has in view this effect of the promise of God, as is clear in his brief concluding statement: "God has not rejected his people, whom he foreknew." His language now recalls his prior statement concerning God's foreknowledge of believers in Christ, whom God predetermined to be conformed to the image of his Son (8:29–30). There, Paul had in view the resurrection from the dead and the sonship that he subsequently names among the divine gifts granted to Israel (8:23; 9:4). As in 8:29, then, "foreknowledge" here is prospective in nature: in speaking of Israel as "those whom God foreknew," Paul has in view the coming salvation of his people.

It is within this framework that Paul elaborates his self-reference in 11:2b–6. He represents the present remnant and thus anticipates future salvation for Israel (see discussion of 9:27–29 above). The Scripture speaks about this hope in the experience of Elijah: God's way with the prophet in the past reveals his way with Israel in the present. The former pattern is eschatologically repeated.

Paul introduces Elijah as "interceding with God against Israel" (11:2b). Elijah, who was sent to the Gentile widow of Zarephath, serves as a counter-example to the apostle to the Gentiles, who, along with the prophet Isaiah, laments Israel's failure and petitions the Lord on behalf of the nation (9:1–5, 27–29; 10:1). Elijah likewise stands in contrast to the exalted Christ, who intercedes for believers (8:34). Elijah's contention against the nation is not finally valid. He does not perceive the work of the merciful God, who in the midst of judgment has preserved a remnant for himself. Elijah's implicit imprecatory petition against Israel is thus implicitly rejected. Hope for Israel remains.

Elijah's complaint appears twice in the biblical narrative in precisely the same wording, taking on the character of a formal witness against Israel in a contention (1 Kings 19:10, 14). The context is Elijah's flight from the threats of Jezebel after the dramatic confrontation with the prophets of Baal. He flees, forty days and forty nights, to Horeb, where the "word of the LORD comes to him." Twice the Lord asks him, "Why have you come here, Elijah?" Twice Elijah voices his complaint. In the second instance he does so while standing on the mountain after encountering the "still, small voice" of the Lord, which comes after the tremendous wind, earthquake, and fire.

Paul makes several alterations that set apart his use of the text from the LXX (and the MT, to

which the LXX closely corresponds). He omits Elijah's opening protest that he had been "extremely zealous for the LORD of hosts" (1 Kings 19:10, 14), limiting the prophet's address simply to "Lord, . . ." Given Paul's usage of *kyrios* in context, this brief introduction perhaps points to the merciful God whom we meet in Christ, about whom the prophet must yet learn.

Paul also rearranges the order of the prophetic complaint. The murder of the prophets appears first, perhaps emphasizing self-concern on the part of the prophet, perhaps reflecting Paul's situation (cf. 1 Thess. 2:15), or perhaps both. Paul's omission of the murder of the prophets "by the sword" suggests that he has his contemporary context in view (in which, of course, the *ius gladii* is limited to the Roman authorities). The reference to Israel's destruction of the Lord's altars in some measure anticipates Israel's present rejection of the gospel (Paul matches the LXX's *kateskapsan* at 1 Kings 19:10; 1 Kings 19:14 LXX has *katheilan*, "remove"). Paul's preceding citation of Isa. 65:2 has hinted already at repetition of the former pattern of idolatry in the present.

The third and fourth lines of the complaint also vary from the LXX. Paul's wording differs in a minor way from the LXX in tense and form (aorist passive instead of a perfect passive of the verb *hypoleipō*; the positive adjective *monos* instead of a superlative). More significantly, he again fronts the prophet's self-reference, "And I, alone, am left," focusing on the person of the prophet. He abbreviates the conclusion, omitting the unnecessary verb: "And they seek [to take] my life."

In reporting the divine response, Paul takes up only the final words of the Lord to Elijah from the biblical narrative, and he does so in a highly interpretive manner. God remains essentially hidden. Paul's introduction of the citation is among the most unusual of his letters: "But what does the oracular instruction [*chrēmatismos* (cf. 2 Macc. 2:4)] say to him?" This characterization of God as hidden corresponds closely to Paul's appeal to the narrative of 1 Kings. In that context the Lord announces the end of Elijah's ministry: he is to anoint Hazael as the new king of Damascus, Jehu as the new king of Israel, and Elisha as a new prophet in Elijah's place. They will execute the judgment for which Elijah has implicitly appealed (1 Kings 19:15–18). Yet the judgment will not be complete, for the Lord will spare "seven thousand in Israel, all the knees which have not bowed to Baal and every mouth that has not kissed him" (1 Kings 19:18). In fact, in the confrontation with the prophets of Baal, the Lord has "turned back (to himself)" the hearts of the people (1 Kings 18:37). Paul leaps over the announcement of judgment and the end of the prophet's ministry to the final word of the Lord. He interprets the text as speaking not merely of the Lord's sparing those innocent of idolatry, but much more as the Lord's keeping for himself seven thousand "who have not bent their knee to Baal" (11:4). The Lord himself has preserved for himself a "remnant" (cf. *b. Sanh.* 102b, which interprets 1 Kings 19:18 as indicating that "there were righteous among them"). Paul thus reads the Elijah passage in the light of the "remnant theology" of the book of Isaiah, to which he already has made reference (9:27–29). His interpretive use of the text corresponds to that of the narrative itself: the purpose and work of God transcend the limited vision and work of the prophet.

Unlike the LXX of 1 Kings 19:18, Paul uses the feminine article with the name of Baal, a male deity. This practice appears elsewhere in the LXX (23x), especially in the book of Jeremiah, where all twelve references to Baal appear with the feminine article. The use of the feminine article very likely reflects the association of the feminine term "shame" with Baal (Heb. *bōšet*; Greek *hē aischynē* [see BDAG, s.v. αἰσχύνη; BDF §53.4]). Paul may very well reflect the context of 1 Kings 19:18 LXX, since only here in the LXX, at 1 Kings 18:19, 25 (in the story of Elijah's confrontation with the prophets of Baal), does the term "shame" substitute for "Baal," as it refers to the "prophets of shame."

The work of God in the present corresponds to that in the past: "Thus also in the present time there has come to be a remnant according to a selection which is of grace" (*kat' eklogēn charitos* [11:5]). Paul recalls his earlier argument concerning the freedom of divine mercy and makes use of it in his argument here (cf. 9:10–13). Again divine "election" is concrete and historical and therefore always comes as an act of "selection." God presently has chosen the "remnant" and rejected the rest of the nation. He has done so entirely by grace. As he does earlier in the letter, Paul here defines

grace over against potential misunderstanding: if God saves a remnant by grace, it is no longer by works, since then grace would no longer be grace (4:4, 16). In his grace God acts freely as Creator; that is Paul's larger message (cf. 11:33–36).

In the final verses of this section (11:7–10) Paul draws together the threads of his discussion in an appeal to the Scriptures that parallels the opening of his discussion of Israel's failure (9:30–33). Whereas his opening affirmation of the freedom of God's mercy led to the description of Israel's failure, his return to the theme of God's freedom in grace appears in the context of the hope of Israel's salvation. Israel's present hardening comes from God, who has not rejected his people.

Paul's conclusion in 11:7 is simple: "What Israel seeks, this it did not reach. The election [*eklogē*] reached (it)." Again Paul has in view Israel's pursuit of the law and righteousness (9:31), at which it did not arrive, because it sought it apart from the God who manifests his righteousness in Christ (10:3–4). Despite its zeal for God, it therefore did not seek God (3:11), but rather sought to establish its own righteousness (10:3). God was found in Christ by those who were not seeking him (10:20); thus "the election" attained that which Israel did not. "The rest," says Paul, "were hardened" (11:7). He again recalls the freedom of God's mercy as displayed in God's contention with Pharaoh: "On whom God wills, he has mercy, and whom he wills, he hardens" (9:18).

Paul's summary consists primarily in his appeal to the witness of Scripture. The present hardening of Israel conforms to the pattern of God's dealings with Israel in the past ("just as it is written" [11:8]). As with his earlier pronouncement concerning Israel's failure, the apostle again presents a twofold witness (cf. 10:19–21).

The first appeal to Scripture is a mixed citation, drawn primarily from Deut. 29:4 (29:3 MT/ LXX) but modified by a distinctive substitution from Isa. 29:10:

> God gave to them a spirit of slumber, eyes not to see and ears not to hear until the present day. (11:8)

The opening of the citation differs significantly from Deuteronomy, where at the outset of the covenant renewal ceremony in Moab Moses declares to the people, "The Lord *has not given* you a heart to understand, or eyes to see, or ears to hear, to this day" (Deut. 29:4 [see *Midr. Deut.* 7:10–11]). Paul inverts the pronouncement, turning the diagnosis into a word of judgment by drawing on Isa. 29:10: "The LORD has poured out upon you a spirit of slumber." The Deuteronomic text thereby comes to serve Paul's purpose as a witness to divine hardening (11:7). The change is not drastic, since "hardening" for Paul represents divine surrender of human beings to their rebellion (see commentary on 9:18 above), the very theology that appears in the Isaianic announcements of the judgment that effects Israel's deafness and blindness (Isa. 6:9–13). Paul implicitly understands the act of judgment pronounced in Isa. 29:10 as coming upon the ignorance and rebellion already present in Israel according to Deut. 29:4.

The Isaianic language at the same time reinforces the hope of future redemption that appears in the narrative of Deuteronomy. Moses' description of Israel's spiritual lethargy is not the end of the story. The promise remains until the time "after the blessings and the curses," when the Lord will gather the people of Israel again and bring them back from exile. He will change them, "circumcising" their heart, "to love the LORD your God with all your heart and all your soul" (Deut. 30:6). The final words of the citation, "until the present day," mark the current state as an anticipation of God's future work (Deut. 29:3 LXX: *heōs tēs hēmeras tautēs*; Rom. 11:8: *heōs tēs sēmeron hēmeras*). The wording of Isaiah that Paul borrows underscores the certainty of this coming salvation. The fact that it is God who has brought slumber, blindness, and deafness upon Israel implies that he also has the power to end that condition. A "spirit of slumber" does not signal death, but rather a future when one finally awakes. The Isaianic prophecy accordingly goes on to announce the day in which "the deaf shall hear the words of a scroll, and out of their gloom and darkness the eyes of the blind shall see" (Isa. 29:18). Paul, too, anticipates the salvation of the nation.

Paul's second witness, David, much like Elijah, utters an imprecatory prayer:

> May their table become a snare and a trap and a stumbling-block and recompense to them. May their eyes be darkened, so as not to see, and may their back be continually bent. (11:9–10)

The apostle cites Ps. 68:23–24 LXX (69:23–24 MT; 69:22–23 ET), which varies from the MT at several places. The MT refers to the opponents' "things of peace" (*šělômîm*); modern versions vary widely in their rendering of the difficult phrase in which the term appears. The LXX opts for the quite plausible reading of the radicals as *šillûmîm*, "recompenses," shifting the term to the Greek singular *antapodosis* (cf. *Tg. Ps.* 69:23: "Let their sacrifice [*šělāmîm*] become an offense" [see Str-B 3:289]). The LXX also alters the final curse. The psalmist prays not that "their loins might continually shake," but rather that "their back might continually be bent" (*kai ton nōton autōn dia pantos synkampson*). The expression, though appearing rather infrequently, clearly signifies oppression and probably servitude (cf. similar language in 2 Sam. 22:40; Ps. 38:6 [37:7 LXX]; Ps. 57:5 [56:7 LXX]; 4 Macc. 3:4; Sir. 7:23; 33:27; also Gen. 49:8; Ps. 66:11 [65:11 LXX]; 81:6 [80:7 LXX]; 129:3 [128:3 LXX]; Philo, *Moses* 1 40:6; *T. Iss.* 5:3). The change heightens the *lex talionis* already present in context. Just as the opponents "gave me poison for food, and vinegar to drink for my thirst" (Ps. 69:21), so their table is to become a trap and snare for them. Just as the psalmist "bent his soul with fasting" (Ps. 69:10 [68:11 LXX: *kai synekampsa en nēsteia tēn psychēn mou*]) and yet was subject to the reproach of the adversaries, so he prays that their "back will be bent."

Paul varies in his own way from the LXX. He omits the words "before them" (*enōpion autōn* [MT: *lipnêhem*]) from the septuagintal "May their table become before them a snare." And whereas the LXX reads, "May their table become before them a snare, and recompense [*antapodosis*] and stick-trap [*skandalon*]," Paul moves the expression of recompense to the final position, accentuating it (*antapodoma*). He also adds a fourth element, "trap," to the curse of Israel's table: "a snare and a trap [*thēra*] and a stumbling-block and recompense." He very likely adds the reference to a "trap" in order to preserve the sense in which he already has used *skandalon*, as "stumbling-block." Had he left the septuagintal reading untouched, the term likely would have been read simply as "stick-trap."

One finds the imprecation of Ps. 69:22–23 applied to the wicked in early Jewish texts (*Odes Sol.* 5:5; *Midr. Esther* 7:9). Paul strikingly uses it to speak of Israel as a whole. The context in Romans already makes clear that it is the proclamation of the crucified and risen Christ that brings the present moment of judgment and hardening upon Israel (cf. 9:30–33; 10:3, 19–21). In appealing to the Davidic psalm, Paul makes the christological moment central. Just as David once pronounced a curse on his enemies, so now the Son of God, of the seed of David (1:3), who, according to Paul's later citation of this very psalm, bore the reproaches of God's own enemies, pronounces a curse on unbelieving Israel (see 15:3, citing Ps. 69:9 [69:10 MT; 68:10 LXX]). Of course, David appears as a witness alongside the mixed citation of Deut. 29:4 and Isa. 29:10. Israel's disobedience has not been confined to a single event, but rather has been repeated in its history with God. The former judgments of God, which have repeatedly come upon his people, have been recapitulated finally in Christ.

The curse upon Israel's "table" bears its own significance in its Pauline context, where it reflects Israel's exclusive table fellowship. The question of table fellowship between Gentile believers and their Jewish brothers and sisters became a burning issue at the inception of the Pauline mission, and it came to a head in Paul's momentous confrontation with Peter in Antioch (Gal. 2:11–21). Already before that encounter the conditions for the acceptance of the Gentiles as full members of God's people were hotly debated (Acts 10:1–11:18) and became a crisis for the earliest church (Acts 15:1–29). "Israel's table," which fenced it off from Gentile idolatry, had to give way to the table of the Lord (on the exclusivity of Jewish table fellowship, see, e.g., *Jos. Asen.* 7:1; 8:5; *Jub.* 22:16; Add. Esth. 14:17; 3 Macc. 3:4, 7; also on purity of foods, see *Let. Aris.* 128–166). The concern of conservative Jewish Christians to maintain purity, to observe the Sabbath, and to avoid any form of association with idolatry had resulted in tensions within the circle of Roman house churches, which Paul addresses later in 14:1–15:13. It is apparent here that Paul treats exclusive Jewish table fellowship as a dimension of Israel's pursuit of the law (9:31), an expression of a commitment to "works" that set it apart from the Gentiles (11:6)—the very point of contention at Antioch (Gal. 2:11–14). The ethnic boundary marker was simultaneously a claim to true piety and godliness. David's pronouncement

of a curse "speaks" (*legei*) to the present because Israel, with its exclusive table, has rejected the crucified and risen Jesus, who is the Messiah.

Consequently, the "spirit of slumber" sent upon Israel, which blinds and deafens the nation (11:8), turns out to be divine judgment upon Israel's refusal to obey the gospel. God has sent that for which David has asked. Blindness comes as "hardening," the surrender of human beings to their own rebellion. Just as the "bending" of the back of the psalmist's enemies represented due recompense for their scorn, so here the "continual bending of Israel's back" signals the divine recompense for their sins. Quite possibly, Paul regards the rejection of Christ as a repetition of Israel's former idolatry, so that the "bending of the back" is recompense for a "bending of the knee" to an idol. Israel remains unaware of this oppression and servitude. It is not outward and visible, but rather inward and spiritual (cf. Gal. 4:21–31).

THE SALVATION OF ISRAEL IN PROMISE AND HOPE (11:11–36)

Just as formerly the hope of the return from exile and the rebirth of the people remained, so Paul awaits the redemption of the nation. He has already made clear that the presence of the remnant, of which he himself is a representative, is itself a hidden promise of the salvation of the nation as a whole (11:1–5). Having described the creation of a remnant by God's grace, he now elaborates the hope of Israel's salvation. Israel retains its priority in the saving purpose of God: its salvation stands at the end of all things.

11:11–16

Israel retains its priority in the saving purpose of God, as Gentile believers must learn. The Davidic imprecation that effects Israel's stumbling is not the end of the story. Paul here, in new form, reaffirms the eschatological salvation of Israel. Whereas in 11:1 he raises the question in terms of God's abiding relation with his people (cf. 10:21), he does so now in terms of Israel's failure itself: "I say, then, they did not stumble so that they might fall, did they? By no means!" Paul already has indicated indirectly that God's preservation of a remnant bears the promise of the salvation of the nation as a whole: the remnant embodies the promise that God has not rejected his people (11:1–10). In the face of Israel's failure he now states the matter directly. Precisely because Israel's fall came from God's hand (11:7–10), Israel has not fallen out of God's hand. Despite the discontinuity in the outward course of events, the continuity of God's saving purpose for Israel, his people, remains. This brief subsection largely consists in an allusive expansion of Paul's earlier citation of Deut. 32:21 in 10:19. Just as in Deut. 32 the redemption of Israel follows its rejection, so it is in the present. The hope of Israel's salvation consequently serves as instruction for Gentiles, warning against pride and bringing true hope.

11:17–24

Paul takes up the natural, creaturely image of the olive tree, into which the Gentiles have been grafted unnaturally and unexpectedly. The Gentiles, as well as Israel, appear again as mere created entities in the hand of the Creator, who does with them as he pleases. Paul reinforces to his Gentile readers the freedom of the merciful Creator, which has effected their participation in the saving benefits granted to Israel. As in 9:19–20, where he speaks to a Jewish interlocutor, Paul now returns to second-person singular usage, addressing Gentiles corporately as an individual person, corresponding to his prior reference to them as "the world" (11:12, 15; see also 10:6–9). Individual identity is found in ethnic identity; ethnic identity is simultaneously individual identity.

The time of mission to the Gentiles will come to an end. Likewise, Israel will be ingrafted again, if it does not remain in unbelief, for God is able to ingraft it again (11:23; cf. 4:21). Indeed, God will ingraft Israel. God's purpose of saving Israel as a people remains unchanged. Gentiles have been afforded a time of God's goodness that will come to an end.

11:25–36

In the first two subsections Paul has described the salvation of fallen Israel as the hope of the world and has drawn out its implications for the life and thought of his Gentile addressees. In this final unit he sets forth the underlying *theo*-logy of this hope, beginning with Scripture (11:25–27), continuing with theological explication (11:28–32), and concluding with a doxology that not only draws the conclusion of this unit but also serves as the conclusion of the whole of his presentation of the gospel (11:33–36). The apostle voices for the

believing community the thanksgiving and praise that belong to the Creator, the thanksgiving and praise that idolatrous humanity refuses to return to God (1:18–23).

Paul does not want the believers in Rome to be ignorant of a certain "mystery," which here he unfolds. As his opening announcement of the gospel (1:16–17) and his closing doxology show (16:25–27), "mystery" here signifies the disclosure of truth to which the Scripture already bears witness. In other words, the knowledge of a "mystery" entails insight into the message of Scripture, which, although present, formerly was hidden and unknown. As is clear from both this text and the other pair, this knowledge of the Scripture entails the knowledge of the ways of God as Creator and Redeemer. Paul's citation of Scripture here, perhaps the most interpretive and theologically dense reading of Scripture in the entire letter, by its very nature reflects Paul's purpose of explaining "this mystery," a "mystery" that is distinct from that of the gospel: it announces the fulfillment of promise and hope in "the coming of the Redeemer from Zion."

Paul's unfolding of this mystery of Scripture reinforces the warning that he has issued already to his Gentile readers: they are not to imagine themselves to be wise (11:25b [cf. 11:18–20]). The claim to possess wisdom, the essence of rebellion and idolatry (1:22), which manifests itself in a false trust and boasting in the law (2:17–29), is alien to the very nature of the gospel (3:27–28). Faith in the gospel, worked by God alone, must not become the basis of a false boast on the part of Gentiles.

The "mystery," Paul explains, is that a hardening, in part, has come upon Israel. This "hardening in part" also has a limited time: "until the fullness of the Gentiles has entered in" (11:25c–d). This statement is most naturally understood as an expression of Paul's argument thus far in chapter 11. The "hardening in part" is something of a litotes that describes the divine judgment on the nation that preserves a not inconsiderable "remnant" as a sign of the coming salvation of Israel as a whole (11:1–9, 14). Paul already has made it clear that Israel's "fall" is not final, that God will finally accept them again (11:11–16). He now makes clear that they will be ingrafted again into "their own olive tree"—that is, into the community of faith that proceeds from Abraham (11:23–24). The Gentiles, too, will be cut off, once their "fullness has entered in" (11:22, 25). Just as "the fullness" of Israel signifies the eschatological salvation of the nation as a whole (11:12), the "fullness of the Gentiles" likely signifies their acceptance by God in full numbers—there had always been proselytes—an eschatological event that has come about through the gospel (11:25). They now are entering into salvation, into the people of God. Perhaps Paul's language of "entering in," which as a soteriological term appears here as a *hapax legomenon* (cf., however, 5:12), suggests that the Gentiles now are entering into Zion, vaguely recalling Isa. 2:2–5; Mic. 4:1–4; and similar passages (cf. Isa. 30:29 LXX; Isa. 26:2; see Wilk 1998: 68–70). However, the Gentiles' time will come to an end, and when it does, the "hardening" of Israel will end as well. Interpreters often suppose that here Paul, under the force of circumstances, inverts the scriptural order of the pilgrimage of the nations and the deliverance of Zion. It is more likely, however, that he regards Israel's salvation as proleptically accomplished in the risen Christ, the seed of David according to the flesh, the root of Jesse, who has risen to rule the Gentiles and in whom the Gentiles hope (1:3; 15:12 [Isa. 11:10]). Indeed, the apostle's appeal to Isa. 52:7 (10:15: "How beautiful are the feet of those who proclaim the good news") and Isa. 53:1 (10:16: "Lord, who has believed our report?") signals the arrival of salvation, the fulfillment of God's promise to Israel in the risen Jesus. Paul's following reference to an altered form of Isa. 59:20 likewise presents the Redeemer coming forth from the heavenly Zion. Israel's salvation has been accomplished. Salvation awaits the nation as a promise already fulfilled. Paul does not cast aside his affirmation of the priority of Israel: salvation remains "for the Jew first, and also for the Greek."

As Paul's subsequent citation of Isaiah will make clear, his next statement is fundamental to the "mystery" that he announces: "And in this manner all Israel shall be saved" (11:26). This contested utterance is most naturally understood in the light of Paul's prior argument. The salvation of the Gentiles serves God's purpose of provoking Israel to jealousy (10:19; 11:11–16). Paul is not concerned to indicate precisely how in human terms this provocation shall work. His present

zeal as apostle to the Gentiles serves only as anticipation of the larger event in which not merely "some" of his own people, but rather the nation as a whole, will believe (11:13–14). It is through delay, through God's temporary preference of the Gentiles, that "all Israel" will be saved. As Paul will make clear, the people of Israel have been rendered disobedient in order that now they might be given mercy (11:31). Paul's point here is not that every last member of Israel in all of time will be saved; if that were the case, his deep lament, with his willingness to suffer his own condemnation for Israel's sake, would be pointless. "All Israel" does not signify every descendent of Abraham for all time; rather, as an allusion to Scripture, it speaks of Israel as a corporate reality (e.g., Deut. 1:1; 5:1; 29:2; 31:11; Josh. 3:7; 1 Sam. 7:5). Paul is concerned instead about Israel as a nation, as a people with a history, as an ethnic reality. Christ alone remains the way to salvation, but Israel's way to Christ will differ from that of the nations that hear the gospel: Israel will see and believe in him as the coming Redeemer, as Paul himself did. The final act in the drama of redemption is not the formation of a church that consists largely of Gentiles, but the creation of salvation for the people of Israel. The gospel of Christ does not stand at odds with his coming as Redeemer, but rather announces it. Before that coming, then, Paul hopes to save "some" of his people. As the larger dynamic of the passage makes clear, the surprising turns in the path of God's purposes are by no means arbitrary. God's untraceable ways reassert his right over us as our Creator, who acts in the freedom of mercy.

This pattern of Israel's final salvation will take place "just as it is written":

> There shall come forth from Zion the Redeemer;
> he shall turn away ungodly deeds from Jacob.
> This shall be the covenant from me for them,
> when I take away their sins. (11:26–27)

Paul draws the first part of his citation from Isa. 59:20–21a LXX, and the latter part from Isa. 27:9 LXX. However, his wording here is his own, a theological distillation rich in echoes and nuance.

The first clause varies from both the MT and the LXX of Isa. 59:20. Whereas the MT speaks of the Redeemer coming "to" Zion (so also *Targum*

Isaiah), and the LXX speaks of the Redeemer coming "on account of" Zion, Paul speaks of the Redeemer coming "from" Zion. F. Wilk (1998: 39–40) argues that Paul is dependent on a septuagintal version that bore *ek* ("from") as a misreading of *eis* (Heb. *lĕ-*, "to") from a prior version. This twofold process is possible, but the text form *eis* is hypothetical, the LXX witnesses to *ek* are likely dependent on Romans (the reading *'al ṣiyyôn* in *1QIsaiah* is not relevant), and Paul's reading is probably theologically motivated, since his entire citation of the text is highly interpretive.

In this case, then, Paul's variation is theologically significant (see Wagner 2002: 284–86). His citation echoes various texts that speak of God sending forth help for Israel from Zion, especially Ps. 14:7 (cf. Ps. 53:6), which speaks of the Lord sending forth from Zion "the salvation of Israel" (*yĕšû'at yiśrā'ēl*; 13:7 LXX: *to sōtērion tou Israēl*), of the Lord "turning back the captivity" of his people (*šûb . . . šĕbût 'ammô*; 13:7 LXX: *en tō epistrepsai tēn . . . aichmalōsian tou laou autou* [cf. Rom. 11:26b: *apostrepsei asebeias apo Iakōb*]), and of the resultant rejoicing of Jacob (cf. Rom. 11:26b). That the Redeemer comes "from Zion" for Israel implies that Israel is in exile, a setting that the allusion to Ps. 14 accentuates: God saves his people who are in captivity. Likewise, the text of Isa. 59:20 describes God as "the Redeemer," who savingly comes to his exiled people—a prominent characterization of God in Isa. 40–55 (MT: *gō'ēl*; LXX: *ho lytroumenos; ho rhyomenos, ho rhysamenos* [see Isa. 43:14; 44:6, 22, 23, 24; 47:4; 48:17; 49:7, 26; 54:5, 8]).

Paul's citation of Isaiah here consequently serves as the conclusion to the story of God's dealings with Israel in the gospel of Christ, a story that Paul introduces in 9:27 with a citation of Isaiah (Isa. 10:22 [with Hos. 1:10]; 28:22; 1:9). The apostle's Isaianic lament speaks of judgment and disaster, and ultimately of exile that has come anew upon Israel (see discussion of 9:27–29 above). The subsequent announcements of judgment and disaster drawn from Isaiah, Deuteronomy, and the narrative of Elijah complement Paul's opening lament (see discussion of 9:33; 10:19–21; 11:1–10 above). Paradoxically, the gospel, the word of God's promise to Abraham come to fulfillment in Christ, has worked not faith in Israel, but rather disobedience. Yet in 9:27 Paul places the hope

of Israel's salvation within Isaiah's lament, inserting Hos. 1:10 ("The number of the sons of Israel shall be as the sand of the sea") into the word of judgment (Isa. 10:22). Now, drawing again on the Isaianic promise of salvation through judgment, Paul announces the "mystery" of God's way with Israel: the present divine judgment and rejection of Israel through the proclamation of the gospel to the nations will finally end in the coming of Israel's Redeemer from Zion.

Paul undoubtedly refers to Christ as the coming Redeemer, whom he here again identifies with God through his use of the Isaianic text (see, e.g., 1 Cor. 11:26; 15:23; 16:22; 1 Thess. 2:19; 3:13; 4:15; 5:23; on redemption, see Rom. 7:24). Christ, the stumbling-stone whom God has placed in "Zion" and with whom God himself is identified (Isa. 8:14; Rom. 9:33), will come forth from the heavenly Zion as the Redeemer of Israel (see Gal. 4:26–27 [Isa. 54:1]; see also discussion at Rom. 9:33). Paul's unique use of the preposition *ek* ("from") is likely intentional. In context the Isaianic promise speaks of conflict between the nations and the Lord, who comes triumphantly to deliver his people (Isa. 59:15b–20). Paul's prior warning to Gentiles, "since you also shall be cut off" (11:22), may also faintly anticipate a final confrontation between the Lord and the unbelieving nations, which would then continue in this citation. One need not imagine a complicated eschatological scenario but only the hostility of the world against the gospel, of which Paul speaks elsewhere (cf. Phil. 1:28; 2 Thess. 1:6–10; 2:3–12). In any case, the salvation of Israel by the coming of the Redeemer from Zion will be, according to Paul, the resurrection of the dead, the final salvation of all who believe (11:15).

Although Paul's reading of the second clause of Isa. 59:20 (11:26b) reflects that of the LXX, his reading of the text differs significantly from that of the LXX. The Hebrew text speaks of the Lord coming to Zion not "to turn away ungodly deeds from Jacob," but rather "for those in Jacob who turn from iniquity." The absence of the LXX's *kai* ("and") at the beginning of the clause, which is perhaps intentional on Paul's part, sets apart the following third clause for particular emphasis (Wilk 1998: 57; see below). Isaiah 59:2 LXX speaks of the Lord "having turned away [*apestrepsen*] his face from you [Israel] on account of your sins so as not to have mercy" (MT: "your sins have hidden his face"). After the prophetic confession of Israel's sins and transgressions, however, when the Lord sees that there is no judgment (*krisis*; MT: *mišpāṭ*), he is said to have "defended them with his arm and established (them) with mercy" (59:16 LXX). The Lord thus repays the adversaries with reproach (59:18 LXX); he will come as a violent river, and wrath from him will come with anger (59:19 LXX). According to 59:20 LXX, when the Lord comes "for the sake of Zion" (*heneken Siōn*) and "turns away ungodly things from Jacob," he brings wrath on Israel's adversaries. The LXX thus reads 59:20 in terms of the monergistic, divine mercy, which it inserts into the text at 59:16; but unlike Paul's text, the "removal of ungodly things" here signals not a change in Israel, but rather the defeat of Israel's enemies. This theme recurs significantly in the latter part of the book of Isaiah (e.g., 45:14–15; 46:1–2; 47:1–15; 49:22–26; 54:1–17; 60:1–22). As we have noted, it may express itself in another way in Paul's own reading of the text: the salvation of Israel brings the resurrection of the dead.

If, as is likely, Paul supposes that his readers are familiar with the septuagintal reading of Isa. 59:20b, he presents an ironic reversal of their usual reading of the passage: the "ungodly deeds" that the Redeemer removes from Jacob are those not of the adversaries, but rather of "Jacob" himself. Nevertheless, Paul's reading of Isa. 59:20b is, in its own way, deeply rooted in the theology of the book of Isaiah, so that his interpretation corresponds remarkably with the Hebrew text. Whereas the septuagintal reading focuses on the Lord's deliverance of Israel from its oppressors, Paul's reading is based on the forgiveness that underlies that deliverance. The theme of forgiveness runs like a scarlet thread through Isa. 40–55 and also informs the reading of Isa. 56–66, reappearing at critical points, including 59:15b–21. The Lord is the one who, for his own sake, blots out Israel's transgressions and does not remember its sins (43:25). He wipes away Israel's transgressions like a cloud and its sins like a fog (44:21–22; see also 40:1–2). These pronouncements of forgiveness by the Lord who is Creator express themselves in the redemption of Israel from exile (43:14–21; 44:23–28). They stand especially close to 59:16, which announces the salvation that the Lord himself effects for Israel in the face of its failure ("his own arm worked salvation for him"). Paul reads Isa. 59:20 in light of these promises. Consequently, insofar as he has the Hebrew text in mind, he interprets the characterization "those in Jacob who turn from transgression" not as a condition, but rather as an effect of the saving action of the Lord. It is also possible that he has in view the following promise, which he omits from his citation: the Lord makes a covenant with his people that he will never remove his Spirit from them (59:21). The announcement of the gift of the Spirit appears earlier in the book of Isaiah, framed by promises of forgiveness (44:1–8). In Romans it represents the arrival of the new creation in Christ, in which the human being is made anew (see 2:25–29; 8:1–11; cf. Deut. 30:6). In his citation of Isa. 59:20b, then, in a distillation of Isaianic theology, Paul compresses new obedience and final redemption into a single divine act in Christ. Consequently, the coming of the Redeemer to Zion brings with it the removal of Jacob's ungodly deeds. This use of Isa. 59:20b LXX may suggest a dramatic reversal of the Lord's pronouncement of judgment on Jerusalem in Ezek. 23:27, 48 LXX, where he promises to "remove its godless deeds" by judgment and exile (cf. Ezek. 18:28, 30). Strikingly, the thought of both Isa. 59:7–8 ("their feet are swift to shed blood") and Ps. 14:1 ("there is no one who does good"), which appears in the context of Isa. 59:20a–b, also appears prominently in Paul's indictment of humanity in 3:10–18 (see 3:10–12, 15–17). Israel's unbelief has left it in its ungodly deeds. Only the coming of the Redeemer will bring deliverance.

In this citation of Isa. 59:20b Paul refers to Israel as "Jacob." Only here and in his citation of Mal. 1:2 in 9:13 does he use this name. This designation, which appears frequently in the book of Isaiah in the context of the Lord's contention with his people and his promises to save them, implies a return to the beginning of the nation, a fresh wrestling with God, as Jacob once contended with him at the river Jabbok (Isa. 43:1–13, 25–28 [see Gen. 32:22–32]). Again in Paul's day, by the wonder of the Lord's grace, this contention will issue in the salvation of the people. The Redeemer who comes from Zion meets Jacob and removes his ungodly deeds, just as the Lord did in the past.

The third clause, the opening clause of Isa. 59:21, stands at the center of interest while serving as a transition to a brief citation of Isa. 27:9. Paul's text corresponds verbatim to Isa. 59:21a LXX, "This shall be the covenant from me for them," and at the same time nearly matches Isa. 27:9a LXX, "This is my blessing of him." We will return to this clause after considering the fourth and final clause.

The texts are linked not only by the shared wording but also by the theology. The septuagintal reading, of which Paul makes use again, differs from the Hebrew text and again takes up a fundamental theme of the larger context. According to Isa. 27:9 MT, atonement will be made for "Jacob's" guilt, and the "fruit" of the removal of his sin will be present, "when he turns all the stones of the altar into crushed chalk, the Asherah poles and the incense altars will not stand." The announcement might be taken to indicate the condition for forgiveness. Yet, as is the case with Isa. 59:20–21, the septuagintal reading here interprets Israel's acts of repentance not as the condition, but rather as the effect, of the Lord's mercy on his people. The opening phrase, "On account of this [*dia touto*] (the lawlessness of Jacob shall be removed)," refers to the prior expression of the Lord's mercy. The Lord was not one concerned with "the hard spirit" to take them away by a spirit of wrath. *"On account of this* the lawlessness of Jacob shall be removed"* (27:8–9a LXX). The LXX further reads the opening clause of 27:9b MT, "And this will be all the fruit," as "And this is his blessing." The remainder of the verse then becomes a temporal clause: "And this is his blessing, *when I take away his sin.*" Israel's acts of repentance appear not as a condition for the atonement of its guilt, but rather as contemporaneous effects of the forgiveness that the Lord grants. In fact, the septuagintal reading of the Hebrew text is the most natural one. The passage falls at the conclusion of the "Isaiah Apocalypse" (chaps. 24–27), wherein emphasis falls on the Lord's redeeming work as Creator. There will come a day when the Lord will "slay (Leviathan), the dragon in the sea" (27:1). In that day Jacob, the Lord's vineyard, will blossom and fill the earth with fruit (27:2–7). The exiles in Egypt and Assyria will return (27:12). The work of salvation rests with the Lord alone. Consequently, Israel's destruction of its former

idols is best understood along with the LXX as the effect of the Lord's redeeming work, as the characterization of it as "the whole fruit of the removal of his sin" (*kol-pĕrî hasir ḥaṭṭāʾtô*) already suggests (cf. 27:6).

Paul draws the fourth and final clause of his citation from Isa. 27:9 LXX, "when I take away their sin." The language recalls not only the Lord's self-revelation to Moses (Exod. 34:5–8) and the forgiveness that Israel obtained in the wilderness (Num. 14:18), but also the prophet Isaiah's encounter with the Lord (Isa. 6:7). Paul now describes substantially the same act as Isa. 59:20b ("He shall turn away ungodly deeds from Jacob") in a temporal clause. Yet the language is not redundant. As we noted above, the omission of the septuagintal "and" (*kai*), which probably is due to Paul, places emphasis on the Lord's promise: "This is my covenant with them." The temporal marker here likewise subordinates the final clause ("*when* I take away their sins") to this preceding promise. The promised covenant stands at the center of attention. In its original context the demonstrative pronoun ("*this* shall be the covenant from me for them") pointed forward to the promise of the eternal presence of the Lord's spirit and words in the repentant ones of Jacob and their children (Isa. 59:21). Paul's substitution of Isa. 27:9b for this promise redirects the demonstrative so that it refers to the prior promise: "the Redeemer shall come from Zion" for Israel. "*This* is the covenant for them" (11:27). In his coming, the Redeemer turns aside Jacob's godless deeds and removes "their" sins.

The language of the citation stresses the one-sided divine initiative in this final covenant. It is, according to the Lord, a "covenant from me" (*hē par emou diathēkē*). Furthermore, it is a covenant "for them" (*autois* as *dativus commodi*), for the benefit of disobedient and unbelieving Israel.

Furthermore, as Paul's final, temporal clause shows, this covenant is a future one, consisting simply in the coming of the Redeemer from Zion for Jacob. Israel, which is in the exile of its sins and unbelief, cannot make its way to God. God must come to it as Redeemer. It cannot run a course to God by the pursuit of the law and works (9:16, 30–33). God in Christ must finally bridge the gap between heaven and earth for it (10:6–13). Without knowing or recognizing it, Israel is in the same situation as the "wretched person" of 7:24, who, unlike Israel, cries out for redemption.

The reference to "covenant" recalls Paul's opening enumeration of the gifts given to Israel, which include "the covenants" (9:1–5). To their number will yet be added a final covenant. The former exodus from Egypt, around which the gifts of 9:1–5 are centered, will have its fulfillment in Israel's new, eschatological exodus from sin. The former gifts have their fulfillment in God's gift of himself to Israel as its Redeemer; the final gift is the Creator, who in Christ comes forth from Zion for Israel (see 9:5).

In this emphasis on God's giving of himself to Israel, Paul stands close to the Isaianic passage that he cites and echoes the very text of Isa. 59:21 that he omits. In the original context the Lord promises to make the covenant that his Spirit will not depart from his people or from their children. In coming to them, the Lord will remain in and with them forever. The rebellious people will be created anew, so that they will freely confess and belong to the Lord (Isa. 44:1–5). The passage recalls Jeremiah's promise of a new covenant and essentially expresses the same promise (see Jer. 31:31–34; cf. Ezek. 11:19; Hos. 2:16–20). Paul's substitution of Isa. 27:9b makes it clear that the new covenant consists in the coming of the Redeemer—that is, the eschatological coming of God in Christ for Israel. At the same time, the continuing text of Isaiah likely played in the background for Paul's first readers, reminding them of the promised gift of the Spirit for Israel.

In the larger context of the book of Isaiah the Lord's promise of a covenant, precisely because it is new, recalls the new Noahic covenant, which the Lord promises his people after the flood of catastrophes and exile that he has brought upon them (54:9–10; see Gen. 8:21–22; 9:11–17). It likewise recalls the new, "everlasting" Davidic covenant of his constant and sure love, which the Lord promises all his people (55:3–5; see 2 Chron. 6:14–17, 42). In some measure, too, the promised covenant of 59:21 brings to mind the Lord's word to the Servant, whom he appoints as a "covenant of the people" (42:6; 49:6, 8). In the Isaianic context the emphasis lies on the universal horizon of the Servant's redemptive work. Yet the first and foremost task of the Servant is to "raise up the tribes of Jacob" and to "establish the survivors of Israel"—

the very work of the Redeemer who comes to (and for) Zion (59:20). Rich christological suggestions lie in the background. Paul's use of Isa. 59:20 is again typological. God's ways with his people in the past will be recapitulated at the eschaton.

As the asyndeton at 11:28 makes clear, in 11:28–32 Paul unfolds the "mystery" (11:25) afresh for his Gentile readers, now employing his own theological categories in light of the Scripture that he has cited. Paul first deals with the earthly, ethnic realities (11:28–29). On account of the gospel, Paul says, God treats those of Israel as enemies for the sake of "you," Gentiles, to whom the gospel is now proclaimed (11:28a). Israel's national pride, bound up with its heritage and works, is brought to nothing by God's call of a new people of both Jews and Gentiles (9:6–9, 10–13, 22–26). Nevertheless, God's love for Israel has not come to an end. According to "the election," Israel remains beloved "for the sake of the fathers," just as the Gentile believers in Rome are beloved by God (11:28b; 1:7). The saving, electing purpose of God remains unchanged by human works (11:11) and, through its own winding way, will yet come to fulfillment for Israel. The word of God has not fallen, and the promises to the patriarchs are still valid; they remain a "root of fatness" for Israel (9:4–5, 6; 11:17). Paul explains: "The gifts and calling of God are unchangeable" (11:29; see 9:1–5). The expression is essentially a hendiadys: the gifts signal God's effective call of his people, while the call, because it is effective, carries divine gifts with it.

A second explanation follows in 11:30–32. Paul here describes, a posteriori, the course of events in terms of the purpose of God. Just as the Gentiles were once disobedient to God and now have been granted mercy by Israel's disobedience, thus also now "they [Israel] are disobedient by means of your mercy in order that they now might be granted mercy" (the omission of "now" [*nyn*] has strong attestation, but so does its presence; it certainly is the *lectio difficilior* and therefore preferable). Only now that Israel has been rendered disobedient in its refusal to acknowledge the righteousness of God may it be granted mercy; otherwise, it is not mercy. Paul summarizes his point in precisely these terms: "For God has shut up all to disobedience in order that he might have mercy on all." Only the disobedient and condemned receive mercy.

In effecting the salvation of Israel and the nations, God acts upon us as our Creator. We are not thereby removed from our earthly place and identity, which inescapably includes a national and ethnic dimension. However—and this is Paul's point—in the freedom of his mercy God the Creator brings us to see ourselves as creatures, whose times and places and reception of mercy are given as gifts in time and space by the Creator alone. In this way our eyes are opened to other human creatures, who also are the objects of God's mercy. Likewise, our fundamental sin, our refusal to glorify and render thanks to our good Creator, is thereby overcome. If in Rom. 1–8 the gospel addresses us as *fallen* creatures, in Rom. 9–11 God's word of promise to Israel, given in the freedom of his mercy, addresses us as fallen *creatures*. God's justifying work in the gospel is an inseparable dimension of his work as Creator. Of course, there have long been different readings of Rom. 11, interpreting "Israel" as referring to the church or to the remnant of Israel throughout the ages (see Hoekema 1994). It is beyond the scope of the present work to engage in detailed debate with such readings, but two observations are appropriate. First, such a reinterpretation of "Israel" can hardly be reconciled with the apostle's opening lament for his people in 9:1–29, which is echoed in the prophet Isaiah. Biblical lament arises only in the face of unanswered promise. Likewise, Paul's sorrow over the nation is hardly answered by a redefinition of the term. Second, and more importantly, such readings remove us from recognizing our limited time and place as Gentiles (as most of us are), which is precisely what the apostle is trying to prevent.

Paul concludes the body of the letter with a profound expression of praise to God as Creator, a doxology that appears as a counterpart to the silent refusal of idolatrous humanity to glorify the Creator and thankfully sing his praise (1:18–23). It likewise implicitly echoes Paul's blessing of Christ as God and sovereign over all things (9:1–5). The doxology uses tripartite hymnic form:

> O, the depth of the riches and wisdom and
>   knowledge of God!
> How unsearchable his judgments and how
>   untraceable his ways!

> For who has known the mind of the Lord?
>   Or who became his counselor?
> Or who gave to him in advance, and (as a
>   result) he shall repay him?
> For from him and through him and unto
>   him are all things.
> To him be glory forever, Amen! (11:33–36)

The hymn undoubtedly is Paul's own composition. Its language is that of Hellenistic Judaism. The central section, which fills out the content of the doxology, contains a rather strong allusion to Scripture followed by two direct citations, first Isa. 40:13 in 11:34 ("Who has known the mind of the Lord . . ."), and then Job 41:3 (41:11 ET) in 11:35 ("Or who gave to him . . .").

The hymn begins with threefold praise of God's riches, wisdom, and knowledge. The exclamatory reference "O, the depth" intentionally employs a creational category in order to underscore the Creator's transcendence (cf. 8:39). Even the depths (of the sea or the earth) were hardly subject to measurement. How much more the Creator! Similar language appears in *2 Bar.* 14:8–10 ("Who can explore the depth of your judgment?") and 1QHᵃ V, 8–12 ("the depth of your knowledge") (see further Str-B 3:294–95). The way to wisdom may be described as a searching of the depths (e.g., Job 28). The metaphor of depth also expresses the inward thought of a person, which the thoughts and purposes of God far exceed in their hiddenness (Jdt. 8:14; 1 Cor. 2:10, "the depths of God").

A threefold string of genitives, "riches and wisdom and knowledge," supplies the content of the metaphorical appeal to "depth." They are thus aspectual descriptives rather than designators of three distinct referents. Quite clearly for Paul, the riches of God speak of the goodness of God and of the saving benefits found in the Creator himself (2:4; 9:23; 10:12; 11:12; see further *Sib. Or.* 2:125; Philo, *Alleg. Interp.* 3.163; *Posterity* 151). The pairing "wisdom and knowledge," which appears in Ecclesiastes (1:16–18; 2:21, 26; 7:12; 9:10), is a way of describing a comprehensive awareness of the end and essence of created things (cf. Dan. 1:4; Col. 2:3). To ascribe the depth of riches, wisdom, and knowledge to God is a reversal of human rebellion, the surrender of the claim that we ourselves are wise (Rom. 1:21–23).

The central section of the hymn contains three paired clauses that more precisely describe the goodness, wisdom, and knowledge of the Creator. The first of these pairings restates the opening exclamation of praise, making it more precise (11:33c–d). Reference to God's "unsearchable judgments" recalls God's repeated saving acts of judgment, the "wonders" that the Lord works (e.g., 1 Chron. 16:12, 14; Pss. 9; 105). God's "untraceable ways" describes the same reality, echoing texts that speak of the ever-surprising nature of God's saving dealings, the constant difference between human calculations and the work of God (e.g., Ps. 77, esp. 11:19, "your way was through the sea"; Isa. 40:3; 42:16; 55:8, "neither are your ways, my ways"). According to Pr. Man. 6, God's mercy is likewise "immeasurable and untraceable."

The second pair of clauses (11:34) is a citation of Isa. 40:13, which reasserts the Lord's identity as Creator in the face of the nations and their idols. The Lord both comforts Israel in exile with the promise of salvation and reprimands it for failing to trust in the Lord, who is Creator. Aside from Paul's addition of the explanatory particle *gar* and omission of the final clause ("Or who instructed him?"), his wording corresponds to that of the septuagintal rendering. Isaiah 40:13 LXX eliminates the play upon the prior rhetorical questions concerning the measure of the waters, the heavens, and the earth found in the Hebrew text. It also interprets *rûaḥ* ("spirit") here as *nous*, "mind" ("Who has measured the Spirit of the Lord, and as his counselor instructed him?"). These rhetorical questions sharpen the doxological confession by introducing the context of contention between the Lord and all idolatry and unbelief. No one has known the mind of the Lord or has been his counselor. As Creator, he acts alone and uniquely (Isa. 40:18). Therefore, his judgments and ways are inscrutable. The human attempt to reduce the ways of God to knowledge that we can manage and comprehend is a violation of God's right as Creator.

The third and final pair of clauses, "Or who gave to him in advance, and he shall repay him?" closely correspond to *Tg. Job* 41:3, which asks, "Who has preceded me in the works of creation, that I must repay (him)?" (for a lengthy citation from *Pesiq. Rab.* 75a, which reflects a similar rendering of Job 41:3, see Str-B 3:295). It may have been that there was a septuagintal version that approximated the reading found in the Targum.

These final rhetorical questions further sharpen the doxology because they again introduce the context of contention between God and fallen humanity. The attempt to domesticate God by reducing his ways to human ways turns out to be the attempt to make him indebted to reward us for our works. If in the former citation there was a warning not to imagine ourselves to be clever, here there is an implicit warning against imagining that our works gain us any privilege with God. The Creator retains the freedom of his mercy and cannot be bound to a mere distributive justice. Our salvation rests in our coming to see God as our Creator in Christ.

The final note of the doxology is a confession of God as the Creator who is active in the world and will yet triumph in it: "For from him and through him and unto him are all things." This is no deistic confession. God appears here as the one who presently sustains all things and guides them to himself and his saving ends (cf. 8:28). Paul employs a similar confession that includes Christ in the divine identity in 1 Cor. 8:6. A similar confession appears in Aristob. 4:5. The language, if isolated from its context, bears a certain proximity to Stoicism, but here it clearly serves to underscore the distinction between Creator and creation (see *NW* 3.1:313–16).

"To him be the glory forever! Amen." The apostle voices the praise of the Creator to whom fallen humanity has refused to yield. With this high note of praise, the body of the letter comes to a conclusion.

The Closing of the Letter: Apostolic Exhortation for the Church at Rome (12:1–16:27)

Call to Life under the Gospel (12:1–15:13)

12:1–2

The opening exhortation stands as a head and summary of Paul's subsequent exhortation to the church at Rome. It takes up the whole of his exposition of the gospel (1:16–8:39) and especially his description of the outworking of the promise of Israel's salvation (9:1–11:36). The call to present our bodies to God as a sacrifice flows out of the Creator's right over us (cf. 9:20–21) and constitutes a reversal of God's judgment on our idolatry (1:24). The exhortation takes up the concrete references to the bodily members that Paul draws from Scripture (3:13–15; 10:6–15; see also 6:12–14, 19). In this context, despite the broad significance of the term *thysia* (which despite its undoubtedly Jewish orientation here would have Hellenistic associations as well), the apostle's appeal that we present our bodies as a "sacrifice" especially recalls sacrifices of thanksgiving (e.g., Lev. 1:1–2:16; Ps. 27:6; 50:14, 23; 96:8; 107:22; 116:17). This sacrifice is not the surrender to God of that which by rights is ours; rather, it is the yielding of the whole of our bodily life in thanksgiving to our Creator, who not only has made us and formed us but also has given himself for us and to us in Christ (see esp. 8:32). This sacrifice is the mere opening of our life to the embrace of God's love in Christ. The concept of surrender of bodily life as a sacrifice, which transcends and supplants any offering of grain or animals, has its roots in the prophets and psalms (see, e.g., Ps. 40:6–8).

12:3–21

Paul now spells out the details of the surrender of our bodily life to God, first of all and particularly within the community of believers, the body of Christ (12:5). The individual reality has its corporate counterpart. The call to refrain from evil and cling to the good (12:9) recalls Amos 5:15; Ps. 37:27 (see also Ps. 97:10; 101; Prov. 3:7). The pattern of obedience remains the same. The exhortation to "rejoice with those who rejoice" (12:15) has a parallel in Sir. 7:34 ("Do not neglect those who weep, and mourn with those who mourn"). The admonition not to be wise in one's own eyes clearly echoes Prov. 3:7 (see also Isa. 5:21).

At the conclusion of these exhortations Paul's attention turns to the relationship of the believing community with outsiders. Christians are to bless those who persecute them, "bless and do not curse" (12:14). As far as possible, we are to be at peace with all people (12:18). Yet such peace is not always possible, as Paul implicitly assumes in his following exhortation: we are not to take vengeance, but rather to leave room "for the wrath of God" (cf. *Apoc. Sedr.* 7:9–10; 1 Thess. 5:15; 1 Pet. 3:9).

Paul couples two explanatory citations of Scripture to this final exhortation, bringing the unit of thought to an emphatic conclusion.

He draws the first citation from the Song of Moses, again applying it to the community of believing Jews and Gentiles (see 10:19; Deut. 32:21). In this case he not only introduces the quotation with a citation formula ("for it is written") but also appends a common biblical pronouncement formula to the biblical text ("says the Lord") (see also 14:11): "For it is written, 'Vengeance is mine, I shall repay,' says the Lord" (12:19 [Deut. 32:35]). Aside from the appended pronouncement formula, Paul's citation corresponds closely to the MT (*lî nāqām wĕšillēm*). As is the case with both the LXX and the Targumim, Paul renders the *hapax legomenon šillēm* as a verb. The septuagintal reading, interpretively drawing on the context, varies from the MT and Paul ("In the day of vengeance I will repay"). It is possible that Paul depends on a septuagintal tradition that stood closer to the Hebrew, but definite evidence is lacking (see, however, Heb. 10:30). His rendering stands quite close to that of *Targum Yerushalmi II* (see Str-B 3:300).

As the citation of Deut. 32:35 in Heb. 10:25 suggests, this passage expressed the expectation of final judgment and retribution from God (*Midr. Esther* 1:6 [23]; 1QS X, 15–20; CD-B XIX, 20–35). Thus the Qumran writer vows not to enter into contention with "the men of the pit" until the day of vengeance (1QS X, 19). Here there is a marked difference from Paul. The rabbinic traditions, like Paul, much more fully recognize the scriptural injunction (as it appears in various texts) to leave judgment to God alone (see Str-B 3:300–301; see also *2 En.* 50:2–4; *T. Gad* 6:7; *Jos. Asen.* 23:9; 28:14).

The text in Deuteronomy that Paul cites appears within the Song of Moses at the point at which the Lord has turned from announcing the judgment that he will bring on Israel (32:1–30) to the recompense that he will bring upon the Gentile nation that he has used as a tool to punish his people (32:31–38). Paul again applies the Song of Moses to the eschatological community of believing Jews and Gentiles. Yet they appear here not as the nation that provokes Israel's jealousy (Rom. 10:19; Deut. 32:21), but rather as the people of God. Paul appeals to biblical texts according to the pattern of God's dealings, not in a systematic fashion. As was the case for Israel in the past, the eschatological people of God must rely on the Lord himself to take vengeance. They are not to usurp God's role as judge by taking matters into their own hands (see Rom. 2:1; 14:1–13).

Paul introduces his second citation in 12:20 with an adversative, so that it stands in parallel with his opening admonition:

> Do not avenge yourselves, beloved,
> but give place to wrath. . . .
> [explanatory citation of Deut. 32:35]
> but should your enemy hunger . . .
> (12:19–20)

Loving action toward the enemy is thus the complement of leaving vengeance to the Lord and the alternative to taking vengeance oneself. Paul calls not for mere passivity, but rather for active love of those who harm us.

Paul does not employ any introductory formula with this second citation. His addition of the biblical pronouncement "says the Lord" in 12:19 provides a sufficient transition to the following citation. He now cites Prov. 25:21–22, varying only slightly from the LXX, which drops the Hebrew reference to the objects of food and drink ("feed him bread"; "give him water to drink"). Paul uses a different verb to describe the act of feeding (*psōmizō*) than does the LXX (*trephō*). The change may be significant: *psōmizō* describes the act of feeding as an act of giving:

> If your enemy should hunger, feed him.
> If he thirsts, give drink to him.
> For if you do this, you shall pile burning
>   coals on his head. (12:20)

Paul noticeably omits the concluding line of the proverb, "and the LORD shall repay you." He already has dealt with the question of recompense in the preceding verse. His attention has now shifted to the call to love one's enemies.

The final part of the biblical proverb, which draws on Egyptian texts and imagery, may be interpreted either as effecting shame and repentance in the opponent or as furthering their condemnation (see Cranfield 1975–1979: 648–50). Rabbinic interpretation recognized that both outcomes were possible, expressing them by the alternative reading of the final clause (which Paul omits). Instead of "he shall repay you" (*yĕšallem lāk*), one may read "he [the enemy] shall be made at peace

with you" (*yašlimēnû lāk* [*b. Sukkah* 52a; see also *b. Meg.* 15b; so also *Targum of the Writings*; see Str-B 3:302–3]). The tradition of giving to the enemy appears also in *T. Job* 7:1–13.

It is altogether likely that Paul plays upon both meanings of the proverb. He has allowed for divine vengeance in his citation of Deut. 32:35. Now he underscores the hope of bringing enemies to repentance by doing nothing but good to them. He already has exhorted his readers, in emphatic form, to bless those who persecute them (12:14). His closing admonition, drawn from the proverb, restates this purpose: "Do not be conquered by evil, but conquer evil with the good" (similar exhortations appear in *T. Benj.* 4:3; *T. Jos.* 18:2; *T. Iss.* 7:6; *T. Zeb.* 7:2–4; see Piper 1979a: 35–49). Subtly, but unmistakably, Paul reminds his readers of the work of God in Christ by which they have been conquered by the good (see 5:6–8; 8:37). They are now to do the same.

13:1–7

Paul here emphatically underscores the eschatological nature of the gospel (12:1–2; 13:11–14). Faith in this gospel brings with it rejection and persecution from the fallen world, which remains in rebellion against its Creator (12:14, 18–21; cf. 5:1–11; 8:17–39). Paul's affirmation that God has ordained earthly government is to be understood in this context; otherwise, his readers might falsely understand the gospel to enjoin the rejection of all secular authority, potentially leading to rebellion or sedition. Within this limiting context the instruction is straightforward. Everyone is to be subject to the governing authorities, since there is no authority except from God. The one who resists such authority resists God (13:1–2). The injunction has deep roots in biblical thought and early Judaism, not least in the Jeremianic injunction to the Judean exiles to "seek the welfare of the city" where the Lord had sent them (Jer. 29:1–23). The narrative of Daniel, which likewise reflects an exilic setting, describes how Nebuchadnezzar had to learn that the Lord gives sovereignty over the "kingdom of human beings" to whomever he wills. Belshazzar, his son, failed to grasp the lesson, to his own loss (Dan. 4:25, 32; 5:21, 22–28). In both of these examples the temporal limits that the Lord places on all earthly government inform the confession of his sovereignty (see also Sir. 10:4–5; *2 Bar.* 82:9). Broad streams of early Judaism understood that rulers were appointed by God (cf., e.g., Wis. 6:1–11; *b. Ber.* 58a; see further Str-B 3:303–5). Early Jewish thought also understood that these rulers also are held accountable by God (Wis. 6:5–8).

13:8–14

This concluding exhortation is a counterpart to Paul's opening call to yield our bodily life to God in response to his mercies toward us. Faith and love toward God have their necessary complement in love toward our neighbor. Just as in the opening exhortation Paul speaks of the fulfillment of Israel's sacrifices through the life of the eschaton, so in his closing exhortation he describes the fulfillment of the duties toward our neighbor that the law requires of us.

Paul explains the unending duty of love toward one another in reference to the law, which here, as elsewhere in Romans, bears universal validity, despite its having been given to Israel (cf. 2:12–16, 25–29; 5:20–21; 7:7–25): "For the one who loves the other has fulfilled the law" (13:8b). Paul follows this explanation with a lengthy interpretive citation (13:9), followed by a summary conclusion that restates his opening explanation (13:10). His declaration that love is the fulfillment of the law is therefore clearly his fundamental point.

The language of the opening explanation is significant. The participle expresses the enduring obligation to love: it is the one who is here and now practicing love (*ho agapōn*) toward the "other" who has fulfilled the law. Paul furthermore sharpens or clarifies the significance of the biblical injunction: here he speaks not of the "neighbor," but rather of the "other," the one who is different from us, whom we are to love. His language thus anticipates his following admonitions concerning the strife between the "weak" and the "strong" (see 14:15). It is also significant that he takes up the language of "fulfillment" that he briefly introduced in 8:4. In that context he spoke of those who believe as passive recipients of the fulfillment of the law, effected in them by the presence of another, the Spirit of God (8:4–11). Here he uses the active voice: the one who is exercising love has fulfilled the law. This statement is clearly a counterpart to his earlier description of the one "by nature" uncircumcised, who completes (*teleō*) the law (2:27).

Paul unpacks his declaration concerning the fulfillment of the law by concrete reference to the law itself:

> For the [commandment] "Do not commit adultery, do not murder, do not steal, do not covet," and if there is any other commandment, (it) is summed up in this word, "You shall love your neighbor as yourself." (13:9)

This citation of the Decalogue corresponds to Exod. 20:13–15, 17a LXX as well as Deut. 5:17–19, 21a LXX, which likewise follow the Hebrew text quite closely: the differences between Exod. 20:17 and Deut. 5:21 do not come into view, given Paul's abbreviated quotation. The commandments appear in biblical order, unlike the Synoptic accounts of Jesus' recitation of the commandments (see below), beginning with the "second table of the law" (duties toward the neighbor). Paul omits the commandment of duty toward parents and the prohibition of false witness. These omissions, together with his abbreviated citation of the prohibition against coveting, undoubtedly reflect his concern with the more important and fundamental commandments.

According to the Synoptic accounts of his exchange with the rich young ruler, Jesus cites the prohibition of murder before the commandment to honor one's father and mother, probably, much like Paul, in order to emphasize the weightier commandments (Matt. 19:18–19; Mark 10:19; Luke 18:20). According to Matthew, Jesus concludes his citation with a summary reference to the commandment to love one's neighbor (Matt. 19:19 [Lev. 19:18]). The interpretive and ethical implications of this interpretation of the Decalogue stand quite close to Paul's thought (see Matt. 22:34–40; cf. Mark 12:28–34; Luke 10:25–28). The same joining of these texts appears with James, who regards the fulfilling of the commandment to love the neighbor as the presence of salvation ("you do well" [James 2:8]) and as the fulfillment of the law. None of the injunctions of the law may be transgressed: neither the prohibition of adultery nor the prohibition of murder, the implicit transgression of which James finds present already in coveting (James 2:8–11; 4:1–2).

Philo likewise singles out three prohibitions, "you shall not commit adultery, you shall not murder, you shall not steal" (*Decalogue* 36), attaching greater significance to them. The opening sentences of Pseudo-Phocylides contain a summary of the Decalogue in which the first table of the law is lacking, except for a final injunction to "firstly honor God, after this your parents." Duties toward parents appear last, as in the Synoptics. Like the early church fathers, Pseudo-Phocylides finds it necessary to elaborate and expand the commandments, obviously with a view to the practices of his Hellenistic environment (Ps.-Phoc. 3–8; see, e.g., already *Did.* 2, which adds yet further instruction in Christian duties toward the neighbor). The Decalogue as a whole appears in Pseudo-Philo, which provides explanatory elaborations (*L.A.B.* 11:1–13).

Paul's citation of the commandment to love one's neighbor likewise corresponds precisely to Lev. 19:18 LXX, which also follows the Hebrew text. Rabbinic Judaism recognized the fundamental importance of the commandment to love one's neighbor. Hillel's response to a Gentile who requested that he teach him the Torah while standing on one foot is perhaps the best-known appropriation of this text: "What is hateful to you, do not to your neighbor: that is the whole Torah, the rest is commentary; go and learn it" (*b. Sanh.* 31a; see also *m. 'Abot* 1:12). Aqiba regards this commandment as the great, all-encompassing commandment of the law (*Midr. Gen.* 24:7; *Sipre Lev.* 19:18). Both Hillel and the later Aqiba appear to have love for all human beings in view (*contra* Str-B 1:357–58; see also Str-B 1:907–8). Nevertheless, there were varying interpretations of the extent of the commandment, which in Lev. 19:34 broadens to include the proselyte. Does it then exclude non-Israelites or implicitly include them (see Str-B 1:353–68)? In the Qumran community the commandment quite clearly was interpreted in terms of the community alone: those outside were to be the objects of godly hatred (CD-A VI, 20–21; CD-B XIX, 18; 1QS I, 10). The restriction of love to the pious or like-minded also appears elsewhere (e.g., Tob. 4:14–17; Sir. 12:1–7).

Alongside the commandment to love God, Jesus likewise ascribed supreme importance to the commandment to love one's neighbor (Matt. 22:39; Mark 12:31; Luke 10:27). According to Matthew's witness, Jesus speaks of these two commandments as the interpretive key to the entire Scriptures: "The entire law and the prophets hang upon these two commandments" (Matt. 22:40). In Luke's account of a lawyer's question as to what he might do to inherit eternal life, Jesus' citation of these two commandments leads to the further question as to who might be counted as "neighbor." Jesus responds with the well-known parable of the Good Samaritan, touchingly and profoundly sweeping away all questions and debate as to the implications of the commandment (Luke 10:29–37).

As we have noted, Paul follows his declaration with an explanatory statement that takes up the language of 13:8: "Love works no evil to the neighbor; love therefore is the fulfillment of the law" (13:10). The apostle understands "love" as a present reality; here he speaks not of the one who loves, but rather of love itself as working (cf. Gal. 5:6). The same perspective is present in his description of Lev. 19:18 not as a "commandment" alongside the others, but rather as a "word" (13:9). As is the case elsewhere in Romans, "word" (*logos*) here signifies an effective utterance of God, which brings its own fulfillment (3:4; 9:6, 9, 28; see also Gal. 5:14). Paul's immediately following reminder of the dawning of the eschatological day and the new person given in Jesus Christ further establishes this reading of the text. The commandment to love the neighbor is a word that has become reality in Jesus Christ. Paul's claim that all the commandments are "summed up in this word" is therefore not merely a theological judgment that asserts the priority of love toward the neighbor and interprets this commandment as informing all the rest (although it is that). The "summing up" (*anakephalaioō* [13:9]) is eschatological and effective: love now has come to reality (cf. similar usage in Eph. 1:10). In this way Paul is decisively different from the later rabbis, who (nevertheless, rightly) saw this commandment as foundational.

In this context Paul interprets the law, or at least the second table of the law, as serving to prevent harm to the neighbor. All the "commandments" that he cites are prohibitions, of course. These other commandments serve the same purpose: his addition "if there is any other commandment" is a comprehensive assertion, which in its conditional form presses the hermeneutical implication on the readers. Any conceivable divine commandment is included within the scope of the apostolic declaration that the law serves to prevent harm to the neighbor. Paul speaks of the divine function of the law in other terms in Romans, particularly its role in effecting sin and divine wrath (4:15; 5:20; 7:7–25). His statement concerning the law here is thus simultaneously comprehensive and perspectival: the law has more than one function.

As we have noted, Paul in his opening reference speaks of the one who loves the "other" (13:8b). He thus implicitly includes the subsequent Levitical injunction to love the alien, the sojourner (*gēr*), as oneself within the commandment to love one's neighbor (Lev. 19:18, 34). In this respect he draws no distinction between those inside the community and those without: he stands, with Jesus, clearly on the universal side of the rabbinic interpretation of the text. His opening injunction bears the same sense: "Owe nothing to anyone, except…" (13:8a). Nevertheless, he speaks here in terms of the practice of love within the believing community: "Owe nothing… except to love one another" (13:8b). It may well be that he recognizes that Christians in Rome already face ostracism; his earlier call to bless persecutors and refrain from vengeance says as much (12:14, 19–21). To be practiced in its fullness, love requires the relationships that are present within the believing community. Furthermore, the limitation likely has a theological dimension. Paul conceives of love as the eschatological reality that now has dawned and continues into eternity: the unending obligation to love (13:1) finds its place on earth only in the community of faith.

Life Together as Jews and Gentiles (14:1–15:13)

The two subsections concerning love and life together are joined by the continuative *de*. The obligation to love takes a concrete form for the Roman Christians in the conflict between those "weak in faith" and those who "believe" (13:2) and thus are "strong" (15:1).

14:1–23

Paul begins with instruction (14:1–12). It is the apostle who characterizes the positions in the dispute, thereby indicating that the gospel supports the practice of those who eat meat and do not mark any day as special. The conflict almost certainly has to do with the avoidance of meat offered to idols and the observance of the Sabbath (see 14:14, where Paul's language reflects the distinction between "clean" and "unclean" foods [on which, see, e.g., Acts 10:14; 1 Macc. 1:63; 4 Macc. 7:6; Josephus, *Ant.* 11.346]). Circumcision is no longer a question. Here those who "believe" are predominant. In fact, Paul directs his opening admonition to them: "Receive the one who is weak in faith, not (entering into) the judging of reasoned views" (14:1). Conservative Jewish Christians are in the minority. The situation differs from that which Paul addresses in Galatians, as well as that in 1 Cor. 8–10, where Hellenistic believers have so intellectualized the confession of the one God that participation in idolatry seems permissible to them. In the Roman church neither the faith of the "strong" nor the practices of "the weak in faith" threaten to violate the gospel. Paul deals with this as an *adiaphoron*, or matter of indifference.

Yet in this *adiaphoron* the gospel is at stake. Christ's lordship comprehends and grasps the life of every believer decisively and completely (14:7–9). None of us lives or dies for ourself. If we live, we live for the Lord; if we die, we die for the Lord. Paul draws the conclusion: "So then, whether then we live or we die, we belong to the Lord" (14:7–8). Indeed, it was to this end that Christ himself entered into our flesh, died, and lived, "so that he might exercise lordship over the living and the dead." Not only Paul's certainty that the Lord will surely cause his own servant to "stand" in judgment (14:4) but also his description of Christ's death and resurrection make it clear that he conceives of Christ's lordship here as gift, not demand. The crucified and risen Christ rules in such a way that our sin, our death, our weakness, our errors have been defeated and overcome, whether we are counted among the "weak" or the "strong."

Against this background Paul takes up his opening admonition against judging one another, now setting aside the metaphor of the household and turning to the sphere of public life: "Why do you judge your brother? Or why do you despise your brother? For we shall all stand at the judgment seat of God" (14:10). As Paul already has made clear in the earlier part of the letter, his gospel does not exclude the judgment of believers, but rather includes it (2:1–11, 12–16). Now he appeals to Scripture to explain his affirmation ("for it is written"):

As I live, says the Lord, to me shall bow every knee, and every tongue shall confess God. (14:11)

Paul draws the substance of the oath from Isa. 45:23. In place, however, of the lengthy asseveration in Isa. 45:23, Paul substitutes a briefer introductory formula that appears elsewhere in Scripture, especially in the book of Ezekiel: "'As I live,' says the LORD" (e.g., Num. 14:28; Isa. 49:18; Jer. 22:24; Ezek. 5:11; 14:16, 18, 20; 16:48). This reflexive form pointedly appropriates the oath "As the LORD [Yahweh] lives" (e.g., Judg. 8:19; Ruth 3:13; 1 Sam. 14:39; Jer. 4:2). In most contexts the Lord's self-binding oath introduces a warning of coming judgment, whereas in Isa. 49:18 it introduces the promise of Zion's salvation. Since the oath that Paul cites is likewise inherently salvific, it is quite possible that the formula recalls this text.

Paul's citation of Isa. 45:23 corresponds verbatim to that of the LXX, aside from the transposition of the verb in the second clause after the subject (*pasa glōssa*), so that it appears just prior to its object (*exomologēsetai tō theō*). Both Paul and the LXX disrupt the Hebrew *parallelismus membrorum* slightly in the second clause by (1) adding the coordinating conjunction *kai* ("and"); (2) supplying the object of the verb, which is left unexpressed in Hebrew because it appears at the outset of the first clause ("that to me shall bow every knee, shall swear every tongue"). Paul's transposition of the subject and verb bring him further out of line with the Hebrew word order. The Hebrew text also contains a parallelism that disappears in the LXX and with Paul: just as the Lord has sworn (*nišba'tî*) by himself, every tongue will swear (*tiššāba'*) to him. Usually to "swear to [*lĕ-*]" someone is to make a promise (e.g., Gen. 24:7; 26:3; Ps. 89:3, 49 [89:4, 50 MT]). Here, however, there is a dramatic reversal: the Lord is the one who has promised. Every knee and tongue responds by acknowledging that "righteousness and strength" are found in Yahweh alone (Isa. 45:24). The septuagintal rendering (*exomologēsetai*), which Paul takes up, stands quite close to the sense of the Hebrew text (on "confession," see commentary on Rom. 15:9 below).

As the content of the human response to the Lord indicates, the divine oath unquestionably bears salvific significance in its Isaianic context. The oath follows the Lord's call, "Turn to me and be saved, all ends of the earth, for I am God, and there is no other!" (45:22). Moreover, the oath that the Lord swears by himself is "righteousness which has gone forth from my mouth, a word, and it will not turn back" (45:23b). As is especially clear from the usage in the context, this "righteousness" is salvific, effecting right order in the creation (45:8, 19, 24; 46:13). The "word" that goes forth and does not turn back is the Lord's effective, saving word—that is, the Lord's promise (45:21; 46:10; 55:10–11). Likewise, as we have seen, the response of every knee and every tongue is the confession that salvation is found in Yahweh alone.

Yet the salvific cast of the Isaianic passage is not unequivocal: "Those who were angry with Yahweh shall come unto him and be put to shame" (45:24c). In contrast, "In Yahweh they shall be vindicated, and shall rejoice all the seed of Israel" (45:25). As is the case elsewhere in the Hebrew Scriptures, here in Isaiah both salvation and judgment are announced for the nations, without final resolution of their relation to one another.

Nevertheless, the note of salvation clearly is primary. The salvific implications of the Isaianic text come to expression in Paul's use of it. He has already affirmed, without qualification, that the one who belongs to the Lord will "stand" because the Lord will cause that one to stand (14:4). Life and death "to the Lord" are the certain expression of his saving death and risen life (14:8–9). Given his usage in context and his substitution of the oath formula, the naming of "the Lord" (*kyrios*) in the citation implicitly identifies Christ with Yahweh. The "Lord" who lives and swears by himself is Christ who died and lives (14:9, 11). The same identification appears in Phil. 2:9–11. In Romans, moreover, the "confession of God" is the saving confession of Jesus as Lord (10:9–10; again, see Phil. 2:9–11). The risen Christ likewise, according to Paul's citation of Ps. 18:49 (17:50 LXX), confesses God among the nations for their salvation (15:9). The God before whom we shall appear is the crucified and risen Lord (cf. 2:16).

Before this one who lives for us we will bend the knee and submit ourselves. The question that Paul implicitly puts to the Roman church is concrete: You who judge your brother, do you not know that you will appear before the judgment seat of this one of whom the Isaianic Scripture speaks, the one who has overcome our judgment? The self-accounting that each person will render to God will be based on nothing other than the gospel (14:12). Paul's concluding warning operates by the same criterion: "Everything that does not proceed from faith is sin" (14:23).

15:1–13

The extensive attention that the apostle devotes to the conflict in the Roman church is indicative of its fundamental theological significance. Paul first presents the Messiah as the pattern to whom believers are to be conformed (15:1–6). "We who are strong" ought to bear the weaknesses of those without strength and not please ourselves (15:1 [on "help in weakness," see Rom. 5:6; 8:3, 26; on "bearing" that of another, see Isa. 53:4–6, 11–12; Matt. 8:17; Gal. 6:2; Col. 3:12; Heb. 9:28; 1 Pet. 2:24]. Paul says that each of us is to please our neighbor (see 13:9), to further "the good" (i.e., the new life worked by the gospel [see 14:16]), for the purpose of edification. It is the Messiah who is our example in this matter. According to Paul, "He did not please himself," but rather, "just as it is written, 'The reproaches of those reproaching you fell upon me'" (15:3). One would have expected the apostle to speak of Christ's love toward human beings, but instead he strikingly speaks of the Messiah's devotion to God. More precisely, and significantly, it is the Messiah himself who speaks in Scripture, as he does again in 15:9–11.

Paul here cites Ps. 68:10 LXX, which does not deviate from Ps. 69:10b MT (69:9 ET). He has already used Ps. 68:23–24 LXX (69:23–24 MT; 69:22–23 ET), which he ascribes to David, to describe Israel's hardening and fall (see 11:9). The words of David concerning his adversaries in the past correspond to the divine judgment on Israel for its rejection of Christ in the present. The Messiah speaks in the words of the psalm, implicitly present in David. Now, in v. 3, the Messiah appears in the psalm directly addressing God. Paul's present appeal to Ps. 69 differs from Rom. 11:9 in another way as well. Whereas in the earlier cita-

tion the enemies of the psalmist anticipate Israel in its rejection of Christ (see discussion of 11:9–10 above), here it is unlikely that Paul has unbelieving Israel in view. On the contrary, it is much more likely that Paul sees in the opponents who appear in the psalm a pattern that will be repeated in the experience of Gentile believers (the "strong") who accept and bear their "weak" Jewish brothers and sisters in the faith. In associating themselves with believing Jews, they expose themselves to hostility from their pagan neighbors. In doing so, according to Paul, they will be following the pattern provided by the Messiah, who likewise bore the reproach directed against God. The hostility that the psalmist experiences comes from his own household and family (Ps. 69:6–8 [69:7–9 MT; 68:7–9 LXX]). Paul likewise may suggest that Gentile believers in Rome may have to experience what both the Messiah and David before him faced: rejection from those close to them.

The immediate context of Paul's citation is quite familiar (see John 2:17): "Zeal for your house has consumed me" (Ps. 69:9a [69:10a MT; 68:10a LXX]). It is just possible that Paul echoes something of this in the idea of the church as God's temple in his references to "building up" one another (14:19; 15:2; see also 15:20).

The larger context of Paul's citation also suggests a connection with the latter part of the chapter, where Paul cites a series of texts of Scripture in reference to the risen Messiah. The psalmist's lament turns finally to the hope of deliverance. He thus announces, "I will praise the name of God with song, and I will magnify him with thanksgiving" (Ps. 69:30 [69:31 MT; 68:31 LXX]). The suffering of Christ anticipates his deliverance. It is altogether likely that the first readers would have caught something of this echo, since in the following verse Paul speaks immediately of the hope that the Scriptures impart to us (15:4). His appeal to Scripture in this way makes sense only if he has in view the turning point in the psalm, which he expects that his readers will see as well.

The fundamental significance of the one church of believing Jews and Gentiles becomes apparent in the following explanation, which again reveals much of the apostle's hermeneutic:

For whatever was written beforehand [*proegraphē*] was written for our instruction, in order that through perseverance and through the comfort of Scripture we might have hope. (15:4)

The statement is a counterpart to Paul's opening description of the gospel, where he also employs a *pro-* compound: the gospel, which God promised beforehand through his prophets in Scripture (1:1b–2). The reference to the past and present of Scripture recurs once more in the closing words of the letter (16:25–27). In the opening verses of the letter Paul makes a statement about the gospel, which here he extends to the purpose and nature of Scripture as a whole. All that has been "written in advance" about the inbreaking of the eschaton has been written for our instruction; even the words of the Davidic psalm speak to believers now, including Gentile readers. This instruction is something larger and greater than mere knowledge. The Scripture has been written in order to impart hope, which does not signify mere intellectual imagination or apprehension: we possess hope "through perseverance and the comfort of Scripture." Paul has already indicated that hope is possessed through perseverance, not in the sense that hope is a result of our own endurance, but rather that through perseverance we come to possess more fully the hope that was already ours (5:1–5; 8:25; see also 2:7; 12:12). The inclusion of "perseverance" within our instruction signals that the passage of time and the endurance of trial are essential to "instruction," which consequently obviously belongs to the sphere of wisdom, not mere knowledge. Paul carefully distinguishes the work of Scripture from the passage of time, repeating the preposition and definite article in order to separate the two ideas: through perseverance and through the comfort of Scripture we have hope (cf. 1 Macc. 12:9). The term *paraklēsis* bears the broad sense of "encouragement," which according to context may signify either "exhortation" or "comfort." Although Paul sometimes uses the verb *parakaleō* in the former sense, his use of the noun in almost every instance clearly signifies the latter sense (e.g., 2 Cor. 1:3–7; 7:4–13; cf. Ps. 119:50), which is to be preferred here not only for this reason but also because of the distinction that Paul has drawn between the work of Scripture and perseverance. The Scriptures impart to us comfort in the midst of our trials so that we might have hope. That is the function and purpose of Scripture, according to the apostle. Again the

direction of Paul's thought indicates that in his citation of Ps. 69:9b (69:10b MT; 68:10b LXX) he has in view the larger context of the psalm: the final vindication implicitly experienced by Christ himself. That vindication is our comfort and hope.

In the second movement of this unit (15:7–13) the apostle presents the risen Christ as the servant of the circumcision who in this very role has become the source of mercy and hope for the nations. The triumph of the Christ that Paul intimates in 15:3 now becomes the central theme of the passage. In his triumph the Messiah brings hope to Israel and the nations. This hope in God, of which the Messiah provides the pattern (15:3), brings with it love for the other, in which the Messiah again is our example: "Therefore welcome one another, just as the Messiah has welcomed you to the glory of God" (15:7). The reality of love is an essential dimension of glory that the believing community renders to "the God and father of Jesus Christ" (15:6). There is no true worship without love, and no true love without worship. Both are given by the hope found in the Messiah.

Paul explains his opening exhortation (15:7) by announcing afresh the service of the Messiah, which effects the reality of hope among Jews and Gentiles: "For, I say, the Christ has become a servant . . ." (15:8–12). The syntactical structure of the explanation in 15:8–9 is unexpected, providing some difficulties in interpretation:

(15:8)
Christ has become a servant
(a) of (the) circumcision for the sake of the truth of God,
(b) in order to establish the promises belonging to the fathers;
(15:9)
(a′) and (has become a servant of [the] circumcision) with respect to the Gentiles for the sake of mercy,
(b′) in order to glorify God.

It is preferable to take 15:9 as a continuation of indirect discourse, in which Christ is the subject of the purpose clause, not the Gentiles (i.e., Christ serves with respect to the Gentiles, for the sake of mercy so as to glorify God). If 15:9a expressed its own subject, the syntax would suggest that the subject is God—an impossibility. The parallelism of the prepositional phrases ("for the sake of the truth of God . . . for the sake of mercy") likewise suggests that 15:8 and 15:9a are to be read in parallel. More significantly, it is the Messiah who is the agent of divine glory in 15:7. Paul explains this thought in 15:8–12. It is the Messiah who is the implicit speaker in the following citation in 15:9, not the Gentiles (see Wagner 2002: 307–15). Indeed, he announces that he will speak to them: "I will confess you among the Gentiles." Of course, in the following citations the Gentiles are called upon to praise God (15:10–11), but the first citation is the primary substantiation of 15:9a and cannot rightly be set aside. To read "the Gentiles" as the subject of this clause is to ignore the opening words of the following citation, "on account of this . . . ," which implicitly speak of the deliverance of the Lord's anointed (see below).

The shift from the genitive ("[servant] of the Gentiles") to the accusative is somewhat unexpected. Yet the accusative surely is to be read as an accusative of respect, so that no real break in the grammar appears. In this way Paul avoids the otherwise confusing sequence "the promises of the fathers and of the Gentiles." He makes a significant theological statement as well. As the servant of the circumcision, the Messiah also acts with respect to the Gentiles—that is, for their benefit. Perhaps there are faint echoes here of the Isaianic Servant Songs, in which the Servant's mission to Israel becomes salvation for the nations (Isa. 42:1–4; 49:1–6; 52:13–53:12). The gospel remains "for the Jew first, and also for the Greek" (Rom. 1:16).

Paul derives his understanding of the mission of the Messiah from Scripture. He follows his explanation in 15:8–9a with a lengthy chain citation (15:9b–12) in which he again treats the Scripture typologically. As in 15:3, it is the Messiah who speaks in the text. He is the subject of the verbs of speaking in the citation of Ps. 17:50 LXX (18:50 MT; 18:49 ET) in 15:9, so that it is natural to understand Paul as attributing the words of the two following citations to him ("and again he says" [15:10]; "and again" [15:11]) before he finally turns to the testimony of Isaiah concerning "the root of Jesse" ("and again Isaiah says" [15:12]).

Paul probably draws his first citation from Ps. 17:50 LXX (18:50 MT; 18:49 ET), which has a close parallel in 2 Sam. 22:50. The entire psalm appears in nearly the same wording in Ps. 18:2–50 (17:2–51 LXX) and 2 Sam. 22:3–51. The wording in Romans stands just a bit closer to Ps. 17:50 LXX than to 2 Sam. 22:50 LXX, where David announces, "I will sing praises *in* your name." Yet in 2 Samuel "the last words of David, the son of Jesse" follow the psalm, which describe David as the ("faithful" [LXX]) man whom the Lord "raised up" (*anestēsen*), the language of which anticipates Paul's following citation of Isa. 11:10 in 15:12. Even if Paul is citing Ps. 17:50 LXX, the context of 2 Samuel resonates in the background.

It is likely that Paul intentionally omits the address "Lord" (YHWH; *kyrios*), which appears at the end of the first clause in the psalm ("I will confess you among the nations, LORD"). Often in Romans, as we have seen, Paul employs the title "Lord" in reference to Jesus in such a way that he is included in the divine identity. That is likely the case in the following citation of Ps. 116:1 LXX (117:1 MT/ET) in 15:11, which calls on all nations to praise "the Lord." But here Paul has in view the confession of God's name by the risen Christ himself. His omission of the appellation from his citation brings clarity to his use of it.

The expression "to confess" (*exomologeō*), which Paul uses along with the LXX, signifies the "praise" of God, but here, as always, it represents a response to him, as is the case with the Hebrew term that it translates (the Hiphil stem of *yādâ*). Often in Scripture such a response is voiced before others, frequently in the context of blessings or deliverance that God has granted, as is the case in our text. This "confession" thus frequently signifies an acknowledgment of the Lord in thanksgiving. It comes very close to the broader usage of the same stem (homologeia), which may more simply denote the "confession" or acknowledgment of God. The verb may well have carried an archaic, biblical overtone, since in the later Hellenistic period diction had shifted to the more individualistic expression "give thanks" (*eucharistō*).

Paul obviously intends that his readers recall the larger context of Ps. 18, since he includes the opening causal clause ("on account of this . . ."), the antecedent of which stands in the psalm. That context is one of thanksgiving. In Ps. 18 David, who is named in 2 Sam. 22:1 and in the heading of the psalm, gives praise to Yahweh for deliverance from his enemies, who threatened him with death (18:1–5). In a dramatic intervention the Lord delivered him from death itself because of his righteousness (18:6–24). As a result, David pursued his enemies and destroyed them (18:31–42). The Lord made him the head of nations, which then came to serve him. God granted him vengeance and by divine pronouncement placed peoples under his rule (18:46–48). "On account of this," David praises the Lord among the nations and sings praise to his name (18:49 [17:50 LXX]). In Paul's citation the risen Christ implicitly stands in the place of David. The nations that opposed this Christ (see 3:9–18) have been defeated in his resurrection; they enter into his saving lordship as conquered enemies (see 1:5). According to Paul's citation, then, the risen Messiah confesses and praises the divine name among the Gentiles, bringing them salvation. Behind and before the single mouth by which believing Jews and Gentiles glorify God (15:6) is the mouth of the Messiah, who makes known the name of God to them (15:9).

The Messiah also speaks in the Song of Moses ("and again he says" [15:10]). Paul draws the second citation in the series from Deut. 32:43 LXX. The text of the MT is rather difficult. As it stands, it reads, "Rejoice, nations, his people." Textual difficulties must have arisen rather early, since a Qumran fragment of Deuteronomy here reads, "Praise, heavens, his people" (*1QDeuteronomy^b*). *Targum Onqelos* likewise shifts to "Praise, Gentiles, his people." The LXX plausibly presupposes a haplography, by which *'im* ("with") has been omitted, and supplies it to the text. Paul, in any case, follows the septuagintal reading: "Rejoice, Gentiles, with his people."

The Deuteronomic context is remarkably similar to that of Ps. 18:50. The Lord will take vengeance on his enemies, making his "arrows drunk with blood" (32:34–42). The call for the nations to rejoice is sandwiched between announcements of their coming destruction (32:42–43). The Lord brings this recompense on the very nations that he has used to judge his people. In 10:19 Paul cited an earlier verse from the Song of Moses in which the Lord warns that he will provoke his people to jealousy by a nation without understanding (32:21). Before the Lord judges the nations, he judges his own people (32:19–33). Thus both the nations and his people are to know this:

> Behold, behold that I am and there is no god but me.
> I put to death and I make alive.
> I smite and I heal, and there is no one who can deliver from my hand. (Deut. 32:39)

The Song of Moses is a mirror of the Isaianic "Book of Consolation" (Isa. 40–55), in which Israel and the nations are to learn this lesson. Salvation follows judgment (see Isa. 45:7). Paul cites the single statement in the Song of Moses that holds out the hope of salvation for the Gentiles: there is salvation for them, too, in the salvation of God's people. This promise of salvation, spoken by Moses in the narrative of the Song, is now spoken to the Gentiles by the risen Christ. Judgment has been passed. The Messiah now invites them to salvation.

In confessing God and singing praises to God's name among the Gentiles (15:9) and inviting them to salvation (15:10), the Messiah also calls them to join in his song of praise (15:11). Paul draws the third citation in the chain from Ps. 117:1 (116:1 LXX). His wording corresponds closely to that of the LXX, which follows the MT. The only variations in Paul's citation (which may well be intentional) are the transposition of the name "Lord" to the end of the first clause and the (probably related) addition of the conjunction *kai* ("and") to the beginning of the second clause. The apostle joins the citation to the preceding one simply, using the elliptical "and again (he says)." The words once more are those of the Messiah, according to Paul:

> Praise the Lord, all Gentiles.
> And let all the people praise him. (15:11)

The psalm goes on to provide the reason and ground for the praise for which it calls. The LXX here announces the "strength of the mercy [MT: *ḥesed*] of the Lord," and that the "truth [MT: *ĕmet*] of the Lord" abides forever. The psalm itself has universal scope: the Lord's saving mercy and enduring faithfulness embrace the nations. The Messiah's call to the Gentiles implicitly rests on this message.

The second clause of the psalm speaks of "all peoples" praising God. Paul most likely intends it as a counterpart to 15:10, which speaks of the Gentiles rejoicing with "his people." All the peoples now appear within the scope of God's saving care alongside his own people, Israel.

Paul's transposed reference to the "Lord" in the final position receives emphasis, recalling the Messiah's song of praise to God's name in 15:9. The identity and name of God, whom the Gentiles are to praise, is fundamental, just as they must know the name of the Lord in order to call on him (see 10:11–17). The identification of Christ with God in the name of the "Lord," which is usual in the latter part of Romans, is perhaps diminished here somewhat, since it is the Messiah himself who calls the Gentiles to praise "the Lord." Yet it is likely not entirely absent, since in the following citation the Messiah himself appears as the hope of the nations.

Paul draws the final citation from the book of Isaiah and attributes it to him: "And again Isaiah says. . . ." The form of the introduction naturally changes, since the Messiah is now the subject of the announcement:

> There shall be a root of Jesse and one who
> arises to rule the Gentiles.
> Upon him the Gentiles shall hope. (15:12
> [Isa. 11:10])

Paul's citation follows the LXX closely. He omits only the opening temporal reference "in that day," which links the prophecy to the promised time of salvation—for Paul, that time has arrived (see Isa. 11:1–9). Along with the LXX, Paul concentrates the passage upon the root of Jesse, rendering the MT participle 'ōmēd ("one standing") as a Greek participle, *anistamenos*: there will be one who arises. Both the LXX and Paul obscure the semantic distinction between 'ammîm ("peoples") in the first clause and *gôyim* ("pagan nations") in the second clause: in both instances the Gentiles are in view. The work of the "root of Jesse" appears differently in the LXX: he arises not as a standard or a signal pole, but rather to rule the nations. This alteration of the text probably represents a messianic interpretation that plays upon the similarity between *nēs* ("standard") and *nāsîk* or *nāśî'* ("prince, ruler") (Wagner 2002: 322). The LXX interprets the "staff" in terms of the righteous rule of this new David, who will rule the nations also. The peoples' "seeking" of the root of Jesse becomes their "hoping upon him." Paul takes up this interpretation of the text.

The verse represents the promise of restoration after judgment. The well-known opening verse of Isa. 11 describes a "shoot" arising from the stump of Jesse and a branch from his roots. Although the entire line of David will be removed by the judgment of the Lord, the Lord will begin afresh and create a new David out of the "stump of Jesse," which will be left behind. Unlike the prior line of David who preceded him, he will judge righteously, defending the poor and needy (11:2–5). This time of salvation will bring the restoration of Eden on earth (11:6–9). The remnant of Israel will be restored from the nations (11:11–16). Even before this final promise, the Lord announces that the nations will seek this new "root of Jesse." According to the MT, he stands as a standard (*nēs*) for the nations.

Various early Jewish texts in some measure echo the promise of the Messiah found in this verse and its context, although there is surprisingly little, if any, citation of it aside from rabbinic literature (see Wagner 2002: 317–23). *Psalms of Solomon* 17:21–46 probably reflects the text most fully, but even so, only allusively. *Genesis Rabbah* 97 cites Isa. 11:10 as confirmation that the Messiah will come from the tribe of Judah (see Gen. 49:8). Proceeding from Gen. 49:10 ("The scepter will not depart from Judah"), both *Midr. Ps.* 21:1 and *Gen. Rab.* 98:9 cite Isa. 11:10 to affirm the hope that the Gentiles will seek the Messiah. Yet even here they find a distinction between Israel and the nations. The Gentiles must be instructed by the Messiah, who will give them thirty precepts. Israel will be taught directly by God (Isa. 54:13). *Genesis Rabbah* 99:8 stresses that the Messiah will enforce obedience from the Gentiles. As is typical of the Qumran writings, 4Q161 8–10 III, 18–25 interprets Isa. 11:10 to speak of the Messiah "ruling" (cf. the LXX) all the Gentiles (*gôyim*) and Magog (see Ezek. 38:2; 39:6). His sword will judge all peoples. Here the Gentiles appear as the enemies of the Lord and his people: the Messiah rules by the sword.

Paul, too, understands the text to speak of the Messiah, the new David, who has arisen to rule over the Gentiles. Yet Jesus rules not by the sword, but rather by his resurrection from the dead (see 1:1–7). The nations enter into the salvation that he brings as they place their hope in him. It is in this way that they submit to him. Paul's mission of effecting the "obedience of faith" (1:5; 15:18; 16:26) is embedded within this citation. His apostolic "priestly service" [*hierourgeō* [15:16–18; cf. 1:9]), by which the Gentiles are reclaimed, is thus an echo of the Messiah's "service" (*diakonos* [15:8]).

15:14–33

The gospel impels the apostle to proclaim Christ where Christ has not been named (15:20). As in the opening, Paul is here explaining to the church in Rome why he has not yet visited them (1:13–15). He has made the same point in his earlier defense of the apostolic mission to the Gentiles: "How shall they call upon him [i.e., with 'the name of the Lord'] in whom they have not believed?" (10:14 [see 10:11–13]). The apostle does not want to "build upon the foundation of another" (15:20b). Here, as elsewhere in Paul's letters, the language of building suggests "temple" imagery: the eschatological temple of the Lord is being constructed out of human beings, Jews and Gentiles, among whom God himself now dwells (e.g., 1 Cor. 3:10–17; 2 Cor. 6:14–18). Those who believe are not merely offerings; they are also, individually and corporately, God's temple. Paul also conceives of the individual churches as instantiations of the temple of God; he thus will not build on the foundation that another has laid (cf. 2 Cor. 10:12–18).

Paul again finds the apostolic mission within Scripture, now expressly in its anticipatory announcements concerning the Christ. His aim corresponds to the witness of Scripture ("but, just as it has been written"):

> (To those) to whom it was not announced
> concerning him, they shall see.
> And those who have not heard, they shall
> understand. (15:21 [Isa. 52:15c–d LXX])

Paul's citation corresponds to the LXX, which shifts the MT *sūppar* ("to be recounted") to *anēngelē* ("to be announced"). As a result, the focus rests on the decisive newness of the Lord's saving action rather than on a rehearsal of his dealings, especially his announcing and fulfilling his promises (see, e.g., Isa. 43:21). But this change is minor.

This second appeal by Paul to this Servant Song as the basis for apostolic mission is a mirror image of his first one in 10:16, which he draws from the following verse in Isaiah (Isa. 53:1). His point in 10:16 is that Isaiah, too, announced the proclamation of good news that calls for faith and, like the apostle, encountered unbelief within Israel. That emphasis is now inverted. According to Isaiah, the "nations" and "kings" who have not heard Yahweh's word will now see in amazement its fulfillment in the exaltation of his Suffering Servant (52:13–15). The reference to the Servant's "sprinkling" (*yazzeh*) the nations suggests a salvific, cultic action. Likewise, the shutting of the mouths of the kings implies that they have been silenced in their contention with the Lord (52:15a–b [see, e.g., 45:20–25; cf. Rom. 3:19]). Paul obviously sees the salvific implications of the text: those who heard no announcement concerning Christ (*peri autou*) now see; those who did not hear now understand. Along with the other NT witnesses, Paul identifies the Isaianic Suffering Servant with Christ. His interest here obviously rests on the message of Isaiah: the nations that did not hear will enter into the salvation that the Servant brings. It is this announcement, in its depth and breadth, that drives his apostolic mission. All those who have not heard must yet see and understand: the understanding of Yahweh as creator of the nations, prominent in the book of Isaiah, operates in the background. Paul echoes here the theme of the Servant Songs: the Servant is to be a "light to the nations" (Isa. 42:6–9; 49:6–7; see Acts 13:47). The larger thematic complex of the promise of salvation for the nations that the Lord has made (e.g., Isa. 44:24; 45:12, 18), clearly informs Paul's thought. The pattern of salvation that appears in Isa. 52:15 is fulfilled in Christ.

Closing Greetings and Call to Guard against False Teaching (16:1–27)

COMMENDATION OF PHOEBE, THE LETTER CARRIER (16:1–2)

The greetings begin with a commendation of the letter carrier, Phoebe, who is both a deacon of the church in Cenchrea and a patron of Paul and of the church. Quite possibly she has business matters to attend to in Rome as well. Paul's words are intended to secure her reception by the church in Rome, to which she otherwise appears to have been unknown.

APOSTOLIC GREETINGS (16:3–16)

The lengthy list of greetings to members of the Roman house churches serves to show the extensive personal contacts that Paul already enjoys with Rome. Paul clearly intends to send the message that he knows and is concerned about many members of the church.

16:17–20

Paul's third and final exhortation is directed against external threats to the church. The church members are to be watchful and guard against those who bring divisions and things offensive to the teaching that they have already learned. Paul clearly has opportunism in view: he describes such persons as "serving their own belly" (i.e., they are out for personal gain) and deceiving the hearts of innocent persons through "pleasing speech and pleasant words." There is a broad circle of churches (where the threat will arise) that know of the obedience of the church at Rome (16:19a).

Paul again describes faith as obedience. Here he allusively sets it over against the serpent's temptation of Eve (cf. 2 Cor. 10:4–6; 11:1–4). He rejoices in the obedience of the believers in Rome, but he wants them "to be wise with respect to the good and pure with respect to evil." The wording clearly echoes Gen. 3:5: "You will be like God, knowing good and evil [*tôb wārā'*; LXX: *kalon kai ponēron*]." Paul's indication that he wants them to be wise in what is good but innocent in what is evil recalls Eve's contemplation: she saw that the tree was desirable to make one wise (Gen. 3:6). It likewise recalls Paul's opening description of idolatrous and fallen humanity (1:22). What they have learned stands in agreement with Paul's gospel. The corruption of this teaching is equivalent to Satan's temptation of Eve. Implicitly, then, the gospel reopens the gates of paradise and brings fallen human beings back to Eden itself. The corruption of the gospel is equivalent to the fall.

Paul's allusion to Genesis continues in his final promise to the Roman church: "The God of peace shall quickly crush Satan under your feet" (16:20). Now Paul takes up the promise that the seed of the woman will "bruise the head" of the serpent (Gen. 3:15). There is an eschatological overtone as well, since various biblical texts describe the Lord as having slain the serpent Leviathan in his work of creation. The image appears in the promise of a new creation, at which the Lord again will slay the serpent, as at the exodus (e.g., Ps. 74:14; Isa. 27:1; 51:9–11; see *T. Levi* 18:12). In establishing the *shalom* of the eschaton, the Lord will crush Satan under the feet of the Roman church. The threat and temptation presented by false teaching will end. Paul follows this promise with a closing grace-wish (16:20).

GREETINGS FROM PAUL'S COMPANIONS AND CO-WORKERS (16:21–23)

Paul's co-workers and companions express their greetings, including some whom he expressly names as his kinspeople; Tertius, his amanuensis; Gaius, his host; and Erastos, city treasurer of Corinth.

16:25–27

The doxology in 11:33–36 has in view the whole of the Creator's saving dealings with humanity. This final doxology, which also answers the guilty silence of idolatrous humanity (1:18–23), is focused upon the church in Rome itself:

> (16:25) To the one who has power to establish you,
>> according to my gospel and the proclamation of Jesus Christ,
>> according to the revelation of the mystery which for long ages was silent
> (16:26) but which now has been manifest
>> and which has been made known
>>> through the prophetic Scriptures, according to the order of the eternal God,
>> for the obedience of faith for all the Gentiles,
> (16:27) to the only wise God, through Jesus Christ,
>> to him be glory forever. Amen.

In this lengthy and complex description of the gospel Paul gives glory to God as the one who is able to "establish" the church at Rome (16:25a). The work of the apostle rests not in himself, but rather in God's power. This power of God is the message of Paul's gospel and the proclamation of Jesus Christ (16:25b; cf. 1:16). Not only is the salvation of Israel a mystery found in Scripture (11:25–27), but now also the gospel is described as a mystery. In contrast with the present proclamation of Jesus Christ, this mystery was silent for long ages (16:25d). Now it has been revealed and made manifest (16:25c, 26a [cf. 1:17; 3:21]). That which was present within Scripture is now revealed (see Bockmuehl 1990). By God's order it has been made known; Paul recalls here the freedom of the Creator to turn the course of human history as he will, including the opening and closing of Scripture (cf. 11:28–32). The eternal God (*aiōnios theos* [see Gen. 21:33; Isa. 40:28; Bar. 4:8; *1 En.* 1:3]) stands above the ages (*chronoi aiōnioi*) (16:25–26). The gospel is now proclaimed in order to effect the obedience of faith for all the Gentiles (cf. 11:30–32).

As Paul's earlier allusion to Gen. 3 implies, his giving glory "to the only wise God" is an expression of salvation received (see Ps.-Phoc. 54; Sir. 1:8). Paul's monotheism is intensely concrete, a confession of God as he reveals himself savingly in Jesus Christ. As a fallen yet redeemed human creature, he voices the praise that belongs to God alone. Precisely in his unexpected work of salvation through Jesus Christ, God has shown himself to be God, who alone is wise. "To him be glory forever! Amen." Of necessity, Paul's theology ends in doxology.

Bibliography

Albl, M. C. 1999. *"And Scripture Cannot Be Broken": The Form and Function of the Early Christian Testimonia Collections.* NovTSup 96. Leiden: Brill.

Avemarie, F. 1996. *Tora und Leben: Untersuchungen zur Heilsbedeutung der Tora in der frühen rabbinischen Literatur.* TSAJ 55. Tübingen: Mohr Siebeck.

Bailey, D. P. 1999. "Jesus as the Mercy Seat: The Semantics and Theology of Paul's Use of *Hilasterion* in Romans 3:25." PhD diss., Cambridge University.

Bauckham, R. 1998. *God Crucified: Monotheism and Christology in the New Testament.* Grand Rapids: Eerdmans.

Bell, R. H. 1994. *Provoked to Jealousy: The Origin and Purpose of the Jealousy Motif in Romans 9–11.* WUNT 2/63. Tübingen: Mohr Siebeck.

Berkley, T. 2000. *From a Broken Covenant to Circumcision of the Heart: Pauline Intertextual Exegesis in Romans 2:17–29.* SBLDS 175. Atlanta: Society of Biblical Literature.

Bockmuehl, M. N. A. 1990. *Revelation and Mystery in Ancient Judaism and Pauline Christianity.* WUNT 2/36. Tübingen: Mohr Siebeck.

Bonhoeffer, D. 1970. *Psalms: The Prayer Book of the Bible.* Minneapolis: Augsburg.

Bovati, P. 1994. *Re-establishing Justice: Legal Terms, Concepts and Procedures in the Hebrew Bible.* Translated by M. J. Smith. JSOTSup 105. Sheffield: JSOT Press.

Cathcart, K. J., and R. P. Gordon, trans. and eds. 1989. *The Targum of the Minor Prophets.* ArBib 14. Wilmington, DE: Glazier.

Collins, J. J. 1997. "The Background of the 'Son of God' Text." *BBR* 7: 51–62.

Cranfield, C. E. B. 1975–1979. *A Critical and Exegetical Commentary on the Epistle to the Romans.* 2 vols. ICC. Edinburgh: T&T Clark.

Davies, G. N. 1990. *Faith and Obedience in Romans: A Study in Romans 1–4.* JSNTSup 39. Sheffield: JSOT Press.

Davies, W. D. 1980. *Paul and Rabbinic Judaism: Some Rabbinic Elements in Pauline Theology.* Philadelphia: Fortress.

———. 1994. *The Gospel and the Land: Early Christianity and Jewish Territorial Doctrine.* BibSem 25. Sheffield: Sheffield Academic Press.

Ebner, M. 1991. *Leidenslisten und Apostelbrief: Untersuchungen zu Form, Motivik und Funktion der Peristasenkataloge bei Paulus.* FB 66. Würzburg: Echter.

Ego, B. 1996. "Abraham als Urbild der Torah Israels: Traditionsgeschichtliche Überlegungen zu einem Aspekt des biblischen Abrahambildes." Pages 25–40 in *Bund und Tora: Zur theologischen Begriffsgeschichte in alttestamentlicher, frühjüdischer und urchristlicher Tradition.* Edited by F. Avemarie and H. Lichtenberger. WUNT 92. Tübingen: Mohr Siebeck.

Fitzmyer, J. A. 1981. "Habakkuk 2:4 and the New Testament." Pages 236–46 in *To Advance the Gospel: New Testament Studies.* New York: Crossroad.

———. 1993. *Romans: A New Translation with Introduction and Commentary.* AB 33. New York: Doubleday.

———. 1995. "The Palestinian Background of 'Son of God' as a Title for Jesus." Pages 567–77 in *Texts and Contexts: Biblical Texts in Their Textual and Situational Contexts; Essays in Honor of Lars Hartman.* Edited by T. Fornberg and D. Hellholm. Oslo: Scandinavian University Press.

Garlington, D. 1991. *The Obedience of Faith: A Pauline Phrase in Historical Context.* WUNT 2/38. Tübingen: Mohr Siebeck.

———. 1994. *Faith, Obedience, and Perseverance: Aspects of Paul's Letter to the Romans.* WUNT 79. Tübingen: Mohr Siebeck.

Gathercole, S. 2002. *Where Is Boasting? Early Jewish Soteriology and Paul's Response in Romans 1–5.* Grand Rapids: Eerdmans.

Gese, H. 1981. *Essays on Biblical Theology.* Translated by K. Crim. Minneapolis: Augsburg.

Haak, R. D. 1992. *Habakkuk.* VTSup 44. Leiden: Brill.

Hays, R. 1985. "Have We Found Abraham to Be Our Forefather according to the Flesh?" *NovT* 27: 76–98.

———. 1989. *Echoes of Scripture in the Letters of Paul.* New Haven: Yale University Press.

———. 2000. "The Letter to the Galatians." Pages 183–348 in vol. 11 of *The New Interpreter's Bible.* Nashville: Abingdon.

Hengel, M. 1981. *Judaism and Hellenism: Studies in Their Encounter in Palestine during the Early Hellenistic Period.* Translated by J. Bowden. 2nd ed. Philadelphia: Fortress.

———. 1986. *The Cross of the Son of God.* Translated by J. Bowden. London: SCM.

———. 1993. "'Setze dich zu meiner Rechten!' Die Inthronization Christi zur Rechten Gottes und Psalm 110,1." Pages 108–94 in *Le trône de Dieu.* Edited by M. Philonenko. WUNT 69. Tübingen: Mohr Siebeck.

Herold, G. 1973. *Zorn und Gerechtigkeit Gottes bei Paulus: Eine Untersuchung zu Röm. 1,16–18.* EUS 23/14. Frankfurt: Lang.

Hoekema, A. 1994. *The Bible and the Future.* Grand Rapids: Eerdmans.

Hofius, O. 1989. "'Rechtfertigung des Gottlosen' als Thema biblischer Theologie." Pages 121–47 in *Paulusstudien.* WUNT 51. Tübingen: Mohr Siebeck.

———. 1994. "Wort Gottes und Glaube bei Paulus." Pages 148–74 in *Paulusstudien*. 2nd ed. WUNT 51. Tübingen: Mohr Siebeck.

———. 2002. "Die Gottesprädikationen Röm 4,17b." Pages 58–61 in *Paulusstudien II*. WUNT 143. Tübingen: Mohr Siebeck.

Hooker, M. D. 1990. "Adam in Romans 1." Pages 73–84 in *From Adam to Christ: Essays on Paul*. Cambridge: Cambridge University Press.

Janowski, B. 1999. "JHWH der Richter—ein Rettender Gott." Pages 92–124 in *Die rettende Gerechtigkeit*. BTAT 2. Neukirchen-Vluyn: Neukirchener Verlag.

———. 2000. *Sühne als Heilsgeschehen: Traditions- und Religionsgeschichtliche Studien zur Sühnetheologie der Priesterschrift*. WMANT 55. Neukirchen-Vluyn: Neukirchener Verlag.

Janzen, J. G. 1980. "Habbakuk 2:2–4 in the Light of Recent Philological Advances." *HTR* 73: 53–78.

Kaiser, O. 1974. *Isaiah 13–39*. OTL. Philadelphia: Westminster.

Käsemann, E. 1980. *Commentary on Romans*. Translated and edited by G. W. Bromiley. Grand Rapids: Eerdmans.

Knittel, T. 2002. *Das griechische "Leben Adams und Evas": Studien zu einer narrativen Anthropologie im frühen Judentum*. TSAJ 88. Tübingen: Mohr Siebeck.

Koch, D.-A. 1985. "Der Text von Hab 2,4b in der Septuaginta und im Neuen Testament." *ZNW* 76: 68–85.

———. 1986. *Die Schrift als Zeuge des Evangeliums: Untersuchungen zur Verwendung und zum Verständnis der Schrift bei Paulus*. BHT 69. Tübingen: Mohr Siebeck.

Kraus, W. 1991. *Der Tod Jesu als Heiligtumsweihe: Eine Untersuchung zum Umfeld der Sühnevorstellung in Römer 3,25–26a*. WMANT 66. Neukirchen-Vluyn: Neukirchener Verlag.

Levenson, J. D. 1993. *The Death and Resurrection of the Beloved Son: The Transformation of Child Sacrifice in Judaism and Christianity*. New Haven: Yale University Press.

Levison, J. R. 1988. *Portraits of Adam in Early Judaism: From Sirach to 2 Baruch*. JSPSup 1. Sheffield: Sheffield Academic Press.

Lichtenberger, H. 2004. *Das Ich Adams und das Ich der Menschheit: Studien zum Menschenbild in Römer 7*. WUNT 164. Tübingen: Mohr Siebeck.

Lohse, E. 1982. "Emuna und Pistis." Pages 88–104 in *Die Vielfalt des Neuen Testaments: Exegetische Studien zur Theologie des Neuen Testaments*. Göttingen: Vandenhoeck & Ruprecht.

Metzger, B. M. 1971. *A Textual Commentary on the Greek New Testament*. New York: United Bible Societies.

Moo, D. J. 1996. *The Epistle to the Romans*. NICNT. Grand Rapids: Eerdmans.

Moore, G. F. 1927. *Judaism in the First Centuries of the Christian Era: The Age of the Tannaim*. Cambridge, MA: Harvard University Press.

Oberhänsli-Widmer, G. 1998. *Biblische Figuren in der rabbinischen Literatur: Gleichnisse und Bilder zu Adam, Noah und Abraham im Midrasch Bereschit Rabba*. JC 17. Bern: Lang.

Piper, J. 1979a. *"Love Your Enemies": Jesus' Love Command in the Synoptic Gospels and in the Early Christian Paraenesis*. SNTSMS 38. Cambridge: Cambridge University Press.

———. 1979b. "Prolegomena to Understanding Romans 9:14–15: An Interpretation of Exodus 33:19." *JETS* 22: 203–16.

Sanders, E. P. 1977. *Paul and Palestinian Judaism: A Comparison of Patterns of Religion*. Philadelphia: Fortress.

Schlatter, A. 1905. *Der Glaube im Neuen Testament*. 3rd ed. Stuttgart: Calwer Verlag der Vereinsbuchhandlung.

Schneider, F., and W. Stenger. 1987. *Studien zum neutestamentlichen Briefformular*. NTTS 11. Leiden: Brill.

Schreiner, T. R. 1998. *Romans*. BECNT 6. Grand Rapids: Baker Academic.

Seifrid, M. A. 2000. *Christ, Our Righteousness: Paul's Theology of Justification*. NSBT 9. Downers Grove, IL: InterVarsity.

———. 2001. "Righteousness Language in the Hebrew Scriptures and Early Judaism." Pages 415–42 in *The Complexities of Second Temple Judaism*. Vol. 1 of *Justification and Variegated Nomism: A Fresh Appraisal of Paul and Second Temple Judaism*. Edited by D. A. Carson, P. T. O'Brien, and M. A. Seifrid. WUNT 2/140. Tübingen: Mohr Siebeck.

———. 2004a. "Paul's Use of Righteousness Language against Its Hellenistic Background." Pages 39–74 in *The Paradoxes of Paul*. Vol. 2 of *Justification and Variegated Nomism: A Fresh Appraisal of Paul and Second Temple Judaism*. Edited by D. A. Carson, P. T. O'Brien, and M. A. Seifrid. WUNT 2/181. Tübingen: Mohr Siebeck.

———. 2004b. "Unrighteous by Faith: Apostolic Proclamation in Romans 1:18–3:20." Pages 105–45 in *The Paradoxes of Paul*. Vol. 2 of *Justification and Variegated Nomism: A Fresh Appraisal of Paul and Second Temple Judaism*. Edited by D. A. Carson, P. T. O'Brien, and M. A. Seifrid. WUNT 2/181. Tübingen: Mohr Siebeck.

Silva, M. 1993. "Old Testament in Paul." *DPL* 630–42.

Sjöberg, E. 1938. *Gott und die Sünder im Palästinischen Judentum nach dem Zeugnis der Tannaiten und der apokryphisch-pseudepigraphischen Literatur*. BWANT 79. Stuttgart: Kohlhammer.

Strobel, A. 1961. *Untersuchungen zum eschatologischen Verzögerungsproblem auf Grund der spätjüdisch-urchristlichen Geschichte von Habakuk 2,2 ff*. NovTSup 2. Leiden: Brill.

Stuhlmacher, P. 1968. *Das paulinische Evangelium: Vorgeschichte*. FRLANT 95. Göttingen: Vandenhoeck & Ruprecht.

———. 1986. "Recent Exegesis on Romans 3:24–26." Pages 94–109 in *Reconciliation, Law, and Righteousness: Essays in Biblical Theology*. Translated by E. Kalin. Philadelphia: Fortress.

———. 1991. "The Pauline Gospel." Pages 1–25 in *The Gospel and the Gospels*. Edited by P. Stuhlmacher. Grand Rapids: Eerdmans.

———. 1992. *Grundlegung: Von Jesus zu Paulus*. Vol. 1 of *Biblische Theologie des Neuen Testaments*. Göttingen: Vandenhoeck & Ruprecht.

———. 2001. "'Christus Jesus ist hier; der gestorben ist, ja vielmehr auch auferweckt ist, der zur Rechten Gottes ist und uns vertritt.'" Pages 351–62 in *Auferstehung—Resurrection: The Fourth Durham-Tübingen Research Symposium; Resurrection, Transfiguration, and Exaltation in Old Testament, Ancient Judaism and Early Christianity*. Edited by F. Avemarie and H. Lichtenberger. WUNT 135. Tübingen: Mohr Siebeck.

Urbach, E. E. 1987. *The Sages: Their Concepts and Beliefs*. Translated by I. Abrahams. Cambridge, MA: Harvard University Press.

Wagner, J. R. 2002. *Heralds of the Good News: Isaiah and Paul "In Concert" in the Letter to the Romans*. NovTSup 101. Leiden: Brill.

Watts, R. E. 1999. "'For I Am Not Ashamed of the Gospel': Romans 1:16–17 and Habakkuk 2:4." Pages 3–25 in *Romans and the People of God: Essays in Honor of Gordon Fee on the Occasion of His 65th Birthday*. Grand Rapids: Eerdmans.

Wilk, F. 1998. *Die Bedeutung des Jesajabuches für Paulus*. FRLANT 179. Göttingen: Vandenhoeck & Ruprecht.

Wright, N. T. 2002. "The Letter to the Romans." Pages 395–770 in vol. 10 of *The New Interpreter's Bible*. Nashville: Abingdon.

Zahn, Theodor. 1925. *Der Brief des Paulus an die Röme*. Leipzig/Erlagen: A. Deichertsche Verlagsbuchhandlung.

Ziegler, J., ed. 1939. *Isaias*. Septuaginta: Vetus Testamentum Graecum 14. Göttingen: Vandenhoeck & Ruprecht.

1 Corinthians

ROY E. CIAMPA AND BRIAN S. ROSNER

The Structure of 1 Corinthians

Many commentators follow Mitchell (1991) in affirming that Paul's main purpose in writing the letter is to unify the congregation (see the thesis statement in 1:10). Most also note that Paul deals with oral reports in chapters 1–6 before addressing matters raised in the Corinthian letter to Paul in chapters 7–16 (7:1: "Now concerning [*peri de*] the matters about which you wrote"; cf. *peri de* repeated in 7:25; 8:1; 12:1; 16:1, 12). Rhetorical and other approaches have also been used to analyze the structure of this letter. However, such summaries and outlines of the letter, though not without some validity, are deficient in that they largely neglect the content of Paul's instructions. In 1 Corinthians Paul deals with two main vices that, according to Jewish moral teaching based on the OT, were typical of pagans: sexual immorality and idolatry. Paul explicitly ties these two vices to OT background in his discussion of Israel's failures in 10:7–8, and their inclusion in the vice list of 5:11 is based on their inclusion in a list of sins associated with a Deuteronomic expulsion formula (see commentary on 1 Cor. 5:9–11 below).

Chapters 5–7 deal primarily with issues related to sexual immorality, first in a negative treatment of its manifestations in Corinth (chaps. 5–6) and then in a positive treatment of marriage and sexual relationships in the church (chap. 7; note how the chapter is introduced in 7:2). This arrangement of ethical material is reminiscent of Hellenistic Jewish parenesis (reported by Niebuhr 1987: 232) that discusses sexual deviations such as incest, homosexuality, and sexual relations in marriage in close proximity.

Chapters 8–14 deal with the issue of idolatry, beginning, again, with a negative treatment of its manifestations in Corinth (chaps. 8–10) and then moving to a more positive treatment of the proper worship of the one true God (chaps. 11–14; note how 12:2 relates the following material back to the issue of idolatry).

Toward the end of each negative section (chaps. 5–6, 8–10) Paul provides both a negative imperative and a positive imperative relating to the broader theme. In concluding the negative section on sexual immorality, Paul exhorts the Corinthians to "flee sexual immorality" (6:18) and to "glorify God" with their bodies (6:20). In concluding the negative section on idolatry, Paul exhorts them to "flee idolatry" (10:14) and to do everything "to the glory of God" (10:31).

Paul's emphasis on true versus false wisdom in 1 Cor. 1–4 suggests that his treatment of sexual immorality and idolatry in this letter is following the logic of his discussion of the same subject in Rom. 1:21–25. There it is the lack of true wisdom (Rom. 1:22) that leads to idolatry and sexual immorality (Rom. 1:23–25). To Paul's way of thinking, true wisdom (1 Cor. 1–4; cf. Rom. 1:22) should keep one from sexual immorality (1 Cor. 5–7; cf. Rom. 1:24) and idolatry (1 Cor. 8–14; cf. Rom. 1:23). As in his treatments of sexual immorality and idolatry, Paul's discussion of wisdom here begins with a negative treatment (1:18–2:5) but then moves to a more positive one (2:6–3:4).

The only other specific vice to be "fled" (*pheugō*) in the NT apart from sexual immorality (1 Cor. 6) and idolatry (1 Cor. 10) is greed (1 Tim. 6:11; in context, *philargyria*, "love of money" [6:10]). Typically, Jews added greed as a third member of the unholy triad of vices that rightly condemn the heathen (see Rosner, forthcoming). Greed (*pleonektēs*) is mentioned alongside sexual immorality and idolatry in each of this letter's three vice lists (5:10, 11; 6:10), and it is likely that greed was a primary motivation for the lawsuit in 6:1–11.

The letter comes to a climax in chapter 15 with Paul's discussion of the resurrection as it relates to the ultimate triumph of Christ over all adversaries and the ultimate transformation of our corruptible humanity into humanity that fully reflects God's glory. It is no surprise that Paul offers the resurrection as the decisive basis for his ethical instruction (see O'Donovan 1986).

Letter Opening (1:1–9)

1:2

Those who "call on the name of the Lord," like "saints," is another name for Christians (Acts 9:14, 21; 22:16; 2 Tim. 2:22). The phrase is used frequently in the OT to refer to one who worships the one true God (Gen. 4:26; 12:8; 13:4; 21:33; 26:25; 1 Kings 18:24; 1 Chron. 16:8; Ps. 75:1; 79:6; 80:18; 99:6; 116:4, 13; Isa. 64:7; Lam. 3:55; Joel 2:32; Zeph. 3:9; Zech. 13:9).

Paul mentions that the Corinthians are united with "all those who call on the name of our Lord in every place." A key theme in Deuteronomy is the Lord's selection of one particular place where people would call on his name (understood to refer to Jerusalem). Repeated reference is made to "the place which the Lord your God will choose to have his name called upon" (cf. Deut. 12:11, 21, 26; 14:23–24; 16:2, 6, 11; 17:8, 10; 26:2).

Rather than refer to that place, however, Paul says that the Corinthians join those who call on the name of our Lord "in every place" (*en panti topō*). He is the only NT author to use the expression (1 Cor. 1:2; 2 Cor. 2:14; 1 Thess. 1:8; 1 Tim. 2:8), and he uses it to refer to the worship of God which is spreading around the world through his ministry to the Gentiles.

The expression echoes Mal. 1:11 LXX, which (in a context of frustration over the way the Lord is being worshiped in Jerusalem) prophesies a future time when God would be worshiped by Gentiles "in every place": "For from the rising of the sun until its setting my name will be glorified among the Gentiles, and in every place [*en panti topō*] incense is offered to my name and a pure offering, for my name is great among the Gentiles, says the LORD Almighty" (see Towner 2000: 333). The echo suggests that the Corinthians are part of the fulfillment of God's eschatological plan that he be worshiped among all the Gentiles.

Censure of Corinthian Factionalism (1:10–4:17)

Introduction

Following an appeal for unity in 1:10, Paul mounts a long and complex argument against divisions in the church (1:10–4:17 is marked off by the repetition of *parakalō hymas*, "I appeal to you" [1:10; 4:16]). The Corinthian church (like Corinthian society in general) was keenly conscious of social status. Caught up in rivalries, they boasted about their own possession of wisdom and rhetorical eloquence or that of their favorite leaders. A point of contention with Paul was his failure to display this status-enhancing rhetoric expected of a "wise" and cultured person worthy of their allegiance.

The Role of Scripture in the Argument

Ellis (1977) and others claim to have found a standard Jewish form of biblical exegesis in the opening chapters of the letter, the "proem midrash," which was used in the synagogue as a kind of homily or sermon. Ellis finds two examples in 1 Cor. 1–2, which have a tripartite structure. The first is 1 Cor. 1:18–31: (1) 1:18–20: theme and initial texts, Isa. 29:14; 19:11–14 (cf. 33:18);

(2) 1:20–30: exposition linked to the initial and final texts by the catchwords *sophos* (1:26–27), *sophia* (1:20, 21, 22, 24, 30), *mōros* (1:25, 27), *mōria* (1:21, 23), *kauchasthai* (1:29); (3) 1:31: final text, Jer. 9:22–23. The second is 1 Cor. 2:6–16: (1) 2:6–9: theme and initial texts, Isa. 64:4; 65:16 (LXX); (2) 2:10–15: exposition linked to the initial and final texts by the catchwords *anthrōpos* (2:11, 14 [cf. 12:3]), *idein* (2:11–12), *ginōskein* (2:11, 14); (3) 2:16: final text, Isa. 40:13, and application.

However, three reservations caution against detecting these structures in 1 Corinthians: (1) the Jewish form in question opened with pentateuchal texts, not texts from Isaiah; (2) the final texts in the above examples are not clearly linked to the initial texts; (3) the Jewish examples are much longer (as in, e.g., Philo). Nevertheless, Ellis's work alerts us to the crucial role of OT texts at every level in these passages.

The summary by Hays (1999: 402–3) of the role of Scripture in the section is accurate: "The backbone of the discussion in 1.18–3.23 is a series of six OT quotations (1.19; 1.31; 2.9; 2.16; 3.19; 3.20) all taken from passages that depict God as one who acts to judge and save his people in ways that defy human imagination." In the following sections the six quotations will be analyzed, along with several allusions and scriptural motifs.

1:17

For Paul, the apostolic work of the ministry of the word is crucial; God sent him to "preach the gospel" (*euangelizesthai*). Paul restricts his usage of *euangelizesthai* in his letters to the activity of duly authorized proclaimers. Key to understanding his perspective is Isa. 40–66. As Dickson (2003: 176) has shown, "Paul's usage of gospel-terminology [esp. *euangelizomai*] was heavily influenced by the particular significations contained in the messenger traditions arising from Isa 40:9, 52:7 and 61:1, wherein 'secular' messenger language had been transposed to a higher, eschatological level, depicting the end-time herald(s) commissioned by Israel's God to announce his salvific reign." Many texts in Palestinian Judaism adopt this interpretation of the word. *Targum Isaiah*, for instance, draws out from the OT the notion that the herald stands for Zion's prophets: "Get you up to a high mountain, prophets who herald tidings to Zion" (*Tg. Isa.* 40:9); "A spirit of proph-ecy before the Lord God is upon me, because the Lord has exalted me to announce good tidings to the poor" (*Tg. Isa.* 61:1). Paul's use of Isa. 52:7 in Rom. 10:15 offers explicit support for making these connections and for taking *euangelizesthai* to refer to Paul's gospel heralding as an eschatological, divinely commissioned activity (Stuhlmacher 1991: 156–65).

1:18–25

Along with announcing the main theme of the paragraph by quoting Isa. 29:14 in 1 Cor. 1:19 (Koch 1986: 273–75), Paul also echoes Isa. 33:18 in 1:20 and Isa. 28:16 in 1:21–24 (Williams 2001: 47–102). All three texts are drawn from the woe oracles of Isa. 28–33.

1:19

A. NT Context: God's Sentence of Judgment on Human Wisdom. Paul shows that there is implacable opposition between human wisdom and the "word of the cross." The quotation in question helps establish that this observation is linked to the OT narrative of judgment and grace and shows that the paradox of the cross—foolishness to some, but in reality power for salvation—is in accord with Scripture.

B. Isa. 29:14 in Its OT Context. Several features of Isa. 29:14 and surrounding verses suggest its attractiveness to Paul and its aptness in relation to his argument. Part of a woe oracle condemning various human practices (cf. 29:1, 3), the preceding verse associates wisdom with "lip service" to God: "These people draw near with their mouths and honor me with their lips, but their hearts are far from me" (29:13).

The first part of 29:14 indicates that the judgment of the "wisdom of the wise" will occur when God will do "shocking and amazing" things. The threefold appearance of the Hebrew root for "wonder" (*pl'*) in this verse may imply messianic involvement. The first name of the messianic figure in Isa. 9:6 is "wonderful" (cf. 25:1), and in 28:29 the Lord, who announces the plan of salvation, is said to be "wonderful in counsel." Furthermore, that the Messiah should be associated with the judgment of human wisdom is suggested by the involvement of Cyrus, a type of the Messiah in the reversal of wisdom in 44:25.

C. Isa. 29:14 in Early Judaism. A wide range of Jewish texts, which have affinities with Isa.

29:14, treat the theme of the absence and judgment of wisdom (Williams 2001: 61–73): Bar. 3:9–14; *2 Bar.* 48:31–37; 70:3–6; *4 Ezra* 5:9–13; 13:29–32; *1 En.* 39:8; 42; 1Q27 1 I, 1–9; 1QH^a XI, 13–18; 3 Macc. 6:19–29; *Tg. Isa.* 29:13–14.

In these texts the absence of wisdom occurs in situations where strife and division are plaguing a community. Under such circumstances God's people are enjoined to appreciate his future intervention in order to help sort out their present difficulties. In particular, a dearth of wisdom is seen as part of a great judgment or as a sign pointing to the final, universal judgment. The absence of wisdom and its ultimate judgment are associated with the work of the coming Messiah.

D. Textual Matters. Paul quotes the LXX text verbatim except that he changes the final word from *krypsō* ("hide") to *athetēsō* ("frustrate"). As Stanley (1992: 186) notes, the latter term serves Paul's purposes better: "Paul's point in 1 Cor. 1.18–29 is not that God has simply 'hidden' understanding from the 'wise,' but rather that he has done a work in the death of Jesus that defies all purely rational understanding. By substituting the stronger *athetēsō*, Paul creates a chiastic parallel with the preceeding *apolō* ["destroy"] that serves to drive home his point to his readers."

E. The Use of Isa. 29:14 in 1 Cor. 1:19. Isaiah 29:14 seems to have exerted an influence on Paul's language and thought at various points in the surrounding verses. "Those who are being destroyed" in 1:18 anticipates the "destruction" (*apolō*) in 1:19. A purely verbal show of piety—the very thing that Paul faults the Corinthians for in chapters 1–4—recalls the superficial "lip service" condemned in Isa. 29:13. The "wonderful" yet "shocking" things (29:13–14) that the prophet foretells, with messianic overtones, are what Paul declares to have now transpired through Christ crucified.

F. Theological Use. Especially when read in the context of its early Jewish interpretation, Isa. 29:14 is used by Paul to announce that God's eschatological judgment and salvation are taking place in the midst of the Corinthians. As Hays (1999: 403–4) puts it, "God has already put the wise to shame through the foolishness of the cross, the apocalyptic event that has shattered the old order of human wisdom." The Corinthians who still value "the wisdom of the wise" have failed

to notice God's apocalyptic judgment on such wisdom through the crucified Messiah. The fact that in 1:18 people are still in the process of being saved (or destroyed) indicates that the unfolding of the drama of salvation is not yet complete. Isaiah's words are for Paul not just a judgment on ancient Judean leaders, but also "an indictment of the rhetorical affectations of the Corinthians" (Hays 1999: 404).

1:20

Robertson and Plummer (1911: 19) label the presence of Isa. 33:18 in 1 Cor. 1:20 "a very free citation from the general sense." Although other commentators have suggested the influence of other texts, both OT and postbiblical, this proposal is the most plausible.

Both Isa. 33:18 and 1 Cor. 1:20 contain three questions beginning with the word "where" (*pou*), the only two places where this structure appears in the LXX and the NT. Both texts refer to the ineffectiveness of individuals who oppose God's people. Both contain rhetorical questions expecting the response "nowhere."

Isaiah 33:18 concerns the whereabouts of the chief officer, the one who weighed the tribute, and the one who counted the towers, a composite reference to the oppressors of God's people. It announces the end of their ascendancy and dominance. The surrounding context refers to an ideal king, probably the Messiah, who will overthrow the oppressors (33:17, 21–22). In related early Jewish texts (see Williams 2001: 73–80) the oppressors disappear following a great judgment. In fact, the end time is characterized by their absence and by the presence of a messianic ruler. Intriguingly, the absence of the oppressors coincides with the failure of human plans and the disappearance of wisdom.

In this light, the echo of Isa. 33:18 in 1 Cor. 1:20 recalls the overthrow by the Messiah of all those who oppose God and his people in the end time, reinforcing the passage's Christology and eschatology.

1:21–24

A number of OT texts claiming that God possesses all wisdom and power are relevant to these verses on a thematic level (e.g., Job 12:13; Jer. 10:12; Dan. 2:23; cf. Bar. 3:9–4:4; see Hübner 1990–1995: 2:114–16).

A more specific connection to another Isaiah text also merits consideration, a prominent text in early Jewish and Christian circles: Isa. 28:16, which concerns "the cornerstone, a sure foundation." Paul uses the text in Rom. 9:33–10:14 (cf. 1 Pet. 2:6), where the themes of dualistic predestination and stern warning are developed: perdition or salvation are the consequence of a person's response to the stone (cf. 1 Cor. 1:23–24). Along with developing these same themes, 1 Cor. 1:21–24 evinces some terminological overlap with the Isaiah text, with 1:21 containing a participial use of *pisteuō*, as does Isa. 28:16 (in both texts God saves "those who believe"). The use of the word *skandalon* ("stumbling block") in 1:23 may also have been picked up from the broader associated "stone" tradition (which emerges in 1 Cor. 3:10–15); the word appears in Rom. 9:33 in connection with Isa. 28:16; 8:14.

1:26–31

Paul cites Jer. 9:23/1 Kgdms. 2:10 in 1:31 and alludes to both texts and their surrounding contexts in 1:26–29. Both texts support his contention that the Corinthians should not evaluate themselves by human criteria before God; God called them by different standards. They should consider themselves in the light of the salvation plan of God in Christ. Both the allusions and the hybrid quotation can be dealt with together, but in reverse order, since the latter provides the clue to the recognition of the former. Further echoes of both OT texts may be heard in 4:6–13, which refers back to 1:31 (Wagner 1998).

1:31

A. NT Context: Boast Only in the Lord. As we noted above, there are two equally likely sources for the scriptural warning in question. The wording of Jer. 9:24 (9:23 LXX) and of 1 Kgdms. 2:10 is virtually identical, and both provide rich subtexts for Paul's argument (note that 1 Kgdms. 2:10 contains material not found in 1 Sam. 2:10, which is based on the MT). We are not forced to choose, for, as Hays (1999: 404) observes, "significant writing often mingles the echoes of multiple precursors."

If 1:18–25 considers those who reject the message of the cross, 1:26–31 shifts the focus to those who accept. Paul uses the Corinthians themselves as an illustration of the pattern of eschatological reversal that characterizes the work of Christ. The low social status of most of the Corinthians itself points to the cross, which was anything but impressive, humanly speaking, and radically overturned expectations.

B. Jer. 9:24/1 Kgdms. 2:10 in Their OT Contexts. The warning in Jeremiah is part of a series of judgment oracles. God's judgment is coming on those people guilty of a variety of sins: lies, oppression, idolatry (specifically, Baal worship) (8:3–9:26). Those who claim to be wise will suffer judgment (e.g., 8:9: "The wise shall be put to shame . . . ; since they have rejected the word of the LORD, what wisdom is in them?"). The climax of the section is 9:23–24, which warns against all boasting save in God. The verb "boast" occurs five times in 9:23–24 in negative and positive senses, the improper boasts being human wisdom, strength, and riches.

First Kingdoms 2:10 concludes Hannah's song of praise, in which God is exalted for reversing the fortunes of the poor and the downtrodden. A celebration of God's gracious blessing, the accent here is on this startling reversal, rather than on eschatological judgment as in Jeremiah.

C. Jer. 9:24/1 Kgdms. 2:10 in Early Judaism. A number of Jewish texts, especially Jer. 9, cite or take up themes from the two LXX texts. Consonant with Paul's use, these place the warning about improper boasting in the broader context of future universal judgment. They also discourage boasting in human attainments and instead promote trust in the plans of God (Williams 2001: 113–24).

D. Textual Matters. Stanley (1992: 188), who considers only the Jeremiah text, labels Paul's use "a generalized appropriation of an attractive phrase from Jer 9.23 LXX by Paul himself." The small differences between the precursor text and Paul's rendition are three: (1) he omits the initial conjunction; (2) he advances "let the one who boasts" to the beginning of the sentence; (3) he changes the object of the boasting from *toutō* ("this," referring to "that the one who boasts understands and knows me, that I am the LORD, who . . .") to *en kyriō* ("in the Lord"). The changes are not substantial. The third one does not change the meaning of the verse, "but it does create a concise and generalized expression that could be adapted to a variety of contexts (cf. 2 Cor. 10:17)" (Stanley

1992: 188). The phrase *en kyriō*, "in the Lord," appears frequently in Paul's letters.

First Kingdoms 2:10 is identical to Jer. 9:23 LXX except that the object of boasting is briefer and in fact closer to Paul's citation: *syniein kai ginōskein ton kyrion*, the one who boasts "understands and knows the Lord."

E. The Use of Jer. 9:24/1 Kgdms. 2:10 in 1 Cor. 1:26–31. The texts in question and their surrounding contexts have influenced the vocabulary, structure, and main theme of the paragraph in 1 Corinthians. The culminating pithy maxim in 1:31 is only the tip of the iceberg of scriptural dependence.

Jeremiah provides the pattern for Paul's threefold dismissal of the wise, the powerful, and the well-born; 1:26–28 recalls Jer. 9:23: "Let not the wise boast of their wisdom, or the strong boast of their strength, or the rich boast of their riches." Further, the reference to Christ in 1:30 becoming "righteousness" echoes the last part of Jer. 9:24 ("I act with mercy, justice, and righteousness").

The connection to 1 Kgdms. 2:10 and the Song of Hannah underscores the reversal of status, a theme that Paul discusses in terms of wisdom and folly and strength and weakness throughout 1:18–31. The first reference to boasting in 1 Kgdms. 2:1–10 is negative and appears in 2:3. It resonates powerfully with Paul's critique of the Corinthians' obsession with rhetoric and could just as easily have been quoted (along with 2:10): "Do not boast [*mē kauchasthe*], and do not speak lofty things; do not let grandiloquence [*megalorrēmosynē*] come out of your mouth, because the Lord is a God of knowledge, and God prepares his own designs" (Hays's [1997: 405] translation).

The allusions and citations in context supply the ideas of shame and role reversal in 1:26–29, help Paul move from past to future judgment in 1:27–29, and indicate how a personified boast in a wise messianic figure could emerge in 1:30.

F. Theological Use. Paul uses the texts in question to support his contention that through the cross God has turned the world's values upside down. As Wagner (1998: 287) concludes, "Far from being an irrelevant reminder, Paul's reference to the Scriptural command, 'Let the one who boasts, boast in the Lord,' undergirds and advances his censure of the Corinthians' behavior." The paradoxical nature of salvation in Christ turns out, no less than his death and resurrection, to be "according to the Scriptures." Paul's disparagement of wisdom, power, and privilege is rooted in the OT. Thus Paul uses the text to sum up a point about the doctrine of salvation that has ethical implications for Corinthian factionalism.

2:3–5

Williams (2001: 133–56) perceives an echo of Zech. 4:6 in 2:3–5 that helps establish the character of Paul's preaching: "Paul's fear and trembling as a weak human being emphasize his cornerstone message of God's power and presence. Therefore, the Corinthians should not despise the day of 'small things' (Zech 4:10)" (Williams 2001: 156).

Intriguingly, both Paul and Zechariah are establishers of foundations of a new temple (Zech. 4:6–10; 1 Cor. 3:10–11; cf. the Corinthians as a temple [1 Cor. 3:16–17; 2 Cor. 6:16–18] and Paul as a temple worker [1 Cor. 9:13–14]). Combined with some shared terms ("spirit," "wisdom," "power") and the importance of the text elsewhere in the NT (esp. Revelation), Zech. 4:6 resonates with Paul's emphasis on his founding work among the Corinthians being in weakness and yet exhibiting divine power: "Not by might, nor by power, but by my Spirit, says the LORD of hosts."

2:6–12

The theme statement of 2:6–3:4 is 2:6a: "But [in contrast to human wisdom] we [the apostles and prophets/preachers at Corinth] speak wisdom [the gospel of Christ crucified in its fullness] among the mature [knowledgeable, discerning, experienced Christians]" (cf. 14:20). Picking up key elements of this statement, Paul expounds "wisdom" in 2:6b–12 negatively and positively, "we speak" in 2:13, and "the mature" in 2:14–3:4.

That Paul is quoting Scripture in 2:9 is suggested by the words "as it is written." Nowhere else does he cite anything but the OT using this formula. However, what follows does not match closely any particular text in the Greek or Hebrew Bibles. In the third century Origen attributed the quotation to the now no longer extant *Apocalypse of Elijah*, and a similar quotation turns up in *Gos. Thom.* 17 as the words of Jesus. In fact, alternative hypotheses suggest that Paul is citing not only an apocryphal source or Jesus, but also a wisdom tradition and his opponents in Corinth. A range of OT texts have also been proposed as his source. After considering the best candidate for the precursor text to 2:9 (see Williams 2001: 157–208), we will also note an echo of Dan. 2:19–23 in 2:6–8, 10–11 (Hübner 1990–1995).

2:9

A. NT Context: No Eye Has Seen. Although we cannot be certain, a loose quotation of Isa. 64:4 (64:3 LXX), "From of old no one has heard or perceived by the ear, no eye has seen a God besides you," in 2:9 has much to commend it. Both texts assert that no human being is able to understand the divine revelation without God's enabling. The fact that the references to the ear and eye in Isa. 64:4 are in the reverse order compared to 1 Cor. 2:9 does not rule out a link between the texts; such alterations were an accepted aspect of citation technique in antiquity (see Stanley 1992).

The Hebrew idiom "go up onto the heart," which appears in 2:9, is not found in Isa. 64:4 but does occur in the Greek of Isa. 65:17. This has led some to suggest that Paul combines Isa. 64:4 and 65:17 in his citation. However, two differences between Isa. 65:17 and 1 Cor. 2:9 weigh against it: (1) whereas the tense of the verb in Isaiah is future, in 1 Corinthians it is aorist; (2) the Isaiah text has "their heart" rather than "the heart of man." The conclusion by Thiselton (2000: 251) is fair: "The widespread suggestion that Paul combines Isa. 64:4 and 65:17, although possible, seems too imprecise for certainty, even if Paul does combine various quotations in a catena or free collection elsewhere (e.g., in Rom. 3:10–18)."

In 2:8–12 Paul discusses the revelation of the wisdom that came to the apostles and prophets through the Holy Spirit. Negatively, it was not known (perceived or grasped) by the rulers of this age (2:8–9); positively, it was revealed by God through the Spirit to the apostles and prophets, who received the Spirit of God (2:10–12).

B. Isa. 64:4 in Its OT Context. Isaiah 64:4 concerns the uniqueness of God's plan of salvation, which remains hidden. Judgment against God's enemies also appears, as in the plea for divine intervention in 64:1 and the appearance of fire in 64:2 (cf. "to make your name known to your adversaries").

C. Isa. 64:4 in Early Judaism. A range of texts associated with Isa. 64:4 stress the inability of humanity to understand God's ways and connect it with the stone tradition and the theme of the new creation (cf. Isa. 65:17; see Williams 2001: 175–84).

D. Textual Matters. The loose form of citation precludes any discussion of textual differences.

E. The Use of Isa. 64:4 in 1 Cor. 2:9. In its new context the text is straightforward with one grammatical exception: semantically, what does the relative pronoun "what" (*ha*) look back to? While Conzelmann is right that the construction is difficult to unravel, Findlay and Ellicott's suggestion makes sense of the connection: "what" looks back to "we speak" in 2:6–7, giving the sense: "we speak God's wisdom . . . what no eye has seen. . . ." Thus Paul, in citing this Scripture, shows that the wisdom that he and other apostles and prophets preach is nothing less than the fullness of God's plan of salvation. What Isaiah promised as part of a dramatic divine intervention (see 64:1), Paul takes to be fulfilled in the message and proclamation of the cross.

F. Theological Use. With this citation Paul develops further the apocalyptic dimension of divine wisdom. Those who love God understand his salvation as true wisdom. Having affirmed that Paul does teach wisdom among the mature, we are reminded by Isa. 64:4 that we relate to God through love, not primarily through wisdom or knowledge: "these things God has prepared for those who love him." Those "in the know" are not there by virtue of their own ingenuity; they receive "what no human mind has conceived." God prepares things beyond human comprehension for those who are his. As Paul will say in 2:16, "the mature" are not those who boast of their superior mind but rather "have the mind of Christ." Paul uses the text to promote systemic humility among the proud Corinthians.

2:6–8, 10–11

When God reveals to Daniel the interpretation of Nebuchadnezzar's dream in Dan. 2:16, Daniel responds in a prayer that shares language and ideas similar to those in 1 Cor. 2:6–8, 10–11. In both passages wisdom (Dan. 2:20–21, 23; 1 Cor. 2:6) from God is associated with a mystery (Dan. 2:19; 1 Cor. 2:7), and both claim that this mystery reaches to the depths: "he reveals deep [*bathys*] and hidden things" (Dan. 2:22); "the Spirit searches all things, even the depths [*bathos*] of God" (1 Cor.

2:10). The similarities, though noteworthy, are insufficient to regard this as more than a possible echo.

2:16

A. NT Context: The Mind of Christ. Having declared that he has received God's wisdom by the Spirit of God (2:10–11), Paul explains in 2:12–3:4 the relationship that the Spirit has to him and to others. In 2:16 he quotes the question from Isa. 40:13: "Who has known the mind of the LORD?" Paul's answer in the same verse is that "we have the mind of Christ."

B. Isa. 40:13 in Its OT Context. One of several rhetorical questions in 40:12–14, Isa. 40:13 expects the answer "no one." Isaiah 40:15–17 stresses further the gulf between humans and God: even "the nations are like a drop in the bucket." In context, the "spirit of the Lord," which no one can know, involves God's plan of salvation (11:2; 40:7; 59:19; 63:14). Likewise, no one is qualified to be God's "counselor" (11:2; 19:3; 30:1). Isaiah 40 itself concerns God's intention to deliver his people, as 40:1–11 indicates. As Williams (2001: 214) observes, 40:13a could be paraphrased, "Who is able to comprehend the salvific plan of God?"

Another dimension to the "spirit of the Lord" in Isaiah is its association with the figure of the servant who acts as God's agent in salvation (42:1; 48:16; 61:1; 63:10).

C. Isa. 40:13 in Early Judaism. The use of this text in Jewish literature anticipates Paul's use in a number of ways (Williams 2001: 216–25). The spirit of the Lord is connected with the mind of the Lord not only in the LXX, but also in Wis. 9:13, 17. Furthermore, the link to God's plan of salvation is clear in various texts from Qumran that emphasize human inability to grasp God's spirit, mind, and ways. Other texts indicate that there is a group of people, effectively a remnant, who due to divine intervention do indeed grasp his plan of deliverance (e.g., Qumran, *2 Baruch*, *1 Enoch*, *4 Ezra*).

D. Textual Matters. The MT reads, "Who has measured the spirit of the LORD? Or what man shows him his counsel?" while the LXX reads, "Who has known the mind of the Lord? And who has become his advisor so as to instruct him?" The MT and LXX differ significantly only in regard to the verbs "measure" and "know" and the nouns "spirit" (*rûaḥ*) and "mind" (*nous*). First Co-

rinthians 2:16 begins exactly as the LXX, with the addition of "for," but omits the middle clause. The change from "spirit" to "mind" is understandable in Paul's case because the two are virtual synonyms in 1 Cor. 2:10–15.

E. The Use of Isa. 40:13 in 1 Cor. 2:16. Introduced with an explanatory *gar* ("for"), the question and answer conclude 2:12–16. That the citation leads into 3:1–4 is indicated by the conjunction *kagō* ("and I") at the beginning of 3:1, since the word is normally used to link its clause or statement (or the author/speaker) with what preceded. Paul's use of the Isaiah text clarifies a number of puzzling features of the passage.

Paul's audacious claim that we have the mind of Christ represents a biting ironic twist against the Corinthian elitists. His identification of Christ with the "spirit"/"mind" of Isa. 40:13 is explicable in the light of its connection in Isaiah with the servant. Paul is not asserting his possession of a spiritual insight above his fellow Christians. The wisdom of which he speaks is not exclusive or esoteric but nothing more or less than the cross and the salvation that it wrought (1:18–25).

The disjunction between the times of Isaiah and of Paul is underscored in the stunning final assertion of 2:16b. "Who has known the mind of the Lord?" The anticipated answer is "no one." Yet Paul follows the question with the answer, "But we have the mind of Christ." "Mind" here is "not an instrument of thought," but rather "a mode of thought" or "mindset" (Thiselton 2000: 275). The "mind of Christ," then, is God's profound wisdom regarding salvation through a crucified Messiah, which was hidden but now revealed by the Holy Spirit. In keeping with earlier uses of the first-person plural pronoun in such statements, "we" here does refer to the apostles specifically, but also to those who are spiritual, for they receive the message of God's wisdom (2:6).

The change from "Lord" to "Christ" is a subtle indication that Paul sees himself and the Corinthians living in the messianic age of fulfillment. As Jewett (1971: 377) puts it, "The change of expression from 'Lord' in 16a to 'Christ' in 16b binds the true divine wisdom to the crucified Christ." The Spirit does not impart wisdom out of thin air, for the Spirit and the cross go together. The mind of Christ is not exercised by thinking about nothing. Rather, those who are spiritual habitually turn to the cross (2:8), as Paul did in the face of divisions in Corinth in 1:18–2:5. For the cross is where we find Christ's mindset on such behavior.

F. Theological Use. Paul's discussion of wisdom is not philosophical, but rather apocalyptic in character. Based on OT and Jewish traditions, and in keeping with his use of other OT texts elsewhere in chapters 1–4, Paul speaks of "this age," a "hidden mystery" "decreed before the ages," and a "glory" that is "revealed." As Hays (1999: 407) notes, "Paul was trying to remake the minds of his readers by teaching them to interpret their lives in light of an eschatologically interpreted Scripture."

3:5–9

In 3:5–9 Paul uses an agricultural image in dealing with the preoccupation of the Corinthians with specific leaders. Hays and Williams have detected an echo here of Isa. 5:1–7, a prominent text in early Jewish interpretation of Scripture. Overlapping features include the planting as the people of God, God's role as the chief worker and owner of the vineyard/field, the relative unimportance of human workers and their role as mediators, and the notion of inappropriate fruit. In particular, like 1 Cor. 3:5–9, Isa. 5:2 mixes building and planting metaphors (cf. Jer. 18:9; 24:6; Ezek. 36:9–10).

3:10–17

Turning to architectural imagery to describe his role in Corinth, Paul echoes Isa. 3:3 in 3:10 (Robertson and Plummer 1911; Hübner 1990–1995, vol. 2) and Mal. 3:2–3 in 3:12–15 (Proctor 1993; Schrage 1991–2001), and he picks up a biblical theme in 3:16–17.

In 3:10 Paul refers to himself as "a wise master builder." Only in Isa. 3:3 and here do we find the combination of *sophos* and *architektōn*. Both passages speak of wisdom and of judgment in relation to the leaders of God's people.

A number of OT and Jewish texts swirling around a general motif of judgment may have influenced Paul in 3:12–15. Malachi 3:2–3 is a specific parallel. The two texts use similar terminology (gold, silver, day, fire). Both envisage a judgment in which fire consumes certain materials. Both "the temple" (1 Cor. 3:16) and its leaders are seen in relation to a judgment that will distinguish valid from ineffectual service.

The motif of temple and holiness (*naos* occurs over sixty times in the LXX; *hagios* over five hundred times) in 3:16–17 is a biblical one that has relevance to 5:1–13 (on which, see commentary below). Descriptions of the temple as God's dwelling and warnings to those who would profane or destroy God's temple are common in Scripture.

The comparisons of the church to "God's field" and "God's building" may in fact be related. Beale (2004: 245–52) lays out the evidence. The "building" in question turns out to be a temple in 3:16, for which the most obvious model is that of Solomon's temple. As Beale states, "The only other place in Scripture where a 'foundation' of a building is laid and 'gold,' 'silver,' and 'precious stones' are 'built' upon the foundation is Solomon's temple" (1 Kings 5:17; 6:20–21, 28, 30, 35; cf. 1 Chron. 29:1–7; 3–4). Indeed, "one hundred thousand talents of gold and a million talents of silver" were prepared for the construction of Solomon's temple (1 Chron. 22:14). Furthermore, the description of Solomon's temple combined precious metals with botanical features, such as wood-carved "gourds and open flowers" (1 Kings 6:18), "palm trees" (1 Kings 6:29, 32), "pomegranates" (1 Kings 7:18–20), "a lily design" (1 Kings 7:22), rows of "gourds" (1 Kings 7:24–26, 42), and lampstands resembling a grove of trees with blossoms (1 Kings 7:49–50). Significantly, later Judaism spoke of Solomon's temple as a "field" (*Tg. Ps.-J.* 27:27; *Pesiq. Rab.* Piska 39). And in the early Christian *Odes of Solomon*, 38:17–21 describes a "saint" being "established" on "foundations [that] were laid" and also as a "cultivation" that was "watered" by God. These traditions build upon the fact that in the OT "the Garden of Eden, Israel's garden-like promised land, and Israel's future restoration in a garden-like land were either equated or associated with a temple" (Beale 2004: 246). All this suggests that in 3:5–18 Paul is comparing the Corinthians not just to any cultivated field and temple, but to nothing less than Solomon's garden temple.

3:19

A. NT Context: Catching the Wise. In order to demonstrate further the futility of human wisdom, Paul appeals to two more OT texts in 3:19–20. Together they offer a pithy summary of Paul's argument in 1:18–3:21 (Koch 1986: 275). The first declares God's ability to frustrate the goals of those claiming to be wise: "He catches the wise in their craftiness."

B. Job 5:13 in Its OT Context. The unit in which the verse appears, part of the first speech of Eliphaz, reinforces the idea of God's superiority over human wisdom and strength. Job 5:8–16, in a passage depicting the God who does "great, unsearchable, and marvelous things" (5:9), sets up an opposition between "the wise" and "the poor." The passage in question develops the theme of God's deliverance of the latter ("he saves the needy from the sword of their mouth . . . so the poor have hope" [5:15–16]) and his frustration of the former ("the schemes of the wily are brought to a quick end" [5:13b]).

C. Job 5:13 in Early Judaism. A number of Jewish texts develop themes arising out of or overlapping with the sentiments of Job 5:13 (Williams 2001: 307–15). For example, Bar. 3:20–28 protests the futility of human striving to attain wisdom, which can be granted only by God's revelation (cf. 3:36–4:4). That God makes certain wise people ineffectual and thwarts their plans is seen in *Pss. Sol.* 8:20 (the wise Jewish leaders when the Romans captured Jerusalem); Wis. 17:7–11 (the wise Egyptians at the time of the exodus); 3 Macc. 1–2 (King Ptolemy planning to enter the holy of holies); Jdt. 2:2–3 (Holofernes and Nebuchadnezzar planning to decimate Judea).

D. Textual Matters. The MT, LXX, and 1 Cor. 3:19 carry an equivalent sense but differ in some details. Compared to the LXX, Paul has *drassomai* rather than *katalambanō* (both meaning "lay hold of"), and *en tē panourgia autōn* ("in their craftiness") instead of *en tē phronēsei* ("in prudence/understanding"). Concerning the latter, the Hebrew is closer to Paul's rendition, using a word that implies a sly and crafty form of wisdom. The differences may be explained as Paul offering his own Hebraizing revision of the present LXX or his own translation of the Hebrew, or that he is quoting a wholly independent translation of the Hebrew text of Job (see Stanley 1992: 188–94).

E. The Use of Job 5:13 in 1 Cor. 3:19. In the book of Job as a whole, Job's friends' advice is shown to be unhelpful, misapplied wisdom. Hays (1997: 59), however, rightly asserts that "Paul cites Job 5:13 here as an authoritative disclosure of the truth about God's debunking of human wisdom." The immediate context of the quotation resonates

with the themes of reversal and the mystery of divine mercy that Paul introduced earlier in the letter (1:18–2:16).

F. Theological Use. See commentary on 1 Cor. 3:20 below.

3:20

A. NT Context: The World's Wisdom Is Folly. If in 1:18–25 Paul says that what God does in wisdom seems foolish to the world, here we have the converse: what the world thinks is wise, God declares to be futile folly (Fee 1987: 152).

B. Ps. 94:11 in Its OT Context. Psalm 94 is a prayer for God to overthrow the wicked oppressors and vindicate the righteous. The summary by Thiselton (2000: 323) is accurate: "Psalm 94 stresses that in spite of manipulative and corrupt leadership by those in authority (Ps. 94:5–7, 16), the 'schemes' of these human persons fail because their best 'thinkers' are fallible (Ps. 94:11)." The psalm also promises that blessing awaits those who depend on God; he will not abandon them, but rather will teach them and aid them in their time of need (94:12–23).

C. Ps. 94:11 in Early Judaism. The contrast between human thinking and God's thoughts is widespread in Jewish literature (Williams 2001: 315–25). The *Targum of Job* contains numerous references to the futility of the human intellect without God's revelation. Likewise, Bar. 3:29–37 asserts the inaccessibility of God's wisdom. In 1 Macc. 2:61–64 the plans (*dialogismos*) of sinners will perish. Other texts emphasize the benefits of cooperating with God's plans and call on people to turn to God asking for wisdom.

D. Textual Matters. The MT, the LXX, and 1 Cor. 3:20 are equivalent except that Paul renders Ps. 94:11 (93:11 LXX) as describing the thoughts of "the wise" instead of "men" (*anthrōpōn*). No OT manuscript has any other reading. A few lesser Pauline manuscripts agree with the MT and the LXX and read *anthrōpōn* instead of *sophōn* in 3:20, but this is probably a deliberate conforming of Paul's wording to the psalm. "There is little reason to doubt that the present modification goes back to Paul himself" (Stanley 1992: 195).

The futility of human wisdom is a central theme for Paul in 1:19–27a; 2:4–6; 3:18–19. However, it is not that he has altered the text in cavalier fashion simply to suit his argument. Paul's allusion to 94:14 in Rom. 11:2 indicates that he knew the psalm well. What makes the form of his quotation in 3:20 explicable is the link that Ps. 94 itself forges between "fools" and the "wise": "Understand, O dullest of the people! Fools, when will you be wise?" (94:8). The "humans" spoken of in 94:11, whose thoughts the Lord knows to be futile, are the same group described as "fools" earlier in the psalm. That Paul feels free to label them, ironically, as "the wise" fits his rhetoric and does no violence to the larger context of the psalm.

E. The Use of Ps. 94:11 in 1 Cor. 3:20. Psalm 94 and early Jewish literature emphasize not only that God thwarts the plans of the wise, but also that there is great blessing for those who are part of and cooperate with God's plans. Thus, not only does the citation of Ps. 94:11 signal the futility of acting or thinking independently of God, but also, as 3:21–23 goes on to celebrate, there are great benefits to those who boast not in human leaders, but rather in God.

F. Theological Use. Together the texts cited in 3:19–20, which testify to the futility of human thoughts apart from God's revelation and the consequent emptiness of human wisdom, support Paul's conclusion in 3:21a: "Let no one boast about human leaders" (NRSV). Paul uses the two citations in 3:19–20 to bolster the paradoxical nature of his doctrine of salvation. The gospel spells the end of human pride.

4:6–13

Described by Conzelmann (1975: 86) as "unintelligible," the words "not [to go] beyond the things which are written" (4:6) are most naturally taken as a reference to Scripture; 4:6 instructs the Corinthians not to transgress the exhortations found in and constructed from the Scriptures, to boast exclusively in the Lord (not in human leaders), and to recognize the unity of the people of God. Hays (1997: 69) defends this interpretation convincingly:

> The phrase "what is written" in Paul always refers to Scripture.... Paul has prominently spotlighted six Scripture quotations in the first three chapters of the letter (1:19, 31; 2:9, 16; 3:19, 20). In the case of the first two and the last two, the application of the texts is explicitly spelled out: No boasting in human beings. First Corinthians 3:21a links the two quotations in chapter 3 back to the quotations in chapter 1. ... Furthermore, the two quotations in chapter

2, though they are not explicit admonitions against boasting, reinforce the same theme by juxtaposing God's gracious ways to all human understanding. The cumulative force of these citations is unmistakable: the witness of Scripture places a strict limit on human pride and calls for trust in God alone. What would it mean to go "beyond" this witness of Scripture? It would mean, quite simply, to boast in human wisdom by supposing that we are, as it were, smarter than God. The last clause of 1 Corinthians 4:6 confirms this interpretation.

Alternatively, Wagner (1998) argues that 4:6a refers back in particular to the citation in 1:31, noting echoes of 1 Kgdms. 2:10 in 4:6–13.

The Case of the Incestuous Man (4:18–5:13)

Introduction

If the Corinthians' fundamental problem is divisions, their most serious and pressing fault is that they are tolerating in their midst the presence of a man committing incest. In 4:18–21, a transitional section, Paul threatens the Corinthians with stern discipline if they do not acknowledge his authority. In 5:1–2 he rebukes the Corinthians for their inaction and tells them to remove the offender. In 5:3–5 he supplies authoritative support for this action. In 5:6–8 he offers further motivation, appealing to the spiritual self-interest of the Corinthians' church: whereas removing the offender will benefit them, allowing him to remain will harm them. In 5:9–11 he further facilitates the offender's removal by correcting a misunderstanding: it is such offenders within, not outside, the household of faith whom they must shun. Finally, in 5:12–13 he asserts the Corinthians' responsibility to act and closes the section with a weighty command from Scripture.

Incest

Whether committed with one's mother or with the wife of one's father, incest is prohibited in the OT and early Judaism. Many commentators mention Lev. 18:8; 20:11 as the critical background to Paul's decision to expel the sinner, noting the shared terminology *gynē* and *patēr*, "woman/wife" and "father" (5:1). Sexual intercourse with the "wife" of one's father is also condemned in Gen. 49:4 (cf. 35:22); Ezek. 22:10–11. However, two verses in Deuteronomy are just as likely to have influenced Paul. First, Deut. 27:20, "Cursed is the man who sleeps with his father's wife," is perhaps the reason Paul "curses" the sinner in chapter 5. Second, Deut. 22:30, "A man must not marry his father's wife," may have been the impetus for Paul to quote the Deuteronomic expulsion formula in 5:13. A variation of that formula appears in Deut. 22:22 ("If a man is found sleeping with another man's wife, both of them must die . . . ; you must purge the evil from Israel" [cf. 22:24]) and presumably carries the penalty for the incest prohibited in Deut. 22:30.

Judaism maintained this Deuteronomic resolve that incest be punished: *m. Sanh.* 7:4 (incest is punishable by stoning); 9:1 and *m. Ker.* 1:1 (incest is one of the first offenses punishable by expulsion); *Jub.* 33:10–13; *t. Sanh.* 10:1; CD-A V; 11Q19 LXVI. Josephus describes incest as "the grossest of sins" and "an outrageous crime" (*Ant.* 3.274), and of incest Philo asks, "What form of unholiness could be more impious than this?" (*Spec. Laws* 3.13–14; cf. 3.20–21).

Expulsion

The rationale that Paul provides for removing the offender recalls teaching from the Pentateuch, where expulsion is administered for (1) breach of the covenant and (2) guilt by association in order to (3) maintain holiness. The three motifs form a package of three perspectives on the identity of Israel: offenders are expelled because Israel is the sanctified (holiness motif) covenant (covenant motif) community (corporate responsibility motif) of the Lord, the holy God. These motifs undergird Paul's teaching throughout the passage (Rosner 1999: 61–93).

4:21

The rod that Paul threatens to brandish reluctantly is what OT wisdom believed a father (cf. 4:15) should use to drive out folly from the heart of his children (Prov. 22:15; 23:13–14).

5:1–2

Paul's rebuke of Corinthian arrogance and his call for the body to show passionate grief that will lead to action indicates that he considered the Corinthians in some sense implicated in the offense of the sinner. The verb *pentheō* ("grieve") is used in the NT of mourning over the death of a loved one (Matt. 9:15; Mark 16:10; cf. Gen. 50:10) and for grief over a great loss (Rev. 18:11, 15, 19). Hence many commentators understand Paul to be enjoining a mourning over the impending loss of the sinning brother. However, the word is used elsewhere by Paul only in 2 Cor. 12:21 (cf. Jas. 4:9; *1 Clem.* 2:6), where its sense closely parallels the concept of godly sorrow or repentance.

The use of "mourn" in the LXX suggests that in 5:2a Paul thought that the Corinthians ought to mourn in the sense of confessing the sin of the erring brother as if it were their own. The word occurs only six times in the LXX with reference to sin. In Ezra 10:6; Neh. 1:4; 1 Esd. 8:72 (8:69 LXX); 9:2; and Dan. 10:2 it refers to sorrow over the sins of others, and in Neh. 8:9 (cf. *T. Reub.* 1:10) it refers to sorrow over personal sin (but still in a corporate context). For example, in Ezra 10:6 Ezra "mourned over the unfaithfulness of the exiles." In the former references the grief is given expression in prayers by Ezra, Nehemiah, and Daniel in which the sins of others are confessed as if they are their own. Ezra 10 in particular is a distinct parallel to 1 Cor. 5. It is an Ezra-like Paul who deals with the expulsion of the sinner. Just as Ezra mourned over the sins of the community, so also Paul enjoined the Corinthians to mourn over the sin of the incestuous man. Just as Ezra demanded that the sinners separate from their foreign partners or else suffer expulsion (10:8), so also Paul demanded the expulsion of the sinner unless he separate from his illicit partner.

In biblical thought, failure to deal with a blatantly sinning member invites the possibility of judgment from God on the whole group (see Rosner 1992a). The corollary of corporate responsibility—the fear of God's judgment on the community—evident in Josh. 7 and other OT texts, is also present in the incidents involving Ezra, Nehemiah, and Daniel. All three assumed that the nation stood under the covenant and that breach of responsibility could jeopardize the whole group before God. A sense of urgency gripped these leaders in their dealings with God and the nation. As Héring (1969: 35) states, "In the OT, belief in the efficacy of mourning and fasting for warding off public misfortune is well attested by 1 Kings 21:9; Amos 5:16; 8:10."

5:3–5

In 5:4 the excommunication is to take place when the Corinthians "are assembled" in the name and power of the Lord Jesus. Whatever else this scene implies, it is comparable to the judgment scene of Deut. 19:16–20, which includes the command quoted in 5:13b. In Deut. 19 the discipline also takes place in the presence of the congregation (19:20a) and of God (19:17). Comparable texts are Lev. 24:14, 16 ("the entire assembly is to stone" a blasphemer); Num. 15:35 ("the entire assembly must stone" the sabbath-breaker); 35:24 ("the assembly must judge" a case of homicide). The forum for the judgment of offenders is the gathered community also in 1QS VI–VII. In biblical criminal law the entire community is involved in judgment.

Paul prescribes the actual judgment in 5:5: the offender is to be handed over to Satan for "the destruction of the flesh." Some hold that Paul here enjoins the pronouncement of a curse on the immoral man that will lead to physical suffering and ultimately death (cf. NEB: "This man is to be consigned to Satan for the destruction of the body"). The word *olethros* ("destruction"), it is argued, is so strong a term that it must refer to death. In the LXX the cognate verb *olethreuō* frequently denotes utter ruin and sudden death (e.g., Exod. 12:23; Josh. 3:10; 7:25; Jer. 2:30), and Paul uses the related term, *olothreutēs*, in 10:10 in referring to loss of life at the hands of "the destroying angel." Supposedly parallel ancient curses appear in secular Greek literature (the Magical Papyri) and Jewish sources, and similar tragic episodes of serious sin leading to loss of life occur in Acts 5:1–11; 1 Cor. 11:30. Conzelmann (1975: 97) states the conclusion that seems to follow: "The destruction of the flesh can hardly mean anything else but death."

However, the "curse/death" view of 5:5 is not the best interpretation. To hand the offender over to Satan is to turn him back out into Satan's sphere, outside the edifying and caring environment of the church, where God is at work (see South 1993). The "flesh" to be "destroyed" is his sinful nature. In other words, 5:5 states metaphorically what Paul says literally in 5:2, 13: the man is to be excluded from the community of faith.

The resemblance of 5:5 to ancient curse formulas is only superficial. The closest parallels are OT formulas using the terms "drive out" and "cut off." Second Temple Judaism regularly replaced execution with excommunication when applying these texts to their communities (see Horbury 1985, esp. 27–30). Also parallel perhaps are Job 1:12; 2:6, where Job is "handed over" to Satan, in which case suffering led to a positive result, and the loss of life was specifically excluded.

Why must the offending man's flesh be "destroyed"? Three groups of observations support the case for reading chapter 5 (esp. 5:5) with 3:16–17 ("Do you not know that you yourselves are God's temple and that God's Spirit lives in you? If anyone destroys God's temple God will destroy him; for God's temple is holy, and that is what you are") with an OT temple/holiness motif in mind. The man must suffer "destruction" because he has destroyed God's holy temple, the church. First, certain features of 3:16–17 suggest its affinity with chapter 5. The characteristic of the temple to which Paul draws attention in 3:16–17 is its holiness, which carries a demand for the maintenance of purity, a thought that Paul develops in 5:6–8. Second, temple imagery is prominent in both Corinthian epistles. In 2 Cor. 6:16 the church is identified as the "temple of God," and in 1 Cor. 6:12–20 the need for sexual purity is linked to Christians being the "temple of the Holy Spirit." Third, Horbury demonstrates that during the Second Temple period the scope of the laws of admission to the assembly found in Deut. 23:1–8 were expanded beyond stipulations of physique and descent to include moral requirements. Biblical evidence for this evolution includes the "entrance-*torot*" (Ps. 15; 24:3–5; Isa. 33:14–17), the exclusion of "rebels" in Ezek. 20:38–40 from the future congregation, and the indictment of Israel in Ezek. 44:6–9 for admitting into the sanctuary aliens who are "uncircumcised in heart." Josephus and Philo build upon this biblical background and "take Deut. 23 to exclude not only aliens and defective Jews, but also gravely-offending Jewish sinners" (Horbury 1985: 26).

The likelihood that Deut. 23:1–8 played a role in the formation of Paul's thinking in 1 Cor. 5 is increased by the fact that Deut. 22:30 addresses the very question that Paul is engaging: "A man must not marry his father's wife; he must not dishonor his father's bed." That Paul linked the two passages has every possibility because, as Horbury

(1985: 25) observes, "The admission-regulations of Deut. 23:2–9 (1–8) were linked in rabbinic exegesis with 23:1 (22:30), and correspondingly understood, as by Targum Pseudo-Jonathan, as marriage laws." This exegesis may even have a basis in Deuteronomy. Fishbane (1985: 120) suggests that Deut. 22:30 and 23:1–8 are linked through the mention of the Ammonites and Moabites, who, according to Gen. 19:31–38, are the offspring of incest (Lot and his daughters).

5:6–8

Having "cleansed the temple," Paul calls upon the congregation to celebrate spiritually the festival of Passover/Unleavened Bread. That this sequence of events occurred to Paul's mind may itself testify to the influence of the OT temple motif, since in the OT there is an observable link between cleansing or restoring the temple and celebrating the Passover. Following the "removal of all defilement from the sanctuary" in order to "reestablish the service of the temple of the LORD" (2 Chron. 29:5, 35), King Hezekiah calls upon the people to celebrate the Passover (2 Chron. 30). Similarly, King Josiah, after removing the articles of idolatry from the temple and repositing the sacred ark in its rightful place, orders the Israelites to celebrate the Passover and observe the Feast of Unleavened Bread (2 Kings 23:1–23; 2 Chron. 35:1–19). In Ezra the same pattern is followed: first the completion and dedication of the temple (6:13–18), then a joyous Passover and Feast of Unleavened Bread (6:19–22).

Paul wants the Corinthians to be free from leaven, "a new batch," without the evil influence of the sinning brother. The sense of "get rid of" (ekkathairō) in 5:7 is paralleled by the use of a similar verb (ekkatharizō) in Judg. 20:13, where the Benjamites are called upon by the other tribes of Israel to execute certain Gibeonite sexual offenders (see 19:22–26) and thereby "get rid of the evil from Israel."

"Leaven" is a "little" portion of a previous week's "batch of dough" that had been allowed to ferment. When added to the next batch, the leaven made the bread rise. It carried with it the slight risk of infection, especially if the process was left to go on indefinitely without starting afresh with a completely new batch. Each year the Israelites, in part perhaps as a health provision, had to cleanse their homes and the temple from all leaven (Exod.

12:14–20; Deut. 16:3–8). The unleavened bread from the Feast of Unleavened Bread would supply some "fresh" leaven and start the process anew for the next twelve months of baking bread. The Israelites left Eygpt in such a hurry that they did not have time to leaven their bread. The Feast of Unleavened Bread, a seven-day festival in which the Jews were forbidden to eat anything leavened, commemorates this event. Paul emphasizes (by emphatic word order in Greek) that although in only a "little" part of the church—one person, in fact—the evil would inevitably, slowly but surely, spread through the whole community if left unchecked. The example of willful sin in the church can have serious effects. Like leaven in bread, unchecked sin in the church spreads through the whole and irretrievably changes it.

With the mention of unleavened bread, Paul's mind turns to Passover, that great founding event for God's people Israel, and the cross, its even more relevant equivalent as a type for the church. Such events and institutions are regarded by Paul as patterns of God's work of salvation in the OT that point to their greater analogue of salvation in Christ. In 5:8 Paul draws out a lesson from the fact that only unleavened bread was eaten during Passover. He broadens out the discussion of the unfortunate case at hand, without losing sight of it, to treat the Christian life as a whole, which he pictures most attractively as a celebration: "Therefore let us keep the festival," a reference to holy living and moral purity in general.

5:9–11

In 5:10 Paul lists four examples of people with whom social contact in the world is unavoidable. Then in 5:11 he gives a representative list of six sinners that the church is to judge in terms of withdrawal of social integration. The verb synesthiō ("eat with") appears in Ps. 100:5 LXX (101:5 MT) in a similar context: "He who slanders his neighbors secretly, he is banished; he who is of haughty looks and of a greedy heart, with him food is not shared [synēsthion]." There, as Newton (1985: 95) observes, "banishment is equivalent to [exclusion from] table fellowship" in comparable fashion to 5:11. In both 1 Cor. 5 and Ps. 100 LXX the faithful are not to eat with those guilty of slander, arrogance, and greed. In Ps. 100:7 LXX (101:7 MT) the presence of God in the temple and evil are said to be incompatible, supplying a further link with the temple theme in 1 Cor. 5: "No one who practices deceit shall dwell in my house; no one who speaks falsehood shall remain in my presence." The psalm again demonstrates the OT roots of Paul's instructions about exclusion from the people of God.

The representative list of sinners that the church is to judge (5:12b) is in one sense a list of covenantal norms that, when broken, automatically exclude the offender. Paul lists "sexual immorality" first, since that is the issue at hand. But what governs his choice of the next five vices in the catalog? Paul gives a clue in 5:13b: the sins to which the Deuteronomic formula "Expel the wicked person from among you," which Paul quotes, is connected in Deuteronomy form a remarkable parallel to the particular sins mentioned in 5:11 (Rosner 1999: 68–70; Hays 1997: 88):

1 Cor. 5:11	Deuteronomy
sexually immoral	promiscuity, adultery (22:21–22, 30)
greedy	(no parallel, but paired with "robber" in 1 Cor. 5:10)
idolater	idolatry (13:1–5; 17:2–7)
reviler	malicious false testimony (19:16–19)
drunkard	rebellious drunken son (21:18–21)
robber	kidnapping, slave-trading (24:7; the LXX uses *kleptēs* ["thief"])

5:12–13

A. NT Context: Expelling the Sinner. In 5:13b Paul quotes a frequent expression of the LXX of Deuteronomy, where it is used on six occasions to signal the execution of a variety of offenders (13:6 [13:5 ET], using *aphanizō* rather than *exairō*; 17:7; 19:19; 21:21; 22:21, 24; 24:7; cf. 17:12; 22:22; Judg. 20:13; 1 Macc. 14:14). The verb *exairō* ("expel") occurs in the NT only here, suggesting Paul's intentional and explicit use of the formula from Deuteronomy. Paul's failure to introduce a quotation in 5:13b with "as it is written" or the like may be explicable on rhetorical grounds; the lack of connection suits the chapter's emotionally charged atmosphere.

B. The Deuteronomic Expulsion Formula in Its OT Context. Deuteronomic expulsion formulas involving the verb "utterly remove" (BDB §129.3) are consistently associated with the idea of a covenant. This word is translated by *exairō* in the LXX of Deuteronomy, and it is one of these formulas that Paul quotes in 5:13b. People are expelled by these formulas in Deuteronomy for

having breached the covenant. Deuteronomy 17:7 makes this clear; the expulsion takes place because a person has "violated the covenant" of Israel's God (17:2). Commenting on Achan's sin, Josh. 7:15 states: "He who is caught with the devoted things shall be destroyed . . . because he has violated the covenant of the LORD" (cf. 23:16: "If you violate the covenant of the LORD your God . . . you will quickly perish").

Another reason for expulsion in this material is to deter a further breach of the covenant in the community. For example, Deut. 19:19b–20 states, "You must purge the evil from among you. The rest of the people will hear of this and be afraid, and never again will such an evil thing be done among you." To dissuade further from sin is also a reason for expulsion in 13:12–18; 17:2–7, 12–13; 21:18–21. In such formulas the offender is expelled in order to maintain Israel's obedience to the demands of the covenant. Read in the light of this material, the vice catalog of 1 Cor. 5:11 takes on new significance.

A second motif is associated with "utterly remove" formulas in Deut. 19:13; 21:9. In both cases the phrase "You must rid Israel of the guilt of innocent blood" expresses the penalty for the crime of murder. That "blood guilt" touches the whole community is made clear in Deut. 19:13, where the motivation for the expulsion is "so that it may go well with you [i.e., the nation]" (cf. Deut. 21:8). The notion of "blood guilt" introduces the motif of corporate responsibility, in which the community is held responsible for the sin of an individual.

C. Expulsion in Early Judaism. In the *Damascus Document* expulsion from the community for a variety of offenses is also consistently associated with the covenant.

As we noted above, in Paul's day many Jews replaced execution with expulsion in applying the teaching from Deuteronomy.

D. Textual Matters. The texts in the LXX of Deuteronomy and 1 Corinthians are identical except for the verb, with the latter using a singular future indicative rather than a plural aorist imperative, presumably to suit Paul's epistolary context.

E. The Use of the Deuteronomic Formula in 1 Cor. 5. The command to expel the sinner closes Paul's instructions on the case of the incestuous man in an unambiguous and uncompromising way. At the end of chapter 5, along with connecting with the vice list of 5:11 (see above), it draws together the threads of covenant and corporate responsibility that run through the passage and complements Paul's own authority with that of Scripture.

Once again we see Paul using Israel as an analogy for the church. If God's people in Israel expelled certain sinners, then God's people in Christ should do no less.

F. Theological Use. In all of Paul's letters no instruction speaks more forcefully about the seriousness of sin, the holiness of God's people, and their corporate standing before him than this passage, which is the longest text in the NT on the subject of church discipline. The church must expel the wicked man in the hope of regaining him and above all to protect the community's standing before God and the world. This teaching is largely based on the Pentateuch, especially Deuteronomy, as 5:13b suggests.

Civil Litigation in the Family of God (6:1–11)

Introduction

Paul turns his attention to another issue that involves judging. He is indignant that "the saints"—that is, members of the church in Corinth—are suing each other in secular courts. His case against lawsuits comprises two points: (1) in 6:1–6 he insists that Christians ought to be able to settle their own disputes; (2) in 6:7–11, going a step further, he contends that Christians ought to be willing to suffer injustice rather than engage in a dispute with another believer (see Rosner 1999: chap. 4).

The Processes of Law

In the OT there is a distinction between civil and criminal processes of law (Buss 1977). The link between 5:1–13 and 6:1–11 becomes clear when the two passages are read in the light of this distinction. Incest, the problem in 5:1–13, falls in the category of criminal law, and the dispute in 6:1–11 is covered by civil law that deals with relations within a group. Criminal cases "were decided by the head of a community on his own

authority or by the people as a corporate whole" (Buss 1977: 53), both of which occur in 5:3–5, where Paul pronounces judgment and calls for the consent of the body corporate. Criminal legislation in the OT "speaks of the offender in the third person and addresses the breaching community in the second" (Buss 1977: 59) (e.g., Exod. 21:14, 23). This is precisely Paul's style in 5:1–13.

Civil cases in the OT, on the other hand, were to be presented to the judges described in Exod. 18/Deut. 1 and related passages. It is the model of these judges that informs Paul's discussion in 6:1–11.

It appears that Paul understood the scriptural distinctions between civil and criminal law and appropriated them in response to Corinthian problems in 5:1–6:11. First Corinthians 5:1–13 and 6:1–11 are related in that they both concern law, criminal and civil respectively.

The Appointment of Judges

Various attempts have been made to compare the Christian "courts" that Paul recommends in 6:1–6 with contemporary Jewish judicial practices.

There can be little doubt that Paul's concern that judicial matters be settled internally was the common Jewish attitude of his day. It is also possible that the administration of justice in ancient Israel as presented in the Scriptures may have influenced Paul's thinking in the appointment of judges. De Vaux (1965: 1:152–55) explains that Israel had three different jurisdictions involving priests, elders, and professional judges instituted by the authority of the king. All three groups are mentioned in the Pentateuch and take part in judicial affairs in other parts of the Scriptures. The third group of judges is relevant to 1 Cor. 6:1–6. Such judges find their prototypes in the competent laymen appointed to dispense justice by Moses upon the advice of Jethro, his father-in-law, in Exod. 18:13–26; Deut. 1:9–17. Deuteronomy 16:18–20; 17:8–13 give further directions for these judges.

The appointment of judges by prominent Israelite leaders is a well-attested practice in the Scriptures. Notices concerning the appointment of judges by Samuel, David, Jehoshaphat, and Ezra also occur in 1 Sam. 8:1; 1 Chron. 23:4, 2 Chron. 19:5–11; Ezra 7:25; 10:14. Contemporary Jewish custom also bears the imprint of the Moses material. Nor did it escape the notice of the early church that Moses appointed judges (see Rosner 1999: 98–99).

The Family of God

Paul emphasizes the inappropriateness and regrettable nature of the Corinthians' behavior in 6:1–6 by depicting the situation as a family altercation between brothers. The generic *adelphos* ("brother") is used three times in 6:5–6 and once in 6:8 for this very purpose. The term "brother" was in standard Jewish use (see, e.g., 1–2 Maccabees and many rabbinic texts) in Jewish communities and may well have enjoyed a relatively technical sense in early Christian communication (cf. "brother" in quasi-legal contexts in Matt. 18:15; Gal. 6:1). Paul's concern that disputes between "brothers" be settled peacefully is shared by Exod. 18; Deut. 1. In Gen. 13:8, a text that records the legal controversy between Abram and Lot over the promised land, Abram says that there should be no strife between Lot and himself, because they are "brothers." Psalm 133:1 captures Paul's sentiment well: "Behold, how good and how pleasant it is for brothers to dwell together in unity." Paul was concerned that "brothers" in the family of God not squabble.

6:1–6

That Paul considers "unrighteous" judges, the *adikōn*, unsuitable—a description that simultaneously identifies them as unbelievers and as unfair judges—is not surprising in terms of the qualifications of judges taught throughout the OT, especially in Exod. 18/Deut. 1 and related passages (note in Deut. 16:18–20a LXX the four occurrences of *dik-* words).

Paul's conviction in 6:2 that the saints will judge the world derives from the Jewish hope that God's people will participate in the judgment of the last days expressed in Dan. 7:22 (Dodd 1953: 68), developed by postbiblical Jewish writings (e.g., Wis. 3:7–8; *Jub.* 24:29; Sir. 4:11, 15; *1 En.* 1:9, 38; 38:5; 95:3; 96:1; 98:12; 108:12; 1QpHab V, 4–5) and picked up in early Christian teaching (e.g., Matt. 19:28; Luke 22:30; Jude 14–15; Rev. 2:26–27; 20:4).

No prior text, to our knowledge, contains the thought of believers judging angels. It may simply

be an extension from 6:2, "the world" including not only humankind on earth, but also heavenly beings. Though the OT does not specifically speak of human beings judging angels, Paul could have deduced the idea from Ps. 8:5 (a psalm that he quotes in 15:27), whereby a person's ultimate destiny in Christ is to be above the angels (although the LXX [8:6] puts human beings a little lower than "the angels," not "God" [cf. Heb. 2:7]), or from Dan. 7:18, whereby sharing the kingdom would involve sharing the king's authority.

The situations in which Moses in Exod. 18/Deut. 1 and Paul in 6:1–6 find themselves are remarkably similar. Both Moses and Paul are overwhelmed by the judicial problems of the people of God. Both leaders decide to handle the more difficult cases themselves, with the Lord's help (cf. Exod. 18:19b and 1 Cor. 5:3–5), and appoint judges to adjudicate the lesser cases (see Exod. 18:21–22; Deut. 1:15; 1 Cor. 6:1b, 4, 5b) by deciding between their brothers.

There are also impressive terminological links between 6:1–11 and Exod. 18/Deut. 1 LXX (and related passages). A total of eight terms, some of which occur rarely in both the LXX and Paul's letters, can be traced from 6:1–8 to the tradition of Moses appointing judges in the Greek OT. There may be an echo of Deut. 1:16 in 6:5b (see Rosner 1991).

In 6:1–6 Paul applies the lessons of Exod. 18/Deut. 1 (and related passages) to the problem of lawsuits in Corinth. He follows the implications of the Moses material (because Moses provided the most important biblical precedent for what he was doing) but finds it unnecessary to signal his use of Scripture to the Corinthians either by quotation or allusion. Just as Moses appointed wise and righteous laity to decide lesser civil cases (including fraud) between their brothers, so also Paul rejected unrighteous judges and told the Corinthians to appoint wise laity to decide such cases between their brothers.

The fact that Paul expects the church to operate judicially like the Israel of old suggests that he views the Corinthian community as the beginning of the true Israel.

6:7–8

Paul is, in effect, calling for believers not only to forgo their rights, but also to suffer injustice and abuse willingly. Christians should avoid secular courts, which are based on the principle of retaliation for wrongs done.

Leviticus 19:13a LXX states, "You shall not wrong [*adikēseis*] your neighbor." Paul is in agreement, contending that it would be better for the Corinthian Christians to suffer wrong (*adikeisthe*). Several commentators confidently ascribe the source of Paul's teaching in these verses to the words of Jesus in Matt. 5:39–42 (cf. 5:40: "If anyone wants to sue you and take your coat, give your cloak as well"). However, the nonretaliatory ethic of Jesus itself stands in the tradition of OT ethics and of early Judaism (see Zerbe 1993).

The biblical theme of the suffering righteous, which can be traced through the intertestamental Jewish literature, forms the dominant background for the various Pauline discussions of suffering, including those found in 1 Corinthians (see Kleinknecht 1984).

Paul applies this theme as a help to understanding not only the sufferings of Jesus, but also his own sufferings, and in this case the sufferings that he advocates for his churches.

6:9–11

Above it was argued that two OT texts play a formative role in 6:1–8, even though they are not explicitly cited: Dan. 7:22 in 6:2–3 and Exod. 18/Deut. 1 in 6:1–6. The broader OT contexts of both may have prompted Paul to refer in 6:9–10 to inheriting the kingdom of God (Rosner 1996b).

Both Deut. 1 and Exod. 18 precede the giving of the law. In Deut. 1–6 the point is made repeatedly that the people of God will inherit the land if they obey the covenant stipulations set forth in the Ten Commandments (see, e.g., Deut. 6:1). Furthermore, in Deut. 3:21 the land that they will inherit is described as "the kingdoms" of the peoples whom they will dispossess. In Exod. 19:6 they are told that keeping this covenant will enable them to become a "kingdom of priests and a holy nation." Paul, in 6:9–10, connects inheritance with a list of ten vices. Although the Ten Commandments and Paul's vice list overlap in content, the similarity is not so marked as to suggest dependence. It is not the case that Paul is giving a second Decalogue. Nonetheless, it is intriguing that both Moses and Paul gave God's people "ten words" to ensure that they would receive their inheritance and become part of a kingdom.

In Dan. 7 "the saints" are said to have been given judgment to exercise (7:22), a function that Paul echoes for "the saints" (6:1) in 6:2–3. In the case of Daniel, in chapter 7 alone there are nine references to "kingdom(s)." In fact, in 7:22 it is stated that not only was "judgment given to the saints," but also "the saints received the kingdom." Whereas in Deuteronomy the inheritance, though desirable and from God, is temporal and limited (the land), in Dan. 7 the kingdom, as in 1 Cor. 6:9–10, is everlasting and universal (see esp. Dan. 7:27). The OT texts that influenced Paul in 6:1–6 continued, it seems, to have influenced him in 6:9–10 when he refers to inheriting the kingdom.

In Exodus, Deuteronomy, and Daniel, the references to inheriting the kingdom are set in the context of suffering. Whereas in the former texts the people have come out from slavery in Egypt (Exodus) or have endured the wilderness wanderings (Deuteronomy), in Daniel the theme of hardship and destruction matches both the courses of the four kingdoms that are narrated in rapid succession and the historical setting of God's people in exile. In both cases inheriting the kingdom is held out as encouragement to fidelity and obedience in difficult circumstances.

This notion provides a bridge between 6:7–8 and the following three verses. Paul states in 6:9 that "the unrighteous will not inherit the kingdom of God." The natural question to ask is, Who *will* inherit the kingdom? The inheritors are those who suffer righteously by refusing to fight disputes with fellow believers (6:7–8). In 6:9–11 Paul provides encouragement to the Corinthians to follow his difficult advice in 6:7–8 (to avoid disputes with one another, even if it means suffering): those who choose to suffer wrong are the kind of people who will inherit the kingdom.

As we noted earlier in reference to 6:1–6, Paul applies categories originally reserved for Israel in ways that suggest that he regards the church to be the true Israel.

The vice list in 6:9–10 contains ten items, six of which are repeated from 5:11. Whereas one new term, "thieves" (*kleptai*), belongs especially to the concerns of 6:1–11, the other three deal with sexual sin and thus are in line with the main subject matter of the rest of chapters 5–7. "Adulterers" (*moichoi*) refers to married persons having sexual relations outside marriage. In the LXX the cognate verb *moicheuō* is employed in the Decalogue (Exod. 20:13 [20:14 ET]; Deut. 5:17 [5:18 ET]) and the Holiness Code (Lev. 20:10).

The two terms *malakoi* and *arsenokoitai* refer to homosexual behavior (of one form or another). Rather than being read as referring to "male prostitutes and homosexual offenders," they are better understood as the passive and active partners in any homosexual act. With *arsenokoitēs* Paul employed a new term (cf. 1 Tim. 1:10) that may have been fashioned on the very basis of the Levitical prohibitions (cf. Lev. 18:22; 20:13; see D. F. Wright 1984). The only other occurrence of the word that is possibly contemporary with Paul (it may be a Christian interpolation) is *Sib. Or.* 2:73. Thus, it seems likely that "the *arsenokoit-* group of words is a coinage of Hellenistic Judaism or Hellenistic Jewish Christianity" (D. F. Wright 1984: 129).

Temple Prostitution (6:12–20)

Introduction

Although sacred prostitution probably was not prevalent in the Corinth of Paul's day, there is evidence that many of the temple precincts hosted dinners after which prostitutes were on offer. It seems that some Corinthian Christians justified participation in such activities with the words "I have the right to do anything" (cf. 6:12; 10:23; see Rosner 1998).

Paul's response underscores the serious nature of sexual union and calls for faithfulness to Christ by quoting Gen. 2:24 in 6:16 (see Rosner 1996a). Further, a possible quotation of *T. Reub.* 5:5 in 6:18 reveals Paul's indebtedness to the Genesis account of Joseph fleeing Potiphar's wife (Rosner 1999: 123–46; 1992b).

6:16–17

A. NT Context: Union with Christ. Paul warns against *porneia* at a number of levels. Central to his argument is a text from Genesis explaining the nature of marriage. He uses it to explore the implications of the statement that "the body is for [service of and communion with] the Lord" (6:13).

B. Gen. 2:24 in Its OT Context. In its original context Gen. 2:24b forms part of a description of the first, prototypical marriage. Its contribution is to emphasize the real and enduring bond that is created in a marriage through sexual union. The text is also used within the OT to prohibit divorce, as in Mal. 2:15–16: "Has not God made them one?"

C. Gen. 2:24 in Early Judaism. The text was used in discussions of marriage (e.g., by Philo) to explain the nature of marital union, as in Matt. 19:5; Eph. 5:31.

D. Textual Matters. "Apart from the intrusion of the introductory formula ['For it is said'] . . . which occurs only here in the Pauline corpus, the quotation in 1 Cor. 6.16 follows the unanimous wording of the LXX tradition of Gen 2.24" (Stanley 1992: 195).

E. The Use of Gen. 2:24 in 1 Cor. 6. Paul's use of Gen. 2:24 in 6:16–17 differs from Matt. 19:5; Eph. 5:31. Whereas the latter two instances appear in discussions of divorce and marriage per se respectively, 1 Cor. 6 discusses the problem of sexual immorality. All three uses pick up the notion of the unique bond created by marriage. In 1 Cor. 6 the quotation functions in three ways. First, Paul uses it to prove that sexual intercourse with a prostitute is not an insignificant or casual matter. The "for" introducing 6:16a indicates that Gen. 2:24 gives a reason for the assertion in 6:15 that "the one who cleaves to a harlot becomes one body [with her]." A compound of the verb *kollaomai* ("cleave") occurs in the part of Gen. 2:24 LXX that is not quoted in the new 1 Corinthians context ("For this reason a man shall leave his father and mother and cleave [*proskollaomai*] to his wife").

Second, Gen. 2:24 draws attention to the spiritual marriage of the believer to Christ, a union that Paul assumes calls for faithfulness and purity. Paul presents two mutually exclusive alternatives in 6:16–17: cleaving to a prostitute or cleaving to the Lord. Thus the text is used not only to prove the seriousness of sexual union with a harlot, but also to introduce the notion of the believer's nuptial union with Christ (cf. 2 Cor. 11:2).

Third, Paul takes up the thought introduced by Gen. 2:24—the intended permanence of sexual relationships—to highlight the uniqueness of the sin of *porneia* in 6:18b.

F. Theological Use. Paul's reflections on the nature of the bond established in sexual relations via Gen. 2:24 are intended to impress upon the Corinthians a high view of the body and behavior involving the body. Throughout the paragraph Paul seeks to demolish Corinthian notions about the transience and consequent insignificance of the body. The text also supports the notion that our bodies are not our own, but rather belong to the Lord (not unlike spouses in marriage [cf. 7:4]). Genesis 2:24 gives credence to Paul's assertions that "the body is for [service of and communion with] the Lord" (6:13b) and "you are not your own" (6:19b).

6:18–20

The paragraph's central command in 6:18, *pheugete tēn porneian*, finds an exact parallel in *T. Reub.* 5:5 (with the addition of the conjunction *oun*). Even though the individual words are not uncommon, the specific injunction occurs only in these two places in ancient Greek literature (along with quotations of 1 Cor. 6:18 in the church fathers).

On the other hand, Gregory of Nyssa suggested a link between Paul's advice in 1 Cor. 6 and the example of Joseph in Gen. 39 (*Contra fornicarios oratio* 9.214–215). Genesis 39:12 LXX uses *pheugō* to describe Joseph's successful escape from Potiphar's wife: "He fled out of her house" (cf. Gen. 39:13, 15, 18). Furthermore, Gen. 39 forms a contrast to Tamar's prostitution in Gen. 38.

It is possible that both sources influenced Paul. As it turns out, *T. Reub.* 5 itself was written with Joseph in mind (see 4:8). The author not only warns his readers to "flee immorality," but also notes the relevance of God's indwelling to the state of chastity (cf. 1 Cor. 6:19) and concluded that Joseph had "glorified" God (cf. 1 Cor. 6:20). The Genesis Joseph account likewise describes Joseph as "one in whom is the Spirit of God" (41:38) and notes that his chief motivation in rejecting the advances of Potiphar's wife was to avoid sinning against God (39:9), akin to glorifying him. Thus *Testament of Reuben* witnesses to a traditional interpretation of Gen. 39 that may also have influenced Paul. Alternatively, Paul perhaps quotes *T. Reub.* 5:5 directly, not as sacred Scripture but as an appropriate ethical maxim, a text to which he was driven because of its effective use of Joseph in its warnings against *porneia*.

Marriage, Divorce, and Singleness (7:1–40)

Introduction

In answer to a number of questions put to him in a letter ("Now for the matters you wrote about" [7:1]), Paul's basic advice to the married, the unmarried, the "virgins," and the widows is to seek no change in status (e.g., 7:2, 8, 10, 11). This guiding principle of contentment with one's situation in life is taken up directly and reinforced in 7:17–24 with reference to circumcision and slavery. Although not made explicit, much of what Paul says here finds its roots in Scripture (Rosner 1999: 147–75).

7:1–7

Paul makes several points regarding marriage in these verses, most of which bear the marks of being influenced by his scriptural inheritance. The notion in 7:2 that sexual relations within marriage ought to act as a check on immorality (*tas porneias*) is reflected in Prov. 5:15, 18, 20 ("Drink water from your own cistern. . . . Rejoice in the wife of your youth. . . . Why should you be infatuated, my son, with a loose woman?") and *T. Levi* 9:9–10 ("Be on your guard against the spirit of immorality [*tēs porneias*]. . . . Take for yourself a wife" (cf. Tob. 4:12). The related idea that the husband and wife are obliged to give themselves sexually to each other derives from Exod. 21:10, where the husband "shall not diminish her [his wife's] food, her clothing, or her marital rights" (the expression "marital rights" being a euphemism for sexual relations).

In 7:4 Paul explains why sexual relations are due in marriage: the spouse's body belongs to his or her partner. While a property ethic applied to sexuality was common in the ancient world, including the OT (e.g., Deut. 20:5–7; 28:30), the distinctive reciprocity of Paul's comments (the husband's body belongs to the wife and vice versa) recalls the notes of mutual belonging in the Song of Solomon (2:16a; 6:3; cf. 7:10).

Finally, periodic abstinence for the purpose of prayer, commended in 7:5, brings to mind similar voluntary deprivation before cultic activities (e.g., Exod. 19:15; Lev. 15:18; 1 Sam. 21:4–6) and finds a specific parallel in *T. Naph.* 8:8: "There is a time for having intercourse with one's wife, and a time to abstain for the purpose of prayer."

7:10–11

Paul's prohibition of divorce for married couples is based on the teaching of Jesus, which later was preserved in Mark 10:2–12 (cf. Luke 16:18). To label this a departure from OT teaching is somewhat misleading, for although Deut. 24:1–4 presupposes the legitimacy of divorce, other texts disallow it under certain circumstances (Deut. 22:19, 28–29; Mal. 2:15–16).

7:12–16

In these verses Paul deals with a problem caused by the intrusion of the gospel. His response is that "mixed marriages are essentially Christian marriages" (Fee 1987: 298). The idea of a "holy family" takes up Jewish ritual language and rests on the presupposition of family solidarity. The notion that God's loving concern extends to the whole family is illustrated in various OT texts (e.g., Gen. 6:18; 17:7–27; 18:19; Deut. 30:19; Ps. 78:1–7). Rabbinic Judaism's view that proselyte children constituted full members of Israel is roughly parallel.

7:17–24

Two great social dividers appear in these verses as examples of Paul's main point in the chapter: "Let each of you remain in the condition in which you were called" (7:20 [cf. 7:24]). The sentiments in 7:18–19 concerning the relative irrelevance of circumcision (cf. Gal. 5:6; 6:15), despite the obvious contradiction of, for example, Gen. 17:10–14, are in effect an amplification of texts such as Deut. 10:16; Jer. 4:4, where membership in the covenant community is a matter of the heart, not an outward sign. Other figurative uses of circumcision (Exod. 6:30; Jer. 6:10; 9:26, which speak of uncircumcised lips, ears, and heart respectively) also point in Paul's direction.

On the topic of slavery, Paul teaches that believers should be content with their lot, but if the chance to go free arises, he advises the slave to take it. This teaching is comparable to the ceremony of piercing the earlobe of a slave who, at the end of seven years service, instead of becoming free chooses to remain with his master (Exod. 21:5–6). Daube (1963: 46) points out that the *Mekilta* commentary on this passage parallels 7:22–23 in that it not only recommends that slaves become free if the opportunity arises, but also cites the notion that God is the master of every Jew because of the exodus event (the Jewish antecedent to the Christ event in 7:23a: "You were bought with a price").

7:25–31

Paul gives two reasons why the "virgins" (probably young women who are betrothed but not yet married to men in the church) are to remain as they are: the present order of the world is going to pass away, and marriage presents hindrances to serving God. Hays (1997: 128) explains the logic of the first, which stands in the tradition of Jewish apocalyptic (for a late parallel, see 2 Esd. 16:40–48): "Paul's teaching on detachment is based on the conviction that the future is impinging upon the present; consequently, 'the present form of this world is passing away' (v. 31b). Under such circumstances, it simply looks illogical to undertake long-term commitments such as marriage."

7:32–35

Paul explains that he prefers singleness because marriage makes life more complicated and can be a distraction from devotion to Christ. The priority of pleasing God in these verses may have been derived from Deut. 6, which Paul alludes to in the next chapter (8:6). McNamara (1972:122–23) has noted the Palestinian Targum to the Pentateuch's treatment of Deut. 6 and its relevance to NT teaching on the undivided heart: "Israel was commanded to love God 'with all her heart' [Deut. 6:5]. In the targum full devotion to God is described as 'a perfect heart,' i.e., one completely set on God, not divided between him and created things." Furthermore, in several rabbinic texts worldly preoccupations, such as a wife, are seen as a potential distraction from the study of Torah (e.g., 'Abot R. Nat. a. 20). It would not be the first time that Christ replaces Torah in Paul's appropriation of traditional teaching (cf., e.g., the use of Deut. 30:12–13 in Rom. 10:6–8).

7:39–40

Paul makes three points regarding the termination of marriage and remarriage for the benefit of Christian widows in Corinth. Tomson (1990: 120–22) argues that all three use "formulations directly related to Rabbinic halakha." Biblical roots are also evident.

In 7:39a Paul indicates that the death of a husband terminates the marriage bond, so that the widow has the right to remarry. Deuteronomy 24:3 stipulates the same provision with the words "if the latter husband dies." In 7:39b Paul states that the widow may marry whomever she wishes. This is similar to *m. Giṭ.* 9:3, in a tractate expounding the halakic implications of Deut. 24:1–4: "You are permitted to marry any man." Finally, in 7:39c Paul adds the restriction "only in the Lord." Similar clauses were in Jewish circulation in Paul's day. For example, a Bar Kokhba divorce deed has an analogous specification: "You may go and be married to any Jewish man you want" (*DJD* 2, no. 19). The exclusion of marriage to a non-Jew has its basis in Scripture (Deut. 7:3; Josh. 23:12; Ezra 9:1–4; Neh. 13:23–27).

Idolatry and True Worship (8–14)

Introduction

Chapters 8–14 are held together by the underlying unifying theme of worship, with 8:1–11:1 focusing on the avoidance of cultic associations with idols, and chapters 11–14 focusing on the proper worship of the one true God.

Love and Edification

Kim (2002: 26n94) suggests, "In 1 Cor 10:14–11:1 Paul summarizes and concludes his long, careful discussion of the problem of eating the meat offered to idols (1 Cor 8–10) in terms of the principles of Christian liberty and the double command of love, the wholehearted devotion to God which excludes idolatry, and the love to neighbors which demands giving up one's right for the sake of the weak brethren." Similarly, Youngman (1987: 128) summarizes the theme of 8:1–11:1 as "Do everything out of love for God and people; restrict the exercise of your rights for the sake of the gospel." The double command of love (Deut. 6:5; Lev. 19:18), though not cited in this book, clearly underlies Paul's thinking here. Given the even more explicit stress on love found in 13:1–14:1 and on edification in chapter 14 (in light of the prior connection Paul established between love and edification in 8:1), it may be asserted that the double command of love undergirds all of chapters 8–14.

That love and edification are closely related in Paul's thought and argument can be seen in Paul's statement in 8:1 that "love builds up" and in the close relationship between Paul's discussion of love in chapter 13 and the theme of edification in chapter 14. These texts signal that the themes of love and edification undergird all of chapters 8–14. (For more OT background on love, see commentary on 1 Cor. 13 below, and for discussion of edification, see commentary on 1 Cor. 14 below.)

Food Sacrificed to Idols

On food sacrificed to idols (8:1–11:1) Paul has three basic things to say: (1) in relation to their fellow Christians (8:1–13), the Corinthians are exhorted via Paul's example not to cause a brother or sister to stumble by allowing themselves to be associated with idol worship (8:13); (2) in relation to God (10:1–22), the Corinthians are warned not to provoke the Lord to jealousy by association with idols (10:22); (3) in relation to their neighbors (10:23–11:1), the Corinthians are told to be careful not to give offense to anyone (10:31–11:1).

The issue of food sacrificed to idols would naturally be expected to be dealt with in the light of OT teaching on idolatry.

In early Judaism concerns regarding idolatry tended to revolve around the issue of eating. The association between eating and idolatry was established in some key OT texts. In chapter 10 Paul will cite the first of those texts, Exod. 32:6, which is found in the middle of the discussion of the fiasco with the golden calf. In that verse the description of Israel's worship of the calf includes a reference to sitting down to eat and then rising up to engage in "play"—the latter generally understood as a reference to pagan revelry. Exodus 34:14–15 discusses the need to destroy pagan altars in terms of the need to eliminate the danger that an Israelite might be invited to eat of the sacrifices that they would otherwise offer. That worst-case scenario came to be realized in the event narrated in Num. 25:1–3, where the daughters of Moab invited the Israelites to their sacrifices, and the Israelites went and ate and worshiped their gods, inciting God's anger against them. Paul's discussion of food offered to idols reflects a similar concern with associations between believers and pagans through invitations to social and religious events in pagan contexts.

8:1–6

Paul is apparently citing from the Corinthians' letter when he says "we all have knowledge" (8:1). It becomes clearer in 8:4 that the knowledge that they are claiming is based on an idiosyncratic interpretation of Deut. 6:4 (and perhaps other idol-rejecting texts of the OT; see, e.g., Deut. 32:17; 2 Kings 19:18; 2 Chron. 13:9; Isa. 37:19; Jer. 2:11; 5:7; 16:20; Hos. 8:6). That all peoples would come to recognize that Israel's Lord is the only God was a basic prophetic and apocalyptic motif of the OT (Isa. 11:9; 37:20; 40:28; 43:10; 44:8; 45:5–6; 49:23, 26; 52:6; Jer. 9:24; Ezek. 6:14; 7:4, 9; 15:7; 20:38; 24:24, 27; 25:5, 7, 11, 17; 26:6; 28:23–24, 26; 29:9, 16, 21; 30:8, 19, 26; 32:15; 33:29; 35:9, 15; 36:11, 23, 38; 37:28; 38:23).

In saying that "there is no idol that really exists" and that "there is no God but one," they evidently are arguing that since there is only one God, idols do not actually represent any spiritual (or other) reality, and therefore there is no reason to fear or avoid contact with their temples or with that which had been offered to them. Those who held to this position considered themselves the "knowing" in comparison to the "weak," who had serious qualms about any association with idolatry or food tainted by it. The "knowing" may have considered their position unassailable because it is based on an interpretation of the most fundamental text of Jewish monotheism, the first verse of the Shema (Deut. 6:4–9; 11:13–21; Num. 15:37–41), which was recited twice daily by faithful Jews and was central to the monotheistic understanding of early Judaism and Christianity. Yet other members of the church obviously were disturbed that some were even accepting invitations to dinners held in pagan temples (8:10).

In responding to the situation, Paul does not attack the theoretical basis of the position of the "knowing," but he redirects their approach to the issue from one based on determining who has the best theological arguments to one based on the most basic issues of love toward God and neighbor (cf. Deut. 6:5; Lev. 19:18; see Hays 1997). In doing so, Paul echoes other parts of the Shema, including Deut. 6:5; 11:13, when he says, "Anyone who loves God is known by him" (8:3). It is loving God, not mere theological knowledge, that is a defining characteristic of

God's chosen people. N. T. Wright (1992: 127) notes the significance of the Shema, pointing out that "Paul's references to humans loving God, as opposed to vice versa, are few and far between, and in this case at least . . . the reason for the reference is that he wishes to allude to, or echo, the Jewish confession of monotheistic faith." The Shema presents two alternatives: God's people either will love and serve him (Deut. 6:5; 11:13) or will "turn aside and serve other gods and worship them" (11:16). In that context it is understood that "loving God" entails an unequivocal rejection of any flirtation with idolatry.

In its original context the Shema does not support the idea that since there is only one God, there is no actual danger associated with idol worship. Rather, proper recognition of God's unique status requires absolute rejection of any association with the worship of other gods, regardless of their ontological status.

The language of Deut. 6:4 ("the LORD our God, the LORD is one") governs Paul's wording and argument in 8:5–6. He expands his opening statement that "there are many so-called gods" so as to allow the plurality of "lords" in the pagan world as well. References to "gods" are common in the OT, but they are not frequently referred to as "lords." Paul is already thinking of the interpretation that he wants to provide of Deut. 6:4, however, so he speaks of "many gods and lords." In that way his interpretive use of Deut. 6:4 in 8:6 is provided with a perfect contrast: "But for us there is one God, the Father, from whom all things came and for whom we exist, and one Lord, Jesus Christ, through whom all things came, and through whom we exist." The key words "Lord," "God," and "one" are taken from Deut. 6:4 ("the LORD our God, the LORD is one"), in which "Lord" and "God" both refer to the deity who is declared to be "one." But now Paul "has glossed 'God' with 'the Father,' and 'Lord' with 'Jesus Christ,' adding in each case an explanatory phrase: 'God' is the Father, 'from whom are all things and we to him,' and the 'Lord' is Jesus the Messiah, 'through whom are all things and we through him'" (N. T. Wright 1992: 129). In this one text Paul has simultaneously reaffirmed strict Jewish monotheism and embedded Christ within the very definition of that one God/Lord of Israel (see Hays 1997; N. T. Wright 1992).

The references to the roles of the Father and of the Lord Jesus Christ in creation ("from whom and through whom") also reflect traditional scriptural affirmations of the roles of God and of Wisdom in creation (for the latter, see Prov. 8:22–31; Wis. 9:4, 9; Philo, *Flight* 109). In prophetic literature Yahweh's absolute power as creator of heaven and earth is what sets him apart from idols, which, on the contrary, are human creations (e.g., Jer. 10:3–16; Isa. 44:9–24). The description of Christ in terms normally attributed to Wisdom (Wis. 8:1–6; 9:1–2, 9; Sir. 24) suggests that just as Jesus takes the place of "the Lord" in the Shema, he also takes the place of "Wisdom" within Hellenistic Judaism: "Paul has indicated that everything one might hope to gain through possessing [*sophia* (Wisdom)] can be gained rather by possessing Christ" (N. T. Wright 1992: 130).

Paul's statement that "there are many so-called gods" and indeed "many gods and many lords" seems to affirm the OT's recognition that pagan gods, while not really being gods in any sense comparable to the God of Israel (and thus are only so-called gods), do represent some reality. This may suggest an echo of Deut. 10:17, where, just a few chapters after the Shema, the Israelites are told "the LORD [MT: *yhwh*; LXX: *kyrios*] your God, he is God of gods and Lord of lords." This is the only text in the Hebrew Bible where "gods" and "lords" appear in the same sentence as in 1 Cor. 8:5, and in that sentence Israel's God is referred to as both Lord and God (as in the Shema), and his superiority over any other hypothetical claimant to that title is strongly affirmed as in 1 Cor. 8:5 (cf. Ps. 136:2–3).

The Shema was important both for its theological affirmation and for its sociological function. Early Judaism rallied around the one God who had redeemed them, and their allegiance to that one God was reflected both by their worship of him and by their rejection of all other claims to deity. It is notable that Paul's christological modification of the Shema comes in a passage where he hopes that this statement might fulfill the very same roles that the Shema did in Judaism. If the Corinthians would rally together in loyalty to God the Father and the Lord Jesus Christ in a way that signaled a radical rejection of all other claims to deity, it would go a long way toward promoting unity within the congregation and toward maintaining a distinct identity in contrast to the pagan environment.

8:9–10

Paul is concerned for the Corinthians that the exercise of the right to eat whatever food is placed before them might become a "stumbling block" (Gk. *proskomma*; Heb. *mikšôl*) to others; that is, it might lead others to fall into idolatry. In the OT idols are identified as, or directly associated with, stumbling blocks. Three verses in Ezek. 14 (vv. 3, 4, 7) repeat a refrain referring to those who "set up idols in their hearts and place the stumbling block [*mikšôl*] of their sin before their faces." The line is alluded to, and the parallelism repeated, in 1QH^a XII, 15 (and 4Q430 1, 3). In Exod. 23:33 LXX the Israelites are told, "And they [the former occupants] shall not dwell in your land lest they cause you to sin against me; for if you serve their gods, they will be a stumbling block [*proskomma*] to you." Exodus 34:12 LXX uses the word in a similar way (seen in the context of 34:11–14). The association between stumbling blocks and idolatry is seen also in *b. 'Abod. Zar.* 6a; 14a and in *b. Menaḥ.* 109a. The texts in *b. 'Abodah Zarah* understand the reference to a stumbling block in Lev. 19:14 to relate to the promotion of idolatry among Gentiles.

By describing the behavior of the "knowing" as a potential stumbling block, Paul may be associating the potential outcome of that behavior with that which is attributed to idolatrous behavior in the OT. As 8:10 suggests, the weak are actually led to commit idolatry, or at least to do something that they understand to be tainted by idolatry.

9:8–12

A. NT Context: Paul's Right to Compensation.

In chapter 9 Paul begins what appears at first sight to be a digression in which he defends himself and some of his rights (9:1–14). He then points out that he has intentionally refused to take advantage of some of his rights (9:15–18). He explains that he does so based on his willingness to make whatever sacrifices are necessary to reach as many people as possible and gain the reward that Christ has in mind for him (9:19–27). This whole section of the letter fits into an A-B-A′ structure similar to those found elsewhere in the letter (most clearly in chaps. 12–14). That is, the Corinthians' approach to dealing with food offered to idols (the issues explicitly addressed in chapters 8, 10) should be based not on their view of their rights, but rather on their concern for the spiritual well-being of those around them. Paul's discussion of his rights in 9:1–14 focuses on his right to be compensated for his work, and he quotes Deut. 25:4 as evidence that the law teaches that workers are entitled to benefit from the fruit of their labor (see 9:7–11).

B. Deut. 25:4 in Its OT Context. Deuteronomy 25:4 says, "You shall not muzzle an ox while it treads out the grain." At first glance, this command seems to have little or nothing in common with the surrounding laws, since they have to do with humans while it deals with the treatment of oxen at work. It is difficult to discern any clear relationship between the surrounding statutes, which are commonly referred to as "miscellaneous laws." The broader context shows a more general concern for the humane treatment of people (Hays 1997: 151). Deuteronomy 24:10–25:3 addresses the need for humane treatment of poor and marginalized people, and Deut. 24:19–22 discusses the need to allow sojourners, orphans, and widows to benefit from what is left in the field at the end of the harvesting process. The command of Deut. 25:4 comes soon after these passages, which are concerned to insure not only that those who work get the benefit of consuming the product of their labor, but also that other, needy and marginalized people be able to eat it. Given that context, it would be natural to understand the command of Deut. 25:4 as a particular extension of an already implied principle that those who work are allowed to partake of the fruit of their labors, since, when it comes to humans, that benefit even extends beyond the margins of those whose labors contributed to the harvest or production of food.

C. Deut. 25:4 in Early Judaism. The reason there is no specific law that states that those who work are free to benefit from the product of their labor is due probably to the fact that the principle was generally understood. Such a principle is in some places assumed and in other places argued in early Jewish literature.

Deuteronomy 25:4 is cited in the *Temple Scroll* of Qumran (11Q19 LII, 12) in the midst of a series of other laws relating primarily animal sacrifices. In fact, Deut. 25:4 and 22:10 are cited side by side and are the only stipulations that do not have to do with sacrifices. While some of the laws relating to sacrificial animals relate to the theme of avoiding excessive cruelty (11Q19 LII, 5–7), Deut. 22:10 is taken from a series of texts dealing with prohibitions of mixing. They are put together probably on the grounds that they both deal with the proper treatment of working livestock. It is possible that by being placed next to Deut. 25:4, Deut. 22:10 is understood to also relate to the theme of avoiding undue hardship on animals that are already worked hard by forcing them not only to do difficult work, but also to do so in tandem with a very different breed of animal.

Philo cites Deut. 25:4 as an example of a law relating to the humane treatment of animals (*Virtues* 145). Like 11Q19, Philo treats Deut. 22:10 immediately after his treatment of Deut. 25:4 and understands both to deal with the issue of the humanitarian treatment of animals (with emphasis given to the different natures of the two animals and the difficulty of one animal having to work with another that is much stronger). Philo's use of Deut. 25:4 must be understood in the light of the way the entire section of *Virtues* 125–147 is introduced. Philo informs us that the section will address the extension of the same principles of humanity and compassion that were applied to all types of people "even to the race of irrational animals" (*Virtues* 125). As Philo concludes this section, he points to the significance of laws concerning the humane treatment of animals and lower forms of life. If we learn how to treat lower forms of life humanely, we will not fail to do likewise with humans (*Virtues* 160).

Josephus discusses Deut. 25:4 in *Ant.* 4.233, where it is both immediately preceded and followed by his discussion of the laws of gleaning (Lev. 19:9; 23:22) and those that allow people who pass through a field to pluck ears with their hands (Deut. 23:25), respectively. By placing Deut. 25:4 in the midst of various laws that provide people with access to food, Josephus may be treating the law concerning work animals as an extension of those that apply to people. That such is the case might be indicated also by the word that he uses to refer to the animals in this context. He says that one is not "to bind the mouth of the oxen treading out the corn on the threshing floor, since it is not right to restrain our co-workers [*tous syneirgasmenous*] of the fruit . . ." (*Ant.* 4.233).

The Mishnah refers to Deut. 25:4 in *Ter.* 9:3 and in *B. Qam.* 5:7. The former text discusses how one can comply with Deut. 25:4 and yet keep the animal from eating any of the grain that is dedicated to the heave offering. The question is raised in the context of a discussion about the importance of respecting the laws of gleaning and the poor person's tithe (Lev. 19:9; 23:22; Deut. 14:28–29) without allowing any of the harvest that is dedicated to the heave offering to end up being diverted from it. In each case the concern to assure that the dedicated part of the harvest is not diverted from that purpose is satisfied without prejudicial effects on the poor (and the beast), who also are supposed to benefit from the harvest.

The Talmud's treatment of Deut. 25:4 reflects some significant (and later) developments in the rabbinic interpretation of the text. In *b. B. Meṣiʿa* 88b the teaching that people may eat from the loose produce of the field in which they work (cf. *m. B. Meṣiʿa* 7:2) is first defended on the basis of an argument from the lesser to the greater (called *kal waḥomer* in rabbinic literature and referred to in Latin as an argument *a minore ad majus* or *a fortiori*) from Deut. 25:4, perhaps influenced by Deut. 23:24 as well (see Tomson 1990: 125–31).

Since oxen are not allowed to eat food that is unplucked (or not loose) but people are, it follows that if even oxen are allowed to eat loose food, people must also be allowed to do so. This argument takes Philo's logic further. The laws that extend humanitarian care to animals are an extension of those that provide for humans. Thus, in the proper context, what is applied to animals can also be applied to people. This is taken a step further on the next page (*b. B. Meṣiʿa* 89a), where Rabina argues, on the basis of the use of the word "ox" both here and in Deut. 5:14, that whatever applies to the muzzled (i.e., the ox and animals in general) applies to the muzzler (i.e., people) as well, since the Sabbath law of Deut. 5:14, which is explicitly applied to the "ox," clearly applies generally to people and animals alike.

In *b. Yebam.* 4a the muzzling of the ox in Deut. 25:4 is applied metaphorically to the issue of levirate marriage, which is treated in the immediately following verses (25:5–10) to support the halakic view that a widow must not be forced to enter into a levirate marriage with a man whom she finds objectionable. The argument is based on relating Deut. 25:4 to the issue discussed in Deut. 25:5–10 through the principle of interpreting one text in the light of another text in close proximity. In doing so, the rabbis seem to be seeing a relationship between the various laws at the beginning of Deut. 25 that is similar to that which we proposed above: if an ox is free to eat and is not to be constrained as it labors, a woman who suffers the loss of her husband is not to be constrained to marry someone against her will. To "muzzle" her would be to force her to endure even greater hardship than she has already experienced.

D. Textual Matters. The MT and the LXX are in close agreement. There is a question about the text of Paul's citation. External support (with 𝔓⁴⁶ ℵ A B² C D¹ Ψ 33 1881 𝔐) favors *phimōseis* ("muzzle"), in agreement with the LXX, but that very agreement strongly suggests that *kēmōseis* ("muzzle" [found in B* D* F G 1739]) is to be preferred as the original reading. Assuming that in 9:9 Paul used the synonym rather than the word found in the LXX, we may conclude that probably he was quoting from memory (of either the Greek or the Hebrew text). There does not appear to be any semantic significance between the synonyms. First Timothy 5:18 quotes the same text but uses *phimōseis* (although D* has *kēmōseis* there as well).

E. The Use of Deut. 25:4 in 1 Cor. 9. Paul quotes Deut. 25:4 to support his argument that he is entitled to compensation for the work of the ministry. He argues that God's overriding concern here is not for oxen (9:9b), but for "us" (9:10). Paul's use of the verse has been categorized in a variety of ways, most frequently as allegorizing (see most commentaries, esp. Schrage 1991–2000: 2:298–300, and the views cited in Kaiser 1978: 11–14). It is probably more accurate to understand it as an argument from the lesser to the greater, as Jewish usage suggests (see above and the discussion in Instone-Brewer 1992: 554).

At first glance, it seems as though the cited text does indeed reflect concern for oxen (rather than people), but as we noted above, the near literary context does in fact reveal an emphasis on concern for human well-being.

Paul has set up the argument from the first verse of this chapter when he argues that the Corinthians are his "workmanship" (*ergon*), which means that just as the vineyard worker gets to eat some of the fruit of the vineyard, and the one who tends a flock gets to have some of the milk (9:7), and even an ox gets to eat some of the grain that it treads out, so also the one whose labor has resulted in the Corinthian community has the right to enjoy some compensation from that which has been produced. They are the field that he has sown, and he has the right to reap some fruit from its harvest (9:11). The logic of Deut. 25:4 clearly fits the logic of the other examples given in 9:7.

Barrett (1996: 206) argues against understanding this text in terms of an argument from the lesser to the greater. In his view, Paul is not saying, "If God cares for oxen, how much more for people," but rather, "God cares not for oxen, but for people." Barrett's argument rests on a common reading of the last clause of 9:9 and the first clause of 9:10. First Corinthians 9:10a probably should not be translated "Does he not speak entirely for our sake?" however, but rather "Does he not surely say it for our sake?" (see BDAG, which gives "by all means, certainly, probably, doubtless" as possible glosses; Thiselton 2000: 686–87). That is, Paul's statement should be taken not as an absolute denial that the law was given for the sake of animals, but rather as a strong assertion that God is even more concerned about humans (and that God was particularly concerned to give guidance for the eschatological community of the church). Martin Luther cleverly quipped that Deut. 25:4 obviously was not written for oxen, since "oxen cannot read." As a general principle, ancient Jewish interpreters agreed that the law was written for human consumption. Philo said, "The law was given not for the sake of unthinking creatures, but for the sake of those who can think and reason" (*Spec. Laws* 1.260).

Hays (1997) argues that "our sake" indicates that Paul has his apostolic team specifically in mind. It may be better to understand the statement in terms of Paul's other affirmations that scriptural texts were written (especially) for the community of the last days (as in 10:6, 11). It seems likely, however, that Paul's use of the argument from the lesser to the greater presupposes a previously established apostolic halakah according to which apostolic missionaries are understood to

be spiritual laborers, sowers, and reapers (Matt. 9:37–38; 10:10; Luke 10:2, 7; John 4:36–38; Rom. 1:13; 1 Cor. 3:6–9; 9:11; 1 Thess. 5:12; 1 Tim. 5:17–18). If so, it would support Hays's argument that the apostolic team is particularly in view. This halakic background may help solve a key question regarding the second half of 9:10. It is unclear whether it is to be understood as a quotation ("for it is for our sake it is written that 'whoever plows should plow in hope and whoever threshes should thresh in hope of sharing in the crop'") or as a justification of Paul's interpretation of Deut. 25:4 ("for [Deut. 25:4] was written for our sake since whoever plows should plow in hope and whoever threshes should thresh in hope of sharing in the crop"). The first option is difficult because we do not know of any text that Paul could be citing. The strongest argument against the second option is the balanced parallel (poetic) nature of the two clauses and the apparently un-Pauline vocabulary (see Stanley 1992: 197n52). But if Paul is summarizing an orally transmitted halakic interpretation of Deut. 25:4, it would explain the formalized language and its relationship to the prior citation (see Instone-Brewer 1992: 558–59; Koch 1986: 42n33).

The suggestion that Paul is thinking in terms of a *kal wahomer* argument in 9:9–10 is strengthened by the observation that 9:11 operates by means of a reversed *kal wahomer* argument: "If a labourer may eat of a valuable crop he is working on, much more should he be allowed to eat from a less valuable crop instead" (Instone-Brewer 1992: 559 [see his fuller discussion]). In 9:12 Paul reveals that his biblical argument establishing his right to be supported through his work served as a foundation to support his observation that he does not exercise his rights if doing so would somehow hinder the work of the gospel.

Paul quotes Deut. 25:4 again in 1 Tim. 5:18, also in support of compensating church leaders. There it is quoted in exact agreement with the LXX (with the exception of D* which reads *kēmōseis* there as well).

F. Theological Use. This is another example of Paul's use of Scripture as a guide for Christian conduct. Paul's argument asserts that we should deduce from a proper interpretation of Deut. 25:4 that Christian leaders have a right to be supported in their ministries. Thus, it is not merely a matter of acceding to an affirmation of Paul's apostolic authority on this subject, but rather of learning to understand how scriptural authority should inform our ethical understanding with respect to such issues.

9:13

Paul's statement that "those employed in the temple service" get to partake of the sacrificial offerings is a principle reflected in the administration of both the Jerusalem temple (e.g., Lev. 6:16–18, 26; 7:6–8; Num. 5:9–10; 18:8–20; Deut. 10:9; 18:1–5; 1 Sam. 2:28; 2 Chron. 31:4) and pagan temples. Paul most likely has the Jerusalem temple and its priests in mind, however, since the connection to the following verse ("so also" [*houtōs kai*]) probably implies not that the Lord's teaching happens to agree with other known religious practices, but that it was based on the scriptural pattern.

9:16–17

Paul's role as preacher of the gospel is not something he has chosen for himself, but rather is a task assigned to him by God. His language is reminiscent of 20:9 (see, e.g., Hays 1997; Thiselton 2000).

Nasuti (1988) has suggested that Paul's language entails an inversion of the self-directed woe that prophets sometimes declared in response to sufferings experienced as a result of their prophetic ministry. During his vision of the throne of God, Isaiah declares a woe on himself due to his sinfulness and that of the people of Israel (Isa. 6:5). Other such woes include Isa. 24:16; Jer. 10:19; 15:10; 45:3.

Like Jeremiah, Paul suffers because of his preaching, but rather than bemoan his suffering, he boasts in it. For Paul, not preaching the gospel would be grounds for lament. "Jeremiah wishes he had never been born because of his suffering (Jer. 15:10); Paul would rather die than give up the suffering which is his grounds for boasting in the gospel" (Nasuti 1988: 258).

Of course, Paul does finds himself at the stage of salvation history not where judgment and exile are the key messages, but rather where restoration and salvation are being preached to all nations. Jeremiah's own message was expressed in terms of the contrasting messages of plucking up or planting, destroying or building (e.g., Jer. 1:10; 24:6;

31:3–4, 28; 33:7), and his hearers experienced plucking up and destruction. Paul's hearers experience planting and building. His message is one that brings salvation (rather than judgment) to all the groups that he mentions in 9:19–22, and he is happy to do whatever he must for the sake of the gospel in order that he "may share with them in its blessings" (9:23).

9:19–23

Elsewhere Paul emphasizes that he is committed to pleasing God rather than humans (Gal. 1:10; 1 Thess. 2:4). Here and in 10:32–11:1 Paul highlights his commitment to making a positive impression on those among whom he lives and works. The first set of passages deals with behaviors that please mortals but are dishonoring to God, while here Paul has in mind a limited accommodation in ways that would not be offensive to God as a strategy to bring people into life-transforming contact with the gospel. The desire to make a good impression on pagan neighbors in order to win them over (and thereby preserve or exalt God's reputation) is an ethical motive found here and in other early Jewish and Christian writings (see van Unnik 1960) based on OT background (e.g., Exod. 32:12, 25; Num. 14:13–19; Deut. 9:25–29; Isa. 52:5 LXX; Ezek. 20:9–22; 36:20–23; cf. Paul's quotation of Isa. 52:5 LXX in Rom. 2:24; see Rosner 1999: 110–11).

10:1–13: Introduction

In chapter 10 Paul explicitly returns to the theme that has been his concern since chapter 8 and that motivated his discussion of the giving up of his rights in chapter 9. He does so through a typological (and ecclesiological) interpretation of the exodus, wilderness wandering, and apostasy of Israel.

Mitchell (1991: 138–40) has pointed out that Philo (*Spec. Laws* 4.129; *Moses* 1.161–164, 305; 2.174, 283; *Posterity* 182–185; *Drunkenness* 95) and Josephus (*Ant.* 3.295; 4.12, 140) refer to the same incidents that Paul mentions in 10:1–13 as notorious instances of factionalism (cf. 1:10–13; 11:18–19; 12:25). Corinth was not the first place where God's people had experienced divisions relating to idolatry and sexual immorality!

In a way similar to that of Pss. 78; 106; Neh. 9:5–37; Deut. 32:1–43, Paul, in 10:1–13, rehearses the consequences of earlier rejections of God's mercy as a warning to the author's own generation of readers (Fee 1987).

In 10:1–4 Paul discusses the redemptive blessings experienced by the whole community of Israel (with "all" [*pas*] repeated five times) as parallels to those blessings experienced by Christians. In 10:5–10 he discusses Israel's experience as a warning for "us" in light of the fact that God's judgment fell on "most" of Israel due to the various things that "some" of them did (with "some of them" repeated four times). Four of the sins that brought God's wrath upon Israel echo texts from Numbers. Paul mentions in 10:6 that they "craved evil things," echoing Num. 11, where 11:4 and 11:34 serve as an *inclusio* around the narrative of Israel's rebellious craving to eat meat (Collier 1994: 63). Collier (1994: 65) also points out that two key verbs from Exod. 32:6, *kathizō* ("sit down") and *anistēmi* ("rise up"), occurred at the beginning (11:4) and end (11:32) of Num. 11 LXX, respectively.

As Collier (1994: 65) suggests, the linguistic ties provided Paul with "a midrashic link to Exod. 32.6 as a kind of summary of Numbers 11. Exodus 32.6 is understood midrashically as Numbers 11 writ small." Paul ties together Exod. 32:6 and the theme of "craving" found in Num. 11 and related OT texts that mention food and the craving of evil things (Collier 1994: 65–66). So "when Israel sat down to eat, they sinned, for they craved the food of their own choosing, rather than what God had provided: (1) in *idolatry* (v. 7) it was eating and drinking in an idol feast in an attempt to fulfill their own desires (Exod. 32.6); (2) in *harlotry* (v. 8), it was a desecration against God himself as 'the people blatantly practiced harlotry' . . . , primarily a forsaking of God in idolatry, since the people 'ate the [Moabite] sacrifices and worshipped their idols' (. . . Num. 25.1–2); and (3) in *testing* (v. 9), it was the speaking against God . . . that was at issue, for the people said, 'there is no food or water' (. . . Num. 21.4–7)" (Collier 1994: 66). In 10:11–13 he concludes the passage with a final warning.

10:1–4

Paul's statement that "our fathers were all under the cloud" suggests that even the Gentile readers of this letter are to think of the Israelites of the exodus as their adopted "fathers" through their inclusion in the covenant community (so Hays 1997: 160). The Israelites' experience of redemption, idolatry, and destruction is used as a lens through which the Corinthians are to view and understand their own situation. The reference to "baptism into Moses" is evidently formulated by Paul in order to make the metaphorical parallel as clear as possible. The fivefold repetition of "all" (*pantes*) in 10:1–4 emphasizes that the experience of God's redemptive acts was common to the community as a whole (both in Israel's experience and, by analogy, in the experience of the Corinthian church).

References to the sea and the cloud are interspersed within Exod. 14:2–27. The fact that the Israelites were "under the cloud" and "passed through the sea" (10:1) is understood to correspond to the baptism experienced by the Corinthian Christians (10:2). The idea that the fathers were "under the cloud" is suggested in Exod. 14:24 when God "looked down" from the pillar of fire and cloud upon the Egyptians trailing the Israelites (see also Exod. 13:21–22; Num. 9:15–23; 14:14; Deut. 1:33; Ps. 78:14). That the Israelites passed through the midst of the sea is indicated in Exod. 14:22, 29. Paul's language facilitates the identification between the experience of the Israelites and that of the Corinthians.

The divine provision of quail and manna is related in Exod. 16; Num. 11 and celebrated in Deut. 8:3, 16; Neh. 9:20; Ps. 78:24; 105:40. The water from the rock is mentioned in Exod. 17:6; Num. 20:8–11 and then celebrated in a series of texts, including Deut. 8:15; Neh. 9:15; Ps. 78:20; 105:41; 114:8; Isa. 48:21. Paul calls the food and drink that was miraculously provided "spiritual" (*pneumatikos*) food and drink, since he understands that they were provided by the Spirit and understands the elements of the Lord's Supper also to be food and drink of the Spirit, who communicates the presence of Christ to his community. The early church's (and Paul's) understanding of Jesus' last supper and the Lord's Supper in terms of the Jewish Passover and the promised second exodus would have made the parallel between the Lord's Supper (see commentary on 1 Cor. 11:23–26 below) and the Israelites' experience in the exodus a natural one for Paul and his readers.

Paul draws on a rich Jewish exegetical tradition (e.g., *L.A.B.* 10:7; 11:15; *t. Sukkah* 3:11, *b. Šabb.* 35a; *b. Pesaḥ.* 54a; *Gen. Rab.* 62:4; *Num. Rab.* 1:2; 9:14; 19:25–26; *Tg. Onq.* Num. 21:16–20) when he speaks in 10:4 of the rock that followed Israel (see Ellis 1978a; Enns 1996). In inquiring how the interpretive tradition of a moveable well developed, Enns (1996: 30) notes that "the miraculous provision of water in the desert is mentioned only at the beginning of the wilderness wandering period (Exod. 17, Rephidim; also the waters of Elim in Exod. 15:22–27; see *Bib. Ant.* 11:15 . . .) and at the end (Num. 20, Kadesh; Num. 21, Beer)." According to the exegetical tradition, the answer to the natural question of what the Israelites had done for water between those times was that "the rock of Exodus 17 and the rock of Numbers 20 are one and the same. Hence, this rock must have accompanied the Israelites through their journey."

This interpretation was facilitated by a potential ambiguity in Num. 21:16–20. Jewish tradition came to understand God's promise to provide Israel water from the well (21:16) to entail giving them not just water from the well, but the well itself. In the following verse the Israelites sing to the well, calling on it to spring up (or go up), using a verbal form that in every other context (Num. 21:17; 1 Sam. 25:35; Isa. 21:2; 40:9; Jer. 22:20; 46:11) entails movement from one place to another. The understanding that the well/rock traveled with Israel was based on an interpretation that Paul and his colleagues evidently inherited from their forebears. Paul's use of the basic conclusion regarding the traveling nature of the rock should be distinguished from suggestions that he is indebted to the fuller (and fanciful) legends found in later rabbinic material. Garland (2003: 456–57) suggests that "Paul may have incorporated a traditional Jewish interpretation of the following rock, but he gives it a uniquely Christian twist: 'The rock was Christ.' He is not thinking of a material rock following them, or a movable well, but of the divine source of the water that journeyed with them. He understands the replenishing rock in a spiritual sense, not a physical sense."

The identification of the rock with Christ involves another hermeneutical step beyond that of a moveable well or rock. Although Hanson (1965: 17–22) argues for the "real presence" of Christ in the well, most scholars hold that Paul establishes an analogy between the role of the rock in Israel's experience and the role of Christ in the church's experience (Koch [1986: 211–16] considers it an allegorical interpretation). Philo identified the rock with God's Wisdom (*Alleg. Interp.* 2.86). Other texts show that Paul's understanding of Christ has parallels with Jewish thinking about the hypostatization of that particular divine attribute (1 Cor. 1:24, 30; 8:6; Col. 1:15–17), and it may be that Philo's understanding of the rock shares some background with Paul's. The identification of Christ with the rock may also be related to Paul's use of Deut. 32 in this chapter, since "Rock" (*ṣûr*) is the preferred name for God in the Hebrew text of that chapter (cf. 32:4, 15, 18, 30, 31; see Meeks 1982). Interestingly, the only other place where *ṣûr* is used in Deuteronomy outside chapter 32 is 8:15, which affirms that God "brought you water out of the flinty rock."

10:6

The Language of Typology. In 10:6 Paul says that the events listed in 10:1–5 happened to serve as warnings or patterns (*typoi*) from which we should learn. The word that Paul uses provides the background for the concept of typology, which is the understanding that patterns found in persons, actions, events, and institutions can be expected to find correspondences in God's future redemptive works (Goppelt 1982: 17–20). The use of "type" (*typos*) and "typical" (*typikōs*) as technical terms for typological interpretation is established by the time of the early church fathers. Goppelt (1982: 4) argues that Paul was the first to use these words for "the prefiguring of the future in prior history" (cf. Hays 1997: 162; Thiselton 2000: 731–32). Two of the key texts for this argument are found in this passage (1 Cor. 10:6, 11; Rom. 5:14). Paul clearly establishes a typological relationship between Israel and Christian experience in 10:1–4. It could be argued, however, that in 10:5–11 he points not to divinely established patterns, but rather to patterns that the Corinthians must avoid fulfilling (see Garland 2003: 459). Some interpreters understand typology to consist merely of retrospective interpretation by NT authors whereby they find correspondences between their own experience and that described in the OT. Many texts seem to reflect such an approach. If the OT text was written as a warning or pattern to guide the church in the last days (cf. 10:6, 11), however, it could be so only if it were understood that the experience of God's eschatological community would follow patterns established in the OT such that one could deduce a lesson from Israel's exodus experience and apply it to a context that was significantly different in its historical particularities. That the second exodus would follow the general pattern of the first exodus was an expectation found already in OT texts. Although Davidson (1981: 193–297), for example, pushes the predictive element of typological exegesis too far, the basic understanding that the church's experience would correspond to patterns found already in Israel's experience seems to be required by Paul's argument.

10:7

A. NT Context: Postredemption Idolatry in Israel and Corinth. In 10:1–10 Paul describes the exodus and desert experience of Israel as a pattern in which idolatry followed on the heels of redemption. Some Corinthians are in danger of falling into the same pattern because of their attitudes and practices involving food sacrificed to idols (especially the practice of eating in pagan temples or participating in certain pagan meals).

B. Exod. 32:6 in Its OT Context. The episode of the golden calf is one of the most notorious in the OT (Exod. 32; cf. Deut. 9:8–21; Judg. 2:17; 1 Kings 12:28; Neh. 9:16–18; Ps. 106:19–23).

Exodus 32:6 depicts a perversion of the covenant-ratifying meal described earlier in 24:5–11. The preceding verse indicates that the behavior described in 32:6 was understood to consist of a "feast to the LORD," but the report that they "rose up to play" suggests that they entered into pagan revelry (see Meeks 1982: 69–70). In 32:4 Aaron suggested that the golden calf represented the gods who delivered the Israelites from Egypt. Rather than properly worship the God who actually had redeemed them from Egypt, Israel now gave credit for the exodus to the gods represented by the calf.

C. Exod. 32:6 in Early Judaism. That the fiasco of the golden calf held a strong place in Jewish thinking is clear (see Childs 1974: 573–81). The story is recounted in Acts 7:39–43 as an example of Israel's hard-heartedness and idolatry.

Philo refers to the event several times (*Moses* 2.161–162, 270; *Drunkenness* 95; *Spec. Laws* 1.79). Josephus does not mention it (cf. *Ant.* 3.99)—"the most glaring exception" to his promise to omit nothing (Thackeray 1930: 363). The story is retold again in *L.A.B.* 12. In *t. Soṭah* 3:10 the focus on eating and drinking is thought to suggest an arrogant, self-absorbed attitude on the part of the Israelites, while in *t. Soṭah* 6:6 the clearly idolatrous reference to "playing" in Exod. 32:6 is used to interpret Ishmael's actions in Gen. 21:9 in a similar manner.

The event left an indelible mark on the history of Jewish thought about idolatry and functioned as the archetypal act of apostasy (see Hafemann 1995: 279–81).

D. Textual Matters. Paul's text reproduces the LXX of Exod. 32:6, which is a literal rendering of the MT text (for minor textual variations in a few manuscripts see Stanley 1992: 197n54).

E. The Use of Exod. 32:6 in 1 Cor. 10. In 10:7 Paul quotes the LXX of Exod. 32:6 as proof that the Israelites committed idolatry. The references to eating and drinking in association with idolatry make Exod. 32:6 an obvious reference point for issues related to food sacrificed to idols. Paul marks Exod. 32:6 as his main text (*pace* Collier 1994) by its explicit citation (and important use of the key words for "eating," "drinking," and "rising up"). Allusions to Num. 11; 14 and other texts fill out the picture by pointing to subsequent situations where the same association between eating, drinking, and idolatry can be seen (along with other temptations that the Corinthians are facing).

F. Theological Use. Paul uses Exod. 32:6 to inform the Corinthians' understanding of the ethical and spiritual danger that they are facing. As Hays (1989: 92) suggests, "By coaxing the reader to recall the golden calf story, he links the present Corinthian dilemma . . . to the larger and older story of Israel in the wilderness. This metaphorical act creates the imaginative framework within which Paul judges—and invites his readers to judge—the proper ethical response to the problem at hand." The text serves as a warning against following in the footsteps of the Israelite ancestors.

10:8

Paul refers to the incident in Num. 25:1–9, where the first verse refers to Israel's participation in gross sexual immorality (LXX: *ekporneuō*) with

Moabite women, and the last verse refers to the consequential death of twenty-four thousand.

Paul highlights the Israelites' involvement in sexual immorality associated with an idolatrous meal. Numbers 25:2 indicates that the incident began when Israelites, having been invited by Moabites to the sacrifices to their gods, ate the sacrifices and then bowed down to those gods/idols. Thus idolatry and sexual immorality are tied together in both Num. 25:1–2 and 1 Cor. 10:8 (not to mention the broader structure of this letter).

Although Paul clearly has the Numbers text in mind, he refers to twenty-three thousand casualties, while Num. 25:9 sets the number at twenty-four thousand. Koet (1996) suggests that Paul has fused together elements of the punishments mentioned in Num. 25:9 and Exod. 32:28 (which, unlike the Numbers text, says that the people died "that day" and that they "fell," using the exact same word, *epesan*, as in 1 Cor. 10:8). Koet thinks Paul may have fused the two texts together so that the reference to Num. 25:9 would still be recognizable but that the echo of Exodus might also be heard. In his view, this explains why there is no mention of a punishment in 10:7: the punishment for the sin of Exod. 32:6 is incorporated into the reference to the punishment for the sin of Num. 25 in the subsequent verse.

Koet's suggestion deserves serious consideration because it not only would clarify the numerical discrepancy (which many feel has not yet found a satisfying solution), but also would explain other features of Paul's text. Still, unless or until other examples of such an intertextual use of numbers can be found in early Jewish or Christian literature, his argument will remain less than compelling.

10:9

The reference to destruction by serpents alludes to Num. 21:5–6, where the Israelites spoke against God, complaining about a lack of food and water. Elsewhere in the OT such complaining is described as "testing the LORD" (Exod. 17:2–3, 7 [concerning water to drink]) or "testing God" (Ps. 78:18 [demanding food that they craved], 41, 56 [provoking him through idolatry]; 106:14 [due to their craving]). Hays (1997: 165) suggests the parallel between the two halves of this verse does not necessarily imply that Israelites had put Christ to the test (on the textual issues for 10:9,

see Metzger 1994: 494). Paul could be understood to say, "We should not put Christ to the test the way some of them tested God." On the other hand, Paul has already identified Christ with the rock in 10:4, and in Exod. 17:2, 7 the people of Israel are described as testing "the LORD" (LXX: *kyrion*). Furthermore, in Num. 21:6 it is "the LORD" who sends the serpents in response to the complaining. Paul has already identified Christ as "the Lord" named in the Shema (see commentary on 1 Cor. 8:1–6 above), making the identification between Christ and the Lord in these texts a natural one. Numbers 21:5–6 probably is being read in the light of Ps. 78:18, where the incident is related to craving food—a theme found throughout this passage (see Hays 1997: 164; Collier 1994). When God's people test his patience by insisting on things that they crave rather than what he provides, such insolence can expect to be met with judgment.

10:10

There is no agreement on what passage(s) Paul has in mind in this verse. Suggestions include Num. 14 (Hays 1997: 165), Num. 11 (Collier 1994: 66), and Ps. 106 (Garland 2003: 464). Numbers 11 begins "And the people were grumbling," while 11:33–34 describes the plague of the Lord, which "takes place in the context of rampant *epithumia* [craving]... described as an insatiable (and deadly) craving for meat" (Collier 1994: 66). Psalm 106 shares several lexical and conceptual links with this passage (including "craving," "testing God," "grumbling," spiritual "adultery," and "destruction"). Thiselton (2000: 742–43) affirms that the reference to "grumbling" serves as a general allusion to the various pentateuchal texts that cite Israel's guilt in this area.

Paul's reference to "the destroyer" (*ho olothreutēs*) may echo Exod. 12:23, but Schneider (1967) is probably correct: "in good OT fashion" Paul has in mind the destroying angel who carries out any divine judgment (cf. Exod. 12:23; 2 Sam. 24:16; 1 Chron. 21:12, 15; 2 Chron. 32:21; Wis. 18:25; Sir. 48:21; see Garland 2003: 463).

10:11–12

Paul says Israel's experiences happened as examples (*typikōs*) and were written down to warn "us" (*pros nouthesian hēmōn*). The understanding that Scripture was always relevant to God's people is common to ancient Jewish and Christian literature (see Rosner 1994: 98–102). The word that Paul uses for instruction or warning only occurs once in the LXX, in Wis. 16:6, which, in fact, speaking of Num. 11, says, "They were provoked as a warning [*nouthesia*] for a short time."

Paul understands, however, that the Scripture has particular relevance "for our instruction, on whom the ends of the ages have come" (cf. Rom. 4:23–24; 15:4; Dan. 8:26; 9:24; 12:4, 9; Isa. 8:16; the pesharim of Qumran; see Hays 1989: 166–68). Paul understands that he and his communities are living in the days of the eschatological fulfillment of the OT promises and prophecies, related to the theme of the "latter days" (Deut. 4:30; Jer. 23:20; 30:24; 48:47; 49:39; Ezek. 38:16; Dan. 2:28; 10:14; Hos. 3:5).

In 10:12 Paul uses the same word, *piptō* ("fall"), to describe the danger risked by those who think that they stand that he used in 10:8 to describe what happened to the Israelites who engaged in sexual immorality. Here the word carries an eschatological connotation as in Ps. 19:9 LXX (20:8 ET); 35:13 LXX (36:12 ET); *Pss. Sol.* 1:5; Rom. 11:11; 14:4; 1 Cor. 13:8.

10:13

The Corinthians are dealing with a temptation that is "common to humanity" (BDAG) (cf. Num. 5:6; Josephus, *Ant.* 1.22). Garland (2003: 467) correctly points out that the temptation should be understood "in the context of the warning examples he has just enumerated and the exhortation to flee idolatry that immediately follows." Evidence suggests that the OT and early Judaism considered idolatry the most human of all temptations.

Paul's reference to God's faithfulness implies a dualistic contrast between the merely human power and origin of the temptation and the divine power of our God, who will provide for us a way through. The fact that only "some" of the Israelites fell into each of the sins listed in 10:7–10 suggests that the temptations were not irresistible. That God does not allow us to be exposed to irresistible temptations is a reflection of his faithfulness to us.

10:14–15

As Paul approaches the end of his treatment on food sacrificed to idols, he provides a summarizing exhortation similar to the exhortation to "flee

from sexual immorality" that he gave near the end of his treatment on that subject (6:18).

10:16

The final cup of the Passover meal (and presumably the Last Supper) was called the "cup of blessing." Just as participation in the Passover celebration entailed participation in the benefits of the Passover sacrifice (cf. Exod. 12:27; 34:25; Deut. 16:2, 5–6; 2 Chron. 35:1, 6, 11), participation in the Lord's Supper entails participation in the benefits of his sacrifice for us. Hanson (1974: 115) suggests that the references to bread and wine (and "blood") in Deut. 32:14 would have been "quite enough to point Paul to the Eucharist." Although links to Deut. 32 in the near context (esp. 10:19–20, 22) make Hanson's suggestion feasible, he goes a bit too far in describing 10:14–21 as "a Christian midrash on Deut. 32:17–21" (Hanson 1974: 115).

10:17

As Exod. 12:43–48 indicates, the Passover was to be celebrated by the whole community of Israel. It was to be a common and unifying experience for the nation. The Lord's Supper should have played a similar unifying role in the Corinthian church, which was suffering from serious divisions (cf. 1:10; 11:18; 12:25).

10:18

The reference to "Israel according to the flesh" points to a distinction between true Israelites and the rest that already had begun to be made in the OT (e.g., Deut. 10:16; Jer. 4:4; 9:24). Elsewhere Paul refers to Christians as the "true circumcision" (Rom. 2:28–29) and as the children of the "Jerusalem above" rather than the present Jerusalem (Gal. 4:25–26).

Paul points to the cultic practices of the Judaism of his day, based on OT teaching. While some sacrifices were consumed only by the priests and others by the whole community (see Reid 2000: 1038–44), to eat the food that had been offered in sacrifice was to participate in the cultic act of the sacrifice.

10:19–20

A. NT Context: The Significance of Pagan Worship. Since 10:16 Paul has been discussing the religious significance of participation in Christian and Jewish cultic meals as part of his argument against participating in pagan religious meals. Earlier (see commentary on 1 Cor. 8:1–6 above) he affirmed (in agreement with some of the Corinthians) that idols are not real and that there is only one real God. In 10:19 he concedes that food itself does not become spiritually contaminated by being sacrificed to idols. Paul's reference to Deut. 32:17 clarifies the nature of his objection to participation in pagan religious meals: "They sacrifice to demons and not to God."

B. Deut. 32:17 in Its OT Context. The Song of Moses in Deut. 32 recounts Israel's unfaithfulness to the Lord. They provoked him to jealousy by strange gods (32:16) and "sacrificed to demons, not God, to gods they had not known; to new ones who had recently appeared, ones your ancestors had not known" (32:17). The "demons" (*šēdîm*) were not deities, but rather were less powerful spirits referred to in Mesopotamian texts as spiritual protectors of persons or places (see *HALOT* 4:1417–18; *TWOT* 2:906). The Israelites offered the worship due to God to inferior spiritual beings.

C. Deut. 32:17 in Early Judaism. In Deut. 32:17 God's "sons and daughters" (32:19) sacrificed to demons (*šēdîm*), but in Ps. 106:37 Israel is condemned for sacrificing their own sons and daughters to demons (*šēdîm*) (the only two places in the OT where this word appears). It refers to later, even more shocking events that are probably understood in the light of Deut. 32:17. In Bar. 4:7 the exile is attributed to the fact that Israel provoked their Creator, "sacrificing to demons and not to God." The reference to God's nursing of Israel in Bar. 4:8 probably reflects the influence of Deut. 32:10–15 (esp. 32:13–14). In *1 En.* 19:1 Enoch is told that the spirits of the angels who cohabited with women in Gen. 6 (see *1 En.* 6) will lead the people to offer sacrifices to demons as though they were gods, and in *T. Sol.* 5:5 a captive demon identifies himself to Solomon as one born of a human mother and an angelic father and tells him that he and his colleagues will be freed and will deceive the human race into worshiping them as gods.

Sacrifices to demons reflect the extreme spiritual corruption of Israel and humanity. *Leviticus Rabbah* 22:8 associates Deut. 32:17 with the sacrifices to goat idols/demons mentioned in Lev. 17:7

and explains that the laws insisting that sacrifices be offered only at the door of the tabernacle (Lev. 17:3–4) were intended to prevent such forbidden sacrifices from taking place in Israel.

D. Textual Matters. The best reading of Paul's text agrees perfectly with the LXX, with the minor difference of using a present-tense verb rather than an aorist ("they worship" versus "they worshiped").

Some manuscripts ($\mathfrak{P}^{46\text{vid}}$ ℵ A C P Ψ 33^{vid} 81 1739 𝔐 and the lectionaries) supply an explicit subject for the verb "sacrifice": "the Gentiles/pagans" (*ta ethnē*). The editors of UBS[4] considered it "an ancient gloss" intended to exclude a reference to the offerings made in Jerusalem (cf. 10:18). Most interpreters understand the words to represent an accurate interpretation of Paul's meaning (even if a later gloss), but some argue that it completely misunderstands Paul (see Thiselton 2000: 773; Kistemaker 1993: 346–47). Hays (1989: 93) thinks that the gloss reflects a failure to recognize Paul's allusion to Deut. 32:17.

E. The Use of Deut. 32:17 in 1 Cor. 10. Although Deut. 32:17 refers to the abhorrent unfaithfulness of Israel, most readers understand Paul to be speaking of the practices of the Corinthian Christians' pagan neighbors (as did many ancient scribes). Paul's other references to the scene of the golden calf in the context (and elsewhere) suggest that "Paul sees the Corinthian controversy about idol meat (v. 19) in double exposure with Israel's wilderness idolatry" (Hays 1989: 93). Thus, while the sacrifices referred to in both Deut. 32:17 and 1 Cor. 10:20 are pagan sacrifices, "Paul's real concern, like that of the Song of Moses, is that *God's own people* are becoming implicated in this 'abhorrent' practice" (Hays 1997: 169). Although the Corinthians may not have been tempted to offer sacrifices to pagan gods, they, by partaking in pagan religious meals, were still considered participants in the sacrifices themselves (thus the relevance of Paul's argument in 10:16–18 to his use of Deut. 32:17).

The concept of "demons" had developed since the time of Deut. 32:17 and "the wraps are taken off the demonic" in the NT (*TWOT* 2:906). Paul and his readers would understand Deut. 32:17 in that fuller light.

F. Theological Use. Paul seems to be drawing a broader theological conclusion (with clear ethical implications) from the statement about Israel's practice in Deut. 32:17. Since Israel's idolatrous sacrifices were offered to demons, idolatrous sacrifices in general should be similarly understood (certainly they could be no better).

10:21

The expression "Lord's table" is used to refer to the altar in the OT (Mal. 1:7, 12; cf. Ezek. 41:22; 44:16). Paul's reference to the Lord's Supper as a participation in the "Lord's table" suggests that the celebration of Christ's sacrifice now serves as the centerpiece for Christian worship as did the altar—the Lord's table in the OT—where the people of Israel went to worship by bringing their sacrifices to the Lord.

In Isa. 65:11 LXX the Lord complains against unfaithful Israelites who "prepare a table for the devil [*daimōn*] and fill up the mixture [of wine as an offering] for Fortune." Paul emphasizes that one cannot worship the one true God and also participate in any other worship. The church remains committed to "the radically *exclusive* character of Israel's monotheistic faith" (Hays 1997: 170).

10:22

Paul's words "Shall we provoke the Lord?" echo the Lord's complaint against Israel in Deut. 32:21 LXX: "They have provoked me with what is no god, angered me by their idols." He essentially asks if he or the Corinthians would be foolish enough to follow in Israel's footsteps by participating in pagan worship, provoking him by engaging in idolatrous associations or actions. Paul's follow-up question, "Are we stronger than he?" probably also reflects Deut. 32 and its emphasis on the strength of the Lord. According to Deut. 32, one of the purposes of the coming judgment will be to impress on the nation their lack of strength and the Lord's great power (cf. 32:30, 36–38). Craigie (1976: 387) comments on Deut. 32:36, "Since Israel's defection was largely a result of the arrogance of believing in their own strength, that arrogance and belief in human strength had to be totally demolished before the people were in a position to realize their need of God's strength. The rhetorical question posed in vv. 37–38 is designed to create awareness that other possible sources of strength were also useless." The motif of God's strength is also seen in the repeated use of the epi-

thet "the Rock" (*ṣûr*) in Deut. 32 (32:4, 15, 18, 30, 31), which the Targumim understand as a figure for God's strength, most frequently translating it as "the Strong One" (see Rosner 1999: 200). The motif relates to the Lord's strength as reflected in his power to protect or punish his people. Paul's question is designed not only to underscore the impotence of believers, but also to stress the omnipotence of God: surely we are not stronger than the Strong One! It entails a frightening threat of judgment upon those Corinthian Christians who provoke God to jealousy.

10:25–26

A. NT Context: Eating Food in Various Contexts. Paul discusses a variety of contexts in which food might be eaten (as part of a pagan religious meal, food purchased in the market for eating at home, food that one is offered when eating as a guest in another's home) and gives advice for each context. One of the questions that Paul addresses is whether food sacrificed to idols becomes inherently inconsumable or if problems arise only when one participates in or is associated with the offering itself.

B. Ps. 24:1 in Its OT Context. Psalm 24 boldly declares that the Lord, the God of Israel (and no other deity) is sovereign Lord over all the earth: "The earth is the LORD's and all of its fullness." The earth does not belong to Baal or to any other god, but to the Lord of Israel. He alone is the glorious king who reigns over all the earth and over all of its inhabitants (see Craigie 1983: 212).

Psalm 24:4 is ambiguous (Broyles 1999: 129), but idol worship may be one of the two offenses listed as precluding one from the worship procession (cf. Ps. 25:1; see Kraus 1993: 1:314).

The Lord's identification as the "King of glory" is mentioned four times in the last five verses of the psalm. Within those verses the motif of the Lord's strength (see commentary on 1 Cor. 10:22 above) is stressed: The King of glory is the Lord "strong and mighty," the Lord "mighty in battle."

C. Ps. 24:1 in Early Judaism. Psalm 24:1 is most commonly cited in rabbinic literature to teach the obligation to thank God for one's food. On the basis of this text it was taught that one should not taste any food until after having recited a benediction over it (*t. Ber.* 4:1; *b. Ber.* 35a; *b. Šabb.* 119a).

D. Textual Matters. The LXX translates the Hebrew quite literally, and Paul's citation follows it exactly, with only the introduction of postpositive *gar* ("for") to connect the citation to the context.

E. The Use of Ps. 24:1 in 1 Cor. 10. Paul is thoroughly Jewish and biblical in his understanding that creation is good and that the food we receive has been provided for us by God and should be received with thanksgiving (cf. 10:30). The doctrine of creation that Paul finds in Ps. 24:1 indicates that there is nothing wrong with the food itself, regardless of the way others have misused it in their religious ignorance. Psalm 24:1 says that it all belongs to the Lord, not to any god or demon to whom it may have been offered (regardless of what the pagans who offered it may have thought). As far as the Christian is concerned, whatever food is found in the market is part of God's gracious provision and should be thankfully received as such.

F. Theological Use. Paul draws an ethical application from the text's statement of God's ownership of and sovereignty over all creation. Since all food belongs to the Lord and comes from him, it can be received with thankfulness regardless of how it has been used by others.

10:27–30

The particular concern regarding food sacrificed to idols and the contamination of idolatry from eating food is based on Exod. 34:15, which, in the midst of a passage preoccupied with the avoidance of contamination from idolatry, warns that the danger of allowing the inhabitants of the land to remain would be that "when they prostitute themselves to their gods and sacrifice to their gods, someone among them will invite you, and you will eat of the sacrifice." This verse was a key text in the development of an important strand of Jewish thinking that condemned (accepting invitations and) eating with Gentiles (cf. *Jub.* 22:16; *t. 'Abod. Zar.* 4:6; *b. 'Abod. Zar.* 8a; *S. Eli. Rab.* 9 [8] 46–48; see Ciampa 1998: 159–63).

Paul's permission to accept an invitation to a meal and to eat whatever is served (10:27) would seem to contradict Exod. 34:15 (so Hübner 1997: 277), but whereas that text refers to an invitation to a sacrifice, Paul's instructions (10:28–30) suggest that he has a simple dinner invitation in mind and that the believer was to be careful to avoid eating any food that was explicitly identified as having been offered to an idol. This clearly does not follow the Jewish tradition cited above, but still it may be understood as a more "liberal" approach to avoiding association with pagan sacrifices (and thus to the spirit of Exod. 34:15) while still allowing believers to maintain and develop social relationships with their nonbelieving neighbors.

10:31–11:1

Paul concludes his discussion of whether to eat food sacrificed to idols by returning to the biblical motif of maintaining a good reputation before outsiders for the dual motives of protecting the honor of God's name and winning over the heathen (see Rosner 1999: 109–11).

Paul says that he seeks not his own benefit, but rather "that of many [*to tōn pollōn*], in order that they might be saved." Such an approach to life is to be expected of anyone who follows the example of the one described in Isa. 53:11–12 LXX as "the righteous one who serves many well [*dikaion eu douleuonta pollois*] . . . who will bear their sins" and "who bore the sins of many [*pollōn*]."

Paul's exhortation to do everything (including eating and drinking) to God's glory as he concludes his section on idol food parallels his exhortation to glorify God with our bodies in the conclusion to his section on sexual immorality (see 6:20).

Glorifying God in Christian Worship (11:2–14:40)

Having dealt with the issue of idolatry in 8:1–11:1, Paul now turns to discuss issues relating to proper Christian worship.

In chapter 11 he deals with commendable and condemnable ways in which the Corinthians are relating to traditions that Paul passed on to them. In chapters 12–14 he focuses on issues related to spiritual gifts and their use in the Christian worship gathering. In 11:2–16 creation traditions are in the foreground as Paul explains the ways in which men and women are to worship together in this new community. In 11:17–34 traditions relating to the (first and second) exodus take center stage as Paul explains the implications of the celebration of the new covenant meal for the way rich and poor are to worship together in the new community. In chapters 12–14 themes relating to the rebuilding of the new restored community and the role of the eschatological Spirit in that edification process are most prominent.

11:2–16

This is one of the most difficult passages in this letter because of statements that Paul apparently expects to be transparent to the Corinthians but that have been opaque to other readers. Some of our difficulty undoubtedly comes from our inability to know exactly what Paul had previously taught the Corinthians on this subject and what they had written to him about it. Most likely, some Corinthians had begun suggesting that all distinctions between men and women were to be avoided in worship, based on a misunderstanding of Paul's teaching that in Christ "there is neither Jew nor Greek, there is neither slave nor free, there is no 'male and female'" (Gal. 3:28; perhaps one of the traditions he delivered to them [cf. 11:2]). The wearing of veils seems to have been a particular issue.

This is one of the passages at the heart of an ongoing debate over biblical teaching on the proper relationship between men and women. Many believe that this passage establishes a functional authority structure between husbands and wives (or men and women) while still underscoring the ontological equality of men and women in 11:11–12 (e.g., Schreiner 1991). This approach holds that with the inauguration of the end-time new creation the same dual reality is maintained (although no longer tainted by the fall), while at the consummation of the eschaton all functional distinctions will be erased.

Others believe that the passage does not establish an authority structure but does emphasize the importance of maintaining distinctions between men and women that reflect their distinctive origins (e.g., Jervis 1993). These also see a stress on ontological equality.

In several passages Paul seems to reflect a tension between a hierarchy that is reflected in creation (and in Gen. 2–3) and the understanding that the eschaton brings an end to authority structures based on gender distinctions. Some hold that 11:3–10 reflects Paul's respect for gender and authority structures reflected in creation (as narrated in Gen. 2), while 11:11–12 reflects his recognition that in Christ we experience the inbreaking of the eschaton, such that the church lives in the tension between the norms of creation and new creation (see D'Angelo 1988).

In this passage Paul seems to point to a hierarchy of status based on the Genesis narrative of human origins, and yet his ultimate conclusion is that women may, in general, participate as freely as men, providing that their attire and comportment are respectful.

Paul's primary concern is that all be done to the glory of God (cf. 10:31) and not to glorify or shame anyone else.

11:3

The language used to describe the husband as the "head" of the wife does not predate this letter (and is not as transparent as many think), but the OT clearly reflects a patriarchal context and understanding of the relationship between husbands and wives (even if a "softer" patriarchalism than in some other cultures). Much debate has taken place over the meanings of the words for "head" in the OT (*rō'š*) and the LXX (*kephalē*) and their relationship to Paul's meaning here. Even if by "head" Paul means "more prominent/preeminent partner" or "one through whom the other exists," his language and the flow of the argument seem to reflect an assumed hierarchy through which glory and shame flow upward from those with lower status to those above them (see Thiselton 2000: 812–22; Watson 2000: 43–44n3; Loader 2004: 100). Our understanding of Paul is complicated by the fact that he engages in wordplay, alternating between literal and metaphorical referents. It may be that Paul reflects the idea that each member originates from the other (8:6 tells us all things are from God and through Christ; that women originated from men is explicitly stated in 11:8), and that each one brings glory or shame to the one from which it came (see Meier 1978: 217–18). The concept of primogeniture (where temporal priority correlates with privilege and preeminence) is implied.

There is significant debate regarding whether or not a patriarchal relationship is understood to exist between Adam and Eve before the fall. Most ancient readers of Gen. 1–2 would have assumed such a relationship (the only kind of marriage that they knew), and those texts make good sense in the light of such a reading. Many readers believe Paul's argument here (and in 11:7–9) reflects a functional authority structure established in Gen. 2. Others think that the same verses are stressing the distinct origins of each gender (as part of a rationale for maintaining gender distinctions).

If some Corinthians were arguing that Christ, as head of the church, was head over men and women in the same way (since there was no longer any "male and female"), Paul affirms that the creation pattern is still significant and cannot be shrugged off. Although there is a tension between creation and new creation (especially fallen creation and new creation), creation is the context in which Christians live out their lives, and it cannot be passed off as irrelevant.

11:4–5

These two verses discuss how men and women can both pray and prophesy in the church without shaming their respective "heads." Although there were female prophets in OT times (Exod. 15:20; Judg. 4:4; 2 Kings 22:14; Neh. 6:14; Isa. 8:3), Joel 2:28 indicated that one of the marks of the last days would be the outpouring of the Spirit on all God's people with the result that Israel's "sons and daughters shall prophesy." Paul indicates that doing so in an inappropriate manner would bring shame (*kataischynei*) on one's head, meaning one's husband (in the case of a woman) or Christ (in the case of a man). Paul's ultimate concern, in the broader context, is with the glory of God and Christ. The immediate concern seems to be that the behavior of some wives would bring shame on their husbands (for an insightful discussion of the relationship between veils, nakedness, and shame, see Watson 2000). The two verses preceding Joel 2:28 stress that in the eschatological time of restoration God would see to it that "my people will never again be put to shame [*kataischynthē/ kataischynthōsin*]" (2:26, 27).

Paul's words in 2 Cor. 3:13–16 may suggest a biblical background for his understanding that men's heads should be uncovered and also for some Corinthians' support for both men and women to be uncovered in God's presence. There Paul says that "we are not like Moses, who put a veil over his face" (3:13), for in turning to the Lord "the veil is removed" (3:16), and as a result "we all with unveiled faces" reflect the glory of the Lord and are transformed into the image by the work of the Spirit (3:18). The conceptual and lexical ties between 1 Cor. 11:4–7 and 2 Cor. 3:13–18 are

remarkable. Paul is referring to Moses' experience as explained in Exod. 34:33–34, when he decided to wear a veil when in the presence of the people but remove it when he went into the presence of the Lord. If the Corinthians were already familiar with Exod. 34:33–34 and had heard Paul express something similar to 2 Cor. 3:13–18, then one could easily see how some might deduce that the women also should act like Moses and remove the veil when entering into God's presence, since Paul indicates we should "all" approach God with "unveiled faces." In the following verses Paul explains why women should continue to wear veils even when in the presence of the Lord.

11:7

First Corinthians 11:7–12 reflects Paul's thinking on men and women in light of creation (as expressed primarily in Gen. 1:26–27; 2:18–23).

First, there is the image and glory of God and man. The traditional (and majority) reading of 11:7–9 takes these verses to reflect Paul's understanding that Gen. 2 establishes a functional hierarchy reflected in the order in which the man and woman were created and in their respective purposes. (For an intriguing study of the translation of the creation narrative in the LXX and its potential importance for understanding the NT texts, see Loader 2004: 27–59, 99–104.) Others think that the point is that gender distinctions are reflected in the distinct origins of men and women (Adam and Eve) and should be maintained in the church.

Jewish interpreters struggled to understand the relationship between Gen. 1:26–27 and the narratives in Gen. 2. Many distinguished between the accounts and applied them in very different ways. Philo distinguishes between "the heavenly man" of 1:26–27 and "the earthly man" of 2:7 (*Alleg. Interp.* 1.31; 2.4–5; *Creation* 134). The former is "born" in the image of God and does not partake of the corruption of earthly existence; the latter is made out of clay and partakes of the vagaries of earthly existence and "has a helpmeet for him."

Paul's statement in 11:7 that the man is "the image and glory of God, but the woman is the glory of the man" suggests to some that Paul understood Adam, but not Eve, to have been created in the image of God. In 15:49, however, Paul says, "Just as we have borne the image of the earthly man, we shall also bear the image of the heavenly one," suggesting that he understands all humanity to share imperfectly in the image of God as it has been passed down to us through Adam and that part of our redemption in Christ entails the restoration of God's perfect image in Christ (cf. Rom. 8:29 and 1 Cor. 15:49; 2 Cor. 3:18 and Col. 3:10; 2 Cor. 4:4 and Col. 1:15).

Paul uses the term "glory" because it is associated with "image" (Hooker 1964: 415) and can substitute for "likeness" or "image" in references to Gen. 1:27 (cf. Ps. 8:5; 4Q504 8, 4). He can move smoothly from "image" to "glory," which "then becomes the key term in 1 Cor. 11:7–9 and counterbalances the notion of 'shame' in 11:4–6" (Garland 2003: 523). The idea that the wife brings glory to the husband is found in Prov. 11:16 LXX; 1 Esd. 4:17.

Understanding 11:7 in the light of 15:49 suggests that for Paul, Adam was created directly in the image of God and that the rest of us (from Eve on) are made in God's image as we inherit it from Adam and our parents (cf. Gen. 5:3; 9:6).

That is similar to a rabbinic way of interpreting Gen. 1:26–27 and understanding the relationships between those verses and the narratives in Gen. 2. As D'Angelo (1988), following Boucher, has shown, some rabbinic debates over the interpretation of Gen. 1:26 suggested that the plural forms in God's speech ("let us," "our") referred to his intention to create the first man and woman in unique manners, after which he would create every other man and woman in conjunction with (through) a human father and mother (thus "our" image would be the image of God and the parents). Thus, "In the past Adam was created from dust and Eve was created from Adam; but henceforth it shall be 'in our image, after our likeness' [Gen. 1:26]; neither man without woman nor woman without man, and neither of them without the Shekinah" (*Gen. Rab.* 8:9; cf. *Gen. Rab.* 22:2; *y. Ber.* 9:1). Thus Adam and Eve were created in different manners, and neither was created in the manner of the rest of humanity (through a mother and father). The rest of humanity, however, was to come about through God working through both a mother and a father (on the variety of Jewish sources that relate to this theme, see D'Angelo 1988: 7–21).

The close relationship between Paul's clear allusion to Gen. 1:26 in 11:7b and his statement in 11:7c that the woman is the glory of the man suggests that he understands Adam to have been uniquely made in God's image (without any other human contribution), while God's image was passed to Eve through Adam. Therefore, 11:7 is probably best understood as an interpretation of Gen. 1:26–27 "through the creation account in Gen. 2" (Garland 2003: 522).

Gundry-Volf (1997: 157) argues that Paul's point is that "man and woman are both *the glory of another* and therefore both have an obligation not to cause shame to their heads." But the question of whose glory each one reflects (and not just that it is of another) seems important to Paul's argument. It is important because it is appropriate for God's glory to be reflected in worship, but not that of man. One of the reasons Paul does not mention that the woman was also created in God's image is probably "because he wants to stress the point that she is the glory of man" (Garland 2003: 523; cf. Gundry-Volf 1997: 156). Thus Paul's point is not that women are not made in God's image, but rather that the way the creation narrative distinguishes between the origin and purpose of the man and the woman suggests that the man (not originating from the woman or being created to complete her) does not reflect the woman's glory (but only God's), while the woman does reflect the glory of the man. In 11:8–9 Paul uses details from Gen. 2 to explain why the man cannot be understood as the glory of the woman, while the woman can be understood as the glory of the man.

Paul's overarching point seems to be that nothing should happen in worship that detracts from God's glory, including behavior that would draw attention to the glory of man. Hooker (1964: 415) points out that the woman's head should be covered "not because she is in the presence of man, but because she is in the presence of God and his angels—and in their presence the glory of man must be hidden."

11:8–9

In these two verses Paul supports the principle that he drew in 11:7 from the creation of Adam and Eve as described in Gen. 2. That man did not come from woman is patent in Gen. 2:7: he was formed from the dust of the earth. That the woman came from man is taught in Gen. 2:23. In fact, it is given as the explanation of her name.

Paul's statement that the woman was created for the sake of the man (*dia ton andra*) is based on Gen. 2:18. The context indicates that the man would have been the only one of God's creatures without a corresponding mate, and that was not good. That the woman originated from the man and that she was made because of him points to the anteriority of the man (see 1 Tim. 2:13; cf. Philo, *Alleg. Interp.* 2.5) and evokes the concept of primogeniture with the implied prominence and precedence. (We should note that in Paul's context wives would have almost always been significantly younger and less mature than their husbands [see Witherington 1995: 170], such that the husband could be expected to share an anteriority similar to that of Adam with regard to Eve.)

11:10

While some interpreters take the word "angels" [*angelous*] to actually refer to human messengers visiting the church rather than to angels overseeing its worship (see Winter 2001: 133–41; Murphy-O'Connor 1988), the majority understand it to refer to angels, which is how the word is used elsewhere in this letter (4:9; 6:3; 13:1; see the discussion in Garland 2003: 526; Thiselton 2000: 839–41). Angels are associated in such diverse ways with creation, worship (including prayer and prophecy), and women in the OT and in Jewish literature that it is difficult to discern which one(s) Paul might have had in mind here. It is also unclear whether he is referring to good angels or evil ones.

According to Jewish tradition, the angels worshiped Adam when he was created (e.g., *L.A.E.* 13–16; *Gen. Rab.* 8:10). It could be that by covering the face of the glory of the man Paul hopes to avoid distracting their attention from the worship of God to the worship of man (Hooker 1964: 415n2). In Isa. 6:2 the seraphs cover their faces in the presence of God, and perhaps Paul thinks that the women should behave in a similar fashion (while men are granted an exception). Some think that Paul may be concerned about the women's vulnerability to angelic attention based on the common Jewish understanding that Gen. 6:2 referred to angels who mated with women. Some think that since, in light of Jewish tradition, angels were the guardians of creation order, Paul was con-

cerned to make sure that nothing in the worship service would offend them.

It may be that Paul was thinking of the angels simply as divinely appointed observers of the community's gathering who, like God, would be offended by any shameful displays during the worship (see Loader 2004: 102). Watson (2000: 71) suggests that the veil "is a prophetic sign to the angels that the new creation has dawned and that their jurisdiction has passed away" and that "the *exousia* [authority] of the woman prophet, represented by the veil, is greater than theirs." It is unclear why the angels would have interpreted the use of the veil in that way without having read Paul's argument. That women would simultaneously respect the men/husbands in the congregation and freely exercise a newly found authority to pray and prophesy alongside them may have served as such a sign for angels observing the scene.

11:11–12

After establishing in 11:8–9 principles for the behavior of men and women in worship from the narrative of the unique creation of the first man and woman, Paul now qualifies the implications of those narratives in light of the origin of every man and woman since that first pair. As we noted in the comments on 11:7, rabbinic tradition also distinguished between the origin of Adam and Eve and that of the rest of humanity. The language that they used is very close to Paul's language here: "In the past Adam was created from dust and Eve was created from Adam; but henceforth it shall be 'in our image, after our likeness' [Gen. 1:26]; *neither man without woman nor woman without man*, and neither of them without the Shekinah" (*Gen. Rab.* 8:9 [italics added]). D'Angelo (1988: 21) sees three features in common between 11:7–12 and the rabbinic statements: "First, Paul advances the formula 'neither woman without man nor man without woman' as an interpretation of Gen. 1:26. Second, Paul also contrasts that phrase with the creations of Adam and Eve (1 Cor. 11:7–9). Third, Paul also makes a temporal distinction between creation and its aftermath, and on that basis rejects the creation of Eve as the basis for prescriptions about women." It is not clear that Paul's statement in 11:11 reflects his interpretation of Gen. 1:26 (although his allusion to the text and the use of his phrase elsewhere as an interpretation of that text raise that possibility). It may be based on a broader understanding of the relationship between Gen. 1 and 2, one that later rabbis based on Gen. 1:26 itself. Also, it is not the case that Paul "rejects the creation of Eve as the basis for prescriptions about women." Paul introduces the verse with *plēn* ("nevertheless"), which introduces a qualification, not a rejection, of the prior statement. Paul is in agreement with other ancient interpreters of Gen. 1–2 in deducing some principles from the creation of Adam and Eve, while qualifying them in light of the recognition that their creation was unique and that other principles may be applied in light of the way all men and women have come into being ever since.

Paul's statement that "neither woman without man nor man without woman" applies "in the Lord" (*en kyriō*) seems strange at first sight, since clearly the same reality applies to all of humanity, not merely to Christians. D'Angelo (1988: 24–25) suggests that Paul has taken the temporal distinction that other interpreters applied between the creation of the first pair and the formation of the rest of humanity and has applied it to the distinction between all creation and new creation in Christ. The point, presumably, would be similar to that made in the rabbinic texts: the community's application of the principle drawn from the narration of the creation of the first human couple is tempered by the way God has determined to bring every other human being into his creation. In Paul's case it is the community established "in the Lord" that is to live in the light of these truths. It may be that "in the Lord" suggests that the new creation in Christ relativizes the distinctions between men and women in a way similar to the observation based on the distinction between Adam and Eve and the rest of us.

If one were to take the final prepositional phrase instrumentally (*en kyriō* = "by/through the Lord"), then Paul's meaning would correspond perfectly to a Jewish exegetical tradition about the Lord's role in the formation of every human being (based in part on Gen. 4:1): "neither of them without the Shekinah" (*y. Ber.* 9:1; *Gen. Rab.* 8:9; 22:2). It would also strengthen the parallel between 11:11 and 11:12:

1. neither woman without man (v. 11)
   ≈ woman is from man (v. 12)
2. nor man without woman (v. 11)
   ≈ the man through the woman (v. 12)
3. *en kyriō* ("by/through the Lord") (v. 11)
   ≈ all things are from God (v. 12)

In this case the only difference between Paul's statement and the rabbinic view would be that "the Lord" in 11:11 refers to Christ.

Watson (2000: 79) sees Paul pointing to an aspect of the new creation in Christ that was foreshadowed in the narratives of Gen. 2:

Having moved forward from the old creation to the situation "in the Lord" (vv. 7–10), Paul is now in a position to look back at the old creation from the new perspective and to see the togetherness of man and woman in the Lord already foreshadowed there. The new creation redresses an imbalance in the old; but, seen retrospectively, the old creation is also prophetic of the new. Anticipations of the togetherness of man and woman in the Lord may be found in the simplest and most obvious phenomena of the first creation.

Paul then summarizes in 11:12 the interpretation of Gen. 1–2. The first clause ("as woman came/comes from man") refers to Eve (or to her and to women in general). The second clause ("so also man comes through woman") points not to the creation of the first man, but rather to that of every man since Adam (perhaps evoking Gen. 4:1 [see Watson 2000: 79]). The final clause ("all things are from God") reminds the reader that God is the ultimate origin of every human being (and all creation), apparently relativizing the significance of other factors in the creation of men and women and clearly emphasizing that it is God's glory and honor that must govern all that is done.

11:17–34

Craigie (1976: 242) points out that "the Passover became the act, symbolically speaking, of the one large family of God" (see also Routledge 2002: 207, 212, 216). Chapter 30 of 2 Chronicles depicts the celebration of Passover as a unifying and sanctifying event that "fit well into Hezekiah's designs to reunify the nation" (Matthews, Chavalas, and Walton 2000: 453). The Lord's Supper, like the Passover meal on which it was based, should serve as an experience that strengthens the unity of God's people.

11:21–22

God's concern for the poor, caring for the poor as a mark of piety, and the oppression of the poor as a mark of the wicked are key themes of the OT (see Ciampa 1998: 153n94).

11:23–26

The verb *paredideto* ("was handed over" or "was betrayed") in 11:23 may be understood as a reference to Judas's betrayal, but more likely Paul is echoing the LXX rendering of Isa. 53:6 ("the Lord gave him up [*paredōken*] for our sins") and 53:12 ("his life was given up [*paredothē*] to death and . . . he was given up [*paredothē*] on account of their sins") (see Hays 1997: 198). Paul understands Jesus' death as the fulfillment of God's plan as foreshadowed in Isa. 53.

Jesus would have broken the unleavened bread served at a Passover meal (cf. Exod. 12:8; see Routledge 2002: 215–17). Paul has already alluded to the unleavened bread and referred to Christ as "our Passover lamb" who has been sacrificed (see commentary on 1 Cor. 5:6–8 above), suggesting that he understood Jesus' words at the Last Supper to mean that he was fulfilling the role of the sacrificial lamb in the establishment of the new covenant.

Deuteronomy 16:3 calls the unleavened bread "the bread of affliction," referring to the sufferings of Israel. Jesus, in saying that the bread represents his body "which is for you," makes it refer to the redemption that he is about to accomplish by his own suffering.

Jesus' statement that the cup "is the new covenant in my blood" fuses together the language of Jer. 31:31 ("a new covenant") and Exod. 24:8 ("the blood of the covenant that the LORD has made with you"). The latter text refers to the establishment of the covenant at Sinai, while the former consists of God's promise to establish a new covenant in the time of postexilic restoration. By fusing the two texts together, Jesus interprets his impending death as the sacrifice that establishes the new covenant associated with the second exodus.

The celebration of the Passover entailed a focused reflection on the exodus redemption, stimulated and structured by discussion of the unusual elements of the Passover meal (*m. Pesaḥ.* 10:4–5; cf. Exod. 13:7–8; Deut. 16:3). Jesus reflects on the redemption that he is about to accomplish and reinterprets two elements of the traditional Passover meal (bread and wine) so that now they can communicate the message of the redemption that he brings.

Jesus' statement that we are to partake of the Lord's Supper in his "remembrance" reflects the nature of the Passover as a "memorial" (Exod. 12:14) during which the Israelites were to remember the day of their exodus redemption (Deut. 16:3).

For the Corinthians to truly celebrate the *Lord's* Supper, they would need to take more seriously its nature as a celebration of new covenant redemption brought about through Christ's *self-sacrificing* death for them on the cross. To recognize it as such would necessarily require a change in the ways the Corinthian Christians were treating each other.

11:27–34

Hugenburger (1998: 209n171) points out that "Paul's threat that whoever eats and drinks unworthily will 'eat and drink judgment upon himself'" reflects the nature of the Lord's Supper "as a covenant-ratifying oath-sign" implying "a self-maledictory symbolism" such that "our infidelity deserves the same dreadful curse which overtook Christ, whose death is symbolized in the elements." This is consistent with Paul's depiction in 10:8–10 of the judgment that fell on Israel as a result of their infidelity to God's covenant.

12:1–14:40

In this section of the letter Paul continues the theme of worship that he had already begun to develop in chapter 11 (chaps. 8–10 dealt with the avoidance of association with *pagan* worship). That this material relates back to chapters 8–10 is suggested by Paul's reference to idols in 12:2. Chapters 12–14 reflect the A-B-A' structure found in chapters 8–10, where an apparent digression turns out to provide a key to the apostle's approach to the issue introduced in the previous chapter and developed in the following chapter. Chapter 12 introduces the issue of spiritual gifts and their function within the body of Christ. Chapter 13 stresses the importance, nature, and permanence of love, which is the only proper basis for the use of the gifts. Chapter 14 returns to the gifts of tongues and prophecy in particular and stresses the superiority of prophecy because of its ability to edify the body (the goal established by love).

The only biblical quotation in this section is Paul's quotation of Isa. 28:11–12 in 14:21. The only other allusion to Scripture that has been identified in this section is one to Isa. 45:14 (cf. Zech. 8:23) in 14:25.

12:2

The OT knows of two types of people: idolaters and those who worship only the God of Israel (cf., from the central section of the Shema, Deut. 11:13, 16; see Meeks 1983: 690).

That idols are "dumb" is an OT theme taken up many times in Jewish sources (e.g., Ps. 115:4–5; 135:15–17; Isa. 46:6–7; Jer. 10:5; Hab. 2:18–19 [cf. 1QpHab XII, 10–17]; *Gen. Rab.* 84:10; *b. Sanh.* 7b). Whereas the idols are dumb, the Lord speaks through Isaiah and the other prophets (Isa. 41:22–42:9).

12:3

The OT teaching that true prophetic speech comes through God's Spirit (Num. 11:25–29; 24:2–3; 1 Sam. 10:6, 10; 19:20, 23; 2 Sam. 23:2; Neh. 9:30; Isa. 61:1; Joel 2:28; Mic. 3:8; Zech. 7:12) was commonplace in early Christian teaching (Luke 1:67; Acts 2:17–18; 19:6; 28:25; Eph. 3:5; 1 Pet. 1:10–12; 1 John 4:1; Rev. 19:10) and is reflected throughout 1 Cor. 12–14.

12:4–6

Prophetic texts that looked forward to the outpouring of the Spirit anticipated a variety of manifestations. Joel 2:28–32, one of the more influential texts, refers to prophesying, dreaming (inspired) dreams, seeing visions, and God-given wonders. Other texts also look forward to a variety of qualities or manifestations (e.g., Isa. 11:1–5; 32:15–17; 44:3–5; 61:1–4).

That all the variety of manifestations must be understood to originate from the one God (rather than from a variety of spiritual beings [cf. 12:2]) is based on the presupposition of biblical monotheism (see commentary on 1 Cor. 8:1–6 above).

12:7

That the Spirit would be manifest in each person is suggested by Joel 2:28–29 as well as Ezek. 36:26–27; 37:14, and this may be understood as the fulfillment of the desire expressed by Moses

in Num. 11:29, which is alluded to and developed by the Joel 2 text (Dillard 2000).

12:8–10

Several of the gifts that Paul mentions were already associated with the Spirit (or were referred to in terms of "a spirit of . . .") in the OT and Jewish thought, including wisdom and knowledge or understanding (Exod. 31:3; 35:31; Isa. 11:2; Dan. 1:4; 5:11–12; 1QS IV, 3–4, 20–22; 4Q161 8–10 III, 11–12), healing (Isa. 61:1; 1QS IV, 6), and prophecy (e.g., Num. 11:29; Joel 2:28; 1 Sam. 10:6, 10; 19:20, 23; 2 Sam. 23:2).

Miracles were especially associated with God's special intervention in the exodus and in the ministries of Elijah and Elisha.

In the OT healing was expected to accompany forgiveness and restoration of God's people (Deut. 32:39; 2 Chron. 7:14; Job 5:18; Ps. 41:4; 103:3; 107:20; 147:3; Isa. 6:10; 19:22; 30:26; 42:4–6; 53:5; 57:18–19; 58:8; 61:1; Jer. 30:17; 33:6; Ezek. 47:12; Hos. 6:1; 14:4; Mal. 4:2). The Gospels (see esp. Matt. 11:4–5/Luke 7:22–23) make it clear that Jesus' ministry of healing was understood as a fulfillment of such prophetic promises (perhaps especially Isa. 42:6–7).

It appears that in Acts and Paul, speaking in tongues (as a manifestation of the Spirit that requires interpretation) has taken the place of dreams and visions in Joel and the rest of the OT (cf. Acts 2:4, 16–19; 19:6; Joel 2:28–32).

12:13–26

There has been much speculation about the source of Paul's identification of the church as the body of Christ. Kim (1984: 252–56) has argued that Jewish mystical (*merkabah*) speculation based on Ezek. 1:26 and Dan. 7 may have played a role. Paul describes the church as both a Spirit-filled temple (3:16; cf. 6:19) and a Spirit-filled body (12:13; cf. 6:19). There may be some relationship between Paul's understanding of the church as the Spirit-indwelt temple of God and Jesus' identification of his body with God's temple (Matt. 26:61; 27:40; Mark 14:58; 15:29; John 2:19–21). Paul's usage of the body metaphor appears to be an interesting variation on an ancient rhetorical commonplace relating to corporate solidarity and unity (see Mitchell 1991: 157–64).

Paul's statement that the Corinthians were all baptized into one body and were all given the one

12:31

Spirit to drink (12:13) echoes his description of Israel's experience in 10:2–4. The Israelites were all "baptized into Moses" and drank the same spiritual drink (cf. Ps. 78:15).

12:31

Paul's promise to show the Corinthians a superior path to follow reflects an OT motif usually associated with the exodus or second exodus (Exod. 13:21; Deut. 1:33; Isa. 48:16–17; Mic. 4:2). Samuel also was committed to showing Israel the good and right way (1 Sam. 12:23).

13:1–13: Introduction

There is a long tradition of unpacking the meaning of the command to love one's neighbor (Lev. 19:18): Tob. 4:13; 2 Macc. 15:14; Matt. 5:43 (Jesus citing a contemporaneous interpretation), 44–46; 19:19; 22:39–40; Mark 10:21; 12:31–33; Luke 6:27–38; 10:25–37; John 15:12–17; James 2:8; 1 Pet. 1:22; 2:17; 4:8; 1 John 2:10; 3:10–18, 23; 4:7, 11–12, 20–21; 5:1; 2 John 5–6; *m. Ned.* 9:4; *Gen. Rab.* 24:7; *Lev. Rab.* 24:5; *b. Pesaḥ.* 75a; *b. Yebam.* 62b; *b. Ketub.* 37b; *b. Ned.* 65b; *b. Soṭah* 8b; *b. Qidd.* 41a; *b. B. Qam.* 51a; *b. Sanh.* 45a, 52a–b, 76b, 84b; *b. Nid.* 17a.

Love is a central theme of Paul's Christian ethical teaching (Rom. 12:9–10; 13:8–10; 14:15; Gal. 5:13–14; Eph. 1:15; 4:2, 16; 5:2), and in Rom. 13:10 Paul makes clear that he understands his teaching on love to be a reflection of Lev. 19:18, which he considers a summary of the law.

Söding (1995: 130–31) highlights "the eschatological and theocentric dimension" of love (*agapē*) in 1 Cor. 13 (see below) and suggests that it represents "God's eschatological power." Paul's discussion of love focuses on qualities that have been lacking in the Corinthians' behavior.

13:1

Forbes (1995) has argued that tongues would have been understood as unknown human languages, but Paul's reference to the ability to speak the "tongues of angels" probably indicates that he and the Corinthians consider glossolalia ("speaking in tongues") to be, or at least to include, the ability to speak angelic languages. D. Martin (1991: 558–61; 1995: 88–90) provides evidence that angels were thought to have their own languages (*T. Job* 48–50; Dio Chrysostom, *Discourses* 10.23; 11.22). The praise that angels give to God is men-

tioned in Ps. 103:20; 148:2, and the Qumran community manifested an extraordinary fascination with the subject (cf. 4Q400; 4Q401; 4Q403).

13:2–3

The eschatological nature of love is reflected in the affirmation that whether or not one "is" anything before God or "gains" anything from one's actions (both of which have soteriological connotations) depends on the presence or absence of love.

The reference to "knowing all mysteries" evokes the portrayal of Daniel in Dan. 2; 4 (esp. 4:9).

The manuscripts of 13:3 are divided as to whether Paul speaks of giving up one's body "to boast" or "to be burned." The latter reading (which is slightly inferior on internal grounds) would echo Dan. 3:95 LXX, where Daniel's friends "gave their bodies to be burned."

13:4–7

The theocentric nature of love in this chapter is reflected in that much of what Paul says about it was previously affirmed of God in the OT and early Judaism (and is said about God by Paul himself elsewhere). Patience is one of God's attributes (in the LXX, see Exod. 34:6; Num. 14:18; Neh. 9:17; Ps. 7:12; 85:15; 102:8; 144:8; Wis. 15:1; Sir. 5:4; 18:11; Joel 2:13; Jon. 4:2; Nah. 1:3; cf. Rom. 2:4; 9:22). The same can be said of kindness (in the LXX, see Ps. 24:7–8; 30:20; 33:9; 67:11; 85:5; 99:5; 105:1; 106:1; 118:68; 135:1; 144:9; Wis. 15:1; *Pss. Sol.* 10:7; Jer. 40:11; Dan. 3:89; 1 Esd. 5:58; cf. Rom. 2:4; 11:22; Titus 3:4). Söding (1995: 131) points out that not keeping count of evil (13:5) "is God's prerogative and salvific will" (cf. Rom. 4:7–8; 2 Cor. 5:19), and that God is the one who supremely "hates injustice (cf. Rom. 1:28; 2:8) and bears all truth in himself (v. 6)."

13:8–10

The eschatological nature of Paul's thinking about love is evident throughout these verses. He uses a variety of images to distinguish between that which is permanent and that which, being temporary, will pass away. Paul's statement that love "never falls/fails [*piptei*]" reflects the eschatological connotations of *piptō*, which can be seen elsewhere (see commentary on 1 Cor. 10:11–12 above).

Paul's references to things that "pass away" in 13:8, 10 employ the word *katargeō*, which consistently has an eschatological connotation in this letter, referring to those things that do not survive the transition from this age to the age to come (1:28; 2:6; 6:13; 13:8, 10; 15:24, 26).

13:12

In 13:12 Paul alludes to Num. 12:6–8, which contrasts Moses' prophetic experience with that of all other prophets. Whereas other prophets receive revelation through visions and dreams (12:6; cf. Joel 2:28), Moses experiences the presence of the Lord face to face (*stoma kata stoma*), not indirectly (*ou di ainigmatōn*) and sees his form (LXX: "glory"): "With him I speak face to face, clearly, and not in riddles, and he beholds the form of the LORD." Paul says, "Now we see in a mirror [*di esoptrou*] indirectly [*en ainigmati*], but then face to face [*prosōpon pros prosōpon*]. Now I know in part; then I shall know fully, even as I am fully known."

According to *Lev. Rab.* 1:14, there was a debate regarding the difference between Moses and the other prophets based on Num. 12:8. Both sides held that Moses, like the other prophets, saw the Lord through a mirror (reading the word for "appearance" [*mar'eh*] in Num. 12:8 as though it meant "mirror," another meaning of the word used for "vision" [*mar'â*] in Num. 12:6 [cf. Exod. 38:8]). Some thought that the difference was that the other prophets saw the Lord through a series of mirrors rather than just one, while others thought that Moses saw the Lord through a polished mirror while the other prophets saw him through a blurred one. Fishbane (1986: 74) argues that this midrashic reading "may have preceded Paul or have been common coin among ancient homileticists." Paul's reference to a mirror in the context of an allusion to the same text would be a strange coincidence if he does not share some interpretive tradition with its authors.

Paul suggests that Christians now share the experience of seeing God indirectly, in a mirror (presumably analogous to his understanding of the prophets' experience), but one day will see him face to face (as did Moses). *Leviticus Rabbah* 1:14 goes on to quote Isa. 40:5 and say that although only a few in this age were able to see God the way Moses did, in the age to come "all flesh shall see the glory of the Lord" (as Moses did).

The contrast between this age and the age to come matches Paul's thinking precisely. The reference to the vision of "the glory of the Lord" (in the citation from Isa. 40:5) brings us to the LXX translation of Num. 12:8. Whereas the Hebrew text says that Moses saw the "likeness" or "form" (*těmûnâ*) of the Lord, the LXX says he saw the "glory" (*doxa*) of the Lord. The LXX both affirms Moses' face-to-face experience with the Lord and interprets it as a vision of his glory (cf. 2 Cor. 3:18).

Fishbane also hints that Paul's alteration of *stoma kata stoma* ("mouth to mouth") in Num. 12:8 LXX to *prosōpon pros prosōpon* ("face to face") may reflect the influence of Deut. 34:10, which refers to Moses as a prophet whom the Lord "knew" (*egnō*) "face to face" (*prosōpon kata prosōpon*). Philo also brought together Num. 12:8 and Deut. 34:10 (*Heir* 262). Deuteronomy 34:10 not only provides a closer parallel to Paul's wording for "face to face," but also supplies another link to the motif of "knowing" and "being known" (see also Num. 12:6 LXX: *autō gnōsthēsomai*), which is prominent in 13:12 (cf. 13:8).

Paul's allusion to Num. 12:8, then, is consistent with other early Jewish interpretations in understanding that in the age to come all God's people will have an experience similar to that which distinguished Moses from the other prophets. We already see the Lord as through a mirror (imperfectly) and know him as well as that experience allows (cf. 2 Cor. 3:18), but the day is coming when we will see him as Moses did, face to face, an experience of knowing him fully, as we are already fully known by him.

13:13

In keeping with his emphasis on the theocentric nature of love in this chapter, Söding (1995: 131) points out that love's quality of enduring, both now and in the future, is a reflection of the fact that "God is the Eternal One, who has no beginning and no end (13:13; cf. Rom. 16:26)." Of all the things said to endure forever in the OT and early Jewish texts, God's *ḥesed*, his loyalty, steadfast love or mercy, is mentioned most often (e.g., 1 Chron. 16:34, 41; 2 Chron. 5:13; 7:3, 6; 20:21; Ezra 3:11; Ps. 100:5; 106:1; 107:1; 118:1–4, 29; 136; 138:8; Jer. 33:11).

14:1–40

14:1

This verse signals a transition between the various themes of chapters 12–14. "Spiritual gifts" in general were the focus of chapter 12. Love was the center of attention in chapter 13 as the key to the significance and use of spiritual gifts and to the nature of new life in Christ. In chapter 14 Paul highlights prophecy as a spiritual gift whose exercise would be more naturally promoted by the principle of love than the gift of tongues because it more clearly serves to edify the church (which is what love seeks).

14:3–4

The motif of "building/edifying" finds its background in OT prophetic promises regarding God's future plans for the redemption and restoration of Israel (with *oikodomeō* or *anoikodomeō* in the LXX: Isa. 44:26, 28; 49:17; 54:14; 58:12; 60:10; 61:4; Jer. 1:10; 12:16; 24:6; 37:18 [30:18 ET]; 38:4, 28, 38 [31:4 ET]; 40:7 [33:7 ET]; 49:10 [42:10 ET]; Ezek. 36:36; Amos 9:11, 14; Zech. 1:16; 6:12, 15; 8:9). In Jeremiah 1:10 "tearing down" (the prophetic ministry associated with judgment and exile) and "building up" (the prophetic ministry associated with salvation and restoration) are ascribed to Jeremiah's own prophetic activity. Jeremiah tears down and builds as he proclaims God's prophetic word, or alternatively, God acts through the prophet to tear down and build up his chosen nation/people.

Michel (1967: 139) points out that in the NT building "is primarily an apocalyptic and Messianic concept. . . . The Messiah will build the future temple and the new community." The edification of the church is an activity for which the Spirit empowers the eschatological community, as Paul will make clear throughout this chapter. As Paul also makes clear, the prophetic ministry of the church carries particular edifying value. It is because Paul is concerned about the edification of the church that he puts such a high value on the prophetic ministry.

14:10–11

The reference to the diversity of languages in the world (14:10) and Paul's reference to a speaker being "a foreigner [*barbaros*] to me" (14:11) suggest that he already has Isa. 28:11–12 in mind (see commentary on 1 Cor. 14:21–24 below). Paul will

cite the text that deals with Israel's experience of not understanding the strange, unknown language of its foreign invaders.

14:20

Paul is about to quote Isa. 28:11–12. In Isa. 28:9–10 the religious leaders complain that the prophet's message is too simple and naïve. The irony is that "those who are 'wise' and 'gifted' in their own eyes dismiss the plain message as 'childish,' when in reality it is the supposedly wise who think and act like children" (Thiselton 2000: 1121). Paul's appeal to the Corinthians to reason as adults rather than as children may echo Isaiah's encounter with childish people who thought they were too wise to heed his message.

14:21–24

A. NT Context: Tongues and Prophecy in Corinth. In chapter 12 Paul argued that God had provided, and the church needed to exercise, a diversity of gifts (probably engaging the church's fascination with one particular gift: tongues). Throughout this chapter Paul has been arguing for the superior value of prophecy over tongues for ministering in the church. That motif will be stressed again at the end of 14:26. In 14:21 Paul quotes Isa. 28:11–12: "'By people of other tongues and by the lips of others I will speak to this people, and even then they will not listen to me,' says the Lord."

B. Isa. 28:11–12 in Its OT Context. Isaiah 28:1–29 consists of an oracle against the political and religious leadership of God's people (Samaria and Jerusalem). They had rejected God's counsel to rest and trust in him as being naïve and had gone ahead in a policy marked by a drunken madness and formed other alliances. The leadership (rulers, priests, and prophets [cf. 28:1, 3, 7, 14–15]) refused to listen when God clearly and plainly explained to them what it meant to rest in him and to give rest to the weary (28:12), so now God's voice of judgment will be heard in the barbarian language of the Assyrian invaders (28:11). The verses immediately preceding our text evidently represent their mockery of Isaiah's message (28:9–10). The word used for "stammering" (*lā'ēg*) usually means "derision" (*HALOT* 2:532), and it may be that Isaiah intends a double entendre involving an ironic reversal: the "stammering" of the Assyrian invaders is God's punishment for the "mocking" perpetrated by the nation's leadership (Kwon 2004: 26). As Kwon (2004: 26) has suggested, "The judgment of unintelligible speech serves as a metonymy for the experience of foreign invasion in general and, perhaps, the experience of exile in particular."

C. Isa. 28:11–12 in Early Judaism. In the *Isaiah Targum* and 1QH^a (X, 19; XII, 16) the strange tongues and lips of Isa. 28:11–12 are those of God's rebellious people (false teachers, according to the Qumran writers; the people in general, according to the Targum) who reject his revelation and his true prophets. In the LXX it is unclear whether the message of 28:12 was spoken by the drunken prophets and priests or by the invading Assyrians (see Johanson 1979: 182). Stanley (1992: 201), following Koch (1986: 64), argues that in the LXX "vv. 10–12 are mistakenly read as continuing the description of the disgraceful deeds of the 'priest and prophet' that begins in v. 7." Lanier (1991) thinks that the LXX has turned 28:12 into a call for endurance in the face of taunting invaders (whose words are found in that verse).

Each text (regardless of which words are attributed to which people) understands the passage to deal with a radical division between faithful and unfaithful Israelites. In some cases the stammering lips and foreign tongue are considered a cause for God's judgment, while in others they appear to be a sign of it.

D. Textual Matters. "Determining the precise relationship between the wording of 1 Cor. 14.21 and the text of the LXX is one of the greatest challenges in the entire corpus of Pauline citations" because of "the distance of the Pauline wording from both the LXX and the Masoretic Hebrew textual traditions" (Stanley 1992: 198).

Paul leaves out most of Isa. 28:12, evidently because he sees those clauses as irrelevant to his argument. His text appears to be an interpretive rendering, perhaps dependent upon an earlier Greek version that sought to conform more closely to the Hebrew text than the LXX (see Stanley 1992).

The Hebrew texts (MT and 1QIsa^a) indicate that God would speak to his people "by stammering [or 'mocking'] lips and by another tongue" because he had spoken to them before "but they were unwilling to hear." The LXX says that it is "because of the contempt of lips and through another tongue they will speak [*lalēsousin*] to this people . . . but they did not want to hear."

Paul follows the Hebrew texts in understanding the speaker to be the Lord, but his text uses the first person rather than the third person (*lalēsō* ["I will speak"]). It is unclear whether Paul's reading is based on an ambiguous form in 28:12b (cf. Stanley 1992: 201–2) or is his adaptation. Whereas both the Hebrew texts and the LXX represent the final clause as a historical observation—"they were not willing to listen"—Paul's text transforms it into a shocking prediction: *oud' houtōs eisakousontai* ("even then they will not listen"). This seems to be his own modification, reflecting his interpretation of the significance of the strange language (in both Isaiah and the history of the nation). He also adds two other elements at the end that reinforce who the speaker is: the object pronoun "to me" (*mou*) followed by the formula "says the Lord" (*legei kyrios*). (For more detailed examination of the textual issues, see Stanley 1992; Lanier 1991.)

E. The Use of Isa. 28:11–12 in 1 Cor. 14. Paul introduces his quotation by identifying it as something "written in the law," probably meaning only that it is a quotation from Scripture (it is not, strictly speaking, from the law). Paul emphasizes the idea of "other" or "foreign" tongues and lips through repetition (*heteroglōssois . . . cheilesin heterōn*). In Paul's case the issue is the use of strange languages in worship. Whereas other early interpretations of the text could gloss over the text's reference to unknown languages (and emphasize the idea of scornful or mocking words [e.g., 1QH^a; *Isaiah Targum*]), Paul is interested in this text precisely due to its reference to God's use of unknown languages to communicate a message to his people.

Paul agrees with the Hebrew texts (MT and 1QIsa^a) in holding that it is the Lord who speaks through the stammering or strange lips and tongue. He emphasizes the point by adding the object pronoun ("to me," referring to the Lord) and the final quotation formula ("says the Lord"). Paul and the Corinthians agree that glossolalia is divine speech. If there is a problem with the gift or its employment, it is not because God does not speak through it.

Paul's greatest interpretive move related to the text form involves his perspective on the significance of the foreign language in the history of God's relationship with his people. Isaiah 28:11–12 indicates God would speak to his people in judgment through a strange language because they did not listen to him earlier when he spoke in clear and simple terms. Paul's rendering of the text indicates that God could not even get his own people to respond to him, even when he spoke to them in that extreme, attention-getting manner. Paul's understanding that unbelieving Jews of his day continued to stand indicted by God and in need of redemption suggests that, in his view, not even exile brought the nation of Israel back to God (cf. Rom. 3:9–20; 9:2–8, 27–33; 10:1–3; Gal. 3:10–13; 4:4–5, 25; 1 Thess. 2:14–16).

The relationship between Paul's quotation of Isa. 28:11–12 in 14:21, the conclusion drawn in 14:22, and the examples given in 14:23–25 has proven to be extremely difficult to unravel (see, besides the commentaries, Hodges 1963; Robertson 1975; Johanson 1979; Lanier 1991; Sweet 1967; Grudem 1979; Smit 1994; Sandnes 1996; Forbes 1995). Part of the solution may be found in the relationship between Paul's quotation of Isa. 28:11–12 in 14:21 and his allusion to Isa. 45:14 and Zech. 8:23 in 14:25. While 14:22 mentions both believers and unbelievers, the illustrations in 14:23–25 focus exclusively on unbelievers and the way they respond to an encounter with a community that is speaking in tongues or one that is prophesying. The focus on unbelievers was signaled in the quotation's reference to Israel's unwillingness to listen to the Lord despite his attention-getting approach. In the OT context the experience of the invading Assyrians was God's execution of the covenant curses on his unbelieving and unfaithful people (see Robertson 1975). Just as the experience in Isa. 28:11–12 did not result in the conversion of the hearers but instead expressed alienation between God and his people, so also Paul indicates that the use of tongues in the church will result not in the conversion of unbelievers but rather in their further alienation.

His allusion to Isa. 45:14, on the other hand, relates to a later phase in God's relationship with his people, one when even Gentiles would come to recognize the presence of God in the midst of his people and would worship him for who he really is. The different responses in the two texts relate to those two consecutive phases in God's relationship with his people. Different modes of communication are associated with each of those two phases.

Unintelligible communication from God was a sign to his unbelieving people that the curses of the Mosaic covenant had fallen on them, while the powerful prophetic ministry of the church is a sign that God's presence has been restored to his redeemed (and believing) people.

F. Theological Use. Paul draws a theological conclusion about the appropriateness (or, rather, the inappropriateness) of the use of tongues in the congregation based on its function in Israel's experience (and in salvation history) as in Isa. 28:11–12. God spoke to his people through unknown languages as a sign and tool of alienation before the age of redemption. Now that Christ has inaugurated the age of salvation, the prophetic message is to be employed (in public) as the means of accomplishing God's purposes.

14:25

Paul's expectation that the prophetic ministry of community gathered for worship will lead to the conversion of outsiders who will respond by bowing down and worshiping God and declaring "God is really here in your midst!" echoes Isa. 45:14 (Hays [1999: 391–93] thinks that it also alludes to Zech. 8:23 and perhaps Dan. 2:46–47; for other texts anticipating the eschatological recognition of the God of Israel, see commentary on 1 Cor. 8:1–6 above). Isaiah prophesies the conversion of Gentile nations in the time of the postexilic restoration of God's people. At that time, he says, the various peoples will become Israel's servants and will bow down to them and pray to them "since God is among you," and they will say that "there is no god besides you, for you are God and we did not know it, the God of Israel, the Savior." Paul has changed the plural verb ("they will worship") to a singular ("he/she will worship") because he is describing the conversion of an individual, and he has changed the pronoun from the singular ("in your [*soi*] midst") to the plural ("in your [*hymin*] midst") because he is describing the gathered community rather than the nation of Israel (see Hays 1999: 393). Paul expects Isaiah's script to be performed and his eschatological vision to be realized in the midst of the gathered community as it exercises its prophetic ministry

(Hays 1999: 393). Hays (1999: 394) points to the dramatic transformation in Paul's intertextual use: in Paul's scenario "it is the church—itself a predominately Gentile community—through which God will accomplish the eschatological conversion of outsiders," and the Corinthian believers have "stepped into the role originally assigned to Israel in Isaiah's eschatological drama." Hence the church is the fulfillment of Isaiah's prophecy about Israel.

14:33–35

Paul says that the women (or wives) should be silent during the church gathering; they are not permitted to speak and should be in submission, "just like the law says" (for the textual issues, see Niccum 1997; Thiselton 2000: 1148–50). Paul cannot mean that women are not allowed to speak at all, since in chapter 11 he discusses their authority to pray and prophesy in the worship service (for evidence that the nature of the silence is expected to be contextually determined, see Grudem 1982: 242–44). He probably means either that women should not participate in the judging/evaluation of the prophetic messages of others (so Grudem 1982; Carson 1987: 229 [cf. 14:29]; or perhaps particularly the messages spoken by their own husbands? [cf. 14:35]), or that they must refrain from disruptive chatter or inappropriate conversations (so Paige 2002), perhaps especially with other men (cf. 14:35: "Let them ask their own husbands [*tous idious andras*]").

Paul's reference to the teaching of "the law" probably has the Genesis creation narratives in mind, with their implications for order and propriety in relationships between men and women (see Thiselton 2000: 1153–54; Bruce 1980: 136; Carson 1987: 129; Keener 1992: 86–87; see also commentary on 1 Cor. 11:2–16 above). Some think that Paul is alluding to Gen. 3:16 and its statement to the woman that her husband will rule over her (cf. 4Q416 2 IV, 1–8). That text, however, deals with a domination resulting from the curse of the fall (though see Grudem [1982: 253–54], who thinks that the source is Gen. 3:16 in conjunction with Gen. 2:18–23). Many take this text to forbid women (then and now) from enjoying "a church-recognized teaching authority over men" (e.g., Carson 1987: 130). Others believe that Paul's point is that Scripture teaches the importance of maintaining respect and order

in the worship setting (here, especially, the respect of women for their husbands), but that this principle might be applied rather differently in cultures where the social expectations of husbands and wives are markedly different from those in Paul's world.

The Resurrection of the Body (15:1–58)

Introduction

The historical situation that gave rise to Paul writing this chapter is difficult to pinpoint with absolute certainty. Common to all mirror readings of the chapter is the recognition, based on 15:12 ("Some of you say there is no resurrection of the dead"), that some within the Corinthian congregation were skeptical about the concept of a future resurrection of believers. It is not that this group did not believe in any postmortem existence, since in 15:29 Paul speaks of a "baptism on behalf of the dead," which, though puzzling for us, apparently was quite acceptable to them. Rather, the notion of *bodily* resurrection seems to have been in dispute. If in 15:1–34 Paul contends that the resurrection of the dead is central to the gospel, in 15:35–58 he explains how the bodily resurrection of believers is neither unintelligible nor inconceivable. Indeed, the double question of 15:35, along with Paul's word of stern rebuke in 15:36, indicates that it was the very possibility of the body's involvement in the afterlife that some in Corinth denied. "With what kind of body do they come?" (15:35) is at the heart of the dispute.

Resurrection Bodies

Unlike Greco-Roman philosophy, which expressed thoroughgoing skepticism regarding any place for the body in the afterlife, Paul's Jewish inheritance affirms a sturdy belief in the resurrection of the body (Rosner 2004; N. T. Wright 2003). Although explicit affirmation is reserved for certain OT prophets, its foundations, as Bauckham (1998) argues, are firmly laid in the OT portrayal of God as Sovereign Creator, Righteous Judge, and Divine Warrior.

Whereas some OT texts use resurrection imagery to refer to national restoration (e.g., Ezek. 37:1–14), at least two texts declare a resurrection of the dead as a personal hope of life after death that is bodily in nature: Isa. 26:19 promises a resurrection ("your dead shall live") that is explicitly corporeal ("their corpses shall rise"), and Dan. 12:1–3 speaks of the awakening of "many who sleep in the dust of the earth . . . some to everlasting life, and some to shame and everlasting contempt." (Other texts, such as Job 14:14, Ps. 16:10; 49:15; 73:24, also seem to imply belief in life after death, although the exegesis of such texts is more controversial.)

Jewish intertestamental writings from almost every quarter include resurrection as central to their beliefs. Among apocalyptic texts, *1 En.* 51:1; 62:14–16; *4 Ezra* 7:32–33a; *2 Bar.* 50:2, 4 describe resurrection in terms of the place where the dead are kept (variously in Sheol, hell, the earth, dust, and the chambers) "giving back" the deceased. In these texts those who rise eat, rest, and are clothed. *Second Baruch* 49:2 poses almost the same question as does Paul in 1 Cor. 15:35b, framed in a prayer: "In what shape will those live who live in your day?"

A prominent example of testamentary literature that reflects on the afterlife is the *Testaments of the Twelve Patriarchs*. For example, *T. Jud.* 25:4–6 affirms the resurrection of those who have died in sorrow, poverty, or on account of the Lord, and *T. Benj.* 10:6–10 mentions a resurrection in which "all are changed," with some to expect glory, and others dishonor.

As an example of historical literature, Josephus, in *Jewish War*, speaks of "the revolution of the ages" in terms of a new habitation of a chaste body (*J.W.* 3.374). In *Jewish War* and *Antiquities* he describes the belief of the Pharisees of a soul passing from one body to another (cf. 2 Macc. 7:10–13).

A marked difference between Paul and this Jewish background is that from Paul's Christian perspective the general resurrection of the dead is preceded, and indeed made possible, by the resurrection of the Christ: "For one man alone to be raised is a great surprise in the Jewish apocalyptic framework" (Hays 1997: 263).

15:3–4

Paul asserts that the death and resurrection of Christ, the central events of his gospel (15:2), are *kata tas graphas* ("in accordance with the Scriptures"). That Paul refers to "the Scriptures" in the plural only rarely (Rom. 1:2; 15:4; 16:26; 1 Cor. 15:3–4; cf. Gal. 3:10) suggests that here

he is speaking generally; the many references to "Scripture" in the singular are used routinely when citing a specific text. Barrett (1996: 338–39) understands Paul's point in 15:3–4 to be that the cross is the climax of the events of salvation history as they are revealed in the OT, and that the message of the cross must be understood through the OT categories of sacrifice, atonement, suffering, vindication, and so forth (cf. Dodd [1953], who expounds this "substructure" of NT theology by observing the OT texts most commonly used by the NT authors, especially those from Isaiah, Jeremiah, and Psalms).

Notwithstanding a reference to the OT in general, the description of Christ's death as being "for our sins" may be an allusion to or echo of the portrayal of the Suffering Servant in Isa. 53:5–6, 11–12. And the psalms are a good candidate for seeing a prefiguring of the resurrection of Christ, especially those that praise God for delivering the righteous sufferer (see the use of Ps. 110 and Ps. 8 in 1 Cor. 15:24–28 [cf. Ps. 16:9b–10 in Acts 2:24–31]).

The reference to "the third day" in 15:4 may bring to mind Hos. 6:2; Jon. 1:17. However, the phrase "according to the Scriptures" modifies "was raised" rather than the temporal reference (cf. similar syntax in 1 Macc. 7:16).

15:14–18

In rehearsing the consequences for the Corinthians if Christ is not raised, Paul effectively reverts to an OT/Jewish view of their condition. If there were no resurrection of Christ, God would judge and condemn them in their sin. They would be, as Eph. 2:12 describes their former life, "excluded from citizenship in Israel and foreigners to the covenants of the promise, without hope and without God" (cf. Eph. 2:1–3, 11–12; 4:17–19).

15:20

The metaphor of the firstfruits is, as de Boer (1988: 109) explains, "derived from the OT where it denotes the first portion of the crop (or flock) which is offered in Thanksgiving to God. As such, the term signifies the pledge of the remainder, and concomitantly, the assurance of a full harvest . . . the first installment of that part which includes, as by synecdoche, the whole." In other words, Paul uses the image to underline the link between our fate and the fate of Christ; Christ's resurrection is not an isolated event, but rather guarantees something even more stupendous.

15:21–22

Moving from metaphor to typology, Paul makes essentially the same point as in 15:20. His reference to Adam without explanation assumes that the Corinthians have some knowledge of the story of Gen. 1–3, which probably he taught to them while in Corinth. As in Rom. 5:12–21, Paul focuses on the differences between Adam and Christ. The consequences of the resurrection of Christ (life for all) correspond antithetically to the consequences of Adam's sin (death for all). The former has broken the power of the latter. However, Paul is not teaching universalism (see 1 Cor. 1:18); the unqualified "all" of 15:22 who will be made alive is clarified by 15:23 with the phrase "those who belong to him."

15:25

Hays (1989: 84) comments that in 15:25–27 Paul "alludes to Ps. 110:1 and Ps. 8:6 as prophecies of Christ's enthronement at the right hand of God and ultimate authority over all creation. Thus Paul offers the earliest documentation of a christological exegesis of these psalms." Together they support Paul's claim that all powers and authorities will be placed under Christ's feet and thus be subjected to God. These two psalms are employed together also in Eph. 1:20–22; Heb. 2:5–8.

First Corinthians 15:25 ("until he has put all his enemies under his feet") alludes to Ps. 110:1 ("until I make your enemies your footstool"). The use of this psalm suggests that the referent of "he has put" is God (cf. 15:28).

15:27

A. NT Context: Everything under His Feet. The words "when it says" (15:27b) make it clear that Paul is citing Scripture (Ps. 8:6) in 15:27a, as most English translations indicate with quotation marks around "has put everything under his feet." In 15:27 Paul explains why death is to be destroyed (15:26), or more accurately, how human beings, through whom death came (15:22), can exercise dominion over all things. If with Ps. 110 authority and dominion is considered in relation to God's right hand, with Ps. 8 it is seen in relation to all of creation.

B. Ps. 8:6 in Its OT Context. Psalm 8 is a psalm of descriptive praise for God's majestic work in creation. The psalm alludes to Gen. 1:26–30 and comments specifically on the creation of humankind in the image of God and their function as God's vice-regent over the earth (8:5–8), and it also carries the theme of the dominion of God over all creation (8:1, 3–5, 9).

C. Ps. 8:6 in Early Judaism. Jewish texts that refer to creation also carry the implication of God's dominion and authority over it (cf. e.g., Sir. 16:17–20; *4 Ezra* 3:1–5; 6:38–59; Philo, *Creation* 88; see Williams 2004: 172). A messianic interpretation of Ps. 8 and Ps. 110 is not evident in the Jewish literature (Koch 1986: 245).

D. Textual Matters. Paul follows the LXX (both textual traditions are united) of Ps. 8:6 (8:7 LXX), but with two differences. First, he changes the second-person verb *hypetaxas* ("you have put") to the third-person *hypetaxen* ("he has put"). The second-person form is present in three of the four other NT citations of the psalm: Phil. 3:21; Heb. 2:6–8; 1 Pet. 3:22 (cf. Eph. 1:22, which conforms to the 1 Cor. 15:27 wording). This suggests that the change is due to literary contexts: whereas second-person verbs run through Ps. 8 in both the MT and the LXX, third-person verbs surround the quotation in 1 Cor. 15.

Second, Paul uses the preposition *hypo* instead of the LXX's *hypokatō*, with no difference in meaning. It may simply be that Paul preferred the former, which is common in his letters, to the latter, which he never uses.

E. The Use of Ps. 8:6 in 1 Cor. 15:27. Garland (2003: 713) explains the contribution of Ps. 8:6 to Paul's argument and the way he connects it to Ps. 110 in 1 Cor. 15:25: "The exegetical principle of *gezerah shavah* (comparing similar expressions) leads Paul to Ps. 8:6 (8:7 LXX): 'And you set him over the works of your hands, having put all things under his feet.' Paul interprets this psalm as applying to the Messiah as the one who brings to fulfillment God's intentions for humanity. The key word he finds in this psalm is *panta* (all things), which he inserts in the allusion to Ps. 110:1 in 1 Cor. 15:25. He interprets 'all things' to include 'death.'"

F. Theological Use. In 15:24–27 Paul deftly conjoins two psalms. His point is that Christ, as the last Adam, retrieved the situation that the first

Adam lost. It is an explicitly christological use of the OT, with the OT notion of corporate representation as its presupposition; Christ represents his people (see 15:22–23). Hebrews 2:5–8 is comparable in its use of Ps. 8 and Ps. 110. There, the glorious destiny of humankind—coronation and dominion—which we failed to grasp, is fulfilled for us through Jesus.

15:30

Paul's remark that the apostles are in constant danger from opponents of the gospel echoes the language of Ps. 44:22; 119:109.

15:32

A. NT Context: A Dissipated Lifestyle. In 15:32–33 Paul cites two sources, an OT text (15:32) and Menander (15:33), to point to the utter futility of a life without the direction and motivation given by the resurrection of Jesus Christ. In 15:30–32a he cites his own positive example of how one ought to live in light of the resurrection. The polar opposite is illustrated in 15:32b, with reference to Isa. 22:13: "Let us eat and drink, for tomorrow we die."

B. Isa. 22:13 in Its OT Context. Isaiah depicts the reaction of the inhabitants of Jerusalem when faced with the Assyrian siege and the grim prospect of their impending annihilation (22:12–14). Instead of repenting, they decide to "party like there is no tomorrow" (Hays 1997: 268).

C. Isa. 22:13 in Early Judaism. This section of Isaiah does not have a distinctive history of interpretation.

D. Textual Matters. The text is quoted verbatim.

E. The Use of Isa. 22:13 in 1 Cor. 15:32. The slogan "Let us eat and drink, for tomorrow we die" is Paul's way of summing up the logical entailment of denying or forgetting about resurrection. Misbehaving by eating and drinking brings to mind Paul's criticism of the Corinthians for these very activities in the context of pagan temples (10:21–22) and the Lord's Supper (11:20–22). Paul effectively accuses the Corinthians who deny bodily resurrection of having a flawed basis for a lifestyle that pleases God, which will lead them to idolatrous and immoral behavior.

F. Theological Use. As Garland (2003: 721) puts it, "Resurrection means endless hope, but no resurrection means a hopeless end—and hopeless-

ness breeds dissipation." In one sense, Paul's use of the OT here is not critical, since the sentiment is widespread—note the words of the rich fool in Luke 12:19. Paul could have even cited a Greek historian such as Herodotus: "After rich men's repasts, a man carries an image in a coffin, painted and carved in exact imitation of a corpse two or four feet long. This he shows to each of the company, saying, 'While you drink and enjoy, look on this; for to this state you must come when you die'" (*Hist.* 2.78.1 [cited in Garland 2003]).

Thus Paul uses Isa. 22:13 to underscore the depravity of the human condition "without hope and without God in the world" (Eph. 2:12).

15:36

The scornful rebuke *aphrōn* ("Fool!") in 15:36 echoes Ps. 14:1: "The fool [LXX: *aphrōn*] says in his heart, 'There is no God'" (Paul quotes from this psalm in Rom. 3:11–12), but the contexts are different. Whereas in the psalm the fool fails to acknowledge any accountability to God, here the derision is occasioned by one's failure to duly regard the power of God in conceiving of a resurrection body.

15:45

A. NT Context. Although 1 Cor. 15:45–49 is a difficult and controversial passage, its use of Scripture is relatively straightforward. Adam and Christ have already been compared in 15:21–22. Paul's purpose in these verses is to explain how the poles of the earthly and heavenly are bridged through Christ.

B. Gen. 2:7 in Its OT Context. Part of the creation account that focuses on the creation of humankind—"the man of dust from the ground"—Gen. 2:7 appears at the beginning of the narrative: "So it is written, 'The first man, Adam, became a living being'" (1 Cor. 15:45a).

C. Gen. 2:7 in Early Judaism. Philo's exegesis of Gen. 2:7 (*Alleg. Interp.* 1.31) is sometimes proposed as relevant to Paul's interpretation. However, the differences outweigh the similarities. Philo takes Adam's becoming a living soul to mean that God breathed into his corruptible, earthlike mind the power of real life. Whereas for Paul the earthly man is Adam and the heavenly man is Christ, for Philo both of these can be found in Genesis (albeit allegorically).

The notion of Adam as an embodied soul in a natural body finds a parallel in Wis. 15:11.

D. Textual Matters. Three changes are evident. First, Paul leaves out the initial *kai* ("and"), a typical omission to conform the quotation to its new context.

Second, he adds *prōtos* ("first") to "the man." As Stanley (1992: 208) notes, "The addition brings to formal expression the fundamental contrast between Adam and Christ as the first and last Adam (v. 45b) that forms the backbone of the ensuing argument." Although the addition finds no textual support, it would not be out of place in the original text.

Third, the addition of "Adam" requires explanation. Paul has "the first man, Adam, became a living being," whereas the LXX has simply "the man became a living being." While none of the LXX manuscripts have the word "Adam," both Theodotion and Symmachus have "the Adam man" (the reverse word order from Paul's) at this point in their texts. The dual rendering in both these texts and in 1 Cor. 15:45 probably is due to the ambiguous sense of Hebrew *'ādām,* which can be a generic noun or a proper name. Paul's wording either reflects a common exegetical tradition or testifies to an earlier written text that he was using.

E. The Use of Gen. 2:7 in 1 Cor. 15:45. In 15:44a Paul introduces the principle that "an opposite presupposes its counterpart" (Garland 2003: 734): "If there is a natural body, then there is also a spiritual one." In 15:45, introduced by *houtōs* ("thus"), the conclusion is drawn from this principle. In 15:45–46 Paul asserts that the terrestrial and celestial opposites are temporally successive, and he cites Gen. 2:7 to prove this point. Just as there is a natural and a spiritual, there is also a first and a last (in the sense of ultimate). Garland (2003: 735) explains (summarizing Asher 2000): "If there is a natural body represented by the first Adam in a sown body, then there must be a spiritual body represented by the last Adam, the risen Christ." In other words, Adam received life as an embodied soul in a natural body, while Christ gives life as a life-giving spirit. Paul uses Gen. 2:7 to set up one side of the contrast and lead into the other.

F. Theological Use. The opening shot in a complex argument in 15:45–49, where Paul alludes to Adam as "the first man" and "the man of dust" (both twice), Paul's use of Gen. 2:7 points to the significance of Jesus Christ, who is of equally universal bearing as our first ancestor. In naming Christ "the second man" and "the last Adam," Paul, characteristically of his use of the OT in 1 Cor. 15, makes a point both christological and eschatological in nature.

15:52

The trumpet as a sign of the day of the Lord in 15:52 recalls Isa. 27:13; Joel 2:1; Zeph. 1:14–16 (cf. 2 Esd. 6:23).

15:54

A. NT Context: Death Gobbled Up. In 15:50–57 Paul fills out his answer to the question of the nature of the resurrection body (see 15:35b) by introducing the theme of transformation: "We will all be changed" (15:51b). In 15:50–53 he explains that the earthly body will become fit for heavenly existence at the parousia. Then in 15:54–57 he declares that at that time God will claim the final victory over death, which is vanquished by the resurrection.

B. Isa. 25:8 in Its OT Context. The text is part of an oracle of salvation in 25:6–10a that envisions God's universal salvation of "all peoples" (25:6–7 [cf. "all nations" in 25:7]) and the ultimate destruction of the power of death.

C. Isa. 25:8 in Early Judaism. Isaiah 25:8 is cited in rabbinic literature as a divine promise that death would be no more in the age to come (*m. Mo'ed Qaṭ.* 3:9; *Exod. Rab.* 15:21; 30:3; *Deut. Rab.* 2:30; *Lam. Rab.* 1:41; *Eccles. Rab.* 1:7; *b. Pesaḥ.* 68a; *b. Ketub.* 30b).

D. Textual Matters. Paul's words "Death has been swallowed up in victory" differ markedly from the LXX, which reads literally, "Death, being strong, swallowed (them) up" (the context suggests that the nations have been swallowed up by death). However, Aquila, Theodotion, and Symmachus have differing variants, some of which are quite close to Paul's citation (for the details, see Stanley 1992: 210–11). Paul probably was following a preexisting Greek text. Revelation 21:4 cites the same tradition.

Alternatively, as Hays (1997: 276) suggests, Paul may have altered *dikē* ("judgment") in Hos. 13:14 LXX to *nikos* ("victory") and inserted it in his quotation of Isa. 25:8 to create a word link with the next verse. It is also possible that the Isaiah citation supplies the word "victory" to the Hosea text (see below).

E. The Use of Isa. 25:8 in 1 Cor. 15:54. In Paul's mind, the final destruction of death requires the resurrection of the dead. In citing Isaiah's eschatological vision, Paul ties God's triumph over death (and God's universal salvation) to the resurrection of the body. For Paul, resurrection is the necessary outcome of what God has done in Christ and what he intends to do for his people.

F. Theological Use. Paul's personification of death, following the lead of both Isa. 25:8 and Hos. 13:14 (see below), depicts death not as the inevitable and benign fate of all humans, but rather as "an alien, inimical power" (de Boer 1988: 184), nothing less than a tragedy. In the words of Isa. 25:7, death is "the shroud that is cast over all peoples, the sheet that is spread over all nations." Death, in Paul's view, is a power that casts its ominous shadow over us all, and it must be not just removed, but defeated.

15:55

A. NT Context: Death Vanquished. Paul celebrates God's final victory over death, both in the resurrection of Christ and in its implications for all humanity.

B. Hos. 13:14 in Its OT Context. The text is part of a prophecy of judgment upon Ephraim: "The iniquity of Ephraim is bound up; his sin is kept in store" (13:12). Four rhetorical questions appear in 13:14. The first two expect a negative answer: "Shall I ransom them from the power of Sheol? Shall I redeem them from Death?" Paul quotes the last two, which act as a summons to personified Death and Sheol: "O Death, where are your plagues? O Sheol, where is your sting?"

C. Hos. 13:14 in Early Judaism. The text does not have a distinctive history of interpretation.

D. Textual Matters. The MT, LXX, and Paul's citation exhibit various differences: (1) Hebrew: "Where, O Death, are your plagues? Where, O Sheol, is your destruction?" (2) LXX: "Where, O Death, is your judgment? Where, O Hades, is your sting?" (3) Paul: "Where, O Death, is your victory? Where, O Death, is your sting?" Aside from minor differences in word order that may be explained on stylistic or rhetorical grounds,

Paul's text, compared to the LXX, has "victory" (*nikos*) instead of "judgment" (*dikē*), and "Death" instead of "Hades." It is difficult to imagine why the LXX translated the Hebrew *deber* ("plague") as "judgment" in the first place. We are left to conjecture. Stanley (1992: 211–15) suggests that the LXX translators had a different non-Masoretic *Vorlage* and/or that Paul's Greek *Vorlage* itself had "victory." We should not rule out the possibility that Paul made the change to "victory" in order to link the present citation to the one in 15:54.

E. The Use of Hos. 13:14 in 1 Cor. 15:55. Interpreting the passage from the perspective of the resurrection of Christ, Paul turns the summons to death into a taunt. The rhetorical questions now sneer defiantly at death's impotence in the face of God's powerful act of mercy and forgiveness in Christ. If in Hosea death is called on to punish sin, Paul shows that such a role is no longer needed (15:3, 17). Death's dominion over the whole earth has been ended, its "sting" (*kentron* [15:55–56]) drained of potency.

F. Theological Use. An eschatological hermeneutic is employed in the use of Hos. 13:14. Paul turns a text about judgment into one declaring salvation, for we are not under the law, and the resurrection of Christ signals the beginning of the new age of redemption. "Paul projects an eschatological vision of a stingless death precisely because Jesus Christ has himself absorbed the sting on the basis of how his death and resurrection addresses the problem of human sin and the law" (Thiselton 2000: 1300).

15:56

Paul's epigrammatic statements in 15:56 consist of two maxims, the second being built upon the first. The nexus between sin and death is prepared for by the allusions to the fall in 15:21–22. Vlachos (2004) argues convincingly that rather than originating from an issue in the Corinthian church, Paul's assertion that "the power of sin is the law" may arise out of an Edenic context. There is evidence that Paul found the triad of law, sin, and death present in the Garden of Eden. That law plays a catalytic role in Eden is implicit in the story depicted in Rom. 7:7–11. There, as in Rom. 5:12–14, the fall is the prototype for sins under the Mosaic law.

Final Instructions and Exhortations (16:1–24)

16:1–10

As Keener (1993: 489) points out, Paul's instruction that each one should give according to his or her prosperity is an application of Deut. 15:14.

Paul's reference to the approach of Pentecost (16:8) may explain some of the biblical texts that have been on his mind as he writes this letter.

16:13–23

Paul's exhortation to "be strong and courageous" (16:13) reflects an OT motif of a call to courage under extremely challenging circumstances (Deut. 31:6–7, 23; Josh. 1:6, 9, 18; 10:25; 2 Sam. 10:12; 1 Chron. 22:13; 28:20; 2 Chron. 32:7; Ps. 27:14; 31:24).

The key motif of love (*agapē*) is given a reprise as the letter comes to a close (16:14).

Paul describes Stephanas's household as the "firstfruits" (*aparchē*) of Achaia (16:15). The OT background suggests the idea of the community as an offering dedicated to the Lord, of which the household of Stephanas is the first part to come to fruition in Achaia.

Paul calls for a curse on anyone who does not love the Lord (16:22). In the OT such a curse formula was "used when the intention was to discourage someone from transgressing . . . a far-reaching legal or ethical demand. In this case the curse formula is the most severe means of separating the community from the evildoer" (Scharbert 1974: 409–10). Here the fundamental demand upon the Christian community—that which distinguishes it as a community—is to love the Lord.

Paul moves right from the curse to the Aramaic expression "Maranatha" ("Our Lord, come!"), which points to "the coming of the Lord in judgment to redress wrong and establish right" (*NIDNTT* 2:897). The expectation that the Lord would come to redress wrong and establish his righteousness in the earth (see commentary on 1 Cor. 13:8–10, 12 above) grew out of OT prophetic and apocalyptic texts and is found throughout early Judaism (*1 En.* 1:9) and the NT (e.g., Matt. 3:7/Luke 3:7; Eph. 5:6; Col. 3:6; 1 Thess. 1:10; 2:14–16; Jude 14–15; Rev. 6:17).

Bibliography

Asher, J. R. 2000. *Polarity and Change in 1 Corinthians 15: A Study of Metaphysics, Rhetoric, and Resurrection.* HUT 42. Tübingen: Mohr Siebeck.

Barrett, C. K. 1996. *The First Epistle to the Corinthians.* BNTC 2. Peabody, MA: Hendrickson.

Bauckham, R. 1998. *The Fate of the Dead: Studies on the Jewish and Christian Apocalypses.* NovTSup 93. Leiden: Brill.

Beale, G. K. 2004. *The Temple and the Church's Mission: A Biblical Theology of the Dwelling Place of God.* NSBT 17. Downers Grove, IL: InterVarsity.

Broyles, C. C. 1999. *Psalms.* NIBCOT 11. Peabody, MA: Hendrickson.

Bruce, F. F. 1980. *1 and 2 Corinthians.* NCBC. Grand Rapids: Eerdmans.

Buss, M. J. 1977. "The Distinction between Civil and Criminal Law in Ancient Israel." Pages 51–62 in *Proceedings of the Sixth World Congress of Jewish Studies: Held at the Hebrew University of Jerusalem, 13–19 August 1973, under the Auspices of the Israel Academy of Sciences and Humanities.* Vol. 1. Edited by A. Shinan. Jerusalem: World Union of Jewish Studies.

Carson, D. A. 1987. *Showing the Spirit: A Theological Exposition of 1 Corinthians 12–14.* Grand Rapids: Baker Academic.

Childs, B. S. 1974. *The Book of Exodus.* OTL. Philadelphia: Westminster.

Ciampa, R. 1998. *The Presence and Function of Scripture in Galatians 1 and 2.* WUNT 2/102. Tübingen: Mohr Siebeck.

Collier, G. D. 1994. "'That We Might Not Crave Evil': The Structure and Argument of 1 Corinthians 10:1–13." *JSNT* 55: 55–75.

Collins, R. F. 1999. *First Corinthians.* SP 7. Collegeville, MN: Liturgical Press.

Conzelmann, H. 1975. *1 Corinthians.* Translated by J. W. Leitch. Hermeneia. Philadelphia: Fortress.

Craigie, P. C. 1976. *The Book of Deuteronomy.* NICOT. Grand Rapids: Eerdmans.

———. 1983. *Psalms 1–50.* WBC 19. Waco: Word.

D'Angelo, M. R. 1988. "The Garden: Once and Not Again; Traditional Interpretations of Genesis 1:26–27 in 1 Corinthians 11:7–12." Pages 1–41 in *Genesis 1–3 in the History of Exegesis: Intrigue in the Garden.* Edited by G. A. Robbins. SWR 27. Lewiston, NY: Mellen.

Daube, D. 1963. *The Exodus Pattern in the Bible.* All Souls Studies 2. London: Faber & Faber.

Davidson, R. M. 1981. *Typology in Scripture: A Study of Hermeneutical τύπος Structures.* AUSDDS. Berrien Springs, MI: Andrews University Press.

de Boer, M. C. 1988. *The Defeat of Death: Apocalyptic Eschatology in 1 Corinthians 15 and Romans 5.* JSNTSup 22. Sheffield: JSOT Press.

de Vaux, R. 1965. *Ancient Israel.* 2 vols. New York: McGraw-Hill.

Dickson, J. P. 2003. *Mission-Commitment in Ancient Judaism and in the Pauline Communities: The Shame, Extent and Background of Early Christian Mission.* WUNT 2/159. Tübingen: Mohr Siebeck.

Dillard, R. B. 2000. "Intrabiblical Exegesis and the Effusion of the Spirit in Joel." Pages 87–94 in *Creator, Redeemer, Consummator: A Festschrift for Meredith G. Kline.* Edited by H. Griffeth and J. R. Muether. Greenville, SC: Reformed Academic Press.

Dodd, C. H. 1953. *According to the Scriptures: The Sub-Structure of New Testament Theology.* New York: Scribner.

Ellis, E. E. 1957. *Paul's Use of the Old Testament*. Edinburgh: Oliver & Boyd.

———. 1977. "How the New Testament Uses the Old." Pages 199–219 in *New Testament Interpretation: Essays on Principles and Methods*. Edited by I. H. Marshall. Exeter: Paternoster.

———. 1978a. "Note on 1 Corinthians 10:4." Pages 209–13 in *Prophecy and Hermeneutic in Early Christianity: New Testament Essays*. Grand Rapids: Eerdmans.

———. 1978b. *Prophecy and Hermeneutic in Early Christianity: New Testament Essays*. Grand Rapids: Eerdmans.

Enns, P. E. 1996. "The 'Moveable Well' in 1 Corinthians 10:4: An Extra-Biblical Tradition in an Apostolic Text." *BBR* 6: 23–38.

Fee, G. D. 1987. *The First Epistle to the Corinthians*. NICNT. Grand Rapids: Eerdmans.

Fishbane, M. 1985. *Biblical Interpretation in Ancient Israel*. Oxford: Clarendon.

———. 1986. "Through the Looking Glass: Reflections on Ezek. 43:3, Num. 12:8, and 1 Cor. 13:8 [*sic*]." *HAR* 10: 63–75.

Fitzmyer, J. A. 1990. "Introduction to the New Testament Epistles." Pages 768–71 in *The New Jerome Biblical Commentary*. Edited by R. E. Brown, J. A. Fitzmyer, and R. E. Murphy. Englewood Cliffs, NJ: Prentice-Hall.

Forbes, C. 1995. *Prophecy and Inspired Speech in Early Christianity and Its Hellenistic Environment*. WUNT 2/75. Tübingen: Mohr Siebeck.

Garland, D. E. 2003. *1 Corinthians*. BECNT. Grand Rapids: Baker Academic.

Goppelt, L. 1982. *Typos: The Typological Interpretation of the Old Testament in the New*. Translated by D. H. Madvig. Grand Rapids: Eerdmans.

Grudem, W. A. 1979. "1 Corinthians 14:20–25: Prophesy and Tongues as Signs of God's Attitude." *WTJ* 41: 381–96.

———. 1982. *The Gift of Prophecy in 1 Corinthians*. Lanham, MD: University Press of America.

Gundry-Volf, J. M. 1997. "Gender and Creation in 1 Corinthians 11:2–16: A Study in Paul's Theological Method." Pages 1151–71 in *Evangelium, Schriftauslegung, Kirche: Festschrift für Peter Stuhlmacher zum 65. Geburtstag*. Edited by J. Ådna, S. J. Hafemann, and O. Hofius. Göttingen: Vandenhoeck & Ruprecht.

Hafemann, S. J. 1995. *Paul, Moses, and the History of Israel: The Letter/Spirit Contrast and the Argument from Scripture in 2 Corinthians 3*. WUNT 81. Tübingen: Mohr Siebeck.

Hanson, A. T. 1965. *Jesus Christ in the Old Testament*. London: SPCK.

———. 1974. *Studies in Paul's Technique and Theology*. Grand Rapids: Eerdmans.

Hays, R. B. 1989. *Echoes of Scripture in the Letters of Paul*. New Haven: Yale University Press.

———. 1997. *First Corinthians*. IBC. Louisville: John Knox.

———. 1999. "The Conversion of the Imagination: Scripture and Eschatology in 1 Corinthians." *NTS* 45: 391–412.

Héring, J. 1969. *First Epistle of Saint Paul to the Corinthians*. Translated by A. W. Heathcote and P. J. Allcock. London: Epworth.

Hodges, Z. C. 1963. "Symposium on the Tongues Movement: The Purpose of Tongues." *BSac* 120: 226–33.

Hooker, M. D. 1964. "Authority on Her Head: An Examination of 1 Cor. 11:10." *NTS* 10: 410–16.

Horbury, W. 1985. "Extirpation and Excommunication." *VT* 35: 13–38.

Hübner, H. 1990–1995. *Biblische Theologie des Neuen Testaments*. 3 vols. Göttingen: Vandenhoeck & Ruprecht.

———. 1997. *Corpus Paulinum*. Vol. 2 of *Vetus Testamentum in Novo*. Göttingen: Vandenhoeck & Ruprecht.

Hugenberger, G. P. 1998. *Marriage as a Covenant: Biblical Law and Ethics as Developed from Malachi*. BSL. Grand Rapids: Baker Academic.

Instone-Brewer, D. 1992. "1 Corinthians 9:9–11: A Literal Interpretation of 'Do Not Muzzle the Ox.'" *NTS* 38: 554–65.

Jervis, L. A. 1993. "'But I Want You to Know . . .': Paul's Midrashic Intertextual Response to the Corinthian Worshipers (1 Cor 11:2–16)." *JBL* 112: 231–46.

Jewett, R. 1971. *Paul's Anthropological Terms: A Study of Their Use in Conflict Settings*. AGJU 10. Leiden: Brill.

Johanson, B. C. 1979. "Tongues, a Sign for Unbelievers? A Structural and Exegetical Study of I Corinthians XIV.20–25." *NTS* 25: 180–203.

Kaiser, W. C., Jr. 1978. "Current Crisis in Exegesis and the Apostolic Use of Deuteronomy 25:4 in 1 Corinthians 9:8–10." *JETS* 21: 3–18.

Keener, C. S. 1992. *Paul, Women and Wives: Marriage and Women's Ministry in the Letters of Paul*. Peabody, MA: Hendrickson.

———. 1993. *The IVP Biblical Background Commentary: New Testament*. Downers Grove, IL: InterVarsity.

Kim, S. 1984. *The Origin of Paul's Gospel*. 2nd ed. WUNT 2/4. Tübingen: Mohr Siebeck.

———. 2002. *Paul and the New Perspective: Second Thoughts on the Origin of Paul's Gospel*. Grand Rapids: Eerdmans.

Kistemaker, S. J. 1993. *Exposition of the First Epistle to the Corinthians*. Grand Rapids: Baker Academic.

Kleinknecht, K. T. 1984. *Der leidende Gerechtfertigte: Die alttestamentlich-jüdische Tradition vom "leidenden Gerechten" und ihre Rezeption bei Paulus*. WUNT 2/13. Tübingen: Mohr Siebeck.

Koch, D. A. 1986. *Die Schrift als Zeuge des Evangeliums: Untersuchungen zur Verwendung und zum Verständnis der Schrift bei Paulus*. BHT 69. Tübingen: Mohr Siebeck.

Koet, B. J. 1996. "The Old Testament Background to 1 Cor. 10:7–8." Pages 607–15 in *The Corinthian Correspondence*. Edited by R. Bieringer. BETL 125. Leuven: Leuven University Press.

Kraus, H.-J. 1993. *Psalms*. 2 vols. Translated by H. C. Oswald. CC. Minneapolis: Fortress.

Kwon, D. L. 2004. "Obfuscation and Restoration: Paul's Use of Isaiah in 1 Corinthians 14:20–25." ThM thesis, Gordon-Conwell Theological Seminary.

Lanier, D. E. 1991. "With Stammering Lips and Another Tongue: 1 Cor. 14:20–22 and Isa. 28:11–12." *CTR* 5: 259–86.

Liefeld, W. 1986. "Women, Submission, and Ministry in 1 Corinthians." Pages 134–54 in *Women, Authority, and the Bible*. Edited by A. Mickelsen. Downers Grove, IL: InterVarsity.

Lindsay, D. R. 1993. *Josephus and Faith: Pistis and Pisteuein as Faith Terminology in the Writings of Flavius Josephus and in the New Testament*. AGJU 19. Leiden: Brill.

Loader, W. 2004. *The Septuagint, Sexuality, and the New Testament: Case Studies on the Impact of the LXX in Philo and the New Testament*. Grand Rapids: Eerdmans.

Martin, D. 1991. "Tongues of Angels and Other Status Indicators." *JAAR* 59: 547–89.

———. 1995. *The Corinthian Body*. New Haven: Yale University Press.

Martin, R. P. 1984. *The Spirit and the Congregation: Studies in 1 Corinthians 12–15*. Grand Rapids: Eerdmans.

Matthews, V. H., M. W. Chavalas, and J. H. Walton. 2000. *The IVP Bible Background Commentary: Old Testament*. Downers Grove, IL: InterVarsity.

McKnight, S. 2000. "Proselytism and Godfearers." *DNTB* 835–47.

McNamara, M. 1972. *Targum and Testament: Aramaic Paraphrases of the Hebrew Bible—A Light on the New Testament*. Grand Rapids: Eerdmans.

Meeks, W. A. 1982. "'And Rose Up to Play': Midrash and Paraenesis in 1 Corinthians 10:1–22." *JSNT* 16: 64–78.

———. 1983. "Social Functions of Apocalyptic Language in Pauline Christianity." Pages 687–706 in *Apocalypticism in the Mediterranean World and the Near East: Proceedings of the International Colloquium on Apocalypticism, Uppsala, August 12–17, 1979*. Edited by D. Hellholm. Tübingen: Mohr Siebeck.

Meier, J. P. 1978. "On the Veiling of Hermeneutics (1 Cor 11:2–16)." *CBQ* 40: 212–26.

Metzger, B. M. 1994. *A Textual Commentary on the Greek New Testament*. 2nd ed. New York: United Bible Societies.

Michel, O. 1967. "οἰκοδομέω." *TDNT* 5:136–44.

Mitchell, M. M. 1991. *Paul and the Rhetoric of Reconciliation: An Exegetical Investigation of the Language and Composition of 1 Corinthians*. HUT 28. Tübingen: Mohr Siebeck.

Murphy-O'Conner, J. 1988. "1 Corinthians 11:2–16 Once Again." *CBQ* 50: 265–74.

Nasuti, H. P. 1988. "The Woes of the Prophets and the Rights of the Apostle: The Internal Dynamics of 1 Corinthians 9." *CBQ* 50: 246–64.

Newton, M. 1985. *The Concept of Purity at Qumran and in the Letters of Paul*. SNTSMS 53. Cambridge: Cambridge University Press.

Niccum, C. 1997. "The Voice of the Manuscripts on the Silence of Women: The External Evidence for 1 Cor. 14:34–35." *NTS* 43: 242–55.

Niebuhr, K.-W. 1987. *Gesetz und Paränese: Katechismusartige Weisungsreihen in der frühjüdischen Literatur*. WUNT 2/28. Tübingen: Mohr Siebeck.

O'Donovan, O. 1986. *Resurrection and Moral Order: An Outline for Evangelical Ethics*. Grand Rapids: Eerdmans.

Paige, T. 2002. "The Social Matrix of Women's Speech at Corinth: The Context and Meaning of the Command to Silence in 1 Corinthians 14:33b–36." *BBR* 12: 217–42.

Proctor, J. 1993. "Fire in God's House: Influence of Malachi 3 in the NT." *JETS* 36: 9–14.

Reid, D. G. 2000. "Sacrifice and Temple Service." *DNTB* 1036–50.

Robertson, A., and A. Plummer. 1911. *A Critical and Exegetical Commentary on the First Epistle of St. Paul to the Corinthians*. ICC. Edinburgh: T&T Clark.

Robertson, O. P. 1975. "Tongues: Sign of Covenantal Curse and Blessing." *WTJ* 38: 45–53.

Rosner, B. S. 1991. "Moses Appointing Judges: An Antecedent to 1 Cor 6.1–6?" *ZNW* 82: 275–78.

———. 1992a. "*Ouchi mallon epenthēsate*: Corporate Responsibility in 1 Corinthians 5." *NTS* 38: 470–73.

———. 1992b. "A Possible Quotation of *Testament of Reuben* 5:5 in 1 Corinthians 6:18a." *JTS* 43: 123–27.

———. 1994. "'Written for Us': Paul's View of Scripture." Pages 81–105 in *A Pathway into the Holy Scripture*. Edited by P. E. Satterthwaite and D. F. Wright. Grand Rapids: Eerdmans.

———. 1996a. "The Function of Scripture in 1 Cor. 5:13b and 6:16." Pages 513–18 in *The Corinthian Correspondence*. Edited by R. Bieringer. BETL 125. Leuven: Peeters University Press.

———. 1996b. "The Origin and Meaning of 1 Corinthians 6:9–11 in Context." *BZ* 40: 250–53.

———. 1998. "Temple Prostitution in 1 Corinthians 6:12–20." *NovT* 40: 336–51.

———. 1999. *Paul, Scripture, and Ethics: A Study of 1 Corinthians 5–7*. Grand Rapids: Baker Academic.

———. 2004. "'With What Kind of Body Do They Come?'" Pages 190–205 in *The New Testament in Its First-Century Setting: Essays on Context and Background in Honour of B. W. Winter on His 65th Birthday*. Edited by P. J. Williams et al. Grand Rapids and Cambridge: Eerdmans.

———. Forthcoming. *Greed: The Second Idolatry*. Tübingen: Mohr Siebeck.

Routledge, R. L. 2002. "Passover and the Last Supper." *TynBul* 53: 203–21.

Sandnes, K. O. 1996. "Prophecy—A Sign for Believers." *Bib* 77: 1–15.

Scharbert, J. 1974. "אָרַר." *TDOT* 1:405–18.

Schneider, J. 1967. "ὀλοθρευτής." *TDNT* 5:169–70.

Schrage, W. 1991–2001. *Der Erste Brief an die Korinther*. 4 vols. EKKNT. Zürich: Benziger; Neukirchener-Vluyn: Neukirchener Verlag.

Schreiner, T. R. 1991. "Head Coverings, Prophecies and the Trinity: 1 Corinthians 11:2–16." Pages 124–39 in *Recovering Biblical Manhood and Womanhood: A Response to Evangelical Feminism*. Edited by J. Piper and W. Grudem. Wheaton, IL: Crossway.

Smit, J. F. M. 1994. "Tongues and Prophesy: Deciphering 1 Cor. 14:22." *Bib* 75: 175–90.

Söding, T. 1995. *Das Liebesgebot bei Paulus: Die Mahnung zur Agape im Rahmen der paulinischen Ethik*. NTAbh 26. Münster: Aschendorff.

South, J. T. 1993. "A Critique of the 'Curse/Death' Interpretation of 1 Cor. 5:1–8." *NTS* 39: 539–61.

Stanley, C. D. 1992. *Paul and the Language of Scripture: Citation Technique in the Pauline Epistles and Contemporary Literature*. SNTSMS 69. Cambridge: Cambridge University Press.

Stuhlmacher, P. 1991. "The Pauline Gospel." Pages 149–72 in *The Gospel and the Gospels*. Edited by P. Stuhlmacher. Grand Rapids: Eerdmans.

Sweet, J. P. M. 1967. "Sign for Unbelievers: Paul's Attitude to Glossolalia." *NTS* 13: 240–57.

Thackeray, H. St. J., trans. 1930. *Flavius Josephus*. Vol. 4. LCL. Cambridge, MA: Harvard University Press.

Thiselton, A. C. 2000. *The First Epistle to the Corinthians*. NIGTC. Grand Rapids: Eerdmans.

Tomson, P. J. 1990. *Paul and the Jewish Law: Halakha in the Letters of the Apostle to the Gentiles*. Minneapolis: Fortress.

Towner, P. H. 2000. "The Pastoral Epistles." *NDBT* 330–36.

van Unnik, W. C. 1960. "Die Rücksicht auf die Reaktion der Nicht-Christen als Motiv in der altchristlichen Paränese." Pages 221–34 in *Judentum, Urchristentum, Kirche: Festschrift für Joachim Jeremias*. Edited by W. Eltester. BZNW 26. Berlin: Töpelmann.

Vlachos, C. A. 2004. "Law, Sin and Death: An Edenic Triad? An Examination with Reference to 1 Corinthians 15:56." *JETS* 47: 277–98.

Wagner, J. R. 1998. "'Not Beyond the Things Which Are Written': A Call to Boast Only in the Lord (1 Cor. 4:6)." *NTS* 44: 279–87.

Watson, F. 2000. *Agape, Eros, Gender: Towards a Pauline Sexual Ethic*. Cambridge: Cambridge University Press.

Williams, H. H. D., III. 2001. *The Wisdom of the Wise: The Presence and Function of Scripture within 1 Cor. 1:18–3:23*. AGJU 49. Leiden: Brill.

———. 2004. "The Psalms in 1 and 2 Corinthians." Pages 163–80 in *The Psalms in the New Testament*. Edited by S. Moyise and M. J. J. Menken. NTSI. London and New York: T&T Clark International.

Winter, B. W. 2001. *After Paul Left Corinth: The Influence of Secular Ethics and Social Change*. Grand Rapids: Eerdmans.

Witherington, B., III. 1995. *Conflict and Community in Corinth: A Socio-Rhetorical Commentary on 1 & 2 Corinthians*. Grand Rapids: Eerdmans.

Wright, D. F. 1984. "Homosexuals or Prostitutes? The Meaning of *Arsenokoitai* (1 Cor. 6:9; 1 Tim. 1:10)." *VC* 38: 125–53.

Wright, N. T. 1992. "Monotheism, Christology, and Ethics: 1 Cor. 8." Pages 120–36 in *The Climax of the Covenant: Christ and the Law in Pauline Theology*. Minneapolis: Fortress.

———. 2003. *The Resurrection of the Son of God*. Christian Origins and the Question of God 3. Minneapolis: Fortress.

Youngman, S. 1987. "Stratificational Analysis of a Hortatory Text: I Corinthians 8:1–11:1." MA thesis, University of Texas at Arlington.

Zerbe, G. M. 1993. *Non-Retaliation in Early Jewish and New Testament Texts: Ethical Themes in Social Contexts*. JSPSup 13. Sheffield: JSOT Press.

2 Corinthians

Peter Balla

Introduction

Second Corinthians was written by the apostle Paul to a predominantly Gentile Christian congregation. Nevertheless, even in this letter he quotes the OT several times, and he does so in different ways. For example, he makes use of a long OT story in chapter 3, and yet he quotes only a short sentence from it in a changed form (at 3:16). He alludes to the creation story in an analogical way (at 4:6), and he makes use of analogy also in 8:15; 9:6–10 (see also commentary on 2 Cor. 5:17 below). There is a christological interpretation of an OT text in 3:14–16; 10:17, the former being also an example of a typological use of the OT. In all the cases when Paul quotes the OT, he does so in order to support what he is saying with an authoritative text (or, indeed, with a chain of OT quotations, as in 6:16–18). The OT has canonical authority for him, and he expects his readers to acknowledge that high authority.

Commentators debate whether 6:14–7:1 might be an interpolation; otherwise the integrity of the letter is not questioned. Many scholars argue for the thesis that 2 Corinthians is compiled from more than one Pauline letter. In the present commentary I side with a growing number of contemporary scholars who regard the whole letter as Pauline and as written in the sequence of the chapters as we have them today (and, indeed, as all the extant manuscripts have them). For a convincing argument concerning the integrity of the alleged interpolation, see Beale 1989; further relevant literature on introductory matters is mentioned in commentary on 2 Cor. 2:14–3:18; 6:16–18; 8:15; 10:17 below.

The ways in which Paul uses the OT is of great significance for the hermeneutics of Christians today. We should learn from him to retain a high respect for the OT Scriptures and to read them from the viewpoint of the Christ-event—to read them as God's word pointing to Christ.

3:16 (2:14–3:18)

A. NT Context: Ministry of the New Covenant. The first quotation in 2 Corinthians occurs in 3:16 (since Paul changes the OT text substantially, Ellis [1957: 153] lists it among the "manifestly intentional" allusions and not among the quotations). We have to examine the longer context of the verse because already the previous verses refer to several OT motifs as well as to the OT context of the words quoted in 3:16. I extend the discus-

I would like to express my gratitude to the Alexander von Humboldt Foundation for scholarships in July 2004 and July 2005, that enabled me to work on this chapter in Heidelberg. I also thank Professor Gerd Theissen (University of Heidelberg) and Professor D. A. Carson (Trinity Evangelical Divinity School) for commenting on parts of the manuscript, and Professor G. K. Beale (Wheaton College) for a number of excellent suggestions to improve my original text.

sion to include the end of chapter 2 because there begins the theme of the defense of Paul's ministry, leading the apostle to discuss the relationship between the two covenants and thus to make use of a wide range of OT references in chapter 3.

Our passage belongs to a long unit (2:14–7:4) discussing "Paul's present ministry to the Corinthians" (Best 1987: 25). Paul discusses his travel plans, his journeys, and Titus's role in them from 1:15 up to 2:13 and then again from 7:5 up to 7:8, and in between he devotes a long section to defend his apostolic ministry (for a discussion of the integrity of the letter, see Lang 1986: 12–14; Best 1987: 25; and especially the detailed argumentation in defense of the unity of the letter in Martin 1986: xxxviii–lii). It seems that he was attacked by some people in Corinth who claimed that he was no true apostle. At the same time they perhaps referred also to Moses as a great minister of God's will, and they emphasized the inferiority of Paul's ministry compared to that of Moses. In his response Paul argues by referring to motifs in the OT. Thus he acknowledges the high value of the OT (which was holy Scripture for the Corinthians as well as for himself), and at the same time he points to the higher glory of the new covenant.

In 2:14–17 Paul gives thanks for God's help in all difficulties: "Thanks be to God, who in Christ always leads us in triumph" (2:14). (Here, as in general, I quote the RSV; on a few occasions I note that I provide my own translation.) In 2:14, 16 he uses the term "fragrance" (*osmē*) for the ministry of Jesus: God spreads the fragrance of knowing Christ through Paul and his fellow missionaries (2:14); they themselves become the "fragrance from death to death" or "from life to life" (2:16). Paul points to the high honor of this ministry by asking, "Who is sufficient [*hikanos*] for these things?" (2:16). Chapter 3 was written probably to answer this question by pointing to God, who made even Paul competent for his ministry. The chapter employs OT references in defense of Paul ministering the new covenant. Paul even states explicitly that his "competence" (*hikanotēs*) is from God (3:5–6).

The term "fragrance" may come from the imagery of a triumphal procession during which incense was burnt to the gods (so, e.g., Kruse 1987: 86), but it is also possible that Paul thinks

of the world of the sacrifice, where the smell of the incense ascends to the deity (so, e.g., Martin 1986: 45). There is no need to choose one and reject the other idea as a possible background. Paul may have used this term (and another noun, *euōdia* ["aroma"], in 2:15) as a continuation of the image of the triumphal procession (*thriambeuō* [2:14]) and at the same time as a preparation for his arguments about his ministry for God in chapter 3. As Martin (1986: 45) puts it, "Such terms are designed to enforce the claim of Paul's work as 'pleasing to God,' as the OT sacrifices were so regarded (Lev., Ezek.)."

Chapter 3 can be divided in two main sections: 3:1–6 deals with Paul's adequacy for the ministry, and 3:7–18 compares two kinds of ministries, that under the old covenant and that under the new covenant. In the first main section he refers to the OT motif of "tablets of stone" contrasted to "tablets of human hearts" (3:3, referring to Exod. 31:18; Ezek. 11:19; 36:26) and to the "new covenant" (3:6, referring to Jer. 38:31 LXX [31:31 MT]).

In 3:7–18, the second main section, the apostle offers an exposition of Exod. 34:29–32 and then of 34:33–35. Paul's primary purpose is "to highlight the glorious character of the ministry with which he has been entrusted and so explain why, despite so many difficulties, he does not lose heart" (Kruse 1987: 93).

The two main sections should not be separated in the exposition, since we not only have a thematic connection in the idea of the ministry, but also possibly a formal link: the verb "to have" (*echō*) in various forms appears in 3:4, 12 (and even in 4:1, 7, 13), which might be a pointer to how Paul structured his line of thought (so Schröter 1998: 242). It is also important to see that the two sections are related in order to understand why and how Paul refers to the OT. My interpretation will emphasize that Paul wanted to address the issue of his own day: his own ministry of the new covenant; and he referred to the old covenant so that by means of a comparison he could highlight aspects of his own ministry—for example, that of openness (as opposed to a veiled glory in the case of Moses). Thus Paul has a certain view of the OT from the outset, as we can see in the very first reference to the ministry of the old covenant, where he already calls it a "ministry of death" (3:7). He refers to the old covenant from the perspective of the new.

B. OT Context. Here we examine only those OT texts that have a main role in Paul's argumentation in this passage. A number of other OT texts are mentioned in the course of our exposition, but probably they are not "referred to" in the proper sense by Paul; only their motifs are used by him.

Paul's key OT passages in 2:14–3:18 come from the books of Exodus, Jeremiah, and Ezekiel. We will look at the texts in the sequence as Paul refers to them.

The motif of the "tablets of stone" (3:3) appears in Exod. 31:18; 32:15–16; 34:1 (and, when the Mosaic law is repeated, in Deut. 4:13; 10:1–2). Exodus 31 is the end of a long section that narrates what God told Moses while he was on Mount Sinai forty days and forty nights (chaps. 25–31). In 31:12–17 God emphasizes the importance of keeping the Sabbath. After God's words to Moses are concluded, we are told, "And he gave to Moses, when he had made an end of speaking with him upon Mount Sinai, the two tables of the testimony, tables of stone, written with the finger of God" (31:18). Chapter 32 begins a new theme, going back in time, telling how the people, having lost patience while Moses was on the mountain, made a golden calf. In 32:15–16 it is said that Moses "went down from the mountain with the two tables of the testimony" and that "the writing was the writing of God, graven upon the tables." According to 32:19, "Moses' anger burned hot, and he threw the tables out of his hands and broke them at the foot of the mountain." In 34:1 we read that God ordered Moses to cut two new tables of stone upon which God would write the words that were on the first tables, which Moses broke. Hafemann (1995: 333, 347) argues that the whole context should be kept in mind when reading 2 Cor. 3 because Paul argues on the basis of Exod. 32–34, not just certain verses from it (Hafemann [1995: 189–254] even devotes a whole chapter to "Exod. 32–34 in Canonical Tradition"). Schröter (1998: 239, 274), however, maintains that in order to understand Paul's text it is sufficient to study how Paul used certain motifs and short texts of the OT, and we should not presuppose that the result of our exegesis of the whole OT context would be the same as Paul understood it.

Since the Ten Commandments were always in the center of Israel's faith, the reference to the two "tablets of stone" points to the very heart of the Mosaic law. We should note that Paul does not criticize the "content" of the two tablets; rather, he contrasts the outward appearance of the tables of stone with the internalized message written on the hearts of people (so, e.g., Grindheim [2001: 99], who also emphasizes, "The means by which this new heart comes about, however, is not the law, but the new covenant, whose character is fundamentally different from that of the law" [2001: 100]).

The expression "tablets of human hearts" appears in the Bible only in 2 Cor. 3:3, but we may suspect that Paul uses it as a reference to the aforementioned Exodus text ("tables") and to passages where writing upon the hearts of people appears (see Schröter 1998: 247–49). The latter idea is found in several passages in Ezekiel. In Ezek. 11:19 we read God's promise: "And I will give them one heart, and put a new spirit within them; I will take the stony heart out of their flesh and give them a heart of flesh." The same idea appears in 36:26: "A new heart I will give you, and a new spirit I will put within you; and I will take out of your flesh the heart of stone and give you a heart of flesh." In both places the context contains the words of God reminding the people of Israel of their sins and the consequence thereof: they were scattered among the nations (Ezek. 11:5–16; 36:16–23). After this reminder God tells his people that he will gather them from the nations (11:17–18; 36:24–25), and this promise is explicated by the reference to the new spirit and to hearts of flesh given by God. After this promise the context contains more promises: God's people will keep his ordinances (11:20; 36:27) when they live again in their homeland (36:28). It may be of significance that the context of 11:19 also contains a reference to God's glory: "Then the cherubim lifted up their wings, with the wheels beside them; and the glory of the God of Israel was over them. And the glory of the LORD went up from the midst of the city, and stood upon the mountain which is on the east side of the city" (11:22–23). We should note that Paul does not polemicize with *this* "glory" in 2 Cor. 3, but only with the "glory" that shone on the face of Moses (to be referred to below).

755

Second Corinthians 3:6 refers to the "new covenant," noting that God "has qualified us to be ministers of a new covenant, not in a written code but in the Spirit; for the written code kills, but the Spirit gives life." The term "new covenant" appears only once in the OT: "Behold, the days are coming, says the LORD, when I will make a new covenant with the house of Israel and the house of Judah" (Jer. 31:31 [38:31 LXX]). This verse is preceded by God's promises to restore the fortune of the land of Judah (Jer. 31:23–28) and the reversal of a previous saying (31:29–30): "In those days they shall no longer say: 'The fathers have eaten sour grapes, and the children's teeth are set on edge.' But every one shall die for his own sin; each man who eats sour grapes, his teeth shall be set on edge." Then 31:31 is followed by a promise that the new covenant will not be like the other covenant that was made with the "fathers" (31:32), but the new covenant will mean that the law will be put "within them" (31:33b): "And I will write it upon their hearts; and I will be their God, and they shall be my people," says the Lord. Thus this passage in Jeremiah was suitable for Paul not only because of its reference to the new covenant, but also because here the law is written upon the "hearts" of people—a theme referred to by Paul just a little earlier in 3:3 (as we saw in connection with the Ezekiel passages; for a discussion of Jer. 31:31–34 as the background of Paul's argument, see Hafemann 1995: 119–40).

The main text that Paul refers to in 2 Cor. 3 comes from Exod. 34:29–35, and the only quotation is from this section (Exod. 34:34, quoted in 2 Cor. 3:16). The OT context is as follows. We have already seen that in Exod. 34:1 the Lord commands Moses to cut two new tables of stone, so that the Lord can write upon them the same words that were on the tables that Moses had broken. Moses had to go up on Mount Sinai again (34:2–4), and the Lord gave him many commands (34:11–26), including the keeping of the Sabbath and other feasts. The last command is "You shall not boil a kid in its mother's milk" (34:26b). Then the Lord said that with these words he has made a covenant with Moses and with Israel (34:27). In 34:28 the reader learns that Moses was with the Lord forty days and forty nights.

Exodus 34:29–30 is the first section of the long narrative that is alluded to in 2 Cor. 3. In 34:29b we read, "Moses did not know that the skin of his face shone because he had been talking with God." Then in 34:30b we learn that because his face was shining, the people "were afraid to come near him." Paul summarizes these motifs by saying: "Now if the dispensation of death, carved in letters on stone, came with such splendor that the Israelites could not look at Moses' face because of its brightness . . ." (3:7).

Then in Exod. 34 we read that Moses insisted that the people come to him, and "Moses talked with them" (34:31). Moses told them all the commandments he had heard from the Lord (34:32). The rest of Exod. 34 is the key example for Paul in 3:13–16, but he uses it in such a way that he adds to it motifs that are not mentioned in the OT passage. Because of the importance of Exod. 34:33–35 for Paul's exegesis, I quote it in full: "And when Moses had finished speaking with them, he put a veil on his face; but whenever Moses went in before the LORD to speak with him, he took the veil off, until he came out; and when he came out, and told the people of Israel what he was commanded, the people of Israel saw the face of Moses, that the skin of Moses' face shone; and Moses would put the veil upon his face again, until he went in to speak with him." In this passage we are first told that Moses put a veil on his face only after he had spoken to the people (34:33), but from the rest of the passage it is clear that later he always put on the veil when he was speaking to his people and took it off when he went in before the Lord (34:34–35 [see the use of "until" in both verses]). This passage implies that the presence of the Lord could be borne only by Moses; Moses could bear it even unveiled, whereas the people only could hear the Lord's commandments in an indirect way; not only could they not go into the presence of God, but even Moses had to veil his face from them because God's splendor shone on his face in such a strength of brightness that the people could not have borne it.

In Exod. 35 Moses goes on to tell the people all that the Lord had commanded him, beginning with the sanctification of the Sabbath (35:2–3). The veil motif does not appear again in this passage.

We will have to examine later how Paul adds to this OT passage when he says that Moses "put a veil over his face so that the Israelites might not see the end of the fading splendor" (3:13). However, we should note here that Hafemann does not think that Paul added to the OT context, and he translates Paul's text in a way that is in harmony with the OT. Hafemann (1995: 353–65) argues that Paul wished to express that Moses wanted to save the Israelites from the judgment of God. Moses put on the veil *in order that* the sons of Israel might not gaze into the outcome of that which was being rendered inoperative" (1995: 365).

We will also have to examine how Paul quotes one sentence from the OT passage cutting it out of its context: whereas in Exod. 34:34 we read, "Whenever Moses went in before the LORD to speak with him, he took the veil off," Paul, in 3:16, says this about anyone who turns to the Lord: "But when a man turns to the Lord the veil is removed" (Schröter [1998: 265] says that this verse is near to Exod. 34:34 in wording but not in meaning). Hafemann (1995: 388) argues that Paul refers to Moses in this verse: to "Moses' experience in the tent of meeting as a *type* of the one whose heart has been changed by the power of the Spirit under the ministry of the new covenant."

C. The Context in Judaism. From the aforementioned OT passages the main expression that surfaces in intertestamental Judaism is "new covenant" (see Jer. 31:31), which occurs in the *Damascus Document* (CD). Fragments of this document were found at Qumran, but the relevant sections are known from medieval copies of this document found in 1896–1897 in the *genizah* (manuscript storeroom) of an old Cairo synagogue. Following the most widely accepted theory, we may say that according to this document, the Qumran community saw itself as people of the "new covenant" just before the time of Jesus (Vermes [1987: 81], who calls this document *The Damascus Rule*, dates it ca. 100 BC). In CD-A VI, 17b–19 we read, "to separate unclean from clean . . . to keep the sabbath day according to the exact interpretation, and the festivals and the day of fasting, according to what they had discovered, those who entered the new covenant in the land of Damascus" (García Martínez 1994: 37). In CD-A VIII, 21 the text breaks off when, after a blank space, we read the words "All the men who entered the new covenant in the land of Damascus. . . ." From another passage we learn that

some members of the community were unfaithful to the precepts of God. About these people the document says: "Thus, all the men who entered the new covenant in the land of Damascus and turned and betrayed and departed from the well of living waters shall not be counted in the assembly of the people and shall not be inscribed in their lists . . ." (CD-B XIX, 33b–35).

It may have special significance that the term "new covenant" appears only in the *Damascus Document*. Other documents from Qumran use the term "covenant" without the adjective "new." Perhaps the community became reluctant to emphasize the element of newness because in antiquity the older generally was considered to be better (see the monograph by Pilhofer [1990] on this theme). However, even these very few references to the "new covenant" (an expression that they could find in Jeremiah) could be looked at as pointers to how they understood themselves, and thus it may be in the background of their thoughts also on occasions when they simply emphasize that they are in a covenantal relationship with God.

It is important for us to see that a little while before the time of Paul there was a Jewish community that held that they were entering a "new covenant." Paul uses this term to describe the Christian community. We may add that the term (Gk. *kainē diathēkē*) does not appear very often in the NT either, but nevertheless it is of great significance for the identity of the early Christians (it occurs in Luke 22:20; 1 Cor. 11:25; 2 Cor. 3:6; Heb. 8:8; 9:15; cf. Heb. 7:22; 8:6, 10, 13; 10:16, 29; 13:20, passages where covenant is mentioned as referring to the covenant in Jesus [e.g., in his "blood"] or as a "better" covenant; Heb. 12:24 also refers to "new covenant," but using a different Greek word for "new": *diathēkē nea*).

D. Textual Matters. In the case of the usage of motifs, we can confine the discussion to the question of whether a term appears in the MT, the LXX, or both. The motif of the "tablets of stone" in Exod. 31:18 is found both in the MT and in the LXX. The LXX uses the same Greek words that Paul uses in 3:3 (LXX: *plakas lithinas* [accusative pl.]; Paul: *plaxin lithinais* [dative pl.]), and whereas the LXX has *gegrammenas* ("written"), Paul's term in 3:2–3 has the prefix *en-*: *engegrammenē* ("written in"). In Exod. 32:15 the LXX uses all three words ("tablets," "stone," "written"), but the MT refers only to "tablets" (RSV: "tables") that were "written" on both sides.

Ezekiel 11:19 and 36:26 contain the contrasting expressions "heart of stone" (*kardia lithinē*) and "heart of flesh" (*kardia sarkinē*); these terms appear also in the MT. In 3:3 Paul wrote *en plaxin kardiais sarkinais* ("on tablets of human hearts"); this makes it likely that he alludes to Ezekiel here (so also Martin 1986: 52). It is significant that the LXX and the MT have a further expression in both verses: "a new spirit" (LXX: *pneuma kainon*). This may have been in Paul's mind when he spoke of the "Spirit" in 3:3 and of the "Spirit" as well as of the "new" covenant in 3:6.

In the case of the term "new covenant," we can say that the LXX's *diathēkē kainē* (Jer. 38:31) is a close translation of the MT's *běrît ḥădāšâ* (Jer. 31:31).

In 3:13 Paul says that "Moses . . . put a veil over his face." This expression appears both in the MT and in the LXX in Exod. 34:33. Paul has a slightly different word order: he places "veil" before "over his face." Paul, for the verb "put," has *etithei* (imperfect of *tithēmi*), whereas the LXX has the compound verb *epethēken* (aorist of *epitithēmi*).

Apart from these phrases, there is one longer expression quoted from the OT in 2 Cor. 3. The MT of Exod. 34:34a (quoted by Paul in 3:16) appears in a close translation in the LXX, but Paul changes the quotation significantly. Belleville (1991: 250–51) argues for "some form of literary dependence" but points out that we do not have "an exact citation" here, adding that "selective citation is more the norm than the exception in the NT." The MT and the LXX both indicate "But whenever Moses went in before the Lord to speak with him, he took the veil off, until he came out." Paul says, "But when he [or, 'a person'] turns to the Lord the veil is removed." The verb of the LXX text, "went in" (*eiseporeueto*), is replaced by Paul in 3:16 with "turns to" (*epistrepsē*), without an expressed subject (for six possibilities for the verb's subject, see Thrall 1994–2000: 1:269–71). The verb referring to the "taking off" of the veil appears in a different form: the LXX has an imperfect middle (*periēreito*), whereas Paul uses the present tense (*periaireitai*) (and probably the passive here, so that a divine activity in the unveiling may be expressed [see Belleville 1991:

253–54; Garland 1999: 194]). This is in accordance with the change that he introduced in the application: "is removed" expresses a general truth. Martin (1986: 70) maintains that the verb "turns to" has a generalized subject: "whenever there is a turning to the Lord." Belleville (1991: 249–50) argues that "the individual Israelite" may be in view here, and Paul himself was "a prime example" of the possibility of such an individual conversion of an Israelite. Whereas the LXX narrated in past tense what happened when Moses went in before the Lord, until he came out, Theissen (1987: 122) argues that the subject of Paul's verb *epistrepsē* in 3:16 is Moses, who "becomes the prototype of the convert." Hafemann (1995: 388–89) sees in Moses a "type": Paul established "a correlation between Moses and the indefinite person from within Israel now in view." Hafemann (1995: 390) paraphrases Paul's text as follows: "Whenever 'he or she' (like Moses) returns to the Lord, the veil is being removed." These interpretations have an element of truth: Moses may be in the background as a type of any convert, but not only of converts from the Israelites. It is better to see (with Martin [1986], referred to above; see also Matera 2003: 95) an even wider generalization here: as Paul writes to the Corinthians, he probably has in view Gentile Christians as well, who in Corinth probably outnumbered the Jewish Christians. Paul's emphasis here is on the necessity of turning to Christ—true for Jews and Gentiles alike. The difference between the OT text and Paul's usage of it has significant theological implications.

E. Paul's Use of the OT in 2 Cor. 3. We must keep in mind that Paul's main aim in this section is to defend his ministry. He achieves this by contrasting the ministries carried out in the old covenant and in the new covenant. In doing so, he nevertheless grants us an insight into his view on the relationship between the two covenants. Thus we inquire about how he uses the OT texts from this double aspect: what does he say about his ministry, and what view does he hold concerning the relationship between the two covenants? It is important to see that it is not Paul's aim here to address the latter issue, but while speaking on his primary theme—the defense of his ministry—he uses the OT and interprets it. As Belleville (1991: 297) puts it, "Paul is not concerned with Moses and the Exodus generation for their own sakes.

They are, instead, tools for developing his opening statement: 'We are very open in our ministerial behavior.'"

We can observe that Paul does not make any long, direct quotation in this chapter. He uses some OT expressions ("new covenant"; "tablets/tables"; "heart of flesh"; "veil"), he combines references to different OT passages (Exod. 31:18; Ezek. 11:19; 36:26 [see Martin 1986: 52]), he refers to a long narrative in the OT (Exod. 34), and he has one longer quotation that he substantially changes (Exod. 34:34a, quoted in 3:16). We can see that the OT is an important source for him, a source that has a high authority. Nevertheless, he does not offer an exegesis of it; rather, he uses it for the support of his argument, and while doing so, he interprets it from the perspective of the Christ-event: "For to this day, when they read the old covenant, that same veil remains unlifted, because only through Christ is it taken away" (3:14). This verse should be seen as a key to the whole chapter, since for "taken away" it uses the same term (*katargeō*) that appears repeatedly concerning the ministry of the old covenant and of its glory (3:7, 11, 13).

Paul applies some direct verbal OT prophecies to his own time and sees them beginning fulfillment in himself and in the Christian community. He claims that he and his readers live in the era of the "new covenant" prophesied by Jeremiah (Jer. 31:31). He further claims that the same "Spirit" of God works in them about whom Ezekiel had prophesied (Ezek. 11:19; 36:26). However, for Paul, the "tablets of stone" in the OT point forward through a contrasting analogy to the "tablets of human hearts" of the Christians (3:3): Whereas God wrote the Ten Commandments on stone tablets, he writes his new covenant on the hearts of his servants (with Ellis [1957: 127], we may see in this usage an example of "typology" as well). Paul and his readers are such servants (3:2–3, 5–6). Bultmann (1976: 82, 93) rightly emphasizes that Paul extends his thoughts from his own apostleship to Christians in general in 3:18: "we all" (so also Theissen 1987: 123, esp. n15; Belleville [1991: 276], however, maintains that only Paul and his co-workers, "all true gospel ministers without exception," are referred to here).

The way Paul refers to the story when Moses put on a veil when going in before God is of high significance for his view on the old covenant. On the one hand, we can see his high regard for the old covenant in his words praising that covenant (e.g., "glory/splendor"); on the other hand, he points out in what way the new covenant is "more glorious." Both aspects are important and must be given due weight in the interpretation.

The old covenant was "carved in letters on stone" (3:7). Paul does not say explicitly, but we can expect that even former "pagan" Corinthian Christians would know, that according to the OT text, it was God who carved those letters on two tables of stone. That dispensation "came with such splendor [*en doxē*] that the Israelites could not look at Moses' face because of its brightness [*dia tēn doxan*]" (3:7). Paul uses the term "splendor/brightness/glory" (*doxa*) repeatedly in the subsequent verses (3:8–11) about the old covenant (more exactly, about that "dispensation" or "ministry," *diakonia* [3:7, 9]). Thus, Paul had a high respect for the old covenant (and for the OT).

However, Paul's high respect serves here as a point of comparison: he says even more words of praise about the new covenant (or dispensation). When doing so, he also says negative words about the old dispensation; these terms highlight the positive side of the comparison, that of the new covenant.

Paul probably uses a rabbinic method of exegesis when he argues from the lesser to the greater (see Kruse 1987: 94; Sampley 2000: 66; so also Martin 1986: 59; see further Martin's [1986: 58] criticism of Windisch's thesis that 2 Cor. 3:7–18 is a Christian midrash on Exod. 34:29–35; for further literature, see Sampley 2000: 63). Paul shows that the new covenant is superior by the way of three comparisons: (1) the old dispensation was a "dispensation of death," while the new one is that of the "Spirit" (3:7–8); (2) the old dispensation was a "dispensation of condemnation," while the new one is that of "righteousness" (3:9); (3) the old dispensation "faded away," while the new one "is permanent" (3:11). In these comparisons it can be seen that the new covenant (dispensation or ministry) has a "greater splendor" (note the comparative "more" [*mallon*] in 3:8, 9, 11). Paul brings the comparison to a summary in 3:11: "For if what faded away [*to katargoumenon*] came with splendor, what is permanent [*to menon*] must have much more splendor." It can be seen, then, that

Paul says positive things about the old covenant; however, he refers to it in order to highlight how much more splendid is the new covenant, in which ministry he himself stands. As Martin (1986: 64) asserts, "The good is now replaced by the better" (so also Witherington 1995: 376: "One good thing is simply eclipsed by something better"; according to the "socio-rhetorical" analysis of Witherington [1995: 375], this passage belongs to the *probatio*, as the first division of the first argument). This idea is expressed also in 3:10: "Indeed, in this case, what once had splendor has come to have no splendor at all, because of the splendor that surpasses it" (Grindheim [2001] sees the law/gospel dualism in this verse, and indeed in the whole passage of 3:5–18, on which, see the title of his article, and esp. p. 102). God has qualified Paul to be a minister of a glorious new covenant (see also 3:6a).

This is to say that from Paul's perspective, the OT law and the old covenant and Moses, their minister, were a prophetic foreshadowing of the new covenant and of Paul, a minister of the new covenant. The glory of the old covenant that was fading suggested, from Paul's vantage point, that another covenant must come to replace it, the glory of which would be permanently unfading and thus greater. Furthermore, Paul has established a correlation between Moses and those turning "to the Lord" from among both Jews and Gentiles: "Whenever a man [on analogy with Moses] returns to the Lord, the veil is taken away" (3:16). Moses appears to be in the background as a type, not just earlier for Paul, but now of any convert (see also, in this respect, 3:18). As Hafemann suggested (1995: 388–90), Paul refers to Moses' experience in the tabernacle as a "type" of the person whose heart has been transformed by the power of God's Spirit under the new covenant ministry.

In the following section of the chapter (3:12–18) Paul quotes the OT and changes it substantially (at 3:16). The aim of the change is to apply the text to his own situation. He claims that he has understood the message of the OT properly because he reads it "in Christ" (see 3:14). In Paul's view, the OT points typologically to Jesus. If the reader of the OT does not understand Jesus, on the basis of that text, to be the promised Messiah, then he or she has read it as if with a veiled face. In

the OT text (Exod. 34) the Israelites were afraid to come near Moses. Paul says that the Israelites could not "fix their eyes on Moses." Most commentators say that Paul clearly changes the OT narrative when he adds in 3:13 that Moses "put a veil over his face so that the Israelites might not see the end of the fading splendor" (as Theissen [1987: 121] puts it, "Paul imputes a brand-new motive"). Some argue that Paul thought that Moses did this deliberately in order to hide the fading of the glory (*doxa*) or that Paul thought that Moses did it to the effect of hiding the fading character of the glory although Moses himself might not have been aware of it (see the views summarized in Thrall 1994–2000: 1:255–61). In either case, Paul contrasted the fading splendor of the old dispensation with the permanent splendor of the new covenant. However, it is unnecessary to see in Paul's words a reference to Moses actually hiding the fading of the glory, because it is *Paul's view* of the character of the old dispensation that it is fading away. Thus Paul does not necessarily add to the OT text any content that was not there (i.e., the motif of fading), but he refers to the OT and at the same time says that from the viewpoint of the permanent new covenant, the old covenant is transitory (a thought that is in line with his view on the law in Gal. 3–4). If Paul adds anything to the OT, it is his interpretation, as if he would say, "Moses put a veil over his face so that the Israelites might not see a glory that has its end, that is fading away in my view, because I already know of the unfading glory of the new covenant." This is a possible inference from the Greek text, because already in 3:7 *tēn katargoumenēn* is added to the end in the manner of the Greek adjectival structure: "glory on his face, (a glory that is) a fading one" (in Paul's opinion). Paul has in mind this view concerning the old covenant from the beginning of 3:7 because he started it by saying that it is a "ministry of death" (see Wendland 1963: 156). The aim of Paul's addition of his interpretation to the OT text is to highlight the ministry that he stands in: the glory of the new covenant is a permanent one (see 3:11).

Concerning the Israelites, Paul goes on to say, "But their minds [*ta noēmata autōn*] were hardened; for to this day, when they read the old covenant, that same veil remains unlifted, because only through Christ is it taken away. Yes, to this day, whenever Moses is read, a veil lies over their minds [*epi tēn kardian autōn*]" (3:14–15). Thus Paul applies the changed OT text to his contemporary fellow Jews who did not believe in Jesus as the Messiah. It is in accordance with this new meaning, expressed by Paul, that the quotation of the OT text is also changed in 3:16: "But when a man turns to the Lord the veil is removed." By now, Paul is far away from the OT narrative: the veil is not the veil on Moses' face that he put on when he came out from the presence of God; rather, it is a veil that prevents some Israelites from seeing Jesus as the Messiah whom the OT had prophesied about (the expression "old covenant" in 3:14 appears only here in the NT). Vielhauer (1979: 211) has pointed to the three ways that Paul refers to the veil in this passage: (1) it is the veil on the face of Moses, as in the OT narrative of Exod. 34 (3:13); (2) it is a veil at the reading of the OT that remains unlifted, because only through Christ is it taken away (3:14); (3) it is on the hearts of the Israelites (3:15). It is interesting to note (with Theissen [1987: 121–22], who writes in even more detail about the threefold use of the veil) that there is a fresco at Dura Europos in which "either the Torah shrine itself or a *capsa*, in which the scroll or several scrolls were transported from the Torah shrine to the synagogue room," is covered by a veil while a scroll is being read out by a man in the synagogue (for sources where the picture can be seen, see Theissen 1987: 121n11). Theissen (1987: 122) suggests, "It is therefore possible that Paul has a concrete practice in view when he speaks of this veil."

The veil is removed "through Christ" (*en Christō* [3:14]) when a person turns to the Lord (3:16). Martin (1986: 73) even adds, "The Christian ministry is meant, by divine intention, to supersede the old Judaic ceremonial order." Paul's aim in referring to the OT has thus gained a further aspect: apart from pointing typologically to his ministry of the new covenant (by the way of a comparison with Moses' ministry of the old covenant), he also claims the necessity of a christological reading of the OT. In order to achieve this aim, Paul not only has quoted the OT, but also has changed an original narrative concerning the "veil" and how the veil is "removed."

F. Theological Use. One of the important theological themes in this passage is that of the

covenant. This passage by Paul is a witness to the early Christians' view of themselves as being in a covenant relationship with God. This can be seen as evidence for an implicit claim that just as God stood in a covenant relationship with his people in the OT, so now the Christians are part of that people: they belong to God's chosen people. They are part of a "new covenant."

Paul uses the motifs of and references to OT texts in order to defend his ministry. While doing so, he also tells us about his relationship to the OT (see Theissen 1987: 118). The defense of his competence is more than a personal issue: "Underlying the debate over ministry is the theological tension of what kind of ministry is it that carries the divine approval" (Martin 1986: 55). Paul makes it clear that the old covenant (the one mediated by Moses) was glorious, but, with an argument "from the lesser to the greater" (Theissen 1987: 120), he claims that the new covenant is even more glorious. It is against this background that Paul can formulate even more sharply: the old ministry is transitory in comparison to the permanent character of the new. "The old ministry is critiqued *by comparison with the ministry of the Spirit*" (Sampley 2000: 66).

Paul uses the occasion of defending his ministry to highlight his christological stand. It is only "in Christ" that people "are given eyes to see and minds and hearts to understand not only what is going on in God's plan, but also that Moses and all of Scripture still disclose God's purpose and God's will and provide guidance to all God's people" (Sampley 2000: 68). In other words, the true meaning of the OT can be understood only when looking back at it from the perspective of the NT. Christ is the key to the understanding of the OT. Christians must hold on to this hermeneutical insight.

Second Corinthians 3:18 may be read as an expression of the "mysticism" of Paul, but it can also summarize the whole chapter inasmuch as the Christians are depicted here as growing "from glory to glory": the OT was glorious, but one has to read it through Christ, and then one is transformed to even greater glory. This can happen only through the Spirit (see also 3:6: the "written code," the OT "letter," does not kill if it is read through the Spirit, who leads us to Christ and to a christological reading of the OT). As Paul formulates in this concluding verse of chapter 3: "And we all, with unveiled face, beholding the glory of the Lord, are being changed into his likeness from one degree of glory to another; for this comes from the Lord, who is the Spirit" (for the idea of "progression from one state of glory to a further state," see also Thrall [1994–2000: 1:286], who holds that this "progressive transformation" is an "aspect of life in the sphere of the new covenant" [1:282]).

4:6

A. NT Context: The Light of the Gospel. Although there is no clear reference to an OT passage in this verse, Paul seems to indicate that he makes a direct quotation from the OT when he writes, "For it is God who said, 'Let light shine out of darkness'" (4:6a); but as NA[27]'s marginal "unde?" indicates, scholars are uncertain as to where the quotation comes from.

This verse belongs to the long unit mentioned at the discussion of 3:16 (2:14–3:18). The "reference" to the OT at 4:6 is embedded in the closer context of 4:1–6, which in turn is a continuation of chapter 3 from the point of view of both content and the key terms. The content is continued by the reference to the ministry in which Paul stands: "Therefore, having this ministry by the mercy of God, we do not lose heart" (4:1 [cf. 3:7–9]). The open character of this ministry is a further point of contact between the chapters: "We have renounced disgraceful, underhanded ways; we refuse to practice cunning or to tamper with God's word, but by the open statement of the truth we would commend ourselves to every man's conscience in the sight of God" (4:2 [cf. 3:12]). The following motifs of section 4:1–6 appear in the preceding chapter: "ministry" (4:1; cf. 3:7–9); the gospel being "veiled" (4:3; cf. 3:13–18); "splendor/glory" (4:4, 6; cf. 3:7–18); "likeness" or "image" (4:4; cf. 3:18); "heart" (4:6; cf. 3:2–3).

Furthermore, some motifs in 4:1–6 can be seen as elements of a "ring-composition" (so Martin 1986: 75; Matera 2003: 98): they complete the ideas referred to in 2:14–17. By describing his own ministry in 4:1–6, Paul rounds off his polemic against the false teachers mentioned in 2:14–17. The following motifs are evidence of this literary device: "those who are perishing" (4:3; cf. 2:15); "knowledge" (4:6; cf. 2:14); "God's word" (4:2;

cf. 2:17) (note that Witherington [1995: 385] assigns 4:1–5:10 to the second division of the first argument in the *probatio*).

Then, from 4:7 on Paul describes the sufferings that he had to undergo during his ministry: "But we have this treasure in earthen vessels, to show that the transcendent power belongs to God and not to us. We are afflicted in every way, but not crushed . . ." (4:7–8a).

B. OT Context. Although "Let light shine out of darkness" does not surface verbatim in the OT, it is likely that Paul refers to the beginning of the OT, to the story of creation, to Gen. 1:3. Genesis 1:2 may also be in his view because of its reference to "darkness." In 1:2–3 we read, "The earth was without form and void, and darkness was upon the face of the deep; and the Spirit of God was moving over the face of the waters. And God said, 'Let there be light'; and there was light." In the first version of the creation story (1:1–2:4a [the second being the rest of chap. 2]) the creation of light happens on the first day, right after God created "the heavens and the earth" (1:1). After God created the light, he "saw that it was good" (1:4), and "God called the light Day, and the darkness he called Night" (1:5). Then follows the narration of creation from the second to seventh days. Thus, Paul's reference to the creation story must imply that the light of the gospel is also a result of the creative act of God (so also Thrall 1994–2000: 1:315; Grässer [2002–2005: 1:157] speaks of an "analogy" with the creation of light).

There are other OT passages where the creation of light is not mentioned but "light" plays a significant role (see Matera 2003: 104). Let us look at some important examples (see Hübner 1997: 340–43). In 2 Sam. 22:29 we read, "Yea, thou art my lamp, O LORD, and my God lightens my darkness." This verse is part of a long song by David in which he thanks the Lord for deliverance from his enemies. Chapter 22 of 2 Samuel is a parallel to Ps. 18 (Ps. 17 LXX). Accordingly, this verse also appears in that psalm, with a slight variation: "Yea, thou dost light my lamp; the LORD my God lightens my darkness" (18:28 [cf. Ps. 112:4]). In these texts it is significant that darkness is referred to directly, while "light" is referred to in an indirect way: the noun "lamp" and the verb "lighten." Even if these verses were in the back of Paul's mind, they probably are not "referred to" in 2 Cor. 4; at most, they colored Paul's thinking in an indirect way.

Another example, again only as a possible coloring of Paul's thinking, is Isa. 9:2 (9:1 MT/LXX), where we read, "The people who walked in darkness have seen a great light; those who dwelt in a land of deep darkness, on them has light shined." In this prophecy the lands of Zebulon and Naphtali are promised recovery and glory after an initial defeat by the Assyrian occupants. Because the preceding verse refers to "the way of the sea, the land beyond the Jordan, Galilee of the nations," this prophecy became significant for the early Christians, as Jesus began his ministry in Galilee (see Matt. 4:13–17). Although Isa. 9:2 has three important terms that appear in 2 Cor. 4:6 ("darkness," "light," "shine on"), God is not mentioned in Isa. 9:2, nor is it God who speaks in that verse; therefore, Thrall (1994–2000: 1:315) concludes that Paul's "primary source is the divine command in Genesis," although "it could be that the phrasing of Paul's allusion has been influenced by the wording of Isa 9:1" (so also Martin 1986: 80).

C. The Context in Judaism. Since we do not have a direct quotation here, it is difficult to look for parallels in Judaism. It might suffice to name some of the key terms in 2 Cor. 4:6 that are important in intertestamental Judaism as well. Although neither Gen. 1:3 nor Isa. 9:2 is directly quoted in the Qumran literature, the antithesis of darkness and light is well attested—for example, in the recurring expressions "sons of light" and "sons of darkness" (e.g., 1QM I, 1, 7–8, 16; 1QS I, 9–10). We also see passages in the Qumran writings that, as Martin (1986: 81) puts it, "emphasize the shining of God's face on his people" (e.g., 1QHª XII, 5–6, 27–29; 1Q28b IV, 24–28; 1QS II, 2–4). There is a section alluding to God's creative activity in 1QM X, 11–15.

If it is correct that Paul alludes to the first verses of the OT creation story in 4:6, then it may be relevant to note that the idea of creation plays a role also in the Wisdom literature (see, e.g., Wis. 6:22; 10:1; 11:17; Sir. 1:4, 9; 16:26; 24:8–9). According to this literature, "Wisdom" takes part in God's work (e.g., Wis. 8:4). Wisdom is further related to the knowledge (and the fear) of God (e.g., Sir. 1:16, 18, 26–27). If Paul alludes to God's creative activity in people's knowing God in Christ, this emphasis on God's new creation (or, to use Thrall's

[1994–2000: 1:316] expression, "fresh creation") may have been prepared by Jewish Wisdom literature before Paul's time (so Lang 1986: 279).

D. Textual Matters. Here we can focus on the few expressions common to 2 Cor. 4:6 and the aforementioned OT passages. In regard to Gen. 1:3–4, we note that the LXX text uses a finite verb form of "say": "God said" (*eipen ho theos*), whereas the NT passage uses a participle: "God who said" (*ho theos ho eipōn*). The nouns "light" and "darkness" appear in both texts, but the OT has "Let there be light" (*genēthētō phōs*), while Paul has "Let light shine" (*phōs lampsei*). Thrall (1994–2000: 1:315) notes that Klauck (1987) sees *ho eipōn* "as decisive for a background in Gen 1:3" (see also the whole volume in which Klauck's essay appears). I side with this view, represented by many others as well (e.g., Best 1987: 39; Kruse 1987: 105; Martin 1986: 80). Concerning Isa. 9:2 (9:1 MT/LXX), it is worth noting that the same Greek future-tense verb appears there as in 2 Cor. 4:6: light "will shine" (*lampsei*).

E. Paul's Use of the OT in 2 Cor. 4:6. Although there is no direct quotation from the OT at 2 Cor. 4:6, Paul makes use of some OT motifs in this verse. Paul probably refers primarily to the creation story (Gen. 1:3). He does not quote it verbatim; nevertheless, his analogical point is clear: just as God acted in creation, "whereby the darkness of the primeval world was banished by the light" (Kruse 1987: 105), so now God shines "the light of the gospel" into the hearts of those who receive Jesus Christ as Savior. This is like a "new creation"—as Paul will use this phrase just a little later in the letter, in 5:17 (see Best 1987: 39). It is possible that Isa. 9:2 is also in the background of Paul's thought (so Martin 1986: 80); if so, then he is in line with the gospel tradition, which applied this verse to the ministry of Jesus (cf. Matt. 4:15–16; Luke 1:79; see Kruse 1987: 105).

F. Theological Use. Paul's purpose with the allusion to the creation story probably is to highlight the extraordinary character of people turning to Christ: it comes not from the initiative of human beings, but only from God's own new intervention in human life. The Greek sentence in 4:6 is difficult from the point of view of sentence structure; as Thrall (1994–2000: 1:314–15n862) puts it, "The syntax is awkward, since there is no main verb." However, the relative pronoun "who" (*hos*) is most likely emphasizing the activity on God's side: "For it is God who said, 'Let light shine out of darkness,' who [*hos*] has shone in our hearts..." (4:6a). God creates the Christian believer by showing a person God's glory on Christ's face. Paul may even have his own conversion experience on the Damascus road in the background of this thought here (see Beale 1989: 580; Martin 1986: 80). The glorious knowledge of God being made accessible in Christ Jesus is expressed by a number of phrases chained together: "to give the light of the knowledge of the glory of God in the face of Christ" (4:6b). The glory of Jesus Christ and that of God belong together. As Best (1987: 40) puts it, "We cannot separate Christ and God. The brightness of God is seen in the face of Christ; Christ is the likeness of God." Thus Paul's allusion to the creation of light serves his christological emphasis: true knowledge of God comes only through Jesus Christ, and God himself made it possible for human beings to know him in this way, and this way only.

4:13

A. NT Context: Courageous Witnessing in Spite of Persecution.
After Paul refers to God's activity in creation as well as in the illumination of Christians (4:1–6), he recalls different kinds of suffering that he had to endure during his ministry (4:7–18). These exemplify that the "treasure" of the gospel is carried in the "earthen vessels" of the bodies of Christ's servants (4:7 [for a discussion of parallels to the idea of the body as an "earthenware container," see Thrall 1994–2000: 1:322–25]). In spite of these sufferings, Paul is bold in ministering the gospel, and he underlines this boldness by quoting from a psalm. The idea of an open and bold ministry was already present in chapter 3 and in the first section of chapter 4. Here in 4:13 Paul writes, "Since we have the same spirit of faith as he had who wrote, 'I believed, and so I spoke,' we too believe, and so we speak." The message of this speaking by Paul is the resurrection: "knowing that he who raised the Lord Jesus will raise us also with Jesus and bring us with you into his presence" (4:14). This courageous witnessing is carried out for the sake of the Corinthians: "For it is all for your sake, so that as grace extends to more and more people it may increase thanksgiving, to the glory of God" (4:15). The theme of God's "glory"

is a further point of contact with the previous passage as well as with chapter 3.

B. OT Context.
The quotation in 4:13 comes from Ps. 115:1 LXX (Ps. 116:10 MT/ET). There is a difference between the MT and the LXX translation not only regarding the chapter numbering, but also in the numbering of the verses. Psalm 114 in the LXX is based on the first nine verses of Ps. 116 MT, and then the MT continues the numbering, whereas the LXX begins a new psalm; thus 116:10 MT = 115:1 LXX. When surveying the contexts of the OT and Judaism, for the sake of clarity I refer to the MT numbering.

In the first nine verses of Ps. 116 the psalmist gives thanks for God's intervention in his need. We do not know who the psalmist is, since no name is given at the beginning of the Hallel psalms, Pss. 113–118 (Dahood [1970: 130] notes that these psalms are sometimes called "the Egyptian Hallel"). He cried for God's deliverance, and God saved him from deep dangers, even from death. It is significant that although Paul quotes only a short phrase from the psalm ("I believed, and so I spoke"), he brings this quotation after listing his sufferings, just as the psalmist did before he uttered the expression quoted by Paul. For example, the psalmist says, "The snares of death encompassed me; the pangs of Sheol laid hold on me; I suffered distress and anguish" (116:3), and he continues, "For thou hast delivered my soul from death, my eyes from tears, my feet from stumbling; I walk before the LORD in the land of the living. I kept my faith, even when I said, 'I am greatly afflicted'" (116:8–10). It is interesting to note that in the psalm the phrase "I said" can be regarded as an introduction to what the psalmist said, but Paul stops at this point, thus emphasizing the act of speaking per se. The English text in the KJV can be understood in this way: "I believed, therefore have I spoken..." (116:10). Then the psalmist gives thanks, using the expression of lifting up "the cup of salvation" (116:13 [cf. Paul's use of "the cup of blessing" in 1 Cor. 10:16]): "I will lift up the cup of salvation and call on the name of the LORD."

C. The Context in Judaism.
Martin (1986: 83) notes that "the substance of the quotation" from Ps. 116 "is without parallel in the use the rabbis make of the OT." Perhaps the general idea of the suffering righteous person as expressed in

this psalm may be in Paul's mind concerning his own ministry as well. If so, then he sees himself in a tradition present in both biblical and extrabiblical Jewish writings (cf., e.g., Pss. 22; 30; 34; 40; 118; 130; *T. Jos.* 1:3–7; see Thrall 1994–2000: 1:329–30).

D. Textual Matters. The three words quoted by Paul in 4:13 are exactly the same as in the LXX (Ps. 115:1 LXX): *episteusa, dio elalēsa* ("I believed, and so I spoke"). We have already seen that in the OT "I spoke" may be the introduction to what the psalmist actually "said" (at the end of the same verse): "I am greatly afflicted." This is not quoted by Paul; however, the whole passage in which the OT quotation appears is describing his afflictions. The whole verse in the LXX (Ps. 115:1) can be seen as a translation of the MT (Ps. 116:10), with one addition: the LXX version adds *allēlouia* at the beginning of the verse, indicating that a new Hallel psalm is beginning. However, it is difficult to be certain about the meaning of the Hebrew text (see the difference between the RSV and the KJV quoted above); it probably is referring to the psalmist's trust in God in spite of the afflictions. Thus we may say that Paul's quotation agrees with the LXX but slightly differs from the MT (in the classification by Ellis [1957: 152] the agreement of the LXX and the MT is registered, but Best [1987: 44] and Martin [1986: 83] point to the difference as well).

The quotation is introduced by a phrase that Paul uses only here: "according to what is written" (*kata to gegrammenon*). Thus the KJV translation of 4:13 is already an exegetical decision when it applies this phrase to the psalmist "who wrote…" (Martin [1986: 82] approves of such a paraphrase, suggesting the following translation: "We possess the same spirit of faith as that shown by the Scripture writer"). Although the Greek text leaves it open as to with whom Paul shares the "same spirit of faith," the context makes it most likely that he refers to the same faith as that of the psalmist (see the detailed argumentation for this exposition in Thrall 1994–2000: 1:339).

E. Paul's Use of the OT in 2 Cor. 4:13. Paul's choice of the psalm passage is excellent from the point of view of content: he shares the sufferings with the psalmist and also his faith that enables him to speak (to bear witness to Christ) boldly (so also Kruse 1987: 108). However, in Paul the

quotation may fulfill two aims: on the one hand, he shows through his comparison to the psalmist's attitude that he shares with the psalmist the reference to his trust ("belief") in God in spite of the afflictions; on the other hand, Paul probably uses *episteusa* ("I believed") with a richer meaning—he also refers to his belief in Christ, and *that* is why he is bold in his witnessing. As we have seen in the context, Paul goes on to bear witness to the resurrection of Jesus and of the Christians (4:14). The quotation in 4:13 shows once again how high an authority the OT is for Paul. This is all the more significant in view of the fact that the majority of the Corinthians were of Gentile origin; the point is that Gentile Christians needed to know the OT as well. As Best (1987: 44) points out, Paul usually quotes the OT from the LXX version, "for it would be the one his Greek-speaking readers would have had available," though there is debate about the educational level and reading ability of the majority of Paul's Gentile readers, as well as what acquaintance pagan Gentiles would have had with the Jewish OT before their conversion. Nevertheless, the more important issue concerns the audience as hearers more than readers and the fact that church leaders most probably would disciple new converts on the basis of the early Christian kerygma and the Bible at the time, which was the Greek OT. Accordingly, on a first hearing, Gentile listeners, who had been recently converted, likely would not have picked up on how the OT context shed light on what Paul was saying, but on subsequent readings and hearings of the letter, they likely would have gained more insight into the OT's significance for Paul's quotations and allusions.

F. Theological Use. It is of great significance that Paul uses a quotation from the OT in order to emphasize his faith shared with the psalmist. His faith is in line with the faith of his ancestors; he stands in continuity with the faith of the OT writers. However, his faith is also faith in Jesus Christ. The early Christians are in continuity with the OT, but they believe in God who sent his Son, Jesus. The faith of the early Christians is bound to Jesus Christ; this is the new element in the faith that they share with, for example, the psalmist.

5:17

Although there is no direct quotation in 5:17, many commentators agree that the "newness" motif in Paul's verse here has its roots in some passages in Isaiah (see Thrall 1994–2000: 1:420–21; Best 1987: 54; also Bultmann 1976: 159; Lang 1986: 300; Martin 1986: 152; Ellis [1957: 153] mentions only Isa. 43:18–19 in his list of "allusions" at 5:17; Shires [1974: 113] says that Paul "is citing the prophecy of Isa. 43:18–19" here). In a detailed article on the OT background of reconciliation in 2 Cor. 5–7, Beale (1989) has argued convincingly that Isa. 43:18–19; 65:17; 66:22 are alluded to in 5:17. Since the limits of the present chapter do not allow a detailed elaboration, I summarize briefly the relevant section of his article.

Beale (1989: 555) points out that the context of these Isaianic passages is "the recreation of the nation through restoring it from exile to its homeland" (see esp. Isa. 43:3–7). Paul alludes to these passages in order to strengthen his point that the Corinthians should be reconciled with God as well with Paul, who is God's apostle (Beale 1989: 552). In 2 Cor. 5:17 we read, "Therefore, if any one is in Christ, he is a new creation; the old has passed away, behold, the new has come." The terms "old" (*ta archaia*), "behold" (*idou*), and "new" (*kaina*) appear both in Isa. 43:18–19 LXX and in 2 Cor. 5:17 (see Beale 1989: 553). Isaiah 43:18–19 reads, "Remember not the former things, nor consider the things of old. Behold, I am doing a new thing; now it springs forth, do you not perceive it?" Isaiah 65:17a has the term "new" twice: "For behold, I create new heavens and a new earth." The "emphasis on restoration as a new creation" is the point of Isa. 65:17–25 "in its context" (Beale 1989: 555). The same is true for Isa. 66:18–23. In Isa. 66:22 we read, "For as the new heaven and the new earth which I will make shall remain before me, says the LORD; so shall your descendants and your name remain." On the basis of the contexts of these Isaianic passages, as well as on the basis of the line of thought in 2 Cor. 5:14–21, Beale (1989: 556) suggests that "'reconciliation' in Christ is Paul's way of explaining that Isaiah's promises of 'restoration' from the alienation of exile have begun to be fulfilled by the atonement and forgiveness of sins in Christ." Thus, once again, we find Paul making a christological application of an important OT motif. Furthermore, the OT allusions have a significant message for the Christian community as a whole.

When Paul applies an OT promise for Israel to the Gentile Christians in Corinth (see Beale 1989: 559), he affirms that the death and resurrection of Jesus (see 5:15) "can be viewed as inaugurating true Israel, the church, into the presence of God" (Beale 1989: 558).

6:2

A. NT Context: The Message of Reconciliation.
In the first part of chapter 5 Paul writes about his "groaning" in the human body, the "earthly tent," and about his desire to "put on" his "heavenly dwelling" (5:1–2). However, while he is still here on earth, he wants to please God by fulfilling the task assigned to him: he wants to "persuade" people about the saving act of the death and resurrection of Christ (5:11–15). This task can be summarized as that of bringing the message of the "new creation" (5:17) and of the reconciliation to all people (5:18–19). In the concluding verses of chapter 5 Paul writes, "So we are ambassadors for Christ, God making his appeal through us. We beseech you on behalf of Christ, be reconciled to God. For our sake he made him to be sin who knew no sin, so that in him we might become the righteousness of God" (5:20–21).

The opening verse of chapter 6 has a participle, *synergountes* ("working together"), begging the question of with whom Paul "works together." In the light of the preceding chapter, it is most likely that Paul works together with God in extending his "appeal" to human beings; thus many translations add the expression "with him," referring back to God, who was mentioned in 5:20–21 (for arguments that Paul refers to God and not to the Corinthians, see Martin 1986: 165; Thrall 1994–2000: 1:451). Paul hopes that the Corinthians are showing fruits of their reconciliation with God: "Working together with him, then, we entreat you not to accept the grace of God in vain" (6:1). In the next verse he quotes part of Isa. 49:8 as supporting his appeal to the Corinthians, with a stress on the urgency of their reaction: "For he says, 'At the acceptable time I have listened to you, and helped you on the day of salvation.' Behold, now is the acceptable time; behold, now is the day of salvation" (6:2). This verse may be seen as a parenthesis (so Martin 1986: 160) supporting what Paul said in 6:1; then from 6:3 on he returns to the theme of his own ministry ("verses 3–10 are tied grammatically to verse 1" [Best 1987: 59]). He has a long list of the sacrifices that he was willing to bring for the recipients of his message. To quote in part: "We put no obstacle in any one's way, so that no fault may be found with our ministry, but as servants of God we commend ourselves in every way: through great endurance, in afflictions, hardships, calamities . . ." (6:3–4).

B. OT Context. The context of the verse that Paul quotes from the OT is relevant to his own ministry (see Lambrecht 1994: 524). Isaiah 49 belongs to the sections that speak about the special role of the suffering "Servant of the Lord." In the first few verses of the chapter the Servant bears witness about his calling (49:1–3). Then he is addressed by the Lord, and he is told that he has to minister not just to Jacob, but to all the nations: "It is too light a thing that you should be my servant to raise up the tribes of Jacob and to restore the preserved of Israel; I will give you as a light to the nations, that my salvation may reach to the end of the earth" (49:6). It is emphasized two more times in the continuation of the passage that it is the Lord who is speaking here: "Thus says the LORD, the Redeemer of Israel. . . . Thus says the LORD: 'In a time of favor I have answered you, in a day of salvation I have helped you; I have kept you and given you as a covenant to the people . . .'" (49:7–8). The ensuing verses describe the saving deeds that Yahweh will carry out for his people; these may be regarded as signs of a messianic age to come (see, e.g., 49:9–11).

C. The Context in Judaism. It is a notoriously difficult question: About whom do the Servant Songs speak? The Servant is called "Israel" in Isa. 49:3, yet the continuation of that verse may be understood also as the words of an individual mentioning Israel: "But I said, 'I have labored in vain. . . .' And now the LORD says, who formed me from the womb to be his servant, to bring Jacob back to him, and that Israel might be gathered to him . . ." (49:4–5). Perhaps we do not have to decide between the "collective" and the "individual" interpretations. It may well be that Israel as a nation is called as the Servant of Yahweh, yet there may have been individuals at times who felt that they were to fulfill that call—for example, the prophet who wrote Isa. 49 (see Garland 1999: 305; Blenkinsopp [2002: 356] argues that "the Servant is none other than the author of the core of these chapters, the so-called Deutero-Isaiah";

passages from "Deutero-Isaiah" are quoted in fragments from Qumran: 4Q176 [see Maier 1995–1996: 2:111–14; García Martínez 1994: 208–9]). The likelihood is that the "servant" in Isa. 49:1–6 is an anonymous individual, identifiable with the "servant" of Isa. 53, since in 49:6a this servant restores not merely the whole nation, but in particular he restores the remnant (the "preserved ones of Israel"), of which Isaiah the prophet presumably would have considered himself a part (see Beale 1989: 561). It is worth noting that in Acts the Ethiopian eunuch asks Philip concerning another Servant Song (from Isa. 53:7–8): "About whom, pray, does the prophet say this, about himself or about some one else?" (Acts 8:34). From the answer we can see that one segment of "Judaism"—that is, early Christianity—understood the Servant Songs as fulfilled in their Messiah: "Then Philip opened his mouth, and beginning with this scripture he told him the good news of Jesus" (Acts 8:35). We note that Isa. 49:8 is not quoted in the Dead Sea Scrolls, but Isa. 49:7, 13–17 are partially referred to immediately after one another in 4Q176 1–2, II, 4–9.

D. Textual Matters. The OT quotation by Paul in 6:2 is introduced by a typical introductory formula: "For it/he says . . ." (*legei gar*). The third-person singular of the verb can have either the Scripture or God as its subject. After the introductory formula the quotation agrees verbatim with the first part of Isa. 49:8 LXX. The LXX "gives substantially the sense of the Hebrew" MT here (Toy 1884: 184): "In a time of favor I have answered you, in a day of salvation I have helped you" (*kairō dektō epēkousa sou kai en hēmera sōtērias eboēthēsa soi*). The LXX has *legei* ("says") in the introduction as well, and the LXX makes it clear that it is the "Lord" who speaks here: *houtōs legei kyrios* ("thus says the Lord" [see Hughes 1962: 219]). Then Paul applies the quotation to his readers (so also Thrall 1994–2000: 1:453): "Behold, now is the acceptable time; behold, now is the day of salvation" (6:2b). In this application he uses a more emphatic word for "acceptable": *euprosdektos.*

E. Paul's Use of the OT in 2 Cor. 6:2. Paul's aim in the quotation here is to support from Scripture what he has said. He uses the OT as a high authority to show that his ministry is also a fulfillment of the OT. Several commentators note that Paul uses the Jewish method of pesher here (we can see many instances of the use of the pesher among the Qumran documents—e.g., the pesher on Habakkuk, 1QpHab [see Martin 1986: 168–69]). The pesher always consists of two parts: first it quotes an OT passage, and then it adds an interpretation that is at the same time an application to the author's own day. In Paul's case the application is made very direct through the emphatic repetition of "now" (*nyn*): "Behold, now is the acceptable time; behold, now is the day of salvation" (6:2b).

As we have seen in the previous sections, Paul expects that even the Gentile Christians in Corinth regard the OT as a high authority. We cannot know whether the Corinthians could recall the context of the verse quoted from Isa. 49, but for Paul it may be a pointer to how he saw his ministry: he probably regarded Jesus as the "Servant" and saw himself called into the ministry of this Servant. His message of reconciliation was a fulfillment of the OT promises.

It is an open question in what sense the Corinthians may have accepted God's grace "in vain" (6:1). On the basis of the two canonical epistles to the Corinthians, we can say that Paul already regarded the Corinthians as "saints" (see, e.g., 1 Cor. 1:2); that is, they were already reconciled with God. They responded with conversion to "Paul's initial proclamation of the gospel at Corinth" (Matera 2003: 149 [see also Kruse 1987: 131]). Yet many areas in their lives were not in agreement with God's will; therefore Paul had to remind them to live in accordance with God's grace shown to them. Telling them not to accept God's grace "in vain" may have been another way of calling them to a way of life that accords with the will of God as their thankfulness for God's grace. As Martin (1986: 169) puts it, "Paul is probably urging the Corinthians to rededicate their lives to the Christian ideal." If they do not obey, then there is a sense, as with the Servant in Isa. 49:4a, that Paul's efforts would be "in vain."

In the larger context of the defense of Paul's ministry this includes the expectation that the Corinthians accept Paul as Christ's ambassador in the work of "reconciliation"; that is, they should accept Paul's apostolic ministry. Just as Isa. 49:8 prophetically affirmed that God would "help" the "Servant" carry out and make effective his mis-

sion, so Paul sees himself corporately identified with the Servant Jesus, who began to fulfill this prophesied mission. Thus, as an apostle, Paul continues to fulfill the mission of the Servant, which Jesus had begun (note also Acts 13:47, where Paul likewise applies Isa. 49:6 to himself; see, similarly, Rom. 15:20–21 in comparison with 15:8–9). The aim of Paul's quotation in 6:2 is to highlight his apostolic authority as the "Servant prophet" and to emphasize the urgency in the Corinthians' response to God's grace by showing loyalty to the apostle (see Beale 1989: 562–63). The "acceptable time" (*kairos dektos*) is the time when God shows his favor (cf. the MT of Isa. 49:8; see Garland 1999: 304). The Corinthians should live their lives in accordance with the "salvation" that God has already shown to them. The application of the quotation sounds as a call to accept God's grace, but in view of the two letters to the Corinthians, it is more likely that the "now" refers to the time of the answer of the Corinthians. They should urgently show their gratitude for God's salvation by leading a way of life in accordance with what is expected from the "saints" of God and also by receiving the apostle as the servant of *the* Servant, Jesus the Messiah. As Beale (1989: 564) puts it, "In that he [Paul] was continuing the mission of Jesus, the Servant, he could easily apply this Servant prophecy to himself."

F. Theological Use. The quotation in 6:2 is an example of the christological reading of the OT on Paul's part: "The eschatological day of salvation that the prophet foresaw has arrived with Christ" (Matera 2003: 149). It is clear from the context that Paul saw the saving act of God in Christ's death and resurrection (5:14–15); this was the means by which God reconciled humanity with himself (5:18–21). This "day of salvation" (6:2) is fulfilled in the Christ event. The Corinthians have accepted this message of reconciliation with God, so they should now also be reconciled with God's messenger, the apostle Paul. The theological notion of corporate solidarity is also in play, as Paul views himself to be identified with the prophesied Servant of Isa. 49, which Jesus had already begun to fulfill (see Beale 1989: 564). The "day of salvation" should urge the Corinthians to receive Paul as the apostle of Jesus, indeed as the continuing fulfillment of the Servant of Isa. 49, for their sake, lest they behave in a way unworthy of those who received God's grace. Thus the soteriological message concerning "God's eschatological act of salvation" has an ethical implication: "The Corinthians must respond to Christ's ambassador 'now'; otherwise they will have received the grace of God in vain" (Matera 2003: 150).

6:16–18

A. NT Context: A Life Worthy of God's People.
Many exegetes regard 2 Cor. 6:14–7:1 as an interpolation in Paul's letter (see, e.g., Lang 1986: 310–11). Among the arguments for this theory is that this passage has a theme different from that of its context. This observation is correct, but it does not lead in a conclusive way to the interpolation theory (for arguments in support of the view that the passage is non-Pauline, see, e.g., Furnish [1984: 376–80], who nevertheless thinks that Paul incorporated it into his own letter [1984: 383]). The origin of the passage is significant because it impacts the question of whether we can find Paul's use of the OT in it (since there are several OT quotations in 6:16–18). However, even if one agreed that a non-Pauline text is used by Paul here, one might argue that he uses the OT at least in a secondary way: he chose to incorporate material that contains OT quotations (so also Matera 2003: 164n64). In any case, without going into further detail, I will treat this passage as a text from Paul (leaving open the possibility that he may have made use of some traditional material, as argued by, e.g., Martin [1986: 192–94]).

Thus we examine the passage in the context of 2 Corinthians as an integral part of it (for argumentation for the passage fitting in the context of Paul's letter, and exegesis regarding the passage as Pauline, showing its relationships to the context, see Thrall 1994–2000: 1:26–28, 472–85). After Paul describes in 6:4–10 the hardships that he had to endure in his ministry (for a discussion of the careful structure of this "hardship list," see Matera 2003: 148; Thrall 1994–2000: 1:453–54), he addresses the Corinthians in a very personal tone. He reminds them how his heart was "widened" toward them (6:11) and asks for a similar response from the Corinthians: "In return—I speak as to children—widen your hearts also" (6:13 [like the RSV here, many translations supply the word "hearts," which occurs in the Greek text in 6:11 in the singular, *kardia*, with the same verb, *platynō*, "enlarge, widen," in the passive voice]). Then Paul

warns the Corinthians not to be "mismated with unbelievers" (6:14a). Five antithetical questions strengthen this warning (6:14b–16a), the last of which leads to an application to the Christian congregation: "What agreement has the temple of God with idols? For we are the temple of the living God" (6:16a). This statement is then supported by several OT quotations, originating in different OT writings (6:16b–18): "As God said, 'I will live in them and move among them, and I will be their God, and they shall be my people. Therefore come out from them, and be separate from them, says the Lord, and touch nothing unclean; then I will welcome you, and I will be a father to you, and you shall be my sons and daughters, says the Lord Almighty." The ensuing verse, 7:1, belongs to this passage as a conclusion drawn by Paul from the OT quotations (as Best [1987: 65] notes, "The chapter division here is certainly incorrect"): "Since we have these promises, beloved, let us cleanse ourselves from every defilement of body and spirit, and make holiness perfect in the fear of God." Then 7:2 takes up the idea that the Corinthians should receive Paul and his companions with good feelings: "Open your hearts to us; we have wronged no one, we have corrupted no one, we have taken advantage of no one." Again in the Greek the word "heart" does not appear here, but it can be understood in the phrase used by Paul: "make room for us" (*chōrēsate hēmas*). Although the Greek verb is different from the one used for "widen" in 6:11, 13 (*platynō*), it is clear that 7:2 refers back to 6:11–13, since in the next verse Paul makes an explicit connection to what he had said about the "heart" in 6:11b. Then Paul says in 7:3, "I do not say this to condemn you, for I said before that you are in our hearts, to die together and to live together." The Greek verb *proeirēka* ("I said before") is more natural after a digression in the line of thought, so we can regard it as a conscious reference back to the theme that Paul left when he included the ethical warning and the OT quotations (so also Matera 2003: 159; Thrall [1994–2000: 1:26n162] rightly notes that this verse "takes up 6.11b–12a").

At 7:4 Paul concludes the long unit (2:14–7:4) about his ministry to the Corinthians (see commentary at 2 Cor. 3:16 above. After this concluding remark, Paul returns in 7:5 to the theme of his travel plans (last mentioned in 2:13).

B. OT Context. We will examine the context of the OT texts in order as they appear in the chain of quotations. In the second half of 6:16 parts from Lev. 26:11–12 are quoted. It is possible that Ezek. 37:27 also is in Paul's thought here, since the Corinthian text is even closer in wording to the text of Ezekiel (Matera 2003: 166). Leviticus 26 lists commandments and promises for those who obey the commandments. The chapter begins with a prohibition of idols and a command to observe the Sabbath (26:1–2). We should note that in the Pauline passage the emphasis lies on the need for the Corinthians to avoid the impure influence of their neighborhood. Even if they may not have known the context of the quotation from Leviticus, on Paul's side even this context fits his main message (see Matera 2003: 165). Leviticus 26 then lists promises of good harvest (26:4–5), of peace in the land (26:6), and of victory over enemies (26:7–8). In 26:9 we read God's promise to confirm his "covenant" with his people, and in 26:10 is a promise of such abundant food that the people can eat "old store" in order to make room for the new. Paul's quotations (with some changes to be discussed later) come from 26:11–12 (the quotations and allusions are in italics): "And *I will make my abode among you*, and my soul shall not abhor you. *And I will walk among you, and will be your God, and you shall be my people*." In 26:13 God reminds the Israelites that he brought them out of Egypt, and from 26:14 onward follows a long section warning against disobedience to God's commandments, with the punishments for the disobedient (26:14–39). The chapter finishes with renewed promises for those who confess their sins committed against God (26:40–45). From the last verse of the chapter we can see clearly that the whole passage is about the relationship between God and his people, Israel; it is important that this is applied to the Corinthians as God's people in the new covenant in the Pauline context. Leviticus 26:46 reads, "These are the statutes and ordinances and laws which the LORD made between him and the people of Israel on Mount Sinai by Moses."

If Ezekiel is also in Paul's mind when he quotes Leviticus, then the Ezekiel context, Ezek. 37:1–15, is also telling: the idea that God lives among his people occurs in the very chapter that promises a new life for God's people, even in the vision of

a valley full of bones coming to life. God's explanation of the vision and also the following verses make it clear that God promises his people that he will bring them home from the exile in Babylon (see, e.g., 37:21, 23). In 37:26 God promises "a covenant of peace" with his people, and then in 37:27 we read, "My dwelling place shall be with them; and I will be their God, and they shall be my people." The last verse of the chapter shows the benefit for all the nations of the presence of God among his people: "Then the nations will know that I the LORD sanctify Israel, when my sanctuary is in the midst of them for evermore" (37:28).

In 6:17 Paul draws on parts of Isa. 52:11 and Ezek. 20:34. Isaiah 52 concerns God's promise to his people that they are to return from the Babylonian exile (see, e.g., 52:3). In 52:7 we read about "good tidings," and in 52:8–9 there sounds a call for singing, "for the LORD has comforted his people, he has redeemed Jerusalem" (52:9b). In 52:10b we read the promise that "all the ends of the earth shall see the salvation of our God." Then follows the verse referred to by Paul (Paul brings the two italicized references in the reverse order): "Depart, depart, go out thence, *touch no unclean thing*; *go out from the midst of her*, purify yourselves, you who bear the vessels of the LORD" (52:11). In 52:12 it is promised that God will go with his people; then from 52:13 onward we read about the Servant. These verses, 52:13–15, belong thematically to chap. 53, as a "servant passage (52:13–53:12) containing comment (53:1–11a)" (Blenkinsopp 2002: 340; see also pp. 344–57).

At the end of 6:17, after a clause from Isa. 52:11 ("touch no unclean thing"), without indicating that a different source is quoted, Paul apparently uses a phrase from Ezek. 20:34: "I will welcome you." In the Ezekiel passage the verb is followed by "out of the countries," which is why the RSV translates the phrase as "I will . . . gather you out of the countries." The Greek verb used by Paul, *eisdexomai*, does mean "I will welcome you" or "I will receive you"; however, the same Greek finite verb is used to translate the Hebrew word for the "gathering" of the people scattered among the nations (e.g., Hos. 8:10; Zech. 10:8, 10; Jer. 23:3; Ezek. 11:17; cf. Zeph. 3:20, where, instead of the future tense, the aorist subjunctive middle *eisdexōmai* is used). However, of special significance are the places where in the LXX this verb is followed by the accusative plural *hymas* ("you") as in the Pauline text: Ezek. 20:34; 22:20. *Hymas* appears also in Ezek. 20:41 after the present infinitive middle *eisdechesthai* (this verse may be in Paul's mind, together with 20:34, as is emphasized by Lang [1986: 310] and by Garland [1999: 339n981], who points to a variant in 20:41 containing *eisdexomai*). In 22:20 the context is not that of gathering from the nations, but rather from different metals: "As men gather silver and bronze and iron and lead and tin into a furnace, to blow the fire upon it in order to melt it; so I will gather you in my anger and in my wrath, and I will put you in and melt you" (in 22:19 the present indicative *eisdechomai* is followed by *hymas* as well). We might add that *eisdexomai* (future tense, as in Paul) is introduced by "and I" [*kai egō*] in Jer. 23:3 (Paul has the contracted form, *kagō*). Ezekiel 20:34 has only the *kai*; nevertheless, because of the addition of "you" (*hymas*) in this verse, we might say (with most of the commentators [e.g., Matera 2003: 166]) that Paul quotes Ezek. 20:34 in 6:17 (Ellis [1957: 152, 179] does not mention this text in his lists of OT passages quoted by Paul; Hübner [1997: 366–67] holds the view that Ezek. 20:34 is quoted here). This conclusion can be supported also by the context of the phrase in Ezekiel. As we have seen in the case of the other quotations that their OT contexts fit the main thought of Paul in 2 Cor. 6 (the Corinthians should avoid the defilement that results from keeping fellowship with unbelievers), so in Ezekiel the immediate context concerns the people of God as distinct from other nations. After the prophet repeated God's words telling the people how God brought them out of Egypt (20:3–10) and how they disobeyed God's ordinances in the wilderness (20:11–27), the disobedience of the prophet's generation is pointed out (20:28–31). Then the contrast between God's people and their surroundings is emphasized: the people should not think of being "like the nations" (20:32–34). Then God warns his people that he will have to "enter into judgment" with them (20:35), and he will "purge out the rebels" from among them (20:38). Thus the context is about God's people being cleansed from the impurity that they acquired from their pagan neighbors.

The last element in Paul's chain of quotations is in 6:18, where a few phrases, with some changes,

are quoted from 2 Kgdms. 7:14 (2 Sam. 7:14 MT/ ET). It is interesting to note that from the same chapter Paul quotes a phrase from an earlier verse, 7:8, with which he rounds off the whole chain of quotations. Second Corinthians 6:18 reads (the phrases quoted by Paul are in italics), "'and *I will be a father* to you, and *you* shall be *my sons* [LXX: 'son'] and daughters,' *says the Lord Almighty*." The reason why Paul changes "son" to the plural is that in the OT the context concerns a promise about David's offspring. In 2 Sam. 7 (2 Kgdms. 7) David says to the prophet Nathan that whereas David as king lives in a house, the ark of the Lord dwells only in a "tent" (7:1–3). The Lord tells Nathan to remind David that the Lord dwelled in a tent throughout the journeys in the desert and also in the time of the judges, so why does David want to build a house for him (7:4–7)? Then in 7:8 God says, "Now therefore thus you shall say to my servant David, 'Thus says the LORD of hosts, I took you from the pasture, from following the sheep, that you should be prince over my people Israel,'" and here the LXX employs the term "Lord Almighty" (*kyrios pantokratōr*) for the common expression "LORD of hosts." The Lord promises David both rest from his enemies (7:9–11) and an offspring who will build a house for the Lord (7:12–13a). The promise continues concerning David's offspring: "And I will establish the throne of his kingdom for ever. I will be his father, and he shall be my son. When he commits iniquity, I will chasten him with the rod of men, with the stripes of the sons of men" (7:13b–14). In this way the promise is for the whole future that there will be a Davidic king on the throne, because at the end of Yahweh's message the promise is for David: "And your house and your kingdom shall be made sure for ever before me; your throne shall be established for ever" (7:16). Thus Paul applies a promise originally uttered for David's royal house—and through it for the whole chosen people—to the new people of God (to whom the Christians in Corinth belong).

C. The Context in Judaism. The idea that God separates his people from the pagan environment and has a special relationship with them (he is their God and their "father") is the main belief of the people of Israel. Second Samuel 7:14a is a promise concerning David's son, "and the text was used at Qumran with reference to the Davidic messiah" (Thrall 1994–2000: 1:478) in 4Q174 1 I, 10–13 (see Maier 1995–1996: 2:102–5). Here is the text as translated by García Martínez (1994: 136 [with his markings in the text]): "'YHWH de[clares] to you that he will build you a house. I will raise up your seed after you and establish the throne of his kingdom *11* [for ev]er. I will be a father to him and he will be a son to me.' This (refers to the) 'branch of David', who will arise with the Interpreter of the law who *12* [will rise up] in Zi[on in] the last days. . . ." It is worth noting that there are passages in Philo concerning God dwelling among his people in a spiritual way. For example, in *Dreams* 1.149 the "soul" is addressed as being the "house of God" and "a holy temple": "Be zealous therefore, O soul, to become a house of God, a holy temple, a most beauteous abiding-place" (see Thrall 1994–2000: 1:476). In the preceding section, *Dreams* 1.148, and in *Dreams* 2.248 the first part of Lev. 26:12 is quoted by Philo: "I will walk in you, and will be your God" (in the latter case with the interpretation that God walks in "the soul of the Sage . . . as in a city" [see Martin 1986: 204]). The other OT references in 2 Cor. 6:16–18 do not appear to be commented on by early Judaism.

D. Textual Matters. Only a few of Paul's words in 6:16 can be seen as verbatim quotation; otherwise he uses different forms of words and even "merges" texts from different parts of the OT (so Ellis 1957: 186; Thrall 1994–2000: 1:35, both of whom list further "merged quotations" [e.g., from Rom. 3:10–18; 11:34–35; 1 Cor. 15:54–55], which shows that this style of quotation does not militate against the Pauline authorship of the passage under discussion here). The quotations are introduced by a formula that does not occur elsewhere in the NT (see Thrall 1994–2000: 1:477): "As God said" (*kathōs eipen ho theos*).

In this verse the Greek for "I will dwell among them" is different in Paul's text and in both of the OT texts that he may have had in mind. Paul uses a verbal form, *enoikēsō en autois* ("I will live in them"), whereas in Lev. 26:11 the LXX translates the MT's "I will set my tabernacle/dwelling place" as *thēsō tēn diathēkēn mou* ("I will set my covenant") (see Martin 1986: 204). It is likely that even instead of the aforementioned Lev. 26:11a, Paul has Ezek. 37:27 already here in mind, since Ezekiel has "my dwelling place shall be with them,"

although with a different Greek term, *kataskēnōsis*, for "dwelling place." Then Paul quotes from Lev. 26:12, *kai emperipatēsō* ("and I will walk [among you]"), and also the rest of the verse, but conflated with Ezek. 37:27, which has a similar content. The pronouns of the Pauline text are nearer to the text of Ezek. 37:27: "And I will be their God, and they shall be my people" (*kai esomai autois theos, kai autoi mou esontai laos* (see Ellis 1957: 179; Thrall 1994–2000: 1:477).

In 6:17 Paul continues the chain of quotations by adding "therefore" (*dio*), a "strong inferential conjunction" (Martin 1986: 205). It is as if Paul said, "Because God dwells among his people, therefore *come out from them*." The italicized words are quoted by Paul from Isa. 52:11. Paul does not quote the whole verse from Isaiah, and he even reverses the order. He also changes the text slightly and adds a closing phrase, probably from Ezekiel. Paul's text reads, "Therefore come out from them, and be separate from them, says the Lord, and touch nothing unclean; then I will welcome you." The last phrase, "I will welcome you," may come from Ezek. 20:34.

Paul's text at 6:17a with the Isaiah quotations reads, *exelthate ek mesou autōn kai aphoristhēte, legei kyrios, kai akathartou mē haptesthe*. It is important to observe that Paul inserts the phrase "says the Lord" (*legei kyrios*) between the quotations and that he uses this formula elsewhere (cf., e.g., Rom. 12:19; see Thrall 1994–2000: 1:35). The formula appears also in the OT in Isa. 52:5, a few verses before the quoted text, so Paul may have taken it from the context in Isaiah (see Thrall 1994–2000: 1:478).

In Isa. 52:11 the people of God are first told to "go out" from the pagan environment, then they are told "not to touch" any unclean thing, but then a second time they are called to "go out" from among them: "Go out thence, touch no unclean thing; go out from the midst of her, purify yourselves." The LXX text reads, *exelthate ekeithen kai akathartou mē haptesthe, exelthate ek mesou autēs, aphoristhēte* (and in Isaiah is added "you who bear the vessels of the Lord," referring to those who brought home the holy vessels at the return from the Babylonian exile; the order and the content in the LXX follows that of the MT). As we can see, Paul not only changes the order, but also writes "from among them" (*ek mesou autōn*) instead of "from the midst of her" (*ek mesou autēs*). With the singular feminine pronoun the LXX refers to the city of Babylon, whereas with the plural pronoun Paul has "an implicit allusion to the unbelievers of v. 14" (Thrall 1994–2000: 1:478, referring to 2 Cor. 6:14).

In the last quotation in the chain Paul uses the first half of 2 Sam. 7:14, changes it, and even adds to it. Then he uses a phrase from 2 Sam. 7:8 to round off the whole series of quotations. In 2 Sam. 7:14a (2 Kgdms. 7:14a) God promises to King David's offspring, "I will be his father, and he shall be my son" (*egō esomai autō eis patera, kai autos estai moi eis huion*). Paul, in 6:18, changes the third-person singular pronouns to second-person plural, referring to God's people in general (including the Corinthian Christians as the addressees of the letter in particular): "And I will be a father to you [*hymin*], and you [*hymeis*] shall be my sons and daughters, says the Lord Almighty." Paul's text has the plural "sons" (*eis huious*), and he even adds "and daughters" (*kai thygateras*). The latter expression may come from Isa. 43:6 (so Hübner 1997: 368), where daughters and sons are mentioned together. By the addition Paul emphasizes the validity of God's promise for the whole community of Christians, including women (Martin 1986: 206–7).

The final clause of the chain of quotations comes from the LXX version of 2 Sam. 7:8 (2 Kgdms. 7:8). In translating the MT's "Thus says the LORD of hosts," the LXX uses "almighty" instead of "hosts," and Paul quotes the resulting phrase verbatim: *legei kyrios pantokratōr*.

E. Paul's Use of the OT in 2 Cor. 6:16–18. In this chain of quotations Paul seems to quote the OT in a free way: he picks certain phrases from longer sentences, on occasion he reverses the order of the OT phrases, and he can even refer to the OT so freely that his wording is different from the LXX, although the LXX is a close translation of the MT. However, in spite of the changes made by Paul, we may say that he refers to the LXX version, since certain short phrases appear only in the LXX (e.g., the expression "almighty" in 2 Kgdms. 7:8, which Paul quotes in 6:18 at the end of the chain). The quotations are well chosen even from the point of view of the context: they speak about the special relationship between God and his people in the OT (Lev. 26:12; Ezek. 37:27;

20:34; 2 Sam. 7:14), and also about the ethical consequences of that relationship (Isa. 52:11). In the case of Ezek. 20:34 and Isa. 52:11, "the context is concerned with Israel's restoration from exile" (Thrall 1994–2000: 1:478). Paul applies the quotations to the Christian community as the people of God; this new community has to be different from the pagan environment as well.

Since all of these OT references are direct verbal prophecies or are set in a direct verbal prophetic context, Paul sees them having inaugurated fulfillment in the Corinthian community. Consequently, the Corinthians are the beginning of the prophesied end-time tabernacle or temple, and they are part of the dawning fulfillment of Israel's restoration prophecies.

F. Theological Use. The OT quotations are rich in theological implications. The primary message of the quotations is that the Christians are the "people of God." Paul and the Corinthian addressees are included, as can be seen from the pronoun "we" (*hēmeis*) in 6:16 and from the verbal form in the first-person plural "let us cleanse ourselves" in 7:1 (see Martin 1986: 202). This section does not address the question of the fate of the OT "people of God"; it simply affirms in a natural way that the followers of Christ are now also the people of God, even if they are of "Gentile" origin. The OT quotations address them now; God is their father as well; they too are now God's people (*laos* [6:16b]).

Connected to this theme is the presence of God, his dwelling among his people (the verb *enoikeō* ["dwell"] is not used of God in the LXX, so it is emphatic here in the Pauline text [Martin 1986: 204]). God dwells now spiritually in his people: they are the temple of God (6:16; cf. 1 Cor. 3:16–17; 6:19; see Garland 1999: 338). The context of the quotations (see, e.g., Ezek. 37:26–27) and also Paul's own thoughts in 2 Cor. 3 as a context within the letter raise the possibility that Paul looks at the Corinthian congregation (as at any Christian) as the new covenant people of God (see Matera 2003: 166–67). In the Christian community can be seen the fulfillments of prophecies about the restoration of God's people. The vision in Ezek. 37 is one of the most beautiful expressions of that restoration theology, and Isa. 43:6, with the emphasis on the "daughters," belongs to that context as well (see Beale 1989: 572;

Thrall 1994–2000: 1:479; but cf. Garland [1999: 340], who supports Olley's proposal that Deut. 32:19 may be the background for Paul adding the reference to "daughters" in his text; however, since the context in Deut. 32 is negative—the Lord was angered by his "sons and daughters" because of their idolatrous behavior—it is more likely that Paul refers to a restoration text rather than simply to an OT passage with warning against idolatry).

Just as in the OT the people of God had to keep themselves clean (separating themselves from their pagan environment), so also the Corinthian addressees have to be different from the non-Christian environment (see esp. 6:17). The quotations have an ethical implication: "They are to live as befits the temple of God" (Martin 1986: 205). Holiness is expected from them, as is seen in the message of the OT quotations in 6:16–18 summarized by Paul in the next verse (which should belong to chap. 6 because it clearly refers back to what has just been said): "Since we have these promises, beloved, let us cleanse ourselves from every defilement of body and spirit, and make holiness perfect in the fear of God" (7:1). The promises of God require a "life of moral holiness that accords with the gift of holiness that God has bestowed upon" the Christian community, including the Corinthians (Matera 2003: 168).

All this is emphasized by Paul through the OT quotations; this shows that the OT writings are "the word of God" for him as well as for his addressees, and that is why he uses "a series of proofs from Scripture to reinforce the main admonition in 6:14" (Garland 1999: 336). It is significant that Paul refers to God as the author of these prooftexts three times, "thereby underscoring the authority of this citation" (Matera 2003: 164): at the beginning of the chain of quotations ("as God said" [6:16]), at the middle, between two quotations ("says the Lord" [6:17]), and at the end of the series ("says the Lord Almighty" [6:18]).

8:15

A. NT Context: Collection for the Christians in Jerusalem.

In chapters 8–9 Paul deals with the issue of the collection for the poor Christians in Jerusalem (concerning the question of whether the two chapters were originally separate letters, see Thrall [1994–2000: 1:36–43], who holds that chap. 8 belongs with chaps. 1–7, but chap. 9 was written later; so also Martin 1986: 249–52; in my view, the timing of the composition of the letter as a whole is not of great significance, so I treat both chapters as Pauline and as integral parts of 2 Corinthians in the historical sequence as they appear in the letter; for a similar view, see Kruse 1987: 31). Chapter 8 begins a new theme in the letter, that of the collection: "We want you to know, brethren, about the grace of God which has been shown in the churches of Macedonia.... For they gave according to their means ..." (8:1, 3a). Paul sends Titus to the Corinthians to complete among them "this gracious work" (*tēn charin tautēn* [8:6]). Paul advises the Corinthians to complete the collection that they had begun a year earlier (8:10–11). He does not want to put an unbearable burden on them; every one has to give "according to what a man has, not according to what he has not" (8:12). Paul does not mean that others should be eased and the Corinthians be burdened (8:13), but one has to discern when to give help and when to receive it: "As a matter of equality your abundance at the present time should supply their want, so that their abundance may supply your want, that there may be equality" (8:14). This argument is strengthened by an OT quotation: "As it is written, 'He who gathered much had nothing over, and he who gathered little had no lack'" (8:15). Then Paul gives further details about the role of Titus in administering the collection carried out by the Corinthian Christians (8:16–23). Paul rounds off the theme with an exhortation at the end of the chapter: "So give proof, before the churches, of your love and of our boasting about you to these men" (8:24).

B. OT Context.

In 8:15 Paul supports his argument concerning the equality among God's people in their care for one another by quoting the major part of Exod. 16:18. Exodus 16 deals with the details of how God provided food for his people during the journey through the desert (during the exodus from Egypt). In the "wilderness of Sin" the people of Israel "murmured against Moses and Aaron in the wilderness" (16:1–2) because they were hungry. God promised to provide "bread from heaven" for them every day of a week, and on the sixth day of the week even a double portion, so that they did not have to gather in food on the Sabbath day (16:4–5). Moses and Aaron conveyed the message of the Lord to the people, and the glory of the Lord appeared to the people (16:6–10). When God's promise was fulfilled, the people were wondering what the special food was (16:15: "What is it?"—to this question in Hebrew the term "manna" as the name of the "flake-like" food is related [see 16:31, 33, 35]). Then Moses explains what God had done: "This is what the LORD has commanded: 'Gather of it, every man of you, as much as he can eat; you shall take an omer apiece, according to the number of the persons whom each of you has in his tent'" (16:16). The people did so, and "they gathered, some more, some less" (16:17). The next verse tells the reader that even though some gathered more, after eating they did not have more, because everyone happened to gather what he or she and the people in their "tent" were able to eat. It is from this detail of the manna story that Paul quotes: "But when they measured it with an omer, he that gathered much had nothing over, and he that gathered little had no lack; each gathered according to what he could eat" (16:18). Moses commanded the people to eat everything that they gathered in on the same day, but some did not trust that they would find new food the following day, so they did not eat up everything; however, on the following morning, what was left over had worms "and became foul" (16:19–20). God kept his promise: when they gathered the double portion on the sixth day, it did not become foul during the Sabbath (16:22–24). Although Moses explained to the people that the manna could not even be found on the Sabbath day, some went out to gather even on the seventh day, but of course they found none (16:25–27). In the rest of the chapter we find the naming of the special food as manna and the commandment that as a remembrance for God's special provision, Aaron had to put a jar of manna "before the LORD" to be kept throughout the generations (16:31–34). The people of Israel ate the manna for forty years, until they reached the border of Canaan (16:35). The final verse of the chapter informs the reader that "an omer is the tenth part of an ephah" (16:36).

C. The Context in Judaism.

In Israel's life the exodus from Egypt was like the "hour of birth" for the nation. Their journey through the wilderness over forty years was remembered already in other parts of the OT as well (see, e.g., Josh. 5:6; Ps. 95:10; Amos 2:10; 5:25). As we have seen in Exod. 16, actions were taken to keep the memory of the events, such as the storing of the manna in a jar for future generations. In *Heir* 191 Philo quotes the same verse that Paul uses, Exod. 16:18, "with regard to the equal distribution of wisdom by the divine Word" (Furnish 1984: 420). It may have been of special significance for the people that the manna story occurred between "Elim and Sinai" (Exod. 16:1), on the way to Sinai, the place of the giving of the law.

D. Textual Matters.

Paul begins 8:15 with an introductory formula, "as it is written" (*kathōs gegraptai*); then he quotes part of Exod. 16:18 from the LXX. The word order of the LXX follows the MT, but Paul changes it slightly. He quotes the middle section of the OT verse: "He who *had gathered* much had nothing over; and he who *had gathered* little had no lack" (*ho to poly ouk epleonasen, kai ho to oligon ouk ēlattonēsen*) (8:15 RSV, supplying a verb [noted here in italics] not present in the Greek). The LXX has *ouk epleonasen ho to poly, kai ho to elatton ouk ēlattonēsen* ("did not superabound who [had] much . . ." [my translation]).

E. Paul's Use of the OT in 2 Cor. 8:15.

Paul uses Exod. 16 in 2 Cor. 8 "to validate the principle of equality" (Thrall 1994–2000: 2:543). He finds a text in Scripture that can strengthen his argument that the Corinthians should support the poor in Jerusalem. In the original setting the phrases "to abound" and "to lack" referred to the individuals in Israel: each person had the right amount for himself or herself (and for the people who belonged to them, who were in their tent). Although some people had gathered more than others, they had no surplus, because they needed just that much (see Furnish 1984: 420; Grässer 2002–2005: 2:35). For Paul, "the concept of equality has scriptural warrant in the story of the manna in Exod 16, where each had enough, no more and no less" (Thrall 1994–2000: 2:542–43 [cf. Lang 1986: 320]). In the Corinthian context the apostle argues that at a certain time God provides some members of the church with more so that they may help those who have less at that time (e.g., as a consequence of a famine [see Martin 1986: 261]). Thus we may say that the important point for Paul in the quotation is the very fact that God provides for his people. For Paul, "the principle of equality" meant that God provides for *all* his people (see Thrall 1994–2000: 2:543). To borrow a picture from another Pauline context: members of the church body should assist each other in times of need (cf. 1 Cor. 12:14–26; see Lang 1986: 320; Matera 2003: 192). The Corinthians should not keep what they have to themselves, because the "saints" at the Jerusalem congregation are in need. It is God's will that every member of his people have sufficient provisions (as the example of the manna in Exod. 16 shows), so the Corinthians should offer their help now. That is why God had given more to the Corinthians at that particular time (see Matera 2003: 193). Thus, Paul uses Exod. 16:18 in an analogical manner.

F. Theological Use. It may well be said that the collection was a practical help in time of need (see Martin 1986: 257); however, it may also have had a symbolic meaning: the Christians of Gentile origin could show their respect to the "mother congregation," the church at Jerusalem, which was of Jewish origin (see the excursus on the Pauline collection in Martin 1986: 256–58). This idea may also be in the background here, but the "eschatological motif" that the Gentile nations bring gifts to Israel is not explicitly emphasized by Paul in 2 Cor. 8, nor other letters where he mentions the collection (Thrall 1994–2000: 2:513). However, the unity among Christians of Gentile origin and those of Jewish origin could be furthered by the collection; this may well be a motivation for Paul in organizing it (so Thrall 1994–2000: 2:514).

Theologically, it remains important that Christians do not keep to themselves what they had received from God. God provides for them; this provision is there also to enable them to help others (so also Garland 1999: 386). Paul made use of an OT quotation to emphasize that even the Corinthians had received from God all that they had. Paul spoke a similar message to them at another place in different words: "What have you that you did not receive? If then you received it, why do you boast as if it were not a gift?" (1 Cor. 4:7).

9:9 (9:6–10)

A. NT Context: The Willingness of the Corinthians at the Collection. In 2 Cor. 9:9 there is a verbatim quotation from a psalm, but in the immediate context there are further short phrases taken from different OT writings, so we examine these quotations together. Although chapter 9 has

the same theme as chapter 8—the collection for the Christians in Jerusalem (see commentary on 2 Cor. 8:15 above; see also Furnish 1984: 446)—9:1 seems to be a new beginning, perhaps because this chapter was written somewhat later: "Now it is superfluous for me to write to you about the offering for the saints." With this introduction Paul nevertheless returns to the theme of collection, urging the Corinthians to carry on with what was begun in Achaia one year previously (9:2). Paul sends some delegates to Corinth to ensure the readiness of the Corinthians for the offering, so that Paul will not be ashamed in his confidence of them (9:3–5). Paul's motif of sowing and reaping in 9:6 probably comes from Prov. 22:8, and this same verse may be the source of his reference to the "cheerful giver" in 9:7: "The point is this: he who sows sparingly will also reap sparingly, and he who sows bountifully will also reap bountifully. Each one must do as he has made up his mind, not reluctantly or under compulsion, for God loves a cheerful giver" (9:6–7). In 9:8 Paul reminds the Corinthians that God provides for them abundantly so that they can give to others in abundance. This idea is strengthened by a quotation from Ps. 112:9 in 9:9: "As it is written, 'He scatters abroad, he gives to the poor; his righteousness endures for ever.'" The following verse is not an explicit quotation as such, yet the idea of God giving "seed to the sower" and "bread for food" may come from Isa. 55:10; the verse concludes what had preceded in 9:6–9 (so Furnish 1984: 449; but see Matera [2003: 206], who holds that this Pauline verse begins a new section). In 9:10 we read, "He who supplies seed to the sower and bread for food will supply and multiply your resources and increase the harvest of your righteousness." In the rest of the chapter Paul motivates the Corinthians' giving by pointing out that there will be even spiritual riches—for example, thanksgiving flowing out of the Corinthians' generosity (9:11–14). The final verse of the chapter rounds off the theme of collection: "Thanks be to God for his inexpressible gift!" (9:15). Then in chapter 10 a new tone begins a completely new theme: the apostle has to defend his apostleship again (chaps. 10–13).

B. OT Context. We look briefly at the OT context of each of the three aforementioned texts to which Paul may refer in chapter 9. Proverbs

22 has several sayings that speak about the rich and the poor. Both groups are led to humility in 22:2: "The rich and the poor meet together; the LORD is the maker of them all." Wealth is not mentioned only in positive terms: "A good name is to be chosen rather than great riches, and favor is better than silver or gold" (22:1); "The rich rules over the poor, and the borrower is the slave of the lender" (22:7). It is interesting to note that 22:8 in the MT is shorter than in the LXX (they also differ slightly even in their common part), and Paul takes motifs from both parts. The MT reads, "He who sows injustice will reap calamity, and the rod of his fury will fail," but the LXX has a further clause: "God blesses the cheerful and giving man, and he will end the futility of his deeds" (my translation). The ensuing verse continues the theme of the additional LXX clause: "He who has a bountiful eye will be blessed, for he shares his bread with the poor" (22:9).

Paul's long verbatim quotation in 9:9 comes from Ps. 111:9 LXX (112:9 MT [in discussing the context, I will use the MT numbering]). Psalm 112 belongs to the frame of the Hallel psalms (Pss. 113–118), which begin with the phrase "Praise the LORD." This psalm concerns the person who "fears the LORD" and declares him "blessed" (112:1). Such a person will have "wealth and riches . . . in his house" (112:3). We may see 112:5 as also fitting the context of the Corinthians' collection: "It is well with the man who deals generously and lends, who conducts his affairs with justice." The "righteous" will have a steady heart (112:6–8). About this "godly man" (Furnish 1984: 448) it is said in 112:9 (the verse quoted by Paul, without the last clause concerning the "horn"), "He has distributed freely, he has given to the poor; his righteousness endures for ever; his horn is exalted in honor." The final verse of the psalm speaks about the wicked person who sees the righteous and "gnashes his teeth" (112:10).

In 9:10 Paul quotes a few words from Isa. 55:10. The beginning of Isa. 55 contains God's promise for those who thirst: "Ho, every one who thirsts, come to the waters; and he who has no money, come, buy and eat! Come, buy wine and milk without money and without price" (55:1). This fits the context of Paul's argument concerning the Corinthians' giving willingly, since God pro-

vides for them as well. God keeps his "everlasting covenant" and "love for David" even toward the addressee of Isa. 55. The phrase quoted by Paul (italicized in the following quotation), with a slight change, is from the promise of the Lord: "For as the rain and the snow come down from heaven, and return not thither but water the earth, making it bring forth and sprout, giving *seed to the sower and bread to the eater*, so shall my word be that goes forth from my mouth; it shall not return to me empty, but it shall accomplish that which I purpose, and prosper in the thing for which I sent it" (55:10–11). Thus it can be seen that in the OT context the main message of the text is about God's powerful, effective word, which will make all his promises come true. The very phrase quoted by Paul is a supporting example within the promise, showing the inevitable consequences of God's provision through the forces of nature: rain brings forth fruit; it brings forth grain and eventually provides bread. The rest of the chapter continues God's promises: the people will "go out in joy" (55:12–13).

C. The Context in Judaism. The idea of a willing and joyful giving (including almsgiving) is widespread in Judaism. See, for example, *Lev. Rab.* 34:8 (131b: "When a man gives alms, let him do so with a joyful heart"; cf. also *m. 'Abot* 5:13); Sir. 4:1–10 (see Martin 1986: 290; see also the references in Str-B 3:525 for "late rabbinic usage" concerning almsgiving [Furnish 1984: 448]). The OT verses referred to by Paul in 9:6–10 do not seem to be quoted in the Dead Sea Scrolls.

D. Textual Matters. Paul quotes only a few phrases from Prov. 22:8. The LXX text reads, "He who sows evil things will reap bad things" (*ho speirōn phaula therisei kaka*). Paul writes in 9:6, "The point is this: he who sows sparingly will also reap sparingly [*ho speirōn pheidomenōs pheidomenōs kai therisei*], and he who sows bountifully will also reap bountifully." In the second half of Paul's parallelism "bountifully" is *ep' eulogiais* in the Greek, which can be rendered as "with blessings" (Martin 1986: 289). The same *eulog-* root is used in the LXX's addition to Prov. 22:8 (referred to by Paul): *andra hilaron kai dotēn eulogei ho theos* ("God blesses a cheerful man and a giver") (see Kruse 1987: 165). Paul uses *agapa* ("loves") (cf. Wis. 7:28: "For God loves nothing so much as the man who lives with wisdom"; see Martin 1986: 290) where the

LXX has *eulogei* ("blesses") (Thrall [1994–2000: 2:576] notes, "It may be that he is quoting from memory, or perhaps from a version of the Greek text different from that of the LXX"). Paul omits *andra* ("man"), thus *hilaron* ("cheerful") becomes the adjective of *dotēn* ("giver"): *hilaron gar dotēn agapa ho theos*. Martin (1986: 290) rightly emphasizes that the order of words in the Greek should be kept in the translation: "It is the cheerful giver whom God loves."

In 9:9 Paul quotes Ps. 111:9 LXX (112:9 MT/ET) in exactly the same words: *eskorpisen, edōken tois penēsin, hē dikaiosynē autou menei eis ton aiōna* ("He has distributed freely, he has given to the poor; his righteousness endures for ever" [Paul's quotation of this same Greek text in 2 Cor. 9:9 is translated differently in the RSV: "He scatters abroad, he gives to the poor; his righteousness endures for ever"]). In between the references to Proverbs and Isaiah (which are not marked as quotations by Paul), the quotation from Ps. 111:9 LXX is introduced by the same formula that Paul used at 8:15: "as it is written" (*kathōs gegraptai*).

The part of Isa. 55:10 quoted by Paul runs like this: "giving seed to the sower and bread to the eater" (*dō sperma tō speironti kai arton eis brōsin*). Paul writes, with a slight change, "He who supplies seed to the sower and bread for food . . ." (*ho de epichorēgōn sporon tō speironti kai arton eis brōsin*). Some commentators see a reference to Hos. 10:12 ("Sow for yourselves righteousness") after the reference to Isa. 55:10 because of Paul's reference to "justification" (*dikaiosynē*) in 9:10 (so, e.g., Lang 1986: 325; Martin 1986: 291; Furnish 1984: 449). This may be so, but *dikaiosynē* occurs in the Pauline quotation from the psalm in the previous verse (9:9), and this may be enough to account for its presence in 9:10 as well: "He who supplies seed to the sower and bread for food will supply and multiply your resources and increase the harvest of your righteousness."

E. Paul's Use of the OT in 2 Cor. 9:6–10. Paul makes use of three different books of the OT: he takes over short phrases from Proverbs and Isaiah that he includes in his own sentences (these are not marked as quotations in UBS[4], nor does Ellis [1957: 178] list them as such), and between these two Paul quotes a whole sentence from a psalm, introduced by a formula. The OT quotations support Paul's request that the Corinthians

be willing to offer generous financial help to the poor "saints" in Jerusalem (see also 9:1, 12, where they are called *hagioi*). By way of an analogical employment of the three OT texts, Paul is saying that just as God exhorted the Israelites to be generous givers, so also the new covenant community of the Corinthians is being exhorted. We cannot know whether the Corinthians recognized the unmarked OT references. They must have understood from the psalm, clearly marked as a quotation, that it is God's will that the righteous openheartedly provide for others (so Matera [2003: 208], who puts it this way: "From start to finish, then, the collection is God's work"). It is important that Paul uses Scripture as authority to support his own request in a matter among Christian congregations.

F. Theological Use. It is significant that already the OT texts connected righteous living with the willingness to provide for the poor (so in Ps. 112). Thrall (1994–2000: 2:580–83) argues that Paul uses "righteousness" here in the sense of the psalm quotation: "The acts of the righteous man continue throughout his life." However, Garland (1999: 410) argues that both the psalm and Paul refer to "God's righteousness" enduring forever; Paul's point here is that "charity comes from God." Furnish (1984: 448) combines the two possibilities by holding that Paul knew that his quotation is "a description of the pious man" in the psalm; however, "*his righteousness* could be a reference to that divine righteousness by which one is held fast in God's covenant." In either case (and in their combination as well), the quotations from the OT serve to highlight the unity of the church, where those who have more can see this abundance as God's blessing. God provides for his people, and his provision is enough for everyone (see Grässer 2002–2005: 2:60). There may perhaps even be a warning in the background that if the Corinthians keep everything to themselves, they will lose their surplus, just as the manna could not be kept for the following day (so Best 1987: 80).

God's provision leads to a certain equality in the church: the members should help each other. This idea is expressed by Paul (probably referring to spiritual gifts as well) in 9:8, the very verse that occurs between the OT quotations: "And God is able to provide you with every blessing in abundance, so that you may always have enough of everything and may provide in abundance for every good work." As Paul notes in 9:13, this mutual care in the church is for the glory of God (see Furnish 1984: 451).

10:17

A. NT Context: Boasting in the Lord. In 1 Cor. 1:31 Paul introduces the same sentence that he has in 2 Cor. 10:17, using the usual formula: "Therefore, as it is written, 'Let him who boasts, boast of the Lord'" (the Greek text of 2 Cor. 10:17 has an additional word, *de* ["but"], which often is left untranslated). Although 2 Cor. 10:17 does not have the introductory formula, we should regard it as an OT quotation here as well (the "quotation" is in fact a new, short sentence formed from elements contained in a longer verse in Jeremiah).

There is a change in Paul's tone and in his attitude to his readers in chapters 10–13 compared to that of chapters 1–9: Paul defends himself even more in the latter part of the epistle than in the earlier. Some scholars argue that chapters 10–13 were written before chapters 1–9 (e.g., as part of the "painful letter"; for a detailed discussion of the various proposals, see Thrall 1994–2000: 1:5–20). Here I follow the view that a long letter such as 2 Corinthians may have been written with intervals in the process of writing; thus Paul may have received news from Corinth that caused him to change his tone of writing from chapter 10 onward (so, e.g., Carson, Moo, and Morris 1992: 271–72; Furnish [1984: 454] regards chaps. 10–13 as "the last of the five letters" that Paul wrote to the Corinthians, and thus he calls this section "Letter E").

In chapter 10 Paul defends himself against some people in Corinth who think that he leads his way of life "according to the flesh" (*kata sarka* [10:2]). The weapons of Paul's warfare are not according to the flesh (*ou sarkika* [10:4]); his aim is to "take every thought captive to obey Christ" (10:5). From 10:8 onward Paul repeatedly refers to "boasting." In 10:8 he says that he boasts with the authority that God gave him for upbuilding the Corinthians, not for destroying them. In 10:10 he quotes those who say that his letters are strong, but his speech is "of no account." Some people "commend themselves," but "they measure themselves by one another" (10:12). In 10:13 Paul says, "But we will not boast beyond limit, but will keep to the limits God has apportioned

us, to reach even to you." Then Paul says that he does not want to work in the field of others, but only in fields that God has apportioned to him (10:14–15), so that he can reach out even beyond the Corinthians, yet "without boasting of work already done in another's field" (10:16) (for Paul's intention "to go to Rome and then on to Spain," see Rom. 15:24 [Garland 1999: 456]; it is generally held that Paul wrote Romans from Corinth). Then 10:17 contains the sentence that is a quotation (according to 1 Cor. 3:31): "Let him who boasts, boast of the Lord." The final verse of the chapter, 10:18, sums up the message of the preceding quotation as well: only those are accepted "whom the Lord commends" (see Matera 2003: 236; Garland 1999: 457).

B. OT Context. The phrases quoted by Paul in 10:17 come from Jer. 9:24 (9:23 LXX): "But let him who glories glory in this, that he understands and knows me, that I am the LORD who practices steadfast love, justice, and righteousness in the earth; for in these things I delight, says the LORD" (Grässer [2002–2005: 2:108] leaves open the question of whether this verse or 1 Kgdms. 2:10 is quoted here, the latter differing from 1 Sam. 2:10 MT by a long addition quite similar in content to Jer. 9:22–23 LXX). Jeremiah 9 is a lamentation of the prophet concerning the way of life of his people, because "they proceed from evil to evil" (9:3). Even the Lord warns them with words of judgment: "Shall I not punish them for these things? says the LORD; and shall I not avenge myself on a nation such as this?" (9:9). The judgments continue in 9:13–15, and they even include the scattering of God's people among the nations (9:16). The Lord calls up women to teach their daughters "a lament" because of their dead (9:20–22). Then the Lord first warns the people against inappropriate boasting: "Thus says the LORD: 'Let not the wise man glory in his wisdom, let not the mighty man glory in his might, let not the rich man glory in his riches'" (9:23). Then in 9:24 (9:23 LXX) he says that those who "glory" (*kauchaomai*, the same Greek word used by Paul, translated in the NT as "boasting") should glory in that they know that their Lord is such a Lord who practices love, justice, and righteousness, as quoted above. The last two verses of the chapter address the uncircumcised nations as well as Israel, who is uncircumcised in heart (9:25–26).

C. The Context in Judaism. Jeremiah 9:24 (9:23 MT/LXX) does not seem to play an important role in intertestamental Judaism. For example, chapter 9 of the book is not quoted in the Qumran documents (but there are copies of Jeremiah as a biblical book among the Dead Sea Scrolls, with more than one text type [see Maier 1995–1996: 3:172]). The idea of boasting ("glorying") "in the fear of the Lord" occurs also in Sir. 9:16; 10:22; 25:6 (see Furnish 1984: 474).

D. Textual Matters. Jeremiah 9:23 LXX has only a short phrase used by Paul (an imperative and a participle of the same root): "Let him who boasts, boast . . ." (*kauchasthō ho kauchōmenos*). Paul writes in 10:17, *ho de kauchōmenos en kyriō kauchasthō.* The OT text does not say that one should boast *en kyriō* (lit., "in the Lord," or as the RSV translates it, "of the Lord"), but rather that one should boast "in this" (*en toutō*), that one understands and knows the Lord. The Greek term for "Lord," *kyrios,* occurs twice in the Greek text of Jer. 9:23. Thus Paul conflates a new sentence from elements of the Jeremiah passage (see also, in the present volume, §D of Rosner and Ciampa's commentary on 1 Cor. 1:31, where Paul has *ho kauchōmenos en kyriō kauchasthō*).

E. Paul's Use of the OT in 2 Cor. 10:17. Paul's sentence is a "reformulation" of Jer. 9:23 LXX, and it is not marked here as a quotation; however, as Thrall (1994–2000: 2:652) points out, since the same sentence is introduced in 1 Cor. 1:31 by "as it is written," the Corinthians "might be expected to remember this" (Furnish [1984: 474] calls it a "free adaptation of a LXX text"; see also Garland 1999: 457). Paul uses the OT here as a *testimonium* (Martin 1986: 317). The aim of the quotation is "to confirm" the only "legitimate form of boasting"; as Best (1987: 99) puts it, "If it has to be, it should be about the Lord (v. 17)" (so also Furnish [1984: 482]: Paul's quotation is "a reminder that faith's only true boast is in Christ" [cf. Phil. 3:3]).

F. Theological Use. It is important to see that the content of the OT quotation in 10:17 is "explicitly substantiated" (Thrall 1994–2000: 2:653 [see also Lang 1986: 334; Grässer 2002–2005: 2:108]) in 10:18, immediately following the quotation: "For it is not the man who commends himself that is accepted, but the man whom the Lord commends" (cf. 1 Thess. 2:4; see Matera 2003:

236). In this last verse of the chapter the "Lord" must be the "exalted Jesus" (Martin 1986: 325; see also Grässer 2002–2005: 2:108). It is Christ who commends also Paul's apostleship through the Spirit, who founded the Corinthian congregation by means of the evangelistic work of Paul (see Thrall 1994–2000: 2:653; Lang 1986: 334), whereas the Corinthians "recommend themselves" (1 Cor. 9:1–2; 2 Cor. 3:1–3; cf. 2 Cor. 10:12; see Martin 1986: 318; Grässer 2002–2005: 2:108). Since in the quotation in 10:17 the term "Lord" (*kyrios*) is the translation of the "divine name" (Martin 1986: 325), we can affirm that Paul uses the OT quotation with a christological application: a text about the Lord, Yahweh, is applied to the Lord Jesus Christ. This is also confirmed by the other occurrence of this OT quotation, at 1 Cor. 1:31, where Christ is referred to in the previous verse, "and one would expect the same application of the term here" (Thrall 1994–2000: 2:653).

13:1

A. NT Context: Paul's Visits as Warnings. In chapter 12 Paul tells the Corinthians that he does not want to boast; he "boasts" only of his weakness—for example, the "thorn" in his body (12:1–10). The Corinthians should have commended Paul, but now he has to remind them of the signs of his apostleship (12:11–12). He says in 12:14 that he is willing to go to them the third time (this theme is mentioned also in 13:1, where the OT quotation occurs [see Grässer 2002–2005: 2:245]). Paul reminds the Corinthians that he did not take advantage of them and did not burden them (12:16–19). If he visits them, he has to point out their sins, some of which he even lists in the final two verses of the chapter (12:20–21). The OT quotation occurs in the first verse of chapter 13: "This is the third time I am coming to you. Any charge must be sustained by the evidence of two or three witnesses." Then in 13:2 Paul probably refers to his second visit, which may suggest that the "two or three witnesses" in the quotation in 13:1 were his own visits to the Corinthians, during which he had to warn them repeatedly: "I warned those who sinned before and all the others, and I warn them now while absent, as I did when present on my second visit, that if I come again I will not spare them" ("visit" is added in the translation; the Greek text has *hōs* *parōn to deuteron,* "when present on the second [occasion]"). In the remaining verses of this last chapter of 2 Corinthians Paul appeals in different ways to the Corinthians that they should "mend their ways" (see, e.g., 13:11) and greets them with brotherly feelings.

B. OT Context. The quotation in 13:1 is taken from Deut. 19:15: "A single witness shall not prevail against a man for any crime or for any wrong in connection with any offense that he has committed; only on the evidence of two witnesses, or of three witnesses, shall a charge be sustained." This verse from Deuteronomy comes in the context of commandments about how the people must conduct their lives in the promised land. There is a section on the establishing of three cities to which people can flee who committed unintentional manslaughter (19:2–10). Then the law deals with those who sin against one another out of hatred (19:11–13). In 19:14 the law orders that one must not remove the landmark at a neighbor's border. After the commandment in 19:15 concerning the necessity of two or three witnesses at any charge comes the prescription of punishment for malicious witnesses, once the various parties have been heard, and it has been established that there was a false witness (19:16–21): the harm that the false witness intended for the unjustly accused person shall instead be meted out to the false witness (19:19).

C. The Context in Judaism. The OT emphasizes the necessity of more than one witness in a case elsewhere, but not in exactly the same words quoted by Paul in 13:1 (see, e.g., Num. 35:30; Deut. 17:6; and for the practice, see 1 Kings 21:10, 13). The Deuteronomic ruling appears in more than one NT writing: in Matt. 18:16, where Jesus is reported to quote Deut. 19:15, and in allusions to the ruling in John 8:17; Heb. 10:28 (for the practice, see 1 Tim. 5:19). In the Judaism before Paul's time, CD-A IX, 17–23; 1QS VI, 1, 25–26 may be evidence for the ruling (see Thrall 1994–2000: 2:873; see also the earlier monograph by van Vliet [1958, esp. 54] on the adoption of Deut. 19:15 into the NT; Best 1987: 128). For rabbinic texts exemplifying this ruling, see the references in Str-B 1:790 (see also Grässer 2002–2005: 2:245).

D. Textual Matters. Paul shortens the LXX text of the clause from which he quotes, omit-

ting the repetition of the words for "mouth" and "witnesses" in the case of the "three" witnesses (by metonymy, "mouth" stands for "utterance" and thus for "evidence" [see Matera 2003: 303]). The MT has the longer wording too (a similar shortened version of this OT commandment is quoted in Matt. 18:16). The fuller LXX text runs as follows: *epi stomatos dyo martyrōn kai epi stomatos triōn martyrōn stathēsetai pan rhēma* (Furnish [1984: 569] notes that the meaning of *rhēma* ["word"] "derives from the context"; thus here it may mean "charge" or "matter"). Paul cites the LXX text "in a slightly abbreviated form" (Garland 1999: 540): *epi stomatos dyo martyrōn kai triōn stathēsetai pan rhēma.* Furnish (1984: 569) argues that even Paul's shorter text must mean "two *or* three witnesses," since the longer OT version requires this translation of *kai* (it was understood thus in Matt. 18:16, whose Greek text has the conjunction *ē* ["or"]; cf. the Greek text of 1 Tim. 5:19).

E. Paul's Use of the OT in 2 Cor. 13:1. Scholars discuss whether "the two or three witnesses" in Paul's quotation should be understood as real witnesses whom he would call to testify when he arrives in Corinth and begins a legal proceeding in the congregation (e.g., Garland [1999: 541], who holds that "Paul will take disciplinary action" on his third visit). Although in the OT context it is clear that the witnesses are real persons (see Kruse 1987: 217), it is unlikely that Paul intended to ask "the members of the Corinthian church to testify against each other" (Thrall 1994–2000: 2:874; however, Garland [1999: 541] would respond that Titus, Timothy, and "even God" can be Paul's witnesses). Some scholars follow the earlier proposal of Bultmann (e.g., Lang 1986: 356) that the witnesses in Paul's application are actually the warnings that he made during his visits in person and in his "painful letter" (so also Matera 2003: 306).

Thrall (1994–2000: 2:876) argues that there is no need to combine visits with letters as a solution. It is more likely that just as "the third time" (*triton*) in 13:1a refers to a visit, so too "the second time" (*to deuteron*) in 13:2 refers to a visit, and these numbers relate to the "two or three witnesses" in the quotation. Concerning the first visit being a witness, Thrall (1994–2000: 2:876) rightly observes that "Paul may well have given his converts warning against slipping back into the heathen vices which he lists in 1 Cor 6.9–10." It seems to be true, then, that "Paul intends his three visits to be understood as the equivalent of three witnesses" (Best 1987: 128). Martin (1986: 470) argues that Paul wanted to say that he offered "ample warning," and the actual numbers of the witnesses do not have to be identified with the visits. This may be so, but even if we accept that the witnesses are the visits, we have to see that on the occasion of the visits Paul issued warnings. The three visits are witnesses in the sense that the Corinthians were warned about the consequences of an immoral lifestyle. Thus Paul uses the idea of "witnesses" in the OT quotation metaphorically (so also Thrall [1994–2000: 2:875], who notes that it is therefore "not relevant" that in this case Paul himself is the only witness and that "his occasions of witness are separated in point of time"; cf. Grässer [2002–2005: 2:247], who speaks of a "very loose" connection between the OT text and its application here). The quotation in the letter "gives an added note of seriousness" to Paul's announcement of his visit, upon which he "intends to settle matters once and for all" with the Corinthians (Matera 2003: 305).

F. Theological Use. The aforementioned NT attestations likely indicate that the early church adhered to the Deuteronomic ruling about the requirement of witnesses (see Thrall 1994–2000: 2:873). From the Pauline usage here we can see that the witnessing did not have to require formal legal proceedings, and it could refer to the warnings given by Paul during his personal visits (see Matera 2003: 305). Thus we can say that it was important for Paul to warn the Corinthians "that sinners will be punished" (cf. 12:20); the aim of the OT quotation is "to add force" to this claim (Thrall 1994–2000: 2:876). The OT serves here not only as an authority, but also as a guideline in dealing with ethical issues in the Christian community. After the quotation Paul draws the consequences (under the basis of his metaphorical reading) of the OT ruling: it is through repeated warnings that he wants to change the Corinthians way of life (cf. 13:2–7; see Martin 1986: 471).

Bibliography

Beale, G. K. 1989. "The Old Testament Background of Reconciliation in 2 Corinthians 5–7 and Its Bearing on the Literary Problem of 2 Corinthians 6.14–7.1." *NTS* 35: 550–81.

Belleville, L. L. 1991. *Reflections of Glory: Paul's Polemical Use of the Moses-Doxa Tradition in 2 Corinthians 3.1–18*. JSNTSup 52. Sheffield: Sheffield Academic Press.

Best, E. 1987. *Second Corinthians*. IBC. Atlanta: John Knox.

Blenkinsopp, J. 2002. *Isaiah 40–55*. AB 19A. New York: Doubleday.

Bratcher, R. G. 1987. *Old Testament Quotations in the New Testament*. 3rd ed. New York: United Bible Societies.

Bultmann, R. 1976. *Der zweite Brief an die Korinther*. Edited by E. Dinkler. KEK. Göttingen: Vandenhoeck & Ruprecht.

Carson, D. A., D. J. Moo, and L. Morris. 1992. *An Introduction to the New Testament*. Leicester: Inter-Varsity; Grand Rapids: Zondervan.

Casciaro, J. M., et al., eds. 1991. *St Paul's Epistles to the Corinthians*. Translated by M. Adams. Navarre Bible. Blackrock, Ireland: Four Courts Press.

Dahood, M. 1970. *Psalms 101–150, with an Appendix, "The Grammar of the Psalms."* AB 17A. Garden City, NY: Doubleday.

Ellis, E. E. 1957. *Paul's Use of the Old Testament*. Edinburgh: Oliver & Boyd.

Furnish, V. P. 1984. *II Corinthians*. AB 32A. New York: Doubleday.

García Martínez, F., ed. 1994. *The Dead Sea Scrolls Translated: The Qumran Texts in English*. Translated by W. G. E. Watson. Leiden: Brill.

Garland, D. E. 1999. *2 Corinthians*. NAC. Nashville: Broadman & Holman.

Grässer, E. 2002–2005. *Der zweite Brief and die Korinther*. 2 vols. ÖTK 8/1–2. Gütersloh: Gütersloher Verlagshaus; Würzburg: Echter.

Grindheim, S. 2001. "The Law Kills but the Gospel Gives Life: The Letter-Spirit Dualism in 2 Corinthians 3.5–18." *JSNT* 84: 97–115.

Hafemann, S. J. 1995. *Paul, Moses, and the History of Israel: The Letter/Spirit Contrast and the Argument from Scripture in 2 Corinthians 3*. WUNT 81. Tübingen: Mohr Siebeck.

Hübner, H. 1997. *Corpus Paulinum*. Vol. 2 of *Vetus Testamentum in Novo*. Göttingen: Vandenhoeck & Ruprecht.

Hughes, P. E. 1962. *Paul's Second Epistle to the Corinthians*. NICNT. Grand Rapids: Eerdmans.

Klauck, H.-J. 1987. "Erleuchtung und Verkündigung: Auslegungsskizze zu 2 Kor 4,1–6." Pages 267–316 in *Paolo, Ministro del Nuovo Testamento (2 Co 2,14–4,6)*. Edited by L. De Lorenzi. SMBen 9. Abbazia di S. Paolo, Rome: Benedictina Editrice.

Kruse, C. G. 1987. *The Second Epistle of Paul to the Corinthians*. TNTC. Leicester: Inter-Varsity.

Lambrecht, J. 1994. "The Favorable Time: A Study of 2 Corinthians 6,2a in Its Context." Pages 515–29 in *Studies on 2 Corinthians*. Edited by J. Lambrecht and R. Bieringer. BETL 112. Leuven: Leuven University Press.

Lang, F. 1986. *Die Briefe an die Korinther*. 16th ed. NTD 7. Göttingen: Vandenhoeck & Ruprecht.

Maier, J. 1995–1996. *Die Qumran-Essener: Die Texte vom Toten Meer*. 3 vols. Munich: Reinhardt.

Martin, R. P. 1986. *2 Corinthians*. WBC 40. Waco: Word.

Matera, F. J. 2003. *II Corinthians*. NTL. Louisville: Westminster John Knox.

Pilhofer, P. 1990. *Presbyteron Kreitton: Der Altersbeweis der jüdischen und christlichen Apologeten und seine Vorgeschichte*. WUNT 2/39. Tübingen: Mohr Siebeck.

Sampley, J. P. 2000. "The Second Letter to the Corinthians: Introduction, Commentary, and Reflections." Pages 1–180 in vol. 11 of *The New Interpreter's Bible*. Nashville: Abingdon.

Schröter, J. 1998. "Schriftauslegung und Hermeneutik in 2 Korinther 3: Ein Beitrag zur Frage der Schriftbenutzung des Paulus." *NovT* 40: 231–75.

Shires, H. M. 1974. *Finding the Old Testament in the New*. Philadelphia: Westminster.

Theissen, G. 1987. *Psychological Aspects of Pauline Theology*. Translated by J. P. Galvin. Philadelphia: Fortress.

Thrall, M. E. 1994–2000. *A Critical and Exegetical Commentary on the Second Epistle to the Corinthians*. 2 vols. ICC. Edinburgh: T&T Clark.

Toy, C. H. 1884. *Quotations in the New Testament*. New York: Scribner.

van Vliet, H. 1958. *No Single Testimony: A Study on the Adoption of the Law of Deut. 19:15 par. into the New Testament*. Utrecht: Kemink en Zoon.

Vermes, G. 1987. *The Dead Sea Scrolls in English*. 3rd ed. London: Penguin.

Vielhauer, P. 1979. *Oikodome: Aufsätze zum Neuen Testament*. Vol. 2. Edited by G. Klein. TB 65. Munich: Kaiser. [In this collection of essays, see esp. "Paulus und das Alte Testament," pp. 196–228.]

Wendland, H. D. 1963. *Die Briefe an die Korinther*. 9th ed. NTD 7. Göttingen: Vandenhoeck & Ruprecht.

Witherington, B., III. 1995. *Conflict and Community in Corinth: A Socio-Rhetorical Commentary on 1 and 2 Corinthians*. Grand Rapids: Eerdmans; Carlisle: Paternoster.

GALATIANS

Moisés Silva

Introduction

Any attempt to understand Paul's use of the OT in the letter to the Galatians requires a full appreciation of the distinctive qualities of this document. As is well known, Paul in Galatians places extraordinary emphasis on the divine origin—and therefore the legitimacy and independence—of his apostleship both in the opening (Gal. 1:1) and elsewhere in the letter (esp. 1:11–17; 2:6–9). A related matter is the unusual tone of this epistle: the typical expression of thanksgiving (or blessing in the case of 2 Cor. and Eph.), which occurs right after the opening in all of Paul's letters to the churches, is replaced in Galatians by an expression of astonishment at the turn of events in the conduct of his readers, followed by a uniquely occurring anathema (Gal. 1:6–9). Moreover, this letter as a whole, while not devoid of affection (e.g., 4:19–20; 6:1), is characterized by rebukes of a type not seen elsewhere (see esp. 3:1; 4:11, 16; 5:2–4, 7–12, 15).

The differences between Galatians and most of Paul's other letters extend to the matter of the apostle's use of the OT. With at least ten formal citations in six chapters, Galatians is second only to Romans, proportionately speaking, in its explicit appeals to Scripture (1 Cor. has some fifteen quotations, but this document is about three times as long: 437 verses as opposed to 149 in Gal.).

Is there a connection between this feature and the matters mentioned above? Undoubtedly. As a general rule, we can say that the apostle makes formal appeals to Scripture in polemical contexts, that is, when he needs to establish the validity of a point (usually doctrinal in nature) over against a contrary opinion—whether that opinion is held or only entertained either by the readers (cf. 1 Cor. 3:18–20) or by a third party that is likely to influence the readers (cf. Rom. 3:8–21). Galatians is easily the most urgent and polemical of Paul's epistles; moreover, the points in dispute focused on nothing less than "the truth of the gospel" (2:5, 14). Accordingly, his explicit dependence on the OT is pervasive, especially in the theological argument of chapters 3–4.

On the basis of these features, some scholars have suggested that Paul depended on the OT only when pressured and cornered by Jewish opponents, who argued that his teaching was a departure from the divine revelation already given in the Hebrew Scriptures. But this is precisely the wrong inference to draw, for Paul's *non*-explicit use of the OT shows how fundamental the Law and the Prophets were for his theological formulations. Interestingly, the first two chapters of Galatians contain no explicit scriptural citations (there is one probable exception [2:16], but even this one is debated). And yet it is immediately apparent that Paul's discussion in this part of the letter moves in the conceptual world of the OT and makes no sense apart from the latter. Indeed, Ciampa (1998) has devoted a substantial monograph to demonstrating *The Presence and Function of Scripture in Galatians 1 and 2*. His attempts to identify specific allusions and links may not always prove persuasive, but questions about individual instances hardly cast doubt on the thesis as a whole. In what follows, we shall look at two allusions in these chapters that are especially significant, then move on to the explicit OT references in the letter.

1:15–16a

In the first part of the body of Galatians, after describing his earlier commitment to Jewish tradition (1:13–14), Paul makes this remarkable statement: "But when he [*v.l.*, God] who separated me from my mother's womb [*ho aphorisas me ek koilias mētros mou*] and called me by his grace was pleased to reveal his Son in me, so that I might preach him among the Gentiles..." (1:15–16a). These words constitute a long subordinate clause that can be summarized briefly and simply as, "When God called me to serve him..." (then the clause in 1:16b–17 describes Paul's course of action upon receiving that call). We should not infer that this statement provides merely a temporal background and that the reference to the revelation he received is "incidental" (*contra* Corsani 1990: 96). The syntax does not necessarily tell us which is the most important conceptual constituent in a sentence.

The very length and complexity of the subordinate clause says something about its significance. Paul plainly wishes to make sure that the reader (or hearer) does not hasten over this passage and miss its point. The primary verbal idea within the subordinate clause ("God was pleased to reveal his Son in me") is clearly an allusion to the Damascus vision and expands on the last clause of 1:12 ("I received [the gospel] through a revelation of Jesus Christ"). The choice of the verb *eudokeō* ("delight in, be pleased, determine") highlights God's sovereign disposition and initiative (cf. 1 Cor. 1:21; 10:5; Col. 1:19; the noun *eudokia* has a similar force in Eph. 1:5, 9; Phil. 2:13), and this notion is reinforced by the verb *apokalyptō* ("reveal"), which refers to a distinctly divine action.

Note, however, that the subject of the verb *eudokē* is expressed by means of two participial phrases: (1) *ho aphorisas me* ("the one who set me apart"), which again calls attention to the divine initiative, further emphasized by means of the prepositional phrase *ek koilias mētros mou* ("from [the time when I was in] my mother's womb" [note the similar language in Isa. 44:2, 24]); (2) *kalesas dia tēs charitos autou* ("[the one] who called [me] by his grace"). Within the long subordinate clause of 1:15–16a this last phrase is the most specific component and thus the key to Paul's concern. Indeed, all the other verbal ideas in this passage may be viewed as illustrations or concretizations of God's gracious call. (It is no coincidence that the same language was used in 1:6 with reference to the Galatians' conversions. Thus the view that we should not speak of Paul's conversion, but only of his call, seems misguided. Although it is true enough that the apostle would not have viewed his Christian experience as a renunciation of his Hebrew faith, here he explicitly distances himself from his previous life and conduct "in Judaism" [1:13–14]. And by drawing a parallel with the Galatians' Christian call, he in effect recognizes a certain analogy between his "conversion" and that of Gentiles who abandon their pagan way of life to serve the living God.)

Our primary concern, however, is with the phrase "who set me apart from my mother's womb," the implications of which are possibly reflected in the way Paul speaks of Jacob and Esau in Rom. 9:11–12 ("Even before they had been born or had done anything good or bad, so that God's purpose of election might remain, namely, not by works but by his call..."). It can hardly be doubted that in Gal. 1:15–16a the apostle is alluding to Jer. 1:5 ("Before I formed you in the womb [*pro tou me plasai se en koilia*], I knew you; before you came out of the womb [*ek mētras*], I sanctified you; I appointed you as a prophet to the nations [*eis ethnē*]") and Isa. 49:1–6 ("Pay attention, you Gentiles... from my mother's womb he called my name [*ek koilias mētros mou ekalesen to onoma mou*]" [49:1]). In the latter passage the Servant is further told, "I have made you a covenant for a race, a light to the nations, that you may be my salvation to the end of the earth" (49:6 LXX, quoted in Acts 13:47). In the view of some scholars (e.g., Fung 1988: 64), the allusion to Isaiah indicates that Paul was selected to continue the work of the Servant (cf. Rom. 15:21). In any case, Paul must have seen his own ministry as integrally related to the work of the OT prophets, and in some sense even as its culmination. Now at last the message of salvation is breaking all national barriers. Light has fallen on the lands of the Gentiles, of whom the Galatians are part.

The significance of this allusion to the prophetic experience, therefore, lies not only in the support it gives to the immediate context—Paul's stress on God's gracious initiative—but also, more broadly, in the light that it sheds on the fundamental eschatological perspective that provides the theological structure for the argumentation of Galatians as a whole (see Silva 2001: 169–86). Some comments on this feature are necessary. In the opening of the letter Paul highlighted Christ's work of delivering us "from the present evil age" (*ek tou aiōnos tou enestōtos ponērou* [1:4]). Although the precise construction is unique, it is no doubt equivalent to the common Pauline phrase "this age" and its semantically related expression "this world" (cf. Rom. 12:2; 1 Cor. 1:20; 2:6, 8; 3:18–19; 5:10; 2 Cor. 4:4; Eph. 1:21; 2:2). The addition of the modifiers "present" and "evil" (note the detached, emphatic position of the latter) serves to highlight the eschatological force of Paul's concept, since it suggests an implicit contrast with some other, presumably future, age that is not present and not evil (see Bruce 1982: 76; Corsani 1990: 60–61; Cook 1992).

Moreover, for Paul to say that we are delivered from a *present* age assumes some kind of overlapping of the old and new ages. If believers, who still live in the present age, are rescued from it, this means that somehow they partake of both the present and the future. The same paradox is reflected in 2:20, where Paul concedes that he lives "in the flesh," even though one of the great concerns of the letter is to persuade the Galatians not to depend on or live according to the flesh, which has already been crucified (3:3; 4:29; 5:13–26). This eschatological thrust is of fundamental significance, since the Galatians' problem was to a large extent one of failing to understand the character of redemptive history (such as the law/covenant contrast and the concept of the fullness of time). Not surprisingly, this theme becomes prominent in the argument of chapters 3–4, particularly insofar as that argument depends on Paul's understanding of the OT and its relationship to the gospel.

2:6

In Paul's account of his meeting with the apostles in Jerusalem (2:1–10) he introduces in 2:6 the outcome of the conference by stating that the pillars of the church—James, Peter, and John (cf. 2:9)—"added nothing" (*ouden prosanethento*) to him; after all, "Whatever they were previously does not matter to me, [for] God shows no partiality" (*prosōpon ho theos anthrōpou ou lambanei* [lit., "God does not accept the face of a man"]). The latter phrase is a "loan translation" of the corresponding Hebrew expression, as in Lev. 19:15, where we find the instruction *lōʾ-tiśśāʾ pĕnê-dāl wĕlōʾ tehdar pĕnê gādôl* (lit., "You shall not lift the face of a poor one, and you shall not honor the face of a great one"; i.e., "Do not be partial to the poor, and do not defer to the great"), which the LXX renders, *ou lēmpsē prosōpon ptōchou oude thaumaseis* ["admire"] *prosōpon dynastou* (on loan translation as a type of lexical borrowing, see Silva 1994: 86–88). That God himself is impartial in his dealings derives specifically from Deut. 10:17 LXX, *ou thaumazei prosōpon* (Sir. 35:13 [35:16 ET] uses *lēmpsetai*), although, of course, this truth is reflected throughout the OT.

Given the polemical character of the epistle as a whole, and of this section in particular, one is not surprised that Paul first summarizes the results of the meeting with a strong negative statement. The emphatic position of the personal pronoun *emoi* ("to me") in the last clause of 2:6 almost suggests, "The leaders may have imposed their authority on others, but that certainly was not true in my case." As in the other negative statements throughout the letter, so also here Paul may be responding to, or at least anticipating, an accusation. Was it true that he was given instructions by the Jerusalem leaders and that therefore the validity of his apostleship was in some sense dependent on their supervision? Paul's unequivocal answer is that the three pillars did not in any way encroach on his distinctive ministry and message.

Perhaps as significant as the negative clause in 2:6c ("they added nothing to me") is the tortuous road that Paul takes to get there. The verse as a whole is a striking example of anacoluthon, for the prepositional phrase in 2:6a ("from those who seemed to be something") begins a new sentence, and after an interruption (the parenthetical comment in 2:6b), the apostle concludes the sentence in a way that is grammatically inconsistent with its beginning. In other words, one would have expected Paul to say, "But from the reputable ones I received/was taught nothing." Instead, he stops in his tracks, writes two unrelated clauses (including the OT allusion), and then resumes the main idea with what is in effect a new sentence. Why such a convoluted form of expression? It is difficult to resist the inference that the apostle is "distracted between the fear of saying too much and the fear of saying too little. He must maintain his own independence, and yet he must not compromise the position of the Twelve. How can he justify himself without seeming to condemn them?" (Lightfoot 1898: 104 [cf. Lightfoot's oft-quoted words on p. 106: "The counsels of the Apostles of the Circumcision are the hidden rock on which the grammar of the sentence is wrecked"]).

The expression *hoi dokountes* ("those who seem [to be important]") acknowledges the high regard in which the Jerusalem apostles were held, but without suggesting that Paul owed any submission to their authority. Yet even this language might be interpreted as implying some kind of subservience, and thus the parenthetical material in 2:6b, with its indirect appeal to Scripture, is intended to remove any doubts about that. One need not infer that Paul saw no value or advantage whatever in the disciples' having received personal instruction from Jesus during his earthly ministry. The question here, however, is the relevance of such an experience for determining "the truth of the gospel." When it comes to preserving the freedom that believers have in Christ, neither status nor previous accomplishment matters at all. The apostle then justifies his assertion by stating the fundamental biblical truth that God is impartial. The use of the expression in the present context is rather unexpected, and it demonstrates the ease with which Paul can take a general OT principle and apply it to situations far removed from its initial articulation. In any case, the apostle's point is obvious: "God does not pay attention to human status, so neither should you as you seek to determine the truth."

2:16

The Function of Gal. 2:15–21. The first two chapters of Galatians (or at least 1:6–2:14) have

often been described as autobiographical in character and contrasted to the doctrinal material in chapters 3–4. Sharp distinctions of this sort can be misleading, and one must appreciate that theology plays a significant role in the first major part of this letter. It remains true, however, that most of chapters 1–2 is written in the form of an apologetic narrative, while the initial articulation of Paul's theological thesis is found in the present paragraph, 2:15–21. Moreover, these verses function as a most effective transition to the argumentation of chapter 3. We would do well, therefore, to devote special attention to this passage, which has significant implications for our understanding not only of 2:16, but also of the other citations in the letter.

This whole paragraph is in fact the arena where some of the most fundamental questions of Pauline theology have to be fought. It is also a passage that bristles with exegetical problems, including difficult lexical questions (e.g., the meaning of "sinners" and of "works of the law") and puzzling syntactical issues (e.g., whether 2:17c negates the immediately preceding conclusion in 2:17b or the earlier premise in 2:17a). To help us get our bearings, we should first seek to identify the overarching concerns of the passage.

Paul himself gives us a clue by the two statements that bracket this section: 2:14 (esp. the last clause) and 2:21 (esp. the first clause). The former makes clear that the argument of 2:15–20 is intended to demonstrate the wrongfulness of any behavior (on the part of Peter and other Jewish Christians) that might coerce Gentile Christians to adopt a Jewish way of life. No less important is 2:21a: "I do not set [or, 'I am not setting'] aside the grace of God" (*ouk athetō tēn charin tou theou*). At first blush, these words sound like a response to some accusation, but what could that be? Burton (1921: 140) suggests that Paul's doctrine of grace over against law was understood by his opponents as "making of no account the special grace of God to Israel in giving them the law" (cf. Betz 1979: 126). But if so, the following sentence does not clearly substantiate his denial (one would need to supply several bridging thoughts to make the argument work). There is, however, a more attractive alternative, and that is to view 2:21a as an emphatic expression of Paul's resolve to uphold the grace through which he was called: "I am determined not to frustrate God's grace—as I would if I had failed to speak up" (cf. the paraphrase in Lightfoot 1898: 119). In any case, this verse clearly indicates that the *whole* passage must be understood as Paul's attempt (1) to guard the doctrine of grace (2) in opposition to a doctrine of "justification through law" (3) on the grounds that the latter renders Christ's death worthless.

The argument of the passage may be summarized as follows. First, Paul points out that he and Peter, along with all other Jewish Christians, by placing their faith in Jesus Christ, had acknowledged that the Jewish law was unable to make them right with God (2:15–16). Second, it follows that Jews no less than Gentiles are sinners, with nothing in themselves to commend them to God; Peter himself fully recognized this fact, for he was willing to relax the ceremonial laws and act like a "Gentile sinner" (2:17a). Third, Paul denies that this abandonment of Jewish observances makes the gospel of Christ an instrument of sin; quite the contrary, it would be a serious transgression if Paul, having set aside those observances through the gospel, were now to follow Peter's playacting and reinstate them (2:17b–18). Fourth, in one of the most profound statements in his letters, Paul asserts that it is the law itself, paradoxically, that has led him to this course of action (2:19). Fifth, the apostle makes crystal clear what has motivated him to speak so strongly: it is the value of the death of Christ, and therefore the principle of grace, that is at stake (2:20–21).

Exegetical Issues in Gal. 2:16. Before we can adequately address the quotation in 2:16, we must try to understand the problems raised by the verse as a whole. It should be noted that the first half of this statement (from *eidotes* ["knowing"] to *episteusamen* ["we believed"]) consists of a participial clause followed by a main clause. (The second half of the verse also consists of two clauses, one indicating purpose, the other providing a reason.) How should the participial clause be construed? Following virtually all commentators and versions, we should construe it with the main clause that follows. Specifically, the participle is taken as causal, while the *kai* introducing the main clause is understood as adverbial: "*since we know* that no one is justified by works of the law but through faith in Jesus Christ, *even we* [*kai hēmeis*] have believed in Christ Jesus, so that . . ." Accord-

ing to this view, 2:16 begins a new thought, which has a mild adversative or qualifying force. (For a different and unusual approach, see Dunn 1993: 131n2.)

It is also true, though, that 2:16 continues the argument begun in 2:15 by bringing in a second agreed-upon premise. The first premise was that Paul and Peter were Jews and did not fall into the category of (Gentile) sinners; the second is that (in spite of their being Jews) they decided that even they should place their faith in Christ. This second premise, however, includes the reason they made that decision: they had come to understand that faith in Christ was necessary because performing the deeds required by the Mosaic law—in other words, their Jewish identity and practice—does not bring about justification.

Unfortunately, the interpretation of the participial clause in 2:16 is complicated by several exegetical questions, two of which require comment. First, prior to the 1970s the construction *pistis Iēsou Christou* was almost universally understood to mean "faith in Jesus Christ" (the so-called objective genitive), but in recent decades many scholars have argued that it should be rendered "the faith/faithfulness of Jesus Christ" (subjective genitive). Elsewhere (Silva 2004: 227–34), I have attempted to show that the arguments usually advanced against the traditional interpretation are either irrelevant (e.g., some scholars point to the absence of *pistis* + objective genitive of a person in classical literature, but this absence is precisely what one would expect in documents that do not otherwise speak about the need for believing in a person) or based on an inadequate understanding of the objective genitive (e.g., that it is not natural, or that it does not apply in this case because *pisteuō* is construed with the dative or with a prepositional phrase). The ambiguity inherent in genitival constructions can be resolved only by examining unambiguous constructions in the immediate and broader contexts, preferably if they use the same or cognate terms. The NT as a whole, and Paul in particular, regularly and indisputably use both *pistis* and *pisteuō* of the individual's faith in God or Christ, but they never make unambiguous statements such as *episteusen Iēsous* ("Jesus believed") or *pistos estin Iēsous* ("Jesus is believing/faithful"). These and other considerations explain why the early fathers who spoke

Greek as their native tongue never seem to have entertained the idea that this genitival construction has Jesus Christ as the subject of the implied action.

Second, the meaning of another genitival phrase, *erga nomou* ("works of law"), is also disputed, but for different reasons. Does Paul have in view God's commands in general or only those (ceremonial) regulations—circumcision, dietary laws, calendrical observances—that served as "national badges" marking the Jewish people as separate from others? Since Paul first uses the phrase against the background of Peter's withdrawing himself from meal-fellowship with Gentiles, it is quite possible that the ceremonial elements of the law are in the forefront. It would be a mistake, however, to suggest that such elements are exclusively in view. As the apostle develops his argument (esp. in 3:15–25), it is patently clear that he speaks about the law as a whole. (For example, the initial statement that we cannot be justified by works of law is paralleled by the comment that the law is not able to give life [3:21], but the latter passage can hardly be restricted to dietary regulations.) A more important disagreement among scholars relates to the question of whether this phrase has a positive or a negative connotation. There is no reason to think that this particular combination of terms had an intrinsically negative meaning, and thus we cannot rule out the possibility that it may have been used (even by Paul himself) in positive contexts. But the point is moot with regard to Galatians, where the phrase is always used in semantic opposition to *pistis* (one cannot be justified by works of law [2:16]; such works come from the flesh rather than the Spirit [3:2, 5]; those who are characterized by such works are cursed [3:10]). This fact, however, does not necessarily mean that Paul views works of law as bad in themselves, nor does it solve the further question of whether he has in mind a "legalistic" attitude. We will return to this problem when examining the citations in 3:10–13.

The Quotation from Ps. 143. The matters we have looked at thus far have an important bearing on the OT quotation at 2:16, since the quoted words ("no flesh shall be justified by works of law") are given as the reason (*hoti* ["because"]; many manuscripts have the synonym *dioti*) for the statement "so that we may be justified by faith in Christ and not by works of law." To be sure, some scholars do not regard the words as a formal quotation, and that for two reasons.

First, the statement is not introduced by *gegraptai* ("it is written") or a comparable formula. By itself, however, this objection has little weight. Although Paul typically uses a more explicit introduction, his practice is hardly uniform, and the use of *hoti* certainly can signal a citation (as it does, e.g., at 3:11).

Second, and more important, there is only a partial correspondence between Galatians and the OT text, Ps. 143:2 (142:2 LXX). Paul writes, *hoti ex ergōn nomou ou dikaōthēsetai pasa sarx* (lit., "because out of works of law all flesh will not be justified"), whereas the Greek text of the psalm reads, *hoti ou dikaiōthēsetai enōpion sou pas zōn* ("because every living [being] will not be justified before you," itself a literal rendering of the Heb. *lōʾ-yiṣdaq lĕpānêykā kol-ḥāy*). However, Paul's use of *pasa sarx* instead of *pas zōn* is hardly surprising: the latter phrase occurs only in this psalm (though *pantōn tōn zōntōn* occurs in Gen. 3:20; Job 12:10, and *pasan sarka zōsan* in Gen. 8:21), whereas *pasa sarx*, which is used over twenty times in the OT, clearly became a common form of expression, occurring eight times in the NT, even when the OT is not being quoted (note also that the word *sarka* was inserted in Gen. 8:21 LXX, where the Heb. has simply *kol-ḥāy*; whether the change is also intended to focus the polemic on the act of circumcision [see Martyn 1997: 253] is difficult to determine). Moreover, Paul, in the parallel passage at Rom. 3:20, more fully reproduces the psalm text: *dioti ex ergōn nomou ou dikaōthēsetai pasa sarx enōpion autou* ("because out of works of law all flesh will not be justified before him"). Although some scholars (e.g., Koch 1986: 18) consider that both of these Pauline references are too loose to be regarded as citations, it seems futile to deny that the apostle is directly appealing to Ps. 143 as providing some kind of evidence for his doctrine of justification (it "is evidently intended to confirm what has been said by the authority of scripture" [Burton 1921: 123]).

But how, then, does one explain Paul's use of Ps. 143 when the crucial phrase "works of law" is absent there? This so-called penitential psalm is usually regarded as an individual lament. The psalmist is dismayed because of the persecution of the enemy (143:3–4), and so he spreads out his hands to God, who alone can save him (143:6). As he pleads with the Lord, however, he appeals not to his own innocence (contrast Ps. 7:8; 73:13) but rather to God's mercy, faithfulness, and righteousness (143:1). Indeed, he is cognizant of his sin and acknowledges that the divine judge can only pronounce him guilty: "Do not bring your servant into judgment" (143:2). This plea suggests that in the next clause, "for no one living is righteous before you," the psalmist is denying not the possibility of justification as such, but rather "the possibility of a man's being justified on the basis of his deserts" (Cranfield 1975–1979: 1:197). Burton (1921: 124) goes so far as to argue that the first part of the verse gives to the second part this meaning: "No man can be justified if judged on a basis of merit, all grace and mercy on God's part being excluded." He further claims that the addition of *erga nomou* is "a correct interpretative gloss. Indeed, the teaching of the apostle on this point is a re-exposition in clearer form of a doctrine already taught by the Hebrew prophets." Burton here is no doubt reading Ps. 143 through Pauline glasses, but the general thrust of his comments can be defended on the basis of the Hebrew text itself.

If the apostle is indeed quoting (or even alluding to) Ps. 143 as confirmation of his teaching, two important points follow. In the first place, this feature casts considerable doubt on the attempt to restrict "works of law" to ceremonial practices. The latter certainly form part of the background to Gal. 2:16, but it is evident that the psalmist was hardly thinking of national "badges" that distinguished him from the Gentiles. Paul's appeal to the psalm, then, confirms what the context of Gal. 2–3 strongly suggests: the apostle is thinking of the dietary regulations and circumcision as part and parcel of the broader concept of the law considered as a whole, and therefore "works of law" designates obedience to the commandments in toto. (Dunn [1993: 140] further suggests that Paul changed "living person" to "flesh" specifically because the latter is "the realm where outward and ethnic distinction is most clearly marked"; however, we have no evidence that the common idiom *pasa sarx*, which is emphatically universal in character, would have been understood as alluding to such a distinction.)

In the second place, the appeal to Ps. 143 lends to Paul's statement a distinctly eschatological force. This inference may come as a surprise, for in the traditional reading of Galatians the apostle's words are, as a matter of course (and not inappropriately), applied to the individual, and thus "subjective," experience of believers. Moreover, most writers are usually so preoccupied by the exegetical problems found in this verse that they tend to ignore the redemptive-historical bedrock on which it lies. Although the future form *dikaōthēsetai* could be understood as a generalizing use of the tense (see Lagrange 1925: 48), a reference to the future judgment is most likely (see Betz 1979: 119). For one thing, the phrasing in the psalm itself (both the Hebrew and the Greek) clearly indicates the finality of the divine judgment. Moreover, the context of Rom. 3:20 (if we may appeal to this parallel) undoubtedly has the final judgment in view (cf. 3:19; note also 2:5–16). In Galatians too Paul speaks of the reception of righteousness in future-eschatological terms (5:5).

To recognize the apocalyptic overtones of this clause, however, is not to undermine the traditional application of the verse, for in this very passage Paul is stressing the significance of faith for his own personal—yes, present—justification and that of his Jewish-Christian contemporaries. The point, nevertheless, is that this truth is set within the context of cosmic, eschatological realities. In other words, the "subjective" experience of justification is not divorced from the "objective" judgment at the end of the age. Quite the contrary, it is grounded in that final judgment, so that our sense of assurance (cf. 4:6–7) is not merely some psychological strategy that bypasses reality, but rather a proleptic manifestation of God's righteous verdict.

3:6–14

(The following material on 3:6–14 reproduces some parts of, but considerably expands, the appendix in Silva 2001 [which, however, contains some details not included here]. Individual articles on this passage are numerous. For an analysis of the OT citations here and elsewhere in Galatians, see the relevant sections in Ellis 1957; Koch 1986; Michel 1929; Stanley 1992; Verhoef 1979; Wakefield 2003; Wilk 1998; for a general discussion, see Silva 1993.) Before examining the individual quotations in this passage, we must look at the section as a whole and note its structure and coherence. Few portions in the Pauline literature have received as much attention as the four quotations in 3:10–14. Thus the numerous exegetical problems that we face here are compounded by the increasingly large number of attempts to solve them. In addition, however, most discussions of 3:10–14 seem to be developed in relative isolation from the immediately preceding paragraph, 3:6–9, which contains two more quotations (one important exception to this trend is Wakefield 2003: 132–37, who sees 3:6–14 as a chiasm). Without denying that 3:10 introduces a new thought, we should do justice to the function of the conjunction *gar* ("for") in that verse. (It is true that Paul can use *gar* as a simple transitional particle and thus without a clear and specific logical connection [Silva 2001: 82–83]. Such a use, however, is not typical, and in this particular case it is highly unlikely, as the discussion below should confirm.)

In any case, the sheer number of citations within such short compass—six of them in the course of seven or eight sentences—is worthy of note. A comparable density is found only in the catena of Rom. 3 and in the torrent of Rom. 9–10; moreover, the way the quotations are strung together in Gal. 3 has its own distinctiveness. The first two citations come from Genesis (15:6 and 12:3/18:18); the third and last are taken from Deuteronomy (27:26; 21:23); the fourth and fifth constitute the (in)famous coupling of Hab. 2:4 with Lev. 18:5. Notice, moreover, that both the initial statement (3:6) and the concluding comment (3:14) highlight the person of Abraham and the function of faith. Thus, while it is probably true that 3:10 begins a new paragraph, special attention should be given to the coherence of the larger section.

In fact, it is quite possible to lay out the structure of this section's argument by using the OT citations as the logical markers. As the following chart indicates, these quotations appear to provide the grounds for five different theses. It is also important to note, however, that in all four cases the logical connection is not at all obvious.

Thesis 1 (implied)
    [God gives you the Spirit by the hearing of faith]
  Grounds (v. 6)
    Abraham believed God, and [his faith] was reckoned to him for righteousness

Thesis 2 (vv. 7, 9)
    the ones who are of faith—these are sons of Abraham . . .
    the ones who are of faith are blessed with believing Abraham
  Grounds (v. 8)
    all the Gentiles will be blessed in you

Thesis 3 (v. 10a)
    as many as are of works of law are under a curse
  Grounds (v. 10b)
    cursed is everyone who does not remain in all the things written in the book of the law in order to do them
  [*Assumed premise:* all are disobedient (this point is disputed)]

Thesis 4 (v. 11a)
    through the law no one is justified before God
  Grounds (v. 11b)
    the righteous one will live by faith
  Stated premise (v. 12a)
    the law is not of faith
  Grounds for premise (v. 12b)
    the one who does them will live by them

Thesis 5 (v. 13a)
    Christ redeemed us from the curse of the law
    by becoming a curse for us
  Grounds (v. 13b)
    cursed is everyone who hangs on a tree

Conclusion (v. 14)
    in order that the blessing of Abraham might come to the Gentiles,
    so that we might receive the promise of the Spirit through faith

Note that the two purpose clauses of 3:14 bring the argument to its climax, and they do so by tying together six crucial concepts: Abraham (3:6–9), Christ (3:1, 13 [both of which mention the crucifixion]), the Gentiles (3:8), the promise/blessing (3:8–9), the reception of the Spirit (3:2, 5), and faith (3:2, 5, 6–9, 11–12). It is difficult not to be impressed, on the one hand, by the care and effectiveness with which these various themes have been interwoven and, on the other hand, by the glaring gaps in the argumentation.

The decision to look at this passage as consisting of five theses, each of which is supported by an OT citation, has certain advantages, though it can also obscure other features. For example, what I am calling the first thesis is much more than just one item (or even the most important item) out of several; in effect, Gen. 15:6 is intended to demonstrate the overarching burden of the whole passage (or even the whole chapter), and so it might be a more accurate representation to view the second through the fifth theses as subordinate arguments. In spite of these concerns, however, the proposed structure can prove useful. As long as we do not think of such an outline (or any other outline) as being right in some exclusive sense, it does highlight important logical elements and therefore can serve us well as a preliminary framework within which to understand Paul's use of Scripture.

3:6–9

The first and, as just noted, foundational quotation in this passage is the programmatic statement in Gen. 15:6 that Abraham's belief was credited to him (by God, surely) as righteousness (or justification). This citation functions not merely as supporting evidence; one can almost say that it takes on a life of its own. The mention of Abraham should not be thought of as an illustration that the writer would set aside once the point of comparison had been made (as perceptively pointed out by Koch 1986: 273). Quite the opposite. By introducing the figure of the patriarch, Paul grounds his argument in redemptive history, which becomes the dominant perspective through the end of chapter 4. To put it differently: the apostle's point is not simply that we should believe as Abraham believed (though that is true enough and critically important), but that those who believe become the recipients of the redemptive blessings associated with the patriarch.

Thus, after quoting Gen. 15:6, Paul does not return to the "experiential" argument that he articulated in 3:1–5. Rather, he (1) goes on to assert (in 3:7, 9) that believers are the true descendants and heirs of Abraham, supporting this statement with another citation (3:8); (2) brings up again the reception of the Abrahamic blessing at the conclusion of the next paragraph (3:14); (3) contrasts the Abrahamic covenant with the Sinaitic covenant (3:15–18), supporting this paragraph with a quotation regarding the seed of Abraham (3:16); (4) expands on the redemptive-historical significance of the Sinaitic covenant (3:19–25); (5) brings this part of the argument to a summation by emphasizing that the true children of God are made up of Abraham's seed (3:26–29); (6) recapitulates his argument on the basis of the history of salvation (4:1–7); and (7) after another appeal to the experience of the Galatians (4:8–20), con-

cludes the theological section of the letter with his tour-de-force appeal to the "free/slave" distinction in Abraham's two children (4:21–31), supporting this final paragraph with two more explicit quotations (4:27, 30).

In short, then, the initial quotation in 3:6 has the effect of pushing the subject matter of 3:1–5 (how did the Galatians receive the Spirit?) into the background. This move was needed because the Galatians' error was, at a fundamental level, historical-theological in character. Misguided regarding the place of the Sinaitic covenant in the plan of salvation, they were hoping for incorporation into the people of God (Abraham's descendants) through the wrong means (works of law). Once the apostle had patiently sorted out the theological issue, he could again address directly the initial question: it is through the Spirit and by faith that we eagerly await the hoped-for righteousness (5:5).

Both of the quotations regarding Abraham in 3:6–9 are relatively straightforward and present no serious problems. The words from Gen. 15:6 are reproduced exactly from the LXX (aside from switching the order of "Abraham" and "believed"), which in turn had translated the Hebrew fairly literally, except that (1) *theos* ("God," rather than *kyrios*, "Lord") renders the tetragrammaton, YHWH—not an uncommon variation in Genesis LXX and elsewhere; (2) the passive *kai elogisthē* ("and [it] was reckoned") renders an active verb plus suffix, *wayyaḥšĕbehā*, ("and he [God] reckoned it"), no doubt because a literal rendering might suggest that Abraham is the subject of the verb (see Wevers 1993: 206); and (3) the translator adds the preposition *eis* ("for"), which is a totally accurate way of representing the simpler Hebrew syntax (indeed, most English translations add "for" or "as"). In 3:8 ("all the Gentiles [nations] will be blessed in you") Paul combines Gen. 12:3, where Abraham is addressed directly (LXX: "all the tribes [Heb. 'families'] of the earth will be blessed in you"), with Gen. 18:18, which contains the crucial term *ethnē*, "nations" (LXX and Heb.: "all the nations of the earth will be blessed in him"). Here the apostle deliberately leaves out the phrase "of the earth" (found in both Genesis passages), an omission that helps to focus attention on the specific sense of *ta ethnē* as the non-Jewish nations, the Gentiles (see Koch 1986: 124, 162–63; Stanley 1992: 236–38).

Although one can hardly object to the very minor textual changes in the citations, it is still proper to ask whether Paul has faithfully used the scriptural passages. It has been suggested that in the Hebrew text the subject of the verb "he reckoned it" remains Abraham, meaning that the patriarch counted his own faith (*lô* ["to himself"]) as his righteousness (see Rottzoll 1994: 25–26). However, nothing in the context—which focuses on what God promises and performs— would lead the reader to think that the narrative is momentarily shifting attention to Abraham's self-assessment (in fact, such a concern with subjective reflection is quite foreign to the patriarchal narratives as a whole). There is, moreover, no hint that anyone in the biblical period or in early Judaism ever understood the text in this fashion.

As we noted earlier, however, Paul does apply the Genesis statement in a peculiar way, namely, as evidence that God supplies the Holy Spirit and works miracles through the hearing of faith rather than through the works of the law (see 3:5; cf. Rom. 4:9, where Paul's use of the same statement takes a different route; see Koch 1986: 221–26). The logic behind this argument apparently is built on three unstated assumptions.

First, Abraham's act of believing had to do with God's having promised him the miracle of a son. This assumption is a rather obvious one, but it is also the least prominent in Paul's argument, although the subject comes up again in 4:21–31.

Second, faith and works are, at least on some level, mutually exclusive categories, so if Abraham's being credited with righteousness came about through faith, it could not have come through the works of the law. The contrast between faith and works had, of course, been expressed previously (in 2:16, and in the rhetorical questions of 3:3, 5), but Paul here seems to assume that the presence of one indicates the absence of the other—hardly an obvious fact. The apostle thus needs to argue this principle, which he will do in 3:10–12. In addition, it is possible that he is already thinking in terms of Abraham's pre-Mosaic status: since the Sinaitic law had not yet been given, Abraham could not be subject to the works of the law (cf. 3:15–17 and also the argument in Rom. 4:9–12

that Abraham had been declared righteous prior to his receiving the covenant of circumcision).

Third, the Holy Spirit was at work in the life of Abraham. One could argue that this assumption is both the least obvious and the most significant for Paul's argument. Three of the rhetorical questions in 3:1–5 explicitly mention the Spirit. Indeed, the fundamental point of contention is, How did the Galatians receive the Spirit? And the evident answer is, By the hearing of faith, *just as* Abraham believed! Moreover, in 3:14 Paul will summarize the blessing of Abraham in terms of reception of "the promise of the Spirit" (i.e., the promised Spirit). It is noteworthy that Paul makes no effort to prove this point; indeed, the next explicit reference to the Holy Spirit is in the key statement of 4:6–7, and later he will, without any qualifications, refer to Isaac as having been born according to the Spirit (4:29). We must infer that the apostle did not anticipate objections to this link between the Spirit and Abraham—a link that is crucial for the legitimacy of his use of Gen. 15:6. Presumably, then, such a connection would have been generally acknowledged among the disputants (the rabbinic literature does contain a few references to the role of the Spirit in the lives of the patriarchs; cf. Ginzberg 1909–1938: vol. 7, s.v. "Holy Spirit"). It is still worth pointing out, however, that the Genesis narrative does not mention the Spirit, and that Paul himself does not even bother to spell out this fundamental premise. In other words, there is a substantial formal gap in his argumentation.

In addition, Paul needs to bring out the relevance of Gen. 15:6 for his non-Jewish readers, and that is the purpose of the next quotation. Note that in 3:7 he first draws a general inference emphasized through both the word order and the use of the pronoun *houtoi* ("these"): "the ones of faith [not necessarily the physical descendants]—*these* are the sons of Abraham." Then in 3:8 he introduces the quotation from Gen. 12:3/18:18 with some remarkable words: "Now the Scripture, foreseeing that God would justify the Gentiles by faith, announced the good news in advance [*proeuēngelisato*, "predeclared the gospel"] to Abraham." Several features here deserve attention. First, Paul in a unique way personifies the Scripture (*hē graphē*) by making it the subject of the verb "announced the good news";

and because the words from the Genesis texts are themselves a direct quotation of what God said to (and about) Abraham, it is plain that, as far as Paul is concerned, what Scripture says, God says (see Warfield 1899). Second, by using the verb *proeuangelizomai* (also unique to this passage), the apostle asserts the fundamental continuity between the Hebrew Scriptures and the gospel of God and his Son (see Rom. 1:1–3); the latter is truly the fulfillment of the former. Third, and most important, Paul identifies that gospel specifically as containing the message that the Gentiles are justified by faith. And although he does not actually say that the OT explicitly taught (but only that it foresaw) such a message, the conclusion is inescapable that the apostle viewed his doctrine of justification (the gospel of the uncircumcision [2:7]) not as an innovation in any sense, but rather as the revelation of a secret kept hidden for long ages (see Rom. 16:25–26; Eph. 3:2–6; Col. 1:25–27).

This understanding of Abraham's faith and the blessing given to him contrasts sharply with the views of Paul's contemporaries. Given the significance of the patriarch in the Genesis narrative, it is understandable that the figure of Abraham looms large in all expressions of Judaism. (For a readable synthesis of Jewish traditions about Abraham, see Ginzberg 1909–1938: 1:185–308; see also Str-B 3:186–201 [on Rom. 4:2]; Hansen 1989: 175–99; Oeming 1998: 27–30; Calvert Koyzis 2004.) And a major concern reflected in the literature is, of course, Abraham's faithfulness in the midst of trials. Interestingly, however, Gen. 15:6 does not play as prominent a role in that literature as one might expect. *Midrash Rabbah* on Genesis, a fifth-century homiletical commentary, has only a very brief paragraph on that verse: merely three sentences that say nothing about Abraham's act of believing or about his faith being counted as righteousness (*Gen. Rab.* 44:13). Moreover, a search for references to Gen 15:6 in the whole of *Midrash Rabbah* yields precious few instances (such as a passing comment in *Exod. Rab.* 3:12 [on Exod. 4:1] and a more significant use of the verse in 23:5 [on Exod. 15:1]; in a number of additional passages Abraham's righteousness is spoken of, sometimes at length). These rabbinic documents, to be sure, are not a precise reflection of Judaism during the Second Temple, but if Gen.

15:6 had played a significantly greater role during that period, it seems unlikely that the later rabbinic tradition would not have preserved it. (With regard to Gen. 12:3/18:18, one does find in Jewish literature considerable material on Abraham as recipient of and channel for God's blessing, but even here the contrast with Paul is especially striking. Whereas Paul highlights the significance of the promise for Gentiles, the midrashic tradition does not at all focus on this specific element of the Abrahamic promise.)

In any case, such allusions as there are to Gen. 15:6 in Jewish tradition are consistently tied to Abraham's faithful obedience, particularly as expressed in the Aqedah (the binding of Isaac), and one recurring concern in Jewish writings is to point out that Abraham obeyed the Torah even though it had not yet been given to the Israelites. This fact immediately suggests a difference between Judaism and Paul. As Hansen (1989: 99) puts it, "In contrast to the use of Abraham in much contemporary Jewish literature, Paul dissociates the Abrahamic promise and its blessing from the law and works of the law. This dissociation is designed to explode any attempt to use Abraham as an example for circumcision and law-observance."

Similarly, Garlington (1997: 94) points out that Paul places Abraham "in the same arena as the Gentiles" even though Abraham, having converted from paganism, "was the perfect model for the Jewish missionaries." He concludes, "It is just this un-Jewishness of Paul's use of Abraham that provides the bridge into his cursing of his opponents; that is, in the salvation-historical purposes of God, the paradigm of eschatological justification is provided not by the Torah, but by Abraham, who had nothing to do with the Torah."

3:10, 13

These two verses are best treated together not only because they share the combined lexical (and conceptual) elements "law" and "curse," but also because both verses quote from the book of Deuteronomy. In addition, it can be argued that these verses form an *inclusio* that brackets the paragraph (i.e., 3:10–14 [note that 3:13–14 forms one sentence]), though from another perspective 3:14 could be thought of as marking an *inclusio* with the larger section that begins at 3:6. Be that as it may, we need to keep in mind the tight contextual connection among the various quotations in 3:6–14. Our treatment of any one citation individually should not be allowed to obscure the logical integrity of Paul's argument as a whole.

Both of the quotations from Deuteronomy contain interesting variations, which are easily displayed through literal renderings in parallel fashion. (In the following translations italics in the LXX are used to highlight its differences from the MT, while italics in Gal. 3 highlight differences between Paul and the LXX. Note also, in the second set of translations, that strictly speaking, English "hanged" [rather than "hung," meaning "suspended"] would indicate a specific method of execution [hanging], but, as pointed out below, the biblical text reflects a different practice.)

> Deut. 27:26 MT: Accursed is the one who does not establish the words of this law to do them.
>
> Deut. 27:26 LXX: Accursed is *every man* who does not *remain* in *all* the words of this law to do them.
>
> Gal. 3:10: Accursed is every*one* who does not remain in all the *things written in the book of the* law to do them.
>
> Deut. 21:23 MT: A curse of God is one hung [on a tree].
>
> Deut. 21:23 LXX: Cursed *by* God is everyone being hung on a tree.
>
> Gal. 3:13: *Accursed* [—] is everyone *who is* being hung on a tree.

How much significance should we attach to these variations? (Although one must keep open the possibility that Paul might have used a Greek translation other than what has come down to us as the LXX, that explanation will not work for the differences in these verses. Some Greek manuscripts of Deuteronomy agree with Paul in a couple of these variations, but the likelihood is great that the LXX scribes were influenced by NT manuscripts. On this general question, see Jobes and Silva 2000: 189–93.) Some of the differences can be set aside quickly. For example, in 3:13 nothing should be made of Paul's "who is" (my attempt to represent in English the mere addition of the Greek definite article *ho*) or of his use of the adjective *epikataratos* (rather than the LXX's perfect participle, *kekatēramenos*, rendering

Heb. *qilĕlat*, construct of *qĕlālâ*); both of these are stylistic changes that have no semantic implications, though the latter serves to tie together the two verses of Deuteronomy more explicitly, thus indicating that both refer to the same curse (LXX uses *epikataratos* in Deut. 27:26, rendering Heb. *ārûr*). In Deut. 21:23 LXX the phrase "cursed by God" (*kekatēramenos hypo theou* [Aquila and Theodotion, more literally: *katara theou kremamenos*]) is a defensible representation of the Hebrew construction (*qilĕlat 'ĕlōhîm* [however, the NJPS translates it as "an affront to God"]), while the addition of "everyone" and "on a tree" simply makes explicit what is implicit in the Hebrew (note that the NIV and the NRSV make comparable additions in Deuteronomy).

In Deut. 27:26 the LXX appears to take greater liberties: it makes the statement more emphatic by adding *pas* (meaning "all, every"), and doing so twice (in the first instance the addition consists of *pas anthrōpos* ["every man"]); moreover, it renders the Hebrew verb *qûm*, which in the Hiphil means "set up, raise up, establish," with the Greek verb *emmenō*, meaning "abide in, abide by, stand by, be true to." Even these variations, however, cannot be said to change the meaning of the text. With regard to the latter, it should be noted that the Hebrew verb *qûm*, when used of promises or intentions, can be rendered "confirm, uphold, accomplish, fulfill, be true to" (e.g., Deut. 9:5; 1 Sam. 3:12), which corresponds rather closely to the metaphorical uses of Greek *emmenō* (see esp. its use with *tois nomois* ["the laws"] and in parallel with *peithō* ["obey"] in Xenophon, *Mem.* 4.4.16). As for the twofold addition of *pas*, we could again argue that such a rendering gives expression to what is implied in the text. This is certainly true of the first addition (the Heb. *'ăšer* connotes "anyone who" or "whoever"); in the case of the second addition, some may object that the phrase "all the words" adds a nuance not present in the Hebrew, but such a phrase is found elsewhere in very similar passages in Deuteronomy (*kol-dibrê hattôrâ hazzō't* ["all the words of this law"] in Deut. 27:3, 8; 28:58; 29:28; 31:12 [note that the LXX inserts "all" also in Deut. 30:10]).

We do find three variations that may have exegetical significance for our understanding of Paul's citations. (1) In 3:10 his change of *pas anthrōpos* to a simple *pas* makes no substantial difference, yet it would seem to indicate that the apostle, rather than thoughtlessly quoting from the LXX, is conscious of the Hebrew/Greek textual variations and has deliberately chosen to preserve the LXX addition of *pas*. This detail in turn suggests that his retention of the second instance of *pas* ("*all* the words"), which may have some theological importance, is also intentional.

(2) Paul changes "the words of this law" to "the things written in the book of the law"; the latter phrase appears to be taken from Deut. 30:10 ("to keep the commandments and statutes that are written in the book of this law" [cf. 28:58]). One cannot rule out the possibility that the apostle has unconsciously (or semiconsciously) merged the language of similar passages, but the change is still of interest. The use of the longer expression, while obviously not altering the meaning, perhaps adds some rhetorical force to the quotation; possibly it also draws attention to "the law of Moses in general and *in toto*, not—as Deut 27:26 does— about a specific part of it" (J. S. Sibinga, quoted in Verhoef 1979: 68). Here again, however, what proves significant is what this modification tells us about Paul's approach to the use of biblical texts. In particular, it is clear that there is nothing mechanical about his method, for he feels no compulsion to quote the LXX verbatim. While "minor" textual details can be very important to him (see commentary on Gal. 3:16 below), he apparently sees no problem in modifying the wording under certain circumstances.

(3) Finally, and most notably, we must address Paul's omission of "by God" in 3:13. Some scholars have attached great importance to this variation. For Burton (1921: 164), it was a major piece of evidence for the view that the curse to which Paul refers "is not the curse of God, but . . . the curse of the law." According to Burton (1921: 165), we need to distinguish throughout the passage "between the verdicts of law and the judgments of God, and to recognise that the former are, for Paul, not judgments which reflect God's attitude now or at any time or under any circumstances, but those which the legalist must, to his own undoing, recognise as those of the law interpreted as he interprets it, and which on the basis of his legalism he must impute to God." And if so, it follows that the deliverance from the curse is not "a judicial act in the sense of release from penalty, but

a release from a false conception of God's attitude, viz., from the belief that God actually deals with men on a legalistic basis" (Burton 1921: 168).

This remarkable interpretation (formulated at the height of Classical Liberalism in America) has not been followed by subsequent commentators, although some agree that, according to Paul, "the voice of God and the voice of the Law are by no means the same" (Martyn 1997: 321, without so much as an attempt to solve the resulting contradiction in Paul, who evidently viewed the book of Deuteronomy as having its origin in God). According to Bruce (1982: 165), Paul is avoiding not "an unseemly collocation of the divine name with the idea of cursing but . . . the implication that Christ in his death was cursed *by God*," an idea that would conflict with his view that Christ's death was an act of obedience. Others think that the omission of "by God" is immaterial; indeed, it might have been simply a consequence of changing the LXX's *kekatēramenos* to *epikataratos*, since the use of the latter, a verbal adjective, with *hypo theou* would be grammatically rough (cf. Hanson 1974: 49, from Verhoef 1979: 229n167; however, Paul could have said simply *epikataratos theou*).

It seems difficult to believe that there is no significance in the omission of the phrase "by God," but it is even more difficult to articulate clearly and convincingly what that significance might be. If Paul had been challenged about this matter, he could not have denied that the words were present in the biblical text, and presumably he would have had an explanation both for that and for his decision to leave the words out. Perhaps he omitted them simply because they would have unnecessarily introduced a complication, and he could not afford to be distracted from the major issue at hand.

The issue in question was that the law does pronounce a curse (this is surely the force of the genitive construction *hē katara tou nomou*) and that Christ has delivered "us" from it by himself falling under that curse (on the significance of the first-person plural, see below). Since the notion of a "cursed Messiah" must have been offensive to many (cf. 1 Cor. 1:23), Paul presents evidence by quoting a clause from Deut. 21:23. In its original context this clause gives the reason why the corpse of a criminal (who would have been executed, probably by stoning, and *subsequently* suspended from a tree or gibbet for public exposure) was not to be left hanging during the night. As is now well known, the Temple Scroll from Qumran alters the word order of Deut. 21:22 (from "he will be put to death, and you will hang him on a tree" to "you shall hang him on the tree, and he shall die" [see 11Q19 LXIV, 7–13]) and thus appears to understand the hanging as a reference to the execution itself. To be sure, the evidence is not conclusive that crucifixion as such was in view (see McLean 1996: 132–33). Even without that evidence, however, many scholars are inclined to think that the reason Paul quotes Deut. 21:23 is that it had previously been employed by Jews in their anti-Christian polemic. (For the interesting but speculative view that Paul is reflecting a Christian midrash on the story of Isaac, see Wilcox 1977.)

Although it is possible, indeed likely, that Paul's use of Deut. 21:23 had points of contact with contemporary Jewish interpretation and therefore was intelligible (and potentially persuasive) to his readers, one needs to acknowledge that this verse, which originally had no messianic overtones, is here applied in a surprising manner. Must we go further and say that it is being misused? Since we are not in a position to interview the apostle so that he can clarify his line of reasoning, our attempts to sort out the logic can only be tentative. We need not assume, however, that the "prooftext" character of this citation (i.e., with the introductory formula *hoti gegraptai* ["because it is written"]) is a clear entrée into Paul's thought patterns, much less deduce from it that he regarded Deut. 21:23 as a direct predictive reference to Christ. Roman crucifixion, though quite different from OT methods of execution, shared with the latter the element of shameful public exposure on some kind of gibbet, and it was such exposure that, according to Deuteronomy, reflected the divine curse. It is hardly to be doubted that first-century Jews as a whole would have seen the connection between the two and therefore that Jesus, by being suspended on a wooden cross for public viewing and ridicule, would have been regarded as falling, in some sense, under a curse.

But Paul's use of this passage faces an additional obstacle. Is it legitimate for him to identify the curse of Deut. 21:23 with that of Deut. 27:26? We cannot attempt an answer to that question, however, until we understand what he is saying in 3:10, one of the most hotly debated verses in the Pauline literature.

If we wish to make sense of Paul's argument in 3:10, a couple of preliminary considerations should be kept in the forefront. In the first place, we ought not to assume (as most students of this verse seem to do) that we have here an exceptional logical problem. The truth is that, as we noticed earlier, every single citation in 3:6–14 is characterized by some kind of logical gap; that is, Paul does not trouble himself with spelling out the premises that make his thinking cogent. One of the most significant gaps is the lack of an explicit connection between the giving of the Spirit and Abraham's faith, yet, strangely, commentators and scholars seldom even mention the problem. (There is thus little weight in the argument that the traditional interpretation of 3:10 *cannot* be right because it has to supply a premise [so Fuller 1980: 90–91]. Similarly unpersuasive is the view that such a premise would be "unintuitive" [so Cranford 1994: 258].) The only time the apostle bothers to give some sort of explanation for his choice of a text is after quoting Hab. 2:4—and in that case it has seemed to most commentators that Paul's cure is worse than the disease!

I should add parenthetically that this feature in Paul's use of Scripture has important points of contact with that of the rabbis. Even the most skeptical rabbinic scholar will agree that the kind of compressed argumentation found in the Mishnah has a very long prehistory. The same is true, mutatis mutandis, of the numerous citations in other rabbinic documents where the connection between the scriptural passage and the point being addressed is not immediately obvious. As I have argued elsewhere (Silva 1992: 159–61), it is a grave mistake to infer that in every case the connection is artificial. That may well be true in some instances, but typically the gap is the result of assumed and agreed-upon premises that need not be spelled out (we ourselves, in ordinary conversation with family and close friends, use this "technique" far more often than we realize).

The second consideration that must guide our thinking here is the pivotal significance of 3:10 for the argument as a whole. Earlier I suggested that the *gar* ("for") in this verse very likely preserves its causal function, and this point needs to be fully appreciated. Earlier, in 3:7, Paul's emphatic form of expression—the word order and, especially, the inclusion of *houtoi* ("these")—implied an opposition between the ones of faith and some other group. It was back then that Paul had thrown down the gauntlet, putting us on notice that there are people around who are *not* of faith and who therefore do not partake of the Abrahamic blessing. But now the apostle must give a reason for his warning and make good on his implicit claim. It is thus not very likely that at this point he would let his guard down or become either careless or arbitrary.

At any rate, these two considerations create the presumption that Paul was counting on his readers' ability to fill in the gaps. Undoubtedly, they shared certain items of information that did not need to be explicitly formulated. Some of these items may have included general beliefs common to early Christianity; others may have consisted of specific communication, especially during Paul's visit(s) to Galatia. Implicit data in any text can usually be inferred from the context—understanding "context" in the most general sense (i.e., including additional knowledge that we have about authors).

Moreover, the very paradox in this verse that troubles scholars—those who *do* the works of the law are cursed because Deuteronomy says that those who *do not do* the works of the law are cursed!—should tell us something about what is motivating Paul. The fact is that the apostle nowhere (in Galatians or in his other letters) characterizes his opponents as people who are obedient to the law. He will admit to no such thing. In this very epistle, as many have pointed out, he specifically accuses them of not keeping the law (6:13). It is also quite possible that the same idea is implied in 5:3, though some dispute the point. (Incidentally, it is obvious that Paul, if pressed, would have had to admit that his Jewish opponents obeyed many specific commands, but that is a different issue from the question whether they could be appropriately *characterized* as people who obey the law.) And in Phil. 3:2–4, when describing a group of opponents who, to say the least, had some affinities with the Judaizers in Galatia, he deliberately depicts them as pagans (see Silva 2005: 147–48).

That general conviction could hardly have been foreign to the Galatian Christians. There is in fact every reason to believe that when they heard Paul describing his opponents as being of the works of the law, these Galatians knew that by that phrase he did not mean something like "these are the people who fulfill the law"! Or, to put it differently, the Galatians could perfectly well understand (whether they agreed or not) why Paul would think of his opponents as people who did not "remain in all the things written in the book of the law to do them."

It would appear, then, that the assumed premise is not precisely the principle that all people fail to keep the law. That Paul believed in such a principle—and that the Galatians knew it—can hardly be disputed. Moreover, this theological truth is not irrelevant to the understanding of 3:10. But the specific item of information that supplies the missing premise was Paul's conviction that his "faith-less" opponents in particular were the ones who failed to fulfill the requirement of Deut. 27:26. (Possibly, Paul means that the Judaizers have not kept the law "because they have not 'upheld' . . . it in its eschatological design, that is, to point Israel to Jesus of Nazareth as the one who has done away with the barriers of separation between nations. . . . In a word, the opponents are apostates in a newly defined eschatological sense" [Garlington 1997: 120].) We could even say that the premise is built into the way Paul introduces the citation: he describes the false teachers as being characterized by works (and therefore as not being children of faithful/believing Abraham). In short, the quotation functions as Paul's way of informing or reminding the Galatians of how the Judaizers should be regarded.

These considerations suggest strongly that when Paul speaks of "as many as are of law-works" (meaning probably "as many as seek to live [= be justified] by the things commanded in the law" [see Silva 2001: 228]), he has primarily in mind neither people in general (Jews and Gentiles) nor Judaism as a whole, but rather the Judaizers whom he opposes and therefore anyone, Jew or Gentile, who followed the Judaizers' teaching. Although scholars are not always explicit about it, this view is held widely (see, e.g., Martyn 1997: 308n76). One difficulty with this position is Paul's use of *hēmas* ("us") in 3:13 (although the shift to the first person is a problem for any interpretation). If the ones under the curse are primarily Paul's opponents, how can the apostle say that Christ has redeemed "us" from the curse? Here too we need to avoid false dichotomies. Although the Judaizers are presented as the prime expression of people who fall under the curse, we need not infer that Paul viewed Deut. 27:26 as having one exclusive application. After all, the apostle goes so far as to include the Gentiles at the end of the paragraph (3:14), even though in the strict sense Gentiles could hardly be conceived of as being under the curse of the law (see Levinson 1997: 139–40; note esp. also the shift in 4:4–7 between the first person and second person).

Another objection has to do with the way in which the curses of Deut. 27–32 were understood by postexilic Jews. Scott (1993), following M. Knibb, has argued forcefully that Daniel's prayer of confession, which alludes to those curses (see esp. Dan. 9:11), gives expression to a point of view widely held in Second Temple Judaism, namely, that as a result of Israel's disobedience, the nation would remain under the curse of exile until the eschatological restoration. Then, building on the work of N. T. Wright, Scott (1993: 198–201, 213–14) infers that this is the point of view that Paul, for whom restoration had already come, is reflecting in 3:10 (cf. more generally Hafemann 1997: 329–71). If so, it would follow that the phrase "those of the works of the law" refers to the nation of Israel as a whole, while the wrongdoing that brings a curse is not some specific sin, but simply disobedience to God in a more general sense. This solution, however, labors under significant difficulties. One of them is the ambiguity of the evidence that Israel's exile functioned as a substantive hermeneutical paradigm for Paul. Although this approach has become increasingly popular, and some scholars seem to regard it as proven fact, the arguments are far from conclusive (see the criticisms in Seifrid 1994, esp. 89, 91). In my opinion, it is not unreasonable to suspect that preoccupation with the exile may have played a role in Paul's thinking, but when drawing exegetical conclusions, one should hesitate to lean heavily on a concept that the apostle never mentions explicitly and to which he does not even clearly allude. But even if it could be proven that Paul shares this understanding, can we assume that he

must be alluding to it in this specific quotation? After all, the apostle frequently uses scriptural texts in ways that differ from, or even contradict, those of his contemporaries, so we can hardly assume that his use of Deut. 27:26 here conforms to theirs.

3:11–12

From a theological point of view, the most difficult problem in the quotations found in Gal. 3:6–14, and perhaps in the whole Pauline corpus, is the opposition between Hab. 2:4 (Gal. 3:11) and Lev. 18:5 (Gal. 3:12). The problem is exacerbated by the way Paul introduces the latter: he states that "the law is not of faith" (*ho de nomos ouk estin ek pisteōs*). It goes without saying that Paul's contemporaries would have viewed Lev. 18:5 ("he who does them will live by them") in a totally positive way, and the thought of pitting this verse against Hab. 2:4 ("the righteous one will live by faith") must have appeared to them every bit as surprising as it does to us. For the latter text we have, of course, the pesher from Qumran, which interprets the passage as a reference to the "doers of the law" in Judah, whom God will deliver from condemnation because of their suffering and their faithfulness to the Teacher of Righteousness (1QpHab VIII, 1–3). Although some have sought to highlight the similarities between this interpretation and Paul's, the fact is that on the most crucial question raised by the apostle's use of this text, the sectarians appear to take exactly the opposite position. For them, Habakkuk does not even suggest a tension between faith(fulness) and obedience to the law; on the contrary, that text serves as grounds for legal observance. Moreover, the Epistle to the Hebrews (10:36–38) uses the verse as an encouragement to perseverance and doing the will of God (thus, faithfulness), not as proof for the doctrine of justification by faith rather than by works. Paul definitely appears as "the odd man out," and his handling of Habakkuk and Leviticus has been severely criticized by many scholars.

In attempting to understand what Paul is doing here, we first need to appreciate the function of these two citations within the argument. The quotation from Deut. 27:26 in 3:10 was intended to prove the accusation that Paul's opponents are under a curse and thus are to be distinguished from those who "are blessed with faithful/believing Abraham" (3:9). But the apostle had so far only assumed, without demonstration, that these opponents are not characterized by faith. That is why he needs to formulate the fourth thesis: "No one is justified by the law." Notice that 3:11, which begins with *de* ("and, now, but") introduces an *additional* piece of information by revealing the principle that allows Paul to characterize his opponents as "faith-less." Thus it would be possible (as we noted earlier) to view 3:11a not as a distinct thesis, but rather as a corollary of the thesis in 3:10.

If so, it may well be that Paul understands 3:10 as already giving expression to the concept spelled out in 3:11a. In other words, to say that those who seek to live or be justified by the works of the law are under a curse is in effect to say that it is impossible to be justified by the law. This negation, embedded in 3:10, is brought into prominence in 3:11a and supported by the combination of Hab. 2:4 and Lev. 18:5. The latter verse is meant to confirm 3:12a ("the law is not of faith"), which in turn may be regarded as a stated premise (see the structural outline above). The other premises in 3:6–14 were left unstated, so it would have been in character for Paul to omit 3:12 altogether, in which case we would be facing the same problem that we face in 3:10: a gap in the argumentation. (One is tempted to wish that the apostle had in fact left it out here as well and to think that it might have been easier to fill the gap ourselves than to figure out what he had in mind by his statement that "the law is not of faith"!)

Turning then more directly to the quotations themselves, we will do well to treat them separately. The citation from Hab. 2:4 raises an interesting textual question. The MT reads, *wěṣaddîq be'ěmûnātô yiḥyeh*, "but the righteous [one] by his faith will live" (on whether the Heb. term really means "faith," see below), whereas the LXX uses the first-person pronoun: *ho de dikaios ek pisteōs mou zēsetai*, "but the righteous [one] by my faith will live" (some LXX manuscripts have the pronoun after *dikaios*, thus "my righteous one by faith will live," and that is the form of the text in Heb. 10:38). In the unvocalized Hebrew writing of biblical times the difference between those two readings comes down to the use of either a final *waw* ("his") or a final *yod* ("my"), two letters that are easily confused. It is theoretically possible that

the Hebrew text used by the Greek translator had a *yod*, but no surviving Hebrew manuscript does. The translator likely either made a visual mistake or altered the text for exegetical reasons (these two options are not mutually exclusive, however, since a theological predisposition might have facilitated an error of sight).

The fact that the pronoun is missing altogether in Paul's quotation can be interpreted in at least two ways. The apostle, while citing the LXX, may have simply omitted the *mou* because this text attributed the faith/faithfulness to God and thus did not fit his purpose in this context. Perhaps more likely, Paul was familiar enough with the Hebrew text to know that the Greek version was not quite accurate. In either case, his quotation has the effect of bringing the quotation closer to the Hebrew. (Some argue that the form that he uses deliberately renders the reference ambiguous, but it is very unclear how his argument would gain anything by leaving open the possibility that the faith/faithfulness in question is God's.)

Another interesting question raised by this citation is whether the words "by faith" should be construed with the verb (as in the traditional rendering, "the righteous will live by faith") or with the subject ("the one who by faith is righteous will live"). The latter is preferred by some scholars as being more consonant with the Pauline doctrine of justification by faith and as answering more appropriately to the immediately preceding thesis: "no one is justified by law" (where certainly the prepositional phrase *en nomō* is construed with the verb *dikaioutai*). As many have pointed out, however, nothing would have prevented Paul from resolving the ambiguity through a simple transposition (*ho ek pisteōs dikaios zēsetai*), and the reply that "Paul is quoting, not formulating something quite independently" (Cranfield 1975–1979: 1:102) seems rather naive in view of the freedom that he obviously felt to alter the Greek text when it suited his purpose (even in the present passage, note the citations in 3:8, 10, 12, 13). In addition, the contrast between Hab. 2:4 and Lev. 18:5 is aided by the structural similarity in the syntax of these two passages: both have an articular subject (*ho dikaios* and *ho poiēsas*), both have a prepositional phrase (*ek pisteōs* and *en autois*), and both have *zēsetai* as the main verb. Now in Lev. 18:5 one cannot possibly construe the prepositional phrase with the subject, and it seems most unlikely that Paul (who has deliberately altered the Lev. 18:5 text [see below]) would have intended the constructions in these two citations to be taken in two different ways. This parallelism also argues against the view that Paul wished to leave ambiguous the syntax of Hab. 2:4 (as though he hoped that his readers would construe the prepositional phrase both ways).

The most significant issue raised by this citation, however, is that the Hebrew word for "faith," *ʾĕmûnâ*, normally means "steadiness, faithfulness," thus implying obedience to the law, yet Paul uses this text precisely to attack the notion of justification by the works of the law. It seems bad enough that Paul should use this verse in a way not originally intended—to propound a distinctively "Pauline" doctrine—but the problem is even more acute, for his meaning appears to be exactly the opposite of the original. And if Paul was being careless or dishonest, how could the Christian church use this text as a fundamental argument for the biblical doctrine of salvation? Indeed, we are faced with a major exegetical and theological problem.

The Hebrew text of Habakkuk, in spite of some textual and interpretive problems, is basically clear. The prophet had uttered a complaint to God regarding wickedness in Judah ("the wicked hem in the righteous" [1:4]). The Lord responded that the Babylonians would destroy Judah, but that response raised an even more serious problem regarding divine justice, and thus we have a second complaint: How can God, who cannot look upon evil, be silent while the wicked swallow up those more righteous than they (1:13)? The answer is delayed by a verse that creates considerable suspense (2:1). The setting is then further dramatized by the instruction to write down the message and by an emphatic promise that in spite of apparent delay, the prophecy will come to pass, and so the prophet must wait for its fulfillment (2:3). Finally, 2:4 discloses the awaited revelation, which we may paraphrase: "Behold, the unrighteous Babylonians are wicked and proud, but the righteous one will live by his faithfulness." The last clause, in which we are primarily interested, may be parenthetical (cf. the NIV), and it is followed by a detailed prophecy of the destruction of the wicked.

It may appear that Paul is using Habakkuk to support a notion of faith that he gets from elsewhere, Gen. 15:6: "And he believed [*wĕheʾĕmīn*] God, and it was credited to him as righteousness [*ṣĕdāqâ*]." But does the Genesis passage address a different issue? A quick look at the Hebrew text suggests that Genesis and Habakkuk may in fact be dealing with the same thought, since the lexical parallels can hardly be a coincidence (the roots *ʾmn* and *ṣdq* appear in both passages). The point to appreciate is that Habakkuk himself was involved in biblical interpretation. Although his method may appear subtle to the English reader, the prophet surely was exhorting the people of Judah to follow in the footsteps of Abraham, whose faith was not a momentary act, but rather a whole life of persevering in obedience (see esp. Gen. 22, which is the basis for James 2:21–24). Faith involves waiting for fulfillment and thus is always in danger of being shaken; therefore, steadiness and constancy are of its essence.

In other words, for Habakkuk, there was no such dichotomy between faith and faithfulness as we often assume (similarly, the Epistle to the Hebrews emphasizes their connection [see Heb. 3–4]). That the apostle Paul did not view justifying faith as excluding obedience to God's commandments is suggested in Galatians itself (see esp. 5:13–26; see also commentary on Gal. 5:14 below), but the organic link between these two concepts is extensively developed in Romans. Indeed, Paul, in his letter to the Romans, after describing his gospel as the fulfillment of the OT promises (1:2) and appealing to Hab. 2:4 as a key to understand that gospel (1:16–17), spends considerable time elaborating on the significance of Abraham's faith (chap. 4; note especially the emphasis on his perseverance in 4:18–21) and then devotes a major section to the doctrine of the believer's sanctification (chaps. 6–8). Far from manipulating the Habakkuk citation as a convenient prooftext for a view that contradicted that of the prophet, Paul was genuinely indebted to that text as a source for his teaching; moreover, his own theological formulations strengthened and advanced the prophetic message.

As for Paul's quotation of Lev. 18:5, the textual variations are also interesting, but not substantial. (1) Since Paul is quoting only part of the sentence, he has to change the LXX's relative pronoun (*ha*) at the beginning of the clause to an independent pronoun (*auta*) after the participle; but the Hebrew has both (relative *'ăšer* plus independent *'ōtām*, a common pleonastic idiom), and so in this respect Paul's quotation does not diverge from the original any more than the LXX does. (2) The two finite verbs in the Hebrew, "which the man *will do* them and *live* by them" (*'ăšer ya'ăśeh 'ōtām hā'ādām wāḥay bāhem*), are properly rendered by the LXX with a participle plus finite verb: "which, *doing*, a man *will live* by them" (*ha poiēsas anthrōpos zēsetai en autois* [the anarthrous "man" also represents accurately the function of the Hebrew articular construction]). Paul, having omitted the relative pronoun, needs a different construction, and he chooses to imitate the syntax of Hab. 2:4 by adding an article to the participle: *ho poiēsas* ("the one doing"). (3) Once that change has been made, the word "man" becomes superfluous, and Paul drops it.

These variations have no substantial semantic import, but many scholars would argue that Paul, by applying the text as he does here (and in Rom. 10:3–8), transmutes its meaning in a fundamental way. After all, the original setting of the passage—punctuated by the refrain "I am Yahweh your God"—far from displaying a "legalistic" mentality void of faith, presents the law as that which the Lord requires of his people for their good (there is also no hint that Lev. 18:5 is viewed negatively in other biblical allusions to it [Neh. 9:29; Ezek. 20:11, 13, 21; Luke 10:28]). The questions raised by Gal. 3:12 have to do not merely with how Paul quotes a specific text of Scripture, but rather with the very roots of his theology as well as its ramifications. A whole volume would be needed to discuss the matter adequately. Nevertheless, it is possible within the confines of this chapter to offer some clarifying comments.

Luther (1963: 271–72) understood Paul's quotation (also Jesus' in Luke 10:28) as ironic: "Yes, just go ahead and do it!" However, this approach was based on his view that Lev. 18:5 itself had a "moral" sense: people who, without faith, keep the commandments will receive earthly rewards and not be punished. The commentary by Calvin (1965: 54) on Gal. 3:12 is rather brief and ambiguous, but when commenting directly on Lev. 18:5 (1989: 2:165), he says, "The hope of eternal life is, therefore, given to all who keep the Law;

for those who expound the passage as referring to this earthly and transitory life are mistaken. The cause of this error was, because they feared that thus the righteousness of faith might be subverted, and salvation grounded on the merit of works. But Scripture therefore denies that men are justified by works, not because the Law itself is imperfect, or does not give instructions for perfect righteousness; but because the promise is made of none effect by our corruption and sin" (I have slightly modified the translation of the last sentence for greater clarity). Earlier, Calvin (1989: 2:162–63) had commented that Paul contrasted law and gospel not because they oppose each other, but because "his controversy was with those who interpreted it [the law] amiss" by asserting that we can be justified by its works.

Calvin undoubtedly was correct that from Paul's point of view, first-century Judaism, and the Judaizers in particular, had a faulty understanding of the role of the law in justification. It is also most likely that the theological perspective of the false teachers in Galatia would have affected the apostle's form of expression and argumentative strategy (see Ridderbos 1975: 154). One should not infer, however, that 3:12, rather than giving expression to Paul's own views, merely echoes the Judaizers' misinterpretation of the law (so esp. Fuller 1980; for a rebuttal, see Moo 1982). The word *nomos* ("law") surely must retain a uniform meaning throughout the passage, and it is evident that in phrases such as "the book of the law" (3:10) and "the curse of the law" (3:13) this term cannot mean "misinterpreted law" or "legalism." In short, for Paul's argument in 3:10–14 to work, 3:11–12 must express his own conviction regarding some kind of contrast between "faith" and "law." To be sure, such a contrast cannot be absolute or comprehensive (cf. 3:21); it must be narrowed, at least, to the issue of how one obtains justification (see Silva 2004: 242).

At any rate, if we wish to understand the logic of Paul's argumentation here, it is not really necessary to solve the conceptual problem of how he viewed the larger question of the relationship between law and faith. In one sense, we ought not to be surprised by 3:12, since it appears to be one more expression of the opposition between works of law and faith—an opposition initially formulated in 2:16, repeated in 3:2, 5, alluded to in 3:3, and restated in the contrast between 3:9 and 3:10. The restatement in 3:10 includes, of course, the quotation from Deut. 27:26, which has the effect of linking the substantive "works" (*erga*) with the verb "to do" (*poieō*). Therefore, when in 3:12 Paul tells us that the "law," which has to do with "doing," is not "of faith," possibly he does not intend to say much more than what the context has already expressed up to this point: works of law and faith are opposing principles with regard to the reception of the Abrahamic promise.

Admittedly, it is difficult to read this bald statement and reduce it to a mere contrast between works of law and the hearing of faith. But there is also an exegetical difficulty involved in thinking that Paul, for no obvious reason, jeopardizes the persuasiveness of his argument by dumping out of the blue a startling, programmatic comment about the non-faith (or even anti-faith) character of the law. Only a few verses later Paul will forcefully deny the inference that the law is against the faith-based promise (and in Rom. 3:31 he affirms just as forcefully that faith establishes the law).

It is also possible, however, that 3:12 does add semantic content to what the previous verses have already expressed. If so, the new element may be this: Paul is now directing us, by way of anticipation, to the chronological, redemptive-historical distinctions that he begins to develop in 3:15 (the law came centuries after the Abrahamic covenant), climaxing in 3:19, 23–25 in his affirmation that the time of the law preceded the time of faith (see Silva 2001: 177–78). If so, to say that "the law" (if this means more than "the works of the law") is not of faith is to claim that the Sinaitic covenant belongs to a different redemptive epoch than does the gospel; in other words, "the former does not occupy . . . the same turf in the salvation-historical continuum as the latter" (Garlington 1997: 101; see also Wakefield 2003: 184).

3:16

After 3:13, the only direct OT quotation in chapter 3 is at 3:16 (and then we have to wait until 4:27 for the next one). It would be a serious mistake, however, to infer that Paul's use of the OT is less prominent or significant in the second half of the chapter than it is in the first. In fact, 3:17–29 (plus what we may call its "coda," 4:1–7) serves as a prime example of the principle that the absence of formal citations is, in itself, no indication whatso-

ever of the degree to which the apostle depends on and interacts with the Hebrew Scriptures. There is hardly a clause in this section (with the exception of 3:25–28) that does not allude to the OT in a fairly explicit manner. Within the confines of the present essay, providing a commentary on Paul's involved argument in this passage is out of the question. Some general remarks, however, are necessary, especially since the citation at 3:16 plays a significant role in the discussion as a whole (the concept of the "seed" makes its first appearance in this verse, reoccurs in 3:19, is implicit in what follows, and makes possible the resounding conclusion in 3:29).

As we noted in the discussion of 3:6–14, Paul brings up the figure of Abraham to point out not only that we should believe as the patriarch did, but also, and more fundamentally, that when we believe, we become recipients of the redemptive blessings that God promised to him. In other words, the apostle grounds his argument in redemptive history. This historical perspective becomes more explicit and takes on a prominent role, beginning at 3:15, where Paul introduces the term *diathēkē*. As is well known, the LXX translators consistently used this word, which in nonbiblical literature means "testament, last will," to render the Hebrew word *běrît*, "covenant" (possibly because the other likely option, *synthēkē* ["agreement"], would have obscured the unilateral aspect of the covenants established by God, who alone sets the conditions [see Jobes and Silva 2000: 200–201]). In the present verse Paul is drawing an analogy with human practice (although which specific custom that may be is unclear), and for that reason many commentators prefer the rendering "last will." As the argument proceeds in 3:16–17, however, it immediately becomes obvious that the apostle is still thinking of the covenant promises made to Abraham, contrasted with the Sinaitic covenant, "which came four hundred thirty years later" (NRSV [note that this version renders *diathēkē* as "will" in 3:15 but as "covenant" in 3:17]; see also Hahn 2005).

The number "four hundred thirty" comes from Exod. 12:40, which in the MT covers only the period during which the Israelites lived in Egypt (cf. similarly the round figure "four hundred years" in Gen. 15:13, quoted in Acts 7:6). The LXX, however, has the additional clause *kai en gē Cha-*

naan ("and in the land of Canaan"), thus including within that time period the patriarchal era as well. This latter reading, which reflects a view attested in other Jewish literature (see Longenecker 1990: 133), considerably shortens the stay in Egypt. The question is of interest for the establishment of OT chronology, but it is totally irrelevant to Paul's purpose. (We do not even know that the apostle was consciously choosing one chronology over against another. If he had come up with a larger number, the statement would have lost rhetorical force, for lack of a specific OT text that had such a number. Perhaps there is an implicit "at least" in his allusion?) What matters is that there was a substantial temporal stretch between the two events, and the use of a specific figure in years highlights the apostle's interest in the historical process.

This interest is, moreover, evident in the very structure of the argument as well as in various explicit comments, such as "until [*achris*] the seed should come" (3:19), "before [*pro*] faith came" (3:23), "for as long a time as [*eph' hoson chronon*] the heir is a child" (4:1), and especially "when the fullness of time [*to plērōma tou chronou*] came" (4:6). Paul, at least in this passage, views history as consisting of three epochs: (1) the period of promise, from Abraham to Sinai; (2) the period of law, from Sinai to the coming of Christ; (3) the period of faith, commencing at the "fullness of time." These characterizations should not be absolutized, as though the promise was no longer operative after Sinai, or as though faith did not exist prior to Christ (after all, Abraham "believed"), or as though "law" in every sense of the term was absent both during Abraham's time and after the coming of Christ. Nevertheless, it certainly is true, and of critical significance for Paul, that the Mosaic "economy"—the law viewed as covenant or administration—was confined to the period between Sinai and the cross.

The primary thesis of this passage (at least 3:15–22) is that the principle of inheritance-by-law (= life-by-law = righteousness-by-law [3:21]) is incompatible with the principle of inheritance-by-promise (3:18). But since the giving of the law cannot annul the prior giving of the promise (3:17), it follows that the law was not given for the purpose of providing inheritance, life, and righteousness (3:21; cf. 2:21). A crucial distinc-

tion must be noted at this point. Paul does not say that the law as such is antithetical to the promise; indeed, he emphatically denies such an opposition (in 3:21 itself: *mē genoito* [NIV: "Absolutely not!"]). The antithesis lies, rather, between two different means by which the inheritance might be received: "If the inheritance is [or, 'comes, results'] by law, it is no longer by promise" (3:18). These considerations probably should inform our understanding of Paul's earlier comment that "the law is not of faith" (3:12). Calvin (1965: 54) is probably not far off the mark when he explains that difficult statement by saying that the law "has *a method of justifying* a man which is completely foreign to faith" (italics added).

If the Sinaitic covenant does not have a justifying (or life-giving or inheritance-providing) function, it is natural to ask why the law was given in the first place (3:19a). Paul's multifaceted response to that question (3:19b–20, 22–24) raises some complex exegetical and theological problems that would take us well beyond the issue of his use of the OT. However, at least the following three issues are relevant to our concerns.

First, Paul states in 3:19 that the law was "put in place through angels" (ESV [the verb is *diatassō*, meaning "appoint, dispose, arrange, order"]). This enigmatic comment undoubtedly reflects the Jewish understanding that angels assisted in the giving of the law at Sinai (a view attested as early as the LXX version of Deut. 33:2, as well as in Acts 7:53; Heb. 2:2; possibly also in Josephus, *Ant.* 15.136, though some take *angeloi* here as indicating prophetic messengers). Such a notion is prominent in later rabbinic documents, and one can reasonably assume that the Jewish teachers in Galatia used it as evidence of the superiority of the law. If so, Paul is here about to turn the tables and suggest that it indicates inferiority (cf. Paul's mention of angels in the anathema of 1:8). How? He adds the clause "by means of [*en cheiri*, 'by the hand of'] a mediator," a clear allusion to Lev. 26:46: "These are the decrees, the judgments, and the laws that Yahweh established [*nātan*, 'gave'] between himself and the children of Israel on Mount Sinai by means of [*bĕyad*, 'by the hand of'; LXX: *en cheiri*] Moses" (cf. Deut. 5:5, where Moses tells the people that he "stood between" Yahweh and them). Then Paul points out, "Now the mediator is not of one, but God is one" (3:20). The precise force of this mystifying (some would say inscrutable) comment eludes us (among many discussions, see Wright 1991: chap. 8; Callan 1980; Riesenfeld 1984; Burchard 1998). Nevertheless, the general thrust is all too clear: Paul's emphasis on the need for twofold mediation (Moses and the angels) suggests that the law is twice removed from God and contrasts sharply with the directness evident in God's dealings with Abraham. Moreover, the obvious allusion to the Shema (Deut. 6:4: "Yahweh is one") may reflect Paul's concern with the universality of God's redemption over against any sense of ethnic exclusiveness (cf. Rom. 3:29–30).

Second, a very important clue to Paul's understanding of the OT is the remarkable statement in 3:22a that "the Scripture hemmed in all [*ta panta*, neuter gender] under sin." The verb used in this clause, *synkleiō*, can be rendered "enclose, shut off, close up, lock in, confine," and several modern translations see here the figure of imprisonment (e.g., NRSV: "the scripture has imprisoned all things under the power of sin"), a notion confirmed by the ensuing verse (*phroureō* ["to guard, keep under watch"]). But in what sense can it be said that the OT does such a thing? The NIV seeks to clarify the concept by translating, "the Scripture declares that the whole world is a prisoner of sin," but this translation, though not necessarily wrong, weakens the force of Paul's language (contrast the TNIV: "Scripture has locked up everything under the control of sin"). According to BDAG 952 (s.v. *synkleiō* 2), "Scripture" here stands for "God's will as expressed in the Scripture," which probably is correct. If so, however, "Scripture" is in effect equivalent to "God," and we are not surprised that in a closely parallel statement, where the same verb is used, Paul puts it this way: "God hemmed in all [*tous pantas*, masculine gender] to disobedience" (Rom. 11:32a).

Some argue strongly that in Galatians the apostle dissociates God from the law (see esp. Kuula 1999: 103), but if there is any truth to that view, it is superficial, applying only to the form of expression. There can be no question that, fundamentally, Paul shared the conviction that Scripture, and thus the law, came from God and expressed his will. In and through the OT, and specifically through the Sinaitic covenant, God not only declared all to be under the power of sin, but also effectively enclosed them in a state of sinful slavery to the law. (If this approach is correct, it gives further support to the view that the difficult clause in 3:19, *tōn parabaseōn charin prosetethē*, should be rendered, "[the law] was added to increase transgressions" [cf. Rom. 5:20].)

But third, and most important, the ultimate purpose of such "hemming in" was that believers might be given the promise (3:22b) (in other words, that God might show mercy to them [Rom. 11:32b]). Paul expands on this idea in 3:23–24 by saying that the period of imprisonment was temporary, "until [*eis*] faith should be revealed"; that is, the law functioned as a "guardian [*paidagōgos*] to Christ [*eis Christon*]." This last expression has traditionally been rendered along the lines of "to lead us to Christ" (cf. KJV, NIV), but many scholars have argued that the context requires us to take the preposition *eis* temporally: "until Christ came" (so NRSV, TNIV). A temporal rendering probably is accurate; it would be a mistake, however, to regard the two notions as antithetical or incompatible. The question is complicated by larger theological issues, as well as by the convoluted discussion concerning the force of the *paidagōgos* metaphor: is the law being compared to a harsh disciplinarian driving us to seek salvation elsewhere, or should we think of it simply in terms of a temporary, kind, protective custodian? Whichever option one prefers, it is hardly possible to think of the "until" as purposeless or as otherwise unrelated to that which comes at the end of the temporary period. At the very least, we must say that Paul views the period of law as preparatory for the period of faith.

Such is then, in broad strokes, the redemptive-historical picture that the apostle presents to his readers. And it is within that history that we must make sense of the quotation in 3:16. The verse reads literally, "Now the promises were spoken to Abraham and to his seed. It does not say, 'and to the seeds,' as [referring] to many, but as [referring] to one, 'and to your seed,' which is Christ." The quotation itself is a four-word phrase (*kai tō spermati sou*; in Heb. one word: *ûlĕzar ʿăkā*) that occurs at several points in Genesis where God speaks to Abraham (Gen. 13:15; 17:8; 24:7 [here the MT has no conjunction]; without the *kai*: 12:7; 15:18; 22:18; the phrase is also used elsewhere with reference to other patriarchs).

It has become commonplace in the modern literature to criticize, and even ridicule, the apostle for his use of the OT here. After all, both the Hebrew *zera'* and the Greek *sperma* are collective singulars, like English "offspring" (notice that the NRSV and the NIV sometimes render with the plural "descendants" [e.g., Gen. 15:18]; the targumic tradition consistently renders with "sons"). And in any case, we are told, the original contexts make clear that the reference is not to one distant descendant, but rather in the first instance to Isaac, and through him to a large family as numerous as the sand on the shore.

One could point out that the Hebrew OT does use the plural of *zera'* (about twenty times [e.g., Gen. 9:9; Exod. 32:13]; the LXX very rarely uses the plural of *sperma*), but such a response, though not totally irrelevant, does not help us much. More significant is the fact that exegetical arguments based on linguistic details of this sort are common in rabbinic literature. The Mishnah, for example, after quoting Isa. 61:11 ("a garden causes its seeds [*zērû'êhā*] to grow"), comments, "It is not said 'its seed,' but 'its seeds' [*zr'h l'n'mar 'l'zrw'yh*]" (*m. Šabb.* 9:2). Similarly, *Gen. Rab.* 22:9 cites Gen. 4:10 ("your brother's blood [*děmê*, plural construct] cries out to me from the ground") and gives Rabbi Judan's explanation: "It is not written, 'your brother's blood' [*dm 'hyk 'yn ktyb*], but 'your brother's bloods' [*dmy*, plural]—his blood and the blood of his descendants" (the same argument is then used regarding 2 Kings 9:26; 2 Chron. 24:25). Now the rabbis knew perfectly well that the Hebrew word for "blood," *dām*, is very commonly used in the plural (especially when the context indicates shed blood), but no one seems to have objected to this kind of argumentation.

It would be ludicrous to suggest that Paul was unaware of the collective sense of *sperma* or that he was hoping that his readers would not detect this "logical flaw." In this very passage—indeed, at its climax—he affirms, "If you are of Christ, then you [plural!] are Abraham's seed, heirs according to the promise" (3:29). The collective meaning of the term is fundamental for Paul's argument, and thus we can hardly read 3:16 as though he were wishing to exclude such a meaning.

Perhaps what confuses us here is the assumption that the apostle is saying something controversial. We should consider the possibility that

Paul's readers, and even his Judaizing opponents (all of whom acknowledged Jesus as the Messiah), would have readily acknowledged this identification between Abraham's seed and the Christ. If so, they would have been offended neither by Paul's exegetical device (with which presumably they were familiar and comfortable) nor by the doctrinal content of his statement. It is even possible, as some have argued, that 3:16 is parenthetical. More likely, we should think of 3:16b (beginning with the words *ou legei* ["it does not say"]) as an explanatory comment that breaks the argument; in other words, 3:15–16a is the integral thought expanded upon in 3:17–18. We might paraphrase thus: "Even a human arrangement, if ratified, cannot be altered; similarly, God ratified his promises to Abraham and his seed (and, by the way, we know that 'the seed' refers to Christ, as the singular should remind us). Let me be clearer: the law cannot alter the Abrahamic covenant."

At any rate, there is much to be said for the idea that in 3:16b Paul is not attempting to prove anything; rather, he is merely bringing to the surface something that his readers already know and accept. He mentions the point here because he is about to show its relevance to the more general argument ("the law was added . . . until the seed should come" [3:19]). The Galatians aspire to be fully included within the fold of Abraham's people, but that can be true only of those who are in corporate union with *the* seed, Christ. And as a matter of fact, the Galatians themselves, by responding to the gospel message with faith, have already received the Spirit, an experience that is integral to the Abrahamic promise (3:3, 5, 14); they have already been baptized into union with Christ (3:27), which means that they belong to Christ and have been incorporated into the Abrahamic seed. What is more, they are now not only the heirs and children of Abraham, but also the children of God himself (3:26, 29; 4:4–7). How mistaken and perverse, then, to alter God's promises to Abraham by adding the later legal requirements that were but a temporary expedient until the arrival of faith!

4:24

Galatians 4:21–31 contains, strictly speaking, only two formal quotations, one from Isa. 54:1 (in 4:27) and the other from Gen. 21:10 (in 4:30). The whole section, however, is a direct "exposition" of the Genesis narrative concerning Sarah (including her son Isaac) and Hagar (including her son Ishmael). Quotation marks are needed around the word "exposition" because considerable disagreement exists regarding Paul's use of Scripture here. The crucial statement is in 4:24, where Paul says that Sarah and Hagar "are two covenants" (*eisin dyo diathēkai*). He then goes on to equate Hagar (who "bears [children] for slavery") with Mount Sinai and with contemporary Jerusalem; by implication, but not expressly, Sarah is identified with the new covenant—that is, with the free Jerusalem from above (4:26). As if that were not enough, Paul proceeds to identify Isaac with the believing Galatian Gentiles (4:28), while Ishmael is said (less directly but not subtly) to stand for his Judaizing opponents (4:29).

Some scholars argue that the passage uses a typological approach to the Genesis narrative, but many others are convinced that the apostle is treating us here to a full-blown allegorical interpretation. After all, he begins 4:24 with the words *hatina estin allēgoroumena*, "which things are spoken [or 'interpreted'] allegorically." We must not simply assume, however, that his use of the verb *allēgoreō* (from *allos* ["other"] and *agoreuō* ["speak"]) corresponds to what modern scholars mean when they speak of "allegorical interpretation" (see Davis 2004). It is true, of course, that this latter semitechnical sense has its roots in pre-Christian Greek literature and that Paul would have been acquainted with it; in other words, we cannot from the start rule out the possibility that he means a nonhistorical type of interpretation similar to that used by Philo and by the Stoics before him.

On the other hand, Paul nowhere in his writings gives any hint that he rejects the historical character of biblical narrative or even minimizes its significance. Moreover, it could be argued that the apostle himself provides a clue to his meaning by using the verb *systoicheō* in the very next verse: "Now Hagar . . . corresponds to [*systoichei*] the present Jerusalem" (4:25). In contrast to Philo, Paul casts no doubts on either the factual nature or the historical value of the Genesis narrative (Philo himself, to be sure, is not as antihistorical as many suppose). Indeed, some of his comments here (e.g., "For it is written that Abraham had two sons, one by the slave woman and the other by the

free woman" [4:22]; "But just as at that time the one born according to the flesh persecuted the one [born] according to the Spirit, so also now" [4:29]) are clear affirmations of factual events upon which the apostle builds his argument.

Thus, if it turns out that Paul is pointing out a correspondence between two historical realities, we may with good reason regard his reading of Genesis as "typological" rather than "allegorical." The central theological truth with which he is concerned is the contrast between Spirit and flesh: God works according to the former, while sinners depend on the latter. This contrast has manifested itself in a notable way at various points throughout (redemptive) history. It did during the patriarchal period, and it does now at the fullness of time (4:4).

In addition to these considerations, one should keep in mind the place of 4:21–31 within the argument as a whole. It can be argued that Paul had completed his scriptural demonstration at the end of chapter 3 and that the present paragraph is intended not as some kind of logical, exegetical proof, but rather as a climactic, forceful finale directed at those who claim to subject themselves to law (4:21). Some have even suggested that the Abraham-Sarah-Hagar narrative had been used by the Judaizers first and that Paul "could not escape it" (Barrett 1982: 162). We have no evidence to confirm this theory, and the text itself gives no clear indication to support it, but the possibility should be left open. In any case, the very fact that Paul nowhere else uses this approach (1 Cor. 10:4 provides only a partial analogy, while 9:9 does not deal with an OT narrative) should be a warning against drawing major conclusions on the basis of Paul's use of the Sarah/Hagar analogy.

4:27

The quotation of Isa. 54:1 in 4:27—an exact transcription of the Greek version—deserves special attention. The LXX rendering, which is mostly literal, represents the original faithfully. The first Hebrew verb, *ronnî* ("shout, cry out" [from *rānan*]), occurs most often in contexts of joy, so the translation *euphranthēti* ("rejoice") is appropriate (cf. the rendering "sing" in most English versions). In the next line, the Hebrew cognate noun *rinnâ* is omitted by the LXX, probably for stylistic reasons, and the meaning is not affected. No other textual issues arise in the rest of the verse.

Paul's use of this verse in the Galatians argument appears, at first blush, to exploit a superficial connection (Sarah as a sterile woman who nevertheless gives birth) for purposes far removed from those of the original context. In Isa. 54 God addresses the nation of Israel, which is pictured as a woman, first forsaken but then restored: "For your Maker is your husband—Yahweh of hosts is his name. . . . Yahweh has called you like an abandoned wife and grieved in spirit. . . . For a brief moment I abandoned you, but with great compassion I will gather you" (Isa. 54:5–7). What does this have to do with Sarah and Hagar, let alone the two Jerusalems, or Isaac and Ishmael, or circumcision and faith? Moreover, the implicit comparison between Sarah and a sterile, abandoned woman who had numerous children is fraught with complications, as is the correspondence between Hagar and the woman who was married.

Curiously, Sarah is mentioned by name in the OT, outside the Genesis narrative, only in Isa. 51:1–2, where she is said to have given birth to those who "pursue righteousness" (Heb. *ṣedeq*; LXX: *to dikaion* ["what is right"]) and who "seek Yahweh." Indeed, it has been argued that in the book of Isaiah the theme of Sarah's barrenness is transformed from a past story of a child to the future "story of a birth of a people" (Callaway 1986: 63). This "development made it exegetically possible for Paul to dissociate the Isaiah proclamation from ethnic Israel exclusively" (Jobes 1993: 308); in other words, Sarah's children include those who truly search for God and his righteousness. Moreover, since it was common to personify a city as a woman (see esp. Ps. 87:5, where the LXX [86:5] translates with *mētēr Siōn* ["mother Zion"]), and since Isaiah portrays Jerusalem as a desolate city (Isa. 64:10, where the city is called "a curse" [cf. Gal. 3:13]!), the prophet manages "to produce female images of two Jerusalems, a barren, cursed Jerusalem and a rejoicing Jerusalem" (Jobes 1993: 309; see Jobes's article for several other intriguing associations and parallels; note also, as suggested by Wilk [1998: 235], that the verb "will inherit," used by Paul in 4:30, frames the Isaianic passage [Isa. 53:12; 54:3]).

Since Isa. 54:1 follows immediately upon the "song" of the Suffering Servant (no doubt alluded to in Gal. 2:20–21; 3:1, 13), Paul evidently expected the Galatians to see the connection between faith in the crucified Christ and incorporation into the numerous people who have the new Jerusalem as their mother. It is true that a direct correspondence between Sarah/Hagar and the sterile/married women of Isa. 54:1 does not work, but as various commentators have pointed out, Paul seems to refrain from actually mentioning Sarah in 4:25–26. The link between a sterile Sarah and a forsaken, cursed Jerusalem had previously been established by Isaiah; this background gives Paul the canonical authority to quote Isa. 54:1 within the context of the Genesis narrative. The point of the quotation, however, is to stress the link that believers enjoy not so much with Sarah precisely, but with the new, redeemed Jerusalem. If that free and heavenly city is the Galatians' true mother, how absurd to regress and become enslaved to a slavish Jerusalem abandoned by God! (Recent treatments of this citation include Boer 2004; Willits 2005; Di Mattei 2006.)

4:30

The specific citation here ("Cast out the slave woman and her son; for the son of the slave woman will not inherit with the son of the free woman") does not require much discussion beyond what has already been said. The LXX of Gen. 21:10 (itself a totally literal rendering of the Hebrew) is quoted here word for word, except that the last two Greek words, *mou Isaak*, are changed to *tēs eleutheras*; thus the original phrase "my son Isaac" appears as "the son of the free woman." In Genesis Sarah is speaking, whereas Paul wants to present the statement as a divine declaration. Since God subsequently instructed Abraham to do as Sarah had said (Gen. 21:12), Paul's readers could have hardly objected to this handling of the text. Moreover, the choice of the word *eleuthera* serves to highlight the central theme of freedom, which the apostle proceeds to develop (e.g., 4:31; 5:1, 13).

5:14

Chapters 5–6 of Galatians contain only one direct citation: "For the whole law is fulfilled in one word, namely, 'You will love your neighbor as yourself'" (5:14, quoting Lev. 19:18). This brief quotation presents no textual problems whatever; in addition, Paul's use of the OT passage is straightforward, and no one has suggested that the apostle's handling of the text is inappropriate. Yet, ironically, the presence of this citation here has baffled commentators. For many of them, it seems almost unimaginable that Paul, in the very letter where he gives his most sustained argument against the law, should now speak about the need to fulfill the law. Indeed, a few scholars (e.g., O'Neill 1972: 71) have resorted to the desperate measure of identifying this section of the letter as an editor's interpolation.

However, the alleged dissonance between this passage and the rest of the epistle rests on the assumption that chapter 3 is an indiscriminate attack on the law. Such an assumption encounters many obstacles, not the least of which is the fact that throughout the argument Paul supports his theses by appealing to statements from the Torah. As suggested above, the focus of Paul's negative statements is narrowly defined to one issue: the role of the law in justification for the reception of the Abrahamic inheritance. It is an unnecessary, and indeed illegitimate, inference to say that the law has been abrogated in every respect.

The question of the role of the law in the life of the Christian is a complicated one and certainly goes beyond the bounds of the present essay. It is worth pointing out, however, the striking parallelism between the following statements:

Gal. 5:6: "Neither circumcision nor uncircumcision has any power, but faith working through love."

Gal. 6:15: "Neither circumcision nor uncircumcision is anything, but a new creation."

1 Cor. 7:19: "Circumcision is nothing and uncircumcision is nothing, but keeping the commandments of God."

It is quite apparent that Gal. 5:13–14, which warns against the abuse of freedom by emphasizing our obligation to love one another, restates and expands the earlier comment that faith works through love. This restatement appeals to the law itself in support and thus reveals its harmony with 1 Cor. 7:19. Finally, the fulfillment of the law through love characterizes the new creation (Gal. 6:15). In short, when Paul calls the Galatians to identify themselves with the eschatological reality inaugurated by Christ (chap. 3), he is not proposing a wholesale abandonment of God's law. On the contrary, to throw off the yoke of the law for justification leads to its true fulfillment by the power of the Spirit (5:22–23; cf. Rom. 8:4).

Conclusion

Several other passages in Galatians appear to contain subtle allusions to the OT. For example, Paul's scathing words in 5:12 perhaps should be understood against the background of Deut. 23:1. The context of 5:18 perhaps reflects the exodus narrative (see Wilder 2001). Paul's reference to the fruit of the Spirit (especially peace) in 5:22 appears to derive from Isa. 32:14–18. Similarly, the figure of sowing and reaping in 6:7 harks back to OT Wisdom literature (Job 4:8; Prov. 22:8). Special interest attaches to 6:16, where Paul, referring to those who follow the rule of the new creation, invokes the blessing "Peace on them, and mercy on the Israel of God." The expression "peace on Israel" occurs in Ps. 125:5; 128:6, but Beale (1999: 208) has cogently argued that Paul here may have been influenced by eschatological passages in Isaiah, especially 54:10 LXX: "Neither shall the mercy [eleos] that comes from me to you fail, nor shall the covenant of your peace [hē diathēkē tēs eirēnēs sou] be removed." Since Paul earlier (4:26) had applied Isa. 54:1 to the Gentile believers in Galatia, and since the letter as a whole focuses on the unity of God's people, it is difficult to believe that at the very end of the document he would introduce an ethnic distinction. Quite the contrary. By means of a final OT allusion the apostle assures his readers that all who belong to the new order, whether Jew or Gentile, are the true seed of Abraham and thus constitute the eschatological Israel of God.

Bibliography

Barrett, C. K. 1982. "The Allegory of Abraham, Sarah, and Hagar in the Argument of Galatians." Pages 154–70 in *Essays on Paul*. Philadelphia: Westminster.

Beale, G. K. 1999. "Peace and Mercy upon the Israel of God: The Old Testament Background of Galatians 6,16b." *Bib* 80: 204–23.

———. 2005. "The Old Testament Background of Paul's Reference to the 'Fruit of the Spirit' in Galatians 5:22." *BBR* 15: 1–38.

Betz, H. D. 1979. *Galatians: A Commentary on Paul's Letter to the Churches in Galatia*. Hermeneia. Philadelphia: Fortress.

Boer, M. C. de. 2004. "Paul's Quotation of Isaiah 54.1 in Galatians 4.27." *NTS* 50: 370–89.

Bruce, F. F. 1982. *The Epistle to the Galatians: A Commentary on the Greek Text*. NIGTC. Grand Rapids: Eerdmans.

Burchard, C. 1998. "Noch ein Versuch zu Galater 3,19 und 20." Pages 184–202 in *Studien zur Theologie, Sprache und Umwelt des Neuen Testaments*. Edited by D. Sänger. WUNT 107. Tübingen: Mohr Siebeck.

Burton, E. de Witt. 1921. *A Critical and Exegetical Commentary on the Epistle to the Galatians.* ICC. Edinburgh: T&T Clark.

Callan, T. 1980. "Pauline Midrash: The Exegetical Background of Gal. 3:19b." *JBL* 99: 549–67.

Callaway, M. C. 1986. *Sing, O Barren One: A Study in Comparative Midrash.* SBLDS 91. Atlanta: Scholars Press.

Calvert Koyzis, N. 2004. *Paul, Monotheism and the People of God: The Significance of Abraham Traditions for Early Judaism and Christianity.* JSTNSup 273. London: T&T Clark.

Calvin, J. 1965. *The Epistles of Paul the Apostle to the Galatians, Ephesians, Philippians and Colossians.* Edited by D. W. Torrance and T. F. Torrance. Translated by T. H. L. Parker. Grand Rapids: Eerdmans.

———. 1989. *Harmony of the Pentateuch.* 2 vols. Vols. 2–3 of *Calvin's Commentaries.* Translated and edited by J. King et al. Grand Rapids: Baker Academic.

Ciampa, R. E. 1998. *The Presence and Function of Scripture in Galatians 1 and 2.* WUNT 2/102. Tübingen: Mohr Siebeck.

Cook, D. 1992. "The Prescript as Programme in Galatians." *JTS* 43: 511–19.

Corsani, B. 1990. *Lettera ai Galati.* Commentario storico ed esegetico all'Antico e al Nuovo testamento: Nuovo testamento 9. Genoa: Marietti.

Cranfield, C. E. B. 1975–1979. *A Critical and Exegetical Commentary on the Epistle to the Romans.* 2 vols. ICC. Edinburgh: T&T Clark.

Cranford, L. L. 1994. "A Rhetorical Reading of Galatians." *SwJT* 37: 4–10.

Davis, A. 2004. "Allegorically Speaking in Galatians 4:21–5:1." *BBR* 14: 161–75.

Di Mattei, S. 2006. "Paul's Allegory of the Two Covenants (Gal. 4.21–31) in Light of First-Century Hellenistic Rhetoric and Jewish Hermeneutics." *NTS* 52: 102–22.

Dunn, J. D. G. 1993. *The Epistle to the Galatians.* BNTC. Peabody, MA: Hendrickson; London: Black.

Ellis, E. E. 1957. *Paul's Use of the Old Testament.* Edinburgh: Oliver & Boyd.

Fuller, D. P. 1980. *Gospel and Law: Contrast or Continuum? The Hermeneutics of Dispensationalism and Covenant Theology.* Grand Rapids: Eerdmans.

Fung, R. Y. K. 1988. *The Epistle to the Galatians.* NICNT. Grand Rapids: Eerdmans.

Garlington, D. 1997. "Role Reversal and Paul's Use of Scripture in Galatians 3.10–13." *JSNT* 65: 85–121.

Ginzberg, L. 1909–1938. *The Legends of the Jews.* Translated by H. Szold and P. Radin. 7 vols. Philadelphia: Jewish Publication Society of America.

Gombis, T. G. 2007. "The 'Transgressor' and the 'Curse of the Law': The Logic of Paul's Argument in Gal. 2–3." *NTS* 53: 81–93.

Hafemann, S. J. 1997. "Paul and the Exile of Israel in Galatians 3–4." Pages 329–71 in *Exile: Old Testament, Jewish, and Christian Conceptions.* Edited by J. M. Scott. JSJSup 56. Leiden: Brill.

Hahn, S. W. 2005. "Covenant, Oath, and the Aqedah: [Diathēkē] in Galatians 3:15–18." *CBQ* 67: 79–100.

Hansen, G. W. 1989. *Abraham in Galatians: Epistolary and Rhetorical Contexts.* JSNTSup 29. Sheffield: JSOT Press.

Hanson, A. T. 1974. *Studies in Paul's Technique and Theology.* London: SPCK.

Jobes, K. H. 1993. "Jerusalem, Our Mother: Metalepsis and Intertextuality in Galatians 4:21–31." *WTJ* 55: 299–320.

Jobes, K. H., and M. Silva. 2000. *Invitation to the Septuagint.* Grand Rapids: Baker Academic.

Koch, D.-A. 1986. *Die Schrift als Zeuge des Evangeliums: Untersuchungen zur Verwendung und zum Verständnis der Schrift bei Paulus.* BHT 69. Tübingen: Mohr Siebeck.

Kuula, K. 1999. *Paul's Polemical Treatment of the Law in Galatians.* Vol. 1 of *The Law, the Covenant and God's Plan.* PFES 72. Helsinki: Finnish Exegetical Society; Göttingen: Vandenhoeck & Ruprecht.

Lagrange, M.-J. 1925. *Saint Paul, Épître aux Galates.* 2nd ed. Paris: Gabalda.

Levinson, B. M. 1997. *Deuteronomy and the Hermeneutics of Legal Innovation.* New York: Oxford University Press.

Lightfoot, J. B. 1898. *Saint Paul's Epistle to the Galatians.* 10th ed. London: Macmillan.

Longenecker, R. N. 1990. *Galatians.* WBC 41. Dallas: Word.

Luther, M. 1963. *Lectures on Galatians 1535: Chapters 1–4.* Vol. 26 of *Luther's Works.* Edited by W. A. Hansen and J. Pelikan. Saint Louis: Concordia.

Martyn, J. L. 1997. *Galatians.* AB 33A. New York: Doubleday.

McLean, B. H. 1996. *The Cursed Christ: Mediterranean Expulsion Rituals and Pauline Soteriology.* JSNTSup 126. Sheffield: Sheffield Academic Press.

Michel, O. 1929. *Paulus und seine Bibel.* BFCT 2/18. Gütersloh: Bertelsmann.

Moo, D. J. 1982. Review of D. P. Fuller, *Gospel and Law. TJ* 3: 99–103.

Oeming, M. 1998. "Der Glaube Abrahams: Zur Rezeptionsgeschichte von Gen 15,6 in der Zeit des zweiten Tempels." *ZAW* 110: 16–33.

O'Neill, J. C. 1972. *The Recovery of Paul's Letter to the Galatians.* London: SPCK.

Ridderbos, H. 1975. *Paul: An Outline of His Theology.* Grand Rapids: Eerdmans.

Riesenfeld, H. 1984. "The Misinterpreted Mediator in Gal 3:19–20." Pages 405–12 in *The New Testament Age: Essays in Honor of Bo Reicke.* Edited by W. C. Weinrich. Macon, GA: Mercer University Press.

Rottzoll, D. U. 1994. "Gen 15,6: Ein Beleg für den Glauben als Werkgerechtigkeit." *ZAW* 106: 21–27.

Scott, J. M. 1993. "'For as Many as Are of Works of the Law Are under a Curse' (Galatians 3.10)." Pages 187–221 in *Paul and the Scriptures of Israel.* Edited by C. A. Evans and J. A. Sanders. JSNTSup 83. Sheffield: JSOT Press.

Seifrid, M. A. 1994. "Blind Alleys in the Controversy over the Paul of History." *TynBul* 45: 73–95.

Silva, M. 1992. "The New Testament Use of the Old Testament: Text Form and Authority." Pages 147–65 in *Scripture and Truth.* Edited by D. A. Carson and J. D. Woodbridge. Grand Rapids: Baker Academic.

———. 1993. "Old Testament in Paul." *DPL* 630–42.

———. 1994. *Biblical Words and Their Meaning: An Introduction to Lexical Semantics.* Rev. ed. Grand Rapids: Zondervan.

———. 2001. *Interpreting Galatians: Explorations in Exegetical Method.* 2nd ed. Grand Rapids: Baker Academic.

———. 2004. "Faith versus Works in Galatians 2–3." Pages 217–48 in *The Paradoxes of Paul.* Vol. 2 of *Justification and Variegated Nomism: A Fresh Appraisal of Paul and Second Temple Judaism.* Edited by D. A. Carson, P. T. O'Brien, and M. A. Seifrid. WUNT 2/181. Tübingen: Mohr Siebeck.

———. 2005. *Philippians.* 2nd ed. BECNT. Grand Rapids: Baker Academic.

Stanley, C. D. 1992. *Paul and the Language of Scripture: Citation Technique in the Pauline Epistles and Contemporary Literature.* SNTSMS 69. Cambridge: Cambridge University Press.

Verhoef, E. 1979. *Er staat geschreven . . . : De Oud-Testamentische citaten in de brief aan de Galaten.* Meppel: Krips Repro.

Wakefield, A. H. 2003. *Where to Live: The Hermeneutical Significance of Paul's Citations from Scripture in Galatians 3:1–14.* AcBib 14. Leiden: Brill; Atlanta: Society of Biblical Literature.

Warfield, B. B. 1899. "'It Says:' 'Scripture Says:' 'God Says.'" *Presbyterian and Reformed Review* 10: 472–510.

Wevers, J. W. 1993. *Notes on the Greek Text of Genesis.* SBLSCS 35. Atlanta: Scholars Press.

Wilcox, M. 1977. "'Upon the Tree'—Deut 21:22–23 in the New Testament." *JBL* 96: 85–99.

Wilder, W. N. 2001. *Echoes of the Exodus Narrative in the Context and Background of Galatians 5:18.* SBL 23. New York: Lang.

Wilk, F. 1998. *Die Bedeutung des Jesajabuches für Paulus.* FRLANT 179. Göttingen: Vandenhoeck & Ruprecht.

Willits, J. 2005. "Isa 54, 1 in Gal 4, 24b–27: Reading Genesis in Light of Isaiah." *ZNW* 96: 188–210.

Wright, N. T. 1991. *The Climax of the Covenant: Christ and the Law in Pauline Theology.* Edinburgh: T&T Clark.

EPHESIANS

FRANK S. THIELMAN

Introduction

Paul wrote Ephesians to a wide audience of Gentile Christians (2:11; 3:1). They lived in a world where evidence of the power that belonged to the "rulers," "authorities," "world rulers," and "spiritual forces of evil in the heavenly places" was all too clear (6:12; cf. 2:2). They could see signs of its strength in the political statuary, friezes, and inscriptions in the markets and on the street corners of their cities. The gods, this propaganda proclaimed, had given Rome the eternal right to rule the universe. To the first readers of Ephesians, perhaps Paul's own troubles were only a grim reminder of the complications the gospel had introduced into their attempts to live in such a world (3:13).

Paul wrote his letter to encourage them that as people who were "in Christ" they worshiped the Creator of the universe (1:4; 3:9). The Creator was their Father and had graciously included them within his family (1:2, 5; 2:18; 5:20), given them an important role in his eternal purposes (1:9–10; 3:10), and blessed them richly with a close relationship to himself (2:16–18; 3:12). Through his anointed king Jesus, he had already triumphed over all the "spiritual forces of evil in the heavenly places" (1:20–22a) and had made available to his people the same power that brought Jesus to this victory (1:19–23; 3:14–19). Paul hoped God

would use his letter to open the eyes of his readers to these spiritual truths (1:15–18; 3:14–19), to call them to live in unity with each other (4:1–6:9), and to encourage them in their battle with the forces of evil around them (6:10–20).

His interaction with the OT played an important role in accomplishing this purpose. He alluded to a range of texts in Psalms and Isaiah to remind his readers that if they were "in Christ," they had joined God's anointed king in the victory God had given to him over the enemies of his people. Because God had raised Christ from the dead, he was enthroned in heaven with his enemies conquered and beneath his feet (1:20–22; 4:8; cf. Ps. 110:1; 8:6; 68:18). These enemies were precisely the rulers, authorities, powers, and dominant forces that Paul's readers might have been tempted to see as triumphing over them (1:21; cf. 2:2; 3:10; 6:11–12; cf. Arnold 1997: 41–69).

Not only had Christ conquered them so that they no longer held his people captive, but as a victorious king he had distributed largess to his people on the heels of this victory. He had given them gifts by which they were able to maintain their unity and guard against continuing danger (4:8; cf. Ps. 68:18). They were clothed in the armor and weaponry of God himself. They were able, therefore, to defend themselves against the dying efforts of the defeated enemy powers to

813

make trouble for God's people (6:10–17; Isa. 59:17; 11:5; 52:7).

Paul probably also tapped themes from Genesis, Isaiah, and possibly Psalms to remind his readers that God was in the process of restoring his creation to its original unity: a unity of peace between peoples and a unity of peace between all humanity and their Creator. The idea of a restored creation may already be present in 1:22 where Paul quotes a line from Ps. 8:6 to describe Christ's defeat of his enemies. Paul may have been aware that, in its original context, the line was part of a couplet that itself recalled the dominion God gave Adam over all creation (Gen. 1:28). Paul clearly refers to the creation narrative in 5:31–32 when he applies Gen. 2:24 to the union of believers with Christ, and here too the idea of a new creation may lie in the background.

Similarly, Isa. 57:19, which Paul uses in 2:13–17, can be understood as a reference to the future peace of the nations and Israel with God, a common theme in Isaiah generally (2:2–4; 11:10; 19:24–25; 45:14, 22; 51:4–5; 52:10; 55:5; 56:6–7; 60:11; 66:18–23). Sometimes in Isaiah this theme is mingled with the motif of a future new creation (66:18–23). The same mixture of themes appears in 2:13–17 when Paul not only speaks of peace between Jews and Gentiles but then describes the union of the two peoples in Christ as fulfilling God's intention to "create . . . one new human being" (2:15). The new creation theme is important in the letter generally (2:10; 3:9; 4:13, 22, 24), and this lends support to the idea that Paul chose his allusions to Ps. 8:6 and Isa. 57:19 because the wider contexts of these OT passages supported that theme.

We need to be cautious here. If these echoes of the creation narrative and Isaiah's pilgrimage of the nations motif are intentional, they are very subtle. Two considerations, moreover, seem to weigh against seeing Ephesians as deeply indebted to major theological themes in the OT. First, where a quotation formula appears in the letter it introduces either a severely altered form of the OT text (4:8; cf. Ps. 68:18) or something that is not from the OT at all (5:14). This may mean that the OT itself was only one of several sources of tradition used in the letter and that the various passages alluded to did not themselves play a major role in forming the letter's thought

(Lincoln 1982: 44–45, 49). Second, according to 3:5, 9 the unity between Jewish and Gentile believers, a theme of critical importance in the letter, was utterly unknown before God revealed it to Paul and other apostles and prophets. This seems to preclude a major role for the OT in the letter's thought (Lincoln 1982: 47).

These are important considerations, and they usefully remind us that the theology of Ephesians is not understandable solely in OT terms. The accent in a description of the letter's use of the OT, however, needs to lie on continuity (cf. Moritz 1996). In particular, the twin themes of God's triumph "in Christ" over the forces of evil and his restoration "in Christ" of creation seem to emerge from the very Scriptures whose language Paul uses.

1:20–23

Paul opens Ephesians with two lengthy prayers. The first is a benedictory prayer in 1:3–14 in which he blesses God for the lavish gifts that he has given to his people. The second prayer is, formally, a "prayer report" in which Paul first tells his readers in 1:15–16a that they are the focus of his thanksgiving prayers and then in 1:16b–23 that they are also at the center of his intercessory prayers. Paul says that when he intercedes with God for them, he asks God to give them a full understanding of what he has done for them. Paul is particularly eager that his readers appreciate how God has used the same power by which he raised Jesus from the dead also to benefit them (1:19–20).

God has put such massive power into effect, Paul insists, "in the Messiah [*tō Christō*], having raised him from the dead and seated him at his right hand [*kathisas en dexia autou*] in the heavenly places" (1:20). He has also "subjected all things under" the Messiah's "feet" (1:22). The language that Paul uses in these statements comes from Ps. 110:1 (109:1 LXX) and Ps. 8:6 (8:7 LXX/ MT).

The original historical setting of Ps. 110 has been widely disputed among scholars. Some have dated it as late as Maccabean times, but most now believe that it describes at least elements of an early enthronement ritual, perhaps reaching back to David's reign or even before (e.g., Kraus 1989: 346–47). Most also envision a court official of some type, perhaps the poet who composed the psalm, reciting it to the king at the time of the king's enthronement (Kraus 1989: 236; Allen 2002: 114). The wide variety of suggestions for the psalm's historical setting make it difficult to deny that it could have come from the time of David himself, and the tendency of recent scholars to date the psalm to the period of the early monarchy (Kraus 1989: 347; Allen 2002: 113) lends plausibility to the idea that David was its author. This certainly was what Jesus thought (Mark 12:35–37 pars.).

The psalm consists of two oracles, both of which seem to be addressed not to a contemporary of the psalmist, but to a special king and priest of some future era. In the first oracle Yahweh instructs the king to sit at his right hand until he conquers the king's enemies: "An announcement of Yahweh to my Lord: 'Sit at my right hand [LXX: *kathou ek dexiōn mou*] until I put your enemies beneath your feet for a footstool'" (110:1). Although some scholars have taken the king's position at the right hand of Yahweh as referring to the location of the king's throne or dwelling relative to the holy place of God's presence, the psalmist probably thinks of a future king who will be exalted to Yahweh's right hand and to whom Yahweh will subject the rulers of all the earth (110:6). The thought is close to Dan. 7:13–14, where the Son of Man is exalted to the presence of God and receives dominion over all the nations of the earth (Moritz 1996: 16).

In the second oracle Yahweh designates the king as a priest: "Yahewh has sworn and will not be sorry, 'You are a priest forever in the manner of Melchizedek'" (110:4). Here too the unusual claim that the king is an eternal priest is enigmatic if we think only of a contemporary coronation ritual. It is true that Melchizedek was the king of Salem (Gen. 14:18), and that "Salem" may be Jerusalem, thus providing a connection to the coronation of David as king over Jerusalem (Kraus 1989: 347). However, if the king in the psalm is merely a king from the psalmist's own period, then the psalmist's reference to his priesthood as "eternal" is puzzling.

The psalm speaks of a king who shares the royal authority of Yahweh, defeats the rulers of the earth, and enters an eternal priesthood. This is an extraordinarily exalted understanding of the king and thus seems to refer not to a king in the psalmist's own experience, but rather to the Messiah, who will one day come to establish God's rule over all the earth.

That some first-century Jews gave the psalm a Messianic reading is implied by the way Jesus uses it. When Jesus taught on the psalm in the temple, he assumed that his hearers would agree with him that it referred to the Messiah (Mark 12:37 pars.). In addition, Jesus' conflation of Dan. 7:13 with Psa. 110:1 at his Jewish trial ("You will see the Son of Man sitting at the right hand of Power" [Mark 14:62]) probably means that Jewish interpreters of Jesus' time had already brought these two texts together as messianic texts (cf. Moritz 1996: 16–17).

Like most other early Christians who used this text (see Hay 1973: 163–66), Paul, when he wrote 1:20, was interested in the first oracle's pronouncement that the king should sit at Yahweh's right hand. Paul believed that this pronouncement had been fulfilled in Jesus Christ in connection with God's powerful action of raising him from the dead (cf. Rom. 8:34; Col. 3:1). Jesus' resurrection led to his exaltation to a place of equal regal authority with the king of the universe, just as the psalm implies that Yahweh shares his authority with the king at his right hand.

In addition, Paul was interested in the first oracle's reference to Yahweh's defeat of the Messiah's enemies (cf. 1 Cor. 15:25; Heb. 10:13). This comes not by means of direct quotation or even by clear allusion, but merely by the conceptual correspondence between Yahweh's defeat of the king's enemies in Ps. 110:1 and Paul's statement in 1:20–21 that Christ's position at God's right hand is "in the heavenly places, far above all rule and authority and power and lordship and every name that is named" (*pace* Lindars 1961: 50). Paul makes clear in 6:12 that these are inimical powers, and with echoes of Ps. 110:1 already in the air, Christ's position "far above" these powers must mean that God has defeated them on his behalf at the resurrection.

It is possible that when Paul quotes Ps. 8:6 in 1:22, he is only making God's defeat of the cosmic powers for Christ explicit: "And he subjected [*hypetaxen*, replacing the LXX's *hypetaxas*, "you subjected"] all things under [*hypo*, replacing the LXX's *hypokatō*] his feet." It is also possible that he relies merely on a traditional association of Ps. 110:1 with Ps. 8:6 (cf. Heb. 1:3, 13; 2:6–8; 1 Pet.

3:22), and that he is not concerned with the wider contexts of these biblical allusions (Lincoln 1982: 42; Best 1998: 181).

It is more likely, however, that Paul taps into another OT theme here to emphasize a point he has just raised in 1:19, 21. There he alluded to Isa. 40:26 and Ps. 147:4 when he spoke of "the might of [God's] strength" in creation, revealed in, for example, his flawless naming and ordering of the stars. Now he quotes a psalm that extols both God's power in creation, especially his creation of all that one can see in the night sky (8:1, 3), and his placement of human beings over the earthly creatures that he has made (8:4–9). Worshipers originally may have sung the psalm in a nighttime worship setting, perhaps during a festival (cf. 1 Chron. 9:33; Ps. 134:1; Isa. 30:29; see Kraus 1988: 179). It echoes Gen. 1:26, where God says that Adam (*ādām*) must "rule" (*rādâ*) the creatures of the earth. The psalm celebrates Adam as a metaphorical king to whom Yahweh has given the right to rule the world, just as in ancient Near Eastern cultures generally, the god ruled the state through the literal monarch (Kraus 1988: 183–84).

Jewish interpreters of Scripture in the Second Temple period believed that Adam's right to rule the world had been transferred to Israel. This seems to be implied in the hope, expressed at Qumran, that God would one day give to the righteous remnant of his people "all the glory of Adam" (1QS IV, 23; CD-A III, 20; 1QHᵃ IV, 15). It also lies beneath the complaint of the seer in *4 Ezra* 6:38–59 that although God had commanded the sun, the moon, and the stars to serve the human being whom he created (6:45–46 [cf. Ps. 8:6–8]) and had selected Israel from all the nations descended from Adam to rule over creation, Israel, nevertheless, does not "possess the world as an inheritance [*hereditatem*]" (6:59).

Paul's use of Ps. 8:6 in 1:22 probably fits within this conceptual framework. What the Qumran covenanters and the seer of *4 Ezra* longed for, Paul claims, has already begun to happen in Christ. He explicitly claims at several points in the letter that God has begun to restore his fallen creation (2:15; 3:9; 4:13, 24), and he probably opens the door to this idea in 1:19–23. God has not simply conquered Christ's cosmic enemies through raising him from the dead and exalting him to

his royal right hand; he also has subjected all creation to him. This subjection of all things to Christ, moreover, is for the benefit of the church, which is Christ's body (1:22–23), and which, as Paul later will say, "was raised and seated together with Christ in the heavenly places" (2:6). In other words, the hegemony that God intended for humanity to have over all creation is in the process of coming to pass through the Messiah's kingly rule over "all things."

The thought is close to Paul's argument in 1 Cor. 15, where he claims that at Christ's resurrection "the last Adam" and "the second man" reversed the curse of death that came to all people through Adam (15:22, 45, 47) and set in motion the events that eventually would lead to the demise of "every rule and every authority and power" (15:24), including death itself (15:26, 54). Here too Paul uses Ps. 110:1 and Ps. 8:6 to speak of the defeat of the powers and the restoration of human hegemony over creation through the Messiah (cf. Rom. 8:19, 29, 34, 38–39; Phil. 3:20–21; see Wright 2003: 333–38). It is true that in 1 Cor. 15, as in Ps. 110:1 itself, the subjugation of the king's enemies is understood as a future event, whereas in Eph. 1:20, 22 it is conceived of as already accomplished (Luz 1998: 124). Later in his letter, however, Paul will tell his readers to "be strong in the Lord and in the might of his power" (6:10 [cf. Isa. 40:26]), to take up the armor of God so that they might stand in "the day of evil" (6:13), and to extinguish "all the flaming arrows of the evil one" (6:16). It thus becomes clear that there is no fundamental difference between the eschatology of 1 Corinthians and the eschatology of Ephesians (see Wright 2003: 236–38). As the description of the Spirit as a "down payment" in 1:14 implies, Christian redemption is not yet complete (Wright 2003: 236).

In his intercessory prayer in 1:17–23, therefore, Paul foreshadows a theme that will grow in prominence in the later portions of the letter. When God raised the Messiah from the dead, he began the process by which he would subdue the enemies of his people and restore to his people their rightful place as rulers of his creation. Just as God has acted on behalf of his Messiah in accomplishing both these goals, so also his Messiah acts on behalf of God's people. Since God has raised the Messiah from the dead and seated him at his right hand, far above all inimical powers, Paul can speak at this point as if this victory is fully accomplished for his people also.

2:13–17

Part of the new creation that God establishes through his Messiah is a new humanity. In 2:11–22 Paul says that this new humanity consists of both Jews and Gentiles, two formerly discrete and hostile groups that Christ has now united and reconciled (2:14–15, 19). Christ has also reconciled this newly created people to God (2:16–17). He has accomplished both these feats through his death on the cross, which abolished the Mosaic law and therefore brought to an end the basis of the enmity between Jews and Gentiles and between both groups and God (2:14–16).

In these descriptions of God's new humanity Paul expresses himself in language that seems intended to recall at least two passages in Isaiah. The clearest allusions come in 2:17, where Paul says that Christ "came and proclaimed [euēngelisato] peace to you who were far away [tois makran] and peace to those who were near [tois engys]." This is reminiscent of two texts: Isa. 52:7, which speaks of "the messenger who proclaims peace, the messenger of good news, who proclaims salvation," and Isa. 57:19, which speaks of lips whose fruit is the message "Peace, peace to the far and to the near." Paul has skillfully combined the wording of these two texts to make the double peace of 57:19 the object of the herald's glad proclamation in 52:7. In addition, he has used separately each member of Isaiah's poetic doubling of the term "peace," pairing one use with the proclamation of good news to those far away and the other use with the proclamation of good news to those nearby (Lincoln 1982: 28; 1990: 149). His handling of the text reveals a reliance on the Hebrew text rather than on the LXX, which has the herald announcing "a report of peace" (euangelizomenou akoēn eirēnēs) rather than "peace" itself in 52:7, and which disrupts the poetry of the Hebrew text's "peace, peace" in 57:19 by inserting a preposition between the two words: "peace upon [epi] peace." Since Paul also uses the terms "far" and "near" in 2:13 to describe the inclusion of his Gentile readers in the people of God, many interpreters believe that he was already thinking of Isa. 57:19 there before he made more explicit reference to it in 2:17 (e.g., Schlier 1957: 121; Best 1998: 245).

Paul probably was also thinking of the broad literary contexts in which both of these quotations occur in Isaiah. This becomes clear from three considerations.

First, since virtually everyone who has examined Eph. 2:17 closely agrees that Paul alludes to Isa. 57:19 when he speaks of "peace" to "the far" and "peace" to "the near," it seems most reasonable to see this text behind Paul's earlier use of the terms "far" and "near" in 2:13. Trips made to the rabbinic literature and Qumran (Lincoln 1982: 27–28) or even to other OT texts (Hoehner 2002: 362) in search of parallels to Paul's language in 2:13 seem to be unnecessarily long journeys when Isa. 57:19 stands so close. If Paul already alludes to Isa. 57:19 in 2:13, however, then this prophetic text stands like a set of matching bookends at the beginning and the end of his claim in 2:14–16 that Christ, through his death, reconciled Gentiles and Jews to one another and a newly created people drawn from both groups to God (Moritz 1996: 28–29). This use of Isa. 57:19 as an *inclusio* implies in turn that the text was important to Paul's thinking as he wrote about the reconciliation of peoples to one another and of both to God. It did not come to mind as an afterthought.

Second, Paul's concern in 2:13, 17 for the coming of Gentiles into the boundaries of God's people captures a thought that is characteristic of Isaiah's theology (Moritz 1996: 45–52). Isaiah frequently refers to a future influx of Gentiles to Jerusalem and to the temple to worship God. He tells Israel that at the time of their eschatological restoration, "peoples that you do not know shall run to you" (55:5). A few paragraphs later the prophet says that God will bring foreigners "to my holy mountain" so that they might "rejoice in my house of prayer . . . because my house will be called a house of prayer for all peoples" (56:6–7).

The text to which Paul alludes in 2:13, 17 comes only a few paragraphs later still, in Isa. 57:18–19, where the Lord speaks of the comfort that will come to his people at the time of their restoration: "'Peace, peace to the far and to the near,' says the LORD, 'and I will heal him [i.e., the people]'" (57:19). Although scholars frequently claim that the terms "far" and "near" in this passage refer to Jews within geographical Israel and to Jews of the Diaspora respectively (e.g., Westermann 1969: 300; Whybray 1981: 211; Lincoln 1982:

27; Hübner 1997: 165; Hoehner 2002: 365), the broader context of the passage indicates that a reference to the Gentiles probably at least stands in the background and may be the primary meaning of the text (see Moritz 1996: 32–34). It certainly is plausible that Paul understood the reference in this way. After all, he knew the text of Isaiah well, and modern distinctions between "Second" and "Third" Isaiah (chaps. 40–55 and 56–66) did not trouble him.

Third, Paul, like Isaiah before him, combined the notion of the eschatological pilgrimage of the nations to Israel with the notion of a new creation. Isaiah could speak of the "new heavens and the new earth" in one breath and of "all flesh" coming to Jerusalem to worship God in the next (66:22–23; cf. 11:6–9; 45:18–19; 62:3–5; 65:17–25; cf. also Hos. 2:18; see von Rad 1965: 240–41; Brueggemann 1997: 546–51; Childs 1993: 114–15). Paul similarly could merge these two ideas and speak of Christ "creating" Jews and Gentiles "into one new humanity" (2:15). Since Paul's indebtedness to the language of Isaiah in Ephesians is clear, it seems likely that this concept, so distinctive of Isaiah's theology, comes from that source also.

In 2:13–17, therefore, Paul reminds his Gentile readers that God worked powerfully among them by including them in his newly created people. Through Christ's death he has also started the process of bringing together in Christ all things in heaven and on earth (1:9–10). Christ's death started this process because it demolished the dividing wall of partition that stood between Jews and Gentiles and also between both groups and God. Christ's death brought in the period of peace that Isaiah said would characterize the time of Israel's restoration, a period when the nations would come from afar and join Israel in the worship of the one "who created the heavens, . . . who fashioned the earth and made it" (Isa. 45:18).

3:1–13

If Paul believed that the death of Christ set in motion the fulfillment of Isaiah's prophetic expectations (see commentary on Eph. 2:13–17 above), then Paul's comments on how God revealed this fulfillment in 3:1–13 pose a problem for the interpreter. Here Paul seems to say that the inclusion of the Gentiles within the eschatological people of God as he has described it in 2:11–22 came

to him and other NT apostles and prophets as a new "revelation" (3:3, 5) or "mystery" (3:3–4, 9). This "mystery," he says, "was not made known to the sons of men in other generations as [hōs] it has now been revealed to his holy apostles and prophets by the Spirit" (3:5). It was "hidden for ages in the God who created all things" (3:9b), but God has now entrusted it to Paul so that he might openly proclaim it to the Gentiles (3:8–9a).

Is the contrast between former ignorance and present insight in this passage too stark to allow the kind of promise-and-fulfillment scheme for Paul's thinking that I have argued is present in 2:13–17? Many interpreters think that it is. Barth (1974: 332) believes that in 3:5 Paul has used a hymnic fragment that varies from his own understanding of the OT. Best (1998: 306) thinks that the author may have overemphasized the element of discontinuity between the testaments in 3:5, but that he corrects this exaggeration in other passages. Lincoln (1982: 44–47 [cf. 1990: 178]) maintains that despite the author's linguistic echoes of Isaiah in 2:13, 17, he was relatively uninterested in the question of how the inclusion of the Gentiles with God's people fulfills prophetic expectations.

A more promising line of interpretation focuses on Paul's use of the conjunction "as" (hōs) in 3:5. Some scholars argue that Paul does not use this conjunction to compare a complete lack of knowledge in previous generations with the present revelation. Instead, he uses it to describe a comparison of degree: the mystery was not made known in former generations "to the extent" that it has now been revealed (see Caragounis 1977: 102). This leaves room for the notion that whereas the OT prophets did not see God's plan for the inclusion of the Gentiles with the same clarity as did the NT apostles and prophets, they did understand its basic outline.

Two considerations, however, weigh against this otherwise attractive reading of 3:5. First, where Paul uses similar expressions elsewhere, he leaves out the critical hōs on which this view depends (Grindheim 2003). In 3:9 he speaks simply of "the mystery hidden for ages in the God who created all things," with no indication that the mystery was only partially hidden. Similarly, in Col. 1:26, a text that closely parallels both Eph. 3:5 and Eph. 3:9, Paul again speaks only of "the mystery hidden for ages and for generations, but now manifested to his saints." The *hōs* is missing here, and with it any idea that the revelation recently given to God's people was illumined more clearly only in recent times.

Second, Paul's use of the terms "revelation" (*apokalypsis* [3:3]), "reveal" (*apokalyptō* [3:5]), and "mystery" (*mystērion* [3:3–4, 9; cf. 1:9; 5:32; 6:19]) in Eph. 3:1–13 seems closely related to the use of similar terms in Daniel 2. There, the dream of Nebuchadnezzar remains utterly inaccessible to the wise men of Babylon, including Daniel and his three Jewish friends, but Daniel and his friends seek the mercy of God concerning this "mystery" (LXX: *mystērion*). "The God in heaven who reveals mysteries [LXX: *ho anakalyptōn mystēria*]" then provides Daniel both with the details of the king's dream and with its interpretation (2:18–19, 27–30, 47; cf. 4:9). The dream's interpretation reveals God's sovereignty over the course of history (2:29, 36–45). For Paul too, God's willingness to reveal the "mystery" of his purposes in history to believers arose from "the wealth of [God's] grace" (1:7–10). It seems likely that, as with Daniel's use of the term, so also with Paul, the revelation of these purposes involved giving information that was utterly inaccessible apart from God's gracious revelation of it to Paul and others who lived after Christ's crucifixion.

How, then, can we explain Paul's implied appeal to Isa. in 2:13–17 in light of his claim in 3:5, 9 that the truths that he explains in that passage were hidden from previous generations? The answer lies in understanding the specific nature of the mystery as Paul describes it in 3:6. The mystery is that "the Gentiles are fellow heirs [*sygklēronoma*] and one body [*syssōma*] and sharers [*symmetocha*] in the promise in Christ Jesus." As the piling up of words compounded with *syn* ("with") shows, the mystery is the equal footing that Gentiles and Jews now have together in the people of God (see Bruce 1984: 314; O'Brien 1999: 232; Hoehner 2002: 440–41). It is true that many OT texts, particularly in Isaiah, speak of the inclusion of Gentiles in the worship of God during the days of Israel's eschatological restoration (e.g., Isa. 2:2–4; 25:6–10; 56:6–8). It is also true that some Jews during the Second Temple period valued this hope (Tob. 13:11; *1 En.* 90:33; *2 Bar.* 72:4). It is not clear from these texts, however, that Gentiles

would occupy a place of equal importance with Jews in those days (*pace* Donaldson 1997: 69–74), and this is precisely what Paul implies in 3:6 (cf. Grindheim 2003).

In conclusion, Paul's implicit claim in 2:11–22 that the unity of Jews and Gentiles in Christ fulfilled Isaiah's expectations for the eschatological inclusion of the nations in the worship of God is not inconsistent with his claim in 3:5 that this mystery was withheld from previous generations only to be revealed to NT apostles and prophets in the present. The mystery of 3:3–4, 9 is not the entire argument of 2:11–22, but rather one element within that argument. Now that the eschatological age has begun, Jews and Gentiles do not merely worship together; they are united with each other, occupying the same level of privilege before God.

4:7–11

A. Paul's Quotation of Ps. 68:18 in NT Context.
Paul's description of God's powerful work on behalf of his Gentile readers in 2:11–22 led him in 3:1–21 to pray that God would give them the power to grasp "the breadth and length and height and depth . . . of the love of Christ" (3:18–19). This prayer included a digression on the importance of Paul's divine commission "to preach to the Gentiles the unfathomable wealth of Christ" (3:8) and to illumine all people about the mystery that Gentiles and Jews who believe in Christ are one body (3:3–9) (see commentary on Eph. 3:1–13 above). He concluded with an ascription of praise to the God "who is able to do far more than all that we ask or imagine" (3:20).

Then, in 4:1, Paul opened the second major part of the epistle (4:1–6:24) with a statement of this part's theme: those for whom God has done so much should live in a way that is consistent with what God has done for them. In 4:1–6:9 Paul describes how his readers should "therefore walk," how they should live on the basis of the truths that he has just described in the letter's first part (Hoehner 2002: 581). They should "walk" in unity (4:1–16), holiness (4:17–32), love (5:1–6), light (5:7–14), and wisdom (5:15–6:9).

In the first of these five sections Paul says that God, through Christ, has brought his readers together from disparate social groups into "one new man" and has reconciled this one new man with himself. Unity and peace should therefore characterize God's new humanity, the church (4:1–6).

In 4:7–16 Paul insists that this unity does not exclude the exercise of diverse gifts. Rather, a diversity of gifts builds up the body of Christ, providing it with the maturity and stability necessary to guard this "perfect man" against the cunning attacks of false teaching. In 4:7–11 Paul begins this argument with the claim that God has graciously distributed gifts to his people. He grounds this claim in a quotation and brief exegesis of Ps. 68:18 (68:19 MT; 67:19 LXX). This is the only biblical quotation in the letter that begins with a quotation formula: *dio legei* ("therefore it says" [4:8]).

B. Ps. 68:18 in OT Context. Ps. 68 is notoriously difficult both to outline and to place in any specific historical setting. Scholars often rank it among the most difficult psalms to interpret (see Albright 1950–1951: 7; Weiser 1962: 481; Kraus 1989: 47), and the wide variety of proposals for its setting are evidence of the truth in this assessment. Weiser (1962: 481–84) believes that the psalm was composed for and used in the corporate worship of God (68:24–27) in the Jerusalem temple (68:29) at the time of an autumn festival (68:9). Kidner (1973: 238) believes that it originated in the transfer of the ark from the house of Obed-Edom to Mount Zion (68:17–18 [cf. 2 Sam. 6:12]). Kraus (1989: 49–51, 55) proposes that the psalm is a collection of traditions: one tradition locates the worship of God on Mount Tabor (68:15), another envisions Jerusalem as the place of worship (68:27), and still another arose during a period of animosity between Egypt and Israel, probably in the fourth century (68:30–31). Perhaps the most unusual theory about the psalm's origin is that of Albright (1950–1951: 7–10), who claims that the psalm is not a coherent composition at all, but rather a catalog of separate psalms, each one identified by its opening lines.

Although almost universally rejected as an explanation for the psalm, this last position usefully highlights the psalm's diversity: it ranges over a wide field historically, geographically, and topically. It speaks of the scattering of God's enemies (68:1–3), God's protection for the poor (68:5–6, 10), and the history of God's dealings with his people from the exodus to the establishment of the temple on Mount Zion (68:7–18). It describes a procession of worshipers (68:24–27) and includes a prayer that God hasten the day when all the kingdoms of the earth would submit to him (68:28–31). Despite this variety of material, the psalm displays a coherent historical movement from God's past faithfulness to Israel to a future in which all the nations of the earth would worship him. At the center of the psalm, between the account of past victory and the expression of future hope, lies an affirmation of God's faithfulness in the present (68:19–20).

In 68:17–18 the psalm reaches the climax of its historical review when it speaks of God as moving from Sinai into the sanctuary on Mount Zion. In 68:17 the psalmist seems to conceive of Mount Sinai as inside the sanctuary in Jerusalem (Weiser 1962: 488; Kidner 1973: 241–42), and this image seems to mean that the God whose power was so much in evidence on Mount Sinai is now present in all this power on Mount Zion. In 68:18 the psalm apparently refers to the victories that God gave to the Israelites as they moved into and occupied Canaan, particularly the victory of Deborah and Barak over the forces of Sisera as it is celebrated in Deborah's song: "You ascended to the heights; you captured captives [*šābîtā šebî*; cf. Judg. 5:12: *ûšăbēh šebyĕkā*]; you received gifts among humanity, even among the rebellious, to dwell there as Yah Elohim."

Thus in 68:17–18 the psalm summarizes the military victories that God gave to his people as he led them from Sinai to Jerusalem. The gifts that God received "among humanity" (*bā'ādām* [sg.]) are the booty of war and the tribute that conquered peoples pay to him. These victories are God's victories over his enemies and for his people. They bring to a triumphant conclusion his march with his people from Egypt to Sinai to Jerusalem.

From this point forward the psalm focuses on God's present (68:19–20) and future (68:21–23, 28–31) salvation of his people and on his dominion over their enemies. It ends with a command to the kings of the earth to sing the praises of God (68:32–35). God's victories over his enemies and faithfulness to his people in the past seem to form the foundation for the hope that in the future God will continue to protect his people from those, whether from east, west (68:22 [Wilson 2002: 1:940]), north, or south (68:30 [Wilson 2002:

1:942]) who would oppress them. It is also the foundation for the hope that one day God will rule over all the peoples of the earth (68:32–35) (see Gunkel [1998: 251, 264], who identifies Ps. 68 as an "eschatological hymn").

C. Ps. 68:18 in Jewish Interpretation. With remarkable consistency, Jewish interpreters of Ps. 68:18 explained it as a reference to Moses' ascent to heaven to receive the Torah from God. The "you" of that verse was not God, but Moses; the ascension was not up Mount Zion, as the psalm probably implies, but up to heaven; and the "captivity" that Moses took captive was the Torah.

This interpretation led to problems when the interpreter encountered the phrase "you received gifts among man," a statement that implies the reception of gifts not from God, but from people, and therefore not in heaven, but on earth. One rabbinic text interprets the phrase to mean that Moses received the Torah "by the virtue Israel" (*Pesiq. Rab.* 47:4); others that Moses received the Torah "because of the merits of the man," meaning the pious Abraham (*Sop.* 16:10; *Midr. Ps.* 22:19; *Exod. Rab.* 28:1); another that Moses received the Torah as recompense for the insult that the heavenly angels gave to him when they called him "man" (*b. Šabb.* 89a); another that Moses received the Torah "as a mere man" (*Pesiq. Rab.* 20:4); and still another that Moses received the Torah "which was bestowed upon Israel as a gift, at no cost" (*Midr. Ps.* 68:11) (see Barth 1974: 475–76; Harris 1998: 77–95). Rashi (Rabbi Shlomo Yitzhaki), writing in the eleventh century in northern France, apparently followed this last interpretation: "YOU WENT UP, you, the prince of My people, Moses son of Amram, and YOU TOOK CAPTIVE the Torah, and YOU RECEIVED TRIBUTE from those on high to give them to human beings" (translation in Gruber 1998: 304 [see also 310nn67–69]).

The interpretation of the phrase in *Midrash Psalms*, which Rashi adopted, says explicitly that Moses received the Torah in order to give it as a gift to Israel. The Targum on Ps. 68:19 MT condenses the action of receiving the Torah in order to give it to Israel by saying simply, "You ascended to the firmament, Prophet Moses; you led captive captivity; you learned the words of Torah; you *gave* them as gifts to the sons of men" (translation in Harris 1998: 65 [italics added]).

Even the earliest of these texts, in their present form, come from centuries after the composition of Ephesians. A plausible argument can be made, however, that the exegetical elements that these traditions hold in common, from the least to the most elaborate, were current in the first century. Three elements of this exegetical tradition meet this criterion and therefore are likely very old: (1) the "you" of the text is Moses rather than God; (2) the ascension in the text refers to Moses' ascension to heaven; (3) Moses went to heaven to take the Torah "captive" (see Harris 1998: 92–93).

Occasionally, scholars take the traditional association of Ps. 68:18 with Moses a step further to suggest that this text was used at Pentecost, the harvest festival at which Jews since the second century BC (*Jub.* 6:11–22) had celebrated the giving of the law to Israel (Lincoln 1982: 20; 1990: 243–44; Harris 1998: 143–70; Moritz 1996: 62–63). It then becomes possible to posit a Jewish-Christian polemic against this tradition in which Christ (not Moses) gave the Spirit (not Torah) on the Christian (not the Jewish) Pentecost (Harris 1998: 171–72; Moritz 1996: 74–76). This Jewish-Christian tradition may be visible in Acts 2:33: "[This Jesus], having been exalted to the right hand of God, and having received the promise of the Holy Spirit from the Father, has poured out this which you both see and hear."

This statement appears in Peter's Pentecost sermon and, in the view of some scholars, is patterned after the Jewish understanding of Ps. 68:18. Like Moses, Jesus ascends to heaven, receives something from God, and bestows it on God's people (Harris 1998: 159–69; cf. Lindars 1961: 53–54).

D. Paul's Text. Paul introduces his quotation with the phrase "therefore, it says" (*dio legei*), a formula that he uses also in 5:14. There, however, the formula does not precede a quotation from Scripture. Since Paul's quotation in 4:8 differs markedly from both the MT and the LXX of Ps. 68:18, some scholars have proposed that, just as in 5:14, Paul does not cite Scripture at all in 4:8, but rather quotes a piece of Christian tradition that is itself related to Ps. 68:18 (Moritz 1996: 56–86; Best 1998: 378–82). The same formula, however, signals a quotation from Scripture elsewhere in the NT (James 4:6) and often in Philo (*Alleg. Interp.* 3.180; *Drunkenness* 138; *Confusion* 182; *Agriculture* 100). It seems more probable, then, that in both 4:8 and 5:14 Paul wanted to alert his readers that he was about to quote from Scripture: here he quotes the OT, and in 5:14 he quotes a piece of early Christian tradition that he believed had scriptural status.

The differences between Paul's quotation of Ps. 68:18 and the text in both the MT and the LXX are dramatic. First, Paul changes "you ascended" (MT: *'ālîtā*; LXX: *anebēs*) to the participle "having ascended" (*anabas*). The LXX text reveals some instability at this point, with the original hand of Codex Sinaiticus reading "he ascended" (*anebē*) and the original hand of Codex Vaticanus reading, like Paul, "having ascended." The second corrector of Sinaiticus and the second and third correctors of Vaticanus, however, agree with the MT that the first verb of the text should be in the second-person singular. The deviations from this reading by the original hands of Sinaiticus and Vaticanus probably reflect a tendency to conform the LXX text to Paul's citation of it (Harris 1998: 97–98).

Paul then changes "you captured"—the reading in the MT and the LXX—to "he captured." Once again, the original hand of Sinaiticus agrees with Paul (against its second corrector and Vaticanus), but there can be little doubt that here too its deviation from the MT stems from a tendency to conform the text to Paul's quotation. A full translation of the original hand of Sinaiticus at this point reveals why: "*He* ascended to the heights; *he* captured captivity; *you* received gifts among humanity." The nonsensical shift from third to second person in the verb "you received" (*elabes*) shows that some influence has disrupted the text. It seems probable that this influence was Paul's change of the last two verbs from the second to the third person. The scribe, perhaps unconsciously, remembered Paul's change in the person of these verbs and applied it inconsistently (see Harris 1998: 98n101).

Paul's most significant change comes in his handling of the third verb, which reads "you received" (MT: *lāqaḥtā*; LXX: *elabes*) but in Paul becomes "he gave" (*edōken*). Paul has not merely changed the verb from the second to the third person; he also has replaced the verb with its antonym. This apparently led Paul to render the difficult phrase "among humanity" (MT: *bā'ādām*; LXX:

en anthrōpō) with the more intelligible words "to human beings" (*tois anthrōpois*).

How can we explain these changes? One of the most popular explanations relies on the Jewish exegetical tradition reviewed above (see §C), and especially the paraphrase of the Targum on Ps. 68:19. In the Targum, just as in Eph. 4:8, we find an ascent to heaven and then not the receiving of gifts from humanity, as in the MT, but rather the giving of gifts to humanity, as in Eph. 4:8. Some scholars think that Paul (or the author) knew the Targum (Barth 1974: 476) or at least appealed to an exegetical tradition on Ps. 68:18 that also stands behind the Targum (Lincoln 1982: 19; 1990: 243; Gnilka 1971: 207; Pokorný 1992: 170; Harris 1998: 64–122). Perhaps Paul even used this tradition in a polemical way to say that Christ, not Moses, ascended not merely to heaven but "far above all the heavens" (4:10) and gave to people not the Torah but "grace" (4:7) (Lincoln 1982: 20; 1990: 243; Bruce 1984: 342–43).

A variant of this last explanation says that in 4:8 Paul is indebted to the early Christian polemic against the association of Moses, the Torah, and Pentecost with Ps. 68:18. For Paul, as for the early Jewish Christians before him, Christ's ascension to heaven and subsequent gift of the Spirit at Pentecost had trumped Moses' ascent to heaven and subsequent mediation of the law to Israel (Harris 1998: 171–72; cf. Moritz 1996: 74–75; Schnackenburg 1991: 177; Best 1998: 381). Some who adopt this understanding of 4:8 believe that in 4:9–10 Paul explains Christ's descent not as his descent into the underworld (e.g., Arnold 1997: 56–58), nor as his incarnation (e.g., Best 1998: 386), but as the coming of the Spirit at Pentecost (e.g., Harris 1998: 171–97).

Several scholars attempt to show that Paul's change of *elabes* ("you received") to *edōken* ("you gave") is consistent with the theology expressed in Ps. 68. One theory claims that Ps. 68:17–18 intentionally echoed the language of Num. 8:6, 14; 18:6, in which Yahweh takes the Levites from among the people and then gives the Levites back to the people as a gift (Smith 1975: 186–88; cf. O'Brien 1999: 292–93). Another theory focuses on the many "gifts" that God gives to his people in the psalm: his active presence, his care for the needy, his faithfulness to Israel throughout its history (especially in giving them victory over their enemies), his entrance into his sanctuary, and his removal of the wicked. Admittedly, Paul has changed the wording of the lines that he quotes from the psalm, but since the psalm speaks of these many divine gifts, the change from "you received" to "he gave" is not arbitrary (Hoehner 2002: 528).

Tracing the origins of the text that Paul cites in 4:8 is fraught with such uncertainty that definitive pronouncements for or against certain theories are probably ill-advised. Nevertheless, it seems necessary to make two cautionary observations about the popular thesis that Paul's citation repeats an exegetical tradition, whether Jewish or Jewish-Christian, that preceded him.

First, the Targum on Ps. 68:19 is the only unambiguous evidence of a Jewish exegetical tradition that actually replaces the verb "received" with the verb "gave." The other ancient Jewish comments on this text retain the verb "received" in the quotation but then imply that Moses received the Torah in order to "give" it to Israel. The Targumim on Psalms in their present form, however, come from the fourth or fifth centuries after Christ. That they existed in the first century and influenced Paul seems unlikely, and even the idea that the Targum on Ps. 68 is indebted to an early tradition that had already changed "you received" to "he gave" in 68:18 remains highly uncertain. Since the Targum comes from such a late period, and the christological reading of Ps. 68:18 was so widespread (e.g., Justin, *Dial.* 39.4–5), it seems at least as likely that the Targum represents a polemical response to the Christian exegesis of Ps. 68:19 MT as that it preserves a three- or four-centuries-old Jewish exegetical tradition that Paul used but that left no other clearly perceptible traces in Jewish exegetical literature.

Second, Paul writes in Greek to Gentiles (2:11; 3:1; 4:17), probably scattered over a wide area, not in Aramaic to Jews, nor even in Greek to Jewish Christians. He may have been able to assume some knowledge of the Greek rendering of the Scriptures among his readers, but he probably did not assume that they were familiar with an exegetical tradition preserved only in an Aramaic paraphrase of the Hebrew Scriptures. Even if some of his readers had heard of the rendering of Ps. 68:19 MT now preserved in the Targum, it seems unlikely that Paul would assume that they would give the

Targum the same status as the Greek Scriptures (see Best 1998: 379–80).

Unless more concrete evidence appears in the future and points in another direction, it seems best to think that Paul himself changed the Greek rendering of the text to suit his argument at this point in the letter. He certainly follows a similar procedure elsewhere (see Best 1998: 381). When he quotes Hab. 2:4 in Gal. 3:11 and in Rom. 1:17, he leaves out the possessive pronoun "his," so that Habakkuk's "the righteous person shall live by his faithfulness" becomes "the righteous person shall live by faith." Similarly, he quotes Deut. 30:12–14 in Rom. 10:6–8 to draw a contrast between the righteousness that comes by faith and the righteousness that comes by the Mosaic law. Deuteronomy 30:12–14 is a description of the ease with which one can obey the law. Paul, however, omits from his quotation any reference to the law, makes the text refer to the universal availability of the righteousness that comes by faith, and contrasts the effortlessness of faith with the impossibility of doing the law. Although in each instance Paul has introduced dramatic changes to the text that he cites, a reasonable case can be made that his overall argument is consistent with the overall argument of the passage out of which his citation comes.

Has Paul also followed this procedure in Eph. 4:7–11? Here too a good case can be made that although Paul's changes to the Greek text of Scripture are dramatic, they are consistent with the overall theological direction of the psalm from which his citation comes.

E. Paul's Use of Ps. 68:18. Commentators usually identify the theme of Christ's gifts to the church as the primary focus of the passage. This certainly is an important theme, as the threefold appearance of the verb "give" (*didōmi*) in the passage reveals. Paul uses "was given" (*edothē*) in 4:7, makes the critical change from "you received" to "he gave" (*edōken*) in the quotation in 4:8, and repeats this form of the verb in 4:11 to refer to the gifts that Christ bestowed on his people.

Another important, perhaps equally important, theme in the passage, however, is the triumph of Christ over the hostile, invisible powers (see Arnold 1997: 56–57). Paul not only describes this triumph explicitly in the quotation's statement that "he captured captivity," but also he hints at Christ's triumph over these powers when, in his interpretation of the quotation, he says that Christ ascended "far above all [*hyperanō pantōn*] the heavens" (4:10). This statement may intentionally recall Paul's earlier claim in 1:20–21 that when God raised Christ from the dead, he seated him "at his right hand in the heavenly places far above all [*hyperanō pasēs*] rule and authority and power and lordship and every name that is named."

Paul's interest in Ps. 68:18, therefore, lay not only in the "gifts" that the psalm mentions and that, according to Paul's change from *elabes* ("you received") to *edōken* ("he gave"), were given to people, but also in the psalm's expression of God's triumph over his enemies. This second theme of triumph, therefore, dominates Paul's exegesis of his quotation in 4:9–10. Paul insists that Ps. 68:18 refers to Christ. He argues first that the quotation's mention of an ascent implies a prior descent (4:9). He then says that the one who both descended and ascended must be Christ, the same person whom God exalted over all invisible and inimical cosmic powers (4:10) after his descent to "the lower regions of the earth."

The notion that God (or, in Paul's thinking, God's agent, Christ) triumphed over the enemies of God's people is a prominent theme in Ps. 68. The psalm begins with a request that God arise and scatter his enemies (68:1–2), continues with a historical review of God's military triumphs over Israel's enemies from the exodus to the battle of Deborah and Barak against the forces of Sisera (68:7–10 [cf. Judg. 5:4–5, 21]), and, as it reaches its climax (Terrien 2003: 486–87, 490, 494; *pace* Moritz 1996: 65–66), pictures God sweeping away all his enemies before him in a dramatic military drive from Mount Sinai to Mount Zion (68:17–18). It concludes with references to God's continued triumph over his enemies and the enemies of his people in the future (68:21–23, 28–30). Paul's quotation comes from the psalm's triumphant climax in 68:17–18.

In Ephesians, Paul is also interested in the theme that God, in Christ, has triumphed over the enemies of God's people (1:20–23; 2:5–6; 3:10; cf. 6:12). Since Paul voices this theme both in his quotation of the climactic paragraph of Ps. 68 and in his interpretation of it, he may have chosen this quotation because it not only used the crucial term "gift," but also articulated the theme of Christ's triumph (*pace* Smith 1975:

182). To make the quotation more suitable to his concern with Christ's giving of gifts to "the saints," he changed "you received" to "he gave," but no change was necessary in the quotation to make it suitable to his theme of Christ's triumph over the inimical powers.

If this is a correct understanding of the passage, then Paul has not made use of a Jewish or Jewish-Christian exegetical tradition that had previously replaced "you received" with "he gave," nor did he use a Jewish-Christian tradition that polemically compared Christ with Moses. Instead, Paul has tied the two principal parts of his letter together in the opening paragraph of the second part by stressing both the theme of God's triumph in Christ over the hostile powers of the universe and the theme of Christian unity. The Christ who in his descent to earth and ascent to heaven triumphed over all his cosmic enemies is the same Christ who from his position of triumph at God's right hand distributes diverse gifts to his people in order to foster their unity.

F. The Theological Implications of Paul's Use of Ps. 68:18. Paul apparently found in Christ's distribution of various gifts to his people for the unity and maturity of the church the fulfillment of the eschatology that he saw in Ps. 68. He also seems to have believed that this eschatology was consistent with the eschatology that he had developed elsewhere in Ephesians of God's triumph in Christ over the inimical cosmic powers of the universe (1:20–23; 2:1–7) and the restoration of humanity to its condition prior to its alienation from God (2:15; 3:9; 4:13, 24).

In the psalm God's past faithfulness to his people reaches a climax in his ascent to Mount Zion, and that ascent holds promise for the salvation of his people in even more glorious ways in the present and future. God will rescue them from death, deal their enemies far and wide a fatal blow, and receive the worship of the earth's rulers. Paul believed that this time of God's salvation had started with the ascent of Christ to the "Mount Zion" of God's right hand. Acting in the role of God himself in Ps. 68:17–18, Christ had triumphed over the cosmic forces arrayed against God's people. From his lofty and newly-won position on the eschatological Zion, he distributed gifts to God's people. These gifts would enable them to become, as a people, the "mature man" (Eph. 4:13) that God created humanity to be.

4:17–5:20

Although Paul's ethical admonitions in 4:17–5:20 frequently speak the language of the OT, Paul never alerts his readers in this section that he is quoting from Scripture. Sometimes he uses the precise wording of an OT passage (4:26a; 5:18). Sometimes his wording is close to something in the OT, but not exact (4:25, 30). At other times he refers merely to a command or principle that also appears in the OT (4:26b, 28a).

This situation has led most scholars to conclude that Paul (or the author) does not use the OT directly here, but is indebted instead to a Jewish tradition of ethical instruction that itself spoke the language of the OT (e.g., Gnilka 1971: 234, 238, 269; Lincoln 1982: 42–43; 1990: 300; Luz 1998: 161). Admonitions not to lie, not to be angry, not to steal, not to grieve the Holy Spirit, not to become drunk, and to avoid debauchery were common in the ethical literature of Second Temple Judaism and Jewish Christianity. These admonitions, moreover, sometimes appear in combination with each other, just as they do in Eph. 4:17–5:20 (e.g., *T. Iss.* 7:3–4 [debauchery, drunkenness, stealing, deceit]; *T. Dan* 2:1, 4; 3:5–6; 4:6–7; 5:1–2, 7; 6:8 [deceit, anger]), and sometimes they use the language of precisely the OT passages to which Paul's admonitions seem indebted (e.g., *T. Dan* 5:2 [cf. Zech. 8:16 and Eph. 4:25]; Herm. *Mand.* 41:2–6; 42:2 [cf. Isa. 63:10 and Eph. 4:30]; *T. Jud.* 14:1 [cf. Prov. 23:31 LXX and Eph. 5:18]).

This understanding of Paul's ethical admonitions in 4:17–5:20 is plausible and may be correct, especially for his advice against stealing (4:28), drunkenness, and debauchery (5:18). Three admonitions (4:25, 26, 30), however, seem to recall the wider biblical context from which they ultimately come.

In 4:25 Paul contrasts the former way his readers lived when they were Gentiles with the way that they should live now that they have put off "the old man" (4:22) and put on "the new man" (4:24). Because of this new situation (*dio*), they should "lay aside falsehood and *speak the truth, each one with his neighbor* [*laleite alētheian hekastos meta tou plēsion autou*]." The italicized phrase duplicates Zech. 8:16 LXX almost exactly. Paul

has simply changed the word that translates the Hebrew preposition 'et ("with") in the LXX from *pros* ("to") to *meta* ("with") and made the necessary change in the case of the article that follows the preposition.

Several scholars have noticed that the context of Paul's admonition parallels the context of Zech. 8:16 in important ways (Yoder Neufeld 1997: 133–34n128; O'Brien 1999: 337–38; Hoehner 2002: 616–17). Just as Eph. 4:25 is concerned with the conduct of the eschatologically formed people of God, so Zech. 8:16 is concerned with the conduct of Israel in the future when God will restore their fortunes (8:2–8, 12–15, 18–23). In that day God will return to Mount Zion and dwell among his people (8:3), whom he will gather from their exile east and west. The nations will stream to Jerusalem to worship Yahweh (8:20–23). Zechariah gives Yahweh's admonition to speak the truth to one another to this future, restored remnant of God's people.

Paul too gives his admonition to speak the truth to the "new man" (4:24)—God's new people gathered from Jews and Gentiles (2:15). Paul has described this new people as God's "holy temple . . . the dwelling place of God by the Spirit" (2:21–22). The conceptual parallels here are close, particularly when we remember that Paul has just used a psalm in 4:8 (Ps. 68) that also speaks about God's eschatological triumph over the enemies of his people and his dominion over the rulers of the earth (see Gunkel [1998: 255n61], who notices a connection between Ps. 68 and Zech. 8).

In the next verse Paul, using language that duplicates exactly Ps. 4:5a LXX (4:4a ET), admonishes his readers not to sin when they are angry (4:26a). Here too Paul may have had the wider context of the psalm in mind when he used these words. He has just forbidden falsehood (4:25), one of the sins in which the psalmist's adversaries were engaged (Ps. 4:2). Paul is also about to recommend that his readers not let the sun set on their anger (4:26b), an idea that may have been prompted by the psalmist's advice to his enemies not to act on their anger, but instead to ponder their feelings in silence on their beds (Ps. 4:4b) (see Moritz 1996: 90).

A few sentences later Paul admonishes his readers not to "grieve [*lypeite*] the Holy Spirit of God" (4:30), a statement that echoes the language of Isa. 63:10, although it neither translates the Hebrew text literally ("they grieved [ʿatsab] his Holy Spirit") nor matches the rendering in the LXX ("they provoked [paroxynō] his Holy Spirit"). Within its context Isa. 63:10 describes how Israel's rebellion against God, even after he had showed them mercy, turned God into their enemy and resulted in their exile. Elsewhere in his correspondence Paul turns God's judgment on a rebellious Israel into an admonition to God's eschatologically restored people not to follow the example of their "fathers" (1 Cor. 10:1–22). He may be doing something similar here in 4:30, although, if so, his exegetical procedure is much less explicit.

How are we to evaluate the evidence both that Paul followed a common Jewish ethical tradition in 4:17–5:20 and that he was aware of the wider context of at least some of the OT passages whose language he uses? It may be unwise to force a choice between these two possible sources for Paul's biblical language. As a Hellenistic Jew himself, Paul probably was aware of the ethical traditions that stand behind products of Hellenistic Judaism such as the *Testaments of the Twelve Patriarchs*, and there is no reason to think that he would have resisted using these traditions. At the same time, there is also evidence, not least from Ephesians itself, that Paul had a detailed knowledge of the content of the Jewish Scriptures, particularly of Psalms and Isaiah. Perhaps Paul used a common ethical tradition with which he had long been familiar but, aware of the roots of this tradition in the OT, also allowed the biblical context of some of the passages used in the tradition to shape his own thinking as he composed 4:17–5:20.

5:31–32

A. Paul's Quotation of Gen. 2:24 in NT Context.
As the final part of his instruction on how Christians should "walk" (4:1–6:9), Paul urges his readers to "walk not as unwise but as wise people" (5:15 in 5:15–6:9). One aspect of walking wisely is "submitting to one another in the fear of Christ" (5:21), and this willingness to submit to each other has particular implications for the Christian household. "Wives," Paul says, should submit "to their own husbands as to the Lord," and they should do this because an analogy exists between the wife's submission to the husband as her head and the church's submission to Christ as its head (5:21–22, 24, 33). Christ qualifies as the head of the church because "he himself is the savior of the body" (5:23).

With this statement Paul introduces the thought that will dominate his description of the husband's responsibility toward the wife (5:25–33). The husband should "love," "nurture," and "cherish" (5:25, 28, 29, 33) his wife because an analogy exists between the husband's love and care for his wife and Christ's love and care for the church (5:25–30). Paul now explains this analogy in detail. By means of an echo of Ezek. 16:9, which describes Israel as the bride of Yahweh whom he "washed . . . with water," Paul implies that the church is the bride of Christ whom he sanctified and cleansed "by the washing of water with the word" (5:26) (O'Brien 1999: 422; *pace* Best 1998: 543, and most others). Just as Christ cared for his bride, so the Christian husband should care for his wife.

In addition, Paul folds into this metaphor the image of the church as the body of Christ that he had already introduced in 5:23. The husband is one body (5:28) or one flesh (5:29) with his wife and thus should care for her as he cares for himself, just as we, the members of the church, are members of Christ's body (5:30). At this point Paul quotes Gen. 2:24, surprisingly not to show that husband and wife are one flesh (5:28–29), but rather to show that Christ and the church are one body (5:30). Paul is fully aware of the surprising nature of his use of Scripture at this point, as 5:32 reveals: "This is a great mystery, but [*de*] I speak with respect to Christ and the church."

B. Gen. 2:24 in OT Context.
The text that Paul quotes is the crowning touch to the story of God's creation of Adam, Eve, and the garden that God gave them to tend (2:4–25). After forming Adam from the earth, God recognized that Adam needed a helper that corresponded to him (2:7, 18). A sense of suspense builds in the narrative as God forms the animals from the earth, like Adam (2:19), but none of them is found to correspond to him (2:20) (see Wenham 1987: 68). The narrative tension is resolved when God builds a woman from Adam's own "bone," closing up the "flesh" afterward (2:21–22). The man expresses his delight: "Now, at last, this is bone from my bone and flesh from my flesh! She will be called woman because she was taken from man" (2:23). The nar-

rator then takes this unique correspondence between woman and man, originating in the unity of their bone and flesh, as the reason (ʿal-kēn) why, in marriage, the man leaves his family, "clings" (dābaq) to his wife, and they "become one flesh." The organic unity of woman and man, ensured by the way in which God created the woman, corresponds to the physical unity of woman and man in marriage (so most interpreters, but *pace* Gunkel [1997: 13], who thinks that the text "does not discuss 'marriage'").

C. Gen. 2:18–25 in Jewish Interpretation.

The point of the Genesis account of God's creation of the woman was not lost on ancient Jewish interpreters. They found the suspense implied in 2:19–20 fascinating, and they expanded it. According to Josephus (*Ant.* 1.35), after parading the animals, both male and female, before Adam so that he could name them, God was surprised to realize Adam himself had no suitable mate (cf. *Gen. Rab.* 17:5). God therefore made Eve from Adam's rib, and Adam, when he saw her, knew that "she had come from him [*ex autou genomenēn*]" (*Ant.* 1.36). Even Philo, who was not happy about the problems that women and sexual desire supposedly introduced into the world, says that when Adam saw "an image like his [*adelphon eidos*] and a kindred form [*syngenē morphēn*]," he was thrilled; the reason for this is that love (*erōs*) fits two divided halves together (*Creation* 151–152; cf. *Alleg. Interp.* 2.44–52). When Jesus used Gen. 2:24, he too focused on the final phrase: "and the two shall be one flesh." This implies, he said, that the husband and wife are "no longer two but one flesh" by God's design and that divorce should be rare (Matt. 19:5–6; Mark 10:7–8). First-century interpreters of Genesis, therefore, clearly understood Gen. 2:21–24 to say that Eve was uniquely suited to Adam because she was made from his substance.

The same assumption appears to govern a debate in the Babylonian Talmud over whether the Jewish laws of marriage apply to Gentiles. At one point in the discussion the question arises of whether a Gentile woman can be executed for adultery when Gen. 2:24 speaks only of a man leaving his father and mother and being joined to his wife. The question is resolved by a quotation from Rabbi Judah: "'And they shall be as one flesh,' so that Scripture went and treated the two as one

[applying the statement to both parties]" (*b. Sanh. 57a* [translation in Neusner 1984]). This comment implies that since the man and the woman are one flesh, and the man must leave his parents and be joined to his wife, then the woman must do the same. Here too the governing assumption is that the man and the woman are united by the identical physical substance that they share.

D. Paul's Text.
Paul's quotation is nearly identical to the LXX rendering of Gen. 2:24, and the LXX itself follows the Hebrew text fairly closely. The future tense verbs in the LXX render the corresponding Hebrew imperfect + perfect construction somewhat woodenly, and this may have given readers of the LXX the impression that God was issuing a command to marry (see also, e.g., NASB, NIV, ESV). The Hebrew text, however, carries a gnomic sense: "Hence a man leaves his father and mother and clings to his wife, so that they become one flesh" (NJPS) (see Mathews 1996: 222). It is possible, however, that the LXX intended its futures in a gnomic sense also, and so the difference may be nonexistent. The LXX also changes the Hebrew phrase "they become one flesh" to make it slightly more explicit: "the two shall be one flesh."

Paul follows the LXX in these changes and adds three of his own. Two of his three changes to the LXX are insignificant: he leaves out *autou* ("his") after both *patera* ("father") and *mētera* ("mother"), perhaps to condense the length of the quotation (cf. Matt. 19:5 with Mark 10:7). His other change is more important: he replaces *heneken toutou* with *anti toutou*. Although both expressions mean "on account of this," Paul's alteration is significant because it shows that he intended the phrase to carry its meaning within the context of his own argument (*pace* Schlier 1957: 262; Best 1998: 552). He did not leave it out (as he might have done had he thought it unimportant), nor did he simply repeat it because it was part of the biblical text (as we might assume if he had reproduced it verbatim from the LXX). For Paul, the phrase made a clear, logical connection between his statement that Christians are members of Christ's body (5:30) and the phrase "the two shall be one flesh" (5:31).

E. Paul's Use of Gen. 2:24.
Like many Jewish interpreters before him, particularly in the first century, Paul was concerned primarily with

the final phrase of Gen. 2:24: "and the two shall be one flesh" (Gnilka 1971: 287; Lincoln 1990: 380; O'Brien 1999: 430). The importance of this phrase to him is clear in the shift he makes from the term "bodies" (*sōmata*) in 5:28 to the term "flesh" (*sarka*) in 5:29a. The most obvious reason for this shift in terminology is that Gen. 2:24 uses the term "flesh" rather than "body" (Lincoln 1982: 31–32).

This shift to the terminology of the OT quotation in 5:28–29a also shows that Paul intended the quotation to support the concern of 5:28–29a, 33. Since husband and wife are "one flesh," the husband should love, nurture, and cherish his wife just as he would his own body or, as Genesis says, his own flesh.

Paul's primary reason for using Gen. 2:24, however, is to support his contention that Christ is one with the church and to introduce the new thought that marriage illustrates this unity. Paul develops the notion of Christ's unity with the church throughout the letter and often uses the "body" metaphor to explain it. God seated Christ in heavenly places as head over all things for his body, the church (1:20–23), and the church is seated in heaven with him and "in" him (2:6); the unified church is attaining "the measure of the stature of the fullness of Christ" (4:13) and, as Christ's body (4:4, 16), is growing up into its "head," Christ (4:15).

Thus it comes as no surprise when Paul speaks about Christ as the head of his body—the church—in 5:23, and about Christians as members of Christ's body in 5:30. It also seems natural when Paul uses this metaphor in various ways in his ethical instruction on marriage (5:21–33). The metaphor's portrayal of Christ's self-giving love for the church shows how the husband should love his wife (5:25b–27, 29b–30), and the unity of husband and wife in marriage further illustrates the unity of Christ and the church in the metaphor (5:30–32).

In 5:31–32, however, Paul takes the metaphor of the church as the body of Christ to a new level in two ways. First, his quotation of Gen. 2:24 in 5:31 and his interpretation of it as referring to Christ and the church in 5:32 indicate that the text speaks as it does because it speaks allegorically of the unity between the "members" and Christ's "body" mentioned in 5:30. This is the force of

Paul's opening words in 5:31: "For this reason ..." (*anti toutou*) (see §D above). The two parties of Gen. 2:24, Paul says in 5:32, are "Christ and the church." Paul calls this interpretation of Gen. 2:24 a great mystery because no one could have understood that the text should be read this way apart from God's gracious revelation of this truth to Paul (cf. Dan. 2:18–19, 30 [see commentary on Eph. 3:1–13 above]).

Second, Paul may find in Gen. 2:24 a happy convergence of his metaphor of the body with his metaphor of the church as God's newly created humanity. Throughout the letter Paul has developed the idea of a "new" (2:15–16; 4:24) or "perfect" (4:13) humanity. This new humanity is created "in" Christ (2:15), and united Christians are growing into this "new man" until they attain Christ's full stature (4:13, 15). Christians should put off the "old humanity" and put on the "new humanity," probably because to do so is to act in a way that is consistent with their status as God's newly created humanity (4:22–24). Genesis 2:24 both comes from the creation narrative and speaks of the unity of two entities in one body, and Paul may have found in this text the meeting place of these two ideas. He does not explicitly say this, however, so it must remain a tentative suggestion.

F. A Hermeneutical Implication of Paul's Use of Gen. 2:24. In his use of the OT at this point Paul employs an allegorical method that may at first seem arbitrary. The way Paul phrases his interpretation in 5:32, however, shows that he understood the problem and did not believe that he had fallen victim to it. The adversative character of his statement "But [*de*] I say ..." shows that he was aware of the unusual nature of his interpretation. His return to the theme of the love and respect that should characterize Christian marriage in 5:33, moreover, shows that he affirmed the normal reading of Gen. 2:24. Nevertheless, he believed that God had revealed to him an allegorical application of the statement in Genesis in a manner similar to the way God revealed to Daniel the allegorical interpretation of Nebuchadnezzar's dream (Dan. 2:18–19, 30). The interpretation was not arbitrary, because it was a "mystery" that God himself had graciously revealed to Paul.

6:1–3

A. Paul's Quotation of Exod. 20:12 in NT Context. As part of his advice to his readers on how to "walk" in wisdom within the household (5:21–6:9), and directly after his advice to wives and husbands (5:21–33), Paul turns to children. He urges them to "obey" their parents and provides three motivations for his command (Lincoln 1982: 37). First, they should obey their parents "in the Lord" (6:1a) because of the unity that all Christians, as "members of" Christ's "body" (5:30), have with Christ. Second, they should obey their parents because it is commonly recognized as the "right" way to behave (6:1b [cf. Phil. 4:8]). Third, children should obey their parents simply because the Scriptures command it, something that is clear from the lack of any conjunction connecting the quotation to what precedes it.

B. Exod. 20:12 in OT Context. The command that Paul cites is the fifth commandment of the Decalogue (or the fourth in Roman Catholic, Lutheran, and Anglican reckoning). It says that every Israelite (second-person singulars appear throughout) should honor his or her parents. The command to honor one's parents stands as a bridge between the first half of the Decalogue, which governs Israel's relationship with Yahweh, and the second half, which governs the Israelites' interpersonal relationships (Sarna 1991: 108, 113). The phrase "Yahweh your God," which is woven throughout the first four commandments (Exod. 20:2, 5, 7, 10) but is absent from the others, also appears in the fifth commandment. In addition, the commandment's initial word, "honor" (*kabēd*), often applied to God in the Scriptures, implies that a parallel exists between the honor owed to one's parents and the honor that one should give to God (cf., e.g., 1 Sam. 2:30; Ps. 22:23; Prov. 3:9; Isa. 24:15; see Durham 1987: 291). At the same time, the fifth commandment governs the first and most basic of human relationships and so appropriately stands at the head of the final five commandments in the Decalogue, which govern relations between people. The fifth commandment, therefore, occupies a place of importance in the second half of the Decalogue equal to that of the first commandment in the first half (Durham 1987: 290).

C. Exod. 20:12 in Jewish Interpretation. First-century Jewish interpreters frequently pointed out the important place within the Decalogue of the command to honor one's parents (Philo, *Decalogue* 106; *Spec. Laws* 2.224; cf. Josephus, *Ag. Ap.* 2.206). They also often linked the command with the law that stipulates a penalty of death for a recalcitrant son (Philo [*Spec. Laws* 2.232, 243] and Josephus [*Ag. Ap.* 2.206], alluding to Deut. 21:18–21; Jesus [Matt. 15:4; Mark 7:10], alluding to Exod. 21:17). In addition, these interpreters of the command reveal a concern that adult children should observe it with respect to their aging parents (Philo, *Decalogue* 115–117; *Spec. Laws* 2.237; Matt. 15:4; 19:9; Mark 7:10; 10:19; Luke 18:20). Occasionally, they spiritualize the command's promise so that it refers to immortality or to long life generally and not, as in the command itself, to long life in the land of Israel (Philo, *Spec. Laws* 2.262 [see Str-B 3:614–15]).

D. Paul's Text. Scholars sometimes have thought that Paul cites the fifth commandment from Deut. 5:16 (e.g., Ellis 1981: 152, 187; Bruce 1984: 397–98), presumably because the MT of Deut. 5:16 shares with Paul's citation the phrase "so that it may go well with you," and this phrase is missing from the MT of Exod. 20:12. It is now generally agreed, however, that this is wrong, and that Paul's citation comes from Exod. 20:12 LXX. The Exodus text of the LXX not only includes the phrase "so that it may go well with you," but also lacks both the "your" (*sou*) after "mother" and the phrase "as the LORD your God commanded you." These two gaps are present in both the Exodus text of the LXX and Ephesians but not in Deut. 5:16 LXX or either version of the command in the MT (see Lincoln 1982: 37–38; Moritz 1996: 154–55; Best 1998: 566; Hoehner 2002: 788). The current consensus on this rather minor issue is therefore correct, and the problem should be laid to rest.

E. Paul's Use of Exod. 20:12. Paul expresses no interest in the features of the command that other first-century interpreters considered important. He does not apply the command to adult children; rather, as 6:4 shows, he speaks only of its relevance for children still under their parents' care (Lincoln 1990: 403). He does not undergird the command's importance with references to the parallels between honoring God and honoring parents, nor does he comment on the central location of the command within the Decalogue.

Instead, Paul focuses on the relationship between the command and the promise that accompanies it. The command is important, he says, because "it is the first command with a promise" (6:2). This statement has puzzled interpreters because at first it seems incorrect. Has Paul failed to see that the second commandment (Exod. 20:4–6) includes God's promise of steadfast love (see Pokorný 1992: 233)? Perhaps Paul meant that the commandment was first in importance (Best 1998: 567), or the most difficult (Schlier 1957: 281n3 [cf. *Deut. Rab.* 6 on Deut. 22:6]), or the first command with a promise in the second part of the Decalogue (Gnilka 1971: 297).

None of these explanations carries much persuasive power. Paul probably understood the promise attached to the second commandment not as a reference to any specific commandment, but to the whole body of divine commands (cf. Exod. 20:6). The fifth commandment is, in fact, the first of the many commandments in the Torah with a promise linked specifically to the action enjoined (Lincoln 1982: 38).

Paul is also interested in the content of the promise. By changing the specific reference to long life in "the land that the Lord your God is giving you" into a more general reference to long life "on the earth," he joins ancient Jewish interpreters who have decoupled the promise from any reference to the land of Israel itself. What, then, does the promise of long life on the earth mean?

F. A Possible Theological Implication of Paul's Use of Exod. 20:12. Paul may simply be referring to the general principle that children who submit to the authority of loving parents are more likely to live longer than those who do not (Hoehner 2002: 793). Some scholars who take this position think that this text reflects a situation in which the eschatological expectation of the early church has dimmed, and the ethic of some Christians has "declined" (Best 1998: 568) into an accommodation of life in the world (see Lincoln 1982: 39–40; contrast Hoehner 2002: 793–94).

In light of Paul's frequent use of the "new creation" theme throughout the letter (2:15; 3:9; 4:13, 24), however, it is possible that the idea of a new creation may also stand behind his thinking here. Paul may be saying that children whose obedience to their parents arises from their commitment to "the Lord" (6:1) will live eternally not

on a particular land with national boundaries such as ancient Israel, but rather on an earth without boundaries, as God created it to be.

As with Paul's use of Gen. 2:24 in 5:31, "new creation" theology is far from explicit in this text, if it is present at all. At the same time, such an idea is consistent with Paul's thinking that in the church God is breaking down national barriers and creating one new humanity (2:14–16).

6:10–17

Paul concludes Ephesians in 6:10–20 with an appeal to his readers to resist the insidious and clever attacks of the devil (6:11, 16) and his evil cosmic allies (6:12). One plausible reading of Ephesians takes this passage as the epistle's climax (Lincoln 1990: 432; Yoder Neufeld 1997: 110; O'Brien 1999: 457–60). Paul has prayed that his readers would understand how the "power" and "mighty strength" of God had been made available to them by their union with the Messiah, who sits at God's right hand, victorious over all his cosmic foes (1:19–20; 2:6). The Messiah has ascended a figurative Mount Zion in a triumphal march after the defeat of his enemies, and God's people have shared in his triumph (see commentary on Eph. 4:7–11 above). Now, Paul urges his readers to defend the position that the Messiah has won for them by putting on the armor of God and standing firm (6:11, 13, 14) against the devil and other invisible evil powers.

Scholars dispute the extent of Paul's indebtedness in this passage to the OT and particularly to Isa. 59:17; 11:4–5; 52:7. All agree that Paul neither quotes these texts explicitly nor uses their imagery in the same way Isaiah uses it. At the same time, virtually all agree that some connection exists between the figurative armor of God (or of his Messiah) described in these OT texts and the armor that Paul exhorts his readers to "put on" (6:11), "take up" (6:13), or "take" (6:17). At one end of the interpretive spectrum stands Lindemann (1975: 64–65 [cf. Gnilka 1971: 310]), who believes that the pseudonymous author of Ephesians relied not on Isaiah itself, but rather on a traditional picture of God's armor that circulated in Jewish Wisdom literature and is clearly visible in Wis. 5:15–23. At the opposite end of the spectrum stand scholars such as Moritz (1996: 178–212) and O'Brien (1999: 473–74, 477–79, 482), who find the broader context of the imagery in Isaiah to be crucial for understanding the full meaning of the imagery in Ephesians.

Between these two poles lies a variety of mediating opinions. Lincoln (1982: 43), for example, suggests that the pseudonymous author of Ephesians first found the creative use of Isaiah's "divine warrior" traditions in 1 Thess. 5:8 and, inspired by the interpretive method of the genuine Paul, creatively appropriated Isaiah's imagery for his own purposes (see Yoder Neufeld 1997: 96–97, 102–3, 105, 117–18, 125). Hoehner (2002: 822–23, 839–40, 841, 843–44, 850) acknowledges that Paul took the imagery directly from Isaiah but does not find the Isaiah contexts of the imagery to be particularly significant for understanding Paul's use of it (cf. Schlier 1957: 294–300).

The evidence for a direct and important link between Eph. 6:10–17 and several passages in Isaiah is impressive. In 6:11 Paul tells his readers to "put on the whole armor of God," in 6:14 to "stand, therefore, having girded [*perizōsamenoi*] your waist with truth, and having put on the breastplate of righteousness," and in 6:17 to take up "the helmet of salvation." Paul's language in these three statements seems to echo Isa. 59:17–18 LXX: "[God] put on righteousness as a breastplate and placed the helmet of salvation upon his head and donned the garment of retributive justice, and [donned] his coat like one who will give disgrace as repayment to his enemies." Paul's language is reminiscent also of Isa. 11:5 LXX: "[A rod from the root of Jesse] will have girded [*estai ... ezōsmenos*] his waist with righteousness and wrapped his sides in truth."

When Paul tells his readers in 6:15 to put on as shoes "the preparation of the gospel of peace [*euangeliou tēs eirēnēs*]," he seems to echo the prominent concern of Isaiah that in the era of Israel's restoration messengers would announce the good tidings of peace from the mountaintops (cf. Isa. 40:9–11; 52:7; see O'Brien 1999: 478). In Isa. 52:6–7 LXX, just as in Eph. 6:15, "foot" imagery mingles with the language of "glad tidings ... of peace": "I myself am he who speaks, for I am present as a season on the mountains, as the feet of one who proclaims [*euangelizomenou*] a report of peace [*eirēnēs*], as one who proclaims [*euangelizomenos*] good things. For I will make your salvation heard, saying, 'Zion! Your God shall reign!'"

Moreover, when Paul tells his readers in 6:17 to take "the sword of the Spirit [*pneumatos*], which is the word [*rhēma*] of God," he seems to reach back again to Isa. 11 LXX, this time to 11:4b: "He will strike the earth with the word [*logō*; MT: *šēbeṭ* ('rod')] of his mouth, and with the breath [*pneumati*] through his lips he will kill the godless one."

Besides the close verbal correspondence between Eph. 6:11, 14–15, 17 and Isa. 59:17; 11:4–5; 52:7, there is also a close conceptual correspondence. In Isa. 59 the iniquity of God's people has separated them from God (59:2). Societal "righteousness" and "truth" have suffered bitterly as Israel has turned its back on its God and embraced "oppression and revolt" (59:12–15a). Everyone is guilty (59:4); justice is wholly absent (59:8, 11); "transgressions" and "sins" are rife (59:12). God responds to this situation by donning the armor of righteousness, salvation, vengeance, and zeal (59:17) and repaying his people according to their deeds (59:18). At the same time, however, he comes in the form of "a Redeemer for Zion" and rescues those who turn from their transgression (59:20) (see Young 1965–1972: 3:440–41). The pattern of sin, punishment, and restoration for the repentant is clear.

This pattern appears in the other two Isaiah passages as well. The deliverance that the "rod" (LXX) or "shoot" (MT) from the stump of Jesse (11:1) brings to God's people in 11:4–5 comes only after their pervasive godlessness (9:17) leads God to punish them by "Assyria, the rod of my anger" (10:5). Similarly, the feet of the one who brings good news of peace appear on the mountains (52:7) only after Israel has drunk to the dregs the cup of God's wrath for its sins (51:17, 22).

Paul's letter has followed this pattern of sin, punishment, and restoration. He has told his readers that at one time they were dead in their "transgressions" and "sins" and that everyone was guilty: "we all ... were by nature children of wrath" (2:1, 3, 5). God, however, because of his rich mercy and great love, graciously rescued them and seated them in heavenly places with God's risen and victorious Messiah (2:5–6). This Messiah, he has said, is "our peace" (2:14).

Now, in 6:10–17, however, he recognizes the other side of the eschatological tension in which believers live: although the victory is sure, believers must still defend the position that Christ has won for them against the last desperate attacks of the devil and his malevolent allies. In 6:10–17 Paul may consciously be borrowing the imagery that Isaiah used of God's battle against evil before the time of Israel's eschatological restoration in order to portray this tension. He urges his readers to take up the armor that, in Isaiah, Yahweh and his Davidic king use to fight for and establish truth and righteousness in the era prior to Israel's restoration (cf. Isa. 11:5; 59:17; see Yoder Neufeld 1997: 135).

The verbal and conceptual parallels between Eph. 6:10–17 and Isa. 59:17; 11:4–5; 52:7, therefore, are strong. When we consider the full use that Paul has made of Isaiah elsewhere in Ephesians, particularly of Isa. 52:7 and its context in 2:13–17 (on which, see commentary above), it begins to seem likely that Paul has consciously and directly used Isaiah in this stirring conclusion to his letter.

It is important, however, before drawing this conclusion, to consider two pieces of mitigating evidence. First, Paul's use of the "armor" imagery differs from Isaiah's use of it in significant ways. Most obviously, Paul speaks not of God or the Messiah, but of God's people wearing the armor that he describes. The armor itself also includes both shield and sword, neither of which is found in Isaiah.

Second, by the time of Paul, Isaiah's imagery of the divine or messianic warrior had already reappeared in various literary contexts. It is possible, therefore, that Paul made use not of Isaiah itself, but only of the literary tradition that incorporated Isaiah's imagery. The author of the Wisdom of Solomon, for example, speaks of the Lord battling his enemies by taking zeal as his "whole armor" (*panoplia* [5:17]). "He will put on," says the author, "righteousness as a breastplate . . . impartial justice as a helmet . . . holiness as an invincible shield . . . stern wrath for a sword" (5:18–20). Although Paul is closer to Isaiah than to Wisdom when he matches the helmet with salvation (Eph. 6:17; Isa. 59:17), he is closer to Wisdom than to Isaiah when he uses the term "whole armor" (*panoplia* [Eph. 6:11; Wis. 5:17]) and includes the "shield" (*aspida* [Wis. 5:19]; *thōraka* [Eph. 6:14]) and "sword" (*rhomphaia* [Wis. 5:20]; *machaira* [Eph. 6:17]) in his list of weapons.

Similarly, Isa. 11:4 reappears in *Pss. Sol.* 17:32–35, where "the Lord Messiah [*christos kyriou*] . . . will strike the earth with the word of

his mouth forever." The language of Isa. 11:4–5 reappears also in 1Q28b V, 24–26, where the writer, addressing "the prince of the congregation" (V, 20), says,

> May [you strike the peoples] with the power of your mouth. With your scepter may you lay waste the earth. With the breath of your lips may you kill the wicked. [May he send upon you a spirit of] counsel and of everlasting fortitude, a spirit of knowledge and of fear of God. May your justice be the belt of [your loins, and loyalty] the belt of your hips. (García Martínez 1994: 433)

The notion that God or his Messiah would put on the gear of war and fight against the wicked seems to have been in common circulation in Paul's time.

Although both Paul's differences from Isaiah and the common currency of the imagery should caution us against hasty or overconfident conclusions about Paul's use of the OT in 6:10–17, the evidence seems slightly weighted in favor of his direct use of Isa. 59:17; 11:4–5; 52:7 and even of his awareness of their literary contexts. We have already seen (see commentary on Eph. 2:13–17; 4:17–5:20 above) how Isaiah's concept of restoration, both of God's people and of all creation, helped to form Paul's eschatology in this letter, and it does not seem unlikely that Paul would again call upon Isaiah's imagery of God's intervention in his world and among his people on behalf of righteousness and truth in this climactic closing passage.

Paul transfers "the whole armor of God" from God himself, or from his Messiah, to God's people in this passage because, despite 1:20–23; 2:6, he knows that the victory of God's people over the devil is not yet complete. God certainly has struck a fatal blow against the rulers, authorities, and cosmic powers of "this present darkness" (6:12), but the flaming arrows of the doomed regime continue to assail God's people.

Between the time of Christ's victory and the consummation of God's purposes in Christ, therefore, believers themselves must imitate God in his role of divine warrior. Paul earlier had said that Christians must "put on [*endysasthai*] the new human being, created in God's image, in righteousness, holiness, and truth" (4:24 [cf. 5:9]). He also had said that they should imitate the Messiah (4:32) and God (5:1) in showing forgiveness and love to one another. Now he depicts this imitation of God in terms of the final eschatological battle in a war that has largely already been won (see O'Brien 1999: 473–75). Before the time of final victory God's people must strap on the armor that in the OT belongs to Yahweh and his Messiah, and, taking their stand on what God has already done for them in the gospel (6:15) (Moritz 1996: 200, 203), they must act as God would act—in truth and righteousness (Schlier 1957: 295; Lincoln 1990: 447–48; *pace* Moritz 1996: 201–3).

Bibliography

Albright, W. F. 1950–1951. "A Catalogue of Early Hebrew Lyric Poems (Psalm LXVIII)." *HUCA* 23: 1–39.

Allen, L. C. 2002. *Psalms 101–50*. Rev. ed. WBC 21. Nashville: Nelson.

Arnold, C. E. 1997. *Power and Magic: The Concept of Power in Ephesians*. Grand Rapids: Baker Academic.

Barth, M. 1974. *Ephesians 4–6*. AB 34A. Garden City, NY: Doubleday.

Best, E. 1998. *A Critical and Exegetical Commentary on Ephesians*. ICC. Edinburgh: T&T Clark.

Bruce, F. F. 1984. *The Epistles to the Colossians, to Philemon, and to the Ephesians*. NICNT. Grand Rapids: Eerdmans.

Brueggemann, W. 1997. *Theology of the Old Testament*. Minneapolis: Fortress.

Caragounis, C. C. 1977. *The Ephesian Mysterion: Meaning and Content*. ConBNT 8. Lund: Gleerup.

Childs, B. 1993. *Biblical Theology of the Old and New Testaments: Theological Reflection on the Christian Bible*. Minneapolis: Fortress.

Donaldson, T. L. 1997. *Paul and the Gentiles: Remapping the Apostle's Convictional World*. Minneapolis: Fortress.

Durham, J. I. 1987. *Exodus*. WBC 3. Waco: Word.

Ellis, E. E. 1981. *Paul's Use of the Old Testament*. Grand Rapids: Baker Academic.

García Martínez, F., ed. 1996. *The Dead Sea Scrolls Translated: The Qumran Texts in English*. 2nd edition. Translated by W. G. E. Watson. Grand Rapids: Eerdmans.

Gnilka, J. 1971. *Der Epheserbrief*. HTKNT 10/2. Freiburg: Herder.

Grindheim, S. 2003. "What the OT Prophets Did Not Know: The Mystery of the Church in Eph 3,2–13." *Bib* 84: 531–53.

Gruber, M. I. 1998. *Rashi's Commentary on Psalms 1–89 (Books I–III), with English Translation, Introduction and Notes*. SFSHJ 161. Atlanta: Scholars Press.

Gunkel, H. 1997. *Genesis*. Translated by M. E. Biddle. MLBS. Macon, GA: Mercer University Press.

———. 1998. *Introduction to Psalms: The Genres of the Religious Lyric of Israel*. Completed by J. Begrich. Translated by J. D. Nogalski. MLBS. Macon, GA: Mercer University Press.

Harris, W. H., III. 1998. *The Descent of Christ: Ephesians 4:7–11 and Traditional Hebrew Imagery*. BSL. Grand Rapids: Baker Academic.

Hay, D. 1973. *Glory at the Right Hand: Psalm 110 in Early Christianity*. SBLMS 18. Nashville: Abingdon.

Hoehner, H. W. 2002. *Ephesians: An Exegetical Commentary*. Grand Rapids: Baker Academic.

Hübner, H. 1997. *An Philemon, an die Kolosser, an die Epheser*. HNT 12. Tübingen: Mohr Siebeck.

Kidner, D. 1973. *Psalms 1–72*. TOTC. Leicester: Tyndale.

Kraus, H.-J. 1988. *Psalms 1–59*. Translated by H. C. Oswald. Minneapolis: Augsburg, 1988.

———. 1989. *Psalms 60–150*. Translated by H. C. Oswald. Minneapolis: Augsburg.

Lincoln, A. T. 1982. "The Use of the OT in Ephesians." *JSNT* 14: 16–57.

———. 1990. *Ephesians*. WBC 42. Dallas: Word.

Lindars, B. 1961. *New Testament Apologetic: The Doctrinal Significance of the Old Testament Quotations*. Philadelphia: Westminster.

Lindemann, A. 1975. *Die Aufhebung der Zeit: Geschichtsverständnis und Eschatologie im Epheserbrief*. SNT 12. Gütersloh: Gütersloher Verlaghaus.

Luz, U. 1998. "Der Brief an die Epheser." Pages 106–80 in *Die Briefe an die Galater, Epheser und Kolosser*. By J. Becker and U. Luz. NTD 8/1. Göttingen: Vandenhoeck & Ruprecht.

Mathews, K. 1996. *Genesis 1–11:26*. NAC 1A. Nashville: Broadman & Holman.

Moritz, T. 1996. *A Profound Mystery: The Use of the Old Testament in Ephesians*. NovTSup 85. Leiden: Brill.

Neusner, J. 1984. *Tractate Sanhedrin Chapters 4–8*. Vol. 23B of *The Talmud of Babylonia: An American Translation*. BJS 84. Chico, CA: Scholars Press.

O'Brien, P. T. 1999. *The Letter to the Ephesians*. PNTC. Grand Rapids: Eerdmans.

Pokorný, P. 1992. *Der Brief des Paulus an die Epheser*. THKNT 10/2. Leipzig: Evangelische Verlagsanstalt.

Sarna, N. M. 1991. *Exodus*. JPSTC. Philadelphia: Jewish Publication Society.

Schlier, H. 1957. *Der Brief an die Epheser*. Düsseldorf: Patmos.

Schnackenburg, R. 1991. *The Epistle to the Ephesians*. Translated by H. Hero. Edinburgh: T&T Clark.

Smith, G. V. 1975. "Paul's Use of Psalm 68:18 in Ephesians 4:8." *JETS* 18: 181–89.

Terrien, S. 2003. *The Psalms: Strophic Structure and Theological Commentary*. ECC. Grand Rapids: Eerdmans.

von Rad, G. 1965. *The Theology of Israel's Prophetic Traditions*. Vol. 2 of *Old Testament Theology*. Translated by D. M. G. Stalker. New York: Harper & Row.

Weiser, A. 1962. *The Psalms*. Translated by H. Hartwell. OTL. Philadelphia: Westminster.

Wenham, G. J. 1987. *Genesis 1–15*. WBC 1. Waco: Word.

Westermann, C. 1969. *Isaiah 40–66*. Translated by D. M. G. Stalker. OTL. Philadelphia: Westminster.

Whybray, R. N. 1981. *Isaiah 40–66*. NCBC. Grand Rapids: Eerdmans.

Wilson, G. H. 2002. *Psalms*. 2 vols. NIVAC. Grand Rapids: Zondervan.

Wright, N. T. 2003. *The Resurrection of the Son of God*. Vol. 3 of *New Testament and the People of God*. Minneapolis: Fortress.

Yoder Neufeld, T. R. 1997. *Put on the Armour of God: The Divine Warrior from Isaiah to Ephesians*. JSNTSup 140. Sheffield: Sheffield Academic Press.

Young, E. J. 1965–1972. *The Book of Isaiah*. 3 vols. Grand Rapids: Eerdmans.

Philippians

Moisés Silva

Introduction

Paul's letter to the Philippians is totally lacking in direct OT quotations, and even its allusions to the OT are subtle enough that they can easily be missed. In this respect, the contrast between Philippians and, say, Galatians is arresting. But other differences between these two documents are no less surprising. In Galatians Paul places very heavy emphasis on his apostolic authority, whereas in Philippians he identifies himself simply as a servant (Phil. 1:1), the word *apostle* is nowhere to be found. Indeed, the very concept of apostleship, though implicit in his authoritative instructions (e.g., 1:27–28; 2:12–15; 3:2, 17–19; 4:8–9), is something Paul never refers to expressly in this letter.

A related matter is the striking difference in tone between the two epistles. As is well known, Galatians is missing an initial thanksgiving and contains a relatively large number of negative comments and rebukes. In contrast, Philippians is generally recognized as the gentlest and warmest of all the Pauline epistles. One should not conclude, as many do, that the church in Philippi was a model community without significant problems. The truth is that the Christians in this city were going through a severe crisis—fear, division, discontent—and the apostle does not hesitate to rebuke them even while he encourages them (see

Silva 2005: 20–22). Nevertheless, one can hardly deny that the letter gives evidence of an unusually close relationship between the author and his readers, and everything Paul says seems tempered by a strong sense of mutual love and understanding (see esp. 1:7–8, 25–26; 2:17–18; 4:1, 4–7, 10, 15–16, 18).

It is very likely that these features account, at least in part, for the differences between the two letters regarding Paul's use of the OT. When writing to the church in Philippi, the apostle was not facing challenges to his authority, nor did he need to correct doctrinal defections within the community. And even though he decided (apparently after some hesitation [cf. 3:1]) to warn the Philippians against a possible threat from false teachers who might make their way into the city (3:2, 18–19), it is clear that the church needed only to be reminded, not persuaded, of the truth of apostolic teaching. As a result, we find no *gegraptai*, "it is written," in his argument (contrast Gal. 3:10, 13; 4:30), nor any direct appeal to *hē graphē*, "the Scripture" (contrast Gal. 3:10, 13; 4:20, 27).

It would be a grave mistake, however, to infer that the Hebrew Scriptures play no role in Philippians. Paul's indirect uses of the OT in this letter demonstrate clearly that even when the apostle does not give a formal quotation, his language and thought patterns are heavily dependent on

Scripture and particularly so in its Greek form. In a number of instances, it is very unlikely that Paul was specifically thinking of the relevant OT passage, much less that he intended to call attention to it. For example, the words *martys gar mou ho theos*, "for God is my witness" (1:8), may or may not reflect acquaintance with the similar phrase in Gen. 31:44 (cf. also Wis. 1:6), but an examination of this OT context would not make an appreciable difference to our understanding of Paul's meaning. The same is true of *karpon dikaiosynēs*, "fruit of righteousness," in 1:11 (see Prov. 3:9 et al.), *homoiōmati anthrōpōn*, "likeness of men," in 2:7 (see Ezek. 1:5), and several others.

The discussion that follows is therefore limited to instances where one can make a reasonable case that Paul was consciously alluding to an OT passage—or at least that the OT passage in question affects our interpretation of the apostle's teaching. Even in these cases, however, it would be misleading to provide extensive comments such as are appropriate in contexts (e.g., Gal. 3) where Paul explicitly cites Scripture, for in the latter he evidently expects his readers to take specific OT statements into account. When he does not explicitly cite Scripture, on the other hand, he apparently assumes that his teaching is directly accessible and thus that its meaning does not depend on the reader's ability to see a connection with a particular OT passage. Nevertheless, understanding that connection can enhance our appreciation of Paul's thought.

1:19

Unless one refers specifically to the LXX text, it is easy to miss the OT allusion in Paul's statement, "What has happened to me will turn out for my deliverance" (NIV, NRSV). The Greek here is *touto moi apobēsetai eis sōtērian* ("this will lead to salvation for me"), which reproduces Job 13:16 LXX verbatim. Most commentators, even if they notice the striking verbal correspondence, appear to see little significance in it (see Hawthorne 1983: 41–44; for the history of the interpretation of this verse, see Reumann 2006). And, to be sure, it is possible that Paul has simply, and perhaps even unconsciously, borrowed the language of Job to express quite a different idea: his hoped-for deliverance from prison (the connection would have been aided by the parallel between Job's accusers

and the individuals whom Paul mentions in 1:17 [see Hays 1989: 21–24]).

There is much to be said, however, for the view that what Paul has in mind is the more profound issue of his relationship with God and thus his spiritual destiny. Since the context of Job 13:13–18 deals precisely with matters of eternal import, Paul's use of that passage may be more than a casual allusion (see O'Brien 1991: 109–10; Fee 1995: 130–32; Bockmuehl 1998: 83). No doubt the word *sōtēria* can sometimes be translated "deliverance," but the view that here Paul is speaking of his expected release from prison runs against insurmountable difficulties. The apostle specifically ties in his adversity with his deliverance: it is not merely that he will be delivered, but that his adversity *will result* in his deliverance (it makes little sense to interpret this as Paul saying that what he has suffered will lead to his release from prison). Moreover, as 1:20 indicates, the deliverance that he speaks about is one that he will experience irrespective of what happens to him in prison: *eite dia zōēs eite dia thanatou* ("whether through life or through death"). In addition, his use of such soteriologically charged terms as *apokaradokia* ("eager expectation" [cf. Rom. 8:19]) and *elpis* (Paul's standard term for the distinctive and certain hope of the believer that will not make him ashamed [cf. Rom 5:4; 8:24–25]) is inexplicable if the apostle is describing his desire to be released from prison. Thus, even if such a desire is indirectly reflected here, the primary reference must be to his perseverance in faith: the magnification of Christ, not his own freedom or even his life, is Paul's salvation. (For further details on Phil. 1:18–20 and other OT allusions in this letter, see the relevant sections in Silva 2005.)

2:6–8

In some instances conceptual rather than strict verbal correspondences suggest that Paul has an OT passage or theme in mind. One such instance is the first part of 2:6–11, a passage now widely referred to as the *Carmen Christi* ("Christ Hymn"). In 2:6 Paul's description of Christ as being *en morphē theou* ("in the form of God") has led to a wide variety of interpretations, one of which is that this phrase bears some correspondence to *eikōn tou theou* ("the image of God" [Col. 1:15]) and thus gives expression to an Adam Christology (cf. Gen. 1:26 LXX; see Martin 1997: 106–19; Kim 1984: 193–205).

The discussion of LXX backgrounds is often affected by fuzzy linguistic arguments and by the implication that the various theses proposed are mutually exclusive. Accordingly, the parallel with Adam has sometimes been pressed beyond the evidence, but there is an undeniable network of associations between Phil. 2 and Gen. 1–3 (reflected also in texts such as Rom. 5:19; 8:29; 1 Cor. 15:41; 2 Cor. 3:18; 4:4; Phil. 3:21; Col. 1:15; 3:10), and the theological coherence of these associations has been especially shown by Ridderbos (1975: 68–78 [see also the recent defense by Hooker 2000]).

In addition, some scholars have argued that the clause "made himself nothing" (lit., "emptied himself") in 2:7 alludes to Isa. 53:12, which says that the Servant of the Lord "poured out his life unto death." The next clause in 2:7, *morphēn doulou labōn* ("taking the form of a servant"), is then thought to mean, "Christ assumed the role of the Suffering Servant." Since Paul definitely uses Isaiah later in the passage (see commentary on Phil. 2:9–11 below), it may well be that this motif has played a role in the formulation of the Christ Hymn (see Heriban [1983: 160–62], who proposes that the Isaianic passage provides the thematic background of humiliation and exaltation; see also Bockmuehl 1998: 135–36). If so, however, the allusion is rather subtle, and therefore one should be cautious about reading too much into Paul's language. In particular, to suggest that the Christ Hymn is primarily an attribution of the "Servant of the Lord" description to Jesus seems an overstatement; much less is it defensible to argue that "he emptied himself" actually means "he suffered the death of the Servant of the Lord" (see further the objections summarized in O'Brien 1991: 268–71; for a different view, see Gundry 1994).

2:9–11

These verses, which form the second part of the Christ Hymn, consist of one sentence: God has exalted Jesus and granted to him a superior name so that all may bow to him and confess that he is Lord. This sentence begins with the conjunction "therefore" (*dio*), and commentators have debated the precise relationship between the two parts of the hymn. Does Paul mean that God rewarded Jesus, or is he simply referring to a natural outcome? Because the notion of reward might suggest that merit is involved, some complicated theological questions arise. For our purposes, we may simply note that although the notion of reward cannot be excluded from this passage, we must restrict its application in view of Jesus' uniqueness (see Gnilka 1968: 125). Martin (1997: 232) helpfully clarifies the issue by accepting in this context the concept of reward while rejecting that of merit: "The obedience of Christ did not force the hand of God, as a doctrine of merit implies. The action of God is but the other side of that obedience, and a vindication of all that the obedience involved."

This passage raises other interesting questions, such as, What is the name that Jesus received: "Lord" or "Jesus"? Moule (1970: 270) gives us a satisfactory answer: "Because of the incarnation, the human name, 'Jesus,' is acclaimed as the highest name; and the Man Jesus thus comes to be acclaimed as Lord, to the glory of God the Father." And is the universal homage spoken of here voluntary or involuntary? Calvin (1965: 252) rightly responds that the devils, for example, "are not, and never will be, subject of their own accord and by cheerful submission; but Paul is not speaking here of voluntary obedience."

Our main concern, however, is the last part of the sentence, where Paul states that the purpose of Christ's exaltation is that "every knee should bow . . . and every tongue confess that Jesus Christ is Lord," a clear allusion to Isa. 45:23 (on the basis of this link, Wilk [1998: 325] suggests that there are further allusions to Isa. 45 in 1:28; 2:12–13). The Isaiah passage as a whole (45:18–25) constitutes one of the most powerful OT affirmations of the uniqueness of God of Israel in the context of his redeeming work:

> I am Yahweh, and there is none else. . . .
> They have no knowledge—
> > those who carry about their wooden idols
> > and pray to a god who cannot save. . . .
> There is no other God besides me,
> > a righteous God and a Savior—
> > there is none except me.
> Turn to me, and be saved, all the ends of the earth,
> > for I am God, and there is no other.
> I have sworn by myself . . .
> > that to me every knee will bow,

every tongue will swear allegiance. (Isa. 45:18–23)

The Hebrew verb behind "swear" here is translated by the LXX with the same verb used by Paul, *exomologeō* ("confess"). Although not an explicit or precise quotation, this use of Isaiah is especially significant because of its profound implications for Paul's conception of Christ. Whether or not Paul composed the Christ Hymn, it patently expresses his own conviction that the worship of Jesus Christ does not compromise Israel's monotheistic faith. On the contrary, Jesus Christ the righteous Savior bears the name of the one Lord, Yahweh, "to the glory of God the Father."

2:14–15

A few verses later, Paul addresses the problem of grumbling and complaining (2:14), a theme reminiscent of the experience of the Israelites in the wilderness. That comment leads him in 2:15 to speak of the Philippians as "blameless children of God in the midst of a crooked and depraved generation" (*tekna theou amōma meson geneas skolias kai destrammenēs*), a phrase that largely reproduces the last part of Deut. 32:5 LXX (*tekna mōmēta genea skolia kai destrammenē*), but with a provocative twist. Since the OT passage speaks of the Israelites themselves as a crooked people and thus not God's children (although some question this reading of the Hebrew), Paul here seems to suggest that it is the Gentile Christians of Philippi, not the unbelieving Jews, who may be regarded as God's children (for a different view, see Bockmuehl 1998: 156–57). Thus the Philippians need not be intimidated by the Jewish-based opposition that they are experiencing (see 3:1–3). (In the light of this use of Deut. 32, it is also possible that Paul's earlier reference to his being present/absent [2:12] was influenced by Moses' language in Deut. 31:27 [so Michael 1928: 101].)

4:18

Finally, a fairly obvious dependence on the OT may be seen in 4:18 in the way Paul describes the monetary gifts he received from the Philippian church: "They are a fragrant scent, an acceptable sacrifice, pleasing to God" (*osmēn euōdias, thysian dektēn, euareston tō theō*). This language, of course, comes from various ceremonial passages, such as Exod. 29:18 (LXX: *osmēn euōdias*); moreover, a

figurative shift is already present in Ezek. 20:41: "With a fragrant scent [LXX: *en osmē euōdias*] I will accept you when I bring you out from the peoples." This detail must be understood against a larger theological framework, for Paul elsewhere uses priestly language to describe Christian service (cf. *leitourgia* ["service"] and related words in 2:17, 25, 30). In effect, the ceremonial system of Israel is viewed as having been transformed and transferred to the Christian church, which properly fulfills the significance of that system. A few scholars have even suggested that Paul sees himself as the priest who, serving in the church as the true temple of God, receives the Christians' offerings (see Newton 1985: 60–68).

Bibliography

Bockmuehl, M. 1998. *The Epistle to the Philippians*. BNTC 11. Peabody, MA: Hendrickson.

Calvin, J. 1965. *The Epistles of Paul the Apostle to the Galatians, Ephesians, Philippians and Colossians*. Edited by D. W. Torrance and T. F. Torrance. Translated by T. H. L. Parker. Grand Rapids: Eerdmans.

Fee, G. D. 1995. *Paul's Letter to the Philippians*. NICNT. Grand Rapids: Eerdmans.

Gnilka, J. 1968. *Der Philipperbrief*. HTKNT 10/3. Freiburg: Herder.

Gundry, R. H. 1994. "Style and Substance in 'the Myth of God Incarnate' according to Philippians 2:6–11." Pages 271–93 in *Crossing the Boundaries: Essays in Biblical Interpretation in Honour of Michael D. Goulder*. Edited by S. E. Porter, P. Joyce, and D. E. Orton. BIS 8. Leiden: Brill.

Hawthorne, G. F. 1983. *Philippians*. WBC 43. Waco: Word.

Hays, R. B. 1989. *Echoes of Scripture in the Letters of Paul*. New Haven: Yale University Press.

Heriban, J. 1983. *Retto [phronein] e [kenosis]: Studio esegetico su Fil 2,1–5.6–11*. BSR 51. Rome: LAS.

Hooker, M. D. 2000. "Adam *Redivivus*: Philippians 2 Once More." Pages 220–34 in *The Old Testament in the New: Essays in Honour of J. L. North*. Edited by S. Moyise. JSNTSup 189. Sheffield: Sheffield Academic Press.

Kim, S. 1984. *The Origin of Paul's Gospel*. WUNT 2/4. Tübingen: Mohr Siebeck.

Martin, R. P. 1997. *A Hymn of Christ: Philippians 2:5–11 in Recent Interpretation and in the Setting of Early Christian Worship*. Downers Grove, IL: InterVarsity.

Michael, J. H. 1928. *The Epistle of Paul to the Philippians*. MNTC 10. London: Hodder & Stoughton.

Moule, C. F. D. 1970. "Further Reflexions on Philippians 2:5–11." Pages 264–76 in *Apostolic History and the Gospel: Biblical and Historical Essays Presented to F. F. Bruce on His 60th Birthday*. Edited by W. W. Gasque and R. P. Martin. Grand Rapids: Eerdmans.

Newton, M. 1985. *The Concept of Purity at Qumran and in the Letters of Paul*. SNTSMS 53. Cambridge: Cambridge University Press.

O'Brien, P. T. 1991. *The Epistle to the Philippians: A Commentary on the Greek Text*. NIGTC. Grand Rapids: Eerdmans.

Reumann, J. 2006. "The (Greek) Old Testament in Philippians 1:19 as Parade Example—Allusion, Echo, Proverb?" Pages 189–200 in *History and Exegesis: New Testament Essays in Honor of E. Earl Ellis for His 80th Birthday*. Edited by S.-W. Son. London: T&T Clark.

Ridderbos, H. 1975. *Paul: An Outline of His Theology*. Grand Rapids: Eerdmans.

Silva, M. 2005. *Philippians*. 2nd ed. BECNT. Grand Rapids: Baker Academic.

Wilk, F. 1998. *Die Bedeutung des Jesajabuches für Paulus*. FRLANT 179. Göttingen: Vandenhoeck & Ruprecht.

Colossians

G. K. Beale

Introduction

Until recently, there had been no book, monograph, or even article dedicated explicitly to a study of the OT in Colossians. An essay on the subject by Fee (2006) was published recently, and not long before that, C. Beetham (2005) completed a doctoral dissertation on the same subject, of which I was the supervisor (Beetham and I did our work independently). The final form of both Fee's and Beetham's studies appeared too late for sufficient interaction with them in the present chapter, although prepublication exposure of their work reveals that their approach is quite similar to mine, and the OT allusions that they have identified overlap with many of those that I discern.

One reason for such little attention to this subject is that there are no formal quotations or citations from the OT in the letter. Many commentators even find difficulty in detecting many allusions in the letter. Nevertheless, there are allusions, and a number of them. Some of the allusions are discussed in the various commentaries, which sometimes agree about the particular OT texts to which the author is alluding. (I am indebted to Beetham for cataloguing the various allusions and echoes recorded by various commentators; of course, I have subsequently consulted the commentary literature

myself. For a large-scale discussion and analysis of allusions in Colossians, see Beetham 2005. In some cases I have detected new allusions.) But even when commentators have observed allusions, there has been little attempt to demonstrate their validity or to reflect on how Paul is using them (for debate over Pauline authorship of Colossians, which I am assuming for purposes of the present chapter, see the commentaries). As far as possible, within the limits of this overall project, the procedure in this chapter on Colossians is generally twofold: to demonstrate the validity of various OT allusions and to discuss their significance. Neither of these tasks has been consistently carried out in past study of Colossians (an expansion of the discussions throughout the following commentary, as well as other OT references that could not be discussed at all due to space limitations, are given in Beale, forthcoming).

Commentators offer various definitions of "allusion" and "echo" and posit various criteria for discernment of both, sometimes defining an echo as unconscious and unintentional and sometimes as conscious and intentional. Whether OT references are referred to as "allusions" or "echoes," the purpose here is to argue the likelihood that Paul, to one degree or another, intended to make the reference. The goal here is to point out, on a case-by-case basis, the clearest cumulative evidence for the presence of an intentional OT reference, regardless of how one wants to categorize it formally.

Nevertheless, readers will make different judgments on the basis of the same evidence, some categorizing a reference to be "probable," and others viewing the same reference to be only "possible" or even so faint as not to merit analysis. I have tried to include for study those OT allusions whose validity are attested by the best evidence and that I consider to be probable. However, some may still wonder whether Paul has intended to make a particular allusion, and they may question that if Paul really intended to convey all the meaning from an OT text for which I am contending, why he did not make the links with that text more explicit. In such cases I would allow for the possibility that Paul merely may have presupposed the OT association in his mind, since he was such a deep and long-experienced reader of the OT Scriptures. This would not mean that there is no semantic link with the OT text under discussion, but rather that Paul perhaps was either unconscious of making the reference or was not necessarily intending his audience to pick up on the allusion or echo. In either case, identification of the reference and the enhancement of meaning that comes from the context of the source text may well disclose the author's underlying or implicit presuppositions, which form the basis for his explicit statements in the text (e.g., texts in the following discussion that may be susceptible to this kind of conclusion are 1:9, 12b–14; 2:11; 3:1).

Colossians 1

After greeting the readers (1:1–2), Paul launches off into his typical introductory thanksgiving (1:3–8).

1:6, 10

The first OT allusion occurs in 1:6, 10, the former a part of the thanksgiving, and the latter a part of a prayer based on the thanksgiving (translations of Scripture quotations are mine or the NASB [1971 edition]):

Gen. 1:28	Col. 1:6, 10
"Increase [auxanō] and multiply [plēthynō] and fill the earth . . . and rule over . . . all the earth [pasēs tēs gēs]." (LXX)	"in all the world [panti tō kosmō] also it [the word of truth, the gospel] is bearing fruit [karpophoreō] and increasing [auxanō]" (1:6)
"Be fruitful and multiply, and fill the earth . . . and rule . . . the earth." (MT)	"in every good work bearing fruit [karpophoreō] and increasing [auxanō]" (1:10)

Note that Gen. 1:26 has "rule over . . . all the earth" in both LXX and MT (also, "all the earth" appears in Gen. 1:29).

Several commentators have noticed that 1:6, 10 are an allusion to Gen. 1:28 (and perhaps 1:22) (R. P. Martin 1974: 49; Wright 1986: 53–54, 59; however, Lohmeyer [1964: 27] and O'Brien [1982: 13] view it as an echo [cf. Schweizer 1982: 36–37], while others merely note similarities to the Genesis passage, although Ernst [1974: 158] sees the wording of 1:6, 10 as too general to posit a precise allusion to Gen. 1:28). It appears that the Hebrew text may be the focus, since the LXX renders pārâ ("bear fruit") with auxanō ("increase"), and rābâ ("multiply") with plēthynō ("multiply"). The LXX is a viable rendering, since auxanō can have the connotation of the "increase" of fruit or of some kind of organic growth (e.g., Isa. 61:11; 1 Cor. 3:6–7). The LXX may be combining the notions of "multiplying" and "bearing fruit" by its choice of auxanō in order to anticipate the directly following reference to "multiplying." Paul appears to give perhaps a bit more of a literal rendering of the verbs by translating pārâ with karpophoreō ("bear fruit"), and rābâ ("multiply") with auxanō, as well as reproducing "all the earth" either from the MT of Gen. 1:26 or 1:29 or plugging the "all" from those two verses into the wording about "earth" in 1:28 (or, perhaps, he could have been influenced by the LXX rendering itself of 1:28).

Paul could well be reproducing "all the earth" from Gen. 1:28 in his phrase "in all the world [en panti tō kosmō]" in 1:6, though the LXX has gē instead of Paul's kosmos, which may reveal further his own rendering independently of the LXX (Gen. 1:26, 29 also have "all the earth," likewise using gē). In addition, the fact that the LXX never translates 'ereṣ with kosmos but only by gē presents no problem, since by the time of the NT kosmos was sometimes used synonymously with gē to indicate the created world or the inhabited world (see

Matt. 5:13–14; John 17:4–5; 2 Pet. 3:5–6), and when used separately, the two words sometimes also refer to the same things—a usage observable elsewhere also in Paul's own writings. It is striking indeed that the phrase "all the world," utilizing *kosmos* to translate *ṣābā'* ("host"), occurs only a few verses away from Gen. 1:28's *gē* in Gen. 2:1: "and the heavens and the earth [*'ereṣ* = *gē*] were finished, and all the world [*pas ho kosmos*] of them" (also of significance may be the phrase *genesis kosmou*, which serves as a summarizing title directly before "the heaven and the earth" [*ton ouranon kai tēn gēn*] in Gen. 1:1 in Codex Alexandrinus, so that "heaven and earth" are summarized by *kosmos*). Could Paul be inserting *kosmos* in place of *gē* in his allusion to Gen. 1:28 under the influence of the directly following *kosmos* in Gen. 2:1? The influence of the all-inclusive *kosmos* from Gen. 2:1 on Paul in 1:6 may well be pointed to further by the observation that he refers to the original creation in Gen. 1 by the phrase "in the heavens [*ouranois*] and upon the earth [*gēs*]" in 1:16 and then refers to the same combination (though in different order) in 1:20. Thus, in 1:6 Paul may have in mind the entire created cosmos, not just the earthly part of it.

Understandably, one might doubt that such an allusion exists in Col. 1, because whereas Gen. 1 refers to the increase of humans on "all the earth" and their dominion over it, Col. 1:6 refers to the word of the gospel "bearing fruit and increasing" "in all the world," and Col. 1:10 refers to good works as "bearing fruit" and to Christians' growth "in the knowledge of God" (i.e., in God's word). In this light, even if one were to persist in concluding that Paul was alluding to the Genesis text, it would still seem perhaps necessary to conclude that the use is noncontextual, since Paul would be "spiritualizing" what Genesis applies to the physical growth of the human race.

There does appear, however, to be sufficient linguistic evidence to posit a probable and conscious allusion to Gen. 1:28 (see the chart of parallels above). The repetition of the wording in Col. 1:10 highlights the earlier identical phrase and points further to Paul's conscious awareness of alluding to Gen. 1:28. Therefore, the question is whether or not Paul used the text to suit his own rhetorical purposes without being interested in the original meaning of Genesis. In order to an-swer this question, more analysis of Gen. 1:28 is needed. (More discussion than elsewhere in the present study is dedicated to this first allusion in Colossians because it is the only repeated allusion in Colossians, and my analysis of the Gen. 1:28 allusion is designed in part to set up the contextual framework for some of the following allusions.)

It may be that Paul's use of the Gen. 1:28 language about the old creation, despite the apparently different application of it, is intended to indicate merely the general notion that a new creation has been inaugurated with believers because of their identification with Christ. But more than this may have been in Paul's mind. I have argued elsewhere that Gen. 1:26–28 was a mandate to Adam to reflect God's image (the following extended discussion on Gen. 1:26–28 and its use elsewhere in the OT is based on a larger study in Beale 2004: 81–121 and secondary sources cited there). This reflection was implicitly ontological and explicitly functional. God created Adam and Eve with the internal equipment (e.g., moral, spiritual, volitional, and rational attributes) to be able functionally to "subdue," "rule," and "fill" the entire earth with the presence and glory of God. The very notion of being in God's "image" likely included reflecting the divine glory, since God himself was essentially a glorious being (for an underscoring of the Adamic role to glorify God, see Ps. 8; see also the use of Ps. 8:2 in Matt. 21:15–16). Being in God's "image" also suggested that Adam was God's "son," just as when Adam's son was born, Adam was said be the "father of [a son] in his own likeness, according to his image" (Gen. 5:3). Part of "ruling and subduing" certainly was to "be fruitful and multiply and fill" the earth with actual physical children who would join Adam in reflecting God's image and join him in his kingly dominion over the earth.

Thus, Adam and Eve and their progeny were to be vice-regents who were to act as God's obedient children, reflecting God's ultimate glorious king-ship over the earth. Even already in Gen. 1–3, and relevant for Col. 1:6, 10, it is apparent that obedi-ence to God's word was crucial to carrying out the task of Gen. 1:26, 28 (and disobedience to it led to their failure; cf. Gen. 2:16–17; 3:2–4, where there are three examples of Eve's apparent misquotation of the divine word in Gen. 2 [on which, see Ross 1988: 133–35]). Likely included in carrying out the mandate was to defeat and rule over the evil serpent partly by remembering and trusting in God's word of command in 2:16–17 (note the emphasis on God "said" or "saying" with reference to 2:16; 3:1b, 3). Nevertheless, the serpent ended up ruling over Adam and Eve by deceiving them with his deceptive word.

Being "fruitful and multiplying" in Gen. 1:28 refers to the increase of Adam and Eve's progeny, who also were to reflect God's glorious image and be part of the vanguard movement, spreading out over the earth with the goal of filling it with divine glory. This assumes that essential to Adam and Eve's raising of their children was spiritual instruction in God's word that the parents themselves were to remember and pass on.

Paul has tapped into one of the most important veins of the redemptive-historical story line of Scripture, albeit allusively. In fact, the mandate of Gen. 1:28 is repeated throughout the OT—for example, Gen. 9:1, 6–7; 12:2; 17:2, 6, 8; 22:17–18; 26:3, 4, 24; 28:3–4; 35:11–12; 47:27; Exod. 1:7; Lev. 26:9; Ps. 8:5–9; 107:38; Isa. 51:2; Jer. 3:16; 23:3; Ezek. 36:10–11, 29–30, most of which contain the actual dual terminology of "increase and multiply," and several of which have the phrase "all the earth" (*pasa* + *gē*) (Gen. 17:8; 26:4; Ps. 8:9 [8:10 LXX]; Isa. 54:2–5; Jer. 23:3; as also in Col. 1:6, albeit with *kosmos*; cf. 1 Chron. 29:10–12; see Wright 1986: 53; and to lesser extent, O'Brien 1982: 13; note also that the subsequent repeated mandate in the OT may be within Paul's purview).

After Adam's failure to fulfill God's mandate, God raises up other Adam-like figures to whom his commission is passed on. Some changes in the commission occur as a result of sin entering into the world. Beginning with Abraham, the repeated mandate also becomes a promise that God eventually will fulfill. In addition, there is more satanic opposition over which to rule than merely the serpent (thus possession of the land held by the enemy or possession of the "gate" of the enemy is spoken of sometimes as a part of the repeated mandate associated with "ruling and subduing"). Adam's descendants, like him, however, fail.

In the repetition of the commission to the patriarchs noted above, the mention of "all the nations of the earth" being "blessed" by Abraham's "seed"

alludes to a renewed human community bearing God's image and "filling the earth" with regenerated progeny who also reflect God's image and shine out its luminosity to others in the "city of man" who do not rebel and also come to reflect God. Thus, these new converts are "blessed" with the favor of God's glorious presence and become a part of God's ever-increasing kingdom and rule, which the first Adam had forfeited. Hence, the "ruling and subduing" of Gen. 1:28 now includes spiritually overcoming the influence of evil in the hearts of unregenerate humanity that has multiplied upon the earth. The implication is that the notion of physical newborn children "increasing and multiplying" in the original Gen. 1:28 commission now includes people who have left their old way of life, have become spiritually newborn, and have come to reflect the image of God's glorious presence and participate in the expanding nature of the Gen. 1:26–28 commission.

It is possible that what we see in Col. 1:6, 10 is the collective impact of these restatements upon Paul's thinking. If Paul is consciously alluding to Gen. 1:28 in 1:6, 10 (for further echoes of Gen. 1:26–28 that may be heard in the nearby context of Col. 1:10, see Beale, forthcoming), how could he be appropriating this material? He appears to be focusing on the role of God's word in Gen. 2–3 in relation to carrying out the Adamic commission. Paul highlights this in 1:5–6, where "the word of truth" has finally begun expansion "in all the world . . . bearing fruit and increasing" in the way the first Adam should have spread it. This expansion is also taking place "in" the Colossians, who have been "delivered from the domain of darkness and transferred . . . to the kingdom" (1:13), which should have happened earlier in the case of the successive recipients of the repeated Adamic commission but did not occur in the way it has with Christ's coming. As believers continue to "bear fruit and increase," the commission of Gen. 1 is growing in them with the inevitable result that it will expand beyond them to others. In 1:10 we are told how they are "bearing fruit and increasing": "in every good work bearing fruit and increasing in the knowledge of God." Reference to "the knowledge of God" is conceptually synonymous in a general way with the earlier mentioned "word of truth." The more one gains a knowledge of God's word, the more one should "bear fruit" in good works.

Thus, we have begun to perceive how Paul, without doing violence to the OT passage, can spiritually interpret the mandate of Gen. 1 to bear physical children and fill the world with them. He sees new Colossian converts as newly born children of God through their identification with Jesus Christ, the last, new Adam (note the readers' "faith in Christ" in 1:4, which no doubt has caused them to be identified with Christ ["transferred to the kingdom of his beloved Son" in 1:13] and even united with him ["in whom" in 1:14] in 1:13–14, which is directly linked to Christ as "the image of the invisible God" in 1:15; the theme of their identification with Christ as their representative continues in 1:22, 24, 27, 28; 2:6, 10–13, 19; 3:1, 3–4, 10). When they place their faith in the Messiah, they become identified with who he is and what he has accomplished as the last Adam, who has regained the image of God for fallen humanity (cf. 1:15) and established the kingdom that the first Adam should have set up (1:13). Since Christ is the "firstborn" of the new creation, those who identify with him also become subsequently born into the beginning of the new creation. They have been born through being raised from spiritual death to spiritual life by means of being identified with Christ's own resurrection (2:12–13). In 3:9–10 Paul explains that this means that they have "laid aside the old man" (i.e., their identification with the old Adam and the fallen, dead world) and "have put on the new man" (i.e., have become identified with the last Adam and new creation [on which, see commentary on Col. 3:9–10 below]).

Recall that even Adam's actual children were to be not merely new physical humans, but new spiritual creatures, the latter of which especially is the implication that they were to be faithful image bearers of God's glory. And, after the fall the repeated commission in the OT age itself likely included new converts being "blessed" with God's presence and becoming spiritually newborn children in God's ever-increasing kingdom and rule. Paul understands that believers have begun to experience new life because of their identification with Christ as God's Son (1:13 [cf. Rom. 8:16–29]) and with his resurrection (2:12–13). Paul likely viewed this resurrection of believers

not in mere metaphorical terms, but as a true, literal resurrection. Their resurrection, however, is occurring in two stages, first spiritually and then physically at the final consummation (see 3:4). Thus, the spiritual phase of resurrection is just as literal as the future physical phase, since the resurrection of the whole person must be both spiritual and physical. If they are experiencing the beginning of literal resurrection, then they are part of the beginning of the new creation and thus also are newborn children of God. Paul underscores that their growth spiritually occurs through feeding not on physical nutrients, but rather on the food of God's word. It is God's word, then, that fuels the inaugurated phase of the expansion of the great commission in Gen. 1. The goal of the renewed commission in Christ is to spread God's glory through a renewed humanity (for a similar conclusion, see Wright 1986: 53–54). According to Paul, the very means for accomplishing this goal of glory is God's "glorious might" itself (1:11).

Consequently, as "new men," they are progressively "being renewed to a true knowledge according to the image of the one who created" them (a direct allusion to Gen. 1:27 in 3:10 [on which, see commentary on Col. 1:15; 3:9–10 below]) (Philo closely links the "Spirit" and "bearing fruit" with "the image of God," which are combined also in Col. 1:8–15, both texts reflecting the direct link in Gen. 1:27–28 between "the image of God" and "bearing fruit": "For the man stamped with the Spirit [*pneumati*] which is according to the image of God differs not a whit . . . from the tree [in context called 'the tree of Life . . . in the midst of the Garden'] that bears the fruit of immortal life [*tou tēn athanaton zōēn karpophorountos*]; for both are imperishable" [*Planting* 44]).

Therefore, believers are the created progeny of the last Adam, who are beginning to fulfill in him the mandate given to the first Adam. The Gen. 1:28 language applied by Paul to them in 1:6, 9–10 indicates that they are a part of the inaugurated new creation and are beginning to fulfill in Christ what has been left unfulfilled in the primordial mandate throughout the ages.

The book of Acts refers four times to Gen. 1:28, and, like Col. 1:6–10, three of these uses appear to refer collectively to the repeated commission later in Genesis and elsewhere together with an interpretative focus on the "word":

Acts 6:7: "And the word of God continued to increase, and the number of the disciples continued to multiply greatly in Jerusalem, and a great many of the priests were becoming obedient to the faith."

Acts 12:24: "But the word of the Lord continued to grow and to be multiplied."

Acts 19:20: "So the word of the Lord was growing mightily and prevailing."

That the repeated commission is most likely in mind in these three verses is evident in that Acts 7:17 actually quotes one of the repeated commissions from Exod. 1:7, 20 and refers to it as a "promise" that appeared to be beginning its fulfillment: "the people increased and multiplied in Egypt" (Pao 2000: 167–69; this makes Pao think that the Exodus restatement of the commission is the focus in the other restatements in Acts). The two verbs for "increase and multiply" in Acts 6:7; 12:24; 19:20 are identical to Gen. 1:28 LXX (except for "prevail" in 19:20, which uses *ischyō* instead of *plēthynō*, though the former verb occurs in Exod. 1:20, and the prefixed form in Exod. 1:7). These passages are virtually identical in sense with Col. 1:6, all of which view the literal commission about progeny to be interpreted in the new age as the increase of the reception of God's word in new believers and the multiplication of believers. And, as we have seen, the notion in Col. 1:10 is quite similar.

If one had to try to classify the particular category of the "use of the OT" here in 1:6, 10, possibly it is a mere analogical use. However, the closest category might be typology: the continued failure to fulfill the Genesis commission pointed to an eschatological humanity that would finally be obedient to the Genesis command. The presupposition underlying such a use is likely the notion of the "last, eschatological Adam," Jesus Christ, who first came as the true "image of the invisible God" (1:15), and who initially carried out the commission so that his people could walk in his steps in continuing to obey the mandate. Or, one could categorize the use as completion of intended design (i.e., God's original design for humanity).

Excursus on the Use of Gen. 1:28 in Early Judaism and Christianity. Such an interpretation of Gen. 1:28 as we have seen in Col. 1, especially with the emphasis on God's word, apparently has not been acknowledged sufficiently as present in early or late Judaism (e.g., see the survey of the uses in the OT and Judaism in Cohen 1989), since there are a number of examples that indicate that Jewish commentators understood Gen. 1:28 "literally" in terms of human reproduction (e.g., *Jub.* 6:5; 10:4; 32:17–19; *Sib. Or.* 1:55–58, 271–274; *1 En.* 67:1–3; 89:49; 2 Esd. 3:12; Sir. 44:21; Bar. 2:34 [for about half of the Jewish references, excluding Dead Sea Scrolls but including CD-A, that develop Gen. 1:28 here and below in this section on 1:6, 10, I am indebted to Beetham 2005: 80–86]).

Nevertheless, the interpretation of Gen. 1:28 that we have noted in Colossians becomes more plausible by observing that it has various kinds of precedents in early Judaism and is attested elsewhere in early Christianity, especially through a combination of the language of Gen. 1:28 together with "growing garden" imagery from Gen. 2 (see *Hel. Syn. Pr.* 12:44–45, 49–52; Philo, *QG* 2.56; *1 En.* 10:16–22; likewise *1 En.* 5:7, 10; *Jub.* 36:6; Josephus, *Ant.* 4.112–117; *T. Levi* 18:9–10, 14; CD-A II, 11–13a; 4Q158 1–2, 7–8; 4Q433a 2; 1QHᵃ XIV, 11–19; 4Q418 81; *Odes Sol.* 11–12; 38; *Barn.* 6:11–19 [for elaboration on how the Jewish texts precisely relate to the use of Gen. 1:28 in Col. 1:6, 10, see Beale, forthcoming]).

1:9

On the basis of Paul's thanksgiving for the readers' growing faith and hope (1:3–8), he says that he had "not ceased to pray" for them and to request that they "be filled with the knowledge of his [God's] will in all wisdom and spiritual understanding." Some commentators (e.g., Wright 1986: 58; MacDonald 2000: 48; Lohmeyer 1964: 33; Ernst 1974: 161) view the concluding phrase, "in all wisdom and spiritual understanding," to reflect a broad OT-Jewish tradition in which the phrase is repeated (e.g., Exod. 31:3; 35:31; Deut. 4:6; 1 Chron. 22:12; 2 Chron. 1:10–12; Job 12:13; 28:20; 39:17; Ps. 49:3 [48:4 LXX]; 111:10 [110:10 LXX]; Prov. 1:7; 2:2, 3, 6; 9:10; 24:3; Isa. 10:13; 11:2; Jer. 51:15 [28:15 LXX]; Dan. 1:17; 2:21; Sir. 1:4; 14:20; 15:3; 39:6; Bar. 3:23; cf. Deut. 34:9; 1QS IV, 3–7; 4Q213a 1 I, 14; 4Q504 8 4–5; CD-A II, 3; 1QS IV, 22; XI, 6; 1QHᵃ IX, 19; 4Q286 1 II, 6). More probably, however, the wording alludes to only a few specific OT passages: Exod. 31:3; 35:31; Isa. 11:2 (in agreement with Fee 1994: 642; cf. Dunn [1996: 70], who includes more texts than does Fee). These are the only texts where the "Spirit" and "filling" (though a different verb in the LXX) are directly linked to "wisdom and understanding" and "knowledge" (but cf. Sir. 39:6; 1QS IV, 3–7; 4Q213a 1 I, 14, which probably allude to these OT passages):

Exod. 31:3; Isa. 11:2 LXX	Col. 1:9–10
"I have filled [*empimplēmi*] him with a divine Spirit [*pneuma*] of wisdom [*sophia*] and understanding [*synesis*] and knowledge [*epistēmē*] in every good work [*en panti ergō*]." (Exod. 31:3 [35:31–32a is virtually identical])	"that you should be filled [*plēroō*] with the knowledge [*epignōsis*] of his will in all wisdom [*sophia*] and spiritual understanding [*synesei pneumatikē*] . . . in order to walk about . . . in every good work [*en panti ergō agathō*]"
"The Spirit [*pneuma*] of God will rest upon him: a spirit of wisdom [*sophia*] and understanding [*synesis*] . . . a spirit of knowledge [*gnōseōs*] . . . will fill [*empimplēmi*] him." (Isa. 11:2–3a)	

One could consider that Colossians is closer to Exodus, since, in contrast to Isaiah, both also view the result of the filling to be accomplishing God's will "in every work" (cf. Exod. 31:3 with Col. 1:10, both reading *en panti ergō*, though Exod. 35:31–32a is not verbatim; cf. also 1 Kings 7:14 MT [3 Kgdms. 7:2 LXX]: Hiram "was filled with wisdom and understanding and knowledge to perform in every work" ["wisdom" is lacking in the LXX]). The phrase "in every good work" in Col. 1:10 does not syntactically modify the clause "that you should be filled with the knowledge . . . in all spiritual wisdom and understanding" (1:9), but it is part of an infinitival purpose clause, "in order to walk about . . ." (and not likely modifying the following participle, "bearing fruit" [the phrase "every good work" occurs also in the Pastoral Epistles five times without allusion to the OT: 1 Tim. 5:10; 2 Tim. 2:21; 3:17; Titus 1:16; 3:1; cf. 2 Thess. 2:17]).

The Exodus texts assert that God filled people with the Spirit so that they would have the skills needed to build the tabernacle and fashion its inner contents (see Exod. 31:1–11). Accordingly, Paul sees God filling Christians with his Spirit so that they can live skillful godly lives. The immediate context does not support the notion

that Christians are being equipped to construct a spiritual temple, though the following context could hint further at this (see commentary on Col. 1:19 below).

On the other hand, Isaiah also has in common with Colossians virtually the same Greek word for "knowledge" (Isaiah, *gnōsis*; Colossians, *epignōsis* [cf. Exodus, *epistēmē*]). What also points to awareness of Isaiah is Eph. 1:17, where, also after the thanksgiving, there is a prayer that God give to the readers "a Spirit of wisdom [*pneuma sophias*] and revelation in the knowledge [*epignōsei*] of him," which some commentators rightly see as an allusion to Isa. 11:2: *pneuma sophias . . . pneuma gnōseōs* (e.g., Fee 1994: 675; more loosely, Hendriksen 1967: 97). Both Ephesians and Colossians refer not so much to a quality of mere human "spiritual understanding" as more primarily to an "understanding" that comes from God's Spirit, since both Isaiah and Exodus explicitly refer to God's Spirit as the originator of the "wisdom and understanding" (on which, see Fee 1994: 642). Paul uses the adjective *pneumatikos* twenty-four times with the sense of something being "of, from, given, or inspired by the Holy Spirit," so that the best rendering in Col. 1:9 is "in all Spirit-given wisdom and understanding" (for a fuller analysis of this point, see Beetham [2005: 91–92], who follows and builds on BDAG 837 and Lohmeyer 1964: 33, as well as on, e.g., Schweizer 1968; Dunn 1975–1985: 706–7; Kremer 1990–1993).

Awareness of Isaiah in Colossians is indicated by three further considerations: (1) the preceding allusion to Gen. 1:28 in Col. 1:6 has in common with Isa. 11:1–2 the botanical metaphor applied to human growth (note the verb *pārâ* in both Gen. 1:28 and Isa. 11:1 in the Hebrew, and *auxanō*, read by the LXX in Gen. 1:28 and Aquila and Symmachus in Isa. 11:1) together with the notion of "filling," so that the wording and theme of the former allusion easily could have led Paul's mind to the Isaiah passage (i.e., perhaps the Gen. 1 allusion led to Isa. 11 via the common word and concept); (2) both the following Isaiah context (11:4) and the preceding Colossians context (1:5) mention the "word" (*logos*) as a crucial instrument in accomplishing the divine will; (3) Judaism repeatedly applied Isa. 11:2 to the coming Messiah and the end-time community, and it is natural that the early Jewish Christian community would have utilized it in like manner (*T. Levi* 18:7, 11; *1 En.* 49:1–4; 61:11 [on which, see further references below]).

Especially noteworthy is that one of the main instruments used by the anointed leader in establishing his rule is "the word of his mouth" (Isa. 11:4 LXX), a crucial element also picked up on from Genesis in Colossians (*T. Levi* 18:6–11 also applies Gen. 1:28, as well as Adam and Eden motifs, to the Isa. 11:2 figure).

In the light of the foregoing data, it appears that both the Exodus tabernacle text and Isaiah are in Paul's mind in 1:9 (and Gen. 1:28 in 1:10). Paul develops both. What could he intend by the reference?

Colossians, like Eph. 1:17, however, goes one step further than Isaiah: the "wisdom and spiritual understanding" is now applied not to one person, as in Exodus or Isaiah, but rather to all of God's people who participate in the new creation. This wider application possibly has been sparked by the presence of the Gen. 1:28 context, which was intended to be applied to all of Adam's progeny. Now, all of the last Adam's progeny have the "wisdom and spiritual understanding" needed "to walk worthily of the Lord" and to "bear fruit in every good work" in the new creation. The Colossian believers can grow in these attributes only as they continue to hear (and heed) God's "word of truth" (1:5), which Adam should have heeded, and which their true Adamic forerunner, Jesus Christ, did heed (Matt. 4:1–11; Luke 3:38–4:12).

Thus, when saints identify with Christ by faith, they begin to possess the attributes of their messianic representative, since, as Paul states in 2:3, "in Christ are hidden all the treasures of wisdom and knowledge [*sophias kai gnōseōs*]." The application to God's eschatological people of what would be true of their king had a precedent in earlier Jewish interpretation of Isa. 11:1–5, 10 (for focus on the individual king or Messiah, see 4Q161 8–10 III, 9–25; *1 En.* 49:1–4; *T. Levi* 18:7, 11; *Pss. Sol.* 17:35–43; *Midr. Rab.* Gen. 2:4; *Midr. Rab.* Num. 13:11; *Midr. Rab.* Ruth 7:2; *Pesiq. Rab.* Piska 33; *Pirqe R. El.* 3; *Tanḥ.* Gen. 9:13; and with respect to application to the corporate people, see *1 En.* 61:11 [cf. 61:8–9], 1QS IV, 3–7; Sir. 39:6; cf. 4Q213a 1 I, 14, 17; see also quotation of Exod. 31:3 in 4Q365 10, 4). Note that both

notions are combined in *T. Levi* 18; *T. Jud.* 24; *1 En.* 49; 61.

Therefore, Paul may apply the Exodus/Isaiah texts merely analogically to the Colossians, though if the Isaiah prophecy is the greater focus, then believers may be seen as continuing to fulfill it by virtue of their identification with Christ (cf. 1:18, 24; 2:10, 19), who has inaugurated the fulfillment of Isa. 11:2. If the latter, then Paul saw in Jesus' first coming the fulfillment of the Isa. 11:2 prophecy, which he is assuming as the basis for the readers' partaking of the Spirit (see Beetham 2005: 95–96). Perhaps there was no explicit link with Isa. 11:2 in Paul's mind, in which case an unintended association with the Isaiah text may still be traceable, revealing that it formed an underlying foundation for the statement that he makes about the readers' "spiritual wisdom and understanding" in 1:9.

1:12–14

This segment of the chapter forms part of the prayer begun in 1:9. Paul began by praying that the readers would be "filled" with God's wisdom "in order to walk in a manner worthy of the Lord, to please him in all respects." This goal is to be reached by means of "bearing fruit and increasing in the knowledge of God . . . being strengthened with all power . . . giving thanks to the Father." In 1:12b–14 Paul gives the reason for the thanksgiving, which is rooted in the language of Israel's exodus and subsequent inheritance of the promised land.

Although it is unlikely that Paul has one OT passage in mind, the broad tradition describing Israel's exodus appears to have influenced the wording of 1:12–14 (see Yates 1993: 12). "In Christ" the believers "have redemption [*apolytrōsis*]" (1:14), and they have been "delivered from" (*rhyomai* + *ek*) bondage to evil (1:13). Likewise, Israel had been "delivered from" the bondage of Egypt (see *lytroō* + *ek* in Exod. 6:6 [*rhyomai ek* + *kai lytroō*]; Deut. 7:8; 13:5 [13:6 LXX]; 24:18 [with *ekeithen* instead of *ek*]; 2 Sam. 7:23; 1 Chron. 17:21; Ps. 106:10 [105:10 LXX]; Add. Esth. 13:16 [Esther 4:17g LXX]; ten other times the LXX also uses *lytroō* to refer to Israel's redemption out of Egypt; cf. Exod. 14:30, with *rhyomai* + *ek*; others who see Israel's deliverance from Egypt as background include Caird 1976: 171–74; Dunn 1996: 77, 80; Wright 1986: 62–63; Wall 1993: 57–61; Hübner

1997a: 53; MacDonald 2000: 51). Interestingly, the "second exodus" prophecies of Israel's deliverance from exile also employ the terminology of "redemption" (see Isa. 44:22, 23, 24; 51:11; 52:3; 62:12; cf. 41:14; 43:1, 14; Barth and Blanke [1994: 188, 190–93] see the background of both the first and the second exodus redemptions behind Col. 1:12–14).

In addition, these prophecies of another exodus use the language of "bringing [Israel] out of darkness [*skotia*]" (cf. Ps. 107:10–14 [106:10–14 LXX], preceded by "redeem" [*lytroō*] in 107:2 [106:2 LXX] as a synonym for "lead"; Isa. 42:7; cf. 42:16; 49:9). These prophecies also picture Israel as being restored from the "darkness" (*skotia*) of exile into "light" (*phōs*) (Isa. 9:2 [9:1 LXX]; 42:6b–7, 16; 58:10; 60:1–3), which may be a development of the contrasting "darkness" (*skotia*) and "light" (*phōs*) that was part of the first exodus narrative (Exod. 10:21–23; 14:20). Israel's deliverance from Egypt also had qualified them to become "saints" (*hagioi*) (Exod. 22:31 [22:30 LXX]; Lev. 11:44–45; 19:2; 20:7, 26; 21:6; Num. 15:40; 16:3) and to receive "a share of the inheritance" in Canaan (note *meris* + *klēros* fifteen times in this respect in the LXX of Numbers, Deuteronomy, and Joshua, often with respect to the Levites, who, unlike the other tribes, had "no portion" or "inheritance" [e.g., Deut. 10:9]; see Lohmeyer 1964: 39).

Just as Israel had been "delivered from" Egyptian slavery and had become "saints," and then had received "a share of the inheritance" in the promised land, so too the church had been "delivered from" (*rhyomai* + *ek*; *apolytrōsis*) a greater bondage than that of Egypt (satanic "darkness" [*skotia*]) and had been "qualified . . . for a share" in a greater "inheritance of the saints in light" (*meris* + *klēros* + *hagioi* + *phōs*) (others who see the phrase "share of the inheritance" in 1:12 to have its background in the allotment of land to Israel in Canaan include, e.g., Lightfoot 1961: 141; Masson 1950: 96; Caird 1976: 171; Patzia 1984: 10; Wright 1986: 60–61; Callow 1983: 30; Hübner 1997a: 52; Lincoln 1990: 593; Melick 1991: 205; E. D. Martin 1993: 49; so also R. P. Martin [1974: 53–54]; Wall [1993: 55]; Vaughn [1978: 179], who include "saints" as part of the background). This inheritance was none other than "the kingdom of the Son" (1:13).

Furthermore, Yahweh's "redemption" (*lytroō*) of Israel out of Babylonian captivity has escalated significance in comparison to the release from Egypt, since it is equated with "wiping out their transgressions" (Isa. 44:22 [likewise 40:2]), which is strikingly comparable to Paul's words in 1:14: "in him we have redemption, the forgiveness of sins" (Barth and Blanke 1994: 192).

What would have fueled Paul's application of exodus imagery to the church's salvation? Presumably, he sees the people of God in Christ as undergoing an exodus like that out of Egypt, but on an escalated scale (beginning spiritually in this age and consummated with physical resurrection). Probably, Paul was directed to such an application also because of Isaiah's second-exodus prophecies, which utilized and developed some of the same language as the first exodus. Elsewhere in his letters Paul views the restoration prophecies of Israel and of its second exodus as having begun fulfillment in Christ's first coming and in the formation of the earliest Christian churches (see Beale 1989; J. M. Scott 1992: 167–71, 179; Keesmat 1994). Indeed, Paul has just made a combined allusion in 1:9 to significant events associated with the first and second exoduses (respectively, Exod. 31:3 and Isa. 11:2 [cf. 11:3–16]). Additionally, Paul's awareness of OT restoration themes is apparent from his description of his own call with the second-exodus language of Isa. 42:7, 16 (noted above) together with wording uniquely similar to 1:12–14 in Acts 26:18: "to open their eyes in order that they may turn from darkness unto light and from the authority of Satan to God, in order that they should receive forgiveness of sins and an inheritance among those who have been made holy by faith in me [Jesus]." In fact, it is probable that Paul is reflecting on this aspect of his call in 1:12–14 (see Moule 1957: 56).

Paul uses the exodus images either analogically or typologically; if the latter, then Israel's redemptive history prefigured that of eschatological Israel, the church. A typological use is pointed to by Paul's awareness elsewhere and in the nearby context of Isaiah's second-exodus prophecies. These prophecies would have been fertile ground from which Paul's typological understanding of the first exodus easily could have grown (it may be more precise to say that Paul *presupposes* a typological approach to the first exodus [so Beetham

2005: 114]). In fact, there appears to be a mixing of the exodus (historical) and second-exodus (prophetic) material in 1:12–14, since, as we noted, the combination of "light and darkness" echoes Isaiah (1 Pet. 2:9 does likewise, combining Exod. 19:6; 23:22 LXX with Isa. 42:6–7, 12, 16; 43:20–21). Paul would have viewed Isaiah's second-exodus prophecies to have begun fulfillment, to the degree that he was conscious of them. And, even if it were concluded that the second-exodus prophecies were not expressly used by Paul, they still likely elicit an association with such prophecies that has become the underlying trigger in his thinking, inspiring his description of the readers' salvation.

Paul does not appear to be the only one of his time to have conducted such a typological exegesis. Early Judaism applied the promise about Israel's "share of an inheritance" in Canaan to an eternal, end-time reward, which likely also was done according to a typological rationale (e.g., Dunn [1996: 76] adduces 1QS XI, 7–8 [God "has given them an inheritance in the lot of the saints"] as a striking parallel to 1:9–12; similarly 1QH^a XIX, 10b–12; so also see Wis. 5:5 ["his inheritance is among the saints"]; *T. Ab.* [A] 13:13 [on which, see Pokorný 1991: 52, including additional references]).

1:13

Some commentators have suggested that "the kingdom of his beloved Son" in 1:13 is an allusion to 2 Sam. 7:12–16 (Barth and Blanke 1994: 190). In the 2 Samuel text, God promises to David that he "will establish" a descendant's "kingdom . . . forever" and that this descendant would be a "son" to God. The Hebrew text of 7:15 says that God's "lovingkindness [*hesed*; LXX: *eleos*] shall not depart from him." In this light, David's statement in 7:18 LXX that this promise shows how much God had "loved [*agapaō*] him" implies that 7:15 indicates that such love would continue with his descendant (see Beetham [2005: 121–23], who views "love" in the LXX passage as part of the 2 Sam. 7 allusion).

Thus, the notion in 1:13 of a "beloved son" with an eternal "kingdom" has unique affinity with the 2 Samuel text and likely alludes to it. Since exodus themes have been interwoven throughout 1:12–14, it is possible that Hos. 11:1 ("When Israel was a child, I loved him, and out of

Egypt I called my son") was the underlying link between the exodus and 2 Samuel passages (see Wright [1986: 63], who sees the Hosea passage as an actual allusion; several commentators, such as Lenski [1964: 43], also see an echo of Matt. 3:17: "my beloved son" [cf. some manuscripts of Luke 9:35]; Lohmeyer [1964: 50] observes that Col. 1:13 may also have been influenced by the repeated reference to Israel as a "son" [*huios*] whom God "loves" [*agapaō*]: Ps. 28:6 LXX; *Pss. Sol.* 13:9 [in parallel with "firstborn"]; 18:3–4 [which has *agapē* and "firstborn son"]; Wis. 16:26 [has plural, "sons"]).

Again, presuming Paul's consciousness of the 2 Samuel allusion, we must ask whether he perceives an analogical, a typological, or a prophetic relationship underlying his linking of the two texts. The context of the 2 Samuel passage points to a typological or prophetic-fulfillment connection. Clearly, 2 Sam. 7:10–16 is a prophetic promise. The question is whether it was completely fulfilled in Solomon or only partially, so that part of the prophecy remained to be fulfilled at a later point. If the former, then the fulfillment itself could become a typological event pointing forward to Christ.

It appears, however, that the prophecy was fulfilled only partially by Solomon. That the promise certainly has Solomon in mind is evident, since the text says that the promised king would commit "iniquity" and be "corrected" for it. However, 2 Sam. 7:10–16 says that the coming kingdom and temple will last forever, which was not true with Solomon's temple and kingdom or that of his descendants (Exod. 15:17 also affirms the eternal character of the coming kingdom and, implicitly, of the temple, to which allusion is made in 2 Sam. 7:10, 12–13). Sometimes the Hebrew word '*ôlām* may connote a long time or an "eternal" period. Although there is debate, when considered in the light of the context of the canon, the word '*ôlām* in 2 Sam. 7:13–29 likely refers to an eternal epoch because of its links with the purposes of Eden that are developed with the patriarchs and because of the links with the eternal eschatological temple and kingdom later in the OT and the NT (cf., e.g., Heb. 1:5; similarly, Acts 2:30; 13:23; 2 Cor. 6:18; Rev. 21:7; cf. also Luke 1:32; John 1:49; 7:42; for further support in these respects, see Beale 2004: chap. 3).

Hence, the Colossians reference sees that what was promised in 2 Sam. 7, and was partially fulfilled by Solomon, was finally fulfilled in Christ (though the consummation even of Christ's fulfillment still remains). The prophesied eternal kingdom of 2 Sam. 7 is also seen elsewhere in the NT to have begun fulfillment in Christ (see Heb. 1:5; Acts 2:30; 13:23 [Acts 13:23 and 2 Cor. 6:18 come from Paul himself]). Thus, Hübner (1997a: 53–54) rightly contends that "the eternal dominion of Christ [in 1:15 is . . . the *messianic fulfillment from 2 Sam 7,16.*" At Qumran too 2 Sam. 7:11–14 was understood to be a prophecy of the coming eschatological Messiah (4Q174 1 I, 10–12), who will deliver "the sons of light" from the onslaughts of Belial (4Q174 1 I, 7–9 [cf. Col. 1:13: "saints in the light"]).

It is possible that Ps. 2:7 ("You are my son; today I have begotten you") is also echoed in the Colossians expression (Wolter [1993: 67] sees 2 Sam. 7:14 = 1 Chron. 17:13; Ps. 2:7; 89:27–28 as part of the background). Nevertheless, perception of the psalm's presence may be only an impression created by the fact that the psalm itself alludes to 2 Sam. 7 (on which, see Delitzsch 1970: 1:96). That a possible echo of the psalm could be heard may be suggested by Heb. 1:5, where the psalm is quoted and then is directly linked to a quotation of 2 Sam. 7:14. If there is any trace of such an echo, it would support a prophetic use of 2 Sam. 7, since the psalm is probably directly prophetic of a coming messianic king (which is the way Paul understood the psalm in Acts 13:33; likewise, Heb. 1:5; 5:5 [for a thorough survey of 2 Sam. 7:12–14 in Judaism, elsewhere in the NT, and in the early fathers, see Beetham 2005: 127–33]).

1:15

The so-called poem of 1:15–20 has been discussed by commentators more than any other passage in Colossians (for significant qualifications about this passage being based on a preformed hymn, see O'Brien 1982: 32–37). Here I can offer only a brief analysis of the passage and some of the main lines of past interpretation (for further discussion of the poem and its background and meaning, see O'Brien 1982: 31–32; Wright 1986: 63–80; Barclay 1997: 56–68; Wolter 1993: 70–71; Dunn 1996: 83–104; Hübner 1997a: 55; for a convenient list of bibliography on the hymn, see Pokorný 1991: 56–57; Lohse 1975: 41). If the widely held

conclusion that Paul has alluded to a preexisting hymn is correct, then he has adapted it to fit into the context of what he is writing. Since we do not have the context of the preexisting hymn against which to interpret Paul's use, we must concentrate only on how Paul is using the wording in its context. As we investigate the hymn, we will see how its themes are developments of the preceding context. Most directly, 1:15–20 is an explanation of the directly preceding verses (1:13b–14): "the son of his love, in whom we have the redemption, the forgiveness of sins."

The unit can be broadly divided into two sections: Christ's supremacy over the first creation (1:15–17), and Christ's supremacy over the new creation (1:18–20).

An Adamic Background for the Portrayal of Christ: "The Image of God." A number of commentators rightly understand that the reference to Christ as the "image of the invisible God" is, at least in part, an allusion to Gen. 1:27: "God created man in his own image, in the image of God he created him"; LXX: "God made man according to the image of God" (seeing an echo of Gen. 1:27 are Kittel 1964: 395–96; Simpson and Bruce 1957: 193; Yates 1993: 22; Wall 1993: 66–67; seeing Gen. 1:27 as part of the background are O'Brien 1982: 43; Masson 1950: 98–99; Hugedé 1968: 52–54; seeing Paul's phrase as rooted in Gen. 1:26 is Furter 1987: 98; a possible variant of this is Burney 1926, arguing that Paul exegeted Gen. 1:1 ["in the beginning"] via Prov. 8:22 [on which, see discussion of Proverbs below]).

Paul's language here is virtually identical with his reference elsewhere to "man" being in "the image and glory of God" (1 Cor. 11:7, where clear allusion is made to Gen. 1:27 [on 1 Cor. 11:7, see Fee 1987: 515]). Paul's thought here may have been led to this reference, not only because of the repeated allusion to Gen. 1:28 in the preceding context (1:6, 10), but also because of the mention of "son" in 1:13 (the relative pronoun *hos* in 1:15, like *hō* in 1:14, has its antecedent in "the son of his love" in 1:13). "Sonship," as we noted, is inextricably linked to the Gen. 1 notion of God's "image." For example, Gen. 5:1–4 implies that Adam's being in God's "image" means that Adam was God's "son," since when Adam's son was born, Adam was said be the "father of [a son] in his own likeness, according to his image."

Early Judaism also closely associated the notions of Adam's sonship and his being in God's image, sometimes even referring to his being the image of the "invisible" God. The *Life of Adam and Eve* (ca. 100 AD) refers to God as Adam's "unseen Father" because "he is your image" (*L.A.E.* 35). Philo (*Planting* 18–19) also underscores that Adam was created "to be a genuine coinage of that dread Spirit, the Divine and Invisible One," and that he "has been made after the image of God, not however after the image of anything created" (likewise, Philo [*Worse* 86–87] says that "the invisible Deity stamped on the invisible soul the impress of itself, to the end that not even the terrestrial region should be without a share in the image of God"). Noah, as a second-Adam figure, is viewed by Philo (*Moses* 2.65) as being given the original Adamic commission from Gen. 1:28 and, accordingly, is said to be "born to be the likeness of God's power and visible image of the invisible [*eikōn tēs aoratou*] nature" of God (cf. Col. 1:15: *eikōn tou theou tou aoratou*, which Lightfoot [1961: 144–46] sees as partly linked to Philo's similar uses).

Paul either independently interprets the OT notion of the Adamic image along the same lines as does Judaism or he follows the interpretive trajectory begun in earlier Judaism. Either way, he sees that Christ was in the image of God before creation and is still in God's image, though now this has been functionally enhanced in a redemptive-historical manner: Christ has come in human form and accomplished that which the first Adam did not; consequently, as divine and ideal human, Christ reflects the image that Adam and others should have reflected but did not.

A clear link to Gen. 1:26–27 in 1:15 is also indicated in that precisely the same phrase, "who is the image of God," occurs in 2 Cor. 4:4, where probably it refers to Christ as in the pristine image in which the first Adam should have been, since 4:6 ("Let light shine out of darkness") alludes to Gen. 1:3 in further explanation of 4:4 (Phil. 2:6–7 apparently has the same significance as 2 Cor. 4:4: Christ "existed in the form of God . . . and coming about in the likeness of men"). And, as in Col. 3:10, so also 2 Cor. 3:18 refers to Christians becoming "transformed" into this "image." Also strikingly similar to Col. 1:15 is Rom. 8:29, which echoes Gen. 1:27 (note the allusion to Gen. 3:17–19 in Rom. 8:20): Christ is both "the image of his son" (to which believers become "conformed") and the "firstborn." Christ's preexistence is not denied, but the emphasis in Col. 1:15a is on his present condition of being in the divine "image" and being "firstborn."

Hence, the stress in this first phrase of 1:15 is on Christ as the incarnate revelation of the invisible God. The incarnational revelatory emphasis is also pointed to by 1:12–14, where the exodus redemption background has been applied to God's redemption of people through his Son; indeed, 1:15 continues to describe the "Son," who accomplished redemption and forgiveness for his people (so also Wright 1991: 109). Likewise, 1 Cor. 15:45–49 portrays Christ possessing the heavenly image of the last Adam, which Christians will fully reflect at his final parousia. To see 1:15 primarily against the background of Genesis is a line of interpretation followed by many commentators, though a few strongly resist it (see, e.g., Aletti 1993: 94–116). Nevertheless, it is unlikely that "image" in 1:15 does not have the same background and meaning of "image" in Rom. 8:29; 1 Cor. 15:45–49; 2 Cor. 4:4.

But even if the thought here is only of Christ being in God's image *before* creation began, the identification with being the ideal Adam would still hold: if the exalted Christ was the full expression of God's image, then he had always been in the divine image. Hence, "the one who can be described in Adamic language (Gen 1:27) can also be held to have existed before Adam and to have been on the side of the Creator as well as on the side of the creation" (Lincoln 1990: 597). This pattern appears to be present in Phil. 2:6–7, where Christ is said to have "existed in the form of God" before his incarnation, and then he "came to be in the likeness of men," both phrases now seen by many commentators to have an Adamic identification (see, e.g., Wright 1991: 56–98, esp. 57–62, 90–97). Wright has noted that it is appropriate that Christ in his preincarnate divine state could be said to be in God's image, since the task of the ideal man who would represent Israel and save the world is a task that the OT also attributes to God; indeed, the glorious authority of the ideal man (in fulfillment of Gen. 1:26–28; Ps. 8; Dan. 7:13–14) is (according to Isa. 45) thoroughly suitable for God himself (Wright 1991: 95). It may well be that describing Christ's preincarnate condition with the word "image" is a way of portraying him "as being, so to speak, a potential man" (Wright 1991: 95 [a conclusion that Wright makes about Christ being in "the form of God" in Phil. 2:6]). Just as 2 Cor. 8:9 can refer to the preexistent Messiah by his subsequent incarnate name of "Lord Jesus Christ," so is the case with calling the preexistent Christ the human "image" of God, "much as we might say 'the Queen was born in 1925'" (Wright 1991: 116) or that "the Prime Minister studied economics at Oxford" (Wright 1991: 98).

It seems best, then, to see Christ as God's "image" in 1:15 to point to his incarnate "revealing of the Father on the one hand and his preexistence on the other—it is both functional and ontological" (O'Brien 1982: 44). The same dual concept occurs in John 1:1–18; Phil. 2:6–11; Heb. 1:2–2:9.

But in the unlikely event that an Adamic/Gen. 1 background is not in mind in 1:15, the second part of the passage (1:18), affirming Christ's role in the new creation, would likely make the point that he is the new Adam and, by implication, representing the divine image the way the first Adam should have. This is pointed to further by 3:10–11, where Christ probably is portrayed as being the image of the "new man," according to which believers are being renewed. If there is a link between 1:15 and 3:10, which is highly probable, then understanding the Adamic nature of the image in 1:15 naturally follows.

An Adamic Background for the Portrayal of Christ: "The Firstborn." The directly following reference in the second line of 1:15 to Christ as the "firstborn [*prōtotokos*] of all creation" highlights further the idea that he was an Adamic figure and "son" of God. The OT repeatedly asserts that the "firstborn" of every Israelite family gained authority by virtue of being given the inheritance rights. This notion was projected back upon the first Adam by early Judaism, since Adam was the "firstborn" of all human creation (see, e.g., *Midr. Rab.* Num. 4:8, where the reason that "firstborn" Israelites were redeemed by Levites and received the "birthright" is that "Adam was the world's firstborn" who served as a priest, as did his representative progeny until the Levites were established). By a similar application, Christ is the last Adam,

who is the "firstborn," not only of all humanity in the new creation (on which, see the comment on Col. 1:18 below in this section), but also of "all [things in the old] creation."

Even Israel was called God's "firstborn" (*prōtogonos*) and his "very first [*prōtistos*] offspring" (see Wall [1993: 68–69], who perceives both the law of primogeniture and Israel as "firstborn" as part of the background for Paul's expression). The reason the nation was given this name probably was that the nation was given the same mandate (Gen. 1:28) as were Adam and Noah, the latter being a second-Adam image (so also Philo, *Flight* 208: "Israel, the son free-born and first-born [*prōtogonos*]"; Israel was also God's "firstborn, only begotten" [*4 Ezra* 6:58], his "beloved son and . . . firstborn" [*Pss. Sol.* 13:9], and "a first-born, only begotten son" [*Pss. Sol.* 18:4]) (see commentary on Col. 1:6, 10 above). Thus, Israel was a corporate Adam figure that was to accomplish the same purposes as Adam, and 1:15 shows Christ summing up the purposes of both OT figures.

In the light of the foregoing, it is understandable that Ps. 88 LXX referred to the coming eschatological messianic king of Israel as having God as his "father" and being "firstborn" (*prōtotokos*) and inheriting a position "higher than the kings of the earth," with a "throne" that lasts "forever" (Ps. 88:27–29, 37 LXX [89:26–28, 36 ET]) (note that in Heb. 12:23, "church of the firstborn" likely connotes the church as being in an exalted position of inheriting eschatological blessings [see Lightfoot 1961: 147]). Paul's use of "firstborn" in 1:15 probably includes allusion to this psalm passage (see Abbott 1905: 210; see also Simpson and Bruce [1957: 194]; O'Brien [1982: 43], who detect an echo of the psalm). Paul affirms that Christ is the fulfillment of the psalm prophecy. Later Judaism understood that Ps. 88 LXX could refer to the coming eschatological king on analogy with Exod. 4:22, where God says of the nation, "Israel is my son, my firstborn" (*Midr. Rab.* Exod. 19:7, the context of which primarily identifies the patriarch Jacob with "Israel," who then is compared by analogy to the coming Messiah). In this respect, there also may be some kind of underlying connection in this psalm with Adam as a firstborn king over the earth. What points further to a Ps. 88 LXX allusion is the use of *christos* twice (88:39,

52 LXX [89:38, 51 ET]) to refer to Israel and the use of the verb *chriō* to refer to David and, implicitly, to the coming Davidic seed who will be the eschatological representative king of the nation (see 88:20–29, 35–37 LXX [89:19–28, 34–36 ET]). Although "Christ" as a name does not occur in the poem in 1:15–20, it does appear repeatedly in the nearby context (1:1–4, 7, 24, 27–28).

Similarly, Philo strikingly refers to the highest ranking angelic figure (one "who holds the eldership among the angels, an archangel as it were") as "God's First-born . . . 'the Beginning' . . . the Man after his image . . . that is Israel," and people who want to be represented by this angelic figure can become "sons of God" (citing Deut. 14:1; 32:18) and "sons of his invisible image . . . [who] is the eldest-born image of God" (*Confusion* 145–147 [see also Philo, *Dreams* 1.215; *Agriculture* 51; *Confusion* 62–63]). The angel probably was conceived to be Israel's heavenly representative.

Paul's additional reference to Christ as "before all things" (1:17a) further highlights his role as "firstborn" of all creation (1:15). The three descriptions for Christ in 1:15–17 ("image of God," "firstborn," "before all things") are thus different ways of referring to Christ as an end-time Adam, since they were common ways of referring to the first Adam or to those who were Adam-like figures and were given the first Adam's task, whether this be Noah, the patriarchs, or the nation Israel. And, just as Adam's temporal priority was not the main point of his purpose but contributed to his ultimate design to be a world ruler, so these names in Colossians were not intended merely to indicate Christ's temporal priority to the old creation but primarily underscored his sovereignty over it (likewise, the significance of "firstborn" Israelites was that they gained authority over the household and inheritance, and each of Philo's references to the highest-ranking angel called "firstborn" also emphasizes this [except *Dreams* 1.215]). The pretemporal connotation indicates not that Christ was the very beginning part of the creation, but that he was "born before it" (rightly according to Moule 1957: 76, in the sense of the "eternal generation of the son"), which places Christ as separate from the rest of the creation; Christ's separateness from creation is underscored by the affirmation that he is the Creator (E. F. Scott 1948: 21).

It is this point of world sovereignty that Ps. 88 LXX underscores about the "firstborn" messianic king. In particular, "I will make him firstborn" in Ps. 88:28 LXX (89:27 ET) is directly followed by the phrase "higher than the kings of the earth," showing, at the least, that the two notions are inextricably linked, if not the latter being a further explanation of the former (as suggested by Theodore of Mopsuestia [cited in Abbott 1905: 211]; likewise, Rev. 1:5, also alluding to Ps. 88:28–30, 37 LXX [89:27–29, 36 ET], highlighting that Christ's resurrection has placed him in a position of rule).

This position of authority is also grounded in Paul's acknowledgment that Christ is the sovereign Creator of the world (1:16 [where an introductory *hoti* occurs]) and sovereignly maintains its ongoing existence (1:17b). Therefore, Christ perfectly embodies the ruling position that Adam and his flawed human successors should have held, and he is at the same time the perfect divine Creator of all things, who is separate from and sovereign over that which he has created, especially underscored by the clause "all things have been created through him and for him" at the end of 1:16 (on which, see Dunn 1996: 90–91).

As is widely recognized, while 1:15–17 refers to Christ's sovereignty over the first creation, 1:18–20 affirms his sovereign position in the second, new creation that has been launched. In this respect, the identical title of "firstborn" is reapplied in order again to indicate Christ's rule over the new order by virtue of his resurrection from the dead (1:18c). His priority in the new creation entails his kingship over it (for a relevant parallel, see Heb. 1:2–5; 2:5–9).

In 1:19–20 Paul states the reasons for Christ's position of rule in the new age: (1) he is the full expression of deity (amplified in 2:9 as "the fullness of deity dwells in bodily form"); (2) he has inaugurated the process of bringing creation back into harmonious relation to itself and to God (i.e., "reconciling"). Paul portrays Christ as God and end-time Adam in the flesh in order to affirm that "Jesus fulfills the purposes which God had marked out *both* for himself *and* for humanity" (Wright 1986: 70–71). The design for humanity originally reaches its completion in the last Adam. The first Adam's failure left a gap of needed obedience for humanity to reach its eschatological completion, so that even the first Adam's disobedience typologically pointed to another Adam's obedience.

A "Wisdom" Background for the Portrayal of Christ? Many commentators believe that the figurative portrayal of "wisdom" in Judaism and in Prov. 8:22–27 (as "the beginning of his [God's] ways" prior to the creation) lies behind 1:15–17. For example, some commentators (Lohse 1975: 46–56; Wright 1986: 66–71; Simpson and Bruce 1957: 197; Wall 1993: 68) highlight Gen. 1 and OT wisdom, especially Proverbs (comparable to Proverbs, note Sir. 24:9: "From eternity, from the beginning [*archē*] he created me [wisdom]"). In the case of Prov. 8, the personification of "wisdom" as being in God's presence directly preceding his creation of the world is to indicate that God's wisdom enabled him to be the perfect artisan in accomplishing this marvelous work. Such a background is certainly possible and plausible, but the allusion is not as clear as so often indicated.

Although further discussion of this issue is not possible here, we may note that, in addition to the various OT influences (especially Gen. 1) and the very few relevant Philo texts noted above, among plausible Jewish backgrounds that may have influenced Paul to one degree or another throughout 1:15–17 is a pastiche of passages from Wisdom of Solomon (see Boring, Berger, and Colpe [1995: 483–84], who mention most of these texts from Wisdom as forming part of the background for 1:15–17):

1. wisdom, which is identified with God's Spirit (in light of 1:6), "holds all things together" (1:7);
2. wisdom is the "reflection of the everlasting light, the unspotted mirror of the power of God, and the image of his goodness" (7:26);
3. wisdom "makes all things new" (7:27) and "she orders all things well" (8:1) and "works all things" (8:5);
4. wisdom "was present when you made the world" (9:9);
5. "you formed man through your wisdom that he should have dominion over the creatures" (9:2), and wisdom "guarded the first-formed father of the world who was created alone, and brought him out of his own transgression [i.e., his 'fall' into sin], and gave him power to rule all things" (10:1–2).

If this particular wisdom background is in mind, then Paul would be affirming that, whereas the fullest manifestation of earthly wisdom in the OT was the Torah, now the Messiah is the greatest expression of divine wisdom on earth, the former pointing to the latter. Such a background is not necessarily mutually exclusive of a Gen. 1 Adam background, though others are adamant that only the "wisdom" background is in mind and not Adam in Genesis (e.g., Aletti 1993: 94–116). That the two backgrounds are compatible is apparent from recalling that one of Wisdom's key roles was to come to dwell in Israel (cf. Proverbs; Sirach; Wisdom of Solomon), the corporate representative of humanity, to enable them to be truly wise humans and to rule over the creation, and this became connected to messianic expectation focused on a coming eschatological king, as in, for example, Ps. 89:27 (88:28 LXX) (following Wright 1991: 112–13). To affirm that only the preexistent Christ, as Wisdom, is in view in 1:15a is also not to give enough credence to the present tense "is" (*estin*). Yes, Christ was in the image of God before creation, but also he is still in that "image," and not to identify that image in the present also with Gen. 1:27 appears implausible, especially in light of the parallels with 2 Cor. 4:4; 1 Cor. 15:45–49, adduced at the beginning of this section.

1:19

This verse explains why Christ should "come to have first place in everything" (1:18b). Some commentators have observed that the combined wording of "well-pleased" and "dwell" in 1:19 may be traced to Ps. 67:17 LXX (68:17 MT; 68:16 ET).

Ps. 67:17–18 LXX	Col. 1:19
"God was well-pleased [*eudokeō*] to dwell [*katoikeō*] in it [*en autō* {Zion}] . . . the Lord will dwell [there] forever . . . in the holy place [MT: *qōdesh*]."	"Because in him [*en autō*] all the fullness of deity was well-pleased [*eudokeō*] to dwell [*katoikeō*]."
	Alternatively: "In him he was well-pleased for all the fullness to dwell."
Most translations render the MT's *qōdesh* as "holy place" or "sanctuary" (KJV, NIV, HCSB, NJB, NLT, RSV, NRSV, ESV; so also 3 En. 24:6–7), though a few translate it as "holiness" (e.g., NASB, NEB).	The LXX's *en tō hagiō* can be taken in the same way. Also, *en autō* of Ps. 67:17 could refer to Sinai instead of Zion, but we take even the reference to "Sinai" in 1:18 as a comparison to "Zion," which is the way, e.g., the NASB and ESV take the verse, and the LXX is just as susceptible to this interpretation as is the MT.

In this respect, Münderlein (1962: 266–70) sees an undoubted connection between Ps. 67:17 LXX (especially the targumic version) and Col. 1:19; Abbott (1905: 219) and Wright (1986: 78) see an echo of the psalm text; Beasley-Murray (1973: 177) says that Ps. 67:17 LXX is a "parallel that is more than a matter of vocabulary"; MacDonald (2000: 63) says that the wording "calls to mind the Jewish Scripture . . . LXX Ps. 67:17, for example"; Wolter (1993: 85) argues that the wording comes from the Jewish-OT background, especially Ps. 68:17 (and, secondarily, Ps. 132:13–14; 2 Macc. 14:35; 3 Macc. 2:16); O'Brien (1982: 52) says only that the combination of the two verbs in both Ps. 67:17 LXX and Col. 1:19 "is of special significance" (see Hay 2000: 62, more tentatively); Wall (1993: 75) sees a reference to the OT temple but does not adduce convincing parallels.

The unique wording in common between Ps. 67 LXX and Col. 1 points to such an allusion: Ps. 67:17a LXX is the only place in the LXX where the verbs "well-pleased" (*eudokeō*) and "dwell" (*katoikeō*) occur together ("dwell" in Ps. 68:17a, as well as "dwell" [*kataskēnoō*] in 68:17b, 19 point further to 68:17 being a reference to the temple, as most English translations render the last phrase of 68:17).

There are other OT passages that are similar to the Ps. 67 LXX passage. Haggai 1–2 contains language and concepts quite close to those of the psalm and Colossians: "build the house, and I will take pleasure in it [*eudokēsō en autō*], and I will be glorified" (1:8); "I will fill [*plēsō*] this house with glory" (2:7). Likewise, 2 Macc. 14:35 affirms, "O Lord of all, who has need of nothing, you were pleased [*ēudokēsas*] that there be a temple for your habitation [*skēnōseōs*] among us." Along the same lines, 3 Macc. 2:15–16 affirms, "For, indeed, your dwelling place [*katoikētērion*], the heaven of heaven, is unapproachable to men; but since you were well-pleased [*eudokēsas*] to set your glory in the midst of your people Israel, you sanctified this place [the temple]."

The Targum to 1 Kings 8 also repeatedly links God's "good pleasure" with his "dwelling" (Shekinah) in Solomon's temple (*Tg.* 1 Kings 8:13–15, 23–24, 27–30; cf. 2 Chron. 6:4–5, 20; 7:16), which also twice says that God's glory cloud "filled the house of the sanctuary" (*Tg.* 1 Kings

8:10–11), language having further affinity with Col. 1:19 (the LXX of 1 Kings 8:10–11 and the parallel in 2 Chron. 7:1–2 use *pimplēmi* for "fill," the latter reading *plēroō* in two manuscripts [ce], which is comparable to the noun form *plērōma* in Col. 1:19. The LXX also reads forms of *katoikētērion* or *katoikēsis* in 1 Kings 8:39, 43, 49 with reference to the heavenly temple in relation to its extension to the earthly temple; so also see *katoikeō* and *katoikēsis* in 2 Chron. 6:18, 21, with reference to the earthly temple, and see *katoikētērion* in 2 Chron. 6:30, 33, 39 with respect to the heavenly temple in parallel to that of 1 Kings 8:39, 43, 49).

At the least, Colossians appears to reflect this general background of God being well-pleased to dwell in and fill the temple. In particular, Colossians may resonate with interpretive rings of the Targum (or perhaps the exegetical tradition that it reflects) together with Ps. 67 LXX, and, at least, the 1 Kings background shows that Paul's allusive language of the psalm is about God's dwelling in the temple (Barth and Blanke [1994: 212] see Ps. 67:17 LXX; *Tg. Ps.* 68:17; *Tg.* 1 Kings 8:27 as "especially close parallels" to Col. 1:19, while also seeing echoes from the LXX of 2 Sam. 7:6; 2 Chron. 6:18; Ps. 21:4 [22:3 ET]; 131:14 [132:14 ET]; 134:21 [135:21 ET]; Isa. 8:18; Lohse [1975: 58] briefly discusses some of this background but never comments on its bearing for Col. 1:19; cf. also *Tg. Ps.* 132:13: "For the Lord is pleased with Zion; he has desired it for his habitation"; the MT of that verse reads, "For the Lord has chosen Zion; he has desired it for his habitation," and 132:14b MT reads, "Here I will dwell, for I have desired it," for which the LXX renders the MT's "desired" [*'āwâ*] with "choose" [*hairetizō*]).

The notion of Christ as the temple of God's presence occurs elsewhere in the NT (e.g., John 2:19–21; Rev. 21:22) and in Paul (Eph. 2:20–22), though he usually highlights the church as the temple, no doubt because of its identification with Christ (as in Eph. 2:20–22; 1 Cor. 3:17; for the church as a temple, see also 1 Cor. 6:19; 2 Cor. 6:16; Rev. 3:12; 7:15; 11:1–2).

Beasley-Murray (1973: 77) explains that the temple background in Col. 1:19 has often been overlooked because there has been too much narrow focus only on *plērōma* ("fullness"), whereas consideration of the language of the whole verse reveals that "Christ is portrayed as fulfilling the role assigned to the Temple in the Old Testament," particularly Ps. 67:17 LXX (so also, almost identically, Wright 1991: 117). If the allusion is intentional, as some rightly think, then the point would be that God's presence on earth is no longer in the earthly temple (the holy of holies), but now is in Christ, who eschatologically instantiates and typologically fulfills all that the temple represented (the subject of "well-pleased" could be God or "all the fulness [of deity]," which amounts to the same thing [see Harris 1991: 49–50]). God's tabernacling presence on earth has now been expressed more greatly in Christ's incarnation than in the old architectural temple, and the Spirit of Jesus continues that earthly presence in the church as the true form of the temple since Christ's ascension. Thus, the reason (*hoti*) Christ should "come to have first place in everything" (1:18b) is that he is the escalated form of God's holy-of-holies presence on earth, and as such, he himself is God.

Excursus on the Relationship of "Wisdom" to the Temple as a Possible Background for Col. 1:19. There is another intriguing observation possibly related to 1:19. It appears to be significant, in light of the acknowledged allusion to "wisdom" in 1:15–18, that early Judaism viewed "wisdom" as having its "headquarters" in the temple, as, for example, Sir. 24:8–10 affirms: "So the Creator of all things gave me [wisdom] a commandment, and he that made me caused my tabernacle to rest, and said, 'Let thy dwelling be in Jacob, and thine inheritance in Israel.' He created me from the beginning before the world, and I shall never fail. In the holy tabernacle I served before him; and I was established in Zion" (for analysis that all of Sir. 24:1–27 focuses on "wisdom" as being in the temple, see Hayward 1999; see also Wis. 9:4–9; cf. *1 En.* 42:1–2 with *1 En.* 39:6–13).

Likewise, Philo says that "God's dwelling-place, the tabernacle" is symbolic of "wisdom," which "is the court and palace of the All-ruler" (*Prelim. Studies* 116–117). This background about the association of "wisdom" and the "temple" points further to a temple reference in 1:19 and may even make more sense of why 1:9 alludes to Exod. 31:3; 35:31, where God filled people with the Spirit in order to have "wisdom" to be able to build the tabernacle. Paul may already subtly be anticipating in 1:9 the OT temple allusion of 1:19. Significantly, 1:9 mentions the "wisdom" of the believer, which ultimately is related to one's identity with Christ, who is "wisdom" of 1:15–18 (since only by growing in "wisdom" can one be "complete in Christ" [1:28], "in whom are hidden all the treasures of wisdom" [2:3]; likewise 3:16).

Conclusion on Col. 1:19. Thus, one reason why Christ should "come to have first place in everything" (1:18b) is that he is God and is the inauguration of the eschatological temple, in which God's fullness and wisdom have begun to dwell (Wright [1991: 117–18] intimates briefly a similar connection between 1:15 and 1:19).

1:26–27; 2:2; 4:3

In 1:24–25 Paul has understood his imitation of Christ's suffering as a "servant" on behalf of the church to be a "fulfillment" of the prophetic "word of God" (for discussion of this point, for which there is insufficient space here, see Beale, forthcoming, *ad loc.*). In 1:26–27 Paul calls this prophetic fulfillment "the mystery [*mystērion*] which has been hidden from the ages and from the generations, but now has been manifested to his saints, to whom God willed to make known what is the richness of the glory of this mystery [*mystērion*] among the nations, which is Christ in you, the hope of glory."

This thought is continued in 2:2, where Paul expresses his desire that the new Colossian believers attain to "all the wealth which comes from the full assurance of understanding, resulting in a knowledge of God's mystery [*mystērion*], which is Christ." Presumably it is this same "mystery of Christ" in 4:3 that Paul wants to "speak forth."

The word "mystery" (LXX: *mystērion*; MT: *rāz*) with a prophetic and eschatological sense occurs in the OT only in Dan. 2 (2:18–19, 27–30, 47 ["mystery" also occurs in Dan. 4:6 with reference to the hidden interpretation of the king's prophetic dream, which Daniel makes known to him, though this dream does not concern explicit eschatological issues]). There, the revelation of the "mystery" refers to the hidden interpretation of the king's dream, and the primary focus of the meaning of the dream was that in the end times God would destroy the kingdom of evil and establish his own eternal kingdom (2:44–45).

The use of "mystery" elsewhere in Jewish apocalyptic and Judaism is associated with eschatological issues in general and with the end-time coming of a messianic figure in particular, sometimes in association with Dan. 2 (e.g., *4 Ezra* 12:37–38; *1 En.* 46; 52; 71; Qumran).

"Mystery" (*mystērion*) occurs twenty-eight times in the NT. A feature noticeable in many of the occurrences is that the word is directly linked with OT quotations or allusions (sometimes from the book of Daniel itself). In almost all of these cases, at least, "mystery" appears in order to indicate two things: (1) OT prophecy is beginning fulfillment, and (2) this fulfillment is unexpected from the former OT vantage point. With respect to this last point, it is apparent that various NT authors understand OT texts in the light of the Christ event and under the guidance of the Spirit, which result in new interpretive developments, though still consistent with the OT idea. Thus, although Daniel may not always be in mind in these uses, the notion of an eschatological prophecy needing further inspired interpretation is. Such a notion appears not always to be directly allusive to Dan. 2, but this idea of "mystery" probably had its ultimate origin there. Perhaps, the NT exhibits at times a stock-in-trade use of "mystery" that has been dislodged from, and no longer directly related to, Daniel, while still retaining the idea of unexpected end-time fulfillment of the OT, which needs further interpretation to understand.

I do not have sufficient space here to elaborate on the uses in Judaism or the majority of uses elsewhere in the NT or to defend the thesis just laid out, though I have done that elsewhere, especially with respect to Qumran and Matt. 13:11; Rom. 11:25–26; 16:25–26; 1 Cor. 4:1; 13:2; 14:2; Eph. 1:9; 3:3, 9; 5:32; Col. 1:26–27; 2:2; 4:3; 2 Thess. 2:7; Rev. 1:19–20; 10:6–7; 17:5, 7 (see Beale 1998: 215–72).

How do these uses of "mystery" in Daniel, Judaism, and especially elsewhere in the NT relate to those in Col. 1? The word "mystery" appears in 1:26, 27; 2:2; 4:3. The wording of the "mystery" phraseology in 1:26–27 appears to be based on the verses in Dan. 2 (for some of these text comparisons, see Hübner 1997b: 530):

Dan. 2 (Theodotion)	Col. 1:26–27
"the <u>mystery</u> [*mystērion*] was revealed . . . [the one] giving <u>wisdom</u> [*sophian*] to the wise and knowledge to ones knowing <u>understanding</u> [*synesin*]" (2:19–21); "he makes known . . . the <u>hidden things</u> [*apokrypha*]" (2:22); "the one revealing <u>mysteries</u> and <u>he made known</u> [*mystēria . . . egnōrisen*]" (2:28) (so virtually identically 2:29 and similarly 2:30, while the following manuscripts of the Theodotionic tradition read, "<u>he made known this mystery</u> [*egnōrisen to touto mystērion*]": 230; same phrase minus *touto*: 106 584 of A, and the Armenian; the Old Greek differs with Theodotion by omitting *apokrypha* in 2:22 and *gnōrizō* in 2:28–30 and replacing them with other words)	"the hidden mystery [*to mysterion to apokekrymmenon*] . . . manifested to his saints to whom God willed <u>to make known</u> [*gnōrisai*] what is the richness of the glory of this mystery [*mystēriou*]" In addition to these parallels, note the use of "<u>wisdom</u>" (*sophia*) and "<u>understanding</u>" (*synesis*) in direct relation to "<u>mystery</u>" (*mysterion*) in Col. 2:2–3; Eph. 3:3–10.

The underlined lexical combinations are found only in Dan. 2 (see Beale 1996: 139–40 for the likelihood of a pre–first century AD date for proto-Theodotionic readings of Daniel, some of which are attested clearly elsewhere in the NT), Col. 1–2; Eph. 3:3–10. And, as in Eph. 3, so also here the wording expresses eschatological realities likewise in line with the end-time focus of the Dan. 2 "mystery" (cf., e.g., Dan. 2:28–29, 44–45; see Aletti [1993: 156–57], who sees Dan. 2 broadly as the background for "mystery" in Col. 1:26–27; cf. Wolter [1993: 104], who understands "mystery" here generally against the background of Jewish apocalyptic and Qumran). Daniel concerns the establishment of the eschatological kingdom, and Ephesians and Colossians focus on the end-time messianic king (*christos*) and the "mystery" revolving around him. The explicit identification of the "mystery" in Col. 1:27 as "Christ in you [the Gentiles]," and the similar identification in Col. 2:2, points to the same kind of mystery as in Eph. 3: Jews and Gentiles are fused together on a footing of complete equality by means of corporate identification in Jesus the Messiah, the true Israel—they are in Christ, and Christ is in them (presumably through the Spirit). This is a "mysterious" fulfillment of Daniel's prophecy because it was not clear in the OT that Israel's theocratic kingdom would be so thoroughly transformed that it would find its continuation only in the sphere of the end-time Israelite messianic king himself (for fuller discussion of this conclusion and of the use of Daniel's "mystery" in Eph. 3, see Beale 1998: 242–47; Caragounis 1977: 123–26).

In this regard, Col. 2:16–23 is parallel with Eph. 2:14–18, the latter underscoring that Christ's advent abolished the former ethnic markers of God's people and replaced them with Christ, which is key to understanding the mystery of Eph. 3. The same thing is emphasized by Col. 2:16–23, where the Mosaic laws pertaining to "food or drink or Jewish festivals or new moons or Sabbath days" are no longer binding because now they must be seen as only "shadows" pointing toward Christ, who is the eschatological "substance" of these things (for further elaboration, see commentary on Col. 2:8–23 below). Believers have "died with Messiah [Christ]" to these things that were so important to Israel's old world but no longer are crucial for membership in God's true end-time people (2:20–22). Salvation of the Gentiles in the latter days was a clear prophetic expectation (e.g., Isa. 2:2–4; Zech. 2:11; 8:22–23), but it would have been assumed that they would come to the land of Israel and convert to the faith of Israel, which would include taking on the nationalistic signs (circumcision, etc.) of becoming Israelites. Revealed in Eph. 3 and Col. 1–2 is that it was formerly a mystery that Gentiles could become a part of latter-day Israel not by submitting to the identification marks of the old theocracy, but only by submitting to and having the Messiah as their sole identification. Thus, the Colossians' "mystery" indicates inaugurated fulfillment not only of Dan. 2, but also of the general prophetic expectation about how Gentiles would become part of the saved people of God in the end time.

Colossians 2

2:3

Paul labors to "present every man complete in Messiah" by teaching "with all wisdom" (1:28–2:1). He has said in 1:26–27 and 2:2 that the "mystery" is Christ. As we saw, the allusion to Dan. 2, first seen in 1:26–27 in relation to the "mystery," probably resurfaces in 2:2–3:

Dan. 2 (Theodotion)	Col. 2:2–3
"the mystery [mystērion] was revealed . . . [the one] giving wisdom [sophian] to the wise and knowledge to ones knowing understanding [synesin]" (2:19–21); "he makes known the hidden things [apokrypha]" (2:22)	"unto all the richness of the full assurance of understanding [syneseōs], unto a knowledge of the mystery [mystēriou] of God, which is Christ, in whom are hidden [apokryphoi] all the treasures of wisdom [sophias] and knowledge"

It is best, however, to see the Dan. 2 allusion as now merged with Prov. 2:3–6 LXX and leading Paul to focus on the latter text in Col. 2:3 (for some of these text comparisons, see Hübner 1997b: 532, 534):

Prov. 2:3–6 LXX	Col. 2:2–3
"For if you should call upon wisdom [sophian], utter your voice for understanding [synesei], and if . . . you should search for her as treasures [thēsaurous] [in place of 'treasures,' Symmachus and Theodotion read, 'hidden things' {apokrypha}], then you will understand [synēseis] . . . and find the knowledge [epignōsin] of God. For the Lord gives wisdom [sophian], and from his presence are knowledge [gnōsis] and understanding [synesis]."	"unto all the richness of the full assurance of understanding [syneseōs], unto a knowledge [epignōsin] of the mystery, which is Christ, in whom are hidden [apokryphoi] all the treasures [thēsauroi] of wisdom [sophias] and knowledge [gnōseōs]"

Although "wisdom" (sophia) and "understanding" (synesis) (and rarely even the additional word "knowledge" [gnōsis]) occur together throughout the LXX (on which, see commentary on Col. 1:9 above), all of the unique word combinations in the chart are found only in Prov. 2 and Col. 2. Furthermore, the validity of the Proverbs reference is to be seen in the prior emphasis on Christ as epitomizing true "wisdom" in Col. 1:15–17 (recall that Prov. 8:22–31 was seen as part of the possible background in Col. 1:15–17; cf. Wolter [1993: 111–12], who sees Paul's "treasures of wisdom" to be reflective of a common metaphor used for "wisdom" in early Judaism, though he includes Prov. 2:3–4 among the list of references that he adduces; some commentators see a parallel to Isa. 45:3—"I will give you dark treasures [thēsaurous], hidden [apokryphous] invisible things I will open to you"—but the Proverbs passage is much closer in wording). That identification resurfaces here. It may even be that Paul's preceding description of the "mystery" in 1:26 anticipates the clearer reference to the "mystery" as "wisdom" here: compare the loose link between "mystery" in 1:26–27 and "wisdom" in 1:28; and compare 1:26, "the mystery hidden from the ages [*apo tōn aiōnōn*]," with Sir. 24:9, 29, God "created me [wisdom] before the age [*pro tou aiōnos*]," and wisdom's "counsels [are] profounder than the great deep."

Believers are able to have genuine "knowledge of the mystery of God, which is Christ" because it has been revealed to them (1:26–27; 2:2). Since Christ is the true fount of "wisdom and knowledge" (2:3), the saints also share in such understanding by virtue of their identification with him (likewise, see 2:3–8). Whereas the Torah was the epitome of "wisdom" in the OT epoch, the Messiah is now the grandest expression of divine "wisdom." In this light, Torah was the typological precursor of the fullest expression of "wisdom," which was to come in the person of the Messiah.

The Nature of the False Teaching in Colossae in Relation to Revelation in the Old and New Testaments (2:8–23)

The False Teaching as Deceptive Philosophy

Paul has told the readers that they are to focus on Christ as the one "in whom are hidden all the treasures of wisdom and knowledge," so that they will not be "deluded by persuasive argument" otherwise (2:3–4). They are to continue to trust Christ, as they had done in the beginning, and become increasingly established in their faith in order that "no one takes you captive through philosophy and empty deception, according to the tradition of men, according to the elements of the world and not according to Christ" (2:6–8). The word "philosophy" (*philosophia*) and the phrases "empty deception," "the tradition of men," and "the elements of the world" must be understood in the light of the following context in chapter 2. In particular, in view is a wrong understanding of the meaning and application of OT law for the new age. This appears to be an erroneous Jewish doctrine that focused on the law instead of Christ as the epitome of divine revelation (see Wright 1986: 23–30). Although there may have been some influence from pagan religion, this is doubtful (but see Arnold [1995: 243], who concludes that the false "philosophy" represents a "combination of Phrygian folk belief, local folk Judaism, and Christianity").

The False Teaching as Idolatry

In 2:22 Paul says that the OT "shadows," particularly the food laws ("do not handle, do not taste, do not touch"), are called "the commandments and teachings of men" (*ta entalmata kai didaskalias tōn anthrōpōn*). This is an allusion to Isa. 29:13 LXX: "This people draws near with their lips [and] they honor me, but they remove their heart far from me, and they worship me vainly by teaching the commandments and teachings of men" (*entalmata anthrōpōn kai didaskalias*) (seeing an allusion to Isa. 29:13 are Lohmeyer 1964: 128; Moule 1957: 108; Lohse 1975: 124; Masson 1950: 137; Caird [1976: 201], who calls it a "quotation"; Wright [1986: 101, 126], who also sees the allusion even in 2:8; see also Dunn 1996: 193–94, including his view of an allusion to Mark 7:7/Matt. 15:9; R. P. Martin 1974: 97; O'Brien 1982: 151; Hübner 1997a: 91; Gnilka 1980: 158; Barth and Blanke 1994: 357; Pokorný 1991: 154; Lindemann 1983: 51; Schweizer 1982: 167; E. F. Scott 1948: 58; Abbott 1905: 275; Lightfoot 1961: 204; Simpson and Bruce 1957: 255; H. M. Carson 1966: 78).

The Colossians' context likely links such "commandments and teachings" to "empty deception" based on "the tradition of men" instead of "on Christ" (2:8). Paul's expansion of the earlier "tradition of men" by Isaiah's "commandments and teachings of men" associates the false teaching with idolatry, since that is the contextual sense in Isaiah.

The Hellenistic Jewish false "philosophy" (2:8) focuses on the keeping of regulations about "food or drink . . . a festival or a new moon or Sabbath days" (2:16), which concern "decrees such as 'do not handle, do not taste, do not touch'" (2:20b–21). That this language is clearly Jewish and not pagan is apparent also from the *Let. Aris.* 142: God "hedged us [Jews] round on all sides by rules of purity, affecting alike what we eat, or drink, or touch, or hear, or see." Likewise, the combination of "feasts" (*heortē*), "sabbaths" (*sabbaton*), and "new moons" (*neomēnia*) occurs repeatedly in the LXX to refer to the festivals that were a part of Israel's law, which every Israelite was to obey (see 1 Chron. 23:31; 2 Chron. 2:4; 31:3;

Neh. 10:33; Isa. 1:13–14; Ezek. 45:17; Hos. 2:11; 1 Esd. 5:51–53; Jdt. 8:6; 1 Macc. 10:34).

In the inaugurated age of fulfillment it is idolatry to substitute the "shadows" for Christ, who is their eschatological substance. Furthermore, among the four times that the tripartite formula "feasts, new moons, and Sabbath days" occurs in the OT, two refer to them as having become idolatrous (see Isa. 1:13–14 and the direct association with *bdelygma* ["abomination"], a common reference to idolatry in Isaiah and the OT; cf. Hos. 2:11 in the context of 2:6–13). Thus there is already a precedent for the transforming of OT festivals into idolatrous activities. In Gal. 4:8–10 virtually the identical phrase ("you observe days and months and seasons and years"), together with the word "elements" (cf. Col. 2:20), is directly linked to objects of idolatry. That Col. 2:16–23 describes idolatrous traditions may also be suggested by 3:3–7, where at least part of the saints' former unbelieving life is summarized as "idolatry" (in this respect, note the verbal and conceptual similarity of "you have died" and "put to death the members [of your body] upon the earth" in 3:3, 5 to "you have died . . . from the elements of the world" in 2:20, the latter closely linked to the Isa. 29:13 allusion in 2:22 and to the "worship of angels" in 2:18).

Isaiah 29:13 is part of a pericope that begins with an allusion to Isa. 6:9–10 (29:9–10: "blind yourselves and be blind . . . the LORD . . . has shut your eyes"), which is a literary taunt against Israel, mocking them because they were becoming like the idols that they worshiped (just as the idols had eyes and ears but could not see or hear, so the Israelites had eyes and ears but could not spiritually see or hear [on which, see Beale 1991; see also Ps. 135:15–18]). Isaiah 29:9–13 views Isa. 6 to be commencing fulfillment. Israel's "removing their heart far from" God and "worship" of God "by teaching the commandments and teachings of men" (29:13) was, thus, part of their idolatry. When Israel is described as "far" from God elsewhere in the OT, they are "far" in the sense that they are "worshiping" idols and not God (Jer. 2:5; Ezek. 44:10); when they are said to worship in "vain," sometimes it is when they are worshiping idols (Isa. 41:29). Isaiah 30:1–5 explains that part of Israel's sin was to trust in Egypt's help against another nation that was about to invade Israel. In particular, Isa. 30:1 MT refers to Israel "pouring

out a drink offering," but not to God (rather, implicitly, to an idol to seal a political pact); Isa. 30:3 also says that Israel sought "refuge in the safety of Pharaoh." This involved some degree of compromise with idol worship, since Pharaoh claimed to be God, the incarnation of the sun god; the divine kingship of Pharaoh was a cornerstone of Egyptian religious beliefs. Also, Isa. 30:22 explicitly refers to Israel's "graven images" and "molten images," which Israel worshiped apparently in some connection to its alliance with Egypt.

Therefore, the words that Paul is quoting from Isaiah concern the sin of idol worship. In Paul's time this sin manifested itself by Israel worshiping not stone or wooden idols, but rather the idol of human tradition (the same reference in Mark 7:7/Matt. 15:9 carries with it in context the same idolatrous notion). An idol, in essence, is anything that is worshiped in place of the true God. For example, in Eph. 5 and Col. 3 Paul says that idol worship can be expressed in other ways than merely bowing down to a literal statue; he says in the latter text that "immorality, uncleanness, passion, evil desire and greed . . . is idolatry" (Col. 3:5).

The reference to "circumcision made without hands" (Col. 2:11) implies a contrast with "circumcision made with hands," which Paul refers to in Eph. 2:11 ("circumcision in the flesh made by hands"). The word "handmade" (*cheiropoiētos*) always refers to idols in the Greek OT and is in the NT, without exception, a negative reference with overtones of idolatry (on which, see Beale 2004: 224–25). Thus, the implied reference to "circumcision made with hands" in Col. 2 further enforces the notion that to continue to trust in the OT "shadows" is an idolatrous trust.

In this respect, quite comparably with Col. 2, Paul says in Phil. 3:2, "Beware of the dogs, beware of the evil workers, beware of the false circumcision," and then in 3:18–19 he calls them "enemies of the cross of Christ, whose end is destruction, whose god is their belly and whose glory is in their shame, who set their minds on earthly things." Paul's statement that the unbelieving Jews had their "belly" as their "god" is most probably a reference to their preoccupation with human traditions concerning all kinds of cleansings associated with eating. Commitment to such traditions, versus trust in Christ, was idolatry.

Paul is saying in Col. 2:22 that to trust in the shadowy dietary laws of the OT more than in Christ (or on the same level as Christ) is to worship an idol. Colossians 2:18–19 also supports an idolatry notion, since it says that trusting in the "old shadows" also involves substituting "the worship of the angels" for worship of Christ (which is "not holding fast to the head" [for succinct argument that the genitival phrase "worship of the angels" refers not to "worshiping with the angels" but to "worshiping angels" and to angelic idolatry, see Hay 2000: 105–9). The reference to Isa. 29:13 in Titus 1:14 is used similarly, since "commandments of men" is parallel to "Jewish myths," both of which result in "turning away from the truth." Elsewhere Paul also understands that Jews who trust only in the law and not in Christ are idolaters (Rom. 2:22; cf. Gal. 4:8–10, where "elements" are equated with false "gods"; note "the elements of the world" used similarly in Col. 2:20).

Isaiah 29:13 probably is used analogically: just as Israel was idolatrous in its past, so again professing Jewish believers (i.e., Jewish Christians) are propagating trust in idolatrous objects (if Col. 2:22 is to be closely identified with the use of Isa. 29:13 in Mark 7:7/Matt. 15:9, then it would have a typological notion, since that is its likely use in the gospel passages).

PAUL'S RATIONALE FOR THE NULLIFICATION OF THE FALSE TEACHING IN 2:17

The context of 2:9–23 must be analyzed in order to understand the rationale in 2:17, which, together with 2:9–15, serves as the basis for refuting the false teaching.

In general, the reason that the external rites (dietary laws, circumcision, etc.) of the law are no longer necessary is that their redemptive-historical purpose was to function as a "shadow of things about to come, that is, the [substantial] body of Christ" (2:17). In one way or another, Paul understood that the various external expressions of the OT law pointed to the coming Messiah, who now has come. Therefore, the law's preparatory adumbrating function has come to an end, since the messianic "substance" to which it pointed has arrived. The idea here is very similar to that in Matt. 5:17: Jesus "fulfilled" the "law" and "the prophets" by fulfilling in his actions and words the OT's direct verbal prophecies, foreshadowing

events (e.g., the Passover lamb) and institutions (e.g., sacrifices and temple), the ultimate meaning of the law, and the true and enduring authority of the OT (for the full argument behind this conclusion, see D. A. Carson 1995: 1:140–45).

Likewise, Heb. 8:5 and 10:1 speak, respectively, of the tabernacle and the sacrifices as a "shadow" pointing forward to the true end-time temple and of Christ's once-for-all sacrifice. Colossians 2:17 and the two Hebrews texts are classic expressions of the NT's typological view of the OT. Especially emphasized in this context are dietary laws (2:16, 21–22), which were designed to make a person clean for participation in worship at the tabernacle or temple (for this view of the original design of the dietary laws, see Kohler 1903: 596; cf., similarly, Rabinowitz 1972). Accordingly, Paul apparently sees that these specific laws foreshadowed the time when believers would be made clean by Christ's redemptive work in order that they could qualify for worship in the true temple, founded upon Christ and built of Christians (see commentary on Col. 1:19 above).

The first clear expression of this "shadow to substance" notion in 2:8–23 is in 2:11–13, which anticipates 2:17. In 2:11–13 Paul appears to view the external rite of circumcision as a pointer to the greater redemptive reality of Christ and his followers being "circumcised" or "cut off" from the old sinful world and set apart to a new one. Accordingly, Paul speaks in 2:11 of believers' redemption consisting of being "circumcised with a circumcision made without hands," which has occurred by means of the "circumcision of Christ" (i.e., his death [2:11]). "Uncircumcision [*akrobystia*] of your flesh [*sarx*]" (2:13a) represented sinful unbelief, from which one needed to be "circumcised." This is likely an analogical allusion to Gen. 17:10–27, where "the flesh [*sarx*] of your [or, 'his'] uncircumcision [*akrobystia*]" appears four times (see also Gen. 34:24 LXX; Lev. 12:3; Jdt. 14:10). There the point of the narrative is that those who are in covenantal relationship with God should express that relationship through being "circumcised in the flesh of his [lit., 'your'] uncircumcison" (e.g., Gen. 17:11). This was a symbol expressing that a true Israelite was one whose heart had been cut apart from unbelief and sin and was regenerated (cf. Deut. 10:16; Jer. 4:4). Similarly, Paul compares this physical circumcision to the spiritual reality of the new covenantal relationship with Christ. When believers are identified by faith with Christ's death, which "cut him off" from the old world and led to his resurrection, they are likewise "cut off" from the old world and subsequently raised (the point of 2:12–13). Paul's reference to the "removal of the body of the flesh" is likely also part of the allusion to Gen. 17, where also "flesh" is part of the description of the symbolic sinful condition directly preceding circumcision.

But Paul seems to be making more than an analogy here. His likely acquaintance with another OT background outside of Genesis suggests that he viewed circumcision in the flesh to be pointing to a coming spiritual "circumcision" to be performed by the Messiah on behalf of eschatological Israel. Paul seems to be developing the forward-looking, end-time meaning of circumcision that had been expressed already in Deuteronomy. The majority of Israel are said to be in need of "circumcising" their spiritual "heart," though they are physically circumcised (Deut. 10:16; cf. Jer. 4:4; 9:25–26). However, at the time of the "latter-day" restoration of Israel, Deuteronomy prophesies that God "will circumcise your heart and the heart of your seed to love the Lord . . . in order that you may live" (Deut. 30:6; for the explicit "latter-day" time of this promise, see Deut. 4:27–31; 31:29; cf., possibly, 32:29; Lev. 26:41; Wolter [1993: 129] sees these texts from Leviticus, Deuteronomy, and Jeremiah, together with what he considers parallel Jewish texts, forming the background for Colossians here [esp. *Jub.* 1:23; 1QpHab XI, 13]).

Thus, it is apparent from Deuteronomy itself that physical circumcision was not to be merely an outer symbol of an inner spiritual reality for Israelite saints (which it was for the faithful remnant, as Rom. 2:25–29 indicates). In addition, circumcision was a pointer to the eschatological time, when spiritual circumcision would occur on a grander scale and result in the life of the age to come. So, in line with this, in 2:11–13 Paul views the circumcision of Christ and of the believer to lead to resurrection life. After Christ's death and resurrection the practice of the physical rite of circumcision is no longer required, since the end-time reality to which it pointed had come, and its proleptic purpose had been accomplished. The presupposition that seems to underlie Paul's reference is that in Christ's death and resurrection the

prophecy of Israel's end-time spiritual circumcision has begun and even included Gentiles in its fulfillment (Beetham 2005: 218). Or, even if Paul did not wish consciously to allude to the Deuteronomy text, does not the wording of 2:11 still reflect an unconscious link with the OT passage, so that the association has become a presupposition for what he says?

Why can Paul conclude that the defeat of demonic forces (2:15) results in the fact that no one can "judge [the Colossian saints] with respect to food and drink or with respect to a festival or a new moon festival or Sabbath observances" (2:16), all of which refer to the rites of the OT Law? Paul does not clearly say. The answer must be supplied by placing 2:17–23 within the wider scope of Paul's other letters, especially Ephesians, and entering into an extensive Pauline biblical-theological consideration, which limits of space do not permit here (although, for elaboration of this, see Beale 1997: 34–38; forthcoming, *ad loc.*).

The following table summarizes how Paul understands Christ's role in relation to various OT institutions that have been discussed so far (for the most part adapted from Beetham 2005: 313–14):

Old Testament Institution and Paul's Presentation of Christ

OT Institution	OT and Jewish Perspective	Paul in Colossians
Torah	Torah is Wisdom	Christ is Wisdom (2:3; cf. 1:15–20)
Temple	Jerusalem temple is the locus of the divine presence	Christ is the new and greater locus of the divine presence (1:19)
Circumcision	Physical circumcision is necessary for incorporation into the people of God	Christ's death "cut him off" from the old world and believers who identify with him (2:11–13)
Festivals, new moons, Sabbath days	Sacred days are to be kept	Reality found in Christ of the new age (2:16–17)
Torah-prescribed dietary regulations	Laws of clean and unclean food are to be maintained	Reality found in Christ of the new age (2:16–17)

Colossians 3

3:1

This verse begins with "therefore" (*oun*), indicating that the basis for the following is in 2:20

(which itself resumes the assertions about Christ's death and resurrection from 2:11–13): believers are to "seek the things above, where Christ is seated at the right hand of God," on the basis that they "have died with Christ" (2:20) and "have been raised with Christ" (3:1a).

The reference to "Christ . . . seated at the right hand of God" is an allusion to Ps. 110:1. This allusion occurs often elsewhere in the NT, where it refers to the exalted position of Christ in heaven, as a result of the resurrection (on which, see explicit citations in Matt. 22:44 pars.; Acts 2:34–35; Heb. 1:13; cf. allusions in Matt. 26:64 pars.; Rom. 8:34; 1 Cor. 15:25; Eph. 1:20; Heb. 1:3; 8:1; 10:12–13; 12:2; 1 Pet. 3:22; see Hay 1973). Psalm 110:1 says, "The Lord says to my Lord: 'Sit at my right hand, until I make your enemies a footstool for your feet.'" The first phrase, "The Lord says to my Lord," appears to indicate that the king being addressed is a divine king, which is pointed to further by his ascription as "a priest forever" (110:4 [also in direct relation to "right hand" in 110:5]). At the very least, David refers to a coming king who is greater than he, since he calls this king "my Lord" (Adonai, not Yahweh or Elohim). This points strongly to the original messianic nature of the psalm, and Jesus interprets it this way (Mark 12:35–37, which also assumes that the psalm is written/spoken by David, not just about David).

Early Judaism applied Ps. 110:1 to pious individuals, human leaders, the future Davidic messiah, or to supernatural beings (the heavenly Melchizedek, Enoch, or the Son of Man). Later Judaism applied the text to pious individuals or the Messiah (for use in Judaism, see Hay 1973: 21–33). The point of Ps. 110:1 is not merely the achievement of a sovereign position of rule ("sit at my right hand"); the focus is on the beginning achievement of that rule ("until I make your enemies a footstool for your feet"). Psalm 110:2 expands further on this inaugurated rule: "The Lord will stretch forth your strong scepter from Zion, saying, 'Rule in the midst of your enemies.'" This fits perfectly into the broad NT notion that Christ commenced his messianic rule during his ministry, death, resurrection, and exaltation.

The notion of an inaugurated rule is also appropriate within the immediate context. In 2:10 Paul said that Christ "is the head over all rule and authority"; similarly, in 2:15 he said that "when he [Christ] had disarmed the rulers and authorities, he made a public display of them, having triumphed over them through it [the cross]." The Ps. 110:1 allusion underscores Christ's exalted position that he has been given as a result of winning the decisive victory over evil angelic powers, which is also how the psalm verse is applied in 1 Cor. 15:25; Eph. 1:20; 1 Pet. 3:22; and possibly Rev. 3:21 (cf. *1 Clem.* 36:5; Pol. *Phil.* 2:1 [see O'Brien 1982: 162]). Although the crucial battle has been won at Christ's cross and resurrection, the enemy is not yet completely defeated. In 1:20 Paul says that God had designed "to reconcile all things ['whether things on earth or things in heaven'] to himself, as a result of having made peace through the blood of the cross." This complete reconciliation has not yet been accomplished by the time Paul writes Colossians, which is clear from observing that he has to warn the readers against the detrimental influence of false teachers (2:8, 18–23), who are part of the "authority of darkness" (1:13) and through whom the unseen demonic "rulers and authorities" still work, even though they have been decisively defeated.

Possibly it is most accurate to say that in 3:1 Paul presupposes that Christ has fulfilled the prophesied king of Ps. 110:1, and the enemies in the psalm are assumed to be the evil spiritual forces of 2:15, which presumably were the inspiration behind the false "philosophy" in 2:16, 18–23 (so Beetham 2005: 285). And, at the least, in the event that Paul did not have Ps. 110:1 foremost in mind, the phrase of 3:1 probably points to a connection with the psalm that Paul had made formally at an earlier time and that forms the stimulus for the present form of the words.

The inextricable link between the invisible "rulers and authorities" and false teaching occurs in Ephesians, where these same forces are referred to as "world [and spiritual] forces of this darkness" and work under the aegis of the devil and through false teachers (cf. Eph. 6:11–12, where "the schemes of the devil" is likely a development of 4:14: "We are no longer to be children, tossed here and there by waves, and carried about by every wind of doctrine, by the trickery of men, by craftiness in deceitful scheming").

The Colossians are to focus on Christ's exalted position ("keep seeking the things above") and to want to be identified with their exalted Lord in order continually to be reminded that worship of other heavenly powers (2:18) is idolatrous and that allegiance to them can only lead away from Christ the "head" (2:19). The "seeking" is a desire to have one's thinking and lifestyle oriented around Christ's kingship over all things (similarly, see the use of *zēteō* in Matt. 6:33; John 5:44; 7:18; Rom. 2:7; cf. Phil. 2:21; 3:19–20; 1 Thess. 2:4–6).

3:9–10

On the basis (*oun* [3:5]) of the believers' identification with Christ's death and resurrection (3:1–4), Paul exhorts the believers to live like resurrected new creatures and not like those who belong to the old world (3:5–4:6).

The Genesis 1 Background of "the Image of God." The first clear OT allusion in this segment appears in 3:10 (though it is possible that 3:6 echoes Isa. 13:3, 9, which refer to God's "wrath" that "comes"). Paul describes true Christians as those who "have donned the clothes of the new man ['man' is implied from *anthrōpos* in 3:9] who is being renewed to a true knowledge according to the image of the one who created him [*kat' eikona tou ktisantos auton*]." This is a reference back to Gen. 1:26–27: "Then God said, 'Let us make man in our image. . . . ' And God created man in his own image, in the image of God he created him" (note 1:27b: *ton anthrōpon kat' eikona theou epoiēsen auton*; whereas Paul uses *ktizō* for "create" in 3:10, Gen. 1:26–27 LXX uses *poieō*, though Aquila, Symmachus, and Theodotion use *ktizō* in 1:27; seeing an allusion to the same Genesis passage in 3:10 are Lohse 1975: 142; Gnilka 1980: 188; NA[27]; so also Lightfoot 1961: 215–16; Robertson 1959: 503; Simpson and Bruce 1957: 272; Hugedé 1968: 175–77; Caird [1976: 205], who calls it a "quotation"; Patzia 1984: 61; Lincoln 1990: 644; MacDonald 2000: 138, 146). The allusion is related to the earlier allusion to Gen. 1:26–27 in 1:15 (Christ as "the image of the invisible God"), as well as to the repetition of the allusion to Gen. 1:28 in 1:6, 10 (e.g., 1:6: "in all the world it is bearing fruit and increasing"). Thus, Gen. 1:26–28 is in Paul's mind at points throughout this epistle.

Genesis 1:26–28 is a reference to Adam and Eve as the crown of creation, created in God's image to be God's vice-regents over the world and to multiply their progeny as bearers of the divine image. The likelihood is that the Genesis passage focuses on humanity being functional reflectors of God's image, though the ontological aspect of the image may secondarily be in mind (see commentary on Col. 1:6, 10 above).

Paul's point in 3:10 is that believers, who have begun to be identified with Christ's resurrection (i.e., they "have donned the clothes of the new man," the resurrected Christ), are those who have begun to be identified with the new creation in Christ. The creation in God's image in order to rule and subdue and to be fruitful and multiply (Gen. 1:26–28) is now applicable not only to Christ, but also to his people, since he and they have entered into the sphere of the new creation and have begun to do what Adam failed to do. Here the emphasis is on new creation in the divine image, but ruling is not far away (cf. 3:1), nor is the notion of multiplying (1:6, 10). It may be important to recall that part of "ruling and subduing" in Gen. 1:26–28 was to "be fruitful and multiply and fill" the earth not only with literal, but also, after the fall, with spiritual children who would join Adam in reflecting God's image and join him in his kingly dominion over the earth. This idea fits quite well with the believers' identification with Christ's resurrection and sovereign kingship in 3:1, which is part of the basis for the paraenetic section beginning in 3:5 and continuing with 3:10.

Thus, the believers have become identified with Christ (the new man) and are no longer identified with the "old man" (3:9–10 [consequently, the participles often translated "putting off" and "putting on" are not imperatives, which would be a very rare use of the participle, but rather are to be understood as adverbial of cause, providing the indicative basis for the imperative "do not lie" in 3:9]). On this basis, Paul exhorts them to stop being identified with the traits of the former life in the "old Adam" (cf. 3:5–9a) and be characterized by those of the new life in the last Adam. Accordingly, the "image" in which they are being renewed is Christ's image, especially in the light of the link back to 1:15, and "the one having created" them in this image is God (following Hugedé 1968: 177; Hay 2000: 126; Furter 1987: 173 [although, the "creator" here may well be Christ, especially in light of 1:16]).

Even the reference to being "renewed unto a true knowledge [*epignōsis*]" in 3:10 may echo the Genesis context, where "knowledge" was at the heart of the fall (cf. Gen. 2:17: "from the tree of the knowledge of good and evil you shall not eat") (following Dunn 1996: 221–22). Humanity's "failure to act according to their knowledge [*epignōsis*] of God by not acknowledging him in worship was the central element in Paul's earlier analysis of the human plight" in Rom. 1 (see 1:21) (Dunn 1996: 222 [followed by MacDonald 2000: 138]).

Related to this is the observation that the second allusion to Gen. 1:28 in Col. 1 (cf. 1:10: "bearing fruit and increasing") is directly appended by "in the knowledge [*epignōsis*] of God." This further connects being in God's image with knowing him and his will, since Gen. 1:28 is part of the functional manner in which humanity was to reflect the divine image. Adam and his wife's "knowledge" of God also included remembering God's word addressed to Adam in Gen. 2:16–17, which Adam's wife failed to recall in Gen. 3:2–3.

Being "renewed unto a knowledge of the image" of God will be the remedy for the Colossian believers not being "deluded with persuasive arguments" (2:4) and not being "taken captive through . . . empty deception" (2:8) in the way Adam and Eve had been through the serpent's deceptive speech (the last time "knowledge" was used in the epistle was, not coincidentally, in this context, 2:2–3 [*epignōsis* followed by *gnōsis*]).

The Genesis 3 Background of Paul's "Clothing" Metaphors.

The portrayal of stripping off old clothing and donning new clothing in 3:9–10 may reflect a background of changing clothes in relation to the rite of baptism (so several commentators), though this is uncertain (the custom of changing clothes as a part of the custom of baptism is not attested until after the middle of the second century AD [on which, see Lincoln 1990: 643], though Lev. 16:23–24 could have influenced the later practice). Also, the portrayal of putting on and putting off garments, though widespread in antiquity, is likely not the background here; even the parallels of the initiation into the Isis mysteries and of Gnosticism are post–first century, belong to a different realm of ideas, and have no literal verbal parallels with Paul's language portraying a person as clothing that is put on or taken off (on which, see O'Brien 1982: 189).

More plausibly, in the light of the two allusions to the divine "image" and "knowledge" in 3:10 from Gen. 1–3, the references to clothing in 3:9–10 may be an allusion to Gen. 3. In Gen. 3:7 we are told that Adam and Eve, directly after their sin, tried to cover their sinful nakedness by their own autonomous efforts: "they sewed fig leaves together and made themselves loin coverings." On the other hand, in an apparent expression of their beginning restoration to God after the fall (especially in light of Gen. 3:20), Gen. 3:21 says that "the LORD God made garments of skin for Adam and his wife, and clothed [*endyō*] them." The clear implication is that their first suit of clothes was removed and replaced by divinely handmade clothing, indicating that the handmade clothing was associated with their alienated condition and sinful shame (Gen. 3:7–11) and was an insufficient covering for those who have begun to be reconciled to God (that Adam's and Eve's "loin coverings" were not proper attire to wear in God's holy presence is clear from the fact that "they hid themselves from the presence of the LORD God" and still considered themselves "naked" [Gen. 3:8–10]; this view of the clothing in Gen. 3:8 is also taken by *Sib. Or.* 1:47–49).

Likewise, Paul, in 3:9–10, refers to believers who have "stripped off the clothes [*apekdyomai*] of the old [sinful] man" and "clothed yourselves [*endyō*] with the new man," which indicates their inaugurated new-creation relationship with God (thus, the clothes consist in the new man; the NRSV and the NLT also have apparel metaphors: "you have stripped off . . . and have clothed yourselves" [similarly, NJB, NETB]; see Eph. 4:22–24 for closely parallel wording; similarly, *Barn.* 6:11–12, which also quotes Gen. 1:26, 28). The imagery is not precisely "laying aside" and "putting on," the usual rendering of the English translations, but rather is sartorial language. Believers have laid aside the clothes of the first Adam (the "old man"), in which they could not come into God's presence, and have "clothed themselves" with the last Adam ("the new" man), in whom they have been "renewed" (so also, seeing a contrast between the first Adam and the last Adam, Calvin 1999: 211; Simpson and Bruce 1957: 272–74; H. M. Carson 1966: 84; O'Brien 1982: 190–91). By donning their new clothing, they have begun to return to God and will do so consummately in the future (so also R. P. Martin [1974: 107]; Wright [1986: 138], who also see a contrast between identification with the old Adam and the new Adam).

Hence, one is in the position either of the old, fallen first Adam, who is the corporate "embodiment of unregenerate humanity," or of the new, resurrected last Adam, who is the corporate "embodiment of the new humanity" (O'Brien 1982: 190–91 [the latter side of the identification is made clear by Rom. 6:5–11; 13:14; Gal. 3:27]).

Some early Jewish and Christian writings express the belief that Adam and Eve were clothed in glorious garments before the fall and lost that glory and then tried in the wrong way to cover their inglorious shame with fig leaves. Some also held that the new set of clothes given to Adam and Eve in Gen. 3:21 actually possessed some degree of glory, or designated Adam as the first high priest, or pointed to a greater inheritance of the final glorious clothing of immortality, the first and third notions plausibly lying behind the clothing picture of Col. 3:10. Others also believed that the glorious clothing that the devil possessed as a holy angel before his fall was given to Adam and Eve. (For the Jewish references supporting the statements in this paragraph, see Beale, forthcoming, *ad loc.*)

Paul refers in 2:11 to the believers' old clothing as "the body of the flesh," which was "unclothed" (*apekdysis*), in contrast to their new condition, which he characterizes as "made without hands" (*acheiropoiētos*)—that is, divinely created by causing them to be "raised" and "made alive with Christ" (2:12–13 [for "flesh" being equivalent to the old age characterized as uncircumcision, see commentary on Col. 2:11–13 under the section "Paul's Rationale for the Nullification of the False Teaching in 2:17" above). This is consistent with the use elsewhere of "handmade" (*cheiropoiētos*) to refer to sinful, idolatrous, and corruptible old-world realities in contrast to an "already and not yet" new-creational reality "made without hands" (e.g., human-made temples of the old age [Mark 14:58; Acts 7:48; 17:24; Heb. 9:11, 24] in contrast to the new, eschatological temple, which is equivalent to God's dwelling in the new creation with his resurrected people [Mark 14:58; 2 Cor. 5:1]) (on the further significance of the verbal

contrasts between *cheiropoiētos* and *acheiropoiētos*, see commentary under Col. 2:8–23 above; Beale 2004: 152–53, 309–12, 375–76).

Early Christian tradition also understands the removal of old clothing and putting on new clothing to represent a new, converted condition in a new creation of a latter-day Eden (*Odes Sol.* 11:10–14; *Ascen. Isa.* 9:6–18; likewise *Apoc. El. (C)* 5:6; *4 Ezra* 2:33–48; *Gos. Truth* 20:28–34; cf., from the Nag Hammadi texts, *Trim. Prot.* 48:6–18, as well as especially the Jewish *T. Levi* 18:10–14; so also the following Jewish texts, though without mention of Eden: *Jos. Asen.* 14:12[13]–15[17]; 15:5[4]–6[5]; *Apoc. Ab.* 13:14; also *2 En.* 22:8–10). In *L.A.E.* 20:1–5 *Apocalypse* (a Jewish work, ca. 100–200 AD) is expressed the belief that after Adam had lost "the righteousness with which he had been "clothed" (*endyō*), he made for himself "skirts" (*perizōma*) from a fig tree to "cover" his nakedness and shame, and at his death he was clothed with divinely given garments, indicating his beginning restoration to God (see also 28:1–4 *Apocalypse*; 43:1–4 *Apocalypse*; Armenian *L.A.E.* 48[40]:2–3, 5b–6; see chaps. 47–48 *Vita*).

Most of the aforementioned uses refer not to a new status alone, but one that also entails an inheritance, whether this is the inheritance of eternal life with God and of rule in a new creation (the focus of the texts associated with Gen. 1–3) or more general eschatological blessings. Even in the ancient Near East or in the OT, to receive a robe from a parent or to be disrobed by a parent indicated, respectively, the rights of inheritance or the state of disinheritance (Hugenberger 1994: 198–99).

This Jewish and early Christian background, especially the Adamic-Genesis and eschatological uses, are very similar to Paul's use of Gen. 3 and enhance the presence of an allusion to the Gen. 3 clothing in Col. 3:9–10 and even its inaugurated application. This is apparent from observing that the majority of the most relevant aforementioned texts related to Gen. 1–3 or new creation also speak of a new spiritual or redemptive-historical status inaugurated, but not consummated, for the people of God, especially speaking in terms of resurrection, new creation, or incorruption. Paul himself elsewhere expresses virtually the same sartorial contrast in relation to Adam and Christ with regard to the consummation (most clearly in 1 Cor. 15:51–54). Is it coincidental that the notion of the believer's "inheritance" from God occurs in the context of Colossians (1:12; 3:24), one of which is sandwiched in between an allusion to Gen. 1:28 (in 1:10b) and Gen. 1:26–27 (1:15)? Virtually the same clothing metaphor occurs in Gal. 3:27 and is even more closely linked to gaining an "inheritance" (Gal. 3:29). (I am indebted to research students Ben Gladd and, especially, Keith Williams for their survey and listing of references to clothing in Judaism, which have alerted me to study the various contextual uses of several of these references and their relationship to Col. 3. Just before submitting the completed manuscript of the present chapter, I discovered the relevant monograph by Kim [2004], who has made all the same essential points that I make about the "clothing" background of 3:9–10 on the basis of most of the same biblical, Jewish, and Christian texts.)

Paul appears to be using the Gen. 3 "clothing" language analogically: believers are seen to have discarded the clothes of the old, fallen Adam (their old nature and position in the old Adam) and been clothed with the attire of the last Adam (the new nature and position in the new Adam), with which Adam himself was proleptically clothed to indicate his restored relationship with God.

Colossians 4

4:5

The text of 4:1–6 continues the segment begun at 3:5, which explains the new-creational living of believers based on their identification with Christ's death and resurrection (3:1–4); 4:2–6 is a concluding subsection of 3:5–4:6, which is dominated by Paul's concern for the gospel message to be communicated to unbelievers. Accordingly, he exhorts his hearers to "walk in wisdom with respect to the ones outside by buying up the time [*ton kairon exagorazomenoi*]" (4:5). Several commentators have observed that the wording (*kairos* + *exagorazō*) derives from Dan. 2:8: "you are buying up time."

That Paul probably has Dan. 2 in mind is apparent from the following considerations. (1) The use of *kairos* + *exagorazō* (even in the same order) occurs only in Dan. 2:8 and Col. 4:5 in all of Hellenistic Greek literature. (2) Paul has just referred to the "mystery" (4:3), which, he prays, he will have opportunity to proclaim and to do so clearly (just as Daniel and his friends prayed that God would reveal the mystery, so that Daniel could understand it and declare it [Dan. 2:16–18]). We noted in the earlier analysis of "mystery" (see commentary on Col. 1:26–27; 2:2; 4:3 above) that Dan. 2 was part of the backdrop against which to understand Paul's earlier uses in the epistle. (3) The use of "wisdom" (*sophia*) in connection with "mystery" (*mysterion*) occurs only in Dan. 2 (cf. 2:20–21, 23 with 2:30); 1 Cor. 2:1 (NA[27] prefers *mysterion* to the *v.l. martyrion*), 7; Col. 2:2–3; 4:3–5; Eph. 3:3–10, and we have already noted the connection of Col. 2:2–3 and Eph. 3:3–10 to Dan. 2 (see commentary on Col. 1:26–27; 2:2; 4:3 above; the word combination also occurs in Wis. 6:22, where it likely also alludes to Dan. 2 [cf. Wis. 6:1–21, which concerns making known "wisdom" and "mysteries" to unbelieving kings]; there are only two other places in Hellenistic Greek where the combination of "wisdom" and "mystery" occurs, and they do not appear in a redemptive-historical framework or in the context of biblical tradition). The combination of these two words in 1 Cor. 2 has also been understood to have its background in Dan. 2 (Williams 2000: 166–68, 173–75, 192–200, 202–8).

Although it is probable that Dan. 2 is reflected in Paul's wording in 4:5, the issue of how he could be using the Danielic language is unclear. Possibly, he uses the wording without concern for its OT meaning. In Dan. 2:8 the Babylonian king tells his soothsaying servants to explain the meaning of his dream and to stop trying to "buy up the time" or "bargain for time." The idea was that the king believed they were trying to delay their own inevitable execution, which he believed was disingenuous. On the other hand, Paul is encouraging his Colossian hearers sincerely to "buy up the time." The uses seem different, but they do have some common features. At the very least, both uses refer to the preciousness of time and that one is to make one's best use of it. In addition, possibly the "wisdom" that the Babylonian soothsayers lacked to proclaim the "mystery," while attempting to delay their punishment, was the same "wisdom" that the Colossians now possess in order to make the best use of their time to proclaim the same eschatological "mystery," which has been fulfilled in Christ. The fact that the "mystery" of Daniel's eschatological prophecy (see Dan. 2:28–45) has been inaugurated in Christ's first coming may enhance the exhortation for the saints to make good use of every moment for spreading the gospel, since the consummation of the last days may come unexpectedly at any time.

Bibliography

Abbott, T. K. 1905. *A Critical and Exegetical Commentary on the Epistles to the Ephesians and to the Colossians*. ICC. New York: Scribner.

Aletti, J.-N. 1993. *Saint Paul, Épître aux Colossiens*. EB. Paris: Gabalda.

Anderson, G. A., and M. E. Stone, eds. 1994. *A Synopsis of the Books of Adam and Eve*. SBLEJL 5. Atlanta: Scholars Press.

Arnold, C. E. 1995. *The Colossian Syncretism: The Interface between Christianity and Folk Belief at Colossae*. WUNT 2/77. Tübingen: Mohr Siebeck.

Barclay, J. M. G. 1997. *Colossians and Philemon*. NTG. Sheffield: Sheffield Academic Press.

Barth, M., and H. Blanke. 1994. *Colossians*. AB 34B. New York: Doubleday.

Beale, G. K. 1991. "Isaiah VI 9–13: A Retributive Taunt against Idolatry." *VT* 41: 257–78.

———. 1989. "The Old Testament Background of Reconciliation in 2 Corinthians 5–7 and Its Bearing on the Literary Problem of 2 Cor. 6:14–18." *NTS* 42: 133–52.

———. 1996. "The Old Testament in Revelation." *NTS* 42: 133–52.

———. 1997. "The Eschatological Conception of New Testament Theology." Pages 11–52 in *Eschatology in Bible and Theology*. Edited by K. E. Brower and M. W. Elliott. Downers Grove, IL: InterVarsity.

———. 1998. *John's Use of the Old Testament in Revelation*. JSNTSup 166. Sheffield: Sheffield Academic Press.

———. 2004. *The Temple and the Church's Mission: A Biblical Theology of the Dwelling Place of God*. NSBT 17. Leicester: Apollos.

———. Forthcoming. *Colossians*. BECNT. Grand Rapids: Baker Academic.

Beasley-Murray, G. R. 1973. "The Second Chapter of Colossians." *RevExp* 70: 469–79.

Beetham, C. A. 2005. "The Scriptures of Israel in the Letter of Paul to the Colossians." PhD diss., Wheaton College Graduate School.

Boring, M. E., K. Berger, and C. Colpe. 1995. *Hellenistic Commentary to the New Testament*. Nashville: Abingdon.

Burney, C. F. 1926. "Christ as the ΑΡΧΗ of Creation." *JTS* 27: 160–77.

Caird, G. B. 1976. *Paul's Letters from Prison*. NClB. Oxford: Oxford University Press.

Callow, J. C. 1983. *A Semantic Structure Analysis of Colossians*. Dallas: Summer Institute of Linguistics.

Calvin, J. 1999. *Commentaries on the Epistles of Paul the Apostle to the Philippians, Colossians, and Thessalonians*. Grand Rapids: Baker Academic.

Caragounis, C. C. 1977. *The Ephesian Mysterion: Meaning and Content*. ConBNT 8. Lund: Gleerup.

Carson, D. A. 1995. *Matthew*. 2 vols. EBCNIV 1, 2. Grand Rapids: Zondervan.

Carson, H. M. 1966. *The Epistles of Paul to the Colossians and Philemon*. 2nd ed. TNTC. Grand Rapids: Eerdmans.

Cohen, J. 1989. *"Be Fertile and Increase, Fill the Earth and Master It": The Ancient and Medieval Career of a Biblical Text*. Ithaca, NY: Cornell University Press.

Delitzsch, F. 1970. *Biblical Commentary on the Psalms*. Translated by F. Bolton. 3 vols. Biblical Commentary on the Old Testament. Grand Rapids: Eerdmans.

Dunn, J. D. G. 1975–1985. "Spirit, Holy Spirit NT." *NIDNTT* 3:693–707.

———. 1996. *The Epistles to the Colossians and to Philemon*. NIGTC. Grand Rapids: Eerdmans.

Dupont-Sommer, A. 1962. *The Essene Writings from Qumran*. Translated by G. Vermes. Cleveland: World Publishing Company.

Ellicott, C. J. 1872. *A Critical and Grammatical Commentary on St. Paul's Epistles to the Philippians, Colossians, and to Philemon*. Philadelphia: Smith, English.

Ernst, J. 1974. *Die Briefe an die Philipper, an Philemon, an die Kolosser, an die Epheser*. RNT. Regensburg: Pustet.

Fee, G. D. 1987. *The First Epistle to the Corinthians*. NICNT. Grand Rapids: Eerdmans.

———. 1994. *God's Empowering Presence: The Holy Spirit in the Letters of Paul*. Peabody, MA: Hendrickson.

———. 2006. "Old Testament Intertextuality in Colossians: Reflections on Pauline Christology and Gentile Inclusion in God's Story." Pages 201–21 in *History and Exegesis: New Testament Essays in Honor of Dr. E. Earle Ellis for His 80th Birthday*. Edited by S.-W. (A.) Son. New York: T&T Clark.

Furter, D. 1987. *Les Épîtres de Paul aux Colossiens et à Philémon*. CEB. Vaux-sur-Seine: Edifac.

García Martínez, F., and E. J. C. Tigchelaar. 1997. *The Dead Sea Scrolls Study Edition*. 2 vols. Grand Rapids: Eerdmans.

Gnilka, J. 1980. *Der Kolosserbrief*. HTKNT 10/1. Freiburg: Herder.

Gorday, P., ed. 2000. *Colossians, 1–2 Thessalonians, 1–2 Timothy, Titus, Philemon*. ACCS 9. Downers Grove, IL: InterVarsity.

Harris, M. J. 1991. *Colossians and Philemon*. EGGNT. Grand Rapids: Eerdmans.

Hay, D. M. 1973. *Glory at the Right Hand: Psalm 110 in Early Christianity*. SBLMS 18. Nashville: Abingdon.

———. 2000. *Colossians*. ANTC. Nashville: Abingdon.

Hayward, C. T. R. 1991. "Sacrifice and World Order." Pages 22–34 in *Sacrifice and Redemption: Durham Essays in Theology*. Edited by S. W. Sykes. Cambridge: Cambridge University Press.

———. 1999. "Sirach and Wisdom's Dwelling Place." Pages 31–46 in *Where Shall Wisdom Be Found? Wisdom in the Bible, the Church and the Contemporary World*. Edited by S. C. Barton. Edinburgh: T&T Clark.

Hendriksen, W. 1967. *Ephesians*. London: Banner of Truth Trust.

Hübner, H. 1997a. *An Philemon, an die Kolosser, und die Epheser*. HNT 12. Tübingen: Mohr Siebeck.

———. 1997b. *Corpus Paulinum*. Vol. 2 of *Vetus Testamentum in Novo*. Göttingen: Vandenhoeck & Ruprecht.

Hugedé, N. 1968. *Commentaire de L'Épître aux Colossiens*. Geneva: Labor et Fides.

Hugenberger, G. P. 1994. *Marriage as a Covenant: A Study of Biblical Law and Ethics Governing Marriage, Developed from the Perspective of Malachi.* VTSup 52. Leiden: Brill.

Keesmat, S. C. 1994. "Exodus and the Intertextual Transformation of Tradition in Romans 8.14–30." *JSNT* 54: 29–56.

Kim, J. H. 2004. *The Significance of Clothing Imagery in the Pauline Corpus.* JSNTSup 268. London: T&T Clark.

Kittel, G. 1964. "εἰκών, F. The Metaphorical Use of Image in the NT." *TDNT* 2:395–97.

Kohler, K. 1903. "Dietary Laws." Pages 596–600 in vol. 4 of *The Jewish Encyclopedia: A Descriptive Record of the History, Religion, Literature, and the Customs of the Jewish People from the Earliest Times to the Present Day.* Edited by I. Singer. New York: Funk & Wagnalls.

Kremer, J. 1990–1993. "πνευματικός, πνευματικῶς." *EDNT* 3:122–23.

Layton, B. 1987. *The Gnostic Scriptures: A New Translation with Annotations and Introductions.* London: SCM.

Lenski, R. C. H. 1964. *The Interpretation of St. Paul's Epistles to the Colossians, to the Thessalonians, to Timothy, to Titus and to Philemon.* Minneapolis: Augsburg.

Lightfoot, J. B. 1961. *Saint Paul's Epistles to the Colossians and to Philemon.* Rev. ed. CCL. Grand Rapids: Eerdmans.

Lincoln, A. T. 1990. *Ephesians.* WBC 42. Dallas: Word.

Lindemann, A. 1983. *Der Kolosserbrief.* ZBK 10. Zürich: Theologischer Verlag.

Lohmeyer, E. 1964. *Die Briefe an die Philipper, Kolosser und an Philemon.* KEK 9/1. Göttingen: Vandenhoeck & Ruprecht.

Lohse, E. 1975. *A Commentary on the Epistle to the Colossians and to Philemon.* Hermeneia. Philadelphia: Fortress.

MacDonald, M. 2000. *Colossians and Ephesians.* SP 17. Collegeville, MN: Liturgical Press.

Martin, E. D. 1993. *Colossians, Philemon.* BCBC. Scottdale, PA: Herald Press.

Martin, R. P. 1974. *Colossians and Philemon.* Rev. ed. NCB. London: Oliphants.

Masson, C. 1950. *L'Épître de Saint Paul aux Colossiens.* CNT 10. Neuchâtel: Delachaux & Niestlé.

Melick, R. R. 1991. *Philippians, Colossians, Philemon.* NAC 32. Nashville: Broadman.

Moule, C. F. D. 1957. *The Epistles of Paul to the Colossians and to Philemon.* CGTC. London: Marshall, Morgan & Scott.

Münderlein, G. 1962. "Die Erwählung durch das Pleroma." *NTS* 8: 264–76.

O'Brien, P. T. 1982. *Colossians, Philemon.* WBC 44. Waco: Word.

Pao, D. W. 2000. *Acts and the Isaianic New Exodus.* WUNT 2/130. Tübingen: Mohr Siebeck.

Patzia, A. 1984. *Colossians, Philemon, Ephesians.* GNC. San Francisco: Harper & Row.

Pokorný, P. 1991. *Colossians.* Peabody, MA: Hendrickson.

Rabinowitz, H. 1972. "Dietary Laws." *EncJud* 6:26–46.

Robertson, A. T. 1959. *Paul and the Intellectuals: The Epistle to the Colossians.* Nashville: Broadman.

Ross, A. P. 1988. *Creation and Blessing: A Guide to the Study and Exposition of the Book of Genesis.* Grand Rapids: Baker Academic.

Ryrie, C. C. 1966. "The Mystery in Ephesians 3." *BSac* 123: 24–31.

Saucy, R. L. 1992. "The Church as the Mystery of God." Pages 127–55 in *Dispensationalism, Israel and the Church: The Search for Definition.* Edited by C. A. Blaising and D. L. Bock. Grand Rapids: Zondervan.

Schweizer, E. 1968. "πνευματικῶς." *TDNT* 6:436–37.

———. 1982. *The Letter to the Colossians.* Translated by A. Chester. Minneapolis: Augsburg.

Scott, E. F. 1948. *The Epistles of Paul to the Colossians, to Philemon and to the Ephesians.* MNTC. London: Hodder & Stoughton.

Scott, J. M. 1992. *Adoption as Sons of God: An Exegetical Investigation into the Background of ΥΙΟΘΕΣΙΑ in the Pauline Corpus.* WUNT 2/48. Tübingen: Mohr Siebeck.

Simpson, E. K., and F. F. Bruce. 1957. *Commentary on the Epistles to the Ephesians and the Colossians.* NICNT. Grand Rapids: Eerdmans.

Vaughn, C. 1978. "Colossians." Pages 161–226 in vol. 11 of *The Expositor's Bible Commentary.* Edited by F. E. Gaebelein. Grand Rapids: Zondervan.

Wall, R. W. 1993. *Colossians and Philemon.* IVPNTC 12. Downers Grove, IL: InterVarsity.

Wallace, D. 1996. *Greek Grammar beyond the Basics: An Exegetical Syntax of the New Testament.* Grand Rapids: Zondervan.

Williams, H. H. 2000. *The Wisdom of the Wise: The Presence and Function of Scripture within 1 Cor. 1:18–3:23.* AGJU 49. Leiden: Brill.

Wolter, M. 1993. *Der Brief an die Kolosser; Der Brief an Philemon.* ÖTK 12. Gütersloh: Mohn.

Wright, N. T. 1986. *The Epistles of Paul to the Colossians and to Philemon.* TNTC. Grand Rapids: Eerdmans.

———. 1991. *The Climax of the Covenant: Christ and the Law in Pauline Theology.* Edinburgh: T&T Clark.

Yates, R. 1993. *The Epistle to the Colossians.* Epworth Commentaries. London: Epworth.

1–2 Thessalonians

Jeffrey A. D. Weima

Introduction

A superficial reading of 1–2 Thessalonians might suggest that the OT had little if any impact on Paul's wording and thinking in these letters. After all, neither letter contains even one explicit citation of the OT. Furthermore, these documents were written to a predominantly Gentile church (see 1 Thess. 1:9b) for whom the OT was a foreign and unknown text. But even though 1–2 Thessalonians differ dramatically from Romans, with its plentiful and evident OT quotations, they share with this and the other Pauline letters a significant indebtedness to the Jewish Scriptures. For as the following analysis demonstrates, Paul's vocabulary, metaphors, and theological framework in the Thessalonian correspondence betray the influence of the OT in both small and significant ways.

Letter Opening and Thanksgiving (1 Thess. 1:1–10)

The letter opening (1:1) has not been altered in any noteworthy way vis-à-vis some of Paul's other letters—a likely reflection of the good relationship that exists between the apostle and this church as well as his overall pleasure at their spiritual condition. The thanksgiving (1:2–10) not only confirms Paul's delight in their "work

of faith, labor of love, and steadfastness of hope" (1:3), but also foreshadows the four major themes taken up in the letter body: the defense of Paul's integrity (2:1–3:10), persecution (3:1–5), proper moral conduct (4:1–12; 5:12–22), and Christ's return (4:18–5:11).

1:1

Paul identifies the readers as "the church of the Thessalonians in God the Father and the Lord Jesus Christ." Although the noun *ekklēsia* ("church") in secular Greek refers to an officially summoned assembly of citizens (see Acts 19:32, 39, 41), in the LXX it describes the people of God, whether they are assembled for worship or not (see, e.g., Deut. 23:2–3; 31:30; 1 Sam. 17:47; 1 Chron. 28:8; Neh. 13:1). In light of Paul's Jewish heritage, as well as his references to the "church(es) of God" both later in the letter (2:14) and elsewhere (e.g., 1 Cor. 1:2; 10:32; 11:16; 15:9; 2 Cor. 1:1; Gal. 1:13), "it seems unreasonable to doubt that in I Thess. 1,1 Paul is thinking of the Christians of Thessalonica as members of the 'Church of God,' and that he is fully aware of the biblical background and theological implications of his use of the term" (Deidun 1981: 11 [cf. Malherbe 2000: 99]). That the term *ekklēsia* reflects Paul's understanding of the predominantly Gentile church of Thessalonica as the new people of God is confirmed by his subsequent reference to them just three verses later as those who are "loved by God" and who know their "election" (1:4)—terms used in the OT to refer to Israel but now applied to NT believers.

1:4

Paul addresses his readers with the striking phrase "loved by God." As with the noun "church" (see commentary on 1 Thess. 1:1 above), here too we have an instance of language originally applied to Israel (e.g., Deut. 32:15; 33:12; Ps. 60:5; 108:6; Isa. 44:2; Jer. 11:15; 12:7; Sir. 45:1; Bar. 3:37) being reapplied to the Christian church. Especially in this context where the emphasis is on God's election ("because we know, brothers loved by God, your election"), there can be little doubt that Paul's application of terms originally reserved for Israel to the predominantly Gentile congregation of Thessalonica is not coincidental, but rather stems from his conviction that the church, consisting of both Jewish and Gentile Christians, now constitutes the renewed Israel of God (on this important concept, see commentary on 1 Thess. 4:1–12 below). As Marshall (1990: 262) observes, "It is clear [from the phrase 'loved by God'] that by this early stage in his thinking Paul has already developed the concept of the church as the Israel of God. The conviction that God's love is now extended to the church composed of Jews and Gentiles is already present, and it does not need to be defended in any way. The church has inherited the position of Israel."

1:9b

Paul describes the conversion of the Thessalonian Christians with terms that appear to reflect the influence of the OT upon his word choice and meaning: "how you turned to God from idols in order to serve a living and true God" (*pōs epestrepsate pros ton theon apo tōn eidōlōn douleuein theō zōnti kai alēthinō*). The correlated actions of "turning to God" from pagan gods and "serving" only God are found in 1 Kgdms. 7:3 (1 Sam. 7:3 MT/ET), where Samuel challenges the Israelites to "turn to the LORD [*epistrephete pros kyrion*], take away the other gods from your midst and your groves, and . . . serve [*douleusate*] him alone." Elsewhere in the LXX, the verb *epistrephō* is frequently used not only of Israel (re)turning to their God (e.g., Hos. 5:4; 6:1; Joel 2:13), but also of Gentiles turning to Israel's God (e.g., Ps. 21:28; Isa. 19:22; Jer.

18:8). The verb *douleuō* similarly occurs with some frequency in the LXX such that it is a common term for expressing total commitment to God (*TDNT* 2:261–68).

The God to whom the Thessalonians have turned and now serve with this total commitment is portrayed as "living" (*zōnti*) and "true" (*alēthinō*). These two adjectives are rarely used by Paul as a description of God: they occur as a word pair nowhere else, and although the adjective "living" is used alone on a few occasions (Rom. 9:26; 2 Cor. 3:3; 6:16; 1 Tim. 3:15; 4:10), the adjective "true" is found only here. However, both are common descriptors of God in the OT ("living": Num. 14:21, 28; Deut. 5:26; 32:40; Josh. 3:10; 1 Sam. 17:36; 2 Kings 19:4, 16; Ps. 42:2 [41:3 LXX]; 84:2 [83:3 LXX]; Isa. 37:4, 17; Jer. 10:10; 23:36; Dan. 6:20, 26 [6:27 LXX]; Hos. 1:10 [2:1 LXX]; "true": Exod. 34:6; Num. 14:18; 2 Chron. 15:3; Ps. 86:15 [85:15 LXX]; Isa. 65:16; Jer. 10:10), and so, like the verbs "turn" and "serve" in the same clause, their meaning originates from this OT background. This conclusion is strengthened by the fact that those few instances where Paul does describe God as "living" are often part of his citing or adapting an OT passage. This OT background indicates, then, that these two adjectives function to highlight the contrast between God and the idols from which the Thessalonians have turned. They previously worshiped idols, dead "gods" who could do nothing, but now they serve the one and only God, who is living and true.

Defense of Paul's Past Visit to Thessalonica (1 Thess. 2:1–16)

In 2:1–16 Paul defends the integrity of his motives and conduct during his mission-founding visit to Thessalonica (see Weima 1997). Non-Christians in that city—the "fellow citizens" (2:14) of the believers—not only oppressed the members of the church, but also raised questions about the integrity of its founder, Paul, claiming that he was interested solely in winning human praise and financial gain. Although the Christians in Thessalonica had not bought into these charges, Paul, in view of the context of a young church separated from its leader and under heavy social pressure to resume former pagan practices, felt the need to answer these accusations. He begins the body of the letter, therefore, with a lengthy autobiographical reminder of how both he and his readers conducted themselves during his past visit to them. The apostle first focuses on his own conduct and that of his co-missionaries (2:1–12) and then shifts to the Thessalonians' response to that past visit (2:13–16).

2:4

Paul claims to speak "not as those who please people, but God, the one who examines our hearts." The apostle thus distinguishes himself sharply from other speakers of his day: whereas they seek to please people and so engage in the kind of speech that originates from "deceit, impure motives, or trickery" (2:3), Paul seeks to please God and so speaks in an honest and selfless manner that meets this goal. The apostle here, as he will again later in the letter (4:1), makes use of the characteristically OT purpose of "pleasing God" (e.g., Num. 23:27; 1 Kings 14:13; Job 34:9; Ps. 19:14; 69:31; 104:34; Prov. 15:26; 16:7; Mal. 3:4). By identifying God as "the one who examines our hearts," Paul may be alluding to Jer. 11:20 (Malherbe 2000: 141), where the Lord is described as one who "judges justly, examining minds and hearts." The notion of God as the tester of human hearts, however, occurs frequently in the OT (e.g., 1 Sam. 16:7; 1 Chron. 28:9; 29:17; Ps. 7:9; 17:3; 139:23; Prov. 17:3; Jer. 11:20; 12:3), and so it seems more probable that the apostle has in mind the general idea of a God who examines hearts rather than any specific text. Paul employs this common OT concept to show that the God who examined him and found him worthy to be entrusted with the gospel (2:4a) also continues to examine him (note the present tense of the participle *dokimazonti*) and thus ensures that the apostle's motives are pure.

2:15

The mention of "the Jews" at the end of 2:14 becomes the occasion for a description (2:15–16) of the role that some members of the Jewish faith have played in hindering the gospel and the consequent judgment that they face. Paul begins this description of certain members of his race by attributing responsibility to them for the death not only of the Lord Jesus, but also of the prophets: "the Jews who killed both the Lord Jesus and the prophets." The apostle is drawing on a well-known tradition concerning the killing of the OT prophets. Paul's familiarity with this tradition is evident from Rom. 11:3, where he cites the complaint of Elijah to God in 1 Kings 19:10: "The sons of Israel have forsaken you . . . and killed your prophets." This tradition is found in several OT texts (1 Kings 18:4; 2 Chron. 36:15–16; Neh. 9:27; Jer. 2:30) that employ the key words *apokteinō* ("kill") and *prophētai* ("prophets") and occurs in contemporary Jewish literature as well (*Martyrdom and Ascension of Isaiah*; *Pesiq. Rab.* 27 [129a]). By NT times, therefore, "killing the prophets" had become a common way to refer to the persecution of the faithful remnant within Israel by the unrighteous. This tradition appears often in Jesus' teaching (Matt. 5:12; 23:29–37; Luke 4:24; 6:23; 11:47–51; 13:33–34) and is found also in the preaching of the early apostles (Acts 7:52). Paul uses this tradition here in 2:15 to highlight the similarity between the persecutions currently experienced by the Thessalonian church, the Judean church, and himself and the persecutions constantly endured in the past by God's righteous prophets.

2:16

This long history of Jewish opposition to the Lord Jesus, the OT prophets, and the Pauline mission (2:15–16a) has a logical outcome: "with the result that they have been constantly filling up the measure of their sins" (*eis to anaplērōsai autōn tas hamartias pantote*). Paul here employs an OT theme that is developed also in later Jewish writings: there exists a fixed amount of sins to be committed, after which punishment will be meted out. The verb *anaplēroō* suggests the picture of a vessel or cup that is in a slow but constant process of being filled up, and once it is completely full, judgment will take place. The same verb is used in Gen. 15:16 LXX to describe the sins of the Amorites, which are said "to be not yet filled up." This theme of "filling up the measure of one's sins" occurs also in Dan. 8:23; Wis. 19:4; 2 Macc. 6:14. In the NT the verb "fill up" (*plēroō*, the unaugmented form of *anaplēroō*) is found in Matt. 23:32, where Jesus uses it to describe the scribes and the Pharisees, who likewise are linked to the killing of the prophets (Matt. 23:31). The notion that humans have a fixed limit to their actions, both good and evil, is widely attested in later Jewish writings as well (*4 Ezra* 4:34–37; 7:74; *2 Bar.* 21:8; 48:2–5; *L.A.B.*

26:1–3). Paul's judgment in 2:16 against his own people, therefore, apparently borrows from a common theme and conventional language, rooted in the OT and developed in later Judaism, used by Jews to express their anger at the faithlessness of certain members of their own race.

Defense of Paul's Current Absence from Thessalonica (1 Thess. 2:17–3:10)

Non-Christians in Thessalonica not only attacked the integrity of Paul in regard to his past visit to the city (2:1–16), but also used the apostle's inability thus far to return to the fledgling church to cast further doubts about the genuineness of his motives. Paul's first key concern in this next section of the letter, therefore, is to reassure the Thessalonian Christians of his continued love and concern for them, despite his failure to return for a second visit (2:17–20). His second key concern focuses on the theme of Christian suffering as he seeks to encourage the Thessalonians to remain steadfast in their newly found faith even in the face of opposition (3:1–5). The apostle concludes his discussion by bringing these two concerns together in the good report about the Thessalonians given by Timothy upon his return to Paul (3:6–10).

2:19

Paul's deep affection for the Thessalonians is expressed in a rhetorical question that involves three elements: "For who is our hope and joy and crown of boasting?" The third member of the triad, "crown of boasting" (*stephanos kauchēseōs*), is an expression that occurs three times in the LXX (Prov. 16:31; Ezek. 16:12; 23:42). The word "crown," though with a different appellation ("crown of glory"), also occurs with a figurative meaning in the LXX (Jer. 13:18; Lam. 2:15) and in later Jewish literature (*2 Bar.* 15:8; *T. Benj.* 4:1; 1QS IV, 7), and this appears to have influenced at least one NT writer ("crown of glory" [1 Pet. 5:4]: cf. "crown of life" [James 1:12; Rev. 2:10]; "crown of righteousness" [2 Tim. 4:8]). Paul's use of the expression "crown of boasting," however, probably stems not from these OT and Jewish texts (contra Lightfoot 1904: 38; Richard 1995: 133–34), but rather from the Hellenistic athletic contests in which the victor received a wreath. The apostle frequently employs the metaphor of the

games to depict the Christian life in general and his apostolic ministry in particular (see Pfitzner 1967).

3:5

Paul expresses his fear that, due to Satan's malevolent activity of tempting the Thessalonian believers, "our labor might have been in vain" (*eis kenon genētai ho kopos hēmōn*). The apostle's language here may echo that of the Suffering Servant of the Lord in Isa. 49:4: "I have labored in vain" (*kenōs ekopiasa*) (see also the eschatological hope of Isa. 65:23, which envisions a time when the Lord's servants "will not labor in vain" [*ou kopiasousin eis kenon*]). This possibility is strengthened by the fact that Paul alludes to this text elsewhere (Phil. 2:16) to demonstrate that his apostolic calling and labor parallel that of the prophets (so Malherbe 2000: 195).

3:7

The good report about the Thessalonians from Timothy caused Paul to be comforted "in all our distress and affliction" (*epi pasē tē anankē kai thlipsei hēmōn*). The nouns *anankē* and *thlipsis* are paired elsewhere in the LXX (Job 15:24; Ps. 25:17 [24:17 LXX]; 119:143 [118:143 LXX]; Zeph. 1:15) and in 2 Cor. 6:4, suggesting that it would be wrong to distinguish them from each other. This is supported here by the presence of only one definite article, which links *anankē* and *thlipsis* together as a collective whole. There is no justification, therefore, for the claim of some earlier commentators that the first term refers to "physical privation" and the second to "sufferings inflicted from without" (Lightfoot 1904: 45; Frame 1912: 133). Still others claim, on the basis of *anankē* and *thlipsis* in 1 Cor. 7:26, 28 and the word pair in Zeph. 1:15, that these two terms have a special eschatological focus as denoting those persecutions and sufferings connected with the last days (e.g., Best 1972: 141; Wanamaker 1990: 135). But although Paul's worldview is one in which he sees all his missionary activities as taking place in the final days, there is nothing to suggest that he uses "all our distress and affliction" in 3:7 with a special eschatological focus. Instead, the two terms are a general description of the hardships that Paul endures for his Christian faith.

Transitional Prayers (1 Thess. 3:11–13)

The two petitions of 3:11–13 function as transitional prayers in which Paul skillfully concludes the apologetic concerns at work in the first half of the letter (2:1–3:10) and also foreshadows three key themes (holy or blameless conduct, mutual love, and the return of Christ) that will be developed in the second half (4:1–5:22).

3:13a

The purpose of the second prayer is for the Lord "to strengthen your hearts" (*eis to stērixai hymōn tas kardias*). The combination of the verb "strengthen" with the noun "heart" (found in Paul only here and in 2 Thess. 2:17) occurs in the OT with a variety of meanings: the strengthening of the physical body (i.e., nourishment: Judg. 19:5, 8; Ps. 104:15 [103:15 LXX]); the strengthening of the mind (i.e., insight: Sir. 6:37; 22:16); the strengthening of the emotions (i.e., courage: Ps. 112:8 [111:8 LXX]; cf. James 5:8). It is this last sense that Paul intends here, as he prays that the Thessalonians will have courage to stand firm in their faith even in the face of persecution.

3:13b

Christ will return accompanied "with all his holy ones" (*meta pantōn tōn hagiōn autou*). Does Paul have in view angels or believers ("saints")? Most commentators support the former option for two reasons. First, there is strong evidence that Paul is dependent on Zech. 14:5 LXX ("And the Lord my God will come, and all the holy ones with him"), a text that refers to angels. In fact, in Matt. 25:31, which borrows from this same OT text, the word "holy ones" is changed to "angels." Second, the term *hagioi* in the OT (e.g., Job 5:1; 15:15; Ps. 89:5, 7 [88:6, 8 LXX]; Dan. 7:18; 8:13; Zech. 14:5) and the intertestamental literature (e.g., Tob. 11:14; 12:15; *1 En.* 1:9) sometimes refers to the presence of angels at the final judgment—a picture of the end times found elsewhere in Paul (2 Thess. 1:7).

There are convincing reasons, however, to adopt the second option, that "holy ones" refers to believers or "saints." First, the plural *hagioi* in every other occurrence in Paul refers clearly to Christians (Rom. 1:7; 8:27; 12:13; 15:25; 1 Cor. 1:2; 6:1–2; 2 Cor. 1:1; Eph. 2:19; 3:8; Phil. 1:1; 4:22; Col. 1:4, 26; 3:12; 1 Tim. 5:10), so there

would need to be weighty grounds to interpret this word differently here in 3:13b. Second, the supposed parallel in 2 Thess. 1:7 is not exact, since the key word "holy ones" does not occur there, but instead the noun "angels." In fact, just a few verses later, in 2 Thess. 1:10, which, like 1 Thess. 3:13, describes the coming judgment at Christ's return, Paul uses "holy ones" to refer to believers (it is parallel to "the ones who believe"). Third, the skillful way in which the second prayer of 3:12–13 anticipates the major themes to be developed in the second half of the letter suggests that the phrase "with all his holy ones" similarly looks ahead to key topics yet to be discussed. This is, in fact, exactly what one finds. The reference to believers as "the holy ones" reinforces the goal of the prayer that the Thessalonians be "blameless in holiness" and foreshadows the discussion of the key word "holiness" in 4:3–8. Similarly, the statement that "all" of the holy ones will be with Jesus at his coming anticipates Paul's claim in 4:13–18 that all believers—not only the living Christians, but also "those who have fallen asleep"—will be present and reunited at Christ's return.

This compelling evidence suggests, therefore, that Paul's allusion to Zech. 14:5 has been reinterpreted in such a way that either (1) this text now refers to believers ("saints") instead of angels (so, e.g., Findlay 1891: 77; Hendriksen 1955: 93; Williams 1992: 67–68); or (2) the "all" in the phrase "with all his holy ones" has been expanded to include both angels and believers (so, e.g., Lightfoot 1904: 50; Milligan 1908: 45; Morris 1991: 111–12; Holmes 1998: 116n5).

Increasing in Conduct That Pleases God (1 Thess. 4:1–12)

In 4:1–12 Paul leaves behind the apologetic concerns developed in the first half of the letter body (2:1–3:10) and begins the exhortative concerns that dominate the second half (4:1–5:22). In this passage he addresses two distinct subjects: the sexual conduct of the Thessalonians (4:3–8), and their practice of mutual love within the church (4:9–12). These disparate subjects are combined in 4:1–12 under the overall theme of increasing in conduct that pleases God (4:1–2).

There is some debate over the background or determining influences of Paul's exhortations in 4:1–12. Some believe that the apostle was impacted most by the Greco-Roman setting of his birthplace, Tarsus (Acts 22:3), and the Hellenistic culture that permeated the ancient world generally, and so they stress the parallels between his exhortations and those found in Cynic and Stoic thought (e.g., Malherbe 2000; Hock 1980: 44–47). A variety of factors, however, clearly indicate the apostle's indebtedness in this passage to the OT and the Jewish moral tradition (so, e.g., Hodgson 1982: 199–215; Carras 1990: 306–15; Rosner 1995: 351–60; Collins 1998: 406–10, 414). This is suggested in a general way by Paul's (1) threefold use of the verb "walk" (4:1 [2x], 12), a common OT and rabbinical term denoting moral conduct; (2) employment of the verb "receive" (4:1), which functions as a technical term in rabbinical writings for the transmission of traditional material; (3) call to "please God" (4:1) as the goal of human conduct, an idea rooted in the OT (see, e.g., Num. 23:27; 1 Kings 14:13; Job 34:9; Ps. 19:14; 69:31; 104:34; Prov. 15:26; 16:7; Mal. 3:4); (4) concern to make a good impression on those outside the community (4:12), an aspiration found throughout the OT (e.g., Exod. 32:12, 25; Num. 14:14–16; Deut. 9:25–29; 1 Kings 20:28). Paul's indebtedness in this passage to the OT is seen in a more specific way, however: his emphasis on the theme of "holiness" in vv. 3–8, which is to be a defining characteristic of Israel as God's covenant people, and his allusions to the OT in vv. 5, 6, 8b, and 9.

The theme of "holiness" (*hagiasmos*) is an OT concept that Paul stresses in 4:3–8. The importance of this concept for the apostle is indicated by his identification of it as the will of God (4:3) and his inclusion of it as the key statement that introduces his discussion of sexual conduct. Its importance is further suggested by the two additional references to "holiness" in the following verses (4:4, 7) and by the closing description of God's Spirit where the unusual word order emphasizes his "holy" character (4:8). The holiness theme is also foreshadowed by Paul in the prayer of 3:13, where he calls upon the Lord to strengthen the hearts of the Thessalonians such that they may be "blameless in holiness" when Jesus comes again "with all his holy ones." The apostle's emphasis on holiness manifests itself finally in his deliberate expansion of the closing peace benediction of

5:23, where, instead of the simple and expected formula "May the God of peace be with you" (see Rom. 15:33; 2 Cor. 13:11; Phil. 4:9b), Paul writes, "May the God of peace himself make you holy through and through; and may your whole spirit, soul, and body be kept blameless at the coming of our Lord Jesus Christ."

This persistent emphasis on holiness reveals an important truth about the theological perspective from which Paul views the Thessalonian believers and issues his exhortations to them (Weima 1996, esp. 101–3). Holiness was the attribute by which Israel, God's covenant people, was to be distinguished from all other nations. This is explicitly stated by God when he constitutes the nation of Israel at Mount Sinai as his chosen covenant people: "You will be to me a distinctive people out of all the nations. . . . You will be to me a kingdom of priests and a holy nation" (Exod. 19:5–6 LXX). This divine command for Israel to let holiness be the distinguishing feature of its existence is repeated in the renewal of the Sinai covenant: "And the Lord has chosen you today that you may be to him a distinctive people . . . in order that you may be a holy people to the Lord your God" (Deut. 26:18–19 LXX). Likewise, the book of Leviticus repeatedly calls on the people of Israel to imitate the holiness of their God: "You shall be sanctified/made holy and you shall be holy, because I, the Lord your God, am holy" (Lev. 11:44 LXX [cf. 11:45; 19:2; 20:7, 26; 22:32]).

The basic concept associated with this call to holiness is that of "separation"—that is, the need for Israel to "come out" and be "distinct" from the surrounding peoples (Snaith 1944: 24–32). Thus holiness is the boundary marker that separates God's people from all other nations: "I am the Lord your God who has separated you from all the nations. You shall therefore make a distinction between clean and unclean. . . . And you will be holy to me, because I, the Lord your God, am holy, the one who separated you from all the nations to be mine" (Lev. 20:24–26 LXX).

Any first-century Jew would have been familiar with all of this, since Lev. 17–26 (the so-called Holiness Code), where God's call to holiness is clearly set forth, was well known among Jews in both Palestine and the Diaspora (Hodgson 1982: 199–215). Paul certainly was familiar with the material in Lev. 17–26, since he had been an active member of the Pharisees, a Jewish movement whose name, "the separated ones" (Gk. *Pharisaioi* comes from the Aram./Heb. *prš*, meaning "separate, make distinct"), reflected their desire to distance themselves from other Jews who did not share their passion for following the Torah's call to holiness. It is not at all surprising, therefore, that Paul viewed holiness as God's desired purpose for and defining characteristic of Israel, his covenant people.

What is surprising, however, even astonishing, is that Paul applies this standard of holiness to predominantly Gentile believers in Jesus at Thessalonica. The holiness that previously has been the exclusive privilege and calling of Israel has now also become God's purpose for Gentiles at Thessalonica who have "turned to God from idols to serve the true and living God" (1:9). The holiness that previously has been the characteristic that distinguished Israel from the Gentile nations has now become the boundary marker that separates the Thessalonian Gentile believers from "the Gentiles who do not know God" (4:5), those who are "outside" God's holy people (4:12). Paul, it seems clear, views his Gentile converts at Thessalonica as the renewed Israel—those who, together with Jewish Christians, are now full members of God's covenant people. And on the basis of their privileged new position, he exhorts them in 4:3–8 to exhibit the holiness that God's people have always been called to possess.

4:5

In contrasting the sexual conduct of the Thessalonian believers with that of their unbelieving fellow citizens, Paul identifies the latter group as "the Gentiles who do not know God" (*ta ethnē ta mē eidota ton theon*). This expression, used in the apostle's other letters as well (Gal. 4:8–9; 2 Thess. 1:8; cf. 1 Cor. 1:21), likely stems from the OT (Job 18:21; Ps. 79:6 [78:6 LXX]; Jer. 10:25) and serves to root immoral sexual conduct in ignorance about God (so also Rom. 1:24–27; cf. Wis. 14:12, 22–26; *Sib. Or.* 3:29–45). The phrase "the Gentiles who do not know God" also immediately places this verse in a covenant context, for "to know God" is a technical reference in the OT, especially in Jeremiah (see Jer. 31:34), to the covenant relationship (Deidun 1981: 19n61). Paul's placement of the Thessalonian Christians, themselves Gentiles, in sharp antithesis to "the

Gentiles who do not know God" is striking and incomprehensible *unless* the apostle views these converts no longer as Gentiles but rather now as full members of God's covenant people. His use of this OT phrase, therefore, provides additional support to two principal claims made above. First, it shows that Paul perceives the Gentile believers at Thessalonica to be members of the renewed Israel, the covenant people of God. Second, it illustrates once again that Paul viewed holiness—here specifically holiness in sexual conduct—as the distinguishing sign or boundary marker of believers that sharply separates them from the world, from "those who do not know God."

4:6b

The exhortations to holiness in 4:3–6a are followed in 4:6b–8 by three causal statements (4:6b: *dioti* ["because"]; 4:7: *gar* ["for"]; 4:8: *toigaroun* ["therefore"]) that provide the reasons why the Thessalonian converts must be holy with regard to their sexual conduct. The first of these causal statements comes in 4:6b: "because the Lord is an avenger concerning all these things" (*dioti ekdikos kyrios peri pantōn toutōn*). These words likely allude to Ps. 93:1 LXX (94:1 MT/ET): "The Lord is a God of vengeance" (*theos ekdikēseōn kyrios*). This possibility is strengthened by the fact that the predicate nominative in both 1 Thess. 4:6b and Ps. 93:1 is located at the head of the sentence in the position of emphasis. The theme of God as a judge who exacts vengeance is widely found in the OT (e.g., Exod. 7:4; 12:12; Deut. 32:35; Ps. 18:47; Jer. 11:20; Amos 3:2, 14; Mic. 5:15; Nah. 1:2) and appears also in the intertestamental literature (e.g., *T. Reub.* 6:6; *T. Levi* 18:1; *T. Gad* 6:7; *T. Jos.* 20:1; *T. Benj.* 10:8–10; *Jos. Asen.* 23:13).

There is some ambiguity as to whom Paul has in view: God or Jesus? The fact that God is being described in the allusion to Ps. 93:1 LXX, as well as the presence of multiple references to "God" in the rest of 4:3–8 (4:3, 5, 7, 8), leads some to conclude that the noun "Lord" here refers to God (e.g., Morris 1991: 124; Richard 1995: 203–4). Against this conclusion, however, are at least three factors. First, the term *kyrios* has occurred twelve times in the letter thus far, eight of which explicitly include the name "Jesus" (1:1, 3; 2:15, 19; 3:11, 13; 4:1, 2). This strongly suggests that the remaining four nonexplicit references (1:6, 8; 3:8, 12), along with *kyrios* here in 4:6, also refer to Jesus.

Second, if *kyrios* refers not to Jesus but to God, it would make the explicit introduction of the subject "God" in the following verse unnecessary. Third, Paul makes several references throughout both Thessalonian letters to the future coming of Jesus, who will punish the wicked and serve as the agent of God's wrath (1 Thess. 1:10; 5:1–11; 2 Thess. 1:7–10; 2:8–10; cf. Rom. 12:19; Col. 3:23–25). If, then, as seems likely, the avenging one to whom Paul refers is Jesus, this text reveals how the apostle attributes to Jesus a role that the OT attributed to God. Paul's allusion in 4:6b to Ps. 93:1 LXX, therefore, reflects his christological reinterpretation of this OT passage such that it now refers to Jesus instead of God.

4:8

The third reason (the first and second reasons are given in 4:6b, 7) why holiness ought to be a distinctive characteristic of the Thessalonians' sexual conduct is that "the one who rejects these exhortations rejects not a human being but God, who indeed gives his Spirit, who is holy, to you." Here Paul picks up the language of the OT prophets, especially Ezek. 36:27; 37:14, about the blessed presence of God's Spirit in the messianic age—language associated with the "new" or "everlasting" covenant—and applies it to the Thessalonian believers (see Deidun 1981: 19, 53–56; Thielman 1994: 76–77; Weima 1996: 110–12).

Jews of the first century were painfully aware that their nation was not living according to the standard of holiness that God had called for when he first established his covenant with them. However, most Jews also believed, on the basis of God's promise given through the prophets, that he would not abandon his people, but would restore their holiness by pouring out his Spirit upon them as part of the covenant blessings to be enjoyed in the messianic era. This eschatological hope for holiness, made possible through the presence of God's Spirit, is most clearly seen in Ezek. 36:25–27 LXX: "I will sprinkle clean water on you, and you will be purged from all your uncleannesses and from all your idols, and I will cleanse you. And I will give you a new heart, and will put a new spirit in you [*pneuma kainon dōsō en hymin*]; and I will take away the heart of stone out of your flesh, and will give you a heart of flesh. And I will put my Spirit in you [*to pneuma mou dōsō en hymin*] and will cause you to walk in

my commands and to keep my judgments and do them" (cf. Ezek. 11:19).

The gift of God's Spirit as a key blessing of the eschatological age is also stressed in Ezek. 37:6, 14: "I will put my Spirit into you" (*dōsō pneuma mou eis hymas*). And although other prophets such as Jeremiah and Isaiah do not highlight the gift of God's Spirit quite as explicitly as Ezekiel does (but see Isa. 59:21), they do hold out the future hope of a "new" or "everlasting" covenant in which God will live in and among his people in such an intimate way that they will be able to obey his commands and live holy lives (see, e.g., Jer. 31:31–34 [38:31–34 LXX]; 32:40; 50:5; Isa. 55:3; 59:21).

Paul takes this new covenant language, which articulates the eschatological hope of the Jewish people, and applies it to Gentile Christians at Thessalonica. The parallels with Ezek. 36:25–27 are especially striking. For as Ezekiel prophesied ("You will be clean from all your uncleannesses" [36:25]), God has cleansed the Thessalonian believers from their "uncleanness/impurity" (4:7), so that their sexual conduct now is to be controlled by "holiness" (4:3, 4, 7). And as Ezekiel prophesied ("I will cleanse you from all your idols" [36:25]), God has cleansed Paul's converts at Thessalonica from their idolatry, with the result that they "turned to God from idols to serve a living and true God" (1:9). Likewise, as Ezekiel prophesied ("I will cause you to walk in my commands, and to keep my judgments and do them" [36:27]), God has enabled Gentile Christians at Thessalonica to "walk" (*peripateō*) according to his commands (4:1 [2x], 12). But most significantly, as Ezekiel prophesied ("I will put my Spirit in you," [36:27; cf. 37:6, 14]), Paul can now say to Gentile believers at Thessalonica that God is the one "who indeed gives his Spirit, who is holy, to you" (4:8).

That Paul did, in fact, quite consciously have in mind the eschatological age envisioned by Ezekiel can be seen in his description of God giving his Spirit "into you" (*eis hymas*). For although this expression is somewhat awkward (the more natural and expected expression is the dative *en hymin* ["in you"]), it echoes exactly the words of Ezekiel: "I will put my Spirit into you [*eis hymas*]" (37:6, 14 LXX). But whereas for Ezekiel and others in Judaism the gift of God's Spirit was only a future hope

("I will give my Spirit"), for Paul it had become a present and ongoing reality, as indicated by the present tense of the participle *didonta*.

It seems clear, therefore, that Paul viewed the conversion of Gentiles at Thessalonica as a fulfillment of the eschatological promises made to Israel. The Thessalonian believers were no longer simply "Gentiles who do not know God"; now they were members of the renewed Israel, the covenant people of God. This privileged status meant that in their sexual conduct they must observe the boundaries of holiness that the new covenant marked out for them. The key to living such lives of holiness is the present and ongoing presence of God's Spirit. So here, as elsewhere in Paul's letters, the Holy Spirit is the power that enables believers to live holy lives.

4:9

After introducing in the first half of 4:9 the new topic of mutual love, Paul in the second half provides the reason for the superfluous nature of writing to the Thessalonians about this subject: "for you yourselves are taught by God [*theodidaktoi*] to love one another." The term *theodidaktos*, an adjective meaning "taught by God," is striking, since there are no known occurrences of this term anywhere in Greek literature prior to its appearance in this verse, thereby suggesting that it is a new word coined by Paul. The remarkable character of this term is evident also in the fact that it occurs nowhere else in the NT, only rarely in later Christian literature, and never in non-Christian writings.

Paul's use, or perhaps even invention, of the term *theodidaktos* is almost certainly an allusion to Isa. 54:13 LXX: "And I will cause all your sons to be taught of God [*didaktous theou*]." Within the context of Isaiah's description of the blessings to be enjoyed in the messianic age, these words refer to a time when God will live so intimately with his people through his Spirit that they will no longer have to be taught by human intermediaries, but rather will be "taught of God." This idea of divine instruction as an eschatological blessing enjoyed by God's covenant people is found elsewhere in the prophetic writings. Jeremiah portrays the new covenant as a period when God's people will not need others to teach them the law but will know it innately, for God will write it on their hearts (Jer. 31:33–34 [38:31–34 LXX]). Isaiah also,

earlier in his prophecy, envisions a future age when all the nations will stream to Mount Zion in order that "[God] may teach us his ways and that we may walk in his paths" (Isa. 2:3). The importance that Jews attached to this idea of divine instruction as an eschatological blessing is further evidenced in the fact that Isaiah's vision of 2:2–4 is repeated in Mic. 4:1–3. This idea also manifests itself in *Pss. Sol.* 17:32, which speaks of the future king who will rule in the messianic age as one who is "taught by God" (*didaktos hypo theou*). That this eschatological blessing was still anticipated in NT times is clear from Jesus' citation of Isa. 54:13 in John 6:45 to show that "all will be taught by God [*didaktoi theou*]" in the messianic age. This expected eschatological blessing probably also lies behind the statement to the readers of 1 John that due to the enlightening grace of the Holy Spirit, "you have no need for anyone to teach you" (1 John 2:27).

Paul's use of the term *theodidaktos*, therefore, is significant. The apostle's allusion in this term, either specifically to Isa. 54:13 (*didaktous theou*) or more generally to the anticipation of divine instruction as an eschatological blessing (an anticipation expressed in several OT, intertestamental, and NT texts), so soon after his clear allusion in the preceding verse (4:8) to Ezekiel's description of the gift of God's Spirit in the messianic age suggests that here too Paul views the Thessalonians' practice of *philadelphia* ("mutual love") as an eschatological blessing of God's covenant people (Deidun [1981: 20–21] observes that "by utilizing the parallel texts of Jeremiah and Ezekiel in I Thess. 4,8b–9, Paul wishes to recall to the Thessalonians their unique Covenant relationship with God," and that the combination of the prophetic texts of Jer. 31:34 [38:34 LXX] and Ezek. 36:27; 37:14 "is widely attested in Jewish tradition in contexts concerning messianic times, and with particular reference to the immediacy of God's teaching"). Though this blessing of divine instruction was originally intended for Israel (but see the reference to "all nations" in Isa. 2:2 and to "many nations" in Mic. 4:2), Paul believes that it extends to the predominantly Gentile believers at Thessalonica. This new-covenant language of being "God-taught," therefore, further supports my earlier claim that Paul's exhortations in 4:1–12 are rooted in his conviction that the Gentile Christians at Thessalonica are included in the renewed Israel, the eschatological people of God who enjoy both the blessings and the challenges of that privileged relationship.

Comfort Concerning Deceased Believers at Christ's Return (1 Thess. 4:13–18)

The Thessalonians feared that fellow church members who had died would be at some kind of disadvantage at Christ's return compared to themselves, who were still alive. After introducing this problem (4:13), Paul presents two arguments in response: (1) he appeals to Christ's resurrection as a guarantee of believers' resurrection such that they will be present at Christ's return (4:14); (2) he appeals to the authoritative "word of the Lord," which emphatically states that deceased believers will share equally with living believers the glory and events connected with Christ's return (4:15–17). The apostle concludes his discussion with an exhortation (4:18).

4:16–17

The description of Christ's return in 4:16–17 is part of Paul's appeal to the "word of the Lord" (4:15a)—that is, an authoritative teaching of Jesus Christ. In these verses the apostle may well be making use of material that had taken shape before his use of it here, and this in turn suggests that he may or may not have been conscious of any allusions to the OT in this quoted material.

The main clause of 4:16, "because the Lord himself will come down from heaven," recalls in a very general way the prophetic literature of the OT that envisions "the day of the Lord," when God will come to judge the wicked and save the righteous (Isa. 2:10–12; 13:6, 9; Ezek. 7:19; 13:5; 30:3; Joel 1:15; 2:1, 11, 31; 3:14; Amos 5:18–20; Zeph. 1:7–8, 14, 18; 2:2–3; Zech. 14:1; Mal. 3:2; 4:5). The circumstances surrounding Christ's return are indicated by three prepositional phrases, the third of which involves the sound of a musical instrument: "with the trumpet call of God." The trumpet in the OT, as in the ancient world generally, functioned primarily not as a musical instrument, but rather as a signal, marking in particular the visible appearance of God not only in the past

(Exod. 19:13, 16, 19; 20:18), but especially at the future day of the Lord (Isa. 27:13; Joel 2:1; Zeph. 1:14–16; Zech. 9:14).

The trumpet as an end-time sign becomes even more prominent in the intertestamental literature (*4 Ezra* 6:23; *Pss. Sol.* 11:1; *Sib. Or.* 4:173–174; 8:239; *L. A. E.* 22:37–38; *Apoc. Zeph.* 9:1; 10:1; 11:1; 12:1; *Apoc. Ab.* 31:1–2; 1QM VII, 12–IX, 6) and so, not surprisingly, appears also elsewhere in Paul (1 Cor. 15:52) and the NT (Matt. 24:31; Rev. 8:2–13; 9:1, 13–14; 10:7; 11:15). As with the apostle's other reference to a trumpet call (1 Cor. 15:52), so also here in 4:16 it is linked with the resurrection of the dead (note the immediately following clause "and the dead in Christ will rise first"). The sound of a trumpet, therefore, not only functions as a codified sign of Jesus' return, but also, more importantly for the specific concern of the Thessalonians, marks the moment when the deceased church members will be brought to life such that they can participate equally in Christ's triumphant coming (for an intriguing but ultimately unconvincing argument that the reference to Christ's descent from heaven with a shout in 4:16 echoes Ps. 46:6 LXX [47:5 ET], see Evans 1993).

Believers will be taken up by God to meet the descending Christ "by means of clouds." Clouds in the OT are so frequently associated with a theophany—the appearance of God (e.g., Exod. 13:21–22; 14:19–20, 24; 16:10; 19:9, 16–17; Lev. 16:2; Num. 9:15–22; 10:11–12; 1 Kings 8:10–12; 2 Chron. 5:13–14; 6:1; Neh. 9:12, 19; Ps. 97:2; Isa. 19:1; Ezek. 1:4–28)—that this meaning is naturally carried over to the NT (Matt. 17:5; Mark 9:7; Luke 9:34–35; 1 Cor. 10:1–2). Clouds as a sign of God's presence become connected not only with the ascension of Christ (Acts 1:9 [cf. the ascension of the two witnesses in Rev. 11:12]), but also with his future return (Matt. 24:30; 26:64; Mark 13:26; 14:62; Luke 21:27; Rev. 1:7; 14:14–16), an image that can be traced back ultimately to Daniel's vision of "one like a son of man coming with the clouds of heaven" (Dan. 7:13). The reference to believers being snatched up "by means of clouds," therefore, highlights the presence of God and the active part that he will play in ensuring the equal presence and participation of both living and deceased believers in Christ's return.

Comfort Concerning Living Believers at Christ's Return (1 Thess. 5:1–11)

Whereas 4:13–18 concerns the fate of deceased Christians at Jesus' return, 5:1–11 focuses on the fate of living Christians at the same eschatological event. A variety of factors suggest that the Thessalonian Christians worried whether they were spiritually and morally worthy to meet the Lord on the day of his coming (Marshall 1983: 132; Holmes 1998: 165). Paul responds to their anxiety by reassuring them that they need not fear the day of the Lord (5:1–3). He then provides two supporting grounds for his claim: (1) their present status as "sons of light and sons of the day" (5:4–5); (2) their past election by God to obtain salvation and eternal life (5:9–10). Sandwiched between these two grounds is an appeal to live vigilantly as those who "belong to the day" (5:6–8). The discussion concludes with an exhortation (5:11).

5:2

The "day of the Lord" concept has its roots in the OT, where it refers to a future time when God will come to punish the wicked and vindicate his people, though the notion of judgment is more commonly stressed than that of deliverance (e.g., Isa. 2:1–4:6; Jer. 46:10; Ezek. 30:2–3; Joel 1:15; 2:1, 11, 31–32; Amos 5:18–20; Obad. 15; Zeph. 1:14–18; Zech. 14). The early Christians, for whom Jesus Christ was their "Lord," naturally applied the NT "day of the Lord" to the future time when Christ will come to punish the wicked and vindicate his followers. The apostle thus far in the letter has used the term "parousia" (2:19; 3:13; 4:15), but now he switches to the phrase "the day of the Lord," most likely because, due to its predominant OT usage, it better conveys the notion of judgment associated with Christ's return—a point made in the following verse ("then sudden destruction comes upon them . . . and they will certainly not escape").

5:3a

The phrase "peace and security" (*eirēnē kai asphaleia*) has traditionally been understood as an echo of the OT prophetic warnings against false claims of peace uttered by wicked leaders or false prophets in Israel. In Jer. 6:14 God accuses the spiritual leaders in Jerusalem of treating "the wound of my people carelessly, saying 'Peace,

peace,' when there is no peace" (so also 8:11 [but not in the LXX]). Similarly, in Ezek. 13:10 God claims that the prophets of Israel are false "because they have misled my people, saying, 'Peace, peace,' and there is no peace" (cf. Mic. 3:5). Consequently, many commentators conclude that in 5:3a Paul is alluding to these OT warnings against false claims of peace.

There exists stronger evidence, however, that the apostle is instead making use of a popular slogan of the imperial Roman propaganda machine (see esp. Hendrix 1991; also Donfried 1985: 334; Gaventa 1998: 70; Holmes 1998: 166–67; Green 2002: 233–34). The Romans vigorously promoted themselves as the providers of "peace" and did so through various public media. They widely issued coins with the word *pax* ("peace") alongside the image of the various emperors, and the phrase *pax Augusti* ("The peace of Augustus") is a characteristic one of the numismatic evidence after the time of Nero. The Romans also erected key monuments and distributed official proclamations celebrating the peace that their rule provided. Many ancient authors further enhanced the notion of the Romans as the restorers and extenders of peace (e.g., Seneca, *Clem.* 1.4.1–2; Ovid, *Epistulae ex Ponto* 2.5.18; Tacitus, *Hist.* 2.12; 4.74). The Romans, however, marketed themselves not merely as those who secured "peace," but as also those who provided "security" (either the Greek *asphaleia* or the Latin *securitas*). Although not occurring as frequently as "peace," the term "security" similarly appears on Roman coins, monuments, and official proclamations and so also functioned as an important part of the imperial propaganda. Finally, there are a couple of texts in which the terms "peace" and "security" are combined in the context of describing Roman rule (see Josephus, *Ant.* 14.247–255; also the first-century historian Velleius Paterculus, *Compendium of Roman History* 2.103.5), thereby providing a closer parallel to Paul's statement in 5:3 than any of the aforementioned OT texts.

5:3b

Paul uses a simile to describe the destruction that will suddenly come upon all those who look to the political power of Rome for peace and security: "as labor pains come upon a pregnant woman." The symbolic or metaphorical use of labor pains is found with great frequency in the OT (e.g.,

Ps. 48:6; Isa. 13:8; 21:3; 26:17–18; 37:3; 42:14; 66:7–8; Jer. 4:31; 6:24; 22:23; 30:4–7; 48:41; 50:43; Hos. 13:13; Mic. 4:9) and in the intertestamental literature (e.g., *1 En.* 62:4; *4 Ezra* 4:40–43; 16:37–39; *Sib. Or.* 5:514; 1QH^a XI, 7–12; XIII, 30–31). The image of labor pains in these texts functions in differing, though related, ways (Gempf 1994): it can be an "intense" pain that makes clear the acuteness of suffering; a "productive" pain that leads to a positive outcome; a "helpless" pain that the sufferer cannot avoid; a "cyclical" pain that, once begun, must run its course.

It is not clear, however, whether Paul's metaphorical use of labor pains fits any of these functions. On the one hand, the fact that the image comes after the adverb "suddenly" (*aiphnidios* is emphasized by its location at the head of the sentence, separated from the main verb and subject) and parallels the simile of a thief's surprise arrival at night in the preceding verse suggests that Paul here in 5:3b is stressing the unexpectedness of the coming judgment—a use of this image that has no exact parallel in the OT. The objection against this view—"To what pregnant woman does labor come as a surprise?" (Martin 1995: 160)—is not necessarily a compelling one, since Paul may be thinking about the unexpected timing of the onset of labor. On the other hand, the immediately following statement, with its emphatic (note the double negative *ou mē*) claim that "they certainly will not escape," suggests that Paul may have in mind the inevitableness of the coming judgment—a use of this image that is paralleled in the OT. In light of the fluidity with which metaphors function, it is perhaps best to allow for both usages to be maintained.

5:4–8

The references in 5:2 to the "day" of the Lord and to the thief's arrival at "night" lead Paul in 5:4–8 to develop, in a metaphorical manner, the contrasts not only between "day" and "night," but also between their corresponding qualities of "light" and "darkness." This metaphorical use of day/night and light/darkness to describe the human condition appears in many religious traditions, including the OT (e.g., Job 22:9–11; Ps. 27:1; 74:20; 82:5; 112:4; Prov. 4:18–19; Isa. 2:5; 5:20; 9:2; 60:19–20) and Jewish writings from the intertestamental period (e.g., *1 En.* 41:8; *4 Ezra*

14:20; *T. Levi* 19:1; *T. Naph.* 2:7–10; *T. Benj.* 5:3; 1QS I, 9–10; III, 13, 19–26; 1QM I, 1, 8–16). This usage undoubtedly influenced the thinking of Paul, who elsewhere makes similar employment of this metaphor (Rom. 1:21; 2:19; 1 Cor. 4:5; 2 Cor. 4:6; 6:14; Eph. 4:18; 5:8–11; 6:12; Col. 1:13). Here in 5:4–8 the apostle uses the metaphor to distinguish sharply the current spiritual condition and future fate of the Thessalonian believers from that of their non-Christian neighbors. The "light" and "day" symbolize the Thessalonians' intimate relationship with God and their knowledge about the imminent arrival of the day of the Lord, whereas the "darkness" and "night" symbolize non-Christians' alienation from God and their ignorance about the impending judgment that they will experience at Christ's return.

5:8b

Paul shifts from the metaphor of day/night and light/darkness to that of military armor (note how the apostle similarly links these two metaphors in Rom. 13:12: "Let us put on the armor of light"). The widespread presence of Roman soldiers meant that military armor could function quite easily as a metaphor for human ethical conduct, and certain philosophers and moralists of that day used it in exactly this way (see the texts cited in Malherbe 2000: 297). Paul's use of this metaphor, however, almost certainly stems from the OT, given the close verbal parallels between his words in 5:8 ("by putting on the breastplate of faith and love and as a helmet the hope of salvation") and Isa. 59:17 ("He put on righteousness as a breastplate and placed a helmet of salvation on his head" [cf. Wis. 5:17–18]). The apostle's indebtedness to Isa. 59:17 explains why he does not add a third piece of armor to better parallel the triad of faith, love, and hope. Paul does adapt this OT text, however, such that it is no longer God who is the divine warrior, but rather the human believer who wears the armor (a similar application to humans is found in a later rabbinic text [*b. B. Bat.* 9b]).

Paul uses the image of military armament several times in his letters (Rom. 13:12; 2 Cor. 6:7; 10:3–5; Eph. 6:11–17; Phil. 2:25; 2 Tim. 2:3–4), and these texts show how diverse he was in identifying the various virtues that the specific pieces of armor represented. That the apostle adapts this OT text so that it better suits the specific new context can be seen also here in 5:8b. Paul modifies the original text such that the breastplate no longer represents the single quality of "righteousness," but rather the two virtues of "faith and love." He also adds the third virtue of "hope" so that the original "helmet of salvation" now becomes "as a helmet the hope of salvation." The result of Paul's reapplication of this OT metaphor is that it now highlights the triad of faith, love, and hope, thereby echoing the same three virtues with which he opened the letter (1:3). In the larger context of the concerns at work in 5:1–11 this means that the Thessalonian believers should not fear the day of the Lord, since they need only put on the armor of faith, love, and hope—virtues of which they have already amply demonstrated their possession (1:3).

Letter Opening and Thanksgiving (2 Thess. 1:1–12)

The brief and unembellished nature of the letter opening (1:1–2), like that of the first letter, likely reflects the good relationship that Paul enjoys with the Thessalonians and his general happiness at their spiritual condition. In the thanksgiving (1:3–12) the apostle commends the Thessalonians for their abundant faith and love even in the midst of persecution (1:3–4), comforts them with the just judgment of God whereby they will be rewarded and their persecutors punished (1:5–10), and challenges them in his closing prayer report to continue their worthy conduct (1:11–12).

A number of terms and theological themes in 1:5–10 appear to have been influenced by the OT. Particularly striking are the several parallels with Isa. 66, the final chapter of that important prophetic book, which describes what the Lord will do in the final days to prosper his chosen people and to punish the wicked. These parallels have led Aus (1971: 113–14; 1976, esp. 266–67) to propose that 1:5–10 is the result of a conscious reflection of Isa. 66, supplemented by a few other OT texts, in order to create an end-time scenario that will comfort the persecuted readers and counter the false claim concerning the day of the Lord (see also Richard 1995: 315–16). The several OT allusions in 1:5–10 prompted Bruce (1982: 148) to suggest that Paul was borrowing here from a

"testimony collection," a pre-Pauline compilation of OT passages that deal with the common subject of eschatological teaching. These two theories, however, have not found wide acceptance, as most commentators view the OT parallels in 1:5–10 to be the result of unconscious allusions that come from the hand of the apostle himself rather than any preformed tradition. The situation is analogous to Christians who are so familiar with the text of the Bible that their prayers unconsciously echo many biblical phrases or passages.

1:6

The claim that it is just for God "to repay [*antapodounai*] those who afflict you with affliction, and you who are being afflicted with rest" involves the OT principle of retribution—the *lex talionis*, "an eye for an eye, and a tooth for a tooth." Although Scripture frequently affirms the theme of divine recompense, at times also using the identical verb "to repay" (Deut. 32:35; Ps. 138:8 [137:8 LXX]; Obad. 15; cf. Isa. 63:4), the allusions to Isa. 66 in the subsequent verses strengthen the possibility that Paul has that same passage in view here. In fact, there are two verses from Isa. 66 that are relevant: "The voice of the LORD repaying [*antapodidontos*] retribution to his enemies" (66:6); "For the LORD will come like a fire, and his chariots like the whirlwind, to repay [*apodounai*] his punishment with anger, and his rebuke with a flame of fire" (66:15). The *lex talionis* is rejected as a principle of human conduct (Matt. 5:38–48; Rom. 12:17), since one may easily act unjustly or out of vindictiveness. These dangers do not exist in divine conduct, however, since "God is just," and so this principle forms an essential aspect of any teaching about God's judgment (see Rom. 2:6–8; 12:19; 2 Cor. 5:10; Col. 3:25). Paul uses this OT principle to comfort the Thessalonians by pointing them to the future judgment as the time when the injustice of their present suffering will be redressed.

1:8a

The occasion at which the Thessalonian believers will be rewarded and their persecutors punished is the return of Christ, who will come "from heaven, with his mighty angels, in a flame of fire" (1:7b–8a). The third and final prepositional phrase likely contains another allusion to the OT. The issue is complicated, however, by a textual problem: did Paul write "in a fire of flame" [*en pyri phlogos*] or "in a flame of fire" [*en phogi pyros*]? Most commentators, as well as the text of NA[27], prefer the first reading on the grounds that it has slightly stronger textual support and is the more difficult reading. The second reading is then explained as a copyist's assimilation either to Isa. 66:15 or other less likely texts such as Ps. 29:7; Isa. 29:6; Dan. 7:9 (so, e.g., Best 1972: 258; Malherbe 2000: 399–400). If this interpretation is correct, then the apostle may well have in view Exod. 3:2 ("And the angel of the LORD appeared to him in a fire of flame out of the bush"), where "fire" refers to a theophany. According to this understanding, Paul portrays Christ's return as the presence of the divine somewhat akin to God's appearance before Moses.

This hardly settles the matter, however, since at least one important manuscript of Exod. 3:2 has the alternate reading "a flame of fire" (the same variation occurs in Acts 7:30, which looks back to this OT text). Furthermore, the frequent allusions to Isa. 66 not only elsewhere in the thanksgiving of 1:3–12 but also particularly in the latter half of this same verse (see commentary on 1:8b below) strongly suggest that here too Paul is drawing from Isa. 66:15 (so, e.g., Aus 1976: 266; Richard 1995: 307). This possibility gains further strength from the fact that the apostle's reference to "fire" is intended to highlight not so much the divine presence as the judgment that will take place—the point that is made not in Exod. 3:2, but in several other OT texts (Ps. 29:7; Isa. 29:6; Dan. 7:9; see also Sir. 21:9), including Isa. 66:15 ("For the LORD will come like a fire, and his chariots like the whirlwind, to repay his punishment with anger, and his rebuke with a flame of fire"). It appears likely, therefore, that the alternate reading "in a flame of fire" is in fact original and that this phrase involves an allusion to Isa. 66:15. Paul uses the imagery of a flaming fire to portray in a powerful manner the frightening judgment that awaits those who have been oppressing the Thessalonian believers.

1:8b

Paul continues to comfort his persecuted readers by picking up again the OT idea of divine retribution that he introduced in 1:6. Whereas that earlier verse balances the punishment of Thessalonians' persecutors with the reward that believers will receive, this verse stresses only the negative half of judgment: "giving vengeance [*didontos ekdikēsin*] to those who do not know God and to those who do not obey the gospel of our Lord Jesus." The phrase "give vengeance" (*didōmi ekdikēsin*), with slight variations, occurs several times in the LXX (Num. 31:3; Deut. 32:35; 2 Kgdms. 4:8; 22:48 [2 Sam. 4:8; 22:48]; Ps. 17:48 [18:47 ET]; Ezek. 25:14, 17). It is striking, however, that this phrase occurs also in Isa. 66:15 (*apodounai . . . ekdikēsin*)—the same text alluded to in the immediately preceding phrase, "a flame of fire." The action of "giving vengeance" in Isa. 66:15, as in the other OT texts containing this phrase, is ascribed to God. In Paul's use of this phrase, however, the divine work of meting out judgment is transferred to the returning Christ (the participle *didontos* modifies *tou kyriou Iēsou*).

This vengeance will be given not only to the persecutors of the Thessalonians, but also to a much larger group: "to those who do not know God, and to those who do not obey the gospel of our Lord Jesus." Several commentators have concluded from this double clause that Paul has two distinct groups in mind, most likely Gentiles and Jews (so, e.g., Dobschütz 1909: 248; Frame 1912: 233; Marshall 1983: 177–78). This "two group" interpretation appeals not only to the repetition of the definite article *tois*, but also to the description of the people in each clause. The first clause refers to "those who do not know God" (*tois mē eidosin theon*), an OT expression that typically refers to Gentiles (Job 18:21; Ps 79:6 [78:6 LXX]; Jer. 10:25) and that has this meaning elsewhere in Paul's letters (Gal. 4:8–9; 1 Thess. 4:5; cf. 1 Cor. 1:21). The second clause refers to "those who do not obey the gospel of our Lord Jesus" (*tois mē hypakouousin tō euangeliō tou kyriou hēmōn Iēsou*), an expression that may well allude to Isa. 66:4, where "they did not obey [God]" (*ouch hypēkousan mou*) refers to the Jewish people.

These two OT expressions, however, do not always refer exclusively to Gentiles and Jews: sometimes Jews are described in the OT as those who do not know God (Jer. 4:22; 9:6; Hos. 5:4), and sometimes Gentiles, along with Jews, are accused of not obeying the gospel (Rom. 10:16; 11:30). Furthermore, the two clauses with their OT allusions are better read as being in synonymous parallelism, whereby the second clause restates or clarifies the first (so Bruce 1982: 151; Wanamaker 1990: 227; Malherbe 2000: 401)—a reading that is supported by the parallelism also found in the immediately following verse ("from the face of the Lord and from the glory of his might"). Finally, it is doubtful whether the predominantly Gentile church at Thessalonica had knowledge of the OT sufficient to discern in Paul's allusions a reference to Gentiles and Jews as distinct groups (Wanamaker 1990: 227). Therefore, it is best to see Paul as describing a single group consisting of all those who will receive divine retribution for their failure to know God and obey the gospel.

1:9

The exact nature of the "affliction" (1:6) or "vengeance" (1:8) or "penalty" that such people "will pay" (1:9) is finally spelled out: "eternal destruction from the presence of the Lord and from the glory of his might" (*olethron aiōnion apo prosōpou tou kyriou kai apo tēs doxēs tēs ischyos autou*). This description clearly echoes the triple refrain of Isa. 2:10, 19, 21, where on the day of the Lord the wicked are commanded to hide themselves behind rocks and in caves "from the presence of the fear of the LORD and from the glory of his might [*apo prosōpou tou phobou kyriou kai apo tēs doxēs tēs ischyos autou*] whenever he will rise to terrify the earth." The omission in Paul's text of Isaiah's reference to "fear" has been interpreted by some (Best 1972: 264; Malherbe 2000: 403) as reflecting the reluctance of the apostle, compared with other apocalyptic writers of his day, to speak in active terms about the punishment of the wicked (the term "fear" might suggest torture). This, however, reads too much into Paul's motives. More likely, the omission stems from his desire to express better the parallelism between "from the presence of the Lord" and "from the glory of his might" (the Hebrew of Isa. 2:10, 19, 21 similarly omits "fear"). Since these two prepositional phrases are in synonymous parallelism (see also 1:8b), it would be wrong to distinguish their meaning too sharply. Instead, these two clauses together express in OT language something of the glorious and powerful presence of Yahweh, which here, significantly, is applied to Jesus. Therefore, the persecutors of the Christians in Thessalonica, along with all those who do know God and obey the gospel, will be forever separated from this glorious and powerful presence of Christ—a sharp contrast to the fate of the Thessalonian believers, who will "always be with the Lord" (1 Thess. 4:17; cf. 5:10).

1:10a

Having spelled out in 1:8–9 the judgment that will fall upon those who are persecuting the Thessalonian believers, Paul shifts in 1:10 to the reward that awaits his Christian readers, again making use of OT language. Whereas Christ's return results in unbelievers having no share in "the glory of his might" (1:9), his coming for believers is an occasion when he will "be glorified in his holy ones" (*endoxasthēnai en tois hagiois autou*). That this phrase involves an allusion to Ps. 88:8 LXX (89:7 ET), "God is glorified in the assembly of the holy ones" (*ho theos endoxazomenos en boulē hagiōn*), is strengthened by the fact that the compound verb *endoxazomai* is relatively rare in the LXX and occurs in the NT only here and two verses later in 1:12. As in many of Paul's other OT allusions, here again we see how texts originally referring to God are now applied to Christ. Another significant change is that in the psalm "the assembly of the holy ones" refers to angels, while here believers are in view, as the parallel phrase "those who believe" clearly indicates (see also 1 Thess. 3:13).

Less obvious, however, is what specific point Paul intends with his claim that the Lord will "be glorified in his holy ones." The issue centers on the meaning of the preposition *en* ("in"), which could be instrumental (Christ is glorified by or through believers), causal (believers are the cause or reason for Christ to be glorified), or locative (Christ's glorification takes place in the presence of believers). Although a case can be made for each option, the locative sense is supported by three factors (see Marshall 1983: 180; Wanamaker 1990: 230–31). The locative meaning (1) agrees with the meaning of *en* in Ps. 88:8 LXX, (2) matches the parallel phrase "to be marveled at in all who believe," and (3) contrasts well the fate of the Thessalonians' tormentors, who will be excluded "from the presence of the Lord" (1:9).

1:10b

The infinitival clause that opens 1:10 ("to be glorified in his holy ones") is synonymously paralleled in the concluding half of the verse by another infinitival clause: "to be marveled at in all who believe" (*thaumasthēnai en pasin tois pisteusasin*). As with the opening half, here too Paul's language echoes the OT, this time Ps. 67:36 LXX (68:35 ET): "God will be marveled at in the presence of his holy ones" (*thaumastos ho theos en tois hagiois autou*). Once again we see how Paul takes an OT text that originally refers to God and applies it to Christ. His pairing of "to be glorified" and "to be marveled" (see also Exod. 34:10; Sir. 38:3, 6) suggests that the latter term refers not so much to the notion of amazement or astonishment as to that of ascribing honor or glory (see Rev. 13:3, where *thaumazō* has the sense of "worship"). Christ's return will be an occasion when he is given his due glory, and this glorification will take place in the presence not just of the Thessalonian Christians, but of "all who believe."

1:12

Paul's thanksgiving closes with a prayer (1:11–12) whose ultimate purpose is "so that the name of the Lord Jesus may be glorified in you and you in him" (*hopōs endoxasthē to onoma tou kyriou hēmōn Iēsou en hymin, kai hymeis en autō*). The apostle's language is similar to that found in Isa. 66:5 LXX: "so that the name of the LORD may be glorified" (*hina to onoma kyriou doxasthē*). Some (e.g., Best 1972: 270–71; Wanamaker 1990: 234–35) have questioned this allusion on the grounds that Paul uses *hopōs* instead of the original *hina*, and the compound verb *endoxasthē* instead of the simple *doxasthē*. These two differences, however, are easily explained. The use of *hopōs* likely stems not merely from stylistic variation after the preceding *hina* in 1:11 (so Turner 1963: 105, and most commentators), but rather from Paul's desire to distinguish the initial purpose of the prayer from its ultimate purpose (see also 1 Cor. 1:28–29; 2 Cor. 8:14). The use of the compound verb *endoxasthē* is influenced by the presence of this form two verses earlier in 1:10, which in turn stems from its allusion to Ps. 88:8 LXX (89:7 ET). Furthermore, Paul has echoed Isa. 66 three times in the preceding verses (1:6, 8a, 8b), thereby strengthening the possibility that he is doing so once again here in 1:12. Finally, even though "the name of the Lord" is a phrase that Paul commonly employs (e.g., Rom. 10:13; 1 Cor. 1:2, 10; 5:4; 6:11; Col. 3:17; 2 Thess. 3:6), "of the six occurrences of *onoma* with *doxazein* in the LXX, only Isa. 66:5 uses *to onoma kyriou*," thereby making "the identification of the allusion certain" (Aus 1976: 267).

The words of Isa. 66:5 were originally addressed to those in Israel who were being despised and mocked for their faith in God: "Speak, our brothers, to those who hate you and detest you, so that the name of the Lord may be glorified, and may be seen in gladness; but they shall be put to shame" (LXX). Paul's prayer for the Thessalonian Christians, who are similarly suffering opposition and ridicule for their newly found faith, is that they may fulfill every good desire and work of faith (1:11) such that "the name of the Lord Jesus may be glorified."

The Day of the Lord (2 Thess. 2:1–17)

The Thessalonian church was badly shaken by a claim that "the day of the Lord"—the events surrounding the return of Christ—had already come. Paul responds to this falsehood first by urging the congregation not to be alarmed by such a counterfeit report (2:1–2). Then he explains why it is impossible for the day of the Lord to have already arrived: there must first occur certain clearly defined events, foremost of which involves the appearance of the "man of lawlessness," who for the present time is being restrained (2:3–12). The apostle concludes his discussion with a thanksgiving (2:13–14), an exhortation (2:15), and a prayer (2:16–17), all of which are intended to comfort those shaken by the false report and to challenge the church to stand firm in the true teaching that he passed on to them.

2:1

The content of Paul's appeal in this section concerns not only "the coming of our Lord Jesus Christ," but also "our gathering to him." The immediate reference to this latter subject is the comforting picture given in the previous letter of how all believers, both those who have died and those who are still alive, will be gathered together to Jesus at his return (1 Thess. 4:16–17). The motif, however, goes back to the widespread OT hope in the gathering together of the scattered exiles to their own land on the day of the Lord (Ps. 106:47 [105:47 LXX]; Isa. 27:13; 43:4–7; 49:12; 56:8; Jer. 29:14; 30:3, 18; 31:8, 23; 33:7; Joel 3:1–2; Zech 2:6; Tob. 14:5; 2 Macc. 1:27; 2:7, 18; *Pss. Sol.* 17:50; *T. Ash.* 7:6–7; *T. Naph.* 8:3). This hope was taken over by Jesus and his scattered followers to refer to the final gathering of God's people with the Messiah (Matt. 24:31 par.; cf. 23:37 par.).

2:2

For the OT roots of the "day of the Lord" concept, see commentary on 1 Thess. 5:2 above.

2:3–4

Paul exhorts the Thessalonians not to allow anyone to deceive them about the arrival of the day of the Lord, because that day cannot take place until two related events occur first: the apostasy comes, and the "man of lawlessness" is revealed. The apostle's description of this individual involves a number of OT allusions, though it is not clear whether these allusions originate from the apostle himself or whether he is drawing from traditional material of early Christian eschatology.

The person is identified in 2:3 by the parallel phrases "the man of lawlessness, the son of destruction" (*ho anthrōpos tēs anomias, ho huios tēs apōleias*), which may be influenced by Ps. 88:23 LXX (89:22 ET): "The enemy shall have no advantage against him, and the son of lawlessness shall not hurt him"; and by Isa. 57:3–4 LXX: "But as for you, come here, you sons of lawlessness. . . . Are you not children of destruction, a lawless seed?" Both phrases involve a Semitic idiom in which a generic personal noun ("son," "man," "master," etc.) followed by an adjectival genitive designates the person's essential condition or quality (BDF §162.6). Paul, therefore, depicts this person as one who is the very personification of lawlessness (note the abbreviation in 2:8: "the lawless one") and destruction.

A third, much longer parallel phrase in 2:4 further identifies this person as "the one who opposes and exalts himself above every so-called god or object of worship [*ho antikeimenos kai hyperairomenos epi panta legomenon theon ē sebasma*], so that he takes his seat in the temple of God, proclaiming himself to be God." The first part of this description appears to be influenced by Dan. 11:36, which describes a king of the north, generally identified as Antiochus Epiphanes, who desecrated the Jerusalem temple during the time of the Maccabees by setting up an altar to the pagan god Zeus. Of this king, Daniel prophesies that he "will exalt and magnify himself above every god" (*hypsōthēsetai . . . kai megalynthēsetai epi panta theon*) (11:36 Θ).

The latter part of this figure's description, with his claim to divine status, similarly stems from the figure of Antiochus and his profanation of the temple as described in Daniel (see 8:9–14; 9:26–27; 11:31, 45; 12:11). There are other OT texts, however, that also address the same subject: Ezek. 28:2 involves a condemnation of the king of Tyre for claiming to be divine, while Isa. 14:13 taunts the king of Babylon for elevating himself to the realm of the divine. And though Paul's language about taking a seat in the temple and claiming to be God goes back to the original plundering and profanation of the temple by Antiochus as prophesied in Daniel, the blasphemous actions of this king were subsequently kept alive in Jewish and early Christian thought through various rulers who also attempted to desecrate the Jerusalem sanctuary: the Roman general Pompey entered the holy of holies in 63 BC; the emperor Gaius Caligula considered himself to be a god and consequently attempted in AD 40 to have his statue erected in the Jerusalem temple. Paul, therefore, employs a familiar theme to portray the evil character of the coming lawless one and his usurpation of God's place in the world.

2:8

Paul cannot refer to the revelation of the man of lawlessness without immediately mentioning in the same sentence this evil one's defeat: "whom the Lord Jesus will destroy with the breath of his mouth." The apostle employs language reminiscent of Isa. 11:4 LXX, where the prince from David's house "will strike the earth with the word of his mouth, and with the breath of his lips he will destroy the ungodly." The allusion to this OT text is strengthened by adopting the more strongly attested indicative *anelei* ("he will destroy")—the same form found in Isa. 11:4—rather than optative *aneloi* or the different verb *analōsei* ("he will consume"). Paul has combined the two phrases from the Isaiah text ("with the word of his mouth and with the breath of his lips") into one ("with the breath of his mouth"). Although some (e.g., Frame 1912: 265; Best 1972: 303) have attributed this compression to an unconscious reminiscence of Ps. 32:6 LXX (33:6 MT/ET), "By the word of the Lord the heavens were established, and all the hosts of them by the breath of his mouth," there are a number of biblical and intertestamental passages that similarly refer to the destruction of the wicked by means of breath or the force of the mouth (Job 4:9; Isa. 30:27–28; *1 En.* 14:2; 62:2; 84:1; *4 Ezra* 13:10–11; *Pss. Sol.* 17:24, 25; Rev. 19:15).

The larger context of Isa. 11:4 was interpreted by the early church as a prophecy about the messiah, and so Paul, not surprisingly, applies this text to the coming of "the Lord Jesus" (even if "Jesus" is a later scribal addition [it is absent in B D² 1739 1881 𝔐 bo^ms], "the Lord" for Paul is Jesus). The "breath" of God is always depicted as something powerful and mighty (see the texts cited at the end of the preceding paragraph). The image that Paul presents with this OT allusion, therefore, is not one whereby the man of lawlessness will be easily blown over by the mere breath of the Lord Jesus (contra Morris 1991: 231), but rather one whereby breath is a potent and fearful weapon used by the returning Christ to destroy this eschatological enemy.

2:11

As a consequence of unbelievers following the false signs and wonders of the man of lawlessness (2:9) and their refusal to love the truth (2:11), God acts: "And for this reason God sends them a work of deception so that they believe the lie" (2:11). Although such divine action may seem perplexing and even troubling, it is similar not only to Paul's statements elsewhere that God gives sinners over to their own sin (Rom. 1:24, 26, 28; 11:8; cf. 2 Tim. 4:4), but also to certain OT texts where God employs evil spirits to inspire false prophets and so carry out his just judgment against the wicked (2 Sam. 24:1 with 1 Chron. 21:1; 1 Kings 22:23; Ezek. 14:9).

2:13

See commentary on 1 Thess. 1:4 above, regarding the phrase "loved by God."

Closing Exhortations (2 Thess. 3:1–15)

Paul brings his second letter to a close (note *to loipon* ["finally"] in 3:1) by issuing some general exhortations about prayer (3:1–5) and then proceeding to specific commands about the "idlers" (3:6–15).

3:5

The general exhortations about prayer in 3:1–5 conclude fittingly with a prayer: "May the Lord direct your hearts to the love of God and to the steadfastness of Christ" (3:5). The opening words of this prayer likely stem from the LXX, where the phrase "direct your hearts" is frequently used to describe people turning their hearts to the Lord (2 Chron. 12:14; 19:3; 20:33; 30:19; Sir. 49:3; 51:20) or, in a closer parallel with 3:5, the Lord turning people's hearts to himself (1 Chron. 29:18; Prov. 21:1). Thus, in keeping with this OT usage, the verb "may he direct" (*kateuthynai*) should not be taken literally (as in 1 Thess. 3:11), but rather metaphorically as referring to the spiritual condition of the Thessalonians.

3:16

The specific exhortations about idleness in 3:6–15 also conclude with a prayer: "May the Lord of peace himself give you peace at all times in every way. The Lord be with you all." The first part of the prayer echoes the Aaronic blessing of Num. 6:26 LXX: "May the Lord lift up his face to you and give you peace." This request for peace fittingly looks back to the two major concerns of the letter: the anxiety within the Thessalonian church over the claim that the day of the Lord had already come and the internal tensions due to the problem of the idlers (see Weima 1994: 189–91). The second part of the prayer involves a typical Jewish greeting: "The Lord be with you" (Judg. 6:12; Ruth 2:4; Luke 1:28). As with the earlier part of the prayer, "the Lord" for Paul is no longer Yahweh, but Jesus, and this reflects the apostle's conviction that the Lord Jesus is always present with his followers (Phil. 4:5; 2 Tim. 4:22; see also Matt. 28:20; Acts 18:10).

Bibliography

Aus, R. D. 1971. "Comfort in Judgment: The Use of the Day of the Lord and Theophany Traditions in Second Thessalonians 1." PhD diss., Yale University.

———. 1976. "The Relevance of Isaiah 66:7 to Revelation 12 and 2 Thessalonians 1." *ZNW* 67: 252–68.

Best, E. 1972. *A Commentary on the First and Second Epistles to the Thessalonians.* BNTC. London: Adam & Charles Black.

Bruce, F. F. 1982. *1 and 2 Thessalonians.* WBC 45. Waco: Word.

Carras, G. P. 1990. "Jewish Ethics and Gentile Converts: Remarks on 1 Thess 4,3–8." Pages 306–15 in *The Thessalonian Corre-*

spondence. Edited by R. F. Collins. BETL 87. Leuven: Leuven University Press.

Collins, R. F. 1998. "The Function of Paraenesis in 1 Thess. 4, 1–12; 5, 12–22." *ETL* 74.4: 398–414.

Deidun, T. J. 1981. *New Covenant Morality in Paul*. AnBib 89. Rome: Biblical Institute Press.

Dobschütz, E. von. 1909. *Die Thessalonicher-Briefe*. KEK 10. Göttingen: Vandenhoeck & Ruprecht.

Donfried, K. P. 1985. "The Cults of Thessalonica and the Thessalonian Correspondence." *NTS* 31: 336–56.

Evans, C. A. 1993. "Ascending and Descending with a Shout: Psalm 47.6 and 1 Thessalonians 4.16." Pages 238–53 in *Paul and the Scriptures of Israel*. Edited by C. A. Evans and J. A. Sanders. JSNTSup 83. Sheffield: JSOT Press.

Findlay, G. G. 1891. *The Epistles to the Thessalonians*. CBSC. Cambridge: Cambridge University Press.

Frame, J. E. 1912. *A Critical and Exegetical Commentary on the Epistles of St. Paul to the Thessalonians*. ICC. Edinburgh: T&T Clark.

Gaventa, B. R. 1998. *First and Second Thessalonians*. IBC. Louisville: John Knox.

Gempf, C. 1994. "The Imagery of Birth Pangs in the New Testament." *TynBul* 45: 119–35.

Green, G. L. 2002. *The Letters to the Thessalonians*. PNTC. Grand Rapids: Eerdmans.

Hendriksen, W. 1955. *Exposition of I and II Thessalonians*. NTC. Grand Rapids: Baker Academic.

Hendrix, H. L. 1991. "Archeology and Eschatology at Thessalonica." Pages 107–18 in *The Future of Early Christianity: Essays in Honor of Helmut Koester*. Edited by B. A. Pearson. Minneapolis: Fortress.

Hock, R. F. 1980. "Paul's Life as an Artisan-Missionary." Pages 26–49 in *The Social Context of Paul's Ministry: Tentmaking and Apostleship*. Philadelphia: Fortress.

Hodgson, R. J. 1982. "1 Thess 4:1–12 and the Holiness Tradition (HT)." *SBLSP* 21: 199–215.

Holmes, M. W. 1998. *1 & 2 Thessalonians*. NIVAC. Grand Rapids: Zondervan.

Lightfoot, J. B. 1904. *Notes on the Epistles of St. Paul*. 2nd ed. London: Macmillan.

Malherbe, A. J. 2000. *The Letters to the Thessalonians*. AB 32B. New York: Doubleday.

Marshall, I. H. 1983. *1 and 2 Thessalonians*. NCB. London: Marshall, Morgan & Scott.

———. 1990. "Election and Calling to Salvation in 1 and 2 Thessalonians." Pages 259–76 in *The Thessalonian Correspondence*. Edited by R. F. Collins. BETL 87. Leuven: Leuven University Press.

Martin, D. M. 1995. *1, 2 Thessalonians*. NAC. Nashville: Broadman & Holman.

Milligan, G. 1908. *St. Paul's Epistles to the Thessalonians*. London: Macmillan.

Morris, L. 1991. *The First and Second Epistles to the Thessalonians*. 2nd ed. NICNT. Grand Rapids, Eerdmans.

Pfitzner, V. C. 1967. *Paul and the Agon Motif: Traditional Imagery in the Pauline Literature*. NovTSup 16. Leiden: Brill.

Richard, E. J. 1995. *First and Second Thessalonians*. SP 11. Collegeville, MN: Liturgical Press.

Rosner, B. S. 1995. "Seven Questions for Paul's Ethics: 1 Thessalonians 4:1–12 as a Case Study." Pages 351–60 in *Understanding Paul's Ethics: Twentieth-Century Approaches*. Edited by B. S. Rosner. Grand Rapids: Eerdmans.

Snaith, N. H. 1944. *The Distinctive Ideas of the Old Testament*. New York: Schocken.

Thielman, F. 1994. *Paul and the Law*. Downers Grove, IL: InterVarsity.

Turner, N. 1963. *Syntax*. Vol. 3 of *A Grammar of New Testament Greek*. By J. H. Moulton, W. F. Howard, and N. Turner. Edinburgh: T&T Clark.

Wanamaker, C. A. 1990. *The Epistles to the Thessalonians*. NIGTC. Grand Rapids: Eerdmans.

Weima, J. A. D. 1994. *Neglected Endings: The Significance of the Pauline Letter Closings*. JSNTSup 101. Sheffield: JSOT Press.

———. 1996. "'How You Must Walk to Please God': Holiness and Discipleship in 1 Thessalonians 4:1–12." Pages 98–119 in *Patterns of Discipleship in the New Testament*. Edited by R. N. Longenecker. Grand Rapids: Eerdmans.

———. 1997. "An Apology for the Apologetic Function of 1 Thessalonians 2:1–12." *JSNT* 68: 73–99.

Williams, D. J. 1992. *1 and 2 Thessalonians*. NIBCNT. Peabody, MA: Hendrikson.

1–2 Timothy and Titus

Philip H. Towner

Introduction

Within these three NT letters the OT text is not explicitly cited in the degree that we find in Paul's letters to churches. According to the techniques of NA[27], in which OT quotations are set out in italics along with their corresponding marginal references, there are just two such explicit engagements with the OT text: 1 Tim. 5:18–19; 2 Tim. 2:19. The first of these is accompanied by an introductory formula, while the second is preceded by a signal word that serves the same purpose. Just outside of the category of the quotation, no one doubts that Titus 2:14, with its more integrated use of the OT, represents "explicit" use of the OT. And 1 Tim. 2:13–14 is also a rather clear intensive adaptation of OT material, though its function remains problematic. But OT usage in the letters extends beyond this handful of texts.

At least in theory no part of a NT text is off limits for an OT allusion, echo, or resonance to occur. Within these letters to Timothy and Titus one repository of OT and other traditional language and formulations is the theological or liturgical constructions that occur at various points in each letter. On the one hand, these syntactically and lexically marked pieces are designed to attract attention. They culminate theological, didactic, and paraenetic discussions (e.g., 1 Tim. 1:15–16; 2:5–6; 3:16; 2 Tim. 1:9–10; 2:8, 11–13;

Titus 2:11–14; 3:4–7), or they invite and lead the way in a liturgical response (e.g., 1 Tim. 1:17; 6:15–16), and they do so by compacting theological and liturgical elements into tradition-like statements that evoke ready affirmation. But the very familiarity of these pieces, which makes them effective repositories of traditional freight, may make them ineffective devices for drawing the audience's attention beyond their function as slogans to a more significant engagement with the OT (or other texts). On the other hand, there is good reason to think that Paul fashioned these set pieces himself—that is, they are more than oft-recited hymns or confessions—and that they serve significant purposes within the arguments of their respective contexts. If so, then the OT materials may have been set into them in anticipation that readers/hearers would explore connections with OT discourses.

The role of the OT in its Greek translation (LXX) within these letters is greater than often is perceived. Setting aside explicit quotations and citations for the moment (often set off by introductory formula), we note that intertextual echoes of OT texts were accomplished by means of lexical choice and the repetition of thematic patterns in a degree sufficient to catch the hearers' attention. But there is no reason to think that NT authors always succeeded at this, however saturated in the OT their audiences may have been. It is therefore possible that in nineteen or so centuries of reflection the modern church has succeeded in hearing intentional OT echoes that the first churches missed. Perhaps, too, some of an author's intertextual play was aimed simply at "amusing" himself—more of a way or habit of expressing his theological/eschatological outlook than an item in the discourse that he urgently wanted his audience to apprehend. The task of detecting intentional echoes (as opposed to either simply subliminal employment of OT diction or mere coincidence) is a cumulative one that includes setting out, assessing, and weighing the degree of contact with the OT and exploring the immediate (and more remote) NT context for clues that intentional engagement with the OT has indeed occurred. Engagement, in this sense, whether initiated overtly by quotation or more subtly by echo, will have as its general purpose the framing of a discourse within another literary setting and inviting readers/hearers to locate a particular discourse and perhaps themselves within that other setting. What the author hoped to achieve by this particular engagement with the OT is the specific purpose. The scope of this study is thus determined by two interrelated questions: Where has the author intentionally engaged the OT, and why?

1 Timothy

2:5

The first potentially significant use of the OT in 1 Timothy comes in the christological statement offered in 2:5–6a. (We should note that 1:1 employs "savior" language with an OT precedent [Ps. 25:5]; 1:17, with "king of the ages," likewise employs a Jewish epithet for God [Tob. 13:7, 11]; and the practice of offering prayers for rulers, as in 2:1–2, has roots in the Jewish Diaspora [Ezra 6:10; Bar. 1:11–12; Jer. 29:7; 2 Macc. 3:11].) In this piece, designed to back the preceding statement about the universal salvific will of God (2:4), which is the unifying theme of 2:1–7, the opening affirmation of God's singularity (= universal access to salvation [cf. Rom. 3:29–30]) opens out into a parallel affirmation of the "mediator's" corresponding singularity. This mediator is then identified with the unusual phrase "[the] man Christ Jesus" (*anthrōpos Christos Iēsous*). This phrase establishes the central thrust of the christological formulation: the association of salvation with the humanity of Christ, which the subsequent appeal to the Jesus tradition (2:6a) complements by stressing the substitutionary and representative nature of Jesus' human death and the universal extent of the results ("for all"). But in describing the mediator with this phrase, Paul also accesses the theme within developing messianism of "a man to rule the nations" (Num. 24:7, 17 LXX) and "a man who will save" (Isa. 19:20) (see Horbury 1998: 44–45).

Several themes and ideas link the two OT discourses together and make the combination an attractive and clever interpretive framework for reflecting on the extent of Christ's work. First, each text reports the contents of a "vision" (*horasis* [Num. 24:4; Isa. 19:1]). Second, whether incidental or not, Egypt and Exodus imagery figure in each discourse (Num. 24:8; Isa. 19 throughout), and so do the Assyrians (Num. 24:22; Isa. 19:23–25), though of course the reflections on events, people, and places are from different historical and theological vantage points. Third, and of obvious interest to Paul, each OT vision explores Israel's role in relation to "the nations." In Numbers, Balaam's third oracle casts Israel in the role, under the leadership of "the man," of subjugator or conqueror of the nations. Isaiah's oracle concerning Egypt resumes this theme but adds the dimension of Egyptian worship of God: God's smiting of Egypt is followed by its healing and coming to know God (Isa. 19:19–22). Finally, the central actor in each drama is "the man" (*anthrōpos*). In Num. 24:7 the man will come out of the seed of Israel to rule the nations; 24:17 employs the apocalyptic-like image of a "star rising out of Jacob" and then returns to the more mundane description of "a man" to describe the ascent of this figure to power and victory over the nations. Isaiah 19:20 records God's promise to the Jews in Egypt: "He will send them a man who will save them; he will judge and save them." The MT at Num. 24:7 lacks completely the first reference to "a man"; at 24:17, where the prophecy of "the star rising out of Jacob" does appear, it is subsequently described with the imagery of a "rod" or "scepter," likewise omitting any reference to "a man." There is closer agreement between the Greek and the

Hebrew of Isa. 19. However, where the LXX has "a man who will save," the Hebrew has "a savior" (*môšîaʿ*). If the OT background suggested here does lie behind Paul's reference to *anthrōpos*, most likely it is the LXX that he accesses.

But what is gained by describing the mediator in a way that recalls this background? First, Paul strengthens the argument for the universal gospel, based on the statement of God's will (2:4) and the *heis theos* ("God is one") formula (2:5), by depicting Christ, the mediator, as fulfiller of this OT promise of "a man." Second, Paul in effect completes the development of the messianic "man" theme by depicting the death of Christ as the means by which "the man" takes up his rule and by transforming early OT images of subjugation and judgment into the picture of salvation for the nations, via the gospel, in terms already emerging in Isaiah. As we will see shortly, in 2:8, it is precisely this sense of the church standing in the midst of salvation's spread to the world that defines not only Paul's mission, but also that of the church. "The man Christ Jesus" resumes and completes the messianic theme initiated in the Greek translation of Numbers and Isaiah. Paul invites the church of Ephesus to view its own location within God's redemptive story and its responsibilities in relation to the appearance of this "man."

2:8

At this point Paul enlarges on the instruction about community prayer in 2:1. First, he addresses men, instructing them to pray and to pay attention to the manner in which they do it (2:8). Second, he addresses women, with the same concerns in mind (2:9–10). It is in the instructions to men that the phrase "in every place" (*en panti topō*), which indicates something about the scope of prayer, occurs. Although this phrase is often understood as a local reference (= "in all the house churches [in Ephesus]"), this fails to notice its role in continuing the theme of the universal gospel initiated in 2:1 and carefully developed with various forms of the term "all" (2:1, 2, 4, 6) and other devices to this point (Brox 1969: 131; Bartsch 1966: 48; Roloff 1988: 130–31; Towner 1989: 205–7; Marshall 1999: 444–45). Paul's hearers would not have failed to note the choice of the thematic term.

In the NT the phrase is Pauline, restricted elsewhere to three occurrences (1 Cor. 1:2; 2 Cor. 2:14; 1 Thess. 1:8). Notably, in each of these instances either Paul's prayer (1 Cor. 1:2) or preaching mission (2 Cor. 2:14; 1 Thess. 1:8) is in view. Both of these features and the sense of universality suggest that the phrase originated in and consciously echoes Mal. 1:11: "For from the rising of the sun to its setting my name is great among the nations, and in every place [LXX: *en panti topō*] incense is offered to my name, and a pure offering; for my name is great among the nations, says the LORD of hosts."

Within Judaism, Mal. 1:11 was associated in the targumic tradition with prayer (cf. *Targum Pseudo-Jonathan*; Justin, *Dial.* 117.2; see Gordon 1974). *Didache* 14:3, perhaps influenced by the interests in 1 Tim. 2:8 and certainly by those of Judaism, later conflated Mal. 1:11 and 1:14 to construct a citation, attributed to the Lord, that instructed those quarreling to reconcile before praying. But in the OT context "prayer"—the offering of incense and declaring of God's name—is not the sole topic; rather, it is symbolic of the gracious outward turn of God to the nations and pronouncement of judgment on the corrupt temple-centered worship. The function of the echo in the Pauline texts intends to explore the implications of this prophetic promise in the new eschatological reality of the church. Viewed within this line of OT promise, the churches' prayer (1 Cor. 1:2; 1 Tim. 2:8) and Paul's apostolic ministry (2 Cor. 2:14; 1 Thess. 1:8; 1 Tim. 2:7) become signs of the fulfillment of God's promise to offer salvation to "the nations." Equally, the church in its proclamation and prayer becomes the vehicle by which promise is fulfilled. This is exactly the eschatological perspective that Paul had of his ministry (cf. Rom. 9–11; 15:9–13; Gal. 1:15–16; see Hengel 1983: 49–54), so it is hardly surprising to find it extended here to a discussion of the church's prayer responsibility within the Pauline mission (Towner 1989: 205–7). Within the broader context of 1 Tim. 2:8, this echo of Mal. 1:11 resonates with the theme of universality and prayer in support of Paul's mission (2:1–6) and Paul's self-understanding of his calling to the Gentiles ("herald, apostle . . . teacher of the Gentiles" [2:7]) to underline the intrinsic place of prayer within the gospel ministry and the ministry of this church.

2:13–15a

The presence of a complex OT allusion in 2:13–14 is recognized by all. There is less agreement whether the allusion continues into 2:15a with the statement "but she shall be saved through childbearing." Grounds for this will be given below. Still more disputed is the intention of drawing on the story of creation and the fall: does it "ground" the prohibition of women from teaching or, rather, "illustrate" by forming a link between the OT story and the church's present dilemma? A pressing question facing any interpreter is whether Paul drew upon the Genesis story in response to a competing interpretation of it by false teachers in the community (who perhaps used it to support their views of women, marriage, childbearing, etc. [cf. 4:3]). Without attempting to solve this riddle, I will proceed on the assumption that the allusion to (1) the creation of Adam and Eve, (2) Eve's temptation, and (3) salvation through childbearing in some way explains or supports the prohibition of women from "teaching and having authority over a man" (2:11–12) (cf. the views in Küchler 1986: 13; Holmes 2000). First we seek to establish the nature and extent of the allusion.

The supporting material alludes to and draws together two parts of the Genesis story, three if 2:15a is allusive: (1) the story of creation of Adam and Eve (2:7–8, 15); (2) the story of Eve's temptation (3:6–13); (3) the pronouncement of judgment on the woman as a result of her role in the event (3:16).

Part one consists of the allusion to the creation account of Gen. 2. In addition to the clear general reference to this familiar account, specific links are established by means of the names "Adam" and "Eve" and by the choice of verb "form" (*plassō*). The name "Adam" occurs first in Gen. 2 at 2:16, and then nine times thereafter in the chapter (cf. Luke 3:23; Rom. 5:14 [2x]; 1 Cor. 15:22, 45 [2x]; Jude 14). In the LXX the name "Eve" (*heua*) does not actually occur until 4:1 (cf. 3:20 MT: *ḥawwâ* [= "life"; LXX: *Zōē*]); thereafter it appears rarely in the OT and the NT (Gen. 4:25; Tob. 8:6; 2 Cor. 11:3; cf. Philo, *Alleg. Interp.* 2.81; Josephus, *Ant.* 1.36, 49; *Sib. Or.* 1.29). But clearly the name was well known, and so, not surprisingly, it is back-read naturally into the creation story here. Apart from the characters and the general content

of the story, it is the verb *plassō* (in the NT only here and Rom. 9:20) that links the reflection to the account in Gen. 2:7–8, 15:

> 1 Tim. 2:13: For Adam was formed [*eplasthē*] first, then Eve.
>
> Gen. 2:7: God formed [*eplasen*] the man from the dust of the ground.
> Gen. 2:8: And there [in Eden] he put the man whom he had formed [*eplasen*].
> Gen. 2:15: The LORD God took the man whom he had formed [*eplasen*] and put him in the garden.

The verb *plassō* is not used in the Genesis account of the process by which Eve came into being, but in later retellings of this story it is typically applied to the creation of both man and woman (2 Macc. 7:23; Josephus, *Ant.* 1.32; *1 Clem.* 33:4). Notably, even though the sequence of creation clearly is important to Paul (*prōtos... eita* = "first ... then" [cf. 1 Cor. 15:46; Mark 4:28]), the notion of woman's creation being derivative (taken up in 1 Cor. 11) is absent.

The second part of the allusion is to the episode of the woman's temptation given in Gen. 3. Sequence of action is again an important feature of the presentation in 1 Tim. 2:14. In the case of the temptation and transgression, however, the sequence is reversed to emphasize the priority of the woman's deception and action in relation to the man's; this is done not by reversing the order of occurrence of the names, but (by means of the negative) by locating the initial deception and transgression with the woman. Again the OT account is accessed generally by simple reference to the well-known episode. Specific access is made by means of a thematic verb, *apataō*, which occurs, as in the LXX account (Gen. 3:13), first in the simplex form and second in reference to the woman (a departure from the OT account, for reasons of stylistic emphasis) in the compound form *exapataō*. The switch to the compound form of the verb is probably stylistic, serving to set the woman and the man apart in the fall and to stress the priority of the woman's deception. Intensification is not the likely force of the change; the compound had already found its way into the traditional account of this scene (2 Cor. 11:3) without any specific added nuance to the deception (i.e., in the sense of sexual deceit). A second intentional verbal connection with the divine interrogation of Gen. 3:12–13 may also be present in the decision to refer for a second time to the personal name "Adam" (as in Gen. 3:12) but in the case of Eve to the impersonal "woman" (*gynē* [as in Gen. 3:13]).

> 1 Tim. 2:14: And Adam was not deceived [*ēpatēthē*], but the woman was deceived [*exapatētheisa*] and became a transgressor.
>
> Gen. 3:12: Adam said, "The woman you gave to be with me, she gave to me from the tree and I ate."
>
> Gen. 3:13: And the LORD God said to the woman, "What have you done?" The woman answered, "The serpent deceived [*ēpatēsen*] me, and I ate."

A third part exists if the allusion extends as far as 2:15a: "But she will be saved through childbearing." The main reason for suggesting this possibility is the term *teknogonia* ("childbearing"), which may well be a refashioning of the idea expressed in the verb-object combination *texē tekna* ("you shall give birth to children") in Gen. 3:16. Also, by extending the allusion to this clause, which retains the singular as in the Gen. 3 account, we may be helped to explain why the shift to the plural (from "she" to "they") is delayed until after the initial clause (see further below).

> 1 Tim. 2:15a: But she will be saved (preserved) through childbearing [*teknogonia*].
>
> Gen. 3:16: And to the woman he said, "I will greatly multiply your pains and your groaning; in pain you shall bring forth children [*texē tekna*], and your submission shall be to your husband, and he shall rule over you."

Far more complicated than establishing the nature and extent of the OT allusion is deciding the way in which it functions in this text. Before looking at the best options for this, we will briefly consider developments in the speculation on these related Genesis episodes in Judaism. The question behind this excursion is whether or not the author of 1 Timothy is indebted to such developments.

A possible Jewish basis for Paul's argumentation in 2:13–15a may be considered in two parts.

First, the basic argument for the superiority of the first created—that is, from the priority of creation—offered in 2:13 (in support of 2:11–12) is found widely in Greek and Jewish and rabbinic sources (for the argument in Greek writers, see Plato, *Resp.* 412c; *Leg.* 11, 917a; for the argument in Judaism particularly linked to creation, see *Exod. Rab.* 21:6; *Midr. Ps.* 114 §9; *Sipre Deut.* 11, 10 §37 [76a]; see Str-B 3:256–57, 626, 645; Jervell 1960: 71–121; and esp. Nauck 1950: 95–97; Küchler 1986: 17–32; Dibelius and Conzelmann 1972: 47; Roloff 1988: 136–38; Oberlinner 1994: 97–99). The rabbinic reasoning "first is best" (cf. 1 Cor. 11:8–9) can be seen in *Exod. Rab.* 21:6: "Moses . . . went to divide the sea, but the sea refused to comply, exclaiming, 'What, before you shall I divide? Am I not greater than you? For I was created on the third day and you on the sixth'" (cf. *Sipre Deut.* 37: "This is also true concerning God's actions—whatever is most precious comes first").

In applying the argument "first is best," Paul does not appear to cite a rabbinic formula that made use of Gen. 2. His literary indebtedness to rabbinic thought is limited to the method of argumentation, and for all we know, his application of it to men and women by way of allusion to Gen. 2 is novel (cf. 1 Cor. 11). It is often pointed out that in Judaism and Greco-Roman cultures the subordinate status of the woman was assumed. Josephus states emphatically, "[The law] says, 'A woman is inferior to her husband in all things.' Let her, therefore, be obedient to him; not so that he should abuse her, but that she may acknowledge her duty to her husband; for God hath given the authority to the husband" (*Ag. Ap.* 2.201 [cf. Philo, *Hypothetica* 7.3]). This being the assumption, the question of why Paul strove to make such a point via Gen. 2 becomes all the more acute.

The tendency among those holding to a biblical feminist perspective has been to play down this element of the argument and focus more on 2:14 (see Towner 1997). This is not particularly helpful and only avoids the question. The point from creation seems too central to bypass; however, the wild card that the heresy and the likelihood of women's involvement in it recommends proceeding with due caution. Here I will simply enumerate the possible explanations for taking up this argument, with its adaptation of Gen. 2, insisting only that 2:13 cannot be sidestepped.

(1) Many understand Paul or a Paulinist to be applying a creation principle with which he was

in full agreement. If it is Paul writing, then here he insists on the view that he uniformly held (cf., e.g., 1 Cor. 11:3–16; 14:33–35; see Knight 1992; Hurley 1981; Moo 1980) that, based on the creative will of God, proscribed women from teaching and holding positions of authority over men in the church. If the letter is regarded as the work of a Paulinist, then application of the Jewish argument is held to reflect the return to a patriarchalism that the Pauline gospel had challenged (cf. Gal. 3:28), a return perhaps designed as an answer to women who (under the influence of an overrealized eschatology or an overly enthusiastic implementation of an equality principle [Gal. 3:28]) had asserted themselves in ways that caused a disturbance in the community (Roloff 1988: 128–30; Schüssler Fiorenza 1983). Although neither variation on this view requires all of the rabbinic chauvinistic assumptions to be in the author's mind, the view suggests that the author drew quite naturally on the assumptions of the day, including the principle that first created is best.

(2) The creation account may have been employed not for its universal applicability to any and all man/woman situations, but rather in order to combat a specific view or correct an interpretation of the creation account somehow linked with the heresy (see Wire 1990: 116–34, esp. 122). This approach takes various shapes that tend to agree that 2:13 must be taken seriously. In one of the more plausible arguments, Schlarb (1990 [for another approach, see Kroeger and Kroeger 1992]) suggests that Spirit-enthusiasm linked with speculation on creation accounts (myths, genealogies, etc. [1:4; 4:1, 7]) contrived a pre-fall paradigm for present Christian living (celibacy, vegetarianism [4:3]) that also supported a revolutionary interpretation of women's roles in the community. In response (2:13–14), the author refers to a correct reading of the Genesis material to reorient the church's thinking around a view of the present that accounts properly for both creation and the realities of sin and redemption. Of course, any attempt to interpret the use of the OT material as a response to a specific misreading of it faces the daunting challenge of plausibility. However, from what can be gleaned about the heretics' speculative approach to the OT and the heresy's influence on women, the challenge would

seem to be unavoidable, even if some questions must remain open in the end.

Once it is recognized that the argumentation and use of Genesis here resemble to some degree rabbinic logic, and that the prevailing Jewish view included the subordinate status of women, something of a sidebar argument is often smuggled into the discussion: the Jewish chauvinistic belief in the inherent gullibility of women (e.g., Philo, *QG* 1.33, 46). However, in view of the roles in which women participated in the early church (teaching [Acts 18:26]; prophesying [1 Cor. 14:26]; some level of leadership/ministry status [e.g., Rom. 16:1, 3, 7; see Keener 1992: 237–57), it is not at all evident that Paul endorsed such a view, which, in any case, would sit rather awkwardly with the positive statement in 2:11 about women's learning. This particular view, however widespread it might have been, is irrelevant to a discussion of the argument in 1 Tim. 2.

Second, the sentiment expressed in 2:14 ("And Adam was not deceived [*ēpatēthē*], but the woman was deceived [*exapatētheisa*] and became a transgressor") bears at least a superficial resemblance to some of the Jewish speculative comments on the fall into sin, and especially the deception of Eve, based on the same Genesis material. These developments led in several directions, not all of which are useful. These developments must be included in order to decide how Paul understood the texts that he cited (cf. 2 Cor. 11:3), but the dating of some of these is far from certain, and a pattern of development is difficult to fix.

(1) Sir. 25:24 ("From a woman sin had its beginning, and because of her we all die") bears no material relation to the form or language of 2:14. However, it offers an interpretive reflection on the origins of sin and death, for which the woman takes full blame, based on the Genesis account, which could be thought to lie behind the second statement of rationale for women not teaching or holding authority over men (Nauck 1950: 96–98; but see Holmes 2000: 268–72).

(2) Philo may not have developed the idea, but he gave a certain elegance to the traditional link between the soft and weak feminine nature and gullibility and susceptibility to deception (*QG* 1.33; cf. *Pirqe R. El.* 13 [see Str-B 1:137–38]). Philo's further reflections on Gen. 3:16–19 in *Alleg. Interp.* 3.59–61 are too allegorical to fit

precisely within the "deception of Eve" motif, but the way he interprets the character of feminine human nature as intrinsic to the process leading from the serpent's deception to the man's eating of the forbidden fruit fits in well with his statement on her inborn susceptibility to falsehood. His thinking is more or less reiterated by certain modern scholars who distinguish between the rationality of men and the relational, nurturing bent of women and draw conclusions about their relative strengths and weaknesses with regard to "preserving the apostolic tradition" (e.g., Schreiner 1995: 145–46).

(3) Far more provocative and exotic is the development in the speculation on the fall by which Eve's temptation and sin came to be regarded as sexual in nature. Such views are widespread, though the dating of these texts is not always certain. Almost certainly, *2 En.* 31:6 and 4 Macc. 18:6–8 reflect the deception of Eve as an event of sexual seduction, and rabbinic and later Christian sources do so as well (cf. *b. Yebam.* 103b; *Gen. Rab.* 18:6; *Prot. Jas.* 13:1; *Barn.* 12:5; *Diogn.* 12:8; see Küchler 1986: 44–50; Hanson 1968: 65–77).

(4) Texts preserved in later gnostic writings demonstrate an interest in Eve as prototype of the superior woman (Rudolph 1983: 211–12, 215–16, 270–72; for the possible relevance, see Kroeger and Kroeger 1992: 105–25).

Those who detect this sort of background, especially the first three of the four given above, behind 2:14, often depend upon the capacity of the verbs *apataō* and especially *exapataō* to refer to sexual deceit (esp. Hanson 1968; Küchler 1986). Although this need not be disputed, the compound verb in question already has a nearer corollary in 2 Cor. 11:3, where in another Pauline use of the deception of Eve motif it served (similarly) to raise the question of the Corinthian church's susceptibility to false teaching. Neither Pauline case reflects the sort of rabbinic elaboration that goes beyond the basic thought of "deception" to something as specific as sexual deception.

Determining the use to which the Genesis material is put in this passage begins with the question of why Paul prohibited women from teaching and holding authority. If the reason was simply Paul's general principle, based on Genesis (the creation order), then one has to correlate this assumption with the evidence that women took

vital roles in ministry elsewhere, and one also has to accept the inescapable implication of 2:14 that Paul believed women to be more susceptible to deception than men or less capable by nature to deal with false teachers. If, however, the instructions and backing were given in response to a particular interpretation of the Genesis account in Ephesus that somehow fueled inappropriate activities of women (teaching in a way that shamed men/husbands, somehow furthering the heresy, eschewing marriage because of the false teaching, etc.), then 2:13–15a supports the measures to be taken (2:11–12) by reproducing a better reading of the Genesis story. There are strong indications that women were involved in the heresy and so were teaching false doctrine; there are strong indications that certain elements of the traditional role of women (marriage and childbearing) were being set aside on the basis of the false teaching or secular cultural developments (Marshall 1999: 466; Towner 2006). If the overrealized views alluded to in 2 Tim. 2:18 were at all within the purview of 1 Timothy (Towner 1989; Schlarb 1990), then all the chemistry necessary to unloose traditional values would have been present. In such an atmosphere of enthusiasm, where the operative concept was "reversal of roles," if women were guilty of teaching in a way that abused authority and disrespected their male counterparts, 2:13 is a reminder that the creation order is still in effect and men are to be respected (omission of the mitigating factor included in 1 Cor. 11 is understandable where women have already stepped over the line). If heretical speculation on the early chapters of Genesis (fueled by mistaken notions of eschatology) somehow influenced women to think that they were free from the constraints and limitations brought on by the fall into sin (or more specifically if they appealed to the Adam-sinner model of Rom. 5 to make their better claim to the right to teach [Marshall 1999: 467]), 2:14 reminds women of their role in the fall and of the present unfinished nature of Christian existence, and it does so in a way that aptly illustrates the deception of women in Ephesus by false teachers (cf. 2 Cor. 11:3).

Finally, 2:15a, with its allusion to Gen. 3:16, serves two related purposes. First, in response to confusion about the times and women's roles, it prolongs the allusion to Gen. 3 in a way that establishes the eschatological "location" of the Ephesian Christian women as still being in that paradoxical place of pain (struggle, tension, sin, etc.) and divine promise. Second, it reinforces the continuing relevance, importance, and value of the traditional role model being subverted by the heresy (cf. 4:3). There is no reason why the reference to "salvation" in the promise—"But she will be saved through childbearing"—cannot strike two (or more) chords at once. In fact, with the tape of Gen. 3 already playing, it is hard to imagine that the attentive hearer or reader would escape reflecting on the Protoevangelion (the promised defeat of the serpent in Gen. 3) or indeed on the pronouncement that the woman was to be under the lordship of the man. But Paul did not bring these things out. Instead, the final fleeting allusion to the Genesis account develops into the instruction to women (plural) generally to "work out their salvation" in the domestic sphere by ensuring that they manifest the marks of authentic Christian existence.

4:3–4

In 4:1–3a comes a prophetic word of the Spirit designed to place the heresy troubling the church into an eschatological framework. In this statement, apostasy is a sign of the last times, and the presence of the heresy in this church is an indication that the last times are underway as the letter is read. (Here Paul draws on the well-known motif of end-time apostasy [see Gaston 1970: 433–68]. His language for accessing this motif includes the tendency to "hold to deceiving spirits" [*prosechontes pneumasin planois*]. In Isa. 19:14 we read of a "spirit of error" [singular: *pneuma planēseōs*], which is said to have been poured into the Egyptians by God. Given the link quite probably already made with Isa. 19:20 in 2:5 ["a man who will save"], and thereby with that broader Isaiah text, a return to that source here is not out of the question. Quite possibly, the motif of end-time apostasy includes the theme of God's intentional [or permissive if not active] "letting go and confusing" of those who have chosen the way of disobedience.) The statement goes on further to describe certain features of the heretics and their views. This is one of the letter's rare glimpses of the actual practices and views of the false teachers. And it is in the course of describing their abstention from (certain) foods that Paul engages the Genesis account again.

In 4:3 Paul denounces the opponents for their "abstinence from certain foods which God created to be received with thanksgiving" (*apechesthai brōmatōn, ha ho theos ektisen eis metalēmpsin meta eucharistias*). The corrective assertion draws upon and in two ways alludes to the story of creation and its elaboration in the early chapters in Genesis. First, the argument adapts Gen. 9:3 specifically, since it negates the erroneous limitations (i.e., *apechesthai brōmatōn*) on the basis that God gave everything for food: "Every living reptile shall be meat for you, as the green vegetables, I have given everything to you [for food]" (*kai pan herepton ho estin zōn hymin estai eis brōsin hōs lachana chortou dedōka hymin ta panta*). It also recalls the stress on divine initiative in the earlier affirmation in Genesis of God's provision ("God gave") of vegetables "for food" (*eis brōsin* [1:29; 2:9]; *brōsei* [2:16]; cf. 3:2; cf. Deut. 26:11). Thus a simple allusion taps into a broader stream of tradition about the source of foods. Second, in the counterassertion about foods, "which God created," the subject/verb combination that asserts God's role as Creator recalls the account of creation. Selection of the verb *ktizō* reflects the preference for this verb (or its cognate noun) in Hellenistic-Jewish (Wis. 9:2; 13:5; 14:11; Sir. 39:25–27; 3 Macc. 5:11) and NT discussions of creation (Rom. 1:25; 1 Cor. 11:9; Eph. 2:10, 15; 3:9; 4:24; Col. 1:16 [2x]; 3:10; Rev. 4:11 [2x]; 10:6; Matt. 19:4; Mark 13:19). In the LXX of Genesis the verb "make" (*poieō*) predominates in the early chapters (in the NT see Matt. 19:4; Mark 10:6; Acts 17:24, 26), with *ktizō* entering only in 14:9. The use of *ktizō* as a replacement to access the early accounts of God's creative activity is not problematic; it prepares the way for the polemical coup de grâce in 4:4a.

In 4:4a we see the foundation for the previous counterassertions: "for the whole creation of God is good" (*hoti pan ktisma theou kalon*). In this statement, which itself quite obviously echoes the divine assessment that closes Gen. 1, the specific connections are made by the adjective "all" (*pan*), by reference to the Creator "God" (*theou*) and by the predicate adjective "good" (*kalon*): "And God saw all the things that he had made, and behold, they were very good" (*kai eiden ho theos ta panta hosa epoiēsen, kai idou kala lian*) (Gen. 1:31).

Again the shift from the *poieō* word group to *ktisma* reflects preferences shaped by the tradition.

The logic of Paul's polemical response to the heretical food asceticism is completed in this statement: "And nothing is to be rejected, if it is received with thanksgiving." The same argument—permitting the consumption of all foods with the proviso of thanksgiving—was made in 1 Cor. 10:26, 30. And the logic here is not hard to follow.

In 4:3–4 Paul undoubtedly has drawn on Gen. 9:3 as a historical-theological precedent for the specific eating of meat, subsequently backing this by allusion to the more fundamental statement in Gen. 1:31 of the goodness of God's creation. The tougher question is, Why has he done so?

To answer that question we need to think creatively about the heretical teaching alluded to in 4:2 (see commentary on 1 Tim. 2:13–15a above). On the assumption that we should link the ascetic tendencies alluded to here to the reference to the heretics' speculative exegesis ("myths and genealogies" [1:4]), in the sense that the former were somehow grounded in the latter, it is likely that Paul is turning an apostolic interpretation of OT Scripture against some novel exegesis of Genesis by the opponents. Other patterns of the heretical outlook, such as an overly enthusiastic (overrealized) eschatology, which led them to anticipate the end time by living according to a pre-fall pattern, could provide the theology that was fueling the asceticism (Schlarb 1990: 123–24). The effect of Paul's counterargument would be: (1) to affirm the ongoing relevance of the pattern of life reflected in Gen. 9:7, (2) to discourage (or deny implicitly) attempts to live beyond the present realities (including the ongoing presence of sin), and yet (3) to affirm the freedom in Christ (note the emphasis on thanksgiving and prayer [4:4b–5]) to partake of all foods because of their created basis. Although it remains conjectural that Paul specifically corrected aberrant exegesis of Genesis texts, it is nonetheless certain that the argument from Genesis intends to counter the practice of abstention from certain foods (= meat).

5:18–19

This section of the letter gives instructions concerning the two administrative matters of remuneration and discipline of elders. In each case Paul cites OT texts (and in the first case also the Jesus tradition) that had already been incorporated into the early church's halakic framework. The citations function separately and we will take them

in order. (We should briefly note that 5:5 employs OT language or images. The image of the devout widow who hopes in God taps into the rich tradition of God's special care for widows and orphans [Jer. 49:11; cf. Deut. 14:29; 26:12–13; Ps. 68:5].)

In 5:17 Paul instructs concerning the compensation ("double honor") of elders, "namely those who are engaged in preaching and teaching" (Marshall 1999: 612). The potential ambiguity of the instruction, which refers literally to "honor" (*timē*) and therefore possibly to something other than payment (i.e., community esteem [cf. 6:1]), is resolved in the subsequent supporting citation of Scripture. The OT prooftext is initiated in 5:18a, connecting it with the preceding instructions, with the formal introductory formula "for the Scripture says" (see Rom. 9:17; 10:11; cf., e.g., 4:3; 11:2; Gal. 4:30).

The content of the quotation, "Do not muzzle the threshing ox," is a slightly reorganized rendering of Deut. 25:4 LXX:

Deut. 25:4 LXX: *ou phimōseis boun aloōnta.*

1 Tim. 5:18a: *boun aloōnta ou phimōseis.*

The shift of the object to the head of the sentence (so also Philo, *Virtues* 145) may simply be in accord with better Greek style, but it probably also corresponds to the different emphasis created in the NT adaptation of the OT command. Whereas the word order of the Greek in Deut. 25:4 rather slavishly copies the Hebrew, which in the legal setting stresses obedience (and therefore the "you"), the rearrangement in 1 Tim. 5:18a allows for stress to be placed on the "threshing ox," which by analogy stands for the laboring elders who are the main topic.

The Mosaic command envisioned one of the processes by which threshing was accomplished. The ox was driven over a threshing floor, the animal's hooves separating the grain from the stalk and chaff.

By the time Paul employs the OT principle in this letter, he can assume that its application (which is nonetheless reinforced by a Jesus logion) is clearly understood. This perhaps was not the case in 1 Cor. 9:9–10, where Paul takes the time to disabuse the Corinthian congregation of any simplistic material notions concerning the true import of the Deuteronomy text by drawing on another development of the agricultural logic that promised the plowman and the thresher a share in the harvest (cf. Sir. 6:19; James 5:7). But in any case, between the original command set down in Deuteronomy, which presumably was in fact given originally out of concern for the proper care of oxen, and the application of the OT text in 1 Tim. 5 and 1 Cor. 9, the text had passed through the grid of Jewish exegesis to yield finally the analogy that Paul employs here. The argument works a fortiori by applying the reasoning of the law concerning provision for working oxen to the situation of those laboring in the gospel ministry.

This commandment had been a well of deeper meaning for the rabbinic scholars (see Str-B 3:382–99). It was used as a particular illustration of the "lesser to greater" logic that urged that God's concern for animals implied far greater concern for people (*b. B. Meṣiʿa* 88b; *b. Giṭ.* 62a; 1 Cor. 9:9; Philo, *Virtues* 145 [for additional references, see Knoch 1988: 40]). Pharisaic interpretation apparently deduced from this text a broader principle: oxen stand for all species of labor, including humans (Brewer 1992), and Paul may have drawn on this halakic rule instead of engaging in creative midrash himself. In any case, on the assumption that 1 Timothy is linked to Paul, this commandment had already been drawn out in the tradition, the NT precedent being 1 Cor. 9:9, and therefore the force of the argument and its Mosaic-to-apostolic authority required no elaboration. In both Pauline texts Paul followed or adapted the Jewish interpretation of the text and applied it to material support of those engaged in ministry. Notably, the same conclusion had been pursued and reached along other related tangents, as the succeeding quotation of the Jesus logion shows (Matt. 10:10; Luke 10:7).

In 5:19 the attention shifts to another administrative concern. Probably as a result of the heresy and its influence on some of the church's leadership, Paul addresses the issue of due process in the examination and (if necessary) discipline of elders. The next quotation occurs in connection with the evidence-gathering step of the procedure. In order to control or avoid the kind of damage that might be caused by rash and unsubstantiated allegations in a situation where leaders were under suspicion and where others may have been vying to move into leadership ranks, Paul again draws on Mosaic legislation with a long history of acceptance in Judaism and in the church to ensure that due process is followed.

The relevant command accessed here is a combination of two texts in Deuteronomy LXX. In reference to sentences of death, Deut. 17:6 stipulates,

> He shall die on the testimony of two or three witnesses [*epi dysin martysin ē epi trisin martysin*]; a man who is put to death shall not be put to death for one witness.

In a more general context, Deut. 19:15 stipulates,

> One witness shall not stand to testify against a man for any iniquity, or for any fault, or for any sin which he may commit; by the mouth of two witnesses, or by the mouth of three witnesses [*epi stomatos dyo martyrōn kai epi stomatos triōn martyrōn*], shall every word be established.

In 5:19 Paul sets out the adversarial setting freely according to the specific situation and "accused" at hand: "Do not accept any accusation against an elder." The adverbial exceptive phrase that introduces the correct procedure to follow ("except" [*ektos ei mē*]) shows the meaning of the proscribed procedure to be precisely that which both Deuteronomic texts disallow: establishment of guilt on the basis of a single witness. In turning then to correct procedure, the phrase "on the basis of two or three witnesses" (*epi dyo ē triōn martyrōn*) reflects certain features of both Deuteronomy texts. The conjunction "or" (*ē*) and the omission of the word "mouth" (*stomatos*) reflect the wording of Deut. 17:6, but the genitive object of the preposition (*dyo ē triōn martyrōn*) corresponds to Deut. 19:15. On the assumption that it is the presence of the word "mouth" in the Greek of Deut. 19:15 that determines the genitives that complete the object (also present in the Hebrew of 17:6 but absent in the Greek translation at that point), Paul's genitive construction in 5:19 may correspond more closely to the more general application of the multiple witness principle in Deut. 19:15, with "mouth" having been omitted to give a smoother expression. Since the death penalty is not under discussion (cf. Heb. 10:28), it is not surprising that the broader application of the witness principle in Deut. 19:15 would be most applicable.

However, the form of the citation/maxim as it occurs here may also have been shaped by the early church's paradosis. Paul clearly cites Deut. 19:15 most closely in 2 Cor. 13:1, dropping only the repeated phrase, *epi stomatos*, but including the subject/verb combination "every matter shall be established" (*stathēsetai pan rhēma*). Though lacking the introductory formula, it is a formal quote, as the syntax shows. The principle was also known within the Jesus tradition, where Matt 18:16 preserves a slightly more attenuated citation of Deut. 19:15, with a change of conjunctions (from *kai* to *ē*) and the change from the future passive to the aorist passive form of the verb (*stathē*). In reference to the death penalty, Heb. 10:28 naturally utilizes the multiple-witness principle (with slight modification) as it occurs in Deut. 17:6 in connection with the death penalty.

In invoking this OT principle by means of quotation, Paul did not teach in a particularly innovative way. Both the Jesus tradition and numerous other allusions to the law of multiple witnesses (e.g., John 8:17) and apparent applications of it in various practical and eschatological situations (Matt. 18:19–20; 27:38; Mark 6:7; Luke 9:30, 32; 10:1; 24:13; John 20:12; Acts 1:10; Heb. 6:18; Rev. 11:3–4) show how deeply rooted the principle had become in the teaching of the early church. This principle governing due process in the giving and weighing of evidence was mediated to the early church from Judaism. Josephus (*Life* 256) and the Qumran writings (CD-A IX, 17–X, 2 [cf. *m. Sanh.* 5:4]) demonstrate how the principle was present and applicable in Jewish life in general and in fact did not need to be quoted to be understood.

Thus Paul gives directions in the two administrative matters in 5:18–19 by drawing explicitly upon OT texts whose principles had already been appropriated in the early church (especially in Pauline churches) and in Judaism. The first principle, concerning the support of laborers, was accessed at some point in the tradition (not necessarily originally by Paul or freshly at this point [cf. 1 Cor. 9:9–10]) by means of allegorical or midrashic techniques. The second principle, concerning requisite witnesses, involved no such exegetical procedures. Direct quotation of the OT was intended to ensure that the authority of the instructions and the gravity of the situation were properly understood.

6:1

In 6:1–2 Paul takes up matters related to the behavior of slaves in relation to their masters. Two situations are envisioned, with 6:1 addressing slaves who belong to unbelieving masters. Although the circumstances occasioning these instructions are not spelled out, they parallel other NT texts that in some cases, at least, probably aimed to restore equilibrium threatened by hasty assumptions made about the gospel and freedom. In Ephesus some expression of that problem (perhaps aggravated in some way by the heresy) probably also lay behind the instructions (Marshall 1999: 626–27).

The instructions in 6:1, where believing slaves are called to respect their unbelieving masters, set out the good testimony as the ultimate objective: "so that the name of God and the teaching may not be blasphemed." Here Paul echoes Isa. 52:5 LXX:

> 1 Tim. 6:1b: that the name of God . . . might not be blasphemed [*hina mē to onoma tou theou . . . blasphēmētai*]

> Isa. 52:5 LXX: Thus says the LORD, "On account of you, my name is continually blasphemed among the Gentiles" [*tade legei kyrios, di' hymas dia pantos to onoma mou blasphēmeitai en tois ethnesin*].

The thought was thematic. Ezekiel says much the same thing in different words (36:20 [cf. CD-A XII, 7–8]). And Paul himself, in Rom. 2:24, had already cited the Isaiah text more fully (including the causal *di' hymas* ["on account of you"] and reference to the Gentiles), making the same change from the original first person to the third person required by his discourse. The only other alteration required here in 6:1b is the shift to the subjunctive form of the verb to suit the preceding conjunction, "in order that" (*hina*).

It is debatable whether Paul accesses the OT directly or rather echoes it indirectly and unconsciously in citing what had become a commonplace in the early church (cf. James 2:7; 2 Pet. 2:2; Rev. 13:6; 16:9, 11, 21; *2 Clem.* 13:2; Pol. *Phil.* 10:3; see Marshall 1999: 630). Either way, the function of the usage is to equate believing slaves with the Jews depicted in the Isaiah text, and the unbelieving masters with the (implied) Gentiles of the OT text/tradition: disobedience on the part of the Christian slaves would complete the equation, making them responsible for provoking unbelievers to slander God's name, while in fact the behavior of God's people should rather adorn God's name and make it attractive to unbelievers.

In the remainder of 1 Timothy several texts employ OT diction or concepts that had become a part of the early church's liturgical lexicon, including 6:11 (the designation "man of God" [*anthrōpos theou*] has OT roots [Judg. 13:6; 1 Sam. 2:27; 1 Kings 13:1]), 6:15 (the lofty language recalls certain Hellenistic-Jewish reflections: for "sovereign" [*dynastēs*], see Sir. 10:24; 16:11; 46:5; 2 Macc. 12:15; for "King of kings," see 2 Macc. 13:4; 3 Macc. 5:35), and 6:16 ("whom no person has seen or can see" [*hon eiden oudeis anthrōpōn oude idein dynatai*] is based on Exod. 33:20 and may be a loose reworking of it: "And he said, 'You shall not be able to see my face; for no one shall see my face and live'" [*kai eipen ou dynēsē idein mou to prosōpon ou gar mē idē anthrōpos to prosōpon mou kai zēsetai*]). Texts in this category apparently have no overt intention of drawing the audience back into the OT narrative world or of appealing to the authority of the OT.

The language of 6:7 ("For we brought nothing into the world, so that we can take nothing out of it") shows some affinity with the wisdom sayings of Job 1:21; Ps. 49:16–17; Eccles. 5:14–16. However, the thought is so well documented in the ancient world (cf. Philo, *Spec. Laws* 1.294–295; Ps.-Phoc. 110–111; *Anthologia Palatina* 10:58; Seneca, *Ep.* 102.25; *m. 'Abot* 6:9; *b. Yoma* 86b; Luke 12:16–21; Herm. *Sim.* 50:6; see Dibelius and Conzelmann 1972: 84–85; Menken 1977: 535–36) that it is impossible to limit the source of the proverbial saying, as it appears here, to the OT, although OT wisdom may indeed have played a seminal role in bringing the opinion into the ethical thought of the early church.

The same is true of the warning in 6:17 against boasting and trusting in one's wealth. The prohibition against hoping in wealth resembles slightly the language and more negatively framed themes of Ps. 61:11 LXX (62:10 ET): "Do not hope in unrighteousness...; if wealth should flow in, do

not set your heart on it"; however, the parallels in Prov. 23:4–5; Jer. 9:23 (cf. Ps.-Phoc. 62) suggest instead the echoing of a theme, and the alternative wisdom of placing hope in God and his provisions in contrast to the illusory benefits of material wealth also has a wider base (cf. Ps. 52:7).

2 Timothy

Second Timothy differs in two distinct ways from 1 Timothy and Titus. First, it exhibits a different genre, more closely resembling the paraenetic letter and more limited in scope to instructing its addressee (Johnson 2001: 320–24). Second, within the Pauline story 2 Timothy serves as the closing chapter. At the center of this conclusion are Paul's suffering and death. These themes are intertwined throughout the letter, finally reaching a climax in 4:16–18. In this closing section a web of OT allusions allows Paul's death to be viewed in a deeply theological way.

2:7

Coming as the conclusion to a well-defined section of paraenesis (2:1–6), 2:7 urges Timothy to "grasp" what has been said. This didactic formula is well known (e.g., Plato, *Ep.* 352c). The preceding paraenesis amounts to an exhortation to faithfulness and perseverance in ministry that begins with the command to be empowered by grace and to transmit Paul's teaching to other capable teachers (2:1–2). Then, a succession of three metaphors (the soldier, the athlete, and the farmer) enjoins single-mindedness, perseverance, and patience (2:3–6). Presumably, 2:7 addresses the challenge of discerning the meaning of the metaphors and their relation both to the initial commands and to Timothy himself. Thus Paul backs up the imperative "Grasp what I am saying" with a statement of promise. And in the promise we may detect an allusion to Prov. 2:6 LXX.

2 Tim. 2:7: For the Lord will give you understanding in all things [*dōsei gar soi ho kyrios synesin en pasin*].

Prov. 2:6 LXX: Because the Lord gives wisdom, and from his presence come knowledge and understanding [*hoti kyrios didōsin sophian kai apo prosōpou autou gnōsis kai synesis*].

The LXX follows the Hebrew closely, substituting "presence" (lit., "face") for "mouth" as the source of knowledge and understanding.

Second Timothy 2:7 parallels Prov. 2:6 in the verb "give" (*didōmi*), in the designation "Lord" (*kyrios*), and in the reference to "understanding" (*synesis*). Differences between the texts are also noticeable: (1) the verb is third-person future in 2 Tim. 2:7, third-person present in Prov. 2:6; (2) 2 Tim. 2:7 personalizes the promise by adding the pronoun "you" as indirect object, while Prov. 2:6 is general; (3) "Lord" has the article in 2 Tim. 2:7 but lacks it in Prov. 2:6; (4) the threefold reference to wisdom, knowledge, and understanding in Prov. 2:6 is reduced to "understanding in all things" in 2 Tim. 2:7.

In view of the reduction, modifications, and proverbial ring, it is possible that 2:7 represents a commonplace distantly linked to a saying like Prov. 2:6 (the idea that "understanding" is a divine gift is widely expressed [Exod. 31:6; 1 Kings 3:11–12; Dan. 1:17; 2:21; *T. Reub.* 6:4; *T. Levi* 18:7; Col. 1:9; 2:2; James 1:5]), but the possibility of intentional interaction with Prov. 2:6 is strengthened by the wider discussion in Prov. 2. There we notice the contrast between the one (singular: "you"; "[my] son" [e.g., 2:1, 2, 3]) who diligently pursues wisdom and "those who have forsaken the upright way" (plural: *hoi enkataleipontes* [2:13]). In the wider discussion of 2 Timothy this latter group could correspond to the opponents and also to those who have forsaken the apostle, whose desertion is described with the language of Prov. 2:13 (4:16: "all have forsaken me" [*pantes me enkatelipon*]; 4:10: "Demas deserted me" [*Dēmas ... me enkatelipen*]; cf. 1:15). If this broader comparison is intended, then in these instructions Paul reconfigures the wisdom tradition's ideal way of wisdom and uprightness (i.e., according to Prov. 2, "the fear of the LORD") as the way of suffering for the gospel that the apostle has exemplified and Timothy is to walk in. In the new context, the promise of the Lord's assistance applies first to understanding the immediate teaching; however, in view of the wide scope implied by "in all things," and if the Proverbs background is considered, the gift of insight extends beyond the immediate passage to the dangerous path of suffering that still lies ahead for Timothy. As the citation is applied

to Timothy, "the Lord" is to be understood as Jesus (Marshall 1999: 731, 720).

The wisdom tradition's way of wisdom thus supplies a template for the way of apostolic suffering. In either articulation, the starting point is "the fear of the Lord" (Prov. 1:7; 2:5–6), which in 2 Timothy is reshaped in terms of the vital concept of a life that is "godly" (*eusebōs* [3:12]). "Godliness" (*eusebeia*) was closely associated with "the fear of the Lord" in Prov. 1:7 LXX (cf. Isa. 11:2; 33:6; see Towner 1996; Marshall 1999: 135–44). Its use in 2 Timothy to define the authentic life of faith incorporates the goal of the pursuit of God from Proverbs and sets in contrast the opponent who forsakes that way. The OT allusion in 2:7 (cf. 3:12) invites Timothy to equate the way of suffering in godliness with the gift of God according to Prov. 2.

2:19

At 2:14 Paul readdresses the matter of the opponents who are troubling the churches. Employing the technique of contrast, he sets the apostolic faith and its ministers into a different category from the opponents. He specifically names two opponents in 2:17 and links the spread of the false view that the resurrection of believers had (in some sense) already occurred to their teaching activities (2:18). The very presence of heresy and heretics in the church apparently had planted in the minds of believers the question about the stability and permanence of the church. In the two images that follow (the church as foundation [2:19a]; the church as a great household [2:20]) Paul addresses the implied question by challenging the present turbulent reality with affirmations of God's control and giving directions for the appropriate Christian response.

In 2:19 Paul presents a potent image of the church's strength and God's control. For convenience, the verse may be broken into two parts, each of which utilizes OT texts. First comes a strong affirmation: "God's firm foundation [*themelios*] stands" (2:19a). Although some scholars detect other backgrounds behind the imagery, the "household" orientation of Paul's earlier uses of this architectural image (cf. 1 Cor. 3:10–13; Rom. 15:20; Eph. 2:20; see Johnson 2001: 386–87; 1996: 77–78; Towner 1989: 132) best explains its application here (2:20). Consequently, this is a depiction of the church, the people of God, which sets the stage for the household image to come. But in making the affirmation, Paul adds potency to it by way of an OT echo.

In the *themelios* imagery an echo of Isa. 28:16 LXX is probable.

2 Tim. 2:19a: Nevertheless, the firm foundation [*themelios*] of God stands.

Isa. 28:16 LXX: Therefore thus says the Lord, "Behold, I lay for the foundations [*themelia*] of Zion a costly stone, a choice, a cornerstone, a precious stone, for its foundations [*themelia*]; and he that believes on him shall by no means be ashamed."

In the early church this OT text became an important OT christological testimony. Its application here as an ecclesiological testimony is thus somewhat of a departure from the trend, but it is not for that reason a less probable adaptation. Paul initiates his reply to the situation facing Timothy by drawing on the part of the well-known OT statement that emphasizes the certainty of God's accomplishments, applying it here to the establishment and stability of the church. The reference to Isa. 26:13 in the next part of the verse strengthens the likelihood that this echo of the Isaiah *themelios* text is intentional, however light.

Paul extends the architectural imagery by inviting the audience to imagine a "seal" that authenticates the "foundation." Seals (*sphragis*) were used commonly to identify legal ownership of property and, like signatures in modern practice, to guarantee authenticity, genuineness, and integrity, or to preserve the secrecy of the contents of a letter or of some product. In this case, "seal" is used in a figurative sense to denote God's ownership of "the foundation" (= the church) just mentioned.

Paul describes the twofold content of the seal by means of two statements of biblical materials. These two statements in effect bring together theology in what is affirmed and ethics in the response that people are called to make in the crisis situation. The first statement is this:

2 Tim. 2:19c: The Lord knows those who are his [*egnō kyrios tous ontas autou*].

This repeats the LXX wording of one part of Num. 16:5, making only one change from "God" (*ho theos*) to "Lord" (*kyrios*):

Num. 16:5 LXX: And he spoke to Korah and all his assembly, saying, "God has visited and known those that are his [*egnō ho theos tous ontas autou*] and who are holy, and has brought them to himself; and whom he has chosen for himself, he has brought to himself."

The Hebrew has the tetragrammaton ("YHWH"), which normally is translated in the LXX with *kyrios*. This tendency may have influenced the shift from *theos* to *kyrios* in the NT adaptation of the OT material. In any case, the reference is probably to God (the anarthrous use is typical for Numbers and throughout the LXX).

The OT context and the present context must be compared in order for us to appreciate the full weight of the citation's claim that God knows his own people. In both cases authority is disputed, and loyalty to God and his appointed servants is in question. The setting in Num. 16 is one of dispute and confrontation: Moses and Aaron, leaders chosen by God, had been challenged by Korah and his companions (Levites to whom the privilege of the priesthood had not been given), who demanded the right to serve God as priests in the community. In response, Moses declared that God knows those who truly belong to him, meaning the people whom God had chosen, and that he would make it known. Korah presented a challenge to Moses' and Aaron's authority, and in so doing, he rebelled against God; God confirmed his choice of Moses and Aaron by the destruction of Korah and all who sided with him.

The reader who is familiar with the OT background is compelled to view the present situation in a similar light: characters such as Hymenaeus and Philetus, with their false teaching, present the apostolic ministry with a leadership challenge. So, the points of contact are apparent. But how much of the paradigm is to be brought across to the situation in Ephesus? The result of the OT story was the dramatic destruction of the unrecognized rebels; it is not hard to see how the story accessed by the citation might function as a warning in the way that the wilderness allusions in 1 Cor. 10 did for the Corinthian community. The statement of Moses quoted here was a statement of vindication, and it pointed forward to judgment. Because God distinguishes, one must ensure one's proper alignment with him. The OT story serves as a paradigm that acknowledges the rebellion of some within the church and God's continued presence within it; however, the statement is both a consolation and a warning that God will distinguish between those who are his and those who are not. God is present as protector and redeemer, but also as judge who will vindicate his truth and his people.

The second segment of OT materials (2:19d) serves a function similar to 1 Cor. 10:14, which follows the OT story there with the admonition to "flee from idolatry." Here the next OT citation completes the content of the "seal":

2 Tim. 2:19d: And "Let everyone who names the name of the Lord turn away from wickedness" [*kai apostētō apo adikias pas ho onomazōn to onoma kyriou*].

Echoes of several OT texts are possible in this statement, and they must be traced as we decide its thrust.

First, "name the name of the Lord" is an idiom occurring in the LXX on several occasions. In our text we have the phrase in participial form (*ho onomazōn to onoma kyriou*). It takes various forms elsewhere (see Lev. 24:11, 16 [2x]; Josh. 23:7; Isa. 26:13; Amos 6:10; *Odes Sol.* 5:13 [echoing Isa. 26:13]; Sir. 23:9–10). The more normal phraseology comes to be "to call upon the name of the Lord" (using *kaleō* or *epikaleō* [see, e.g., Acts 2:21; Rom. 10:13; 1 Cor. 1:2; cf. 2 Tim. 2:22; see *TDNT* 5:263]). Although presumably the basic sense was to make entreaty to the Lord (more typically expressed with "call upon [the name of] the Lord"), it denotes acknowledging the name of YHWH (Isa. 26:13 LXX: "O Lord our God, take possession of us: O Lord, we know no other beside you: we name your name [*to onoma sou onomazomen*]"), or mentioning the name as if to summon him (Amos 6:10 LXX: "Be silent, that you do not name the name of the Lord" [*siga, heneka tou mē onomasai to onoma kyriou*]). And in one case the phrase is used to describe blasphemy of the Lord (Lev. 24:16 LXX: "And he that names the name of the Lord, let him die the death" [*onomazōn de to onoma kyriou thanatō thanatousthō*]); however, here the phrase acquires this negative meaning from 24:11, where the naming of the Name is accompanied by "cursing" ("And the son of the Israelite woman named the Name and cursed"

[*kai eponomasas ho huios tēs gynaikos tēs Israēlitidos to onoma katērasato*]).

This variety of usage leads to two suggested sources of the phrase cited here. Most interpreters regard the reference as an echo of Isa. 26:13 LXX, where a positive acknowledgment of God is implied:

Isa. 26:13 LXX: O Lord our God, take possession of us: O Lord, we know no other beside you: we name your name [*to onoma sou onomazomen*].

In this case the statement, extending the thought of the previous line, calls on the faithful to separate themselves from evil and so show their allegiance to God. If, however, "naming the name" intends an echo of Lev. 24:16 (in the context of 24:11), where the phrase is descriptive of blasphemy, then the reference would be to the false teachers in the community, who are then to heed Paul's warning in 2:19d and repent before judgment is executed:

Lev. 24:16 LXX: And he that names the name of the Lord, let him die the death [*onomazōn de to onoma kyriou thanatō thanatousthō*].

The context of opposition and false teaching makes this latter view possible (cf. 1 Tim. 1:20), but the former view seems more likely, primarily because of the renewed contact made with the story in Num. 16 at its point of climax (see below). It occurs where the people are instructed to choose sides. The command added to the "naming" text in 2:19d is "turn away from wrongdoing" (*apostētō apo adikias*).

This command in itself recalls several similar LXX texts (see Pss. 6:9 [6:8 ET]; 33:15 [34:14 ET]; Prov. 3:7; Isa. 52:11; Sir. 17:26) but, due to the choice of *adikia* over *anomia*, might seem at first glance closest in form to the citation of Ps. 6:9 preserved in Luke 13:27. Three differences from our text should be noted: (1) Ps. 6:9 LXX (Luke 13:27) addresses the command to evildoers; (2) the speaker (David [in Luke it is Jesus describing eschatological judgment]) is concerned to be separated from them; (3) both Luke and 2 Timothy have chosen *adikia* instead of *anomia*:

Ps. 6:9 LXX: Depart from me all you who do lawlessness [*apostēte ap' emou pantes hoi ergazomenoi tēn anomian*].

Luke 13:27: Depart from me all you workers of injustice [*apostēte ap' emou pantes ergatai adikias*].

2 Tim. 2:19d: Turn away from wickedness [*apostētō apo adikias*].

However that lexical choice is to be explained, the main difference is one of perspective. The personal perspective adopted in Ps. 6:9 LXX ("Depart from *me* all *you* who do lawlessness" [also Luke 13:27]) equates separation with judgment. The perspective adopted in 2 Timothy, however, compares more closely with that of Ps. 33:15; Prov. 3:7; Sir. 17:26, which equate separation with purity and a return to the Lord, so that separation from wickedness preserves God's people from judgment:

Sir. 17:26: Return to the Most High and turn away from wickedness [*apostrephe apo adikias*].

The sharp focus on God's people, and indeed on their identity as God's people, as well as on their preservation is produced by the allusion to Isa. 26:13 and the image of "naming the Name." The command of separation, although paralleled in various OT texts, is without a precise textual match. But bearing in mind the essential matter of perspective, we see that the climactic command at the end of the story in Numbers (which would have been well known), which orders the people to separate from the rebels, does provide both the thematic (perspective) and verbal contact point (in the verb "turn away" [*apostētō*]). Numbers 16:26–27 reports the visit of Moses and the elders of Israel, at the Lord's command, to Dathan and Abiram, companions of Korah, to urge the people to get away from the rebels before judgment:

He said to the congregation, "Separate yourselves [*aposchisthēte*] from the tents of these wicked men, and touch nothing of theirs, or you will be swept away for all their sins." So they got away [*apestēsan*] from the dwellings of Korah, Dathan, and Abiram; and Dathan and Abiram came out and stood at the entrance of their tents, together with their wives, their children, and their little ones.

This concern—the people of God must demonstrate their purity—exactly parallels Paul's concern in the "seal"-response portion of 2:19c–d.

The initial allusion to Num. 16:5 draws the audience into that dramatic OT story of identity where the specter of impending judgment has been raised. The two situations are sufficiently close, and the Korah story was well enough known in Judaism (applied to enforce proper recognition of authority [e.g., 4Q423 5; Sir. 45:18–19]) and the early church (as here, as a template for rebellious heretics [Jude 11]). The parallels are obvious: challengers to God's representatives (Moses/Paul) have been named, and the people must choose sides, thereby establishing their identity. Consequently, the verbal contact in "turn away"/"depart from" should be taken seriously as an echo of the climax of the Korah story: the OT story provides a narrative illustration of the concept of "wickedness" (*adikia*) and the narrative source that gives meaning to the command in 2:19d.

Thus following on from the warning that supplies the first part of the "seal," the second citation calls the faithful of the congregation ("all who name the name of the Lord") to dissociate themselves completely from the opponents and their teachings (*adikia*). What the rest of the passage confirms, however, is that the fate of the false teachers is not yet fixed, for they too may turn from evil. The general call to separate from evil that occurs throughout the OT is given specific shape in this instance by the intertextual play between the apostasy faced by Timothy and the story of Korah's rebellion in the wilderness. As in the use of wilderness motifs in 1 Cor. 10, the present passage issues a dire warning by way of Israel's experience of God's wrath; the equal need for his grace and kindness is not passed over, but is left to a later point (2:25).

3:8

In a section of the letter designed to place the heretics into the traditional framework of the evil of "the last days," Paul taps into the story of Moses and the magicians of Egypt (Exod. 7–9) to draw an analogy between those who resisted Moses and those who resist Paul and his gospel ("the truth"). In doing so, he does not access Scripture directly, but rather draws on the story somewhere downstream of Exodus in the oral and literary tradition of Judaism.

2 Tim. 3:8: As Jannes and Jambres opposed Moses, so also these people . . . oppose the truth.

The derivation of the names "Jannes" (*Iannēs*) and "Jambres" (*Iambrēs*) is debated (Pietersma 1994: 36–42; 1995–1997; Dibelius and Conzelmann 1972: 117; Schürer 1973–1987: 3.2:781–83; Thackeray 1900: 220–21). "Jannes" may be the Greek transliteration of "Johana," which is possibly derived from the Hebrew verb *ḥānâ*, meaning "oppose, contradict." "Jambres" may be a misspelling of an original "Mambres" (as some Latin and Greek versions have it), which in turn may be derived (via the spelling "Mamrey") from the Hebrew verb *mārâ*, meaning "rebel." Whatever the derivation of the names, they emerge first in the tradition in CD-A V, 17–19: "For formerly Moses and Aaron arose by the hand of the Prince of Lights; but Belial raised up Jannes and his brother, in his cunning, when Israel was saved for the first time." Subsequent references are numerous and spread among Jewish (e.g., *Tg. Ps.-J.* on Exod. 1:15; 7:11; Num. 22:22; *Exod. Rab.* 9; *b. Menaḥ.* 85a [see further Str-B 3:660–64]), Christian (e.g., *Acts Pil.* 5:1; Origen, *Comm. Matt.* 23:37; 29:9; *Cels.* 4.51), and secular Latin and Greek writers (e.g., Pliny the Elder, *Nat.* 30.1.11; Apuleius, *Apol.* 90). What is noticeable, apart from variances in spelling and in single versus double mention of the two characters, is the way the tradition elevated their roles to archetypal status. They came to represent Moses' archnemeses who would counter his displays of divine power with various tricks of their own; and by their association with various stories (as Balaam's servants or sons, trailing Israel through the wilderness and instigating the rebellion embodied in the golden calf [see *TDNT* 3:192–92]), they acquired symbolic status as opponents of the truth.

The source for this tradition remains uncertain (Spicq [1969: 779] suggests that Paul learned it from the Targum). The NT attests to the fact that other expansions of OT stories were common currency in the early church's tradition (Acts 7:22–23, 53; 1 Cor. 10:2, 4; Gal. 3:19; Heb. 2:2; Jude 9). Paul alludes to these figures generally in the way that the rabbinic writers did. His readers presumably know the developments surrounding these two characters in tradition. The function of the reference is to link the present (eschatological) adversaries—the false teachers—with the age-old spirit of deception and opposition embodied in these two figures. In this appropriation of the traditional symbol the unity of God's story is understood: what has gone around is now (again, in "the last days") coming around. The pattern established in the early stage of God's story of redemption finds new yet continuous expression in the opposition of "the last days." Equally present in the adoption of the analogy, though more implicit, is a comparison of Moses' authority with Paul's. As in the seminal story, so in the latter days God's representatives and people will triumph over all opposition.

3:11

Paul next takes up again the renewal of Timothy's calling. The apostle's faithfulness and obedience (3:10), well known by Timothy, form the paradigm for the co-worker's life. But also paradigmatic are the apostolic persecutions and sufferings as well as God's rescue from them (3:11). In the recollection of God's intervention, Paul echoes the OT:

2 Tim. 3:11: . . . what persecutions [*diōgmous*] I endured, yet the Lord rescued me from them all [*kai ek pantōn me errysato ho kyrios*].

The wording of this statement corresponds closely to the second half of Ps. 33:18 LXX (34:16–18 MT; 34:17 ET):

The righteous ones cried out and the Lord heard them and delivered them from all their afflictions [*ekekraxan hoi dikaioi kai ho kyrios eisēkousen autōn kai ek pasōn tōn thlipseōn autōn errysato autous*].

Psalm 33:20 LXX (34:20 MT; 34:19 ET) resumes the language, stating the principle (in the future tense) underlying the act of deliverance celebrated two verses earlier:

Many are the afflictions [*thlipseis*] of the righteous, and yet he will rescue them from them all [*kai ek pasōn autōn rhysetai autous*]. (Cf. 33:5 LXX [34:5 MT; 34:4 ET]; 141:7 [142:7 MT; 142:6 ET].)

The theme of "deliverance" begins in Ps. 33:5 LXX, but Paul seems to have made his entrance at the point where it is applied specifically to God's intervention on behalf of "the righteous" in 33:18–20 LXX. Thus he makes explicit his interest in a theology of suffering built on the OT theme of the righteous sufferer. This theme—the suffering of the righteous and God's promise to vindicate them—was already present in some Jewish circles (Pss. 22; 38; 69; Wis. 2:12–20; 5:1–7), and it was taken by the early church in reference to Christ (see Ruppert 1972). Paul had already extended the pattern to include Christians (Rom. 8:36; cf. Acts 14:22), and here he interprets his experience according to that pattern. In place of the term "righteous" is the statement in 3:12 that associates "godly living" with "persecution," which is essentially a contextualized form of Ps. 33:20a LXX (the association of *eusebeia* ["godliness"] with *dikaios* ["the righteous"] was also taking place in the later OT literature [Prov. 13:11; cf. Isa. 33:6; 4 Macc. 9:24; see Towner 1996]). Given the importance of the "godliness" language in these letters to co-workers, this transposition is almost predictable. Other changes are minor: replacement of the psalmist's term "afflictions" (*thlipseis*) with "persecutions" (*diōgmoi*) and "sufferings" (*pathēmata*) is incidental and occasioned by Paul's discourse; instead of the feminine form of "from all" (*ek pasōn*), required by the object "afflictions" (*tōn thlipseōn*), Paul uses the masculine form (*ek pantōn*) in connection with the masculine term "persecutions" (*diōgmous*).

Consequently, by means of the echo, Paul assumes the role of the OT righteous sufferer and links his sufferings closely to the suffering of Jesus. He allows the theme to interpret his apostolic ministry and extends it to explain the missiological dimension of the church's existence. The appearance of the theme foreshadows Paul's conclusion in 4:16–18, where there is, however, a significant difference in accent. Here, looking backward and toward Timothy's ongoing ministry, Paul's experience of "deliverance" (*rhyomai* [4:17–18]) relates to temporal, physical rescue ("from all of them" [i.e., the aforementioned sufferings]). These rescues stand as evidence not only of the Lord's (here Christ; in the psalms Yahweh) love, but also of the apostle's status as one who stands in the line of righteous sufferers, along with OT prophets, the Suffering Servant, and Messiah. Seen in this light, suffering is neither meaningless nor hopeless. Consequently, Paul's suffering (in prison at present or in the past) confirms rather

than denies (as some might have been alleging; cf. 1:16) his divine calling. Sufferings come, but the Lord rescues. Why? The answer comes in the OT background: the suffering ones are God's righteous; his pledge is to rescue them completely ("from all of them").

3:15a

Paul's comment in 3:15a about how Timothy, from his youth, has had knowledge of the Scriptures taps into the rich and widely developed value and practice in Judaism of instruction in Torah from childhood (see the references and discussion in Str-B 3:664–66). The following description of the Scriptures as being "able to make you wise for salvation" (*ta dynamena se sophisai eis sōtērian* [3:15b]) possibly owes a debt to the language of Ps. 118:98 LXX (119:98 MT/ET), "You have made me wiser [*esophisas*] than my enemies in your commandment, for it is mine forever"; however, beyond the sharing of the verb and the interest in God's word, the resemblance is slight.

4:8

Here Paul employs the figure of "the crown of righteousness" (*ho tēs dikaiosynēs stephanos*). This bears a resemblance to the reward promised to the righteous ones in Wis. 5:15–16: "But the righteous [*dikaioi*] live forever, and their reward is with the Lord. . . . Therefore they will receive a glorious crown [*to basileion tēs euprepeias*] and a beautiful diadem [*to diadēma tou kallous*] from the hand of the Lord." A closer verbal correspondence is seen in *Let. Aris.* 280: "God having granted you a crown of righteousness" (*theou soi stephanon dikaiosynēs dedōkotos*). But although these texts indicate the currency of the imagery (reward expressed in terms of a crown, and specifically the phrase "crown of righteousness"), it is doubtful that Paul consciously echoed either text.

4:14

The treacherous actions of Alexander in the events that Paul describes (possibly some part in Paul's arrest by Roman authorities [Quinn and Wacker 2000: 819–20; Fee 1988: 295–96]) elicited a severe pronouncement of judgment. Although there may be no conscious attempt on Paul's part to quote or allude to an OT text or texts directly, he does have in mind a well-known Jewish principle enunciated variously in a series of OT and Jewish texts. The language of this pronouncement may actually echo Rom. 2:6, as other links to that letter in 2 Timothy may suggest (1:7; 2:11). In Romans the principle is invoked to illustrate the preceding statement about God's fairness of judgment. Here in 2 Timothy it is invoked because that very "fairness" of God determined that Alexander would get his just deserts. In both texts it is probably the formulation of the principle in Psalms and Proverbs that would be most in mind (LXX: Pss. 27:4 [28:4 ET]; 61:13 [62:11 ET]; Prov. 24:12; see also Job 34:11; Jer. 17:10; Hos. 12:2; Sir. 16:12–14; 35:24; *1 En.* 100:7; *L.A.B.* 3:10; Matt. 16:27).

Ps. 61:13 LXX: Strength is God's, and mercy is yours, Lord, because you repay each one according to his deeds [*sy apodōseis hekastō kata ta erga autou*].

Ps. 27:4 LXX: Give them according to their deeds [*dos . . . kata ta erga autōn*], and according to the evil of their ways, give them according to the deeds of their hands [*kata ta erga . . . dos*], repay them the recompense due them [*apodos to antapodoma*].

Prov. 24:12 LXX: But if you should say, "I do not know this person," know that the Lord knows the hearts of all, and he that formed the breath for all, he knows all things, who pays back each one according to his deeds [*hos apodidōsin hekastō kata ta erga autou*].

Rom. 2:6: He will repay each one according to his deeds [*hos apodōsei hekastō kata ta erga autou*].

2 Tim. 4:14: The Lord will pay him back according to his deeds [*apodōsei autō ho kyrios kata ta erga autou*].

Matt. 16:27: For the Son of Man shall come in the glory of his Father with his angels, and then he will pay back to each one according to his deeds [*apodōsei hekastō kata tēn praxin autou*]. (Cf. Sir. 35:22 LXX [35:24 ET]: "until he repays a person according to his deeds" [*heōs antapodō anthrōpō kata tas praxeis autou*]. The textual tradition of Matt. 16:27 [א* et al.] corrects *tēn praxin* to the more dominant *ta erga*.)

Contact with the tradition in 4:14 is clear from the characteristic verb (*apodidōmi*) and the standard or criterion of recompense ("according to his/her deeds" [*kata ta erga autou*]). This applica-

tion is somewhat unusual among the various expressions of the principle because it takes the form of a specific pronouncement (*apodōsei* is future indicative) of judgment on an individual. In this it inclines to the application of the principle in Ps. 27:4 LXX, and we hear in Paul's pronouncement the sentiments of the oppressed there (almost an imprecation, and it would be if the verb were subjunctive or optative, as a few manuscripts weakly attest; but it is hardly a "curse" [*pace* Dibelius and Conzelmann 1972: 123]): appeal is made to God to mete out to the oppressors what their evil deeds deserve.

The rabbis discussed the principle of judgment or payback on the basis of deeds at length (see the numerous references in Str-B 3:78–79; cf. Yinger 1999). And the acceptable "deeds" would have been those acts that expressed faithfulness to the covenant. Paul does not develop the positive side of this principle here, but he has created a contrast by means of the same verb and same tone of certainty, with the statement of his reward in 4:8: "the Lord will recompense me" (*apodōsei moi ho kyrios*) versus "the Lord will recompense him" (*apodōsei autō ho kyrios*). We may assume that in Paul's adaptation of the principle, authentic faithfulness to God (= faith in Christ and the life that this engenders) receives the reward. Although the pronouncement of judgment may hint at Paul's authority (cf. 1 Cor. 16:22; Gal. 1:8–9), it is hedged about with the appropriate recognition of divine prerogative. And the standard of judgment paid out that ensures impartial justice consists precisely of the deeds of the one judged (cf. 2 Cor. 11:15; 1 Pet. 1:17; Rev. 2:23; 18:6; 20:12–13).

4:16–18

In the self-reflection of 4:6–8 Paul has placed the matter of his impending death openly on the table. In 4:16–18, however, his death receives its clearest interpretation. In this closing statement Paul is operating on two levels. The first is the historical level that describes what is ostensibly the apostle's present situation and historical framework. To interpret these circumstances Paul seeks a second theological level by connecting consciously to a dominant OT template. The reflections on suffering already viewed (3:11; cf. 1:8–12; 2:8–10) prepare the reader for the connections to be made in this climactic interpretation; however, this interpretive reflection could not have been fully anticipated. Attention must be paid to each level for the impact of Paul's conclusion to be felt. We will see that the theological interpretation that Paul achieves depends upon a cumulative web of allusions to Ps. 21 LXX, a psalm that figures prominently in the evangelists' depiction of Jesus' passion. Subtler echoes that might be passed over (and indeed have been ignored by most commentators) fall into alignment around the overt reference to rescue "from the lion's mouth." And the likelihood that Paul adopted the psalm as an interpretive compass is further strengthened by the close associations already made in the letter between his experiences of suffering and those of Jesus (1:8; 2:8–10) and the righteous sufferer (3:11).

At the historical level, Paul reflects on his court case, which has progressed through an initial hearing and has gone badly for the accused (see Sherwin-White 1963: 49–52, 112–17; Marshall 1999: 822–24). This assessment emerges in his only explicit comment about it: "At my first defense no one came to my support, but everyone deserted me." That is, apparently those whom he expected to come forward to speak in his behalf decided rather to abandon the apostle. The adversative phrase "but everyone abandoned me" serves two purposes. On the historical level it creates a double contrast—with the statement just made and in the juxtaposing of "everyone" with "me" (*alla pantes me*)—that serves to escalate the theme from the sense of isolation and negligence just expressed to the more shocking sense of culpable abandonment. Also on the historical level the verb *egkateleipō* ("desert"), the same verb used to describe Demas's desertion in 4:10, invites the readers to draw a connection between the two events of abandonment and to place this reference to abandonment within the framework of the statement made about the desertion of the Asian co-workers in 1:15.

This historical reflection on abandonment does not exhaust the contrast statement's function; rather, it initiates the sequence of allusions to the psalms, and especially Ps. 21 LXX (22 MT), that will form an interpretive grid for a theological reading of Paul's final sufferings.

The verb used to tell of the abandonment is the same one that occurs in Ps. 21:2 LXX ("My God, my God, why have you forsaken me?"), a text

that occurs on the lips of Jesus at the climax of the passion, by which the suffering of Jesus came to be understood (Mark 15:34 par.):

> 2 Tim. 4:16: But everyone deserted me [*me egkatelipon*].

> Ps. 21:2 LXX: My God, my God, why have you forsaken me? [*ho theos ho theos mou, prosches moi; hina ti egkatelipes me?*]

> Mark 15:34: *elōi elōi lema sabachthani . . . ho theos mou ho theos mou, eis ti egkatelipes me?*

With but a single term serving as the initial cue to an intertextual connection, the question of a Greek or Hebrew source text is, in principle, open, although Paul's preference for the LXX will be demonstrated again as he extends the OT web. With this allusion Paul (however obliquely) taps into the psalmist's puzzled question and the theme of the messianic sufferings. His intention is to link up the somber statements of abandonment in the letter, identifying this experience as being symbolic of the cruciform path walked by the Messiah. But the interpretive grid is broader than this, and Paul will incorporate several other items from the psalm before he is finished.

Following a brief prayer for the deserters (4:16b), Paul uses the strong statement of his experience of betrayal and abandonment as a contrastive backdrop for his presentation of the climax of his ministry (4:17–18). The conclusion of the sequence initiated at 4:16 brings together four important elements, each of which is rooted in some way in Ps. 21 LXX, before the doxology is reached.

First, Paul stresses that abandonment by people was more than compensated for by the Lord's presence and empowerment. The first phrase, "the Lord stood by me" (*ho de kyrios moi parestē*), describes an experience of divine presence. The tradition surrounding Paul's ministry made note of similar divine interventions in the apostle's life (Acts 18:9–10; 27:23; cf. 13:2; 16:7; 20:22–23; 21:11), accompanied in one case by the Lord's personal promise of support for his ministry in Rome (23:11); so in itself this is not an unusual feature.

In making this claim, however, Paul introduces a strong image that evokes a cluster of dominant ideas fundamental to the OT expression of Israel's belief in God. Here again historical reflection opens a door to a deeper theological level of the text. The language of Paul's claim first transports the reader back to the beginnings of Israel's existence. The verb *parestē* first describes the dramatic descent of the Lord in a cloud to "stand by" Moses (Exod. 34:5), and Moses' experience becomes one to be enjoyed by any of God's people (Ps. 108:31 [109:31 ET]; Wis. 10:11), reenacted within the community in the tabernacle and then the temple (*TDNT* 5:838–39). Moreover, God's "presence" with his people becomes symbolic of Israel's uniqueness among the nations—a relationship with the Creator God that is characterized by divine "help" and "deliverance" (Exod. 15:2; 18:4; Deut. 32:38; 33:7, 29; with the key word groups being *boētheō, sōzō,* and later *rhyomai*). These elements become the trademarks of God's presence with his people in the very early going, and their absence, the sign of his displeasure (Deut. 28:29, 31).

These concepts of divine help and deliverance permeated the Psalter as the liturgists of Israel's middle and later periods shaped the nation's worship on the basis of remembrance of past help and present need (e.g., LXX: Pss. 7:11 [7:10 ET]; 20:2 [21:1 ET]; 21:12, 20 [22:11, 19 ET]; 53:6 [54:4 ET]; 69:2 [70:1 ET]; 70:12 [71:12 ET]). It becomes typical to find the prayer for God's help and deliverance linked closely to the question of his proximity. This brings us again to Ps. 21 LXX, where this cry for help and God's presence is raised twice (21:12, 20) and where the Lord's past deliverance of the nation (21:5) becomes the basis for the prayer for his deliverance from present dangers (21:9, 21). And all of this is occasioned by the psalmist's perplexed opening question to God: "Why have you abandoned me?" (21:2).

The likelihood that Paul arranged the themes of his closing reflection around Ps. 21 LXX might be questioned if he were limited to explicit quotation to lure his readers to a deeper level. However, the theme of the "nearness and help of the Lord" is central in the psalm, and, as we saw, it is fundamental to the broader OT story; and the evidence will accumulate as we continue. At this point, by saying "the Lord stood by me," Paul says in effect that in his experience the psalmist's prayers were answered. Paul, like Jesus, entered the psalm of messianic travail (indeed, several times, though

with the advantage of a postresurrection perspective) and came out on the other side of it (or would do so) in the strength of the Lord's presence. His experiences follow the pattern established by Jesus (1:8; 2:8–10; cf. Col. 1:24), and his vindication, made certain by Jesus' resurrection (2:8), cannot be far off.

In Paul's situation, divine presence/help was experienced as "empowerment" (2:1 [cf. Phil. 4:13]) that resulted in an event of proclamation that symbolized the completion of his mission (4:17b). Historically, this probably is a reference to his day in court (the first *apologia*), which, as in the past (Acts 22; 25; 26), he was able to exploit for the gospel (Towner 1999: 166–67; Marshall 1999: 824).

But how can Paul interpret this court appearance with such boldness? In what sense have all the Gentiles heard? The phrase "all the Gentiles/nations" (*panta ta ethnē*), which certainly need not exclude the Jews (Prior 1989: 115–24; Towner 1999: 167), is a loaded term in Pauline thought (Rom. 15:11; 16:26; Gal. 3:8). It sums up the universal scope of the salvation plan of God, from the Abrahamic promise and institution of the covenant (Gen. 18:18; 22:18; 26:4; Deut. 7:6; 28:10) to its full unveiling in the psalms and the prophets (Pss. 46:2 LXX [47:1 ET]; 71:11, 17 LXX [72:11, 17 ET]; 85:9 LXX [86:9 ET]; Isa. 2:2; 66:18; Ezek. 38:16; Hag. 2:7; Dan. 7:14), from which Paul clearly took his cue (Rom. 9–11; 15:9–13; Gal. 1:15–16). It is this deeply theological meaning that suggests the symbolic nature of this statement about his Roman proclamation. Thus what Paul says figuratively in 4:7, "I have competed well, finished the race, kept the faith," now on the historical (and missiological) plane translates into "I have fully accomplished my mission to the Gentiles."

Is the messianic psalm still in mind? Again historical reflection finds theological resonance in the background text. As Ps. 21 LXX turns from the desperate prayer for help (21:21–22 [see also below]) to the beleaguered one's promise to proclaim the Lord's faithfulness (21:23–27), the psalmist announces the same promise to the nations that Paul claims here to be fulfilled: "All the ends of the earth [*panta ta perata tēs gēs*] shall remember and turn to the Lord; and all the families of the nations [*pasai hai patriai tōn ethnōn*] shall worship before him, for dominion belongs to the Lord, and he rules over the nations" (21:28–29). The universal scope of salvation ("all...all" [*panta ...pasai*]) and the language ("all ... the nations" [*pasai...tōn ethnōn*]) suggest that this is more than a chance allusion.

In rapid succession come three final links to Psalm 21 LXX: a distinctive metaphor, verbs of rescue, and kingdom language. The second element of the story's conclusion (4:17c) completes the sentence with a metaphorical description of deliverance: "And I was delivered from the lion's mouth." The phrase "lion's mouth" was a strong metaphor for death (Ps. 21:22 LXX [22:21 ET]; Judg. 14:8–9; Amos 3:12; Dan. 6:21 Θ [6:20 ET]; 1 Macc. 2:60), and it functions in this way here. It is a close match with Ps. 21:22 LXX, and it is the definitive echo of the psalm in this section and the literary magnet that attracts and orientates the other allusions:

Ps. 21:22 LXX: Save me from the mouth of the lion [*sōson me ek stomatos leontos*].

2 Tim. 4:17c: And I was delivered from the mouth of the lion [*kai errysthēn ek stomatos leontos*].

The psalmist's verb (*sōzō*) is different (but note *sōsei* ["he will save"] in 4:18b), but the one occurring here (*rhyomai*) and repeated in 4:18a is a dominant feature of the vocabulary of the psalm (21:5, 9, 21 LXX), fortifying the connection. In fact, the verb pair in the first two clauses of 4:18 (*rhyomai/sōzō*) replicates the alternating pattern of the psalm: 21:5–6, 9, 21–22 LXX (this particular pattern, which corresponds to the parallelism of Hebrew poetry, is restricted mostly to the psalms [LXX: Ps. 6:5; 7:2; 30:2–3, 16–17; 58:3; 59:7; 68:15; 70:2; 107:7; Job 33:28, 30; cf. Ps. 50:16; 85:2; 108:26]):

4:17c: And I was delivered [*errysthēn*] from the mouth of the lion.
4:18a: The Lord will deliver [*rhysetai*] me from every evil deed,
4:18b: and he will save [*sōsei*] me into his heavenly kingdom.

21:5: Our fathers hoped in you; they hoped, and you delivered [*errysō*] them.
21:6: To you they cried and were saved [*esōthēsan*].

21:9: He hoped in the Lord; let him deliver [*rhysasthō*] him, let him save [*sōsatō*] him because he takes pleasure in him.

21:21: Deliver [*rhysai*] my life from the sword.
21:22: Save [*sōson*] me from the mouth of the lion.

In 4:18a–b the second statement of salvation is parallel to the first, and in supplying the positive measurement of salvation ("into"), it complements the negative measurement ("from" [cf. 4:17c]) as it also completes the verb pairing. The Hebrew-type parallelism and the orientation of thought indicated in this second part make it clear that the future acts of rescue (4:18a) and saving (4:18b) are meant in a final sense (Marshall 1999: 826); and with the thought of impending death, the accent on salvation is shifted to the future consummation (as in 1 Cor. 15:40, 48 [2x]; Eph. 1:3, 20; 2:6; 3:10; 6:12; Col. 1:13; also John 3:12; Heb. 9:23 [see *TDNT* 5:538–42]). This salvation is ultimately described as entry into "his heavenly kingdom." The two-part affirmation of the Lord's salvation is, in Paul's historical context, a thorough rejection of the dominion of evil (rulers or opponents) in view of the reality and supremacy of the Lord's dominion ("kingdom" [*basileia*]). In both the term and the tone, Paul makes his final reference to the psalm. There, in Ps. 21:29 LXX, a claim about God's dominion establishes the certainty that all nations will turn to the Lord:

Ps. 21:29 LXX: For dominion [*basileia*] is the Lord's, and he rules the nations [*tōn ethnōn*].

Consequently, Paul's discourse moves from the historical level to the theological level by making various connections with Ps. 21 LXX. The purpose is to interpret his final episode of suffering for the gospel in terms of the tradition of Jesus' passion. By incorporating the psalmist's vision for the Gentiles, this interpretive application of the suffering figure of the psalm to his apostolic ministry actually takes Paul to a place that Jesus would go fully only through the apostolic mission—to the Gentiles. This is in keeping with the place at which the Pauline story begins and ends and the distinctive role that he plays in relation to God's promise to save the nations. Paul's suffering, the abandonment he experienced, and his impending death all fit the Jesus mold. Yet his experience in no way supersedes that of Jesus; rather, it is the complementary outworking of one who has taken to himself the cruciform character and behavior of the Lord.

Titus

Written with much the same purpose and tone as 1 Timothy, this letter instructs the Pauline co-worker Titus in matters related to organizing the leadership and community life of churches on Crete.

2:14

The only extensive interaction with the OT occurs in 2:14. (We should note that the use of the *bdelyktos* ["detestable"], a NT *hapax legomenon*, as a denunciation in 1:16 compares with the use of the cognate verb in Ps. 13:1 LXX [14:1 ET], a text that expresses the same sentiment of denying the existence of God by acts of abominable behavior: "The fool has said in his heart, 'There is no God.' They have corrupted themselves and become abominable [*ebdelychthēsan*] in their devices; there is none that does goodness, there is not even so much as one" [cf. Rom. 3:10–12]. For use of the adjective, see Prov. 17:15; 2 Macc. 1:27.) This verse concludes a christological statement inserted to explain the nature of the appearance of God's grace in the world (2:11–14). The explicit identification that closes 2:13—"our Savior, Jesus Christ"—returns Paul to the past event of salvation with which the statement began (2:11). He interprets this event in two ways: (1) by means of a relative clause that incorporates a Pauline interpretation of Jesus' death; (2) by means of a purpose clause that reflects on the significance of that event. The whole statement is a thoughtful combination of intertextual echoes of his own use elsewhere of a Jesus saying and OT texts and imagery.

The traditional character of the opening clause ("who gave himself for us") is indicated by the relative pronoun that attaches this statement to the name Jesus Christ (cf., e.g., Rom. 8:32; Phil. 2:6; 1 Tim. 3:16; 1 Pet. 2:22–24; 3:22). The comment often is traced to the Son of Man logion in Mark 10:45, but Paul clearly had picked up and adapted this saying for other teaching contexts (cf.

Gal. 1:4; 2:20; Eph. 5:2; 1 Tim. 2:6; see Towner 2005; Johnson 2001: 191).

The purpose clause that follows (*hina*) identifies two effects of Christ's death, and it is in drawing out the purpose that OT texts are woven together. First, Christ's self-offering accomplished the removal of believers ("us") from the sphere of sin. To express this aspect, Paul draws on the metaphor of redemption. Behind the metaphor was the practice of purchasing the freedom of a slave or captive by the payment of a ransom (*lytroō* [Luke 24:21; 1 Pet. 1:18]; see *TDNT* 4:349–51; *TLNT* 2:423–29; Hill 1967: 49–81). But the verb "redeem" was used widely in the biblical tradition of the action taken by God to set his people free (Ps. 106:2 [107:2 MT]; 118:134 [119:134 MT]; 1 Macc. 4:11; Sir. 50:24), and it was already closely associated with his deliverance of the people from Egypt (Exod. 6:6; Deut. 7:8; 2 Sam. 7:23). It was another way of speaking of God's saving act, and it would have primarily called to mind the OT story of deliverance from Egypt.

But a more specific intertextual cue is given as the verse goes on to name the hostile environment from which people are redeemed—"from all iniquity/lawlessness":

Ps. 129:8 LXX: It is he who will redeem Israel [*lytrōsetai ton Israēl*] from all its iniquities [*ek pasōn tōn anomiōn autou*].

Titus 2:14b: in order that he might redeem us [*lytrōsētai hēmas*] from all iniquity [*apo pasēs anomias*]

The contact points suggest that the primary scriptural echo is the Greek text of Ps. 129:8 (130:8 ET). The changes are basically cosmetic: from "Israel" to "us" (= followers of the Messiah, and thus the substitution of the plural for the collective singular; doctrine-like sayings are often applied to believers by means of personal pronouns [cf., e.g., Rom. 5:6; 8:32; 2 Tim. 1:9–10; Titus 3:5; see Cranfield 1982]), and from the plural formulation ("from all its iniquities") to a generalizing singular ("from all iniquity").

In both cases redemption is "from all lawlessness." The term *anomia* was used frequently in the OT to depict opposition to God's law, and in the singular it denotes "wickedness" or "sinfulness," which is set in opposition to the concept of righteousness (cf. Rom. 6:19; 2 Cor. 6:14). Paul uses the term occasionally to describe the state of sinfulness (as here, in the singular: Rom. 6:19; 2 Cor. 6:14; 2 Thess. 2:3, 7) and seems to avoid the plural usage (= "acts of lawlessness" [Rom. 4:7]). Paul's choice of the phrase was naturally determined by the OT text in mind at this point. But the term *anomia* rings into consciousness the next web of OT texts to be engaged. To this point, the effects of Christ's self-offering are interpreted in terms of redemption from sin's enslavement, which is associated in the OT with God's powerful intervention.

Reflection on Christ's death continues in Titus 2:14c, where the metaphor of "washing/cleansing" echoes another cluster of OT covenantal texts linked to the preceding by the term *anomia*: "and to cleanse for himself a people of his own." The new metaphor, "cleansing" (*katharizō*; for the cognate adjective, *katharos*, see 1:15 [3x]; see *TDNT* 3:413–26), leads some to think of baptism (cf. Titus 3:5; Eph. 5:25–26; note other symbolic cleansings in Heb. 9:14, 22–23; 1 Pet. 1:2; 1 John 1:7, 9). But the sense is that of cultic purification (in relation to the preparation for making sacrifices and so on), which the OT already extended figuratively to describe God's action of purifying his people, so that they may be his people. The "cleansing" imagery gives access to a catena of Greek texts from Ezek. 36–37, already anticipated in the *anomia* of the last clause:

Ezek. 37:23: They will no longer defile themselves with their idols and vile images or with any of their offenses, for I will save them from all their sinful backsliding [*apo pasōn tōn anomiōn autōn*], and I will cleanse them [*kathariō autous*]. They will be my people [*esontai moi eis laon*], and I will be their God.

Ezek. 36:25: I will sprinkle clean [*katharon*] water upon you, and you will be cleansed [*katharisthēsesthe*] from all your uncleannesses [*tōn akatharsiōn*] and from all your idols, and I will cleanse [*kathariō*] you.

Ezek. 36:29: I will save you from all your uncleannesses [*tōn akatharsiōn*].

Ezek. 36:33: Thus says the Lord God, "In the day wherein I will cleanse [*kathariō*] you from all your iniquities [*ek pasōn tōn anomiōn hymōn*] I will also cause the cities to be inhabited, and the waste places will be built upon."

Titus 2:14c: and to cleanse for himself a people of his own [*kai katharisē heautō laon periousion*]

Paul's intertextual play may have begun with Ezek. 37:23, but the spread of the term *anomia* and the *katharos* word group make a single text source impossible to establish. And in the closing reference to "a people of his own," Paul strikes another rich thematic vein that incorporates the Ezekiel context but also reaches back to the seminal reflections on the covenant made on Mount Sinai:

Ezek. 37:23: They will be my people, and I, the Lord, will be their God [*esontai moi eis laon, kai egō kyrios esomai autois eis theon*].

Ezek. 36:28: You will be my people, and I will be your God [*esesthe moi eis laon, kagō esomai hymin eis theon*].

Exod. 19:5: You will be a people of my possession out of all the nations [*esesthe moi laos periousios apo pantōn tōn ethnōn*].

Deut. 7:6: The Lord your God has chosen you out of all the nations on the earth to be a people of his possession [*se proeilato kyrios ho theos sou einai se autō laon periousion para panta ta ethnē*]. (Cf. 14:2.)

Paul's adaptation draws together the concepts of cleansing (from *anomia*) and election. The defilement in mind in Ezek. 37:23 and 36:25 is that of exilic and postexilic idolatry, and the application of this to the Cretan context is not hard to see (1:10–16 and the use of the *katharos* word group in 1:15). The wider textual network that Paul contacts also associates purification from idolatry with the event of "becoming" God's people and the ongoing act of "being" God's people by way of the Godward covenant commitments required of his people.

The event of "becoming" is God's covenantal and creative act, and the uniqueness of this people is first seen in this light. Paul sets the identity of the church into the OT context specifically focused on the promise of the new (or renewed) covenant (cf. Ezek. 36:26–28). The textual network, beginning with Ezek. 37:23, superimposes Christ's purifying act over God's act in the OT. The result is a people whose messianic identity is uniquely imprinted upon them. In the OT covenantal transaction, by Yahweh's action of cleansing (Ezek. 37:23) and electing (Deut. 7:6; 14:2), and upon the condition of the people's faithfulness (Exod. 19:5), Israel would be known as "a people for his own possession" (for the phrase *laos periousios*, see also Exod. 23:22 LXX; Deut. 26:18; cf. *peripoiēsis* in Eph. 1:14; 1 Pet. 2:9; see *TDNT* 4:50–57)—that is, the unique possession of Yahweh, bearing the imprint of his holiness. The quality of uniqueness is emphasized by the selectivity with which Israel was chosen (Deut. 7:6); the Greek phrase behind "people for his possession" adds the sense of preciousness or costliness to this identity (*TDNT* 6:57–58; Marshall 1999: 286). The historical event that marked this development was the exodus. Now, in the messianic age, the death of the Messiah replicates the exodus event and replaces it as the new historical benchmark; and it is the Messiah, who, acting in God's behalf, possesses this human treasure and imprints it with a renewed, unique identity.

The act of "being" belongs to the category of response. Paul closes the christological statement in 2:14d with the phrase "zealous for good deeds" (*zēlōtēn kalōn ergōn*). This loosely attached phrase links this christological statement to the preceding ethical teaching (2:2–10), ensuring the close relationship between theology (as anchored in the historical Christ event) and ethics (the life that this event "teaches" [2:12]). "Good deeds" (1:16; 2:7; 3:8, 14) is Pauline shorthand (particularly in these letters to co-workers [see Towner 1989: 153–54; Marshall 1999: 227–29]) for the visible, outward dimension of Christian existence (cf. Eph. 2:10).

We should recall that Paul insists that this dimension of Christian identity is something that the opponents lack (1:16), since, as we make the connections implied by Paul's logic, they have not been "cleansed" (1:15). Thus, with this closing phrase Paul lifts the web of OT reflections into the contemporary situation, rounding off the theological rationale of Christian existence by returning to the ethical vocabulary most familiar to the readers. From the perspective of cause and effect, authentic Christian identity involves a creative act of "becoming" (redemption, purification) that makes a unique quality of "being" possible. With a distinct framework of OT covenant and new covenant already established by Paul, "zeal for good deeds" can be understood within that frame. The appropriate response to grace was to be devotion to Torah (Exod. 19:5; Deut. 26:18). From Paul's eschatological Spirit-perspective, the faith response to covenant grace is the Spirit-generated fulfillment of Torah. His web of Ezekiel echoes (linked by the key themes and word groups of "cleansing," "lawlessness," "nationhood") encompasses this new Spirit-reality, even if he delays explicit reference to the Spirit until 3:5–6:

36:25: I will sprinkle clean [*katharon*] water upon you, and you will be cleansed [*katharisthēsesthe*] from all your uncleannesses [*tōn akatharsiōn*] and from all your idols, and I will cleanse [*kathariō*] you.

36:26: I will give you a new heart, and will put a new spirit in you; and I will take away the heart of stone out of your flesh, and will give you a heart of flesh.

36:27: I will put my Spirit in you, and will cause you to walk in my ordinances, and keep my judgments, and do them.

36:28: You will dwell in the land which I gave to your ancestors; and you will be my people, and I will be your God.

36:29: I will save you from all your uncleannesses [*tōn akatharsiōn*].

36:31: Then you will remember your evil ways and your practices that were not good, and you will be hateful in your own sight for your transgressions [*tais anomiais hymōn*] and for your abominations [*tois bdelygmasin hymōn*]. (Cf. Titus 1:16.)

36:33: Thus says the Lord God, "In the day wherein I will cleanse [*kathariō*] you from all your iniquities [*ek pasōn tōn anomiōn hymōn*] I will also cause the cities to be inhabited, and the waste places will be built upon."

Making the conceptual shift from "keeping the law" (e.g., Ezek. 36:27) to being "zealous for good deeds," Paul has established an OT hermeneutical line that allows Christ's death to be viewed as Yahweh's ultimate act of deliverance, and the results to be seen in terms of the new-covenant perspective that emerged especially in Ezekiel. The eschatological wildcard, surely latent—as the Ezekiel texts themselves and Pauline theology in general would suggest—but not yet breaking the textual surface, is the Holy Spirit, whose dynamic role in authentic Christian existence will finally be explored in the subsequent section of Titus.

3:4–6

Before looking at 3:4–6 as a unit, we should note that 3:4 initiates the description of the epiphany of God's "kindness [*chrēstotēs*] and love for people [*philanthrōpia*]" with a striking pair of terms (frequently linked in extrabiblical literature) that here coalesces OT and Hellenistic concepts. God's *chrēstotēs* (cf. Rom. 2:4; 11:22 [3x]; Eph. 2:7) is a quality mentioned in numerous texts in the OT and the deuterocanonical writings (e.g., LXX: Ps. 30:20 [31:19 ET]; 84:13 [85:12 ET]; 118:65 [119:65 ET]; *Pss. Sol.* 5:18; 9:7; 18:1; for the adjective *chrēstos*, see, e.g., LXX: Ps. 99:5 [100:5 ET]; 105:1 [106:1 ET]; 106:1 [107:1 ET]; Jer. 40:11 [33:11 ET]). The second term of the pair, *philanthrōpia*, occurs only here as a description of God's character (cf. Wis. 1:6; 7:23, where the adjective *philanthrōpos* is used to describe wisdom) and is more typically a virtue to be found in rulers (cf. Philo, *Embassy* 67; 73; *Spec. Laws* 3.155; Plutarch, *Luc.* 18.9; see *TLNT* 3:512–13).

We should also note that the language in which the negation of human effort in divine salvation is framed in 3:5 has a Pauline ring (cf., e.g., Rom. 9:12; Eph. 2:8–9), and this wider Pauline reflection is the more significant background to the statement. However, the structure and theme of Deut. 9:5 may have influenced the presentation of 3:5a (as well as Paul's theology of justification):

> Deut. 9:5: Not for your righteousness [*ouchi dia tēn dikaiosynēn sou*] . . . do you enter to inherit the land, but [*alla*] . . .

> Titus 3:5a: He saved us, not out of works done in righteousness [*ouk ex ergōn tōn en dikaiosynē*], but [*alla*] . . .

Turning our attention to 3:4–6 as a unit, we note that the Pauline character of this closing theological piece is widely acknowledged. In it, Paul comes closest to reaching the level of emphasis on the role of the Spirit in salvation expressed elsewhere in his letters. Within the poem he draws explicitly on traditional language (Joel 3:1 LXX [2:28 ET]; Acts 2:17–18) to describe the Spirit's "outpouring":

> Titus 3:6a: whom [God] poured out richly upon us [*hou execheen eph' hēmas plousiōs*]

> Joel 3:1: It will come to pass afterwards that I will pour out my Spirit on all flesh [*kai echeō apo tou pneumatos mou epi pasan sarka*].

> Acts 2:17: And it will be in the last days, God says, I will pour out my Spirit on all flesh [*kai estai en tais eschatais hēmerais, legei ho theos, echeō apo tou pneumatos mou epi pasan sarka*].

As a comparison of the three texts suggests, the theme of the Spirit and the image of "pouring out," stated in all three with the same verb (*echeō*), determine the link to the tradition. What cannot be said is whether Paul draws directly from the OT text of Joel or rather accesses it as it has already been incorporated into the early church's paradosis (there is no reason to think that Acts 2 is the source of the allusion). Either way, the verb (shifted from first person to third person to suit the context) and the theme invoke Joel's promise of the Spirit's outpouring in order to establish the redemptive historical moment of salvation in Christ in relation to the ministry of the Spirit.

However, the OT background to this teaching about the Spirit is quite possibly more expansive. In so short a space of discourse the catena of Ezekiel texts recently summoned will not have been forgotten. The epicenter of that network of texts is the promise of renewal by the "ingiving" of the Spirit (36:27).

Even before the mention of the outpouring of the Spirit, this description of the Spirit's activity in 3:5d–e echoes the OT texts that speak of the new covenant. Given the potency of the Spirit tradition and some verbal and conceptual cues, this language ("the washing [*loutron*] of regeneration," "renewal by the Holy Spirit") would call to mind the vivid images of the promise of the Spirit in Ezek. 36:25–27 (which included the imagery of sprinkling with water, renewal of the heart, and gift of the Spirit) and other such texts (cf. Ps. 103:30 LXX [104:30 ET]). And the thought of new life implicit in this poem (see 3:1–2; 2:14d)—the Spirit-enabled "doing of the law"—cannot be far from mind.

When the OT promise of the Spirit's "outpouring" is subsequently echoed in 3:6, what must be observed is that in the Ezekiel text's broader context (esp. 36:18), the verb that links the prophetic past as expressed in Joel with the eschatological present as expressed here, "pour out" (*ekcheō*), is in Ezekiel overwhelmingly used of God's wrath (LXX: 7:5 [7:8 ET]; 9:8; 14:19; 20:8, 13, 21; 21:36 [21:31 ET]; 22:22, 31; 30:15; 36:18; 39:29 [cf. Jer. 6:11; Lam. 2:4; 4:11]). If we allow for the continuing resonance of the Spirit texts in Ezekiel, then Paul possibly is creating a striking "reversal of fortunes" theme. In Ezek. 36 the readers are to imagine themselves first as victims of the outpouring of God's wrath (in exile for defiling the land) and then as recipients of God's cleansing, of new hearts, and of the indwelling Spirit. And Paul called up this scenario in 2:14 to dramatize, in Ezekiel's prophetic terms, the changes that have taken place for the Christians in Crete. Now, with the readers already immersed in the Ezekiel background, the echo of Joel's prophecy strikes a chord that is simultaneously harmonious and dissonant. The promise of the Spirit links firmly to Ezekiel, but the verb describing this glad event, "pour out," clangs against the dominant use of "outpouring" for wrath in Ezekiel. The newly sounded OT text does not supplant the first; rather, it creates an atmosphere of climax: Paul paints a picture of dramatic reversal. God himself has brought his people from wrath to blessing, from immorality to godliness, by the provision of his Spirit. What was promised to God's people in exile is "now" being enjoyed by God's people in Christ. And in a way continuous with 2:14, the promise of the Joel text is combined creatively with the the Spirit texts in Ezekiel and new-covenant prophecy to locate the Cretan Christians within redemptive history.

Bibliography

Bartsch, H.-W. 1966. *Die Anfänge urchristlicher Rechtsbildungen: Studien zu den Pastoralbriefen*. TF 34. Hamburg: Reich.

Brewer, D. I. 1992. "1 Corinthians 9:9–11: A Literal Interpretation of 'Do Not Muzzle the Ox.'" *NTS* 38: 554–65.

Brox, N. 1969. *Die Pastoralbriefe*. RNT. Regensburg: Pustet.

Cranfield, C. E. B. 1982. "Changes of Person and Number in Paul's Epistles." Pages 280–89 in *Paul and Paulinism: Essays in Honour of C. K. Barrett*. Edited by M. D. Hooker and S. G. Wilson. London: SPCK.

Dibelius, M., and H. Conzelmann. 1972. *The Pastoral Epistles*. Hermeneia. Philadelphia: Fortress.

Fee, G. D. 1988. *1 and 2 Timothy, Titus*. NIBCNT. Peabody, MA: Hendrickson.

Gaston, L. 1970. *No Stone on Another: Studies in the Significance of the Fall of Jerusalem in the Synoptic Gospels*. NovTSup 23. Leiden: Brill.

Gordon, R. P. 1974. "Targumic Parallels to Acts XIII and Didache XIV 3." *NovT* 16: 285–89.

Hanson, A. T. 1968. *Studies in the Pastoral Epistles*. London: SPCK.

Hengel, M. 1983. *Between Jesus and Paul: Studies in the Earliest History of Christianity*. London: SCM.

Hill, D. 1967. *Greek Words and Hebrew Meanings: Studies in the Semantics of Soteriological Terms*. SNTSMS 5. Cambridge: Cambridge University Press.

Holmes, J. M. 2000. *Text in a Whirlwind: A Critique of Four Exegetical Devices at 1 Timothy 2.2–15*. JSNTSup 196. Sheffield: Sheffield Academic Press.

Horbury, W. 1998. *Jewish Messianism and the Cult of Christ*. London: SCM.

Hurley, J. B. 1981. *Man and Woman in Biblical Perspective*. Leicester: Inter-Varsity.

Jervell, J. 1960. *Imago Dei: Gen 1,26f. im Spätjudentum, in der Gnosis und in den paulinischen Briefen*. FRLANT 76. Göttingen: Vandenhoeck & Ruprecht.

Johnson, L. T. 1996. *Letters to Paul's Delegates: 1 Timothy, 2 Timothy, Titus*. NTC. Valley Forge, PA: Trinity Press International.

———. 2001. *The First and Second Letters to Timothy*. AB 35A. New York: Doubleday.

Keener, C. S. 1992. *Paul, Women and Wives: Marriage and Women's Ministry in the Letters of Paul*. Peabody, MA: Hendrickson.

Knight, G. W., III. 1992. *A Commentary on the Pastoral Epistles*. NIGTC. Grand Rapids: Eerdmans.

Knoch, O. 1988. *1. und 2. Timotheusbrief, Titusbrief*. NEchtB 14. Würzburg: Echter.

Kroeger, R. C., and C. C. Kroeger. 1992. *I Suffer Not a Woman: Rethinking 1 Timothy 2:11–15 in Light of Ancient Evidence*. Grand Rapids: Baker Academic.

Küchler, M. 1986. *Schweigen, Schmuck und Schleier: Drei neutestamentliche Vorschriften zur Verdrängung der Frauen auf dem Hintergrund einer frauenfeindlichen Exegese des Alten Testaments im antiken Judentum*. NTOA 1. Freiburg: Universitätsverlag.

Marshall, I. H. 1999. *The Pastoral Epistles*. ICC. Edinburgh: T&T Clark.

Menken, M. J. J. 1977. "hoti en 1 Tim 6, 7." *Bib* 58: 532–51.

Moo, D. J. 1980. "1 Timothy 2:11–15: Meaning and Significance." *TJ* 1: 62–83.

Nauck, W. 1950. "Die Herkunft des Verfassers der Pastoralbriefe: Ein Beitrag zur Frage der Auslegung der Pastoralbriefe." Diss., University of Göttingen.

Oberlinner, L. 1994. *Kommentar zum Ersten Timotheusbrief*. Vol. 1 of *Die Pastoralbriefe*. HTKNT 11. Freiburg: Herder.

Pietersma, A. 1994. *The Apocryphon of Jannes and Jambres the Magicians: P. Chester Beatty XVI, with New Editions of Papyrus Vindobonensis Greek Inv. 29456 + 29828 Verso and British Library Cotton Tiberius B. v f. 87*. RGW 119. Leiden: Brill.

———. 1995–1997. "Jannes and Jambres." *ABD on CD-ROM*. Version 2.1a.

Prior, M. 1989. *Paul the Letter-writer and the Second Letter to Timothy*. JSNTSS 23. Sheffield: Sheffield Academic Press.

Quinn, J. D., and W. C. Wacker. 2000. *The First and Second Letters to Timothy*. ECC. Grand Rapids: Eerdmans.

Roloff, J. 1988. *Die Erste Brief an Timotheus*. EKK. Zürich: Benziger; Neukirchen-Vluyn: Neukirchener Verlag.

Rudolph, K. 1983. *Gnosis: The Nature and History of an Ancient Religion*. Edinburgh: T&T Clark.

Ruppert, L. 1972. *Jesus als der leidende Gerechte? Der Weg Jesu im Lichte eines alt- und zwischentestamentlichen Motivs.* SBib 59. Stuttgart: KBW Verlag.

Schlarb, E. 1990. *Die Gesunde Lehre: Häresie und Wahrheit im Spiegel der Pastoralbriefe.* MTS 28. Marburg: Elwert.

Schreiner, T. R. 1995. "An Interpretation of 1 Timothy 2:9–15: A Dialogue with Scholarship." Pages 105–54 in *Women in the Church: A Fresh Analysis of 1 Timothy 2:9–15.* Edited by A. J. Köstenberger, T. R. Schreiner, and H. S. Baldwin. Grand Rapids: Baker Academic.

Schürer, E. 1973–1987. *The History of the Jewish People in the Age of Jesus Christ (175 B.C.–A.D. 135).* Revised and edited by G. Vermes, F. Millar, and M. Goodman. 3 vols. Edinburgh: T&T Clark.

Schüssler Fiorenza, E. 1983. *In Memory of Her: A Feminist Theological Reconstruction of Christian Origins.* New York: Crossroad.

Sherwin-White, A. N. 1963. *Roman Society and Roman Law in the New Testament.* Oxford: Oxford University Press.

Spicq, C. 1969. *Les Épîtres Pastorales.* 4th ed. Paris: Gabalda.

Thackeray, H. St. J. 1900. *The Relation of St. Paul to Contemporary Jewish Thought.* London: Macmillan.

Towner, P. H. 1989. *The Goal of Our Instruction: The Structure of Theology and Ethics in the Pastoral Epistles.* JSNTSup 34. Sheffield: Sheffield Academic Press.

———. 1996. "Piety in Chinese Thought and in the Biblical Tradition: *Li* and *Eusebeia.*" *Jian Dao* 5: 95–126.

———. 1997. "Feminist Approaches to the New Testament" *Jian Dao* 7: 91–111.

———. 1999. "The Portrait of Paul and the Theology of 2 Timothy: The Closing Chapter of the Pauline Story." *HBT* 21: 151–70.

———. 2005. "Christology in the Letters to Timothy and Titus." Pages 219–46 in *Contours of Christology in the New Testament.* Edited by R. N. Longenecker. MNTS 7. Grand Rapids: Eerdmans.

———. 2006. *The Letters to Timothy and Titus.* NICNT. Grand Rapids: Eerdmans.

Wire, A. C. 1990. *The Corinthian Women Prophets: A Reconstruction through Paul's Rhetoric.* Minneapolis: Fortress.

Yinger, K. L. 1999. *Paul, Judaism, and Judgment according to Deeds.* SNTSMS 105. Cambridge: Cambridge University Press.

Philemon

There are no OT quotations or clear allusions to discuss in Philemon, though some have proposed an OT and Jewish background for Paul's desire that the slave, Onesimus, not be punished but be accepted as a brother by Philemon (see Deut. 23:15–16 and the Jewish commentary that grew up around it in rabbinic, targumic, philonic, and Qumranic literature). On the other hand, not only was Onesimus not a Jewish slave, but a Gentile, a pagan who was converted to Christ in the midst of his fleeing, but Paul was returning him to his owner—the very thing that Deut. 23:15–16 forbids. See Joseph A. Fitzmyer, *The Letter to Philemon*, AB 34C (New York: Doubleday, 2000), 30–31, 110; contra, Craig A. Evans, *Ancient Texts for New Testament Studies: A Guide to the Background Literature* (Peabody, MA: Hendrickson, 2005), 395.

HEBREWS

George H. Guthrie

Introduction

At the end of a group of parables on things gathered into the kingdom of heaven, Matthew records these words of Jesus: "For this reason every scholar who has become a disciple of the kingdom of heaven is comparable to a man with property who brings out of his storeroom both new and old things" (Matt. 13:52). Whatever the identity of the scholar who wrote the NT book of Hebrews, he fulfills this description admirably, bringing to his task a rich mix of skills, both rhetorical and rabbinic, drawing from the ancient texts at his disposal and presenting them in light of his received christocentric tradition, with the intention of offering strong encouragement to a beleaguered community. With good reason, the book recently has been called the "Cinderella" of NT studies (McCullough 1994: 66), but its astute scholar has crafted what might be called the "Queen" when it comes to the use of the OT in the NT. No NT book, with perhaps the exception of Revelation, presents a discourse so permeated, so crafted, both at the macro- and microlevels, by various uses to which the older covenant texts are put, and his appropriation of the text is radically different from the book's apocalyptic cousin. (For a more complete introduction to the use of the OT in Hebrews than follows here, see G. H. Guthrie 1997; 2003.)

As we come to the task of analyzing in detail the appropriation of the OT text by Hebrews, we immediately are presented with striking challenges. To a great extent Hebrews marks overt quotations well, but the exact line between quotation and allusion is not always perfectly clear (e.g., the use of Gen. 15:5 at 11:12, which has no introductory formula). With recent work on OT echoes in the NT (e.g., Hays 1989), identifying echoes and distinguishing them from allusions also has become a factor. Furthermore, Hebrews is so permeated with general references to OT topics, allusions to historical events, and repetition or exposition of those passages that have been introduced overtly, that the task of exact enumeration of the author's uses of the OT has taxed the efforts of many a student of the book. Longenecker (1975: 164), for instance, counted thirty-eight quotations, whereas Westcott (1909: 472) and Caird (1959: 47) each found only twenty-nine. Michel (1986: 151) discerned thirty-two, Spicq thirty-six (1952–1953: 1:331), and Bratcher (1969: 57–67) forty.

Based on the treatment of the OT in Hebrews that follows, I count roughly thirty-seven quotations, forty allusions, nineteen cases where OT material is summarized, and thirteen where an OT name or topic is referred to without reference to a specific context. As for echoes, Hays's tests have been utilized (for an explanation of these tests see Hays 1989: 29–32). Yet, while cognizant of these criteria, as a methodological approach I have given special weight to aspects of the third test: recurrence. In light of the extent and pervasiveness of Hebrews' uses of the OT, I suggest that the tracking of echoes might best begin with a consideration of the broader contexts of the book's citations. Of course, there are places where an author uses echoes not originating in the contexts of his or her direct quotations, as is demonstrated below. However, when one is stepping out on uncertain ground, it is better to step first on the firmer parts of a path rather than the softer spots of a wide-open field, and the contexts of the quotations are, at least, an appropriate place to begin our search, for here we are assured both of Hays's first and third criteria: availability and recurrence.

As Hays (1989: 20) points out, "Allusive echo functions to suggest to the reader that text B should be understood in light of a broad interplay with text A, encompassing aspects of A beyond those explicitly echoed." In his study on the influence of Isa. 7–9 on Matthew's soteriology, Carter (2000: 505), following Lars Hartman, suggests that intertextual elements invoke the authority of the source text, using the words of that text but at times pointing beyond the intertextual element to a larger complex of ideas. In line with Hartman, Carter (2000: 506) is concerned to move away from atomistic treatments of citations, which detach them from any scriptural context and ignore "the audience's knowledge of a larger common tradition." This is much in line with the suggestions of Dodd (1961), who proposed that a quotation from the OT serves to bring to mind a broader OT context. It also makes sense in communication contexts, such as the preaching of sermons today. Imagine, for instance, a preacher, expounding on the theme of the need for love in the church, who exhorts, "Let's not be clanging cymbals!" This reference calls to mind, of course, the whole of 1 Cor. 13. That chapter is so foregrounded in the conscience of most Christian congregations, both by its distinctiveness and its popularity, that the allusion would be readily identifiable.

In line with this dynamic, it may be suggested that the author of Hebrews, rather than taking an atomistic approach to citations from Israel's Scriptures, had in mind, and at times used, OT references in light of their broader contexts. For

instance, the author's reasons for using the brief quotation from Isaiah at 2:13 are barely discernible until one considers the broader, messianic context from which the quotation hails. The broader contexts of many of Hebrews' quotations, moreover, would have been familiar to the hearers, stemming from their Scriptures, though some contexts certainly would have been more familiar than others, depending on the level of popularity and use. Such a circumstance, therefore, challenges us not to be atomistic in our analysis of the OT citations and allusions. In my study of the uses of the OT in Hebrews, therefore, I have systematically examined the broader contexts of every quotation (as presented in the LXX), looking for elements that might be echoed elsewhere in Hebrews.

There are a number of places where interpreters have already noted what might be considered echoes of the OT text. For instance, Lane (1991) points to Ps. 92:1 LXX (93:1 MT) and Ps. 95:10 LXX (96:10 MT) as the source for *tēn oikoumenēn* in Heb. 1:6; 2:5, which he equates with the age to come (6:5) and the city to come (13:14). Both psalm passages proclaim that this "world," established with the reign of God, "shall not be shaken," a part of these psalms alluded to overtly at 12:28. Lane (1991: 1:46) comments, "The explicit allusion to 'a kingdom that cannot be shaken' in Heb. 12:28 indicates that these passages were not far from the writer's mind when he penned v. 5." Thus, the uses of *tēn oikoumenēn* at 1:6; 2:5 echo these two psalms.

Elsewhere I have argued that the author's use at 3:16–19 of *subiectio*—a rhetorical pattern of asking and answering a series of questions in rapid-fire manner—takes its questions from Ps. 95:7b–11 and its answers from a network of passages bemoaning the wilderness rebellion (G. H. Guthrie 1998: 131). That those who came out of Egypt with Moses were the ones who rebelled against the Lord (3:16) may be concluded from Ps. 106, Num. 14:1–38, or Deut. 9. That it was "those who sinned, whose bodies fell in the desert" with whom God was upset (3:17) echoes either Ps. 106 or Num. 14:1–38. The concept of the disobedient ones as those to whom God swore that they would not enter his rest (3:18) finds expression in Deut. 9:7, 24. Finally, the unit concludes with a summary statement in 3:19, explaining that at its core the wanderers' inability to enter God's rest stemmed from their unbelief, thus linking the concepts of unbelief and disobedience. This important "unbelief" motif occurs in Deut. 9:23; Num. 14:11; Ps. 78:22, 32. These allusions, rather than being overt—some of them cannot be pinpointed as to location—constitute recollections (to use Hays's word) of prominent concepts. Thus, these interrelated passages form somewhat a hall of echoes from which the author draws.

Other examples could be given. My interest in Hebrews research originates from a 1954 article by August Strobel in which he suggests that the "cries and tears" of 5:7, although not part of the Gethsemane accounts, probably stem from Ps. 116, a "prayer of righteous suffering" (Strobel 1954). The faintness of the allusion, however, would suggest that these be considered echoes expressing, however faintly, reflection on Jesus' experience in Gethsemane in light of early Christian appropriation of "righteous sufferer" psalm material.

More recently, Mathewson (1999) has offered a highly suggestive article entitled "Heb 6:4–6 in Light of the Old Testament." Mathewson (1999: 214) argues that "the author's language in 6:4–6 is colored by OT references by means of allusion and echo apart from direct citation." Thus, the descriptions of those who have fallen away—descriptions so elusive and divisive in the history of interpretation—stem from the passages about wilderness wandering, continuing an exhortation dynamic begun in 3:7–19. For instance, Mathewson (1999: 216–17) suggests that those who were "enlightened" echoes the pillar of fire by which the Israelites were "enlightened" on their way (Neh. 9:12, 19; Ps. 105:39). The "heavenly gift" that those under consideration had tasted echoes those passages that refer to the heavenly gift of manna, which the Lord gave to people of the wilderness generation. In texts such as Exod. 16:15; Neh. 9:15; Ps. 78:24 (77:24 LXX) the heavenly bread is said to have been given (*edōken*) to them. For Mathewson, that those who have fallen away had become companions of the Holy Spirit (6:4c) echoes the experience of the wilderness wanderers, who had extensive interaction with the Spirit of God, as witnessed in numerous passages (e.g., Neh. 9:20; 11:17, 25; Isa. 63:11). Having considered the elements describing the fallen in 6:4–6, Mathewson (1999: 223) concludes, "The author

is not just alluding to snippets of texts and isolated vocabulary for rhetorical color, but by alluding to texts which belong to a larger matrix of ideas he is evoking the entire context and story of Israel's experience in the wilderness." Thus, the author of Hebrews utilizes the language of the OT to describe a particularly grievous abandonment of the Christian community in his day.

In a few cases I will add to this list in the pages that follow. The identifiable echoes in Hebrews are not many, the author wishing rather to carry forward his discourse on the strength of his considerable quotations and overt allusions. Nonetheless, a couple of the echoes have import for interpretation at key points (e.g., 1:4; 3:3–6).

In terms of his employment of different parts of the Scriptures, the author of Hebrews depends most heavily by far on Psalms, drawing from this well especially in support of his christological proclamations. Nineteen of the quotations and another fifteen allusions come from this portion of the OT. The Pentateuch is accessed via nine quotations (three from Genesis, two from Exodus, four from Deuteronomy) and another fifteen allusions (eight from Genesis, one from Exodus, two from Leviticus, two from Numbers, two from Deuteronomy), often in relation to redemptive history. Among the prophets, Isaiah holds pride of place with three quotations and four allusions, and Jeremiah follows closely with two quotations and three allusions. Habakkuk, Haggai, Proverbs, and 2 Samuel each are quoted once, and Joshua is alluded to a single time, as possibly are Proverbs and Job.

The quotations are introduced normally as falling from the lips of God, forms of the verb *legō* being employed most often. In fact, twenty three of the quotations in Hebrews have God as the speaker. Four passages put the words of the OT on the lips of Christ, and four others are attributed to the Holy Spirit. In addition, Moses speaks a command of God at 9:20 and is terrified at God's revelation at 12:21. Yet, the context is still that of divine revelation. The introductory formula at 2:6 is an anomaly ("But somewhere one has testified, saying . . ."). The ambiguity of the formula, which acknowledges this messianic psalm as framed from a human perspective, may serve to keep the focus on God as the primary speaker of Scripture.

The issues surrounding the text form used by Hebrews have been studied extensively since the middle part of the last century and have increasingly focused on the differences that we find between the author's form of quotation and known forms of the Old Greek text. With rare exception, the assumption is that a Greek, rather than a Hebrew, text was used by the author. Bleek initiated the format for the debate in the nineteenth century. In his commentary Bleek (1828) argued against Pauline authorship of Hebrews, partly on the basis that Paul used a text similar to Codex Vaticanus (Codex B) when quoting a Greek text. According to Bleek, Hebrews gives evidence of its author's partiality to a text similar to Codex Alexandrinus (Codex A). However, scholars such as Katz (1958) questioned Bleek's observations about LXX A, and discussions for most of the twentieth century focused on how the author's text related to one, or both, of these major codices. Arguing that Hebrews follows neither Codex A nor Codex B exclusively, Thomas (1965) suggested that Hebrews combines the more primitive elements of each, probably utilizing an earlier form of the Greek text. Howard (1968), on the other hand, proposed that Hebrews reflects a form of the Hebrew text earlier than the MT that was used in the revision or standardization of the LXX, a suggestion mentioned also by Barth (1962) and others.

McCullough, in his 1971 dissertation and later in a 1979–1980 article, concluded that for several books of the OT, such as Jeremiah and Psalms, the recension from which the text quoted is taken is fairly clear, whereas definite conclusions concerning other OT books were elusive. Therefore, he emphasized the need to study the Greek text forms on a book-by-book basis rather than drawing wide-ranging conclusions concerning specific recensions of the Old Greek text. All these explanations, of course, have to do with issues of textual transmission. Other explanations of the form of the OT quotations in Hebrews are possible: (1) corruption of the Epistle to the Hebrews; (2) adjustments based on prior tradition of interpretation (e.g., in the Christian community); (3) a lapse of memory on part of the author as he is quoting the OT text; (4) the author accommodated himself to the Greek text form at hand for his audience; (5) a freedom on the part of the author to make adjustments to the Greek text for stylistic reasons; (6) a freedom on the part of the author to make slight adjustments or paraphrases that are theologically motivated.

The last two of these suggestions form the dominant view in discussions of the past two decades. Silva (1983: 155) moves in this direction by suggesting that the NT authors exercise freedom in paraphrasing the OT text as they interpret and apply it. He also leaves open the possibility that the author of Hebrews exercises freedom in proactively using the LXX form for theological reasons. Leschert (1994: 245–47) suggests that the author handled his *Vorlage* as authoritative and generally followed it consistently. Yet, the author may have altered the *Vorlage* slightly to improve on its literary style or to emphasize points of theology, but it is difficult, Leschert notes, to determine which departures from the septuagintal texts that we have were actually in his form of the Greek text and which were his own adjustments. Bateman (1997: 240) concludes the same, that in keeping with his historical milieu, the author freely edits his OT both for stylistic balance and for theological emphasis. G. Hughes (1979: 59) suggests that by doing new-covenant reflection on the old-covenant text, the author of Hebrews creates a new *logia*, and this process may, in line with the techniques utilized by exegetes of the day, involve altering the text to suit the author's interpretation. Very similar is the conclusion by Enns regarding the author's use of Ps. 95 in chapter 3. Enns (1997: 362) states, "Apparently, the author seems to have no difficulty in taking certain liberties with the text in order to make his theological point. His exegetical technique is similar to what we find, for example, in the commentaries of the Qumran community." Jobes (1992: 183–85) proposes that the changes that we find in the author's quotation of Ps. 40 create a phonetic assonance, a pleasing style, and she notes similar dynamics in five other quotations in Hebrews. Further, Jobes (1992: 191) suggests that such changes accomplish a theological purpose: they highlight the discontinuity between the old and the new eras.

These authors feel varying degrees of comfort in suggesting that the author of Hebrews is making substantive changes in the message of the OT text. Most argue that he makes interpretive renderings that in essence are in line with the basic meaning of the OT text but bring out the greater significance of that meaning as fulfilled in Christ. At the same time, they acknowledge that the variants in the textual histories of both the Hebrew and Old Greek texts may account for some of these changes. Thus, one rather substantial current in research on Hebrews' use of the OT consists of a move away from focus on the question of a specific textual form behind the book and a move toward consideration of the author's own minor adjustments in presentation of the text for stylistic and theological purposes.

All issues concerning the OT in Hebrews come down to the author's uses or appropriations of the text for specific ends, and I offer the following as a brief summary on that topic. There are striking uses of the OT that assimilate numerous OT texts in an overarching method, such as the use of *ḥāraz* (the "string of pearls" method) at 1:5–14 and the beautiful *exempla* (example list) of chapter 11. These treatments rest on the building up of an impressive amount of evidence for the point being made. In the case of 1:5–14, the superiority of the Son to the angels comes through forcefully by the number of quotations offered. The *exempla*, on the other hand, by providing concisely expressed example after example, drives home the necessity of a life of faith for one who would please God. To these uses of a method that takes in numerous texts may be added, for instance, the running exposition on Ps. 95:7–11 that extends from 3:7 to 4:11. The exposition of the psalm is aided by the echoes from other "wandering" passages of the OT (3:16–19) and the addition of Gen. 2:2 at 4:4. On the other end of the spectrum, some of the author's arguments turn on a minute detail of the text in question, such as his seizing on the word "new" (*kainē*) from Jer. 38 LXX (31 MT) at 8:13 or the temporal logic inherent in Ps. 39 LXX (40 MT) at 10:8–9.

Of Hillel's principles or guidelines for appropriating the Scriptures, the author uses both verbal analogy and a fortiori argument consistently. The former serves to bring together sibling texts for support of a topic (such as those paired in the catena of 1:5–14) or to make a transition in the argument at hand (e.g., the move from exaltation in chap. 1, which culminates in the quotation of Ps. 110:1, to the focus on incarnation facilitated by the quotation of Ps. 8 at 2:5–9, these two psalms

having a key phrase in common). The latter technique forms a basis for the author's harsh warnings, for instance, and thus does much to support the hortatory purpose of the book.

More than any other technique, and sometimes in conjunction with other techniques, the author of Hebrews uses "reinforcement" (G. H. Guthrie 1997: 843–44) either to support a theological point just made or to bolster a word of exhortation (2:5–8a, 12–13; 3:15; 4:7; 5:5–6; 7:17, 21; 8:5, 7; 10:16–17, 30, 37–38; 12:26; 13:5–6). The form normally followed is that of the theological point or exhortation immediately followed by the reinforcing quotation. This technique highlights a general orientation in Hebrews' use of the OT, one that certainly is related to the book's genre. For, more than any other NT book, Hebrews, from beginning to end, *preaches* the OT. The author's explanations of the text serve ultimately to communicate a forceful message aimed at convincing the hearers/readers to respond by persevering in following Christ and standing with his church. His Christology vies for a christocentric life. His hortatory material has one aim: to present a resolute call to endurance and holy living. This is the task that he takes up in taking up the OT, and he carries it out with rhetorical power and artistry.

Hebrews 1

The book of Hebrews begins with a ceremonious, beautifully constructed period concerning the climax of revelation (1:1–2a) and the person, work, and status of God's Son (1:2b–4). The sentence begins by contrasting the revelation given during the time prior to the coming of the Messiah, expressed with "formerly" (*palai*), with that given "in these last days" (*ep' eschatou tōn hēmerōn toutōn*). Then the author turns to a series of three relative clauses describing the Son.

1:2

The first relative clause in the book's introduction (1:2b) concerns the Son's appointment as "heir of all things" (*klēronomon pantōn*), an allusion to Ps. 2:8. Just a few verses later, at 1:5, the author quotes Ps. 2:7, which should be taken as God's induction of the Messiah to his position as king of the universe upon his exaltation to the right hand. The allusion to the eighth verse of the psalm, however, is eschatological in force, pointing ultimately to Christ's total rule (e.g., Heb. 2:5–9), and is balanced with a confession of the Son's role as agent of creation in the following clause ("through whom he made the universe"). The author has taken the "nations" and "ends of the earth" of the psalm verse and interpreted them expansively as "all things." Inheritance serves as a key theme of Hebrews (1:14; 6:12, 17; 9:15; 11:7–8; 12:17).

1:3

The introduction's third relative clause (1:3–4) forms the climax of the introduction, and at the heart of this third clause is "he sat down at the right hand of the majesty on high," an overt allusion to Ps. 110:1 (109:1 LXX). Whereas "God" is the subject of the sentence prior to this third relative clause, the sentence now shifts to the Son as subject, which some have seen as an indication that traditional material is in play (e.g., Martin 1967: 19; Sanders 1971: 19). Further, this third relative clause is supported by four subordinate clauses, three in 1:3 ("being..., bearing..., having made...") and one in 1:4 ("having become..."), which point to the Son's person, work, and status. These all have the exaltation to the right hand as their central reference. In this way the author brings the Son's exaltation into sharp focus. Psalm 110:1 serves as a key to the structural development of the book, being quoted at 1:13 and alluded to here and at 8:1; 10:12; 12:2 (see commentary on Heb. 1:13 below).

1:4

At 1:4 the author speaks of the superior "name" (*onoma*) inherited by the Son. Recent commentators have given various interpretations of this *onoma*, but most understand it as a stylistic replacement for the title "Son." Others have suggested the title "Lord" or even "High Priest" is in mind. Still others have understood the term *onoma* to be a title in and of itself connoting the Messiah's power, divinity, and superior rank (e.g., G. H. Guthrie 1998: 50).

Interpretations of the use of *onoma* at 1:4 typically overlook the broader context of several of the OT passages in the "string of pearls" found in 1:5–14, among them 2 Sam. 7:14 (2 Kgdms. 7:14 LXX), quoted by the author in his next breath at 1:5. The Nathan oracle of 2 Sam. 7 and 1 Chron.

17 plays a vital role in OT thought concerning the house of David. In the Samuel version the passage is introduced saying, among other things, that the Lord had given David an inheritance on every side (7:1). The passage continues with God telling David, "I made a name for you according to the names of the great ones of the earth" (7:9 = 1 Chron. 17:8). In 7:13, the verse immediately prior to the quotation used by the author of Hebrews in 1:5, we find this promise concerning David's son: "He shall build a house for me for my name [*tō onomati mou*], and I will establish his throne forever." Here the OT author associates the name of the Lord and the throne of David's son, as is the case in Heb. 1:3–4. At 7:23 David says to the Lord, "What other nation on earth is like your people Israel, in that God guided him, to redeem for himself a people, to make himself a name, to accomplish greatness and visibility?" and in 7:26, "Let your name be magnified forever." In each of these last two uses of *onoma* the name of the Lord is emphasized. Thus, the author of 2 Sam. 7 uses *onoma* four times (7:9, 13, 23, 26), the name of David and the name of the Lord both coming into play. At Heb. 1:6 there also may be an association of Ps. 88 (89 MT) with the Nathan oracle of 2 Sam. 7/1 Chron. 17, that psalm offering a possible origin for the use of *prōtotokon* in the introductory formula. That psalm also places emphasis on the name of the Lord in 88:17, 25 (89:17, 25 MT; 89:16, 24 ET). In 88:25 (89:25 MT; 89:24 ET) God says of David, "And my truth and my mercy will be with him, and in my name [*en tō onomati mou*] his horn will be exalted."

The proposition that the *onoma* of 1:4 echoes 2 Sam. 7 finds further support by the occurrence of *megalōsynē* in both 1:3–4 and 2 Sam. 7. In 1:3 the author makes an allusion to Ps. 110:1 with the words "he sat down at the right hand of majesty." At this position at the right hand of majesty Jesus has been exalted, having become as much better than the angels as his inherited name is superior to theirs.

The term *megalōsynē*, found in the NT twice in Hebrews (1:3; 8:1) and at Jude 25, occurs fairly infrequently in the Greek version of the Jewish Scriptures as well. It occurs only in about nine contexts in some form of association with the name of God (Deut. 32:3; 1 Chron. 17:19–21; 22:5; 29:11–13; Prov. 18:10; Dan. 2:20; Odes

2:3; Sir. 39:15, and, in our text under consideration, 2 Sam. 7:21–23). At 2 Sam. 7:21–23, in the prayer in which David answers the oracle of God given through Nathan, David praises God for having brought about all this greatness (*megalōsynēn* [7:21]), speaking of the establishment of David's royal house, his kingdom, and his throne. Indeed, according to the passage, God has made a name for himself by accomplishing the greatness (*megalōsynēn*) of David's reign (7:23). Further, the cognate verb is used in 7:22, 26. In 7:22 David proclaims that God has worked great things on David's behalf that he might magnify (*megalynai*) the Lord, and in 7:26 David, speaking to the Lord, says, "Let your name be magnified [*megalyntheiē*] forever." The greatness of a name also is expressed at 7:9, where God says to David, "I will make your name like the names of the great ones [*tōn megalōn*] of the earth." Although the evidence should not be pressed too far, it may be that the descriptor of God's right hand as *tēs megalōsynēs* by the author of Hebrews in 1:3 is picked up from this context and used by him to describe God's work in the exaltation.

Thus, the use of *onoma* in 1:4, in association with God's right hand as *tēs megalōsynēs*, could be understood as an anticipatory echo of that broader messianic context of 2 Sam. 7 to which our author immediately will point in 1:5. The inherited "name," then, mentioned in 1:4, is, on this reading, not to be understood as an allusion to the title "Son," but rather as an honor conferred by God on the Messiah as the Davidic heir at the establishment of his throne and in association with God himself. This fulfills Hays's criteria of availability, volume (especially in terms of source text), recurrence, thematic coherence, historical plausibility, and satisfaction.

1:5

A. The Immediate NT Context: A Chain Quotation on the Son's Superiority to the Angels.
Teachers in broader Judaism, among both the rabbis and the interpreters of Qumran, at times used "catchwords" to string together OT texts revolving around a particular theme. These chain quotations, or *hāraz*, brought to bear a quantity of scriptural evidence to support the teacher's topic. The text of 1:5–12 consists of three movements, each one having a pair of OT quotations from the Septuagint that supports the superiority of the Son

over the angels. The Son's unique relationship to the Father, and his enthronement, constitute the focus of Ps. 2:7 and 2 Sam. 7:14 at 1:5, joined by the catchwords *huios* ("son") and *egō* ("I"), as well as, perhaps, the pronoun *mou/moi* ("my," "to me") and the verb of being. The second pair of texts, Deut. 32:43/Ps. 96:7 LXX (97:7 MT/ET) and Ps. 103:4 LXX (104:4 MT/ET) at 1:6–7, treat the angels, who worship the Son and function as servants, in terms of their inferior status and are joined by their common use of *angeloi/angelous*. The Son's eternal reign and role in relation to the cosmos is the concern of the third pair of texts, Ps. 44:7–8 LXX (45:7–8 MT; 45:6–7 ET) and Ps. 101:26–28 LXX (102:26–28 MT; 102:25–27 ET), at 1:8–12. These are joined by the various forms of the second-person personal pronouns in both passages. The climax of the chain occurs with the quotation of Ps. 110:1 (109:1 LXX) at 1:13, capping off a chain of OT texts that speak eloquently of the superiority of God's Son. Moreover, the chain functions to set up the argument "from lesser to greater" (*qal wahomer*) found in 2:1–4. Thus, the quotation of Ps. 2:7 introduces the chain quotation on the superiority of Christ to the angels.

Psalm 2:7, moreover, is introduced at 1:5 with the rhetorical question "For to which of the angels did God ever say . . . ?" (*tini gar eipen pote tōn angelōn*), an approximation of which is repeated at 1:13. These rhetorical questions, along with these conceptually related psalms, form an *inclusio* that brackets the chain quotation. Further, Ps. 2:7 stands at the front of the first main christological movement of the book, which concerns the position of the Son in relation to the angels (1:5–2:18), and is used also at 5:5 to introduce the book's second main christological movement, which concerns the position of the Son in relation to the earthly sacrificial system. These two uses of Ps. 2:7 form "parallel introductions" to these two great christological movements of the book.

B. The Original OT Context.
In its original context Ps. 2 speaks of the rebellion of the nations and their rulers against God and his Anointed One. This rebellion, however, will be smashed by the awesome, overwhelming power of the king whom God has enthroned on Mount Zion. The first movement of the psalm (2:1–3) depicts the insolence of the heathen nations. They rage

against the Lord, make empty plots (2:1), take a united stand (2:2), and proclaim their desire to get out from under the rule of the Lord and his Anointed One (2:3). The second movement of the psalm (2:4–6) constitutes the Lord's response. He laughs at and ridicules these rebellious kings (2:4), and then he speaks harshly to them (2:5). In 2:6, the MT has the Lord's proclamation that he has installed his choice of king on Mount Zion, while the LXX places the confession in the mouth of the king himself ("I have been appointed [*katestathēn*] king" [aorist passive indicative of *kathistēmi*]). The passage then shifts to a confession of confidence based on the Lord's decree. God has proclaimed that the Davidic king is his heir and that the nations, even to the ends of the earth, are his inheritance (2:7–8). The "I have begotten you" does not refer to the king being physically born of God, as might be expected in ancient eastern Mediterranean mythology; rather, "the father-son relationship so expressed connotes divine sponsorship, support, or assistance for the king, and by implication for his dynasty" (Fitzmyer 2000: 66). Consequently, being supported by God, the king's rule will constitute victory over the rebellious nations (2:9). The final movement (2:10–12), therefore, expresses a warning to the leaders of the earth. They should serve the Lord in fear and rejoice in trembling (2:11). They should accept his correction (LXX) or submit to the son (MT) and allow themselves to find refuge in him. Thus, the psalm displays a resounding confession of the Lord's support of his vicegerent, the Davidic king.

Finally, we should note a number of lexical parallels between the broader context of this psalm and Ps. 110 (109 LXX), which is alluded to at 1:3 and quoted at 1:13. The two, both royal psalms, are connected by the following: "Lord" (110:1; 2:2, 4, 7, 11); the concept of "sitting" or "dwelling" (110:1; 2:4); the concept of "enemies" (110:1–2; 2:2); "scepter" (110:2; 2:9); "Zion" (110:2; 2:6); the concept of "shattering" (110:5–6; 2:9); "wrath" (110:5; 2:12); "judge" (110:6; 2:10); "nations" (110:6; 2:1).

C. Relevant Uses of the OT Reference in Jewish Sources. Appendix A of *The Manual of Discipline* describes the "last days" as an ideal period in the future. In this appendix is described a feast that will take place upon the arrival of Messiah (1Q28a

II, 11–12), which is reminiscent of the marriage feast of the Lamb in the NT (Rev. 19:6–9). God is said to "beget" the Messiah of Israel, who comes from the line of David, although this reading is disputed (Wise, Abegg, and Cook 1996: 144). If it is authentic, as many conclude, it constitutes an allusion to Ps. 2:7.

Although not specifically alluding to Ps. 2:7, both 4Q174 1 I, 10–II, 5 and *Pss. Sol.* 17:14–20 deal with the broader context of Ps. 2 as a whole. 4QFlor174 1 I, 18–II, 2 quotes Ps. 2:1–2, speaking of the nations raging and setting themselves against the Lord and his anointed. *Psalms of Solomon* 17:14–20 also speaks of the Lord raising up a king for his people, and it contains a plea that the king have the strength to destroy the unrighteous rulers, driving them from the inheritance. This destruction is described in the words of Ps. 2:9 and concerns the "shattering" of the sinners with a rod of iron.

Both Ps. 2:7 and Ps. 110:1 seem to be alluded to at *T. Levi* 4:2, where the concepts of "son" and "priest" occur together. In this passage "son" refers to the anointed priest, and the statement constitutes a parallel to the king as God's son (*OTP* 1:789 note 4a).

Much later, *b. Sukkah* 52a reads, "Our Rabbis taught, The Holy One, blessed be He, will say to the Messiah, the son of David (May he reveal himself speedily in our days!), 'Ask of me anything, and I will give it to thee,' as it is said, *I will tell of the decree etc. this day have I begotten thee, ask of me and I will give the nations for thy inheritance*" (italics added). Here Ps. 2:7 is used to reinforce that the Holy One will give the Messiah anything he asks, with the line from the psalm "I will give the nations for thy inheritance" understood as expressing God's limitless giving to the Davidic heir.

Thus, Ps. 2:7 is applied consistently to the Messiah in the Jewish literature through several centuries. For the most part, the psalm is associated with hearty anticipation of Messiah's coming and the vindication of God's people before the unbelieving nations.

D. The Textual Background. At Ps. 2:7 there exists a one-to-one correspondence between the Hebrew and the Septuagint texts (the text of the Greek OT seems very stable at this point), and between the Septuagint text and the quotation as found in Hebrews. This seems to point to Hebrews' use of the Septuagint, since the two would be unlikely to translate the Hebrew in exactly the same way. Two interesting dynamics in the immediate context of Ps. 2:7, however, might be mentioned. First, at 2:6, the Qal perfect in the Hebrew text, "I have installed," has become an aorist passive in the LXX, "I have been appointed." Thus, in the Hebrew the Lord speaks of his appointment of the king, whereas in the Greek the king himself speaks of his appointment by the Lord. Also, in 2:12 the Hebrew text presents an exhortation to the earthly rulers to submit themselves reverently to the son, the appointed king, and it is the son who is the subject of the rest of the verse. In the Greek translation, however, the rulers are to accept correction and seek refuge from the Lord.

E. How Ps. 2:7 Is Understood and Used at Heb. 1:5. On one level, as indicated in our consideration of the use of Ps. 2 in broader Judaism, and certainly in the case of early Christianity, Ps. 2 was read at times as messianic. The psalm builds on the 2 Sam. 7 promise to David regarding the world dominance to be accomplished by his dynasty. Yet, of course, such dominance was not realized by any of the kings of David's line. Thus, Ps. 2:7 must have anticipated a greater fulfillment. At both Acts 13:33 and in Heb. 1:5; 5:5 the psalm seems to be understood as a direct verbal prophecy fulfilled in the resurrection and exaltation of Christ.

On another level, the psalm is used rhetorically to reinforce the central proclamation of the chain quotation: the Son of God is superior to the angels. The rhetorical question that opens the chain constitutes a proclamation of that superiority, and the quotations that follow, given with no elaboration, are to be taken at face value as witnesses to the Son's supremacy from various vantage points. Further, this psalm, along with 2 Sam. 7:14, to which it is tethered by verbal analogy, is programmatic due to the concept of sonship, a concept that has great influence in Hebrews from the introduction through 5:11.

Of the seven interpretive principles attributed to Hillel (*t. Sanh.* 7:11; *'Abot R. Nat.* [A] §37), verbal analogy (*gezerah shavah*) is one of two that the author of Hebrews uses extensively in appropriating the OT. The principle of verbal analogy suggests that two passages having the same or similar wording may be interpreted one in light of the other. Psalm 2:7 and 2 Sam. 7:14, appearing together in 1:5, are joined by catchwords: *huios* ("son") and *egō* ("I"), as well as, perhaps, the pronoun *mou/moi* ("my," "to me") and the verb of being. Both have the form of proclamations, and both work to speak of God's open proclamation of the Son, as Messiah, heir of all creation, upon his exaltation to the right hand (Heb. 1:3; Ps. 110:1).

F. The Theological Use of the OT Material. It seems clear from the uses of Ps. 2:7 in broader Jewish literature that the concept of the Messiah as God's Son was an aspect of Jewish thinking in some quarters even prior to the Christian era. A plethora of passages in the Gospels speak of Jesus' unique relationship to God, describing that relationship as Son to Father (e.g., Mark 1:9–11; Luke 1:32; 2:41–50; 3:21–22; 4:1–13). In both overt statements and inferences Jesus defines himself as God's Son, and as used by other characters in the divine drama, the title often is closely associated with the title "Christ" ("Messiah") (Matt. 16:16; 26:63; Mark 8:29; Luke 4:41; John 11:27; 20:31). This title, "Son," became an important aspect of early Christian preaching about Jesus (e.g., Acts 9:20–22). Early Christian preachers specifically applied Ps. 2:7 to Jesus as Messiah and saw in it the promise of victory over those earthly forces opposed to the church (e.g., Acts 4:23–31; 13:33–34). Although this certainly is in play in the broader context of Hebrews (e.g., 2:5–9), the author, in using the psalm, has exaltation theology at the center of his thought. His primary point in 1:5 is that Jesus has been shown to be the Son of God by his exaltation to the right hand, his enthronement over all creation demonstrating his unique relationship to the Father.

What, then, of the temporal imagery communicated by the psalm? What does it mean that God has "begotten" the Son "today"? These cannot be references to bringing the Son into existence, since the reference in early Christian usage is associated with the exaltation to the right hand, and the Son has already been praised as the Father's agent in creation of the world (1:2; also 1:10). Thus, Jesus was considered "the Son" prior to creation itself. Nor can the use of the psalm here be considered a statement of adoption as Son, for Jesus is referred to as "Son" with reference to the incarnation (e.g., 2:10–18; 5:8). Rather, the early church understood Ps. 2:7 to refer to Jesus' induction into his royal position as king of the universe at the resurrection and exaltation. In these events God vindicated Jesus as Messiah and established his eternal kingdom (see Acts 13:32–34; Rom. 1:4). God becoming the Son's father, then, refers to God's open expression of their relationship upon Christ's enthronement—an interpretation that fits the OT context well.

1:5

A. The Immediate NT Context: A Chain Quotation on the Son's Superiority to the Angels. See §A of commentary on Heb. 1:5 (quoting Ps. 2:7) above.

B. The Original OT Context. In terms of the broader OT context, this passage has a number of parallels with Ps. 110 (109 LXX) and Ps. 2 considered above, parallels related to the theme of a royal heir being invested to rule. The context of 2 Sam. 7 begins by stating that the Lord had given King David "an inheritance" (2 Sam. 7:1; cf. Ps. 2:8) and provided freedom from "his enemies" (2 Sam. 7:1, 9, 11; cf. Ps. 2:2 [in concept]; 110:1–2). Further, David's seed would be given a throne (2 Sam. 7:13, 16; cf. Pss. 2; 110 [implied]) forever (2 Sam. 7:13, 16; cf. Ps. 110:4). Each of the passages also mentions a "rod" (2 Sam. 7:14; Ps. 2:9; 110:2). Thus, the connections between these psalms extend beyond the verbal analogy between 2 Sam. 7:13 and Ps. 2:7.

As to the context of 2 Sam. 7, the chapter has an introduction (7:1–3) and two main divisions: the Lord's oracle to David through the prophet Nathan (7:4–17) and David's response, given in the form of a prayer (7:18–29). It is in the oracle that God makes the proclamation quoted at Heb. 1:5. In the introduction to 2 Sam. 7, David's security as king gives him time for reflection on the incongruity between the quality of his house of cedar and the quality of the Lord's dwelling, a dwelling made of tents (7:1–2). Initially, Nathan tells David to act on his instincts, but then the prophet receives a word from the Lord (7:4). The oracle begins with God's reasons for not allowing David to build him a house (7:5–7). It has not been God's habit to dwell in a house when among the Israelites, and he has never given a command to build him a house of cedar (7:6–7). In 7:8–11 the narrative recounts God's goodness to David.

The king was taken from very humble beginnings and made a prince over God's people, and God supported David against his enemies and made his name great in the earth (7:8–9). The oracle shifts to a future orientation in 7:10–11 (use of Qal *waw* consecutive perfect in the MT and future tense in LXX), the Lord promising a place for his people in which they will find security and freedom from enemies. At a future time the Lord will grant David's desire to build a house for the Lord. The house, however, will be built by a son in David's line rather than by David himself (7:12–17). The Lord will establish the kingdom of David's son, and that son will have a throne that will be established forever (7:12–13). In the primary verse under our consideration, 7:14, the oracle proclaims that God will be a father to David's heir, and that son will be adopted as God's heir. Also in 7:14 God promises accountability to the son, saying when the son sins, he will correct him with "the rod of men." In the parallel, 1 Chron. 17:13, these words of accountability do not occur. There, as in 2 Sam. 7:15, the relationship is stated more positively, giving the assurance that God will not remove his mercy from the heir as he had removed it from Saul. The oracle concludes with God's triple promise that the heir's kingdom would endure forever (7:16). Therefore, 7:14 occurs as part of a series of promises to King David concerning one of his descendants. God will adopt David's son as heir, the heir will build a house for God's name, and God will establish that son's kingdom irrevocably. The proclamation here fits the pattern of early Hittite promissory grants by which the property gained in the establishment of a dynasty could not be revoked (Bateman 1997: 157).

C. Relevant Uses of the OT Reference in Jewish Sources. With 2 Sam. 7 as a foundation, subsequent writings of the OT focused on the father-son relationship between Yahweh and the Davidic heir (1 Chron. 17:13; 22:10; 28:6; Ps. 2:7), the permanence of David's dynasty (Ps. 89:30–34, 49; 132:11–12), and the certainty of the Lord's covenant love toward David's house (Ps. 89:28–35). The permanence of God's covenant with David formed the basis for Israel's hope in a future king who would carry on David's line and be the inheritor of covenant promises (Isa. 11:1–5; Jer. 23:5; 33:15; Amos 9:11; Zech. 3:8;

6:12) (Bateman 1997: 158–59). Thus, it is understandable that 2 Sam. 7 would be appropriated by later generations as a vital messianic text. For instance, the reference in 7:12 to God raising up David's "seed" (LXX: *sperma*) fostered messianic interpretations of the passage in broader Judaism (Lane 1991: 1:25), and 7:12 is alluded to in John 7:42: "Has not the Scripture said that the Christ comes from the descendants of David, and from Bethlehem, the village where David was?" The dominant use of 2 Sam. 7 in Jewish sources seems to be to emphasize especially the dynastic permanence of David's line (4Q252 V, 1–6; Sir. 47:11, 22; *Pss. Sol.* 17:4).

Further, in the context of this messianic passage, in the words of our passage under consideration, some in ancient Judaism found a basis for the belief that Messiah would be God's son. At 4Q174 1 I, 10–11 we read,

[And] YHWH [de]clares to you that "he will build you a house. I will raise up your seed after you and establish the throne of his kingdom [for ev]er. I will be a father to him and he will be a son to me." This (refers to the) "branch of David," who will arise with the Interpreter of the law who [will rise up] in Zi[on in] the [l]ast days, as it is written. . . .

The author of 4Q174 wrote an interpretation of the last days that involved the coming of Messiah along with "the Interpreter of the law." The Messiah is described by the writer in words taken from 2 Sam. 7. Yahweh will fulfill the promise to build David a house and raise up his descendant, whose throne will be permanently established. Further, God promises, "I will be a father to him, and he will be a son to me." It is significant that here this king whose kingdom will last forever, who is declared God's son, is identified with the "branch of David" (cf. Jer. 33:15), a designation used elsewhere in the Dead Sea Scrolls, but nowhere else in connection with the declaration that the branch is God's son.

D. The Textual Background. There exists a fairly direct correspondence between the Hebrew of 2 Sam. 7:14, the LXX, and the quotation as found in Hebrews. Once again this offers evidence of Hebrews' use of the LXX, for it would be highly unlikely that the LXX and Hebrews would translate the Hebrew with exactly the same wording and word order. Therefore, as broad evidence in the book constantly affirms, Hebrews uses the LXX text rather than translating from the Hebrew.

E. How 2 Sam. 7:14 Is Understood and Used at Heb. 1:5. As is the case with the author's use of Ps. 2:7 in 1:5, 2 Sam. 7:14 serves to reinforce the central proclamation that the Son of God is superior to the angels. Thus, it constitutes a direct confession of Christ's unique relationship to the Father as Son. This verse from 2 Samuel offers scriptural grounding for the concept of sonship, which plays a prominent role in this first main movement of Hebrews and in the theology of the book as a whole.

Further, we have already noted that 2 Sam. 7:14 is joined to Ps. 2:7 by virtue of verbal analogy (*gezerah shavah*), an interpretive principle that Hebrews uses extensively in appropriating the OT. The principle of verbal analogy suggests that for two passages having the same or similar wording, one may be interpreted in light of the other. Psalm 2:7 and 2 Sam. 7:14, appearing together in 1:5, are joined by catchwords: *huios* ("son") and *egō* ("I"), as well as, perhaps, the pronoun *mou/moi* ("my," "to me") and the verb of being. Both have the form of proclamations, and both address God's investment of the Son, as Messiah, on the throne of the universe, upon his exaltation to the right hand (Heb. 1:3; Ps. 110:1).

What, then, of the author's basis for appropriating this passage? In what sense is the Christ event a fulfillment of the OT text? First, as was the case with Ps. 2, 2 Sam. 7 was read as messianic by some Jews of the day. They certainly understood aspects of the prophecy to have been fulfilled in Solomon (i.e., the building of the original temple [see, however, commentary on Heb. 3:2–5 below]). Yet, in other respects, notably the establishment of a perpetual rule for the Davidic heir (2 Sam. 7:13), the prophecy was not realized by any of the kings of David's line and therefore must have anticipated a greater fulfillment. The OT context of 2 Sam. 7 clearly constitutes a prophetic oracle offered by the prophet Nathan. Thus, it is most likely that the author of Hebrews read the quotation as having a double fulfillment, aspects of the prophecy being fulfilled in the more immediate Davidic heir but finding its ultimate fulfillment in the exaltation of the Messiah.

F. The Theological Use of the OT Material. As we saw in the theological use of Ps. 2:7 in 1:5, that psalm, along with 2 Sam. 7:14, provided one scriptural basis for the confession that the Messiah was to be God's son. Also as noted in our discussion of Ps. 2:7, the Gospels speak extensively of Jesus' sonship in relation to God the Father, and that relationship constitutes a central focus for treatments of key events—for instance, Jesus' birth (Matt. 2:15; Luke 1:32), baptism (Matt. 3:17 pars.), transfiguration (Matt. 17:5 pars.), and crucifixion (Matt. 27:54 par.). Further, Jesus defines himself as the Son of God, and other characters in the Gospels define him as such. This title, "Son," became an important aspect of early Christian preaching about Jesus.

In Heb. 1:5, the quotation of 2 Sam. 7:14 plays at least a dual role theologically. First, it underscores this unique relationship the Son shares with the Father, which is a filial relationship, over against the status of the angels, who the author will go on to demonstrate are mere servants who worship this Son and serve him (1:6–7). Continuing on with emphases first found in the book's introduction (1:2–3), the quotation thus serves to highlight closeness of relationship and identity between the Father and Son. Second, it joins Ps. 2:7, along with the other passages in the chain quotation of Hebrews 1, in celebrating the Son's exaltation to the right hand of God. For the author of Hebrews, the passage constitutes, therefore, the Father's bold proclamation that the Son, as the Davidic heir, is indeed heir of the whole universe. The passage from 2 Samuel 7:14 should be seen, therefore, as a statement of induction of the Son into the position as ruler of the universe, rather than a statement of adoption.

1:6

A. The Immediate NT Context. The chain quotation at 1:5–14 builds overwhelming biblical support for the superiority of the Son of God to the angels (see commentaries on Heb. 1:5 above). Contributing to the chain quotation of 1:5–14 in this way, the quotation of Deut. 32:43 LXX in 1:6 comes as the first in a pair of passages focusing on the unique role of the angels, as that role is set over against the superior status of the Son. It is joined by verbal analogy to the quotation of Ps. 104:4 (103:4 LXX), which follows, by virtue of their common reference to "the angels" (ange-

los). Several aspects of the introductory formula require attention. First, some have suggested that the term rendered "again" (*palin*) should be given temporal significance and associated with the verb "he brings into" (*eisagō*) (e.g., Michel 1986: 113), referring to a second entrance into the "world" by the Son. Rather, *palin* should be read as a connective of which the author is fond in his introductory formulae. As such, he uses it simply to communicate "and here is another passage." Second, the reference to the "firstborn" (*prōtotokos*) may stem from Ps. 89:27 (88:28 LXX), which refers to God exalting David above the kings of the earth. Significantly, in light of Hebrews' use of Ps. 2:7 and 2 Sam. 7:14 in 1:5, God says that David will call him "Father," and he will make David *prōtotokos* (Ps. 89:26–27 [88:27–28 LXX]). This, then, continues the theme of the unique relationship of the Messiah as God's Son, established thus far in Hebrews. Third, although the term for "world" (*oikoumenē*) most often refers to the world inhabited by humans, here it probably refers to the heavenly realm, as it does in 2:5 (Lane 1991: 1:27; *contra* Attridge 1989: 56). The author does not turn to a consideration of the incarnation until the transition effected by the quotation of Ps. 8:4–6 at 2:5–9, and not with full force until 2:10–18. Reading *oikoumenē* in 1:6 as referring to the heavenly realm keeps the emphasis of the chain quotation on the exaltation of Christ and thus fits better with the immediate context. The point of the introductory formula is that the angels react a certain way upon the Son's entrance into the heavenly realm: they worship him. This posture of worship demonstrates the stark contrast between the person of the Son and the angels.

B. The Original OT Context. Traditionally, Deut. 32:1–43 is referred to as the Song of Moses. The passage, called "hauntingly beautiful" by one scholar (Christensen 2002: 785), has received more attention by both ancient scribes and modern researchers than any other passage in Deuteronomy and more than most other passages of the OT. The song was used for liturgical purposes in the temple, synagogue, and early church, and its popularity among Greek-speaking Jews is evidenced by its presence in the Odes at the end of the Greek version of Psalms (Lane 1991: 1:28). In the Talmud, rules are given that require two hymns from the Pentateuch, Exod. 15 and Deut.

32, to be written in a specific way (*b. Meg.* 16b). Thus, Deut. 32 was a very important text to the Jews of the ancient world. The Song of Moses occurs near the end of the book of Deuteronomy, in a final movement (Deut. 31:1–34:12) in which Moses anticipates the Israelites' entrance into the promised land. The song is situated in the narrative, just after the law is finished (31:24–29) and just prior to Moses' final exhortation to the people (32:44–47) and God's command for Moses to ascend Mount Nebo to view the land (32:48–52).

The song constitutes Moses bearing witness to heaven and earth concerning the people (31:28; 32:1–3). Aspects of the chapter recount God's experience thus far with his people, and other parts, including 32:43, are a mixture of exhortation and prophecy, anticipating what is to come. The song has three main movements. The first concerns the past blessings of God on the people (32:1–14), the second addresses Israel's provocation of God's anger by their sin (32:15–29), and the third proclaims God's judgment and salvation (32:30–43) (Christensen 2002: 788, 799, 809). Therefore, our quotation from 32:43 occurs in the final movement of the LXX version of the song, indeed, its last verse. In this final movement Moses proclaims the downfall of God's enemies (32:30–35) and his ultimate deliverance of his people (32:36–43). This final verse of the song constitutes a climactic celebration of God's victory over the enemies and just treatment of his people. The exhortation to worship is in parallel with an exhortation to find strength, but the subject of the verbs depends on the textual tradition with which one is dealing (see §D below). The basis for the exhortations, however, is clear: God's judgment on his enemies provides a basis for worship and strength. Therefore, the theme of "the defeat of enemies," seen also in Ps. 2 and 2 Sam. 7, is continued and serves as a basis for exhorting to worship.

C. Relevant Uses of the OT Reference in Jewish Sources. As we noted, the Song of Moses in Deut. 32 was widely published as a liturgical piece in ancient Judaism. The song is cited or alluded to in, for example, 4 Macc. 18:18–19; Rom. 10:19; 11:11; 12:19; 15:10; 1 Cor. 10:20, 22; Phil. 2:15; Luke 21:22; Rev. 6:10; 10:5; 15:3; 18:20; 19:2; Justin, *Dial.* 130. It later was used in an Easter vigil liturgy (Attridge 1989: 57; Thomas 1965: 304; Kistemaker 1961: 22). Given the popularity of

the song as a whole, it is not surprising that Deut. 32:43 finds a place in various Jewish traditions and in a variety of forms.

D. The Textual Background. Here we encounter one of the most interesting and most difficult histories of the quotations in Hebrews. In 1:6 the quotation reads, "And let all the angels of God worship him" (*kai proskynēsatōsan autō pantes angeloi theou*). First, the part of Deut. 32:43 that finds expression in 1:6 is not found in the MT at all (*Tg. Onq.* Deut. 32:43 is very similar to the MT). Additionally, at the beginning of Deut. 32:43 the MT reads, "Rejoice, O nations" (*gôy*), whereas the LXX reads, "Rejoice, O heavens" (*ouranoi*); and where the MT says that the Lord will avenge the blood of his "servants" (*'ebed*), the LXX says "sons" (*tōn huiōn*). With reference to these elements, the LXX parallels a reading from Qumran (4Q44) rather than the MT or the Samaritan Pentateuch. Yet, neither does the LXX form of our quotation match Hebrews' form of the text, but rather reads as follows:

> O heavens, rejoice together with him,
>   and let all the sons of God worship him.
> Rejoice, O Gentiles, with his people,
>   and let all the angels of God regain their
>   strength.

Note that in this form of the text "the sons of God" (*huioi theou*) are those exhorted to worship. Of course, it is possible that Hebrews has conflated the parallel second and fourth lines, so that "angels" in the fourth line replaces "sons" in the second, especially since the designation "sons of God" at times is interpreted as referring to angels (e.g., Gen. 6:2, 4; Job 1:6; 2:1; 38:7). Yet, there are other possibilities to be considered.

It has been pointed out that the wording of the Hebrews quotation also resembles Ps. 97:7 (96:7 LXX), which reads, "Worship him, all his angels" (*proskynēsate autō, pantes hoi angeloi autou*). In this reading, and unlike a conflated reading from Deut. 32:43 LXX, no conjunction (*kai*) is found before the verb, the form of the verb is different, and the "of God" (*theou*) of the quotation is "of him" (*autou*). Motyer (1999: 18–19), while affirming that the Hebrews quotation is influenced by Deut. 32:43, prefers the psalm reading, since, given the context and the heading of Ps. 96 LXX, it moves "into the orbit of the David ideology of

Psalm 2." Other scholars have suggested that the quotation in 1:6 results from the conflation of this psalm with the Greek form of Deut. 32:43 (e.g., Thompson 1976: 356; D. Guthrie 1983: 74–75); yet, this solution, although possible, has no advantages over a conflation within the Greek form of Deut. 32:43, and it has several liabilities.

To complicate matters further, however, the reading from Qumran associated with Deut. 32:43 (4Q44), mentioned above, parallels the wording of Ps. 97:7c MT: "and bow down to him, all you gods" (Skehan 1954). The term here for "gods" (*ĕlōhîm*) at times was interpreted by the LXX as referring to angels, as the Greek translation of the psalm (96:7 LXX) demonstrates (cf. Ps. 137:1 LXX [138:1 MT/ET]). Thus, it may be that some scribes of ancient Judaism associated the passage from Deuteronomy and Ps. 97:7c.

More promising still is the insight that the quotation in 1:6 matches very well the representation of the Song of Moses found in Odes 2:43: "and let all the angels of God worship him" (*kai proskynēsatōsan autō pantes hoi angeloi theou*). The only difference between the two is the article (*hoi*) prior to "angels" (*angeloi*) in Odes. Thus, some hold this to be the source for Hebrews' quotation (e.g., Kistemaker 1961: 22; Spicq 1952–1953: 1:336). It is, therefore, quite possible that the author of Hebrews accessed this form of Deut. 32:43, which would have been widely known among Greek-speaking Jews of the day, due to its reference to the angels and its emphasis on worship. This form seems to have been widely published in a liturgical tradition and, for instance, is reflected in Justin, *Dial.* 130 (Lane 1991: 1:28). Beyond this suggestion, it is also possible that Hebrews is reading a variant form of the LXX in which "angels" are the subject of the exhortation to worship.

E. How Deut. 32:43 Is Understood and Used Theologically at Heb. 1:6. A strand of rabbinic tradition recounts that when the first man, Adam, was created, God called the angels to worship him. This strand is reflected in the first-century AD pseudepigraphical work *The Life of Adam and Eve* (13:1–16:3), and it explains that Satan's failure to worship Adam was the reason he and the angels under his influence were expelled from glory and cast to the earth. In this work we read the devil's account:

And Michael himself worshiped first, and called me and said, "Worship the image of God, Yahweh." And I answered, "I do not worship Adam." And when Michael kept forcing me to worship, I said to him, "Why do you compel me? I will not worship one inferior and subsequent to me. I am prior to him in creation; before he was made, I was already made. He ought to worship me." (14:2–3)

Satan declares further that he will set his throne above the stars of heaven and will be like God. Because of the great grief of being cast down to the earth and seeing the bliss of Adam and Eve, the devil tempted Eve to make sure that humans also fell and were expelled from God's presence (16:1–3).

This interesting strand of Jewish thought may be placed in contradistinction to the clear strand of Christian teaching on the worship of the "second Adam," Christ, upon his exaltation. For when the author of Hebrews quotes "and let all the angels of God worship him," he understands the "him" (*autō*) to refer to Christ and this scriptural passage, Deut. 32:43, to have been explicitly fulfilled, as a prophetic portion of the chapter, at his exaltation to the right hand of God (Bruce 1990: 57–58). Thus, the quotation parallels that aspect of exaltation theology in the NT, also supported by Ps. 8:4–6 (quoted at Heb. 2:5–9), in which all things, including the angelic beings, are subjected to Christ upon his enthronement (see, e.g., Phil. 2:5–11; Eph. 1:20–21).

Deuteronomy 32:43 is the third of the texts used by the author to build his "string of pearls" chain quotation and is appropriated specifically for its reference to the angels' posture of worship vis-à-vis the Son of God. It is also by virtue of its reference to "angels" that it is paired with Ps. 104:4 (103:4 LXX) based on the principle of verbal analogy. These texts focus on fundamental differences between the Son and the angels. This form of Deut. 32:43 specifically proclaims that the angels worship the Son as God. In this way, the quotation reinforces the author's primary agenda for the chain quotation.

Yet, it may also be significant to note several points about the broader context of this quotation as it relates to Hebrews. Deuteronomy 32, as we stated, constituted a highly significant passage in broader Judaism and was an aspect of liturgical readings. It was originally given as a powerful word just prior to Israel's entrance to the promised land, and "entrance into the rest" or "the inheritance" is an important theme for Hebrews (3:7–4:11). In that chapter Moses, leader of the people of God, confronts the people concerning the consequences of a lack of faithfulness to covenant with God. Hebrews too is concerned with a lack of faithfulness to covenant and even utilizes parts of Deut. 32 (32:35–36), later in the book (10:30), to speak of judgment against those who have "regarded the blood of the covenant as common" (10:29). Therefore, this significant OT passage works, by virtue of its broader context, to demonstrate the status—the Son, as equal with God, is worthy of worship—and cost of rejecting the Son of God. He is one with the God of radical judgment, who, through Moses, warned those about to cross into the promised land concerning dire consequences of such a rejection.

1:7

A. The Immediate NT Context. Psalm 104:4 continues the chain quotation begun in 1:5, the author continuing to build impressive scriptural evidence for the superiority of Jesus over the angels. It is the fourth in this series of OT quotations and specifically is paired with the previous quotation, Deut. 32:43 LXX, due to their common reference to the angels. This required use of the LXX form of the text, since the use of the term "angels" (*angelous*) is the LXX's interpretive rendering of the Hebrew text, a text that constitutes a hymn of praise to God for his lordship over all creation (see §D below).

The introductory formula setting up this OT quotation reads, "On the other hand, with reference to the angels, he says" (*kai pros men tous angelous legei*), the *pros* plus the accusative form being read as indicating reference, speaking about the angels, rather than addressing them directly. The particle *men* probably should be understood as indicating an element of contrast with the previous introductory formula, which suggests that Deut. 32:43 LXX, a text about the angels' act of worship, was spoken with reference to the Son of God. Here, by contrast, the author has the angels themselves squarely in view and is interested in their specific ministry and perhaps their mutability. So the contrast built into the pairing of these texts has to do with the status of the Son of God,

whom the angels worship, and that of the angels themselves.

Finally, we should note that in the context of Ps. 104:4 (including 103:18–22) there are terms and concepts also found in Ps. 45:6–7 (44:7–8 LXX) and Ps. 102:25–27 (101:26–28 LXX), the next two passages in the Hebrews chain quotation (1:8–12). The establishment of a throne in heaven and a kingdom occurs at 103:19, as well as 45:6; 102:19, and we have seen that it plays a significant role in the contexts of other passages in the chain quotation (Ps. 2:7; 2 Sam. 7:14; Ps. 110:1). In addition, the phrase "as a garment" (*hōs himation*) is found at 104:2, 6; 102:26, and the term *himation* is also found at 45:8. Further, the emphasis on the "heavens" (*ouranos*) is found in 104:2; 102:25, and the establishment of the earth's foundations (*themelioō*) occurs at 104:5; 102:25. These connections suggest once again that the broader context of these psalms had an influence on the author's choice of which passages to include in the chain, or perhaps that they had been grouped prior to the author's use of them.

B. The Original OT Context. Psalm 104 is part of a group of psalms that are songs of praise to God (Pss. 103–106). As indicated by the self-exhortations in the song, it is most likely that Ps. 104 was used by a worship leader at the temple as he led the community in worship. In this hymn the writer mixes imperatival and participial forms with addressing the Lord directly (Allen 2002: 39). Attridge (1989: 57) notes that the psalm, similar to a Mesopotamian hymn and to an Egyptian sun hymn, has a long prehistory. Craigie (1974: 19–21), who understands the psalm to have been written for the dedication of Solomon's temple, takes the connection with Egyptian and Mesopotamian materials to indicate that the psalm was written for apologetic purposes, to demonstrate the Lord God's transcendence with respect to the sun and to express the cosmic significance of Solomon's temple (cf. Allen 2002: 39).

The psalm divides into three main movements bracketed by a prologue and an epilogue, with a final self-exhortation. The prologue (104:1–4), at the end of which our quotation occurs, extols God's greatness with a string of participles on the cosmic dimensions of his dwelling and his power. God is clothed with "praise" and "beauty," according to the LXX ("majesty" and "splendor" in the

MT). Further, God puts on light like a robe and stretches out heaven like a huge tent (lit., a "skin" [Gk. *derris*]). In 104:3 there is variation between the LXX and the MT. The latter says that God places the roofbeams of his upper chamber in (*bĕ*) or on the waters, while the LXX suggests that he covers his upstairs room in or on the waters. Both senses suggest that God has built his true dwelling place in the heavens, where the heavenly reservoir of water exists (cf. Gen. 1:6–7; Ps. 29:10; Amos 9:6). Moreover, he uses the clouds as a chariot and the wings of the wind as his pathway. Finally, in our focal verse the MT says that God either makes "winds his messengers and flaming fires his servants" or makes "his messengers winds and his servants flaming fires." The LXX has narrowed the choice to the latter and interpreted the "messengers" (*mal'āk*) as "angels" (*angelos*). Therefore, the prologue introduces Ps. 104 by proclaiming God's greatness in light of his awesome presence and his dominion over creation.

Following the prologue, the three main movements of this extensive psalm of praise address the creation of the world as it relates to water (104:5–13), God's provision for human beings and animals (104:14–23), and the wonder of God's creatures, both of the land and of the sea, for whom he provides the necessities of life (104:24–30). The author closes with an epilogue of praise (104:31–35b) and a brief self-exhortation to praise the Lord (104:35c–d).

C. Relevant Uses of the OT Reference in Jewish Sources. *Genesis Rabbah* 1:3 quotes Ps. 104:4 in a discussion about when the angels were created: "R. Johanan said, 'They were created on the second day, as it is written, *Who layest the beams of Thine upper chambers in the waters* (Ps. CIV, 3), followed by, *Who makest the spirits Thine angels* (*ib.* 4).'" Here 104:3 is taken as alluding to the dividing of the waters on the second day of creation, and 104:4 shows that the angels were created on the same day. It is significant that here 104:4 is interpreted as referring to the angelic beings. The same is true in *Gen. Rab.* 21:9; *Exod. Rab.* 15:6, 22; 25:2; *Deut. Rab.* 9:3. In the Jewish sources, furthermore, there exists an association between angels and fire (or at points, lightning) and angels and the winds. For instance, *Jub.* 2:2 gives the account of God creating angels on the first day of creation. Among these are "the angels of the spirit

of fire" (mentioned in manuscripts B C D but lacking in A and the Greek text of Epiphanius) and "the angels of the spirit of the winds." *Testament of Adam* 1:12 speaks of the heavenly powers as "all the ranks of fire and wind," and elsewhere in the pseudepigrapha angels are associated with fire (*1 En.* 17:1; *2 En.* 29:1; *2 Bar.* 21:6). Further, in the Latin version of *4 Ezra* 8:21–22 we read of God, "before whom the hosts of angels stand trembling, they whose service takes the form of wind and fire," but in the Syriac and other eastern versions, "before whom the hosts of angels stand trembling and at whose command they are changed to wind and fire" (*OTP* 1:542). Bruce (1990: 58–59) suggests that this may be behind the thought of the author of Hebrews, as he contrasts "the evanescence of angels with the eternity of the Son, which is stressed in the two quotations that follow." Lane (1991: 1:28) agrees, pointing out the description of the angels in 1:7 is placed in contrast to the eternality of the Son in 1:8–12, with Ps. 104:4 functioning to tell of the mutability of the angels.

In 1QH^a IX, 9–12 this association between the angels and the forces of nature is expressed:

> You have stretched out the heavens for your glory. Everything [which it contains] you have [es]tablished according to your will, and powerful spirits, according to their laws, before they became h[oly] angels [. . .] eternal spirits in their realms: luminaries according to their mysteries, stars according to [their] circuits, [all the stormy winds] according to their roles, lightning and thunder according to their duties and well-designed storehouses.

These thoughts are in line with a strand of OT tradition in which the elemental forces are associated with angels. Kraus (1993b: 299–300) suggests that the "winged winds" of Ps. 104:3–4 and the winds as messengers/flames of fire as servants may have the angels in mind, who attend God around his throne (see also Anderson 2000: 719; Attridge [1989: 58] points to Exod. 3:2; 19:16–18; Dan. 7:10). It is therefore not surprising that the translators of the LXX interpret the winds and fires of Ps. 104:4 as angelic beings, and their interpretation also has a basis in the immediate context of the psalm, as we will see next in §D.

D. The Textual Background. As we noted, it is the LXX form of Ps. 104:4 (103:4 LXX) that serves the author's purpose in 1:7, due specifically to the use of the term "angels" (*angelos*), since it is that term that warrants the association of Ps. 104:4 with the previous quotation (Deut. 32:43 LXX) by verbal analogy. There is a slight variation between the LXX and the form of the quotation in Hebrews. The *pyr phlegon* ("flaming fire") of the LXX has the accusative noun *pyr* ("fire") plus *phlegō* in its present active participle form. The reading in Hebrews, on the other hand, has *pyros phloga* ("a flame of fire" [also found in Bo, Sa, *L*ᵇ]), *phloga* being an accusative noun and *pyros* a genitive noun (perhaps an attributed genitive). The change could be due to the influence of liturgical readings of the psalm (Kistemaker 1961: 23) or to the use of a nonextant form of the LXX (Thompson 1976: 357n21), but it is more likely that Hebrews' slight adjustment of the wording is for stylistic, and perhaps theological, reasons (so Bateman 1997: 129). If it is a stylistic adjustment, Hebrews' reading balances *pneumata* with *phloga* at the end of each line. Nevertheless, the meaning of the passage does not change.

A more difficult question, on the surface, is the difference between the LXX and the MT, since the former seems to focus on heavenly beings, while the latter relates to God's interaction with the forces of nature, which he has created, specifically winds and lightning. The Hebrew text is ambiguous, and either "winds" (*rûaḥ*) and "fire" (*'ēš*) or "messengers" (*mal'āk*) and "ministers" (Piel participle of *šrt*) could be read as the objects of the Qal participle "makes" (*'śh*). Most translations of the MT go with the former, and this reading of the text is alluded to also in 1 QHᵃ IX, 9–12 (quoted above), where the winds are changed into angels. Yet, the Hebrew also could be read as having "messengers" and "ministers" as the object: "He makes his messengers winds and his ministers flaming fire." Further, *rûaḥ* could be translated as "spirits" as well as "winds." This latter approach to which words in the verse are considered the objects is adopted by the LXX, and a parallel reading of the passage is, perhaps, found in *Tg. Onq.* Ps. 104:4, which renders the psalm, "Who made his messengers *as swift as* wind; his servants, *as strong as* burning fire" (translation in Cook 2001).

An aspect of the broader context sheds light on why the LXX translated the passage with reference to angelic beings. In addition to the strata of tradition in the OT associating angels with the elemental forces of wind and lightning (see above), aspects of the immediate context point in this direction as well. The close association of Ps. 103 and Ps. 104 may be seen, in part, by the concatenation joining the end of the former with the beginning of the latter ("Bless the Lord, O my soul"). At Ps. 103:20–21 (102:20–21 LXX) we read,

> Bless the LORD, you His angels,
> Mighty in strength, who perform His
> word,
> Obeying the voice of His word!
> Bless the LORD, all you His hosts,
> You who serve Him, doing His will.
> (NASB)

In this passage, which clearly speaks of the angelic beings, we find the Hebrew terms *mal'āk* (rendered "angels" in the NASB) and *šrt* ("you who serve him") in the exact same forms in which they occur in Ps. 104:4 MT. It may be, therefore, that the translators of the LXX provided a translation of Ps. 104:4 (103:4 LXX) in keeping with the broader context of that verse, interpreting the "messengers" and "servants" as angelic beings.

E. How Ps. 104:4 (103:4 LXX) Is Understood and Used at Heb. 1:7. The author of Hebrews reads this psalm passage as reinforcing his proclamation of the Son's superiority to the angels. It is drawn together with Deut. 32:43 LXX by virtue of their common reference to the angelic beings (verbal analogy), and yet, it is the only OT quotation of the chain (1:5–14) that does not have the Son of God as its subject. The author is interested in what is taught in the psalm concerning the angels' role vis-à-vis their creator. He focuses on the fact that they are ministering spirits sent out to do the Lord's will (cf. 1:14, which is a reiteration of the psalm passage). They contrast dramatically with the Son of God, who has sat down at the position of highest authority in the universe (1:3, 5, 13). In other words, the angels are servants, and the Son is Lord.

Although the author is not primarily interested in the proclamation that the angels are made into winds and lightning at this point, Bruce and Lane may be correct that Hebrews reads Ps. 104:4

(103:4 LXX) as indicating the evanescent nature of the angels; that is, they can be changed to wind and lightning and therefore are not like the Son of God, who is "the same yesterday, today, and forever" (13:8; cf. 1:10–12).

F. The Theological Use of the OT Material. In the biblical literature the angels are created, heavenly beings who function as God's messengers, revealing his will or announcing key events (e.g., Gen. 19:1–22; Exod. 3:2–6; Judg. 2:1–5; Matt. 1:20–24). They also work to give God's people protection from harm (e.g., Exod. 14:19–20; 1 Kings 19:1–8; Acts 12:7–11). As with Deut. 32:43 LXX, quoted at 1:6, angels are found worshiping God or attending his throne.

Some have misjudged 1:5–14 as an indication that the audience was flirting either with the worship of angels (e.g., Manson 1949–1950) or with a form of aberrant Christology in which Christ himself was considered subordinate to an angel (Yadin 1958). Although speculation about angels seems to have had some influence on specific churches in the first century (e.g., at Colossae), as well as in some Jewish and gnostic circles (Ellingworth 1993: 103), Hebrews should not be read in light of a deficient angelology; rather, the author goes to great lengths to drive home the unrivaled superiority of Jesus for specific rhetorical reasons, which indeed have a fuzzy Christology as their impetus. Specifically, with the chain quotation of 1:5–14, the author of Hebrews lays the foundation for his argument "from lesser to greater" (*qal wahomer*) in 2:1–4. This method of argumentation, used by the rabbis, held that if something is true in a lesser situation, it certainly is true in a greater, or more important, situation and has greater implications. The text of 1:5–14 establishes beyond question that Jesus, the Son of God, is far superior to the angels. Then, in 2:1–4 the author argues that those who rejected the word of God given through the angels faced dire consequences (the "lesser" situation), and since the Son is greater than the angels, the argument "to the greater" reasons that those who reject the word of God given through the superior Son deserve even greater punishment than those who rejected the word given through angels. Rather than casting the angels in a negative light, as if the readers held too high an angelology, Hebrews actually builds on a common aspect of Jewish theology—the an-

gels were mediators of the OT law—in order to demonstrate the responsibility of the hearers to take most seriously the word of salvation delivered through the superior Son. The audience's respect for the role of angels as mediators of God's revelation provided a reference point from which to speak of the much higher status (and, therefore, authority) of the Son of God. This, then, is the purpose of the comparison between Jesus and the angels in 1:5–14: the author is establishing a firm foundation upon which to argue for unreserved obedience to the word delivered through Jesus. As part of this process, the author's quotation of Ps. 104:4 contributes to this end by showing the inferior status and nature of the angels themselves.

1:8–9

A. The Immediate NT Context: The Son Is Greater Than the Angels by Virtue of His Eternal Reign. The quotation of Ps. 45:6–7 (45:7–8 MT; 44:7–8 LXX) begins to move the reader toward the climax of the author's chain of OT quotations, which will occur with the quotation of Ps. 110:1 (109:1 LXX) at 1:13. It is paired with Ps. 102:25–27 (101:26–28 LXX) by virtue of the fact that both are read as proclamations concerning the Son and formally connected by forms of the pronoun *sy* ("you"). This fifth quotation in the author's chain supports the overall program of driving home the Son's decisive superiority to the angels by focusing on the status of the Son as the exalted and reigning Lord. Thus, it well picks up an emphasis of the quotations of Ps. 2:7 and 2 Sam. 7:14 at 1:5, both of which are read as enthronement announcements, and it anticipates the presentation of Ps. 110:1 (109:1 LXX), the exaltation psalm par excellence for the early church.

The formula introducing Ps. 45:6–7 in 1:8 reads, "But to the Son" (*pros de ton huion*), and the understood verb is *legei* ("he says") from 1:7a. This introductory formula contrasts with the one introducing Ps. 104:4 (103:4 LXX) in the previous verse. Whereas *pros* plus the accusative was read as "reference" in 1:7, the *pros* in our verse at hand should be translated "to," since it introduces two quotations addressing the Son (i.e., "But [he says] to the Son").

Once again, it should be pointed out that the context of Ps. 45:6–7 (44:7–8 LXX) demonstrates links with other passages in the author's chain of quotations. The mention of a throne and God's rule occurs at 45:6 and Ps. 103:19, and it forms a dominant theme in the contexts of Ps. 2:7; 2 Sam. 7:14; Ps. 110:1 (2 Sam. 7:13, 16; implied in Pss. 2; 110). The term *himation* ("garment") is found at 45:8, as well as Ps. 104:2, 6; 102:26. Further, the "scepter" referred to in 45:6 is mirrored at Ps. 110:2; 2:9; 2 Sam. 7:14, and the king's enemies are mentioned in 45:5, as well as Ps. 110:1–2; 2:2; 2 Sam. 7:1, 9, 11. Also, that the Lord's reign is "forever," reflected in 45:2, is seen also at 2 Sam. 7:13, 16; Ps. 110:4, and the Lord's eternality is also seen at Ps. 102:26–27, which the author quotes in 1:10–12. Finally, Allen (1982: 235) has raised the possibility of a link between the "anointed one" of Ps. 2:2 and the *echrisen* ("the anointed") of 45:7 (44:8 LXX).

B. The Original OT Context. The interpretation of Ps. 45:7–8 MT (44:7–8 LXX; 45:6–7 ET) has generated a good deal of discussion. These verses are part of a royal psalm (see §B of commentary on Heb. 1:5 [quoting Ps. 2:7] above; other royal psalms are Pss. 20; 21; 72; 89; 101; 132; 141), more specifically, a love song apparently crafted for the wedding of the king. Suggestions as to its exact setting have ranged from the marriage ceremony of a specific king, such as Solomon or Ahab, to an annual cultic enthronement ritual. Kraus (1993a: 453) rejects both, suggesting that the wording of the psalm does point in the direction of a royal wedding, but the attempts to tie it to a specific occurrence miss the formulaic nature of the psalm and underestimate "the prophetically formulated expressions of perfection," which "overreach any historical portrait of a king."

Following the title (45:1 [44:1 LXX; 45:1a ET]), the psalm divides into four movements. The introduction given by the psalmist describes his inspiration and the handsomeness of the king to whom the psalm is addressed (45:2–3 [44:2–3 LXX; 45:1b–2 ET]). In 45:4–9 is a description of the king as groom, and this divides into sections on the king as a glorious warrior (45:4–6 [44:4–6 LXX; 45:3–5 ET]) and as an enthroned monarch ruling in prosperity (45:7–10 [44:7–10 LXX; 45:6–9 ET]). An address encouraging the bride to joy and submission, and in praise of the bride, follows in 45:11–16 (44:11–16 LXX; 45:10–15 ET). Finally, the king is addressed again, with an expression of hope for the endurance of his dynasty and the effectiveness of his rule (45:17–18 [44:17–18 LXX; 45:16–17 ET]).

The most difficult phrase for interpreters has been *kis'ăkā 'ĕlōhîm*, traditionally translated as "Your throne, O God" (45:7 [44:7 LXX; 45:6 ET]). Other prominent suggestions include "Your throne is God's for ever and ever," argued by Mulder (1972: 73–80) on the basis of the psalm's structure, syntax, and ideological backdrop (followed by Allen 1982: 221–30); "Your throne is like God's throne" (Emerton 1968, following Driver); and "The eternal and everlasting God has enthroned you" (Craigie 1983: 336, following Dahood 1966–1970: 1:273), based on the difficulty of the king being addressed with the vocative as God. Yet, the punctuation and syntax of the MT support the reading "Your throne, O God, is for ever and ever" (Kraus 1993a: 451; J. R. Porter 1961; Couroyer 1971; Harris 1992: 190–202), a word of prophecy concerning the perpetual nature of the king's rule. Perhaps the most prominent difficulty for reading *'ĕlōhîm* as vocative is the earthly king being addressed as "God" or a "divine one." Although this was somewhat common in ancient Egypt, for instance, this would be the sole occurrence in the Hebrew Scriptures where the king is addressed directly in this way. Yet, in connection with Ps. 2:7 and 2 Sam. 7:14, we have seen the king adopted by God as "son," and in other places the earthly king is very closely associated with Yahweh via metaphorical language (cf., e.g., 2 Sam. 14:17, 20; Zech. 12:8; see Kraus 1993a: 455; Vanhoye 1969: 180). Further, the king, according to Ps. 45, has divine characteristics, such as "glory and majesty" (45:3–4a ET), a posture defending truth and righteousness (45:4b, 7a ET), an ability to judge equitably (45:6b ET), and an eternal rule (45:6a ET). The term *'ĕlōhîm*, finally, has a great deal of fluidity in the Hebrew Scriptures, being used variously of heavenly beings (Ps. 8:6 [8:5 ET]; 97:7), judges (Ps. 82:1, 6), Moses (Exod. 7:1), and the specter of Samuel (1 Sam. 28:13) (see Harris 1992: 200–202; Leschert 1994: 50–78). Thus, I agree with those who opt for the traditional view.

The author of the psalm continues by saying that because of the king's love of righteousness and hatred of wickedness, God has anointed him with the oil of gladness (45:8 [44:8 LXX; 45:7 ET]). Here the Lord God is referenced as "God, your

God" (LXX: *ho theos ho theos sou*), maintaining the "insurmountable distinction between Yahweh and the king, between God and man" (Weiser 1962: 363). Thus, whereas the preceding verse addresses the close association of the king with Yahweh by addressing the king as "God," this verse notes that it is by the blessing of Yahweh that the king has been exalted to his position.

C. Relevant Uses of the OT Reference in Jewish Sources. In broader Judaism Ps. 45 occurs rarely. Our passage may be alluded to at 4Q252 V, 1–4, where, speaking of the hope for a Davidic king and alluding to Gen. 49:10, the author describes the "scepter" that represents his rule (V, 1), and the messiah is called "the messiah of righteousness" (V, 3), for whom the kingship will be "for everlasting generations" (V, 4). Similarly, *T. Jud.* 24:1–6 emphasizes the coming of the Messiah and the "scepter of righteousness." Both passages understand the psalm from an eschatological standpoint, as pointing to the coming of the future king. Also, in the Targum on the psalm, 45:3 MT (45:2 ET) reads, "Your beauty, O King Messiah, is greater than the sons of men," and 45:7 MT (45:6 ET), "The throne of your glory, O Lord." Thus, the psalm is again interpreted as messianic, and the difficult phrase in 45:7 MT is understood as a vocative. Further, in the rabbinic literature, Rabbi Eliezer, quoting 45:4 MT (45:3 ET), proclaims that in the messianic age the Messiah will still wear a sword, but it will be ornamental rather than martial (*b. Šabb.* 63a). Consequently, the application of the psalm by the author of Hebrews, to Jesus as the Messiah, is much in keeping with traditions within Judaism that apply the psalm to the Messiah and his kingdom.

D. The Textual Background. The LXX translation of Ps. 45 (44 LXX) corresponds very directly to the MT, so much so that Harris (1984: 88–89) sees it as a "literal" rendering, maintaining the Hebrew word order and personal pronouns, even when Greek language convention would not require them. In 44:7–8 LXX (45:7–8 MT) we might expect the vocative form of *theos* ("God"), but at this point the vocative is being supplanted by the nominative form, with the vocative form, *thee*, being used rarely in either the LXX or the NT (Attridge 1989: 58).

There are, however, several differences between the LXX and the quotation in Hebrews that need

to be considered (see Allen 2002: 231; Bateman 1997: 131; Thomas 1965: 305, 321–23). At 1:8 the author of Hebrews apparently adds *kai* ("and") prior to the *hē rabdos* ("the scepter") in the quotation. This probably is a stylistic addition meant to balance the two clauses (Allen 2002: 231) and highlight the two distinct thoughts inherent in the verse: the Son has an eternal throne (first clause), and the Son rules in righteousness (Kistemaker 1961: 25–26). Second, the word *rabdos* ("scepter") occurs twice in 1:8. In the Hebrews quotation articles appear before the first *rabdos* and its accompanying descriptive genitive, *euthytētos* ("righteousness"), and the second *rabdos* is anarthrous. In the LXX it is the second *rabdos* that has the article, and both *rabdos* and *euthytētos* in the first part of the clause are anarthrous. Hebrews in effect reverses the subject and predicate of the LXX rendering. Once again, this may have been done to balance stylistically this clause with the previous one, both clauses now beginning with an articular noun plus the genitive (*ho thronos sou* in the first clause, *hē rabdos tēs euthytētos* in the second). Hebrews' form of the passage also serves to highlight attention on the Son's rule as one of righteousness (Bateman 1997: 132). The third variation in Hebrews' form of Ps. 45 is a bit more difficult and involves the question of whether following *basileias* ("kingdom") in 1:8 the reading *sou* ("your") or *autou* ("his") is correct. If the former, then Hebrews aligns with the LXX, and this has been argued for by Metzger (1994: 592–93), primarily on two grounds: (1) the witnesses in support of *sou* are ancient and geographically diverse; (2) the internal difficulty of the reading *autou*, which would conflict with reading *ho theos* as vocative. Further, the variant *sou* aligns with the LXX, the author's text, and matches the four other occurrences of the second-person singular pronoun in the quotation, and scribes, understanding *ho theos* in 1:8a as nominative, may have changed the pronoun to *autou* (Harris 1992: 210–11). On the other hand, the reading *autou* has impressive early witnesses in its favor ($\mathfrak{P}^{46}$ ℵ B), is the more difficult reading in terms of scribal motivation (Thomas 1965: 305; Bateman 1997: 133–34), and helps to explain the insertion of the conjunction *kai* ("and") as a means of easing the transition from the second-to third-person address. Yet, I side with Metzger and

Harris, regarding the arguments in favor of *sou* as slightly winning out. Finally, there is a question as to whether *anomian* or *adikian* should follow *emisēsas* in Ps. 44:8 LXX = Heb. 1:9a. In the LXX B'' R *L*'' 1219' have *anomian*, while 2013' A have *adikian*. In manuscripts of Hebrews a similar split occurs, with *anomian* found in 𝔓⁴⁶ B D² et al., and *adikian* in ℵ A.

E. How Ps. 45:6–7 MT Is Understood and Used Theologically at Heb. 1:8–9. The quotation of Ps. 45:6–7 (44:7–8 LXX) is the fifth quotation in the chain, being paired with Ps. 102:25–27 (101:26–28 LXX) on the basis of verbal analogy, by forms of the pronoun *sy* ("you"). It is clear that the author of Hebrews walks the path of other Jewish interpreters of the era in understanding the psalm as messianic, and thus, for him, as christological. As such, the passage reinforces his rhetorical program of proclaiming the Son as superior to the angels, and with this aim he uses it to affirm Jesus as "God," making a clear demarcation between the nature of the Son and the angels. Yet, the author also understands Ps. 45:6–7 as a direct verbal prophecy concerning the perpetual nature of the Son's reign, having been explicitly fulfilled (indeed, which could only be fulfilled) in the exaltation of Jesus to the right hand of God (Heb. 1:3, 13; Ps. 110:1). Finally, the reference to "God, your God" in the quotation's final verse also reinforces the distinction, present everywhere thus far in Hebrews, between the Son and the Father, thus communicating an implicit Trinitarian perspective that affirms the Son as God but makes a distinction between him and the Father.

This quotation continues certain emphases that the author has already presented in the book and extends his treatment of the Son's superiority. With Ps. 110, Ps. 2, and 2 Sam. 7, Ps. 45 focuses on the kingdom of God, inaugurated by the Son of God. This is a kingdom that will put down God's enemies, involve the eternal establishment of the Son's throne, give the Son an inheritance over all, and now, via Ps. 45, is said to be characterized by righteousness. The eternality of the Son, expressed in the phrase "for ever and ever" (*eis ton aiōna tou aiōnos*) (Heb. 1:8; Ps. 45:6 [44:7 LXX]), joins the proclamation, taken from Ps. 102:26–27 (101:27–28 LXX) at 1:10–12, that the Son "remains" (*diamenō*) and that his years do not fail (*ekleipō*). The eternality of the Son is

critical to the author's argument in the rest of the book, being supported by the "forever" priesthood of the Son, based on Ps. 110:4 (5:5; 6:20; 7:3, 17, 21, 24, 28). He is a priest who does not die, who offers a sacrifice that never needs to be repeated (10:1–14). Further, the *ho theos* of 1:8, understood as vocative, and the *ho theos* of 1:9, a nominative, proclaim the deity of Christ, on the one hand, and the distinct persons of Son and Father, on the other (so Harris 1985).

1:10–12

A. The Immediate NT Context: The Son Is Greater Than the Angels by Virtue of His Role in Relation to the Cosmos. Psalm 102:25–27 (102:26–28 MT; 101:26–28 LXX) participates with Ps. 45:6–7 (45:7–8 MT; 44:7–8 LXX) in bringing a resounding crescendo to the chain of OT quotations in 1:5–14, and it leads to the climax embodied in the quotation of Ps. 110:1 (109:1 LXX) at 1:13. It is paired with Ps. 45:6–7, the author reading both as proclamations concerning the superior Son. The two passages are joined formally by forms of the second-person pronoun *sy* ("you"). The sixth quotation in the author's chain, Ps. 102:25–27 trumpets the decisive superiority of the Son, when compared to the angels, by presenting his role in both the creation and consummation of the universe. The author already has noted the Son as the Father's agent in creation (1:2c), as well as the heir of all things (1:2b [cf. the quotation of Ps. 2:7 in 1:5]), and these themes are reiterated and expanded here.

Psalm 102:25–27 is introduced simply with *kai* ("and"), demonstrating its close association with the previous quotation (Ps. 45:6–7), while at the same time setting it off as distinct. That close association includes a share in the formula introducing 1:8, *pros de ton huion* ("But to the Son"), which carries over to the quotation under consideration here, as a second proclamation addressed to the Son.

The broader context of Ps. 102 evinces links with other texts of the chain quotation (1:5–14). There is emphasis in the chapter on the name of the Lord (102:15, 21 [cf. Deut. 32:3; 2 Sam. 7:9, 13]), Zion as God's special interest (102:13 [cf. Ps. 2:6; 110:2]), kings of the earth (102:15, 22 [cf. 2:2, 10; 110:5]), earth (102:19, 25 [cf. 2 Sam. 7:9, 23; Ps. 2:2, 8, 10; 45:16; 104:5, 9]), heaven(s) (102:19, 25 [cf. Deut. 32:1, 40, 43; Ps. 2:4; 103:19;

104:2]), the earth having a foundation (102:25 [cf. Deut. 32:22; Ps. 104:5]), and the eternality of God's rule or his king's rule (102:12, 24, 26–27 [cf. 2 Sam. 7:13, 16; Ps. 45:2; 110:4]).

B. The Original OT Context. Psalm 102 has generated a plethora of complex speculations as to its exact genre, its unity of form, its setting, and its appropriate interpretation (see Allen 2002: 16–18). For example, 102:1b–11 and 102:23–24a seem to be an individual lament, while 102:12–22 and 102:24b–28 appear much more communal in nature. Suggestions have varied as to whether we have here the conflation of two separate psalms, the reworking of an individual psalm of lament to make it useful in public worship (Brunert 1996: 287–92), or the crafting of a unified composition (Mays 1994: 323). The title to the psalm characterizes it as a song of a troubled person who pours out a complaint to the Lord. This person, in the throes of suffering, seems to be terminally ill (102:23), his physical resources wasting away as he is assaulted by enemies (102:3–9) and the knowledge that in some way he is experiencing God's wrath (102:10). With 102:12 the focus shifts to God, who, being eternal, transcends the problems and devastation of the moment. God is a God of mercy who cares for and identifies himself with Zion. Moreover, he is a God who hears the groaning of the oppressed (102:13–22). Finally, the author appeals to the Lord for a life that will endure on the basis of God's everlasting nature (102:23–28).

In terms of context, the MT and the LXX differ significantly. As we noted, 102:26–28 MT (102:25–27 ET) points to the immutability of God, who lives above the changing chaos of the earth and is seen in bold contrast to the psalmist's own experiences of trouble and the temporal nature of life. In 102:24 MT (102:23 ET), however, we read the Piel perfect third-person masculine singular *'innâ* ("he weakened" or "he broke"), while the LXX (101:24) has understood the word as *'ānâ* ("he answered") and translated it with the Greek *apekrithē* ("he answered"). Thus, in the LXX the words of our quotation can be taken as the words of Yahweh spoken to one addressed as "Lord," and in that case they must refer to divine Wisdom or the Messiah (Lane 1991: 1:30; Bruce 1990: 61–63).

C. Relevant Uses of the OT Reference in Jewish Sources. Various portions of Ps. 102 are transcribed in the Qumran literature (11Q5 Frag. C ii; 4Q84). Bateman (1997: 200–202) notes a few changes in 11Q5 from the MT, but these are minor, and it basically is a textual reproduction. The Targum on the psalm parallels the MT, although there are minor additions related to exile (102:23, 28?) and the world to come (102:24), and creatures are included in the reference to creation (102:25).

Our passage is alluded to in *Lad. Jac.* 7:35, but there are several problems in regard to this allusion. First, the work has survived in highly unsatisfactory form, known only from the Slavonic *Explanatory Palaia*, the editors of which took great liberty with the texts that they utilized, removing text, rearranging texts, melding disparate works, and changing the wording to make their products anti-Jewish. Chapter 7, in which our allusion occurs, probably should be seen as a separate work, juxtaposed to the end of the book. This chapter contains various oracular prophecies on the birth and crucifixion of Christ (*OTP* 2:401–2). Alluding to 102:27 in *Lad. Jac.* 7:35, and speaking of Christ, it reads, "His own dominion and years will be unending forever." Thus, as in Heb. 1:10–12, the allusion to Ps. 102 is used in support of an aspect of Christology.

D. The Textual Background. When we compare the MT and the LXX texts, we see that the latter makes three changes to the passage under consideration. (1) The LXX adds the vocative *kyrie* ("O Lord") in 101:26 (cf. 102:26 MT; 102:25 ET), a term used of Yahweh eight times thus far in the psalm (LXX: 101:2, 13, 16, 17, 19, 20, 22, 23), though here, as we saw, the referent seems to have changed either to divine Wisdom or the Messiah. (2) The singular "work" (*ma'ăśēh*) is rendered as plural "works" (*erga*) in 101:26 LXX (cf. 102:26 MT; 102:25 ET), perhaps because of a developing cosmology that understood the heavens as multifaceted. Or, perhaps the singular form in the MT is corrupt, discerned so on the basis of grammar, as well as the fact that the reading in 4Q84 and a targumic reading have the plural. On the other hand, the translator may have rendered the term in the plural to facilitate a concordance with "the heavens" in the verse (Bateman 1997: 137). (3) The LXX adds *kai* ("and") before *hōsei* *peribolaion allaxeis* ("as a cloak you will change them") in 101:27 (cf. 102:27 MT; 102:26 ET). The Hebrew parallelism is thereby disrupted, but a heightened sense of progression comes with the addition of *kai*, each of the final three clauses in the verse driving home the mutability of the created order (Bateman 1997: 138).

The author of Hebrews once again uses the LXX text, mirroring that text in its deviations from the MT, but he does so with a few modifications of his own. First, the second-person personal pronoun *sy* ("you") is moved from the third word in the parent text to the first in the quotation. However, the LXX manuscripts show several variations of word order at the beginning of 101:26, with almost every possible combination of the first seven words, partially under the influence of 101:2, 13 in the Greek text (see McCullough 1971: 100). Lane (1991: 1:31) notes that the position of *sy* in Hebrews' use of the quotation accomplishes a hookword effect with the ending of the previous quotation (*sou* at the end of 1:9), thus making a smooth transition between the quotations. We might add that it also heightens the sense of proclamation accomplished by the quotation as the primary referent, the Son, constitutes the first utterance of the passage. Second, the future active indicative *diameneis* ("you will remain") in 101:27 LXX is changed to present tense. The author of Hebrews executes the entirety of the chain quotation from the vantage point of the Son in his exalted glory (1:3, 5, 13). Perhaps, then, he changes the tense form to rivet attention on the eternality of the Son's nature, now revealed in his session at the right hand. The change, then, brings the assertion in parallel thought with the proclamation "you are the same" (also having a present tense verb) in 1:12. Third, the verb *allassō* ("change" [LXX S La Ga et Tert. have *allaxeis*]) in 101:27 LXX is replaced in Hebrews with *helixeis* ("you roll up," also found in LXX B' *L*'' A''), a more vivid and specific term, which perhaps the author adopts under the influence of Isa. 34:4 LXX (Kistemaker 1961: 26–27; Attridge 1989: 61). Finally, in 1:12 Hebrews adds the phrase *hōs himation* ("as a garment") to the quotation, repeating the same phrase from the previous verse. This works to balance the last clause quoted in 1:11 with the first two in 1:12, the three clauses reiterating rhythmically the analogy utilizing the temporary usefulness of clothing, thus driving home the temporality of the created order (Attridge 1989: 61n131).

E. How Ps. 102:25–27 Is Understood and Used Theologically at Heb. 1:10–12. The quotation of Ps. 102:25–27 (101:26–28 LXX), the sixth quotation in the chain quotation of 1:5–14, is paired with Ps. 45:6–7 (44:7–8 LXX) on the basis of verbal analogy, by forms of the second-person personal pronoun *sy* ("you"). It is brought into the chain quotation as a resounding conclusion to the chain's body, just prior to the climactic quotation of Ps. 110:1 (109:1 LXX) at 1:13. In tandem with Ps. 45, Ps. 102 extends an emphasis on the Son's status, Ps. 45 focusing on the reign of the Son as messianic ruler and Ps. 102 on his lordship in creation and consummation of the universe. With other NT authors, the author of Hebrews holds the Son as the agent of God the Father in the creation of the universe (1:10; cf. John 1:3; 1 Cor. 8:6; Col. 1:16). Also, the Son is the one to whom all of creation will be subjected in the end (e.g., 1:13; 2:5, 8; cf. 1 Cor. 15:28). The quotation in 1:10–12 foreshadows the day of the Lord (9:28; 10:36–39) and the shaking of the earth, the eschatological judgment to be visited upon the earth at the end of the age, when the material universe will pass away (12:25–29; cf. 1 Cor. 7:31; 1 John 2:8; Rev. 21:1). On that day only the kingdom of God will remain, the kingdoms of this world having been utterly destroyed. Of all things, then, the Son is "Lord," a basic element of early Christian confessions about Christ (e.g., Acts 2:36; Rom. 1:4; 1 Cor. 1:2; Phil. 2:11), and so the author of Hebrews recognizes this divine name from the LXX version of the psalm (101:26) as referring to him.

Psalms 45 and 102 primarily work together, however, to demonstrate the eternality of the Son, over against the transitory nature of the angels. The eternality of the Son has already been expressed in 1:8 in the phrase "for ever and ever" (*eis ton aiōna tou aiōnos*) from Ps. 44:7 LXX (45:7 MT; 45:6 ET), and this motif is critical to a number of primary themes in the book, mainly expressed in the "forever" priesthood of the Son, based on Ps. 110:4 (5:5; 6:20; 7:3, 17, 21, 24, 28). This aspect of Christology, however, extends in the book to the "remaining" of those who, on the basis of new covenant, inherit the heavenly city (10:34;

12:22–24; 13:14) (Lane 1991: 1:31; Thompson 1976: 360–61). The "forever" status of the Son, therefore, has a direct implication for the forever stability of those who are believers in him.

1:13

A. The Immediate NT Context: The Person, Work, and Status of the Son. The allusion to Ps. 110:1 (109:1 LXX) at 1:3 launches a section on the Son's superiority over the angels (1:4) that reverberates through the chain quotation in which our passage under consideration is found (1:5–14). It also anticipates the quotation at 1:13, which serves as the climax of the chain begun at 1:5. The introductory formula for the quotation of Ps. 110:1 at 1:13 forms the closing of an *inclusio* opened in 1:5. This rhetorical question concerning the angels in reality constitutes an assertion that such a proclamation as embodied in Ps. 110:1 has never been said with reference to an angelic being.

It should be noted that the quotation of Ps. 110:1 at 1:13 is the only quotation in the chain that is not paired with another passage. This is because the author places special focus on this passage in particular, for the quotation of Ps. 110:1 at 1:13 is programmatic for the book, moving the discussion spatially between heaven and earth (G. H. Guthrie 1994: 121–24). The allusion to the passage at 1:3 functions to start the book with a focus on the Son as "higher than" or superior to the angels (1:4, 5–14). At 1:13 the psalm serves both as the climax of the section on the Son's superiority and to make a transition to the discussion of incarnation (2:10–18), by its verbal analogy with Ps. 8:4–6, quoted at 2:5–9. Again at 8:1 an allusion to Ps. 110:1 functions to move the discussion back to a focus on the heavenly realm, since a cornerstone of the author's treatment of Christ's superior offering has to do with its location "in heaven" (8:1–2, 4–6; 9:11, 23–24). Also, at 10:12 the author utilizes the psalm spatially, emphasizing the Son's session as indicating the decisiveness of his sacrifice for sins, and at 12:2 to show the outcome of the Son's endurance, as he was exalted to heaven.

B. The Original OT Context. The concept of the "right hand" (*yāmîn*) is used in the OT to represent either superior power or ultimate honor, though it also carries the derivative meanings of "greatness" or "favor." For instance, the right hand

as a symbol of honor is used for the bestowal of a blessing (Gen. 48:18). Bathsheba was given the honor of sitting at Solomon's right hand (1 Kings 2:19), and the right-hand position is occupied by the bride at the marriage ceremony of an unnamed monarch (Ps. 45:9). At Yahweh's right hand are an abundance of pleasures (Ps. 16:11), learning (Ps. 45:4), and righteousness (48:10). In this broad conceptual context Ps. 110:1 makes a straightforward assertion: Yahweh pronounces an oracle concerning the author's "lord," commanding him to sit at his right hand, until this lord's enemies are brought into submission. The original setting of Ps. 110 is a matter of ongoing scholarly debate (Allen 2002: 112–13), with most commentators now opting for an early date associated with the monarchy rather than a late date during the Maccabean era (Kraus 1993b: 346–47). That the psalm is a royal psalm is supported by references to "my Lord," the exhortation "sit at my right hand," the footstool motif, and the reference to a "scepter" (Bateman 1997: 175), and many commentators hold that it constitutes the utterances of a court prophet, perhaps upon the coronation of the Davidic monarch.

In Ps. 110, which is constructed around two divine oracles (110:1, 4), the king is presented as Yahweh's vicegerent. The second oracle (110:4) proclaims the monarch a priest, a sacred mediator between Yahweh and the people, according to the order of Melchizedek (thus an appointed successor to the Jebusite priest-kings), which the author of Hebrews develops extensively in treating the appointment of Jesus as high priest (5:1–10; 7:1–28). This second oracle is amplified in 110:5–7 and marked by the repetition of the preposition *'al* ("on, over, therefore"), and it elaborates on the significant position of the king (110:5). Further, Yahweh will use the king's rule to execute judgment on the nations (110:5–6) (Allen 2002: 113–14). The first oracle, however, to which the author of Hebrews alludes, and the amplification of the oracle in 110:2–3, are given cohesion by the pronominal suffix "your," repeated eight times. This proclamation assures the king of victory in war against his enemies (110:2) and of having the necessary personnel to carry out the battles. The army of Israel is pictured here as the blessing of God on the king (110:3).

C. Relevant Uses of the OT Reference in Jewish Sources. In *T. Job* 33:3 Job speaks of his majestic throne, saying, "My throne is in the upper world, and its splendor and majesty come from the right hand of the Father." In the broader context of this apparent allusion to Ps. 110:1 Job parallels certain concerns also present in Heb. 1:1–14. Job speaks of the world as passing away and contrasts it with the eternal nature of God and heaven (1:8–12). Further, rulers of the earth are temporary, whereas the kingdom of which Job is a part is "for ever and ever." At the end of the book Job's reward for his piety is his elevation to heaven by the chariots of God so that he may receive his throne. Consequently, he is vindicated by his exaltation to God's right hand.

In rabbinic materials the "lord" addressed in Ps. 110:1 is interpreted variously as Abraham, Hezekiah (according to Justin Martyr, *Dial.* 33), David, and the Messiah. In *Midr. Ps.* 18:29, for instance, Rabbi Yudan, in the name of Rabbi Hama, speaks of the Holy One seating the lord Messiah at his right hand and Abraham at his left! In these Jewish texts, the session of a person beside God is seen as honorific and, at times, indicating passivity. For example, *Midr. Ps.* 110:5 suggests passivity on the part of David, who, seated at God's right hand, was to wait until the end of Saul's reign (Hay 1973: 30), and this interpretation is also reflected in the rendering of Ps. 110:1 in *Tg. Ps.* 110:1 (McNamara 2000: 20–21). It may be suggested that the rabbinic interpretations of the psalm as referring to the Messiah probably existed in the NT era. Jesus' reference to the psalm in Mark 12:35–37 and Peter's use of the psalm on the day of Pentecost (Acts 2:32–36) suggest that the Jews of their day were familiar with messianic interpretations of the passage.

D. The Textual Background. The form of the allusions to Ps. 110:1 in Heb. 1:3; 8:1; 10:12; 12:2 all compose a reflective look back at the exaltation of Christ as having fulfilled Ps. 110:1. Only the session at the right hand of God is mentioned, the verb form is changed, and *dexiōn* of the quotation has become *dexia* in the allusions, but the allusion to this verse is unmistakable. At 1:3 the "at my right hand" (*ek dexiōn mou*) of the psalm is alluded to as "at the right hand of the majesty in heaven" (*en dexia tēs megalōsynēs en hypsēlois*). Of necessity, the personal pronoun *mou* ("my")

has been changed because God, rather than the speaker, is now made the point of reference. In terms of the quotation of Ps. 110:1 at 1:13, there exists an exact correspondence of words between the MT, the LXX, and Hebrews. This, among much other evidence, suggests that the author of Hebrews used the LXX as his Scripture, since it is unlikely that he and the translators of the OT into Greek would have used exactly the same words and word order to render a translation of the MT (Bateman 1997: 125–26). The allusion at 1:3, however, along with the other allusions to the verse in Hebrews, is shaped in form by christological reflection on the psalm as fulfilled by the exaltation of the Son to the right hand of God.

E. How Ps. 110:1 Is Understood and Used Theologically at Heb. 1:13. Psalm 110:1 is the OT passage most frequently cited in the NT, being quoted or alluded to twenty-two times. Five of these occurrences appear in Hebrews. The psalm accomplishes a number of theological objectives, showing the supremacy of Christ to all earthly rulers and at the same time demonstrating the ongoing relationship of Jesus to God the Father. There are at least four distinct ways this psalm is used in the NT: (1) as a preexaltation messianic text (e.g., Mark 12:36 pars.); (2) as a text showing God's vindication of Jesus before unbelievers (e.g., Mark 14:62 pars.; Acts 2:32–36; 5:31); (3) as a reference to Christ's intercession on behalf of believers (e.g., Rom. 8:34); (4) as a proclamation of Christ's lordship or superiority (e.g., 1 Cor. 15:25; Eph. 1:22; 1 Pet. 3:22) (for the development of use in the NT, see Loader 1977–1978).

The quotation of Ps. 110:1 at Heb. 1:13 most immediately fits the last of these uses, since the focus of chapter 1 is the superiority of Christ over the angels; yet, the quotation also anticipates Christ's role as high priest (e.g., 1:3; 7:11–28; 10:1–18), as he intercedes for his new-covenant people. In the NT generally, as here in Hebrews, the psalm passage is understood as a directly fulfilled word of prophecy. At Mark 12:35–37 pars., Jesus notes that David, "in the Spirit," calls the Messiah "Lord." At Acts 2:30–35, Peter proclaims David a prophet and Ps. 110:1 as a prophecy of the exaltation. For the author of Hebrews as well, the passage speaks of the exaltation of Christ, and the exaltation has great significance for the people of God in strengthening their endurance. Christ, as exalted, will utterly defeat the enemies of God and his people (2:5–9), and this gives a struggling people hope of vindication. Yet, as exalted to the presence of the Father, the Son also functions as high priest, who has made a sacrifice that has dealt with sin decisively, opening a way for the new-covenant people to "draw near" (10:19–25), and the extent of his priesthood is described, in the words of Ps. 110:4, as "forever."

2:6–8a

A. The Immediate NT Context: The Superior Son Became Incarnate.

The first main movement of Hebrews begins at 1:5 and ends at 2:18 and addresses the status of the Son in relation to the angels (G. H. Guthrie 1994: 144). There are three main christological subsections of 1:5–2:18. The author begins, in 1:5–14, by focusing on the superiority of the Son to the angels, and he does so in the form of a "string of pearls" chain quotation. Using this form, a rabbi would link together a number of OT passages to drive home a point by weight of evidence. Here the author asserts that the exalted Son is superior to the angels by virtue of his unique relationship to the Father (1:5), the angels' inferior role (1:6–7), and his eternal reign and role vis-à-vis the created order (1:8–12). In the third subsection, 2:10–18, the focus is on the incarnation and the Son's solidarity with God's people. A critical role is played by 2:5–9, which moves the discussion from the first of these expositions on the Son of God to the third, since it contains elements of exaltation ("you have crowned him with glory and honor") as well as incarnation ("you have made him lower than the angels for a little while").

In terms of immediate context, three points should be noted. First, the theological statement of 2:5 is significant, hinting at the theological framework with which the author of Hebrews approaches Ps. 8:4–6. That statement is expressed negatively—"for he has not submitted the coming world to angels"—and leads into the quotation, which the author understands as supporting, or reinforcing, his statement in 2:5. Thus, with the quotation from Ps. 8, the author has in mind the submission not only of the world, but also of the world to come, and this is vital to our understanding of how he uses this passage from the OT. Second, the introductory formula here is somewhat unusual (2:6). The author normally introduces Scripture as falling from the lips of God, utilizing forms of *legō* ("say") with God, or the Son, or the Spirit as the subject. The introductory formula at 1:6, however, is stated ambiguously, not because the author has forgotten who spoke this psalm or where it occurs in Scripture, but to keep the focus on God, rather than a human agent, as the primary speaker of Scripture. He does not present this quotation as God speaking, of course, because this portion of Scripture is spoken to God—he is the one being addressed. Third, as Ellingworth (1993: 144) points out, this is the first place in Hebrews in which the author does midrashic commentary on the text, 2:8b–9 comprising a clear application of the passage to Jesus.

B. The Original OT Context.

In its OT context Ps. 8 follows several psalms of lament, which contain requests for deliverance (Pss. 3–7), and offers a beautiful praise-filled counterpoint to these, a song of God's glory and the dignity of human beings. The psalm is framed by an *inclusio*, a refrain celebrating the majesty of the Lord's name: "O Yahweh, our Lord, how magnificent is your name in all the earth." The body of the psalm develops in two primary movements. The Hebrew of 8:1b–2 (8:2b–3 MT) is notoriously difficult to understand because of a grammatical conundrum (see the summary in Kraus 1993a: 178), but the psalmist seems to proclaim that Yahweh has placed his glory on, or above, the heavens. The image of infants and toddlers, who are immensely vulnerable, is placed in sharp relief with that of powerful enemies. God is able to build up a people of weakness as a force to oppose his enemies (Wilson 2002: 202). In 8:3–8, from which our quotation is taken, the author expresses wonder at God's dealings with humanity, for whom God has ordained a special role in the created order. Thus, these verses concern humanity's astonishing dignity. In light of God's awesome creation of his heavens, the moon and stars that he has put in their places, the psalmist reflects on the relative insignificance of people in the vast scope of God's purposes (8:3–4). In 8:4 a question is posed in synonymous parallelism, in essence asking, "Why do you even spare a thought for people?" The term here for humanity (*ĕnôš*) is used most often to focus on "human frailty, weakness, and mortality" (Wilson 2002: 204), the earthbound nature of the creature under God's heavens (Kraus 1993a: 182).

Yet, the wonderful mystery is that God thinks of and cares for people. In 8:5–8 we find a reflection on Gen. 1:26–28, where God commissions human beings, created in the image of God, to rule over the fish of the sea, birds of the air, and over all living creatures. Humans have been made a little lower than *ʾĕlōhîm*, which can be translated as a reference to angels, gods, or God himself. The LXX translates the term with *angelous* ("angels"), and on that reading human beings have their place in the created order, just below those who serve around God's throne. It may well be that *ʾĕlōhîm* referred to the angels in the Hebrew original of the psalm, for the "let us" in Gen. 1:27 can be read as a reference to the angelic council (see Waltke and Fredricks 2001: 64). This place of humans in the created order emphasizes the surprising dignity of people in spite of their being dwarfed by the massive reaches of God's creation. Yet, the stewardship given to humanity over other works of God's hands extends the emphasis on human dignity. In its original context the critical phrase "you laid everything at his feet" refers to the animals, as is made clear in Ps. 8:7–8, over whom the human has been installed as a king (Kraus 1993a: 183). At the end of the psalm the author repeats the word of praise with which it opened.

It is vital to understand the ideal relationship communicated here, Adamic kingship being squarely in focus. The passage communicates a divine, ongoing commission. The OT story in many ways reflects a repeated failure to fulfill that commission by Adam, Noah, Israel, and so forth, and it is interesting that Jewish sources through the ages have seized on this psalm to emphasize the insignificance of people rather than their exalted roles as "kings" over the created order.

C. Relevant Uses of the OT Reference in Jewish Sources. Among Jewish sources, the most prominent appropriation of Ps. 8:4–6 seizes on the question "What is man . . . ?" in order to emphasize the insignificance of human beings. 1QS III, 17–18 plays part in a discussion of God's sovereign design of all things and asserts, "He created humankind to rule over the world," a possible allusion to Ps. 8. Later in the same work it says, "Who can measure your glory? Who, indeed, is man among your glorious works?" (1QS XI, 20). This latter verse emphasizes the insignificance of human beings, and the author goes on to state, "His body is but

the bread of worms; he is so much spit, mere nipped-off clay" (1QS XI, 21–22a).

Several late works also use Ps. 8 to emphasize the insignificance of human beings. In *3 Enoch*, a work probably from the fifth or sixth century AD, the ministering angels bring a complaint to God: "Lord of the Universe, what business have you with men, as it is written, 'What is man [*ĕnôš*] that you should spare a thought for him?'" (*3 En.* 5:10 [cf. *Gen. Rab.* 8:6]). Given Hebrews' use of the psalm to make a transition to the topic of incarnation, it is interesting that this passage goes on to say, "Why did you leave the heaven of heavens above, the abode of your glory, the high and exalted throne which is in the height of Arabot, and come and lodge with men who worship idols?" (*3 En.* 5:11). Similar to *3 Enoch*'s use of the psalm, *b. Šabb.* 88b says that upon Moses' ascension to heaven, angels questioned why a human being has been allowed to be among them. In *b. Sanh.* 38b angels, using the form of the psalm's question, ask God about why he would want to create people in the first place. Later, when the flood generation does not turn out well, the angels, in effect, say to the Lord, "We told you so!" Also speaking of Moses, but with an emphasis on the dignity of this man, *b. Ned.* 38a and *b. Roš Haš.* 21b take the psalm's statement "you have made him a little lower than God" to refer to Moses as having all but one of the "fifty gates of understanding."

One of the most significant allusions to Ps. 8 in relation to Hebrews is in *4 Ezra* 6:53–54, part of a larger section on God's work in creation. The book of *4 Ezra*, perhaps written by a first-century Palestinian Jew, proclaims that God is just in spite of the evil in the world (Evans 1992: 11). The passage speaks of God placing Adam as ruler over all his created works. Yet, in 6:55–59, the writer goes on to ask God why, if the world was created for his people, the evil nations are being allowed to rule over and devour the people of God. He asks, "If the world has indeed been created for us, why do we not possess our world as an inheritance?" As we will see momentarily, the same concern may be in view in Heb. 2:8–9.

D. The Textual Background. Three primary differences between our author's text, the LXX, and the Hebrew version need to be addressed. First, the meaning of the Hebrew of Ps. 8:5 (8:6 MT/LXX) can be rendered in various ways. As we noted in the discussion of Ps. 45 at Heb. 1:8–9, the term *'ĕlōhîm* has a broad semantic range in the OT, referring to God, heavenly beings (Ps. 97:7), judges (Ps. 82:1, 6), Moses (Exod. 7:1), and the specter of Samuel (1 Sam. 28:13). At first blush, the context of the psalm seems to favor the translation "God," by virtue of the contrast in the psalm between the creator/ruler of all and humanity, his stewards, as well as the strong allusion to Gen. 1:26–28 (Craigie 1983: 108). The term could also refer to "heavenly beings" generally, including both God and his angels. Yet, the LXX, along with the Syriac OT and a Targum on the psalm, translates *'ĕlōhîm* with "angels" (*angelos*). On this reading, the angels are a point of reference in the created order and fit the context, which has to do with humanity's place in God's creation. For Hebrews, the presence of "angels" in the OT text serves the greater purpose in 1:5–2:18: to show the Son's relation to these beings as a way of emphasizing both his superiority to the angels and his solidarity with human beings.

Second, a textual variant in the quotation at 2:7, "and appointed him over the works of your hands," occurs in the Hebrew and LXX texts but has been omitted from the standard NT Greek texts of Hebrews in spite of a wealth of witnesses in the variant's favor (e.g., ℵ A C D*; it is omitted in 𝔓⁴⁶ B D² 𝔐). Metzger (1994: 594) notes the impression made "by the probability that the longer reading may be the result of scribal enlargement of the quotation." However, it may be the case that scribes dropped this portion of the text because of an apparent contradiction with the quotation of Ps. 101:26–28 LXX in 1:10, where the created order is spoken of as the work of the Son's hands. Further, the word *katestēsas* ("appointed") plays a crucial role in the structure of Hebrews, speaking of the appointment of the Son as high priest (cf. 5:1; 7:28; 8:3; see G. H. Guthrie 1994: 82). Of course, it also may be that the author of Hebrews left out the clause in question to avoid confusion with Ps. 101:26–28 LXX as well (see McCullough 1971: 70–72).

Finally, the quotation in Hebrews begins with *ti* in the best manuscript evidence, but 𝔓⁴⁶ C* P and a few other witnesses have *tis*. This mirrors the situation in the LXX, where *ti* is found in most manuscripts, but *L^pau* A read *tis*.

E. How Ps. 8:5–7 Is Understood and Used at Heb. 2:5–9. In 2:5–9 the use of Ps. 8 suggests that the divine commission of Adam as king over God's creation ultimately has been fulfilled in Christ, the eschatological last Adam. Christ, in his solidarity with humanity (2:10–18), had been for a little while lower than the angels but now has been crowned with glory and honor as a result of his suffering. This approach, of course, assumes that the author is using the passage christologically rather than primarily anthropologically, and I suggest that this is the case for the following reasons. First, this quotation from Ps. 8 is introduced, in part by its verbal analogy with the quotation of Ps. 110:1 (109:1 LXX), at the end of chapter 1, the two passages speaking of subjugation as placing something or someone under "the feet" (*tōn podōn*). Thus, the quotation and exposition at 2:5–9 continue the christological discussion of 1:5–14 carried out vis-à-vis the angels. The introductory formula of 2:5 refers back to the exaltation heralded through the quotation of Ps. 110:1 at 1:13. The submission of the world to come (2:5) alludes to Ps. 110:1, speaking of all the enemies being placed under the feet of Christ at a future time (cf. Eph. 1:20–22). These two OT texts, Ps. 110:1 and Ps. 8:4–6, are brought together also elsewhere in the NT to speak of the subjection of all things to Christ at his exaltation (1 Cor. 15:25–27; Eph. 1:20–22). Christ, then, in his solidarity with human beings, was able to bring about the ultimate fulfillment of the psalm's intention. Thus, "It is a natural development of the thought of the psalm, for the dominion of which the psalmist spoke may have had theological reality, yet it did not always appear to have historical reality in the developing history of the human race. The historical reality, according to Paul and the author of the Epistle to the Hebrews, is—and will be—fulfilled in the risen Christ" (Craigie 1983: 110).

But this raises an important issue for the first readers of Hebrews: a seeming confusion between Ps. 110:1 and Ps. 8:4–6. The former seems to suggest that the submission of all things is a future event, while the latter would indicate that the submission is an accomplished fact. When confronted with an apparent contradiction between two passages, the rabbis would seek to "dispel confusion" by explaining how the two passages relate

(G. H. Guthrie 1997: 843), and this is exactly what the author of Hebrews does in 2:8–9. He explains that all things have indeed been placed under the feet of Christ (quoting Ps. 8:4–6), but we do not yet see all things placed under his feet (quoting Ps. 110:1). The reality has been inaugurated, but its consummation will come at a time in the future.

For the first hearers of Hebrews, this theological point was crucial. Perhaps they were questioning whether Ps. 8:4–6 had indeed been fulfilled in Christ, given the persecution that they were facing (see the discussion of *4 Ezra* 6:53–59 in §C above). The author assures them that Christ really is in control, but that the full subjugation of all things lies in the future. Thus, he dispels their confusion concerning the passage and at the same time leads them into his discussion of the incarnation. This is the beauty and genius of the author's use of Ps. 8:4–6.

F. The Theological Use of the OT Material.

The use of Ps. 8:4–6 in 2:5–9 incorporates several aspects of Christology, but two central aspects are primary: exaltation and incarnation. Thus, it provides a concise expression to what some have called "the way of the Son," by which the Son of God leaves heaven, adds humanity to his deity and walks among us, suffers, and is raised and exalted to the right hand of God (see, e.g., Phil. 2:5–11). The author takes the psalm to tell of the exaltation in the statements "you have crowned him with glory and honor" and "you have submitted all things, placing them under his feet." The Son's incarnation, on the other hand, is expressed with "you have made him lower than the angels for a little while." This solidarity with people, this becoming human, made it possible for Christ to fulfill the original intention of the psalm. In him the full dignity and destiny of humanity find their ultimate expression, as all things, not just the animal world, are submitted to him. Thus, although not expressed overtly, we also have a "last Adam" Christology in play. The original context of the psalm, echoing the creation account in Gen. 1:26–28, points both to human frailty, in the earthly nature of our existence, and to human dignity, in the power and stewardship bestowed on us in Adam. In adding humanity to his deity via the incarnation, Christ joined us in our frailty, our smallness in the scope of the vast

creation. He moved from his preincarnate sphere of the power and authority that he wielded in creating the world, and he assumed a lower place in the created order. The frailty consequent of this move terminated in the Son's death for everyone (2:8–9). Yet, because of suffering and death, he was "crowned with glory and honor," in the words of the psalm. The dignity of humans, granted to Adam in his place in the world, comes to ultimate fulfillment and expression in the Son as he is made Lord of all things, all things having been placed under his feet.

2:12

A. The Immediate NT Context. Thus far in Hebrews' exposition on "the Son" (1:1–14; 2:5–9), the author has capitalized on a comparison between Christ and the angels to highlight the unquestionable superiority of the Son. In 1:5–14 the author uses a chain quotation to drive home that superiority on several bases, with the intention of setting up the a fortiori argument in 2:1–4. The discussion of the Son picks up with 2:5–9, a transitional unit that exploits Ps. 8:4–6, which contains elements that speak to Christ's exaltation, as well as elements that speak to his incarnation. Thus, the OT passage facilitates movement from the theme of superiority to that of the humiliation of the Son, the theme of 2:10–18, in which our passage under consideration here is quoted. In 2:10–18 the author wishes to demonstrate the Son's solidarity with believers ("the sons"). "It was fitting" (*prepō* [2:10]) for the Father, in accomplishing salvation for those of the new covenant, to perfect the Son through sufferings (2:11). That is, the Son had to take on flesh and blood in order to die and thus to break the power of the devil (2:14). In this way salvation was bought and a way was made for believers to be brought to glory (2:10). This solidarity between the Son and the heirs of God results in a gracious identification on the part of Christ: he is not ashamed to call "the sons" "brothers" (i.e., "family"). In 2:12–13 the author sets forth two texts, Ps. 22:22 (22:23 MT; 21:23 LXX) and Isa. 8:17b–18 as OT reinforcement for Christ's solidarity with believers. At first blush, the psalm and the text from Isaiah might seem to provide minimal support for the author's discussion. However, in the choice of these OT texts, the author of Hebrews tapped into a well of messianic teaching with which his audience probably would have been readily familiar. Further, the proclamation of solidarity between the Son of God and the people of God anticipates a requirement for Christ's high priesthood—he must be taken from among people (2:17–18; 5:1–3)—to which the author turns shortly.

B. The Original OT Context. Psalm 22 (21 LXX) is one of the "prayer songs" in the Psalter, and 22:22 initiates a "thanksgiving" portion of that psalm (Kraus 1993a: 293). In the first eleven verses of the psalm the writer grapples with the silence and apparent absence of God (22:1–11). The passage begins with the familiar words "My God, my God, why have you forsaken me?" taken up by Jesus on the cross (Matt. 27:46 par.). The psalmist feels that God has become remote and does not listen to his groaning (22:1b); his incessant crying goes unanswered (22:2). Yet, history has shown that God can be trusted, since the fathers cried out to him in trust and experienced his deliverance (22:3–5). The writer's pitiful existence, despised and mocked by people (22:6–8), is balanced with the strong personal history that he has with God, and this is the basis for his appeal for help (22:9–11). In 22:12–21 he recounts vicious attacks by human enemies. Like one surrounded and harassed by wild or violent animals, the psalmist is depleted of strength (22:12–15), and evil people have pierced (or perhaps bound [Strawn 2000: 448]) his hands and feet, gloated over him, and divided his clothes (22:16–18). So, the writer makes an urgent plea for deliverance (22:19–21a). The turning point in the psalm begins in 22:21b (22:22b MT), where the psalmist exclaims, "You have heard me!" (Qal perfect of *'nh*). This interjection functions as an abrupt transition from the lament of 22:1–21a, with the thanksgiving that follows. Some interpreters conceive of this as an "oracle of rescue" (an expression that God has now brought the sufferer deliverance), while others see it as an expression of trust, understanding that the sufferer hopes for rescue (Kraus 1993a: 293, 298). Nevertheless, it paves the way for 22:22, the first expression of thanksgiving in the chapter. "The name" in that verse represents God's power to save, proclaimed to other worshipers in the community. Thus, with 22:22 the psalm turns to a confession of trust in which the righteous sufferer expresses joy and praise for God's answer to his cry for help. The balance of the chapter constitutes a hymn of praise and thanksgiving that perhaps moves from the individual (22:23–26) to the whole congregation (so Craigie 1983: 198), for God has listened to the sufferer's cry for help; all the nations of the world will be compelled to worship this wonderful God, as will future generations (22:27–31).

C. Relevant Uses of the OT Reference in Jewish Sources. Psalm 22 (21 LXX) is used rarely in the Jewish sources. The material from the Dead Sea Scrolls does not quite extend to the portion of the psalm in which our quotation is found (5/6Ḥev 40 has 22:3–8, 14–20; 4Q88 has 22:14–17, see Abegg, Flint, and Ulrich 1999: 518–19), but it is interesting that the psalm scroll from Naḥal Ḥever matches the LXX at 22:16 ("they have pierced my hands and feet" [21:17 LXX]) over against the MT and the Targum on the psalm (Abegg, Flint, and Ulrich 1999: 518–19). There is, however, possibly a very faint echo of our passage at 1QHᵃ XIII, 15b, where the writer proclaims, "And to show your greatness /through me/ before the sons of Adam, you did wonders." This portion of 1QHᵃ seems to echo a number of themes from Ps. 22.

In the Talmud the immediate context of our passage (though not the verse itself) is found at *b. Meg.* 15b, where, recounting the plight of Queen Esther, Rabbi Levi says that when she entered the king's house, the Divine Presence left her, and she said, "My God, my God, why hast thou forsaken me?" She reasoned that it may be because she had called her enemy a dog (cf. 22:20), and so she changed her words to "Save me from the lion's mouth" (cf. 22:21). Thus, the psalm is used to speak of righteous suffering in the face of evildoers.

D. The Textual Background. There exists a direct, almost rigid, correspondence between the MT and the LXX at Ps. 22:22 (22:23 MT; 21:23 LXX). Furthermore, the only difference between the LXX and the quotation as it stands in Hebrews is that the NT author replaces a future indicative form of *diēgeomai* ("tell, relate, describe") with a future indicative form of *apangellō* ("tell, proclaim"). Although Howard (1968: 215) suggests that here we have a possible example of Hebrews' direct use of the Hebrew text, Attridge (1989) surely is correct that the semantic overlap between *diēgeomai* and *apangellō* is too great to make such a determination on the basis of Hebrews' use of the latter. Rather, it may be that the author felt *apangellō* "better suited to emphasize Christ's mission" (Attridge 1989: 90), or it may be that the change was stylistic, the *ō* sound now found near the beginning of each of the four quoted lines in 2:12–13: *apangelō..., en mesō..., egō...,* and *idou egō*. The meaning, however, is not altered by the change in terminology.

E. How Ps. 22:22 is Understood and Used at Heb. 2:12. Given the original context of Ps. 22:22, and the numerous points of contact that its chapter has with the passion of Jesus, the author of Hebrews certainly understood the verse to have been part of a direct verbal prophecy explicitly fulfilled in the person of Christ. Numerous details, in which Jesus' suffering parallels that of this righteous sufferer in the psalm, point to a striking relationship between the OT passage and Jesus' experience. Yet, this relationship is more than merely analogical, and NT writers, including the author of Hebrews, understood those details in the psalm specifically to be anticipating the sufferings of Christ. Indeed, the final movements of this psalm anticipate a future and universal impact of the sufferer's experience, and these anticipatory proclamations give the psalm a prophetic tenor (note esp. 22:27–31).

In this vein, Jesus "proclaimed the name" to his "brothers" in the preaching of the gospel of the kingdom (e.g., Luke 4:18–19) and offered praise to God in the midst of the assembly. As the turning point in the psalm, 22:22 offers a strong note of victory coming out of suffering, and this accords with the vindication of Christ through resurrection and exaltation. Yet, the author utilizes this verse primarily to reinforce the idea of solidarity between "the Son" and "the sons." That he makes a proclamation "to my brothers" speaks of closeness of relationship, picking up on the term "brothers" in 2:11. This closeness is also communicated by the phrase "in the midst of the assembly." This is not a proclamation from the heavens; rather, it is "down to earth." Consequently, the psalm reinforces the statement in 2:11 that "he is not ashamed to call them brothers."

F. The Theological Use of the OT Material. As we noted, Ps. 22:22, quoted in 2:12, comes from a section of Scripture containing a number of significant prophecies of Christ's suffering (see P. E. Hughes 1977: 107). The psalm begins with the familiar words of suffering used by Jesus when he cried from the cross, "My God, my God, why have you forsaken me?" (Matt. 27:46 par.). In 22:7–8 the righteous sufferer is mocked by evil people saying, "He trusts in the LORD; let the LORD rescue him," words taken up by the religious leaders around the cross (Matt. 27:43). In 22:16–18 the psalm speaks specifically of the piercing (or, in the MT, perhaps the binding) of the righteous one's hands and feet, the wholeness of his bones, and the division of his garments through the casting of lots (cf. Matt. 27:35; John 19:23–24, 31–37). The psalm's first twenty-one verses, on the anguish of the righteous sufferer, present stark parallels to events surrounding Christ's crucifixion. Consequently, the psalm as a whole fits precisely into the author's broader theme of Jesus' "suffering of death" on the cross, a suffering that would bring "many sons to glory" (2:10). Yet, as we noted, Ps. 22:22 works to reinforce the solidarity of the Son with the people he came to save, thus bringing the incarnation squarely into focus, and it is clear from this passage that this aspect of Christology is soteriological. Why was it "fitting" (2:10) for God to accomplish salvation the way that he did, in Christ? The suffering of Christ certainly was in line both with God's righteousness—sacrifice for sin was required—but also it was much in line with God's love. In this way, the incarnation is directly related to Christ's high-priestly work (2:17–18). Simply put, Christ came to help sinners (2:16, 18). That help could be given only if he was "one of us," for ultimately that help came through his death, and only by becoming fully human could he die. This is the significance of the solidarity expressed via Ps. 22. The Son came to be "in the midst," and he died and rose there.

2:13

A. The Immediate NT Context. (See §A of commentary on Heb. 2:12 above.) Isaiah 8:17–18, two parts of which are quoted in 2:13, has been drawn together with Ps. 22:22 (22:23 MT; 21:23 LXX) in the immediate context. The joining of the psalm passage with the one from Isaiah may be on the following bases. First, the *mou/moi* in the two passages quoted provide a degree of verbal analogy, and these pronouns are closely related to the terms of family relationship in each of the respective passages (*adelphos/paidion*). Second, in each OT context there occurs a turning of God's face. In Isa. 8:17 LXX, from which the first Isaiah quotation is taken, the prophet writes, "I will wait for God, who has turned his face away from the house of Jacob." In Ps. 21:25 LXX (22:25 MT; 22:24 ET) the psalmist proclaims that the Lord "has not turned his face away from me." Beyond these bases, both quotations are confessions of trust occurring in broader contexts that the church found laden with messianic prophecies.

B. The Original OT Context. Isaiah 8 is part of a larger section of the book that concerns whether the people of God will trust God or earthly political powers (7:1–12:6). The immediate context of our quotation involves 8:11–9:7 ET (8:11–9:6 MT/LXX) and addresses a stark contrast between walking in the way of a rebellious people and walking in the way of the Lord. These verses reflect on the content of 7:1–8:10 (Oswalt 1986: 231), which includes the threat of war by Aram and Israel on Judah (7:1–9), the sign of Immanuel (7:10–17), the threat of Assyria (7:18–25), the sign of Maher-shalal-hash-baz (8:1–4), and the onslaught of Assyria, which will come like a flood (8:5–10). Thus, 8:11–23 poses the question of how the people will respond to such an imminent threat. Will they call it "conspiracy" and live in fear of earthly powers (8:12), or will they fear the Lord (8:13)? The Lord can be a sanctuary or a stumbling block, a snare and a trap (8:14). It is clear that many of the people have chosen a path of stumbling and captivity (8:15), and so Isaiah commands that the testimony be bound up and sealed, perhaps meaning that Isaiah here steps out of public proclamation of the word of God (8:16) (see Wildberger 1991: 365–69). In response to the impending devastation, the prophet takes a different path than do the people, a path of resolute trust, he and his children serving as "signs" (MT: 'ôt; LXX: sēmeion) to the rebellious generation of the correct way to follow the Lord (8:17–18). When the people seek the word of mediums rather than the word of God, it means imminent destruction, and they will end up cursing both the king and their god (8:19–22). Yet, there still exists the promise of future redemption, when war will be done away with, the ideal ruler having come (9:1–7 [8:23–9:6 MT/LXX]). In this way, Isa. 8:17–18, which occurs at Heb. 2:13, immediately follows and precedes potent messianic passages, the first on the stone of stum-

bling (8:14), and the second on the coming of "the Prince of Peace" (9:1–7), and it portrays the prophet and his children in a posture of trust as they follow the ways of God.

C. Relevant Uses of the OT Reference in Jewish Sources. The passage under consideration does not seem to appear in Jewish sources other than as transcriptions at Qumran (1QIsa^a) and in targumic form (*Targum Isaiah*). The former, very close in form to the MT (with the exception that "sign" and "wonder" are singular), maintains the focus on trust in the Lord, while the Targum is greatly embellished and has transformed into a prayer that, in the face of God's threat to remove his Shekinah from the house of Jacob, the people might be spared exile if they repent. There are other passages that draw on elements of the broader context (e.g., 4Q174 III, 15–16a; *Odes Sol.* 31:4; *Sib. Or.* 1:346; *2 En.* 46:3; *3 En.* 26:8), but they are not especially relevant to the meaning of the passage as used in Heb. 2:13.

D. The Textual Background. The first quotation in 2:13 almost certainly comes from Isa. 8:17. The exact wording of the Isaiah passage in the LXX, *pepoithōs esomai ep' autō*, occurs in two other places in the LXX (2 Sam. 22:3; Isa. 12:2). Yet, in Heb. 2:13 the author follows immediately with a portion of Isa. 8:18, the *kai palin* ("and again") functioning as a stock introductory formula separating the two parts of Isa. 8:17–18; consequently, that 8:17 is the parent text of our quotation is clear, given its association with 8:18. This approach, separating two parts of a passage with *kai palin*, occurs also at Heb. 10:30, where the author presents two parts of Deut. 32:35–36. The separation of the two portions of Isa. 8:17–18 in two distinct quotations highlights the exact phrases from this portion of Scripture and their respective theological points. The first focuses on the Messiah's trust in the Father and the second on the Messiah's solidarity with the children.

The first quotation, from Isa. 8:17, is slightly altered from the LXX form of the text. An emphatic *egō* has been added, attracting the verb *esomai*, which has moved forward, now preceding *pepoithōs* (Kistemaker 1961: 33). The second quotation, from Isa. 8:18, matches the LXX perfectly, as the LXX matches the MT (even in word order), with one exception. Whereas the LXX says that it is God (*ho theos*) who has given the children, the MT uses the name "Yahweh" (*yhwh*).

E. How Isa. 8:17–18 is Understood and Used at Heb. 2:13. Grounded in a context that contained explicit prophecies about Christ's life, death, and significance, the author of Hebrews understood Isa. 8:17b–18 to be messianic, and he appropriated the passage to reinforce scripturally the integral relationship between the Son's posture of trust in the Father and the impact of that posture on others (i.e., "the sons"). In fact, taken together with Ps. 22:22, the quotations are arranged in a chiastic structure meant to highlight both of these dynamics:

A I will proclaim your name to my brothers
  B I will sing your praise in the midst of
    the assembly
  B′ I will place my trust in him
A′ Behold, I and the children God has given
  to me

Thus, Hebrews presents Isa. 8:17b–18 in a two-step fashion in order to clarify these points. First comes 8:17b: "I will place my trust in him." This prophecy expresses Jesus' trust toward the Father. He then offers the next part of the Isaiah passage: "Behold, I and the children God has given me," which demonstrates that the Messiah is in solidarity (or family relationship) with the people of God. Finally, both Ps. 22:22 and Isa. 8:17b–18 allow the author to emphasize that the Son came to be human, expressed in the words "in the midst of the assembly," in the former passage, and "I and the children" in the latter.

F. The Theological Use of the OT Material. As we noted, Isa. 8:17b–18, in its original context, was in proximity to passages of great messianic import for the early church. Isaiah 8:14 describes the Lord as "a stumbling stone," words applied to Christ by other NT writers (Rom. 9:33; 1 Pet. 2:8). Paul specifically describes the crucifixion as that aspect of Christian teaching that causes the unbelieving to stumble (1 Cor. 1:23). It is not surprising, therefore, that the author of Hebrews would use the quotations from Isa. 8:17b–18 to describe Christ's posture of trust and his solidarity with his followers. The Son and his special group of people constitute the remnant prepared by God for himself. Bruce (1990: 83) writes,

Certainly, in Isaiah's prophetic ministry there is a close association between the coming King and the remnant—or, to use the language of Hebrews, between the Son and his brothers. Moreover, there is reason to believe that Isaiah himself took steps to give a conscious corporate existence to the embryonic remnant of his own day, partly in the circle of his disciples of whom he speaks in Isa. 8:16 and partly in his own family.

Consequently, our passage at hand also supports and extends the idea of the righteous remnant. It is a remnant, in Hebrews' estimation, however, led by the Son, who in faithful obedience to the Father suffered and in this way brought the remnant "to glory" (2:10). Therefore, as is the case with the quotation of Ps. 22:22 at 2:12, the incarnation is front and center in the author's intention for this section of Hebrews, and the incarnation was meant to accomplish something relationally between God and his people. The Son's suffering gave a context for his posture of trust, and it accomplished the relationship between the Father and those who would embrace the new covenant.

It is interesting that one point of the quotation—God has given the children to the Son—seems to play a part in Johannine theology. At John 6:37; 10:27–29; 17:6 Jesus says that his followers are given to him by the Father, and this seems to parallel Isa. 8:18 quite closely (Attridge 1989: 91).

2:16–18

With his reference to "the seed of Abraham" (*spermatos Abraam*) at 2:16, the author of Hebrews makes an allusion to Isa. 41:8 LXX: "But you, Israel, my child Jacob, whom I chose, the seed of Abraham [*sperma Abraam*], whom I loved . . ." Yet, there are three other echoes from this passage woven into Hebrews' discourse at this point. The term *epilambanomai* ("take hold of, help, assume the nature of") may echo the use of *antilambanomai* ("help, take hold of") in Isa. 41:9 LXX, the prefix change perhaps taking place under the influence of the use of the former term at Jer. 38:32 LXX (31:32 MT/ET), quoted at 8:9. Second, the exhortation "do not fear" (*mē phobou*) in Isa. 41:10 LXX is mirrored in the observation in Hebrews that the Son has delivered those bound under fear of death (2:15). Finally, the Isaiah passage points to God's "help" (*boētheō*) as an assurance in the face of the Assyrian crisis, the same verb being used in Hebrews at 2:18 with reference to the high-priestly ministry of Jesus. Thus, Hebrews weaves allusions to a passage on God's help for his people, a passage of comfort in the face of difficult circumstances, into a passage (2:10–18) concerning the particular role of the Son, who offered help in the form of deliverance, through his incarnation and suffering.

3:2–5

At 3:2, 5 the author of Hebrews makes an allusion to Num. 12:7, where God says of Moses, "He is faithful in all my house." This affirmation of the great deliverer occurs in a passage on the rebellion of Miriam and Aaron, who spoke against Moses. Here God rebukes the rebels by pointing out the uniqueness of Moses. With mere prophets, God communicates in visions or dreams or dark sayings, but with Moses, openly and face to face. The *synkrisis*, or comparison, between Moses and Jesus, found in 3:1–6 capitalizes on the high esteem with which the former was held in the Judaism of the day. They are comparable in that they both were appointed by God over a people (3:2) and that they were faithful in their ministries (3:5–6).

In drawing the analogy of building a "house," the author possibly is pulling this analogy out of thin air, or there is a parallel to Philo's truism, "That which has made is superior to the thing made" (*Migration* 193). But, we must consider the argument in light of 2 Sam. 7/1 Chron. 17 (see D'Angelo 1979: 70–93; see also commentary on Heb. 1:5 [quoting 2 Sam. 7:14] above). In 2 Sam. 7 we are told that David's son would build a house for God's name (7:13) and that the son's house would be made sure forever. The term *oikos* is prominent in this chapter, used fourteen times by the author to speak variously of the Lord's house, David's house, and the house of David's heir. Further, the chapter proclaims that the Lord would build the son's house and that the son would build a house for the Lord (7:13).

However, this is not all. In 2 Sam. 7:16, 25 God promises to "confirm" or "show faithful" the house of David's son, the author using the verb *pistoō*, and this is the same verb used in Ps. 77:8, 37 (78:8, 37 ET) to speak of the unfaithfulness of the wilderness wanderers. In 2 Sam. 7:25–26 LXX we read, "And now, O my Lord, the Almighty Lord God of Israel, show faithful the word forever which you have spoken concerning your servant and his house; and now, as you have said, let your name be magnified forever." This fact is notable in light of the emphasis on faithfulness in Heb. 3:1–6. Further, in the parallel passage, 1 Chron. 17:23, we find the phrase *epi ton oikon autou*, which is mirrored exactly in Heb. 3:6. In light of the broader context of Heb. 3–4, it also is interesting that 2 Sam. 7 speaks of the promised rest for the people of Israel in 7:11. In addition, D'Angelo (1979: 65–93) sees an allusion here to 1 Sam. 2:35, where God promises to raise up a faithful priest for whom God will raise up a house.

Part of the difficulty of unraveling the logic of Heb. 3:3–4 has been the fact that both Jesus (by analogy) and God the Father are spoken of as builders. Yet, this mix of both God and the Messiah spoken of as builders of a house is exactly what we find in 2 Sam. 7. It could be that the author is echoing that chapter (or its parallel in 1 Chron. 17), which also speaks of the concept of faithfulness. In light of Hays's tests for echoes, this suggestion meets the criteria of availability, volume, recurrence, thematic coherence, historical plausibility, and satisfaction (see Hays 1989: 29–32).

3:7–11, 15–19; 4:3–7

A. The Immediate NT Context. The first two chapters of Hebrews primarily present an exposition on Jesus, in relation to the angels, as the superior (1:5–14) and incarnate (2:10–18) Son of God. With chapter three, the author turns in earnest to a different genre, exhortation, and the extended exhortation running from 3:1 to 4:16 varies as to methods used. The first unit, 3:1–6, presents a *synkrisis*, or comparison, of Jesus with Moses. Rather than disparaging Moses, the comparison plays off the high esteem with which the hearers held the OT figure to show the even greater esteem due Jesus. At the center of the author's intention is the theme of faithfulness, which, by contrast, sets up the theme of unfaithfulness that the author draws from the quotation of Ps. 95:7c–11 (94:7c–11 LXX). The psalm is introduced with a formula presenting the Holy Spirit as the speaker of this portion of Scripture ("Therefore, as the Holy Spirit says . . ."). The psalm itself is offered as a hortatory word to Hebrews' recipients, and the author follows with a midrashic exhortation, using various terms from the psalm for the content of the exhortation to the community (3:12–14: "heart," "day," "today," "hear," "enter," "test," "rest," and "swear"), and quoting once again Ps. 95:7c–8b at 3:15. This midrashic exhortation concludes the section with a rhetorical technique known as *subiectio*, by which an author or orator asks and answers a series of questions (3:16–19). In this *subiectio* the rhetorical questions are taken from the content of Ps. 95, and the answers from other OT passages on the wilderness wanderings (Num. 14:1–38; Deut. 9; Ps. 78:22, 32; 106).

In 4:1–2 the author executes a transition that moves the discussion from the topic of the faithlessness of those who failed to enter God's rest (3:7–19) to the proclamation of the continuing promise of rest for the new-covenant people of God (4:3–11). Here again parts of the quotation from Ps. 95 play a prominent role. At 4:3 the author quotes Ps. 95:11, drawn together with Gen. 2:2 on the basis of verbal analogy to help define the "rest" of which the psalm speaks (4:3–5). Then, Ps. 95:7c–8a is quoted again at 4:7 to demonstrate that the "rest" was not limited to the physical entrance into Canaan by the people of Israel (4:6–9). Thus, Ps. 95 plays a dominant role in the author's discussion extending from 3:7 to 4:11.

B. The Original OT Context. Psalm 95 divides into two distinct movements, the first a celebratory song of thanksgiving (95:1–7b), the second a prophetic word of exhortation to the psalmist's community (95:7c–11). Most scholars associate the psalm with a worship setting, perhaps, with Pss. 50; 81, a festival context (Tate 1990: 498). Some have envisioned a cultic-liturgical service in which the worshiping community moves in procession into the place of worship with loud praises of joy (95:1–2), praising God for his mighty works (95:3–5). The procession climaxes with the worshipers prostrating themselves before Yahweh: "Come, let us worship and bow down . . . for he is our God, and we are . . . the sheep of his hand" (95:6–7b). Then the prophetic voice rings out with the words of 95:7c–11, challenging the people to obedience (Kraus 1993b: 246). The prophetic word has three movements. The exhortation "Do not harden your hearts" lies at the center of the first movement. This warning

follows a temporal frame of reference ("today" [MT: *hayyôm*; LXX: *sēmeron*]) and a conditional clause ("if you hear his voice"). The second movement of the exhortation, beginning with "as you did . . ." and running through the end of 95:9, offers an example or illustration. This illustration is expressed differently in the MT and the LXX. In the Hebrew text the author points to the water incident at Meribah (*mĕrîbâ*) and Massah (*massâ*) (Exod. 17:1–7), which at Num. 20:1–14 is identified with Kadesh, the location where God earlier gave an oath that the people would not enter the land of promise (Num. 14:20–23, 28–35). The LXX, on the other hand, interprets the psalm with Num. 14 more squarely in focus, transforming the names "Meribah" and "Massah" into meanings behind the names, "revolt" (*parapikrasmos*) and "trial" (*peirasmos*), and a similar approach occurs in the Targum on the psalm. The final movement of the psalm's prophetic word reminds the worshipers of the judgment experienced by that rebellious generation. God "was disgusted" (MT: *qwṭ*) or "very angry" (LXX: *prosochthizō*) with them because of their wandering hearts and their failure to walk in his ways. Therefore, God swore that they would not enter his rest. Thus, the psalm is what might be called a "prophetic liturgy" (Kraus 1993b: 245) in which people are called to worship God and soften their hearts to his "voice."

C. Relevant Uses of the OT Reference in Jewish Sources. The ruinous moment of rebellion recounted at Num. 14 and reiterated in Ps. 95 left an indelible mark on Jewish memory and prompted widely published reflection, as the rebels of the wilderness became a symbol for disobedience (cf., e.g., Neh. 9:15–17; Ps. 106:24–26; CD-A III, 6–9; *L.A.B.* 15; *Sipre Num.* 82 to 10:33; *4 Ezra* 7:106; 1 Cor. 10:5–10; see Lane 1991: 1:85). Some researchers believe that Ps. 95 was used liturgically in the preamble of synagogue services in Hebrews' era (Lane 1991: 1:85; Kirkpatrick 1917: 572; Tate 1990: 499); if so, the first hearers of our book would have been thoroughly familiar with it. Furthermore, the "exodus" and "wilderness" motifs form a prominent network of images appropriated by the writers of the NT (see §F below).

Some rabbis understood the "rest" to refer to the temple (as does *Tg. Ps.* 95:11), and some associated it with the land more broadly (Laansma

1997: 124–27). Yet, others associated the "rest" of the psalm with eschatological realities. For instance, at *b. Sanh.* 99a the forty years of the psalm are interpreted by Rabbi Eliezer as the days of the Messiah. In *b. Sanh.* 110b the question is addressed of whether the wilderness generation would have any portion in the world to come—evidently a popular point of discussion among the rabbis in the post–New Testament era. Psalm 95 was used by some rabbis to teach that the wilderness wanderers had no portion in the world to come. Rabbi Eliezer, however, maintained that they did, explaining that God "swore" in his "wrath" but then changed his mind.

An interesting, highly soteriological interpretation of the "rest" is found in *Jos. Asen.* 8:9, where Joseph prays to God for Aseneth:

> Renew her by your spirit, and form her anew by your hidden hand, and make her alive again by your life, and let her eat your bread of life, and drink your cup of blessing, and number her among your people that you have chosen before all (things) came into being, and let her enter your rest [*katapausis*] which you have prepared for your chosen ones, and live in your eternal life for ever (and) ever.

Here, the *katapausis* is "not a state of body or mind, but a place in heaven prepared for the saved" (*OTP* 2:213nf2).

In light of Hebrews' discussion, it is interesting that at *Num. Rab.* 14:19, commenting on Ps. 95:11, the rabbi suggests that God's oath, "they should not enter into my rest," means that when God's wrath turns away, they may "enter into my rest," which the rabbi associates with entering the tent of meeting.

D. The Textual Background. Hebrews either follows an alternative form of the Greek text or, more likely, makes several adjustments to the form that the author has at hand. A few of these are of little consequence. The *eidon* ("they saw" [also in LXX S *L'* A'']) in 1:9b constitutes a form common to the writer's era, rather than *eidosan* (LXX B R *L*pau), and the Hellenistic *eipa* of Ps. 94:10 LXX has been updated in 1:10 to *eipon* (also in LXX *L*bTThtpHe* A'). The *kai* ("and") in that same line of the psalm is changed in 1:10 to *de*—a minor adjustment, perhaps to smooth the style a bit. Style concerns may also have affected the change from the aorist active indicative form of

the verb *dokimazō* ("to test" [LXX B '' Sa R '', with *me* added in Ga(sub 13) *L* ''A ']) in Ps. 94:9 LXX to the prepositional phrase *en dokimasia* in 1:9. The prepositional phrase in Hebrews' expression parallels *en tō parapikrasmō* ("in the rebellion") of 94:8a LXX and *en tē erēmō* ("in the wilderness") of 94:8b LXX, and the passage is made to read more smoothly. Another possibility is that a theological concern was in play, the author of Hebrews wishing "to avoid the unusual idea of human beings testing God" (Ellingworth 1993: 218), the prepositional phrase being read as the testing of those who fell in the wilderness. Yet, the stylistic concern seems more likely.

More significant is the addition of *dio* in 1:10. In the MT and LXX God's anger characterizes the forty-year period of wilderness wandering. In Hebrew's addition of *dio*, the forty years is now grammatically associated with testing God and seeing his works. Enns (1997) suggests that the author wants to separate the wilderness period, which he conceives of as positive, from the time of judgment that followed. According to Enns (1997: 354), the analogy conceived in this way provides a more exact parallel to the situation of the church. In short, the church's "wilderness period" is a season not of punishment, but rather of blessing, which parallels another strand of tradition (e.g., Ps. 78:15–20; 105:41; 107:6; 114:8; Wis. 11:4–14). Yet, as Enns (1997: 355) himself points out, Hebrews recognizes the wilderness period as a time of God's anger (3:17); Enns reads this as the author giving the psalm an entirely different meaning than he did at 3:10 because in 3:10 he has the church that he addresses utmost in mind, whereas the wilderness generation is squarely in view at 3:17. Rather, it may be argued that the *dio* does not necessarily indicate a temporal distinction between two periods, but rather serves to highlight the causal relationship between disobedience and God's wrath. The *dio* is not necessarily an indicator of time.

Finally, the LXX's *tē genea ekeinē* ("with that generation") becomes *tē genea tautē* ("with this generation") in Hebrews. Enns (following Spicq 1952–1953: 1:357) suggests that the change "concretizes" the psalm for the readers, making the impact of the psalm immediate, more urgent for them. However, the author does not play off the term *tautē* in the exhortation that follows in

3:12–19, and this change is found in the psalm's word of judgment. The term *sēmeron*, found in the psalm's call to obedience, seems, rather, to be the term used to focus attention on the psalm's immediate relevance. This change from *ekeinē* to *tautē*, rather, once again may be stylistically driven, accomplishing a phonetic assonance with *etē* in the previous line (Jobes 1992: 191).

E. How Ps. 95:7c–11 Is Understood and Used at Heb. 3:7–11, 15–19; 4:3–7. It is clear how the author of Hebrews understood Ps. 95:7c–11 at 3:7–11 from his explication in 4:3–11, which constitutes one of the most tightly knit arguments in the book. For him, the fact that God, through David, generations after the wilderness wanderers failed to enter the land of Canaan, set a "day" for entering the "rest" (i.e., "today") gives assurance that this rest was not limited to entrance into Canaan (4:6–9). Rather, the author reasons, in light of Gen. 2:2, that God's rest is a spiritual reality in which one ceases from one's own work (4:10). Nevertheless, we must strive to enter that rest and keep from falling short of it (4:11). On this basis the author offers a strong warning concerning the awesome power and penetrating nature of God's inescapable word (4:12–13). This familiar warning—"the word of God is living and effective and sharper than a two-edged sword"—echoes the "voice" of Ps. 95, providing a fitting conclusion to the discourse on the "rest" into which believers may still enter.

Therefore, the author understood Ps. 95 as a perennially pertinent word from God to people. Rather than being primarily concerned with the wilderness generation, the author uses that generation as an exemplar on how people should not respond to God and his revelation. The force of the example works by way of analogy and consists of people in relationship with God, to whom God speaks his word, and who will respond in some way; but this also, therefore, is an analogy of potential situation. They have the potential of following the bad pattern, and the challenge to choose another path constitutes the exhortation. The analogous nature of the wilderness situation to the experience of Hebrews' addressees is clearly expressed in places such as 4:2—"just as those" (*kathaper kakeinoi*)—and it works because there is both continuity and discontinuity between the old- and new-covenant situations. The ad-dressees of Hebrews also are the people of God to whom the good news has been preached, but they, when juxtaposed to the wilderness generation, hear the voice of God at another time and in another situation.

Notice that the author's logic in 4:3–11 is based on the specific historical context in which Ps. 95 was written (i.e., David's time). This is the rabbinic principle of appropriation (*dabar halamed me'inyano*)—a meaning is established by its context (Longenecker 1975: 182). In addition, the verbal analogy with Gen. 2:2 (as with all the author's uses of verbal analogy) speaks to the unity of revelation. A word used in two different passages indicates a connection between the passages, each passage able to shed light on the meaning of the other.

It may be that the *subiectio* of 3:16–19, in which the author asks and answers a series of questions about those who fell in the wilderness, is an example of Hillel's *binyan ab mikathub 'ehad* (building up a family from a single text). This appropriation principle said that when the same phrase is found in several passages, a consideration in one applies to all. In the case of 3:16–19, the wilderness passages speak with a single voice on the nature of the wanderers' situation.

F. The Theological Use of the OT Material. The theological framework into which Hebrews' use of Ps. 95 fits has varied expression in the NT, as Bruce (1990) has shown. Jesus' redemptive work on the cross is referred to as a new "exodus" (*exodos* [Luke 9:31]), and he himself is the Passover lamb (1 Cor. 5:7; 1 Pet. 1:19; John 1:29, 36; 19:33–36). His followers, moreover, spiritually parallel Israel in the wilderness (Acts 7:38), having passed through baptism, as the OT people of God passed through the Red Sea (1 Cor. 10:1–2). Christ is the guide through the wilderness, as a spiritual rock (1 Cor. 10:4) (Bruce 1990: 96–97). In fact, Paul points out that this analogical relationship is instructive, offering an example not to be followed, the things that happened to the wilderness generation serving to warn followers of Christ against idolatry, immorality, testing God, and grumbling (1 Cor. 10:5–10). Hebrews uses the psalm similarly. The author uses the wanderers as a negative example, a basis for exhorting the hearers in a number of directions.

First, for our author, the psalm's term "today" (*sēmeron*) refers to an era of opportunity rather than to a twenty-four-hour period, as 3:13 clearly demonstrates. "Today" then is a time for encouragement among believers to follow God's ways, forsaking the path of unbelief. It is a time, therefore, to "hold fast" one's assurance, and this "today" will cease with "the end" (*telos* [3:14]). It also is said to be the era in which the promise to enter God's rest is still in force (4:1). Second, failure in relation to God during this era of opportunity results from "an evil heart of unbelief" that falls away from the living God (3:12). In Hebrews' conception, unbelief and disobedience go hand in hand (3:12, 18–19). Unbelief leads to sin, and sin leads to a hardened heart that does not believe in the living God (3:13). Assurance of one's relationship with Christ, therefore, results from perseverance in holding firmly to one's posture of belief and a life characterized by obedience to Christ (3:14). Thus, the author of Hebrews exhorts his hearers that the word heard must be united with belief (4:1–3). The promise for the obedient people of God, who believe him, hearing his "voice" is that they enter his "rest" (*katapausis*). The negative tone of the psalm, therefore, is turned inside out. That the wilderness generation was not allowed to enter God's rest means that there is a rest to be entered by those who take the opposite path, that of belief and obedience. (On the theology of "rest," see §F of commentary on Heb. 4:4 below.)

4:4

A. The Immediate NT Context. The unit of 4:1–11 plays a significant role in the extended exhortation from 3:1 to 4:16. This unit offers a counterpoint to the negative example of the wilderness period by proclaiming a promise of rest to those who will believe God's word, responding in faith. In 4:1–2 the author executes a transition that moves the discourse from the topic of the faithless, disobedient wanderers (3:7–19), who are used as a negative example, to the promise of rest for the new-covenant people of God (4:3–11). The author's main point in this transition is that there is a "rest" of which the psalm speaks that some of the hearers will miss if they do not respond appropriately (4:1). In 4:2 the analogy between the community addressed and those who fell in the wilderness is reiterated. Both communities have had the "good news" preached

to them, but the preached word is not enough; faith must come into play. The implication is that the first hearers of Hebrews must respond in faith in order to avoid the situation of the disobedient of the desert.

In 4:3–5 the author proclaims that it is the believing who enter the rest of which Ps. 95:11 (94:11 LXX) speaks, and this rest has been around since God finished the creation. Thus, the author associates the "rest" of Ps. 95:11 with God's "rest" on the seventh day of creation, spoken of in the creation account (Gen. 2:2). The author draws the two passages together on the basis of verbal analogy and introduces the verse from Genesis to help define the "rest" more clearly. The fact that long after the original entrance into the land of promise was achieved under Joshua's leadership David spoke of a rest that might be entered (or missed!) "today" demonstrates that God had more in mind than physical entrance to the land (4:6–8). The author reasons, therefore, that a Sabbath rest is still available for God's people (4:9). The quotation from Gen. 2:2 figures prominently into 4:10. In light of the quotation from Genesis, the "rest" of Ps. 95:11 involves resting from one's own works, even as God rested from his works on the seventh day. The unit ends with an exhortation to diligence so that no one in the community will miss this rest through disobedience.

B. The Original OT Context. Certainly one of the most familiar sections of the OT, Gen. 1:1–2:3 presents a majestic hymn of praise to God for his creation. The passage, as the first word (*běrē'šît*) of the Hebrew canon suggests, is about beginnings. It introduces God as creator and human beings as the pinnacle of his creation and simultaneously opens the Torah, the first five books of the canon. This will lay the foundation for the calling out of a people with whom God will make covenant. Within the book of Genesis, 1:1–2:3 is unique both in style and content, forming an "overture to the whole work" (Wenham 1987: 5). Many scholars have identified the boundary of the book's opening unit as extending to 2:4a rather than 2:3, primarily based on a vocabulary typical of the priestly stratum. Yet, the clause "This is the story of" (2:4) is used consistently elsewhere in Genesis at the beginning of new movements in the narrative. As Wenham (1987: 6, 55–56) points out, 2:4 also has a tightly knit chiastic structure quite distinct from 2:1–3. Furthermore, as we will see below, elements of 2:1–3 provide a closing to an *inclusio* opened at 1:1. For these reasons, the unit should be marked as extending from 1:1 to 2:3 (Wenham 1987: 5–6; Hamilton 1995: 3–5; Waltke and Fredricks 2001: 55–58).

The six days of creation are the dominant aspect in the structure of Gen. 1, with days one and three marked uniquely with a double announcement of God's command ("and God said" [1:9, 11, 24, 26]), and pairs of days—one and four, two and five, three and six—corresponding in content. In all, God gives ten different commands, and eight works of creation are enumerated. Throughout the chapter the author follows a consistent pattern: announcement ("and God said"), commandment ("let there be"), separation (e.g., day from night), fulfillment or report ("and God made"), approval ("God saw that it was good"), naming or blessing, and chronological framework (Wenham 1987: 6; Waltke and Fredricks 2001: 56–57).

In contradistinction to the other six days of creation, the number of the seventh is marked three times, setting it apart as especially significant. Here the author breaks the patterns established with the first six days of creation. In the first six days "space is subdued; on the seventh, time is sanctified." It may be that evening and morning are not mentioned because from the beginning humans were intended to take part in the rest of the Sabbath, as Hebrews argues. The seventh day is made holy—the first thing of God's creation to be made so. Whereas other gods set apart temples as memorials of their creative work, the God of Israel set apart a day (Waltke and Fredricks 2001: 67). The "heaven and earth" of 2:1 and "which God created" of 2:3 are linked chiastically with 1:1 (Wenham 1987: 34). Thus, 2:1–3 is crafted specifically to provide a conclusion to the whole of the creation hymn, a conclusion in which "rest" is the climax of the passage.

C. Relevant Uses of the OT Reference in Jewish Sources.

Given the foundational nature of the Genesis passage, it is somewhat surprising that it is not quoted or alluded to more often in the primary Jewish sources. It is reported that at the beginning of the Sabbath, in the synagogue liturgy, the recitation of Ps. 95:1–11 was followed by Gen. 2:1–3 (Lane 1991: 1:100), though this sug-

gestion is based on very late materials (Laansma 1997: 350).

Odes of Solomon, a thoroughly Jewish-influenced Christian hymn collection from the late first or early second century AD, contains a straightforward allusion to Gen. 2:2 in a psalm of praise to God for his creation, proclaiming, "And he set the creation and aroused it, then he rested from his works. And created things run according to their courses, and work their works, and they are not able to cease and be idle. And the hosts are subject to his word" (16:12–14). Josephus, in his account of the creation of the world (*Ant.* 1.33), explains that God's rest on the seventh day of creation is the source of the Jewish practice of the Sabbath.

Philo comments extensively on Gen. 2:2. For instance, he is intent on the philosophical significance of the numbers of the days of creation. Using the Greek version of the OT (see §D below), he notes, "When, then, Moses says, 'He finished His work on the sixth day,' we must understand him to be adducing not a quantity of days, but a perfect number, namely six" (*Alleg. Interp.* 1.3). Further, speaking of the significance with which God vested the seventh day, Philo calls that blessed, dignified day "the birthday of the world" (*Moses* 2.210) and a "festival, not of one city or country, but of all the earth" (*Creation* 89). More significantly for the use in Hebrews, he comments on the nature of the rest mentioned in Gen. 2:2. At *Alleg. Interp.* 1.16 he notes that Moses says "caused to rest" rather than "rested" in order to make clear that God never ceases from activity. Philo goes on to explain that this means that God quit shaping the mortal and began to craft the divine things. Elsewhere Philo explains that Moses named the Sabbath "God's Sabbath" (e.g., Exod. 20:10), for God, being free from any imperfection and therefore any weariness, is the only thing in the universe that truly can be said to rest. This does not mean that he is inactive; rather, "God's rest is a working with absolute ease, without toil and without suffering," and so "rest belongs in the fullest sense to God and to Him alone" (*Cherubim* 87–90). Finally, the implications of God's rest for human beings is that it is the most nourishing, most enjoyable thing in the world, providing great peace in life (*Flight* 173–174).

What is clear is that the "rest," though not always tied directly to the Genesis passage, generally took on an eschatological slant in Jewish exegesis (see Attridge [1989: 129n85], who cites, e.g., *Gen. Rab.* 10:9; *m. Tamid* 7:4; *Pirqe R. El.* 18; *'Abot R. Nat.* 1 [1c]). For instance, *2 Baruch*, a Jewish work reflecting on the destruction of the temple in AD 70, gives "rest" an eschatological bent, saying that after God "has brought down everything which is in the world, and has sat down in eternal peace on the throne of the kingdom, then joy will be revealed and rest will appear" (7:31).

D. The Textual Background. The textual differences between Gen. 2:2 LXX and Hebrews are minor, the author adding *ho theos en* ("God on"), just as Philo does in *Posterity* 64. Moffatt (1924: 51–52) suggests that this may have been done "as a proof that the *katapausis* had originated immediately after the six days of creation." However, for Hebrews, it may simply be a way to make the subject clear, since the author was interested in quoting only this part of the passage, and the subject of both compound verbs, *ho theos*, had been given in the first half of the sentence.

Yet, the alteration of the Hebrew form of Gen. 2:2 by the LXX offers a conspicuous example of the influence of an exegetical tradition on text forms. In the MT the Hebrew text reads, "On the seventh day God ended his work." This identification of the seventh day as the day on which God completed, or finished, his work is followed in a transcription of the passage at Qumran (4Q10) and in the Targumim (*Tg. Ps.-J.*; *Tg. Neof.*). The LXX, however, reads, "On the sixth day God ended his work." This change in the day, which alters the important threefold repetition of "seventh" in 2:2–3, came about because the Hebrew could be interpreted as God doing some work on the seventh day prior to his rest (though this certainly is not implied in the grammar [see Wenham 1987: 35]). The same change is made in, for instance, the Samaritan Pentateuch and the Peshitta. The wording has been changed in these texts to avoid misunderstanding, due to the importance of the passage for Sabbath-keeping. God ending his work on the sixth day suggests that he worked up to the end of that day, but the seventh day was completely a day of rest (Jobes and Silva 2000: 98).

E. How Gen. 2:2 Is Understood and Used at Heb. 4:4. It is quite clear that Gen. 2:2 functions to add information that the author of Hebrews wishes to access to help him define the "rest" into which the wilderness wanderers were not permitted to enter, and which, by contrast, remains open to the people of God. He draws from the Genesis passage on the basis of verbal analogy, an appropriation technique used extensively in Hebrews. The quotation of Ps. 95:7c–11 (94:7c–11 LXX) climaxes with God's proclamation that the desert generation would not enter his "rest" (*katapausis*). Notice that in the psalm God refers to the rest as "my rest" (*katapausin mou*). So, the author of Hebrews, in good rabbinic style, thinks of another place in Scripture that speaks specifically of God's rest. He finds it in Gen. 2:2, where it says that "God rested" (*katepausen ho theos*) from his work of creation. Here the cognate verb *katapauō* ("rest") is used. On the basis of this family of terms the author interprets these two OT passages, one in light of the other. In 4:3–5 he quotes parts of Ps. 95:11 both immediately before and after the quotation of Gen. 2:2. Thus, additional information on the meaning of the psalm comes out.

First, the "rest" of which the psalm speaks was available to the wilderness generation and, in fact, had been around since the creation of the world. In other words, their failure to enter was not because the rest was unavailable. The *gar* ("for") used as part of the introductory formula in 4:4 indicates that the quotation itself is employed to reinforce the proposition in 4:3 that God's rest was initiated with the foundation of the world. Therefore, the "rest" of which the psalm speaks should not be thought of as limited to the time during which the people of Israel were to enter the land of promise; rather, it is a rest that transcends any specific time and place. Second, since the "rest" of the psalm passage should be identified with that of God on the seventh day, it is a Sabbath rest (4:9). This means, therefore, that this rest involves resting from one's works, "as God did from his." Consequently, the author's interpretation of the "rest" in Ps. 95 is that it is a rest that still is available, since it was not limited to the time for entering Canaan, and it is a Sabbath rest that involves the cessation from one's works.

F. The Theological Use of the OT Material. Scholars have spilled much ink in attempting to discern what the author of Hebrews means by the "rest" into which one may enter. In 4:10 he defines this rest minimally as ceasing from one's own works; yet, he presents no specifics as to where or when this takes place. Some have suggested that it involves an eschatological destination, perhaps the heavenly holy of holies, entered at the end of the age (Hofius 1970). This interpretation finds consonance with the pilgrimage motif of the book and the exhortations to persevere to the end. Others suggest that this rest is a spiritual state that the believer enters in this present life (Theissen 1969), pointing to the association of rest with God's rest on the seventh day. As we noted, in Gen. 1–2 all of the first six days of creation have an end; the seventh, however, is an "open-ended day." This suggests that this rest must not be limited to a location and a point in time, and on this interpretation, God's rest must be seen as a present reality. In favor of this interpretation, the present context, in which the author exhorts the listeners to respond "today" and emphasizes the current availability of this rest, seems to point to a present time of opportunity. Moreover, the author is concerned that some of those in the community perhaps have fallen short of this rest. How could this be so if it is only a future reality? Thus, the present appropriation of God's rest must be considered an aspect of our author's concern.

A third position is that the writer of Hebrews speaks of a "now and not yet" reality, the "rest" being something that a believer enters (and thus experiences) now, but that in its fullness remains a promise to be consummated in the future (Hurst 1990: 71; Leschert 1994: 168–70). In this vein, Attridge (1989: 128) writes,

> Thus the imagery of rest is best understood as a complex symbol for the whole soteriological process that Hebrews never fully articulates, but which involves both personal and corporate dimensions. It is the process of entry into God's presence, the heavenly homeland (11:16), the unshakeable kingdom (12:28), begun at baptism (10:22) and consummated as a whole eschatologically.

Similarly, A. T. Lincoln (1982: 212), in discussing "rest" in the NT, suggests that Gen. 2:2 offers a broad eschatological significance to the discussion in Heb. 4, taking us beyond the apocalyptic resting place. The "rest" mentioned in Gen. 2:2 is, in the words of von Rad (1966: 102), "an eschatological expectation, a fulfillment of the prophecies of redemption." A. T. Lincoln (1982: 212) perceives that this rest of Gen. 2:2 shows "the consummation of God's purposes for creation." What are those purposes? They are redemption of his people and a rest ultimately consummated in the heavenly locality. Thus, Lincoln interprets this rest in terms of inaugurated eschatology. The "today" of the psalm, read in conjunction with Gen. 2:2, brackets the period of the "now" and "not yet" for the people of God. Since it is God's rest, it is both present and future; people enter it and must strive to enter it.

This third position is valid but requires greater specificity. The "rest" should be interpreted as entrance into the new covenant via the great Day of Atonement sacrifice of the great high priest, Jesus.

First, Lev. 16:29–31; 23:26–32 speak of the Day of Atonement as "a Sabbath of rest" during which a person must not do any work, and the people will be cleansed from their sins. In these passages the Sabbath ordinance finds direct association with the high priest's offering on the Day of Atonement, and this offering constitutes a central focus for the author of Hebrews (2:17–18; 4:14–5:4; 7:26–28; and esp. 8:3–10:18). Second, researchers generally have failed to notice that extensive lexical connections exist between 3:1–4:13 and the epistle's two most important summaries on Christ's high-priestly work, 4:14–16; 10:19–25, passages that form an *inclusio* around the author's discourse on the appointment and superior offering of the heavenly high priest (G. H. Guthrie 1994: 79–82). When carefully considered, the summary of 10:19–25 reaches back and connects with this section of exhortation (3:1–4:13) by means of the terms having to do with "brethren" (3:1; 10:19), the name *Iēsous*, "Jesus" or "Joshua" (3:1; 4:8; 10:19), "considering" (3:1; 10:24), Christ as a great high priest (3:1; 10:19, 21), "entering in" (4:1, 3, 5, 6, 10, 11; 10:19–20), "confidence" (3:6; 10:19), being "his house" (3:6; 10:21), "God" (3:4, 12; 4:4, 10, 12), "living" (3:12; 10:20), "heart" (3:12; 4:7, 12; 10:22), "faith" (4:2; 10:22), "evil" (3:12; 10:22), "bodies" (3:17; 10:22), "holding fast" (3:6, 14; 10:23), "our confession" (3:1; 10:23), "hope" (3:6; 10:23), God as one who promises (4:1; 10:23),

Christ as "faithful" (3:2; 10:23), "works" (3:9; 4:4, 10; 10:24), "encouragement" (3:13; 10:25), and "day" (3:7, 13; 4:7–8; 10:25). Thus, there are no fewer than twenty-one verbal parallels between the climactic summary on Christ's work in the heavenly tabernacle in 10:19–25 (a mere seven verses) and 3:1–4:13. This demonstrates that in the author's crafting of the book he builds toward the climactic summary of 10:19–25, on Christ's high-priestly work, beginning at 3:1–4:11, which includes our passage on rest.

Therefore, it may be suggested that the "rest" of which the author of Hebrews speaks is entrance into the new covenant. Some in the community are in danger of rejecting it, not combining faith with their hearing of the "good news" (4:1–2). It is a rest that one must strive to enter (4:11)—the entrance into the new covenant involves taking a bold stand with Christ and his people—but at the same time involves ceasing from one's own works (4:10). In context, this seems to point to a life of faith and obedience to God, in which a person turns away from a "wandering" way of life in order to embrace the proclaimed word of God. Finally, it is a rest that may be entered now by believing (4:3) and will be consummated at the end of the age.

5:5

(For a fuller analysis, see commentary on Heb. 1:5 [quoting Ps. 2:7] above.) The use of Ps. 2:7 at 5:5 plays a strategic role in the structure of the book. At 1:5 the author uses this psalm text to introduce the first major movement of his christological exposition. In that section, dealing with the relationship of the Son to the angels (1:5–2:18), Ps. 2:7 opens the chain quotation at 1:5–14, which demonstrates that the Son is superior to the angelic beings. Specifically, Ps. 2:7 is juxtaposed with 2 Sam. 7:14 to show that the Son is superior by virtue of his unique relationship to the Father, a uniqueness shown in part by his enthronement as God's Messiah.

The reiteration of this quotation at 5:5 comes as the author is launching the second major movement of his christological exposition. Now he treats the relationship of the Son, our high priest, to the earthly sacrificial system (4:14–5:10; 7:1–10:25). To introduce this extended embedded discourse, the writer first recounts universal principles, or requirements, for high priests

(5:1–4). He concludes these principles by noting that only those appointed, or called, by God may occupy the office (5:4). The two quotations at 5:5–6 follow this assertion, reinforcing it. The author quotes Ps. 2:7 first in order to draw the connection between this new subdiscourse on Christ's appointment and ministry as high priest and all that he has already said about the superior Son of God in 1:5–2:18. This is the significance of the introductory formula, which reads, "the one having said to him" (5:5), the author using the participial clause to hark back to that earlier section. Thus, the two quotations of Ps. 2:7 form a type of transition called "parallel introductions" (G. H. Guthrie 1994: 104–5), since each serves a vital role in the initiation of the author's two main christological movements in the book.

By verbal analogy with Ps. 2:7, the writer of Hebrews now introduces Ps. 110:4 (109:4 LXX), a verse that plays a dominant role in the section on the Son's appointment to high priesthood (especially 7:1–28). The two psalms are drawn together by their common use of the second-person personal pronoun and their form as proclamations, the author interpreting both as messianic pronouncements concerning Christ, as is made clear by the commentary of 5:7–10. Therefore, Ps. 2:7 plays more of a structural role than a theological role at 5:5. Its primary function is to aid in introducing Ps. 110:4, which then becomes a focus in the author's discussion on Christ's appointment as a superior, Melchizedekian high priest.

5:6

A. The Immediate NT Context. See commentary on Heb. 5:5 above.

B. The Original OT Context. See §B of commentary on Heb. 1:13 above.

C. Relevant Uses of the OT Reference in Jewish Sources. Speculation about the enigmatic OT figure Melchizedek exists in Jewish literature before, during, and after the first Christian century, though there are few specific allusions to Ps. 110:4. The Qumran community seems to have understood Melchizedek as a heavenly figure. The fragmentary scroll 11Q13 interprets, among other texts, Lev. 25:9–13, a passage dealing with the Jubilee Year. In 11Q13 the last "Jubilee" is called the "year of grace of Melchizedek," in which Melchizedek is said to bring freedom from the debt of sins and atonement to the sons of light, defeating Belial and his evil spirits. Here we read, "But Melchizedek will carry out the vengeance of Go[d's] judgments, [and on that day he will fr]e[e them from the hand of] Belial and from the hand of all the sp[irits of his lot]" (11Q13 II, 13). It seems that Melchizedek is some type of heavenly figure in this scroll fragment from the Qumran community, perhaps an exalted angel, and the Qumran literature uses Melchizedek quite differently than does Hebrews (Lane 1991: 1:160–61). In the first-century book of *2 Enoch* (71–72) Melchizedek also is a heavenly figure. In this work Melchizedek is saved from the flood so he can continue a line of priests started with Seth. Michael takes the child Melchizedek to paradise, where he is to be a priest forever.

In a different vein, 1QapGen ar XXII, 14–17 simply recounts the story of Melchizedek from Gen. 14:17–20. Similarly, Josephus recounts the story in *Ant.* 1.179–181, and he interprets Melchizedek's name as meaning "righteous king" (also in *J.W.* 6.438) and takes "Solyma" (Salem) as a reference to Jerusalem. At *Alleg. Interp.* 3.79–82 Philo interprets the reference to Salem as Melchizedek being "king of peace," as does Heb. 7:2. Here Melchizedek is the ideal priest-king—a priest who has his own priesthood and a king who rules by righteousness, and, finally, a symbol for the Logos.

The eschatological interpretation of Melchizedek also finds expression in later Jewish works (*b. Sukkah* 52b), but the priest-king more often is downplayed, being identified with Noah's son Shem (e.g., *Num. Rab.* 4:8). In another twist of exegesis that diminishes the role of Melchizedek, *b. Ned.* 32b, for instance, interprets the events of Gen. 14 and Ps. 110:4 as the priesthood being given to Abraham (Ps. 110:1; also in *Gen. Rab.* 55:6). They suggest that it is "because of the words of Melchizedek" that Abraham was made a priest.

D. The Textual Background. There exists a very direct, almost wooden, correspondence between the Hebrew and the Greek texts of Ps. 110:4 (109:4 LXX). The quotation in Hebrews matches the LXX, with the exception that it drops the *ei* before *hiereus* (*ei* is included in, e.g., LXX S R and in 𝔓⁴⁶ P among the manuscripts of Hebrews; it is omitted in LXX *L*' A'). Interestingly, in the Targum on Ps. 110:4 the figure of Melchizedek

drops out, and the verse is presented in eschatological terms. McNamara (2000: 21) renders the verse: "The LORD has sworn and will not relent: 'You are appointed as chief for the world to come, on account of the merit that you have been a righteous king.'" He notes that the Targum "is modeled on the Hebrew text." For instance, *kōhēn* ("priest") is rendered as *rb* ("prince"), a term often used for *kōhēn* when referring to a respected, non-Jewish priest (e.g., Gen. 41:45, 50; 46:20; Exod. 3:1). The Targum rendering paraphrases *lĕʿôlām* ("forever") as "the world to come." The Hebrew *ʿal-dibrātî* ("according to the order of") is understood as meaning "because," and Melchizedek's name is paraphrased as "a just king" (McNamara 2000: 21).

E. How Ps. 110:4 Is Understood and Used Theologically at Heb. 5:6. As we noted, the quotation of Ps. 110:4 at 5:6 serves an important role in the structure of the book. Paired with Ps. 2:7 by verbal analogy, Ps. 110:4 (109:4 LXX) introduces the author's major discourse on the appointment of the Son of God as a superior high priest (5:1–10; 7:1–28). In line with this function, the psalm passage reinforces the idea of appointment, to which the author now begins to turn his attention, and provides numerous elements that will be significant for his argument in chapter 7.

Psalm 110 portrays an ideal relationship between God and the Davidic monarch, and this relationship serves as the basis for a typological construct appropriated by the author of Hebrews. The psalm has intrinsic aspects that could not have been completely fulfilled in one of the Davidic monarchs and, consequently, anticipated a later fulfillment in Christ. A key element in this regard, and one seized upon by the author of Hebrews, is that the king has been proclaimed a "priest forever." Thus, the writer of Hebrews understands the verse to be an indirect typological prophecy about Jesus' appointment to a unique form of priesthood, fulfilled perhaps at Christ's resurrection and exaltation to the right hand of God (Ps. 110:1 [109:1 LXX]). Several dynamics inherent in Ps. 110:4 have great theological significance for the author. First, an implicit trinitarian perspective is in play, as one member of the Godhead (the Father) addresses another (the Son) with a proclamation. Thus, God's word is spoken not only to and concerning his people, but also to and concerning his Son. Second, that the psalm verse expresses an oath, made by God, is vital for our author. God has made promises concerning the Son that will not be revoked—he is a priest "forever"—and this provides strong encouragement for those who commit to the new covenant (e.g., 7:17–22, 28). This oath, rather than ancestry, provides the basis for Jesus' high priesthood (7:11–16). Yet, though marked out for appointment, the path to that appointment lay along the way of suffering. Although he was a son (Ps. 2:7; Heb. 5:5), he "learned obedience" and was made completely "fit" for the office of high priest by his passion (5:7–11).

5:7–9

The interpretation linking this passage to the Gethsemane accounts in the Gospels has been criticized by some scholars; however, others have understood "the one who could save him from death" as a clear allusion to Jesus' plea in the garden (e.g., Montefiore 1964: 97–98; Kistemaker 1961: 136; Bruce 1990: 127). Nevertheless, the "cries and tears" of Jesus are not found in the Gethsemane accounts, but probably stem from one or more "prayers of the righteous sufferer" found in Psalms. For instance, Strobel (1954) suggests that Ps. 116 forms the basis for 5:7–8. That psalm states,

> I love the LORD, for he heard my voice; he heard my cry for mercy. . . . The cords of death entangled me, the anguish of the grave came upon me; I was overcome by trouble and sorrow. . . . You, O LORD, have delivered my soul from death, my eyes from tears, my feet from stumbling. (Ps. 116: 1, 3, 8)

Psalm 22, taken by the early church as referring to Christ's passion, offers another possible backdrop, emphasizing the "cry" of the righteous sufferer.

6:4–6

Mathewson (1999: 214) rightly argues that "the author's language in 6:4–6 is colored by OT references by means of allusion and echo apart from direct citation." Thus, the descriptions of those who have fallen away, descriptions so elusive and divisive in the history of interpretation, stem from the "wilderness wandering" passages, continuing an exhortation dynamic begun in 3:7–4:2. For instance, Mathewson (1999: 216–17) suggests

that the reference to those who were "enlightened" echoes the pillar of fire by which the Israelites were "enlightened" on their way (Neh. 9:12, 19; Ps. 105:39). The "heavenly gift" that those under consideration had tasted echoes those passages that refer to the heavenly gift of manna, which the Lord gave to people of the wilderness generation. In passages such as Exod. 16:15; Ps. 78:24 (77:24 LXX); Neh. 9:15 the heavenly bread is said to have been given (*edōken*) to them. For Mathewson, that those who have fallen away had become companions of the Holy Spirit (Heb. 6:4c) echoes the experience of the wilderness wanderers, who had extensive interaction with the Spirit of God, as witnessed in numerous passages (e.g., Neh. 9:20; 11:17, 25; Isa. 63:11). Having considered the elements describing the fallen in Heb. 6:4–6, Mathewson (1999: 223) concludes, "The author is not just alluding to snippets of texts and isolated vocabulary for rhetorical color, but by alluding to texts which belong to a larger matrix of ideas he is evoking the entire context and story of Israel's experience in the wilderness." Thus, the author of Hebrews utilizes the language of the OT to describe a particularly grievous abandonment of the Christian community in his day and to craft a stern warning to those who would turn their backs on Christ and his church. Moreover, the warning harks back to the earlier hortatory section on those who fell in the wilderness (3:7–4:2), who heard the good news preached but did not profit by it (4:2).

6:7–8

The agricultural imagery in 6:7–8 offers a striking picture of God's blessing for those who respond to his word and God's curse on those who do not. Several passages have been proposed as possible OT origins for the imagery, including Gen. 3:17–18 for the curse of the ground, Isa. 5:1–5 for the image of the failed crop and thorns growing up, Hos. 10:8, 12 also for the thistles coming up, and Ezek. 19:10–14, which depicts a vine being torn down and burned. To this list should be added several passages from Deuteronomy, which establishes a context of blessings for those who receive and live out the covenant or curses for those who reject it. First, earlier in the book, at Deut. 11:11, the blessing of the promised land is described as follows: "But the land into which you go to inherit it is a land of mountains and plains; it shall drink water of the rain of heaven," and the terms used are *gē, hyetos,* and *pinō.* To my knowledge, this is the only place in the LXX that speaks of the land drinking rain using these terms, the same terms used at Heb. 6:7.

Second, the dichotomy of land that either is blessed or cursed is prominent in Deuteronomy. For example, at Deut. 28:12 the rain from God is a gift and works with the blessing of the works of one's hands. On the other hand, there are those passages that emphasize curse, such as Deut. 29:17 LXX (29:18 ET) alluded to at Heb. 12:15. That passage continues a few verses later,

> All its land is brimstone and salt, a burning waste, unsown and unproductive, and no grass grows in it, like the overthrow of Sodom and Gomorrah, Admah and Zeboiim, which the LORD overthrew in His anger and in His wrath. All the nations will say, "Why has the LORD done thus to this land? Why this great outburst of anger?" Then men will say, "Because they forsook the covenant of the LORD, the God of their fathers, which He made with them when He brought them out of the land of Egypt. They went and served other gods and worshiped them, gods whom they have not known and whom He had not allotted to them. Therefore, the anger of the LORD burned against that land, to bring upon it every curse which is written in this book." (Deut. 29:23–27 NASB)

Thus, the curse on the land is brought on by a rejection of the covenant, and that curse consists of burning.

Third, the image of fire as a form of judgment occurs in Hebrews at three places. At Heb. 10:27 the author proclaims that for those who keep on sinning after receiving a knowledge of the truth there remain only imminent judgment and a jealousy of fire, perhaps alluding to Isa. 26:11 or Zeph. 1:18, but also consonant with Deut. 29:20, where God's inflamed jealousy burns against those cursed ones who turn away from the covenant. At Heb. 12:29 we find a second reference to fire as a form of judgment in Hebrews, here in an overt allusion to either Deut. 4:24 or 9:3, where God is called a "consuming fire." Again we are moved decisively back into the orbit of Deuteronomy. The third place where fire occurs as a form of judgment is Heb. 6:8. The unproductive land ends up being burned. The burning of land also occurs in

Deut. 32. Moses quotes God as saying, "For a fire has been kindled out of my wrath, it shall burn to hell below; it shall devour the land, and the fruits of it" (Deut. 32:22).

Finally, Heb. 6:8 says that such land is *katara engys,* "about to be cursed." There are a number of places in the LXX where the term *engys* is used to speak of the imminence of judgment—all but two of these are in the prophets, who speak of the nearness of the day of the Lord (e.g., Joel 1:15; 2:1; 4:14; Obad. 15; Zeph. 1:7, 14; Isa. 13:6; Ezek. 30:3). The only other places where the imminence of judgment is mentioned, using *engys,* is Deut. 32:35, where God says of his enemies that "the day of their calamity is near," and the restatement of this verse in Odes 2:35. This small portion of Scripture from Deut. 32:25 happens to be wedged between the two parts of Deut. 32:35–36 quoted at Heb. 10:30: "Vengeance is mine, I will repay," and again, "The Lord will vindicate his people." Therefore, a case can be made that Hebrews has in mind this Deuteronomy passage specifically at 6:8, and the nearness of a curse fits the context of Deuteronomy, with its "blessing or curse" framework.

Thus, several elements from Deuteronomy seem to be echoed in the proverbial imagery of Heb. 6:7–8, including the earth that drinks the rain, the blessed over against the cursed land, burning of the land as an image of judgment, and the nearness of God's judgment.

What, then, of the "thorns and thistles" of Heb. 6:8? The exact form of the words as they occur in 6:8 (*akanthas kai tribolous*) occurs also in Gen. 3:18, the statement of judgment on Adam, which involved the curse on the ground. It would grow thorns and thistles for him. It seems that Hebrews may be utilizing the material about the curse on the land in Deuteronomy and incorporating into it the curse on the ground from Gen. 3:18. Indeed, a number of Pentateuch scholars suggest that the Genesis passage is one wellspring from which the curse on the land in Deuteronomy flows, and a rabbi of the first century certainly would have seen the verbal analogy between the curse on the earth in Gen. 3:18 and the terminology of curse and land in Deuteronomy. Therefore, it may be that Hebrews borrows from both sources to craft the proverbial statement in 6:7–8. This identification of Deuteronomy echoes behind 6:7–8 fulfills

Hays's criteria of availability, volume, recurrence, thematic coherence, historical plausibility, and satisfaction.

What difference does this make to interpretation? It places the harsh warning of 6:7–8 squarely in the context of Deuteronomy's blessing-and-curse framework. Moreover, if Mathewson (1999) is correct about the wilderness echoes in 6:4–6, the agricultural imagery of 6:7–8 provides a culmination of that imagery in the immediate context, much as Deuteronomy generally and its Song of Moses in chapter 32 provide for the Pentateuch. Moreover, the ambiguous language of 6:4–8 now has a grounding in the scriptural text and the imagery from Israel's history, much like and in line with the other warnings in 2:1–4; 3:7–19; 10:26–31; 12:25–29.

6:14

A. The Immediate NT Context: God as a Keeper of Oaths.
An interconnected series of exhortations forms the broader context for the quotation at 6:14 (5:11–6:20). Assessment of the recipients' spiritual immaturity (5:11–6:3) precedes the harsh warning of 6:4–8. The author mitigates this warning with a word of encouragement concerning the positive evidence of their spiritual commitments and the need to imitate great exemplars of true faith as they look to the future (6:9–12). The wider unit of 6:13–20, to which 6:14 belongs, plays two distinct roles.

First, as part of the hortatory material extending from 5:11 to 6:20, the unit offers encouragement derived from the logic of the author's argument. The argument has three main movements, each with an assertion or action and a result. In the first movement the writer offers an illustration, using Abraham as the exemplar of faith (6:13–15). God swore, making a promise to Abraham, and as a result the patriarch received what was promised. A truism forms the second movement. People swear in legal situations (the action), and as a result disputes are ended (6:16). Again, an action produces a result. Finally, the author comes to his main point (6:17–20). God gave an oath, and strong encouragement is provided. The quotation at 6:14 serves to support the first of these movements, the illustration of 6:13–15, by giving a scriptural basis for that illustration. The quotation of Gen. 22:17 provides clear evidence of God's oath to Abraham.

Second, 6:13–20 plays the role of an ingressive intermediary transition (G. H. Guthrie 1994: 110). At 5:1–10 the author quotes Ps. 110:4, introducing the key passage that forms the basis for his argument in 7:1–28 on the appointment of Jesus as a high priest in the order of Melchizedek. In this way the author's discussion of Melchizedek, begun in 5:1–10 and developed in 7:1–28, is strategically interrupted by the hortatory material of 5:11–6:20. Yet, the author's treatment of the hearers' immaturity extends only to 6:12. At 6:13–20 the author begins to move back to his discussion of Melchizedek by alluding to Ps. 110:4 (see the allusion "two things" at 6:18 below), the key text that he uses in 7:1–28. At the heart of the psalm is God's oath: "The Lord swore and will not change his mind!" Thus, the author begins to prepare for the further explication of Christ's appointment as a superior priest by demonstrating the significant encouragement provided by the great God, who offers such oaths. In this way 6:13–20 wraps up the hortatory material begun at 5:11 and provides a smooth transition to the discussion of Melchizedek in chapter 7.

B. The Original OT Context: The Binding of Isaac.
Abraham perhaps serves as the greatest exemplar of faith in Jewish tradition, and the greatest example of his faith is the Aqedah, the binding of Isaac on Mount Moriah, narrated in Gen. 22:1–19 (see Swetnam 1981). The setting of the event opens with the comment that following the birth of Isaac and Abraham's covenant with Abimelech (chap. 21), "God tested Abraham" (22:1). The form of the test follows in 22:2–10. In 22:2 God instructs the patriarch to sacrifice his son as a burnt offering on the mountain. In 22:3–10 Abraham responds to God's command by going to the mountain and preparing to offer his son. The moment of crisis intensifies when Abraham, knife in hand, prepares to kill Isaac (22:10). But in 22:11–14 God intervenes, providing a ram for the sacrifice in place of Isaac and prompting Abraham to name the place in memorial of God's provision.

Thus, Abraham, caught in a crisis, loving his son, yet fearing God more, obeyed. Hebrews interprets the event, saying that Abraham believed that the promises of God would not fail (Heb. 11:17–19). The second main movement of the passage involves God's response to Abraham's faithfulness, God calling to Abraham a second time (Gen. 22:15–19). In this part of the narrative God swears to bless Abraham and multiply his descendants because of his obedience (22:15–17). In fact, God says that Abraham's seed will be multiplied innumerably and have victory over their enemies, and in them all the nations of earth will be blessed (22:18). This embedded discourse ends with Abraham going to Beersheba to live (22:19).

This passage has two components upon which the author of Hebrews focuses. The first, the Lord's declaration "I swear by myself," constitutes the main concern of 6:13–20, God's oath, and leads nicely back to a discussion of Ps. 110:4 in chapter 7. The second component, God's pledge to bless Abraham and give him numerous descendants, illustrates the result of faith in response to God's oath. That Abraham, who waited patiently, received what was promised made him a fitting model for our author's hearers, who were in great need of reassessing the rewards of perseverance (6:12).

C. Relevant Uses of the OT Reference in Jewish Sources. The promise of blessing to Abraham and the multiplication of his seed find various expressions and touted significances in the Jewish sources. In the Targumim the blessing of Abraham is stated similarly to that in the MT, though the broader context is greatly expanded, with an emphasis placed on Isaac's amazing willingness to be slaughtered ("Tie me well lest I struggle") and Abraham's perfect, joyful heart in the offering of his son (*Tg. Ps.-J.* Gen. 22:1–19; *Tg. Neof.* Gen. 22:1–19).

In *Jub.* 18:15 we have a retelling of the story in approximation to the Genesis passage, but the backdrop is given of the many different ways God had already tested the patriarch (e.g., with the land, famine, wealth, his wife's death, and circumcision [17:15–18]). The blessing is alluded to or noted in a number of other places in the Pseudepigrapha, including *L.A.B.* 14:2; *T. Ab.* 3:6; 4:11; 8:6–7; *T. Mos.* 3:9; *Gk. Apoc. Ezra* 3:10. In *T. Mos.* 3:9 is mentioned "the oath" that God swore to the patriarchs that their seed would always be in the land.

In *Exod. Rab.* 44:10 there is an interesting parallel to the use of Gen. 22:16–17 in Heb. 6:13–20, which, through mention of the two unchange-able things in which it is impossible for God to lie, foreshadows the focus on Ps. 110:4 in Heb. 7 (see 7:21–25). The passage explains that the reason God swore by himself was that the eternality of God's oath is tied to the eternality of God himself.

Philo, however, presents the closest parallel to the use of the quotation found in Hebrews. In *Alleg. Interp.* 3.203–208 the Alexandrian scholar presents a discourse using Abraham as an example of a "diligent soul" (*tē spoudaia psychē*) upon whom God pours good things. Philo states, "It is good both that he confirmed the promise with an oath and by an oath fit for God. For notice that God does not swear by something else, for there is nothing better than him; but he swears by himself, who is best" (*Alleg. Interp.* 3.203). Here the writer uses two terms (*bebaioō*, "confirm"; *kreittōn*, "better") belonging to families of words of which the author of Hebrews is fond, and he makes the point that God swears by himself, having nothing greater by which to swear (cf. Heb. 6:13). The parallel could not be more plain.

D. The Textual Background. One pattern followed by various translators and in some LXX documents is the translation of the Hebrew infinitive absolute plus a verb with which it is cognate, using cognates also in Greek, often a participial form with a finite verb, to craft a powerful assertion or oath (Lane 1991: 1:148). In Gen. 22:17 the Piel infinitive absolute *bārēk* ("bless") precedes the Piel imperfect of the same verb, and the Hiphil imperfect of *rbh* ("multiply") follows the Hiphil infinitive absolute of the verb. The LXX translators rendered this Hebrew construction with present active participles followed by future active indicative forms.

There are two noticeable changes as Hebrews' author appropriates the LXX form of the text. First, the *ē mēn* construction with which the quoted portion begins in the LXX has been changed by our author to read *ei mēn* (Attridge [1989: 178], contra UBS⁴/NA²⁷, suggests that the addition of a circumflex over the iota is preferable). The LXX form translates the Hebrew *kî* with a classical assertive meaning "surely." Hebrews' *ei* is simply a later Hellenistic form, the author updating the form to the more common idiom of his day. Second, in the LXX form of the text the object of the verb *plēthynō* ("multiply") is Abraham's "seed" (*to sperma sou* ["your seed"], found in most of the LXX manuscripts, with the exception of the Bohairic and the Dialogue of Timothy and Aquila). Hebrews adjusts this object to the accusative singular form of the second-person personal pronoun *sy* ("you"). With this change, the author accomplishes two things, one stylistic and the other rhetorical. Stylistically, the two parts of the quotation now are fully balanced in form: a participle, followed by a future verb, which has the personal pronoun as its object:

> *eulogōn eulogēsō se . . .*
> *plēthynōn plēthynō se.*

Rhetorically, the whole of the quotation now focuses with pinpoint intensity on Abraham himself, keeping the topic narrowly defined to God's oath, Abraham's faith, and the resulting effect on the patriarch. In the OT text the second part of the quoted portion begins the transition to the implications of Abraham's faith for his descendants (admittedly, corporate identity is in play, so we do not want to make too sharp a distinction between Abraham and his descendants), yet the author of Hebrews does not wish to go there. For him, Abraham is the exemplar whom he wishes to exploit for his current purpose. The adjustment of the text at this point does not change the sense of the original forms of the passage (Abraham obviously was indeed multiplied via the multiplication of his descendants), but the focused purpose of appropriating this OT quotation is maintained.

E. How the OT Reference Is Understood and Used Theologically at Heb. 6:14. The author of Hebrews, in his appropriation of Gen. 22:17, builds on theological presuppositions even while developing a theological statement. On one level, the quotation supports the building of an illustration that serves in the development of a strong word of encouragement. This illustration (6:13–15) and the ensuing truism (6:16) serve to highlight how both divine and human oaths give a heightened sense of certainty, and therefore encouragement, in relationships—relationship with God, and even relationships in human contexts such as legal situations. The author once again uses an argument "from lesser to greater" (*qal wahomer*), suggesting that if this dynamic is true in human situations, such as a court, it certainly is even more sure and has greater implications in

relationship to God. In other words, if human oaths can give certainty, God's oath should give even more certainty.

Yet, on another level, the promise to Abraham is the theological basis for ultimate fulfillment of that promise in "the heirs" (6:17)—that is, the new-covenant community. The oath of God, expressed in Ps. 110:4, gives great assurance to the people of God that he will fulfill the blessing of Abraham through Christ's redemptive work as superior high priest (6:17–20).

Of course, one of the primary theological presuppositions here concerns the nature and trustworthiness of God. In contradistinction, for example, to process theology or aspects of Mormon theology, the biblical understanding of God is his nature does not change. He is eternal (Ps. 102:26–27) and unchanging (Mal. 3:6), and therefore his words are constant (Ps. 33:11). His nature being what it is, therefore, his oaths carry a lasting certainty. Specifically for Hebrews, since God has sworn an oath in the form of Ps. 110:4 (109:4 LXX), therefore, Jesus has become the guarantor or guarantee of a better covenant (7:22), being a "permanent" high priest (7:24). He is the same—yesterday, today, and forever (13:8). This provides strong encouragement for those of the new covenant, because their relationship with God could not be more stable. This stability provides help for walking through a world of turmoil, sifting circumstances, and even persecution, since the ultimate outcome of a life lived faithfully is certain. Since God does not change, the fundamental nature of Christianity does not change. Therefore, a stable future is infused with hope (6:19–20). A changing god, of questionable character, whose words cannot be trusted, provides no basis for a sure future and therefore no basis of true hope. Thankfully, this is not Hebrews' understanding of God. Hebrews proclaims the great God, whose oaths can be trusted and therefore provide hope for his covenant people.

6:18, 20

Psalm 110:4 is in the forefront of the author's mind as he moves toward resumption of Christ's high priesthood according to the order of Melchizedek in 7:1–10. The "two unchangeable things in which it is impossible for God to lie" are the two parts of Ps. 110:4, which will comprise the author's arguments in chapter 7. That Christ is "a priest forever" constitutes the author's argument in 7:15–28 and focuses on the perpetual nature of Christ's priesthood. That the Son is a priest "according to the order of Melchizedek" is addressed in 7:11–14. Why are these two facts about Christ "unchangeable"? Because "The Lord has sworn and will not change his mind." It is impossible for God to lie (6:18). Why do these two facts give encouragement to those who have fled to God to take hold of hope (6:18–19)? Christ has become our high priest according to the order of Melchizedek (6:20) in fulfillment of the psalm's prophetic oath.

7:1–4

The enigmatic priest Melchizedek is mentioned in the OT only at Ps. 110:4 and Gen. 14:17–20, the passage to which the author of Hebrews alludes at 7:1–10. The author seeks to demonstrate decisively that Melchizedek's priesthood is superior to the Levitical priesthood, for this will lay the foundation for an argument for the superiority of the Son's Melchizedekian high priesthood. In 7:1–3 he teases out typological connections between Melchizedek and the Son of God. Melchizedek is a king of righteousness and peace, and the lack of reference in the Scriptures to his parents, or a beginning or ending of his life, is taken as consonant with immortality. Thus, he is "made like [*aphōmoiōmenos*] the Son of God" (7:3), and at the same time his life points to, anticipates, the type of high priesthood to be embodied by the Son of God. Thus, the author's interpretation of the passage has a compact style with which he quickly highlights certain key points that strengthen the association, suggested by Ps. 110:4, between Jesus and Melchizedek.

Melchizedek was a priest-king from the city Salem whom Abraham encountered after defeating a group of invading kings. Genesis 14 tells of the four kings from the east—Amraphel king of Shinar, Arioch king of Ellasar, Chedorlaomer king of Elam, Tidal king of Goiim—who attacked a confederation of five kings from Sodom, Gomorrah, Admah, Zeboiim, and Bela. The latter were defeated and their cities plundered. In the process Lot, Abraham's nephew, was captured, and Abraham pursued the invaders to Dan, where he staged a nighttime attack, putting the enemies to flight and recovering their stolen goods. Upon his return home, Abraham was met by the king of Sodom

and Melchizedek. The author of Hebrews focuses on Abraham's encounter with the latter, in which Abraham gave a tithe and received a blessing.

As for extrabiblical literature, Philo mentions Melchizedek at points, mostly using Melchizedek as a symbol—for instance, of the Logos (*Alleg. Interp.* 3.79–82). As shown by a scroll fragment on Melchizedek found in Qumran Cave 11, which dates from around the time of Christ's birth, the Qumran sectarians considered the priest a heavenly figure. A passage dealing with the Jubilee Year, Lev. 25:9–13, forms the focus of the fragment, the last "Jubilee" being called the "Year of Melchizedek," in which Melchizedek is said to bring deliverance and salvation to the people of God by defeating Belial and his evil spirits: "And Melchizedek will exact the ven[geance] of E[l's] judgments [and he will protect all the sons of light from the power] of Belial and from the power of all [the spirits of] his [lot]" (11Q13 II, 13). In this document Melchizedek seems to be some type of heavenly figure, perhaps an exalted angel. The enigmatic priest also is a heavenly figure in the first-century work *2 Enoch*, in which Melchizedek is saved from the flood so that he can continue a line of priests started with Seth. Michael transports the child Melchizedek to paradise, where he is to be a priest forever (see Attridge 1989: 192–95).

Focusing on the mention of Melchizedek in Ps. 110:4, the author of Hebrews brilliantly crafts a high-priestly Christology unique to the NT. Jesus is proclaimed as Son of God, who has been appointed by God as a superior priest according to the order of Melchizedek (5:5–6).

In light of the "argument from silence" at 7:3, it is interesting that in *Apoc. Ab.* 17:10 Abraham recites a song that says of God, in part, "without mother, without father, ungenerated, exalted." Also, one of the *Hellenistic Synagogal Prayers*, likely altered by later Christian interpolation, calls the divine Word, God's Son, a "high priest; both king and lord of all intelligible and perceptible nature" (*OTP* 2:690).

7:17, 21

(For a fuller treatment of Ps. 110:4 [109:4 LXX] and the way in which the author conceives it as fulfilled in Christ, see commentary on Heb. 5:6 above.) In 7:11–28 the author of Hebrews offers a culmination, his treatment of Christ's appointment as superior high priest (5:1–10; 7:1–28). He develops his argument along several lines, the first two of which involve reiteration of Ps. 109:4 LXX. First, that Jesus was appointed to high priesthood suggests that the regulations for worship, found in the law and centered on the old-covenant priests, have been exchanged for something better (7:11–19). As part of his logic, the author points out in 7:16 that unlike the old-covenant priests, who were appointed on the basis of their ancestry, the Son of God was appointed on the basis of "a life that cannot be destroyed" (*zōēs akatalytou*). This thought the author reinforces in 7:17 with the quotation of the last part of Ps. 109:4 LXX. The key phrase in the quotation for the author, at this point, is that translated "forever" (*eis ton aiōna*), which demonstrates immortality. Second, the superiority of Jesus' high priesthood is demonstrated by God's use of an oath in bringing about his appointment (7:20–22). The earthly priests were not appointed with an oath. Yet, Ps. 110:4 clearly shows God's oath concerning the Melchizedekian high priest: "The Lord has sworn and will not change his mind." Here again a quotation from Ps. 110:4 is used, this time with focus on the first part of the verse, to reinforce the idea (7:21). The author understands this to imply that Jesus guarantees a better covenant.

8:1

The allusion to Ps. 110:1 (109:1 LXX) at 8:1 plays a critical role in the development of the book (G. H. Guthrie 1994: 123). Here, the *en hypsēlois* ("on high") of the allusion to the same verse at 1:3 has become *en tois ouranois* ("in the heavens"), a more overt reference to the heavenly realm. With the allusion at 8:1 the author has moved the focus of Christ's ministry to the heavenly realm. The author argues, in part, that the new-covenant offering of Christ is superior to the old-covenant offerings because the former took place in the heavenly tabernacle rather than in the earthly one (e.g., 9:23–24).

8:5

A. The Immediate NT Context. The quotation of Exod. 25:40 occurs in the introduction to Hebrews' extensive treatment of Christ's superior high-priestly offering (8:3–10:18). This treatment has three movements: the introduction (8:3–6), an explanation of the superiority of the new cov-

enant (8:7–13), and a discourse on the superiority of Jesus' new-covenant offering (9:1–10:18). The introduction in 8:3–6 begins with an axiom asserting that "every high priest is appointed to offer gifts and sacrifices." This statement forms a parallel introduction with 5:1, which makes an approximate statement. In 8:3b, however, the author points out an implication that Jesus, who has been appointed as superior high priest (7:11–28), must therefore also have an offering to bring. Then, with 8:4–5 the writer makes a point that is critical for his argument that Christ's new-covenant offering is superior to those made by the Levitical priests. Here he vies for the superiority of the heavenly realities over the earthly. First, he reiterates that Jesus is not like the earthly priests, since the law dictates the requirements for the Levitical priesthood, which is an earthly institution. He already has made clear that Jesus is of another tribe (7:13) and his priesthood based on appointment rather than ancestry (7:16–22). Second, in 8:5 the distinction between the earthly and heavenly is made clearer. The institutions of earth, the Levitical priesthood, and all the material aspects of their worship practices are "a sketch and a shadow" of the heavenly realities. This is very important to the author's argument for the superiority of the new-covenant offering, for he proclaims Jesus' offering superior in part because of it being offered in the true tabernacle in heaven (9:11, 23–24). The quotation of Exod. 25:40 serves to support the idea that the earthly things were made as copies of the true heavenly realities. Moses was given a pattern to follow, the verse says. Therefore, the author of Hebrews reasons, the heavenly tabernacle served as the prototype for what would become the earthly place of worship.

B. The Original OT Context. Exodus 25:40 occurs in that section of the book of Exodus having to do with God's revelation to his covenant people at Mount Sinai (19:1–31:18). Within this broader section God calls Moses up to the mountain, where the leader spends forty days (24:12–18). There, God commands Moses to raise a heave offering of various materials for the construction of the tabernacle and its furniture, the ark of the covenant, the table of showbread, and the lampstand (25:1–39). In 25:9 Moses is told to make everything according to the "pattern" (*tabnît*) of the tabernacle and its furniture, a pattern that God would show him. This thought the writer of Exodus reiterates in 25:40, God commanding Moses to make the tabernacle and its furniture "according to the pattern" that God showed him on the mountain. From this point in Exodus the narrative continues with the description of the specifics concerning construction of various articles to be used in conjunction with the tabernacle worship (26:1–31:18).

C. Relevant Uses of the OT Reference in Jewish Sources. There are a number of places where Exod. 25:40 is quoted or alluded to overtly in the ancient Jewish sources and other sources that bear witness to the belief in the heavenly temple, often in the context of a discussion on the heavenly city, Jerusalem. In *QE* 2.82, Philo asks, "What is the meaning of the words, 'You shall make (them) according to the pattern which has been shown to you on the mountain'?" He answers, in terms of his Platonic idealism, that the word "pattern" points to "the incorporeal heaven, the archetype of the sense-perceptible." Further, Philo suggests that the word "see" from the passage constitutes an exhortation to perceive incorporeal forms with the soul, since there would be no need for an exhortation to see a sense-perceptible form with one's physical eyes. In *Alleg. Interp.* 3.102, furthermore, Philo uses Exod. 25:40 to argue that Moses received instructions concerning the tabernacle directly from God himself.

That there are heavenly items used in worship finds expression in *b. Menaḥ.* 29a, a passage that tells of an ark, table, and candlestick made of fire and coming down from heaven. Rabbi Jose b. Judah suggests that Moses saw these and reproduced them, quoting Exod. 25:40 as his prooftext. Then Exod. 26:30, a parallel passage, is quoted in support of the tabernacle itself being copied by Moses. In a more obscure use of the passage, Rabbi Shimi b. Hiyya says that Exod. 25:40 means that God's revelation will be given "in future generations" (*b. Šebu.* 14b–15a; *b. Sanh.* 16b). In addition to these, a number of other rabbinic passages point to the relationship between the earthly and heavenly places of worship (cf., e.g., *b. Ḥag.* 12b; *Gen. Rab.* 55:7; *Midr. Songs* 4:4; see Cody 1960: 23–26).

Texts in the Pseudepigrapha point to the heavenly city or its temple in a number of places. In *2 Bar.* 4:2–6 the author speaks of the heavenly Je-

rusalem, with its heavenly temple, which was created even before Adam sinned, shown to Abraham upon his covenant-making, and shown again to Moses on Mount Sinai when he saw the image of the tabernacle and its vessels, and is with God even to this day. Thus, the heavenly temple has been a reality from the creation. In *1 En.* 14:15–20 Enoch's heavenly vision of the great "second house," with God's throne, almost certainly is a reference to a heavenly temple. Similarly, *T. Levi* 3:2–5 describes different levels of the heavens, in the uppermost of which "dwells the Great Glory in the Holy of Holies superior to all holiness." Finally, *Sib. Or.* 4:10 proclaims that the temple of God cannot be seen from earth and was not made by human hands, a sentiment expressed also at Heb. 8:2; 9:11, 24.

This idea of the heavenly temple also seems to be reflected in the Apocrypha at Wis. 9:8: "You have given command to build a temple on your holy mountain, and an altar in the city of your habitation, a copy of the holy tent that you prepared from the beginning."

D. The Textual Background. The LXX follows the pattern of the Hebrew text in a fairly literal fashion. Hebrews shows at least two adjustments to the Greek text. The first, the addition of *panta*, occurs also in Philo's paraphrase of the verse at *Alleg. Interp.* 3.102 and in the LXX witness F, and Attridge (1989: 220) suggests that the word may have been added to accentuate how totally the copy of the tabernacle was dependent on the heavenly tabernacle. Second, the participle from *deiknymi* has changed from a perfect passive (*dedeigmenon*) to an aorist passive (*deichthenta*). Following Thomas (1965: 309), Attridge (1989: 220) thinks that this might indicate for the author that the relationship between the earthly and heavenly tabernacles was impermanent. Yet, it is quite doubtful that the change in verbal aspect can bear the weight of such a temporally oriented nuance. Rather, the author may once again make the change for stylistic reasons, the alteration in this case achieving a more pleasing rhythm as well as the assonance of its final syllable with the final syllables of *hora*, *panta*, and *kata*.

E. How Exod. 25:40 Is Understood and Used Theologically at Heb. 8:5. Primarily, the author of Hebrews uses the quotation of Exod. 25:40 to reinforce the theological thought that there is a heavenly tabernacle. At one time there existed almost a consensus in Hebrews scholarship that the writer's thought was Platonic, and this view found its most ardent supporter in Ceslas Spicq, who marched through extensive parallels between Hebrews and Philo in the areas of interpretive method, vocabulary, and worldview (see Spicq 1952–1953: 1:39–91). But this position came under attack from several directions. First, the finding and study of the Qumran scrolls brought to light another Jewish backdrop against which Hebrews could be considered, one that offered alternative explanations for some of Hebrews' concepts. Second, Spicq's research was challenged in a series of studies. Barrett (1956) began to shift the focus to the influence of apocalyptic thought as a significant backdrop for the book. Spicq's position was further weakened by Hanson (2002), Schröger (1968), and, most extensively, Williamson (1970), who showed Spicq's research and logic to be flawed. More recently, Hurst (1990) has extended Barrett's and Williamson's work by further demonstrating the cogency of Hebrews' use of terminology with the spatial and temporal dualism of Jewish apocalyptic. In his conclusion on the matter Hurst (1990: 42) states, "In all of this there is nothing *distinctly* 'Platonic,' 'philosophical' or 'noumenal'; much of it is drawn from the OT. Enough indications exist to point to a reasonable conclusion that *Auctor* developed certain OT ideas within the Jewish apocalyptic framework, while Philo developed the same themes within a Platonic framework."

In Jewish apocalyptic there exist both temporal and spatial dualisms. The temporal dualism, for instance, places emphasis on the distinction between the present age and the age to come and is manifested in Hebrews extensively (e.g., 9:28; 10:25; 12:25–29). The spatial dualism is so prominent in apocalyptic literature that some scholars distinguish those works with a heavenly journey from those without such a journey. In the NT we have heaven breaking into earth, for instance, at the birth, baptism, transfiguration, and resurrection of the Messiah, the stoning of Stephen, and Paul's experience on the Damascus Road. Earth breaks into heaven at the death of the saints and the ascension/exaltation, and there in heaven, according to Hebrews, Paul, and Revelation, is

the Jerusalem above (Gal. 4:26; Rev. 3:12; 7:15; 11:19; 14:15, 17; 15:5; 16:1, 17; 21:2, 10).

Thus, Hebrews' reference to the heavenly tabernacle, from which the earthly tabernacle was copied, concerns the permanent heavenly dwelling place of God over against the earthly tabernacle, which was merely temporary and provisional. There is no hope in the earthly, which is in the process of passing away, for it is part of the earthly realm, a realm that will be "shaken" at the end in such a way that only that which is incapable of being shaken will remain (9:11; 12:25–29). Jesus has established a new covenant that is lasting and involves the transformation of people as well as their transference to an eternal kingdom. Both are effected by the new covenant, a covenant that, according to Hebrews, was established by Christ's superior sacrifice. That sacrifice, moreover, is superior in part because it was made in the true tabernacle in heaven (9:23–24), the eschatological tabernacle in which Jesus now serves as superior high priest. This tabernacle, according to Hebrews, is the fitting context for the new-covenant offering of Christ, for it is "greater" and "more perfect" than the earthly tabernacle (9:11). Christ's entrance into the heavenly tabernacle is synonymous with his entrance into the very presence of God in the heavenly realm, where he intercedes for us (7:25; 9:24). The heavenly tabernacle, therefore, is eschatological for Hebrews in that it is the context for the new-covenant relationship established between God and his people via the sacrifice of Christ as our high priest. Thus, new-covenant people have already come to Mount Zion, the living God's city, the heavenly Jerusalem, where Jesus' blood speaks a better word on their behalf (12:22–24). Further, these new-covenant realities will be consummated when Christ brings salvation at the end of the age (9:28).

8:8–12

A. The Immediate NT Context. The quotation of Jer. 31:31–34 (38:31–34 LXX), the longest OT quotation in the NT, plays a vital role in the book's discourse on Christ's superior high-priestly offering (8:3–10:18), laying the groundwork for the climax of the book's christological exposition. Through use of this rich prophetic passage, the author establishes the superiority of the new covenant (8:7–13) prior to addressing the superiority of the new-covenant offering (9:1–10:18). The development from one to the other follows the pattern identified in chapter 7, where he first asserts the superiority of Melchizedek's priesthood and builds on that assertion by proclaiming the superiority of Jesus' Melchizedekian appointment as priest. The superiority of the institution is followed by the superiority of the new-covenant expression of the institution. The author primarily establishes the superiority of the new covenant by pointing out that (1) the first covenant was not faultless (*amemptos*) and thus gave rise to a second covenant (8:7), and (2) the term "new" (*kainē*) in the quotation (8:8) means that the old covenant "has been made obsolete" (*palaioō*) (8:13).

In chapters 9–10 the author utilizes the passage from Jeremiah to focus on the forgiveness of sins promised in the quotation, thus associating the new covenant with cultic ideas of priesthood and sacrifice (e.g., 9:14–15; 10:15–18).

The introductory formula for this quotation contains an important textual variant, which reads "for faulting them, he says" (*memphomenos gar autous legei*). The *autous* reads as a direct object and a reference to the people who were under the old covenant, and this is reflected overtly in some translations (e.g., NIV, NASB). However, based on the context, which deals with the inadequacy of the old covenant itself, the variant *autois* ("to them"), supported by witnesses $\mathfrak{P}^{46}$ B, among others, is preferable and is understood as an indirect object of the verb *legei* ("he says"). On this reading, the clause introduces the quotation with, "for finding fault (with the old covenant) he says to them . . . ," and, it may be suggested, this reading flows more naturally from 8:7, which implies that the first covenant was flawed. Furthermore, it matches the author's concluding assertion in 8:13. The discussion emphasizes the defective nature of the older arrangement.

B. The Original OT Context. Jeremiah 31:31–34 is part of a larger section of Jeremiah known as the Book of Consolation (30:1–31:40), a section that promises future salvation for those who are suffering at present. The question of how God can both wield judgment and promise deliverance finds an answer in his covenant love for Israel and Judah. Jeremiah brings this section of consolation to a close with five brief oracles that pronounce salvation and form a chiasm structurally. At the center of the chiasm is the section

quoted in Heb. 8:8–12 (Keown, Scalise, and Smothers 1995: 83, 126–27).

Jeremiah 31:31–34 falls into three movements. First, in 31:31 the Lord promises a time when he will make a new covenant with the people of God. The clause "the days are surely coming" is an eschatological formula used also in 31:27–30, 38–40. Second, this promise is qualified negatively in 31:32: the new covenant will not be like the Sinai covenant made at the time of the exodus. God's rejection of the old covenant is explained in terms of the lack of faithfulness to the covenant on the part of its recipients. Third, the characteristics of the new covenant are detailed in 31:33–34. The laws of God will be internalized, placed on the minds and hearts of God's people. The relationship between God and his followers will be firmly established, and everyone within the covenant will know the Lord (31:33–34a). This relationship with God is connected to his decisive forgiveness of the sins of the covenant people (31:34b).

C. Relevant Uses of the OT Reference in Jewish Sources. In line with the wording of Jer. 31:31–34, the Qumran community understood itself as a new-covenant community (Charlesworth 1992: 12). This is expressed most overtly in the *Damascus Document*, which in part challenges the congregation to endure in faithfulness to the covenant with others who have retreated to the "land of Damascus," which many scholars understand as a code name for the Qumran headquarters. Passages such as CD-A VI, 19; VIII, 21 (= CD-B XIX, 33b–34a); CD-B XX, 12 speak of those who "entered the new covenant in the land of Damascus." The context of rigorous faithfulness to the practices of the law, for instance, is the context for CD-A VI, 19. Here the members of the community are exhorted, in part, to "keep the Sabbath day according to specifications, and the holy days and the fast day according to the commandments of the members of the new covenant in the land of Damascus" (CD-A VI, 18–19). Further, 1QS I, 16, 18, 20, 24; II, 10 speak of entering the covenant.

There are possible allusions to our passage in the Pseudepigrapha, but they are rare. For instance, *L.A.E.* 13:5 makes a possible allusion to Jer. 31:33, saying, "And there shall not be any more sinners before him, for the evil heart shall be removed

971

from them, and they shall be given a heart that understands the good and worships God alone." Also making reference to the condition of the heart, *T. Jud.* 20:3–4 proclaims that both truth and error are written in a person's affections, and that a person's works are written on the heart.

Ecclesiastes Rabbah 2:1 says that God's promise to put his law "in their inward parts" is related to the world to come, for there it will not be forgotten as it is in this world, and the evil inclination will be dissolved before the good inclination.

D. The Textual Background. The LXX (38:31–34) varies from the MT (31:31–34) at several points. In 31:34 the *nĕ'um yhwh* ("declares the LORD") has been dropped by the LXX, and the singular references to "guilt" (*'āwôn*) and "sin" (*haṭṭā't*) in the MT have converted to plural forms in the LXX. More significantly, at 31:32 the MT reads "although I was a husband [Qal perfect of *b'l*] to them," whereas the LXX has "and I did not care [*ameleō*] for them" (variants of the LXX text include "and I am the one who ruled among them" and "I was restraining them"). It seems that the translator of the LXX read *b'l* as *g'l* (Swete 1900: 338). In *Tg. Jer.* 31:32 it reads, "although I took pleasure in them," thus removing the anthropomorphic reference to marriage in the MT.

Hebrews generally follows the form of the LXX, but it does diverge at points. Minor variations include the following. Hebrews reads *legei* for *phēsin* ("he says") at 8:8, 9, 10; *kagō* for *kai egō* ("and I") at 8:9; *epigrapsō* for *grapsō* ("I will write" [Heb. follows LXX A]) at 8:10; and Hebrews omits *autōn kai* ("of them and") following *mikrou* ("the least") at 8:11. Hebrews makes a change at 8:8 from *diathēsomai* ("I will arrange" [the form of all the Greek manuscripts except Aquila]) to *syntelesō* ("I will accomplish" [also found in Symmachus and Syʰ]). All the ancient Greek manuscripts have *tō oikō* ("with the house"), while Hebrews reads *epi ton oikon* ("over the house"). Further, there is a change in 8:9 from *diethemēn* ("I arranged") in the LXX to *epoiēsa* ("I made" [the form also found in Qᵗˣᵗ]). The use of *syntleō* with *diathēkē* has a scriptural basis (cf., e.g., Jer. 41:8 [34:8 ET]; see Attridge 1989: 227). Yet, against Thomas (1965: 310–13) and following Kistemaker (1961: 40–42), Lane (1991) understands these changes as stylistic rather than theologically

motivated and as communicating a qualitative difference in the establishment of the old covenant and the establishment of the new (see also McCullough 1979–1980: 364–67).

E. How Jer. 31:31–34 Is Understood and Used Theologically at Heb. 8:8–12. The quotation of Jer. 31:31–34 (LXX 38:31–34) is the longest quotation in the NT, yet the author of Hebrews follows with a surprisingly brief comment, focusing solely on the word "new" (*kainos*). This method of appropriation involves drawing out implications of a text, often focusing on a word's meaning, and the practice was common in rabbinic exegesis. In 8:13 the author reasons that since God referred to the second covenant as "new," he has made the first covenant "obsolete" (*palaioō*), communicating that it has lost its usefulness. Earlier, at 1:11, the author quotes Ps. 102:26 (LXX 101:26), which uses the same term: "they will all wear out [*palaiōthēsontai*] like a garment." Similarly, at 8:13 the writer speaks of the old covenant as having passed its time of usefulness; its demise is a foregone conclusion. The author focuses on this point to lay a foundation for discussion of the new-covenant offering made by Jesus, and he wraps up the section on that offering (9:1–10:18) by repeating the last part of the quotation at 10:16–17. In short, the author understands this rich passage from Jeremiah as a direct verbal prophecy, fulfilled by the inauguration of the new covenant in Christ's sacrificial death and his triumphant exaltation to service as superior high priest. It is that new covenant, established by a superior offering, by which people can know God, have his laws written on heart and mind, and have their sins decisively forgiven.

The concept of the new covenant occurs elsewhere in the NT at Luke 22:20; 1 Cor. 11:25; 2 Cor. 3:6. The reference in 2 Cor. 3:6 speaks of the nature of Christian ministry and uses the "new covenant" as a designation for being in relationship with God through Christ. In the passages from Luke and 1 Corinthians, however, the new covenant is associated with Christ's sacrificial death, as is the case in Hebrews, where it is the new covenant in Christ's "blood" (*haima*) (9:12, 14; 10:19, 29; 12:24; 13:12, 20). Hebrews, however, uniquely develops the theme of the new covenant and uses it for theological and hortatory purposes.

9:20

A. The Immediate NT Context. The quotation of Exod. 24:8 occurs in a broader section of Hebrews (9:1–10:18) on the superiority of Christ's sacrifice over those of the old-covenant system. In 9:1–10 the author explains regulations (9:1) of old-covenant worship, focusing on three aspects: the place of worship—the earthly tabernacle—(9:1–5), the recurrent or continual nature of the sacrifices (9:6–7), and that the sacrifice involved blood (9:7). These three regulations of the old system are compared to the new-covenant sacrifice of Christ, which is shown to be superior at every point: (1) the place of Christ's offering was in heaven rather than on earth (9:11, 23–25; 10:12–13); (2) the blood of the offering was Christ's blood rather than the blood of animals (9:12–28); (3) Christ's sacrifice was made once for all time rather than continually (9:25–26; 10:1–18).

In the more immediate context of our quotation the author focuses on how a covenant is established (9:15–22). Christ is the mediator of the new covenant (9:15 [cf. 8:6; 12:24]), bringing the people to God in a holy agreement. Interpreters often have read 9:16–17 in terms of a "will" or "testament," but these verses should be read, in their context, as speaking of the establishment of the covenant (L. Lincoln 1999). "The one arranging [*diatithēmi*] it," occurring in participial form in 9:16–17, refers to the sacrificial animal that must die for a covenant to be established (G. H. Guthrie 1998: 313). This fits perfectly the argument of 9:18–22, which deals with Moses' inauguration of the Sinai covenant with the sprinkling of blood (Exod. 24:3–8). In 9:18 the author asserts that the first covenant was inaugurated with blood. A summary of this OT event is provided in 9:19–21. Having informed the people of the Lord's words concerning the law (Exod. 24:3, 7), Moses took the blood of the calves sacrificed as fellowship offerings and sprinkled it on the people, saying, "This is the blood of the covenant, which God has commanded you to keep" (Exod. 24:8). The elements of water, scarlet wool, and branches of hyssop are not found in the Exodus text, but their use in ceremonial sprinkling seems to have been common (Exod. 12:22; Lev. 14:4–7, 51–52; Num. 19:6, 18). Hebrews alone among ancient references to this event states that Moses also sprinkled the book of the covenant. Thus, the quotation of Exod. 24:8 helps to reinforce the point that covenants are established by the spilling of a sacrifice's blood.

B. The Original OT Context. Having given the people of Israel various laws and commands at Sinai (Exod. 20–23), the Lord called Moses and other leaders—Aaron, Nadab, Abihu—and seventy elders up on the mountain to worship (24:1–2). Before going up, however, Moses recounted all of God's words, the commands and laws, to the people of Israel, and the people responded, proclaiming their obedience to God's will (24:3). So, Moses wrote down all of the words of the covenant and then built an altar at the foot of Sinai on which burnt offerings and peace offerings would be made to the Lord (24:4–5). Half of the blood from the sacrifices was put in bowls, and half was sprinkled on the altar (24:6). Then, in formal presentation, Moses read the Book of the Covenant to the people, and they responded by confessing their enduring obedience (24:7). At this point in the narrative Moses sprinkled the blood on the people, calling it the "blood of the covenant" that God had established with the people (24:8). After the ratification of the covenant, Moses and the other leaders went up to the mountain and fellowshiped with God (24:9–11). Then God called Moses himself up on the mountain so that he might receive the commandments written on stone (24:12–18).

C. Relevant Uses of the OT Reference in Jewish Sources. At *QE* 2.36 Philo asks, "Why does he say further, 'Behold the blood of the covenant which the Lord commanded you concerning all these words'? He answers: '(He does so) because the blood is a symbol of family kinship. And the form of kinship is twofold: one is that among men, which has its origin in ancestors, while that among souls has its origin in wisdom.'" Thus, Philo moves away from the ratification of the covenant to a consideration of blood as a symbol of close physical or intellectual relationship.

At *Tg. Onq.* Exod. 24:8, however, the Targum maintains the focus on establishment of the covenant, but an element not found in the MT or LXX is added. The Targum says that Moses sprinkled the blood "on the altar to atone for the people." This interpretive rendering of the Hebrew understands the blood to have been sprinkled on the altar, on behalf of the people, rather than on the people themselves, an interpretation also found in the *Mekilta* to Deuteronomy in *Midrash Tannaim* on the book of Deuteronomy. In the Babylonian Talmud Exod. 24:8 finds expression in discussions of the requirements for proselytes. At *b. Yebam.* 46b one encounters a discussion on circumcision and ritual ablution. Some rabbis argued that both were required to make a proper proselyte. Exodus 24:8 is quoted in support of the tradition that there must be no sprinkling without ritual ablution. Also concerning a proselyte entering the covenant, *b. Ker.* 9a deals with circumcision, immersion, and the sprinkling of blood. In the immediate context of the quotation, circumcision is affirmed on the basis of Josh. 5:5; Ezek 16:6. Exodus 24:8 then is quoted to reinforce the idea of immersion: "But whence do we know the immersion?—It is written, *And Moses took the blood, and sprinkled it on the people*, and there can be no sprinkling without immersion."

D. The Textual Background. Once again the LXX corresponds almost woodenly to the Hebrew text. There are, however, several points at which Hebrews' form of the quotation differs from the LXX. The word *idou* ("behold") at the beginning of the LXX rendering has been changed in Hebrews' form to *touto* ("this" [also the reading in the LXX Sahidic version, 88, and Dialogue of Timothy and Aquila]). Second, the verb *diatithēmi* ("arrange") has been replaced by a form of *entellō* ("command"), a change also found in Philo (*QE* 2.36). Finally, the *kyrios pros hymas* ("the Lord . . . with you") has become *pros hymas ho theos* ("God . . . for you" [the LXX manuscripts 24, 44, 88, Sahidic, and Dialogue of Timothy and Aquila also read *ho theos*]). It is a broadly published opinion that the first of these changes is due to the influence of traditional eucharistic material (Christ's words "This is my blood of the covenant" [Matt. 26:28; Mark 14:24]; so Spicq 1952–1953: 2:264; Thomas 1965: 313–14; McCullough 1979–1980: 375). Lane demurs, suggesting that all three changes result from the carefully structured argument in the immediate context. For Lane, the presence of *touto* in the quotation "underscores the fact that the old covenant was ratified by means of sacrificial blood obtained from slain animals" (Lane 1991: 2:245). The second change to the text was done to avoid

ambiguity, since the author used *diatithēmi* to refer to the ratifier of the covenant (8:10; 9:16; 10:10). Lane believes that the use of *eneteilato* in 9:20 removes the sense that God ratified the former covenant, suggesting rather that Hebrews' form communicates that the people ratified God's authoritative word to them. Finally, Lane (1991: 2:245) proposes, Hebrews' common use of *kyrios* for Jesus prompted the author to substitute *ho theos* to avoid the misunderstanding that the Sinai covenant was commanded by Jesus.

E. How Exod. 24:8 Is Understood and Used Theologically at Heb. 9:20. Very simply, the quotation of Exod. 24:8 at 9:20 serves to reinforce the idea that the covenants are established with blood sacrifice. The author is doing more than establishing a helpful analogy, for the broader context of the discussion has to do with "regulations" for worship (9:1, 10). The establishment of a covenant necessitates a sacrificial death (9:16–18), for cleansing and forgiveness come only with the shedding of blood (9:22).

At least since the time of B. F. Westcott the blood motif in the NT has been misconstrued by some commentators as representing the communication of "life" (Stibbs 1978). In his commentary on John, for instance, Westcott (1966: 34–37) states,

> Thus, in accordance with the typical teaching of the Levitical ordinances, the Blood of Christ represents Christ's life (1) as rendered in free self-sacrifice to God for men, and (2) as brought into perfect fellowship with God, having been set free by death. The Blood of Christ is, as shed, the Life of Christ given for men, and as applied, the Life of Christ now given to men, the Life which is the spring of their life (John xii. 24). . . . The Blood always includes the thought of the life preserved and active beyond death.

Speaking specifically of 9:18–22, Westcott (1909: 266) writes, "By the use of the words 'not without blood' the writer of the Epistle suggests the two ideas of atonement and quickening by the impartment of a new life which have already connected with Christ's work." In this way, Westcott suggests that the idea of "blood" communicates the idea of life being given. Rather, however, the biblical evidence strongly suggests that sacrificial blood in Scripture points to the death of the victim, not the bestowal of life. Specifically for Hebrews,

Christ's blood speaks of Christ's death, the death that cleanses us, brings us freedom (9:15), and inaugurates the new covenant (9:16–18).

Consequently, the establishment of the new covenant through the death of Christ functions as part of a larger theological complex on the effectiveness of his death on behalf of his new-covenant people.

9:23

In 9:19–21 the author of Hebrews reviews the inauguration of the old covenant, found in Exod. 24. In connection with that inauguration, he suggests that the law required various elements related to the earthly tabernacle to be purified with blood from the animal sacrifices (on the problems surrounding the assertion that the tabernacle and ceremonial vessels were sprinkled with blood [9:21], see G. H. Guthrie 1998: 314). What, then, does he mean, in 9:23, that the heavenly tabernacle and vessels of ministry had to be cleansed with Christ's blood? The answer is found in the instructions on the Day of Atonement in Lev. 16:16–19. There, Leviticus explains that atonement had to be made for the holiest place and the tent of meeting because of the impurity and rebellion of the Israelites. Thus, in the case of the new-covenant offering of Christ, the heavenly tabernacle had to be cleansed because of the sins of the people who would be brought into the covenant. The heavenly tabernacle is cleansed in conjunction with the cleansing of God's people.

9:28

At 9:28 the author of Hebrews makes an allusion to Isa. 53:12, found in the Song of the Suffering Servant. In 53:12 the prophet says that the Servant "bore the sins of many" (*autos hamartias pollōn anēnenken*). This allusion comes in a broad section in Hebrews on the superiority of Christ's new-covenant sacrifice (9:1–10:18). That sacrifice is superior because of where it was made (in the heavenly tabernacle [e.g., 9:24]), when it was made (once for all time rather than perpetually [e.g., 9:25]), and with whose blood (Christ's own blood rather than the blood of animals [e.g., 9:13–14]). When the author says that as the new-covenant sacrifice he "bore the sins of many," the sacrificial, Day of Atonement imagery of the section is reinforced by appropriation of a key "sacrifice for sins" prophecy. In its broader context Isa.

53 speaks of the one who "carried our sickness" (LXX: "carries our sins") and "was wounded for our transgressions," who was "a guilt offering" and bore "iniquities" (53:4–5, 10–11).

10:5–9

A. The Immediate NT Context. In 10:1–18 the author of Hebrews moves to the climax of his treatment of Christ's superior, new-covenant offering for sins (8:3–10:18). That treatment, in part, highlights three aspects of the earthly regulations for worship under the Levitical system, placing them in stark contrast to the offering accomplished by the heavenly high priest: the Levitical sacrifices were made in an earthly tabernacle (9:1–5); (2) the old-covenant priests used the blood of animals (9:7); (3) the sacrifices had to be made year after year (9:6–7). By contrast, Christ's sacrifice was offered in the heavenly tabernacle (9:11, 23–25; 10:12–13), involved his own blood (9:12–28), and had to be made only one time (9:25–26; 10:1–18). This final point dominates the author's attention in 10:1–18, the immediate context of the quotation of Ps. 40:6–8a (39:7–9a LXX). In 10:1–4 he asserts that the old-covenant sacrifices, offered year after year, are unable to perfect (*teleioō*) the worshipers (10:1), and the perpetual nature of the sacrifices supports the assertion. If the offerings provided complete cleansing from sins, further sacrifices would not be needed, and the worshipers would have no sense of barrier between themselves and God (10:2). However, this is not the case, and indeed the sacrifices themselves serve to remind the worshipers that they are sinful, shut off from the presence of God (10:3). Why are the old-covenant sacrifices ineffectual in dealing with sins? Because they involve the blood of bulls and goats (10:4), which by its nature is unable to eradicate sins. Thankfully, Christ came, as superior high priest, and brought a superior offering. The author supports this assertion by quoting Ps. 40:7–9. The use of the conjunction "therefore" (*dio*) at 10:5 shows the coordination of thought between the discussion of 10:1–4 and the discussion of Christ's sacrifice in 10:5–10, the inability of the law's sacrificial system being set in stark contrast to the offering of Christ.

B. The Original OT Context. Psalm 40 has two distinct movements, the first ten verses (40:1–11 MT; 39:1–11 LXX) forming an individual thanksgiving song, and 40:11–17 (40:12–18 MT; 39:12–18 LXX) a song of lament. The distinct forms of the two parts, and the duplication of 40:14–18 MT in Ps. 70, apparently pointing to those verses' circulation as an independent psalm, have led a number of scholars to suggest that two distinct psalms have been made into one (e.g., Kraus 1993a: 423–24). Craigie (1983), however, disputes this based, in light of similar dynamics in Ps. 27, on the psalm's language and form. He notes that the language in the two parts of Ps. 40 "is intimately interrelated." Formally, the two parts form a portion of a liturgy, according to Craigie (1983: 314), and the distinction between the two parts can be explained on the basis of progression in that liturgy. This liturgy may be read as a "royal liturgy of supplication" (Eaton 1976: 42–44).

Our quotation from Ps. 40 stems from the "thanksgiving" portion of the psalm (40:1–10). In 40:1–3 (40:2–4 MT) the author expresses thanks to God for deliverance. God heard his cry and raised him from the pit, setting his feet in a firm place (40:1–2). The nature of the peril from which the psalmist was delivered is unclear, perhaps a military threat or an illness, but the result of the deliverance is both the writer's hymn of praise to God and the witness to others of the Lord's trustworthiness (40:3). The psalm continues with an affirmation of the blessedness of the person who places trust in the Lord, for he is a God of wonders and great plans for those who follow him (40:4–5).

If indeed part of a royal liturgy of supplication, the verses quoted at Heb. 10:5–9 (Ps. 40:6–8) may refer to the king's submission to the Lord as part of his royal duties and recall Samuel's pronouncement upon Saul's grand failure (1 Sam. 15:22–23 [so *Midr. Ps.* 40:7]). The appropriate performance of God's worship must be grounded in his faithful service in his role as king. The offering of sacrifices, in and of itself, was not the most basic of God's requirements; rather, commitment to the will of God held the place of primacy. The "digging of the ears" in 40:6 refers to a posture of obedient submission. Craigie (1983: 315) suggests that the backdrop for these verses is the "law of kings," found in Deut. 17:14–20, and the reference to the scroll of the book in 40:7 points to the Deuteronomic law, with its requirements for kings (so *Midr. Ps.* 40:8). In living out

his responsibilities in light of this law, the king has internalized the Lord's instruction (40:8b) and has been outspoken concerning God's faithfulness and salvation in the assembly of the people (40:9–10).

C. Relevant Uses of the OT Reference in Jewish Sources. *2 En.* 45:3 (J) has an allusion to our quotation: "Does the Lord demand bread or lamps or sheep or oxen or any kind of sacrifices at all? That is nothing, but he [God] demands pure hearts, and by means of all those things he tests people's hearts." The context speaks of worship that is acceptable to God. If a person offers an oblation appropriately or multiplies lamps before the Lord, these acts are blessed (45:1–2). However, foundational to true worship is a pure heart, and this is reckoned above the offering of sacrifices (45:3). The reference to the "heart" alludes to Ps. 40:8b, a part of the passage left off by the author of Hebrews.

The Targum on the psalm ties it directly to observance of Torah, the "coming" (40:8 MT [40:7 ET]) having to do with entering eternal life on the basis of focus on the scroll of the Torah. The "scroll" of the psalm is also interpreted in the Talmud as referring to the Torah, in a discussion concerning the writing of scrolls (*b. Git.* 60a). The question is raised of whether Torah should be transmitted on one scroll or on separate scrolls. Rabbi Johanan, in the name of Rabbi Bana'ah, quoting Ps. 40:8 MT (40:7 ET), suggests that it can be written on separate scrolls. His dialogue partner replies that the reference to the scroll in the psalm refers to a single scroll. In *b. Yebam.* 77a, in a discussion of whether Ammonite and Moabite women may be permitted to marry into the congregation of Israel, the question is asked, "What was meant by the Scriptural text *Then said I: 'Lo, I am come with the roll of a book which is prescribed for me'*?" The explanation is given that David said that he thought he had come only now to his kingship and did not know that the Pentateuch had spoken about him. The Talmud then brings together two texts referring to "finding": Gen. 19:15, which refers to the two daughters of Lot from whom Ammon and Moab descended, and Ps. 89:21 MT (89:20 ET), which speaks of David.

Beyond these references, Jdt. 16:16 seems to be cast in the direction that love is greater than cultic sacrifices, and Sirach suggests that good works serve as acceptable sacrifices before God (Sir. 34:18–35:12). After the destruction of the temple, the rabbis worked out a system of social practices and rituals that they understood to replace the offering of sacrifices (Neusner and Green 1999: 540).

D. The Textual Background. It is possible that the Hebrew of Ps. 40 has become disordered (Kraus 1993a: 426), yet the LXX translation of the Hebrew parallels the MT in terms of both word meanings and word order. Hebrews quotes the Greek version but introduces four variations. In 10:5c we find *sōma* ("body") rather than the LXX's *ōtia* ("ears" [also in LXX La^G Ga]). Although it is true that LXX B S A have *sōma*, these probably should be read as corrections by scribes wishing to bring the manuscripts in line with Hebrews' quotation. The LXX's singular *holokautōma* ("whole burnt offering" [also in 𝔓^46 D of Hebrews]) has become plural (*holokautōmata*) in 10:6. Also, the aorist active indicative form of *aiteō* ("ask for") in the LXX has been changed in Hebrews to an aorist active indicative form of *eudokeō* ("be pleased"). The text at this point in the LXX, however, presents various options: B has *ētēsas*, S R *L'' A'* have *ezētēsas*, 55 has *ēthelēsas*, and Bo 2013' have *ēudokēsas*. McCullough (1971: 83) suggests that *eudokēsas* has been introduced under the influence of Ps. 50:18 LXX (51:16 ET). Finally, the LXX's *to thelēma sou* and *ho theos* have become transposed in 10:7c and the remainder of the verse omitted.

Jobes (1992) has offered perhaps the most compelling explanation for these changes, and her suggestion is much in line with the pattern of stylistically motivated adjustments to OT quotations seen in a number of places in Hebrews. Jobes notes that the changes, perhaps with the exception of the transposition at the end of the passage, achieve phonetic assonance between the variant as presented in Hebrews and another word in the quotation. For instance, *sōma de* has phonetic assonance with the final three syllables of *holokautōmata*, both changes to the text being needed to attain this rhetorical effect. The same can be said for the relationship between *ouk ēthelēsas* and *ouk eudokēsas*, which form a phonetic *inclusio* in part of the passage. Finally, assonance is discerned between the *emou* and the *sou* in the

last two lines of the quotation. Jobes notes that the truncation and transposition that occur with the last verse of the quotation (LXX 39:9a) cannot be explained on the basis of phonetic assonance being achieved. She goes on to suggest that the paronomasia crafted by Hebrews' slight changes to the text also focus attention on theological nuances that give the passage distinct christological force. For example, the use of *eudokeō* has a rich tradition in the NT in relation to Christ.

E. How Ps. 40:6–8a Is Understood and Used at Heb. 10:5–9. First, it may be that the author of Hebrews was mindful of Ps. 40:6–8 in part because of its verbal analogy with Jer. 31:33 (38:33 LXX), the key passage bracketing the whole of 8:7–10:18. Both emphasize the internalization of the law, rivet attention with *idou* ("behold"), have something "written," contain references to "sin" (*harmartia*), and refer to God (*theos*). On the first of these points, the author of Hebrews does not present the analogous portion of the psalm (39:9b LXX: *ton nomon sou en mesō tēs koilias mou* ["your law is in the midst of my heart"]) in the quotation, perhaps because it does not fit his immediate purpose, which is to focus on the obedience of Christ.

Second, the author appropriates the psalm as being explicitly fulfilled by Christ "when he comes into the world" (10:5). This language is distinct from that used as an introductory formula in 1:6, where the author employs *oikoumenē* ("world"), which can be interpreted as a reference to the heavenly realm. The use of *kosmos* ("world"), along with the context, suggests here that the incarnation is in mind (Lane 1991: 2:262–63). The psalm presents the posture of obedience and resolute intention to die on the cross, embraced by Christ in the incarnation. This fulfillment, moreover, probably should be seen as a fulfillment of indirect typological prophecy, the experience of David the king being understood as a pointer to the experience of Christ. Some might find an element of double fulfillment here by seizing on the original author's reference to his place in the scroll of the book, but, as we noted, the original context may simply be alluding to the role of kings as mentioned in the law.

Third, Hebrews understands the order of the parts of the quotation to be significant. The first part, speaking of sacrifices and offerings, alludes to the sacrificial system of the old covenant, according to the author. The quotation, taken as the very words of Christ, follows with "Then I said, 'Here I am . . . I have come to do your will.'" The wording here demonstrates that there is a temporal sequence inherent to the psalm, indicating, "He annuls the first to establish the second" (10:9). Using a rabbinic technique by which the literal meaning of a word rivets attention, the author of Hebrews interprets the "then" (*tote*) in the text as indicative of that sequence. God annuls one covenant in order to establish the second (10:9).

F. The Theological Use of the OT Material.
There are at least three primary theological motifs expressed in the quotation of Ps. 40:6–8. First, the use of this psalm reiterates the discontinuity between the old and new covenants. From the perspective of the author of Hebrews, Christ is at the center of the purposes of God, and he has facilitated the replacement of one covenant with another. All the promises of God are "yes" in him (2 Cor. 1:20). The election of Israel would ultimately be fulfilled in Christ (Gal. 3:16). The old covenant, therefore, has been superseded by the new. When Paul speaks of the salvation of the Jewish people (Rom. 11:25–26) and notes that God loves them for the sake of the patriarchs and from the standpoint of God's choice (Rom. 11:28), he means that the proclamation of the gospel is for Jews first, if they will accept it, and then for the Gentiles. The Jews' history with God lays the foundation, but it is not the whole picture of the ultimate Israel, which includes all those incorporated into the new covenant.

Second, and related to the first point, the psalm picks up a theme that exists in both biblical and, as we have seen, extrabiblical Jewish literature. The author uses this quotation to emphasize that the sacrifices of the old system were, by their nature, unsatisfactory in attaining God's ultimate goal of relationship with a covenant people. The inadequacy of the sacrifices in and of themselves finds expression elsewhere in the OT (e.g., 1 Sam. 15:22; Ps. 50:8–11; Isa. 1:10–13; Jer. 7:21–24; Hos. 6:6), pointing rather to heartfelt devotion as the most foundational aspect of true worship. The practice of cultic rituals, apart from heart obedience, misses God's intention for the sacrificial system. "Perfection," on the other hand, when speaking of Christ's work in his new-covenant

people, carries a sense of typological fulfillment in Hebrews, in that the Son of God, revealed in the last days (1:2), has brought to realization those things foreshadowed in the old covenant (10:1, 14) (Silva 1976: 68).

Third, in his passion Christ has submitted himself fully to the Father's will, offering himself perfectly as the new-covenant sacrifice for sins. Hebrews emphasizes the path of obedience in suffering that the Son of God was called to walk and his "perfection"—that is, his completion of the task to which he was assigned and, through his new stage of experience as a human being, his being made fit for the role of high priest (2:10; 5:7–10). Here too we have a typological fulfillment of those things existing as shadow in the old-covenant era, Christ filling out completely God's ultimate intention for the role of high priest and also that of sacrifice. At the heart of his obedience was the task of dying for sins (2:9; 5:7; 9:12–14, 26–28; 10:12, 20, 29; 13:12, 20), the high-priestly offering of his body as the supreme, new-covenant sacrifice.

10:12–13
The fourth allusion to Ps. 110:1 (109:1 LXX) in Hebrews occurs at 10:12–13 (for a fuller discussion, see commentary on Heb. 1:13 above). The original context of this verse portrays an ideal relationship between God and the Davidic monarch, and this relationship serves as the basis for a typological interpretation according to which the psalm is fulfilled in the exaltation of Christ. Specifically, the psalm verse serves here to emphasize the sacrifice of Christ as decisive. Whereas every earthly priest "stands daily" (*hestēken kath' hēmeran*) offering sacrifices over and again (10:11), Christ demonstrates the finality of his sacrifice by sitting down at the right hand of God upon his exaltation (10:12). Now until the end of the age, when his enemies will be placed under his feet, he waits (10:13). The psalm text is used here to underscore that Christ's sacrifice needs no repetition.

10:16–17
(See the fuller treatment of the passage in commentary on Heb. 8:8–12 above.) The author once again quotes Jer. 31:33–34 (38:33–34 LXX) for two reasons. Structurally, the quotation closes an *inclusio* marking 8:3–10:18, a section on the su-

periority of Christ's high-priestly offering. As for his theological purposes at this point, he argues for the decisiveness of Christ's sacrifice, seizing especially on Jer. 31:34, which proclaims of those who belong to the new covenant that God will no longer remember their sins.

The author has introduced several changes to the form of the quotation, when compared to its earlier iteration in 8:7–12. The "to the house of Israel" (*tō oikō Israēl*), quoted at 8:10, has become "to them" (*pros autous*) in 10:16, perhaps to deemphasize national Israel, thus making the promise more universal in our passage at hand. Second, the terms for "minds" (*dianoian* [the accusative singular normally is translated as plural because of the plural possessive pronoun that follows]) and "hearts" (*kardias*) have been inverted. Kistemaker (1961: 41–42) suggests that this construction juxtaposes "heart" and "law," both of which have been shown to be inadequate, the former in chapters 3–4 and the latter in chapters 9–10. Attridge (1989: 281), however, disagrees, though he does admit the possibility that the new order of the words in 10:16–17 may be intended to give prominence to "heart" in anticipation of the following unit (10:22). It may be, however, that the author's inversion of the words is stylistic and serves to highlight the opening and closing of an *inclusio*. The same happens, for instance, with the inversion of "holding fast" and "drawing near" in the book's grand *inclusio*, opened at 4:14–16 and closed at 10:19–25. Further, in place of the preposition *eis* before *tēn dianoian*, as at 8:10, the author has written *epi tēn dianoian* at 10:16, perhaps because the phrase is now positioned with the verb *epigrapsō* ("I will write").

At this point in the quotation the author skips the portion of the Jeremiah passage dealing with God's relationship with the people—he will be their God, and they will know him (Jer. 38:33d–34 LXX)—and moves to the forgiveness of sins. In the earlier version of the quotation there exists a parallelism between "I will be merciful to their wrongdoings" and "I will no longer remember their sins." Yet, at 10:17 the first of these verbal ideas ("I will be merciful" [*hileōs esomai*]) is dropped out, and the "sins" (*hamartiōn*) is in the foreground. Further, the word *adikiais* ("wrongdoings") has now been replaced with *anomiōn* ("lawless acts"), achieving rhythm and assonance

between the *kai tōn hamartiōn autōn* and the *kai tōn anomiōn autōn*. Finally, the aorist subjunctive form of *mimnēskomai* ("remember") has now become a future indicative, making the idea of the decisive eradication of sins more emphatic.

10:27

In perhaps the harshest warning in the book (10:26–31), the writer of Hebrews, alluding to Isa. 26:11, notes that those who reject the truth concerning Christ face terrifying judgment, and that judgment probably should be understood as in the future, on the day of the Lord (10:25, 36–39; 12:26–27). The Greek form of that prophecy reads "and now fire will eat up the enemies" (*kai nyn pyr tous hypenantious edetai*). Examples of the final judgment as a conflagration for the unrighteous are found elsewhere in the OT literature (Isa. 66:15–16, 24; Zeph. 1:18) as well as in eschatological works (*2 Bar.* 48:39–40) and the NT (2 Thess. 1:7–8; Rev. 11:5; 20:14).

10:28

In 10:28–29 the author of Hebrews builds an a fortiori argument. The "lesser" situation, which he assumes that the audience will affirm as true, is stated with an allusion to Deut. 17:2–7. This passage from the Pentateuch announces the penalty for rejecting the Lord's covenant and worshiping other gods, and that penalty is death. That this judgment is to be executed "without mercy" alludes to a second text, Deut. 13:8. Having established the "lesser situation," the author moves to the "greater situation" articulated in 10:29: those who reject the new-covenant sacrifice of the Son of God deserve a punishment even more severe than death.

10:30

A. The Immediate NT Context. The quotation of Deut. 32:35–36 at 10:30 comes at the climax of perhaps the harshest warning in the book. Having concluded the great extended discourse of 4:14–10:25, comparing Christ and his offering to the earthly priesthood and sacrificial system (see G. H. Guthrie 1994: 144), the author presents a stark warning built around an a fortiori argument (*qal wahomer*). The writer cautions that high-handed sin, in this case rejection of the new covenant, has no hope for forgiveness, for Christ's new-covenant sacrifice has done away with all other sacrifices

(10:18, 26). While such a sinner cannot expect forgiveness, he can anticipate terrifying judgment (10:27). The "lesser" situation in the a fortiori argument concerns a person under the old covenant who laid aside the law and therefore was sentenced to death. Pointing to a "greater" situation, the author argues that an even more severe punishment awaits one who has rejected the new covenant, trampling the Son of God, regarding his blood as common, and insulting the Holy Spirit (10:28–29). Now comes the two-part quotation from Deut. 32:35–36, a quotation that reinforces the author's strong statement concerning the severity of the judgment awaiting those who have rejected Christ. The introductory formula is a bit unusual here, the author writing, "we know the one who said" (*oidamen gar ton eiponta*). The statement "suggests that Christians know the character of God who speaks in scripture and who has acted in Christ and that an essential attribute of this God is a negative attitude toward sin" (Attridge 1989: 295). He concludes the warning by saying, "It is frightful to fall into the hands of the living God." In 10:32–39 the writer mitigates the warning by reminding his hearers of their own example of past faithfulness.

B. The Original OT Context. See §B of commentary on Heb. 1:6 above.

C. Relevant Uses of the OT Reference in Jewish Sources. One of the primary ways our quotation is used in broader Jewish literature is to exhort people to leave vengeance to God. Perhaps the earliest of the allusions to Deut. 32:35, *T. Gad* 6:7 is found in a broader passage on loving one's brother. The writer gives the exhortation to "love one another from the heart" (6:3) and forgive. If an adversary refuses even to admit his guilt, he will be brought to repentance. Even if he persists in wickedness, the appropriate course of action is to forgive "and leave vengeance to God." Similarly, *2 En.* 50:4 exhorts the reader not to take vengeance on a neighbor. The longer recension reads, "And if you are able to take vengeance with a hundredfold revenge, do not take vengeance, neither on one who is closest to you nor on one who is distant from you. For the Lord is the one who takes vengeance, and he will be the avenger for you on the day of the great judgment, so that there may be no acts of retribution here from human beings,

but only from the Lord" (the shorter recension carries the same basic meaning).

Philo makes a clear allusion to Deut. 32:35 at *Alleg. Interp.* 3.105. In the context of offering a prayer to God, that he might open good things to us, not evil, Philo writes of God's treasuries. He notes there God has both treasuries of good things and treasuries of evil things, and then he points the reader to "the great song," a common way he refers to Deut. 32. In that song, Philo notes, God says that he has sealed up his treasuries for the day of vengeance, when the foot of the evil "shall have slipped." In the Qumran writings there are faint allusions to God's vindication or judgment, in passages such as 1QS I, 11; X, 18–19, the latter of which notes that God is the sole proprietor of judgment.

In the Talmud *b. 'Abod. Zar.* 2a discusses whether it is appropriate to interact, on any level, with idolaters three days prior to pagan festivals. There is a question whether the correct reading from the Mishnah is *ed* (a metonymy for "festivity") or *'ēd* ("testimony"). In support of the former reading, Deut. 32:35 is quoted, "for the day of their calamity is at hand," the term "calamity" being a translation of the Hebrew *'ēd*. In one of the only quotations of Deut. 32:36, *b. Sanh.* 97a offers a messianic interpretation of the passage. The quotation occurs in a discussion of the Messiah's coming, a discussion that suggests that the son of David will not come until the whole world is converted to the belief system of the heretics. The rabbis taught, "For the Lord shall judge his people, and repent himself of his servants, when he seeth that their power is gone, and there is none shut up, or left." The various interpretations focus on the meaning of "their power is gone," and the passage is offered in support of the idea that denunciators will abound in the world at the great coming.

D. The Textual Background. In the portion of the text quoted from Deut. 32:35, Hebrews' reading parallels that of the MT, syr[p], and *Targum Onqelos* and is also found at Rom. 12:19. However, it is more likely that Hebrews follows an alternate Greek version, perhaps conformed to the Hebrew, rather than depending on the MT (so Lane 1991: 2:295; Ellingworth 1993: 542). The readings of the portion from 32:36 are the same in Hebrews, the LXX, and Ps. 135:14 (134:14 LXX), but Hebrews drops the *hoti* that introduces the clause in the LXX, thus making the quotation read as an assertion of fact.

E. How Deut. 32:35–36 Is Understood and Used Theologically at Heb. 10:30. The quotation of two phrases from Deut. 32:35–36 should be understood as reinforcing the idea that God severely judges those who reject his covenant in Christ. Although 32:36 in its original context could be taken as a reference to the Lord's vindication of those who truly are his (so Christensen 2002: 818), it seems that the author of Hebrews is reading the verse, and specifically the word *krinō* in the LXX version, as a statement of judgment. First, as explained above, the context is one of harsh warning. The two-part quotation is used to reinforce the idea of severe punishment in the warning, and it is followed immediately by the statement in 10:31: "It is frightful to fall into the hands of the living God." Second, when the author uses the connecting phrase *kai palin* ("and again") to join two portions of Scripture, he normally is connecting parallel ideas (1:5; 2:13; 4:5), and the first part of this two-part quotation clearly has God's wrath in view.

Therefore, theologically, the quotation plays a part in the warnings of Hebrews, warnings that call the reader to take with utmost seriousness the consequences of disobedience to God and that emphasize divine judgment (2:1–4; 4:12–13; 6:4–8; 12:25–29). The original context of the passage treats the downfall of the enemies of God and also hints of the salvation of God's people. That context gives, in part, a prophetic word from Moses concerning the future of his people, but the exact time of the fulfillment is unclear, since the prophetic word is stated more in terms of a general promise. However, it is easy to see how this promise would come to be associated with "the day of the Lord." So it is with Hebrews' use, for with this quotation, the author almost certainly has in mind eschatological judgment, similar to the use of the passage at *2 En.* 50:4. In Hebrews, that judgment will come on "the day" (10:25) and will be for those who "shrink back" to their destruction (10:39).

The theme of God's just punishment of the wicked plays a major role in both Testaments of the Bible. People are judged by God in accordance with their works (Job 34:11; Ps. 62:12; Prov. 24:12; Ezek. 7:3, 27), and as in Heb. 2:1–4, there is no escape for those who have turned away from God (Job 11:20; Prov. 1:24–31; Jer. 11:11). Jesus, in his teaching, also emphasized God's judgment (Matt. 5:22; 16:27; 23:14; 25:41–46), and the theme is common in the rest of the NT as well (Rom. 2:3; Col. 3:25; Rev. 14:10–11). Thus, Hebrews is in agreement with earliest Christianity (6:2; 10:28–31) and uses the theme rhetorically to challenge those who are considering abandoning Christ and the Christian community.

10:37–38

A. The Immediate NT Context. The conflated quotation of Isa. 26:20 and Hab. 2:3, found at 10:37–38, occurs in an extended section of hortatory material that spans the final third of Hebrews. Beginning that hortatory section, 10:19–25 serves as an overlapping transition, at once providing a fitting climax to the author's grand discourse on the appointment and superior offering of the heavenly high priest (4:14–5:10; 7:1–10:25) and introducing what follows (G. H. Guthrie 1994: 103). The most severe warning in Hebrews follows the transition of 10:19–25, and the warning describes those who have abandoned the faith as trampling the Son of God, treating his sacrificial blood as unfit for sacrifice, and outraging the Holy Spirit of grace (10:26–31). Having given this sharp warning, the author presents 10:32–39, a passage that mitigates, or softens, the warning by reminding the hearers of their own past resolve to stand with those who were suffering for the faith. Thus, the author uses the congregation itself as a positive example of how to respond to their current struggles. The first three verses of this unit focus on reminding them of a former time when they had such spiritual resolve. In 10:35–39 the author exhorts the hearers to respond appropriately to the current crisis by not throwing away their "confidence" (*parrēsia*), reminding them of their need for endurance in doing the will of God, so that they might receive what God had promised (10:35–36). This exhortation finds reinforcement in the conflated quotation of 10:37–38, placing the hearers' need for endurance in the light of Christ's second coming. The appropriate response to crisis, as defined by the quotation, is to be a righteous person (*dikaios*) who lives by faith (*ek pisteōs*). By contrast, the one who "shrinks back" (*hyposteilētai*) gives God no pleasure.

Two other points can be made about the broader literary context in which the quotation is found. First, this quotation shares two prominent elements with the quotation of Ps. 39:7–9a LXX (40:7–9a MT; 40:6–8a ET), quoted at 10:5–8. Both concern one who is "coming" and that which does not give God pleasure. As we have seen, the quotation from Ps. 39 LXX concerns Christ's first coming, the incarnation, and God's lack of pleasure in the old-covenant sacrifices. Here, Christ's second coming is in view, and it is those who shrink away from perseverance who fail to give God pleasure. These two quotations may form somewhat of a chain, since they link the expositional material on Christ's superior offering with the hortatory material that follows. Second, the author uses the quotation at 10:37–38, which focuses on the righteous living "by faith," in anticipation of the great *exempla* (example list) that follows in chapter 11. There the term that we translate as "by faith" (*pistei*) is used, via anaphora, to drive the point home with relentless repetition: those who please God live *by faith*.

B. The Original OT Context. The quotation in 10:37–38 conflates parts of two OT texts, Isa. 26:20–21 and Hab. 2:3–4, and communicates a contrast between the righteous person, who lives by faith, and the wicked person, who shrinks back from doing the will of God. The two passages probably were brought together by virtue of their common reference to "the coming," the author again working on the principle of verbal analogy. In Isaiah it is the Lord who is coming to punish the wicked. Isaiah 26:20–21 sits within a broad section on God's rule over the nations, a section that extends from 13:1 to 35:10 (Oswalt 1986: 296). More immediately, 26:20–21 follows on the heels of a psalm of dependence (26:7–19) and introduces an oracle on salvation (26:20–27:1) in which the people of God are invited to enter their hiding places for a time while the wrath of God falls upon the wicked of the earth. Thus, the context for Isaiah's part of the quotation orients the proclamation to the day of the Lord, especially as a day of judgment, but also as a day in which the people of God are protected. The context of Isaiah's part of the conflated quotation also mentions resurrection (26:19) and has eschatological overtones (Attridge 1989: 301). It is easy to understand, therefore, why Hebrews has appropri-

ated this passage, understanding it as a prophecy concerning the second coming of Christ, that "day of the Lord" that will come at the end of the age, bringing with it vindication for the true people of God and judgment for God's enemies.

As for the portion of the quotation from Habakkuk, it occurs in a passage on Yahweh's second response in the book (2:2–5) and follows Habakkuk's second lament (1:12–17). The response constitutes the revelation of judgment that will come both to reward the person who lives by faith and to deal with the unrighteous. The Isaiah text, as we noted, carries with it strong overtones of the "end time," since it involves both resurrection and comprehensive judgment and so has been adopted by our author to speak of Christ's second coming. The Habakkuk passage also lends itself to application to that eschatological event, speaking, as it does, of "the end." The vision of Habakkuk points to a future appointed time (2:3) that may seem slow in coming, but its coming is certain. Originally, the prophecy concerned the destruction of Israel at the hands of the Chaldaeans. Therefore, this OT text might be considered to have a double fulfillment, being originally fulfilled in Habakkuk's era but also pointing to an ultimate fulfillment at the second coming of Christ. The passage climaxes with a focus on the contrast between the wicked person, who has a crooked soul, and the righteous person, who lives by faith (2:4). The Hebrew text at 2:4 is difficult, but it may be taken to refer to the fainthearted person who recoils at the vision offered by God. This is the person who is not "right in the eyes of" the Lord (Roberts 1991: 111) or perhaps is "not straight" or "upright" in soul (Andersen 2001: 208–10; Robertson 1990: 177). This person is contrasted with the righteous person, who is faithful (Robertson 1990: 177) or understands the trustworthiness of the vision itself (Andersen 2001: 198).

C. Relevant Uses of the OT Reference in Jewish Sources. Attempts have been made to trace the use of this important passage in pre-Christian and other extracanonical sources (Strobel 1961; Betz 1979: 147). For example, 1QpHab VI, 12b–VIII, 3 presents a pesher on Hab. 2:1–4. In this passage the writer explains that when Habakkuk writes that the vision should be written down on tablets to be read, the prophecy concerned the Teacher of Righteousness, "to whom God made known all the mysterious revelations of his servants the prophets" (1QpHab VII, 4–5). The "appointed time" refers to the last days, which, according to the interpretation, will be a very long time indeed (1QpHab VII, 7–8). The Qumran scroll uses Hab. 2:3–4 quite similarly to the way Hebrews appropriates Habakkuk's prophecy—that is, to encourage the true people of God to remain faithful in spite of the delay of the end's coming. For the Qumran sectarians, those who are faithful are the loyal ones, obedient to the law of God even in the face of a protracted endurance in suffering, and loyalty is interpreted specifically as loyalty "to the Teacher of Righteousness" (1QpHab VIII, 2–3). These loyal ones are contrasted with those who will be condemned in the judgment.

The Habakkuk passage may be alluded to at *4 Ezra* 4:26–27, which emphasizes, for instance, that the age is moving swiftly to its conclusion (4:26). This passage and the reflections that follow concern how long the end will be in coming. Interestingly, in 4:27 the writer notes that the righteous will not receive all of the promises in the current age, which sounds much like a note in Heb. 11:13, 39. These reflections on the eschaton are rejoined at *4 Ezra* 16:35–78.

Also, in *2 Bar.* 54:17, a work from the early second century AD written in response to the destruction of the temple, the writer exhorts, "But now, turn yourselves to destruction, you unrighteous ones who are living now, for you will be visited suddenly, since you have once rejected the understanding of the Most High." This may constitute an allusion to our passage.

As for the rabbinic literature, *b. Sanh.* 97b, which involves a discussion on those who predict the time of the end of the age, addresses how the person of God should live. In line with Hab. 2:4, the proper posture is to "wait." Reflecting on Hab. 2:4, the rabbi notes the most essential principle in living for God: "But it is Habakkuk who came and based them all on one [principle], as it is said, *But the righteous shall live by his faith.*"

D. The Textual Background. The first line of the quotation comes from Isa. 26:20 and the remainder from Hab. 2:3–4 LXX. The *mikron hoson hoson* of 10:37a (Isa. 26:20) translates *kimʿaṭ-regaʿ* ("for a little while") in the Hebrew text.

A number of adjustments are made by the LXX to the Hebrew text of Hab. 2:3–4, which together

make for a different emphasis. In the Hebrew version God exhorts the hearer to be patient, for, in accordance with the vision, the oppressor would be punished in due course, and the righteous person would live by trusting in God. The Greek OT places emphasis on the coming of a deliverer. If he (the deliverer? a person anticipating the fulfillment?) shrinks back, God takes no pleasure in him, but the righteous one lives by faith (or faithfulness).

At 2:3 the translation of the Hebrew infinitive absolute *bōʾ* ("come") with *erchomenos* ("coming") makes the subject of the verbs for "shall come and not tarry" ambiguous, since the masculine participle cannot modify "vision" (*horasis*), which is feminine in form (Attridge 1989: 302).

In 2:4 the Pual perfect form of *ʿpl* ("swell") has been rendered by the Greek text as *hypostellō* ("shrink back"). Bruce (1990: 272) suggests that this might be due to a *Vorlage* that had *ʿulləpâ* ("faints"), which occurs in some manuscripts. The third-person singular masculine suffix on *napšô* has been translated as *hē psychē mou* ("my soul") by the Greek version, and the Hebrew *yāšrâ* ("be straight") has been replaced with the Greek *eudokei*. Finally, the third-person singular masculine suffix added to *ʾĕmûnâ* ("his faithfulness") has been translated rather with the pronoun *mou* ("my").

As for the form of Hebrews' quotation, two changes from the LXX version are most significant. First, Hebrews has added the definite article to the participle *erchomenos*, now reading "the coming one," providing definite messianic connotations to the passage. Second, the last two parts of the quotation are inverted. The inversion makes "my righteous one" (*ho dikaios mou*) the subject of both parts, and in Hebrews' context this is applicable to the person in the Christian community, who either will live by faith or will shrink back (Bruce 1990: 274). In the LXX it is the coming one who might be understood as shrinking back. Also, there is a question of the placement of *mou* ("my"). Hebrews follows the A- and C-group readings of the LXX, placing *mou* after *dikaios* rather than after *pisteōs*, a reading found in LXX B.

E. How Isa. 26:20/Hab. 2:3 Is Understood and Used Theologically at Heb. 10:37–38. As with the quotation of Deut. 32:35–36 at 10:30, the conflated quotation at 10:37–38 serves to reinforce the exhortation that immediately precedes it. The encouraging word "Do not throw away your confidence" first finds its basis in 10:35b–36. The hearers should not cast off this confidence, gained in the superior person and work of Christ (4:16; 10:19), because it leads to "great reward" (*megalē misthapodosia*). That they should not jettison their confidence corresponds to the "need of endurance," so that having conformed to God's will, they might, in time, receive what God has promised. A key component here involves the tension between the "now" and the "not yet," inherent in the author's inaugurated eschatology. This theological orientation, stressing the challenge to faith of living in a present time of tension, reflects a prominent perspective of the NT and has everything to do with the introduction of the conflated quotation at hand. The quotation stresses a posture of waiting and thus the need for living "by faith." Also, this inaugurated eschatology is oriented to a person, for the theology here is overtly messianic. It is the Coming One who will be at hand in "a little while." Correspondingly, "the coming one" finds expression as a messianic title elsewhere in the NT (Matt. 3:11; 11:3; 21:9; Luke 7:19; 19:38; John 1:15, 27; Rev. 1:4). Thus, in Hebrews' appropriation of the quotations from Isaiah and Habakkuk, Christology, eschatology, and Christian living in community are wed.

Of course, Paul quotes Hab. 2:4 twice (Rom. 1:17; Gal. 3:11), omitting the personal pronoun, using the passage with the sense "It is the one who is righteous by faith that will live" (Bruce 1990: 274), thus forming a significant basis for Paul's doctrine of justification by faith. Hebrews, rather than supporting a theological argument on the basis of the Habakkuk passage, as does Paul, has a more hortatory significance here, one that anchors present posture toward God in the future hope of the coming (Attridge 1989: 304). Thus, both Isa. 26:20–21 and Hab. 2:3–4, in their conflated form, are used in 10:36–39 by the author to orient endurance in the Christian faith in both the promises and the warnings associated with Christ's second coming.

11:1–40

Hebrews 11:1–40 may be divided as follows: (1) prologue (11:1–3); (2) movement 1: first examples of faith (11:4–12); (3) interlude: a faith of pilgrims (11:13–16); (4) movement 2: more examples of faith (11:17–31); (5) crescendo and conclusion (11:32–40). The intention is to challenge hearers to live lives of faith as seen in those who by faith had followed God in various aspects of life.

The writer uses two literary devices in his challenge in this chapter. First, he uses the phrase "by faith" (*pistei*) repeatedly, focusing attention on the primacy of faith. Second, he follows the form of an *exempla* (example list), a rhetorical tool employed by ancient authors to challenge hearers to action. This device worked by impressing the audience with overwhelming evidence that a desired pattern of action is best (Cosby 1998a; 1988b; Bulley 1996). Chapter 11 forcefully argues that people of God must be people of faith, even in the face of disheartening difficulties. The general pattern used with each example in the chapter is (1) the term *pistei* ("by faith"), followed by (2) the name of the person used as an example, (3) the action or event by which faith is expressed, and (4) the result. Sometimes the positive result is omitted, as in each of the examples at 11:20–22, and at other times the author includes a concession (the "even though" of 11:11) or a rationale for the act of faith (e.g., 11:10, 19, 23, 26).

Eisenbaum (1997a; 1997b) has sought to demonstrate that the use of the heroes in Heb. 11 was intended to denationalize biblical history. She perceptively raises the question concerning the criteria by which these heroes, and their specific characteristics highlighted, were chosen. Eisenbaum concludes that the key criterion in a profile of these people is their marginalization in relation to the nation of Israel. Thus, they are "transvalued"; that is, the value normally placed on these people as national heroes has been transformed into another value: they were faithful as the marginalized. Thus, the author of Hebrews uses them as good examples to Christians who are struggling with marginalization, giving them a biblical ancestry without national identity.

Since the uses of allusion and the two overt partial quotations in Heb. 11 serve essentially the same function, the material is presented here in tabular form:

Hebrews Reference	OT Allusion (* = quotation)	Description
11:3	Ps. 33:6, 9 (32:6, 9 LXX); Gen. 1	The creation accomplished by the word of God
11:4	Gen. 4:1–10	Abel offered a better sacrifice than Cain, obtained God's witness that his gifts were superior, and spoke via his blood crying from the ground
11:5	Gen. 5:24	Enoch taken by the Lord
11:7	Gen. 6:13–22	Noah prepared an ark
11:8–11	Gen. 12–17	Abraham called to a new land, and Sarah given ability to have a son
11:12	Gen. 22:17*	God promised Abraham numerous descendants
11:17	Gen. 22:1–10	The binding of Isaac
11:18	Gen. 21:12*	The promise of descendants through Isaac
11:20	Gen. 27:27–29	Isaac blessed Jacob and Esau
11:21	Gen. 47:31	Jacob blessed his sons
11:22	Gen. 50:22–26	Joseph foretold the exodus and gave orders concerning his bones
11:23–26	Exod. 2	Moses' parents hid him at birth; when he grew up, he chose solidarity with God's people
11:30–31	Josh. 6	The walls of Jericho fell, and Rahab was protected

12:2

Hebrews' fifth use of Ps. 110:1 (see the allusions to it at 1:3; 8:1; 10:12; and the initial full discussion of its quotation in commentary at Heb. 1:13 above), the occurrence at 12:2, challenges the hearers to focus on Jesus (cf. 3:1), who thought little of the shame of the cross and, enduring, "sat down at the right hand of God." The movement of Christ from heaven to earth, to death and resurrection, to exaltation has been called the "Way of the Son" and is used variously by Hebrews. Here, the culmination in his exaltation provides strong encouragement for those who are suffering under persecution by demonstrating the outcome of Christ's perseverance. Immediately following this allusion, 12:3–4 makes somewhat an argument from a greater situation to a lesser: if Christ endured, shedding his blood, then the hearers, who have not yet resisted to the point of martyrdom, likewise can endure.

12:5b–6

A. The Immediate NT Context. The extensive *exempla* of Heb. 11 confronts the reader with copious evidence that it is the life of faith that pleases

God and is effective spiritually. In response, the believer should cast off sin, which hinders running the race of the Christian life (12:1), and look to Jesus, who endured suffering, scoffed at the shame of the cross, and has been exalted to the right hand of God (12:2). Building on the example of Jesus' endurance, 12:3–17 forms a cohesive unit on the need for endurance in the face of life's challenging circumstances. The author addresses the issue of endurance by utilizing an analogy in which hardship is compared to parental discipline (12:3–11), the metaphor of running a race (12:12–13), and the OT example of Esau, which illustrates the negative effect in the community of faith of a base disregard for the value of one's spiritual inheritance (12:14–17). The disunity hinted at in 12:14–17 seems to stem from friction caused by those who are not remaining faithful to the new covenant. From these various angles, the difficult circumstance of the hearers and their need to persevere are addressed.

More particularly, 12:3–11 develops the analogy of parental discipline in the following ways. At 12:3 a smooth transition is effected from the material on Jesus' endurance in 12:1–2. The verse begins with an admonition to "consider" (*analogizomai*) Jesus, restating the exhortation offered in 12:2a, but then gives the basis for the admonition: "in order that you might not get discouraged by being emotionally worn out." Thus, the author hints at the difficulty of the hearers' present circumstance. Unlike Jesus, however, these believers had yet to shed blood in their struggle (12:4).

In 12:5–6 the author addresses the congregation in the words of the quotation under consideration, Prov. 3:11–12. Their despondence has prompted his gentle rebuke, "Have you forgotten the word of encouragement?" which also could be read as a statement of fact. The author reads the proverb as a word of encouragement (*paraklēsis*) because of its content—the difficulties they are facing are an expression of God's love and acceptance. Also, the address in the proverb, "my son," speaks of intimacy of relationship, mirroring the material in 2:10–18 on the solidarity of Christ with "the sons"—that is, members of the new covenant.

An exposition of the proverb is presented in 12:7–11 and involves three primary movements. First, 12:7–8 suggests that discipline serves to validate the hearers' relationship with God as Father. Second, in 12:9 the author explains proper response to God's discipline. Third, 12:10–11 gives encouragement by pointing out the benefit of discipline: it leads to holiness.

B. The Original OT Context. The first two main sections of Proverbs generally may be divided between the instructional literature of 1:1–9:18 and the so-called sayings, or shorter-sentence literature, of 10:1–22:16 (Waltke and Diewert 1999: 310). Several scholars, moreover, on the basis of various factors, have asserted that 3:1–12, in which the quotation from Heb. 12:5–6 occurs, should be considered a cohesive unit set apart from the surrounding material (Overland 2000: 425–27). First, the material before and after the passage celebrates the great value of wisdom, while 3:1–12 expresses how wisdom might be lived out. Second, throughout the passage the author presents a series of exhortations followed by the bases of these exhortations. Third, the passage is framed by the repetition of *kî* ("for," "because") and the occurrences of *bēn* ("son").

The unit of 3:1–12 begins with a double introduction—an exhortation, from a father to a son, to be committed to sound instruction. Each part of this double introduction is followed by the basis, or an incentive, for doing so. Living by his father's commands, the son might have a long life characterized by peace (3:1–2). Holding tightly to "goodness" and "faithfulness," which should be bound around the neck and written on the heart, will lead to a good reputation (3:3–4). Then follows a series of four exhortations related to Yahweh. The son should "trust the LORD" (3:5–6), "fear the LORD," which corresponds to not being wise in one's own eyes (3:7–8), and "honor the LORD" from his wealth (3:9–10). Obeying each of these admonitions has a corresponding benefit: straight paths (3:6), healing and refreshment (3:8), and full barns and vats (3:10). The passage reaches its climax with the fourth exhortation related to Yahweh: "My son, do not refuse the LORD's discipline or dread his reproof." The basis for this final exhortation is that such reproof expresses Yahweh's love, even as a father's discipline is a manifestation of a father's delight in his son (3:11–12). Thus, the verses quoted by the author of Hebrews serve as the crowning exhortation of the unit in Proverbs.

C. Relevant Uses of the OT Reference in Jewish Sources. First, both the form and the use of the quotation in 12:5–6 are quite similar to that found in Philo, *Prelim. Studies* 175–177. There, Philo touts the benefits and blessings of falling into life's difficulties, even so egregious a difficulty as slavery. In this regard, he uses Esau as an example, but in a way different from Hebrews' use of that OT character at 12:14–17. Rather, he points out that Isaac prayed for the problems that Esau experienced at the hands of his brother, Jacob. Why? Because Isaac knew that it would be good for Esau to live in subjection to a man of temperance! Philo then uses Prov. 3:11–12 to reinforce the idea that difficulties may be a blessing to the one experiencing them. After quoting the passage, Philo remarks that chastisement and correction are shown to be good because they lead to intimacy with God, for there is no closer relationship than that between father and son. The parallels with Heb. 12:5–11 are obvious.

The idea that discipline might be beneficial is found in other works, such as *Pss. Sol.* 3:4; *2 Bar.* 13:9–10. In the former, the righteous person takes the Lord's discipline seriously because righteousness is associated with the Lord's presence; in the latter, the Most High is said to have inflicted his own sons as enemies because of their sin, and their punishment led to forgiveness.

Also, the rabbinic literature uses Prov. 3:11–12 to make a similar point. For example, *b. Ber.* 5a reads,

> If a man sees that painful sufferings visit him, let him examine his conduct. For it is said: *Let us search and try our ways, and return unto the Lord* [Lam. 3:40]. If he examines and finds nothing [objectionable], let him attribute it to the neglect of the study of the Torah. For it is said: *Happy is the man whom Thou chastenest, O Lord, and teachest out of Thy law* [Ps. 94:12]. If he did attribute it [thus], and still did not find [this to be the cause], let him be sure that these are chastenings of love. For it is said: *For whom the Lord loveth He correcteth* [Prov. 3:12].

Further, at *b. Meg.* 31b, Prov. 3:11 is quoted in support of the thought that on days of fasting when Scripture is read, with its blessings and curses, "there must be no break in [the reading of] the curses." Where did this rule come from? "Because Scripture says, *My son, despise not the chastening of the Lord* [Prov. 3:11]." Thus, curses are associated with the Lord's loving discipline.

D. The Textual Background. Hebrews clearly follows the LXX form (LXX B reads *elenchei* instead of *paideuei* in the first line of 3:12), which differs slightly from the MT. The last part of the passage from the MT reads, "as a father [corrects] the son in whom he delights," whereas the LXX reads, "and chastises every son whom he accepts." The MT has *kĕ'āb* ("as a father"), which the LXX understands as a verb, *k'b*, meaning "to cause pain" (in the Hiphil). Bruce (1990: 343) suggests that the LXX "may well represent the original sense," pointing to *Midrash Psalms* on Ps. 94, which makes reference to Prov. 3:12. The only difference between the reading in Hebrews and that of the majority of LXX witnesses is the addition of *mou* ("my") following *huie* ("son"), which, though in line with the Hebrew text, should be read as a natural addition rather than owing to the MT.

E. How Prov. 3:11–12 Is Understood and Used Theologically at Heb. 12:5b–6. As we noted, the author of Hebrews offers the quotation from Prov. 3 as a word of encouragement, which at the same time is a mild rebuke. Therefore, it is rhetorical, but in some ways a milder form of exhortation than we normally find in Hebrews. This may be due to the hearers' weariness of spirit, which serves as a special focus of this section (12:3, 12–13).

The author begins his exposition of the proverb with the exhortation: "With reference to discipline, endure." Outside of Hebrews (12:5, 7, 8, 11), the term translated "discipline" (*paideia*) occurs in the NT only at Eph. 6:4 and 2 Tim. 3:16. The Ephesians passage mentions a father training his children, and the one from 2 Timothy speaks of Scripture as being effective for training in righteousness. Thus, the author of Hebrews uses the proverb to associate the situation of the hearers with God's discipline. In short, with reference to their difficulties, they are to discern the Lord's hand lovingly training them in right character. Croy (1998: 217) demonstrates that the use of *paideia* in 12:4–13, rather than punitive, is a nonpunitive, educational notion that has precedent in both Jewish and Greco-Roman writings and is found especially in the later Stoics. Further, Croy shows that the athletic imagery in the context and nonpunitive forms of moral discipline often were used together as mutually reinforcing concepts.

Rather than evidence of God's inattention, therefore, the difficulties that the hearers face are actually a sign that they are true children of the Father. Assuming that discipline is a normal part of the father-son relationship, the author asks, "What son is not disciplined by his father?" On the contrary, it is the person who does not experience the Lord's rebuke who is marked as illegitimate (12:8).

Using an a fortiori argument (12:9), the author comments that since human fathers are given respect in response to their discipline, God deserves a great deal more. This is all the more true because God "disciplines us for our good," the term *sympheron* meaning "something done for the advantage of another." Specifically, his discipline is given "that we may share in his holiness." The whole context suggests that right parental discipline involves training or instructing in right living. So the discipline of God, when received in the right manner, trains the Christian in right character, purifying the heart. This theme, of course, is found elsewhere in the NT. Paul told the believers at Thessalonica that their sufferings had a dual effect: condemning their persecutors and showing those persecuted to be worthy of the kingdom of God (2 Thess. 1:4–8). Suffering, therefore, can be celebrated because it has a positive effect on the believer's character and relationship with God (James 1:2–4; 1 Pet. 3:14; 4:14).

12:12–13

In 12:12 the author of Hebrews uses an image of weak hands and feeble knees to connote discouragement. The allusion brings to mind several OT passages. For instance, in a context in which Eliphaz the Temanite rebukes Job for his impatience, Job is said to have strengthened the hands of the weak and provided help to those with weak knees (Job 4:3–4). The language of 12:12 finds closer verbal analogy with Sir. 25:23, which also speaks of *cheires pareimenai* (Heb. 12:12 reads *pareimenas cheiras* ["weakened hands"]) and *gonata paralelymena* (Heb. 12:12 reads *paralelymena gonata* ["paralyzed knees"]), but the context, which focuses squarely on the problems associated with an evil wife, is much out of step with the concerns of Hebrews. Much more in line with those concerns is Isa. 35:3, an exhortation to strengthen the limp hands (*cheires aneimenai*) and the paralyzed knees (*gonata paralelymena*). The exhortation occurs in a context that encourages the readers to hope in the salvation of God, looking to his way of holiness as the way of life (35:3–8). This focus matches well with the allusion to Prov. 4:26a that follows in 12:13, which also concerns choosing the right path or way. The proverb reads, *orthas trochias poiei sois posin* ("make straight paths for your feet"), whereas Hebrews reads, with the same meaning but slightly altered form, *trochias orthas poieite tois posin hymōn*.

12:15

The "bitter root" mentioned in 12:15 alludes to Deut. 29:17 LXX (29:18 ET), a warning against rejecting the covenant due to idolatry. The Israelites are challenged, "Lest there is among you a man, or a woman, or a family, or a tribe, whose heart has turned away from the Lord your God, having left to serve these nations' gods; lest there is in you a root springing up in gall and bitterness." In this OT context Moses renews the covenant prior to the crossing into the land of promise. The author of Hebrews uses the imagery to challenge the hearers not to turn away from the superior, new covenant offered by Christ.

12:18–21

Hebrews does not mention Mount Sinai (Horeb) by name in 12:18–21, but clearly the author has in mind this site of the establishment of the old covenant. The descriptive language in this passage stems from the Israelites' encounter with God as told in Exodus and Deuteronomy (e.g., Exod. 19:16–22; 20:18–21; Deut. 4:11–12; 5:23–27). Israel draws near to God in solemn assembly for the covenant to be established (Deut. 4:10–14). The visual and aural elements of the passage (fire, darkness, gloom, storm, trumpet blast, and the voice) communicate awe and distance between God and the people; this mount is a place of terror and is impersonal in nature. The trumpet blast filled the air around Mount Sinai on the morning of the third day at the mountain, growing increasingly loud, causing the hearers to shake with fear (Exod. 19:16, 19; 20:18). God's disembodied voice came from the fire (Deut. 4:12), and the people begged that the voice would stop speaking (Exod. 20:18–19; Deut. 5:23–27). Thus, they rejected the word of God. At 12:20 the author of Hebrews condenses Exod. 19:13, which sug-

gests that anyone, whether human or animal, who touches the mountain will be put to death.

At 12:21 the author concludes the description of the encounter at Sinai by remarking that even Moses was overawed by the event. Rather than drawing this fact from the passages to which he has been alluding thus far, the author seems to allude here to Deut. 9:19a, where Moses confesses, "I feared the LORD's anger and wrath." The context of Deut. 9 addresses the people's idolatry with the golden calf. Yet, one may discern several connections between Deut. 9 and the establishment of the covenant in Deut. 4. Both experiences happen at Mount Sinai (4:11; 9:8), and both focus on the Ten Commandments (4:13; 9:9–11). In both passages the mountain burns with fire (4:11; 9:15), and Moses speaks with the Lord (4:14; 9:19). Thus, the author of Hebrews seems to draw the two passages together on the basis of verbal analogy.

The author of Hebrews uses the images of Sinai, drawn from these OT passages, to communicate the relational inadequacies, indeed the terrible inapproachability of God, under the old-covenant system. The whole scene is dark and frightening, communicating the need to stay away from the mountain and God. This striking picture of the old covenant sets up the beautiful contrast seen in the description of the new-covenant mountain, Zion, in 12:22–24, a mountain of joyful celebration, community, and relational closeness to God himself.

12:26b

A. The Immediate NT Context. God's "speaking" constitutes a major theme for Hebrews, as is seen in the first assertion in the book (1:1–2a), the many introductory formulae using forms of *legō* with which the author introduces his OT quotations (e.g., 1:5, 6, 7, 13), and various exhortations throughout the book (e.g., 3:7; 4:12). The text of 12:18–24, a striking passage contrasting old and new covenants, involves both the terror of the disembodied voice at Sinai (12:19) and the blood of Jesus, which speaks better than the blood of murdered Abel (12:24 [see Gen. 4:10]). This theme continues in 12:25–29, where the author begins the warning by saying, "Be sure that you do not reject the one speaking." This last warning passage of the book (cf. 2:1–4; 4:12–13; 6:4–8; 10:26–31) uses an argument from lesser to greater, moving from the warning spoken at Mount Sinai (i.e., on earth) to God's warning from heaven. In that argument there is a move from the certain fate of those who refused to listen at that old-covenant mountain to those who will not escape if they reject the word of salvation (cf. 2:1–4), and from the shaking of the earth to the shaking of the whole cosmos. What, then, should the response of the hearers be? Since those of the new covenant receive a kingdom that cannot be shaken, even by a shaking of heaven and earth, they should respond with thankfulness and appropriate reverent worship (12:28), for "our God is a devouring fire."

B. The Original OT Context. The book of Haggai presents a series of exhortations to Zerubbabel the son of Shealtiel and to Joshua (LXX: *Iēsous*) the son of Jehozadak the high priest (LXX: *ho hiereus ho megas*), along with the remnant of God's people. They are to rebuild the Lord's temple, both in light of their present difficult situations and in light of God's promised blessings for the future. The book is organized around four messages, marked by *dĕbar-yhwh* (1:3; 2:1; 2:10; 2:20). The first (1:3–15) constitutes an exhortation to build the Lord's house and includes sobering words of warning and the reflection that their current poverty stems from their apathy toward the needed project. In 1:12–15 the people respond obediently to the exhortation (1:12, 14), and God responds with approval (1:13). The second message (2:1–9) presents words of encouragement that speak of God shaking the world. The people are discouraged because the temple does not approach its former glory (2:3), but the Lord is with them (2:4) and his Spirit among them (2:5). Furthermore, he will shake the heavens and earth, sea and dry land—indeed, the nations of the earth, so that the riches of the nations will be used to restore the temple to an even greater state than its former glory (2:6–9). Haggai received a third message (2:10–19) concerning the need for purity in worship of the Lord and the deleterious effect of impurity. Their barrenness and poverty stem from their impurity, which God calls them to abandon. Finally, the fourth message (2:20–23) parallels the second, also proclaiming that God will shake the nations, destroying their power (2:22).

The quotation of Hag. 2:6 at 12:26 comes from the second of these messages in Haggai. God promises to shake heaven and earth in order to advance the glories of the temple and provide encouragement to his people. It is at once a word of encouragement to the covenant people and a word of judgment on the nations, which God will plunder in divine wrath. Some understand this word of prophecy, with its shaking of the heavens and earth, of sea and dry land, to be figurative, referring to the restoration of the glory of the nation and its temple. Others suggest that the prophecy should be understood to refer to the end times, for the aspects of this cataclysm are universal in scope, indeed cosmic in scope, covering all the nations and all of creation. The language well serves Hebrews' appropriation of the passage to refer to Christ's second coming as a cataclysmic event, and this use of the passage as referring to the end times has consonance with similar interpretations in broader Judaism.

C. Relevant Uses of the OT Reference in Jewish Sources. The book of *2 Baruch*, written in response to the destruction of the second temple, capitalizes on the encouragement of Haggai, taking the prophet's words to have eschatological import. In chapter 2 we read, "You, however, if you prepare your minds to sow into them the fruits of the law, he shall protect you in the time in which the Mighty One shall shake the entire creation. For after a short time, the building of Zion will be shaken in order that it will be rebuilt. That building will not remain; but it will again be uprooted after some time and will remain desolate for a time. And after that it is necessary that it will be renewed in glory and that it will be perfected into eternity" (*2 Bar.* 32:1–4). Here Baruch gives encouragement in two directions. First, as with Haggai, the people are encouraged to keep the law, and this obedience is key to their protection when the entire creation is shaken. Second, whereas in Hebrews it is the kingdom that will not be shaken, Baruch suggests that the temple will be renewed and in fact will be an eternal structure.

The rabbinic literature also utilizes the OT passage, tying it to the end of the world. At *b. Sanh.* 97b Rabbi Akiba is said to have expounded upon "Yet once, it is a little while, and I will shake the heavens, and the earth." He explained, "But the first dynasty [the Hasmonean] shall last seventy years, the second [the Herodian] fifty-two, and the reign of Bar Koziba two and a half years." Rabbi Akiba's words are given in the context of an end-time discussion of how long the world will last. In this same type of context occurs a quotation of Hab. 2:3 at Heb. 10:37.

D. The Textual Background. Hebrews quotes only a part of Hag. 2:6, the part dealing with the shaking of heaven and earth. The Hebrew form of the text has the concept normally translated as "a little while" (*mĕ'aṭ*), found neither in the LXX nor in Hebrews' quotation, and the concept is found also in the Targum on the verse. Further, the term for "heavens" is plural in the MT and the Targum rather than singular as in the Greek versions. The change when moving from the LXX to the quotation in Hebrews has to do with a transposition of the portions of the verse involving heaven and earth and the addition of *ou monon . . . alla* [*kai*] ("not only . . . but also"). The *kai*, already present in the verse with conjunctive force, has been brought into a new, adjunctive sense by its juxtaposition with *alla*.

E. How Hag. 2:6 is Understood and Used at Heb. 12:26. Here we have a rare occurrence in Hebrews of what has been called "implicit midrash" (Ellis 1978: 152–57), by which an interpretation is woven into the form of the text quotation. As we noted, in Hebrews two parts of the Haggai text are transposed, with the shaking of the earth placed before the shaking of heaven. The author does this to bring out the significance of the text for his present discussion. He has already discussed the shaking of the earth in relation to the Sinai theophany (12:18–21; 26a): "And his voice shook the earth then." Thus, the shaking of the earth from the Haggai text is presented first by our author because he understands it as referring to an event that he has already discussed and one that is foundational for the rhetoric of his current exhortation. Moving from a focus on "earth" to a focus on "heaven," he warns that the coming "shaking" will be cosmic in scope.

In 12:25–29 we also encounter again the author's often-used technique of argument "from lesser to greater" (*qal wahomer*). The "lesser" situation in this passage is that of the people of the wilderness generation, who, refusing to listen to God's word, were judged (3:7–19). That God "warned them on earth" is a reference to his manifestation at Mount Sinai.

Now the author moves to the "greater" situation, which, according to the logic of the rabbinic technique, has greater implications for the hearers. The central point involves their receptivity to the voice of God from heaven. If those at Mount Sinai were judged by God for rejecting his word, then judgment is even more certain for those who reject the word of salvation (2:1–3) received in the era of the new covenant. The author quotes Hag. 2:6, weaving an interpretation into his quotation to speak of the coming judgment. The shaking of the earth ties the warning back to the terrible confrontation at Sinai. Thus, at the Sinai event God "shook the earth," but he has promised a cosmic "shaking" for the future, a shaking that will include the heavens. For the author, the "once more" (*eti hapax*) of the quotation points to the cataclysmic judgment coming on the earth at the end of the age, when Christ returns. In light of that coming event, believers should reverently serve God.

F. The Theological Use of the OT Material. Conceptions of cataclysmic manifestations at the end of the age varied somewhat in Second Temple Judaism. The book of 2 Peter, for instance, builds on the disaster of the flood as prefiguring the destruction, or perhaps transformation, of the world at the day of judgment by use of fire (2 Pet. 3:6–7)—a thought that occurs also in Josephus (*Ant.* 1.70 [cf. *L.A.E.* 49:3]) and apocalyptic texts (*Sib. Or.* 2:187–213; 3:83–92; *1 En.* 1:6–9; 2 Esd. 13:10–11) but is unique in the NT. In the OT certain passages point to the use of fire in dealing with the enemies of God (e.g., Isa. 30:30; Nah. 1:6; Zeph. 1:18), and this thought is echoed in the NT in passages such as 2 Thess. 1:7, which asserts that when Jesus is revealed from heaven, he will come with his angels "in flaming fire" (cf. Rev. 8:5–7). Indeed, Peter, on the day of Pentecost, quoted Joel 2 to speak of salvation, but also of cosmic disturbances associated with the day of the Lord, including "fire" (Acts 2:19).

Another strand of tradition, however, points to the shaking of the earth at its end, and it is this manifestation on which Hebrews capitalizes. At Matt. 24:29 and its parallels (Mark 13:25; Luke 21:26), Jesus quotes Isa. 13:10 and then alludes, perhaps, to Isa. 13:13, which refers to the shaking of the heavens and the earth. Jesus says, "And the powers of the heavens will be shaken." Hebrews, as we noted, plays off the shaking of the earth at Mount Sinai. Although God's presence as causing the earth to shake is not mentioned in the Exodus or Deuteronomy accounts that lie behind Heb. 12:18–21, other passages do mention this manifestation (e.g., Judg. 5:5; Ps. 68:8; 77:18). The author of Hebrews then builds on this terrestrial shaking to move to a cosmic shaking that he finds in Hag. 2:6. The theological framework to which this belief relates has to do with the present order of the creation passing away, which is found in texts such 1 Cor. 7:31; 1 John 2:8; Rev. 21:1 and serves an important foundational belief for NT hortatory material. If the world is going to experience such a dramatic change, one needs to be ready for that change. The way to be ready is to be in right relationship to Jesus, for he is the one who laid the earth's foundations in the beginning and who, in contrast to the creation, which grows old and will be packed away by Christ himself, will remain (1:10–12). Thus, he and his kingdom, and those who are of the kingdom, transcend the present state of the created order. Those who are of the world will perish with it at its shaking when Christ returns.

13:5

A. The Immediate NT Context. The context for the tandem quotations at 13:5–6 is a series of practical exhortations on how the hearers might serve God. The first five of these (13:1–6) provide common general guidelines that would have been familiar throughout the churches of the first century. The seven that fill out the balance of the section (13:7–19) concern the community's relationship with their leaders. The more immediate context involves the exhortation not to be a lover of money, but rather to be content. In several treatments of NT ethics sexual immorality and covetousness are treated in tandem, as they are in 13:4–6 (2 Cor. 5:10–11; Eph. 4:19; 1 Thess. 4:3–6). Both sins involve a gross self-centeredness that inherently disparages God's care and provision. It is probable that the love of money, treated in 13:5, stems from the atmosphere of persecution in which the hearers find themselves, since such persecution can involve loss of property or even basic needs (10:32–36; 13:3). Thus, the author of Hebrews uses the quotations as words of encouragement, reinforcing his exhortation to contentment. Contentment is found in the presence and help of the Lord, as is confidence. People cannot harm those whose helper is the Lord.

B. The Original OT Context. The passage from Genesis presents God's assurance to Jacob at Bethel, given in the dream about the ladder. God assured Jacob that he would not leave him until he had accomplished all of his word to the patriarch. The context of Deut. 31:6, on the other hand, comes just after the covenant ceremony of 27:1–30:20 and just before the Song of Moses (on Deut. 32, see §B of commentary on Heb. 1:6 above). Deuteronomy 31 is a word of encouragement about crossing into the land of promise. Moses gives encouragement first to the people (31:6) and then to Joshua, to whom he is handing over leadership (31:8). The people should not be afraid, because the Lord is with them and will not abandon them.

Psalm 118 (117 LXX), on the other hand, from the Hallel (Pss. 113–118), deals with confidence in the face of persecution and was "the Passover psalm par excellence" (Lane 1991: 2:520). The first four verses of the psalm repeat the confession that God "is good and his mercy endures forever," grounding the believer's hope in the character of God. Then the psalm moves to testimony as a basis for confidence. The psalmist recalls how, in affliction, he called on the Lord and was delivered (118:5). This testimony serves as the basis for our focal passage, 117:6 LXX: "The Lord is my helper, and I will not fear what man will do to me." Following that verse, the psalmist continues with a confession that the Lord's help is to be desired above the help of people. Because of the Lord's help, enemies are overthrown (118:7). One should trust, or place hope, in the Lord rather than in people (118:8–9). Even when a believer is hemmed in on all sides, seemingly in an overwhelming situation, victory may be found "in the name of the Lord" (118:10–12), for he is the God of great deliverance (118:13–16). The broader context also contains the striking messianic text of 118:22: "The stone that the builders rejected has become the main cornerstone" (cf. Matt. 21:42 pars.; Acts 4:11; 1 Pet. 2:7).

C. The Textual Background. Although the quotation from Ps. 117:6 LXX at 13:6 matches exactly the LXX form, the quotation in the previous verse presents a challenge.

Approximate parallels to the first of the quotations (13:5) are found at Gen. 28:15; Deut. 31:6,

8; 1 Chron. 28:20; Josh. 1:5 (see Lane 1991: 2:519).

Heb. 13:5	ou mē se anō oud' ou mē se enkatalipō
Gen. 28:15c	ou mē se enkatalipō
Deut. 31:6	ou mē se anē oute mē se enkatalipē
Deut. 31:8	ouk anēsei se oude mē enkatalipē se
1 Chron. 28:20	ouk anēsei se kai ou mē se enkatalipē
Josh. 1:5	ouk enkataleipsō se oude hyperopsomai se

Yet, none of these matches exactly the form of the quotation found in Hebrews. The exact form found in Hebrews, however, does occur in Philo. The text is used by the Alexandrian to speak to the dangers of having a liberated soul. It is, rather, the lovers of discipline who are blessed by God and whom God will never abandon. Several options have been put forward regarding the source of the text as it stands in Hebrews and vis-à-vis Philo. It may be that the author of Hebrews takes his form from Philo, but the text is used quite differently by each author. More likely is the suggestion that Hebrews and Philo both depend on a form (perhaps from the Alexandrian synagogues) of Deut. 31:6 LXX that is no longer extant (Michel 1986: 483–84; Schröger 1968: 194–96). Katz (1958: 223) suggested that this form started with Gen. 28:15 and then was enlarged by interaction with Deut. 31:6, 8. Others have proposed Josh. 1:5 as the foundational text, which was changed under the influence of Deut. 31:8 (Montefiore 1964: 240–41; Williamson 1970: 570). All in all, it seems likely that Hebrews and Philo both depend on a common text form that in some way conflates the texts from Genesis and Deuteronomy.

D. How Gen. 28:15c/Deut. 31:6, 8; Ps. 118:6 Is Understood and Used Theologically at Heb. 13:5. Earlier in Hebrews great assurance was offered on the basis of God's oath-keeping. It is God's word that has exalted Jesus (1:5, 8–13) and appointed him as superior high priest (5:5–6). This appointment offers believers the greatest possible security, for Ps. 110:4 says, "The LORD has sworn and will not change his mind," a fact made much of by the author (7:20–25). Indeed, we have hope, procured by God's oath, as a sure anchor to the soul, for it enters behind the veil (6:17–20). The quotation at 13:5, in which God says, "I will never leave you, nor will I ever abandon you," offers another promise of God, which the author has appropriated as a word of assurance to new-covenant believers. The contexts of the

approximations of this quotation in Genesis and Deuteronomy (see §C above) are instructive. In Gen. 28 Jacob is sent out from his father's house to find a wife among his mother's people. At Bethel he has his dream of the ladder, and God speaks to him. God promises him the land and that he will have innumerable descendants, and in those descendants all the families of the earth will be blessed. Then God promises Jacob that he will be with him (28:15), and this is the climax of the dream. Jacob, in a position of uncertainty, is offered assurance. In Deut. 31, in the context of God's covenant faithfulness, the people of Israel are challenged to be strong and full of courage and not to fear the people of the land that they are about to enter. They and Joshua are given strong encouragement that the Lord is with them and will by no means abandon them. Thus, in the face of uncertainty they are offered assurance tied to the certain presence of the Lord. So, the first hearers of Hebrews, in their persecution, their position of uncertainty, are offered hope along the same lines. God will not abandon them to their difficulties.

This word of assurance is answered with a confident confession in the words of Ps. 117:6 LXX, and this confession, that God is a helper to his people, is echoed throughout the OT and especially the psalms. God gave help at the exodus (Exod. 15:2). In a final blessing Moses reminded the people that they were unique, for they had been saved by the Lord their helper (Deut. 33:29). In the songs of Israel God is praised as a generous helper to people in a variety of difficult situations (e.g., Ps. 9:9; 18:2; 27:9; 28:7; 30:10; 33:20; 40:17; 59:17; 62:8; 63:7; 70:5). In these songs confidence is expressed in the character of God. He will be true to his word not to abandon or forsake his people. Therefore, there is no reason to fear what humans can do. God's presence as helper negates the worst that people can put forward.

13:11

Leviticus 16:27 directs that the bodies of the Day of Atonement sacrifices, including the hides, the flesh, and their waste, be taken outside the camp and burned. This practice was associated with other sacrifices (4:12, 21; 9:11; Exod. 29:14). The author of Hebrews draws an analogy between the Day of Atonement sacrifices of the old covenant and Jesus' new-covenant sacrifice for sins, which he accomplished "outside the gate" of Jerusalem (13:12).

Bibliography

Abegg, M. G., P. W. Flint, and E. C. Ulrich. 1999. *The Dead Sea Scrolls Bible: The Oldest Known Bible.* San Francisco: HarperSanFrancisco.

Allen, L. C. 1982. "Psalm 45:7–8 (6–7) in Old and New Testament Settings." Pages 220–42 in *Christ the Lord: Studies in Christology Presented to Donald Guthrie.* Edited by H. H. Rowdon. Leicester: Inter-Varsity.

———. 2002. *Psalms 101–150, Revised.* 2nd ed. WBC 21. Nashville: Nelson.

Andersen, F. I. 2001. *Habakkuk.* AB 25. New York: Doubleday.

Anderson, B. W. 2000. *Out of the Depths: The Psalms Speak for Us Today.* 3rd ed. Louisville: Westminster John Knox.

Attridge, H. W. 1989. *The Epistle to the Hebrews.* Hermeneia. Philadelphia: Fortress.

Barrett, C. K. 1956. "The Eschatology of the Epistle to the Hebrews." Pages 363–93 in *The Background of the New Testament and Its Eschatology.* Edited by W. D. Davies and D. Daube. Cambridge: Cambridge University Press.

Barth, M. 1962. "The Old Testament in Hebrews: An Essay in Biblical Hermeneutics." Pages 65–78 in *Issues in New Testament Interpretation.* Edited by W. Klassen and G. F. Snyder. New York: Harper & Row.

Bateman, H. 1997. *Early Jewish Hermeneutics and Hebrews 1:5–13: The Impact of Early Jewish Exegesis on the Interpretation of a Significant New Testament Passage.* AUS 7/193. New York: Lang.

Beale, G. K. 1994. "Did Jesus and His Followers Preach the Right Doctrine from the Wrong Texts? An Examination of the Presuppositions of Jesus' and the Apostles' Exegetical Method." Pages 387–404 in *The Right Doctrine from the Wrong Texts? Essays on the Use of the Old Testament in the New.* Edited by G. K. Beale. Grand Rapids: Baker Academic.

Betz, H. D. 1979. *Galatians: A Commentary on Paul's Letter to the Churches in Galatia.* Hermeneia. Philadelphia: Fortress.

Bleek, F. 1828. *Der Brief an die Hebräer.* Berlin: Dümmler.

Bratcher, R. G. 1969. *Old Testament Quotations in the New Testament.* HT 3. London: United Bible Societies.

Bruce, F. F. 1990. *The Epistle to the Hebrews.* Rev. ed. NICNT. Grand Rapids: Eerdmans.

Brunert, G. 1996. *Psalm 102 im Kontext des Vierten Psalmenbuches.* SBB 30. Stuttgart: Katholisches Bibelwerk.

Bulley, A. D. 1996. "Death and Rhetoric in the Hebrews 'Hymn to Faith.'" *SR* 25: 409–23.

Caird, G. B. 1959. "The Exegetical Method of the Epistle to the Hebrews." *CJT* 5: 44–51.

Carter, W. 2000. "Evoking Isaiah: Matthean Soteriology and an Intertextual Reading of Isaiah 7–9 and Matthew 1:23 and 4:15–16." *JBL* 119: 503–20.

Charlesworth, J. H. 1992. *Jesus and the Dead Sea Scrolls.* New York: Doubleday.

Christensen, D. L. 2002. *Deuteronomy 21:10–34:12.* WBC 6B. Nashville: Nelson.

Clements, R. E. 1985. "The Use of the Old Testament in Hebrews." *SwJT* 28: 36–45.

Cobrink, H. 1971. "Some Thoughts on the OT Citations in the Epistle to the Hebrews." *Neot* 5: 22–36.

Cody, A. 1960. *Heavenly Sanctuary and Liturgy in the Epistle to the Hebrews: The Achievement of Salvation in the Epistle's Perspective.* St. Meinrad, IN: Grail Publications.

Cohn-Sherbok, D. 1982. "Paul and Rabbinic Exegesis." *SJT* 35: 117–32.

Cook, E. M. 2001. "The Psalms Targum: An English Translation." No pages. Cited 3 January 2007. Online: http://www.drsbrady.com/ntcs/pss/tg_ps_index.htm.

Cosby, M. R. 1988a. *The Rhetorical Composition and Function of Hebrews 11 in the Light of Example Lists in Antiquity.* Macon, GA: Mercer University Press.

———. 1988b. "The Rhetorical Composition of Hebrews 11." *JBL* 107: 257–73.

Couroyer, B. 1971. "Dieu ou roi? Le vocative dans le Psaume XLV (vv. 1–9)." *RB* 78: 233–41.

Craigie, P. C. 1974. "The Comparison of Hebrew Poetry: Psalm 104 in the Light of Egyptian and Ugaritic Poetry." *Semitics* 4: 10–21.

———. 1983. *Psalms 1–50.* WBC 19. Waco: Word.

Croy, N. C. 1998. *Endurance in Suffering: Hebrews 12.1–13 in Its Rhetorical, Religious, and Philosophical Context.* SNTSMS 98. Cambridge: Cambridge University Press.

Dahood, M. 1966–1970. *Psalms.* 3 vols. AB 16, 17, 17A. Garden City, NY: Doubleday.

D'Angelo, M. R. 1979. *Moses in the Letter to the Hebrews.* SBLDS 42. Missoula, MT: Scholars Press.

DeSilva, D. A. 2000. *Perseverance in Gratitude: A Socio-Rhetorical Commentary on the Epistle "To the Hebrews."* Grand Rapids: Eerdmans.

Dodd, C. H. 1961. *According to the Scriptures: The Sub-Structure of New Testament Theology.* London: Nisbet.

Eaton, J. H. 1976. *Kingship and the Psalms.* Naperville, IL: Allenson.

Eisenbaum, P. 1997a. "Heroes and History in Hebrews 11." Pages 380–96 in *Early Christian Interpretation of the Scriptures of Israel: Investigations and Proposals.* Edited by C. A. Evans and J. A. Sanders. JSNTSup 148. Sheffield: Sheffield Academic Press.

———. 1997b. *The Jewish Heroes of Christian History: Hebrews 11 in Literary Context.* SBLDS 156. Atlanta: Scholars Press.

Ellingworth, P. 1977. "The Old Testament in Hebrews: Exegesis, Method and Hermeneutics." PhD diss., University of Aberdeen.

———. 1993. *The Epistle to the Hebrews: A Commentary on the Greek Text.* NIGTC. Grand Rapids: Eerdmans; Carlisle: Paternoster.

Ellis, E. E. 1978. *Prophesy and Hermeneutic in Early Christianity: New Testament Essays.* Grand Rapids: Eerdmans.

———. 1981. *Paul's Use of the Old Testament.* Grand Rapids: Baker Academic.

Emerton, J. A. 1968. "Syntactical Problem of Psalm 45:7." *JSS* 13: 58–63.

Enns, P. 1997. "The Interpretation of Psalm 95 in Hebrews 3.1–4:13." Pages 352–63 in *Early Christian Interpretation of the Scriptures of Israel: Investigations and Proposals.* Edited by C. A. Evans and J. A. Sanders. JSNTSup 148. Sheffield: Sheffield Academic Press.

Evans, C. A. 1992. *Noncanonical Writings and New Testament Interpretation.* Peabody, MA: Hendrickson.

Filson, F. 1967. *"Yesterday": A Study of Hebrews in Light of Chapter 13.* SBT 4. Naperville, IL: Allenson.

Fitzmyer, J. A. 1963. "'Now This Melchizedek' (Heb. 7:1)." *CBQ* 25: 305–21.

———. 2000. *The Dead Sea Scrolls and Christian Origins*. SDSSRL. Grand Rapids: Eerdmans.

France, R. T. 1996. "The Writer of Hebrews as a Biblical Expositor." *TynBul* 47: 245–76.

Georghita, R. 2003. *The Role of the Septuagint in Hebrews: An Investigation of Its Influence with Special Consideration to the Use of Hab. 2:3–4 in Heb. 10:37–38*. WUNT. Tübingen: Mohr Siebeck.

Grässer, E. 1990–1997. *An die Hebräer*. 3 vols. EKKNT 17/1–3. Braunschweig: Benzinger; Neukirchen-Vluyn: Neukirchener Verlag.

Guthrie, D. 1983. *The Letter to the Hebrews*. TNTC. Grand Rapids: Eerdmans; Leicester: Inter-Varsity.

Guthrie, G. H. 1994. *The Structure of Hebrews: A Text-Linguistic Analysis*. NovTSup 73. Leiden: Brill.

———. 1997. "Old Testament in Hebrews." *DLNTD* 841–50.

———. 1998. *Hebrews*. NIVAC. Grand Rapids: Zondervan.

———. 2003. "Hebrews' Use of the Old Testament: Recent Trends in Research." *CBR* 1 (2003): 271–94.

———. 2004. "Hebrews in Its First Century Contexts: Recent Research." Pages 414–43 in *The Face of New Testament Studies*. Edited by G. Osborne and S. McKnight. Grand Rapids: Baker Academic.

Hamilton, V. P. 1995. *The Book of Genesis*. NICOT. Grand Rapids: Eerdmans.

Hanson, R. P. C. 2002. *Allegory and Event: A Study of the Sources and Significance of Origen's Interpretation of Scripture*. Louisville: Westminster John Knox.

Harris, M. J. 1984. "The Translation of *Elohim* in Psalm 45:7–8." *TynBul* 35: 65–89.

———. 1985. "The Translation and Significance of *ho theos* in Hebrews 1:8–9." *TynBul* 36: 129–62.

———. 1992. *Jesus as God: The New Testament Use of Theos in Reference to Jesus*. Grand Rapids: Baker Academic.

Hay, D. M. 1973. *Glory at the Right Hand: Psalm 110 in Early Christianity*. SBLMS 18. Nashville: Abingdon.

Hays, R. B. 1989. *Echoes of Scripture in the Letters of Paul*. New Haven: Yale University Press.

Hofius, O. 1970. *Katapausis: Die Vorstellung vom endzeitlichen Ruheort im Hebräerbrief*. WUNT 11. Tübingen: Mohr Siebeck.

Howard, G. 1968. "Hebrews and the OT Quotations," *NovT* 10: 208–16.

Hughes, G. 1979. *Hebrews and Hermeneutics: The Epistle to the Hebrews as a New Testament Example of Biblical Interpretation*. SNTSMS 36. Cambridge: Cambridge University Press.

Hughes, P. E. 1977. *A Commentary on the Epistle to the Hebrews*. Grand Rapids: Eerdmans.

Hurst, L. 1990. *The Epistle to the Hebrews: Its Background of Thought*. SNTSMS 65. Cambridge: Cambridge University Press.

Jobes, K. H. 1992. "The Function of Paronomasia in Hebrews 10.5–7." *TJ* 13: 181–91.

Jobes, K. H., and M. Silva. 2000. *Invitation to the Septuagint*. Grand Rapids: Baker Academic.

Katz, P. 1958. "The Quotations from Deuteronomy in Hebrews." *ZNW* 49: 213–23.

Keown, G. L., P. J. Scalise, and T. G. Smothers. 1995. *Jeremiah 26–52*. WBC 27. Waco: Word.

Kirkpatrick, A. F. 1917. *The Book of Psalms*. CBSC. Cambridge: Cambridge University Press.

Kistemaker, S. 1961. *The Psalm Citations in the Epistle to the Hebrews*. Amsterdam: W. G. van Soest.

Koester, C. R. 1994. "The Epistle to the Hebrews in Recent Study." *CR* 2: 123–45.

———. 2001. *Hebrews*. AB 36. New York: Doubleday.

Kraus, H.-J. 1993a. *Psalms 1–59*. CC. Minneapolis: Fortress.

———. 1993b. *Psalms 60–150*. CC. Minneapolis: Fortress.

Laansma, J. 1997. *"I Will Give You Rest": The "Rest" Motif in the New Testament with Special Reference to Mt 11 and Heb 3–4*. WUNT 2/98. Tübingen: Mohr Siebeck.

Lane, W. L. 1991. *Hebrews*. 2 vols. WBC 47A, 47B. Dallas: Word.

Leschert, D. 1994. *Hermeneutical Foundations of Hebrews: A Study in the Validity of the Epistle's Interpretation of Some Core Citations from the Psalms*. NABPRD 10. Lewiston, NY: Mellen.

Lincoln, A. T. 1982. "Sabbath, Rest, and Eschatology in the New Testament." Pages 205–20 in *From Sabbath to Lord's Day: A Biblical, Historical, and Theological Investigation*. Edited by D. A. Carson. Grand Rapids: Zondervan.

Lincoln, L. 1999. "Translating Hebrews 9:15–22 in Its Hebraic Context." *JOTT* 12: 1–29.

Lindars, B. 1991. *The Theology of the Letter to the Hebrews*. NTT. Cambridge: Cambridge University Press.

Loader, W. R. G. 1977–1978. "Christ at the Right Hand: Ps. cx.1 in the New Testament." *NTS* 24: 199–217.

Longenecker, R. N. 1975. *Biblical Exegesis in the Apostolic Period*. Grand Rapids: Eerdmans.

Manson, T. W. 1949–1950. "The Problem of the Epistle to the Hebrews." *BJRL* 32: 1–17.

Martin, R. P. 1967. *Carmen Christi: Philippians ii.5–11 in Recent Interpretation and in the Setting of Early Christian Worship*. London: Cambridge University Press.

Mathewson, D. 1999. "Reading Heb 6:4–6 in Light of the Old Testament." *WTJ* 61: 209–25.

Mays, J. L. 1994. *Psalms*. IBC. Louisville: John Knox.

McCullough, J. C. 1971. "Hebrews and the Old Testament: A Comparison of the Use Which the Author of the Epistle to the Hebrews Makes of the Old Testament with the Use Made by Other Writers of His Day." PhD diss., University of Belfast.

———. 1979–1980. "The Old Testament Quotations in Hebrews." *NTS* 26: 363–79.

———. 1980. "Some Recent Developments in Research on the Epistle to the Hebrews." *IBS* 2: 141–65.

———. 1981. "Some Recent Developments in Research on the Epistle to the Hebrews: II. *IBS* 3: 28–43.

———. 1994. "Hebrews in Recent Scholarship." *IBS* 16: 66–86, 108–20.

McNamara, M. 2000. "Melchizedek: Gen 14,17–20 in the Targums, in Rabbinic and Early Christian Literature." *Bib* 81: 1–31.

Metzger, B. M. 1994. *A Textual Commentary on the Greek New Testament*. 2nd ed. Stuttgart: Deutsche Bibelgesellschaft and United Bible Societies.

Michel, O. 1986. *Der Brief an die Hebräer*. 8th ed. KEK. Göttingen: Vandenhoeck & Ruprecht.

Moffatt, J. 1924. *A Critical and Exegetical Commentary on the Epistle to the Hebrews*. New York: Scribner.

Montefiore, H. 1964. *A Commentary on the Epistle to the Hebrews*. HNTC. New York: Harper.

Motyer, S. 1999. "The Psalm Quotations of Hebrews 1: A Hermeneutic-Free Zone?" *TynBul* 50: 3–22.

Mulder, J. S. M. 1972. *Studies on Psalm 45*. Oss: Offsetdrukkerij Witsiers.

Neusner, J., and W. S. Green, eds. 1999. *Dictionary of Judaism in the Biblical Period: 450 B.C.E. to 600 C.E.* Peabody, MA: Hendrickson.

Oswalt, J. N. 1986. *The Book of Isaiah: Chapters 1–39.* NICOT. Grand Rapids: Eerdmans.

Overland, P. 2000. "Did the Sage Draw from the Shema? A Study of Proverbs 3:1–12." *CBQ* 62: 424–40.

Porter, J. R. 1961. "Psalm XLV.7." *JTS* 12: 51–53.

Porter, S. 1997. "The Use of the Old Testament in the New Testament: A Brief Comment on Method and Terminology." Pages 79–96 in *Early Christian Interpretation of the Scriptures of Israel: Investigations and Proposals.* Edited by C. A. Evans and J. A. Sanders. JSNTSup 148. Sheffield: Sheffield Academic Press.

Roberts, J. J. M. 1991. *Nahum, Habakkuk, and Zephaniah.* OTL. Louisville: Westminster John Knox.

Robertson, O. P. 1990. *The Books of Nahum, Habakkuk, and Zephaniah.* NICOT. Grand Rapids: Eerdmans.

Sanders, J. T. 1971. *The New Testament Christological Hymns: Their Historical Religious Background.* SNTSMS 15. Cambridge: Cambridge University Press.

Schröger, F. 1968. *Der Verfasser des Hebräerbriefes als Schriftausleger.* BU 4. Regensburg: Pustet.

Silva, M. 1976. "Perfection and Eschatology in Hebrews." *WTJ* 39: 60–71.

———. 1983. "The New Testament Use of the Old Testament: Text Form and Authority." Pages 147–65 in *Scripture and Truth.* Edited by D. A. Carson and J. W. Woodbridge. Grand Rapids: Zondervan.

Skehan, P. W. 1954. "A Fragment of the 'Song of Moses' (Deut 32) from Qumran." *BASOR* 136: 12–15.

Spicq, C. 1952–1953. *L'Épître aux Hébreux.* 2 vols. EBib. Paris: Gabalda.

Stibbs, A. M. 1978. *The Meaning of the Word "Blood" in Scripture.* Leicester: Theological Students' Fellowship.

Strawn, B. A. 2000. "Psalm 22:17b: More Guessing." *JBL* 119: 439–51.

Strobel, A. 1954. "Die Psalmengrundlage der Gethsemane-Parallele Hbr. 5,7ff." *ZNW* 45: 252–66.

———. 1961. *Untersuchungen zum eschatologischen Verzögerungsproblem auf Grund der spätjüdisch-urchristlichen Geschichte von Habakuk 2,2ff.* NovTSup 2. Leiden: Brill.

Swete, H. B. 1900. *An Introduction to the Old Testament in Greek.* Cambridge: Cambridge University Press.

Swetnam, J. 1981. *Jesus and Isaac: A Study of the Epistle to the Hebrews in the Light of the Aqedah.* AnBib 94. Rome: Biblical Institute Press.

Tate, M. E. 1990. *Psalms 51–100.* WBC 20. Dallas: Word.

Theissen, G. 1969. *Untersuchungen zum Hebräerbrief.* SNT 2. Gütersloh: Mohn.

Thomas, K. J. 1965. "The Old Testament Citations in Hebrews." *NTS* 11: 303–25.

Thompson, J. W. 1976. "Structure and Purpose of the Catena in Heb 1:5–13." *CBQ* 38: 352–63.

Übelacker, W. G. 1989. *Der Hebräerbrief als Appell: Untersuchungen zu Exordium, Narratio und Postscriptum.* ConBNT 21. Stockholm: Almqvist & Wiksell.

Van der Ploeg, J. 1947. "L'exégèse de l'Ancien Testament dans l'Épître aux Hébreux." *RB* 54: 187–228.

Vanhoye, A. 1969. *Situation du Christ: Épître aux Hébreux 1–2.* LD 58. Paris: Cerf.

———. 1976. *La structure littéraire de l'Épître aux Hébreux.* 2nd ed. StudNeot 1. Paris: Desclée de Brouwer.

von Rad, G. 1966. "There Remains Still a Rest for the People of God: An Investigation of a Biblical Conception." Pages 94–102 in *The Problem of the Hexateuch and Other Essays.* Translated by E. W. Trueman Dicken. Edinburgh: Oliver & Boyd.

Walters, J. 1996. "The Rhetorical Arrangement of Hebrews." *AsTJ* 51: 59–70.

Waltke, B. K., and D. A. Diewert. 1999. "Wisdom Literature." Pages 295–328 in *The Face of Old Testament Studies: A Survey of Contemporary Approaches.* Edited by D. W. Baker and B. T. Arnold. Grand Rapids: Baker Academic.

Waltke, B. K., and C. J. Fredricks. 2001. *Genesis: A Commentary.* Grand Rapids: Zondervan.

Weiser, A. 1962. *The Psalms: A Commentary.* Translated by H. Hartwell. OTL. Philadelphia: Westminster.

Weiss, H.-F. 1991. *Der Brief an die Hebräer.* KEK 13. Göttingen: Vandenhoeck & Ruprecht.

Wenham, G. J. 1987. *Genesis 1–15.* WBC 1. Waco: Word.

Westcott, B. F. 1909. *The Epistle to the Hebrews: The Greek Text with Notes and Essays.* London: Macmillan.

———. 1966. *The Epistles of St. John: The Greek Text with Notes.* 4th ed. Abingdon: Marcham Manor Press; Grand Rapids: Eerdmans.

Wilcox, M. 1979. "On Investigating the Use of the Old Testament in the New Testament." Pages 231–44 in *Text and Interpretation: Studies in the New Testament Presented to Matthew Black.* Edited by E. Best and R. Wilson. Cambridge: Cambridge University Press.

Wildberger, H. 1991. *Isaiah 1–12.* Translated by T. H. Trapp. CC. Minneapolis: Fortress.

Williamson, R. 1970. *Philo and the Epistle to the Hebrews.* ALGHJ 4. Leiden: Brill.

Wilson, G. H. 2002. *Psalms–Vol. 1.* NIVAC. Grand Rapids: Zondervan.

Wise, M. O., M. G. Abegg, and E. M. Cook. 1996. *The Dead Sea Scrolls: A New Translation.* San Francisco: HarperSanFrancisco.

Yadin, Y. 1958. "The Dead Sea Scrolls and the Epistle to the Hebrews." *ScrHier* 4: 36–55.

JAMES

D. A. CARSON

Introduction

The use of the OT in the Epistle of James is characterized by several features that we should note before moving to the individual passages. First, in almost all quotations from the OT the text quoted is the LXX. This is particularly noticeable in 2:23 (quoting Gen. 15:6), where the passive *elogisthē* ("it was reckoned") follows the LXX, while the Hebrew deploys a verb in the active voice; and in 4:6 (quoting Prov. 3:34), where the LXX differs significantly from the Hebrew. Almost all of the allusions to the OT (1:10–11; 3:9; 5:4, 7) also seem to align with the LXX. Second, James's handling of themes has particular resonance with the Wisdom literature of the OT, not least the straightforward counsel on how to live, cast in polarities: better this than that; live like this, not like that. James shares vocabulary and concepts with early Jewish literature of the Second Temple period, not least *Testaments of the Twelve Patriarchs*, but also Sirach, Philo, and Wisdom of Solomon. Third, while wisdom themes percolate steadily through this literature, they also surface repeatedly in the teaching of Jesus, not least in the Sermon on the Mount, with which James has many resonances. Yet the popularity of such instruction is what makes determination of direct dependence particularly difficult: one suspects that sometimes James is using biblical categories

that have been filtered through the common heritage of the early church's teaching and preaching. The following quotations and allusions stand out most dramatically.

1:1

James addresses his readers by making reference both to their status and to their location: they are "the twelve tribes" "scattered among the nations." Both expressions allude to OT realities. The former stems from the fact that the nation of Israel was descended originally from the twelve patriarchs; the latter reminds the reader of the impact of the exile under the Assyrian and Babylonian regional superpowers, with countless thousands of Jews still scattered all over the Mediterranean world and beyond. Through the OT prophets, however, God promised, both before the exile and after the initial return from exile, that he would regather his exiled people and reconstitute the twelve tribes (e.g., Isa. 11:11–12; Jer. 31:8–14; Ezek. 37:21–22; Zech. 10:6–12)—promises that lived on in the expectations of later Judaism (e.g., *Pss. Sol.* 17:26–28; *T. Benj.* 9:2). Jesus himself links his choice of twelve apostles to the twelve tribes of Israel (Matt. 19:28; cf. Luke 22:30), and the last book of the Bible pictures the people of God in the last days as the sum of twelve thousand drawn from each of the twelve tribes (Rev. 7:5–8). These themes prove to be enormously evocative, and debates rage over (1) the extent to which these references to the twelve tribes refer to empirical, racial Israel or, in typological fashion, to the eschatological Israel of the new covenant; (2) the extent to which the years of exile ended with Cyrus's decree or continued until the time Jesus as the Davidic king introduced the long-promised kingdom, or continue yet until the consummation (see the well-researched and nuanced assessments in Wood 2005).

If the Epistle of James was written early (in the 40s), then it may well be that James, by these expressions, betrays that he has Jewish Christians in mind—Jewish Christians who have been "scattered" not only as the heirs of the exile but also as a result of persecution (cf. Acts 11:19).

1:9–11

The contrast between the lowly person (*ho tapeinos* [NIV: "in humble circumstances"]) and the wealthy person (*ho plousios*) is common fare in biblical tradition. This lowly or humble person may, of course, be financially poor (e.g., Amos 2:7; 8:6), but the word is used in the LXX to refer to someone who counts for little in the world, someone who may be oppressed (e.g., Ps. 10:18 [9:39 LXX]; 18:27 [17:28 LXX]; 34:18 [33:19 LXX]; 138:6 [137:6 LXX]). Used in this fashion, the word is often linked with "widow" and "orphan." From such usage it is a small step to focus less on the world's evaluation than on the individual's attitude: these are the humble, to be contrasted with the proud and haughty (see Prov. 3:34, quoted in both James 4:6 and 1 Pet. 5:5). Since James draws the distinction between "lowly" people and the rich, something of the socioeconomic status of the former must be presupposed.

Yet there is a crucial interpretive uncertainty in these verses whose resolution depends in part on what OT antecedent James likely has in mind. The lowly person whom James has in mind is a Christian, a brother or sister (*ho adelphos*); they are "believers" (TNIV). Is the rich person also a Christian, a believer? Initially, at least, the parallelism suggests that this is so. In that case, James is giving practical advice to both Christian groups: the lowly are to take pride in their high position in Christ, while the same gospel teaches the rich Christians that material blessings are ephemeral and not to be trusted. The OT conceptual background, then, probably is a passage such as Jer.

9:23–24: "This is what the LORD declares: 'Let not the wise man boast of his wisdom or the strong man boast of his strength or the rich man boast of his riches, but let him who boasts boast about this: that he understands and knows me, that I am the LORD, who exercises kindness, justice and righteousness on earth, for in these I delight,' declares the LORD." On the other hand, if the rich person whom James has in mind in 1:10 is not a Christian, he may be playing with the sharp contrast that sometimes identifies the rich with the wicked, not least in the teaching of Jesus (e.g., Luke 6:23–24). Certainly elsewhere in James the rich do not appear in a good light (2:1–6; 5:1–6): they are portrayed as people who wickedly oppress the people of God.

Although some have strongly supported this second interpretation (e.g., Dibelius 1975: 85–86; Moo [2000: 66–67] is uncertain), quite a lot of evidence stands against it, prompting most commentators to side with the first interpretation. Jesus himself brings salvation to Zacchaeus, a rich man (Luke 19:1–10). Not a few of the writings of Second Temple Judaism with which James surely was familiar offer quite nuanced views of the rich: they are prone to selfishness and arrogance, and they may exploit the poor, but they are redeemable and often encouraged to honor their Creator with their wealth (e.g., Sir. 31:5–11). Moreover, although James can say some scathing things about the wealthy (possibly outsiders [5:1–6]), he certainly recognizes that wealthy people made up part of the Christian community, for he warns against the partiality that shows them undue deference (2:1–4). Elsewhere in the NT Paul can warn against loving money, which love brings a catalog of evils (1 Tim. 6:6–10), while nevertheless not banishing all wealthy people from the assembly of believers but rather teaching them to put their hope in God, not wealth, and to learn to be generous (1 Tim. 6:17–19).

What is clear is that James likens rich people in this passage to grass—a favorite image in the OT and in later Jewish literature for transitoriness (e.g., Job 14:2; Ps. 37:2; 90:5–6; Isa. 40:6–8; *2 Bar.* 82:7).

2:8

A. NT Context: Avoiding Favoritism. In general terms, the argument of James is clear: over against favoritism, love is cast as the mandated antithesis that makes all forms of partiality repugnant. Yet the connection between 2:8 and what precedes is slightly uncertain because of the connecting Greek particle *mentoi*, which some render as an emphatic ("really" [NIV, ESV]; "indeed" [NLT]), and others as an adversative ("however" [NASB, REB]). In its other seven NT occurrences (John 4:27; 7:13; 12:42; 20:5; 21:4; 2 Tim. 2:19; Jude 8) the word is invariably adversative, though the emphatic use is known outside biblical literature (LSJ 1102). Some preserve the adversative force by linking 2:8 with 2:6a: "But you have insulted the poor. . . . *However*, if you fulfill the royal law. . . ." Note the continuity between the two second-person plural pronouns: "you . . . you." Most interpreters accept that *mentoi* has emphatic force: "If you *really* keep the royal law" or the like. But perhaps some attenuated adversative force can be maintained between 2:7 and 2:8 if we emphasize the shift in pronouns: "*They* slander the noble name of him to whom you belong; *however*, if *you* keep the royal law. . . ."

B. OT Context. On first reading, the command found in Lev. 19:18 occurs in the context of a bewildering diversity of commandments. A key to understanding is found in the repeated clause "I am the Lord (your God)." This has both a theological function and a literary function. The theological function establishes that the ultimate ground of all of these commandments is God himself—not (in the first instance) the utilitarian nature of each commandment or its social benefits, but God himself. The literary function of the clause marks the end of each topic/paragraph (see Wenham 1979: 263–64). Our commandment, then, is found in a block that enjoins good relations with neighbors: honesty, freedom from exploitation, justice in court, and love for neighbor. The latter is cast over against hate, the secret silence that does not rebuke with kindness and candor and nurtures bitterness.

C. The Context in Judaism. At Qumran, Lev. 19:17–18a was applied to members of the sect who spotted an offense in another and instead of offering a reproof the same day did so later in anger or by simply denouncing the culprit to the elders. Those who act in this way are themselves guilty of violating the prohibition against vengeance; they themselves are nurturing a grudge. Over against this is the command to love one's

neighbor as oneself (see CD-A IX, 2–8). If one were to ask how it is possible for love to be commanded, the assumption here, as elsewhere (e.g., Deut. 10:18–19; 11:1), is that love encompasses both emotion and deeds. That the verb "love" (*'āhab*) brings deeds along with it is taught by both Rabbi Hillel and by Jesus: "Hillel, negatively, '*What is hateful to you do not do to others*' (*b. Šabb.* 31a; *y. Ned.* 9; cf Sir. 28:4), and Jesus, positively, '*Do unto others as you would do unto yourselves*' (Matt 7:2; Luke 6:13; Rom 13:8–10)" (Milgrom 2000: 1653). Many scholars, Jewish and Christian, view the two forms, negative and positive, as ethically equivalent. That may strike some as a bit too convenient.

D. Textual Matters. James follows the LXX, which uses the future tense to convey command. In fact, all instances of the Greek future tense in the NT functioning to convey command are quotations from the Greek OT.

E. James's Use of the OT in 2:8. What is initially surprising is that James quotes Lev. 19:18 instead of Lev. 19:15, which on first reading is more directly pertinent to his topic: "Do not pervert justice; do not show partiality to the poor or favoritism to the great." In fact, Spitta (1896) argues, rather implausibly, that Lev. 19:15 is what James really has in mind but merely lumps it under the rubric of the better-known passage. But there is a far more plausible reason for James's choice of OT quotation, as we will see.

Many have argued that there is no distinctively Christian use of Lev. 19:18 in this passage. After all, the ensuing verses cite two more commandments, lumping them all together in such a way (it is argued) that no commandment takes precedence over others: if you break any one of them, you break the whole law (see below). Certainly the immediate application of Lev. 19:18 is to combat favoritism, as the contrasting pair of conditional sentences in James 2:8–9 shows:

If you really keep the royal law . . .	you are doing well.
But if you show favoritism . . .	you sin and are convicted by the law. . . .

There are several bits of evidence, however, that, when taken together, suggest that James presupposes a profoundly Christian understanding of the law. First, the verb for "keep" the royal law, *teleō*, is not the common one. This verb has this meaning only here and in Luke 2:39; Rom. 2:27. It is perhaps possible that there is some overtone of bringing things to their appointed *telos*, "end." Second, James speaks of "the royal law" (*nomon ... basilikon*). Some take "royal" (*basilikos*) to mean "governing" or "supreme" (e.g., NJB: "The right thing to do is to keep the supreme Law of scripture: 'you will love your neighbor as yourself'"). That accords superficially with Jesus' insistence that all the law and the prophets "hang" on the first and second commandments—the commandment to love God with heart and soul and mind and strength, and the commandment to love one's neighbor as oneself (Matt. 22:40). Yet *basilikos* means "pertaining to the king" or "belonging to the king," "royal" in that sense. Several commentators draw attention to a usage found in Philo, who, commenting on Num. 20:17, compares the "royal road" in that verse (NIV: "the king's highway") to the law of God: the road is "royal" because it belongs to the king and leads to him, in exactly the same way in which the law belongs to God and leads to him (*Posterity* 101–102). The use of *basilikos* elsewhere in the NT likewise suggests the rendering "royal." Some scholars therefore argue that "the royal law" in this context is simply James's way of referring to the love commandment that immediately follows (e.g., Laws 1980: 108–9). But, third, the word "law" (*nomos*) in the NT usually refers to an entire corpus of law, such as the law of Moses, rather than to a single commandment. That comprehensiveness is suggested by the way that further individual commandments within the law are cited in the ensuing verses (see below). That in turn suggests that the expression "royal law" does not refer to the specific love commandment but rather to some larger corpus. Fourth, the concatenation of "royal" (*basilikos*) with the cognate word "kingdom" (*basileia*) in 2:5 ("to inherit the kingdom he promised to those who love him") strongly suggests that what James has in mind is the law that belongs to the kingdom of God. So "royal law," like "the perfect law that gives freedom" (1:25), is James's way of referring to the demands of God mediated through Jesus—the commands bound up with the kingdom that Jesus introduces. This is "the whole law as interpreted and handed over to the church in the teaching of Jesus" (Davids 1982: 114; cf. Frankemölle 1994 1:400–402). "Understood in this sense, the 'royal

law' may well extend beyond the Mosaic law as fulfilled and reinterpreted by Jesus to include the teaching of Jesus" (Moo 2000: 112). To complete God's will for his people means more than obeying an isolated commandment from Lev. 19:18; it means living in conformity with what Jesus himself, using the words of Lev. 19:18, insists lies at the center as the controlling core of that love: love for one's neighbor. Fifth, this interpretation is strengthened when we recall that the NIV's "found in Scripture" is perhaps an unfortunate rendering of *kata tēn graphēn*. That rendering suggests that the royal law actually refers to a single commandment "found *in* Scripture"—a rendering that we have already seen is an unlikely use of *nomos* ("law"). But the Greek expression here more literally means "according to Scripture" or "according to the Scripture" (ESV, NRSV) (see Johnson 1995: 230–32). Certainly Jesus always insisted that what he was preaching and accomplishing was "according to the Scripture." Indeed, elsewhere Paul insists that the matters "of first importance" regarding the gospel are "according to the Scriptures" (1 Cor. 15:3–4).

What James is saying, then, might be paraphrased thus: If you really keep the royal law, the law of the dawning kingdom, the law which is according to Scripture—Scripture as it has been magnificently fulfilled in all that Christ has taught and effected, and that is rightly summarized in "Love your neighbor as yourself"— you are doing well. In other words, it appears that James, even while quoting Lev. 19:18, simultaneously uses a number of Gospel categories that remind us of Jesus' own instruction on the centrality of the first and second commandments (Matt. 22:37–40; Mark 12:28–34), which had substantive impact on how early Christians understood the relationship of their new covenant obligations with respect to the OT law (e.g., Rom. 13:8–10; Gal. 5:13–14; cf. Matt. 5:17–20).

F. Theological Use. In addition to the obvious and powerful voice against favoritism that this citation generates, it is of a piece with many other related themes scattered throughout the NT. Not least is Jesus' new commandment (John 13:34–35): Jesus' followers are to love one another even as Christ has loved them, for by this all people will recognize his disciples. The emphasis on love as the distinguishing mark of Christian unity is ultimately tied to love among the persons of the Godhead (John 17). Equally, this way of seeing that the force of an OT commandment is tied to the way in which Jesus brings such stipulations to new-covenant fulfillment is of a piece with many strands of both eschatology and ethics in the NT.

2:11

A. New Testament Context: Why the Law Is an Indivisible Unity. James has been arguing that favoritism is a great evil. If some were to imagine that they are, on the whole, very faithful believers in every other domain of life, with the implication that favoritism is not such a very bad thing after all, James resorts to a commonplace in Jewish thought: in his own words, "Whoever keeps the whole law and yet stumbles at just one point is guilty of breaking all of it" (2:10). This is not an affirmation that some in fact do keep the law perfectly, save for one point: James casts his argument hypothetically, and for his readers his logic would be self-evident. Nevertheless, in order to justify the point James here cites two further commandments, both drawn from the Decalogue, to make the point that one voice stands behind both of these commandments (see Johnson 1995: 232) and, implicitly, behind everything that he commands. Thus to break one of them is to defy God himself—a foundational breaking of the whole.

B. OT Context. The prohibitions against adultery and murder are found in both versions of the Decalogue (Exod. 20:13–14; Deut. 5:17–18). By contrast with the order of James, the Decalogue in Exodus and Deuteronomy places the prohibition against murder before the prohibition against adultery (see discussion below). After the relatively elaborated commandments of the first part of the Decalogue, these two are brief and punchy.

The precise meaning of *rāṣaḥ* ("kill, murder") is disputed. Occasionally the verb refers to accidental killing (e.g., Num. 35:11; Deut. 19:4; Josh. 20:3), which is not "murder" in the English sense. It is regularly used to refer to the killing of one human being by another (or by others), but never in judicial or military contexts. Clearly accidental killing is not in view in this passage, in the very nature of the case (see Zimmerli 1978: 134–35). "The command corresponds to a concern to promote the life and well-being of other members of

the covenant community, as its ramifications in the code (e.g., 22:1–4) make plain" (McConville 2002: 129). Certainly the prohibition against the taking of life is found in longer forms (e.g., Gen. 9:6; Exod. 21:12; Lev. 24:17; Deut. 27:24). The prohibition against adultery is only one aspect of broader stipulations dealing with sexual relations (see Deut. 22:9–30). Although either married partner may be guilty of committing adultery, in the Hebrew idiom, "The man can only commit adultery against a marriage other than his own, the woman only against her own" (Stamm and Andrew 1967: 100; cited also in Childs 1974: 422).

C. The Context in Judaism. The Decalogue certainly enjoyed a special place even within OT tradition. The Ten Commandments had a special name, the "Ten Words" (e.g., Exod. 31:18; Deut. 4:13; 9:9), were uniquely written on stone, and, especially in Deuteronomy, they are set within a narrative framework that stresses their finality: "These words Yahweh spoke . . . and added no more" (Deut. 5:22). They are sometimes referred to in the prophets (Hos. 4; Jer. 7) and in the psalms (Ps. 50; 81). Within the Judaism of the first century Philo certainly assigned preeminence of place to the Decalogue (*Decalogue* 154)—a view shared by some writers in the Tannaitic tradition. Apparently it was incorporated into Jewish literature (*m. Tamid* 5:1), though this was discontinued at a later period. And if there are voices that delight in the Ten Words (see the later *Midrash on the Ten Words*), there are also voices directed against using the Ten Words at the expense of other laws (*Sipre* on Deut. 1:3). Moreover, when Jews distinguished different kinds of law, their typical distinction was between "light" and "heavy" law—a distinction that Jesus himself invokes (Matt. 23:23)—not "moral" versus "civil" and "ceremonial" law, which categories arrived on the scene a little later and came to be important in Christian circles in the patristic period, though even so they did not serve as the fundamental explanation of the continuities and discontinuities between the Testaments until Thomas Aquinas. Some strands of Judaism around the time of Christ, happy to distinguish between "light" and "heavy" laws, nevertheless insisted that breaking either is equally serious: "Do not suppose that it would be a petty sin if we were to eat defiling food; to transgress the law in matters either small or great is of equal seriousness, for in either case the law is equally despised" (4 Macc. 5:19–21 [cf. *b. Hor.* 8b; *b. Šabb.* 70b; 1QS VIII, 16–17; *T. Ash.* 2:5–10]).

D. Textual Matters. The verbal forms in James are aorist subjunctive (*moicheusēs* and *phoneusēs* respectively, as opposed to the future-tense form found in the LXX). Of greater interest is the fact that James puts the prohibition against adultery before the prohibition against murder, which is the opposite of the order in both Exodus and Deuteronomy. This may reflect nothing more than the order in which they came to James's mind. Yet it is worth noting that Codex B (Vaticanus) of the LXX of Deut. 5:17–18 preserves the same order as does James, as do also some miniscules of the LXX of Exod. 20:13–14 and a handful of other sources. Moreover, there may be another reason why James chose the order he did (see discussion in the next section).

E. James's Use of the OT in 2:11. James cites these two commandments, as we have seen, to demonstrate the indivisible unity of the law: one lawgiver stands behind the lot, so that breaking any one of them is still defiance against the seamless fabric of his authority. It is in that sense that the whole law is broken by the transgression of any part of it. Two further observations will clarify James's use of these two OT prohibitions.

First, both the examples of law that James cites are also referred to by Jesus in the Sermon on the Mount, a passage with which James has numerous affinities. Both the prohibition against adultery and the prohibition against murder come from the second table of the Decalogue, whose "horizontal" commandments were closely associated in early Christian teaching with the love commandment (Matt. 19:18–19; Rom. 13:8–10) to which James has already referred. Some have argued that James is so Jewish that he would have applied his principle to every single law found in the Mosaic code, including food laws, laws relating to the Day of Atonement sacrifices, and so forth. But strictly speaking, James does not stipulate every statute in the Mosaic covenant, but rather "the royal law" (2:8 [see commentary above]), "the law that gives freedom" (2:12 [cf. 1:25]). This is in line with Jesus' approach: Jesus could express unqualified endorsement of the law (Matt. 5:18–19) even while insisting that he himself is the one who fulfills it (Matt. 5:17), and in this fulfillment he treats even the prohibitions against murder and adultery to significant reshaping (Matt. 5:21–30). So also James: he "applies this standard point about the law's unity to the law as reinterpreted by Jesus" (Moo 2000: 116).

Second, this interpretation of James may be confirmed by his choice of these two laws. His argument for the indivisible unity of law under one lawgiver would have been equally effective regardless of which pair of laws he chose to cite. Yet these two "happen" to be two of the laws that Jesus himself insisted pointed in the direction of the heart, of one's motives and thoughts and emotions: murder is irrefragably bound up with hate, and adultery with lust. The suggestion that reference to the law prohibiting murder may have been called up because Christians themselves needed to be reminded of it in the most literal sense because they were caught up in the Jewish internecine warfare that preceded the Jewish revolt of AD 66–70 (so Martin 1988: 70) is speculative. It is far more likely that James recalls Jesus' teaching on the true direction in which these Mosaic laws point and perceives the close parallel with his own immediate purpose in writing. Proper response to God ultimately probes the heart and motives, and a command such as "Love your neighbor as yourself. . . . I am the LORD" not only addresses nasty problems of favoritism but also turns out to be the crucial point on which all of God's demands hang.

F. Theological Use. Although it would be profitable at this point to explore further the ways in which this passage in James might contribute to the extraordinarily complex questions surrounding the continuity and discontinuity of "law" from the OT to the NT, it is perhaps even more fundamentally important to reflect on how this passage helps clarify the nature of idolatry. Idolatry "degods" God. It replaces him with a substitute that cannot be other than a horrific insult. Idolatry begins in the Bible with the temptation to create our own good and evil, with the desire to be like God himself in this regard (Gen. 3). Yet to cut ourselves off from God, who alone gives life, can mean only death. One does not cut oneself off from only part of the blessing of God. So also here: the breaking of what God enjoins is worse than the breach of one specific commandment (whether that commandment is the prohibition against eating the fruit of a certain tree or the prohibition against committing murder)—it is defiance of God himself. Whatever the specific transgression, we become transgressors of the law, and thus we declare ourselves to be in rebellion against God, and thus idolaters.

2:23

A. NT Context: The Nature of Abraham's Faith.
The quotation of Gen. 15:6 occurs within James 2:14–26, the section of the letter that is by far the most challenging theologically. To provide a full accounting of James's understanding of the OT passage would require a thorough exegesis of all of James's discussion—a task manifestly beyond the parameters of this commentary. The issue is complicated not only by unavoidable comparisons with Paul's discussion (on which we will see more below) but also by the fact that the one particular work in Abraham's life to which James points, the so-called Aqedah, the offering of Abraham's son Isaac (Gen. 22), occurs a long time after Gen. 15:6, when, we are told, Abraham's faith was credited to him as righteousness.

The least that must be said is that in this part of his argument James is responding to the thesis that faith and works are separable (2:18a). James replies that genuine faith is demonstrated in works (2:18a–19); indeed, the kind of "faith" that merely believes that certain propositions are true is the kind of "faith" that the demons themselves demonstrate (2:19). They certainly "believe" that there is but one God, and they have sense enough to shudder. But that kind of "faith" is not faith at all in any sense that James recognizes. James is not arguing that works must be added to some such "faith" as the demons have; his argument, rather, is that genuine faith inevitably entails works, such that the faith is demonstrated in the works. The first exhortation is humbly to "accept the word implanted in you, which can save you" (1:21), but such faith will inevitably "show" itself in works. Is biblical evidence for this thesis required (2:20)? Then consider Abraham, whose remarkable obedience in the offering of Isaac (2:21) powerfully attests that "his faith and his actions were working together, and his faith was made complete by what he did" (2:22). The verb rendered by the NIV as "was made complete" (eteleiōthē [from teleioō]) does not mean (despite Calvin's sup-

port) that the actions revealed Abraham's faith to be perfect (teleioō never has that sense); nor does it mean that works were somehow tacked onto a faith that otherwise would have been incomplete, for James's point is that such faith does not really count at all, it is simply useless. Rather, to follow James's argument we must recognize that although the expression teleioō linked with ek (i.e., Abraham's faith "was made complete . . . [lit.] out of" works) is found nowhere else in the NT, parallels found elsewhere are illuminating. Philo tells us that Jacob "was made perfect as the result of [ek] discipline" (Agriculture 42); alternatively, he "was made perfect through [ek] practice" (Confusion 181). In other words, he grew in maturity as a result of the stresses laid on him. In Philo, however, the maturation takes place in a human being, Jacob; here in James this "maturation" takes place in an inanimate object, faith. This prompts Moo (2000: 137) to suggest that the closest conceptual parallel is 1 John 4:12: "if we love one another, God lives in us and his love is made complete [teteleiōmenē estin] in us." Transparently, God's love is not somehow lacking something, intrinsically deficient, until we love one another; rather, "God's love comes to expression, reaches its intended goal, when we respond to his grace with love toward others. So also, Abraham's faith, James suggests, reached its intended goal when the patriarch did what God was asking him to do" (Moo 2000: 137).

James 2:23, where the crucial quotation from Gen. 15:6 occurs, is connected with the preceding argument by a simple kai ("and," not "thus" as in the NRSV or "and so" as in the NLT): "And the Scripture was fulfilled that says, 'Abraham believed God, and it was credited to him as righteousness'" (NIV). Whatever the fine points, James is using the OT text to justify his thesis that faith without works is dead.

B. OT Context.
After Abraham's decisive defeat of the five kings (Gen. 14:8–22), God appears again to Abraham to renew the promise given him while he was still in Ur of the Chaldees, to the effect that he would make a great nation of him, and that through his seed all the nations of the earth would be blessed (Gen. 12: 1–3). Now God assures him that his progeny will be as countless as the stars of the heavens. Abraham, Gen. 15:6 tells us, "believed the LORD, and he [the LORD]

credited it to him as righteousness." Three points require brief comment. First, in the context Abraham's faith has as its object God and the utter reliability of his promises. "The Hebrew [*'āman*] is better translated 'trusted.' Abraham considers God true, reliable, and trustworthy" (Waltke 2001: 242). Second, although some Jewish interpreters have argued that this "crediting" that God undertakes effectively means that in God's sight Abraham's faith *was* his righteousness (see below), this is highly unlikely. Although we may doubt his thesis that the verb "credit" or "impute" took its meaning from priestly judgments in the cult, von Rad's insistence that Abraham's righteousness here is not "the result of any accomplishments, whether of sacrifice or acts of obedience" (von Rad 1972a: 185) surely is right. "Normally righteousness results in acquittal by the divine judge. Here faith, the right response to God's revelation, counts instead" (Wenham 1987: 330). Detailed examination of the context has repeatedly shown that God is depicted as accounting to Abraham "a righteousness that does not inherently belong to him" (Robertson 1980; see also von Rad 1951). Of particular interest are parallels in which something is reckoned as something else to someone's account—for example, "Your offering will be reckoned to you as grain from the threshing floor or juice from the winepress" (Num. 18:27 NIV); compare "He who blesses his neighbor with a loud voice, rising early in the morning, will be counted as cursing" (Prov. 27:14 RSV) (see Ziesler 1972: 181). Third, when the Akedah (Gen. 22) is introduced, God treats it as revealing Abraham's faith ("for now I know that you fear God, since you have not withheld your son, your only son, from me," 22:12) not somehow making up for what is lacking in the faith. Fourth, it should be noted in passing that this certainly is Paul's understanding of Gen. 15:6 when he cites the passage in Rom. 4 and Gal. 3. Note especially Paul's further inference in Rom. 4:5 that this means that God here is justifying the wicked (see Carson 2004).

C. The Context in Judaism. One of the striking features about the wealth of evidence—too great a wealth to canvass adequately here—is the esteem in which Abraham is held, not only because of his obedience in the Aqedah, the test concerning Isaac, but also (it is sometimes asserted) because he is believed to have obeyed Torah before it was formally revealed. Some Jews concluded that Abraham's exercising of faith was itself an act of righteousness. Abraham was regularly seen as righteous (e.g., *Jub.* 23:10; *Pr. Man.* 8; Sir. 44:19; *2 Bar.* 57:2; 58:1). Of particular interest is 1 Macc. 2:52, "Was not Abraham found faithful when tested, and it was reckoned to him as righteousness?" for here the latter part of Gen. 15:6 is attached, out of sequence, to the offering of Isaac in Gen. 22:15–18. The kind of faith that Abraham displays is often portrayed as particularly virtuous, even as justice toward God—so, for example, Philo (*Heir* 94–95; *Virtues* 216–218; *Abraham* 270). *Genesis Rabbah* virtually understands Abraham's faith to be his faithfulness in keeping the whole Torah before it was given (cf. *b. Qidd.* 82a; *b. Yoma* 28b; *y. Qidd.* 58a–b; *Mek. Exod.* 14:31; see Ziesler 1972: 125).

D. Textual Matters. The only point of interest to note here is that the LXX, which James follows, puts the verb into the passive, "was credited to him," as opposed to the active voice in which God himself is the subject, "God credited it to him" (Hebrew). Yet there is no doubt, in either the LXX or James, that God is the one doing the crediting (it is not for nothing that some have dubbed such passive-voice verbs "divine passives").

E. James's Use of the OT in 2:23. One cannot help but discern a bifurcation between, on the one hand, the fairly obvious meaning of Gen. 15:6 in its immediate context, along with the very similar way it is taken up by Paul and others, and, on the other hand, the way in which major voices within Judaism interpret Abraham's faith as a virtuous or righteous deed, or read back into Gen. 15:6 his obedience in the episode of the offering of Isaac. On the face of it, James sides with the latter tradition, and in its strongest form that tradition is hard to square with either Gen. 15:6 or with Paul. Yet a closer reading shows how James qualifies the kind of tradition found in 1 Macc. 2:52 (quoted above): he argues that faith is the ultimate cause of the works that justify Abraham. They "complete" the faith in the fashion already described. It is true that James reads Gen. 22 back into Gen. 15:6. However, he does so not to demonstrate that Abraham's faith is particularly virtuous or is in itself a righteous deed but rather to argue that that faith was completed in the obedience of the Aqedah. The timing of the crediting of righteousness is not, for James, the issue so much as the irrefragable connection between genuine faith and "completing" obedience (see Rakestraw 1986: 50).

The last line of James 2:23 depicts a further result of the peculiar cooperation of Abraham's faith and Abraham's works: "he was called the friend of God." This title doubtless derives from Judaism, where it is found in many sources (e.g., *Jub.* 19:9; 20:20; Philo, *Abraham* 273; *Testament of Abraham*); it is not found in the OT. Nevertheless, the title within Judaism probably derives from the biblical description of Abraham as the "beloved" of God (Isa. 41:8 [NIV: "Abraham my friend"]; 2 Chron. 20:7; see also Isa. 51:2; Dan. 3:35 LXX).

F. Theological Use. In one sense, the distance between Paul and James is not great. After all, Paul, who insists so emphatically that a person is justified by faith apart from the works of the law (Rom. 3:28), insists as forcefully as does James that a so-called believer whose conduct does not change will never inherit the kingdom of God (e.g., 1 Cor. 6:9–10). One must conclude that Paul would not recognize as valid any purported faith that did not result in the transformation that he expects the gospel to effect. At this fundamental pastoral level it is hard to detect any great difference between James and Paul.

Yet in their respective handlings of Gen. 15:6 the differences between James and Paul are substantial and must not be obliterated. Paul reads Gen. 15:6 within its immediate context, is careful to observe its chronological placement, and seizes upon the verse as evidence that Abraham attained a declaration that he was righteous on the basis of his faith alone. James reads Gen. 15:6 within the cycle of the Abrahamic narrative and carefully observes how the kind of faith displayed in that verse is "completed" by the kind of obedience displayed in Gen. 22, thereby demonstrating that genuine faith is never alone. Although the foci of their respective concerns are slightly different, along with their use of formally similar terminology, it would be obtuse not to see that both are right.

Although Gen. 15:6 is not explicitly quoted in Heb. 11, there the "faith of Abraham" theme is explored in yet another context to stress not only Abraham's willingness to trust God's prom-

ises but also the persevering nature of his faith, demonstrated in his willingness to live the life of a nomad while he waited for a fulfillment of the promises that stretched far beyond his own lifespan. Thus there are at least three distinctive "faith of Abraham" lessons drawn by NT writers (see Longenecker 1977). It is a salutary exercise to trace the differences, observe carefully how each is genuinely grounded in the OT text, and think through the kind of theological synthesis that celebrates the contribution of each voice while delighting in the unity and wholeness of the counsel of God. The "faith of Abraham" theme, not least the passages that explicitly cite Gen. 15:6, contributes by example to the careful reflection needed to avoid the obverse errors of turning complementary witnesses into mutual contradictions, and of turning deep and nuanced theological synthesis into exegetically irresponsible reductionism that flattens all distinctions.

2:25

The term *homoiōs* ("similarly, in the same way") ties 2:25 not to 2:24 but rather to the example of Abraham in 2:20–23. The OT account of Rahab (Josh. 2) does not explicitly mention her faith (the way Gen. 15 mentions the faith of Abraham), although the narrative flow leaves little doubt: she had heard the accounts of the mighty acts of the God of Israel, and her trust in him led her to concrete actions, just as Abraham's faith in God led him to concrete actions. Both the Hebrew and the LXX identify Rahab as a prostitute, and James does not hesitate to affirm the same (she is a *pornē*). According to the best texts, however, he changes "spies" in the LXX of Josh. 2 to "messengers" (*angeloi*).

The slightly puzzling question that arises is why James decided to choose Rahab to stand beside Abraham as premier exemplars of faith working out in action, when many other illustrious examples from the OT readily spring to mind. Later rabbinic traditions identify Abraham and Rahab as shining examples of the classic proselyte—that is, the Gentile who identifies with the people of Israel. It is not clear, however, that that tradition extends back to the first century. Others have proposed that Abraham and Rahab belong together because both serve as models not only of faith but also of hospitality. That tradition is preserved in *1 Clement* (end of the first century). That is possible, but in that case one wonders why James does not mention Gen. 18, the crucial passage where Abraham displays hospitality to three "men" who bring him predictions regarding his family. Perhaps James simply wants maximum diversity: both the ultimate ancestor of all of Israel and an obscure Gentile prostitute woman exemplify the importance of the truth that genuine faith works itself out in actions. In any case, James is using the Rahab narrative for exemplary moral purposes.

3:7, 9

James 3:7 almost certainly alludes to the Genesis account of creation, in which human beings are given the stewardship of the entire creation. More telling, yet equally drawn from the creation account, is the allusion in 3:9: "With the tongue we praise our Lord and Father, and with it we curse human beings, who have been made in God's likeness" (TNIV), an obvious allusion to Gen. 1:27. The unit of this epistle in which this passage is embedded is concerned with the tongue, and vv. 9–12 focus on the inconsistency of the tongue. For God to bless and curse, based on responses to his graciously given revelation (e.g., Deut. 30:19), is one thing; however, for people to take on this divine prerogative simply to vent their own likes and dislikes is a form of idolatry, for it usurps the place of God. Worse, the "blessing" of God that we undertake with our tongue is not very sincere or honorable if the same tongue is happy to curse those who are made in God's image.

The long and rich discussions on the nature of the *imago Dei* (image of God) need not detain us here, as James sheds little light on them. The likeness that human beings have to God must be, in James's mind, close enough to make this awful polarity in the use of our tongues simply appalling. James was not the only one to make this point. Later rabbis taught that no one should say, "'Let my neighbor be put to shame'—for then you put to shame one who is in the image of God" (*Gen. Rab.* 24 on Gen. 5:1).

4:5

Although this verse promises to give us what "Scripture says," there is no transparently obvious OT reference, and in any case the substance of the verse is bound up with a number of interpretive difficulties. These difficulties are both narrowly syntactical and broadly contextual. The two prin-

cipal syntactical possibilities (though there are many minor variations) of what "Scripture says" in this verse are these:

1. "He jealously longs for the spirit he has caused to dwell in us." (TNIV [similarly ESV: "He yearns jealously over the spirit that he has made to dwell in us," though the ESV makes this a direct quotation, within quotation marks])
2. "The spirit he caused to live in us envies intensely." (NIV)

There are three exegetical issues that must be decided. (1) The case of *to pneuma* ("the spirit"). The first of the two interpretations takes it to be in the accusative case, functioning as the direct object of the verb *epipothei* ("he [jealously] longs for the spirit"); the second takes *to pneuma* to be in the nominative, functioning as the subject of the verb ("the spirit [he caused to dwell in us] envies [intensely]" or "the spirit [he caused to dwell in us jealously] longs for"). The latter is usually understood to refer to the human spirit, the spirit that God breathed into Adam to make him a living creature (Gen. 1:27); in this sense, God caused this spirit to dwell in us. A few, however, understand "the spirit" to refer to the Holy Spirit, whom God caused to dwell in us at our conversion (so the NLT). If this is the human spirit, then the text is saying that we humans (i.e., our spirits) either jealously long for God (in a positive sense) or envy intensely (in a negative sense); if "the spirit" refers to the Holy Spirit, then the text is saying that the Holy Spirit jealously longs for us, and this, of course, is akin to the first interpretation except that it specifies the Holy Spirit in particular as the one who jealously longs for us instead of simply saying that God jealously longs for us. Indeed, it is syntactically likely that God is the subject of *epipothei* ("longs for" or "desires"), not least since God is transparently the subject of the other finite verb, *katōkisen* ("he caused to dwell"). (2) The meaning of *phthonos*, which might be taken in a negative sense to refer to human envy (second reading, above) or in a positive sense to God's righteous jealousy. Since the word is almost always negative in connotation, and in fact James has used it that way in 3:13–4:3, on the whole we must infer that *phthonos* favors the second interpretation, which speaks of human envy. Yet it does not quite rule out the second interpretation, for *phthonos* is sometimes used interchangeably with *zēlos* (e.g., 1 Macc. 8:16; *T. Sim.* 4:5; *T. Gad* 7:2), and the latter regularly refers to divine jealousy. Further, even *phthonos* is sometimes used by pagan Greek writers to refer to the jealousy of the Olympian gods. So it is at least possible that James deploys the word to describe the nature of God's desire for his own people. (3) The meaning of the verb *epipothei*, which I have been rendering "longs for" or "desires" or the like, is here linked to the preposition *pros* ("toward"). The problem is that the "human envy" interpretation demands something like "tends toward"—for example, "the human spirit tends toward envy [*pros phthonon epipothei*]," which the NIV renders paraphrastically with "envies intensely." But although the "toward" part of "tends toward" seems to be preserved in *pros*, "tends" is never an obvious meaning of *epipothei*. Conversely, if *epipothei* carries its normal meaning of "desires" or "longs for," the first interpretation is favored: God longs for the spirit he has caused to dwell in us. But then what is the force of *pros phthonon*? If this is an unusual adverbial construction describing the nature of the desire, we may render it "God longs jealously for the spirit. . . ." But God's jealousy, in Scripture, is always a good thing, and, as we have already observed, *phthonos* is normally a bad thing.

In short, of these three exegetical details, (1) favors the first reading, (2) favors the second, and (3) is ambiguous. But when we consider the contextual arguments, the evidence decisively shifts in one direction. It is true that James does sometimes talk about the human sin of envy (e.g., 3:14, 16; 4:2). Nevertheless, in the immediate context James has been extrapolating from the OT depiction of God as the husband of his people (even as, in the NT, Christ is the bridegroom of the church); that is the conceptual framework in which James charges his readers with being "an adulterous people" (4:4). Verse 5 follows and thus most naturally reads as talking about God's righteous jealousy in the light of such betrayal. On balance, then, the first rendering is to be preferred.

So we are now at the place where we must consider afresh what "Scripture" James has in mind when he writes, at the beginning of the verse, "Or do you think Scripture says without reason that. . . ?" No OT passage qualifies, despite various attempts to stipulate allusive references (e.g., Schlatter [1956: 249] and Laws [1980: 174–79] suggest Ps. 42:1 [Laws also adds Ps. 84:2]). Some have therefore trawled through the noncanonical Jewish literature, but no suggestion has been convincing. Others have supposed that James has a lost apocryphal text in mind (e.g., Dibelius 1975: 220–23). Such speculation is unnecessary. Sometimes the singular "Scripture says" refers to a theme rather than to a specific quotation (e.g., John 7:37–39; possibly Matt. 2:23). So, most likely, here: the God of the Bible is a jealous God, a point established not only in the Decalogue but also in many passages, perhaps most movingly in the prophecy of Hosea. For this reason, then, the ESV is ill-advised to use direct quotation marks: in Greek there is no orthographically unambiguous distinction between a direct quotation and an indirect quotation, and in this context it would be wiser to side with the latter because the former, with its quotation marks, falsely signals the preservation of the actual words of a quotation when none appears to be present.

Theologically speaking, the theme of God's jealous love for his people is tied to the exclusiveness of his claims (like the exclusiveness of a spouse's claims in marriage), ratcheted up because God is not only the (metaphorical) husband of his people but also their God. God alone is God. For his creatures to betray this first allegiance is not freedom; it is the most horrific idolatry. Precisely because this God is personal, his response cannot possibly be dispassionate: he yearns for his image-bearers still and is outraged at their adultery. He longs for them with jealous longing.

4:6

A. NT Context: God's Grace Is Given to the Humble. The end of James 3 finds James distinguishing between two kinds of wisdom. Yet this contrast is not general or theoretical. The focus of the wisdom that James has in mind is its ability to bring integrity and peace to human relationships. Thus the "wisdom that comes from heaven" (3:17) is characterized by the virtues that make for peace. The beginning of James 4, then, is not changing the subject but rather analyzes what does *not* make for peace. The evil, James insists, lies within us: we covet more things, more power, more victories, and we do not even begin to recognize that genuine good gifts come from our heavenly Father and are ours for the asking (4:1–3). That we are so slow to perceive this reflects our own wayward hearts: our relationship with the world is simply adulterous, a betrayal of the covenant relationship that we have entered into with God (4:4). Do we not recognize that Scripture teaches us that this God jealously longs for the spirit that he himself placed within his image-bearers (4:5)?

Our understanding of the relationship of 4:6 to the five verses that precede depends, inevitably, on our interpretation of 4:5 (on which, see above). If it is our spirit that envies intensely, then the mild adversative that introduces 4:6 should be understood as follows: we have this spirit of evil envy within us, but God gives us more [*meizona*, "greater"] grace to enable us to overcome it. On the other hand, if the correct interpretation of 4:5 is (as I have suggested) that God jealously longs for the spirit that he himself caused to live in us, then the flow reads as follows: God's longing for us is driven by his own holy jealousy, but God is as gracious as he is holy, and he supplies us with all the grace we need to meet his own holy demand.

Either way, although 4:6a comes across as an encouragement, James, quite typically, will not permit grace to stand by itself, without consideration of the appropriate response. That response is humility, and its antithesis is pride—a point that James makes by quoting Prov. 3:34: "God opposes the proud but gives grace to the humble."

B. OT Context. The poem of Prov. 3:21–35 begins with parental encouragement to the son to retain possession of "sound judgment and discernment" (NIV)—what Longman (2006) interprets as "resourcefulness and discretion." Verses 23–25 establish the motivation for pursuing values, though in v. 26 it is Yahweh himself who protects. Verses 27–31 introduce five prohibitions, all having to do with relationships that the young man characterized by "sound judgment and discernment" will want to avoid, and vv. 32–35 set out the motivations behind such prohibitions—indeed, behind the appeal of the entire poem. The controlling thought in these motivations is the distinction between Yahweh's attitude toward the wicked and his attitude toward the righteous. In our verse, 3:34, the distinction is plain: "He mocks proud mockers but gives grace to the humble" (NIV). Mockers inevitably

think of themselves as strong and sneer with condescending derision at those whom they judge to be weak. But God, who is immeasurably strong, holds them in derision and mocks them, giving grace to the humble, who alone are wise. The mockers "will get from God exactly what they give others: as they tear everything down with their mouths, so the Lord will tear them down with his curse (see v. 34); as they cover others with reproach, so the Lord will cover them with shame (cf. 1:24–33; Ps. 18:25–26 [26–27])" (Waltke 2004: 273).

C. The Context in Judaism. Although Prov. 3:34 does not appear to have played a major role in Judaism at the turn of the eras, it is of a piece with a widespread wisdom tradition that thought in polarities, distinguished between the wise/righteous and the fool/wicked, and stressed the importance of dependence on God for the kind of wisdom that brings life (see von Rad 1972b; Perdue 1994; Hempel, Lange, and Lichtenberger 2001).

D. Textual Matters. The Hebrew text reads *'im-lallēṣîm hû'-yālîṣ wĕla'ănāwîm yitten-ḥēn* ("Surely he mocks the mockers, but he gives grace to the humble"). The "he" who gives this grace is, contextually, YHWH, "the LORD." The LXX preserves this reference to "the LORD" but reads *kyrios hyperēphanois antitassetai tapenois de didōsin charin*, which James follows exactly, except for his change of *kyrios* to *ho theos*: "God [not 'the LORD'] opposes the proud but gives grace to the humble." The general idea is the same, of course, but the LXX (and therefore also James) loses the specificity of the manner of God's opposition: God mocking the mockers.

E. James's Use of the OT in 4:6. The same OT passage is quoted in 1 Pet. 5:5, one of the many close connections between James and 1 Peter. The grace that we require (4:6a) to face God's jealous longing for us (4:5b) is given to the humble. God sets himself against the proud (a common theme in the OT—e.g., Ps. 18:27; 34:18; Isa. 61:1; Zeph. 3:11–12). James applies a common wisdom contrast to the particular situation that he is addressing, but this particular situation is embedded in the fundamental problematic of how sinful human beings are established in relationship with their Creator—a challenge that runs throughout the Bible, finding ready exposition in the Wisdom literature and in this embodiment of it.

F. Theological Use. The antithesis bound up with this quotation is so common in Scripture that it would take a very long essay merely to canvass the conceptual parallels. See, for instance, the Beatitudes (Matt. 5:3–10). The first responsibility of the creature is to recognize his or her creatureliness and therefore live in dependence upon, and with worship toward, the Creator and Sovereign of all. The only alternative is the proud independence that is nothing other than utterly destructive idolatry, the arrogance that finally brings down God's displeasure. This theme lies at the heart of the Bible's storyline and of God's plan of redemption brought to fulfillment in the cross and resurrection of Jesus Christ and to consummation at the end.

5:4

A. NT Context: God's Attentiveness to Those Oppressed by the Rich. James 5:1–6 directly addresses the unrighteous wealthy. They are busily storing up physical wealth and do not realize that they are storing up wrath that will fall upon them at the end (5:1–3). Here in 5:4 James charges them more directly with actual injustice: they have defrauded workers of their pay (with the reading of the verb *apostereō*), or perhaps they have simply withheld their wages in some way (with the reading of the verb *aphystereō*)—a decision between the two is difficult but fortunately makes little difference for our purposes. The sins against which OT writers inveighed (see Lev. 19:13; Deut. 24:15; Mal. 3:5) are taking place in James's day. Day-workers apparently expected to receive their wages at the end of each day (cf. Matt. 20:1–16), and in a subsistence economy the failure to meet this expectation might well cause desperate hardship for the worker and his family. Not only does the unpaid wage cry out, but also the cries of the harvesters reach "the ears of the LORD Almighty" (see Isa. 5:9).

B. OT Context. The notion of God hearing the cries (*boai*) of the oppressed is a common one. It first springs from Abel's blood crying to God for justice (Gen. 4:10). Often God's people, when oppressed, cry to him for relief (e.g., Exod. 2:23; 1 Sam. 9:16; 2 Chron. 33:13). God is often said to hear their cry.

Nevertheless, in Isa. 5:9, the OT passage that most scholars detect behind James 5:4, the Hebrew assigns the "ears" not to God but rather to the prophet Isaiah. The Hebrew of the verse is a bit clipped (the verb is missing), but the NIV doubtless captures the thought: "The LORD Almighty has declared in my hearing [lit., 'ears']." What he declares, in the ensuing lines, is his judgment on the wicked rich who have oppressed the poor.

C. The Context in Judaism. The literature of Second Temple Judaism includes many passages in which the prayers or the cries or the blood of the righteous or oppressed call out to God (e.g., *1 En.* 22; 47:1; 3 Macc. 5:7), and God hears them. Dibelius (1975: 238) surely is correct in asserting that "unto the ears of the LORD Sabaoth" (both LXX and James) springs from a traditional style that adds gravitas to the notion of God hearing such cries.

D. Textual Matters. Whereas the Hebrew of Isa. 5:9 attaches the ears to Isaiah's head, the LXX reads *ēkousthē gar eis ta ōta kyriou sabaōth tauta* (lit., "these things were heard unto the ears of the Lord of hosts"). The idea is that the cries extended that far. James picks up the words *eis ta ōta kyriou sabaōth*, though his verb is not *ēkousthē* ("were heard") but rather *eiselēlythasin* ("have come unto" or "have reached"), and his subject is not *tauta* ("these things") but rather the actual cries of the harvesters. The expression *kyrios sabaōth* means literally "Lord of armies" or "Lord of hosts," the second word being a transliteration of the Hebrew for "army" into Greek. The choice of "the LORD Almighty" (NIV) captures the general sense, but not the form. The ESV's "the LORD of hosts" preserves the traditional English but also a religious overtone probably not present if we render the expression more literally as "the Lord of armies."

E. James's Use of the OT in 5:4. It is not altogether certain that James intends us to detect a reference to Isa. 5:9. The strongest point in favor of supposing that James intends us to think of Isa. 5 is that in the OT reference the cries for justice have to do with the oppression caused by the unrighteous rich. But it is equally plausible to suppose that James, steeped in OT text (most in the form of the LXX or something like it), would naturally gravitate in his linguistic usage to the texts that have shaped his mind. It is easy to think of contemporary parallels in which older Christians brought up on the Bible drop biblical expressions into their conversations without any self-conscious intention of drawing attention to particular biblical passages, even while they remain gratefully conscious of the biblical themes to which they are alluding.

F. Theological Use. As important as it is to understand how the NT writers regularly use OT texts in distinctive theological ways, it is no less important to recognize the numerous instances when their categories, vocabulary choices, and even turns of expression are steeped in OT usage without necessarily establishing theological links between the Testaments. The theme of this verse—God is a God of justice and hears the cries of his oppressed people—is a mainstay of both Testaments, of course; however, that point does not turn on some obscure typology or fulfillment motif but happily picks up the verbal expressions of the biblical writers.

5:5

A. NT Context: The Theme of Reversal on the Last Day. James continues his indictment of the unrighteous wealthy. They have lived "in luxury and self-indulgence" (5:5), while their condemnation of the innocent has resulted in the death of the latter (5:6). This belongs to a lengthy tradition of condemnation of those, like the citizens of Sodom, who were "overfed and unconcerned; they did not help the poor and needy" (Ezek. 16:49). One recalls the similar contrast in Jesus' parable about the rich man and Lazarus (Luke 16:25). Implicitly there is a reversal theme: James says that these unrighteous rich folk lived "on earth in luxury and self-indulgence" (5:5), which hints at a reversal on the last day. That in turn has a bearing on how we understand the words quoted from the OT: "You have fattened yourselves in the day of slaughter" (5:5b NIV). Before probing the matter more closely, we must unpack the OT context.

B. OT Context. Jeremiah is having a hard time understanding the justice of God. He happily confesses God's justice, but cannot understand why the evil flourish (Jer. 12:1–4). If they flourish, it can only be because God has planted them, even though their religion is merely formal and their hearts are far from God (12:2b)—in sharp contrast to Jeremiah's own heart (12:3a). As the nation collapses around him, Jeremiah's prayer with respect to the wicked is very pointed: "Drag them off like sheep to be butchered! Set them apart for the day of slaughter" (12:3b). This may mean that

Jeremiah wants the wicked to receive their due punishment, without much thought being given to the question of when this will take place; he may imagine specific temporal punishments; alternatively, he may have final judgment in mind. Isaiah 30:25 reflects at least something of a similar ambiguity: "In the day of great slaughter, when the towers fall, streams of water will flow on every high mountain and every lofty hill"—although, here the ultimate day of the Lord most probably is in view. In other words, the same day of the Lord that brings the most appalling judgment brings blessing and prosperity for the Lord's own people.

C. The Context in Judaism. The Bible frequently uses the imagery of slaughter in a battle to depict the day of judgment. The phrase "in the day of great slaughter" is picked up in *1 En.* 90:4 to describe the ultimate judgment, and indeed that chapter of *1 Enoch* boasts several parallels to James 5:1–6. Compare somewhat similar language in *1 En.* 16:1 (Greek) and a similar theme of judgment on the unrighteous wealthy, though without this particular phrase, in *1 En.* 100:7.

D. Textual Matters. This passage is remarkable in that the LXX nowhere has the expression "in [or 'for'] the day of slaughter," and certainly not in Isa. 30:25 or Jer. 12:3). If James is picking up the expression from the biblical text itself, and not from the surrounding environment of Judaism, he is picking it up from the Hebrew.

E. James's Use of the OT in 5:5. The expression *en hēmera sphagēs* ("in the day of slaughter" [NIV]) could, by itself, refer to any time of horrible, widespread death. James could be using it in one of two ways. (1) He could be applying the expression to the deaths of the righteous poor: the rich indulge themselves, while the poor suffer in horrific ways (so, e.g., Dibelius 1975: 238–39). (2) If the reversal theme is understood, a theme hinted at both by the words "on earth" (5:5) and by the clause "You have hoarded wealth in the last days" (5:3), then "the day of slaughter" refers to the day of eschatological judgment, and the unrighteous rich are the ones who face it. A subset of this interpretation holds that the "eschatological day" that James has in mind is the destruction of the Jews in Jerusalem in AD 70 (so Feuillet 1964), but this seems unlikely in the light of the exhortation in 5:7: "Be patient, then, brothers, until the Lord's coming." James's point, then, is that while the rich are fattening themselves, they are like cattle awaiting the day of slaughter; the eschatological day of judgment could break in at any time, and their self-indulgence and total unconcern for others will end in slaughter. But whether James is self-consciously drawing on an expression found in Jer. 12:3 and Isa. 30:25, in which case he is dependent on the Hebrew, or simply using a stock expression not unknown in the Judaism of his day cannot be determined.

F. Theological Use. One cannot speak of the "use" of the OT, theological or otherwise, if the OT is not actually quoted or alluded to. Yet the OT Scriptures are the ultimate fount from which many of the religious expressions in Second Temple Judaism derive. Certainly the reversal theme is a commonplace of both Testaments.

5:6

Most scholars have detected a reasonably clear allusion to Abel in the crying out to God depicted in James 5:4: the first instance of injustice crying out to God in the Bible is the death of Abel, his blood crying out. This has prompted Byron (2006) to suggest that if Abel is on James's mind, then it is not difficult to imagine that his brother Cain is too, and in this verse, Byron claims, an allusion to Cain cannot be ruled out. From the time of the writings of Josephus and Philo, and continuing on through the midrashim, Cain appears as a stock figure who in his time oppressed the poor and the righteous. If that connection was understood, then the condemnation of the unrighteous rich articulated in 5:6 would in fact be charging them with the sin of Cain. Byron's suggestion cannot be disproved, of course, but it presupposes a strong affinity between the OT reading habits of James and those of Josephus and Philo that is not secure.

5:11

James has encouraged his readers to persevere in the face of suffering by appealing to the example of the prophets (5:10). Here he adds the example of Job (5:11). Job is numbered with Noah and Daniel in Ezek. 14:14, 20. In later Judaism he is held up as a model prophet along with Ezekiel (Sir. 49:9; see also *T. Ab.* 15:20; *T. Job*, esp. 1:2; 4:5–6; 27:3–10; 39:11–13).

The most difficult part of 5:11 is the clause "you have seen the *telos* of the Lord." The ESV renders this "you have seen the purpose of the Lord," and the NIV "you have seen what the Lord finally brought about." The former understands *telos* to refer to the "end" that God had in mind—that is, God's "purpose"—presumably in refining Job as well as in displaying his own mysterious "compassion and mercy" (to use James's language). The latter understands *telos* to refer to the "end" of Job's experience, brought about by God—the restoration of his family and vast wealth. Commentators are approximately evenly divided between the two. Both meanings are found within Job: in Job 42:5–6 Job confesses that he has learned a fundamental lesson about the majestic sovereignty and goodness of God (hence "purpose"), while the narrative itself tells of Job's restoration, which is a way of saying that the "end" is not in the suffering but rather in what God brings about finally. What is clear is that James is using Job as a moral example under the providence of God. It is less clear that Job is being held up as an example throughout James's epistle (so Richardson 2006).

5:17

Just as James has already cited Abraham, Rahab, and Job as examples of various kinds (2:21, 25; 5:11), so here he introduces Elijah as the capstone of his encouragement of his readers to pray (cf. 5:13–16). Elijah's miracles were spectacular, his denunciation of sin in his own day was courageous, and his departure from this world was unique. As a result, he became an enormously popular figure in Judaism. Even within the OT he appears as the one who paves the way for the final messianic age (Mal. 4:5–6; cf. Sir. 48:1–10; see also Mark 9:12; Luke 1:17). Here, however, what is celebrated is that he was "a man like us" (*homoiopathēs*), even though his prayers were wonderfully effective. The moral lesson is clear: our prayers can be wonderfully effective too. The event to which James refers, found in 1 Kings 17–18, sets the stage for the confrontation on Mount Carmel (1 Kings 19).

Two details require further probing. First, the OT account does not actually mention that Elijah prays for the drought to begin, though it mentions his prayers that it would end (1 Kings 18:42). Doubtless his prayers at the beginning are an understandable inference. Certainly others in

Second Temple Judaism drew the same inference (Sir. 48:2–3; 2 Esd. 7:109). Second, James's mention of "three and a half years" instead of the "three years" specified by 1 Kings 18:1 may be an instance of an odd "rounding up" to bring in the symbolism associated with three and a half years as a period of judgment (see Dan. 7:25). Luke makes a similar adjustment (Luke 4:25), and the symbolism recurs in Revelation (Rev. 11:11; 12:14).

5:20

A. NT Context: The Reward of Service. In line with more "formal" letters, James ends his not with final greetings and benedictions but rather with a call to action (5:19–20). If someone (presumably a fellow believer) wanders from the truth, and if someone brings that person back, James says, remember this: "Whoever turns a sinner from the error of his way will save him from death and cover over a multitude of sins" (5:20 NIV). The words "cover over a multitude of sins" constitute at least an allusion to, and perhaps a deliberate quotation of, Prov. 10:12, where hate and love are contrasted: "Hatred stirs up dissension, but love covers all wrongs."

The point of ambiguity in the quotation is this: many scholars (e.g., Dibelius 1975: 257–60; Laws 1980: 239; Mussner 1981: 233) think that the first result of rehabilitating a sinner is saving that person from death (i.e., a benefit that accrues to the converted), while the second result, covering over a multitude of sins, accrues to the converter. This is far from implausible. Both Testaments promise those with the ministry of the word that in the discharge of their ministry they will save not only their hearers but also themselves (Ezek. 3:21; 1 Tim. 4:16). This probably is an outworking of the fact that God finally treats us as we treat others (cf. Matt. 6:14–15; 18:23–25). But although this interpretation is not intrinsically implausible, the syntax is a bit awkward. It is probably better to think of the second result as nothing other than the blotting out of sins that is often portrayed as one of the benefits of salvation, both results applying to the restored sinner (so Davids 1982: 201; Martin 1988: 220; Moo 2000: 250–51).

B. OT Context. The OT text in question occurs in a unit that considers the effects of speech on self and others, Prov. 10:6–14 (the analysis is that of Waltke 2004: 456–62). Here the effect on others is in view (10:11–14). In 10:11 the health-giving speech of the righteous is contrasted with the destructiveness of the mouth of the fool. In 10:12 hatred expressed in speech, not least where that hatred has been stirred up by the speaker's revulsion of the other's sin (which is suggested by the parallel line "Hatred stirs up dissension / But love covers all wrongs"), achieves nothing more than strife and division. By contrast, articulated love wins the sinner as a friend and "covers over all wrongs"; the idea is not that the wrongs are concealed but not dealt with, but rather that the love itself reconciles the alienated offender and changes everything.

C. The Context in Judaism. Normally, to "cover sin" means to procure forgiveness, both in biblical texts (e.g., Ps. 32:1; 85:2) and in later Judaism (e.g., Sir. 5:6). The notion of a multitude of sins has a similar range of precedents (e.g., Ps. 5:10; 85:2; Ezek. 28:18; Sir. 5:6; 1QHᵃ IV, 19). Proverbs 10:12 is quoted also in 1 Pet. 4:8 and is picked up in early post-NT documents as well (*1 Clem.* 49:5; *2 Clem.* 16:4).

D. Textual Matters. Although the allusion to Prov. 10:12 is clear, the wording of James 5:20 is close to neither the Hebrew nor the LXX; the LXX is least similar. This has prompted many to wonder if James is dependent for the form of his expression on common early Jewish Christian tradition. That is plausible enough, but the justifying sources are meager.

E. James's Use of the OT in 5:20. Where Proverbs preserves the antithesis between speech of hate and speech of love, James applies the second part of the proverb, the part including the expression "and cover over a multitude of sins," to what he views as the most loving act of all: warning people from the errors of their ways and bringing them into a robust repentance.

F. Theological Use. This exhortation is of a piece with the recurring NT theme that evil is not overcome merely by refraining from doing it: we are to overcome evil with good. It is not enough to break a bad habit; it is essential to love Jesus more, to want eternal things more. It is not enough not to retaliate against an enemy; it is essential to love one's enemy. So too here at the end of James's epistle: it is not enough to try to be faithful ourselves; rather, it is essential to try to secure the faithfulness of others. We overcome evil with good.

Bibliography

Byron, J. 2006. "Living in the Shadow of Cain: Echoes of a Developing Tradition in James 5:1–6." *NovT* 48: 261–74.

Calvin, J. 1948. *Commentaries on the Catholic Epistles*. Translated by J. Owen. Repr., Grand Rapids: Eerdmans.

Carson, D. A. 2004. "The Vindication of Imputation: On Fields of Discourse and Semantic Fields." Pages 46–78 in *Justification: What's at Stake in the Current Debate*. Edited by M. Husbands and D. J. Treier. Downers Grove, IL: InterVarsity Press.

Childs, B. S. 1974. *Exodus*. OTL. London: SCM Press.

Davids, P. H. 1982. *The Epistle of James: A Commentary on the Greek Text*. NIGTC. Grand Rapids: Eerdmans.

Dibelius, M. 1975 [1964]. *A Commentary on the Epistle of James*. Revised by Heinrich Greeven. Hermeneia. Philadelphia: Fortress.

Feuillet, A. 1964. "Le sens du mot Parousie dans l'Évangile de Matthieu: Comparaison entre Matth. xxiv et Jac. v.1–11." Pages 261–88 in *The Background of the New Testament and Its Eschatology*. Edited by W. D. Davies and D. Daube. Cambridge: Cambridge University Press.

Frankemölle, H. 1994. *Der Brief des Jakobus*. 2 vols. ÖTK 17. Gütersloh: Gütersloher Verlagshaus; Würzburg: Echter Verlag.

Hempel, C., A. Lange, and H. Lichtenberger, eds. 2001. *The Wisdom Texts from Qumran and the Development of Sapiential Thought*. BETL 159. Leuven: Peeters.

Johnson, L. T. 1995. *The Letter of James*. AB 37A. New York: Doubleday.

Laws, S. 1980. *A Commentary on the Epistle of James*. HNTC. New York: Harper & Row.

Longenecker, R. N. 1977. "The 'Faith of Abraham' Theme in Paul, James and Hebrews: A Study in the Circumstantial Nature of New Testament Teaching." *JETS* 20: 203–13.

Longman, T., III. 2006. *Proverbs*. BCOT. Grand Rapids: Baker Academic.

Martin, R. P. 1988. *James*. WBC 48. Waco: Word.

McConville, J. G. 2002. *Deuteronomy*. ApOTC. Leicester: Apollos.

Milgrom, J. 2000. *Leviticus 17–22*. AB 3A. New York: Doubleday.

Moo, D. J. 2000. *The Letter of James*. PilNTC. Grand Rapids: Eerdmans.

Mussner, F. 1981. *Der Jakobusbrief*. 4th ed. HTKNT 13/1. Freiburg: Herder.

Perdue, L. G. 1994. *Wisdom and Creation: The Theology of Wisdom Literature*. Nashville: Abingdon.

Rakestraw, R. V. 1986. "James 2:14–26: Does James Contradict the Pauline Soteriology?" *CTR* 1: 31–50.

Richardson, K. A. 2006. "Job as Exemplar in the Epistle of James." Pages 213–29 in *Hearing the Old Testament in the New Testament*. Edited by S. E. Porter. MNTS. Grand Rapids: Eerdmans.

Robertson, O. P. 1980. "Genesis 15:6: New Covenant Exposition of an Old Covenant Text." *WTJ* 42: 265–66.

Schlatter, A. 1956. *Der Brief des Jakobus*. Stuttgart: Calwer.

Spitta, F. 1896. "Der Brief des Jakobus." Pages 1–239 in *Zur Geschichte und Litteratur des Urchristentums*. Vol. 2. Göttingen: Vandenhoeck & Ruprecht.

Stamm, J. J., and M. E. Andrew. 1967. *The Ten Commandments in Recent Research*. SBT 2. London: SCM Press.

von Rad, G. 1951. "Die Anrechnung des Glaubens zur Gerechtigkeit." *TLZ* 76: cols. 129–32.

———. 1972a. *Genesis*. 3rd ed. London: SCM Press.

———. 1972b. *Wisdom in Israel*. London: SCM Press.

Waltke, B. K. 2001. *Genesis*. Grand Rapids: Zondervan.

———. 2004. *Proverbs 1–15*. NICOT. Grand Rapids: Eerdmans.

Wenham, G. J. 1979. *The Book of Leviticus*. NICOT. Grand Rapids: Eerdmans.

———. *Genesis 1–15*. 1987. WBC 1. Waco: Word.

Wood, T. R. 2005. "The Regathering of the People of God: An Investigation into the New Testament's Appropriation of the Old Testament Prophecies Concerning the Regathering of Israel." PhD diss., Trinity Evangelical Divinity School.

Ziesler, J. A. 1972. *The Meaning of Righteousness in Paul: A Linguistic and Theological Enquiry*. SNTSMS 20. Cambridge: Cambridge University Press.

Zimmerli, W. 1978. *Old Testament Theology in Outline*. Translated by D. E. Green. Edinburgh: T&T Clark.

1 Peter

D. A. Carson

Introduction

The OT is cited or alluded to in 1 Peter in rich profusion. In a handful of instances quotations are introduced by formulae: *dioti gegraptai*, "wherefore it is written" (1:16, citing Lev. 19:2), *dioti periechei en graphē*, "wherefore it stands in Scripture" (2:6–8, citing Isa. 28:16; Ps. 118:22; Isa. 8:14), or, more simply, by *dioti*, "wherefore" (1:24–25a, citing Isa. 40:6–8) or by *gar*, "for" (3:10–12, citing Ps. 34:13–17). About twenty quotations are sufficiently lengthy and specific that there is little doubt regarding their specific OT provenance. For a book of only five short chapters, there is a remarkable record of quotation. Yet the quotations tell only a small part of the story, for 1 Peter is also laced with allusions to the OT. How many there are is disputed, depending on the tightness of the definition of allusion: Osborne (1981: 65) sees thirty-one, while Schutter (1989: 43) finds forty-one. If one were to extend beyond allusions (however defined) to echoes picking up OT language and themes, scarcely a verse in this epistle would be exempt. For example, just within chapter 1 (and even this list is partial) one finds the Diaspora theme in v. 1, the sanctifying work of the Holy Spirit and "sprinkling" language in v. 2, the inheritance theme in v. 4 (which becomes hugely important in the Epistle to the Hebrews), mention of gold refined by fire in v. 7, a collection of reflections on what the prophets knew and did not know in 1:10–12, a lamb without blemish in v. 19, mention of the creation in v. 20, and so forth. This surfeit of connections with the OT means that a thorough treatment of the subject would require a full-length commentary on the entire epistle. Since that is not feasible, we must restrict ourselves here to the quotations and to only the most important or evocative allusions.

Although quotations in 1 Peter are drawn from all three divisions of the Hebrew OT (Torah, Prophets, Writings), the books with the greatest number of quotations are, in descending order, Isaiah, Psalms, and Proverbs. Although he overstates the point, Achtemeier (1996: 12–13) correctly observes that by and large Peter cites the OT for illustrative or supporting purposes rather than as fundamental proof.

1:1

Peter addresses his letter to those who have been "scattered [*diasporas*] throughout Pontus, Galatia, Cappadocia, Asia, and Bithynia"—literally, "foreigners of the diaspora." That one Greek word forces us to reflect on the Diaspora (see also commentary on James 1:1). The word reminds the reader of the impact of the exile under the Assyrian and Babylonian regional superpowers, with countless thousands of Jews still scattered all over the Mediterranean world and beyond. Through

1015

the OT prophets, however, God promised, both before the exile and after the initial return from exile, that he would regather his exiled people and reconstitute the twelve tribes (e.g., Isa. 11:11–12; Jer. 31:8–14; Ezek. 37:21–22; Zech. 10:6–12)—promises that lived on in the expectations of later Judaism (e.g., *Pss. Sol.* 17:26–28; *T. Benj.* 9:2).

Most contemporary commentators treat the expressions "strangers in the world" and "scattered throughout Pontus . . ." to be evocative ways of referring to the transitoriness of life in this broken world, of an ongoing spiritual exile that will not be finally brought to an end until the return of Christ. Recently, however, Jobes (2005: 28–41, 63–66) has convincingly argued that although the sense of spiritual pilgrimage and transition is certainly present, a concrete setting can be responsibly envisaged in which physical scattering plays a part. All five of the regions named in 1:1 were recolonized by Rome under the reign of Claudius. A circumstantial case can be made for the thesis that Christians, both Jews and Gentiles, were among those forcibly sent. If this is correct, then Peter's readers were Christians (both Jews and Gentiles) who had been converted elsewhere, perhaps in Rome, but whose forceful relocation guaranteed their sense of dislocation, setting them up to feel very much like a new generation of exiles in a strange land.

1:2

Although there is widespread acknowledgment that the words "and sprinkling by his blood" (NIV) allude to Exod. 24:3–8, the exact force of the expression in 1 Peter depends on a difficult exegetical problem. To appreciate it, we must begin by understanding the OT text on its own terms. The scene in Exod. 24 is the confirmation of the covenant, the sealing of the covenant: by Moses' instructions, an altar is set up at the foot of Mount Sinai, and young Israelite men (the formal legitimate priesthood had not yet been instituted) offer burnt offerings and sacrifice young bulls as fellowship offerings to God. Moses collects the blood, sprinkling half on the altar, which speaks of God's forgiveness grounded in his acceptance of this sacrifice. Moses then takes the Book of the Covenant and reads it to the people, who vow, "We will do everything the LORD has said; we will obey" (Exod. 24:7), whereupon Moses takes the other half of the blood, collected in bowls, and

sprinkles it on the people, making this a blood oath, a solemn covenant commitment to the effect that their blood will be required if they break the covenant.

How, then, does Peter pick up on this theme? Christians, Peter asserts, have been "chosen . . . through the sanctifying work of the Spirit, *eis hypakoēn kai rhantismon haimatos Iēsou Christou*," commonly rendered "for obedience to Jesus Christ and sprinkling through his blood" (NIV) or "for obedience to Jesus Christ and for sprinkling with his blood" (ESV). We may, with almost all commentators, accept that *eis* has a telic sense, "for" (i.e., "for the purpose of"), not the causal sense suggested by Agnew (1983). The English translations, however, give the impression that the words "Jesus Christ" modify both "obedience" and "sprinkling" or "blood" (since "his" is included), whereas this easy twofold understanding of the words "Jesus Christ" masks an exegetical problem. If the genitive expression *Iēsou Christou* ("Jesus Christ") modifies *hypakoēn* ("obedience"), presumably it is an objective genitive; that is, Jesus Christ is the one to be obeyed. We have been chosen for the purpose of obeying Jesus Christ, whether this obeying Jesus Christ is understood as the initial response to the gospel (so Best 1982: 71) or as ongoing submission to the lordship of Christ (so Davids 1990: 48). Unfortunately, however, it is difficult to construe *Iēsou Christou* as an object genitive with *rhantismon haimatos* ("sprinkling of blood"). Many therefore take the words to be an objective genitive with respect to "obedience" but a possessive genitive with respect to "blood"—that is, "sprinkling through [or 'of'] the blood of Jesus Christ" or, more simply, using the possessive pronoun, "sprinkling of his blood" (so, more or less, NRSV, NLT, NIV, TNIV, ESV). Occasionally, commentators see this as a second, higher stage: first the initial response to Christ in obedience to the gospel, and then a higher stage of conformity to Christ, signaled, perhaps, by suffering and referred to obliquely by this "sprinkling of his blood" (so Bigg 1901: 93). Syntactically, however, it is extraordinarily difficult to suppose that the one pair of words *Iēsou Christou* could be functioning as an objective genitive with respect to one noun and as a possessive genitive with respect to another.

It seems wiser, then, to take "obedience and sprinkling" as a hendiadys (two words expressing a single idea) alluding to the scene in Exod. 24:3–8 (so Achtemeier 1996: 87–89; Jobes 2005: 72). There, as we have seen, the people pledge their obedience, and then they are sprinkled with the blood of the sacrifice. So also here: Christians have been chosen "for (the purpose of) obedience and sprinkling of the blood of Jesus Christ"—that is, to enter into this new covenant relationship in which we pledge our obedience while the covenant is sealed by Jesus' death. The genitive *Iēsou Christou* is, then, possessive, modifying "blood"—a way of referring to Jesus' death while understanding that this is a new-covenant commitment modeled on the type of the old-covenant confirmation ceremony.

It must be admitted that although many commentators detect the allusion to Exod. 24:3–8, their conclusions are usually much more attenuated. Goppelt (1993: 74) does not see more than a remote allusion to Exod. 24; Michaels (1988: 12) suggests that Num. 19, the red-heifer ceremony, is the primary OT background; several find in "sprinkling" an allusion to water baptism, though that theory is less in vogue today than when the theory that 1 Peter was part of a baptismal liturgy dominated scholarly enthusiasm. Yet the covenantal connection seems strong on the face of it, and stronger yet when we recall that in the ensuing words Peter reminds his readers how this "new birth" (1:3 [redolent of "the sanctifying work of the Spirit" in 1:2]) grants to us a living hope grounded in the resurrection of Jesus from the dead, a hope to be certainly fulfilled in "the coming of the salvation that is ready to be revealed in the last time" (1:5), "when Jesus Christ is revealed" (1:7).

1:16

A. NT Context: Holiness in Conformity with Torah's Stipulation.

In previous verses Peter has explained the manner in which OT prophets looked forward beyond their immediate horizons to the fulfillment of their words (1:10–12). The salvation that they longed for has now been disclosed in the coming of Christ—a salvation that Peter's readers are now enjoying, even as they await its consummation (1:3–9). In the light of all this (*dio*, "wherefore" [1:13]), his readers must set their hope, their expectation, fully on the end,

"on the grace to be given you when Jesus Christ is revealed" (1:13). As obedient children—that is, obedient to Jesus Christ and to the stipulations of the new covenant—they are no longer to conform to the evil desires that dominated them before their conversion (1:14). Rather (*alla*), "Just as he who called you is holy, so be holy in all you do" (1:15 NIV). "Wherefore [*dio*] it is written: 'Be holy, because I am holy'"—the quotation drawn from Leviticus. Michaels (1988: 59) observes that the application of the verse is in this case given before the quotation itself, but this happens elsewhere in 1 Peter (see commentary on 1 Pet. 2:6 and 2:8 below).

B. OT Context.

The commandment "Be holy because I am holy" occurs, with slight variations, four times in Leviticus (11:44; 19:2; 20:7–8, 26). The words that Peter uses are drawn from Lev. 19:2 (see §D below). That means the context in Peter's mind as he quotes these words is not the Passover or exodus theme (as would have been the case had he quoted from Lev. 11:44 [cf. Lev. 11:45]) but rather is the so-called Holiness Code (Lev. 17–26). The instructions in Lev. 11–20 are not just for the priesthood; they are for the entire nation of Israel.

C. The Context in Judaism.

The OT frequently insists that God's people must be holy, for the holy God dwells among them (cf. Exod. 32–34; Isa. 6). Not infrequently this holiness included cultic purity (e.g., Exod. 28:2; Deut. 7:6; 26:19; Ezra 9:2; Ps. 50:13)—a theme picked up and developed among the sectarians at Qumran (e.g., 1QM III, 5; XII, 7; XVI, 1). Yet although there is within Judaism a reservoir of moral exhortation grounded in the holiness of God, the tendency to attach holiness to the temple and all its rituals guarantees that there is a rich emphasis on the theme in the *Temple Scroll*. But the community at Qumran is itself a "holy community" (1Q28a I, 12–13), a "holy council" (1QS II, 25; V, 20; 1Q28a II, 9; 1QHᵃ XV, 10; CD-B XX, 24–25), a "holy fellowship" (1QS IX, 2), and its men are "men of holiness" (1QS V, 13; VIII, 17, 23; IX, 8), even "men of perfect holiness" (1QS VIII, 20; CD-B XX, 2, 5, 7).

D. Textual Matters.

Peter follows the LXX of Lev. 19:2 exactly: *hagios esesthe, hoti hagios [eimi]*, a fine rendering of the Hebrew. Note the use of the future tense (*esesthe*, "you shall be") to convey imperatival force.

E. Peter's Use of the OT in 1:16. Although the OT commandment is given to the Israelites, Peter unhesitatingly applies it to the new-covenant people of God, Jews and Gentiles alike. Yet neither he nor anyone else in the NT systematically applies all of the stipulations of Lev. 17–26 directly to Christian believers. In short, the OT remains the word of God for NT believers, and Peter and others can sometimes appeal to its commandments directly, yet the application of OT texts is never undifferentiated. What is certain is that however disputed the principles of continuity and discontinuity between the commandments of the old and new covenants might be, the commandment to be holy because God is holy crosses the line between the covenants in an unqualified way—though even here some nuance must be introduced, for the manifestation of holiness is more detached from ritual concerns than it is, say, in Qumran.

F. Theological Use. The word "holy" and its cognates are used in the Bible in a series of concentric semantic distinctions. Toward the center, "holy" is almost an adjective for "God": God alone is God; God alone is holy. Things that are then reserved for God's use, or peculiarly possessed by God, are said to be holy—whether it be the shovel that removes the ash from God's altar, or the priests that serve him, or his covenant people as a whole. Of course, the implications of what "holy" means will differ for shovel and people. For the latter, belonging exclusively to the Lord soon takes on an array of moral, cultic, and behavioral overtones, not because such moral stances are independent of God but precisely because they are what this holy God requires of his people. Farther out, the word can refer vaguely to the domain of the sacred. In that sense, a pagan priest can be considered a "holy man."

Inevitably, God's holiness is tied to his wrath. Not to revere God as holy is not to revere God as God; it is to "de-god" him, to displace him with non-gods, with idols. The complex sacrificial system of Leviticus is bound up with the ways in which people become unholy, dirty, and then how they can become holy again. Some of this drama is bound up with matters of ritual purity; some of it is bound up with obligations that

God's covenant people have toward each other and toward him. Insofar as these God-provided sacrifices, which made people holy again under the stipulations of the Mosaic covenant, point forward to the ultimate sacrifice of Christ, they anticipate the way in which Christ by his death and resurrection makes people of the new covenant holy by dealing with their sin. The theme is nowhere more powerfully expounded than in Heb. 9. But that never means that NT writers are unconcerned about the actual conduct of new-covenant believers. The expectation is that the gospel not only fits God's people for the presence of the holy God but also powerfully transforms them. Jobes (2005: 113) provides a useful chart to remind us of how Peter contrasts the "before conversion" and "after conversion" experience of the people to whom Peter writes:

Formerly	Now
ignorance of God	knowledge of Christ and of God
are not God's children/people	are God's children/people
controlled by desires	controlled by obedience to God
futile way of life	holy way of life
affirmed by society	misunderstood and maligned by society

1:19

The preceding verse, 1:18, discloses the nature of the redemption that Peter's readers had experienced in the gospel: "For you know that it was not with perishable things such as silver or gold that you were redeemed from the empty way of life handed down to you from your forefathers"—and then our verse, with its OT allusion: "but with the precious blood of Christ, a lamb without blemish or defect."

Two things need to be sorted out before we look at the OT allusion itself. First, the redemption language has deep roots in both the Greco-Roman and the Jewish worlds. The verb rendered "redeemed" (*lytroō* [cognate with the noun *lytron*]) was used, for instance, for the manumission of slaves in Greco-Roman culture. The slave's price could be deposited (by the slave or by some kind benefactor) in the temple of a local god or goddess, which money, minus a commission for the temple, would be paid out of the temple's treasury to the slave's owner, with the result that ownership of the slave passed, nominally, to the god of the temple. The former slave was then free from his former master and would be viewed as a slave of the god or goddess, which for all intents and purposes meant that the slave was free. The purchase price for this redemption was referred to as a *timē* ("price"). Of course, manumission could also take place in Jewish culture; see, for instance, Ps. 34:22 (34:23 MT; 33:23 LXX), in a psalm that Peter will allude to in his next chapter (1 Pet. 2:3) and quote at length another chapter later (1 Pet. 3:10–12): "The Lord will redeem the lives of his slaves; none who hope in him will go astray" (LXX). Indeed, redemption also refers to the deliverance of God's people from foreign domination, whether from exile or from the original enslavement in Egypt (e.g., Deut. 7:8; Isa. 52:3). Clearly Peter is using this language to talk about how Christians have been redeemed from their own captivity. Now they are free, but they are slaves to God (cf. 1 Pet. 2:16).

Second, just as the manumission of the slave or the rescue of the people from captivity meant that they had been rescued from a former way of life that was empty, so Peter picks up the same terminology and applies it to the Christian converts whom he is addressing: You have been redeemed "out of [*ek*] the useless [*mataios*] way of life you inherited from your ancestors" (1:18). Certainly the ancestral "way of life" (*patroparadotos*) normally has very positive associations (see van Unnik 1969). Possibly Peter is the first person to use the word in an essentially negative way, referring to pre-Christian existence. Many commentators think that this means that Peter's readers must be primarily Gentiles, for not only is the adjective *mataios* often used in the LXX to describe pagan idols (e.g., 1 Kings 16:2; Hos. 5:11; Jon. 2:9 [2:8 ET]; Isa. 44:9; Jer. 2:5), but also, it is argued, surely Peter would not paint Jewish life before conversion to Christ in such dark hues. Yet that conclusion is far from certain. After all, Paul can elsewhere describe his own Jewish life before conversion in astonishingly negative categories (Phil. 3:4–9). In short, it is unwise to use Peter's language to infer too much about his readership.

With what, then, are Christians purchased, redeemed? Not with the *timē* ("price") of silver and gold but rather with the *timios* ("precious") blood of Christ, a lamb without blemish or defect. It is impossible to specify one concrete OT antecedent text, but the redemption by the blood of a lamb is rooted in Exodus, Leviticus, Isaiah, and Psalms (see Achtemeier 1996: 128–29)—books that Peter quotes, some of them often. Nothing from their old life could have redeemed them, certainly not silver and gold; rather, they have been redeemed by God's own powerful act in the death and resurrection of his Son (1:20–21; cf. 1 Cor. 6:20; 7:23; Heb. 9:12).

1:24–25

A. NT Context: The Living and Enduring Word of God.

In his exhortation to his readers to live in holy community, Peter has already urged them to set their hope fully on God's grace (1:13) and to be holy because their heavenly Father is holy (1:15–16). Now he urges them to love one another earnestly (1:22). By obeying the truth— that is, by submitting to the gospel and coming to faith in Jesus Christ—"they have set themselves apart from the ways of the world and how they used to treat people" (Jobes 2005: 123). As Peter puts it, "You have purified [*hēgnikotes*] yourselves by obeying the truth" (1:22 NIV). This perfect participle indicates that the people are in the state of consecration, of having been set apart (that is the idea, rather than purification) by their obedience to the gospel. The verb *hagnizō* ("consecrate, make holy") consistently appears in the LXX and in the Gospels and Acts to refer to a ceremonial ritual in which one willingly and intentionally devotes oneself to God (e.g., Exod. 19:10; Josh. 3:5; 2 Chron. 30:17; John 11:55; Acts 21:24; 24:18). This consecration to God by obedience to the gospel is for the purpose (the NIV's "so that" suggests result, but *eis* here is almost certainly telic) of having "sincere love for your brothers" (1:22 [*eis philadelphian anypokriton*, lit., "unhypocritical brotherly love"]). Hence the exhortation itself: in the light of all this, "love one another deeply, from the heart" (1:22). After all, they "have been born again, not of perishable seed, but of imperishable, through the living and enduring word of God" (1:23). In other words, the command to love is coherent because the very nature of Peter's hearers has been transformed. The new birth generates life from imperishable seed, the word of God, which implicitly is contrasted with ordinary life generated by normal human procreation, life that is fragile, temporary, and frequently vile. The quality and enduring character of this new life, over against all the ephemeral qualities of mere mortal life, is grounded in the quality and enduring character of the "seed" that engendered it, the word of God. "Peter's logic here is that the new birth given by God to those who enter the new covenant of Christ's blood in faith is conceived from the imperishable seed of God's word, which generates eternal life" (Jobes 2005: 125). To validate this point, Peter introduces a scriptural quotation from Isaiah, introducing it with *dioti* ("for, wherefore"), to demonstrate that the sharp contrast that he has in mind is biblically warranted:

> All men are like grass,
>   and their glory is like the flowers of the field;
>   the grass withers and the flowers fall,
>   but the word of the LORD stands forever.

This word Peter connects with the gospel itself: "And this is the word that was preached to you" (1:25).

B. OT Context. The larger context is so important that a translation of all of Isa. 40:1–11 is provided here. This translation is by Childs and is of the MT:

> ¹Comfort, comfort my people,
>   says your God.
> ²Speak tenderly to Jerusalem
>   and say to her
> that her term of service is over,
>   that her iniquity has been pardoned,
> that she has received from the LORD's hand
>   double for all her sins.
> ³A voice cries:
> "In the wilderness prepare the way of the LORD,
>   make level in the desert a highway for our God.
> ⁴Let every valley be raised up,
>   every mountain and hill made low.
> Let the uneven ground become smooth
>   and the rugged places a plain.
> ⁵And the glory of the LORD will be revealed,
>   and all flesh as one will see it,
>   for the mouth of the LORD has spoken."
> ⁶A voice says, "Cry!"
>   Another asks, "What shall I cry?"
> All flesh is grass,
>   and all its strength like a wildflower.
> ⁷The grass withers, flowers fade

> when the breath of the LORD blows on them.
> Surely the people are grass.
> ⁸The grass withers, flowers fade,
>   but the word of our God stands forever.
> ⁹Get up to a high mountain,
>   O Zion, herald of good tidings,
> Lift up your voice with might,
>   O evangelist Jerusalem.
>   Lift it up, do not fear.
> Say to the cities of Judah,
>   "Behold, your God."
> ¹⁰See, the Lord GOD comes in power,
>   and his arm triumphs for him.
> See, his reward is with him,
>   and his retribution before him.
> ¹¹Like a shepherd he will feed his flock,
>   gathering them in his arms;
> he will carry them in his bosom,
>   gently leading those with young.

The prophet envisages the Israelite exiles under the Babylonian superpower and knows full well that they have sunk into massive discouragement. This proclamation is characterized by comfort, hope, and promise of deliverance and is addressed to a discouraged covenant community exiled in the Diaspora and uncertain about the validity of God's covenant promises—and God says, "Comfort, comfort my people" (40:1). "Without question this is the language of the covenant (Exod. 6:7; 19:5; Lev. 26:12; Deut. 26:17–18; etc.). . . . The descendants of Abraham and Jacob need not fear that God will forget his promises to their ancestors" (Oswalt 1998: 49). How could it be otherwise? God's word stands forever, unlike the ephemeral grass and flower. God's promise to lower the hills and raise the valleys and smooth the uneven places (40:4) is a powerful metaphorical way of saying that anything that could be construed as a barrier to the return of the exiles will be removed. This is picking up language from Isa. 35, which also anticipates a highway, "the Way of Holiness," designed only "for those who walk in that Way" (35:8). Apparently, then, removing the barriers and hindrances is equivalent to making this a way of holiness. The moral dimensions to preparing the way for the Lord would be well understood, six centuries later, by John the Baptist (e.g., Matt. 3; cf. Mark 1:1–3).

The promise is of a worldwide theophany, a glorious display of the glory of God to "all flesh" (40:5). Some of the glory theme of Isa. 6 is taken up here. The promise is sure, "for the mouth of the LORD has spoken" (40:5), and God's word stands forever (40:6–8). Yet again the prophet reminds the exiles that the Lord God himself is coming in power, bringing both reward and retribution (40:10), coming as the shepherd of his flock (40:11).

C. The Context in Judaism. The Qumran scrolls preserve evidence of slightly different readings of this passage, readings sometimes a little closer to the LXX (see §D below). Danker (1967) reminds us that just as this quotation from the OT triggers in 1 Peter the discussion in 1 Pet. 2:1–17 (so also Westermann 1969: 42), so also in 1QHᵃ it triggers a consoling discussion with similar themes designed for a suffering people.

D. Textual Matters. To begin with simplest matters first, the syntax of *mĕbaśśeret ṣîyyôn* (40:9) is disputed. The LXX, Targum, Vulgate, and many contemporary commentators take it as an accusative object: "good tidings to Zion" (cf. 41:27; 52:7). Others read it in apposition: "herald of good tidings" (cf. 41:14). This decision influences a further decision two lines later. Since these have little bearing on Peter's quotation, these alternatives are not probed here. Moreover, the rendering "Another asks" (second line of 40:6) reflects the MT. Both 1QIsaᵃ and the LXX have "And I said."

On the whole, 1 Peter follows the LXX more closely than it does the MT. Isaiah 40:7 is missing from both the LXX and 1 Peter, and both the LXX and the MT omit the definite article before *pasa sarx* ("all flesh"). Further, the LXX changes MT's "flower of the field" to "flower of grass," which is followed by the best reading of 1 Peter (even though the NIV arbitrarily translates "flowers of the field"; the ESV has "flower of grass"). The MT tells us that the flowers "fade"; both the LXX and 1 Peter say that they "fall." On the other hand, while the LXX reads *pasa doxa anthrōpou* ("all human glory"), 1 Peter follows the MT in reading *pasa doxa autēs* ("all its glory," with "its" pointing to "all flesh"; and because the NIV has rendered *pasa sarx* ["all flesh"] as "all men," it necessarily changes "its" to "their").

But 1 Peter introduces three changes unsupported by the MT or the LXX. (1) Peter inserts *hōs* ("as" or "like") between "flesh" and "grass." This merely makes the metaphor explicit, and it is something that Peter does elsewhere (e.g., 1:14; 2:2, 5 [see Schutter 1989: 125]). (2) Peter omits *hēmōn* ("our") in v. 25a; that is, he reads "but the word of the Lord stands forever" instead of "but the word of our Lord stands forever." The meaning of the citation is not thereby altered. (3) Over against both the MT and the LXX, which have "word of our God," Peter substitutes *kyrios* for *theos* ("Lord" for "God"). The possible reasons for the change are much disputed (see Achtemeier 1996: 141–42).

E. Peter's Use of the OT in 1:24–25. Although the promises of Isa. 40 were first given to encourage Israelites in exile after the Babylonian captivity, they are so generous—including the promise of a worldwide theophany—that it is hard to imagine that anyone thought that the promises had been exhausted in the small-scale return to the promised land under the leadership of men such as Zerubbabel, Ezra, and Nehemiah. God's covenant people needed to persevere in quiet confidence in their God, for his word, unlike ephemeral glories such as flowers and grass, endures. Peter recognizes the stark similarities between those who were initially comforted by Isa. 40 and those who are going to read his epistle. Almost certainly he expects them to pick up on all of Isa. 40, not just the two verses that he actually cites, and to detect the parallels in their own situation. Selwyn (1955: 152) astutely comments,

> Every leading thought here [in Isa. 40] fits in with what our author [Peter] has been saying. He too is addressing readers who are exiled . . . and oppressed; and he has the same message for them, the contrast between the perishability of all mortal things (cf. φθαρτός in verses 18, 23) and the incorruptibility of the Christian inheritance and hope. . . . The passage quoted is, therefore, the focal point of a much longer passage which must have been often present in the Apostle's mind.

Peter's readers, too, are in exile, at least spiritually, and perhaps (as we saw above) physically as well if they have recently been forcibly transported by the Roman government. Achtemeier (1996: 142) comments (also cited in Jobes 2005: 129),

The contrast between what is transitory and what is permanent embodied in the quotation would be highly appropriate for a beleaguered community of Christians facing what gave every appearance of being the permanent, even eternal, power and glory of the Roman Empire. In such a situation, the announcement that the glitter, pomp, and power of the Roman culture was as grass when compared to God's eternal word spoken in Jesus Christ, available through the gospel preached to and accepted by the Christians of Asia Minor, would give them courage to hold fast to the latter while rejecting the former. Even the hostility of that overwhelming power becomes more bearable when its ultimately transitory nature is revealed and accepted.

F. Theological Use. At one level, Peter is applying Isa. 40:6–8 to his own readers in a direct fashion, for their circumstances are remarkably similar to those to whom Isa. 40 was designed to bring comfort. Yet by his final sentence in 1:25 Peter introduces another dimension: "And this is the word that was preached to you." He thus insists that the gospel word preached to his converts is in fact the word that Isaiah had in mind. Of course, this might mean nothing more than that God's word is forever secure, and the same sort of stability found in God's word at the time of the Babylonian exile is no less stable in Peter's day under the Roman Empire. In other words, the message may not be exactly the same, but the stability is the same: God's word is always trustworthy. Yet Peter apparently is claiming something more. If he is expecting his readers to bring the content of Isa. 40 along with the actual lines quoted, then the word preached to them is doubtless the word promising the visitation by Yahweh, the promised worldwide theophany—manifested in the gospel itself and still to be fulfilled at the end of the age. Precisely because God's word is reliable, Peter's readers can rest assured that the fulfillment that has not yet taken place will come—and "this is the word that was preached to you."

So Peter's Christian readers must press on and be faithful. Not only the first chapter of 1 Peter, but also the ensuing verses, demonstrate what has already been achieved by Christ, even while they exhort the readers to persevere in the light of the promises still to come. This is a not uncommon way for OT prophecies to be picked up by NT writers: substantial fulfillment has already taken

place, but more is to come, so faithful perseverance is all the more needed.

2:3

A. NT Context: Crave Spiritual Nourishment. We come to the fourth of Peter's exhortations to his readers. He has already urged them to set their hope fully on God's grace (1:13), to be holy because their heavenly Father is holy (1:15–16), and to love one another earnestly (1:22). Now he enjoins them to crave spiritual nourishment.

Christians are to rid themselves of the vices listed in 2:1, all of which interrupt godly relationships with others and with the Master himself. Like newborn babies, they are to "crave pure spiritual milk" (2:2). The majority of contemporary commentators take this to be a symbolic way of referring to the word of God, so prominent in the closing lines of the previous chapter. That certainly is possible, though Calvin (1963: 256), Michaels (1988: 89), and especially Jobes (2005: 130–41) argue forcefully that Peter has now left the focus on the word of God behind and uses "milk" to refer to the sustaining life of God. That interpretation becomes the more plausible on a certain reading of the OT quotation with which Peter brings this section to a close: "now that you have tasted that the Lord is good." So to the OT we must turn.

B. OT Context. Once again Peter probably has the entire chapter in his mind (Ps. 34), as later in his letter he will quote from it extensively (1 Pet. 3:10–12), and some have found further allusions to the psalm in 1 Pet. 1:15; 2:4 (Snodgrass 1977–1978). The superscription asserts that the psalm was written by David when he feigned madness in the court of Abimelech. One cannot read the psalm without feeling the sense of euphoric relief from having escaped—an escape that must finally be credited to the Lord himself. Hence: "This poor man called, and the LORD heard him; he saved him out of all his troubles" (34:6 TNIV); "Taste and see that the LORD is good; blessed are those who take refuge in him" (34:8 TNIV). The small changes in the psalm introduced by the LXX translation tend to contextualize the psalm for the Diaspora setting.

C. The Context in Judaism. Normally the Hebrew verb *ṭāʿam* ("taste") is used in conjunction with real food, so the corresponding occurrences of this verb and Greek *geuomai* in the literature of Second Temple Judaism, not surprisingly, most commonly have to do with tasting food, or perhaps not tasting it because of some vow or cultic restriction (see Tob. 7:11; 2 Macc. 6:20; Josephus, *Ant.* 6.119, 126, 377; 7.42). But the figurative use of the verb in Ps. 34:8 (34:9 MT), "where the very present reality of god's goodness is so vivid to the psalmist that he is able to describe it as actually perceptible to the senses of taste and sight" (*ISBE* 4:738), is echoed in Sir. 23:27 as well as in 1 Pet. 2:3.

D. Textual Matters. When Peter quotes Ps. 34:8 (33:9 LXX), he changes the mood of the verb from the (plural) imperative *geusasthe* ("[you] taste") to the (aorist) indicative, *egeusasthe* ("you have tasted"). He also drops the second verb, *kai idete* ("and see"), which omission may stem from his application to the milk metaphor in the preceding verse, since "seeing" milk is not only unnecessary for his purpose but also potentially confusing.

E. Peter's Use of the OT in 2:3. The logic between 2:2 and 2:3, then, is straightforward: "Crave spiritual milk, since you have [already] tasted that the Lord is good." Five observations will clarify some of the details. First, 2:3 is presented as a first-class condition, which does not necessarily assume the reality of the protasis, but clearly does in this case. Second, Peter, like others in the NT, does not hesitate to use the expression "the Lord" to refer to Jesus Christ (as is clear from the following verses) even when the OT expression, in Hebrew, is the Tetragrammaton, YHWH. Third, the word "good" here, as in the LXX, is *chrēstos*. The word occurs frequently in the LXX to refer to God, to God's name, to God's mercy, and to God's law (see the many references in Jobes 2005: 137). Many writers (e.g., Goppelt 1993: 137) detect a play on words with *christos* ("Christ"), since there is only one vowel difference. Fourth, this reading of Peter's use of Ps. 34:8 (33:9 LXX) tends to confirm the view expressed above, that "milk" has a broader experiential reference than simply the word of God. The milk is their experience of the Lord himself, which they have already tasted. Now they are to abandon all sin and crave more of the experience of the Lord that they have already tasted and enjoyed, for "there can be no food beyond Christ" (Best 1982: 97). Fifth, if the context of Ps. 34 is in Peter's mind, he wants his readers

to think of more than the mere verbal expression of tasting the Lord. He wants to remind them of the enormous sense of relief and pleasure in the Lord that they enjoyed when they came to know him in the context of the gospel, and to encourage them to pursue more of the same.

F. Theological Use. There are many biblical passages, of course, that urge believers to press on in obedience and conformity to Christ (e.g., Phil. 3). One of the more interesting features of Peter's argument here, however, is the way in which he appeals to the experience of his readers as a kind of ground for his appeal for them to press on. Precisely because they have already tasted that the Lord is good, they are urged to crave pure spiritual milk and thus grow up into their salvation. One recalls other passages in which biblical writers make a legitimate appeal to experience. Not least notable is Paul, who reminds the Galatians that they received the Spirit not by observing the law but rather by believing in the gospel message that they heard (Gal. 3:2)—that was their experience. So why, then, should they think that they can go on to gospel maturity by seeking nothing more than conformity to law?

2:6

A. NT Context: Jesus the Precious Cornerstone. The move from the "milk" metaphor to "stone" imagery has prompted not a few suggestions regarding possible verbal or conceptual links. Hillyer (1969: 126) suggests that, quite naturally in Hebraic thought, the stones are used to build a house, and "to become a house is to obtain children." Jobes (2005: 145) thinks that Ps. 34 (33 LXX) is still in play: Peter recalls two earlier verses in the psalm that capture where his thought is now going (here I have added italics to the NETS translation in order to highlight the thematic connections):

> I *sought* the Lord, and he hearkened to me,
>   and delivered me from all my
>   sojournings.
> *Come to him*, and be enlightened;
>   and your faces *shall never be put to shame*.
>   (Ps. 33:5–6 LXX NETS)

For other suggestions regarding Peter's movement of thought, see Achtemeier 1996: 153.

More important, perhaps, is the number of expressions that Peter uses in 2:4–5 that anticipate where he is going in his series of OT quotations in 2:6–10 (for a list, see Bauckham 1988: 311). As Peter tells his readers how they are to understand themselves with respect to the Lord Jesus, he asserts that Jesus, to whom his readers "come," is "the living Stone, rejected by human beings but chosen by God and precious to him" (2:4 TNIV), while they themselves are "like living stones" who "are being built into a spiritual house" (2:5). This is then warranted (*dioti*, "wherefore") by a quotation from Isa. 28:16:

> See, I lay a stone in Zion,
>   a chosen and precious cornerstone,
> and the one who trusts in him
>   will never be put to shame.

What precisely is being warranted by this quotation is still to be explored. For the moment we must observe that there are three OT passages that reflect this stone imagery (Ps. 118:22–23; Isa. 8:14–15; 28:16), and all three are quoted in our passage, 1 Pet. 2:6–8. Elsewhere, in his speech in Acts 4:11–12, Peter identifies Jesus as the rejected stone that nevertheless becomes the cornerstone. Doubtless Peter learned the identification from Jesus himself: all three Synoptic Gospels bear witness that Jesus prophetically identified himself with the rejected stone (Matt. 21:42–44; Mark 12:10–11; Luke 20:17–18). In the seven places where stone imagery is picked up in the NT (in addition to the present text and those cited in the Synoptics and Acts, see Rom. 9:32–33; Eph. 2:20–22) the rejected stone is always identified as Jesus. The multiplicity of witnesses, which cannot be explained by literary dependence, testifies that this was a common Christian tradition, finally warranted by Jesus' own teaching. In the past this impressive list of NT passages has sometimes been taken as evidence of a written document of stone *testimonia*. Although that is not an impossible conclusion, it is simpler to suppose that the links could have been forged in common oral tradition, not least when we recall that some strands of Second Temple Judaism had already identified the stone in the OT stone passages with the Messiah (see §B below). All the NT writers had to do was identify Jesus as the Messiah.

B. OT Context. A recurring dynamic tension between hope and despairing condemnation characterizes Isa. 28. Thus 28:5–6 anticipates the day when "the LORD Almighty will be a glori-ous crown, a beautiful wreath, for the remnant of his people" (28:5), while the next unit, 28:7–13, pictures a confrontation between the prophet Isaiah and the drunken priests and prophets of Judah. They "stagger from beer and are befuddled with wine" (28:7). "All the tables are covered with vomit, and there is not a spot without filth" (28:8). In their drunken stupor they loudly protest against this wretched prophet who presumes to teach them (28:9). They hear him uttering what is to them incomprehensible gibberish: *ṣaw lāṣāw ṣaw lāṣāw* (28:10 [strangely rendered by the NIV as "Do and do, do and do"]). But the prophet protests that if they will not listen to his words, God will finally speak to them in catastrophic judgment. Invading troops will trample them down, and through them God will speak to this people "with foreign lips and strange tongues." Instead of the land of Judah being a place of rest (28:12), the message of judgment will be couched in genuinely incomprehensible speech: *ṣaw lāṣāw ṣaw lāṣāw* (28:13).

Similarly in the next section: a dynamic tension continues between hope and catastrophic condemnation. The oracle opens with judgment pronounced against the scoffers, now identified with the rulers of the people (28:14). Once again there is a caustic quotation of their own words. This "covenant with death" or "pact with Sheol" may simply be twisting the highly foolish decisions of the leaders; they probably have entered into an alliance with Egypt, an alliance that they think will spare them but actually will prove to be a covenant with death, a device that will ultimately bring down the devastating power of Babylon on their heads. They think that their pact will save them from the "overwhelming scourge" (28:15), yet in reality they will be overwhelmed by that scourge and swept away.

Yet, in the midst of this blistering denunciation there is promise of hope: "So this is what the Sovereign LORD says: 'See, I lay a stone in Zion, a tested stone, a precious cornerstone for a sure foundation; the one who trusts will never be dismayed'" (28:16). In consequence, God will establish justice (28:17), and this justice will include the violent overthrow of the rulers and the people whom they lead (28:18–19).

Apart from the challenges cast up by certain textual variants (see §D below), there are three exegetical decisions to be taken with respect to 28:16. First, there are disputes regarding certain architectural terms in the verse. Some have identified *bōḥan*, one of the words for "stone" (NIV: "a tested stone"), as an Egyptian loanword referring to schist gneiss, a very hard stone, but this remains conjectural. More plausible is the suggestion that the word derives from another Egyptian loanword signifying "fortress," not least because this appears to be the meaning in Qumran sources that cite this passage (Roberts 1987, followed by Childs 2001: 208). Childs (2001: 202) renders this as "Behold, I am laying in Zion a stone, *a massive stone*, a precious cornerstone of sure foundation." Second, the last verb of the verse, *ḥyš*, is usually translated "be in haste," but probably the verb refers to "the one who trusts," not the foundation, and means that the one who trusts will not be alarmed (NIV: "will never be dismayed"). Third, this brings us to the most important exegetical questions of all: To what does this stone refer? What is its theological significance within the book of Isaiah? Suggestions include the temple, the Davidic monarchy, the remnant, Zion, faith, the Messiah (see Oswalt 1986: 518). Most of the suggested options seem too narrow, unable to fill the strength of the promise here made or inappropriate in the parallel passages. Childs (2001: 209–10) convincingly argues that the key to the passage lies in the book of Isaiah as a whole. Isaiah 1:26 had already spoken of a restored city and its connection with righteousness, just as here in 28:16 this massive stone constitutes a foundation for the righteousness in the next verse. The dialectic in Isa. 7–8 between King Ahaz's rejection of the challenge to establish himself in faith in God's promise to the house of David and God's gracious provision of a sign for the remnant (8:8, 10) is echoed in the dialectic between searing judgment and gracious intervention found in 28:5–13 and again in 28:14–22. The same dialectic recurs in another "stone" passage in Isaiah: God is both a stalwart sanctuary and a stone that causes people to stumble, "a trap and a snare" (8:14–15). Childs (2001: 209–10) concludes,

> The effect of this intertextual interaction of passages is that the initially ambiguous foundation stone of 28:16 serves as a metaphor unifying central themes that have been nuanced in different ways throughout the book.... The symbolism

of the stone encompasses the reality of the new community, a faithful remnant, which is a foretaste of the coming righteous reign of God and which is ushered in by the promised messianic rule of Zion. Within this organic whole various aspects of the promise have been highlighted in a variety of ways in different texts. Isaiah 14:32 spoke of Zion as having been established in the past as a refuge for the remnant, whereas 28:16 envisions the establishment in Zion of a sure foundation, which extends into the future. At times the stone is a pledge of security for faith; at other times it is a rock of stumbling for unbelief (8:11ff.). Some texts of the corpus lay emphasis on the remnant as a creation of God, others on the remnant as a sign of the eschatological community. The error of earlier interpreters has been in trying to isolate only one feature from within this larger whole without adequate attention to the dynamic interplay of texts that together comprise the truth of the prophetic proclamation.

C. The Context in Judaism. *Targum Jonathan* on Isa. 28:16 understands the stone to refer to a Davidic king. This is part of an extensive tradition in which various texts referring to a "stone" were applied to the Messiah and to the eschatological age (see Elliott 1966: 26–33). Of particular interest is 1QS VIII, 7–8, which may well depend on the Targum (so de Waard 1965: 54), and where the council of the eschatological community is the foundation. Almost certainly the LXX presupposes a messianic reading (see §D below). Just as 1 Pet. 2:5–6 connects Christians as "living stones" to Christ, who is the stone of 2:6, thereby picturing the church as a temple (for discussion regarding those who think that this building is a house but not a temple, see Achtemeier 1996: 158–59), so also the community at Qumran could think of themselves as some kind of spiritual house—for example, "those in Israel who have freely pledged themselves to the House of Truth" (1QS V, 6); "a House of Holiness for Israel, an Assembly of Supreme Holiness for Aaron" (1QS VIII, 5–6); or passages where the Teacher of Righteous himself seems to constitute the house in which the Qumran community is built (1QHᵃ XIV, 25–28; 4Q171 III, 15–16) (see Davids 1990: 87).

D. Textual Matters. The MT points the verb *yāsad* ("lay a foundation") as a Piel perfect, preceded by the particle *hinnî*: "Behold, I am the one who laid a stone for a foundation." This is possible, but the syntax is very rare. More commonly, the *hinnēh* particle calls for a participle, and that is found in Qumran texts (1QIsa[a]: *mysd*; 1QIsa[b]: *ywsd*). Both the Targum and the Greek translations presuppose the participle. I have opted for the participial construction.

The LXX apparently preserves a messianic identification of the stone: note the italicized *in him* carefully inserted by the second-century BC translator and preserved in the NETS translation:

> Therefore thus says the Lord,
> See, I will lay for the foundations of Sion
> [Zion]
> a precious, choice stone,
> a highly valued cornerstone for its
> foundations,
> and the one who believes *in him* will not
> be put to shame.
> And I will turn judgment into hope. (Isa.
> 28:16–17 LXX NETS)

But while it is clear that 1 Pet. 2:6 derives from Isa. 28:16, it does not accurately reproduce either the MT or the LXX. With the LXX, 1 Peter includes the words *ep' autō* ("in him") after *ho pisteuōn* ("the one who believes"), but it omits *egō* ("I" [relying on the morphology of the verb]), replaces *embalō* ("will lay") with *tithēmi* ("lay" or "place"), omits *eis ta themelia* ("for the foundations"), adds *en* ("in") before "Zion," and omits *polutelē* ("precious") and *eis ta themelia autēs* ("for its foundations"). None of these changes affects the fundamental meaning of the passage, and certainly 1 Peter preserves the messianic hint by holding on to "in him." Nevertheless, the differences have prompted some to wonder if Peter is borrowing from Paul's use of the same text in Rom. 9:32–33. The differences between Peter and Paul, however, are as striking as the similarities. Perhaps both are adapting the LXX freely; perhaps both borrow from a common exegetical tradition but in different ways. We have no way of knowing.

E. Peter's Use of the OT in 2:6. Before we look at the big picture, we must pause to evaluate what *akrogōniaion* (NIV: "cornerstone") means, found in both the LXX and Peter. The word is unknown to secular Greek writers of the period. It appears only in the LXX of Isa. 28:16, in 1 Peter, and then in other Christian authors (see Hillyer 1971: 69). Some have argued that it is the capstone or key-

stone of an arch, or even the highest stone of the building. Yet the theme of foundation is so strong in both the MT and the LXX that even though 1 Peter omits the two *themelia* ("foundations") found in the LXX, it is far from clear that he is disavowing the identity of the stone found in his source. Moreover, if the location of the stone in 2:6 is preserved into 2:8, it is difficult to imagine anyone stumbling over a capstone. It seems best to think of this as the cornerstone, even while we admit (with Spicq 1966: 87) that Peter's focus is less on the stone's location than on its function.

Peter's quotation of Isa. 28:16 in 2:6 reintroduces, reinforces, and establishes by scriptural authority the themes of 2:4. If the Isaiah quotation itself does not explicitly pick up on all the themes in 2:4—it does not explicitly mention the rejection of this stone by many, nor does it establish how other living stones "come" to him to construct the whole building—Peter may have thought that those connections were obvious enough, if he read Isa. 28:16 within the context of the entire prophecy of Isaiah, along the lines suggested above. In any case, these other points are largely established by the further biblical quotations that Peter will immediately introduce. What is quite clear is that Peter understands Christ to be the fulfillment of the prophecy of Isa. 28:16, in common with NT insistence that Christ himself is the stone rejected by the builders but given the place of foundational importance by God.

F. Theological Use. We too readily overlook how fundamentally divisive Jesus Christ is, even though that point is repeatedly made not only in the NT but also in OT prophecies concerning him. Peter here (2:4–12) insists that everyone is affected by the coming of Christ, positively or negatively, depending on whether they too are "living stones" or, alternatively, simply reject him or stumble over him. They will find that he crushes them. That point is not quite made by this quotation from Isa. 28:16, but the links with the other "stone" quotations in the ensuing verses make the conclusion inescapable.

Yet Peter's first readers might find this peculiarly encouraging. For those who may have suffered major physical dislocation, and who certainly have suffered social rejection, Peter's quotation, in its context, would reassure them that their painful situation did not reflect the displeasure of God.

Far from it: God's plan includes a division of people around his Son, this cornerstone rejected by so many, and the most important thing, both for this life and for the life to come, is to be living stones along with him in the temple of which he is the cornerstone.

Perhaps it should also be mentioned that Peter leaves no hint that he saw himself as in some way a special or foundational stone in the church, despite the name that Jesus himself had given him (see Matt. 16:17–18).

2:7

A. NT Context: The Stone That the Builders Rejected Has Been Vindicated. The preceding quotation (2:6) specified that Jesus, the chosen cornerstone, is "precious" or, better, "honored" (*entimon*). Picking up on the simple form of that word, Peter says that "the honor [*hē timē*] is for you who believe" (ESV). This is a more plausible rendering than that of the NIV and the TNIV, "to you who believe, this stone is precious," as there is no mention of the stone in the Greek text, and the Greek most naturally reads, "Therefore honor is to you who believe" (so, among others, Achtemeier 1996: 160; Beare 1970: 124; Goppelt 1993: 145; Jobes 2005: 152; McKnight 1996: 109; Reicke 1964: 92). Probably this is picking up on the fact that Isa. 28:16 LXX asserts that those who trust in the stone "will not be put to shame," and, reading the expression as a litotes, affirms that they will be honored (Beare 1970: 124). The theme is important when the people of God feel under such dislocation and threat, demeaned by the culture in which they are embedded (see Elliott 2000: 117).

But 2:7 is set up as a contrast between two groups. On the one hand, to those who do believe that Jesus is the chosen honored stone, there is honor; on the other hand, to those who do not believe, Jesus does not stop being the stone, but, in words drawn from Ps. 118:22 (117:22 LXX), "The stone the builders rejected has become the cornerstone," regardless of what they think. But there is no honor for them (and worse, as the next verse will show, this stone will destroy them).

B. OT Context. Psalm 118 is a psalm celebrating deliverance (see Constant 2001: 27–102). Many units of the psalm describe the terrible plight in which the psalmist found himself, answered by the sheer joy of articulating the deliverance that

the Lord effected. Small wonder that this psalm was sung by the Levites during Passover, a feast that celebrates deliverance. To give some examples that include our text:

> [5]When hard pressed, I cried to the LORD;
> he brought me into a spacious place.
> [6]The LORD is with me; I will not be afraid.
> What can human beings to do me?
>
> [10]All the nations surrounded me,
> but in the name of the LORD I cut them down.
>
> [21]I will give you thanks, for you answered me;
> you have become my salvation.
> [22]The stone the builders rejected
> has become the cornerstone:
> [23]The LORD has done this,
> and it is marvelous in our eyes.
> [24]The LORD has done it this very day;
> let us rejoice and be glad.
> [25]LORD, save us!
> LORD, grant us success! (TNIV)

The LXX (117:22), reflecting the Hebrew, says that the stone that the builders rejected has become *eis kephalēn gōnias* (lit., "the head of the corner"). The TNIV, just cited, renders this "cornerstone"; the NIV renders it "capstone." The philological arguments are complex but inconclusive. Cahill (1999) contends that the word cannot mean "cornerstone," primarily because the builders seem to be rejecting the stone in the course of their building, yet the stone is used at the end of the project—but if at the end, then it cannot be the cornerstone. It must be thought of as the capstone or top stone. Yet this argument is hardly conclusive, as it may be making the metaphor walk on all fours. The psalmist is interested in the vindication of the stone that was rejected; the sequence of the building project may not be more than the scaffold of his metaphor (see McKelvey 1969: 195–204).

C. The Context in Judaism. Psalm 118 is part of the Hallel, more precisely the Egyptian Hallel (Pss. 113–118). Thus it is not surprising that parts of Ps. 118 are discussed in *m. Sukkah* (esp. 3:9; 4:6, 8; 5:4). Verse 22 achieves no special prominence in these paschal settings.

D. Textual Matters. Peter cites the LXX exactly, which is an accurate reflection of the MT.

E. Peter's Use of the OT in 2:7. Regardless of how one understands "head of the corner" in Ps. 118:22 (117:22 LXX), in Peter's deployment of the quotation the rock in 2:7 becomes, in 2:8, a stone that causes people to stumble, and it is difficult to imagine how a capstone could do that. More importantly, Jesus himself quotes this verse from Ps. 118 and applies it to the rejection that he suffered (Matt. 21:42; Mark 12:10; Luke 20:17); Peter also refers to the passage in Acts 4:11. This is not much of a surprise when one remembers how central the rejection and passion of Jesus Christ are to the early Christian understanding of the gospel. It was important to establish biblical warrant. In the Gospels those who reject Christ are Jews; here in 1 Peter they are the unbelieving pagan neighbors and authorities who subject Christians to the kind of social harassment that the readers of this letter have been facing. In any case, already Ps. 118 associates the cornerstone rejected by the builders with salvation, "implying that to reject the stone is to jeopardize one's salvation" (Jobes 2005: 153).

F. Theological Use. In the other NT uses Ps. 118:22 directly contributes to the argument for Jesus' vindication. That is most explicit in Acts 4:11; it is implicit in the Synoptic Gospels in its consistent attachment to the parable of the vineyard. Here, the vindication is limited to the quotation itself, and the addition of the next quotation will move the discussion in the direction of the judgment that the unbelievers will face.

2:8

A. NT Context: The Rock That Makes Them Fall. To the previous quotation (2:7) Peter adds a quotation from Isa. 8:14: "A stone that causes people to stumble and a rock that makes them fall." The logic is simply an extension of the preceding verses: the same honored cornerstone, Christ Jesus himself, whom Peter's readers have trusted but who has been rejected by so many others, not only has become the cornerstone even if they have rejected him but also will end up destroying them. With this quotation, 1 Pet. 2 becomes the NT passage with the highest number of "stone" quotations in one location.

B. OT Context. Isaiah 8:11–15 has an autobiographical flavor (as in 8:1, 5): God speaks to Isaiah with his strong hand on him and tells him and his followers not to fear what the people fear: the

conspiracies that are swirling around Jerusalem. No, their fear must lie elsewhere: "The LORD Almighty is the one you are to regard as holy, he is the one you are to fear, he is the one you are to dread" (8:13). There follows, then, "the familiar double-edged form of prophetic proclamation" (Childs 2001: 75): the Lord will be a sanctuary for those who regard him as holy and who fear him, "but for both houses of Israel he will be a stone that causes people to stumble and a rock that makes them fall" (TNIV). In this context Yahweh himself, transparently, is the stone.

C. The Context in Judaism. Because this is a further "stone" oracle, it is swept up into other OT "stone" passages in some discussions in Second Temple Judaism (see commentary on 1 Pet. 2:6 above).

D. Textual Matters. The Hebrew unambiguously makes God out to be the stone that causes people to stumble; the LXX is a trifle more ambiguous: "Sanctify the Lord himself; and he himself will be your fear. If you trust in him, he will become your sanctuary, *and you will not encounter him as a stumbling caused by a stone, nor as a fall caused by a rock*" (NETS [italics added]). Peter reverts to making God—more precisely, Christ himself—the one who causes the stumbling (as does Paul in Rom. 9:33). On the whole, the text of 1 Peter follows the LXX so loosely that some prefer to think of this as an allusion rather than a citation (e.g., Brox 1975: 79). Paul combines his quotation of Isa. 8:14 with words drawn from Isa. 28:16, but because Peter has separated out the two quotations and slips Ps. 118:22 between them, it is unlikely that Peter is borrowing from Paul. Both Peter and Paul omit *synantēsesthe autō oude hōs* ("you will not encounter him as") between the two references to stone in the Isa. 8:14 passage and change *petras ptōmati* ("rock of falling") to *petra(n) skandalon* ("rock of falling/temptation to sin")—the latter word more familiar in the Christian tradition (e.g., Matt. 11:6; 26:11; Mark 6:3; Luke 7:23; 1 Cor. 1:23; Gal. 5:11) and supported, if not by the LXX, by the later Greek versions of Aquila, Symmachus, and Theodotion. Jobes (2005: 153) points out that there is some irony in the fact that Peter himself was accused by Jesus of being a *skandalon* when he tried to deflect his Master from the predicted path to suffering and death (Matt. 16:23). Many have pointed out that the difference between the two words for stone/ rock, *lithos proskommatos* and *petra skandalon*, is usually the difference between a (loose) "stone" (*lithos*) and native rock (*petra*) (e.g., Hort 1898: 121).

E. Peter's Use of the OT in 2:8. Peter does not quote the "positive" parts of Isa. 8:14, though doubtless he presupposes them, because similar positive emphases have been made in the previous two or three verses. In other words, he fully recognizes that some do sanctify Christ in their hearts and fully put their trust in him; he does not need to repeat the point. But those who do not are not making a morally neutral decision; Christ remains the cornerstone regardless of what they do, but now he becomes, for them, "a stone that causes people to stumble and a rock that makes them fall." In the original context of Isa. 8 these people were primarily the leaders of Jerusalem and those who followed them, over against the faithful remnant, the two groups responding very differently to Yahweh and his revelation. But the reality is that wherever God discloses himself, people respond very differently. Those who do not fully put their trust in this rock in Peter's day include a much wider constituency.

The logical link that Peter establishes (2:7–8) between the quotation from Ps. 118:22 and the quotation from Isa. 8:14 simultaneously establishes that Jesus Christ is the only means of salvation and the one by whom all will be judged, and that the OT had already established a predictive pattern of division around God's revelation—a division between trust and unbelief (Marshall 1991: 73). The people whom Peter has in view by this quotation from Isa. 8:14, he explains, "stumble because they disobey the message" (lit., "the word" here and in 3:1; "the gospel" in 4:17).

> Christ is laid across the path of humanity on its course into the future. In the encounter with him each person is changed: one for salvation, another for destruction.... One cannot simply step over Jesus to go on about the daily routine and pass him by to build a future. Whoever encounters him is inescapably changed through the encounter: Either one sees and becomes "a living stone," or one stumbles as a blind person over Christ and comes to ruin, falling short, i.e., of one's Creator and Redeemer and thereby of one's destiny (Goppelt 1993: 144, 146).

So they stumbled because they disobeyed the message, "which," Peter adds, almost in a throwaway line that in fact has generated massive discussion, "is also what they were destined for" (*etethēsan*)—a divine passive that certainly means that God himself appointed them to this end. The nub of the debate asks whether the "which" refers only to their rejection or to their disobedience and rejection. In other words, did God appoint those who disobeyed to judgment, perhaps as a necessary part of his appointment (*tithēmi*) of Christ to be the cornerstone in 2:6 as people divide around him (e.g., Elliott 2000: 433–34; Hillyer 1992: 64; Panning 2000; Michaels 1988: 107), or did he appoint some to disobedience and to judgment (e.g., Achtemeier 1996: 162–63; Beare 1970: 126; Best 1982: 106; Calvin 1963: 264–65; Grudem, 107–8; Kelly 1969: 94)? The syntax does not settle the issue. All will agree with McKnight (1996: 109): "God's act of appointing Jesus as the living Stone has become both honor for believers and judgment for unbelievers; this was God's design, and everything happens according to his will." The question that such a formulation does not address is whether in some sense even the unbelief and disobedience of those who stumble at the stone is by God's determination. It draws some of the sting from the debate, however, if those who answer in the affirmative insist with equal rigor that however sweeping God's sovereignty may be, it never functions in Scripture in such a way as to mitigate human responsibility and thus human guilt. Peter has no trouble simultaneously insisting, "They stumble because they disobey the message." Our theological problems arise when we imagine that such guilty actions hold God's sovereignty in abeyance, or when we imagine that an affirmation of God's sovereignty somehow diminishes human responsibility and guilt.

F. Theological Use. Two observations should be made. First, the pattern in which Jesus Christ is the dividing line is endemic to the NT. These "stone" passages are not unusual in their division of humankind into two groups; otherwise put, the exclusiveness of Jesus Christ is a common theme apart from "stone" quotations, such that all either come to him for forgiveness and life or face condemnation and death. Acts 4:11 may depict Peter citing one of the OT "stone" passages, but that leads directly to 4:12: "Salvation is found in no one else, for there is no other name given under heaven by which we must be saved" (TNIV). But that is thematically not far removed from Jesus claiming that he himself will be the judge on the last day (Matt. 7:21–23) or saying, "I am the way and the truth and the life. No one comes to the Father except through me" (John 14:6). Nor is it conceptually very far from the vision of Rev. 4–5, in which the only one who is able to bring to pass all of God's purposes for blessing and for judgment, and redeem for himself a new humanity drawn from every tongue and tribe and people and nation, is the lion/lamb who emerges from the very throne of God.

Second, the idea that God sovereignly remains in control of all things is common in the OT (e.g., Neh. 9:6; Prov. 21:30; Dan. 4:34–35; Isa. 40:22–24; 44:7–8; 45:1–7; Jer. 18:5–11), the NT (e.g., Mark 4:10–12; Luke 2:34; Rom. 8:29; 9:18, 22; Eph. 1:4–5; 1 Thess. 5:9; 1 Pet. 1:2) and in some strands of Second Temple Judaism (e.g., 1QH^a V, 1–10; IX, 7–8; X, 23–25; XII, 38; XIX–XX; 1QS III, 15–16; CD-A II, 6–11; 1 En. 62:10). The commonness of this theme, combined with the Bible's insistence on God being exclusively good and on human beings being genuinely culpable, is what generates complex theological discussion on the notion of compatibilism (see Carson 1981). But Peter's dominant concerns, as he works out this affirmation of God's sovereignty, are, first, that God himself had anticipated and predicted the sufferings of the Messiah, which were no accident and should have been no surprise; and second, that God himself had anticipated and predicted the rejection of the Messiah, as well as his triumph, so that these were no accident and should be no surprise.

2:9–10

After reflecting on the shame and destruction of those who reject Christ, Peter returns to his Christian readers, marking the change with an adversative: "But you," he writes, are (1) a chosen race, (2) a royal priesthood, (3) a holy nation, (4) God's special possession, (5) those who have been constituted the people of God by God's remarkable mercy. The language in these verses is drawn from Exod. 19:6; Isa. 43:20–21; Hos. 2:25. Scholars disagree on how much is quotation and how much is allusion, but even those who insist

on some direct quotations cannot find more than two words at a time that apparently spring from specific texts. We briefly survey each in turn and then reflect on what this string of allusions signals regarding Peter's reading of the OT.

First, "a chosen race" (genos eklekton). The language is drawn from Isa. 43:20–21; Exod. 19:5–6. The former passage is located in a chapter in which Yahweh announces that he is Israel's Savior; he is the one who will bring them out of the exile (43:3). In 43:20, in his promise to redeem his people, he affirms that he provides water in the wilderness, "to give drink to my people, my chosen" (potisai to genos mou to eklekton). Here, of course, genos ("race" or "people") refers to Abraham's descendants. Peter boldly applies it to his Christian readers in Asia Minor, regardless of race; or, better put, he applies it to them because their commonalities in Christ, regardless of physical background, constitute them the true "race" that God redeems. Exodus 19:5–6 also speaks of God's covenant community being his special people, at least in the LXX. Whereas the Hebrew has "you shall be my treasured possession among all peoples," the LXX has "you shall be to me a people special above all nations" (NETS). Nevertheless, the words "a people special" in the LXX are laos periousios. In other words, the linguistic links with 1 Pet. 2:9–10 are at this point much closer to Isa. 43 than to Exod. 19. But the exodus is so common a type in the NT for the ultimate release from slavery that it is impossible not to see that Peter understands his brief reference to be an affirmation of (typological) prophetic fulfillment.

Second, "a royal priesthood" (basileion hierateuma). This picks up one of the controlling themes of 1 Pet. 2:4–5. Although the language of the first allusion, "a chosen race" (above), is drawn from Isa. 43:20–21 and not from Exod. 19:5–6, this category, "a royal priesthood," draws the exact terminology from the latter (LXX). In the OT context the people so designated are the Hebrews, located between the escape from Egypt and the giving of the law; here in 1 Peter the people so designated are Christians, in particular Christians who have experienced their own "exodus" from slavery to sin, coming now under the dominion of the high king of the universe. That is what makes them "royal" (regardless of whether we render the Greek "kingdom and priests" or "royal priests").

Davies (2004: 238) has rightly shown that the words of declaration "denote primarily how the nation is to relate to God, rather than how it is to relate to the other nations as is often supposed, though it is not denied that there may be implications for human relationships of what it means to be the chosen and treasured people of God." In both cases, the priestly function of the whole people of God is to be holy and offer sacrifices to God, and only in that context to mediate between God and fallen humanity. Christians are to offer themselves in loyal consecration to God, offer spiritual sacrifices that are "coextensive with the lives of the faithful," by which the church "brings the kingdom of God into being here below" (Congar 1952: 178–79).

This passage in 1 Peter has often been used in connection with discussions over the priesthood of all believers. Certainly it has some important bearing on that subject, but we cannot overlook that in the OT context the designation of all Israel as a "royal priesthood" did not preclude, a few chapters later, the establishment of the Levitical priesthood. One must infer that the designation of Christian believers as a "royal priesthood" does not preclude the existence of pastors/elders/overseers (see France 1998: 38). The debate over the precise status of such people under the terms of the new covenant finally turns on an array of other passages. More importantly, both in Exod. 19 and in 1 Pet. 2 the notion of a royal priesthood has less to do with establishing the authority of the covenant people of God (old covenant or new) than with themes of obedience, holiness, privilege, mission, self-identity under the good purposes of God. "The kingdom of God is composed of believers who must think of themselves as holy with respect to the world, set apart for purity and a purpose demanded by God. This is the priesthood that serves the King of the universe" (Jobes 2005: 161).

Third, "a holy nation" (*ethnos hagion*). Here too the exact wording is from Exod. 19:6 LXX. As it occurs in Exod. 19, the expression announces the fact that the descendants of Abraham, just released from slavery in Egypt, were on the verge of becoming constituted as a "tribe," a "nation," with their own constitution, land, and covenant with their God. As Peter applies the expression to his Christian readers, the "tribe" or "nation" that

he has in mind is made up of Jews and Gentiles alike but are constituted one people, one "nation," under the terms of a new covenant. Some of the theological implications of this identification will be teased out a little more below; once again the exodus typology is presupposed.

Fourth, "God's special possession" (*laos eis peripoiēsin*), literally, "a people for [God's] special possession." The exact wording is found neither in Exod. 19:5–6 nor in Isa. 43:20–21, but the idea is transparent in both OT texts. The former promises that if the Israelites, at the time of the exodus, obey Yahweh and keep his covenant, then out of all the nations of the earth they alone will be his "treasured people" (LXX: *laos periousios*), which is then unpacked in terms of being a royal priesthood and a holy nation. The latter envisages God rescuing his exiled people (LXX: *laos*), "whom I formed that they may make known my excellencies/mighty acts" (LXX: *hon periepoiēsamēn tas aretas mou diēgeisthai*). Peter says that his readers are God's people (*laos*) for his own possession, "that you may proclaim the excellencies [*hopōs tas aretas exangeilēte*] of him who called you out of darkness into his marvelous light" (2:9). The excellencies of God that Isaiah has in view are manifested in the deliverance of his people from the exile; the excellencies of God that Peter has in view are manifested in the salvation and transformation of his people, along with the hope that they enjoy for the consummating transformation—all of which was achieved by the ministry, death, and resurrection of God's own Son.

Fifth, those who have been constituted the people of God by God's remarkable mercy. This is an allusion to Hos. 2:23 (2:25 LXX). The OT context is extraordinarily important to a right understanding of the passage to which Peter alludes. God has already disowned the northern kingdom of Israel because of its adulterous relationships with other gods, and the kingdom of Judah will soon follow in the same wretched course (cf. Hos. 1:11). Hosea is to name his own child "Lo-Ammi," "Not My People," because God no longer views his covenant people, the entire people of Israel (northern kingdom and southern alike), as his people. Then, almost as if Yahweh cannot bear the thought, he announces that they will one day flourish again: "In the place where it was said to them, 'You are not my people,' they will be called 'children of the living God'" (Hos. 1:10). The same theme is continued in Hos. 2:23, to which Peter alludes. This passage is part of an oracle in which God in mercy overturns his own sentence against his adulterous people:

> I will plant her for myself in the land;
> I will show my love to the one I called
> "Not my loved one."
> I will say to those called "Not my people,"
> "You are my people";
> and they will say, "You are my God."
> (TNIV)

In other words, a superficial reading of Hos. 2:23 may lead one to think that the oracle is promising that Gentiles, who surely merit the label "Not my people," are now in mercy being received by God as his people. But in fact, the context shows that the people designated "Not my people" are Israelites who have broken the covenant so badly that God declares them no longer his—and then he goes ahead and shows mercy to them anyway.

The apostle Paul quotes Hos. 1:10; 2:23 in Rom. 9:23–26, part of his complex discussion on the relationships between Jews and Gentiles under the aegis of the new covenant. Paul understands that in a very deep sense Israel "has not only lost her privileged position among the peoples of the earth, she has become just another one of the Gentile nations . . . , entirely cut off from the promises of God (cf. Hos. 8:8; 9:17; Zeph. 2:1)" (Wood 2005: 298). But if God nevertheless promises to show mercy to this people now declared Gentile (i.e., not-his-people), then what is to stop the merciful God from showing mercy to other Gentile people? That seems to be Paul's reasoning: what if God wished to "make the riches of his glory known to the objects of his mercy, whom he prepared in advance for glory—even us, whom he also called, not only from the Jews but also from the Gentiles?" (Rom 9:23), followed by the quotations from Hosea. From this perspective, then, all those who have entered into the new covenant by the mercy of God in Christ Jesus were in fact "Gentiles" in need of mercy. Indeed, Wood (2005: 299) suggests that this may be the reason why John the Baptist calls his fellow Jews to undergo baptism, a rite more commonly associated with Gentile conversion; this becomes one of the appropriate things to do to prepare for the coming Messiah.

These details are not spelled out in 1 Pet. 2:10, of course, but the allusion to Hosea is unmistakable: "Once you were not a people, but now you are the people of God; once you had not received mercy, but now you have received mercy" (1 Pet. 2:10 TNIV). If Peter's reading of Hosea is as straightforward as that of Paul, and if he has adopted similar reasoning, then his application of Hos. 2:23 to his readers may be grounded in two complementary lines of thought. First, Hos. 2:23 is a straightforward prophecy whose fulfillment takes place when the Israelites who are now "Gentiles" once more become the people of God. Nevertheless the context of Hosea shows that the (natural) descendants of Abraham are in view. Still, the logic of the situation—that if the ancient covenant people have become "Gentiles," then perhaps God's mercy may extend to those who are (racially) Gentiles—breeds a second line of thought: God's merciful handling of his own "Gentile" people becomes an action, a pattern, a "type," of his handling of even more Gentiles. In other words, what one finds in Peter's reference to Hosea is more than a type/antitype set of assumptions (i.e., the way God works with the people of God under the old covenant is the way he works with the people of God under the new covenant), but it may be a meditation on God's great mercy to Jew and Gentile alike, once both are declared to be guilty "Gentiles" (see Jobes 2005: 163–64).

Some further theological reflections on this string of OT allusions in 1 Pet. 2:9–10 may prove helpful. By reassuring his readers that they constitute a chosen race, a royal priesthood, a holy nation, God's special possession, those who have received God's mercy, Peter is simultaneously accomplishing several things. He is, of course, showing how he understands the true line of continuity to run from the people of God under the old covenant to the people of God under the new covenant. But equally, he is giving his readers a distinctive identity that is bound up tightly with God's mercy to them in Christ Jesus, and with their response in obedient faith and holiness. One of the effects, of course, was to make them sufficiently different as a "people" or "race" or "nation" that first-century pagan society would not be long in resenting them. Christians were widely perceived to repudiate some of the widely accepted "pleasures" of the Roman world—for example, the Roman theater, gladiatorial combat, the races. They abandoned pagan religious observance, and, where pagan ritual was tied to civic duty, they abandoned civic duty (see Colwell 1939; Judge 1960). Moreover, by thinking of themselves as a "nation" under King Jesus, they had to work out a distinction introduced by their Master: what did they owe to Caesar, and what did they owe to God? Precisely because they were an international "people" and "race" and "nation" who were without the kind of territory that was part of being a "nation" in the eyes of the Romans (and in the assumption of OT writers), Christians found themselves in an eschatological tension that has been both an unavoidable challenge and a glorious privilege throughout two millennia of church history.

2:12

Although Peter wants his Christian readers to be a distinctive people, he doubtless understands that being aliens and foreigners, both in their own perception and in that of their pagan neighbors, might well cause painful opposition. The Roman writer Suetonius (*Nero* 16) considered Christianity to be not only a mischievous superstition but also one that deserved punishment for this class (*genus*) of people. Tacitus (*Ann.* 44) thought of Christians as a race rightly detested for its evil practices. How, then, should Christians respond? Peter displays quite extraordinary sophistication: he does not think in simple antithetical terms, "them" versus "us," but rather keeps two *desiderata* in view. First, Christians must live differently from the surrounding pagan culture (2:11); second, they must live such exemplary lives that, however many charges are leveled against them, the quality of their Christian living will change opinions. The aim is that the surrounding pagans "may see your good deeds and glorify God on the day of visitation" (2:12).

It is this last expression, *en hēmera episkopēs* ("on the day of visitation"), that has OT roots. Within the NT the expression is found only here and in Luke 19:44, "the time of your visitation," which refers to the "visit" of God in the incarnation of God in Christ and all the surrounding events. The verbal form of the expression is found in Luke 1:68. Some have argued that the expression in 1 Pet. 2:12 refers to the moment of individual conversion, when God "visits" unbelievers with

salvation (e.g., Beare 1970: 164; Calvin 1963: 268; Kelly 1969: 106; Reicke 1964: 94; Selwyn 1955: 171). Overwhelmingly, however, this and related expressions refer to final eschatological judgment. This use is common both in the OT (e.g., Isa. 10:3; Jer. 6:15) and in the literature of Second Temple Judaism (e.g., 1QS III, 18; IV, 6–8, 11–12, 18–19; CD-A VII, 9). Instances where the expression is ostensibly only positive in overtone (e.g., Gen. 50:24–25; Job 10:12) turn out on inspection to mention "visitation" (*episkopē*) but have no time expression constructed with it. Taken together, this evidence strongly suggests that 1 Pet. 2:12 has the day of judgment in view. This is intrinsically the more likely meaning when we recall how often 1 Peter mentions the day of judgment elsewhere, using other forms of expression (e.g., 1:5, 7, 13; 4:7, 13, 17; 5:1 (see Achtemeier 1996: 178; Michaels 1988: 118).

In short, here Peter is simply picking up common biblical terminology to refer to the day of judgment. If that day promises blessing and vindication for God's holy people (1:5–7) and judgment against those who refuse the gospel, here it will also provide an opportunity to pagans to bear witness to the good, even exemplary, transformed lives of Christians, and this will glorify God.

2:22–25

A. NT Context: The Unique Example of the Suffering Messiah. These verses in 1 Peter include four quotations from, and at least four further allusions to, Isa. 52:13–53:12, the fourth of the so-called Servant Songs of Isaiah. At first glance, it appears strange to find this theme in a household table dealing with slaves, wives, and husbands. Readers freshly converted out of paganism would have found it doubly strange, for the pagan household codes said nothing whatsoever about appropriate suffering. In the immediate context Peter insists that slaves, and in principle all Christians (cf. 3:9), are called upon to suffer unjustly and still to act righteously, for they follow the example of the Lord Jesus. Even if there are unique elements in Jesus' suffering and death, Peter here melds together theology and ethics so powerfully that it becomes impossible to abstract one from the other. Because the culmination of Christ's sufferings was crucifixion, a form of execution reserved for slaves, noncitizens, and other undesirables, perhaps the usefulness of Jesus' ex-

ample even for slaves was a little more obvious to thoughtful first-century Christian readers than it might be for some contemporaries who live with an extraordinarily domesticated cross. Many commentators note that these lines from Peter are the more moving when one remembers how Peter once rebuked his Master for saying that the Messiah had to suffer, be crucified, and rise again (Matt. 16:21–23; Mark 8:31–33).

An earlier generation of scholars frequently argued that Peter here (2:21–25) is quoting from and perhaps adapting an earlier Christian hymn, but that theory has been successfully refuted (see Achtemeier 1996: 192–93). Arguably, Peter himself was the first of the apostles to develop Suffering Servant Christology. It has frequently been pointed out that of the five instances in the NT where Jesus is referred to as the *pais* ("servant"), two are found in a speech attributed to Peter (Acts 3:13, 16) and "two more are found in a prayer of the early Jerusalem church when Peter is in leadership (Acts 4:27, 30)" (Jobes 2005: 193).

B. OT Context. The Suffering Servant figure in Isaiah is remarkably fluid. In Isa. 41:8–11, the Servant is transparently Israel as a whole. Williamson (1998) has nonetheless demonstrated the subtle relationships in Isaiah among King, Messiah, and Servant. Many have concluded that the Servant in Isa. 52:13–53:12 refers to Israel, and certainly early Christians sometimes thought of Jesus as somehow recapitulating Israel's existence (the theme is especially strong in Matthew). On the whole, however, it is more straightforward to detect an individual in the fourth Servant Song. If the song is read in its Isaianic context, one cannot fail to note two things: (1) this is part of God's promise to restore his exiled people to himself; (2) the Servant himself is declared to be exalted at the beginning and end of the song, though most of the focus is on his appalling suffering.

C. The Context in Judaism. There does not seem to be an unambiguous pre-Christian source within Judaism that identifies the Suffering Servant of Isa. 53 with the anticipated Messiah. The Targum to Isa. 52:13 adds the words "the Messiah" after "my servant," but the date of the Targum is disputed. Even the notion of vicarious suffering appears to be relatively late within Judaism (e.g., 4 Macc. 6:27–29; 17:22; 18:4; less clearly, 2 Macc. 7:37–38). But segments of the fourth

Servant Song are echoed in other Jewish literature, even where the song is not quoted. For instance, the Servant not opening his mouth even when he was oppressed (Isa. 53:7) finds echoes in Josephus, *Ant.* 2.60 (the example of Joseph), and in *T. Benj.* 5:4 ("The pious man shows mercy to the one who abused him, and maintains silence"). On the other hand, such silence can be contrasted with the loud threats made by the famous Jewish martyrs of 2 Macc. 7:17, 19, 31, 35; 4 Macc. 10–13.

D. Textual Matters. The text of 1 Peter follows the LXX for the quotations. There is little purpose in providing here a detailed comparison of the MT and the LXX for the entire fourth Servant Song, but where the song is quoted (LXX) and it differs slightly from the MT, it will be noted in the exposition that follows.

E. Peter's Use of the OT in 2:22–25. Slaves (and, as we have seen, other Christians) are called to suffer for doing good, "because," Peter tells them, "Christ suffered for you, leaving you an example, that you should follow in his steps" (2:21). What follows is a Christology of suffering, with words or lines from Isa. 52:13–53:12 sprinkled through the description. The order is roughly the order of the passion narrative, with the words of the Servant Song drawn into the exposition as appropriate, rather than the order of the song itself, with 1 Pet. 2 serving as commentary. In what follows there is no attempt at an exposition of the entire passage in 1 Pet. 2:22–25 but rather only of those lines that either cite or allude to the fourth Servant Song.

(1) "He did not commit sin, neither was deceit found in his mouth" (1 Pet. 2:22). This is a direct quotation from Isa. 53:9 LXX. The text follows the Hebrew parallelism of the MT, so it is possible that the second clause is meant to be a more precise specifying of the first.

(2) The four allusions are found in 2:23 and are marked by italics font in the following sentence, with the source inspiration included in square brackets: "When he was reviled, *he did not retaliate*, when he suffered *he did not make threats* [Isa. 53:7c–d], but instead *trusted* [Isa. 53:4a, 12] *the one who judges justly* [Isa. 53:8a]." So far, Peter's emphasis has largely been on Jesus' speech. Peter's readers, of course, were suffering verbal abuse (2:15; 3:9, 16; 4:14), and the temptation to retaliate in kind must have been overwhelming. In

fact, Peter will later say, "Do not repay evil with evil or insult with insult" (3:9). In some instances the soundest advice is to keep silent, not least if the opponents are so obsessed that whatever you say will be turned against you. This is not the silence of fear, resentment, or even resignation but rather of courage, compassion, confidence, and patient endurance.

(3) "He himself bore our sins in his own body on the tree" (1 Pet. 2:24). If Jesus' silence tells us what Jesus did not do—he did not speak—Peter now tells us what Jesus did in fact accomplish. The quoted words conflate a phrase from Isa. 53:12 LXX, *autos . . . anēnenken* ("he himself . . . bore"), with a phrase from Isa. 53:4 LXX, *tas hamartias hēmōn* ("our sins"). This amalgam uses "our sins" from 53:4 instead of "the sins of many" in 53:12, thereby preserving a personal feel. The MT of 53:4 speaks of the Servant carrying our sickness. This may, of course, be a metaphor for sin, but certainly it is not less than an identification of the outworking of sin in the "sickness" of the entire Israelite nation in its estrangement from the God of the covenant. Peter's addition of the two phrases "in his body" and "on the tree" specify Jesus' crucifixion as the locus of the sacrifice that he has in mind, and the latter expression, "on the tree," may call to mind Deut. 21:23, which promises God's curse on the one who hangs on a tree (cf. 2 Sam. 21:9).

(4) "By his wounds you have been healed" (1 Pet. 2:24). These words, drawn from Isa. 53:5, accurately reflect both the LXX and the MT, including the reference to healing. But both the LXX and the MT deploy the first-person plural, "we"; Peter, typically, changes this to second-person plural, "you" (used eighty-three times in 1 Peter, with first-person plural pronouns occurring only four times). The reason for the shift here may be bound up with the form of the household code, which prefers direct address, but it may be meant to say, quite forcefully, that the wounds of the Suffering Servant were for the healing not only of the Jews but also of "you"—Gentile Christian readers. Here Peter draws no immediate moral inference for his readers: he does not suggest that they too by their wounds might heal others. The implied inference, rather, is gratitude: Jesus' suffering is in some ways unique, for it is atoning, achieving our healing, our forgiveness. That, surely, hints that

appropriate response is thankfulness, and at that point if we recall the exemplary character of his suffering, then one way in which we display our gratitude for the salvation that we have come to enjoy because of his suffering on our behalf is by displaying similar refusal to retaliate and speak harshly when we ourselves are attacked.

(5) "For you were like wandering sheep" (1 Pet. 2:25). The language is drawn from Isa. 53:6a, again changing the first-person plural to the second-person plural. The point is that Jesus' suffering was not merely exemplary, offered as a fine example to generally good people; rather, his suffering was aimed at rescuing lost people, lost sheep, and it succeeded wonderfully. The person to whom these sheep have come and by whom they have been rescued is "the Shepherd [*poimēn*] and Overseer [*episkopos*] of your souls" (1 Pet. 2:25). That language does not spring directly from the fourth Servant Song, but Peter may have in mind passages such as Isa. 40:10–11; Ezek. 34; Ps. 23, in all of which it is Yahweh himself who is the shepherd of his flock. The terminology of Ezek. 34:11–13 LXX is especially suggestive: there the shepherd seeks out "and will oversee [*episkepsomai*] them" and bring them back from every place "where they were scattered [*diesparēsan*]." Peter does not hesitate in identifying this Shepherd and Overseer as the Lord Jesus (see also 5:1–4). Here he joins John, who insists that Jesus is the good Shepherd (John 10).

F. Theological Use. This is far from being the only NT passage where a writer simultaneously emphasizes the unique death of Jesus Christ and its exemplary moral significance. Indeed, the link doubtless goes back to Jesus himself (see Matt. 20:20–28; Mark 8:31–38) and was well understood by Paul (see Phil. 2:1–11). Once again Peter's high Christology enables him to identify OT passages describing Yahweh's activity as the activity of none other than Jesus Christ. Peter's reading of Isa. 52:13–53:12 and its outworking in Jesus' passion and vindication is of a piece with his understanding of God's prophetic purpose to call out a new Israel bound together and redeemed by the Suffering Servant, whose wounds are alone sufficient to effect the healing of the nations.

3:6

This allusion to Sarah and Abraham occurs in the part of the household code that deals with wives

(1 Pet. 3:1–6). It appears as if the wives that Peter has particularly in mind are Christians whose husbands have not yet been converted (3:1). In brief, his instruction to them, akin to what he has told the slaves, is to live their lives with such integrity, submission to their husbands, and the "unfading beauty of a gentle and quiet spirit" (3:4) that the husbands "may be won over" (3:1) by such becoming conduct. For Peter to address wives and slaves regarding ethical and moral matters was already a breach of the social order, for such address was uncommon in the Greco-Roman world. It gives to wives and slaves a moral responsibility and significance that few in the empire would have acknowledged. Yet the unconverted husbands are hardly in a position to complain, since the conduct advocated by the apostle as he addresses their wives actually affirms the husband's authority. The motivation that Peter insists upon, however, is not the preservation of Roman social structure but rather what is "of great worth in God's sight" (3:4). The authority and example of the crucified and risen Redeemer was thus making an impact in Roman culture, but in a strangely anomalous fashion. "In a masterful move, Peter both upholds and subverts the social order" (Jobes 2005: 204).

As models for his women readers, Peter appeals to "holy women of the past who put their hope in God" (3:5) and who "submitted themselves to their own husbands, like Sarah, who obeyed Abraham and called him her lord" (3:5–6). The source for the "lord" reference is Gen. 18:12 LXX, where Sarah refers to Abraham as her *kyrios* ("lord," "master"). Although this passage does not say that she addressed him in such terms, certainly that is to be inferred. What passage Peter has in mind when he writes that Sarah "obeyed" Abraham is less than clear. There is no passage in Genesis where that verb is used of Sarah. Martin (1999) has argued that the most likely text that Peter has in mind is *Testament of Abraham*, but the judicious examination of Martin's thesis by Allison (2003) considers that such literary dependence has not been demonstrated. Most likely, 1 Peter and *Testament of Abraham* share something of the first-century *Zeitgeist*. Other commentators make much of the fact that in at least three texts in Genesis (16:2, 6; 21:12) Abraham defers to Sarah. But this brute detail is misleading. The fact that he must make the decision to defer to his wife's wishes shows that those wishes cannot stand apart from his sanction: he has the final authority in the home.

Some have suggested that either Gen. 12:13 or Gen. 20:5, 13 are in view. In both places Sarah submits to the morally questionable and selfish requests of her husband, even though it puts her at risk (so Spencer 2000; Kiley 1987). This puts the women among Peter's readers who are married to unconverted husbands into a somewhat analogous position: they should submit to the unjust demands of their husbands. On the whole, however, it is best to conclude that we cannot be certain what was in Peter's mind when he penned these words, except for the explicit allusion to "lord" in Gen. 18:12 LXX, and the general way in which that form of address is in line with the rest of the account of Abraham and Sarah. What is clear is that just as Christians are rightly called "sons of Abraham" (regardless of gender) if they share Abraham's faith (Rom. 4:1–12; Gal. 3:6–29), so also these women become Sarah's daughters if they share her submission (1 Pet. 3:6). Moreover, they must "not give way to fear" (3:6 [cf. Prov. 3:25 LXX]). The expression *agathopoiousai kai mē phoboumenai mēdemia ptoēsin* probably should not be taken as a conditional: "if you do what is right and do not give way to fear." One alternative—not certain, but attractive—suggests that the participles enjoy the imperatival force that all present participles have in this household code: "You have become Sarah's children, so do good and do not give way to fear" (see Michaels 1988: 166–67; Forbes 2005). In any case, these Christian women "are subordinate, but their subordination is revolutionary in that they are subordinate not out of fear or desire for social position or other human advantage but out of obedience to Christ, who treats them as full persons and allows them to rise above the threats and fears of this age" (Davids 1990: 121).

3:10–12

A. NT Context: The Lord Is against Those Who Do Evil. Earlier in his letter Peter had given instruction to his readers as to how Christians should interact with the hostility of the pagan, unbelieving society in which they found themselves. This he had followed up with specific counsel for slaves, wives, and husbands (2:18–3:17), which roles necessarily interlace with societal structures all the time. In 3:8–9 Peter provides a list of qualities that should be reflected in all relationships, not least those that Christians maintain with the wider unbelieving community. Above all, Christians learn not to "repay evil with evil or insult with insult" (3:9). They are called to repay evil with blessing, Peter tells them, "so that you may inherit a blessing" (3:9). For God himself has made it abundantly clear that he does not finally pour out his blessings on those who do evil, for the eyes of the Lord are on the righteous, and this point is so important to Peter as he brings this part of his argument to a close that he grounds it in an extensive and somewhat adapted citation from Psalm 34 (33 LXX).

B. OT Context. Peter likes to quote Psalm 34 (33 LXX) as a foundation passage for Christian ethics (see commentary on 1 Pet. 2:3 above, where Ps. 34:8 [33:9 LXX] is cited). In a convenient chart Jobes (2005: 221–22) lists the numerous places in the first half of the letter where the language in some way mirrors the language of Ps. 33 LXX: 1 Pet. 1:3 (Ps. 33:2 LXX [34:1 ET]); 1:6 (Ps. 33:20 LXX [34:19 ET]); 1:17 (Ps. 33:5, 8 LXX [34:5, 7 ET]); 1:18; 2:16 (Ps. 33:23 LXX [34:22 ET]); 2:6 (Ps. 33:6 LXX [34:5 ET]); 2:17 (Ps. 33:10, 12 LXX [34:9, 11 ET]); 3:12 (Ps. 33:18 LXX [34:11 ET]).

For more on the substance of the psalm, see commentary on 1 Pet. 2:3 above. As much as the psalm reverberates with relief that God has provided, the psalmist (David, according to the superscription) turns his relief and gratitude to God into a moral lesson: the Lord himself distinguishes between those who do good and those who do evil, between the righteous and the unrighteous (34:12–16 [33:13–17a LXX]).

C. The Context in Judaism. See commentary on 1 Pet. 2:3 above. The linguistic patterns of early Judaism shed some light on several expressions in the quotation. In particular, "life" and "good days" clearly refer in the psalm to the blessings of *this* life, and this is the common usage in the LXX, including Tob. 4:5; Sir. 14:14; 41:13; 1 Macc. 10:55 (see Schelkle 1970: 95).

D. Textual Matters. By and large the LXX faithfully follows the MT, and Peter follows the LXX in an adaptive fashion. For the many small changes that Peter introduces, see Achtemeier 1996: 225n70. The most important two are these: (1) Whereas the psalm (LXX) uses the second

person—David begins, "Come, my children, listen to me; I will teach you the fear of the LORD" (34:11 [33:12 LXX]) and then addresses them in the second person—Peter writes in the third person. (2) It is often argued that while "life" and "good days" refer to the blessings of this present life in the OT text, in 1 Pet. 3:10 these expressions take on an eschatological dimension owing to the expression "coheirs of the grace of life" in 3:7 (so Piper 1980: 226–27; Michaels 1988: 180; Reicke 1964: 105). Yet Goppelt (1993: 230) points out that only a few verses earlier, in 2:24, mention of living does in fact pertain to this present life, and, more broadly, Peter emphasizes that eschatological life is already present because of the rebirth accomplished by Christ's resurrection (cf. 1:3–5, 22–24). Moreover, the immediately succeeding verses (3:13–16) focus on this present life. These factors combine to drive Goppelt to resolute insistence that we are not to decide between this life and the life to come in 3:10 (similarly Bigg 1901: 157; Achtemeier 1996: 226).

E. Peter's Use of the OT in 3:10–12. Although Ps. 34 originally applied to David and his readers and surely was read with appreciation in the LXX version by Jews in the Diaspora, Peter directly applies these verses to his readers. The logic that he assumes is not hard to find: just as God delivered David from the dangers implicit in his sojourn among the Philistines, so also God will deliver Peter's Christian readers from their sojourn among their pagan communities. But they are to make no mistake: God cherishes righteousness and promises ultimate judgment on the wicked.

F. Theological Use. Whether under the terms of the old covenant or the new, the privilege of belonging to God's redeemed people brings with it the grateful, grace-driven responsibility to pursue righteousness and holiness, not to presume on God's grace while trying to live no differently from the world.

3:14–15

A. NT Context: What Suffering Christians Are to Fear and Revere.
Continuing his exhortation to his readers to expect suffering—of course, the suffering that he has in mind is not generic, such as chronic illness or bereavement, but rather is focused on opposition, persecution, and abuse for being a Christian—Peter recognizes that stability depends in part on the things we choose to fear:

"Do not fear their threats; do not be frightened" (3:14), Peter writes, citing Isa. 8:12.

B. OT Context. On the context of Isa. 8, see §B of commentary on 1 Pet. 2:8 above.

C. The Context in Judaism. See §E of commentary on 1 Pet. 2:8 above. The combination of proscribing the kind of fear from which unbelievers suffer and mandating the fear of the Lord is not unknown in early Judaism (e.g., *1 En.* 96:3).

D. Textual Matters. The two quotations can be usefully compared in the LXX and in 1 Peter by means of the following chart:

LXX	1 Peter
ton de phobon autou ou mē phobēthēte	*ton de phobon autōn me phobēthēte*
oude mē tarachthēte (Isa. 8:12b)	*mēde tarachthēte* (1 Pet 3:14a)
kyrion auton hagiasate kai autos estai	*kyrion de ton Christon hagiasate en tais*
sou phobos (Isa. 8:13)	*kardiais hymōn* (1 Pet. 3:15a)

Several details stand out. (1) There is a move from *autou* (sg.) to *autōn* (pl.) in the first line: literally, "do not fear its [referring to the people as a whole, the *laos*] fear" becomes "do not fear their fear." At one level this move to the plural is merely *ad sensum* ("according to the sense"), but the context in 1 Pet. 3 means the "their" now refers to the people who surround Peter's Christians in Asia who are offering increasing opposition. (2) In Isa. 8:12b, the "fear" that Isaiah and his followers are not to share is the fear that held their opponents captive, the fear of being taken over by foreign forces from the northeast, prompting the leaders to make an unwise coalition with Egypt. In 1 Pet. 3:14, however, the fear in which Peter's readers are not to indulge is not the fear that their opponents feared but rather the opponents themselves. "Do not fear their fear" must now mean "Do not fear the fear they engender": the expression is difficult enough that the TNIV paraphrases, "Do not fear their threats," while the ESV paraphrases, "Have no fear of them." (3) In Isa. 8:13 the LXX says, "Consecrate the Lord himself and he will be your fear." The quotation in 1 Pet. 3:15a preserves the words *kyrion* ("Lord") and *hagiasate* ("sanctify" or "consecrate"), but the expression as a whole is difficult to translate. Perhaps the most common rendering is "Sanctify Christ as Lord in your hearts," or, in more contemporary English, "Revere the Christ as Lord in your hearts." But the

verb *hagiazō* ("sanctify, consecrate") is not used for "revering X as Y" or the like. Thus it is better to render the clause as "But *sanctify* the Lord Christ in your hearts" or "But *revere* the Lord Christ in your hearts *as holy*," where the italicized words are attempts to render the verb—that is, either "sanctify" or "revere . . . as holy" (see Kuykendall and Collins 2003). In other words, if the Lord Christ is rightly sanctified in the hearts of his people, they will fear him, and no other. (4) Once again, of course, the move from *kyrios* ("Lord") in Isa. 8 to "the Lord Christ" (or, more euphoniously, "Christ the Lord") in 1 Pet. 3 (there is an unimportant textual variant) testifies to the willingness of first-century Christians to see in many OT expressions about God's activity expressions equally suitable to the Lord Jesus.

E. Peter's Use of the OT in 3:14–15. Although there is considerable difference between Isa. 8 and 1 Pet. 3 with respect to the nature of the fear that the respective believers were to avoid, the heart of the quotation, both in Isaiah and in Peter where he adapts it, is the contrast between fearing humans and what they may bring and revering God.

F. Theological Use. "Fear God, and fear no other": this oft-repeated slogan has bred courage in moral conflict and in Christian witness and has invested in Christian commitment an eternal perspective that is not easily seduced by opinion polls and social fads. This is precisely the kind of spiritual backbone that Peter is trying to build into his readers. At the end of the day, it depends utterly on a view of God that brooks no rivals.

3:18–22

This is not the place to undertake a detailed exegesis of this passage, as that would immediately double the length of the 1 Peter essay in the present volume. All the major commentaries include useful surveys of the options. In addition, one may usefully consult the major work by Dalton (1989) and the more recent (and lengthy) dissertation by Yoshikawa (2004), who patiently and systematically examines how the flood narrative of Gen. 6–9 is used in the OT, in the literature of Second Temple Judaism, and in the NT. For our purposes, it is enough to acknowledge the general line of interpretation that seems most persuasive and then identify how Noah is being used within that framework.

Some limitations on interpretive options are achieved when one recalls (1) that vv. 18–22 are linked with the preceding verses (vv. 13–17) by *hoti kai*, "because also" (3:18), indicating that vv. 18–22 are meant to justify the claim of the preceding verses that it is better to suffer for doing good than for doing evil; and (2) that when Christ suffered for doing good, his suffering and death were not the last word, for he was gloriously vindicated, achieving authority over all "angels, authorities, and powers" (3:22). That suggests that if Peter's readers suffer in appropriate ways (i.e., for doing good), they will be vindicated at the end, like their Master. In other words, a reading of 3:18–22 that nicely suits the larger context of 1 Peter is more likely to be right than one that ignores these contextual constraints.

However one decides what is meant by Christ making proclamation to the imprisoned spirits (3:19), the flood in the days of Noah is a type of God's catastrophic judgment after a long period of self-restraint and patience with respect to the anarchic rebels. But the flood waters also "save" Noah and his family, thus becoming a type of Christian baptism, which regularly stands by metonymy for salvation (e.g., "For all of you who were baptized into Christ have clothed yourselves with Christ" [Gal. 3:27 TNIV]). The same flood waters that destroyed many saved the few; the same visitation that brings catastrophic judgment on unrepentant sinners brings glorious salvation to the relatively few in Asia Minor. Even when the numbers are small, God is perfectly able and willing to save his people. The pagans of Noah's time did not repent, and it should come as no surprise that many in the first century will similarly remain unrepentant. In other words, the reference to Noah and his family, not least the mention of small numbers, is meant to be a substantial encouragement to small numbers of believers in Christ Jesus who are facing ridicule from unbelievers in their own time. After all, they experience grace from the same God who showed grace to Noah.

4:8

A. NT Context: Loving One Another in Light of the End. In the previous verses (4:1–6) Peter has again been telling his readers how to arm themselves (4:1) with the same attitude that Christ had, if they plan on withstanding the opposition of those who heap abuse on them (4:4). Above

all, they must recognize that this present state of affairs is not the last word. The abusers "will have to give account to him who is ready to judge the living and the dead" (4:5). Of course, that is also true for believers, who likewise must remember that the "end of all things is near" (4:7). What that means for their conduct is spelled out in the ensuing verses (4:7b–11), and the most important ingredient is articulated in 4:8: "Above all, love each other deeply, because love covers over a multitude of sins." This last expression, "covers over a multitude of sins," apparently derives from Prov. 10:12.

B. OT Context. The OT text in question occurs in a unit that considers the effects of speech on self and others, Prov. 10:6–14 (the analysis is that of Waltke 2004: 456–62). Here the effect on others is in view (10:11–14). In 10:11 the health-giving speech of the righteous is contrasted with the destructiveness of the mouth of the fool. In 10:12 hatred expressed in speech, not least where that hatred has been stirred up by the speaker's revulsion of the other's sin (which is suggested by the parallel line: "Hatred stirs up dissension / But love covers all wrongs"), achieves nothing more than strife and division. By contrast, articulated love wins the sinner as a friend, and "covers over all wrongs"; the idea is not that the wrongs are concealed but not dealt with, but rather that the love itself reconciles the alienated offender and changes everything.

C. The Context in Judaism. Normally "to cover sin" means to procure forgiveness, both in biblical texts (e.g., Ps. 32:1; 85:2) and in later Judaism (e.g., Sir. 5:6). The notion of a multitude of sins has a similar range of precedents (e.g., Ps. 5:10; 85:2; Ezek. 28:18; Sir. 5:6 1QH XII, 19). Proverbs 10:12 is also quoted in James 5:20 and is picked up in early post-NT documents as well (*1 Clem.* 49:5; *2 Clem.* 16:4).

D. Textual Matters. Although it is difficult to miss the allusion to Prov. 10:12, the wording of 1 Pet. 4:8 (*agapē kalyptei plēthos hamartiōn*) is close to neither the Hebrew nor the LXX; the LXX is least similar (*pantas de tous mē philoneikountas kalyptei philia*). This has prompted many to wonder if Peter is dependent for the form of his expression on common early Jewish Christian tradition (e.g., Achtemeier 1996: 295; Boring 1999: 150; Davids 1990: 158; Goppelt 1993: 297; Jobes 2005: 279).

That is plausible enough, but the justifying sources are meager.

E. Peter's Use of the OT in 4:8. When James 5:20 quotes this same passage, it is only the second half of Prov. 10:12 that interests him. Here, however, although once again only part of the second half is quoted, the context shows how apt the entire proverb is for Peter's readers. A community that is suffering abuse from outsiders may become a little frayed internally as well. But if they display hatred to one another, they will merely stir up dissension; by contrast, loving one another will "cover over" the many wrongs that inevitably take place in any community, and this is the stance that they must adopt in the light of the imminence of the end, and also because they are Christ's holy nation and therefore different from the surrounding pagans, and because they follow the example of Christ.

It follows, then, that the love that Peter has in mind is the patient forbearance that nips in the bud wrong actions and attitudes that, if allowed to fester, will attract retaliation, virulent animosity, and ultimately dissension and division. It is the kind of love that "does not dishonor others, it is not self-seeking, it is not easily angered, it keeps no record of wrongs.... It always protects, always trusts, always hopes, always perseveres" (1 Cor. 13:4–7 TNIV). In other words, Peter (any more than Prov. 10:12) is not making a theological statement about sins being forgiven by God, "covered" in that sense; still less is he saying it is all right to "cover up" sins by refusing to deal with offenses that must on occasion be confronted. Rather, this is the love that breaks the downward spiral of wounded sensibilities, hard feelings, nurtured bitterness, dissension, and vendetta. At the end of the first century Clement of Rome (*1 Clem.* 49:5) already rightly understood 1 Pet. 4:8 this way (see Achtemeier 1996: 296; Boring 1999: 150; Davids 1990: 158; Jobes 2005: 278–79; Reicke 1964: 122). The love that Peter has in view is far more than warm sentimentality; indeed, its relational mandate is a point that he has repeatedly underscored (e.g., 1:22; 2:1; 3:9), entirely in line with the wisdom of the quoted proverb.

F. Theological Use. This exhortation is of a piece with the recurring NT theme that evil is not overcome merely by refraining from doing it; we must overcome evil with good. It is not enough to break a bad habit; it is essential to love Jesus more, to want eternal things more. It is not enough not to retaliate against an enemy; it is essential to love one's enemy. So too here in 1 Pet. 4:8: it is not enough to try to be faithful ourselves, to put up with abuse from outsiders, and if necessary assume a defensive posture with fellow believers. That will merely fester into hatred. Because we belong to Christ, we are to overcome evil with good.

4:14

A. NT Context: The Spirit of God Rests on Those Who Suffer for Christ's Sake. Suffering quite often takes us by surprise. Peter tells his readers not to be surprised by the "fiery ordeal" that has befallen them (4:12–19). This ordeal is more specific than the sufferings that are part of this broken world, of course: Peter has in mind the abuse and opposition of a world that detests Christ and his followers. Nevertheless, the perception that suffering is "not the way it's supposed to be" (to borrow the title from Plantinga 1994) is at one level a reminder that sin and all its nefarious effects are abnormal.

> Misfortune and death are certainly "normal" in the sense that they are universally experienced, but they are not normal when viewed from God's intention in creation and his plan in redemption. The idea that normal life should always be harmonious and free from suffering, despite universal suffering and death, remains a lingering echo of life in Eden as God created it before the fall. It is also a longing for the time where there will be no more tears, suffering, pain, and death (Rev. 21:4). (Jobes 2005: 286)

Nevertheless, to participate in "the sufferings of Christ" should bring joy (4:13). "If you are insulted because of the name of Christ, you are blessed" (4:14). The blessing that Peter has in mind is not the suffering itself, nor is it alone the potential for character improvement (note the "testing" in 4:12); rather, it is the very presence of God: "you are blessed, for the Spirit of glory and of God rests on you" (4:14, citing Isa. 11:2). The theme is tied to what Peter says earlier: suffering with Christ rather than sliding into moral and spiritual compromise in a pagan world is a sign of the transforming work of the Spirit (1:2), evidence that one has become a living stone in the spiritual house of God (2:5).

B. OT Context. Isaiah 11 is a glorious messianic passage. The movement of thought begins in Isa. 6: Isaiah is charged to announce that God has determined in his holiness to cut his covenant people back to a mere stump (6:13). Just as God destroys the insufferable Assyria, so also he cuts down the arrogant and corrupt house of David (10:5–34). Nevertheless, God promises a coming messianic ruler (Isa. 7), a righteous messianic king who sits on David's throne and is recognized as the mighty God (Isa. 9). In other words, from the stump there springs a new shoot (11:1, thus harking back to 6:13). The following verse, 11:2, promises the endowment that will be on this messianic figure, "The Spirit of the LORD will rest on him," and then Isaiah describes the consequent charismata that this Messiah will enjoy, set out in three pairs: wisdom and insight, counsel and might, knowledge and fear of the Lord.

C. The Context in Judaism. The notion of being tested and thereby purified by suffering is very common in early Judaism (e.g., Wis. 3:1–6; Sir. 2:1–6; Jdt. 8:25–27; 1QS I, 17–18; VIII, 3–4; 1QM XVII, 8–9; 1QH^a XIII, 16). The messianic reference is made unmistakable in the Targum to Isa. 11:1, where the "shoot" now becomes a king: "A king shall come forth from the sons of Jesse, and the Messiah shall be anointed from among his children's children" (see Fitzmyer 2007: 165).

D. Textual Matters. Isaiah 11:1–3 LXX follows the MT fairly closely, except for inserting *eusebeia* ("piety") in place of "the fear of the LORD" in 11:2 (see Fitzmyer 2007: 74–75), though this has no impact on what Peter picks up. Because the wording of 1 Pet. 4:14 (*hoti to tēs doxēs kai to tou theou pneuma eph' hymas anapauetai*, "because the Spirit of glory and of God rests on you") differs significantly from the LXX (*kai anapausetai ep' auton pneuma tou theou*, "And the spirit of God shall rest on him" [NETS]), many take this to be an allusion, not a quotation. Perhaps this is a quibble over the appropriate label. Nevertheless Moyise (2005: 185) is right to point out that Isa. 11:2 is the only verse in the LXX where *pneuma* ("spirit"), *theos* ("God"), and *anapauō* ("to rest") come together, and come together in this way.

E. Peter's Use of the OT in 4:14. Where Isaiah promises the Spirit on the Messiah, Peter applies the prophecy of Isa. 11:2 directly to his Christian readers. Their suffering is precisely the context in which God visits them by his Spirit. But to understand what prompts Peter to apply Isa. 11:2 to his readers, one needs to reflect on wider theological use.

F. Theological Use. At first glance, it is more than a little strange to discover a prophecy made in so unambiguously a messianic setting transferred to the Messiah's followers. Yet perhaps it is not so strange after all. In Acts 9:4 the ascended Christ certainly identifies with his persecuted followers, which of course is another way of saying that they are identified with him. In Paul's writings the "union with Christ" theme ensures that Christians are said to be crucified with Christ, dead with him, raised with him, and seated on the right hand of the Majesty with him (e.g., Gal. 2:20; Col. 3:1, 3; Ephesians—indeed, Isa. 11:2 is cited in Eph. 1:17 and, as here, applied to believers). Paul elsewhere insists that if we endure suffering with him, we will reign with him (2 Tim. 2:12). So perhaps it is not so strange to conclude that the Spirit of the Lord, poured out on the Messiah, who suffered for their redemption, will also be poured out on Messiah's people when they too suffer on the Messiah's behalf. What all this suggests is that Peter's application of Isa. 11:2 to believers is not some metaphorical extension, still less an argument by analogy, but an application to believers grounded in their real participation in the end-time prophetic fulfillment inaugurated by Christ.

4:17–18

A. NT Context: Judgment Begins with God's Household. In words largely borrowed from Ezek. 9:5–6; Zech. 13:9; Mal. 3:1–3, Peter in 4:17 insists that it is time for judgment to begin at God's household. The context of 1 Pet. 4, however, shows that this is referring to what his Christian readers are currently suffering at the hands of pagan oppressors. Their suffering is unjust. So how can this be thought of as in any sense a mark of God's eschatological judgment, which is what Ezekiel, Zechariah, and Malachi have in mind? For that judgment is utterly just, and if it brings punishment, such punishment is deserved. Could Peter really be saying that his Christian readers actually deserve the oppression that they are forced to endure at the hands of pagans?

Several explanations have been advanced, but the most credible is that the word for "judgment" (*krima*) in this context refers not to condemnation and punishment, as it often does (e.g., Rom. 3:8; Gal. 5:10; 2 Pet. 2:3), but rather to the process of judgment, "the action of a judge" (BDAG 567). God begins his process of judging humanity, of sifting humanity, with his own people. Jobes (2005: 293) draws attention to the parallel in the parable of the sheep and goats (Matt. 25:31–46): God first judges the sheep and then the goats. Thus although some of the words from Ezekiel, Zechariah, and Malachi have been drawn into 1 Pet. 4:17, and with them the notion of eschatological judgment, the conceptual background of the OT passages, which is bound up with condemnation, is absent. In its place is the notion of a current "fiery ordeal" that in God's sovereign pleasure is sent along to "test" the believers (4:12). But if God's process of judging begins with his own people, "what will the outcome be for those who do not obey the gospel of God?" (4:17 TNIV). This a fortiori argument is reinforced by Peter's quotation from Prov. 11:31: "If it is hard for the righteous to be saved, what shall become of the ungodly and the sinner?" (1 Pet. 4:18).

B. OT Context. Proverbs 11:31 occurs in a unit that treats riches and payments in some detail, and this final proverb is "a climactic assertion that crime does not pay" (Waltke 2004: 513): "If the righteous person is repaid in the earth, how much more the wicked and the sinner!" Waltke (2004: 514) argues that "in the earth . . . probably implies a distinction between the present remedial punishment of the righteous 'in the earth' and the future penal punishment of the wicked, the theme of this section." In other words, if God's justice is not relaxed even for his own people but metes out assorted temporal judgments (one thinks of such passages as Deut. 3:23–26; 1 Sam. 2:27–36; 2 Sam. 12:9–12; 1 Kings 11:9–13), how can the wicked imagine that they will escape the severity of the justice of God?

C. The Context in Judaism. On the developing and complex understanding within early Judaism of God's grace and God's judgment toward his own people, see Carson, O'Brien, and Seifrid 2001.

D. Textual Matters. The LXX replaces "is repaid" by "is saved" but nevertheless retains the a fortiori form of argument. The LXX replaces "in the earth" with *molis*, usually rendered "with difficulty" or "scarcely," a word picked up by 1 Peter:

"If the righteous person is scarcely [*molis*] saved, what will become of the ungodly and the sinner?" On this point the Peshitta and one Arabic version follow the LXX, while the Vulgate and the Targum follow the MT. Various explanations for the difference have been preferred (see, e.g., Barr 1975), but none is certain.

E. Peter's Use of the OT in 4:18. To say that salvation is difficult for the righteous is not to say that God finds it terribly difficult to save them (though one should never downplay the cost of the atonement) but rather that God's people, in line with Jesus' own instruction, enter the narrow gate (Luke 13:23–24) and face the opposition of the world from which they have sprung (cf. Matt. 10; Mark 13:20). Implicitly this is a challenge to Peter's readers to follow through to the end, to persevere to the end. Earlier the motive that Peter offered his readers was their opportunity to glorify God by their suffering, their pleasure in being associated with the name of Christ (4:16). Here he provides a different motive: they are never to feel envious of the oppressors and persecutors, for those who reject the gospel will suffer much more than anything Christians have had to face in this life.

F. Theological Use. It is difficult to overestimate the importance, especially in the NT, of establishing one's priorities on the basis of an eternal perspective that never forgets that God is the final judge.

5:5

A. NT Context: The Priority of Humility. After instructions to the "elders" among his readers (5:1–4), Peter addresses those who are younger (5:5). He tells them to submit to the elders; doubtless under times of stress brought about by external pressure, there will be no shortage of suggestions, frequently advanced by the young, offering alternative courses of action, and this in itself could easily erupt into dissension and strife. Peter then universalizes the argument: "All of you," he writes, "clothe yourselves with humility toward one another" (5:5). The reason is that God himself declares that he opposes the proud but shows favor to the humble and oppressed—words cited from Prov. 3:34, also cited in James 4:6.

B. OT Context. The poem of Prov. 3:21–35 begins with parental encouragement to the son to retain possession of "sound judgment and discernment" (NIV)—what Longman (2006) interprets as "resourcefulness and discretion." Verses 23–25 establish the motivation for pursuing values, though in v. 26 it is Yahweh himself who protects. Verses 27–31 introduce five prohibitions, all having to do with relationships that the young man characterized by "sound judgment and discernment" will want to avoid, and vv. 32–35 set out the motivations behind such prohibitions—indeed, behind the appeal of the entire poem. The controlling thought in these motivations is the distinction between Yahweh's attitude toward the wicked and his attitude toward the righteous. In our verse, 3:34, the distinction is plain: "He mocks proud mockers but gives grace to the humble" (NIV). Mockers inevitably think of themselves as strong and sneer with condescending derision at those whom they judge to be weak. But God, who is immeasurably strong, holds them in derision and mocks them, giving grace to the humble, who alone are wise. The mockers "will get from God exactly what they give others: as they tear everything down with their mouths, so the Lord will tear them down with his curse (see 3:34); as they cover others with reproach, so the Lord will cover them with shame (cf. 1:24–33; Ps. 18:25–26 [26–27])" (Waltke 2004: 273).

C. The Context in Judaism. Although Prov. 3:34 does not appear to have played a major role in Judaism at the turn of the eras, it is of a piece with a widespread wisdom tradition that thought in polarities, distinguished between the wise/righteous and the fool/wicked, and stressed the importance of dependence on God for the kind of wisdom that brings life (see von Rad 1972; Perdue 1994; Hempel, Lange, and Lichtenberger 2001).

D. Textual Matters. The Hebrew text reads *'im-lallēṣîm hû'-yālîṣ wĕla'ănāwîm yitten-ḥēn* ("Surely he mocks the mockers, but he gives grace to the humble"). The "he" who gives this grace is, contextually, YHWH, "the LORD." The LXX preserves this reference to "the LORD" but reads *kyrios hyperēphanois antitassetai tapenois de didōsin charin*, which Peter follows exactly, except for his change of *kyrios* to *ho theos*: "God [not 'the LORD'] opposes the proud but gives grace to the humble." The general idea is the same, of course, but the LXX (and therefore also Peter) loses the specificity of the manner of God's opposition: God mocking the mockers.

E. Peter's Use of the OT in 5:5. Peter's insistence on humility is not an arbitrary or whimsical piece of counsel designed only for the immediate cultural context. Far from it: it is grounded in God's deepest commitments. Indeed, the instruction would have seemed positively countercultural to Peter's readers, as humility was so often seen in Greco-Roman culture as a mark of a slave (see Elliott 2000: 847; Goppelt 1993: 253). Peter's readers, however, are to see themselves as strangers and aliens (1:1; 2:11) with primary allegiance to another kingdom.

> True humility, as opposed to a contrived, self-degrading humiliation, flows from recognizing one's complete dependence on God and is expressed by the acceptance of one's role and position in God's economy. With such humility one is freed from attempts to gain more power or prestige. Instead, humility expresses itself in the willingness to serve others even beyond one's self-interest. (Jobes 2005: 309)

F. Theological Use. The antithesis bound up with this quotation is so common in Scripture that it would take a very long essay merely to canvass the conceptual parallels. See, for instance, the Beatitudes (Matt. 5:3–10). The first responsibility of the creature is to recognize his or her creatureliness and therefore live in dependence upon, and with worship toward, the Creator and Sovereign of all. The only alternative is the proud independence that is nothing other than utterly destructive idolatry, the arrogance that finally brings down God's displeasure. This theme lies at the heart of the Bible's storyline and of God's plan of redemption brought to fulfillment in the cross and resurrection of Jesus Christ and to consummation at the end.

5:8

A. NT Context: The Devil as a Roaring Lion. The real enemy of Peter's Christian readers is the devil himself. Christians must resist him (5:9), and to do so effectively demands that they recognize how dangerous he is. Here he is likened to "a roaring lion looking for someone to devour" (5:8).

B. OT Context. The figure of a lion appears in various OT contexts to describe the opponents of Israel (e.g., Jer. 50:17 [27:17 LXX]; 51:34–38 [28:34–38 LXX]), and specifically as "a roaring lion" in Ps. 22:13 (21:14 LXX), even juxtaposing animals:

> Many bulls encompass me;
> strong bulls of Bashan surround me;
> they open wide their mouths at me,
> like a ravening and roaring lion.
> (22:12–13 ESV)

In other words, in a usage such as this the rapacious and savage characteristics of human opponents are in view, not the devil himself.

C. The Context in Judaism. The figure of the lion to describe Israel's opponents continues at Qumran (e.g., 1QH^a XIII, 5–7, 9, 13–14, 18–19; 4Q167 2, 1–2; 4Q169 3+4 I, 4–6) (see Kelly 1969: 210).

D. Textual Matters. In the LXX the singular "roaring lion" referring to an enemy is found only at Ps. 21:14 (22:13 ET). It is also found in the MT of Ezek. 22:25, but the LXX there has a plural, "roaring lions." In other words, if Peter is self-consciously alluding to any one passage, it must be the psalm passage.

E. Peter's Use of the OT in 5:8. This usage merely picks up a colorful metaphor from the OT and applies it to the devil. It is not obvious that Peter is attempting any other associative transfer.

F. Theological Use. A somewhat parallel description is found in 2 Tim. 4:17 (see also Heb. 11:33), but it is not applied directly to the devil himself. A full-scale summary of what the Bible says about the devil would soon unveil the fact that the one who is here envisaged as a savage and threatening lion also masquerades on occasion as an angel of light (2 Cor. 11:14). Finally, it is important to remember that the lion is not a standard technical symbol suitable only for the devil. Because the lion is regal ("the king of the beasts"), Jesus' kingship can be displayed under the figure of the lion—indeed, under the mixed symbolism of the lion and the lamb (Rev. 5).

Bibliography

Achtemeier, P. J. 1996. *1 Peter*. Hermeneia. Minneapolis: Fortress.

Agnew, F. H. 1983. "1 Peter 1:2—an Alternative Translation." *CBQ* 45: 68–73.

Allison, D. C., Jr. 2003. *Testament of Abraham*. CEJL. Berlin: de Gruyter.

Barr, J. 1975. "באר‎ ~ ΜΟΛΙΣ: Prov. XI.31, I Pet. IV.18." *JSS* 20: 149–64.

Bauckham, R. 1988. "James, 1 and 2 Peter, Jude." Pages 303–17 in *It Is Written: Scripture Citing Scripture; Essays in Honor of Barnabas Lindars, SSF.* Edited by D. A. Carson and H. G. M. Williamson. Cambridge: Cambridge University Press.

Beare, F. W. 1970. *The First Epistle of Peter: The Greek Text with Introduction and Notes.* 3rd ed. Oxford: Blackwell.

Best, E. 1982 [1971]. *1 Peter.* NCB. Repr., Grand Rapids: Eerdmans.

Bigg, C. A. 1901. *Critical and Exegetical Commentary on the Epistles of St. Peter and St. Jude.* ICC. New York: Scribner.

Boring, M. E. 1999. *1 Peter.* ANTC. Nashville: Abingdon.

Brox, N. 1975. "Zur pseudepigraphischen Rahmung des ersten Petrusbriefes." *BZ* 19: 78–96.

———. 1979. *Der erste Petrusbrief.* EKKNT. Zurich: Benziger.

Cahill, M. 1999. "Not a Cornerstone! Translating Ps 118,22 in the Jewish and Christian Scriptures." *RB* 106: 345–57.

Calvin, J. 1963. *The Epistle of Paul the Apostle to the Hebrews and the First and Second Epistles of St. Peter.* Translated by W. B. Johnson. Grand Rapids: Eerdmans.

Carson, D. A. 1981. *Divine Sovereignty and Human Responsibility: Biblical Themes in Tension.* London: Marshall, Morgan & Scott.

Carson, D. A., P. T. O'Brien, and M. A. Seifrid, eds. 2001. *The Complexities of Second Temple Judaism.* Vol. 1 of *Justification and Variegated Nomism.* WUNT 140. Tübingen: Mohr Siebeck.

Childs, B. S. 2001. *Isaiah.* OTL. Louisville: Westminster John Knox.

Colwell, E. C. 1939. "Popular Reactions against Christianity in the Roman Empire." Pages 53–71 in *Environmental Factors in Christian History.* Edited by J. T. McNeill, M. Spinka, and H. R. Willoughby. Port Washington, NY: Kennikat.

Congar, Y. M.-J. 1952. *The Mystery of the Temple, or, The Manner of God's Presence to His Creatures from Genesis to the Apocalypse.* Translated by R. F. Trevett. London: Burns & Oates.

Constant, P. 2001. "Le Psaume 118 et son emploi christologique dans Luc et Actes: Une étude exégétique, littéraire et herméneutique." PhD diss., Trinity Evangelical Divinity School.

Dalton, W. J. 1989 [1965]. *Christ's Proclamation to the Spirits: A Study of 1 Peter 3:18–4:6.* 2nd ed. AnBib 23. Rome: Pontifical Biblical Institute.

Danker, F. W. 1967. "1 Peter 1,24–2,17—A Consolatory Pericope." *ZNW* 58: 93–102.

Davids, P. H. 1990. *The First Epistle of Peter.* NICNT. Grand Rapids: Eerdmans.

Davies, J. A. 2004. *A Royal Priesthood: Literary and Intertextual Perspectives on an Image of Israel in Exodus 19:6.* London: T&T Clark.

de Waard, J. A. 1965. *Comparative Study of the Old Testament Text in the Dead Sea Scrolls and in the New Testament.* STDJ 4. Leiden: Brill.

Elliott, J. H. 1966. *The Elect and the Holy: An Exegetical Examination of 1 Peter 2:4–10 and the Phrase βασίλειον ἱεράτευμα.* NovTSup 12. Leiden: Brill.

———. 1981. *A Home for the Homeless: A Sociological Exegesis of 1 Peter, Its Situation and Strategy.* Philadelphia: Fortress.

———. 2000. *1 Peter.* AB 37B. New York: Doubleday.

Fitzmyer, J. A. 2007. *The One Who Is to Come.* Grand Rapids: Eerdmans.

Forbes, G. 2005. "Children of Sarah: Interpreting 1 Peter 3:6b." *BBR* 15: 105–9.

France, R. T. 1998. "First Century Bible Study: Old Testament Motifs in 1 Peter 2:4–10." *JEPTA* 18: 26–48.

Goppelt, L. 1993 [1978]. *A Commentary on 1 Peter*. Edited by F. Hahn. Translated by J. E. Alsup. Grand Rapids: Eerdmans.

Grudem, Wayne A. 1988. *The First Epistle of Peter: An Introduction and Commentary*. TNTC 17. Grand Rapids: Eerdmans.

Hempel, C., A. Lange, and H. Lichtenberger, eds. 2001. *The Wisdom Texts from Qumran and the Development of Sapiential Thought*. BETL 159. Leuven: Peeters.

Hillyer, N. 1969. "Spiritual Milk . . . Spiritual House." *TynBul* 20: 126.

———. 1971. "'Rock-Stone' Imagery in 1 Peter." *TynBul* 22: 58–81.

———. 1992. *1 and 2 Peter, Jude*. NIBCNT 16. Peabody, MA: Hendrickson.

Hort, F. J. A. 1898. *The First Epistle of St. Peter: I.1–II.17: The Greek Text with Introductory Lecture, Commentary, and Additional Notes*. London: Macmillan.

Jobes, K. H. 2005. *1 Peter*. BECNT. Grand Rapids: Baker Academic.

Judge, E. A. 1960. *The Social Pattern of Christian Groups in the First Century*. London: Tyndale.

Kelly, J. N. D. 1969. *A Commentary on the Epistles of Peter and of Jude*. HNTC. New York: Harper & Row.

Kiley, M. 1987. "Like Sara: The Tale of Terror behind 1 Peter 3:6." *JBL* 106: 689–92.

Kuykendall, C., and C. J. Collins. 2003. "1 Peter 3:15A: A Critical Review of English Versions." *Presbyterion* 29: 76–84.

Lea, T. 1980. "How Peter Learned the Old Testament." *SwJT* 22: 96–102.

Longman, T., III. 2006. *Proverbs*. BCOT. Grand Rapids: Baker Academic.

Marshall, I. H. 1991. *1 Peter*. IVPNTC. Downers Grove, IL: InterVarsity.

Martin, T. W. 1999. "The TestAbr and the Background of 1 Pet 3,6." *ZNW* 90: 139–46.

McKnight, S. 1996. *1 Peter*. NIVAC. Grand Rapids: Zondervan.

McKelvey, R. J. 1969. *The New Temple: The Church in the New Testament*. Oxford: Oxford University Press.

Michaels, J. R. 1988. *1 Peter*. WBC 49. Waco: Word.

Moyise, S. 2005. "Isaiah in 1 Peter." Pages 175–88 in *Isaiah in the New Testament*. Edited by S. Moyise and M. J. J. Menken. London: T&T Clark.

Osborne, T. P. 1981. "L'utilisation des citations de l'Ancient Testament dans le première épître de Pierre." *RTL* 12: 46–77.

Oswalt, J. N. 1986. *The Book of Isaiah: Chapters 1–39*. NICOT. Grand Rapids: Eerdmans.

———. 1998. *The Book of Isaiah: Chapters 40–66*. NICOT. Grand Rapids: Eerdmans.

Panning, A. J. 2000. "Exegetical Brief: What Has Been Determined (ἐτέθησαν) in 1 Peter 2:8?" *WLQ* 98: 48–52.

Perdue, L. G. 1994. *Wisdom and Creation: The Theology of Wisdom Literature*. Nashville: Abingdon.

Piper, John. 1980. "Hope as the Motivation of Love: 1 Peter 3:9–12." *NTS* 26: 212–31.

Plantinga, C., Jr. 1994. *Not the Way It's Supposed to Be: A Breviary of Sin*. Grand Rapids: Eerdmans.

Reicke, B. 1964. *The Epistles of James, Peter and Jude*. AB 37. Garden City, NY: Doubleday.

Roberts, J. J. M. 1987. "Yahweh's Foundation in Zion (Isa. 28:16)." *JBL* 106: 27–45.

Schelkle, K. H. 1970. *Die Petrusbriefe, der Judasbrief*. 3rd ed. HTKNT. Freiburg: Herder.

Schutter, W. L. 1989. *Hermeneutic and Composition in 1 Peter*. WUNT 30. Tübingen: Mohr Siebeck.

Selwyn, E. G. 1955. *The First Epistle of St. Peter*. 2nd ed. London: Macmillan.

Snodgrass, K. R. 1977–1978. "1 Peter II.1–10: Its Formation and Literary Affinities." *NTS* 24: 97–106.

Spencer, A. B. 2000. "Peter's Pedagogical Method in 1 Peter 3:6." *BBR* 10: 107–19.

Spicq, C. 1966. *Les Épîtres de Saint Pierre*. SB. Paris: Librairie Lecoffre.

van Unnik, W. C. 1969. "The Critique of Paganism in 1 Peter 1:18." Pages 129–42 in *Neotestamentica et Semitica: Studies in Honour of Matthew Black*. Edited by E. E. Ellis and M. Wilcox. Edinburgh: T&T Clark.

von Rad, G. 1972. *Wisdom in Israel*. London: SCM Press.

Waltke, B. K. 2004. *Proverbs 1–15*. NICOT. Grand Rapids: Eerdmans.

Westermann, C. 1969. *Isaiah 40–66*. OTL. Philadelphia: Westminster.

Williamson, H. G. M. 1998. *Variations on a Theme: King, Messiah and Servant in the Book of Isaiah*. Exeter: Paternoster.

Wood, T. R. 2005. "The Regathering of the People of God: An Investigation into the New Testament's Appropriation of the Old Testament Prophecies Concerning the Regathering of Israel." PhD diss., Trinity Evangelical Divinity School.

Yoshikawa, S. T. 2004. "The Prototypical Use of the Noahic Flood in the New Testament." PhD diss., Trinity Evangelical Divinity School.

2 Peter

D. A. Carson

Introduction

The study of the use of the OT in 2 Peter is beset with several challenges.

(1) Clearly, either 2 Peter borrows from Jude, or Jude borrows from 2 Peter. Though in briefer compass, the challenge is not unlike the way 1–2 Chronicles uses antecedent material or the way the Synoptic Gospels display interdependencies. Most scholars today accept that Jude was written first, and that 2 Peter quotes extensively from it. Although that is probably correct, I will nevertheless present the material in canonical order. More important, perhaps, is the fact that Jude clearly cites extrabiblical material (as do some other NT books), and this has prompted a preponderance of scholars to read the OT allusions through the lenses of those extrabiblical books. The case is more plausible in Jude than in 2 Peter (though even there it needs some qualification), but because most scholars hold that 2 Peter depends on Jude, tendencies ostensibly found in Jude are then too easily read back into 2 Peter. The following commentary tries to avoid the worst of these pitfalls.

(2) A related but broader perception is that the OT allusions in 2 Peter, regardless of any influence from Jude, are largely mediated through the lenses of the literature of Second Temple Judaism; that is, that literature's interpretation of the foundational OT passages becomes the interpretation of those OT passages found in 2 Peter. That is not intrinsically improbable, of course, but dependence is frequently not an easy thing to demonstrate. At the very least, one must make an effort to see if 2 Peter is developing a parallel interpretation or an interpretation somewhat modified from the one found in other sources of early Judaism.

(3) Some scholars insist that there are no OT quotations at all in 2 Peter, but only allusions. Others classify some words in 2 Pet. 3:13 a quotation—the only one in the letter. Terminological disputes aside, the allusive nature of Peter's use of the OT in this epistle means that sometimes the reader is uncertain as to which passage or passages Peter has in mind, let alone precisely how he reads them. The peculiar challenges of this document mean that the procedure adopted in the commentary on 1 Peter will be modified here. In the case of 1 Peter, quotations were treated to the full sweep of the recommended editorial structure: NT context, OT context, context in Judaism, textual matters, and so on. Allusions were handled more briefly and discursively. Here in 2 Peter, however, some allusions will receive the full gamut of steps. But as in 1 Peter, the interests of brevity demand that we skip over a handful of passages treated as allusions or echoes by some scholars.

1:19

The "word of the prophets made more certain" (NIV) almost certainly refers to the OT Scriptures. Since no particular Scripture is mentioned, it is best to think of the OT Scriptures as a whole (which may suggest that there was more canonical awareness than many are willing to concede). We should pay attention to this word, Peter writes, "as to a light shining in a dark place, until the day dawns and the morning star rises in your hearts" (TNIV). God's word is often compared to a light, both in the OT (e.g., Ps. 119:105) and in other Jewish literature (e.g., Wis. 18:4). The expression "dark place" is not found elsewhere in either the LXX or the NT, but Davids (2006: 208) draws attention to *4 Ezra* 12:42: "For of all the prophets you alone are left to us, like a cluster of grapes from the vintage, and like a lamp in a dark place, and like a haven for a ship saved from a storm." There is no direct dependence, of course, but the parallel shows that the image was a natural one waiting to be called up by both authors.

The imagery of the morning star probably derives from Num. 24:17: "I see him, but not now; I behold him, but not near. A star will come out of Jacob; a scepter will arise out of Israel." The oracle in which it is set (Num. 24:15–19) is introduced with Balaam's announcement of what Israel will do to Balak's people "in the latter days" (ESV; "in days to come," NIV). The phrase regularly signals not only something in the future but also something with eschatological overtones, even on occasion more immediate events that themselves point to the future. Certainly the coming of a "star" is widely connected in early Judaism with the coming of a messianic figure, sometimes understood to be a new priest, sometimes a ruler (e.g., "a prince of the congregation")—for example, *T. Levi* 18:3; *T. Jud.* 24:1; CD-A VII, 18–20; 1QM XI, 6–7; 4Q175 9–13. None of these texts modifies "star" with "morning" (though see Rev. 22:16, which speaks of Jesus as the "bright morning star"), but this is doubtless Peter's way of signaling the coming of the eschatological age, in line with the way other NT writers deploy the night/day contrast (e.g., Rom. 13:12; 1 Thess. 5:4–9). What is in view is Jesus' return, a theme certainly of interest to Peter (cf. 2 Pet. 3:10–13). In that light, the phrase "and the morning star rises in your hearts" most likely does not refer to inner enlightenment (Mayor 1979; Spicq 1966). Nor should we think that the expected apocalyptic parousia has been transmuted into an individual experience (Schelkle 1980; Kelly 1969), but that at the "dawn," at the parousia, we will no longer see through a glass darkly, we will no longer need the mediating revelation of Scripture, for Christ will rise in our hearts (so Bauckham 1988; Davids 2006).

2:4

A. NT Context: "Angels" Not Spared. This is the first of five allusions compressed into 2:4–10a, the general purpose of which is to demonstrate that God has always been perfectly willing and able "to rescue the godly from trials and to hold the unrighteous for punishment on the day of judgment" (2:9 TNIV). Yet the interpretation of who these angels are depends on a matrix of several interlocking interpretive challenges: (1) what Gen. 6:1–4 means (on which, see below); (2) the relationship of this passage to 1 Pet. 3:18–22, and the interpretation of the latter; (3) how this passage relates to Jude, what the latter means, and whether 2 Peter means the same thing.

Despite the view of some interpreters, 2 Peter does not simply take over Jude 4–18 in a block quotation. Close comparison shows that the former is "a rather free paraphrase" of the latter (see Sidebottom 1967: 95, 112; Callan 2004). Peter and Jude both mention judgment on "angels" and on Sodom and Gomorrah, but only the former mentions the flood, only the latter mentions judgment on Israel after the exodus, and the latter does not set things out in chronological order. More importantly, Peter interweaves into his list the preservation of the righteous, in particular Noah and Lot, while Jude omits all mention of the righteous. The result is that where the two documents substantially overlap, each nevertheless develops its own distinctive rhetorical emphases (see Charles 2005). Schreiner (2003: 335) helpfully sets forth the logic of 2 Pet. 2:4–10 that distinctively incorporates mention of the righteous:

> If God judged the angels (v. 4)
> and if he judged the flood generation (v. 5),
>   while at the same time sparing Noah (v. 5),

and if he judged Sodom and Gomorrah (v. 6), while at the same time preserving Lot (vv. 7–8)

then it follows that the Lord will preserve the godly in the midst of their trials (drawing this conclusion from the examples of Noah and Lot)

and it also follows that the Lord will punish the ungodly on the day of judgment (drawing this conclusion from the three examples of the angels, the flood, and Sodom and Gomorrah).

B. OT Context. Under the assumption that the OT background to 2 Pet. 2:4 is Gen. 6:1–4, we must ask what the latter passage means. There have been three primary interpretations: (1) the "sons of God" are angels who crossed species lines and married human women, producing "Nephilim," who were "heroes of old, men of renown" (Gen. 6:4); (2) the "sons of God" were kings, judges, and other members of aristocratic nobility who displayed their own greatness by indulging in polygamy and creating harems; (3) the "sons of God" were human males from the putatively godly line of Seth who freely married women from ungodly lines.

Nowadays the majority of interpreters from across the theological spectrum accept the angel interpretation (the list of supporters is very long, but see esp. the discussion in Dexinger 1966; see also Wenham 1987: 138–41). This interpretation is assumed by the LXX and is supported by most early Jewish exegesis, though not quite all (see below), as well as by all the earliest church fathers and some later ones (including Justin Martyr, Clement of Alexandria, Tertullian, Cyprian, Ambrose, and Lactantius), but not by some later fathers (Chrysostom, Augustine, Theodoret). "Sons of God" (in the plural) refers elsewhere in the OT to angels—certainly so in Job 1:6; 2:1; 38:7, and probably so in Ps. 29:1; 89:7; Dan. 3:25 (where *bar-ʾĕlāhîn* underlies the traditional rendering "mighty ones" or the like found in most English versions). Yet the interpretation does not easily fit the context of the flood, since that judgment is pronounced against humanity (cf. Gen. 6:3–5; note "flesh" in 6:3 [NIV: "mortal"]). According to Jesus, angels do not marry (Matt. 22:30; Mark 12:25), and although excellent efforts have been

undertaken to avoid this and other objections to the angel interpretation (e.g., Brown 2002: 52–71; vanGemeren 1981), the niggles make it less than a sure thing.

Those who take the view that the expression "sons of God" refers to kings, nobles, and other aristocrats (e.g., Cassuto 1973; Kline 1961–1962) understand them to be lusting after power, the multiple women being the signs of their success. Kline suggests that they are "divine kings"—that is, kings viewed as in some sense divine owing to the dominant religious commitments of the time. In other words, instead of administering justice under God, they forsook their proper place, claimed deity for themselves, violated God's will by forming royal harems, and lusted after power. Their children were the Nephilim-heroes (6:4), "evidently characterized by physical might and military-political dominance" (Kline 1993: 115). On the face of it, this explanation makes best sense of "and they took any of them they chose" (Gen. 6:2) and admirably sets the stage for the pronouncement of judgment against "flesh" in the flood. Negatively, however, there is no linguistic warrant outside Gen. 6:1–4 for supposing that "sons of God" refers to "divine kings" or, more generally, to aristocratic ruling figures, whereas the reading of "angels" has a long track record, including the LXX.

The view that "sons of God" refers to the line of Seth, while "daughters of human beings" refers to non-Sethian women, not only suffers from an absence of philological support but also has few elements in its favor compared with the "divine kings" view.

A few scholars have suggested the possibility that the first and second interpretations might be combined; that is, human rulers (the second interpretation) who claimed some sort of divine status might still fit the requirement of some kind of "angelic" encroachment (the first interpretation) if they were viewed as somehow demon possessed (so Clines 1979; Waltke 2001: 115–17; Gispen 1974: 221).

A few scholars over the years, however, have argued that Gen. 6:1–4 is not the OT background to 2 Pet. 2:4, but rather that Peter has in mind the prehistoric fall of angels. Some sort of prehistoric fall of the embodied serpent (Gen. 3) is doubtless presupposed by Genesis, but one is hard-pressed to find explicit discussion of the event. This interpretation of Gen. 6:1–4 sounds a bit like the interpretation of the scarcely known by the still yet more unknown.

C. The Context in Judaism. The interpretation of Gen. 6:1–4 that takes "the sons of God" to be angels (often called "Watchers") who have sexual intercourse with women is widespread in early Judaism (e.g., *1 En.* 6–19; 21; 86–88; *Jub.* 4:15, 22; 5:1; CD-A II, 17–19; 1QapGen ar II, 1; *Tg. Ps.-J.* Gen. 6:1–4; *T. Reub.* 5:6–7; *T. Naph.* 3:5; *2 Bar.* 56:10–14). True, a minority rabbinic tradition pronounces a curse on those who take the angel view (*Gen. Rab.* 26:5; cf. R. Simeon b. Yohai), but this probably does not go back earlier than the mid-second century AD.

Three further comments on this literature should be addressed. First, although various themes are emphasized by these assorted texts from early Judaism, the most extensive tradition is found in *1 En.* 6–19. Bauckham (1988: 51) argues that originally the fall of the Watchers in this tradition "was a myth of the origin of evil" but became detached from such mythology about the middle of the first century AD. The account tells how, in the days of Jared (Gen. 5:18), two hundred angels, under the leadership of Šemiḥazah and 'Aša'el, rebelled against God, lusted after the beautiful daughters of men, descended to Mount Hermon, and took human wives. Their children were giants who ravaged the earth. The fallen angels themselves taught human beings things that they should not know and many kinds of sin. Ultimately, then, the fallen angels were responsible for the corruption and degradation that brought down from the hand of God the punishment of the flood. The fallen angels, the Watchers, were punished by being bound under the earth until the final judgment; the giants were condemned by being abandoned to destroy each other in incessant battle, and their spirits became the evil spirits finally responsible for the evil in the world between the flood and the day of judgment. What is striking about these accounts is the attempt to shift blame for the flood from human beings to fallen angelic beings.

Second, Both Jude and 2 Peter apparently pick up on at least some of these themes. Yet what is picked up is not the entire "package" taught by *1 Enoch* but rather only that these "angels" (*an-geloi*) are kept in darkness, bound in eternal chains awaiting the day of judgment (see further below). Jude picks up on one further factor (see §C of commentary on Jude 6).

Third, some have suggested that Peter (and Jude before him) knows of, and is perhaps dependent on, the Greek myth of the Titans, recounted in Hesiod's *Theogony*. Certainly some Jewish writers identified the Titans with fallen angels or with their giant progeny (see Josephus, *Ant.* 1.73; Sir. 16:7; Jdt. 16:6). In this myth the Titans were imprisoned in "Tartarus," the word that Peter here uses for "hell." This may be nothing more than the vocabulary choice of someone influenced by Hellenistic Judaism; it is hard to be sure, for already the word is used in the LXX of Job 40:20; 41:24 (Tartarus of the abyss); Prov. 30:16 (apparently parallel to Hades). In other words, appeal to ostensible Petrine knowledge of Hesiod is premature. The issue is compounded by a difficult textual variant, to which we now turn.

D. Textual Matters. However we understand "the sons of God" in the Hebrew of Gen. 6:1–4, the LXX refers to them as *angeloi*, which word is picked up in 2 Pet. 2:4 and, in the NT, is almost always used of angels, rarely of "messengers," and never of aristocratic figures such as kings and nobles. In other words, on the basis of philology alone, the angel interpretation seems most credible, unless one accepts the synthesis of Waltke and others who see that the "divine kings" are "possessed" by fallen angels, combining the strengths of the first two interpretations.

In 2 Pet. 2:4 there is a very difficult decision between *seirais* ("bonds, ropes, chains") and *seirois/sirois* ("pits"). Jude 6 uses *desmois* ("bonds"). Peter may have chosen a more elegant word than Jude's (he makes this sort of change elsewhere), thus opting for *seirais*, and a later scribe "corrected" it to *seirois*, perhaps because it seems to fit better with *zophou* ("of darkness"). Alternatively, Peter wrote *seirois zophou* ("pits of darkness"), whether under the influence of Hesiod or not, and a scribe "corrected" it to *seirais zophou* ("bonds of darkness," "chains of darkness" [TNIV], obviously understood metaphorically) under the influence of Jude 6. The external evidence is evenly divided.

E. Peter's Use of the OT in 2:4. The nature of the sin is less specific in 2 Pet. 2:4 than in Jude 6–7, which mentions that the "angels" not only abandoned their place but also, apparently by analogy with Sodom, engaged in sexual sin. Crossing the species line is central to the sin in *Jub.* 5; that is not explicit in either Jude or 2 Peter. Peter is interested in the inevitability of the judgment of these "angels," whoever they are, rather than in the precise nature of their sin.

F. Theological Use. "The point of this verse is that these fallen angels await eternal judgment.... The eschatological judgment of the angels who sinned is sure. They are already in prison. How much more sure is the judgment of those who have denied the Christ who purchased them" (Davids 2006: 226). That is entirely right, even if there remains some uncertainty regarding the referent of "angels."

2:5

A. NT Context: The Flood and Noah—a Bad Example and a Good One. The next two allusions, the second and third, one negative and one positive, are packed into this verse. God did not spare the antediluvian world but rather brought catastrophic judgment on its ungodly people; on the other hand, God did spare Noah, "a preacher of righteousness," and his family (Gen. 6–9). Unlike Jude, Peter, by giving a positive example as well as a negative one, shows that "the Lord knows how to rescue the godly from trials" as well as how "to hold the unrighteous for punishment on the day of judgment" (2:9).

B. OT Context. There is no doubt that Peter is referring to the flood narrative of Gen. 6–9. Brown (2002: 94–98) usefully lists the minor linguistic connections, but they shed little light on how Peter is reflecting on this passage for his own use. Genesis 6:11–12 establishes that the reason why God sent this devastating judgment was the unmitigated violence and corruption on the earth. The singular exception was Noah. At the end of it, God promises with a covenant sign that he will never destroy the earth the same way again, which in the narrative reads as a singular mark of divine grace, for the earth surely will deserve the destruction.

Since the world is destroyed because of its corruption, and Noah and his family are saved, it is a fair inference that they are, by contrast, righteous; and that point is made the more explicit when God tells Noah to build an ark, and Noah does so, simply because he is committed to doing what

God commands. The OT text nowhere explicitly states that Noah is "a preacher of righteousness," though probably imaginative reading of the narrative presupposes that Noah would have to provide some sort of rationale for his activity before the ungodly watching world. The literature of Second Temple Judaism, as we will see, makes the inference explicit.

Other writers in the OT refer back to the flood to testify to Yahweh's omnipotent rule over creation (Ps. 29; perhaps Ps. 104:3–4) in order to provide imagery to depict the judgment of God that will overtake the wicked (Isa. 24:1, 4, 18; cf. Job 22:15–17; Nah. 1:8 LXX) and to depict trials and tribulations that the righteous must face and from which only God can save them (e.g., Ps. 18:16; 46:1–3; 65:5–8). For a full trajectory of flood imagery through the OT and early Judaism, see Yoshikawa 2004.

C. The Context in Judaism. Mention of the flood narrative is extraordinarily frequent in the literature of early Judaism. It shows up in Wisdom literature and historical books (e.g., Wis. 10:4; 14:6–7, connecting the flood with the time of the giants; 3 Macc. 2:4; 4 Macc. 15:31, where Noah's ark is a metaphor for the guardian of the law) and very often in apocalyptic literature (*Jubilees, 1 Enoch,* 2 Esdras), where quite commonly the fallen angels of Gen. 6:1–4 contribute to the corruption of humankind before the flood. The Dead Sea Scrolls preserve many references (CD-A II, 17–21; V, 1; 1QapGen ar; 1Q19 + 1Q19 bis; 4Q176; 4Q244; and numerous other passages [for which, see García Martínez 1999]). The tendency in this literature is to correlate Noah with the righteous remnant that the community constituted, while associating the rebellious Watchers of the flood generation with the corrupt Jewish priestly line in Jerusalem, all the while fostering an awareness of the end times. Philo can deal with Gen. 6–9 as straightforward historical narrative (e.g., *Abraham* 41–45; *Confusion* 23–24; *Moses* 2.54, 59), use it to promote moralizing stances under the threat of judgment (e.g., *On Dreams* 1.74; *Moses* 2.59), and interpret it in several allegorical ways—for example, the flood stands for a rush of evil passions and lust that wash over the soul (*Flight* 191–193; *QG* 2.15, 18, 45; *Confusion* 23–25).

The most interesting use for our purposes is the interpretation of Josephus (esp. *Ant.* 1.72–119), for here we have the longest imaginative description of Noah pleading with his compatriots to change their ways and then becoming afraid of them because they are so displeased with him (*Ant.* 1.74; elsewhere, see also *Sib. Or.* 1:128–129, 150–198; *Jub.* 20–29; *Eccles. Rab.* 9:15; *b. Sanh.* 108).

D. Textual Matters. Probably *kataklysmon kosmō asebōn epaxas* ("when he brought the deluge on the world of ungodly people") echoes Gen. 6:17 LXX: *epagō ton kataklysmon hydōr epi tēn gēn* ("I am bringing the flood of water upon the earth").

E. Peter's Use of the OT in 2:5. The thrust of Peter's appropriation of the flood narrative, the account of Noah's part in it included, is plain enough: it is part of his controlling bifurcation throughout these verses, to the effect that God knows how to rescue the godly and punish the ungodly. Moreover, by moving on from "angels"—however they are understood—to ordinary human beings, he is bringing the threat closer to the false teachers whom he is opposing. Two further comments are in order. First, the righteousness of righteous Noah, in this context, surely has to do with his behavior, not with imputed righteousness or the like (contra Schreiner 2003: 339). Second, the slightly odd expression *ogdoon Nōe*, "Noah the eighth person" (contrast the form of language in 1 Pet. 3:20; Jude, of course, does not mention Noah), is a classical construction (see BDAG, s.v. "ὄγδοος") meaning "Noah along with seven others," clearly his wife, three children, and their respective spouses.

F. Theological Use. A moralizing use of the OT by the NT is far from unknown (e.g., 1 Cor. 10:1–13; Heb. 3:7–19). Here the failure of the Israelites to enter the promised land, even though God had saved them from slavery in Egypt, is ascribed to their unbelief and disobedience. In short, the people of Israel did not *persevere*—and Christians who have been saved from their former slavery to sin need to *persevere* in faith and obedience to the end if they are to enter the consummated kingdom. Of course, this reading of both 1 Cor. 10:1–13 and of Heb. 3:7–19 depends also on a typological connection between Israel and the church, while the former passage also includes

a complex analogy of the "rock" (1 Cor. 10:4) and the latter rushes on to develop a salvation-historical argument (Heb. 4:1–13). Here in 2 Pet. 2:5, however, none of these complexities is present. The language is simply moralizing by way of analogy: if God distinguished between Noah (including those with him) and the rest of the ancient world and brought judgment on the latter, how can we escape the conclusion that at the end judgment will fall but that some will be saved? And what does that say about the kind of people we ought to be?

2:6–8

A. NT Context: The Contrast between Sodom and Lot. These final two allusions (the fourth and the fifth) to the OT—one to Sodom and one to Lot—must be taken together because the interpretation of each is linked with the interpretation of the other, as we will see. The general point that Peter is making, however, is again clear: he contrasts the judgment that fell on the twin cities of Sodom and Gomorrah because of their wickedness ("an example of what is going to happen to the ungodly" [2:6]) with the rescue of Lot ("a righteous man who was distressed by the depraved conduct of the lawless" [2:7]). Moreover, by going on from water to fire, he is advancing to consideration of the final day of judgment.

B. OT Context. There have been two long-standing exegetical debates concerning the interpretation of Gen. 19 that have a bearing on our understanding of how 2 Peter may be reading this OT chapter. First, what, precisely, is the nature of the Sodomites' sin? The dominant alternatives are sexual perversion (both homosexual and heterosexual) and betrayal of ancient Near Eastern hospitality codes. Second, is there any reasonable ground in the OT text itself for thinking that Lot's behavior is honorable? In particular, his willingness to sacrifice his daughters to protect his visitors strikes many contemporary readers as sexist, selfish, weak, and thoughtless, regardless of how important hospitality was to the culture of the time. So does the claim that Lot is "righteous" depend far more on later Jewish traditions about Lot than on the OT text itself? Is Peter's "use" of the OT really in this instance a twisting of it based on the wishful thinking of interpreters who promulgated their views under Second Temple Judaism?

Recently Morschauser (2003) has attempted a reconstruction and interpretation of Gen. 19 that attempts to address both of these exegetical points simultaneously (I am indebted to Scott J. Hafemann for the reference). Morschauser attaches voluminous ancient Near Eastern parallels to the points that he makes; here I can do no more than sketch the most important elements of his thesis. (1) According to Gen. 19:1, Lot was sitting in the gateway of the city when the two visitors showed up. In the social structure of the day this meant that Lot was one of the elders, possibly sitting there in some sort of official capacity. In other words, when he invited the visitors into the city and into his home, he was not acting in the capacity of a private citizen. (2) The throng that gathered before Lot's house, specifically described as "young and old," is not made up of all the men of the town (otherwise 19:12 would make little sense) but rather constitutes the representative ruling elite; that is the overtone of "young and old." (3) This event occurs only a few chapters after the raid against Sodom described in Gen. 14. Doubtless some people were nervous about the possibility of visitors being spies. Lot's strong insistence that the visitors spend the night not in the square but rather with him in his house (19:2–3) not only displays generous hospitality but also might well be understood as Lot making sure that his visitors did not roam through the city freely. As an official in the gate, Lot, by bringing them into his home, was also keeping an eye on them. (4) When the crowd, "young and old," demands that the visitors be sent outside so that the crowd might "know" (*yāda'*) them, we are not to think of sexual assault (TNIV: "Bring them out so that we can have sex with them" [19:5]). Certainly this Hebrew verb for "know" can be a euphemistic way of referring to sexual intercourse—indeed, that is unmistakably the meaning in 19:8—but the verb itself has a broad semantic range, and can be used in other contexts. In Ps. 139:1–2, 23 it is parallel to *ḥāqar* ("search out"). In the present context the crowd is asking to "get to know" these visitors, to "interrogate" them, not least to find out if they are spies. Of course, "interrogation" in those days could itself be a fairly brutal business. (5) The one dramatic exception to the ethics of generous hospitality in the culture of the time was the visit of spies. If the visitors were spies, then obviously

they could not claim protection under the "rules" of hospitality (note Gen. 42:5–14, where Joseph can handle his visiting brothers roughly once he "determines" that they are spies; Josh. 2–3 and the demand to Rahab to turn over her visitors). But what makes the demand of this crowd so inappropriate is that Lot is not now a private citizen. He is an official in the gate, he has exercised his judgment in good faith, and they have no right to question him this way. (6) What Lot proposes, then, is not that his daughters be sent outside to satisfy the lust of the perverted throng but rather that his daughters be temporarily held, overnight until the strangers leave town, as a kind of pledge, a hostage exchange. The arrangement was both legal and humane. Providing a kind of hostage was the course that Reuben and Judah took at a later period (Gen. 42:37; 43:9). Even the expression "And you can do what you like with them" is, Morschauser asserts, formulaic for "They are in your hands [and of course the protocol is that you keep them safe until this matter is resolved by the departure of my visitors in the morning]." (7) What happens, however, is that this mob of ruling elite will have none of the arrangement and wants to bring about their proposed interrogation by force. Instead of treating Lot with the respect that he deserves, they respond with atavistic rage, dismiss him as a foreigner, and challenge his authority (19:9). What they are trying to do, against a recognized official, is simply anarchic, and God judges them for it. But Lot himself comes out as a righteous man who acts honorably throughout.

It will be interesting to see how this proposal fares when all of Morschauser's parallels are scrutinized closely by experts in ancient Near Eastern literature and culture. My impression at this juncture is that there may well be something to Morschauser's reconstruction, but several elements of it make one pause. First, the proximity of the verb *yāda'* ("know") in 19:8 with an unambiguously sexual sense colors the meaning of the verb in 19:5 more than Morschauser admits. Second, and more importantly, the narrative relating the separation of Abraham and Lot (Gen. 13) depicts the latter as selfish and materialistic. He chooses Sodom and the well-watered plains, even though 13:13 specifies clearly that this is a wicked city terribly offensive to God. The account of Abraham's intercession in Gen. 18:16–33 also presupposes that Sodom is notoriously wicked. If Lot had become an official in the city, sitting in the gate in his official capacity, what does this say about his moral course? At the very least, he is living a terribly compromised existence even before the events of Gen. 19. Third, the parallels of Reuben and Judah offering themselves as substitute "hostages" prompt another reflection: why does not Lot offer himself as hostage, the way Reuben and Judah do, instead of his daughters, until the morning? Fourth, the parallel account in Judges of the estate owner who takes in the Levite and his concubine in the town of Gibeah cannot be set aside as quickly as Morschauser attempts to do. He thinks that the big difference is that the crowd banging on the door is described as "sons of Belial"—they are already a dangerous lot. Their initial demand, that they may "know" the visitor (Judg. 19:22), was also, as in Gen. 19, a demand to interrogate the man. But one wonders if this is a naive reading. The entire account shows how threatened the Levite and his concubine were as they traveled, and even how unsafe staying in the town square of Gibeah was likely to be. In other words, the estate owner's insistence that they spend the night with him and not remain in the square has nothing to do with preventing them from casing the city but rather with trying to keep them safe. Similarly with respect to Gen. 19: granted that the city is already declared to be wicked, and granted that there is not a hint that Lot is trying to prevent the visitors from roaming freely through the city to prevent any possible spying activity, Morschauser's reconstruction sounds too neat, not to say naive. Here and there it feels like exegesis by knowledge of comparable social custom that has to be read into the text rather than a straightforward reading of the text.

What must be said, however, is that even if part of Morschauser's reconstruction is correct, and even if in consequence Lot appears more righteous than he otherwise would, he remains a flawed figure. But why should that surprise us? Abraham is a man of faith, beloved by God, but he is also a liar, and the latter does not undo the former. Despite his faith, he sleeps with Hagar because he cannot at that point see how God will provide him with the promised progeny by any other means. David is repeatedly said to be a man after God's own heart, yet this man after God's

own heart seduces his neighbor's wife and arranges for the death of her husband. One wonders what he would have done had he not been a man after God's own heart! So also Lot: he is sufficiently a man of faith, a righteous man, that he joins his uncle Abraham in following the Lord, leaving Ur to travel they know not where. Although he makes the flawed decision to settle in the cities of the plains despite their reputation, there is no evidence that he becomes morally indistinguishable from them, and two important pieces of evidence suggest that he maintains some God-centered and righteous distinctions: (1) he listens to the angelic visitors when he is told to flee; (2) when Abraham pleads for the cities (Gen. 18) by appealing to the number of "righteous" people who may still be there, clearly he is including Lot in their number.

Sodom becomes proverbial for wickedness and judgment in the rest of the OT (see Isa. 1:9–10; Jer. 23:14; 50:40; Ezek. 16:46–56; Amos 4:11; Zeph. 2:9).

C. The Context in Judaism. The literature of early Judaism boasts a very high number of references to Sodom (for summaries, see Brown 2002: 185–92; Loader 1990: 75–117). Some of the references spell out the sins of Sodom, primarily homosexuality and arrogance (e.g., 3 Macc. 2:5; Sir. 16:8; *T. Levi* 14:6; *T. Naph.* 3:4; *Jub.* 16:5–6; *2 En.* 10:4. Wisdom 10:7 points to the barren wasteland of the Dead Sea plain as "evidence" (*martyrion*, "witness") of God's judgment, and 3 Macc. 2:5 specifically asserts that the destruction of the city makes them "an example to those who should come afterward" (RSV). By and large, the theme of Sodom's judgment is not developed in the Dead Sea Scrolls, but it plays a major role in the thought of Philo and of Josephus. The NT likewise mentions Sodom in an almost proverbial way (e.g., Matt. 10:15; Luke 10:12; 17:29), though quite remarkably Jesus appeals to Sodom in Matt. 11:20–24 to argue that the city proverbial for its wickedness will have an easier time on the day of judgment than will the towns of Galilee in which Jesus disclosed himself in word and deed—a powerful way of making the point that in God's accounting there are degrees of responsibility grounded in how much access to revelation we enjoy.

No less important for our purposes is how the literature of early Judaism refers to Lot. In some references Lot merely locates the Sodomites (e.g., they are "neighbors of Lot" [Sir. 16:8]). More commonly, however, Lot's righteousness is emphasized. In Wis. 10:6 we are told that Wisdom "rescued" (*errysato*) this "righteous man" (*dikaion*)—terminology close to what is found in 2 Pet. 2:7. The same chapter puts Lot into a "righteous" category along with Adam, Noah, Abraham, Jacob, Joseph, and Israel under Moses (see also Wis. 19:17). Elsewhere, *Jub.* 12:30 puffs Lot a bit by making him Abraham's adopted son and heir; in 1QapGen ar XX, 22–24 it is Lot who intercedes for Abraham when the latter is down in Egypt, and the same book refuses to mention Sodom's wickedness when Lot and Abraham separate. Philo presents Lot as a thoroughly flawed individual (often in contrast to Abraham [e.g., *Abraham* 211–238; *Moses* 2.58]). His drunkenness and consequent incestuous relations with his daughters are categorized as willful ignorance (*Drunkenness* 162–164). By contrast, although Josephus's account of Lot (largely scattered through *Ant.* 1.151–205) is fairly faithful to the biblical text, there is a tendency to make him a little more righteous than he is, primarily on the grounds that he is Abraham's nephew and David's ancestor.

D. Textual Matters. If the words *katastrophē katekrinen* ("he condemned them to extinction" [ESV]) are original, then it is quite possible that Peter is quoting Gen. 19:29 LXX directly. The combination of *dikaion* ("righteous man") and *errysato* ("he rescued") in 2 Pet. 2:7 (*kai dikaion Lōt kataponoumenon hypo tēs tōn athesmōn en aselgeia anastrophēs errysato*, "he rescued Lot, a righteous man, who was distressed by the depraved conduct of the impious") makes it at least possible that Peter is relying on Wis. 10:6 (where the same two Greek words appear [on which, see §C above], though the two words are such obvious choices in this narrative that one cannot be sure.

E. Peter's Use of the OT in 2:6–8. Whereas Jude appeals to the example of Sodom to underscore its eternal destruction, Peter again (as in the case of the flood and Noah) underscores a contrast—this time the contrast between the destruction of Sodom and the rescue of Lot. The differentiation between the two depends on Lot's righteousness, of course, and so that point is elabo-

rated in 2:8. Lot's rescue ultimately was not from the Sodomites but rather from the wrath of God that befell the city. How much Peter's emphasis on Lot's righteousness is influenced by parallel Jewish sources from early Judaism we cannot ascertain. Peter's emphasis may have been a parallel development based on similar inferences.

F. Theological Use. Peter's concern is not only to show that God has made a distinction between the righteous and the unrighteous in the past but also thereby to argue that "the Lord knows how to rescue the godly from trials and to hold the unrighteous for punishment on the day of judgment" (2:9) in the future and thus to influence behavior.

2:11

A brief note may be introduced here, rather exceptionally, to rule out an OT allusion. The parallel passage in Jude (v. 9) introduces the archangel Michael disputing with the devil over the body of Moses. At the very least, that requires today's readers, when studying Jude, to think about the relationship between Deut. 34 (on the death of Moses) and later Jewish literature, in particular the lost *Assumption of Moses* (see commentary on Jude). Yet although 2 Pet. 2:11 is related to Jude 9 in some way, it makes no explicit mention of either Michael or Moses. Moreover, the passage has been so thoroughly rewritten that it is far from clear that Peter is duplicating Jude's argument (for the options, see Davids 2006: 234–35). Even if Peter is following Jude's general line of thought, however, because of the omission of Michael and Moses the most that can be said is that Peter is generalizing what Jude says. Since the allusion in Jude depends on the specificity of the mention of Moses, it follows that on any interpretation of 2 Pet. 2:11, where Moses has been dropped, the allusion is lost.

2:13

On the day of judgment the false teachers will be paid back (*adikoumenoi*) for the wrong (*adikias*) that they have done (2:13), although the false teachers themselves apparently deny that there will be any final day of judgment (3:3–5). Peter then adds a further charge: adapting the language of Jude 12, he accuses them of self-indulgence: "Their idea of pleasure is to carouse in broad daylight." This phrase "in broad daylight" is one of the factors that seem to make their offense particularly odious (the other is that they engage in their reveling even at the meal that some early Christians enjoyed together in connection with the Lord's Supper: "reveling in their pleasures while they feast with you" [NIV]). Several OT writers view carousing during the daylight hours as particularly worthy of denunciation: "Woe to you, O land . . . whose princes feast in the morning" (Eccles. 10:16); "Woe to those who rise early in the morning to run after their drinks" (Isa. 5:11). Similar denunciations can be found in the literature of early Judaism (e.g., *T. Mos.* 7:4).

2:15–16

A. NT Context: Wandering from the Truth toward Greed.
Peter has already charged the false teachers with greed. Now he fleshes out this charge by providing an OT counterpart. Worse yet, these teachers were at one point faithful. Now "they have left the straight way and wandered off to follow the way of Balaam son of Bezer, who loved the wages of wickedness" (TNIV). The Greek behind "wandered off" (*eplanēthēsan*) is cognate with Jude's mention of Balaam's "error" (*planē*), although Balaam is the only one of the three persons whom Peter picks up from Jude 11 (the others are Cain and Korah). The rebuke that Balaam received from the donkey (2:16) was the result of miraculous intervention by God, but Peter emphasizes the ironic symbolism: Balaam's sin was irrational, and he was rebuked by an irrational beast.

B. OT Context.
The initial account of Balaam (Num. 22–24) provides such grist that Balaam's name is picked up in many later OT texts (Num. 31:8, 16; Deut. 23:4–5; Josh. 13:22; 24:9–10; Neh. 13:2; Mic. 6:5). Most of these texts stress how God intervened so that Balaam was unable to pronounce the curses on Israel that Balak wanted to hear. The hint of the bad advice that Balaam gave Balak anyway comes in Num. 31:16. That bad advice, advocating the kind of enticement to sin that would bring God's wrath down on Israel's head, is what is picked up in Rev. 2:14 (though not, as we will see, in 2 Pet. 2).

C. The Context in Judaism.
Balaam's love for money surfaces in the work of Philo (*Moses* 1.268; *Cherubim* 33–34). Especially in the rabbinic literature one finds a strong emphasis on the view that Balaam ultimately received the appropriate

"wages" of his wickedness: he was killed by Israel (Num. 31:8; cf. *Sipre Num.* 157 on Num. 31:9; *Num. Rab.* 22:4). For the rich lore of rabbinic tales on Balaam, most and perhaps all of which are later than 2 Peter, see the chart in Davids 2006: 253–56. Many of them assert that Balaam himself was sexually perverted—an interpretation grounded in the advice that he gave Balak to encourage cross-religious (and thus, from the perspective of the covenant, highly illegal) marriages.

D. Textual Matters.
Several commentators (e.g., Neyrey 1993: 211–12; Bauckham 1988: 268; Davids 2006: 242–43) note that in the three Targumim on Numbers (*Pseudo-Jonathan/Yerušalmi, Neofiti, Fragmentary Targum*) the donkey actually rebukes Balaam instead of merely asking why he is being beaten (the biblical narrative leaves the actual rebuke for Balaam's actions to the angel).

E. Peter's Use of the OT in 2:15–16.
When Peter says that the false teachers whom he is opposing have left "the straight way," he is picking up on a locution not uncommon in the LXX (1 Kgdms. 12:23 [1 Sam. 12:23 ET]; Ps. 106:7 [107:7 ET]; Prov. 2:13, 16; Isa. 33:15; Hos. 14:10 [14:9 ET]), though it is not obvious that he is thinking of any particular passage. Apparently, what has made these false teachers wander away is greed, as Jude (11) also asserts with respect to those whom he is confronting. Many commentaries suggest that when Peter asserts, "But he was rebuked for his wrongdoing by a donkey" (2:16 [Jude does not make this point]), he is in fact either relying on some source now unknown to us or reflecting the kind of tradition found in the Targumim (see above), the rabbis, and even in Philo (*Names* 203). This may be inferring too much. Compared with some of these accounts, Peter's prose is remarkably sparse, and the words just cited need not require us to think that Peter holds that the entire content of the rebuke came from the donkey.

F. Theological Use.
It is easy enough to compile a list of biblical warnings against a focus on wealth (see the admirable balance in Blomberg 1999). Closest in theological conception to this passage is perhaps 1 Tim. 6:3–10, where false teachers are denounced not only for the content of their instruction but also because they seem to think that godliness is a means to financial gain (6:5).

"For the love of money is a root of all kinds of evil. Some people, eager for money, have wandered [*apeplanēthēsan*] from the faith and pierced themselves with many griefs" (6:10). This is of a piece with Peter's insistence that believers must live in the light of the prospect of a new heaven and a new earth (2 Pet. 3:8–13)—an emphasis that goes back to the teaching of the Lord Jesus himself (e.g., Matt. 6:19–21).

2:17

While Jude 12 asserts that the false teachers are "clouds without rain," he probably is alluding to Prov. 25:14: "Like clouds and wind without rain is a man who boasts of gifts he does not give." In 2 Pet. 2:17 Peter modifies "clouds without rain" and says the false teachers are "springs without water." Both images picture promise without delivery, spiritual charlatans. The false teachers promise nurturing, refreshing "water" but provide none. The Bible is replete with images that connect water with wisdom, the law, instruction from God, and blessing, whereas aridity is linked to fruitlessness, chaff that must be burned, and forsaking God (e.g., Ps. 1:3–4; Prov. 13:14; 18:4; Jer. 2:18–19; 14:3; 17:5–8).

2:22

A. NT Context: The Unclean Return to the Unclean. Although Peter is making just one point—the false teachers are returning to their own unclean domain—he uses two proverbs to do so: (1) "A dog returns to its vomit"; (2) "A sow that is washed returns to her wallowing in the mud." Only the first is drawn from the OT (Prov. 26:11). Neither animal would have enjoyed a host of pleasant associations in the ancient world. For both pagans and Jews, dogs sometimes were used for various things (Isa. 56:10 can speak of a watchdog, and Job 30:1 of a sheepdog), but they were not regarded as pets or as "man's best friend," and most of the thirty-two OT occurrences of "dog" hold the animal in contempt. Pigs were kept and eaten in pagan circles but were regarded as ritually unclean by Jews, who therefore did not keep pigs at all. Jesus himself can link them in a highly negative context (Matt. 7:6). Here what makes them disgusting is that their very nature makes them return to what is disgusting or dirty.

B. OT Context. Proverbs 26 largely focuses on the behavior of the fool (vv. 1–12) and the sluggard (vv. 13–16), with the remainder of the chapter canvassing various forms of wicked and foolish behavior. Regarding 26:11, Murphy (1998: 200) writes, "The comparison to the dog's action underlines the continuousness and sameness of the actions of fools; they never get out of the rut they are in, and they keep on making the same gaffes." The proverb "juxtaposes a fool with the contemptible dog; his destructive folly with the dog's vomit; and the fool's incorrigibility with the dog's repulsive nature to return to its vomit, to sniff at it, to lick it, and finally to eat it" (Waltke 2005: 354).

C. The Context in Judaism. Dogs continue with their unsavory reputation in the literature of early Judaism. More interesting perhaps for our investigation is the second proverb, "A sow that is washed returns to her wallowing in the mud." We have no direct source, but there are comparable sentiments elsewhere. In *Ahiqar*, the Arabic version addresses the son: "Thou hast been to me like the pig who went into the hot bath with people of quality, and when it came out of the hot bath, it saw a filthy hole and it went down and wallowed in it" (cited in Bauckham 1988: 279).

D. Textual Matters. The second of the two proverbs in 2 Pet. 2:22 is missing the finite verb "returns" or "has returned," which means that it is just barely possible to read *eis kylismon borborou* ("to wallow in the mud") with *lousamenē* ("after washing") to produce "a sow that washes herself by wallowing in the mire." But this is as unnecessary as it is awkward, for proverbs often omit the main verb, which in any case is here presupposed from the first proverb.

E. Peter's Use of the OT in 2:22. Peter does not have in view people who have been enthusiastic false teachers from the beginning of their professional lives, nor is he thinking of genuine Christians who, sadly, have slipped into some sort of temporary backsliding. The context shows (esp. 2:20–22) that these people once lived sinful and perhaps debauched lives but then for a time "escaped the corruption of the world by knowing our Lord and Savior Jesus Christ" (2:20), but now they are again entangled in the world and all its corruptions. This is so serious a retrogression that Peter can declare, "It would have been better for them not to have known the way of righteousness, than to have known it and then to turn their backs on the sacred command that was passed on to them" (2:21 TNIV). And so the two proverbs prove true (2:22), which means that the true nature of these people never changed. A dog may leave its vomit for a while but will return to it; a sow might well be spruced up and look clean but will still find a mud pit enticing.

F. Theological Use. A widespread NT theme insists that genuine believers persevere to the end (e.g., John 8:31; 1 Cor. 15:2; Col. 1:23; Heb. 3:6, 14; cf. 2 Pet. 1:10). Indeed, 1 John 2:19 makes it clear that if some leave the Christian community, their departure shows that at some deep level they never really belonged. One of the themes of the Epistle to the Hebrews is that the failure to persevere (see 3:14) is equivalent to apostasy (6:4–6; 10:26–31; cf. 1 Kings 21:27–29; 22:8, 37; Matt. 12:43–45). The two proverbs that Peter deploys in 2 Pet. 2:22 powerfully make the same point by insisting that the fundamental nature of such people remains unchanged.

3:5–6

This pair of verses refers to two huge events: the creation (Gen. 1–2) and the flood (Gen. 6–9). These two references make the same point, and that point is a little removed from the conclusion that Peter draws from his reference to the flood in the preceding chapter (2:5). There the distinction between what happened to people at large and what happened to Noah and his family establishes that God is perfectly willing and able to bring about a decisive judgment that makes crucial distinctions among people. Here the double reference to creation and flood is set in the context of scoffers who mock the notion of a second coming and disavow that there ever will be a catastrophic judgment. They hold to what would today be called uniformitarianism: "everything goes on as it has since the beginning of creation" (3:4). But Peter says this sneering derision shows they "deliberately forget" (KJV, RSV, NRSV, NIV, TEV, TNIV—almost certainly the correct rendering; the ESV has "deliberately overlook") the creation and flood. When God made everything by his powerful word (Ps. 33:6; 148:5; cf. Heb. 11:3—a point also confessed by Wis. 9:1), heaven, water, earth all appeared, the latter apparently by the water withdrawing (Gen. 1:6–10). Lest anyone respond by saying, "Yes, yes—but *since* the creation, everything continues as it was," Peter rushes on to

add the flood: this creation that God made, God himself has already destroyed once. The Greek of 3:6 begins with *di' hōn* (lit. "by these"), probably referring to the waters. This seems more plausible than the view that the deluge came about by water and word (Bauckham 1998: 298); although that is true, the point does not seem to be made until 3:7. Peter here seems to argue that by the same waters that were part of the creation, God brought about the deluge (recall Gen. 7:11 with two groups of waters combining to form the deluge; cf. similarly *1 En.* 83:8). By the same powerful word by which God brought about creation and flood, Peter goes on to aver, the present heavens and earth are heading for the final destruction (3:7). In other words, God has not left himself without witness that he is willing and able to bring his own creation to decisive judgment, so sneering condescension is the very antithesis of a wise attitude to take when God announces that that is what is coming.

3:8

A. New Testament Context: God's Timing Is Not Ours. Instead of refuting the false teachers directly, who have apparently been sneering at the notion of a second coming (3:3–7), Peter now turns to his Christian readers (note the "dear friends") who, influenced perhaps by the skepticism of their opponents, are at least troubled by the delay: "But do not forget this one thing, dear friends: With the Lord a day is like a thousand years, and a thousand years are like a day" (3:9). Apparently there is an allusion to Ps. 90:4 (89:4 LXX): "A thousand years in your sight are like a day that has just gone by, or like a watch in the night."

B. Old Testament Context. Psalm 90 (89 LXX) is described in the superscript as a "prayer of Moses the man of God." The quoted words about a thousand years are part of a winsome and colorful argument to remind readers of God's eternality and therefore his utterly stable reliability: "Lord, you have been our dwelling place throughout all generations. Before the mountains were born or you brought forth the whole world, from everlasting to everlasting you are God" (90:1–2). In comparison, human life is utterly transient: "Yet you sweep people away in the sleep of death—they are like the new grass of the morning: In the morning it springs up new, but by evening it is dry and withered" (90:5–6 TNIV). None of this powerful and colorful imagery, of course, is meant to establish an exact equivalence, as if Moses were interested in establishing that one thousand of our years is precisely equivalent to one day of God's experience.

C. The Context in Judaism. Early Judaism (much of it later than 2 Peter) and early Christianity appealed to Ps. 90:4 "(1) to define the length of one of the days of creation, (2) to explain why Adam lived one thousand years after his sin, (3) to calculate the length of the Messiah's day, and (4) to explain the length of the world" (Neyrey 1993: 238, with appropriate references). Some scholars have appealed to such passages as *2 En.* 33:1–2 to suggest that our passage, 2 Pet. 3:8, is asserting that the day of judgment will be one thousand years long (e.g., von Allmen 1966: 262). Bauckham (1988: 308–9) links a number of passages together (*Pirqe R. El.* 28; *Apoc. Ab.* 28–30; *2 Bar.* 43:12–13; *L.A.B.* 19:13) to argue that Ps. 90:4 was used in apocalyptic contexts to encourage believers to recognize that the End could be long delayed, even if in God's time it was short, and that therefore the argument in 2 Pet. 3:8 plausibly derives from a Jewish apocalypse. Davids (2006: 276–77), rightly, is more cautious: there is no convincing evidence of dependence by Peter on any Jewish apocalypse, but the argument that Peter advances was "in the air," and seems like a reasonable enough inference from Ps. 90:4 that more than one exegete could have drawn it at about the same time.

D. Textual Matters. As is common with allusions, the point of connection between these texts is so brief that textual matters do not come into play.

E. Peter's Use of the OT in 3:8. Although Ps. 90:4 is designed to underscore God's eternality and therefore his unfailing reliability over against human transience and without reference to the End, Peter's application of this truth to how one thinks about God's own perspective on how "soon" or "quickly" the End will come does not seem like much of a reach. It is an obvious inference, and is mirrored in others drawing a similar inference. Certainly it is far removed from the highly speculative literal inferences, without literary sensitivity, drawn from Ps. 90:4 by others about the length of creation days and the like.

F. Theological Use. Two further things must be said. First, the theological conclusion that the return of the Lord may be long delayed is of a piece with a large strand of NT evidence. For example, in Matthew's version of the Olivet Discourse (Matt. 24–25), Jesus can on the one hand tell a parable to warn his hearers that the coming of the Son of Man could be at any time, so they should always be ready (Matt. 24:36–43), and on the other tell a further parable to warn them that they need to make preparations *for a long delay* (Matt. 25:1–13). Second, God's motives in what appears to us to be delay (2 Pet. 3:9) are tied with his desire that "everyone come to repentance"—and here, too, there is complementary NT witness (e.g., Rom. 2:4).

3:10

The expression "day of the Lord" appears about twenty times in the OT, especially in the prophets where it signals a visitation by God that brings in both salvation and judgment. It is impossible to nail down any one OT passage here as the background that Peter had in mind. It is more likely that he is picking up terminology that was standard by the time he wrote. In the NT, "the day of the Lord" is equivalent to "the day of Christ" (1 Cor. 1:8; 2 Cor. 1:14; Phil. 1:6, 10; 2:16).

3:12–13

A. NT Context: Waiting for the Consummation. These verses come at the end of a unit (3:3–13) in which Peter exhorts his readers to live in the light of the anticipated consummation. Living one's life as if this world is all that matters is both shortsighted and stupid; worse, it belongs to the scoffers who "deliberately forget" (3:5) the patterns of God's thorough judgment in the past, not least in the deluge. The only reason that the final judgment has not already taken place is that God "is patient with you, not wanting anyone to perish, but everyone to come to repentance" (3:9 [cf. Rom. 2:4]). But "the day of the Lord" (3:10) will come. Christians who live in the light of that anticipated judgment and consummation understand that it shapes how they live right now: "Since everything will be destroyed in this way, what kind of people ought you to be? You ought to live holy and godly lives as you look forward to the day of God and speed its coming. That day will bring about the destruction of the heavens by fire, and the elements will melt in the heat. But in keeping with his promise we are looking forward to a new heaven and a new earth, where righteousness dwells" (3:11–13 TNIV). In these lines Peter has picked up at least three OT allusions. One of them, "day of the Lord" or "day of God" (and the NT adds "day of Christ"), as we have seen, is so common that it cannot be traced to a single OT text, but the other two found in the present passage are distinctive.

B. OT Context. The two distinctive OT allusions are as follows. (1) Peter says that his readers "look forward to" the day of God, but he also says that they "speed its coming" (3:12). This latter clause ultimately depends on Isa. 60:22. The entire chapter of Isa. 60 has been promising the future glory of Israel, God's covenant people. The language is spectacularly evocative. And at the end of it God promises, "I am the LORD; in its time I will hasten it." Here, of course, it is the Lord who is hastening the day, not his obedient people. (2) Peter says that the day of the Lord brings both catastrophic judgment and triumphant renewal. On the one hand is the conflagration that burns up everything (3:12b); on the other hand is the promise of "a new heaven and a new earth, where righteousness dwells" (3:13). Here too Peter is drawing from Isaiah: "'Behold, I will create new heavens and a new earth. The former things will not be remembered, nor will they come to mind. . . .' 'As the new heavens and the new earth that I make will endure before me,' declares the LORD, 'so will your name and descendants endure'" (Isa. 65:17; 66:22 NIV).

C. The Context in Judaism. (1) The notion of God hastening the day of judgment or vindication is picked up in the literature of early Judaism, for the most part making it clear that God, not the believers, is hastening the day (e.g., Sir. 36:10; *2 Bar.* 20:1–2; 54:1; 83:1; *L.A.B.* 19:13). In rabbinic circles another tradition affirms that God hastens or delays the day based on Israel's repentance or lack of repentance (see esp. *b. Sanh.* 97b–98a; see also *y. Ta'an.* 1:1; *b. Yoma* 86b), though it is uncertain that any of these traditions reach back to Peter's time. Some have interpreted Acts 3:19–20 in the same light: "Repent, then, and turn to God, so that your sins may be wiped out, that times of refreshing may come from the Lord, and that he may send the Messiah. . . ." (2) The need for a renewal of creation is also widely recognized in this literature, though usually not with the terminology of "a new heaven and a new earth" or the

like (e.g., *Jub.* 1:29; *1 En.* 45:4–5; 91:16; *2 Bar.* 32:6; 47:2; *4 Ezra* 7:71; *L.A.B.* 3:10). For a fuller discussion, see Bauckham 1988: 326.

D. Textual Matters. (1) The notion of hastening is found in the MT. It appears that the LXX translator had difficulty with the notion of God "hastening" the day, and gave an entirely different meaning ("I the Lord will gather them according to the time"). Nevertheless the "hastening" idea reverberates (as we have seen) through later Jewish thought. It should be remembered that the context of the Isaiah reference includes descriptions of cosmic phenomena (60:18–21, overlapping with, though not identical to, those found in 2 Pet. 3:10–13) and mention of the people's eternal righteousness (cf. 2 Pet. 3:13, which thinks of the new heaven and the new earth, promises in Isa. 65 and 66, as "the home of righteousness"). The verb rendered "look forward to" or "wait for" in 2 Pet. 2:12 is *prosdokeō*; the corresponding verb in Isa. 60:22 LXX is *hypomenō*. Aquila's Greek translation of the verb, however, coincides with that of 2 Peter, as does the usage in *2 Bar.* 83:4. Peter may be relying on a Greek translation other than the LXX. (2) In 2 Pet. 2:13 Peter follows the LXX's singular "heaven" rather than the Hebrew plural "heavens."

E. Peter's Use of the OT in 3:12–13. The appeal to the OT to point forward to the consummation of the kingdom is in line with the structure of NT eschatology elsewhere. That Isa. 60—a passage filled with promises for the restoration of Israel—can be cited in this regard and applied to the consummation of the entire church presupposes one of the commonest typologies that link the OT and the NT.

It may go beyond the evidence to argue that Acts 3:19–20 argues for a set of assumptions to the effect that Christians can actually hasten the time of Christ's coming by their conduct (see §C above); strictly speaking, it does no such thing but instead simply insists that certain things must take place before the return of Christ, including the wiping out of the sins of many. There is no hint that if a greater number repent, or repent more quickly, then the times of refreshing and the return of Christ will thereby be expedited. Here in 2 Pet. 3:11–12, however, the notion of hastening the day of the Lord's return is unavoidable. In one sense, of course, this is the corollary of God's delaying the parousia in order to give more people time to repent (Rom. 2:4; 2 Pet. 3:9). "Their repentance and holy living may therefore, from the human standpoint, hasten its coming. This does not detract from God's sovereignty in determining the time of the End . . . , but means only that his sovereign determination graciously takes human affairs into account" (Bauckham 1988: 325 [cf. Moo 1996: 198–99]).

F. Theological Use. The Isaianic promise of "a new heaven and a new earth" (LXX) is also picked up by Revelation's final vision: Rev. 21:1, with its promise of a new heaven and a new earth, introduces the glorious description of the final state that follows the millennium and the judgment of God. The same vision can be cast without using the same words that Peter uses: the apostle Paul talks about the anticipated liberation of the entire creation from its bondage to decay (Rom. 8:18–25). It is doubtful that either Christian steadfastness or Christian morality, let alone Christian spirituality and Christian eschatology, can long be maintained without the dominance of this vision.

Bibliography

Avioz, M. 2006. "Josephus's Portrayal of Lot and His Family." *JSP* 16: 3–13.

Bauckham, R. J. 1988. *Jude, 2 Peter.* WBC 50. Waco: Word.

Begg, C. 1901. *A Critical and Exegetical Commentary on the Epistles of St. Peter and St. Jude.* ICC. Edinburgh: T&T Clark.

Blomberg, C. L. 1999. *Neither Poverty Nor Riches: A Biblical Theology of Possessions.* NSBT 7. Downers Grove, IL: InterVarsity.

Brown, D. E. 2002. "The Use of the Old Testament in 2 Peter 2:4–10A." PhD diss., Trinity Evangelical Divinity School.

Callan, T. 2004. "Use of the Letter of Jude by the Second Letter of Peter." *Bib* 85: 42–64.

Calvin, J. 1979 [1551]. *Commentaries on the Catholic Epistles.* Translated by J. Owen. Grand Rapids: Baker Academic.

Cantinat, J. 1973. *Les Épîtres de Saint Jacques et de Saint Jude.* SB. Paris: Gabalda.

Cassuto, U. 1973. "The Episode of the Sons of God and the Daughters of Man." Pages 29–40 in *Biblical and Oriental Studies.* Vol. 1. Translated by I. Abrahams. Jerusalem: Magnes.

Charles, J. D. 2005. "The Angels under Reserve in 2 Peter and Jude." *BBR* 15: 39–48.

Clines, D. J. A. 1979. "The Significance of the 'Sons of God' Episode [Genesis 6:1–4] in the Context of the 'Primeval History' [Genesis 1–11]." *JSOT* 13: 33–46.

Davids, P. H. 2006. *The Letters of 2 Peter and Jude.* PNTC. Grand Rapids: Eerdmans.

Dexinger, F. 1966. *Sturz der Göttersöhne; oder, Engel vor der Sintflut? Versuch eines Neuverständnisses von Genesis 6, 2–4 unter Berücksichtigung der religionsvergleichenden und exegesegeschichtlichen Methode.* WBT 13. Vienna: Herder.

Elliott, J. H. 1982. *I–II Peter, Jude.* ACNT. Minneapolis: Augsburg.

García Martínez, F. 1999. "Interpretations of the Flood in the Dead Sea Scrolls." Pages 86–108 in *Interpretations of the Flood.* Edited by F. García Martínez and G. P. Luttikhuizen. TBN 1. Leiden: Brill.

Gispen, W. H. 1974. *Genesis 1–11.* COT. Kampen: Kok.

Green, E. M. B. 1968. *The Second Epistle of Peter and the Epistle of Jude.* TNTC. Grand Rapids: Eerdmans.

Grundmann, W. 1974. *Der Brief des Judas und der zweite Brief des Petrus.* THKNT 15. Berlin: Evangelische Verlagsanstalt.

Hillyer, N. 1992. *1 and 2 Peter, Jude.* NIBCNT. Peabody, MA: Hendrickson.

James, M. R. 1912. *The Second Epistle General of Peter and the Epistle of Jude.* CGTSC. Cambridge: Cambridge University Press.

Kelly, J. N. D. 1969. *The Epistles of Peter and of Jude.* BNTC. London: Black.

Kline, M. G. 1961–1962. "Divine Kingship and Genesis 6:1–4." *WTJ* 24: 184–204.

———. 1993. *Kingdom Prologue.* South Hamilton, MA: M. G. Kline.

Kraftchick, S. J. 2002. *Jude, 2 Peter.* ANTC. Nashville: Abingdon.

Loader, J. A. 1990. *A Tale of Two Cities: Sodom and Gomorrah in the Old Testament, Early Jewish and Early Christian Tradition.* CBET 1. Kampen: Kok.

Mayor, J. B. 1979 [1901]. *The Epistles of Jude and II Peter.* Repr., Grand Rapids: Eerdmans.

Moffatt, J. 1928. *The General Epistles: James, Peter and Jude.* MNTC. London: Hodder & Stoughton.

Moo, D. J. 1996. *2 Peter, Jude.* NIVAC. Grand Rapids: Zondervan.

Morschauser, S. 2003. "'Hospitality,' Hostiles, and Hostages: On the Legal Background to Genesis 19.1–19." *JSOT* 27: 461–85.

Murphy, R. E. 1998. *Proverbs.* WBC 22. Nashville: Nelson.

Neyrey, J. H. 1993. *2 Peter, Jude.* AB 37C. New York: Doubleday.

Reicke, B. 1964. *The Epistles of James, Peter, and Jude.* AB 37. Garden City, NY: Doubleday.

Schelkle, K. H. 1980. *Die Petrusbriefe, der Judasbrief.* 5th ed. HTKNT. Freiburg: Herder.

Schreiner, T. R. 2003. *1, 2 Peter, Jude: An Exegetical and Theological Exposition of Holy Scripture.* NAC. Nashville: Broadman & Holman.

Sidebottom, E. M. 1967. *James, Jude and 2 Peter.* NCB. London: Nelson.

Spicq, C. 1966. *Les Épîtres de Saint Pierre.* SB. Paris: Gabalda.

vanGemeren, W. H. 1981. "The Sons of God in Genesis 6:1–4 (An Example of Evangelical Demythologization?)." *WTJ* 43: 320–48.

Vögtle, A. 1994. *Der Judasbrief, der 2. Petrusbrief.* EKKNT 22. Solothurn: Benziger; Neukirchen-Vluyn: Neukirchener Verlag.

von Allmen, Daniel. 1966. "L'apocalyptique juive et le retard de la parousie en II Pierre 3:1–13." *RTP* 16: 255–74.

Waltke, B. K. 2001. *Genesis.* Grand Rapids: Zondervan.

———. 2005. *Proverbs 15–31.* NICOT. Grand Rapids: Eerdmans.

Wenham, G. J. 1987. *Genesis 1–15.* WBC 1. Waco: Word.

Yoshikawa, S. T. 2004. "The Prototypical Use of the Noahic Flood in the New Testament." PhD diss., Trinity Evangelical Divinity School.

1–3 JOHN

D. A. CARSON

Introduction

In an essay on the use of the OT in John and the Johannine Epistles, published some twenty years ago, I asserted, "The most striking feature relevant to our subject in these epistles is the absence not only of OT quotations but even of many unambiguous allusions to the OT" (Carson 1988: 256). John did mention Cain, of course (1 John 3:12, with possible connections elsewhere in the letter). Since then, I have wondered about two or three other possibilities, briefly considered below. But the riposte by Lieu (1991: 87; 1993) turns on asking a slightly different set of questions. In addition to the Cain reference, she proposes that Isa. 6:10 stands behind 1 John 2:11, "and other passages too may go back to OT passages and their exegesis, while, as we have seen, many of the images have Old Testament roots" (Lieu 1991: 87). But that was not the focus of my 1988 essay, and it is not the focus of this volume. In both places I have included direct quotations and clear or reasonably clear allusions to specific texts or events. The fact remains that there is no quotation of the OT in these epistles, and the number of allusions, real or potential, is extremely limited: there are not "many unambiguous allusions to the OT." Extending background searches in the OT to massive theological themes (e.g., the relationship between God and the world; knowledge of

God; the sacrificial system; idolatry; appeals for love; mention of law) or to biblical images (e.g., contrasts between light and darkness) usefully reminds us of the historical, social, literary, and theological matrix out of which the biblical books emerged, for the Jewish dimension of these letters is striking. Nevertheless, such sweeping work, as valuable as it is, does little to enable us to tie down specific NT texts to specific OT quotations, specific OT allusions, and specific OT events (e.g., the exodus).

To make matters still more complicated, the manner in which these epistles may or may not refer to the OT is tied to the extraordinarily disputed subject of their relation to the Gospel of John. In common with Brown (1982) and many others, I take it that the Johannine Epistles were penned after John's Gospel. What, then, shall we do with epistolary passages that seem to refer to some crucial passage in the Fourth Gospel where there *is* an allusion to the OT? For example, the precise connection between *logos* ("word") in 1 John 1:1–3 and the same word in the Johannine prologue (John 1:1–18) is highly disputed, owing not least to the fact that, on the surface at least, in 1 John it appears to be "the life" that is incarnated, rather than "the word." Moreover, in the prologue to the Gospel one is impelled to look into the OT background of *logos* ("word") because of the immediate connection with creation (John 1:3) and, by the end of the prologue, mention of Moses and the giving of the law. Again, does the reference to water and Spirit in the text-critically complicated verses 1 John 5:6–8 connect in some way with the reference to water and Spirit in John 3:3, 5, which almost certainly does allude to Ezek. 36:25–27?

Regardless of whether one thinks that these two epistolary passages refer to specific passages in John—my own judgment is that the first one does and the second one does not—it seems fairly clear that where there is indeed a connection with John, the author of the epistles is thinking of that connection, not of possible antecedent connections with the OT itself. This is not to deny that OT thought frequently stands behind all of the Johannine texts in some fashion or other; it is merely to assert that the focus here on quotations and allusions requires tighter controls.

So why are there so few OT quotations and allusions in the Johannine Epistles? It is often perilous to give reasons for what is absent from a NT document, for that is a form of appeal to the argument from silence, and such an argument is usually convincing only if one has unusually strong reasons for believing that there should be noise (like Sherlock Holmes's dog that did not bark in the night). The issue becomes all the more complicated if there are numerous possible reasons that could account for the silence. For instance, the suggestion some decades ago by Smith (1972: 58) to the effect that the relative paucity of the OT in these epistles represents progressive attenuation of the Johannine community's interaction with Jewish communities is unconvincing. Moreover, as Smith himself points out, other NT writings normally considered late (e.g., Hebrews, Revelation), and a noncanonical work such as *1 Clement*, boast a very high number of OT quotations and allusions. Doubtless Hebrews can be easily accounted for by supposing that its readers are strongly tempted to turn (back?) to Judaism, but it is not so easy to find an equivalent reason for the multitude of allusions in Revelation.

If we adopt the majority view that holds (1) that the Johannine Epistles were written after John's Gospel, and (2) that at least part of the matrix in which these epistles are embedded is the rising dispute with incipient Gnosticism, which in turn generated debates over the true meaning of the Fourth Gospel (see discussion in Schnackenburg 1992; Brown 1982; Smalley 1984), then a plausible solution is at hand. The Epistles of John are disputing, at least in part, what *John* means, especially as various elements of his thought have come under attack from incipient Gnosticism. To the extent that this re-creation of the epistolary settings is correct, we should not be surprised by the relative paucity of references to the OT, any more than we should be surprised by the abundance of references to Johannine themes.

1 John 2:11

I include this one "test case" of a verse in the Johannine Epistles that fairly clearly depends on a passage from the Gospel of John, a passage that in turn quotes the OT. At this point in 1 John the author is still teasing out the implications of 1:5: "This is the message we have heard from him and declare to you: God is light; in him is no darkness at all." Among the necessary signs of light is love for fellow believers (2:9–10). "But those who hate a fellow believer are in the darkness and walk around in the darkness; *they do not know where they are going, because the darkness has blinded them*" (2:11 TNIV). The italicized words quite clearly hark back to John 12:40, which is in fact a quotation from Isa. 6:10: "He has blinded their eyes and hardened their hearts, so they can neither see with their eyes, nor understand with their hearts, nor turn—and I would heal them." If one were studying John 12:37–41, of course, it would be necessary to unpack the quoted words from Isaiah and trace their meaning in the context of the OT prophet's writing. Yet the epistolary author's brief reference in 1 John 2:11 is most likely to John, not Isaiah, judging by the way he so frequently alludes to passages in the Fourth Gospel. Such allusions back to John, who alludes back to or quotes the OT, are so extraordinarily common that we must reluctantly set such tantalizing trajectories aside in favor of more immediate connections with the OT.

1 John 2:18

In a private communication, G. K. Beale has suggested to me that this reference to "the last hour" may go back to Dan. 12:1–2. John's evidence that it is the last hour is tied to the presence of many deceivers ("antichrists") who anticipate the ultimate antichrist: "This is how we know it is the last hour" (1 John 2:18). This connection is almost certainly drawn from the teaching of the Lord Jesus, who announced that false christs and false prophets would arise (Mark 13:22; Matt. 24:24), and this teaching has palpable links with Dan. 7:25; 8:12, 23–25; 11:30–34. In other words, Jesus is developing the prophecy of the latter-day deceiver from Daniel (Matthew 24 is saturated with allusions to Dan. 7–12, including such expressions as "abomination of desolation" and "great tribulation"). If so, and if John is drawing his thought from that of Jesus, the link between John's "last hour" and Dan. 12:1–2 becomes plausible. What it means, of course, is that John holds that at least many of the end-time phenomena that Jesus describes in the Olivet Discourse have already begun in his own day. Elsewhere I have argued that that is precisely how the Olivet Discourse itself is to be read: the envisaged tribulation stretches from Jesus' first coming to his second, with one sharp "birth-pang" of the Messiah tied to the destruction of Jerusalem (Carson 1984: 488–507).

1 John 2:27

A. NT Context: Why Christians Do Not Need Anyone to Teach Them.
The context shows that John is trying to repel the influence of false teachers who, John avers, "are trying to lead you astray" (2:26). The assumption seems to be that these teachers claim a certain inside knowledge (*gnōsis?*) that they wish to impress on the believers. But John's riposte, at this juncture, is that the believers are so well endowed that they do not need teachers: "As for you, the anointing you received from him remains in you, and you do not need anyone to teach you" (2:27). After all, "His anointing teaches you about all things and is true and is not a lie—just as it has taught you, remain in him" (2:27). One may well ask why John words his warning against false teachers in this way. On the face of it, he does not merely warn against false teachers but formally warns against Christian need for *any* teachers, despite the fact, of course, that John himself is transparently a teacher, and elsewhere he is prepared to warn his readers not to depart from his teaching (2 John 10). But John's meaning is less problematic once the OT allusion is clarified.

B. OT Context.
Jeremiah 31 looks forward to a time when God will not only restore both Israel and Judah (31:27–30) but also will deal radically with their cycles of sin. The exile under which they are suffering at the time of writing was brought on by the ancestors of those then in exile; the old proverb is transparently operating very well: "The fathers have eaten sour grapes, and the children's teeth are set on edge" (31:29). The "fathers" are the ancestors whose sin was the cause of the exile, and their children are still suffering. (Here and in other places I have modified my earlier paper on this passage [Carson 2004], influenced by private correspondence with Andrew Shead. Doubtless he will forgive me if I have not followed him entirely.) In the future, God says, he will not bring about this kind of tribal punishment: "Instead, everyone will die for his own sin; whoever eats sour grapes—his own teeth will be set on edge" (31:30). In part, however, the old pattern stemmed from the tribal-representative nature of the old covenant itself. What is required, therefore, is a new covenant. Mirroring the antithesis between 31:29 and 31:30 is the antithesis built into the following verses, 31:31–33: the antithesis between the old covenant and the new one that Yahweh now promises. The new covenant will not be like the old covenant. No, this will be the pattern, overcoming not only the tribal-representative structure that brought the sins of the fathers down on the heads of the children but also the guilt of individuals: "I will put my law in their minds, and write it on their hearts. I will be their God, and they will be my people. No longer will a man teach his neighbor, or a man his brother, saying, 'Know the LORD,' because they will all know me, from the least of them to the greatest.... For I will forgive their wickedness and will remember their sins no more." In other words, the logic of the oracle runs like this: (1) God forgives the sin of his people, concomitantly with God's Torah being written on their hearts, (2) establishing an abiding new-covenant relationship (3) in which all who are under this covenant genuinely know God (4) with genuine knowledge independent of the mediating teachers that characterized the old covenant (e.g., Levites were "brothers" and "neighbors" of the rest of the people of God, yet they had peculiar mediatorial teaching roles in this regard, as did the schools of the prophets).

C. The Context in Judaism.
The "anointing" language of 1 John 2:27 is introduced first in 2:20;

indeed, the word *chrisma* ("anointing") is found only in these two verses in the NT. But it is sometimes found in the OT in connection with literal anointing of people with oil (e.g., Exod. 29:7), while in the literature of early Judaism it occasionally takes on more metaphorical color. It can be understood as the oil of life that flows from the tree of life in paradise (e.g., *2 En.* 22:8–9; *L.A.E.* 9:13), although of course it can be used of the oil utilized at consecrations of various sorts (e.g., Josephus, *Ant.* 3.197; Philo, *Moses* 2.146, 152) (see Strecker 1996: 65–66).

D. Textual Matters. The allusion is so clipped that detailed textual comparison between 1 John 2:27 and the OT is impossible, although probably John is relying on Jer. 38:34 LXX (31:34 MT). Because *chrisma* ("anointing") is such a rare word in the NT, the usual variants are expected: *charisma* ("grace gift") replaces *chrisma* ("anointing") in some manuscripts of 1 John.

E. John's Use of the OT in 2:27. Assuming (rightly with, e.g., Brown 1982: 341–48) that the "anointing" is "an *anointing with the Holy Spirit*, the gift *from Christ* which constituted one a Christian" (Brown 1982: 348), then the fourfold structure that we saw in the Jeremiah oracle (see §B above) is nicely paralleled here in 1 John. This anointing, (1) whereby one becomes a Christian, is bound up with the forgiveness of sins (1:8–2:2), such that Christians do come to know the truth (2:20–21), (2) establishing an abiding new-covenant relationship in which we remain in Christ (2:24), (3) and in which all who enjoy this relationship genuinely know God (2:23–3:1) (4) with knowledge independent of what must be passed on by mediating teachers. In other words, for John's readers to rely on these (false) teachers is to admit that their own knowledge of God is somehow faulty or inadequate, which is to undercut all the power and reality of the new covenant. John is not denying the proper place of teachers; rather, he is denying the place of mediating teachers under some tribal-representative structure of covenant, for under the new covenant, in direct fulfillment of the promise articulated by Jeremiah, the place of mediating teachers is forever passed.

F. Theological Use. John warns against ostensibly Christian teachers who claim to have some sort of inside track with God that others do not, and

perhaps cannot, enjoy. No one denies that there are various degrees of maturity and experience, but a categorical distinction between Christian teachers and all other Christians overlooks not only passages such as this but also OT promises about the pouring out of the Spirit on all of God's people, cited by Peter at Pentecost (Acts 2:17–21; cf. Joel 2:28–32).

1 John 3:12

A. NT Context: The Negative Example of Cain. This is the only undisputed direct reference to the OT in the Johannine Epistles. This reference is found in a unit that emphasizes the importance of love among Christians (3:10b–24). The inverse of loving is hating, which in the worst case issues in murder, like Cain's murder of his brother.

B. OT Context. The OT passage is Gen. 4:1–25. Cain, we are told, was angry with his brother Abel because the latter's sacrifice was accepted by God, while Cain's was not. One must infer from Gen. 4:6–7 that the reason for the rejection of Cain's sacrifice was that he was an evildoer. God challenges him: "Why are you angry? Why is your face downcast? If you do what is right, will you not be accepted? But if you do not do what is right, sin is crouching at your door; it desires to have you, but you must rule over it" (TNIV).

C. The Context in Judaism. The literature of early Judaism is extraordinarily rich in references to Cain (e.g., *Apoc. Ab.* 24:3–5; *1 En.* 22:5–7; *L.A.E.* 2:1–4; 3:1–3; 4 Macc. 18:6–19; *L.A.B.* 2:1–4; *Jub.* 4:1–6; *T. Benj.* 7:1–5 [for a convenient and fuller summary, see Kruse 2000: 235–42]). In both *T. Benj* 7:1–5 and *Apoc. Ab.* 24:3–5 Cain's murder of Abel is viewed as an act inspired by the devil (Beliar).

D. Textual Matters. The allusion to Gen. 4 is accomplished through one word, the name of Cain, so textual matters do not come directly into play. Moreover, where 1 John goes beyond Gen. 4, the difference does not turn on something that the LXX says is not retained by the MT.

E. John's Use of the OT in 3:12. John's comment that Cain "belonged to the evil one" is not drawn from Gen. 4. It echoes parallels in early Judaism (see §C above), but is not demonstrably dependent on any of them. The statement may be seen as little more than an inference from Gen. 3 and Gen. 4 taken together: the evil one who seduced his parents now seduces Cain. When

John read Gen. 3 and 4, there were of course no chapter divisions, so he may well have seen the serpent's sway extending from Adam and Eve to Cain. Certainly John elsewhere in this chapter establishes that any performance of sin inevitably shows that the sinner is "of the devil" (1 John 3:7–8). When John states that the reason Cain murdered Abel was that his own actions were evil and his brother's righteous, this is no more than thoughtful unpacking of Gen. 4:6–7 (see §B above). In other words, John uses the Cain episode as a powerful negative moral example, a historical account not to emulate.

Because of this mention of Cain in 3:12, a few scholars have detected in *dikaion* ("just") in 2:1 an allusion to Abel. But that word is so common that it seems far-fetched to see Abel pointing to Jesus in this passage.

F. Theological Use. The connection that John draws between murder and underlying emotions—hate and jealousy—is reminiscent of similar connections drawn by the Lord Jesus (Matt. 5:21–24), delivered in a context (Matt. 5:17–20) in which Jesus insists that his assessment of the law prohibiting murder points in the direction of, and is fulfilled by, a heart free of hate.

Bibliography

Brown, R. E. 1982. *The Epistles of John*. AB 30. Garden City, NY: Doubleday.

Carson, D. A. 1984. "Matthew." Pages 3–599 in vol. 8 of *The Expositor's Bible Commentary*. Edited by F. E. Gaebelein. Grand Rapids: Zondervan.

———. 1988. "John and the Johannine Epistles." Pages 245–64 in *It Is Written: Scripture Citing Scripture; Essays in Honor of Barnabas Lindars, SSF*. Edited by D. A. Carson and H. G. M. Williamson. Cambridge: Cambridge University Press.

———. 2004. "'You Have No Need That Anyone Should Teach You' (1 John 2:27): An Old Testament Allusion That Determines the Interpretation." Pages 269–80 in *The New Testament in Its First Century Setting: Essays on Context and Background in Honour of B. W. Winter on His 65th Birthday*. Edited by P. J. Williams et al. Grand Rapids: Eerdmans.

Klauck, H.-J. 1991. *Der erste Johannesbrief*. EKKNT. Zürich: Benziger.

Kruse, C. G. 2000. *The Letters of John*. PNTC. Grand Rapids: Eerdmans.

Lieu, J. M. 1991. *The Theology of the Johannine Epistles*. Cambridge: Cambridge University Press.

———. 1993. "What Was from the Beginning: Scripture and Tradition in the Johannine Epistles." *NTS* 39: 458–77.

Schnackenburg, R. 1992. *The Johannine Epistles*. Translated by R. Fuller and I. Fuller. Tunbridge Wells: Burns & Oates.

Smalley, S. S. 1984. *1, 2, 3 John*. AB 51. Waco: Word.

Smith, D. M. 1972. "The Use of the Old Testament in the New." Pages 3–65 in *The Use of the Old Testament in the New and Other Essays: Studies in Honor of William Franklin Stinespring*. Edited by J. M. Efird. Durham, NC: Duke University Press.

Strecker, G. 1996. *The Johannine Letters: A Commentary on 1, 2, and 3 John*. Hermeneia. Minneapolis: Fortress.

JUDE

D. A. Carson

Introduction

As is the case with 2 Peter (see the introduction to the commentary there), the study of the use of the OT in Jude is beset with several challenges.

(1) Clearly, either 2 Peter borrows from Jude, or Jude borrows from 2 Peter. Though in briefer compass, the challenge is not unlike the way 1–2 Chronicles uses antecedent material or the way the Synoptic Gospels display interdependencies. Most scholars today accept that Jude was written first, and that 2 Peter quotes extensively from it. Although that is probably correct, I will nevertheless present the material in canonical order. More important, perhaps, is the fact that Jude clearly cites extrabiblical material (as do some other NT books), and this has prompted a preponderance of scholars to read the OT allusions through the lenses of those extrabiblical books. This is not unreasonable, but some care needs to be taken not to read too much into Jude. For example, if Jude overlaps in content with one element found in, say, *1 Enoch*, it does not necessarily follow that Jude buys into all that *1 Enoch* says on the subject.

(2) There is only one passage where, some scholars say, Jude quotes the OT (Jude 9); others call even this an allusion. In light of the number of allusions, however, it is mildly surprising that Jude does not depend to any substantial degree

on the LXX. He picks up some of the LXX's expressions, of course, but frequently the snippets are so brief that one is unclear as to whether these expressions are simply part of the common stock of Jewish-Christian idiom (see commentary on Jude 11, 12 below). More interesting yet is the fact that Jude may on occasion be dependent on the MT rather than the LXX (see commentary on Jude 13 below).

(3) Once again it is necessary to avoid consideration of such common expressions as "mercy, peace, and love" (Jude 2), for although they enjoy deep rooting in the OT, it is impossible to link such expressions to one or two passages or to a specific event.

Verse 4

The opening of the body of the letter finds Jude urging his readers to "contend for the faith that the Lord has once for all entrusted to the saints" (v. 3). The verb "contend," not to mention the thrust of this brief letter, shows that this contention is not with unbelievers outside the church but rather with false teachers within the church. That is why v. 4 draws attention to the way these false teachers have "slipped in among you." Of the four charges that Jude lays on them in this verse, one is of interest to us here: Jude asserts that their "condemnation was written about long ago." To what is he referring?

Some have argued that Jude has in mind earlier Christian writing, perhaps passages such as Acts 20:29–30; 1 Tim. 4:1–3; 2 Tim. 3:13; 2 Pet. 2:1–3:4. This view is sometimes said to be confirmed by Jude 17–18 (see Moo 1996: 230; Vögtle 1994: 26–27; Bauckham 1988: 36). But it is far from clear that "long ago" (*palai*) would have been used for references so recent. A few have argued that Jude is thinking of heavenly books that already have the judgment of sinners written down (e.g., Kelly 1969: 250–51), but the evidence for this view is far from persuasive (see Bauckham 1988: 35–36). The most plausible interpretation of Jude 4 is that the author has in mind ancient Jewish prophecies found in the Scriptures, for these are the examples that he proceeds to list in vv. 5–7, 11. Taken together, they demonstrate that, at least typologically, the judgment that befell certain people in ancient times points to similar judgment falling on those with similar failings in Jude's own day. These ancient prophecies may, in Jude's mind, include prophetic words from *1 Enoch* (see commentary on Jude 14–16 below).

Verse 5

Jude mentions the exodus, but 2 Peter does not. Yet Jude's mention of the exodus does not focus on the manner in which it often functions in the NT in some positive typological way to point toward the "new exodus" from the slavery of sin. The positive thing that this text says about the exodus is primarily a setup for what follows: "I want to remind you that the Lord at one time delivered the people out of Egypt, but later destroyed those who did not believe" (v. 5 TNIV). As in 1 Cor. 10:1–13; Heb. 3:7–13, the appeal to the exodus is here primarily a cautionary moral lesson: the people experienced great deliverance given by God, but because they did not persevere in faith, they fell in the wilderness and never entered the promised land (cf. Num. 14; Exod. 32). Implicitly, then, we learn that just because people belong to the right community does not mean that they can escape the judgment of God, any more than could the Israelites after God had delivered them from Egypt and before they had been brought into the promised land. Implicitly, of course, there is a further typological connection between Israel as the people of God at the time of the exodus and the Christians to whom Jude is writing. See further, above, on 2 Pet. 2:5.

Verse 6

A. NT Context: "Angels" Not Spared. Peter and Jude both mention judgment on "angels" and on Sodom and Gomorrah, but only the former mentions the flood, only the latter mentions judgment on Israel after the exodus, and the latter does not set things out in chronological order. More importantly, Peter interweaves into his list the preservation of the righteous, in particular Noah and Lot, while Jude omits all mention of the righteous. The result is that where the two documents substantially overlap, each nevertheless develops its own distinctive rhetorical emphases (see Charles 2005). Whereas 2 Peter presents God as making a distinction, in the final judgment, between the righteous and the unrighteous, Jude's focus in vv. 5–7 is on compiling a list that provides examples "of those who suffer the punishment of eternal fire" (v. 7) and thus functions as a warning to false teachers and those who might wish to follow them in Jude's day.

B. OT Context. Under the assumption that the OT background to Jude 6 is Gen. 6:1–4, we must ask what the latter passage means. There have been three primary interpretations: (1) the "sons of God" are angels who crossed species lines and married human women, producing "Nephilim" who were "heroes of old, men of renown" (Gen. 6:4); (2) the "sons of God" were kings, judges, and other members of aristocratic nobility who displayed their own greatness by indulging in polygamy and creating harems; (3) the "sons of God" were human males from the putatively godly line of Seth who freely married women from ungodly lines.

Nowadays the majority of interpreters from across the theological spectrum accept the angel interpretation (the list of supporters is very long, but see esp. the discussion in Dexinger 1966; see also Wenham 1987: 138–41). This interpretation is assumed by the LXX, and supported by most early Jewish exegesis, though not quite all (see below), as well as by all the earliest church fathers and some later ones (including Justin Martyr, Clement of Alexandria, Tertullian, Cyprian, Ambrose, and Lactantius), but not by some later fathers (Chrysostom, Augustine, Theodoret). "Sons of God" (in the plural) refers elsewhere in the OT to angels—certainly so in Job 1:6; 2:1; 38:7, and probably so in Ps. 29:1; 89:7; Dan. 3:25

(where *bar-'ĕlāhîn* underlies the traditional rendering "mighty ones" or the like found in most English versions). Yet the interpretation does not easily fit the context of the flood, since that judgment is pronounced against humanity (cf. Gen. 6:3–5; note "flesh" in 6:3 [NIV: "mortal"]). According to Jesus, angels do not marry (Matt. 22:30; Mark 12:25), and although excellent efforts have been undertaken to avoid this and other objections to the angel interpretation (e.g., Brown 2002: 52–71; vanGemeren 1981), the niggles make it less than a sure thing.

Those who take the view that the expression "sons of God" refers to kings, nobles, and other aristocrats (e.g., Cassuto 1973; Kline 1961–1962) understand them to be lusting after power, the multiple women being the signs of their success. Kline suggests that they are "divine kings"—that is, kings viewed as in some sense divine owing to the dominant religious commitments of the time. In other words, instead of administering justice under God, they forsook their proper place, claimed deity for themselves, violated God's will by forming royal harems, and lusted after power. Their children were the Nephilim-heroes (6:4), "evidently characterized by physical might and military-political dominance" (Kline 1993: 115). On the face of it, this explanation makes best sense of "and they took any of them they chose" (Gen. 6:2), and admirably sets the stage for the pronouncement of judgment against "flesh" in the flood. Negatively, however, there is no linguistic warrant outside Gen. 6:1–4 for supposing that "sons of God" refers to "divine kings" or, more generally, to aristocratic ruling figures, whereas the reading of "angels" has a long track record, including the LXX.

The view that "sons of God" refers to the line of Seth, while "daughters of human beings" refers to non-Sethian women, not only suffers from an absence of philological support but also has few elements in its favor compared with the "divine kings" view.

A few scholars have suggested the possibility that the first and second interpretations might be combined; that is, human rulers (the second interpretation) who claimed some sort of divine status might still fit the requirement of some kind of "angelic" encroachment (the first interpretation) if they were viewed as somehow demon possessed

(so Clines 1979; Waltke 2001: 115–17; Gispen 1974: 221).

A few scholars over the years, however, have argued that Gen. 6:1–4 is not the OT background to Jude 6 and 2 Pet. 2:4, but rather that Jude and Peter have in mind the prehistoric fall of angels. Some sort of prehistoric fall of the embodied serpent (Gen. 3) is doubtless presupposed by Genesis, but one is hard-pressed to find explicit discussion of the event. This interpretation of Gen. 6:1–4 sounds a bit like the interpretation of the scarcely known by the still yet more unknown.

C. The Context in Judaism. The interpretation of Gen. 6:1–4 that takes "the sons of God" to be angels (often called "Watchers") who have sexual intercourse with women is widespread in early Judaism (e.g., *1 En.* 6–19; 21; 86–88; *Jub.* 4:15, 22; 5:1; CD-A II, 17–19; 1QapGen ar II, 1; *Tg. Ps.-J.* Gen. 6:1–4; *T. Reub.* 5:6–7; *T. Naph.* 3:5; *2 Bar.* 56:10–14). True, a minority rabbinic tradition pronounces a curse on those who take the angel view (*Gen. Rab.* 26:5; cf. R. Simeon b. Yohai), but this probably does not go back earlier than the mid-second century AD.

Three further comments on this literature should be addressed. First, although various themes are emphasized by these assorted texts from early Judaism, the most extensive tradition is found in *1 En.* 6–19. Bauckham (1988: 51) argues that originally the fall of the Watchers in this tradition "was a myth of the origin of evil" but became detached from such mythology about the middle of the first century AD. The account tells how, in the days of Jared (Gen. 5:18), two hundred angels, under the leadership of *Šemiḥazah* and *'Aśa'el*, rebelled against God, lusted after the beautiful daughters of men, descended to Mount Hermon, and took human wives. Their children were giants who ravaged the earth. The fallen angels themselves taught human beings things that they should not know and many kinds of sin. Ultimately, then, the fallen angels were responsible for the corruption and degradation that brought down from the hand of God the punishment of the flood. The fallen angels, the Watchers, were punished by being bound under the earth until the final judgment; the giants were condemned by being abandoned to destroy each other in incessant battle, and their spirits became the evil spirits finally responsible for the evil in the world between the flood and the day of judgment. What is striking about these accounts is the attempt to shift blame for the flood from human beings to fallen angelic beings.

Second, Jude apparently picks up on at least some of these themes, as does 2 Peter. Yet what is picked up is not the entire "package" taught by *1 Enoch* but rather only that these "angels" (*angeloi*) are kept in darkness, bound in eternal chains awaiting the day of judgment. The point, in Jude, is that their judgment is certain. In 2 Peter the exact nature of the angels' sin is not specified; Jude initially says nothing about this either, at least while he is talking about the angels themselves, but clearly he links the sexual debauchery of Sodom and Gomorrah, in the next verse, with the debauchery of the "angels" in this verse. Yet Jude's dominant point is that both groups end up in final judgment under God.

Third, some have suggested that Jude (and Peter after him) knows of, and is perhaps dependent on, the Greek myth of the Titans, recounted in Hesiod's *Theogony*. Certainly some Jewish writers identified the Titans with fallen angels or with their giant progeny (cf. Josephus, *Ant.* 1.73; Sir. 16:7; Jdt. 16:6). In this myth the Titans were imprisoned in "Tartarus," the word that Peter (but not Jude) uses for "hell." This may be nothing more than the vocabulary choice of someone influenced by Hellenistic Judaism; it is hard to be sure, for already the word is used in the LXX of Job 40:20; 41:24 (Tartarus of the abyss); Prov. 30:16 (apparently parallel to Hades). In other words, appeal to ostensible Petrine knowledge of Hesiod is premature, and in any case it is irrelevant for Jude unless one were to adopt the unlikely position that Jude is dependent on 2 Peter rather than the other way around.

D. Textual Matters. However we understand "the sons of God" in the Hebrew of Gen. 6:1–4, the LXX refers to them as *angeloi*, which word is picked up in both Jude 6 and 2 Pet. 2:4 and, in the NT, is almost always used of angels, rarely of "messengers," and never of aristocratic figures such as kings and nobles. In other words, on the basis of philology alone, the angel interpretation seems most credible, unless one accepts the synthesis of Waltke and others who see that the "divine kings" are "possessed" by fallen angels, combining the strengths of the first two interpretations.

E. Jude's Use of the OT in Verse 6. Crossing the species line is central to the sin in *Jub.* 5; that is not explicit in either Jude or 2 Peter. Jude is interested in the inevitability of the judgment of these "angels," whoever they are, rather than in the precise nature of their sin.

F. Theological Use. "The point of this verse is that these fallen angels await eternal judgment.... The eschatological judgment of the angels who sinned is sure. They are already in prison. How much more sure is the judgment of those who have denied the Christ who purchased them" (Davids 2006: 226). That is entirely right, even if there remains some uncertainty regarding the referent of "angels."

Verse 7

A. NT Context: The Destruction of Sodom and Gomorrah. Jude briefly mentions the "sexual immorality and perversion" of "Sodom and Gomorrah and the surrounding towns"; the latter reference, of course, is to Admah, Zeboiim, and Bela or Zoar (Gen. 14:8; 19:25, 29), Zoar was spared as a concession to Lot.

B. OT Context. There has been a long-standing exegetical debate concerning the interpretation of Gen. 19 that has a bearing on our understanding of how Jude may be reading this OT chapter. What, precisely, is the nature of the Sodomites' sin? The dominant alternatives are sexual perversion (both homosexual and heterosexual), and betrayal of ancient near eastern hospitality codes.

Recently Morschauser (2003) has attempted a reconstruction and interpretation of Gen. 19 that offers a fresh reading and, incidentally, attempts to exonerate Lot as well—a subject of more interest to readers of 2 Peter than of Jude (I am indebted to Scott J. Hafemann for the reference). Morschauser attaches voluminous ancient Near Eastern parallels to the points that he makes; here I can do no more than sketch the most important elements of his thesis. (1) Genesis 19:1 asserts that Lot was sitting in the gateway of the city when the two visitors showed up. In the social structure of the day this meant that Lot was one of the elders, possibly sitting there in some sort of official capacity. In other words, when he invited the visitors into the city and into his home, he was not acting in the capacity of a private citizen. (2) The throng that gathered before Lot's house, specifically described as "young and old," is not made up of all the men of the town (otherwise 19:12 would make little sense) but rather constitutes the representative ruling elite; that is the overtone of "young and old." (3) This event occurs only a few chapters after the raid against Sodom described in Gen. 14. Doubtless some people were nervous about the possibility of visitors being spies. Lot's strong insistence that the visitors spend the night not in the square but rather with him in his house (19:2–3) not only displays generous hospitality but also might well be understood as Lot making sure that his visitors did not roam through the city freely. As an official in the gate, Lot, by bringing them into his home, was also keeping an eye on them. (4) When the crowd, "young and old," demands that the visitors be sent outside so that the crowd might "know" (*yāda'*) them, we are not to think of sexual assault (TNIV: "Bring them out so that we can have sex with them" [19:5]). Certainly this Hebrew verb for "know" can be a euphemistic way of referring to sexual intercourse—indeed, that is unmistakably the meaning in 19:8—but the verb itself has a broad semantic range and can be used in other contexts. In Ps. 139:1–2, 23 it is parallel to *ḥāqar* ("search out"). In the present context the crowd is asking to "get to know" these visitors, to "interrogate" them, not least to find out if they are spies. Of course, "interrogation" in those days could itself be a fairly brutal business. (5) The one dramatic exception to the ethics of generous hospitality in the culture of the time was the visit of spies. If the visitors were spies, then obviously they could not claim protection under the "rules" of hospitality (note Gen. 42:5–14, where Joseph can handle his visiting brothers roughly once he "determines" that they are spies; or Josh. 2–3 and the demand to Rahab to turn over her visitors). But what makes the demand of this crowd so inappropriate is that Lot is not now a private citizen. He is an official in the gate, he has exercised his judgment in good faith, and they have no right to question him this way. (6) What Lot proposes, then, is not that his daughters be sent outside to satisfy the lust of the perverted throng but rather that his daughters be temporarily held, overnight until the strangers leave town, as a kind of pledge, a hostage exchange. The arrangement was both legal and humane. Providing a kind of hostage was the course Reuben and Judah took at a later period (Gen. 42:37; 43:9). Even the expression "And you

can do what you like with them" is, Morschauser asserts, formulaic for "They are in your hands [and of course the protocol is that you keep them safe until this matter is resolved by the departure of my visitors in the morning]." (7) What happens, however, is that this mob of ruling elite will have none of the arrangement and wants to bring about their proposed interrogation by force. Instead of treating Lot with the respect that he deserves, they respond with atavistic rage, dismiss him as a foreigner, and challenge his authority (19:9). What they are trying to do, against a recognized official, is simply anarchic, and God judges them for it. But Lot himself comes out as a righteous man who acts honorably throughout.

It will be interesting to see how this proposal fares when all of Morschauser's parallels are scrutinized closely by experts in ancient Near Eastern literature and culture. My impression at this juncture is that there may well be something to Morschauser's reconstruction, but several elements of it make one pause. First, the proximity of the verb *yāda'* ("know") in 19:8 with an unambiguously sexual sense colors the meaning of the verb in 19:5 more than Morschauser admits. Second, and more importantly, the narrative relating the separation of Abraham and Lot (Gen. 13) depicts the latter as selfish and materialistic. He chooses Sodom and the well-watered plains, even though 13:13 specifies clearly that this is a wicked city terribly offensive to God. The account of Abraham's intercession in Gen. 18:16–33 also presupposes that Sodom is notoriously wicked. If Lot had become an official in the city, sitting in the gate in his official capacity, what does this say about his moral course? At very least, he is living a terribly compromised existence even before the events of Gen. 19. Third, the parallels of Reuben and Judah offering themselves as substitute "hostages" prompt another reflection: why does not Lot offer himself as hostage, the way Reuben and Judah do, instead of his daughters, until the morning? Fourth, the parallel account in Judges of the estate owner who takes in the Levite and his concubine in the town of Gibeah cannot be set aside as quickly as Morschauser attempts to do. He thinks that the big difference is that the crowd banging on the door is described as "sons of Belial"—they are already a dangerous lot. Their initial demand, that they may "know" the visitor

(Judg. 19:22), was also, says Morschauser, as in Gen. 19, a demand to interrogate the man. But one wonders if this is a naive reading. The entire account shows how threatened the Levite and his concubine were as they traveled, and even how unsafe staying in the town square of Gibeah was likely to be. In other words, the estate owner's insistence that they spend the night with him and not remain in the square has nothing to do with preventing them from casing the city but rather with trying to keep them safe. Similarly with respect to Gen. 19: granted that the city is already declared to be wicked, and granted that there is not a hint that Lot is trying to prevent the visitors from roaming freely through the city to prevent any possible spying activity, Morschauser's reconstruction sounds too neat, not to say naive. Here and there it feels like exegesis by knowledge of comparable social custom that has to be read into the text rather than straightforward reading of the text.

Sodom becomes proverbial for wickedness and judgment in the rest of the OT (see Isa. 1:9–10; Jer. 23:14; 50:40; Ezek. 16:46–56; Amos 4:11; Zeph. 2:9).

C. The Context in Judaism. The literature of early Judaism boasts a very high number of references to Sodom (for summaries, see Brown 2002: 185–92; Loader 1990: 75–117). Some of the references spell out the sins of Sodom, primarily homosexuality and arrogance (e.g., 3 Macc. 2:5; Sir. 16:8; *T. Levi* 14:6; *T. Naph.* 3:4; *Jub.* 16:5–6; *2 En.* 10:4. Wisdom 10:7 points to the barren wasteland of the Dead Sea plain as "evidence" (*martyrion,* "witness") of God's judgment, and 3 Macc. 2:5 specifically asserts that the destruction of the city makes them "an example to those who should come afterward" (RSV). By and large, the theme of Sodom's judgment is not developed in the Dead Sea Scrolls, but it plays a major role in the thought of Philo and of Josephus. The NT likewise mentions Sodom in an almost proverbial way (e.g., Matt. 10:15; Luke 10:12; 17:29), though quite remarkably Jesus appeals to Sodom in Matt. 11:20–24 to argue that the city proverbial for its wickedness will have an easier time on the day of judgment than will the towns of Galilee in which Jesus disclosed himself in word and deed—a powerful way of making the point that in God's accounting there are degrees

of responsibility grounded in how much access to revelation we enjoy.

D. Textual Matters. Jude does not deploy peculiar expressions that enable the reader to draw direct links to either the LXX or to Wis. 10:6 (unlike 2 Pet. 2:6–8, on which, see commentary).

E. Jude's Use of the OT in Verse 7. Jude appeals to the example of Sodom and Gomorrah to underscore their eternal destruction, the inevitability of judgment under God. These towns "serve as an example of those who suffer the punishment of eternal fire" (v. 7), not least since, as Jude goes on to say, the false teachers themselves have been indulging in the pollution of their own bodies (v. 8). As in v. 4 (above), the reading is typological in the sense that Jude is concerned to demonstrate a pattern of divine retribution that anticipates the final judgment.

F. Theological Use. Jude's concern is to emphasize the inevitability and finality of God's coming judgment on the last day. This is entirely in line with many texts that promise judgment to come (e.g., Matt. 25:31–46; Acts 17:31; 1 Thess. 5:1–11; Rev. 14:14–20), apart from the saving grace of God.

Verse 9

A. NT Context: The False Teachers' Lust for Authority Not Rightly Theirs. According to Jude 8, not only do these teachers "pollute their own bodies" but also they "reject authority" and "slander celestial beings." There is good reason to think that the "authority" that they rejected was that of Christ or of God (see Bauckham 1988: 56–57). But what does it mean to say that they slandered the *doxas* (NRSV: "glorious ones")? In the MT the Hebrew equivalent can on occasion refer to famous people (e.g., Ps. 149:8; Isa. 3:5; 23:8; Nah. 3:10; similarly 1QM XIV, 11; 4Q169 3–4 II, 9; 3–4 III, 9), but the LXX never uses *doxas* ("glorious ones") to refer to famous people. If these "glorious ones" are angels (cf. the usage in Exod. 15:11 LXX), they are unlikely to be evil angels (only good angels are in view when the expression crops up in passages such as 1QHᵃ XVIII, 8; 11Q5 XXII, 13; *2 En.* 22:7, 10). The verb for "slander" (*blasphēmeō*) has to do with dishonoring or shaming someone, speaking insultingly about someone, or the like. Angels sometimes are seen as the guardians of God's established order and thus his authority, or the ones who have mediated

God's revelation to us (e.g., Acts 7:38, 53; 1 Cor. 11:10; Heb. 2:2). To "slander" them, then, looks like rebellion against God's authority, which not only admirably fits the context but also is in line with the rebellious tendencies of the false teachers. So Jude goes on in our verse (v. 9) to give an example of a dispute in which even the archangel Michael is careful not to outstrip his authority.

B. OT Context. The short comment is that there is no OT context. When the burial of Moses is described (Deut. 34:1–8), no mention is made of Michael or the devil. Michael the archangel is mentioned only in Dan. 10:13, 21; 12:1. The words quoted at the end of the verse, however, and placed on Michael's lips as he addresses the devil, are "The Lord rebuke you!" and this expression is indeed found in the OT, in Zech. 3:2. There, however, it is the Lord himself who utters them, rebuking Satan in defense of the high priest Joshua as he stands before "the angel of the Lord." In the vision in question the high priest Joshua is in the temple courts in the presence of God and represents the Jews. His (and their) accuser is Satan, but if God rebukes Satan, then Joshua (and thus the Jews) is secure before the Lord.

C. The Context in Judaism. The incident that Jude (9) describes we know about from the church fathers, beginning with Clement of Alexandria (*Fragments on the Epistle of Jude*), who claims that Jude is quoting *Assumption of Moses*, an apocryphal work. But no extant manuscript preserves the story. There is, however, a manuscript (the Milan manuscript) that preserves another apocryphal book called *Testament of Moses*, whose ending has been lost. In a long excursus Bauckham (1988: 65–76 [cf. more briefly Davids 2006: 59–63]) argues that this lost ending is what originally preserved the story (that Jude here briefly relates) of Michael disputing with the devil over the body of Moses. The tradition of angels disputing with the devil goes back to Zech. 3:2 (referred to in §B above) and grows stronger in the literature of early Judaism (e.g., CD-A V, 17–18; 1QS III, 18–25; *T. Ash.* 6:4–6). The idea seems to be that when Moses dies, Satan wants to claim or destroy the body of Moses rather than bury him, perhaps on the grounds that Moses was a failure (just as Satan wants to claim Joshua, in some sense, in Zech. 3:2).

D. Textual Matters. Since we do not have the original source of the narrative, close textual comparisons are impossible.

E. Jude's Use of This Tradition. The critical expression *ouk etolmēsen krisin epenengkein blasphēmias* literally means "he did not dare to bring a judgment of slander," and it could be taken two ways. It could be rendered "he did not dare to bring a slanderous accusation" against the devil (NIV), but it is difficult to comprehend how it is possible to slander the devil. It is better to render it "he did not dare to bring a condemnation of slander against him" (NRSV) or, slightly more paraphrastically, "he did not himself dare to condemn him for slander" (TNIV). (The ESV's "he did not presume to pronounce a blasphemous judgment" is misleading because it takes Greek *blasphēmia* to mean English "blasphemy.") The flow of thought, then, is as follows:

> The false teachers slander angels, probably accusing them of foisting the law with is moral requirements upon Moses. By way of contrast, Michael, whose position was indisputable, when disputing with the devil in a narrative in which the devil was slandering the character of Moses, would not accuse this fallen angel, whom all agree is evil, of slander. In doing this Michael refused to overstep his proper boundaries and take the place of God in judging evil. (Davids 2006: 62)

It has been suggested that Jude does not himself actually believe the story to be true but cites it to illustrate the moral point that the story makes (in much the same way that someone might cite a *Harry Potter* book or the film *West Side Story* to illustrate a point). That may or may not be so, but it is wonderfully difficult to demonstrate.

F. Theological Use. That God jealously preserves his prerogatives in the rebuke of Satan in the latter's role as "the accuser of our brothers and sisters" (Rev. 12:10) is finally extended, in Rev. 12, to those who overcome the devil not in their own name but rather on the basis of the blood of the Lamb.

Verse 11 (Cain)

A. NT Context: The Hatred of Cain. Cain is the first of three individuals in this verse who are held up as negative examples.

B. OT Context. The OT passage is Gen. 4:1–25. Cain, we are told, was angry with his brother Abel because the latter's sacrifice was accepted by God, while Cain's was not. One must infer from Gen. 4:6–7 that the reason for the rejection of Cain's sacrifice was that he was an evildoer. God challenges him: "Why are you angry? Why is your face downcast? If you do what is right, will you not be accepted? But if you do not do what is right, sin is crouching at your door; it desires to have you, but you must rule over it" (TNIV).

C. The Context in Judaism. The literature of early Judaism is extraordinarily rich in references to Cain (e.g., *Apoc. Ab.* 24:3–5; *1 En.* 22:5–7; *L.A.E.* 2:1–4; 3:1–3; 4 Macc. 18:6–19; *L.A.B.* 2:1–4; *Jub.* 4:1–6; *T. Benj.* 7:1–5 [for a convenient and fuller summary, see Kruse 2000: 235–42]). In both *T. Benj.* 7:1–5 and *Apoc. Ab.* 24:3–5 Cain's murder of Abel is viewed as an act inspired by the devil (Beliar).

D. Textual Matters. The allusion to Gen. 4 is accomplished through one word, the name of Cain, so textual matters do not come directly into play.

E. Jude's Use of the OT in Verse 11. It is doubtful that Jude thinks that the false teachers whom he excoriates are actual murderers, like Cain. But to say that they followed "the way of Cain" probably calls to mind how Cain's murder of his brother already stands as the primal example of hatred (cf. *T. Benj.* 7:5; 1 John 3:11–12).

F. Theological Use. Jude's assumption that murder and hatred are so tightly connected is worked out in greater detail in 1 John 3:11–12, and it is reminiscent of similar connections drawn by the Lord Jesus (Matt. 5:21–24), delivered in a context (Matt. 5:17–20) in which Jesus insists that his assessment of the law prohibiting murder points in the direction of, and is fulfilled by, a heart free of hate. In the immediate context of Jude, the false teachers do not love the truth "once for all entrusted" to Christ's people, and this works itself out in animus to the Christians themselves (very much as in 1 John).

Verse 11 (Balaam)

A. NT Context: Wandering from the Truth toward Greed. The false teachers have "rushed for profit into Balaam's error." The Greek behind the word "error" (*planē*) is cognate with "wandered off" (*eplanēthēsan*) in 2 Pet. 2:15–16. Peter goes

into more detail, including reflection on the role of the donkey. Jude is brief and pungent: Balaam's desire for money is what he condemns, not the subtlety of the advice that he eventually gave Balak, or his confrontation with the angel, or the speech of the donkey.

B. OT Context. The initial account of Balaam (Num. 22–24) provides such grist that Balaam's name is picked up in many later OT texts (Num. 31:8, 16; Deut. 23:4–5; Josh. 13:22; 24:9–10; Neh. 13:2; Mic. 6:5). Most of these texts stress how God intervened so that Balaam was unable to pronounce the curses on Israel that Balak wanted to hear. The hint of the bad advice that Balaam gave Balak anyway comes in Num. 31:16. That bad advice, advocating the kind of enticement to sin that would bring God's wrath down on Israel's head, is what is picked up in Rev. 2:14 (though not in 2 Pet. 2).

C. The Context in Judaism. Balaam's love for money surfaces in the work of Philo (*Moses* 1.268; *Cherubim* 33–34). Especially in the rabbinic literature one finds a strong emphasis on the view that Balaam ultimately received the appropriate "wages" of his wickedness: he was killed by Israel (Num. 31:8: cf. *Sipre Num.* 157 on Num. 31:9; *Num. Rab.* 22:4). For the rich lore of rabbinic tales on Balaam, most and perhaps all of which are later than Jude, see the chart in Davids 2006: 253–56. Many of them assert that Balaam himself was sexually perverted—an interpretation grounded in the advice that he gave Balak to encourage cross-religious (and thus, from the perspective of the covenant, highly illegal) marriages.

D. Textual Matters. Several commentators (e.g., Neyrey 1993: 211–12; Bauckham 1988: 268; Davids 2006: 242–43) note that in the three Targumim on Numbers (*Pseudo-Jonathan/ Yerušalmi*, *Neofiti*, *Fragmentary Targum*) the donkey actually rebukes Balaam, instead of merely asking why he is being beaten (the biblical narrative leaves the actual rebuke for Balaam's actions to the angel).

E. Jude's Use of the OT in Verse 11. Apparently, one of the motives that has encouraged these false teachers into their "error" is simply greed.

F. Theological Use. It is easy enough to compile a list of biblical warnings against a focus on wealth (see the admirable balance in Blomberg 1999). Closest in theological conception to this passage is perhaps 1 Tim. 6:3–10, where false teachers are denounced not only for the content of their instruction but also because they seem to think that godliness is a means to financial gain (6:5). "For the love of money is a root of all kinds of evil. Some people, eager for money, have wandered [*apeplanēthēsan*] from the faith and pierced themselves with many griefs" (6:10).

Verse 11 (Korah)

A. NT Context: The Rebellion of Korah. Jude's list of three bad examples is not chronological, for if it were, Korah would precede Balaam. Here is another "bad character" who finally meets destruction at God's hands.

B. OT Context. The Korah in question is not the man whose name appears in the titles of eleven psalms, associated with the temple officials mentioned in 1 Chron. 1:35; 2:43; 6:22, 37; 9:19, nor any of the several descendants of Esau mentioned in Gen. 36, but rather is the Levite leader first mentioned in Exod. 6:21, 24 who, along with Dathan and Abiram, led a rebellion in Num. 16 and is mentioned one final time in Num. 26:10–11. His attack on Moses and Aaron is motivated by lust for their authority and is defended by the argument that since all the people of Israel are holy, therefore Moses and Aaron have no right to take on special authority that other Israelites cannot enjoy. The leaders of the rebellion (Korah and his friends, plus Reubenite leaders) and their households were destroyed by God (Num. 16:31–35).

C. The Context in Judaism. Korah became proverbial for a divisive or rebellious person (e.g., Josephus, *Ant.* 4.14–21; *L.A.B.* 16).

D. Textual Matters. Once again, the one-word link to an OT chapter (Num. 16) does not allow for lengthy textual comparisons.

E. Jude's Use of the OT in Verse 11. Two points are established in Jude's brief reference to Korah. First, he rebelled against Moses and Aaron and therefore against God and the leaders whom he had appointed. Second, he was destroyed by God. Implicitly, Jude is saying that the false teachers with whom he is dealing are rebelling against properly constituted spiritual authority, and he is announcing that, on analogy with Korah's fate, they too will be destroyed.

F. Theological Use. The primal sin is the desire to be God (Gen. 3)—that is, to claim an authority that is not ours. The first responsibility of the creature is to recognize his or her creaturely status. Jude's point is that God is not mocked: sooner or later rebellion against God's authority will always be judged.

Verse 12

Jude picks up at least two expressions that may well be alluding to OT texts. His accusation that the false teachers are "shepherds who feed only themselves" probably springs from Ezek. 34:2–3, coming in a chapter that delivers a blistering attack against the false "shepherds" of Ezekiel's day and redolent of the fundamental sin of Balaam as well. Ezekiel 34 also underscores Yahweh's own promise that he himself would come and shepherd his people. The charge that the false teachers are "clouds without rain" springs from Prov. 25:14: "Like clouds and wind without rain is a man who boasts of gifts he does not give." Whereas Jude 12 asserts that the false teachers are "clouds without rain," 2 Pet. 2:17 says they are "springs without water." Both images picture promise without delivery, spiritual charlatans. The false teachers promise nurturing, refreshing "water" but provide none. The Bible is replete with images that connect water with wisdom, the law, instruction from God, and blessing, whereas aridity is linked to fruitlessness, chaff that must be burned, and forsaking God (e.g., Ps. 1:3–4; Prov. 13:14; 18:4; Jer. 2:19; 14:3; 17:5–8). For discussion as to whether Jude here is following the MT or merely using inherited linguistic expressions (for certainly he is not citing the LXX in either of these OT allusions), see Bauckham 1988: 87–88; Davids 2006: 71.

Verse 13

Jude develops his series of metaphors from four spheres of nature: land (trees), air (clouds), sea, and heaven (stars), which, Davids (2006: 72) points out, parallel the four spheres of *1 En.* 80. Here we have reached the third metaphor: the false teachers are "wild waves of the sea, foaming up their shame," possibly an echo of Isa. 57:20: "But the wicked are like the tossing sea, which cannot rest, whose waves cast up mire and mud." The ancient Israelites were not a seafaring people, so "sea" images were unlikely to be associated with adventure or mystical communion with nature. Rather, "sea" words conjure up chaos, wickedness, danger, which is one of the reasons why the final biblical vision of the consummation not only announces a new heaven and a new earth but also promises that there will be no more sea (Rev. 21:1). This no more establishes an absence of all hydrological principles in the eschaton than the insistence that God and the Lamb constitute the "sun" or the "light" of the new heaven and the new earth means that we thereby gain insight into the astronomical principles of the eschaton.

Verses 14–16

The longest and only unambiguous quotation in the Epistle of Jude is not from an OT book but rather from *1 Enoch*. There are a couple of OT allusions in the Jude text. Enoch is acknowledged to be "seventh from Adam" (14), and, according to the OT, counting inclusively, he is. The image of God coming with his angelic hosts (14) is drawn from Deut. 33:2: "The LORD came from Sinai and dawned over them from Seir; he shone forth from Mount Paran. He came with myriads of holy ones from the south, from his mountain slopes." This is a colorful metaphorical description of the theophany at Sinai. The "holy ones" probably are angels, though this is less than certain because "holy ones" in the ensuing verse (33:3) clearly refers to God's people. Nevertheless, the language is picked up by *1 En.* 1:9 and then cited here in Jude to conjure up the divine court coming for final judgment. Indeed, the language of *1 En.* 1 anticipates determined, irrevocable judgment and refers to the saints as "elect": that is how it reads Deut. 33:2, possibly because it reads the Sinai theophany as a type, an anticipation, of culminating revelation to come at the end of the age. In much the same way, Jude anticipates determined, irrevocable judgment (e.g., vv. 4–7), and speaks of believers as the "called" and the "kept" (vv. 1, 24 respectively).

Several brief notes may be helpful. First, in its totality the book of *1 Enoch* has come down to us only in Ethiopic, but that version had not yet been created in Jude's day. What version he did use is debated. His own summary is fairly close to the Aramaic version. Second, Jude says that Enoch "prophesied" about these wicked people and their fate in the judgment that he then describes, quoting the lines from *1 En.* 1:9. This suggests that Jude saw this text as preserving genuine prophecy; it does not necessarily imply that he thought all of *1 Enoch* was prophetic (a point recognized by

Augustine, *Civ.* 15.23 [cf. Moo 1996: 271–74; Schreiner 2003: 469–70]). In a private communication David R. Jackson, author of the important book *Enochic Judaism*, suggests that Jude expects his words to be read in some ironic sense. But I have not seen that view defended anywhere in print, convincingly or otherwise, so at this juncture the claim still strikes me as odd. The book of *1 Enoch* was also valued by those in the Qumran community. It has been suggested that Jude's opponents may not have accepted those Scriptures that do speak of final judgment, so Jude cites a book they would accept (Vögtle 1994: 84). In any case, third, we do not find *1 Enoch* grouped with the scrolls of Scripture, nor is it ever referred to as *graphē* (lit., "writing," but commonly used as a technical expression for "Scripture").

Bibliography

Bauckham, R. J. 1988. *Jude, 2 Peter.* WBC 50. Waco: Word.

Blomberg, C. L. 1999. *Neither Poverty Nor Riches: A Biblical Theology of Possessions.* NSBT 7. Downers Grove, IL: InterVarsity .

Brown, D. E. 2002. "The Use of the Old Testament in 2 Peter 2:4–10A." PhD diss., Trinity Evangelical Divinity School.

Callan, T. 2004. "Use of the Letter of Jude by the Second Letter of Peter." *Bib* 85: 42–64.

Calvin, J. 1979 [1551]. *Commentaries on the Catholic Epistles.* Translated by J. Owen. Grand Rapids: Baker Academic.

Cassuto, U. 1973. "The Episode of the Sons of God and the Daughters of Man." Pages 29–40 in *Biblical and Oriental Studies.* Vol. 1. Translated by I. Abrahams. Jerusalem: Magnes.

Charles, J. D. 2005. "The Angels under Reserve in 2 Peter and Jude." *BBR* 15: 39–48.

Clines, D. J. A. "The Significance of the 'Sons of God' Episode [Genesis 6:1–4] in the Context of the 'Primeval History' [Genesis 1–11]," *JSOT* 13 (1979): 33–46.

Davids, P. H. 2006. *The Letters of 2 Peter and Jude.* PNTC. Grand Rapids: Eerdmans.

Dexinger, F. 1966. *Sturz der Göttersöhne; oder, Engel vor der Sintflut? Versuch eines Neuverständnisses von Genesis 6, 2–4 unter Berücksichtigung der religionsvergleichenden und exegesegeschichtlichen Methode.* WBT 13. Vienna: Herder.

Elliott, J. H. 1982. *I–II Peter, Jude.* ACNT. Minneapolis: Augsburg.

García Martínez, F. 1999. "Interpretations of the Flood in the Dead Sea Scrolls." Pages 86–108 in *Interpretations of the Flood.* Edited by F. García Martínez and G. P. Luttikhuizen. TBN 1. Leiden: Brill.

Gispen, W. H. 1974. *Genesis 1–11.* COT. Kampen: Kok.

Green, E. M. B. 1968. *The Second Epistle of Peter and the Epistle of Jude.* TNTC. Grand Rapids: Eerdmans.

Grundmann, W. 1974. *Der Brief des Judas und der zweite Brief des Petrus.* THKNT 15. Berlin: Evangelische Verlagsanstalt.

Hillyer, N. 1992. *1 and 2 Peter, Jude.* NIBCNT. Peabody, MA: Hendrickson.

Jackson, D. R. 2004. *Enochic Judaism: Three Defining Paradigm Exemplars*. LSTS 49. London: T&T Clark.

Kelly, J. N. D. 1969. *The Epistles of Peter and of Jude*. BNTC. London: Black.

Kline, M. G. 1961–1962. "Divine Kingship and Genesis 6:1–4." *WTJ* 24: 184–204.

———. 1993. *Kingdom Prologue*. South Hamilton, MA: M. G. Kline.

Kraftchick, Steven J. 2002. *Jude, 2 Peter*. ANTC. Nashville: Abingdon.

Kruse, C. G. 2000. *The Letters of John*. PNTC. Grand Rapids: Eerdmans.

Loader, J. A. 1990. *A Tale of Two Cities: Sodom and Gomorrah in the Old Testament, Early Jewish and Early Christian Tradition*. CBET 1. Kampen: Kok.

Mayor, J. B. 1979 [1901]. *The Epistles of Jude and II Peter*. Repr., Grand Rapids: Eerdmans.

Moffatt, J. 1928. *The General Epistles: James, Peter and Jude*. MNTC. London: Hodder & Stoughton.

Moo, D. J. 1996. *2 Peter, Jude*. NIVAC. Grand Rapids: Zondervan.

Morschauser, S. 2003. "'Hospitality', Hostiles, and Hostages: On the Legal Background to Genesis 19.1–19." JSOT 27: 461–85.

Neyrey, J. H. 1993. *2 Peter, Jude*. AB 37C. New York: Doubleday.

Reicke, Bo. *The Epistles of James, Peter, and Jude*. AB 37. Garden City, NJ: Doubleday, 1964.

Schelkle, K. H. 1980. *Die Petrusbriefe, der Judasbrief*. 5th ed. HTKNT. Freiburg: Herder.

Schreiner, T. R. 2003. *1, 2 Peter, Jude: An Exegetical and Theological Exposition of Holy Scripture*. NAC. Nashville: Broadman & Holman.

Sidebottom, E. M. 1967. *James, Jude and 2 Peter*. NCB. London: Nelson.

vanGemeren, W. H. 1981. "The Sons of God in Genesis 6:1–4 (An Example of Evangelical Demythologization?)." *WTJ* 43: 320–48.

Vögtle, A. 1994. *Der Judasbrief, der 2. Petrusbrief*. EKKNT 22. Solothurn: Benziger; Neukirchen-Vluyn: Neukirchener Verlag.

Waltke, B. K. 2001. *Genesis*. Grand Rapids: Zondervan.

———. 2005. *Proverbs 15–31*. NICOT. Grand Rapids: Eerdmans.

Wenham, G. J. 1987. *Genesis 1–15*. WBC 1. Waco: Word.

REVELATION

G. K. BEALE AND SEAN M. MCDONOUGH

Introduction

No other book of the NT is as permeated by the OT as is Revelation. Although its author seldom quotes the OT directly, allusions and echoes are found in almost every verse of the book. Revelation's message remains thoroughly "New Testament." The church universal is called to maintain a faithful witness in the midst of persecution, following in the footsteps of the Lamb, who died to free them from their sins. Having conquered through faith, they are promised the blessing of eternal life in the presence of God in the new heaven and new earth, all with the purpose that they worship him and that he receive the glory forever. However, the imagery is drawn almost exclusively from the OT, thus reminding the reader that redemption in Christ is the fulfillment of God's eternal plans.

Recent Discussion on the Use of the Old Testament in Revelation

In comparison with the rest of the NT, the use of the OT in Revelation had not received a proportionate amount of attention up through the early 1980s. Only two books had been published (Schlatter 1912; Jenkins 1972). In addition, six significant articles had been dedicated to the topic between the 1950s and the 1970s (Van-

hoye 1962; Lancellotti 1966; Trudinger 1966; Gangemi 1974; Marconcini 1976; Goulder 1981 [see also, of more limited value, Cambier 1955; Lohse 1961]).

Otherwise, during roughly the first three-quarters of the twentieth century important discussion of the subject was found only in portions of books and commentaries, the more valuable of which were Swete 1906, esp. cxl–clvi; Charles 1920, esp. lxv–lxxxii; Vos 1965: 16–53; Caird 1966; van der Waal 1971: 174–241; Beasley-Murray 1974; D. Ford 1979: 243–306; and to somewhat lesser degree, Comblin 1965; Farrer 1964; Holtz 1971.

From the mid-1980s to the mid-1990s, however, six significant books and an important dissertation were written on the topic: Beale 1984; Vogelgesang 1985; Paulien 1988a; Ruiz 1989; Bauckham 1993a (see also 1993b); Fekkes 1994; Moyise 1995. Space limitations do not allow evaluation of these works (for which, see Beale 1999b: 15–59; see also discussion of literature up to the early 1990s in Murphy 1994). In addition, during the same approximate ten-year period a number of articles on the same subject appeared, among which, see Beale 1988; Bøe 1992; McComiskey 1993.

Since the mid-1990s the following substantive books (including major commentaries) on the subject have appeared: Aune 1997–1998; Beale 1999a; 1999b; Osborne 2002; Mathewson 2003. Among the noteworthy articles published during that same period are Beale 1999c; 2001; Moyise 1999b; 2000; 2001a; 2001b; Paulien 2001a; 2001b.

The Degree of Old Testament Influence and Key Old Testament Books

It is generally recognized that Revelation contains more OT references than does any other NT book, although past attempts to tally the total amount have varied (UBS³ = 394; NA²⁶ = 635; British and Foreign Bible Society Greek text = 493; Hühn 1900 = 455; Dittmar 1903 = 195; Swete 1906 = 278; Charles 1920 = 226; van der Waal 1971 = approximately 1000 [for a listing of statistics from other commentators, see Fekkes 1994: 62]). For an example of the varying lists of allusions in a particular segment of Revelation (8:7–9:21; 11:15–18), see Paulien (1988b: 37–38); see also Paulien 2001a, in which are compared the varying lists of allusions in Aune 1997–1998; Beale 1999a.

The variation in statistics is due to the different criteria employed to determine the validity of an OT reference and the fact that some authors include echoes and parallels of a very general nature together with allusions and citations (see Vos 1965: 17–19; Vanhoye 1962: 438–40). The range of OT usage includes the Pentateuch, Judges, 1–2 Samuel, 1–2 Kings, Psalms, Proverbs, Song of Solomon, Job, major prophets, and the minor prophets. Roughly more than half the references are from Psalms, Isaiah, Ezekiel, and Daniel, and in proportion to its length, Daniel yields the most (so Swete [1906: cliii], who gives numerical statistics for many of the OT books used).

The evaluation of Daniel as most influential is supported by recent study (see Beale 1984), though there is more agreement that Ezekiel exerts greater influence in Revelation than does Daniel. Proportionally, Ezekiel ranks second as the most used OT book (see Vanhoye 1962: 473–75), although in terms of actual numbers of allusions Isaiah is first, followed by Ezekiel, Daniel, and Psalms (although statistics cited by commentators differ—e.g., Swete 1906: Isaiah = 46 [although Fekkes 1994: 280–81 finds 50 "certain and probable" allusions to Isaiah], Daniel = 31, Ezekiel =

29, Psalms = 27). The OT in general plays such a major role that a proper understanding of its use is necessary for an adequate view of Revelation as a whole.

John leaves almost no OT stone unturned in the course of Revelation, but six OT books in particular have overarching conceptual significance for the composition of his work. The creation/fall accounts of Genesis are foundational for Revelation, in terms of both antithesis (the dissolution of the created order in John's visionary material) and fulfillment (the blessings of the new Jerusalem as eschatological fulfillment of Eden). The accounts of the plagues in Exodus are the source of some of the most startling imagery in Revelation, and the theme of liberation from oppressive rulers is the predominant motif in both books.

In regard to the prophets, Isaiah and Ezekiel contribute significantly to John's vision of the heavenly throne room in Rev. 4–5, and the promises of eschatological blessing in Isa. 40–66 permeate the vision of the new heaven and new earth (itself an Isaianic phrase) in Rev. 21–22. Ezekiel provides the primary background for John's prophetic self-understanding (see esp. Rev. 1:10, 17; 10:9–11), and John models his narrative of the final battle, judgment, and new Jerusalem precisely on Ezek. 37–48 (see commentary on Rev. 20 below). Zechariah provides some crucial imagery for John, notably the four horseman, the lampstands, and (in one of the rare OT quotations in Revelation) the statement that "every eye will see him, even those who pierced him" (Rev. 1:7; Zech. 12:10).

Finally, the book of Daniel—chapter 7 in particular—provides a mother lode of material for John (e.g., it is likely the dominant influence in the vision of Rev. 4–5). Revelation's central theme of faithful witness in the midst of persecution derives directly from the stories in Daniel, as does the particular note that these witnesses triumph over the beast (Dan. 7; Rev. 13). John's themes of judgment and the reign of the saints, though present elsewhere in the OT, arguably find their closest parallels in the vision of Dan. 7.

The Text Form of Old Testament References in Revelation

The text form of the OT references in Revelation requires in-depth discussion because there are no formal quotations and most are allusive, a phenomenon often making textual identification more difficult. The complex relationship of the Hebrew text to early Greek versions, the history of which is largely unknown to us, makes it difficult to know whether John depends on the Hebrew or the Greek (so Vogelgesang 1985: 19–22). Unfortunately, the scope of the present discussion precludes thorough analysis of this important subject. The majority of commentators have not followed the assessment by Swete (1906: clv–clvi) that John depends mainly on the LXX but apparently have embraced the conclusion by Charles (1920: 1:lxvi–lxvii, also lxviii–lxxxii) that John was influenced more by the Hebrew than by the Greek OT (Ozanne 1965; Trudinger 1966; S. Thompson 1985: 1–2, 102–8). This conclusion is based mainly on the observation that John's allusions depart from the wording of the LXX (Charles 1920: 1:lxvi); however, the wording also departs from the Hebrew at significant points (see Moyise 1995: 17). The likelihood is that John draws from both Semitic and Greek biblical sources and often modifies both (so, e.g., Moyise 1995: 17; although, this is a conclusion reached already in the mid-nineteenth century by Stuart [1845: 231–32] and the beginning of the twentieth century by Laughlin [1902: 21]). Charles (1920: 1:lxvii) himself acknowledged that even though John's pattern was to translate from the Hebrew text and not to quote from the Greek version, "he was often influenced in his renderings by the LXX and another Greek version" (proto-Theodotion).

Problematic Use of Combined Allusions and the Issue of Literary Consciousness

We have already acknowledged the nonformal character of the OT references in Revelation. Not only does this make OT textual identification more difficult but it also renders it problematic to determine whether or not the author is consciously or unconsciously referring to an OT text. This problem is compounded since many, indeed most, of the OT reminiscences are found in combination with one another. Sometimes four, five, or more different OT references are merged into one picture. Good examples are the descriptions of Christ (1:12–20), God on the throne and the surrounding heavenly host (4:1–11), and the dia-

bolic beast (13:1–8) (for a thorough list of other examples, see Vos 1965: 39–40). How are such combined allusions to be studied? This phenomenon would be particularly hard to analyze if, as some contend, it is less intentional and more the result of a memory so saturated with OT language and ideas that they are unconsciously organized in the author's visions "like the changing patterns of a kaleidoscope" (Swete 1906: cliv and Vos 1965: 38–39). In this case, the OT contextual meanings of the allusions need not be examined to better comprehend John's use, since he himself did not consciously reflect on such OT contexts. Indeed, many have concluded that the lack of formal citation in the Apocalypse points in the same direction.

However, some see conscious effort in such allusive combinations for the purpose of expressing evocative and emotive power (e.g., Caird 1966: 25–26). Therefore, it is unnecessary to attempt to comprehend the meaning of each reference in its OT and NT context since the whole picture must be kept together without separating and analyzing various strands in order to evoke the desired emotional effect. Of course in these mosaics there is always the possibility of a mixture of conscious intention with unconscious activity.

But often a greater understanding is gained and emotive effect felt when the various allusive parts of these visionary amalgamations *are* studied separately in their OT contexts. Vos cites Rev. 4:2–9 as a fitting illustration of unconscious mixing of OT allusions. However, when the OT context of each allusion is studied one finds that, without exception, they are all from descriptions of theophany scenes that function as introductory sections to an announcement of judgment either upon Israel or the nations: cf. Vos's parallels of (1) Rev. 4:2 = Isa. 6:1 and/or 1 Kgs. 22:19; (2) Rev. 4:3–4 = Ezek. 1:28; (3) Rev. 4:5a = Ezek. 1:13 and/or Exod. 19:16; (4) Rev. 4:5b = Ezek. 1:13 and Zech. 4:2, 6 [omitted from Vos]; (5) Rev. 4:6a = Ezek. 1:22; (6) Rev. 4:6b = Ezek. 1:5 and 1:18; (7) Rev. 4:7 = Ezek. 1:10; (8) Rev. 4:8a = Isa. 6:2; (9) Rev. 4:8b = Isa. 6:3; (10) Rev. 4:9 = Isa. 6:1.

This common denominator of a theophany-judgment theme is enhanced when one notes also the dominant influence of Dan. 7:9–13 throughout Revelation 4–5 (see the commentary below on Rev. 4–5). This clearly common motif in all the OT allusions points toward a more intentional thematic formation of texts to describe a similar theophany in Revelation. This seems even more likely when one considers that in the immediate contexts of three of the OT allusions there appears the image of a "book" associated with judgment, as in Rev. 5:1 (cf. Dan. 7:10; Ezek. 2:9–10; Zech. 5:1–3). All of the common scenes and themes of these OT contexts intensify the cognitive and emotive aspects of the picture in Rev. 4:2–9.

The same thing can be illustrated through Rev. 1:12–20; 13:1–8; and 17:1ff. and other examples cited by Vos to support his proposal of unconscious clustering, which this chapter will argue against (this is presented in even more detail in Beale 1984: 154–270).

Therefore, caution must be used in making claims of unconscious activity on the author's part, although this is a possibility. For example, it is possible, though speculative, to propose that the above-mentioned exegetical links were already intact in some previous tradition to which John makes unconscious allusion (e.g., a synagogue or Christian liturgical tradition). Such unconscious activity is more likely to have occurred with the less clear or non-clustered allusions, although exegetical analysis must determine this in each case. Furthermore, as Vanhoye (1962: 467) has concluded, it is not typical for John to use OT allusions in isolation but to fuse them together on the basis of their affinity with one another, as illustrated above in Revelation 4–5.

Although space does not permit elaboration, it may be helpful to briefly discuss in this section whether or not the Apocalypse is a mere literary composition, or if it can be traced to a visionary experience, or is a combination of both (cf. further, e.g., Beale 1984: 7–9). If there was an experiential basis, which is highly probable (see further Rissi 1966: 18–21), descriptions of a number of such visions were probably colored both unconsciously and consciously by the traditions which had exerted a formative influence on the author's thinking. Accordingly, actual visions would have been experienced in the author's own learned thought forms, so that it might be difficult to distinguish description of a visionary experience from that of a retelling of the experience through unconscious or conscious appeal to various traditions (OT, Jewish, etc.).

Therefore, John had genuine visions, and he subsequently recorded those visions in literary form. On the one hand, the written references to the OT are often the result of a mere recording of the actual visions and auditions themselves, though some of these would have come to him through the lens of his own learned OT traditions (much like students taking first year intensive Greek in the summer might testify that they dream in Greek or about Greek class, though this is a pedestrian illustration to compare with the prophet John's experience). On the other hand, some of the visions and auditions received are described and interpreted as a result of John's subsequent conscious reflection on the OT during the writing down of the vision, one of the telltale signs of which are the various OT versions that are discernible in the text of the Apocalypse. No doubt, John would have associated some of his visions and auditions with similar OT passages and employed the language of those passages to record what he saw and heard. What better way for John to record his experience, especially those visions and auditions difficult to describe, than by using OT references that had already portrayed similar difficult visions that he believed were related in one way or another to what he heard and saw?

Consequently, there may be cases where it is hard to know when John is merely recording what he saw in a vision, which itself contains clear reference to the OT, or when he is intentionally using the OT to describe further the visions which he has seen and the things he has heard in conjunction with those visions. But even if John was always only recording what he saw and heard directly from his visionary and auditory experience, he likely still would have been conscious of the OT links and associations inherent in those visions and apocalyptic declarations which he received, since he considered himself to be in a long line of prophets stretching back into the OT.

Indeed, John's implicit self-identification with the line of OT visionaries (cf. 1:1–3, 10; 4:1–2; 17:3; 21:10) implies that he would be conscious of receiving and writing down visions closely related to his OT prophetic forerunners, which develop in various ways those prior revelations (e.g., by designating inaugurated fulfillment or by prophesying the same or similar thing but in more apocalyptic detail). Furthermore, to the degree that John makes use of the OT, he would also be conscious of developing the ideas of the earlier prophets. Consequently, John likely would have understood his own recording of the clear OT references in his work to be the result either of (1) an intentional activity by God in revealing OT related visions to him, or (2) his own intentional activity in using the OT to describe further the visions or auditions that he experienced. Whichever is the case, John would have considered himself as recording and interpreting under divine prophetic inspiration (note again the texts cited at the beginning of this paragraph, in addition to which see also the "hearing-Spirit" formula at the conclusion of each of the seven letters, as well as Rev. 19:9; 21:5; 22:6–7, 9, 18–19). Furthermore, the chain of associated texts in Revelation 1, 4–5, 13, and 17 discussed above, and evident elsewhere, confirms an intentional appeal to and use of the OT. This conclusion is enhanced by the evidence of the remainder of this chapter. The perspective of the authors of this chapter is aligned with John's own presuppositions about his revelatory experience and writing.

The Particular Ways That John Uses the Old Testament

As will become clear in the course of the following commentary, John makes use of the OT in a number of ways. Prophecies from the OT are fulfilled in Revelation, but they may be fulfilled in various ways. None of these are prefaced with any kind of fulfillment formula, so we may refer to them as informal direct prophetic-fulfillment uses. Some are relatively straightforward, such as the promise that Christ will come again in Rev. 1:7, quoting Zech. 12:10 (though for qualifications of this passage, see Beale 1999a: 196–99). Others may be fulfilled, but with an "eschatological enhancement." Thus, whereas Ezekiel is led to a mountain and sees a vision of a renewed but recognizable temple, John is led to a mountain and sees a mammoth garden-city like a temple that apparently dwarfs the earlier vision. A particular feature of Revelation is the universalization of prophetic fulfillment. Designations or descriptions ("all the tribes of the earth will mourn over him," "his people") and promises (ruling over the nations, restoration and the end-time temple) once associated exclusively with Israel are now

seen to apply to God's people from every nation (see, respectively, Rev. 1:7; 21:3; 2:26–28; 7:9–17; 21:1–22:5).

John often uses the OT analogically. In this respect, he is intent on placing an OT text in a comparative relationship to something in his book, usually well-known persons, places, and events. The pictures undergo creative changes (expansions, condensations, supplemental imagery, etc.) and, of course, are applied to different historical situations. Nevertheless, a key idea in the OT context is usually carried over as the main characteristic or principle to be applied in the NT situation. Therefore, even though John handles these OT figures with creative freedom, almost always these pictures broadly retain an essential OT association and convey principles of continuity between the OT and the NT (so Cambier 1955: 116–20).

The following is a sampling of some analogies with a brief description of the primary point of correspondence or continuity:

(1) *Judgment*—theophanies introducing judgment (Isa. 6; Ezek. 1; Dan. 7; Rev. 4–5), books of judgment (Ezek. 2; Dan. 7; 12; Rev. 5:1–5 and Ezek. 2; Rev. 10), lion from Judah exercising judgment (Gen. 4:9; Rev. 5:5), "Lord of lords and King of kings" exercising judgment (Dan. 4:37 LXX; Rev. 17:14; 19:16), horsemen as divine agents of judgment (Zech. 1; 6; Rev. 6:1–8), exodus plagues inflicting judgment (Exod. 8–12; Rev. 8:6–12; 16:1–14), locusts as agents of judgment (Joel 1–2; Rev. 9:7–10), prophets giving testimony through judgment (Exod. 7:17; 1 Kings 17:1; Rev. 11:6), "Babylon" judged by God in "one hour" (Dan. 4:17a LXX; Rev. 18:10, 17, 19).

(2) *Tribulation and persecution of God's people*—ten days of tribulation (Dan. 1:12; Rev. 2:10), three-and-a-half years of tribulation (Dan. 7:25; 12:7; Rev. 11:2; 12:1; 13:5), Sodom, Egypt, and Jerusalem as infamous places where persecution occurs (Gen. 19:5–9; Exod. 1:8–22; Matt. 23:27; Rev. 11:8), persecuting rulers symbolized as beasts (Dan. 7; Rev. 11–13; 17) and "Babylon the Great" (Dan. 4:30, etc.; Rev. 14:18; 16:19; 17:5; 18:2).

(3) *Seductive, idolatrous teaching*—Balaam (Num. 25; 31:16; Rev. 2:14) and Jezebel (1 Kings 16:31; 2 Kings 9:22; Rev. 2:20–23).

(4) *Divine protection*—the tree of life (Gen. 2:9; Rev. 2:7; 22:2, 14, 19), the "sealed" Israel-

ites (Ezek. 9; Rev. 7:2–8), the wings of the eagle (Exod. 19:4; Deut. 32:11; Rev. 12:14).

(5) *Victorious battle of God's people over the enemy*—Armageddon (Zech. 2:11; Rev. 16:16 [19:19]; cf. Gog and Magog in Ezek. 38:1–39:16; Rev. 20:8).

(6) *Apostasy*—the harlot (Ezek. 16:15, etc.; Rev. 17).

(7) *The divine Spirit as the power for God's people*—Zech. 4:1–6; Rev. 1:12–20; 11:4.

Some analogies are repeated in the book and creatively developed in different ways, though always anchored in some significant manner to the broad parameters of the OT context.

It is also viable to consider that there are OT texts that John understands as prophetic but that do not appear as such in the OT. These uses also are not part of formal OT quotations (with introductory formulae), but are in the form of allusions. It is worth considering whether parts of certain OT historical narratives are viewed as indirect typological prophecies. Many of the OT passages listed above in the discussion of analogical uses are potential candidates in this category. That is, are all of these texts merely analogies? We have already found that the essence of the analogies has to do with a basic correspondence of meaning between OT prophecy or historical narrative and something in the NT. It is the historical material in the OT that has the potential to be considered as "types" for various things in the NT. Some of these OT historical elements have also undergone an escalation, even a universalization, under John's hand (e.g., the church as a "kingdom of priests" [1:6], the seven golden lampstands [1:12], and the exodus plagues [16:1–21]). Perhaps there was a prophetic rationale in escalating these historical texts. At any rate, such uses are worth further inquiry in this regard, especially against the background of John's and the NT's awareness that the "latter days" had been inaugurated, that the church was the latter-day Israel, and that the whole OT pointed toward this climax of salvation history (for language of inaugurated eschatology, see Mark 1:15; Acts 2:17; Gal. 4:4; 1 Cor. 10:11; 2 Cor. 6:2; 1 Tim. 4:1; 2 Tim. 3:1; 1 Pet. 1:20; Heb. 1:2; 9:26; James 5:3; 1 John 2:18; Jude 18; Rev. 1:1, 19; 4:1; 22:6, 10). The precedent of overt typological-prophetic uses in Matthew, Hebrews, and elsewhere in the NT should leave open the

same possibility in Revelation. Indeed, such typological uses definitely can be found in Revelation (e.g., see commentary on Rev. 3:7–8 below).

One can even find inverted or ironic uses of the OT in Revelation. For example, promises given to Israel, who are prophesied to be persecuted by the nations, are now ironically applied to and understood to be fulfilled in Gentile believers persecuted by Israel (Rev. 3:9). Finally, the imagery of the book is furnished almost exclusively from the OT. The exodus plagues, now universalized through the judgments of the trumpets and bowls, form the background for the end-time woes upon the earth; the vision of four living creatures worshiping God in heaven combines images from Ezekiel and Isaiah; the association of stars and angels (Rev. 1:20) hearkens back to OT texts such as Judg. 5:20. Examples could be multiplied.

As is partly apparent already in this introductory discussion, John uses OT themes of creation, covenant faithfulness, end-time redemption, and judgment, which lie at the heart of the book of Revelation (e.g., for the latter two themes, see Fekkes [1994: 70–103], who conducts in-depth discussion of these kinds of uses of the OT throughout). Likewise, among other themes that occur are that of "the day of the Lord" and holy war. These themes may involve directly prophetic themes, indirect typological themes, mere analogies, or inverted uses.

John sometimes uses segments of OT Scripture as a literary prototype on which to pattern his creative compositions. Such modeling can become apparent by (1) observing a thematic-structure that is uniquely traceable to only one OT context, or (2) discerning a cluster of clear allusions from the same OT context. Sometimes both are observable, thus enhancing the clarity of the OT prototype. It has been argued in some depth that broad patterns from Daniel (especially chaps. 2; 7) have been followed in Rev. 1; 4–5; 13; 17, the former two sections in particular exhibiting both allusive clusters and structural outlines from segments of Daniel (for thorough discussions of these uses of the OT, see Beale 1984: 154–305, 313–20; for debate and discussion about some of these uses, see Beale 1999b: 75–93).

In a somewhat similar vein, Goulder (1981: 343–49) has argued that broad portions of Ezekiel have been the dominant influence on at least twelve major sections of Revelation (Rev. 4; 5; 6:1–8; 6:12–7:1; 7:2–8; 8:1–5; 10:1–7; 14:6–12; 17:1–6; 18:9–24; 20:7–10; 21:22). Goulder (1981: 353–54) observes that these uses of Ezekiel are a dominant influence on the structure of Revelation, since they are placed to a marked extent in the same order as they occur in Ezekiel itself (though he proposes a liturgical rather than a literary explanation to account better for the parallel order of Ezekiel and Revelation). Virtually identical to Goulder, though not positing a liturgical background, is Vogelgesang, who has gone so far as to conclude that John used Ezekiel as the model for the book's overall structure and this "is the key to understanding the message of the book altogether" (1985: 394 [see also 16, 66–71]). Others have also recognized Ezekiel's influence, especially in Rev. 20–22, where the order of events appears to have been taken from Ezek. 37–48. The broad structure of the new Jerusalem in Rev. 21:12–22:5 is based on the vision of Ezek. 40–48, which prophesies the pattern of the final temple (chaps. 40–44), as well as the arrangement of the eschatological city and divisions of the land around the temple compound (chaps. 45–48). Revelation 21:12–22:5 further interprets the yet future fulfillment of Ezekiel by collapsing temple, city, and land into one end-time picture portraying the one reality of God's communion with his people.

There is a consensus that the plagues of the "trumpets" in Rev. 8:6–12 and those of the bowls in 16:1–9 follow the paradigm of the exodus plagues (Exod. 8:12), although creatively reworked and applied.

All of the foregoing proposed OT models have woven within them allusions from other parts of the same OT book and from elsewhere in the OT corpus, and many of these are based upon common themes, pictures, catchphrases, and so on. Often these other references serve as interpretive expansions of an OT prototype. They are used in an "already and not yet" sense to indicate either indirect typological fulfillment or fulfillment of direct verbal prophecy. Sometimes they refer exclusively to fulfillment yet in the future.

Attention also should be directed to what might be called John's stylistic use of OT language. It has long been recognized that Revelation contains a multitude of grammatical solecisms.

Charles claimed that Revelation contained more grammatical irregularities than any other Greek document of the ancient world. He accounted for this with his famous dictum, "While he writes in Greek, he thinks in Hebrew, and the thought has naturally affected the vehicle of expression" (Charles 1920: 1:cxliii).

But was this intentional on the author's part or an unconscious by-product of his Semitic mind? It seems that his grammatical "howlers" are deliberate attempts to express Semitisms and septuagintalisms in his Greek, the closest analogy being that of the LXX translations, especially Aquila (Sweet 1979: 16; see also S. Thompson 1985: 108 and *passim*). The fact that most of the time the author does keep the rules further points to the solecisms being intentional.

Why did John write this way? Sometimes his purpose was deliberately to create a "biblical" effect in the hearer and thus to demonstrate the solidarity of his work with that of the divinely inspired OT Scriptures (Sweet 1979: 16). A polemical purpose may also have been included. John may have been expressing the idea that OT truth via the church as the new Israel was uncompromisingly penetrating the Gentile world and would continue to do so until the final parousia.

It may be that the best way to approach these grammatical solecisms is to see many of them being used as signals for the presence of OT allusions (for the full argument, see Beale 1999b: 318–55). Apparently unrecognized for the most part previously, a significant number of these irregularities occur in the midst of OT allusions. Accordingly, a number of the expressions appear irregular because John is carrying over the exact or nearly exact grammatical form of the OT wording or intentionally reproducing a septuagintalism in order to create syntactical dissonance. This dissonance appears to be one of the ways that John gets the readers' attention, causing them to pause and focus on the phrase and to recognize more readily the presence of an OT allusion.

Perhaps one of the reasons for the high degree of OT influence in Revelation is that John could think of no better way to describe some of his visions, which were difficult to explain, than with the language already used by the OT prophets to describe similar visions.

A Principal Hermeneutical Concern: Old over New, or Old into New?

There are three basic views regarding John's use of the OT. The first is that John simply grabs whatever lies at hand in the OT to make his own theological pronouncements. This, however, fits poorly within the first-century Jewish milieu, where the integrity of a movement such as early Christianity would be judged by its coherence with the OT message. The two more viable options recognize that John uses the OT with utmost care and concern. Given this common ground, these two views can be distinguished as follows: should Revelation be interpreted in the light of the OT, or should the OT be interpreted in the light of Revelation? Put more pointedly, Which body of material takes interpretive precedence?

One typical evangelical version of the first scenario is that Revelation provides supplementary information for the events (particularly events involving Israel) foretold in the prophets, which are taken in a more or less "literal" fashion. Thus, for example, when the interpreter comes to Rev. 20, the promises of physical blessings to Israel in the Holy Land ought to be read into the text of Revelation, even though John makes no explicit mention of these things. In the second approach, John is seen as interpreting the promises to (ethnic) Israel and understanding them to have begun fulfillment in the experience of the Jewish and Gentile church of the new covenant, the true eschatological people of God. Of course, even in the second approach the OT remains the foundation for John's proclamation, and it is assumed that John fully respects the theological contours of OT texts in interpretively developing them. Indeed, the reader unfamiliar with the OT is hard pressed to make any sense of Revelation. In this respect, one certainly should read Revelation in the light of the OT, but not in a pedantically "literal" fashion. Nevertheless, while the old interprets the new, the new also interprets the old—Scripture interprets Scripture. In terms of the "cash value" of a given prophecy, this approach argues that John ought to have the final word, since he is interpreting from a redemptive-historical stance of greater progressive revelation and "unpacks" the earlier revelation. This is merely to say that "progressive revelation" is crucial in understanding the OT and John's book, as it is for all of the NT. On the other hand, of course, such "progressive revelation" must not be separated from prior revelation, since it builds on and develops the earlier revelation with hermeneutical integrity.

Conclusion

John's use of given OT texts must be examined on a case-by-case basis, with careful attention to the contexts of the book of Revelation and the OT texts themselves (for an expansion of the preceding introductory section, see Beale 1999a: 76–99; 1999b: 60–128, as well as the numerous references to other secondary sources therein).

The following commentary seeks to investigate as much as possible, within the limits of this overall project, the OT references in Revelation, paying attention to the contexts of the OT passages and those in Revelation (for an expansion of the discussions throughout the following commentary on Revelation, as well as for many OT references that could not be discussed at all due to space limitations, see Beale 1999a).

The Prologue: Rev. 1:1–20

Chapter 1 introduces the book as a "revelation of Jesus Christ," while the greeting from John to the churches marks it as a letter. It concludes with John on the island of Patmos, where he receives the inaugural vision of the glorious risen Christ.

1:1

The word *apokalypsis* ("apocalypse") is part of an allusion to Dan. 2, since the whole of 1:1 is patterned after the broad structure of Dan. 2:28–30, 45–47 (cf. Θ), where *apokalyptō* ("reveal") appears five times (cf. also 2:19, 22), *ha dei genesthai* ("what must come to pass") three times, and *sēmainō* ("signify") twice (cf. also 2:23 LXX). The words *en tachei* ("quickly") are a conscious substitution for Daniel's "in the latter days" (e.g., Dan. 2:28) and connote the definite, imminent time of fulfillment. But whereas Daniel expected this fulfillment to occur in the distant future, the "latter days," John expects it to begin in his own generation. Indeed, it has already started to happen, as the references to beginning fulfillment of OT prophecy in chapter 1 bear out (cf. 1:5, 7, 13, 16).

The use of *sēmainō* in Dan. 2:45 LXX indicates the symbolic nature of the Babylonian king's dream (a statue symbolizing four world empires, somewhat like a political cartoon drawing). The appeal to this Daniel reference in the title and programmatic statement of the entire book indicates that symbolic vision is going to be part of the warp and woof of the means of communication throughout Revelation. Thus, rather than producing the expectation that the majority of the book will be "literal" in nature, this verse is asserting that the expectation is for most of the material to be understood symbolically (on which, see Beale 1999b: 295–99). This is one among a number of reasons that chapters 4–21 especially should be viewed predominantly as symbolic communication (particularly the visions of seals, trumpets, and bowls [on which, see Beale 1999a: 50–69]).

1:4a

The number "seven" is the favorite number of Revelation. In the OT the number was used to denote "fullness" (e.g., Lev. 4–16; 26:18–28). The idea of completeness originates from the account of creation in Gen. 1, where six days of creating are followed by the consummation. It is thus likely that the seven churches of Asia function representatively for the whole church.

The description of God as "the one who is and was and is to come" is an interpretation of the name "YHWH," based on reflection on Exod. 3:14 together with twofold and threefold temporal descriptions of God in Isaiah (cf. Isa. 41:4; 43:10; 44:6; 48:12), which themselves likely are reflections on the divine name in Exod. 3:14. The name in Exod. 3:14 was also expanded in a threefold manner by later Jewish tradition, most notably *Tg. Ps.-J.* Deut. 32:39, "I am he who is and who was, and I am he who will be." The first element, "the one who is" (*ho ōn*), derives from Exod. 3:14 LXX (*egō eimi ho ōn*), and although the preposition *apo* calls for the genitive, John keeps *ho ōn* in the nominative in order to highlight it as an allusion to Exodus (for a full account of the phrase, see McDonough 1999). It is possible that John employs such kinds of constructions here and elsewhere as Hebraisms (in Hebrew the noun in the indirect cases is not inflected [see Charles 1920: 1:13]) in order to create a "biblical" effect upon the reader and so to show the solidarity of

his work with that of God's revelation in the OT (for further examples of such kinds of intended solecisms, see commentary on Rev. 1:5; 2:20; 3:12; 9:14 in Beale 1999a; see also Beale 1997b).

1:4b

This prophetic epistle is also from "the seven spirits who are before the throne." The wording is likely a figurative designation of the Holy Spirit, expressing the diversity of God's work in the church and the world. The expression "seven spirits" is part of a paraphrased allusion to Zech. 4:2–7 (as is evident from 4:5; 5:6), which identified the "seven lamps" as God's one Spirit, whose role was to bring about God's grace (cf. Zech. 4:7: "Grace, grace to it") in Israel through the successful completion of the rebuilding of the temple (see commentary on Rev. 1:12; 4:5; 5:6 below). It is possible that Isa. 11:2–10 LXX is included along with Zechariah in the background of the "seven spirits," since this text is alluded to in 5:5–6 (cf. the "root" of Isa. 11:1 in 5:5, and the mention of "the seven spirits of God" in 5:6 [see Farrer 1964: 61]; note also the use of Isa. 11:4 in 1:16 [for agreement about the presence of both OT influences, see Skrinjar 1935: 114–36]).

1:5

Psalm 88:28, 38 LXX (89:27, 37 ET) is the basis for the statement that Christ is "faithful witness," "firstborn," and "ruler of the kings of the earth," since all three of the phrases uniquely occur there (cf. Isa. 55:4). The immediate context of the psalm speaks of David as an "anointed" king who will reign over all his enemies and whose seed will be established on his throne forever (Ps. 88:20–38 LXX [89:19–37 ET]; Judaism understood Ps. 89:28 messianically [*Midr. Rab.* Exod. 19:7; perhaps *Pesiq. Rab.* 34:2]). Although the "faithful witness" in Ps. 88:38 LXX refers to the unending witness of the moon, this is by way of comparison to the unending reign of David's seed on his throne, and accordingly it is applied here to Christ (on "faithful witness," see also Isa. 43:10–13). John thus views Jesus as the ideal Davidic king, whose death and resurrection have resulted in his eternal kingship and in the kingship of his "beloved" children (cf. 5:5b). "The firstborn" refers to Christ's privileged position as a result of the resurrection from the dead (Ps. 89:27–37, developing this idea from 2 Sam. 7:13–16; Ps. 2:7–8).

Also in 1:5 is an allusion to Christ's priestly function ("loosed us from our sins by his blood"), since OT priests accomplished sanctification and atonement for Israel by sprinkling the blood of sacrificial animals (cf. Exod. 24:8; Lev. 16:14–19; see Loenertz 1947: 43). This may be a typological fulfillment of Israel's redemption from Egypt by the blood of the Passover lamb, as is evident from the clear allusion to Exod. 19:6 in 1:6. Here, as in Hebrews, Christ is portrayed as both a priest and a sacrifice.

1:6

The phrase "a kingdom, priests" is based on the similar phrase in Exod. 19:6 (*basileion hierateuma* [cf. MT]). There is some ambiguity about whether this phrase in Exodus is to be understood as a "royal priesthood" or as a "priestly kingdom," but the difference is insignificant, since both can include reference to kingly and priestly elements (for discussion of alternative meanings in Exod. 19:6; Rev. 1:6, see Gelston 1959; Dumbrell 1985: 124–26, 159–60).

The expression from Exodus is a summary of God's purpose for Israel. This primarily meant that they were to be a kingly and priestly nation mediating Yahweh's light of salvific revelation by witnessing to the Gentiles (e.g., Isa. 43:10–13), a purpose that the OT prophets repeatedly observed went unfulfilled by Israel (e.g., Isa. 40–55). The priestly nature of the whole nation of Israel was also shown by the fact that Moses consecrates them in precisely the same manner as Aaron and his sons, by the sprinkling of sacrificial blood (cf. Exod. 29:10–21 with Exod. 24:4–8). The appointing of all the saints to be priests in 1:6 probably draws from this background (so Düsterdieck 1980: 124). Like OT priests, the entire people of God now have unmediated access to God's presence (I. T. Beckwith 1919: 430) because Christ has removed the obstacle of sin by his substitutionary blood (Vanhoye 1986: 289). Such unmediated access receives some qualifications elsewhere in the NT, particularly in the sense that Christ is the high-priestly mediator in the heavenly temple for all of God's people (cf., e.g., Heb. 8–10; for further qualifications of this "unmediated access," see Beale 2004 [the chapters on the temple in the NT]).

1:7

This verse is composed of two OT citations. The first is from Dan. 7:13, which in its OT context refers to the enthronement of the "son of man" over all the nations (cf. Dan. 7:14) after God's judgment of evil empires (Dan. 7:9–12). The following citation is from Zech. 12:10, which in its context pertains to the end-time period when God will defeat the enemy nations around Israel and when Israel will be redeemed after repenting of their sinful rejection of God and his messenger (i.e., "the one they have pierced").

The identical combination of Dan. 7 and Zech. 12 in Matt. 24:30 may have influenced John to do the same here (the same combination occurs also in Justin Martyr, *Dial.* 14.8; Matt. 24:30 may also refer to repentance, in light of 24:31). That the one "mourned" for is compared to a "firstborn son" in Zech. 12:10 is also not a coincidence, since the same word (*prōtotokos*) is used to describe the king in Ps. 88:28 LXX (89:27 ET) and Jesus in Rev. 1:5.

The Zechariah text has been altered in two significant ways. The phrases "every eye" and "of the earth" (cf. Zech. 14:17) have been added to universalize its original meaning. This probably is a reference not to every person without exception, but rather to all among the nations who believe, as is indicated clearly by 5:9; 7:9 (cf. the plural "tribes" as a universal reference to unbelievers in 11:9; 13:7; 14:6). The word *gē* ("earth, land") cannot be a limited reference to the land of Israel; rather, it is a universal denotation, since this is the only meaning that the phrase *pasai hai phylai tēs gēs* ("all the tribes of the earth") has in the OT (LXX: Gen. 12:3; 28:14; Ps. 71:17; Zech. 14:17). The phrase "all the tribes of Israel" occurs repeatedly in the OT (approximately twenty-five times), which highlights the different wording of Rev. 1:7b. This implies an extension of the OT concept of Israel, since what applied to that nation in Zech. 12 is now transferred to the peoples of the earth, who assume the role of repentant Israel. Some believe that the Zechariah quotation is utilized contrary to its original intention to denote the grief of the nations over their impending judgment. However, John typically adheres to and consistently develops the contextual ideas of his OT references, and proposed exceptions to this rule must bear the burden of proof. The nations in 1:7b mourn not over themselves, but over Jesus, which fits better into an understanding of repentance than judgment.

That the "son of man" figure is applied to Jesus twice in the space of only seven verses (1:7, 13) is highly appropriate, since the "son of man" in Dan. 7 was a corporate representative for the saints with respect both to suffering trial and to ruling, and this title was used by Jesus in the Gospels to indicate his veiled, inaugurated kingship amidst suffering. In *Midr. Ps.* 2:9, Dan. 7:13–14 is interpreted as referring corporately to the nation of Israel, though other sectors of Judaism applied it to an individual messianic figure (e.g., *4 Ezra* 13:1–39; *1 En.* 37–71; *2 Bar.* 36–40). Jesus in his present identification as "son of man" (1:13) and the progressive nature of the present tense in 1:7a ("he is coming") suggest that here the Dan. 7:13 prophecy is seen as beginning in the first century, continuing throughout the church age, and culminating at the very end of history.

1:8

The "Alpha and Omega" merism could well have been formulated through reflection on the similar clauses in Isa. 41–48, since "the First and the Last" in 1:17b is based on the same Isaianic wording (cf. Isa. 41:4; 44:6; 48:12) and since the threefold phrase of 1:8b also has a link with Isaiah (see commentary on Rev. 1:4a above ["the one who is and the one who was and the one who is coming"]). God, who transcends time, guides the entire course of history because he stands as sovereign over its beginning and end. The phrase "says the Lord God Almighty" (*pantokratōr*), which is repeatedly used by the prophets (e.g., Haggai, Zechariah, Malachi), likewise here represents God's sovereignty.

1:10–11

The introduction of John's commission is coined in the language of the prophet Ezekiel's repeated rapture in the Spirit, thus identifying John's revelation with that of the OT prophets (cf. Ezek. 2:2; 3:12, 14, 24; 11:1; 43:5). His prophetic authority is enforced by the description of the voice that he heard as "a great voice as a trumpet," evoking the same voice that Moses heard when Yahweh revealed himself to him on Mount Sinai (Exod. 19:16, 19–20). This idea is emphasized further by the command to "write in a book," which is

reflective of the charge given by Yahweh to his prophetic servants to communicate to Israel the revelation that they had received (LXX: Exod. 17:14; Isa. 30:8; Jer. 37:2; 39:44; Tob. 12:20). Note that all such commissions in the prophets were commands to write testaments of judgment against Israel (LXX: Isa. 30:8; Jer. 37:2; 39:44; cf. also in the LXX: Exod. 34:27; Isa. 8:1; Jer. 43:2; Hab. 2:2).

1:12

The first image that John sees in his initial vision is that of "seven golden lampstands" (1:12b), which has its general background in Exod. 25; 37; Num. 8, but which is drawn more specifically from Zech. 4:2, 10. This is borne out by three observations: (1) the mention of "seven spirits" in 1:4 (cf. Zech. 4:6); (2) the lampstand vision of 1:12b is interpreted in 1:20, which follows the same vision-interpretation pattern of Zech. 4:2, 10; (3) clear allusions to Zech. 4:2, 10 are found in 4:5; 5:6 in close association with allusions to Daniel.

The "seven lampstands" represent the church (cf. 1:20). In Zech. 4:2–6 the lampstand with its seven lamps is a figurative synecdoche by which part of the temple furniture stands for the whole temple. This by extension also represents faithful Israel (cf. Zech. 4:6–9), which is required to live "'not by [earthly] might nor by power, but by my Spirit' says the LORD" (Zech. 4:6). The lampstand in the tabernacle and temple was placed directly in front of the holy of holies, which contained the glorious presence of God, and the light that emanated from it apparently represented the presence of God (see Num. 8:1–4; in Exod. 25:30–31 the lampstand is mentioned directly after the "bread of the Presence"; see also 40:4; 1 Kings 7:48–49). Likewise, the lamps on the lampstand in Zech. 4:2–5 are interpreted in 4:6 as representing God's presence or Spirit, which was to empower Israel (= "the lampstand") to finish rebuilding the temple, despite resistance (cf. Zech. 4:6–9). So the new Israel, the church, as a "lampstand" is a part of the temple and is to draw its power from the Spirit, the divine presence, before God's throne in its drive to stand against the resistance of the world. This is highlighted by 1:4 and chapter 4.

The unusual expression "see the voice" may be related to Exod. 20:18, where "all the people saw the voice . . . and the voice of the trumpet" (cf. in the LXX: Ezek. 3:12–13; 43:5–6; Dan. 7:11).

1:13–16

An analysis of OT allusions in 1:13–16 shows that the predominant features of the "son of man" are drawn from Dan. 7; 10, with other texts contributing to the depiction. Most commentators agree that the significance of this is that Christ is portrayed as a kingly and priestly figure, since the figure in the two Daniel texts has the same features. Although the clothing in 1:13 could also resemble kingly attire, its use here evokes the image of a priest because of the temple atmosphere of the lampstands in 1:12 and also because of the angels coming out of the heavenly temple, who wear the same clothing in 15:5–8. The ambiguity may be due to the possibility that both a king and a priest are in mind, which has precedent in the two figures of Zech. 4:3, 11–14 (see commentary on Rev. 11:4 below; cf. 1 Macc. 10:88–89; 14:30, 32–47).

The transferal of the attributes from the judicial figure of the Ancient of Days (cf. Dan. 7:9–12) to Christ also evokes his role as latter-day divine judge, which is clear from 19:12. This is underscored further by the observation that Dan. 10 is also behind the "son of man" image: the primary purpose of the heavenly man in Dan. 10 is to reveal the divine decree that Israel's persecutors would assuredly be judged (see 10:21–12:13). Daniel 10:6 even depicts the "son of man" as having "eyes . . . like flaming torches." The application of the attributes from the Ancient of Days to Christ also points to the eternal life that he has together with his Father (so Sickenberger 1942: 49).

The portrayal of the "son of man's" head and hair (1:14a) is taken from that of the Ancient of Days in Dan. 7:9, while the description of his eyes and feet again follow Dan. 10:6 LXX. The mention of the "furnace" that follows (1:15b) echoes the description from Dan. 3:26 (3:93 Θ), although Ezek. 1:27 perhaps also is in view. The conclusion of 1:15 mentions the roar of the "son of man's" voice, in the same way as Dan. 10:6, although the actual language describing the voice is taken from Ezek. 1:24; 43:2 MT, where God's voice is compared to the roar of many waters, so that this enhances the portrait so far of Christ as a divine being.

Like the seven lampstands, the number of "seven stars" may also have arisen in part from the "seven lamps" of Zech. 4. In later Judaism the Zech. 4:2 lampstand is said to symbolize the righteous in Israel and is equated with the wise who will shine like the stars in Dan. 12:3 (*Midr. Rab.* Lev. 30:2; *Sipre Deut.* Piska 10; *Pesiq. Rab Kah.* Piska 27:2; *Pesiq. Rab.* Piska 51:4). McNamara (1966: 197–99) sees the Palestinian Targum to Exod. 40:4 as the background for 1:20a, where the "seven lamps" of the tabernacle are viewed as "corresponding to the seven stars which resemble the just that shine unto eternity in their righteousness," the latter phrase being a clear allusion to Dan. 12:3.

The fact that the stars are explicitly identified with angels in 1:20a (cf. the apparent identification of stars and angels in, e.g., Judg. 5:20) does not preclude the influence of Daniel. The angels may be seen as representatives of the people of God, in keeping with texts such as Dan. 10:13; 12:1.

The "sharp two-edged sword" proceeding from Jesus' mouth is based on the prophecies of Isa. 11:4; 49:2, which add further to his depiction as the fulfillment of the eschatological judge. The last description of the "son of man" as having a face "like the sun shining in its strength" (1:16c) still follows the Dan. 10 outline, although the actual wording is derived from Judg. 5:31 LXX (B). The link with Judges may lie in the descriptions of the bright appearance of the victorious Israelite warrior in Judg. 5:31 and of the "son of man" in Dan. 10, and the immediately preceding portrayal of Jesus as a warrior with a sword.

1:17

In 1:17 is exhibited the same fourfold pattern found in, for example, Dan. 10:8–20: (1) the prophet observes a vision, (2) falls on his face in fear, (3) subsequently is strengthened by a heavenly being, and (4) then receives further revelation from him, which is introduced by a form of *laleō* ("speak"). This is another clue identifying John and his message with OT prophetic authority (cf. 1:10).

The "son of man" calls himself the "first and last," a clear reference to the self-predications of Yahweh in Isa. 41:4; 44:6; 48:12. These texts are linked by catchword phrases and common pictures: (1) the Isa. 41:4 context contains the picture of God's servant defeating the enemy with a sword (41:2), and the key phrase "do not fear" immediately followed by divine words of comfort that God will "strengthen" and "uphold" the righteous one with his right hand (41:10); (2) the Isa. 44:6 context also has the phrase "do not fear" (cf. 44:2); (3) Isa. 48:12 is directly followed by a picture like that of Isa. 41:10; Dan. 12:6–7; Rev. 1:17: "Surely, my hand founded the earth, and my right hand spread out the heavens" (48:13). These common elements provided the associative bridge leading from the Dan. 10 picture of prophetic comfort to that of the three Isaiah passages concerning Yahweh's comfort of Israel. If, with some commentators, we link "the living one" (*ho zōn* [cf. the very similar *ho ōn* in 1:4]) in 1:18 with "the first and the last" in 1:17, we have a tripartite formula parallel to that used of God in 1:4. This would further underscore Christ's divine status (note also the expression "the one living unto the ages of the ages" in 1:18, which is repeatedly used for God in the OT [Deut. 32:40; Dan. 4:34 Θ; 12:7; Sir. 18:1]).

1:19

The third part of the formula in 1:19, like 1:1a, has been composed with terminology from Dan. 2 and should not be seen as the last part of a three-fold literal sequential chronology of the book. The phrase *meta tauta* ("after these things") may have an end-time nuance, since Dan. 2 employs the same phrase synonymously with *eschatōn tōn hēmerōn* ("latter days" [cf., similarly, the use of Joel 3:1 in Acts 2:17]). These "latter days" probably are to be viewed as having already begun in John's time (for the argument, see Beale 1999a: 152–70).

1:20

The expression *to mystērion* ("the mystery") occurs in the OT only in Daniel and twelve times in the Apocrypha. Since "mystery" occurs with an eschatological sense only in Daniel, its appearance in 1:20 in such a context confirms its link to Daniel. John's vision will depict the fulfillment of Daniel's prophecies concerning the latter days (on the significance of "mystery" here, see Beale 1999b: 255–59).

Revelation 2

Chapter 2 introduces the first four messages (recalling that the genre of Revelation includes

the notion that the book is a letter; on the genre of Revelation, see Beale 1999a: 37–43). These messages are sent to the churches in Asia Minor: Ephesus, which is zealous for truth but has "lost its first love"; small but faithful Smyrna; Pergamum, which has endured persecution faithfully but is in danger of succumbing to compromise with idolatry; and Thyatira, where similar compromise is being condoned by the prophetess "Jezebel."

2:7

The admonitory phrase "the one having ears, let him hear" is based on virtually the same wording found in the Synoptics, which itself alludes to Isa. 6:9–10 (cf. also Jer. 5:21; Ezek. 3:27; 12:2). Part of the point of the exhortation in Isa. 6 was a warning to the remnant not to participate in idolatry, and the context of Rev. 2–3 indicates that this warning still applies (cf., e.g., the letters to Pergamum and Thyatira; see further Beale 1997a).

"To eat of the tree of life, which is in the paradise of God" is alluded to again at the conclusion of the book as a picture of forgiveness and consequent experience of God's intimate presence (22:2–4). The same end-time hope is referred to with virtually identical language in several early Jewish texts (see *T. Levi* 18:10–11; *Pss. Sol.* 14:2–3, 10; *4 Ezra* 8:52; *2 En.* 8:3–7; cf. also *1 En.* 25:4–7; *3 En.* 23:18; *4 Ezra* 2:12; *L.A.E.* 28:2–4; *Odes Sol.* 20:7). In Gen. 2–3, as here, the image of the "tree of life" together with the "paradise of God" symbolizes the life-giving presence of God, from which Adam and Eve are separated when they are cast out of the garden paradise (cf. 2:9; 3:23–25 LXX; Ezek. 28:13; 31:8–9).

2:10

The mention that the saints in Smyrna "will have ten days of tribulation" is an allusion to Dan. 1:12–15, where the "testing" of Daniel and his three friends for "ten days" is mentioned three times. The emphasis is on a fixed, limited period of suffering that those in Smyrna must endure in a similar manner to Daniel and his friends as they underwent trial and were tempted.

2:11

Those who suffer the "second death" will participate neither in the resurrection of the saints (cf. "second death" in *Tg. Jer.* 51:39, 57) nor in the life of the new world to come, but rather will experience unending punishment (cf. this sense of "second death" in *Tg. Deut.* 33:6; *Tg. Isa.* 22:14; 65:6, 15; see McNamara 1966: 117–25; Philo, *Rewards* 67–73; cf. also Rev. 19:20; 20:6, 14; 21:8).

2:14

Some within the church at Pergamum had compromised with the idolatrous society around them, and this is explained through reference to the compromising relationship that Balaam had with Israel as recorded in Numbers (cf. Num. 22:5–25:3; 31:8, 16). Israel was led to worship idols and commit immorality as a result of his deceitful counsel, and the church was being led in the same direction by the Nicolaitans. Balaam became proverbial for the false teacher who for financial gain influences believers to enter into relationships of compromising unfaithfulness. He is warned by God to stop and finally is punished for continuing to disobey (cf. Num. 22:7; Deut. 23:4; Neh. 13:2; 2 Pet. 2:14–16; Jude 5–12; Philo, *Moses* 1.264–314; *Migration* 114; see Ginzberg 1967: 3:361, 370). For the association of idolatry and fornication, see, for example, Acts 15:29; 21:25 (cf. Acts 15:20; Rev. 9:20–21).

The word *porneuō* ("fornicate") may have both a literal and a metaphorical idea, since it is employed in such a double manner in both Testaments, especially in the story of Baal-Peor, in which Israelites committed both physical fornication with foreign woman and spiritual fornication with their gods (cf. Num. 25:1 with 25:2–3). The emphasis probably is on spiritual fornication, which is further supported by the reference to Jezebel in 2:20 (on which, see commentary below), where it is shown that the spiritual or figurative sense of *porneia* (and its word group) as idol worship is the predominant use elsewhere in Revelation.

2:15–16

Balaam was threatened with being "killed by the sword" of "the angel of the Lord" if he continued to oppose Israel (Num. 22:23, 31; cf. Josh. 13:22). When he did not heed the warning, he was indeed "killed by the sword," which in Jewish tradition sealed his destiny of exclusion from the "world to come" (*b. Sanh.* 90a; 105a; *'Abot R. Nat.* 31b–32a). The Christians in Pergamum were threatened with judgment in a similar fashion.

The teachings of Balaam and the Nicolaitans are identified further by observing that the etymology of their names has essentially the same meaning: "Nicolaitan" (*nika laon*) means "overcomer of the people," and the rabbis conjectured that "Balaam" (*bl' 'm* or *blh 'm*) meant "consume the people" (e.g., *b. Sanh.* 105a); it could also be construed as "rule over the people" (*b'l 'm*). We have no further secure historical information on the precise identification of the Nicolaitans.

2:17a

Those who refuse to participate in the pagan feasts will be rewarded with participation in Christ's end-time feast, represented by the "manna," which presently is "hidden" but then will be revealed. The manna was an eschatological expectation also in Judaism (so *b. Ḥag.* 12b; *2 Bar.* 29:8; *Sib. Or.* 7:149; *Midr. Rab.* Eccles. 1:9; cf. Exod. 16:32–36 with 2 Macc. 2:4–7). This promise sometimes was addressed to those who did not worship idols (*Sib. Or.* Frag. 3:46–49). The manna given to Israel in the wilderness was also said to have been "hidden in the high heavens ... from the beginning" of creation (*Tg. Ps.-J.* Exod. 16:4, 15) and was ultimately to prosper Israel "at the end of days" (*Tg. Neof.* 8:16) (see Malina 1995: 75–77). The church has begun to taste this eschatological food, but not consummately.

2:17b

The "white stone" also enforces the idea of the "manna" as a heavenly salvific and end-time reward, since the OT describes the heavenly manna as a white bdellium stone in appearance (cf. Exod. 16:31; Num. 11:7; see Chilton 1987: 110). The LXX of Num. 11:7 compares it to "the appearance of rock-crystal." In *b. Yoma* 75a it is said that the manna was "round ... and white like a pearl." This reward probably had already begun to be enjoyed, but its consummation was yet to come. The white color of the stone portrays the righteousness of the saints in not compromising and "soiling" themselves (cf. 3:4).

2:17c

To know someone's name in the ancient world and the OT often meant to enter into an intimate relationship with that person and to share in that person's character or power. To be given a new name was an indication of a new status. When God's name was applied to a place in the OT (notably the temple [see, e.g., Deut. 12:5, 11]), it often indicated that his presence was there. When someone gave a name to another person or thing, it meant that the giver possessed that person or thing (for these associations of "name" see, e.g., *TDNT* 5:253–58, 277; Eichrodt 1967: 2:40–45, 310–11; Jacob 1958: 82–85; Johnson 1981: 442). These connotations of "name" from the OT probably are in view here to one degree or another.

The description of the name as "new" is an allusion to the prophecies of Isa. 62:2; 65:15 about Israel's new standing in the future (cf. *kaleō* ["call"] + *onoma kainon* ["new name"] in both texts). There, the "new name" designates Israel's future kingly status (62:3), restoration to Yahweh's covenantal presence (62:4a [cf. the same significance for "name" in 56:4–8; 65:15–19]) and especially new "married" relationship with the Lord (cf. 62:4b–5, which also refers to Israel as a "bride" and God as the "bridegroom"; also note the "new name" given to the posterity of Levi in *T. Levi* 8:12–14). In sum, the "new name" in 2:17c represents the eschatalogical new identity of the redeemed in the new heaven and new earth.

2:20

Jezebel incited King Ahab and Israel to compromise and "fornicate" by worshiping Baal (cf. 1 Kings 16:31–32; 21:25–26; 2 Kings 8:18; 9:22). Similarly, the false teachers in the church were arguing that some degree of participation in idolatrous aspects of Thyatiran culture was permissible. Although Baal worship, and some pagan worship in John's day, included literal fornication, the emphasis on spiritual fornication here is supported by 2 Kings 9:22 LXX, where *porneia* ("immorality") is applied to Jezebel to emphasize her efforts to entice Israel into syncretistic idolatry (cf. 1 Kings 16:31–32). The following equation of *porneuō* and *porneia* in 2:20–21 with *moicheuō* ("to commit adultery") shows that a more general spiritual idea is included, since in 2:22 this clearly connotes the metaphorical sense of believers married to Christ who are flirting with spiritual intercourse with pagan gods. The spiritual sense of *porneia* as idol worship is attested in the LXX also in Wis. 14:12 ("For the devising of idols was the beginning of fornication [*porneia*]"); Ps. 105:39 (106:39 ET); Isa. 47:10; Nah. 3:4. The spiritual nuance is also borne out in the light of John's figurative use of *porneuō* (and

its word group) elsewhere in the book (thirteen times outside of chap. 2 in contrast to the literal sense only in 9:21; 21:8; 22:15, though even the last two are questionable).

2:23

Jezebel's followers are also called her "children," and their tribulation will involve their death, which was also the punishment of Jezebel and Ahab's seventy sons because of his sin against Naboth at Jezebel's instigation (cf. 1 Kings 21:17–29; 2 Kings 9:30–37; 10:1–11 [for the phrase "kill with death," see Ezek. 33:27 LXX]).

God's knowledge of "minds and hearts" (*nephrous kai kardias*) is a common idea for his ability to judge righteously (LXX: Ps. 7:10 [7:9 ET]; Jer. 11:20; 17:10; 20:12; cf. Rom. 8:27; 1 Thess. 2:4; also 1 Sam. 16:7). The same notion is expressed through the typical phrase "I [God] will give ... to each according to [his] works" (e.g., LXX: Ps. 27:4 [28:4 ET]; 61:13 [62:11 ET]; Prov. 24:12; Jer. 17:10; also Matt. 16:27; Rom. 2:6; 2 Cor. 11:15). Foremost in mind here is Jer. 17:10, since both expressions together appear only in that text. Furthermore, the statement in Jeremiah is especially suitable because it refers to God's judgment of those within the Israelite community who practice idolatry out of economic motives (see Jer. 17:3, 11; cf. 11:10–17, 20). Believers in the province of Asia may have been tempted to worship idols to maintain their status in local trade guilds, which often had pagan gods as patrons.

2:26–27

Concluding with the promise from Ps. 2:9 is fitting because Christ introduced himself at the beginning of the letter as "the Son of God" (2:18) a title derived from Ps. 2, which affirms further that he has already begun to fulfill the prophecy of the psalm. Whereas the LXX and Revelation have "shepherd" (*poimainō*), Ps. 2:9 MT has "smite." Either reading is possible from the unpointed Hebrew text. John may in fact have both meanings in mind: compare 19:15 (12:5?), where he uses *poimainō* to mean "judge" or "destroy" (cf. the parallelism of "strike" in 19:15); in 7:17 it has the positive nuance of "shepherd." Accordingly, the "authority" that Jesus received in fulfillment of the psalm is understood to be the authority that a king wields in protecting his subjects and defeating his enemies.

2:28

The statement that Christ also will give the overcomer "the morning star" reaffirms the climactic promise just made. The star most likely is representative (by metonymy) of messianic rule, as is evident from its use in 22:16 as a further explanation of the Isa. 11:1 prophecy, which has begun fulfillment in Jesus. This meaning of the image is confirmed from Num. 24:14–20, where the future eschatological ruler of Israel is described as a "rising star" and "scepter" (cf. *šēbeṭ* in Num. 24:17; Ps. 2:9) who will "crush the princes" of the "nations" (so also Ps. 2:9), "rule" over them, and receive them as an "inheritance" (so also Ps. 2:8) (see Gangemi 1978). In addition to the parallels between the Ps. 2 and Num. 24, the Numbers prophecy is a natural fit to combine with that of Ps. 2 in Rev. 2:26–28, since the prophecy was issued by Balaam, and Balaam is a symbol in Rev. 2:14 for the same heresy as is mentioned in Rev. 2:20. Numbers 24:17 is also interpreted messianically in Judaism (cf. *T. Levi* 18:3; *T. Jud.* 24:1 [in combination with Isa. 11:1–4 in 24:4–6]; CD-A VII, 18–21; 1QM XI, 6–7; 4Q175 9–13; *y. Taʿan.* 4:5).

Revelation 3

The messages to the seven churches continue. Sardis is warned that its failure to persevere could lead to sudden trouble; Philadelphia is encouraged to endure the slanders of the local synagogue and to maintain faithful witness; lukewarm Laodicea is chastised for its pitiable spiritual state in the midst of apparent prosperity.

3:4–5

The "white robes" signify the purification of the end-time tribulation in Dan. 11–12, where the saints are "made white" through the fire of persecution; a similar meaning fits well here. Compare Rev. 6:11; 7:14 with Dan. 11:35; 12:1, 10, and in the latter book note the Hebrew *lāban* ("make white") in 11:35; 12:10 and *ekleukainō* ("make white") in 12:10 Θ (for priests clothed in white, see *m. Mid.* 5:4; *b. Yoma* 19a).

The second expression of the promise to the overcomer is that Christ "will not erase his name from the book of life." The dual idea of a "book of life" and "books" of judgment respectively for believers and unbelievers has been derived from the same dual conception in Dan. 12:1–2; 7:10 (cf. Rev. 13:8; 17:8; 20:12). We also see allusions to Exod. 32:32–33; Ps. 69:28, both of which refer to "erasing" the names of unbelievers "from a book" of salvific blessing (cf. Isa. 4:3; *Jos. Asen.* 15:4). In the latter OT texts only one book is in mind, whereas in Revelation there are clearly two. The book motif in Rev. 3:5b and elsewhere in Revelation has been modeled more on the Danielic notion of two books, one in which only believers' names are written and one in which the deeds of all are written, which becomes the basis of judgment for unbelievers (cf. Dan. 7:10; 12:1–2). John's use of the "book of life" elsewhere suggests that the promise here not to erase a name from the book of life does not imply the opposite (for fuller discussion, see Beale 1999a: 278–82).

3:7–8

Whereas the keys in 1:18b are called the "keys of death and of Hades," in 3:7b a quotation from Isa. 22:22 is substituted for "of death and of Hades": "the one having the key of David, who opens and no one shuts, and who shuts and no one opens." The substitution is meant to amplify the idea of the original phrase in 1:18b by underscoring the sovereignty that Christ holds over the sphere "of death and Hades." Isaiah 22 describes Eliakim's absolute control over the kingdom of Israel, though eventually he is deposed from his office. The reference to Eliakim as "my servant" in Isa. 22:20 would have been easily associated with Isaiah's servant prophecies of chaps. 40–53, since the phrase occurs there thirteen times (the same phrase occurs only twice elsewhere in Isaiah, in reference to the prophet himself [20:3] and to David [37:35]). The description of placing "the key of the house of David [= administrative responsibility for the kingdom of Judah] on his [Eliakim's] shoulder," the allusion to him as a "father" to those in "Jerusalem and to the house of Judah," and the reference to him as "becoming a throne of glory" would have facilitated such a typologically prophetic understanding of Isa. 22:22, since this language is so strikingly parallel to that of the prophecy of the future Israelite ruler of Isa. 9:6–7 ("the government will be on his shoulders . . . and his name will be called . . . Eternal Father," who sits "on the throne of David"). Thus, Eliakim's temporary control of the kingdom as "prime minister" to the king of

Israel was a prophetic historical pattern pointing forward to Jesus Christ's greater and eternal sovereignty over a greater kingdom.

In view of the heavy influence of Isa. 40–60 in 3:7–9, allusion to Isa. 45:1 can also be recognized in 3:8: compare "I shall open to him doors and cities shall not be closed" (Isa. 45:1) with "I have given before you an opened door, which no one is able to shut" (Rev. 3:8). Just as Israel was weak in comparison to its opponents but would be made strong by God's restoring work through Cyrus (cf. Isa. 45:2–7), so also would God make the witness of the small church in Philadelphia effective among its opponents (so Lövestam 1965).

3:9

The clause "I will make them in order that (or 'so that' [Dana and Mantey 1957: 249]) they will come and bow down before your feet" is a collective allusion to Isa. 45:14; 49:23; 60:14 (see Göttingen LXX apparatus); Ps. 86:9. These OT texts predict that the unbelieving Gentiles would come and bow down at Israel's feet and to Israel's God in the last days. This prophecy has been fulfilled in an apparent ironic fashion in the Gentile church, which has become true Israel by virtue of its faith in Christ. In contrast, the ethnic Israelites in Philadelphia fulfill the role of the Gentiles.

Likewise, the prophecy that God would demonstrate his love for persecuted Israel before the nations seems to be fulfilled in an ironic manner: "and [they will] know that I have loved you" in 3:9b is applied to the Gentile-dominated church instead of ethnic Israel, as apparently in Isa. 43:4 (and LXX of Isa. 41:8; 44:2; 60:10; 63:9; cf. 48:14; *Jub.* 1:25).

The force of the Isaiah allusions shows that this is not a begrudging recognition by the Jews (*contra* Mounce 1977: 118–19; Beasley-Murray 1974: 101); rather, it is an acknowledgment that leads to the very salvation of the ethnic Jews themselves (*contra* I. T. Beckwith 1919: 480–82). The focus on salvation derives from the Isaiah prophecies, which refer not only to the judgment of some Gentiles, but also the salvation of many others who acknowledge Israel as God's true people (see, likewise, Caird 1966: 52–53; cf. Isa. 42:6; 45:22; 49:1, 6; 49:13 LXX; 51:4; Acts 13:47; 26:17–18, 23). The conclusion is also apparent from observing that the similar Isa. 60:11 prophecy is understood in Rev. 21:25–26 as referring to redemption; indeed, the Isa. 60 context refers to redeemed Gentiles offering voluntary worship (see commentary on Rev. 21:24–26 below).

3:10

That John has in mind a spiritual protection of Christians as they go through tribulation is evident from noticing that 3:10 may well be alluding to Dan. 12:1, 10 LXX, where "that hour" is immediately described as "that day of tribulation" (cf. Rev. 7:14) when "many are tested and sanctified and sinners sin." This suggests that the "testing" here in 3:10 has the double effect of purifying and strengthening believers while being at the same time a divine punishment on unbelievers (likewise Alford 1866: 586).

3:12

The Philadelphians are promised a permanent place in God's temple. This is likely an evocation of Isa. 56:3–5 (together with 62:2; 65:15): "Let not the foreigner who has joined himself to the LORD say, 'The LORD will surely separate me from his people.' . . . To [those who] hold fast my covenant I will give in my house and within my walls a memorial and a name better than that of sons and daughters; I will give them an everlasting name which shall not be cut off." For "memorial" the LXX has the Gentile being given "a named place," which is suitable to the threefold repetition of a name being written on the "pillar" or overcomer in 3:12.

Christ's statement that he would write upon the overcomer "the name of my God and the name of the city of my God" recalls Ezek. 48:35 (cf. 1 Macc. 14:26–49). There, the "name of the city" of the new Jerusalem is called "the Lord is there" because he has established his latter-day temple in its midst, where his glory will reside forever (so Ezek. 40–47; 48:10, 21; *Tg. Ezek.* 48:35; *b. B. Bat.* 75b renders Ezek. 48:35 as "the Lord is its name" by changing the Hebrew pointing; cf. Rev. 21:2).

3:14

The promise of a new creation by the faithful God of Israel in Isa. 65:15–16 stands behind the title "the Amen, the faithful and true," as well as behind the concluding "the beginning of the creation of God." The notion of God and of Israel as a "faithful witness" to the new creation in Isa.

43:10–12 forms the background for "witness." This Isa. 65:15–16 allusion is used to indicate that Christ is the divine "Amen, the faithful and true witness" to his own resurrection as "the beginning of the new creation of God," in inaugurated fulfillment of the Isaianic new-creation prophecies (see Beale 1996). Isa. 43:10–12 underscores Jesus as fulfilling the prophesied role of the true and faithful Israel.

Introductory Overview of the Visions of Revelation 4–5

Chapter 4 begins the glorious vision of God's throne room that is at the theological heart of Revelation. God is worshiped by the heavenly beings for his mighty acts of creation. God's sovereignty in creation (chap. 4) is the basis for his sovereignty in judgment and in redemption (chap. 5), which is new creation. The parallels between the hymns of 4:11a and 5:9, 12–13, which interpret respectively the main point of both chapters, indicate that God's work as creator is continued through Christ's work of redeeming fallen creation, which is new creation, inaugurated by his resurrection.

An overview of the two chapters together reveals that they exhibit a unified structure that corresponds more to the structure of Dan. 7 than to any other vision in the OT. If we begin with Dan. 7:9–28 and observe the elements and order of their presentation that are in common with Rev. 4–5, a striking resemblance is discernible:

1. Introductory vision phraseology (Dan. 7:9 [cf. 7:2, 6–7]; Rev. 4:1)
2. The setting of a throne(s) in heaven (Dan. 7:9a; Rev. 4:2a [cf. 4:4a])
3. God sitting on a throne (Dan. 7:9b; Rev. 4:2b)
4. The description of God's appearance on the throne (Dan. 7:9c; Rev. 4:3a)
5. Fire before the throne (Dan. 7:9d–10a; Rev. 4:5)
6. Heavenly servants surrounding the throne (Dan. 7:10b; Rev. 4:4b, 6b–10; 5:8, 11, 14)
7. Book(s) before the throne (Dan. 7:10c; Rev. 5:1–7)
8. The "opening" of the book(s) (Dan. 7:10d; Rev. 5:2–5, 9)
9. A divine (messianic) figure approaches God's throne in order to receive authority to reign forever over a "kingdom" (Dan. 7:13–14a; Rev. 5:5b–7, 9a, 12–13)
10. This "kingdom" includes "all peoples, nations, and tongues" (Dan. 7:14a MT; Rev. 5:9b)
11. The seer's emotional distress on account of the vision (Dan. 7:15; Rev. 5:4)
12. The seer's reception of heavenly counsel concerning the vision from one among the heavenly throne servants (Dan. 7:16; Rev. 5:5a)
13. The saints are also given divine authority to reign over a kingdom (Dan. 7:18, 22, 27a; Rev. 5:10)
14. A concluding mention of God's eternal reign (Dan. 7:27b; Rev. 5:13–14)

Both visions also contain the image of a sea (Dan. 7:2–3; Rev. 4:6). From the comparison it can be seen that Rev. 4–5 repeats the same fourteen elements from Dan. 7:9–28 in the same basic order, but with small variations that result from the expansion of images. For example, Rev. 5 places the messianic figure's approach to the throne after the mention of the seer's emotional distress and reception of angelic counsel and before the actual opening of the books. On the other hand, Dan. 7 has the approach of the "son of man" before the seer's distress and reception of counsel and has the opening of books before the approach of the "son of man." Further, Rev. 4–5 contains more description of the heavenly throne servants than does Dan. 7 and repeatedly portrays their presence around the throne, whereas they are mentioned only three times in Daniel.

However, if only the first section of the vision in 4:1–5:1 were considered, then it is evident that one other OT vision, Ezek. 1–2, is the source of an even larger number of allusions and has many of the same elements seen in the outline given above. Consequently, many have seen it to be the dominant influence in chapters 4–5. However, there are more variations in order, and five important elements are lacking: (1) the opening of books; (2) the approach of a divine figure before God's throne in order to receive authority to reign forever over a kingdom, (3) which consists of all peoples of the earth; (4) the reign of the saints over a kingdom; (5) mention of God's eternal reign. Therefore, it probably is the structure of Dan. 7 that dominates the whole of the Rev. 4–5 vision. In 5:2–14 the structure of Ezek. 1–2 and allusions to it fade out.

Although some of the proposed allusions from Daniel in Rev. 4 may appear questionable, they become more plausible when seen within the larger Danielic framework of the whole vision. The presence of allusions to Dan. 7 and other chapters of Daniel in Rev. 4–5 serve to corroborate the presence of the Danielic pattern (for details, see Beale 1984: 181–228; 1999a: 316–66). Of the various allusive references from Daniel (approximately twenty-three), about half are from Dan. 7 and half from other chapters in Daniel. When the latter are studied, it becomes clear that they have parallels and themes associated with Dan. 7 and therefore may have been employed to supplement the interpretive significance of the scene of Dan. 7. If Dan. 7 was the controlling pattern of John's thought in these two chapters, other Danielic material would have lain close in the field of association and would have been convenient to draw on for supplementary purposes.

The same supplementary approach probably was taken with respect to the other OT allusions outside of Daniel that were drawn into the portrayal (cf. Ezek. 1; Isa. 6; Exod. 19). What better way to interpret the Dan. 7 scene than by drawing in parallel elements (themes, images, wording) from other theophanic, messianic, and eschatological sections of the OT? In this regard, other OT texts appear to have been linked with Daniel because of common overall pictures or themes and sometimes by keywords or catchphrases.

Such dependence on Dan. 7 here is quite possible because that chapter was an interpretive model used by Jewish apocalyptists around the time of John's writing (cf. *1 En.* 46–48; 69–71; *4 Ezra* 11–12; 13; *2 Bar.* 39–42; see Beale 1984: 96–106, 108–12, 153). Thus, at this time it may have been a commonly used framework through which to understand eschatological issues. It is certainly true that John records what he has seen and heard about Dan. 7 and other OT books, but it is plausible that he then adds his own allusions

or stylistic glosses from Daniel and elsewhere for interpretive purposes, the latter of which is apparent from the unique correspondence of his language to different Greek versions and the Hebrew and early Jewish traditions.

Consequently, Rev. 4–5 should be interpreted primarily within the conceptual framework of Dan. 7. This has the following significant interpretive and theological implications.

(1) John intends chapters 4–5 to depict the initial fulfillment of the Dan. 7 prophecy of the reign of the "son of man" and of the saints, which has been inaugurated by Christ's death and especially by his resurrection—that is, his approach before the throne to receive authority.

(2) The combination of scenes such as Isa. 6 and Ezek. 1–2 with the predominant one of Dan. 7 expresses a judgment nuance in the vision, since these scenes serve as introductions to an announcement of judgment upon sinful Israel or the nations. Although it is true that these OT contexts are also associated with ideas of redemption and creation, as Jewish tradition and Rev. 4:11–5:14 show, the thought of judgment should be kept in mind (*contra* Collins 1976: 23, 214). More precisely, these OT scenes present a vision of God's cosmic reign and dominion that issues first in judgment and then redemption. It is this which is the theological background of chapters 4–5.

(3) The idea of judgment is also connoted by the image of the "book," which has been described in language from Ezek. 2; Isa. 29; Dan. 7; 12. Each of these contexts has the central idea of judgment but again together with ideas of salvation or blessing. Since Dan. 7:10 is the predominant influence for the image of the "book," the nuance of judgment probably is more dominant, especially when seen in relation to the following chapters, which announce judgment.

(4) The universal significance that Dan. 7 has in common with Rev. 4–5 points to a theological dominance of Daniel over Ezek. 1–2, since the latter's message is concerned only with the nation Israel. The Dan. 7 idea of a kingdom in which all peoples will serve the "son of man" (7:14) and God (7:27b) is seen by John as being fulfilled in the church. Yet the church is also the ongoing fulfillment of the Danielic reign of the saints of Israel.

Revelation 4

4:2

The introductory section of 4:1–2 is a reproduction of similar angelic council visions in the OT prophets (e.g., Isa. 6:1–13; 1 Kings 22:19–23 in 4:2b, 8a, 8b, 9a, 10a). John catches a glimpse of Yahweh's heavenly council and thereby is invested with prophetic authority. The OT theophanies form the general background for 4:2, although Ezek. 1 is foremost in mind, since clear reference is made to it in the following phrases.

4:3

References from Ezek. 1:26, 28 and from Ezek. 9:2 LXX; 10:1 LXX; 28:13 have been combined, although reflections of Exod. 24:10 and especially Exod. 28:17–20 are also included. These later chapters of Ezekiel and Exodus have been thought of in relation to Ezek. 1:26 because they are associated with a theophany scene and contain the mention of a "sapphire" stone in association with it. The "rainbow" implies, as probably also in Ezek. 1:28, that God's actions of judgment portrayed in the following visions will be tempered with considerations of mercy (cf. the same implication of the rainbow in relation to the Noahic covenant; see *TDNT* 3:342). Above all, the rainbow evokes thought of God's glory, since Ezek. 1:28 metaphorically equates it with "the appearance of the surrounding radiance . . . the appearance of the likeness of the glory of the Lord" (likewise *Midr. Ps.* 89:18; *Midr. Rab.* Num. 14:3; *b. Ḥag.* 16a, all citing Ezek. 1:28 in support; cf. *Midr. Rab.* Gen. 35:3).

4:5

Daniel 7:9–28 and Ezek. 1:26–28 are in the background, since both portray fire metaphors following the mention of a throne and its occupant. The actual wording of 4:5a is influenced by the fiery theophanic descriptions of Ezek. 1:13 (cf. LXX), although the similar scene of Exod. 19:16 is evident to a secondary extent.

The second half of 4:5 clearly is patterned after Zech. 4:2–3, 10, where there is a vision of seven lamps followed by their interpretation (cf. Rev. 1:12, 20) and associated with the Spirit of Yahweh (Zech. 4:6). The wording from Ezek. 1:13 has merged with the description in Zechariah. The first reference to Ezek. 1:13 in 4:5a has given rise to the thought of Zech. 4, since both have visionary imagery of "lamps" (cf. the LXX).

4:6a

The most prominent background for the image "like a sea of glass like crystal" is that of Ezek. 1:22 (which is confirmed by the wording "as the firmament, as the appearance of crystal," and by the preceding Ezek. 1 allusions already observed). This crystal sea forms the floor before God's heavenly throne. In view of the use of "sea" elsewhere in the OT as representing evil (see esp. Dan. 7; cf. Ps. 74:12–15; Isa. 51:9–11; Ezek. 32:2), there may also be a hint that John sees the chaotic powers of the sea as calmed by divine sovereignty, which has been expressed through Christ's resurrection (as chap. 5 indicates).

4:6b–8a

In describing the living beings in 4:6b–8a, John continues to draw from the picture of Ezek. 1 (1:5–21), although probably this had become merged in his mind with the same portrait of the "living beings" in Ezek. 10:12–15, 20–22. In addition, the six wings of the seraphim from Isa. 6 have been used to supplement the Ezekiel picture. The various portraits of the living creatures in Revelation and within the OT (cf. 1 Kings 6:24–28; 2 Chron. 3:13; Ezek. 1:6) argue against a strictly literal understanding of these beings. They likely are heavenly angelic representatives of the created order that continually give praise to God (cf. Pss. 19; 104).

4:8b

The influence of Isa. 6 continues in 4:8b, since the Trisagion finds its background in Isa. 6:3, where the seraphim chant, "Holy, holy, holy is the Lord Almighty; the whole earth is full of his glory." Note that the living creatures here replace "the whole earth is [no copular verb in Hebrew] full of his glory" with "who was and is and is to come," the last three words certainly including an anticipation of God's future coming to earth to fill it with his glory in an unprecedented way.

4:9

In 4:9a the living beings are portrayed as giving praise "to the one sitting on the throne." This description of praise offered by heavenly beings to God on his throne is a general recollection of the similar description in a series of OT theophanies, especially Isa. 6:1 (cf. also theophanic scenes in 1 Kings 22:19; 2 Chron. 18:18; Ps. 47:8 [46:9 LXX]; Dan. 7:9; Sir. 1:8).

In the last phrase of 4:9 the throne description of God is expanded by an attribute of eternity: the praise is offered "to the one living unto the ages of the ages." About five times different forms of this phrase occur in the OT outside of Daniel and in the Apocrypha, but the closest verbal parallels appear in Dan. 4:34 Θ; 12:7, where the dative participial form of *zaō* ("live") followed by a temporal *aiōn* ("eternity") clause is unique. These phrases from Daniel form the most probable collective influence on 4:9b.

Revelation 5

The throne vision continues, with the focus now on the resurrected and exalted Christ and his redemptive activity. Only Christ is found worthy to "open the scroll"—that is, to inaugurate God's kingdom on earth. The chapter concludes with all creation giving worship "to the one who sits on the throne and to the Lamb."

5:1

Most interpreters have rightly identified the phrase of 5:1b, "a scroll/book written on the front and back," as evoking the image of Ezek. 2:9b–10. John's scroll, like Ezekiel's, will contain "lamentations, mourning, and woe" (Ezek. 2:10). The *biblion* ("book") is further described by the phrase "having been sealed with seven seals," which appears to be a merging of Dan. 12:1, 4, 9 with Isa. 29:11.

5:2

The phrase "to loose the seals" in 5:2c reveals more inspiration from the "sealing" of Dan. 12 (although cf. Isa. 29). The idea of sealing and opening books in connection with end-time happenings is unique in the OT to Dan. 12:1–13. Daniel 12:8–9 implies the future unsealing of the book in a latter-day period. This is yet another indication that John's prophecy contains the fulfillment of the latter-days prophecies of Daniel.

5:5

The descriptions of Christ as "the lion that is from the tribe of Judah" and as "the root of David" in

5:5b–c derive respectively from Gen. 49:9; Isa. 11:1, 10 (cf. Jer. 11:19; 23:5; 33:15; Zech. 3:8). The word *nikaō* ("overcome") serves as an introduction to these OT titles and brings out their "conquering" significance, since both concern the prophecy of a messianic figure who will overcome his enemies through judgment.

5:6

There are two different proposals for the background of the "slain lamb" in 5:6. Some see it as a reference to the OT Passover lamb, while others favor Isa. 53:7: "he was led as a sheep to the slaughter" (cf. Isa. 53:8–12). However, neither should be excluded, since both have in common with the metaphorical picture in 5:6 the central idea of a lamb's sacrifice that accomplishes redemption and victory for God's people (see Comblin 1965: 26, 31; Swete 1906: cxxxix). The Isa. 53 background especially highlights the atoning aspect of the lamb's sacrificial death and also applies the metaphors of "root" (cf. Rev. 5:5) and "lamb" to the sacrificial victim. In fact, "root" occurs also in Isa. 11:1, 10 (alluded to in Rev. 5:5), which may have inspired attraction to the same metaphor in 53:2. The Passover and Isa. 53 backgrounds are also suggested by the use of *arnion* ("lamb"), behind which could lie the Aramaic *talja*, meaning not only "lamb," but also "servant" and "boy" (see *TDNT* 1:338–41; Kraft 1974: 109). The sacrificial victim's prophesied sinlessness in Isa. 53:9 partly underlies the "worthiness" of Jesus in 5:9 ("worthy are you . . . because you were slain").

The picture of the lamb with horns is best explained against the background of the Jewish tradition found in *1 En.* 90; *T. Jos.* 19 concerning a conquering messianic lamb (although some see the latter text as a Christian interpolation); for "horns" as representing power, see Deut. 33:17; 1 Kings 22:11; Ps. 89:17; Dan. 7:7–8:24; *1 En.* 90:6–12, 37.

The last phrase of 5:6 ("having seven eyes which are the seven Spirits of God having been sent out into all the earth") is dependent on Zech. 3:4. In Zech. 3:9 the "seven eyes" are bound up with a divine inscription set before Joshua, the high priest, concerning the "removing of iniquity of the land in one day." In Zech. 4 the symbols of the "seven lamps" (4:2) and the "seven eyes" (4:10) are associated with Yahweh's omnipotent Spirit. Indeed, in 2 Chron. 16:9 the phrase "the eyes of the LORD move to and fro throughout the earth" highlights not just omniscience, but especially divine sovereignty: "that he may strongly support those whose heart is completely his." The preceding mention of "seven horns" underscores further the notion of omnipotence (on both points, see Bauckham 1993a: 164).

John has interpreted the "seven eyes" in Zechariah as Yahweh's Spirit and has identified both as a possession of the lamb. It is only by the Spirit of Yahweh's "Servant the Branch," the messianic lamb, that iniquity has been removed from the world (Zech. 3:9) and resistance to the kingdom overcome (cf. Zech. 4:6–7). The seven spirits of God (= the seven burning lamps) have formerly been confined to the heavenly throne room (1:4, 12; 3:1; 4:5), implying that they are agents only of God operating throughout the earth (cf. Zech. 4:10; also 1:8–11; 6:5). But, as a result of Christ's death and resurrection these spirits also become his agents in the world (see Caird 1966: 75). The Spirit carries out the sovereign plan of the Lord (see commentary on Rev. 1:12 above and 11:4 below; for the use of Zech. 4, see Bauckham 1993a: 162–66).

5:7

The Lamb approaches the throne. Daniel 7:13 is the only text in the OT where a divine messianic figure is portrayed as approaching God's heavenly throne in order to receive authority. The description of "the one sitting on the throne" is now related specifically to Dan. 7:9–28. Thus, Christ is the fulfillment of the prophetic portrayal of the "Son of man" coming to God's throne to be granted authority over an eternal kingdom.

5:9

The content of the "new song" is expressed in 5:9–10. In the OT the "new song" was always an expression of praise for God's victory over the enemy, which sometimes included thanksgiving for his work of creation (cf. Ps. 33:3; 144:9 [which combine playing a harp and singing a new song]; also Ps. 40:3; 96:1; 98:1; 149:1; Isa. 42:10). Therefore, the "new song" is used analogically or even typologically here, since the powers of evil and sin have been conquered. Note that the "new song" in some of the aforementioned OT passages is related by Judaism to the coming messianic age

(e.g., *Midr. Rab.* Num. 15:11; *Midr. Tanhuma* Gen. 1:32; *b. ʿArak.* 13b).

5:10

The prophesied kingdom of the saints of Israel in Daniel 7:22b, 27a may stand behind the idea of ruling in 5:10. However, in 5:10 the influence of Exod. 19:6 ("a kingly priesthood") is also present in the phrase "a kingdom and priests." In this regard, 5:9b–10 is also a reworking of 1:5c–6a in the light of Exod. 19:6 and the Passover idea of the slain lamb (so Schüssler Fiorenza 1972: 276–77, 281–82). This means that the Exodus idea of the kingdom and priesthood has been universalized and woven in with the concept of the saints' universal kingdom of Dan. 7, which has been inaugurated in the church.

5:11

The description "myriads of myriads and thousands of thousands" is taken from Dan. 7:10 (cf. *1 En.* 40:1; 60:1; 71:8, which also are allusions to Dan. 7:10; see also *1 En.* 14:22; Gen. 24:60; Num. 10:36).

5:12

Standing behind the combination of "power," "wealth," "might," and "glory" is 1 Chron. 29:11–12, while the use of *sophia* ("wisdom") goes back to Dan. 2:20 (so Milling 1972: 181–82, 215 [in Dan. 2:23 Θ "wisdom" is coupled with "power"]). It probably is not accidental that "might," "glory," and "honor" are found together in Dan. 2:37 LXX; 4:30 LXX (cf. 4:31 LXX), a combination occurring only twice elsewhere in the LXX.

5:13

The fivefold expression of praise in 5:13a may be a collective reflection of Exod. 20:11; Neh. 9:6; Ps. 146:6 (cf. Dan. 2:38; 4:37 LXX). In these OT contexts God is praised both as creator and as king of Israel who has delivered his people from bondage. God and the Lamb now receive this praise because they have accomplished an even greater deliverance.

Revelation 6

Christ begins to unseal the scroll, and scenes of devastating judgment (including the famous "four horsemen of the apocalypse") begin to unfold on earth. These climax with a depiction of the day of God's wrath, as the heavens are opened and the hills and islands are "removed from their places" (for the predominantly symbolic nature of the seal visions, see Beale 1999a: 50–55).

The most obvious background for the four horsemen is Zech. 6:1–8 (cf. 1:8–15). There, four groups of horses of different color are commissioned by God to patrol the earth and to punish those nations on earth that they find to have oppressed his people (6:5–8). By analogy, the horses in Rev. 6:1–8 may signify that the natural and political disasters throughout the world are caused by Christ in order to judge unbelievers who persecute Christians and to vindicate his people. The colors of the horses in both Zechariah and Revelation are almost all identical (see Charles 1920: 1:168–69). The colors in Revelation, however, clearly are metaphorical for the respective plague delivered by each horseman (see Mounce 1977: 152; Haapa 1968: 217–18): white (conquering), red (bloodshed [e.g., 2 Kings 3:22–23]), black (famine [cf. *Tg. Jer.* 14:2]), and pale green (death). The clearest difference between these texts is that Rev. 6 describes four individual horses and horsemen, whereas Zech. 1 pictures four groups of horses, and Zech. 6 depicts four groups of horses pulling chariots. However, the difference is insignificant, since John may have deduced by implication from Zech. 6 that four riders were in the chariots. Zechariah's summarizing of the four sets of horses as "the four winds of heaven" may be another factor in John's depicting only four horses (Ezek. 14:12–23 is also formative for this section [cf. Deut. 32:23–25], on which, see commentary on Rev. 6:7–8 below).

6:5

In the ancient world food was distributed by rationed amounts (using scales) when it became scarce (see the metaphorical use of scales indicating famine also in Lev. 26:26; 2 Kings 7:1; Ezek. 4:10, 16). Severe food shortages are in view.

6:6

I. T. Beckwith (1919: 521–22) correctly argues for no specific historical background in 6:5–6. For grain, wine, and oil being not luxury items but basic food staples typically available during nonfamine times, see Deut. 7:13; 11:14; 28:51;

2 Chron. 32:28; Neh. 5:11; Ps. 104:14–15; Jer. 31:12; Hos. 2:8, 22; Joel 1:10; 2:19; Mic. 6:15; Hag. 2:12; see further references in Burchard 1983: 212n8i.

6:7–8

Possibly echoed here are Hos. 13:8, 14 LXX, where "Hades [*hadēs*] and . . . Death [*thanatos*]" and "beasts of the field" are divine judgments to come upon Israel for idolatry from which God subsequently will redeem them (cf. Isa. 28:15). Hades is the sphere that imprisons the dead. The LXX uses "Death" and "Hades" in combination almost synonymously in reference to the region of the dead (e.g., Ps. 6:6 [6:5 ET]; 48:15–16 [49:14–15 ET]; Prov. 2:18; 5:5; Song 8:6; Job 17:13–16; 33:22). Since the four judgments are specific ways in which death is executed, the use of *thanatos* in 6:8b refers to "pestilence, disease" rather than death in the general sense (see I. T. Beckwith 1919: 523). In fact, *thanatos* in the LXX translates the Hebrew *deber* ("plague, pestilence") over thirty times (see Court 1979: 64; Mayer 1978). Strikingly, two of these renderings of *deber* occur in Ezek. 14:19–21 and one in Lev. 26:25, two contexts providing the model for Rev. 6:1–8. Ezekiel 14 is alluded to directly here in 6:8. The same word, *thanatos*, in 6:8a has the more general meaning, although it certainly includes the specific nuance of "pestilence."

The calamities that Death and Hades inflict are described through a citation from Ezek. 14:21. The fourth rider generally summarizes the previous three (conquering, the sword, and famine would all include "death") and adds one more (plague of beasts). The four judgments from Ezek. 14 are found elsewhere in the prophets, usually as fourfold constructions and developments of the covenantal curse formulas of Lev. 26:18–28; Deut. 32:24–26 (for fourfold developments of these formulas, see Jer. 15:1–4; 16:4–5; 34:17, 20; Ezek. 5:16–17; *Frg. Tg.* Deut. 32:22–26; *Pss. Sol.* 13:1–3; Sir. 39:28–31 [cf. 40:8–10]; see also *Pss. Sol.* 15:8–11; *Pirqe 'Abot* 5:11; *Sipre Deut.* Piska 43; three of the judgments occur in formulaic phraseology in Jer. 14:12–18; 21:7, 9; 24:10; 29:17–18; 42:17; 43:11; Ezek. 5:12; 6:11–12; 7:15; 12:16; 33:27; Bar. 2:25; 4Q171 III). The curse formula in the Ezek. 14 context (14:13–23) indicates judgment on unbelievers outside and inside the covenant community and suffering for the true remnant; the same groups are in mind here, though the latter is the focus, as the following vision confirms.

6:9

The mention of the "altar" in association with those slain evokes the sacrificial nature of their suffering. The altar alluded to is the golden altar of incense, which stood in the vicinity of the holy of holies (this clearly is the reference in 8:3–5; 9:13; and 11:1; 14:18; 16:7 are developments of these references in chaps. 8–9). Upon this altar sacrificial blood was poured for the Day of Atonement, and incense was burned (Exod. 30:1–10; Lev. 4:7; cf. Heb. 9:4).

6:10

The expression "how long?" (*heōs pote*) is typically used throughout the Greek OT for questions about when God will finally punish persecutors and vindicate the oppressed (see Ps. 6:4 [6:3 ET]; 12:2 [13:1 ET]; 73:10 [74:10 ET]; 78:5 [79:5 ET]; 79:5 [80:4 ET]; 88:47 [89:46 ET]; 89:13 [90:13 ET]; 93:3 [94:3 ET]; Dan. 8:13 Θ; 12:6–13 Θ). John's emphasis on God defending his own reputation by judging sinners who have persecuted the righteous is also evoked by the clause "will you not vindicate our blood?" which is an allusion to Ps. 78:10 LXX (79:10 ET): "Let the vindication of your servants' blood that has been poured out be known." In the psalm this expression of vindication is introduced earlier by the question of "how long" it would be until God acted against the enemy (78:5–6 LXX). In 78:9–10 LXX is a plea for God to uphold his glorious name and to demonstrate the truth of his existence by judging sinners because they have not called on his name and have wrongly oppressed his people (see 78:6–7 LXX). Also, 78:2 LXX mentions that as a result of persecution from the nations, the saints' bodies were given as food "for the wild beasts of the earth" (*tois thēriois tēs gēs*), a phrase virtually identical to the one in Rev. 6:8b. Those who have persecuted the saints have done so because they rejected their testimony about the truth of God. Therefore, part of the appeal is for God to judge these persecutors in order to demonstrate that he is the only true God. Note also (with Court 1979: 58) that the same question, "How long?" is asked in Zech. 1:12

after the four groups of horses have patrolled the earth and reported that the nations that had persecuted Israel were enjoying peace. God then responds by proclaiming that he will remove this peace and judge these nations (Zech. 1:13–16), and the same horses become the agents of this judgment in Zech. 6:1–8.

For the background of God avenging the blood of saints against their persecutors, who are referred to as "ones dwelling on the earth," compare Hos. 1:4, "I will avenge the blood," with Hos. 4:1–2, "The LORD has a judgment against the ones dwelling upon the earth" partly because "they mingle blood with blood" (cf., more broadly, Isa. 26:21).

6:12–14

The judgment of the world is depicted with stock-in-trade imagery from the OT that describes the dissolution of the cosmos. The most important texts that form a part of the apocalyptic quarry of passages influencing the dramatic portrayal in 6:12–14 are Isa. 13:10–13; 24:1–6, 19–23; 34:4; Ezek. 32:6–8; Joel 2:10, 30–31; 3:15–16; Hab. 3:6–11 (cf., secondarily, Ps. 68:7–8; Jer. 4:23–28; Amos 8:8–9). The same OT texts are also influential for the portrayals in Matt. 24:29; Mark 13:24–25; Acts 2:19–20 (= Joel 2:30–31) (standing in the same OT tradition are *T. Mos.* 10:3–6; *4 Ezra* 5:4–8 [cf. 7:39–40]). All of these texts mention at least four of the following elements also found in the Revelation text: the shaking of the earth (including mountains); the darkening or shaking of the moon, stars, sun, heaven; the pouring out of blood. The most formative influence among these texts is Isa. 34:4: "And the powers of the heavens shall melt, and the heaven shall be rolled up like a scroll; and all the stars shall fall . . . as leaves fall from a fig tree."

In Isa. 34:3–4 "blood" is directly linked with "the power of the heavens melting," and 34:5–6 refers to God's sword being "drunk" with blood "in heaven," which may be related to the moon becoming like blood in Rev. 6:12b. Also included in the Isaianic depiction is the mention in 34:12 LXX that judgment will fall on "the rulers . . . the kings and the great ones," which is nearly identical to the first three groups of people undergoing judgment in Rev. 6:15a: "the kings of the earth and the great ones and the rulers of a thousand" (cf. Ps. 2:2).

Joel 2:31 (3:4 LXX = Acts 2:20) also stands behind the picture in 6:12b of the sun becoming darkened and the moon becoming like blood (though for the former depiction, see also Joel 2:10; 3:15; Isa. 13:10 [cf. Matt. 24:29; Mark 13:25]). Likening the darkening of the sky to "sackcloth" was suggested by Isa. 50:3: "I will clothe the sky with darkness, and I will make its covering as sackcloth [LXX: *sakkon*]."

There is debate about whether the description depicts an actual dissolution of the cosmos (allowing room for metaphorical language to describe this dissolution) or whether it is a purely figurative description of the fall of ungodly kingdoms. The OT often uses such language in a hyperbolic manner to depict the fall of kingdoms: note the defeats of Babylon (Isa. 13:10–13), Edom (Isa. 34:4), Egypt (Ezek. 32:6–8), enemy nations of Israel (Hab. 3:6–11), and Israel itself (Joel 2:10, 30–31 [cf. *Sib. Or.* 3:75–90]). Other examples in the OT of figurative cosmic disruption language include 2 Sam. 22:8–16 (= Ps. 18:7–15), figuratively referring to David's victory over his enemies; Eccles. 12:1–7, referring to human death; Isa. 2:19–21; 5:25, 30; Jer. 4:23–28; Ezek. 30:3–4, 18; Amos 8:7–10; Mic. 1:4–6 (*Midr. Ps.* 104:25 says, "Wherever the term 'earthquake' occurs in Scripture it denotes the chaos between [the fall of] one kingdom and [the rise of] another"). Revelation 6 itself emphasizes the judgment upon "the kings of the earth" (6:15) followed by other representatives of humanity.

On the other hand, some OT texts seem to use the language of cosmic catastrophe in a more "literal" fashion (see, e.g., Ps. 102:25–26; Isa. 24:1–6, 19–23; 51:6; 64:1; Ezek. 38:19–20; Hag. 2:6–7). A radical renovation of the cosmos is certainly envisioned elsewhere in Revelation, most notably in 20:11–22:5. If, as many commentators hold, the scene in Revelation is a depiction of the beginning of final judgment, a more "literal" understanding of the imagery might be preferable, or, alternatively, this is a figurative scene of the beginning of the literal final judgment. Whichever is the case, the OT dissolution language is analogically applied to the final judgment of the cosmos. These OT depictions may even be foreshadowings of the final judgment.

6:15

The only place in the OT (LXX) where the combination "the rulers . . . the kings and the great ones" occurs is in Isa. 34:12 LXX, which, as we noted, is nearly identical to the first three groups mentioned in 6:15a (cf. Ps. 2:2). As in Isa. 34, so also here these groups of people undergo divine judgment because they are an essential part of the corrupt world system that must be destroyed. In both cases the precise reason for punishment is the persecution of God's people (cf. Isa. 33:1–34:13; 35:1–4; Rev. 6:9–12). That they are judged also because of idolatry is evident from the mention of them "hiding themselves in the caves and the rocks of the mountains [6:15b] . . . from the presence of the one sitting on the throne and from the wrath of the Lamb [6:16b]," which is based on a typological understanding of God's judgment of Israelite idolaters in Isa. 2:10, 18–21 (a similar description from Jer. 4:29 may be included in this typological inference [cf. Jer. 4:23–28; 5:7]; see also Isa. 24:21).

6:16

The earth dwellers desperately appeal to "the mountains and the rocks, 'Fall on us and hide us.'" The petition is an allusion to Hos. 10:8b, which, like Isa. 2, speaks of judgment on idolaters and portrays them seeking refuge from divine wrath in mountains and rocks: "They shall say to the mountains, 'Cover us,' and to the hills, 'Fall on us'" (cf. Hos. 10:1–3, 8; 11:2). The similar imagery of Jer. 4:29 is also included in the allusion, which enforces further in Rev. 6:16 the idea of judgment on idolaters who try to hide from God's anger (cf. Jer. 4:23–30; 5:7). Behind Rev. 6:16, and even the Hosea and Jeremiah references, stands an allusion to the incident in Gen. 3 in which Adam and Eve "hid themselves from the presence of the Lord God" (3:8). God has thus designed history to end as it began.

6:17

Since the cosmic conflagration imagery of Joel 2:10, 31 is partially behind the picture introducing the segment of 6:12–17 (6:12), it is appropriate that the segment should conclude with an allusion that also concludes the description of Joel 2:10: "For the day of the Lord is great . . . and who will be able to resist it?" (Joel 2:11). The description from Joel is supplemented in 6:17 by a phrase from the oracle of judgment on Nineveh in chapter 1 of Nahum, which likewise concludes a figurative depiction of the cataclysmic fall of the world: "The mountains quake because of him . . . the earth recoils from his presence. . . . Who shall stand before his anger? And who shall withstand the anger of his wrath?" (1:5–6 [cf. 1:4]). The judgment in Nahum is linked to that nation's idolatry (Nah. 1:14; likewise *Midr. Rab.* Exod. 29:9).

These OT allusions are figurative expressions in their respective contexts for divine judgment on Israel or Nineveh, which were historically fulfilled; here they are taken as foreshadowings of the last judgment (for the same contextual use, cf. Isa. 13:9; Zeph. 1:14, 18; 2:2–3; Mal. 4:5, which could be additional background behind the phrase in Rev. 6:17a, "the great day of their wrath came").

Revelation 7

Chapter 7 answers the question that concludes chapter 6: "The day of their wrath has come, and who can stand?" Who can stand? Only those who are sealed by God—those who have trusted in him and maintain their faithful witness. This sealing is strategically located just prior to the consummate judgment depicted in the opening of the seventh seal (8:1–5) and illustrates the progress of the gospel through the ages.

7:1

John first sees "four angels." That they are "standing on the four corners of the earth" refers to their authority over the whole world (so Isa. 11:12; Ezek. 7:2; Rev. 20:8; cf. *2 Bar.* 6:4–7:2; *T. Ash.* 7:1–7; *Gk. Apoc. Ezra* 3:6; cf. also *3 En.* 48A:10). The phrase "the four winds" likewise refers to the entire known world, as is clear from the use of the same phrase in Jer. 49:36; Dan. 8:8; 11:4; *1 En.* 18:2; *4 Ezra* 13:5; Matt. 24:31; Mark 13:27 (*Tg. Isa.* 11:12 renders the MT's "four corners of the earth" as "four winds of the earth").

"The four winds of the earth" are best identified as the four horsemen of 6:1–8, who clearly were modeled on the horsemen of Zech. 6:1–8. The four horsemen in Zech. 6:1–8 are also identified in Zech. 6:5 as "the four winds of heaven" (see Carrington 1931: 139; Kiddle and Ross 1940:

131–32; Caird 1966: 94; Beasley-Murray 1974: 142; Morris 1987: 113; Wilcock 1975: 79; cf. Josephus, *J.W.* 6.297–301). This identification becomes clearer when we see that the sealing of believers in 7:3–8 explains how they are able to be protected spiritually from the woes of the four horsemen, which they must endure. That the winds have to be held back to prevent their harmful activity is evidence of their rebellious and wicked nature (Caird 1966: 94; note also that the four winds in Jer. 49:36 [cf. *1 En.* 76] are divine agents of judgment). If there is any significance in the change from Zechariah's "winds of heaven" to "winds of the earth," it may lie in an attempt to emphasize the earthly havoc that these heavenly agents accomplish. For "winds" in general as agents of divine judgment elsewhere in the OT, see Ps. 18:10; 104:3–4; Isa. 19:1; 66:15; Jer. 4:11–12; 23:19; 51:1; Hos. 13:15–16 (cf. also *Jub.* 2:2). Of relevance for comparison to Rev. 7:1 is Josephus, *J.W.* 6.297–301, where heavenly chariots purportedly were seen as warning signs of Jerusalem's impending destruction, followed by a reference to "a voice from the four winds" also as a warning sign.

7:2–3

The vision in Ezek. 9 provides the best background for understanding the activity of divine sealing. In anticipation of the coming Babylonian sack of Jerusalem, God commands an angel to put a mark on all genuine believers but instructs other angels to slay unfaithful Israelites (note the parallels with the mark of blood over the Hebrews' doors at Passover [Exod. 12:7, 13, 22–28]). That this vision has a one-to-one correspondence with the actual events of the fall of Jerusalem wrought by the Babylonians is most unlikely. The angels begin killing in the temple and move outward, whereas the Babylonians presumably moved in the opposite direction, from the outside of the city inward. It is likewise difficult to assume that only the wicked were killed and all the righteous were spared in the invasion. Ezekiel himself seems dubious of the spiritual status of many exiles (see, e.g., Ezek. 36:20; cf. also Jeremiah's scathing denunciation of some of the "remnant" [42:2] in Jer. 43–44). Keeping in mind that this is a vision, the "sealing" of the Ezekiel portrayal likely refers either to spiritual protection of the remnant faithful at the time of the destruction or to the preservation of the remnant who symbolize a future hope for Israel in captivity and, especially, in the restoration from captivity.

John himself clearly is concerned not with physical security but with the protection of the believers' faith and salvation in the midst of the various sufferings and persecutions that are inflicted upon them, whether by Satan or by his demonic and earthly agents (as, e.g., enumerated in 6:1–11; the Qumranians applied Ezek. 9:4 to themselves as the true, faithful remnant of Israel living in the last days [CD-B XIX, 12]). John likely views the Ezek. 9 passage as typological of the remnant faithful within the church community and God's spiritual preservation of it in the midst of trials and persecutions.

It is likely that the "seal" on the forehead is to be equated with the "name" of God that elsewhere marks his servants (e.g., Rev. 14:1). We may compare Exod. 28:11–21 (= 36:13–21), where most of the same precious stones as found in Rev. 21:19–20 are mentioned and the name of one of the twelve tribes is written on each stone to show who is a member of the Israelite covenant community. The twelve precious stones with the tribal "names" in Exod. 28:10–11, 21 are said to be "seals" worn on the high priest's shoulders; the OT Greek textual tradition of Exod. 28:11 has various participial forms like Rev. 7:4–8 (e.g., *sphragismenōn* in manuscript 552 [cf. other like variants in the apparatus in Wevers 1991]). These seals correspond to the "seal" placed on Aaron's forehead, which also represented Israel, described in Exod. 28:31–38 (cf. *epi tou metōpou Aarōn* ["upon the forehead of Aaron"] in Exod. 28:38 with *epi tōn metōpōn autōn* ["upon their foreheads"] in Rev. 7:3). The seal in Exod. 28:36 has written, in place of the names of Israel, the phrase "consecration of the Lord" (*hagiasma kyriou*), which carries the idea of Israel as Yahweh's consecrated possession (so Exod. 19:6). Revelation 7:2–3 has in mind that the sealed believers are God's own consecrated possession.

7:4–8

Bauckham (1993a: 217–29) has argued convincingly that in Rev. 7:4–8 those numbered are God's eschatological army—not a literal army of Israelites, but a symbol of the "church militant," which wages war against its spiritual foes and overcomes the devil through faithful witness to Jesus.

The evidence for the view may be summarized as follows.

(1) The purpose of numbering for a census in the OT was always to count up the military force of the nation, as seen in, for example, Num. 1:3, 18, 20; 26:2, 4; 2 Sam. 24:1–9; 1 Chron. 27:23 (the use of "thousand" in Rev. 7 may also have a military connotation, as in, e.g., Num. 1; 31:14, 48 [so Boring 1989: 131]). The repetition of *ek phylēs* ("from the tribe") in Rev. 7:5–8 may echo the almost identical repeated phrase *ek tēs phylēs* ("from the tribe") from Num. 1:21–43 (note also "of the sons of Israel" in Num. 2:32 and the same phrase in Rev. 7:4).

(2) Those counted in the OT were males of military age, and the 144,000 in Rev. 14:1–4 are "male virgins."

(3) The military census of Num. 1 has influenced the account in 1QM of the Qumran community's understanding of the future, imminent messianic war, when they would reconquer the land of promise. For instance, 1QM organizes the army of the Qumran sect into the traditional grouping of twelve tribes (II, 2–3, 7; III, 13–14; V, 1–2).

7:5

The fact that Judah is listed first in the register of tribes in 7:5–8 is striking, since out of the many OT lists of the twelve tribes it is rarely cited first (see Num. 2:3–32; 34:19; Josh. 21:4; 1 Chron. 12:23–37; likewise *L.A.B* 25:4; cf. Judg. 1:2–4). The priority of Judah here emphasizes the precedence of the messianic king who was to come from the tribe of Judah (cf. Gen. 49:10; 1 Chron. 5:1–2; see also *Midr. Rab.* Gen. 98:2). This portrays a fulfillment of the prophecy in Gen. 49:8 that the eleven other tribes would "bow down" to Judah. Ezekiel 37:15–19 develops Gen. 49:8 by asserting that at the time of the restoration all "the tribes of Israel" will be incorporated into "the tribe of Judah," and then 37:24–25 indicates that all Israel, including Ephraim, will have Judah as their representative head. In particular, 37:24–25 says that a latter-day David from Judah will reign as king over all the tribes (likewise 34:23–25). Therefore, Rev. 7:5 is a continuation of 5:5, where Jesus is identified as the fulfillment of the promised leader from Judah.

7:9–17

The relationship between the group in 7:4–8 and the group in 7:9–17 has occasioned much comment. It is possible that they may constitute two distinct groups, but the points adduced above concerning the "census" argue for an identification of the two groups. Bauckham (1993a: 215–16) observes that the relation between the two segments is precisely parallel to the relationship between the lion and the lamb in 5:5–6. Just as John hears about a lion and sees its meaning through the symbolism of a lamb, so also he hears about the 144,000 and then understands its meaning through seeing a vision of the innumerable multitudes. "To the Lion *of the tribe of Judah* (5:5) . . . corresponds a list of the sealed of the tribes of Israel, headed by those *of the tribe of Judah* (7:5). . . . To the Lamb *standing* (5:6), who has ransomed people from *every tribe, tongue, people and nation* (5:9), corresponds the multitude from all *nations, tribes, peoples and tongues, standing* before the Lamb (7:9)" (Bauckham 1993a: 216). The parallelism between chapter 5 and chapter 7 is confirmed further by Bauckham's earlier suggestion that 7:4–8 depicts the numbering of an army for holy war, led by Judah, which 7:9–14 pictures as fighting ironically by persevering faith in the midst of suffering and worldly defeat (similarly Valentine 1985: 219–23). That the group in 7:9–17 is the same group of warriors as in 7:4–8 is suggested further by the observation that in 7:9 *ochlos* ("multitude") can be translated "army" and that white robes and palm branches are associated elsewhere with a military victory (see, respectively, 2 Macc. 11:8; 1 Macc. 13:51; cf. *T. Naph.* 5:4; see commentary on Rev. 7:9 below); the viable translation of *sōtēria* in 7:10 as "deliverance, victory" seems to confirm this conclusion (Bauckham 1993a: 225–26).

7:9

The phrase "a great multitude which no one was able to number" evokes the promise to Abraham and Jacob that God would multiply their descendants, "which shall not be numbered for multitude" (see esp. Gen. 16:10; 32:12; also Gen. 13:16; 15:5; 22:17; 26:4; Hos. 1:10; *Jub.* 13:20; 14:4–5; Heb. 11:12 [seeing the link are D'Aragon 1968: 478; Mounce 1977: 171; Sweet 1979: 150; Hughes 1990: 95; Bauckham 1993a: 223; Ulfgard

1989: 94; cf. Prigent 1981: 123]). As throughout Revelation, this promise to Israel is applied to the church from all nations.

In reflecting on the promise to Abraham, Jewish tradition even questions how it is that some OT texts can affirm that the people of Israel can be counted, yet the Abrahamic promise affirms that Israel will multiply so much as to be uncountable. Among the answers offered is that only God is able to know the exact number of the true remnant in Israel, yet no human is able to count the total number when considered from the eternal or heavenly perspective (e.g., *Midr. Rab.* Num. 2:14, 18–19; *Sipre Deut.* Piska 47; *b. Yoma* 22b). Another answer offered by Jewish exegetical tradition is that during any particular generation when the majority of Israel is disobedient, one is able to count the faithful remnant; however, when the nation is faithful (in the messianic era, when all the obedient are gathered together [so *Midr. Rab.* Num. 2:14]), they are too numerous to be counted (so *Midr. Rab.* Num. 2:18; 20:25; *Sipre Deut.* Piska 47; *b. Yoma* 22b). Something like this is going on in Rev. 7:9: from God's perspective, which John hears about in 7:4–8, Abraham's elect seed is known as a countable remnant; yet, they are uncountable from John's human perspective and especially in line with the language of the promised multiplication of Abraham's seed.

The saints wear "white robes" (see commentary on Rev. 3:4–5 above) and hold "palm branches in their hand" as they stand before the throne of God and before the Lamb. The reference to "palm branches" is an allusion to the Festival of Tabernacles (cf., e.g., Lev. 23:40, 43; Neh. 8:15; 2 Macc. 10:7; see Ulfgard 1989: 89–92, 95). In the OT this was an annual occasion for the nation to rejoice and to thank God for the fruitfulness of their crops. The feast was also to commemorate Israel's dwelling in tents under divine protection during their pilgrimage in the wilderness after the redemption from Egypt (Lev. 23:40, 43). This reminded them that their continued existence as a nation was traceable ultimately to God's redemption at the Red Sea and victory over the Egyptians (in 1 Macc. 13:51, and included in 2 Macc. 10:7, palm branches signify victory over an enemy; likewise Philo, [*Alleg. Interp.* 3.74] refers to a "palm tree [as] a symbol of victory"; cf. Suetonius, *Cal.* 32). The same imagery is now applied by John to people from all nations, who rejoice in their latter-day exodus redemption, in their victory over their persecutors, and in the fact that God has protected them subsequently during their wilderness pilgrimage (cf. 12:6, 14) through the "great tribulation." The eschatological celebration of tabernacles in Zech. 14:16–19 may lie in the background here.

7:14

Daniel 12:1 LXX is acknowledged as the likely origin for the idea of "the great tribulation": "There will be a time of tribulation, such tribulation as has not come about from when a nation was upon the earth until that time." The phrase "great tribulation" (*thlipsis megalē*) occurs elsewhere in the NT only in Matt. 24:21 and Acts 7:11. In Matt. 24:21, the phrase is part of a fuller, explicit reference to Dan. 12:1 (cf. Mark 13:19). The tribulation in Daniel consists of the eschatological opponent persecuting the saints because of their covenant loyalty to God (see Dan. 11:30–39, 44; 12:10). Some will apostatize and also persecute those remaining loyal, especially by attempting to cause the faithful to forsake their loyalty (Dan. 11:32, 34; 12:10). In John's view, this tribulation has already begun (cf. 1 Macc. 9:27, which understands that the "great tribulation" of Dan. 12:1 had already begun in the second century BC as a result of the chaos produced by Judas Maccabaeus's death at the hands of Israel's enemy).

7:15

The reference to the multitudes being "in his temple" where God "tabernacles over them" is a clear echo from the prophecy of Israel's restoration in Ezek. 37:26–28 LXX. There God says, "I will establish my sanctuary in the midst of them forever. And my tabernacle [*kataskēnōsis*] shall be over them . . . when my sanctuary is in the midst of them forever." The link with Ezekiel is confirmed by the parallel in Rev. 21:3, where Ezek. 37:27 is quoted more fully and is immediately followed in 21:4, 6b by the same OT allusions found in 7:16–17 directly following 7:15. Yet again, the innumerable multitudes of redeemed in the church are viewed as the fulfillment of a prophecy concerning Israel's latter-day restoration. The application of the Ezek. 37:27 prophecy to the church is striking because Ezekiel emphasizes that when this prophecy takes place, the immediate result will

be that "the nations will recognize that I am the LORD, who sanctifies *Israel*, when my sanctuary is in their midst" (37:28). Thus, the church appears to be the continuation of true Israel.

7:16–17

The saved multitudes from all peoples (cf. 7:9) who enjoy God's presence continue to be described as a fulfillment of Israel's prophesied restoration. They enjoy the comforts of the divine presence that were promised as a part of the restoration. John appeals to Isa. 49:10, which affirms, "They shall not hunger, neither shall they thirst; neither shall the heat nor the sun smite them . . . and by fountains of waters shall he lead them" (cf. John 6:35). The "fountains of waters" from Isaiah have now become the "fountains of the waters of life." The word *zōēs* ("of life") could be either an appositional genitive ("fountains of waters which are life") or, more likely, an adjectival genitive ("fountains of living waters"). These "living waters," which picture eternal life, have their origin in God and the Lamb (so 21:6; 22:1, 17) (*1 En.* 48:1–4 is a development of the Isaiah text together with Isa. 49:6; see also Ps. 36:8–9; 46:4–5; Prov. 14:27; Isa. 12:3; 33:21; 55:1–3; Jer. 2:13; Joel 3:18; *1 En.* 96:6; John 4:14; 7:38; in contrast, 1QH^a XVI, 4–10 identifies the Teacher of Righteousness from Qumran as the fount of living waters from which the saints should drink). This is the life of eternal fellowship with God and Christ.

Even the image of the Lamb "shepherding them" in 7:17 comes from Isa. 49:9, where the Lord says that "in all the paths they will be pastured" (so also 49:10; cf. Ps. 23:1–2). Both Isa. 49 and Ps. 23 portray God as the shepherd, so that Christ's shepherding role here enhances his position as a divine figure.

An additional allusion to a restoration promise from Isa. 25:8 is appended at the end of the Isa. 49:10 wording: "God will wipe away every tear from their eyes." The reason there will no longer be any mourning is that God "will swallow up death for all time," which is the introductory phrase of Isa. 25:8. Although John omits the initial line about the cessation of death, he probably assumes it as the basis for the promise that there will be no more weeping (since he does include this part of Isa. 25:8 in 21:4: "death will be no longer," which is placed directly after "He will wipe away every tear from their eyes").

Revelation 8:1–12

The chapter begins with a depiction of final judgment—the "silence" of judgment that accompanies the opening of the seventh seal. A septet of trumpet judgments then commences, with a depiction of the devastation of the natural order modeled on the plagues that accompanied Israel's exodus from Egypt.

8:1

The silence after the opening of the seventh seal should be understood as the silence attending the final judgment of the world. The following considerations support this conclusion.

Although *sigē* ("silence") occurs only twice in the LXX, silence is often associated with divine judgment in the OT (see, e.g., 1 Sam. 2:9–10; Ps. 31:17; 115:17; Isa. 47:5; Lam. 2:10–11; Ezek. 27:32; Amos 8:2–3; as well as 1 Macc. 1:3; *4 Ezra* 7:30; cf. *4 Ezra* 6:39; *2 Bar.* 3:7). Especially relevant for consideration are Hab. 2:20; Zech. 2:13, where the Lord is pictured as being in "his holy temple" in heaven, from which he executes judgment upon the ungodly (i.e., Babylon). That the temple in these OT texts is in heaven is to be assumed from other texts in the OT (e.g., Ezek. 1:1–28) and Jewish apocalyptic, where Yahweh's temple is located in heaven. The anticipated response (or the subsequent response) to the judgment in these two texts is that "all the earth" and "all flesh" stand in silent awe (cf. Isa. 23:2; 41:1–5). Jewish commentators affirmed that the Song of Moses, which predominantly predicts the judgment of Israel because of idolatry, caused the whole creation to respond in silence (Ginzberg 1967: 6:947).

Temple imagery is evoked again in Zeph. 1:7, where people are to "be silent" because God is about to slay them like a cultic sacrifice (cf. Zeph. 1:11: "All the people of Canaan will be silenced"). These three announcements of judgment from the Minor Prophets are perceived as cosmic eschatological expectations from the perspective of the writers, which may be implicitly expressed in the pregnant word "all" (see D. Stuart 1987; cf.

the note of universal eschatological judgment in Zeph. 1:2–3, 14).

Also in 8:1 may be an echo of the "primeval silence" expected to occur at the end of history when all earth's inhabitants die; this immediately precedes the final judgment (*4 Ezra* 7:30). Silence was understood to precede the first creation in Gen. 1, according to *4 Ezra* 6:39; *2 Bar.* 3:7; *L.A.B.* 60:2. In *Midr. Rab.* Exod. 39:9 it is said that immediately before the judgment of the Baal prophets at Mount Carmel there was silence over the entire creation. It compares this to the "waste and void" that preceded the first creation.

In OT and Jewish tradition "silence" is associated both with Egypt's defeat and Israel's redemption at the Red Sea. This likely derives from Exod. 14:14 LXX, where Moses commands the Israelites to "be silent" [*sigaō*] and not fight, because the Lord would destroy the Egyptians. Wisdom 18–19 is especially interesting. A "quiet silence" (18:14) immediately precedes God's judgment of the firstborn in Egypt—this just after Moses' intercessory prayer, which appears to be equated with a propitiation of incense (18:21). The deliverance of Israel is then repeatedly described as a new creation (19:6–8, 11, 18–21). For related descriptions of the judgment of Egypt, we may compare *Tg. Exod.* 15; Ps. 76:6–9; *Mek. R. Ish. Shir.* 7:20–23.

Finally, there is a Jewish tradition that in the fifth heaven angelic servants praise God at night but become silent during the day so that the praises offered by Israel could be heard by God (*b. Ḥag.* 12b; *b. ʿAbod. Zar.* 3b). A partial basis for both this Jewish tradition and Rev. 8:1 may be Ps. 65:1–2: "There will be silence before Thee, [even] praise in Zion ... O Thou who dost hear prayer" (cf. *Midr. Ps.* 65:1; *b. ʿErubin* 19a; *Midr. Ps.* 31 on Ps. 31:18; *T. Adam* 1:11–12; 4Q405 20 II, 7). A variant of this theme is reflected in *Tg. Ezek.* 1:24–25, which asserts that when the guardian cherubs were in motion, they "were blessing and thanking" God, but "when they stood still, [they] became silent" in order to hear God's revelatory word, which in the context of Ezek. 1–2 is a pronouncement of judgment on Israel.

Why the silence lasts "for about a half hour" is unclear. The prefixing of *hōs* ("as, about") to *hēmiōrion* ("half hour") shows that this was only an approximation, so that it could be almost equivalent to *hōra* elsewhere in the book. A "half hour" emphasizes the suddenness and unexpectedness of a decreed judgment, and the crisis that it introduces. The most comparable parallel is Dan. 4:19 Θ, where Daniel stood speechless, "his thoughts troubled him," and he was "amazed about one hour [*hōsei hōran mian*]" after hearing the dream foretelling Nebuchadnezzar's doom.

8:2

The seven angels may be identified with the seven well-known archangels of Jewish apocalyptic (so I. T. Beckwith 1919: 550–51; see Tob. 12:15; *1 En.* 20:1–8; 81:5; 90:21–22; *T. Levi* 3:5; *Pirqe R. El.* 4; cf. *1 En.* 40; 54:6; 71:8–9; see also commentary on Rev. 1:4b above). It is tempting to identify them with the seven guardian angels of the seven churches in chapters 2–3 (cf. 1:20). Angels as divine agents executing the plagues follows the trajectory of biblical and Jewish tradition that angels were appointed by God to perform the judgments against the Egyptians, especially at the Red Sea (Exod. 12:23; Ps. 78:49–50; *Tg. Jerus. Frag.* Exod. 4:25; 12:42; 15:18; *Jub.* 49:2; *Mek. R. Ish.* Beshallah 7:30–35, 40–45).

8:4

The "much incense . . . with the prayers" that "went up . . . before God" is metaphorical of acceptance by God: "prayer . . . as incense" in the OT connotes a prayer accepted by God (e.g., Ps. 141:1–2; cf. *Midr. Rab.* Num. 13:18). Divine acceptance was also indicated by the fragrant "smoke of incense" in the OT temple (e.g., Lev. 16:12–13). In the OT and the NT incense was always associated with sacrifices. Incense was added to the burning of the sacrifice in order to make it acceptable to God (such as that on the Day of Atonement [e.g., Lev. 16:11–19; cf. Exod. 29:18, 25; Lev. 2:1–2; Eph. 5:2; see Weisberg 1970]). Revelation 8:3–5 echoes Lev. 16:12–13 LXX: the priest "will take his censer full of coals of fire off the altar, which is before the Lord; and he will fill his hands with . . . incense . . . and he will put the incense on the fire before the Lord, and the smoke of the incense will cover the mercy seat." Similarly, Exod. 30:8–10 virtually equates "incense" with "burnt offering" and "meal offering" and links it directly with the Day of Atonement. The point here is that the Lord hears the prayers of his priestly people (cf. Rev. 1:5; 5:10) and answers with devastating judgment. Consequently, the Leviticus and Exodus portrayals serve as analogical precursors for Rev. 8:4.

8:5

This is the last judgment. The fire results in "thunders and sounds and lightnings and quaking," which is an almost identical expression for a description of consummate judgment in 11:19; 16:18. This fourfold metaphorical chain of cosmic disturbance has a precedent in the OT, where also it refers to divine judgment (e.g., esp. Exod. 19:16, 18; also Ps. 77:17–18; Isa. 29:6; Esther 1:1d LXX; cf. Ps. 18:7–13). Since the formulaic phrase concludes the series of trumpets and bowls by referring to the last judgment, the same formula here likewise must conclude the series of seals. The Sinai theophany of Exod. 19:16–18 is partly in mind in 8:5, since it was part of the allusion, if not the primary one, in 4:5 (cf. Ps. 68:8; 77:17–18; Hab. 3). Sometimes the earthquake is found listed as part of a series of cataclysmic signs that are woes preliminary to the final cosmic destruction but are not part of it (*2 Bar.* 27:7; 70:8; *4 Ezra* 9:3; *Apoc. Ab.* 30:6; Matt. 24:7 pars.). But whenever there is explicit allusion to the Sinai or Exodus earthquake as an eschatological event, it is a sign of the climactic destruction of the world. The same is true when the earthquake is mentioned as the sole eschatological sign.

Not only are the virtually identical phrases in 4:5; 8:5; 11:19; 16:18–21 all Sinai allusions, but also they are linked together by the theme of final judgment. Bauckham (1977: 228) has observed that these phrases form a progressive sequence of allusions to Exod. 19 that systematically build upon one another:

4:5: "lightnings and sounds and thunders"

8:5: "thunders and sounds and lightnings and quaking"

11:19: "lightnings and sounds and thunders and quaking and great hail"

16:18–21: "lightnings and sounds and thunders and great quaking . . . and great hail"

This OT background, especially that of Sinai, functions as an adumbration of the climactic eschatological punishment.

The portrayal of 8:3–5 is modeled to a great extent on Ezek. 10:1–7. There also an angelic figure stands in the heavenly temple (cf. Ezek. 1:1–28) and is told, "Fill your hands with coals of fire from between the cherubim [presumably from the altar] and scatter them over the city [Jerusalem]" (10:2; cf. 10:6–7). This comes immediately after the narrative of Ezek. 9, in which the angels are commanded to slay all the unfaithful in Jerusalem upon whose foreheads God's angel did not place a protective mark. Again, the Ezekiel description is viewed as containing a pattern that corresponds to the greater judgment at the end of history.

In 8:6–12, the first four trumpets clearly are modeled on the exodus plagues that came against Egypt (for the predominantly symbolic nature of the trumpet visions, see Beale 1999a: 50–55). This is a systematic dismantling of the created order of Gen. 1, though not in the same order: the elements affected are light, air, vegetation, sun, moon, stars, sea creatures, and humans (Paulien 1988a: 229–30; cf. McDonough 2000). The notion of a "de-creation" (Ellul 1977: 74, 76) is supported by the fact that the book climaxes in new creation (21:1–22:5) and that the trumpet series has begun a new overview of history. This spins out of the seventh seal, which partly evoked the silence following the destruction of the old creation (for a similar view on the exodus plagues themselves, see Philo, *Moses* 1.96–97). The Exodus plagues prefigure the escalated judgments seen in the first four trumpets, and other OT allusions in Rev. 8:6–12 are woven in to enhance the Exodus framework.

Although some commentators affirmed that the plagues brought some Egyptians to repentance (e.g., Josephus, *Ant.* 2.293–295; Philo, *Moses* 1.147), God's overall intention in the plague narratives was to demonstrate his incomparable omnipotence to the Egyptians (Exod. 7:5, 17; 8:6, 18; 9:16, 29; 10:1–2). The exodus plagues also had the function of demonstrating the hardness of heart in Pharaoh and in the majority of the Egyptians. In light of the failure of the inhabitants of the world to repent (Rev. 9:20–21), the trumpets may signify hardening judgment more than a call to repentance, although the latter is not to be excluded completely.

The trumpet imagery works in a similar way. Trumpets were obvious signs of warning that bat-

tle is near (see, e.g., Judg. 7:16–22; Jer. 4:5–21; 42:14; 51:27; Ezek. 7:14; Hos. 8:1; Joel 2:1; Zeph. 1:16), and thus they might be appropriate symbols of a call to repentance. On the other hand, because the trumpets are generally sounded in holy war, they are equally susceptible to be taken as signs of certain, destructive judgment. This certainly is the case in the fall of Jericho, which forms the primary background for the seven trumpets of Revelation.

8:7

This verse is patterned after the Egyptian plague of hail and fire in Exod. 9:23–25 LXX: "And the Lord gave . . . hail, and fire ran upon the land [*gē*]. And the Lord rained hail upon all the land [*gē*]. . . . And there was hail and flaming fire mingled with the hail. . . . And the hail struck in all the land [*gē*]. . . . And the hail struck all the vegetation in the field, and the hail shattered all the trees in the field." Both Exod. 9 and Rev. 8:7 present an affliction of hail together with fire sent from heaven against three parts of creation: the earth or land, the trees, and the grass. Although the trial from Exodus has been limited in Revelation in two of its effects to "one-third," it has also undergone universalization. Now the affliction has effect throughout the inhabited earth. The parts of the earth affected are associated with food supplies, as is clear from Exod. 9:25, 31–32. But the exodus plague destroys only part of the food supply (Exod. 9:31–32: "Now the flax and barley were smitten . . . but the wheat and the rye were not smitten"). This is strikingly similar to the description in Rev. 6:6, where there is famine, and wheat and barley are scarce but still available.

The limitation of the tribulation to one-third of the land is above all due to the influence of Ezek. 5:2, 12 (cf. Zech. 13:8–9). There, the effect of the coming judgment is determined metaphorically by using "scales for weighing." Israel is pictured as being divided into thirds and judged accordingly. One-third is to be burned with fire, one-third struck by sword, and one-third scattered into captivity (Ezek. 5:2). Ezekiel 5:12 repeats the verdict virtually verbatim except that the precise judgment of fire from 5:2 is omitted and interpreted by "plague and famine." Ezekiel 5 concludes the prediction of coming judgment with an emphasis on famine (so 5:16–17). Fire may similarly be a metaphor for famine in Rev. 8.

8:8–9

The second trumpet continues the judgment theme of the first. The seer has a vision of something "like a great mountain burning with fire thrown into the sea." The likeness of a mountain could be metaphorical for a kingdom, as elsewhere in Revelation (14:1; 17:9; 21:10) and in the OT and Jewish apocalyptic. This meaning is supported by 18:21, which is based on Jer. 51:63–64 (cf. *1 En.* 18:13; 21:3; *Sib. Or.* 5:512–531), where similarly the prophet commands Seraiah to tie a stone to a book and cast it into the Euphrates to represent Babylon's fall. The angel immediately interprets the symbolism of his action by saying, "Thus will Babylon, the great city, be thrown down with violence, and will not be found any longer." It is likely that this same background is in view in Rev. 8 and that the second trumpet indicates the judgment of Babylon, the "great city" of Rev. 11–18.

The mention that "a third of the sea became blood" is a direct allusion to Exod. 7:20, where Moses turns the water of the Nile into blood. And as in Exod. 7:21 the fish in the Nile died, likewise in Rev. 8:9 "a third of the creatures which were in the sea died."

8:10–11

The allusion in 8:8–9 to Exod. 7:15–24 may still stand in the background, as is evident from the statement in 8:10 that the "rivers and the springs of waters" were affected (cf. Exod. 7:19). The similarity is enhanced by Ps. 78:44, which paraphrases the exodus plague thus: God "changed their rivers into blood, so that they should not drink of their streams."

In keeping with Rev. 1's equation of stars and angels, the "burning star" likely indicates the judgment of an angel (cf. esp. *1 En.* 18:13; 21:3; 108:3–6, the first two of which describe the judgment of fallen angels as "stars like great burning mountains"; the last borrows the same image to picture the punishment of sinful people; see also *1 En.* 86–88). The identification of the star as being Babylon's representative angel becomes more convincing if 8:10 is an allusion to Isa. 14:12–15 (so also Caird 1966: 115; J. M. Ford

1975: 133; Sweet 1979: 163; Buchanan 1993: 215; cf. *Sib. Or.* 5:158–160).

The star is called "Wormwood," a bitter herb, and one-third of the waters that it strikes are turned into wormwood. This scene of judgment is based on Jer. 9:15; 23:15. Both texts affirm that God "will feed them [Israel] . . . with wormwood and give them poisoned water to drink." This judgment in Jeremiah is part of a description of coming famine, alluded to earlier in 8:13–14: "There will be no grapes on the vine, and no figs on the fig tree, and the leaf shall wither; and what I have given them shall pass away. . . . For the LORD has doomed us and given us poisoned water to drink." There too the woe of famine occurs because of idolatry (8:19). A figurative understanding of wormwood as a metaphor for the bitterness of punishment is confirmed from the indisputable metaphorical use elsewhere in the OT, where it also represents severe affliction as a consequence of divine wrath (see Deut. 29:17–18 [again in connection with idolatry]; Prov. 5:4; Lam. 3:15, 19; Amos 5:7; 6:12 [cf. Hos. 10:4]).

8:12

The fourth trumpet is partly based on Exod. 10:22 (cf. Amos 8:9), where God sent darkness over Egypt for three days. Early Jewish tradition understood the plague of darkness to have symbolic significance—for example, as representing estrangement from God and eternal judgment (Wis. 15–17), and a similar meaning is likely in mind here.

Revelation 8:13–9:21

The trumpet judgments continue, culminating with the gathering of the great army at the Euphrates. As with the previous plagues, judgments focused in the OT on Egypt or Israel are universalized here, at least in an analogical sense, and it may be that the OT judgments are understood to contain a forward-looking aspect to that in Rev. 8:13–9:21.

8:13

This verse is in keeping with the image of an "eagle" (*aetos*, which can be translated also as "vulture") as a metaphor of destruction in OT announcements of coming judgment (see esp.

Hos. 8:1; Jer. 4:13; cf. Deut. 28:49; Job 9:26; Jer. 4:13; 48:40; 49:22; Lam. 4:19; Ezek. 17:3; Hab. 1:8; for Judaism, see Ginzberg 1967: 6:100; see also Luke 17:37).

9:1

The abyss in the LXX is always related to water, whether it be the chaotic waters—the "primeval deep"—of the creation account (Gen. 1:2; Ps. 103:6 [104:6 ET]), the waters of the sea (Isa. 63:13), or the waters below the earth (Ezek. 31:15). Because all of these could be symbolically associated with evil forces, however, by NT times the abyss was spoken of more broadly as the place of punishment and/or confinement for wicked spirits (in addition to Revelation, see Luke 8:31; *1 En.* 10:4–14; 18:11–16; 19:1; 21:7; 54:1–6; 88:1–3; 90:23–26; *Jub.* 5:6–14; 2 Pet. 2:4; cf. *4 Ezra* 7:36; *Pr. Man.* 3). This clearly is what is in view here.

9:2

Dense smoke arises from the abyss when the angel opens it. The smoke darkens both the sun and air. Partly included is Exod. 10:15, which describes a swarm of locusts so great "that the land was darkened." Note also the theme of darkness in the account of the locust plague in Joel 2:2, 10.

9:4

The locusts in Exod. 10:15 destroyed "the land, and they devoured the vegetation, and all the fruit of the trees . . . [and] there was no green thing left on the trees" (so also Ps. 105:33–35). In contrast to the locusts in Exodus, these are commissioned "not to harm the grass of the earth nor any green thing nor any tree." They are to harm only unbelievers, who do "not have the seal of God upon their foreheads." Just as the plagues did not harm the Israelites but only the Egyptians (Exod. 8:22–24; 9:4–7, 26; 10:21–23), so likewise true Christians are protected (spiritually [cf. Rev. 7]) from the fifth plague.

9:5

Deuteronomy 28 predicts that "in the latter days" (Deut. 4:30) Israel would suffer the plagues of Egypt (28:27, 60), including that of locusts (28:38–39, 42), because of their idolatry (e.g., 28:14; 29:22–27; 30:17; 31:16–20). This latter-day affliction includes "plagues" (28:61)

of "madness and . . . bewilderment of heart, and groping at noon, as the blind man gropes in darkness" (28:28–29), being "driven mad" (28:34), "trembling heart . . . despair of soul" (28:65); their "life shall hang in doubt," and they would have "dread of heart" (28:66–67). Revelation 9:6 explains the torment of 9:5 in a similar psychological manner.

9:6

As elsewhere in Scripture, so here severe suffering often causes a desire for death rather than a life of torment (see, e.g., 1 Kings 19:1–4; Job 3; 6:8–9; 7:15–16; Jer. 8:3; 20:14–18; Jon. 4:3, 8; Luke 23:27–30).

9:7

The portrayal in 9:7–9 is based on Joel 1–2, which describes a plague of locusts devastating Israel's land (cf. Jer. 51:27). The locust judgment in Joel 2 is introduced and concluded with the phrase "sound the trumpet" (2:1, 15). This judgment in Joel is modeled on the plague of locusts in Exod. 10 (note the clear allusions in Joel 1:2; 2:2 [= Exod. 10:6, 14]; 1:3 [= Exod. 10:2]; 2:9 [= Exod. 10:6]; 2:27 [= Exod. 10:2; cf. 8:22]). It is thus natural that Joel would be used to supplement the description of the exodus locusts already alluded to in 9:3–5.

9:8

The statement that "their teeth were as [those] of lions" is based on Joel 1:6: the locusts were like "a nation" whose "teeth are the teeth of a lion." Later Judaism compared the teeth of the locusts that plagued Egypt to the teeth of lions (see Ginzberg 1967: 2:345).

9:9

Partial allusion may be made to Job 39:19–25 (LXX + MT), which describes the war horse as going forth only at the "trumpet sound," clothed "in terror" and "in perfect armor," and "leaping like the locust" (see Kraft 1974: 141–42). Again, the phrase "the sound of their [the locusts'] wings as the sound of chariots, of many horses running unto battle" is an allusion to Joel 2:4–5: "Their appearance is like the appearance of horses, and like war horses, so they run, like the sound of chariots they leap on the tops of the mountains . . . arranged for battle."

9:10

Jewish tradition held that in Sheol and Abaddon there were "angels of destruction," who were in authority over thousands of scorpions. The sting of the scorpions was lethal (Ginzberg 1967: 1:11–16). However, some of the stings do not kill, but only torment the inhabitants of hell (Ginzberg 1967: 2:312).

9:11

The name of the angel who controls the realm of the demons is "Abaddon" (Hebrew for "destruction") and "Apollyon" (Greek for "destroyer"). In the OT "destruction" is sometimes synonymous with "hell" (Sheol) or "death," the realm of the dead (Job 26:6; 28:22; Ps. 88:11; Prov. 15:11; 27:20).

9:14

That the four (presumably wicked) angels are held back at the "great river Euphrates" evokes the OT prophecy of a northern enemy beyond the Euphrates whom God would bring to judge sinful Israel (cf. Isa. 7:20; 8:7–8; 14:29–31; Jer. 1:14–15; 4:6–13; 6:1, 22; 10:22; 13:20; Ezek. 38:6, 15; 39:2; Joel 2:1–11, 20–25), as well as other ungodly nations around Israel (Isa. 14:31; Jer. 25:9, 26; 46–47; 50:41–42; Ezek. 26:7–11 [from Israel's vantage point, the Euphrates ran north as well as east]). In both cases the invaders were characterized as a terrifying army on horses/chariots arising from the north (Isa. 5:26–29; Jer. 4:6–13; 6:1, 22; 46–47; 50:41–42; Ezek. 26:7–11; 38:6, 15; 39:2; Hab. 1:8–9; cf. *As. Mos.* 3:1; in Amos 7:1 LXX an army like locusts is pictured "coming from the east"). The echoes of Jer. 46 are especially strong.

9:17

In the OT the metaphor of "fire and sulphur," sometimes together with "smoke," indicates a fatal judgment (Gen. 19:24, 28; Deut. 29:23; 2 Sam. 22:9; Isa. 34:9–10; Ezek. 38:22).

9:19

The description of the creatures in the sixth trumpet echoes Job's portrait of the sea dragon, the symbol of cosmic evil (Job 40–41). This enhances the identification of these creatures with Satan and his deceptive work. The implication of deception, along with spiritual and physical death, is suggested by the fact that the saints cannot be harmed by these plagues. The essence of the saints' seal is not immunity from physical death, but rather protection against being deceived and losing their covenantal relationship with God.

9:20

Despite the plagues, the ungodly do not repent from idolatry, "from the work of their hands." The typical OT list of idols according to their material essence is stated (cf. Deut. 4:28; Ps. 115:4–7; 135:15–17; Dan. 5:4, 23). The catalog of sins is prefaced by a summary of the idols' spiritual essence: they are demonic (as is seen also in Deut. 32:17; Ps. 95:5 LXX [96:5 ET]; 106:36–37; *Jub.* 11:4; *1 En.* 19:1; 99:6–7; 1 Cor. 10:20).

Revelation 10

Just as the sixth seal was followed by an image of God's "sealing" of the saints, so also the sixth trumpet will be followed by a similar scene of God's spiritual protection of his people (the "measuring of the temple" [see commentary on Rev. 11 below]). This interlude between the sixth and seventh trumpets begins with the dramatic appearance of an angel who commissions John in terms drawn from the commissioning of the prophet Ezekiel.

10:1

The angel in chapter 10 has some unmistakable features of divinity. The first sign of this is that he is "clothed with a cloud." In the OT God alone comes in heaven or to earth in a cloud. In Exod. 19:9–19 God's descent on Sinai "in a thick cloud" and "in fire" is announced by "thunder" and "the sound of a trumpet," which reflects the pattern of Rev. 10, where "thunder" and a "trumpet sound" follow in 10:3–4, 7 (Philo [*Decalogue* 44] paraphrases Exod. 19:18 as "the descent of a cloud which like a pillar stood with its foot planted on the earth"). During Israel's wilderness wanderings God dwelt among them in the form of a "pillar of cloud" and "pillar of fire" (Exod. 13:20–22; 14:24; Num. 14:14; Neh. 9:12, 19; cf. Exod. 40:38; Num. 9:15–16; 14:14; Deut. 1:33; 4:11; 5:22; Ps. 78:14; 105:39; Isa. 4:5; Ezek. 1:4). Sometimes God was spoken of as dwelling among the nation in only a "pillar of cloud" (Exod. 14:19; 33:9–10; 34:5;

Num. 12:5; Deut. 31:15; Ps. 99:7). Even when reference is made merely to a "cloud" in connection with a heavenly being's advent, that being is always God (Exod. 14:20; 16:10; 19:9, 16; 24:15–16, 18; 40:34–37; Lev. 16:2; Num. 9:17–22; 10:11–12, 34; 11:25; 12:10; 16:42; 2 Sam. 22:12; 1 Kings 8:10–11; 2 Chron. 5:13–14; Ps. 18:11–12; 68:4; 97:2; 104:3; Isa. 19:1; Jer. 4:13; Ezek. 1:28; 10:3–4; Dan. 7:13; Nah. 1:3; Matt. 17:5 pars.). The only possible exception to this may be Dan. 7:13, where the "one like a son of man" comes on the clouds to receive authority from the Ancient of Days; however, in light of the cloud imagery everywhere else being linked to God's presence, the "son of man" probably should be seen as a divine figure representing Israel (which is the way the earliest interpretation of Dan. 7:13 takes it: the old LXX [versus Theodotion] reads, "and as [not 'unto'] the Ancient of Days he came").

The angel in 10:1 thus is probably equivalent to "the angel of Yahweh" in the OT, who is referred to as Yahweh himself (e.g., Gen. 16:10; 22:11–18; 24:7; 31:11–13; Exod. 3:2–12; 14:19; Judg. 2:1; 6:22; 13:20–22; cf. Zech. 3:1–3 with Jude 9; see also Dan. 3:25; Acts 7:30, 35, 38). This is confirmed further by two allusions to Dan. 7:13 in chapter 1, where the one "coming with the clouds" in 1:7 is identified further in 1:13 as "like a son of man" who is given the attributes of the divine Ancient of Days, an interpretation of the "son of man" along the lines already given in the old LXX. Since the "son of man" figure in Rev. 1 clearly is Jesus, he is also to be identified with the "angel of the Lord" figure in 10:1. The pattern here of a divine angel of the Lord appearing in order to commission a prophet is a reflection of the same repeated pattern in the OT (e.g., Exod. 3:2–12; Judg. 6:22; 2 Kings 1:3–15; 1 Chron. 21:18).

Another indication that the angel of 10:1 is a divine being is the following description that "the rainbow was upon his head." Especially near in thought is Ezek. 1:26–28, where "the glory of the LORD" is described as being like a rainbow. The only other reference to "rainbow" (*iris*) in the NT is Rev. 4:3, where "a rainbow is around the [divine] throne." Consequently, the rainbow of 4:3 is applied intentionally to the heavenly being of 10:1.

The portrait of the angel in chapter 10 is based on the portrait of the heavenly being in the vision of Dan. 10–12. This is a significant observation because the being in Dan. 10 is referred to "as the likeness of a son of man" (Dan. 10:16 Θ [cf. LXX of 10:6, 18; MT of 10:18]). This substantiates further the link between the "son of man" vision of chapter 1 and the depiction of the angel here, especially in view of the fact that the inaugural vision of chapter 1 is also based partly on Dan. 10 (see commentary on Rev. 1:13–16, 17 above). Note also the small change in wording between the clause of 1:15 and here (the heavenly being in Dan. 10:6 MT/LXX likewise has "feet as the appearance of polished bronze"): the feet of the heavenly being are now called "pillars of fire" instead of "bronze as having been fired in a furnace." The reason for the change is to evoke the presence of Yahweh with Israel in the wilderness, where he appeared as "a pillar of cloud . . . and a pillar of fire" to protect and guide them.

10:3–4

Since there is clear allusion to Amos 3:7 in 10:7, it is probable that reference to the roar of a lion in 10:3 is an allusion to Amos 3:8: "A lion has roared! Who will not fear? The LORD God has spoken! Who can but prophesy?" (Bauckham 1993a: 259). This underscores the divine aspect of the angelic speaker in 10:3 (God's voice is also compared to that of a lion in Isa. 31:4; Hos. 11:10).

Thunder in the OT and Revelation is a clear signal of judgment (cf. Exod. 9:23–34 [5x]; 19:16, 19; 1 Sam. 7:10; 12:17; Ps. 29:3; 77:17–18; 81:7; Isa. 29:6; Rev. 4:5; 6:1). The seven thunders may be based on Ps. 29, where God's thunders of punishment are equated with "the voice of the LORD," the latter of which is repeated seven times in the psalm (see Kiddle and Ross 1940: 169; Wilcock 1975: 101; Sweet 1979: 178; also Feuillet [1964: 219], who lists others in support).

The command in 10:4b to "seal up" the seven thunders reflects the similar command given to Daniel by the angel, who is the model for the angel here and in 10:5–6 (Dan. 12:4, 7, 9 Θ; note the common use of *sphragizō* ["seal"] in Daniel and Revelation; see also Dan. 8:26). Many commentators take this to mean a revocation of judgments that would have come had God not "shortened the time." This fits with the fact that John not only is to "seal up" this portion of the vision/audition, but also is not even to write the words down. On the other hand, "seal up" in Daniel refers not to the cancellation of future events, but rather to the obscurity of their fulfillment.

10:5–6

The description of the angel and his address to God is a direct allusion to Dan. 12:7, a text that is a development of Deut. 32:40, which also may be secondarily in mind here in the Revelation text. The verse in Deut. 32 is an oath by God that he will judge the ungodly. God swears oaths elsewhere throughout the OT (see Gen. 22:16; Exod. 32:13; Isa. 45:43; Jer. 49:13; Ezek. 20:5; Amos 6:8; cf. Heb. 6:13; see Chilton 1987: 264).

The content of the oath here follows the parenthetical description of God as creator. The oath continues to follow that of Dan. 12:7, though the idea has been altered somewhat. In Dan. 12:7 the oath is "that it would be for a time, times and half a time"; in contrast, the oath in Rev. 10:6 reads "that time shall be no longer." This phrase in Revelation expresses the idea that there is a predetermined time in the future when God's purposes for history will be completed (see Barr 1962: 76). The expression could be translated "there will be delay no longer" (*chronizō* has the meaning of delay in Hab. 2:3 LXX, where the fulfillment of the prophetic vision "will not delay" when the appointed time arrives for its execution; likewise Matt. 24:48; 25:5; Heb. 10:37). The point is that when God decides to terminate history, there will be no delay in doing so.

10:7

Daniel 12:7 goes on to say that after the "time, times, and half a time," God's prophetic plan would "be completed." The occurrence of *etelesthē* ("completed") here in 10:7 manifests the continuing influence of Dan. 12:7 (cf. *syntelesthēsetai* ["will be completed"] in Dan. 12:7 LXX). John views Daniel's prophecy about "times, time, and half a time" as fulfilled in the church age leading up to the final judgment (see commentary on Rev. 11:2; 12:6; 13:5 below).

The phrase "the mystery of God" is best taken as a genitive of source or a subjective genitive, since God is the revealer of the mystery in Daniel. Amos 3:7 is combined with the Danielic mystery idea, further confirming the genitive as source or subjective: Amos says that God "reveals his secret counsel to his servants the prophets" (the same Daniel-Amos combination appears also in

1QpHab 7:4–5 [see Beale 1984: 35–37]). The wider context of Amos 3:4–8 contains the triple mention of God as a lion roaring (1:2; 3:4, 8 [cf. Rev. 10:3]) and a trumpet blowing (3:6 [cf. Rev. 10:7]), all of which betoken judgment, as in Rev. 10 (so Farrer 1964: 124).

The word *mystērion* ("mystery") is chosen because of its Danielic flavor. The word is used in the Greek OT with a latter-day notion only in Daniel, and it refers to the interpretation of end-time prophecy as a mystery needing revelation to be understood (so Dan. 2:19, 27–30, 47; cf. 4:6 Θ) and often indicates elsewhere in the NT apparent unexpected (from the OT vantage point) inaugurated fulfillment (see Beale 1999b: 215–72, including discussion of the unexpected element in Rev. 10).

10:9–10

The precise reference for eating the scroll is clearly Ezek. 2:8–3:3. Ezekiel is called to warn Israel about their impending doom if they do not repent of their unbelief and idolatry (3:17–21; 5–14). He is to preach so that the nation will "know that a prophet has been among them," but also he is told that "Israel will not be willing to listen" to his message because "the whole house of Israel has a hard forehead and a stiff neck" (2:2–8; 3:4–11). Therefore, his message is primarily one of judgment. This is explicitly emphasized by the description of the scroll: "it was written on the front and back, and written on it were lamentations and mourning and woe" (2:10). However, there will be a remnant who will respond and repent (3:20; 9:4–6; 14:21–23). The prophet's eating of the scroll signifies his identification with its message.

The sweet taste of the scroll alludes to the life-sustaining attribute of God's word that empowers the prophet to carry out his task (e.g., Deut. 8:3), and to the positive and joyous effect that God's words have in instructing and guiding those who submit to them (e.g., Ps. 19:7–11; 119:97–104; Prov. 16:21–24; 24:13–14). Although Ezekiel's task is a sober one, he takes pleasure in the message of woe because it is God's will, which is good and holy. However, he does not contemplate this pleasure for long, since he focuses on the overall purpose of his call to announce judgment. Although Ezekiel does not refer to the scroll as being bitter in his stomach, he does refer to the scroll's "lamentations and mourning and woe" (2:10), which elicited in him a "bitter" response (3:14) after he ate it (cf. 3:3a). The bitterness is in response to either his grief over Israel's impending doom or his anger over their refusal to repent. Notable parallels are found in Jer. 6:10b–11a and, especially, 15:16–17: "Your words were found, and I ate them, and your words became for me a joy and the delight of my heart. . . . You filled me with anger." In context, the delight and anger of God's words that Jeremiah eats refer respectively to the prophet's own comfort and to the judgment of his enemies (the LXX of Jeremiah has, instead of "anger," the word *pikria* ["bitterness"], which is the nominal form of the verb used in Rev. 10:9–10). Like the prophets of old, John will preach a message that is sweet for those who heed God's word but carries bitter judgment for those who refuse it.

Revelation 11

God's spiritual protection of the saints is illustrated by the measuring of the temple in 11:1–2. The prophetic witness of the church is then given parabolic expression in the ministry of the two witnesses, whose faithful testimony and mighty works earn them the wrath of the beast. After their death and resurrection, the city of Babylon is devastated by an earthquake at the blowing of the seventh trumpet.

11:1

The measuring of the temple in 11:1 is best understood as a beginning fulfillment of the prophecy of the temple in Ezek. 40–48, where the sure establishment and subsequent protection of the temple is metaphorically pictured by an angel measuring various features of the temple (so also Lohmeyer 1970: 89–91; Ernst 1967: 130; Kraft 1974: 152; Prigent 1981: 159). In Rev. 11 the measuring (analogous to the "sealing" in chap. 7) connotes God's presence, which is guaranteed to be with the "temple" community (the church) living on earth before the consummation. This spiritual security is contrasted with the persecution of the church, which is symbolized by the trampling of the outer court (see commentary on Rev. 11:2 below). Such an apparent "spiritualizing" of the temple has ample precedent in the

NT (cf. John 2:21; 1 Cor. 3:16–17; 6:19; Eph. 2:21; 1 Pet. 2:5) as well as in early Judaism (cf. 1QS V, 5–6; VIII, 4–10; IX, 3–6; XI, 7–8; CD-A III, 19–IV, 6; 4Q174 1 I, 2–9) (so Gärtner 1965: 16–44; McKelvey 1969: 45–53), and it fits well with the generally symbolic nature of the images in Revelation. Rather than "spiritualizing," however, it is probably better to refer to a literal eschatologically escalated conception of the essential meaning of the OT temple, which is the architecturally unlimited and expanded end-time presence of God with his people (on which, see Beale 2004).

11:2

Both the outer court and the holy city represent the people of God who will be persecuted. This is the time when Daniel predicted that "the holy place [*to hagion*] and the host [were] to be trampled under foot [*sympatēthēsetai*]" (Dan. 8:13 Θ [so also 1 Macc. 3:45, 51; 4:60; 2 Macc. 8:2, which use *katapateō*; Isa. 63:18 uses the same wording as Daniel to speak of how Israel's "adversaries trampled down your sanctuary"; cf. Ps. 79:1]). Zechariah 12:3 LXX, possibly paralleling the idea of "trampling" in Dan. 8:13, may also partially be alluded to: "I will make Jerusalem a stone trampled by all the nations; every one who tramples it will utterly mock at it" (Bauckham 1993a: 270–71). For the nations to "trample down the city" is equivalent to them "trampling down the altar" and the temple (as also in *Pss. Sol.* 2:2, 19; 7:2; 17:22). The unusual language of "casting out the court outside the temple" may come from John's translation of Dan. 8:11 as "the place of his sanctuary was cast out" (Bauckham 1993a: 267–73).

The number "forty-two" months is not precisely literal, but rather is figurative for the extended eschatological period of tribulation repeatedly prophesied by Daniel (7:25; 9:27; 12:7, 11–12). The use of "forty-two" here and in 13:5 recalls the same time of Elijah's ministry of judgment (see commentary on Rev. 11:6 below) and Israel's wilderness wandering after the exodus, which encompassed a total of forty-two encampments (so Num. 33:5–49; see Morris 1987: 147). One may also reckon forty-two years as Israel's total sojourn in the wilderness, since it appears that they were in the wilderness for two years before incurring the penalty of remaining there for forty years until the death of the first generation (so Farrer 1964: 132). In 12:6 the messianic community (= the "woman") is protected from the dragon's onslaught during the three and a half years by taking refuge in "the wilderness, where she has there a place prepared by God." The picture in 12:14 is virtually identical. This "place" (*topos*) in which Christians are kept safe from the devil is likely none other than the invisible sanctuary of God, since that is to be the object of attack during the three and a half years in Daniel, and since that is the idea in Rev. 11:1–2; 13:5–6. This is pointed to by the fact that *topos* can be a synonym for the "sanctuary" in the NT and is a widespread synonym for the "sanctuary" in the LXX, including Dan. 8:11 (on which, see commentary on Rev. 12:6 below). The three and a half years is thus a symbolic representation of the time from Christ's death and resurrection to his second coming, which is considered to be a fulfillment of the prophesied three and a half year tribulation in Dan. 7, 9, and 12.

11:3

Why are the two witnesses referred to as two lampstands instead of the expected seven (see chap. 1)? The OT law demands that a minimum of two witnesses be required for just judgment (Num. 35:30; Deut. 17:6; 19:15). Thus the two witnesses are not two actual individual prophets; rather, they symbolize the corporate prophetic witness of the church.

The witnesses are "clothed in sackcloth," reflecting mourning over the judgment in which their message will result, possibly with the hope that some may repent. In the OT the wearing of sackcloth primarily refers to such mourning in the face of judgment, though sometimes repentance is also in mind. Twenty-seven out of approximately forty-two occurrences of the word "sackcloth" in the OT refer only to mourning, and an additional thirteen include mourning together with repentance (see, e.g., Gen. 37:34; 2 Sam. 3:31; Isa. 37:2; Dan. 9:3).

11:4

The two pictures of olive trees and lampstands together with the concluding clause of 11:4 come from Zech. 4:14 (cf. 4:2–3, 11–14). In Zechariah's vision the lampstand represented the second temple (the part for the whole), for which Zerubbabel had laid the foundation. On either

side was an olive tree, which provided the oil to light the lamps. The olive trees are interpreted to be "the anointed ones who are standing before the Lord of the whole earth" (4:14). In context, "the anointed ones" in 4:14 must refer to Joshua the high priest and Zerubbabel the king. The establishment and preservation of the true temple despite opposition has been introduced in Rev. 11:1–2, and Zech. 4:14 is a climax to a section concerning the very same topic. Just as the priest and king there were the key vessels used by the Spirit for the establishment of the temple against opposition, so here the two witnesses are empowered by the Spirit to perform the same role for the inaugurated latter-day temple in 11:1–2. As such, the witnesses as "lampstands" are viewed as conducting their luminescent ministry in the spiritual holy place of the invisible temple, since that is where the lampstands were positioned in the OT temple. In this respect, 11:4 continues the theme in 11:1–2 of believers being part of the true eschatological temple. The image of lampstands suggests strongly the corporate nature of the witnesses, since the only prior use of the lampstands in the book (chaps. 1–3) has referred to churches (part of the reason for only two here may be that only two churches in the letters did not receive criticism by Christ), so that the remnant faithful church is in mind.

The broader context of Zech. 4 shows the richness of the connection to the present context: (1) in Zech. 1:16–17; 2:1–5 an angel "measures" Jerusalem to signify that it surely will be reestablished in order that "God's house will be built in it," and that God "will be the glory in her midst" (cf. Rev. 11:1–2); (2) Satan, however, together with the world powers, opposed the reestablishment of God's temple in Jerusalem (Zech. 3:1–2; 4:7), just as the beast and the world oppose the invisible temple-building work of the witnesses (Rev. 11:5–10), part of whose task is to increase the size of the temple by causing others to be added to it through preaching and living the gospel (cf. the role of the churches as "lampstands" in Rev. 2–3, which includes "faithful witness" [2:13]).

11:5

The word of God's judgment can be spoken of as a fire in the mouths of the OT prophets. Note especially Jer. 5:14: "Because you have spoken this word, behold, I have given my words in your

mouth [as] fire . . . and it will consume them."
The Messiah's righteous judgment is spoken of
in a similar way in Isa. 11:4: "He will strike the
earth with the rod of his mouth, and with the
breath of his lips he will slay the wicked." The
messianic judgment is likewise figuratively portrayed elsewhere in Judaism (*4 Ezra* 13:25–39;
Pss. Sol. 17:24–26; cf. *1 En.* 62:2; *m. 'Abot* 2:10).
Similarly, in the OT God's judgment is pictured
as fire coming from his mouth and devouring
(2 Sam. 22:9; Ps. 18:8; cf. Ps. 97:3 with *Mart.
Isa.* 4:18). Elijah repeatedly called down fire that
consumed King Ahaziah's soldiers and led to the
king's death (note 2 Kings 1:10–17: *katebē pyr
. . . kai katephagen* ["fire descended . . . and consumed"]; note also Joseph in *Jos. Asen.* 25:5–6;
Abraham in *T. Ab.* [A] 10:11–12). Elijah calls
this fire down in order "to prove . . . he was a true
prophet" (Josephus, *Ant.* 9.23 [cf. 2 Kings 1:10]).
The echo of Elijah here anticipates the explicit
reference to him in the next verse. Moses' prophetic office was also demonstrated by his ability
to call down fire from heaven to judge the ungodly.
Moses and Elijah sometimes are compared partly
on the basis of their ability to call down fire (Philo,
Moses 2.282–284; *Pesiq. Rab* Piska 4). Hence, the
word of the two witnesses becomes an instrument
of judgment among those who reject it (at least in
the sense that it becomes part of the basis of judgment, but probably more is involved than this).

11:6

Shutting up the sky alludes to Elijah's prevention
of rain in Israel (1 Kings 11). It is noteworthy
that in Luke 4:25 and James 5:17 this period is
described as being three and a half years. The water
turning to blood obviously points toward Moses
(Exod. 7:17–25). It is possible that the coupling
of Elijah (perhaps symbolizing the prophets) and
Moses (symbolizing the law) points toward the
witnesses' faithful testimony to the whole OT
message. It is critical to note that the same types
of plagues inflicted on earth in chapters 6–11 are
here seen as emerging from the ministry of the two
witnesses in 11:5–6. In keeping with the symbolic
understanding of the witnesses argued for here,
this would indicate that the prayers of the faithful saints call down judgment on their oppressors
(cf. 6:9; and esp. 8:1–5). The resemblance to the
pattern of Moses' confrontations with Pharaoh is
clear. This is reinforced by the last clause of 11:6,

which says that the city of God "strikes the ungodly community with every manner of plague."
This follows the wording of the summary of all
the Egyptian plagues given in 1 Sam. 4:8. Hence,
Elijah and Moses are conceived of as presaging the
judicial witness of the eschatological covenant
community.

There was a deeply rooted OT-Jewish expectation that the prophets Moses and Elijah were to
come again before the end of history to restore Israel
and to judge the ungodly. For Moses in this respect,
see, for example, Deut. 18:15; John 1:21; 6:14;
7:40; Acts 3:22–23; 4Q175 4–8; 1 Macc. 4:44–46;
Josephus, *Ant.* 20.97–99; *Midr. Rab.* Exod. 2:4;
for Elijah, Mal. 3:1–5; 4:1–6; Sir. 48:1–10; Matt.
11:10–14; 27:47, 49; Mark 9:11–13; 15:35–36;
Luke 1:15–17; *L.A.B.* 48:1; *m. 'Ed.* 8:7; *b. Menaḥ.*
45a. For the expectation that both would come,
see *Midr. Rab.* Deut. 3:17; *4 Ezra* 6:26 (though
the latter may refer to Elijah and Enoch); also *Pesiq.
Rab.* Piska 4, which likewise draws out extensive
comparisons between the two.

11:7–8

The defeat of the saints is coined in language from
Dan. 7. In Dan. 7:3 the vision says that "four great
beasts came up out of the sea" (*tessara thēria megala
anebainon ek tēs thalassēs*), while Rev. 11:7 speaks of
"the beast coming up out of the abyss" (*to thērion to
anabainon ek tēs abyssou*) (see also Dan. 7:8, 21).

Daniel 7:21 is a prophecy of a final kingdom on
earth that will persecute and defeat God's people.
Afterward, the persecutors themselves will be
judged, and the saints will inherit the kingdom
of the world (Dan. 7:22–27). Since Dan. 7:21
refers to an attack on the Israelite saints, here also
the beast makes war not on two individuals, but
rather on the community of the faithful. That
this multiple view of the witnesses is probable is
shown by the use of the same Dan. 7:21 allusion in
13:7, where "saints" is substituted for "witnesses":
"to make war with the saints and to overcome
them." The futuristic depiction in Rev. 11:7 is a
fulfillment of Dan. 7:21.

The city in 11:8 is like Sodom because it is
wicked and will be destroyed in judgment (see
Deut. 32:28–33; Isa. 1:9–15; Jer. 23:14–15;
Mart. Isa. 3:10). The city is like Egypt because
it persecutes the saints. According to Joel 3:19,
Egypt is the place where "violence [was] done
to the sons of Judah, in whose land they have

shed innocent blood." Egypt and Sodom appear to be compared together in this manner in Wis. 19:14–17 (likewise with respect to Sodom alone in Deut. 29:22–26; Isa. 3:9). The two nations have a seductive influence on God's people (Ezek. 16:26, 44–57). Egypt became a symbol for all nations that persecuted Israel (see *Midr. Rab.* Gen. 16:4; *Midr. Rab.* Lev. 13:5; cf. *Mek. R. Ish.* Beshallah 6). Just as Israel had become like Sodom and Egypt and would be punished accordingly (Amos 4:10–11), so also Rev. 11:8 portrays the world as resembling Israel, Sodom, and Egypt, and subject to the same fate.

11:11

The picture of the resurrection of the witnesses is taken directly from Ezek. 37:5, 10, a prophecy of God's restoration of Israel out of Babylonian captivity. John applies Ezekiel to the restored church because he sees them finally released from their earthly pilgrimage of captivity and suffering. This demonstrates that they are God's true people (cf. Ezek. 37:12–13), the realization of the prophecy about Israel in Ezek. 37.

"Great fear fell upon the ones perceiving" the deliverance of the witnesses. The fear of the earth dwellers is like that of the Egyptians when they beheld the unexpected plagues and the Israelites' deliverance through the afflictions: "great fear fell upon them" (cf. Rev. 11:11b with Ps. 105:38). The same description is applied to the ungodly inhabitants of the promised land (Exod. 15:16; cf. Jon. 1:10).

11:12

The acceptance of the witnesses into the cloud shows divine approval. The validity of Elijah's prophetic authority was confirmed by God at the end of his ministry in the same manner (2 Kings 2:11). Likewise, the NT and Jewish tradition maintained that Moses' ministry was concluded with his "assumption" to heaven (see Philo, *Sacrifices* 8; Josephus, *Ant.* 4.320–326; *Midr. Rab.* Deut. 9:5; *Sipre Deut.* Piska 357; *As. Mos.* 10:11–13; and the implication of Jude 9, which probably are based on interpretation of Deut. 34:5–6; see also the ascension of Jesus in Acts 1:9, 11).

11:13

The wording "great earthquake" actually derives from Ezek. 38:19, where *seismos megas* refers to the final judgment on Gog at the end of history when it attempts to exterminate restored Israel (see Hughes 1990: 130). The reference to Ezek. 38 is natural because it comes directly after Ezek. 37, which explains Israel's restoration through the picture of resurrection. The same pattern is followed in Rev. 11:11–13, indicating future accomplishment of the Ezekiel prophecy.

The last part of the verse poses the difficult question of whether the survivors of the earthquake became genuine believers or remained antagonistic though compelled to acknowledge the power of God. Their reaction of "fearing" and "giving glory to the God of heaven" could easily be understood positively on analogy with Dan. 4:34 (cf. Isa. 42:12; Jer. 13:16; Matt. 5:16; possibly also Dan. 5:21–23; Luke 7:16; 17:18; 18:43; 1 Pet. 2:12; *T. Ab.* 18:11), especially because of the parallel language and because both contexts concern inhabitants of Babylon the "great city" (cf. Dan. 4:27–30; Rev. 11:8). A figurative understanding of the "tenth of the city" that fell and the "seven thousand" people who died conform to this viewpoint. The tenth that is judged could be an ironic counterpart to the tenth that is spared in the OT (cf. Isa. 6:13, which most view as referring to a faithful remnant), while the seven thousand who die would again be an ironic counterpart to the seven thousand faithful worshipers of 1 Kings 19:18 (cf. Rom. 11:4). In addition, the exhortation in 14:7 that unbelieving nations "fear God and give to him glory" and the expression in 15:4 applied to the nations, "Who will not fear, O Lord, and glorify your name?" are the strongest evidence suggesting that the similar language of 11:13 alludes to saving faith (as urged especially in Bauckham 1993a: 273–83; W. J. Harrington 1993: 123; Krodel 1989: 228; Schüssler Fiorenza 1991: 79). Finally, it may be of significance that the city falls *before* the blowing of the seventh, consummate trumpet, in contrast to the picture of the fall of Jericho in Josh. 6.

On the other hand, the response of Nebuchadnezzar in Dan. 4 may not express true conversion to the faith of Israel. Elsewhere in the OT "giving glory to God" does not always indicate the response of true Israelites, but rather sometimes of unbelievers who are forced to acknowledge the reality of God's sovereignty (e.g., Josh. 7:19; 1 Sam. 6:5; cf. 1 Pet. 2:12; the use in John 9:24 could be taken either way; see, similarly, Prov. 1:24–32; cf.

Acts 12:23). This is also pointed to by the precedent of Dan. 2:46–47, where the king's recognition of God's sovereignty is only temporary, since it is followed in Dan. 3 by his attempt to force the saints to worship an idol. Also, the parallel of Rev. 14:7 could well be taken to refer to the "fear and glorification" of God by those about to be judged, as it does with respect to Nebuchadnezzar in Dan. 4:34 LXX, to which 14:7 alludes (on which, see Beale 1999a: 750–54).

The concluding phrase "God of heaven" in 11:13 refers without exception in the OT to the heavenly sphere where God holds sway over events on earth (so the Hebrew text of Gen. 24:7; 2 Chron. 36:23; Ezra 1:2; 6:9–10; 7:23; Neh. 1:4–5; 2:20; Ps. 136:26; Dan. 2:18–19, 37, 44; Jon. 1:9; probably also Gen. 24:3; Ezra 5:11; 7:12, 21). The title occurs three times in the LXX expansion of the account of Nebuchadnezzar's praise of God in Dan. 4:37. Together with the four other uses in Dan. 2, this use shows further evidence of the Dan. 4 background.

The OT background alone may not be sufficient to determine whether this is an image of terrified subjection or of genuine repentance. If one did wish to see genuine repentance here, it would be difficult to take the passage as a literal last-minute turning to God just prior to the final judgment (a judgment signaled by the earthquake), since this is nowhere else envisioned in Revelation. It might represent the ongoing repentance of unbelievers through history in the face of the church's faithful witness and God's acts of judgment, but such a view would not fit the eschatological finality of the scene.

11:18

The judgment of the nations, as in 8:8; 19:2, is clearly patterned after Jeremiah's announcement of the judgment of historical Babylon. Babylon is a type of the eschatological world community that will be judged at the end. This ties in 11:18 with Babylon, "the great city," which is destroyed in 11:13. By contrast, there is blessing for "the ones fearing the LORD, the small and the great" (Ps. 115:13). This may suggest further that the language reminiscent of Dan. 4:34 LXX in 11:13 (in parallel to 14:7) refers to judgment and not salvation.

11:19

The appearance of the ark of the covenant may stem from the account of the fall of Jericho, where the ark plays a prominent role along with the trumpets. The ark also symbolizes God's gracious presence in his redeemed community.

Revelation 12:1–17

Chapter 12 begins a new section of Revelation, with the focus on the conflict between the dragon (Satan) and the woman (God's people). Jesus' sacrificial death assures and actually commences victory for all who hold to his name, a victory whose consummation is anticipated as God protects the woman from the dragon's onslaughts.

12:1

The picture of the woman is based on Gen. 37:9 (cf. *T. Naph.* 5:3), where sun, moon, and eleven stars are metaphorical respectively for Jacob, his wife, and the eleven tribes of Israel. All these bow down to Joseph, representing the twelfth tribe. The depiction could also reflect the portrayal in Judaism of Abraham, Sarah, and their progeny as sun, moon, and stars (*T. Ab.* [B] 7:4–16); in *Midr. Rab.* Num. 2:13 the sun symbolizes Abraham, the moon Isaac, and the stars Jacob and the seed of the patriarchs.

The twelve stars represent the twelve tribes of Israel. The woman's appearance may also connote Israel's priestly character (cf. 1:6; 5:10), since in Philo's and Josephus's explanations of Exod. 28; 39 they use the imagery of a crown, the sun, moon, and twelve stars in describing the vestments of the Israelite high priests because they represented the twelve tribes before Yahweh in the temple service (see Josephus, *Ant.* 3.164–172, 179–187; Philo, *Moses* 2.111–112, 122–124; *Spec. Laws* 1.84–95). In fact, in these same texts the parts of the priestly garment symbolizing sun, moon, and stars are explicitly said to symbolize the twelve tribes of Israel. Such dual imagery was meant to indicate that Israel on earth also had an inviolable heavenly identity. In fact, Judaism interpreted the twelve signs of the zodiac to symbolize the twelve tribes of Israel (*Midr. Rab.* Exod. 15:6; *Midr. Rab.* Num. 2:14; cf. *b. Ber.* 32b). Thus, in 12:1 the covenant community's unbreakable link to a heavenly identity is pictured.

12:2

There are allusions in 12:2 to OT metaphors representing Israel as a pregnant mother whose birth pangs refer to the suffering of foreign captivity, with the imminent birth alluding to her future deliverance from foreign oppression and salvation: Isa. 26:17–18 LXX; 66:7–9; Mic. 4:9–10; 5:3, where either Judah or Jerusalem is depicted as a woman in labor ready to deliver (cf. Holtz [1971: 103], who sees allusion to the same OT texts; see also Hos. 13:13). Also noteworthy is Isa. 51:2–3, 9–11, which speaks of "Sarah, who gave birth . . . in pain" to her child the woman Zion, whom God promised to "comfort" in "all her desert places," redeeming her out of captivity, as he did at the exodus when he "cut Rahab in pieces . . . and pierced the dragon" (note also that Zion is viewed as a mother with "seed" [*sperma*] in Isa. 54:1–3; 61:9–10; 65:9, 23; 66:10, 22). These prophetic texts themselves and Rev. 12:2 were inspired by Gen. 3:15–16, where it is prophesied that Eve will bear in the pain of birth a future seed who will smite the head of the serpent (see commentary on Rev. 12:17 below), which, of course, in Rev. 12 refers to Jesus Christ as the fulfillment. The Qumran text 1QH^a XI, 7–12 makes use of similar imagery of a woman enduring the agonies of childbirth in order to bring forth a child who appears to be a messianic deliverer.

12:3

The imagery of the dragon is used throughout the OT to represent evil kingdoms that persecute God's people, and this is in mind here. "Dragon" (*drakōn*) is another word in the OT for the sea monster that symbolizes wicked kingdoms that oppress Israel. Often the wicked kingdom of Egypt is portrayed by this emblem. God is spoken of as defeating Pharaoh as a sea dragon at the exodus deliverance and at later points in Egypt's history (Ps. 74:13–14; 89:10; Isa. 30:7; 51:9; Ezek. 29:3; 32:2–3; Hab. 3:8–15; *Pss. Sol.* 2:29–30; see Ps. 87:4, where "Rahab" is a synonym for Egypt; cf. Jer. 51:34, where Babylon is the subject; see also Amos 9:3). The use of "a great dragon" is an allusion to Ezek. 29:3: "Pharaoh . . . the great dragon." In *Pss. Sol.* 2:29–30 the sea monster is identified as Rome (the commander Pompey) lying "on the mountains of Egypt." Sometimes there is allusion to, perhaps at the dawn of history, God's past defeat of a more sinister, malevolent force behind

Egypt and other evil kingdoms: God "shattered the sea monster . . . his hand has pierced the apostate dragon" (Job 26:12–13 LXX [cf. chap. 41; see also 7:12; 9:13]). The image of the dragon in Rev. 12:3 represents the devil (so see confirmation of this in 12:9) who instigates the evil kingdoms of the world to persecute God's people. In the light of the comments on 12:2 and together with 12:4–5, 12:3 indicates the beginning fulfillment of Gen. 3:15–16.

12:4

The picture of the dragon's tail sweeping away a third of the stars and casting them to the earth is taken from Dan. 8:10, which describes an end-time enemy persecuting the forces of God: "And it [the horn] grew up to the host of heaven and caused some of the host and some of the stars to fall to the earth, and it trampled them down." Although Dan. 8:10 first had application with respect to Antiochus Epiphanes, it now comes to be applied by John in an escalated way to the devilish power behind Antiochus. There is debate about whether the "host and some of the stars" in Daniel refers to angels or to Israelite saints. The debate may be moot, since both are likely true. In Daniel angels represent peoples (see 10:20–21; 12:1; cf. *As. Mos.* 10:8–10). The "stars" in Dan. 8 signify angels who represent saints on earth (so also Lacocque 1979: 161–62; see the excursus on Rev. 1:20 in Beale 1999a: 218–19). The same representational link is true between the "son of man," Michael, angels, and the "saints" in Dan. 7 (Lacocque 1979: 126–28, 152). That stars can represent Israelite saints, not just angels, is apparent from Dan. 12:3, where the righteous are compared to "the firmament and . . . the stars" (for this application of Dan. 12:3, see Matt. 13:43; cf. Gen. 15:5; 22:17; *1 En.* 43:1–4). Israelite saints have their true identity in heaven before the divine throne, so that when they are persecuted, the angels and God himself are seen also as being attacked (so Keil 1971: 296–97; Young 1980: 171; Leupold 1969: 346; Lacocque [1979: 130–34, 153], who also shows that "saints" in Daniel and Qumran include reference both to saints and angels; cf. 2 Macc. 7:1–8:15 with 9:10). Daniel 8:11 LXX/Θ interprets the falling "to the earth [of] some of the host of heaven and of the stars" and their being "trampled" in 8:10 to represent "the captivity" of Israel, which will be "delivered" in the future. Thus, here in 12:4 both good heavenly beings and the saints whom they represent are portrayed as being attacked by the devil. Perhaps, the reference to a "third of the stars" being swept away indicates that only a portion of the covenant community was suffering attack from the devil's forces at the time of Christ's life (see 12:2, 4b–5), whereas at the very end of the age the attack will reach universal proportions (as in 11:7–10; 20:7–9).

12:6

The fleeing into the wilderness is an allusion both to Israel's exodus from Egypt and the anticipated end-time exodus, which was to occur during Israel's latter-day restoration from captivity. First, it refers to the time when Israel fled from Egypt into the wilderness and was protected and nourished by Yahweh (Exod. 16:32; Deut. 2:7; 8:3, 15–16; 29:5; 32:10; Josh. 24:7; Neh. 9:19, 21; Ps. 78:15, 19; 136:16; Hos. 13:5). The same pattern of fleeing into the wilderness is observable in the cases of Elijah (1 Kings 17; 19:3–8) and Moses (Exod. 2:15; Josephus, *Ant.* 2.256), who symbolize the church in 11:5–6. The woman's flight into the wilderness also recalls the end-time exodus or restoration when Israel would return in faith to the Lord and again be protected and nourished by him in the wilderness (Isa. 32:15; 35:1; 40:3; 41:18; 43:19–20; 51:3; Jer. 31:2; Ezek. 34:25; Hos. 2:14). For Jewish application of these verses, especially Hos. 2:14, see *Midr. Rab.* Exod. 2:4; *Sipre Deut.* Piska 313; 1QM I, 2–3; 1QS VIII, 12–15; IX, 18–21; 4Q171 37.

Judaism developed the belief that the Messiah would gather his people in the wilderness at the end time partly on the basis of the aforementioned OT eschatological texts, and especially via a typological interpretation of Israel's exodus wilderness experience (see *TDNT* 2:659; cf. Matt. 24:24–26; Acts 21:38). Revelation 12:6 is to be understood likewise. This belief is reflected in the writings of Josephus, where there is explicit identification of first-century messianic movements with the desert and exodus themes (*J.W.* 2.259–262; 7.438; *Ant.* 20.168–172; see also *Ant.* 20.97–99; *J.W.* 6.351–352). The association of the wilderness with the Zealots and similar groups probably is part of this larger messianic expectation (Josephus, *J.W.* 2.433, 508; 4.508). Moses was also to appear in the desert in the latter days and lead

his people into the promised land (see Ginzberg 1967: 2:302, 373). Since here this flight takes place immediately after the ascension of Christ (12:5), the woman's representative function now extends beyond ethnic Israel to all those who call upon the name of the Lord—that is, all Christians, whether Jew or Gentile.

The "place" (*topos*) in the desert where Christians are kept safe from the devil is the invisible, spiritual sanctuary of God, since that is to be the object of attack during the three and a half years in Daniel (8:11–13; 9:27), and since that is the idea in Rev. 11:1–2; 12:14; 13:5–6. The word *topos* ("place") in 12:6, 14 is synonymous elsewhere in the NT for the "temple" and is a widespread synonym for the "sanctuary" in the LXX. This observation points further to the nature of the "wilderness" as being closely associated with a protective sanctuary (although, strictly speaking, the sacred "place" is not coterminus with the wilderness, but rather is *in* the wilderness). Matthew 24:15 identifies the "abomination of desolation" of Dan. 9:27 as occurring "in the holy place" (*en topō hagiō*), as does Dan. 8:11 LXX. The use of *topos* in the same Daniel texts to which the three and a half years alludes in Revelation makes the cultic appearance of *topos* in 12:6, 14 all the more natural. John may have identified the "sanctuary" with the "wilderness" because the Jerusalem "sanctuary" (*hagiasmos*) in the LXX is likened to a "wilderness" (*erēmos*), as a result of the attacks by Babylon (Dan. 9:17 Θ) and Antiochus Epiphanes (1 Macc. 1:39). In the same texts of Dan. 9 and 1 Macc. 1 the wilderness of the sanctuary is also identified with the three and a half years of trial predicted by Daniel to be directed against the sanctuary and the saints.

12:7

In 12:7 is developed Daniel's heavenly combat imagery between Michael and the "son of man" against the wicked angels of Persia and Greece (Dan. 10:13, 21; cf. 10:6, 18 LXX; 10:16, 18 Θ). In Daniel, Michael is closely associated with the "son of man," since both are set forth as heavenly representatives of Israel (cf., respectively, Dan. 12:1; 8:11 LXX/Θ and 7:13–27). This is why they are identified as fighting together for Israel against the forces of evil in Dan. 10:20–21. The two figures are not the same heavenly being, since the one in the "likeness of a son of man" in Dan.

1124

10:16 is distinguished from Michael. Michael helps the "son of man" fight against malevolent angelic forces. On the basis of this evidence, a plausible conclusion is that Michael is a heavenly representative for Israel as is the "son of man," although, in light of Dan. 10:20, he is a subordinate helper of the "son of man." The link with Daniel is confirmed further from Dan. 8:10–11 LXX/Θ, where, after mention of the stars falling as a metaphor for Israel's suffering (cf. Rev. 12:4), Michael is said to be the "chief captain" who will "deliver" Israel's "captivity" in the end time (the "chief captain" of Dan. 8:11 is likely to be identified with "Michael the great prince" of Dan. 12:1).

Likewise, Dan. 12:1 has Michael as Israel's latter-day deliverer. This text from Daniel may well have given rise to other formulations in Judaism of Michael as guardian angel of Israel and of Jacob (cf. *1 En.* 90:14; 1QM XIII, 9–10; XVII, 5–8; *T. Levi* 5:7; *T. Dan.* 6:1–7; see Ginzberg 1967: 7:312).

The defeat of Satan's forces is described through the precise wording of Daniel. In Dan. 7:21 Θ (cf. 10:20) we read that the horn "was making war with the saints and was too powerful for them" (*epoiei polemon meta tōn hagiōn kai ischysen pros autous*), and in Rev. 12:7–8 that "Michael . . . made war [*tou polemēsai*] against the dragon . . . and he [the dragon] made war . . . and he was not strong enough [*ouk ischysen*]."

Daniel 10:20 refers to the "son of man" who makes war, but Michael is included with him in this battle. The "ruler" of the Persians and Greeks of the Daniel text is identified as Satan. The allusion to Dan. 7:21 has already been made in 11:7 and appears again in 13:7, both referring to the beast's attacks against the saints (see commentary on Rev. 11:7–8 above and 13:7a below). The language of Dan. 7:21 is now applied to the defeat of the dragon. Like the woman, Michael now represents not simply ethnic Israel, but rather the church as a whole, which triumphs through Christ's sacrifice (12:11). The overall context of Daniel 7 itself prophesied the final defeat of the beastly kingdoms. What better language to use to portray the devil's defeat than that which Dan. 7:21 used to prophesy the evil kingdom's victory over the saints. The reversed application of the wording of Dan. 7:21 appears to connote a parody whereby the devil is mocked by having his defeat described in the same way his own victory over God's people

was depicted. The heavenly struggle of v. 7 pictures the beginning of the earthly and celestial battle predicted by Daniel to occur in the last days (Dan. 7:21; 8:10; 12:1), an expectation also featured in Jewish tradition (*Sib. Or.* 3:796–808; cf. 2 Macc. 5:1–14, which may be related to Daniel). Since the woman, the dragon, the serpent, the wilderness, the wings of the eagle, and other descriptions throughout chapter 12 are clearly symbolic, so also is the war of angels here. The remainder of chapter 12 elucidates the manner in which the devil was defeated by Christ's resurrection and the meaning of the symbolism in v. 7.

12:8

An immediate consequence of the defeat of the devil and his hosts is that "a place was not found for them any longer in heaven." This is based on the nearly identical wording of Dan. 2:35, which also prophetically describes the immediate consequence of the destruction of the hostile world kingdoms in the latter days (cf. 2:28, 45), which is seen in Rev. 12:8 as a beginning realization of Christ's resurrection.

12:9–10

The description of the dragon as the "ancient serpent" identifies him as the same diabolical character of Gen. 3:1, 14. The ancient foe of God's people here in 12:9 is also "called devil and Satan," meaning, respectively, "slanderer" and "adversary." He is a slanderous adversary in two ways. Genesis 3 attributes to him the two functions of slanderer and deceiver. After the fall, the serpent and his agents do on a worldwide scale what he began in the garden (cf. *Jub.* 11:5; *1 En.* 54:6; *2 En.* 7; 18). Here in 12:9 he is called "the one deceiving the whole inhabited earth" and in 12:10 "the accuser" of God's people.

On the basis of this description and the description of Satan in Job 1:6–11; 2:1–6; Zech. 3:1–2, it can be concluded that the devil was permitted by God to come before him in heaven and "accuse" his people of sin. The OT texts portray Satan accusing saints of unfaithfulness, with the implication that they did not deserve God's salvation and gracious blessings (Zech. 3:1–5, 9; cf. *Midr. Rab.* Num. 18:21). Implicit also in the accusations was the charge that God's own character was corrupt.

The emphasis on Satan's accusatorial role here in 12:10 reveals that the angelic battle of 12:7–9 was figurative for a courtroom battle between two opposing lawyers, with one losing the argument and being disbarred for employing illegal tactics (so Caird 1966: 154–56). In addition to Satan's accusatorial role in Job 1:6–11; 2:1–6; Zech. 3:1–2, the devil also had the role of a legal "accuser" in early Judaism (*Jub.* 1:20; 17:15–16; 18:9–12; 48:15–18; *1 En.* 40:7; *T. Levi* 5:6; *T. Dan* 6:2), and Michael played the part of an advocate defending Israel from the accusations made by Satan in the heavenly court (*T. Levi* 5:6; *T. Dan.* 6:1–6; *Midr. Rab.* Exod. 18:5). Particularly interesting is *Jub.* 48:10–19, which says that essential to Israel's victory over Egypt at the exodus was that Satan "was bound and imprisoned behind the children of Israel that he might not accuse them." Christ's death has freed Christians at a greater exodus from the devil's accusations.

12:14

The image of the woman flying with "the two wings of a great eagle . . . into the wilderness" to a "place of nourishment" alludes to two OT pictures and adopts them analogically. First, 12:14 reflects the picture of God as an eagle protecting Israel in the wilderness, which is an allusion combining Exod. 19:4; Deut. 1:31–33; 32:10–15. This well-known image is also attested in the psalms, where David repeatedly alludes to the exodus figure by praying that God's wings will shelter him from persecutors and slanderers, the same protection needed by the "woman" in Rev. 12:13–17 (see, e.g., the contexts of Ps. 17:8–9; 36:7–8; 63:1–2, 7; 91:4, 11–13; also Ps. 57:1; 61:4). Especially instructive for Rev. 12:14–18 is Ps. 54 LXX, where David prays for protection against "crafty men" arising from the covenant community who "oppress" him with "words . . . smoother than oil . . . [as] darts": "Who will give to me wings as a dove? Then I would fly away, and be at rest. Behold, I have fled far away, and lodged in the wilderness. I waited for him [God], the one saving me from distress of soul and tempest" (Ps. 54:7–9 LXX [55:6–8 ET]; cf. Isa. 40:3).

12:15

The metaphor of an overflowing flood can have at least three ideas in the OT: (1) an army spreading out to conquer a country (Dan. 11:10, 22, 26, 40), sometimes as an indication of divine judgment (Ps. 88:7, 17; Isa. 8:7–8; 17:12–13; Jer. 46:8; 47:2; 51:55; Hos. 5:10; cf. Isa. 10:22; 59:19;

Mic. 1:4; Nah. 1:8); (2) a more general reference to divine judgment (Ps. 32:6; 90:5); (3) persecution of God's people by enemies from which God delivers them (2 Sam. 22:5; Ps. 18:4, 16; 46:3; 66:12; 69:1–2, 14–15; 124:4–5; 144:7–8, 11; Isa. 43:2). The third idea clearly is in view in 12:15. In Ps. 18:4 David describes Saul's pursuit of him explicitly as "the torrents of Belial . . . assailing me." Also noteworthy is Ps. 144:7–8, 11 because it is a prayer that God would deliver David "out of many waters," which is a picture of those who speak "deceit and . . . falsehood"; likewise, "in a deluge of many waters" in Ps. 32:6 refers to threatening persecution from the ungodly.

12:16

The swallowing of the flood by the earth is a further allusion to the exodus and Israel's wilderness experience. The "earth swallowed" the Egyptians when they pursued Israel through the Red Sea (Exod. 15:12). The *Tg. Ps.-J.* to Exod. 15:12 expands on the MT and repeats that "the earth opened its mouth and consumed them." Also, later in the wilderness "the earth opened its mouth and swallowed" the families of Korah, Dathan, and Abiram because of their rebellion against Moses' leadership. This OT background is analogically applied to the church's wilderness sojourn in the world.

12:17

That the "rest of her seed" of 12:17 is to be linked with Christ in 12:5, 13 is probable because those two verses are the only ones in 12:1–16 that refer to a firstborn offspring. Such a contrast between individual and corporate seeds is supported by the fact that 12:17 is an allusion to Gen. 3:16, where John would have seen that Eve's messianic seed has both individual and corporate meaning.

Also, 12:17 is a partial fulfillment of the promise in Gen. 3:15, where God prophesies that the individual (messianic) and corporate seed of the woman will fatally bruise the head of the serpent. The Gen. 3 background also confirms the conclusion in 12:15–16 that the "serpent" opposes the "woman" not only through persecution, but also through deception, as in the Garden of Eden. This is but another instance of the end being modeled on the beginning (cf. 12:9, where "serpent" is derived primarily from Gen. 3 [see commentary on Rev. 12:9–10 above]).

Revelation 12:18–13:18

The dragon, having been thwarted in his attempt to destroy the woman, enlists the aid of two beasts, creating a "satanic trinity" in mockery of the triune God. The two beasts are seen here in terms of the Roman state and its accompanying propaganda machine in the local governments of the province of Asia, though until the final parousia other states succeeding Rome could be included in the beast images. The apparent success of the beast in its wars leads people to worship and revere it, but God's people are warned to worship God alone.

13:1

The depiction of the two beasts in chapter 13 is based in part on Job 40–41, which is the only place in the OT that portrays two satanic beasts that oppose God. The sea monster of the Job passage also has a companion classified as a land "beast" (*thērion* [40:15–32]). Both beasts are described with demonic attributes and are said to have been "made to be mocked by the angels" (LXX: 40:19; 41:25 [on the two demonic beings in Job 40, see Day 1985: 62–87]). The two beasts of Job 40–41 (cf. esp. LXX) are echoed throughout Rev. 13: one is called a "dragon" from the sea (40:25); the land beast is to be slain by God with a "sword" (40:19 MT); the sea dragon conducts a "war waged by his mouth" (40:32 LXX), and "burning torches" and "a flame goes out of his mouth" (41:11, 13 LXX); "there is nothing upon the earth like him" (41:25 LXX).

Job 40–41 alludes to a primordial defeat of the dragon by God (see 41:8 MT [so also *Midr. Rab.* Exod. 15:22]) but also implies a future battle (40:19 MT; 41:9 MT), which is necessitated by the sea beasts' continued attitude of defiance (e.g., 41:33–34 MT). Although the beast was defeated, he continues to exist in a subdued condition (Job 7:12 MT; Amos 9:3; cf. *Apoc. Ab.* 10; 21). Jewish tradition held that on the fifth day of creation God created Leviathan to be in the sea and Behemoth to dwell on land (*1 En.* 60:7–10; *4 Ezra* 6:49–52; *2 Bar.* 29:4; *b. B. Bat.* 74b–75a; *Pesiq. Rab Kah.* Suppl. 2:4). These two beasts were symbolic of the powers of evil and were to be destroyed at the final judgment (explicitly in *2 Baruch*; *Midr. Rab.* Lev. 13:3; *b. B. Bat.* 74b, and implicitly in the other three texts above [for further references to the two beasts in later Judaism, see Ginzberg 1967:

5:26–27, 43–46]). This tradition may have developed because people in Asia Minor associated whatever came "of the sea" as foreign and whatever came from the land as native. That is, one of the initial expressions of the first beast was Rome, whose governors came repeatedly by sea to Ephesus. The second beast represented native political and economic authorities (Ramsay 1904: 103–4). The Roman ships literally seemed to be rising out of the sea as they appeared on the horizon off the coast of Asia Minor.

The material in 13:1–2 is a creative reworking of Dan. 7:1–7. The "beast coming up from the sea" and his "ten horns" are based respectively on Dan. 7:2–3 and 7:7, 20, 24. Many understand the "seven heads" as a reference to an ancient Near Eastern sea-monster myth from before the time of Daniel (cf. Leviathan with seven heads in *CTA* 5.I.1–3; 3.III.37–39; cf. also Job 40–41; Ps. 74:13–14; 89:10; Isa. 27:1; 51:9; see also *Odes Sol.* 22:5). This is possible, but it is better to view the "seven heads" as a composite of the heads of all four of the beasts of Dan. 7 (so Hengstenberg 1853: 2:20; Farrer 1964: 152; Ernst 1967: 132; Kraft 1974: 175; Prigent 1981: 201). This view is preferable because other features of the Danielic beasts are also applied to the one beast in Rev. 13:2 (the ancient Near Eastern image could still be in mind secondarily). In addition, the "ten diadems" upon the "ten horns" are a reference to Daniel's fourth beast, whose "ten horns" are interpreted as "ten kings" (Dan. 7:24). Likewise, the "blasphemous names" are connected with the blaspheming figure of Dan. 7:8, 11, who is also associated with the fourth kingdom (cf. Rev. 13:5–6).

For Judaism's identification of Rome with the fourth beast of Dan. 7:7–8, 11, 23, see, for example, *Midr. Rab.* Gen. 44:17; 76:6; *Midr. Rab.* Exod. 15:6; 25:8; cf. Matt. 24:15 with Luke 21:20; see also *4 Ezra* 12:10; *2 Bar.* 39:5–8; *As. Mos.* 10:8; cf. Josephus, *Ant.* 10.203–210 with *Ant.* 10.272–278; *Pss. Sol.* 2:25 identifies a Roman ruler as "the dragon."

13:2

Whereas in Dan. 7:3–8 the images of the lion, bear, leopard, and "terrifying" beast represent four successive world empires, in Rev. 13:1–2 all four of these images are applied to the one beast. This probably includes a connotation of Rome as the fourth beast, which Daniel predicted would be more powerful and dreadful than the previous three beasts of Dan. 7:4–6 (for specific allusions to Daniel's fourth kingdom, see commentary on Rev. 13:1 above). At the least, the gathering up of four beasts into one highlights the extreme ferocity of this beast. Since the prophesied fourth beast of Dan. 7 is the focus in Rev. 13:1–2, these introductory verses show inaugurated accomplishment of that prophesy (for more on this see 13:3).

Various exegetical traditions in Judaism also understood Daniel's fourth kingdom as transtemporal (and the combination of Daniel's four beasts into one might also suggest such a notion). In *4 Ezra* 12:12–13 God tells the seer that the interpretation given to Daniel that the fourth kingdom was Greece is not wrong, but now that kingdom is to be identified as Rome. *Midrash Rabbah* Gen. 76:6 applies the horns of the fourth kingdom in Dan. 7:8 to numerous world empires: the eastern Palmyran-Roman kingdom under the reign of Odaenathus, Babylon, Persia (Media), Greece, and Rome. The same midrash goes on to state that Dan. 7:2–8 "informs us that every nation that rules in the world hates Israel and subjugates them." The ten horns of Dan. 7:7 are taken by *Midr. Ps.* 75:5 to prove "that the [heathen] nations of the world are symbolized by the beasts described in Daniel, and that as long as the horns of the wicked endure, the horns of Israel remain cut off."

13:3

John now sees the beast with a wound on one of his heads. God must be the unmentioned agent of the beast's head "wound" (*hē plēgē*), since everywhere else in Revelation *plēgē* (usually rendered "plague") is a punishment inflicted by God (so eleven times + the cognate verb in 8:12). Such a wound on the head of the grand nemesis of God's people reflects Gen. 3:15, especially when seen together with Rev. 12:17 (cf. 12:17 with respect to *Tg. Neof.* Gen. 3:15; see Sweet 1979: 210). In Rev. 13:14 it is added that it was a sword that struck the beast's head. The added mention of the sword in this connection recalls the prophecy of Isa. 27:1 LXX: "In that day God will bring the sword, the holy and great and mighty [sword] upon the dragon, the fleeing serpent, upon the dragon, the crooked serpent. He will destroy the dragon" (cf. Job 40:1; Rev. 13:14). The fact that Isa. 27:1 is also echoed in Rev. 12:3, 9 points further to the conclusion that the beast's "death stroke" came through Christ's death and

resurrection in initial fulfillment of Isa. 27 (see Rev. 12:7–12). Also included in the OT reflection upon God's defeat of the sea monster may be Ps. 74:13; Hab. 3:8–15. The healing of his wound constitutes a counterfeit of Christ's resurrection.

13:4

The phrase denoting transferal of authority is based on Dan. 7:6, where authority is given to the third beast to rule over the earth and to persecute God's people who live on it.

The multitudes worship the beast because of his purported incomparability: they proclaim in their worship, "Who is like the beast, and who is able to make war with him?" The expression of satanic incomparability is an ironic use of the same OT phraseology applied to Yahweh (esp. Exod. 8:10; 15:11; Deut. 3:24; Isa. 40:18, 25; 44:7; 46:5; see also Ps. 35:10; 71:19; 86:8; 89:8; 113:5; Mic. 7:18). This is a further attempt at satanic imitation of God.

13:5

The reference in 13:5 to the beast expressing his authority through speech for a period of three and a half years is a collective allusion to Dan. 7:6, 8, 11, 20, 25—for example: "a tongue was given to it . . . a mouth speaking great things" (7:6, 8 LXX).

13:6

Daniel 7:25 is referred to again in 13:6a to describe the effect of the beast's authorization (cf. Dan. 11:36 LXX). Both texts speak of an eschatological fiend who speaks out against God, equates himself with God (implicitly in Rev. 13:4, 6), and persecutes the saints, which is likewise the case in Dan. 8:10, 25; 11:36 (cf. Dan. 8:11, 13; see also *Mart. Isa.* 4:6; *Sib. Or.* 5:33–34; *As. Mos.* 8:5). That "he blasphemes God's name" implies speaking out against God through self-deification (as with the Roman emperors [see Suetonius, *Dom.* 13]). Also included in the blaspheming are accusations or actions against Christians, who have God's name written upon them (3:12; 14:1; 22:4; cf. 7:3).

In 13:6b "his tabernacle" immediately followed by "the ones tabernacling in heaven" is a recollection of, respectively, the "sanctuary" and the heavenly "host" in Dan. 8:10–13: the end-time tyrant "caused some of the host [of heaven] and some of the stars to fall to the earth" and "magnified himself to be equal with the Prince of the host and . . . the place of his sanctuary was thrown down" (8:10–11). This continues the theme in Revelation of Christians being a part of the invisible end-time heavenly temple that extends to earth, who are attacked and persecuted but cannot be separated from God's tabernacling presence despite whatever physical harm they may suffer (11:1–4; 12:6, 14), all in partial fulfillment of the Dan. 8:10–13 prediction.

13:7a

In 13:7a the focus shifts back again to the prophecy of Dan. 7 (i.e., 7:8 LXX, 21 MT/Θ) and the persecuting activities of the "horn" in order to show that the same activity of the beast is a beginning fulfillment and affects all classes of people throughout the earth. The phrase "to make war with the saints and to overcome them" is virtually identical to 11:7; both of these verses are based on Dan. 7:8b LXX, 21 MT/Θ. After the statement that the evil king had "a mouth speaking great things," the Greek of Dan. 7:8 immediately adds that the tyrant "was making war with the saints." The same pattern is followed here.

13:7b–8a

Influence from Dan. 7 continues through allusion to Dan. 7:14, which describes the "son of man's" reception of universal worship as a result of the conferral of sovereign authority but here is ironically applied to the beast who attempts to usurp proper divine, messianic authority.

13:10

"If anyone [is destined] for captivity, to captivity he [must] go. If anyone by the sword is to be killed, by the sword he must be killed." This is a paraphrase combining Jer. 15:2; 43:11. Jeremiah prophesies to Israel that God has destined them to go into "captivity" and suffer from the "sword." This is a penalty for their unbelief and sin. In the present context, it appears to apply to genuine believers who suffer persecution for their witness. Nevertheless, this appears not to be inconsistent with Jeremiah's thought, where it can be assumed that the remnant faithful of Israel would have experienced the same suffering as the unfaithful majority, although for the former group the trials would have had a refining effect on their faith (see the same idea in Ezek. 14:21–23 and its use in Rev. 6:8, on

which, see commentary on Rev. 6:7–8 above; Beale 1999a:704–5). Revelation 13:10 now sees that the same is true of the faithful Christian remnant.

13:11

As in 13:1, this vision begins with the image of an ascending beast, which is a collective recollection of the beasts of Dan. 7, especially 7:17 LXX: "These great beasts are four kings who will arise from the earth" (cf. 7:3a, 4b, 5a).

The two horns, in addition to parodying the two witnesses, lampstands, and olive trees, also reflect the evil ruler of Dan. 8. Just as the first beast was described with attributes from the beasts of Dan. 7, so also the description of the second beast as having "two horns as a lamb" is taken from Dan. 8:3 MT: "a ram that had two horns" (cf. Dan. 7:7 LXX).

13:13

The idea of imitation is carried on in 13:13. First, the beast's activities are described by an ironic echo of the acts of Moses, whose prophetic authority was validated by "doing great signs" (e.g., Exod. 4:17, 30; 10:2; 11:10). Even in the Exodus narrative (7:11) Pharaoh's magicians "did the same [signs] with their secret arts." This is reinforced by Daniel, where God is praised for "doing signs and great wonders" (cf. Dan. 4:37a LXX with Rev. 13:13a). The casting down of fire from heaven in the presence of people recalls the prophetic demonstration by Elijah (1 Kings 18:38–39; 2 Kings 1:10–14), though now it describes a pseudoprophetic action.

13:14

The deception causes the earth dwellers to acquiesce to his command to "make an image to the beast" (for *legōn* as "order, command, demand," cf. 10:9; Acts 21:21). The concluding command of 3:14c anticipates the explicit reference to Dan. 3 in 13:15. In the light of the influence from Daniel in 13:1–11, the beast "who deceives" in 13:14a may be an echo of the end-time king of Daniel, who "causes deceit to succeed by his influence" (Dan. 8:25 MT) and "by smooth words will turn to godlessness those who act wickedly" (Dan. 11:32 MT). Also "the signs" that are "given" to the beast to "perform" are a repeated expression of the authorization pattern from Dan. 7, which is viewed as recapitulated again during the church age.

13:16–17

In the OT God told Israel that the Torah was to be "as a sign on your hand, and as a reminder on your forehead" in order to remind them continually of their commitment and loyalty to God (Exod. 13:9; so also Exod. 13:16; Deut. 6:8; 11:18). This was done with phylacteries (leather pouches) containing portions of Scripture worn on the forehead and arm. The NT equivalent is the invisible seal or name of God (see commentary on Rev. 7:2–3 above). The "forehead" represents their ideological commitment and the "hand" the practical outworking of that commitment.

13:18

The response of "wisdom" (*sophia*) and "understanding" (*nous*) needed to comprehend the "number of the beast" is best understood as having its background in the "wise insight" (*śākal*) and "understanding" (*bîn*) required in Daniel to comprehend latter-day visions and events. Especially in Dan. 11:33; 12:10 the combination of these two Hebrew words refers to the same thing as *sophia* and *nous* in the present chapter: (1) the requirement for the saints to have spiritual perception in order to comprehend (2) end-time events of tribulation (3) brought about by an evil king who persecutes the saints, (4) deceives others into acknowledging his purported sovereignty, and convinces them to spread the deception; (5) furthermore, in both Daniel and Revelation this message is communicated through the medium of a vision to a prophet (on the full background in Daniel for the combined use of *sophia* and *nous*, see Beale 1980). If the saints have such perception, they will not be deceived.

The same response in 17:9 (with *hōde* ["here"] + *sophia* ["wisdom"] and *nous* ["mind"]) has precisely the same meaning as here. It serves to exhort Christians not to be taken in by the beast's deceptions like the rest of "the earth dwellers" (17:8). It also functions to exhort them to perceive the symbolic meaning of the beast's "seven heads," which continues the idea from 17:7–8 about the state's deception (see commentary on Rev. 17:9a, 9b below). Outside of 13:18; 17:9, *sophia* ("wisdom") occurs only in 5:12; 7:12, where "wisdom" is attributed to the Lamb's ability to plan and execute redemptive history. In 13:18; 17:9 believers are to have "wisdom" that enables them to know God's wise plan and be prepared

to discern divine imposters and their propagandists, which have been prophesied by Daniel (see Ruiz 1989: 207). Since the same exhortation in 17:9 refers to understanding the figurative meaning of a number, so the exhortation and number in 13:18 are to be understood likewise. John is exhorting saints to spiritual and moral discernment, not intellectual ability to solve a complex math problem. Unbelievers as well as spiritual Christians are mentally capable of solving a purely mathematical problem.

Consequently, the proper spiritual application of the 666 to wicked rulers and compromising institutions, as well as to false teachers, will reveal to believers their seductive and imperfect nature. "Wherever there is blasphemy, there the beast's name is found" (Minear 1968: 260). Christians must be aware that the spirit of the antichrist can express itself in the most unexpected places, even, indeed especially, in the church (so 1 John 2:18, 22; 4:1–3; 2 John 7). The prophecy of Dan. 11:30–39 already warned that apostates from the covenant community would be allies of the ungodly state and infiltrate the believing community. They must be spiritually on the alert to discern such prophesied manifestations, which are unexpected by those not cultivating divine wisdom. Therefore, an interpretive approach must be rejected that attempts only a literal calculation of the number 666 in an effort to identify only one historical individual.

Fourth Ezra 12:37–38 alludes to Dan. 12:10 in saying that true saints will need "wisdom" and "understanding" to discern truth in the end-time trial caused by the Dan. 7 beast from the sea. The same thing is said in *2 Bar.* 28:1 with respect to the last tribulation in direct connection with "Leviathan [who] will ascend from the sea" (cf. *2 Bar.* 29:1–5). In *4 Ezra* 14:13–17 the author is to "instruct those that are wise" not to love "the life that is corruptible, [to] let go from thee the cares of mortality," presumably because of the same kind of economic persecution in view in Rev. 13. The readers of *4 Ezra* 14 need such discernment because "truth . . . and falsehood be nigh at hand: for already the Eagle [the beast of Dan. 7] is hastening." These parallels confirm the Daniel background. The parallels also support the idea that the exhortation in Rev. 13:18 concerns discernment of truth in the midst of Daniel's predicted falsehood and not a calculation pinpointing only one specific evil individual. Nevertheless, an individual could be the embodiment of evil at any particular period of history, and Christians would need spiritual wisdom to discern the danger that such a person posed.

If John's readers have spiritual perception, they will remain faithful and "come off victorious from the beast and from his image and from the number of his name" (15:2). To identify with the beast by worshiping his image is to identify with his imperfect nature, which is symbolized by the triple six. Not to identify with him is "to come off victorious" from his deceptive influence. The victory in 15:2 must not be understood as winning a game by solving a riddle through intellectual cleverness, despite the fact that the NEB and the JB render the verse in a manner approaching such a perspective—for example, the JB translates, "There is need for shrewdness here; if anyone is clever enough he may interpret the number of the beast."

Revelation 14

Chapter 14 shows us the godly counterpart to the beast worshipers of chapter 13. These are the 144,000 followers of the Lamb, a symbol of the spiritually faithful saints of God. These faithful ones will see the overthrow of the beast's counterfeit kingdom and the destruction of all who cling to this deception. In chapter 15 they celebrate the triumph of God's kingdom just as the children of Israel celebrated the exodus deliverance, the former as an antitypical escalation of the latter.

14:1

In the OT "Zion" occurs approximately 155 times. Rarely does the name refer to a place of sin and judgment, "Jerusalem" being the term usually reserved for that reference. It can refer to God's dwelling in the temple or be a symbol for the people of God. However, it most commonly refers to the city that God will establish and rule over at the end of the age, which subsumes and escalates the prior two ideas (*TDNT* 7:300, 312–17). Here it is symbolic for the place where God's new-covenant people receive this eschatological promise.

The fuller name "Mount Zion" in distinction to "Zion" by itself occurs only nineteen times in the OT, at least nine of which allude to a remnant being saved, in connection with either God's name or God's sovereign rule, and sometimes both (2 Kings 19:31; Ps. 48:2, 10–11; 74:2, 7; Isa. 4:2–3; 10:12, 20; 37:30–32; Joel 2:32 [3:5 MT]; Obad. 17, 21; Mic. 4:5–8).

It is beyond coincidence that a "new name" is repeatedly associated with eschatological Zion. The city is to be given various new names (Isa. 62:2; 65:12; cf. 56:5), all of which express the new nature of the restored people and city—for example, note the names "my delight is in her" (Isa. 62:4), "city that is not forsaken" (Isa. 62:12), "throne of Yahweh" (Jer. 3:17), "Yahweh our righteousness" (Jer. 33:16), and "Yahweh is there" (Ezek. 48:35) (for further OT references, see *TDNT* 7:315).

14:4a

The word "virgin" is repeatedly applied to the nation of Israel in the OT (see "virgin of Israel" and other similar variant phrases in 2 Kings 19:21; Isa. 37:22; Jer. 14:17; 18:13; 31:4, 13, 21; Lam. 1:15; 2:13; Amos 5:2). The Hebrew for "virgin" in the majority of these passages is rendered in the LXX by *parthenos*. As is typical in Revelation, this description of Israel is now applied to the church.

In the OT Israel's idolatries, as well as their political and economic practices, were pictured as "harlotry" (Ezek. 23; Jer. 3:1–10; cf. Hos. 1:2). Their worship of idols also was referred to as "defilement" (Isa. 65:4; Jer. 23:15; 44:4; 1 Esd. 8:83). The picture of preventing "pollution" occurred earlier in Revelation to refer to Christians who have not identified with idolatrous institutions such as emperor worship or trade guild idolatry (cf. 3:4 with 14:4; see commentary on Rev. 2:14, 20; 3:4–5 above). The same notion is conveyed here.

14:5

The expression of the saints' guilelessness is also an allusion to Zeph. 3, which itself may be an allusion to Isa. 53 (see Fekkes 1994: 191–92):

Isa. 53:9: "he did not do lawlessness, nor was guile in his mouth"

Zeph. 3:13: "and by no means was a deceitful tongue found in their mouth"

Rev. 14:5: "and a lie was not found in their mouth"

In addition to the parallel language with Revelation, Zeph. 3:11–14 speaks of God in the last days saving a remnant, who are identified with his "holy mountain" and "Zion." This prophecy has become reality in the faithful Christian remnant. Also relevant is Ps. 15:1–3 (14:1–3 LXX), where those fit to dwell on God's holy mountain are the "blameless" (*amōmos*) who speak truth in their hearts and do not lie with their tongues. Those who maintain a faithful witness will live with God.

14:8

The phrase "fallen, fallen is Babylon" derives from Isa. 21:9, and it is equivalent to the ensuing statement there that the idols of Babylon are destroyed. The destruction of the idolatrous system of the world is also in mind here, as chapter 13 and the immediately following verses 14:9, 11 bear out. The Isaiah allusion is merged with another OT reference. The title "Babylon the Great" is based on the identical name of the city in Dan. 4:30 (LXX/Θ [4:27 MT]). In Dan. 4 the name forms part of an expression of the king's self-glorification, for which he is about to be judged. Now in Rev. 14:8 the latter-day Babylon meets its end.

Just as Babylon destroyed the first temple and sent Israel into exile, so Rome came to be called Babylon in some sectors of Judaism because it also destroyed the temple in Jerusalem and exiled Israel (cf. *Midr. Rab.* Num. 7:10; *Midr. Ps.* 137:8; see Hunzinger 1965). In fact, contemporary and later Jewish sources equated the name "Babylon" with Rome (see *2 Bar.* 11:1; 33:2; 67:7; 79:1; *Sib. Or.* 5:140–143, 158–61, 434; 1 Pet. 5:13; *Midr. Rab.* Lev. 6:6; *Midr. Rab.* Song 1:6, 4; cf. 1QpHab II, 11–12; *b. Sanh.* 21b). "Babylon" is a symbolic name for Rome also in *4 Ezra* 3:2, 31, especially in relation to *4 Ezra* 12:10–39, where the metaphor of the eagle for Babylon from Dan. 7:4 is applied to Rome as the "fourth kingdom."

The metaphor of drunkenness comes from Jer. 51:7–8: "Babylon has been a golden cup in the hand of the LORD, intoxicating all the earth. The nations have drunk of her wine; therefore, the nations are going mad. Suddenly Babylon has fallen and been broken." The intoxicating madness here appears to result from the terror of Babylon's op-

pressive measures (so also in Hab. 2:15–16). This is borne out by Jer. 25:15–16, which also is included in John's allusion: "Take this cup of the wine of wrath from my hand, and cause all the nations . . . to drink it. And they shall drink and stagger and go mad because of the sword that I will send among them." Since Jer. 25:15 (32:15 LXX) is alluded to also in 14:10, its language is likely borrowed here. This intoxication of the nations may refer to Rome/Babylon's idolatrous economic activity, which will continue to express itself in all evil political and economic systems until Christ's return. Such an interpretation of 14:8 is supported by Isa. 23:15–18, where Tyre's economic domination of the nations is portrayed as immorality. Tyre's benefiting from the wealth of the nations is pictured as a "harlot" receiving "harlot's wages" (see Isa. 23:1–18; so also Nineveh is regarded in Nah. 3:4). Likewise, Ezek. 16:1–36 portrays as harlotry Israel's political and economic dependence on other nations, as well as the idolatry that infected them from those nations (see 16:33–34).

14:10

The picture of pouring out wine resulting in intoxication indicates the unleashing of God's wrath at the final judgment (Ps. 60:3; 75:8; Isa. 51:17, 21–23; 63:6; Jer. 25:15–18; 51:7; cf. Job 21:20; Obad. 16). Sometimes the drunken stupor ends in physical death and destruction (Jer. 25:27–33; Obad. 16; Rev. 18:6–9). This imagery is inspired especially by the wording of Ps. 75:8; Jer. 25:15; 51:7, all three of which are grouped together and applied by Jewish exegetical tradition to the wicked who will "drink in the time to come" (*Midr. Rab.* Gen. 88:5; *Midr. Ps.* 11:5; 75:4; cf. *Midr. Rab.* Gen. 16:4).

The thorough and enduring effect of the judgment is expressed through the portrayal of the divine draught being "mixed undiluted," in allusion to Jer. 32:15 LXX (cf. Ps. 74:8 LXX [75:8 ET]; *Pss. Sol.* 8:14; 3 Macc. 5:2).

The apocalyptic belief was that the wicked would be punished, often by fire, in the presence of the righteous (*1 En.* 48:9; 62:12; 108:14–15; Wis. 5:1–14; *4 Ezra* 7:93; *Tg. Isa.* 33:17) forever (Isa. 66:22–24; *1 En.* 27:2–3 [cf. with *1 En.* 21]).

14:11

Together with the conclusion of 14:10, the portrait of 14:11a is drawn from Isa. 34:9–10, which describes God's judgment of Edom. Isaiah pictures the historical annihilation of Edom because of its sin. Once destroyed by God's judgment, Edom would never rise again. Likewise, the judgment of unbelievers at the end of time would be as absolute.

14:17–20

The imagery of the harvest is developed from Joel 3:13: "Put in the sickle, for the harvest is ripe. Come, tread, for the wine press is full; the wine vats overflow, for their wickedness is great." The Joel passage is the only one in the OT where images of both harvest and treading the wine press occur, and there they connote judgment. Accordingly, the final judgment of evil earthly forces is pictured in 14:1–20. Since Joel 3:13 is a prophecy of God's judgment of the evil nations, the same theme of judgment is expressed in both metaphors here (so Kiddle and Ross 1940: 285–95; *contra* Swete [1906: 190], who believes that John has transformed Joel's punitive harvest image into a redemptive one; cf. *Midr. Rab.* Song 8:14, which also takes Joel 4:13 positively to refer to Israel's redemption). "Reaping" is an image associated with judgment elsewhere, though God or his agents are not specified as the reapers (Job 4:8; Prov. 22:8; Jer. 12:13; Hos. 8:7; Gal. 6:7–8). Likewise, "harvesting" can be a picture of judgment (Jer. 51:33; Mic. 4:12–13; Matt. 3:12/Luke 3:17).

The overthrow of the nations implicitly takes place outside the holy city, not in it. Outside Zion there will be only destruction, as predicted by the prophets (Zech. 14:2–5, 12–16 affirm that the rebellious nations will be defeated in the vicinity of Jerusalem, as do other texts [e.g., Dan. 11:45; *4 Ezra* 13:34–39; *2 Bar.* 40:1–3; *Sib. Or.* 3:667–697; 1QM VII, 3–4; *Midr. Rab.* Song 2:2, 5]). Perhaps uppermost in thought is Joel 3:2, 11–12, 14, which say that God will enter into judgment with the "surrounding nations" outside of Jerusalem in the nearby "valley of Jehoshaphat."

Revelation 15

15:2

The sight of what appeared to be "like a sea of glass like crystal" could include allusion to the reflection of the laver in Solomon's temple and the heavenly splendor of God's holy separateness (see Beale 1999a: 327–28, 789–92). But uppermost in mind is the heavenly analogue to the Red Sea in connection with the new exodus. This identification is confirmed beyond doubt by the following mention of the new "song of Moses," which is the latter-day counterpart of Moses' song recounted in Exod. 15 (*Mekilta* to Exod. 14:16 and *'Abot R. Nat.* 30a say, on the basis of Exod. 15:8 ["the deeps were congealed"], that one of the miracles at the Red Sea episode was that the sea became congealed and appeared like glass vessels [see McNamara 1966: 203–4]; *'Abot de Rabbi Nathan* adds that fire was present in the midst of the glass; again on the basis of Exod. 15:8, *Midr. Ps.* 136:7 says that the sea appeared as a "crystallized . . . kind of glass"; for a sea in heaven, cf. *T. Levi* 2:7a; *2 En.* 3:3). The exodus atmosphere is discernible through the prior mention of "plagues" (15:1), which clearly are modeled after the plagues of Egypt (so chap. 16), and by the subsequent mention of the "tabernacle of testimony" (so Caird 1966: 197). The first exodus, out of Egypt and out from under Pharaoh's tyrannical power, will be recapitulated by divine design in a final, end-time exodus of God's people out from under the tyrannical oppression and rule of the "beast" over the world.

Daniel 7:10 pictures similarly a "river of fire" in heaven before the divine throne, with multitudes of angels standing around it. This prophetic picture in Dan. 7 indicates God's decision to judge "the beast," who was "slain and destroyed, and his body was given to be burnt with fire" (Dan. 7:11) (on the Dan. 7 background for the "sea of glass" in Rev. 4:6, see Beale 1999a: 327–28). The certainty of the beast's prophesied demise is underscored in Rev. 15:2.

15:3a

Like God's people of old, God's new-covenant people will praise him by singing "the song of Moses," extolling his end-time judgment of their oppressors. Their song is a hymn of deliverance and praise of God's attributes like that in Exod. 15:1–18.

Deuteronomy 32 is also called a song of Moses (Deut. 31:19, 22, 30; 32:44), which is included in the allusion to Exod. 15, since it also describes judgment. Wrath against apostate Israelites because of idolatry is the focus in Deut. 32, as here judgment on apostate Christians together with the nations is in view. Just as "the song of Moses" includes reference to the earlier deliverance by Moses, so also "the song of the Lamb" includes reference to the fact that the deliverance of the saints from the beast will have been decisively led by Jesus himself.

15:3b

The content of the song itself comes not directly from Exod. 15, but rather from passages throughout the OT extolling God's character. All of these are combined to explain the new exodus, which will happen again on a grander scale than the first. The first line of the song expresses God's "great and marvelous works." This is an OT allusion derived from Deut. 28:59–60 LXX, which predicts that Israel's future judgment will be patterned after the Egyptian plagues. Also echoed is Ps. 110:2–4 LXX (111:2–4 ET), which glorifies God for his "great works" and "marvelous doings" when he redeemed Israel at the Red Sea. The psalm itself may be alluding to Exod. 34:10 (where God promises that the nations "will see that the works of the LORD [in his dealings with Israel], that they are great"; so also Exod. 15:11: God is "marvelous in glories, doing wonders").

Just as the God of the exodus generation was praised as one whose "works are true" and "all his ways just" (Deut. 32:4), so he will be lauded again. The passage from Deuteronomy is introduced in 31:30 as a "song" by Moses, and it is applied by *b. Ta'an.* 11a to the judgment and reward "in the world to come," which is further evidence that Deut. 32 also lay behind the "song" mentioned here in 15:3 (*L.A.B.* 19:4 affirms that Deut. 32:1 includes the idea that God "revealed the end of the world").

15:4

Together with the last clause of 15:3 ("king of the nations"), the opening statement of this verse recalls Jer. 10:7: "Who would not fear you, O King of the nations?"

Psalm 86:9–10 is the basis for most of the language in 15:4: "Who will not . . . glorify your name? For you alone are holy, so that all the nations will come and worship before you." Like Jeremiah, the description from the psalm explains further how God is incomparable in contrast to false gods (in addition to 86:10, cf. "there is no one like you among the gods" in 86:8; the eschatological prophecy of Isa. 2:2 could also be an in-

cluded echo: "all the nations will come to" Zion). The prophetic theme of the nations streaming into Zion to worship God in the end time occurs elsewhere in the OT (Isa. 2:3; 49:22–23; 60:14; 66:23–24; Mic. 4:2; Zech. 8:20–22; 14:16, where language similar to Ps. 86:9–10 occurs). This prophetic theme is seen to achieve its fulfillment in the futuristic depiction of Rev. 15:4.

Bauckham (1993a: 296–307) provides a good analysis of how the OT allusions in Rev. 15:3–4 are used to fill out the themes of Exod. 15:1–18; the latter is best seen as typological of the former.

15:7

The image of bowls comes partly from the OT, where "bowls" are used (approximately thirty times) in conjunction with the priestly service at the altar in the tabernacle or temple. The bowls probably were used to carry out the ashes and fat of sacrifices. Sometimes these bowls are directly connected with "the tabernacle of witness" (Exod. 38:3; Num. 4:14–15; 7:13–89) and are referred to as "golden bowls" (1 Chron. 28:17; 2 Chron. 4:8, 21).

The image is derived also in part from Isa. 51:17, 22, where twice it is said that "the bowl of the cup of [God's] wrath," formerly poured out on sinful Israel, is now to be poured out on their pagan "tormentors," which in context is Babylon. As in Isa. 51, the bowls in Rev. 16 are directed against end-time Babylon and its inhabitants and are also called a "cup" (16:19; as in 14:10).

15:8

God's presence in the temple is highlighted as it is "filled with the smoke of God's glory and from his power" (as in Exod. 40:34–35; 1 Kings 8:10–11; 2 Chron. 5:13; Isa. 6:1, 4 LXX). The description may be a collective echo of similar OT descriptions of God's presence in the earthly temple, though the focus may be more on Ezek. 10:2–4, where an angelic being "clothed in linen" stands close to the four cherubim in the heavenly temple, and "the temple was filled with the cloud, and the court was filled with the brightness of the glory of the LORD." The Ezek. 10 scene is an introduction to an announcement of judgment, which brings it even closer to the function of the similar vision in Rev. 15 so that the former becomes analogous to the latter.

Revelation 16

Chapter 16 concludes the series of seal, trumpet, and bowl judgments with the outpouring of the seven bowls, signifying God's consummate judgment of the wicked. The sixth bowl features the decisive battle of Armaggedon (for the predominantly symbolic nature of the bowl visions, see Beale 1999a: 50–55). The bowls, like the trumpets, are modeled on the Exodus plagues that John views to be typological for the events described in the bowls. Some of these plagues occur throughout the church age (bowls 1–5) and others happen only at the very end of history (bowls 6–7).

16:1

That God is the speaker in 16:1 is confirmed by the fact that God has just been mentioned as being in his heavenly temple (15:5–8) and by the allusion to Isa. 66:6 (so also Holtz 1971: 132): "a voice from the temple, a voice of the LORD rendering recompense to his adversaries" (which is applied to judgment of Rome in *Midr. Ps.* 18:11).

The phrase "pour out God's wrath" (*ekcheō* + *thymos*) in the LXX is used to indicate judgment, either against covenant breakers or against those who have persecuted God's people (cf. Ezek. 14:19; Jer. 10:25; similarly, Ps. 68:25 [69:24 ET]; Zeph. 3:8 [in substantial agreement with Kraft 1974: 204–5; Prigent 1981: 243; Roloff 1993: 161]). Sometimes the formula includes "fire" as the figurative destructive effect of the pouring, which enforces a figurative interpretation of the bowls (e.g., Jer. 7:20; Lam. 2:4; 4:11; Ezek. 22:21–22; 30:15–16; Zeph. 3:8; so also Ps. 78:5–6 [79:5–6 ET]; Ezek. 21:36–37 [21:31–32 ET]).

Standing also in the background is the "pouring out" of sacrificial blood by the priest at the base of the altar in direct connection twice with "the priest [who] ... will sprinkle it [the blood] seven times ... in front of the sanctuary" (Lev. 4:6–7, 17–18 [see J. M. Ford 1975: 265]). Just as the pouring out of sacrificial blood represented the cleansing of the tabernacle from defilement of sin, so also the pouring out of the bowls cleanses the earth from the defilement of sin through judgment.

16:2

The description of the first bowl's effect is based on the Egyptian plague of boils (Exod. 9:9–11), which is summarized in Deut. 28:27, 35 as an "evil sore" (*helkos ponēros*). The punishment matches the crime: those who receive an idolatrous mark will be chastised by being given a penal mark (see Beasley-Murray 1974: 240).

16:6

Note the echo of Ps. 79:3, 10, 12: "They have poured out their [Israel's] blood as water. . . . Let the vindication of your servants' blood that has been poured out be known among the nations before our eyes. . . . Repay to our neighbors sevenfold into their bosom their reproach with which they have reproached you, O LORD." The same truth is applied to the people of God during the interadvent age.

16:12

The woe of the sixth bowl is depicted according to the description of God's judgment of Babylon and Israel's restoration, which itself was patterned after the drying up of the Red Sea at the exodus (cf. Exod. 14:21–22 with Isa. 11:15; 44:27; 50:2; 51:10; cf. also Josh. 3:16; 4:23). The OT prophesies that this judgment would include the drying up of the Euphrates River (Isa. 11:15; 44:27; Jer. 50:38; 51:36; cf. Zech. 10:11). The prophecy was fulfilled by Cyrus, who diverted the waters of the Euphrates (cf. Isa. 44:27–28). This allowed his army to cross the now shallow waters of the river, enter the city unexpectedly, and defeat the Babylonians (Herodotus, *Hist.* 1.190–191; Xenophon, *Cyr.* 7.5.1–36 [see also *Tg. Jer.* 51:36, 41–44; 4Q169 Frags. 1+2, 3–9). Against this background, it can be seen that the battle in Revelation will end in the absolute destruction of all the opponents of God.

16:13

Mention of a woe of frogs again recalls the exodus plagues. In fact, the only places in biblical literature where the word *batrachos* ("frog") appears are in the LXX of Exod. 8:2–13; Ps. 77:45 (78:45 ET); 104:30 (105:30 ET); Wis. 19:10, all of which describe the exodus plague (so likewise the accounts of the exodus in Josephus, *Ant.* 2.296–298; Philo, *Sacrifices* 69; *Migration* 83; *Moses* 1.103–106, 144). Here in Revelation the frogs are expressly said to be symbols for deceptive demonic spirits (16:14) that plague unbelieving humanity.

16:14

In this case, the deception is aimed at "the kings." Likewise, in the exodus plagues the frogs were first to affect the king (Exod. 8:3–4), and Ps. 104:30 LXX (105:30 ET) says only that "kings" in Egypt were struck by the frogs.

The three synonymous phrases "gather together for war" with minor variants in 16:14; 19:19; 20:8 are based on OT prophecy, especially from Zech. 12–14 and possibly Zeph. 3, which foretold that God would gather the nations together in Israel for the final war of history (strikingly, Zech. 13:2 LXX says that the activity of "false prophets and the unclean spirit" will be active in Israel contemporaneously with the gathering of the nations). Revelation 16:14 continues this prophetic forecast.

That the battle is called "the war of the great day of God" indicates that the battle is one in which God will decisively judge the unrighteous. This is the meaning of the phrase "great day of God" in Joel 2:11; Zeph. 1:14, and especially of the eschatological prophecy of judgment in Joel 2:31. The nations are deceived to think that they are gathering to exterminate the saints, but they are gathered together ultimately by God in order to meet their own judgment at the hands of Jesus (19:11–21) (see Beasley-Murray 1974: 244–45). A striking parallel is 1 Kings 22:22–23, 30–31: a demonic spirit before the heavenly throne says, "I will go forth, and I will be a false spirit in the mouth of all the prophets" of Ahab, which results in the king "entering into war" and being slain.

16:16

That "Armageddon" (Heb. *har měgiddô* ["mount of Megiddo"]) is not literal is evident from the fact that OT prophecies of the final battle of history place its location, without exception, in the immediate vicinity of the city of Jerusalem and Mount Zion or its surrounding mountains. However, the Plain of Megiddo is about a two-day walk north of Jerusalem. Furthermore, John himself places the location directly outside of Jerusalem (14:20; 20:8–9), though he universalizes the OT references and speaks in spiritual rather than literal geographical terms. A figurative view

of "Armageddon" is apparent also from the fact that no "mountain" of Megiddo has ever existed, although even in OT times the city of Megiddo sat prominently on a tell. It is possible that the Hebrew *har* could refer to a tell, since the word sometimes refers to settlements on hills. However, the word predominantly refers to "mountain" in the usual sense of the word (see *TDOT* 3:429–34). It is likely that the use of "mountain" is meant to provoke associations with the destruction of Israel's enemies on mountains (e.g., Ezek. 38:21; Zech. 14:4).

Megiddo is the place where righteous Israelites were attacked by wicked nations (Judg. 5:19; 2 Kings 23:29; 2 Chron. 35:20–22, the latter two of which occur in connection with "the River Euphrates" [cf. 2 Kings 9:27]). The Judges 5 passage provides the most probable OT typological pattern for Rev. 16:16, since there God defeats an overwhelmingly powerful foe who had formerly oppressed defenseless Israel (cf. Judg. 4:3; 5:8; see Düsterdieck 1980: 423; Hendriksen 1962: 196; Morris 1987: 200); see Rev. 16:12–14, 16, and note Judg. 4:7, where God prophesies that he "will bring" to Israel "the captain of the host of Jabin . . . and his multitude . . . and I will deliver them into your hand," and compare Judg. 5:19: "The kings set themselves in array, then they battled . . . at the waters of Megiddo" (see also *Midr. Rab.* Num. 23:7). Likewise, compare the striking wording of 2 Chron. 35:20–22 LXX: "Pharaoh went up . . . to the river Euphrates. . . . And he [Josiah] came to do battle [*tou polemēsai*] in the plain of Megiddo." The end-time attack by the nations against Jerusalem is also compared in some way to the incident of Josiah's defeat at Megiddo (Zech. 12:1–14), the latter of which, together with Ahab's defeat in the same vicinity, had become almost proverbial in Judaism (*Tg. Lam.* 1:18; *Tg. Zech.* 12:11; *b. Meg.* 3a; *b. Mo'ed Qat.* 28b). And, if Armageddon is associated with nearby Mount Carmel, then the name might also include allusion to Elijah's defeat of the prophets of Baal during the reign of Ahab and Jezebel (1 Kings 18:19–46) (so Shea 1980).

All of the aforementioned passages recording events occurring in the vicinity of Megiddo may stand behind the reference in 16:16, so that John's reference to this place name may ring with the following typological and prophetic associations: the defeat of kings who oppress God's people (Judg. 5:19–21); the destruction of false prophets (1 Kings 18:40); the death of misled kings, which led to mourning (2 Kings 23:29; 2 Chron. 35:20–25); and the future expectation that in direct connection with the one "whom they have pierced," there would be destruction of "all the nations that come against Jerusalem" and a mourning by all of Israel's tribes (Zech. 12:9–12) (so D. Ford 1979: 303; LaRondelle 1989, following Farrer 1964: 178).

For further discussion and overview of the history of interpretation of Armageddon, see Paulien 1992; Day 1994.

16:17

The seventh bowl describes the final destruction of the corrupt world system, which follows on the heels of the battle of Armageddon. The bowl being poured out on the "air" is best understood as part of the exodus plague imagery used already in the trumpets and preceding bowls and alluded to in reference to "the plague of hail" in 16:21. Therefore, 16:21 makes allusion to the plague of "hail" from Exod. 9:22–34. Similarly, Philo (*Moses* 1.129) calls the hail in Egypt, together with other trials, "plagues of heaven and air" (see also *Moses* 1.114, 119–120).

16:21

Why does hail come last in the presentation of bowl plagues? Bauckham (1977: 228) argues plausibly that the Exod. 9 plague of hail is being combined with the cosmic phenomena surrounding the Sinai theophany of Exod. 19, alluded to in Rev. 16:18. Furthermore, the placement at the end has been influenced by Ezek. 38:19–22, where hail and earthquake mark the final stage of judgment on the end-time enemy. The identification of the plague with that of the plague of hail in Egypt is evidenced further by the fact that both Rev. 16:21 and the Exodus account emphasize the severity or large size of the hail. If both Exodus 9 and Ezekiel 38 are in mind, the latter points forward to the events of Rev. 16:21 and the latter prophesy is underscored as still to happen in the future.

Revelation 17

The destruction of Babylon, emblem of the anti-God forces in the world, is described in graphic detail. It becomes clear that Babylon is the great "counterfeit city," a mockery and perversion of God's new Jerusalem.

17:1

The description of end-time Babylon's judgment is taken from Jer. 51:13 (28:13 LXX), where Jeremiah predicts absolute judgment on historical Babylon: "For his [God's] wrath is against Babylon, to destroy it utterly . . . against the inhabitants of Babylon dwelling upon many waters" (28:11–13 LXX). This judgment, which occurred in the OT epoch, prefigures that which begins to be described in 17:1.

17:3a

The mention of the seer's transport "into the desert" is an allusion to Isa. 21:1–2, where a vision from God (see 21:10) is revealed to the prophet Isaiah and is described as "coming from a desert [*erēmos*]" (as in Rev. 17:3). That this is an allusion and not coincidental language is borne out not only by the fact that Isa. 21:1–10 is a vision of judgment against Babylon, but by the fact that the phrase "fallen, fallen is Babylon" of Isa. 21:9 appears in Revelation in the following context of 18:2, as well in the preceding text of 14:8, which itself looks ahead to chaps. 17–18. Isaiah 21:1 uniquely combines the apparently disparate images of desert and sea ("the burden of the wilderness of the sea") and associates them with Babylon (see MT and various LXX witnesses). Likewise, Rev. 17:1, 3 picture latter-day Babylon in a wilderness and as "sitting on many waters."

17:4

The Israelite whore in the book of Jeremiah has "scarlet dress" (4:30 LXX), and on her "skirts is found the lifeblood of the innocent" (2:34 LXX). Likewise, the book of Isaiah portrays faithless Israel as a "harlot" whose sin is "as purple . . . and as scarlet," which represents its sin of "murder," her "hands" being "full of blood" and her "wine merchants mixing wine with water" (1:15–22 LXX). Nor is it accidental that in the LXX the high priest's garments are also described as adorned with "gold, purple, scarlet, linen, and [precious] stones," which is the identical combination of words used to describe the Babylonian harlot's attire here in 17:4; 18:16 (for the significance of this, see commentary on Rev. 17:16 below). Thus

Babylon may appear from one perspective to be religiously good, but she is, in reality, evil.

17:6

John's response, "I marveled greatly," is similar to Daniel's response to the angelic revelation about the Babylonian king's imminent demise in the LXX of Dan. 4. The metaphor of "being drunk with blood" is developed from Isa. 34:5–7; 49:26; Jer. 46:10, where it describes God's judgment of the wicked. The imagery is applied now in reverse manner to show that Babylon will be punished by means of its own sin, as 16:6 reveals. In describing the judgment of wicked oppressors, *1 En.* 62:12 also alludes to the passages in Isa. 34; Jer. 46.

17:9a

In 17:9a is a further development of Daniel's prophecy that in the end-time tribulation true saints would need spiritual "understanding" and "wisdom" to keep from being deceived by an evil king who exalts his sovereignty over God and persecutes God's people who do not acknowledge him (so Dan. 11:33; 12:10 [for further discussion of background, see commentary on Rev. 13:18 above; Beale 1980]). The beast that John has seen in the vision in 17:3 is none other than the wicked state force prophesied in Daniel.

17:9b

"Mountains" are symbolic for kingdoms in the OT and Judaism (e.g., Isa. 2:2; Jer. 51:25; Ezek. 35:3; Dan. 2:35, 45; Zech. 4:7; *1 En.* 52; *Tg. Isa.* 41:15 (see commentary on Rev. 8:8–9 above; for the interchangeableness of "kings" and "kingdoms," see Dan. 7:17, 23). The identification is also confirmed by Dan. 7:4–7, where seven is the total number of heads of the four beasts (= kingdoms), which also is the source for the seven heads in Rev. 13:1 (on which, see commentary above). That kings who represent kingdoms are thought of is apparent from Dan. 7:17 LXX ("the great beasts are four kings") and Dan. 7:23 LXX ("the fourth beast will be a fourth kingdom"). The presence of allusions to Dan. 7 shows that its prophecy of an end-time persecuting foe is being developed in Rev. 17:9b.

17:12

As Dan. 7:4–7 was the source of the seven heads, so Dan. 7:7–8, 20, 24 are the source of the "ten horns." Daniel identifies the horns with kings, and Rev. 17:12 does the same in beginning to reveal further details about how that prophecy will be fulfilled.

The kings' future reign with the beast will last for a period referred to as "one hour." The time period echoes that in Dan. 4:17a LXX, where it refers to the period during which God caused King Nebuchadnezzar to become like a beast. Here also God is sovereign even over the authority of ungodly kings who ally with the beast in order to prepare to oppose the Messiah (cf. 17:13–14). The phrase "one hour" is repeated in chap. 18 with reference to the time in which "Babylon the Great" was judged by God (18:10, 17, 19), which is a combined allusion to the "one hour" from Dan. 4:17a LXX with "Babylon the Great" from Dan. 4:30 LXX.

17:14

The purpose of forming the strong coalition mentioned in 17:13 is to do "battle with the Lamb." However, "the Lamb will conquer them." This battle phraseology in the first clause of the verse is from Dan. 7:21:

Dan. 7:21 Θ (cf. the MT)	Rev. 17:14a
"That horn was making war with the saints, and he overpowered them."	"These will make war with the Lamb, and the Lamb will conquer them."

The allusive connection is enhanced by the fact that, as in Daniel, here also it is kings who are portrayed as horns (17:12) who conduct the war (although in Dan. 7:21 it is a singular "horn" [for the parallel Greek with 17:14, see Beale 1999a: 880]). However, there is a change in the wording from Daniel that does not invalidate its allusive nature but reveals an ironic interpretive alteration like that already made with the Dan. 7:21 allusion in chap. 12 and in *1 En.* 90:12, 13b (see further Beale 1999a: 652–54, 880–82 on 5:6; 12:7b–8a; 17:14). The last part of Daniel's wording is reversed and applied to the champion of the "saints" instead of to the beast's victory.

The same language by which the beast was described in Dan. 7:21; Rev. 11:7; 13:7a as defeating the saints is now applied to the portrayal of the Lamb overcoming the forces of the beast and his horned allies (for the allusion to Dan. 7:21, see Beale 1999a: 880 on 11:7; 13:7a). The reversal of language is not a result of random Scripture twisting, but rather is intended to express irony. The prediction of the beast's victory over the saints in Dan. 7:21 becomes an ironic type of his own final defeat. His defeat must occur fittingly according to the same warlike method by which he attempted to oppress. The reversed portrayal shows that he must be punished by means of his own sin.

Revelation 17:14 is the answer to the concluding question of 13:4: "Who is able to make war with him [the beast]?" (so Ruiz 1989: 452). The "called and elect and faithful" (17:14c) who accompany the Lamb fight alongside him and represent the vindication of the persecuted saints of Dan. 7:21 and of Rev. 6:9–11; 12:11; 13:10, 15–17. Strikingly, Dan. 7:22 promises that after the horned beast attempts to conquer the saints, God will "give the judgment to the saints of the Most High." This became the basis for the expectation that the saints would judge the wicked in the end time (see 1 Cor. 6:2; *1 En.* 38:5; 91:12; cf. Wis. 3:8; *1 En.* 90:19; 95:3; 96:1; 98:12). Perhaps the Dan. 7:22 prophesy is echoed here.

The basis for the Lamb's victory in 17:14 is that "he is Lord of lords and King of kings." The same title occurs only twice in biblically related material prior to the NT (*1 En.* 9:4; Dan. 4:37 LXX). It is possible that *1 Enoch* is in mind here, since its context concerns eschatological judgment (i.e., of the fallen Watchers), as does that of Rev. 17. However, Dan. 4:37 LXX is the more likely influence (on which, see Beale 1999a: 881):

Dan. 4:37 LXX	Rev. 17:14b
"because he himself is God of gods and Lord of lords and King of kings"	"because he is Lord of lords and King of kings" (cf. *1 En.* 9:4: "Lord of lords, God of gods, King of kings")

Just as the Babylonian king was addressed by this title, so the king of latter-day Babylon (Rome) in John's day was similarly addressed. The title refers to God in Dan. 4 as the one who demonstrated his true divine sovereignty and revealed Nebuchadnezzar as an empty parody of the name by judging the beastly king of "Babylon the Great." Now the title is applied typologically to the Lamb. The Lamb demonstrates his deity on the last day by judging the beast that carries "Babylon the Great." And he exposes as false the divine claims of the emperor and others like him.

17:15

Isaiah 17:12–13 also uses the metaphor of "many waters" for "many nations" (cf. Isa. 8:7; 23:10; Jer. 46:7–9; 47:2; in Judaism, see *Tg. Ps.* 18:16; 4Q169 Frags. 1+2, 4; 3–4 III, 10). The "many waters" have already been seen to be an allusion to Jer. 51:13 (28:13 LXX), where they refer to the waters of the Euphrates and the channels and canals that surrounded the city. These waters helped Babylon to flourish economically and provided security against outside attack. The multitudes of humanity that the waters now represent are the basis for Babylon's economic trade and security.

17:16

The portrayal of the harlot's desolation is sketched according to the outlines of the prophesied judgment of apostate Jerusalem by God in Ezek. 23:25–29, 47: "your survivors will be devoured by the fire [23:25] . . . they will also strip you of your clothes [23:26] . . . and they will deal with you in hatred . . . and leave you naked and bare, and the nakedness of your harlotries will be uncovered [23:29] . . . they will burn their houses with fire [23:47]" (cf. Ezek. 16:37–41). Also, Ezek. 23:31–34 portrays the harlot as having a cup in her hand and becoming drunk, strikingly similar to Rev. 17:4.

The portrait of the whore throughout Rev. 17 draws also from Israel's depiction as a harlot in Jer. 2:20–4:30 (so D. Ford 1979: 270): there Judah is a harlot (2:20) who has "a harlot's forehead" (3:3) and causes others to sin (2:33), on whose "skirts is found the lifeblood of the innocent" (2:34), whose "dress (is) in scarlet," who "decorates herself with ornaments of gold" (4:30), and whose lovers will despise her and try to kill her (4:30). Israel is called a harlot because although she is supposedly committed to Yahweh, she has spiritual intercourse with idols.

However, "harlot" can also refer to other ungodly nations in the prophets, as in Isa. 23:15–18; Nah. 3:4–5 (although 4Q169 Frags. 3–4 II, 7–11 applies the Nahum text to the apostate leaders of Jerusalem). The "harlot" metaphor has the essential idea of an illicit relationship, whether that be religious, economic, political, or a combination of these. In both Nah. 3:4–5 and especially Isa. 23:15–18 Nineveh and Tyre are called harlots because they cause ruin and uncleanness among the nations by economically dominating them and influencing them by their idolatry (see Glasson 1965: 95). Furthermore, the whore in Rev. 17 is called "Babylon the Great," which refers to the proud, pagan Babylonian city in Dan. 4. Therefore, "Babylon" refers both to the pagan world and apostate Israel and to the apostate church that cooperates with it.

Revelation 18

The description of Babylon's fall continues, with an emphasis on its idolatry and worldwide economic exploitation as a basis for its judgment. Except for 18:1, the clear OT allusions discussed in this chapter serve as foreshadowings of the fall of Babylon the Great.

18:1

"The earth shone with a light from the glory around" God when Ezekiel saw a vision of the end-time restoration of Israel to its land and temple (Ezek. 43:2, also in conjunction with a loud "voice," as in Rev. 18:1–2). The OT prophecy provides an appropriate allusion to introduce a chapter in which one of the major themes is an exhortation to God's true people to separate from the world and be restored to the Lord (so also Caird 1966: 222; see commentary on Rev. 18:4 below).

18:2

The description of desolation most approximates the portrayal of Babylon's and Edom's judgment in Isa. 13:21; 34:11, 14. These judgments are viewed as anticipations of universal Babylon's judgment at the end of history. The final stripping away of Babylon's luxurious facade (17:4; 18:16) reveals her skeleton, within which sit only demonic bird-like creatures. Jewish interpretation of the creatures in Isa. 13:21; 34:11, 14 understood them to be demonic (e.g., *Tg. Isa.* 13:21; *Midr. Rab.* Lev. 5:1; 22:8; *Midr. Rab.* Gen. 65:15; and likely *2 Bar.* 10:8).

18:3

This recalls Ezek. 27:12 LXX: "The Carthaginians were your merchants because of the abundance of your power" (cf. Ezek. 27:33 LXX: Tyre "enriched all the kings of the earth"). This is the first reference in this chapter from Ezek. 26–28.

Tyre's destruction is the model for the destruction of the latter-day Babylon, Rome and her evil descendants. Tyre's demise looked forward implicitly to Babylon the Great's fall.

18:4

The exhortation to separate from Babylon's ways is patterned after the repeated exhortations of Isaiah and Jeremiah, especially that of Jer. 51:45: "Come forth from her midst, my people" (cf. Gen. 12:1; 19:15; Isa. 48:20; 52:11; Jer. 50:8; 51:6). As here, in Jer. 51 and the other OT parallels the coming judgment that Babylon must suffer forms the basis for the prophets' exhortation to God's people to separate (see esp. Jer. 51:35–45). Strikingly, the judgment that elicits the exhortation from Jer. 51 is portrayed with similar metaphors of desolation as in Rev. 18:2—Jer. 51:37 reads, "Babylon will become . . . a haunt of jackals, an object of horror, without inhabitants."

That the exhortation of 18:4 also strongly echoes that in Isa. 52:11 is evident from the immediately following phrase in the Isaiah text: "do not touch the unclean," which refers to the idols of Babylon. The exhortation in Jeremiah also includes separating from idol worship (see Jer. 51:44, 47, 52).

18:5

The reason that Babylon will be punished with such "plagues" is that "her sins have reached up to heaven." Again, appeal is made to Jer. 51: "For her [Babylon's] judgment has reached to heaven, it is lifted up to the skies" (Jer. 51:9 [note also an echo of Gen. 18:20; 19:13]). This foreshadows the judgment of the worldwide system, Babylon the Great. In some passages of the OT and early Judaism the expression becomes an idiom for an extreme degree of corporate sin (cf. Ezra 9:6; Jon. 1:2; 1 Esd. 8:75; *4 Ezra* 11:43).

God "remembering unrighteous acts" is an expression of judgment found elsewhere in the OT (e.g., Ps. 109:14; Hos. 9:9).

18:6

Babylon's punishment is commensurate with its crime. This is first expressed through wording that evokes Ps. 136:8 LXX (137:8 ET): "Blessed is he who will give back the recompense to you [Babylon] which you have given back to us [Israel]." Similarly, Jer. 27:29 LXX (50:29 ET) says of Babylon, "Render [*antapodote*] to her according to her works; according to all that she has done, do to her." Likewise, in Jer. 28:24 LXX (51:24 ET) God says, "I will repay [*antapodōsō*] Babylon and all the inhabitants . . . for all their evil that they have done" (cf. Jer. 27:15 LXX [50:15 ET]; Ezek. 23:31–35). The punishment of historical Babylon prefigures that of the end-time Babylonian system.

18:7

The basis for Babylon's judgment as a world system is reiterated (cf. 18:5a), this time patterned after the prediction of historical Babylon's judgment in Isa. 47, which portends eschatological Babylon's sinful arrogance.

Isa. 47:7–8 LXX	Rev. 18:7b
"She has said, 'I will be a princess [MT: "queen"] forever'; you did not understand these things in your heart. But now hear these words, you luxurious one, who sits securely, who says in her heart . . . 'I will not sit as a widow nor will I know bereavement.'" (Cf. Zeph. 2:14–15 LXX, concerning Nineveh: ". . . ravens in her porches . . . This is the scornful city which dwells securely, that says in her heart, 'I am, and there is no longer any after me'; how she is become desolate, a habitation of wild beasts.")	". . . because she says in her heart, 'I sit as a queen, and I am not a widow, and I by no means will see mourning.'"

18:8

The political and economic arrogance noted in 18:7b is emphasized as the cause for Babylon's sudden destruction, which "will come in one day." This is a continued typological reference to Isa. 47 (47:9: "but now these . . . things will come upon you suddenly in one day"), as is the statement that Babylon "will be burned by fire" (47:14: "they all will be burned in fire").

The prediction of Tyre's judgment in Ezek. 26–27 forms the model for the prophecy of Babylon's judgment in 18:9–19, although the cargo lists have been adapted to fit the realities of economic exploitation in the Roman Empire (see Bauckham 1993a). The past downfall of Tyre and those who mourn over it is a prophetic foreshadowing of the fall of the last great economic system (which needs to be kept in mind in the following explanation of these verses). Note the parallel of kings, merchants, and mariners in Ezek. 27:29–30, 35–36 (see Mounce 1977: 328).

18:9

The earthly rulers express despair in response to the destruction of Babylon, echoing Jer. 51:8: "Suddenly Babylon has fallen . . . wail over her," which continues the allusion to Jer. 50–51 in Rev. 18:4–8. They weep because they have lost their lover. This idolatrous involvement allowed "the kings of the earth" to "live in luxury," which is a partial allusion to Ezek. 27:33. The close connection between idolatry and economic prosperity was a fact of life in Asia Minor, where allegiance to Caesar and to the patron gods of the trade guilds was essential for people to maintain good standing in their particular trades.

18:10

In 18:9–10 we see the pattern of Ezek. 26:16–18 LXX, where, in response to the fall of prosperous Tyre, "princes of the nations . . . fear . . . and will groan . . . and they will take up a lamentation . . . and they will speak" in sorrow about how the city has been judged (likewise Ezek. 27:28–32). The Ezekiel background confirms the suggestion that the kings' lament over Babylon's desolation is grounded in the fear of their own imminent economic loss. The LXX of Ezek. 26:16b, adding to the Hebrew text, says that "they will fear their own destruction," which is to be understood economically in the light of Ezek. 27:33–36. Likewise, the LXX of Ezek. 27:27–28 (which is partly formative for Rev. 18:17–19) narrates that "the rowers . . . and the pilots of the sea," who "will wail over you . . . and cry bitterly, and put earth on their heads," will also "perish in the heart of sea" together with Tyre and its "traders" and "they that traffic" with the city.

18:12–13

The list of products is based partly on Ezek. 27:7–25, where fifteen out of twenty-nine of the same items are listed together along with the repetition of *emporoi* ("merchants") (so Rev. 18:11a, 15). Repeated allusion to Ezek. 26–27 in the immediately preceding and following contexts confirms reference to this segment of Ezek. 27.

18:16

The city's apparel is composed of six prosperous trade products. This follows the same pattern of Ezek. 27, where a full list of goods is found (27:12–24) and where part of the list is metaphorically applied to Tyre's clothing, "to clothe you with blue and purple from the islands," with the clause "fine linen … from Egypt became your couch" (27:7 LXX).

The picture of an ungodly economic system as a person dressed in luxurious clothing made of trade products has been partly inspired also by the same figurative portrayal of the king of economically prosperous Tyre in Ezek. 28:13: "Every precious stone was your covering: the ruby, the topaz, and the diamond; the beryl, the onyx, and the jasper; the lapis lazuli, the turquoise, and the emerald; and the gold." In *Tg. Ezek.* 28:13 it is explicitly said that the stones were on clothing: "your robe was adorned with all kinds of jewels" (see Rist 1957: 502).

18:17b–19

The pattern of Ezek. 27 continues to be followed, since there too those who conduct the business of sea trade lament and throw dust on their heads because the demise of Tyre means the demise of the sea commerce by which they make their living (Ezek. 27:28–33).

18:20

That believers in general, not particular groups of the Christian community, are addressed is evident from the allusion to Jer. 51:48, which also refers to heaven and earth in order to represent the whole Israelite community: "Then heaven and earth and all that is in them will shout for joy over Babylon, for the destroyers of the earth will have come to her." Jeremiah's reference to "heaven" is repeated, but the reference to "earth" is now substituted by "the saints and the apostles and the prophets," who compose the new people of God (so Jörns 1971: 141). It is not by chance that Jer. 51:49a states that "the slain of Israel" form part of the basis for Babylon's fall and consequent rejoicing in 51:48 (cf. the following phrase in 51:49b: "the slain of all the earth").

18:21

The judgment of Babylon here is based on Jer. 51:63, where Jeremiah commands his servant Seraiah to "bind a stone upon" a book that contains the prophecy of Babylon's judgment and to "cast it into the midst of the Euphrates." The angel in 18:21 interprets his symbolic action to mean that "in the same manner will Babylon the Great

City be thrown down and will not be found any longer."

18:22–23b

The allusion to Isa. 24:8 ("the sound of the harp has ceased") and its context underline both economic loss and resulting loss of joy (Isa. 24:6 LXX: "the dwellers in the earth will be poor"; Isa. 24:8 LXX: "the joy of timbrels has ceased"). The reference to Isa. 24:8 in 18:22a has been combined with Ezek. 26:13 (cf. Jer. 25:10).

18:23c–23d

The implication of self-glorification as the basis for condemnation in 18:23c is suggested from the context of the OT allusion, where the judgment of Tyre includes overturning its merchants because they had become proud about their economic achievements and consequent power: "The Lord of hosts has purposed to bring down all the pride of the glorious ones, and to disgrace every glorious thing on the earth" (Isa. 23:9 LXX). About Tyre itself the prophet says, "Your heart is lifted up because of your riches," which is equated with saying "I am a god" (cf. Ezek. 28:5 with 28:2–10). Tyre's economic self-idolatry was the cause of its eventual judgment. Likewise, the evil world system will be judged because of human self-glorification.

Revelation 19

The heavenly beings rejoice in God's mighty judgments, and the destruction of the wicked is seen from yet another angle. This time the imagery is drawn from the destruction of the eschatological adversaries Gog and Magog in Ezek. 38–39.

19:7–8

The language of the marriage supper echoes the prophesy of Isa. 61:10: "I will rejoice in the LORD, my soul will exult in my God; for he has clothed me with garments of salvation, he has wrapped me with a robe of righteousness; as a bridegroom decks himself with a garland, and as a bride adorns herself with jewels."

19:10

For angels refusing worship, see *Mart. Isa.* 7:21; 8:5; Tob. 12:16–22; *Apoc. Zeph.* 6:11–15; *Ps.-Mt.* 3; Cairo Genizah Hekhalot A/2, 13–18 (see Bauckham 1993a: 118–49).

19:12b

The statement that "no one knows" the name "except himself" does not mean that it is a secret to all others, as is commonly held (e.g., Swete 1906: 252; Kittel 1967: 126; Rissi 1972: 23; Mounce 1977: 345; Hailey 1979: 382–83). At issue is not the mysterious essence of the divine being, but rather his actions of judgment (Kraft 1974: 247–48). The expression could refer to the tetragrammaton (YHWH = "Lord" in the LXX), which the Jews would not pronounce (see McDonough 1999). This is supported by the fact that the name may be written on Christ's head or diadems, just as the name "Yahweh" was written on a gold plate on the high priest's forehead (M. Stuart 1845: 346, followed by, e.g., Farrer 1964: 198; Prigent 1981: 293). For example, Wis. 18:24 says, "Your majesty [= YHWH] [was written] on the diadem of his [the high priest's] head."

19:13

The rider is portrayed as "clothed with a garment sprinkled with blood," an allusion to God judging the nations in Isa. 63:1–3 (cf. *Tg. Ps.-J.* Gen. 49:11): "with garments of red colors . . . garments like the one who treads in the wine press . . . their juice sprinkled on my garments." The prophecy of God as a warrior in Isa. 63 is reaffirmed, and Christ is identified as that divine warrior. In Isaiah the warrior judges to achieve "vengeance" and "redemption" on behalf of his people (so Isa. 63:4), and the same goal is implicit in Rev. 19. Therefore, the stained garments symbolize an attribute of justice that will be exercised in the coming judgment (see Kiddle and Ross 1940: 384–85). Allusion to Isa. 63:2–6 is picked up again in 19:15.

In the OT "word" (LXX: *logos*) can take on the idea of "promise" or "prophecy" (e.g., 1 Kings 8:56 LXX). The fall of Babylon will "fulfill" the prophetic "words of God" about the final judgment found in both Testaments. Perhaps the title in 19:13 alludes to Christ's execution of final judgment upon the remaining enemies of God in fulfillment of OT and NT prophecy. Such an understanding is confirmed from the phrase "these are true words of God" in 19:9, which has primary reference to the future fulfillment of OT prophecy, especially of Isa. 61:10, as do the nearly identical phrases in 21:5; 22:6. This is another of the various links between 19:7–9 and 19:11–19.

19:14

Elsewhere in the NT angelic armies accompany Christ from heaven in executing the final judgment (Matt. 13:40–42; 16:27; 24:30–31; 25:31–32; Mark 8:38; Luke 9:26; 2 Thess. 1:7; Jude 14–15 [cf. *T. Levi* 3:3; *Apoc. El. (C)* 3:4; *1 En.* 102:1–3; *2 En.* 17]). If the armies here in 19:14 are angelic, there may be no question of God's people taking part in their own vindication. Nevertheless, 17:14 supports the initial suggestion that it is Christ himself who conquers the beast as a representative act on behalf of the "called and chosen and faithful" who accompany him.

The saints' garments here and throughout the book should also be understood as priestly garments, since the same garments worn by the heavenly beings are also likely conceived of as priestly in Rev. 15:6; Ezek. 9:2; Dan. 10:5; 12:6. Note also the similar garments worn by Christ in 1:13 (for the full argument in favor of this, see Kline 1980: 47–50). The saints with white robes in 7:9, 14–15 also have a priestly function. Likewise, the "bright, pure linen" of 19:8 has priestly associations. Christ's followers reflect their representative's priestly character as they accompany him when he executes judgment.

19:15

The picture of the "sharp, two-edged sword proceeding from his mouth" (cf. 1:16; 2:12, 16) is based on Isa. 49:2, where the figurative language refers to the ability of "servant Israel" (Isa. 49:3) to accomplish God's mission of restoring Israel and saving the nations (Isa. 49:6) by means of his word (*Tg. Isa.* 49:2 reads, "He placed his words in my mouth like a sharp sword"). Here in 19:15 the Isaiah prophecy is reaffirmed, and Jesus is identified implicitly as the "servant Israel" (as in Luke 2:32; Acts 26:23). An echo from the prophecy of Isa. 11:4 completes the depiction here: "in order that he should strike the nations." The Hebrew text's "he will strike the earth with the rod of his mouth" is interpreted by the LXX as smiting with the "word of his mouth," which supports the idea that "the word of God" in 19:13 is a name expressing the means by which Christ executes judgment. Likewise, *4 Ezra* 13 alludes to Isa. 11:4 and interprets the instrumentality of the Messiah's punishment to be the words of the "law," which "shall reprove the nations . . . with their evil thoughts" (*4 Ezra* 13:10–11, 37–38 [cf. *1 En.* 62:2]).

An allusion to Ps. 2:9 fills out the portrayal of judgment. In Ps. 2:8–9, 12 is foretold how God's "son" (2:7) will overthrow the ungodly "kings of the earth" who "take their stand . . . and take counsel against the Lord and his Messiah" (2:2). The "rod" here in 19:15, like the "sword proceeding from the mouth," connotes God's word of accusation, which will condemn the ungodly and consign them to perdition.

The trampling of the grapes in the winepress is a continued allusion to the OT prediction of God's last great act of judgment (Isa. 63:2–6) begun in 19:13, again applied to Christ.

19:16

Yet another name is adduced to explain further the ambiguous name of 19:12. The name is written on the rider's garment and thigh. The thigh was the typical location of the warrior's sword (e.g., Exod. 32:27; Judg. 3:16, 21; Ps. 45:3) and the symbolic place under which the hand was placed to swear oaths (e.g., Gen. 24:2, 9; 47:29). Christ's victory over the wicked will be a fulfillment of God's promise to judge.

The name for Christ in 19:16 is "King of kings and Lord of lords," which is intended as a title expressing the idea of "ultimate ruler over all kings" (cf. Moulton, Howard, and Turner 1906–76: 2:443). The name is taken from Dan. 4:37 LXX, where it is a title for God, and which has already been applied to Christ in 17:14 (on which, see commentary above), underscoring his role as divine judge.

19:17–18

The angel announces the coming destruction of the beast, false prophet, and their troops through the same imagery by which the defeat of Gog and Magog was announced in Ezek. 39:4, 17–20: "I will give you as food to every kind of predatory bird. . . . Speak to the bird of every wing . . . , 'Gather yourselves together and come . . . so that you may eat flesh. . . . You will eat the flesh of mighty ones and the blood of princes. . . . And you will be satisfied at my table with horses and chariots, mighty ones and all the men of war.'" Rev. 19:17–18 continues this prophetic portrayal and reaffirms that it will assuredly occur.

The portrayal from Ezek. 39 is included because its main point is that God will "make known" his "holy name" both to Israel and to their oppressors during captivity by means of defeating Gog and Magog. The goal of revelation of the divine name introduces (39:7) and concludes (39:21–25) the description of the slaughter (39:8–20).

19:19

In addition to Ezek. 39, Ps. 2:2 rings in the background. The prophetic picture in 19:19 of the final war develops and stresses that the Psalms prophecy will still certainly take place. "The kings of the earth stood up, and the rulers gathered themselves together against the Lord and against his Anointed" (Ps. 2:2 LXX). The earlier undoubted reference in 19:15 to Ps. 2:9 substantiates the further allusion here.

19:21

The armies following the beast and false prophet will be "killed by the sword proceeding from the mouth of the one sitting upon the horse." This is an allusion, repeated from 19:15, to the prophecy of Isa. 49:2 and 11:4, which will find accomplishment in the future.

Revelation 20

The triumph of the saints is vividly depicted in the vision of the millennium, which is followed by another depiction of the final battle. Heaven and earth flee before the Lord seated on his glorious throne, making way for the new heaven and earth in chapter 21.

There is much debate about whether chapter 20 follows chapter 19 in historical chronological terms or whether it recapitulates the final battle narrated at the end of 19:17–21 and thus also narrates events leading up to that battle in 20:1–7. The overarching use of Ezek. 38–48 in chapters 19–22 deserves special mention. In 20:8–10 there is a repeated allusion to Ezek. 38–39 concerning the battle of Gog and Magog against the covenant community. This repeated allusion points to the likelihood that 20:8–10 is a recapitulation of the same battle narrated in 19:17–21, where allusions are made to the same battle of Ezek. 38–39 together with the virtually identical expression "gather them together unto the war" (see commentary on Rev. 20:8, 9–10 below; for corroboration, see White 1989: 326–28). Indeed, both 19:17–21 and 20:8–10 recount the same battle as 16:12–16, which is highlighted by the same phrase "gather them together unto *the* war" (cf. 16:14; 19:19). If 20:1–6 precedes the time of 20:7–10, and if 19:17–21 is temporally parallel to the battle of 20:7–10, then 20:1–6 is temporally prior to the battle of 19:17–21.

That John has in mind a specific prophecy-fulfillment connection with Ezek. 38–39 is borne out by the broader context of chapters 20–21, where a fourfold ending of the book reflects the ending of Ezek. 37–48: resurrection of God's people (Rev. 20:4a; Ezek. 37:1–14), messianic kingdom (Rev. 20:4b–6; Ezek. 37:15–28), final battle against Gog and Magog (Rev. 20:7–10; Ezek. 38–39), and final vision of the new temple and new Jerusalem, described as a restored Eden and sitting on an exceedingly high mountain (Rev. 21:1–22:5; Ezek. 40–48) (for references to those observing the pattern, see Lust 1980: 179; similarly, White 1994: 543–44).

Note also that Ezek. 39 recapitulates the same battle narrated in Ezek. 38. This would suggest that if John is following any model in 19:17–21 and 20:7–10, it would be the generally acknowledged pattern of recapitulation in Ezek. 38–39. Indeed, recapitulation is typical elsewhere in Ezekiel, as well as in the other prophetic books of the OT (for other arguments in favor of recapitulation at this point in Revelation, see Beale 1999a: 972–1026).

Part of the thesis of this section (although there is not enough space to argue it thoroughly) is that the "binding" of Satan in 20:1–3 is not complete in every way but refers primarily to an inability to deceive the nations, so that they could mount an attack to annihilate the covenant community. This attack, indeed, will be mounted briefly after the "millennium," but the effort will fail (20:8–10). Thus, Satan can still deceive during the "millennial" period, but he cannot deceive to accomplish the purpose of destroying the community of faith and its expansion.

20:1–3

Isaiah 24:21–22 is the basis for 20:2–3 (see Kraft 1974: 256) and finds its fulfillment there: "In that day the LORD will punish the host of heaven on high, and the kings of the earth on earth. They will be gathered together like prisoners in the pit, and they will be confined in prison, and after many days they will be punished." This fulfillment was inaugurated at Christ's death and resurrection and will be culminated when Christ returns at the climax of history. The prophetic connection of Isa. 24 with Rev. 20 is suggested also by Isa. 27:1, which appears to be a further explanation of the punishment of 24:21–22 (the Hebrew "in that day Yahweh will visit" occurs only in 24:21 and 27:1): "In that day Yahweh will visit the sea monster . . . with his . . . sword" (the LXX of 27:1 has "the dragon, the serpent," which is almost identical to Rev. 20:2: "the dragon, the ancient serpent").

Typically, early Judaism spoke of evil spirits, not Satan, imprisoned in an absolute manner either at the time of or prior to the Noahic deluge or subsequently in the OT epoch (cf. *1 En.* 10:4–16; 18:11–19:3; *Jub.* 5:6–14; *1 En.* 88:1–3; 2 Pet. 2:4; Tob. 8:3; see also Jude 6). Even the NT sees demonic spirits as absolutely imprisoned, while Satan and other spirits are on the loose (e.g., contrast 2 Pet. 2:4; Jude 6 with 1 Pet. 5:8). In *1 En.* 54 is depicted the end of the age, when good angels will "cast into the abyss of complete condemnation" forever (53:2) human, and possibly demonic, subjects of Satan who were "leading astray those who dwell on the earth."

The only apparently explicit references to the binding of Satan in Judaism speak of a "binding" that is not absolute, since immediately subsequent to the binding his "evil spirits" continue to exist in some form of opposition to the saints; we note *T. Levi* 18:12, "Beliar shall be bound by him [the Messiah], and he shall give power to his children to tread upon the evil spirits," a text with such striking similarities to Luke 10:18–20 that the two probably are organically related in some way. In this respect, both of these texts appear to be developing the prophecy in Gen. 3:15 that Eve's "seed" would fatally "bruise" the "serpent" (see *T. Levi* 18:9–14 and the margin of NA[27] of Luke 10:19). In this light, it is likely not coincidental that Rev. 20:2 makes allusion to the same "ancient serpent," so that the "binding" is part of the fulfillment of the primeval promise in Gen. 3:15 (on which, see Beale 1999a: 994, 998).

Jubilees 48:15–17 portrays Mastema, prince of demons, as being restrained only so that he could not accuse the Israelites at the time of their exodus from Egypt: "Mastema was bound and imprisoned behind the children of Israel that he might not accuse them." Then he is "let loose" so that again he could work against and accuse Israel. So also 48:18: Mastema was "bound . . . that he might not accuse the children of Israel" (see also 48:9–11). Since the exodus theme dominates so much of the book of Revelation (e.g., the trumpet and bowl plague series), perhaps there is also a similar reflection here of Satan's inability to keep Israel in Egyptian captivity but now applied to a limited binding of Satan in 20:1–3, so that he cannot stop the latter-day exodus of the church and its expansion during the church age. That the notion of "binding" with respect to an inability to "accuse" may be in mind is apparent because the parallel account of Satan's defeat in 12:7–11 also refers to Satan twice as "the [former] accuser" of the saints and once as "the great dragon, the ancient serpent." In some way (which limits of space do not allow us to expand upon here), Satan's inability to "accuse" because of Christ's death and resurrection is part of his "binding" (for the parallels with chap. 12, see Beale 1999a: 992–94). Reference to the fulfillment of the Gen. 3:15 promise also occurs in 13:3, again with notions of a continuing activity of the devil after his decisive defeat and also including allusion to the Isa. 27:1 prophecy of the slaying of the "sea monster" by the "sword" (which, as we saw, is likely also alluded to in 20:1–2 [on the significance of 13:3 in relation to Gen. 3:15; Isa. 27:1 and on other associated issues, see Beale 1999a: 677–80, 688–93; and for a full discussion of 20:1–9, see Beale 1999a: 972–1028]).

In wording strikingly similar to that in Rev. 20:2–3, *Pr. Man.* 3 speaks of God restraining the evil chaos powers at the beginning of creation: "he who bound the sea and . . . who closed the bottomless pit and sealed it." Nevertheless, a complete restraint is likely not in view, since the OT portrays the sea monster as still being able to wreak havoc with the nations throughout history (see commentary on Rev. 12:3; 13:1 above). And if the "angels" who were "chained" in "pits of darkness" at the beginning of history or at the Noahic deluge (2 Pet. 2:4; Jude 6) were subsequently allowed to be active on earth (including, presumably, Satan), then the binding in Rev. 20 might also be so qualified.

20:4

There is much debate about whether this verse envisions physically resurrected saints reigning on earth during the "millennium" (the "premillennial" view) or whether it understands their reign as spiritual in heaven (part of an inaugurated millennial reign, typically know as "amillennialism"); for a more in-depth argument on this issue, see Beale 1999: 972–1031. The OT background for 20:4 appears to bear upon this issue.

The "thrones" and those who "sat on them" appear to represent the angelic court of Dan. 7 that declares the final judgment against the satanic fiend in vindication of the saints whom he oppressed; this would be in correspondence to Dan. 7:9–11: "thrones were set up . . . the court sat . . . the beast was slain" (cf. Dan. 7:26; *Midr. Ps.* 4:4 identifies the court as angelic; but see also Ps. 122:5, where the thrones are for human judges: "There thrones for judgment were set, the thrones of the house of David").

The inaugurated judgment against Satan (20:1–3) has been executed on behalf of God's people. The judgment presumably has already been passed by the divine court in heaven. This is suggested by Dan. 7:9–27, where the heavenly court seems to be distinct from the saints on whose behalf the court declares the judgment. The vindication in Dan. 7 was a necessary condition enabling the saints to assume kingship together with the "son of man" (cf. 7:13–14, 18, 27). The judgment of the evil kingdoms paves the way for the "son of man" and his saints to reign (7:11–14, 18, 27). As in Rev. 20:4, so also in Dan. 7:22 the "judgment" is followed by the mention of "saints possessing the kingdom."

The same pattern of Dan. 7 is evident in Rev. 20:1–4, where the casting down of Satan is the inaugurated judgment enabling the saints to commence their reign in incipient fulfillment of Dan. 7:22. Though in Dan. 7 the heavenly court may be distinct from the saints in whose favor the court announces the judgment, the saints' inaugurated reign in Rev. 20:4 appears also to take place in heaven, since the court in 20:4 probably includes exalted believers along with angels, and since the same scene of figures ("elders") sitting on heavenly thrones in 4:4 included angels, who corporately represent exalted saints (cf. 4:4; 11:16). This receives support from the fact that the only places outside of 20:4 in the book where the plural "thrones" (plural of *thronos*) occurs are 4:4; 11:16, where it is elders who sit on the thrones.

Indeed, the heavenly location of the thrones in 20:4 is apparent from the fact that forty-two of the forty-six times "throne[s]" (*thronos*) occurs elsewhere in the book, it is clearly located in heaven (so Hendriksen 1962: 230; Morris 1987: 236 [although the throne in 22:1, 3 is located in the new heaven and new earth]). The remaining three uses refer either to Satan's or the beast's throne, which likewise is not earthly, but rather is located in a spiritual dimension. Furthermore, the "thrones" of Dan. 7:9 are clearly also set in heaven (cf. *b. Sanh.* 38b, which views the court of Dan. 7:9–10 as consisting of God, angels, and the Davidic Messiah, while *b. Ḥag.* 14a sees only God and the Messiah sitting on the plural thrones). The focus on saints sitting on the thrones is evident from the third phrase of 20:4: "judgment was passed for them [*autois*]," where "them" refers to saints (see above the allusion to Dan. 7:22). The antecedent of "them" in 20:4 must be in "they sat," which clearly places the saints on the "thrones." That the word "them" appears abruptly without any antecedent is improbable.

One of the most substantial arguments in favor of the premillennial interpretation is based on the observation that the coming to life of "the rest of the dead" mentioned in 20:5a is clearly a physical resurrection (about which there seems to be nearly unanimous agreement among commentators). If the physical resurrection of the wicked is described with "they came to life" (*ezēsan*), and the identical word describes the resurrection of the saints in 20:4, then the resurrection of 20:4 must also be a physical resurrection. Mounce (1977: 356) notes likewise that if "they came to life" in 20:4 "means a spiritual resurrection . . . then we are faced with the problem of discovering within the context some persuasive reason to interpret the same verb differently within one concise unit. No such reason can be found."

A word study of *anastasis* ("resurrection") is adduced in further support of the literal interpretation of the initial resurrection in 20:4, which is formally called "the first resurrection" (*hē anastasis hē prōtē*) in 20:5–6. The word *anastasis* appears forty-one times in the NT, and it indicates a physical resurrection with but two exceptions (Luke 2:34; John 11:25). In this light, it appears probable that the term has a literal meaning in Rev. 20:5–6 (so Deere 1978: 71). According to

this perspective, the word *zaō* ("live"), found in both 20:4 and 20:5, should also be understood literally in the same way. Indeed, it also can be found with the literal meaning both inside and outside of the book.

The design of the present commentary does not allow a full response here, though this has been carried out elsewhere (Beale 1999a: 1002–17; in counterreply, see Osborne 2002: 703–9, 718). Nevertheless, brief response is given here, including how the OT may bear on the issue. Before discussing the OT background, we should survey some of the relevant uses of *zaō* in the NT and in Hellenistic Greek.

The use of "live" (*zaō*) or the cognate noun "life" (*zōē*) referring to the intermediate heavenly state prior to physical resurrection is found elsewhere in the NT and Judaism and indicates that the range of meaning allows for this meaning in Rev. 20:4, 6. In Luke 20:37–38 Jesus quotes Moses, who calls "the Lord the God of Abraham and the God of Isaac and the God of Jacob. He is not God of the dead, but of the living, for all are living to him." The statement that God presently "is not the God of the dead" suggests that the patriarchs are living presently since their death and prior to their physical resurrection and that God is presently their God. Furthermore, the last clause, "for all are living to him," utilizes the present tense of *zaō* ("live") apparently to underscore the reality that if God is God of all the believing dead, then "all [who have died in the faith] are [presently] living to [before] him." This is confirmed by the fact that the quotation is part of Jesus' argument against the Sadducees, "who say that there is no resurrection of the dead" (Luke 20:27). Josephus (*Ant.* 18.16 [likewise *J.W.* 2:165]) says that the Sadducees not only denied bodily resurrection but also affirmed "that the soul perishes along with the body," so that Jesus' words are a polemic against both Sadducean heresies (so Hoekema 1979: 233–34). If this is a correct understanding of *zaō* ("live") in Luke 20:38, then *anastasis* ("resurrection") in Luke 20:35–36 also includes the idea of resurrection of the soul, as well as of the body.

Jubilees 23:27–31 speaks of the eternal bliss of the godly and figuratively refers to it as "one thousand years" when "they shall . . . live in joy and . . . they shall rise up and see great peace . . . rejoice with joy forever and ever . . . and their bones shall rest in the earth, and their spirits shall have much joy." Significantly, this clearly speaks of a resurrection of the "spirit" (following Charles 1963: 240). Like Rev. 2:8; 20:4–5, 4 Maccabees portrays the same ironic picture of being translated to heavenly life through physical death by using forms of *zaō* ("live"). By persevering in faith through suffering unto death, the Maccabean martyrs win "victory over death" (7:3), which is referred to as the beginning of "eternal life" (17:12); though they die physically, "to God they die not, for they live to God" at the point of physical death (7:19; so also 16:25), receive "immortal souls," and are gathered together with the deceased patriarchs (13:17; 18:23) in heaven (17:4–5). This "life" is termed "blessed" and is associated with being "crowned" (17:15–18). In 4 Macc. 17:17–18 it is said explicitly that unbelievers "admired their [the martyrs'] endurance, through which, also, they now stand beside the divine throne and live a blessed life" (even though *zaō* is not used, the cognate noun *zōē* does occur in 17:12, which introduces the paragraph and is equated with "endurance"). See also 2 Macc. 7:8–36; *T. Ab.* [A] 20:9–15; *T. Isaac* 7:1. Meanwhile, *2 Baruch* can speak of "treasuries of souls" of saints that God "preserves" and "sustains" until they will be reunited with their bodies at the last resurrection (21:9; 30:1–3; 85:11–12) and that also are identified with "Abraham and Isaac and Jacob" (21:23–24). Wisdom 3:1–8 also attests clearly to the soul's existence after death, the highlights of which are as follows: "But the souls of the righteous are in the hand of God.... In the sight of the unwise they seemed to die ... but they are in peace.... God ... tried them and received them as a burnt offering.... They will judge the nations and have dominion ... and their Lord will reign forever" (so also *4 Ezra* 7:75–101).

Also of relevance is the observation made earlier that the broader fourfold ending of Revelation reflects the ending of Ezek. 37–48: resurrection of God's people (Rev. 20:4a; Ezek. 37:1–14), messianic kingdom (Rev. 20:4b–6; Ezek. 37:15–28), final battle against Gog and Magog (Rev. 20:7–10; Ezek. 38–39), and final vision of the new temple and new Jerusalem (21:1–22:5; Ezek. 40–48). In the light of the structural parallelism, the word *ezēsan* ("they came to life") in Rev. 20:4 is to be seen as an echo of Ezek. 37:10, where the identical word is used (so also Ezek. 37:6, 14, though

using a future-tense form). If the parallelism is intentional, then it would support a spiritual resurrection in Rev. 20:4–6, since the resurrection of Ezek. 36–37 is also spiritual, or at least metaphorical (on this point, see Feuillet 1965: 121; Brütsch 1970: 2:340; White 1991). Revelation 20:4 would then reflect the "already and not yet" fulfillment of Ezek. 7:10 throughout the church age.

The understanding of 20:4–6 as a spiritual reality is consistent with the view reflected elsewhere in both the OT and the NT that there will be only one physical resurrection, which will occur at the conclusion of history (see Isa. 26:19–21; Dan. 12:2; John 5:28–29; Acts 24:15; 2 Thess. 1:7–10; cf. John 6:39–40, 44, 54; so also *1 En.* 51:1–5; *4 Ezra* 7:32; 14:35; *2 Bar.* 42:8; *Sib. Or.* 4:179–182; *L.A.B.* 3:10). Thus, the "first" resurrection of 20:4–6 apparently refers to a spiritual resurrection of saints followed later by their final, physical resurrection.

Note the use of the number "one thousand" both as a literal temporal indicator and as a nontemporal indicator in the OT and the NT. See nontemporal figurative uses in Deut. 1:10–11; 32:30; Josh. 23:10; Job 9:3; 33:23; Ps. 50:10; 68:17; Song 4:4; Isa. 7:23; 30:17; 60:22; Dan. 7:10; Amos 5:3; for temporal figurative uses, see Deut. 7:9; Ps. 84:10; Eccles. 6:6; 7:28; *Jub.* 30:20. Especially noteworthy is 1 Chron. 16:15–17 (= Ps. 105:8–10), where God's "covenant forever" and his "everlasting covenant" are equated with "the word which he commanded to a thousand generations."

In Judaism there are numerous traditions about the nature and length of the future messianic reign. Some speculated that there would be no messianic reign at all, while others proposed periods of an intermediate reign from forty to 365,000 years. Only two rabbis calculate the period to be one thousand years (Rabbi Eliezer ben Hyrcanus, cited in *Midr. Ps.* 90:17; Rabbi Eliezer ben Jose the Galilean, cited in *Pesiq. Rab.* Piska 1 [cf. *b. Sanh.* 97a, where a thousand-year reign is implied from the teaching of Rabbi Kattina]). Rabbi Eliezer ben Hyrcanus (ca. AD 90) represents the earliest attested view of a thousand-year reign, a conception that he likely learned from earlier rabbinic tradition (so Str-B 3:826–27; cf. *b. Sukkah* 28a). Samaritan tradition also held to a thousand-year messianic reign (see Bailey 1934: 179–80).

The only other use of the millennial period is clearly figurative for the complete perfection of the eternal time of blessing for God's people: "And the days shall begin to grow many and increase among those children of men till their days draw near to one thousand years, and to a greater number of years than (before) was the number of the days. And there shall be no old man. . . . And all their days they shall complete and live in peace and joy . . . and rejoice with joy for ever and ever" (*Jub.* 23:27–30). The number "one thousand" is derived from an earlier passage in *Jubilees* (4:29–30), which alludes to Isa. 65:22 LXX ("For as the days of the tree of life shall be the days of my people, they shall long enjoy the fruits of their labors"): "Adam died. . . . He lacked seventy years of one thousand years; for one thousand years are as one day [= Ps. 90:4] in the testimony of the heavens, and therefore was it written concerning the tree of knowledge, 'On the day you eat thereof you shall die.' For this reason he did not complete the years of this day, for he died during it." *Jubilees* understands that the ideal life of the probationary period ("day") in Eden should have been one thousand years (so also *Midr. Rab.* Gen. 19:8; *Midr. Rab.* Num. 5:4; *Midr. Ps.* 25:8 on the basis of Ps. 90). Therefore, the *Jubilees* text concludes that the future messianic reign must achieve what Adam did not. *Jubilees* bases this on three pieces of evidence: (1) Adam's age at death, which did not quite last one thousand years; (2) Isa. 65:22, which prophesies that the messianic age will last as long as the ideal meant for the first paradise (likewise *T. Levi* 18:8–13); (3) Ps. 90:4 (the *Jubilees* tradition of the ideal millennial span of the first paradise is reflected in Irenaeus [*Haer.* 5.23.2]). At least in part, *Jub.* 23:27–30 was influenced to conceive of this millennium figuratively because of the Ps. 90 formula, whereas early fathers such as Justin (*Dial.* 81) used the same reasoning to formulate a literal premillennial perspective (likewise Hippolytus, *Comm. Dan.* 2.4–6).

20:8

The assembling of these antagonistic forces against God's people is seen as a fulfillment of the prophecy in Ezek. 38–39, which foresaw that "Gog and Magog" and the nations would "gather together for war" against Israel. Ezekiel 38–39 distinguishes the enemy "Gog and Magog" from the other nations of the earth that ally with them

(38:2–7, 15, 22; 39:4). In particular, the language of "gathering together" the nations derives from Ezek. 38:2–8; 39:2, together with passages from Zech. 12–14; Zeph. 3, which also stand behind the parallel phrases in Rev. 16:14; 19:19. All of these OT texts foretell that *God* would gather the nations together in Israel for the final war of history (see commentary on Rev. 16:14; 19:19 above and the introduction to this section on Rev. 20).

That the "number" of the nations assembled is "as the sand of the sea" underscores their innumerability and the overwhelming odds in their favor against the saints; in Josh. 11:4; Judg. 7:12; 1 Sam. 13:5 the same metaphor is used for the multitudinous forces of the nations arrayed to fight against Israel at various times.

20:9–10

In 20:9–10 there continues allusion to Ezekiel, where we find the unique parallel of the multitudinous end-time enemy (38:15, 22) who will "ascend [*anabainō*] upon the land" (38:11 [see also 38:16; 39:2; *Tg. Ezek.* 38:9]) and be judged by "fire" from heaven (39:6) and by "fire and brimstone" (38:22).

In its attack against Israel, Babylon was described as "going forth on the plain of the earth in order to inherit tabernacles not his own" (Hab. 1:6 LXX). The same wording is drawn on now to depict the end-time foe's attack against the saints. The former OT episode foreshadowed the latter.

Next in John's prophetic vision he sees that the enemy nations "surrounded the camp of the saints and the holy city." In the OT the "camp" referred often to the wilderness encampment of Israelite tribes around the tabernacle (esp. Exodus, Leviticus, Numbers, Deuteronomy). Those remaining in the camp had to be ritually clean because of God's presence residing in its midst (e.g., Num. 9:18–23; 2 Chron. 31:2; see Hamilton 1980: 300). Most comparable among OT texts is Deut. 23:14: "Because the LORD your God walks in the midst of your camp to deliver you and to defeat your enemies before you, therefore your camp must be holy" (cf. 1QM III, 5–9; 1QM X).

The attacking nations will be destroyed by God before they can annihilate the saints: "fire descended from heaven and consumed them." This follows the pattern of Ezekiel's prophecy (noted just above on Rev. 20:9–10) where the demise of Israel's enemy is by fire, which is also reflected upon in Judaism (see *Tg. Ps.-J.* Num. 11:26, where the destruction of Magog by fire is noted, also in allusion to Ezek. 39; similarly, in 1QM XI, 16–17 God "will battle against them [Gog] from heaven above").

The actual wording of the fiery defeat is drawn from 2 Kings 1:10–14, which describes God's deliverance of Elijah from the armies of the ungodly king Ahaziah.

20:11

The vision of "a great white throne and one sitting on it" harks back to 4:2; 5:7 (on which, see commentary above), where God is pictured "sitting on a throne," which is an allusion primarily to Dan. 7:9; Ezek. 1:26–28. Both there and here Dan. 7 is the focus, since the "opening of books" from Dan. 7:10, as well as other allusions to Daniel, directly follow in the two contexts. The phrase "a place was not found for them" is taken from Dan. 2:35 Θ, where it describes the destruction of the wicked kingdoms at the end time. Revelation 12:8 makes the same allusion to underscore the inaugurated defeat of the devil and his forces by the death and resurrection of Christ. Now the same Danielic wording is applied to the complete destruction of the entire evil world system. Thus Rev. 20:11 pictures the future fulfillment of both Dan. 2:39 and 7:9.

20:12

"The books were opened, and another book was opened, which is of life" combines allusion to Dan. 7:10 ("the books were opened") and Dan. 12:1–2 ("everyone who is found written in the book . . . will be rescued . . . to everlasting life"). The point of the books in Dan. 7 is to focus on the evil deeds of the end-time persecutor of God's people, for which the persecutor(s) would be judged. The book in Dan. 12:1 also concerns the end time, but it is an image of redemption. Those written in the book will be given life, but those excluded from the book will suffer final judgment (12:1–2). These two Daniel prophesies are depicted to find realization at the time of the last judgment.

Revelation 21:1–22:5

The last vision of Revelation is a magnificent view of the new creation, which is, we will argue, portrayed as equivalent to the new Jerusalem, the eschatological cubic temple, and to end-time Eden, the eternal home of God's people.

21:1

The new cosmos will be an identifiable counterpart to the old cosmos and a renewal of it (Harrisville 1960: 99–105), just as the body will be raised without losing its former identity (Farrer 1964: 213; Sweet 1979: 297 [see *b. Sanh.* 92a–b; *Midr. Ps.* 104:24, which see the future resurrection of the body as a part of the larger "renewal" of the earth]). The qualitative antithesis between the first world and the second one is highlighted by Isa. 65:17; 66:22, which stand behind the wording of Rev. 21:1; note Isa. 65:17 LXX: "For there shall be a new heaven and new earth; and they will by no means remember the former" (cf. 66:22). Isaiah 65:16–18 makes a qualitative contrast between the "former" earth, where the "first affliction" of captivity occurred, and "a new heaven and a new earth," where there will be only enduring "joy and exultation." Isaiah 66:22 affirms that one of the qualitative differences is that "the new heaven and new earth" will "remain" forever, in contrast to the old, which passed away. Revelation 21:1 portrays the future fulfillment of the two Isaianic new creation prophecies.

Judaism also conceived of the new creation as a renewal or renovation of the old creation (see *Jub.* 1:29; 4:26; *1 En.* 45:4–5; *2 Bar.* 32:1–6; 57:2; *4 Ezra* 7:75; *Tg. Ps.-J.* Deut. 32:1; *Tg. Hab.* 3:2).

21:2

The new world that 21:1 portrays as replacing the old is now, in 21:2, called "the holy city, new Jerusalem." Not surprisingly, the language comes from another Isaiah passage, "Jerusalem, the holy city" (52:1b). The marital imagery in the OT contexts of the prior two Isa. 52 and 62 allusions comes to the fore at the end of 21:2: the city is now seen "as a bride adorned for her husband." Isaiah 61:10 LXX personifies Zion speaking in prophetic perfect style: "He adorned me with ornaments as a bride" (Isa. 62:5 also uses "bride" as a metaphor for the people of Israel). This second verse of Rev.

21 gives assurance that these Isaiah promises will find consummation in the new cosmos.

21:3

In the light of the following references to the Ezek. 40–48 temple (cf. 21:9–22:5), the promise in Ezek. 43:7 is echoed and fulfilled in 21:3: the end-time temple would be "where" God "will dwell [*kataskēnōsei*] among the sons of Israel forever." Leviticus 26:11–12 and Ezek. 37:26–28 (cf. Zech. 2:10–11) equate this final dwelling of God among his people with the coming latter-day tabernacle, and following suit are *Jub.* 1:17, 29; 2 Cor. 6:16; Rev. 7:15; 21:3a, 22. Thus, 21:3 now interprets the vision of the new creation in 21:1 and the vision of the new Jerusalem in 21:2 to be the "the tabernacle of God among men [all believing inhabitants in the new creation]."

21:4

In 21:4 is a fulfillment of prophecy from Isa. 25:8: "The LORD God has taken away every tear from every face" (see commentary on Rev. 7:16–17 above). The same verse in Isaiah says that this will be a comfort from "death," which formerly "prevailed" during Israel's captivity in the world, which gives rise to the directly following mention of "death" being done away with in 21:4 (see Fekkes 1994: 254). Also in mind are Isa. 35:10; 51:11 LXX, which predict that "pain and grief and groaning" will have "fled away." It is more than coincidental that only one verse earlier in Isa. 51 the prophet reflects on the first exodus, when God caused the "sea" to pass away (on which see Rev. 21:1): "Was it not you who dried up the sea, the waters of the great deep, who made the depths of the sea a pathway for the redeemed to pass over?" (51:10).

The conclusion of 21:4, that "the first things have passed away," continues the Isa. 35; 51 allusions while at the same time calling to mind again the wording of Isa. 65:17 (together with Isa. 43:18). The parallelism between 21:1 and 21:4 is further confirmed by noticing that both expressions of cosmic dissolution serve as the cause (respectively, *gar* and *hoti*) of the new world conditions. In this light, Isa. 65:19 is likely combined with Isa. 35; 51, since it also says that in the new creation "there shall no more be heard in her the voice of weeping or the voice of crying" (see commentary on Rev. 21:1 above). Similarly, Isa.

65:20a says that "no longer will there be" unnecessary death, as in the old age. Consequently, even the formula "there will be [is] no more" derives from Isa. 65:19–20 (see Fekkes [1994: 254], who apparently understands that the formula is based on the Hebrew of Isa. 65:19–20). These Isaiah predictions again find their realization in the new creation.

21:5

God says, "Behold, I am making all things new," which repeats for a third time the Isaiah prophecies about the coming new creation. In 21:1 appeal is made to Isa. 65:17; 66:22, in 21:4b is an allusion to Isa. 65:17; 43:18, and 21:5 draws from Isa. 43:19 LXX: "Behold, I make new things" (cf. Isa. 66:22).

21:6

Isaiah 49:10 continues a prior string of Isaiah prophecies and is the basis for the reward of being given water for sustenance, which is metaphorical for eternal life.

21:7

The reference to "inheriting" the blessings promised in the Davidic prophecy of 2 Sam. 7:14 shows a hint of further inspiration from the promise of Isa. 55:1–3, where God promises those who "thirst" (55:1) that he will make with Israel "an everlasting covenant, the sure mercies of David" (55:3) (so Kraft 1974: 265).

21:9–10

In 21:10 is a combination of Ezek. 43:5 LXX ("And the Spirit took me up") and 40:1–2 LXX ("the hand of the LORD was upon me and brought me . . . and set me on a very high mountain, and upon it there was, as it were, the edifice of a city before me"). This combination indicates beyond doubt that the following vision in Rev. 21:10–22:5 is to be identified with the prophetic culmination of the blissful vision of the future temple in Ezek. 40–48, which was located "on a very high mountain." The angel transports John to a "great and high mountain," where also the new city-temple is likely located, since OT prophecy understood the coming Jerusalem to be situated on a high mountain (Isa. 2:2–3; 4:1–5; 25:6–26:2; Mic. 4:1–2; cf. Ps. 48:2; *Jub.* 4:26).

21:11

In the light of the clear allusions to Isa. 40–66 in 21:1–22:5, the reference to "the glory of God" must derive from Isa. 58:8; 60:1–2, 19, where there is the prophetic portrayal of "the glory of the LORD" residing in the latter-day Jerusalem (for allusions to Isa. 40–66, see, e.g., 21:1–2, 4–5, 19–21, 23–26; 22:5).

That "the city, the holy Jerusalem" is described as "having the glory of God" and "its luminary like a precious stone, as a jasper stone shining like crystal" continues the prophetic portrait of Ezek. 43.

21:12–13

The broad structure of the city from 21:12 through 22:5 is based on the vision of Ezek. 40–48, which prophesies the pattern of the final temple (chaps. 40–44), as well as the arrangement of the eschatological city and divisions of the land around the temple compound (chaps. 45–48). Also, 21:12–22:5 further interprets the yet-future fulfillment of Ezekiel by collapsing temple, city, and land into one end-time picture portraying the one reality of God's presence and communion with his people in the unending new creation.

That the first part of the city structure that John sees is a "wall" and "gates" continues the allusion to Ezek. 40 begun in 21:10–11; note Ezek. 40:5–6: "And behold, there was a wall on the outside of the temple all around. . . . Then he went to the gate. . . ." The multiple gates of the Ezekiel temple in chap. 40 and the twelve gates of the city listed in 48:31–34 are, in John's vision, merged into one group of twelve gates arranged around the one city-temple. Like Ezekiel's city in 48:31–34, there are four groups of three gates, with each trio of gates facing respectively east, north, south, and west (though Ezekiel's list begins with north and then east). Furthermore, each of both Ezekiel's and John's gates has one of the names of the twelve tribes of Israel written on it. John is also influenced by Ezek. 42:15–19, where the angel measures first at the east gate, then the north, south, and lastly at the west gate (see Kiddle and Ross 1940: 427; Caird 1966: 271–72).

21:15

The image of an angelic figure measuring parts of the city-temple with a measuring rod is a continued allusion to Ezek. 40:3–5. This shows yet further influence by the model of the Ezek. 40–48 vision, where measuring signifies the future establishment and security of the new city, which is portrayed as finally achieved here.

21:16

John next sees that the "city lies square [lit., 'four-cornered']." He also sees an angel who "measured the city with the rod . . . the length and width and height of it are equal." The scene again resonates with the Ezekiel portrayal. In particular, Ezek. 45:2–3 asserts that the whole temple complex will be a "square" and that the prophet was "from this area . . . [to] measure a length . . . and a width." Throughout the description of measuring the area of the temple in Ezek. 45:1–5 and the area of the city in Ezek. 48:8–13 is the repeated refrain of measuring by "a length and a width" (similarly Ezek. 40 [for a description of the square structure of Ezekiel's temple, see McKelvey 1969: 9–10]; cf. Zech. 2:2).

Also striking is the equal measurement of the "length . . . and the breadth . . . and the height" of the holy of holies in the temple (see 1 Kings 6:20; cf. 1QS VIII, 5–9; *Jub.* 8:19), which, together with Ezekiel, could form part of the background here (so Caird 1966: 272–73). The dimensions of the holy of holies in 1 Kings 6:20 may be foremost in mind.

21:18–20

The gold intensifies the attribute of the city as reflecting God's glory. This feature is partly based on 1 Kings 6:20–22, where not only were the inner sanctuary and altar overlaid with gold, but also Solomon "overlaid the whole house [= temple] with gold" (Farrer 1964: 218; Beasley-Murray 1974: 324).

The list of the twelve jewels adorning the foundation stones of the wall is based on the list in Exod. 28:17–20 (so also 39:8–14), which describes the twelve stones on the high priest's "breastpiece of judgment." The breastpiece was the pouch containing the Urim and Thummim. Eight of the stones are identical to the precious stones here in 21:19–20, while the other differently named stones are semantic equivalents of the ones in Exodus (for the rationale, see Caird 1966: 274–75). Written on each stone of the breastpiece was one of the names of the twelve tribes of Israel (Exod. 28:21; 39:14). The priest was "to carry the names of the sons of Israel in the breastpiece of judgment . . . when he enters the holy place, for a memorial before the LORD continually." Therefore, these stones symbolized all Israel, so that the priest in his cultic actions represented all Israel before the presence of God in the temple. As in the rest of Revelation, imagery formerly applied to Israel is now applied to the church of Jews and Gentiles who are part of the city-temple complex.

The notion that the foundations are composed of precious stones, not just decorated with them, is pointed to by Isa. 54:11–12, which is alluded to in 21:18–19, 21: "I prepare sapphire for your foundations, and I make your buttresses jasper and your gates stones of crystal . . . and your wall precious stones."

21:22

The OT prophesied that a temple would be rebuilt along with the renovation of Jerusalem. However, John says, "I saw no temple" in the new Jerusalem. It is not that John saw no temple at all, but only that he saw no material temple like Israel's old temple. The reason that he saw no material temple in the city is that "the Lord God, the Almighty, and the Lamb are its temple (or 'sanctuary' [naos])." Or, more precisely, God and the Lamb have filled the entire new creation with their glorious presence, a glorious presence formerly sequestered in the holy of holies and in the heavenly temple. This is why the new Jerusalem is portrayed as a cube, since that was the shape of the holy of holies in Israel's former temple; and now God's glorious presence, formerly limited to that back room of the temple, has burst forth and filled the entire new cosmos (on which, see below the excursus "The Worldwide Extent of the Paradisal City-Temple"). The temple pictured in four detailed chapters of Ezekiel's prophecy (chaps. 40–43) is now summarized and interpreted by a brief statement affirming that God and the Lamb are the temple (see Glasson 1965: 120).

Haggai 2:9 prophesied that "the latter glory of this house will be greater than the former," and Jer. 3:16–17 predicted, "They shall say no more, 'The ark of the covenant of the LORD.' And it shall not come to mind, nor shall they remember it, nor shall they miss it, nor shall it be made again. At that time they shall call Jerusalem 'The throne of the LORD,' and all the nations will be gathered to

it, for the name of the LORD in Jerusalem." Thus, the Jeremiah text affirms that in the eschatological future God's holy of holies presence will extend out over Jerusalem and become coequal with it.

In the light of the portrayal in 21:22, John probably would have understood these OT prophecies as being fulfilled in the future by God and Christ replacing the former material temple and ark with their glorious habitation, which will make the glory of the former temple fade in comparison.

21:23

The wording of the entire verse is based directly on the forecast of Isa. 60:19 (though the similar prophetic depiction of God's glory in Isa. 24:23 could be secondarily in mind): "No longer will you have the sun for light by day, and the brightness of the moon will not give light to you; but the LORD will be to you an everlasting light, and your God will be your glory." See also Isa. 60:20; 24:23.

21:24–26

These verses continue to allude to Isa. 60, with the mention of the nations walking by (or in) the light of the city (60:3), the nations bringing their wealth/glory (60:5), and the city gates being open continuously (60:11). Isaiah 60 develops further Isa. 2:2, 5—"all the nations will stream" to Zion, and devout Israelites will "walk in the light of the Lord"—which also stand in the background of 21:24 (see Bauckham 1993a: 314–15). The scene envisions a time when all nations will devote their gifts and energies to the worship of the one true God and not to idols in completion of the Isaiah 60 forecast.

22:1–2a

The opening verse of chapter 22 combines the prophetic pictures of a spring or river of "living water" flowing out of latter-day Jerusalem (Zech. 14:8) and its temple (Ezek. 47:1–9).

The introductory verse of chapter 22 reaches farther back even than the OT prophecies of Ezekiel, Joel, and Zechariah to the description of the primeval garden in Gen. 2:10: "a river was going forth from Eden." In association with the first Eden's river, the "gold . . . the bdellium and the onyx stone" were features around one of the river's tributaries, which compares to the precious stones surrounding the river of Rev. 22:1

(cf. 21:18–21). The point is that God "will make the end like the beginning" (*Barn.* 6:13), though the consummated garden will exist on an escalated scale in comparison to the first (see Beasley-Murray, 330).

As in Ezek. 47, the living water flows from the temple, though now God and the Lamb are the temple (21:22). Although the Holy Spirit may be in mind, the water metaphor primarily represents the life of eternal fellowship with God and Christ, which is borne out by the way 22:3–5 develops 22:1–2 (for water as symbolic of the Spirit in the OT, Judaism, and the NT, see Ezek. 36:25–27; John 3:5; 4:10–24; cf. 1 John 5:7–8; 1QS IV, 21; in *Pesiq. Rab.* Piska 1:2 water from the earthly temple is interpreted as being the Holy Spirit).

22:2b

The scene of a future, permanent fertile land with a river and trees whose leaves have healing properties is based on Ezek. 47:12: "And by the river . . . on one side and on the other, will grow all trees. . . . They will bear [fruit] every month . . . their leaves [will be] for healing." The scene in Ezekiel itself is modeled partly on the primal garden and its adjacent river of Gen. 2:9–10, so that both Ezekiel and Revelation envision an escalated reestablishment of the garden of the first creation, in which God's presence openly dwelt. Even the decorative palm trees and cherubim portrayed as part of the Ezekiel temple (41:18–26) allude to the garden setting of Eden; the depiction in the Ezekiel temple was anticipated earlier in the Solomonic temple, which also included carvings of flowers (e.g., 1 Kings 6:18, 29, 32, 35; 7:18–19) (see Kline 1980: 42).

The river in Ezek. 47:8–9, 12 "purifies" (lit., "heals") much water (cf. the "[pure] river" in Rev. 22:1), gives "life" to the creatures swimming in it and causes trees to grow whose "leaves are for healing." Ezekiel's river is the source that renovates the natural world and symbolizes God's fellowship with his people (cf. Isa. 35:6–9; 41:17–20; 43:18–20; Joel 3:18).

Elsewhere in the OT the waters of the new creation are designed not merely to renew the natural world, but to be given to God's people so that they may refresh themselves (Isa. 41:17–20; 43:18–20).

22:3

The "healing of the nations" is further explained by 22:3. First, "there will no longer be any curse." The phrase is taken from Zech. 14:11 and applied to the eternal new order in which it finds its final attainment. Although for "curse," the LXX of Zechariah has *anathema* and Revelation has *katathema*, both are legitimate renderings of the Hebrew *ḥerem* (cf., possibly, Isa. 34:1–2). In the OT *ḥerem* typically referred to people being put under a ban for complete destruction because of sin (cf. the Canaanites in the Hexateuch). Likely echoed also is the curse in the first Eden, which will be removed here.

Second, the earlier observation in 7:15 that the saints serve God as priests in his heavenly temple shows that here also they are performing priestly service in the temple of the end-time city. This echoes the prophecy of Isa. 61:6 ("you will be called priests of the LORD . . . the ministers of God"), which will be fulfilled in the new cosmic temple. That Isa. 61:6 is in mind is evident from the fact that allusions to Isaiah have been woven throughout 21:1–22:5 (especially note Isa. 61:10 in 21:2 and allusions to Isa. 60 in 21:23–26; 22:5).

22:4

The divine presence fully permeates the eternal temple and dwelling place of the saints, since "they will see his face," a hope expressed by OT saints (Ps. 11:4–7; 27:4; *4 Ezra* 7:98; cf. Ps. 42:2; *T. Zeb.* 9:8). The whole community of the redeemed are considered as priests serving in the temple and privileged to see God's face in the new holy of holies, which now encompasses the entire city-temple (see Schüssler Fiorenza 1972: 375–89).

22:5

The repeated prayer of OT saints was that God would reveal his presence by "shining the light of his countenance" upon them (Num. 6:25–26; Ps. 4:6; 31:16; 67:1; 80:3, 7, 19; 119:135; *Pesiq. Rab.* Piska 1:2). This prayer is consummately answered here in 22:5 (as promised in *T. Zeb.* 9:8; *4 Ezra* 7:97–98). Uppermost in thought is the blessing in Num. 6:25–27, since there the shining of God's face is to result in preservation and "peace" for the saints, which is equated with the Aaronic blessing of "putting my name on the Sons of Israel" (following Sweet 1979: 312).

Excursus: The Worldwide Extent of the Paradisal City-Temple

The paradisal city-temple appears to encompass the entirety of the newly created earth. That is, John does not see a city and a gardenlike temple in a particular geographical location in the new earth, but rather he depicts the new creation as equivalent to the city and temple. Such an equation is implicit from, for example, 21:27, which declares that "nothing unclean . . . shall ever come into" the urban temple (which receives further support from 22:15 together with 21:8, where, respectively, the ungodly cannot enter into the city and are in "the lake of fire," all of which must be outside the new creation, the city, and the temple [for reasons in favor of this equation, see Beale 1999a: 1111]). The rationale for the worldwide encompassing nature of the paradisal temple lies in the ancient notion that the OT temple was a microcosmic model of the entire heaven and earth (see Fletcher-Lewis 1997: 156–62). One of the most explicit texts affirming this is Ps. 78:69: "And he built the sanctuary like the heights, like the earth which he founded forever."

Josephus understood the tripartite structure of the tabernacle to signify "the earth [= outer court] and the sea [= inner court], since these . . . are accessible to all, but the third portion [= holy of holies] he reserved for God alone, because heaven also is inaccessible to men" (*Ant.* 3.181 [cf. *Ant.* 3.123; see also *Midr. Rab.* Num. 19:19]). Josephus and Philo discuss various ways in which the tabernacle or temple or parts of it symbolically reflect the cosmos (Philo, *Moses* 2.71–145; Josephus *Ant.* 3.123, 179–187; Josephus [*J.W.* 4.324] refers to priests as leading the "cosmic worship" [*kosmikē thrēskeia*]). They also observe that the veil of the tabernacle and temple was made to reflect the four elements of the cosmos: earth, air, water, and fire (Philo, *QE* 2.85; *Moses* 2.87–88; Josephus, *J.W.* 5.212–213; *Ant.* 3.183). The curtains of the temple were woven of things that resembled the elements of which the world was made, since the created world itself was "the universal temple which existed before the holy temple [of Israel]" (Philo, *QE* 2.85). Likewise, both writers understand the garments of the high priest to symbolize the cosmos (Philo, *Moses* 2.117–126, 133–135, 143; Josephus, *Ant.* 3.180, 183–187). Philo (*Moses* 2.135) even says explicitly that the high priest "represents the world" and is a "micro-cosm" (or "small world" [*brachys kosmos*]). Also, the seven lamps on the lampstand were viewed as cosmic symbols (see commentary on Rev. 1:12; 1:13–16 above). It is true that Philo and Josephus had varying particular interpretations of this symbolism, but it is probable that they both testify to a general cosmological understanding of the temple held by mainstream contemporary Jewish thought, as well as by the OT itself (see Kline 1980: 41–47; Poythress 1991: 13–35). For similar notions in the ancient Near East, see Niehaus 1995: chap. 5; Fletcher-Lewis 1997: 159n47.

This cosmic reflection of the temple implicitly suggested that its purpose was to point to a future time when it would encompass the whole world (much like an architect's model of a newly planned building is but a small replica of what is to be built on a much larger scale). Since the OT temple was the localized dwelling of God's presence on earth, the temple's correspondence with the cosmos pointed to an eschatological goal of God's presence tabernacling throughout the earth, an eschatological goal that 21:1–22:5 appears to be developing (cf. 21:3). This imagery ultimately appears to be traceable back to the garden of Eden itself (note the proliferation of Eden imagery in chaps. 21–22), if one accepts the likely argument that the garden was understood as a kind of proto-temple that was to be expanded to cover the whole earth (see esp. Beale 2004, the thesis of which is to support this idea; see also Kline 1989: 31–32, 54–56; 1980: 35–42; Wenham 1994; to lesser degree, Poythress 1991: 19, 31, 35).

This particular interpretation finds striking parallel in Qumran (4Q418 Frag. 81). The members of the Qumran community are those who are the true "sons of Adam" who will "walk" in an "eter[nal] plantation" (lines 13–14), and who are to "honour" God "by consecrating yourself to him, in accordance to the fact that he has placed you as a holy of holies [over all] the earth, and over all the angels" (line 4 [following the rendering of García Martinez and Tigchelaar 1997–1998, on which, see Beale 2004: chap. 4]). It appears that John and Qumran are not dependent on one another, but rather are on parallel trajectories in interpreting the OT in this manner, though both may have been familiar with a common earlier tradition that interpreted the OT like this (for further analysis in support of an equation between the new creation, the new Jerusalem, the new temple, and the new Eden in the OT and in Rev. 21:1–22, see Beale 2004: chap. 12 [beginning segment]).

Revelation 22:6–21

The vision ends with a warning that its words must be heeded because Jesus is coming soon.

22:10

The prohibition "Do not seal the words of the prophecy" is linked to the command to Daniel at the conclusion of his prophecy: "Close the words and seal up the book until the time of the end" (Dan. 12:4 Θ; so also 8:26; 12:9 [cf. LXX readings]). Daniel prophesied about a final tribulation for God's people, the consummate defeat of wicked kingdoms, and the eternal establishment of God's kingdom. However, Daniel did not understand precisely how these events would transpire or when in history the final end would occur and the prophecies at last be fulfilled (Dan. 8:27; 12:8–9), though he was assured that the end had not yet come (Dan. 12:13). Therefore, the "sealing" of Daniel's book meant that its prophecies would neither be fully understood nor be fulfilled until the end.

What Daniel prophesied can now be understood because the prophecies have begun fulfillment and the latter days have begun, but they have not been consummated. "Do not seal up the words of the prophecy" here in 22:10 means that now, at last, the end-time prophecies of the OT, especially those in Daniel, have begun fulfillment, and, in the light of this fulfillment, these prophecies can now much more fully be understood. Therefore, the language about not sealing up the book indicates not only *beginning* fulfillment, but also the revelation of greater insight into the prophecies that was kept from OT saints (so likewise Eph. 3:4–5). In particular, Christ's death, resurrection, and reign over history, as well as the saints' tribulation, are the inaugurated fulfillment of OT prophecies. Through Christ's initial fulfillment and teaching, saints can have greater insight into OT prophecy and better obey God's word for their generation not only with respect to how OT prophecies have commenced fulfillment but also to how they will finally be completed.

22:11

Again the angel appeals to the conclusion of Daniel's prophecy:

Dan. 12:10	Rev. 22:11
"Many will be purged, purified, and refined, but the wicked will act wickedly, and none of the wicked will understand, but those who have insight will understand." (Cf. Ezek. 3:27.)	"Let the one doing unrighteousness [or 'harm'] continue to do unrighteousness [or 'harm'], and let the filthy one continue to be filthy; and let the righteous one continue to be righteous, and let the holy one continue to be holy."

How does the Daniel allusion contribute to the theological background of dual exhortations in Rev. 22:11? The Daniel text predicts that during the latter days false members of the covenant community will not understand the dawning fulfillment of prophecy (alluded to in Rev. 22:10), and consequently they will continue to disobey God's laws; the godly, however, will have insight and discern the beginning fulfillment of prophecy occurring around them, and they will respond by obeying God's word. The change from prediction in Daniel to imperatives in Rev. 22:11 expresses awareness that Daniel's prophecy is commencing fulfillment in John's own time and that genuine believers should discern this revelation and respond positively.

22:12a

The theme of unexpected, quick execution of judgment in the end time occurs already in the OT (see Isa. 47:11; Mal. 3:1; cf. Jer. 6:26). Perhaps the ideas of "nearness" and of a swift, "unexpected" appearance are both included, the latter with respect to the possibility that Jesus could come at any time, as in Matt. 24:36–25:13 (cf. Acts 1:7; 1 Thess. 1:9–10; 2 Tim. 4:8; Titus 2:13).

22:12b

Jesus' second assertion in 22:12 is an allusion to Isa. 40:10; 62:11:

Isa. 40:10 LXX	Rev. 22:12
"Behold, the Lord comes with strength . . . behold, his reward is with him, and his work is before him." (Isa. 62:11 LXX is virtually identical; see also Wis. 5:15–16.)	"Behold, I come quickly, and my reward is with me to render to each as his work is."

What is prophesied of the Lord in Isaiah is now prophesied by Jesus to be fulfilled by himself, another of the many affirmations of Jesus' deity found in the book (see Gill 1811: 382). The last clause in Isaiah concerning the "work" defines "reward" further and refers to God's work of bestowing blessings of salvation on his faithful people, though judgment of the unfaithful is likely implicit.

22:14

The language about a tree of life and open gates picks up on the Isa. 60 and Gen. 3 imagery in 21:24–22:3, where the worshiping nations file through the opened gates of the holy city and have access to the "tree of life," in contrast to the unholy, who are not able to enter (see commentary on Rev. 21:24–26; 22:1–2a, 2b, 3 above). Here appeal is made specifically to Isa. 62:10 LXX ("Go through my gates"), possibly together with Isa. 26:2 LXX ("Open the gates; let a people enter that keeps righteousness"). This clause from Isa. 62:10 is further explained with salvation metaphors in Isa. 62:11, one of which already has been alluded to in 22:12, only two verses prior to the present one. At the end of history true saints will inherit the reward of "the tree of life" that Adam and his unbelieving progeny did not inherit, and they will enjoy the realization of Isaiah's prophetic anticipations.

Perhaps Ps. 118:20 is included in the allusion ("the righteous shall enter by it [the gate]"), since Ps. 118:22 is one of the most frequently used messianic prophecies elsewhere in the NT: the rejected stone that became the chief cornerstone (see also Ps. 100:4).

22:15

The phrase "everyone practicing a lie" in Jer. 8:10 may lie behind Revelation's "everyone loving and practicing a lie." The wording is applied to idolatrous Israelites (Jer. 8:2) and equated with "apostasy" and "deceit" (8:5). Similarly, Ps. 101 identifies "those who practice apostasy" (101:3) with those who practice deceit, lying, and iniquity, and who therefore must be excluded from God's city (101:7–8): "He who practices deceit will not dwell within my house; he who speaks falsehood will not be established before me.... [I will] cut off from the city of the LORD all those who do iniquity."

Likewise, "dogs" in the OT can refer to Israelites who violate God's covenant (Ps. 59:6, 14). In Deut. 23:19 LXX (23:18 ET) "the wages of a dog

[*kynos*]" are equated with "the hire of a harlot" and refer to Israelites making votive offerings in the temple bought with money, which apparently they have earned from being a cult prostitute in the temple of an idol (cf. Deut. 23:17: "None of the daughters of Israel shall be a cult prostitute, nor shall any of the sons of Israel be a cult prostitute").

Thus, the "liars" and "dogs" primarily portray those who claim to be part of the true covenant community of the church but are, in reality, counterfeit, just as many professing to be part of Israel's covenant community were not true Israelites by faith.

Malachi 3:5 has a sin list similar to that in 22:15 in conjunction with the statement that God would be a "quick witness" against such sinners by "sending his angel" (Mal. 3:1), which is alluded to in the directly following verse ("I have sent my angel to witness" [22:16a]). The list of sinners in Malachi is "sorcerers . . . adulterers . . . ones swearing falsely in my name" and ones committing economic sins by "keeping back the wage of the hireling . . . oppressing the widow . . . afflicting orphans . . . perverting the judgment of the stranger." This continues the theme of counterfeit in the prior two images of "liars" and "dogs."

22:16–17

In 5:5 the title of Jesus was "root of David"; now "offspring" is combined with the name. "Root and offspring of David" may well be a shorthand paraphrase for the fuller Greek clause of Isa. 11:1 ("a rod [Heb. 'shoot'] from the root of Jesse and a blossom [Heb. 'branch'] from his root"). The point may be to identify Jesus generally with the fulfillment of the Davidic messianic hope as expressed in Isa. 11:1.

Even more explicitly than in 21:6, here the thought of Isa. 55:1 is drawn on (perhaps together with John 6:35; 7:37): "Ho! Everyone who thirsts, come to the waters; and you who have no money, come, buy and eat. Come, buy wine and milk without money and without cost." The three imperatives "Come" to people in Isaiah are likely the model for the three in 22:17 with the same prophetic hope in mind (see Lang 1945: 391–92; for further validation of the Isaiah allusion, see Fekkes 1994: 260–64).

22:18–19

These verses summarize the book of Revelation as a new law code to a new Israel, which is patterned on the old law code to ethnic Israel. Although many commentators note only Deut. 4, John alludes to a series of warning passages throughout Deuteronomy:

Deut. 4:1–2; 29:19–20	Rev. 22:18–19
"Hear the statutes.... You shall not add to the word . . . nor take away from it" (4:1–2 [likewise 12:32]). "And it will be when he hears the words . . . every curse which is written in this book will rest on him, and the LORD will blot out his name from under heaven" (29:19–20).	"I testify to everyone who hears the words . . . : If anyone adds to them, God will add to him the plagues which have been written in this book, and if anyone takes away from the words of the book . . . , God will take away his part of the tree of life and of the holy city. . . ."

What is the meaning of "adding to" and "taking away from" the revelatory words? The answer must be sought in Deuteronomy. In Deut. 4:1–2; 12:32 the language serves as a twofold warning against deceptive teaching that affirmed that idolatry was not inconsistent with faith in the God of Israel (see Deut. 4:3 [which alludes to the Baal-Peor episode of Num. 25:1–9, 14–18]; 13; see also *1 En.* 104:11). Those who deceive in this way are false prophets (so Deut. 13:1–18). Such false teaching amounts to "adding to" God's law; furthermore, it is tantamount to "taking away from" God's law, since it violates the positive laws against idolatry (for the theological problem of God taking away someone's "part of the tree of life and of the holy city," see Beale 1999a: 1150–54). Revelation 22:18–19 applies Deuteronomy analogically to the situation of the Christians.

Bibliography

Alford, H. 1866. *The Greek Testament IV.* Cambridge: Deighton.

Aune, D. E. 1997–1998. *Revelation.* WBC 52A, 52B, 52C. Dallas: Word.

———. 1999. "Qumran and the Book of Revelation." Pages 622–48 in vol. 2 of *The Dead Sea Scrolls after Fifty Years: A Comprehensive Assessment.* Edited by P. W. Flint and J. C. VanderKam with A. E. Alvarez. Leiden: Brill.

Bailey, J. W. 1934. "The Temporary Messianic Reign in the Literature of Early Judaism." *JBL* 53: 170–87.

Barr, J. 1962. *Biblical Words for Time.* SBT 33. London: SCM.

Bauckham, R. 1977. "The Eschatological Earthquake in the Apocalypse of John." *NovT* 19: 224–33.

———. 1993a. *The Climax of Prophecy: Studies in the Book of Revelation.* Edinburgh: T&T Clark.

———. 1993b. *Theology of the Book of Revelation.* Cambridge: Cambridge University Press.

Beale, G. K. 1980. "The Danielic Background for Revelation 13:18 and 17:9." *TynBul* 31: 163–70.

———. 1984. *The Use of Daniel in Jewish Apocalyptic Literature and in the Revelation of St. John.* Lanham, MD: University Press of America.

———. 1988. "The Old Testament in Revelation." Pages 318–36 in *It Is Written: Scripture Citing Scripture; Essays in Honour of Barnabas Lindars, SSF.* Edited by D. A. Carson and H. G. M. Williamson. Cambridge: Cambridge University Press.

———. 1996. "The Old Testament Background of Rev 3.14." *NTS* 42: 133–52.

———. 1997a. "The Hearing Formula and the Visions of John in Revelation." Pages 167–80 in *A Vision for the Church: Studies in Early Christian Ecclesiology in Honour of J. P. M. Sweet.* Edited by M. Bockmuehl and M. B. Thompson. Edinburgh: T&T Clark.

———. 1997b. "Solecisms in the Apocalypse as Signals for the Presence of Old Testament Allusions: A Selective Analysis of Revelation 1–22." Pages 421–46 in *Early Christian Interpretation of the Scriptures of Israel: Investigations and Proposals.* Edited by C. A. Evans and J. A. Sanders. JSNTSup 148. Sheffield: Sheffield Academic Press.

———. 1999a. *The Book of Revelation: A Commentary on the Greek Text.* NIGTC. Grand Rapids: Eerdmans.

———. 1999b. *John's Use of the Old Testament in Revelation.* JSNTSup 166. Sheffield: JSOT Press.

———. 1999c. "Questions of Authorial Intent, Epistemology, and Presuppositions and Their Bearing on the Study of the Old Testament in the New: A Rejoinder to Steve Moyise." *IBS* 21: 151–80.

———. 2001. "A Response to Jon Paulien on the Use of the Old Testament in Revelation." *AUSS* 39: 23–33.

———. 2004. *The Temple and the Church's Mission: A Biblical Theology of the Dwelling Place of God.* NSBT 17. Downers Grove, IL: InterVarsity.

Beasley-Murray, G. R. 1974. *The Book of Revelation.* London: Marshall, Morgan & Scott.

Beckwith, I. T. 1919. *The Apocalypse of John.* New York: Macmillan.

Beckwith, R. 1985. *The Old Testament Canon of the New Testament Church and Its Background in Early Judaism.* Grand Rapids: Eerdmans.

Bøe, A. S. 1992. "Bruken av det Gamle Testamente i Johannes' Åpenbaring." *TTKi* 63: 253–69.

Boring, M. E. 1989. *Revelation.* Louisville: John Knox.

Briggs, R. A. 1999. *Jewish Temple Imagery in the Book of Revelation.* New York: Lang.

Brütsch, C. 1970. *Die Offenbarung Jesu Christi: Johannes-Apokalypse.* 2nd ed. 3 vols. ZBK. Zürich: Zwingli.

Buchanan, G. W. 1993. *The Book of Revelation: Its Introduction and Prophecy.* MBCNTS 22. Lewiston, NY: Mellen Biblical Press.

Burchard, C. 1983. "Joseph and Aseneth." *OTP* 2:177–247.

Caird, G. B. 1966. *A Commentary on the Revelation of St. John the Divine.* BNTC. London: Black.

Cambier, J. 1955. "Les images de l'Ancien Testament dans l'Apocalypse de Saint Jean." *NRTh* 77: 113–22.

Carrell, P. R. 1997. *Jesus and the Angels: Angelology and the Christology of the Apocalypse of John.* SNTSMS 95. Cambridge: Cambridge University Press.

Carrington, P. 1931. *The Meaning of the Revelation.* London: SPCK.

Charles, R. H. 1920. *A Critical and Exegetical Commentary on the Revelation of St. John*. 2 vols. ICC. Edinburgh: T&T Clark.

———. 1963. *Eschatology: The Doctrine of a Future Life in Israel, Judaism, and Christianity; A Critical History*. 2nd ed. New York: Schocken.

Chilton, D. C. 1987. *The Days of Vengeance: An Exposition of the Book of Revelation*. Ft. Worth, TX: Dominion Press.

Collins, A. Y. 1976. *The Combat Myth in the Book of Revelation*. HDR 9. Missoula, MT: Scholars Press.

Comblin, J. 1965. *Le Christ dans l'Apocalypse*. BTh 3/6. Paris: Desclée.

Court, J. M. 1979. *Myth and History in the Book of Revelation*. Atlanta: John Knox.

Dana, H. E., and J. R. Mantey. 1957. *A Manual Grammar of the Greek New Testament*. New York: Macmillan.

D'Aragon, J.-L. 1968. "The Apocalypse." Pages 467–93 in vol. 2 of the *Jerome Biblical Commentary*. Edited by R. E. Brown, J. A. Fitzmeyer, and R. E. Murphy. Englewood Cliffs, NJ: Prentice-Hall.

Davila, J. R. 1996. "Melchizedek, Michael, and War in Heaven." *SBLSP* 35: 259–72.

Day, J. 1985. *God's Conflict with the Dragon and the Sea: Echoes of a Canaanite Myth in the Old Testament*. COP 35. Cambridge: Cambridge University Press.

———. 1994. "The Origin of Armageddon: Revelation 16:16 as an Interpretation of Zechariah 12:11." Pages 315–26 in *Crossing the Boundaries: Essays in Biblical Interpretation in Honour of Michael D. Goulder*. Edited by S. E. Porter, P. Joyce, and D. E. Orton. BIS 8. Leiden: Brill.

Decock, P. B. 1999. "The Scriptures in the Book of Revelation." *Neot* 33: 373–410.

Deere, J. S. 1978. "Premillennialism in Revelation 20:4–6." *BSac* 135: 58–73.

Dittmar, W. D. 1903. *Vetus Testamentum in Novo: Die alttestamentlichen Parallelen des Neuen Testaments im Wortlaut der Urtexte und der Septuaginta*. Göttingen: Vandenhoeck & Ruprecht.

Dochhorn, J. 1997. "Und die Erde tat ihren Mund auf: Ein Exodusmotiv in Apc 12,16." *ZNW* 88: 140–42.

Dumbrell, W. J. 1985. *The End of the Beginning: Revelation 21–22 and the Old Testament*. Homebush West, N.S.W.: Lancer.

Düsterdieck, F. 1980. *Critical and Exegetical Handbook to the Revelation of John*. Translated by H. E. Jacobs. KEK 11. Repr., Winona Lake, IN: Alpha Publications.

Eichrodt, W. 1967. *Theology of the Old Testament*. 2 vols. London: SCM.

Ellul, J. 1977. *Apocalypse: The Book of Revelation*. New York: Seabury.

Ernst, J. 1967. *Die eschatologischen Gegenspieler in den Schriften des Neuen Testaments*. BU 3. Regensburg: Pustet.

Farrer, A. 1964. *The Revelation of St. John the Divine*. Oxford: Clarendon.

Fekkes, J. 1994. *Isaiah and Prophetic Traditions in the Book of Revelation: Visionary Antecedents and Their Development*. JSNTSup 93. Sheffield: JSOT Press.

Fenske, W. 1999. "Das Lied des Mose, des Knechtes Gottes, und das Lied des Lammes (Apokalypse des Johannes 15,3f): Der Text und seine Bedeutung für die Johannes-Apokalypse." *ZNW* 90: 250–64.

Feuillet, A. 1964. *Johanine Studies*. New York: Alba House.

———. 1965. *The Apocalypse*. New York: Alba House.

Fletcher-Lewis, C. H. T. 1997. "The Destruction of the Temple and the Relativization of the Old Covenant: Mark 13:31 and Matthew 5:18." Pages 145–69 in *The Reader Must Understand: Eschatology in Bible and Theology*. Edited by K. E. Brower and M. W. Elliott. Leicester: Apollos.

Ford, D. 1979. *The Abomination of Desolation in Biblical Eschatology*. Washington, DC: University Press of America.

Ford, J. M. 1975. *Revelation*. AB 38. Garden City, NY: Doubleday.

Gangemi, A. 1974. "L'utilizzazione del Deutero-Isaia nell'Apocalisse di Giovanni." *Euntes Docete* 27: 109–44, 311–39.

———. 1977. "La manna nascosta e il nome nuovo." *RivB* 25: 337–56.

———. 1978. "La stella del mattino (Ap 2,26–28)." *RivB* 26.

Garrow, A. J. P. 1997. *Revelation*. NTR. London: Routledge.

Gärtner, B. 1965. *The Temple and the Community in Qumran and the New Testament: A Comparative Study in the Temple Symbolism of the Qumran Texts and the New Testament*. SNTSMS 1. Cambridge: Cambridge University Press.

Gelston, A. 1959. "The Royal Priesthood." *EvQ* 31: 152–63.

Gill, J. 1811. *An Exposition of the New Testament III: The Revelation of St. John the Divine*. Philadelphia: Woodward.

Ginzberg, L. 1967. *The Legends of the Jews*. Translated by H. Szold and P. Radin. 7 vols. Philadelphia: Jewish Publication Society.

Glasson, T. F. 1965. *The Revelation of John*. CBC. Cambridge: Cambridge University Press.

González, C. G., and J. L. González. 1997. *Revelation*. WestBC. Louisville: Westminster John Knox.

Goulder, M. D. 1981. "The Apocalypse as an Annual Cycle of Prophecies." *NTS* 27: 342–67.

Haapa, E. 1968. "Farben und Funktionen bei den apokalyptischen Reitern." *Teologinen Aikakauskirja* 73: 216–25.

Hailey, H. 1979. *Revelation*. Grand Rapids: Baker Academic.

Hamilton, V. P. 1980. "חֲנָה (taḥănâ) encamping or encampment." Page 300 in *Theological Wordbook of the Old Testament* I. Edited by R. L. Harris. Chicago: Moody Bible Institute.

Harrington, D. J. 1999. *Revelation: The Book of the Risen Christ*. Hyde Park, NY: New City.

Harrington, W. J. 1993. *Revelation*. SP 16. Collegeville, MN: Liturgical Press.

Harrisville, R. A. 1960. *The Concept of Newness in the New Testament*. Minneapolis: Augsburg.

Hendriksen, W. 1962. *More Than Conquerors: An Interpretation of the Book of Revelation*. Grand Rapids: Baker Academic.

Hengstenberg, E. W. 1853. *The Revelation of St. John*. 2 vols. New York: Carter.

Hoekema, A. A. 1979. *The Bible and the Future*. Grand Rapids: Eerdmans.

Holtz, T. 1971. *Die Christologie der Apokalypse des Johannes*. TU 85. Berlin: Akademie-Verlag.

Hughes, P. E. 1990. *The Book of the Revelation*. Grand Rapids: Eerdmans.

Hühn, E. 1900. *Die alttestamentlichen Citate und Reminiscenzen im Neuen Testament*. Tübingen: Mohr Siebeck.

Hunzinger, C. H. 1965. "Babylon als Deckname für Rom und die Datierung des I. Petrusbriefes." Pages 67–77 in *Gottes Wort und Gottes Land: Hans-Wilhelm Hertzberg zum 70. Geburtstag am 16. Januar 1965 dargebracht von Kollegen, Freunden und Schülern*. Edited by H. G. Reventlow. Göttingen: Vandenhoeck & Ruprecht.

Jacob, E. 1958. *The Theology of the Old Testament*. London: Hodder & Stoughton.

Jenkins, F. 1972. *The Old Testament in the Book of Revelation*. Marion, IN: Cogdill Foundation Publications.

Johnson, A. 1981. "Revelation." Pages 397–603 in vol. 12 of *The Expositor's Bible Commentary*. Edited by F. E. Gaebelein. Grand Rapids: Zondervan.

Johnston, R. M. 1987. "The Eschatological Sabbath in John's Apocalypse: A Reconsideration." *AUSS* 25: 39–50.

Jörns, K.-P. 1971. *Das hymnische Evangelium: Untersuchungen zu Aufbau, Funktion und Herkunft der hymnischen Stücke in der Johannesoffenbarung*. SNT 5. Gütersloh: Mohn.

Keil, C. F. 1971. *Biblical Commentary on the Book of Daniel*. Grand Rapids: Eerdmans.

Kiddle, M., and M. K. Ross. 1940. *The Revelation of St. John*. MNTC. London: Hodder & Stoughton.

Kistemaker, S. J. 2000. "The Temple in the Apocalypse." *JETS* 43: 433–41.

Kittel, G. 1967. "λέγω." Pages 91–136 in vol. 4 of *TDNT*. Grand Rapids: Eerdmans.

Kline, M. G. 1980. *Images of the Spirit*. BBMS. Grand Rapids: Baker Academic.

———. 1989. *Kingdom Prologue*. South Hamilton, MA: Gordon-Conwell Theological Seminary.

Knight, J. 1999. *Revelation*. Readings. Sheffield: Sheffield Academic Press.

Kraft, H. 1974. *Die Offenbarung des Johannes*. HNT 16A. Tübingen: Mohr Siebeck.

Krodel, G. A. 1989. *Revelation*. ACNT. Minneapolis: Augsburg.

Lacocque, A. 1979. *The Book of Daniel*. Translated by D. Pellauer. London: SPCK.

Lancellotti, A. 1966. "L'Antico Testamento nell'Apocalisse." *RivB* 14: 369–84.

Lang, G. H. 1945. *The Revelation of Jesus Christ: Select Studies*. London: Oliphants.

LaRondelle, H. K. 1989. "The Etymology of Har-Magedon (Rev 16:16)." *AUSS* 27: 69–73.

Laughlin, T. C. 1902. *The Solecisms of the Apocalypse*. Princeton, NJ: Princeton University Press.

Leupold, H. C. 1969. *Exposition of Daniel*. Grand Rapids: Baker Academic.

Loenertz, R. J. 1947. *The Apocalypse of St. John*. London: Sheed and Ward.

Lohmeyer, E. 1970. *Die Offenbarung des Johannes*. HNT 16. Tübingen: Mohr Siebeck.

Lohse, E. 1961. "Die alttestamentliche Sprache des Sehers Johannes: Textkritische Bemerkungen zur Apokalypse." *ZNW* 52: 122–26.

Lövestam, E. 1965. "Apokalypsen 3:8b." *SEÅ* 30: 91–101.

Lust, J. 1980. "The Order of the Final Events in Revelation and in Ezekiel." Pages 179–83 in *L'Apocalypse johannique et l'Apocalyptique dans le Nouveau Testament*. Edited by J. Lambrecht. BETL 53. Gembloux: Duculot; Leuven: Leuven University Press.

Malina, B. J. 1995. *On the Genre and Message of Revelation*. Peabody, MA: Hendrickson.

Marconcini, B. 1976. "L'utilizzazione del TM nelle citazioni isaiane dell'Apocalisse." *RivB* 24: 113–36.

Martínez, F. C., and E. J. C. Tigchelaar (eds.). 1997–1998. *The Dead Sea Scrolls Study Edition*. 2 Vols. Leiden: Brill.

Mathewson, D. 2001. "A Re-Examination of the Millennium in Rev 20:1–6: Consummation and Recapitulation." *JETS* 44: 237–51.

———. 2003. *A New Heaven and a New Earth: The Meaning and Function of the Old Testament in Revelation 21.1–22.5*. JSNTSup 238. Sheffield: Sheffield Academic Press.

Mayer, G. 1978. "debher." Pages 125–27 in *TDOT* 3. Grand Rapids: Eerdmans.

McComiskey, T. E. 1993. "Alteration of OT Imagery in the Book of Revelation: Its Hermeneutical and Theological Significance." *JETS* 36: 307–16.

McDonough, S. 1999. *YHWH at Patmos: Rev. 1:4 in Its Hellenistic and Early Jewish Setting*. WUNT 2/107. Tübingen: Mohr Siebeck.

———. 2000. "Of Beasts and Bees." *NTS* 46: 227–44.

McKelvey, R. J. 1969. *The New Temple: The Church in the New Testament*. OTM. Oxford: Oxford University Press.

McNamara, M. 1966. *The New Testament and the Palestinian Targum to the Pentateuch*. AnBib 27. Rome: Pontifical Biblical Institute.

Michaels, J. R. 1997. *Revelation*. IVPNTC 20. Downers Grove, IL: InterVarsity.

Milling, D. H. 1972. "The Origin and Character of the New Testament Doxology." PhD diss., University of Cambridge.

Minear, P. S. 1968. *I Saw a New Earth: An Introduction to the Visions of the Apocalypse*. Washington, DC: Corpus Books.

Morris, L. 1955. *The Apostolic Preaching of the Cross*. London: Tyndale.

———. 1987. *Revelation*. TNTC. Leicester: Inter-Varsity.

Morton, R. 2001. "Glory to God and to the Lamb: John's Use of Jewish and Hellenistic/Roman Themes in Formatting His Theology in Revelation 4–5." *JSNT* 83: 89–109.

Moulton, J. H., W. F. Howard, and M. Turner. 1906–1976. *A Grammar of New Testament Greek*. 4 vols. Edinburgh: T&T Clark.

Mounce, R. H. 1977. *The Book of Revelation*. NICNT. Grand Rapids: Eerdmans.

Moyise, S. 1995. *The Old Testament in the Book of Revelation*. JSNTSup 115. Sheffield: Sheffield Academic Press.

———. 1999a. "The Language of the Old Testament in the Apocalypse." *JSNT* 76: 97–113.

———. 1999b. "The Old Testament in the New: A Reply to Greg Beale." *IBS* 21: 54–58.

———. 2000. "Intertextuality and the Study of the Old Testament in the New Testament." Pages 14–41 in *The Old Testament in the New Testament: Essays in Honour of J. L. North*. Edited by S. Moyise. JSNTSup 189. Sheffield: Sheffield Academic Press.

———. 2001a. "Authorial Intention and the Book of Revelation." *AUSS* 39: 35–40.

———. 2001b. "Seeing the Old Testament through a Lens." *IBS* 23: 36–41.

———. 2002. "Does the Author of Revelation Misappropriate the Scriptures?" *AUSS* 40: 3–21.

Murphy, F. J. 1994. "The Book of Revelation." *CurBS* 2: 181–225.

———. 1998. *Fallen Is Babylon: The Revelation to John*. Harrisburg, PA: Trinity Press International.

Niehaus, J. J. 1995. *God at Sinai: Covenant and Theophany in the Bible and Ancient Near East*. Grand Rapids: Zondervan.

———. Forthcoming. *No Other Gods*. Grand Rapids: Baker Academic.

Olson, D. C. 1997. "'Those Who Have Not Defiled Themselves with Women': Revelation 14:4 and the Book of Enoch." *CBQ* 59: 492–510.

Osborne, G. R. 2002. *Revelation*. BECNT. Grand Rapids: Baker Academic.

Ozanne, C. G. 1965. "The Language of the Apocalypse." *TynBul* 16: 3–9.

Pate, C. M. 1998. *Four Views on the Book of Revelation*. Counterpoints. Grand Rapids: Zondervan.

Paul, I. 2000. "The Use of the Old Testament in Revelation 12." Pages 256–57 in *The Old Testament in the New Testament: Essays in Honor of J. L. North*. Edited by S. Moyise. JSNTSup 189. Sheffield: Sheffield Academic Press.

Paulien, J. 1988a. *Decoding Revelation's Trumpets: Literary Allusions and the Interpretation of Revelation 8:7–12*. AUSDDS 21. Berrien Springs, MI: Andrews University Press.

———. 1988b. "Elusive Allusions: The Problematic Use of the Old Testament in Revelation." *BR* 33: 37–53.

———. 1992. "Armageddon." *ABD* 1:394–95.

———. 2001a. "Criteria and Assessment of Allusions to the Old Testament in the Book of Revelation." Pages 113–29 in *Studies in the Book of Revelation*. Edited by S. Moyise. Edinburgh: T&T Clark.

———. 2001b. "Dreading the Whirlwind: Intertextuality and the Use of the Old Testament in Revelation." *AUSS* 39: 5–22.

Peachey, B. F. 1999. "A Horse of a Different Colour: The Horses in Zechariah and Revelation." *ExpTim* 110: 214–16.

Poythress, V. S. 1991. *The Shadow of Christ in the Law of Moses*. Brentwood, TN: Wolgemuth & Hyatt.

Prigent, P. 1981. *L'Apocalypse de Saint Jean*. CNT 14. Paris: Delachaux et Niestlé.

Provan, I. 1996. "Foul Spirits, Fornication and Finance: Revelation 18 from an Old Testament Perspective." *JSNT* 64: 81–100.

Ramsay, W. M. 1904. *The Letters to the Seven Churches of Asia and Their Place in the Plan of the Apocalypse*. London: Hodder & Stoughton.

Rissi, M. 1966. *Time and History: A Study on the Revelation*. Richmond: John Knox.

———. 1972. *The Future of the World: An Exegetical Study of Rev. 19:11–22:15*. SBT 2/23. London: SCM.

Rist, M. 1957. *The Revelation of St. John the Divine*. Pages 347–613 in vol. 12 of *The Interpreter's Bible*. Edited by G. A. Buttrick. New York: Abingdon.

Roloff, J. 1993. *Revelation*. Translated by J. E. Alsup. CC. Minneapolis: Fortress.

Ruiz, J.-P. 1989. *Ezekiel in the Apocalypse: The Transformation of Prophetic Language in Revelation 16:17–19:10*. EUS 23/376. Frankfurt: Lang.

Schlatter, A. 1912. *Das Alte Testament in der johanneischen Apokalypse*. BFCT 16/6. Gütersloh: Mohn.

Schüssler Fiorenza, E. 1972. *Priester für Gott: Studien zum Herrschafts-und Priestermotiv in der Apokalypse*. NTAbh 7. Münster: Aschendorff.

———. 1991. *Revelation*. Proclamation. Minneapolis: Fortress.

Shea, W. H. 1980. "The Location and Significance of Armageddon in Rev. 16:16." *AUSS* 18: 157–62.

Sickenberger, J. 1942. *Erklärung der Johannesapokalypse*. 2nd ed. Bonn: Hanstein.

Skrinjar, A. 1935. "Les sept Esprits (Rev 1,4; 3,1; 4,5; 5,6)." *Bib* 16: 1–24, 113–40.

Stuart, D. 1987. *Hosea–Jonah*. WBC 31. Waco: Word.

Stuart, M. 1845. *Commentary on the Apocalypse*. Vol. 2. Andover, MD: Allen, Morrell & Wardwell.

Sweet, J. P. M. 1979. *Revelation*. London: SCM.

———. 1996. "Revelation." Pages 160–73 in *Early Christian Thought in Its Jewish Context*. Edited by J. Barclay and J. P. M. Sweet. Cambridge: Cambridge University Press.

Swete, H. B. 1906. *The Apocalypse of St. John*. London: Macmillan.

Thompson, L. L. 1998. *Revelation*. ANTC. Nashville: Abingdon.

Thompson, S. 1985. *The Apocalypse and Semitic Syntax*. SNTSMS 52. Cambridge: Cambridge University Press.

Trudinger, L. P. 1966. "Some Observations Concerning the Text of the Old Testament in the Book of Revelation." *JTS* 17: 82–88.

Ulfgard, H. 1989. *Feast and Future: Revelation 7:9–17 and the Feast of Tabernacles*. ConBNT 22. Lund: Almqvist & Wiksell.

Valentine, J. 1985. "Theological Aspects of the Temple Motif in the Old Testament and Revelation." PhD diss., Boston University.

van der Waal, C. 1971. *Openbaring van Jezus Christus: Inleiding en vertaling*. Groningen: de Vuurbaak.

Vanhoye, A. 1962. "L'utilisation du livre d'Ezéchiel dans l'Apocalypse." *Bib* 43: 436–76.

———. 1986. *Old Testament Priests and the New Priest: According to the New Testament*. Translated by J. B. Orchard. Petersham, MA: St. Bede's Publications.

Vogelgesang, J. M. 1985. "The Interpretation of Ezekiel in the Book of Revelation." PhD diss., Harvard University.

Vos, L. H. 1965. *Synoptic Traditions in the Apocalypse*. Kampen: Kok.

Weisberg, D. B. 1970. "Incense." Page 421 in *The New Westminster Dictionary of the Bible*. Edited by H. S. Gehman. Philadelphia: Westminster.

Wenham, G. J. 1994. "Sanctuary Symbolism in the Garden of Eden Story." Pages 19–25 in *"I Studied Inscriptions from before the Flood": Ancient Near Eastern, Literary, and Linguistic Approaches to Genesis 1–11*. Edited by R. S. Hess and D. T. Tsumura. Winona Lake, IN: Eisenbrauns.

Wevers, J. W., ed. 1991. *Exodus*. Vol. 2/1 of *Septuaginta: Vetus Testamentum graecum*. Göttingen: Vandenhoeck & Ruprecht.

White, R. F. 1989. "Reexamining the Evidence for Recapitulation in Rev 20:1–10." *WTJ* 51: 319–44.

———. 1991. "Millennial Kingdom-City: Epic Themes, Ezek. 36–39, and the Interpretation of Rev. 20:4–10." Paper presented at the annual meeting of the Evangelical Theological Society, Kansas City, MO, 21 November 1991.

———. 1994. "Making Sense of Rev. 20:1–10? Harold Hoehner versus Recapitulation." *JETS* 37: 539–51.

Wilcock, M. 1975. *I Saw Heaven Opened: The Message of Revelation*. London: Inter-Varsity.

Willis, J. T. 1997. "An Interpretation of Isaiah 22:15–25 and Its Function in the New Testament." Pages 334–51 in *Early Christian Interpretation of the Scriptures of Israel: Investigations and Proposals*. Edited by C. A. Evans and J. A. Sanders. JSNTSup 148. Sheffield: Sheffield Academic Press.

Young, E. J. 1980. *The Prophecy of Daniel*. Grand Rapids: Eerdmans.

Index of Scripture and Other Ancient Writings

Dead Sea Scrolls and Related Texts

Qumran

CD-A